# ROYAL NAVY AIRCRAFT SERIALS AND UNITS 1911 TO 1919

RAY STURTIVANT, I.S.O.
AND GORDON PAGE

AN AIR-BRITAIN PUBLICATION

ISBN 0 85130 191 6


Printed by Unwin Brothers Ltd,
The Gresham Press
Old Woking
Surrey GU22 9LH

The cover painting by Dugald Cameron depicts Sopwith 2F.1 Camel N6812 piloted by Lt S.D.Culley climbing to successfully attack Zeppelin *L53* after taking off from a towed lighter in the North Sea on 11th August 1918.

Maps by Mick Davis

# CONTENTS

*Sopwith 2F.1 Camel N6606 (named 'SHALL US') being hoisted aboard HMS Renown, probably in February 1918*
*(FAA Museum)*

# INTRODUCTION

British naval aviation originated in July 1908 when proposals were made for the construction of a rigid airship for Fleet reconnaissance. Naval Airship No.1, or *Mayfly*, eventually had its maiden flight in May 1911, but the saga of naval lighter-than-air flying is outside the scope of this book.

In the meantime, Frank McLean, an early aviation pioneer with his own locally-built fleet of Short biplanes, had in February 1911 made two of these available at his school at Eastchurch, in the Isle of Sheppey, for instructing naval officers. In November of that year a naval flying school was officially opened at Eastchurch, by which time four Shorts were in use for this purpose, and on 13 April 1912 the service became formally known as the Naval Wing of the Royal Flying Corps.

A seaplane station was commissioned at nearby Grain in December 1912, this being mainly used for experimental and trials purposes, and three months later another seaplane base was opened at Calshot. These were followed by similar stations at Felixstowe, Yarmouth, Cromarty (later Fort George) and Dundee.

On 1 July 1914 the service was restyled the Royal Naval Air Service, and seventeen days later a formation of naval aircraft flew over the Fleet at Spithead during a review by His Majesty King George V.

By the outbreak of war on 4 August 1914, the service had grown to a strength of 130 officers and around 700 other ranks, its aircraft now comprising 39 landplanes and 52 seaplanes, in addition to seven airships. There was soon to be a rapid and ever-increasing expansion. Following German minelaying operations off the Suffolk coast on 8 August, regular coastal patrols were instigated between the Humber and the Thames, as well as across the English Channel between Westgate and Ostende.

A naval element, initially known as the Eastchurch (Mobile) Squadron, soon joined the British Expeditionary Force in France and Belgium. By the following month there was a headquarters at Dunkerque with Nos.1, 2 and 3 Squadrons in operation, each nominally with 12 aircraft. At home, the first of a series of bases was being set up for training purposes, as well as coastal operations including defence against Zeppelins.

On 3 September 1914 the Royal Naval Air Service officially took over the air defence of Great Britain, and a series of small detachments was established at various airfields around the coast.

The first ever bombing raid on Germany was made on 22 September by naval aircraft based at Antwerp, but German forces were soon to advance, reaching the Belgian coast by 15 October. The R.N.A.S. retreated to Dunkerque, and Nos. 1 and 2 Squadrons ceased to exist for a time. However, they soon reformed in England.

From June 1915 numbered Wings appeared, initially by retitling the squadrons, which were then gradually expanded. Each Wing was divided into lettered squadrons, which in turn were sub-divided into numbered flights (e.g. 3 Flight B Squadron 1 Wing). Squadron letters could be duplicated within different wings, but there was no such duplication of flight numbers, which were allocated between 1 and 15. 1 Wing also had an Eastchurch Group.

In the meantime, following a few experiments in operating fixed-wing aircraft from ships, the Admiralty had requisitioned three cross-Channel steamers, *Empress*, *Engadine* and *Riviera*. These were fitted out at Chatham dockyard with an improvised arrangement to carry four seaplanes each. The origins and subsequent history of this method of operating are too detailed to be covered here, but are dealt with very comprehensively in Dick Cronin's companion work *'Royal Navy Shipboard Aircraft Developments 1912 - 1931'*.

By 1915 the R.N.A.S. was engaged in a variety of tasks, in addition to its small but growing rôle in France. The force had a significant success when on 7 June Flight Sub-Lieutenant R.A.J. Warneford brought down Zeppelin *LZ37* in flames after catching it over Bruges, a feat for which he gained the Victoria Cross.

At home the service was beginning to take a part in defence against U-boat attacks on merchant shipping in coastal waters, as well as helping to defend against Zeppelin attacks. It also played a part in the unsuccessful attempt to force the Dardanelles, 3 Wing being sent out to the Aegean for this purpose in March 1915, to be followed by 2 Wing in August. It was in this campaign that the service gained another Victoria Cross, this being awarded to Squadron Commander R.Bell-Davies for his courage on 19 November in landing in his Nieuport single-seater to successfully pick up Flight Sub-Lieutenant G.F.Smylie, who had just been brought down within sight of Turkish forces.

The R.N.A.S. also played a major rôle in the search for the German battlecruiser *Königsberg*, and its subsequent detection and destruction in the Rufiji river delta in German East Africa in July 1915. Operations in this theatre were later based at Zanzibar and Mombasa, a small detachment being sent to Mesopotamia in August 1915 to assist the Royal Flying Corps for a time.

By the time the war had been under way for twelve months, the R.N.A.S. had expanded considerably. To augment home production of aircraft, a variety of machines had been purchased in France, Canada and the United States, for both operational and training purposes. A significant development was the introduction of Curtiss "America" flying boats to help combat the U-boat menace in the North Sea. Various Short seaplanes, many built by sub-contractors, continued to be the mainstay of coastal operations. Defence against the Zeppelin had a welcome success when on 28 November 1916 two B.E.2c's from the Yarmouth group shot down *L21* into the North Sea.

In France, fighter and reconnaissance operations were now undertaken by numbered squadrons administered by 1 and 4 Wings, whilst 5 Wing was a bomber force based at Coudekerque. The original 3 Wing had merged into 2 Wing to continue Aegean operations, and a new 3 Wing began to form at home, later going over to France to carry out strategic bombing attacks from bases near Nancy. Bombing aircraft at this stage mainly comprised Sopwith 1½ Strutters and Short Bombers, the latter being a landplane derivative of the Short 184 Type seaplane. These were soon to be joined by the first successful British heavy bomber, the Handley Page O/100.

In October 1916 the R.N.A.S., which until then had operated mainly in coastal regions of northern France, was called upon to assist the Royal Flying Corps on the Western Front. A small detachment of Pups and 1½ Strutters was attached to the 22nd Wing, soon becoming 8 Squadron, this being the forerunner of a number of squadrons to fight alongside the R.F.C., equipped later with Sopwith Triplanes and then Sopwith Camels. These had distinguished careers, though few of their original pilots survived the war. 3 Wing, which had been due to re-equip with O/100s, disbanded, and this type was issued instead to 5 Wing at Coudekerque.

Towards the end of 1916 an Anti-Submarine Division of the Naval Staff was established to co-ordinate and expand operations against U-boats. The following Spring activities in the Western Approaches came under a new South-Western Group and mid-channel operations were controlled by a Portsmouth Group with headquarters at Warsash, whilst a Milford Haven Group was set up in November for the Irish Sea area.

By early 1918 seaplane and flying boat coastal patrols were being augmented by the Airco D.H.4, a sturdy aircraft capable of use for anti-submarine reconnaissance work in addition to light day bombing and reconnaissance operations in France. By the Spring of that year these had been joined by a series of D.H.6-equipped flights based at small airfields all around the British coast and undertaking "scarecrow" patrols against U-boats.

On 1 April 1918 both the Royal Flying Corps and the Royal Naval Air Service ceased to exist, on being merged to form the Royal Air Force. By that time the R.N.A.S. had been built up to strength of 2,900 aircraft, with 55,000 officers and men. The existing squadrons, which now included some equipped with D.H.4s for bombing duties, had 200 added to the numbers. This 200-series was gradually expanded by giving squadron numbers to other sizeable operational units, such numbers eventually running as high as 274. Training units were similarly given numbered designations.

The Royal Naval Air Service attracted quite a number of Canadians to its ranks, several of them achieving distinction, especially in France. With the entry of the United States into the war, numbers of U.S. Navy personnel were attached to the R.N.A.S. and later the R.A.F., mostly serving with coastal formations in the United Kingdom and day bomber squadrons in France. In addition, R.N.A.S. Killingholme was taken over by the U.S.Navy in July 1918 for flying boat operations, as were similar stations in southern Ireland. Many feats of bravery were performed by both Canadians and Americans, and it is noteworthy that the achievements of two of the latter led to U.S. Navy ships being later named after them - one being a near-namesake of the primary author of this book.

A new development at sea was the birth of the aircraft carrier as we know it today. Experiments with HMS *Furious* had proved that it was possible for wheeled aircraft to both land and take-off from a moving deck, though sadly Squadron Commander E.H. Dunning lost his life during pioneer landing attempts in August 1917. Later, many battleships and cruisers were fitted with turret platforms from which to operate small landplanes.

In the Eastern Mediterranean, seaplanes were operated throughout much of the war, often embarking on small seaplane carriers and other ships from their bases at Port Said and later Alexandria. Aircraft operations in the Aegean and Adriatic theatres were expanded considerably in the final year of war. At Mudros, the former 2 Wing broke up to form 62 and 63 Wings at the same base on the formation of the Royal Air Force, whilst 6 Wing, which had formed at Otranto in March 1917, became 66 and 67 Wings, regular supplies of more modern aircraft now being received by all of these.

Despite the merger, there remained a distinct naval element in the new service. Naval uniforms were still much in evidence, and most of the controlling organisation continued much as it had been for quite some time. Weekly disposition lists of "naval" units and aircraft, daily summaries of operations and other regular reports and listings continued to be issued separately to at least the beginning of 1919. The only gap of any size in surviving documentation relates to the former naval training organisation after the merger, though this may be due to the criteria adopted for preservation in the post-war years, as there is, regrettably, a similar paucity of records relating to contemporary R.F.C. and non-naval R.A.F. training units.

Another area in which "naval" aircraft were engaged was Russia, where British forces operated from 1918 in support of the White Russians against the Bolsheviks. After the Armistice on 11 November 1918, units from 66 and 67 Wings operated in the Caspian and Black Sea areas, and seaplane carriers ferried out aircraft to both the Baltic and Northern Russia. Numerous operations were carried out before all British forces were withdrawn in the early part of 1920.

Even that was not really the end of the story, as a few small "naval" units still existed, and in 1923 these formed the nucleus of what was to become the Fleet Air Arm, a worthy successor to the pioneering Royal Naval Air Service.

## ROYAL NAVY AVIATION FIRSTS

2.5.12  First recorded flight from a moving ship (HMS *Hibernia* steaming at 10½ knots): Lt CR Samson, in a Short S.38 biplane.

28.7.14  First successful torpedo drop: Sqdn Cdr AM Longmore, in a Short 81 Type carrying a 14-in torpedo.

22.9.14  First British air raid on Germany (on the Düsseldorf airship sheds): aircraft of 3 Sqdn, based at Antwerp.

8.10.14  First destruction of a Zeppelin by an aircraft (the newly delivered Z9 in the Düsseldorf airship sheds): Flt Lt RLG Marix of 3 Sqdn.

21.11.14  First long-range strategic bombing raid (on the Friedrichshafen airship sheds on the shores of Lake Constance): three Avro 504s based in eastern France at Belfort near the German-Swiss border.

21.12.14  First night bombing raid (on Ostende): Wing Cdr CR Samson in a Maurice Farman.

25.12.14  First attempt to exert sea power upon land by means of the air (an attack on Cuxhaven on the north German coast): Short seaplanes from the seaplane carriers *Empress*, *Engadine* and *Riviera*.

7.6.15  First victory over a Zeppelin in the air (*LZ37*, shot down near Bruges): Morane-Saulnier monoplane flown by Flt Sub-Lt R Warneford, who was subsequently awarded the Victoria Cross.

12.8.15  First occasion a ship torpedoed from the air (a 5,000-ton Turkish supply vessel): a Short 184 piloted by Flt Cdr CHK Edmonds during the Dardanelles campaign.

6.6.17  First landplane torpedo-carrier completed: the Sopwith Cuckoo.

28.6.17  First successful flight from a turret platform: by Flt Cdr FJ Rutland in a Sopwith Pup from HMS *Yarmouth*.

2.8.18  First carrier deck landing: Sqdn Cdr EH Dunning on HMS Furious.

15.3.18  First carrier with lifts re-enters service: HMS *Furious*.

14.9.18  First flush deck carrier enters service: *HMS Argus*.

# FOREWORD

During the compilation of this book the authors learned a considerable amount about the structure, equipment, operations and other aspects of the Royal Naval Air Service. The achievements of that service have largely tended not to gain the appreciation they deserve. It is hoped our efforts will go some way towards redressing the balance, and provide a basis from which other researchers can investigate particular aspects.

The format of the book gradually evolved as increasing amounts of contemporary documentation came to light. The serial lists follow the same general lines as "Royal Air Force Aircraft J1 - J9999 and WW1 Survivors", the primary author's co-authored work on RAF aircraft of the 1920s. The wealth of available material, however, made it possible for most of the individual histories to be much more detailed than in any previous work in this Air-Britain series. Some explanation follows of the general format and the main sources used.

## DATES

Wherever possible, precise dates are given. Where a date is without any form of qualification, it will be the actual date of the event in question - such as initial delivery; movement between units, stations or ships; operations; deletion or struck off charge; a particular incident.

In the absence of a precise date, especially in relation to movements, the first known date with that particular unit is prefixed "by" (e.g. "by 28.7.16"), and the last known date is prefixed "@" (e.g. "@28.7.16"). In some instances it is possible to be more precise than that, even where the exact date is unknown. This is especially the case, for instance, where the source is a series of regular returns, and the change could only have taken place within a few days either way. In such cases the date may be marked either "FM" (first mention) or "LM" (last mention); very often these dates have turned out to be the actual date of a movement or incident when further information has been found in contemporary records.

Alternatively, the date of a movement or event may be prefixed "W/E" (e.g. W/E 29.7.18), indicating that the change took place in the week ending the date given, but the precise date has not been traced. In practice, particularly after the formation of the RAF, it has been found that the event may have actually been up to 10 or 11 days earlier, generally because a composite or summarising return was based on individual returns compiled a few days earlier (see under "Sources").

In the case of shipborne aircraft, especially towards the end of the war, there were often several moves within a week, and as far as possible these have been listed in the correct sequence, even though some or all of the actual dates may be unknown. However, in some instances, the precise date of one of those moves may have been established, making it appear in the lists as if it is shown out of sequence when this is not really so.

Where a date is incomplete, this is because no surviving record has been found which can pin-point the actual date. It will therefore be expressed as, for instance, "6.18" or occasionally just ".18". If this is known to be the actual month of the incident or change it will be shown a such, e.g. "to Dundee 6.18" or "Deleted 7.15".

A word of caution on dates. Daily returns were generally made up in the early evening, very often effectively at 18.00 hrs, though at least one home station is known to have used 12.00 noon as the cut-off point. In many instances this is not made clear on individual returns, so the earliest events listed may actually have occurred late the previous day, but not noted as such. Another problem is that an aircraft which was still out on patrol, for instance, at the time of the return, would be marked as 'not yet returned'. In most such cases the aircraft simply returned later the same day, or in some instances the following day if had landed away from the aerodrome for some reason, such as the onset of dusk or engine trouble. Subsequent returns do not always make it clear when this has been the case, although we have tried to account for all such instances.

## TIMES

If time is considered important, this is given, if known, usually immediately before the relevant date, the 24-hour clock system being used. Times can be useful in relation to aerial combats since, taken in conjunction with locations, they may help to identify the enemy pilot(s) involved from German records. They have also been found useful in discounting published information, such as where the supposed enemy victim or victor was actually involved in an incident at a quite different time on the same date.

Care had to be exercised over times quoted in official documents. These sometimes gave only the time of departure, with no indication of actual combat times. Where actual combat times were recorded, these are given, but they were often very approximate, and may only relate to the commencement of the fight, which could have lasted some time, especially if it was part of a general combat. Where an aircraft is seen to crash, the time is more likely to be accurate, though not always so if noted by someone who was busy with his own combat.

## LOCATIONS

Locations are given where known. The location of an accident is given where it occurred away from the base, but to save space the aerodrome name is not given in the many instances, especially at training establishments, where it occurred on or around the aerodrome. In the case of a squadron or other titled unit, the base at the time of the accident can be found from the lists of units.

With regard to combats or losses, it should be borne in mind that in many cases the location can only be approximate. A combat, particularly a general one involving numbers of aircraft on both sides, could drift some distance. It is therefore quite possible for two reports to give different locations for the same combat. Similarly an aircraft may be seen to go down, or may have been last seen, in one location, but to have crashed some distance away. Place names were often mis-spelt, but the majority of such errors have been identified. Where an aircraft crashed in enemy territory, any location quoted in surviving German records is likely to be the more accurate.

Maps are provided indicating the location of many of the place names associated with successes and losses, the spelling being that used on current maps, which in some instances will differ from contemporary spelling.

Nautical locations, such as those for attacks on U-boats, are expressed as four digits, of which the first two represent degrees and the second two represent minutes. For example a location 05° 27' North (or 5° 27' North) 18° 22' West would be expressed as 0527N 1822W.

## NAMES AND RANKS

Names are given wherever possible in relation to specific activities or incidents, though many documents do not record these. Where relevant names are recorded, it is quite common for these to consist only of rank and surname, especially in the case of other ranks, and often the names are wrongly spelt or initials given incorrectly.

Every effort has been made to overcome such shortcomings from contemporary records. In the case of officers, the most useful sources have been Navy Lists, of which a comprehensive set is available on open shelves in the Reference Room of the Public Record Office at Kew, and also the weekly lists of officers with each RNAS station or unit, available there in files AIR.1/2108/207/49/1 to AIR.1/2111/207/49/9. Other useful documents in this respect are squadron Daily Routine Orders, field returns and record books. Unfortunately contemporary Air Force Lists, of which a number are held by the RAF Museum, give no details as to an officer's station or unit. Initials of ratings or other ranks are much more difficult to identify, there being usually no equivalent documentation, especially in relation to units other than squadrons.

With regard to naval officers prior to 1.4.18, these were generally RN, though some were RNR or RNVR, but only a limited attempt has been made to distinguish these. A few Marine officers are shown as RMLI (Royal Marine Light Infantry). More precise details of the relevant service may be found in contemporary Navy Lists. From 1.4.18 the majority of these officers were given corresponding Army ranks as previously used by the Royal Flying Corps. There was some reluctance to adopt the new ranks, and naval uniforms were in evidence for many months after the change, so it is not uncommon to see officers referred to by the old rankings for some months afterwards. The new RAF rankings were not adopted until some time after the war.

Where an aircraft involved in an incident carried two or more aircrew, the pilot's name is always given first. The second name will be that of the observer, followed by the names of any other crew, where relevant.

## CASUALTIES

All known casualties are listed against the relevant or likely serial. Separate lists gives casualties, mainly fatalities, where no serial has been traced. Where a crew comprises both casualties and uninjured personnel, all are listed, as far as records allow.

It will usually be apparent from the entry whether the casualty is due to combat or an accident. In the case of a non-fatal casualty, this is referred to as "injured" in the case of an accident, and "wounded" if in combat. Where the man concerned died of his injuries, the actual date of death is quoted if this is later than the incident concerned.

Contemporary records often failed to record the ultimate fate of aircrew who were posted as missing. As far as possible the authors have ascertained from later records whether each individual was killed, taken prisoner or interned in Holland. Where taken prisoner or interned, it is noted if the person concerned was known to have been wounded or injured.

## AIRCRAFT FATES

Where relevant records have been traced, the fate of each individual aircraft has been listed, and also the cause, if known. Such information has been derived from varied sources with consequent variation in the amount of detail. The normal RNAS procedure was for a

Board of Survey to visit each station at intervals to inspect any relevant paperwork and the aircraft concerned, or its wreckage, and make recommendations to the Air Department of the Admiralty. A recommendation for deletion would generally be accepted at a later date, though there are instances where it was not accepted and the aircraft was subsequently rebuilt. Very occasionally an aircraft would be rebuilt even where deletion had been authorised.

It seems likely that as the war progressed the system was streamlined, and deletions often authorised on the basis of local recommendations. In the case of aircraft lost in battle, deletions were made in the field, though these had to be ratified by higher authority at home. Most Admiralty documentation relating to deletions has failed to survive, but a number of such lists can be found in file AIR.1/301/15/226/151 Part II [Nos.60 to 70, covering the period September to December 1917], and file AIR.1/308/15/226/186 [Nos.69 to 92 covering December 1917 to May 1918], though with gaps. It is interesting to note from these that a Board of Survey was required even where an aircraft had been lost in action. As one might expect, paperwork relating to surveys of aircraft in the Mediterranean or Aegean generally took some time to arrive and deletion be authorised.

Where no such relevant lists survive, we have had to rely on such other documentation as could be found. Some U.K. stations, for instance, were very good at showing deletion on the date they received the necessary authorisation. Others simply stopped listing the aircraft concerned, and these deletions could only be worked out by comparing returns from day to day, or later from week to week.

The phraseology relating to crashed aircraft was somewhat unsophisticated, with none of the designated categories and sub-categories of later years. Terms such as "wrecked", "smashed", "completely wrecked", "totally wrecked" and "struck off strength" though repeated in these tables, were no real indication of whether an aircraft was repairable or a write-off. With the formation of the RAF, the term "deleted" gradually gave way to "struck off charge" (usually abbreviated to "SOC") or "written off charge" ("WOC"), but lesser damage remained relatively vague until the introduction of official categories in the 1920s, these becoming more refined during World War II.

During 1918, numerous RAF aircraft, including those belonging to the naval element, were completely rebuilt at depots, and given fresh serial numbers, even where, in some instances, such rebuilding was completed within only a few days. A hiatus occurred, however, when batch F5801 to F6300 was exhausted, as numbers continued to be allocated as far as F6513 before the error came to light. The offending aircraft were then retrospectively renumbered in the H6843 to H7293 range, though a few had already been in service using their incorrect numbers.

## DEPOTS

In support of the RNAS units in the Dunkerque area, an Aeroplane Depot was set up at St.Pol to receive aircraft from England and to provide storage and repair facilities for RNAS aircraft in that area, this being generally referred to as AD Dunkerque. However, an increasing number of aircraft were attached to the RFC, and their aircraft were supported instead by corresponding RFC Aircraft Depots. By late 1917 the naval depot was referred to as the Naval Aeroplane Park (NAP) until late in March 1918 when it was absorbed into a new No.4

Aeroplane Supply Depot sent out from England and established at Guines, a satellite being set up at Audembert (otherwise No.69 Aerodrome).

## SOURCES
The majority of the information contained in this book originated in records deposited in the Public Record Office at Kew, nearly 3,000 of which have been examined. Most useful was the AIR.1 category, of which Daily Reports of activities of naval squadrons serving in France, numbered between AIR.1/40/15/9/7 (for 1 Squadron) and AIR.1/48/15/9/26 (for 16 Squadron), were found to be particularly helpful.

For home stations and home-based ships, the series of Daily Reports numbered mainly AIR.1/186/15/226/3 to AIR.1/233/15/226/55 and AIR.1/310/15/226/196 to AIR.1/328/15/226/227 proved equally useful. The standard of compilation varied, however, the reports from some stations giving very detailed information, whilst others were very sketchy. There was provision on the form, for instance, for listing aircraft arriving or departing, but some stations failed to use this properly, and in many cases it has only been possible to determine such dates by comparing consecutive Daily Reports.

Regrettably, these Daily Reports for home stations mostly gave way to Weekly Reports from September 1917, these being numbered AIR.1/333/15/226/238 to AIR.1/336/15/226/245. Again, the standard of compilation varied, far too many stations ignoring the requirement to record all changes, with dates. Accidents and deletions were now seldom recorded, and hardly any names. There are no such surviving returns after May 1918.

These returns were, however, summarised in printed Weekly Disposition Lists, a near complete run of which for the period January 1918 to January 1919 can be found in file AIR.1/670/17/124, earlier returns in this series having failed to survive. Up until 31 March 1918 they covered all Royal Naval Air Service units, but from 1 April 1918 they related only to naval elements of the Royal Air Force. From that date training units for land-based aircraft were no longer listed, and naval squadrons on the Western Front were only listed until 25 May 1918 and even then were increasingly based on out-of-date information. It should be noted also that these lists only contained information extracted from the most recent returns then available to the compilers, which could be out of date by that time. This is especially so with listings for units in the Mediterranean and Aegean theatres, which often reflected returns which were several weeks old, seemingly updated with available information.

Other sources of information researched at the PRO included records in the ADM and MUN series, these relating to the Admiralty and Ministry of Munitions respectively. Particularly useful were the numerous Ships Logs in the ADM.53 series, though it should be borne in mind that these were basically concerned with the movements and activities of the ship, and therefore vary in the amount of detail devoted to aircraft activities, though serial numbers were sometimes quoted.

In addition, much useful information has been obtained from the Royal Air Force Museum, Fleet Air Arm Museum, National Maritime Museum, Imperial War Museum and the Liddle Collection at the University of Leeds, who have all been most helpful. Each has numbers of relevant flying log books, and the RAF Museum also has many RFC and RAF casualty records. The RAF Museum have in addition permitted access to the comprehensive collection of W.W.1 records recently donated by the family of the late Paul Chamberlain. The Air Historical Branch (Ministry of Defence) has also been very helpful.

Private individuals who have kindly made records and photographs available, or otherwise helped, include Chris Ashworth, Rod Ashton, Rick Barker, Chaz Bowyer, Robin Brown, Gordon Bruce, Jack Bruce, Mick Burrow, Frank Cheesman, H.S.Clarke, Ernie Cromie, Major John Cross, Dick Cronin, Peter Dalloso, Mick Davis, Mike Goodall, Peter Green, Jim Halley, Harm Hazewinkel, Ian Huntley, Philip Jarrett, Kevin Kelly, Stuart Leslie, Len Lovell, Tim Mason, Bill Morgan, Graham Mottram, Mike O'Connor, Jim Oughton, Ron Pankhurst, Bruce Robertson, Mike Schoeman, Ken Smy, Robert H. Sturtevant, Ray Vann, Jerry Vernon, Colin Waugh and Peter Wright. The cover design has kindly been drawn by Dugald Cameron, and Mick Davis has been good enough to contribute a large number of detailed maps. The authors are especially grateful to Frank Cheesman for his considerable help in checking our manuscript.

## ANOMALIES
Many anomalies have come to light during our researches, especially in relation to serial numbers, which were particularly prone to error. A major difficulty was the tendency of some units (notably 208 Sqdn) to omit serial prefixes. This was also frequently to be found in individual flying log books. Another common difficulty arises with transposed digits, either in typing or in entering a serial number from memory, and on occasion they were simply misread. Every effort has been made to eliminate these and other types of error, but in a relatively small number of instances this has not proved possible. In such cases both alternatives have been entered in the lists.

A particular source of confusion is to be found in Combat Reports, a relatively high proportion of which have been found to contain typing and compilation errors, presumably due to the adverse conditions in which clerks had to work. If a pilot flew more than one sortie, especially if in different aircraft, the clerk would often extract the wrong serial from the Daily Report when subsequently compiling the individual Combat Report. In the case of a Combat Report for a shared victory, the pilots names were quite often typed in a different sequence from those of the aircraft serials as shown in the relevant Daily Report. Times were also occasionally prone to typing error, and did not always distinguish between a.m. and p.m., leading, for example, to some researchers quoting times which would have been most unlikely, being during the hours of darkness.

Such numerous errors have regrettably led to some confusion in the past, but we have done our best to put the record straight in as many cases as possible.

Many Combat Reports have either failed to survive, or were not available to us. The complete set of No.208 Squadron reports, for instance, is shown in the AIR.1 index as having been wanting when that series was transferred to the original Air Historical Records. More recently a very large number of aviation documents, including many World War I Combat Reports, were stolen from the Public Record Office, being the subject of a subsequent prosecution and conviction; quite a number of these had not been recovered at the time of writing.

To some extent it has been possible to reconstruct the

essential details of such missing Combat Reports from other records. Often no serial is quoted, but in the majority of such cases it has been possible to trace or deduce this from squadron Daily Reports. In doing this, we have found sometimes that compilation from miscellaneous sources appears to have resulted in dubious or duplicated references to victories oon the same or adjacent days. In such cases we have endeavoured to eliminate the extraneous references from our own lists.

Generally speaking, we have found Daily Reports to be more accurate than Combat Reports in respect of serials and times, this being generally borne out when it has proved possible to study a pilot's own flying log book. The latter, incidentally, will also sometimes show victory claims not readily available in surviving official material, and on occasion show no claim on days when the pilot concerned has been quoted as having had a victory.

We have come across quite a number of instances where pilots are supposed to have had victories, but where the squadron record for the day in question does not support this. Sometimes there was no flying at all, usually due to weather conditions, and in other cases the day is clearly marked as having been uneventful. In either such circumstances we have felt justified in discounting supposed claims, unless we have been able to establish that the date was incorrect.

We have done our best to resolve such problems, but no doubt there are other surviving records not available to us which would have thrown up similar anomalies if we had been able to inspect them.

It is not always apparent from surviving Combat Reports whether a claim has been allowed, many being officially recorded as indecisive on investigation by higher authority. Where squadron diaries or similar records are available we have regarded these as being most likely to be correct, and consequently, where such a record does exist, we have excluded from our own lists any claim not supported by such records. Where there is no such record we have had to use our own judgment based on such evidence as is available. We have also noted a number of instances where a Combat Report would lead one to believe that a shared victory was involved, but this was not necessarily supported by the squadron record, which might credit it to only one or sometime two of the pilots, and here we have followed the squadron's apparent intentions as regards credit and made no reference to the other pilots involved in the engagement.

We have not usually included the numerous "driven down" claims, as being indecisive, though we have made small number of exceptions to this rule where we feel it might be helpful.

It follows from the foregoing that our own findings will quite often differ from those of other researchers. Despite all our efforts, however, we are well aware that we have not always discovered the whole truth. Readers must form their own views as whether our approach is a sensible one. Interpretation of surviving papers is an inexact science, made more difficult by the loss of relevant records over the years, and compounded by the recent thefts.

## GERMAN VICTORS AND VICTIMS

Wherever possible the names, ranks and units of German victors and victims are given. These are based mainly on German sources, including Den Toten zur Ehrung (Ehrentafel der gefallen Flieger), a list of German casualties produced shortly after the First World War by Major Wilhelm Haehnelt, and extracts from official German victory claims.

Any conclusions we have drawn by comparisons between these German lists and contemporary British records are our own. In a small number of cases we tend to disagree with previously published identities of such victims or victors, since the place and/or times in respective records appear to us not to fit each other. Our knowledge of German aspects is, however, somewhat limited, and we are therefore open to correction.

German aircraft which fell on the British side of the lines were given G-numbers for record purposes. Most such aircraft were wrecks, but a few were reasonably intact and the G-number was painted on the fuselage of these. The original series of numbers, started in early in 1917, extended from G.1 to G.167, but later HQ RAF and the Brigades each had its own series (e.g. G/5Bde/8). All such numbers are given where known or deduced.

## CIVILIAN PILOTS

Many deliveries and official acceptance tests were carried out by civilian pilots, some in respect of the firm by which they were employed and others for a number of firms. Such pilots in respect of naval aircraft included A.E.Barrs, Gordon Bell, Rowland Ding, E.C.Gordon England, Harry Hawker, A.Dukinfield Jones, Ronald Kemp, Victor Mahl, Marcus Manton, F.Warren Merriam, J.Lankester Parker, Sidney Pickles, Clifford Prodger, F.P.Raynham and Sydney Sippe. Some of these later received commissions.

## UNITS

The Royal Flying Corps (Military Wing), following Army practice, numbered its units from the very early days, the original balloon and airship squadron numbers being adopted for use in a straightforward aeroplane squadron numbering system, from No.1 onwards, this being continued to the present day by the Royal Air Force. Similarly, training units were numbered 1 onwards, these being mostly known at first as Reserve Aeroplane Squadrons, later abbreviated to Reserve Squadrons, then changed to Training Squadrons and finally grouped as Training Depot Stations.

The Royal Navy, however, being ship and shore based, had no similar tradition, and its aeroplanes were simply attached to Royal Naval Air Stations, the first of which was at Eastchurch, this soon becoming known as the Eastchurch Naval Flying School. There was never any numbering system for RN Air Stations up until the time of their absorption into the Royal Air Force on 1 April 1918, though many stations or sub-units were styled according their function, such titles including War Flight, War School, Flying School, Observers School Flight, Repair Depot and the like.

This rather vague system has led to some confusion in identification of such units, and was certainly impractical for operational units sent overseas to join the naval element of the British Expeditionary Force. The first such unit, set up at Eastchurch just before the outbreak of war, was known as the Eastchurch (Mobile) Squadron, but this title soon lapsed, and instead numbered squadrons were set up, starting at No.1 in the same fashion as the Military Wing. As operations expanded, these were grouped into naval Wings, also numbered from 1 onwards.

With the absorption into the Royal Air Force, it was not practicable to have duplicated unit numbers, so from

1 April 1918 all the naval squadrons had 200 added to their numbers, whilst the naval wings had 60 added to their numbers. Training stations were absorbed into the RFC system of Training Depot Stations, each station being allocated one or more numbers from 200 onwards, some of these being renumbered in the 50 series in July 1918, and the remainder restyled to more precisely reflect the particular role they had acquired.

## ATTACKS ON U-BOATS
During the course of World War I an increasing number of attacks were made by coastal aircraft on German U-boats. Brief details of all such attacks have been included in the lists, to the extent that surviving records allow, but it is apparent that many of the claims made at the time were somewhat optimistic.

## HOME DEFENCE
Brief details are given of all known United Kingdom-based flights against German attacks by Zeppelins or aeroplanes, including seaplanes. Comparatively few of these achieved any worthwhile result, but readers wishing to learn more on this aspect of naval activities are commended to read the comprehensive account given in *'The Air Defence of Great Britain 1914 - 1918'* (see Bibliography)

## ADMIRALTY TYPE NUMBERS
In the absence, in most cases, of a standard system of type names, the Admiralty adopted a practice of referring to production aircraft by type numbers. Such numbers could be based on the prototype, as for instance Admiralty 179 Type, otherwise the Avro 504, or on an early production machine, an example of the latter being Admiralty 9901 Type, more generally known as the Sopwith Scout (later the Pup). The system lapsed on the formation of the R.A.F.

## SERIAL NUMBERS
Identification numbering of naval aircraft initially went through several stages. The first four aircraft, all Shorts, were given naval numbers 1 to 4 in November 1911. Three month later the system was expanded and divided into three categories, B1 onwards for biplanes, M1 onwards for monoplanes and H1 onwards for hydro-aeroplanes (later changed to seaplanes). The B-series was short lived, as it clashed with a similar Army numbering system, so in April 1912 it was changed to T1 onwards, possibly standing for "twin planes", though that is pure conjecture in the absence of any known official documentation.

As an increasing number of aircraft came into service with both the Naval and Military Wings, it was realised that a more simple system was required. This was promulgated on 1 August 1912, and consisted of blocks of numbers allocated to each service. The Naval Wing initially had block 1 to 200 and, as the advent of war produced an ever increasing intake of aircraft, this was followed by blocks 801 to 1600, 3001 to 4000 and 8000 to 10000, the intervening blocks being taken up by the Military Wing.

By 1916 this series was becoming exhausted, and unwieldy to operate, so the system was divided, Military Wing aircraft being then numbered A1 to A9999, B1 to B9999 and so on. Naval needs being less, it was considered that only the series N1 to N9999 was needed, though even this was nearing exhaustion by the time of the Armistice. Unlike the military series, however, the N-series was sub-divided into blocks for different categories of aircraft, as shown in the lists.

From the earliest days, aircraft originally intended for the Military Wing were transferred to the Naval Wing (or RNAS), or vice versa, as requirements or priorities changed. At first such aircraft tended to be re-serialled to conform with the numbering system of their new service, but after a while this practice came to be regarded as cumbersome and unnecessary, especially when large numbers of machines were involved. Thus complete batches of RFC-serialled Camels, for instance, would enter service with the RNAS bearing their RFC serials. On the other hand, there are examples of late batches of aircraft such as Cuckoos being renumbered before delivery to conform with the standard system. Also, there was sometimes a switch between categories, some flying boats being initially allocated serials in the N1000 series, then renumbered to fit into the N4000 series, occasionally after they had already been painted up.

In addition to these official categories, a number of aircraft, mostly of French origin, went into service with constructor's numbers and the like as their only identification. It is probable that most, if not all, of these were actually allocated RNAS serial numbers, though never painted on. Such aircraft are listed separately.

It should be borne in mind that recording numbers correctly, other than in accounting documents, was not likely to have much priority in the heat of battle. As a consequence Western Front squadron reports contain many incorrect serials. We believe, however, that we have established virtually all the correct serials of aircraft flown by each squadron, and in the vast majority of cases this has enabled us to deduce the correct serial where an error has occurred.

## SHIPBORNE AIRCRAFT
A variety of aircraft, both landplanes and seaplanes, were carried on warships and merchant vessels during the period covered by this book. Space considerations preclude detailed listing of such vessels, but readers wishing to know more of this aspects of RNAS and RAF operations are recommended to read the companion Air-Britain publication, *'Royal Navy Shipboard Aircraft Developments 1912-1931'* by Dick Cronin, which covers the subject comprehensively.

## CONSTRUCTOR'S NUMBERS
Several large aircraft manufacturers allotted their own sequence numbers to individual aircraft and these are given where known. French-built aircraft usually carried these on the tail, and it was not uncommon for such aircraft to be referred to by these constructor's numbers, rather than the official serial number, particularly if the latter had not been painted on the machine.

During research into this aspect, it became apparent that previously published information regarding Short's constructor's numbers was unreliable. We were very fortunate, therefore, shortly before our book went to the printers, in having the benefit of Gordon Bruce's own substantial researches into this subject. Gordon has spent many years at Shorts, the Public Record Office and elsewhere working out a definitive list, with a view to eventual publication. Notwithstanding his intentions, he readily agreed to allow us to have the benefit of this information for incorporation in our own work. We are most grateful to him for his generosity.

## BIBLIOGRAPHY

Numerous books and other publications were consulted during the compilation of this work. The following were particularly useful:

Above the Trenches. Christopher Shores, Norman Franks & Russell Guest (Grub Street)

Aeroplanes of the Royal Flying Corps, The (Military Wing). J.M.Bruce. (Putnam)

Aircraft Carriers of the World. Roger Chesneau. (Arms & Armour Press)

Aircraft of the Royal Air Force since 1918. (Putnam)

Air Defence of Great Britain 1914 - 1918, The. Christopher Cole & E.F.Cheesman. (Putnam)

Air Force List, April 1918. (Brian Strudwick reprint)

Air Power and the Royal Navy 1914 - 1945. Geoffrey Till. (Jane's)

Britain's First Warplanes. J.M.Bruce. (Arms & Armour Press)

British Aeroplanes 1914 - 1918. J.M.Bruce (Putnam)

British Military Aircraft Serials 1878 - 1987. Bruce Robertson (Midland Counties Publications)

British Naval Aircraft since 1912. Owen Thetford. (Putnam)

British Naval Aviation. Ray Sturtivant. (Arms & Armour Press)

British Warships 1914 - 1919. Dittmar Colledge. (Ian Allan)

Cross & Cockade International Journals (various).

Den Toten zur Ehrung (Ehrentafel de gefallen Flieger). Major Wilhelm Haehnelt.

Fairey Aircraft since 1915. H.A.Taylor. (Putnam)

Fortnightly Summaries of No.5 Group, Dover Patrol, April 1918 to November 1918.

German Aircraft of the First World War. Peter Gray & Owen Thetford. (Putnam)

German Victory Claims, January 1917 to August 1918.

History of the RAF and USNAS in Ireland 1913 - 1923 Karl E.Hayes.

Nachrichtenblatt der Luftstreiträste.

Officers Died in the Great War 1914 - 1919. (J.B.Hayward & Son reprint)

Over the Front magazine (various).

R.A.F. Squadrons. Wing Cdr C.G.Jefford. (Airlife)

Royal Air Force Aircraft J1-J9999 and WW1 Survivors. Dennis Thompson & Ray Sturtivant. (Air-Britain).

Royal Naval Air Service Communiques, January 1917 to March 1918.

Royal Navy Shipboard Aircraft Developments 1912 - 1931. Dick Cronin. (Air-Britain)

Shorts Aircraft since 1900. C.H.Barnes. (Putnam)

Sopwith Camel - King of Combat. Chaz Bowyer. (Aston)

Squadrons of the Royal Air Force & Commonwealth 1918 - 1988, The. James J.Halley (Air-Britain).

Supermarine Aircraft since 1914. C.F.Andrews & E.B.Morgan. (Putnam)

War in the Air, The, 6 Vols. Walter Raleigh & H.A.Jones. (Oxford University Press)

*Naval seaplanes at Calshot for the Royal Review of July 1914. Aircraft visible in the photograph include Short Type Nos.74, 76 and 77, and Sopwith Bat-Boat No.118 (FAA Museum)*

# GLOSSARY OF TERMS AND ABBREVIATIONS

| | |
|---|---|
| A | Acting |
| AA | Anti Aircraft |
| AAM | Acting Air Mechanic |
| AAP | Aeroplane Acceptance Park |
| A/B | Able seaman |
| AC | Aircraftman |
| A/c | Aircraft |
| AD | Aeroplane Depot/ Acceptance Depot/ Air Department (Admiralty) |
| ADD | Aeroplane Depot Dunkerque (at St.Pol) |
| Adv | Advanced |
| AEG | Allgemeine Elektrizitäts Gesselschaft |
| AES | Aeroplane Experimental Station |
| A/F/Cdr | Acting Flight Commander |
| A/G | Air Gunner |
| AG&FS | Aerial Gunnery and Fighting School |
| AGL | Acting Gunlayer |
| AGP | Anti-Gotha patrol |
| AI | Air Issues (otherwise Issues Section) |
| Airco | Aircraft Manufacturing Co Ltd |
| AM | Air Mechanic |
| AMC | Armed Merchant Cruiser |
| AMF | Aviation Militaire Française |
| AP | Aeroplane Park/ Air Pilotage |
| ARD | Aeroplane Repair Depot |
| AR&ED | Aeroplane Repair and Engine Depot [at Pizzone] |
| Arr | Arrived |
| ARS | Aeroplane Repair Section |
| A.S. | Armament Supplies (contracts) |
| A/S | Anti-submarine |
| ASD | Aeroplane Supply Depot |
| ASIPOP | Anti-Submarine Inshore Patrol Observers School |
| Assd | Assembled |
| Asst Payr | Assistant Paymaster |
| ASU | Aeroplane Storage Unit |
| AZP | Anti-Zeppelin Patrol [enemy intruder identified as Zeppelin] |
| Bde | Brigade |
| BO | Burnt out |
| Bois | Wood (French) |
| BR | British Requisition/Beyond repair |
| BST | Boat Seaplane Training |
| BU | Broken up/broke up |
| C | German two-seat aeroplane |
| CAAD | Coastal Area Aircraft Depot |
| CAF | Canadian Air Force |
| Capt | Captain |
| Cdr | Commander |
| Cdt | Cadet |
| CFS | Central Flying School (Upavon) |
| COL | Crashed on landing |
| Comms | Communications |
| Convtd | Converted |
| C.O.W. | Coventry Ordnance Works |
| C.P. | Contract & Purchase Branch (contracts) |
| CPO | Chief Petty Officer |
| Cpl | Corporal |
| CSD | Central Supply Depot |
| C/Sgt | Colour Sergeant |
| CTD | Committee for Technical Development? |
| CW | Completely wrecked |
| D | German single-seat scout |
| DBR | Damaged beyond repair |
| DC | Dual control |
| DD | Driven down (not necessarily crashed) |
| Deld | Delivered |
| Dest | Destroyed |
| Devt | Development |
| DFC | Distinguished Flying Cross |
| DFM | Distinguished Flyng Medal |
| DFW | Deutsche Flugzeug-Werke |
| DL | Deck landing |
| DLG | Day Landing Ground |
| DoI | Died of Injuries |
| DoW | Died of Wounds |
| DR | Daily Report |
| DRO | Daily Routine Orders |

| | |
|---|---|
| DSC | Distinguished Service Cross |
| DSM | Distinguished Service Medal |
| DSO | Distinguished Service Order |
| EAD | Experimental Armament Department |
| EAFF | East Africa Field Force |
| EC&AD | Experimental Constructive & Armament Department |
| ECD | Experimental Constructive Department |
| ECNFS | Eastchurch Naval Flying School |
| EF | Engine failure |
| EI&ESS | East Indies and Egypt Seaplane Squadron |
| Elec | Electrician |
| Eng Lt | Engineer Lieutenant |
| Ens | Ensign (US Navy) |
| ERA | Engine Room Artificer |
| Exptl | Experimental |
| FAA | Fleet Air Arm |
| FB | Flying boat |
| F/Cdr | Flight Commander |
| F/Cdt | Flight Cadet |
| FF | First flew |
| FIS | Flying Instructors School |
| FL | Force landed |
| F/L | Flight Lieutenant |
| Fl.Abt | Flieger Abteilung (German reconnaissance unit) [or FLA] |
| Fl.Abt(A) | FliegerAbteilung (German artillery spotting unit)[or Fla(A) ] |
| Flgm | Flugmaat (German Naval Flying Mate) |
| FlgObm | FlugObermaat (German Naval Flying 1st Mate) |
| Flt | Flight |
| F/Sgt | Flight Sergeant |
| FM | First mention |
| F/O | Flight Sergeant |
| FS | Fighting School/Flying School |
| FSL | Flight Sub-Lieutenant |
| ft | Foot/feet |
| FTR | Failed to return |
| Fw | Feldwebel (German sergeant) |
| FwLt | FeldwebelLeutnant (German Master Sergeant) |
| FW&T | Fair wear and tear |
| G | German multi-engined aircraft |
| Gen | General |
| GHQ | General Headquarters |
| GI | Ground instructional (airframe) |
| G/L | Gunlayer |
| Gnr | Gunner |
| Govt | Government |
| Grp | Group |
| GRW | Gregory-Riley-White (beaching gear) |
| GS | Gunnery School |
| GW | Grahame-White |
| HA | Hostile aircraft |
| HACP | Hostile Aircraft Patrol [enemy intruder of unknown type] |
| HAPP | Hostile Aeroplane Patrol [enemy intruder identified as aeroplane] |
| Haupt | Hauptmann (German Captain) |
| HD | Home defence |
| HF | Henry Farman |
| HLI | Highland Light Infantry |
| HMA | His Majesty's Airship |
| HMAS | His Majesty's Australian Ship |
| HMFA | His Majesty's Fleet Auxiliary |
| HMS | His Majesty's Ship |
| HMT | His Majesty's Trawler |
| HMY | His Majesty's Yacht |
| HP | Handley Page |
| hp | Horsepower |
| HQ | Headquarters |
| Hrs | Hours |
| HSMP | Hostile Submarine Patrol [reported U-boat] |
| HSPP | Hostile Seaplane Patrol [enemy intruder identified as seaplane] |
| IAF | Independent Air Force |
| IS | Issues Section (otherwise Air Issues) |

| | |
|---|---|
| IWM | Imperial War Museum |
| Jasta | Jagdstaffel (German scout unit) |
| KB | Kite balloon |
| LAM | Leading Air Mechanic |
| L/Artificer | Leading Artificer |
| lb | Pound weight |
| L/Col | Lieutenant Colonel |
| LFG | Luftfahrzeug Gesellschaft |
| LM | Leading Mechanic/Last mention |
| L-S | Long-stroke |
| Lt | Lieutenant |
| 2/Lt | Second Lieutenant |
| L/Tel | Leading Telegraphist |
| Ltn | Leutnant (German 2nd Lieutenant) |
| LtzS | Leutnant zur See (German Naval Lieutenant) |
| L/Tel | Leading Telegraphist |
| LV | Light vessel |
| LVG | Luft-Verkehrs Gesellschaft |
| MAD | Marine Aeroplane Depot |
| MAEE | Marine Aircraft Experimental Establishment |
| MAES | Marine Aircraft Experimental Section |
| MB | Motor boat |
| MC | Military Cross |
| M/c | Machine |
| Mech | Mechanic |
| MF | Maurice Farman |
| m/g | Machine gun |
| Mid | Midshipman |
| Min | Minute |
| Misc | Miscellaneous |
| Mjr | Major |
| Mk | Mark |
| Mkrs | Makers |
| ML | Motor Launch |
| MM | Military Medal |
| Mod | Modified |
| Mods | Modifications |
| MOS | Marine Operators School |
| MPK | Missing presumed killed |
| MU | Maintenance Unit |
| NAD | Naval Aeroplane Depot/ Naval Air Division |
| NADD | Naval Aeroplane Depot Dunkerque |
| NAP | Naval Aeroplane Park |
| NARD | Naval Aeroplane Repair Depot |
| NFS | Naval Flying School |
| NFT | No further trace |
| NLG | Night Landing Ground |
| (N)MAD | (Northern) Marine Aeroplane Depot |
| NPL | National Physical Laboratory |
| nr | Near |
| NTO | Naval Transport Officer |
| NTU | Not taken up |
| NWR | Not worth repair |
| NZPAF | New Zealand Permanent Air Force |
| Oblt | Oberleutnant (German 1st Lieutenant) |
| Obs | Observer |
| Offstlvtr | OffizierStellvertreter (German Warrant Officer) |
| O/L | Officer Lieutenant |
| OOC | Out of control |
| Op | Operator |
| OS | Observers School |
| OSL | Observer Sub-Lieutenant |
| o/t | Overturned |
| PD | Packing Depot |
| Pdr | Pounder |
| PFO | Probationary Flying Officer |
| PFSL | Probationary Flight Sub-Lieutenant |
| PoW | Prisoner of War |
| PRO | Public Record Office |
| Pte | Private |
| PVRD | Port Victoria Repair Depot (Grain) |
| PVRS | Port Victoria Repair Station (Grain) |
| Q/M | Quartermaster |
| RAE | Royal Aircraft Establishment |
| RAF | Royal Air Force/Royal Aircraft Factory |
| RAF(R) | Royal Air Force (Russia) |
| RCNAS | Royal Canadian Naval Air Service |
| RD | Repair Depot |
| Rec Pk | Reception Park |
| Refd | Reformed |
| Rep Pk | Repair Park |
| Retd | Returned |
| RFA | Royal Fleet Auxiliary/Royal Field Artillery |
| RFC | Royal Flying Corps (Military Wing) |
| RHNAS | Royal Hellenic Naval Air Service |
| Rittm | Rittmeister (German Cavalry Captain) |
| Rly | Railway |
| RM | Royal Marines |
| RMA | Royal Marines Artillery |
| RMLI | Royal Marines Light Infantry |
| RN | Royal Navy |
| RNAS | Royal Naval Air Service/Royal Naval Air Station |
| RNASTE | Royal Naval Air Service Training Establishment |
| RNR | Royal Naval Reserve |
| RNVR | Royal Naval Volunteer Reserve |
| RR | Rolls-Royce |
| RS | Reserve Squadron/ Royal Scots |
| RTP | Reduced to produce |
| SAAC | South African Air Corps |
| (S)ARD | (Southern) Aeroplane Repair Depot |
| SCAW | South Coast Aviation Works |
| S/Cdr | Squadron Commander |
| SD | Special Duties/ Stores Depot |
| SDF | Seaplane Defence Flight |
| SDS | Seaplane Defence School |
| Sgt | Sergeant |
| Sig | Signalman/Signaller |
| S/L | Sub-Lieutenant |
| S/Ldr | Squadron Leader |
| (S)MAD | (Southern) Marine Aeroplane Depot |
| SMOP | School for Marine Operational Pilots |
| SoAF&G | School of Aerial Fighting and Gunnery |
| SOC | Struck off charge |
| SoN&BD | School of Navigation and Bomb Dropping |
| SoNC | School of Naval Co-operation |
| Spec | Specification |
| Sqdn | Squadron |
| SS | Steam ship/Salvage Section |
| SSF | School of Special Flying |
| Staffel | [German Unit] |
| Stn | Station |
| TB | Torpedo boat |
| TBD | Torpedo boat destroyer |
| TD | Test Depot |
| TDS | Training Depot Station |
| T/F/Cdr | Temporary Flight Commander |
| T/F/L | Temporary Flight Lieutenant |
| TFSL | Temporary Flight Sub-Lieutenant |
| TL | Total loss |
| TO | Take-off |
| TPFO | Temporary Probationary Flight Officer |
| TPFSL | Temporary Probationary Flight Sub-Lieutenant |
| TS | Training Squadron |
| T/S/L | Temporary Sub-Lieutenant |
| TW | Totally wrecked |
| U-boat | Unterseeboot (German submarine) |
| u/c | Undercarriage |
| Uffz | Unteroffizier (German corporal) |
| u/s | Unserviceable |
| US | United States |
| USAS | United States Air Service |
| USMC | United States Marine Corps |
| USMCR | United States Marine Corps Reserve |
| USN | United States Navy |
| VC | Victoria Cross |
| Vzfm | Vizeflugmeister |
| Vzfw | Vizefeldwebel (German Sergeant Major) |
| W | Wasser [= water] (German water aeroplanes) |
| W/Capt | Wing Captain |
| W/Cdr | Wing Commander |
| W/E | Week ending |
| WR | Weekly Report |
| W/T | Wireless Telegraphy (equipment/ operator) |
| W&T | Wear and tear |
| WO | Written off/ Warrant Officer |
| WOC | Written off charge |
| Yds | Yards |

# RNAS SERIAL RANGES

**A.D. Scout**
1452-1453, 1536-1537
**A.D.Pusher Flying Boat**
1412-1413, N1290-N1299, N1520-N1529,
N1710-N1719, N2450-N2499
**A.D.Navyplane Pusher Seaplane**
9095-9096, N1070-N1074
**Airco D.H.2**
8725
**Airco D.H.3**
3696-3697
**Airco D.H.4**
3696-3697, N5960-N6009, N6380-N6429
**Albatros B.II**
890
**Armstrong-Whitworth Fighter**
**Reconnaissance Biplane**
N513
**Armstrong-Whitworth F.K.10**
**Quadruplane**
N511-N512, N514
**Armstrong-Whitworth F.K.12 Triplane**
3684-3685
**Astra Seaplane**
25, 106-107
**Avro 500 (Type E) Biplane**
41, 150, 939
**Avro 501**
16
**Avro 503**
51-53
**Avro 504 (179 Type)**
179, 873-878
**Avro 504B**
1001-1050, 9821-9830, 9861-9890,
N5250-N5279, N6010-N6029,
N6130-N6159, N6650-N6679
**Avro 504C**
1467-1496, 3301-3320, 8574-8603
**Avro 504E**
9276-9285
**Avro 504G**
N5310-N5329, N5800-N5829
**Avro 504 Seaplane**
889
**Avro 509**
94
**Avro 510**
130-134, 881
**Avro 519**
8440-8441
**Avro 523 Pike**
N523
**Avro 529/529A**
3694-3695
**Beardmore W.B.1**
N525
**Beardmore W.B.III**
N6100-N6129, N6680-N6749
**Beardmore W.B.IV**
N38-N40
**Beardmore W.B.V**
N41-N43
**Blackburn School Machine**
1414
**Blackburn G.P.**
1415-1416
**Blackburn T.B.**
1509-1517
**Blackburn N.1b Flying Boat**
N56-N58
**Blackburn Blackburd**
N113-N115
**Blackburn Triplane**
N502
**Blackburn Kangaroo**
N1720-N1739
**Bleriot XI-2 Monoplane**
39, 908, 3214-3238, 3890-3893,

3947-3952
**Bleriot XI-BG Parasol Monoplane**
902, 903, 907, 1538-1549
**Borel Monoplane Seaplane**
37, 48, 83-88
**Breguet Tractor Biplane**
T6/6
**Breguet "Tin Whistle" Seaplane**
110-112
**Breguet de Bombe**
3888-3889
**Breguet de Chasse**
1390-1394, 3209-3213, 3883-3887
**Breguet Type V Concours**
1398-1399, 3946, 9175-9200, 9426-9455
**Bristol T.B.8**
43, 153, 916-917, 948, 1216-1227
**Bristol T.B.8H**
H5/15
**Bristol Boxkite**
24, 35, 942-947, 8442-8453, 8562-8573
**Bristol Seaplane**
147-148
**Bristol Scout C**
1243-1266, 3013-3062
**Bristol Scout D**
8951-9000, 9500, N5390-N5419
**Bristol Scout S.2A**
3692-3693
**Bristol Scout**
N6610-N6649
**Burgess Type O**
3657-3681, 8258-8268
**Caproni Ca4**
N526-N531
**Caudron Amphibian Seaplane**
55-57
**Caudron G.II**
1320
**Caudron G.III**
40, 45, 1372, 1592-1597,
3264-3288, 3863-3882, 8941-8950,
N3050-N3099, N3240-N3269, N3280-
N3299
**Caudron G.IV**
3289-3300, 3333-3344, 3894-3899,
9101-9131, 9286-9305
**Coventry Ordnance Works Tractor**
**Seaplane**
54
**Curtiss B.2**
1323-1324
**Curtiss H.1 Small America**
950-951
**Curtiss H.4 Small America**
1228-1235, 1236-1239, 3545-3594
**Curtiss H.8 'Large America'**
8650-8699
**Curtiss H.12 'Large America'**
N1160-N1174, N2330-N2353
**Curtiss H.12B 'Large America'**
N4330-N4353
**Curtiss H.16 'Large America'**
N1890-N1949, N4060-N4074,
N4890-N4999
**Curtiss 'Large America'**
N1505-N1519
**Curtiss 'Improved America'**
N1510-N1529
**Curtiss J.N.3**
3345-3423, 8392-8403
**Curtiss J.N.4/J.N.4 (Improved)**
3424-3444, 8802-8901, N5660-N5709
**Curtiss N (Modified)**
1362-1367
**Curtiss R.2**
3445-3544
**Curtiss T**
3073-3092

**Curtiss Canada Model C**
3700, 9501-9600
**Delauney-Belleville Pusher Biplane**
1395-1399
**Deperdussin Monoplane**
M1/7, 22, 36, 885, 1375, 1376-1379
**Deperdussin Monoplane Seaplane**
30, 44
**D.F.W. Military Arrow**
154
**D.F.W. B.2**
891
**Donnet L'Eveque Seaplane**
H7/18
**Dyott Tractor Monoplane**
1598
**Dyott Twin-Engined Fighter**
3687-3688
**Etrich Taube Monoplane**
M4/9
**Fairey AD Tractor Biplane**
3702-3703
**Fairey AD Pusher Biplane**
3704-3705
**Fairey N.2a Biplane**
N76-N81
**Fairey F.2a**
N88-N89
**Fairey Atalanta I**
N118, N119
**Fairey III**
N9-N10
**Fairey IIIA**
N2850-N2899
**Fairey IIIB**
N2230-N2259
**Fairey IIIC**
N9230-N9259
**Fairey Campania**
N1000-N1009, N1840-N1889,
N1890-N1959, N2360-N2399,
N2580-N2629
**Fairey Hamble Baby**
N1190-N1219, N1320-N1329,
N1330-N1339, N1450-N1479,
N1960-N1985
**Fairey Hamble Baby Convert**
N1986-N2059
**Henry Farman Pusher Biplane**
31, 108, 189, 940, 1368, 1374,
1454, 1518-1533, 1599, 3150, 3682,
3998
**Henry Farman Pusher Seaplane**
H4/11, 96-100, 102, 110, 139-144, 156,
886, 887, 915
**Henry Farman F.27**
1550-1555, 3617-3636, 3900-3919,
8238-8249, 9099, 9134-9153, 9251-9275,
N3000-N3049
**Henry Farman F.40/F.56**
9155-9174, N3210-N3239
**Maurice Farman Gun-carrying Seaplane**
125
**Maurice Farman Pusher Biplane**
146, 888, 1240-1241
**Maurice Farman Pusher Seaplane**
29, N1530-N1579
**Maurice Farman S.7 Longhorn**
23, 67, 69-70, 91-92, 109, 188,
909-914, 949, 3001-3012, 3954-3955,
8474, 8604-8605, 8921-8940,
N5000-N5029, N5030-N5059, N5330-
N5349, N5720-N5749, N5750-N5759
**Maurice Farman S.7 Longhorn Seaplane**
71-73, 95, 113-117
**Maurice Farman S.11 Shorthorn**
1127, 1134, 1369-1371, 1380-1387,
3932-3939, 8106-8117, 8466-8473,
N5060-N5079, N6310-N6329

**Maurice Farman F.37 Pusher Biplane**
9133
**F.B.A. Type A**
3113-3114, 3199-3208, 3637-3656,
9601-9610
**F.B.A. Type B**
9612-9635, N1040-N1059, N2680-N2709,
N2710-N2739
**F.B.A. Type H**
N1075-N1078 (and N1079 not delivered?)
**Felixstowe F.2a**
N1260-N1274, N2280-N2304,
N2530-N2554, N4080-N4099,
N4280-N4309, N4430-N4479,
N4480-N4504, N4510-N4519,
N4520-N4529, N4530-N4554,
N4555-N4559, N4560-N4579
**Felixstowe F.2c**
N64, N65
**Felixstowe F.3**
N1950-N1959, N2160-N2179,
N2305-N2307, N2310-N2321,
N2400-N2429, N4000-N4037,
N4100-N4101, N4160-N4179,
N4180-N4191, N4230-N4279,
N4310-N4321, N4360-N4397,
N4400-N4429
**Felixstowe F.5**
N90, N4038-N4049, N4112-N4149,
N4192-N4229, N4580-N4629,
N4630-N4679, N4680-N4729,
N4730-N4779, N4780-N4829,
N4830-N4879
**Felixstowe Fury**
N123
**Flanders B.2**
918
**Grahame-White XV**
1321, 1600, 3151-3162, 3607-3616,
8305-8316, 8752-8801
**Grain Griffin**
N100-N106
**Hamble River Luke H.L.1 Pusher
Seaplane**
105
**Handley Page Type G**
892
**Handley Page O/100**
1372-1375, 1455-1467, 3115-3142
**Handley Page P/320**
N519-N520
**Handley Page R/200**
N27-N32
**Handley Page T/400**
N62-N63
**Hewlett & Blondeau Biplane**
8317-8320
**Kingsbury Davis-Gun Triplane**
N51-N52, N75
**Mann Egerton Type F**
N2
**Mann Egerton Type H Shipboard Scout**
N44-N49
**Morane-Saulnier Type G Monoplane**
941, 1242
**Morane-Saulnier M.S.3 Parasol**
3239-3263
**Morane-Saulnier M.S.7 Biplane**
3683
**Nieuport Monoplane**
M3/13
**Nieuport Twin Biplane**
1395-1397
**Nieuport Twin Tractor Biplane**
3940-3945, 3953, 3995-3997, 8475-8486
**Nieuport Monoplane Seaplane**
3187-3198
**Nieuport Scout**
3149, 9154-9155
**Nieuport Type 10 Scout**
3163-3186, 3962-3973, 8516-8517

**Nieuport Type 11 Two-seater**
3974, 3975-3979, 3980-3994
**Nieuport Type 12 Two-seater**
3920-3931, 8510-8515, 8524-8529,
8708-8713, 8726-8744, 8902-8920,
9201-9250, N3170-N3173, N3174-N3183,
N3188
**Nieuport Type 17bis Scout**
N3100-N3104, N3184-N3187,
N3189-N3197, N3198, N3199-N3209,
N5860-N5909, N6030-N6079,
N6530-N6579
**Nieuport Type '17B' Scout**
3956-3958, 8745-8751
**Nieuport XV Bomber**
N5560-N5599
**Nieuport Triplane**
N521-N522, N532
**Norman Thompson N.T.2b**
N2260-N2359, N2400-N2429,
N2500-N2523, N2555-N2579,
N2760-N2784, N3300-N3374
**Norman Thompson N.T.4/4A**
8338-8343, 9061-9064, N2140-N2159,
N2740-N2759
**Norman Thompson Cruiser Flying Boat**
N18-N19
**Norman Thompson Flying Boat**
N26
**Norman Thompson Tandem Fighter
Flying Boat**
N37
**Norman Thompson N.2c**
N82-N83
**Norman Thompson School Biplane**
N107-N109
**Parnall Panther**
N91-N96, N7400-N7549, N7680-N7841
**Parnall Zepp Straffer**
N505-N506
**Pemberton Billing P.B.9**
1267
**Pemberton-Billing P.B.23E**
8487
**Pemberton-Billing P.B.25**
9001-9020
**Pemberton Billing P.B.31E Night Hawk**
1388-1389
**Perry Tractor Biplane**
1322
**Phoenix P.2**
N22
**Phoenix Pusher Seaplane**
N23
**Phoenix P.5 Cork**
N86-N87
**Porte F.B.2 Baby**
9800-9820
**Port Victoria P.V.2**
N1
**Port Victoria P.V.4**
N8
**Port Victoria P.V.5**
N53-N54
**Port Victoria P.V.7 Grain Kitten**
N539
**Port Victoria P.V.8 Eastchurch Kitten**
N540
**Port Victoria P.V.9**
N55
**R.E.P. Parasol**
8454-8465
**Robey-Peters Gun-Carrier**
9498-9499
**Robey Seaplane**
N33-N35
**Royal Aircraft Factory B.E.2a**
46-47, 49-50, 101
**Royal Aircraft Factory B.E.2c**
952-963, 964-975, 976-987, 988-999,
1075-1098, 1099-1122, 1123-1146,

1147-1170, 1183-1188, 1189-1194,
1424-1435, 3999, 8293-8304, 8326-8337,
8404-8409, 8410-8433, 8488-8500,
8606-8629, 8714-8724, 9456-9475,
9951-10000, N5570-N5594,
N5770-N5794
**Royal Aircraft Factory C.E.1 Flying Boat**
N97-N98
**Royal Aircraft Factory F.E.8**
3689-3690
**Royal Aircraft Factory H.R.E.2**
17
**Royal Aircraft Factory H.R.E.3**
26
**Royal Aircraft Factory H.R.E.6**
68
**Royal Aircraft Factory R.E.5**
26
**Royal Aircraft Factory S.E.5a**
N6030-N6079
**Royal Aircraft Factory Two-seat
Seaplane**
30
**Royal Aircraft Factory Seaplane**
199
**Sage 4**
N116-N117
**Sage N.3**
N5280-N5309
**Short S.27 Tandem Twin**
No.4
**Short S.34**
No.1/T1/1
**Short S.38**
No.2/T2/2, 3, 28, 34, 62-66, 152, 904,
1580-1591, 3143-3148, 8434-8439,
8530-8536
**Short S.39 Triple Twin**
No.3/T3/3
**Short S.41 Seaplane**
H1/10
**Short Improved S.41**
H8-H9/20-21
**Short S.42 Monoplane**
M2/8
**Short S.45**
T5/5, 1268, 1279
**Short S.46 "Double Dirty"**
H2/12
**Short S.47 "Triple Tractor"**
T4/4
**Short S.52 4-Seater Hydro Monoplane**
14
**Short S.54 Seaplane**
H3/19
**Short S.60 Tractor Biplane**
42
**Short S.79 Pusher Seaplane**
80
**Short S.81 Gun-carrying Seaplane**
126
**Short Single-Seater Biplane**
145
**Short 126 Type Gun-carrying Machine**
1268-1279
**Short 74 Type Seaplane**
74-77, 81-82, 183
**Short 81 Type Seaplane**
89-90, 119-122
**Short 184 Type Seaplane**
7184-185, 841-850, 8001-8030, 8031-
8105, 8344-8355, 8356-8367, 8368-8379,
8380-8391, 9041-9060, 9065-9084,
9085-9094, N1080-N1099, N1130-N1139,
N1140-N1149, N1220-N1229,
N1230-N1239, N1240-N1249,
N1250-N1259, N1260-N1271,
N1272-N1279, N1340-N1759,
N1580-N1589, N1590-N1599,
N1600-N1620, N1621-N1624,
N1630-N1659, N1660-N1689,

N1760-N1774, N1780-N1799,
N1820-N1839, N2600-N2629,
N2630-N2659, N2790-N2819,
N2820-N2849, N2900-N2949,
N2950-N2999, N9000-N9059,
N9060-N9099, N9100-N9139,
N9140-N9169, N9170-N9199,
N9200-N9229, N9260-N9289,
N9290-N9349, N9350-N9399,
N9400-N9449

**Short 827 Type Seaplane**
822-827, 3063-3072, 3093-3112,
3321-3332, 8218-8229, 8230-8237,
8250-8257, 8550-8561, 8630-8649

**Short 135/830 Type Seaplane**
135-136, 819-821, 828-830, 1335-1346,
9781-9790

**Short Tractor Seaplane**
78-79

**Short Type A (320) (310-A4) Seaplane**
8317-8318, N1150-N1159, N1300-N1319,
N1360-N1389, N1390-N1409,
N1480-N1504, N1690-N1709

**Short Type B Seaplane**
178, 190-198, 8319-8320

**Short Type C (166 Type) Seaplane**
161-166, 811-818, 9751-9770

**Short Two-seat Biplane**
180

**Short Two-seat Pusher Biplane**
181

**Short Dual-control Seaplane**
182

**Short 186 Type Folder Torpedo-
carrying Seaplane**
186, 1441-1449

**Short Nile Seaplane**
905

**Short Bomber**
3706, 9306-9355, 9356-9375, 9477-9495,
9771-9776, 9831-9840

**Short Day Bomber**
N507-N508

**Short Scout N.3**
N1079

**Short Improved Navyplane**
N20-N21

**Short Experimental Scout No.1 Seaplane**
N36

**Short N.2b Seaplane**
N66-N73

**Short School Seaplane**
N97-N98

**Short Shirl**
N110-N112, N7550-N7649

**Short Cromarty**
N120-N122

**Sloane-Day H.1**
3701

**Sloane-Day Tractor Biplane**
4000

**Sopwith School Biplane**
27

**Sopwith Three-Seater Biplane**
33

**Sopwith Bat Boat**
38, 118, 127, 879

**Sopwith HT Seaplane**
58-60

**Sopwith Type S Hydro-aeroplane**
61

**Sopwith Gunbus Seaplane**
93

**Sopwith D.1 Three-seat Seaplane**
103-104

**Sopwith Pusher Seaplane**
123-124

**Sopwith 137 Type Tractor Seaplane**
137

**Sopwith Sociable**
149

**Sopwith Tractor Seaplane**
151

**Sopwith 1½ Strutter**
3686, 9376-9425, 9651-9750, 9892-9897,
N4-N5, N5080-N5119, N5120-N5169,
N5170-N5179, N5200-N5219, N5220-
N5249, N5500-N5549, N5550-N5559,
N5600-N5624, N5630-N5654, N5910-
N5934, N5940-N5954

**Sopwith Type C Biplane**
157-159

**Sopwith Single-seat Tractor Biplane**
160

**Sopwith Tabloid**
167-168, 169, 904-905, 1201-1212

**Sopwith Tabloid R**
1213

**Sopwith Special Tractor Seaplane**
170

**Sopwith Three-seater**
906

**Sopwith 'Spinning Jenny'**
1051-1074

**Sopwith Gordon Bennett Racer**
1214-1215

**Sopwith Schneider**
1436-1447, 1556-1579

**Sopwith Tractor Biplane**
3698-3699

**Sopwith Modified Schneider**
3707-3806

**Sopwith 806 Type 'Gunbus No.1'
Biplane**
801-806, 3833-3862

**Sopwith 807 Type Folder Seaplane**
807-810, 919-926

**Sopwith 860/151 Type Seaplane**
851-860, 927-938, 1347-1350

**Sopwith 880 Type Seaplane**
880, 896

**Sopwith Pusher Seaplane**
897-901

**Sopwith Baby**
8118-8217, N4, N300, N1010-N1039,
N1060-N1069, N1100-N1129,
N1410-N1449, N2060-N2134

**Sopwith Pup**
N503, 3691, 9496-9497, 9898-9900,
9901-9950, N5180-N5199, N6100-N6129,
N6160-N6209, N6460-N6529

**Sopwith Ships Pup**
N6430-N6459

**Sopwith B.1**
N50

**Sopwith F.1 Camel**
N517-N518, N6330-N6379, N6530-N6579

**Sopwith 2F.1 Ship's Camel**
N5, N6600-N6649, N6750-N6799,
N6800-N6849, N7100-N7139, N7140-
N7149, N7200-N7299, N7300-N7349,
N7350-N7399, N7650-N7679, N7850-
N7979, N8130-N8179, N8180-N8229

**Sopwith School**
9891

**Sopwith T.1 Cuckoo**
N74, N6900-N6929, N6930-N6949,
N6950-N6999, N7000-N7099,
N7150-N7199, N7980-N8079

**Sopwith 'Daily Mail' Seaplane**
N1340-N1359

**Sopwith Triplane**
F1-F17, N500, N504, N524, N533-N538,
N541-N543, N5350-N5389,
N5420-N5494, N5550-N5559,
N5910-N5934, N6290-N6309

**Sopwith Triplane** (a different design)
N509-N510

**Spad S.7C.1**
9611, N3399, N6030-N6079,
N6080-N6129, N6210-N6284,
N6580-N6604

**Spencer Biplane**
200

**Sunbeam Bomber**
N515-N516

**Supermarine Patrol Seaplane**
N24-N25

**Supermarine Baby**
N59-N61 (N61 not built)

**Tellier Flying Boat**
N84-N85

**Thomas T.2**
3809-3820, 8269-8280

**Vickers F.B.5 Gunbus**
32, 861-872, 1534-1535, 3595-3600,
3601-3606

**Vickers Valentia**
N124-N126

**Voisin Type B**
1390-1394

**Voisin Biplane**
3821-3832

**Voisin Type III LA.S**
8501-8509, 8518-8523, 8700-8707, 9154

**Voisin Canon**
N544-N545

**Westland Scout Seaplane**
N16-N17

**White Dual Control Machine**
1267

**White & Thompson/Curtiss Bat Boat**
882

**White & Thompson/Curtiss H.4 "Small
America"**
883

**White & Thompson 'Bognor Bloater'**
1171-1182

**White & Thompson No.3 Flying Boat**
1195-1200, 3807-3808

**White & Thompson Biplane**
1280-1299

**White & Thompson Flying Boat**
1497-1508

**White & Thompson Pusher Flying Boat**
N1180-N1189

**Wight 1914 Navyplane Pusher Seaplane**
128-129, 155

**Wight Seaplane**
186

**Wight Navyplane Seaplane**
884

**Wight Type A.I. Improved Navyplane
Pusher Seaplane**
171-177

**Wight Twin Fuselage, Twin-engined
Seaplane**
187, 1450-1451

**Wight 840/177 Type Seaplane**
831-840, 1300-1319, 1351-1354,
1400-1411, 8281-8292, 8542-8549,
9021-9028, 9029-9040

**Wight Pusher Seaplane**
893-895

**Wight Trainer Seaplane**
8321-8322

**Wight Admiralty 1000 Type**
1000, 1355-1361

**Wight Baby Seaplane**
9097-9098, 9100

**Wight 'Converted' Seaplane**
9841-9860, N1280-N1289, N2180-N2229

**Wight Quadruplane**
N14

**Wight Quadruplane Fighter**
N546

**Wight Flying Boat**
N15

**Wight Landplane**
N501

**Wright Pusher Biplane**
1373

*Short S.27 "Tandem-Twin"(later Naval Biplane No.4) in 1911. (via Philip Jarrett)*

*Deperdussin Monoplane M1 (later 7) in landplane form. (J.M.Bruce/G.S.Leslie collection)*

*Short Monoplane M2 (later 8). (via Philip Jarrett)*

*Short S.38 Hydroplane T2 (later 2) on HMS Hibernia in May 1912. (MAP)*

*Short Tractor T5 (later 5) in single-float form at Portsmouth for Royal Review, July 1912. (MAP)*

*Short S.47 "Triple Tractor" T4 (later 4) at Eastchurch, August 1912 . (via Philip Jarrett)*

## ADMIRALTY SERIALS. FIRST SYSTEM.
### November 1911

No.1    Short No S.34
No.2    Short No S.38
No.3    Short No S.39 (Triple Twin)
No.4    Short No S.27 (Tandem Twin)

## ADMIRALTY SERIALS. SECOND SYSTEM.
### February 1912

**B-series (Biplanes)**
| | | |
|---|---|---|
| B1 | Short No S.34 | |
| B2 | Short No S.38 | |
| B3 | Short S.39 | |
| B4 | Short S.27? | |

**M-series (Monoplanes)**
| | | |
|---|---|---|
| M1 | Deperdussin | Later 7 |
| M2 | Short No S.42 | Later 8 |
| M3 | Nieuport | Later 13, then 409 at CFS |
| M4 | Etrich Taube | Later 9 |

**H-series (Hydro-aeroplanes)**
| | | |
|---|---|---|
| H1 | Short No S.41 | Later 10 |
| H2 | Short No S.46 | Later 12 |
| H3 | Short No S.52? (to have been 14) | |
| H4 | Henry Farman | Later 11 |
| H5 | Bristol T.B.8H | Later 15 |
| H6 | Short No S.54? | Later 19 |
| H7 | Donnet L'Évêque | Later 18 |
| H8 | Short No S.56 | Later 20 |
| H9 | Short No S.57 | Later 21 |

**T-series (Twin planes?) [Replaced B-series April 1912]**
| | | |
|---|---|---|
| T1 | Short No S.34 (ex No.1/B1) | Later 1 |
| T2 | Short No S.38 (ex No.2/B2) | Later 2 |
| T3 | Short No S.39 (ex No.3/B3) | Later 3 |
| T4 | Short No S.47 | Later 4 |
| T5 | Short No S.45 | Later 5 |
| T6 | Breguet | Later 6 |

## RNAS SERIALS
### Promulgated 1 August 1912 and used from late that month

### FIRST SERIES (1 to 200)

**1 SHORT "LONG RANGE" PUSHER BIPLANE numbered 1 & built Eastchurch. (50-hp Gnome)** [Gordon Bruce's researches show correct c/n to be S.34]

1    (Originally Naval Biplane No.1, then B1, then T1). Made available to RNAS at Eastchurch by Frank McClean (No.6 in his Fleet) as No.1 8.3.11; Bounced landing, damaged propeller, lower mainplane and skid 22.3.11 (Lt CR Samson); Flying again 30.3.11; Lt EL Gerrard RMLI with Lt GV Wildman-Lushington RMA made world record cross-country flight with passenger of 4 hrs 13 min 16.8.11; Station became ECNFS 2.12; Collided with No.2 and damaged 2.10.12; Fitted new wings 7.11.12; Damaged 3.12.12; Damaged 22.1.13; S/L R Bell-Davies flew his first solo in this aircraft 26.2.13;

**1 SHORT S.38 NACELLE TYPE PUSHER BIPLANE numbered 1 (50-hp Gnome)** [Gordon Bruce's researches show corect c/n S.86]

1    Deld ECNFS 8.12.13; Tested 13.12.13; Float u/c fitted 3.14 and tested GRW Wheel Attachment; ECNFS defence by 11.8.14; Engine burst during ground test, fuselage & wings damaged 31.8.14; C Flt Eastchurch 3.11.14; 2 Sqdn Eastchurch 1.15; Fitted 70-hp Gnome by 11.3.15; ECNFS 1.7.15; Damaged 11.9.15; Damaged by fire 22.9.15; FL 2.11.15 (FSL N Keeble);

Damaged 13.11.15; Deleted 22.2.16 FW&T [supposedly a reconstruction of S.34, but see Gordon Bruce's notes]

**1 SHORT-SOMMER PUSHER BIPLANE numbered 2 & built Eastchurch. (50-hp Gnome)** [Gordon Bruce's researches show correct c/n to be S.38]

2    (Originally Naval Biplane No.2 at Eastchurch, then B2, then T2). Tested by Samson after rebuild 23.5.11; With flotation gear was successfully landed on River Medway by Lt AM Longmore 1.12.11; Flown at Sheerness from platform of HMS *Africa* 10.1.12 (Lt CR Samson); Flown for 15 minutes on 22.1.12 by Cdr CR Samson and described by him as "very nasty"; Station became ECNFS 2.12; Refitted 70-hp Gnome by 20.4.12 when flown by Lt CR Samson; Flown off HMS *Hibernia* under way by Lt CR Samson 2.5.12; Mkrs, rebuilt to late Farman style with 70-hp Gnome and lower weight, flying in this form by 22.6.12; Wrecked hoisting aboard HMS *London* 9.7.12; FF Eastchurch after renovation 30.8.12 (JL Parker & Eng Lt E Featherstone Briggs, later Lt CR Samson); One of earliest night flights made by Lt W Parke 7.9.12; Collided with No.1 and damaged 2.10.12; Flying again by 12.10.12; Damaged 21.11.12; Lower wing repairs 1.2.13 to at least 29.3.13; Tested with 50-hp Gnome after repaired and rebuilt by naval ratings 2.5.13 (Lt CR Samson & Eng Lt E Featherstone Briggs); Damaged 19.7.13; Converted to Farman-type; Samson's first night flight, carrying Asst Payr EB Parker 11.9.13; Fitted DC when flown by Eng Lt E Featherstone Briggs 17.9.13; Flew Winston Churchill 29.11.13 (Lt GV Wildman-Lushington); C Flt Eastchurch 3.11.14; Crashed, CW 28.1.15 (FSL AG Shepherd); Surveyed 1.2.15; Deleted 20.2.15

**1 SHORT "TRIPLE-TWIN" TRACTOR/PUSHER BIPLANE numbered 3 & built Eastchurch. (Two 50-hp Gnome)** [Gordon Bruce's researches show correct c/n to be S.39]

3    (Two 50-hp Gnome driving three propellers, but unsuccessful as twin and later converted to No.2 type with single 50/70/80-hp Gnome). (Originally Naval Biplane No.3, then T3). Original cost £1400. FF 18.9.11 (Frank McClean's Fleet No.10); Made available to RNAS at Eastchurch and first flown by Samson 22.11.11; Station became ECNFS 2.12; Retd Mkrs for overhaul 27.11.12; Completely rebuilt instead

**1 SHORT S.38 NACELLE TYPE PUSHER BIPLANE rebuilt from c/n S.39 under Cont No C.P.31105/13/X.2087 dated 15.2.13, to same standard as c/n S.38 with 2-str pusher nacelle, new wings, transparent windscreen and DC (80-hp Gnome)** [Gordon Bruce's researches show correct c/n to be S.78]

3    Flown by Lt CR Samson & Eng Lt E Featherstone Briggs 4.6.13; Tested 24.7.13 (Pickles); Refitted 70-hp Gnome and tested by Eng Lt E Featherstone Briggs by 6.8.13; Flown 8.8.13; Flown several times at night by Cdr CR Samson 9.13; To Daventry for Army manoeuvres 18.9.13; Retd ECNFS 26.9.13; Cdr CR Samson flew Winston Churchill to Grain 23.10.13; Climbed to 10,000 ft 23.2.14; Allotted Maxim gun 2.8.14; Eastchurch patrol 8.14; To Thurso by rail 13.8.14 (flew patrol 25.8.14); Eastchurch 3.9.14; ADD 30.9.14; 3 Sqdn 1.10.14; Detailed for night lookout 9.10.14; Burst propeller, badly damaged in crash, Poperinghe 31.10.14 (W/Cdr CR Samson); To Sheerness in SS *Princess* 3.11.14; Cedric Lee Co/SCAW repair 5.1.15 (now 70-hp Gnome); Eastbourne 7.6.15; ECNFS 26.8.15; Damaged 3.9.15; Damaged 15.9.15; Deleted 26.4.16

**1 SHORT "TRIPLE-TRACTOR" TRACTOR BIPLANE numbered 4 & built Eastchurch. (Two 50-hp Gnome)** [Gordon Bruce's researches show correct c/n to be S.47]

4    "Triple Tractor" [or "Field Kitchen" - due to amount of heat under cowling]. (Two 50-hp Gnome driving three tractor airscrews). Deld ECNFS 24.7.12; Accepted (Lt CJ L'Estrange Malone); Participated Army manoeuvres

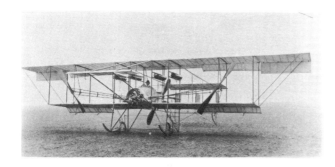

*Short "Triple Twin" (T3, later 3) in modified form with four fuel tanks and upper wing extensions, December 1911. (via J.D.Oughton)*

*Crashed Breguet Tractor Biplane with naval personnel, possibly 6. (J.M.Bruce/G.S.Leslie collection)*

*Short S.41 10 converted to landplane, being inspected by Wing Cdr Gerrard, the CO of 2 Wing at Imbros in 1915. (via J.D.Oughton)*

*Henry Farman Seaplane 11 (ex H4) at Carlingnose piloted by Lt F.E.T.Hewlett RN. (J.M.Bruce/G.S.Leslie collection)*

*Etrich Taube Monoplane 9 (ex M4). (J.M.Bruce/G.S.Leslie collection)*

7-20.8.12; New curved tail fitted 9.11.12; Rouzet wireless experiments 11.12; Fuselage fabric repaired 9.1.13; New tail skid fitted 15.1.13; New extension tube fitted 16.1.13; Damaged on W/T trials 22.1.13. Deleted early 1913

**1 SHORT TRACTOR BIPLANE numbered 5 & built Eastchurch. (70-hp Gnome)** [Gordon Bruce's researches show correct c/n to be S.45]

5      Cost £1184. Deld ECNFS 23.5.12; FF 24.5.12 (Cdr CR Samson); Operated as single-float seaplane by 2.7.12 (flown by Lt Spenser DA Grey); Participated Naval Review, Portsmouth 3.7.12; Attempted return from Eastney but failed to TO, ribs broke on touching water 13.7.12 (Lt Spenser DA Grey & Eng Lt E Featherstone Briggs); Possibly retd by road; Marked "5" by 2.9.12; Reverted to wheels for Army manoeuvres 7-20.9.12; From 2.10.12 operated again as single float seaplane at temporary seaplane station Carlingnose (Port Laing), near north end of Forth Railway Bridge, capsized there 4.10.12 (Mjr R Gordon RM), deleted

**1 BREGUET TRACTOR BIPLANE numbered 6 and purchased in France. Built at Douai. (80-hp Chenu)**

6      Purchase recommended by Lt CR Samson 1.12. Cost £1400. Deld ECNFS in crate 2.8.12 (Originally T6); FL in marshes and damaged 22.4.13 (dismantled and to shed at Eastchurch); Deleted 1913; Presume repaired/rebuilt; Felixstowe by early 1914; At Hendon 11.8.14; Fitted 110-hp Canton-Unné 6.15; Shown on Eastchurch daily returns without engine 6.15 - @15.8.15 [no type given, and appears as "1373" from 8.9.15]
[Some reservations have been expressed about the Canton-Unné engine in the absence of photographic proof, even though it appears in official disposition list as early 11.12 which notes it as still being on order]

**1 DEPERDUSSIN TRACTOR MONOPLANE purchased in France & numbered 7. Built Paris. (70-hp Gnome)**

7      Purchase recommended by Lt CR Samson 1.12. Cost £1080. (Initially M1). Flown from Paris to ECNFS by Maurice Prevost 13.4.12. Flown by Cdr CR Samson 24.4.12; Still as M1 arrived Windermere to be fitted with a Gnosspelius float; Accepted 24.7.12; Reverted to wheels at Eastchurch by "7" by 29.8.12; Participated Army manoeuvres 6-20.9.12 (flown by Lt Spenser DA Grey and Cdr CR Samson); Flown by Draper. Tested after new wings made and fitted by naval ratings 24.4.13 (Eng Lt E Featherstone Briggs); Probably the Deperdussin run into on ground and damaged by BE 46 24.4.13 (but could be 22); Fitted new wings 4.13 (and/or 5.14); Eastchurch patrol 8.14; ADD 27.9.14; Dover (crated) 24.10.14; Deleted 12.14

**1 SHORT TRACTOR MONOPLANE built Eastchurch for McClean and later numbered 8. (50-hp Gnome)** [Gordon Bruce's researches show correct c/n to be S.42]

8      (Initially M2). Cost £820. RN's first single-seater. Acceptance test ECNFS, spun round after landing, wheels damaged 24.2.12 (Cdr CR Samson); Fitted with floats 27.2.12 (to be flown from HMS *Actaeon* at Sheerness); Possibly the seaplane which left HMS *Actaeon* for Harwich 3.6.12; Marked "8" 8.12; Flown by Samson, also by Lt W Parke (9.12) and Capt R Gordon RMLI; Flown to 26.9.12; Shorts repair and fit 2-ft longer wings 10.12; Retd RNAS Eastchurch; Pancaked and damaged landing gear and propeller 19.4.13 (Cdr CR Samson); Taxying only by 6.13; Cleaned, doped and varnished 9.13, but soon deteriorated; flying badly by 5.14; deleted 6.14

**1 ETRICH TAUBE TRACTOR MONOPLANE built by Etrich near Vienna & numbered 9. (65-hp Austro-Daimler)**

9      Purchase recommended by Lt CR Samson 1.12. Cost £1500. (Initially M4); Left factory 29.5.12; Arrived

ECNFS circa 15.6.12; Test flown 15.6.12 by Herr Steugler with Lt Spenser DA Grey as passenger; Subsequent flying mostly by Lt R Gregory; Unfit for flying by 3.13; Shorts estimated repairs £150; Overhauled late 4.13/early 5.13; Failed to TO 23.5.13 (Eng Lt E Featherstone Briggs); Flown successfully 29.5.13 (Eng Lt E Featherstone Briggs); Dismantled W/E 11.10.13

**1 SHORT TRACTOR BIPLANE HYDRO AEROPLANE built Eastchurch & numbered 10. (100-hp Gnome)** [Gordon Bruce's researches show correct c/n to be S.41]

10     Deld Eastchurch by 27.3.12; FF as "H1" 2.4.12 (Cdr CR Samson); Fitted twin float u/c early 5.12 and participated Fleet Review at Weymouth; Flown Sheerness to Eastney (Portsmouth) 4.7.12; Folkestone 13.7.12; Dover to Harwich 14.7.12; Reverted to landplane; Participated Army manoeuvres 9.12 flown by Cdr CR Samson; Refitted floats and after reassembly operated from temporary seaplane station at Carlingnose (Port Laing), Firth of Forth 2.10.12 to 15.10.12; Dismantled and retd Sheerness 16.10.12; Damaged 9.11.12, repaired by Shorts; Reverted landplane early 1913; New tailskid fitted 15.1.13; Mounting for Maxim gun fitted mid 1.13, and gun fired 10 & 27.2.13; New ailerons 17.4.13; Overhauled 5.13 and gap in centre section filled; Flown with new ailerons 30.5.13; Larger new wings with bigger ailerons fitted by Mkrs 9.13; Eastchurch by 11.13; Fitted 140-hp Gnome 1.14; Patrols from Eastchurch 8.14; Mkrs repair 27.8.14; Eastchurch 12.14; Mkrs repair by 11.3.15; 2 Sqdn Eastchurch 3.15; Became 2 Wing Eastchurch 21.6.15; Remained Eastchurch for engine overhaul on departure of 2 Wing to France 4.8.15; Mkrs 31.8.15 for near-total reconstruction with airframe similar to Improved Type 74; fitted 135-hp Canton-Unné 8.15; To Aegean in SS *Venetian* by 1.10.15; 2 Wing Imbros late 1915; Probably lost in fire 4.11.15

**1 HENRY FARMAN PUSHER BIPLANE SEAPLANE ordered 5.12 & numbered 11. Imported by The Aircraft Manufacturing Co Ltd, Hendon. (70-hp Gnome)**

11     Deld ECNFS 21.6.12 (Initially H4); FF 28.6.12; Flown in exercises with submarines at temporary seaplane station Carlingnose (Port Laing), Firth of Forth 10.12; Nacelle fitted 1.13; Tested 15.1.13 (Cdr CR Samson); Airco 9.13; Eastchurch retest 19.9.13; Grain 11.13; To Felixstowe but wrecked 1.4.14; Wreckage salved, to Eastchurch & surveyed; U/s until deleted 24.8.14 (80-hp Gnome by then)

**1 SHORT TWIN-ENGINED TRACTOR/PUSHER MONO-PLANE built Eastchurch & numbered 12. (Two 70-hp Gnome)** [Gordon Bruce's researches show correct c/n to be S.46)

12     (Nicknamed "Double Dirty"). Deld ECNFS 21.9.12; FF 23.9.12 (Lt CR Samson); Damaged landing, towed to Grain 24.10.12 (Lt CR Samson & Eng Lt E Featherstone Briggs); Repaired Grain 30.12.12, then retd Eastchurch; Dismantled W/E 2.8.13

**1 NIEUPORT IV.G TRACTOR MONOPLANE purchased from France & numbered 13. Built Issy-les-Moulineaux. (50-hp Gnome)**

13     Purchase recommended by Lt CR Samson 1.12. Cost £1040. (Originally M3). Probably never used by ECNFS before transferred to CFS (as 409), initially on loan

**1 SHORT TWIN-ENGINED TRACTOR HYDRO MONOPLANE to be built at Eastchurch & numbered 14. (Two 140-hp Gnome)** [Gordon Bruce's researches show correct c/n to be S.52]

14     Intended as four-seater but not built.
[NB Aircraft No.14 mentioned twice in records as going from UK to ADD 27.9.14 could not have been this machine]

*Bristol T.B.8 (later T.B.8H 15) with twin floats at Dale, 1913. (via J.D.Oughton)*

*Nieuport IV.G, believed to be the machine intended for the RNAS as M3 (later 13) but which went to the Central Flying School as 409 instead. (J.M.Bruce/G.S.Leslie collection)*

*Avro 501 16 at Eastchurch. (J.M.Bruce/G.S.Leslie collection)*

*Royal Aircraft Factory H.R.E.2 17 at Calshot, 1914. (J.M.Bruce/G.S.Leslie collection)*

*Believed to be the Donnet-L'Évèque received at Eastchurch in October 1912 and numbered 18. (J.M.Bruce/G.S.Leslie collection)*

**1 BRISTOL T.B.8H TRACTOR BIPLANE HYDRO AEROPLANE built at Filton by The British & Colonial Aeroplane Co Ltd & numbered 15. (80-hp Gnome)**

15    (c/n 205). Rebuild of Bristol Coanda Monoplane c/n 121. Converted as prototype T.B.8; Tested Larkhill 7.13; Two floats made by sawing in half the original Gnosspelius floats of Coanda c/n.120; FF Dale, Pembs 20.9.13; To Filton 12.13, stripped, modified and rebuilt as T.B.8H c/n 205 (serial No.15); Failed test at Cowes 1.14; Deld Calshot 2.1.14 and accepted 13.1.14; Mkrs mods to make it fly with tail lower 23.2.14; Calshot 24.7.14; floats poorly rigged; Grain 3.8.14; 1 Sqdn Ostende 3.9.14; Westgate to Grain 9.9.14; For conversion to landplane by 29.9.14; Eastchurch 28.10.14; Deleted 5.15

**1 AVRO 501 TRACTOR BIPLANE SEAPLANE built under Cont No C.P.33177/13 at Manchester & numbered 16. (100-hp Gnome)**

16    Deld Grain by 23.1.13 as centre-float amphibian; Failed test at Grain 1.13; Retd Mkrs, fitted narrow-track wheeled u/c; Accepted ECNFS 28.8.13; Farnborough 19.5.14; ECNFS 21.5.14; Engine caught fire on ground, badly burnt 22.5.14; Mkrs repair 5.14; 2 Sqdn Eastchurch late 1914; Dover for raids on Zeebrugge and Ostende 10.2.15; Attd 2 Sqdn Dunkerque 11-20.2.15; Carried bombs for attack on Ostende but failed to reach objective 16.2.15; ECNFS 22.2.15; Damaged 15.7.15, repaired; Detling 19.8.15 (expts); ECNFS 20.8.15; Damaged 7.11.15; Deleted 22.2.16

**1 ROYAL AIRCRAFT FACTORY H.R.E.2 HYDRO TRACTOR BIPLANE built Farnborough & numbered 17. (70-hp Renault)**

17    Fitted NPL floats; First flown mid 1913 as landplane with 70-hp Renault; Abortively tested with floats on Fleet Pond but insufficient length for TO; Flown from Frensham Ponds 7.13; Fitted 100-hp Renault by 10.13; Flown as landplane to Calshot 3.11.13; Floats fitted at Hamble 4.11.13; Floats smashed in crash on Solent 23.11.13 (Ronald Kemp and passenger unhurt); Mkrs 12.13, rebuild with R.E.5 wings and ailerons in place of warping wings (with both 70 and 90-hp Renault; as both landplane and seaplane); FF 1.9.14; Flown to Calshot 6.9.14; Floats fitted by 15.9.14 but many maintenance problems; Acceptance tests 19.9.14; Fitted land chassis 20.11.14; Fitted new wings 11.14; Refitted floats by 11.1.15 when defects in damaged main float and tail float being made good. Flew reconnaissance 1.2.15; Fitted bomb gear 2.2.15; Crashed, CW Calshot 10.2.15 (FSL WL Welsh); Deleted 2.15

**1 DONNET L'ÉVEQUE PUSHER FLYING BOAT built by Aeros Ltd, London & numbered 18. (80-hp Gnome)**

18    (Initially H7); Deld ECNFS 22.10.12, brief test before dusk by Conneau then flown to Grain; Acceptance test 23.10.12; Damaged float landing 24.12.12 (S/L FET Hewlett & Eng Lt E Featherstone Briggs); Very poor controls, regarded as dangerous by 5.13; Repairs abandoned, tent collapsed on it in gale Spring 1913; Deleted 6.13

**1 SHORT TRACTOR BIPLANE SEAPLANE orderd 2.8.12, built Eastchurch & numbered 19. (140-hp Gnome)** [Gordon Bruce's researches show correct c/n to be S.54]

19    (may initially have been H3); FF 4.11.12 & deld ECNFS; Tested Grain 28.11.13; Accepted 1.12.13, fitted W/T; With No.79 to Felixstowe with 1st Lord 24.4.14 (Winston Churchill); To go Felixstowe to Grain, but not ready 27.4.14; Flown by Lt JW Seddon with Winston Churchill as passenger 15.5.14; Grain 29.5.14; 160-hp Gnome by 6-7.14; Spare m/c for Royal Review 7.14; Westgate by 11.8.14; Damaged on TO Westgate 14.8.14; Mkrs repair 24.8.14; Grain 6.11.14; Tested 27.11.14; Wrecked on patrol near Felixstowe 14.12.14 (Lt HG Wanklyn & L/Tel Hartley picked up by SS

*Orange Nassau*); Aircraft found by trawler *Ocean Rambler* and to Harwich on board destroyer HMS *Brazen*, arrived Shotley Barracks (HMS *Ganges*) but TW; Engine salvaged 15.12.14; Deleted 22.12.14

**2 SHORT IMPROVED TYPE S.41 TRACTOR BIPLANE SEAPLANES built under Cont No C.P.43037/13 at Eastchurch & numbered 20 & 21. (100-hp Gnome)** [Gordon Bruce's researches show correct c/n's to be S.56 & S.57]

20    (Initially to have been H8) On order 11.12; Floats ordered 29.11.12; Deld Grain 21.4.13 (Gordon Bell); Accepted 23.4.13 (Gordon Bell); Fitted with wireless 5.13; Yarmouth for manoeuvres 23.7.13; Grain 27.7.13; Just managed to TO with W/T fitted 10.13; First test of GRW amphibious gear 2.5.14; Patrols from outbreak of war; In need of erection by 8.14, completed 1.9.14; Fitted sight to drop 20-lb bombs 18.11.14; Handley Page overhaul 15.12.14; Yarmouth by rail 12.2.15 (W/T expts); Re-erected by HP 14.2.15; Tested after repair 25.2.15; HSMP 9.6.15 (F/L CHC Smith & PO Mech Jones); For overhaul 20.6.15; HSMP 29.7.15 (F/L EJ Cooper & PO Mech Notley); Calshot by road & rail 20.8.15 (arr 25.8.15); Tested 4.9.15; Chassis wrecked by 1.10.15; Badly damaged 31.1.16; Deleted 14.2.16

21    (Initially to have been H9) Floats ordered 29.11.12; To be fitted with wireless 21.4.13; Deld Grain 22.4.13 (Gordon Bell); Acceptance tests by Gordon Bell; W/T expts; Mkrs repair 9.13; "Old and soggy" by 2.14; Ready at Mkrs after reconstruction for Grain 6.4.14; Fitted land chassis 7.14; Grain defence 8.14; Fitted with parachute flares loaded with lead after airship sighted nr Gorleston, not sent up 14/15.8.14; Fitted with release gear (presumably for Holt parachute flares) 29.8.14 but u/c carried away on test flight and lower plane wrecked; Damaged 8.9.14; Dismantled 9.9.14; tested 23.11.14 (F/L S Pickles); Flown as Home Defence aircraft at Grain 25.12.14; Slightly damaged in storm 29.12.14; Dropped live 100-lb bomb from 1,000ft on adjoining land (S/Cdr PA Shepherd), also 60-lb bomb (S/Cdr DA Oliver), both 18.1.15; Deleted 7.2.15 deteriorated

**1 DEPERDUSSIN TRACTOR MONOPLANE (built by British Deperdussin?), numbered 22. (80-hp Anzani)**

22    Deld Eastchurch by 1.13 but flew very little; Pancaked landing 31.5.13 (S/L R Bell-Davies); "no use" by 8.14; Earmarked by Expeditionary Force 29.9.14 (NTU); ECNFS by 6.10.14; Deleted 20.2.15 [One report suggests originally at CFS, then to Farnborough for mods, then to Eastchurch]

**1 MAURICE FARMAN S.7 LONGHORN PUSHER BIPLANE built by The Aircraft Manufacturing Co Ltd, Hendon & numbered 23. (70-hp Renault)**

23    Deld ECNFS 12.1.13; Flown 14.1.13 (Lt PA Shepherd & Eng Lt E Featherstone Briggs); Flown 15.1.13 (Cdr CR Samson); Sideslipped in 2.12.13 (Capt GV Wildman-Lushington RMA killed & Capt Fawcett killed)

**1 BRISTOL BOXKITE PUSHER BIPLANE built by The British & Colonial Aeroplane Co Ltd, Filton & numbered 24. (50-hp Gnome)**

24    (c/n 99) Tested ECNFS 8.10.12 and in use to at least 11.8.14; Deleted 1.10.14 [later 80-hp Gnome?]

**1 ASTRA TWO-SEATER SEAPLANE to be purchased from France & numbered 25, to be built Billancourt. (100-hp Renault)**

25    On order by 11.12, but cancelled on/by 1.7.14

**1 ROYAL AIRCRAFT FACTORY H.R.E.3 TRACTOR BIPLANE reconstructing from Cdr Oliver Schwann's Avro Type D seaplane at Farnborough by 11.12 & numbered 26. (90-hp Green, changed to 120-hp Austro-Daimler)**

26    Flown Farnborough as landplane 18.11.13 (or 3.12.13). RE.5 substituted for delivery to RN

*Short S.54 Tractor Biplane 19 at Felixstowe, 1914.*
*(J.M.Bruce/G.S.Leslie collection)*

*Short S.56 Tractor Biplane 20 at Yarmouth, 1914.*
*(J.M.Bruce/G.S.Leslie collection)*

*Royal Aircraft Factory H.R.E.3 26. (J.M.Bruce/G.S.Leslie collection)*

*Maurice Farman Seaplane 29 at Yarmouth, July 1913 (FAA Museum)*

**1 ROYAL AIRCRAFT FACTORY R.E.5 TRACTOR BIPLANE built Farnborough & numbered 26. (120-hp Austro-Daimler)**

26    Flown Farnborough by 20.7.14; Deld Hendon by Geoffrey de Havilland 2.9.14; Eastchurch in transit 26.9.14 (S/Cdr AM Longmore); 3 Sqdn France 27.9.14; Bombed Cambrai railway junction 30.9.14 (S/Cdr AM Longmore and F/L E Osmond); Grain arrived in crate 24.10.14; Pemberton Billing for repair 21.11.14; Fort Grange, Gosport to Eastchurch 24.11.14; Engine repaired by Pemberton Billing under Cont No C.P.72199/14/X d/d 15.12.14; 4 Wing Eastchurch 3.8.15; Not to be flown by 1.10.15; Surveyed 22.11.15; CSD White City 23.11.15 and deleted

**1 SOPWITH SCHOOL TRACTOR BIPLANE built Kingston & numbered 27. (To have been 50-hp Gnome but fitted 70-hp Gnome)**

27    Deld by Harry Hawker from Brooklands to ECNFS 23-24.11.12; Tested 27.11.12 (Lt CJ L'Estrange-Malone & Eng Lt E Featherstone Briggs); Only suitable for taxi-ing by 5.13; Sopwith 1.6.13; Reconstructed as Sopwith D.1 three-str; Flown by Harold Barnwell to ECNFS 6.11.13; Fitted with gun mounting mid 3.14; Shoreham 14.4.14; ECNFS 17.4.14; Southampton 25.4.14; Shoreham 27.4.14; FL, overturned nr Shoreham 4.5.14 (FSL TA Rainey); Deleted 5.14

**1 SHORT S.38 NACELLE TYPE PUSHER BIPLANE built Eastchurch & numbered 28. (To have been 50-hp Gnome but fitted 70-hp Gnome) [Gordon Bruce's researches show correct c/n to be S.55]**

28    Deld ECNFS 2.11.12; Accepted 4.11.12 (Lt W Parke); Flown Shoeburyness to Eastchurch for NFS 23.12.12 (Cdr CR Samson); Fitted bomb-dropping gear early 5.13 (visited Brooklands with this 12.5.13); Inspected Hendon 11.6.13; Retd Eastchurch by 30.6.13; Fitted "automatic bomb-dropping gear" mid 1.14; Accident 28.3.14; Surveyed 2.4.14; Fitted W/T by 5.14; Patrols 8.14; To Yarmouth but blown over in gale on arrival 9.8.14; Wreckage returned Eastchurch 11.8.14; Shorts repair 13.8.14; Eastchurch by 17.10.14 - @11.3.15; To Eastbourne FS 3.15; Blown over after landing 7.4.15 (FSL G Donald); Crashed 16.6.15; SCAW Shoreham repair 28.6.15; Still 70-hp Gnome 8.15, but 80-hp Gnome by 10.15; Eastbourne FS 24.11.15; SCAW 31.12.15 (rebuilding); Eastbourne FS 16.5.16; Deleted 17.8.16

**1 MAURICE FARMAN PUSHER BIPLANE HYDRO AEROPLANE built Buc & numbered 29. (70-hp Renault)**

29    (Possibly the Maurice Farman 70-hp Hydro in which Samson & Briggs flew round Southend Pier 30.5.13, but seems too early); Tested Buc 4.6.13 (100-hp engine?); Deld Yarmouth (ex Sheerness?) 18.7.13; Participated Fleet manoeuvres 1913; To Grain for instructional purposes 29.6.14; Felixstowe 11.8.14; Airco 31.8.14 (repair); Calshot 14.10.14; Fitted bomb sight 25.11.14; EF, crashed Southampton Water 19.1.15 (FSL EIM Bird); Repaired; Bembridge 6.7.15; Calshot 13.7.15; Crashed, wrecked 24.7.15 (FSL FJ Bailey unhurt); Deleted 4.8.15.

**1 ROYAL AIRCRAFT FACTORY TWO-SEAT BIPLANE SEAPLANE ordered in/by 11.12, to be built Farnborough & numbered 30.**

30    Cancelled, serial reallocated

**1 DEPERDUSSIN TRACTOR MONOPLANE SEAPLANE purchased from France through Aircraft Manufacturing Co & numbered 30. (100-hp Anzani)**

30    (Possibly the 80-hp Deperdussin deld Eastchurch by Gordon Bell 7.3.13) Believed tested Grain early 1913; unsatisfactory floats; Deleted by end of 1913 [One report says initially 80-hp Anzani]

**1 HENRY FARMAN PUSHER BIPLANE built by the Aircraft Manufacturing Co Ltd at Hendon and purchased 2.13, & numbered 31. (80-hp Gnome)**

31    Tested off Eastchurch 15.3.13; Flown by Cdr CR Samson 17.3.13; EF, FL in marshes and overturned, nr Queenborough, Kent on delivery from Farnborough to Eastchurch 11.4.13 (Capt CE Risk RMLI & Chief ERA Susans both injured); Airco repairs; ECNFS 3.11.13; Fitted W/T early 1914; FL going to assist 103, ran into hole, badly damaged, Elmley Marshes 6.7.14 (F/L ET Newton Clare & Carpenter Brownridge unhurt); Eastchurch defence 8.14; Ostende for patrols 27.8.14; 1 Sqdn Belgium 1.9.14; Wrecked in gale Ostende 12.9.14; Wreck burnt 13.9.14; Serviceable bits retd Eastchurch without engine; Deleted 14.10.14

**1 VICKERS F.B.5 GUNBUS PUSHER BIPLANE built Crayford & numbered 32. (100-hp Gnome Monosoupape)**

32    Mkrs flew extensively before delivery; On order for Eastchurch 7.14; Test for Eastchurch 6.8.14, fitted Vickers belt-fed machine gun with parallel-motion sights; 13.8.14, due for delivery to Eastchurch in few days time; RN Maxim gun fitted 20.8.14; Eastchurch defence by 28.8.14; Retd Mkrs Dartford 16.9.14; Eastchurch 16.10.14; Sent for by W/Cdr CR Samson for Dunkerque 31.10.14; Delayed by weather 2.11.14 and evidently NTU; Engine taken down 11.11.14; Tested with new type of engine with longer propeller, but flew badly, no power, rudder modifications needed adjustment 26.1.15 (F/L HA Buss); 2 Sqdn Eastchurch by 1.15; Deleted 6.15

**1 SOPWITH THREE-SEATER TRACTOR BIPLANE built Kingston and purchased 2.13, to be numbered 33. (80-hp Gnome)**

33    Olympia Show 2.13; Flown at Hendon 1.3.13 but criticised by RN; Retd Mkrs Brooklands for mods 13.3.13; Flown by S/L R Bell-Davies 21.4.13 - @2.5.13; Flown at Eastchurch by Eng Lt E Featherstone Briggs 22.5.13; Mkrs (repair & overhaul); Deld Eastchurch 12.10.13 (Gordon Bell); Eastchurch (Mobile) Squadron 8.8.14; Killingholme 9.8.14; Immingham 10.8.14; Skegness 11.8.14; EF, FL Great Warley en route Eastchurch 24.8.14; Eastchurch 25.8.14; Ostende 27.8.14; Became 3 Sqdn St.Pol 1.9.14; COL, wings damaged, Morbecque 10.9.14 (S/Cdr R Bell-Davies); Eastchurch 18.9.14; Recommended total rebuild with ailerons instead of warping wings 21.9.14 (NTU); Deleted 14.10.14

**1 SHORT S.38 NACELLE TYPE PUSHER BIPLANE built Eastchurch and purchased 2.13, to be numbered 34. (50-hp Gnome) [Gordon Bruce's researches show correct c/n to be S.61]**

34    Deld ECNFS for armament training 14.4.13; Fitted 80-hp Gnome when tested after repairs by naval carpenters 4.7.13 (Eng Lt E Featherstone Briggs); Hendon 2.8.13; ECNFS 4.8.13; Bomb-dropping gear fitted mid 11.13; "Sighting arrangement" added by 6.12.13; Many bombs dropped by Lt RH Clark Hall with S/L REC Peirse as pilot 15.12.13, 17.12.13, 13.1.14 & 21.1.14; Front of nacelle covered by transparent Cellon sheet mid 2.14 (removed by 25.4.14); FL, structure wire carried away, north side Minster station 22.4.14; Tail damaged at Farnborough 10.6.14, retd by road; Eastchurch defence 8.14; Hendon 27.8.14; Grain 3.9.14; Bombs dropped experimentally 11.9.14; Fitted DC 15.9.14, then used for bombing and armament training until 1.15; Deleted 7.2.15 deteriorated

**1 BRISTOL BOXKITE PUSHER BIPLANE built Filton and purchased 2.13, to be numbered 35. (70-hp Gnome)**

35    (c/n 139). Deld ECNFS 20.2.13; frequently unserviceable; Deleted 8.14

**1 DEPERDUSSIN TRACTOR MONOPLANE purchased from France 2.13 & numbered 36. (80-hp Anzani)**

*Sopwith Three-seater (became 33).*
*(J.M.Bruce/G.S.Leslie collection)*

*Sopwith Bat-Boat 38. (FAA Museum)*

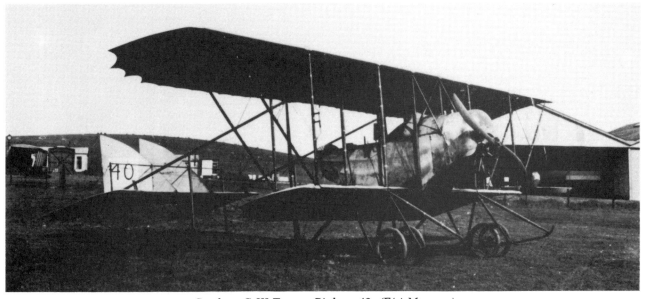

*Caudron G.III Tractor Biplane 40. (FAA Museum)*

*Short S.60 42 after conversion to landplane. (FAA Museum)*

36     Deld ECNFS 4.13; Flown 24.4.13 (Eng Lt E Featherstone Briggs); Tested after trueing up 20.5.13 (Eng Lt E Featherstone Briggs); High chassis unpopular; To Shoreham but smashed 12.5.14; Deleted 1.15

**1 BOREL TRACTOR MONOPLANE SEAPLANE purchased from Borel, France 2.13 & numbered 37. (80-hp Gnome)**

37     Purchased at Olympia Show 2.13; Accepted Grain 11.3.13 (Georges Chemet & Lt JW Seddon); Flown 13.3.13 (Cdr CR Samson & Eng Lt E Featherstone Briggs); Crashed landing in the Swale, Harty Ferry, Sheppey 18.3.13 (Cdr CR Samson & Lt JW Seddon); Deleted 8.13?

**1 SOPWITH BAT BOAT PUSHER BIPLANE AMPHIBIAN FLYING BOAT ordered 2.13 under Cont No.32098/13 & built Kingston, to be numbered 38. (90-hp Austro-Daimler)**

38     Ordered after Olympia Show 2.13; Left works 8.6.13 for assembly Hamble River, Luke & Co; Handed over to Naval Wing at Calshot 8.6.13; To Brighton 23.8.13; Sank at moorings in bad weather, Brighton 24.8.13; Extensively damaged while being salvaged; Sopwith for rebuild; Never bore No.38

38     Numbered 38, probably used hull of earlier aircraft but had revised tail unit; Calshot 23.11.13; Crashed 17 or 18.5.14 [Doubts expressed on this. May have been the machine tested 28.6.14 by Lt AW Bigsworth, though could have been after repair]; Grain 6.14 - 7.14; Felixstowe by 1.8.14; Reported wing fabric rotted through 11.8.14; To Yarmouth 20.8.14; Patched 21.8.14; Shipped to Scapa Flow in SS *Indraini* 24.8.14; Hull in store at Scapa 29.8.14; Serviceable on 30.8.14; Taxied into some wreckage 11.9.14; Serviceable by 15.9.14; Bows stoved in while taxying, CW 29.9.14 (F/Cdr H Fawcett & passenger unhurt); Destroyed in gale Scapa Flow 21.11.14; Deleted 12.14

**1 BLERIOT XI-2 TRACTOR MONOPLANE purchased from France 2.13 & numbered 39. (80-hp Gnome)**

39     Bought by Admiralty at Olympia Show 2.13; Acceptance trial ECNFS 26.2.13 (Gustav Hamel with Eng Lt E Featherstone Briggs, who subsequently flew it frequently); While returning from Shoreham, EF, FL, on nose in ditch nr Tunbridge Wells, retd by road 30.6.13 (Eng Lt E Featherstone Briggs); To Lilbourne for Army manoeuvres 17.9.13 (Eng Lt E Featherstone Briggs); Flew 13½ hours, retd Eastchurch 26.9.13; New wings fitted by 11.10.13; Gun firing trials 10.12.13 (Eng Lt E Featherstone Briggs & Lt RH Clark-Hall); Fitted 80-hp Le Rhône 3.14; Climbed to 14,920 ft to set new British altitude record 11.3.14 (Eng Lt E Featherstone Briggs); CFS 25.4.14; Farnborough 27.4.14; ECNFS 8.5.14; U/c smashed on TO for flight over King of Denmark's yacht, FL nr Grain, damaged, dismantled and taken to Grain 9.5.14 (Eng Lt E Featherstone Briggs); Repaired Eastchurch; Patrols from Eastchurch 8.14; Ostende 27.8.14; Crashed Dunkerque 30.8.14 (F/L Lord EA Grosvenor); Became 3 Sqdn Dunkerque 1.9.14; To England in HMS *Empress*, apparently in CW condition 6.9.14; Badly damaged on TO in strong wind, Morbecque, 20.9.14; ADD 22.9.14; Unsafe, for deletion by 27.9.14; In bits to Sheerness in SS *Princess* 3.11.14; Deleted 4.11.14

**1 CAUDRON G.III TRACTOR BIPLANE purchased from France 2.13 under Cont No C.P.32194/13, built Rue & numbered 40. (80-hp Gnome)**

40     Left Paris 8.3.13; Flown to England by Philippe Marty 9.3.13; Reached W.H.Ewen Aviation Co Ltd at Hendon 12.3.13; Deld ECNFS 3.13; Extensive overhaul mid 7.13 - mid 8.13; Flew 7½ hrs in Army manoeuvres at Lilbourne 9.13 (Lt RLG Marix); Still 80-hp Gnome 28.3.14; Deleted 6.14

**1 AVRO TYPE E TRACTOR BIPLANE ordered 2.13 under Cont No C.P.32188/13, built Manchester & numbered 41. (50-hp Gnome)**

41     Deld ECNFS 4.3.13; Proof-loaded for training duties mid 3.13; Fitted wireless aerials week ending 24.5.13; Extensively repaired and overhauled 7.13 - 9.13; Tested after alterations 4.2.14; Minor accident 28.2.14; Nose skid caught hummock while landing, o/t, Eastchurch 7.3.14 (L/Artificer Bradford); repaired Eastchurch; Flown to Portsmouth by F/L HA Littleton for Royal Review 13.7.14; EF, FL, then FL on TO, dived in, badly damaged Shoreham 22.7.14 (F/L HA Littleton); Mkrs repair; Hendon by rail 18.9.14 - LM11.3.15; Deleted 3.15

**1 SHORT TRACTOR BIPLANE SEAPLANE built Eastchurch for 1913 Olympia Show. Sold Admiralty 11.2.13 & numbered 42. (80-hp Gnome) [Gordon Bruce's researches show correct c/n to be S.60]**

42     Main floats and tail built 4.2.13; Deld ex Port Laing to temporary station Leven 12.7.13; Heavy landing, burst two floats, Leven 27.7.13 (Mjr R Gordon, RMLI); Repaired; Tested 26.8.13; Port Seton 26.8.13; Retd Leven; Unable to TO with W/T 10.1.14; Port Laing 1.14; Damaged float u/c at St.Andrews 20.1.14 (Mjr R Gordon, RMLI); Dysart aerodrome 21.1.14; new Broomfield Aerodrome, Montrose 22.1.14; Temp converted to landplane ("lash-up") 1.14; Dundee 2.14; Refitted floats for Fleet manoeuvres 3.14 - 4.14; Leven 18.3.14; Dundee 21.4.14; Reverted to landplane; Eastchurch (Mobile) Sqdn Skegness 23.8.14; Eastchurch 24.8.14; Ostende 27.8.14; Became 3 Sqdn Belgium 1.9.14 - @14.9.14; RNAS HQ Flight Morbecque by 21.9.14; EF on TO, hit tree, Morbecque 28.9.14 (Cdr CR Samson); Deleted 14.11.14 BR

**1 BRISTOL T.B.8 TRACTOR BIPLANE ordered 2.13 under Cont No C.P. 32096/13, built Filton & numbered 43. (80-hp Gnome)**

[70-hp Renault per official 1.17 list, seems doubtful]

43     (c/n 225). Converted from Coanda monoplane? FF 12.8.13; Deld Eastchurch c.1.10.13; Accepted ECNFS (Sydney Sippe) 13.10.13; Eastbourne 17.1.14; ECNFS 19.1.14; Stalled from 50 ft and crashed, Leigh-on-Sea, Essex 3.2.14 (FSL TA Rainey); Bristol rebuilt 3.14 (cost £385); tested at ECNFS 7.5.14; Eastchurch (Mobile) Squadron 8.8.14; Felixstowe 9.8.14; Immingham 10.8.14; Skegness by 11.8.14; Immingham 24.8.14; Left for Eastchurch 2.9.14, but FL, damaged chassis and lower wings 3.9.14; Very poor condition by 9.14; Packed at Grain for repairs by Cedric Lee & Co/SCAW 14.11.14; ECNFS 9.6.15; Wrecked 4.7.15; Test after alterations 6.8.15; Damaged 22.10.15; Eastbourne FS by 1.3.16; Dismantled and held as spares 3.3.16; Deleted 13.3.16

**1 DEPERDUSSIN TRACTOR MONOPLANE SEAPLANE purchased from France under Cont No C.P.32688/13 dated 2.13, to be numbered 44. (100-hp Anzani)**

44     Deld 4.13; Twin floats and probably ailerons; Deleted .13

**1 CAUDRON G.III TRACTOR BIPLANE purchased under Cont No C.P.32926/13 from France through W.H.Ewen Aviation Co Ltd, Hendon, built Rue & numbered 45. (80-hp Gnome) [50-hp Gnome at first?]**

45     Possibly the Caudron deld Hendon by Gordon Bell 28.2.13; Tested Hendon 12.3.13 (Philippe Marty & Lt ER Berne); ECNFS 1.4.13; Rebuilt; Ready for test 27.6.14; Accepted 29.6.14; Hendon 7.8.14; Run into by a Grahame-White aircraft 31.8.14; Grahame-White repair 31.8.14; Hendon 10.14?; Caudron by 11.3.15, rebuilding and fitting 70-hp Gnome; Chingford 11.6.15; Overturned 12.6.15 (F/L FW Merriam unhurt); Re-erecting by 4.8.15; Deleted 12.15

**2 ROYAL AIRCRAFT FACTORY B.E.2a TRACTOR BIPLANES built Farnborough, purchased 2.13 & numbered 46 & 47. (70-hp Renault)**

*Royal Aircraft Factory B.E.2a 49 and 50 at Cosham, Portsmouth for Royal Review, July 1914. 50 was Cdr C.R.Samson's favourite aircraft, 49 being flown by Lt E.Osmond. (FAA Museum)*

*Caudron Amphibian 55 while attached to HMS Hermes, July 1913. (M.H.Goodall)*

46 Tested at Farnborough 31.3.13; Accepted 9.4.13; Eastchurch 13.4.13 (Cdr CR Samson); Run into by Deperdussin (No.7?) on ground, damaged 24.4.13 (S/L R Bell-Davies); Flown after tuning up 23.5.13 (Eng Lt E Featherstone Briggs); Royal Aircraft Factory extensive overhaul by 7.6.13; RNAS banned B.E.2 flying 6.13; RAF fit new wings mid 8.13; ECNFS by 5.14 to 7.14; Royal Aircraft Factory, second conversion to B.E.2c 8.14; Eastchurch (Mobile) Sqdn 8.8.14; Immingham 9.8.14; Wrecked Skegness 20.8.14; EF, FL Faversham 22.9.14; Eastchurch by 25.9.14; Eastchurch to HQ Flight RNAS Morbecque (via Dunkerque), badly damaged landing on arrival 27.9.14; ADD repair, to be completed 4.10.14; 3 Sqdn by 8.10.14; Deleted 12.14

47 Test at Farnborough 31.3.13; Brooklands 4.13; Accepted 9.4.13; Farnborough to Eastchurch 9.4.13; Flown by Cdr CR Samson 9.4.13; RAF repairs and overhaul 3.5.13; Flown Eastchurch 19.5.13 (Eng Lt E Featherstone Briggs); RNAS banned BE2 flying 6.13; RAF fit new wings mid 8.13; RAF conversion to B.E.2c 8.14; Eastchurch (Mobile) Sqdn 8.8.14; en route Skegness 11.8.14; Eastchurch 24.8.14; Dunkerque 27.8.14; Became 1 Sqdn Belgium 2.9.14; Crashed in FL, Dunkerque 11.9.14 [probably the aircraft FL by Lt R Bell-Davies in field near Roulers and damaged by Belgians to prevent capture by approaching Germans 11.9.14]; Wrecked in gale Ostende 12.9.14; Serviceable parts to Eastchurch 9.14; 3 Sqdn Belgium by 12.10.14; Hendon by 20.12.14 (rebuilt?); detd Dover for raid on Zeebrugge or Ostende 10.2.15; Dunkerque 11.2.15; Took part in mass raid on Zeebrugge and other targets; Dover 22.2.15 (transit); Hendon 23.2.15; Chingford 21.5.15; AZP 31.5.15/1.6.15 (F/Cdr WG Sitwell); Wrecked 27.1.16 (PFSL RG Gregory injured); Deleted 5.5.16

**1 BOREL TRACTOR MONOPLANE SEAPLANE purchased under Cont No C.P.37126/13 through agents DelaCombe & Maréchal & numbered 48. (80-hp Gnome)**

48 Probably the aircraft erecting at Hamble on/by 6.6.13 and due for acceptance test 9-10.6.13; HMS *Hermes* at Sheerness 5.7.13; Grain 14.7.13; HMS *Hermes* 18.7.13 (for Fleet manoeuvres); Wrecked on board in heavy seas when its canvas shelter was blown away 22.7.13; Grain Repair Station 25.7.13 (subsequently used for training); Wheeled u/c by 10.14; Deleted 9.12.14

**2 ROYAL AIRCRAFT FACTORY B.E.2a TRACTOR BIPLANES built under Cont No C.P.37126/13 by Hewlett & Blondeau, Clapham & numbered 49 & 50. (70-hp Renault)**

49 Transferred from RFC (Military Wing); Deld ECNFS 22.1.14; Tested by Ronald Kemp 26-27.1.14; Flown by F/L E Osmond to Portsmouth for Royal Review 13.7.14; EF, FL, through hedge, on nose nr Tatsfield, Surrey 27.7.14 (F/L E Osmond), retd by rail; Eastchurch (Mobile) Sqdn 8.8.14; arr Maldon 9.8.14; Immingham 10.8.14; Skegness 11.8.14 (wrecked en route); Landbeach 25.8.14 (en route Eastchurch); Eastchurch 26.8.14; Dunkerque 27.8.14; Became 3 Sqdn Belgium 1.9.14; EF, FL safely near Antwerp 20.9.14; 1 Sqdn Belgium 27.9.14; Lost in retreat, faulty engine, Antwerp 9.10.14; Deleted 14.10.14

50 Transferred from RFC (Military Wing); Deld ECNFS circa 12.2.14; Flown 13.2.14; New lower wing fitted end 2.14; Additional fuel tank in front cockpit; Cdr Samson's favourite aircraft; Flown by Cdr CR Samson to Portsmouth for Royal Review 13.7.14; Eastchurch (Mobile) Sqdn 8.8.14; Long Sutton 9.8.14 (patrols); Wrecked en route Skegness 11.8.14; Eastchurch 24.8.14; Dunkerque 27.8.14; Became 1 Sqdn Belgium 1.9.14; Attacked Düsseldorf airship sheds 22.9.14 (Mjr EL Gerrard RMLI); Still 1 Sqdn 27.9.14; 3 Sqdn Belgium by 8.10.14; arr Ostende 9.10.14; Wings renewed 1.15; Dover (packed) 20.2.15 (arr 28.2.15); Shipped from Plymouth 19 or 20.3.15 in SS *Inkosi* or SS *Moorgate*; 3 Squadron Dardanelles, first flown 28.3.15 (first landplane to fly there); Renamed 3 Wing 21.6.15; Sometimes flown as bomber; Last recorded flight

10.12.15 when Bell-Davies visited 3 Wing; Broken up 1.16 on unit's return to UK as unfit to travel

**3 AVRO 503 TRACTOR BIPLANE SEAPLANES built Manchester under Cont No C.P.36208/13 & numbered 51 to 53. (100-hp Gnome or Gnome Monosoupape)**

51 (100-hp Gnome); Deld Grain for erection 8.9.13; Acceptance test including W/T 25.9.13 (FP Raynham); Converted landplane trainer 9.14; ECNFS 9.14; Hendon by 31.12.14; Tested 2.1.15 (Merriam); Chingford 24.5.15; Crashed reservoir bank, TW 11.8.15 (PFSL NWG Blackburn); Deleted 18.8.15

52 (100-hp Gnome). Deld Grain 2.10.13; Acceptance test including W/T 7.10.13 (FP Raynham); W/T test 19.11.13; Floats moved, plus 30% increase in rudder; Retested Grain 17.2.14; Convtd landplane trainer 9.14; ECNFS 9.14; Hendon dismantled 29.10.14; Tested 7.12.14 (F Warren Merriam); Damaged 12.1.15 (FSL GF Breese); Mainly u/s by 6.15 when fitted 100-hp SPA; Later fitted 60-hp Le Rhône; To Chingford but EF, FL Watford en route 18.9.15; Surveyed 19.1.16; Deleted 21.1.16

53 (100-hp Gnome Monosoupape, later 60-hp Le Rhône). Deld Grain 15.10.13 (Raynham); Accepted 20.11.13 (Raynham); Little flying prewar; Convtd landplane trainer; Hewlett & Blondeau rebuild by 2.1.15; ECNFS by 7.2.15; Grain 5.4.15 (W/T expts); Eastchurch 4.15; General overhaul 4.9.15; Surveyed and to CSD White City 22.11.15

**1 COVENTRY ORDNANCE WORKS TRACTOR BIPLANE SEAPLANE ordered under Cont No C.P.40688/13 to be built Coventry & numbered 54. (160-hp Gnome)**
[also officially listed to have 80-hp Gnome]

54 To be fitted with W/T (call sign No.6 allotted 8.13). ["Caudron" 54 ready for test after repair 25.4.14]; On order for Grain 7.14, but never delivered. Still on order 1.9.15

**3 CAUDRON TRACTOR BIPLANE AMPHIBIAN SEAPLANES purchased from France 3.13 under Cont No C.P.36526/13 for delivery through W.H.Ewen & Co Ltd & numbered 55 to 57. Built at Rue. (80-hp Gnome or 100-hp Gnome Monosoupape)**

55 (80-hp Gnome). Flown from Le Crotoy to Grain by Philippe Marty 12.6.13; HMS *Hermes* 19.7.13; Yarmouth 19.7.13; Ex reserve to HMS *Hermes* 25.7.13 to replace Borel No.48; Flown from trackway on ship while making 10 knots into wind 28.7.13 (F/L FW Bowhill); Yarmouth 29.7.13; (Reported flown off platform 6.8.13 but from Ships Log it does not appear to have been on board then); Grain to HMS *Hermes* 20.8.13; Grain 9.10.13; Sideslipped in on TO River Medway 15.10.13 (Lt AB Gaskell & ERA Rees uninjured); Deleted 25.6.14

56 (80-hp Gnome). Flown from Le Crotoy to Grain by Pickles 30.6.13; Acceptance test 1.7.13 (Pickles with Lt JW Seddon); HMS *Hermes* 5.7.13; Fell in sea 1m from shore 14.7.13 (F/L FW Bowhill clung to wreckage, rescued by motor launch); Wreckage salved & to Yarmouth but BR

57 (100-hp Gnome Monosoupape). Single vertical tail surface. Delivery by Sidney Pickles beset by engine problems. Delivered Grain 6.8.13; Crashed on acceptance flight Grain 25.8.13; Repaired; Retested, but struck buoy on TO, sank, o/t, River Medway 15.10.13 (F/L EB Bauman); Retrieved but not repaired and not accepted

**3 SOPWITH HT TRACTOR BIPLANE SEAPLANES built Kingston under Cont No C.P.36209/13 & numbered 58 to 60. (100-hp Anzani)**

58 Fitted W/T; Passed acceptance tests at Calshot 28.6.13 and taken over by Lt Spenser DA Grey; Churchill flown 28.8.13; Various experiments early 1914 at Calshot; Tested by Howard Pixton new lifting tailplane 3.3.14; W/T removed to improve performance 4.4.14; Bomb-

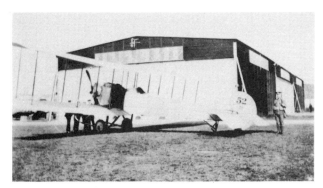

*Avro 503 52 in landplane trainer form, photographed at Cranwell. (J.M.Bruce/G.S.Leslie collection)*

*Short S.38-type Biplane 66 used for gun trials at Eastchurch, during a visit by Winston Churchill, 15 May 1914. Cdr C.R.Samson is on the left. (via J.D.Oughton)*

*Maurice Farman S.7 Longhorn 67 at Felixstowe. (via Frank Cheesman)*

*Short 74 Type Seaplane 75. (J.M.Bruce/G.S.Leslie collection)*

*Sopwith HT Seaplane 60 piloted by Harry Hawker with Courtney as passenger, probably at Yarmouth. (J.M.Bruce/G.S.Leslie collection)*

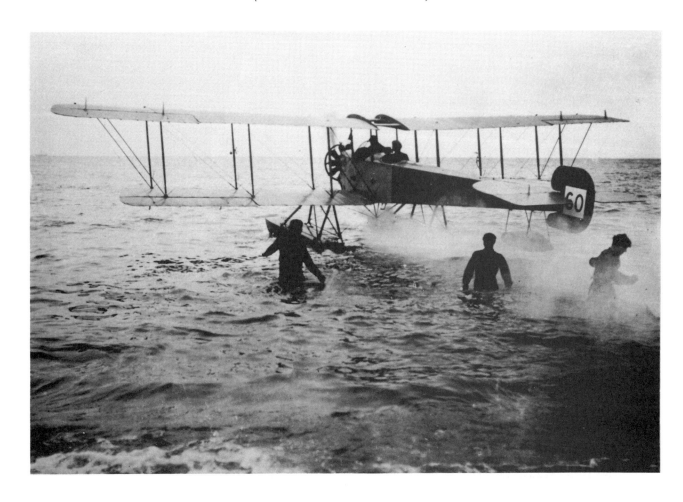

dropping gear fitted 6.5.14; Demonstrated with new floats designed at National Physical Laboratory 25.6.14; Calshot to Hamble repair 29.6.14 (presume this was 58); Still Calshot to 7.14; Sopwith by 8.14; Fitted wheeled u/c; Hendon 18.9.14; Eastchurch 26.9.14; 3 Sqdn Morbecque (via Dunkerque) 27.9.14; ADD 9.10.14; Reported by W/Cdr CR Samson as unsuitable for active service 31.10.14; To Sheerness in SS *Princess* 3.11.14; ECNFS 3.11.14; FL Tollesbury, Essex, then to Yarmouth 18.11.14; FL in sea off Winterton, wrecked, drifted ashore 19.11.14 (2 crew picked up by trawler); Wreckage salved and retd Yarmouth from California, Norfolk; Surveyed 1.1.15; Deleted 9.1.15

59   Fitted W/T; Arrived Cromarty by lorry 19.7.13 for Naval manoeuvres (second aircraft to arrive on station); First flown there but damaged 23.7.13; Caught by gust of wind on turn, dived into water, towed ashore 3.9.13 (Lt DA Oliver); Major parts left Cromarty for repair by Mkrs; Became landplane; Grain by 2.14; W/T removed to improve performance 4.4.14; Grain defence 8.14; Tested by F/Cdr HR Busteed as landplane 21.8.14; Used for experiments with Holt parachute flares fitted with release gear 29.8.14; Crashed en route France, TW Deal 7.9.14 (F/L AC Barnby injured); Deleted 1.10.14 BR

60   Passed tests at Yarmouth W/E 5.8.13; had W/T 4.14; Float damaged on TO 1.4.14 (F/L RJ Bone); Presume other damage as finally burnt 5.14 [later 80-hp Gnome ??]

**1 SOPWITH TYPE S PUSHER BIPLANE HYDRO AEROPLANE built Kingston under Cont No C.P.36209/13 & numbered 61. (Two 120-hp Austro-Daimler)**

61   Ordered for Calshot, to carry a gun. To Sopwith, Hamble 3.14; Erection started 5.14; Awaiting sand (strength) tests at Sopwith, Woolston by 7.8.14, APU and wireless installation now removed and at Calshot, engines to be removed; Never accepted and probably never reached Calshot

**5 SHORT S.38 NACELLE TYPE PUSHER BIPLANES built Eastchurch under Cont No C.P.36191/13 & numbered 62 to 66. (50 or 80-hp Gnome) [Gordon Bruce's researches show correct c/n's to be as listed]**

62   (C/n S.66). (50-hp Gnome) (DC) Acceptance test, engine stopped 3,500 ft, landed safely 12.7.13 (Pickles); Flown ECNFS 25.7.13; New wings fitted mid 9.13; Continued Benzol tests 28.10.13 (Eng Lt E Featherstone Briggs); Went to assistance of 65 at Dunkirk Hill, then EF on TO, landed heavily avoiding fence 10.11.13 (S/L R Bell-Davies); Experimental floats made 12.13 but probably transferred to 65; O/t in gale 6.2.14; Shorts repair; Accepted ECNFS 13.5.14; Eastchurch (Mobile) Sqdn, Immingham 28.7.14; ECNFS 2.9.14; Earmarked for Dunkerque 6.9.14 but never sent; C Flt Eastchurch 3.11.14; Re-engined with 70-hp Gnome some time between 12.14 and 11.3.15; FL outside aerodrome 3.6.15; minor crash 30.7.15; Wrecked 25.9.15; Deleted 22.2.16 (after 4 rebuilds)

63   (C/n S.67). (50-hp Gnome, later 70-hp Gnome by 11.3.15). Acceptance tests ECNFS 11.8.13; Army manoeuvres Lilbourne 9.13; Tested W/T 4.14; ECNFS by 8.14; Bomb experiments 16.8.14; Earmarked for Dunkerque 3.9.14 but not sent; C Flt Eastchurch 3.11.14; Damaged 26.5.15; Wrecked 21.6.15; Deleted 6.9.15

64   (C/n S.76). (80-hp Gnome). ECNFS by 9.13; Fitted W/T; Army manoeuvres Lilbourne 17-26.9.13; Flown by F/L DG Young to Portsmouth for Royal Review 13.7.14; Eastchurch (Mobile) Sqdn, Immingham 28.7.14; Crashed 14.8.14; Repair attempted, but deleted 19.8.14 [BUT Shorts to deliver set of wheels 27.8.14 !] [Reported 50-hp Gnome at first]

65   (C/n S.75). (80-hp Gnome). Accepted Eastchurch 16.9.13 (Pickles with Capt IT Courtney); Army manoeuvres Lilbourne 17.9.13 (Asst Payr EB Parker) - 10.13; Floats under construction mid 10.13; FL Dunkirk Hill as landplane 19.11.13 (S/L RLG Marix); (further?) pair of floats in hand by 6.12.13; Still flying as landplane 8.1.14 & 20.2.14; On floats by 2.14 - 5.14; To

Kingsnorth & return 13.4.14 (presumed as landplane); Visited Dover & Deal 19.4.14; Work begun on installation of GRW Wheel Attachment [Gregory-Riley-White beaching gear] 2.5.14; Still floats and wheels 28.8.14; Reverted to wheel u/c 9.14; C Flt Eastchurch 3.11.14; Damaged 8.6.15; Wrecked 15.6.15; Flying by 19.7.15; Wrecked 1.8.15; Repaired; Mid-air collision with Caudron G.III 3282 at Eastchurch and wrecked 12.9.15 (FSL M Keith Johnston killed); Deleted 11.15

66   (C/n S.77). (80-hp Gnome). Rebuild of c/n S.28 "Sommer" type biplane (McClean No.5, ex Moore-Brabazon No.6). First flown by Gordon Bell at Eastchurch 24.9.13 (passenger Lt RH Clark Hall); Tested gun and wireless installations; Acceptance test with 265-lb ballast at ECNFS 22.10.13; Fired Vickers and .45 Maxim guns 21.1.14; Fitted 50-hp Gnome 6.14 - 7.14; Eastchurch patrol 8.14; Eastchurch (Mobile) Sqdn, Immingham 9.8.14 (arr 10.8.14); Skegness 11.8.14; Immingham 25.8.14; Armed with grenades and bombs 8.14; Mkrs 28.8.14; Eastchurch 25.9.14; 2 Sqdn Eastchurch 10.14; B Flt Eastchurch 3.11.14; Deleted 4.15

**1 MAURICE FARMAN S.7 LONGHORN PUSHER BIPLANE built under Cont No C.P.35945/13 by Aircraft Manufacturing Co Ltd, Hendon & numbered 67. (70-hp Renault)**

67   In use at Yarmouth by 7.13; Participated Navy manoeuvres from 23.7.13; Felixstowe by 2.14; Bomb racks fitted 15.8.14; En route Yarmouth to Felixstowe 28.8.14; Crashed Hendon 29.8.14; Probably to Airco for repair; Hendon as trainer 15.11.14; Chingford 1.5.15; Wrecked 17.5.16; Still Chingford 29.9.17; Deleted by 29.12.17

**1 ROYAL AIRCRAFT FACTORY H.R.E.6 TRACTOR BIPLANE SEAPLANE ordered 10.13, to be built Farnborough under Cont No C.P.41589/14 & numbered 68. (150-hp Salmson)**

[was to be 100-hp Renault per 1.17 official list]

68   On order 10.13 to 9.15 but never delivered; Detail construction 11.13, but design never finalised

**2 MAURICE FARMAN S.7 LONGHORN PUSHER BIPLANES built by The Aircraft Manufacturing Co Ltd, Hendon under Cont No C.P.359945/13 & numbered 69 & 70. (70-hp Renault)**

69   Deld by Lt CL Courtney to Yarmouth 31.5.13 (first landplane at Yarmouth); FL, damaged 3.14; Mkrs repair 4.14; Yarmouth 10.8.14; ECNFS 25.9.14; C Flt Eastchurch 3.11.14; still Eastchurch 11.3.15; Eastbourne NFS 3.15; EF, FL and wrecked Eastbourne 7.5.15 (F/L RH Jones); Deleted 17.5.15

70   (later 120-hp Renault). Possibly the Admiralty aircraft which arrived Hendon 26.7.13. No.70 flown at Hendon by Lt Spenser DA Grey 6.9.13; ECNFS by 30.9.13 with signalling apparatus; Flown by F/L C Draper to Portsmouth for Royal Review 13.7.14? [or may have been 146]; Felixstowe War Flt 28.7.14; Fitted bombs by 15.8.14; Fitted bombs and rifle 16.8.14; Eastchurch 22.9.14; Mkrs repair 9.10.14; ECNFS by 1.1.15; Crashed 6.4.15; Damaged 29.7.15; Wrecked 25.8.15; Crashed 6.10.15 (FSL HC Jevons); Bomb Flight Eastchurch 17.3.16; Damaged 31.3.16; Gun Flight Eastchurch 24.5.16; School Flight Eastchurch 31.5.16; Deleted 6.9.16

**3 MAURICE FARMAN S.7 LONGHORN PUSHER BIPLANE SEAPLANES built by The Aircraft Manufacturing Co Ltd, Hendon under Cont No C.P.35945/13 & numbered 71 to 73. (70-hp Renault)**

71   Arrived Leven 7.13; Tested 8.8.13; Accident while flying across Forth 25.8.13; No flying after 11.13; Wings to Mkrs 11.13; Remainder to Dundee 2.14; Pieces to Calshot 19.8.14; Deleted 13.1.15

72   Delivered Grain 15.8.13; Acceptance test 19.8.13; many faults; Crashed and wrecked off Dover pier while searching for Gustav Hamel 23.5.14 (Lt FG Brodribb);

*Short Tractor Seaplane 78 at Westgate, August 1914.
(J.M.Bruce/G.S.Leslie collection)*

*Short Pusher Seaplane 80. (J.M.Bruce/G.S.Leslie
collection)*

*Borel Monoplane Seaplane 83, Sub-Lt J.L.Travers'
aircraft. (via P.H.T.Green)*

*Henry Farman F.22H Seaplane 97 at Yarmouth.
(J.M.Bruce/G.S.Leslie collection)*

*Sopwith D.1 Three-seater 103 at Shoreham. (via Philip Jarrett)*

Deleted 25.6.14

73 Delivered Grain 15.8.13; Passed acceptance tests 22.8.13 (Lt JW Seddon); Accepted by Admiralty 9.9.13; Used in experiments in shooting at "aerial targets" (i.e. wild ducks, of which 2 bagged); Calshot by road without engine 9.9.14; Flying 10.14; damaged 5.11.14; Repaired; Fitting 70-hp Renault 2.4.15; Bembridge 4.15; Calshot 24.4.15; Bembridge 28.4.15; Calshot 5.7.15; Deleted 1.1.16

**4 SHORT ADMIRALTY 74 TYPE TRACTOR BIPLANE SEAPLANES built Eastchurch under Cont No C.P.38479/13 & numbered 74 to 77. (100-hp Gnome Monosoupape)** [Gordon Bruce's researches show correct c/n's to be S.69 to S.72]

74 Flown by Gordon Bell from Eastchurch to Grain 19.1.14; Acceptance test Grain 23.1.14; Possibly retd Eastchurch before final delivery to Grain 27.1.14; retested after 20.3.14; erected Leven W/E 21.3.14 (W/T fitted); Took part in Fleet manoeuvres; Dundee 21.4.14; Dismantled for transport by rail to Calshot for Royal Review end 6.14; With "B" Flight Calshot for Royal Review Flypast 13.7.14; Left for Grain 28.7.14; FL Grain with float trouble 29.7.14; Westgate by 11.8.14; Grain 18.8.14; Shipped from Sheerness in SS *Indraini* 23.8.14; Scapa 29.8.14; Shipped to Grain 20.11.14; Handley Page repair 12.14; Grain 29.12.14; Re-erecting 11.3.15; Tested after reconstruction 20.3.15; Aileron jammed, went out of control, smashed 29.3.15 (F/L BF Fowler & F/L GE Livock unhurt); Deleted 30.3.15

75 Probably the Short tractor flown by Gordon Bell at Eastchurch 31.1.14 and to Grain 2.2.14. No.75 to Grain 2.14; Leven by 23.3.14 (W/T fitted); Dundee 21.4.14; Dismantled for transport by rail to Calshot for Royal Review end 6.14; With "B" Flight Calshot for Royal Review Flypast 13.7.14; Left for Grain, but EF, FL Dover 28.7.14; arr Grain 29.7.14; arr Clacton Adv Base for Grain 3.8.14 (patrols); Westgate by 11.8.14 (patrols); Grain 18.8.14; Patrol to Ostende, EF, FL, damaged by tug 8.14 (F/Cdr CF Kilner & F/Cdr ETR Chambers); Shipped back to Sheerness in SS *Empress* 23.8.14; Shorts repair 24.8.14; To Dundee by rail 22.9.14 (arr 25.9.14); Granton by 11.11.14; Dundee 19.11.14; Granton by 24.11.14; Dismantling 6.12.14; Blackburn 8.12.14 (repair & overhaul); Dundee for re-erection 25.1.15; Test after overhaul, accepted then sideslipped turning, wrecked 24.2.15 (F/L HA Busk & AM Vobe); Deleted 3.15

76 Grain 2.14; Rebuilt by 4.14 with W/T; Re-acceptance tests at Grain 9.6.14; (S/Cdr CR Samson and Winston Churchill at Grain); EF, beached Dover 18.6.14; Dismantled for transport by rail to Calshot for Royal Review end 6.14; With "B" Flight Calshot for Royal Review Flypast 14.7.14; Left for Grain 28.7.14; EF, FL Littlehampton 29.7.14; Clacton Adv Base 2.8.14; to Westgate but engine trouble 13.8.14; Grain 18.8.14; to Ostende but split float 19.8.14; Shipped back to Sheerness in SS *Empress* for repair 22.8.14; Grain 23.8.14; Dundee by rail 22.9.14 (arr 25.9.14); Granton by 11.11.14; Dismantled 6.12.14; Blackburns 8.12.14 (repair & overhaul); Dundee 25.1.15 (re-erection); Accepted 15.2.15; Wrecked 22.2.15 (F/L H Stewart & AM Groucott); Deleted 3.15

77 Deld Grain 16.2.14; Leven for Fleet manoeuvres 3.14 (W/T fitted); Erected week ending 21.3.14; Dundee 20.4.14 (fitted W/T); With "B" Flight Calshot for Royal Review Flypast 13.7.14; Grain 28.7.14; Clacton Adv Base 2.8.14 & 11.8.14; Westgate 13.8.14; Ostende 14.8.14 (weather); Grain 19.8.14; Shipped from Sheerness in SS *Indraini* 23.8.14; Scapa 29.8.14; Dundee 25.9.14; FTR North Sea patrol 29.9.14 (F/L HD Vernon & F/L BD Ash killed); Deleted 4.1.15 [74-77 all arrived Calshot 30.6.14?]

**2 SHORT TRACTOR BIPLANE SEAPLANES built Eastchurch under Cont No C.P.38479/13 & numbered 78 & 79. (160-hp Gnome)** [Gordon Bruce's researches show correct c/n's to be S.73 and S.74]

78 Possibly the 160-hp Short in which Lt JW Seddon flew Winston Churchill from Tilbury Fort to Grain 7.2.14

[but could be "19"]; Grain 16.2.14 ["100-hp" per Samson]; Flew patrol to Ostende 9.8.14; Westgate by 18.8.14; EF, FL Middelkerke, towed in to Ostende 18.8.14; Grain 2.9.14; Preparing for shipment 12.9.14; Dundee by rail 22.9.14 (arr 25.9.14); Beached, damaged chassis 6m SE of Dunbar 16.12.14; Overhaul 2.15; EF, FL Thornton Lough 15.3.15; EF, beached Pea Sand 16.3.15; Seriously damaged in storm 17.3.15; Dismantling Dunbar 18.3.15; Dundee by rail 19.3.15; Test after reconstruction 23.7.15; Flown 1.10.15 (FSL EAdeL de Ville & CPO Jones), then to repair; Deleted 9.5.16

79 Probably the 160-hp Short which first flew Leysdown then deld by Gordon Bell to Grain 11.3.14 (passenger CR Fairey); Felixstowe 1.4.14; With No.19 to Felixstowe with 1st Lord (Winston Churchill) 24.4.14; Grain 27.4.14; EF on cross-Channel patrol, FL Dunkerque 10.8.14; Ostende 10.8.14; Grain 20.8.14; Westgate 8.14; Grain 2.9.14; Dundee by rail 22.9.14 (arr 25.9.14); Granton by 11.11.14; EF, FL, BU in heavy seas 2m N of Fifeness 1.1.15 (Lt HA Busk & Lt LH Strain RNVR rescued); Wreckage washed ashore Sanmuir 2.1.15; Deleted 17.1.15

**1 SHORT TWO-SEAT PUSHER BIPLANE SEAPLANE built Eastchurch under Cont No C.P.38479/13 & numbered 80. (100-hp Gnome Monosoupape)** [Gordon Bruce's researches show correct c/n to be S.79]

80 (100-hp Gnome Monosoupape). Side-by-side, DC. Grain 1.14; Probably stored 8.14 - 12.14; Re-erected Grain 30.12.14; Completed 4.1.15; Broke u/c and port lower wing landing 31.3.15 (F/L HM Cave-Browne-Cave & F/L JH Lidderdale); Calshot 29.5.15; CW 24.8.15 (FSL LER Murray); Deleted 9.15

**2 SHORT ADMIRALTY 74 TYPE FOLDER TRACTOR BIPLANE SEAPLANES built Eastchurch under Cont No C.P.35829/13 & numbered 81 & 82. (160-hp Gnome)** [Gordon Bruce's researches show correct c/n's to be S.64 and S.65]

81 First Short Folder. Passed acceptance tests Eastchurch 17.7.13; HMS *Hermes* 18.7.13 for Naval manoeuvres; Slightly damaged when gale blew down its canvas shelter 22.7.13; Broke struts 27.7.13; Grain repair 29.7.13; HMS *Hermes* 31.7.13; EF, FL in English Channel, recovered by SS *Clara Mennig* of Rostock 1.8.13 (Cdr CR Samson and Lt R Fitzmaurice); Grain repair 4.8.13; HMS *Hermes* 19.8.13; Rudder jammed at 1,000 ft, dived into sea, badly damaged Cromarty 4.9.13 (F/L FW Bowhill & Mech); Mkrs repair 9.13; Grain 4.14; Wrecked 5.14; Deleted 25.6.14

82 Tested by Gordon Bell 2.10.13; Grain 11.13; By rail to Plymouth 21.1.14; Grain by 7.2.14; Calshot by road 27.6.14; Erected 30.6.14; Tested 6.7.14 (Gordon Bell); Participated Royal Review 18.7.14; EF in the Down, towed into Dover 22.7.14; Grain 22.7.14 - @30.7.14; Chassis to be modified by Mkrs for torpedo 8.14; Grain by 11.8.14 (later Westgate); Mkrs 14.9.14; Tested Grain 2.10.14; HMS *Hermes* 10.14; HMS *Riviera* 17.10.14; HMS *Hermes* 18.10.14; Damaged by 905's bombs on HMS *Hermes* 28.10.14; Went down with ship when it was torpedoed by a U-boat in the Straits of Dover 31.10.14 [another unidentified Short Folder also went down with it?]

**6 BOREL TRACTOR MONOPLANE SEAPLANES ordered 5.13 through agents DelaCombe & Maréchal under Cont No C.P.38160/13 & numbered 83 to 88. (80-hp Gnome)**

83 Left Paris 23.6.13, arrived Dunkerque 27.6.13, then held up in dock strike; Calshot by/from 23.7.13 (earlier in month?); Tested Levasseur propeller 11.13; New wings fitted week ending 6.12.13; Grain by rail 12.2.14; Calshot 6.14 - 8.14; Land chassis fitted 9.14; Eastchurch 9.14; Deleted 9.12.14

84 Deld Grain 17.7.13; Yarmouth 17.7.13; Leven 18.7.13; Grain 9.8.13; Used in Fleet manoeuvres 21.9.13; Painted blue/grey 8.14; Land chassis fitted 9.14; Rifle fitted 11.14; Deleted 9.12.14

85 Deld Cromarty 23.7.13; Passed acceptance tests 31.7.13;

Fleet manoeuvres 1913; Flown with Winston Churchill early 10.13; Fort George 4.11.13; Flown by Mjr R Gordon, RMLI from Queensferry to Dundee 9.2.14; Dundee by early 1914; Fort George 2.14, 6.14 - 8.14; Land chassis fitted 9.14; Eastchurch by rail 5.9.14; Hendon 11.9.14; Deleted 9.12.14

86    Deld Leven 24.7.13; Tested by Georges Chemet 8.8.13 (passenger/observer Mjr R Gordon, RMLI); Flown to Fleet manoeuvres 9.13; Port Laing .13; Leven 9.13 - 9.2.14; Dundee 9.2.14; Leven 25.3.14; Dundee 15.4.14 - 8.14; Land chassis fitted; Eastchurch 9.14; Deleted 9.12.14

87    Left Paris 24.7.13, delayed by strike; Arrived Grain 25.8.13; Tested Grain 29.8.13; [Stationed Lewis & Cromarty?]; Grain 6.14; Deleted 6.14

88    Arrived Grain 25.8.13; Accepted 27.8.13 (PH Daucourt); Badly smashed when dived into sea nr Harwich shortly after TO Felixstowe 22.10.13 (Lt CEH Rathborne & Capt CE Risk, RMLI); Deleted 12.1913

**2 SHORT ADMIRALTY TYPE 81 THREE-BAY FOLDER TRACTOR BIPLANE SEAPLANES to be built Eastchurch under Cont No C.P.34603/13 & numbered 89 & 90. (160-hp Gnome)**

89 and 90 cancelled by 1.14

**2 MAURICE FARMAN S.7 LONGHORN PUSHER BIPLANES ordered under Cont No C.P.01720/13 from the Aircraft Manufacturing Co Ltd, Hendon to be numbered 91 & 92. (70-hp Renault)**

91 and 92 cancelled

**1 SOPWITH GUNBUS PUSHER BIPLANE SEAPLANE built Kingston under Cont No C.P.01717/13) & numbered 93. (200-hp Salmson)**
[120-hp Austro-Daimler per 1.17 official list, but this is doubtful]

93    Deld Calshot by 25.2.14; Fired 12-pdr Vickers gun 29.4.14; Fired Maxim gun 26 & 28.5.14; Passed tests 30.5.14; Sopwith 25.6.14 (alterations under Cont No C.P.02114/14/X); Calshot 10.7.14; Fired 1½-pdr Vickers gun 20.8.14; Deleted 26.8.14; 1½-pdr EOC gun fitted 9.14 after deletion due to fin deficiency

**1 AVRO 509 TRACTOR BIPLANE SEAPLANE ordered 1.14 under Cont No C.P.10760/13 dated 6.13 & numbered 94. (Two 120-hp Austro-Daimler or 100-hp Gnome)**

94    To carry a heavy calibre gun. On order for Grain to at least 6.14 but never built.

**1 MAURICE FARMAN S.7 LONGHORN PUSHER BIPLANE SEAPLANE purchased from France under Cont No C.P.37276/23 through The Aircraft Manufacturing Co Ltd, Hendon & numbered 95. (110-hp Canton-Unne)**

95    Flown by Louis Gaubert in Monaco seaplane contest 4-14.4.13; Bought by Admiralty & deld Calshot via Southampton 23.6.13; Crashed autumn 1913; Airco rebuilt with new wings and rudders 23.1.14; Calshot 2.14; Flown by Farman pilot at Calshot 13.2.14 [200-hp Salmson per *The Aeroplane* 19.2.14, but seems unlikely]; Lt AM Longmore flew with Winston Churchill as passenger 23.2.14; Felixstowe (via Grain) 22.7.14 (now 130-hp Salmson); Yarmouth by 11.8.14; Took part in searchlight experiments; Last flown 13.10.14; Deleted 24.11.14; Dismantled as spares 26.1.15

**5 HENRY FARMAN PUSHER BIPLANE SEAPLANES purchased from France under Cont No C.P.50395/13 & numbered 96 to 100. (80 or 160-hp Gnome)**

96    (160-hp Gnome). Three-str. Flown by Jules Fischer at Monaco seaplane contest 4-14.4.13; Bought by Admiralty, but crashed by Fischer at Monaco; Repaired; Deld Calshot via Southampton but FL on acceptance test 28.8.13 (Jules Fischer with Lt AW Bigsworth and Mech as passengers); Repaired; Still Calshot 2.14 but no

longer in use; Deleted 25.6.14
[NB. Curiously, official lists dated 1.17 and 2.18 show this as having been a Maurice Farman, supposedly 110-hp Canton-Unné, to Cont No C.P.37276/13 with No.95]

97    (80-hp Gnome). Probably the first Naval Wing Henry Farman with "Deauville" sprung floats; Deld Yarmouth W/E 24.1.14 and flight from France counted as acceptance flight; Tested Yarmouth 1.14; To Grain 7.14; Yarmouth 10.8.14 - @11.8.14; Scapa (Kirkwall) by 27.8.14; shipped to Grain 20.11.14; Grain 11.14; Yarmouth by 28.2.15; Airco rebuild 11.3.15; Yarmouth 3.4.15; Re-erected 9.4.15; Accepted 19.4.15; AZP 30.4.15 (F/Cdr deCWP Ireland & LM C Notley); HSMPs 12.6.15 (F/L V Nicholl & PO Mech C Notley), 19.6.15 (F/L V Nicholl & PO Mech Litton), 13.7.15 (F/L V Nicholl & PO Mech Litton), 29.7.15 (F/L V Nicholl & PO Mech C Notley) & 30.7.15 (S/Cdr deCWP Ireland & PO Mech Brownlee, later S/Cdr de CWP Ireland & PO Mech Litton); HSMP, EF, FL in heavy sea, towed back by trawler but chassis collapsed 1.8.15 (F/L V Nicholl & PO Mech C Notley); Repaired; Seaplane School Calshot by rail 9.11.15 (arr 16.11.15); Deleted 17.7.16

98    (80-hp Gnome). Deld Yarmouth 2.14; Tested by Henry Farman and Jules Fischer at Yarmouth 11.2.14; Accident at Felixstowe 10.3.14 (pilot & PO Tel JC Hendry unhurt); Unserviceable 3.8.14; Deleted 24.8.14

99    (80-hp Gnome). Not delivered

100   (80-hp Gnome). Not delivered

**1 ROYAL AIRCRAFT FACTORY B.E.2a TRACTOR BIPLANE to be built Farnborough & numbered 101. (70-hp Renault)**

101   Possibly temporary allotment. Reported Eastchurch 8.14

**1 HENRY FARMAN F.22H PUSHER BIPLANE SEAPLANE purchased France through Aircraft Manufacturing Co Ltd under Cont No C.P.50395/13 & numbered 102. (70-hp Gnome)**

102   Possibly never entered service

**2 SOPWITH D.1 THREE-SEAT TRACTOR BIPLANES built Kingston under Cont No C.P.45488/13 & numbered 103 to 104. (80-hp Gnome)**

103   Deld Eastchurch by 9.13; Flown by Lt Spenser DA Grey 1.9.13 - @25.10.13; Calshot 1.14 (& 6.14 - 7.14?); Sopwith overhaul; Brooklands to ECNFS & accepted 17.6.14; EF, FL Elmley Marshes, damaged 6.7.14 (F/L HA Littleton unhurt); Mkrs repair; Hendon 27.8.14; ECNFS 30.8.14; Left for Dunkerque but FL Dover, took off again but FL on beach, slightly damaged Calais 8.9.14 (F/L HA Littleton unhurt); 3 Sqdn Morbecque by 19.9.14 to replace Sopwith 33, but unsuitable; For ADD by 27.9.14; ECNFS 10.11.14; Eastbourne by air 7.1.15; COL, damaged 20.1.15 (FSL WS Newton-Clare); retd Eastchurch to at least 20.4.15; RD Grain by 31.5.15; Deleted 9.15

104   Deld ECNFS 9.13; Accepted 8.9.13 (Hawker & F/L R Bell-Davies); Flew 12 hrs on Army manoeuvres Lilbourne 9.13; Flown by F/L RLG Marix to Portsmouth for Royal Review 7.14; Eastchurch patrol by 8.8.14; To Thurso by rail 13.8.14; Thurso/Scapa (patrols) 16.8.14; Eastchurch 5.9.14; 2 Sqdn Eastchurch 2.1.15; ECNFS by 1.15; EF, FL mud flats River Blackwater 11.1.15 (F/L IGV Fowler); Surveyed 14.1.15; Deleted 1.15

**1 HAMBLE RIVER, LUKE & CO LTD H.L.1 PUSHER BIPLANE SEAPLANE built Southampton under Cont No C.P.54199/13 & numbered 105. (150-hp BRITISH N.A.G. F.4)**

105   Designed by F.Murphy. Shown at Olympia 2.14 with 150-hp N.A.G. engine. Ordered by Admiralty with 160-hp Gnome; Launched 5.14, but much out of balance, tail partly sank and aircraft badly damaged; Repaired and tested with pontoon-type floats without success by EC Gordon England 11/12/17.8.14; Never accepted; Sold at auction for £30 in 6.15, wings bought by Pemberton Billing Ltd for five shillings

*Hamble River, Luke & Co H.L.1 Seaplane, exhibited at Olympia in March 1914 was to have become 105, but was never accepted. (J.M.Bruce/G.S.Leslie collection)*

*Breguet "Tin Whistle" Seaplane with racing number 15 is possibly the machine intended to have become 110. (J.M.Bruce/G.S.Leslie collection)*

*Maurice Farman Shorthorn Seaplane 115. (J.M.Bruce/G.S.Leslie collection)*

*Short 81 Type Folder Seaplane 119. (via Philip Jarrett)*

*Sopwith Pusher Seaplane, possibly 124. (RAF Museum)*

**2 ASTRA CM SEAPLANES ordered from France & numbered 106 and 107. (70-hp Renault)**

106   ) No evidence of completion
107   ) or delivery

**1 HENRY FARMAN PUSHER BIPLANE ordered from France & numbered 108.**

108   No evidence of completion or delivery

**1 MAURICE FARMAN S.7 LONGHORN PUSHER BIPLANE ordered from France & numbered 109.**

109   No evidence of delivery. Possibly the 120-hp Renault seaplane erected Grain 11.8.13 which failed its acceptance test

**1 HENRY FARMAN F.22H PUSHER BIPLANE SEAPLANE purchased from France & numbered 110. Built Douai. (100-hp Gnome)**

110   Deld Grain by 3.14; EF, FL in sea and overturned near Clacton, Essex 1.4.14 (F/L EB Bauman & Ldg Seaman Marchant)
[Appears to be based on report in *The Aeroplane* of 9.4.14, but probably mistaken identity as 110 officially listed as Breguet seaplane - could it really be 140?] [not in official lists 1.17 or 2.18]

**3 BREGUET "TIN WHISTLE" BIPLANE SEAPLANES ordered from France & numbered 110 to 112, to be built Douai. (200-hp Canton-Unné)**

110   Possibly the unidentified machine at Brighton 7.13; first flown by Henri Brégi 25.7.13; Damaged 6.8.13; Tested Calshot early 10.13, but probably not accepted
111 & 112   Not delivered

**5 MAURICE FARMAN PUSHER BIPLANE SEAPLANES purchased in France & numbered 113 to 117. (100 or 120-hp Renault)**
[Per official list 1.17, 113 was Maurice Farman (120-hp Renault) under Cont No C.P.4889/13, 114 - 116 were Henry Farmans and 117 was Maurice Farman under Cont No C.P.45117/13]

113   (100-hp Renault). Deld Felixstowe 18.12.13; Grain 19.5.14; Felixstowe by 7.14; Grain 9.7.14 (transit); Calshot for Royal Review 11.7.14; With "C" Flight for Royal Review Flypast 18.7.14; left 22.7.14; Re-erected Felixstowe 11.8.14; Dunkerque 1.11.14; Shipped to UK 12.14; Airco 7.12.14 (repair); Grain by road 21.1.15; Re-assembled by Airco 26.1.15; Dismantled for transport 4.2.15; HMS *Empress* 5.2.15; 3 Sqdn St.Pol 5.2.15; Dunkerque Seaplanes 26.2.15; Dropped 2x20-lb bombs on U-boat 5m off Middelkerke 16.5.15 (S/Cdr CEH Rathborne); Calshot (via Eastbourne) 2.7.15; EF, FL, stranded on sands Bembridge 4.7.15 (FSL WH Dunn & Asst Payr TA Batchelor unhurt); Accident 9.7.15 (S/L JBP Ferrand & S/L CH Dolling-Smith unhurt); No engine 8.15; Extensive repairs; Re-erecting 16.1.16; Collided with Owers Lake buoy taxying, wreckage salved 11.6.16 (FSL HA Peck & FSL HA Bower unhurt); Deleted 17.7.16

114   (100-hp Renault). Deld Felixstowe 20.12.13; Accepted 25.2.14; W/T in 1914; Damaged 18.5.14; Serviceable by 6.8.14; Dunkerque 5.11.14; Airco 7.12.14 (repair); Allocated Dunkerque 3.2.15; Re-assembled Dunkerque Seaplanes 12.2.15; Flown 16.2.15; Broke tail boom leaving slipway 27.2.15; Flying again 31.3.15; Hit off Ostende by enemy AA guns, dived into sea from about 3,000ft after being severely shelled, wreckage towed base by French TB then burned 31.5.15 (Lt HG Wanklyn saved); Deleted 6.15

115   (100-hp Renault). Deld Felixstowe by 1.14; Grain 19.5.14; Felixstowe by 7.14; Grain 9.7.14 (transit); Calshot for Royal Review 10.7.14; With "C" Flight for Royal Review Flypast 18.7.14; Returning Felixstowe developed engine trouble, o/t, CW on alighting off West Worthing, Sussex 22.7.14 (F/Cdr CEH Rathborne, RMLI & Tel Stirling rescued by boat); Deleted 18.8.14

116   (120-hp Renault). Deld Leven and Tested; Crashed Leven 25.8.13; Deleted 9.13? [but see 71]

117   (120-hp Renault). Deld Calshot (via Southampton) 6.13; Cromarty by 7.13; Assembled by 12.7.13; Tested by Lt AM Longmore & Lt DA Oliver 14.7.13; Used on Fleet manoeuvres 7.13; Flew around HMS *Hermes* 3.9.13; Flown by Longmore with Winston Churchill as passenger 2.10.13; CW 7.10.13; Deleted 11.13

**1 SOPWITH BAT-BOAT (TYPE 1) PUSHER BIPLANE AMPHIBIAN FLYING BOAT built Kingston under Cont No C.P.54578/13 & numbered 118. (90-hp Austro-Daimler)**

118   (No.1). Completed 1.13; At Olympia Show 2.13; Retd Kingston 22.2.13; Wrecked in gale, Whippingham, nr Cowes IoW; Fitted 110-hp Green E6 and temp land u/c, tested Brooklands 25.5.13; Won Mortimer Singer prize for first flight by an all-British amphibian 8.7.13; Purchased by Admiralty and serial allocated; Prepared at Hamble River 1.14; Acceptance tests by Howard Pixton at Calshot 27.2.14; Used for experimental work; Twin fins fitted, tested 10.5.14; Successful night flight using headlight 25.6.14 (Lt AW Bigsworth); Propeller accident Portsmouth 29.6.14 (ERA Parrott injured); "E" Flight Calshot for Royal Review on 18.7.14; To Grain but towed back to Calshot after EF at Hayling; Remained Calshot, occasional flying from 8.14; New wings fitted 10.14; Bomb-dropping gear fitted 11.14; Crashed 14.2.15; Dismantling 2.3.15; Deleted 3.15

**4 SHORT ADMIRALTY 81 TYPE FOLDER TRACTOR BIPLANE SEAPLANES ordered 30.10.13 under Cont No C.P.53783/13/X/16128 intended for the Forth Area, built Eastchurch & numbered 119 to 122. (160-hp Gnome)** [Gordon Bruce's researches show correct c/n's to be S.82 to S.85]

119   Second test at Mkrs 5.5.14; Deld Grain & tested 28.5.14; Calshot for Royal Review 9.7.14; With "A" Flight for Royal Review Flypast 18.7.14; Grain 24.7.14 - @30.7.14; Westgate by 11.8.14; Damaged 13.8.14; Shorts 16.8.14 (repair and fit modified chassis for torpedo carrying); Grain 21.9.14; On HMS *Hermes* 14.10.14; Calshot to HMS *Riviera* 19.10.14; Dover 21.10.14; HMS *Riviera* 22.10.14; Damaged by 905's bombs going off on HMS *Hermes* 28.10.14; Grain 28.10.14; Flew from Westgate with 100-lb bombs 11.14; HMS *Engadine* 20.11.14; Felixstowe 27.11.14; HMS *Engadine* 16.12.14; Felixstowe 22.12.14; HMS *Engadine* 23.12.14; In Cuxhaven raid, towed in afterwards by HMS *Lurcher* 24-25.12.14 (F/Cdr RP Ross); Felixstowe 4.1.15; To Grain in SS *Stamfordham* 21.1.15; Assembling Grain 25.1.15; Propeller expts 7.3.15; Shorts Rochester in tow to pack for shipment 14.3.15; To Durban in SS *Laconia*, arrived early 4.15; To Niororo Island for *Königsberg* operation 4.15 (poor performance in tropics); Flown 27.4.15; Fired on from Ras T Wara, rudder shot away, FL in sea, capsized and broke up, crew clung to wreckage for 3 hours 5.5.15 (F/L HEM Watkins and Mech rescued by F/Cdr JT Cull in Short 122); Attempted to salve but sank; Deleted 6.15

120   Deld and accepted Grain 15.6.14 (G Bell); Westgate 15.6.14; Grain 19.6.14; Calshot for Royal Review 9.7.14; With "A" Flight Spithead (via Eastbourne and Newhaven) for Royal Review Flypast 18.7.14 (F/L JT Babington & AB Clarke); Flown at Calshot with dummy torpedo lashed to floats; Grain (via Dover) 24.7.14; Westgate 2.8.14; Bomb dropping gear fitted 25.8.14; HMS *Engadine* 26.8.14; Adrift all night in North Sea in slight swell 7.9.14 (F/L AB Gaskell & Lt R Erskine Childers); Grain 5.10.14; HMS *Engadine* 6.10.14; Calshot 15.10.14; HMS *Engadine* 17.10.14; Grain 28.10.14 (overhaul); Tested after overhaul 9.11.14; HMS *Engadine* 20.11.14; Felixstowe 27.11.14; HMS *Engadine* 16.12.14; Felixstowe 22.12.14; HMS *Engadine* 23.12.14; Participated in Cuxhaven raid, bombed by Schütte-Lanz, forced down by shortage of fuel 10m N of Nordeney Gat LH, taken in tow near Nordeney Gat by submarine *E.11*, but had to be abandoned and sunk by gunfire 25.12.14 (F/L AJ Miley)

121   Deld Grain 7.14; EF, FL, salved by SS *Algeibo*, to Newhaven 9.7.14; Calshot for Royal Review 11.7.14;

With "A" Flight for Royal Review Flypast 18.7.14; Officially taken over by Calshot 23.7.14; Fitted torpedo-dropping gear 23-25.7.14; First British aircraft to successfully launch torpedo 28.7.14 (S/Cdr AM Longmore); Grain 3.8.14; Painted blue 25.8.14; HMS *Engadine* 26.8.14; Grain 5.10.14; HMS *Engadine* 13.10.14; Grain 29.10.14; HMS *Engadine* 20.11.14; Tested Grain 27.11.14; Felixstowe 5.1.15; Grain 6.1.15; Fitted bomb-dropping gear 11.2.15; FL off Kentish Knock, damaged floats, towed Harwich 12.2.15; Retd Grain from Felixstowe 15.2.15; Flown to Shorts Rochester to pack for shipment 14.3.15; Shipped Durban in HMS *Laconia*, arrived early 4.15; To Niororo Is for *Königsberg* operation 4.15 (poor performance); Flown 24.4.15. Last flown 15.6.15; Condemned and burnt Mafia Island 13.7.15

122 Fitted W/T; Delivered Grain by 30.7.14 (CO's aircraft); Westgate by 11.8.14; Bomb dropping gear fitted 25.8.14; HMS *Engadine* 26.8.14; Grain 5.10.14; HMS *Engadine* 13.10.14; Grain 29.10.14; HMS *Engadine* 20.11.14; Felixstowe 27.11.14; HMS *Engadine* 16.12.14; Failed to start for Cuxhaven raid 24.12.14 (F/Cdr AB Gaskell); Damaged aboard ship in storm 28.12.14; Felixstowe 4.1.15 (instructional flying); Dismantled for shipment 20.1.15; To Grain in SS *Stamfordham* 21.1.15 (arr 22.1.15); Tested after re-assembly 10.2.15; Fitted bomb-dropping gear 11.2.15; Floats burst on TO 12.2.15; Damaged landing 15.2.15; Shorts Rochester to pack for shipment 11.3.15; Shipped Durban in HMS *Laconia*, arrived early 4.15; To Niororo Island for *Königsberg* operation 4.15; Tested 24.4.15; Recce of *Königsberg* 25.4.15; FL 5m off Ras T Wara, towed to ship by MB 14.6.15 (last flight); Burnt Mafia Island 13.7.15

**2 SOPWITH PUSHER BIPLANE SEAPLANES built Kingston under Cont No C.P.54578/13 & numbered 123 & 124. (100-hp Anzani)**

123 Deld Grain by 31.5.14; Poor controls 7.14; Felixstowe 14.8.14; Grain for conv to landplane 29.9.14 (NTU?); [Wings swept 11.14 ?]; Fitted bomb-dropping gear 20-22.11.14; Some instructional use; Flew patrol on 14.1.15; Dismantled 20.1.15; Shipped in SS *Stamfordham* 21.1.15; Grain 22.1.15; Re-assembling 25.1.15; RD Grain 30.1.15; Deleted 2.15 (poor design)

124 Deld Grain 5.14; Tested 29.5.14; Poor controls 7.14; [Sopwith mods 7.14?]; Felixstowe 27.8.14; Fitted bomb-dropping gear 20-22.11.14; New rudder fitted 12.14; Dismantled 20.1.15; Shipped in SS *Stamfordham* 21.1.15; Grain 22.1.15; Re-assembling 25.1.15; RD Grain 30.1.15; Deleted 2.15 (poor design)

**1 MAURICE FARMAN GUN-CARRYING PUSHER BIPLANE SEAPLANE ordered 2.14 under Cont No C.P.01769/13, to be built by Aircraft Manufacturing Co Ltd, Hendon & numbered 125. (100-hp Mercedes)**

125 Not delivered

**1 SHORT GUN-CARRYING PUSHER BIPLANE SEAPLANE built Eastchurch under Cont No C.P.01764/13 & numbered 126. (160-hp Gnome) [Gordon Bruce's researches show correct c/n to be S.81]**

126 Deld Calshot 25.5.14; Accepted 2.6.14 (Gordon Bell); With "E" Flight for Royal Review Flypast 18.7.14; Carried 1½-pdr Vickers quick-firing gun mid 7.14; Grain 30.7.14; Packed Ramsgate for Shorts by rail 3.8.14; Grain 26.9.14; Lewis gun fitted 10.14; Fired Vickers 1½-pdr quick-firing gun 11.12.14; Single central rudder by 1.15; Tested 1½-pdr gun 24.1.15; To Yarmouth but landed Felixstowe due to fuel shortage, then continued, but came down off Kessingland and drifted ashore, badly damaged, hauled up on beach nr Southwold 26.1.15 (Lt CF Lan Davis); Yarmouth 29.1.15 (repair); Fitted dynamo, searchlight and landing lamp 3.15; Fired 6-pdr Davis recoilless gun 13/15/16.4.15 (Lt RH Clark-Hall); Grain 5.5.15; Deleted 20.10.15

**1 SOPWITH BAT BOAT (TYPE 2) PUSHER BIPLANE FLYING BOAT ordered 2.14 under Cont No C.P.57961/13, built Woolston & numbered 126. (200-hp Canton-Unné)**

127 Under construction 9.13 intended for 200-hp Anzani engine; Possibly at Olympia Show 3.14; W/T 5.14; Deld Calshot by 15.5.14; Passed acceptance tests but damaged hull on alighting and could not be accepted 20.5.14; Sold to Greece and left Calshot 7.7.14; Deleted 10.14

**2 WIGHT 1914 NAVYPLANE PUSHER BIPLANE SEAPLANES ordered 1.14 under Cont No C.P.57922/13, to be built East Cowes & numbered 128 & 129. (200-hp Salmson)**

128 FF 7.4.14 (E.C.Gordon England); Arrived Calshot 3.2.14 [??] (good W/T, very carefully insulated); Accepted Warsash 17.4.14 (E.C.Gordon England); New flying controls fitted by 24.4.14; Crashed into Solent off Calshot 4.6.14 (Lt TS Creswell, RMLI & Cdr A Rice both killed); Deleted 10.14

129 Exhibited Olympia Show from 16.3.14; Fitted wheel control system and W/T; First flew Calshot 1.5.14 (EC Gordon England); Fitted extra tanks and bomb-dropping gear; Deld Calshot 7.14; Accepted 22.9.14; Shipped in HMS *Argus* from Newhaven for Dundee (crated) 9.10.14; arr Fort George 12.10.14; No engine by 20.12.14; HSMP, damaged float landing Cromarty at dusk, wrecked in tow by steamboat 29.1.15 (F/L AR Arnold); Deleted 7.2.15

**5 AVRO 510 TRACTOR BIPLANE SEAPLANES ordered under contract No C.P.30654/14, built Manchester & numbered 130 to 134. (150-hp Sunbeam Crusader)**

130 Deld Killingholme for erection 6.12.14; First trial flight 21.12.14; Poor performance, failed repeatedly to TO and mostly u/s; Tested 14.2.15; Dismantled 7.4.15; Grain 10.4.15; New non-standard u/c awaited 19.5.15; Tested 26.7.15; Refit called for 29.7.15; Wings to Mkrs 27.8.15; Fuselage to Pemberton Billing 28.10.15 (rebuild); Calshot 23.1.17 (training); Deleted W/E 14.9.17

131 Deld Killingholme for erection 5.2.15; Accepted 15.4.15 (Raynham); Mostly u/s; Standby for Zeppelin raids 5.15; Dismantled 18.10.15; Pemberton Billing by sea 21.10.15 (rebuild); Calshot 14.5.16; Deleted 9.2.17

132 Deld Killingholme for erection 17.2.15; Accepted test 15.4.15 (Raynham); Mostly u/s; Standby for Zeppelin raids 5.15; Still Killingholme late 8.15, being modified; Pemberton Billing 22.10.15 (rebuild); Calshot 23.9.16; Deleted 9.2.17

133 Deld Dundee for erection 25.3.15; Preliminary trials 31.3.15; Failed acceptance test 2.4.15; Made solo flights but could not TO with passengers 10.4.15, not accepted; Floats reconstructed 6.15; Tested 20.6.15; Declared of negligible value 3.9.15; Pemberton Billing 26.10.15 (rebuild); Calshot W/E 11.10.16; Deleted 9.2.17

134 Deld Dundee for erection 3.4.15; Failed acceptance test 12.4.15; Occasionally managed to TO; 35 minutes flying in 8.15; Flew a few operational patrols but only without observer; Longest patrol was 1½ hrs by F/L C Draper 3.5.15; F/L C Draper flew under Tay Bridge 17.5.15 & 23.5.15; Pemberton Billing repair 23.10.15; Calshot under tow 8.6.16; Deleted 9.2.17

**2 SHORT ADMIRALTY 135 TYPE FOLDER TRACTOR BIPLANE SEAPLANES ordered 12.2.14 under Cont No C.P.30774/14/X.2461 & numbered 135 and 136. Identities to be transposed 12.9.14. (135 or 200-hp Canton-Unné) [Gordon Bruce's researches show correct c/n's to be as shown]**

135 (c/n S.88). (135-hp Salmson). [166 Type] Deld HMS *Riviera* 9.9.14; Grain 9.9.14; Accepted 15.9.14; HMS *Riviera* 22.9.14; Grain 8.10.14; HMS *Riviera* 9.10.14; Calshot 18.10.14; HMS *Riviera* by 24.10.14; Grain 28.10.14; New wings fitted 10.14; Wider floats fitted 11.14; HMS *Riviera* 21.11.14; Felixstowe 27.11.14; HMS *Riviera* 16.12.14; Felixstowe 20.12.14; HMS *Riviera* 21.12.14; Felixstowe 22.12.14; HMS *Riviera* 23.12.14; EF, forced down on Cuxhaven raid, last

*Short Gun-carrying Seaplane 126 fitted with 1½-pdr Vickers quick-firing gun. (J.M.Bruce/G.S.Leslie collection)*

*Wight 1914 Navyplane 128 at Calshot, piloted by Longmore. (J.M.Bruce/G.S.Leslie collection)*

*Sopwith Tractor Seaplane 137. (via J.D.Oughton)*

*Short Folder Seaplane 136 hoisting HMS Ark Royal 1915. (Hadfield/FAA Museum)*

*Sopwith "Sociable" 149 side-by-side two-seater with Lt Spenser D.A. Grey at Hendon. He flew Winston Churchill several times in this machine in February 1914. (J.M.Bruce/G.S.Leslie collection)*

seen sinking 8m W of Heligoland 24-25.12.14 (F/L FET Hewlett interned by Dutch at Ymuijden); Deleted 1.15

**136**   (c/n S.87). (200-hp Canton Unné Type 2.M.7). [830 Type] Deld Grain and accepted 28.8.14 (S/Cdr JW Seddon & Mr Fairey); HMS *Riviera* 16.9.14; AZP 12.10.14 (F/L CF Kilner & F/L CHK Edmonds); Calshot 14.10.14 (new floats fitted); HMS *Riviera* 17.10.14; Calshot 18.10.14; Damaged chassis on landing when 100-lb bomb exploded in water 25.10.14 (F/L CF Kilner); Towed to Sheerness for Mkrs repair and overhaul 30.10.14; Grain 6.12.14; Re-accepted 17.12.14 (F/L HR Busteed); Felixstowe 21.12.14; HMS *Riviera* 23.12.14; Participated Cuxhaven Raid, chased Schütte-Lanz airship, sighted and recovered by HMS *Riviera* 24-25.12.14 (F/Cdr CF Kilner & Lt R Erskine Childers); Suffered weather damage 28.12.14; Towed Felixstowe 7.1.15 (repairs); HMS *Riviera* 14.1.15; Felixstowe 18.1.15; HMS *Riviera* 22.1.15; Felixstowe 31.1.15; HMS *Ark Royal* and sailed for Dardanelles 31.1.15; Flown on arrival Valetta, Malta 13.2.15; Flown on arrival Tenedos 17.2.15; First recce over Dardanelles 19.2.15; Engine test at Port Mudros; Spotted for HMS *Triumph* on Turkish battleship in Narrows, badly damaged by rifle fire, landed in rough sea with port chassis strut and lower wing shot through 27.4.15 (Lt EH Dunning & Lt W Parke); Flown again 2.5.15; Chassis struts collapsed on TO, capsized 2.5.15 (Lt EH Dunning & Lt AG Brown RNR unhurt); Flown again 17.5.15; Floats collapsed landing, believed struck wreckage, salved 23.5.15 (F/L EH Dunning & Lt W Park); Flown again 25.5.15; Mudros 18.6.15; Towed to HMS *Ark Royal* for engine repairs 24.6.15; Damaged, retd in tow 29.6.15 (Lt EH Dunning); Bottom of floats burst taxying for TO, taken in tow by a Fleet Sweeper 17.8.15 (F/L R Whitehead & Lt LH Strain RNVR); Reconstructed; Retd HMS *Ark Royal* in tow 26.9.15; Flown again but poor 21.12.15; Various work, then tested 8.1.16 (LM) "she will not be successful as a dual control machine"; Completely dismantled for destruction and WO owing to age 9.6.16

**2 SOPWITH ADMIRALTY 137 TYPE TRACTOR BIPLANE SEAPLANES built Kingston under Cont No C.P.30775/14 & numbered 137 & 138.**

**137**   (120-hp Austro-Daimler) Deld Calshot and accepted 21.8.14; Wrecked 3.9.14 (Pickles & FSL Lord Carbery unhurt); Pemberton Billing 8.9.14 (repair); Calshot 23.4.15; Retested 26-29.4.15; Damaged 11.5.15; Engine removed 21.5.15; Flew again with 200-hp Canton-Unné 19.8.15; Deleted 1.1.16

**138**   (200 Canton-Unné) Deld Calshot 7.8.14; Accepted 12.8.14; Managed TO with W/T and 810-lb torpedo 25.8.14; Stagger altered 28.8.14; Successful torpedo drops 29-30.8.14 & 12-13.9.14; Fitted 4-blade Lang propeller 17.10.14; Damaged attempting to put it on board HMS *Hermes* 28.10.14; Damaged landing 21.2.15; Tested with camera sights 25.6.15; Bembridge 1.7.15; Calshot 3.7.15; Deleted 1.1.16

**6 HENRY FARMAN F.22H PUSHER BIPLANE SEAPLANES built by The Aircraft Manufacturing Co Ltd, Hendon under Cont No C.P.36585/14 & numbered 139 to 144. (120-hp Gnome)**

**139**   Deld Grain by 14.5.14 - @3.6.14; Passed W/T test 5.14; Yarmouth by early 7.14; Calshot for Royal Review 11.7.14; With "D" Flight for Royal Review Flypast 18.7.14; flown by S/Cdr CL Courtney & PO Hendry 23.7.14; Yarmouth 29.7.14; Flew patrol with orders to destroy enemy seaplanes 9.8.14; still Yarmouth 11.8.14; Scapa 8.14; Crashed and wrecked on or shortly after arrival at Scapa 8.14; Deleted 24.8.14

**140**   Deld Grain 5.14; Tested 20.5.14 (Jules Fischer); Passed W/T test 5.14; EF, FL while searching for Gustav Hamel, floats came off, wrecked Dover 23.5.14 (Cdr CR Samson); Remains to Grain; Deleted 25.6.14

**141**   Deld Felixstowe by 5.14; Passed W/T test 5.14; Still Felixstowe 15.6.14; Calshot to Yarmouth but EF, FL off Yarmouth, o/t, wrecked, towed ashore 28.7.14 (F/L RJ Bone slightly injured & PO Tel JC Hendry unhurt);

Engine salved 8.14; Deleted 24.8.14

**142**   Deld Yarmouth 4.4.14; Passed W/T test 22.5.14 (Jules Fischer & Tel Hendry); Calshot for Royal Review 11.7.14; With "D" Flight for Royal Review Flypast 18.7.14; Yarmouth 28.7.14; Left for Hunstanton, EF, FL Burnham Overy Staithe, retd Yarmouth 10.8.14 (F/L H Fawcett); still Yarmouth 11.8.14; Scapa 8.14; EF while on patrol, FL in sea, swell broke up aircraft Scapa 24.8.14; Wreckage recovered, but deleted 18.9.14

**143**   Deld Yarmouth 4.4.14; Passed W/T test 5.14; Calshot for Royal Review 11.7.14; With "D" Flight for Royal Review Flypast 18.7.14 (marked "C4"); Retd Yarmouth, EF at 650-ft, FL, capsized Dover en route; Crashed 11.8.14 (engine lost); Deleted 24.8.14

**144**   Deleted by 31.5.14

**1 SHORT SINGLE-SEATER BIPLANE to be built Eastchurch & numbered 145. (65-hp Austro-Daimler)**

**145**   Allocated to Eastchurch by 6.14 - 8.14, not delivered

**1 MAURICE FARMAN PUSHER BIPLANE purchased from Maurice Farman under Cont No C.P.57643/13, built in France & numbered 146. (80-hp de Dion-Bouton)**

**146**   Believed the aircraft flown to Hendon by the Marquis Jules de Lareinty Tholozan 18.10.13, and to Farnborough by early 11.13; Deld Eastchurch by M.Verrier 9.12.13; Yarmouth 24.2.14; Eastchurch 3.14; Wrecked on arrival Hendon 7.8.14; Repaired; Hendon 16.9.14; Airco repair and overhaul 10.14; Fitted 70-hp Renault by 11.3.15, possibly by 11.14; Hendon by 1.12.14; Tested, hit trees on TO, landed in rough ground, damaged 26.5.15 (F/L DM Barnes); Crashed 26.5.15; Airco repair 30.5.15; Hendon to Chingford 11.8.15; Ran into 1549 22.8.15 (FSL L Briffault unhurt); Deleted 1.11.16 [then listed as LONGHORN]

**2 BRISTOL SEAPLANES to be built Filton & numbered 147 & 148. (80-hp Gnome, changed to 200-hp Salmson)**

147 and 148 cancelled by 9.14

**1 SOPWITH "SOCIABLE" TWO-SEATER SIDE-BY-SIDE TRACTOR BIPLANE built under Cont No C.P.30680/14 at Kingston & numbered 149. (100-hp Gnome Monosoupape)**

**149**   Fitted DC. FF Brooklands 17.2.14; Deld Hendon 19.2.14; Flown by Lt Spenser DA Grey with Winston Churchill as passenger 20.2.14, 25.2.14 & 28.2.14; Spun in from 250-ft on TO to return from visit to Eastchurch 25.3.14 (Lt Spenser DA Grey & Lt WS Aldwell); Sopwith repair 3.14; Ready 27.8.14; Eastchurch 9.14; 3 Sqdn Belgium 16.9.14; Additional fuel tank and bomb-dropping gear fitted 19.9.14; Flown by L/Cdr Spenser DA Grey in abortive attempt to bomb airship shed at Cologne 22.9.14; 1 Sqdn, broke axle on TO, capsized landing, upper wings badly damaged, Antwerp 26.9.14 (F/L ET Newton Clare); Left at Antwerp while under repair at local aeroplane works 12.10.14; Had to be abandoned; Deleted 14.10.14

**1 AVRO TYPE E/500 TRACTOR BIPLANE built Manchester under Cont No C.P.30057/14 & numbered 150. (50-hp Gnome)**

**150**   Deld ECNFS by F.P.Raynham and tested with Lt R Bell-Davies 23.2.14; Provisionally accepted 7.5.14; Flown by S/Cdr R Bell-Davies to Portsmouth for Royal Review 13.7.14; Retd to ECNFS but EF, FL 2m S of Salisbury, sideslipped in from 40ft avoiding tree on TO again, TW 27.7.14 (F/L C Draper); Deleted 1.10.14

**1 SOPWITH TRACTOR BIPLANE SEAPLANE built Kingston under Cont No C.P.31415/14 & numbered 151. (100-hp Green)**

**151**   Built for Daily Mail Seaplane Trial 1913 with Racing Number 1; Crashed nr Dublin 27.8.13; Rebuilt and flew as landplane 4.10.13; Crashed 8.10.13; Flying again 10.13; Purchased by Admiralty; Tested Calshot 29.4.14; Accepted 12.5.14; With "E" Flight for Royal Review

Flypast 18.7.14; Left for Grain en route Yarmouth, but EF, FL Felpham 30.7.14; Deleted 19.8.14

**1 SHORT "SOCIABLE" [S.38 NACELLE TYPE] TRACTOR BIPLANE built Eastchurch under Cont No C.P.38688/14 & numbered 152. (80-hp Gnome) [Gordon Bruce's researches show correct c/n to be S.89]**

152     Fitted DC; Accepted at Mkrs 9.6.14, retained for alterations; Accepted ECNFS 26.6.14 (Gordon Bell); Yarmouth War Flt 28.7.14 (coastal patrols); Wrecked Yarmouth 27.8.14; Rebuilt Yarmouth; ECNFS 22.9.14; Due for night lookout with 3 Sqdn Belgium 9.10.14, (presume NTU); B Flt Eastchurch 3.11.14; Engine removed Eastchurch by 18.2.16; Deleted 27.4.16

**1 BRISTOL T.B.8 TRACTOR BIPLANE built under Cont No C.P.36217/14/X at Filton & numbered 153. (80-hp Gnome)**

153     (c/n 198). Deld Eastchurch by 3.14; Flown by S/L R Bell-Davies 31.3.14; Eastchurch without u/c by 11.4.14; U/c made and fitted early 5.14; Flying 15.5.14; Flown by S/Cdr IT Courtney to Portsmouth for Royal Review Flypast 13.7.14; Eastchurch (Mobile) Sqdn, Immingham 28.7.14; Spares ordered 5.8.14; En route Ostende, FL, broken rib Faversham 27.8.14 - @28.8.14; arr 1 Sqdn Belgium 1.9.14; New wings fitted 9.14; Wrecked in gale Ostende 12.9.14; Dismantled, then damaged when Henry Farman fell on it 13.9.14; Deleted 2.10.14

**1 D.F.W. MILITARY ARROW TRACTOR BIPLANE purchased from Germany 3.14 under Cont No C.P.36909/14 & numbered 154. (100-hp Mercedes)**

154     Brooklands 17.3.14; Accepted at Brooklands 25.3.14 (Lt CH Collet RMA who became its regular pilot); With supplementary fuel tank flew 7½ hours non-stop from Portsmouth to Immingham (objective was Wick), but EF, FL Jenning's Farm, near Donna Nook, Lincs 13.5.14 (Lt CH Collet, RMA); Deld Eastchurch 3.6.14; Re-engined 120-hp Beardmore; Eastchurch defence by 8.8.14; Eastchurch (Mobile) Sqdn, Skegness by 11.8.14; Killingholme by 23.8.14; Immingham by 28.8.14 (flown by Lt CH Collet RMA); Dismantled 6.10.14; Eastchurch 8.10.14; Deleted 20.2.15 and parts sent to Killingholme; Wormwood Scrubs 19.6.15

**1 WIGHT 1914 NAVYPLANE PUSHER BIPLANE SEAPLANE built under Cont No C.P.40814/14 by J.Samuel White & Co Ltd, East Cowes & numbered 155. (200-hp Canton-Unné)**

155     Deld Calshot by 3.14; Tested 1.3.14; W/T fitted 4.14; Tested Calshot 5.5.14; Damaged; Mkrs 25.6.14; Calshot 6.10.14; Shipped crated in HMS *Argus* from Newhaven 9.10.14; arr Fort George 12.10.14; COL due to heavy ground swell 24.10.14; Without engine to 2.15; Wrecked and lost in rough sea during strong gale Fort George 8.4.15 (F/L AR Arnold & PO Mech JW Rose); Deleted 11.4.15

**1 HENRY FARMAN F.22H PUSHER BIPLANE SEAPLANE purchased from France under Cont No C.P.40917/14 & numbered 156. (80-hp Gnome)**

156     W/T test 5.14; Accepted Yarmouth 28.7.14; Scapa 24.8.14; Led the Battle Fleet to sea 27.8.14; Grain 25.11.14; To Airco 2.15; Yarmouth by road 11.4.15; Accepted 19.4.15; HSMP 12.6.15 (S/Cdr de CWP Ireland & LM Hooks); HSMP, chassis collapsed in heavy sea, salved 22.6.15 (not repaired); Calshot by rail 11.11.15 (arr 16.11.15); Deleted 28.3.16

**3 SOPWITH ADMIRALTY TYPE C TRACTOR BIPLANE SEAPLANES ordered 7.14 under Cont No C.P.37385/14, built Kingston & numbered 157 to 159. (200-hp Canton-Unné)**

157     Deld Calshot 11.14; Failed test 21.11.14; Accepted 12.14; Could not carry 14" Whitehead torpedo in test (S/Cdr AM Longmore); some flying to 3.15; but engine removed by 4.15; Ready by 12.5.15; Deleted 20.11.15

158     Deld Calshot by 11.11.14 (poor performance); Mkrs 24.11.14; Redeld Calshot but failed test 21.12.14 (V Mahl); Re-tested, accepted 4.2.15 (V Mahl); Trial, EF, FL ½m W of Calshot Spit LV, sank attempting tow, TW 8.2.15 (F/L TW Elsdon & FSL EF Bray); Deleted 2.15

159     Deld Calshot 11.14; Tested 26.1.15 & 20.2.15; Poor performance; No engine 3.15 (engine in by 10.15); Deleted 1.1.16

**1 SOPWITH SINGLE-SEAT TRACTOR BIPLANE built Kingston under Cont No C.P.37385/14 & numbered 160. (80-hp Gnome Monosoupape)**

160     Possibly used as Hawker's private "taxi". On order for Eastchurch 7.14; Still on order 1.12.14; No evidence of delivery

**6 SHORT TYPE C TRACTOR BIPLANE SEAPLANES (Later 166 TYPE) ordered 1.14 under Cont No C.P.37385/14, built Rochester & numbered 161 to 166. (200-hp Canton-Unné) [Gordon Bruce's researches show correct c/n's to be S.90 to S.95]**

161     Prototype, fitted to carry torpedo. Allocated HMS *Ark Royal* by 11.3.15; Shipped in SS *Carrigan Head*; Arr HMS *Ark Royal* 19.4.15; Tested 23.4.15; Chassis damaged taking off in rough sea 13.5.15 (S/Cdr CF Kilner & Lt W Park RNVR); Ready 15.5.15; Port Mudros 25.6.15; HMS *Ark Royal* 23.7.15; Port Mudros 24.7.15; HMS *Ark Royal* 10.8.15 (repair); Port Mudros 14.8.15; Both floats burst landing, salved by ship's whaler 18.8.15 (Capt CF Kilner & Lt W Parke); Port Mudros 18.8.15 (repair); HMS *Ark Royal* 1.9.15; Port Mudros 16.9.15; HMS *Ark Royal* 19.9.15; Last flown 12.6.16; To 2 Wing Mudros 21.6.16 [aircraft log ends]; To be fitted land chassis 15.9.16 (NTU?); NFT

162     Fitted to carry torpedo. Deld Grain in tow 15.5.15; Shorts Rochester for packing 20.5.15; En route to Aegean 20.6.15; Arrived HMS *Ark Royal* 14.7.15; Tested after erection then to Kephalo 2.8.15; HMS *Ark Royal* 5.9.15; Monitor HMS *Earl of Peterborough* 30.1.16; HMS *Ark Royal* 6.2.16; Stavros 29.2.16; HMS *Ark Royal* 8.4.16; HMS *Earl of Peterborough* 23.4.16; Mudros 7.5.16; HMS *Ark Royal* by 7.6.16; Handed over for conversion to land machine 22.6.16 (NTU?); NFT

163     Deld Grain 18.6.15; Accepted 19.6.15 (Kemp); Shipped to Aegean; Arrived HMS *Ark Royal* 7.15; Tested after erection then to Port Mudros 20.8.15; HMS *Ark Royal* 10.10.15; Shipped from Salonika in Fleet Messenger SS *Princess Ena*, at Mudros transferred to HMS *Doris* and carried to Port Iero where transferred to Monitor HMS *Earl of Peterborough* but in transit exposed to rain and suffered in consequence 19.2.16; Flown at Port Iero and hoisted HMS *Earl of Peterborough* 21.2.16; Bombing and spotting for HMS *Earl of Peterborough* at Scalanueva 23.2.16, then hoisted on board HMS *Earl of Peterborough* 15.30 to return to Salonika; HMS *Ark Royal* 25.2.16; Stavros 13.3.16; HMS *Ark Royal* in tow 14.3.16; cruiser HMS *Lowestoft* 13.4.16; HMS *Earl of Peterborough* 22.4.16; HMS *Ark Royal* 23.4.16 (still seaplane); HMS *Roberts* 29.5.16; HMS *Ark Royal* 29.5.16 - @15.8.16; Conv landplane at Thasos 1916; HMS *Ark Royal* 28.11.16; NFT

164     Fitted to carry torpedo. Deld Grain by 7.15; Tested but engine trouble, then left for Mkrs Rochester 10.7.15 (Kemp); Shipped to Aegean in SS *Elden Hall* 7.15; arr HMS *Ark Royal* 7.15; Tested after erection 31.8.15; From base at Aliki Bay to HMS *Roberts* 9.9.15; Damaged on deck of HMS *Roberts* by blast from her 14-in guns 28.9.15; Flown again 3.10.15; Last flown 9.11.15 (only 10 flights with HMS *Roberts*); Remains brought back to HMS *Ark Royal* from HMS *Roberts* after being dropped 30 ft from a crane in transhipping to the Mudros Ferry for passage to Salonika; Tested after rebuild 27.2.16; Stavros 29.2.16; Possibly the HMS *Ark Royal*/Imbros a/c in which F/L V Nicholson & Mid BW Davy RNVR accidentally killed 10.7.16; Burnt by order on Ispatho Island 11.7.16

165     (c/n S.94) Deld Grain by 8.15; Mkrs Rochester for packing 16.8.15; Shipped to Aegean in SS *Joshua Nicholson* 9.15; arr HMS *Ark Royal* 9.15; Tested after

*D.F.W. Military Arrow 154, piloted by Lt C.H.Collett RMLI after forced landing on its way to Immingham, 13 May 1914. (Grimsby Public Library via P.H.T.Green)*

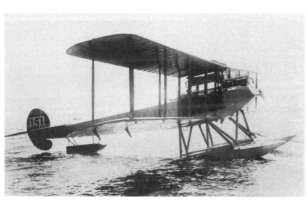

*Sopwith Tractor Seaplane 151 at the Royal Review, Spithead, 20 July 1914. (J.M.Bruce/G.S.Leslie collection)*

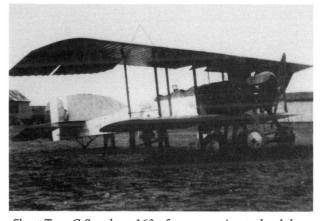

*Short Type C Seaplane 163 after conversion to landplane at Thasos in 1916. (via Frank Cheesman)*

*Sopwith Special Seaplane 170 at Cowes (via P.H.T.Green)*

*Wight A.I. Improved Navyplane 176 at Kephalo, 1915. (RAF Museum)*

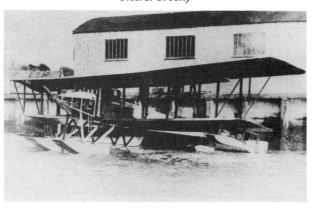

erection 1.10.15; Thasos by 8.10.15; HMS *Ark Royal* to Monitor HMS *Raglan* 10.10.15; HMS *Ark Royal* 16.10.15; HMS *Empress* 6.11.15; Thasos 11.11.15; HMS *Ark Royal* to Stavros 29.2.16; Fired on by submarine 20.6.16 (F/L FW Gamwell & S/L AEH Roberts RNVR); HMS *Ark Royal* to Thasos 27.6.16; HMS *Ark Royal* by 29.6.16 (tested); HMS *Ark Royal*, tested 10-19.1.17; Imbros 17.2.17; HMS *Ark Royal* 3.3.17; Mudros to Imbros harbour 3.17; HMS *Ark Royal* by 24-30.5.17; NFT

166    (c/n S.95). Deld Grain in tow 26.8.15; Shipped to Dardanelles in SS *Norman Prince* 9.15; arr HMS *Ark Royal* 10.15; Tested after erection 10.10.15; EF, FL, drifted 4 hrs then picked up by HMS *Euryalus'* picket boat 5.11.15 (Lt CW Pulford & Lt LH Strain); Flown again 16.11.15; Stavros 29.2.16; Briefly in HMS *Roberts* 29.5.16; Conv landplane at Thasos 1916; Tested HMS *Ark Royal* 5.10.16 (seaplane); HMS *Empress* (ex Mudros) 6.10.16; Mudros 28.12.16; NFT

**2 SOPWITH S.S.1 TABLOID TRACTOR BIPLANES built Kingston & numbered 167 & 168. (80-hp Gnome)**

167    (Ex RFC 394, was to have been serialled 904). Deld Eastchurch 9.9.14; Dunkerque 16.9.14; Damaged landing in soft ground 20.9.14; 2 Sqdn Belgium 25.9.14; EF, FL near Lierre 4.10.14 (S/Cdr Spenser DA Grey), retd by road; Bombed Cologne railway station 8.10.14 (S/Cdr Spenser DA Grey) [now 1 Sqdn?]; Damaged by groundfire Antwerp 9.10.14; Abandoned in retreat; Deleted 14.10.14

168    (Ex RFC 395, was to have been serialled 905). Deld Eastchurch 9.9.14; Dunkerque 16.9.14; 2 Sqdn Antwerp by 20.9.14; Damaged Antwerp 27.9.14 (FSL Lord Carbery); Repaired Antwerp; Engine overhauled 29.9.14; Attacked Düsseldorf Zeppelin sheds and destroyed *Z.IX*, petrol ran out, FL 20m from Antwerp on return journey 8.10.14 (F/L RLG Marix) [now 1 Sqdn?]; Abandoned Antwerp in retreat 9.10.14; Deleted 14.10.14

[One of these two wrecked u/c and lower wing landing on delivery to Eastchurch 9.9.14 (F/L RLG Marix) ]

**1 SOPWITH TABLOID TRACTOR BIPLANE built Kingston & numbered 169. (80-hp Gnome)**

169    (Ex RFC 604). Prototype. Deld Eastchurch 13.9.14; Dunkerque 22.9.14; 1 Sqdn, EF on TO, turned back, spun in from 100 ft 25.9.14 (FSL Lord Carbery injured & The Prince de Ligne unhurt); 1 Sqdn dett Antwerp being rebuilt as single-str with bigger tanks and a covered fuselage with a small tail fin 27.9.14; Deleted 14.10.14

**1 SOPWITH SPECIAL TRACTOR BIPLANE SEAPLANE ordered 2.14 under Cont No C.P.02007/14, built Kingston & numbered 170. (200-hp Canton-Unné)**

170    First British aircraft ordered specially as a torpedo carrier; Deld Calshot 1.7.14; Failed to fly 6.7.14; Flown by S/Cdr AM Longmore 9.7.14 without observer and with little fuel; Never flew with intended weapon; Mkrs Woolston for modifications 7.8.14; Calshot 22.8.14; Tested Calshot 7.11.14; Bomb-dropping gear fitted by 1.12.14; Hamble 19.1.15; Deleted 11.4.15; Dismantled Hamble 15.4.15

**7 WIGHT TYPE A.I IMPROVED NAVYPLANE PUSHER BIPLANE SEAPLANES ordered 14.5.14 under Contract No C.P.37385/14/X.7333, built East Cowes & numbered 171 to 177. (200-hp Canton Unné)**

171    FF 18.9.14 (Gordon England); Deld Calshot by 10.14; Fitted W/T 14.10.14; Tested 6-13.11.14; Dover 19.11.14; HSPP 24.12.14; Trials without torpedo; Damaged propeller and engine landing, towed back to harbour 10.1.15; Cedric Lee/SCAW repair 21.1.15; retd Dover 8.15; Wrecked 10.11.16; To SCAW for repair, but later deleted

172    Deld Blyth direct to HMS *Ark Royal* 16.12.14; Accepted 19.12.14 (Gordon England & F/Cdr GR Bromet); Ship sailed from Sheerness 1.2.15; Flew on arrival Tenedos 17.2.15; Recd 28 bullet holes 4.4.15 (F/L GR Bromet & Lt AG Brown RNR); Recd 16 bullet holes and shrapnel damage 25.4.15; Dismantled and stored SS *Penmorvah* pending engine stores 12.5.15; Repairing HMS *Ark Royal* 1.6.15; To be re-erected with parts from 175 and known as 175 in future 16.7.15

173    Deld Blyth direct to HMS *Ark Royal* 16.12.14; Ship sailed from Sheerness 1.2.15; Flew on arrival Tenedos 17.2.15; Poor performance; Dismantled at Tenedos 27.3.15 (replaced by 176)

174    Larger fin than 173, and additional drag bracing to wings; Tested Calshot 29.1.15 (Gordon England & Lt FH Bramwell); En route 1 Sqdn, EF, FL outside Dover Harbour, rescue TBD collided with it, broke up 8.2.15 (F/L ERC Nanson & AM rescued unhurt by TBD)

175    Shipped to Dardanelles 1.15; HMS *Ark Royal* at Imbros by 7.15 (used bits from 172 and 176 from 7.15); Hoisted on deck 23.7.15 (never flown); Deleted 1.16

176    Accepted 2.3.15; Packed for shipment under Cont No C.P.67772/15/X.12396 dated 1.3.15; Arr HMS *Ark Royal* at Mudros 5.4.15, but reported in poor condition, damaged en route due to poor packing; Erected and tested, then flown over town of Gallipoli 11.4.15; Hit in wings and floats by bullets while spotting for HMS *Lord Nelson*, u/c broken on landing 16.4.15 (F/L R Whitehead & Lt W Parke); Flown after repair 18.4.15; EF attempting to spot for HMS *Prince of Wales* 28.4.15 (F/L R Whitehead & S/L W Park); Kephalo 14.6.15; Condemned on overhaul and inspection 14.7.15; HMS *Ark Royal* 15.7.15; Deleted 21.7.15 FW&T

177    Single seat. Deld Calshot 24.10.14; Dover 18.11.14; Crashed when rudder bar broke, CW, sank in tow of HM steam trawler *St. George* 16.12.14 (F/L ERC Nanson and passenger unhurt), engine salved

**1 SHORT TYPE B TWO-SEAT TRACTOR BIPLANE ordered 6.14, to be built at Eastchurch & numbered 178. (200-hp Canton-Unné or 200-hp Le Rhône)**

178    Ordered for Eastchurch, but cancelled 7.14

**1 AVRO 504 (ADMIRALTY 179 TYPE) TRACTOR BIPLANE built under Cont No C.P.46635/14 at Manchester & numbered 179. (80-hp Gnome)**

179    Avro Flight, shipped to France from Southampton in SS *Manchester Importer* 10.11.14; Then by rail, arr Belfort 13.11.14; Damaged taxying Belfort 17.11.14 (Cdr PA Shepherd); Fitted bombs for Friedrichshaven raid but broke tail skid and could not TO 21.11.14 (FSL RB Cannon); Eastchurch (via Queenborough) 29.11.14; Removed to Eastchurch; Dunkerque 8.12.14; 3 Sqdn Dunkerque 10.12.14; Dover 1.3.15; 1 Sqdn Dunkerque by 11.3.15 - @12.3.15; Dunkerque to RD Grain 30.4.15; Tested and fitted with bombing gear 19.6.15; Landed in marsh in error for aerodrome and damaged 21.6.15 (FSL ON Walmesley injured); Tested after repair 2.7.15; Brought down by gunfire at Canvey Island 13.7.15 (FSL JC Croft); Tested after repair 24.7.15; Test after overhaul 6.9.15; Broke u/c in bomb dropping practice 11.10.15 (FSL EM Morgan); Eastbourne 9.2.16; Damaged 28.2.16 (S/L WM Tait & S/L HW Mortimore); Ringmer 10.5.16; Damaged in ground collision with 9822 19.5.16 (PFSL PG McNeil); retd Eastbourne; Deleted 12.6.16

**1 SHORT TWO-SEAT TRACTOR BIPLANE ordered under Cont No C.P.46634/14 & numbered 180 (100-hp Gnome)**

180    "Short 10" for Eastchurch 7.14, but no record of delivery. Possibly unused renumbering of No.10, Short S.41

**1 SHORT TWO-SEAT PUSHER BIPLANE ordered under Cont No C.P.46634/14 & numbered 181. (50-hp Gnome or 80-hp Le Rhône)**

181    "Short 3" for Eastchurch 7.14, but no record of delivery. Possibly unused renumbering of No.3, Short S.78

**1 SHORT DUAL CONTROL SEAPLANE ordered under Cont No C.P.46634/14 & numbered 182. (100-hp Gnome)**

182      Possibly DC version of 74 Type. On order for Grain 6.14 - 12.14, then for Felixstowe by 28.2.15, but never delivered

**1 SHORT ADMIRALTY 74 TYPE TRACTOR BIPLANE SEAPLANE built under Cont No C.P.46634/14 at Eastchurch & numbered 183. (100-hp Gnome Monosoupape) [Gordon Bruce's researches show correct c/n to be S.128]**

183      Originally allocated to Dundee, but deld Grain 24.11.14; Accepted 20.12.14; Slightly damaged in gale 29.12.14; Repaired 5.1.15; Left for Felixstowe but engine trouble and broke strut on TO 14.1.15 (F/L VG Blackburn); Left for Felixstowe but EF, FL West Mersea 18.1.15 (F/L VG Blackburn); arr Felixstowe 19.1.15; HMS *Empress* 22.1.15; Felixstowe 23.1.15; Wing buckled 1.15; Instructional flying 2.15; HMS *Aurora* 4.3.15; Felixstowe 4.3.15; Damaged landing 5.3.15 (F/L JMD'A Levy); Awaiting spares 1.6.15; Dismantled 4.6.15; Left for Gibraltar 5.6.15; In transit by 20.6.15; arr Gibraltar 6.15; Overhaul 16.7.15; Tested over overhaul 1.8.15; still listed there 30.11.15, but not by 3.16; NFT

**2 SHORT ADMIRALTY 184 TYPE TRACTOR BIPLANE SEAPLANES ordered 7.14 for Grain under Cont No C.P.46634/14, built Rochester & numbered 184 & 185. (To be 200-hp Salmson, but deld with 225-hp Sunbeam) [Gordon Bruce's researches show correct c/n's to be S.106 and S.107]**

184      Built to carry 14-inch torpedo; Deld Grain 21.4.15; Accepted 22.4.15 (Kemp); Felixstowe 30.4.15; HMS *Riviera* 3.5.15; Felixstowe 5.5.15; HMS *Riviera* 7.5.15; HMS *Ben-my-Chree* 21.5.15; HMS *Roberts* 1.8.15; HMS *Ben-my-Chree* 9.8.15; Successful torpedo attack against a steam tug off Gallipoli (F/Cdr GB Dacre) 17.8.15; SS *Tringa* for shipment to UK 5.9.15; Fuselage from CSD White City to Grain for exptl purposes 15.8.16
185      Deld by SS *Upcerne* to HMS *Campania* 20.6.15; Assembled, test flown then taken ashore Scapa 5.7.15; HMS *Campania* 8.7.15; FL bad weather, damaged wings and elevator 9.7.15; Macduff Harbour 17.8.15 (mine spotting); Banff 18.8.15; Macduff Harbour 23.8.15; HMS *Campania* 24.8.15; Port wing damaged hoisting aboard 3.9.15; Repaired Scapa 28.9.15; HMS *Campania* 16.11.15; Scapa 8.12.15; Deleted 3.16 BR

**1 WIGHT BIPLANE SEAPLANE to be  numbered 186 and built East Cowes. (200-hp Canton-Unné)**

186      Cancelled and serial reallocated

**1 SHORT FOLDER TORPEDO-CARRYING TRACTOR BIPLANE SEAPLANE ordered 7.14 for Calshot under Cont No C.P.02112/14, to be built at Eastchurch & numbered 186. (Variously to be two 200-hp Salmson, 160-hp Le Rhône or 180-hp Gnome)**

186      On order to at least 10.14, but not delivered

**1 WIGHT TWIN FUSELAGE, TWIN-ENGINED TRACTOR BIPLANE SEAPLANE ordered 7.14 under Cont No C.P.02108/14, built East Cowes & numbered 187. (Two 200-hp Canton-Unné)**

187      Built to carry 18-inch Mark IX torpedo; Awaiting test at Cowes 25.9.15; Deld Felixstowe 15.7.16; type tested 8.16 but underpowered; Surveyed 1.9.16; Deleted 3.10.16

**1 MAURICE FARMAN S.7 LONGHORN TRACTOR BIPLANE ordered under Cont No C.P.45317/14 from The Aircraft Manufacturing Co Ltd, Hendon & numbered 188. (70-hp Renault)**

188      Deld ECNFS 2.6.14; Ordered to be at Grain for 1st Lord (Winston Churchill) 4.6.14; Skid smashed Calshot 1.9.14 (F/L HA Buss & FSL A Nickerson); Crashed on cross-country, CW 24.10.14 (FSL L Gresley); FL, crashed, wrecked 24.6.15; Repaired; Deleted 1.11.15

**1 HENRY FARMAN F.20 PUSHER BIPLANE built by Eastbourne Aviation Co under Cont No C.P.45317/14 & numbered 189. (80-hp Gnome)**

189      Deld Eastchurch by 6.14 - 8.14; Hendon  by 13.9.14; Flown 12.3.15 & 31.3.15; Officially reported as 70-hp Renault by 11.3.15; Deleted 4.15

**9 SHORT TYPE B TWO-SEAT TRACTOR BIPLANES ordered 7.14, to be built Eastchurch & numbered 190 to 198. (200-hp Canton-Unné)**

190 to 198 On order for Eastchurch to 12.14, but never delivered

**1 ROYAL AIRCRAFT FACTORY SEAPLANE (designation?) ordered 7.14 under Cont No C.P.41589/14 & numbered 199.**

199      Still on order 9.15, but never delivered. For construction by Short Bros

**1 SPENCER "HENRY FARMAN TYPE" PUSHER BIPLANE bought 9.14 & numbered 200. (50-hp Gnome)**

200      Deld Hendon by 30.9.14; Flown 3.10.14 (Merriam); Still listed 11.3.15; NFT

-------------------------------------------------------------------------------

### ROYAL FLYPAST 18th July 1914

20 aircraft were allocated, plus 10/20 reserves at Calshot.

A Flight: War Flight from Grain (Seddon)
        3 Short Folder (160 hp Gnôme) - 119, 120, 121 + 82?

B Flight: Dundee machines plus 2 new a/c (Gordon)
        3/4 Short Tractor (100 Gnôme) - 74, 75, 77 + 76

C Flight: Felixstowe machines (Risk)
        4 Maurice Farman Seaplanes (3 with 210 hp Renault and the Monaco machine with 130 hp Salmson) - 70, 113, 115 (crashed) plus Monaco m/c

D Flight: Yarmouth machines plus 1 from Felixstowe (Courtney)
        3/4 Henry Farman (120 hp Gnôme) - 139, 142, 143 (and 141 from Felixstowe?)

E Flight: at Calshot (Longmore)
        3/4 Sopwiths and Bat-boats :
        Sopwith Gun Carrier (200 hp Salmson) - 93, did not fly
        Short Gun Carrier (160 hp Gnôme) - 126
        Sopwith Tractor, ex Circuit (100 hp Green) - 151
        Sopwith Bat Boat (90 hp Austro-Daimler) - 118

*Short Seaplane 184 prototype, later to be produced in large numbers. (R.C.Sturtivant collection)*

*Spencer Pusher Biplane 200.*

*Short Type C Folder Seaplane 818. (FAA Museum)*

**6 SOPWITH ADMIRALTY 806 [or 804] TYPE "GUNBUS No.1" PUSHER BIPLANES** ordered under Cont No C.P.02133/14, numbered 801 to 806 & built Kingston. (110-hp Sunbeam or 150-hp Sunbeam Crusader)

801     (110-hp Sunbeam). Tested Brooklands 6.10.14; Defence Flight Hendon 11.10.14; Sopwith by 11.3.15 (repair and fit 150-hp Sunbeam); Chingford (via Hendon) 21.7.15; Dismantled for stowing 8.15; CSD White City by lorry 3.12.15, later deleted

802     (110-hp Sunbeam). Deld Hendon by 28.10.14; Mkrs by 12.3.15 (alterations and fit 150-hp Sunbeam); Hendon 8.5.15; AZP, COL Theobalds Park, Herts 1.6.15 (F/L DM Barnes killed and FSL B Travers injured); remains to Pemberton Billing for reconstruction 15.7.15; Hendon for erection 28.10.15; Deleted 6.12.15

803     (150-hp Sunbeam). Deld Hendon by 8.12.14; Mkrs Brooklands by air 20.3.15; Accident while under repair 19.4.15; Sopwith repair to at least 1.10.15; CSD White City by 30.6.16; Deleted 9.16

804     (150-hp Sunbeam). Deld Hendon 4.1.15 (Hawker); Dunkerque in crate 20.1.15; 1 Sqdn 28.2.15; Dismantled by 11.3.15; To Pemberton Billing 5.15 (repair); Hendon for erection 14.8.15; Clement Talbot Works for repair 16.11.15, later deleted

805     (150-hp Sunbeam). Allocated Hendon by 1.1.15; Deld Hendon 16.3.15; Chingford 13.7.15; Dismantled for stowing 16.8.15; CSD White City by road 29.10.15, later deleted

806     (150-hp Sunbeam). Deld Hendon 5.11.14 - @9.2.15; Mkrs by 11.3.15 (alterations); Hendon 21.6.15 (Hawker); Chingford 19.7.15; Dismantled for stowing by 31.8.15; Clement Talbot Works by lorry 1.11.15 for mechanic training
        [One report suggests that the first two were fitted with 100-hp Gnome Monosoupape, not 110-hp Sunbeam]

**4 SOPWITH ADMIRALTY 807 TYPE FOLDER TRACTOR BIPLANE SEAPLANES** ordered under Cont No C.P.02142/14, numbered 807 to 810 & built Kingston. (100-hp Gnome Monosoupape)

807     Deld Calshot for acceptance by 12.14; Mkrs 4.12.14; Blyth 10.12.14; HMS *Ark Royal* 23.12.14; HMS *Empress* 14.1.15; HMS *Ark Royal* 19.1.15; Sailed from Sheerness for Dardanelles 31.1.15; Flown on arrival at Tenedos 17.2.15; Crane accident 4.3.15 (PO Thornton injured); Used as single seater 10.3.15 - 16.4.15, but of little use; Damaged float on TO 16.3.15 (FSL EH Dunning); Dismantled 17.4.15; Unable to climb, so tail and wings fitted to 922 for HMS *Doris* 22.4.15; Re-erected 14.5.15 (with 80-hp Gnome?) but still failed to climb so dismantled and used as spares for 922; Retd HMS *Ark Royal* 11.6.15; Kephalo 23.6.15; HMS *Ark Royal* 7.15; Kephalo 17.7.15; HMS *Ark Royal* 7.15; Last flight as single-seater 26.7.15; Kephalo 27.7.15; Still in HMS *Ark Royal* to 11.15, but soon deleted

808     Deld Blyth 10.12.14; Failed tests 17.12.14; HMS *Ark Royal* 4.1.15; HMS *Engadine* 14.1.15; HMS *Ark Royal* 19.1.15; HMS *Engadine* 22.1.15; HMS *Empress* 26.1.15; HMS *Ark Royal* 28.1.15; Towed to Felixstowe 1.2.15; HMS *Ark Royal* 1.2.15; Ship sailed from Sheerness for Dardanelles 2.2.15; While climbing to observe fire from HMS *Queen Elizabeth*, propeller broke at 3000ft, broke starboard wing tip, OOC in spiral dive into sea 3m W of ship 5.3.15 (F/L WHS Garnett slightly injured & F/Cdr HA Williamson seriously injured, rescued by HMS *Usk*)

809     Deld Calshot by 9.14; tests planned 15.9.14; Not accepted 12.14; Frequent flying 1.15; Chassis damaged Southampton Water 8.1.15 (FSL EH Dunning); Crashed in sea, CW 13.3.15; Deleted 3.15

810     Deld Calshot by Mahl 21.12.14 but not accepted; 3½-in extension to lower wings; instructional flying 1.15; Damaged in tow from St.Helen's 2.2.15 (F/L EVS Wilberforce); Caught fire while taxying, remains salved 5.4.15 (FSL CB Dalison); Wings to 919 4.15; Deleted 13.5.15

**8 SHORT TYPE C FOLDER (IMPROVED ADMIRALTY 74 TYPE) TRACTOR SEAPLANES** ordered under Cont No C.P.02129/14, numbered 811 to 818 & built Eastchurch. (100-hp Gnome) [ [Gordon Bruce's researches shown correct c/n's to be S.108 to S.115]

811     Fitted Rouzet W/T. Deld Grain 10.14; Tested 20.10.14; HMS *Riviera* 21.11.14; Felixstowe 27.11.14; HMS *Riviera* 16.12.14; Felixstowe 20.12.14; HMS *Riviera* 21.12.14; Felixstowe 22.12.14; HMS *Riviera* 23.12.14; Took part in Cuxhaven raid, sighted and recovered by ship 24-25.12.14 (F/L CHK Edmonds); Suffered weather damage 28.12.14; Felixstowe 6.1.15 (repair); HMS *Riviera* 1.15; Felixstowe 18.1.15 (some instructional flying); HMS *Riviera* 26.1.15; Felixstowe 28.1.15; Crashed and badly damaged 29.6.15; Not repaired; Deleted 9.8.15

812     Deld Grain and accepted 8.11.14; HMS *Riviera* 21.11.14; Felixstowe 27.11.14; HMS *Riviera* 16.12.14; Felixstowe 20.12.14; Grain 20.12.14; Failed to start on Cuxhaven raid, engine trouble 24.12.14 (F/Lt R Bone & AM Waters); HMS *Empress* 14.1.15; Felixstowe 18.1.15; HMS *Empress* 22.1.15; Felixstowe 1.2.15; HMS *Empress* 3.2.15; Dunkerque 10.2.15; HMS *Empress* 28.2.15; Felixstowe 3.3.15; HMS *Arethusa* 18.3.15; Felixstowe 18.3.15; HMS *Empress* 20.3.15; Felixstowe 22.3.15; HMS *Empress* 23.3.15; Felixstowe 25.3.15; Grain 14.4.15; Converted DC 13-19.5.15; Calshot 29.5.15; Bembridge 10.8.15; Calshot 15.9.15; Chassis wrecked 24.9.15 (FSL G Smethurst); Deleted 14.2.16

813     Deld Grain 5.11.14; Accepted 8.11.14; HMS *Empress* 6.12.14; HMS *Riviera* 14.1.15; Felixstowe 18.1.15; HMS *Empress* 22.1.15; Felixstowe 1.2.15; HMS *Empress* 3.2.15; Dunkerque 10.2.15; Missing on operations 16.2.15 (F/L The Hon Desmond O'Brien or FSL T Spencer killed - see also 817)

814     Deld Grain 18.11.14; Tested 20.11.14 & 27.11.14; W/T taken out and 4x20-lb bombs fitted 4.12.14; HMS *Empress* 6.12.14; Abandoned nr Norderney Gat on Cuxhaven raid, bombed by Schütte-Lanz 25.12.14 (FSL V Gaskell-Blackburn & CPO Bell saved by submarine *E.11*)

815     Deld Grain 18.11.14; flown 1.12.14; W/T taken out and 4x20-lb bombs fitted 4.12.14; HMS *Empress* 6.12.14; Abandoned nr Norderney Gat on Cuxhaven raid 25.12.14 (F/Cdr DA Oliver and CPO Budds saved by submarine *E.11*)

816     Fitted Rouzet W/T. Deld Grain 25.11.14; Tested 5.12.14; To Blyth 8.12.14; HMS *Ark Royal* 15.12.14; Blyth 17.12.14; HMS *Empress* 14.1.15; Felixstowe 19.1.15; HMS *Empress* 22.1.15; Felixstowe 1.2.15; HMS *Empress* 3.2.15; Dunkerque 10.2.15; Temp missing at Dunkerque 16.2.15; HMS *Empress* 28.2.15; Felixstowe 3.3.15; Grain 20.3.15; Drifted into buoy, smashed tailplane and elevator 2.5.15 (FSL AC Saw); Tested after repair 20.5.15; Calshot 26.5.15; Bembridge 10.7.15; Calshot 13.7.15; Bembridge 14.8.15; Calshot 6.9.15; Deleted 16.5.16

817     Fitted Rouzet W/T. Deld Grain 12.14; Tested 5.12.14, climbed to 3,000 ft in 40 min; To Blyth 7.12.14; HMS *Ark Royal* 18.12.14; HMS *Engadine* 14.1.15; Felixstowe 19.1.15; HMS *Empress* 20.1.15; HMS *Riviera* 22.1.15; Felixstowe 26.1.15; HMS *Ark Royal* 26.1.15; HMS *Empress* 28.1.15; Felixstowe 1.2.15; HMS *Empress* 3.2.15; Dunkerque 10.2.15; Missing on operations 16.2.15 (F/Lt The Hon Desmond O'Brien or FSL T Spencer killed - see also 813); Deleted 12.3.15

818     Fitted Rouzet W/T. Deld Grain 1.12.14; Tested 22.12.14 (Kemp); Accepted 22.12.14 (Kemp); Slightly damaged in gale 29.12.14; Accepted 2.1.15; Felixstowe 5.1.15; Felixstowe 5.1.15; HMS *Riviera* 14.1.15 (fitted W/T); Felixstowe 18.1.15; HMS *Riviera* 22.1.15; HMS *Engadine* 30.1.15; Felixstowe 1.2.15; Detd Dover for raids on Zeebrugge and Ostende 10.2.15; Dunkerque 11.2.15; Felixstowe 20.2.15; HMS *Aurora* 6.3.15; Felixstowe 6.3.15; HMS *Aurora* 20.3.15; Felixstowe 22.3.15; HMS *Aurora* 23.3.15; Felixstowe 27.3.15; For HMS *Empress* by 30.3.15 (NTU?); Grain 5.4.15;

Calshot 2.5.15; Bembridge 7.6.15; Calshot 23.6.15 (clean engine); Bembridge 29.6.15; Calshot 1.7.15; TW 8.8.15 (FSL R Souray & AM AC Lewis); Deleted 11.8.15

**3 SHORT ADMIRALTY 830 TYPE TRACTOR BIPLANE SEAPLANES ordered 25.9.14 under Cont No C.P.57105/14/X.18826, numbered 819 to 821 & built Rochester. (135-hp Canton-Unné; was to be 110-hp Sunbeam)** [Gordon Bruce's researches shown correct c/n's to be S.119 to S.121]

819      Deld Grain 1.12.14; Tested 22.12.14; Accepted 12.1.15 (Kemp); HMS *Engadine* (via Felixstowe) 14.1.15; Tested 14.1.15 (Kemp); Felixstowe (via Grain) 14.1.15; HMS *Engadine* 21.1.15; HMS *Riviera* 30.1.15; Felixstowe 31.1.15; Detd Dover for raids on Zeebrugge and Ostende 10.2.15; Dunkerque 11.2.15; Felixstowe 20.2.15; HMS *Arethusa* 3.3.15; Felixstowe 3.3.15; HMS *Arethusa* 4.3.15; Grain 15.3.15; Felixstowe 15.3.15; HMS *Arethusa* 20.3.15; Felixstowe 22.3.15; HMS *Arethusa* 23.3.15; Felixstowe, towed in by MB *Hatasoo* 27.3.15; HMS *Empress* 31.3.15; Grain 3.4.15; Felixstowe 4.4.15; HMS *Riviera* 18.4.15; Felixstowe 19.4.15; HMS *Riviera* 20.4.15; Grain 19.5.15; HMS *Engadine* 21.5.15; Beardmore (via Granton Harbour) 24.1.16 (overhaul); Dover 6.6.16; Dunkerque 1.7.16; Shot down by U-boat N of Zeebrugge and afterwards picked up by German TBD 24.7.16 (FSL FJ Bailey & O/L FW Mardock RNVR PoWs)

820      Deld Grain 13.1.15; Flown 14.1.15 (Kemp); Accepted 21.1.15 (Kemp); Felixstowe 24.1.15; HMS *Engadine* 26.1.15; Damaged when ship's mast smashed 29.1.15; Bits to Harwich 4.2.15; Shorts repair 5.2.15; HSPP 26.2.15; Grain in tow 5.3.15; Tested 6.3.15; Felixstowe 7.3.15; HMS *Empress* 19.3.15; Felixstowe 22.3.15; HMS *Empress* 23.3.15; Felixstowe 25.3.15; HMS *Empress* 31.3.15; Grain 2.4.15; Felixstowe 26.4.15; HMS *Ben-my-Chree* 1.5.15 (to Dardanelles); Mudros 15.6.15; HMS *Ben-my-Chree* 22.7.15 - 10.15 (to go to HMS *Ark Royal*); Transit to UK 4.16, then deleted

821      Deld Grain 23.1.15; Tested 24.1.15 (Kemp); Felixstowe 28.1.15; HMS *Riviera* 28.1.15; Felixstowe 31.1.15; HMS *Arethusa* 25.2.15; Felixstowe 25.2.15; HMS *Empress* 19.3.15; Felixstowe 22.3.15; HMS *Empress* 23.3.15; Felixstowe 25.3.15; HMS *Empress* 31.3.15; Grain 3.4.15; Felixstowe 26.4.15; HMS *Ben-my-Chree* 1.5.15 (to Dardanelles); Mudros 15.6.15; HMS *Ben-my-Chree* 23.7.15 - 10.15; HMS *Ark Royal* 11.15; transit to UK 4.16, then deleted

**6 SHORT ADMIRALTY 827 TYPE TRACTOR BIPLANE SEAPLANES ordered under Cont No C.P.57105/14, numbered 822 to 827 & built Rochester. (150-hp Sunbeam Crusader; was to be 110-hp Sunbeam)** [Gordon Bruce's researches shown correct c/n's to be S.122 to S.127]

822      Fitted W/T. Deld Grain 5.2.15; Accepted 10.2.15; HAPP 20.3.15 (S/L DA Oliver & FSL WG Moore); Mkrs packing for shipment 19.5.15; Shipped to Gibraltar 6.15; Arr RFC Force D Mesopotamia 5.9.15; Erecting as seaplane from 22.10.15; Tested 31.10.15; EF, FL 10m N of Bgailah 5.11.15 (Mjr R Gordon & Gen Kemball); Retd by lighter; Land chassis fitted 15.11.15; U/s by 6.12.15; Crashed Orah, 10m S of Kut 14.2.16 (FSL WH Dunn), later deleted

823      Fitted W/T. (Deld Grain?); HMS *Campania* 17.4.15; Landed with side drift, damaged u/c 7.5.15; Repairs completed 9.6.15; Struck wreckage on TO, broke starboard float 11.6.15; Exptl firing at balloon 13.9.15; Towed ashore 24.9.15; HMS *Campania* by 10.15; Scapa 13.11.15 (spare machine, no engine); U/c damaged by propeller breaking in rough sea 17.9.16; HMS *Campania* by 8.3.17 (u/s); Deleted 7.7.17

824      Fitted W/T. Deld Grain 7.1.15; Scapa by 28.2.15; Accepted 17.4.15; HMS *Campania* 17.4.15; Scapa (overhaul) 7.12.15; Deleted 8.5.16

825      Fitted W/T. Deld Grain 22.3.15; Failed test 23.3.15; Re-tested and passed 14.4.15; Mkrs packing for shipment 11.5.15; Shipped to Gibraltar 6.15; Arr RFC Force D Mesopotamia 5.9.15; Hit native boat on TO,

chassis seriously damaged 29.9.15 (Mjr R Gordon); Fitted land chassis 6-16.10.15; Flown 19.10.15; Fuselage too badly warped for repair in Mesopotamia by 6.12.15; Reconv seaplane by 4.16 - 5.16; Deleted 1916

826      Fitted W/T. (Deld Grain?); In transit to Scapa for HMS *Campania* by 11.3.15; HMS *Campania* 17.4.15; Tested 19.4.15; Scapa in tow for trueing up 28.5.15; HMS *Campania* 31.5.15; Scapa 15.7.15; HMS *Campania* 9.8.15; O/t hoisting out, CW 14.8.15; remains taken ashore by 28.8.15; Deleted 31.8.15

827      Fitted W/T. Deld Grain 10.4.15; Accepted 16.4.15 (Kemp); Mkrs Rochester 11.5.15 (pack for shipment); Shipped to Gibraltar 6.15; Arr RFC Force D Mesopotamia 3.9.15; Tested after erection 25.9.15; EF, FL, flown to lee shore when elevator and aileron badly damaged 29.9.15; Tested after repair 4.10.15; Land chassis fitted, tested 13.10.15; U/s by 6.12.15; Reconverted to seaplane 2.1.16; Tested 5.1.16; Deleted 1.1.17
[Reported fitted experimentally with 135-hp Samson at one time]

**3 SHORT ADMIRALTY 135 [or 830] TYPE TRACTOR BIPLANE SEAPLANES ordered under Cont No C.P.57105/14, numbered 828 to 830 & built Rochester. (135-hp Canton-Unné)** [Gordon Bruce's researches shown correct c/n's to be S.116 to S.118]

828      (C/n S.116). Deld Grain 10.11.14; Accepted 20.11.14; HMS *Engadine* 11.14; Westgate to Grain 20.12.14; To Felixstowe but propeller broke, FL Foulness 21.12.14; Towed back to Grain via Sheerness 25.12.14; Sideslipped on turn after TO, CW 2.1.15 (Lt HG Wanklyn & AM Goldsmith unhurt); Deleted 19.1.15

829      (C/n S.117). Deld Grain 11.14; Accepted 20.11.14; FL Hook of Holland 17.12.14 (S/Cdr JW Seddon & LM RL Hartley picked by Norwegian ship SS *Orn* 11m NE of Galloper LV, taken to Holland; aircraft interned)

830      (C/n S.118). Failed test when FL with oil leak 2.1.15 (Kemp); Accepted and delivered Grain 5.1.15 (Kemp); Felixstowe 6.1.15; HMS *Engadine* 14.1.15; Felixstowe 18.1.15; HMS *Engadine* 22.1.15; Wrecked when ship's mast fell on it 29.1.15; Bits taken off at Harwich for Shorts 4.2.15; Deleted 2.15

**10 WIGHT ADMIRALTY 840 TYPE TRACTOR BIPLANE SEAPLANES ordered 2.9.14 under Cont No C.P.02143/14/X.16079, numbered 831 to 840 & built East Cowes. (225-hp Sunbeam)**

831      Deld 2.1.15; Cowes 2.3.15 (Gordon England); Tested Calshot 13.3.15 (type trials); Visited Bembridge 17.3.15; Torpedo trials 22.3.15; Camera sight tested 10.6.15; Accident 15.6.15 (FSL WH Dunn unhurt); Under repair to at least 31.8.15; Deleted 1.1.16

832      Deld Calshot 14.4.15; Tested 15.4.15; Dunkerque but hit post of breakwater while taxying into harbour, left lower main spar broken 18.4.15 (FSL CB Dalison & AM Currie); Test after repair 23/24.5.15; Started for England but retd with propeller trouble 2.7.15 (last entry in aircraft flying log); Deleted by 12.15

833      Tested 7.7.15; Accepted Cowes 9.7.15; Deld Calshot 15.7.15 (Gordon England); For overhaul 19.7.15; Tested but would not leave water 6.9.15; Dismantled 1.12.15

834      Deld Calshot by 11.5.15; Tested Wells bombsight 12-13.6.15; Bomb sight trials; unserviceable by 8.15; Deleted 1.1.16

835      Tested Calshot 26.4.15, very poor; Emergency use only 4.15 - 5.15; Mkrs 29.6.15; Accepted Calshot 29.7.15; To HMS *Campania* 7.8.15 (arr 25.8.15, erecting in collier alongside); Erected Scapa 1.9.15; HMS *Campania* 14.9.15; Scapa 1.12.15 - @8.12.15; Possibly then Mkrs for rebuild; Scapa 7.5.16; Deleted 12.6.16

836      Failed to take off 4-7.1.15, poor performance; Still Mkrs 30.4.15; Deld HMS *Campania* by collier 22.5.15; Unpacked 25.5.15; Scapa 28.5.15 - 28.6.15 (for trueing up); HMS *Campania* by 2.7.15; Sideslipped landing and broke wings struts 9.8.15; Still ship 11.8.15; Mkrs for repair 2.9.15 - @30.11.15; CSD White City by 1.16; Seaplane School Calshot 3.1.16; to makers 30.4.16; Arr Scapa in collier *Dalewood* 31.5.16; HMS *Campania*

4.8.16; Scapa 5.8.16; Deleted 5.4.17

**837** Deld *Campania* by collier for erection 22.5.15; Scapa for test 2.6.15; HMS *Campania* 14.6.15 - @28.6.15; Scapa by 1.7.15; HMS *Campania* 5.7.15; Banff Harbour 16.8.15 (mine spotting); Macduff Harbour 17.8.15; Banff Harbour 18.8.15; Macduff Harbour 22.8.15; HMS *Campania* 23.8.15; Wight's for repair 31.8.15; Calshot 5.2.16; Wrecked Calshot 1.4.16; Deleted 16.5.16

**838** Deld Scapa in crate by collier 30.5.15; HMS *Campania* 3.7.15; Scapa 6.7.15; Wights for mods 9.9.15; Arr Scapa in collier *Dalewood* 31.5.16; HMS *Campania* in tow of trawler HMS *Cuckoo* 16.9.16; Damaged by 21.9.16; Deleted 2.10.16

**839** Deld Dundee by boat 28.5.15; Wights in SS *J.Duncan* for repair 3.9.15; Arrived Scapa in collier *Dalewood* 31.5.16; HMS *Campania* 20.6.16; Scapa 30.6.16; HMS *Campania* 6.7.16; Scapa 10.9.16; EF, FL in sea, damaged 16.9.16 (FSL R Davies & OSL AO Jones); Deleted 9.4.17

**840** Tested Cowes 29.5.15; Deld Calshot 24.6.15; Deleted 14.2.16

**10 SHORT ADMIRALTY 184 TYPE TRACTOR BIPLANE SEAPLANES ordered under Cont No C.P.57105/14, numbered 841 to 850 & built Eastchurch. (225-hp Sunbeam, originally to be 200-hp Canton-Unné)** [Gordon Bruce's researches shown correct c/n's to be S.129 to S.138]

**841** Embarked from Felixstowe to HMS *Ben-my-Chree* 28.5.15; HMS *Roberts* 11.8.15; HMS *Ben-my-Chree* 3.9.15; To SS *Tringa* for shipment to UK 5.9.15 and later deleted

**842** Tested Grain 14.7.15; Transit in HMS *Merchant Prince* 8.15; HMS *Ben-my-Chree* 10.8.15; Made world's first successful torpedo attack 12.8.15 (F/Cdr CHK Edmonds); Made second successful torpedo attack 17.8.15; HMS *Euryalus* 3.10.15; HMS *Ben-my-Chree* 10.10.15; Left ship at Kephalo 7.11.15; Shipped to UK; PVRD by 22.3.16; Deleted 29.3.16

**843** Deld Grain 24.6.15 (Kemp); HMS *Riviera* 22.8.15; Dunkerque 18.9.15; HMS *Riviera* 1.10.15; Dunkerque 3.10.15; HMS *Riviera* 27.10.15; Aileron and wingtip damaged passing through lock 22.12.15; Dunkerque for trueing up 28.12.15; HMS *Riviera* 1.1.16; Dover 19.1.16; HMS *Riviera* 25.1.16; Dunkerque 28.1.16 (repair); HMS *Riviera* 1.2.16; Dover 20.2.16; Parnall 31.5.16 (overhaul and repair); Killingholme 28.11.16; South Shields 13.12.16; Deleted 8.2.17

**844** Deld Grain 13.7.15 (Kemp); Tested 14.7.15; AZP 10.8.15 (F/L BS Fowler); HMS *Riviera* 17.9.15; Dunkerque 18.9.15; HMS *Riviera* 1.10.15; Dunkerque 2.10.15; HMS *Riviera* 27.10.15; Grain 18.1.16; HMS *Riviera* 25.1.16; Chased hot air balloon 9.2.16; Damaged taking ashore in snowstorm to Dunkerque 22.2.16; HMS *Riviera* 2.3.16; Was to participate in Zeebrugge raid but failed to rise 20.3.16 (FSL N Gregory); Elevator submerged and damaged 28.3.16 (FSL N Gregory & OSL OH Crowther); Grain 2.4.16; Felixstowe 9.6.16; Deleted 14.11.16

**845** Accepted Rochester 1.7.15; Erecting aboard collier *Boukadra* for HMS *Campania* 22.7.15; Scapa by 25.7.15 (erecting); HMS *Campania* 2.9.15; Scapa 14.9.15; HMS *Campania* 14.9.15; Scapa 1.12.15; HMS *Campania* 2.5.16; Scapa 28.5.16; HMS *Campania* 3.6.16; Scapa 8.6.16; HMS *Campania* 15.6.16; Scapa 4.7.16; HMS *Campania* 27.7.16; Sage 2.9.16 - @28.2.17 (to be ready 18.1.17); HMS *Campania* by 17.3.17 (not ready); Houton Bay 19.1.18 (storage); NFT

**846** Accepted Rochester 1.7.15; Transit via SS *Merchant Prince* 8.15; HMS *Ben-my-Chree* 20.8.15; Port Said 11.3.16; HMS *Ben-my-Chree* 4.16; Lost 3.4.16

**847** Deld and accepted Grain 21.7.15 (Kemp); Bomb gear fitted 7.15; HMS *Riviera* 29.7.15; Grain 18.8.15; Dover 23.8.15; HMS *Riviera* 8.9.15; Dover 19.9.15 (due to go to HMS *Riviera* 26.9.15); Started for ship at Dunkerque, but propeller split on TO, FL, o/t in sea 4.10.15 (F/L EIM Bird); Towed back to Dover; Dismantled 5.10.15; Saunders 21.10.15 - @31.5.16, later deleted

**848** Deld and accepted Grain 29.7.15 (Kemp); HMS *Riviera* 12.8.15; Grain 18.8.15; Dover 23.8.15; HMS *Riviera* 21.9.15; Dunkerque 2.10.15; Bombed U-boat 14m

NNW Ostende 2.10.15 (F/L H Stewart & OSL OH Crowther); HMS *Riviera* 16.10.15; Dover 18.10.15; HMS *Riviera* 23.10.15; EF, FL off Edinburgh LV, capsized astern of HMS *Electra*, salved, badly damaged hoisting in 17.11.15 (FSL R Souray & S/L N Lea); Wreckage landed Grain 20.11.15 and deleted

**849** Deld and accepted Grain 30.7.15 (Kemp); Shorts Rochester for packing 4.8.15; Shipped in SS *Merchant Prince* 8.15; HMS *Ben-my-Chree*, tested 21.9.15; Milo 20.11.15; HMS *Ben-my-Chree* 13.12.15; Damaged starboard float and chassis on landing 20.1.16; Petrol failure, FL in heavy sea, capsized and lost off Sollum 11.2.16 (F/Cdr CHK Edmonds DSO & Lt R Erskine Childers saved by HMT *Charlsen*); Deleted 3.16

**850** Accepted Rochester 17.8.15; shipped in SS *Joshua Nicholson* 8.15; HMS *Ben-my-Chree* 10.10.15; HMS *Ark Royal* 21.10.15; HMS *Ben-my-Chree* 25.10.15; Port Said 11.3.16; HMFA *Raven II* 18.3.16; Port Said 24.4.16; HMS *Ben-my-Chree* 27.4.16; Port Said 11.5.16; HMS *Ben-my-Chree* 26.5.16; Port Said 18.7.16 to 2.17; Deleted 1917

**10 SOPWITH ADMIRALTY 860 TYPE TRACTOR BIPLANE SEAPLANES ordered under Cont No C.P.02140/14, numbered 851 to 860 & built Kingston. Originally ordered as 157 Type. Delivered from Woolston. (225-hp Sunbeam)**

**851** Sank on FF when OOC due to rough weather off Netley [Date N/K] (Mr Alston, Sopwith's Chief Designer drowned); A/c found after 6 days of salvage operations, presume rebuilt; Tested Calshot 24.3.15 (Hawker); Lifted torpedo 2.4.15; Without engine 5.15 - 8.15; Dismantled by 9.15; CSD White City by lorry 28.10.15, later deleted

**852** Prepared for trials at Woolston 11.3.15; Calshot by 4.15 (but no mention in DRs); HMS *Ben-my-Chree* 17.4.15; HMS *Engadine* 21.5.15; Felixstowe 2.7.15 (stowed for HMS *Engadine*); HMS *Engadine* 8.7.15; Grain 9.7.15; Test aileron propeller for No.1000 8.15; Grain RD 9.10.15; Became PVRS 11.16 (fitted high lift wing); Became ECD Grain 1.2.17; Deleted 5.3.17

**853** Deld Calshot 21.12.14 (Mahl), 2-blade Lang propeller (no acceptance test); Mkrs Woolston by 11.3.15 (rebuild); Grain by 13.5.15; CSD White City 10.11.15, later deleted

**854** Deld Calshot 6.1.15 (Wing area 100 sq ft more than 853); Mkrs Woolston in tow for new engine 12.1.15; Tested Calshot with torpedo 27.1.15 (last mention) (Mahl); Accepted 4.2.15 (Mahl); Mkrs Woolston by 30.4.15; Calshot 17.5.15; Air Dept test 3.7.15 "nothing good about type"; FL outside Eastbourne seaplane sheds 1.8.15; Grain 2.8.15; CSD 11.9.15; Mkrs repair by 1.10.15 - @28.2.17, presume then deleted

**855** As landplane at Brooklands by 31.1.15; Preparing for trial by 30.4.15; To seaplane 5.15; Deld Calshot 16.5.15; Failed test 17.5.15 (Hawker); CSD White City by road 12.9.15; Deleted 10.15

**856** Tested Calshot 30.1.15; Tested 20 & 23.3.15 (Mahl); Detd Bembridge 3.15; HMS *Ben-my-Chree* (ex Calshot) 18.4.15; Calshot 24.4.15; W/T test 6.15; Dismantling from 10.9.15; CSD White City by lorry 28.10.15, then deleted

**857** 4 hr duration Flight at Calshot 10.3.15 (Mahl) [first mention]; Shipped to Aegean in case; arr HMS *Ark Royal* 19.4.15 but transferred to SS *Aragaz* as proper oil not arrived; To SS *Penmorvah* for erection 8.5.15; Erected 16.5.15; Tested 17.5.15; Kephalo 24.6.15; HMS *Ark Royal* 25.6.15; Kephalo 26.7.15; HMS *Ark Royal* in tow 27.7.15; Reported as useless, boxed up for passage to UK 6.8.15, then deleted

**858** Tested Calshot 11.2.15; Tested 20.2.15 (Mahl); Mkrs Woolston 22.2.15 (Mahl); HMS *Ben-my-Chree* (at Calshot) 22.4.15; Felixstowe 7.5.15; HMS *Engadine* 25.5.15; Felixstowe 2.7.15; HMS *Engadine* 8.7.15; Grain 9.7.15; CSD White City by road 12.9.15; Mkrs repair by 1.10.15 - @28.2.17, later deleted

**859** Deld Calshot 9.2.15; Mkrs 28.2.15 (Mahl); Calshot by 11.3.15 (not ready); Dover 15.4.15; AZP 17.5.15 (FSL TV Lister); Tested with microphone on aircraft 21.5.15; HACP but capsized on water and wrecked 23.5.15 (F/L RP Cannon & 2AM McSorley); Deleted by 2.6.15

*Sopwith 860 Type seaplane 852 after fitted at Grain with high lift wing. (via Philip Jarrett)*

*Vickers F.B.5 863 of No.1 Squadron at St.Pol, Spring 1915.*

*Sopwith Bat Boat (Type 2) 879 at Calshot, 1914 (J.M.Bruce/G.S.Leslie collection)*

*Avro 504s 873, 874 and 875 at Belfort before setting out for the Friedrichshafen raid, 21 November 1914. (J.M.Bruce/G.S.Leslie collection)*

Aircraft log book to HMS *Ark Royal* 11.4.15 - possibly in error for 860

860   Shipped to Aegean; Arr HMS *Ark Royal* 19.4.15 but transferred to SS *Aragaz* as proper oil not arrived; To SS *Penmorvah* for erection 8.5.15; Erected 22.5.15; Tested 23.5.15; Last flight 27.7.15 (4 hrs 38 min on HMS *Ark Royal*); Deleted

**12 VICKERS F.B.5 GUNBUS (ADMIRALTY 32 TYPE) PUSHER BIPLANES ordered under Cont No C.P.02132/14/X(A) & numbered 861 to 872. (100-hp Gnome Monosoupape)**

861   Deld Eastchurch 14.11.14; To Killingholme but FL Clacton 27.11.14; Awaiting new engine 28.11.14; Saxmundham 3.12.14; Yarmouth with damaged propeller 8.12.14; Dissembled for packing at Walcot, nr Bacton 1.1.15; To Military Wing 6.1.15, probably as 2462

862   Deld Eastchurch mid 11.14; To Killinghome but landed Yarmouth 27.11.14; Awaiting new engine 28.11.14; Landed Preston 16.12.14; Tested 3.1.15; To Military Wing at Joyce Green 5.1.15, probably as 2464

863   Deld Yarmouth 27.11.14; Acceptance approved 8.12.14; To Military Wing at Joyce Green 5.1.15
[One source suggests 864 to 872 handed over to Military Wing, probably as 2340-2347, 4736 respectively, though another official source quotes 4736 as being a renumbering of 2346]

**4 VICKERS F.B.5 GUNBUS PUSHER BIPLANES transferred from Military Wing & numbered 861 to 864. (100-hp Gnome Monosoupape)**

861   Ex ??? of Military Wing; 1 Sqdn Dover 11.2.15; 1 Sqdn St.Pol 26.2.15; 4 Sqdn Dover 1.5.15; ex Dunkerque, damaged landing Folkestone 19.6.15 (FSL R Lord); Deleted 26.6.15

862   Ex 747 of Military Wing; RFC Netheravon to 1 Sqdn Dover 9.2.15 (still as 747 until renumbered 21.4.15); Dover Defence Flt 21.3.15; Became 4 Sqdn Dover 25.3.15; HACP 16.4.15; AZP 17.5.15 (FSL R Lord & CPO Gott); HACP 23.5.15 (FSL LH Hardstaff & LM Marden); Rebuilding wrecked chassis 10.6.15; 5 Wing Dover 3.8.15; Condemned 30.9.15

863   Ex 1633 of Military Wing; Dover 21.3.15; 1 Sqdn St.Pol 21.3.15 - @2.5.15; Deleted 5.15

864   Ex 1634 of Military Wing; Dover 21.3.15; 1 Sqdn St.Pol 21.3.15; Last flown 29.3.15; Deleted 4.15

**6 AVRO 504 (ADMIRALTY 179 TYPE) TRACTOR BIPLANES ordered under Cont No C.P.50788/14, numbered 873 to 878 & built Manchester. (80-hp Gnome)**

873   Deld for Avro Flight, shipped in SS *Manchester* from Southampton 10.11.14; Then by rail, arriving Belfort 13.11.14; Bombed Friedrichshafen 21.11.14 (F/Cdr JT Babington); 1 Sqdn Grange Field (Gosport) 17.12.14; 1 Sqdn Dover 12.1.15; 1 Sqdn St.Pol 26.2.15; Eastbourne 12.5.15; Chassis crashed 22.6.15 (FSL F Warner injured); Deleted 30.6.15

874   Deld for Avro Flight, shipped in SS *Manchester* from Southampton 10.11.14; Then by rail, arriving Belfort 13.11.14; Shot down by ground fire on Friedrichshafen raid 21.11.14 (S/Cdr E Featherstone Briggs DSO PoW); Aircraft exhibited in German markings by Germans in 1917)

875   Deld for Avro Flight, shipped in SS *Manchester* from Southampton 10.11.14; Then by rail, arriving Belfort 13.11.14; Bombed Friedrichshafen 21.11.14 (F/L SV Sippe); Eastchurch (via Queenborough) 29.11.14; 1 Sqdn Grange Field (Gosport) 17.12.14; A Flt 1 Sqdn Dover 29.12.14; HACP 10.1.15; 1 Sqdn Dover 28.1.15; 1 Sqdn St.Pol 11.2.15; FTR from raid 16.2.15 (F/L EG Riggall killed); Deleted 18.2.15

876   Accepted Eastchurch 1.12.14; 3 Sqdn Dunkerque 8.12.14; 1 Sqdn St.Pol 26.2.15; Hendon for erection 3.5.15; AZP 9/10.5.15 (F/L H Rosher); Hendon 15.5.15; Chingford 17.5.15; Wrecked on cross-country 29.7.15 (PFSL GH Jackson); Packed 18.8.15; SCAW, Shoreham repairs

19.8.15; Chingford 16.5.16 (Prodger); Rolled into bank and damaged 2.6.16 (pilot unhurt); Surveyed 13.6.17; Deleted 19.6.17

877   Deld 1 Sqdn Grange Field (Gosport) circa 11.12.14; A Flt 1 Sqdn Dover, but FL nr Lewes 29.12.14; arr Dover 30.12.14; 1 Sqdn Dover 28.1.15; HACP 5.2.15; Lost at sea en route Dunkerque 12.2.15; Deleted 2.15

878   Deld 1 Sqdn Grange Field (Gosport) circa 11.12.14; A Flt 1 Sqdn Dover 29.12.14; Dover 28.1.15; Wrecked at Dover 4.2.15 (F/Cdr JT Babington slightly injured & Lt E Sassoon RNVR seriously injured); Deleted 2.15

**1 SOPWITH BAT BOAT (TYPE 2) TRACTOR BIPLANE AMPHIBIAN FLYING BOAT impressed 8.14 under Cont No 50567/14 & numbered 879. (225-hp Sunbeam Mohawk)**

879   "Circuit of Britain" aircraft (No.3); Sopwith Woolston 5-7.8.14; Deld Calshot 7.8.14 [9.8.14?]; Sopwith mods 11.8.14; Calshot 13.9.14; Mostly unserviceable by 11.14; Proposed fit two 100-hp Gnome Monosoupape not pursued; Deleted 11.4.15

**1 SOPWITH ADMIRALTY TYPE 880 TRACTOR BIPLANE SEAPLANE impressed 8.14 under Cont No 50567/14 & numbered 880. (100-hp Gnome Monosoupape)**

880   "Circuit of Britain" aircraft (No.1); Deld Calshot by 11.8.14; Westgate to Grain 18.8.14 (71 mph on test 8.14); en route Yarmouth to Grain 28.8.14; Yarmouth 29.8.14 (mostly unserviceable); 100-lb bomb fittings 11.14; HACP 22.1.15; AZP 23.1.15; Damaged tailplane and rudder in surf 25.1.15; Hit buoy taxying, damaged lower wing 11.2.15; Hit sandbank taking off to chase *L6* and damaged landing 16.4.15 (F/Cdr deCWP Ireland & LM C Notley); CW 17.5.15; Deleted 5.15 [Also flown as landplane?]

**1 AVRO 510 TRACTOR BIPLANE SEAPLANE purchased 6.8.14 & numbered 881. (150-hp Sunbeam)**

881   "Circuit of Britain" aircraft (No.7); Purchased from manufacturers for £2,500 6.8.14; Tested Calshot 6-10.8.14; Tested at 68 mph, and to 3,000 ft in 20 min; Various mods 8.14 - 9.14 (new "funnel" and cowlings removed); Deleted 24.10.16

**1 WHITE & THOMPSON BUILT CURTISS BAT BOAT TRACTOR BIPLANE FLYING BOAT impressed 8.14 under Cont No 53624/14 & numbered 882. (120-hp Austro-Daimler)**

882   "Circuit of Britain" aircraft (No.6); FF 1.8.14; Deld Calshot 10.8.14; Grain 27.8.14; Tested to 3,000 ft in 8½ min; Bomb fittings 3.11.14; Felixstowe 10.11.14; Wrecked 8.1.15; Rebuilt 15.1.15; Tested 19.1.15; Dismantled for rebuilding 22.1.15; Tested 3.6.15; Sideslipped landing, CW 8.6.15 (F/L AW Clemson)

**1 WHITE & THOMPSON BUILT CURTISS H.4 "SMALL AMERICA" TRACTOR BIPLANE FLYING BOAT impressed 8.14 under Cont No 53624/14 & numbered 883. (Two 100-hp Curtiss)**

883   "Circuit of Britain" aircraft (No.9); Not delivered by 31.8.15

**1 WIGHT "NAVYPLANE" PUSHER BIPLANE FLOAT SEAPLANE impressed 8.14 under Cont No 53665/14 & numbered 884. (160-hp Gnome)**

884   Conv DC 9.14; Deld Calshot 19.9.14; Wrecked (not flying) 15.5.15 (FSL WH Dunn); Trials Cowes 29.5.15; Deleted 6.15

**1 DEPERDUSSIN TRACTOR MONOPLANE built by British Deperdussin, impressed 8.14 under Cont No 57016/14 & numbered 885. (100-hp Anzani)**

885   Deld Hendon 1.9.14 (much used for Zeppelin standbys; Tested gun firing 30.9.14; Chingford 30.4.15; Felixstowe 8.5.15; In wrecked condition by 8.7.15; Deleted 7.15

*Avro 510 "Circuit of Britain" Seaplane 881 at Calshot. (RAF Museum)*

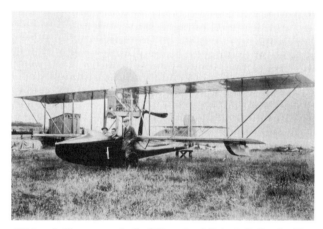

*Sopwith "Circuit of Britain" Seaplane 880 at Yarmouth. (J.M.Bruce/G.S.Leslie collection)*

*White & Thompson-built "Circuit of Britain" Curtiss Bat Boat (later 882). (J.M.Bruce/G.S.Leslie collection)*

*White & Thompson-built "Circuit of Britain" Curtiss H.4 Flying Boat (was to have become 883). (J.M.Bruce/G.S.Leslie collection)*

*Wight Navyplane Seaplane 884 at Calshot, September 1914. (J.M.Bruce/G.S.Leslie collection)*

**1 HENRY FARMAN PUSHER BIPLANE SEAPLANE built by Aircraft Manufacturing Co Ltd, impressed 8.14 & numbered 886. (80-hp Gnome)**

886    Impressed from Eastbourne Aviation Co for £1,200 6.8.14; Deld Calshot 28.8.14; Damaged 23.9.14; Engine removed 11.14; Deleted 2.3.15; Remains to Hamble by 3.5.15

**1 HENRY FARMAN PUSHER BIPLANE SEAPLANE built by French Farman, impressed for £600 from Eastbourne Flying School 6.8.14 & numbered 887. (80-hp Gnome)**

887    (c/n B.35) Deld Calshot 7.9.14 but under repair then; Seldom flown; Blown over under tow to Hamble 2.12.14 (FSL The Hon Desmond O'Brien); Deleted 7.12.14

**1 MAURICE FARMAN PUSHER BIPLANE impressed from Flying School 8.14, probably from Cummings, & numbered 888. (120-hp Sunbeam)**

888    Deld Hendon 24.8.14; FL in mist Manningtree 8.11.14; Yarmouth 9.11.14; Accident 24.11.14; Deleted 7.12.14; Parts to Eastchurch 9.1.15

**1 AVRO 504 TRACTOR BIPLANE SEAPLANE impressed for £900 from Daily Mail newspaper 6.8.14 & numbered 889. (80-hp Gnome)**

889    . Prototype 504. Crashed at Shoreham on delivery to Calshot 10.8.14 (Raynham); Deleted 8.14
["W/Cdr C.R.Samson sending for 888 (Shoreham) 31.10.14" - 889 intended? - NTU?]

**1 A.B.W. ALBATROS B.II TRACTOR BIPLANE impressed 8.14 under Cont No 49959/14 & numbered 890. (100-hp Mercedes)**

890    Arrived Hendon by lorry 27.3.14 for tests at Farnborough; Impressed at Immingham on/by 5.8.14; Retd Eastchurch 9.8.14; Delivered Grain for defence 13.8.14; Chased Friedrichshafen seaplane 25.12.14; EF on TO, ran into dyke, o/t 7.2.15 (F/L HR Busteed slightly injured); To Grain Island Repair Station 11.3.15; Fitted floats for a time; Grain by 13.5.15; AZP 26.5.15 (FSL EdeC Hallifax & AM Bunn); Fell into harbour and badly damaged 24.6.15 (FSL WG Moore unhurt); Tested ARD Port Victoria after extensive repair 4.4.16; Retd Grain 5.4.16; Kingsnorth 11.5.16; Grain 12.5.16; Detling 8.2.17 (visit); to Grain, FL, damaged 28.7.17; Grain Type Test Flight 26.9.17; Deleted 7.4.18

**1 D.F.W. B.2 TRACTOR BIPLANE bought from Germany by Beardmore, impressed 8.14 under Cont No.49959/14 & numbered 891. (100-hp Mercedes)**

891    Brooklands to Admiralty on outbreak of war; Eastchurch (Mobile) Sqdn, Immingham by 11.8.14; Killingholme by 24.8.14; Immingham by 28.8.14; Climbed 160 ft/min on test; Crashed on TO, hit edge of ditch 12.14 (FSL WH Elliot); Patrols up to 3.1.15; Damaged u/c landing 3.1.15; Deleted 23.1.15

**1 HANDLEY PAGE TYPE G TRACTOR BIPLANE impressed 8.14 under Cont No.58787/14 & numbered 892. (100-hp Anzani)**

892    FF 5.11.13; No.8 in 1914 Aerial Derby; Impressed 8.14; At Hendon by 30.9.14 (mostly unserviceable); Mkrs 2.15 (repair); Hendon 27.4.15; Chingford 18.6.15 (not used); Ran into J.N.3 3347 2.8.15 (F/L LD McKean); Deleted 24.8.15 [pilot carried Webley revolver]

**3 WIGHT PUSHER BIPLANE SEAPLANES impressed from German order 8.14 under Cont No C.P.50257/14, numbered 893 to 895 & built East Cowes. (200-hp Canton-Unné)**

893    Fitted fixed fins, 20% longer than those 895. Deld Calshot 9.8.14; Grain 14.8.14; Lewis gun fitted 9.14; Tested 24.9.14; Dover 9.14; Grain 28.9.14; New tail

boom 11.14; Arr Grain from Westgate in tow of HMS *Riviera* 24.11.14; Slightly damaged in gale 29.12.14; No engine from 3.15; Deleted 9.6.15

894    Two fins on tailplane; Deld Calshot 12.8.14; EF, FL Rye harbour 14.8.14; Grain 20.8.14; COL on water 29.9.14 (F/L DH Hyde-Thomson); Eastchurch to Grain 29.10.14; Dunkerque 29.10.14 (via Dover and Calais) - S/Cdr JW Seddon to establish a seaplane station; Slightly damaged under tow after landing 17.11.14 (S/Cdr JW Seddon & PO Mech W Burnett unhurt); Arr Grain ex *Princess Victoria* 7.12.14; Dover for raids on Zeebrugge and Ostende 10.2.15; 3 Sqdn Dunkerque 16.2.15; 1 Sqdn 26.2.15; To Eastbourne Aviation Co for partial rebuild 4.15; To Calshot but EF, FL, damaged 26.1.16; SCAW 27.1.16, later deleted

895    Modified fins; Trials at Cowes 25.8.14; Deld Calshot 26.8.14; To Grain but EF, FL Newhaven 2.10.14; Shipped HMS *Argus* (picked up at Newhaven) 9.10.14; Fort George 12.10.14 (little flying); Broken up for examination 5.2.15, then deleted

**1 SOPWITH ADMIRALTY 880 TYPE FOLDER TRACTOR BIPLANE SEAPLANE impressed from Greek Government order 8.14 under Cont No C.P.50330/14 & numbered 896. (100-hp Gnome Monosoupape)**

896    Retained Sopwith 6.8.14; Not ready 13.8.14 (with 893?); Maxim gun fitted 8.14; Eastchurch by 6.10.14; Dunkerque 29.10.14; COL 29.10.14 (F/Cdr de CWP Ireland); Tested speaking tube intercom 14.11.14; Retd England in SS *Invicta* for repair by Handley Page 7.12.14; Eastchurch NFS 1.2.15; Deleted 26.6.15

**5 SOPWITH PUSHER BIPLANE SEAPLANES impressed from Greek Government order 8.14 under Cont No C.P.50330/14 & numbered 897 to 901. (100-hp Gnome Monosoupape)**

897    Deld Calshot 10.8.14; Fired Lewis gun 31.8.14; Grain 15.9.14 (arr 16.9.14); Yarmouth (en route Killingholme) 23.9.14; Sutton-on-Sea 2.10.14; Immingham by road 4.10.14; Killingholme 4.10.14; EF, FL damaged by wind after landing Stallingborough Marshes 12.1.15 (FSL WH Elliot); Retd 15.1.15; Tested 29.1.15; AZP 31.3.15 (FSL JC Brooke & CPO Roberts); U/c caught barbed wire on TO, o/t, wrecked 5.5.15 (F/L HS Adams & Lt Maulhauser unhurt); Grain Repair Depot 15.5.15 (repairs abandoned); Deleted 2.6.15

898    Deld Calshot 31.8.14; Fitted Lewis gun 9.14; Grain 15.9.14; Yarmouth (en route Killingholme) 23.9.14; Continued but landed Sutton-on-Sea for fuel 1.10.14; Yarmouth 2.10.14; Broke adrift, CW Hunstanton 27.10.14 (FSL JP Wilson); Deleted 19.11.14

899    Deld Calshot 11.9.14; EF en route Grain, retd Calshot 15.9.14; embarked SS *Stanfordham* for Killingholme 27.10.14; arr Killingholme 6.11.14; CW 19.11.14; Deleted 12.14

900    Retained Sopwith 8.14; Converted landplane 9.14; Deld Eastchurch 27.9.14; Dunkerque 30.9.14; 3 Sqdn Belgium by 8.10.14; Left at Antwerp in retreat 9.10.14, but back with 3 Sqdn in Belgium by 12.10.14; Badly damaged 8.11.14 (F/Cdr deCWP Ireland); Retd England in SS *Invicta* for repair by Handley Page 7.12.14; Eastchurch NFS 22.1.15; Deleted 26.6.15

901    Converted to landplane 9.14 (by Hewlett & Blondeau?); Deld Hendon 25.9.14; 3 Sqdn Morbecque (via Dunkerque) 27.9.14; Deleted 14.10.14

**1 BLERIOT PARASOL TYPE XI-BG TRACTOR MONOPLANE SEAPLANE built by Bleriot, impressed for £1,400 from Lord Edward Grosvenor 5.8.14 & numbered 902. (50-hp Gnome)**

902    Under repair 1.8.14; Deld Calshot 7.8.14; Presume converted to landplane; Eastchurch NFS 18.8.14; Damaged 24.9.15; Deleted 13.1.16

**1 BLERIOT PARASOL TYPE XI-BG TRACTOR MONOPLANE presented by Miss Trehawke Davies 8.14 & numbered 903. (70-hp Gnome)**

52

Henry Farman Amphibian 886 at Calshot, 1914.
(J.M.Bruce/G.S.Leslie collection)

Henry Farman Seaplane at Weymouth around May 1914.
Inscribed "Frank Hucks Waterplane Co Ltd", it is
believed to have become 887. (J.M.Bruce/G.S.Leslie
collection)

Albatros B.II 890 spent most of the war at Grain before
deletion in April 1918. (RAF Museum P.15603)

Handley Page Type G Biplane became 892. (MAP)

D.F.W. B2 on 22 July 1914, probably became 891. (W.Jacobs)

903      Allocated Eastchurch 25.8.14; Deld Eastchurch ex Sandgate 20.9.14; ADD 27.9.14; 3 Sqdn Ostende by 8.10.14; Deleted circa 22.10.14 (unsuitable for either Eastchurch or Dunkerque)

**2 SOPWITH TABLOID TRACTOR BIPLANES to have been transferred from RFC Military Wing) (ex 384 and 395) & numbered 904 and 905, but became 167 and 168 instead**

**1 SHORT S.38 NACELLE TYPE SIDE-BY-SIDE SCHOOL PUSHER BIPLANE impressed from Sir Francis McClean (No.14) 8.14 under Cont No C.P.65176/14 & numbered 904. (70-hp Gnome)** [McClean No.8 (S.32) rebuilt to 70½ft span] [Gordon Bruce's researches shown correct c/n to be S.58]

904      (C/n S.32 rebuilt as c/n S.58). Deld Eastchurch for defence 28.8.14; ECNFS by 29.9.14; U/c and wings broken 4.10.14 (pupil unhurt); Mkrs 9.10.14; Fitted standard 52-ft span wings; Bombing expts at Grain 7.2.15 & 12.2.15; Deleted by 30.6.15

**1 SHORT NILE PUSHER BIPLANE SEAPLANE impressed 1.8.14 from Sir Francis McClean (No.16) under Cont No C.P.65176/14 & numbered 905. (140-hp Gnome)** [160-hp according to Shorts records] [Gordon Bruce's researches shown correct c/n to be S.80]

905      (c/n S.80) Grain 1.8.14 as DC trainer; Fitted for torpedo and 100 lb bomb; Allotted HMS *Riviera* 17.8.14 (NTU); re-allocated HMS *Hermes* 28.9.14 (Mkrs to fit bomb gear), onboard later; Re-engined 100-hp Gnome 10.14; Deleted 11.14

**1 SOPWITH THREE-SEATER TRACTOR BIPLANE impressed 8.14 under Cont No C.P.50330/14 & numbered 906. (80-hp Gnome)**

906      Allocated Expeditionary Force 1.8.14; Deld Eastchurch 29.8.14; Dunkerque 7.9.14; 1 Sqdn Belgium by 15.9.14 - @5.10.14; Attacked Düsseldorf airship sheds 22.9.14 (Lt CH Collet); 3 Sqdn Ostende by 8-12.10.14; Deleted 10.14

**1 BLERIOT PARASOL TYPE XI-BG TRACTOR MONOPLANE built by Bleriot, purchased 5.8.14 for £1,400 from Bleriot Company & numbered 907. (90-hp Le Rhône)** [80hp Gnome per official 1.17 list]

907      Allocated Expeditionary Force 1.8.14; Deld Eastchurch 18.8.14; To go to Dunkerque 27.8.14, but delayed 28.8.14; 3 Sqdn St.Pol 1.9.14; Wrecked 1.9.14; Eastchurch repair 6.9.14; 3 Sqdn Belgium 22.9.14; FL in small field nr Bailleul (F/L Lord EA Grosvenor & S/L BA Isaacs), wings taken off, removed by road, arr Morbecqe 27.9.14; ADD 27.9.14; Due Ostende 11.10.14; EF, crashed nr enemy lines, shelled into wreck 27.10.14 (Lt CH Collet DSO & Cpl Brewe RMLI unhurt); Deleted 11.14

**1 BLERIOT TYPE XI TRACTOR MONOPLANE built by Bleriot and purchased from France 8.14 & numbered 908. (80-hp Le Rhône)**

908      Deld Calshot 17.8.14; Eastchurch 5.9.14; EF, FL Latchingdon 17.1.15 (F/L IGV Fowler); retd but FL Colchester 18.1.15; arr Eastchurch 20.1.15; temp 1 Sqdn Dover 10.2.15; 2 Sqdn Eastchurch 2.15; Detd Dover for raids on Zeebrugge & Ostende 10.2.15; Eastchurch NFS by 11.3.15; Damaged 22.8.15; Damaged 12.11.15; Deleted 19.11.15

**6 MAURICE FARMAN S.7 LONGHORN PUSHER BIPLANE purchased from The Aircraft Manufacturing Co Ltd under Cont No C.P.63521/14 & numbered 909 to 914. (70-hp Renault)**

909      Deld Hendon 24.8.14; Fell from 150ft, CW 24.12.14 (FSL BO Ffield killed); Deleted 13.1.15
910 to 914 Ordered for Hendon but transferred to RFC (Military Wing) [not renumbered?]

**1 HENRY FARMAN PUSHER BIPLANE SEAPLANE built by The Aircraft Manufacturing Co Ltd at Hendon, purchased under Cont No C.P.55055/14 & numbered 915. (80-hp Gnome)** [80-hp Le Rhône per official 1.17 list]

915      Deld Calshot 30.8.14; Dover 17.11.14; Damaged by sea 20.11.14; Calshot 25.11.14; Damaged 7.12.14; Airco repairs 12.14; Dover for re-erection 21.4.15; 80-hp Le Rhône replacing 80-hp Gnome 28.5.15; To Yarmouth but EF, FL and wrecked nr South Shingles, remains landed RD Grain from TB No.7 5.8.15 (S/Cdr deCWP Ireland unhurt), then deleted

**2 BRISTOL T.B.8 TRACTOR BIPLANES ordered under Cont No C.P.53505/14/X, numbered 916 and 917 & built Filton. (90 or 80-hp Gnome)** [916 to 918 under Cont No C.P.54557/14 per official 2.18 list !]

916      (C/n 197). (90-hp Le Rhône)[80-hp Gnome per official list]. Deld Eastchurch 17.9.14; Dunkerque 22.9.14; 3 Sqdn Belgium by 24.9.14; EF, FL undamaged between Tournai & Lille 29.9.14 (Lt TA Rainey unhurt); Left Lille, petrol tank holed by cavalry fire, FL in field, nothing salved owing to enemy fire 1.10.14 (Lt TA Rainey); Considering rebuilding from spares 8.10.14; Deleted 14.10.14

917      (C/n 227). (80-hp Le Rhône). (Ex Military Wing No.620 but rejected 19.8.14). Deld Eastchurch 17.9.14; Dunkerque 22.9.14; 3 Sqdn Belgium by 27.9.14; Fired on nr Rouex during bombing attack, FL, damaged, 10m off Calais, salved 27.9.14 (F/L CF Beevor); Hardinghil to ADD 29.9.14 - @22.11.14 [at Ostende 8.10.14]; 3 Sqdn by 19.1.15; Last flown 10.2.15; U/s at Dunkerque 28.2.15; Dismantled by 11.3.15 (80-hp Gnome); Deleted 4.15

**1 FLANDERS B.2 TRACTOR BIPLANE bought from Gaskell Blackburn 30.8.14 & numbered 918. (70-hp Gnome)**

918      Originally Military Trials No.14; On delivery from Filey to Eastchurch (via Immingham, Yarmouth and Felixstowe) by FSL V Gaskell Blackburn but EF, FL Hornsea, dismantled and deld in pieces after several forced landings 2.9.14; Packed for rail to Yarmouth 11.9.14; Condemned by survey, but under reconstruction 1.1.15; Larger elevator fitted 19.1.15; AZP, FL in fog, smashed wing, Ormesby 23.1.15 (dismantled and retd Yarmouth); Deleted 1.15 (not efficient, 3 yrs old)

**8 SOPWITH ADMIRALTY 807 TYPE TRACTOR BIPLANE SEAPLANES ordered under Cont No C.P.02155/14, numbered 919 to 926 & built Kingston. (100-hp Gnome Monosoupape)**

919      Deld Calshot on/by 14.1.15; Tested 29.1.15 (E.C.Gordon England); Bembridge 20.4.15; Calshot 22.4.15; Bembridge 15.5.15; Calshot 5.15; Bembridge 31.5.15; Deleted 14.7.15
920      Deld Calshot packed 9.1.15; Mkrs Woolston 11.1.15; shipped in SS *Persia* 16.1.15; Transferred to HMS *Kinfauns Castle* for *Königsberg* operation; First trial flight at Niororo Island after erecting at Bombay 11.2.15 (F/L JT Cull & CPO Norrington); Flown again but pancaked on landing, port wing slightly damaged 11.2.15 (F/L HEM Watkins & Mid AN Gallehawk); Flown after repair 21.2.15; EF, FL in sea, started to settle, salved and hoisted on board *Kinfauns Castle* 28.2.15 (F/L JT Cull & AM Cornelius unhurt); Flown after repair 4.3.15; Started to settle on landing, bottom of starboard float damaged 9.3.15 (F/L JT Cull); at Zanzibar by 16.3.15; Bottom ripped off starboard float, sank in 4 ft of water at head of Kilcudini Bay, Mombasa, salved 22.3.15; Flown after repair 1.4.15; Last flight, left at Mombasa when party left in SS *Chakdara* 2.4.15; Condemned, left in shed at Mombasa 13.7.15; still Mombasa 8.15; RFC Force D Mesopotamia at Basra by 1.10.15; FL, wrecked landing 1.1.17
921      Deld Calshot packed 9.1.15; shipped in SS *Persia* 16.1.15; Transferred to HMS *Kinfauns Castle*; Arrived Niororo Island 13.2.15; Erected for *Königsberg*

*Short Side-by-side School machine after modification as c/n S.58 (904). (J.M.Bruce/G.S.Leslie collection)*

*Sopwith Three-seater 906 is just visible in this photogaph of lighter and heavier than air craft at Dunkerque early in the war. In the foreground are B.E.2a 50 and Short 42. (J.M.Bruce/G.S.Leslie collection)*

*Short S.80 Nile Seaplane at Khartoum, 1914 (later 905). (J.M.Bruce/G.S.Leslie collection)*

*Henry Farman Pusher Seaplane 915 at Calshot, September 1915. (J.M.Bruce/G.S.Leslie collection)*

*Flanders B.2 Biplane (became 918). (via Philip Jarrett)*

*Sopwith 807 Type Seaplane 920 at Niororo Island with Lt H.E.M.Watkins in the cockpit (J.M.Bruce/G.S.Leslie collection)*

*Avro 500 Biplane 939 at Chingford. (Gwilym Lewis via Philip Jarrett)*

*Morane-Saulnier Monoplane, reputedly 941, crashed near Maidstone 26 February 1915 by Sidney Pickles and Jack Alcock (mechanic). (J.M.Bruce/G.S.Leslie collection)*

operation, but wrecked 24.2.15, 4th day of attempted flight, only 2 hrs in air; Deleted 2.15

922 Deld HMS *Ark Royal* at Chatham 28.1.15; Fitted armoured seat; Ship sailed from Sheerness for Dardanelles 31.1.15; First flight in Dardanelles 19.2.15 (flown at Mudros by F/L EH Dunning and F/L N Sholto Douglas); Hit by rifle fire 5.3.15 (F/L N Sholto Douglas wounded); lent HMS *Minerva* 9.4.15; HMS *Ark Royal* 20.4.15 (repair); HMS *Doris* 23.4.15 (fitted with wings and tail of 807); Fabric seriously damaged by gunfire in ship, retd HMS *Ark Royal* 29.4.15; Damaged on landing 12.5.15 (Lt N Sholto Douglas & Lt LH Strain); Ready 18.5.15; Tested on re-erection 21.5.15; HMS *Minerva* 21.5.15; HMS *Doris* 22.5.15; HMS *Ark Royal* 25.5.15; Kephalo 13.6.15; EF, FL, u/c collapsed in tow by trawler 18.6.15 (F/L N Sholto Douglas & CPO Brady); U/c collapsed landing Kephalo 28.6.15 (F/L N Sholto Douglas); HMS *Ark Royal* 11.7.15; Kephalo 31.7.15; HMS *Ark Royal* in tow 7.8.15; EF on TO, BO Kephalo 18.8.15 (F/Cdr CH Collet DSO DoI & CPO Mech Lacey injured); Deleted 8.15

923 Deld Calshot .15; Tested 10.2.15; Bembridge 27.3.15; In wrecked condition at Calshot 25.4.15; Deleted 4.15

924 Allocated HMS *Campania* by 31.1.15; Transit to HMS *Campania* by 11.3.15; HMS *Campania* 4.5.15; CW 7.5.15 (WO2 T O'Connor); Deleted by 5.15

925 Transit to HMS *Campania* 3.15; Scapa for HMS *Campania* by 11.3.15; HMS *Campania* by 6.5.15; Packing for despatch 4.6.15; Calshot for erection (in TBD HMS *Peterel*) 5.6.15; Bembridge 13.7.15; Calshot 1.8.15; Wrecked 14.9.15 (FSL LER Murray); Deleted 24.9.15

926 Transit to HMS *Campania* by 11.3.15; HMS *Campania*, temp dismantled 6.5.15; Re-erected 6.6.15; Badly damaged alighting in swell, broke off both floats, hoisted inboard 14.6.15 (FSL RD Sibley & Mid DS Earp); Surveyed, remains to Grain Repair Station 15.6.15, deleted

## 12 SOPWITH ADMIRALTY 860 [or 851] TYPE TRACTOR BIPLANE SEAPLANES ordered under Cont No C.P.02155/14 dated 13.10.14 (revised 5.12.14), numbered 927 to 938 & built Kingston. (225-hp Sunbeam) [On order 9.14 as 12 Admiralty Type 801 with 110-hp Sunbeam; Cancelled as such?] [Balance of contract in abeyance by 28.8.16, and cancelled W/E 22.9.16 as resources needed for production of fighting aircraft]

927 Retained Mkrs Woolston preparing for trials; Never delivered

928 Deld Calshot 24.4.15; HMS *Ben-my-Chree* 26.4.15; Crashed and burnt alongside ship on test flight 26.4.15 (F/L S Medlicott & AM1 HG Hughes both killed); Deleted 4.15

929 AW/CN 28.4.15; Deld Dundee for erection 17.5.15; Completed 21.5.15; Tested 26.5.15 (Hawker); HSMP 16.6.15 (F/Cdr C Draper & CPO Harris); Unsuccessful type, being dismantled by 31.8.15; Retd CSD White City 12.10.15, deleted

930 AW/CN 5.5.15; Deld Dundee for erection 17.5.15; Completed 21.5.15; Tested 26.5.15 (Hawker); HSMP 9.6.15 (Lt C Draper & Pte Gamble); EF taxying out for HSMP 10.6.15 (Lt C Draper); HSMPs 16.6.15 (F/L ERC Nanson & FSL TK Young), 18.6.15 (F/L CS Iron & LAM Wellbourn), 19.6.15 (F/L CS Iron & LAM Wellbourn) & 23.6.15 (F/L CS Iron & Cpl Phelps); FL in sea, towed back to Dundee, but o/t and nearly totally submerged, CW 7.8.15 (FSL AH Sandwell); Deleted 9.8.15

931 AW/CN 12.5.15; Deld Calshot ex Woolston 29.5.15; Taxied to Sopwith Woolston 5.6.15; Grain by road for erection 9.6.15; Tested after erection 20.6.15; Yarmouth but broke chassis landing 20.6.15 (S/Cdr deCWP Ireland); CSD White City 8.9.15; Mkrs repair by 1.10.15; Reduced to spares at Mkrs 1917

932 AW/CN 19.5.15; Retained Mkrs Woolston preparing for trials, never delivered; Reduced to spares at Sopwith Works 1917

933 AW/CN 26.5.15; Deld Killingholme 6.6.15; Failed test after engine trouble 16.6.15; Awaiting acceptance trials 31.8.15; CSD White City 9.9.15; Sopwith repair by 10.15; Never re-delivered; ordered cancelled by 1918

934 AW/CN 21.6.15; Retained Mkrs Woolston preparing for trials; Never delivered, order cancelled 9.16

935 Deld Grain by 7.15; Ready 10.7.15; CSD White City by lorry 16.11.15 and then deleted

936 Order cancelled 9.16

937 Order cancelled 9.16

938 Retained Mkrs Woolston by 30.11.15 preparing for trials; Never delivered, order cancelled 9.16

## 1 AVRO 500 TRACTOR BIPLANE believed impressed from C.F.Lan Davis (whose aircraft was reported as cmpletely wrecked at Hendon 6.8.14) & numbered 939 (50-hp Gnome)

939 RNAS service at Hendon from/by 10.10.14; Chingford 30.4.15; AZP 9.10.15 (F/L EB Bauman); Taken down & completely refitted & recovered 7.11.15; Deleted 22.7.17

## 1 HENRY FARMAN PUSHER BIPLANE (Airco built) impressed, number 940 allocated 1.9.14. (80-hp Gnome)

940 Deld Hendon 1.9.14; AZP, COL 10.9.14 (F/L RT Gates DoI 14.9.14); Grahame-White repair 12.9.14; Hendon by 8.11.14; Detd Dover for raids on Zeebrugge and Ostende 10.2.15; En route 1 Sqdn Dunkerque, crashed in sea off Nieuport 11.2.15; Deleted 22.3.15

## 1 MORANE-SAULNIER (TYPE G?) TRACTOR MONOPLANE impressed from Lord Carbery (10.14?) & numbered 941. (80-hp Le Rhône)

941 Tested Eastchurch and issued 2 Sqdn 5.11.14 (later to NFS Eastchurch?); EF, FL Westgate 31.1.15 (stayed overnight); Wrecked 31.5.15; Deleted 11.10.15

## 6 BRISTOL BOXKITE TRACTOR BIPLANES built at Filton under Cont No C.P.56037/14/X & numbered 942 to 947. (50-hp Gnome) [C/n's 394 to 399]

942 Deld Hendon 15.10.14; Deleted 5.15

943 Deld Hendon 26.10.14; Crashed 10.5.15 (WO Bowen); Chingford by road for erection 15.5.15; Damaged 18.7.15 (F/L A Keiller); Crashed 28.7.15 (PFSL L Morgan); Still erecting 4.8.15; Deleted 11.10.15

944 Tested Hendon 27.10.14; Crashed and wrecked 20.3.15; Deleted and bits to 943

945 Deld Eastchurch 10.14; Hendon by lorry 23.3.15; Chingford 22.4.15; Crashed 6.7.15 (PFSL C Perrett); Taxied into Shorthorn 8108 7.9.15 (Lt GS Allfree RNVR); Deleted 21.1.16

946 Deld Eastchurch by 31.12.14; Eastbourne by road 7.1.15; Deleted by 11.5.15

947 Deld Eastchurch by 31.12.14; Eastbourne by road 7.1.15; Tested after repair 12.6.15; Engine trouble, smashed u/c 21.6.15 (S/L WAK Dalzell); Propeller and chassis damaged landing 14.7.15 (WO2 PV Fraser); Deleted 10.8.15

## 1 BRISTOL T.B.8 TRACTOR BIPLANE built from spares by Short Bros at Eastchurch and purchased under Cont No. C.P.56037/14, allotted number 948 14.9.14. (80-hp Gnome)

948 (C/n 196) Ex Military Wing 614 but rejected 19.8.14; Deld ECNFS 12.9.14; EF, FL St.Margaret's Bay en route Dunkerque, o/t by wind, badly damaged 16.9.14 (F/L TA Rainey); Retd Eastchurch 18.9.14; Damaged 24.10.14; Eastbourne 26.1.15; Unserviceable by 11.3.15; Deleted 5.15

## 1 MAURICE FARMAN S.7 LONGHORN PUSHER BIPLANE purchased under Cont No 52840/14 & numbered 949. (100-hp Renault)

949 Eastchurch Sqdn Dunkerque 18.9.14; Deleted 18.11.14; Engine used as spares for No.17

## 2 CURTISS H.1 SMALL AMERICA TRACTOR BIPLANE FLYING BOAT ordered under Cont No C.P.52840/14 from Curtiss, Hammondsport & numbered 950 to 951. (Two 90 or 100-hp Curtiss)

950     (Two 90-hp Curtiss). Deld Felixstowe 13.10.14; Tested 29.10.14; limited flying; FP Kentish Knock, towed by destroyer HMS *Lance* 11.2.15; Packing for despatch to Caudron 3.4.15 (not sent?); AZP 10.5.15 (F/Cdr WR Crocker & FSL ER Moon); Rebuilding 5.15 - 6.15 with two 125-hp Anzani; Tested 16.6.15; AZPs 3.7.15 (FSL PEH Wakeley & FSL LP Openshaw) & 10.8.15 (F/L ER Moon); Serviceable by 1.10.15 (fitted two 100-hp Curtiss); Modified by S/Cdr JC Porte; Dismantled 27.1.16; Deleted 28.1.16 FW&T

951     (Two 100-hp Curtiss by 20.6.15). Deld Felixstowe 25.11.14; Exptl foot operated ailerons 12.14; Many exptl modifications 1.15 - 12.15; (Two 125-hp Anzani by 1.10.15); HACP 13.4.15 (F/Cdr WR Crocker & FSL ER Moon); HSMP 9.6.15 (F/L RJJ Hope-Vere); Deleted 2.5.16

**12 ROYAL AIRCRAFT FACTORY B.E.2c TRACTOR BIPLANES ordered under Cont No C.P.57016/14 from Vickers & numbered 952 to 963. (70-hp Renault)**

952 to 963 transferred to 8 Sqdn, RFC (Military Wing). Not renumbered

**12 ROYAL AIRCRAFT FACTORY B.E.2C TRACTOR BIPLANES ordered under Cont No C.P.57016/14/X18604 dated 23.9.14 from Blackburn Aeroplane & Motor Co Ltd, numbered 964 to 975 & built Leeds. (70-hp Renault)**

964     Deld by rail to Devonport 13.3.15; Shipped in SS *Inkosi* or SS *Moorgate* 19 or 20.3.15; 3 Sqdn Dardanelles 4.15; Renamed 3 Wing 6.15; Deleted by 30.6.15

965     Deld by rail to Devonport 13.3.15; Shipped in SS *Inkosi* or SS *Moorgate* 19 or 20.3.15; 3 Sqdn Dardanelles 4.15; Renamed 3 Wing 6.15 - 10.15; Deleted 1916

966     Deld and tested Hendon 10.5.15 (Ding); Chingford 15.5.15; AZP, hit tree top landing, CW 1.6.15 (F/L CWH Pulford unhurt); Deleted 10.6.15

967     Deld and accepted 15.4.15 (Ding); Chingford for erection 24.4.15; Ready 15.8.15; Yarmouth 25.4.16; Retd Chingford but EF, FL Thaxted 26.4.16; Deleted 20.8.16

968     Left UK 3.4.15 to join 26 Sqdn in SW Africa. Damaged on test flight after arrival; Attd South Africa Air Corps by 20.6.15 - 12.15; Transferred to South African Government

969     Left UK 3.4.15 to join 26 Sqdn in SW Africa; Badly damaged on test flight and took no part in campaign; South African Air Corps by 20.6.15 - 12.15; Transferred to South African Government

970     Deld Grain by 13.5.15; Accepted 30.5.15 (Ding); Test after overhaul 13.7.15; Ranken Dart experiments 3.11.15; Bomb dropping test 27.11.15; Tested Batchelor instructional mirror 5.1.16; Tested poroscope 29-30.3.16; Became Grain Experimental Flight by 14.4.16; Deleted 23.5.16

971     Deld Whitley Bay 18.4.15; Accepted 30.4.15 (Ding); O/t landing, broke chassis, in new and unsuitable field 13.5.15; Deleted 5.15

972     Deld Whitley Bay 2.5.15; Accepted 15.5.15 (Ding); HSMP 23.5.15 (F/Cdr CE Robinson & AM Maskell); Fell in sea 12.8.15 (F/Cdr CE Maude shock); Deleted 28.9.15

973     Deld Hendon by 5.15; Tested but not accepted 6.5.15 (Raynham); Accepted 10.5.15 (Ding); 1 Sqdn St.Pol 11.5.15; Renamed 1 Wing St.Pol 6.15; D Sqdn 1 Wing St.Pol by 20.6.15; still 1 Wing by 31.8.15 - 9.15; Deleted late 1915

974     (80-hp Renault) Deld Hendon by 10.5.15; Tested 19.5.15 (Ding); Dunkerque (via Folkestone) 29.5.15; Attacked Zeppelin 31.5.15 (F/L BL Huskisson); 1 Sqdn St.Pol 6.15; Loaned 3 Sqdn RFC Auchel 11.6.15; Damaged propeller, wing and u/c landing 14.6.15 (Lt H Rosher & Lt DC Cameron); Flown again 19.6.15 (fitted 80-hp Wolseley); Retd 1 Sqdn St.Pol 20.6.15; Became B Sqdn 1 Wing 21.6.15; Last flight 21.6.15; Deleted 8.15

975     In transit to Gibraltar by 20.6.15; Gibraltar 6.15 - 10.15; EF, FL neutral territory, smashed, dismantled & retd 10.8.15 (F/L T England & passenger); Arrived Eastchurch Workshops by rail for GI work 19.9.16

**12 ROYAL AIRCRAFT FACTORY B.E.2c TRACTOR BIPLANES ordered under Cont No C.P.57016/14 from Hewlett & Blondeau Ltd, numbered 976 to 987 & built Clapham. (70/75-hp Renault-Wolseley)**

976     Deld Hendon 27.4.15; Tested 17.5.15; 1 Sqdn St.Pol (via Folkestone) 17.5.15; Became B Sqdn 1 Wing Furnes 21.6.15; 4 Sqdn 1 Wing St.Pol by 1.10.15 (80-hp Renault); Still 1 Wing 12.15; Deleted early 1916?

977     Deld Hendon by 5.15; Tested 25.5.15 (Raynham); Yarmouth 29.5.15 (used by S/Cdr de CWP Ireland for night flying); AZP 7.6.15 (F/L V Nicholl & LM JS Philip); HSMP 23.6.15 (S/Cdr deCWP Ireland); AZP, chased L9, wiped off u/c on landing 9.8.15 (S/Cdr deCWP Ireland), repaired; AZPs 17/18.8.15 & 9.9.15 (S/Cdr de CWP Ireland); EF, FL Wrentham, nr Southwold en route Chingford 7.10.15 (F/L JMR Cripps); Felixstowe 22.11.15; EF, FL Covehithe 23.11.15 (F/L AQ Cooper); Yarmouth by 1.16; Covehithe 30.1.16; Yarmouth 1.2.16; Bacton 5.2.16; Yarmouth 5.2.16; Holt 14.3.16 (fog en route); Sedgeford 18.3.16; EF, FL Barham 8.4.16 (FSL FN Halstead); Yarmouth 13.4.16; Bacton 29.4.16; Burgh Castle 17.10.16; U/c wrecked landing 18.10.16 (FSL CS Nunn); Yarmouth 10.11.16; War Flight Burgh Castle 12.12.16; Yarmouth 19.12.16; War Flight Burgh Castle 8.2.17; Yarmouth 14.2.17; War Flight Burgh Castle 24.2.17; Yarmouth 26.2.17; EF, FL nr Covehithe 26.2.17; Burgh Castle 1.3.17; HACPs 10.3.17 & 25.3.17 (FSL CS Nunn); Deleted 16.4.17

978     Deld and tested Hendon 10.6.15 (Raynham); Chingford 11.6.15; CW, Barnet, Herts 8.10.15 (FSL RS Dallas); Deleted 12.10.15

979     Deld and accepted Chingford 28.6.15; to 4 Wing Dover 6.7.15; Arr via Folkestone 10.7.15 ; 1 Wing St.Pol 6.7.15 (sic); Retd Dover for packing 13.8.15; Shipped from London to Aegean in SS *Nyanza* 26.8.15; Arr 3 Wing 10.15; 2 Wing by 8.11.15 - @6.8.15 (sic); Missing from Narrows-Helles area 8.12.15; Probably the a/c from Tenedos which left to bomb Chanak & in which F/Cdr CE Robinson killed (remains retd in tow of a monitor?); Deleted 1916

980     Deld Chingford 3.7.15; Tested 8.7.15 (Raynham); 4 Wing Dover 15.7.15; HACP 29.7.15 (FSL CE Brisley & AM McCandless); 2 Wing Eastchurch 31.7.15; 4 Wing Eastchurch 3.8.15; Detd Westgate 20.8.15 (HD duties); 1 Wing St.Pol 21.9.15; Eastchurch 23.9.15; Kingsnorth 18.10.15; 4 Wing Eastchurch 19.11.15; Grain 19.11.15 [PVRD repair by 22.3.16]; ARD Grain 14.5.16 (became PVRS); Chingford 24.8.16; Cranwell 13.4.17; EF, FL, CW nr Bardney 27.10.17 (PFO FW Pearson), and deleted

981     Tested Brooklands 31.7.15; Shipped SS *Nankin* 8.15; 3 Wing Imbros 9.15; 2 Wing by 13.11.15 - @19.6.16; Deleted 1916

982     Deld Chingford for erection 18.8.15; Tested 24.8.15 (Raynham); 2 Wing dett Westgate 1.9.15; 1 Wing Dunkerque 21.9.15; 4 Wing Eastchurch 23.9.15; Eastbourne 24.9.15; 4 Wing Eastchurch 25.9.15; Visited Kingsnorth for expts 18.10.15; 4 Wing Eastchurch by 31.10.15; Kingsnorth for erection 16.11.15; Erecting by 16.1.16; Fitted to airship *AP1* at Kingsnorth 16-21.1.16; Under repair 22.1.16; Deleted 8.5.16

983     Deld Chingford for erection 18.8.15; Tested 24.8.15 (Raynham); 4 Wing Eastchurch 1.9.15; 1 Wing Dunkerque 21.9.15; 4 Wing Eastchurch 23.9.15; Rochford 20.3.16; 4 Wing Eastchurch 27.3.16; War Flight Eastchurch 16.4.16; AZP 25/26.4.16 (FSL DG Fleming); Chingford 29.4.16; Damaged 30.4.16 (F/L F Fowler); Hit by 2983 and badly damaged 23.6.16; Cranwell 23.5.17; Deleted 28.7.17 BR

984     Deld Chingford for erection by makers 6.9.15; Tested 10.9.15 (Raynham); Felixstowe 15.9.15; Trimley 13.10.15; Felixstowe 14.10.15; Aldeburgh 29.10.15; Felixstowe 3.11.15; Aldeburgh 8.11.15; Felixstowe 9.11.15; Aldeburgh 15.11.15; Felixstowe 16.11.15; Aldeburgh 5.12.15; Felixstowe 7.12.15; Aldeburgh 12.12.15; Trimley 19.12.15; Aldeburgh 19.12.15; Felixstowe 11.1.16; Trimley but EF, FL, badly damaged 26.1.16 (FSL CE Fox); Deleted 11.3.16

*A.D.Admiralty Seaplane 1000. (via E.Cromie)*

*Bristol Boxkite 947, probably at Eastbourne.*
*(J.M.Bruce/G.S.Leslie collection)*

*Avro 504B 1029, probably after crashing at Tenedos.*
*(J.M.Bruce/G.S.Leslie collection)*

*Sopwith "Spinning Jenny" 1062, probably at Chingford.*
*(J.M.Bruce/G.S.Leslie collection)*

*White & Thompson "Bognor Bloater" 1172.*
*(J.M.Bruce/G.S.Leslie collection)*

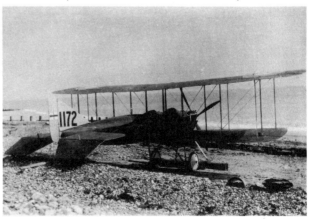

| | |
|---|---|
| 985 | Deld Chingford 7.9.15; Tested 10.9.15 (Raynham); Felixstowe 15.9.15; Trimley 8.11.15; Felixstowe 9.11.15; Ran into shed on landing and slightly damaged 15.11.15 (FSL LP Openshaw & Mjr Horsfield); Repaired; Tested 26.11.15; Levington Heath 8.2.16; Trimley 2.16; Felixstowe 20.2.16; HACP 19.3.16 (F/Cdr RJJ Hope-Vere); Deleted 2.5.16 |
| 986 | Erected by Mkrs at Chingford 23.9.15; Tested 30.9.15 (Raynham); 4 Wing Eastchurch 6.10.15; Grain 8.11.15; 4 Wing Eastchurch 14.11.15; Damaged landing 20.1.16 (FSL N Sholto Douglas); HACPs 20.2.16 (FSL M Birkbeck & AM Briggs), also 6.3.16 & 19.3.16 (FSL CC Wyllie); War Flight Eastchurch 16.4.16; Chingford 28.4.16; Cranwell 13.4.17; Deleted W/E 5.9.17 |
| 987 | Erected by Mkrs at Chingford 23.9.15; Tested 30.9.15 (Raynham); 4 Wing Eastchurch 6.10.15; AZP 6.3.16 (FSL CC Wyllie); HACPs 19.3.16 (F/L FT Digby) & 31.3.16/1.4.16 (FSL N Sholto Douglas); War Flight Eastchurch 16.4.16; HACP 25.8.16 (FSL W Tesh); Eastchurch Workshops for examination 24.9.16; Deleted 16.1.17 |

**12 ROYAL AIRCRAFT FACTORY B.E.2C TRACTOR BIPLANES ordered under Cont No C.P.58232/14 from Martin & Handasyde, numbered 988 to 999 & built Brooklands. (70-hp Renault)**

| | |
|---|---|
| 988 | Deld 2 Sqdn Eastchurch by 31.5.15; AZPs 1.6.15 (F/Cdr JRW Smyth-Pigott); HACP 4.6.15 (F/Cdr JRW Smyth-Pigott); AZP 5.6.15; AZP 9.6.15 (F/Cdr JRW Smyth-Pigott); Grenade dropping experiments 13.6.15 & 15.6.15; Grain Island Repair Depot 14.7.15; Nominally transferred 4 Wing Eastchurch 3.8.15; Grain 7.10.15; 4 Wing Eastchurch, transferred back to Grain 10.12.15; Port Victoria Repair Dept by 22.3.16; Chingford 19.7.16; Eastchurch 9.2.17; Crashed 12.2.17; Eastchurch Workshops 13.2.17; Chingford 29.4.17; Cranwell 9.5.17; EF at low altitude, sideslipped and crashed, CW 16.8.17 (TPFO LE Forman & F/L CV Arnold both killed); Deleted W/E 5.9.17 |
| 989 | Fitted to airship *AP.1* at Kingsnorth 1-13.1.16; Flight in *AP.1* 16.2.16; Aircraft lost when *AP.1* crashed and destroyed 21.2.16 (W/Cdr NF Usborne & S/Cdr deCWP Ireland both killed); Deleted 2.16 |
| 990 | Deld Yarmouth 24.6.15 (Raynham); Tested 30.6.15; HSMP 1.8.15 (FSL GW Hilliard); AZP, slightly damaged landing after pursuing *L.10* 12.8.15 (FSL GW Hilliard); AZP 17.8.15 (FSL GW Hilliard); AZP, u/c collapsed landing in field nr Bacton, bombs exploded, blown to bits 8.9.15 (FSL GW Hilliard killed); Deleted 15.9.15 |
| 991 | Deld Chingford 9.7.15 (en route Yarmouth); Yarmouth 19.7.15; AZP, EF, FL short of aerodrome, badly damaged 12.8.15 (S/Cdr deCWP Ireland); AZP, EF, FL Caistor Marshes, little damage 8.9.15 (F/L JMR Cripps); Bacton 30.12.15; Whitley Bay 31.12.15; Yarmouth 1.1.16; Bacton 5.1.16; Yarmouth 6.1.16; Bacton by 10.1.16; Yarmouth 11.1.16; Bacton 26.1.16; Yarmouth 27.1.16; Kessingland 28.1.16 (overnight, mist); Yarmouth 30.1.16; Covehithe 1.2.16; Yarmouth 4.2.16; Covehithe 5.2.16; Yarmouth 7.2.16; Covehithe 7.2.16; Yarmouth 10.2.16; Covehithe 20.2.16; Yarmouth 26.2.16; To Eastbourne NFS but FL and wrecked Gestingthorpe, Essex 8.4.16 (FSL TR Hackman unhurt); Undamaged parts to Hendon 12.4.16 then deleted |
| 992 | Deld Yarmouth 20.7.15 (Raynham); Tested 21.7.15; Fitted bombing gear early 8.15; AZP, lost u/c after landing 12.8.15 (F/L V Nicholl); Bacton 11.11.15; Yarmouth 16.11.15; Holt 1.12.15; Yarmouth 7.12.15; Bacton 29.12.15; Yarmouth 1.1.16; Bacton 5.1.16; Yarmouth 6.1.16; Bacton 9.1.16; Yarmouth 10.1.16; Damaged landing 25.1.16 (FSL EL Pulling); Covehithe 23.3.16; Sedgeford 6.4.16; Yarmouth 8.4.16; Eastbourne NFS 8.4.16; Eastchurch Workshops 14.10.16; War Flight Eastchurch 15.10.16; Eastchurch Workshops 5.1.17; Eastchurch Flying School 12.1.17; Eastchurch Workshops 28.3.17; Cranwell 30.3.17; Damaged 11.9.17; Surveyed 3.1.18; Deleted 17.1.18 W&T |
| 993 | Deld 4 Wing Eastchurch 6.8.15; 1 Wing St.Pol 21.9.15; 4 Wing Eastchurch 23.9.15; Wrecked 20.1.16 (FSL CH Darley & AM Wynter); Deleted 22.2.16 |
| 994 | (75-hp Renault) Deld 5 Wing Dover 16.8.15 (Raynham); Tested 18.8.15; AZP 14.9.15 (F/L LD McKean); Dover 3.3.16; Wrecked 4.6.16 (FSL WH Hope); Deleted 13.6.16 |
| 995 | (75-hp Renault) Transferred RFC (Military Wing); 12 Sqdn RFC Netheravon 8.15 - 9.15 for training; Retd RNAS; Brooklands to 5 Wing Dover 9.9.15 (HD duties); Dover 3.3.16; Chassis damaged 23.8.16; War Flight Eastchurch 24.9.16; Deleted 1.1.17 |
| 996 | Deld 5 Wing Dover 15.9.15 (HD duties); Wrecked 25.9.15 (FSL AS Ince & Lt HE Cramford); Deleted 15.10.15 |
| 997 | Deld 5 Wing Dover 25.9.15 (HD duties); Dunkerque 19.11.15; 1 Wing Dunkerque by 12.15 [D Group 12.15; B Group by 5.12.15; HQ Sqdn by 19.12.15 - @15.1.16; 4 Flt B Sqdn 1.3.16]; Testing new type of bomb 3.5.16; ADD by 11.5.16; Dover 18.6.16; Deleted 6.3.17 |
| 998 | Deld 5 Wing Dover for training 1.10.15; HACP 5.2.16 (S/Cdr CE Risk); HSPP 19.3.16 (FSL JP Coleman); Deleted 6.3.17 |
| 999 | Deld 5 Wing Dover for training 16.10.15; Wrecked 5.5.16 (FSL PW James); Deleted 6.5.16 |

**1 A.D. ADMIRALTY 1000 TYPE BIPLANE SEAPLANE ordered 24.2.15 under Cont No.P.10516/14 from J.Samuel White & Co Ltd, numbered 1000 & built East Cowes. (Three tractor/pusher 310-hp Sunbeam)**

| | |
|---|---|
| 1000 | Deld Felixstowe 4.6.16; Completed 26.1.17; Preliminary trials 27.1.17; Calshot 12.3.17; Mkrs instructed to repair aircraft, damaged in type trials at Cowes W/E 9.3.17; Wrecked Calshot 18.12.17; Surveyed at Cowes 18.12.17; Deleted 28.12.17 DBR |

**50 AVRO 504B (ADMIRALTY 179 TYPE) TRACTOR BIPLANES ordered under Cont No C.P.58282/14, numbered 1001 to 1050 & built Manchester. 10 transferred to RFC (Military Wing). (85-hp Gnome unless otherwise stated)**

| | |
|---|---|
| 1001 | Deld 1 Sqdn Grange Field (Gosport) 12.14; 1 Sqdn Dover 23.1.15; A Flt 1 Sqdn Westgate 3.2.15; 1 Sqdn Dover 5.2.15; 1 Sqdn St.Pol 11.2.15; EF after attack on Hoboken U-boat depot nr Antwerp, FL Kruiningen, Zeeland 24.3.15 (F/L B Crossley-Meates interned); Deleted 4.15; Taken over by Dutch Air Force as LA14 (later A22) |
| 1002 | (DC) Deld 1 Sqdn Grange Field (Gosport) 12.14; 1 Sqdn Dover, damaged u/c on arrival 23.1.15; A Flt 1 Sqdn Westgate 3.2.15; 1 Sqdn Dover 5.2.15; 1 Sqdn St.Pol by 24.2.15; 4 Sqdn Dover 17.6.15; HACPs 29.7.15 (FSL FT Digby & LM Hill) & 1.8.15 (FSL RGA Baudry & AM Wildbore); Remained when 4 Sqdn left Dover 3.8.15; EF, FL cornfield, chassis carried away 9.8.15 (FSL GH Jackson); Wrecked 22.8.15; Supermarine repair 25.8.15; Dover by road 13.1.16; Accepted 15.1.16; Mkrs Manchester by rail for repair 13.4.16; to Chingford W/E 10.6.16; EF, FL downwind in field, into hedge, on nose 21.4.17 (FSL GF Hyams); Deleted W/E 8.9.17 |
| 1003 | Deld 1 Sqdn Grange Field (Gosport) 12.14 (poorly finished off); COL Dover 30.1.15; HAPP 5.2.15; 1 Sqdn St.Pol 11.2.15; AZP 17.5.15 (F/Cdr JT Babington); Eastbourne FS (via Folkestone) 24.5.15; EF, U/c damaged 6.7.15 (S/L LA Hervey & S/L SD Felkin unhurt); Chassis damaged landing 14.7.15 (S/L SD Felkin); COL 20.7.15 (FSL RH Jones & Lt DG Broad unhurt); COL 25.8.15 (FSL JB Cusson unhurt); Avro for repair 8.15, but later deleted |
| 1004 | Deld 1 Sqdn Grange Field (Gosport) 12.14; 1 Sqdn St.Pol 29.1.15; AZP 17.5.15 (F/L FK Haskins); Became 1 Wing St.Pol 21.6.15 - 10.15; [BUT 4 Sqdn Dover by 20.6.15 (allocated Dover); en route 1.10.15; NFT] |
| 1005 | [Allocated Dover by 28.2.15 - NTU]; 1 Sqdn RFC by 3.15; Transferred to RFC (Military Wing) as 2857 16.3.15 |
| 1006 | [Allocated Dover by 28.2.15 - NTU]; 1 Sqdn RFC by 3.15; 2 Wing RFC 11.3.15; Transferred to RFC (Military Wing) as 2858 16.3.15 |
| 1007 | [Allocated Dover by 28.2.15 - NTU]; 1 Sqdn RFC by |

3.15; Transferred to RFC (Military Wing) as 2859 16.3.15

1008 [Allocated Dover by 28.2.15 - NTU]; 1 Sqdn RFC by 3.15; Transferred to RFC (Military Wing) as 2860 16.3.15

1009 Deld Dover by 11.3.15 (packing); To Dunkerque in crate; 1 Sqdn St.Pol 22.3.15; Attacked and damaged Zeppelin with a bomb over Ostende 17.4.15 (F/Cdr A.W.Bigsworth); EF, FL on sands La Panne 19.4.15 (F/L FG Andreae & 2/Lt AR Collen RM); AZP 17.5.15 (F/Cdr A.W.Bigsworth); Became A Sqdn 1 Wing St.Pol 21.6.15; Dropped 2x20-lb bombs on U-boat off Zeebrugge Mole 3.7.15 (FSL GH Bland & OSL FD Casey); HQ Sqdn 1 Wing St.Pol by 1.10.15; (5 Wing ?) Dover 11.11.15; Wrecked 28.1.16 (FSL KM Van Allen); Deleted 14.2.16

1010 Deld Eastchurch by 11.3.15; 2 Sqdn Eastchurch 12.3.15; 2 Sqdn Defence Flt Westgate by 11.4.15; EF over R.Swale, FL, hit ditch, smashed chassis 19.4.15 (F/L HA Buss & F/L AF Bettington); 2 Sqdn Eastchurch by 19.4.15; AZP 31.5.15/1.6.15, 5.6.15 & 7.6.15 (all F/L PA Johnston); Operated from Rochford 7.6.15, 11-12.6.15 & 18-19.6.15; Became 2 Wing Eastchurch 21.6.15; Eastchurch FS 15.6.15 (nominally 4 Wing); Wrecked 16.8.15; Deleted 9.9.15

1011 Deld Eastchurch by 11.3.15; 2 Sqdn Eastchurch 12.3.15; EF, FL Eastling, nr Faverham 26.3.15 (F/L HA Buss); HACPs 16.4.15 (F/L HA Buss & AM Gardner) & 17.5.15; 2 Sqdn Defence Flt Westgate 2.6.15; Became 2 Wing dett Westgate 21.6.15; 4 Wing dett Westgate 3.8.15; 5 Sqdn Dover 25.8.15; 4 Wing Eastchurch by 9.15; Wrecked 15.9.15; War Flight Eastchurch 16.4.16; AZP 25/26.4.16 (S/Cdr C Draper); EF, FL 14.5.16 (S/Cdr C Draper); Eastchurch School Flight 8.6.16; Deleted 26.4.17

1012 Deld Eastchurch by 11.3.15; 2 Sqdn Eastchurch 12.3.15; HACPs 7.6.15 (F/Cdr BF Fowler) & 2.7.15 (F/L PA Johnston); detd Rochford 12.7.15; Became 2 Wing Eastchurch 13.7.15; 4 Wing Eastchurch 3.8.15 (on departure of 2 Wing for France); War Flight Eastchurch 16.4.16; Eastchurch School Flight 26.5.16; Eastchurch Workshop repair by 1.1.17; Eastchurch FS 10.3.17; Eastchurch Workshops 29.3.17, retd FS; Surveyed 18.3.18; Deleted 27.3.18 W&T

1013 Deld 2 Sqdn Eastchurch in/by 1.4.15; 2 Sqdn detd flt Westgate 4.15; HACP 16.4.15; AZP, chased LZ38 17.5.15 (FSL RH Mulock); HSPP 23.5.15; 2 Sqdn Eastchurch 2.6.15; Surveyed 17.6.15; Deleted 26.6.15

1014 Deld 2 Sqdn Eastchurch (via Gravesend & Grain) 28.4.15; Flown partly coverd in black lead 7.5.15 (F/L HA Buss); Damaged 10.5.15; Retd 2 Sqdn Eastchurch 8.6.15; 2 Sqdn Defence Flt Westgate 13.6.15; Became 2 Wing dett Westgate 21.6.15; 4 Wing dett Westgate 3.8.15; SCAW for repair 10.10.15; Chingford 1.12.17; Surveyed 18.12.17; Deleted 21.12.17 for Lady Drogheda's exhibition in USA (via CSD)

1015 Deld 4 Sqdn Dover by rail 7.4.15; Tested 21.4.15 & 6.5.15; HACP 24.6.15 (FSL RC Hardstaff & AM Pritchard); To Chingford but EF, FL, wrecked Blethingley, nr Redhill 5.7.15 (FSL FT Digby & FSL RC Petter both injured); Deleted 30.7.15

1016 Deld 4 Sqdn Dover by rail 7.4.15; Tested 21.4.15; HACPs 23.5.15 (FSL R Lord & AM Wynter), 21.6.15 (FSL R Lord & AM Witcher), 29.7.15 (FSL CT MacLaren & AM Witcher) & 1.8.15 (FSL FT Digby & AM Witcher); 5 Sqdn Dover 3.8.15; AZP, chased L12 unsuccessfully 10.8.15 (FSL CE Brisley); Wrecked 30.12.15 (FSL CFB Penley); Deleted 1.16

1017 Deld 2 Sqdn Eastchurch 4.15; 2 Sqdn dett Westgate 19.4.15; FL outside aerodrome 11.5.15 (F/L HA Buss); Wrecked 1.6.15; Supermarine for repair 5.6.15; Surveyed; Deleted 24.4.16

1018 Deld 2 Sqdn Eastchurch 4.15; A Flt (= Defence Flt) 2 Sqdn Westgate, by 30.4.15; AZP 17.5.15; HSPP 23.5.15; AZP, chased LZ38 31.5.15 (F/L AF Bettington); Became 2 Wing dett Westgate 21.6.15; HSPP 3.7.15; 4 Wing dett Westgate 3.8.15; Wrecked 6.8.15; Deleted 23.8.15

1019 (DC) (80-hp Le Rhône) Deld Hendon 4.5.15; Accepted 11.5.15 (Raynham); Chingford 19.5.15; 2 Wing Eastchurch 25.7.15 (transit); 1 Wing St.Pol 25.7.15

[with HQ Sqdn by 9.15]; 5 Wing Dover 11.11.15; Mkrs Manchester by rail for repair 22.3.16; Chingford 5.8.16; Deleted W/E 6.4.18

1020 to 1025 transferred to RFC (Military Wing) 1915 as 4221 to 4225 and 4255

1026 (DC) Deld 2 Sqdn Eastchurch 5.15; Grain 28.5.15; Tested 29.5.15; detd Eastchurch 21.6.15; Grain 30.6.15; AZP 10.8.15 (FSL EdeC Hallifax); Grenade and flechette experiments 22.9.15; HSPP 19.3.16 (FSL EdeC Hallifax & Cpl Grant); Cranwell 24.4.16; Deleted 25.2.17

1027 Deld 2 Sqdn Eastchurch 5.15; Damaged u/c visiting Rochford 2.6.15 (F/L DK Johnston & PO Thomas); HSPP 3.7.15; Grain RD 9.10.15; Grain 28.1.16; Hit soft ground landing, broke propeller, visiting Eastchurch 31.3.16 (F/L P Legh & S/Cdr EDM Robertson); Cranwell 24.4.16; Deleted 1.12.16

1028 (DC) Deld 2 Sqdn Eastchurch 5.15; Tested 3.6.15; Grain 5.6.15; Cranwell (via Chingford) 29.5.16; Crashed 7.8.17; Deleted W/E 9.11.17

1029 Deld 2 Wing Eastchurch 31.5.15; Eastchurch 3.6.15; Detd Rochford 12-13.6.15, 16-18.6.15, 20-21.6.15; HACP 13.6.15 (FSL RB Munday); Grenade dropping expts 15.6.15; Became 2 Wing Eastchurch 21.6.15; Detd Rochford 30.6.15 - 1.7.15; 2 Wing dett Westgate 29.7.15; 2 Wing St.Pol 1.8.15; Dropped bomb on Zeppelin, Ostende Harbour 10.8.15 (F/L HA Buss); 2 Wing Folkestone 12.8.15; 2 Wing Dover 13.8.15; Packed for Dardanelles; transit to 3 Wing in SS Nyanza 27.8.15; 3 Wing by 1.10.15 - @30.11.15; Crashed Tenedos; Deleted

1030 (DC) Deld Chingford for erection 20.6.15; Accepted 27.6.15; Smashed 8.7.15; Crashed 13.7.15 (F/L LD McKean); FL and damaged en route visit to Hainault Farm 24.3.16; Deleted 29.6.16

1031 (DC) Deld Chingford by rail 18.6.15; Tested 22.6.15 (Raynham); Accepted 25.6.15; Cranwell 8.2.16; Deleted 5.5.17

1032 (DC) Deld Chingford by rail 18.6.15; Tested 22.6.15 (Raynham); Accepted 25.6.15; Fast landing, u/c & lower wings wrecked 13.7.15 (PFSL MA Simpson); Skid caught ground landing, fuselage broke in two 19.7.15; Packed for transport 5.8.15; Supermarine repair 18.8.15; Chingford 11.11.15; Deleted 22.4.16

1033 (80-hp Le Rhône). Deld Chingford for erection 20.6.15; Tested 27.6.15; 2 Wing Eastchurch 25.7.15 (transit); 1 Wing St.Pol 25.7.15; Deleted by 31.10.15

1034 Deld Chingford for erection 29.6.15; Tested 4.7.15 (Raynham); To 4 Sqdn Dover but EF, FL en route at Smarden 6.7.15; 4 Wing Eastchurch 3.8.15; Wrecked 26.11.15 (FSL RE Greensmith); FL Leysdown 28.12.15 (FSL C Perrett & FSL HL Wood); Visited Folkestone 31.1.16 - 8.2.16; War Flight Eastchurch 16.4.16; Wrecked 21.4.16; Deleted 25.4.16

1035 Deld Chingford by rail 30.6.15; Tested 8.7.15 (Raynham); Accepted 10.7.15; 4 Sqdn Dover 14.7.15; HACP 1.8.15 (FSL R.Lord & AM Howard); AZP 10.8.15 (FSL CE Brisley); 5 Sqdn Dover 11.8.15; Wrecked 14.1.16 (FSL KM Van Allen unhurt); Deleted 27.1.16

1036 (DC) Deld Chingford for erection 30.6.15; Tested 4.7.15; Grain 9.7.15 ("dipped" fuselage for experiments); EF, FL NNE Shoeburyness 23.4.16 (F/L GF Smylie); Under repair Barking 24.4.16; Rochford 24.4.16; Grain 25.4.16; EF, FL Hawksworth 27.4.16 (F/L GF Smylie), retd safely; Cranwell 29.5.16; Deleted 14.1.17

1037 Deld Chingford by rail 2.7.15; Tested 8.7.15 (Raynham); Accepted 10.7.15; Dunkerque 15.7.15; HQ Sqdn 1 Wing St.Pol 18.7.15 - 12.15; Deleted 1916

1038 (DC) Deld Grain for erection 18.7.15; Accepted 27.7.15 (Raynham); 4 Wing dett Westgate 10.8.15; Cranwell 12.3.16; Deleted 15.5.16

1039 (DC) Deld Grain for by 18.7.15; Accepted 27.7.15 (Raynham); Tested with 8x20-lb bombs; Tested 65-lb bomb gear 17.8.15; Convtd to 1-str, tested 6.4.16; Chingford 4.5.16; Collided with 8305, smashed 2.6.16 (pilot unhurt); Deleted 9.9.16

1040 Deld Grain for erection for packing 26.7.15; To Royal Albert Docks by lorry 29.7.15; Accepted 31.7.15, apparently without flight test; Sailed from Dover in SS

*Nankin* 5.8.15; 3 Wing Imbros by 31.8.15; 2 Wing Imbros by 26.10.15, EF after recce, FL in sea 9.12.15 (F/L HA Buss & Lt CA Bourne RFA picked up by monitor HMS *Earl of Peterborough*); Deleted 3.16

1041    To docks 29.7.15; Accepted 31.7.15, apparently without flight test; Sailed from Dover in SS *Nankin* 5.8.15 ; 3 Wing Imbros by 31.8.15; 2 Wing Imbros by 8.11.15 - @30.11.15; Retd UK and to CSD White City; Parnall for repair W/E 19.1.17; Chingford 28.2.17; Deleted 23.7.17

1042    To docks 29.7.15; Accepted 31.7.15, apparently without flight test; Sailed from Dover in SS *Nankin* 5.8.15; 3 Wing Imbros by 31.8.15; 2 Wing Imbros by 4.11.15; O/t in lagoon on return from bombing raid on the narrows 4.12.15 (Mjr H Fawcett RM & Lt WD Jones RM both unhurt); Crashed & o/t in salt lake on TO 9.2.16 (Mjr H Fawcett RM); Deleted 3.16

1043    To docks 29.7.15; Accepted 31.7.15, apparently without flight test; Sailed from Dover in SS *Nankin* 5.8.15; 3 Wing Imbros by 31.8.15; Front cockpit faired over; C Flt A Sqdn 2 Wing Imbros by 25.9.15; Deleted 7.16

1044    (DC) Deld Chingford for erection 4.8.15; Tested 8.8.15; Grain 17.8.15 (Raynham); Chingford 24.8.15; Propeller and wings broken on/by 27.11.15; Crashed 8.1.16 (PFSL AL Thorne); EF, FL badly wrecked by telephone wires Angel Rd, Tottenham 30.5.16 (PFSL CH Butterworth unhurt); Deleted 29.6.16

1045    (DC) Deld Chingford for erection 13.8.15; Tested 20.8.15 (Raynham); Smashed u/c 28.12.15 (PFSL PSJ Owen); Broke u/c landing 5.7.16 (FSL CHM Chapman); EF, FL in reservoir 1.2.17 (FSL AB Hill); Deleted 8.12.17

1046    (DC) Deld Chingford for erection 13.8.15; Tested 20.8.15 (Raynham); Grain 27.8.15; Landed outside aerodrome, damaged 10.4.16 (F/L GF Smylie); Chingford 4.5.16; Became 207 TDS Chingford 1.4.18

1047    (DC) Deld Chingford for erection 17.8.15; Tested 21.8.15 (Raynham); To Yarmouth but EF, FL, damaged en route at Colchester 26.8.15 (FSL CE Wood); Holt 11.11.15; Yarmouth 28.11.15; Bacton 29.12.15; EF, FL Palling 11.1.16 (FSL GWR Fane); Yarmouth 12.1.16; FL Caister 1.3.16 (FSL SG Beare); Erecting Yarmouth 13.4.16 after repair; Bacton 15.4.16; Cranwell 28.4.16; Deleted 25.2.17

1048    (DC) Deld Chingford for erection 17.8.15; Tested 21.8.15 (Raynham); Yarmouth 27.8.15; Grenade gear fitted 10.15; Bacton 29.3.16; Yarmouth 31.3.16; Bacton 2.4.16; Yarmouth 3.4.16; Cranwell 27.4.16; Crashed 30.6.17; Surveyed 14.9.17; Deleted 8.10.17 wrecked

1049    (DC) Deld Chingford for erection 23.8.15; Tested 26.8.15 (Raynham); Yarmouth 2.10.15; Holt 24.11.15; Bacton 1.12.15; EF, FL Palling 1.12.15 (FSL FN Halstead); Yarmouth 2.12.15; Bacton 3.12.15; Yarmouth 7.12.15; Bacton 17.12.15; Yarmouth 18.12.15; Bacton 12.4.16; Holt 25.4.16; Yarmouth 26.4.16; Cranwell 27.4.16; Wrecked 8.11.16 (TFSL W Stewart killed); Deleted 21.11.16

1050    (DC) Deld Chingford for erection 23.8.15; Tested 26.8.15 (Raynham); Deleted 8.2.16

## 24 SOPWITH "SPINNING JENNY" TWO-SEATER SCOUT TRACTOR BIPLANES numbered 1051 to 1074 & built Kingston. (80-hp Gnome)

1051    Deld Eastchurch NFS 26.12.14; Yarmouth by 7.1.15; Damaged on TO Eastchurch 10.1.15; 2 Sqdn Eastchurch by 30.1.15; Damaged 16.3.15; Deleted 10.7.15

1052    Deld Eastchurch & accepted NFS 30.12.14; To Yarmouth but EF, FL Sizewell Gap 17.1.15; dissembled Leiston 19.1.15; Re-erected Yarmouth 21.1.15; EF, FL, badly damaged 22.1.15 (F/L JMR Cripps); EF, FL Southtown Marshes, retd by lorry 13.3.15 (F/L CHC Smith); AZPs 16.4.15 (FSL V Nicholl & PO Lytton) & 30.4.15 (F/L CHC Smith & AM Collins); Bacton 30.4.15; Yarmouth but o/t landing 1.5.15 (FSL CHC Smith); AZPs 10.5.15 (F/L CHC Smith & LM Caple), 11.5.15 (FSL CHC Smith & 1AM Latta); Bacton by 5.15; Yarmouth 20.5.15; HSMP 23.6.15 (FSL CHC Smith & PO Mech Brownlee); AZP 8.9.15 (F/L EJ Cooper); Deleted 16.12.15

1053    Deld Eastchurch NFS 6.1.15 (Hawker); Yarmouth 17.1.15; EF, FL ploughed field, on nose, damaged nr Sherington 22.1.15 (Lt FM Barr); Dismantled, to Yarmouth 22.1.15; FL, broke propeller, wheel and longeron, Winterton 16.2.15; retd by lorry 17.2.15; Engine trouble, damaged landing 5.3.15 (F/L FML Barr); AZPs 30.4.15 (F/L V Nicholl & AM Harrison), 10.5.15 (F/L V Nicholl & 1AM Latta), 7.6.15 (FSL CHC Smith & PO Lytton) & 10.8.15 (FSL E Cadbury); EF, FL Kessingland 8.8.15 (FSL E Cadbury & AM Hazell); Bacton 15.9.15; EF, FL Gorleston 17.9.15 (F/L EJ Cooper); Yarmouth 18.9.15; Deleted 16.12.15

1054    Deld Eastchurch NFS 2.1.15; Killingholme for erection 6.1.15; Tested 9.1.15 (Hawker); Slightly damaged 23.2.15; AZP 31.3.15 (F/L HS Adams & CPO Bradley); O/t landing, slightly damaged 16.4.15 (FSL WH Elliott & CPO Roberts); Dismantled 20.9.15 to make way for newer aircraft; Deleted 11.12.15

1055    Deld Killingholme for erection 6.1.15; Tested 18.1.15; EF, FL ploughed field, broke propeller Scartho 21.1.15; Re-tested 9&10.2.15; AZPs 31.3.15 (FSL WH Elliott & CPO Thompson) & 7.6.15 (FSL JC Brooke & AM Bager); Smashed 25.8.15; Deleted 4.9.15

1056    Deld Yarmouth by train 26.1.15; Erected by Mkrs; Accepted 28.1.15 (Hawker); FL in squally weather, undamaged, Caistor Marshes 28.2.15 (Lt JMR Cripps); retd 2.3.15; O/t landing 10.3.15 (F/L FML Barr & AM Shoote shaken); AZPs 30.4.15 (F/L FML Barr & 1AM Latta); Went on nose taxying after landing, slightly damaged 30.7.15 (F/L EJ Cooper & 1AM Bunn); AZPs 10.8.15 (FSL CHC Smith) & 17.8.15 (FSL E Cadbury); Deleted 16.12.15

1057    AW/CN 26.1.15; Deld Yarmouth for erection 3.2.15; Accepted 8.2.15; EF, FL, CW on TO, Cromer 31.3.15 (FSL CHC Smith & passenger unhurt); Remains to Grain RD 10.4.15; Deleted 4.15

1058    AW/CN 26.1.15; Deld Yarmouth for erection 3.2.15; Accepted 10.2.15; Fitted bomb gear 27.4.15; Bacton 28.9.15; Engine removed 6.10.15; Deleted 16.12.15

1059    Deld 1 Sqdn Dover for erection 8.2.15; Failed initial acceptance test, EF, FL near aerodrome 18.2.15; Accepted 22.2.15; Dover Defence Flt by 11.3.15; Became 4 Sqdn Dover 25.3.15; 5 Sqdn Dover 4.8.15 (transferred when 4 Sqdn left); Packing for CSD 5.12.15; Deleted 20.12.15 and to CSD White City

1060    Deld 1 Sqdn Dover for erection 8.2.15; Accepted 23.2.15; Dover Defence Flt by 11.3.15; Became 4 Sqdn Dover 25.3.15; O/t landing 30.4.15 (pilot unhurt); Grain Island RD by rail 6.5.15 and deleted

1061    Deld Hendon by air 7.3.15; To Chingford but FL en route and damaged Hackney Marsh 14.3.15 (F/L EB Bauman & PFSL RH Routledge) (War machine); Crashed nr reservoir 6.7.15 (F/L GW Price); Smashed 31.7.15; Navigation School Portsmouth by lorry 8.11.15

1062    Deld Hendon by air 20.3.15 (modified tail surfaces); Chingford 16.6.15; Doped in blotchy camouflage; Recovered 21.10.15 - 4.11.15; Deleted 13.12.15; Finally at Navigation School Portsmouth (presume as ground instructional)

1063    Deld Hendon 27.3.15 (Hawker); Chingford 16.6.15; Crashed and wrecked on cross-country 2.7.15 (FSL EAdeL de Ville unhurt); Repairs planned, but deleted and sent to CSD White City 4.8.15

1064    Deld Hendon 3.4.15 (Hawker); Chingford 26.4.15 (War machine); Crashed and wrecked 25.5.15 (F/L CWH Pulford); Grain Island RD 11.6.15; Tested 20.8.15; Chingford 20.8.15; EF at Hendon, left there 24.8.15 (F/L D Arnold) - @27.8.15; EF, FL, chassis wrecked Chingford 19.9.15 (F/L D Arnold); Deleted 13.12.15

1065    Deld Hendon 20.4.15 (Hawker); Chingford 23.4.15; Crashed 1.7.15 (PFSL GF Smylie); Deleted 13.12.15

1066    Deld Eastchurch NFS 4.15; 2 Sqdn Eastchurch 31.5.15; Became 2 Wing Eastchurch 21.6.15; NFS Eastchurch, wrecked 22.8.15; Deleted 22.2.16

1067    AW/CN 1.5.15; Deld Fort George for erection 16.5.15; Montrose by road 27.5.15; HACP 2.6.15 (FSL G Donald); Dismantled 5.9.15; Dundee 13.9.15; Collided with tree and CW 14.9.15 (FSL AH Sandwell slightly injured & LM Lamb unhurt); Deleted 16.9.15

1068    Deld Fort George for erection 16.5.15; Montrose by road 27.5.15; Tested 3.7.15; Dismantled 5.9.15; East

Fortune 14.9.15; Dismantled 22.12.15; Deleted 8.1.16

1069    Deld Barry for erection 24.5.15; Montrose 27.5.15; HACP 2.6.15 (Lt C Draper); HSPP 16.6.15 (F/L G Donald & LAM Groucott); To Barry but overshot into ditch, damaged u/c and propeller 18.8.15 (Lt G Donald & CPO Harris unhurt); Dismantled 5.9.15; East Fortune 13.9.15, but EF, FL, u/c damaged (S/L JEB MacLean & CPO Noonan); Damaged wings, propeller and nose 6.10.15 (S/L AR Cox); Deleted 23.10.15

1070    Deld Killingholme in crate 7.6.15; Tested 9.6.15; AZP 15.6.15 (F/L HS Adams); Deleted 11.12.15

1071    Deld Killingholme in crate 9.6.15; Provisionally accepted 13.6.15; AZP 15.6.15 (FSL WH Elliott); Deleted 11.12.15

1072    Deld Eastchurch NFS by air 14.6.15; Damaged 5.1.16; CW, Eastbourne 8.2.16; Deleted 22.2.16

1073    Deld Eastchurch NFS ex Brooklands 25.6.15; Tested 28.6.15; Wrecked 29.6.15; Damaged 31.1.16; Deleted 2.2.16

1074    Deld Chingford 28.6.15 (Hawker); Wrecked 3.7.15 (PFSL HCG Allen); Repaired by 16.9.15; to CSD White City by lorry 15.12.15, later deleted

**24 ROYAL AIRCRAFT FACTORY B.E.2C TRACTOR BIPLANES ordered from Vickers Ltd & numbered 1075 to 1098. (70-hp Renault)**

1075 to 1098 transferred to RFC (Military Wing). Presume renumbered

**24 ROYAL AIRCRAFT FACTORY B.E.2C TRACTOR BIPLANES ordered from Sir William Beardmore & Co Ltd, numbered 1099 to 1122 & built Dalmuir. (70-hp Renault)**

1099    (75-hp Wolseley-Renault) AW/CN 27.2.15; Deld Gosforth 5.3.15; Tested 8.3.15 (Dukinfield Jones); Whitley Bay 9.3.15; Badly damaged 17.5.15; HSMPs 5.7.15 (FSL P Legh & CPO Ashton) & 21.5.15 (FSL P Legh & AM Worsley); COL 7.6.15 (FSL RG Mack); AZP 15/16.6.15 (FSL KS Savory); Dismantled in bad state of repair 1.9.15; Mkrs repair 29.9.15; En route by road 12.10.15; Whitley Bay 18.10.15; Spun into sea 20.12.15 (FSL GH Bettinson slightly injured); Deleted

1100    Deld Whitley Bay 22.4.15; FL, badly damaged near aerodrome 5.5.15 (FSL RE Nicholl); To Northern Aircraft Co for repair 17.5.15; Repairs abandoned; Deleted 7.15

1101    Deld Montrose by 1.4.15; Barry 17.4.15; Montrose 21.4.15; Whitley Bay 28.4.15; U/c damaged landing 8.6.15 (F/L KS Savory & AM Lewis); AZP, landed, damaged u/c on rifle butts, TO again, COL, wrecked 15/16.6.15 (F/Cdr CE Robinson & LM HJL Hinkler); Deleted 17.6.15

1102    Deld 4 Sqdn Dover 20.5.15; Tested 21.5.15; Became 4 Wing Dover 21.6.15; 4 Wing Eastchurch 2.8.15; Eastchurch FS 25.8.15 (Beardmore pilot); Crashed and wrecked 31.8.15; Grain 23.1.16; Norwich to Yarmouth 25.1.16; Eastchurch 26.1.16; attd Misc Flt Eastchurch by 9.6.16; Eastchurch Workshops 26.6.16; Deleted 16.1.17

1103    Deld 4 Sqdn Dover for erection 22.5.15; Erected 8.6.15; Became 4 Wing Eastchurch; 2 Wing Eastchurch 2.8.15; 4 Wing Eastchurch 3.8.15; AZP 10.8.15 (F/Cdr RJ Bone); Reserve Sqdn 1 Wing St.Pol 21.9.15; Damaged Calais 23.9.15 (burnt after taking out engine 24.9.15); Deleted 4 Wing 11.10.15

1104    Deld 4 Sqdn Dover for erection 5.6.15; 1 Sqdn St.Pol 12.6.15 (Reserve machine); Became 1 Wing 21.6.15; Attd 3 Sqdn RFC 13-26.6.15 & 14-30.7.15; To 5 Wing Dover but wrecked en route at Folkestone 6.9.15; Deleted 31.10.15

1105    Deld 4 Sqdn Dover by 12.6.15; Became 4 Wing 21.6.15; HACP 22.6.15 (F/Cdr RJ Bone); HSPP 3.7.15 (FSL RC Hardstaffe & AM Robson); 4 Wing Eastchurch 4.8.15; To Grain but damaged landing and returned Eastchurch by lorry 10.11.15 (FSL Daniels & FSL Kinsay unhurt); War Flight Eastchurch 16.4.16; Miscellaneous Flight Eastchurch 28.4.16; Spotting Flight Eastchurch 15.9.16; Deleted 16.1.17

1106    Tested Dalmuir 25.6.15; Deld Whitley Bay by rail 26.6.15; Accepted 27.6.15 (Dukinfield Jones); Carried 4

petrol bombs; HSMP 5.7.15 (F/Cdr CE Robinson & AM Hodges); Crashed 22.7.15 (F/L V Nicholl); CSD White City 14.8.15, then deleted

1107    Tested Dalmuir 1.7.15; Deld Chingford by road 7.7.15; Tested 10.7.15 (Dukinfield Jones); EF, FL and smashed Muddley Farm, Edgwarebury Lane, Elstree 6.4.16 (PFSL AR Brown); Deleted 24.4.16

1108    Tested Dalmuir 7.15; Deld Chingford by road 8.7.15; Tested 11.7.15 (Dukinfield Jones); Damaged on visit to Eastchurch (F/L LD McKean unhurt); retd Chingford 27.7.15; Hendon but COL 30.9.15 (FSL F Fowler & S/L RW Gow); FL, minor damage, Crouch End 5.11.15 (FSL LG Sieveking); Chingford 6.11.15; Wrecked 28.12.15 (PFSL PSJ Owen); Deleted 21.1.16

1109    Deld Redcar 31.7.15; Tested 5.8.15 (Dukinfield Jones); Scarborough 25.8.15; Redcar 27.8.15; FL near Whitby 2.9.15 (S/Cdr CEH Rathborne & F/L CB Dalison); AZP 8.9.15 (S/Cdr CEH Rathborne); Scarborough 8.11.15; Hornsea 11.11.15; Scarborough 14.11.15; Redcar 15.11.15; AZPs 10.2.16, 9.8.16 & 27/28.11.16 (all F/L BPH de Roeper); Cranwell 26.5.17 (arr 27.5.17); Deleted W/E 2.11.17

1110    Tested Dalmuir 13.7.15; Deld 4 Sqdn Dover 21.7.15; Tested 24.7.15 (Dukinfield Jones); Crating for transport 25.7.15; To Dover docks 1.8.15; Shipped Aegean in SS *Nankin* 5.8.15; arr 3 Wing Imbros by 31.8.15; 2 Wing Imbros by 9.11.15; Deleted 3.16

1111    Tested Dalmuir 13.7.15; Deld 2 Wing Dover 19.7.15; Packing for transport 25.7.15; To Dover docks 1.8.15; Shipped Aegean in SS *Nankin* 5.8.15; 2 Wing Imbros by 1.10.15 - @8.12.15; Deleted 1916

1112    Deld Redcar 31.7.15; Tested 5.8.15 (Dukinfield Jones); AZP 9.8.15 (F/L CB Dalison); Sideslipped, CW, Middlesbrough 19.8.15 (F/L CB Dalison slightly injured); Deleted 20.10.15

1113    Tested Dalmuir 15.8.15; Killingholme 17.8.15; Accepted 20.8.15 (Dukinfield Jones); Wrecked 18.12.15; Deleted 20.12.15

1114    Tested Dalmuir 15.8.15; Whitley Bay 17.8.15; Accepted 18.8.15; Redcar 1.12.15; Whitley Bay 8.12.15; HSMPs 27.1.16, also 28.1.16, FL, broke chassis (both patrols F/L P Legh & FSL GA Gooderham); HACP 2.4.16 (FSL GA Gooderham); AZP 2/3.5.16 (FSL KF Sanders); Scarborough & Sedgeford 26.5.16 (transit); Chingford 27.5.16; Cranwell 26.1.17; CW 27.6.17; Deleted 28.7.17

1115    Tested Dalmuir 15.8.15; Whitley Bay in crate 21.8.15; Test after erection 25.8.15 (Dukinfield Jones); Accepted 28.8.15; Armstrong Whitworth repair 29.9.15; Whitley Bay 8.10.15; AZP 13.10.15 (FSL P Legh); Armstrong Whitworth Gosforth (temp housed) 10.2.16; Whitley Bay 5.3.16 but EF, FL on moor en route (FSL P Legh); Repaired, arrived Whitley Bay 6.3.16; Chingford 3.6.16; Turned, sideslipped in, wrecked Angmering en route Cranwell 24.3.17 (PFSL AF Harvey killed); Cranwell 27.3.17 (repairs); U/c damaged 27.7.17; Wrecked 16.8.17; Crashed 5.9.17; Surveyed 9.11.17; Deleted 23.11.17 wrecked

1116    Tested Dalmuir 18.8.15; Deld Whitley Bay for erection 22.8.15; Tested 25.8.15 (Dukinfield Jones); Damaged landing 1.5.16 (FSL GB Taylor); Chingford 1.6.16; Cranwell 23.5.17 (80-hp Wolseley-Renault); Deleted W/E 9.3.18

1117    Tested Dalmuir 18.8.15; Deld Redcar 6.9.15; Hornsea 7.9.15; Scarborough 4.11.15; Hornsea 11.15; Scarborough 7.11.15; Hornsea 19.11.15; Scarborough 20.11.15; Hornsea 2.12.15; Scarborough 3.12.15; Hornsea 5.2.16; CW when Bessoneau hangar blown away in gale 16.2.16; Deleted 13.3.16

1118    Deld Redcar and tested 15.9.15 (Dukinfield Jones); Scarborough 8.11.15; Redcar 11.11.15; Scarborough 8.12.15; Whitley Bay 13.12.15; Redcar by 1.16; HSMP 28.1.16 (F/L CB Dalison); AZP 10.2.16 (FSL MJ Golding); To Cranwell but en route FL Grathorne 24.5.17 (F/L RM Everett); retd Redcar 25.5.17; Cranwell 26.5.17; Crashed and damaged 18.7.17; U/c damaged 2.10.17; Still Cranwell 4.18

1119    Deld Redcar and tested 15.9.15 (Dukinfield Jones); COL Whitley Bay 24.9.15 (FSL GA Gooderham); FL, smashed, 8m N of Scarborough 19.1.16; Whitley Bay 28.4.16; AZP 2/3.5.16 (FSL AA Wallis); Redcar

1.7.16; Deleted 4.5.17

1120    Deld Redcar and tested 15.9.15 (Dukinfield Jones);
Scarborough 22.9.15; FL and damaged N of aerodrome
14.1.16 (FSL AS Goodwin); Crashed on TO 30.8.16
(FSL JC Tanner); Deleted 22.9.16

1121    Deld CSD White City; Chingford by lorry 6.4.16; EF,
FL, Damaged 19.6.16 (F/L JS Mills DSC); Visited
Kingsnorth 21.4.17; Cranwell 26.10.17; Flattened out
too late, smashed u/c and lower starboard wing 24.12.17
(PFO NH Witter); Became 201/2 TDS Cranwell 1.4.18

1122    Deld CSD White City; Chingford 13.12.15; AZP, heavy
landing at Joyce Green, broke skid 31.1.16 (FSL H
McLelland), returned; Rochford 5.4.16; Chingford
9.4.16; Crashed through hedge landing, damaged
Rochford 10.4.16 (PFO RF Redpath), retd by lorry;
Cranwell 9.5.17; Smashed 20.8.17 (PFO L Code killed);
Surveyed 3.1.18; Deleted 17.1.18 W&T

**24 ROYAL AIRCRAFT FACTORY B.E.2C TRACTOR
BIPLANES ordered 29.9.14 under Cont No
C.P.58282/14/X/19112 from Blackburn Aeroplane & Motor Co
Ltd, numbered 1123 to 1146 & built Leeds. (70-hp Renault to
1141, then 75-hp Renault)**

1123    In transit to Gibralter by 20.6.15; arr Gibralter 6.15 -
12.15; Deleted 1916

1124    Deld Hendon and accepted 17.6.15 (Ding); 4 Sqdn
Dover 29.6.15; Became 4 Wing Eastchurch 2.8.15;
Grain 7.8.15; Eastchurch 9.8.15; AZP 10.8.15 (F/Cdr
REC Peirse); Wireless experiments 8.15 (FSL JED Boyd
& F/L B Binyon); EF, FL Chingford 7.9.15 (FSL CC
Wyllie & AM Robson); Retd 8.9.15; Hendon 9.9.15
(repair); 4 Wing Eastchurch 5.10.15; Visited
Kingsnorth for expts; Rochford 7.4.16; War Flight
Eastchurch 23.4.16; Misc Flight Eastchurch 1.5.16;
Chingford 23.5.16; Crashed 24.3.17; Deleted 4.4.17

1125    (80-hp Renault) Deld Hendon and accepted 19.6.15
(Ding); 2 Wing Eastchurch 28.6.15; U/c smashed
landing 21.7.15 (F/Cdr REC Peirse); 2 Wing St.Pol
4.8.15; Dover for packing 13.8.15; Shipped 20.8.15;
Transit to Aegean in SS *Joshua Nicholson*; Assembled 2
Wing Imbros 2.10.15; Tested 3.10.15; Fitted for
photography at Mudros 4.10.15; Fitted bomb droppers at
Mudros 1.11.15; D Flt 2 Wing Imbros by 8.11.15 -
@1.16; C Flt A Sqdn 2 Wing Imbros by 14.4.16 -
@16.5.16; Deleted 1916

1126    Deld Hendon and tested 1.7.15; 2 Wing Eastchurch
6.7.15; EF, FL, damaged chassis and wings 27.7.15
(F/L AF Bettington); 2 Wing St.Pol 4.8.15; Dover for
packing 13.8.15; Packed 20.8.15; Shipped from London
to Aegean in SS *Nyanza* 26.8.15; 2 Wing Imbros,
crashed nr aerodrome in gusty conditions 12.10.15 (pilot
seriously injured & CPO Mech3 W McLellan killed);
Deleted 1916

1127    Deld Hendon and tested 1.7.15; Folkestone 10.7.15
(transit); 4 Sqdn Dover 11.7.15; Became 4 Wing Dover
13.7.15; 1 Wing St.Pol 14.7.15; Deleted 8.15 on
transfer to Belgian Government in exchange for
Shorthorn which was also given serial number 1127 (see
below)

1128    Deld Grain for erection 20.7.15; Accepted without flying
test; Packed 24.7.15; To Royal Albert Docks 28.7.15;
Shipped to Aegean in SS *Nankin* 5.8.15; 3 Wing Imbros
by 31.8.15 - @30.11.15; Deleted 1916

1129    Deld Grain for erection 7.15; Packing 26.7.15; To Royal
Albert Docks 28.7.15; To Dover docks 1.8.15; Shipped
to Aegean in SS *Nankin* 7.8.15; 3 Wing Imbros by
31.8.15; 2 Wing Imbros by 14.10.15 - @3.17; Deleted
1917

1130    Deld Grain for erection 7.15; Packing 26.7.15; To Royal
Albert Docks 28.7.15; Shipped to Aegean in SS *Nankin*
5.8.15; 3 Wing Imbros by 31.8.15; 2 Wing Imbros by
16.10.15 - @29.12.15; Deleted 1916

1131    Deld 2 Wing Eastchurch for erection 1.8.15; 4 Wing
Eastchurch 3.8.15; Tested 14.8.15; Felixstowe 22.8.15;
Trimley 10.9.15; Felixstowe 11.9.15; Aldeburgh
17.11.15; Felixstowe 18.11.15; Aldeburgh 19.11.15;
Trimley 23.11.15; Aldeburgh 27.11.15; Felixstowe
29.11.15; Aldeburgh 30.11.15; Felixstowe 3.12.15; CW
5.12.15 (FSL HGR Malet); Deleted 17.12.15

1132    Deld 2 Wing Eastchurch for erection 1.8.15; 4 Wing

Eastchurch 3.8.15; Tested 15.8.15; Felixstowe but badly
damaged landing 22.8.15 (FSL LP Openshaw unhurt);
AZP, EF, FL in dark 8.9.15 (F/Cdr RJJ Hope-Vere);
Aldeburgh 5.2.16; Felixstowe 10.2.16; Aldeburgh
13.2.16; Felixstowe 13.2.16; Trimley 2.16; Felixstowe
20.2.16; Aldeburgh 21.2.16; Levington Heath 22.2.16;
Felixstowe 1.3.16; Aldeburgh 4.3.16; Felixstowe
5.3.16; Aldeburgh 8.3.16; Felixstowe 9.3.16; Aldeburgh
16.3.16; Felixstowe 17.3.16; Sideslipped on turn and
wrecked 31.3.16 (FSL PSJ Owen unhurt); Deleted
2.5.16

1133    Deld Whitley Bay for erection 31.7.15; Tested 11.8.15;
Accepted 18.8.15; Chassis wiped off in landing 4.9.15
(FSL ER Moon); Repaired and tested 7.9.15; Crashed
19.9.15 (FSL DA Hay killed); Deleted 4.10.15
["1133" Beardmore WB.II (development of BE.2) from
Martlesham to Grain EAD 22.12.17 - @25.5.18]
(became F2995?)

1134    (80-hp Renault) Deld 1 Wing Eastchurch 1.8.15; 1
Wing St.Pol 2.8.15; Deleted 8.15 on transfer to Belgian
Government in exchange for Shorthorn which was also
given serial number 1134 (see below)

1135    Deld Redcar and tested 21.8.15 (Ding); AZP 8.9.15
(FSL PA Johnson); Scarborough 4.10.15; U/c badly
damaged on landing 4.10.15 (FSL TFN Gerrard);
Repaired 6.10.15; Redcar 13.10.15; Scarborough
26.11.15; Redcar 29.11.15; Scarborough 8.12.15;
Redcar 16.12.15; Scarborough 8.1.16; En route Redcar,
EF, FL, damaged Brompton, N.Yorks 11.1.16 (FSL HG
Ford); Deleted 3.2.16 DBR

1136    (70-hp Rolls-Royce). Deld Chingford for erection
18.8.15; Tested 23.8.15 (Ding); 4 Wing Eastchurch
1.9.15; Hendon 9.9.15 (repair); 1 Wing Dunkerque
21.9.15; 4 Wing loan to Westgate 23.9.15; Westgate (ex
loan from 4 Wing Eastchurch) 11.10.15; Manston
7.4.16; Deleted 3.10.16

1137    Deld Killingholme 3.9.15; Nosedived into Humber
7.11.15 (F/L JC Brooke & FSL AB Spencer saved);
Deleted 13.11.15

1138    Deld Killingholme 9.9.15; Accepted 18.9.15; Deleted
17.3.16

1139    Deld Killingholme 15.9.15; Awaiting acceptance
1.10.15; to Redcar but FL, smashed wings and u/c
Lackenby 27.2.16 (FSL NR Davenport); AZP, EF, FL,
smashed 1.4.16 (FSL BPH de Roeper); Deleted 14.4.16

1140    Deld Killingholme 20.9.15; Awaiting acceptance
1.10.15; Wrecked 14.11.15 (FSL GG Hodge); Deleted
20.11.15

1141    Deld Hendon and tested 16.12.15; Cranwell 29.2.16;
Fitted DC 4.16; Damaged landing 14.6.16; Deleted
5.7.16

1142    Deld Hendon and tested 16.12.15; AZP, u/c collapsed
landing in fog 31.1.16 (FSL FP Reeves); Cranwell
6.4.16; Eastchurch FS 29.7.16; Eastchurch Workshops
15.3.17 (overhaul); Cranwell 3.5.17; Manston NFS
23.3.18 (75-hp Rolls-Royce); Became 203 TDS Manston
1.4.18

1143    Deld ex York to Whitley Bay 23.10.15; Blackburn repair
27.10.15; Whitley Bay 20.12.15; Tested 24.12.15;
Redcar 26.12.15 (weather); Whitley Bay 10.1.16; Hit
hedge on TO, stalled, sideslipped, wrecked 25.4.16
(FSL AA Wallis & Writer Danskin unhurt); Deleted
23.5.16

1144    Deld Whitley Bay by 11.15; EF en route, FL in
rainstorm, o/t landing and CW Thirsk 4.11.15 (FSL AM
Waistell); Dismantled and by rail to makers 10.11.15;
Re-erecting 24.1.16; Scarborough, COL 28.1.16;
Hornsea 1.2.16; Scarborough 10.2.16; AZP 11.2.16;
Redcar 29.3.16; Scarborough 30.3.16; AZP 5.4.16
(S/Cdr C Draper); Damaged in gale at Hornsea 16.4.16;
Scarborough, AZP 2/3.5.16 (FSL JF Roche shaken);
AZP, COL 27/28.11.16 (FSL JF Roche); Redcar 5.2.17;
Deleted 4.5.17

1145    Deld Redcar 19.12.15; AZP 2.4.16 (FSL HC Vereker);
AZP, hit searchlight landing, crashed 2/3.5.16 (F/L
BPHde Roeper); Cranwell 24.5.17 (arr 25.5.17);
Crashed and damaged 18.7.17; Deleted 2.11.17

1146    Due for delivery to Barrow but not arrived by 2.11.15;
Grain 22.12.15 (expts); To Eastchurch but sideslipped,
wrecked 17.1.16 (FSL LAT Pritchard slightly injured &
Lt HHM Northcott killed); Deleted 18.1.16

## 2 MAURICE FARMAN S.11 SHORTHORN PUSHER BIPLANES received from Belgium in exchange for B.E.2Cs 1127 and 1134. (80-hp Renault)

1127 Belgian built, steel frame. Recd HQ Sqdn 1 Wing St.Pol 8.15; Dover 21.11.15; Deleted 16.8.16

1134 Recd HQ Sqdn 1 Wing St.Pol 8.15 - @30.11.15

## 24 ROYAL AIRCRAFT FACTORY B.E.2C TRACTOR BIPLANES ordered from The Grahame-White Aviation Co Ltd, numbered 1147 to 1170 & built Hendon. (70-hp Renault)

1147 Deld Hendon 4.7.15; Accepted 21.7.15; Chingford 12.8.15; Hendon 13.8.15; Yarmouth 15.8.15; AZP 8.9.15 (F/Cdr RJJ Hope-Vere); Holt 30.12.15; CW in gale 1.1.16; Yarmouth repair 2.1.16; Deleted 30.1.16

1148 Accepted 31.7.15, probably without test; Shipped to Gibraltar in SS *Nankin* 1.8.15; arr Gibraltar 6.8.15 - @12.15; Deleted 1916

1149 Shipped to Gibraltar in SS *Nankin* 1.8.15; Gibraltar by 31.8.15 - 12.15; Retd UK; Erecting Howden from 8.7.16

1150 Deld Hendon and accepted 18.8.15 (Marcus Manton); Yarmouth 25.8.15; Covehithe 29.10.15; Holt 14.11.15; Bacton 17.11.15; Yarmouth 18.11.15; Sedgeford 20.11.15; Holt 11.15; Bacton 30.11.15; Yarmouth 3.12.15; Bacton 17.12.15; Yarmouth 18.12.15; Bacton 18.1.16; Yarmouth 19.1.16; Holt 26.1.16; Bacton 27.1.16; AZP, FL, wings sheared off by tree tops, Starworth Park, Spixworth, nr Norwich 31.1.16 (F/L CE Wood shaken); Retd Yarmouth for repair; Deleted 9.3.16

1151 Deld Yarmouth 18.9.15 but en route FL near Stowmarket; Arrived by lorry Yarmouth 19.9.15; Sedgeford 11.11.15; Damaged when tent collapsed in gale Sedgeford 13.11.15; Yarmouth 15.11.15; Bacton 19.12.15; Yarmouth 22.12.15; AZP 31.1.16 (S/Cdr deCWP Ireland); Bacton 1.2.16; AZP 1.2.16 (FSL CHC Smith); Yarmouth 3.2.16; Bacton 2.16; Yarmouth 18.2.16; Sedgeford 20.2.16; Yarmouth 21.2.16; Bacton 16.3.16; AZP 20.3.16 (FSL CHC Smith); Yarmouth 28.3.16; Bacton 16.4.16; Yarmouth 29.4.16; Bacton 11.5.16; Damaged chassis landing during night flying 12.5.16; Retd Yarmouth; Holt 17.7.16; Yarmouth 19.7.16; Holt 20.7.16; Yarmouth 21.7.16; Chingford 1.9.16; Crashed 24.9.16; Cranwell 24.4.17 (repair); Broke u/c landing 25.6.17 (PFO HH Costain); Deleted W/E 5.9.17

1152 Deld Chingford 25.9.15; Deleted 24.4.16

1153 Deld Felixstowe 15.9.15; Badly damaged when EF, FL in sea just ahead of slipway 25.9.15 (F/L ER Moon); Aldeburgh 8.1.16; Felixstowe 10.1.16; EF, FL Thorpe le Soken 10.2.16 (F/L AW Clemson); Damaged landing 8.4.16 (F/L AW Clemson); Deleted 2.5.16

1154 Deld Chingford 29.9.15; Hendon 8.10.15 (night flying); Graham-White for repair 7.12.15; Deleted 9.16

1155 Deld Yarmouth 29.10.15; Sedgeford 14.11.15; Yarmouth 20.11.15; Fitting dart droppers 7.12.15; AZP, landed Bacton 31.1.16 (F/L V Nicholl); Yarmouth 1.2.16; AZP 14.3.16 (F/L CE Wood); Holt 1.4.16; Yarmouth 13.4.16; Sedgeford 14.4.16; Yarmouth, HACP 24.4.16, landed Sedgeford (FSL SR Watkins); Holt 9.5.16; Sedgeford 10.5.16; Yarmouth 11.5.16; Bacton 12.5.16; Holt 13.5.16; Sedgeford 19.5.16; Yarmouth 20.5.16; Holt 31.5.16; Sedgeford 1.6.16; Yarmouth 7.6.16; Holt 29.6.16; Bacton 30.6.16; Yarmouth 4.7.16; Bacton 20.7.16; AZP 3.8.16 (FSL AV Robinson); Yarmouth 4.8.16; Chingford 1.9.16; Crashed 24.9.16; Cranwell 13.4.17; Deleted 19.5.17

1156 Deld Westgate 3.11.15; Visited Dover but FL and damaged u/c and lower mainplanes 18.1.16 (FSL JS Browne & AM Wilkinson unhurt); HAPP 24.4.16 (FSL ES Boynton); 3 Wing Manston 14.5.16; Manston camp 27.9.16, then deleted

1157 Deld Westgate 27.10.15; Grain 30.10.15; Westgate 3.11.15; To NLG 1.3.16; HACP 18.3.16 (FSL JS Browne); HSPP 19.3.16 (FSL EE Deans & LM R Frater); Thrown against hangar wall in gale, and wrecked 25.3.16; Deleted 5.4.16

1158 Deld Westgate 3.11.15; HSPP 19/20.5.16 (FSL JS Browne & AM H Phipps); Deleted 3.10.16

1159 Deld Westgate 8.11.15; HACP 17.3.16 (FSL JS Browne & AM Sommerville); 2 HSPPs 19.3.16 (F/L HA Buss & AM Speck, later FSL EE Deans & AM H Phipps); Deleted 25.8.17

1160 Deld Yarmouth 8.11.15; Holt 14.11.15; Sedgeford 17.11.15; Yarmouth 20.11.15; Sedgeford 28.11.15; Yarmouth 3.12.15; Fitting dart droppers 1.1.16; Holt 27.1.16; To Yarmouth but FL in fog, wrecked on TO, Gresham, nr Cromer 29.1.16 (F/L FGD Hards slightly injured), to Yarmouth for repair; Bacton 23.4.16; AZP 25.4.16 (FSL BS Wemp); Yarmouth 26.4.16; Covehithe 27.4.16; Yarmouth 19.5.16; Holt 23.5.16; Yarmouth 26.5.16 (allocated Chingford 28.5.16); Holt 31.5.16; Yarmouth 1.6.16; Bacton 8.6.16; Yarmouth 14.6.16; Bacton 16.6.16; Yarmouth 17.6.16; Bacton 19.6.16; Holt 21.6.16; Chingford 1.9.16; CW 18.9.16; Deleted 3.10.16

1161 Deld and tested 20.11.15; Badly damaged by grenade explosion on ground 2.12.15; Tested after repair 23.1.16; Yarmouth 21.2.16; Bacton by 7.3.16; Yarmouth 9.3.16; Covehithe 14.3.16; AZP 14.3.16 (FSL S Kemball); Yarmouth 23.3.16; AZP 31.3.16 (FSL EL Pulling); Covehithe 1.4.16; AZP, FL 4.4.16 (FSL EL Pulling); Yarmouth for repair 8.4.16; Covehithe 14.4.16; Bacton 4.16; Yarmouth 18.4.16; AZP 25.4.16 (FSL S Kemball); Holt 12.5.16; Sedgeford 16.5.16; Holt 18.5.16; Yarmouth 19.5.16; Covehithe 21.5.16; Yarmouth 22.5.16; Eastbourne 18.6.16; Deleted 26.9.16

1162 Deld Chingford 22.11.15; Hendon 1.12.15 (night flying); Caught by gust of wind on TO, dived in, BO 11.12.15 (FSL S Kemball seriously injured & PFSL GGA Armitage DoI); Deleted 2.1.16

1163 Deld Experimental Flight Grain 19.12.15; Tested experimental bomb sight 26.12.15; Dropped new type converted Hales 20 lb bomb 8.1.16 & 20.1.16; Tested Ranken Dart trajectory 4-5.3.16; Tested poroscope 23.3.16; Kingsnorth 5.4.16; Experimental Flight Grain 14.5.16; Hythe 25.5.16; Experimental Flight Grain 26.5.16; Visited Kingsnorth 31.5.16, 3.7.16, 20.9.16 & 26.9.16 (bomb dropping trials); Became Gunnery Experimental Flight Grain 5.12.16; PVRS 20.1.17 (landing trials); Manston 22.4.17; Deleted 25.8.17

1164 Deld 4 Wing Eastchurch 19.12.15; Rochford 23.12.15; 4 Wing Eastchurch 31.12.15; Rochford 1.3.16; AZPs 1.4.16 (FSL GLE Stevens) & 2/3.4.16; Misc Flt Eastchurch 13.7.16; Became Spotting Flt Eastchurch 15.9.16; Eastchurch Workshops 7.12.16; Deleted 15.1.17

1165 Deld Chingford 21.12.15; Parachute fittings (RAF Museum photo); COL 10.4.16; Cranwell 13.4.17; Bounced and COL 16.10.17 (PFO G Cowdell); For deletion by 1.3.18

1166 Deld Yarmouth but EF, FL Aldeburgh 5.1.16; arr Yarmouth 6.1.16; Holt 30.3.16; Yarmouth 30.3.16; Left to bomb German High Seas Fleet off Scarborough, landed Bacton, hit telephone wires, CW 24/25.4.16 (FSL EL Pulling slightly hurt); Deleted 28.4.16

1167 Deld Yarmouth 17.1.16; AZPs 31.1.16 (S/Cdr deCWP Ireland), 20.3.16 (F/L BD Kilner) & 4.4.16 (F/L FGD Hards); Holt 14.4.16; Yarmouth 12.5.16; Bacton 16.5.16; Holt 19.5.16; Yarmouth 20.5.16; Sedgeford 20.5.16; Yarmouth 26.5.16; Eastbourne 17.6.16; Eastchurch Workshops 26.10.16; Eastchurch FS 31.10.16; Eastchurch Workshops 28.3.17; Cranwell 30.3.17; Deleted W/E 23.11.17

1168 Deld 4 Wing Eastchurch 22.1.16; Grain 5.2.16; War Flight Eastchurch 16.4.16; Eastchurch 28.4.16; Chingford 3.5.16; Cranwell 9.5.17; U/c damaged 27.7.17; Deleted W/E 16.11.17

1169 Deld Yarmouth 28.1.16; Sedgeford 9.2.16; Bacton 13.2.16; Yarmouth 14.2.16; Sedgeford 4.3.16; Yarmouth 18.3.16; AZP 4.4.16 (F/L CE Wood); Covehithe 8.4.16; Yarmouth 14.4.16; Bacton 16.4.16; Yarmouth, wrecked 25.4.16; Deleted 3.5.16

1170 Deld Trimley but blew over and damaged on landing 7.2.16 (FSL JJde laT Fox); Felixstowe 13.2.16 (repaired); HSPP 20.2.16; Supermarine repair 6.3.16; Chingford 1.7.16; FL N of Bishops Stortford 6.2.17 (FSL LFW Smith); Fell in reservoir 14.3.17; Cranwell 26.10.17; Became 201/2 TDS Cranwell 1.4.18

**12 WHITE & THOMPSON "BOGNOR BLOATER" TRACTOR BIPLANES, numbered 1171 to 1182 & built Bognor Regis. (70-hp Renault-Wolseley)**

1171    FF Bognor 8.3.15; Mkrs repair by 31.5.15; Tested 25.6.15; Deld 2 Sqdn Eastchurch (via Eastbourne) 25.6.15; Eastchurch FS 27.6.15; Wrecked 30.6.15; Deleted 9.7.15

1172    Deld 2 Sqdn Eastchurch 30.4.15; Eastchurch NFS 27.6.15; Dismantled 13.10.15; Surveyed and to CSD White City 22.11.15

1173    Tested from beach Bognor 22.4.15; Deld Eastbourne FS (via Eastchurch) 16.5.15; Dismantled 5.10.15; Deleted 10.12.15

1174    Deld Killingholme 11.5.15; Tested 15.5.15; Retd Mkrs; Killingholme and tested after alterations 4.6.15 (Gordon England); Chingford for erection 8.6.15; Dismantled as unfit 15.7.15; Deleted 20.7.15

1175    Tested from beach Bognor 5.5.15; Deld Eastbourne FS 15.6.15; Dismantled by 1.10.15; Deleted 10.12.15

1176    Deld Yarmouth by rail 26.6.15; Tested 2.7.15 (Gordon England); Damaged chassis landing 12.7.15 (FSL GW Hilliard & AM Williams); Engine removed 14.7.15; Repair 16.7.15; Deleted 28.7.15

1177    Deld Yarmouth by rail 12.8.15; Acceptance test 7.9.15, out of true (Gordon England); Killingholme, awaiting fresh acceptance 16.9.15 to 2.10.15; Yarmouth, awaiting acceptance 16.11.15; Accepted 19.12.15 (Pickles); CSD White City by rail 4.1.16 (arrived 10.1.16); To Survey Dept 17.1.16

1178    Deld Killingholme 16.9.15 but not accepted; retd Mkrs; CSD White City 14.2.16, later deleted

1179    Deld Grain by road 28.9.15 but not accepted; retd Mkrs 29.10.15 - 11.15; Kingsnorth by 1.16; Deleted 4.16

1180    Retained Mkrs as spares

1181    Accepted as spares only 9.15

1182    Accepted as spares only 9.15

**6 ROYAL AIRCRAFT FACTORY B.E.2C TRACTOR BIPLANES ordered from The Eastbourne Aviation Co Ltd, numbered 1183 to 1188 & built Eastbourne (70-hp Renault)**

1183    Deld and accepted Eastbourne FS 30.7.15; Smashed 22.11.15 (FSL WG McMinnies); U/c carried away 19.3.16; HD duties at Eastbourne 4.16; Crashed Ewell, Surrey 17.7.16; Hendon by road 18.7.16; CSD White City 19.7.16; Deleted 1916

1184    Deld and tested Eastbourne FS 20.8.15; FL nr Canterbury, Kent 6.9.15 (FSL HK Thorold); Mkrs repair 16.9.15; FL nr aerodrome 15.10.15 (FSL N Keeble); Wrecked during night flying 24.11.15 (FSL N Keeble & Lt FE Hast); Mkrs repair 11.15; Upavon 12.12.15; Eastbourne FS 18.12.15; Crashed, CW, Burwash, Sussex 6.3.16 (FSL JD Scott); Deleted 30.3.16

1185    Deld Eastbourne 10.9.15; 5 Wing Dover 15.9.15; Eastchurch 5.1.16; Dover (via Brooklands) 8.2.16; ADD 24.5.16; 7 Flt B Sqdn 5 Wing 26.5.16 - @11.6.16; DBR Dunkerque; Deleted ADD 15.6.16

1186    Deld Eastbourne and tested 20.9.15 (Fowler); 5 Wing Dover 28.9.15; Wrecked 30.12.15 (FSL AS Todd); Deleted 16.1.16

1187    Deld Eastbourne FS 6.10.15; Deleted 13.3.16

1188    Deld Eastbourne FS 15.11.15; 5 Wing Dover (via Westgate) 18.11.15; Westgate 20.11.15; HSPP 19.3.16 (F/L FML Barr & LM R Frater); HACP 24.4.16 (FSL CW Greig & LM R Frater); 3 Wing Manston 14.5.16; Eastchurch 4.7.16; Deleted 25.8.17

**6 ROYAL AIRCRAFT FACTORY B.E.2C TRACTOR BIPLANES ordered from Hewlett & Blondeau Ltd, numbered 1189 to 1194 & built Clapham. (75-hp Renault)**

1189    Deld Chingford and tested 5.10.15 (Raynham); Rochford 13.12.15 (night flying); Eastchurch 14.1.16; Rochford 31?.1.16; Attacked Zeppelin, landed Thameshaven marshes 31.1.16 (FSL JE Morgan); Retd next day; 4 Wing Eastchurch 28.2.16; HSPP 19.3.16 (FSL EP Hicks); AZP 31.3.16 (FSL EP Hicks); Rochford repairs 1.4.16; 4 Wing Eastchurch 3.4.16; Rochford 4.4.16; 4

Wing Eastchurch 6.4.16; War Flight Eastchurch 16.4.16; Rochford 24.4.16; War Flight Eastchurch 4.6.16; Detling 5.6.16; Misc Flight Eastchurch 13.7.16; Spotting Flight Eastchurch 18.9.16; Crashed 1.11.16; Deleted 8.11.16

1190    Deld Chingford for erection 29.9.15; Tested 30.9.15 (Raynham); Wrecked 2.4.16 (PFSL KC Buss); FL rough ground, smashed u/c 29.5.16 (pilot unhurt); Deleted 28.7.16

1191    Deld Hendon 22.10.15; Badly damaged in grenade explosion 2.12.15; Cranwell 29.2.16; Hendon 11.6.16; Eastchurch School Flight 14.6.16 (painted blue); Eastchurch Workshops overhaul 19.1.17; Eastchurch FS 4.3.17; Cranwell but FL en route at Cambridge 25.3.17; Arr Cranwell 30.3.17; Became 202 TDS Cranwell 1.4.18; Propeller accident 11.4.18 (AC2 TS Frazer slightly injured)

1192    Deld Hendon 22.10.15; COL 3.11.15 (FSL S Kemball); Grahame-White repair 12.11.15; Hendon 19.7.16; FL, lost wheel on TO, damaged landing 30.7.16 (F/L PA Johnston & FSL KR Munro); Ranken incendiary bomb expts 1.3.17 (F/Cdr TD Hallam DSC); COL 13.3.17 (FSL RB Freeland); Deleted 23.3.17

1193    Deld Chingford Defence Flt 26.10.15; Tested 2.11.15 (Raynham); Sideslipped, nosedived, CW 19.6.16 (PFSL C Huddy); Deleted 29.6.16

1194    Deld Chingford Defence Flt 28.10.15; Tested 2.11.15 (Raynham); Hendon 6.11.15 (for night flying); Badly damaged in grenade explosion 2.12.15; Yarmouth 21.2.16; Bacton 1.3.16; Covehithe 4.3.16; Yarmouth 14.3.16; Bacton 28.3.16; Yarmouth 29.3.16; Bacton 30.3.16; AZP 31.3.16 (FSL FP Reeves); Yarmouth 16.4.16; Bacton 24.4.16; AZP 24/25.4.16 (FSL FP Reeves); Yarmouth 11.5.16; Bacton 12.5.16; Damaged landing Bacton 16.5.16 (PFSL BS Wemp); retd Yarmouth; FL on marshes between Acle and Yarmouth 10.8.16 (FSL CHM Chapman); Deleted 15.8.16

**6 WHITE & THOMPSON No.3 TRACTOR BIPLANE FLYING BOATS ordered under Cont No C.P.60401/14, numbered 1195 to 1200 & built Bognor Regis. (120-hp Austro-Daimler/Beardmore)**

1195    Fitted Lewis gun on port side of cockpit and modified bracing; Deld 1 Sqdn Dover 7.2.15 (Gordon England); Wrecked 15.2.15; Mkrs repair by 11.3.15; Fitted Type 2A hull during repairs; Dover 12.6.15; EF on TO, FL, damaged tailplane strut 29.6.15 (FSL CN Leeston Smith); EF, FL in rough sea, badly damaged, for survey 2.7.15 (PFSL TV Lister & PO Boyd); Test after repair 31.7.15; HMS *Riviera* 16.9.15; Dunkerque 16.9.15; Dover 8.10.15; Calshot FS 8.10.15; Deleted W/E 11.7.18

1196    Deld Fort George by 28.2.15; Ready for test 6.3.15; Ready for examination by Admiralty Overseer 30.3.15; New hull fitted by mid 5.15; Dundee 12.11.15 (erecting); Deleted 7.1.16

1197    Deld 1 Sqdn Dover, bows slightly damaged on arrival 8.2.15 (F/L ER Whitehouse); Propeller damaged in ground engine test 11.2.15; Remained Dover when 1 Sqdn to France 22.2.15; Defence Flt Dover by 3.15; HSPP 20.3.15 (F/Cdr SDA Grey); Damaged landing 11.4.15; Dismantled 5.15 and fitted new hull; Tested 30.7.15; AZP 19.8.15 (FSL TV Lister & LM McSorley); HMS *Riviera* 16.9.15; Dunkerque 16.9.15; Dover 4.11.15; Bembridge 6.11.15; Deleted 24.10.16

1198    COL 27.2.15; Allocated Fort George by 11.3.15 (NTU); Still Bognor 31.8.15; probably fitted new hull; Deld Dover 14.9.15; Calshot 17.12.15; Deleted 24.10.16

1199    Deld 1 Sqdn Dover 11.2.15; 1 Sqdn France 14.2.15; Hit by AA over Flanders, FL in Wester Schelde, Vlissigen, Zeeland 17.2.15 (F/L DG Murray interned); To Dutch Navy as *G1*; Crashed 17.7.16; At Schellingwoude by 21.8.17; At De Mok by 4.9.17 - @1.11.17

1200    Deld Fort George for erection 27.3.15; Tested after erection 15.4.15; EF, FL Balintore 23.4.15 (FSL FW Gamwell); FL, crashed off Chanonry Point 1.5.15 (FSL FW Gamwell); Remains to Bognor; Deleted 5.15

*Sopwith Tabloid 1205 with 3 Wing Tenedos.
(R.F.Collins)*

*Sopwith "Gordon Bennett" Racer 1215.*

*Bristol T.B.8 1216 at Eastchurch, March 1915. (via J.D.Oughton)*

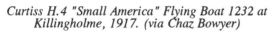

*Curtiss H.4 "Small America" Flying Boat 1232 at
Killingholme, 1917. (via Chaz Bowyer)*

*Maurice Farman Shorthorn 1241. (FAA Museum)*

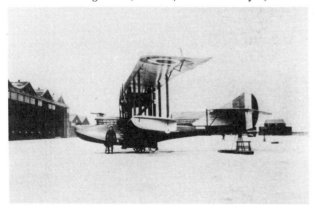

**12 SOPWITH S.S.2 TABLOID TRACTOR BIPLANE SCOUTS ordered under Cont No C.P.58295/14, numbered 1201 to 1212 & built Kingston. (80-hp Gnome)**

| | |
|---|---|
| 1201 | Tested Brooklands 21.12.14 then packed; HMS *Ark Royal* at Blythe for Dardanelles 9.1.15 (intended to fly off forecastle, but never used as such); still HMS *Ark Royal* 31.11.15 (no flying, probably retd UK in crates); Deleted 1916 |
| 1202 | Tested Brooklands 12.14 then packed; HMS *Ark Royal* at Blythe for Dardanelles 3.1.15 (intended to fly off forecastle, but never used as such); still HMS *Ark Royal* 12.15 (no flying, probably retd UK in crates) [BUT reported flown Imbros]; transit to UK 1.16; Deleted 1916 |
| 1203 | Tested Brooklands 12.14; HMS *Ark Royal* at Chatham for Dardanelles 26.1.15 (intended to fly off forecastle, but never used as such); still HMS *Ark Royal* 12.15 (no flying, probably retd UK in crates); Deleted 1916 |
| 1204 | Tested Brooklands 29.12.14; HMS *Ark Royal* at Chatham for Dardanelles 26.1.15 (intended to fly off forecastle, but never used as such); still HMS *Ark Royal* 12.15 (no flying, probably retd UK in crates); Deleted 1916 |
| 1205 | Tested to 3,200 ft in 5 min; Deld 1 Sqdn by 1.1.15 (temp to Dunkerque?); Dover by 28.2.15; Shipped from Plymouth in SS *Inkosi* or SS *Moorgate* 19 or 20.3.15; 3 Sqdn Tenedos 3.15; Tested 9.5.15; Became 3 Wing Tenedos 21.6.15; Retd UK in SS *Liverpool* by 1.10.15, then deleted |
| 1206 | Tested to 3,200 ft in 6 min; Deld 1 Sqdn by 1.1.15 (temp to Dunkerque?); Dover by 28.2.15; Shipped from Plymouth in SS *Inkosi* or SS *Moorgate* 19 or 20.3.15; 3 Sqdn Tenedos 3.15; Became 3 Wing Tenedos 21.6.15; Retd UK in SS *Liverpool* 10.15, then deleted |
| 1207 | Deld Yarmouth by rail 16.3.15; Sopwith 24.3.15 (repair ailerons); Tested but o/t landing 8.4.15 (Hawker); Sopwith 12.4.15 (repair); Yarmouth for erection 27.4.15; Accepted 2.5.15 (Hawker); EF, FL en route Bacton 15.9.15 (FSL E Cadbury); Engine trouble, FL Haisboro 24.3.16 (FSL EB Thompson); Deleted 17.4.16 |
| 1208 | Deld Yarmouth by rail 16.3.15; Sopwith 24.3.15 (repair ailerons); Yarmouth 7.4.15; Accepted 9.4.15 (Hawker); Buckled wheel landing and o/t 21.6.15 (S/Cdr deCWP Ireland unhurt); Bacton 16.9.15; Yarmouth 27.10.15; EF, FL Gorleston 18.1.16 (S/L GWR Fane); Deleted 17.3.16 |
| 1209 | Deld 2 Sqdn Eastchurch 3.15; HSPP 23.5.15 (F/L S Pickles) [4 Sqdn!]; 2 Sqdn dett Rochford 3-4.6.15, 4-5.6.15, 7-11.6.15, ?-18.6.15; HSMPs 7.6.15 (F/L AF Bettington); HACP, EF, FL 9.6.15 (F/L AF Bettington); Became 2 Wing Eastchurch 21.6.15; St.Pol 1.8.15; Shipped to Dardanelles from Dover in SS *Nankin* 5.8.15; 3 Wing Imbros by 31.10.15; Retd UK 12.15; Deleted Dover 20.12.15 and to CSD White City |
| 1210 | Deld 2 Sqdn Eastchurch 3.15; AZPs 26/27.5.15 (crew?) & 1.6.15 (F/L S Pickles); Became 2 Wing Eastchurch 21.6.15; 4 Wing Eastchurch 3.8.15; Wrecked Westgate 9.8.15; Eastchurch NFS 7.10.15; Damaged 23.10.15; 4 Wing Eastchurch 10.3.16; War Flt Eastchurch 16.4.16; Misc Flt Eastchurch 12.5.16; Bomb Flt Eastchurch 16.5.16; Misc Flt Eastchurch 23.5.16; Bomb Flt Eastchurch 6.6.16; Misc Flt Eastchurch 23.6.16; Deleted 1.7.16 |
| 1211 | Deld 2 Sqdn Eastchurch 3.15; Became 2 Wing Eastchurch 21.6.15; 4 Wing Eastchurch 3.8.15; Deleted 31.10.15 |
| 1212 | Deld 2 Sqdn Eastchurch 3.15; 2 Sqdn dett Westgate (Defence Flt) 14.5.15; HSPP 23.5.15; AZPs 31.5.15 (F/Cdr AF Bettington); Damaged Westgate 3.6.15; [listed as on dett at Rochford by 30.6.15]; Became 2 Wing dett Westgate 21.6.15; 4 Wing dett Westgate 3.8.15; AZP, tried to intercept *L12* but crashed and o/t in night landing 10.8.15 (FSL R Lord killed); Deleted 21.8.15 |

**1 SOPWITH "TABLOID R" [TABLOID RACER?] SCOUT TRACTOR BIPLANE ordered under Cont No C.P.60619/14, numbered 1213 & built Kingston. (80-hp Gnome) [Possibly 80-hp Le Rhône at first]**

| | |
|---|---|
| 1213 | Deld Hendon for "Fast Flight" 10.11.14; 80-hp Gnome by 11.3.15; 1 Sqdn St.Pol 6.5.15; 5 Wing Dover by 5.15; C Sqdn by 20.6.15; 1 Sqdn St.Pol 30.6.15 - @9.15; Deleted 1915 |

**2 SOPWITH GORDON BENNETT RACER TRACTOR BIPLANES ordered under Cont No C.P.60619/14, numbered 1214 and 1215 & built Kingston. (80-hp Gnome)**

| | |
|---|---|
| 1214 | Deld Hendon for "Fast Flt" 19.10.14; Dover by road 4.4.15; 1 Sqdn St.Pol 24.4.15; Became 1 Wing St.Pol 21.6.15; C Flt by 20.6.15; Fitted with deflector plates for Lewis gun; probably remained Dunkerque 8.15; still 1 Wing St.Pol 9.15; 5 Wing Dover by 11.9.15; Deleted 3.16 |
| 1215 | Deld Hendon for "Fast Flt" 25.11.14; Chingford 9.6.15 - @23.7.15; Rigging out of true; Deleted 7.15 |

**12 BRISTOL T.B.8 TRACTOR BIPLANES numbered 1216 to 1227 & built under Cont Nos C.P.63528 & C.P.73046/14 at Filton. Transferred from RFC (Military Wing), Farnborough order 691 to 702 (c/n's 331 to 342) and renumbered out of sequence. (80-hp Gnome)**

| | |
|---|---|
| 1216 | Deld Farnborough 18.11.14; C Flt 1 Sqdn to Newcastle (Elswick) by rail 21.11.14; 1 Sqdn Gosport (Grange Field) 12.14; A Flt 1 Sqdn to Dover 29.12.14, but EF, FL Lewes (arr Dover 2.1.15, via Hastings); Slightly damaged 1.2.15; 1 Sqdn St.Pol 24.2.15 - @14.3.15; attd 2 Sqdn Eastchurch 16.4.15; Grain Island RD 4.15; Tested after repair 6.5.15; 4 Sqdn Dover 14.5.15; Westgate 8.6.15; 4 Sqdn Dover 9.6.15; HACP 1.8.15 (FSL JED Boyd & AM Sanders); 5 Wing Dover 3.8.15; SCAW repair 21.9.15; Eastbourne 28.6.16 - @13.4.17; Deleted by 30.4.17 |
| 1217 | Deld Farnborough 18.11.14; C Flt 1 Sqdn Newcastle (Elswick) by rail 20.11.14 (arr 21.11.14); Fitted lights 6.1.15; Whitley Bay 24.1.15; Elswick 29.1.15; Whitley Bay 6.3.15; Slightly damaged taxying Gosforth 10.3.15; retd Whitley Bay 12.3.15; AZP, chased *L9* without success 14.4.15 (FSL P Legh & LM HJL Hinkler); Montrose 28.4.15; Barry 23.5.15; Fitted Armstrong Whitworth wings from 1227 21.6.15; Dismantled Montrose 1.8.15; Redcar 4.8.15; Hornsea (Atwick) 8.8.15; AZP, smashed on TO 9.8.15 (F/Cdr C Draper & FSL AS Goodwin); Scarborough 13.10.15; Hornsea 30.10.15; Deleted 30.11.15 |
| 1218 | Deld 1 Sqdn Gosport (Grange Field) by 3.12.14; 2 Sqdn Eastchurch 20.12.14; Lost returning from Shoreham, FL nr Stelling Maris, 2m SW of Canterbury 2.2.15 (FSL FG Andreae); Blown into wood in gale, crashed and wrecked 2m SW of Canterbury 2.2.15, retd by breakdown party 3.2.15; Dover 20.3.15; 2 Sqdn Eastchurch 26.3.15; Visited Kingsnorth 8.6.15; Rochford 9.6.15; 2 Sqdn Eastchurch 12.6.15; Visited Kingsnorth 15.6.15; Grenade dropping expts 16.6.15; Rochford 18.6.15; 2 Sqdn Eastchurch 19.6.15; Eastchurch NFS 27.6.15; Crashed 29.7.15; Wrecked 9.8.15; Damaged 20.8.15; Wrecked 2.9.15; Repairs to at least 1.16; Damaged 10.2.16; Eastbourne 25.2.16; Deleted 19.4.16 |
| 1219 | Deld Farnborough to 1 Sqdn Gosport (Grange Field) 21.10.14; Slewed, hit tree top on TO with bombs, CW 14.12.14 (F/L GM Dyott & WO2 FW Scarff); Deleted 12.14 |
| 1220 | Deld 2 Sqdn Eastchurch 5.11.14; To Dunkerque but shot down in sea en route 5.11.14 (F/L CF Beevor & S/L The Earl of Annesley RNVR both killed) |
| 1221 | (Ex 700). Deld 2 Sqdn Eastchurch 31.10.14; Dunkerque 5.11.14; Blown over in gale, badly damaged 28.12.14; Last flown 23.1.15; Left behind dismantled at Dunkerque 2.15 - @11.3.15; Deleted circa 3.15 |
| 1222 | (Ex 701). Deld 2 Sqdn Eastchurch but EF en route, FL Croydon 31.10.14; EF, FL Kenley 2.11.14; Arr Eastchurch 3.11.14; COL Calais en route Dunkerque 10.11.14; Repaired and on to Dunkerque to at least 26.12.14; 1 Sqdn St.Pol 2.15 - @11.3.15; Eastbourne by 31.3.15; Deleted 4.15 |
| 1223 | (C/n 342). Modified tail; Deld & tested 2 Sqdn Eastchurch 5.11.14; 2 Sqdn Defence Flt Dover |

24.12.14; 2 Sqdn Eastchurch 2.1.15; detd 2 Sqdn Dover 10.2.15 for raids on Zeebrugge and Ostende; 2 Sqdn Eastchurch by 12.3.15; 2 Sqdn Defence Flt Dover 20.3.15; 2 Sqdn Eastchurch 26.3.15; Visited Rochford 31.5.15; AZP 5.6.15 (F/L F Benson); Eastchurch FS 19.6.15; Wrecked 4.7.15; Wrecked Headcorn 19.7.15; Deleted 2.8.15

1224     (C/n 340). Deld and tested 2 Sqdn Eastchurch 5.11.14; 2 Sqdn Defence Flt Dover 24.12.14; HSPPs 24.12.14 (F/L HA Buss & AM Makin) & 25.12.14 (F/L HA Buss & AM Andrews); 2 Sqdn Eastchurch 2.1.15; detd 2 Sqdn Dover 10.2.15 for raids on Zeebrugge and Ostende; 2 Sqdn Defence Flt Dover 20.3.15; Eastbourne FS 26.3.15 (First aircraft at Eastbourne); Crashed 8.6.15 (repaired); With B Flt to Ringmer 17.9.15; Eastbourne 23.9.15; EF landing, o/t, CW 30.3.16 (FSL HP Watson); Deleted 17.4.16

1225     (C/n 341). Deld Eastchurch 11.14; Tested 5.11.14 and issued to 2 Sqdn Eastchurch; detd 2 Sqdn Dover 10.2.15 for raids on Zeebrugge and Ostende; 2 Sqdn Defence Flt Dover 20.3.15; 2 Sqdn Eastchurch 27.3.15; Smashed 4.4.15; Deleted 4.15

1226     Deld C Flt 1 Sqdn Farnborough 18.11.14; C Flt 1 Sqdn Newcastle (Elswick) 23.11.14; C Flt 1 Sqdn Whitley Bay 18.12.14; Became separate unit at Whitley Bay 1.15; Caught by gust landing, slightly damaged 28.3.15 (FSL KS Savory); HSMP 13.4.15 (FSL KS Savory & LM Gibson); Dundee 14.4.15; Barry 16.4.15; Montrose 17.4.15; Left for Barry but EF, FL, o/t, damaged 1m W of Montrose 20.4.15 (FSL CS Iron); Retd Montrose for repair; Crashed and badly damaged 22.5.15; Badly damaged 24.6.15; Supermarines by road 25.6.15 (repair); Hendon for test 9.10.15; Very badly damaged in grenade explosion on ground 2.12.15; Chingford 12.1.16; Taxied into by Avro 8592, rudder damaged 26.1.16; Badly smashed and CW Edmonton 19.5.16 (FSL MWH Evans unhurt); Deleted 5.6.16

1227     Deld C Flt 1 Sqdn Farnborough 18.11.14; C Flt 1 Sqdn Newcastle (Elswick) by rail 20.11.14 (arr 23.11.14); Armstrong Whitworth Gosforth 29.1.15 (engine trouble); Whitley Bay 4.2.15; Fitting lights 22.2.15; Armstrong Whitworth Gosforth 5.3.15 (fit special wings); Whitley Bay 21.5.15; HSMP 23.5.15 (FSL P Legh & LM HJL Hinkler); Right longeron collapsed landing, m/c wrecked 1.6.15 (FSL P Legh & AM Taylor); Deleted 21.6.15 (wings to Montrose for 1217)

## 8 CURTISS H.4 'SMALL AMERICA' FLYING BOAT ordered 23.12.14 under Cont No C.P.65070/14 from Aircraft Manufacturing Co Ltd & numbered 1228 to 1235. (Two 90-hp Curtiss OX-5 to 1230, then two 100-hp Anzani)

1228     Deld Felixstowe 20.6.15; Tested 3.7.15 & 6.7.15; Accepted 18.7.15; Awaiting wing extensions 31.8.15; Two 100-hp Anzani fitted 11.15; Deleted 28.1.16 FW&T

1229     Deld Felixstowe 19.7.15; Erected but not tested by 31.8.15; Two 100-hp Anzani fitted 9.15 - 1.16; Deleted 2.5.16

1230     Deld Felixstowe 31.10.15; Fitted two 100-hp Anzani 11.15; Hull shape experiments 1.16; Tested 10.1.16 (F/L RJJ Hope-Vere & F/L AQ Cooper); Lost in English Channel off North East Stit 1.3.16; Towed to Sheerness 12.3.16; Grain 15.3.16; Felixstowe 27.3.16; Deleted 2.5.16

1231     Erected Felixstowe 18.7.16; Tested with modified hull of Saunders, Porte design; Deleted 3.10.16

1232     Deld Killingholme School 1.8.16; Deleted W/E 20.4.18

1233     Deld Killingholme School 12.8.16; Deleted W/E 20.4.18

1234     Deld Killingholme for erection 9.10.16; Crashed 23.7.17; Deleted 22.8.17

1235     Deld Killingholme Seaplane School for erection 15.1.17; Deleted W/E 12.9.18

## 4 CURTISS H.4 "SMALL AMERICA" TRACTOR BIPLANE FLYING BOATS built by Curtiss Aeroplane & Motor Co Inc at Hammondsport, New York & numbered 1236 to 1239. (Two 90 or 100-hp Curtiss)

1236     (90-hp Curtiss) Deld Felixstowe for erection 17.1.15; Tested 16.2.15; (Re-?)erecting 16.4.15; Tested 6.5.15;

Dismantling for shipment 31.5.15; In transit by 20.6.15; Gibraltar 6.15 - @30.11.15 (Mediterranean patrols); Deleted 1915 or 1916

1237     (90-hp Curtiss) Deld Felixstowe for erection 24.2.15; Erection completed 29.4.15; Tested 5.15; Dismantled for shipment 25.5.15; In transit by 20.6.15; Gibraltar 6.15 - @30.11.15 (Mediterranean patrols); Deleted 2.16

1238     (100-hp Curtiss, later two 150-hp Sunbeam). Deld Felixstowe for erection by 11.3.15; Airco by 30.6.15; Felixstowe 18.9.15; Fitting 125hp Anzani from 31.1.16; Deleted 3.7.16

1239     (100-hp Curtiss) Deld Felixstowe for erection 18.3.15; Still erecting 29.6.15; Two 160-hp Anzani fitted 9.15 - 10.15; Bottom damaged by 20.12.15 (repaired); Re-erecting from 31.3.16; Deleted 2.5.16

## 2 MAURICE FARMAN PUSHER BIPLANES ordered under Cont No C.P.62662/14 from Aéroplanes Farman, Paris & numbered 1240 and 1241.

[1.17 official list says both with 100 Canton-Unné]

1240     (100-hp Renault). Deld Dunkerque 25.11.14; FTR from raid on submarine sheds at Bruges, engine believed damaged by shell fire, FL near Breskens, Zeeland 17.12.14 (F/L TA Rainey interned); Aircraft interned and dismantled by Dutch; Deleted 1.15

1241     (135-hp Canton-Unné). Deld Dunkerque 27.11.14; 3 Sqdn St.Pol by 15.12.14; First ever night bombing raid, on Ostende 21.12.14 (Cdr CR Samson & F/L WH Wilson); Damaged in attacks on Ostende 10.1.15 (Lt CH Collet DSO & F/L WH Wilson); Damaged in attack on submarines at Zeebrugge 23.1.15 (S/Cdr R Bell-Davies wounded); Dunkerque to Calais 26.2.15; Dover 1.3.15; Shipped to Dardanelles from Plymouth in SS *Inkosi* or SS *Moorgate* 19 or 20.3.15 (remained with Samson's squadron); 3 Sqdn Tenedos (No.2 aerodrome) 3.15; Became 3 Wing Tenedos 21.6.15; Still awaiting wings 27.6.15; Deleted 8.15

## 1 MORANE-SAULNIER TYPE G TRACTOR MONOPLANE ordered under Cont No C.P.63082/14 from The Graham-White Aviation Co Ltd as their Type XIV, numbered 1242 & built Hendon. (80-hp Gnome)

1242     Deld Eastchurch by 12.14; Hendon by 28.2.15; To Grain Repair Station by 5.15 (ex Hendon); Deleted 12.15

## 24 BRISTOL SCOUT TYPE C TRACTOR BIPLANES ordered under Cont No C.P.67209/14/X from The British & Colonial Aeroplane Co Ltd, numbered 1243 to 1266 & built Brislington. (80-hp Gnome)

1243     (C/n 450). Inspected Bristol 1.2.15 (F/L HR Busteed); Deld Grain for erection 16.2.15; Tested 21.2.15; Tested after repairs to u/c 1.5.15; AZPs 17.5.15, 5.6.15 & 9.8.15 (both FSL WG Moore); Still Grain 31.8.15; Grenade and flechette experiments 22.9.15; Ranken Dart dropping tests 28.9.15, 5.10.15 & 14.10.15; Refabricated, ready 12.3.16; Deleted 17.1.17

1244     (C/n 463). Deld 2 Sqdn Eastchurch for erection 5.6.15; EF, FL on grenade dropping expts, o/t by wind, damaged 14.6.15 (W/Cdr EL Gerrard); Became 2 Wing Eastchurch 21.6.15; attd Eastchurch NFS 28.7.15 (2 Wing aircraft); Wrecked 29.8.15; Deleted 1.9.15

1245     (C/n 464). Deld 2 Sqdn Eastchurch for erection 7.6.15; Became 2 Wing Eastchurch 21.6.15; Fire balloon expts Leysdown 2.7.15; Grain to 2 Wing Eastchurch 5.7.15; Visited Rochford 5-6.7.15; 4 Wing Eastchurch 3.8.15; 5 Wing Dover 15.8.15; Crashed 23.8.15; SCAW repair by 21.9.15; War Flt Eastchurch 29.6.16; Manston 30.6.16 (Prodger); 3 Wing Manston but CW when lost control in loop at 1,500ft, sideslipped and went into spinning nose dive 20.7.16 (FSL DH Whittier killed); Deleted 21.7.16

1246     (C/n 465). (Fitted overwing Lewis gun at Eastchurch) Deld 2 Sqdn Eastchurch for erection 14.6.15; 1 Wing St.Pol 20.6.15; 2 Wing Dover 13.8.15; 5 Wing Dover 15.8.15; 4 Wing Eastchurch 21.9.15; Eastchurch NFS 7.10.15; Tested tail guide trestle strop 7.10.15 (F/Cdr BF Fowler); Damaged 31.10.15; Damaged 5.1.16; 4

*Bristol Scout C 1258. (via J.Bagley)*

*Pemberton Billing P.B.9 (later 1267). (via J.D.Oughton)*

*Perry Biplane at Brooklands, 1914 (later 1322). (via Philip Jarrett)*

Wing Westgate 30.3.16 (temp loan); War Flt Eastchurch 15.5.16; Eastchurch Workshops, after crashed 23.9.16; Deleted 25.10.16

1247   (C/n 466). Deld 2 Sqdn Eastchurch for erection 20.6.15; Became 2 Wing Eastchurch 21.6.15; 1 Wing St.Pol 2.7.15; Transferred to French Govt for evaluation 6.15 (sic); Retd Paris to Mkrs 10.16 (overhaul and repair); Chingford by lorry 11.12.16; Cranwell 28.3.17; Wrecked 30.4.17 (TPFO HE Grundy DoI 1.5.17); Crashed, u/c damaged 17.12.17 (pilot unhurt); Crashed Brauncewell 2.4.18 (pilot unhurt)

1248   (C/n 467). Deld 2 Wing Eastchurch for erection 21.6.15; Accepted 25.6.15 (Raynham); Grain 1.7.15; FL and damaged near Rochford 22.7.15 (FSL ON Walmesley unhurt); Grain Island RD 4.8.15; Grain, tested after repair 2.12.15; HSPPs 20.2.16 (F/L ON Walmesley) also 18 & 19.3.16 (both F/L P Legh); Cranwell (vis Chingford) 30.7.16 (arr 31.7.16); Deleted 1.10.16

1249   (C/n 468). Deld 2 Wing Eastchurch 21.6.15; Accepted 25.6.15. (Raynham); 2 Wing St.Pol 4.8.15; 2 Wing Dover 13.8.15; 5 Wing Dover 15.8.15; Damaged wings 11.9.15 (FSL SB Joyce); SCAW repair 21.9.15; Dover 26.4.16; FL, damaged 26.12.16 (FSL HF Beamish unhurt); Deleted W/E 6.8.17

1250   (C/n 469). Deld 2 Wing Eastchurch for erection 24.6.15; Accepted 25.6.15 (Raynham); Yarmouth 3.7.15; Hornsea 19.9.15; Redcar 22.9.15; Tested 19.10.15; Cranwell 26.4.17; Became 201/2 TDS Cranwell 1.4.18

1251   (C/n 470). Deld 2 Wing Eastchurch 24.6.15; Yarmouth 19.7.15; Hornsea 22.9.15; Scarborough 27.1.16; Hornsea 1.2.16; CW when Bessonneau tent blown away in gale 16.2.16; Deleted 13.3.16

1252   (C/n 471). Deld 2 Wing Eastchurch 26.6.15; Accepted 11.7.15 (Raynham); Yarmouth 15.7.15; HACPs 23.4.16 (F/L CE Wood); AZP 25.4.16 (F/L CE Wood later FSL E Cadbury); HACPs 26.5.16, 28.5.16, 2.7.16 & 22.7.16 (all F/L CE Wood); EF, FL on beach, damaged 22.12.16 (FSL S Kemball); Repair 2.17; Burgh Castle 5.4.17; HACP 17.4.17 (F/L FW Walker); Covehithe 21.4.17; HSPP 11.5.17 (F/L GH Simpson); Burgh Castle 12.5.17; CW 24.5.17; retd Yarmouth 24.5.17; Deleted 2.6.17

1253   (C/n 472). Deld 2 Wing Eastchurch for erection 28.6.15; Accepted 11.7.15 (Raynham); Yarmouth 12.7.15; Fitted grenade gear early 8.15; HACPs 31.3.16 (F/L CE Wood), 21.5.16 (F/L CHC Smith), 26.5.16 (F/L BD Kilner), 28.5.16 (F/L CHC Smith) & 31.7.16 (F/L CHC Smith); Bacton 23.11.16; O/t landing crosswind on rough ground Bacton 26.11.16 (FSL EL Pulling); retd Yarmouth; Deleted 2.2.17

1254   (C/n 473). Deld 2 Wing Eastchurch 1.7.15; Accepted 11.7.15 (Raynham); 2 Wing St.Pol 10.8.15; 2 Wing Dover 13.8.15; 5 Wing Dover 15.8.15; AZP 14.9.15 (FSL RFS Leslie); HACPs 8.1.16 (FSL FG Andreae), 15.1.16 (F/L BL Huskisson), 8.2.16 (FSL JF Potts later F/L CE Wood), 9.2.16 (F/L FG Andreae, 24.4.16 (FSL CD Booker) & 23.10.16; Deleted W/E 6.8.17

1255   (C/n 474). Deld 2 Wing Eastchurch for erection 2.7.15; Accepted 11.7.15 (Raynham); 2 Wing St.Pol 5.8.15; 2 Wing Dover 13.8.15; 5 Wing Dover 15.8.15; 4 Wing Eastchurch 21.9.15; Eastchurch NFS 7.10.15; Grain 3.11.15 (F/Cdr BF Fowler); HMS *Vindex*, first landplane launching from deck of a naval vessel specifically equipped for the purpose, in the vicinity of Mouse LV 3.11.15; Eastchurch NFS 11.15; Damaged 10.11.15; Damaged 2.12.15; Wrecked 5.12.15; 4 Wing Eastchurch 23.3.16; War Flt Eastchurch 16.4.16; Misc Flt Eastchurch 28.7.16; Bomb Flt Eastchurch 19.8.16; Crashed 11.9.16

1256   (C/n 475). Deld 2 Wing Eastchurch 6.7.15; Accepted 11.7.15 (Raynham); Yarmouth 24.7.15; AZP, chased Zeppelin 25.4.16 (FSL BD Kilner); Cranwell 8.8.16; Wrecked 24.7.17; CW 7.8.17; Crashed, badly damaged Cranwell South 21.1.18 (pilot injured); Crashed and slightly damaged 22.3.18 (pilot unhurt); Became 201/2 TDS Cranwell 1.4.18

1257   (C/n 476). Deld 2 Wing Eastchurch 9.7.15; Accepted 11.7.15 (Raynham); Yarmouth 29.7.15; AZP 25.4.16 (FSL CEC Smith); HACP, landed Covehithe, retd

Yarmouth 28.5.16 (F/L BD Kilner); War Flt Burgh Castle 12.12.16; HACP 18.12.16 (F/L BD Kilner); Yarmouth 13.1.17; Burgh Castle 9.3.17; Yarmouth 25.3.17; Burgh Castle 7.6.17; Covehithe 12.6.17; AGP 4.7.17; HACP 4.9.17; Written off Yarmouth 22.12.17; Deleted 27.12.17 wreck

1258   (C/n 477). Deld 2 Wing Eastchurch 21.7.15; 2 Wing St.Pol (via Folkestone) 4.8.15; 1 Wing St.Pol by 31.8.15; 5 Wing Dover for erection 16.9.15; HACP 8.1.16 (F/L BL Huskisson) & 15.1.16 (F/L CE Wood); Nosedived in from about 260 ft 27.2.16 (F/L H Rosher killed); Deleted

1259   (C/n 478). Deld 2 Wing Eastchurch 20.7.15; Shipped from Dover to Dardanelles in SS *Nankin* 5.8.15; 3 Wing Imbros by 9.15; C Flt A Sqdn 2 Wing Imbros by 16.12.15; EF after TO, o/t landing, CW 18.3.16 (FSL FDH Bremner)

1260   (C/n 479). Deld 2 Wing Eastchurch for erection 4.7.15; Accepted 11.7.15 (Raynham); HACP 1.8.15 (F/Cdr BF Fowler); 2 Wing St.Pol 5.8.15; 5 Wing Dover 13.8.15; Wingtip slightly damaged 12.10.15 (FSL WH Peberdy); HACPs 24.1.16 & 9.2.16 (FSL RFS Leslie); RNAS Dover 3.3.16; O/t by high wind on TO for Dunkerque, wrecked 29.6.16 (FSL RA Little); Wrecked 10.8.16; Deleted 4.9.16

1261   (C/n 486). Deld for flight trials 26.7.15; Shipped from Dover to Dardanelles in SS *Nankin* 5.8.15; 3 Wing Imbros 9.15; C Flt A Sqdn 2 Wing by 2.12.15 - @8.16; Crashed on nose 1916. Came to grief 12.16?

1262   (C/n 487). Shipped from Dover to Dardanelles in SS *Nankin* 5.8.15; 3 Wing Imbros 9.15; O/t landing 18.1.16 (FSL FDH Bremner); 2 Wing, crashed on TO c.3.16 (FSL H Biscoe); Deleted 3.16

1263   (C/n 488). Shipped from Dover to Dardanelles in SS *Nankin* 5.8.15; 3 Wing Imbros 9.15; 2 Wing, EF, FL 4m NE of Kephalo, sank attempting to hoist in to Trawler *No.83* 16.12.15 (F/Cdr HA Busk rescued by lighter); Deleted 3.16

1264   (C/n 489). Shipped from Dover to Dardanelles in SS *Nankin* 5.8.15; 2 Wing Imbros 9.15; C Flt A Sqdn 2 Wing 1.12.15; Crashed on nose, Imbros 20.3.16 (FSL FDH Bremner); Rebuilt; C Flt A Sqdn 2 Wing Thasos 29.5.16 - @8.6.16; To Malta 6.16 for recovering, but lost on return to Thasos when ship sunk; Deleted 8.16

1265   (C/n 490). Tested Bristol 18.8.15; Transferred to French Government 8.15; Retd Paris to Mkrs 10.16 (overhaul and repair); Chingford by lorry for erection 4.12.16; Cranwell 28.3.17; Crashed near East Gate, propeller and wing damaged 20.12.17 (pilot unhurt); O/t, badly damaged Cranwell South 23.1.18 (pilot unhurt); Became 201/2 TDS Cranwell 1.4.18

1266   (C/n 491). Deld 4 Wing Eastchurch 8.15; Grain 26.9.15; Grain Repair Depot 1.10.15 (50-hp Gnome); Chingford 8.11.15; Cranwell 28.3.17; Wrecked 16.8.17; Crashed near Rauceby Gun Station, CW 24.12.17 (pilot unhurt); Became 201/2 TDS Cranwell 1.4.18; SE Area FIS Shoreham .18 (coded "46"?)

## 1 WHITE DUAL CONTROL FLYING BOAT on order by 12.14

1267   Presume cancelled and serial reallocated

## 1 PEMBERTON BILLING P.B.9 TRACTOR BIPLANE built Woolston & numbered 1267. (50-hp Gnome)

1267   FF 8.14 (Victor Mahl). Flown Hendon 13.1.15 - @31.5.15 (numbered 28.1.15); Chingford by 6.15; Deleted 7.15
[Presumably the PB Scout at Chingford which EF, FL in cornfield 1m from aerodrome 6.9.15 (S/Cdr JT Babington DSO), wreckage to Southampton by road]

## 12 SHORT GUN-CARRYING TRACTOR BIPLANES ordered under Cont No C.P.04901/15, to be numbered 1268 to 1279. (200-hp) [Gordon Bruce's researches show c/n's S.139 to S.150]

1268 to 1279 cancelled. Serials partially reallocated.
[It has been suggested that serials 1268 and 1279 were also allocated at one stage to 2 Short S.45 Type pusher biplanes of the Central Flying School (Nos.423 and 424), to have been transferred

to RNAS Eastchurch in 1915, but this seem unlikely on present evidence]

**20 WHITE & THOMPSON BIPLANES ordered under Cont No C.P.67552/15 & numbered 1280 to 1299, to be built Bognor Regis.**

1280 to 1299 cancelled

**20 WIGHT ADMIRALTY 840 TYPE TRACTOR BIPLANE SEAPLANES ordered 8.2.15 under Cont No C.P.68765/14, numbered 1300 to 1319 & built East Cowes. (225-hp Sunbeam)**

| | |
|---|---|
| 1300 | Accepted 26.7.15 at Cowes; Despatched HMS *Campania* 7.8.15 (arr 25.8.15) and erected in collier alongside; HMS *Campania* 2.9.15; Damaged when hit side of ship while taxying 12.11.15; Scapa in tow 1.12.15; Deleted 10.6.16 |
| 1301 | Accepted 26.7.15 at Cowes; Despatched HMS *Campania* 7.8.15 (arr 25.8.15) and erected in collier alongside; Scapa 1.12.15; Deleted 3.16 |
| 1302 | Accepted Cowes 17.8.15; Shipped to Dundee in collier 29.8.15 (arr 2.9.15); Tested 14.9.15; Deleted 17.1.16 |
| 1303 | Accepted at Cowes 18.8.15; Deld Dover 30.8.15; Awaiting contractors by 16.9.15; Grain 18.9.15; Yarmouth 22.9.15; EF, FL taxying, sank while MB and HMS *Aurora* salving 10.12.15 (F/L FE Sandford unhurt); Deleted 16.12.15 |
| 1304 | Accepted Cowes 21.8.15; Deld Grain 17.9.15; Yarmouth 23.9.15; Deleted 26.3.16 |
| 1305 | Ready Cowes by 31.8.15; Deld Grain 8.9.15; Deleted 14.3.16 |
| 1306 | Cowes preparing for trials 1.10.15; Deld Calshot 17.3.16; Deleted 15.6.16 |
| 1307 | Cowes preparing for trials 1.10.15; Grain 3.10.15; Tested 11.10.15; Deleted 14.3.16 |
| 1308 | Deld Grain by 15.11.15; Felixstowe 19.11.15 (intended for Yarmouth); Deleted 26.11.15 |
| 1309 | Deld Grain (via Newhaven) 8.11.15; Yarmouth 13.11.15; Grain RD repair then storage 14.11.15 - @15.3.16; Port Victoria RD for type trials by 22.3.16; Deleted 31.5.16 |
| 1310 | Deld Calshot 11.1.16; Tested 22.1.16; Sideslipped and wrecked landing, salved 28.1.16 (FSL EL Pralle & FSL H Tether rescued); Deleted 1.2.16 |
| 1311 | Deld Calshot 16.1.16; Deleted 15.6.16 |
| 1312 | Deld Calshot 25.1.16; Deleted 15.6.16 |
| 1313 | Deld Calshot 9.2.16; Deleted 15.6.16 |
| 1314 | Deld Calshot 19.2.16; Deleted 15.6.16 |
| 1315 | Deld Calshot 17.3.16; Deleted 15.6.16 |
| 1316 | Deld Calshot 24.3.16; Deleted 15.6.16 |
| 1317 | Deld Calshot 11.5.16; Deleted 15.6.16 |
| 1318 | (High chassis) Deld Grain 27.11.15; Deleted 14.3.16 |
| 1319 | (High chassis) Deld Calshot 14.11.15; W/T experiments 8.1.16; Deleted 15.6.16 |

**1 CAUDRON G.II TRACTOR BIPLANE ordered under Cont No C.P.65511/14 & numbered 1320, built by British Caudron Co. (60-hp Anzani)**

| | |
|---|---|
| 1320 | Taken over at Hendon by 21.11.14; Wrecked 30.1.15 (FSL M Marsden); Repaired; Crashed by 1.6.15; Deleted 15.6.15 |

**1 GRAHAME-WHITE XV HENRY FARMAN TYPE PUSHER BIPLANE ordered under Cont No C.P.62775/14, numbered 1321 & built Hendon. (60-hp Le Rhône)**

| | |
|---|---|
| 1321 | Taken over at Hendon by 1.12.14; (First mention 12.12.14); Tested 21.2.15; Accepted 23.4.15 (F/L FW Merriam); Chingford 23.4.15; 70-hp Gnome by 20.6.15; (80-hp Gnome by 10.15); Wrecked 14.10.15 (PFSL KV Hooper); Deleted 25.10.15 |

**1 PERRY TRACTOR BIPLANE ordered under Cont No C.P.62775/14, numbered 1322 & built Twickenham. (45-hp Anzani)**

| | |
|---|---|
| 1322 | FF Brooklands 26.6.14. Taken over at Hendon by 1.12.14; Tested 21.2.15 (poor performance); Wrecked 21.3.15; Deleted 3.15 |

**12 CURTISS B.2 TRACTOR BIPLANES ordered under Cont No C.P.68387/14 to be built Hammondsport & numbered 1323 to 1334. (160-hp Curtiss)**

1323 to 1334 cancelled

**12 SHORT ADMIRALTY 830 TYPE TRACTOR BIPLANE SEAPLANES ordered under Cont No. C.P.37639/15, numbered 1335 to 1346 & built Rochester. (135-hp Canton-Unné, mostly later refitted 140-hp Canton-Unné) [Gordon Bruce's researches show correct c/n's to be S.151 to S.162]**

| | |
|---|---|
| 1335 | Allocated *HMS Ben-my-Chree* by 11.3.15 (NTU); Deld Grain ex Eastchurch in tow 28.4.15; Bomb gear fitted 1.5.15; Tested 2.5.15 (failed initially); Felixstowe 2.5.15; HMS *Riviera* 3.5.15; EF, FL in rough sea, chassis and wings damaged, towed back by HMS *Falconer* 17.6.15 (F/L EIM Bird & S/L OH Crowther); Grain 12.8.15; Dover 16.8.15; A/S patrol 3.10.15 (F/L RP Cannon & AM2 Smith); Dunkerque 8.10.15; Dover 22.10.15; Sideslipped in wind off cliff and crashed in harbour, badly damaged 15.11.15 (S/Cdr FET Hewlett & FSL W Perham); Rebuilt; Fitted Lewis gun 14.2.16; Flown again 15.2.16 with 140-hp Canton Unné; Fitted 2 heavy bomb gear racks 26.2.16; HSPP 19.3.16 (FSL FJ Bailey & AM Smith); EF, FL in sea, sank, TL 25.3.16 (F/L JBP Ferrand & F/L JC Brooke saved) |
| 1336 | (later 140-hp) Deld Grain .15; Accepted 1.5.15; HMS *Riviera* 5.5.15; Felixstowe 6.5.15; HMS *Ben-my-Chree* 8.5.15; HMS *Engadine* 21.5.15; Felixstowe 2.7.15 (stowed); HMS *Engadine* 6.7.15; Broke chassis struts on TO with heavy load in big swell 22.2.16; Dover 23.2.16; HMS *Engadine*, dismantling 24.3.16; Parnall 30.3.16 (overhaul and modification); Dunkerque (via Dover) 21.6.16; ADD 17.9.16; Deleted by 1.17 |
| 1337 | (later 140-hp) Deld and accepted Grain 19.5.15 (Kemp); AZP 26/27.5.15 (F/L F Fowler & AM Barrett); HMS *Riviera* 31.5.15; Grain 11.6.15; HMS *Riviera* 12.6.15; Grain 21.6.15 (overhaul); HMS *Riviera* 25.6.15; Dover (via Grain) 20.8.15; Dunkerque 25.8.15; Dover 23.9.15; Dunkerque 5.10.15; FL in fog, broke port forward chassis strut, Calais 14.10.15 (F/L EIM Bird); Retd 15.10.15; Damaged propeller and chassis alighting rough seas 20.11.15 (FSL CB Gasson); EF, FL, collided with breakwater towing in by MB 10.1.16 (FSL GG Hodge & AM Alford); Dover 24.11.16 (by destroyer for repair); Test after rebuilding 9.5.17; AGP 25.5.17 (FSL LC Pincott & CPO Hanna, later FSL LC Pincott & AM WA Coppins); EF, FL in sea, capsized, towed to Ramsgate, TW 18.8.17 (FSL HR Dyke & LAC Thaxter); Deleted 22.8.17 DBR |
| 1338 | (later 140-hp) Deld and accepted Grain 21.5.15 (Kemp); HMS *Riviera* 31.5.15; Grain 1.6.15; HMS *Riviera* 3.6.15; Felixstowe 12.6.15; Grain Island RD 13.6.15 (overhaul); Tested A.D.Mk.II 4-bladed propeller 18-22.6.15; HMS *Riviera* 28.6.15; Grain Island RD 9.7.15 (overhaul and engine trouble); HMS *Riviera* 15.7.15; Grain 15.7.15 (for swinging); HMS *Riviera* by 20.7.15 - @19.8.15; Grain 9.15; Dover 8.9.15; Dunkerque 12.9.15; Dover 13.9.15; Dunkerque 18.9.15; Dover 23.9.15; Dunkerque 30.9.15; Dover 7.10.15 (overhaul); Fitted 140-hp Canton-Unné 20.10.15; Dunkerque 26.10.15; Dover 29.10.15; Dunkerque 3.11.15; Dover 4.11.15; Dunkerque 8.11.15; Dover 10.11.15; Dunkerque 18.12.15; Dover 22.12.15; Dunkerque 30.12.15; Dover 2.1.16; Dunkerque 8.2.16; Dover 9.2.16; Dunkerque 24.2.16; Dover 29.2.16; Dunkerque 16.4.16; HACP 21.4.16 (FSL BC Tooke & AM Clarke); Damaged hostile destroyer off Blankenberge 21.4.16 (FSL FJ Bailey & AM Fryer); Damaged chassis taking off in heavy sea 23.4.16 (FSL BC Tooke & LM Alford); Dover 12.5.16; Dunkerque 14.5.16; Dover 23.5.16; Dunkerque 26.5.16; Dover 23.7.16; Deleted 22.2.17 |
| 1339 | Deld Grain and accepted 16.6.15 (Kemp); HMS *Riviera* 21.6.15; Grain 22.6.15; HMS *Riviera* 24.6.15; Sunk off Terschelling 4.7.15 |
| 1340 | (later 140-hp) Deld Grain but failed test 25.6.15 (Kemp); Shorts Rochester 25.6.15; Accepted Grain 26.6.15 (Kemp); Dundee for erection 8.7.15; Tested 15.7.15 (Kemp); HMS *Engadine* 15.7.15; Dismantling 24.3.16; |

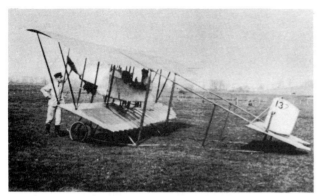

*Caudron G.II 1320, probably at Hendon.*
*(J.M.Bruce/G.S.Leslie collection)*

*Short 830 Type Seaplane 1335. (MAP)*

*Wight A.D. Type 1000 Seaplane 1358. (via Philip Jarrett)*

*Curtiss Type N (Modified) Biplane 1365. (FAA Museum)*

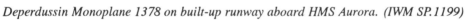

*Deperdussin Monoplane 1378 on built-up runway aboard HMS Aurora. (IWM SP.1199)*

Parnall 30.3.16 (overhaul and modification); Arrived Dover for erection 3.7.16; Tested 8.7.16 (Pickles); Dunkerque 11.7.16; Dover 17.10.16; HACP 22.10.16 (FSL C Laurence & AM Norris); Deleted 9.4.17

1341    (later 140-hp) Deld Grain 6.15; Accepted 26.6.15 (Kemp); Tested "Admiralty slot" 7.15; HMS *Engadine* 9.7.15; Dismantling 24.3.16; Parnall 30.3.16 (overhaul and modification); Dover 18.8.16; Tested 24.8.16 (Pickles); HACP 22.9.16 (FSL MR Buckland & PO Hanna); Dunkerque 1.10.16; Dover 20.4.17; Calshot training 5.7.17; Fitted DC 19.7.17; Deleted W/E 14.9.17

1342    (later 140-hp) Deld Grain and accepted 9.7.15 (Kemp); Calshot 24.7.15; HMS *Empress* 24.7.15; Calshot (via Eastbourne) 27.7.15; HMS *Empress* 2.8.15; Calshot 26.12.15; Dover 11.1.16; Dunkerque 20.1.16; Dover 23.1.16; Dunkerque 2.4.16; AZP 3.4.16 (FSL W Perham & S/L LH Slatter); Dover 3.4.16; Dunkerque 6.4.16; Damaged in rough sea 8.4.16 (FSL BC Tooke & S/L LH Slatter); To Dover but on arrival wrecked off harbour entrance while in tow 7.6.16 (FSL BC Tooke & F/L W Peer-Groves both unhurt); HACP 14.11.16 (S/L LH Slatter & PO Hanna); HSPPs 1.3.17 (FSL LC Pincott & LM GR Hodgson, later FSL AW Farquhar & AM Lawson, later FSL HH Gonyou & LM GR Hodgson); Dunkerque 1.3.17; Dover 3.3.17; HSPP 16.3.17 (FSL AW Farquhar & AM Morris); HACPs 24.3.17 (FSL HH Gonyou & PO Winstone); AZP 21.4.17 (FSL AW Farquhar & FSL GP Paine); Calshot 26.6.17; Deleted W/E 14.9.17

1343    (later 140-hp) Deld Grain by 9.7.15; Accepted 21.7.15 (Kemp); Arrived Seaplane shed Eastchurch en route HMS *Empress*, damaged landing 24.7.15; Calshot (via Eastbourne) 28.7.15; HMS *Empress* 31.7.15; Top mainplane extension damaged 12.10.15; Ready 14.10.15; Calshot 26.12.15; Dover 23.1.16; Dunkerque 20.6.16; Dover 20.10.16; Calshot 6.7.17; Deleted W/E 14.9.17

1344    (later 140-hp) Deld Eastchurch to 24.7.15; Accepted 29.7.15 (Kemp); Calshot 4.8.15 (weather delay); HMS *Empress* 5.8.15; Seaplane School Calshot 26.12.15; Parnall 23.3.16 (overhaul and repair); Dover 1.17; Accepted 12.1.17 (Prodger); Struck TBD on TO and wrecked 31.1.17 (F/L LG Sieveking & AM Anthony unhurt); Calshot 29.6.17; Deleted W/E 14.9.17

1345    Deld Grain in tow and accepted 30.7.15 (Kemp); Calshot 4.8.15; HMS *Empress* 5.8.15; Calshot 26.12.15; Deleted 1.1.16

1346    (later 140-hp) Deld Grain in tow and accepted 11.8.15 (Kemp); Yarmouth 18.8.15; Packing for transport 2.4.16; Parnall Bristol by rail 8.4.16; Dover by rail 27.5.16; Accepted 5.6.16 (Pickles); Dunkerque 7.6.16; Dover 16.11.16; HSPP 1.3.17 (FSL AW Farquhar & AM Lawson); St.Margaret's Bay to Dover 13.4.17; Surveyed 19.11.17; Deleted 23.11.17 W&T

**4 SOPWITH 860 TRACTOR BIPLANE SEAPLANES ordered under Cont No C.P.67552/15 & numbered 1347 to 1350, to be built at Kingston.**

1347    to 1350 cancelled

**4 WIGHT ADMIRALTY 840 TYPE TRACTOR BIPLANE SEAPLANES ordered under Cont No C.P.68765/14 from J.Samuel White & Co Ltd, numbered 1351 to 1354 & built East Cowes. (225-hp Sunbeam)**

1351    (High chassis) Deld Calshot 25.11.15; W/T experiments 9.3.16; Damaged 12.4.16; Deleted 15.6.16
1352    Deld Calshot 21.11.15; Deleted 15.6.16
1353    Deld Gibraltar 1.16; Missing in action 11.2.16; Deleted 2.16
1354    Deld Gibraltar 1.16 - @8.16; Still in commission 1.17

**7 ADMIRALTY A.D. 1000 TYPE SEAPLANES ordered 24.2.15 under Cont No C.P.10516/15 from J. Samuel White & Co Ltd & numbered 1355 to 1361, to be built East Cowes. Work stopped W/E 14.3.17 after only one delivered. (Ordered with three 225-hp Sunbeam, to be delivered with three tractor/pusher 310-hp Sunbeam)**

1355    Not completed. To have been fitted with 12-pdr gun. Five seats
1356    Not completed. To have been fitted with 12-pdr gun. Five seats
1357    Not completed. To have been fitted with 12-pdr gun. Five seats
1358    FF Cowes 13.5.16; To Grain but EF en route, FL Seaford Bay, near Newhaven 31.5.16; EF, FL Colne Point, grounded on Gunfleet mudbank 3.6.16; Towed Harwich to Felixstowe by MB 4.6.16; Felixstowe 4.6.16 (repair); Reconstructing 8.16; Deleted 8.3.17
1359 to 1361 Not completed

**6 CURTISS N (MODIFIED) TRACTOR BIPLANES ordered 1914 under Cont No C.P.72702/14 from The Curtiss Aeroplane Co, numbered 1362 to 1367 & built Toronto. (90-hp Curtiss OX-5)**

1362    Deld Hendon 14.2.15; Dover 20.3.15 (transit); 1 Sqdn St.Pol 21.3.15; Chingford for erection 25.5.15; Not erected; Deleted 6.8.15
1363    Deld Hendon 14.2.15 for Dover (NTU); Eastchurch NFS by 11.3.15; Deleted by 31.4.15 (useless)
1364    Deld Hendon 14.2.15; Dover 20.3.15 (transit); 1 Sqdn St.Pol 21.3.15; Chingford for erection 25.5.15; Not erected; Deleted 28.8.15
1365    Deld Hendon 14.2.15; Dover 20.3.15; 1 Sqdn St.Pol 21.3.15 - @2.4.15; 2 Sqdn Eastchurch by 19.5.15; Ready by 31.5.15; Flying banned 10.6.15; Became 2 Wing Eastchurch 13.7.15; 4 Wing Eastchurch 3.8.15 (still banned); Deleted 27.8.15
1366    Deld Hendon by 28.2.15; 1 Sqdn St.Pol by 31.3.15; 2 Sqdn Eastchurch by 30.4.15; Erecting by 31.5.15; Flying banned 10.6.15; Became 2 Wing Eastchurch 13.7.15; 4 Wing Eastchurch 3.8.15 (still banned); Deleted 27.8.15
1367    Deld Hendon by 28.2.15; 1 Sqdn St.Pol by 31.3.15; Eastchurch by 30.4.15; Erecting by 31.5.15; Flying banned 10.6.15; Became 2 Wing Eastchurch 13.7.15; 4 Wing Eastchurch 3.8.15 (still banned); Deleted 27.8.15
[1362, 1364-1367 - 1 Sqdn Special Flt on detd service under S/Cdr Spenser DA Grey]

**1 HENRY FARMAN PUSHER BIPLANE purchased from Aéroplanes Farman under Cont No C.P.7209/14, deld through Aircraft Manufacturing Co Ltd & numbered 1368. (80-hp Gnome)**

1368    Dunkerque 1.1.15; Dover circa 25.1.15; arr Eastchurch en route Yarmouth 25.1.15; Packing 26.1.15; arr Yarmouth by rail 28.1.15; Tested after erection 10.2.15; Wrecked at Bradwell 6.11.15 (FSL AE Hawker); Deleted 24.11.15

**3 MAURICE FARMAN S.11 SHORTHORN PUSHER BIPLANES purchased under Cont No C.P.7209/14 from Aéroplanes Farman & numbered 1369 to 1371. (100-hp Renault)**

1369    Tested Buc?; Deld ADD, fitted up 12.14; 3 Sqdn St.Pol by 31.1.15; [Dover by 28.2.15]; Shipped 19 or 20.3.15 from Plymouth in SS *Inkosi* or SS *Moorgate*; 3 Sqdn Tenedos (No.1 aerodrome) 3.15; Became 3 Wing Tenedos 6.15; Deleted 8.15
1370    Tested Buc?; Deld ADD, fitted up 12.14; 3 Sqdn St.Pol by 31.1.15; Shipped from Marseilles in SS *Abda* 17.3.15; 3 Sqdn Tenedos 3.15; Became 3 Wing Tenedos 6.15 - @10.15; Deleted 1916
1371    Tested Buc; Deld ADD, fitted up 12.14; 3 Sqdn St.Pol by 31.1.15; Was to be shipped from Marseilles in SS *Abda* 17.3.15 (NTU); 1 Sqdn St.Pol by 9.4.15; Became 1 Wing St.Pol 21.6.15 - @10.15; Deleted 1916

**4 HANDLEY PAGE TYPE O (LATER O/100) TRACTOR BIPLANE PATROL BOMBERS ordered 28.12.14 from Handley Page Ltd, numbered 1372 to 1375 & built Cricklewood. (Two 150-hp Sunbeam)**

1372 to 1375 cancelled 4.2.15 and replaced by 1455 to 1458. Serials reallocated

**1 CAUDRON G.III TRACTOR BIPLANE ordered under under Cont No C.P.34953/14 from The W.H.Ewen Aviation Co Ltd, numbered 1372 & built Hendon. (50-hp Gnome)**

1372     Accepted Hendon 11.2.15; To Chingford early 5.15; Deleted 6.15

**1 WRIGHT PUSHER BIPLANE purchased at Eastchurch under Cont No C.P.66325/15 from Sqdn Cdr Ogilvy & numbered 1373. (35-hp Wright)**

1373     (ex Ogilvie's Short-Wright No.6) Deld Eastchurch NFS 6.8.15; Damaged 2.10.15; Deleted 13.1.16

**1 HENRY FARMAN TYPE III PUSHER BIPLANE purchased under Cont No C.P.34377/15 from Pemberton Billing Ltd & numbered 1374. (50/60-hp Gnome)**

1374     Hendon by 28.2.15 (50-hp Gnome); Chingford 18.4.15; Extensions fitted 5.15; Fell 50-ft, crashed, TW 1.7.15 (L/Cdr PFM Fellowes); Deleted 14.7.15 as spares

**1 DEPERDUSSIN TRACTOR MONOPLANE ordered under Cont No C.P.35518/15**

1375     Purchase cancelled

**4 DEPERDUSSIN TRACTOR MONOPLANES purchased from Armand Deperdussin, Paris & numbered 1376 to 1379. (100-hp Gnome Monosoupape)**

1376     Deld Hendon by 28.2.15; Allocated Chingford 5.15, but 1377 sent in lieu; Wings damaged 9.11.15; Damaged when Bessoneau tent blew away 28.3.16; Deleted 31.3.16

1377     Deld Hendon by 28.2.15; Chingford for erection 22.5.15; Flown 26.5.15; AZP, broke propeller landing 31.5/1.6.15 (F/L FW Merriam); Trimley 5.6.15; Felixstowe 5.6.15; HACP 18.6.15 (F/L RJJ Hope-Vere); Sideslipped in on aerodrome, CW 10.7.15 (F/L ER Moon & AM Terry both injured); Deleted 7.15

1378     Deld Hendon by rail 22.4.15; Chingford for erection 22.5.15; Awaiting nosepiece from 6.15; Felixstowe 25.9.15; to HMS *Aurora*, successfully slipped from built-up runway on board 07.00 4.11.15 (F/L RJJ Hope-Vere); Felixstowe 4.11.15; Levington Heath 8.2.16; Trimley 9.2.16; Felixstowe 9.2.16; Trimley 13.5.16; Deleted 23.1.17

1379     Deld Deld Hendon by rail 22.4.15; Chingford by road for erection 26.5.15; Felixstowe 21.6.15; HSPP 3.7.15 (F/L RJJ Hope-Vere); Trimley 9.2.16; Felixstowe 9.2.16; FL, slightly damaged, Dovercourt 21.2.16 (F/L AW Clemson); Deleted 23.1.17

**8 MAURICE FARMAN S.11 SHORTHORN PUSHER BIPLANES purchased from Aéroplanes Farman, Paris, numbered 1380 to 1387 & built Paris. (110-hp Renault)**

1380     Shipped to Dardanelles 8.15; 3 Wing Aegean by 31.8.15; Deleted 12.15

1381     Shipped to Dardanelles 8.15; 3 Wing Aegean by 31.8.15; 2 Wing Imbros 18.1.16; Deleted by 1.17

1382     Shipped to Dardanelles 8.15; 3 Wing Aegean by 31.8.15; 2 Wing Imbros 18.1.16 ; Deleted 3.16

1383     Shipped Dardanelles 8.15; 3 Wing Aegean (coded 'M5') @31.8.15; D Sqdn 2 Wing Imbros 18.1.16;Deleted 7.16

1384     Shipped to Dardanelles .15; 3 Wing Aegean by 31.8.15; 2 Wing Imbros 18.1.16; Deleted 3.16

1385     Shipped to Dardanelles .15; 3 Wing Aegean by 31.8.15; D Sqdn 2 Wing Imbros 18.1.16 - @8.16; still in commission 1.17

1386     Shipped to Dardanelles .15; 3 Wing Aegean by 31.8.15; D Sqdn 2 Wing Imbros 18.1.16 - @8.16; Deleted 1916

1387     Shipped to Dardanelles .15; 3 Wing Aegean by 31.8.15; 2 Wing Imbros 18.1.16; Deleted 3.16

**2 SUPERMARINE P.B.31E NIGHT HAWK TRACTOR QUADRUPLANES later ordered by Admiralty W/E 24.11.16 under Cont No C.P.130778/16 from Pemberton Billing Ltd, numbered 1388 and 1389 & built Woolston, Southampton. (Two 125-hp Anzani)**

1388     Deld Chingford by lorry 1.1.16 but not on RN strength; Tested 16.1.16; Crashed Chingford; Retd Mkrs for repair; Mkrs dismantling to cover wings W/E 16.9.16; Deld Design Flt Eastchurch W/E 1.12.16; FF 2.17 (Prodger); Deleted 3.3.17

1389     Not completed

**5 VOISIN TYPE B PUSHER BIPLANES to be numbered 1390 to 1394. (200-hp Canton Unné)**

1390 to 1394 cancelled and serials reallocated

**5 BREGUET DE CHASSE TRACTOR BIPLANES purchased from Breguet, numbered 1395 to 1399 & built Villacoublay. (various engines)**

1390     (200-hp Canton Unné). Deld Dunkerque 2.15; Dover by 28.2.15; Packing for 3 Sqdn by 11.3.15; 3 Sqdn Tenedos 3.15; Became 3 Wing Tenedos 6.15; To UK in SS *Liverpool* by 1.10.15; Transit to UK 4.16 then deleted

1391     (200-hp Canton Unné). Deld Dunkerque 2.15; Shipped from Marseilles in SS *Abda* 17.3.15; 3 Sqdn Tenedos 3.15; Became 3 Wing Tenedos/Imbros 6.15; Transit to UK 1.16 then deleted

1392     (225-hp Sunbeam). 1 Wing St.Pol by 30.11.15 - @12.15 [Deleted by 1.17]

1393     (200-hp Canton Unné). [Deleted by 1.17]

1394     (225-hp Sunbeam per 12.15 list) (220-hp Renault by 1.17 list). Deld Dover 5.2.16; HSPP 19.3.16 (FSL S Cotton & FSL RR Soar); To Westgate but FL on arrival 16.4.16; Retd Dover; Deleted 12.7.16

**5 DELAUNEY-BELLEVILLE PUSHER BIPLANES (ST.CHAMOND TYPE) ordered in France & numbered 1395 to 1399.**

1395 to 1399 cancelled and serials reallocated

**3 NIEUPORT TWIN BIPLANES ordered in France & numbered 1395 to 1397. (Two 110-hp Clerget)**

1395 to 1397 cancelled (not received by 12.15)

**2 BREGUET TYPE V CONCOURS TRACTOR BIPLANES airframes, purchase authorised 1.10.15 from Breguet, numbered 1398 and 1399 & built Villacoublay. (Ordered with 225-hp Sunbeam but fitted 250-hp Rolls-Royce)**

1398     Deld from Paris to Hendon 9.7.16 (FSL PA Johnston); Flown 1.9.16; ADD 20.10.16; 7 Flt B Sqdn 5 Wing 1.11.16 - @4.11.16; ADD by 9.11.16; Dover 15.11.16; Deleted 1.2.17

1399     Still on order 1.17; Surveyed by 3 Wing Luxeuil 9.2.17 (only entry in records)

**12 WIGHT ADMIRALTY 840 TYPE TRACTOR BIPLANE SEAPLANES ordered under Cont No C.P.30564/15 from William Beardmore & Co Ltd, numbered 1400 to 1411 & built Dalmuir. (225-hp Sunbeam)**

1400     Deld HMS *Engadine* 12.9.15; Granton Harbour 13.9.15; Dundee 17.9.15; Tested 21.9.15; FL in sea, towed back by trawler, damaged by heavy sea 26.10.15 (FSL EAdeL de Ville & LM Johnston); Wrecked off Dundee 5.4.16 (FSL EM King & AM Ketley unhurt); Deleted 6.4.16

1401     Deld Dundee 22.9.15; Badly damaged near Newport 26.9.15 (FSL EAdeL de Ville); To Beardmore 19.10.15; Deld and tested Dundee 11.2.16; Chassis damaged 22.2.16; Deleted 23.3.16

1402     Deld Dundee (via Grangemouth) 30.9.15; Damaged 12.10.15 (F/L TK Young & LM Bebbington); Deleted 7.1.16

1403     Deld Dundee 11.10.15; Wrecked landing in heavy sea nr Bell Rock, o/t, lost in tow HMT *Thomas Young*, BU 1.11.15 (FSL AH Sandwell & PO Peach); Deleted

1404     Deld Dundee 15.10.15; Deleted 7.2.16 FW&T

1405     Deld Mkrs to HMS *Campania* in SS *Singleton Abbey* 3.11.15; Tested 8.11.15; Scapa 9.11.15 - @8.12.15; HMS *Campania* 12.15; Deleted 29.2.16 FWT

*Supermarine P.B.31E Night Hawk Quadruplane 1388. (RAF Museum P.18131)*

*Wight 840 Type Seaplane 1400. (via Philip Jarrett)*

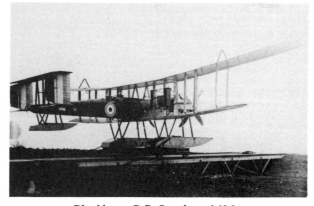

*Blackburn G.P. Seaplane 1416.*

*Sopwith Schneider Seaplane 1445 hoisting aboard HMS Ben-my-Chree, 1915. (FAA Museum)*

*Wight Twin Fuselage Seaplane 1451. (via Philip Jarrett)*

1406 Shipped to Gibraltar by 31.1.16 - @31.7.16; Deleted 1916

1407 (High chassis) Shipped to Gibraltar by 31.1.16; Deleted 6.16

1408 (High chassis) From Beardmore by rail to Dundee 30.11.15; War Flt Dundee 7.3.16; Just TO for A/S patrol when 2x100-lb bombs dropped off, one exploded under water, TW 29.3.16 (FSL EM King & AM); Deleted 1.4.16

1409 (High chassis) Deld Dundee 2.12.15; Dropped Ranken Darts then bombs exploded while taxying, TW 21.12.15 (Lt D Iron & S/L G Gilmore RNVR missing); Deleted 21.12.15

1410 (High chassis) Deld Dundee 31.12.15; Accepted 22.1.16; Deleted 11.7.16

1411 (High chassis) Deld Dundee 31.12.15; Tested 22.2.16; War Flt Dundee 7.3.16; Deleted 11.7.16

**2 A.D. TYPE PUSHER BIPLANE FLYING BOATS ordered 23.10.15 under Cont No C.P.109611/15 from Pemberton Billing Ltd, numbered 1412 and 1413 & built Woolston. (Ordered with 150-hp Hispano-Suiza but deld with 200-hp Hispano-Suiza 8B)**

1412 Hull constructed by May, Harden & May; FF 1916 with Sunbeam Nubian engine - preliminary trials at Southampton 28.6.16 - @15.1.17; Refitted 150-hp Hispano-Suiza; FF Southampton 12.3.17; Type Test Dept Grain 4.4.17; 200-hp Arab by 29.12.17; Surveyed 25.3.18; Deleted 27.3.18 FW&T

1413 Deld Calshot for trials 14.6.17 (for a day or two); Southampton to Grain TD (via Westgate) 27.6.17; left for HMS *Furious* in Scapa Flow 26.7.17; Yarmouth 26.7.17 (transit); Killingholme 28.7.17; Left for South Shields 1.8.17; Hartlepool to South Shields 13.8.17; Grain 13.8.17; Dundee 16.8.17; Scapa 23.8.17; HMS *Furious* 26.8.17; Rosyth 1.9.17; Tested Southampton 5.9.17; South Shields to Seaton Carew 15.9.17; HMS *Furious* W/E 22.9.17; Rosyth (repair) W/E 5.10.17; Scapa 6.10.17; Rosyth W/E 20.10.17; HMS *Furious* W/E 3.11.17; Rosyth W/E 3.11.17; Surveyed 9.1.18; SOC 15.4.18 W&T

**1 BLACKBURN TWO-SEATER SCHOOL MACHINE TRACTOR BIPLANE ordered by 12.15 under Cont No C.P.151627/15 from Blackburn Aeroplane & Motor Co Ltd, numbered 1414 & built Leeds. (130-hp Canton-Unné)**

1414 Cancelled 1916

**2 BLACKBURN G.P. TRACTOR BIPLANE SEAPLANES put forward 7.16 and ordered under Cont No C.P.111708/16 from Blackburn Aeroplane & Motor Co Ltd, numbered 1415 and 1416 & built Leeds. Fitted to carry torpedo between floats**

1415 (Two 150-hp Sunbeam Nubian) FF at Grain 7.16; PVRS, tested 28.7.16; Seaplane Design Flt Grain, 5.12.16; Exp Design Flt Grain 1.2.17; Type Test Dept Grain 4.4.17; Deleted 27.6.17

1416 Erecting Brough by 15.1.17; Deld Exp Design Grain 19.3.17; TW 22.3.17; Surveyed 19.11.17; Deleted 26.11.17 unsatisfactory experimental type
[The second machine is sometimes referred to as Type S.P., but this is very likely a misreading of G.P.]

**7 serials not allotted (cancelled order?)**

1417 to 1423 blank numbers

**12 ROYAL AIRCRAFT FACTORY B.E.2c NIGHT FLYING TRACTOR BIPLANES ordered 1.5.15 from South Coast Aviation Works. & numbered 1424 to 1435. Put forward to cancel 11.16, overdue by nearly two years. (75-hp Renault later 100-hp RAF)**

1424 to 1435 cancelled

**12 SOPWITH SCHNEIDER TRACTOR BIPLANE SEAPLANES ordered under Cont No C.P.31834/15 from Sopwith Aviation Co Ltd, numbered 1436 to 1447 & built Kingston. Deld from Woolston. (100-hp Gnome Monosoupape)**

1436 Deld Calshot 2.15; Tested 12.2.15 (Mahl); Grain 26.2.15; Felixstowe 1.5.15; RD Grain by 16.5.15; Tested 2.7.15; Tested 7.8.15; Mods to ailerons and tail; Experimental test flight 7.10.15; Grain station 10.1.16; Felixstowe 28.4.16; Deleted 3.7.16

1437 Packing by 11.3.15; To Dardanelles in SS *Moorgate* 3.15; HMS *Ark Royal* at Mudros 9.4.15; Erected 9-11.4.15; Tested 16.4.15; HMS *Doris* 29.4.15; Floats damaged on landing, slowly started to sink but salved by HMS *Doris*, Gulf of Smyrna 2.5.15 (F/L WHS Garnett); Retd HMS *Ark Royal* 8.5.15; CW and retd HMS *Ark Royal* in dilapidated condition 21.5.15; SS *Penmorvah* 22.5.15 (overhaul); Completely re-covered and new floats fitted 1.6.15; Dismantled for storage in SS *Penmorvah* 8.6.15; HMS *Ark Royal* and assembled for Mudros, but EF on way to shore 22.6.15 (F/L WHS Garnett); Operations from shore base from 25.6.15; Retd HMS *Ark Royal* but while taxying damaged propeller and both floats in Kephalo Harbour 3.7.15 (F/L CF Lan Davis); Unrigged for repair; Wireless set fitted 12.8.15; Test after repair but engine vibration 3.9.15; (briefly in HMS *Roberts* 9.15?); EF on turn after TO, FL downwind, o/t, salved by Trawler *No.362* 29.9.15 (F/L CW Pulford unhurt); Deleted

1438 Packing by 11.3.15; To Dardanelles in SS *Moorgate* 3.15; HMS *Ark Royal* at Mudros 9.4.15; Erected 10-15.4.15; Tested 16.4.15; Scouted over Gallipoli then damaged chassis landing 25.4.15 (F/L RH Kershaw); HMS *Doris* 9.5.15; HMS *Ark Royal* 28.5.15; Dismantled for overhaul and stowed in SS *Penmorvah* 3.6.15; Flown again HMS *Ark Royal* 3.7.15; Mudros 25.7.15; Taxying in choppy water for TO, u/c submerged then o/t and sank, Kephalo 28.7.15 (F/L CF Lan Davis); Salved but deleted [briefly in HMS *Minerva* 1915?]

1439 Deld Calshot and tested 25.3.15 (Hawker); HMS *Engadine* 28.3.15; Calshot 11.4.15; HMS *Engadine* 27.4.15; Felixstowe 2.5.15; HMS *Engadine* 15.5.15; Felixstowe 16.5.15; HMS *Arethusa* 21.5.15; Felixstowe 21.5.15; HMS *Arethusa* 31.5.15; HMS *Penelope* 4.6.15; Felixstowe 9.6.15; CW on landing 29.6.15 (F/L JMD'A Levy & FSL JF Hay unhurt); Deleted 29.6.15

1440 Tested Grain 31.3.15; Calshot 4.15; New propeller fitted 9.4.15; HMS *Engadine* 26.4.15; Felixstowe 21.5.15; HMS *Penelope* 24.5.15; Felixstowe 28.5.15; HMS *Undaunted* 29.5.15; Felixstowe 4.6.15; HMS *Aurora* 4.6.15; Felixstowe 5.6.15; HSMP 9.6.15 (F/L ER Moon); Float broke on TO 12.6.15 (FSL GW Price); Deleted 13.6.15

1441 Deld Calshot by 4.15; HMS *Engadine* 26.4.15; Felixstowe 24.5.15; HMS *Penelope* 24.5.15; Felixstowe 28.5.15; HMS *Arethusa* 31.5.15; Felixstowe 4.6.15; HMS *Arethusa* 5.6.15; Felixstowe but nosedived in on landing, CW 9.6.15 (F/L JMD'A.Levy); Deleted 9.6.15

1442 Deld Calshot by 21.4.15; Crashed 21.4.15; Sopwith repair 21.4.15; Dover for erection 8.5.15; AZP 16.5.15 (FSL TV Lister); Accepted 19.5.15 (Hawker); HACP but capsized on water 23.5.15 (FSL TV Lister); Test after repair 13.8.15; HACP 20.8.15 (FSL JBP Ferrand); Tail float smashed by wreckage in harbour 24.8.15 (FSL JBP Ferrand); temp Dunkerque 28.9.15; Dover 15.10.15; CSD White City by road 19.1.16; Deleted

1443 Deld Calshot 4.15; HMS *Engadine* 27.4.15 (for anti-Zeppelin duties); Smashed on launch to chase Zeppelin and lost at sea 11.5.15

1444 Deld Felixstowe; HMS *Vindex* by 30.4.15; HMS *Engadine* 2.5.15; TO to chase Zeppelin, wrecked and salved 11.5.15; Surveyed 13.5.15; Deleted 14.5.15

1445 Deld Felixstowe by Hawker then to HMS *Ben-my-Chree* 3.5.15; Bombed Trouges then fell in sea, retd in tow TBD HMS *Wear* 25.6.15 (FSL T Bankes-Price); Retd after recce on Port Sighajik, o/t by wind, CW in rough sea after landing, forward end of fuselage salved 3.8.15; Fuselage remains returned UK in SS *Tringa* 29.8.15, England, but lost in wreck of ship

1446 Deld Yarmouth by road 9.5.15; Accepted 11.5.15 (Hawker); HMT *Kingfisher* 5.6.15; Yarmouth 7.6.15; HMT *Kingfisher* 22.6.15; Yarmouth 22.6.15; HMT *Kingfisher* 26.6.15; Yarmouth 28.6.15; HMT *Kingfisher* 9.7.15; Yarmouth 9.7.15; HMT *Kingfisher* 10.7.15; Yarmouth 10.7.15; HMT *Kingfisher* 11.7.15; Yarmouth

12.7.15; HMT *Sir John French* but damaged wingtip, tailplane, elevator and float while getting her in water from the trawler 30.7.15; Yarmouth 31.7.15; CW on landing 20.1.16 (FSL FGD Hards)

1447     Deld Dover and accepted 19.5.15 (Hawker); HMT *St.Germain* 31.5.15; Dover 31.5.15; HMT *St.Germain* 1.6.15; Dover 2.6.15; Grenade and bomb gear fitted 9.9.15; CSD White City by road 26.1.16

## 2 SHORT ADMIRALTY 186 TYPE TWO-SEAT FOLDER TRACTOR BIPLANE SEAPLANES ordered from Short Bros & numbered 1448 to 1449. (Two 200-hp Canton-Unné)

1448 to 1449 postponed by 12.15 and later cancelled

## 2 WIGHT TWIN-ENGINED ADMIRALTY 187 TYPE TWIN FUSELAGE TRACTOR BIPLANE SEAPLANES ordered 2.3.15 under Cont No C.P.66259/15 from J.Samuel White & Co Ltd, numbered 1450 and 1451 & built East Cowes. (Two 200-hp Canton-Unné)

1450     (Fitted for 18" Mk.IX torpedo)   Deld Felixstowe 28.4.16; Retd Mkrs 3.7.16 and deleted

1451     Deld Felixstowe on *HMS Golden Eagle* 15.7.16 (type tests); Deleted 25.4.17

## 2 A.D. PUSHER BIPLANE SCOUTS (NICKNAMED "THE SPARROW") ordered under Cont No C.P.38552/16 from Hewlett & Blondeau Ltd, numbered 1452 to 1453 & built Leagrave, Beds. (100-hp Gnome Monosoupape)

1452     Deld Chingford 15.11.15; Tested 2.12.15; Dismantled by 18.3.16; CSD White City 14.4.16; Deleted 7.6.16

1453     Tested Chingford (by mkrs?); Deld CSD White City by 21.1.16; Deleted 7.6.16

## 1 HENRY FARMAN PUSHER BIPLANE purchased from Aéroplanes Farman & numbered 1454. (80-hp Gnome)

1454     Equipped for W/T; Left Paris in crate by rail 15.1.15; left Southampton 3.2.15; Arr Gosforth for erection by Airco 8.2.15; Erected and tested 11.2.15; To Whitley Bay but hit telegraph wire and damaged propeller and wings 23.2.15; Repaired by Armstrong Whitworth, Gosforth; [Elswick by 28.2.15]; Whitley Bay ex Gosforth 7.3.15; HACP 14.4.15; Dundee 29.4.15; Barry 19.5.15; AZP 24.5.15 (Lt C Draper); Montrose 26.5.15; Barry 19.8.15 (mine spotting); East Fortune 14.9.15 (arr 16.9.15); Re-erecting 2.16; Dived into sea from 100ft 17.3.16 (F/L C Johnson & 2/Lt EA Abigail both killed)

## 12 HANDLEY PAGE O/100 TRACTOR BIPLANE BOMBERS ordered 4.2.15 under Cont No C.P.65799/15 from Handley Page Ltd, numbered 1455 to 1467 & built Cricklewood. (Two 322-hp Eagle VII unless otherwise stated) [1455-1458 prototypes replacing 1372-1375; 1459-1466 production aircraft]

1455     Completed 11.15; Deld Hendon 9.12.15; FF 17.12.15 (F/Cdr JT Babington); Eastchurch 10.1.16; Type trials until serious engine defect 9.2.16; Damaged 5.3.16, to storage; Handley Page (via Hendon) 15.9.16 (overhaul and rebuild of fuselage); Kingsbury to Hendon 14.3.17 (Prodger) and retd Kingsbury; Same 15.3.17; To Hendon and accepted 18.3.17 (Prodger); HP Sqdn Manston 7.4.17; Hendon 13.4.17; Hendon to Chingford for bomb dropping tests 24.4.17; Tested with 4 passengers & 16x12-lb bombs, climbed to 5,000 ft in 35 min 26.4.17 (F/Cdr KS Savory); Visited Eastchurch 1.5.17; Hendon to HP Sqdn Manston 9.5.17; 7 Sqdn 22.5.17; A Sqdn 13/14.10.17 (275-hp RR); Became 16 Sqdn Ochey 8.1.18 ("arrived Ochey 28.1.18"); Destroyed when an F.E.2b blown into it during German raid on Ochey 19.2.18; 6 AP for repair 22.2.18; Dismantled 22-24.2.18, then deleted

1456     Lengthened nose, strengthened fuselage and wing roots; Second HP to Hendon - arrived 20.4.16 at 13.30 and left 14.30; Flown Hendon 23.4.16; Climbed to 10,000 ft in just under 40 min with 10 volunteers aboard 23.4.16; Accepted 7.5.16; Gunnery School Flt Eastchurch 27.5.16; HP Sqdn Manston 9.7.16; Ready 17.7.16; AZP, damaged tail skid landing 1.8.16 (S/Cdr JT Babington, F/LL HC Vereker, PO Reece & AM

Kennedy); Performance trials 2.8.16; Fabric burnt off starboard side of fuselage and other areas 26.5.17; Transported Hendon for reconstruction 6.8.17; HP Sqdn Manston 22.10.17 (Eagle VI/VII); HP Sqdn 2 TDS Stonehenge 16.2.18 - @31.3.18; 1 SoN&BD Stonehenge by 22.4.18 - @25.5.18

1457     Redesigned fuselage and tail unit; FF Hendon 24.6.16; Flown 26.6.16 (S/Cdr JT Babington) & 1.7.16 (Prodger); HP Sqdn Manston, overhaul by 16.7.16; S/Cdr JT Babington from HP Sqdn Manston to Hendon to fetch aircraft 17.7.16; Flown at Hendon 20.7.16 (Prodger); HP Sqdn Manston 21.7.16 (S/Cdr JT Babington); Tail skid damaged by 1.8.16; Controls lashed on TO, CW 28.12.16 (FSL DK Denham & AM/E Rubie); Deleted 22.1.17

1458     First with frontal radiator and 320-hp RR Mk.III/Eagle; Deld Hendon 19.8.16; HP Sqdn Manston 20.8.16; Eastchurch 21.10.16; HP Sqdn Manston 22.10.16; Extension damaged by hitting telegraph pole while taxying 18.3.17; Wings badly damaged 16.6.17; Dismantled and re-erected; Hendon 15.7.17 (for reconstruction by Mkrs at Kingsbury); Ex Kingsbury Works to Hendon 10.10.17 (275-hp RR); HP Sqdn Manston 15.10.17 (Eagle VI/VII @29.12.17; Eagle VIIIs by 19.1.18); HP Sqdn Stonehenge (coded '5') 1.2.18 - @31.3.18 (Eagle VIII); Crashed and wrecked Salisbury Plain

1459     Deld Hendon 9.16; HP Sqdn Manston 11.9.16; Paris 16.10.16/ferried Dunkerque 4.11.16 (first O/100 in France); HP Sqdn 3 Wing Luxeuil by 27.10.16; HQ Flt Luxeuil 10.11.16; Detd Auxerre 24.12.16 - 15.2.17; Allocated to French Govt 26.3.17 (NTU); ADD 21.4.17; 7 Sqdn Coudekerque 23.4.17; HP Sqdn Manston 25.5.17 (for reconstruction); [5 Wing Coudekerque 30.6.17 (Fitted 6-pounder Davis Gun)]; HP Sqdn Manston 11.7.17; 7A Sqdn (via/ex Dunkerque) 26/27.10.17; Davis gun removed 2.18; Became 207 Sqdn 1.4.18; 214 Sqdn loan 5.4.18; TOC 214 Sqdn 17.4.18; 216 Sqdn (named 'LE TIGRE') 15.5.18 (arr 16.5.18); Returning from attempted raid, FL, partly burnt Bois le Viques [Maron, NW of Pont St.Vincent] 14.9.18 (Lt H Castle, USAS & Lt BA Levy both slightly injured; 1/Lt GSL Hubbell, USAS unhurt); 3 ASD 15.9.18

1460     Deld Hendon 25.9.16 (Prodger); Tested 30.9.16 (Prodger); HP Sqdn Manston 1.10.16; To Villacoubley (via Clermont) but FL in small field on TO for Luxeuil 26.10.16 (S/Cdr JT Babington); Repaired on site (took some weeks); Tested 18.12.16; HP Sqdn 3 Wing Luxeuil 24.12.16; Bombed railway junction nr Metz 16/17.3.17 (S/Cdr JT Babington); Allocated to French 26.3.17 (NTU); Dunkerque 21.6.17; 7 Sqdn 30.6.17; Hit by AA in night raid, FL Baizerais 18.7.17

1461     The first with increased tankage; Deld HP Sqdn Manston (via Eastchurch) 21.10.16 (Prodger); ferried to Villacoublay but EF, FL near Abbeville en route 15.11.16 (FSL EB Waller); HP Sqdn 3 Wing Luxeuil 21.12.16; To 7 Sqdn Coudekerque 4.17; Paris to HP Sqdn Manston 21.6.17 for reconstruction; 7 Sqdn, crashed on TO Coudekerque 18.7.17; To 7A Sqdn Coudekerque 28.7.17 (Fitted 6-pdr Davis Gun 8.17); HP Sqdn Manston [by 11.7.17]; 7 Sqdn Coudekerque 23.11.17; Davis gun removed 2.18; Crashed near Calais 27.3.18; Became 207 Sqdn 1.4.18; 215 Sqdn loan 5.4.18 (still under reconstruction); Left behind when sqdn to UK 23.4.18; 214 Sqdn by 4.5.18; 216 Sqdn 19.5.18 (fitted with Davis gun); Crashed on TO Ochey 18.7.18 (Lt AC Kilburn, Sgt Obs CH Symonds & Pte G Hall); 216 Sqdn by 30.8.18

1462     (Eagle VII/VI) Deld Hendon 2.11.16 (Prodger); HP Sqdn Manston 6.11.16; Allocated 3 Wing 16.11.16 (NTU); Villacoublay 1.1.17; 7 Sqdn 13.4.17; HP Sqdn Manston 26.5.17 for reconstruction; Fitted 6-pdr Davis Gun 8.17; 7 Sqdn Coudekerque 16.9.17; Davis gun removed 2.18; Renamed 207 Sqdn 1.4.18; 215 Sqdn loan 5.4.18; Raid on Zeebrugge, crashed in sea off Ostende, sank 10.30 11.4.18 (Capt JR Allen DSC drowned; Capt T Bewsher DSC wounded; 2/Lt MC Purvis unhurt)

1463     Deld Hendon 25.11.16 (Prodger); Overhaul for overseas 1.12.16; HP Sqdn Manston (named 'L'AMAZONE')

*Handley Page O/100 1463 in German markings after being captured when it inadvertently landed in enemy territory on its way to France, 1 January 1917. (RAF Museum P.7700)*

*Blackburn T.B. Twin-boomed Zeppelin fighter 1510 at Grain, 1916. (via Philip Jarrett)*

*Henry Farman F.22 Pusher Biplane 1528. (MAP)*

26.11.16; Two attempts to fly to France but retd each time due to engine trouble 24.12.16; ferried Villacoublay en route to Luxeuil, but lost way and landed behind German lines at Chalandry, north of Laon 1.1.17 (F/Lt HC Vereker, Lt SR Hibbard RNVR, AM Kennedy, AM Wright, AM Higby all PoW); Flown by Germans but crashed when aileron cables inadvertently crossed during maintenance work

1464   Deld Hendon 7.12.16 (Prodger); Chingford 10.12.16 (Prodger, delayed due to weather); Hendon 11.12.16; Chingford 22.12.16 (en route France); To France but CW landing Dunkerque 1.1.17 (FSL BA Millson injured)

1465   Deld Hendon 22.12.16; Tested 24.12.16 & 5.1.17 (both Prodger); Mkrs 7.1.17; Hendon 13.1.17; Accepted 15.1.17; HP Sqdn Manston 23.1.17; Landed Calais on delivery 5.4.17; 7 Sqdn 26.4.17; HP Sqdn Manston 20.7.17; HP Sqdn 2 TDS Stonehenge 16.2.18 (Eagle VI/VII); For deletion by 30.3.18 (wrecked)

1466   (Eagle VI 10.17. To Eagle VII 2.18) Deld Hendon 6.1.17 (Prodger); HP Sqdn Manston 10.1.17 (trials); 7 Sqdn Coudekerque 5.4.17; Dropped bombs on 5 destroyers 4m off Blankenberghe, then attacked by small green a/c off Ostende 23.4.17 (F/Cdr HA Buss); A Sqdn Manston (via Paris) 4.12.17; A Sqdn Ochey W/E 6.12.17; arr 16 Sqdn Ochey 28.1.18; Became 216 Sqdn Villesneux 1.4.18; FL, damaged 9.5.18 (FSL CEV Wilkins, Sgt Mech GS Keen, Sgt Obs G/L SF Mills, Sgt Mech WJ Darley & Lt J Henry unhurt); Returning from raid on Frankfurt-am-Main, FL one mile short of Ochey, caught fire, BO, Autreville 21.5.18 BO (Lt TEW Browne, Lt JW Adams, 2/Lt CN Yelverton unhurt); SOC in field 22.5.18

**30   AVRO 504C NIGHT FIGHTER AND TRAINER TRACTOR BIPLANES ordered 12.5.15 under Cont No C.P.32600/15 by Brush Electrical Engineering Co, numbered 1467 to 1496 & built Loughborough. (80-hp Gnome)**

1467   Deld Yarmouth 19.11.15; To Covehithe, damaged landing 27.11.15 (FSL WTS Williams); Yarmouth by rail 26.12.15; HACP 20.2.16 (F/L FGD Hards); HACPs 16.4.16. 23.4.16 & 24.4.16 (all FSL JC Northrop), also 24.4.16 (later FSL BS Wemp); EF, FL Gorleston, undamaged 26.4.16; HACPs 2.7.16 (FSL S Kemball) & 30.7.16 (FSL NH McDiarmid x 3, later FSL AV Robinson, later FSL CE Wood); Wrecked 24.8.16; Deleted 28.8.16

1468   Deld Yarmouth and accepted 9.1.16 (Barrs); 3 HACPs 23.4.16 (FSL JC Northrop, later FSL BS Wemp later FSL FP Reeves); To Bacton but EF, FL Walcott Church, near Bacton 21.5.16; Yarmouth 22.6.16; Bacton 23.6.16; Deleted 5.7.16

1469   Deld Redcar for erection 10.12.15; Tested 16.12.15 (Barrs); Deleted 21.3.16

1470   Deld Redcar for erection 10.12.15; Tested 16.12.15 (Barrs); FL Yarm 16.4.16; Retd but EF, smashed u/c 17.4.16 (FSL WE Robinson); FL, CW 8.5.16 (FSL JF Roche slightly injured); Deleted 19.5.16

1471   Deld Chingford by lorry 29.1.16; Cranwell 8.2.16; Wrecked 16.7.16; Deleted 18.7.16

1472   Deld East Fortune for erection 18.12.15; Tested 4.3.16; Deleted 25.8.16

1473   Deld East Fortune for erection 12.1.16 ; Tested 16.1.16 (Barrs); Re-erecting 2.16; Tested 2.3.16 & 1.4.16; Damaged landing 5.6.17; Surveyed 24.12.17; Deleted as spares 3.1.18

1474   Deld Yarmouth by rail for erection 26.12.15; Accepted 9.1.16 (AE Barrs); Hit flare landing and damaged wing 21.2.16 (FSL SG Beare); Bacton 16.3.16; Yarmouth 29.3.16; HACP 31.3.16 (FSL EB Thompson); HACP, wrecked on landing 23.4.16 (F/L CJ Galpin); Deleted 20.5.16

1475   Deld Whitley Bay for erection 3.2.16; Accepted 8.2.16 (Barrs); Redcar 4.3.16; EF, FL, hit ditch, wrecked u/c landing 22.6.16 (FSL R Collishaw); Deleted 14.7.16

1476   Deld Killingholme 13.2.16; Deleted 13.3.16

1477   Deld Redcar for erection 27.2.16; Tested 31.3.16 (Barrs); Wrecked u/c landing 23.1.17 (PFO HC Nutt unhurt); Deleted 4.5.17

1478   Deld Dover by rail 5.2.16; visited Westgate 8.4.16

(engine trouble, stayed); EF, FL into wind, damaged Eastchurch 14.5.16 (FSL RA Little slight concussion); Retd Dover 25.5.16; Parnall 31.5.16 (repair); Cranwell 26.10.16; Deleted 5.4.17

1479   Deld Chingford by lorry 18.2.16; Tested 25.2.16; FL and damaged en route visit to Hainault Farm 24.3.16; Deleted 24.4.16

1480   Deld Chingford by lorry 18.2.16; Tested 25.2.16; Taxied into mud, o/t 5.4.16 (PFSL HL Hitch); Deleted 10.6.16

1481   Deld Chingford 28.2.16; EF on TO, turned left to avoid telegraph wires, hit trees 15.7.16 (PFSL AH Pearce unhurt); Deleted 21.7.16

1482   Deld Felixstowe 1.4.16; War Flt Eastchurch 11.5.16; Eastchurch Gunnery School 5.10.16; Eastchurch Workshops 22.10.16 (storage); Deleted 12.1.17

1483   Deld Grain for erection 14.3.16; Accepted 17.3.16 (Barrs); Westgate 2.4.16; Manston 20.6.16; Wrecked landing 23.2.17 (FSL LD Dainty); Deleted 16.3.17

1484   Deld Grain for erection 14.3.16; Accepted 27.3.16 (Barrs); War Flt Eastchurch 16.6.16; Grain 17.6.16; visited Kingsnorth 24.7.16; To Manston but taxied into Bristol N5398 after landing, wings damaged 16.3.17 (F/L EP Hardman), retd Grain; War Flt Manston 23.9.17; Surveyed 26.10.17; Deleted 29.10.17 W&T

1485   Deld Grain for erection 14.3.16; Accepted 17.3.16 (Barrs); visited Kingnorth 24.7.16; Lent ECD Grain 26.2.17 (landing trials on dummy deck; U-shaped hook beneath fuselage); Grain 3.3.17; Manston 24.5.17; Wrecked landing 31.8.17 (F/L RE Darnton); Deleted W/E 15.9.17

1486   Deld Redcar 13.3.16; Tested 31.3.16 (Barrs); COL 16.4.16 (FSL WE Traynor); COL, damaged u/c and wings 29.10.16 (PFSL MO Fairhurst unhurt); EF, FL, outside aerodrome, badly damaged 24.1.17; Deleted 14.2.17

1487   Deld Redcar 13.3.16; Tested 31.3.16 (Barrs); EF, FL in crops, lost u/c, badly damaged 14.7.16 (FSL R Collishaw slightly injured); Deleted 23.2.18

1488   (80-hp Le Rhône) Deld Dover (via Chingford) 27.4.16 (Barrs); 10 Flt A Sqdn 4 Wing 14.5.16; Into ditch on landing, wrecked 28.5.16 (FSL CR Mackenzie unhurt); DBR Dunkerque, deleted ADD 15.6.16

1489   Deld Dover by rail for erection 18.5.16; ADD 3.6.16; Dover for erection 6.9.16; Damaged 19.9.16; Deleted 8.3.17

1490   Deld Dover 10.5.16 (Barrs); ADD 26.5.16; 10 Flt A Sqdn 4 Wing 29.5.16 - @20.6.16; ADD by 29.6.16; Dover for erection 6.9.16; Deleted 23.5.17

1491   Deld Dover by rail 18.5.16; ADD 29.5.16; Wrecked 11.4.17; Deleted 27.4.17

1492   Deld CSD White City without engine W/E 27.5.16; Cranwell 23.11.16; Crashed 6.7.17; COL 8.12.17 (pilot unhurt); Surveyed 10.12.17; Deleted 14.12.17

1493   Deld CSD White City without engine W/E 27.5.16; Cranwell for erection 21.11.16 (at Freiston 5.17); Crashed 2.10.17; Surveyed 16.10.17; Deleted 18.10.17 wrecked

1494   Deld CSD White City without engine W/E 10.6.16; Cranwell 23.11.16; Crashed 11.9.17; Crashed Brauncewell Gate House 6.12.17 (pilot unhurt); Crashed and damaged 23.2.18 (pilot unhurt); Surveyed 28.2.18; Deleted 13.3.18 DBR

1495   Deld CSD White City without engine W/E 17.6.16; Cranwell for erection 21.11.16; Crashed 11.9.17; Deleted W/E 8.2.18

1496   Deld CSD White City without engine by 18.6.16; Cranwell for erection 1.1.17 - 4.17; Freiston by 6.17; Cranwell by 10.17; EF, stalled on turn, nosedived in and crashed near aerodrome 26.11.17 (PFO GW Stallard); Surveyed 27.11.17; Deleted 6.12.17 wrecked

**12 WHITE & THOMPSON FLYING BOATS to be numbered 1497 to 1508 & built Bognor Regis**

1497 to 1508 cancelled

**9 BLACKBURN T.B. TWIN-BOOMED TWIN-ENGINED TRACTOR BIPLANE ZEPPELIN FIGHTERS ordered 14.4.15 (amended 21.7.15) under Cont No C.P.04903/15 from Blackburn Aeroplane & Motor Co Ltd, numbered 1509 to 1517**

**& built Leeds. (Two 100-hp Gnome Monosoupape 9B) (6.16 Blackburn contracted to fit 140-hp Smith in lieu of 100-hp Monosoupape and to store in meantime, except one to be fitted with Clerget [= 1517]) (all to store without engines W/E 26.3.17)**

1509    (Two 100-hp Gnome Monosoupape 9B). Deld Grain 13.1.16; Accepted 16.3.16 (S/Cdr JW Seddon & FSL GS Abbott); ARD Grain 14.5.16; Port Victoria Repair Section, dismantled for packing 27.11.16; CSD White City by rail 3.12.16; Killingholme 21.3.17 (stored without engine); Deleted 28.4.17

1510    (Two 100-hp Gnome Monosoupape 9B). Deld Grain 5.16; Accepted 2.6.16; Port Victoria Repair Section, dismantled for packing 27.11.16; CSD White City by rail 3.12.16; Killingholme for erection 21.3.17; Deleted 28.4.17

1511    (Refitted two 140-hp Smith). Deld RNAS Air Depot Crystal Palace 6.16 - @14.8.16 (100hp Monosoupape); CSD White City by 4.5.17; Unpacked by 15.6.17 (no engine); Deleted and broken up 7.17

1512    (Refitted two 140-hp Smith). Deld RNAS Air Depot Crystal Palace 6.16 - @14.8.16 (100hp Monosoupape); CSD White City by 4.5.17; Unpacked by 15.6.17 (no engine); Deleted and broken up 7.17

1513    (Refitted two 140-hp Smith). Deld Killingholme in parts for storage by 4.17; Broken up 8.17; Deleted 15.9.17

1514    (Refitted two 140-hp Smith). Deld Killingholme in parts for storage by 4.17; Broken up 8.17; Deleted 15.9.17

1515    (Refitted two 140-hp Smith). Deld Killingholme in parts for storage by 4.17; Broken up 8.17; Deleted 15.9.17

1516    (Refitted two 140-hp Smith). Deld Killingholme in parts for storage by 4.17; Broken up 8.17; Deleted 15.9.17

1517    (Refitted two 110-hp Clerget 9B). Deld Design Flt Grain in makers hands for erection 10.12.16; Dismantled and awaiting Smith engine by 2.17; Tender accepted to fit 110 Clerget instead of 100-hp Monosoupape W/E 16.3.17 (not yet accepted); CSD White City by rail 28.3.17; Killingholme store 9.5.17; Deleted 15.9.17
[2 Blackburn T.B.s were unpacked at CSD 26.7.16 - 1511 & 1512?]

**16 HENRY FARMAN F.20 PUSHER BIPLANES purchased under Cont No C.P.66967/15 from Aéroplanes Farman, Paris & numbered 1518 to 1533. (80-hp Gnome)**

1518    Deld Paris to Marseilles Docks 11.3.15; Shipped to Aegean in SS *Abda* 17.3.15; 3 Sqdn Tenedos 3.15; en route UK 21.6.15; Eastbourne FS 18.8.15; Deleted 1916

1519    Deld Paris to Marseilles Docks 11.3.15; Shipped to Aegean in SS *Abda* 17.3.15; 3 Sqdn Tenedos 3.15; en route UK 21.6.15; Eastbourne FS for erection 19.8.15; EF, FL 2.3.16 (FSL RW Gow & FSL PMJ Grove); Ringmer 26.4.16 (retd?); Ringmer 5.5.16; Eastbourne 6.6.16; Ringmer 10.5.16; Awaiting deletion Eastbourne 18.9.16; Deleted 26.9.16

1520    Deld Paris to Marseilles Docks 11.3.15; Shipped to Aegean in SS *Abda* 17.3.15; 3 Sqdn Tenedos 3.15; en route UK by 20.6.15; Possibly CSD White City by 8.15; Deleted by 12.15

1521    Deld Paris to Marseilles Docks 11.3.15; Shipped to Aegean in SS *Abda* 17.3.15; 3 Sqdn Tenedos 3.15; en route UK by 20.6.15; Possibly CSD White City by 8.15; Deleted by 12.15

1522    Deld Paris to Marseilles Docks 11.3.15; Shipped to Aegean in SS *Abda* 17.3.15; 3 Sqdn Tenedos 3.15; en route UK by 20.6.15; Possibly CSD White City by 8.15; Deleted by 12.15

1523    Deld Paris to Marseilles Docks 11.3.15; Shipped to Aegean in SS *Abda* 17.3.15; For 3 Sqdn Tenedos 3.15; en route UK 21.6.15; Possibly White City by 8.15

1524    Deld Paris to Marseilles Docks 11.3.15; Shipped to Aegean in SS *Abda* 17.3.15; For 3 Sqdn 3.15; en route UK 21.6.15; Possibly White City by 8.15; Deleted by 12.15

1525    Deld Paris to Marseilles Docks 11.3.15; Shipped to Aegean in SS *Abda* 17.3.15; For 3 Sqdn Tenedos 3.15; en route UK 21.6.15; Chingford 10.8.15; Surveyed 13.6.17; Deleted 19.6.17

1526    For 3 Sqdn Tenedos 3.15; Not listed by 30.4.15; en route UK by 20.6.15; Chingford 10.8.15; FL, slightly damaged 28.12.15 (FSL GWR Fane); TW 23.6.16; Deleted 29.6.16

1527    For 3 Sqdn Tenedos 3.15; en route UK by 20.6.15; Chingford 10.8.15; Westgate 19.11.15; retd Chingford but EF, FL Herne Bay 24.11.15 (FSL L Gresley); Grain 26.11.15 (en route); Chingford 27.11.15 TW 23.6.16; Deleted 15.7.16

1528    For 3 Sqdn 3.15; en route UK by 20.6.15; Chingford 10.8.15; Surveyed 13.6.17; Deleted 19.6.17

1529    For 3 Sqdn Tenedos 3.15; Became 3 Wing Tenedos 6.15; en route UK in SS *Annam* by 20.6.15; Presume to CSD White City; Deleted by 12.15

1530    For 3 Sqdn Tenedos 3.15; Became 3 Wing Tenedos 6.15; en route UK in SS *Annam* by 20.6.15; Presume to CSD White City; Chingford by 12.15; Deleted by 1.17

1531    For 3 Sqdn Tenedos 3.15; Became 3 Wing Tenedos 6.15; en route UK in SS *Annam* by 20.6.15; Presume to CSD White City; Deleted by 1.17

1532    For 3 Sqdn Tenedos 3.15; Became 3 Wing Tenedos 6.15; en route UK in SS *Annam* by 20.6.15; Presume to CSD White City; Deleted by 1.17

1533    For 3 Sqdn 3.15; Became 3 Wing Tenedos 6.15; en route UK in SS *Annam* 21.6.15; Presume to CSD White City; Deleted by 1.17

**2 VICKERS F.B.5 GUNBUS (ADMIRALTY 32 TYPE) PUSHER BIPLANES ordered under Cont Nos C.P.145394/15 & 47886/15/X(A), numbered 1534 and 1535 & built Crayford. (140-hp Smith)**

1534    Prototype armoured version; Preparing for (Mkrs?) trials at Joyce Green 31.5.15; Deld 4 Wing Eastchurch 8.8.15; Tested 14.8.15; Eastchurch NFS by 10.15; Damaged and engine out by 22.2.16; Deleted 27.4.16

1535    Second prototype armoured version; CSD White City by 30.6.16; Deleted 8.16

**2 A.D. SCOUT PUSHER BIPLANES (NICKNAMED "THE SPARROW") ordered 3.16 under Cont No C.P.104662/16 from Blackburn Aeroplane & Motor Co Ltd, numbered 1536 and 1537 & built at Leeds. (100-hp Gnome Monosoupape)**

1536    Erecting Chingford by makers from 23.9.15; Ready for test 6.10.15 - @1.1.16; Dismantled by 17.3.16; CSD White City 14.4.16; Deleted 7.6.16

1537    Tested Chingford; To CSD White City; Deleted 7.6.16
[An AD Scout (80-hp Gnome) from Leeds to CSD 21.1.16]

**12 BLERIOT XI-BG PARASOL TRACTOR MONOPLANES purchased from Blériot Aéronautique & numbered 1538 to 1549. (80-hp Gnome)**

1538    Deld Eastchurch by 28.2.15 - @31.3.15; 2 Wing Eastchurch by 30.4.15; AZP 31.5/1.6.15 (F/L GG Dawson); detd Rochford 3-4.6.15 & 15-16.6.15; Damaged Rochford 3.6.15; Became 2 Wing Eastchurch 21.6.15; 4 Wing Eastchurch 3.8.15; u/s by 10.15; War Flt Eastchurch 16.4.16; Miscellaneous Flt Eastchurch 28.4.16; Eastchurch FS 14.7.16; Eastchurch Workshops 31.10.16; Deleted 8.11.16

1539    Deld Eastchurch by 28.2.15; Defence Flt Dover 26.3.15 (attd 2 Sqdn); Left for Eastchurch but wrecked 4.4.15 (FSL AF Bettington unhurt); Deleted 4.15

1540    Deld Eastchurch by 28.2.15; Defence Flt Dover 26.3.15 (attd 2 Sqdn); Eastchurch 9.4.15; Wrecked 11.5.15 (FSL HJ Batchelor killed); Deleted 5.15; Remains still at Eastchurch 31.8.15

1541    Deld Eastchurch by 28.2.15; Defence Flt Dover 27.3.15 (attd 2 Sqdn); HACP, crashed 16.4.15; 2 Sqdn Eastchurch 4.15 (repair); Rebuilding by 7.6.15; Became 2 Wing Eastchurch 21.6.15; 4 Wing Eastchurch 3.8.15; Deleted 13.1.16

1542    Deld Eastchurch 28.2.15; Defence Flt Dover 31.3.15 (attd 2 Sqdn); HACP 16.4.15; 4 Sqdn Dover by 30.4.15; 2 Sqdn Eastchurch 25.5.15; HACP 9.6.15 (FSL RB Munday); Became 2 Wing Eastchurch 21.6.15; 4 Wing Eastchurch 3.8.15; War Flt Eastchurch 16.4.16 for re-erection; Eastchurch FS 26.6.16; Deleted 29.6.16

1543    Deld Eastchurch by 28.2.15; Defence Flt Dover 5.4.15 (attd 2 Sqdn); 2 Sqdn Eastchurch 11.4.15; Defence Flt

Dover by 11.5.15; 4 Sqdn Dover to Eastchurch but FL Canterbury and damaged 22.5.15; Rebuilding by 7.6.15; 2 Sqdn became 2 Wing Eastchurch 21.6.15; 4 Wing Eastchurch 3.8.15; Condemned 8.15; Deleted 13.1.16

1544    Deld Eastchurch by 28.2.15 - @31.3.15; 2 Sqdn Eastchurch by 30.4.15; Detd Rochford 2.6.15, 4.6.15, 7.6.15; Became 2 Wing Eastchurch 21.6.15; Detd Rochford 2-5.7.15; 4 Wing Eastchurch 3.8.15 (remains left on departure of 2 Wing); War Flt Eastchurch 16.4.16; Misc Flt Eastchurch 28.4.16; Deleted 20.5.16

1545    Deld Eastchurch by 28.2.15; 2 Sqdn Eastchurch by 30.4.15; HACP 11.6.15 (FSL GG Dawson); Detd Rochford 14-15.6.15 & 19-20.6.15; Became 2 Wing Eastchurch 21.6.15; Detd Rochford 7-8.7.15; 4 Wing Eastchurch 3.8.15; Condemned by 8.15; Reconstructed?; Still 4 Wing 10.15; Slightly damaged 4.1.16 (FSL RJO Compston); Flying again 15.1.16; Wings condemned 29.2.16; War Flt Eastchurch 25.4.16; Deleted 25.4.16

1546    Deld Eastchurch 28.2.15; Defence Flt Dover (attd 2 Sqdn) 17.4.15 - @30.4.15; 4 Sqdn Dover by 22.5.15 (trial); 2 Sqdn Eastchurch 25.5.15; AZP, COL 26.5.15; To Rochford for AZP, chased LZ38, EF, FL in mud and wrecked, Leigh-on-Sea, Essex 31.5.15; Became 2 Wing Eastchurch 21.6.15; 4 Wing Eastchurch 3.8.15 (wreckage left on departure of 2 Wing); Deleted 13.1.16

1547    Deld 1 Sqdn St.Pol by 21.3.15; Became 1 Wing St.Pol 21.6.15 (D Sqdn); 2 Wing Eastchurch 2.7.15; 4 Wing Eastchurch 3.8.15; U/s (condemned) by 8.15; War Flt Eastchurch 16.4.16; Deleted 2.10.16

1548    Deld 1 Sqdn St.Pol by 4.15; Became 1 Wing St.Pol 6.15; 2 Wing Eastchurch 2.7.15; 4 Wing Eastchurch 3.8.15; War Flt Eastchurch 16.4.16 (awaiting re-erection); Deleted 2.10.16

1549    (c/n 204) Deld Chingford for erection 21.5.15; Run into by 146 and badly damaged 29.8.15; Under repair 9.15 - 10.15; Deleted 21.1.16

**6 HENRY FARMAN F.27 STEEL-FRAMED PUSHER BIPLANES ordered from Brush Electrical Engineering Co, numbered 1550 to 1555 & built Loughborough. (135-hp Canton-Unné)**

1550    On order 1.17 (tropical). Never delivered
1551    to 1555 cancelled 1.16

**24 SOPWITH SCHNEIDER TRACTOR BIPLANE SEAPLANES ordered on Cont No C.P. 38624/15, numbered 1556 to 1579 & built Kingston. (100-hp Gnome Monosoupape)**

1556    Deld Calshot 22.4.15; HMS Engadine 26.4.15; Felixstowe 20.5.15; HMS Aurora 29.5.15; Felixstowe 29.5.15; HACP 3.6.15; HMS Penelope 4.6.15; Felixstowe 4.6.15; Deleted 7.15

1557    Deld Felixstowe and tested 2.5.15; Tested 3.5.15 (Hawker); HMS Riviera 3.5.15 (at Grain); Felixstowe 5.5.15; HMS Riviera 5.5.15; Felixstowe 16.5.15; HMS Penelope 17.5.15; Felixstowe 17.5.15; HMS Aurora 24.5.15; Felixstowe 28.5.15; HMS Arethusa 29.5.15; Felixstowe 30.5.15; HMS Undaunted 31.5.15; Felixstowe 4.6.15; Badly damaged on landing 6.6.15 (FSL LP Openshaw); Deleted 7.6.15

1558    Deld Yarmouth by road 9.5.15 (Fitted rifle and pistol packs); Accepted 11.5.15 (Hawker); HMT Kingfisher 21.5.15; Felixstowe 21.5.15; Wrecked on TO Yarmouth 3.6.15 (S/Cdr deCWP Ireland); Deleted 19.6.15

1559    Deld HMS Campania for erection 11.6.15; Tested but wings out of true 5.7.15; Re-tested 16.7.15; Taxied to Scapa on wheels 31.7.15; HMS Campania 1.8.15; Flew off deck steaming at 18 knots 6.8.15 (F/L WL Welsh); Scapa 2.12.15; HMS Campania 17.4.16; Scapa 7.5.16; Damaged 11.5.16; Surveyed 13.5.16; Deleted 6.6.16

1560    Deld HMS Ben-my-Chree by 20.6.15; Tested 25.6.15; Caught fire 25.6.15 (F/L MEA Wright); Flew again 10.7.15; Damaged float 17.7.15; Wrecked 24.8.15; Retd UK in collier SS Tringa 29.8.15; Arr UK for rebuild by CSD Wormwood Scrubbs 5.9.15; Later deleted, not rebuilt

1561    Deld HMS Ben-my-Chree by 20.6.15; LM 20.8.15; Retd UK in collier SS Tringa 29.8.15; Arr UK for rebuild by CSD Wormwood Scrubbs 5.9.15; Later deleted, not rebuilt

1562    Deld Dover for erection by 8.6.15; Tested 11 & 14.6.15; Failed acceptance test 30.6.15; AZP 10.8.15 (FSL JBP Ferrand); EF, FL outside harbour Dover 25.8.15 (FSL JBP Ferrand unhurt); Deleted 5.9.15

1563    Deld by SS Vocturnus to HMS Campania for erection 22.6.15; Only partly erected by 1.9.15; Scapa 27.9.15; HMS Campania 2.10.15; Flew off deck with ship steaming full speed 3.11.15 (F/L WL Welsh), then damaged; Being stripped 4.11.15; Deleted 2.16 DBR

1564    Deld Yarmouth by road 23.6.15; Engine trouble on acceptance flight, beached Corton, damaged float, towed back 29.6.15 (Hawker); Accepted 20.7.15 (Hawker); Deleted 17.3.16

1565    Deld Felixstowe 26.6.15; Tested 9.7.15 (Hawker); Fitted experimental floats 7.15; Tested 27.7.15; Deleted 28.1.16 FW&T

1566    Shipped to Aegean; HMS Ark Royal by 7.15 - 12.15; Imbros Depot with HMS Ark Royal .15; ashore?; HMS Ark Royal by 4.16 - 7.16; Deleted 1917

1567    Deld Yarmouth road 28.6.15; Accepted 30.6.15 (Hawker); Broke float after TO 6.7.15; Float gave way taxying in, o/t and sank, CW, salved, beached near scenic railway 15.7.15 (F/L V Nicholl); engine removed from remains 19.7.15

1568    Deld Yarmouth by road 3.7.15; Accepted 20.7.15 (Hawker); HMT Sir John French 13.9.15; Yarmouth 15.9.15; Deleted 17.3.16

1569    Deld Dover by road 4.7.15; Accepted 10.8.15 (Hawker); temp at Dunkerque 29.9.15; Dover 7.10.15; Grain 15.10.15; Felixstowe 27.4.16; Deleted 3.7.16

1570    Deld Yarmouth by rail 19.7.15; floats not fitted by 31.8.15; Dismantled 2.12.15; Deleted 17.3.16

1571    Deld Felixstowe 22.7.15; Deleted 15.3.16

1572    Deld Dover by rail 12.7.15; Erected 16.7.15; Tested 28.7.15; CSD White City by road 15.1.16, later deleted

1573    Deld Dover by rail 12.7.15; Erected 16.7.15; Accepted 10.8.15 (Hawker); Temp Dunkerque 1.9.15; Dover 5.10.15; Deleted 15.5.16

1574    Deld Felixstowe 22.7.15; Tested 24.7.15 (Hawker); Lost control, nosedived into water, CW 1.8.15 (FSL LH Hardstaff unhurt); Deleted 2.8.15

1575    Deld Felixstowe 22.7.15; Accepted 24.7.15; Capsized and wrecked off Orfordness, brought in by HMS Lydard 7.8.15 (F/L PEH Wakeley unhurt); Deleted 18.8.15

1576    Deld Dover by rail 23.7.15; Accepted 6.8.15; AZP 10.8.15 (FSL JPB Ferrand); Grain 15.10.15; Felixstowe 28.4.16; Deleted 3.7.16

1577    Shipped to Aegean; Imbros Depot with HMS Ark Royal by 9.15 - 4.16; Tested after erection 2.10.15; Flown until 19.11.15; Flown again 7.1.16 until 1.2.16; Tested again 17.4.16; Cruiser HMS Lowestoft 2.5.16; Capsized and wrecked landing Stavros 3.5.16; Retd HMS Ark Royal but sideslipped, nosedived from 100ft, wrecked 8.5.16 (F/L CWH Pulford injured)

1578    Shipped to Aegean; Imbros Depot with HMS Ark Royal by 9.15; Tested HMS Ark Royal after erection 9.5.16; HMS Snaefell 21.6.16; Disembarked when ship at

*Sopwith Schneider 1557 being hoisted out from HMS Undaunted probably around the time of the Battle of Jutland 31 May - 1 June 1915.*

Kavalo 17.7.16; HMS *Ark Royal* by 8.16; Deleted 1916

1579  Shipped to Aegean; Imbros Depot with HMS *Ark Royal* by 9.15; HMS *Ark Royal* to cruiser HMS *Lowestoft* 2.5.16; Tested HMS *Ark Royal* after erection 9.5.16; Deleted 1916

**12 SHORT S.38 TYPE PUSHER BIPLANES ordered on Cont No C.P.50249/15 from Pemberton-Billing Ltd, numbered 1580 to 1591 & built Woolston. (80-hp Gnome)**

1580  Deld Chingford for erection 1.12.15; To Clement Talbot Works 15.4.16, later deleted
1581  Deld Chingford on lorry 4.11.15; Erected 12.15; CSD Crystal Palace 4.5.16, later deleted
1582  Deld Chingford by lorry 8.11.15; Tested 23.1.16; Tested 1.2.16 (Prodger); CSD Crystal Palace 4.5.16, later deleted
1583  Deld Chingford by lorry 10.11.15; Tested 23.1.16; Tested 1.2.16 (Prodger); Deleted 22.4.16
1584  Deld Chingford by lorry 15.11.15; Tested 1.2.16 (Prodger); Deleted 22.4.16
1585  Deld Chingford by lorry 6.12.15; CSD Crystal Palace 4.5.16, later deleted
1586  Deld Chingford by lorry 14.2.16; Deleted 22.4.16
1587  Deld Chingford by lorry 18.2.16; CSD Crystal Palace 4.5.16, later deleted
1588  Deld Chingford by lorry 17.2.16; Deleted 22.4.16
1589  Deld Chingford by lorry 16.3.16; Awaiting erection 5.5.16; Deleted 9.6.16
1590  No evidence of delivery, possibly to Chingford as spares
1591  No evidence of delivery, possibly to Chingford as spares

**6 CAUDRON G.III TRACTOR BIPLANES purchased under Cont No C.P.40361/15 from Aéroplanes Caudron at Rue & numbered 1592 to 1595. (100-hp Anzani)**

1592  Deld Hendon 4.15; Ready for test 20.4.15; Tested 23.4.15; Accepted 27.4.15 (F/L FW Merriam); Chingford 6.6.15 (stayed due to fog); Chelmsford 10.6.15; HD duties 18.8.15; EF, FL Fairlop 30.10.15 (FSL RM Blake), repaired; Chingford 1.11.15; Chelmsford 6.11.15; Chingford 8.11.15; Chelmsford 11.11.15; Chingford 19.2.16; Deleted 28.2.16
1593  Deld Hendon 4.15; Ready for test 27.4.15; Accepted 29.4.15 (Desoutter); Chingford by lorry 14.5.15; Chelmsford 16.5.15; AZP 31.5.15/1.6.15 (FSL HH Square); Chased Zeppelin for 2½ hrs, COL, CW

18.8.15 (FSL HH Square); Deleted 6.9.15

1594  Deld Hendon on/by 24.4.15; Erecting 27.4.15; Tested by Caudron pilot 20.5.15; Chingford 31.5.15 (overnight due to fog); Chelmsford 5.6.15; HSPP, engine trouble, landed Felixstowe Golf Course 3.7.15 (FSL EV Reid); from there to Trimley but engine trouble 24.7.15 (FSL EV Reid); retd Chelmsford 30.7.15; AZP 12.9.15 (FSL RM Blake); Deleted 27.11.15
1595  Deld Hendon and accepted 16.6.15 (Desoutter); Chingford 20.8.15 (transit); Felixstowe 21.8.15; Trimley 6.9.15; Felixstowe 9.9.15; Accident 24.9.15; Deleted 23.1.17
1596  Deld Hendon and accepted 1.7.15; Chingford 2.7.15; Chelmsford 5.7.15; Chingford 10.7.15 (temp); Chelmsford 13.7.15); AZP, three or four 20 lb Hales bombs exploded in heavy landing on return, machine blown to pieces 18.8.15 (FSL CD Morrison seriously injured); Deleted 1.9.15
1597  Deld Hendon 19.7.15; Chingford 7.8.15 (transit); Chelmsford 8.8.15; AZP 12.9.15; Chingford 7.10.15; Chelmsford 15.10.15; Chingford 20.2.16; Deleted 28.2.16

**1 DYOTT TRACTOR MONOPLANE built under Cont No C.P.44330/15 by Hewlett & Blondeau & numbered 1598. (50-hp Gnome)**

1598  Deld 5 Wing Dover 16.9.15; Deleted 27.1.16 FW&T

**1 HENRY FARMAN F.20-TYPE PUSHER BIPLANE built under Cont No C.P.44879/15 by South Coast Aviation Works & numbered 1599 28.6.15 after delivery from Shoreham. (80-hp Gnome)**

1599  Deld Eastbourne FS 26.6.15; Tested 4.7.15; FL Bethesden 6.9.15 (FSL N Keeble); Retd Eastbourne FS 8.9.15; EF, FL outside aerodrome, u/c smashed 5.1.16 (FSL WG McMinnies); Deleted 30.3.16

**1 GRAHAME-WHITE XV (ADMIRALTY 1600 TYPE) PUSHER BIPLANE ordered under Cont No C.P.70934/15, numbered 1600 & built Hendon. (70-hp Gnome)**

1600  (C/n 183). Hendon by 31.5.15; Repairs by 16.8.15; Eastbourne FS 27.8.15; Rebuilt 8.15; flying again 10.15; Under repair by 1.1.16; Dismantling by 15.1.16; Deleted 13.3.16

## RNAS SERIALS - THIRD SERIES (3001 to 4000)

**12 MAURICE FARMAN S.7 LONGHORN PUSHER BIPLANES ordered on Cont No C.P.43555/15 from The Brush Electrical Engineering Co Ltd, numbered 3001 to 3012 & built Loughborough. Delivered from Hendon. (70-hp Renault)**

3001  Deld Hendon 27.10.15; Eastbourne FS 27.10.15; EF, FL Folkestone, 26.11.15 (FSL HK Thorold); retd 28.11.15; Eastchurch Workshops 20.10.16 (80-hp Renault); Eastchurch FS 3.2.17; Eastchurch Workshops 5.3.17 (repair); Deleted 26.4.17
3002  Deld Hendon 22.10.15; Eastbourne FS 27.10.15; EF, FL 12.3.16, retd (FSL TR Hackman & FSL KR Munro uninjured); Damaged 14.5.16 (FSL JLA Sinclair); Dismantled for Eastchurch FS (NTU) 29.10.16 (80-hp Renault); Station temp closed 9.11.16; NFT
3003  Deld Hendon 29.10.15; Eastchurch NFS 4.11.15; Wrecked Eastchurch 6.11.15; Deleted 15.11.15
3004  Deld Hendon 15.11.15; Eastchurch NFS but damaged on arrival 17.11.15; High Halstead to Grain 29.11.15; Eastchurch NFS 2.12.15; Gun Flt Eastchurch 17.3.16; Cranwell 25.5.16; Wrecked 4.10.16; Deleted 25.10.16
3005  Deld Hendon 18.12.15; Eastchurch NFS 19.12.15; Bomb Flt Eastchurch 17.3.16; Damaged 1.4.16; School Flt Eastchurch 31.5.16; Eastchurch Workshops 23.3.17 (overhaul); EF in circuit, u/c broken landing 11.6.17 (PFO WF Crundall); Deleted 21.6.17
3006  Deld Hendon 22.11.15; Chingford by lorry 7.12.15; Into ditch on TO 19.7.16; Deleted 8.9.17 BR
3007  Deld Hendon 14.1.16; Eastbourne 22.1.16; Deleted 17.8.16

3008  Deld Hendon 25.1.16; Chingford 25.1.16; DC fitted 7.2.16; Cranwell by 7.16; Crashed 15.8.16; Deleted 3.10.16
3009  Deld Killingholme 22.1.16; Cranwell 8.5.16; Wrecked 22.10.16; Deleted 25.10.16
3010  Deld Hendon 10.2.16; Chingford 10.2.16 (75-hp Renault by 10.17); Eastbourne 27.10.17; Crashed and burnt 4.1.18 (pilot unhurt); Deleted W/E 19.1.18
3011  Deld Hendon 9.2.16; Tested Chingford 10.2.16 (arrived 1.2.16); Cranwell 3.5.16; To repair 13.3.17; Deleted 17.5.17
3012  Due Chingford for Cranwell, ready 11.3.16; NFT

**50 BRISTOL SCOUT TYPE C TRACTOR BIPLANES ordered 14.8.15 under Cont Nos C.P.46106/15 & C.P.74782/15/X, numbered 3013 to 3062 & built Filton. (80-hp Gnome) [C/n's 524 to 560, 771 to 783]**

3013  Deld Grain 5.9.15; Accepted 22.9.15; HMS *Vindex* 19.10.15; Grain 31.10.15 (for expts at Eastchurch); Eastchurch NFS 3.11.15; Grain 14.11.15; HMS *Vindex* 14.11.15; Trimley 13.12.15; Eastchurch 26.6.16; Eastchurch Workshops 30.10.16 for War Flt; Chingford 9.2.17; Cranwell 5.4.17; CW 17.7.17; Became 201/2 TDS Cranwell 1.4.18
3014  Deld Grain for erection 12.10.15; HMS *Vindex* 12.11.15; Trimley 27.11.15; War Flt Eastchurch 26.6.16; School Flt Eastchurch after repair in carpenters shop 12.7.16; Eastchurch Workshops for War Flt 30.10.16; Crashed 4.11.16; Eastchurch Workshops

*Blackburn-built A.D. Scout 1536 "The Sparrow" at Chingford*

*Bleriot XI-BG Parasol Monoplane 1548 at Eastchurch. (J.M.Bruce/G.S.Leslie collection)*

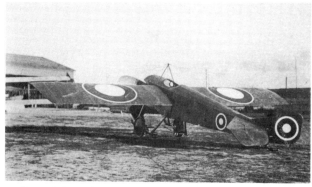

*Dyott Monoplane 1598 with 5 Wing at Dover, 1915. (J.M.Bruce/G.S.Leslie collection)*

*Curtiss Type T flying boat 3073 at Felixstowe. (J.M.Bruce/G.S.Leslie collection)*

*Handley Page O/100 3124 just after landing at Mudros after its flight from the United Kingdom. (Frank Cheesman)*

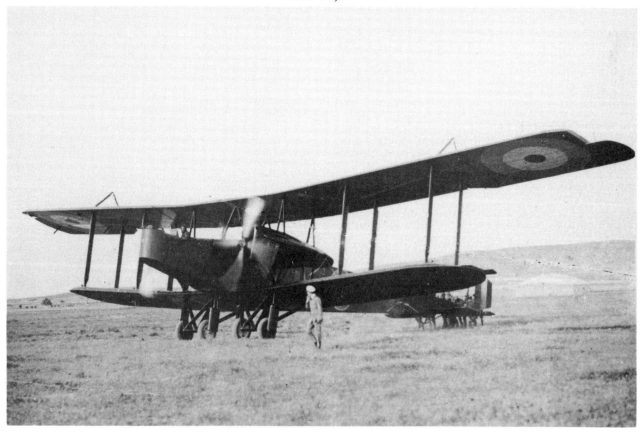

5.11.16; Deleted 16.3.17

**3015** Deld CSD White City to 4 Wing Eastchurch 30.9.15; HACP 20.2.16 (F/L BF Fowler); HSPP 19.3.16 (FSL C Perrett); Westgate loan 27.3.16; Wrecked in gale at Westgate 29.3.16; Retd 4 Wing Eastchurch by road 29.3.16; War Flt Eastchurch 16.4.16; Wrecked 26.4.16 (FSL HW Evens); Deleted 24.5.16

**3016** Deld CSD White City by 30.6.16; Cranwell 16.7.16; AZP 3.8.16 (FSL AHH Gilligan); Deleted 25.10.16 [Possibly the a/c in which TFSL PS Kennedy killed 26.9.16]

**3017** Shipped to Mediterranean by 4.16 ; Retd UK, and to SV Section White City 17.6.16; Later deleted

**3018** Deld and tested Grain 3.11.15; Lewis gun experiments 3.11.15, 11.11.15 & 16.11.15; Shipped to 2 Wing Aegean by 4.16; Retd UK by 6.16 and deleted

**3019** Shipped to 2 Wing by 4.16; Retd UK 6.16; CSD White City 6.16; Cranwell 12.9.16 - 1.17; Freiston 1.17; Deleted Cranwell 12.3.17

**3020** Shipped to Mediterranean by 4.16 ; Retd UK, and to SV Section White City 17.6.16; Cranwell 15.9.16; Crashed, slightly damaged Cranwell South 17.1.18 (pilot uninjured); Crashed, wing damaged Cranwell South 23.1.18 (pilot unhurt); Became 201/2 TDS Cranwell 1.4.18

**3021** Shipped to Mediterranean by 4.16; Retd UK (6.16?); To CSD White City; E Flt Cranwell 13.9.16; FL on Lincoln road 5.11.17; Crashed and damaged Cranwell 9.12.17 (pilot uninjured); Became 201/2 TDS Cranwell 1.4.18

**3022** Shipped to Mediterranean by 4.16; Retd UK (6.16?); To CSD White City; Cranwell 30.9.16; Wrecked by 16.4.17; Crashed 2.10.17; O/t landing, slight damage 13.1.18 (pilot uninjured); Became 201/2 TDS Cranwell 1.4.18

**3023** Deld Chingford 11.10.15; Westgate 5.11.15; HSPP 19.3.16 (FSL JS Browne); Went over cliffs landing, DBR 24.3.16 (FSL RE Bush unhurt); Deleted 27.3.16

**3024** Deld Chingford 20.10.15; Allocated Westgate 20.10.15 (NTU); Wrecked 3.11.15; Deleted 11.15

**3025** Deld Redcar for erection 23.10.15; Hendon (via Cranwell) 3.6.16; Damaged 6.11.16; For deletion 10.11.16, but repaired instead; Re-erecting by 2.17; Damaged after landing 23.2.17 (F/Cdr T Hinshelwood); Deleted 8.3.17

**3026** Deld Redcar for erection 23.10.15; Scarborough 30.3.16; Hendon (via Cranwell) 3.6.16; Grain 26.10.16; Became PVRS 11.16 (for deck landing trials); Deck landing expt 3.1.17 (F/L FE Sandford); Became ECD Grain 26.2.17; EAD Grain 9.3.17; Repair 25.5.17; War Flt/School Manston 13.6.17; Surveyed 26.10.17; Deleted 29.10.17 W&T

**3027** Deld Chingford and tested 3.11.15 (Raynham); Eastchurch 14.11.15 (transit); Westgate 15.11.15; Fitted Ranken Darts 12.15; Damaged landing 12.3.16 (F/L HA Buss); to Clement Talbot Works 30.3.16 for repair but later deleted

**3028** Deld Chingford by lorry 2.11.15; Tested 3.11.15 (Raynham); Trimley 19.11.15; HMS *Vindex* 29.11.15; Trimley 4.12.15; Felixstowe 21.1.16; Used in expts to fly off Porte Baby 6.4.16; Trimley 14.4.16; Levington NLG 2.7.16; Sideslipped and damaged on TO 20.7.16 (FSL MJG Day); Fairey to repair wings 12.8.16; Felixstowe 21.2.17; Cranwell 20.1.18; Crashed, slightly damaged NE of aerodrome 11.3.18 (pilot unhurt); Became 201/2 TDS Cranwell 1.4.18; Crashed, propeller and wings damaged 5.4.18 (pilot unhurt)

**3029** Deld Redcar 14.11.15; AZP 10.2.16 (FSL HC Vereker); COL 3.4.16 (FSL HC Vereker injured); Deleted 1.5.16

**3030** (later 60-hp Le Rhône) Deld Redcar 11.15; Erecting 27.11.15; Scarborough 19.12.15; Hornsea 22.12.15; To Scarborough, COL in strong wind 23.1.16 (F/Cdr C Draper); AZP 1/2.4.16 (F/Cdr C Draper); Redcar 30.1.17; Cranwell 23.3.17; FL, propeller and wing damaged, Kirkby, Lincs 27.3.18 (pilot unhurt); Became 201/2 TDS Cranwell 1.4.18

**3031** Deld Chingford by lorry 24.11.15; Tested 30.11.15 (Raynham); Trimley 8.12.15; HMS *Vindex* 17.12.15; Felixstowe 18.6.16; Cranwell 22.6.16; U/c and propeller broken 13.8.17; Crashed and damaged 4.12.17 (pilot unhurt); Became 201/2 TDS Cranwell 1.4.18

**3032** Deld Chingford by lorry 24.11.15; Trimley 8.12.15;

HMS *Vindex* 17.12.15; Felixstowe 18.6.16; Cranwell 26.6.16; Freiston 6.16; Cranwell 28.6.16; Freiston 12.7.16; Retd Cranwell; U/c repaired 2.17; Crashed and wrecked 19.2.18 (pilot unhurt); Became 201/2 TDS Cranwell 1.4.18

**3033** Deld Chingford by lorry 30.11.15; Erecting 3.12.15; Dover 27.1.16 (arr in damaged condition by lorry from Slough 30.1.16); EF, FL, wrecked 30.7.16 (FSL AV Bowater unhurt); Deleted 29.8.16

**3034** Deld Redcar 6.12.15; Whitley Bay 9.1.16; Redcar 28.5.16; Cranwell 29.7.16; Crashed 9.3.17; Deleted 3.4.17

**3035** (80-hp Clerget). Deld Grain 15.12.15; RD Grain 29.1.16; Tested 29.5.16; Defence Flt Dover (via Folkestone) 19.7.16; ADD 20.7.16 - @3.8.16; C Sqdn 1 Wing by 24.8.16; ADD by 14.9.16; Dover 16.9.16; Deleted 26.4.17 [100-hp Mono per official 1.17 list]

**3036** (80-hp Le Rhône) Shipped to Dardanelles 12.15; A Sqdn 2 Wing Thasos by 5.16 - @28.11.16; Deleted 1917

**3037** (80-hp Le Rhône) Shipped to Dardanelles 12.15; C Flt A Sqdn 2 Wing Imbros by 4.5.16 - @31.8.16; Deleted 1917

**3038** Deld Redcar for erection 19.12.15; FL, damaged 5.2.16; EF, FL, CW 19.8.16 (FSL HT Mellings unhurt); Deleted 29.8.16

**3039** Deld Chingford by lorry 22.12.15; Accepted 5.1.16 (Raynham); For HMS *Vindex* 17.1.16 (NTU); Dover 26.1.16; HACP 5.2.16 (F/L BL Huskisson); HACP 9.2.16 (F/L H Rosher); 2 HACPs 20.2.16 (F/L H Rosher); Westgate 18.3.16 (landed Folkestone); Retd Dover; HACP, EF, FL badly damaged 19.3.16 (F/L GRH Talbot); HACP 9.7.16 (FSL EW Norton); Damaged landing 31.7.16 (FSL CHBJ Parson); HACP 22.9.16 (F/L JP Coleman); HACP 27.10.16 (FSL NT Bailey); Deleted 20.3.17

**3040** (80-hp Le Rhône) Shipped to Dardanelles 12.15; C Flt A Sqdn 2 Wing Imbros by 29.4.16 - @31.8.16; Deleted 1917

**3041** (later 60-hp Le Rhône) Deld Redcar for erection 23.12.15; Erecting 1.1.16; AZP 10.2.16 (F/L CB Dalison); Cranwell 26.4.17 (at Freiston 8.17); Crashed, CW 22.3.18 (pilot unhurt); Became 201/2 TDS Cranwell 1.4.18

**3042** Deld Chingford by rail 30.12.15; Tested 8.1.16 & 20.1.16 (Raynham); 4 Wing Eastchurch 24.1.16; Damaged 30.1.16 (F/L RC Hardstaff); War Flt Eastchurch 16.4.16; EF, FL, repaired 11.9.16 (FSL EP Hicks); Crashed 30.10.16, to Workshops; Eastchurch FS 16.12.16; For deletion by 30.3.18

**3043** Deld Chingford by lorry 11.1.16; Dover Defence Flt 27.1.16; HACP 8.2.16 (FSL RFS Leslie); HACP 9.2.16 (F/Cdr SV Sippe); HSPPs 20.2.16 and 19.3.16 (both FSL RFS Leslie); HD duties 20.3.16 (FSL JH Thompson); HACP 24.4.16 (FSL ER Grange); Dunkerque 29.6.16 (temp); 5m W of Ypres engaged HA which was forced down inside German lines 9.7.16 (FSL RA Little); ADD by 3.8.16; Dover 31.8.16; Deleted 26.2.17

**3044** Deld Chingford by lorry 4.2.16; Tested 7.2.16 (Raynham); Dover 9.3.16; Deleted 23.5.17

**3045** Deld Chingford by lorry 2.2.16; Dover 8.2.16; HACP 20.2.16 (F/L FG Andreae); Patrol nr aerodrome 16.5.16 (FSL ER Pritchard); HSPP 19/20.5.16 (FSL SJ Goble); HACP 22.10.16 (FSL FJ Bailey); HACP 28.11.16 (FSL NDM Hewitt); Deleted 11.12.16

**3046** Deld Chingford by lorry 4.2.16; Grain 10.2.16; Slightly damaged 24.2.16, repaired (FSL FUY Weldon); EAD Grain 12.5.17 (fixed mg interrupter gear); Acceptance Dept Grain W/E 15.12.17; Became 201/2 TDS Cranwell 1.4.18

**3047** Deld Chingford by lorry 2.2.16; Grain 10.2.16; War Flt Eastchurch 27.11.16; Wrecked 28.11.16, to Workshops; Chingford 8.2.17; Cranwell by lorry 9.5.17; Crashed 15.5.17; Crashed 11.7.17; Crashed 7.8.17; Crashed, slightly damaged Cranwell South 16.2.18 (pilot uninjured); Became 201/2 TDS Cranwell 1.4.18

**3048** Deld Chingford by lorry 12.2.16; Yarmouth 20.2.16; Dart droppers fitted 24.2.16; Damaged by 1.4.16; Deleted 13.4.16

**3049** Deld Chingford by lorry 9.2.16; Westgate 21.2.16; HACP 18.3.16 (FSL JA Carr); HACP 24.4.16 (F/Cdr

CH Butler); War Flt Manston 23.6.16; EF, FL in wheat field 8.7.16; HACPs 2 x 22.10.16 & 23.10.16 (all FSL ES Boynton); HACP 28.11.16 (FSL HA Pailthorpe); Crashed 18.10.17; Surveyed 26.10.17; Deleted 29.10.17 W&T

3050    Deld Chingford by lorry 14.2.16; Supermarine repair 13.3.16; Westgate 26.4.16; Manston 21.6.16; Deleted 2.3.17

3051    Deld Chingford by lorry 22.2.16; Grain 5.3.16; Dropped Ranken Darts 3.4.16; HACP 9.7.16 (FSL EM Morgan); Chingford 8.2.17; E Flt Cranwell 28.3.17; FL, slightly damaged near Brauncewell Gun Station 5.12.17 (pilot uninjured); Became 201/2 TDS Cranwell 1.4.18

3052    Deld Chingford by lorry 27.2.16; Tested 26.3.16; Grain 23.4.16; Eastchurch War Flt 27.11.16; Detling 20.12.16; Hit by 8990 24.12.16; Deleted 16.1.17

3053    Deld Chingford by lorry 26.2.16; Grain 23.4.16; Chingford 7.2.17; Cranwell by lorry 31.3.17 (arr 3.4.17); Crashed 7.8.17; Wrecked 25.9.17; COL Cranwell South 29.1.18 (pilot unhurt); Became 201/2 TDS Cranwell 1.4.18

3054    Deld Chingford by lorry 17.3.16; Tested 26.3.16; Westgate 31.3.16; HACP, FL, damaged propeller wheel and wing 24.4.16 (FSL JA Carr); HACP 3.5.16 (FSL JA Carr); Manston 20.6.16; Chingford 23.1.17; Cranwell by lorry 31.3.17 (arr 3.4.17); Wrecked 7.8.17; Crashed, TW Cranwell South 3.1.18 (pilot uninjured); Crashed, CW nr Cranwell 20.3.18 (PFO CC Franklin killed)

3055    Deld Chingford by lorry 2.3.16; Westgate 31.3.16; HACPs 28.4.16 & 3.5.16 (both FSL JS Browne); HSPP 3.5.16 (FSL JS Browne); War Flt/School Manston 23.6.16; HACPs 9.7.16 (FSL CW Greig), 12.8.16 & 16.9.16 (FSL JS Browne); Surveyed 26.10.17; Deleted 29.10.17 W&T

3056    Deld Chingford by lorry 4.3.16; Tested 26.3.16; Yarmouth 8.4.16; HACP 28.5.16 (FSL EL Pulling); FL near Gorleston Cemetery 22.8.16 (F/L BD Kilner); Burgh Castle 31.8.16; Yarmouth, HACP 9.9.16 (FSL S Kemball); War Flt Burgh Castle 12.12.16; HACP 18.12.16 (FSL CS Iron); Yarmouth 10.1.17; Burgh Castle 15.1.17; HACP 26.1.17 (FSL CS Iron); Broke propeller and damaged wings landing 26.2.17 (FSL TGC Wood); Yarmouth 1.3.17; Burgh Castle 27.4.17; Yarmouth 5.5.17; Burgh Castle 1.6.17; Yarmouth 1.7.17; Holt W/E 15.9.17; Deleted W/E 23.3.18

3057    Deld Chingford by lorry 7.3.16; Tested 26.3.16; Yarmouth 8.4.16; Deleted 20.5.16

3058    Deld Chingford by lorry 11.3.16; Tested 26.3.16; 4 Wing Eastchurch 1.4.16; War Flt Eastchurch 16.4.16; Misc Flt Eastchurch 15.7.16; Bomb Flt Eastchurch 21.8.16; Deleted at Workshops 24.12.17

3059    Deld Chingford by lorry 3.16; Tested 26.3.16; Eastchurch 31.3.16; War Flt Eastchurch 16.4.16 HSPP by 19/20.5.16 (F/L HG Henley); HACP 25.8.16 (FSL AF Buck); Crashed 3.11.16 (FSL GT Bysshe); Eastchurch Workshops 3.11.16 - @1.1.17; Gunnery School Flts Eastchurch by 2.17; Gun Flt Eastchurch by 15.3.17; Gunnery School Flts 25.4.17; Gun Flt Eastchurch by 13.5.17; Surveyed 12.3.18; Deleted 16.3.18

3060    Deld Eastbourne 4.4.16; Tested 8.4.16; HACP, crashed 24.4.16 (F/L MS Marsden); Damaged 24.5.16 (FSL A Durston); Vendôme 25.12.16; Became 205 TDS Vendôme 1.4.18; Tyre came off landing, o/t, slightly damaged 24.7.18 (PFO WA Hammerton)

3061    Deld Eastbourne 4.4.16; Ready 8.4.16; U/c wrecked 9.4.16 (FSL RJ McMinnies); Vendôme 25.12.16; Became 205 TDS Vendôme 1.4.18; EF, FL, badly damaged, football ground 26.6.18 (PFO AJ O'Neil)

3062    Deld Eastbourne for erection 25.3.16; Packed for Vendôme by 12.10.16; Vendôme 11.16; Flew into ground, CW 5.12.16 (2/Lt TS Mann); Deleted 26.1.17

3063    Presentation a/c 'Britons Overseas No.1' (named 7.15); Deld Grain 16.9.15; Accepted 23.9.15; HMS *Vindex* 30.9.15; Grain 20.10.15; HMS *Vindex* 20.10.15; Grain 26.10.15; HACP from Grain 20.2.16 (F/L AR Arnold & PO Mech WH Hodgson); Nore War Flt Grain 24.4.16; Calshot 21.7.17; Surveyed 28.9.17; Deleted 6.10.17 W&T

3064    Presentation a/c 'Britons Overseas No.2' (named 7.15); Deld Grain 16.9.15; Accepted 23.9.15; HMS *Vindex* 2.10.15; Grain 29.10.15; HACP from Grain 20.2.16 (F/L AR Arnold & PO Mech WH Hodgson); Damaged float chassis landing 19.3.16 (F/L EdeC Hallifax & PO Mech WH Hodgson); Nore War Flt Grain 24.4.16; Deleted 8.11.16

3065    Presentation a/c 'Britons Overseas No.3' (named 7.15); Deld Grain 16.9.15; HMS *Vindex* 1.10.15; Grain 26.10.15; Came down on patrol, towed to Felixstowe by TBD2, 10.4.16; Nore War Flt Grain 24.4.16; Dover 4.11.16; Calshot but EF, FL en route at Bognor 6.11.16; A Flt Lee-on- Solent W/E 30.12.17; Became 209 TDS Lee-on-Solent 1.4.18; Deleted W/E 27.6.18

3066    Presentation a/c 'Hong Kong Britons No.2'; Deld Grain 16.9.15; Accepted 28.9.15 (Kemp); To HMS *Vindex* capsized on arrival 5.10.15; Deleted 7.10.15

3067    Presentation a/c 'Hong Kong Britons No.3 - Britons Overseas No.8' (presented 1.16, named 16.5.16 - SIC); Deld Grain for Westgate 17.9.15; Accepted 28.9.15; Westgate 2.10.15; Missing on patrol to West Hinder 14.12.15 (FSL AJ Nightingale PoW)

3068    Presentation a/c 'Shanghai Britons No.1' (named 7.15); Deld Grain 22.9.15; Accepted 1.10.15; HMS *Vindex* and W/T test 2.10.15; W/T test Grain 4.10.15; Westgate 7.10.15; HSPP 19.3.16 (FSL BA Millard); Experiments with wheels on floats for taking up seaplane from shore 17.6.16 (S/Cdr RP Ross); Calshot W/E 20.10.17; Lee-on-Solent W/E 1.11.17; Total loss W/E 15.11.17, deleted

3069    Presentation a/c 'Hong Kong Britons No.1'; Deld Scapa by puffer for erection 8.9.15; HMS *Campania* 24.9.15; Damaged u/c landing, beached, TW 12.11.15; Remains salved 13.11.15, deleted

3070    Deld Scapa by puffer for erection 8.9.15; HMS *Campania* 1.10.15; Scapa 8.12.15; HMS *Campania* 17.4.16; Scapa 1.5.16; HMS *Campania* 2.5.16; Scapa 1.7.16; HMS *Campania* 26.7.16; Scapa 8.8.16; HMS *Campania* 25.8.16; FL beach, damaged u/c 26.8.16 (FSL JF Horsey & OSL AO Jones); Scapa 30.8.16; HMS *Campania* 8.3.17; Scapa 16.7.17; Houton Bay by 10.18; Surveyed 11.1.18; Deleted 18.1.18 W&T

3071    Presentation a/c named 'New York Britons No.2 - Britons Overseas No.7' (named 11.1.16); Deld Grain 18.9.15; Accepted 1.10.15; Westgate 4.10.15; HACP 17.3.16 (FSL BA Millard & CPO Boyle); Wrecked Westgate 16.5.16; Deleted 29.5.16

3072    (160-hp Sunbeam) Presentation a/c 'Shanghai Britons No.2' (named 7.15); Deld Grain 30.12.15; Accepted 7.1.16; Type trials 18.6.16; Felixstowe 20.6.16; PVRS by 9.16; Westgate 2.9.16; HACP 28.11.16 (FSL RE Spear & AM Lewis); Damaged on TO, towed into Margate, then by road to Westgate 23.1.17 (FSL LG Maxton & AM2 GO Wright unhurt); EF, FL in sea returning from AZP, later sank 24.5.17 (FSL HM Morris & AM2 GO Wright); Crew picked up from wreckage in North Sea by H12 from Felixstowe 29.5.17; Deleted 8.6.17

**20 CURTISS TYPE T TRACTOR TRIPLANE FLYING BOATS ordered 5.16 under Cont No C.P.102967/16, to be numbered 3073 to 3092 and built in America. (Ordered with four 250-hp Curtiss but fitted four 240-hp Renault instead)**

3073    Deld Felixstowe 1.10.16; Flown 10.11.16 (W/Cdr JC Porte); Tail gave way landing 13.11.16 (F/L RJJ Hope-Vere); Dismantled by 1.4.17; Deleted W/E 10.10.18

3074 to 3092 cancelled 11.16

**20 SHORT ADMIRALTY 827 TYPE TRACTOR BIPLANE SEAPLANES ordered 13.5.15 under Cont Nos C.P.49441/15 & C.P.70484/15 from The Sunbeam Motor Car Co Ltd, numbered 3093 to 3112 & built Wolverhampton. (150-hp Sunbeam-Coatelen)**

**10 SHORT ADMIRALTY 827 TYPE TRACTOR BIPLANE SEAPLANES ordered under Cont No C.P.43399/15, numbered 3063 to 3072 & built Rochester. (150-hp Sunbeam) [Gordon Bruce's researches show correct c/n's to be S.163 to S.172]**

3093 Deld Grain 8.11.15; Accepted 14.11.15 (Kemp); Shorts Rochester 17.12.15; Shipped to East Africa; 8 Sqdn Zanzibar; Transferred to Belgian Government for use in Belgian Congo

3094 Deld Grain 21.11.15; Shorts Rochester 18.12.15; Grain 12.15; Westgate 24.3.16; 8 Sqdn Zanzibar; Transferred to Belgian Government for use in Belgian Congo

3095 Deld Grain by lorry 4.12.15; Accepted 11.12.15; Shipped to East Africa; 8 Sqdn Zanzibar; Transferred to Belgian Government for use in Belgian Congo

3096 Presentation a/c 'Britons Overseas No.4' (named 7.15); Deld Grain by road 10.12.15; Left for shipment to 7 Sqdn 18.1.16; Shipped to Mombasa from Avonmouth Docks in SS *Clan MacPherson* 7.2.16; Chukwani 8.7.16; HMS *Manica* 7.16; Chukwani 30.7.16; Arrived 17.8.16; Cape Station/8 Sqdn Zanzibar by 8.16: HMS *Manica* 1.9.16; Zanzibar 26.9.16; Overhaul 11.16; HMS *Manica* to HMS *Princess* 1.3.17; Lindi 12.3.17; HMS *Manica* 26.3.17; Chukwani 19.4.17; Lindi 21.4.17; still 8 Sqdn 28.12.17; For deletion by 16.3.18

3097 Presentation a/c 'Britons Overseas No.5' (named 7.15); Deld Grain, erected and tested 23.12.15; Accepted 8.1.16; Left for shipment to 7 Sqdn 18.1.16; Shipped to Mombasa from Avonmouth Docks in SS *Clan MacPherson* 7.2.16; Arrived 17.3.16; arr Cape Station/8 Sqdn Zanzibar 1.4.16: HMS *Laconia* 10.4.16; Tanga 11.4.16; Chukwani 13.4.16; Zanzibar 15.4.16; Dar es Salaam 3.6.16; Kokotoni 12.6.16; HMS *Manica* 13.6.16; Chukwani 14.6.16; HMS *Himalaya* 26.6.16; Chukwani 27.6.16; Zanzibar 30.6.16; HMS *Himalaya* 12.7.16; Chukwani 6.8.16; HMS *Himalaya* 14.8.16; Bagomoya 15.8.16; Mikindani 18.8.16; Kilwa Kiswani 19.8.16; Lindi 21.8.16; Sudi (engine failure) 24.8.16; Chukwani 27.8.16; Zanzibar 1.9.16; HMS *Himalaya* 7.9.16; Mikindani 13.9.16; Lindi 16.9.16; Chukwani 20.9.16; HMS *Himalaya* 26.9.16; Lindi 1.10.16; HMS *Himalaya* in tow 1.11.16; Chukwani 3.11.16; Zanzibar 8.11.16 (overhaul); Tested Chukwani after overhaul 27.4.17; Flying until 24.8.17; Next flown 1.3.18; Deleted 15.3.18 [HMS *Manica* to 9.2.17 ??]

3098 Presentation a/c 'Britons Overseas No.6' (named 7.15); Grain, erected and tested 29.12.15; Left for shipment to 7 Sqdn 18.1.16; Shipped to Mombasa from Avonmouth Docks in SS *Clan MacPherson* 7.2.16; Arrived 17.3.16; Cape Station/8 Sqdn Zanzibar 3.16: movements: HMS *Manica* 8.10.16; HMS *Himalaya* 2.11.16; Chukwani overhaul 3.11.16; Deleted 28.3.17 BR
[NB 4 a/c shipped in SS *Clan MacPherson* 7.2.16. 3096/8 plus another]

3099 Deld Grain by lorry 19.1.16; Tested with 4-blade propeller 28.1.16; Accepted 21.2.16; Dover 16.3.16; Dunkerque 2.4.16; AZP 3.4.16 (FSL FJ Bailey & T/S/L RM Inge); Patrol to Zeebrugge 25.4.16 (FSL W Perham & AM Clarke); HMS *Vindex* 26.4.16; Grain 27.4.16; Dover 27.4.16; Dunkerque 29.4.16; Dover 3.5.16; Felixstowe 17.6.16; Condemned 4.7.16

3100 Deld Grain 14.1.16; Accepted 29.2.16; Dunkerque 29.2.16; Grain 17.3.16; Dover 19.3.16; Dunkerque 29.3.16; Fitted 4x16-lb bomb gear 1.4.16; Dover 6.4.16; Wrecked on TO outside Dover harbour 20.6.16 (FSL A Durstan unhurt); Deleted 22.6.16

3101 Deld Grain 18.1.16; Accepted 21.2.16; Dover, chassis damaged on slipway 17.3.16 (FSL CF Latimer); Dunkerque 5.4.16; Patrol to Zeebrugge 25.4.16 (FSL GG Hodge & AM Fryer); Dover 22.5.16; Dunkerque 23.5.16; Dover 3.6.16; Dunkerque 9.6.16; Dover 17.6.16; Dunkerque 18.6.16; Dover 26.6.16; Dunkerque 27.6.16; EF in mid-Channel, towed to Dover 7.7.16 (F/Cdr FET Hewlett & CPO EJ Wright); Hit, damaged floats and propeller, repairs 17.9.16 (FSL LH Slatter); Fighting patrol (last flight) 24.9.16 (FSL LH Slatter), then deleted

3102 Deld Grain 1.2.16; Portland 11.9.16; Grain 22.9.16; HACP 28.11.16 (FSL CV Bessette & CPO Hartley); Deleted 17.1.17

3103 Deld Grain 2.16; Accepted 2.3.16; Portland 11.9.16; Dover 21.9.16 (transit); Grain 22.9.16; Calshot 22.7.17; Deleted W/E 14.9.17

3104 Deld Grain 18.2.16; Yarmouth 19.3.16; HSMP 23.5.16 (FSL A Gammon & CPO Holmes); Damaged on TO

15.7.16 (FSL JW Hobbs & CPO Hayward); Tested but unsatisfactory 26.10.16; Deleted 31.10.16

3105 Deld Grain 25.2.16; Accepted 9.3.16; Yarmouth 27.3.16; Beached, float damaged Aldeburgh 29.4.16 (FSL WA Davies & OSL DC Evans); AZP 19.6.16 (FSL JW Hobbs & CPO Holmes); Deleted 31.10.16

3106 Deld Grain 3.3.16; Accepted 24.3.16; Nore War Flt Grain by 24.4.16; HSPP 19/20.5.16 (FSL FUY Weldon & AM Daly); Deleted 17.1.17

3107 Deld Grain 3.16; Accepted 24.3.16; Nore War Flt Grain by 24.4.16; Trials with Bellars-Noyes bombsight and Lewis Gun Rake sight 27.5.16; Deleted 8.11.16

3108 Deld Grain 14.3.16; Accepted 24.3.16; Yarmouth 23.4.16; Badly damaged by shellfire from German High Seas Fleet raiding Scarborough 16.00-17.00 25.4.16 (FSL HG Hall seriously wounded & OSL DC Evans); Repaired; Capsized off Southwold 29.6.16 (FSL FP Reeves & AM Hains landed safely); Deleted 11.7.16

3109 Deld Grain 21.3.16; Yarmouth 28.4.16; HSMP 21.7.16 (FSL JW Hobbs & CPO Rose); Deleted 31.10.16

3110 Deld Grain 29.3.16; Westgate 27.4.16; Struck mooring and wrecked on TO 31.7.16 (FSL CFM Chambers); Retd Westgate from Dover 1.8.16; Deleted 9.8.16

3111 Deld Grain 5.4.16; Accepted 28.4.16; Westgate 11.5.16; Re-fitted 160-hp 2.17; HSPP 16.2.17 (FSL WN Tees); Felixstowe 10.5.17 (overhaul); Westgate 11.5.17; AZP 24.5.17; EF, adrift, CW off Tongue LV 9.6.17; Deleted 15.6.17

3112 Deld Grain 11.4.16; Accepted 5.5.16; While manoeuvring to engage U-boat, fell in sea, towed to Westgate, crew rescued by trawler 2.8.16 (FSL GN Moore & PO Mech WH Hodgson); Deleted 11.8.16

**2 FBA (TYPE A?) PUSHER BIPLANE FLYING BOATS ordered from Louis Schreck, numbered 3113 and 3114 & built Argenteuil. (100-hp Gnome Monosoupape)**

3113 Deld Seaplane Base 1 Wing Dunkerque 14.4.15; FF 15.4.15; Mkrs 30.4.15 (fit new hull); 1 Wing Dunkerque 21.5.15; AZP, retd engine trouble 21.5.15 (S/Cdr CEH Rathborne); Taxied into ship in harbour, broke elevator 18.6.15 (F/L JJ Petre); Wing damaged landing in rough sea (by?) 1.12.15; Damaged wing on TO 24.12.15 (FSL JBP Ferrand & FSL GG Hodge); Attacked 4 enemy seaplanes 3m N of Westende, 1 Albatros seaplane with long floats nosedived into water and sank 28.12.15 (FSL JBP Ferrand & AM1 Oldfield); EF, FL in North Sea on anti-submarine patrol, drifted 30 hrs 23.1.16 (FSL JBP Ferrand & AM2 Fanshawe); a/c and crew towed from mouth of Meuse by Swedish steamer, then transferred to HM Supply Ship *Couden Bay* for Ramsgate 26.1.16; Arrived Dover but badly damaged in tow, CW 27.1.16; Awaiting deletion 16.2.16; Deleted 7.3.16

3114 Deld Seaplane Base 1 Wing Dunkerque by 23.4.15; Engine trouble, nosedived and damaged 24.5.15 (FSL JJ Petre injured); Struck tow rope on TO, wrecked and hull damaged 5.12.15 (FSL W Perham unhurt), being surveyed; Deleted 22.1.16 FW&T

**28 HANDLEY PAGE 0/100 TRACTOR BIPLANE BOMBERS ordered 11.4.15 on Cont No C.P. 69522/15 & numbered 3115 to 3142. (Two Eagle variants)**

3115 (250-hp RR) Deld Hendon 15.1.17; Accepted 16.1.17; HP Sqdn Manston 28.2.17; Allocated French Govt 22.3.17 (NTU); 7 Sqdn Coudekerque 5.4.17; While bombing German destroyer, shot down in sea by large German seaplane 3m NNW of Nieuport 25.4.17 (FSL TSS Hood drowned, G/L LM RH Watson PoW died, AM2 WC Danzey PoW [died 6.12.17], G/L AM1 FC Kirby wounded, rescued by one of two French FBA, the other being shot down by flak then towed into Ostende by German destroyer); Deleted 3.6.17

3116 (250-hp RR) Deld Hendon 22.1.17 (Prodger); Accepted 23.1.17 (Prodger); HP Sqdn Manston 6.2.17; 5 Sqdn HP Flt 4.3.17; 7 Sqdn Coudekerque (coded 'B3') 2.4.17 (first HP to land at Coudekerque); FL after raid on Thorout Railway Station 15.7.17 (FSL G Andrews); HP Sqdn Manston 27.7.17; A Sqdn Manston 5.10.17; Wrecked when burst into flames just before landing

Manston 3.11.17 (PFO TR Weston, FSL JG Joseph & FSL WA Isaacs all killed + 3 severely injured)

3117 Allocated for engine trials [Became engine testbed for V/1500]; Fitted 310-hp Sunbeam Cossack; Re-engined 260-hp RAF 3a; Deld Hendon 18.5.17 (Prodger); Cranwell 14.7.17; Hendon 16.7.17; HP Sqdn Manston 19.7.17 (engine trials); Retd Hendon for Mkrs 6.8.17; Hendon 12.9.17 (Prodger); Manston 23.9.17; Dismantled and to Mkrs after EF 29.9.17; [RAE Farnborough from 15.9.17 (sic) - 3.18 (engine trials) ??]; Experimentally fitted four 200-hp Hispano-Suiza in two tandem pairs 10.17; 320-hp Sunbeams by 3.18

3118 (Eagle VIII by 10.17) Deld Hendon 30.1.17 but damaged chassis landing (Prodger); Accepted 31.1.17 (Prodger); HP Sqdn Manston 8.2.17; 7 Sqdn Coudekerque 5.4.17; HP Sqdn Manston 3.7.17; Engine caught fire, broke tail skid landing 28.7.17; HP Sqdn Stonehenge 16.2.18; Merged into 1 SoN&BD Stonehenge (coded '2') 4.18 - @5.7.18

3119 (Eagle VI) Deld Hendon and tested 9.2.17 (Prodger); Accepted 1.3.17 (Prodger); HP Sqdn Manston 27.5.17; 7 Sqdn Coudekerque 28.5.17; Believed shot down HA on return from attack on St.Denis Westrem 18/19.2.18 (F/L ER Barker DSC & S/L FD Hudson); Became 207 Sqdn 1.4.17; After attack on Zeebrugge, FL, then crew burnt a/c, Vlissingen, Zeeland 11.4.18 (Capt ER Barker DSC, Lt FD Hudson, 2/Lt DC Kinmond interned)

3120 (275-hp RR) Deld Hendon and accepted 15.2.17; Failed acceptance test, water boiling 8.5.17 (Prodger); Failed test both engines 12.5.17 (Prodger); Two radiator tests 15.5.17 (Prodger); HP Sqdn Manston 22.5.17; 7 Sqdn Coudekerque 23.5.17; 7A Sqdn by 27.9.17; Tested exptl night landing apparatus 30.9.17 - 1.10.17 (Capt Jenkins); A Sqdn 13/14.10.17; FTR from raid on Saarbrücken, shot down nr Handzaeme by Flakzug 47 24/25.10.17 (FSL A McDonald, FSL JM Smith, & LM G/L EE Smith all PoWs); Deleted 26.11.17

3121 (Eagle VI, later Eagle VII by 9.17) Deld Hendon 19.4.17 (Prodger); Accepted 22.4.17; 7 Sqdn Coudekerque (via Manston) 5.5.17; 7A Sqdn by 10.9.17; Became 14 Sqdn (coded 'A3') 9.12.17; Returning from raid on Bruges docks, crashed, o/t 1m NE of Coudekerque 12.12.17 (F/Cdr CH Darley DSC, W/Cdr JT Cull DSO & Capt G Gilmour); Deleted 17.12.17

3122 (Eagle VII) Deld Hendon and accepted 15.4.17 (Prodger); HP Sqdn Manston 20.4.17; 7 Sqdn 23.5.17; 7A Sqdn Coudekerque by 21.9.17; Shot down on night bombing raid on St.Denis Westrem/Ghent 26/27.10.17 (FSL G Andrews PoW, 2/Lt WW Hutton killed & G/L LM GA Kent PoW); Deleted 24.11.17

3123 (275-hp RR) Deld Hendon and tested 4.4.17 (Prodger); HP Sqdn Manston 8.4.17; 7 Sqdn Coudekerque 9.5.17; Manston 3.9.17; 7 Sqdn flt Redcar (Coded 'D3'; named 'SPLIT PIN' = Sieveking's nickname) 5.9.17 (HSMPs); dropped bomb on U-boat 5m NE of Long Nab 10.9.17; Dropped 6 bombs on U- boat 3m N of Redcar 11.9.17; Dropped 4x100-lb bombs on U-boat lying on sea-bed 3m E of North Cheek 21.9.17 (all F/L LG Sieveking); Manston 2.10.17; Became A Sqdn Manston 5.10.17 (still coded 'D3'); Villacoublay 14.10.17 (transit); Ochey 16.10.17; Shot down on attempted raid on Mannheim 30.10.17 (F/L LG Sieveking, AM1 G/L E Brooks, AM1 G/L HL Dodd all PoW's); Deleted 26.11.17

3124 Deld Hendon 1.5.17 (Prodger); Accepted 8.5.17 (Prodger); HP Sqdn Manston 10.5.17; Flown out 22.5.17 from UK (32½ hrs in air) [55 hrs per Barnes]; Arrived Mudros and joined 2 Wing 8.6.17; Dropped 8x112-lb bombs on German battlecruiser *Goeben* in Stenia Bay, nr Constantinople, hit claimed but ship undamaged 00.15 10.7.17 (S/Cdr KS Savory DSO awarded bar to DSO, F/L H Maclelland awarded DSC & Lt PT Rawlings awarded DSC); Dropped 2 bombs on U-boat 5/10m NE of Samothraki Island 2.9.17 (F/L JW Alcock & FSL SH Gaskell); Hit by AA fire, EF, FL in Gulf of Xeros near bombing Haida Pasha (Constantinople) 30.9.17 (F/L JW Alcock, FSL HR Aird & WO2(F) SJ Wise swam ashore and POW)

3125 (Eagle VII, to Eagle VIII 2.18, to Eagle VII 4.18) Deld Hendon 10.5.17 (Prodger); Accepted 23.5.17 (Prodger); HP Sqdn Manston 25.5.17; C Flt 7 Sqdn Coudekerque

26.5.17; 7 Sqdn flt Redcar 5.9.17 (HSMPs); 7 Sqdn flt Manston 2.10.17; Became A Sqdn Manston 5.10.17; 7 Sqdn Coudekerque by 25.10.17; Became 207 Sqdn 1.4.18; 214 Sqdn loan 5.4.18; Stbd EF after bombing Roulers Rlwy Stn, FL in ploughed field on return, hit small hay rick, wrecked Millain, nr Watten 24/25.4.18 (Lt GP Armstrong, Sgt LA Dell & AG AW Murphy); Local repair; Re-assembling by 18.5.18; EF on raid, FL in water at edge of beach nr Bray Dunes 25.6.18 (Lt HA McCormick slightly hurt, Cpl EA Barber both slightly injured & 2/Pte WJ Baker unhurt); Deletion recommended 28.6.18 (CW); 4 ASD 31.7.18

3126 (Eagle VI) Exp Stn Orfordness .17 (trials with special "invisible" dappled colour scheme); Instructions given week ending 2.3.17 to fit 6-pdr Davis gun; Deld Hendon 23.5.17 (Prodger); HP Sqdn Manston 27.5.17 (transit); 7 Sqdn Coudekerque 28.5.17; HP Sqdn Manston 4.9.17; A Sqdn Redcar 5.9.17; A Sqdn Manston 5.10.17; Villacoublay 15.10.17 (transit); Ochey 16.10.17; Redesignated 16 Sqdn Ochey 8.1.18; EF, FL, wrecked Moutrot, 3m NW of Ochey 17.2.18 (F/L TC Angus, S/L AR Clark & AC1 G/L C Hall all unhurt); 6 AP 16.2.18; ADD 18.2.18; Deleted 18.2.18

3127 (Eagle VII) Deld Hendon and accepted 24.5.17 (Prodger); 7 Sqdn Coudekerque 26.5.17 (fitted with Davis gun) (via Eastchurch, engine trouble); HP Sqdn Manston 4.9.17; A Sqdn Redcar 5.9.17 (Anti U-boat trials with Davis gun in nose turret); Martlesham 11.10.17; Manston 12.10.17; Villacoublay 15.10.17 (transit); Ochey 17.10.17; Became 16 Sqdn Ochey 8.1.18; Led raid on Mannheim 24/25.1.18 (F/Cdr FT Digby); Damaged removing from hangar Ochey 19.2.18; Led raid on Cologne, damaged in FL 24/25.3.18 (F/Cdr FK Digby awarded DSO); Became 216 Sqdn RAF 1.4.18 [& @4.5.18 & @8-22.6.18]; Forced landed; Repaired; retd 216 Sqdn (coded 'R') 19.7.18; Bombed Frescaty aerodrome during last heavy bombing raid of war 18.00 10.11.18 (Lt L Tilden-Smith, Lt CJ Clarke & 2/Lt GJ Holdcroft); 3 ASD Courban 14.11.18

3128 (Eagle VI in 10.17, to Eagle VIII 2.18) Deld Hendon 5.6.17 (Prodger); Accepted 6.6.17 (Prodger); HP Sqdn Manston 6.6.17; 7 Sqdn Coudekerque (coded 'C1') 13.6.17; Became 207 Sqdn 1.4.18; 215 Sqdn loan 5.4.18; 214 Sqdn 17.4.18; Stuck in mud Mardyke 15.6.18 (Lt JM Nichol & Sgt LA Dell); EF on TO for raid on Ostende, crashed on Calais road 17.6.18 (Lt JM Nichol, Sgt LA Dell & Pte Thorne)

3129 (Eagle VI+VII, later Eagle VI) Deld Hendon and accepted 9.6.17 (Prodger); HP Sqdn Manston 10.6.17; 7 Sqdn Coudekerque 15.6.17; 7A Sqdn by 10.9.17; Became 14 Sqdn 9.12.17; Became 214 Sqdn 1.4.18; Badly shot about in night raid on Zeebrugge, EF, FL in sea, Fort Mardyke, CW 11/12.4.18 (Lt EF McIlraith, Lt WH Matthews, Lt A Clark); 5 Group 12.4.18

3130 (Eagle VI, to Eagle VII 2.18, then Eagle VII+VI by 5.18) Deld Hendon and accepted 16.6.17 (Prodger); Eastchurch 19.6.17 (transit); HP Sqdn Manston 20.6.17; 7 Sqdn Coudekerque 23.6.17; 7A Sqdn by 10.9.17; Became 14 Sqdn Coudekerque 9.12.17; Became 214 Sqdn 1.4.18; FL, ground fog returning from raid on batteries at Ostende, crashed Mont-Lemaitre, nr Therouanne 11.5.18 (Lt JV Ould & Lt WH Matthews both injured); 2 ASD 11.5.18

3131 (Eagle VII) Deld Hendon and accepted 23.6.17 (Prodger); HP Sqdn Manston 27.6.17; 7 Sqdn Coudekerque 2.7.17; 7 Sqdn flt Redcar 5.9.17 (HSMPs); 7 Sqdn flt Manston 2.10.17; Became A Sqdn Manston 5.10.17; 7 Sqdn by 13.10.17; Became 207 Sqdn 1.4.18; 215 Sqdn loan 5.4.18; 216 Sqdn 20.4.18; 214 Sqdn 4.18; 216 Sqdn 20.5.18; Shot down over Metz 14/15.9.18 (Lt RW Heine, Lt FF Jewitt USAS, 2/Lt EA Marchant & 2/Lt WM London all PoWs)

3132 (Eagle VI, to Eagle VI+VII 1.17, to Eagle VI 2.17) Deld Hendon 30.6.17 (Prodger); HP Sqdn Manston 4.7.17; 7 Sqdn Coudekerque 5.7.17; 7A Sqdn by 9.9.17; Became 14 Sqdn 9.12.17; Became 214 Sqdn 1.4.18; Shot down near Bruges 15/16.5.18 (Capt CG Rushton, Mjr JI Harrison & Lt WJ King killed); SOC 16.5.18

3133 (Eagle VI+VII, to Eagle VI 2.17) Deld Hendon and FF 9.7.17 (Prodger); HP Sqdn Manston 11.7.17; 7 Sqdn

Coudekerque 12.7.17; 7A Sqdn 9.9.17; Became 14 Sqdn 9.12.17; Became 214 Sqdn 1.4.18; 216 Sqdn 16.5.18; 1 AD Guines 13.8.18; 100 Sqdn 13.8.18; 3 ASD 1.10.18; 1 AD Guines by 11.18; 3 AD Courban 4.11.18; 8 TDS Netheravon by 12.18; Top centre section folded up when landing, landed safely 9.12.18 (Lt CF Fyfe & 7 passengers unhurt)

3134   (Eagle VI) Deld Hendon and tested 17.7.17 (Prodger); HP Sqdn Manston 21.7.17; 7 Sqdn Coudekerque 21.7.17; 7A Sqdn by 10.9.17; Became 14 Sqdn (coded 'A1') 9.12.17; Became 214 Sqdn 1.4.18; 216 Sqdn (coded 'B3') 19.5.18; In raid on Thionville brought down intact by AA fire nr Kroppen 21.5.18 (2/Lt HL Le Roy, 2/Lt RW Peat, & 1/Pte WJL Twite POW); SOC 22.5.18; also coded 'A1'

3135   (Eagle VI+VII) Deld Hendon and accepted 24.7.17 (Prodger); HP Sqdn Manston 24.7.17; 7A Sqdn Coudekerque 25.7.17 (coded 'B3'); Badly damaged landing after raid 4.9.17; Repaired; Became 14 Sqdn Coudekerque 9.12.17; Became 214 Sqdn Coudekerque 1.4.18; 216 Sqdn 13.5.18; COL 8.7.18; Repaired; Bombed Stuttgart, lost, FL with nose in bed of River Doubs, nr Swiss border 30.7.18 (Lt AC Kilburn unhurt?, Sgt Mech R Adair injured & Lt RW Heine unhurt?); 3 ASD 4.8.18; NFT

3136   (Eagle VII) Deld Hendon and accepted 30.7.17 (Prodger); Manston 6.8.17 (via Dover); 7 Sqdn Coudekerque 10.8.17; Manston 4.9.17; 7 Sqdn flt Redcar 5.9.17 (HSMPs); Dropped 4 bombs on suspected U-boat off Runswick Bay 24.9.17 (FSL JW Beebee); A Sqdn Manston 5.10.17; Villacoublay 15.10.17 (transit); A Sqdn Ochey 17.10.17; Became 16 Sqdn Ochey 8.1.18; Became 216 Sqdn Ochey 1.4.18; FTR from raid on Saarbrücken 19/20.7.18 (Lt AR Jones, Sgt G Harvey & Sgt JS Ayre all PoWs)

3137   (275-hp RR Mk.III) Hendon 3.8.17 almost complete, ex works (Prodger); HP Sqdn Manston 10.8.17; 7A Sqdn Coudekerque 10/11.8.17; Shot down by flak near Ghent while bombing St.Denis Westrem aerodrome 25-26.8.17 (FSL HH Booth PoW, AM1 G/L SA Canning missing & ACM2 G/L PM Yeatman killed)

3138   (Eagle VI, later VII) Deld Hendon 25.8.17 (Prodger); Testing Sqdn Martlesham Heath 4.9.17 (performance tests); Hendon 11.9.17 (Eagle VII); Manston 16.9.17; 7 Sqdn Coudekerque 10/11.10.17 (transit); A Sqdn Autreville 14.10.17; 16 Sqdn Ochey 8.1.18; Damaged by enemy bombs Ochey 19.2.18; Body remained in sqdn, wings to 6 AP; Became 216 Sqdn RAF 1.4.18; Reconstructing in sqdn by 4.5.18; COL 8.7.18; En route Vancoulers-Roville, port engine caught fire, a/c burst into flames, FL nr Azelot aerodrome, port engine, lower port mainplane and fuselage burnt 18.10.18 (Lt HRAV Puncher, Sgt EC Carpenter & Lt MP Jones all unhurt); 2 AD (Vron) 19.10.18; SOC 11.18

3139   (Eagle VI) Deld Hendon 30.8.17 (Prodger); Manston 3.9.17; 7 Sqdn Coudekerque 10/11.10.17 (transit); A Sqdn Autreville 14.10.17; Crashed on TO for delivery to 7 Sqdn Coudekerque 3.11.17 (NTU); Became 16 Sqdn 8.1.18; COL 17.3.18; Became 216 Sqdn 1.4.18; Repairs completed 14.5.18; After raid on Saarbrücken, FL Blainville-sur-l'Eau, nr Luneville 18.7.18 (Lt JA Stronech, Sgt EC Carpenter & Lt B Norcross)

3140   (Eagle VI) Deld Hendon 8.9.17 (Prodger); HP Sqdn Manston 15(10?).9.17; 7 Sqdn Coudekerque 10/11.10.17 (transit); A Sqdn Autreville 14.10.17; Returning from raid, crashed in middle of wood Chancenay, nr St.Dizier 24/25.10.17 (FSL R Halley & FSL GA Flavelle); Deleted 9.11.17
BUT 16 Sqdn, shot down in error near Nancy by French, landed safely 12.1.18 [serial presumably incorrect]

3141   (Eagle VI) Deld Hendon 10.9.17 (Prodger); HP Sqdn Manston 21.9.17; 7 Sqdn Coudekerque 10/11.10.17 (transit); A Sqdn Autreville 14.10.17 (coded 'A'); On way to raid Burbach Steel Works, Saarbrücken, shot down, FL near Pirmasens 24/25.10.17 (FSL HGB Linnell PoW & TFSL GS Smith killed)

3142   Fitted two 260-hp FIAT A.12bis engines at request of Russian Govt 7.17, but allocation to Russian Govt cancelled; Deld Hendon by 10.11.17; Testing Sqdn

Martlesham Heath 20.11.17; Crashed Martlesham Heath W/E 1.12.17; Repaired and refitted Maori from 1.18 by Handley Page personnel; FF by 4.5.18; Netheravon 4.7.18

**6 SHORT S.38 TYPE PUSHER BIPLANES ordered on Cont Nos C.P.59218/15 & C.P.75962/15 from White & Thompson, numbered 3143 to 3148 & built Middleton-on-Sea, Bognor Regis. (80-hp Gnome)**

3143   Deld Eastbourne FS 29.11.15; Deleted 9.4.16
3144   Deld Eastbourne FS (via Shoreham) 27.11.15; Tested 2.1.16 (WO2 PV Fraser); Wrecked by wind 26.3.16; Deleted 9.4.16
3145   Deld Eastchurch FS (via Eastbourne) 16.12.15; Deleted 27.4.16
3146   Deld Eastchurch FS (via Eastbourne) 13.12.15; Wrecked 19.3.16; Deleted 16.4.16
3147   Deld Eastbourne FS 11.12.15; Damaged 9.4.16 (Mr James & Mr Campbell); Surveyed 15.4.16; Deleted 19.4.16
3148   Deld Eastbourne FS 21.12.15; Crashed while low flying, wrecked 10.1.16 (PFSL GE Duke and WO2 PV Fraser both killed); Deleted 31.1.16

**1 NIEUPORT TRACTOR BIPLANE SCOUT purchased from Nieuport, numbered 3149 & built Issy-les-Moulineaux. (100-hp Gnome)**

3149   Deld 4 Wing Eastchurch 31.8.15; Deleted 11.15

**1 HENRY FARMAN PUSHER BIPLANE purchased from Aéroplanes Farman, Paris and numbered 3150. (125-hp Anzani)**

3150   Deld 4 Wing Eastchurch for erection 6.9.15; Detling 14.12.15; To 3 Wing Detling 4.16; Deleted 28.6.16

**12 GRAHAME-WHITE XV (ADMIRALTY 1600 TYPE) BOXKITE PUSHER BIPLANES ordered under Cont No C.P. 69521/15, numbered 3151 to 3162 & built Hendon. (60-hp Le Rhône except 3151)**

3151   (50-hp Gnome). Deld and tested Hendon 7.8.15; Chingford 12.8.15; Deleted 24.10.16
3152   Deld Chingford 7.8.15; In wrecked condition 16.8.15; Repaired by 1.10.15; Deleted 1.2.16
3153   Deld Chingford 23.8.15; Deleted 12.3.16
3154   Deld Eastbourne FS 25.8.15; Deleted 19.4.16
3155   Deld Eastchurch NFS 8.15; Wrecked 4.10.15; Deleted 12.10.15
3156   Deld Eastchurch NFS 1.9.15; Damaged 9.9.15; Chingford 29.12.15; Deleted 24.10.16
3157   Deld Eastbourne FS 6.9.15; Slight damage 4.11.15 (Mr Fraser & Mr Edwards); Damaged by wind 26.3.16; Deleted 19.4.16
3158   Deld Eastbourne FS 6.9.15; Crashed 7.9.15 (FSL MJM Bryan); Deleted 24.9.15
3159   Deld Chingford 13.9.15; Wrecked 6.10.15; Deleted 31.1.16
3160   Deld Eastbourne FS 24.9.15; Deleted 7.12.15
3161   Deld 4 Wing Eastchurch 24.9.15; Chingford 18.10.15; Wrecked 28.10.15 (FSL B Travers); Damaged 17.5.16; Deleted 22.5.16
3162   Deld Chingford 28.9.15; Damaged 17.5.16; Deleted 24.10.16

**24 NIEUPORT TYPES 10 TWO-SEATER TRACTOR BIPLANE SCOUTS purchased from Nieuport, numbered 3163 to 3186, built Issy-les Moulineaux & deld from Paris. (80-hp Le Rhône)**

[3162   (Type 12) 1 Wing by 3.2.16 - @29.2.16; 2 Flt A Sqdn 1 Wing St.Pol by 4.16. Serial outside batch, but several reports that actually used]
3163   Deld 1 Sqdn St.Pol 23.5.15 [C Sqdn by 20.6.15]; Became 1 Wing St.Pol 21.6.15; Deleted by 12.15
3164   Deld 1 Sqdn St.Pol 25.5.15; Became 1 Wing St.Pol 21.6.15 - 8.15; Deleted late 1915
3165   (80-hp Gnome). Deld 1 Sqdn St.Pol 25.5.15; With B Sqdn 1 Wing temp detd Furnes by 20.6.15; Became 1

*Nieuport Type 10 3170. (J.M.Bruce/G.S.Leslie collection)*

*Nieuport Seaplane 3187, probably at Calshot. (S.Taylor)*

*Bleriot XI-2 Monoplane 3217 at Eastchurch. (J.M.Bruce/G.S.Leslie collection)*

*Brush-built Avro 504C 3315, seen here fitted with a small bomb, was flown at Chingford. (via Philip Jarrett)*

Wing St.Pol 21.6.15; Attd 3 Sqdn RFC Auchel 21.7.15; 1 Wing St.Pol 29.7.15; 5 Wing Dover 12.9.15; War Flt Dover by 2.16; HACPs 20.2.16 (F/L HL Wood) & 24.4.16 (F/L FJE Feeney); Deleted 30.10.16

3166  Deld 1 Sqdn St.Pol 27.5.15; Became 1 Wing St.Pol 21.6.15 [A Sqdn by 20.6.15; A Group by 10.10.15]; to 5 Wing Dover but wrecked at Folkestone 6.9.15; Deleted 25.9.15

3167  Deld 1 Sqdn St.Pol by 21.6.15 [C Sqdn by 20.6.15]; Became 1 Wing St.Pol 21.6.15 - @27.9.15; Deleted by 12.15 BUT 2 Wing Mudros; Shot down by Oblt von Lyncker, Jasta 25 18.2.17

3168  (c/n 120?) Deld 1 Sqdn St.Pol by 14.5.15; Became 1 Wing St.Pol 6.15 - @22.8.15 (sic); Shipped to Mudros; 3 Wing Tenedos 31.7.15 - 31.8.15; A Flt 2 Imbros by 10.15; 3 Wing Tenedos by 31.10.15; 2 Wing Imbros by 9.11.15 - @7.16; Missing in Anzac-Suvla-Imbros area 20.12.15 (FSL F Besson killed & observer possibly PO Mech W Auger wounded); Presume m/c recovered and repaired; 2 Wing Long Island, Asia by 5.17; G Sqdn 2 Wing Marsh by 8.17; Surveyed 21.9.17; Deleted 2.10.17 DBR

3169  Shipped to Mudros .15; 3 Wing Tenedos by 31.7.15 - @31.8.15; 2 Wing Imbros by 10.15 - 4.16; Deleted 1916

3170  Shipped Mudros to .15; 3 Wing Tenedos by 31.7.15; 2 Wing Imbros 18.1.16 - @4.16

3171  Shipped to Mudros .15; 3 Wing Tenedos by 31.7.15; A Flt 2 Wing Mudros 18.1.16 - @5.16

3172  Shipped to Mudros .15; 3 Wing Tenedos by 31.7.15 (possibly coded '26' from 8.15. Coded 'N1' by 11.15); F/Cdr R Bell-Davies gained VC for rescuing FSL GF Smylie in Henry Farman 'H5' 19.11.15; A Flt 2 Wing Imbros 18.1.16; detd B Sqdn 2 Wing Mitylene 8.5.16; Dived in from 200ft 24.6.16 (FSL KV Hooper); Deleted 7.16

3173  Deld 1 Wing St.Pol by 7.15; temp with 2 Wing St.Pol 1.8.15; 1 Wing St.Pol 13.8.15; HACP 26.8.15 (F/L H Rosher); 4 Sqdn 1 Wing Dunkerque by 9.15; 5 Wing Dover 11.11.15 - 12.15; War Flt Dover by 1.16; HACPs 8.1.16 (FSL CH Potts) & 15.1.16 (F/L H Rosher); Sideslipped from 150-200 ft attempting night landing 23.4.16 (FSL JD Marvin injured); Deleted 24.4.16

3174  Shipped Mudros .15; 3 Wing Tenedos by 7.15; 2 Wing Aegean by 10.15 - @8.16

3175  Shipped to Mudros .15; 3 Wing Tenedos by 31.7.15 - @31.8.15; A Flt 2 Wing Imbros by 18.1.16 - @8.16 [still in commission 1.17]

3176  Deld CSD White City to 4 Wing Eastchurch for erection 30.9.15; Tested 5.10.15 & 7.10.15; 1 Wing St.Pol by 31.10.15 - @30.11.15 [HQ Sqdn by 19-20.11.15; B Group by 22-28.11.15; HQ Sqdn by 28.12.15] HACP 9.1.16 (F/L CT MacLaren); From 4 Wing to Expeditionary Force 27.3.16 for special duty with 29 Sqdn RFC; 9 Flt A Sqdn 4 Wing St.Pol 16.4.16; Hit in fight with HA, FL Abeele 1.6.16 (FSL IdeB Daly injured); Flying again 20.6.16; Tested after repair 6.8.16; ADD 25.9.16; Deleted 24.3.17 for use as test bench

3177  Deld 1 Wing St.Pol by 22.8.15 [Reserve Sqdn by 1.10.15; Eastchurch Group by 17.10.15]; Bombed U-boat with 5x20-lb bombs 20m off Nieuport, claimed as probably sunk 6.9.15 (FSL RH Mulock); After raid on airship sheds at Berchem Ste.Agathe, near Brussels, EF, FL on sands near Bray Dunes 18.10.15 (FSL JT Bone killed); Deleted

3178  Temp with 2 Wing St.Pol by 8.15; 1 Wing St.Pol by 13.8.15 - @1.2.16 [3 Sqdn by 1.10.15; A Group by 6-19.11.15; B Group by 22.11.15; A Group by 30.11.15; Eastchurch Group by 2.12.15; B Group by 8-15.12.15; Eastchurch Group by 19.12.15; HQ Sqdn by 25.12.15]; Seaplane forced to land 7m off Nieuport 08.00 25.1.16 (FSL N Keeble); ADD, deleted 15.4.17

3179  Shipped to Mudros .15; 3 Wing Imbros by 31.7.15 - @31.8.15; 2 or 3 Wing Aegean 10.15 - 4.16 [Retd UK 1.16 - or burnt in fire 4.11.15?]

3180  Temp with 2 Wing St.Pol 1.8.15; 1 Wing St.Pol 13.8.15 [Reserve Sqdn by 1.10.15 - @9.2.16; B Group by 30.12.15 - @9.1.16]; AZP, FL in sea 20m NW of Dieppe, partially salved 1.2.16 (FSL BC Clayton); To

ADD; Deleted 15.4.16 DBR

3181  Deld 1 Wing St.Pol by 8.8.15 (Temp with 2 Wing @8.8.15); HAP, smashed u/c 9.8.15 (FSL MA Simpson) ) [4 Sqdn by 1.10.15; A Group by 7-18.10.15; B Group by 17-20.1.16; 2 Flt A Sqdn from formation 1.3.16; Experimental Flt by 11-19.5.16]; ADD 2.6.16; C Sqdn 1 Wing St.Pol by 4.6.16; FL in sea, sank 18.7.16 (FSL HG Travers); ADD 20.7.16; Deleted 30.7.16

3182  Deld/allocated 1 Wing St.Pol by 31.7.15; temp with 2 Wing St.Pol by 5.8.15; 1 Wing St.Pol 13.8.15 [Reserve Sqdn by 10.15 - 12.15; A Group by 25-28.11.15; B Group by 8.12.15]; Dropped 16-lb bomb on U-boat previously bombed by 3963 10-12m W of Ostende 23.1.16 (FSL EW Norton); Deleted ADD 15.4.16 DBR;

3183  Deld 1 Wing St.Pol by 18.8.15 [3 Sqdn by 10.15; Eastchurch Group by 19.10.15; A Group by 26.10.15; B Group by 23.12.15]; Accident Dunkerque; Deleted ADD 15.4.16

3184  Deld 1 Wing St.Pol by 20.8.15; 3 Sqdn by 1.10.15; HACP 2.10.15 (FSL CW Graham); A Group by 10.10.15 - @30.12.15; B Group by 5.1.16 - @17.1.16; 1 Flt A Sqdn from formation 1.3.16; Exptl Flt by 18.5.16; C Sqdn by 22.6.16; 4 Flt B Sqdn by 7.8.16; ADD by 28.9.16; 2 Flt A Sqdn 1 Wing Furnes by 30.9.16; ADD by 19.10.16; For survey 9.11.16; Deleted 5.1.17 general fatigue

3185  Deld 1 Wing St.Pol by 18.8.15 - 12.3.16 [3 Sqdn by 1.10.15; A Group by 18.10.15 - @1.12.15; B Group by 7-30.12.15; 2 Flt A Sqdn from formation 1.3.16]; EF, FL on sands La Panne 23.12.15 (FSL EW Norton); Crashed, WO Abeele 2.4.16 (FSL HG Henley); Exptl Flt 1 Wing by 11.5.16; 14 Flt B Sqdn 1 Wing by 24.5.16; 9 Flt A Sqdn 4 Wing by 1.6.16; Brooklands by 6.16; Retd 9 Flt A Sqdn 4 Wing 11.6.16; Run into by Hartgill (9124?) landing 2.8.16; Test after repair 12.8.16; 10 Flt A Sqdn 4 Wing 28.9.16; Furnes 23.10.16 (visit?); 9 Flt A Sqdn 4 Wing 16.11.16 (ex 10 Flt); Became 6 Sqdn 12.16; Crashed 3.2.17 (FSL VR Gibbs); For survey by 8.2.17; Deleted ADD 24.3.17 DBR

3186  Deld 1 Sqdn St.Pol by 29.5.15; Became 1 Wing St.Pol 6.15 [4 Sqdn by 1.10.15; A Group by 7.10.15 - @10.11.15]; Deleted ADD 21.4.16

**12 NIEUPORT TRACTOR MONOPLANE SEAPLANES purchased from Nieuport, numbered 3187 to 3198 & built Issy-les-Moulineaux. Controls modified. (3187 - 3192 ordered with 80-hp Le Rhône, but all delivered with 100-hp Gnome)**

3187  Deld Calshot 2.10.15; Deleted 2.7.16
3188  (C/n 1671) Deld CSD Wormwood Scrubbs; Calshot 27.9.15; Wrecked Calshot 13.10.15 (FSL CB Gasson); Deleted 19.10.15
3189  (C/n 1672) Deld CSD Wormwood Scrubbs; Calshot 27.9.15; Wrecked 16.1.16; Deleted 21.1.16

[Another Nieuport Seaplane arrived at Calshot by lorry on 30.9.15]

3190  Deld CSD White City; Deld by lorry to Calshot 3.11.15; Bembridge by 1.12.15; FL in sea, picked up by hospital ship *St.Andrew*, but broke adrift under tow 8.2.16 (FSL TGM Stephens & LM Kent); Deleted 6.3.16
3191  (c/n 337) Deld Walney Island 16.10.15; Northern Aircraft FS Windermere (incomplete) 27.4.16; Deleted 21.8.16
3192  Deld CSD White City; Calshot by lorry 3.11.15; Deleted 2.7.16
3193  Deld Walney Island 16.12.15; Stripped for packing 13.3.16; Northern Aircraft FS Windermere 27.4.16; Out of commission 29.5.16; Became RNAS Windermere 29.6.16; Deleted 21.8.16
3194  Deld CSD White City .15; Calshot 21.11.15; Packed 23.12.15; Northern Aircraft FS, Windermere 1.1.16; Became RNAS Windermere 29.6.16; Deleted 21.8.16
3195  Deld CSD White City .15; Calshot by lorry 3.11.15; Bembridge 22.11.15; Calshot 1.4.16; Deleted 21.7.16
3196  Deld CSD White City .15; Calshot for erection 21.11.15; Tested 13.12.15; Deleted 21.7.16
3197  Deld CSD White City .15; Calshot for erection 21.11.15; Packed for Windermere 23.12.15; Northern Aircraft FS, Windermere 1.1.16; Fitted DC 1.5.16;

*Lt Richard Bell-Davies in the cockpit of Nieuport 3172 of 2 Wing, Imbros in which he won the Victoria Cross for rescuing Lt Smiley on 19 November 1916. (via EF Cheesman)*

*Lt G.F.Smiley amusing his fellow officers by demonstrating how he thought the picture papers should have shown him being rescued by Flt Cdr Bell-Davies in the Gallipoli Peninsular. (via Frank Cheesman)*

*Morane-Saulnier Parasol 3253, the machine in which FSL R.S.J.Warneford shot down Zeppelin LZ37 on 7 June 1915, for which he was awarded the Victoria Cross. (RAF Museum P.19903)*

Became RNAS Windermere 29.6.16; Deleted 21.8.16

3198   Deld Westgate for erection 13.12.15; Capsized and CW off Westgate 16.3.16 (S/Cdr RP Ross); Deleted 18.3.16

## 10 F.B.A. TYPE A PUSHER BIPLANE FLYING BOATS purchased from Louis Schreck, numbered 3199 to 3208 & built Argenteuil. (100-hp Gnome Monosoupape)

3199   Deld Seaplane Base 1 Wing Dunkerque 7.15; Left for Dover but FL in harbour entrance, broke nose 2.12.15 (WO S Freeman); Being surveyed 3.12.15; Deleted ADD 21.4.16

3200   Deld Seaplane Base 1 Wing Dunkerque 7.15; Port upper wing damaged on TO 14.12.15 (FSL H Leigh); Lower wing slightly damaged 12.1.16 (FSL BC Tooke); Dover 9.2.16; HACPs 12.2.16 (FSL ATN Cowley) & 20.2.16 (FSL ATN Cowley & AM Clarke); Dunkerque 12.3.16, but FL in sea en route, towed into Dover by armed trawler *Raglan Castle* (FSL BC Tooke & S/L RM Inge uninjured); Deleted 12.3.16

3201   Deld Grain 15.9.15; Tested fitting of Lewis gun 13.10.15; HACPs 9.2.16 & 20.2.16 (both F/L BF Fowler & Cpl Grant RMLI); left for Windermere 26.8.16; arr Windermere for erection 4.9.16; Damaged, for survey by 10.12.16; Packing for Bognor 30.1.17; Norman Thompson by 28.2.17 (rebuild); Calshot School 23.7.17; Lee-on-Solent W/E 12.10.17; Surveyed 30.10.17; Deleted 6.11.17 W&T

3202   Deld Grain for erection 25.8.15; Calshot 11.9.15; Bembridge 15.9.15; Wrecked 27.9.15; Deleted 2.10.15

3203   Deld Calshot and tested 11.9.15; Wrecked 13.9.15 (S/L FS McGill); Deleted 23.9.15

3204   Deld CSD by 9.15; Dover 8.9.15; Dunkerque 26.9.15; Grain by road 30.9.15; Seaplane Base 1 Wing Dunkerque 5.10.15; HSPPs 8.1.16 (FSL JBP Ferrand & AM Tooke) & 9.2.16 (W/O S Freeman & FSL LH Slatter RNVR); Dover 29.2.16; HACP 18.3.16 (F/L JBP Ferrand & CPO Slapp); HSPPs 19.3.16 (FSL FJ Bailey & S/L RM Inge) also (F/L JBP Ferrand & AM Fanshawe); HSMP 24.3.16 (F/L JBP Ferrand & AM Penn); Wrecked 2.4.16; Deleted 7.4.16

3205   Deld CSD White City by 9.15; Calshot 8.9.15; Erected 5.10.15; Sideslipped and nose-dived from 600 ft, wrecked off Calshot 13.2.16 (FSL N McDiarmid injured, AM FG Haynes drowned); Deleted 14.2.16

3206   Deld CSD White City by 9.15; Grain 8.9.15; Test 4.10.15; HSPP 19.3.16 (F/L BF Fowler & Lt J Kilner-Wells); Erecting Windermere 4.9.16; Wrecked 5.12.16 (PFO RB Picken), to survey; Packing for Bognor 30.1.17; Norman Thompson by 28.2.17 (rebuild); Calshot School 14.8.17; Hull smashed 21.8.17 (beyond repair); Deleted W/E 14.9.17

3207   Deld Dover 1.10.15; temp Dunkerque 11.10.15; Dover 14.10.15; Seaplane Base 1 Wing Dunkerque 17.10.15; Dover 29.2.16; HACPs 24.3.16 (F/L JBP Ferrand & AM McCredie), 27.3.16 (FSL GG Hodge & AM Searley), 29.3.16 (FSL AH Sandwell & LM Claydon) & 23.4.16 (FSL HV German & AM2 Smith); HSPP 3.5.16 (F/L JC Brooke & AM2 Fanshawe); Deleted 15.6.16

3208   Deld Dover 1.10.15; Erected 7.10.15; HSPP 11.1.16 (F/L RP Cannon & AM2 Smith), 23.1.16 (F/L TFN Gerrard & FSL GG Hodge) & 24.1.16 (FSL ATN Cowley & F/L TFN Gerrard); HACP 26.1.16 (FSL W Perham & AM Clark); HACP, EF, FL off St.Margarets Bay, towed in by trawler 5.2.16 (FSL BC Tooke & AM2 Smith); HACP 8.2.16 (F/L TFN Gerrard & AM Clark); HSPP 9.2.16 (F/L TFN Gerrard & S/L RM Inge); HACPs 12.2.16 (FSL W Perham), 20.2.16 (FSL BC Tooke & AM Pearson), 19.3.16 (FSL GG Hodge & AM Manning x 2), 18.3.16 (FSL GG Hodge & S/L RM Inge, 30.3.16 (FSL TGM Stephens & AM Geater), 31.3.16 (F/L JC Brooke & AM Fanshawe, later FSL CL Scott & AM Fanshawe), 23.4.16 (F/L JB P.Ferrand & AM Abbott); Deleted 9.5.16

## 5 BREGUET DE CHASSE TRACTOR BIPLANES purchased from Breguet, numbered 3209 to 3213 & built at Villacoublay. (225-hp Sunbeam) [Originally ordered as Breguet BUC with 200-hp Salmson]

3209   Deld 6 Flt A Sqdn 5 Wing 11.3.16; Tested 2-pdr Davis Gun with fused and unfused cartridges from 13.3.16 (F/Cdr WS Newton-Clare); Last mention 2.6.16; ADD 6.16; Deleted 15.6.16 NWR

3210   Deld 6 Flt A Sqdn 5 Wing 20.3.16; Wrecked Coudekerque 23.4.16 (FSL GL Hughes & AM P Tomkins); For survey by 11.5.16; Deleted ADD 5.16

3211   [Deld 5 Wing 3.16?]; ADD by 18.5.16; Deleted 15.6.16 NWR

3212   Deld 6 Flt A Sqdn 5 Wing 11.3.16; Tested 22.3.16; Last mention 2.6.16; Deleted ADD 15.6.16

3213   Deld 1 Wing (via ADD?) 3.16; 1 Wing, Lifting trials with bombs 27.3.16 & 16.4.16; 6 Flt A Sqdn 5 Wing by 10.4.16; Hit by gunfire after raid on Ostende aerodrome, FL Coxyde Bains 23.4.16 (FSL CR Blagrove unhurt); retd 6 Flt 2.5.16; ADD by 11.5.16; Deleted 15.6.16

## 25 BLERIOT XI-2 TANDEM TRACTOR MONOPLANES purchased from Bleriot & numbered 3214 to 3238. (80-hp Gnome)

3214   Deld CSD White City by 20.6.15; Chingford for erection 1.7.15; To Eastbourne FS by 14.9.15; To Ringmer with B Flt for manoeuvres with SW Mounted Brigade 15.9.15; Damaged u/c at Ringmer 17.9.15 (FSL DG Broad & FSL RD Delamere); Eastbourne 23.9.15; Arrived Eastchurch 6.11.15 ex Dymchurch nr Burmarsh; FL and damaged 16.11.15 (FSL JS Bolas); Eastbourne, EF, FL and damaged Rye en route Lewes 23.1.16 (FSL AJ Long); CSD White City 14.5.16, later deleted

3215   Deld CSD White City by 20.6.15; Chingford for erection 1.7.15; To Eastbourne FS tested 7.9.15; To Ringmer with B Flt for manoeuvres with SW Mounted Brigade 15.9.15; Retd Eastbourne 23.9.15; Damaged u/c 19.12.15 (FSL WM Tait); Ringmer 5.5.16, broke propeller landing (S/L W Arnbolt); Eastbourne 6.5.16; Ringmer 11.5.16; Badly damaged landing Eastbourne 12.5.16 (FSL HD Smith); Deleted 12.6.16

3216   Deld CSD White City by 20.6.15; Chingford for erection 4.7.15; Eastchurch FS by road 7.9.15; FL and damaged Canterbury, Kent 16.9.15; Damaged 12.10.15; Damaged 4.12.15; Eastbourne 19.3.16; Ringmer 10.5.16; Dismantled 14.5.16; Deleted 12.6.16

3217   Deld CSD White City by 20.6.15; Chingford for erection 7.7.15; Eastchurch FS by road 7.9.15; Smashed wing landing Ringmer 17.9.15 (FSL N Keeble & AM Knott); Damaged 17.11.15; Eastbourne 4.3.16; Deleted 19.4.16

3218   Deld CSD White City by 20.6.15; Chingford for erection 30.6.15; Deleted 22.4.16

3219   Deld CSD White City by 20.6.15; Chingford for erection 1.7.15; Dover 1.2.16; Ran into Nieuport Scout on landing 20.5.16 (FSL RA Little); Surveyed 26.5.16; Deleted 9.6.16

3220   Deld Eastchurch NFS for erection 1.7.15; Damaged 22.8.15; Wrecked 27.8.15; Deleted 21.9.15

3221   Deld Eastchurch NFS for erection 1.7.15; Damaged 27.8.15; Wrecked 18.9.15; Wrecked 5.12.15; Deleted 13.1.16

3222   Deld Eastchurch NFS for erection 8.7.15; Damaged 29.7.15; Wrecked on cross country 6.9.15; Damaged 4.10.15; Deleted 26.4.16

3223   Deld Eastchurch NFS for erection 8.7.15; Wrecked 3.12.15; Deleted 13.1.16

3224   Deld Eastbourne for erection 17.6.15; Damaged 9.7.15 (FSL TE Viney); FL 24.8.15 (FSL CA Maitland-Heriot); Deleted 27.8.15

3225   (c/n 252 or 275) Deld Eastbourne by road 15.6.15; Tested 18.6.15; EF, FL, damaged 29.7.15 (FSL CL Trower); Held as spares from 1.10.15

3226   Deld Eastbourne for erection 20.6.15; Under repair, retained as spares from 10.9.15; Damaged 14.1.16 (FSL C Williams); Damaged landing Shoreham 8.2.16 (S/L JG Scott & FSL RA Campbell); Deleted 13.3.16

3227   (c/n 252 or 275) Deld Eastbourne by road 15.6.15; Chassis damaged landing 14.7.15 (FSL HK Thorold); Tested 19.8.15; Damaged 23.8.15 (FSL CHM Chapman unhurt); Held as spares from 10.9.15; Deleted 28.10.15

3228   Deld Redcar 5.7.15; D Flt Hornsea 16.7.15; AZP, crashed landing in fog at night trying to find Atwick LG 9.8.15 (FSL RG Mack); Deleted 11.8.15

| | |
|---|---|
| 3229 | Deld Redcar 9.7.15; Nosedived and CW 18.2.16 (FSL TC Angus severely injured); Deleted 11.3.16 |
| 3230 | Deld Redcar for erection 7.8.15; COL, CW 5.2.16; Deleted 1.3.16 |
| 3231 | Deld Scarborough 5.7.15; FF 26.7.15; Tested after overhaul 13.10.15; Hornsea 23.10.15; Scarborough 30.10.15; Hornsea 30.10.15; Scarborough 3.12.15; Redcar 17.3.16; FL and damaged 21.8.16 (FSL GE Nash); Deleted 4.5.17 |
| 3232 | Deld Redcar 7.15; D Flt Hornsea by road 14.7.15; Fuselage and engine damaged on test flight Hornsea 16.7.15; Redcar 17.7.15 (repair); Scarborough 19.10.15; Hornsea 30.10.15 - 12.15; Scarborough by 27.1.16; AZP 11.2.16; FL and damaged 31.7.16 (FSL AWC Kidner); Deleted 15.8.16 |
| 3233 | (c/n B.L.237) Deld Redcar for erection 7.8.15; Scarborough 11.8.15; Hornsea 9.9.15; Deleted 2.10.15 |
| 3234 | Deld Eastbourne 20.9.15; probably never erected and used as spares |
| 3235 | Deld Eastbourne 20.9.15; probably never erected and used as spares |
| 3236 | Deld CSD White City 8.15; Eastbourne FS 8.9.15; To Ringmer with B Flt for manoeuvres with SW Mounted Brigade 15.9.15; retd Eastbourne 23.9.15; Crashed in dyke on landing 1.10.15 (FSL W Perham); Deleted 13.4.16 |
| 3237 | Deld CSD White City 8.15; Eastbourne FS 8.9.15; To Ringmer with B Flt for manoeuvres with SW Mounted Brigade 15.9.15; Eastbourne 23.9.15; Dover 27.10.15 but FL Ham Street, Kent (FSL GWR Fane & FSL NC Blanch), repaired, retd 30.10.15; FL near aerodrome and damaged 10.11.15 (S/L WG McMinnies & Mechanic); Deleted 10.12.15 |
| 3238 | In store 8.15; Probably never erected but used as spares |

## 25 MORANE SAULNIER M.S.3 (TYPE L) PARASOL TRACTOR MONOPLANES purchased from Aéroplanes Morane Saulnier, numbered 3239 to 3263 & built Villacoublay. (80-hp Le Rhône)

| | |
|---|---|
| 3239 | (c/n MS.304) Deld 1 Sqdn St.Pol on/by 18.4.15 (reserve machine by 20.6.15); Became 1 Wing St.Pol 21.6.15; 5 Wing Dover in store 3.9.15; Eastbourne by rail 11.12.15; Erected 13.12.15; Deleted 12.6.16 |
| 3240 | Deld 1 Sqdn St.Pol on/by 18.4.15; AZP 17.5.15 (FSL M Marsden); Became 1 Wing St.Pol 21.6.15; Deleted 8.15 |
| 3241 | (c/n MS.311) Deld 1 Sqdn St.Pol by 18.4.15 (reserve machine by 20.6.15); Became 1 Wing St.Pol 21.6.15; 5 Wing Dover in store 3.9.15; Eastbourne by rail 11.12.15; 4 Wing Eastchurch 3.4.16; Eastchurch NFS 7.4.16; Deleted 26.4.16 |
| 3242 | Deld C Sqdn 1 Wing St.Pol on/by 20.6.15; Attd 3 Sqdn RFC Auchel 25.7.15; 1 Wing St.Pol 28.7.15; 5 Wing Dover 7.10.15; Dover 15.11.15; Deleted 16.8.16 |
| 3243 | Deld 1 Sqdn St.Pol on/by 27.4.15; Became 1 Wing St.Pol 21.6.15 (reserve machine by 20.6.15); 5 Wing Dover 7.10.15; Packing for CSD 6.12.15; Deleted and to CSD White City 16.12.15 |
| 3244 | Deld 1 Sqdn St.Pol on/by 28.4.15; Became 1 Wing St.Pol 21.6.15 - @3.10.15 [reserve machine by 20.6.15; HQ Sqdn by 10.15]; HACP 2.10.15 (FSL JED Boyd); Deleted by 12.15/Deleted ADD 21.4.16 |
| 3245 | (c/n MS.305) Deld 1 Sqdn St.Pol on/by 18.4.15 (reserve machine by 20.6.15); Became 1 Wing St.Pol 21.6.15; 5 Wing Dover in store 3.9.15; Packing for CSD 6.12.15; Deleted and to CSD White City 16.12.15 |
| 3246 | (c/n MS.255?) Deld 1 Sqdn St.Pol on/by 30.4.15 (reserve machine by 20.6.15); Became 1 Wing St.Pol 21.6.15; Attd 3 Sqdn RFC Auchel 25.7.15; 1 Wing St.Pol 28.7.15; 5 Wing Dover in store 3.9.15; Eastbourne by rail 11.12.15 (arr 14.12.15); Deleted 13.3.16 |
| 3247 | (c/n MS.300?) Deld 1 Sqdn St.Pol on/by 30.4.15 (reserve machine by 20.6.15); Became 1 Wing St.Pol 21.6.15; Deleted 1915 |
| 3248 | Deld 1 Sqdn St.Pol by 6.15 (reserve machine by 20.6.15); Became 1 Wing St.Pol 21.6.15 (Reserve Sqdn by 10.15); 5 Wing Dover 7.10.15; HACP 24.1.16 (F/L HL Wood); Damaged 25.5.16; Deleted 3.7.16 |
| 3249 | (c/n MS.302) Deld 1 Sqdn St.Pol by 6.15; Became 1 |

| | |
|---|---|
| | Wing St.Pol 21.6.15; 5 Wing Dover 3.9.15 (in store); Grain 23.5.16; Dover 20.7.16; Deleted 16.8.16 |
| 3250 | (c/n MS.303) Deld 1 Sqdn St.Pol by 6.15; Became 1 Wing St.Pol 21.6.15; 5 Wing Dover 3.9.15 (in store); Deleted for spares 31.12.15 |
| 3251 | Deld 1 Sqdn St.Pol on/by 17.4.15; Became 1 Wing St.Pol 21.6.15; Deleted 8.15 |
| 3252 | Deld 1 Sqdn St.Pol 17.4.15; Warneford Zeppelin attack 26.5.15; Became 1 Wing St.Pol 21.6.15 [D Sqdn by 20.6.15; 3 Sqdn by 1.10.15]; still 1 Wing 12.15 |
| 3253 | (c/n MS.27x) Deld 1 Sqdn St.Pol on/by 30.4.15; Became 1 Wing St.Pol 21.6.15; FSL RAJ Warneford won VC for destroying Zeppelin LZ37 over Bruges 7.6.15; [C Sqdn by 20.6.15; 3 Sqdn by 1.10.15]; HACP 2.10.15 (FSL JT Bone & AM Hall); still 1 Wing 12.15; Deleted 2.16 (fair wear and tear) but preserved for exhibition Hendon to at least 3.18 |
| 3254 | Deld 1 Wing St.Pol on/by 30.4.15; Possibly used as spares; Deleted by 31.8.15 |
| 3255 | Deld 1 Wing St.Pol on/by 30.4.15; Possibly used as spares; Deleted by 31.8.15 |
| 3256 | Deld 1 Wing St.Pol on/by 30.4.15; Possibly used as spares; Deleted by 31.8.15 |
| 3257 | (90-hp Le Rhône) Left works 4.5.15; arr Dover for erection 5.5.15; Ready 20.6.15; FF 24.6.15 (several flights but left wing down, unsatisfactory); Last flown Dover 24.7.15; Packing for transport 27.7.15; To Dover docks 1.8.15; Shipped to Aegean in SS Nankin 5.8.15; Used by 3 Wing Imbros as spares for 3259 - 3262 on arrival 25.8.15; Deleted 23.11.15 |
| 3258 | Deld for erection Dover 5.5.15; 4 Sqdn Dover by 10.5.15; To Dover docks 1.8.15; Shipped to Aegean in SS Nankin 5.8.15; arr 3 Wing Imbros on/by 25.8.15 - @10.15; 2 Wing by 5.11.15 - @4.16; Deleted 1917? |
| 3259 | Deld Dover for erection 5.5.15; 4 Sqdn Dover by 11.5.15; To Dover docks 1.8.15; Shipped to Aegean in SS Nankin 5.8.15; arr 3 Wing Imbros on/by 25.8.15 - @10.15; 2 Wing by/from 18.1.16 - @4.16; Disbanded 1917? |
| 3260 | (90-hp Le Rhône) Deld Dover for erection 5.5.15; 4 Sqdn Dover by 10.5.15; Flown Dover 29.6.15 (only flight there); Examined 22-24.7.15; To Dover docks 1.8.15; Shipped to Aegean in SS Nankin 5.8.15; Recd 2 Wing Mudros 18.8.15; Shipped to 3 Wing; Recd Imbros and tested 26.8.15; Used for reconnaissance and photo work, last flight 30.9.15; Deleted 10.15 |
| 3261 | Deld Dover for erection 5.5.15; 4 Sqdn Dover by 10.5.15; To Dover docks 1.8.15; Shipped to Aegean in SS Nankin 5.8.15; arr 3 Wing Imbros on/by 25.8.15; 2 Wing by 25.10.15; Deleted 2.16 |
| 3262 | Deld Dover for erection 5.5.15; 4 Sqdn Dover by 10.5.15; To Dover docks 1.8.15; Shipped to Aegean in SS Nankin 5.8.15; arr 3 Wing Imbros on/by 25.8.15; 2 Wing by 25.10.15 - @4.16; Deleted 1917? |
| 3263 | Deld 2 Wing Eastchurch for erection 5.6.15; Fire balloon expts at Leysdown 2.7.15; Became 2 Wing Eastchurch 3.7.15; To Kingsnorth, smashed u/c, retd by lorry 15.7.15 (F/L DK Johnston & FSL RB Munday unhurt); Grain Island RD 16.7.15 (for 4 Wing Eastchurch from 3.8.15, repairs not completed?); Deleted 25.12.15 |

## 25 CAUDRON G.III SCHOOL TRACTOR BIPLANES purchased from Caudron, numbered 3264 to 3288 & built Le Crotoy (80-hp Gnome)

| | |
|---|---|
| 3264 | (c/n C.539?) Deld Eastbourne FS 12.5.15; Wrecked 5.15; Deleted 1.6.15 |
| 3265 | (c/n C.529?) Deld Eastbourne FS 16.5.15; Wrecked 7.6.15; Eastbourne Aviation Co 19.6.15 (repair); Eastbourne FS 6.9.15; Tested 6.9.15 but FL on TO (F/L RH Jones); Deleted 21.10.15 |
| 3266 | (c/n C.527?) Deld Eastbourne FS 16.5.15; Erected 30.5.15; Convtg DC 5.6.15; Skid broke landing, o/t 12.6.15 (FSL B Travers unhurt); Crashed nr Cross-in-Hand, nr Heathfield, Sussex 30.6.15 (TFSL PA Watson killed); Deleted 17.7.15 |
| 3267 | (C/n C.576) Deld Eastbourne FS 16.5.15; Convtg DC 6.15; FL and damaged 13.9.15 (FSL HGR Malet); FL 30.9.15 (S/L JD Newberry & FSL GWR Fane); Deleted 28.1.16 |

3268 (c/n C.538?) Deld Eastbourne FS 21.5.15; Erecting 5.6.15; Tested 12.6.15; Shipped to East Indies 15.6.15; Mombasa by 8.15 - 3.16; Deleted by 30.6.16

3269 Deld Eastbourne FS 21.5.15; Shipped to East Indies 15.6.15; Mombasa by 8.15 - @3.16

3270 Deld Eastbourne FS 15.6.15; Crashed and wrecked 22.6.15; Deleted 29.6.15

3271 Deld Eastbourne FS 18.6.15; Tested 23.6.15; COL 25.6.15 (FSL HA Bower injured); Repaired; FL 9.9.15 (FSL HK Thorold); to repair 10.10.15; Wrecked 20.12.15 (FSL C Williams); Deleted 21.1.16

3272 Deld CSD Wormwood Scrubbs by 6.15; Chingford 19.6.15; Crashed and wrecked 22.6.15 (FSL RM Everitt & PFSL EAdeL de Ville unhurt), dismantled; Hendon 6.15 (repair); Chingford 4.7.15; Deleted 6.7.15 but retained for spares; Deleted 3.3.16 (CW)

3273 Deld CSD Wormwood Scrubbs by 6.15; Chingford 19.6.15; Collided with fence at Hendon 3.7.15 (FSL B Travers); retd Chingford 4.7.15; Awaiting re-erection by 4.8.15; Re-erected 24.9.15; Dover 10.2.16; FL, slightly damaged 18.3.16 (FSL INC Clarke); Detling 23.5.16 (transit); Cranwell 24.5.16; Redcar 26.5.16; Deleted 15.7.16

3274 (DC) Deld CSD Wormwood Scrubbs by 6.15; Chingford 19.6.15; still awaiting erection 4.8.15; Crashed 17.9.15 (PFSL FEP Barrington); British Caudron, Cricklewood by lorry for repair 27.9.15; Chingford by lorry 8.2.16; Redcar 11.5.16; Deleted 25.6.17

3275 Deld CSD Wormwood Scrubbs by 6.15; Chingford 19.6.15; Erecting 27.6.15; EF, damaged 29.6.15 (FSL RM Everitt); Crashed, CW 31.7.15 (PFSL CW Graham badly shaken); Deleted 18.8.15

3276 Deld Chingford for erection 24.6.15; Fitted DC 30.6.15 (described as leaky); Flown 11.7.15; Wrecked 16.1.16; Deleted 28.1.16

3277 (C/n C.584) Deld Chingford for erection 25.6.15; Eastchurch NFS 26.11.15; Damaged landing 12.1.16; Redcar 23.1.16; FL smashed Marske 14.5.16 (PFSL WH Chisam injured); Deleted 4.6.16

3278 Deld Chingford by road 25.6.15; Landed in river, TW 22.6.15 (PFSL EAdeL de Ville); Deleted 7.7.15 as spares

3279 Deld Chingford by road 25.6.15; Awaiting erection 3.7.15; Wrecked 24.7.15 (PFSL EP Hardman); Deleted 18.8.15 as spares

3280 Deld Eastchurch NFS for erection 26.6.15 (Coded 'O'); Convtg DC 21.7.15; Redcar 2.3.16; EF, FL, hit hedge, wrecked 28.9.16 (F/L VG Blackburn & FSL TV Lister both injured); Wrecked landing 12.10.16; Deleted 25.10.16

3281 Deld Eastchurch NFS for erection 26.6.15; Conv dual; Damaged landing 13.7.15; Damaged 29.7.15; Wrecked 17.8.15 (FSL CA Eyre injured); Deleted 6.9.15

3282 Deld Eastchurch NFS 2.7.15 (Coded '2'); Wrecked 17.8.15; Mid-air collision with Short S.38 No.65, wrecked 12.9.15 (FSL JM Alexander killed); Deleted 10.10.15

3283 (c/n C.559) Deld Eastchurch NFS 2.7.15 (Coded '3'); EF, FL Harty 9.8.15; Wrecked 9.10.15; Deleted 1.11.15

3284 Deld Eastchurch NFS for erection 2.7.15 (Coded '4'); Wrecked 20.8.15; Damaged 9.10.15; Damaged 3.11.15; Damaged 12.11.15; Wrecked 5.12.15; Wrecked 9.12.15 (pilot unhurt); Deleted 16.12.15

3285 Shipped to East Indies 7.15; East Indies 8.15; Shipped from Liverpool in SS *Bulgarian* to Mombasa 25.9.15; East Africa by 12.15 to 2.16; Deleted 1916

3286 Shipped to Gibraltar by 9.15; Deleted 1916

3287 Shipped to Gibraltar by 20.6.15; Gibraltar by 15.7.15 - @12.15; Retd UK; Hendon for erection 7.7.16; Redcar 7.16; Howden 25.7.16; Deleted Redcar 7.9.16

3288 Shipped to Gibraltar by 20.6.15; FF 25.6.15; DC fitted 15-21.7.15; EF, FL in sea 22.7.15 (F/L FW Gamwell & passenger saved); To storage, unfit 7.8.15; Deleted 4.9.15

**12 CAUDRON G.IV TRACTOR BIPLANES purchased authorised 1.10.15 from Caudron, numbered 3289 to 3300 & built Le Crotoy (Two 100-hp Anzani)**

3289 Deld Eastchurch NFS for erection 1.8.15; 4 Wing Eastchurch 3.8.15; attd Reserve Sqdn 1 Wing St.Pol 23.9.15 [Eastchurch Group by 17-25.10.15; B Group by 14-28.12.15; Eastchurch Group by 30.12.15]; transferred 4 Wing to 1 Wing charge 6.11.15 [Bombing Flt A Sqdn from formation 1.3.16]; 7 Flt B Sqdn 5 Wing 24.3.16 - 5.16; 6 Flt A Sqdn 5 Wing by 29.6.16; DBR Coudekerque 2.7.16 (FSL AM Hughes); For survey 6.7.16; Deleted ADD 30.7.16 wrecked

3290 Deld CSD White City; 4 Wing Eastchurch by road 13.10.15; Wrecked on patrol Gravesend 17.12.15 (FSL HG Brackley & FSL HGR Rees); Deleted 7.1.16

3291 Deld CSD by 9.15; 4 Wing Eastchurch for erection 22.9.15; attd Reserve Sqdn 1 Wing St.Pol 23.9.15 [Eastchurch Group by 12.10.15 - @22.11.15; B Group by 12.12.15]; Crashed on TO for raid with 2x65-lb bombs 13.12.15 (FSL HR Simms unhurt); Hit telegraph pole landing, wing broken 20.12.15 (F/L GW Price & FSL HR Simms both unhurt); Deleted 3.16 (DBR)

3292 Deld CSD White City; 4 Wing Eastchurch by lorry 25.9.15; attd 1 Wing St.Pol 6.10.15 [Eastchurch Wing by 10-12.10.15]; transferred 4 Wing to 1 Wing charge 6.11.15; Crashed St.Pol 13.12.15 (FSL HR Simms); Deleted ADD 21.4.16

3293 Deld CSD White City; 4 Wing Eastchurch by lorry 22.9.15; attd Reserve 1 Wing St.Pol 23.9.15; HACP 2.10.15 (FSL ADW Allen) [Eastchurch Group by 8.10.15 - @20.11.15; B Group by 14.12.15] [Reserve Sqdn 6.11.15 - 12.15]; still 1 Wing 20.3.16; 8 Flt B Sqdn 5 Wing by 10.4.16; 1 Wing 27.4.16; 8 Flt B Sqdn 5 Wing 5.5.16; ADD 17.5.16 - @6.7.16; 4 Wing by 9.7.16; ADD 12.8.16; Wrecked 26.10.16 (F/L CR Blagrove); Deleted 30.10.16

3294 1 Wing St.Pol by 10.15 - 12.15 [Eastchurch Group by 10.10.15 - 30.11.15]; Seriously damaged by double fuselage a/c 12.10.15 (FSL HG Henley & AM Rose unhurt); B Group 14.12.15 - @19.12.15; EF, FL Furnes aerodrome 19.12.15 (F/L GW Price & AM Lush); Deleted 2.16

3295 (Experimentally fitted with Davis gun) Deld CSD White City by 9.15; 4 Wing Eastchurch by lorry 25.9.15; Dover 18.10.15 (transit); 1 Wing St.Pol 19.10.15; [Eastchurch Group by 12.10.15 - @22.11.15; B Group by 12.12.15 - @12.1.16; Bombing Flight A Sqdn from formation 1.3.16]; 5 Wing 15.3.16; 4 Wing, damaged on landing from test flight, out of true, almost uncontrollable 28.4.16 (FSL N Keeble); ADD by 11.5.16; Deleted 15.6.16

3296 Deld CSD White City by 9.15; 4 Wing Eastchurch by lorry 25.9.15; 1 Wing St.Pol 8.11.15 - 12.15; Deleted ADD 21.4.16

3297 Deld CSD White City by 10.15 ; 4 Wing Eastchurch 3.10.15; Damaged 9.2.16 (FSL CR Mackenzie) [BUT Bombing flight A Sqdn 1 Wing from formation 1.3.16]; Dunkerque 11.4.16 (4 Wing move to Petite Synthe?); French aerodrome to 11 Flt B Sqdn 4 Wing 16.4.16 - @2.6.16; u/s, deleted ADD 15.6.16

3298 Deld CSD White City by 10.15; 4 Wing Eastchurch 3.10.15 - 1.16 (u/s); Rochford by 24.2.16; HACP, o/t landing, damaged 9.4.16 (FSL EP Hicks & LM A Ward); 212 TDS Vendôme by 11.18; Stalled and dived into hangar Vendôme 19.11.18

3299 (Allocated?) Dunkerque by 30.11.15 (1 Wing?); Bombing Flt A Sqdn 1 Wing from formation 1.3.16; 5 Wing by 10.4.16

3300 Deld 4 Wing Eastchurch by lorry 4.11.15; Dunkerque 24.2.16; Retd 4 Wing from Folkestone 1.3.16; Dunkerque 11.4.16 (4 Wing move?); French aerodrome to 11 Flt B Sqdn 4 Wing 16.4.16; Became 7 Sqdn 1.11.16; Test after repair 16.11.16; 10 Flt A Sqdn 4 Wing by 16.11.16; 7 Sqdn by 18.1.17; ADD for survey by 1.2.17; Deleted 24.3.17 general fatigue

**20 AVRO 504C TRACTOR BIPLANES ordered on Cont No C.P.32600/15 from Brush Electrical Engineering Co, numbered 3301 to 3320 & built Loughborough. (80-hp Gnome)**

3301 Deld CSD White City 5.16; Cranwell 29.12.16; Crashed 5.9.17; Deleted 22.2.18

3302 Deld CSD White City 5.16; Cranwell 29.12.16; Crashed

| | |
|---|---|
| | 9.10.17; Surveyed 16.10.17; Deleted 18.10.17 wrecked |
| 3303 | Deld CSD White City 7.6.16; Cranwell 20.12.16; Crashed 2.7.17; Deleted 28.7.17 BR |
| 3304 | Deld Redcar 10.5.16; Run into by N5037 and damaged 21.12.16; Badly damaged landing 22.1.17 (FSL BH Bridge unhurt); EF, FL, COL 2.3.17 (PFO MG Woodhouse slightly injured); Deleted 4.5.17 |
| 3305 | Deld Redcar 10.5.16; Deleted 7.9.16 |
| 3306 | Deld Redcar 14.5.16; FL 3.8.16 (FSL ATO Mann unhurt); EF, FL damaged 29.1.17 (PFO AC Jones unhurt); Wrecked by 21.8.17; Deleted 8.9.17 |
| 3307 | Deld Redcar 14.5.16; FL, damaged 24.6.16 (FSL EV Reid unhurt); Deleted 14.7.16 (fin fitted to 2930) |
| 3308 | Deld East Fortune 7.6.16; Tested 2.7.16 (Barrs); FL, Broke longerons and chassis landing 14.6.17 (FSL JP Hales); Surveyed 24.12.17; Deleted 3.1.18 as spares |
| 3309 | Deld East Fortune 7.6.16; Tested 2.7.16 (Barrs); Deleted 31.12.17 as spares |
| 3310 | Deld East Fortune 19.6.16; Tested 2.7.16 (Barrs); FL, u/c smashed 28.9.16 (FSL WH Chisam); CW 10.7.17; Surveyed 24.12.17; Deleted 3.1.18 as spares |
| 3311 | Deld East Fortune 12.6.16; Tested 2.7.16 (Barrs); Chingford 6.10.16; Deleted 27.2.17 |
| 3312 | Deld East Fortune 12.6.16; Tested 2.7.16 (Barrs); Chingford 28.9.16; Deleted 28.12.16 |
| 3313 | Deld Chingford 12.7.16; Avro 2.10.16 (repair); Chingford 7.12.16; Crashed 26.2.17; DBR by 5.7.17; Deleted W/E 29.9.17 |
| 3314 | Deld Chingford 12.7.16; Avro 2.10.16 (repair); Chingford 7.12.16; Deleted 4.4.17 |
| 3315 | Deld Cranwell 23.9.16; Crashed, CW 13.7.17; Deleted 16.8.17 |
| 3316 | Deld Cranwell 29.9.16; Wrecked by 2.2.17; Deleted 28.7.17 |
| 3317 | Deld Cranwell 26.9.16; Deleted 18.6.17 |
| 3318 | Deld Cranwell 3.10.16; Surveyed 16.10.17; Deleted 18.10.17 wrecked |
| 3319 | Deld Cranwell 20.7.16; Deleted 18.6.17 |
| 3320 | Deld Cranwell 24.7.16; CW 14.8.17 (TPFO RE Bray killed); Deleted W/E 5.9.17 |

**12 SHORT ADMIRALTY 827 TYPE TRACTOR BIPLANE SEAPLANES ordered 12.2.15 on Cont No C.P.32600/15 from Brush Electrical Engineering Co Ltd, numbered 3321 to 3332 & built Loughborough. (150-hp Sunbeam-Coatlen)**

| | |
|---|---|
| 3321 | Deld Yarmouth 30.4.16; Accepted 13.5.16 (Pickles); Deleted 5.11.16 |
| 3322 | Deld Yarmouth for erection 29.5.16; Accepted 3.6.16 (Pickles); Deleted 5.11.16 |
| 3323 | Deld Grain 20.6.16; Accepted 30.6.16 (Pickles); Windermere 25.10.16; Calshot by rail 15.2.17; Possibly the aircraft in which TFSL G Towers killed when flew into a steam barge, DoI 7.11.17 (or could be 8225); Surveyed 10.12.17; Deleted 14.12.17 DBR |
| 3324 | Deld Felixstowe Nore Flight 12.7.16; AZP 24.8.16 (FSL AB Helbert & PO RWA Ivermere); FTR patrol, damaged float 3m N of Galloper 28.11.16 (FSL GL Davies & O/L AC Stevens both PoW); Deleted 2.12.16 |
| 3325 | Deld CSD White City by 31.8.16; To Calshot and tested 16.10.16 (Pickles); Portland 18.10.16; Calshot 22.11.16; Wrecked 27.2.17; Deleted 16.7.17 |
| 3326 | Deld Exptl Flight Grain 6.9.16; Accepted 7.9.16 (Pickles); Became Gunnery Exptl Flight Grain 5.12.16 (awaiting refit); Awaiting trial 2.17; EAD Grain to Calshot FS (via Dover) 15.7.17 (arr 17.7.17); Fuselage damaged 13.8.17; Surveyed 10.3.18; Deleted 16.3.18 wrecked |
| 3327 | Deld Calshot 18.10.16; Portland 22.11.16; Bombed U-boat 50m SW of Portland 20.12.16 (FSL JR Ross); Calshot 9.3.17 (general repair); Deleted 11.7.17 |
| 3328 | Deld Windermere 16.10.16; Accepted 15.11.16; Deleted 10.1.17 |
| 3329 | Deld and erected Calshot then to Portland 8.12.16; Calshot FS 11.2.17; Deleted 26.3.17 badly damaged |
| 3330 | Deld Nore War Flight Felixstowe 8.11.16; Killingholme school 4.7.17; Fitted DC 5.7.17; Surveyed 9.11.17; Deleted 17.11.17 DBR |
| 3331 | Deld and accepted Westgate 3.12.16; EF on acceptance test 3.12.16; U/c damaged on TO 13.2.17 (FSL HG Leslie); Attacked U-boat nr Kentish Knock 23.5.17 (FSL |

| | |
|---|---|
| | EB Drake & AM East); AZP 24.5.17; Lee-on-Solent School 1.11.17; Became 209 TDS Lee-on-Solent 1.4.18; Deleted W/E 12.9.18 |
| 3332 | Mkrs to fit tropical radiators for Cape Station 11.16 (NTU); Deld Grain 30.11.16; Tested 19.12.16 (Prodger); Packed 24.3.17; Calshot by lighter 7.4.17; Deleted W/E 14.9.17 |

**12 CAUDRON G.IV TRACTOR BIPLANES ordered on Cont No C.P.44098/15 from British Caudron Co & numbered 3333 to 3344. (Two 80-hp Le Rhône)**
[Two 100-hp Anzani per official 1.17 list]

| | |
|---|---|
| 3333 | Deld Hendon 2.12.15; 4 Wing Eastchurch 11.12.15; Deleted 14.3.16 |
| 3334 | Deld Hendon 1.1.16, flown 3.1.16; 4 Wing Eastchurch 25.1.16; HACP 20.2.16 (FSL HG Henley & AM Turner); War Flight Eastchurch 16.4.16; CSD White City 22.5.16 - @31.8.16, later deleted |
| 3335 | Deld from Cricklewood to CSD White City 31.1.16; Sailed from Tilbury Docks in SS *Khiva* 19.2.16; arr Aegean by 4.16 - @8.16; Transferred to French Government |
| 3336 | Deld from Cricklewood to CSD White City 2.2.16; Tilbury Docks 3.2.16; Sailed in SS *Khiva* 19.2.16; arr Aegean by 4.16 - @8.16; Transferred to French Government |
| 3337 | Deld Hendon 12.2.16; Accepted 9.3.16; Dover 19.3.16; ADD 31.3.16; 7 Flt B Sqdn 5 Wing Coudekerque 9.4.16 - @2.6.16; ADD 6.16 (u/s); Deleted 15.6.16 |
| 3338 | Deld Hendon 30.3.16; Accepted 31.3.16 (Desoutter); Dover 1.4.16; ADD 3.4.16; 8 Flt B Sqdn 5 Wing Coudekerque 15.4.16 - @2.6.16; ADD 6.16 (u/s); Deleted 15.6.16 |
| 3339 | Deld Hendon 30.3.16; Grain 6.7.16 (with Experimental Flight by 7.9.16); Became Gunnery Exptl Grain 5.12.16; Eastchurch Workshops 6.12.16; Deleted 12.1.17 |
| 3340 | Deld CSD White City without engine W/E 6.5.16; Deleted 14.2.17 |
| 3341 | Deld CSD White City without engine W/E 13.5.16; Deleted 14.2.17 |
| 3342 | Deld CSD White City without engine W/E 20.5.16; Deleted 14.2.17 |
| 3343 | Deld CSD White City without engine W/E 27.5.16; Deleted 14.2.17 |
| 3344 | Deld CSD White City without engine W/E 3.6.16; Deleted 14.2.17 |

**79 CURTISS J.N.3 TRACTOR BIPLANES ordered 3.15 under Cont No C.P.61533/15 from Curtiss 1915, numbered 3345 to 3423 & built Toronto (90/100-hp Curtiss OX-2) [From 6.16 to Fairey in batches of four for conversion to J.N.3 (Improved)]**

| | |
|---|---|
| 3345 | Deld Hendon and tested 10.7.15 (Pickles); Ready Hendon 23.7.15; Supermarine repair by 1.10.15 - 11.15; To Fairey 2.16 for conversion to J.N.3 (Improved); Hendon for re-erection 24.9.16; Hendon @2.2.17; 3 Wing Luxeuil for training by 3.17; Transferred to French Govt for AMF 20.4.17; Fairey by 7.17 - 10.17 |
| 3346 | Deld Hendon and tested 19.7.15; Chingford 28.7.15; CSD White City by lorry 1.11.15, then deleted |
| 3347 | (DC) Deld Hendon 20.7.15; Accepted 22.7.15; Chingford 24.7.15; Run into by Handley Page 892 2.8.15; Machine ran away when starting up own propeller, flew over river, hit bump, crashed 8.8.15 (PFSL WH Peberdy); Fairey, Hayes by road for repair 5.9.15; Hendon 29.11.15; Accepted 30.11.15 (Pickles); Eastbourne FS 19.12.15; O/t 22.2.16 (FSL BN Harrop); Retd Ringmer 1.5.16; Eastbourne, bent axle landing 17.5.16 (Lt GH Millar); Fairey 18.6.16 - conv J.N.3 (Imp); Hendon for erection 24.9.16; Tested 16.10.16; Redcar 22.10.16; Deleted 30.4.17 |
| 3348 | Deld Hendon for erection 20.7.15; Accepted 24.7.15; Farnborough 30.7.15 (transit); Chingford 31.7.15; Damaged landing 7.9.15 (WO Allen); Damaged by wind 1.1.16; Fairey 9.4.16 - conv J.N.3 (Improved); Hendon 17.11.16; Accepted 2.1.17; FL Hatfield en route Cranwell 26.2.17 (F/Cdr RB Munday); arr Advanced School Cranwell 27.2.17; Chingford 31.5.17; Surveyed 27.11.17; Deleted 5.12.17 W&T |
| 3349 | Deld Hendon for erection 20.7.15; Accepted 24.7.15; |

Chingford 28.7.15; Damaged by wind 1.1.16; Deleted 19.1.16

3350  Deld Hendon for erection 20.7.15; Tested 29.7.15 (Pickles); Chingford 30.7.15; Deleted 20.3.16

3351  Deld Hendon for erection 22.7.15; Tested 29.7.15 (Pickles); Chingford 31.7.15; CSD White City by lorry 15.11.15, then deleted

3352  Deld Hendon for erection 22.7.15; Chingford 11.8.15; CSD White City by lorry 1.11.15, then deleted

3353  Deld Hendon for erection Hendon 22.7.15; Chingford 12.8.15; Damaged by wind 1.1.16; Deleted 19.1.16

3354  Deld Hendon for erection 22.7.15; Accepted 11.8.15; Alterations 10.15; Westgate 12.10.15; Deleted 24.2.16

3355  Deld Hendon for erection 28.7.15; Tested 5.8.15; Chingford 6.8.15; Completely wrecked 6.8.15 (PFSL WH Peberdy); Deletion recommended but rebuilt instead; Wrecked 29.8.15; To CSD White City; Tilbury Docks for Mediterranean 4.2.16; Deleted 1916

3356  Deld Hendon for erection 29.7.15; Tested 13.8.15; Eastbourne FS (via Sandhurst) 16.8.15; SCAW, Shoreham repair 17.9.15; Eastbourne FS 12.3.16; Fitting DC 31.3.16; Deleted 12.6.16

3357  Deld Hendon for erection 2.8.15; Accepted 5.8.15; Chingford 11.8.15; EF, FL near Great Bardfield 16.12.15; Deleted 21.1.16

3358  Deld Hendon for erection 2.8.15; Tested 9.8.15 (Pickles); Chingford 11.8.15; CSD White City by road 1.11.15; Walney Island 7.2.16; Stripped for packing 13.3.16; Howden 24.4.16; Deleted 9.7.16

3359  Deld Hendon for erection 3.8.15; Accepted 10.8.15; Chingford 12.8.15; Wrecked 17.9.15 (PFSL LG Sieveking); at Westgate re-erecting 11.11.15 - 12.15; Chingford, damaged by 1.1.16; Deleted 19.1.16

3360  Deld Hendon for erection 5.8.15; Tested 11.8.15; Chingford 13.8.15; CSD White City by road 11.11.15, then deleted

3361  Deld Hendon for erection 5.8.15; Tested 11.8.15; Accepted 26.8.15 (Pickles); Alterations 10.15; Eastchurch NFS 11.11.15; Misc Flight Eastchurch 1.5.16 (Ogilvy Improved convert); Spotting Flight Eastchurch 15.9.16; Eastchurch Workshops 14.11.16; Deleted 16.1.17

3362  Deld Hendon for erection 5.8.15; Tested 13.8.15; 5 Wing Dover 21.8.15 - 1.16; Fairey from 13.6.16 to conv J.N.3 (Improved) but deleted W/E 8.12.16 (not worth repair)

3363  Deld Hendon for erection 6.8.15; Tested 11.18.15; Chingford 11.8.15; Crashed, CW 20.10.15 (PFSL E Potter); Surveyed 21.10.17; Deleted 29.10.15

3364  Deld Hendon for erection 6.8.15; Chingford 13.8.15; CW 30.8.15 (PFSL BPH de Roeper); Deleted for spares 16.9.15

3365  Deld Hendon for erection 9.8.15; Tested 16.8.15 (Pickles); To 5 Wing Dover but EF, FL, o/t and damaged Cherkley Court, 2½m from Leatherhead 21.8.15 (FSL JR Potts unhurt); Hendon 31.8.15; Fairey Aviation at Hendon 3.9.15; Killingholme 3.11.15; Scarborough (via Hornsea) 14.11.15; Damaged landing Scarborough 20.4.16 (FSL HCG Allen); Deleted 13.9.16

3366  Deld Hendon for erection 10.8.15; Tested 13.8.15; Tested 25.8.15 (Pickles); Westgate 27.10.15; EF, FL nr Acol, Kent, dismantled and retd in pieces 14.12.15 (FSL RE Bush unhurt); Deleted 24.5.16

3367  Deld Hendon for erection 10.8.15; Ready 16.8.15; Tested 23.8.15 (Pickles); Eastbourne FS 24.8.15; FL nr Harrietsham, Kent 6.9.15 (FSL HGR Malet); Held as spares from 19.9.15; Deleted 13.3.16

3368  Deld Hendon for erection 11.8.15; Tested 13.8.15; Eastbourne FS 24.8.15; detd Ringer with B Flt 15-23.9.15; FL Lydd 27.10.15 (FSL LFB Penley); Deleted 13.3.16

3369  Deld Hendon for erection 12.8.15; Ready 16.8.15; Tested 24.8.15 (Pickles); Eastchurch NFS 26.9.15; Damaged 4.10.15; Deleted 20.10.15

3370  Deld Hendon for erection 13.8.15; Accepted 16.8.15 (Pickles); Eastbourne FS 24.8.15; Damaged landing 26.8.15 (FSL N Keeble unhurt); Retained as spares 5.9.15; Deleted 13.3.16

3371  Deld Hendon for erection 13.8.15; Ready 16.8.15; Tested 23.8.15 (Pickles); Eastbourne FS 24.8.15; Deleted 21.10.15

3372  Deld Hendon for erection 13.8.15; Tested 16.8.15 (Pickles); 4 Wing Eastchurch 13.9.15 but FL en route in field at Grain (FSL CC Wyllie unhurt); Deleted 1.10.15

3373  Deld Hendon for erection 14.8.15; Erecting 16.8.15; Tested 24.8.15 (Pickles); Alterations 10.15; 5 Wing Dover 1.10.15; Deleted 7.3.16

3374  Deld Hendon for erection 14.8.15; Tested 17.8.15; Accepted 24.8.15 (Pickles); Eastbourne FS 19.9.15; Damaged landing 25.9.15 (FSL N Keeble); Converting DC by 14.4.16; Detd Ringmer 1.5.16; Eastbourne 10.5.16; Fairey 18.6.16 conv J.N.3 (Improved) - @3.17; CSD White City by 4.6.17; Packed by 15.6.17; Vendôme 28.6.17; Surveyed 19.12.17; Deleted 31.12.17 W&T

3375  Deld Hendon for erection 16.8.15; Accepted 18.8.15 (Pickles); Grain 18.9.15 (experimental); Modifications ordered 1.10.15; Eastchurch NFS 9.2.16; Damaged 12.2.16; Conv "Eastchurch type" from 24.2.16; Fairey 26.6.16 for conv J.N.3 (Improved), but deleted W/E 8.12.16 (not worth repair)

3376  Deld Hendon for erection 16.8.15; Accepted 18.8.15; Alterations at Hendon 10.15; 5 Wing Dover 4.10.15; Fairey for conversion to J.N.3 (Improved) 13.6.16; Hendon for re-erection 29.10.16; Accepted 9.11.16; Eastchurch Workshops 9.11.16 then to Eastchurch FS; Eastchurch Design Flight 23.11.16 (alterations and trials); Eastchurch Workshops 23.12.16; Deleted 11.1.17

3377  Deld Hendon for erection 19.8.15; Tested 23.8.15 (Pickles); Grain 25.8.15; Under repair by 31.8.15; Test after repair 5.9.15; Wrecked on TO Grain 6.10.15 (FSL JC Croft); Surveyed 7.10.15; Deleted 21.10.15

3378  Deld Hendon for erection 17.8.15; Tested 24.8.15 (Pickles); 5 Wing Dover 24.9.15; Deleted 7.3.16

3379  Deld Hendon for erection 18.8.15; Tested 23.8.15 (Pickles); Grain 25.8.15; Under repair by 31.8.15; Tested bomb sight 7.10.15; Modifications ordered 11.10.15; To CSD White City 14.3.16; Fairey for conversion to J.N.3 (Improved) 7.16; Retd CSD White City 4.17; East Fortune 4.4.17 (arr 8.4.17); Redcar by rail 16.5.17; Deleted 8.9.17

3380  Deld Hendon for erection 19.8.15; Accepted 26.8.15 (Pickles); 5 Wing Dover but FL, chassis wrecked 24.9.15; Deleted 15.10.15

3381  Deld Hendon for erection 19.8.15; Tested 13.9.15 (Pickles); Grain 13.9.15; 4 Wing Eastchurch 18.9.15; Eastchurch NFS 7.10.15 (Ogilvie Improved convert); Damaged 5.1.16; Ran into fence at Westgate 12.2.16 (pilot unhurt); Dismantled and retd; with Misc Flight Eastchurch by 2.5.16; Spotting Flight Eastchurch 15.9.16; Eastchurch Workshops 24.12.16; Eastchurch FS 26.12.16; Eastchurch Workshops 5.6.17; Deleted 31.8.17 BR

3382  Deld Hendon for erection 19.8.15; Accepted 25.8.15 (Pickles); 4 Wing Eastchurch 20.9.15; Eastchurch NFS 24.9.15; Wrecked 2.10.15; Deleted 27.10.15

3383  Deld Hendon for erection 19.8.15; Accepted 24.8.15 (Pickles); 4 Wing Eastchurch 20.9.15; u/s by 1.16; Eastchurch NFS 2.3.16; Dismantled for storage 28.5.16; Fairey 26.6.16 for conversion to J.N.3 (Improved) - @3.17; CSD White City by 4.6.17; Packed for Vendôme by 15.6.17; Vendôme 28.6.17; Surveyed 19.12.17; Deleted 31.12.17 W&T

3384  Deld Hendon for erection 20.8.15; Tested 13.9.15 (Pickles); Grain 17.9.15 (experimental) (Ranken Dart experiments 3.11.15); Modifications ordered 11.10.15; Eastchurch NFS 9.2.16; Dismantled for storage 28.5.16; Fairey 29.6.16 conv J.N.3 (Improved); Hendon for re-erection 12.10.16; Accepted 10.11.16; Eastchurch Workshops 15.11.16; Eastchurch FS 23.11.16; Deleted 11.1.17

3385  Deld Hendon for erection 20.8.15; Tested 13.9.15 (Pickles); Grain 17.9.15 (experimental); Modifications ordered 11.10.15; To Westgate 6.11.15 but FL Queenborough (FSL WG Moore); Retd Experimental Flight Grain from Eastchurch in lorry 10.11.15; CSD White City 14.3.16; To Fairey 7.16 conv J.N.3 (Improved) - @3.17; CSD White City by 4.6.17; arr Vendôme 16.7.17; Surveyed 19.12.17; Deleted 31.12.17 W&T

3386  Deld Hendon for erection 20.8.15; Accepted 26.8.15 (Pickles); 5 Wing Dover 25.9.15; Fairey 13.6.16 conv

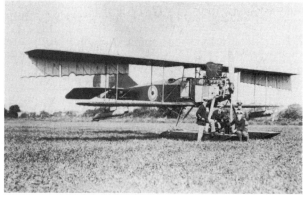

*Short 827 Type Seaplane 3331 at Lee-on-Solent School.
(J.M.Bruce/G.S.Leslie collection)*

*Curtiss J.N.3 3416 in flames at Redcar, May 1916.
(J.M.Bruce/G.S.Leslie collection)*

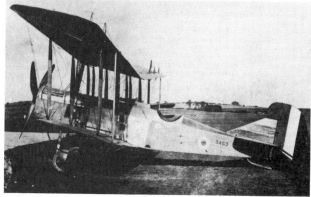

*Curtiss R.2 3453 under going trials at Eastchurch fitted
with a 200-hp Sunbeam engine and four-bladed
propeller. (via Frank Cheesman)*

*Felixstowe F.1 (Porte 1) 3580 after conversion from
Curtiss H.4. (MAP)*

*Henry Farman F.27 3626 with 5 Wing at Coudekerque 1916. (J.M.Bruce/G.S.Leslie collection)*

J.N.3 (Improved); Accepted Hendon 9.11.16; Eastchurch Workshops 15.11.16; Deleted 12.1.17

3387 Deld Hendon for erection 21.8.15; Tested 8.9.15 (Pickles); Eastbourne FS 8.10.15; Dover but COL 5.11.15 (FSL J Robinson); Awaiting deletion at Eastbourne by 28.11.15; Deleted 7.12.15

3388 Deld Hendon for erection 24.8.15; Tested 13.9.15 (Pickles); Grain 18.9.15 (experimental); Modifications ordered 5.10.15; Eastchurch 13.2.16; Dismantled for storage 28.5.16; Fairey 26.6.16 conv J.N.3 (Improved) to 2.17; CSD White City by 4.6.17; Vendôme for erection 26.6.17; Wrecked beyond repair 20.8.17; Deleted W/E 21.9.17

3389 Deld Hendon for erection 24.8.15; Experimental Flight Grain 5.11.15; CSD White City 14.3.16; To Fairey 7.16 conv J.N.3 (Improved) to @3.17; CSD White City by 4.6.17; Vendôme 25.6.17; Surveyed 12.10.17; Deleted 16.10.17 wrecked

3390 Deld Hendon for erection 24.8.15; Tested 10.9.15 (Pickles); 4 Wing Eastchurch 16.9.15; Eastchurch NFS 2.3.16; Fairey 26.6.16 conv J.N.3 (Improved); Hendon for erection 22.11.16; Accepted 2.1.17; Advanced School Cranwell 4.1.17; Wrecked BR 21.7.17; Deleted W/E 5.9.17

3391 Deld Hendon for erection 25.8.15; Tested 9.9.15 (Pickles); Grain but damaged landing 18.9.15 (FSL ON Walmesley); Tests after repair 28.9.15; Modifications ordered 11.10.15; CSD White City 14.3.16; To Fairey 7.16 conv J.N.3 (Improved) to 3.17; CSD White City by 4.6.17; Vendôme 16.7.17; Surveyed 19.12.17; Deleted 31.12.17 W&T

3392 Deld Hendon for erection 25.8.15; Tested 17.9.15 (Pickles); Eastbourne FS 25.9.15; Damaged landing 7.10.15 (FSL RP Minifie); Damaged 13.12.15 (FSL GD Smith unhurt); O/t in bad ground 9.2.16 (FSL BN Harrop); Ringmer 4.5.16; Eastbourne 6.5.16; EF, FL, badly damaged 6.5.16 (FSL JLA Sinclair); Deleted 12.6.16

3393 Deld Hendon for erection 25.8.15; Tested 16.9.15 (Pickles); Dover (via Chingford) 28.9.15; Hendon 28.10.15; Eastchurch 5.1.16; Detling 31.12.15 (sic); Eastchurch NFS 20.3.16 (later Gunnery School); Fairey 13.8.16 conv J.N.3 (Improved); Allocated 3 Wing after trials at Hendon 9.12.16; 3 Wing Luxeuil for training by 12.1.17; Transferred to French Government for AMF 20.4.17

3394 Deld Hendon for erection 25.8.15; Tested 11.9.15 (Pickles); 4 Wing Eastchurch 18.9.15 (mod here at some time to Ogilvie converted); Eastchurch NFS 24.9.15; Damaged 1.10.15; Gunnery School Flights Eastchurch 4.5.16; Misc Flt Eastchurch 21.6.16; Spotting Flight 15.9.16; Eastchurch FS 26.11.16; Deleted 31.8.17

3395 Deld Hendon for erection 25.8.15; Tested 14.9.15 (Pickles); Damaged landing 20.9.15 (FSL GRH Talbot); Westgate 18.10.15; Deleted 24.5.16

3396 Deld Hendon for erection 25.8.15; Grain 18.9.15; Westgate 28.9.15; Deleted 24.2.16

3397 Deld Hendon for erection 26.8.15; Tested 10.9.15 (Pickles); 4 Wing Eastchurch 18.9.15; Eastchurch NFS 26.9.15; Mod to Ogilvie converted by 15.3.16; Misc Flight Eastchurch 1.5.16; Spotting Flight Eastchurch 15.9.16; Eastchurch FS 26.11.16; Convtd to "Eastchurch Type" 24.2.17; Deleted 31.8.17

3398 Deld Hendon for erection 26.8.15; Tested 11.9.15 (Pickles); 4 Wing Eastchurch but EF, FL Cobham en route 18.9.15 (repaired); Deleted 24.9.15

3399 Deld Hendon for erection 11.9.15; Tested 24.9.15 (Pickles); 5 Wing Dover 28.9.15 but EF, FL Tilsey, Surrey; Continued to Dover (ex Westenhangar) 30.9.15; Deleted 7.3.16
BUT UK to Vendôme 29.6.17; Deleted 19.12.17 W&T

3400 Deld Hendon for erection 15.9.15; Tested 16.9.15 (Pickles); Westgate 1.10.15; Eastbourne FS 16.10.15 but damaged chassis landing (FSL WG McMinnies); Damaged landing 13.12.15 (FSL HAJ Wilson unhurt); dett Ringmer 1.5.16; Eastbourne FS 8.5.16; Deleted 9.10.16

3401 To be transferred RFC (Military Wing) 9.15 as 6116 (NTU?); Deld Hendon for erection 15.9.15; Tested 17.9.15 (Pickles); Westgate 8.10.15; Deleted 24.2.16

3402 Deld Hendon for erection 15.9.15; Tested 17.9.15 (Pickles) & 5.10.15 (Pickles); Chingford 15.10.15 (transit); Westgate 17.10.15; EF, FL in field 13.11.15; Dismantled by 2.12.15; Transferred RFC (Military Wing) 9.15 as 6117

3403 Deld Hendon for erection and tested 17.9.15 (Pickles); Chingford 11.11.15; Wrecked 14.11.15 (PFSL RJ McDougall unhurt); Deleted 13.2.16

3404 Deld Hendon for erection 17.9.15; Tested 18.9.15 (Pickles) & 7.10.15; Eastbourne FS 12.10.15; FL Camp Hill, nr Eastchurch 14.10.15 (repaired); Retd 18.10.15; Landed in dyke, broke propeller 20.10.15 (FSL WG McMinnies); Awaiting deletion by 28.11.15; Deleted 7.12.15

3405 Deld Hendon for erection 17.9.15; Tested 22.9.15 & 9.10.15 (both Pickles); Killingholme 23.10.15; Hornsea by 11.15; Scarborough 4.11.15; Redcar 7.11.15; Deleted 7.5.16

3406 Deld Hendon for erection 20.9.15; Tested 22.9.15 (Pickles); Westgate 1.10.15; Practice Paradox Gun 23.12.15 (FSL RE Bush & Lt ST Panther); Manston 7.4.16; Deleted Westgate 9.4.16

3407 Deld Hendon for erection 20.9.15; Tested 22.9.15 (Pickles); Westgate 2.10.15; FL, damaged, retd by road 24.1.16 (FSL RE Bush); Deleted 24.5.16

3408 Deld Hendon for erection 20.9.15; Tested 14.10.15 (Pickles); Killingholme 23.10.15; Deleted 18.3.16

3409 Deld Hendon for erection 21.9.15; Tested 22.9.15 (Pickles); Eastbourne FS 11.10.15; Damaged 15.10.15 (FSL EL Ford); FL Folkestone 27.10.15 (FSL WG McMinnies); Deleted 7.12.15

3410 Deld Hendon for erection 21.9.15; Tested 22.9.15 (Pickles); Westgate 4.10.15; Fairey 3.1.16 conv J.N.3 (Improved); Hendon for erection 15.4.16; Flown 24.4.16; Advanced School Eastbourne 15.6.16; Fairey 29.8.16 - @31.12.16; CSD White City by 4.6.17; Packed for Vendôme by 15.6.17; RNASTE Vendôme 29.6.17; Surveyed 19.12.17; Deleted 31.12.17 W&T

3411 Deld Hendon for erection 22.9.15; Tested 24.9.15 (Pickles); Chingford 6.10.15 (transit); 5 Wing Dover 8.10.15; CSD White City 7.3.16; Fairey by 31.7.16 - conv J.N.3 (Improved); Deleted 6.17

3412 Deld Hendon for erection 9.15; Tested 24.9.15 (Pickles); Experimental Flight Grain 12.10.15 (alterations); CSD White City 14.3.16; To Fairey 7.16 - conv J.N.3 (Improved) - @3.17; CSD White City by 4.6.17; Vendôme 16.7.17; Surveyed 12.10.17; Deleted 16.10.17 wrecked

3413 Deld Hendon for erection 22.9.15; Grain 12.10.15; Eastchurch 27.10.15; Grain by 1.11.15 (repair); Eastchurch NFS 10.3.16; Fairey conv J.N.3 2.6.17 (Improved); RNASTE Vendôme 16.7.17; Surveyed 19.12.17; Deleted 31.12.17 W&T

3414 Deld Hendon for erection 22.9.15; Tested 27.9.15 (Pickles); 5 Wing Dover 4.10.15; HACP 24.1.16 (FSL JR Potts); Fairey 13.6.16 conv J.N.3 (Improved); Hendon for erection 29.9.16; Tested 18.10.16; To Eastchurch but FL and damaged Alexandra Park 4.11.16 (pilot unhurt); Deleted 11.11.16

3415 Deld Hendon for erection and tested 8.10.15 (Pickles); Killingholme 16.11.15; Deleted 15.3.16

3416 Deld Hendon for erection 8.10.15; Tested 11.10.15 (Pickles); Killingholme 23.10.15; Scarborough 30.10.15; Redcar 31.10.15; Deleted 7.5.16 Burnt

3417 Deld Hendon for erection 19.11.15; Tested 19.11.15 (Pickles); Eastbourne FS 19.12.15; Damaged u/c 26.4.16 (FSL KR Munro); Taxied into by 3426 and damaged 19.5.16 (FSL KR Munro); Deleted 12.6.16

3418 Deld Hendon for erection 15.10.15; Accepted 2.11.15 (Pickles); Killingholme 3.11.15 but EF, FL Spilsby, Lincs (FSL DG Broad); arrived by breakdown party 5.11.15; Deleted 18.3.16

3419 Deld Hendon for erection 15.10.15; Accepted 18.10.15 (Pickles); Killingholme 26.10.15; Deleted 1.2.16

3420 Deld Hendon for erection 19.10.15; Tested 3.11.15 (Pickles); Eastchurch NFS by 30.11.15; Wrecked 17.12.15; Damaged 25.1.16; Misc Flight Eastchurch 6.5.16; Detling (coded '5') 13.7.16; Hit tree tops and nosed dived into field 31.8.16 (FSL JA Harman & AC2 BR Carter both injured); Deleted 11.9.16

3421 Deld Hendon for erection 1.11.15; Accepted 11.11.15

(Pickles); Killingholme 25.11.15; Deleted 18.3.16

3422    Deld Hendon for erection 15.11.15; Tested 24.11.15 (Pickles); Detling 27.11.15; Surveyed 8.12.15 (wrecked); Damaged chassis and wings landing 14.12.15; Dismantled 7.4.16; CSD White City 28.6.16; To Fairey - conv J.N.3 (Improved) - @2.17; CSD White City by 4.6.17; Vendôme for erection 26.6.17; U/c damaged 18.8.17; U/c damaged 21.9.17; Surveyed 19.12.17; Deleted 31.12.17 W&T

3423    Deld Hendon for erection and tested 17.11.15 (Pickles); To Detling but became lost and crashed in marshes 2m from Wrotham 27.11.15 (FSL LE Smith); Bits returned to Hendon in lorry 28.11.15; Eastchurch Workshops by lorry 16.12.15 (repair); Detling 30.12.15; EF, FL 20.1.16 (FSL AB Shearer); EF, FL, propeller and chassis wrecked 30.1.16 (FSL AB Shearer); Deleted 9.3.16

**21 J.N.4 TRACTOR BIPLANES ordered 26.3.15 under Cont No C.P.61533/15 from Curtiss 1915, numbered 3424 to 3444 & built Toronto (90-hp Curtiss OX-2)**

3424    Deld Hendon 17.3.16; Fitted DC 15.4.16; Preliminary test 25.4.16 (Pickles); Deleted 21.1.17

3425    Deld Hendon 4.4.16; Fitted DC; Cranwell 25.4.16; Chingford 26.3.17; Redcar 1.12.17; Deleted W/E 23.1.18

3426    Deld Hendon 4.4.16; Tested 8.4.16 (Pickles); Eastbourne FS 14.4.16; Taxied into 3417 and damaged 19.5.16 (S/L RF Bellamy); Dismantled for packing 9.10.16; Vendôme for erection 3.12.16; Deletion recommended 29.1.17

3427    Deld Hendon 4.4.16; Fitted DC; Cranwell 25.4.16; Deleted 3.7.16

3428    Deld Hendon 5.4.16; flown 17.4.16; Tested 19.4.16; Cranwell 20.4.16; Landed too slowly and pancaked Cranwell 16.8.16 (FSL WL Anderson); Deletion authorised 27.8.16; Repaired instead; Wrecked by 1.3.17; Deleted 18.6.17

3429    Deld Hendon 5.4.16; Fitting DC 15.4.16; Accepted 16.4.16; Cranwell 20.4.16; Deleted 30.8.16

3430    Deld Hendon 11.4.16; Flown 24.4.16; Grain 6.5.16; Eastchurch Workshops 7.5.17; Eastchurch FS 27.6.17; Chingford W/E 22.9.17; Deleted 9.1.18 W&T

3431    Deld Hendon 13.4.16; Tested 20.4.16; Chingford 25.4.16; Crashed while attempting a loop, on to Angel Railway Station Goods Yard, Edmonton 30.4.16 (PFSL TR Liddle killed); Deleted 30.5.16

3432    Deld Hendon 14.4.16; Fitted DC; Preliminary test 28.4.16 (Prodger); Accepted 1.5.16; Grain 6.5.16; Rebuilding by 28.2.17; Chingford 28.3.17; Deleted 22.8.17

3433    Deld Hendon 20.4.16; Tested 25.4.16 (Pickles); Cranwell 1.5.16; Chingford 7.4.17; Badly damaged 8.8.17; Redcar W/E 1.12.17; For deletion by 9.3.18; RN College Greenwich W/E 23.3.18, presumed for ground instructional purposes

3434    Deld Hendon 19.4.16; Fitted DC; Accepted 7.5.16; Chingford 9.5.16; East Fortune by rail 26.9.16; Deleted 7.2.17

3435    Deld Hendon 19.4.16; Tested 27.4.16; Cranwell 1.5.16; Chingford 31.5.17; Surveyed 19.12.17; Deleted 9.1.18 W&T

3436    Deld Hendon 19.4.16; Fitted DC; Chingford 1.5.16; Eastbourne 4.8.16; Dismantled for packing by 29.10.16; Vendôme for erection 23.11.16; Surveyed 26.2.17; Deleted 10.3.17

3437    Deld Hendon 24.4.16; Tested 28.4.16; Cranwell 1.5.16; Crashed, damaged 13.7.16 (FSL HS Broad); Chingford by lorry 8.5.17 (arr 9.5.17); Deleted 22.8.17

3438    Deld Hendon 24.4.16; Fitted DC; Tested 12.5.16 (Prodger); Chingford 24.5.16; RNASTE Vendôme 23.11.16; Damaged tail and wingtip landing 30.4.17; U/c damaged 2.5.17; Became 205 TDS Vendôme 1.4.18

3439    Deld Hendon 24.4.16; Flown by 1.5.16; Cranwell 4.5.16; Deleted 18.6.17

3440    Deld Hendon 25.4.16; Fitted DC; Accepted 1.5.16 (Prodger); Chingford 1.5.16; Redcar 8.9.16; Run into by N5037 21.12.16; Leeds to Redcar 26.12.16; COL 6.7.17; Deleted 8.9.17 BR

3441    Deld Hendon 26.4.16; Accepted 2.5.16; Cranwell

4.5.16; Chingford 1.7.17 (damaged); Surveyed 20.12.17; Deleted 9.1.18 W&T

3442    Deld Hendon 27.4.16; Fitted DC; Tested 6.5.16; Redcar 10.5.16 (arr 11.5.16); For deletion by 9.3.18; Tregantle store W/E 23.3.18

3443    Deld Hendon 29.4.16; Redcar 10.5.16 (arr 11.5.16); FL in mist, o/t, severely damaged, Northallerton 22.7.16 (FSL NWG Blackburn); Deleted 25.6.17

3444    Deld Hendon 3.5.16; Fitted DC; Tested 11.5.16; Eastchurch FS 14.5.16; Eastchurch Workshops 10.5.17; Deleted 11.5.17

**100 CURTISS R.2 TRACTOR BIPLANES ordered 26.3.15 under Cont No C.P.01535/15 from Curtiss in 1915, numbered 3445 to 3544 & built Toronto. (Ordered as 200-hp Sunbeam in 3446, 3455-3459, 3461, 3462, 3465, 3466, remainder 160-hp Curtiss VX, delivered as 150-hp Sunbeam to 3468, then 160-hp Curtiss VX)**

3445    Deld Hendon 24.12.15; Tested 16.1.16; Damaged when Bessonneau hangar blew away 28.3.16; Re-erecting Hendon with Sunbeam engine 11.7.16; Deleted 23.8.16

3446    Deld Hendon 5.3.16; Fitting DC 11.7.16; Dismantled for storage 2.17; Deletion recommended 3.4.17; For re-erection by 13.5.17 as 200-hp bomber, but deleted 23.5.17 instead

3447    Deld Hendon 14.4.16; Accepted 4.5.16; Detling 18.5.16; 3 Wing Manston 9.6.16; Deleted 13.9.16

3448    Deld Hendon 4.5.16; Tested 25.5.16 (Prodger); Deleted 23.8.16

3449    Deld Hendon 12.5.16; Grain 1.11.16; Became Gunnery Experimental Grain 5.12.16; Became EAD Grain on/by 1.2.17; Surveyed 25.3.18; Deleted 27.3.18 DBR

3450    Deld Hendon 20.5.16; Preliminary test 31.5.16 (Prodger); Dismantled for storage 2.17; Deleted 15.6.17

3451    Deld Hendon 22.5.16; Flown 5.9.16; Dover 7.9.16; Design Flight Eastchurch 8.9.16; Spotting Flight Eastchurch 13.10.16; Observers School Flight Eastchurch 23.12.16 - @23.2.18

3452    Deld Hendon 23.5.16; Fitting Sunbeam engine 11.7.16; Flown 18.7.16; visited Kingsnorth 23.7.16; Felixstowe 1.1.17; Burgh Castle 3.1.17; Yarmouth 4.1.17; Cranwell 5.1.17 (detd from Hendon); Deleted W/E 5.9.17

3453    Deld Hendon 21.7.16; Fitted 200-hp Sunbeam engine; Flown 15.9.16; Detling 21.9.16 (transit); Design Flight Eastchurch 24.9.16 (type trials); Hendon 14.11.16; Work suspended 16.6.17 until reconstruction of 3473 proved satisfactory; Surveyed 27.12.17; Deleted 3.1.18

3454    Deld Hendon 21.7.16; Flown 1.9.16; Dismantled for storage 2.17; Deleted 3.4.17

3455    Deld Hendon and erecting 31.8.16; Fitting 200-hp Sunbeam engine by 10.11.16; Chingford 9.12.16; Hendon 11.12.16; Design Flight Eastchurch 22.12.16; Hendon for trials 14.2.17; Accepted then dismantled for packing 17.2.17; 3 Wing Luxeuil by rail 21.2.17; ADD by 17.5.17; Deleted 27.6.17 (u/s)

3456    Deld Hendon and erecting 1.9.16; Fitting 200-hp Sunbeam 24.10.16; Fitting bomb gear 17.11.16; Accepted 29.1.17; Dismantled for packing; 3 Wing Luxeuil by rail 9.2.17 - @13.4.17; ADD by 17.5.17; Deleted 27.6.17 (u/s)

3457    Deld Hendon for erection 23.9.16; Fitting bomb gear 17.11.16; Accepted 8.2.17; 3 Wing Luxeuil by road 17.2.17 - @13.4.17; ADD by 17.5.17; Deleted 27.6.17 (u/s)

3458    Deld Hendon 14.10.16; Fitting 200-hp Sunbeam by 10.11.16; Accepted 22.1.17; 3 Wing Luxeuil by rail 9.2.17; ADD by 12.4.17; Deleted 27.6.17 (u/s)

3459    Deld Hendon 16.10.16; Fitting bomb gear 17.11.16; Fit 200-hp Sunbeam, accepted 29.1.17; 3 Wing Luxeuil by rail 9.2.17; ADD by 19.4.17; Deleted 27.6.17 (u/s)

3460    Deld Hendon 17.10.16; Fitting bomb gear 17.11.16; Deleted 2.4.17

3461    (200-hp Sunbeam) Deld Hendon for erection 24.10.16; Fitting bomb gear 17.11.16; Accepted 1.3.17 (Prodger); Cattewater 6.5.17 (via Bournemouth); Prawle Point 15.5.17 - @15.9.17; NFT

3462    Deld Hendon for erection 24.10.16; Fitting bomb gear 17.11.16; Accepted 17.3.17; Manston 30.3.17; Dover 2.4.17; ADD 9.4.17; 7 Sqdn by 12.4.17 - @12.7.17;

Deleted ADD 16.7.17 (u/s)

3463 Deld Hendon for erection 24.10.16 (and fit 160-hp Curtiss VX); Accepted 26.10.16; Fitting bomb gear 17.11.16; Cranwell 21.2.17; Surveyed 21.11.17; Deleted 5.12.17 as spares

3464 Deld Hendon for erection 20.10.16; Fitting bomb gear 17.11.16; Accepted 17.3.17, then packed; Left for Aegean 30.3.17; Mudros (200-hp Sunbeam)

3465 Deld Hendon for erection 20.10.16; Fitting bomb gear 17.11.16; Accepted 3.2.17; Allocated 3 Wing Luxeuil 17.2.17, but not arrived by 16.4.17; ADD by 17.5.17; Deleted 27.6.17 (u/s)

3466 Deld Hendon for erection 30.10.16; Fitting bomb gear 17.11.16; Prawle 12.5.17 - @15.9.17; Fate unknown

3467 (Fitted 200-hp Sunbeam); Deld Hendon for erection 14.11.16; Fitting bomb gear 17.11.16; Work suspended 16.6.17 until reconstruction of 3473 proved satisfactory; Surveyed 25.10.17; Deleted 29.10 17 as spares

3468 (Fitted 200-hp Sunbeam); Deld Hendon for erection 17.11.16; Fitting bomb gear 17.11.16; Accepted 3.6.17; Work suspended 16.6.17 until reconstruction of 3473 proved satisfactory; Surveyed 25.10.17; Deleted 29.10 17 as spares

3469 (Fitted 200-hp Sunbeam); Deld Hendon for erection 20.11.16; Work suspended 16.6.17 until reconstruction of 3473 proved satisfactory; Surveyed 25.10.17; Deleted 29.10 17 as spares

3470 (Fitted 200-hp Sunbeam); Deld Hendon for erection 21.11.16; Work suspended 16.6.17 until reconstruction of 3473 proved satisfactory; Surveyed 25.10.17; Deleted 29.10 17 as spares

3471 Deld Hendon for erection 21.11.16; Removing Curtiss VX engine 22.11.16; Prawle by lorry (via Bournemouth) 9.6.17 - @15.9.17; Fate unknown

3472 Deld Hendon for erection 21.11.16; Removing Curtiss VX engine 22.11.16; Fitted 200-hp Sunbeam; Work suspended 16.6.17 until reconstruction of 3473 proved satisfactory; Eastchurch Gunnery School 15.9.17; Surveyed 26.11.17; Deleted 5.12.17 as spares

3473 Deld Hendon for erection 22.11.16; Fitted 200-hp Sunbeam; Being reconstructed by 16.1.17; Cranwell 15.8.17 (for gunnery training Freiston); Eastchurch Workshops early 11.17; Surveyed 8.11.17; Deleted 17.11.17 W&T

3474 Deld Hendon for erection 23.11.16; Fitted 200-hp Sunbeam; Work suspended 16.6.17 until reconstruction of 3473 proved satisfactory; Surveyed 25.10.17; Deleted 29.10.17 as spares

3475 Deld CSD to Hendon 2.6.17; Work suspended 16.6.17 until reconstruction of 3473 proved satisfactory; Observers School Flight Eastchurch 30.8.17 - @30.3.18

3476 Deld CSD to Hendon for erection 13.6.17; Work suspended 16.6.17 until reconstruction of 3473 proved satisfactory; Observers School Flight Eastchurch 5.9.17 - @30.3.18

3477 Deld CSD to Hendon for erection 13.6.17; Work suspended 16.6.17 until reconstruction of 3473 proved satisfactory; Observers School Flight Eastchurch 7.9.17 - @30.3.18

3478 Deld CSD to Hendon for erection 13.6.17; Work suspended 16.6.17 until reconstruction of 3473 proved satisfactory; Cranwell storage by 16.8.17; Observers School Flight Eastchurch 15.9.17 - @30.3.18

3479 Deld Hendon for erection 13.6.17; CSD 25.6.17; Cranwell storage 18.7.17 - @25.9.17; Observers School Flight Eastchurch by 10.17 (not by 29.9.17) - @30.3.18

3480 Deld Hendon for erection 13.6.17; CSD 25.6.17; Cranwell storage 18.7.17- @30.3.18

3481 Deld Hendon for erection 13.6.17; CSD 25.6.17; Cranwell storage 18.7.17- @30.3.18

3482 Deld Hendon for erection 13.6.17; CSD 25.6.17; Cranwell storage 18.7.17- @30.3.18

3483 Deld Hendon for erection 13.6.17; CSD 25.6.17; Cranwell storage 18.7.17- @30.3.18

3484 Deld Hendon for erection 13.6.17; CSD 25.6.17; Cranwell storage 18.7.17- @30.3.18

3485 Deld Hendon for erection 13.6.17; CSD 25.6.17; Cranwell storage 18.7.17- @30.3.18

3486 Deld Hendon for erection 13.6.17; CSD 25.6.17; Cranwell storage 18.7.17- @30.3.18

3487 Deld Hendon for erection 16.6.17; CSD 25.6.17; Cranwell storage 18.7.17- @30.3.18

3488 Deld Hendon for erection 16.6.17; CSD 25.6.17; Cranwell storage 18.7.17- @30.3.18

3489 Deld Hendon for erection 16.6.17; CSD 25.6.17; Cranwell storage 18.7.17- @30.3.18

3490 Deld Hendon for erection 16.6.17; CSD 25.6.17; Cranwell storage 18.7.17- @30.3.18

3491 Deld Hendon for erection 16.6.17; CSD 25.6.17; Cranwell storage 18.7.17- @30.3.18

3492 Deld Hendon for erection 16.6.17; CSD 25.6.17; Cranwell storage 18.7.17- @30.3.18

3493 Deld Hendon for erection 16.6.17; CSD 25.6.17; Cranwell storage 18.7.17- @30.3.18

3494 Deld Hendon for erection 16.6.17; CSD 25.6.17; Cranwell storage 18.7.17- @30.3.18

3495 Deld Hendon for erection 16.6.17; CSD 25.6.17; Cranwell storage 18.7.17- @30.3.18

3496 Deld Hendon for erection 16.6.17; CSD 25.6.17; Cranwell storage 18.7.17- @30.3.18

3497 Deld Hendon for erection 16.6.17; CSD 25.6.17; Cranwell storage 18.7.17- @30.3.18

3498 Deld Hendon for erection 16.6.17; CSD 25.6.17; Cranwell storage 18.7.17- @30.3.18

3499 CSD to Cranwell storage 18.7.17- @30.3.18

3500 CSD to Cranwell storage 18.7.17- @30.3.18

3501 CSD to Cranwell storage 18.7.17- @30.3.18

3502 CSD to Cranwell storage 18.7.17- @30.3.18

3503 CSD to Cranwell storage 18.7.17- @30.3.18

3504 CSD to Cranwell storage 18.7.17- @30.3.18

3505 CSD to Cranwell storage 18.7.17- @30.3.18

3506 CSD to Cranwell storage 18.7.17- @30.3.18

3507 CSD to Cranwell storage 18.7.17- @30.3.18

3508 CSD to Cranwell storage 18.7.17- @30.3.18

3509 Deld CSD to Hendon for erection 25.6.17; Cranwell storage W/E 15.9.17; Flying by 11.17 - @17.6.18

3510 Deld CSD to Hendon for erection 25.6.17; D/F experiments; Fitted 200-hp Sunbeam engine; Cranwell 28.9.17 (arr 2.10.17); D/F experiments (fitted 160-hp Curtiss VX); Became 201/2 TDS Cranwell 1.4.18 - @30.6.18

3511 Deld CSD to Hendon for erection 25.6.17; Deleted 6.9.17

3512 Deld CSD to Hendon for erection 25.6.17; Cranwell (or Gunnery Flight Freiston) 15.9.17 (arr 2.10.17); Surveyed 3.1.18; Deleted 17.1.18 wreck

3513 Deld CSD to Hendon for erection 25.6.17; Eastchurch 6.10.17 - @30.3.18

3514 Deld CSD to Hendon for erection 25.6.17; Cranwell 2.10.17; D/F experiments; Became 201/2 TDS Cranwell 1.4.18; Netheravon 20.5.18

3515 Deld CSD to Hendon for erection 25.6.17; Eastchurch OS 29.9.17 (arr 1.10.17) - @30.3.18

3516 Deld CSD to Hendon for erection 25.6.17; Eastchurch OS W/E 20.10.17 - @30.3.18

3517 Deld CSD to Hendon for erection 25.6.17; Eastchurch OS W/E 30.9.17 - @30.3.18

3518 Deld CSD to Hendon for erection 25.6.17; Eastchurch OS W/E 13.10.17 - @30.3.18

3519 Deld CSD to Hendon for erection 25.6.17; Eastchurch OS W/E 13.10.17 - @30.3.18

3520 Deld CSD to Hendon for erection 25.6.17; Eastchurch OS W/E 20.10.17 - @30.3.18

3521 Deld CSD to Hendon for erection 25.6.17; Eastchurch OS W/E 9.11.17 - @30.3.18

3522 Deld CSD to Hendon for erection 25.6.17; Eastchurch OS W/E 3.11.17 - @7.18

3523 Deld CSD to Hendon for erection 25.6.17; Eastchurch OS 15.2.18 - @23.2.18

3524 Deld CSD to Hendon for erection 25.6.17; Cranwell W/E 9.10.17; Eastchurch OS W/E 9.11.17 - @30.3.18

3525 Deld CSD to Hendon for erection 25.6.17; Eastchurch OS 28.2.18 - @30.3.18

3526 Deld CSD to Hendon for erection 25.6.17; Eastchurch W/E 14.2.18 - @30.3.18

3527 Deld CSD to Hendon for erection 25.6.17; Eastchurch 26.2.18 - @30.3.18

3528 Deld CSD to Hendon for erection 25.6.17; Surveyed 13.10.17; Deleted 16.10.17 DBR

3529 Deld CSD to Hendon for erection 29.7.17; Eastchurch OS W/E 27.10.17; British & Colonial 27.10.17; Eastchurch by 29.12.17 - @30.3.18

3530     Deld CSD to Hendon for erection 29.7.17; Eastchurch 6.3.18

3531 to 3544 not delivered

## 50 CURTISS H.4 "AMERICA" (LATER "SMALL AMERICA") TRACTOR BIPLANE FLYING BOATS ordered 3.15 under Cont No C.P.01535/15 from Curtiss, numbered 3545 to 3594 & built Toronto. All delivered to Felixstowe. (Two 100-hp Curtiss, mostly re-engined with 100-hp Anzani)

3545     Deld Felixstowe for erection 17.7.15; FF 25.7.15 (probably with Curtiss engines); Fitted Anzani engines 8.15; Stbd extension smashed landing after patrol at Landguard Point 9.10.15 (FSL AQ Cooper & PO Mech Amiss); Tested with night landing lights 15.11.15; Disabled, to Harwich by TB.No.20 21.11.15; Salved by HMS *Riviera* in wrecked condition 22.11.15; Grain 23.11.15; Presume rebuilt; Restored to commission Felixstowe 19.10.17; Felixstowe Seaplane School by 4.18; Deleted W/E 21.11.18

3546     (Two 100-hp Clerget). Deld Felixstowe for erection 21.7.15; FF 31.7.15; Hull experiments (known as "The Incidence Boat"); Tested with two 100-hp Gnome Monosoupape, accepted for bombing practice (10.15?); Fitted Anzani engines 10.15 - 11.15; Dismantled by 27.2.17; Deleted 25.4.17

3547     Deld Felixstowe for erection 31.7.15; Fitted Anzani engines 11.15 - 1.16; Deleted 31.7.17

3548     Deld Felixstowe for erection 31.7.15; Two 150-hp Anzani engines fitted 10.15; Surveyed 2.11.17; Deleted 8.11.17 DBR; Hull originally for preservation

3549     Deld Felixstowe for erection 31.7.15; Fitted Anzani engines 11.15 - 1.16; For deletion by 29.12.17; Presume rebuilt; Felixstowe Seaplane School by 23.2.18; Deleted W/E 29.8.18

3550     Deld Felixstowe for erection 7.8.15; Fitted Anzani engines 11.15 - 1.16; Night reconnaissance, landed Yarmouth 19.5.16; Surveyed 15.8.16; Deleted 29.8.16

3551     Deld Felixstowe for erection 7.8.15; Fitted Anzani engines 9.15 - 10.15; Tested 13.10.15; Packing for Malta 19.4.16; CSD Crystal Palace 9.6.16; To Gibraltar 8.16; Calafrana W/E 10.10.17; Surveyed 26.10.17; Deleted 14.11.17 DBR

3552     Deld Felixstowe for erection 14.8.15; Fitted Anzani engines 11.15 - 12.15; CSD Crystal Palace 9.6.16; To Gibraltar 8.16; Calafrana W/E 10.10.17; Surveyed 26.10.17; Deleted 14.11.17 DBR

3553     Deld Felixstowe for erection 19.8.15; Fitted Anzani engines 11.15 - 12.15; Westgate 5.2.16 but damaged lower plane landing (F/L RH Routledge & AM Langford); Felixstowe 24.4.16; Deleted 3.7.16

3554     Deld Felixstowe for erection 19.8.15; Fitted Anzani engines 11.15; Deleted 14.6.17

3555     Deld Felixstowe for erection 4.9.15; Fitted Anzani engines 11.15 - 12.15; To Calshot but FL off Dungeness 17.12.15 (F/L AW Clemson & FSL GN Geale); Towed to Dover by TBD *Amazon* 18.12.15; Calshot 20.12.15; Tested 8.2.16; Deleted 9.2.17

3556     Deld Felixstowe for erection 4.9.15; Packing for Malta 19.4.16; CSD Crystal Palace 9.6.16; To Gibraltar 8.16; Tested after erection 14.11.16; Calafrana W/E 10.10.17; Surveyed 19.12.17; Deleted 3.1.18 DBR

3557     Deld Felixstowe for erection 14.9.15; Fitted Anzani engines 9.15 - 10.15; EF, towed to Grain 5.11.15 (F/L AW Clemson & LM Farrell); Retd Felixstowe 7.11.15; Re-erected 1.12.15; To Calshot 12.1.16, arrived in tow via Littlehampton 14.1.16; Deleted 9.2.17

3558     Deld Felixstowe for erection 14.9.15; Fitted Anzani engines 9.15 - 1.16; Packing for Malta 19.4.16; CSD Crystal Palace 9.6.16; To Gibraltar 8.16; Calafrana W/E 10.10.17; Surveyed 26.10.17; Deleted 14.11.17 DBR

3559     Deld Felixstowe 23.4.16; Shipped to Malta (via CSD) 14.7.16; Deleted Calafrana 1917

3560     Deld Felixstowe 14.2.16; Tested 1.3.16; Tested night landing appliances 12.3.16; Towed into Grain with engine trouble 8.4.16 (FSL RA Little & FSL WHS Aplin); retd Felixstowe 23.4.16; Surveyed 15.8.16; Deleted 29.8.16

3561     Deld Felixstowe 24.4.16; Shipped to Malta (via CSD) 6.7.16; Surveyed Calafrana 19.9.17; Deleted 27.9.17 DBR

3562     Deld Felixstowe 24.4.16; Shipped to Malta (via CSD) 14.7.16; Deleted Calafrana 1917

3563     Deld Felixstowe for erection 14.1.16; Packing for Malta 19.4.16; CSD Crystal Palace 9.6.16; Shipped 8.16; Deleted Calafrana 1917

3564     Deld Felixstowe 24.4.16; Shipped to Malta (via CSD) 14.7.16; Deleted Calafrana 1917

3365     Deld Felixstowe for erection 24.12.15; Deleted 2.5.16

3566     Deld Felixstowe for erection 24.4.16; Shipped to Malta (via CSD) 6.7.16; Deleted Calafrana 1917

3567     Deld Felixstowe for erection 3.12.15; Tested 29.1.16; Deleted 2.5.16

3568     Deld Felixstowe but never erected; Surveyed 12.10.17; Deleted 19.10.17 as spares

3569     Deld Felixstowe for erection 22.12.15 (fitted Anzanis); Tested 29.1.16; Dismantled on/by 14.3.16; Tested 30.5.16 (L/Cdr JC Porte & F/L RJJ Hope-Vere); Used for hull experiments; Deleted 25.4.17

3570     Deld Felixstowe for erection 14.4.16; Tested 26.7.16; Deleted 25.4.17

3571     Deld Felixstowe for erection 7.1.16 (fitted Anzanis); Ready 1.2.16; EF, FL, towed to Grain by TB No.113 9.4.16 (FSL J Gorman & FSL AL Greer); Retd Felixstowe 10.4.16; Surveyed 15.8.16; Deleted 29.8.16

3572     Deld Felixstowe but never erected; Surveyed 12.10.17; Deleted 19.10.17 as spares

3573     Deld Felixstowe but never erected; Surveyed 12.10.17; Deleted 19.10.17 as spares

3574     Deld Felixstowe for erection 1.5.16; Tested 20.5.16; Wrecked 12.7.16 (FSL LA Rees & FSL SS Benson); Deleted 22.7.16

3375     Deld Felixstowe for erection 31.12.15; Westgate 12.1.16; Felixstowe 24.4.16; Deleted 3.7.16

3576     Deld Felixstowe for erection 29.6.16 ; Deleted 14.11.16

3577     Deld Felixstowe for erection 15.7.16; Deleted 23.1.17

3578     Deld Felixstowe for erection 21.7.16; Deleted 23.1.17

3579     Deld Felixstowe for erection 30.7.16; Deleted 14.11.16

3580     Deld Felixstowe for erection and tested 1.8.16; Fitted modified hull and two 150-hp Hispano to become F.1 (Porte 1); Seaplane School Felixstowe by 29.12.17 - 1.19

3581     Deld Felixstowe for erection 3.11.16 (fitted Anzani); Surveyed 29.11.17; Deleted 8.12.17 DBR

3582     Deld Felixstowe for erection 19.11.16; Deleted 25.4.17

3583     Deld Felixstowe for erection 16.1.17; Deleted 31.7.17

3584     Deld Felixstowe for erection 16.1.17 (fitted Anzani); Fitting sub detection 26.5.17; Seaplane School Felixstowe by 12.17; Deleted W/E 29.8.18

3585     Deld Felixstowe for erection 16.1.17; Fitted 100-hp Anzani; Deleted 12.1.18 BR

3586     Deld Felixstowe for erection 16.3.17 (fitted Anzani); Seaplane School Felixstowe by 29.12.17; Deleted W/E 29.8.18

3587     Deld Felixstowe for erection 16.3.17; Wrecked in harbour 17.12.17; Deleted 12.1.18 BR

3588     Deld Felixstowe for erection 14.6.17; Yarmouth training W/E 15.9.17; Deleted W/E 9.3.18

3589     Deld Felixstowe for erection 14.6.17; Yarmouth training 22.8.17; Deleted W/E 9.3.18

3590     Deld Felixstowe for erection 28.7.17 (fitted Anzani); Seaplane School Felixstowe by 29.7.17; Deleted W/E 23.2.18

3591     Deld Felixstowe for erection by 26.8.17 (fitted Anzani); Seaplane School Felixstowe by 29.9.17; Deleted W/E 29.8.18

3592     Deld Felixstowe for erection by 26.8.17 (fitted Anzani); Seaplane School Felixstowe by 29.9.17; Deleted W/E 29.8.18

3593     Deld Felixstowe for erection by 26.8.17 (fitted Anzani); Seaplane School Felixstowe by 29.9.17; Deleted W/E 29.8.18

3594     Deld Felixstowe for erection by 26.8.17 (fitted Anzani); Seaplane School Felixstowe by 29.9.17; Deleted W/E 29.8.18

## 6 VICKERS F.B.5 (ADMIRALTY 32 TYPE) "GUNBUS" PUSHER BIPLANE SCOUTS ordered under Cont No C.P.58733/15/x(A), built by Darracq in Paris, numbered 3595 to 3600. (100-hp Gnome Monosoupape)

3595     Deld Mkrs to 4 Sqdn Dover in box 15.6.15 (arr 17.6.15); Erected by 22.6.15; Became 4 Wing

Dover; HSPP 3.7.15 (F/Cdr CM Murphy & LM Marsden); U/c, wings and propeller damaged (by) 15.7.15; 5 Wing Dover 3.8.15; Packing for CSD 5.12.15; To CSD White City 20.12.15; PVRD Grain by 22.3.16; Deleted 17.7.16

3596 Taken over by CSD White City from Spares Dept 11.2.16; Deld Experimental Flight Grain 28.4.16; Deleted 27.6.16

3597 Taken over by CSD White City from Spares Dept 11.2.16; Eastchurch, survey re deletion 8.7.16 [BUT no trace in Eastchurch DRs]

3598 Taken over by CSD White City from Spares Dept 11.2.16 - @30.6.16

3599 Taken over by CSD White City from Spares Dept 11.2.16; Transferred to RFC (Military Wing) less engine

3600 Taken over by CSD White City from Spares Dept 11.2.16; Transferred to RFC (Military Wing) less engine

**6 VICKERS F.B.5 "GUNBUS" PUSHER BIPLANE SCOUTS ordered on Cont No 87A/A/210 (M.A.3) & numbered 3601 to 3606. (100-hp Gnome Monosoupape)**

3601 CSD White City by 30.6.16; Deleted 8.16
3602 Transferred to RFC (Military Wing) less engine
3603 Transferred to RFC (Military Wing) less engine
3604 CSD White City by 30.6.16; Deleted 8.16
3605 Transferred to RFC (Military Wing) less engine
3606 CSD White City by 30.6.16; Deleted 8.16

**10 GRAHAME-WHITE XV (ADMIRALTY 1600 TYPE) PUSHER BIPLANES ordered on Cont No C.P. 101607/16, numbered 3607 to 3616 & built Hendon. (80-hp Gnome)**
[60-hp Le Rhône per official 1.17 list]

3607 Deld Chingford 1.3.16; Deleted 24.4.16
3608 Deld Chingford 1.3.16; Cranwell 5.3.16; Chingford 20.7.16; Deleted 18.8.16
3609 Deld Cranwell 25.3.16, but FL en route at Peterborough, crashed on TO, TW (FSL CA Rea); Deleted 14.4.16
3610 Deld Hendon 30.3.16; Damaged in storm 30.3.16; Repaired Mkrs; Cranwell 26.4.16; Chingford 13.7.16; EF on TO, FL, o/t 15.4.17 (F/L L Lavigne killed & F/L FW Merriam unhurt); Deleted W/E 22.9.17
3611 Deld Chingford 16.3.16; Damaged 29.4.16; Deleted W/E 22.9.17
3612 Deld Hendon 30.3.16; Tested, then damaged in storm 30.3.16; Repaired Mkrs; Chingford 3.5.16; Deleted 9.5.17
3613 Deld Hendon 30.3.16; Tested 31.3.16; Cranwell 6.4.16 (arr 8.4.16); Deleted 9.5.16
3614 Deld Eastbourne 6.4.16; At Northolt en route with engine change 15.4.16; FL Uckfield 21.4.16 and dismantled; Deleted 12.6.16
3615 Deld Eastbourne 8.4.16; Deleted 14.5.16
3616 Deld Hendon and tested 19.4.16; Eastbourne 26.4.16; Damaged 16.5.16 (FSL A Durston); Wrecked by wind 6.6.16; Deleted 12.6.16

**20 HENRY FARMAN F.27 PUSHER BIPLANES purchased from Aéroplanes Farman and numbered 3617 to 3636. (140-hp Canton-Unné M.9)**

3617 Shipped to East Indies; Deleted 8.15 (en route or on arrival?)
3618 Shipped to East Indies 8.15; Mombassa by 1.10.15. Niororo Island; To SAAC as No.7; East Africa to 2.16 [Deleted by 1.17]
3619 Deld 1 Wing St.Pol 8.15; Deleted 9.15
3620 Deld 1 Wing St.Pol 7.15 [Reserve Sqdn 1 Wing St.Pol 8.15 - @30.11.15; A Group by 17.10.15 - @28.11.15]; Dropped 65-lb bomb on U-boat (another failed to explode), hit amidships, broke its back, believed sunk 6m W of Middelkerke 28.11.15 (FSL TE Viney & Lt Comte de Sincay)
3621 Deld 1 Wing St.Pol 7.15 [Reserve 1 Wing St.Pol 8.15 - 12.15]; 5 Wing Coudekerque 3.3.16; Participated in attack on Houttave aerodrome, Zeebrugge, dropped 3x65 lb bombs 20.3.16 (FSL SJ Woolley); Damaged in gale Coudekerque 29.3.16; ADD 9.4.16; Dover 2.6.16; Deleted 28.2.17

3622 Deld 1 Wing St.Pol 8.15 [HQ Sqdn by 8.15 - 11.15; A Group by 5-7.11.15]; Deleted ADD 21.4.16
3623 Deld 1 Wing St.Pol on/by 26.8.15; Dropped 3 x 65 lb bombs on U-boat, claimed completely destroyed "seen to sink" 4m NNW of Nieuport 26.8.15 (S/Cdr AW Bigsworth); 1 Wing St.Pol @1.10.15 [4 Sqdn by 1.10.15; HQ Sqdn by 7-20.10.15; Eastchurch Group by 27.10.15; HQ Sqdn by 14.12.15]; 5 Wing Coudekerque 3.3.16; Wrecked in gale Coudekerque 29.3.16; Deleted ADD 9.4.16 BUT For survey by 11.5.16; 1 Wing pilot tested 4-bladed propeller for AD 14.5.16; Not listed by 18.5.16
3624 Deld 1 Wing St.Pol on/by 16.8.15 - @26.9.15; 4 Sqdn 1 Wing Dunkerque by 1.10.15; A Group 1 Wing St.Pol by 10.10.15; EF, FL La Panne 10.10.15 (FSL ECR Edwards & AM Salisbury unhurt); Last flown 19.10.15
3625 Deld HQ Sqdn 1 Wing St.Pol 8.15 [A Group by 7.10.15 - @2.12.15]; Deleted 2.16 FW&T
3626 Deld 1 Wing St.Pol 7.15 [Reserve Sqdn 8.15 - 12.15]; 5 Wing Coudekerque 11.3.16; ADD 24.4.16; Dover 24.4.16; Eastchurch 11.6.16; Dover 31.6.16; Deleted 30.10.16
3627 Ready in France by 31.8.15; Shipped to Dardanelles in SS Castilia 10.15; Retd UK 2.16, then deleted
3628 Ready in France by 31.8.15; Shipped to Dardanelles in SS Castilia 10.15; Retd UK 1.16, then deleted
3629 Ready in France by 31.8.15; Shipped to Dardanelles in SS Castilia 10.15; Deleted 3.16
3630 Ready in France by 31.8.15; Shipped to Dardanelles in SS Castilia 10.15; 3 Wing by 1.16; 2 Wing 18.1.16; Deleted by 1.17
3631 Ready in France by 31.8.15; Shipped to Dardanelles in SS Castilia 10.15; Deleted by 1.17
3632 Deld 1 Wing St.Pol 31.8.15 [Reserve Sqdn by 1.10.15; A Group by 6.10.15; HQ Sqdn by 7-10.10.15; A Group by 12.10.15; HQ Sqdn by 13-21.10.15; A Group by 4.11.15; HQ Sqdn by 19.11.15 - @23.1.16]; 5 Wing Coudekerque 3.3.16; Participated in attack on Houttave aerodrome, Zeebrugge, chased by German aircraft on return, flew out to sea, then retd Coudekerque safely 20.3.16 (FSL AM Hughes); Wrecked in gale Coudekerque 29.3.16; Deleted ADD 9.4.16
3633 Shipped to Dardanelles 9.15 - 10.15; 3 Wing by 1.16; 2 Wing 18.1.16; Deleted by 1.17
3634 Shipped to Dardanelles 9.15 - 10.15; 3 Wing by 1.16; 2 Wing 18.1.16; Deleted by 1.17
3635 Shipped to Dardanelles 9.15 - 10.15; 3 Wing by 1.16; 2 Wing 18.1.16; Deleted by 1.17
3636 Deleted by 1.17

**20 F.B.A. TYPE A FLYING BOATS authorised 1.10.15 for purchase from F.B.A., numbered 3637 to 3656 & built Argenteuil. (100-hp Gnome Monosoupape)**

3637 (c/n 110) Deld CSD White City; Calshot 9.2.16 (arrived 10.2.16); Tested 11.3.16; Fitting aperture valve for photographic experiments 2.17; classified as beyond repair by 23.6.17 but later rebuilt; Lee-on-Solent W/E 30.11.17; Deleted W/E 31.1.18
3638 Deld CSD White City; Calshot 9.2.16 (arrived 10.2.16); Bembridge 14.3.16; Deleted Calshot 24.10.16
3639 Deld CSD White City 5.1.16; Calshot 9.2.16 (arrived 10.2.16); Tested 23.3.16; Bembridge 30.3.16; Calshot 14.5.16; Bembridge 16.10.16; Dropped 2 bombs after U-boat submerged 35m S of Culver, landed near destroyers, wings fouled 10.11.16 (FSL AH Pearce); FTR from patrol 4.12.16 (FSL CT Brimer killed)
3640 Deld CSD White City; Calshot 9.2.16 (arrived 10.2.16); Tested 23.3.16; Deleted 9.2.17
3641 Deld CSD White City 10.1.16; Seaplane Flight Dover 9.3.16; Tested 16.4.16; Wrecked landing in harbour 30.4.16; Deleted 27.7.16
3642 (c/n 115) Deld CSD White City 10.1.16; Killingholme 2.2.16; Wrecked 16.10.16
3643 Deld CSD White City 10.1.16; Killingholme 2.2.16; Deleted 7.3.17
3644 Deld CSD White City 17.1.16; Calshot 22.3.16 (training); Damaged 24.3.17; Deleted 8.4.17
3645 Deld CSD White City 27.1.16; Calshot 22.3.16; Bembridge 7.6.16; Calshot 7.1.17; Deleted 9.2.17
3646 (c/n 122) Deld CSD White City 27.1.16; Calshot

22.3.16; Badly damaged landing 9.11.16 (FSL CRH Stewart unhurt); Deleted 9.2.17

3647    Deld CSD White City 21.1.16; Calshot 22.3.16; Bembridge 24.4.16; Deleted 17.7.16

3648    (c/n 121) Deld CSD White City 25.1.16; Northern Aircraft Co, Windermere for seaplane training by 31.3.16; RNAS Windermere 29.6.16; COL, wrecked 2.9.16 (F/L HA Bower drowned, FSL EGF Thompson shock); Deleted 19.9.16

3649    Deld CSD White City 8.2.16; Northern Aircraft Co, Windermere for seaplane training by 31.3.16; Fitting DC by 1.5.16; Tested 4.5.16; RNAS Windermere 29.6.16; Deleted 1.8.16

3650    Deld Felixstowe 15.2.16; FL, towed in by *TB.114* to Grain 19.2.16, then retd to Felixstowe; Not listed by Felixstowe by 16.3.16; Northern Aircraft Co, Windermere for seaplane training from 5.6.16; Fitted DC; Nosed into lake 15.6.16 (FSL PO Gadbois); Deleted 1.7.16

3651    Deld CSD White City 2.2.16 (and 8.2.16); Calshot 19.4.16; Bembridge 12.9.16; Calshot 10.1.17; Deleted 9.2.17

3652    Deld CSD White City; Calshot 24.4.16 (training); Deleted 27.4.17

3653    Deld CSD White City; Calshot 19.4.16; Deleted 24.10.16

3654    Deld CSD White City 22.3.16; Calshot 23.4.16 (training); Wrecked 17.6.17; Deleted 23.6.17

3655    Deld CSD White City 22.3.16; Dover by rail 16.5.16; Wrecked on TO 15.7.16 (FSL A Durston & LM Fenn); HACPs 9.7.16 (FSL EJ Cuckney & PO Wood), 22.9.16 (FSL AH Sandwell), 23.9.16 (FSL MR Buckland, later FSL LH Slatter twice), 24.9.16 (FSL LH Slatter twice), 28.9.16 (FSL W Perham, later FSL C Laurence, later FSL W Perham); HACPs 1.10.16, 19.10.16, 20.10.16, 21.10.16, 22.10.16 (all FSL LH Slatter); Tested Dover 10.2.17; Calshot 13.2.17 (training); Portland 30.4.17; Surveyed 8.11.17; Deleted 17.11.17 W&T

3656    Deld CSD White City 22.3.16; Seaplane Flight Dover by rail 16.5.16; AZP 3.8.16 (FSL JC Watson & AM Pearson); HACP 12.8.16 (F/L GG Hodge & LM White); Hull collapsed on TO 18.8.16 (FSL MB Walker & LM Robinson); Deleted 5.9.16

## 25 BURGESS TYPE O ("GUNBUS") PUSHER BIPLANES purchased from Burgess, numbered 3657 to 3681 & built Marblehead, Mass. All condemned 5.16. (140-hp Sturtevant)

3657    Deld CSD White City; Hendon for erection 28.7.15; FF 26.8.15; Ready for trials by 21.9.15; visited Northolt 27.10.15 & 30.10.15; Flown 3.11.15 & 8.12.15; Grain 24.12.15; CSD White City 27.4.16; Deleted 5.16

3658    Deld CSD White City; Hendon for erection 10.8.15; Flown 3.11.15; Tested 22.1.16; CSD White City by lorry 22.3.16; Hendon, 29.5.16 now not to go to Eastchurch; Stored White City Depot; Deleted 5.16

3659    Deld CSD White City; Ready Hendon 2.11.15; Flown 3.11.15; Slightly damaged in grenade explosion on ground 2.12.15; Accepted 8.12.15; Detling 5.1.16 (transit); Eastchurch 6.1.16; 4 Wing Eastchurch 7.2.16; Deleted 22.2.16

3660    Deld CSD White City; Hendon 20.11.15; Collided with shed 21.11.15; Surveyed 22.11.15; CSD White City; Deleted 5.16

3661    Deld CSD White City; Hendon 30.11.15; Slightly damaged in grenade explosion on ground 2.12.15; Flown 8.12.15; Tested 19.12.15; 4 Wing Eastchurch 31.12.15; Eastchurch NFS 4.2.16; Dismantled 10.2.16; Deleted 22.2.16

3662    Deld CSD White City; Hendon 30.11.15; Slightly damaged in grenade explosion on ground 2.12.15; Tested 10.1.16; 4 Wing Eastchurch 23.1.16; Eastchurch FS 4.2.16; Deleted 22.2.16

3663    Deld CSD White City; Hendon 10.1.16; 4 Wing Eastchurch 23.1.16; Eastchurch NFS 4.2.16; Deleted 22.2.16

3664    Deld CSD White City; Hendon 13.1.16; 4 Wing Eastchurch 25.1.16; Surveyed 22.2.16 and retd CSD White City; Deleted 29.5.16

3665    Deld CSD White City; Hendon 18.1.16; 4 Wing Eastchurch 25.1.16; Surveyed 4 Wing Eastchurch 22.2.16 and retd CSD White City; Deleted 29.5.16

3666    Deld CSD White City; Hendon 21.1.16; Flown 28.1.16; Accepted 5.2.16; 4 Wing Eastchurch 13.2.16; Deleted 22.2.16

3667    Deld CSD White City; Hendon 21.1.16; Flown 28.1.16; Accepted 8.2.16; 4 Wing Eastchurch 13.2.16; Deleted 22.2.16

3668    Deld CSD White City; Hendon 3.2.16; Accepted 19.2.16; CSD White City by lorry 27.3.16; Deleted 5.16

3669    Deld CSD White City; Hendon 12.2.16; Accepted 19.2.16; CSD White City 14.3.16; Deleted 5.16

3670    Deld CSD White City; Hendon 13.2.16; Preliminary test 1.3.16; CSD White City 22.3.16; Deleted 5.16

3671    Deld CSD White City; Hendon 18.2.16; Tested 9.3.16; CSD White City 29.3.16; Deleted 5.16

3672    Deld CSD White City; Hendon 18.2.16; Preliminary test 16.3.16; Tested 24.3.16; CSD White City 14.4.16 (less wings); Deleted 5.16

3673    Deld CSD White City; Hendon 18.2.16; Preliminary test 17.3.16; Tested 24.3.16; dismantling for CSD White City 14.4.16; Deleted 5.16

3674    Deld CSD White City; Hendon 4.3.16; Preliminary test 17.3.16; Tested 24.3.16; Repacked for CSD White City 24.4.16; Deleted 5.16

3675    Deld CSD White City; Hendon 4.3.16; Accepted 18.3.16; Dismantled for CSD White City 1.4.16; CSD White City by lorry 3.4.16; Deleted 5.16

3676    Deld CSD White City; Hendon 4.3.16; Accepted 18.3.16; Dismantled for CSD White City 1.4.16; CSD White City by lorry 5.4.16; Deleted 5.16

3677    Deld CSD White City; Hendon 8.3.16; Preliminary test 27.3.16; Damaged when Bessonneau tent blown away 28.3.16; CSD White City by lorry 8.4.16; Deleted 5.16

3678    Deld CSD White City; Hendon 8.3.16; Preliminary test 23.3.16; Dismantled 1.4.16; CSD White City by lorry 11.4.16; Deleted 5.16

3679    Deld CSD White City; Hendon 8.3.16; Accepted 18.3.16; Dismantled 1.4.16; CSD White City by lorry 12.4.16; Deleted 5.16

3680    Deld CSD White City; Hendon 14.3.16; Tested 31.3.16; Dismantling 14.4.16; Packed 24.4.16; CSD White City; Deleted 5.16

3681    Deld CSD White City; Hendon 14.3.16; Finished testing 10.4.16; Dismantling 14.4.16; Packed 24.4.16; CSD White City; Deleted 5.16

## 1 HENRY FARMAN PUSHER BIPLANE purchased from Aéroplanes Farman, Paris & numbered 3682. (140-hp Canton-Unné)

3682    (Allocated?) Dunkerque by 30.11.15; Shipped from Paris to Mudros but lost in transit 1915; Deleted 28.11.17 (sic) BUT 1 Wing @18.3.16?

## 1 MORANE-SAULNIER M.S.7 (TYPE BB) TRACTOR BIPLANE purchased from Morane Saulnier, numbered 3683 & built Villacoublay. (110-hp Le Rhône)

3683    Deld 3 Sqdn 1 Wing by 1.10.15 [Eastchurch Group 1 Wing by 4-30.11.15]; 2 Flt A Sqdn 1 Wing (formed) 1.3.16; 5 Flt A Sqdn 5 Wing Coudekerque 27.3.16; For survey, smashed 18.5.16; Dunkerque 5.16 for deletion; Deleted by 22.6.16

## 2 ARMSTRONG WHITWORTH F.K.12 TRACTOR TRIPLANES put forward for ordering 11.16 as the second and fourth machines of a War Office order dated 4.16 for 4 machines to be numbered 7838 to 7841, to be diverted to the Admiralty and renumbered 3684 and 3685, built Newcastle. (250-hp Eagle)

3684    (Ex 7839) Cancelled by War Office 1.17
3685    (Ex 7841) Cancelled by War Office 1.17

## 1 SOPWITH TYPE A1/ADMIRALTY TYPE 9400 TRACTOR BIPLANE ordered on Cont No C.P.101030/16, numbered 3686 & built Kingston. (110 or 130-hp Clerget)

3686    Prototype of 1½ Strutter (Sopwith designation LCT). Passed by Sopwith Experimental Dept 12.12.15;

*F.B.A. Type A Flying Boat 3646 at Calshot 1916. (via E.Cromie)*

*Nose of Burgess Type O Pusher Biplane. (J.M.Bruce/G.S.Leslie collection)*

*Morane-Saulnier Type BB Biplane 3683 in France. (J.M.Bruce/G.S.Leslie collection)*

*Sopwith 1½ Strutter prototype 3686 at Eastchurch. (W.J.Evans)*

*Dyott Type XXX Fighter 3687, fitted with C.O.W. gun, at Grain 22 November 1916. (J.M.Bruce/G.S.Leslie)*

*Avro 529 Biplane 3694. (RAF Museum P.19896)*

*Curtiss Columbia T "Twin-Canada" Biplane 3700 at Farnborough. (J.M.Bruce/G.S.Leslie collection)*

Completed 16.12.15; 4 Wing Eastchurch by road 26.3.16; Serial allotted 10.4.16; War Flight Eastchurch 16.4.16; Grain 22.7.16; Observers School Flight Eastchurch 23.12.16; AZP 16/17.3.17 (F/L LP Openshaw & Lt AN Hansford); AGPs 5.6.17 (F/L GA Cox & Obs Lt FJ Dean) & 13.6.17; For repair, but classified as beyond repair 7.7.17; Deleted 12.7.17

**2 DYOTT TWIN-ENGINED TRACTOR FIGHTER BIPLANES ordered on Cont No C.P.106417/16 from Hewlett & Blondeau, numbered 3687 and 3688 & built Luton. Put forward to fit Vickers 2-pdr gun 8.16. (Two 120-hp Austro-Daimler)**

3687     Under erection Hendon from 12.4.16; Testing engines 15.4.16; Flown 28.4.16 & 12.5.16 (F/L GM Dyott); Flown 10-11.8.16 (F/L PA Johnston); Officially deld RNAS Hendon 17.8.16; Flown 1.9.16 (F/L TD Hallam); Height test 6.9.16 (F/L TD Hallam); Exptl Flt Grain 16.10.16; For repair by 20.10.16; Fitted C.O.W. gun by 11.16; Became Gunnery Experimental Grain 5.12.16; Gunnery Experimental Dept Grain by 22.2.17; Deleted by authy d/d 19.3.17; also EAD Grain, deleted 13.4.17, but repaired instead; Overhauling fuselage 17-22.5.17; Still EAD Grain 25.5.18

3688     Deld Hendon for erection 25.8.16; Flown 5.10.16, 16.10.16 & 31.10.16 (F/L TD Hallam); Development Flight Eastchurch 18.10.16 (mods and prepare for service trials); To Dunkerque but retd 16.11.16; Design Flight Eastchurch to ADD for service trials 7.1.17; Deleted 24.3.17 (endorsed "This machine is devoid of the necessary flying qualities on this station. This machine to be ~~either transferred to another Station or~~ [THIS WORDING CROSSED OUT!] deleted from commission: useful parts and arisings to be taken on charge at Station if deleted. Engine to be returned to Survey Section. Signed S/Cdr FK McClean)

**2 ROYAL AIRCRAFT FACTORY F.E.8 PUSHER BIPLANES to be transferred from War Office 3.16 and renumbered 3689 and 3690. (100-hp Gnome Monosoupape)**

3689 to 3690 cancelled

**1 SOPWITH PUP (ADMIRALTY TYPE 9901) TRACTOR BIPLANE SCOUT ordered on Cont No C.P.109458/16, numbered 3691 & built Kingston. (80-hp Le Rhône)**

3691     Prototype. Deld Chingford 10.5.16; Grain 25.5.16; Chingford via Dover to ADD for service trials 28.5.16 (F/L LH Hardstaff); 5 Flt A Sqdn 5 Wing Coudekerque 1.6.16 - @22.6.16; 6 Flt A Sqdn 5 Wing by 29.6.16; 2 Flt A Sqdn 1 Wing Furnes 10.7.16; C Sqdn 1 Wing St.Pol by 7.9.16; LVG C OOC nr Ghistelles 15.30 24.9.16 (FSL SJ Goble); ADD 24.9.16; Tested 2.11.16; C Sqdn 1 Wing 4.11.16; 8 Sqdn (coded 'B') 16.11.16; Halberstadt shot down Bapaume shared with N5197 26.12.16 (FSL NE Woods); 3 Sqdn 3.2.17; ADD 10.2.17; Dover 30.4.17; HACP, attacked Gotha 25.5.17 (FSL RFS Leslie); AGP 4.7.17; AP Dover, for another station by 10.17; CSD White City W/E 8.12.17; Deleted 21.12.17 and to USA for Lady Drogheda's exhibition; For preservation 9.18, but evidently not preserved

**2 BRISTOL S.2A SCOUT TRACTOR BIPLANES ordered from British & Colonial Aeroplane Co, numbered 3692 to 3693 & built Filton. Firm declined to tender W/E 14.7.16. Transferred to Military Wing under Cont No 87/A/372. (110-hp Clerget)**

3692     (C/n 1379). Transferred to RFC (Military Wing) as 7836
3693     (C/n 1380). Transferred to RFC (Military Wing) as 7837

**2 AVRO 529 TRACTOR BIPLANES ordered on Cont Nos C.P.114876/16 & C.P.122495/16/X/23723 from A.V.Roe & Co Ltd, numbered 3694 & built Manchester. Final assembly Hamble. Put forward to fit folding wings 8.16. Type declared obsolete 1.18. (Two 190-hp Falcon I)**

3694     Hamble by 19.2.17; FF 3.17; Deld Hendon 24.5.17 (F/L RFS Leslie); Lilbourne 26.5.17 (S/Cdr Master of

Sempill); Testing Sqdn Martlesham Heath 5.17; Hendon 29.5.17 (S/Cdr the Master of Sempill); Testing Sqdn Martlesham Heath 8.6.17; Became AES Martlesham Heath 16.10.17; Comparative trials with Kangaroo B9970 19.1.18

3695     (Completed as 529A with 230 BHP to Cont No A.S.15292 (BR.94) dated 18.6.17) Deld AES Martlesham Heath 31.10.17; Wrecked when rudder gave way in air 7.11.17; Deleted 21.11.17 wrecked

**2 AIRCO D.H.3 DAY BOMBER TRACTOR BIPLANES to be numbered 3696 and 3697 & built Hendon. (Two 190-hp Rolls-Royce)**

3696     Awaiting engine W/E 27.5.16, then cancelled and substituted D.H.4
3697     In hand 2.2.17. Later cancelled and substituted D.H.4

**2 AIRCO D.H.4 DAY BOMBER TRACTOR BIPLANES ordered on Cont No C.P.151348/16, numbered 3696 and 3697 & built Hendon**

3696     (Eagle V) Almost ready 2.2.17; Tested Exp Stn Orfordness; ADD by 1.3.17; 2 Sqdn 6.3.17 (only mention); 2 Sqdn St.Pol by 5.17; ADD 25.10.17 - @1.11.17 (for 2 Sqdn); NADD by 29.12.17; 2 Sqdn 15.2.18; ADD 22.2.18 - @21.3.18; Dover by 28.3.18; Became 491 Flt Dover by 25.5.18; 4 ASD Audembert 18.6.18; 202 Sqdn Bergues by 6.18; 4 ASD 23.6.18; Pilots Pool; 4 ASD, deleted 31.8.18 general fatigue [Was to become B394 for RFC (Military Wing) but allotment cancelled]
3697     (230-hp B.H.P.?); Deld Hendon to 2 Sqdn 24.3.17 - @29.7.17; ADD by 2.8.17 (for service); Destroyed by fire on night of 1.10.17; Surveyed 17.10.17; Deleted 23.10.17 burnt

**2 SOPWITH SINGLE-SEATER TRACTOR BIPLANES fitted with special bomb dropper ordered from The Sopwith Aviation Co Ltd, to be numbered 3698 and 3699 & built Kingston. (150-hp Sunbeam)**

3698 and 3699 cancelled

**1 CURTISS CANADA MODEL C TRACTOR BIPLANE purchased from Curtiss & numbered 3700. (Two 160-hp CURTISS VX)**

3700     Erecting at Hendon by 6.6.16; Ready 20.6.16; Altering wings by 11.7.16; Fitted Sperry-Curtiss automatic stabilising gear. Accepted Hendon 11.11.16; Deleted 21.1.17

**1 SLOANE-DAY H.1 TRACTOR BIPLANE purchased from Sloane Aircraft Co Inc., numbered 3701 & built New York. (Ordered with 160-hp Sloane-Day but fitted with 130-hp Hall-Scott A)**

3701     Deld Hendon for evaluation 19.11.15; Erected by 20.11.15; Tested 24.11.15 (Pickles); Crashed into parked GW Boxkite of GW School on TO and badly damaged 14.1.16 (FSL PA Johnston); Fairey repair 10.2.16; Scrapped under repair at Faireys 26.2.17

**2 FAIREY A.D. HEAVY BOMBER TRACTOR BIPLANES ordered 30.5.16 & numbered 3702 and 3703, to be built at Hayes. (Two 200-hp Brotherhood)**

3702     (C/n F.2). Cancelled 3.16 (and 11.16)
3703     (C/n F.3). Cancelled 3.16 (and 11.16)

**2 FAIREY A.D. PUSHER BIPLANES ordered 1916 on Cont No C.P.110731/16 & numbered 3704 and 3705, to be built at Hayes. (Two 190-hp Falcon)**

3704     (C/n F.4). Completed as AD Tractor. Deld Design Flight Eastchurch by road 28.2.17; Erected by Mkrs; Flown 15.3.17; ECD Grain 17.3.17; Grain Test Dept 18.4.17; EAD Grain 4.6.17; Repair chassis 6.8.17; Deleted W/E 23.2.18
3705     (C/n F.5). Not completed, wings only built

*Bristol S.2A of the School of Special Flying at Gosport in March 1916, either 7836 or 7837 (were to have been 3692 and 3693). (Capt D.S.Glover via P.H.T.Green)*

*Sloane-Day H.1 Biplane 3701 at Eastchurch, October 1915. (RAF Museum)*

*Sopwith Modified Schneider Seaplane 3736, possibly hoisting aboard HMS Brocklesby. (via Philip Jarrett)*

*Fairey A.D. Tractor Biplane 3704 at Grain 1917. (J.M.Bruce/G.S.Leslie collection)*

*Port Victoria P.V.1 conversion from Sopwith Schneider 3742. (via Philip Jarrett)*

**1 SHORT BOMBER TRACTOR BIPLANE ordered on Cont No C.P.63683/16, numbered 3706 & built Eastchurch. (225-hp Sunbeam Mohawk later 250-hp Rolls-Royce) [Gordon Bruce's researches show c/n to be S.248)**

3706 Landplane version of Admiralty Type 184. Wingspan extended and increased from 2-bay to 3-bay wings after test. Deld Gunnery School Flight Eastchurch 3.4.16 (fitted overwing Lewis gun); HP Sqdn Manston 7.8.16 ("ex Exp M.III RR motor" = 250-hp Rolls-Royce); Awaiting erection 8.10.16; Deleted 22.1.17

**100 SOPWITH MODIFIED SCHNEIDER TRACTOR BIPLANE SEAPLANES ordered 7.5.15 on Cont No C.P.45562/15/X26993, numbered 3707 to 3806, built Kingston & assembled Woolston. (100-hp Gnome Monosoupape)**

3707 Deld Calshot and tested 30 5.15 (Hawker); HMS *Campania* 11.6.15; Erected by 23.6.15; Flew off flying deck with ship steaming full speed 3.11.15 (F/L RE Penny); Flew off deck with 2¼ hrs petrol and 2x16-lb bombs with ship steaming full speed 4.11.15 (F/L RE Penny); Then flew off deck with 2¼ hrs petrol and 4x16-lb bombs with ship steaming full speed 4.11.15 (F/L RE Penny); Scapa 2.12.15; HMS *Campania* 17.4.16; Scapa 7.5.16; to HMS *Campania* but damaged, retd Scapa 21.8.16; HMS *Campania* 3.9.16; Blackburn repair 10.9.16 - 3.17; To RCNAS without engine

3708 Deld Dover by road 8.6.15; Accepted 11.6.15; hoisted *St.Germain* 19.6.15; Dover 20.6.15; To *St.Germain* but wings, floats and propeller damaged hoisting 30.6.15 (FSL TV Lister), retd Dover; Test after repair 20.7.15; EF, FL 26.7.15 (FSL JBP Ferrand); Re-erecting 10.15; CSD White City by road 20.1.16 and deleted

3709 Deld HMS *Campania* by SS *Vocturnus* 22.6.15; Not erected by 1.8.15; To go ashore for tuning up 27.9.15; Test flight 3.11.15; Flew off deck with 2¼ hrs petrol and ship steaming full speed 4.11.15 (F/L WL Welsh); Scapa 2.12.15; Tested 29.4.16; HMS *Campania* 29.5.16; Scapa 4.7.16; Blackburn 21.8.16 - 3.17; To RCNAS without engine

3710 Deld Yarmouth 20.6.15; Accepted 30.6.15 (Hawker); HMT *Kingfisher* 13.8.15; Yarmouth 15.8.15; HMT *Kingfisher* 17.8.15; HACP 17.8.15 (FSL CH Chichester-Smith); Yarmouth 19.8.15; HMT *Jerico* 20.8.15; Yarmouth 30.8.15; HMT *Jerico* 9.9.15; Yarmouth 10.9.15; HMT *Sir John French* 18.9.15; Yarmouth 20.9.15; Dismantled 2.12.15; Deleted 17.3.16

3711 Deld Felixstowe for erection 25.6.15; Accepted 1.7.15; HMS *Engadine* 2.7.15; Wrecked hoisting out to chase Zeppelin and lost in sea 4.7.15

3712 Deld Felixstowe for erection 25.6.15; Accepted 1.7.15; HMS *Engadine* 2.7.15; Wrecked hoisting out to chase Zeppelin and lost in sea 4.7.15

3713 Shipped to Aegean; HMS *Ark Royal* by 7.15; Tested Kephalo 9.8.15; Capsized and salved 13.8.15; HMS *Ark Royal* for repair 4.9.15; Flown again 2.10.15; Stavros 29.2.16; still HMS *Ark Royal* at Imbros 7.16 (then deleted?)

3714 Deld Felixstowe for erection by 7.15; HMS *Engadine* 3.7.15; Wrecked hoisting out to chase Zeppelin and lost in sea 4.7.15

3715 Deld Yarmouth by rail 7.7.15; Accepted 21.7.15 (Hawker); Accepted 26.7.15; HMT *Jerico* 15.8.15; Yarmouth 17.8.15; HMT *Kingfisher* 20.8.15; Yarmouth 21.8.15; HMT *Jerico* 25.8.15; Yarmouth 28.8.15; HMT *Kingfisher* 5.9.15; Yarmouth 9.9.15; HMT *Jerico* 2.10.15; Yarmouth 6.10.15; HMT *Jerico* 13.10.15; Yarmouth 14.10.15; Dismantled 2.12.15; Re-erecting by 20.12.15; Deleted 17.8.16; Reported also HMT *Sir John French*

3716 Deld Yarmouth by rail 19.7.15; Not accepted by 31.8.15; Deletion recommended 25.4.17

3717 Deld Felixstowe 22.7.15; AZP 10.8.15 (FSL JMd'A Levy); Shot down by AA after attacking Zeebrugge Mole, FL, sank 12.8.15 (FSL JMd'A Levy PoW); Salved and rebuilt by Germans and flown at Zeebrugge; Later in DECKA travelling exhibition of captured Allied aircraft

3718 Deld Dover by rail 23.7.15; Accepted 19.8.15; Temp Dunkerque 14.9.15; Dover 11.10.15; Grain 15.10.15;

Wrecked 17.10.15, landed from lighter; Deleted 27.10.15

3719 Deld Calshot 3.9.15; Bembridge 6.9.15; Chassis strained 13.9.15; Calshot 3.10.15; Wrecked Bembridge 11.10.15; Supermarine repair 11.11.15; Calshot 24.3.16; Dismantled by 2.17; Deleted 9.2.17

3720 Deld Yarmouth by rail 28.7.15; Accepted 13.8.15 (Hawker); HMT *Sir John French* 7.9.15; Yarmouth 8.9.15; HMT *Kingfisher* 16.9.15; Yarmouth 18.9.15; HMT *Sir John French* 2.10.15; Yarmouth 2.10.15; HMT *Jerico* 5.10.15; Yarmouth 6.10.15; HMT *Sir John French* 14.10.15; Yarmouth 17.10.15; HMT *Jerico* 5.11.15; Yarmouth 5.11.15; Deleted 7.3.16

3721 Shipped to Aegean; HMS *Ben-my-Chree* 30.8.15; Port Said 11.3.16; HMS *Raven II* by 31.3.16 - @2.4.16; HMS *Ben-my-Chree* by 29.4.16 (tested); Towed to HMS *Raven II* 10.5.16; HMS *Ben-my-Chree* 6.16; Port Said by 8.16 - 3.17; Deleted 1917

3722 HM Submarine *E.7* by 3.9.15; Shipped to Aegean; HMS *Ben-my-Chree* 30.8.15; HMS *Raven II* 11.3.16; Port Said 11.3.16; HMS *Raven II* 18.3.16; Badly damaged by falling derrick at Port Said 17.4.16; Deleted 1916

3723 Deld Yarmouth 8.15; Accepted 13.8.15 (Hawker); HMT *Jerico* 7.9.15; Yarmouth 10.9.15; HMT *Kingfisher* 12.9.15; Yarmouth 15.9.15; HMT *Jerico* 2.10.15; Yarmouth 4.10.15; Crashed on TO, CW, hoisted on to HMT *Kingfisher* 9.12.15 (FSL E Cadbury unhurt); Deleted Yarmouth 16.12.15; Reported also *Sir John French*

3724 Deld Felixstowe 17.8.15; detd Blackwater River 24.9.16; Badly damaged 25.9.16 (FSL GA Magor); Deleted 3.10.16

3725 Deld Felixstowe 17.8.15; Damaged on TO, salved 14.10.15 (F/L AW Clemson unhurt); Deleted 24.10.15

3726 Deld Calshot 23.8.15 (Hawker); Dived into sea from 2,000 ft and CW Southampton Water 24.8.15 (FSL J MacLarty killed); Dismantling 10.9.15; Supermarines 11.10.15 (rebuild); Calshot 26.3.16 [fitted with overwing Lewis gun]; Deleted 27.4.17

3727 Shipped to Aegean 9.15; HMS *Ben-my-Chree* by 3.3.16; Port Said 11.3.16; HMS *Raven II* 31.3.16; - @2.4.16; HMS *Ben-my-Chree* 4.16 - 6.16; Port Said by 8.16 to 10.16; Deleted by 1.17

3728 Deld Killingholme for erection 9.8.15; Accepted 1.9.15; Wrecked 8.4.16; Deleted 26.4.16

3729 Deld Felixstowe 16.8.15; O/t landing 5.4.16 (F/L AW Clemson unhurt); Deleted 3.7.16

3730 Deld Felixstowe 16.8.15; Flown from HM Submarine *E22* 24.4.16; detd Blackwater River 24.9.16; Killingholme 29.9.17; Deleted 2.10.17 BR

3731 Deld Killingholme for erection 18.8.15; Accepted 1.9.15; Deleted 5.5.16

3732 Deld Killingholme for erection 29.8.15; Accepted 1.9.15; Deleted 12.3.16

3733 Deld Killingholme for erection 29.8.15; Wrecked 28.4.17; Deleted 20.5.17

3734 Deld Calshot 10.9.15;. Retd Mkrs 18.7.17; Calshot Training W/E 21.9.17; Lee-on-Solent W/E 12.10.17; Surveyed Calshot 3.1.18; Deleted 15.1.18 W&T

3735 Deld Calshot 3.9.15; Bembridge 20.10.15; FL, capsized and sank off Nab LV 28.2.16 (FSL C McLaurin saved); Deleted 10.3.16

3736 Deld CSD 2.16; Sopwith Kingston 18.2.16; Yarmouth by road 17.6.16; HMS *Brocklesby* 29.7.16; AZP, unable to get above *L33* as engine missing 2.8.16 (FSL HB Smith); Yarmouth 3.8.16; HACP 6.9.16 (FSL GH Bittles); Surveyed 25.4.17; Deleted 2.5.17

3737 Deld CSD 2.16; Sopwith Kingston 18.2.16; Yarmouth by rail 17.6.16; Erecting 9.7.16; Tested 16.8.16; HACP 24.4.17 (FSL GH Bittles); Deleted 1.9.17

3738 Deld CSD 2.16; Sopwith Kingston 18.2.16; Yarmouth by rail 17.6.16; HACP 30.3.17 (FSL HB Brenton); Fell from 1000 ft, CW off Gorleston 27.4.17 (FSL FG Brown injured); Deleted 9.5.17

3739 Deld Dover by road 24.8.15; Acceptance test 26.8.15 (Hawker); temp Dunkerque 14.9.15; Dover 4.10.15 [fitted overwing Lewis gun]; Wrecked 24.1.16 (F/L EJ Cooper); CSD White City by road 24.1.16, then deleted

3740 Deld Calshot 2.9.15; Wrecked off Hamble Buoy 11.11.15 (FSL LER Murray); Retd Calshot by road 24.11.15; Mkrs Woolston by road 24.11.15 (repair);

Calshot 20.2.16; Bembridge 1.3.16; Calshot 7.1.17; Deleted 9.2.17

3741 Deld Calshot 3.9.15; Wrecked at Bembridge 23.10.15; Deleted 5.11.15

3742 (Modified to become Port Victoria P.V.1) Deld CSD White City 9.15; Port Victoria ARD 1.10.15; Four short trials but badly out of longitudinal balance 7.2.16; Tested 5.8.16 (experimental purposes); Became PVRS 11.16; Seaplane Design Flt Grain, test after erection at PV 12.12.16; Calshot 18.3.17 (4-bladed propeller); Beyond repair by 23.6.17; Surveyed 8.11.17; Deleted 17.11.17 W&T

3743 Deld Felixstowe 30.3.16; Tested 31.3.16 (Hawker); Flown from HM Submarine *E22* 24.4.16; Deleted 2.5.16

3744 Deld Yarmouth 19.7.16; CW on TO 5.1.17 (FSL EJ Crisp); Deleted 5.2.17

3745 Deld Calshot 10.4.16; Deleted 9.2.17

3746 Deld CSD White City by 30.6.16; Nore War Flight Felixstowe 14.8.16; To Killingholme but fell in sea, CW off Yarmouth 22.8.17 (TFSL AS Woodall killed); Deleted 28.8.17

3747 Deld Felixstowe 19.9.15; Tested 21.9.15 (Hawker); Deleted 15.9.17

3748 Deld Felixstowe 19.9.15; Tested 21.9.15 (Hawker); HMS *Vindex* by 14.12.15; Felixstowe 9.2.16; HMS *Vindex* 4.4.16; Felixstowe 15.4.16; First flight for 4 months, EF, FL in water, towed in by TBD's motor boat 19.7.16; Deleted 5.4.17

3749 Deld Grain by road 23.9.15; Accepted 28.9.15 (Hawker); HMS *Vindex* 16.10.15; Grain 21.10.15; HMS *Vindex* 12.11.15; Felixstowe 22.11.15; To HMS *Vindex* 16.1.16; Felixstowe 24.1.16; Wrecked 13.7.16; Deleted 22.7.16

3750 Deld Grain by road 25.9.15; Accepted 28.9.15 (Hawker); HMS *Vindex* but sideslipped in harbour, nosedived into water, CW 9.10.15 (FSL JF Hay); Deleted 10 10.15

3751 Deld Calshot 12.10.15; Tested 14.10.15 (Hawker); Wrecked 19.11.15 (FSL JD Hume); Deleted 9.12.15

3752 Deld Seaplane School Calshot and tested 14.10.15 (Hawker); Stalled and dived in sea 1½m N of Cowes, CW 21.4.16 (FSL AC Saw DoI); Deleted 15.5.16

3753 Deld Dover by road 6.10.15; Accepted 21.10.15 (Hawker); Grain 29.10.15; HSPP 9.2.16 (F/L EdeC Hallifax); Nore War Flight Grain by 4.16 (replaced 8123); Deleted 7.4.17

3754 Deld Dover by road 8.10.15; Accepted 21.10.15 (Hawker); Westgate 30.10.15 (transit); to Grain but EF, FL near East Swale 6.11.15 (FSL ON Walmesley); Towed to Grain from Leysdown by motor boat 7.11.15; CSD Crystal Palace 18.5.17, later deleted

3755 Deld Grain 14.10.15; Accepted 19.10.15 (Hawker); HMS *Vindex* 12.11.15; Felixstowe 4.12.15; HMS *Vindex* 12.12.15; Felixstowe 9.2.16; HMS *Vindex* 4.4.16; Felixstowe 7.4.16 (repair); Deleted 2.8.17

3756 Deld Grain by lorry 14.10.15; Accepted 19.10.15 (Hawker); Westgate 27.10.15; Grain 28.10.15; Crashed and wrecked 22.1.17 (FSL RM Hughes); Deleted 2.3.17

3757 Deld Grain by lorry 14.10.15; Accepted 19.10.15 (Hawker); Westgate 27.10.15; Grain 1.11.15; Deleted 14.6.17

3758 Deld Grain by road 17.10.15; Accepted 20.10.15 (Hawker); Westgate 6.11.15; Deleted 27.1.16

3759 Deld Grain by road 17.10.15; Accepted 20.10.15 (Hawker); Westgate by 30.10.15; Deleted 9.8.16

3760 Deld Grain 16.11.15; Tested 24.11.15; Westgate 9.12.15; Put forward to be converted to Baby by Mkrs 1.17 (NTU?); HACP 22.7.17; O/t landing in strong wind, wreckage salved by *ML546* 17.8.17; Deleted, BR

3761 Deld Grain 16.11.15; Westgate 9.12.15; HSPP 19.3.16 (FSL BA Millard); HACP 22.9.16 (FSL CFM Chambers); Wrecked off Westgate 7.1.17 (FSL WN Tees)

3762 Deld Calshot 19.11.15; Deleted 9.2.17

3763 Deld Calshot 19.11.15; Wrecked 25.1.16 (F/L EJ Cooper unhurt); Deleted 8.2.16

3764 Deld Calshot 19.11.15; to Bembridge but wrecked 11.12.15 (FSL N Gregory); Left 2.1.16 (to Blackburn?); Blackburn by 31.8.16; Deleted 10.16

3765 Deld Calshot 31.12.15; Collided with Calshot pier taxying 9.7.16 (2/Lt A Nelidow, Russian Cavalry

unhurt); Blackburn 3.8.16 - 3.17 (repair); To RCNAS without engine 1918, then to US Navy as *A394*

3766 Deld Grain by lorry 24.11.15; For CSD White City 30.12.15 (NTU?); Accepted 2.2.16 (Hawker); Nore Flight Westgate 8.2.16; HSPP 3.5.16 (FSL AJ Nightingale); HACPs 9.7.16, 23.10.16 x 2 (all FSL MC Wood); AGP 25.5.17 (FSL EB Drake); Still Nore Flight Westgate @30.3.18

3767 Deld Grain 26.11.15; For CSD White City 30.12.15 (NTU?); Accepted 2.2.16 (Hawker); Westgate 8.2.16; HSPP 3.5.16 (FSL BA Millard); HACPs 22.5.16 (FSL HV Worrall), 9.7.16 (FSL CFM Chambers), 17.7.16 (FSL CFM Chambers), 28.11.16; For deletion 9.2.17

3768 Deld Kingston to Killingholme for erection 29.11.15; deleted 29.8.16

3769 Deld Kingston to Killingholme for erection 29.11.15; Seriously damaged 1.9.17

3770 Shipped to EI&SS; HMS *Ben-my-Chree* by 4.16 - 6.16; Port Said by 8.16; HMS *Ben-my-Chree* 13.9.16; Port Said 17.9.16; HMS *Ben-my-Chree* 21.12.16; Flown by S/Cdr CR Samson DSO on ops against Turks 27.12.16; Damaged aboard ship by Turkish shellfire at Castelorizo 9.1.17; Flying again by 27.1.17; Deleted 1917

3771 Shipped to EI&SS 1.16; Port Said by 7.16; HMS *Ben-my-Chree* 21.7.16; Port Said 26.7.16; Deleted 12.16

3772 Deld Calshot 23.12.15; Shipped to EI&SS in HMS *Empress* 3.1.16; Port Said 21.1.16; HMS *Empress* 9.3.16; Test after re-assembly 11.4.16; ashore for compass swinging 12.4.16; HMS *Ark Royal* (for storage) 18.4.16; Tested after erection 12.5.16; HMS *Empress* 19.6.16 (loan in lieu of 3772 repairing in HMS *Ark Royal*) - @12.7.16; HMS *Ark Royal* by 8.16; Talikna 29.8.16; HMS *Empress* @ 11.10.16 & @13.11.16; HMS *Ark Royal* 29.12.16; Talikna 11.2.17; HMS *Ark Royal* @4-5.5.17; Mudros by 1.6.17; G Sqdn 2 Wing Marsh by 8.17; Mitylene by 1.12.17 - @1.1.18

3773 Shipped to EI&SS in HMS *Empress* 3.1.16; Lewis gun fitted 18.2.16; Surveyed 15.3.16; Port Said 2.4.16 (damaged); HMS *Ben-my-Chree* by 5.16; HMS *Empress* by 6.16; DBR 16.3.17; Surveyed 16.3.17; Deleted 1.10.17

3774 Shipped to EI&SS in HMS *Empress* 3.1.16; Port Said 19.3.16 (for HMS *Raven II*); HMS *Raven II* 19.3.16; Port Said by 5.16; HMS *Ben-my-Chree* 17.5.16 - @26.5.16; Port Said 15.7.16; HMS *Ben-my-Chree* 20.7.16; Port Said by 3.17; Deleted 1917

3775 Shipped to EI&SS; in HMS *Empress* 3.1.16; Port Said 21.1.16; HMS *Raven II* 30.3.16; Badly damaged by falling derrick Port Said 17.4.16; Deleted 1916

3776 Deld Yarmouth 24.1.16; Accepted 27.1.16 (Hawker); HMT *Brocklesby* 20.4.16 (no daily returns 21/22.4.16); Yarmouth by 23.4.16; FTR AZP 2.8.16, picked up by Belgian steamer SS *Alberbircke* and taken to Killingholme 3.8.16 (F/L CJ Galpin); Retd Yarmouth 5.8.16; still on strength 31.12.16; Deleted 1917

3777 Shipped to EI&SS; HMS *Ben-my-Chree* by 4.16 - 5.16; Port Said by 7.16; HMS *Anne* 8.8.16 - @25.8.16; Port Said by 9.16; HMS *Ben-my-Chree* 13.9.16; Escorting 8372 spotting for HMS *Espiègle*, FL on sea, chassis collapsed, o/t 6m NE of El Arish, Syria 17.9.16 (FSL W Man picked up by ST *Ronania*)

3778 Shipped to EI&SS; HMS *Ben-my-Chree* by 4.16 - 6.16; HMS *Ark Royal* by 6.16; HMS *Empress* 19.6.16; Port Said by 8.16; HMS *Ben-my-Chree* 13.9.16; Port Said by 10.16; HMS *Ben-my-Chree* 21.12.16; Damaged aboard ship by Turkish shellfire at Castelorizo 9.1.17; Flying again by 27.1.17; Deleted 1917

3779 Deld Calshot 25.1.16; O/t on TO, badly damaged 7.4.16 (FSL AG Woodward); Deleted 25.4.16

3780 Deld Calshot 26.1.16; Bembridge 8.4.16; O/t landing in rough sea, salved 11.10.16 (F/L C McLaurin unhurt); Deleted 24.10.16

3781 Deld CSD White City 29.1.16; Northern Aircraft FS Windermere by 31.3.16; Windermere 29.6.16; Calshot by rail 15.2.17 (arr 21.2.17); Bembridge 7.4.17; Calshot Training 10.7.17; Surveyed 28.9.17; Deleted 6.10.17 W&T

3782 Deld CSD White City 29.1.16; Issued to Mudros 20.5.16; HMS *Ark Royal*, tested after erection 14.8.16; Mudros 15.8.16; HMS *Ark Royal* by 20.8.16; Thasos 18.8.16; HMS *Ark Royal* by 30.4.17; HMS *Peony* by

1.6.17; Surveyed Mudros 24.9.17; Deleted 16.10.17 DBR

**3783** Deld CSD White City 29.1.16; Issued to Mudros 20.5.16; HMS *Ark Royal* by 8.16; Mudros 18.8.16; HMS *Ark Royal* for erection 27.8.16; HMS *Empress* on/by 29.8.16; Fitted Lewis gun and other fitments 29.8.16; Tested 29.8.16; Fitted 4x16-lb bomb rack 2.9.16; Anti-submarine patrol at Stavros 28.9.16; Forced down a FF seaplane which was later destroyed by gunfire from HM ships Yukyeri Bay, E of Tenedos 21.11.16 (FSL AF Brandon); To overhaul 5.2.17; Test after overhaul 30.3.17; Dismantled 28.5.17; HMS *Peony* 29.5.17; Re-erected Thermi 12.6.17; Engine changed in HMS *Peony* 23.6.17; HMS *Ark Royal* for overhaul 13.8.17; Surveyed Mudros 24.9.17; Deleted 16.10.17 DBR

**3784** Deld CSD White City 29.1.16; Issued to Mudros 20.5.16; HMS *Ark Royal* by 8.16; Mudros 18.8.16; Thasos by 10.11.16; HMS *Ark Royal* 5.1.17 - @22.4.17; HMS *Peony* by 1.6.17; G Sqdn 2 Wing Mudros by 8.17; HMS *Ark Royal* by 1.12.17; Surveyed 8.3.18; Deleted 27.3.18 W&T

**3785** Deld Calshot 25.1.16; Tested 8.2.16; Bembridge 8.3.16; Deleted 25.9.16

**3786** Shipped to EI&SS; HMS *Ben-my-Chree* by 4.16; ashore .16; HMS *Raven* by 22.6.16; EF, FL in sea ½m W of Acre, abandoned, sunk by gunfire 2.7.16 (FSL W Man rescued by Short 8091)

**3787** Shipped to EI&SS; Deld HMS *Empress* in case 2.4.16; Tested 8.5.16; HMS *Ark Royal* for repair 19.6.16; Tested HMS *Ark Royal* 20.7.16; HMS *Empress* 27.8.16; HMS *Ark Royal* by 4.12.16; Thasos 10.12.16; HMS *Ark Royal* 28.5.17; Mudros by 1.6.17; Deleted 1917

**3788** Shipped to EI&SS; Deld HMS *Empress* in case 2.4.16; Tested 18.4.16 - @4.5.16; HMS *Ark Royal* by 8.16; Talikna 29.8.16; HMS *Endymion* 9.16; Tested HMS *Ark Royal* 22.11.16; Thasos by 3.17; HMS *Ark Royal* 30.3.17; Thasos 12.6.17; Thasos by 1.12.17 - @14.1.18; Thasos repairs by 3.18 (fitted Lewis gun); HMS *Ark Royal* 3.18; Talikna 12.3.18

**3789** Shipped to EI&SS; Port Said by 5.16; HMS *Ben-my-Chree* 17.5.16; Port Said 29.5.16; HMS *Ben-my-Chree* 2.6.16; Port Said 22.7.16; HMS *Ben-my-Chree* 13.9.16; Front fuselage collapsed taxying back to ship 14.9.16 (S/Cdr CR Samson DSO unhurt); Port Said 17.9.16 - 3.17; Also HMS *Empress*?; Deleted 1917

**3790** Deld CSD White City 2.2.16; To Tilbury Docks 2.2.16; Shipped in SS *Khiva* 19.2.16; Port Said by 3.16; HMS *Ben-my-Chree* 8.3.16 - @10.3.16; HMS *Raven II* by 31.3.16 - @2.4.16; HMS *Ben-my-Chree* by 23.5.16; Port Said 29.5.16; HMS *Ben-my-Chree* 2.6.16; Port Said 17.7.16 - @3.17; Also HMS *Empress*; Deleted 1917

**3791** Deld CSD White City 3.2.16; To Tilbury Docks 3.2.16; Shipped in SS *Khiva* 19.2.16; Presume retd UK; arr Yarmouth by road 17.6.16; Deleted 16.4.17

**3792** Deld CSD White City 11.2.16; Shipped to Aegean by 7.16; Tested HMS *Ark Royal* 1.7.17; Nosedived and damaged landing 3.7.17 (F/L CE Moore); Deleted 1917

**3793** Deld CSD White City 11.2.16; Shipped to Aegean, arr 8.16; HMS *Ark Royal* by 22.4.17; Suda Bay by 1.6.17; HMS *Peony* at Port Iero 21.7.17; Ashore at Port Iero 7.8.17; Retd HMS *Peony* 8.8.17 - @31.8.17; Mitylene by 1.12.17 - @4.3.18

**3794** Deld CSD White City 19.2.16; Nore War Flight Felixstowe 15.8.16; 2 AGPs 13.6.17 (FSL HA Wilson later FSL CC Purdy); Killingholme 31.8.17; Surveyed 12.1.18; Deleted 19.1.18 TL

**3795** To Beardmore for repair 9.16 - @1.17; Deleted in/by 1.17

**3796** Deld Scapa 31.3.16; [lost from HMS *Campania* 27.5.16 per ship's log!]; HMS *Campania* 28.5.16; Flown off deck while ship steaming 19-20 knots 29.5.16; Scapa 4.7.16; HMS *Campania* 7.7.16; HSMP 15.7.16 (F/L RE Penny); Scapa 16.7.16; HMS *Campania* 26.7.16; Scapa 21.8.16; HMS *Campania* 23.8.16; Flown off deck 8.9.16; Scapa 21.12.16; HMS *Campania* 8.3.17; Scapa 16.7.17; Houton Bay by 10.17; Surveyed 11.1.18; Deleted 17.1.18 W&T

**3797** Deld HMS *Campania* for erection by 29.4.16; Scapa 15.5.16; HMS *Campania* 17.5.16; Scapa 23.5.16; HMS *Campania* 30.5.16; Scapa 26.7.16; HMS *Campania*

1.8.16; Scapa 4.8.16; HMS *Campania* 14.8.16; Scapa 23.8.16; FL, wrecked by heavy sea, towed to HMS *Campania* 9.9.16 (F/L LH Wilkins); Surveyed 12.9.16; Deleted 20.9.16

**3798** Deld Scapa for erection by 29.4.16; HMS *Campania* 23.5.16; Scapa 21.8.16; HMS *Campania* 7.10.16; Flown off deck, EF, FL in sea with wheels on, capsized 23.10.16 (FSL LS Breadner), Deleted 3.11.16

**3799** Deld Killingholme 17.4.16; Deleted 29.11.16

**3800** Deld Killingholme for erection 13.4.16; EF, spun into water 2.6.17 (FSL DA Duncan drowned); Deleted 20.6.17

**3801** Deld Killingholme for erection 14.4.16; For HMS *Killingholme* 15.9.16 - 26.9.16; Surveyed Killingholme 7.12.17; Deleted 13.12.17 wrecked

**3802** Deld Killingholme for erection 13.4.16; Deleted 10.6.16

**3803** Deld CSD White City 4.16; Nore War Flight Felixstowe 11.8.16; Killingholme 22.8.17; Deleted 7.9.17

**3804** Deld CSD White City by 30.6.16; Grain 28.7.16 (Enlarged fin, wing warping controls replaced by ailerons, new tail and float); Nore Flight Westgate 20.7.17; Totally destroyed by fire 11.9.17

**3805** Deld CSD White City 4.16; Deleted 8.16

**3806** Deld HMS *Campania* for erection 29.4.16; Scapa 30.5.16; HMS *Campania* 3.6.16; Scapa 5.7.16; Taxied into boat, seriously damaged 30.8.16 (FSL A Gammon); Blackburn repair 9.16 - 3.17; To RCNAS without engine 1918

## 2 WHITE & THOMPSON No.3 TRACTOR BIPLANE FLYING BOATS ordered on Cont No C.P.45183/15, numbered 3807 and 3808 & built Bognor Regis. (120-hp Austro-Daimler)

**3807** Deld Calshot but CW Havant 16(14?).9.15; Modified engine bearers and forward firing Lewis gun; Trials at Bognor 10.15; Calshot 3.11.15; Damaged 19.11.15 (F/Cdr RH Kershaw & FSL N Gregory); AZP, EF, FL, slightly damaged nr Calshot 25/26.9.16 (S/Cdr AW Bigsworth); Calshot training by 2.17; Deleted 11.7.17

**3808** (Fitted DC) Deld Calshot 12.10.15; Calshot training by 2.17; Deleted 27.4.17

## 12 THOMAS T.2 TRACTOR BIPLANE TRAINERS purchased from Thomas Bros Aeroplane Co, Ithaca, New York & numbered 3809 to 3820. (90-hp Curtiss OX-5)

**3809** Deld Hendon for erection 10.8.15; Deleted unerected 11.12.15

**3810** Deld Hendon for erection 10.8.15; Deleted unerected 11.12.15

**3811** Deld Hendon for erection 10.8.15; Deleted unerected 11.12.15

**3812** Deld CSD White City; Hendon for erection 13.12.15; Flown 7.1.16; Chingford 24.1.16; Deleted 28.2.16 DBR

**3813** Deld CSD White City by 31.8.15; Hendon 10.12.15; Accepted 8.2.16; Engine returned CSD 16.2.16; Deleted 3.16

**3814** Deld CSD White City by 31.8.15; Hendon 10.12.15; Chingford 24.1.16; Surveyed 29.2.16; Deleted 3.3.16 DBR

**3815** Deld CSD White City by 31.8.15; Hendon 10.1.16; Awaiting test 29.1.16; Engine returned CSD 16.2.16; Wrecked when Bessoneau hangar blew away 28.3.16; Deleted 31.3.16

**3816** Deld CSD White City by 31.8.15; Hendon 10.1.16; Flown 25.1.16; Engine returned CSD 16.2.16; Deleted 3.16

**3817** Deld CSD White City by 31.8.15; Hendon 26.1.16; Accepted 5.2.16; Engine returned CSD 16.2.16; Wrecked when Bessonneau hangar blew away 28.3.16; Deleted 31.3.16

**3818** Deld CSD White City by 31.8.15; Hendon 26.1.16; Flown 29.1.16; Engine returned CSD 16.2.16; Wrecked when Bessonneau hangar blew away 28.3.16; Deleted 31.3.16

**3819** Deld CSD White City by 31.8.15; Hendon 29.1.16; Engine returned CSD 16.2.16; Deleted 3.16

**3820** Deld CSD White City by 31.8.15; Hendon 1.2.16; Engine returned CSD 16.2.16; Wrecked when Bessonneau hangar blew away 28.3.16; Deleted 31.3.16

*White & Thompson No.3 Flying Boat 3807 at Calshot. (via Philip Jarrett)*

*Thomas T.2 Training Biplane 3812, used at Chingford, 1916. (J.M.Bruce/G.S.Leslie collection)*

*Sopwith 806 Type "Gunbus" 3833, used at Detling early 1916. (J.M.Bruce/G.S.Leslie collection)*

*Breguet de Chasse 3885 Pusher Biplane fitted with Davis gun. (B.Turpin)*

**12 VOISIN PUSHER BIPLANES purchased from Voisin & numbered 3821 to 3832 (140-hp Canton-Unné)**
[3821-3826 probably ex V.551-2, 555-8 q.v.]

3821    Left Villacoublay for 1 Sqdn St.Pol but EF, FL, wing damaged Beauvais 26.4.15; arr by 30.4.15; Probably deleted without use 2.16

3822    Deld Villacoublay to 1 Sqdn St.Pol 26.4.15; Became 1 Wing St.Pol 21.6.15; Reserve machine 1 Wing St.Pol by 20.6.15 - 12.15; Deleted ADD 21.4.16

3823    Deld Villacoublay to 1 Sqdn St.Pol by 30.4.15; Probably V.557 which FTR from HAP to intercept Zeppelins returning from England, came down in German lines at Dixmude 12.5.15 (F/L JO Groves & L/Cdr H Dobell RNVR both PoW)

3824    Deld Villacoublay to 1 Sqdn St.Pol by 30.4.15 - 5.15; Dover by 1.6.15; 2 Sqdn Eastchurch 8.6.15; Became 2 Wing Eastchurch 21.6.15; 4 Wing Eastchurch 3.8.15 (Fitted W/T for expts); Deleted 20.10.15

3825    Deld Villacoublay to 1 Sqdn St.Pol by 30.4.15; Became 1 Wing St.Pol 21.6.15 [D Sqdn by 20.6.15]; attd 3 Sqdn RFC Auchel 17.6.15; 1 Wing St.Pol 10.7.15; 3 Sqdn RFC Auchel 21.7.15; 1 Wing St.Pol 29.7.15 - @9.15; Reserve Sqdn 1 Wing St.Pol by 10.15 - @12.15; Deleted ADD 21.4.16

3826    Deld Villacoublay to 1 Sqdn by 30.4.15; Became 1 Wing 21.6.15; Deleted 7.15

3827    Shipped to Aegean; 3 Wing Tenedos by 6.15 - @31.8.15 [Deleted by 1.17]

3828    Shipped to Aegean; 3 Wing Tenedos by 6.15 - @30.11.15; [Destroyed by fire 4.11.15?]; Deleted by 1.17

3829    Shipped to Aegean; 3 Wing Tenedos by 6.15 - @31.8.15 [Deleted by 1.17]

3830    Shipped to Aegean; 3 Wing Tenedos by 6.15 - @31.8.15 [Deleted by 1.17]

3831    Shipped to Aegean; 3 Wing Tenedos by 6.15 - @31.7.15; Deleted by 8.15

3832    Shipped to Aegean; 3 Wing Tenedos by 6.15 - @31.8.15 [Deleted by 1.17]

**30 SOPWITH ADMIRALTY 806 TYPE "GUNBUS" PUSHER BIPLANES ordered 30.6.15 on Cont No C.P.51744/15 from Robey & Co, numbered 3833 to 3862 & built Lincoln. Only 15 completed by 2.16, balance considered for Rumanian Govt but NTU. (150-hp Sunbeam)**

3833    Deld Brooklands to Detling 10.2.16; TW in gale while pegged out 16.2.16; Deleted 9.3.16

3834    Deld Eastchurch 3.4.16; Deleted 26.6.16

3835    (ex 806) Deld Detling 13.12.15; Chassis and one wing smashed 28.12.15; Wrecked in gale while pegged out 16.2.16; Deleted 9.3.16

3836    Deld Brooklands to Detling 3.1.16; Chassis and propeller damaged 3.1.16 (FSL DE Smith); Deleted 9.3.16

3837    Deld Hendon for erection 13.7.16; Deleted 23.8.16

3838    Deld Brooklands to Detling 10.2.16; Totally wrecked in gale while pegged out 16.2.16; Deleted 9.3.16

3839    Deld Eastchurch 8.4.16; Dismantled on/by 28.5.16; Deleted 26.6.16

3840    Deld ECNFS for erection 8.3.16; Misc Flight Eastchurch 9.5.16; Bomb Flight Eastchurch 16.5.16; Misc Flight Eastchurch 23.5.16; Deleted 29.6.16

3841    Deld Brooklands to Detling 9.2.16; Tested 12.2.16; Wrecked in gale while pegged out 16.2.16; Deleted 9.3.16

3842    Deld ECNFS, erecting by firm 9.3.16; Dismantled on/by 28.5.16; Deleted 29.6.16

3843    Deld Eastchurch 8.3.16; Deleted 26.6.16

3844    Deld Eastchurch 8.4.16; Deleted 1.6.16

3845    Deld CSD White City W/E 6.5.16; Deleted 9.16

3846    Deld CSD White City W/E 13.5.16 probably as spares

3847    Deld Eastchurch Gunnery School 8.3.16; Deleted 15.9.16; presume rebuilt; Deleted 5.12.17 as spares

3848    Deld CSD White City W/E 27.5.16; Deleted 9.16

3849    Deld 4 Wing Eastchurch and accepted 13.2.16; ECNFS 8.3.16; Deleted 26.6.16

3850    Deld CSD White City as spares W/E 3.6.16; Deleted 6.16

3851    Deld CSD White City as spares 6.16 - @30.11.16

3852    Deld CSD White City as spares 6.16; Deleted 6.16

3853    Deld CSD White City as spares 6.16; Deleted 6.16

3854    Deld CSD White City as spares 6.16; Deleted 6.16

3855    Deld CSD White City as spares .16; Deleted by 30.6.16

3856    Deld CSD White City as spares .16; Deleted by 30.6.16

3857    Deld CSD White City as spares .16; Deleted by 30.6.16

3858    Deld CSD White City as spares 7.1.16; Deleted by 30.6.16

3859    Deld CSD White City as spares .16; Deleted by 30.6.16

3860    Deld CSD White City as spares .16; Deleted by 30.6.16

3861    Deld CSD White City as spares 6.16; Deleted 9.16

3862    Deld CSD White City as spares by 30.6.16; Deleted 9.16
        [A Gun Bus was delivered from Kingston to 4 Wing Eastchurch by road 26.3.16]

**20 CAUDRON G.III TRACTOR BIPLANES purchased from Aéroplanes Caudron & numbered 3863 to 3882. (80-hp Gnome)**

3863    (c/n C.521) Deld Killingholme 20.6.15; Deleted 30.1.16

3864    (c/n C.591) Deld Killingholme by rail 22.6.15; Redcar 19.2.16; Damaged avoiding collision 2.4.16 (F/L CL Startup); COL 26.5.16 (FSL GRG Daglish); Deleted 22.6.16

3865    (c/n C.536) (DC) Deld Whitley Bay 24.6.15; Tested 25.6.15; AZP, COL 29.6.15 (FSL RG Mack injured, LM HJL Hinkler concussed); British Caudron Co, Cricklewood 15.7.15 (repair); Redcar 16.1.16; Nose-dived in on landing, CW 16.1.17 (PFO HW Lee injured); Deleted 31.1.17

3866    (c/n C.528) Deld Whitley Bay ex London for erection 22.6.15; Flown 24.6.15; Redcar 20.7.15 (weather); Whitley Bay 22.7.15; Side-slipped and nose-dived in 7.9.15 (F/Cdr CE Maude); Deleted 24.9.15

3867    Deld Redcar 29.7.15; Scarborough 4.8.15; Tested 8.8.15; AZP 10.8.15 (FSL JF Roche); Hornsea 11.8.15; Scarborough 10.9.15; Hit ground landing, o/t 14.9.15 (FSL SR Watkins); Redcar 21.10.15; FL, CW 8.9.16 (FSL JM Mapplebeck unhurt); Deleted 19.9.16

3868    Deld Redcar 7.15; Ran through fence landing 4.7.15 (FSL TFN Gerrard); Scarborough 18.7.15; Hornsea 26.7.15; To Scarborough 26.9.15 but FL near aerodrome on delivery; Hornsea 26.10.15; Deleted 20.12.15

3869    Deld Redcar 7.15; AZP 4.7.15 (FSL AJ Jacob); EF, FL, smashed Robin Hoods Bay 25.7.15 (FSL AJ Jacob); Repaired; Scarborough 28.8.15; Tested 8.9.15; Redcar 30.1.16; FL, smashed 17.3.16; Deleted 21.3.16

3870    Deld Redcar by 14.7.15; Scarborough 19.8.15; AZP 8.9.15 (FSL AJ Jacob);Damaged Redcar 15.9.15 (FSL PA Johnston & FSL MJ Golding); FL, smashed 20.2.16 (FSL BPH de Roeper unhurt); Deleted 11.3.16

3871    Deld Scarborough by 4.7.15; EF, FL in barley field near racecourse, o/t, badly damaged 14.7.15 (F/Cdr A Nickerson slightly injured); Packed 25.7.15; British Caudron Co repair 5.8.15; Redcar 19.8.15; FL 18.10.16; Repaired and flown back to Redcar 19.10.16; Deleted 31.1.17

3872    Deld Redcar 12.7.15; Tested 13.7.15; AZP 6.8.15 (FSL AJ Jacob); Flew into ground on night flying, CW 17.8.15 (FSL EP Hardman badly shaken); Deleted 5.9.15

3873    Shipped Mombassa 7.15; East Africa by 31.8.15 - @30.4.16; Deleted by 31.5.16

3874    Shipped Mombassa 7.15; East Africa by 31.8.15 - @12.15; Deleted 1916

3875    Shipped Aegean in SS *Huntridge* 27.7.15; 3 Wing Tenedos 7.15; Retd UK 1.16 and deleted

3376    Shipped Aegean in SS *Huntridge* 27.7.15; 3 Wing Tenedos 7.15; Retd UK 1.16 and deleted

3877    Shipped Aegean in SS *Huntridge* 27.7.15; 3 Wing Tenedos 7.15; Retd UK 1.16 and deleted

3878    Shipped Aegean in SS *Huntridge* 27.7.15; 3 Wing Tenedos 7.15; Retd UK 1.16 and deleted

3879    Shipped Aegean in SS *Huntridge* 27.7.15; 3 Wing Tenedos 7.15; Probably destroyed in fire 4.11.15

3880    Shipped Liverpool to Mombasa in SS *Bulgarian* 25.9.15; East Africa Field Force by 31.10.15 - @30.4.16; Deleted by 31.5.16

3881    Shipped Liverpool to Mombasa in SS *Bulgarian* 25.9.15; East Africa Field Force by 31.10.15 - @30.4.16; EF on

TO, FL, Maktau, repairable 2.2.16 (FSL NG Stewart-Dawson); Deleted by 31.5.16

3882    Shipped Liverpool to Mombasa in SS *Bulgarian* 25.9.15; East Africa by 31.10.15; Mafia Island .15; Niororo Island; Coded 'C' in 1.16; EF over Salaita on bombing raid, fired at by enemy, FL, CW 27.1.16 (FSL LO Brown); Deleted 2.16 [Two others were coded 'A' and 'B'; believed known as 11 Sqdn for a time]

## 5 BREGUET DE CHASSE PUSHER BIPLANES purchased from Breguet, Villacoublay & numbered 3883 to 3887. (225-hp Sunbeam)

3883    Deld Dunkerque by 30.11.15; 6 Flt A Sqdn 5 Wing Coudekerque by 5.4.16 - @2.6.16; ADD Dunkerque u/s; Deleted 15.6.16 NWR

3884    Deld Dunkerque by 12.15; B Group 1 Wing St.Pol by 8.12.15; Crashed Bourbourg 4.16; Deleted ADD 15.4.16

3885    (fitted Davis gun) Deld 5 Wing Coudekerque 2.4.16; Deleted 5.4.16 (i.e. left Wing?); War Flight Eastchurch 1.5.16; Grain 10.5.16; Kingsnorth 11.5.16 (gunnery test); PVRS 14.5.16 (alterations); Hendon 13.7.16, then deleted

3886    Deld 4.16?; 8 Flt B Sqdn 5 Wing Coudekerque by 5.4.16 - @2.6.16; Dunkerque u/s; Deleted ADD not worth repair 15.6.16

3887    Deld 5 Wing Coudekerque 2.4.16; 1 Wing (ADD?) to 6 Flt A Sqdn 5 Wing Coudekerque 24.4.16 - @2.6.16 [listed as de Bombe !]; Dunkerque u/s; Deleted ADD 15.6.16 NWR

## 2 BREGUET DE BOMBE TRACTOR BIPLANES purchase authorised 1.10.15 from Breguet, Villacoublay & numbered 3888 and 3889. (225-hp Sunbeam)

3888    Deld 6 Flt A Sqdn 5 Wing Coudekerque by 23.4.16 - 5.16; ADD u/s; Deleted 15.6.16 NWR

3889    Not delivered

## 4 BLERIOT XI-2 TRACTOR MONOPLANES purchased from Bleriot, Paris & numbered 3890 to 3893. (80hp Gnome)

3890    (ex RFC 2850) Arr CSD White City 17.1.16; Dover by rail 15.5.16; Damaged 3.6.16; Deleted 13.6.16

3891    (ex RFC 2854) Deld Dunkerque in/by 1.16; B Group 1 Wing St.Pol by 15.1.16 - @17.1.16; arr CSD White City 22.1.16; Dover by rail 15.5.16 (not erected); Eastbourne by road 8.9.16; Station temp closed 9.11.16, aircraft later deleted

3892    Arr CSD White City 22.1.16; Deld Eastbourne by rail 12.5.16; Dismantled 29.10.16; U/s by 13.4.17; Deleted by 30.4.17

3893    (ex RFC 2855) Arr CSD White City 22.1.16; Dover by rail 15.5.16; Awaiting test 8.6.16; Eastbourne 3.9.16; Deleted 18.5.17

## 6 CAUDRON G.IV TRACTOR BIPLANES purchase authorised 1.10.15 from Caudron at Rue & numbered 3894 to 3899. (Two 80-hp Le Rhône)

[1.17 official list says all two 100-hp Anzani]

3894    (Two 100-hp Anzani) Deld Dunkerque; 1 Wing St.Pol by 6.11.15 - @14.12.15 [Eastchurch Group by 6-10.11.15; B Group by 16.11.15 - @8.12.15]; Deleted 2.16 BR

3895    (Two 100-hp Anzani) Deld Dunkerque; 1 Wing St.Pol by 4.11.15 [Eastchurch Group by 4-7.11.15; B Group by 23.1.16]; Deleted ADD 21.4.16

3896    Deld Dunkerque; Eastchurch Group 1 Wing St.Pol by 10.11.15; Shipped to Aegean by 4.16 - @8.16; Transferred to French Govt

3897    Deld Dunkerque; 1 Wing by 10.1.16 [B Group by 10.1.16]; 7 Flt B Sqdn 5 Wing Coudekerque 24.3.16; Shot down Coudekerque 11.5.16 (FSL RR Soar seriously injured); Deleted 15.6.16

3898    Deld Dunkerque?; Shipped to Aegean; C Flt A Sqdn 2 Wing Imbros by 8.2.16 - @8.16; Deleted 1916

3899    Deld Dunkerque; 1 Wing by 10.1.16 [B Group by 10.1.16 - @8.2.16]; 7 Flt B Sqdn 5 Wing Coudekerque 24.3.16; Repair 1.4.16; Lost en route Dover, FL Deal,

continued for Dover but o/t landing and broke tail 25.4.16 (FSL SJ Woolley injured); For survey at Dover by 11.5.16; Deleted 3.6.16

## 20 HENRY FARMAN F.27 PUSHER BIPLANES purchased from Aéroplanes Farman & numbered 3900 to 3919. (150-hp Canton-Unné) [for overseas service]

3900    Shipped from Portsmouth in SS *Hunts Castle* 9.1.16; RFC Force D Mesopotamia by 4.16 - @6.16; Deleted 1916

3901    Shipped from Portsmouth in SS *Hunts Castle* 9.1.16; RFC Force D Mesopotamia by 4.16 - @5.16; Deleted 1916.

3902    Shipped to Aegean by 4.16; C Flt A Sqdn 2 Wing Imbros by 17.5.16 - @22.6.16; Still Aegean 8.16; Deleted 1916

3903    Shipped to Aegean 1916; A Sqdn 2 Wing Thasos by 6.16 - @6.7.16; Deleted 8.16

3904    Shipped to Aegean 1916; 2 Wing Imbros by 8.3.16 - @7.6.16; Deleted 8.16

3905    Shipped to Aegean 1916; 2 Wing Imbros by 16.2.16; C Flt A Sqdn 2 Wing Imbros by 16.5.16; A Flt 2 Wing Thasos by 10.16; FTR raid on Geraviz Seaplane Base 1.12.16 (F/L EJ Cooper & Lt Lord Torrington PoWs)

3906    Shipped to Aegean 1916; 2 Wing Imbros by 28.2.16 - @15.3.16; to East Africa Field Force; 7 Sqdn Kondora Irangi by 7.16; Deleted 1916

3907    Shipped to Aegean by 4.16; Deleted by 30.6.16

3908    Shipped to Aegean; Recd 2 Wing Imbros 4.16; Tested 20.4.16; Mitylene 28.5.16; Imbros 31.5.16; Thasos 14.6.16 (many bombing raids); Repair Base Mudros 1.9.16 (re very bad vibration); 'I' Flight and tested 24.1.17; Last flown 25.1.17; Badly damaged when Bessonneau hangar collapsed in gale 8.3.17; Deleted 8.4.17

3909    Shipped to Aegean 1916; 2 Wing Imbros by 28.2.16; Tested Mitylene, then to Imbros 27.7.16 - @8.16; Deleted 1916

3910    Shipped to Aegean 1916; 2 Wing by 4.16 - @8.16; Deleted 1917

3911    Shipped to Aegean 1916; 2 Wing by 4.16; Deleted by 30.6.16

3912    Shipped to Aegean 1916; 2 Wing by 4.16- @8.16; Deleted 1916

3913    Shipped to Aegean 1916; 2 Wing Imbros by 21.3.16; FL in sea 5.5.16 (FSL CA Maitland-Heriot); Deleted 6.16

3914    Shipped to Aegean by 4.16; Deleted 1916

3915    Shipped to Aegean by 4.16; C Flt 2 Wing Imbros by 13.12.16; COL from bombing raid on Kuleli Bridge 13.12.16 (FSL AM Waistell & O/L WC Jameson); still C Flt 2 Wing @4.1.17

3916    Shipped to Aegean 1916; 2 Wing Imbros by 13.5.16; Wrecked when airfield shelled 16.5.16; 2 Wing Thasos 6.16; A Flt 2 Wing Thasos by 28.11.16; FTR raid on Geravitz Seaplane Base 1.12.16 (FSL CW Greig & O/L RW Frazier RNVR PoWs)

3917    Shipped to Aegean 1916; 2 Wing Imbros by 4.16; ; First flown from Thermi to Iero Island 5.5.16; Thermi 18.5.16; Returning from flight to Chios, fell in harbour and wrecked 21.6.16 (F/L LA Hervey, FSL CA Maitland-Heriot & Lt P Blair); Deleted 7.16

3918    Deld 1 Wing St.Pol; by 2.4.16 - @9.4.16; Shipped to Aegean by 4.16, arr 7.16; Mitylene by 13-17.12.16; Surveyed Mudros 14.10.17; Deleted 29.10.17 W&T

3919    Shipped to Aegean 1916; 2 Wing Imbros by 12.5.16 - @7.16; Mitylene by 20.11.16 - @10.11.17; B Sqdn 2 Wing 13.2.17

## 12 NIEUPORT TYPE 12 TWO-SEATER TRACTOR BIPLANES purchased from Nieuport, numbered 3920 to 3931 & built Issy-les-Moulineaux. (110-hp Clerget 9Z)

3920    Shipped to Aegean 1916; 2 Wing Imbros by 23.2.16 - @25.5.16; B Sqdn 2 Wing Mitylene by 6.16; Mudros (110-hp Clerget with modified engine fitting); 2 Wing Long Island, Asia by 5.17

3921    Shipped to Aegean 1916; arr 2 Wing Imbros 7.2.16; First test flight 10.2.16; During recce to Gallipoli, badly shot about by Fokker 17.3.16 (FSL HK Thorold unhurt & S/L RH Portal wounded); Deleted 8.16

*Nieuport Type 21 3956 of No.3 Squadron, named 'BINKY', early 1917. (RAF Museum P.10897)*

*A Caudron G.IV of 5 Wing Coudekerque. Believed by R.R.Soar to be 3897, the machine in which he was shot down on 11 May 1916, remaining unconscious in hospital for three days. (via Frank Cheesman)*

*Lt Bettington in Nieuport 11 3978 of B Flight 2 Wing, Thermi over the Gulf of Smyrna (Turkey), 1916. (via Frank Cheesman)*

| | |
|---|---|
| 3922 | Shipped to Aegean 1916; 2 Wing Imbros by 4.2.16; COL 15.2.16 (FSL HV Reid); Still flying 1.3.16 |
| 3923 | (Single seater) Deld Dunkerque; 1 Wing St.Pol by 17.1.16 [HQ Sqdn by 17.1.16 - @23.1.16; 3 Flt B Sqdn by 4.16 - 5.16]; ADD 29.6.16; 6 Flt A Sqdn 5 Wing Coudekerque 23.8.16; 8 Sqdn W/E 15.2.17; 10 Sqdn 27.2.17; 8 Sqdn 21.3.17; 10 Sqdn by 29.3.17; Crashed and wrecked 16.4.17; Deleted ADD 27.4.17 |
| 3924 | Deld Dunkerque; 1 Wing St.Pol by 10.1.16 [B Group by 10-15.1.16]; EF, FL 7m N of Dunkerque 7.2.16 (Mid DS Earp); 3 Flt B Sqdn 1 Wing St.Pol by 4.16; Exptl Flt 1 Wing by 11.5.16; ADD by 2.6.16; 4 Flt B Sqdn 1 Wing St.Pol by 16.6.16 - @10.8.16; Recce/Comm Flt C Sqn 1 Wing by 17.8.16; still 1 Wing by 17.9.16; ADD 21.9.16 (repair); to UK 28.12.16; Cranwell 29.12.16; Surveyed 15.10.17; Deleted 26.10.17 DBR |
| 3925 | Deld Dunkerque; B Group 1 Wing St.Pol by 19.1.16; Shipped Aegean by 4.16; C Flt A Sqdn 2 Wing Imbros, tested 11.6.16 - @8.16 ("Gunbus"); Deleted 1916 |
| 3926 | Shipped to Aegean by 4.16; Deleted by 6.16 |
| 3927 | Deld 1 Wing St.Pol by 20.2.16 [3 Flt B Sqdn 1 Wing from formation 1.3.16] [not listed 11.5.16]; Shipped to Aegean by 6.16 - @8.16; Deleted 1916 |
| 3928 | Deld Dunkerque; 2 Flt A Sqdn 1 Wing St.Pol by 5.2.16 - @26.5.16; 4 Flt B Sqdn 1 Wing St.Pol by 2.6.16 - @3.8.16; ADD by 10.8.16; Dover 12.11.16; Surveyed 16.10.17; Deleted 19.10.17 W&T |
| 3929 | (c/n N634 or N654) Shipped to Aegean by 4.16; D Sqdn 2 Wing Stavros by 2.17 ("The Gun Machine"); EF, FL behind enemy lines, recovered undamaged at night 20.2.17; Deleted 1917 |
| 3930 | (Single seater) Deld 1 Wing St.Pol by 2.16; 3 Flt B Sqdn 1 Wing St.Pol from formation 1.3.16; Crashed, CW 7.16; ADD by 20.7.16; Deleted 17.9.16 |
| 3931 | Deld Dunkerque; B Group 1 Wing St.Pol by 19.1.16; Shipped to Aegean by 4.16; A Flt 2 Wing by 8.16; Deleted 1916 |

**8 MAURICE FARMAN S.11 SHORTHORN PUSHER BIPLANES ordered from Aéroplanes Farman & numbered 3932 to 3939. (70-hp Renault)**

| | |
|---|---|
| 3932 | Shipped to Aegean; 3 Wing Imbros by 31.7.15; Retd to France 1.16; HQ Sqdn 1 Wing St.Pol by 19.1.16 |
| 3933 to 3939 on order for 3 Wing 11.15, but later cancelled |

**6 NIEUPORT TWIN TRACTOR BIPLANES ordered from Nieuport & numbered 3940 to 3945, to be built Issy-les-Moulineaux. (Two 110-hp Clerget 9Z)**

3940 to 3945 cancelled

**1 BREGUET TYPE V COUNCOURS TRACTOR BIPLANE purchase authorised 1.10.15 from Breguet, Villacoublay & numbered 3946. (Ordered with 225-hp Sunbeam)**

| | |
|---|---|
| 3946 | Supplied as airframe, British engine fitted (250-hp Rolls-Royce) |

**6 BLERIOT XI-2 TRACTOR MONOPLANES ordered from Bleriot, France & numbered 3947 to 3952. Delivered to UK from Paris (70-hp Gnome)**

| | |
|---|---|
| 3947 | (ex RFC 2852 or 2853) Deld CSD 21.1.16; Scarborough 16.5.16; Redcar 28.7.16; Damaged fuselage landing 21.11.16 (FSL N Black); Deleted 4.5.17 |
| 3948 | Deld CSD 21.1.16; Eastbourne by rail 12.5.16; Dismantled by 16.2.17; Deleted 4.17 |
| 3949 | Deld CSD 22.1.16; Eastbourne by rail 12.5.16; Ringmer 18.5.16; Eastbourne 19.5.16; Dismantled by 16.2.17; Deleted 30.4.17 |
| 3950 | (ex RFC 2852 or 2853) Deld CSD 21.1.16; Scarborough 16.5.16; Deleted 5.8.16 |
| 3951 | Deld CSD 25.1.16; Eastbourne by rail 12.5.16; Ringmer 18.5.16; Eastbourne 19.5.16; FL and damaged nr Hailsham 21.5.16 (FSL DG Donald); Dismantled 29.10.16; Presume deleted when station temp closed 9.11.16 |
| 3952 | Deld CSD 25.1.16; Eastbourne 28.12.16; Deleted 4.5.17 |

**3953 TO 3961 RESERVED FOR FRENCH MACHINES**

**1 NIEUPORT TWIN TRACTOR BIPLANE ordered from Nieuport & numbered 3953, to be built Issy-les-Moulineaux. (Two 110-hp Clerget)**

3953 Cancelled

**2 MAURICE FARMAN S.7 LONGHORN PUSHER BIPLANES ordered from Aéroplanes Farman & numbered 3954 and 3955. (70-hp Renault?)**

| | |
|---|---|
| 3954 | No record of service |
| 3955 | No record of service |

**3 NIEUPORT "TYPE 17B" (probably 21) TRACTOR BIPLANE SCOUTS purchased from Nieuport, numbered 3956 to 3958 & built at Issy-les-Moulineaux, France. (80-hp Le Rhône)**

| | |
|---|---|
| 3956 | [To be transferred to RFC (Military Wing) as A8738, but NTU] Deld ADD by 10.8.16; 2 Flt A Sqdn 1 Wing Furnes 15.8.16; Shot down twin-engined seaplane 2m off Ostende 20.10.16 (F/L GV Leather); A Flt Detd Sqdn/8 Sqdn 26.10.16; Albatros DI shot down NE of Bapaume shared 8750 4.12.16 (FSL GG Simpson); 3 Sqdn (named 'BINKY') 5.1.17; 9 Sqdn 1.2.17; 11 Sqdn 28.3.17; Hit trees while in circuit 12.5.17 (FSL AE Hall injured); ADD 12.5.17; Deleted 16.5.17 ['Baby' Nieuport = 15 metres] |
| 3957 | [To be transferred to RFC (Military Wing) as A8742, but NTU] (Type 11) Deld ADD by 10.8.16; 4 Flt B Sqdn 1 Wing St.Pol 20.8.16; [To 4 Wing 23.10.16]; A Flt Detd Sqdn/ 8 Sqdn 26.10.16; Shot down near Delville Wood 4.12.16 (FSL The Hon AC Corbett killed); Deleted 5.1.17 |
| 3958 | [To be transferred to RFC (Military Wing) as A8743, but not taken up] Deld ADD by 10.5.16 - @17.8.16; 4 Flt B Sqdn 1 Wing St.Pol by 24.8.16; 9 Flt A Sqdn 4 Wing Dunkerque 25.9.16; Furnes 23.10.16; A Flt Detd Sqdn/8 Sqdn 26.10.16; Albatros DI OOC NE of Bapaume 4.12.16]; 3 Sqdn (named 'BUBBLES') 20.12.16; 9 Sqdn 1.2.17; 11 Sqdn 28.3.17; COL after practice flight 5.5.17 (FSL AE Hall); Deleted 14.5.17 |

**3 UNIDENTIFIED purchases in France**

3959 to 3961 probably not taken up

**12 NIEUPORT TYPE 10 TWO-SEATER TRACTOR BIPLANE SCOUTS ordered from Nieuport, numbered 3962 to 3973 & built Issy-les-Moulineaux. (80-hp Le Rhône)**

| | |
|---|---|
| 3962 | Deld Dunkerque; 1 Wing St.Pol by 1.10.15 [Reserve aircraft by 1.10.15; HACP 2.10.15 (FSL RC Hardstaff); Eastchurch Group by 6.10.15; B Group 8.12.15 - @17.12.15; Eastchurch Group by 19.12.15 - @30.12.15; B Group by 8.2.16]; 1 Flt A Sqdn 1 Wing St.Pol/Furnes from formation 1.3.16 - @10.6.16; ADD by 22.6.16; 9 Flt A Sqdn 4 Wing by 1.7.16 - @21.9.16; Collided with Caudron 9125 when landing at dusk, both partially wrecked 8.7.16 (FSL CC Wyllie); Tested after repair 30.7.16; 10 Flt A Sqdn 4 Wing Dunkerque 28.9.16; Damaged when petrol cap flew off and blinded pilot 2.11.16; Became 6 Sqdn 12.16 - @12.3.17; 11 Sqdn by 15.3.17 - @24.4.17; ADD by 6.17; Deleted 27.6.17 general fatigue |
| 3963 | Deld Dunkerque; 1 Wing Dunkerque by 16.9.15 [A Group by 17.10.15; to Eastchurch Group 1.12.15 - @2.12.15; B Group by 12.12.15 - @8.2.16]; With 3182 attacked U-boat 10-12m W of Ostende with 4x16-lb bombs 23.1.16 (FSL HR Simms); HSPP 9.2.16 (FSL RGA Baudry); 2 Flt A Sqdn 1 Wing from formation 1.3.16; Lost in thick mist between Nieuport and Dixmude, FL in sea nr Boulogne 13.3.16 (FSL AS Todd & S/L CL Hains RNVR picked up by French trawler); Presume salved; To ADD, listed as beyond repair 15.4.16, but evidently rebuilt; 3 Flt B Sqdn 1 Wing St.Pol by 4.16 - 5.16 [by 11.5.16]; 2-str destroyed Mariakerke 14.00 21.5.16 (F/Cdr RH Mulock); 4 Flt B Sqdn 1 Wing by 24.5.16; Albatros or LVG shot down at |

12,500ft 1m out to sea between Wenduyne and Blankenberghe 10.30 22.6.16 (F/L T Hinshelwood); Seaplane in flames 10m off Ostende about c16.00 15.7.16 (FSL DMB Galbraith); Became C Sqdn 1 Wing St.Pol by 7.16; Became 3 Sqdn St.Pol 5.11.16 - @25.1.17; 9 Sqdn by 1.2.17; Crashed and DBR, deleted ADD 24.3.17

3964   Deld CSD White City; 4 Wing Eastchurch by lorry 30.9.15; Caught wire fence landing, o/t 28.12.15 (FSL CC Wyllie & S/L WD Wain); HSPP 8.1.16 (FSL ADW Allen); HACP 20.2.16 (FSL ADW Allen); Detling 12.3.16; HSPP, forced down Friedrichshafen FF33 No.537 (Flugmeister Ponater & Leut Herrenkrecht) 19.3.16 (F/Cdr RJ Bone); 4 Wing Eastchurch 26.3.16; Expeditionary Force for special duty with RFC 27.3.16; Attd 29 Sqdn RFC St.Omer/Abeele 3.16; 9 Flt A Sqdn 4 Wing Dunkerque 16.4.16; Run into by Hartgill (9124?) landing, CW 2.8.16; For survey 3.8.16 (ADD by 9.16, wrecked); ADD 1.11.16; Deleted 4.12.16

3965   (Conv single seater). Deld Dunkerque; 1 Wing by 16.9.15; Reserve Sqdn 1 Wing St.Pol by 1.10.15 (in transit) [Eastchurch Group by 10.10.15 - @30.12.15; B Group by 12.1.16]; Westgate to Eastchurch 10.1.16; 1 Wing St.Pol by 9.2.16 - @23.3.16; Attd 29 Sqdn RFC St.Omer/Abeele 3.16; 9 Flt A Sqdn 4 Wing Dunkerque 16.4.16 - 9.16; EF after TO for patrol, FL, wrecked 8.7.16 (FSL C Perrett); Flying again 14.7.16; Became 6 Sqdn 31.12.16; 9 Sqdn 2.2.17 - @1.3.17; For survey by 8.3.17; Deleted ADD 24.3.17

3966   Deld Dunkerque; Reserve Sqdn 1 Wing St.Pol by 1.10.15 [Eastchurch Group by 5.10.15 - 11.11.15]; 5 Wing Dover 11.11.15; Dover 3.3.16; HACPs 9.7.16 (FSL R Young) & 12.8.16 (FSL FCC Calder); Damaged 2.9.16; Convtd single-seater, completed 24.9.16; HACP 23.10.16 (F/L SB Joyce); Wrecked by 11.16; HACP 15.2.17 (FSL CHB Jenner-Parson); Deleted 30.4.17

3967   Deld Dunkerque; 1 Wing St.Pol by 10.15 [HQ Sqdn by 19.10.15 - @10.11.15]; 5 Wing Dover 11.11.15 - @31.12.15; RNAS Dover by 1.16 [5 Wing left Dover 3.3.16]; HACPs 8.1.16 (F/L H Rosher), 8.2.16 x 2 (FSL JP Coleman later FSL FJE Feeney), 9.2.16 (F/L JCP Wood), 20.2.16 (FSL GRH Talbot), 19.3.16 (FSL CA Eyre), 24.4.16 (F/L GRH Talbot), 12.8.16 (FSL AD Carey), 23.10.16 (FSL FCC Calder); Deleted 30.4.17

3968   Deld Dunkerque; 1 Wing St.Pol by 1.10.15 - @3.2.16 [Reserve Sqdn by 1.10.15; A Group by 12.10.15 - @8.11.15; B Group by 12.12.15 - @23.1.16]; Folkestone to Dover 7.2.16; Westgate 18.3.16; Dover, HSPP 19.3.16 (FSL FCC Calder) & 3.5.16 (F/L FJE Feeny & AM Black); EF on TO for Dunkerque, caught by gust of wind, stalled on turn, sideslipped, crashed and CW 29.6.16 (F/L GRH Talbot killed & AM1 A Hampson DoI 30.6.18); Deleted 3.7.16

3969   Deld Dunkerque; 1 Wing St.Pol by 1.10.15 [Reserve Sqdn by 1.10.15; Eastchurch Group by 19.10.15 - @14.11.15; 2 Flt A Sqdn from formation 1.3.16]; LM by 1 Wing 12.3.16; Not listed (presume deleted) by 11.5.16

3970   Deld Dunkerque; 1 Wing St.Pol by 30.10.15 [A Group by 4.11.15; HQ Sqdn 7.11.15 - @18.2.16]; Accident Dunkerque, Deleted ADD 15.4.16

3971   Deld Dunkerque; Eastchurch Group 1 Wing St.Pol by 30.11.15; Shot down large German seaplane in sea in flames NE of Le Panne, then FL in sea, o/t, sank, CW 14.12.15 (FSL CW Graham & FSL AS Ince rescued by *Balmoral Castle*)

3972   Deld Dunkerque; 1 Wing St.Pol by 26.10.15 - @18.3.16 [Eastchurch Group by 26.10.15; HQ Sqdn by 25.11.15 - @8.2.16; 3 Flt B Sqdn from formation 1.3.16]; 9 Flt A Sqdn 4 Wing Dunkerque by 28.4.16; Accident; ADD 22.5.16; Deleted ADD DBR 15.6.16

3973   Deld Dunkerque; 1 Wing St.Pol 26.10.15 [A Group by 26.10.15 - @30.11.15; HQ Sqdn by 5.12.15; B Group 12.12.15 - @20.1.16]; Fuel shortage, FL beach, capsized 1.2.16 (FSL CFB Penley slightly injured); 1 Wing by 12.3.16 - @15.3.16; Deleted ADD 15.4.16

## 1 NIEUPORT TYPE 11 SINGLE-SEATER TRACTOR BIPLANE SCOUT purchased from Nieuport, Issy-les-Moulineaux & numbered 3974. (110-hp Clerget) [Two-seater per 1.17 official list]

3974   Shipped to Aegean; A Flt 2 Wing Imbros by 2.16 - @4.16; O/t Imbros 7.3.16 (Lt CH FitzHerbert unhurt); Deleted 1916

## 5 NIEUPORT TYPE 11 SINGLE-SEATER TRACTOR BIPLANE SCOUTS purchased from Nieuport, Issy-les-Moulineaux & numbered 3975 to 3979. (80-hp Le Rhône)

3975   Shipped to Aegean; Aegean by 4.16 - @8.16; Transferred to Roumania [still commission 1.17?]

3976   (c/n N565) Deld Dunkerque; 1 Wing St.Pol by 20.10.15 - 16.3.16 [HQ Sqdn by 20.10.15 & 20-23.1.16; 1 Flt A Sqdn from formation 1.3.16]; Accident Dunkerque; Deleted ADD 15.4.16

3977   (Type 11). Deld Dunkerque; 1 Wing St.Pol by 19.12.15 [HQ Sqdn by 19.12.15 - @10.1.16; 3 Flt B Sqdn from formation 1.3.16]; 2-str forced to land nr Westende 24.1.16 (FSL RH Mulock); 2-str biplane destroyed Nieuport 15.00 26.1.16 (FSL RH Mulock); Accident DBR [last mention 30.4.16]; ADD by 11.5.16; Deleted 15.6.16

3978   (c/n N570). 1 Wing St.Pol by 1.2.16; Shipped to Aegean; A Flt 2 Wing Imbros by 3.16; B Flt 2 Wing Thermi by 6.16; Crashed 25.6.16 (FSL KV Hooper); Tested Mitylene 5.7.16; Imbros to Thasos 27.7.16; Chased HA in raid on Xanthi aerodrome, smashed tailskid landing 1.8.16 (FSL MA Simpson); Imbros to Roumanian Flight, Bucharest 25.11.16, but EF, FL Marsa, 16m SSW of Bucharest, contd by lorry (F/Cdr S Adams)

3979   Shipped to Aegean; Aegean by 4.16; 2 Wing Mudros 7.16; During bombing attack on Drama aerodrome, forced down over Bojran by von Eschwege, near target 18.11.16 (FSL AJ Whetnall killed)

## 15 NIEUPORT TYPE 11 SINGLE-SEATER TRACTOR BIPLANE SCOUTS purchased from Nieuport, Issy-les-Moulineaux & numbered 3980 to 3994. (80-hp Le Rhône)

3980   Deld ADD; 1 Wing St.Pol by 1.16 - @2.2.16 [B Group by 23.1.16]; Accident, deleted ADD 15.4.16

3981   Deld ADD; 1 Wing St.Pol by 12.15 - @30.4.16 [B Group by 15.1.16 - @8.2.16; 1 Flt A Sqdn from formation 1.3.16]; HA destroyed, observer probably killed Nieuport 20.2.16 (FSL RS Dallas); LVG C shot down in flames in front of Belgian trenches in flooded area nr Dixmude 10.30 29.2.16 (FSL HR Simms); 2-str destroyed Westende-Middelkerke, own a/c damaged 04.35 23.4.16 (FSL RS Dallas); ADD by 18.5.16 - @2.6.16; 2 Flt A Sqdn 1 Wing by 10.6.16; St.Pol 1.7.16; Crashed and damaged Furnes 7.16 or 8.16 (FSL CA Eyre); A Sqdn 1 Wing Furnes by 30.7.16; ADD on/by 3.8.16 - @31.8.16; 1 Flt A Sqdn 1 Wing by 7.9.16; Became 1 Sqdn 1.12.16; ADD 28.12.16 - @4.1.17; 6 Sqdn Petite Synthe by 11.1.17; FTR from Zeebrugge raid, FL Cadzand, Zeeland 26.2.17 (FSL GP Powles interned in Holland); Deleted 24.3.17; To Dutch Air Force as *LA40*, becoming *N213* then *N230*

3982   (C/n 594) Deld ADD; Wrecked Furnes 1.1.16 (FSL AW Kay); 1 Wing by 23.1.16 [B Group by 23.1.16; 1 Flt A Sqdn from formation 1.3.16 - 7.16; 2 Flt A Sqdn 1 Wing Furnes by 9.16]; Crashed, damaged Furnes 1.1.17 (FSL AW Kay); ADD 5.1.17 (deleted?)

3983   Deld ADD; Eastchurch Group 1 Wing St.Pol by 2.12.15; Shipped to Aegean; A Flt 2 Wing Imbros (later Thasos) by 3.16; Became A Sqdn 2 Wing Thasos 1.1.17; Engine trouble, FTR scouting flight 14.1.17 (F/L WH Peberdy killed)

3984   (c/n N595?) Shipped to Aegean; C Flt A Sqdn 2 Wing Imbros by 7.3.16 - @8.16; Captured and exhibited by Germans as war trophy 1917

3985   Deld ADD; 1 Wing St.Pol by 8.2.16 [3 Flt B Sqdn from

formation 1.3.16 - @10.3.16]; Shipped to Aegean; A Sqdn 2 Wing Imbros by 3.16; Crashed 1916; Deleted 7.16

3986 [Was to be transferred to RFC as A8741, but NTU] Deld ADD; 1 Wing St.Pol by 8.2.16 [1 Flt A Sqdn by 24.4.16]; ADD by 11.5.16; C Sqdn 1 Wing St.Pol 29.6.16; ADD by 14.8.16; 4 Flt B Sqdn 1 Wing 17.8.16; Seaplane dived into sea 2½m off Blankenberghe 15.30 22.10.16 (FSL DMB Galbraith); 4 Wing 23.10.16; A Flt detd Sqdn 26.10.16 (became 8 Sqdn); 1 probable (unconfirmed) 9.11.16 (FSL RJO Compston); 3 Sqdn 20.12.16; 9 Sqdn 1.2.17; ADD 21.4.17; Deleted 27.4.17 general fatigue

3987 Deld Dunkerque; 1 Wing St.Pol by 8.2.16 [1 Flt A Sqdn by 16.4.16]; EF, FL after practice firing Le Prieur rocket into corner of aerodrome, Furnes 18.8.16 (F/L P Legh); ADD by 24.8.16; 1 Flt A Sqdn 1 Wing Furnes 9.10.16; Became 1 Sqdn Furnes 1.12.16; ADD 2.1.17; 6 Sqdn 1.2.17; 11 Sqdn 8.3.17; COL 30.4.17 (FSL ND Hall); Surveyed 17.5.17; Deleted 27.5.17 general fatigue

3988 Deld ADD; 1 Wing by 2.16 [A Sqdn by 4.16; 2 Flt by 2.6.16; 1 Flt by 22.6.16]; Practising with Le Prieur rockets 12.11.16; ADD by 16.11.16; 1 Sqdn 18.12.16; ADD by 28.12.16 - @4.1.17; 6 Sqdn (coded '7') by 11.1.17; Collided with another Nieuport 4.2.17; Deleted by ADD 24.3.17

3989 Deld ADD; 1 Flt A Sqdn 1 Wing St.Pol by 29.4.16; 2-str in flames N of Westende 21.5.16 (FSL RS Dallas); ADD; 2 Flt A Sqdn 1 Wing Furnes by 22.6.16; Fokker E OOC 2m off Ostend 14.05 8.7.16 (F/L TFN Gerrard); ADD by 13.7.16; 1 Flt A Sqdn 1 Wing by 14.7.16; 2 Flt A Sqdn 1 Wing by 24.8.16; St.Pol 1.9.16; 1 Wing Dunkerque by 11.16; Crashed and damaged Furnes 27.12.16 (F/L JA Carr); ADD 28.12.16 - @25.1.17; 6 Sqdn by 1.2.17 - @11.3.17; 11 Sqdn by 15.3.17 (formed 8.3.17) - @29.4.17; Deleted ADD 14.5.17 general fatigue

3990 Deld ADD by 11.5.16; 9 Flt A Sqdn 4 Wing Dunkerque 10.6.16; FTR after hit by AA fire 4m N of Ypres 2.8.16 (F/L RGA Baudry killed); Surveyed 3.8.16

3991 Deld ADD; 2 Flt A Sqdn 1 Wing by 13.3.16; 1 Flt A Sqdn 1 Wing St.Pol by 4.16 (Sqdn to Furnes 10.6.16); Hit by flak 17.6.16; ADD 9.10.16 (overhaul); Tested 2.11.16; A Sqdn 1 Wing Furnes 4.11.16 (fitted Le Prieur rockets); Became 1 Sqdn 1.12.16; ADD 24.12.16; 6 Sqdn by 11.1.17 - @25.1.17; ADD by 1.2.17 (repair); 6 Sqdn by 4.3.17 - @13.3.17; 11 Sqdn by 15.3.17; Crashed and wrecked 20.4.17 (FSL DH Masson killed); Deleted ADD 27.4.17

3992 (13m span) Deld ADD; 1 Flt A Sqdn 1 Wing St.Pol by 11.5.16; Exptl Flt ADD by 11.5.16; 2 2-strs OOC off Nieuport 14.00 21.5.16 (FSL RH Mulock); (became?) 14 Flt B Sqdn 1 Wing by 24.5.16; C Sqdn 1 Wing St.Pol 27.6.16; 4 Flt B Sqdn 1 Wing St.Pol W/E 17.8.16 - ?9.11.16; Seaplane OOC 10m off Calais c.11.00, own m/c damaged 28.9.16 (FSL DMB Galbraith); C Sqdn 1 Wing by 16.11.16; Became 3 Sqdn 12.16 - @26.1.17; 9 Sqdn by 1.2.17; Wrecked 4.17; ADD by 5.4.17; Deleted 27.4.17

3993 Deld ADD; 1 Wing by 2.16; 1 Flt A Sqdn 1 Wing by 11.5.16; Exptl Flt ADD by 18.5.16; Seaplane shot down and sunk 4m off Blankenberghe 07.00 20.5.16 (FSL RS Dallas); Chingford 20.5.16; Dover 24.5.16; Dunkerque 26.5.16; 1 Flt A Sqdn 1 Wing St.Pol by 2.6.16; To Furnes with A Sqdn 10.6.16; 2 Flt A Sqdn 1 Wing Furnes by 24.8.16 - @30.11.16; ADD by 7.12.16; 3 Sqdn (named 'BUBBLES' - but see 3958) by 28.12.16 - @26.1.17; ADD to 9 Sqdn 16.2.17; ADD 21.4.17; Deleted 27.4.17 general fatigue; Once coded '1'?

3994 Deld ADD; 1 Wing St.Pol by 4.16; 1 Flt A Sqdn 1 Wing by 18.5.16; Sqdn to Furnes 10.6.16; Fokker E.III shot down, pilot killed Mariakerke aerodrome 15.10 9.7.16 (FSL RS Dallas); KB shot down in flames in Le Prieur rocket attack at 800ft nr Ostend 11.35 20.10.16 (F/L EW Norton); Became 1 Sqdn Furnes 5.11.16; Wrecked on practice flight 26.12.16; 6 Sqdn by 6.2.17 - @6.3.17; 11 Sqdn by 25.3.17 (sqdn formed 8.3.17); ADD 4.6.17; Deleted ADD 27.5.17 (sic) general fatigue

## 3 NIEUPORT TWIN TRACTOR BIPLANES ordered from Nieuport, Issy-les-Moulineaux & numbered 3995 to 3997. (Two 110-hp Clerget)

3995 to 3997 cancelled

## 1 HENRY FARMAN PUSHER BIPLANE ordered from Aéroplanes Farman & numbered 3998. (140-hp Canton-Unné)

3998 Deld ADD; 1 Sqdn St.Pol from/by 25.5.15; Became 1 Wing St.Pol 6.15 [A Sqdn by 20.6.15; HQ Sqdn by 19.12.15]; 5 Wing Coudekerque 3.3.16; Participated in attack on Houttave aerodrome, Zeebrugge 20.3.16 (FSL HG Blagrove saw numerous flashes from bombs); Wrecked in gale Coudekerque 29.3.16; Deleted ADD 15.4.16

## 1 ROYAL AIRCRAFT FACTORY B.E.2c TRACTOR BIPLANE ordered under Cont No C.P.75805/15 from Blackburn Aeroplane & Motor Co Ltd, numbered 3999 & built Leeds. (80-hp Renault)

3999 Built specially for Marconi W/T experiments. Deld Grain for erection 20.7.15 (experiments); Preliminary test 13.8.15 (Ding); Accepted 18.8.15; COL, broke lower wings and propeller 9.9.15 (F/L PL Holmes & S/L FJ Linnell); Eastbourne Aviation Co by lorry for repair 21.9.15; Chingford 19.11.15; Cranwell 15.1.16; To instructional use 8.5.16; Deleted 24.8.16

## 1 SLOANE-DAY TRACTOR BIPLANE purchased in USA. (160-hp Sloane-Day)

4000 Ordered for evaluation, but believed cancelled [see also 3701]

## RNAS SERIALS - FOURTH SERIES (8001 to 10000)

**30 SHORT ADMIRALTY 184 TYPE TRACTOR BIPLANE SEAPLANES ordered 21.5.15 (amended 30.10.15) under Cont No C.P.71756/15 from S.E.Saunders Ltd, numbered 8001 to 8030 & built East Cowes. Type "A" armament from 8015. (225-hp Sunbeam Mohawk to 8013, remainder 240-hp Sunbeam)**

8001    Deld Seaplane School Calshot 2.3.16 (tested and accepted same day); Hit Black Jack Buoy on TO, CW, salved 1.4.16 (FSL AG Woodward unhurt); Deleted 17.4.16

8002    Deld Calshot 1.4.16; Deleted 27.4.17

8003    Deld Calshot 1.4.16; Accepted 2.4.16; Dover 16.4.16; Seaplane Flt Dunkerque 8.6.16; Dover 29.6.16 (reconstruction); Rebuilt 17.8.16 (240- hp Sunbeam); Dunkerque 25.8.16; Dover 19.12.16; Grain 22.12.16; HMS *Riviera* 23.12.16; Dover in tow 1.1.17; HMS *Riviera* 2.1.17; Night flying trials 15.1.17; Dover 16.1.17 (overhaul); HMS *Riviera* 18.1.17; Dover 3.2.17; HMS *Riviera* 14.2.17; To Dunkerque but EF, FL Calais 8.4.17; arr Dunkerque 9.4.17; HMS *Riviera* 13.4.17; Dover 4.6.17; HMS *Riviera* 8.6.17; Dover 15.7.17 (for doping); HMS *Riviera* 17.7.17; EF, FL, sank 6.8.17

8004    (240-hp Sunbeam) Shipped to Mediterranean 4.16; Port Said to HMS *Anne* 12.4.16 - @24.4.16; Port Said by 8.16; HMS *Anne* 1.9.16; AMC *Dufferin* 21.9.16 - @26.9.16; HMS *Anne* by 10.10.16; HMS *Raven II* 11.10.16; Port Said 3.11.16; HMS *Raven II* 29.11.16; HMS *Anne* 1.1.17 - @25.1.17; Attacked by Turkish rifle fire 23.1.17 (FSL E King unhurt; Observer, Lt NW Stewart 7th RS & RFC killed DoW 23.1.17); Port Said 31.3.17 (overhaul); HMS *Empress* 12.5.17; Port Said 13.5.17; HMS *Empress* 18.6.17; HMS *Empress* 22.6.17; Port Said 23.6.17; Port Said 5.7.17; HMS *Empress* 12.7.17; Port Said 16.7.17; HMS *Empress* 9.8.17; Port Said 18.8.17; For deletion by 1.12.17

8005    Deld Felixstowe (via Calshot) 3.5.16; Accepted 11.5.16; Deleted 14.6.17

8006    Tested at Cowes 4.5.16, then to CSD White City; Grain 14.8.16; Smashed on patrol flight by 24.3.17; Deleted 4.6.17

8007    Deld Killingholme 8.8.16; South Shields 7.9.16; FL in sea, damaged, towed in by motor boat 30.1.17 (F/L RE Dean & LM Connor); Re-erecting 16.2.17; HSMP 1.5.17 (FSL FH Wallers & AM2 Jolley); Deleted 11.7.17 for use by Armstrong [Whitworth?] for catapult trials

8008    Accepted Cowes 30.5.16 (by Calshot pilot); Killingholme for South Shields by 14.8.16; South Shields 25.9.16; FL and wrecked in harbour 24.10.16 (FSL TC Wilkinson & FSL PC Moynihan); To Mkrs 11.16, then deleted

8009    Deld Nore War Flt Felixstowe 18.8.16; FL, tail damaged, towed in 8.1.17 (F/L CF Latimer & AM RA Lucas); Killingholme W/E 2.11.17; Deleted W/E 22.2.18

8010    Tested Cowes 9.6.16; Calshot 22.6.16; Deleted 27.4.17

8011    Accepted Cowes 15.6.16; Deld Calshot 22.6.16; Deleted W/E 14.9.17

8012    Accepted Cowes 22.6.16; Deld Calshot 24.6.16; FL in sea, wrecked 23.1.17 (FSL SD Scott & Lt HM Airey RNVR); Deleted 25.1.17

8013    Tested Calshot 14.7.16; Deld HMS *Riviera* 20.7.16; Spotting for HMS *Terror* at Zeebrugge 24.9.16 (F/L H Stewart & S/L GPF Greene); Dunkerque 8.10.16; HMS *Riviera* 2.11.16; Dunkerque 12.11.16; Dover 7.2.17; Deleted 25.7.17

8014    Tested Cowes 24.8.16 (by Calshot pilot); Deld PVRS Grain 4.10.16 with underslung bomb racks; Seaplane Design Flt Grain 5.12.16; Calshot 5.1.17; Stalled and side-slipped landing, wreck salved 10.2.17 (2 crew OK); Deleted 15.2.17

8015    Deld & tested Calshot 1.8.16; Dover 28.9.16; Dunkerque 15.10.16; Bombed Zeebrugge Mole 4.4.17, 5-6.4.17 & 7-8.4.17, also Submarine Repair Works Ostende 8-9.4.17 and Zeebrugge Seaplane Station 30.4.17 (all F/L R Graham DSC); Attacked Ostende Seaplane Station 1.5.17 (F/L GW Price) & 10.5.17 (F/L R Graham DSC); Attacked Zeebrugge Mole 31.5.17 -

1.6.17 (F/L GW Price) & 3.6.17 (F/L R Graham DSC); Dover 17.8.17 (conv reconnaissance type); Dunkerque 24.9.17; Dover 30.11.17; Became 407 Flt Dover by 25.5.18; Under chassis damaged 29.7.18 (Lt GA Wright & Cpl Fox); Became 407 Flt 233 Sqdn 31.8.18; detd Dunkerque 23.10.18; 407 Flt 233 Sqdn Dover 30.10.18 - @30.1.19

8016    Allocated HMS *Riviera* 2.7.16 after trials at Cowes; Tested Calshot 5.8.16; Cowes to Dover 18.8.16; Dunkerque 8.9.16; Lost during raid on Ostende and captured intact 10.11.16 (F/L GGG Hodge PoW)

8017    Tested Cowes 23.8.16 (by Calshot pilot) [then to store?]; Dunkerque 10.11.16; Bad visibility, o/t, CW landing Dunkerque Harbour 5.8.17 (FSL HH Gonyou); Deleted ADD 24.8.17

8018    (Tropical radiators) Deld Calshot 21.11.16; Shipped to Mediterranean; arr EI&SS Port Said 6.2.17; HMS *Raven II* 10.3.17 [convtd 2-str when on special service in Indian Ocean, reconverted single-seater bombing on return to Port Said]; FL Male Island 21.4.17 (F/L GD Smith & Lt WCA Meade); HMS *Raven II* by 13.5.17; Port Said 11.6.17; HMS *Empress* 4.7.17; Port Said 16.7.17; HMS *Empress* 9.8.17; Port Said 18.8.17; HMS *Empress* 25.9.17; Port Said 28.9.17; HMS *Empress* 8.10.17; Remaining bombs exploded in heavy landing off Famagusta after TO to attack Adana, Turkey, when dropped some bombs and towed back 9.10.17 (F/L MC Wood killed); Surveyed 13.10.17; Deleted 8.11.17 TL

8019    Deld Calshot 21.11.16; Shipped to Mediterranean; EI&SS Port Said; HMS *Raven II* 10.3.17; Port Said 11.6.17; HMS *Empress* 14.6.17; Port Said 5.7.17; HMS *Empress* 12.7.17; Port Said 16.7.17; HMS *Empress* 9.8.17; Port Said 18.8.17; HMS *Empress* 4.9.17; Port Said 15.9.17; HMS *Empress* 24.9.17; Port Said 28.9.17; HMS *Empress* 4.10.17; Port Said 13.10.17; HMS *City of Oxford* 10.17; Port Said 10.17; HMS *Raglan* 28.10.17; HMS *City of Oxford* 30.10.17; Port Said 9.11.17 - @31.3.18 (as single-seater by 12.17); EF 14.2.18; Petrol trouble, beached 1m NW of Damiette, towed in by *ML242* 20.4.18 (Lt JW Simpson & Lt A Copley); HMS *City of Oxford* by 5.18; Port Said by 8.6.18; For deletion by 29.6.18; Repaired instead; HMS *City of Oxford* by 23.8.18; Port Said 3.9.18; Deleted at Alexandria 10.18

8020    Shorts to fit streamlined wires 10.16; Shipped to Mediterranean; EI&SS Port Said, tested & satisfactory 17.3.17; HMS *Anne* 21.3.17; Port Said 23.3.17; HMS *Empress* 17.4.17; Port Said 19.4.17; HMS *Empress* 12.5.17; Port Said 13.5.17; HMS *Empress* 22.6.17; Port Said 23.6.17; HMS *Empress* 14.7.17; Port Said 16.7.17 (as single seater by 12.17) - @6.2.18; Suez 2.18; HMS *City of Oxford* 13.2.18; Suez 29.3.18; HMS *City of Oxford* by 5.18 - @8.6.18; Port Said by 29.6.18 (repair); Stalled avoiding vessel on TO, crashed into another ship, Alexandria 15.7.18 (Lt CH Biddlecombe & 2/Lt CW Dobbs both injured)

8021    Accepted at Cowes 4.11.16; Shipped to Mediterranean; EI&SS Port Said; HMS *Anne* 26.2.17; Port Said 1.3.17; HMS *Raven II* 10.3.17; Port Said 12.6.17; HMS *Empress* 22.6.17; Port Said 23.6.17; HMS *Empress* 15.9.17; Port Said 28.9.17; HMS *Empress* 4.10.17; Crashed on operations between Karatash Burnu & Adana, Turkey 11.10.17 (F/Cdr AW Clemson PoW & 2/Lt EA Newton ASC killed); Surveyed 13.10.17; Deleted 8.11.17 TL

8022    Accepted at Cowes 4.11.16; Shipped to Mediterranean; EI&SS Port Said; HMS *Anne* 26.2.17; Port Said 1.3.17; HMS *Empress* 9.8.17; Port Said 18.8.17; HMS *Empress* 16.9.17; Port Said 24.9.17; HMS *Raven II* 31.10.17; Port Said 3.11.17; HMS *City of Oxford* 28.11.17; Port Said @8.12.17; HMS *City of Oxford* (via Suez) 13.2.18; Suez 29.3.18; HMS *Empress* 6.4.18; Port Said 7.4.18 - 9.18; Deleted at Alexandria 10.18

8023    Tested Cowes 28.11.16; Deld Calshot 1.12.16; FL, CW, wreck salved, off St.Leonards 19.12.16 (FSL PH Mackworth & FSL P Brend unhurt); Deleted 23.2.17

8024    Deld Calshot and tested 20.12.16; Bembridge 3.3.17; Calshot 11.5.17; Portland 24.5.17; Calshot 16.8.17; Surveyed 28.9.17; Deleted 6.10.17 W&T

8025 Tested Cowes 7.2.17; Accepted 9.2.17; Deld Cattewater 26.2.17 (transit); Newlyn 27.2.17; U/c damaged on TO 26.5.17; Reported sinking off Longships, drifter assisting 4.6.17; Salvaging by divers 6.6.17; Deleted 14.6.17 BR

8026 Deld Scapa 1.3.17; HMS *Campania* 8.3.17; Wrecked, remains hoisted in 4.5.17; Yarmouth, wrecked by 26.5.17; Deleted 31.5.17

8027 Accepted Cowes; Calshot 13.2.17; Bembridge 3.3.17; HSMP, bombed U-boat 5.4.17 (FSL A Durston); Calshot 29.5.17; Surveyed 28.9.17; Deleted 6.10.17 W&T

8028 Deld Scapa 1.3.17; HMS *Campania* 8.3.17; Flew off deck to test mono-rail 17.4.17 (FSL ART Pipon); Houton Bay 19.2.18 (storage); Deleted W/E 27.4.18

8029 Tested Calshot 15.3.17; Dunfermline to Dundee by rail 25.4.17; HMS *Engadine* 23.5.17; Rosyth 6.8.17; HMS *Engadine* 10.9.17 (ship at Buncrana 27.9.17-18.11.17); Crashed 13.11.17; Surveyed 13.11.17; Deleted 21.11.17

8030 Deld Calshot 28.2.17; HMS *Campania* for erection 8.5.17; Houton Bay W/E 29.12.17; HMS *Campania* W/E 5.1.18; Houton Bay 2.18; HMS *Campania* 7.2.18; Houton Bay 17.3.18 (storage); Became 430 Flt Houton Bay by 25.5.18; Deleted W/E 29.8.18

**75 SHORT ADMIRALTY 184 TYPE TRACTOR BIPLANE SEAPLANES** ordered 12.6.15 (amended 12.8.15) under Cont No C.P.48014/15 from Short Bros, numbered **8031 to 8105** & built Rochester. 8095 to 8103 had Type 'A' armament (except 8103?) (225-hp Sunbeam Mohawk) [Gordon Bruce's researches show correct c/n's S.173 to S.247]

8031 Deld Grain 4.10.15; Calshot 18.10.15; HMS *Empress* 26.12.15; Wrecked 16.2.16 (FSL RM Clifford & Lt Williams, East Yorks Regt); Dismantled 18.2.16; Deleted 27.3.16

8032 Deld Grain 7.10.15; HMS *Vindex* 29.10.15; Grain 30.10.15; Accepted 4.4.16 (Kemp); Westgate 24.4.16; Dunkerque 16.5.16; HMS *Riviera* 16.5.16, fitting roller blinds for sighting; Attacked by 2 enemy seaplanes 7/8m NW of Zeebrugge, wrecked landing in swell 3.6.16 (F/L H Stewart & OSL OH Crowther unhurt); Deleted 4.6.16

8033 Deld Grain and accepted 11.10.15; HMS *Vindex* 26.11.15; Felixstowe 2.12.15; HMS *Vindex* 4.12.15; Felixstowe 9.2.16; HMS *Vindex* 22.2.16; Felixstowe repair 1.3.16; Felixstowe 21.6.16; Damaged on TO 12.7.16 (FSL JA Sadler & LM Fazey); HMS *Vindex* 4.12.16; Felixstowe 5.12.16 (bomb expts); HMS *Vindex* 11.12.16; Dismantling by 9.1.17; Parnall by rail for rebuilding 22.1.17; Dundee by rail 10.5.17; HMS *Manxman* 5.7.17; Otranto (loan) 21.1.18; HMS *Manxman* 2.18; Otranto 27.2.18; Deleted W/E 8.3.18

8034 Accepted Grain 19.10.15 (Kemp); HMS *Vindex* 29.10.15; Crashed in river 7.11.15 (FSL FS McGill & F/L HF Towler both slightly injured); Remains to Grain and hoisted aboard HMS *Vindex* 8.11.15, then scrapped

8035 Deld Grain and accepted 16.10.15; HMS *Vindex* 8.11.15; Felixstowe 4.12.15; HMS *Vindex* 24.12.15; Felixstowe 2.2.16 HMS *Vindex* 22.2.16; Felixstowe 1.3.16; HMS *Vindex* 14.3.16; Arrived Dover in tow, then to HMS *Vindex* 20.3.16; Participated Zeebrugge raid, dropped 2x65-lb bombs 20.3.16 (FSL CG Knight & Mid FH Isaac); Felixstowe 23.3.16; Dunkerque (via Dover) 12.5.16; Felixstowe; Dover 15.5.16; Dunkerque 10.6.16; Dover 25.6.16; Dunkerque 8.7.16; Dover 10.7.16; Deleted 27.7.16

8036 Deld Grain 17.10.15; HMS *Vindex* 22.11.15; Felixstowe 4.12.15; CW on Felixstowe Cliffs in fog 4.12.15 (FSL G Donald & Mid DL Risdon both injured); Deleted 16.12.15

8037 Deld Grain and accepted 27.10.15 (Kemp); HMS *Riviera* at Dover 29.10.15; Grain 18.1.16; HMS *Riviera* 25.1.16; Broke strut landing 3.2.16 (FSL GA Maclean & OSL OH Crowther); Dunkerque 21.2.16; HMS *Riviera* 26.2.16; Participated in Zeebrugge raid, EF, FL Nieuport, taxied back 20.3.16 (F/L GW Price); Hoisted out but slipped too soon, damaged 28.3.16 (FSL N Gregory & OSL OH Crowther); Grain 2.4.16; HMS *Riviera* 26.4.16; Leaking radiator, pancaked landing, badly damaged 28.4.16 (FSL NR Davenport & PO Mech Stirling); Wrecked machine to Dover on board *C65*

30.4.16; Deleted 1.5.16; Parnall for repair by 31.5.16, later deleted

8038 Deld Grain 30.10.15; Dover 19.12.15; Attempted to TO with torpedo 5.1.16; HACP 25.1.16 (FSL ATN Cowley); HSPP 9.2.16; (FSL ATN Cowley & AM Smith); Seaplane Flt Dunkerque 26.2.16; HMS *Riviera* 12.3.16; Dunkerque 12.3.16; HACP 19.3.16 (FSL ATN Cowley & OSL LH Slatter); Night raid 20.3.16 (FSL W Perham & OSL RM Inge); Dover 31.3.16; Dunkerque, badly damaged towing into harbour on/by 14.4.16; Dover 15.4.16; Dunkerque 27.4.16; Dover, FL, captured by German torpedo boat 6.5.16 (FSL ATN Cowley & OSL RM Inge RNVR both PoW); Deleted 19.5.16

8039 Deld Grain and accepted 3.11.15; Dover 5.12.15; Dunkerque 26.2.16; HMS *Riviera* 12.3.16; Dunkerque 12.3.16; Bombed U-boat, results uncertain 10.4.16 (FSL W Perham & OSL LH Slatter); Badly damaged towing into harbour 13.4.16 (FSL FJ Bailey & OSL RW Gow unhurt); Badly damaged 6.5.16 (FSL BC Tooke & OSL LH Slatter); Dunkerque 9.6.16; Crashed on TO 20.6.16 (FSL HV German & OSL LH Slatter rescued)

8040 Deld Grain and accepted (Kemp) 19.11.15; Felixstowe 5.12.15; HMS *Vindex* 5.12.15; Participated in Zeebrugge raid and dropped 3x65-lb bombs 20.3.16 (F/L GH Reid & CPO Mullins); Participated in raid on Hoyer airship base and dropped 3x65-lb bombs then forced down off Belgian coast by Ltn Ratazzi & Ltn Schurer and captured intact by German Air Service 25.3.16 (F/L GH Reid & CPO Mullins PoWs)

8041 Deld Grain and accepted 21.11.15 (Kemp); HMS *Riviera* 23.11.15; Thrown over and damaged on TO 15.1.16 (FSL N Gregory & AM Waters); Towed to Shorts 19.1.16 (repair); HMS *Riviera* 24.1.16; Collided with trawler on TO, damaged wing tip 2.2.16 (FSL GA Maclean & OSL OH Crowther); Dunkerque 22.2.16, but damaged taking ashore in snowstorm; HMS *Riviera* 26.2.16; TW landing 9.3.16 (F/L GW Price); Deleted 11.3.16

8042 Deld Grain and accepted 22.11.15 (Kemp); RD Grain by 27.11.15; Killingholme 3.8.16; Came down off Sunderland en route South Shields to Killingholme, FL Allendale 31.8.16; South Shields by 2.17; Dismantled for transit by 14.2.17; Cattewater by rail 16.2.17; Newlyn 25.3.17; Mylor, Falmouth 31.3.17; Newlyn 5.4.17; Cattewater 22.4.17; Surveyed 19.6.17; Parnall by rail 12.7.17, later deleted

8043 Shipped from Devonport in SS *Hunts Castle* 9.1.16; arr RFC Force D Mesopotamia 2.16 - 6.16; Port Said from 8.16 - 10.16; Retd to UK; CSD White City by 31.12.16; Deleted 1.17

8044 Shipped from Devonport in SS *Hunts Castle* 9.1.16; arr RFC Force D Mesopotamia 2.16; Shot down while dropping food into Kut 26.4.16 (F/L CB Gasson wounded & 2/Lt AC Thouless killed)

8045 Shipped from Devonport in SS *Hunts Castle* 9.1.16; arr RFC Force D Mesopotamia by 5.16 to 6.16 [no record?]; Port Said by 8.16; HMS *Raven II* 24.8.16; Port Said 28.8.16 to 1.17

8046 Shipped from Devonport in SS *Hunts Castle* 9.1.16; HMS *Vindex* by 16.2.16; RFC Force D Mesopotamia by 5.16 to 6.16; Port Said from 8.16 - 10.16; Deleted by 1.17

8047 Shipped from Devonport in SS *Hunts Castle* 9.1.16; RFC Force D Mesopotamia from 2.16 (to 6.16?); Used for supply dropping during siege of Kut al Imara; Port Said from 8.16 to 10.16; Deleted by 1.17

8048 Deld Grain 18.1.16; Dover 28.1.16; Dunkerque 29.1.16; HMS *Riviera* 29.1.16; Dunkerque, damaged taking ashore in snowstorm 21.2.16; HMS *Riviera* 2.3.16; Damaged landing 9.3.16 (FSL N Gregory); EF, FL, damaged in night bombing practice 15.3.16 (F/L GW Price); Removed from drifter to Dover and housed for survey 17.3.16; repaired; Rebuilding with 240-hp Sunbeam at Dover by 28.2.17; Dunkerque 5.5.17; Damaged on ground 25.5.17; Dover 3.6.17 (reconstruction with 260-hp Sunbeam); Wrecked in harbour, towed to slipway 19.1.18 (pilot unhurt); Deleted 1.3.18

8049 Deld Grain 18.1.16 (Kemp); Felixstowe 5.2.16; Tested 8.2.16; To Newlyn for erection 4.1.17 (arr 20.1.17);

Penzance 2.2.17; Newlyn by 18.2.17; Damaged float on slipway trolley 26.2.17 (FSL HW Found & AM2 SH Bromhead); HSMP 8.3.17 (FSL AT Sketchley); Newlyn but EF, FL, elevator damaged, towed into Falmouth 29.3.17 (FSL HW Found & LM S Bremner); Damaged in snowstorm at Falmouth 1.4.17; Newlyn 5.4.17; Deletion recommended 9.4.17; Deleted 9.5.17

8050   Deld Dundee for erection 2.3.16; HMS *Engadine* 7.3.16; AZP 6.4.16 (F/L FJ Rutland & F/L FH Schwann) Killingholme 10.5.16 (storage); HMS *Engadine* 14.5.16; Sideslipped at 250 ft and nose dived, CW 25.5.16 (F/L GE Livock & F/L FH Schwann both injured, picked up by HMS *Lion*'s picket boat); Deleted 26.5.16

8051   Shipped to Mediterranean; EI&SS Port Said by 4.16; HMS *Empress* by 4.16; Deleted by 11.16

8052   Deld Grain 26.2.16; RD Grain 15.3.16 (bombing expts; Fitted racking for 4x16-lb bombs under wings); Dropped 4x100-lb bombs on armoured roof using CFS Trombone bomb sight at Kingsnorth 16.4.16; Dropped 500-lb bomb on armoured roof from 4,000-ft at Kingsnorth 9.5.16; Felixstowe 20.5.16; Grain 6.6.16; Felixstowe 14.7.16; Exp Flt Grain 15.7.16; Felixstowe 24.8.16; Exp Flt Grain 25.8.16; Became Gunnery Experimental Grain 5.12.16; Felixstowe 14.8.17; EAD Grain 15.8.17; Surveyed 25.3.18; Deleted 27.3.18 W&T

8053   (Dual control) Deld Grain 1.2.16 (Kemp); Accepted 10.2.16 (Kemp); HMS *Riviera* 24.2.16; Grain (via Dunkerque) 1.3.16; HMS *Riviera* 18.3.16; Zeebrugge raid but failed to rise off water 20.3.16 (F/L ON Walmesley); Dunkerque 24.3.16; Grain 25.3.16; Yarmouth 7.4.16; Grain 23.4.16; Felixstowe 18.12.16 (for HMS *Vindex* but NTU); Grain 3.2.17 (repair); Westgate 14.6.17 (Nore Flt); Deleted 6.4.18

8054   Shipped to Mediterranean; EI&SS Port Said .16; HMS *Anne* 18.4.16 - @24.4.16; Port Said 4.16; HMS *Ben-my-Chree* 27.4.16; Port Said 6.5.16; HMS *Ben-my-Chree* 8.5.16; Port Said 19.5.16; HMS *Ben-my-Chree* 2.6.16; EF, FL in sea, lost 25.8.16 (F/L GB Dacre PoW)

8055   Deld Scapa, tested after erection 29.4.16; HMS *Campania* 13.5.16; Scapa 15.5.16; HMS *Campania* 8.6.16; Scapa 30.6.16; HMS *Campania* 10.7.16; Scapa 26.7.16; HMS *Campania* 30.7.16; Scapa 10.8.16; HMS *Campania* 14.8.16; Scapa 16.8.16; HMS *Campania* then AZP 19.8.16 (FSL LS Breadner); Sage 2.9.16 (repair); Killingholme 24.2.17; AZP 24.5.17; Surveyed 20.12.17 wreck; Deleted 28.12.17

8056   Deld RD Grain by 17.3.16; Tested after erection 29.4.16; HMS *Campania* 10.5.16; HSMP 15.5.16 (F/Cdr L Tomkinson & F/L FJ Linnell); Scapa 15.5.16; HMS *Campania* 16.5.16; HSMP 15.7.16 (FSL JF Horsey & FSL FAR Malet); Scapa 10.8.16; HMS *Campania* 21.8.16; Sage 12.9.16 (repair); HMS *Campania* by 13.3.17; Rosyth 16.8.17 (repair and overhaul); HMS *Campania* 16.9.17; Scapa W/E 5.1.18 (storage); HMS *Campania* to Scapa W/E 2.2.18 (storage and overhaul); Deleted 9.3.18

8057   Ready by 4.3.16; Transferred to Japanese Govt. Stationed Yokohama 16.8.16

8058   Ready by 4.3.16; Deld Scapa by 31.3.16; Tested after erection 29.4.16; HMS *Campania* 2.5.16; HSMP 15.5.16 (WO T O'Connor & Mid DS Earp); Flew off deck five times with ship under way 3.6.16; Scapa 30.6.16; HMS *Campania* 6.7.16; Sideslipped on TO from deck, remains hoisted in 19.7.16 (F/L RDG Sibley & FSL FAR Malet); Scapa for repair 30.7.16; Sage 21.8.16; Deleted 12.16

8059   Ready by 4.3.16; Deld Long Hope, Orkney, tested after erection 29.4.16; HMS *Campania* 2.5.16; HSMP 30.5.16 (F/L GF Breese & S/L S Owler RNVR); Scapa 4.7.16; HMS *Campania* 1.10.16; EF, FL, towed but sank in rough 24.10.16 (FSL JF Horsey & Mid DS Earp unhurt); Sage 8.11.16 (for repair but later deleted)

8060   Deld Scapa for erection 29.4.16; HMS *Campania* 20.6.16; Scapa 30.6.16; HMS *Campania* 10.7.16; Scapa 28.8.16; HMS *Campania* 29.8.16; Scapa 17.10.16; HMS *Campania* 8.3.17; Scapa 16.7.17 (Houton Bay by 10.17); Surveyed 11.1.18; Deleted 17.1.18 W&T

8061   Deld Scapa for erection 29.4.16; HMS *Campania* 21.7.16; Flew off deck 21.8.16; Sideslipped on TO, nose dived into water, CW, salved 22.9.16 (FSL LH

Wilkins & S/L WR Abbott both injured); To Scapa; Deleted 20.10.16

8062   Deld Grain and accepted 30.3.16 (Kemp); Yarmouth 23.4.16; AZP 31.7.16 (F/L BD Kilner & CPO Heywood); 2 AZPs 19.10.16 (FSL GH Simpson & AM Haines, later FSL GH Bittles & S/L JE Maxwell); Felixstowe 24.10.16; Deleted 10.12.17 W&T

8063   Deld Grain and accepted, but EF, FL 5.4.16 (Kemp); Shorts Rochester 2.8.16; PVRS Grain 14.9.16; Nore War Flt Felixstowe 18.10.16; Wrecked 8.6.17; Deleted 9.6.17

8064   Deld Grain 3.4.16; Accepted 4.4.16 (Kemp); HMS *Engadine* (via Yarmouth) 16.4.16; Killingholme 10.5.16; HMS *Engadine* 14.5.16; Dundee 7.8.16; HMS *Engadine* 8.9.16; Elevator smashed hoisting out 28.11.16; Dundee 4.2.17; HMS *Engadine* 10.2.17; Dundee 27.2.17; HMS *Engadine* 7.5.17; Hawk Craig 28.6.17; Rosyth 23.7.17; Hawk Craig by 27.12.17; Surveyed 1.1.18; Deleted 15.1.18 DBR

8065   Deld Grain and accepted 31.3.16 (Kemp); Killingholme 5.4.16; HMS *Engadine* 6.4.16; Killingholme 10.5.16; HMS *Engadine* 13.5.16; Dundee 16.5.16; HMS *Engadine* 26.5.16; Dundee 7.8.16; HMS *Engadine* 16.8.16; Dismantled for transport 14.1.17; Dundee 6.2.17; Parnall for overhaul 21.2.17; Dover 16.6.17; FF with new 250-hp Sunbeam engine 30.8.17; Wrecked and sank 9.11.17; Surveyed 19.11.17; Deleted 23.11.17 TL

8066   Deld Grain and accepted 4.4.16 (Kemp); Yarmouth 23.4.16; AZP 24/25.4.16 (F/L BD Kilner); HACP 31.5.16 (FSL A Gammon & CPO Rose); 2 HSMPs 30.4.17 (F/L GE Livock & AM Gibbs); Bombed U-boat at Outer Gabbard, missed by 300 yds 3.5.17 (F/L GE Livock & AM Gibbs); AZP 24.5.17 (F/L GE Livock & AM Gibbs); Dropped 2x100-lb bombs on U-boat 15m E of Smith's Knoll 12.7.17; Killingholme 24.7.17; South Shields 25.7.17; Dundee 26.7.17; HMS *Engadine* 26.7.17; Rosyth 27.7.17 (repair); HMS *Engadine* W/E 7.9.17; Hawk Craig .17; Rosyth 2.10.17; Surveyed 2.11.17; Deleted 6.11.17 W&T

8067   Deld Grain and accepted 5.4.16 (Kemp); Dover 15.4.16; Parnall 12.5.16 (repair); Dover 22.10.16; Tested 8.11.16; HMS *Riviera* 5.1.17; Dover 3.2.17; HMS *Riviera* 4.2.17; Night patrol, thick mist, FL off Calais, towed to Dover, TW by rough sea 18.3.17 (FSL BN Harrop & S/L ET Travers)

8068   Deld Grain 26.4.16; Accepted 28.4.16 (Kemp); Killingholme 23.5.16; Calshot (via Yarmouth and Dover) 16.5.18; 209 TDS Lee-on-Solent 5.18; Deleted W/E 12.9.18

8069   Deld Grain and accepted 28.4.16 (Kemp); Killingholme 20.5.16 (transit); Yarmouth 28.5.16; Killingholme 21.8.16 (extensive repair); Yarmouth 16.2.17 (engine trouble); retd Killingholme 23.2.17; Deleted 1.7.17

8070   [Type B]. Deld Grain 18.7.16 (exptl); Tested 28.7.16; Dover 20.4.17 (transit); Calshot 22.4.17; Portland 28.4.17; Bembridge 30.4.17; Deleted 11.7.17 BR

8071   Deld Grain and accepted 20.4.16 (Kemp); Westgate 5.5.16; HACP 31.7.16 (FSL EE Deans); Calshot 10.12.16; Portland 10.1.17; Beached, damaged float, Seatown 19.1.17 (FSL JR Ross); Broke up under tow by destroyer 8m W of Portland Bill 20.1.17 (S/L JR Ross unhurt); Deleted 11.3.17

8072   Presentation a/c "Shanghai Britons No.2". Deld Grain and accepted 1.5.16 (Kemp); Nosedived and wrecked 23.6.16 (F/Cdr HM Cave-Browne-Cave & LM Butcher slightly injured); Deleted 27.6.16

8073   [Type D conversion to single-seater]. Deld Grain and accepted 21.4.16; Dropped 9x65-lb bombs from 2,000 ft at Kingsnorth 9.5.16; Deleted 31.5.16

8074   Deld Grain and accepted 11.5.16 (Kemp); Yarmouth 19.5.16; Attacked Zeppelin 45m E of Yarmouth, then FL in sea 23.9.16 (F/L BD Kilner & CPO Rose); Retd under tow by patrol boat 24.9.16; AZP 28/29.9.16 (F/L BD Kilner & CPO Rose); Damaged on slipway by heavy seas 10.7.17 (FSL AM FitzRandolph); Deleted W/E 8.9.17

8075   Refitted 260-hp Sunbeam Maori; Shipped to Mediterranean 5.16; HMS *Ben-my-Chree* by 5.16; Port Said to HMS *Raven*; 11.7.16; HMS *Anne* 1.9.16; HMS *Northbrook* 18.9.16; HMS *Anne* 27.9.16; HMS *Raven II* 26.10.16; Port Said 3.11.16; HMS *Raven II* 21.11.16;

HMS *Anne* 1.1.17 - @25.1.17; Port Said W/E 24.3.17 (repair & overhaul); HMS *Empress* 12.5.17; Port Said 13.5.17; HMS *Empress* 22.6.17; Port Said 2.7.17; For deletion 1.12.17

8076    Deld Grain 5.5.16; Unsafe, towed to Shorts Rochester 7.6.16; Exp Flt Grain 14.8.16; Awaiting erection 22.9.16; (tested Martin stabilisers on upper wings, a device for lateral control; also Whitehouse gun mounting); Became Gunnery Experimental Grain 5.12.16; Tested Davis 6-pdr gun 11.12.16; Towed to Shorts for reconstruction 28.12.16; Type Test Dept Grain 28.9.17; Fitted 260-hp Sunbeam Maori III; Surveyed 21.12.17; Deleted 3.1.18 DBR

8077    Shipped to Mudros 6.16; Arr 2 Wing 7.16; Tested HMS *Ark Royal* 12.8.16; Mudros by 1.6.17; Surveyed 18.10.17; Deleted 23.10.17 DBR

8078    Shipped to Mudros 6.16; HMS *Ark Royal* by 8.16; Mudros 12.8.16; Thasos to HMS *Empress* 25.9.16; HMS *Ark Royal* by 18.2.17; Exptl firing of Davis Gun 10.3.17 (F/Cdr RM Field & F/Cdr AP MacKilligan); Thasos by 1.6.17; HMS *Ark Royal* 24.6.17; EF, FL 22.7.17; LM 1.10.17; Surveyed Mudros 18.10.17; Deleted 23.10.17 DBR

8079    Deld Grain & tested 26.5.16; Shorts Rochester 10.6.16 (packing for Dundee); Dundee (overhaul) 2.7.16; HMS *Engadine* 7.8.16; Dundee 15.8.16; HMS *Engadine* 11.9.16; retd Port Laing 16.10.16 then to Dundee; HMS *Engadine* by 12.16; Dundee 1.1.17; HMS *Engadine* 12.1.17 - @28.2.17; Dundee to HMS *Engadine* 27.3.17; COL 22.5.17 (FSL GCB Cotterell rescued, slightly injured); Deleted 4.6.17

8080    Shipped to Mediterranean 5.16; EI&SS Port Said 5,16; HMS *Ben-my-Chree* 17.5.16; Port Said 17.5.16; HMS *Ben-my-Chree* 14.8.16; HMS *Ben-my-Chree* 13.9.16; Port Said 17.9.16; HMS *Ben-my-Chree* 2.11.16; Port Said 11.11.16; HMS *Ben-my-Chree* 1.12.16; Went to look for 8372, float pierced by AA 2.12.16 (F/Cdr TH England DSC & Capt J Wedgwood Benn unhurt); HMS *Ben- my-Chree* 21.12.16; Lost with ship 9.1.17

8081    Deld Grain 15.10.15; Accepted 21.10.15 (Kemp); HMS *Vindex* 14.11.15 (tested Felixstowe 14.12.15); Felixstowe 2.1.16 (engine repair); Deleted 9.5.16

8082    Deld Grain 11.11.15; Shorts Rochester and tested en route 12.11.15 (Kemp); Shipped to Mediterranean c.20.11.15; EI&SS Port Said; HMS *Ben-my-Chree* 1.5.16; Port Said 8.5.16; HMS *Ben-my-Chree* 10.5.16; Port Said 26.5.16; HMS *Ben-my-Chree* 1.6.16; Port Said 15.6.16 - @10.16; Deleted 1916

8083    Deld Grain 19.11.15; Shorts Rochester and accepted en route 27.11.15 (Kemp); For Dardanelles 11.15; Transferred to French Govt

8084    Deld Grain by 30.11.15; Shorts Rochester 20.12.15; Grain by 2.16; HMS *Riviera* 24.2.16; Grain (via Dunkerque) 1.3.16; Transferred to French Govt

8085    Deld Shorts Queenborough to Nore Patrol Flt Grain 9.12.15; Accepted then to Shorts Rochester 18.12.15 (Kemp); Shipped from Devonport in SS *Hunts Castle* 9.1.16; RFC Force D Mesopotamia by 4.16 - @6.16; Port Said from 8.16 - @1.17 for HMS *Anne* & HMS *Raven II*

8086    Deld Grain 18.12.15; Accepted 8.1.16 then housed for Repair Depot; HMS *Riviera* 24.2.16; Grain (via Dunkerque) 1.3.16; RD Grain 15.3.16; HMS *Riviera* 18.3.16; Zeebrugge raid 20.3.16 (FSL CV Arnold); Dunkerque 21.3.16; Grain 25.3.16; Nore War Flt Grain by 24.4.16; Dover 11.9.16 (damaged float en route Portland); Portland 12.9.16; Dover 21.9.16; Westgate 22.9.16 (transit); Dover 23.9.16; Deleted 30.9.16

8087    Deld Grain 23.12.15 (for HMS *Ben-my-Chree*); Accepted 10.1.16 (Kemp); Rochester 25.1.16; Shipped to Mediterranean; HMS *Empress* by 4.16; Port Said to HMS *Ben-my-Chree* 19.5.16; Sank after floats smashed on TO 23.5.16 (Cdr CR Samson & Lt J Wedgwood Benn rescued unhurt), deleted

8088    Deld in tow from Eastchurch to Grain 5.1.16; Accepted then to Rochester 24.1.16 (Kemp); HMS *Empress* in crates 21.2.16; Tested 26.2.16; Port Said by 4.16; HMS *Empress* by 4.16; Dismantling for survey 12.6.16; Deleted 19.6.16

8089    Deld Grain, awaiting acceptance 8.2.16; HMS *Riviera* (via Dover) 22.2.16; Accepted Grain 24.2.16 (Kemp);

HMS *Riviera* (via Dover) 24.2.16; Grain (via Dunkerque) 1.3.16; Felixstowe 2.3.16; Deleted 3.7.16

8090    Deld Grain 2.2.16 (towed from Queenborough); Tested en route Rochester 12.2.16; Shipped to Mediterranean; EI&SS Port Said by 4.16; HMS *Raven II* by 5.16; Port Said to HMS *Raven II* 29.6.16 - @7.16; Port Said to HMS *Anne* 8.8.16; HMS *Ben-my-Chree*; Port Said 10.16; Mods to wings, fin and wingtip floats, FF 23.11.16; HMS *Ben-my-Chree* 21.12.16; HMS *Raven II* 10.3.17; Crashed and WO 15m N of Kalpeni 28.3.17 (FSL TGM Stephens and Capt REC Knight-Bruce); Surveyed 12.9.17; Deleted 25.9.17 wrecked

8091    Deld Grain and accepted en route from Shorts Rochester 10.2.16 (Kemp); Shipped to Mediterranean; EI&SS Port Said by 4.16; HMS *Raven II* by 5.16; ashore .16; HMS *Raven II* 29.6.16; Water in float, unable to TO, beached Tersana Bay, retd ship by trawler *Laborieux* 7.7.16 (FSL W Man & Lt JW Brown RFA); Spotting for Monitor *No.21*, attacked by LVG, FL beside monitor, towed to HMS *Raven II* in sinking condition 10.8.16 (F/L J Brooke & 2/Lt AK Smith unhurt); HMS *Anne* by 25.8.16; Port Said by 8.16 to 1.17; HMS *Ben-my-Chree* by 1.12.16 - @27.12.16; HMS *Empress* by 10.17; Port Said, for deletion 1.12.17

8092    Deld Grain 29.2.16; Accepted 1.4.16 (Kemp); Westgate by 7.4.16; HACP 28.11.16 (FSL RE Bush & FSL LG Maxton); Calshot 9.12.16; Deleted 11.7.17

8093    Deld Grain 29.2.16; Accepted 17.3.16 (Kemp); HMS *Riviera* 18.3.16; Zeebrugge raid 20.3.16 (F/L H Stewart); Hoisted out but elevator submerged and damaged, drifted towards 8037 and further damaged 28.3.16 (F/L H Stewart & S/L N Lea RNVR); Grain 2.4.16; HMS *Riviera* 26.4.16; Dropped 3x65-lb bombs on 2 German destroyers off Westende but missed 28.4.16 (F/L GW Price & S/L N Lea); Attacked German submarine off Dutch coast but missed 5.5.16 (F/L H Stewart & S/L OH Crowther); HMS *Riviera* 30.5.16 (fitting roller blinds for sighting); Capsized while hoisting in 17.6.16 (F/L H Stewart & Asst Payr GSN Carter); Dover in HMT *Warbler* for repair 18.6.16, but deleted

8094    Deld Grain 1.3.16; Accepted 17.3.16 (Kemp); Westgate by 31.3.16; Deleted 7.6.17

8095    Deld Grain 21.3.16; Accepted 30.3.16 (Kemp); Shorts Rochester 4.4.16; HMS *Empress* 17.6.16; Test after assembly 25.6.16; Mudros 18.8.16; Thasos by 1.6.17 - @5.18; Phelarin by 6.18; HMS *Ark Royal*, tested 12.7.18; Phelarin 7.8.18 - @1.19

8096    Deld Grain 27.6.16 (Kemp); Dover 19.7.16; Deleted 29.8.16

8097    Deld Grain 4.7.16; Dover 6.7.16; Dunkerque 20.7.16; Dover 22.8.16; Dunkerque 23.8.16; ADD 17.9.16 then deleted

8098    Felixstowe to Shorts Rochester 4.7.16 (Kemp); Dover 6.7.16; Grain 10.7.16 (Exp Flt by 7.9.16); Became Gunnery Experimental Grain 5.12.16; Dover 16.2.17; To HMS *General Craufurd* and return 16.2.17; Deleted 25.7.17

8099    Deld Grain 5.7.16 (Kemp); Dover 22.7.16; Dunkerque 12.8.16; Dover 22.8.16; Dunkerque 11.9.16; Dover 17.10.16; Dunkerque 1.9.17; Dover 4.9.17; Dunkerque awaiting rebuild by 3.10.17; LM 17.10.17; Surveyed 13.12.17; Deleted 17.12.17 wrecked

8100    Deld Grain and accepted 6.7.16 (Kemp); Dover 19.7.16; Dunkerque 6.9.16; Dover 16.10.16; Dunkerque 4.11.16; Dover 7.1.17; Collided with steam pinnace while landing 5.2.17 (FSL LC Pincott); Surveyed 31.10.17; Deleted 6.11.17 W&T

8101    (240-hp Sunbeam) Deld Grain 14.7.16 (Kemp); Dover 22.7.16; Dunkerque 12.8.16; Dover 22.8.16; Dunkerque 1.9.16; Dover, but FL 3m off Dover, tail damaged 5.9.16 (FSL MR Buckland); Dunkerque 3.11.16; Dover 16.2.17; Dunkerque 2.5.17; Dover 4.5.17; Calais 6.3.18; Dover 8.3.18; Surveyed 6.5.18; Deleted 11.5.18 W&T

8102    Deld Grain 22.7.16; Dover 26.7.16; Dunkerque 12.8.16; Dover by 22.8.16; AZP 24.9.16 (FSL C Laurence); Dunkerque 14.11.16; Dover 19.12.16; Grain 20.12.16; HMS *Riviera* 22.12.16; towed to Dover 1.1.17; HMS *Riviera* 2.1.17; Night flying trials on HMS *Riviera* at Dover 4.1.17; Dover 6.1.17; HSMPs 1.3.17

(F/L R Graham & CPO Hanna) & 17.3.17 (F/L MR Buckland & LM GR Hodgson); HSMP, chased 3 German seaplanes off Dungeness 24.3.17 (F/L MR Buckland & CPO Hanna); Dunkerque by 3.17; Dover 20.4.17; Dunkerque 20.4.17; Dover 21.4.17; AZP 21.4.17 (F/L MR Buckland & CPO Hanna); HACP 28.4.17 (FSL HH Gonyou & CPO Hanna); HACP 2.5.17 (FSL AW Farquhar & LM McCredie); Dunkerque 26.5.17; Dover 27.5.17; AGP 5.6.17 (FSL SE Ball & CPO Martin); Damaged floats 13.6.17; Wrecked 11.7.17 (pilot unhurt); Deleted 20.7.17

8103   [Type D conversion to single-seater, fitted to carry 9x65-lb bombs] Deld Grain and accepted 21.7.16 (Kemp); to Dunkerque but CW nr Calais 3.9.16 (FSL WR Dainty), deleted [Type A per official 1.17 list]

8104   [Type D conversion to single-seater, fitted to carry 9x65-lb bombs]. [Fitted experimentally 250-hp Eagle IV with square front radiator]. Deld Grain 10.11.16; Seaplane Design Flt Grain 14.12.16; Due Shorts Rochester W/E 2.2.17 to re-engine with 240-hp Sunbeam; Damaged on TO 9.4.17; Deleted 6.5.17

8105   [Type D conversion to single-seater].   Deld Grain 1.8.16; Mods by Shorts 8.16; Yarmouth (ex PVRS, via Felixstowe) 27.11.16 (experimentally fitted with tall u/c and tail float struts); Wrecked 6.11.17; Surveyed 6.11.17; Deleted 14.11.17 wrecked

**12 MAURICE FARMAN S.11 SHORTHORN PUSHER BIPLANES purchased in France, numbered 8106 to 8117. (70/75-hp Renault)**

8106   Deld Eastbourne FS for erection 10.7.15; Damaged landing 20.8.15 (S/L CR Blagrove); Detd with B Flt to Ringmer 17-23.9.15; COL 8.10.15 (S/L JHDM Campbell); to Dover but FL, broke u/c and propeller, Fatherston 27.10.15 (FSL WM Tait); Repaired; Retd ex Folkestone 4.11.15 (FSL WM Tait); Deleted 13.3.16

8107   Deld Eastbourne FS for erection 10.7.15; Shoreham 15.9.15 (manoeuvres); Crashed Shoreham 24.9.15; Deleted 21.10.15

8108   Chelmsford, repacking for delivery to Airco 7.7.15; Deld Chingford 8.7.15; Still awaiting erection 4.8.15; Run into by Bristol 945 7.9.15; Repaired 15.9.15; Gunnery School Flts Eastchurch 20.5.16; Gun Flt Eastchurch 8.8.16 - @8.3.17; Gunnery Flt Eastchurch by 25.4.17 (ex Bomb Flt) - @1.6.17; Observers School Flt Eastchurch by 8.17; Surveyed 8.11.17; Deleted 12.11.17 W&T

8109   Deld CSD White City .15; Chingford by lorry 7.7.15; Still awaiting erection 4.8.15; Bomb Flt Eastchurch 26.5.16 - @22.9.16; Gun Flt from/by 6.11.16; Eastchurch Workshops 1.12.16; Bomb Flt Eastchurch 3.2.17; Wrecked 6.3.17, to Workshops; Deleted 26.4.17

8110   Deld Eastchurch for erection 8.7.15; 2 Wing Eastchurch 13.7.15; Eastchurch NFS 19.7.15; FL, damaged, Dargate, Kent 20.8.15; retd 6.9.15; Damaged 13.10.15; Gun Flt Eastchurch 12.3.16; Damaged 10.4.16; Wrecked 31.8.16; Deleted 5.9.16

8111   Deld 2 Sqdn Eastchurch 9.7.15; Eastchurch NFS by 25.7.15; Damaged 22.8.15; Wrecked 23.9.15; Gun Flt Eastchurch 17.3.16; Damaged 20.3.16; Fitting gun 7.4.16; Crashed 20.10.16 and to Workshops; Gun Flt Eastchurch 9.12.16; Gunnery Flt Leysdown 25.4.17; Deleted 19.8.17 badly deteriorated

8112 to 8117 transferred to RFC (Military Wing)

**100 SOPWITH BABY (ADMIRALTY 8200 TYPE) TRACTOR BIPLANE SEAPLANES ordered 8.6.15 (amended 7.8.15) under Cont No C.P.48013/15 from Sopwith Aviation Co Ltd, numbered 8118 to 8217 & built Kingston, assembled Woolston. (100-hp Gnome Monosoupape to 8122, then 110-hp Clerget 9Z 8123 to 8186, then 100-hp Gnome Monosoupape 8187 to 8217)**

8118   Deld Grain by road 25.9.15; Accepted 28.9.15 (Hawker) - 4.16 (special type trials); Nore War Flt Grain by 24.4.16; HACP 16.2.17 (FSL RJ Paul); AGP 25.5.17 (FSL FI Jacks); Westgate 16.6.17; CW 16.7.17; Deleted 30.7.17 BR

8119   Deld Grain by road 29.9.15; Accepted 3.10.15; Nore War Flt Grain by 24.4.16; HACP 14.11.16 (F/L EdeC Hallifax); Westgate 15.6.17; TO downwind, left wing

rose, bounced on to left float and cartwheeled, wrecked 21.8.17 (FSL GF Hyams unhurt); Deleted W/E 8.9.17 BR

8120   Deld Grain by road 30.9.15; Accepted 1.10.15; Yarmouth 13.10.15; HMT *Jerico* 14.10.15; Yarmouth 19.10.15; HMS *Campania* 29.10.15 & by 28.11.15; Yarmouth to HMT *Kingfisher* 28.11.15; Yarmouth 29.11.15; HMT *Kingfisher* 28.1.16; Yarmouth 30.1.16; HMT *Cantatrice* 23.3.16; Yarmouth 25.3.16; Deleted 3.5.16

8121   Deleted Dover by road 6.10.15; Erected 7.10.15; Accepted 20.10.15 (Hawker); Dismantled for CSD White City 21.12.15; Westgate 5.1.16; Deleted 12.11.16

8122   Deld Felixstowe 10.10.15; Yarmouth 23.11.15; HMT *Cantatrice* but badly damaged hoisting aboard 23.3.16 (FSL FN Halsted); Yarmouth 25.3.16; HMT *Cantatrice* 31.3.16; Yarmouth 2.4.16; Deleted 5.7.16

8123   Deld Grain by road 26.9.15; Accepted 1.10.15; RD Grain 6.10.15 - @23.3.16; Nore War Flt Grain by 24.4.16 (replaced 3753); HACP 30.7.16 (FSL HGR Malet); Exp Flt Grain 7.9.16; Became Gunnery Exp Flt Grain 5.12.16; Became EAD Grain on/by 1.2.17; to Calshot but EF, FL Whitstable en route, towed into Westgate 13.7.17; arr Calshot 18.7.17; Deleted W/E 14.9.17

8124   Deld HMS *Campania* in SS *Helmsman* 2.12.15; Sopwith for repair by 31.5.16; put forward to cancel repair 8.16; Deleted by 1.17; BUT Transferred crated to Royal Canadian Naval Air Service less engine 1918

8125   Deld HMS *Campania* 22.11.15; Scapa 6.12.15; HMS *Campania* 10.5.16; Scapa 28.5.16; HMS *Campania* 30.5.16; Broke propeller taxying, severely damaged 21.6.16 (F/L RE Penny); Blackburn repair 11.7.16 - 3.17; Transferred crated to RCNAS less engine 1918

8126   Deld CSD White City 11.15; Dover 24.8.16; Erecting 20.10.16; Dunkerque 15.11.16; Hit mainsail of sailing boat on TO and wrecked Dunkerque 11.12.16 (FSL R Graham)

8127   Deld Scapa in HMS *Helmsman* 2.12.15; HMS *Campania* 6.7.16; Tail float burst, chassis strut damaged 6.9.16 (F/Cdr L Tomkinson); Scapa 21.12.16; HMS *Campania* by 3.7.17; Scapa 16.7.17; Deleted W/E 13.6.18

8128   Deld CSD White City 11.15; Sopwith by 31.5.16 - @30.6.16; Transferred to French Govt 4.16

8129   Deld CSD White City 11.15; Sopwith by 31.5.16 - @30.6.16; Transferred to French Govt 4.16

8130   Deld CSD White City 11.15; Killingholme 12.5.16; AZP 24.5.17; HACP 27.5.17; 1 SD store, King Street, Hammersmith W/E 27.5.18 - @25.7.18

8131   Deld CSD White City 11.15; Killingholme 12.5.16; AZP 2.8.16 (FSL GH Simpson); Attacked Zeppelin off Spurn Head 19.8.16 (FSL CE Fox); For HMS *Killingholme* 24.9.16 - 8.10.16; Wrecked, deleted 5.11.16

8132   Deld CSD White City 11.15; Yarmouth 7.6.16; AZP 2.8.16 (F/L CE Wood); AZP 24.9.16 (F/L CJ Galpin); Stalled landing and CW 28.9.16 (FSL GH Simpson unhurt); Deleted 17.10.16

8133   Deld Yarmouth for erection 25.7.16; Damaged float 8.8.16 (FSL GH Bittles); HMS *Halcyon* 19.12.16; Yarmouth 19.12.16; HMS *Halcyon* in tow 27.12.16; Yarmouth 27.12.16; HMS *Halcyon* 10.1.17; Yarmouth 31.1.17; HMS *Halcyon* 23.2.17; HSMP 23.2.17 (FSL HB Smith); Petrol shortage, towed into Harwich from HM 'P' boat *No.20* 24.2.17 (FSL HB Smith); Yarmouth (via Felixstowe) 24.2.17; HMS *Halcyon* 24.3.17; Yarmouth 25.3.17; HACP 30.3.17 (FSL GH Bittles); AZP 22.7.17 (FSL AM FitzRandolph); Deleted 23.2.18

8134   Retained Fairey Hamble by 31.5.16; Tested 26-28.6.16; For repair 23.10.16; Conv Hamble Baby prototype, completed 10.16 with c/n F.129; Tested 11.16; Design Flt Eastchurch for erection 19.1.17; Eastchurch Workshops by 3.17; Eastchurch FS 6.3.17; Gunnery School Flts Eastchurch 14.3.17; Eastchurch Workshops 2.6.17 and deleted

8135   To Sopwith 7.6.16 (fit 110-hp Clerget); CSD White City by 31.7.16; Shipped to Mediterranean; Port Said to HMS *Ben-my-Chree* 13.9.16; Shot down in flames by enemy aircraft E of El Arish 17.9.16 (F/L JT Bankes-Price killed)

8136   Deld CSD; Retd 7.6.16; 12.16 order Sopwith fit 110-hp

8137   Clerget; Deleted by 1.17

8137   Blackburn by 30.6.16; Deld Nore War Flt Felixstowe 17.11.16; HACP 21.4.17 (FSL JL Gordon); AGP 25.5.17; AZP 17.6.17; Killingholme 8.9.17; 1 SD store, King Street, Hammersmith W/E 24.5.18 - @25.7.18

8138   Deld CSD White City by 30.6.16; Dover 19.8.16; Dunkerque 1.9.16; HMS *Riviera* 20.10.16; Dunkerque 3.11.16; Lost 10 miles N of Ostend 16.11.16

8139   Deld Yarmouth and accepted 2.12.15 (Hawker); Fitting dart droppers 12.15; HACP 31.3.16 (FSL E Cadbury); HMT *Kingfisher* 31.3.16 (FSL E Cadbury); Yarmouth 1.4.16; HACPs 21.5.16 (F/L CE Wood), 24.5.16 (FSL FN Halsted) & 26.5.16 (FSL JC Northrop); Wrecked on patrol, towed to harbour but sank 26.5.16 (FSL JC Northrop? unhurt); Deleted 9.6.16

8140   (100-hp Clerget 9Z) Deld Yarmouth and accepted 2.12.15 Hawker; Tested 17.12.15; HMT *Cantatrice* 21.2.16; Yarmouth 22.2.16; HMT *Cantatrice* 2.3.16; Yarmouth 3.3.16; AZP, FL 40m off Dutch coast and brought ashore by Dutch trawler *Sch 187* to Scheveningen, Zuid Holland 25.4.16 (FSL SG Beare retd later); M/c interned in Holland and used by MLD as 'T-1'

8141   Deld Kingston to Killingholme for erection 29.11.15; For HMS *Killingholme* 7.4.16 - 4.6.16, 8.16, 15-20.9.16 & 23.9.16; Under repair 24.9.16; Damaged by 1.4.17; O/t on water 23.5.17; Deleted 2.6.17

8142   Deld Killingholme for erection 7.12.15; Tested 5.1.16 (Pickles); HMS *Engadine* (loan) 23.4.16; Killingholme 25.4.16 (for HMS *Killingholme*); COL, wrecked Scarborough 20.7.16 (pilot unhurt); Deleted 20.7.16

8143   Deld Grain by rail 3.12.15; HSPP 19.3.16 (F/Cdr HM Cave-Browne-Cave); HMS *Vindex* 13.4.16; TO for Tondern raid, crashed into mast of HMS *Goshawk* off Schleswig-Holstein, 4.5.16 (F/L ON Walmesley killed), deleted

8144   Deld Grain by rail 3.12.15; Accepted 6.1.16 (Hawker); Exp Flt Grain 1.4.16; Tested 21.6.16 & 8.7.16; Instructional airframe, RNAS Experimental Workshop Battersea 26.7.16 - @28.2.17

8145   Deld Grain by lorry 5.12.15; HACP 20.3.16 (F/L AR Arnold); HMS *Vindex* 13.4.16; Grain 4.16; Eastchurch 17.4.16 (transit); Felixstowe to HMS *Vindex* 18.4.16; EF on TO for Tondern raid, recovered 4.5.16 (FSL WR Mackenzie); Grain to HMS *Vindex* 22.5.16; Killingholme 25.5.16; HMS *Vindex* 17.6.16; Dunkerque 24.6.16; Dover 14.8.16 (reconstruction); Dunkerque 16.10.16; HMS *Riviera* 3.11.16; Dunkerque 12.11.16; Dover 4.4.17; AGPs 4.7.17 & 7.7.17 (FSL HH Gonyou); Damaged 12.8.17; Capsized Dover harbour, salved 4.12.17 (pilot unhurt); Westgate 6.2.18 (Grain pilot); Deleted W/E 9.5.18

8146   Deld Grain by lorry 4.12.15; Accepted 5.1.16 (Hawker); Westgate 28.4.16; HACPs 9.7.16 (F/L NS Douglas), 30.7.16 (F/L EJ Burling), 22.9.16 (F/L EJ Burling), 23.9.16 (F/L EJ Burling), 23.10.16 (F/Cdr NS Douglas also FSL WN Tees x 2), 28.11.16 (FSL CG Bronson x 2) & 14.2.17 (FSL CG Bronson); HSPPs 16.2.17 (FSL CG Bronson), 1.3.17, 16.3.17 (FSL CG Bronson); AGPs 25.5.17 (FSL LG Maxton) & 1.6.17 (FSL HC Lemon later FSL EB Drake); AGP, aircraft damaged alighting off Margate 21.8.17 (FSL LG Maxton unhurt); Deleted W/E 8.9.17

8147   Deld Killingholme for erection 10.12.15; Tested 5.1.16 (Pickles); For HMS *Killingholme* 7.4.16; Wrecked 27.4.16 (TFSL DG Broad & TFSL AJ Boddy both killed); Deleted 5.5.16

8148   Deld Killingholme for erection 10.12.15; For HMS *Killinghome* 25.4.16; For HMS *Killinghome* 21-22.9.16; Under repair 23.9.16; AZP 31.7.17 - 1.8.17; AZP 3.8.17 (FSL KN Smith); Seriously damaged 8.8.17; Surveyed 17.10.17; Deleted 26.10.17 TL

8149   Deld Yarmouth 25.1.16; Accepted but EF 27.1.16 (Hawker); HMS *Christopher* 28.5.16 & 31.5.16; HACP 4.7.16 (F/L CE Wood); HACP 10.7.16 (FSL GH Bittles); HAP 21.7.16 (FSL CJ Galpin); AZP from HMS *Brocklesby* 2.8.16 (FSL GH Bittles); HACP 17.9.16 (FSL GH Simpson); Attacked Zeppelin (possibly *L21*) 30m E of Lowestoft, returned due to darkness 23.9.16 (F/L CJ Galpin); HMS *Halcyon* 4.4.17; Yarmouth 4.17; HMS *Halcyon* 18.4.17; Yarmouth (via Southwold)

24.4.17; HSMPs 12.5.17 & 23.5.17 (FSL HB Smith); AZP 24.5.17 (FSL HB Smith); AZP 4.7.17; HACP 13.11.17 (FSL JC Grant); still Yarmouth @30.3.18

8150   Deld Yarmouth 24.1.16; Accepted 27.1.16 (Hawker); HMT *Brocklesby* 26.4.16; Yarmouth 27.4.16; HMS *Brocklesby* 29.4.16; Yarmouth 30.4.16; HMT *Kingfisher* 31.5.16; Yarmouth 31.5.16; Dismantling Yarmouth 18.8.16; Re-erecting 31.8.16; HSMP 17.12.16 (F/L CJ Galpin); HMS *Halcyon* 10.2.17; HSMPs 10&11.2.17 (FSL GH Bittles); Yarmouth 13.2.17; HMS *Dryad* 13.3.17; Yarmouth 15.3.17; HMS *Dryad* 15.3.17; Yarmouth 16.3.17; HMS *Dryad* 17.3.17; Yarmouth 18.3.17; AZP 24.5.17 (FSL HB Brenton); HMS *Dryad* 3.6.17; Yarmouth 5.6.17; Deleted W/E 29.9.17

8151   Deld Grain 11.12.15; Accepted 5.1.16 (Hawker); Nore Flt Grain by 24.4.16; HSPPs 24.4.16 (F/L EdeC Hallifax), also 3.5.16 & 20.5.16 (both F/Cdr HM Cave-Browne-Cave); Felixstowe (exptl installation of synchronised Lewis gun on upper starboard longeron); Capsized and wrecked returning from patrol 21.5.16; Deleted 17.6.16

8152   Deld Felixstowe 24.12.15; Ready for test 10.1.16; Tested 26.1.16 (Hawker); HMS *Vindex* 9.2.16; Felixstowe 22.2.16; HMS *Vindex* 1.3.16; Felixstowe 14.3.16; HMS *Vindex* 23.3.16; Dropped 4x16-lb bombs in raid on Hoyer Airship Base but shot down off Schleswig-Holstein and badly damaged 25.3.16 (F/L LP Openshaw); Salved (deletion recommended 28.3.16); Felixstowe 3.4.16; retd ship but seriously damaged 11.4.16; Retd Felixstowe, to be deleted 19.5.16

8153   Deld Felixstowe 24.12.15; Ready for test 10.1.16; Tested 26.1.16 (Hawker); HMS *Vindex* 9.2.16; Felixstowe 22.2.16; HMS *Vindex* 2.3.16; Felixstowe 14.3.16; HMS *Vindex* 23.3.16; Dropped 4x16-lb bombs in raid on Hoyer Airship Base, FTR to ship 25.3.16 (FSL JF Hay PoW)

8154   Deld Killingholme 21.12.15; Tested 5.1.16 (Pickles); For HMS *Killingholme* 25.4.16 & 30.4.16; AZP 19.8.16 (FSL KN Smith); Deleted 12.12.16

8155   Deld Killingholme 21.12.15; To HMS *Killingholme* but lost in Humber 21.4.16 (TPFSL W Hocking killed); Deleted 5.5.16

8156   Deld Yarmouth by rail 27.12.15; Accepted 27.1.16 (Hawker); Wrecked hoisting aboard HMT *Cantatrice* in tideway 23.3.16 (S/L E Cadbury); Deleted 15.4.16

8157   Deld Yarmouth by rail 27.12.15; Accepted 27.1.16 (Hawker); HMT *Kingfisher* 5.3.16; Yarmouth 7.3.16; Felixstowe 16.4.16; HMS *Vindex* 16.4.16; Felixstowe 17.4.16; HMS *Vindex* 28.4.16; HMS *Engadine* (temp loan) 2.5.16; Killingholme 6.5.16; Yarmouth 8.5.16; Felixstowe 10.5.16; HMS *Vindex* 10.5.16; Killingholme 25.5.16; HMS *Vindex* 16.6.16; Dunkerque 24.6.16; Dover 1.11.16 (reconstruction); Dunkerque 9.2.17; Dover 28.4.17; Dunkerque 4.6.17; HMS *Riviera* 5.6.17; Dover 8.6.17; AGP 13.6.17; Deleted 25.7.17 beyond repair

8158   Deld Grain by lorry 29.12.15; Accepted 5.1.16 (Hawker); HMS *Vindex* 13.4.16; Participated Tondern raid, EF, FL, capsized, recovered wrecked 12m NE of Nieuport 4.5.16 (FSL CW Scott) [but Dunkerque operations report says FSL R Graham]; Deleted 13.5.16

8159   Deld Grain by lorry 29.12.15; HMS *Vindex* 13.4.16; EF, FL damaged chassis after bombing submarine, Thorpeness, towed to shore 25.4.16 (FSL JA Sadler); Capsized after TO for Tondern raid, off Schleswig-Holstein 4.5.16 (FSL JA Sadler picked up by destroyer HMS *Goshawk*); Deleted 5.5.16

8160   Deld Grain 6.1.16; Accepted 7.1.16 (Hawker); HMT *Brocklesby* (via Yarmouth) 27.4.16 & 29-30.4.16; Nore Flt Grain by 4.16 (exp armament installation - upward 45 degrees firing Lewis gun attached to port centre section strut); HACPs 9.7.16 (F/Cdr HM Cave-Browne-Cave), 22.9.16 (FSL FE Sandford) & 28.10.16 [friendly] (S/Cdr HM Cave-Browne-Cave); HACP 16.2.17 (F/L JSF Morrison); HSPP 1.3.17 (F/L FE Sandford); AGP but EF, FL nr Nore LV 13.6.17 (FSL JM McCleary); Nore Flt Westgate 15.6.17; AGP 22.7.17; Deleted W/E 2.3.18

8161   Deld Killingholme for erection 7.1.16; AZP 1.7.16; Hornsea sub-stn 16.8.17; Killingholme by 8.9.17 (still

8162    Hornsea really?); Deleted W/E 22.2.18

8162    Deld Killingholme for erection 7.1.16; Wrecked en route HMS *Engadine*, hoisted in 17.4.16; Deleted 15.5.16

8163    Deld Yarmouth 24.1.16; Tested 28.1.16 (Hawker); HMT *Cantatrice* 5.3.16; Yarmouth 7.3.16; HMT *Cantatrice* 23.3.16; Yarmouth 25.3.16; HACP 31.3.16 (F/L HB Smith); AZP 1.4.16 (F/L CE Wood); HACP, wrecked landing in fog 3.4.16 (F/L HB Smith); Deleted 24.4.16

8164    Deld Yarmouth 25.1.16; Tested 28.1.16 (Hawker); Accepted 20.4.16 (Ding); HMPS *Brocklesby* 20.4.16; Yarmouth 23.4.16; HMT *Kingfisher* 28.4.16; HMPS *Brocklesby* 29.4.16; Yarmouth 1.5.16; HMT *Killingholme* 28.5.16 only; HACPs 3.7.16 (F/L CE Wood), 9.7.16 (F/L FGD Hards), 10.7.16 (F/L CE Wood) & 10.7.16 (FSL EL Pulling); HACPs from HMPS *Brocklesby* 29.7.16 & 1.8.16 (FSL GH Bittles); U/c crashed landing, salved, CW 1.8.16 (FSL GH Bittles); Deleted 16.8.16

8165    Deld Felixstowe & tested 8.2.16 (Hawker); Fitted centrally mounted synchronised Lewis gun; Reconnaissance 25.4.16 (landed Yarmouth); Deleted 2.5.16

8166    Deld Felixstowe & tested 8.2.16 (Hawker); Nore War Flt Felixstowe 15.8.16; Killingholme 6.9.17 (crashed on arrival); Deleted W/E 15.9.17

8167    Deld Grain by lorry 28.1.16; Accepted 3.2.16 (Hawker); HMS *Vindex* 13.4.16; Felixstowe 16.4.16; HMS *Vindex* 17.4.16; Felixstowe 25.4.16; HMS *Vindex* 27.4.16; Left for Tondern raid but propeller broke on TO, recovered 4.5.16 (FSL HF Towler); Killingholme 25.5.16; HMS *Vindex* 16.6.16; Dunkerque 24.6.16; Dover 22.10.16; HACP/fighting patrol to Dunkerque, stayed there 23.10.16 (FSL HGR Malet); Deleted by 1.17

8168    Deld Grain by lorry 28.1.16; Accepted 3.2.16 (Hawker); Nore War Flt Grain by 24.4.16; HACP 3.5.16; HSPP 20.5.16 (FSL HGR Malet); HACP [friendly] 28.10.16 (F/L LP Halpin); HACP 28.11.16 (F/L EdeC Hallifax); AGPs 25.5.17 & 13.6.17 (both FSL WF Dickson); Nore Flt Westgate 15.6.17; Deleted W/E 2.3.18

8169    Deld ex Sopwith Southampton to Calshot 19.2.16; to Armstrong Whitworth 21.7.16

8170    Deld Calshot 5.2.16; CW 15.5.17 [see 8362]; Deleted 24.5.17

8171    Unpacked and erected Felixstowe 4.4.16; Wrecked en route HMS *Vindex* 7.4.16 (F/L ON Walmsley); Repaired; Flown at Felixstowe 15.5.16; Dover 20.6.16; Dunkerque 1.7.16; Dover 31.8.16; Dunkerque 24.12.16; Shot down 6m NE of Dunkerque 23.4.17 (F/Cdr WL Welsh unhurt); Deleted 1.6.17

8172    Deld HMS *Campania* for erection by 29.4.16; Scapa 10.5.16; HMS *Campania* 30.5.16; Scapa 26.7.16; Collided with seagull and damaged wing by 1.8.16; HMS *Campania* 14.8.16; Scapa 30.8.16; HMS *Campania* 19.10.16; Scapa 20.10.16; HMS *Campania* 23.10.16; Scapa 21.11.16; HMS *Campania* 8.3.17 - @31.3.17; Scapa by 4.17; HMS *Campania* 17.4.17; Wrecked 24.4.17 (and 1.5.17); LM 31.5.17; Rosyth to CSD White City by 3.11.17 for deletion

8173    Deld Yarmouth by road 6.2.16; Accepted 31.3.16 (Hawker); [Felixstowe to Killingholme 6.4.16]; Fitting dart droppers 25.4.16; HMT *Kingfisher* 26.4.16 & 29.4.16; HACP 26.5.16 (FSL GH Bittles); Capsized off slipway on TO, engine salved 6.7.16 (FSL CJ Galpin unhurt); Deleted 15.7.16

8174    Deld Killingholme 18.3.16; To HMS *Killingholme* 22.4.16; For HMS *Killingholme* 25.4.16 & 30.4.16; Deleted 10.6.16

8175    Deld CSD White City 16.2.16; Killingholme for erection 6.4.16; HMS *Engadine* 11.4.16; Dundee store 13.5.16; HMS *Engadine* 16.5.16; Dundee 7.9.16; HMS *Engadine* 8.9.16; Damaged and to Port Laing 20.9.16; Severely damaged by gale by 24.10.16; HMS *Engadine* 3.7.17; Hawk Craig 25.7.17; Rosyth 3.8.17; Surveyed 11.10.17; Deleted 13.10.17 W&T; Remains to CSD White City

8176    Deld CSD White City 16.2.16; Killingholme for erection 6.4.16; HMS *Engadine* 11.4.16; Dundee store 13.5.16; HMS *Engadine* 23.8.16; Dundee 7.9.16; HMS *Engadine* 8.9.16; Dundee 30.3.17; Rosyth by rail 9.8.17; Surveyed 11.10.17; Deleted 13.10.17 W&T; Remains to

CSD White City

8177    Deld CSD White City 18.2.16; Killingholme for erection 6.4.16; HMS *Engadine* 11.4.16; Dundee store 13.5.16; *Engadine* 20.9.16; Wrecked on landing by 24.10.16; Deleted, gale damage 28.11.16

8178    Deld Killingholme for erection 10.4.16; HMS *Engadine* 11.4.16; O/t on TO 16.4.16 (F/L FJ Rutland); Deleted 20.4.16

8179    Unpacked and erected Felixstowe 4.4.16; HMS *Vindex* 11.4.16; Felixstowe 16.4.16; HMS *Vindex* 18.4.16; Dropped 2x65-lb bombs in Tondern Raid, results unknown 4.5.16 (F/L LP Openshaw); Killingholme 25.5.16; HMS *Vindex* 16.6.16; Dunkerque 24.6.16; EF, FL alongside HMS *Riviera*, capsized hoisting aboard 16m N of Zeebrugge 13.9.16 (FSL FAR Malet); Deleted 17.9.16

8180    Deld without engine for assembly HMS *Engadine* 25.4.16; Dundee store 13.5.16; HMS *Engadine* 21.8.16 (repair); Dundee 6.2.17 (repair); HMS *Engadine* 30.3.17; Capsized, brough in by yacht *Vigilant* 25.5.17 (FSL GCB Cotterell); Deleted 5.6.17

8181    Deld Felixstowe by 22.4.16 for erection of HMS *Vindex*; Deld without engine for assembly HMS *Engadine* 25.4.16; Felixstowe 9.5.16 for HMS *Vindex*; HMS *Vindex*, packing for Dover 29.6.16; Dover for erection 17.7.16; Dunkerque 25.7.16; HMS *Riviera* 20.10.16; To Dunkerque, but flew into sea 300yds from ship, believed non-synchronised bullet hit propeller 12.11.16 (FSL FAR Malet killed); Deleted by 1.17

8182    Deld HMS *Engadine* 26.4.16; Dundee store 13.5.16; HMS *Engadine* 16.5.16; Dundee 23.8.16; HMS *Engadine* from/by 15.1.17; Dundee 3.5.17; HMS *Engadine* 25.5.17; Hawk Craig 2.7.17; Rosyth 3.8.17; Surveyed 11.10.17; Deleted 13.10.17 W&T; Remains to CSD White City BUT Dover, crashed in sea off Grain, lost 4.12.17 (FSL JA Morell picked up by TBD) [incorrect serial - or rebuilt?]

8183    Deld CSD White City by rail .16; Scapa for erection 10.5.16; HMS *Campania* 23.5.16; Scapa 30.5.16; HMS *Campania* 3.6.16; Scapa 26.7.16; HMS *Campania* 14.8.16; Scapa 16.8.16; HMS *Campania* 21.8.16; Scapa 21.11.16; HMS *Campania* 13.3.17; Scapa 28.3.17 (for compass adjustment); HMS *Campania* 28.3.17; Scapa W/E 13.10.17 - @19.1.18 (overhaul)

8184    Deld CSD White City by rail .16; Scapa for erection 10.5.16; HMS *Campania* 23.5.16; Scapa 3.6.16; HMS *Campania* 30.6.16; Scapa 5.7.16; HMS *Campania* 12.7.16; Arrange to go from *Campania* to Blackburns W/E 22.9.16 (NTU?); Scapa 21.11.16; HMS *Campania* 8.3.17; Pierowall 16.6.17; HMS *Campania* 19.6.17; Houton Bay/Scapa 13.10.17; Surveyed HMS *Campania* 10.12.17; Deleted 22.12.17 wrecked

8185    Transferred to French Govt less engine

8186    Deld CSD White City .16; Felixstowe 23.6.16; to Westgate but FL, floats and engine damaged, towed back from Felixstowe 4.7.16 (FSL WR Mackenzie), then deld Westgate; 2 HAPPs 23.10.16 (F/Cdr NS Douglas); HACP 1.3.17 (FSL WN Tees); AZP 23/24.5.17 (FSL HM Morris); AGPs 25.5.17 (FSL LG Maxton later FSL WJ de Salis); AGP, damaged by rough seas on landing 5.6.17 (FSL LG Maxton); Propeller burst and cut floats taking off in rough seas, machine o/t and badly damaged 7.7.17 (pilot unhurt); Deleted 8.7.17

8187    Deld CSD White City 4.16; Felixstowe 21.6.16; HACP 9.7.16 (FSL AB Helbert); AZP 2.8.16; Nore War Flt Felixstowe 15.8.16; AGP 13.6.17 (FSL AL Simms); Killingholme 8.9.17; Deleted 19.12.17 TL

8188    Deld CSD White City 4.16; Shipped to Mediterranean; EI&SS Port Said by 5.16; HMS *Ben-my-Chree* 17.5.16; Port Said 19.5.16; HMS *Ben-my-Chree* 21.12.16; Destroyed aboard ship by Turkish shelling at Castelorizo 9.1.17

8189    Deld CSD White City 4.16; Shipped to Mediterranean; EI&SS Port Said by 5.16; HMS *Ben-my-Chree* 17.5.16; Port Said 19.5.16; HMS *Ben-my-Chree* 2.6.16; Port Said 15.6.16; HMS *Raven II* 29.6.16; Port Said 28.8.16 - 1.17

8190    Deld CSD White City 4.16; Killingholme for erection 25.8.16; Fuselage to CSD White City 30.8.16; Blackburn 30.9.16 (modify and fit 110-hp Clerget); Killingholme for erection 3.2.17; HMS *Campania* for erection 17.3.17; Houton Bay 2.1.18 (storage); Scapa W/E 23.2.18 (storage); Surveyed 25.3.18; Deleted 11.5.18 W&T

**8191** Deld CSD White City 22.3.16; Killingholme for erection 25.8.16; Fuselage to CSD White City 30.8.16; Blackburn 30.9.16 (modify and fit 110-hp Clerget); Killingholme for erection 3.2.17; HMS *Campania* for erection 13.3.17; Scapa 16.7.17 - @28.9.17; Houton Bay by 10.17; Surveyed 25.3.18; Deleted 11.5.18 W&T

**8192** Deld CSD White City 22.3.16; Killingholme for erection 25.8.16; Fuselage to CSD White City 30.8.16; Blackburn 30.9.16 (modify and fit 110-hp Clerget); Killingholme for erection 3.2.17; HMS *Campania* for erection 14.3.17; HMS *Campania* by 9.17; COL, salved 4.9.17 (pilot unhurt); Scapa 17.12.17; Houton Bay by 29.12.17 - @19.1.18 (storage); HMS *Campania* to Scapa by 2.2.18 (overhaul); Deleted W/E 9.3.18

**8193** Deld CSD White City 4.3.16; Put forward for Fairey to convert for flying off deck W/E 27.10.16; to Fairey 12.16; Calshot 1.7.17; Surveyed 28.9.17; Deleted 6.10.17 W&T

**8194** Deld CSD White City 4.3.16; Grain 7.16; Eastchurch 20.7.16; CSD White City by 30.9.16; To Parnall 1.17; Calshot School by rail 24.7.17; Lee-on-Solent W/E 12.10.17; Surveyed 30.10.17; Deleted 6.11.17 wrecked

**8195** Deld CSD White City 3.16; Dover by 9.16; Dunkerque 19.9.16: Dover 7.1.17; Crashed and wrecked on TO in English Channel 14.1.17 (F/L VE Sieveking); Deleted 23.1.17 TL

**8196** Deld CSD White City 3.16; Yarmouth 23.5.16; Erecting 9.8.16; AZP, crashed and CW on beach off Coast Defence Station 24.9.16 (F/L E Cadbury slightly injured); Deleted 17.10.16

**8197** Deld CSD White City 3.16; to Blackburn 9.16 - @3.17 (modify and fit 110-hp Clerget); Transferred RCNAS less engine

**8198** Deld CSD White City by 6.16; Felixstowe 24.6.16; Wrecked 4.4.17 (FSL deCWP Ireland); Deleted 25.4.17

**8199** Deld CSD White City by 6.16; Felixstowe 24.6.16; HACP 21.4.17 (FSL GR Hodgson); Killingholme W/E 15.9.17; 1 SD Store, King Street, Hammersmith W/E 24.5.18 - @25.7.18; Yarmouth by 29.9.18 - @10.18

**8200** Tested Felixstowe 31.3.16; AZP 2.5.16; Nore War Flt Felixstowe by 8.16; Wrecked 8.8.16 (F/L JE Scott); Surveyed 15.8.16; Deleted 31.8.16

**8201** Deld CSD White City 3.16; Transferred to Japanese Govt 7.16

**8202** Deld CSD White City 3.16; Shipped to Mudros 7.16; Tested HMS *Ark Royal* 26.12.16; HMS *Empress* 29.12.16; Thasos 19.1.17; HMS *Ark Royal* 25.2.17 - @11.5.17

**8203** Deld CSD White City 3.16; Shipped to Mudros 7.16; HMS *Ark Royal* by 11.4.17; Surveyed 24.9.17; Deleted 16.10.17 DBR

**8204** Deld CSD White City 3.16 - @23.9.16; Blackburn by 30.9.16 - @3.17; Transferred to RCNAS less engine

**8205** Deld CSD White City 4.16; to Blackburn 9.16 - @3.17; Calshot FS for erection 29.6.17; Surveyed 15.10.17; Deleted 16.10.17 wrecked

**8206** Deld Killingholme 12.5.16; AZP 30-31.7.16; Deleted 29.8.16

**8207** Deld Killingholme 12.5.16; For HMS *Killingholme* 21.9.16 - 8.10.16; Wrecked 18.6.17; Deleted 24.6.17 BR

**8208** Deld CSD White City 4.16; to Blackburn 9.16; Calshot for erection 11.7.17; Deleted W/E 14.9.17

**8209** Deld CSD White City 4.16; to Blackburn 9.16 - @3.17; Transferred to RCNAS less engine; Later to US Navy as *A407*

**8210** Deld CSD White City 4.16; Calshot FS 1.12.16 - @23.9.16; Lee-on-Solent by 10.17; Surveyed 25.11.17; Deleted 3.12.17 wrecked

**8211** Deld CSD White City 4.16; Calshot FS for erection 24.11.16; Badly damaged 6.6.17; Deleted 19.6.17

**8212** Deld CSD White City 4.16; Calshot FS 5.12.16; Deleted W/E 14.9.17

**8213** Deld CSD White City 4.16; Calshot FS for erecting 24.11.16; Badly damaged landing 12.4.17; Deleted 25.4.17

**8214** Deld CSD White City 4.16; Transferred to Italian Govt as pattern 7.16

**8215** Deld CSD White City 4.16; Transferred to Italian Govt as pattern 7.16

**8216** Deld CSD White City W/E 3.6.16; Dismantled there for spares 7.17

**8217** Deld CSD White City W/E 3.6.16; Dismantled there for spares 7.17

[A new Baby tested Dardanelles 17.5.16. Not identified]

**12 SHORT ADMIRALTY 827 TYPE TRACTOR BIPLANE SEAPLANES** ordered under Cont No C.P.48104/15 from George Parnall & Co [Parnall & Sons], numbered 8218 to 8229 & built Bristol. (150-hp Sunbeam Crusader)

**8218** (High chassis) Presentation a/c "Shanghai Britons No.3" 7.15. Deld Grain 28.11.15; Accepted 5.12.15; Packing by Mkrs 30.12.15; Shipped to Mombasa for 7 Sqdn 18.1.16; Arrived 3.16; SS *Clan MacPherson* to 8 Sqdn Zanzibar 5.16; At Zanzibar 1.5.16; Operations from HMS *Manica* to 9.2.17 and from HMS *Laconia*; Deleted by 13.11.16 (sic)

**8219** Shipped to East Africa; 8 Sqdn Zanzibar; Transferred to Belgian Govt and served in Belgian Congo; later to Calais .18

**8220** Presentation a/c "New York Britons No.1" 7.15. Deld Yarmouth by rail 21.1.16; Accepted 26.1.16; FTR HSPP 15.2.16 (FSL BR Lee & TFSL HJ Page both drowned); Deleted 2.16

**8221** Deld Yarmouth by rail 28.1.16; Tested 1.2.16 (Pickles); To Killingholme, but EF, FL NE of Winthorpe, nr Skegness 8.2.16; Returned Yarmouth in tow of drifter, wings and tail badly damaged 9.2.16 (FSL CA Eyre spent two nights drifting in machine); Calshot by rail and lighter 17.4.16; Accepted 29.4.16; Portland 16.10.16; Calshot 13.1.17; Deleted 9.2.17

**8222** Deld Yarmouth for erection 3.2.16; Accepted 9.2.16 (Pickles); HSMP 24.3.16 (F/L CE Wood & LM Hooks); Left to bomb German High Seas Fleet raiding Scarborough, returned in tow 25.4.16 (FSL GH Bittles); HSMP 12.7.16 (F/L BD Kilner & AM Money); Deleted 5.1.18

**8223** Deld Yarmouth for erection 11.2.16; Accepted 13.2.16 (Pickles); EF, FL Winterton 3.8.16; AZP 26.9.16 (F/Cdr V Nicholl & S/L VH Ridewood); Calshot 8.9.17; Lee-on-Solent by 1.11.17; Surveyed 10.12.17 wrecked; Deleted 14.12.17

**8224** Deld by rail to Yarmouth 14.2.16; Accepted 20.2.16 (Pickles); Grain 7.4.16; Deleted 18.6.16

**8225** (DC for training) Deld by rail to Yarmouth 25.2.16; Accepted 2.3.16 (Pickles); Grain 29.3.16; Calshot 23.4.16 - @28.9.17; Lee-on-Solent by 10.17; Surveyed Calshot 10.12.17; Deleted 14.12.17 DBR [Possibly the aircraft which flew into a steam barge, TFSL G Towers DoI 7.11.17 - or could be 3323]

**8226** (DC for training). Deld Yarmouth 1.3.16; Accepted 17.3.16 (Pickles); Killingholme 23.3.16 (160-hp Sunbeam 4.17); Felixstowe (via Yarmouth) 10.5.18; Calshot TS 11.5.18; 209 TDS Lee-on-Solent W/E 7.6.18; Deleted W/E 11.7.18

**8227** (DC for training). Deld by rail to Yarmouth 9.3.16; Accepted 17.3.16 (Pickles); Killingholme 30.3.16; Crashed 13.6.17; Deleted 18.6.17

**8228** (DC for training). Deld by rail to Yarmouth 18.3.16; Accepted 30.3.16 (Pickles); Westgate 3.5.16 (transit); Calshot TS 4.5.16; Float and chassis damaged 7.6.17; Deleted W/E 13.6.18

**8229** (Dual control for training). Deld by rail to Yarmouth 23.3.16; Accepted 30.3.16 (Pickles); Calshot 21.4.16, remaining Portland 24.9.16; Calshot 25.9.16 - @28.9.17; A Flt Lee-on-Solent by 9.17; Became 209 TDS Lee-on-Solent 1.4.18; Deleted W/E 27.4.18

**8 SHORT ADMIRALTY 827 TYPE TRACTOR BIPLANE SEAPLANES** ordered under Cont No C.P.32600/15 dated 12.2.15 from Brush Electrical Engineering Co Ltd, numbered 8230 to 8237 & built Loughborough. (150-hp Sunbeam Crusader)

**8230** (160-hp) Deld HMS *Campania* by 13.3.17 - @22.3.17; Scapa .17 (true up W/T set); HMS *Campania* 6.4.17; Dismantled for transport to Fraserburgh 5.5.17; Scapa 16.7.17; Calshot 24.12.17; HMS *Campania* by 12.17;

Scapa by 1.18; HMS *Campania* W/E 26.1.18; Calshot by 23.2.18; HMS *Campania* by 3.18; Calshot by 3.18; Lee-on-Solent W/E 6.3.18; Became 209 TDS Lee-on-Solent 1.4.18; Beached with broken float [no date]; Deleted W/E 29.8.18

8231 (160-hp) Deld HMS *Campania* by 13.3.17; Tested Scapa 24.3.17; Calshot 24.12.17; HMS *Campania* by 29.12.17 - @2.18; Calshot by 23.2.18; Lee-on-Solent W/E 6.3.18; Became 209 TDS Lee-on-Solent 1.4.18; Deleted W/E 27.6.18

8232 Deld Grain by 23.2.17; Design Flt Grain & accepted 23.2.17; Westgate 10.6.17 (engine trouble en route Calshot); Calshot training 12.6.17 - @28.9.17; Lee-on-Solent by 9.17; Surveyed 30.10.17; Deleted 6.11.17 wrecked

8233 Deld Grain by rail 15.2.17; Design Flt Grain and accepted 23.2.17; Experimental Design Grain 2.3.17; Dover 7.6.17 (transit); Calshot training 8.6.17; Deleted W/E 14.9.17

8234 Deld Grain by 20.2.17; Calshot training 9.6.17 (arr 10.6.17); Deleted W/E 14.9.17

8235 Deld Grain by rail 23.2.17; Calshot training 11.6.17 (arr 12.6.17) - @28.9.17; Lee by 10.17 - @1.11.17; Calshot, Surveyed 10.12.17 DBR; Deleted 14.12.17

8236 Deld Dundee for erection 26.2.17; Accepted 3.3.17; Deleted W/E 8.9.17

8237 (150-hp) Modified (how?); Deld Calshot by lorry 24.2.17 - @28.9.17; Seaplane Training School Lee-on-Solent by 10.17; Became 209 TDS Lee-on-Solent 1.4.18; Deleted W/E 16.1.19

**12 HENRY FARMAN F.27 "ALL STEEL" PUSHER BIPLANES purchase authorised from Aéroplanes Farman in France & numbered 8238 to 8249. (140-hp Canton Unné)**

8238 to 8243 transferred to RFC and left England 3.4.15 for SAAC. All in use by 9.15 - 12.15

8244 In transit to East Indies 5.15 - 6.15; 3 Sqdn/Wing Tenedos/Imbros by 31.7.15 - @31.10.15; Transit to UK 1.16, then deleted

8245 In transit to East Indies 5.15 - 6.15; 3 Sqdn/Wing Tenedos/Imbros by 31.7.15 - @30.11.15 BUT lost in transit from Paris to Mudros 1915; Deleted 28.11.1<u>7</u> (sic - presume original paperwork lost in transit)

8246 A Sqdn 1 Wing St.Pol by 20.6.15; Deleted 8.15

8247 A Sqdn 1 Wing St.Pol by 20.6.15; Deleted 9.15

8248 A Sqdn 1 Wing St.Pol by 20.6.15; Deleted 9.15

8249 Shipped to Aegean; 3 Wing Tenedos/Imbros by 6.15 - @30.11.15 BUT lost in transit from Paris to Mudros 1915; Deleted 28.11.1<u>7</u> [VERY later paperwork!]

**8 SHORT ADMIRALTY 827 TYPE TRACTOR BIPLANE SEAPLANES ordered 14.10.15 under Cont No C.P.48104/15 from George Parnall & Co [Parnall & Sons], numbered 8250 to 8257 & built Bristol. (150-hp Sunbeam Crusader)**

8250 (Fitted DC for training) Deld Yarmouth by rail 25.3.16; Calshot and accepted 20.4.16; Deleted 1.12.16

8251 Deld Grain 8.4.16 (gunnery trials); Exptl Flt Grain, awaiting acceptance 16.6.16; Accepted 1.8.16 & 18.8.16 (Pickles); Exptl Flt Grain by 20.10.16 (awaiting erection); PVRS Grain 3.12.16; Felixstowe 15.4.17 (engine trouble); Ventnor Bay overnight, lost 20.4.17; Grain 21.4.17; Dover 25.1.18; Newhaven & Hastings 27.1.18 en route Calshot; Lee-on-Solent School W/E 7.2.18 (ex Calshot); Became 209 TDS Lee-on-Solent 1.4.18 (160-hp Sunbeam); Deleted W/E 27.6.18

8252 Deld Felixstowe 20.5.16; Tested 25.5.16 (Pickles); Nore Flt Felixstowe by 14.8.16; EF, FL, damaged 29.9.16 (FSL JC Railton & AM Mortimore); Parnall 18.10.16 (overhaul and repair); Westgate & tested 23.2.17 (Prodger); Westgate Repair Base by 13.10.17; Calshot 4.11.17; Surveyed 10.12.17 ; Deleted 14.12.17 wrecked

8253 Deld 5.16; Transit to Cape Sqdn by 30.9.16; arr 8 Sqdn Zanzibar 6.11.16 (Chukwani by 8.3.17; to Lindi 6.17; retd Zanzibar 13.6.17); For deletion by 16.3.18

8254 Deld Calshot 29.5.16; Transit to Cape Sqdn by 30.9.16; arr 8 Sqdn Zanzibar 6.11.16; HMS *Manica* 23.11.16; Slightly damaged hoisting aboard 30.11.16 (FSL EE Deans & Lt ECW Fitzherbert RNVR unhurt); Chukwani

22.12.16; HMS *Manica* 23.12.16; HMS *Himalaya* 6.1.17; EF, FL in creek, set on fire, nr Kiombini 6.1.17 (F/L ER Moon swam ashore POW, Cdr The Hon OBR Bridgeman DSO drowned 9.1.17); Wreckage to HMS *Himalaya* from whaler *Salamander* 7.1.17; Put ashore 8.1.17

8255 Deld Calshot FS 10.6.16; 209 TDS Lee-on-Solent W/E 17.5.18; Deleted W/E 12.9.18

8256 Deld by rail to Dundee 25.6.16; Tested 6.7.16; COL, submerged, salving 30.3.17 (FSL TA Gladstone unhurt, S/L DG McGregor slightly injured); Deleted 10.4.17

8257 Deld by rail to Dundee 30.6.16; Tested 6.7.16; Deleted 25.8.17

**11 BURGESS TYPE O ("GUNBUS") PUSHER BIPLANES purchased from Burgess, numbered 8258 to 8268 & built Marblehead, Mass. (140-hp Sturtevant)**

8258 Deld CSD White City; Hendon 17.3.16; Preliminary test 30.3.16; Dismantled for CSD White City 15.4.16 (repacked 26.4.16); Condemned 5.16

8259 Deld CSD White City; Hendon for erection 24.3.16; Tested; Packed for CSD White City 24.4.16; Condemned 5.16

8260 Deld CSD White City; Hendon for erection 29.3.16; Tested; Packed for CSD White City 24.4.16; Condemned 5.16

8261 Deld CSD White City; Hendon for erection 1.4.16; Tested; Packed for CSD White City 24.4.16; Condemned 5.16

8262 Deld CSD White City; Hendon for erection 12.4.16; Tested; Packed for CSD White City 24.4.16; Condemned 5.16

8263 Deld Hendon 15.4.16; Tested; Packed for CSD White City 24.4.16; Retd unpacked to CSD White City 29.5.16 for deletion

8264 Deld Hendon and to CSD White City by lorry 25.4.16; Condemned 5.16

8265 Deld CSD White City; Condemned 5.16
8266 Deld CSD White City; Condemned 5.16
8267 Deld CSD White City; Condemned 5.16
8268 Deld CSD White City; Condemned 5.16

**12 THOMAS T.2 TRACTOR BIPLANE TRAINERS purchased from Thomas Bros Aeroplane Co Inc, Ithaca, New York, numbered 8269 to 8280. All deleted by 1.17. (90-hp Curtiss OX-5)**

8269 Deld CSD White City by 8.15; Hendon 3.2.16; Engine retd CSD by 16.2.16; Wrecked when Bessonneau tent blown away 28.3.16; Deleted 31.3.16

8270 Deld CSD White City by 8.15; Hendon, awaiting erection 5.5.16; Flown 31.5.16

8271 Deld CSD White City by 8.15

8272 to 8280 Deld CSD White City?
[2 Thomas biplanes at Hendon by 7.12.15, 1 more on 8.12.15, 2 from CSD on 10.12.15, 2 on 10.1.16 and 1 on 1.2.16. No serials quoted]

**12 WIGHT ADMIRALTY 840 TYPE TRACTOR BIPLANE SEAPLANES ordered 14.11.15 under Cont No C.P.78421/15 from Portholme Aerodrome Ltd, numbered 8281 to 8292 & built Huntingdon. All due for delivery to CSD 20.5.16. Contract stopped 5.16, remaining aircraft to be delivered without engines at maker's works. (225-hp Sunbeam Mohawk)**

8281 (High chassis) Allocated Grain 13.11.15 but NTU; Allocated Gibraltar but NTU; Deld as spares

8282 Deld Calshot 9.6.16; Deleted 15.6.16

8283 J.S.White, Cowes to Calshot 8.4.16; Deleted 15.6.16

8284 Ready by 4.16; Allocated Calshot, but NTU; Then allocated Gibraltar but NTU; Delivered as spares

8285 Ready 25.3.16; Deld CSD White City as spares by 29.5.16; Deleted 17.6.16

8286 Deld CSD White City as spares by 29.5.16
8287 Deld CSD White City as spares by 29.5.16
8288 Deld CSD White City as spares by 7.6.16
8289 Deld CSD White City as spares by 29.5.16
8290 Deld CSD White City as spares by 29.5.16
8291 Deld CSD White City as spares by 7.6.16
8292 Deld CSD White City as spares by 29.5.16

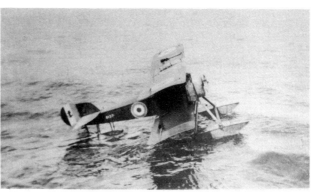

*Fairey Hamble Baby 8134 prototype conversion at Eastchurch 1917. (RAF Museum P.16153)*

*Sopwith Baby 8157 seen here with fouled anchor emblem on the rudder, was R. Graham's first aircraft, at Dunkerque Seaplane Base. (via Frank Cheesman)*

*Wight School Pusher Seaplane 8321, used at Calshot. (J.M.Bruce/G.S.Leslie collection)*

*Short Type B North Sea Scout Seaplane 8319 at Grain. (J.M.Bruce/G.S.Leslie collection)*

*Grahame-White G.W.XV 8305 at Chingford. (Wing Cdr G.H.Lewis)*

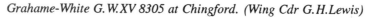

**12 ROYAL AIRCRAFT FACTORY B.E.2c TRACTOR BIPLANES ordered 24.6.15 under Cont No C.P.145397/15 from The Grahame-White Aviation Co Ltd, numbered 8293 to 8304 & built Hendon. Mkrs contracted to modify this batch W/E 23.6.16. (90-hp R.A.F.1a)**

8293    Deld & accepted Hendon 1.4.16; Grain 2.4.16; Deleted 23.5.16

8294    (Single-seater conversion for HD duties) Deld & tested Hendon 14.4.16; Eastchurch 17.4.16; War Flt Eastchurch 26.5.16; 3 Wing Manston 30.6.16; Grain 16.7.16; War Flt Eastchurch 17.7.16; EF, FL in River Swale 28.7.16 (pilot unhurt); Salved; AZP 23.9.16 (FSL AF Buck); Manston to War Flt Eastchurch 12.10.16; CSD White City to fit gun mounting 28.10.16; Wormwood Scrubbs to War Flt Eastchurch (FL Allhallows en route) 6.11.16; Observers School Flt Eastchurch 23.12.16 (100-hp); AZP 16/17.3.17; Deleted 5.12.17 W&T

8295    Deld War Flt Eastchurch 26.4.16; HSPP 3.5.16 (F/L HG Henley); AZP 25.8.16 (FSL ET Bradley); AZP, FL, badly damaged nr Sandwich 24.9.16 (F/L HG Henley); Eastchurch Workshops 24.9.16 (repair); War Flt Eastchurch 4.10.16; Deleted 15.10.16

8296    Tested Hendon 4.5.16; Grain 10.5.16; AZP 24.8.16; Manston 17.3.17; FL, wrecked 27.6.17 (FSL CH Fitzherbert)

8297    Deld Hendon to Grain 14.5.16; Tested 17.5.16; Manston War Flt/School 17.3.17; Deleted W/E 30.3.18

8298    Deld Westgate 11.6.16; Chased *LZ8* 25.4.16 (F/L CH Butler); Manston 20.6.16; AZP 31.7/1.8.16 (F/Cdr CH Butler); Chased *L31* 25.8.16 (F/L CH Butler); AZP 23.9.16 (F/Cdr CH Butler x 2); AZPs 16/17.2.17, 16/17.3.17, 23/24.5.17 & 26.6.17 (all S/Cdr CH Butler); AGPs 9.9.17, 25.9.17, 29.9.17 & 30.9.17 (all S/Cdr CH Butler); War School/Flt Manston by 10.17; Paris NAS by 29.12.17; War School/Flt Manston 1.18 - @30.3.18

8299    Deld Chingford 9.6.16; Cranwell (via Hendon) 28.9.17; Crashed Theringham 4.1.18 (pilot unhurt); FL in fog Bedford 5.1.18 (to return 6.1.18); Crashed, CW Cranwell North 11.3.18 (PFO FB Shaw injured); Surveyed 12.3.18; Deleted 16.3.18

8300    (Fitted with bomb racks under engine cowling. Later used for training) Deld Chingford 14.6.16; Cranwell 2.10.17; FL, crashed and slightly damaged Branston 8.12.17 (pilot unhurt); Surveyed 8.1.18 wrecked; Deleted 17.1.18

8301    Deld Yarmouth & tested 16.6.16; Hendon 6.16; Felixstowe 25.6.16; AZP 31.7.16; Yarmouth 7.9.16; Covehithe 15.9.16; Bacton 21.9.16; Yarmouth 23.9.16; AZP 26.9.16 (FSL CV Halford Thompson); Bacton 26.9.16; Burgh Castle 28.9.16; Yarmouth 29.9.16; Covehithe 8.10.16; Holt 16.10.16; Yarmouth 23.10.16; Covehithe 26.10.16; Yarmouth 2.11.16; Covehithe 8.11.16; Yarmouth 15.11.16; Covehithe 29.11.16; Yarmouth 15.12.16; Covehithe 28.12.16; Yarmouth 6.1.17; Bacton 13.1.17; Yarmouth 31.1.17; Holt 3.2.17; Yarmouth 11.2.17; Burgh Castle 12.2.17; Holt 28.2.17; Bacton 9.3.17; Burgh Castle 1.4.17; FL nr Gorleston, retd Burgh Castle by lorry 7.5.17 (FSL CS Nunn & G/L Ratcliffe); AZP 17.6.17 (FSL CV Halford Thompson); Covehithe 22.6.17; Holt, AZP 21/22.8.17 (FSL CV Halford Thompson); Bacton W/E 8.9.17; Yarmouth W/E 15.9.17; Deletion recommended by 16.2.18

8302    Hendon, tested by Mkrs 22.7.16; E Flt Cranwell 25.7.16; AZP 3.8.16 (F/Cdr the Master of Sempill); Wrecked 30.4.17; Wrecked 1.8.17; Spun in nr RFC Spittlegate 27.2.18 (PFO AWG Crosby DoI 10.3.18); Surveyed 1.3.18; Deleted 13.3.18

8303    Hendon, tested by Mkrs 22.7.16; Cranwell 25.7.16; Deleted 15.2.17 wrecked

8304    Erecting Hendon 11.7.16; Tested by Mkrs 24.7.16; By rail en route Mudros 8.8.16; Surveyed 11.10.17; Deleted 16.10.17 wrecked

**12 GRAHAME-WHITE XV (ADMIRALTY 1600 TYPE) PUSHER BIPLANES ordered under Cont No C.P.59745/15, numbered 8305 to 8316 & built Hendon. (Ordered with 60-hp Le Rhône per official list 12.15, but deld with 50-hp Gnome)**

8305    Deld Chingford 27.11.15; Under repair 21.4.16; Collided with 1039 and smashed 2.6.16 (pilot unhurt); Deleted 9.6.16

8306    Deld Chingford, flown 1.16; Allocation to Chingford cancelled 12.8.16, to CSD White City for survey instead

8307    Deld Eastbourne 24.1.16; Wrecked 9.2.16; Deleted 13.3.16

8308    Deld Chingford 24.1.16; to Eastchurch FS but EF, FL en route nr Chingford 31.5.16; Eastchurch Workshops to dismantle for deletion 24.10.16; Deleted 8.11.16

8309    Deld Chingford (via Cuffley) 31.1.16; Ran into tree, CW 17.5.16; Deleted 30.5.16

8310    Deld Chingford 5.2.16; Deleted 3.3.16 CW

8311    Deld Chingford 5.2.16; Hendon 19.4.16; via Chingford to Eastchurch FS 2.6.16 but EF en route, FL Laindon; Eastchurch Workshops to dismantle for deletion 24.10.16; Deleted 8.11.16

8312    Deld Chingford 10.2.16; After landing, attempted to TO again to avoid running into another aircraft, stalled, wrecked 10.5.16 (PFSL CH Butterworth); Deleted W/E 8.9.17

8313    Deld Chingford 10.2.16; Deleted 1.2.17

8314    Deld Chingford 21.2.16; Wheel came of while landing, u/c wrecked 19.6.16 (PFSL NMD Hewitt); Deleted W/E 22.9.17

8315    Deld Chingford 20.2.16; Cranwell 5.3.16, but EF, FL Bassinghurst cn route; arr Cranwell 6.3.16; arr Hendon by road 18.7.16; To CSD White City 8.16; Chingford by lorry for erection 8.11.16; CW landing 5.5.17; Deleted 15.5.17

8316    Deld Chingford 20.2.16; Deleted 30.3.16

**4 HEWLETT & BLONDEAU BIPLANES to be numbered 8317 to 8320. (Two 100-hp Clerget)**

8317 to 8320 cancelled and serials reallocated

**2 SHORT 320 (SEAPLANE TYPE A) (SHORT TYPE 310-A) TORPEDO CARRIER TRACTOR BIPLANE SEAPLANES ordered under Cont No C.P.11543/16, numbered 8317 and 8318 & built Rochester. Put forward to fit both with experimental radiators W/E 6.10.16. Put forward to fit both with exptl mainplanes 1.17. (310-hp Sunbeam) [Gordon Bruce's researches show correct c/n's S.299 & S.300]**

8317    (Fitted for launching 18-inch torpedo) Deld Grain 26.7.16 (Kemp); Shorts Rochester 1.8.16; PVRS 6.8.16; Shorts Rochester 24.8.16 (mods); PVRS 13.9.16; Tested 16.10.16; Felixstowe 22.10.16; Experimental Design Grain 8.2.17 (fit gun mounting); Became Type Test Dept Grain; Packed, then left by transport for shipment Malta 19.4.17; erecting Torpedo School Malta by 19.5.17; Crashed and written off during trials 11.6.17 (TFSL JR Bibby killed); Repairing 22.6.17 - @6.7.17, then deleted

8318    (Fitted for launching 18-inch torpedo) Deld Test Depot Grain by 31.3.17; Packed, then left by transport for shipment Malta 19.4.17; Torpedo School Malta (not arrived by 19.5.17); Wrecked, deleted by 22.6.17

**2 SHORT SEAPLANE TYPE B (NORTH SEA SCOUT) (SHORT TYPE 310-B) RECONNAISSANCE AND ZEPPELIN ATTACK TRACTOR BIPLANE SEAPLANES ordered under Cont No C.P.11543/16, numbered 8319 to 8320 & built Rochester. Order to fit DC 7.16. (310-hp Sunbeam Cossack) [Gordon Bruce's researches show correct c/n's S.311 & S.312]**

8319    Deld Grain 26.9.16; Shorts Rochester 17.10.16; Grain 20.4.17 (JL Parker) (for trials with 6- pdr Davis gun; also fitted Lewis gun); Calshot but EF, FL Bognor 4.5.17; arr Calshot 5.5.17; Deleted 10.7.17

8320    Converted to 310 Type A-4. Grain by 10.17; To Yarmouth on/by 27.10.17; Crashed 14.1.18 (painted as "N8320"); Deleted W/E 23.2.18 [Curiously, the c/n appears to be S.380 or S.390 in a photo in the Samson archives]

**2 WIGHT ELEMENTARY DC SCHOOL PUSHER BIPLANE SEAPLANES ordered under Cont No C.P.12272/16, numbered 8321 and 8322 & built East Cowes**

8321 (100-hp Anzani). Deld Calshot for trials 21.10.16; Makers for alterations 29.11.16; Calshot FS 2.2.17; Deleted 6.7.17 BR

8322 (100-hp Gnome Monosoupape). Completed 10.16; Deld Calshot for trials 24.10.16; Mkrs for repair 2.2.17; Calshot 31.3.17; Deleted 6.7.17 BR

**Serials 8323 to 8325 not allotted - blank numbers**

**12 ROYAL AIRCRAFT FACTORY B.E.2c TRACTOR BIPLANES ordered under Cont No C.P.53937/15 from Sir William Beardmore & Co Ltd, numbered 8326 to 8337 & built Dalmuir. (90-hp R.A.F. 1a)**

8326 Deld Yarmouth (via Grain) 13.2.16; AZP 14.3.16 (F/L V Nicholl); Attacked Zeppelin L9 with bombs and darts 25.4.16 (F/L FGD Hards); AZP 25.4.16 (FSL CJ Northrop); Holt 7.9.16; Yarmouth 14.9.16; Holt 15.9.16; Bacton 17.9.16; Yarmouth 21.9.16; Burgh Castle 10.10.16; Yarmouth 23.10.16; Holt 1.11.16; Yarmouth 10.11.16; Burgh Castle 12.12.16; Yarmouth 20.12.16; Burgh Castle 1.1.17; HACP 25.3.17 (FSL HB Smith); Yarmouth 27.6.17; Deleted W/E 8.9.17

8327 Deld Dover by rail 24.1.16; Tested 30.1.16 (Beardmore pilot); ADD 5.2.16; 1 Wing St.Pol by 10.2.16; 4 Flt B Sqdn 1 Wing St.Pol 1.3.16 - @18.5.16; ADD by 24.5.16; Eastchurch Workshops (via Dover) 9.11.16; War Flt Eastchurch 10.11.16 (ex Dover); Spotting Flt Eastchurch 23.11.16; Observers School Flt Eastchurch 23.12.16; Wrecked Laindon, nr Billericay 31.12.16 (FSL HJ Arnold & S/L AF Wilson unhurt); Deleted 11.1.17

8328 Deld Dover 23.1.16; Tested 30.1.16 (Beardmore pilot); ADD 5.2.16; 1 Wing St.Pol by 13.2.16; 4 Flt B Sqdn 1 Wing St.Pol 1.3.16 - 5.16; 3 Flt B Sqdn 1 Wing St.Pol by 2.6.16; ADD by 29.6.16 (held for 3 Flt); 3 Flt B Sqdn 1 Wing 30.9.16; ADD 4.11.16; Dover 9.11.16; Crashed and BO 20.4.17 (FSL AC Kermode); Deleted 25.4.17

8329 Deld CSD White City 27.1.16; Sailed from Tilbury in SS Khiva for Eastern Mediterranean 19.2.16; 2 Wing Aegean by 4.16 - @8.16; Deleted 1916

8330 Deld CSD White City 27.1.16; Sailed from Tilbury in SS Khiva for Eastern Mediterranean 19.2.16; 2 Wing Aegean by 4.16 - @8.16; Deleted 1917

8331 Deld CSD White City 5.2.16; To Eastern Mediterranean 5.2.16; 2 Wing Aegean by 4.16; Crashed on nose Imbros .16 (W/Cdr EL Gerrard); Deleted 1916

8332 Deld CSD White City 8.2.16; SS Soldier Prince for Eastern Mediterranean 8.2.16; 2 Wing Aegean by 4.16; Mitylene by 2.4.17 - @12.4.17

8333 Deld CSD White City 5.2.16; To Eastern Mediterranean 5.2.16; 2 Wing Aegean by 4.16; Marsh by 5.7.17; Surveyed 21.9.17; Deleted 6.10.17 DBR

8334 Deld CSD White City 5.2.16; To Eastern Mediterranean 5.2.16; 2 Wing Imbros, tested 28.4.16 - @8.16; Deleted 1916

8335 Deld by rail to Dover 9.2.16; Tested 29.2.16; ADD 9.3.16; 4 Flt B Sqdn 1 Wing St.Pol by 18.3.16; 3 Flt B Sqdn 1 Wing St.Pol 2.6.16 - @22.6.16; ADD by 29.6.16 (held for 3 Flt); 3 Flt B Sqdn 1 Wing 10.8.16; ADD 4.11.16; Dover 6.11.16; Deleted 6.8.17

8336 Deld Dover 19.2.16; Tested 29.2.16; ADD 9.3.16; 4 Flt B Sqdn 1 Wing St.Pol by 23.3.16; ADD W/E 2.5.16; 9 Dover 21.10.16 (transit); Eastchurch Workshops 22.10.16; Observers School Flt Eastchurch 23.12.16; To Eastbourne, COL 29.1.17 (F/L MJM Bryan & F/L AA Wallis); Eastchurch 28.5.17; Crashed 29.5.17, to Workshops; Deletion recommended 11.6.17

8337 Deld by rail to Dover 28.2.16; ADD 9.3.16; 4 Flt B Sqdn 1 Wing St.Pol by 9.4.16 - @11.5.16; 3 Flt B Sqdn 1 Wing St.Pol by 2.6.16; ADD to Chingford 22.6.16; ADD 25.6.16 (held for 3 Flt); 3 Flt B Sqdn 1 Wing St.Pol 10.8.16; ADD 30.9.16 - @19.10.16; 3 Flt B Sqdn 1 Wing by 23.10.16; FL Gravelines en route Dover 3.11.16; Dover 5.11.16 (night fighter, painted all-black, searchlight on top for night flying); Crashed and BO Dover 28.4.17 (F/L LO Brown unhurt & possibly AM1 A Weaver killed)

**NORMAN THOMPSON N.T.4 "SMALL AMERICA" PUSHER BIPLANE FLYING BOATS ordered 28.12.15 under Cont No C.P.45396/15, numbered 8338 to 8343 & built Middleton-on-Sea. (Originally ordered with two 100-hp Green and 6-pdr Davis gun, changed 7.16 to two 140-hp Hispano-Suiza)**

8338 (Exptl Davis 2-pdr gun in nose) On trial Bognor by 20.10.16 - @15.12.16; Deld Calshot 5.4.17 (Calshot School by 10.17); Surveyed 3.11.17; Deleted 8.11.17 W&T

8339 (Fitted to carry 2x230-lb bombs for anti U-boat patrols) Erected 15.12.16; Deld Killingholme for erection 15.1.17 (arr 22.1.17); Dundee by lorry 29.6.17 (arr 5.5.17); Deleted W/E 25.5.18

8340 (Fitted to carry 2x230-lb bombs for anti U-boat patrols) Erected 15.12.16; Deld Killingholme for erection 15.1.17 (arr 22.1.17); Dundee by lorry 29.4.17 (arr 5.5.17); Large fins fitted, tested 15.5.18; Deleted W/E 18.7.18

8341 (Fitted to carry 2x230-lb bombs for anti U-boat patrols) Erected 15.12.16; Deld Killingholme for erection 15.1.17 (arr 22.1.17); Surveyed 8.1.18; Deleted 17.1.18 TL

8342 (150-hp) (Fitted to carry 2x230-lb bombs for anti U-boat patrols) Deld Killingholme Seaplane School for erection 22.3.17 (storage by 19.1.18); Deleted W/E 3.5.18

8343 (150-hp) (Fitted to carry 2x230-lb bombs for anti U-boat patrols) Deld Killingholme Seaplane School for erection 22.3.17 (to Reserve) (in store by 19.1.18); Deleted W/E 3.5.18

**12 SHORT ADMIRALTY 184 TYPE TRACTOR BIPLANE SEAPLANES ordered 27.10.15 under Cont No C.P.79176/15 from Mann Egerton & Co Ltd as their Type A, numbered 8344 to 8355 & built Norwich. (225-hp Sunbeam Mohawk)**

8344 Completed 11.15; Deld Grain c.4.12.15; Accepted 17.12.15 (Kemp); Calshot 23.12.15; Newhaven 11.5.17; Calshot 11.7.17 (repair); Surveyed 28.9.17; Deleted 6.10.17 W&T

8345 Deld Felixstowe and tested 8.1.16 (Pickles); HMS Vindex 22.2.16; Felixstowe 1.3.16; Dover 19.3.16; Felixstowe 23.3.16; Dover 27.4.16 (for repair, but deleted)

8346 Deld Felixstowe 16.1.16; HMS Vindex 2.2.16; Dropped 3x65-lb bombs in Zeebrugge raid 20.3.16 (F/L HF Towler & S/L EG Hopcroft); Participated in raid on Hoyer Zeppelin Base, dropped bombs 25.3.16 (F/L HF Towler & S/L EG Hopcroft), damaged in raid, repaired; Felixstowe 4.4.16; Dover 27.4.16; Dunkerque 13.5.16; Lost 1.6.16; For deletion by 2.6.16

8347 Deld Felixstowe and tested 8.2.16 (Pickles); To Calshot but FL Ramsgate in fog, damaged float 18.1.17; Repairs at Ramsgate by 2.2.17; deleted 9.2.17

8348 Deld Felixstowe 28.2.16; AZP 24/25.4.16 (FSL CJ Galpin & AM Pinn); To Calshot School but FL Eastbourne in fog en route 18.1.17 (arr 20.1.17); Newhaven by 6.6.17; Dropped 2x100-lb bombs on U-boat 17m SSE of Beachy Head 15.7.17 (FSL RM Stirling); Calshot 21.8.17; Deleted W/E 1.3.18

8349 Deld Felixstowe and tested 14.3.16 (Pickles); Grain 19.3.16 (transit); Dover 20.3.16; Felixstowe 25.3.16; (used for torpedo experiments); Deleted 3.7.16

8350 Deld Felixstowe and tested 14.3.16 (Pickles); Left for Newlyn 4.1.17; arr and tested 20.1.17; Bombed U-boat 10m SSE of Dodman Point 16.3.17 (FSL VE Dean & AM2 SH Bromhead); EF, FL off Cape Cornwall, taken in tow by French cargo boat, relieved by ML359 10m off Newlyn, capsized, wreckage brought in by drifter Gardiner 17.3.17 (FSL HW Found & AM2 UG Tongue); Deleted 24.3.17

8351 Deld Felixstowe and tested 31.3.16 (Pickles); AZPs 24.4.16 (FSL FD Till & AM Ayling) & 2.5.16; HMS Vindex 6.4.16 (entry deleted 7.4.16); HMS Riviera, spare machine at Felixstowe to be flown to Dunkerque 4.6.16; To go from Felixstowe to HMS Riviera 7.6.16, but FL en route and wrecked 20.6.16 (reported by

*Norman Thompson N.T.4 8343 at Killingholme Seaplane School, 1917. (RAF Museum)*

*Canadian-built Curtiss J.N.3 prototype 8392 after being extensively repaired and modified by Faireys to bring it up to J.N.4 standard, in which form it was known as the J.N.3 (Improved). At the time of this photograph the conversion had not quite been completed, but an engine run was possible. It is seen here at the firm's North Hyde Road factory site, with the drawing office and main building in the left centre background. On the right can just be seen the fabric/dope shop and underneath the engine and propeller the female staff sitting in a row with backs to the camera.*
*(via Ian Huntley)*

Grain), deleted

8352 Deld Felixstowe 3.4.16; HMS *Vindex* but damaged port wing towing from slipway 3.4.16; Felixstowe 4.4.16; HMS *Vindex* 6.4.16; Felixstowe 7.4.16; Calshot 28.9.16; Portland 1.10.16; Dropped 2x65-lb bombs on U-boat 28.11.16 (FSL JJde laT Fox & AM Redman); FL, temp repair, towed back from Beer Harbour but CW under tow 24.2.17, deleted

8353 Deld Felixstowe 20.4.16; Nore War Flt Felixstowe 15.8.16; Dismantled for Malta 19.2.17; Packed 16.3.17; arr Torpedo School Malta by 19.5.17 but damaged on arrival; Deleted by 22.6.17

8354 Deld Grain 19.4.16; Killingholme 14.8.16 (transit); Yarmouth 15.8.16 (transit); Dundee 16.8.16 (transit); Scapa 17.8.16; HMS *Campania* 8.3.17; Lost at sea 12.6.17; Deleted 24.6.17

8355 Deld Felixstowe 1.6.16; Tested 2.7.16; Deld Newlyn to erect for Scillies, temp stored Trinity House Shed, Penzance 20.1.17; Erected Newlyn by 18.2.17; Tresco 24.2.17; Deleted 21.3.17

**12 SHORT ADMIRALTY 184 TYPE TRACTOR BIPLANE SEAPLANES ordered 28.10.15 under Cont No C.P.79176/15 from Westland Aircraft Works (Petters Ltd), numbered 8356 to 8367 & built Yeovil. (225-hp Sunbeam Mohawk)**

8356 Deld Seaplane School Calshot, erected by Mkrs; Accepted 23.1.16; Taxied into buoy, damaged starboard float and wing 24.3.16 (FSL RA Courtnage); BR by 27.6.17; Surveyed 12.10.17; Deleted 13.10.17 W&T

8357 Deld Calshot and tested 5.2.16 (Pickles); to Dunkerque to join HMS *Riviera* but en route FL at Eastbourne 12.3.16 (FSL N Gregory); Repaired by Eastbourne Aviation Co; Grain 1.4.16; HMS *Riviera* 26.4.16; Patrol to Zeebrugge, EF, FL in fog nr Gravelines, damaged propeller and chassis, towed to ship 17.5.16 (FSL N Gregory & PO Mech Stirling); Fitting roller blinds for sighting 30.5.16; Attacked submarine from 4,500 ft but missed 12m NE Zeebrugge 9.6.16 (FSL JH Woolner & PO Mech Stirling); 4 unsuccessful attacks on destroyer 4m off Belgian coast nr Ostende 18.6.16 (FSL JH Woolner & FSL JA Yonge); Engine cut, FL in German minefield 8m N of Ostende, put fire out, attacked by 3 enemy seaplanes which were driven off by Lewis gun fire, towed home by *ML105* 18.6.16 (F/L GW Price & CPO Mech3 Ellen); Dunkerque 8.10.16; HMS *Riviera* 20.10.16; Dunkerque 12.11.16; Dover 11.12.16; Dunkerque 28.2.17; Sideslipped into water on TO 9.3.17 (FSL SE Ball & OSL DC Evans unhurt); Dover 4.4.17; Dunkerque 16.6.17; Fitted 240-hp Renault-Mercedes by 10.17; Dover 13.1.18; Became 407 Flt Dover 25.5.18; 209 TDS Lee-on- Solent 9.8.18; Deleted W/E 12.9.18

8358 Deld Killingholme 9.2.16; AGP 7.4.16 (FSL WM Tait & PO Wybrow); Wrecked off Bridlington 24.10.16; Deleted 7.11.16

8359 Deld by rail to Grain 22.2.16; Accepted 4.3.16 (Pickles); Killingholme then HMS *Engadine* 30.3.16; Killingholme 10.5.16 (storage); HMS *Engadine* 13.5.16; Dundee 16.5.16; HMS *Engadine* 26.5.16; Reconnoitred before Battle of Jutland 31.5.16 (F/Cdr FJ Rutland & Asst Payr GS Trewin RNR); Dundee 23.8.16; HMS *Engadine* 7.9.16; Dundee 1.3.17 (240-hp); HMS *Engadine* 26.3.17; Dundee 7.5.17; HMS *Engadine* 28.6.17; Rosyth 30.7.17; HMS *Furious* 16.9.17; HMS *Engadine* 23.9.17 (ship at Buncrana 27.9.17-18.11.17, to Liverpool 19.11.17); Packed at Buncrana by 2.12.17; Despatched to Imperial War Museum store W/E 29.12.17; Exhibited pre-WWII

8360 Deld Grain 10.3.16; Accepted 16.3.16 (Pickles); Shipped from London to Mudros via Malta in SS *Khiva* 2.6.16; 2 Wing Aegean from 6.16; Mudros by 6.12.16; HMS *Ark Royal* by 20.2.17; Thasos 19.5.17; Imbros to HMS *Ark Royal* 27.5.17; Mitylene 21.6.17; HMS *Ark Royal* 23.6.17; Thasos 29.6.17; EF, retd HMS *Ark Royal* in tow 30.6.17; Thasos 1.7.17; Deleted 1917

8361 Deld Grain 14.3.16; Accepted 23.3.16 (Pickles); to Scapa (via Yarmouth & Killingholme) 15.8.16 (arr 20.8.16); HMS *Campania* 23.8.16; Damaged in transit, to Scapa 23.11.16; To Shorts for re-engining by 1.17; HMS *Campania* 8.3.17; Scapa 16.7.17; Houton Bay by 10.17; Deleted W/E 4.5.18

8362 Deld Calshot 29.3.16; Accepted 10.4.16; CW 15.5.17; Deleted 24.5.17 [possibly the aircraft which crashed in English Channel, TFSL GG Avery & AM1 WE Elliott both killed 14.5.17 - or could be 8170]

8363 Deld Calshot 29.3.16; Accepted 10.4.16; Deleted 11.7.17

8364 Deld Grain 4.16 (trials of 2-pdr Davis gun with Hamilton sights); Fired 2-pdr Davis gun 23.5.16; to Westgate, fuselage damaged 14.8.17 (Nore Flt by 10.17); Became 406 Flt Westgate 25.5.18; Deleted W/E 19.9.18

8365 Deld Calshot and accepted 27.4.16; Deleted 11.7.17

8366 Deld Calshot and accepted 1.5.16; Portland 2.12.16; Calshot 3.1.17; Deleted 9.2.17

8367 Deld Calshot and accepted 11.5.16; EF, FL Poole 26.2.17 (F/L HA Peck), repaired; retd Portland 28.2.17; FTR from patrol in English Channel 8.3.17 (FSL JJ de laT Fox & AM2 RE Gorman both drowned); Deleted 28.3.17

**12 SHORT ADMIRALTY 184 TYPE TRACTOR BIPLANE SEAPLANES ordered 28.10.15 under Cont No C.P.79176/15 from Phoenix Dynamo Manufacturing Co Ltd, numbered 8368 to 8379 & built Bradford. (225-hp Sunbeam Mohawk)**

8368 Deld by rail to Yarmouth 13.1.16; Accepted 13.2.16 (Kemp); HSPP 24.3.16 (F/L V Nicholl & PO Knotley); HSMP, EF, drifted into St.Nicholas LV 26.7.16 (F/L FGD Hards & FSL EB Thompson); HSPP 11.11.16 (F/Cdr V Nicholl); Deleted 20.6.17

8369 Deld by rail to Yarmouth 9.3.16; Accepted 24.3.16 (Pickles); HSPP 11.11.16 (F/L CJ Galpin); Deleted 3.5.17

8370 Deld by rail to Yarmouth 22.3.16; Accepted 30.3.16 (Pickles); HSMP 28.6.16 (FSL E Cadbury); Reported down off Mundsley 17.10.16 (F/L CJ Galpin); HSMP 30.4.17 (F/L LER Murray); Deleted 3.5.17

8371 Deld by rail to Yarmouth 1.4.16; To Grain but broke down 10m off Orfordness, taxied to Aldeburgh, towed to Grain by *ML28* 18.5.16; Killingholme 18.6.16; Deleted 8.4.17

8372 Deld Felixstowe and accepted 23.4.16 (Pickles); Packing 14.5.16; Left for Port Said 12.6.16; EI&SS Port Said by 7.16; HMS *Ben-my-Chree* 18.7.16; Port Said 26.7.16; HMS *Ben-my-Chree* 14.8.16; Port Said 30.8.16; HMS *Ben-my-Chree* 13.9.16; Port Said 17.9.16; HMS *Ben-my-Chree* 1.12.16; Shot down by AA fire over Ramleh 2.12.16 (FSL AJ Nightingale & Lt PM Woodland RNVR PoWs)

8373 Deld Yarmouth for erection 9.5.16; Accepted 23.5.16 (Pickles); FL in sea, pilot sank his aircraft 24.10.16 (FSL HB Smith picked up by Dutch lugger); Deleted 16.11.16

8374 Deld Killingholme 19.4.16; Crashed on alighting, crew rescued by Scarborough Air Station 20.10.16; Deleted 7.11.16

8375 Deld Killingholme 6.5.16; AZP 19.8.16 (FSL HH Arundel & PO Homer); FL and CW Scarborough Bay 20.10.16; Overhaul by 20.1.17; To Killingholme Seaplane School 2.17; 209 TDS Lee-on-Solent W/E 25.7.18; Deleted W/E 12.9.18

8376 Deld by rail to Dover 23.5.16; Tested 1.6.16; Dunkerque 21.7.16; Deleted 17.9.16

8377 Deld Felixstowe 25.6.16 (for HMS *Vindex*, but never embarked); Calshot FS 30.1.17; Bembridge 3.3.17; HSMP 5.4.17 (FSL PH Mackworth); Calshot 26.4.17; Newhaven 17.7.17; Calshot FS W/E 5.10.17; Surveyed 8.11.17; deleted 17.11.17 W&T

8378 Deld Yarmouth for erection 16.5.16; Accepted 23.5.16 (Pickles); (FL?) Towed in to Yarmouth from Lowestoft 5.5.17; Deleted W/E 8.9.17

8379 Deld Felixstowe and accepted 11.6.16 (Pickles); HMS *Vindex* 5.7.16; Felixstowe 19.7.16; Calshot 28.9.16; Portland 1.10.16; Dropped 65-lb bomb on U-boat, landed to report to British patrol vessel, stalled on TO, sideslipped, CW, abandoned, sank during salvage owing to attack by U-boat, which was sunk by patrol vessel and crew captured 1.12.16 (FSL JR Ross & AM Redman picked up by HM ship)

*Royal Aircraft Factory B.E.2c 8328 of 1 Wing at St.Pol. (via Frank Cheesman)*

*R.E.P. Parasol Monoplane 8454 of 1 Wing at St.Pol, 1915. (via Frank Cheesman)*

*Short S.38 Type Pusher Biplane 8437, used at Chingford, 1916. (R.C.Sturtivant collection)*

*Pemberton-Billing P.B.23E Pusher Scout 8487 at Grain with modified fins of the type later fitted to the P.B.25. (P.T.Capon via Philip Jarrett)*

*Voisin Type III LA.S 8521 was used for armament training at Eastchurch. (via Frank Cheesman)*

**12 SHORT ADMIRALTY 184 TYPE TRACTOR BIPLANE SEAPLANES ordered 28.10.15 under Cont No C.P.79176/15 from Fredk Sage & Co Ltd, numbered 8380 to 8391 & built Peterborough. (225-hp Sunbeam Mohawk)**

8380   (High chassis) Completed 9.15; Deld Calshot and tested 17.11.15; Deleted 9.2.17 FW&T

8381   Deld Grain for erection 4.12.15; Accepted 14.12.15; Calshot 23.12.15; HMS *Empress* 1.1.16; Port Said 9.3.16; HMS *Empress* 12.3.16; HMS *Ark Royal* 12.6.16; HMS *Empress* 16.6.16; Mudros 18.8.16; HMS *Ark Royal* by 18.3.17; Imbros 17.5.17; HMS *Ark Royal* 27.5.17 - LM17.7.17; Deleted 1917

8382   Deld Grain 17.12.15; Dover 8.2.16; Damaged float in torpedo lifting trials 8.4.16 (FSL ATN Cowley); Dunkerque 16.4.16; Wings damaged by gunfire 22.4.16; Night raid on Zeebrugge 25.4.16 (FSL FJ Bailey & OSL LH Slatter); Dover 22.12.16; Dunkerque 7.2.17; Dover 9.2.17; Dunkerque 3.3.17; HMS *General Craufurd* 13.3.17 (FSL C Laurence); Dover 15.3.17; Dunkerque 21.3.17; Dover 24.3.17; Dunkerque 1.4.17; Dover 5.6.17; Dunkerque 7.6.17; Dover 15.6.17; Dunkerque 23.6.17; Dover 15.7.17; Dunkerque 17.7.17; Dover 16.8.17; Dunkerque 17.8.17; Dover W/E 8.11.17; Dunkerque 5.12.17; Dover 19.12.17; Retd ex Calais in tow 9.3.18; EF, FL Folkestone 7.4.18 (Capt AC Reid & 3AM Ball) (fitted 260-hp by then); Deleted W/E 27.4.18

8383   Deld Grain 6.1.16 for erection by makers; Accepted 14.1.16 (Pickles); Felixstowe 26.1.16; Felixstowe 8.2.16; HMS *Vindex* 9.2.16; Dropped 3x65-lb bombs in Zeebrugge raid 20.3.16 (F/L LP Openshaw & Mid SE Hoblyn); FTR from raid on Hoyer Airship Base 25.3.16 (FSL CG Knight & Mid SE Hoblyn PoWs)

8384   (DC) Deld Grain 31.1.16; Tested 8.2.16; HMS *Riviera* 24.2.16; Grain (via Dunkerque) 1.3.16; PVRD mid 3.16; HMS *Riviera* 26.4.16; Attacked U-boat 10-12m NE Zeebrugge with 5x65-lb bombs but missed 28.4.16 (F/L H Stewart & OSL OH Crowther); Straddled U-boat with 5x65-lb bombs from 700 ft 8m N of Zeebrugge, U-boat submerged 3.5.16 (S/L N Lea RNVR); Dropped 3 bombs from 4,000 ft on destroyer 10m NW of Zeebrugge, AA fire at 1,500 ft 28.5.16 (F/L GW Price & PO Mech Stirling); Damaged while coming alongside after patrol 31.5.16 (F/L GW Price & CPO Mech3 Ellen); Dover 1.7.16 (repair); HMS *Riviera* 10.7.16; Dunkerque 8.10.16; Deleted 4.12.16

8385   Deld by lorry to Grain 12.2.16; Accepted 4.3.16 (Pickles); Yarmouth 16.3.16; Left to bomb German High Fleet raiding Scarborough 25.4.16 (S/Cdr DA Oliver); While on patrol, stalled from 200 ft and dived into sea, bombs exploded, CW 8.9.16 (F/L CW Graham DSO killed); Deleted 19.9.16

8386   Deld Grain 9.3.16; Accepted 23.3.16 (Pickles); Tested 23.6.16; Yarmouth 30.6.16 (transit); Killingholme 1.7.16; Damaged off Cleethorpes by 24.10.16; Deleted 2.6.17

8387   Deld Grain 13.3.16; Accepted 27.3.16 (Pickles); Surveyed 8.4.17; Deleted 26.4.17

8388   Deld Grain 29.3.16; Accepted 4.4.16 (Pickles); Calshot 25.4.16; Deleted 9.2.17

8389   Deld Grain 6.4.16; Tested 4.5.16; Yarmouth 27.5.16; HSMP 30.4.17 (FSL AM FitzRandolph); Deleted 13.5.17

8390   Deld Killingholme 19.4.16; Crashed 22.6.17 ; Deleted 2.7.17

8391   Deld Killingholme 6.5.16; AZP 31.7/1.8.16; AZP 19.8.16 (FSL GH Simpson & PO Kershaw); Damaged off Killingholme 29.10.16; Deleted 30.8.17

**12 CURTISS J.N.3 TRACTOR BIPLANES ordered from Curtiss, Toronto, numbered 8392 to 8403. (90-hp Curtiss OX-5)**

8392   (DC) Prototype, FF Long Branch 14.7.15; Shipped to UK; Deld Hendon for erection 20.10.15; Chingford 3.11.15; Fairey for repair and conv J.N.3 (Improved) 20.3.16; Hendon 28.8.16; To Redcar but FL Bunsby, nr Sleaford 11.11.16 (FSL FP Reeves unhurt); Redcar (via Killingholme) 12.11.16; Skidded on soft earth landing, damaged u/c, broke propeller 8.12.16 (PFSL JA Piquet); Wings came off in dive, CW 7.9.17 (TPFO JM Dawson DoI); Deleted W/E 15.9.17

8393   Deld Hendon for erection 20.10.15; Chingford 3.11.15; Deleted 21.1.16

8394   Deld Hendon and accepted 23.10.15 (Pickles); Killingholme 27.10.15; CW 19.11.15 (PFSL BS Wemp); Deleted 7.12.15

8395   Deld Hendon 29.10.15; Ready for test 1.11.15; Chingford by 11.15; Wrecked at Crystal Palace 17.11.15 (FSL AO Brissenden); Deleted 22.12.15

8396   Deld Hendon and erected 27.10.15; Tested 1.11.15 (Pickles); Killingholme 9.11.15; Wrecked 6.2.16; Deleted 12.3.16

8397   Deld Hendon 27.10.15; Accepted 29.10.15 (Pickles); Killingholme 21.2.15; Deleted 18.3.16

8398   Deld Hendon for erection 29.10.15; Tested 15.11.15 (Pickles) Eastchurch NFS 16.11.15; Detling 23.11.15; EF, FL 2m W of aerodrome 28.11.15 (FSL DH Whittier); Surveyed 8.12.15; Chassis wrecked landing 20.12.15 (FSL GK Williams, FSL LE Smith & FSL TW Webber); Ran into hedge landing and damaged u/c 9.2.16 (FSL GK Williams); Deleted 9.3.16

8399   Deld Hendon 15.11.15; Accepted 16.11.15 (Pickles); Detling 31.12.15; Eastchurch 12.3.16; Detling 16.3.16; Fairey 28.6.16 - conv J.N.3 (Improved), to 2.17; CSD White City (packed) by 4.6.17 (for Vendôme); Vendôme, for deletion by 29.12.17; Deleted W/E 25.1.18

8400   Deld Hendon 11.11.15; Allocated Chingford but EF smashed 11.11.15; Preliminary test 7.12.15 (Pickles); Climb test 3.1.16 (Prodger); Chingford 5.1.16; CSD Wormwood Scrubbs 21.3.16, later deleted

8401   Deld Hendon and accepted 11.11.15 (Pickles); Chingford 15.11.15; Deleted 3.3.16 CW

8402   (DC) Deld Hendon and tested 15.11.15 (Pickles); Chingford 15.11.15; Fairey 20.3.16 - repair and conv J.N.3 (Improved); Hendon 18.8.16; Tested 15.10.16; Left for Redcar 2.11.16; FL Sledmer 3.11.16; Scarborough 4.11.16; Redcar 12.11.16; Damaged fuselage landing 21.11.16 (PFO MH Rattray); COL 15.3.17; Deleted 3.4.17

8403   Deld Hendon and tested 15.11.15 (Pickles); Eastchurch NFS 16.11.15; Detling 23.11.15; Low cloud, landed Birling, 10m W of Detling, EF on TO, into hedge, smashed u/c 5.12.15 (FSL LE Smith unhurt); Retd by lorry 6.12.15; Surveyed 8.12.15; Detling 12.2.16; 4 Wing Eastchurch 12.3.16; Detling 16.3.16; Eastchurch NFS 20.3.16; Fairey 29.6.16 - conv J.N.3 (Improved) to 2.17; 3 Wing Luxeuil by 30.3.17; Transferred to French Govt for AMF 20.4.17

**6 ROYAL AIRCRAFT FACTORY B.E.2c TRACTOR BIPLANES ordered under Cont No C.P.63855/15 from Eastbourne Aviation Co Ltd, numbered 8404 to 8409 & built Eastbourne. (90-hp R.A.F.1a) [C/n's 118 to 123]**

8404   Deld Eastbourne 14.7.16; Brooklands 19.7.16; Eastbourne 20.7.16; Chingford 9.9.16; D Flt Cranwell 14.10.16; Wrecked 1.4.17; Became 201/2 TDS Cranwell 1.4.18

8405   Deld Misc Flt Eastchurch 24.7.16; Became Spotting Flt Eastchurch 15.9.16; Observers School Flt Eastchurch 23.12.16; Eastchurch Workshops 23.1.17 (repair); Observers School Flt Eastchurch 22.3.17; Throwley 8.4.17; Observers School Flt Eastchurch 9.4.17; AGP, FL, damaged u/c and propeller, nr Ipswich 5.6.17 (FSL RJM St.Leger & A/Payr GS Trewin RNR); Oxford, repair 10.6.17; Observers School Flt Eastchurch 11.6.17; Surveyed 12.12.17; Deleted 21.12.17 W&T

8406   Fitted for Le Prieur rocket firing and tested Eastchurch. Deld Cranwell (via Chingford) 23.9.16; Deleted 19.6.17

8407   Deld East Fortune 27.12.16 (Night); Transported to Cranwell and arr via Leeds W/E 15.2.18; Became 201/2 TDS Cranwell 1.4.18; Became 58 TS Cranwell 27.7.18; Spun in from gliding turn 16.9.18 (2/Lt AAE Voght)

8408   Deld Eastchurch Workshops 20.10.16; Detling 21.11.16; En route Grain during cross-country, FL in ploughed field nr Stockburn 7.2.17 (FSL AF Buck & FSL RH Horniman)(repaired); War School Manston 31.3.17; AZP, FL Orfordness 24.5.17; EF, FL in sea between North Foreland and Manston, propeller damaged but repairable, dismantled and retd 26.5.17 (occupants unhurt); Damaged landing 23.8.17 (FSL JB White unhurt); Surveyed 26.10.17; Deleted 29.10.17

8409     Deld Chingford 26.10.16; Observers School Flt Eastchurch 12.1.17; Manston 13.1.17; Chingford 23.1.17; U/c damaged Easthorpe 6.6.17 (W/Cdr CR Dane); Cranwell 3.10.17; Became 201/2 TDS Cranwell 1.4.18; Became 58 TDS Cranwell 27.7.18; Mid-air collision with 504 D8916 4.11.18 (F/Cdt J Hops & Capt K Sutherland both injured)

**24 ROYAL AIRCRAFT FACTORY B.E.2c TRACTOR BIPLANES ordered under Cont No C.P.63855/15 from Hewlett & Blondeau, numbered 8410 to 8433 & built Leagrave. 11.16, all to be modified by Mkrs (not clear whether this actually happened) (90-hp R.A.F.1a)**

8410     Deld Hendon 22.2.16; Accepted 9.3.16 (Pickles); Dover 16.3.16; Under repair 9.11.16; Deleted 26.11.16

8411     Deld Hendon and accepted 25.3.16 (Pickles); Dover 29.3.16; ADD 31.3.16; 4 Flt B Sqdn 1 Wing St.Pol by 24.4.16; ADD by 11.5.16; 12 Flt B Sqdn 4 Wing Petite Synthe 27.5.16; ADD 12.8.16; Yarmouth 6.9.16; Burgh Castle 13.10.16; AZP 28.11.16 (F/Cdr V Nicholl); War Flt Burgh Castle 12.12.16; Yarmouth 13.3.17; AZP 24.5.17 (F/L E Cadbury); Pulham 19.10.17; Yarmouth, AZP, landed Burgh Castle 19/20.10.17 (F/L E Cadbury); Became 490 Flt Yarmouth by 25.5.18; CW on TO 25.5.18 (2/Lt IM Johnson injured)

8412     Deld Hendon and accepted 25.3.16 (Pickles); Dover 29.3.16; ADD 9.4.16; 10 Flt A Sqdn 4 Wing 15.4.16; EF during raid on Mariakerke aerodrome, FL in Holland 4.5.16 (FSL RE Greensmith interned); For deletion by 18.5.16

8413     Deld Hendon and accepted 25.3.16 (Pickles); Westgate 27.3.16; 2 HAPPs 24.4.16 (F/L HA Buss & AM H Phipps, later F/L HA Buss & LM Tinsley); Chased LZ87, landed Manston 25.4.16 (F/L HA Buss); HSPP 3.5.16 (F/L HA Buss & LM Tinsley); HACP 22.5.16 (F/L HA Buss); Manston 14.5.16; HACPs 9.7.16 (F/L HA Buss) & 12.8.16; AZP 31.7/1.8.16 (FSL JS Browne); AZPs 23/24.9.16 & 25.9.16 (both F/L HA Buss); HAPP 23.10.16 (F/L HA Buss); HAPP, EF, FL Sandwich 28.11.16 (F/L JA Carr); AGP 29.9.17 (S/Cdr CH Butler); War Flt/School Manston by 6.10.17 - @18.5.18; EF, FL RFC Leadenham 23.2.18; Waddington by 29.7.18

8414     Deld Hendon 30.3.16; Accepted 1.4.16; To Mkrs for despatch to Eastern Expeditionary Force 5.4.16; 2 Wing by 6.16; C Sqdn 2 Wing Imbros by 10.1.17 - 9.17; Marsh by 1.12.17 - @1.1.18; Transferred to Greek Government; Greek Training Mudros by 3.18 - 1.19

8415     (90-hp Curtiss OX-2) Deld Hendon 30.3.16; Accepted 3.4.16 (Pickles); Grain 5.4.16; Kingsnorth 5.4.16; Grain 7.4.16; Eastchurch 9.4.16; Grain 9.4.16; visited Brooklands 7.6.16; Visited Kingsnorth 5.7.16; Visited Detling 8.7.16; Visited Manston 14.7.16 & 21.7.16; Yarmouth 5.8.16; Exp Flt Grain 6.8.16; Oakley Ltd 30.9.16 (arr 3.10.16, overhaul and modifications); Cranwell (via Hendon) W/E 1.12.17; Became 201/2 TDS 1.4.18

8416     (90-hp Curtiss OX-2) Deld Hendon for erection 3.4.16; Grain 19.4.16; War Flt Eastchurch 27.4.16; Exp Flt Grain 6.5.16; Visited Kingsnorth 2.6.16 and 3.7.16 (bomb dropping trials 3.7.16); Oakley Ltd 30.9.16 (arr 3.10.16 - overhaul and modification); Hendon W/E 13.10.17; Cranwell W/E 1.12.17; Fitted 90-hp RAF 2.18; Crashed and damaged Cranwell North 12.2.18 (pilot unhurt); Surveyed 11.3.18 wreck; Deleted 16.3.18

8417     Deld Hendon 7.4.16; Tested 20.4.16; Yarmouth 25.4.16; Night flight to test wingtip flares & Lewis gun firing at fire balloon 29.5.16 (F/L V Nicholl); AZP 31.7.16 (F/Cdr V Nicholl & AM Maintail); AZP 2.8.16 (F/Cdr V Nicholl); Martlesham 24.3.17; Yarmouth 26.3.17; Burgh Castle, AZP 13.4.18 (FSL LL King); 490 Flt Yarmouth 25.5.18; 273 Sqdn Burgh Castle by 6.18; Attacked by 5 enemy seaplanes 5m SE of Cross Sands 05.35, escaped and landed Yarmouth 7.6.18 (Lt GF Hodson); retd Burgh Castle 9.6.18; HSMP and HACP 10.6.18; still Burgh Castle 8.18

8418     Deld Hendon 17.4.16; Tested 27.4.16 (Prodger); Yarmouth 29.4.16; Covehithe 19.5.16; Yarmouth 26.5.16; Covehithe 6.6.16; Yarmouth 18.6.16;

Covehithe 19.6.16; Yarmouth 27.6.16; Bacton 5.7.16; Yarmouth 6.7.16; Bacton 7.7.16; Yarmouth 21.7.16; Bacton 29.7.16; AZPs 30/31.7.16 & 31.7/1.8.16 (both FSL EL Pulling); Yarmouth 2.8.16; Attacked L17, landed downwind in error, hit fence, CW Burgh Castle 2.8.16 (FSL EJ Pulling); Wreckage to Yarmouth 3.8.16; Deleted 16.8.16

8419     Deld Hendon 27.4.16; Tested 28.4.16 (Prodger); Yarmouth 29.4.16; Holt 26.5.16; Yarmouth 28.5.16; Bacton 18.6.16; Yarmouth 20.6.16; Bacton 2.7.16; Yarmouth 3.7.16; Bacton 21.7.16; HACP 21.7.16 (FSL CJ Galpin); Yarmouth 21.7.16; AZP 3.8.16 (F/Cdr CHC Smith); Bacton 11.8.16; Yarmouth 12.8.16; AZP, engaged Zeppelin 30m E of Lowestoft 23.9.16 (F/L CJ Galpin); HACP 26.9.16 (FSL AV Robinson); CW on landing at night 17.10.16 (FSL EL Pulling); AZP 19.10.16 (FSL FW Walker); Burgh Castle 21.10.16; Yarmouth 22.10.16; Burgh Castle 23.10.16; Yarmouth 24.10.16; Burgh Castle 26.10.16; Yarmouth 10.11.16; Covehithe 21.11.16; Yarmouth 29.11.16; Tested Brock's rockets 1.12.16 & 7.12.16; War Flt Burgh Castle 12.12.16; Yarmouth 28.12.16; Burgh Castle 1.1.17; HACP 24.1.17 (F/L CE Wood); Yarmouth 29.1.17; Martlesham 26.4.17; Yarmouth to Burgh Castle 1.5.17; Yarmouth 2.5.17; Deleted W/E 2.2.18

8420     Deld Hendon 2.5.16; Tested 3.5.16 (Prodger); Detector trials at Wormwood Scrubbs 3.5.16 (F/Cdr HR Busteed); Yarmouth 16.5.16; Covehithe 26.5.16; Yarmouth 31.5.16; Covehithe 1.6.16; Yarmouth 6.6.16; Holt 20.6.16; Sedgeford 21.6.16; Yarmouth 27.6.16; AZPs 30.7.16 & 2.8.16 (F/L BD Kilner); Covehithe 9.8.16; Yarmouth 16.8.16; Covehithe 1.9.16; AZP 2/3.9.16 (FSL S Kemball); Bacton 7.9.16; Yarmouth 21.9.16; AZP 25.9.16, landed Burgh Castle (F/L CHC Smith); Bacton 28.9.16; Yarmouth 9.10.16; Bacton 14.10.16; Covehithe 16.10.16; Burgh Castle 21.10.16; Yarmouth 23.10.16; Burgh Castle 26.10.16; Yarmouth 29.10.16; Covehithe 1.11.16; Yarmouth 8.11.16; Bacton 14.11.16; Covehithe 15.11.16; Burgh Castle 21.11.16; Yarmouth 22.11.16; Burgh Castle 26.11.16; AZP 26/27.11.16 (FSL GWR Fane); AZP, chased L21 but guns jammed 27/28.11.16 (FSL GWR Fane awarded DSC); Yarmouth 29.11.16; Bacton 30.11.16; Yarmouth 6.12.16; Covehithe 16.12.16; HACP 28.12.16 (FSL GWR Fane DSC); Yarmouth 28.12.16; Covehithe 4.1.17; Yarmouth 14.1.17; Covehithe 29.1.17; Yarmouth 10.2.17; Covehithe 23.2.17; Yarmouth 9.3.17; HACP 10.3.17 (F/Cdr GWR Fane DSC), landed Covehithe then retd Yarmouth; Bacton 9.17; Yarmouth 24.9.17; Deleted W/E 23.2.18

8421     Deld Hendon for erection 20.5.16; Tested 25.5.16 (Prodger); Eastbourne 28.5.16; Brooklands 19.7.16; Eastbourne 20.7.16; Eastchurch 26.7.16; Eastbourne 25.8.16; E Flt Cranwell (via Chingford) 14.10.16; Deletion recommended 27.11.16; Deleted 16.1.17

8422     Deld Hendon for erection 20.5.16; Tested 25.5.16 (Prodger); Eastbourne 28.5.16; Eastchurch 21.6.16; Eastbourne 24.6.16; Cranwell 14.10.16; Crashed Cranwell 10.9.17; At Freiston 11.17; Became 202 TDS Cranwell 1.4.18; Flat spin on turn, nosedived, caught fire, BO 13.7.18 (Lt GP Armstrong & 2/Lt H Higgins killed)

8423     Deld Hendon for erection 16.6.16; Tested 20.6.16 (Pickles); Eastbourne 30.6.16; D Flt Cranwell 14.10.16 (at Freiston 10.16 - 1.17); O/t Cranwell 14.2.17; Deleted 19.5.17

8424     Deld Hendon for erection 16.6.16; Tested 20.6.16 (Pickles); Dismantling by Oakley Ltd 11.7.16; Despatched by rail for East Africa Field Force 26.7.16; recd 7 Sqdn East Africa 10.16; Kilossa by 7.12.16; to Alt Iringa 7.12.16, retd same day; Ubena 20.12.16; Alt Iringa 5.1.17 (overhaul); To 26 Sqdn RFC 30.1.17; Flown by 26 Sqdn 4.17

8425     Deld Hendon for erection 21.6.16; Dismantling by Oakley Ltd 11.7.16; Despatched by rail for East Africa Field Force 26/27.7.16; 7 Sqdn East Africa by 10.16; Iringa by 7.11.16; Kilossa by 11.16; Iringa 18.11.16; Ubena (Njombe) 20.12.16; Iringa 8.1.17; To Royal Flying Corps (Military Wing); To 26 Sqdn RFC 30.1.17

8426     Deld Hendon for erection 6.7.16; Accepted 8.7.16 (Prodger); Misc Flt Eastchurch 14.7.16; War Flt

Eastchurch 12.8.16; Misc Flt Eastchurch 18.8.16; AZP 24/25.8.16 (F/Cdr AK Robertson); Misc Flt Eastchurch 3.9.16; Became Spotting Flt Eastchurch 15.9.16; Observers School Flt Eastchurch 23.12.16; Fitted 100-hp RAF by 12.17; Became part of 204 TDS Eastchurch 1.4.18 - @25.5.18

8427 Deld Hendon for erection 8.7.16; Tested 14.7.16 (Prodger); Despatched for East Africa Field Force 27.7.16; Recd 7 Sqdn East Africa 21.11.16; To 26 Sqdn RFC 1.17

8428 Deld Hendon and erecting 11.7.16; Tested 14.7.16 (Pickles); Despatched for East Africa Field Force 29.7.16; Recd 7 Sqdn East Africa 10.16; To 26 Sqdn RFC 1.17; SOC 14.12.17

8429 Deld Hendon 14.7.16; Accepted 8.8.16 (Prodger); Cranwell 11.8.16; Howden 13.8.16; Cranwell 14.8.16; Wrecked 5.10.16; Deleted 24.3.17

8430 Deld Hendon 24.8.16; Grain 7.9.16; Yarmouth 20.3.17; Bacton 24.5.17; Yarmouth 6.6.17; Burgh Castle 29.6.17; Yarmouth 24.7.17; Surveyed 14.12.17; Deleted 21.12.17 wrecked

8431 Deld Hendon and accepted 14.9.16 (by makers); 3 Wing Manston 17.9.16; Gunnery Flt Grain 18.9.16; Exp Flt Grain 9.16; To Kingsnorth for bomb dropping experiments but crashed and CW on landing 20.9.16 (S/Cdr EDM Robertson); Deleted 27.9.16

8432 Deld Hendon and accepted 14.9.16 (by makers); Exp Flt Grain 15.9.16; Visited Kingsnorth 20.9.16 (Bomb dropping experiments); Tested Drummond traverse sight 1.11.16, 6.11.16 & 8.11.16; Bomb dropping experiments at Kingsnorth 8.11.16 & 9.11.16; Tested Collimator sight 2.12.16; Became Gunnery Experimental Grain 5.12.16; visited Kingsnorth 11.12.16; Dropped Gidino bombs at Kingsnorth 22.1.17; Dropped bomb at Kingsnorth 23.1.17; EAD Grain to Hendon 28.4.17; EAD Grain 23.5.17; COL 24.5.17; U/c smashed landing 12.7.17; Surveyed 25.3.18; Deleted 27.3.18 W&T

8433 Deld Hendon for erection 24.9.16; Chingford 24.10.16 (transit); D Flt Cranwell 25.10.16 (at Freiston 11.16 - 3.17); Crashed 11.9.17; FL Langrick 24.1.18; COL Harrogate, CW 19.3.18 (pilot unhurt)

**6 SHORT S.38 TYPE PUSHER BIPLANES ordered under Cont No C.P.59218/15 from Norman Thompson Flt Co Ltd, numbered 8434 to 8439 & built Middleton-on-Sea, Bognor Regis. (80-hp Gnome)**

8434 Deld Eastbourne NFS 30.12.15; CW 3.4.16 (FSL JA Ramsay); Deleted 14.4.16

8435 Deld Eastbourne NFS 8.1.16 (transit at Eastbourne 5.1.16); Deleted 27.4.16

8436 Deld Chingford 4.4.16; Dismantled 8.4.16; Deleted 22.4.16

8437 (Mod u/c) Deld Chingford 27.1.16 (Prodger); Dismantled 8.4.16; Deleted 22.4.16

8438 Deld Chingford 9.2.16; Deleted 22.4.16

8439 Deld Chingford 21.2.16; Wrecked by wind 28.3.16; Deleted 24.4.16

**2 AVRO 519 BOMBER TRACTOR BIPLANES with folding wings ordered under Cont No C.P.101234/16, numbered 8440 and 8441 & built Manchester. (150-hp Sunbeam Crusader)**

8440 Deld Exptl Flt Grain by rail 2.2.16; Retd Mkrs 5.5.16 (repair); Design Flt Eastchurch for erection 27.8.16; Preliminary test 1.10.16; Deleted 8.2.17

8441 Deld Dover by rail 28.2.16; Grain 1.4.16 (arrived ex Whitstable 3.4.16); Retd Mkrs Hamble 28.7.16 (fit 200-hp Sunbeam in lieu of 150-hp); Re-erected W/E 7.11.16; Design Flt Eastchurch 22.12.16 (Raynham); Damaged 12.3.17; Eastchurch FS 14.3.17; Observers School Flt Eastchurch 18.3.17; Deleted 31.8.17

**12 BRISTOL BOXKITE TRACTOR BIPLANES ordered under Cont No C.P.57306/15/X from British & Colonial Aeroplane Co Ltd, numbered 8442 to 8453 & built Filton. (50-hp Gnome) [Per official list 1.17, all fitted 60-hp Le Rhône] [C/n's 870 to 881]**

8442 Deld Chingford by lorry 27.9.15; Erecting by makers 11.10.15; Wrecked 19.11.15; Deleted 1.12.15

8443 Deld Chingford & erecting by makers 6.10.15; Retd CSD White City 18.1.16, later deleted

8444 Deld Chingford for erection 11.10.15; Deleted 14.1.16

8445 Deld Chingford 1.11.15; Awaiting test by 1.1.16; Deleted 14.1.16

8446 Deld Killingholme 6.11.15; Deleted 1.2.16

8447 Deld Killingholme 4.11.15; Crashed, extensive damage 11.11.15 (F/Cdr E Osmond); Deleted 18.3.16

8448 Deld Redcar for erection 9.11.15; EF, FL, smashed 9.12.15 (S/Cdr CEH Rathborne unhurt); Deleted 22.12.15

8449 Deld Redcar for erection 15.11.15; Broke skid 1.2.16; Deleted 3.2.16, brought forward as spares

8450 (60-hp Le Rhône) deld Redcar for erection by Mkrs 22.12.15; CW at night in gale 15.2.16; Deleted 1.3.16

8451 (60-hp Le Rhône) Deld Killingholme 24.12.15; Deleted 18.3.16

8452 (60-hp Le Rhône) Deld Walney Island 29.12.15; Flown 2.2.16; Stripped for packing 13.3.16; Howden 24.4.16; Dismantled at Barrow by 7.7.16; Howden 10.7.16 to 3.9.16 (then not listed), later deleted

8453 (60-hp Le Rhône) Deld Kingsnorth for erection 10.1.16; Dismantling by 28.6.16; Despatched 29.6.16, later deleted

**12 R.E.P. PARASOL TRACTOR MONOPLANES purchased in France from Robert Esnault-Pelterie & numbered 8454 to 8465. (110-hp Le Rhône)**

8454 Deld 4 Wing Eastchurch 26.8.15; attd Reserve Sqdn 1 Wing Dunkerque 23.9.15; transferred 4 Wing to 1 Wing charge 6.11.15; 4 Wing Eastchurch 2.3.16; Detling 20.3.16; Damaged 10.4.16; 4 Wing Eastchurch 12.4.16 (repairs to wings); War Flt Eastchurch 16.4.16; Deleted 19.4.16

8455 Deld 4 Wing Eastchurch 4.9.15; attd Reserve Sqdn 1 Wing Dunkerque 23.9.15; transferred 4 Wing to 1 Wing charge 6.11.15

8456 Deld CSD White City; 4 Wing Eastchurch for erection 30.9.15; War Flt Eastchurch 16.4.16; Deleted 1.5.16

8457 Deld CSD White City; 4 Wing Eastchurch for erection 30.9.15; HACP 20.2.16 (FSL HL Wood); HSPP 19.3.16 (F/L FT Digby & PO Smale); Westgate loan but wrecked in gale 25.3.16; Retd 4 Wing Eastchurch in lorry 1.4.16; War Flt Eastchurch 16.4.16; Wrecked Westgate 28.4.16; Deleted 29.4.16

8458 Deld CSD White City; 4 Wing Eastchurch for erection 30.9.15; Westgate 31.3.16; War Flt Eastchurch 21.4.16; HSPP 3.5.16 (FSL HL Wood); HAPP 4.5.16 (FSL HL Wood); Deleted 19.5.16

8459 Deld CSD White City; 4 Wing Eastchurch for erection 30.9.15; HSPP 9.2.16 (FSL RE Greensmith); HACP 20.2.16 (FSL HG Brackley & AM Peachey); War Flt Eastchurch 16.4.16; Deleted 19.5.16

8460 Deld CSD White City; 4 Wing Eastchurch for erection 22.9.15; Reserve Sqdn 1 Wing Dunkerque 23.9.15; FTR attack on Zeebrugge seaplane sheds, FL Zuidgarde 3.10.15 (FSL JED Boyd interned); Aircraft interned and became Dutch *LA-23* later *REP-3*

8461 Deld CSD White City; 4 Wing Eastchurch for erection 22.9.15; attd Reserve Sqdn 1 Wing Dunkerque 23.9.15; 4 Wing Eastchurch 2.3.16; War Flt Eastchurch 16.4.16 (awaiting test); Deleted 19.4.16

8462 Deld CSD White City; 4 Wing Eastchurch for erection 22.9.15; to Reserve Sqdn 1 Wing Dunkerque but FL in sea and sank nr Dunkerque 23.9.15 (FSL CT McLaren)

8463 Deld CSD White City; 4 Wing Eastchurch for erection 25.9.15; Wrecked 21.4.16 (repaired); War Flt Eastchurch 16.4.16; Deleted 19.4.16

8464 Deld CSD White City; 4 Wing Eastchurch for erection 22.9.15; FL Sittingbourne 25.12.15 (FSL C Perrett & AM Palmer); War Flt Eastchurch 16.4.16; Deleted 19.4.16

8465 Deld CSD White City; 4 Wing Eastchurch for erection 30.9.15; War Flt Eastchurch 16.4.16; Deleted 19.4.16

**8 MAURICE FARMAN S.11 SHORTHORN PUSHER BIPLANES purchased from Aéroplanes Farman, Paris, numbered 8466 to 8473. (70/75 hp Renault)**

8466 Deld Eastbourne FS 5.9.15; Chingford 21.9.15; Bomb

Flt Eastchurch by lorry 4.5.16; Damaged 10.8.16; Damaged 28.11.16, to Workshops; Eastchurch Gunnery Flts 1.6.17; Surveyed 8.11.17; Deleted 14.12.17

8467 Deld Chingford for erection 27.8.15; Bomb Flt Eastchurch 30.5.16; Crashed 4.11.16, to Eastchurch Workshops; Deleted 8.11.16

8468 Deld Eastbourne FS for erection 27.8.15; Eastchurch NFS for erection 9.9.15; Damaged landing 7.10.15 (FSL CFB Penley); Eastchurch Workshops 20.10.16; Eastchurch 2.1.17; Gunnery Flt Eastchurch 25.4.17; Surveyed 8.11.17; Deleted 14.12.17 W&T

8469 Deld Eastchurch NFS for erection 21.9.15 (Longhorn?); Wrecked 23.1.16 (FSL CG Ward killed); Deleted 12.2.16

8470 Deld Eastchurch NFS for erection 21.9.15 (Longhorn?); Wrecked 17.12.15; Gun Flt Eastchurch 17.3.16 - @2.11.16; Bomb Flt Eastchurch by 19.12.16; Gunnery Flt Eastchurch 25.4.17 - @26.6.17; Observers School Flt Eastchurch by 6.17; U/c damaged 24.7.17; Surveyed 8.11.17; Deleted 14.12.17 W&T

8471 Deld Eastchurch NFS for erection 21.10.15 (Longhorn?); Damaged 28.11.15 (Longhorn, repaired); Bomb Flt Eastchurch 17.3.16; Damaged 28.4.16; U/c broken on/by 8.2.17; Gunnery Flt Eastchurch 25.4.17; Surveyed 8.11.17; Deleted 14.12.17 W&T

8472 Deld Chingford for erection 15.10.15; 4 Wing Eastchurch 21.2.16; Gun Flt Eastchurch 13.3.16; Wrecked 19.7.16 (repaired); Gunnery Flt Eastchurch 25.4.17; Surveyed 8.11.17; Deleted 14.12.17 W&T

8473 Deld Chingford for erection 15.10.15; Eastchurch 21.2.16; Chingford to Gun Flt Eastchurch by lorry 8.5.16; Bomb Flt Eastchurch 3.6.16; Eastchurch Workshops 12.12.16; Bomb Flt Eastchurch 23.2.17; Gunnery Flt Eastchurch 25.4.17 - @26.6.17; Observers School Flt Eastchurch by 8.17; Surveyed 8.11.17; Deleted 14.12.17 W&T

**1 MAURICE FARMAN S.7 LONGHORN PUSHER BIPLANE purchased from Aéroplanes Farman, Paris, numbered 8474. (75 hp Renault)**

8474 Deld Eastchurch NFS for erection by 27.10.15; Damaged 14.1.16; Bomb Flt Eastchurch 17.3.16; War Flt Eastchurch to Chingford 4.5.16; Deleted 28.7.16

**12 NIEUPORT TWIN TRACTOR BIPLANES ordered by 12.15 from France & numbered 8475 to 8486. (Two 110-hp Clerget)**

8475 to 8486 cancelled

**1 PEMBERTON-BILLING P.B.23E SCOUT PUSHER BIPLANE ordered under Cont No C.P.62042/15 from Supermarine Aviation Works, numbered 8487 & built Woolston. (80-hp Le Rhône 9c)**

8487 Deld Chingford 6.9.15; EF, FL in cornfield 1m from aerodrome 6.9.15 (S/Cdr JT Babington); Wreckage by lorry to Southampton (unserialled); to Grain; Refitted 80-hp Gnome; Hendon; Grain 24.9.15 (awaiting constructors); Grain Repair Depot 6.10.15; Became PVRD in/by 3.16; Tested 3.10.16; Mods by 27.11.16; Renamed ECD Grain 26.2.17; Deleted 7.3.17

**13 ROYAL AIRCRAFT FACTORY B.E.2c TRACTOR BIPLANES ordered under Cont No C.P.79587/15 from Sir William Beardmore & Co Ltd, numbered 8488 to 8500 & built Dalmuir. (90-hp R.A.F.1a)**

8488 Shipped from London to Aegean in SS *Khyber* 11.4.16; 2 Wing Aegean by 4.16 - @8.16

8489 Shipped to Mombasa for East Africa Field Force W/E 24.6.16; 7 Sqdn Iringa by 10.16; Wrecked on TO Iringa 7.11.16

8490 Shipped from London to Aegean in SS *Khyber* 11.4.16; 2 Wing Aegean by 4.16; Surveyed Mudros 12.10.17; Deleted 29.10.17 wrecked

8491 Shipped from London to Aegean in SS *Khyber* 11.4.16; 2 Wing Aegean by 4.16 - @8.16; Deleted 1916

8492 Deld by rail to Yarmouth 22.3.16; Erected 17.4.16; Tested 18.4.16; Awaiting 100-hp RAF and acceptance

by 16.6.16; Accepted 3.7.16 (Dukinfield Jones); Holt 21.7.16; Yarmouth 26.7.16; 3 AZPs 30/31.7.16 (F/L E Cadbury, then FSL AV Robinson, then F/L CHC Smith); AZP, EF, FL wrecked Wymondham 1.8.16 (FSL EB Thompson); Holt 15.12.16; Yarmouth 28.12.16; Holt 5.1.17; Yarmouth 14.1.17; Bacton 10.2.17; Yarmouth 23.2.17; Burgh Castle 28.3.17; Yarmouth 30.3.17; Bacton 21.4.17; Yarmouth 6.5.17; Burgh Castle 11.5.17; Holt 25.5.17; Bacton 6.6.17; Yarmouth 22.6.17; Burgh Castle 29.6.17; Yarmouth 6.7.17; Holt 7.7.17; Burgh Castle 21.7.17; Yarmouth 30.7.17; Burgh Castle 6.8.17; AZP, EF at 3,000ft, o/t landing 19/20.10.17 (F/L CS Nunn); still Burgh Castle 19.1.18; Yarmouth by 23.2.18; Became 490 Flt Yarmouth by 25.5.18

8493 Deld Yarmouth by road for erection 29.3.16; Accepted 18.4.16; Attacked *L9* with bombs 25.4.16 (F/Cdr V Nicholl); Bacton 11.5.16; Yarmouth 16.5.16; Holt 1.6.16; Yarmouth 18.6.16; Holt 19.6.16; Yarmouth 21.6.16; Holt 28.6.16; Yarmouth 21.7.16; Holt 3.8.16; Yarmouth 16.8.16; Holt 23.8.16; Covehithe 7.9.16; Yarmouth 14.9.16; Covehithe 21.9.16; AZP 23/24.9.16 (FSL S Kemball); HACP 25.9.16 (FSL JC Northrop); Yarmouth 28.9.16; Burgh Castle 2.10.16; Holt 3.10.16; Holt 9.10.16; Covehithe 16.10.16; Yarmouth 10.16; Holt 23.10.16; Yarmouth but FL in fog and damaged ½m from aerodrome 24.10.16; Holt but FL en route at Letheringsett 28.12.16 (FSL JC Northrop); Yarmouth 5.1.17; Holt 14.1.17; Yarmouth 31.1.17; Holt 10.2.17; Yarmouth 27.2.17; Holt 13.3.17; Yarmouth 31.3.17; Holt 1.4.17; Yarmouth 4.4.17; Holt 21.4.17; Yarmouth 25.4.17; Holt 28.4.17; Yarmouth but EF, FL Baconsthorpe 6.5.17; Yarmouth 10.5.17; Holt W/E 8.9.17; Yarmouth W/E 15.9.17; Deleted 23.2.18

8494 Deld Dover for erection for overseas 3.4.16; Tested 15.4.16 (Dukinfield Jones); ADD 21.4.16; 12 Flt B Sqdn 4 Wing Petite Synthe by 24.5.16; ADD 1.11.16; Dover 10.11.16; Surveyed 16.10.17; Deleted 19.10.17 W&T

8495 Deld Dover for erection for overseas 3.4.16; Tested 15.4.16 (Dukinfield Jones); ADD 21.4.16; 4 Flt B Sqdn 1 Wing by 11.5.16; ADD 2.6.16; War Flt Eastchurch 23.9.16; Crashed 14.11.16; Eastchurch Workshops 15.11.16; Observers School Flt Eastchurch 10.2.17; O/t on TO 8.5.17 (PFO LGleB Croke); Fitted 100-hp by 10.17; Surveyed 20.12.17; Deleted 28.12.17 DBR

8496 Erecting Westgate 7.4.16; Tested 16.4.16; HAPPs 26.4.16 (FSL EE Deans & LM R Frater) & 28.4.16 (FSL EE Deans & AM Sommerville); Grain 11.5.16; Smashed landing Eastchurch 21.5.16; Deleted 24.5.16; Rebuilt and recommissioned; Handley Page Sqdn Manston 26.3.17; Surveyed 30.10.17; Deleted 2.11.17 wrecked

8497 Deld Westgate for erection 6.4.16; Tested 16.4.16; Chased *LZ87* 26.4.16 (F/Cdr CH Butler); Chased *LZ93* 26.4.16 (F/Cdr CH Butler); HSPP 20.5.16 (F/Cdr CH Butler); AZP 3.8.16 (S/Cdr RLG Marix); Holt but FL in mist at Leatheringsett 28.12.16; Handley Page Sqdn Manston by 26.2.17; Grain 18.8.17; Chingford 19.8.17; Hendon 20.8.17; St.Pol 20.8.17; Hendon 22.8.17; Manston 22.8.17; War Flt/School Manston by 6.10.17; For deletion by 30.3.18

8498 Deld Trimley 1.9.16; Yarmouth 12.9.16; HACP 1.10.16 (FSL JC Northrop); Burgh Castle, AZP 1.10.16 (FSL JC Northrop); Yarmouth 2.10.16; Burgh Castle 5.10.16; Yarmouth 17.10.16; HACP 19.10.16 (F/L CJ Galpin); Bacton 26.10.16; Holt 27.10.16; Yarmouth 1.11.16; Bacton 8.11.16; Holt 10.11.16; Yarmouth 21.11.16; Bacton 28.11.16; Holt 30.11.16; Yarmouth 6.12.16; Bacton 22.12.16; Yarmouth 28.12.16; Bacton 5.1.17; Yarmouth 13.1.17; Covehithe 14.1.17; HACPs 24.1.17 & 26.1.17 (FSL AV Robinson); Yarmouth 29.1.17; Bacton 31.1.17; Burgh Castle 10.2.17; Yarmouth 13.2.17; Bacton 18.2.17; Burgh Castle 9.3.17; HACP 25.3.17 (F/L FW Walker); Covehithe 28.3.17; Bacton 4.4.17; Holt 5.4.17; HACP 7.4.17 (FSL HD Smith); Yarmouth 21.4.17; Holt 25.4.17; Yarmouth 4.17; Burgh Castle 28.4.17; Holt 8.5.17; AZP, missing, probably ran out of fuel chasing *L40* and FL in sea 24.5.17 (FSL HD Smith killed); Deleted 25.5.17

8499 Deld Felixstowe 4.5.16; Yarmouth 7.9.16; HAPP,

landed Burgh Castle 23.9.16 (F/L CHC Smith); Holt 28.9.16; Yarmouth 8.10.16; Bacton 26.10.16 (overnight for Holt); Yarmouth 1.11.16; Holt 21.11.16; AZP 28.11.16 (FSL AV Robinson); Yarmouth 30.11.16; Holt 6.12.16; Yarmouth 15.12.16; Bacton 28.12.16; Yarmouth 5.1.17; Burgh Castle 8.1.17; Yarmouth 10.1.17; Burgh Castle 6.2.17; Covehithe 10.2.17; Yarmouth 24.2.17; Burgh Castle 1.3.17; Covehithe 9.3.17; HACP 10.3.17 (FSL GH Simpson) (at Burgh Castle); COL 27.3.17 (FSL AV Robinson); Yarmouth, BR 28.3.17; Deleted 6.4.17

**8500** Deld Grain by road 18.4.16; AZP 25.8.16 (F/L EdeC Hallifax); Fitted for night flying 2.17; HP Sqdn Manston 8.2.17; FL All Hallows 12.7.17; Surveyed 30.10.17; Deleted 2.11.17 W&T

## 9 VOISIN TYPE III LA.S PUSHER BIPLANES purchased from Aéroplanes Voisin, numbered 8501 to 8509 & built Issy-les-Moulineaux. (140/150-hp Canton Unné)

**8501** (140-hp) Shipped to Aegean; Deld 3 Wing Imbros 7.15; C Flt A Sqdn 2 Wing Imbros by 13.11.15 - @30.12.15; Deleted 1916

**8502** (140-hp) Shipped to Aegean; Deld 3 Wing Imbros 7.15; C Flt A Sqdn 2 Wing Imbros by 29.11.15 - @17.12.15; Attacked by enemy aircraft while spotting, FL nr Helles aerodrome, crew destroyed aircraft with picks, shovel and sledgehammers 8.1.16 (FSL FDH Bremner & Mid HE Burnaby); Deleted 1916

**8503** (140-hp) Shipped to Aegean; Deld 3 Wing Imbros 7.15; 2 Wing Imbros by 18.12.15; EF, FL in salt lake, crashed 17.1.16 (FSL LA Hervey)

**8504** (140-hp) Deld Eastchurch NFS 2.11.15 for erection; Miscellaneous Flt Eastchurch 5.5.16; Wrecked 11.8.16; Deleted 28.8.16

**8505** (150-hp) Dunkerque by 11.15; Shipped to Mesopotamia 2.11.15; Left in SS *Chantara* 9.11.15; Transferred RFC Force D Mesopotamia, arr 17.1.16; Crashed and wrecked Basra Air Park 31.1.16 (Lt TO Clogstoun RFC); Deleted 11.3.16; Wreckage to UK 14.3.16 (also wreckage of another RNAS Voisin)

**8506** (150-hp) Shipped to Mesopotamia 2.11.15; Left in SS *Chantara* 9.11.15; Transferred to RFC Force D in Mesopotamia, arrived 17.1.16; Food drops in Kut siege; Landed under telegraph wires, broke u/c 5.5.16 (F/L WH Dunn); SOC 11.10.16

**8507** (150-hp) Deld CSD White City; Redcar for erection 11.11.15; Tested 19.11.15; Damaged on landing 17.1.16; Deleted 3.2.16

**8508** (150-hp) Deld CSD White City; Redcar for erection 12.11.15; Eastchurch 28.3.16; Rochford (transit) 31.3.16; Exptl Flt Grain 1.4.16; 4 Wing Eastchurch 3.4.16; Tested 7.4.16; Eastchurch 8.4.16; Grain 9.4.16; Gun Flt Eastchurch, erecting and fitting gun 24.4.16; Deleted 27.6.16

**8509** (150-hp) Deld Redcar for erection 18.11.15; Eastchurch NFS for erection 20.3.16; Misc Flt Eastchurch 12.5.16; Gun Flt Eastchurch 8.9.16; Eastchurch Workshops 23.12.16; Gun Flt Eastchurch 17.1.17; Deleted W/E 15.9.17

[9501-8503 & 2 other Voisins with 3 Wing by 31.8.15]

## 6 NIEUPORT 12 FIGHTER RECONNAISSANCE TWO-SEATER TRACTOR BIPLANES ordered by 12.15 from Établissements Nieuport, numbered 8510 to 8515 & built Issy-les-Moulineaux. (110-hp Clerget 9Z)

**8510** Deld ADD by 22.6.16; 4 Flt B Sqdn 1 Wing St.Pol by 25.6.16; ADD by 3.8.16; Dover 31.8.16; War Flt Eastchurch 24.10.16; Dover 1.11.16; Surveyed 16.10.17; Deleted 19.10.17 W&T

**8511** Deld ADD by 22.6.16; "Dover Sqdn" by 2.7.16 (later called Dover Defence Flt); ADD by 27.7.16; Dover 6.9.16 - @31.12.16

**8512** Deld ADD by 22.6.16 (Convtd single-seater); Blown over by wind after landing, damaged 26.8.16 (F/L EM Pizey); 11 Flt B Sqdn 4 Wing Dunkerque 28.11.16; Became 6 Sqdn 12.16 - @8.3.17; 11 Sqdn by 15.3.17; ADD by 10.5.17; Deleted 14.5.17 general fatigue

**8513** Shipped to Aegean; Arr 2 Wing Mudros 7.16; Rumanian Flt Bucharest 21.11.16 - 11.16; Deleted 1917

**8514** Shipped to Aegean; Arr 2 Wing Mudros 7.16; Imbros to Rumanian Flt Bucharest 25.10.16 (S/L HV Reid) - 11.16; Deleted 1917

**8515** Shipped to Aegean; 2 Wing Mudros by 7.16; Surveyed Mudros 10.10.17; Deleted 26.10.17 W&T

## 2 NIEUPORT 10 TWO-SEATER TRACTOR BIPLANES purchased from Établissements Nieuport, numbered 8516 and 8517 & built Issy-les-Moulineaux. (80-hp Le Rhône)

**8516** Deld 4 Wing Eastchurch 27.8.15; to be attd Reserve Sqdn 1 Wing Dunkerque 23.9.15, but engine trouble at Dover en route; Missing 26.9.15; Deleted 21.4.16

**8517** Deld 4 Wing Eastchurch 31.8.15; attd Reserve Sqdn 1 Wing Dunkerque 23.9.15 - @3.10.15; Eastchurch Group 1 Wing by 18.10.15; 1 Flt A Sqdn 1 Wing 1.3.16 - @2.3.16; ADD to Dover 31.3.16; ADD 29.6.16; 2-str OOC at 9,000ft 3m E of Dixmude 18.00 21.7.16 (FSL SJ Goble); ADD by 27.7.16; C Sqdn 1 Wing by 9.8.16 - @26.10.16; Dover Defence Flt 1 Wing, large 2-str seaplane left wing collapsed 4-5m off Ostende 07.30 15.8.16 (FSL SJ Goble); ADD by 2.11.16; For survey 9.11.16; Deleted 5.1.17

## 6 VOISIN TYPE III LA.S PUSHER BIPLANES purchased from Aéroplanes Voisin, numbered 8518 to 8523 & built Issy-les-Moulineaux. (150-hp Canton Unné)

**8518** Shipped to Mesopotamia (requested 13.11.15); Transferred RFC for Force D Mesopotamia; Tested after arrival 24.6.16; SOC 25.11.16

**8519** Deld Eastchurch NFS for re-erection 22.11.15; Wrecked at Eastbourne 8.2.16; Deleted 2.3.16 DBR

**8520** Deld Redcar for erection 13.11.15; Scarborough 26.12.15; Hornsea 26.12.15; Wrecked when Bessonneau tent blown away in gale 10.2.16; AZP 11.2.16; Hornsea 12.2.16; Scarborough, awaiting survey 1.3.16; Deleted 13.3.16

**8521** Deld Redcar for erection 18.11.15; Gunnery School Flts Eastchurch 6.5.16; Eastchurch Workshops 23.12.16; Eastchurch FS 31.1.17; COL 2.2.17, to Eastchurch Workshops; Deleted 15.3.17

**8522** Deld CSD White City by 1.16; Left for 8 Sqdn East Africa 26.1.16; arr Durban by 31.3.16 - @30.4.16; Could be the Voisin which arrived 15.3.16 (FSL LG Sieveking - or 8700); 8 Sqdn Chukwani by 1.5.16; to 8 Sqdn Lindi early 6.16; 8 Sqdn Lindi, erected early 6.17; Under overhaul 9.17; Tested after overhaul 2.10.17; still 8 Sqdn 17.11.17

**8523** Shipped to Mesopotamia (requested 13.11.15); Transferred to RFC for Force D in Mesopotamia; Tested Basra on arrival 10.6.16; Crashed 26.10.16 (Lt S Haywood & Lt LH King-Harman killed)

## 6 NIEUPORT TYPE 12 TWO-SEATER TRACTOR BIPLANE SCOUTS purchased from Établissements Nieuport, numbered 8524 to 8529 & built at Issy-les-Moulineaux. (110-hp Clerget 9Z)

**8524** (C/n N1421). Shipped to Aegean; Arr 2 Wing Mudros 7.16; Imbros 24.10.16 (transit); To Bucharest but FL Dragaeuusti 40m SW of city 25.10.16 (F/L GA Cox); Rumanian Flt Bucharest, tested 3.11.16

**8525** (C/n N1422). Shipped to Aegean; arr 2 Wing Mudros 7.16; Imbros 10.16 (transit); To Rumanian Flt Bucharest but FL 20m N of Ismail, Russia 25.10.16 (F/L AFF Jacob); Reached Bucharest 30.11.16

**8526** Deld ADD 6.7.16; 10 Flt A Sqdn 4 Wing Dunkerque by 9.7.16; 9 Flt A Sqdn 4 Wing by 3.8.16 - @6.8.16; Crashed and CW; ADD by 10.8.16; For survey by 17.8.16; Deleted 17.9.16

**8527** Deld ADD 6.7.16; 6 Flt A Sqdn 5 Wing Coudekerque 7.9.16; Crashed and damaged 1.10.16 (FSL CPO Bartlett); ADD by 14.12.16; Crashed and DBR 24.12.16; For survey by 28.12.16; Deleted 5.1.17

**8528** Deld ADD by 20.7.16; 10 Flt A Sqdn 4 Wing by 6.8.16; 9 Flt A Sqdn 4 Wing Dunkerque by 20.9.16 (Single-seater); ADD 17.10.16; Dover 11.12.16; Deleted 8.4.17

**8529** Shipped to Aegean; arr 2 Wing Mudros 7.16 - @8.16; Deleted 1917

**12 SHORT S.38 TYPE PUSHER BIPLANES ordered under Cont No C.P.77567/15 from White & Thompson, numbered 8530 to 8541 & built Middleton-on-Sea. All due for delivery to CSD 1.4.16. (Ordered 60-hp Le Rhône. Deld 80-hp Gnome)**

| | |
|---|---|
| 8530 | Deld Chingford 1.3.16; Deleted 22.4.16 |
| 8531 | Deld Chingford 5.3.16; Deleted 22.4.16 |
| 8532 | Deld Chingford 10.3.16; Wrecked by gale 28.3.16; Deleted 24.4.16 |
| 8533 | Deld Chingford 27.3.16; Wrecked by gale 28.3.16; Deleted 24.4.16 |
| 8534 | Deld Chingford 9.4.16; Deleted 21.4.16 |
| 8535 | Deld Hendon to Chingford 1.4.16; Dismantled 15.4.16; Deleted 21.4.16 |
| 8536 | to 8541 due for delivery 4.16 - to store? |

**8 WIGHT ADMIRALTY 840 TYPE TRACTOR BIPLANE SEAPLANES ordered 16.8.15 (later 14.11.15) from Portholme Aerodrome Ltd, Huntingdon under Cont No C.P.78421/15, numbered 8542 to 8549 & built East Cowes. Delivery due 20.5.16, but contract closed 5.16, aircraft to be delivered without engines at makers works.**

8542 to 8549 delivered to CSD White City as spares by 11.9.16

**12 SHORT ADMIRALTY 827 TYPE TRACTOR BIPLANE SEAPLANES ordered 29.8.15 under Cont No C.P.57387/15 from Fairey Aviation Co Ltd, numbered 8550 to 8561 & built Hamble. Some initially to store. (150-hp Sunbeam Crusader) [C/n's F.4 to F.15]**

| | |
|---|---|
| 8550 | Deld Calshot FS for assembly 28.3.16; Deleted W/E 14.9.17 |
| 8551 | Deld Hamble to Calshot 24.10.16; Portland 12.3.17; Calshot 7.4.17; Survey 8.11.17; Deleted 17.11.17 W&T |
| 8552 | Deld Calshot FS, test postponed 14.4.16 due to weather; Fitted DC 12.16; Lee-on-Solent W/E 12.10.17; Deleted W/E 21.3.18 |
| 8553 | Deld and accepted Calshot 5.5.16; Deleted W/E 14.9.17 |
| 8554 | Deld Calshot and accepted 16.6.16; Portland 7.9.16 (detd for special anti-submarine patrols); Calshot 18.9.16; Attacked U-boat 10/12m N of the Casquets 24.9.16 (F/L EJ Cooper); AZP 25/26.9.16 (F/L EJ Cooper); Deleted 9.2.17 |
| 8555 | Deld Calshot 14.4.16; Surveyed 28.9.17; Deleted 6.10.17 W&T |
| 8556 | Deld Calshot 2.6.16; Hit mast of a transport ship on landing and dived onto its deck in Southampton Water 20.7.16 (FSL IN Carmichael & FSL A Wallace both killed); Deleted 20.8.16 |
| 8557 | Accepted Cowes and deld Calshot 23.6.16; CW off Calshot 16.7.16 (FSL TC Wilkinson); Deleted 17.7.16 |
| 8558 | Deld Calshot 6.16; to Westgate but EF, FL, propeller smashed, Folkestone Harbour 27.6.16 (FSL CFM Chambers); arr Westgate 28.6.16; EF, FL nr Sunk LV 23.10.16 (FSL MH Stephen & AM Gregory rescued by friendly vessel); Deleted 24.10.16 |
| 8559 | Deld Calshot 8.8.16; Portland 25.9.16; Calshot FS 1.10.16; Deleted 2.6.17 |
| 8560 | Fairey ordered to fit tropical radiators 5.16 (NTU?); Allocated Cape Station W/E 24.7.16 (NTU); Windermere from 13.10.16; To be tested by Pickles but bad weather 27.10.16; Acceptance tests 16.11.16 & 14.12.16; Fairey again ordered to fit tropical radiators 12.16 (NTU?); Transferred to RFC (Military Wing) early 1917 for School of Aerial Gunnery Loch Doon, becoming A9920 [in store at Bogton by 26.9.18; 6 AAP Renfrew W/E 9.1.19 - @30.1.19] |
| 8561 | Fairey ordered to fit tropical radiators 5.16 (NTU?); Allocated Cape Station W/E 24.7.16 (NTU); Fairey again ordered to fit tropical radiators 12.16 (NTU?); Accepted at Hamble 26.2.17; Deld Calshot 24.3.17; 225-hp by 5.17 per a logbook, but 150-hp @23.1.18 - @23.2.18; Became 210 TDS Calshot 6.18 - 8.18; ARS Calshot W/E 22.8.18; 209 TDS Lee-on-Solent W/E 5.9.18 - @30.1.19 |

**12 BRISTOL BOXKITE TRACTOR BIPLANES ordered under Cont No C.P.57306/15/X, numbered 8562 to 8573 & built Filton. (Ordered with 50-hp Gnome, but deld with 80-hp Le Rhône) (60-hp Le Rhône per 1.17 list) [C/n's 882 to 893]**

| | |
|---|---|
| 8562 | Deld Walney Island for rigging 18.1.16; Awaiting test 3.2.16; Broke propeller on TO 4.3.16; Stripped for packing 13.3.16; Howden (dismantled) 24.4.16; Deleted 4.9.16 |
| 8563 | Deld Killingholme 17.1.16; Deleted 18.3.16 |
| 8564 | Deld Kingsnorth 10.1.16; Deleted 13.4.16 |
| 8565 | Deld Kingsnorth and flown 26.4.16; Dismantling by 28.6.16; Despatched 29.6.16, later deleted |
| 8566 | Deld Walney Island and awaiting test 3.2.16; Stripped for packing 13.3.16; Howden 24.4.16; Deleted 3.9.16 |
| 8567 | Deld Redcar for erection 5.2.16; Deleted 21.3.16 |
| 8568 | Deld Redcar for erection 5.2.16; Deleted 1.4.16 |
| 8569 | No evidence of delivery, probably to spares |
| 8570 | Deld Eastchurch NFS for erection 1.10.15; Probably to spares |
| 8571 | Deld CSD White City and stored less engine. |
| 8572 | Deld CSD White City and stored less engine |
| 8573 | No evidence of delivery, probably to spares |

**30 AVRO 504C ("SCOUT") TRACTOR BIPLANES ordered 21.10.15 under Cont No C.P.61138/15, numbered 8574 to 8603 & built Manchester. (80-hp Gnome)**

| | |
|---|---|
| 8574 | Deld Chingford by rail 8.10.15; Erected by makers; Tested 17.10.15 (Raynham); 4 Wing Eastchurch 22.10.15; EF, FL Peckham 24.11.15 (repaired); still 4 Wing 1.1.16; Deleted Detling 7.4.16; War Flt Eastchurch 6.5.16; Gunnery School Flts Eastchurch 11.5.16; Eastchurch FS 14.7.16; COL, propeller and u/c WO 1.2.17 (PFO WL Jordan); to Eastchurch Workshops; Eastchurch FS 19.1.17; Crashed 2.2.17; to Eastchurch Workshops; Deleted 26.4.17 |
| 8575 | Deld Chingford by rail 8.10.15; Erected by Mkrs; Tested 17.10.15 (Raynham); Trimley 13.11.15; Felixstowe 24.1.16; War Flt Eastchurch 12.5.16; School Flt Eastchurch 26.5.16; Eastchurch FS to Eastchurch Workshops 2.1.17 (repair); Eastchurch FS 19.1.17; Eastchurch Workshops 7.5.17 (repair); Eastchurch FS 30.5.17; Chingford W/E 10.11.17; Deleted W/E 23.2.18 |
| 8576 | Deld Chingford 12.10.15; Tested 28.10.15 (Raynham); Yarmouth 3.11.15; To Bacton but EF, FL Bradwell 22.11.15 (FSL FN Halsted); Retd Yarmouth 23.11.15; HACPs 20.2.16 (F/L CHC Smith), 31.3.16 (FSL AF Marlowe), 15.4.16 (FSL EB Thompson), 16.4.16 (FSL CJ Galpin also FSL SG Beare), 23.4.16 (FSL BS Wemp), 29.5.16 (F/L JW Hobbs, later FSL BS Wemp) & 2.7.16 (FSL CJ Galpin); Deleted 5.7.16 |
| 8577 | Deld Chingford 11.10.15; 4 Wing Eastchurch 22.10.15; Wrecked 23.12.15 (FSL J Robinson); War Flt Eastchurch 16.4.16; Misc Flt Eastchurch 28.4.16; Eastchurch FS 14.7.16; Eastchurch 22.11.16; Observers School Flt Eastchurch 23.12.16; Detling 24.12.16; Observers School Flt Eastchurch 28.2.17; Eastchurch Workshops 14.3.17 (alterations); Observers School Flt Eastchurch 13.4.17; Eastchurch Workshops, deletion recommended 10.5.17; Observers School Flt Eastchurch 14.6.17; Damaged by 29.9.17; Surveyed 18.3.18; Deleted 27.3.18 W&T |
| 8578 | Deld Chingford 14.10.15; Felixstowe 29.10.15; U/c smashed 30.12.15 (F/L AW Clemson); Chingford by lorry 15.2.16; Erected 13.3.16; FL Golf course, damaged 12.7.16; Deleted 18.7.16 |
| 8579 | Deld Chingford 22.10.15; Tested 28.10.15 (Raynham); Yarmouth 3.11.15; Sedgeford 20.11.15; Yarmouth 26.11.15; Sedgeford 27.11.15; to Yarmouth but EF, FL, CW Docking 7.12.15 (FSL WTS Willimans unhurt); Deleted Yarmouth 16.12.15 |
| 8580 | Deld Chingford 22.10.15; Tested 3.11.15 (Raynham); Trimley 13.11.15; Felixstowe 14.11.15; Trimley 9.2.16; War Flt Eastchurch 14.5.16; Eastchurch FS 26.5.16; Gunnery School Flts Eastchurch 4.10.16; Eastchurch Workshops 22.11.16; Eastchurch FS 8.1.17; Manston FS 31.8.17; Deleted W/E 23.2.18 |
| 8581 | Deld Chingford 29.10.15; Tested 15.11.15 (Raynham); To Yarmouth but FL en route at Albury, nr Bishops Stortford 19.11.15 (FSL FE Sandford); HACP 23.1.16 (FSL JA Page); Bacton 18.1.16; Yarmouth 19.1.16; Anti-Zeppelin a/c fitted with upward firing Lewis gun; HACP 20.2.16 (FSL E Cadbury); Bacton 24.3.16 (retd?); Yarmouth, HACPs 31.3.16 (FSL WA Davies) & |

16.4.16 (FSL BS Wemp); Covehithe 21.5.16; Deleted 5.7.16

8582 Deld Felixstowe, tested 21.11.15 (Raynham); Trimley 13.12.15; Felixstowe 23.12.15; Trimley 9.2.16; War Flt Eastchurch 12.5.16; Eastchurch School Flt 26.5.16; Detling 9.6.16; Eastchurch Workshops 16.9.16 (fit new engine); Detling 22.9.16; Eastchurch Workshops 20.12.16 (overhaul); Eastchurch FS 7.4.17; Crashed 7.4.17; Eastchurch Workshops 8.4.17; Deleted 26.4.17

8583 Deld Felixstowe and tested 21.11.15 (Raynham); Trimley 12.12.15; Aldeburgh 13.12.15; Felixstowe 14.12.15; Trimley 9.2.16; Eastchurch FS 25.8.16; Erecting Eastchurch Workshops 27.11.16; Eastchurch FS 8.1.17; Eastchurch Workshops 6.3.17 (repair); Eastchurch FS 28.3.17; Eastchurch Workshops 11.5.17; Chingford W/E 9.11.17; Deleted W/E 9.3.18

8584 Deld Hendon and accepted 19.11.15 (Raynham); Repaired 3.12.15; Flown 13.12.15; Cranwell 25.4.16; Deleted 1.7.16

8585 Deld Chingford for erection 25.11.15; Tested 30.11.15 & 22.12.15 (Raynham); Cranwell 15.4.16 (arr 16.4.16); Deleted 18.6.17

8586 Deld Chingford by lorry 6.12.15; Wrecked Cirencester 6.4.16 (PFSL HL Hitch); Deleted 24.4.16

8587 Deld Chingford by lorry 14.12.15; Tested 25.12.15 (Raynham); Crashed and caught fire 21.2.16 (PFSL FH Toms killed); Deleted 30.3.16

8588 Deld East Fortune 7.12.15; Tested 15.12.15 (Raynham); Dismantled by 29.12.15; Re-erected; Attempted to intercept Zeppelin approaching Edinburgh, COL 2.4.16 (FSL CA Cox); Deleted 4.4.16

8589 Deld East Fortune 8.12.15; Tested 15.12.15 (Raynham); Dismantled 29.12.15; Tested 27.3.16; HSMP 21.4.16 (FSL HG Holden); Chingford for erection 22.9.16 (arr 3.10.16); Deleted 13.6.17

8590 Deld East Fortune 14.12.15; Tested 15.12.15 (Raynham); Dismantled 29.12.15; Tested 8.2.16; Chingford 28.9.16; Deleted 13.6.17

8591 Deld Chingford by lorry 20.12.15; Tested 22.12.15 (Raynham); Cranwell 12.2.16; Deleted 9.11.16

8592 Deld Chingford by lorry 22.12.15; Tested 25.12.15 (Raynham); Taxied into Bristol 1226, propeller cracked 26.1.16 (PFSL RG Gardner); Cranwell 18.2.16; Deleted 20.1.17

8593 Deld East Fortune 24.12.15; Accepted 1.1.16 (Raynham); Dismantled after temporary shed blown down 7.1.16; Retd Avro for re-doping 20.2.16; East Fortune, fitted dart droppers 6/7.4.16; Tested 22.4.16; Chingford 8.9.16; Deleted 13.6.17

8594 Deld Whitley Bay by lorry 29.12.15; Accepted 2.1.16 (Raynham); Brought back from Gosforth 12.1.16; Redcar 4.3.16; Smashed landing 31.3.16; Redcar School by 11.16; For deletion by 30.3.18

8595 Deld Whitley Bay by lorry 29.12.15; Tested 8.1.16; EF, FL smashed 5.2.16 (F/L P Legh); Redcar 28.5.16; EF, FL, smashed u/c 23.6.16 (FSL R Collishaw); Deleted 14.2.17

8596 Deld Chingford by lorry 13.1.16; Tested 20.1.16 (Raynham); Wrecked 17.5.16; Deleted 23.2.18

8597 Deld Chingford by lorry 27.1.16; Tested 1.2.16 (Raynham); Damaged by 9.4.16; EF, FL 19.6.16 (PFSL N Bawlff); BO on landing (pilot unhurt); Deleted 18.7.16

8598 Deld Dover (via Eastchurch) 12.2.16; Brush by road for repair 26.3.16; Dover 1.8.16; Deleted 27.3.17

8599 (Monosoupape) Deld Grain 23.2.16; Housed for Port Victoria Repair Depot from 5.3.16; 4 Wing Eastchurch 28.3.16; War Flt Eastchurch 16.4.16; Crashed 26.10.16; Eastchurch Workshops 27.10.16; Deleted 8.11.16

8600 Deld Scarborough for erection 31.1.16; Damaged in gale at Hornsea 16.4.16; Detd Scarborough AZPs 3.5.16 (FSL JC Croft); Damaged landing Scarborough 3.8.16 (FSL LMB Weil); Redcar 30.1.17; Deleted 8.9.17

8601 Deld Scarborough for erection 31.1.16; EF, FL Robin Hoods Bay 13.2.16 (F/Cdr C Draper); retd Scarborough 15.2.16; Killingholme 18.2.16; Scarborough 19.2.16; HACP, EF, FL in dark and wrecked Speeton, 6m N of Flamborough 24.2.16 (FSL JF Roche); Damaged in gale at Hornsea 16.4.16; Deleted 1.5.16

8602 Deld 4 Wing Eastchurch 19.2.16, awaiting test; War Flt Eastchurch 16.4.16; Dived in on turn nr aerodrome

20.4.16 (FSL NS Douglas severely injured); Deleted 19.5.16

8603 Modified to 504F 8.16 (fit 75 hp RR Hawk); Deld PVRS 31.8.16; Tested 1.10.16; Design Flt Grain 5.12.16 - Became Experimental Design Grain 1.2.17; Hendon 17.3.17; Grain 19.8.17; Hendon 3.9.17 (for use of Air Department officers); Dover 10.5.18 (maybe visit only)

**2 MAURICE FARMAN S.7 LONGHORN PUSHER BIPLANES built from spares under Cont No C.P.79931/15 by Aircraft Manufacturing Co Ltd at Hendon & numbered 8604 and 8605. (70-hp Renault)**

8604 Deld and tested Hendon 29.3.16; Chingford 30.3.16; Fitted DC 5-10.4.16; Deleted 17.12.16

8605 Deld and accepted Hendon 2.5.16; Cranwell 4.5.16; Went into wall on landing 23.5.16 (pilot unhurt); Deleted 5.6.16

**24 ROYAL AIRCRAFT FACTORY B.E.2c TRACTOR BIPLANES ordered under Cont No C.P.60949/15 from Blackburn Aeroplane & Motor Co Ltd, numbered 8606 to 8629 & built Leeds. (90-hp R.A.F.1a)** [7.16 put forward to fit Ranken Dart Boxes. 9.16 put forward to fit bomb dropping attachments]

8606 Deld Dover, tested 26.3.16 (Ding); ADD 1.4.16 (FSL RS Dallas); 10 Flt A Sqdn 4 Wing Dunkerque 15.4.16; Slightly damaged on landing 17.5.16; Hit telegraph wires landing and wrecked 21.5.16 (FSL R Darley unhurt); 12 Flt B Sqdn 4 Wing Petite Synthe by 5.16; Deleted ADD 30.7.16 DBR

8607 Deld Dover, accepted 11.3.16 (Ding); Experimental Flt 1 Wing 16.3.16; 1 Wing by 28.4.16; Exptl Flt 1 Wing by 11.5.16; ADD 24.5.16; 6 Flt A Sqdn 5 Wing Coudekerque 25.6.16; 8 Flt B Sqdn 5 Wing by 20.7.16; ADD by 8.8.16 (for UK); Dover 17.10.16; Chingford 20.10.16 (transit); Yarmouth 22.10.16; Holt 29.9.17 - @6.10.17; Yarmouth by 9.10.17; AZP, COL 19.10.17 (FSL CV Halford Thompson unhurt); Deleted 10.12.17 W&T (now 100-hp RAF)

8608 Deld Dover by 3.16; ADD 19.3.16; 10 Flt A Sqdn 4 Wing Dunkerque by 4.16; 12 Flt B Sqdn 4 Wing Petite Synthe 15.4.16 - 7.16; ADD by 9.16; Yarmouth 7.9.16; Covehithe 15.9.16; Holt 21.9.16; AZP 25/26.9.16 (FSL FW Walker); Covehithe 28.9.16; Yarmouth 8.10.16; Covehithe 23.10.16; Yarmouth 26.10.16; Burgh Castle 4.11.16; Bacton 10.11.16; CW on landing 12.11.16 (FSL LH Brett); Yarmouth for repair 13.11.16; HACP 25.3.17 (FSL TGC Wood); Burgh Castle 26.3.17; Yarmouth by 4.17; Bacton 3.4.17; Burgh Castle 4.17; HACP 7.4.17 (FSL TGC Wood); Yarmouth 4.17; Yarmouth 21.4.17; Bacton 9.5.17; AZPs 23/24.5.17 (FSL TGC Wood) & 17.6.17 (FSL TGC Wood); still Bacton 15.9.17; Yarmouth 9.17; Bacton 25.9.17; Deleted W/E 15.12.17

8609 Deld 4 Wing Eastchurch 25.3.16; AZPs 31.3/1.4.16 (FSL CC Wyllie) & 1.4.16 (F/Cdr REC Peirse); War Flt Eastchurch 16.4.16; HSPP 3.5.16 (FSL ET Bradley & AM Casting); Smashed on night TO 13.5.16 (FSL HL Wood); Deleted 6.6.16

8610 Deld 4 Wing Eastchurch and tested 1.4.16 (Ding); War Flt Eastchurch 16.4.16; Rochford 23.4.16; AZP 25/26.4.16 (FSL EP Hicks); War Flt Eastchurch 4.6.16; AZPs 31.7/1.8.16 (FSL EP Hicks & AM Greenwood) & 23.9.16 (crew unknown); Joyce Green 4.10.16; War Flt Eastchurch 12.10.16; Suttons Farm to Chingford (via Hendon) 28.11.16; Eastchurch 4.12.16; Observers School Flt Eastchurch 23.12.16; Crashed 3.5.17, to Eastchurch Workshops; Surveyed 26.11.17; Deleted 5.12.17 as spares

8611 Shipped to Aegean; Aegean by 4.16; 2 Wing Aegean by 10.16; still commission 1.17

8612 Deld Yarmouth for erection 5.4.16; Accepted 9.4.16 (Ding); Left to bomb German High Fleet raiding Scarborough 25.4.16 (FSL BS Wemp); Bacton 23.5.16; Yarmouth 26.5.16; Sedgeford 26.5.16; Holt to Sedgeford 27.5.16; Yarmouth, awaiting 100-hp RAF by 16.6.16; Covehithe 12.7.16; Yarmouth 18.7.16; Covehithe 28.7.16; AZPs 31.7.16 (FSL JC Northrop) & 3.8.16 (FSL S Kemball); Repairing Covehithe 3.8.16;

Yarmouth to Bacton 4.8.16; Yarmouth 9.8.16; [Gorleston to Yarmouth 23.8.16]; Covehithe to Yarmouth but FL giving assistance to 3056 23.8.16 (F/Cdr V Nicholl); FL and wrecked Gorleston 6.9.16 (FSL CS Nunn); Deleted 19.9.16

**8613** Deld Yarmouth 10.4.16; Accepted 14.4.16 (Dring); Bacton 26.5.16; Yarmouth 19.6.16; Covehithe 19.7.16; Yarmouth 26.7.16; Holt 28.7.16; 2 AZPs 30/31.7.16 (FSL GWR Fane); Yarmouth 2.8.16; AZP 3.8.16 [Holt!] (FSL GWR Fane); Burgh Castle 12.8.16; Yarmouth 16.8.16; Holt 17.8.16; Yarmouth 23.8.16; HACP 17.9.16 (F/L CJ Galpin); Burgh Castle 10.10.16; CW 16.10.16 (pilot slightly injured); Deleted Yarmouth 5.11.16

**8614** Deld Yarmouth by rail 17.4.16; Left to bomb German High Fleet raiding Scarborough 25.4.16 (F/L CHC Smith); Accepted 26.4.16; Bacton 11.5.16; Yarmouth 19.6.16; Bacton 20.6.16; Yarmouth 27.6.16; Sedgeford 28.6.16; Bacton 1.7.16; Yarmouth 26.7.16; Wrecked 23.8.16; Deleted 1.9.16

**8615** Deld Cranwell 8.5.16; Deleted 10.1.17

**8616** Deld Dover 17.5.16; Accepted 7.6.16; Dunkerque 9.7.16; Eastbourne 19.7.16 (transit); Dover 20.7.16; Night flying experiments 7.1.17; Deleted 6.8.17

**8617** Deld Dover 20.5.16; ADD 8.6.16; 6 Flt A Sqdn 5 Wing Coudekerque 24.6.16; 8 Flt B Sqdn 5 Wing by 20.7.16; 7 Flt B Sqdn 5 Wing Coudekerque by 21.9.16 - @23.10.16; ADD by 16.11.16 - @30.11.16; B Flt C Sqdn 1 Wing ferry to ADD 7.12.16; To French on/by 28.12.16 - @25.1.17; ADD by 1.2.17; Deleted ADD 3.9.17 general fatigue

**8618** Deld Yarmouth 2.6.16; Tested 5.6.16 (Ding); Accepted 15.6.16 (Ding); Holt 23.6.16; Yarmouth 24.6.16; Holt 25.6.16; Yarmouth 27.6.16; Covehithe 5.7.16; Yarmouth 11.7.16; 2 AZPs 31.7.16 (FSL EB Thompson); Bacton 2.8.16; AZPs 2/3.8.16 (F/L E Cadbury); Yarmouth 3.8.16; Covehithe 5.8.16; Bacton 9.8.16; Yarmouth 16.8.16; Holt to Bacton with spares 18.8.16; Yarmouth 23.8.16; Sedgeford 24.8.16; Yarmouth 1.9.16; HACP 6.9.16 (FSL GWR Fane); CW on TO 18.9.16 (FSL EB Thompson & AM Carter injured); Deleted 10.10.16

**8619** Deld Grain and accepted 10.6.16 (Ding); Yarmouth 24.3.17; Covehithe 4.4.17; Burgh Castle 7.4.17; Covehithe by 10.4.17; Burgh Castle 21.4.17; Yarmouth 1.5.17; Burgh Castle 3.5.17; Covehithe 11.5.17; AZP 23/24.5.17 (FSL CS Iron); Burgh 11.6.17; AZP 17.6.17 (FSL CS Iron); Yarmouth 28.6.17; Holt 5.7.17; Yarmouth 6.7.17; Covehithe 12.7.17; Yarmouth 24.9.17; AZP 19/20.10.17 (F/L CS Iron); still Covehithe 19.1.18; Yarmouth, FL on beach and damaged, Palling 31.1.18 (pilot unhurt); Deleted 23.2.18

**8620** Deld Cranwell (ex York) 29.6.16; Wrecked 1.3.17 (TFSL GRG Daglish killed); Rebuilt; FL, damaged 9.10.17; FL Gipsey Bridge, 5m NW of Boston 8.12.17; Freiston by 25.3.18; Vertical bank nr ground, crashed and CW 1.4.18 (FSL JE Philbrick & FSL ND Lansdown both injured)

**8621** Deld Cranwell (ex York) 28.6.16; Crashed in plantation, damaged 18.7.16 (pilot unhurt); at Freiston 3.17; Deleted W/E 5.9.17

**8622** Deld Cranwell 11.7.16; Deleted 23.7.16

**8623** Deld D Flt Cranwell 23.8.16 (at Freiston 5.17 until 13.7.17); Deleted W/E 5.9.17

**8624** (Wing tip flares, used as single seater) (100-hp RAF by 12.17) Deld War Flt Eastchurch 21.9.16; Observers School Flt Eastchurch 23.12.16; Deleted W/E 16.2.18

**8625** Deld Yarmouth for erection 16.7.16; Accepted 22.7.16 (Ding); Bacton 24.8.16; Yarmouth 27.8.16; Bacton 28.8.16; 3 AZPs 2/3.9.16 (FSL EL Pulling); Yarmouth 3.9.16; AZP, landed Burgh Castle 23/24.9.16 (F/L E Cadbury); Yarmouth to Bacton 23.10.16; Yarmouth 26.10.16; Burgh Castle, AZP, assisted in destruction of L.21, retd Yarmouth 28.11.16 (F/L E Cadbury awarded DSC); Covehithe 23.3.17; HACP 25.4.17 (FSL GH Simpson); Yarmouth 2.5.17; Covehithe 3.5.17; Yarmouth 11.5.17; AZP 23/24.5.17 (F/L GH Simpson); Damaged 26.5.17; Covehithe 6.6.17; AZP 16/17.6.17 (F/L GH Simpson); Yarmouth 22.6.17; Burgh Castle 26.8.17; Covehithe W/E 15.9.17; Burgh Castle W/E 6.10.17; Deleted W/E 23.2.18

**8626** Deld Yarmouth for erection 16.7.16; Covehithe 3.8.16; Yarmouth 5.8.16; Bacton 23.8.16; Yarmouth 28.8.16; AZP, attacked Zeppelin L11 or L30 at 6,000 ft nr Lowestoft, closed to 20-30 ft 2/3.9.16 (F/L E Cadbury); Bacton 3.9.16; Yarmouth 7.9.16; Bacton 23.9.16; AZP 23/24.9.16 (FSL EL Pulling); AZP, landed Yarmouth 25.9.16 (FSL EL Pulling); Bacton 9.10.16; Capsized landing in high wind and slightly damaged 12.10.16 (FSL EL Pulling); Bacton 1.11.16; Yarmouth 8.11.16; Burgh Castle 10.11.16; Yarmouth 11.11.16; Bacton 21.11.16; Credited with shooting down Zeppelin L21 which fell into sea 8m E of Lowestoft 28.11.16 (FSL EL Pulling awarded DSO); Yarmouth 1.12.16; Bacton 6.12.16; Yarmouth 22.12.16; Burgh Castle 13.1.17; HACPs 24.1.17 & 26.1.17 (FSL TGC Wood); Yarmouth 10.2.17; Burgh Castle 13.2.17; To Yarmouth, but broke up in loop and CW 2.3.17 (F/L EL Pulling, DSO & FSL JE Northrop both killed); Deleted 14.3.17

**8627** Deld Grain 28.8.16; Accepted 4.9.16 (Ding); U/c smashed 12.12.16 (FSL Mostyn Lewis); Deleted 17.1.17

**8628** Deld Grain by rail for erection 12.9.16; Fitted for night flying 1.17; To Detling but FL Four Elms 27.2.17 (FSL GMF O'Brien); arr Detling 28.2.17; War School Manston 2.4.17; AGPs 25.9.17, 29.9.17, 30.9.17 & 19.10.17 (all F/L AF Brandon); 8 Sqdn Walmer (via Eastchurch) 8.3.18 - @25.3.18; War School Manston by 30.3.18; still Manston 9.7.18

**8629** Deld Grain 20.9.16; Tested 25.9.16 (Ding); Yarmouth 24.3.17; Burgh Castle 30.3.17; Yarmouth 5.4.17; Burgh Castle 6.4.17; Yarmouth 13.4.17; Yarmouth 4.5.17; Burgh Castle 10.5.17; AZPs 24.5.17 (F/L FW Walker), 16/17.6.17 (FSL CV Halford Thompson later FSL FW Walker) & 25.9.17; Burgh Castle, AZP, landed Bacton 19.10.17 (F/L FW Walker); Surveyed 14.12.17; Deleted 21.12.17 wrecked

**20 SHORT ADMIRALTY 827 TYPE TRACTOR BIPLANE SEAPLANES ordered 29.5.15 under Cont No C.P.78661/15 from Sunbeam Motors, numbered 8630 to 8649 & built Wolverhampton. (150-hp Sunbeam Crusader)**

**8630** Deld Grain 1.4.16; Accepted 4.5.16; Felixstowe 12.5.16; Nore War Flt Felixstowe 15.8.16; Deleted 1.7.17

**8631** Deld Grain 10.5.16; Felixstowe 31.5.16; Nore War Flt Felixstowe 13.8.16; AZP 25.8.16 (FSL CE Fox & AM AE Shorter); Killingholme School 4.7.17; Deleted W/E 22.9.17

**8632** Deld Grain 13.4.16; Accepted 10.5.16; Felixstowe 14.5.16; AZP 30.7.16; Nore War Flt Felixstowe 15.8.16; Deleted 3.10.16

**8633** Deld Grain 13.4.16; Westgate 29.5.16 (160-hp); HACPs 31.7.16 (FSL CFM Chambers & CPO Wise) & 11.9.16 (FSL WN Tees & observer); Wrecked on landing 3.3.17 (FSL HG Leslie unhurt); Deleted 20.3.17

**8634** Deld Felixstowe 5.16; Accepted 26.5.16; Grain, tested 30.5.16; Nore War Flt Felixstowe 14.8.16; Killingholme School 4.7.17; Deleted W/E 22.2.18

**8635** Deld Yarmouth by road 18.4.16; Erected 19.5.16; Accepted 25.6.16; AZP 31.7.16 (FSL S Kemball & AM Haines); Deleted 5.11.16

**8636** Deld Yarmouth by road 23.4.16; Erected 19.5.16; Accepted 21.6.16; Deleted W/E 8.9.17

**8637** Deld Yarmouth by road 23.4.16; Erected 19.5.16; Accepted 21.6.16; CW on landing 5.10.16 (FSL R Leckie & CPO Holmes unhurt); Deleted 17.10.16

**8638** Deld Grain 2.5.16; Accepted 15.7.16; Tested 10.8.16; To Calshot but FL en route and CW off Dover 4.12.16 (FSL H Tether & AM Neate unhurt), deleted

**8639** Deld Grain 10.5.16; Tested 18.6.16; Damaged float Westgate 2.8.16; retd Grain 3.8.16; Portland 11.9.16; Grain 28.9.16; Stalled and sideslipped on TO into River Medway opposite Grain pier 12.10.16 (FSL Mostyn Lewis injured & PO Mech WH Hodgson drowned); Deleted 15.10.16

**8640** Deld Grain 25.5.16; Tested 18.6.16 & 4.8.16; Deleted 3.9.16

**8641** Deld Grain 5.6.16; Accepted 11.6.16; Shorts Rochester (for packing) 16.6.16; Shipped to Cape Station 6.16; 8 Sqdn Zanzibar by 8.16; HMS *Manica* by 3.8.16; HMS *Laconia* .16; HMS *Himalaya* by 1.11.16; HMS *Manica*

*Curtiss H.8 "Large
America" Flying Boat
8650 at Felixstowe.
(J.M.Bruce/G.S.Leslie
collection)*

*A Voisin 5 "New Type",
serialled in the range
8700 to 8707, flown from
M'buyuni in East Africa
by Canadian pilot Lt
R.D.Delamere of 7 Sqdn
against Colonel von
Lettow-Vorbeck's Force,
1916. (via Frank
Cheesman)*

*Curtiss J.N.4 Trainer
8821. (RAF Museum
P.3196)*

2.11.16; Chukwani 19.11.16; HMS *Manica* to 9.2.17; Chukwani by 7.3.17 - @24.4.17; Overhaul 6.17; Still 8 Sqdn 19.11.17; Deleted 12.17

8642 Deld Grain 5.16; Accepted 14.6.16; Shorts Rochester 16.6.16 (for packing); Shipped to Cape Station 6.16; So badly damaged in transit to Zanzibar that rebuilt, tested 5.10.16 (satisfactory); 8 Sqdn Zanzibar from 11.16; [possibly the a/c ex HMS *Manica* to HMS *Himalaya* in exchange for 8641 2.11.16]; HMS *Himalaya* by 9.11.16; Zanzibar 20.11.16; CW flying Zanzibar to Dar-es-Salaam 8.1.17

8643 Deld Grain by road 14.6.16; Accepted 22.6.16; EF, FL, wrecked 15.9.16 (F/L MEA Wright & LM Daly unhurt); Deleted 29.9.16

8644 Deld Grain by road 14.6.16; Accepted 26.6.16; Wrecked 24.8.16 (F/Cdr AR Arnold & CPO Hartley); retd Grain 22.11.16; Deleted 27.1.17

8645 Deld by rail to Dundee 3.7.16; Tested 24.7.16; HSMP 28.2.17 (FSL deCWP Ireland & LM Jenkins); HSMP, attacked U-boat 6m E of Bell Rock 12.3.17 (FSL C McNicoll & LM Jenkins); EF, FL off Aberdeen, retd Dundee for repair 23.5.17; Deleted 25.8.17

8646 Deld by rail to Dundee 3.7.16; Tested 31.7.16; EF, FL 2m off Bell Rock, towed in by HMS *Agatha* 24.3.17; Wrecked on patrol, towed in by trawler 31.7.17; Deleted 7.8.17

8647 Deld by rail to Dundee 3.7.16; Tested 27.7.16; Sunk and wrecked 1.2.17 (FSL WE Foster & AM Jobson); Not listed from 2.2.17, presume rebuilt; Shipped to Cape Station 1.4.17; Arr 8 Sqdn in SS *Berwick Castle* 13.6.17; Erected by 26.6.17 but not flown as in poor condition

8648 Deld CSD 6.16; Fuselage to Mkrs 7.16; Grain 29.8.16; Accepted 8.9.16; EF, FL wrecked 16.9.16 (F/L MEA Wright & LM Daly); En route Dover, wrecked in Dover harbour, engine salved 1.1.17 (FSL H Tether & LM Neate unhurt); to Portland but EF, FL Milford Bay 23.1.17 (to proceed 24.1.17); Dover 2.2.17 (repair); 160-hp Sunbeam by 12.17; Newhaven 31.1.18 (transit); Calshot 1.2.18; Lee-on-Solent School by 23.2.18; Nose-dived in on TO 8.3.18 (PFO R Dobson killed); Deleted W/E 3.4.18

8649 Deld Grain by lorry 20.10.16; For Cape Station 23.2.17; Mkrs instructed to fit tropical radiators W/E 2.3.17; Shipped in SS *Berwick Castle* 1.4.17; landed and erected 8 Sqdn Zanzibar 13.6.17 - @16.3.18 [to go to Lindi 7.17]; HMS *Trent* 4.18; To Port Said 5.18 - @29.6.18; HMS *City of Oxford* by 6.18 - 9.18; 269 Sqdn Port Said by 28.10.18; Deleted 22.12.18

**50 CURTISS H.8 "LARGE AMERICA" (IMPROVED TYPE) TRACTOR BIPLANE FLYING BOATS ordered 5.16 from Curtiss, Toronto under Cont No C.P.77117/15 & numbered 8650 to 8699. (Two 160-hp Curtiss). Re-engined with 250-hp Eagle VIII, except 8650, to became H.12**

8650 Deld Felixstowe 24.3.16; Tested 30.3.16; Propeller burst, badly damaged 9.6.16 (F/L AQ Cooper & FSL WL Graham); Tested with RR engines 15.7.16 [acted as Felixstowe F.2 prototype]; Sunk nr Sunk LV 30.9.16; Deleted 1.10.16

8651 Deld Felixstowe 4.10.16; Tested 1.11.16; To H.12 Convert; Felixstowe by 31.12.16; Calshot 7.1.17; EF, FL, beached, Selsey 5.4.17; Towed to Calshot 6.4.17; Hull damaged 16.8.17; For deletion by 12.10.17, but to repair instead; Reconstructing Saunders, Cowes 7.12.17 - @30.1.19

8652 Deld Felixstowe for erection 31.10.16; Tresco 26.2.17; Engine trouble, started to sink, beached, tail damaged Newlyn 11.3.17 (FSL JC Railton, FSL JEA Hoare & LM DJ Birse); Deleted 30.3.17

8653 Deld Felixstowe 18.11.16; EF, to Calshot (towed from Newhaven) 3.3.17; transit, fitting cylinders Calshot 27.3.17; Tresco 1.4.17; EF, FL outside Plymouth Sound, towed in 2.4.17; Cattewater, wrecked, survey report 11.4.17; Dismantling 12.4.17; Deleted 1.5.17 CW

8654 Deld Felixstowe for erection 18.11.16; Cattewater 26.2.17 (transit); Tresco 27.2.17; Attacked by U-boat, disabled and unable to drop bombs 27.4.17; Lost in fog, landed off Trevose Head, towed into New Grimsby,

wings and tail damaged 5.6.17 (crew saved); Hit and damaged by 8686 taking off 21.7.17; to Newlyn, but retd petrol pump failure 15.3.18; Became 350/3 Flts Tresco 31.5.18; Deleted W/E 25.7.18

8655 Deld Felixstowe for erection 13.12.16; Calshot 7.2.17; Portland to Calshot, bombed U-boat 5016N 0221W, oil seen 24.4.17; Calshot, bombed U-boat 5028N 0115W and later 5018N 0130W 26.4.17 (FSL CL Scott & FSL FE Fraser); Surveyed 18.12.17; Deleted 28.12.17 W&T

8656 To H.12 Convert; Deld Felixstowe 14.12.16; Newhaven (26.2.17 (transit); Cattewater 27.2.17 (transit); Tresco 28.2.17; Cattewater 14.4.17 (weather); Tresco 17.4.17; Dropped 4x100-lb bombs on U-boat which was incorrectly reported as sunk, radiator damaged 27.5.17 (Lt WL Anderson & CPO Tadman); Dropped 4x100-lb bombs on U-boat, oil seen 29.5.17 (Lt WL Anderson); Newhaven to Tresco 17.6.17; Dropped 4x100-lb bombs on U-boat 35m SW of Bishops Rock 18.10.18 (F/L FS McGill, FSL W Morgan Smith, AM1(E) EJA Hopkins & AM2(WT) GT Newbold); Surveyed 19.11.17; Deleted 23.11.17 DBR; Presume rebuilt; 234 Sqdn Tresco by 8.18 - @1.19/Cattewater @30.12.18

8657 To H.12 Convert (Eagle VIII); Deld Felixstowe for erection 15.12.16; Flown 1.3.17; Lower wings and hull damaged in mid-air collision with Baby N1102 17.7.17; Seaplane School Felixstowe by 10.17; Deleted W/E 9.1.19

8658 Deld Felixstowe 21.12.16; Flown 1.3.17; Bombed suspected U-boat 30.4.17 (F/Cdr TD Hallam DSC, FSL BD Hobbs, CPO Rose & AM Bate); Bombed U-boat 20m SE of North Hinder LV then aileron wire failed 3.5.17; Towed in 4.5.17 (FSL SP Martin, FSL FH Prime, AM2 WH Grey & AM Marsden); Dropped 4 bombs on U-boat 10m SE of North Hinder 22.5.17; AZP 24.5.17 (F/Cdr PL Holmes); AGP 25.5.17; Felixstowe School 7.8.17; Deleted 31.8.17

8659 Deld Felixstowe for erection 21.12.16 for Yarmouth; Pilot lost bearings, came down off Haisboro, while being towed to Yarmouth by HMT *Volesus* both wings broke off, o/t, sank 29.4.17 (F/L WHS Asplin & FSL LA Rees to Yarmouth in *ML338*); Deleted 8.5.17

8660 Deld Felixstowe by 22.1.17; Yarmouth 13.4.17; Felixstowe 1.5.17; Yarmouth 22.5.17; Felixstowe 23.5.17; Attacked Zeppelin *L46* 25.5.17 (F/L CJ Galpin & F/L R Leckie); Yarmouth 30.5.17; Dropped 4x100-lb bombs on U-boat 35m E of Smith's Knoll 21.8.17 (FSL SJ Fetherston & FSL CV Halford-Thompson); Dropped 2x100-lb bombs on U-boat 10m SE of Smith's Knoll 29.10.17 (F/L R Leckie & FSL EA Bolton); Wrecked 6.11.17; Deleted 14.11.17 DBR; Fitted with F.2A hull and restored to commission 23.1.18; Became 324/6 Flts by 25.5.18; Attacked by enemy seaplanes when boat alighted due to engine trouble 30.5.18 (Capt CT Young, Ens JT Roe USN, Pte JN Money, Pte WF Chase all killed & Cpl F Grant PoW); Deleted W/E 27.6.18

8661 To H.12 Convert (Eagle VI) Deld Felixstowe 21.1.17; Servo motor test 23.3.17; HACP 21.4.17 (F/Cdr AQ Cooper, F/Cdr PL Holmes, PO Coates & AM Stoyle); HSMP, sighted U-boat 22.4.17 (FSL LCW Trend & F/Cdr TD Hallam DSC); Bombed U-boat 20m ESE of North Hinder LV, reported believed sunk 23.4.17 (F/Cdr TD Hallam DSC, F/Cdr PL Holmes & AM Clements); Attacked by 4 1-str seaplanes 5m E of Shipwash LV 10.12.17; For deletion by 29.12.17; Instead fitted new F.2A hull, completed 6.1.18; With 8677 encountered enemy seaplane 17m SW of North Hinder LV, attacked by 5 seaplanes and gunner Robinson shot down one of them, a single-seater, which was seen to crash 14.00 5.2.18 (F/L CJ Clayton, F/L A Adamson, AM2 GH Robinson & AM2 FC Callen); FL in sea, towed back 25.2.18; With N4282 met 5 enemy seaplanes on water 7m E of old position of North Hinder, W/T operator Nicol shot down a two-seater 12.3.18; To Exptl Stn Felixstowe 1.6.18; Became 230 Sqdn Felixstowe 20.8.18; Worn out, dismantled 30.10.18; Deleted W/E 9.1.19

8662 Deld Felixstowe 21.1.17; AZP 24.5.17 (F/L BD Hobbs) & 26.6.17; Dropped 3 bombs on U-boat 10m W of North Hinder LV 28.6.17 (F/L WR Mackenzie & FSL RFL Dickey); With 8689, dropped 2x100-lb bombs on U-boat 10m NW of Hinder LV 23.7.17 (F/L CJ Galpin

& FSL GF Moody); Dropped bomb on U-boat 2m W of Outer Gabbard 26.7.17 (F/L W Perham & FSL AT Barker); With 8676, dropped bomb on *UB20*, which sank, 7m NW of North Hinder 29.7.17 (FSL CL Young DSC, FSL AT Barker, AM2(E) WJ Priest & L/Tel HT Wilks); To H.12 Convert (Eagle VII) at Felixstowe by 7.17; Felixstowe School 1.9.17; Yarmouth 3.2.18; Dropped 2x230-lb bombs on British submarine *E41* 5m SE of Smith's Knoll Pillar Buoy 21.3.18 (F/L SJ Fetherston, F/L AM FitzRandolph, LM Crook, AM Gibbs & AM G/L Jupp); Felixstowe 27.3.18; Yarmouth by 30.3.18; Dazzle painted red and green; Became 324/6 Flts Yarmouth 25.5.18 (in 228 Sqdn from 20.8.18); Deleted W/E 5.12.18

8663 Deld Felixstowe 25.1.17; HSMP, sighted U-boat 22.4.17 (FSL LCW Trend, FSL CR Morrish & AM2 WH Grey); Sighted U-boat which dived 26.4.17; Bombed U- boat 22m S of North Hinder LV 19.5.17; Helped sink *UC36*, dropped 2 bombs, direct hit, 10m NE of North Hinder LV 20.5.17 (FSL CR Morrish DSC, FSL HG Boswell, AM1(E) WP Caston & LM (W/T) AE Shorter); CW landing in harbour 20.5.17 (crew saved); Deleted 23.5.17

8664 Deld Felixstowe for erection 25.1.17; Tresco 20.4.17; Bombed U-boat 7.5.17; Fell in sea, explosion 1m SW of Gush Island, Scilly 9.5.17 (FSL JC Railton, FSL RS Wigham & LM DJ Birse all killed); Deleted 23.5.17

8665 Deld Felixstowe for erection 25.1.17; Cattewater 15.4.17 (transit, weather); Tresco 17.4.17 (arr 20.4.17); Badly damaged 3.5.17; Dropped 3x100-lb bombs on U-boat which was about to attack hospital ship 10m N of Cape Cornwall 25.6.17; O/t at moorings in gale, CW 16.12.17 (now Eagle V); Surveyed 29.12.17; Deleted 15.1.18

8666 Deld Felixstowe for erection 3.2.17; Yarmouth 5.5.17; Pegged down for night, brought in 10.5.17; Zeppelin *L22* shot down into sea and BO 14.5.17 (F/L CJ Galpin, FSL R Leckie, CPO VF Whatling & AM JR Laycock); Fired at Zeppelin *L40* 10m NE of Terschelling but range too great 24.5.17 (F/L CJ Galpin, FSL R Leckie, CPO VF Whatling & AM JR Laycock); AZP 17.6.17 (FSL R Leckie); Attacked *L44* unsuccessfully, then rescued crew of ditched D.H.4 (crew F/L AHH Gilligan & Lt GS Trewin) 5.9.17 (F/L R Leckie); Landed to rescue crew of forced landed D.H.4, unable to TO, towed back to Yarmouth by HMS *Halcyon*, arrived 8.9.17 (all 6 crew of both aircraft unhurt); AZP 22.12.17; Saw 2 U-boats 5m N of Smith's Knoll Pillar Buoy, one submerged, dropped 2x230-lb bombs on other 5309N 0208E, stern rose 60° and disappeared leaving 50 ft diameter patch of oil 20.2.18 (F/Cdr R Leckie, F/L SJ Fetherston, AM(E) F Grant & PO (W/T) Thompson); Deleted W/E 9.1.19

8667 Deld Felixstowe for erection 3.2.17; Bombed U-boat 15m SE of Hinder LV 10.5.17 (FSL GR Hodgson, FSL HJ Bath, AM2 Millichamp & AM2 W Blacklock); FL, sank in tow 6.7.17; Deleted 11.7.17

8668 Deld Felixstowe for erection 4.2.17; Sighted U-boat which dived 26.4.17; Killingholme 11.5.17; Wing tip smashed 30.5.17; Dropped 4x100-lb bombs on U-boat 14m E of Flamborough 27.6.17 (F/L FGD Hards DSC, F/L Robinson & crew); Deleted W/E 22.2.18

8669 (To Eagle VI) Deld Felixstowe for erection 7.2.17; War Flt Killingholme 22.6.17; AZP 22.8.17; Dropped 3x100-lb bombs on U-boat 5½m NE of Kilnsea 3.9.17 (S/Cdr CR Finch-Noyes, FSL Cutter & crew); Propeller accident 9.3.18 (F/L DF Ellis seriously injured); Killingholme Seaplane School by 3.18; USNAS Killingholme 20.7.18; Left (or deleted) W/E 5.9.18

8670 Deld Felixstowe for erection 9.2.17; For Brest by 25.3.17 (NTU); Calshot 11.6.17; Dropped 230-lb bomb on U-boat 15m ESE of St.Catherines 22.10.17 (F/L DF Ellis & FSL PH Mackworth); Dropped 2x230-lb bombs on U-boat 23m S of Needles 18.11.17 (P/F/L GS Shaw & FSL AGB Ellis); Surveyed 18.12.17; Deleted 28.12.17 W&T

8671 Deld Felixstowe for erection 16.2.17; For Brest by 25.3.17 (NTU); Calshot 17.6.17; Wrecked 16.7.17; Deleted 17.7.17

8672 Deld Felixstowe for erection 16.2.17; For Brest by 25.3.17 (NTU); Killingholme 9.6.17 (transit); to Houton Bay 20.6.17 (arr via Scapa 26.6.17); Hull damaged

1.8.17 (2 x 275 hp RR); To Houton Bay Reserve; Surveyed 10.1.18; Deleted 17.1.18 DBR

8673 Deld Felixstowe for erection 16.2.17; For Brest by 25.3.17 (NTU); To H.12 Convert (Eagle VI); Dundee 9.6.17; Scapa 15.6.17; Houton Bay Reserve (for HMS *Campania*) 15.7.17 - 3.18; Port wings and tail broken 22.9.17 (at Stenness store by 30.3.18); Deleted 11.18

8674 Deld Felixstowe for erection 24.2.17; Convtd H.12; Left for Cattewater 12.5.17; arr Cattewater (via Calshot) 29.5.17 (transit); Tresco 30.5.17; Slightly damaged at moorings in gale 16.12.17; For deletion by 20.3.18

8675 Deld Felixstowe for erection 24.2.17; HACP 14.5.17 (FSL LA Rees & FSL HJ Bath); Dover 15.5.17; Felixstowe in tow 20.5.17; Cattewater 26.5.17; Starboard wingtip float slightly damaged 21.6.17; Hull damaged, awaiting survey 2.7.17; HMS *Riviera* for repair 1.8.17; Cattewater 27.9.17; Tresco 11.5.18; Became 350/3 Flts Tresco by 25.5.18; EF, FL in swell, BU, caught fire just off Scillies 14.6.18 (Lt MO Fairhurst saved & AM2 WTE Pike drowned); Deleted W/E 11.7.18

8676 (V-hull fitted after 147 hrs) Deld Felixstowe for erection 15.3.17; With 8689 & N65, dropped bomb on *UC1* 6m SSW of North Hinder LV , sunk 24.7.17 (F/L EJ Cuckney, FSL CJ Clayton, AM1 JA Mortimer & W/T Barrett); With 8662 sank *UB20* 29.7.17 (F/L WR Mackenzie awarded Bar to DSC; FSL GE Ball; AM1(E) HL Curtiss awarded DSM; AM2(W/T) WH Grey awarded DSM); With 8689, dropped 230-lb bomb on U-boat 14m 210° North Hinder LV 3.9.17 (F/L EJ Cuckney, FSL CJ Clayton & crew); Dropped 2x230-lb bombs, direct hit on *UC6* which was sunk nr North Hinder LV 28.9.17 (F/L BD Hobbs, FSL RFL Dickey, AM(E) EM Nicol & AM1 JA Mortimer); Dropped 2x230-lb bombs on U-boat 17m E of North Hinder LV 22.12.17 (F/L WR Mackenzie, FSL GE Ball & crew); EF, FL nr Shipwash LV, sank in tow by TBD *Meteor* 27.12.17 (F/L CJ Galpin, FSL GF Moody & crew saved); Surveyed 4.1.18; Deleted 15.1.18 TL

8677 Deld Felixstowe for erection 15.3.17; Dropped 230-lb bomb on U-boat, failed to explode, 10m NW of North Hinder LV 11.6.17; Shot down *L43* in flames off Vlieland 14.6.17 (FSL BD Hobbs DSC, FSL RFL Dickey, AM2 HM Davis & AM1 AW Goody); AZP 17.6.17; Convtd H.12 by 8.17; Dropped 2x230-lb bombs on U-boat 4m SW of North Hinder 13.9.17 (FSL BD Hobbs DSC, FSL RFL Dickey & crew); Dropped 2x230-lb bombs on U-boat 10½m 130° North Hinder 15.9.17 (FSL CL Young & FSL AT Barker); For deletion by 29.12.17; With 8661 (q.v.) encountered enemy seaplane 17m SW of North Hinder LV 5.2.18 (F/L LWS Cutler, Ens F Fallon USN & crew unhurt); With N4282 (q.v.) & N4513 sighted 2 seaplanes at 08.31, 1 shot down in flames 19.3.18; To H.12 Convert at Felixstowe (Eagle VIII) by 30.3.18; Shot down in sea at 17.00 in fight with 7 enemy seaplanes off North Hinder LV, claimed by Oblt RMA Christianson & Vizeflugmeister Wladicka 24.4.18 (Capt NA Magor, Ens S Potter USN, LM G/L RA Lucas & AM1 JG Strathearn all killed); Surveyed 10.5.18; Deleted 15.5.18 TL

8678 Deld Felixstowe for erection 17.3.17; Cattewater (via Calshot) 2.7.17; Tresco 30.7.17 (repair aileron controls); Cattewater for overhaul 1.8.17; Deleted W/E 19.1.18

8679 Deld Felixstowe for erection 17.3.17; Destroyed by bomb 4.7.17

8680 Hull deld Felixstowe 23.3.17; Tresco 7.7.17; Dropped 3x100-lb bombs on U-boat 55m SSW of Scilly 21.8.17 (F/L JEA Hoare & FSL WECBC Forsyth); Dropped 4x100-lb bombs on U-boat 15m SW of St.Mary's 14.10.17 (F/L FS McGill, Lt WL Anderson, Lt JC Atkinson RNVR & AM2 AL Pike); O/t at moorings in gale, CW 16.12.17 (now Eagle VI/VII); Surveyed 29.12.17; Deleted 15.1.18

8681 Hull deld Felixstowe 23.3.17; Expts with towed lighters; Calshot 6.7.17 (for RN Signal School Portsmouth); EF, FL 7m E of Hurst Castle, hull badly damaged, beached, to be towed back 14.1.18 (crew safe); Deleted W/E 21.1.18

8682 Hull deld Felixstowe 30.3.17; Dropped 4 bombs on U-boat nr North Hinder LV 14.6.17; Surveyed 20.8.17,

| | |
|---|---|
| | hull worn out; Deleted 31.8.17 |
| 8683 | (V-hull fitted after 53 hrs); Hull deld Felixstowe 30.3.17; Dunkerque 11.7.17; Felixstowe 22.7.17; Dunkerque 30.7.17; Felixstowe 14.8.17 (overhaul); Dunkerque 19.8.17; Felixstowe 3.9.17 (repair); Damaged landing Dovercourt 1.1.18 (pilot unhurt); To H.12 Convert at Felixstowe by 6.4.18; FL on land nr Orfordness, CW 30.6.18 (Capt CJ Galpin, Capt M Faux, Capt Walters all slightly injured); Deleted W/E 18.7.18 |
| 8684 | Deld Felixstowe for erection 7.4.17; Killingholme patrol 13.7.17; Deleted W/E 23.2.18 |
| 8685 | Deld Felixstowe for erection 7.4.17; Killingholme patrol 22.7.17; USNAS Killingholme 20.7.18; Dundee 29.10.18; USNAS Killingholme by 28.11.18; RAF Killingholme by 30.1.19 |
| 8686 | Deld Felixstowe for erection 12.4.17; Tresco (via Calshot & Falmouth) 13.7.17 (fit bomb gear); Hit 8654 on TO and damaged 21.7.17; Cattewater 24.7.17 (loan); EF, FL. towed in by HMS *Porpoise* & HMS *Christopher* 25.7.17 (F/L JEA Hoare & FSL LGleB Croke); Tresco 4.8.17; Dropped 4x100-lb bombs on U-boat 30m SW of Bishop Rock 18.10.17 (F/L FS McGill & FSL W Morgan Smith); O/t at moorings in gale, CW 16.12.17 (now Eagle VI/VII); Surveyed 29.12.17; Deleted 15.1.18 |
| 8687 | Deld Felixstowe for erection 12.4.17; Calshot 15.8.17; S.E.Saunders Cowes W/E 21.12.17 (reconstruction); Deleted W/E 5.4.18 |
| 8688 | (To Eagle VI) Deld Felixstowe for erection 19.4.17; Scapa 14.8.17; Killingholme by 10.17; Dundee 11.10.17 (for trials on Loch Strathbeg); Killingholme 30.10.17; To H.12 Convert after badly damaged landing; USNAS Killingholme 20.7.18; Left (or deleted) W/E 5.9.18 |
| 8689 | (Fitted V-hull after 200 hrs) Hull deld Felixstowe patrol 15.5.17; With 8662, dropped 2x230-lb bombs on U-boat, 1 failed to explode, 13-15m SSE of North Hinder LV 21.7.18 (F/L W Perham & F/L EJ Cuckney); Bombed U-boat with 2x230-lb bombs, missed by 30 ft, 10m W of North Hinder LV 23.7.17 (FSL BTH Batford & FSL EW Keesey & crew); With 8676 & N65, dropped 2x230-lb bombs on *UC1*, sunk 6m SSW of North Hinder LV 24.7.17 (F/L TH Newton, FSL TC Trumble, AM2 W Blacklock & L/Tel TE Jacques); With 8676, dropped 230-lb bomb on U-boat 14m 210° North Hinder LV 3.9.17 (F/Cdr TD Hallam DSC, FSL RFL Dickey & crew); Dropped 2x230-lb bombs on U-boat 8m ESE of North Hinder LV 29.9.17 (Lt BD Hobbs DSO DSC, FSL RFL Dickey & crew); For deletion by 2.2.18; To H.12 Convert (Eagle VIII) by 3.18; Shot down by Germans, FL in North Sea off northern tip of Vlieland and picked up by Dutch trawler 4.6.18 (Lt MJR Duff-Fyfe, FSL JR Pattison, Ens JA Eaton USNRF, 1AM EJ Strewthers & W/T Sgt AJ Brown interned); Become *L-1* with Dutch Navy |
| 8690 | Deld Felixstowe for erection 21.5.17; To H.12 Convert; Calshot patrol 13.8.17; S.E.Saunders, Cowes W/E 7.12.17 - @30.1.19 (reconstructing) |
| 8691 | Deld Felixstowe for erection 21.5.17; Fitted with telescopic W/T mast; Modified hull to H.12b standard (275 hp Rolls-Royce); Calshot patrol 20.7.17; Felixstowe 1.8.17; Calshot 20.8.17; EF, FL, beached Worthing Pier 14.12.17 (crew unhurt); Surveyed 17.12.17; Deleted 22.12.17 wrecked |
| 8692 | Deld Felixstowe for erection 21.5.17; Boat Flt Yarmouth W/E 8.9.17; Broke back on TO in heavy seas, valuable parts salved Yarmouth 3.2.18; Deleted W/E 16.2.18 |
| 8693 | Hull deld Felixstowe 3.6.17; With 8694, dropped 2x230-lb bombs on U-boat 3m NW of North Hinder 25.9.17 (F/L TD Hallam DSC, FSL J Hodson & crew); EF, FL in Deurloo, nr Vlissingen, Zeeland destroyed by crew 24.10.17 (F/L W Perham, FSL HC Gooch, LM CW Sivyer & AM2 BM Millichamp rescued by Dutch torpedo boat *G15* and interned); Surveyed 31.10.17; Deleted 12.11.17 |
| 8694 | Hull deld Felixstowe 3.6.17; With 8693, dropped 2x230-lb bombs on U-boat 3m NW of North Hinder LV 25.9.17 (F/L JL Gordon & FSL M Faux); Dropped 2x230-lb bombs on U-boat 10m NW of North Hinder LV 1.10.17 (F/L GR Hodgson, FSL HA Wilson, AM1 J Watts & AM2 FC Callen); Dropped 2x230- lb bombs on |

| | |
|---|---|
| | U-boat 7m NNE of North Hinder LV 3.11.17 (F/L CJ Galpin, FSL GF Moody & crew); EF, FL, towed in, DBR 5.11.17; Deleted W/E 17.11.17 |
| 8695 | Deld Felixstowe for erection 21.7.17; Dunkerque 10.9.17; Dropped 2x230-lb bombs on U-boat 8½m NE of northern end of East Hinder Bank 22.9.17 (FSL NA Magor, FSL CES Lusk, CPO EA Boyd & Eng LM RA Lucas) [Identified as *UC72* but this had been sunk 2 days earlier; possibly *UB32* which had FTR from North Sea operations around that time]; Bombed U-boat 30m N of Dunkerque 29.9.17 (FSL NA Magor, FSL CES Lusk, O/L DC Evans & AM Reid); Surveyed by ADD 17.11.17 unserviceable; Deleted 24.11.17 |
| 8696 | (H.12A) Deld Felixstowe ex Curtiss 9.11.17; Calshot 6.1.18; Cattewater W/E 19.1.18; Deleted W/E 23.2.18 |
| 8697 | Shipped to UK 22.11.17; no further record |
| 8698 | Deld Yarmouth W/E 14.11.17; Deleted W/E 12.12.17 as spares |
| 8699 | Deld Yarmouth W/E 14.11.17; Deleted W/E 12.12.17 as spares |

**8 VOISIN 5 "NEW TYPE" [TYPE LA.S ?] PUSHER BIPLANES purchased in France, numbered 8700 to 8707 & built Issy-les-Moulineaux. (150-hp Canton Unné)**
[Possibly 4 each for 7 & 8 Sqdns, East Africa]

| | |
|---|---|
| 8700 | Deld CSD White City; Left for 8 Sqdn 26.1.16; Sailed to Durban from Avonmouth in SS *Clan Macpherson* for EAFF 7.2.16; Could be the Voisin which arr 15.3.16 (FSL LG Sieveking - or 8522); For overhaul 2.10.17; 8 Sqdn East Africa 10.17 - @17.11.17 |
| 8701 | Deld Hendon 3.16; Damaged when Bessonneau hangar blew away 28.3.16; Sailed to Durban from Avonmouth in SS *Clan Macpherson* for EAFF 7.2.16 (sic); 8 Sqdn Kilwa Kiswani by 1.17; Kivinga 2.1.17; Kiswani for dismantling 1.2.17; Chukwani by 1.5.17; Tested and flown to Lindi 2.6.17 - @7.17; Tested after overhaul 8.17; Dar-es-Salaam by 10.17; Crashed |
| 8702 | Deld CSD White City; Left for 8 Sqdn 26.1.16; Sailed to Durban from Avonmouth in SS *Clan Macpherson* for EAFF 7.2.16; 8 Sqdn Zanzibar by 11.16; Dar-es-Salaam in HMS *Himalaya* 7.11.16; Tested on arrival 9.11.16; EF on TO, turned to avoid hangar, port wing hit ground, wrecked, Dar-es-Salaam 27.11.16 (F/L WH Dunn & Lt DTE James unhurt); Deleted |
| 8703 | Deld CSD White City; Left for 8 Sqdn 26.1.16; Sailed to Durban from Avonmouth in SS *Clan Macpherson* for EAFF 7.2.16; 8 Sqdn Zanzibar by 12.16; Dar-es-Salaam in HMS *Himalaya*, tested 3.12.16; Zanzibar by 7.17; To Lindi in SS *Carlow Castle*, arr 8.7.17; EF, FL, badly damaged Tandamuti Hill 24.9.17, taken in hand for repair 2.10.17; still Lindi @17.11.17 |
| 8704 | Deld CSD White City; Left for Avonmouth Docks for 8 Sqdn 29.1.16; Sailed to Durban from Avonmouth in SS *Clan Macpherson* for EAFF 7.2.16; arr Mombasa 26.3.16; 7 Sqdn East Africa by 17.5.16; Dar-es-Salaam by 12.16 |
| 8705 | Deld CSD White City; Left for Avonmouth Docks for 8 Sqdn 29.1.16; Sailed to Durban from Avonmouth in SS *Clan Macpherson* for EAFF 7.2.16; arr Mombasa 26.3.16; 7 Sqdn East Africa by 17.5.16 - @8.16; 8 Sqdn Zanzibar |
| 8706 | Deld CSD White City; Left for Avonmouth Docks for 8 Sqdn 29.1.16; Sailed to Durban from Avonmouth in SS *Clan Macpherson* for EAFF 7.2.16; arr Mombasa 26.3.16; 7 Sqdn East Africa by 17.5.16 - @8.16; Possibly the aircraft which FL Kigonigoni, nr Mombasa 29.4.16 (TFSL CR Terraneau & Italian Capt Bruno killed by German Askari troops) |
| 8707 | Deld CSD White City; Left for Avonmouth Docks for 8 Sqdn 29.1.16; Sailed to Durban from Avonmouth in SS *Clan Macpherson* for EAFF 7.2.16; arr Mombasa 26.3.16; 7 Sqdn East Africa by 17.5.16 - @1.17 |

**6 NIEUPORT TYPE 12 TWO-SEATER FIGHTER RECONNAISSANCE TRACTOR BIPLANES purchased from Nieuport, numbered 8708 to 8713 & built Issy-les-Moulineaux. (110-hp Clerget 9Z)**

| | |
|---|---|
| 8708 | Shipped to Aegean; 2 Wing from 8.16; C Sqdn 2 Wing trash |

Termi by 3.17; EF, FL, o/t Salt Lake, Kephalo 3.3.17 (FSL AF Marlowe seriously injured & Mid ER Snow killed)

8709   Deld ADD by 27.7.16; Surveyed, for spares 28.9.16; Crashed and CW, to ADD 1.11.16; Deleted 4.12.16

8710   Deld ADD 27.7.16; 6 Flt A Sqdn 5 Wing 2.9.16 - @23.10.16; ADD by 12.16; Dover 17.12.16; Under repair by 22.3.17; Surveyed 16.10.17; Deleted 19.10.17 W&T

8711   Deld ADD by 3.8.16; 6 Flt A Sqdn 5 Wing Coudekerque 9.10.16 - @8.11.16; ADD by 30.11.16 - @22.2.17; 10 Sqdn by 1.3.17; Wrecked 26.3.17; ADD by 29.3.17; Deleted 27.4.17

8712   Deld ADD by 3.8.16; 6 Flt A Sqdn 5 Wing 23.10.16; 11 Flt B Sqdn 4 Wing 27.11.16; Became 6 Sqdn by 12.16 - @8.3.17; 11 Sqdn by 15.3.17 (formed 8.3.17); General fatigue 7.5.17; ADD 14.5.17; For survey by 17.5.17, deleted

8713   Deld ADD by 3.8.16; 6 Flt A Sqdn 5 Wing 16.8.16; EF, FL, damaged 21.10.16 (FSL WE Orchard & G/L SD Sambrook); ADD by 2.11.16; Cranwell 29.12.16; Surveyed 18.9.17; Deleted 8.10.17

**11 ROYAL AIRCRAFT FACTORY B.E.2c TRACTOR BIPLANES ordered under Cont Nos C.P.60949/15 & C.P.153401/15 from Sir William Beardmore & Co Ltd, numbered 8714 to 8724 & built Dalmuir (90-hp R.A.F.1a)**

8714   Shipped to East Africa 4.16; arr Durban 4.16; EAFF by 31.5.16; Deleted 1917

8715   Shipped to East Africa 4.16; arr Durban 4.16; EAFF by 31.5.16; 7 Sqdn East Africa by 8.16; Kilossa by 11.16; Iringa 8.11.16; Kilossa 17.11.16; Lost en route Alt Iringa, FL Ntanangan, TW, 15m from destination 5.12.16 (FSL RD Delamere); Parts retd Iringa 9.12.16; LM 25.12.16; Transferred to 26 Sqdn RFC East Africa 1.17

8716   Shipped to East Africa 4.16; arr Durban 4.16; EAFF by 31.5.16; 7 Sqdn East Africa by 7.16; Kilossa to Alt Iringa 19.12.16 - @31.12.16LM; Transferred 26 Sqdn RFC East Africa 30.1.17 [7.2.17? ](BE2d); CSD White City, packed by 15.6.17

8717   Deld East Fortune 26.4.16; Tested 28.4.16; AZPs 19.8.16 (F/Cdr EB Beauman & AC2 Robinson later FSL WE Traynor & AC2 Whiting); Morse signalling from airship 19.2.17; Surveyed 11.12.17; Deleted 19.12.17 W&T

8718   Deld East Fortune 28.4.16; AZPs 19.8.16 (FSL RH Horniman & AM Rapley later FSL DW Gray & Lt A Carrol-Marx RNVR); FL St.Abbs Head, FL on taking off again, CW 22.8.16 (FSL RH Horniman & AM1 Gridley); deleted 25.8.16

8719   Deld East Fortune 21.5.16; Tested 23.5.16 (Dukinfield Jones); Cross-country to Newcastle, EF, FL nr Drem 5.8.16 (FSL DW Gray); transported back to aerodrome; Longside for anti-Zeppelin defence 28.8.16; Slightly damaged 9.9.16; Flown again 11.9.16; East Fortune 7.12.16 (Night flying); Cranwell by road, arr 15.2.18; Freiston 26.3.18; 201/2 TDS Cranwell by 29.4.18 - @24.7.18

8720   Deld East Fortune 19.5.16; Tested 23.5.16 (Dukinfield Jones); AZP 19.8.16 (FSL DW Gray & Lt A Carrol-Marx); Longside for anti-Zeppelin defence 28.8.16; East Fortune 7.12.16; CW 20.3.17 (FSL GHG Smith injured)

8721   Deld Cranwell 22.5.16; Deleted 29.7.16

8722   Deld Cranwell 24.5.16; At Freiston 7.16; Cranwell 12.7.16; Freiston 7.16; Cranwell 19.7.16; Freiston by 10.16; Wrecked 24.4.17; Dismantled 27.7.17 (at Freiston 7.17); Cranwell 10.17; Surveyed 21.11.17; Deleted 5.12.17 wrecked

8723   Deld Cranwell 24.5.16; Deleted 22.8.16

8724   Deld East Fortune 27.5.16; Tested 11.6.16; AZP 19.8.16 (F/L RH Routledge); Damaged landing Montrose 1.12.16; retd East Fortune; Crashed at Edinburgh 10.11.17 (TFSL RD Clive & PO TCM Reardon both killed)

**1 AIRCO D.H.2 PUSHER BIPLANE transferred from RFC (Military Wing) and numbered 8725. (100-hp Gnome Monosoupape)**

8725   (Ex 6014). For evaluation. Tested Hendon 28.5.16; Farnborough 10.6.16 on re-transfer to RFC (Military Wing) [supposedly as A2562, which seems unlikely] [6013 also allotted RNAS Dover for Dunkerque W/E 20.5.16 - NTU?]

**19 NIEUPORT TYPE 12 TWO-SEATER FIGHTER RECONNAISSANCE TRACTOR BIPLANES purchased from Établissements Nieuport, numbered 8726 to 8744 & built Issy-les-Moulineaux. (110-hp Clerget 9Z)**

8726   Deld ADD by 17.8.16; Tested 29.9.16; 11 Flt B Sqdn 4 Wing 28.11.16; Became 6 Sqdn 12.16 - @8.3.17; 11 Sqdn by 15.3.17; ADD 6.5.17; Deleted 14.5.17 general fatigue

8727   Deld ADD by 10.8.16; Tested 29.9.16; 6 Flt A Sqdn 5 Wing 23.10.16; 4 Wing 28.11.16; ADD by 30.11.16 - @1.2.17; 8 Sqdn by 8.2.17; Wrecked 10.2.17; ADD by 15.2.17; For survey 19.4.17; Deleted 27.4.17

8728   Deld ADD by 17.8.16; Tested 28.9.16; 6 Flt A Sqdn 5 Wing by 17.10.16; ADD 16.12.16 - @1.2.17; 8 Sqdn by 8.2.17; 10 Sqdn 25.2.17; Wrecked 27.3.17; ADD by 29.3.17; Deleted ADD 27.4.17

8729   Deld ADD 17.8.16; Tested 28.9.16; Dover by 11.1.17; Deleted 28.2.17

8730   Shipped to Aegean; 2 Wing Mudros, tested on arrival 10.10.16; Surveyed 21.9.17; Deleted 6.10.17 DBR

8731   (C/n N1592). Shipped to Aegean; 2 Wing Mudros, tested on arrival 8.10.16; To Roumanian Govt, Bucharest 21.11.16

8732   Deld ADD by 21.9.16; Dover 20.12.16; Chingford 7.1.17 (transit); Cranwell 8.1.17; Surveyed 18.9.17; Deleted 18.10.17 to GI

8733   Deld ADD by 24.8.16; C Sqdn 1 Wing St.Pol 19.9.16; ADD by 16.11.16; Tested 6.2.17; Deleted 24.3.17 obsolete

8734   Deld ADD by 24.8.16; 9 Flt A Sqdn 4 Wing RNAS 17.10.16; Lost port wheel on TO, landed safely 26.11.16 (F/L ADW Allen); Became 6 Sqdn 31.12.16; 11 Sqdn 8.3.17; Crashed, o/t 9.5.17; ADD 10.5.17; Deleted 14.5.17 general fatigue

8735   In transit to Aegean 8.16; Deleted 1917

8736   Shipped to Aegean; Surveyed Mudros 21.9.17; Deleted 6.10.17 DBR

8737   Deld ADD by 7.9.16; C Sqdn 1 Wing 19.9.16; ADD 30.11.16; 1 Sqdn by 2.1.17 - @10.2.17; ADD by 15.2.17; 10 Sqdn by 26.2.17; ADD 9.5.17; Deleted 14.5.17 general fatigue

8738   In transit to Aegean 8.16; Deleted 1916

8739   In transit to Aegean 8.16; Deleted 1916

8740   Deld ADD by 24.8.16; C Sqdn 1 Wing St.Pol by 17.9.16; ADD by road 30.11.16; Tested 6.2.17; Deleted 24.3.17 obsolete

8741   Deld ADD by 24.8.16; 10 Flt A Sqdn 4 Wing 8.9.16; 9 Flt A Sqdn 4 Wing by 28.9.16; 11 Flt B Sqdn 4 Wing by 14.11.16; 5 Wing Coudekerque 27.11.16; Dover 20.12.16; Cranwell 5.1.17 (arrived via Chingford 13.1.17); Tested with 130-hp Clerget 6.11.17 - @12.17; Freiston by 1.18; Cranwell 15.2.18; Crashed, slightly damaged Cranwell South 4.3.18 (pilot unhurt); For deletion by 30.3.18

8742   Deld ADD by 7.9.16; 10 Flt A Sqdn 4 Wing Dunkerque by 14.9.16; 11 Flt B Sqdn 4 Wing by 16.11.16; 6 Flt A Sqdn 5 Wing 28.11.16; Dover 24.12.16; Damaged 3.2.17 (FSL D Plaistowe); Surveyed 16.10.17; Deleted 19.10.17 W&T

8743   Deld ADD by 7.9.16; 10 Flt A Sqdn 4 Wing Dunkerque by 14.9.16; 9 Flt A Sqdn 4 Wing by 23.9.16; 11 Flt B Sqdn 4 Wing by 16.11.16; 6 Flt A Sqdn 5 Wing 28.11.16; Dover 20.12.16; Cranwell 7.1.17 (arrived 8.1.17); Surveyed 16.10.17; Deleted 18.10.17 to GI

8744   Deld ADD by 7.9.16; Dover 4.1.17 (repair by 23.3.17); Surveyed 16.10.17; Deleted 19.10.17 W&T

**7 NIEUPORT "TYPE 17B" (probably 11 & 17bis) TRACTOR BIPLANE SCOUTS purchased from Établissements Nieuport, numbered 8745 to 8751 & built Issy-les-Moulineaux. (80-hp Le Rhône)**

8745   1 Flt A Sqdn 1 Wing St.Pol by 4.16; 2 Flt A Sqdn 1 Wing Furnes; In action, EF at 7,000 ft, FL in sea and

8746 sank 1m W of La Panne 9.7.16 (FSL GV Leather swam ashore); Deleted 16.8.16

8746 (Type 11) Deld ADD by 6.16; 4 Wing 25.6.16; 9 Flt A Sqdn 4 Wing Dunkerque by 7.16 - 9.16; still 4 Wing 12.16; 6 Sqdn by 1.2.17; 11 Sqdn 8.3.17; ADD 24.3.17; 11 Sqdn 27.3.17 - @24.4.17; Deleted ADD 14.5.17 general fatigue

8747 (Type 11) Deld Furnes 20.6.16; 2 Flt A Sqdn 1 Wing St.Pol by 7.16 - 9.16; 1 Flt A Sqdn 1 Wing St.Pol by 9.16; Became 1 Sqdn 5.11.16; ADD 24.12.16; 6 Sqdn by 8.2.17; 11 Sqdn 8.3.17 (Clerget); COL 28.4.17 (FSL AE Hall); Deleted ADD 14.5.17 general fatigue

8748 (Type 11) 2 Flt A Sqdn 1 Wing St.Pol by 9.7.16; Returning in fog from raid on Zeebrugge Mole, attempted to find Furnes, but FL among houses in Adinkerque village, CW 27.11.16 (FSL NW Frames DoW 28.11.16); Deleted ADD 5.1.17 DBR

8749 Deld Furnes 1.7.16; 2(?) Flt A Sqdn 1 Wing, destroyed a Fokker monoplane at 10,000 ft 1m off Middelkerke 15.00, then attacked by HA biplane, EF, FL on beach Nieuport Bains 9.7.16 (FSL LH Irving), shelled on beach, engine and guns salvaged; Deleted 16.8.16

8750 (Type 17bis) 10 Flt A Sqdn 4 Wing Dunkerque 7.8.16; Tested Le Prieur rocket 17.8.16; Destroyed KB 1m SE of Steene 7.9.16 (F/L CR Mackenzie); A Flt Detd Sqdn (later 8 Sqdn) 26.10.16; Albatros DI shot down NE of Bapaume, shared 3956 11.00 4.12.16 (F/L CR Mackenzie); Albatros Scout OOC 2m W of Cambrai 26.12.16 (FSL RJO Compston); ADD 15.1.17; 9 Sqdn 10.2.17; 11 Sqdn 28.3.17; COL 5.5.17 (FSL NS Hall); Deleted ADD 27.6.17 general fatigue

8751 (Type 17bis) (Was to have been 8739). 1 Flt A Sqdn 1 Wing by 28.8.16; Aviatik LVG shot down nr Nieuport 21.10.16 (F/Cdr JJ Petre, DSC); A Flt Detd Sqdn (later 8 Sqdn) 26.10.16; 3 Sqdn 20.12.16 - @29.1.17; 9 Sqdn by 12.2.17; Probably the aircraft wrecked on aerodrome 16.2.17 (FSL CA Narbeth); AP 2.17; 9 Sqdn 26.2.17; 11 Sqdn 28.3.17 - @9.5.17; Deleted ADD 27.6.17 general fatigue

**50 GRAHAME-WHITE XV BOXKITE (ADMIRALTY 1600 TYPE) PUSHER BIPLANES ordered under Cont No C.P.62650/15, numbered 8752 to 8801 & built Hendon. (60-hp Le Rhône)**

8752 To Australian Govt; Shipped to Australia W/E 11.3.16; Stationed CFS Point Cook .16 - 1.18 as CFS11

8753 To Australian Govt; Shipped to Australia W/E 11.3.16; Stationed CFS Point Cook .16 - 1.18 as CFS12

8754 Deld Hendon and tested 19.4.16; Eastbourne 26.4.16; EF, FL Warninglid Olds Park, CW 1.5.16 (S/L AM Proctor); Deleted 12.6.16

8755 Deld Hendon and tested 20.4.16; Eastbourne 26.4.16; TW 16.5.16 (S/L JP White); Deleted 12.6.16

8756 Deld Hendon 5.5.16; School Flt Eastchurch 11.5.16; Deleted 28.8.18 and used to help rebuild 8758

8757 Deld Hendon 5.5.16; School Flt Eastchurch 11.5.16; Dismantled for storage 2.1.17

8758 Deld Hendon 5.5.16; School Flt Eastchurch 11.5.16; Rebuilt from parts of 8756 & 8758 28.8.16; Dismantled for storage 2.1.17, then deleted

8759 Deld Hendon 12.5.16; School Flt Eastchurch 17.5.16; Crashed 21.6.16 (PFSL EA Freeman); Deleted 26.6.16

8760 Deld Hendon for erection 14.5.16; Flown 16.5.16; Chingford 17.5.16; Deleted W/E 22.9.17

8761 Deld Hendon 12.5.16; Eastbourne 17.5.16; Wrecked by wind 6.6.16; Deleted 12.6.16

8762 Deld Hendon 18.5.16; School Flt Eastchurch 26.5.16; Crashed 17.10.16; Eastchurch Workshops 20.10.16; Deleted 23.10.16

8763 Deld Hendon 18.5.16; Redcar 21.5.16; Deleted 31.1.17

8764 Deld Hendon 26.5.16; School Flt Eastchurch 30.5.16; Crashed by 22.6.16; Eastchurch Workshops, deleted 8.11.16

8765 Deld Hendon and tested 26.5.16; Redcar 28.5.16 (arr 3.6.16); Deleted 31.1.17

8766 Deld Hendon and tested 31.5.16; School Flt Eastchurch 6.6.16; Dismantled for storage by 1.1.17, then deleted

8767 Deld Hendon for erection 2.6.16; Chingford 9.6.16 (repair); Deleted 12.1.17

8768 Deld Hendon for erection 2.6.16; Chingford 9.6.16; Damaged chassis landing (pilot unhurt); Deleted 27.2.18

8769 Deld Hendon for erection 2.6.16; Chingford 9.6.16; Wrecked 28.6.17; Deleted 23.8.17

8770 Deld Hendon for erection 2.6.16; Chingford 9.6.16; Deleted 23.8.17

8771 Deld CSD White City 6.16; Eastchurch Workshops for erection 11.9.16; Eastchurch FS 4.10.16; Deleted 12.1.17

8772 Deld CSD White City 6.16; Eastchurch Workshops for erection 11.9.16; Eastchurch FS 24.9.16; Deleted 12.1.17

8773 Deld CSD White City 6.16; Eastchurch Workshops for erection 22.9.16; Eastchurch FS 17.10.16; Deleted 12.1.17

8774 Deld CSD White City 6.16; Chingford by lorry 24.9.16; Wings and chassis damaged 6.7.17; Deleted W/E 22.9.17

8775 Deld CSD White City 6.16; Chingford by lorry 24.9.16; Deleted W/E 22.9.17

8776 Deld Hendon and accepted 29.6.16 (Mkrs); Eastbourne 4.7.16; Deleted 26.9.16

8777 Deld Hendon and accepted 29.6.16 (Mkrs); Eastbourne 4.7.16; Deleted 9.11.16

8778 Deld Hendon and tested by Mkrs 29.6.16; Eastbourne 4.7.16; Deleted 17.8.16

8779 Deld CSD White City by 30.6.16; Chingford 5.10.16; Deleted W/E 22.9.17

8780 Deld CSD White City by 30.6.16; Chingford 5.10.16; Deleted 16.8.17

8781 Deld CSD White City 7.16; Hendon and tested by Mkrs 8.7.16; Chingford 8.7.16; Deleted 24.10.16

8782 Deld CSD White City 7.16; Hendon and tested by Mkrs 8.7.16; Chingford 8.7.16; Deleted 1.11.16

8783 Deld CSD White City 7.16; Chingford 5.10.16; Deleted W/E 22.9.17

8784 Deld CSD White City 7.16; Chingford 5.10.16; Deleted W/E 22.9.17

8785 Deld CSD White City 7.16; Chingford by lorry 7.12.16; Deleted W/E 22.9.17

8786 Deld CSD White City 7.16; Deld Chingford by lorry 7.12.16; Deleted W/E 22.9.17

8787 Deld CSD White City 7.16; Deld Chingford by lorry 7.12.16; Deleted W/E 22.9.17

8788 Deld CSD White City 7.16 - @28.2.17

8789 Deld CSD White City 7.16; Chingford 1.6.17; Badly damaged 7.8.17; Deleted 23.8.17

8790 Deld CSD White City 7.16 - @28.2.17

8791 Deld CSD White City 7.16; Chingford for erection 22.5.17; Deleted W/E 22.9.17

8792 Deld CSD White City 7.16; Chingford for erection 22.5.17 ; Deleted W/E 15.9.17

8793 Deld CSD White City 7.16; Chingford for erection 22.5.17; For disposal by 13.10.17

8794 Deld CSD White City 7.16; Chingford for erection 22.5.17; For disposal by 13.10.17

8795 Deld CSD White City 7.16; Chingford for erection 22.5.17; For disposal by 13.10.17

8796 Deld CSD White City 7.16; Chingford for erection 22.5.17; For disposal by 13.10.17

8797 Deld CSD White City 7.16; Chingford for erection 22.5.17; For disposal by 13.10.17

8798 Deld CSD White City 26.7.16; Chingford for erection by 22.5.17; For disposal by 13.10.17; For Mkrs by 24.11.17

8799 Deld CSD White City 7.16; Chingford for erection 22.5.17; For disposal by 13.10.17; For Mkrs by 24.11.17

8800 Deld CSD White City 26.7.16; Chingford for erection 22.5.17; For disposal by 13.10.17; For Mkrs by 24.11.17

8801 Deld CSD White City 26.7.16; Chingford for erection 22.5.17; For disposal by 13.10.17; For Mkrs by 24.11.17

**100 CURTISS J.N.4 TRACTOR BIPLANES ordered under Cont dated 26.3.15 from Curtiss, Toronto & numbered 8802 to 8901. (90-hp Curtiss OX-2)**

8802 (DC). Deld Hendon 3.5.16; Detling 17.5.16; Eastchurch 19.5.16 (transit); Redcar 21.5.16; Sideslipped on TO, wrecked 13.7.16 (FSL EM Morgan & Lt RMS Veal slightly injured); Deleted 21.8.16

8803 Deld Hendon 29.4.16; Chingford 10.5.16; Design Flt Eastchurch 6.9.16; Dismantling 23.10.16; Re-erected, flown 21.2.17; ECD Grain 16.3.17; Surveyed 22.9.17; Deleted 26.9.17 DBR

8804 (DC). Deld Hendon 3.5.16; Flown 15.5.16; School Flt Eastchurch 16.5.16; Swerved on landing, broke propeller and half u/c 25.10.16 (FSL EJK Buckley); War School Manston 8.9.17; Deleted 9.1.18 W&T

8805 Deld Hendon 1.5.16; Tested 6.5.16; Chingford 10.5.16; Crashed by 7.8.16; East Fortune by rail 21.9.16 (arr 26.9.16); U/c damaged 21.6.17; RNASTE Vendôme by transport via Southampton 12.9.17 (arr 28.9.17); Bad landing in soft ground 19.1.18 (PFO RW Welsh); Stalled landing 26.1.18 (PFO G Heath); Became 205 TDS Vendôme 1.4.18; Heavy landing, bounced, damaged, lower aerodrome 23.4.18 (PFO MD Macpherson); Damaged u/c landing on edge of aerodrome 30.4.18 (PFO FW Boddy); To 212 TDS Vendôme 5.18; Taxied into Avro, slightly damaged 18.6.18 (F/Cdt DH Jones & Capt NM Scott); To US Forces

8806 (DC). Deld Hendon 3.5.16; Flown 12.5.16; Deleted 17.8.16

8807 Deld Hendon 1.5.16; Chingford 11.5.16 (transit); School Flt Eastchurch 12.5.16; COL 11.8.16; O/t taxying 13.4.17 (PFO TLD Silwood); to Eastchurch Workshops; Eastchurch FS 21.5.17; Chingford 7.9.17; ECD Grain 22.12.17; Fitted flotation gear by 6.18

8808 (DC). Deld Hendon 5.5.16; Tested 17.5.16; Eastbourne 17.5.16; CW by 6.7.16; Deleted 17.8.16

8809 Deld Hendon 4.5.16; Eastchurch School Flt 11.5.16 (arr 12.5.16); Chingford 6.9.17; ECD Dept Grain 22.12.17; Fitted skid u/c by 6.18; Successful landing on water with hydrovanes 25.6.18; EF, FL in Medway, air bags leaked, half sank 19.9.18 (Capt WW Wakefield)

8810 (DC). Deld Hendon 8.5.17; Eastbourne 14.5.16; Dismantled 29.10.16 - @6.4.17 (damaged), then deleted

8811 Deld Hendon 4.5.16; Eastbourne 13.5.16; Dismantled for packing 29.10.16; RNASTE Vendôme for erection by 23.11.16; Tested 8.12.16; Fuselage, wings and u/c damaged 3.7.17; Deleted BR

8812 (DC). Deld Hendon 4.5.16; Tested 17.5.16; Eastbourne 17.5.16; Dismantled Eastbourne, FL and damaged Faversham 22.7.16 (S/L JOR Gibeault); Design Flt Eastchurch 21.9.16; Eastbourne; Dismantled for packing 29.10.16; RNASTE Vendôme for erection by 23.11.16; Tested 8.12.16; Wrecked 24.5.17; Deleted 29.6.17 BR

8813 Deld Hendon 4.5.16; Eastbourne 10.5.16; Dismantled for packing 29.10.16; arr RNASTE Vendôme for erection 9.12.16; COL 6.4.17; Damaged 14.9.17; For deletion by 18.11.18

8814 (DC). Deld Hendon 9.5.16; Tested 22.5.16; Chingford 22.5.16; East Fortune rail 21.9.16 (arrived 26.9.16); FL 14.8.17; Transport to RNASTE Vendôme via Southampton 22.9.17 (arr 28.9.17); Became 205 TDS Vendôme 1.4.18; To US Forces

8815 Deld Hendon 4.5.16; Accepted 6.5.16 (Prodger); Eastbourne 10.5.16; Dismantled for packing 29.10.16; RNASTE Vendôme by 2.17; U/c damaged by 30.4.17; BR by 1.6.17; Deleted 29.6.17

8816 (DC). Deld Hendon 9.5.16; Tested 19.5.16; Eastbourne 20.5.16; Dismantled for packing 29.10.16; RNASTE Vendôme for erection by 9.12.16; Tested 18.12.16; U/c damaged by 30.4.17; Damaged 14.9.17; Hit bump landing and stalled 13.1.18 (PFO LE Pocock); Deleted W/E 1.2.18

8817 Deld Hendon 9.5.16; Tested 11.5.16; Chingford 17.5.16; Eastbourne 5.8.16; RNASTE Vendôme 1.11.16; Stalled and FL, CW 19.1.18 (PFO H Bricker); Deleted 8.2.18

8818 (DC). Deld Eastchurch FS 26.5.16; Crashed 20.7.16; Lost in low cloud, FL, hit fence, badly damaged, nr Sittingbourne 14.11.16 (PFO WL Jordan); Deleted 16.1.17

8819 Deld Hendon 9.5.16; Tested 12.5.16 (Prodger); Chingford 17.5.16; Eastbourne 4.8.16 (arr 5.8.16); Eastbourne, Dismantled for packing 29.10.16; For deletion by 16.2.17, then deleted

8820 (DC). Deld Hendon 11.5.16; Tested 22.5.16; Chingford

23.5.16; Cranwell 27.8.16 (transit); Scarborough 28.8.16 (transit); Redcar 30.8.16; U/c and propeller wrecked landing 3.1.17 (F/L BS Wemp & PFO JW Pinder unhurt); Deleted 25.6.17

8821 Deld Hendon 12.5.16; Tested 3.6.16; Chingford 8.6.16; East Fortune (via Cranwell & Redcar) 6.9.16 (arr 7.9.16); FL on A/S patrol and damaged 5.2.17 (FSL FJ Hosking), repaired; Transport via Southampton to RNASTE Vendôme 22.9.17 (arr 28.9.17); Stalled landing 5.2.18 (PFO GH Clarke); Became 205 TDS Vendôme 1.4.18; Stalled short of aerodrome, CW 4.4.18 (PFO GH Clarke)

8822 (DC). Deld Hendon 11.5.16; Tested 17.5.16 (Prodger); Chingford 18.5.16; East Fortune by rail 21.9.16 (arr 26.9.16); Crashed 1.3.17 (FSL SF Ingram unhurt; AC2 WA Maxwell injured); deleted 13.3.17

8823 Deld Hendon 15.5.16; Tested 17.5.16 (Prodger); Grain 20.5.16; Chingford 18.3.17; Redcar W/E 1.12.17; Deleted W/E 2.2.18

8824 (DC). Deld Hendon 17.5.16; Tested 25.5.16; To Dover but wrecked Grain 3.6.16 (FSL MB Walker); flew to Villacoublay 15.12.17 (damaged); RNASTE Vendôme W/E 19.1.18; Became 205 TDS 1.4.18; Bounced and stalled landing, lower aerodrome 16.4.18 (PFO GR Grange); To 212 TDS Vendôme 5.18; Stalled, damaged u/c 20.5.18 (PFO EM Lomax); To US Forces

8825 Deld Hendon 15.5.16; Flown 19.5.16; Dover 3.6.16; Dunkerque 20.7.16; Retd Dover; Slightly damaged by bomb dropped by German aircraft 12.8.16; still Dover 31.12.16

8826 (DC). Deld Hendon 15.5.16; Flown 23.5.16; Grain (via Chingford) 24.5.16; Chingford 17.3.17; Damaged 23.8.17; Redcar W/E 1.12.17; Deleted W/E 23.2.18

8827 Deld Hendon 15.5.16; Flown 19.5.16; Eastbourne 8.6.16; Deleted 17.8.16

8828 (DC). Deld Hendon for erection 21.5.16; Flown 26.5.16; School Flt Eastchurch 28.5.16; FL, damaged u/c and propeller Minster 28.7.16 (PFSL AM FitzRandolph); COL 11.8.16; FL in fog, damaged, Tadworth, Surrey 28.9.16 (PFSL FSG Lewis); Chingford 24.12.16; Eastchurch FS 26.12.16; Eastchurch Workshops 9.6.17 (tune up); Manston FS 8.9.17; HP Sqdn Manston W/E 1.12.17; RNASTE Vendôme W/E 8.12.17 - @30.3.18; To US Forces

8829 Deld Hendon 18.5.16; Flown 26.5.16; Grain 30.5.16; Visited Manston 6.7.16; Visited Kingsnorth 20.7.16; Visited Hendon 8.9.16; Visited Blackwater River 25.9.16; Chingford 8.3.17; Observers School Flt Eastchurch 7.5.17; Crashed 21.8.17; Dover 23.1.18 (transit); RNASTE Vendôme 24.1.18; Stalled landing 12.3.18 (PFO SG Burgess); Became 205 TDS Vendôme 1.4.18; Damaged on TO, lower aerodrome 1.5.18 (PFO RH Cross); To US Forces

8830 (DC). Deld Hendon 19.5.16; Flown 25.5.16; Eastchurch School Flt 26.5.16; Eastchurch Workshops 13.3.17 (repair); Eastchurch FS 10.4.17; Manston FS W/E 15.9.17; St.Pol 9.11.17; RNASTE Vendôme 11.11.17; Heavy landing, lower aerodrome 8.1.18 (PFO GES McLeod); O/t on TO 16.3.18; Became 205 TDS Vendôme 1.4.18; To 212 TDS Vendôme 5.18; Bounced and stalled, slightly damaged 13.6.18 (PFO GS Black); To US Forces

8831 Deld Hendon for erection 19.5.16; Tested 24.5.16; Grain 24.5.16; Brooklands 27.8.16; Grain, tests after repair 21.9.16; Chingford but FL Lodge Park en route 18.3.17 (FSL PO Gadbois); Surveyed 20.12.17; Deleted 9.1.18 W&T

8832 (DC). Deld Hendon for erection 19.5.16; Tested 26.5.16; Eastchurch School Flt 27.5.16; Deleted 11.8.16

8833 Deld Hendon 19.5.16; Tested 24.5.16; Dover 28.5.16 (via Manston); To Westgate, EF, FL on beach, damaged, dismantled and retd in tow 9.6.16 (FSL RA Little); Slightly damaged by bomb dropped by enemy aircraft 12.8.16; Deleted 6.3.17

8834 (DC). Deld Hendon 21.4.16; Accepted 28.5.16; Eastchurch School Flt 29.5.16; Eastchurch NFS by 10.16; Manston FS 8.9.17; HP Sqdn Manston W/E 1.12.17; RNASTE Vendôme W/E 8.12.17 (arr by rail W/E 21.12.17); Became 205 TDS Vendôme 1.4.18; To US Forces

8835 Deld Hendon 23.5.16; Accepted 28.5.16 (Prodger);

Dover (via Manston) 28.5.16; Surveyed 20.11.17; Deleted 26.11.17 DBR

**8836** (DC). Deld Hendon 22.5.16; Tested 7.6.16; Eastbourne 8.6.16; Design Flt Eastchurch 21.9.16; Eastbourne, Dismantled for packing 29.10.16; Arr RNASTE Vendôme for erection 3.12.16; Hit telegraph wire on TO, o/t nr Blois 19.1.18 (PFO JH Brown); Stalled and sideslipped landing, nr Vendôme road 9.3.18 (PFO JH Knight); Surveyed 1.4.18; Deleted 15.4.18 wrecked

**8837** Deld Hendon 31.5.16; Tested 6.6.16 (Prodger); Eastchurch School Flt 1.7.16; Misc Flt Eastchurch 19.7.16; Spotting Flt Eastchurch 15.9.16; Observers School Flt Eastchurch 23.12.16; Eastchurch FS 18.3.17; Eastchurch Workshops 26.6.17 (repair); Manston 8.9.17; Down at Dunkerque by 29.12.17; RNASTE Vendôme by 19.1.18; Became 205 TDS Vendôme 1.4.18; Heavy landing, CW 12.4.18 (PFO JM Johnstone slightly injured)

**8838** (DC). Deld Hendon 22.5.16; Tested 2.6.16; Eastbourne 5.6.16; Dismantled for packing 29.10.16; RNASTE Vendôme 1.11.16; Became 205 TDS Vendôme 1.4.18; Hit by 8876 14.5.18 (Lt SH McCrudden); To US Forces

**8839** Deld Hendon 27.5.16; Accepted 28.5.16 (Prodger); FL in field en route, Wittersham, Kent 1.6.16; arr Eastbourne by road 2.6.16; Dismantled for packing 29.10.16; arr RNASTE Vendôme 1.11.16; FL, dismantled 8.6.17; Damaged 26.7.17; Repaired by 5.8.17; Deleted W/E 21.9.17

**8840** (DC). Deld Hendon 24.5.16; EF, FL, damaged wings and propeller 31.5.16 (F/Cdr HR Busteed and passenger unhurt); Eastchurch 12.8.16; Erecting Hendon 8.9.16; Flown 1.1.17; Damaged taxying in 27.2.17 (F/Cdr CCR Edwards); Damaged chassis landing 24.3.17 (FSL AL Melhado); Martlesham 15.9.17; Hendon 22.9.17; Deleted W/E 2.2.18

**8841** Deld Hendon 28.5.16; Tested 1.6.16; Cranwell 21.6.16; Chingford 24.3.17; Damaged Easthorpe 6.6.17 (PFO AA Bishop); Deleted 22.7.17

**8842** (DC). Deld Hendon 24.5.16; Tested 10.6.16; Cranwell 21.6.16; Deleted 8.1.17

**8843** Deld Hendon 28.5.16; Tested 6.6.16 (Prodger); Cranwell 25.6.16; Chingford 9.6.17; Redcar W/E 1.12.17; Deleted W/E 23.2.18

**8844** (DC). Deld Hendon 24.5.16; Tested 3.6.16; Cranwell 25.6.16; Chingford 23.3.17; Badly damaged 7.8.17; ECD Grain 23.12.17 - @6.18

**8845** Deld Hendon 28.5.16; Tested 1.6.16; Cranwell 15.7.16; Redcar 15.8.16; Tregantle store W/E 23.3.18

**8846** (DC). Deld Hendon 24.5.16; Tested 7.6.16; Cranwell 21.6.16 (arr 25.6.16); Wrecked 5.10.16; Chingford 13.5.17; Redcar for erection W/E 1.12.17; Tregantle store W/E 23.3.18

**8847** Deld Hendon 7.6.16; Tested 15.6.16; Cranwell 15.7.16; Redcar 18.7.16; Severely damaged 6.7.17; Wings damaged 8.9.17; Surveyed 7.12.17; Deleted 14.12.17 wrecked

**8848** (DC) Deld Hendon 28.5.16; Flown 16.6.16; Cranwell 25.6.16; Chingford 23.3.17; Eastchurch Workshops 7.5.17; Eastchurch FS 9.5.17; Chingford W/E 15.9.17; Redcar W/E 1.12.17; For deletion by 9.3.18; Tregantle store W/E 23.3.18

**8849** Deld Hendon 16.6.16; Endurance test 15.8.16; Design Flt Eastchurch 22.8.16; Eastchurch FS 1.9.16; Eastchurch Workshops 25.10.16; Design Flt Eastchurch 9.11.16; Eastchurch Workshops 20.11.16; Eastchurch FS 28.11.16; Eastchurch Workshops 10.4.17 (repair); Deleted 24.4.17

**8850** (DC). Deld Hendon 28.5.16; Accepted 8.6.16; Eastbourne 14.7.16; Dismantled as spares 29.10.16; Deleted 4.17

**8851** Deld Hendon 13.7.16; Preliminary test 31.7.16; Tested 3.8.16; Cranwell 10.8.16; Deleted 1.10.16

**8852** (DC). Deld Hendon 28.5.16; Tested 9.6.16; Clement Talbot Works for 3 Wing 15.7.16; 3 Wing Luxeuil by 4.17; Transferred to French Govt for AMF 20.4.17

**8853** Deld Hendon 13.7.16; accepted 20.8.16; Cranwell 23.8.16; Deleted 8.1.17

**8854** (DC). Deld Hendon 30.5.16; Packing 11.7.16; 3 Wing Manston 17.7.16; Surveyed 30.11.16 wrecked

**8855** Deld Hendon and accepted 16.8.16; Cranwell 20.8.16; Chingford (coded '16') 4.4.17; O/t, badly damaged

1.6.17; Deleted 22.7.17

**8856** (DC). Deld Hendon and tested 8.6.16; Packing 11.7.16; 3 Wing Luxeuil (coded '4C') 18.7.16; Transferred to French Govt for AMF 20.4.17

**8857** Deld Hendon 31.7.16; Accepted 11.8.16; Cranwell 13.8.16; Deleted 8.1.17

**8858** (DC). Deld Hendon and tested 10.6.16; desp 3 Wing Luxeuil (coded '2C') by 11.16; Transferred to French Govt for AMF 20.4.17

**8859** Deld Hendon 21.8.16; Flown 5.9.16; Dover 13.9.16; War Flt Eastchurch 15.9.16 (visit); Dover 16.9.16; J.N.4 (Improved) by 29.12.17; Surveyed 23.2.18; Deleted 1.3.18

**8860** (DC). Deld Hendon and tested 16.6.16; Eastbourne 14.7.16; Dismantled for packing 29.10.16; RNASTE Vendôme for erection by 23.11.16; Tested 28.11.16; Fast landing, o/t, CW 14.1.18 (PFO FEC Benstead); For deletion by 1.2.18

**8861** Deld Hendon 22.8.16; Accepted 28.8.16; Eastchurch FS 5.9.16; Manston 8.9.17; St.Pol 9.11.17; RNASTE Vendôme 11.11.17; Stalled landing 26.1.18 (PFO WT Owen); Bad landing 6.2.18 (PFO W Nesbitt); Became 205 TDS Vendôme 1.4.18; Heavy landing, damaged 11.4.18 (PFO JP Corkery); 84 Wing Vendôme by 8.18; 2nd Aviation Centre, American Air Service, Tours 18.8.18

**8862** (DC). Deld Hendon 31.7.16; Accepted 8.8.16; Cranwell 9.8.16; Chingford 25.5.17; Dived in from 300 ft while landing 12.6.17 (PFO WG Parry and TPFO K Stuart both killed); Deleted 22.7.17

**8863** Deld Hendon for erection 28.8.16; Preliminary test 5.9.16; Dover 7.9.16; Eastchurch War Flt 17.10.16; Dover 9.11.16; Lost way, FL, chassis and propeller damaged Silverhill, Hastings 9.7.17 (pilot unhurt); Surveyed 16.10.17; Deleted 19.10.17 W&T

**8864** (DC). Deld Hendon 1.8.16; Accepted 8.8.16; Cranwell 9.8.16; FL Hendon 5.2.17 (S/Cdr PFM Fellowes); Repaired and retd Cranwell; Crashed 22.8.17; Surveyed 3.10.17; Deleted 6.10.17 wrecked

**8865** Deld Hendon 8.9.16; Fitting Fairey tail 29.9.16 (modified to JN4/Improved); Tested 9.10.16; Chingford 24.10.16 (transit); Cranwell 25.10.16; Chingford 26.3.17; Eastchurch Workshops 7.5.17; Manston FS W/E 22.9.17; HP Sqdn Manston W/E 1.12.17; Deleted 9.1.18 W&T

**8866** (DC). Deld Hendon 21.8.16 and fitted DC; Tested 31.8.16; Felixstowe 17.3.17; Martlesham to Hendon 18.3.17; Grain 24.5.17; Hendon to Grain 13.6.17; Hendon 14.6.17; COL 16.6.17; Surveyed 1.12.17; Deleted 8.12.17 W&T

**8867** Deld Hendon 8.9.16; Fitting Fairey tail 29.9.16 (modified to JN4/Improved); Tested 16.10.16; Chingford 24.10.16 (transit); Cranwell 25.10.16; Wrecked 31.1.17; Chingford 24.3.17; Engine missing, stayed up too long at dusk, COL 11.6.17 (PFO AM Alexander); ECD Grain 22.9.17 - @7.9.18

**8868** (DC). Deld Hendon 25.8.16 and fitted DC; Accepted 1.9.16; Eastchurch Workshops 18.9.16; then to FS; Crashed 23.10.16 and to Workshops; Deleted 8.11.16

**8869** Deld Hendon for erection 3.2.17; Accepted 12.2.17; RNASTE Vendôme 11.4.17; Surveyed 15.11.17; Deleted 21.11.17 wrecked

**8870** (DC). Deld Hendon 28.8.16; Preliminary test 5.9.16; Eastbourne 13.9.16; Dismantled for packing 29.10.16; RNASTE Vendôme for erection by 23.11.16; Tested 8.12.16; U/c damaged by 30.4.17; Wings and u/c damaged 7.6.17; Became 205 TDS Vendôme 1.4.18

**8871** Deld Hendon for erection 3.2.17; Accepted 12.2.17; Accident 14.2.17; Despatched 24.2.17; In transit to Vendôme by 31.3.17; RNASTE Vendôme for erection by 25.4.17; Wings damaged 10.7.17; Stalled landing, damaged 18.2.18 (PFO GW Wilson); Became 205 TDS Vendôme 1.4.18

**8872** (DC). Deld Hendon 8.9.16; Fitting Fairey tail 29.9.16; Preliminary test 1.10.16; Completed tests 5.10.16; Dismantling 2.11.16; Despatched 10.11.16; RNASTE Vendôme by 23.11.16 (erecting); Tested 28.11.16; U/c damaged by 30.4.17; Became 205 TDS Vendôme 1.4.18; Bounced and stalled landing 4.4.18 (PFO HF Mulhall)

**8873** Deld Cranwell 1.4.17; RNASTE Vendôme 25.8.17;

Became 205 TDS Vendôme 1.4.18

8874 (DC). Deld Hendon for erection 3.2.17; Accepted 17.2.17; RNASTE Vendôme 5.4.17; Stalled landing, o/t in ditch, CW 14.1.18 (PFO LE Pocock); Became 205 TDS Vendôme 1.4.18; 212 TDS Vendôme from 5.18; Damaged wings and chassis landing 23.6.18 (PFO RG Spencer & Capt NM Scott); 84 Wing Vendôme by 8.18; 2nd Aviation Centre, American Air Service, Tours 18.8.18

8875 Deld Hendon 28.4.17; Flown 9.6.17; Deleted W/E 2.2.18

8876 (DC). Deld Hendon for erection 3.2.17; Flown 18.2.17; RNASTE Vendôme for erection 21.4.17; Wings damaged 21.5.17; Became 205 TDS Vendôme 1.4.18; Collided with 8838, lower aerodrome 14.5.18 (Capt F Fowler); 212 TDS from 5.18; Slightly damaged TO in grain field nr aerodrome 21.6.18 (Capt NM Scott); To US Forces

8877 Deld CSD White City; RNASTE Vendôme W/E 14.9.17; Failed to flatten out landing 22.1.18 (PFO WA Bridge); Stalled on steep turn, dived in, TW 12.3.18 (PFO WJ Kelly); Deleted W/E 30.3.18

8878 (DC). Allocated CSD for Hendon 18.4.17; Deld White City; RNASTE Vendôme by 10.17; Taxying out hit by 3267, badly damaged 9.2.18 (F/L HER Nelson & PFO HL Burley); Became 205 TDS Vendôme 1.4.18; To US Forces

8879 Deld CSD White City; RNASTE Vendôme W/E 14.9.17; Became 205 TDS Vendôme 1.4.18; To US Forces

8880 (DC). Deld CSD White City; Chingford W/E 10.11.17; Redcar for erection W/E 1.12.17; For deletion by 16.2.18

8881 to 8900 retained in store in USA

8901 To RFC (Military Wing)

**19 NIEUPORT TYPE 12 TWO-SEATER FIGHTER RECONNAISSANCE TRACTOR BIPLANES** purchased from Établissements Nieuport, numbered 8902 to 8920 & built Issy-les-Moulineaux. (110-hp Clerget)

8902 Deld 1 Wing by 20.3.16; 2 Flt A Sqdn 1 Wing St.Pol by 25.4.16 - @11.5.16; 4 Flt B Sqdn 1 Wing by 2.6.16; ADD 10.8.16 - 9.16; Dover by 12.11.16; Damaged 3.2.17 (FSL H Lawson); Surveyed 16.10.17; Deleted 19.10.17 W&T

8903 Deld 1 Wing by 18.2.16; 1 Flt A Sqdn 1 Wing from formation 1.3.16; Shipped to Aegean; C Flt A Sqdn 2 Wing Imbros by 30.4.16 - @9.5.16 ('Gunbus'); Transferred to French Govt

8904 Deld 1 Wing St.Pol by 29.2.16; Fleet patrol over Fleet, Friedrichshafen FF33E seaplane at 9,000ft shot down 5m NE of Zeebrugge while attacking British ships, dived into water, pilot slumped forward, passenger jumped out from 3,000ft rolling horizontally, its bombs blew up on hitting water 24.4.16 (FSL HR Simms & FSL HA Furniss) (LtzS Kurt Faber & Flugmeister Paul Reutter both killed); Shot down at sea 5.5.16 (FSL HR Simms & S/L CJA Mullens RNVR both killed); For survey 11.5.16; For deletion by 18.5.16

8905 Shipped to Aegean 1916; 2 Wing Imbros by 4.16 - @8.16; Deleted 1917

8906 Shipped to Aegean 1916; 2 Wing Imbros by 4.16 - @8.16; Deleted 1916

8907 Deld 1 Wing by 1.4.16; 2 Flt A Sqdn 1 Wing St.Pol by 11.5.16; ADD 2.6.16; 10 Flt A Sqdn 4 Wing Dunkerque 11.8.16 - @9.11.16; 11 Flt B Sqdn 4 Wing by 16.11.16; 2 Flt A Sqdn 5 Wing 28.11.16; Dover 20.12.16; Cranwell 7.1.17; Crashed Hornchurch 8.1.17 (PFO JC De Wilde of Cranwell); Chingford by road 8.1.17; Deleted 5.2.17

8908 Deld 1 Wing by 10.3.16; 2 Flt A Sqdn 1 Wing St.Pol by 4.16 - @18.5.16; 4 Flt B Sqdn 1 Wing by 2.6.16; C Sqdn 1 Wing by 27.6.16; ADD by 13.7.16; 6 Flt A Sqdn 5 Wing 10.8.16; ADD 24.8.16; Dover 12.11.16; Crashed Coudekerque 24.8.17 (FSL CJ Moir); ADD 24?.8.17; Dover by 10.17; For deletion by 13.10.17

8909 Shipped to Aegean; 2 Wing Imbros by 4.16; Mitylene 12.7.16 - @8.16; Deleted 1916

8910 Shipped to Aegean 1916; C Flt A Sqdn 2 Wing Imbros by 2.5.16 - @8.16 ('Gunbus'); Deleted 1917

8911 Shipped to Aegean 1916; 2 Wing Aegean by 4.16 - @8.16; Deleted 1916

8912 Shipped to Aegean 1916; A Flt 2 Wing Imbros by 7.5.16; C Flt A Flt 2 Wing Thasos 30.5.16 - @8.16 ("Gunbus"); Deleted 1916

8913 Shipped to Aegean 1916; 2 Wing Aegean by 4.16; Thasos by 10.16; Recce towards Buk, shot down nr Drama 23.10.16 (FSL GK Bands wounded & Lt RG Blakesley unhurt, both PoW)

8914 Deld 1 Wing by 21.4.16; 2 Flt A Sqdn 1 Wing St.Pol by 4.16 - @11.5.16; 4 Flt B Sqdn 1 Wing by 29.6.16 - 7.16; C Sqdn 1 Wing by 17.8.16 - @2.9.16; ADD by 7.9.16; to Dover but CW on arrival 20.12.16; Deleted 31.12.16

8915 Deld 1 Wing by 10.4.16; 3 Flt B Sqdn 1 Wing St.Pol by 12.4.16 - @11.5.16; 4 Flt B Sqdn 1 Wing by 7.6.16; 3 Flt B Sqdn 1 Wing by 29.6.16; 4 Flt B Sqdn 1 Wing by 10.8.16; ADD by 21.9.16; 1 Wing by 9.16 - 10.16; Cranwell for GI by 29.12.16; Surveyed 18.9.17; Deleted 8.10.17

8916 Deld 1 Wing 4.16; 3 Flt B Sqdn 1 Wing St.Pol by 29.4.16 - @11.5.16; 14 Flt B Sqdn 1 Wing by 24.5.16; 4 Flt B Sqdn by 2.6.16 - @8.6.16; C Sqdn 1 Wing by 22.6.16; C Sqdn 1 Wing by 9.7.16 - @19.7.16; ADD by 20.7.16; Crashed, DBR; For survey 23.11.16; Deleted ADD 5.1.17

8917 Deld ADD by 11.5.16; Damaged, for survey by 2.6.16; Deleted 15.6.16

8918 (Fitted W/T) Deld 1 Wing 4.16; 3 Flt B Sqdn 1 Wing by 10.4.16 - @3.8.16; 4 Flt B Sqdn 1 Wing by 10.8.16; C Sqdn 1 Wing by 17.8.16; ADD by 28.9.16; Dover 22.11.16; Surveyed 16.10.17; Deleted 19.10.17 W&T

8919 Shipped to Aegean; 2 Wing Aegean by 4.16; Deleted by 7.16

8920 Shipped to Aegean; 2 Wing Imbros by 4.16 - @8.16; Deleted 1916

**20 MAURICE FARMAN S.7 LONGHORN PUSHER BIPLANES** ordered under Cont No C.P.145457/15 from Brush Electrical Engineering Co, numbered 8921 to 8940 & built Loughborough. (75 or 80-hp Renault)

8921 Deld Chingford 19.5.16; Deleted W/E 8.9.17

8922 Deld Cranwell 8.5.16; Under repair 2.17; to Redcar but FL and wrecked nr Ormesby 29.6.17 (FSL A Frauenfelder & Lt RMS Veal unhurt); Deleted 15.9.17

8923 Deld Hendon (via Chingford) 28.5.16 (transit); Eastchurch School Flt 29.5.16 (arr 30.5.16); COL 14.7.16 (TPFSL EA Freeman killed); Deleted 11.8.16

8924 Deld Chingford by rail 7.6.16; Deleted W/E 8.9.17

8925 Deld Eastbourne 17.6.16; Deleted 26.9.16

8926 Deld Eastbourne (via Hendon) 29.6.16 (Barrs); Eastchurch Workshops 2.11.16; Eastchurch FS 9.11.16; EF, FL and damaged nr Rochester 13.5.17; Retd by lorry and to Eastchurch Workshops for repair; Eastchurch FS 5.7.17; Damaged in heavy landing 24.7.17; Surveyed 26.11.17; Deleted 5.12.17 as spares

8927 (75-hp) Deld Eastchurch School Flt 6.7.16; Caught fire in air 20.4.17; Little damage, repaired; U/c smashed 5.6.17; Manston FS 6.7.17; Deleted W/E 23.2.18

8928 Deld Chingford 8.7.16; Possibly the aircraft in which T/F/Cdr JD Newberry killed & a PFO injured 28.9.17; Surveyed 3.10.17; Deleted 6.10.17 W&T

8929 Deld Eastbourne 12.7.16; Eastchurch Workshops 15.10.16; Eastchurch FS 17.10.16; Crashed 17.2.17; Eastchurch Workshops 19.2.17; Deleted 13.3.17

8930 Deld Eastbourne 14.7.16; Eastchurch FS 11.3.17; Crashed 10.5.17; Eastchurch Workshops 11.5.17; Deleted 5.6.17

8931 Deld Cranwell 21.7.16; Deleted 25.2.17

8932 (DC) Deld Redcar 23.8.16 (Barrs); EF, FL, damaged 23.8.16 (FSL LA Sands unhurt); Deleted 25.6.17

8933 Deld Eastchurch FS 3.8.16; Deleted 4.9.16

8934 Deld Cranwell 5.8.16; Redcar by rail 3.7.17; Surveyed 7.12.17; Deleted 14.12.17 as spares

8935 Deld Eastbourne 11.8.16; Eastchurch Workshops 16.10.16; Eastchurch FS 24.10.16; Eastchurch Workshops 15.2.17 (repair after crash); Eastchurch FS 13.3.17; Eastchurch Workshops 5.6.17 (repair); Crashed 8.8.17; Surveyed 26.11.17; Deleted 5.12.17 as spares

8936 Deld Eastchurch Workshops 20.10.16; Eastchurch FS

*Bristol Scout Type D
8955 being hoisted
aboard HMS Vindex.
(IWM Q. 73688)*

*Pemberton-Billing P.B. 25
Pusher Biplane 9001.
(via Philip Jarrett)*

*Supermarine-built
.A.D. Navyplane Seaplane
9095.
(J.M. Bruce/G.S. Leslie
collection)*

24.10.16; Crashed 3.11.16 and to Workshops; Eastchurch FS 30.11.16; Eastchurch Workshops 5.3.17 (repair); Deleted 26.4.17

**8937** Deld Eastchurch FS 21.8.16; FL, fog, broke propeller nr Sittingbourne 28.9.16; Crashed 2.3.17; Eastchurch Workshops 5.3.17 (repair); Deleted 26.4.17

**8938** Deld Redcar 30.8.16 (Barrs); Crashed, damaged 8.11.16 (PFSL GW Hemming unhurt); Deleted 29.1.17

**8939** Deld CSD 10.16; Cranwell 9.11.16; Redcar by rail 2.7.17 (arr 3.7.17); Wrecked 21.8.17; Surveyed 7.12.17; Deleted 14.12.17 as spares

**8940** (DC) Deld CSD Crystal Palace 9.16; Redcar 31.10.16; Surveyed 7.12.17; Deleted 14.12.17 as spares

**10 CAUDRON G.III TRACTOR BIPLANES ordered under Cont No C.P.145456/15 from the British Caudron Co Ltd, numbered 8941 to 8950 & built Hendon. (80-hp Gnome)**

**8941** Deld Hendon 7.4.16; Tested 26.4.16 (Desoutter); Accepted 2.5.16; Redcar by rail 4.5.16; Tested 5.7.16; Deleted 25.8.16

**8942** Deld Hendon 6.5.16; Tested 10.5.16 (Desoutter); Redcar 11.5.16 (arr 14.5.16); EF, FL, damaged tail 20.10.16 (FSL FG Browne unhurt); COL and CW 23.12.16 (PFO DA Lancaster shock); Deleted 29.1.17

**8943** (DC) Deld Hendon 11.5.16; Tested 16.5.16; Redcar 16.6.16 (arr 22.6.16 via Killingholme and Scarborough); FL, damaged 21.8.16 (FSL CBdeT Drummond); Deleted 25.6.17

**8944** Deld Hendon 23.5.16; Tested 26.5.16; Redcar by rail 11.7.16; EF, FL, o/t, slight damage 11.9.16 (FSL HRG Whates); Damaged landing 26.10.16 (FSL LCJ Barlow); Deleted 29.1.17

**8945** (DC) Deld Hendon 24.5.16; Tested 26.5.16; Redcar by rail 11.7.16; Tested 2.8.16; EF, FL, damaged 23.8.16 (FSL LA Sands unhurt); EF, FL, ran into hedge and damaged 24.10.16 (FSL RF Hallon unhurt); Flown into ground on landing 11.12.16 (PFO JP Everitt injured); FL, CW 21.1.17 (PFSL RV Power unhurt); Deleted 31.1.17

**8946** Deld Hendon 17.6.16; Tested 20.6.16; Redcar by rail 12.7.16 (arr 15.7.16); Tested 3.8.16; Overshot landing, ran into cottages, CW 15.8.16 (FSL BS Wemp & FSL W Buckley unhurt); Deleted 25.8.16

**8947** Deld CSD 6.16 - @31.7.16 (not by 31.8.16); GI at CSD Crystal Palace by 31.12.16; Surveyed 1.10.17; Deleted 2.10.17 DBR

**8948** Deld CSD White City 6.16; Surveyed 1.10.17; Deleted 2.10.17 DBR

**8949** (DC) Deld Hendon 30.6.16; Accepted 4.7.16 (Desoutter); Redcar School 8.8.16 (arrived 10.8.16); EF, FL, CW 23.3.17 (PFO AS Redgate unhurt); Deleted 3.4.17

**8950** Deld Hendon 10.7.16; Accepted 13.7.16; En route Redcar, EF, FL Shipton, 5m N of York, damaged 18.7.16 (FSL H Rampling); arr Redcar 8.8.16; COL, CW 5.10.16 (FSL AE Taylor unhurt); Deleted 16.10.16

**50 BRISTOL SCOUT TYPE D TRACTOR BIPLANES ordered under Cont No C.P.145461/15/X, numbered 8951 to 9000, to be built at Filton. (Ordered with 110-hp Clerget, delivered with 100-hp Gnome Monosoupape)**
[C/n's 1124 to 1173]

**8951** Deld Westgate 4.5.16; Tested 5.5.16; Manston 23.6.16; HACPs 30.7.16 x 2, 22.9.16, 22.10.16 & 23.10.16 (all F/Cdr JA Carr); HSPPs 16.2.17 (FSL RR Thornely later FSL HA Pailthorpe), 1.3.17 (FSL CB Wincott) & 16.3.17 (FSL ES Arnold); Left for Walmer but engine cut, ran into Bessonneau hangar, wrecked 29.4.17 (FSL EJK Buckley unhurt); Crashed 2.5.17 (F/Cdr JA Carr); Deleted 8.5.17

**8952** At Filton 9.4.16, allocated Dover; Deld Dover by rail 14.5.16; FL 18.6.16 (FSL ER Grange); ADD 16.7.16 (dismantled); Shipped to Dover 20.9.16; Deleted 11.10.16

**8953** Deld Felixstowe 23.5.16; Trimley 20.6.16; HMS *Vindex* 21.6.16; Attacked Zeppelin *L17* with Ranken Darts but to no effect, EF, ditched nr North Hinder LV 2.8.16 (FSL CT Freeman picked up by Belgian steamer SS *Anvers*, taken to Holland, retd 6.8.16)

**8954** Deld Felixstowe 23.5.16; Trimley 18.6.16; Levington 2.7.16 - @1.8.16; COL Trimley 10.7.16 (FSL MJG Day); Fairey 6.8.16 (repair); Felixstowe for erection 15.2.17; HMS *Vindex* 23.3.17; Felixstowe by 1.4.17; Cranwell 15.9.17 - @30.3.18

**8955** Deld Felixstowe 23.5.16; Trimley 18.6.16; HMS *Vindex* 21.6.16; Martlesham Heath 4.4.17; Yarmouth 14.7.17; Martlesham Heath 16.7.17; Hendon 25.7.17 - @13.10.17; Manston on/by 20.10.17; Surveyed 26.11.17; Deleted 3.12.17 DBR

**8956** Deld Westgate 1.5.16; Tested 2.6.16 (Raynham); Manston 22.6.16; HACPs 17.7.16 (FSL JA Carr), 12.8.16 (FSL CW Greig) & 23.10.16 (FSL JM Ingham); HSPPs 16.2.17 (FSL ES Arnold x 2, later FSL CB Wincott who fired 30 rounds at 1500 yds without result); Walmer 29.4.17; Dover 19.5.17; War Flt Manston 11.6.17; FL, slightly damaged u/c Broadsalts 8.8.17 (FSL HR de Wilde), retd 9.8.17; Damaged 15.9.17; U/c damaged landing 29.9.17 (FSL AG Beattie); Surveyed 18.11.17; Deleted 23.11.17 wrecked

**8957** Deld Westgate 1.5.16; Tested 2.6.16 (Raynham); War School Manston 23.6.16; HACPs 9.7.16 (FSL FS Mills), 30.7.16 (FSL CW Greig), 23.10.16 (FSL MWH Evans), 1.3.17 (FSL JE Scott); HACP, damaged u/c and engine landing 17.3.17 (FSL JE Scott); Walmer 2.5.17; Damaged 11.5.17 (FSL WH Chisam), to Dover for repair; Walmer 25.5.17; HACP 25.5.17 (FSL WH Chisam); Dover 3.6.17; War Flt Manston 5.7.17; Surveyed 26.10.17; Deleted 29.10.17 W&T

**8958** Deld Exp Flt Grain 27.5.16; PVRS 17.9.16; Grain 20.11.16; HACP 28.11.16 (F/Cdr AR Arnold); Tested Grain 9.2.17; Manston 22.3.17; Walmer 2.5.17; HACP 23.5.17 (FSL WM Lusby); Dover 28.5.17; War Flt Manston 20.6.17; COL 20.8.17 (FSL JA Piquet); Deleted W/E 30.3.18

**8959** (C/n 1132). Deld by rail and erected Yarmouth 29.5.16; Burgh Castle 14.1.17; HACP 26.1.17 (FSL EL Pulling); Burgh Castle by 25.2.17; Covehithe 8.4.17; HACP 17.4.17 (FSL CS Iron); Burgh Castle 22.4.17; Yarmouth 27.4.17; Badly damaged 24.5.17; AZP 29.5.17 (FSL GWR Fane); AGP 5.6.17 (FSL HRde Wilde); Burgh Castle 19.6.17; DBR 11.7.17; Deleted W/E 8.9.17

**8960** Deld Westgate and tested 2.6.16 (Raynham); War Flt/School Manston 23.6.16; HACPs 9.7.16, 22.9.16 & 28.11.16 (all F/Cdr CH Butler); FL Grove Ferry 23.1.17; HACP, EF, FL Canterbury, Kent 29.1.17 (FSL CB Wincott), retd safely; HACP 16.2.17 (FSL RR Thornely); Crashed 10.9.17; Surveyed 10.11.17; Deleted 14.10.17 DBR

**8961** Deld Yarmouth 1.6.16; Erected 3.6.16; HACP 30.3.17 (F/L GWR Fane); Burgh Castle 5.5.17; HSPP 11.5.17 (F/Cdr CS Iron); Bacton 11.5.17; Covehithe 12.5.17; Yarmouth 1.6.17; Covehithe 4.6.17; Yarmouth 30.6.17; Damaged u/c and wing 20.8.17; Deleted W/E 8.9.17

**8962** Deld Westgate by rail 3.6.16; Accepted 11.6.16; Manston 22.6.16; O/t landing, damaged 8.7.16 (FSL CW Greig); Deleted 31.3.17

**8963** Deld Westgate 5.6.16; Manston 21.6.16; HACPs 7.1.17 (FSL RR Thornely) & 15.3.17 (FSL CB Wincott); Wrecked, wings and chassis damaged leaving Walmer 30.4.17 (FSL AR Brown unhurt); Deleted 14.6.17

**8964** Deld War Flt Eastchurch 8.6.16; HACP 25.8.16; Crashed 19.10.16; Eastchurch Workshops 20.10.16; Deleted 8.11.16

**8965** Deld War Flt Eastchurch 12.6.16; Detling 22.12.16; War School Manston 18.3.17; AGPs 25.5.17 & 5.6.17 (both FSL RH Daly); Surveyed 26.10.17; Deleted 29.10.17 W&T

**8966** Deld Dover 11.6.16; Tested 19.6.16 (Raynham); Dunkerque 30.6.16; Dover Sqdn (later Defence Flt, then C Sqdn 1 Wing) 2.7.16; (1 Wing) EF, FL La Panne 3.9.16, retd 6.9.16; ADD by 28.9.16; To Dover in SS *Mersey* 12.10.16; Deleted 26.4.17

**8967** (80-hp Gnome) Deld Dover 11.6.16; Tested 19.6.16 (Raynham); Dunkerque 30.6.16; Dover Sqdn (later Dover Defence Flt, then C Sqdn 1 Wing) 2.7.16; ADD by 14.9.16; Dover 20.9.16 (retd badly damaged); Cranwell for erection 23.8.17; Surveyed 12.9.17; Deleted 8.10.17 W&T

**8968** Deld Dover 12.6.16; Tested 19.6.16 (Raynham); ADD 30.6.16; Dover Defence Flt (later C Sqdn 1 Wing) by

8.7.16; For survey, crashed and wrecked by 24.8.16; Deleted ADD 17.9.16

8969    Deld War Flt Eastchurch 17.6.16; Detling 20.12.16; Manston War Flt 24.3.17; AGP 25.5.17 & 13.6.17 (both FSL HRde Wilde); Damaged on TO 4.7.17 (FSL EB Drake); Deleted W/E 2.3.18

8970    Deld Eastchurch War Flt 20.6.16; Accepted 21.6.16 (Raynham); Eastchurch Workshops 23.12.16; Detling 15.2.17; Manston 30.3.17; Crashed 21.5.17; Deleted 14.6.17

8971    Deld Dover for erection 18.6.16; Dover Defence, Dunkerque 16.7.16; FL Sandgate 16.7.16; EF, FL on beach Bray Dunes 3.8.16 (FSL SJ Goble); Dover 17.9.16; HACP, damaged landing 22.9.16 (FSL FCC Calder); Deleted 6.8.17

8972    Deld Eastchurch War Flt 23.6.16; Wrecked 29.11.16 (FSL HM Ireland); Observers School Flt Eastchurch 23.12.16; Eastchurch FS 17.2.17; Eastchurch Workshops 14.4.17 (repair); Eastchurch FS 9.5.17; Fitted Lewis gun 10.6.17; AGP 13.6.17 (S/Cdr AF Bettington); War School Manston W/E 24.11.17; Surveyed 23.11.17 DBR; Deleted 28.11.17

8973    Deld Eastchurch War Flt 24.6.16; Eastchurch Workshops 23.12.16; Detling 15.2.17; Manston 1.3.17 but retd Detling bad weather; Manston 1.4.17; U/c damaged 18.6.17; U/c damaged landing 29.6.17 (FSL MA Harker); Propeller and u/c damaged on TO 7.7.17 (FSL HC Lemon unhurt); COL, badly damaged 24.7.17 (FSL HRde Wilde unhurt); War School Manston by 6.10.17; Surveyed 26.10.17; Deleted 29.10.17 W&T

8974    Deld Eastchurch War Flt 26.6.16; Crashed 23.10.16, to Eastchurch Workshops; Deleted 8.11.16

8975    Deld Cranwell 5.7.16; Crashed 8.9.16 (presumably the collision with 5574 coming out of cloud, in which S/Cdr I-HWS Dalrymple-Clark killed); Deleted 3.10.16

8976    Shipped to Australian Govt 6.16; Arrived 28.9.16; Flown at CFS Point Cook 1916/18 as *CFS10*, later *CFS4*

8977    Deld Eastchurch War Flt 6.7.16; HACP 22.10.16 (F/Cdr EH Dunning); Observers School Flt Eastchurch 23.12.16; Grain 7.6.17 (deck trials); War School Manston 28.7.17; Surveyed 1.12.17; Deleted 5.12.17 wrecked

8978    Deld Eastchurch War Flt 17.7.16; Eastchurch Workshops 29.10.16; Eastchurch War Flt 1.12.16; Eastchurch Workshops 6.12.16; Observers School Flt Eastchurch 8.1.17; AGPs 25.5.17 & 5.6.17; AGP, engaged enemy aircraft 10m out to sea 6.6.17 (F/Cdr JCP Wood); AGP 8.6.17 (F/Cdr JCP Wood); AGPs 13.6.17 & 14.6.17 (F/L GA Cox); HACP 16.6.17 (FSL PFT Luckham); For deletion by 30.3.18

8979    Deld Trimley for erection 31.8.16; Levington 2.9.16; Tested Trimley 4.9.16 (Pickles); HMS *Vindex* 9.9.16 (Lewis gun above centre section); Martlesham 4.4.17; Yarmouth 16.7.17; Deleted W/E @23.3.18

8980    Deld Trimley for erection 31.8.16; Levington NLG 2.9.16; Tested 4.9.16 (Pickles); Fitted Lewis gun above centre section; Felixstowe 21.2.17; Burgh Castle 16.7.17; Yarmouth by 29.9.17; Burgh 15.11.17; Yarmouth 20.11.17; HACP 24.12.17; Deleted W/E 2.3.18

8981    (80-hp Gnome) Deld CSD 9.16; Cranwell for erection 11.12.16; Wrecked 25.9.17; EF, FL 20.11.17 (FSL JH Pearson); Became 201/2 TDS Cranwell 1.4.18
[8981 to 8985 were to become RFC A2376 to A2380, but allotment not effected]

8982    Deld CSD 9.16; Cranwell 8.12.16; Redcar 30.3.17; Dismantling 21.7.17; East Fortune NFS by rail 24.7.17 (arr 26.7.17) - @30.3.18

8983    Deld CSD 9.16; Cranwell 11.12.16; Redcar 30.3.17; Dismantling 21.7.17; East Fortune NFS by rail 24.7.17 (arr 26.7.17); For deletion by 18.1.18

8984    Deld CSD 9.16; Cranwell 8.12.16; To Redcar but o/t landing, badly damaged 17.3.17 (S/Cdr PFM Fellowes unhurt); Deleted 3.4.17

8985    Deld CSD 9.16; Chingford by lorry 8.12.16; Grain by rail 22.12.16 (arr 30.12.16) (to test); to Manston 21.3.17; Wrecked on arrival, broken camshaft 22.3.17 (F/L HS Neville); Deleted 28.4.17

8986    Deld CSD 9.16; Chingford by lorry 8.12.16; Grain by rail 22.12.16 (to test); Manston 22.3.17; FL, damaged 21.5.17 (FSL HRde Wilde); Deleted 25.8.17

[8986 to 9000 were to become RFC A3006 to A3020, but allotment not effected]

8987    Deld Chingford for erection 25.10.16; Fitted 60-hp Le Rhône by 12.17; Surveyed 18.3.18; Deleted 27.3.18 wrecked

8988    Deld Chingford for erection 25.10.16; Fitted 80-hp Gnome by 10.17; 50-hp Le Rhône by 12.17; 60-hp Le Rhône by 1.18; Deleted W/E 23.2.18

8989    Deld Design Flt Eastchurch by rail 4.11.16; Detling 7.12.16; War Flt/School Manston 16.3.17; AGPs 5.6.17 (FSL HRde Wilde) & 4.7.17; Surveyed 26.10.17; Deleted 29.10.17 W&T

8990    Deld Design Flt Eastchurch by rail 4.11.16; Eastchurch Workshops awaiting test 27.11.16; Detling 22.12.16; Collided with 3052 while landing, propeller and both wings damaged 24.12.16 (FSL EA Bennetts unhurt); Eastchurch Workshops repair by 1.1.17; Detling 29.1.17; HACP 16.2.17 (FSL RH Horniman); Manston 1.4.17; AGP 25.5.17 (FSL RH Daly); AGP 13.6.17 (F/Cdr GL Thomson, HP Sqdn CO); Damaged on TO 19.6.17 (FSL S Quayle unhurt); EF, FL, damaged nr aerodrome 12.7.17 (FSL CH Fitzherbert unhurt); Deleted 23.7.17

8991    Deld East Fortune NFS for erection 30.10.16; Damaged landing 9.4.17; Tyre burst landing, o/t, wing and propeller damaged 23.5.17 (FSL AB Hill unhurt); Damaged chassis landing 6.7.17; still East Fortune NFS 30.3.18

8992    Deld East Fortune NFS for erection 30.10.16; Chassis CW, propeller and nosepiece broken 13.6.17 (FSL HG Leslie); U/c and propeller broken 31.7.17; still East Fortune NFS 30.3.18

8993    Deld Redcar School by transport 28.10.16 (fighter); Became SoSF Redcar 1.4.18; Became 2 SoSF Redcar 5.18; Became NE Area FIS Redcar 1.7.18 - @8.18

8994    Left Filton for shipment to Mudros in SS *Trojan Prince* 8.16; 2 Wing Imbros, o/t in lagoon 1.17; Deleted 1917

8995    Left Filton for shipment to Mudros in SS *Trojan Prince* 8.16; 2 Wing Mudros, on nose landing .17 (FSL EP Hicks); G Sqdn 2 Wing Mudros by 8.17; Surveyed 21.9.17; Deleted 6.10.17 DBR

8996    Left Filton for shipment to Mudros in SS *Trojan Prince* 8.16; C Flt 2 Wing Imbros by 13.12.16; Attacked by two enemy seaplanes off Imbros 11.2.17; While escorting Sopwith bomber in attack on gunboat, shot down by Ltn Meinecke nr Chanak 17.2.17 (FSL GT Bysshe PoW)

8997    Left Filton for shipment to Mudros in SS *Trojan Prince* 8.16; 2 Wing Imbros by 1.12.17; Thasos by 1.1.18 (repair) - @4.3.18; Deleted 4.18

8998    Left Filton for shipment to Mudros in SS *Trojan Prince* 8.16

8999    Left Filton for shipment to Mudros in SS *Trojan Prince* 8.16; 2 Wing Imbros 1916; B Sqdn 2 Wing Thermi by 2.17; Fuel shortage, FL bad ground, damaged (not wrecked) 4m NW of aerodrome (Mitylene) 13.2.17 (FSL JS Browne)

9000    Deld Redcar by transport 28.10.16; Hangar accident 22.1.17 (F/L SJ Woolley injured); U/c wrecked landing 12.6.17 (FSL A Frauenfelder); Deleted 25.6.17

**20 PEMBERTON-BILLING P.B.25 "PUSH-PROJ" PUSHER BIPLANES ordered under Cont No C.P.134727/16 from Supermarine Aviation Works, numbered 9001 to 9020 and built Woolston. (110-hp Clerget or 100-hp Gnome Monosoupape)**

9001    (110-hp Clerget). Deld Chingford 6.6.16; Tested 11.6.16; Eastchurch Workshops 22.1.17; Deleted 31.8.17

9002    (100-hp Gnome Monosoupape). Deld Design Flt Eastchurch for erection 3.9.16; Ready 11.9.16; Accepted 15.9.16 (Prodger); To be transferred to War Flt Eastchurch (and to CO Workshops for inspection before transfer); War Flt Eastchurch to Design Flt Eastchurch 10.10.16; Chassis test 17.10.16; Gunnery School Flts Eastchurch 19.10.16; Eastchurch Workshops 23.12.16; Deleted 31.8.17

9003    (100-hp Gnome Monosoupape). Deld Design Flt Eastchurch for erection 7.9.16; Ready 11.9.16; Eastchurch Workshops 23.12.16; Ready 26.2.17, to Eastchurch FS; Eastchurch Workshops 28.5.17; Deleted

31.8.17
9004     (100-hp Gnome Monosoupape). Deld Dover for erection 23.10.16; Accepted 3.11.16 (Prodger); Deleted 2.10.17 DBR

9005     (100-hp Gnome Monosoupape). Deld Eastchurch Workshops by lorry 7.11.16; Spotting Flt Eastchurch 27.11.16; Eastchurch Workshops 23.12.16; Eastchurch FS 28.5.17; Deleted 31.8.17

9006     (100-hp Gnome Monosoupape). Deld Eastchurch Workshops by lorry 11.11.16; Spotting Flt Eastchurch 17.11.16; Eastchurch Workshops 23.12.16 - @31.5.17; Eastchurch FS by 27.6.17; Deleted 31.8.17

9007     (110-hp Clerget?). Deld Killingholme without engine 24.2.17; Surveyed 10.10.17; Deleted 6.11.17 as spares

9008     (110-hp Clerget?). Deld Killingholme without engine 24.2.17; Surveyed 10.10.17; Deleted 6.11.17 as spares

9009     (110-hp Clerget?). Deld Killingholme without engine 24.2.17; Surveyed 10.10.17; Deleted 6.11.17 as spares

9010     Deld Killingholme without engine 24.2.17; Surveyed 10.10.17; Deleted 6.11.17 as spares

9011     Deld Killingholme less engine for spares by 26.2.17; Surveyed 10.10.17; Deleted 6.11.17 as spares

9012     Deld Killingholme for erection 24.2.17; Ready 26.5.17; Cranwell 28.5.17 (for Freiston); Surveyed 21.11.17; Deleted 5.12.17 W&T

9013     Deld Killingholme less engine for spares 26.2.17; Surveyed 10.10.17; Deleted 6.11.17 as spares

9014     Deld Killingholme less engine for spares 26.2.17; Surveyed 10.10.17; Deleted 6.11.17 as spares

9015     Deld Killingholme less engine for spares 26.2.17; Surveyed 10.10.17; Deleted 6.11.17 as spares

9016     Deld Killingholme less engine for spares 26.2.17; Surveyed 10.10.17; Deleted 6.11.17 as spares

9017     Deld Killingholme less engine for spares 21.3.17; Surveyed 10.10.17; Deleted 6.11.17 as spares

9018     Deld Killingholme less engine for spares 21.3.17; Surveyed 10.10.17; Deleted 6.11.17 as spares

9019     Deld Killingholme less engine for spares 21.3.17; Surveyed 10.10.17; Deleted 6.11.17 as spares

9020     Deld Killingholme less engine for spares 21.3.17; Surveyed 10.10.17; Deleted 6.11.17 as spares

**8 WIGHT ADMIRALTY 840 TYPE TRACTOR BIPLANE SEAPLANES ordered 24.11.15 under Cont No C.P.145459/15 from Sir William Beardmore & Co Ltd, numbered 9021 to 9040 and built Dalmuir. Contract closed 5.17, remaining machines to be delivered at Mkrs works without engines. (225-hp Sunbeam)**

9021     Shipped to Gibraltar W/E 1.4.16; Damaged on trials 8.4.16; Missing off Gibraltar 26.4.16

9022     Shipped to Gibraltar W/E 1.4.16; Deleted 6.16

9023     Deld Dundee by rail 17.1.16; Awaiting test by 1.2.16; Tested 22.2.16; War Flt Dundee 8.3.16; Deleted 9.5.16

9024     Deld Dundee by rail 9.2.16; Tested 22.2.16; War Flt Dundee 7.3.16; Deleted 19.7.16

9025     Deld War Flt Dundee by rail 2.16; Tested 22.2.16; War Flt Dundee 7.3.16; Inchkeith 2.5.16; Dundee 3.5.16; CW 14.6.16 (FSL EM King & AM Jenkins); Deleted 18.7.16

9026     Deld War Flt Dundee by rail 24.3.16; Tested 25.4.16 (Dukinfield Jones); Inchkeith 2.5.16; Dundee 3.5.16; Deleted 9.5.16

9027     Deld War Flt Dundee by rail 13.4.16; Tested 25.4.16 (Dukinfield Jones); Deleted 11.7.16

9028     Deld War Flt Dundee 8.5.16; Erected 13.5.16; Tested 24.5.16 (Dukinfield Jones); Delivered 17.7.16

9029 to 9040 delivered as spare parts after construction stopped 5.16

**20 SHORT ADMIRALTY 184 TYPE TRACTOR BIPLANE SEAPLANES ordered 23.11.15 under Cont Nos C.P.102693, C.P.146460/15 & A.S.3610 from Robey & Co Ltd, numbered 9041 to 9060 and built Lincoln. Type "A" armament from 9045. (225-hp Sunbeam Mohawk to 9045, then 240-hp Sunbeam Gurkha)**

9041     Deld Dundee by rail 12.6.16 (War Machine); Wrecked 23.8.16 (not flying); Deleted 5.9.16

9042     Deld Dover 30.6.16; Accepted 5.7.16 (Pickles);

Dunkerque 14.7.16; Damaged in fight with enemy seaplane off Nieuport 24.7.16 (Lt OH Crowther); Dover 19.12.16; Fitted 240-hp Gurkha 2.17; Dunkerque 29.4.17; With N1011 & N1024 attacked U-boat, dropped 2x100-lb bombs 15m NNE of Nieuport 15.6.17 (F/L GW Price & O/L DC Evans RNVR); Spun into sea on approach to bomb enemy destroyer, which then approached the sinking aircraft 24.9.17 (FSL AW Phillips & CPO EA Boyd PoWs); Surveyed 3.10.17; Deleted 8.10.17 wrecked

9043     Deld CSD 7.16; Scapa for erection 31.8.16; HMS *Campania* 17.10.16; Accepted 2.11.16; Scapa 21.11.16; HMS *Campania* 28.2.17; Scapa 17.4.17; HMS *Campania* by 1.5.17 - @7.9.17; Houton Bay by 10.17 (overhaul); HMS *Campania* 26.10.17; Houton 30.1.18; Deleted W/E 4.5.18

9044     Deld Calshot by road 24.7.16; Bembridge 3.3.17; Calshot Patrol 1.5.17 (awaiting engine); Calshot FS by 29.9.17; Surveyed 8.11.17; Deleted 17.11.17 W&T

9045     Deld CSD White City 8.16; HMS *Campania* 5.10.16; Retd CSD White City 7.10.16 - @31.10.16; Shipped to Mediterranean; Port Said from 12.16 - @3.17

9046     Deld Dover 17.8.16; Tested 24.8.16 (Pickles); Dunkerque 7.1.17; Bombed Zeebrugge Mole 4.4.17 & 5-6.4.17 (both FSL EJ Cuckney) and 7.4.17 (FSL SE Ball); Dover 8.4.17; Damaged Dunkerque 26.4.17 (F/L R Graham); Dunkerque (ex Calais) 2.5.17; Bombed Ostende Seaplane Station 10.5.17 & Ostende Docks 31.5.17 (both FSL EJ Cuckney); Dover 11.7.17; AGP 22.8.17 (landed Westgate); Dunkerque 22.9.17; Dover 15.10.17; Dunkerque 18.10.17; Dover 21.10.17; Dunkerque 22.10.17; Dover 13.1.18; Calshot FS 6.3.18; Became 210 TDS Calshot 1.4.18; 209 TDS Lee-on-Solent W/E 20.6.18; Deleted W/E 12.9.18

9047     Deld Dover 22.8.16; Dunkerque 11.9.16; HMS *Riviera* 20.10.16; Dunkerque 2.11.16; After TO off to bomb Ostende, EF, FL outside Dunkerque Harbour, beached among ice and snow 9.2.17 (FSL JC Watson); Salved, towed back 10.2.17; Dover 5.5.17; HMS *Riviera* 14.7.17; Cattewater 28.9.17; HMS *Riviera* 29.9.17; Stalled and crashed on patrol 11.11.17; Wreckage and crew picked up 40-45m S of Start Point, retd ship 13.11.17 (S/L RJ Stallard & OSL AD Rogers both injured)

9048     (Type D: Single-seat version) Deld Dover 30.8.16; Grain 22.9.16; Tested PVRS 6.11.16; Seaplane Design Flt Grain 5.12.16; Lent G Flt Grain 18.1.17; Dover 15.2.17 (instal bomb fittings); Dunkerque 4.4.17; Bombed Zeebrugge Mole 5/6.4.17 (twice) & 7/8.4.17, also Zeebrugge Seaplane Station 30.4.17 (all FSL LH Slatter); Bombed Ostende Seaplane Station 1/2.5.17 (FSL JE Potvin) & 10.5.17 (FSL LH Slatter); Dover 2.6.17; Dunkerque 4.6.17; Dover 22.9.17; Dunkerque 23.9.17; Dover 11.1.18; Calshot 1.2.18; Deleted W/E 11.5.18

9049     Deld Dover for erection 8.9.16; Dunkerque 17.9.16; EF, FL 25.9.16 (FSL JC Watson), found adrift next day; Caught fire on TO, towed in badly damaged 28.11.16 (FSL AH Sandwell rescued by French vedette boat); Deleted 17.12.17 wrecked

9050     Deld Dover 14.9.16; Awaiting acceptance 15.10.16; Accepted 3.11.16 (Prodger); Robey 8.11.16; Dover for re-erection 28.11.16; Dunkerque 7.1.17; Port wing hit buoy landing 11.3.17; Bombed Zeebrugge Mole 4.4.17 (FSL JE Potvin) & 7/8.4.17 (S/Cdr HM Cave-Brown-Cave); Bombed Ostende Seaplane Station 10.4.17 (S/Cdr HM Cave-Brown-Cave); Bombed Zeebrugge Seaplane Station 30.4.17 (S/Cdr HM Cave-Brown-Cave); Bombed Ostende Seaplane Station 1/2.5.17 (F/L WR Welsh); Bombed Zeebrugge Mole 3.6.17 (S/Cdr HM Cave-Brown-Cave); Dover for reconstruction 31.8.17; FL off South Goodwin LV, towed in by drifter 8.5.18; Became 407 Flt Dover 5.18; EF, FL in sea 3m SE of Folkestone en route Dover to Lee-on-Solent, badly damaged by fire, towed back to Dover 9.8.18; Deleted 14.8.18

9051     Deld Killingholme for erection 1.11.16; South Shields 4.11.16; Dismantled by 15.2.17; Cattewater by rail 16.2.17; EF, FL Dartmouth 11.4.17; Surveyed at Dartmouth and deletion recommended 14.4.17; Deleted 26.4.17

9052     Deld Grain for erection 19.10.16; Accepted 7.11.16

(Prodger); HMS *Manxman* 15.12.16; Crashed when tail float came away on TO, lost at sea 4.3.17 (FSL HL Hitch rescued); Deleted 8.6.17

9053    Deld Dundee by rail 5.12.16 (War Machine); Dismantled for Malta 16.2.17; Desp by rail to Royal Albert Docks 19.3.17 for SS *Navara*; Shipped 26.3.17; Torpedo School Calafrana by 8.5.17; Surveyed 25.3.18; Deleted 15.4.18 W&T

9054    Deld Westgate for erection 1.11.16; Tested 14.11.16 (Prodger); Dived into sea from considerable height while on patrol nr Tongue LV 10.12.16 (F/L JD Hume & CPO Mech2 WE Bradley DSM both drowned); Wreckage to Sheerness by minesweeper

9055    Deld Killingholme for erection 15.11.16; HMS *Manxman* 20.12.16; Dundee 17.6.17; HMS *Manxman* 5.7.17; Deleted W/E 16.2.18

9056    Deld and accepted 26.11.16 (Prodger); War Flt Yarmouth by 12.17; Became 324/6 Flts Yarmouth 25.5.18; Deleted W/E 25.7.18

9057    Deld Dover for erection 6.12.16; Tested 17.12.16; Accepted 24.12.16; Dunkerque 7.2.17; HMS *General Craufurd* 13.3.17; Dover 15.3.17; Dunkerque 21.3.17; Dover 24.3.17; Dunkerque 1.4.17; HMS *General Craufurd* 8.4.17 (FSL EJ Cuckney); Dover 9.4.17; Dunkerque 13.4.17; Dover 7.6.17; Dunkerque 9.6.17; Hit U-boat (*U33–U49* type) amidships with 100-lb bomb 18m NNE of Ostende 15.6.17 (FSL GP Paine & CPO EA Boyd); Shot down by enemy seaplanes 8m NNE of Nieuport 05.30, captured by Germans, taken in tow by TBD 19.6.17 (F/L GP Paine DSC PoW & OSL T Rogers killed)

9058    Deld Westgate 11.1.17; Dived into sea 1m off Cliftonville 13.3.17 (FSL R Birks & LM EAA Rawson both killed); Deleted 8.4.17

9059    (Tropical radiators) Deld Killingholme for erection 15.12.16; to Dover 12.3.17 (arr 16.3.17); HMS *Riviera* 4.4.17 (night flying expts); Float damaged 22.5.17 (FSL JH Woolner & LM R Thornborrow); Experimental flight 23.5.17; Dover 4.6.17; HMS *Riviera* 8.6.17; Cattewater 3.9.17 (change float and true up); HMS *Riviera* 4.9.17; Damaged on TO 13.9.17; Cattewater 6.12.17; HMS *Riviera* 8.12.17; Cattewater 28.1.18; HMS *Riviera* 30.1.18; Newlyn 27.2.18 (ship refit); Deleted W/E 20.6.18

9060    Deld Killingholme 3.2.17; Awaiting acceptance 26.2.17; to Dover 12.3.17 (arr 16.3.17); Dunkerque 30.3.17; HMS *General Craufurd* 8.4.17 (FSL JA Yonge); Dover 9.4.17; Dunkerque 13.4.17; EF, FL ½m from U-boat which dived, later seen with submarine alongside which then submerged, crew vanished, also its Lewis gun, 20m N of Dunkerque 25.5.17 (F/L C Laurence & S/L LJ Bennett PoWs)

**4 NORMAN THOMPSON N.T.4A "LITTLE AMERICA" TRACTOR BIPLANE FLYING BOATS ordered 28.12.15 under Cont No C.P.145936/15, numbered 9061 to 9064 and built Middleton-on-Sea. All fitted to carry two 230-lb bombs. (Ordered with two 100-hp Green and 6-pdr Davis gun. Delivered with two 150-hp Hispano)**

9061    Deld Calshot School W/E 21.9.17; Surveyed 2.11.17; Deleted 6.11.17 wrecked

9062    Deld Killingholme store (later AD) 21.3.17 - @30.3.18; Killingholme Seaplane School by 27.4.18; Felixstowe Seaplane School 8.5.18; Deleted W/E 5.9.18

9063    Deld 23.6.17; Grain Test Depot 14.7.17 (experiments with Type 52B Wireless Transmitter); Became Type Test Flt Grain by 29.12.17; To Westgate, but sprang leak, moored to buoy and sank, wreck towed ashore 7.1.18; Surveyed 11.1.18; Deleted 17.1.18

9064    Deld 21.6.17; Westgate 3.9.17; Calshot en route Killingholme 12.9.17; Hull and wings damaged in bad weather at Westgate 13.9.17; Mkrs by 29.12.17 - @30.3.18 (repair, then allocated Killingholme); By 6.4.18 expected for trials after repair by Mkrs; NFT

**20 SHORT 184 TYPE TRACTOR BIPLANE SEAPLANES ordered 28.7.15 (later 28.10.15) under Cont Nos C.P.15073/15, C.P.100495/16, C.P.138004, A.S.218 & A.S.4247 from Fredk Sage & Co Ltd, numbered 9065 to 9084 and built Peterborough. (9065 to 9071 & 9082 to 9084 with 225-hp**

Sunbeam Mohawk. 9072 to 9081 with 240-hp Sunbeam Gurkha; Sage to fit larger radiators to these 11.16)

9065    Deld Dover 16.5.16; Tested 19.5.16 (Pickles); Dunkerque 7.6.16; Dover 17.6.16; Dunkerque 18.6.16; Dover 19.8.16; Fighting patrol, then smashed propeller and elevator, heavy sea 20.8.16 (FSL WR Dainty & AM WA Coppins); HACPs 27.11.16 (FSL W Perham & AM Fanshawe) & 28.11.16 (FSL JE Potvin & OSL EJ Travers); Parnall W/E 2.3.17 (repairs and modifications); Dover for erection 30.5.17; Dunkerque 6.7.17; Dover 6.7.17; Dunkerque 14.9.17; Dover 12.1.18; Surveyed 6.5.18; Deleted 11.5.18 W&T

9066    Deld Dover 19.5.16; Tested 24.5.16 (Pickles); Dunkerque 7.6.16; HMS *Riviera* 8.6.16; Dunkerque 8.10.16; Spotting for HMS *Terror* (Zeebrugge?) 24.9.16 (FSL JA Yonge & S/L NP Playford); Dover 20.12.16; Parnall for reconstruction 4.2.17; South Shields for erection 28.4.17; Bombed U-boat 7m E of Newbiggin 14.5.17 (FSL FH Wallers & LM Cornell); Surveyed 8.12.17; Deleted 22.12.17 W&T

9067    Deld Dover for erection 26.5.16; Tested 1.6.16; For HMS *Riviera* 16.6.16 (NTU?); Dunkerque 19.6.16; Shot down by gunfire while spotting for monitor HMS *General Craufurd* off Belgian coast 20.8.16 (F/L BC Tooke PoW & T/Lt OH Crowther both killed)

9068    Deld Felixstowe 15.6.16; AZP 3.8.16; Nore War Flt Felixstowe by 3.17; AZP 24.5.17 (FSL HA Wilson); AGP 25.5.17; Killingholme 22.8.17; 209 TDS Lee-on-Solent 19.5.18; Sideslipped at 700ft and dived into sea 23.5.18 (Probtr OM Armstrong injured); Deleted W/E 11.7.18

9069    Deld CSD 6.16; HMS *Campania* for erection 10.9.16; Accepted 2.11.16; Damaged in transit to Scapa 23.11.16; EF, FL and damaged SE of Pentland Skerries, towed to Scapa Bay by MB from HMS *Nonsuch* 12.1.17 (FSL LS Breadner & Mid DS Earp unhurt); FL in sea, towed by destroyer HMS *Restless*, crashed on TO, CW 12.2.17 (FSL ER Pritchard & Mid DS Earp); Deleted 13.2.17

9070    Deld Dundee by rail for erection 17.6.16 (War Machine); Wrecked 23.8.16 (not flying); Dismantled and packed for Malta from 16.2.17; desp by rail to Malta 19.3.17 (for Otranto); Shipped to Otranto 20.3.17; 66 Wing Otranto by 17.8.17; Surveyed 9.10.17; Deleted 19.10.17 wrecked

9071    Deld Dundee by rail 24.6.16; Tested 29.6.16; Dismantled and packed for Malta 16.2.17; desp Royal Albert Docks by rail 19.3.17 for SS *Navara*; Shipped 26.3.17; Torpedo School Calafrana 19.5.17; Repairing by 6.7.17; Tested 16.8.17; Surveyed 30.11.17; Deleted 13.12.17 DBR

9072    Deld Dundee by rail 29.6.16; Tested 5.7.16; South Shields 16.12.16; Dundee 27.12.16; Visited HMS *Engadine* 12.2.17; Dismantled for Malta 16.2.17; desp Royal Albert Docks by rail 19.3.17 for SS *Navara*; Shipped 26.3.17; Torpedo School Calafrana by 19.5.17; EF, FL, damaged on rocks Cape Scalambri, towed back by motor launch 30.7.17 (FSL GW Hellmuth & LM Lewis unhurt); still Calafrana 18.8.17

9073    Deld Dundee 10.7.16; Tested 2.8.16; HMS *Engadine* 7.8.16; Damaged in gale 20.11.16; Sage for repair 30.12.16; Dundee by rail 31.3.17; HMS *Manxman* 24.4.17; Dundee by rail 5.7.17 (arr 9.7.17); Surveyed 6.4.18; Deleted 15.6.18 DBR

9074    Deld Dundee 17.7.16; Tested 2.8.16; HMS *Engadine* 23.8.16; Dundee 7.9.16; Port Laing 1.3.17; Dundee 24.3.17; HMS *Engadine* 26.3.17 (visited HMS *Yarmouth* 28.6.17); Rosyth 24.7.17; HMS *Engadine* 6.8.17; Rosyth 5.9.17; Surveyed 11.10.17; Deleted 13.10.17 W&T, remains to CSD White City

9075    Deld CSD White City 26.7.16; recd HMS *Campania* for erection 10.9.16; Tested 15.9.16; Accepted 16.9.16; HSMP, EF, FL rough sea, broke up, sank 24.10.16 (WO2 T O'Connor & OSL AO Jones rescued by HMS *Mons* suffering from exposure); Deleted 8.11.16

9076    Deld Killingholme 21.8.16; HMS *Manxman* 20.12.16; Deleted W/E 13.3.18

9077    Deld Killingholme 12.9.16; Scarborough Bay 19.10.16 (en route Rosyth, delayed by bad weather); Still unable to leave harbour 24.10.16; Packing 28.10.16; Brought

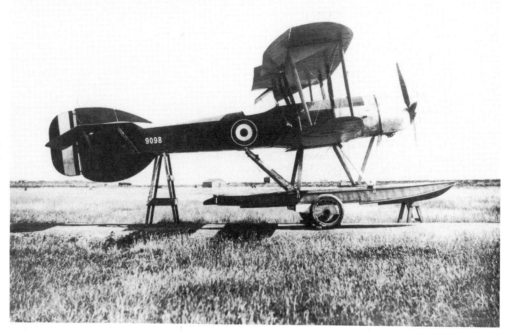

*Wight Baby 9098 Single-seater Seaplane at Grain. (via E. Cromie)*

*Toothy looking Maurice Farman F.37 9133, variously named 'GOO GOO' and 'THE BOGEY MAN', with 2 Wing at Imbros, June 1916 (Frank Cheesman)*

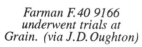

*Farman F.40 9166 underwent trials at Grain. (via J.D. Oughton)*

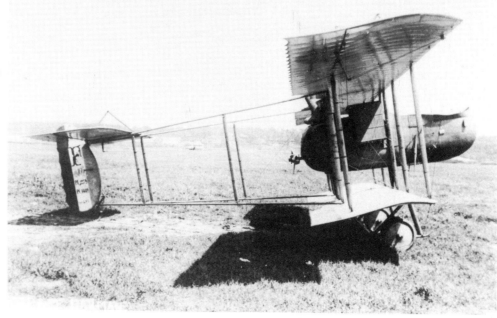

up on harbour jetty for CSD White City 1.11.16 (NTU?); For HMS *Campania* by 9.11.16; Erecting Scapa by 1.12.16; HMS *Campania* 8.3.17; To Scapa 4.17; HMS *Campania* 17.4.17; Scapa 16.7.17 - @24.11.17, later Houton Bay; Deleted W/E 4.5.18

9078    Deld Killingholme 16.9.16; Scarborough 19.10.16; Rosyth 21.10.16; Dundee 21.10.16; Scapa 22.10.16; HMS *Campania* 24.10.16; Tested 2.11.16; Scapa 23.11.16 (damaged in transit); HMS *Campania* 8.3.17; EF, capsized, sank during salvage, occupants taken off by destroyer 20.5.17; Deleted 9.6.17

9079    (250-hp Maori) Deld Killingholme 22.9.16; Felixstowe 10.12.16; HMS *Vindex* 11.12.16; Felixstowe 8.4.17; HMS *Vindex* 12.4.17; Felixstowe 9.5.17; HMS *Vindex* 10.5.17; Killingholme 23.5.17 (storage); HMS *Vindex* 11.6.17; Felixstowe W/E 15.12.17; En route Calshot, EF, FL at Westgate 21.1.18; Dover 22.1.18 (transit); Calshot TS 24.1.18; Deleted W/E 13.6.18

9080    Deld South Shields by rail 6.10.16; Crashed and TW on acceptance test by Sage pilot 4.11.16; To be salved by HMS *Bonaventure* 5.11.16; HMS *Riviera* 13.3.17; Dover 4.4.17; HMS *Riviera* 5.4.17; Dunkerque 8.4.17; Dover 13.4.17; HMS *Riviera* 13.4.17; Retd with damaged float, badly damaged when capsized in folding 23.4.17 (F/Cdr TW Elsdon & AM1 ES Pryor); Dover 4.6.17; HMS *Riviera* 8.6.17; Capsized on landing, wreck salved 21.6.17 (F/Cdr TW Elsdon & Payr HN Carter rescued unhurt)

9081    (225-hp Mohawk) Deld South Shields by rail 9.10.16; HMS *Vindex* 12.11.16; Felixstowe for acceptance test 15.11.16; Accepted and to HMS *Vindex* 16.11.16; Felixstowe 9.5.17; HMS *Vindex* 10.5.17; Killingholme 23.5.17 (storage); HMS *Vindex* 11.6.17; Felixstowe 1.9.17; HMS *Vindex* by 2.11.17; Felixstowe 11.17; HMS *Vindex* W/E 1.12.17 [& @19.1.18]; Felixstowe by 22.12.17; Calshot TS 25.1.18; Deleted W/E 11.7.18

9082    Deld Killingholme for HMS *Campania* (NTU) 22.10.16; Wrecked at sea 3.2.17 (FSL AY Wilks); Deleted 24.2.17

9083    Deld Killingholme 9.11.16; HMS *Manxman* 20.12.16; Badly damaged 2.6.17 (FSL W Lodge & WO2 EJ Withers); Dundee 5.6.17 (repair); Erecting 5.7.17; Deleted 15.9.17

9084    Deld South Shields for erection 12.10.16; Accepted 29.1.17; Cattewater by rail 16.2.17; Tested 26.2.17; Wrecked on patrol 18.4.17

**10 SHORT ADMIRALTY 184 TYPE (MODIFIED) TRACTOR BIPLANE SEAPLANES ordered 10.4.16 under Cont Nos C.P.101871/16 & C.P.107549/16 from Mann Egerton & Co Ltd as their Type B, numbered 9085 to 9094 and built Norwich. (225-hp Sunbeam Mohawk)**

9085    Deld Nore War Flt Felixstowe, tested 1.8.16; Deleted 5.7.17 and to CSD Crystal Palace for GI by rail

9086    Deld Felixstowe 15.6.16; Shorts Rochester 20.6.16; PVRS Grain and tested 4.8.16 (deck landing expts?); Packed 24.3.17; Fishguard by rail 7.4.17 (arr 13.4.17); Crashed 24.4.17 (T/F/L RE Bush killed); Deleted 5.5.17

9087    (Improved B); Deld Dundee by rail 3.7.16; Tested 5/6.7.16; Dismantled for Malta 16.2.17 (practice machine); Changed to Otranto by 9.3.17; By rail to Matthwin & Sons, Cardiff for shipment 10.3.17; Shipped to 6 Wing Otranto 10.3.17; 6 Wing Otranto by 29.6.17; Surveyed 22.10.17; Deleted 2.11.17 W&T

9088    Deld CSD White City 7.16; Westgate for erection 6.1.17; Deleted 22.7.17

9089    Deld Calshot 9.8.16; Deleted 10.7.17

9090    Deld Killingholme 15.8.16; Erected 1.1.17; Deleted 6.3.17

9091    (Improved B) Deld Dundee by road 15.11.16; Accepted 6.1.17; Dismantled for Malta 14.2.17; Changed to Otranto by 9.3.17; By rail to Matthwin & Sons, Cardiff for shipment 10.3.17; Tested 6 Wing Otranto 18.6.17. Beyond repair by 17.8.17

9092    (Improved B) Deld Newlyn 20.1.17 to erect for Tresco but temp stored Trinity House Shed Penzance; Tresco by 29.3.17 (not ready); Newlyn 17.4.17; Tested 9.6.17; Deleted 26.7.17

9093    Deld Nore Flt Grain for erection 8.12.16; Accepted 20.12.16 (Prodger); Calshot 2.5.17; Deleted W/E 14.9.17

9094    Put forward for Mann Egerton to fit tropical radiator 11.16; Supermarine by 31.1.17; Calshot 26.2.17; Badly damaged 6.6.17; Deleted 10.7.17

**2 A.D. NAVYPLANE PUSHER BIPLANE SEAPLANES ordered 1.16 under Cont Nos C.P.113726/16 (and A.S.18936 & A.S.14491?) from Supermarine Aviation Works Ltd, numbered 9095 and 9096 and to be built Woolston. (150-hp Smith Static)**

9095    Preliminary trials abandoned W/E 2.9.16 (engine trouble); Accepted 12.16; Re-engined 150-hp A.R.1; Deld Test Depot Grain 23.4.17; Retested 5.17; Deleted 27.8.17

9096    Cancelled 16.6.17

**2 WIGHT BABY SINGLE-SEATER TRACTOR BIPLANE SEAPLANES ordered 9.16 under Cont No C.P.110634/16, numbered 9097 and 9098 and built East Cowes. (100-hp Gnome Monosoupape)**

9097    Deld Calshot 13.7.16; O/t taxying and badly damaged off Calshot Spit, salved 14.7.16 (F/Cdr RH Kershaw unhurt); Deleted 17.7.16; Put forward for Mkrs repair W/E 18.8.16 but presume NTU

9098    Deld Grain 20.6.16 (Gordon England); Tested PVRS 24.7.16; Flown after mods 27.11.16; Design Flt Grain 5.12.16; Became Exp Design Grain 2.3.17 (alterations); Test Depot Grain 30.3.17; Wings replaced by B.I.R.31 section planes, tested 1917; Deleted 27.8.17 BR

**1 HENRY FARMAN F.27 PUSHER BIPLANE purchased in France, numbered 9099. (160-hp Canton Unné)**

9099    Transferred to RFC (Military Wing) as A8974

**1 WIGHT BABY TRACTOR BIPLANE SEAPLANE ordered 9.16 under Cont No C.P.110634/16, numbered 9100 and built East Cowes. (100-hp Gnome Monosoupape)**

9100    Deld Calshot by lorry 10.4.16; Deleted SOC 25.9.16

**9101 to 9200 reserved for French machines**

**31 CAUDRON G.IV TRACTOR BIPLANES purchased in France (authorised 1.10.15?), numbered 9101 to 9131 & built at Rue. All to be delivered to Dunkerque. (Two 100-hp Anzani)**

9101    Shipped to Aegean; 2 Wing Aegean by 4.16 - @8.16; Transferred to French Govt

9102    Bombing Flt A Sqdn 1 Wing when formed 1.3.16; 7 Flt B Sqdn 5 Wing Coudekerque from 20.3.16 - @14.5.16; ADD by 18.5.16 - @2.6.16; Deleted before 22.6.16

9103    Shipped to Aegean; 2 Wing Aegean by 4.16; Deleted by 6.16

9104    Shipped to Aegean; 2 Wing Aegean by 4.16 - @8.16; Transferred to French Govt

9105    Shipped to Aegean; 2 Wing Aegean by 4.16 - @8.16; Transferred to French Govt

9106    Shipped to Aegean; 2 Wing Aegean by 4.16 - @8.16; Transferred to French Govt

9107    Deld Dunkerque; Accident; Deleted ADD 15.4.16 DBR

9108    1 Flt A Sqdn 1 Wing when formed 1.3.16; 8 Flt B Sqdn 5 Wing Coudekerque from 24.3.16; Landed at night in mist, spun round on touchdown, wrecked when swing and port u/c 15.4.16 (F/L JP Coleman); ADD by 18.5.16; 7 Flt B Sqdn 5 Wing Coudekerque by 21.6.16; FL in sea 8.7.16 (F/L CB Sproatt & G/L Darby saved); For survey by 13.7.16

9109    Shipped to Aegean; Aegean by 4.16; To UK; CSD White City by 30.9.16; Deleted 14.2.17 as spares

9110    Shipped to Aegean; Aegean by 4.16; To UK; CSD White City by 30.9.16; Deleted 14.2.17 as spares

9111    Shipped to Aegean; Aegean by 4.16; To UK; CSD White City by 30.9.16; Deleted 14.2.17 as spares

9112    Deld 1 Wing by 3.16; 7 Flt B Sqdn 5 Wing Coudekerque 27.3.16 - @1.4.16; 8 Flt B Sqdn 5 Wing Coudekerque by 5.16; 7 Flt B Sqdn 5 Wing Coudekerque 18.5.16; ADD 29.6.16; 7 Flt B Sqdn 5 Wing Coudekerque 1.7.16 - @23.9.16; Crashed, badly smashed and burned 9.16; ADD by 28.9.16 - @9.11.16 (for survey after crash)

9113    Deld 5 Wing 2.4.16; 11 Flt B Sqdn 4 Wing Petite Synthe by 24.4.16 - 9.16; 10 Flt A Sqdn 4 Wing Petite Synthe by 16.11.16; Became 7 Sqdn 12.16 - @25.1.17; ADD by 1.2.17 (for survey); Deleted 24.3.17 general fatigue

9114    Deld 8 Flt B Sqdn 5 Wing Coudekerque 28.4.16; ADD 22.6.16; 7 Flt B Sqdn 5 Wing Coudekerque by 29.6.16; Left 12.06, FTR from raid on St.Denis Westrem 7.9.16 (F/Cdr GH Beard drowned); Deleted in field 7.9.16

9115    Deld 5 Wing Coudekerque, but COL 2.4.16 (FSL GCV Hewson); Deleted ADD 15.4.16

9116    Deld 7 Flt B Sqdn 5 Wing Coudekerque 23.4.16; Crashed and DBR 3.7.16 (F/L GH Beard & Lt R St.John); 8 Flt B Sqdn 5 Wing Coudekerque by 6.7.16 (instructional use, DC); 7 Flt B Sqdn 5 Wing Coudekerque by 13.7.16; ADD by 20.7.16; Deleted 30.7.16

9117    While on delivery flight from Paris to Coudekerque, hit by AA fire over Westende then attacked by Fokker, FL nr Oost Dunkerque Bains 16.4.16 (FSL R Souray injured); Deld ADD by 5.16; 8 Flt B Sqdn 5 Wing Coudekerque by 16.5.16 - @22.6.16; 7 Flt B Sqdn 5 Wing Coudekerque by 29.6.16 - @9.16; Deleted ADD 4.1.17 general fatigue

9118    Deld 5 Wing Coudekerque 23.4.16; FTR raid on Mariakerke aerodrome 4.5.16 (FSL KM Van Allen PoW, died 11.5.16); For deletion by 2.6.16

9119    Deld ADD by 22.6.16; 11 Flt B Sqdn 4 Wing Petite Synthe 24.9.16 - @9.11.16; 10 Flt A Sqdn 4 Wing Petite Synthe by 16.11.16; Became 7 Sqdn 12.16; ADD 1.2.17 (for survey); Deleted 24.3.17 general fatigue

9120    Deld ADD by 22.6.16; 11 Flt B Sqdn 4 Wing Petite Synthe 10.7.16; 10 Flt A Sqdn 4 Wing Petite Synthe by 16.11.16; Became 7 Sqdn 12.16; ADD 1.2.17 (for survey); Deleted 24.3.17

9121    Deld ADD by 18.5.16; 8 Flt B Sqdn 5 Wing Coudekerque 20.5.16; 11 Flt B Sqdn 4 Wing Petite Synthe 21.5.16 - @9.11.16; 10 Flt A Sqdn 4 Wing Petite Synthe by 16.11.16; Became 7 Sqdn 12.16; ADD 1.2.17 (for survey); 4 Wing by 2.2.17; Night raid on TBDs in Bruges harbour, FL on Malo beach on return, lumps of ice on beach caused a/c to o/t, slightly damaged 2/3.2.17 (FSL VE Sieveking injured); Deleted ADD 24.3.17 general fatigue

9122    Deld ADD by 24.5.16; 8 Flt B Sqdn 5 Wing Coudekerque 22.6.16; 7 Flt B Sqdn 5 Wing Coudekerque by 29.6.16 - @9.16; Deleted ADD 5.1.17 general fatigue

9123    Deld ADD by 24.5.16; 11 Flt B Sqdn 4 Wing Petite Synthe 23.6.16 - @9.11.16; Severely shot about in raid on Ghistelles aerodrome 3.9.16 (FSL AL Thorne); 10 Flt A Sqdn 4 Wing Petite Synthe by 16.11.16; Became 7 Sqdn 12.16; ADD 1.2.17 (for survey); Deleted 24.3.17 general fatigue

9124    Deld ADD by 2.6.16; 11 Flt B Sqdn 4 Wing Petite Synthe 9.6.16 - @2.8.16; Crashed, CW 8.16; Probably the a/c which ran into 3964 & 3185 2.8.16 (FSL GL Hartgill); For survey by 3.8.16; Deleted ADD 17.9.16 damaged

9125    Deld ADD by 2.6.16; 11 Flt B Sqdn 4 Wing Petite Synthe 20.6.16; Partially wrecked when hit by Nieuport 3962 which was landing at dusk 8.7.16; ADD by 13.7.16; Deleted 7.16

9126    Deld ADD by 22.6.16; 7 Flt B Sqdn 5 Wing Coudekerque by 6.7.16 - @14.12.16; Deleted ADD 5.1.17 general fatigue

9127    Deld ADD by 22.6.16; B Flt 4 Wing Petite Synthe by 10.8.16; Tested after repair 19.8.16; Raid on St.Denis Westrem aerodrome, hit by shellfire from Knocke, then attacked by small enemy seaplane and badly damaged 7.9.16 (FSL HG Brackley); ADD by 14.9.16; Deleted 17.9.16

9128    Deld ADD by 22.6.16; 7 Flt B Sqdn 5 Wing by 20.7.16; Crashed, CW 21.7.16; ADD by 28.7.16; Deleted Board of Survey 30.7.16, but continued at AD by 10.8.16 to at least 14.9.16; Crashed, CW 9.16 (F/L HL Wood & AM G/L Symonds); Deleted ADD 17.9.16

9129    Deld ADD by 6.7.16; 7 Flt B Sqdn 5 Wing Coudekerque by 31.8.16; Deleted ADD 5.1.17

9130    Deld ADD by 10.8.16; 11 Flt B Sqdn 4 Wing Petite Synthe by 12.9.16 - @9.11.16; Slightly damaged on landing from raid on Handzaeme aerodrome 23.9.16; 10

Flt A Sqdn 4 Wing Petite Synthe by 16.11.16; Became 7 Sqdn 12.16; Tested after repair 27.12.16; ADD 1.2.17 (for survey); Deleted 24.3.17 general fatigue

9131    Deld ADD by 10.8.16; Deleted 24.3.17 general fatigue

**1 UNIDENTIFIED TYPE to be numbered 9132**

9132    Cancelled

**1 MAURICE FARMAN F.37 PUSHER BIPLANE purchased from Aéroplanes Farman, numbered 9133. (110-hp [130-hp?] Renault)**

9133    Shipped to Aegean 1916; 2 Wing Imbros by 3.3.16 (Teeth painted on nose; named 'GOO GOO', also 'THE BOGEY MAN'); COL night raid 6.16; Deleted 7.16

**20 HENRY FARMAN F.27 (TROPICAL) PUSHER BIPLANES purchased (authority 1.1.16) from Aéroplanes Farman, numbered 9134 to 9153, all shipped to Aegean. (160-hp Canton Unné)**

9134    Shipped to 2 Wing Aegean; Surveyed Mudros 11.9.17; Deleted 25.9.17 W&T

9135    Shipped to 2 Wing Aegean; Thasos by 1.12.17 - @10.18; To Greek service

9136    Shipped to 2 Wing Aegean; Surveyed Mudros 11.9.17; Deleted 25.9.17 TL

9137    Shipped to 2 Wing Aegean; A Sqdn 2 Wing Thasos by 10.2.17 - @12.2.17; Surveyed Mudros 19.10.17; Deleted 29.10.17 W&T

9138    In transit to 2 Wing Aegean 8.16; Deleted 1916

9139    In transit to 2 Wing Aegean 8.16; Mudros Base by 1.12.17 - @2.18; G Sqdn 2/62 Wing Mudros by 3.18 - 5.18

9140    In transit to 2 Wing Aegean 8.16; 2 Wing Thasos from 11.9.16; A Sqdn 2 Wing Thasos by 5.1.17 - @5.2.17

9141    (155-hp Canton-Unné) In transit to 2 Wing Aegean 8.16; Mitylene by 13.12.16; B Sqdn 2 Wing Thermi by 13.2.17; Damaged chassis landing 21.2.17 (FSL JLA Sinclair & AM Corder unhurt);

9142    Shipped to Aegean; NFT

9143    Shipped to Aegean; NFT

9144    Shipped to Aegean; NFT

9145    Deld Eastchurch Gun Flt 16.8.16; Damaged 7.9.16; Put forward for Brush to fit new tail booms on site 10.16; Deletion recommended by 1.1.17; Dunkerque by 8.17; War Flt Eastchurch 16.8.17; Misc Flt Eastchurch 18.8.17; Deleted on/by 10.7.17?

9146    Shipped to Aegean; Surveyed Mudros 14.10.17; Deleted 29.10.17 W&T

9147    Shipped to Aegean; NFT

9148    (155-hp Canton-Unné) Shipped to Aegean; Surveyed Mudros 3.11.17; Deleted 26.11.17 wrecked

9149    Shipped to Aegean; NFT

9150    Shipped to Aegean; Marsh by 13-20.1.18 & 14-23.1.18

9151    Shipped to Aegean; G Flt 2 Wing by 1.12.17; Marsh by 1.1.18; Mudros by 2.18; HMS *Ark Royal* by 15.2.18; G Sqdn 2 Wing Mudros by 3.18; Became G Sqdn 62 Wing Mudros 1.4.18 - 5.18; To Greek service for training by 6.18 - @30.1.19

9152    To RFC (Military Wing) as A8975. Serial B3958 also allotted but NTU

9153    Shipped to Aegean; Mudros; Deleted 28.11.17 TL

**2 NIEUPORT TRACTOR BIPLANE SCOUTS to be numbered 9154 & 9155, but transferred to RFC (Military Wing) and renumbered. Serials reallotted.**

9154 & 9155 renumbered

**1 VOISIN LA (or LA.S) CANON PUSHER BIPLANE purchased from Voisin (authorised 2.5.16), numbered 9154, built Issy-les-Moulineaux. (150-hp Canton Unné)**

9154    (c/n V1602) Recd Grain ex Paris 9.6.16; Experimental Flt Grain 7.9.16; Renamed Gunnery Experimental Grain 5.12.16; Tested Davis 12-pdr gun 7.12.16; still Exp G Grain 3.17; EAD Grain, deleted 21.4.17

156

**20 HENRY FARMAN F.40 (otherwise F.56) PUSHER BIPLANES purchased from Aéroplanes Farman (authorised 1.4.16), numbered 9155 to 9174. (150-hp Renault-Mercedes)**

| | |
|---|---|
| 9155 | Deld Paris to 1 Wing 30.7.16; 12 Flt B Sqdn 4 Wing from 1.8.16; ADD 9.11.16; Dover 1.3.17; EAD Grain 5.4.17 |
| 9156 | Deld Paris to 1 Wing 30.7.16; 12 Flt B Sqdn 4 Wing 31.7.16; ADD 10.8.16; 3 Flt B Sqdn 1 Wing 10.8.16; Became 2 Sqdn 5.11.16 - @10.11.16; ADD by 10.12.16; 2 Sqdn 15.1.17; Dover 14.2.17; Eastchurch Workshops 16.2.17; Deleted 31.8.17 |
| 9157 | Deld Paris to 1 Wing 30.7.16; 3 Flt B Sqdn 1 Wing St.Pol by 23.8.16; Became 2 Sqdn 5.11.16; ADD 15.12.16; Manston 18.3.17; EAD Grain 22.3.17 (via Dover); New extensions fitted 16.6.17; Eastchurch GS 2.9.17; Surveyed 8.11.17; Deleted 17.11.17 W&T |
| 9158 | (c/n 2414) Deld ex Paris to Cranwell 3.8.16; Yarmouth 23.9.16; en route Grain 24.9.16; Experimental Flt Grain 1.10.16; Yarmouth 28.10.16; Visited Pulham 9.12.16; Burgh Castle 1.2.17; Yarmouth repair 8.2.17; Burgh Castle 13.2.17; Deleted 30.4.17 |
| 9159 | Deld Paris to ADD on/by 5.8.16; Crashed, CW by 10.8.16, probably on delivery; Deleted ADD 17.9.16 |
| 9160 | Deld ex Paris via Grain to Cranwell 4.8.16; Yarmouth 18.9.16 (arrived 19.9.16, transit); Experimental Flt Grain 21.9.16; Yarmouth 4.11.16; Bacton 26.11.16; Yarmouth 29.11.16; Burgh Castle 1.2.17; Yarmouth 3.2.17; Burgh Castle 1.3.17; AZP 16.6.17; Yarmouth to Eastchurch GS 14.9.17; Surveyed 8.11.17; Deleted 17.11.17 W&T |
| 9161 | Deld ex Dunkerque to War Flt Eastchurch 3.8.16 (transit); Cranwell 4.8.16; Deleted 2.5.17 |
| 9162 | Deld ex Paris to Cranwell 3.8.16; Chingford 28.9.16; Experimental Flt Grain 30.9.16; Yarmouth 28.10.16; Bacton 10.11.16; Yarmouth 14.11.16; Bacton 15.11.16; Yarmouth 21.11.16; Bacton 22.11.16; Yarmouth 23.11.16; Eastchurch GS 30.8.17; Surveyed 8.11.17; Deleted 17.11.17 W&T |
| 9163 | Deld Villacoublay to Le Crotoy 2.8.16 (transit); War Flt Eastchurch 3.8.16 (transit); Cranwell 4.8.16; Experimental Flt Grain 19.9.16; Yarmouth 21.10.16; Eastchurch GS 30.8.17; Surveyed 8.11.17; Deleted 17.11.17 W&T |
| 9164 | Deld Dunkerque 8.16; Crashed, CW 8.16; ADD by 10.8.16, for survey, wrecked; Deleted 4.12.16 |
| 9165 | Deld ADD by 10.8.16; 3 Flt B Sqdn 1 Wing by 6.9.16; Became 2 Sqdn 5.11.16; ADD 18.1.17; Dover 12.2.17; Eastchurch Workshops 16.2.17 - @8.3.17; Observers School Flt Eastchurch by 4.17; Deleted 31.8.17 |
| 9166 | Deld ADD by 17.8.16; Dover 26.2.17; EAD Grain 15.3.17; Hendon 21.5.17; EAD Grain 25.5.17; Hendon (via Brooklands) 4.6.17; EAD Grain 5.6.17; Manston 17.6.17 (transit); Hendon 18.6.17; Farnborough 23.6.17; Hendon 24.6.17; Martlesham 7.7.17; EAD Grain 11.7.17; Surveyed 25.3.18; Deleted 27.3.18 DBR |
| 9167 | Deld Misc Flt Eastchurch 21.8.16; Grain Gunnery School Flt 28.8.16; Eastchurch 1.9.16; Grain, AZP, COL in ploughed field, o/t nr Broomfield Court NLG, Chelmsford 3.9.16 (F/Cdr AR Arnold); Deleted 30.9.16 |
| 9168 | Deld ADD 8.16; Intended for England, but crashed on aerodrome, CW by 10.8.16; Deleted 17.9.16 |
| 9169 | Deld Eastbourne (via Eastchurch) 31.8.16; Experimental Flt Grain, ready 22.9.16; Became Gunnery Experimental Grain 5.12.16; Deleted 11.3.17 |
| 9170 | Deld ADD 8.16; Damaged by 10.8.16; War Flt Eastchurch 13.8.16; Misc Flt Eastchurch 8.9.16; Spotting Flt Eastchurch 15.9.16 - @6.12.16, then not flown until Gun Flt Eastchurch by 24.1.17; Gunnery School Flts Eastchurch by 15.2.17; Observers School Flt Eastchurch 9.4.17; Surveyed 8.11.17; Deleted 17.11.17 W&T |
| 9171 | (c/n 302 or 502) Shipped to 2 Wing Aegean; Fitted floats at Thasos |
| 9172 | Deld Paris to ADD 2.9.16; B Sqdn 1 Wing 10.12.16; Became 2 Sqdn 12.16; Dover 14.2.17; Eastchurch Workshops 16.2.17; Eastchurch 13.4.17; COL, o/t, ploughed field 13.4.17 (PFO LGleB Croke slightly injured); Deleted 26.4.17 |
| 9173 | Deld Paris to 1 Wing (AD?) 17.8.16; ADD by 24.8.16; |
| | 3 Flt B Sqdn 1 Wing St.Pol by 28.9.16; Became 2 Sqdn 5.11.16; Burnt at St.Omer 1.3.17; Deleted ADD 24.3.17 |
| 9174 | Deld ADD 3.9.16 - @14.12.16; B Sqdn 1 Wing by 24.12.16 [but became 2 Sqdn 5.11.16]; 2 Sqdn to Dover 14.2.17; EAD Grain 15.3.17; COL 5.4.17; Deleted 26.4.17 BR |

**26 BREGUET TYPE V CONCOURS TRACTOR BIPLANES purchased from Breguet for No.3 Wing, numbered 9175 to 9200, built at Villacoublay. (225-hp Renault)**

| | |
|---|---|
| 9175 | Deld 3 Wing Luxeuil 29.8.16; Raid on Mauser factory, Oberndorf, EF, FL, crashed Buc 12.10.16 (FSL LH Parker & G/L Allen); Surveyed for deletion 25.10.16 |
| 9176 | Deld 3 Wing Luxeuil W/E 25.8.16; Shot down by AA nr Buggingen, 3km N of Mulheim on Oberndorf raid 12.10.16 (F/L CD Newman PoW & G/L Vitty PoW?); Surveyed 18.10.16 |
| 9177 | Deld 3 Wing Luxeuil W/E 22.9.16; Surveyed 18.12.16 |
| 9178 | Deld 3 Wing Luxeuil W/E 19.6.16; Wrecked 22.9.16; Surveyed 27.9.16; Deleted 23.10.16 |
| 9179 | (c/n BR509) Deld Paris to Chaumont 20.8.16; 3 Wing Luxeuil 21.8.16; Damaged in raid by 10.11.16; Surveyed 10.11.16 |
| 9180 | Tested Paris 11.8.16; Deld 3 Wing Luxeuil W/E 25.8.16; Surveyed 4.12.16 wrecked |
| 9181 | Deld 3 Wing Luxeuil W/E 6.10.16; Shot down nr Oberenzen, 15km S of Colmar on Oberndorf raid 12.10.16 (FSL JSN Rockey & G/L Sturdee PoWs); Surveyed 12.10.16 |
| 9182 | Deld 3 Wing Luxeuil W/E 15.9.16; Surveyed 18.12.16 |
| 9183 | Deld 3 Wing Luxeuil W/E 6.10.16; Surveyed 18.12.16 |
| 9184 | Deld 3 Wing Luxeuil W/E 6.10.16; Surveyed 18.12.16 wrecked |
| 9185 | Deld 3 Wing Luxeuil W/E 6.10.16; Loaned to French, FTR Oberndorf raid 12.10.16 |
| 9186 | Deld 3 Wing Luxeuil; Surveyed 26.12.16 (only entry) |
| 9187 | Deld 3 Wing Luxeuil; Surveyed 26.12.16 (only entry) |
| 9188 | Deld 3 Wing Luxeuil; Surveyed 26.12.16 (only entry) |
| 9189 | Deld 3 Wing Luxeuil 10.16; Surveyed 26.12.16 (only entry) |
| 9190 | Deld 3 Wing Luxeuil; Surveyed 3.2.17 (only entry) |
| 9191 | Deld 3 Wing Luxeuil; Surveyed 3.2.17 (only entry) |
| 9192 | Deld 3 Wing Luxeuil; Surveyed 26.1.17 (only entry) |
| 9193 | Deld 3 Wing Luxeuil; Surveyed 22.1.17 (only entry) |
| 9194 | Deld 3 Wing Luxeuil; Surveyed 22.1.17 (only entry) |
| 9195 | Deld 3 Wing Luxeuil W/E 15.9.16; Surveyed 18.12.16 |
| 9196 | Deld 3 Wing Luxeuil W/E 15.9.16; Flown in Oberndorf raid 12.10.16 (FSL PE Beasley & G/L Perks); Surveyed 18.12.16 |
| 9197 | Deld 3 Wing Luxeuil; Surveyed 3.2.17 (only entry) |
| 9198 | Deld 3 Wing Luxeuil W/E 13.10.16; Surveyed 10.11.16 (wrecked) |
| 9199 | Deld 3 Wing Luxeuil; Surveyed 26.1.17 (only entry) |
| 9200 | Deld 3 Wing Luxeuil W/E 15.9.16; Surveyed 19.1.17 (only entry) |
| "9202" | Breguet (RR engine) Deld 3 Wing Luxeuil; Surveyed 22.1.17 (only entry) ["Useless, broken up on site, engine buried under new road"] [NB. It is reported that a number of Breguet engines were buried under this road. Could they be still there?] |

**50 NIEUPORT 12 TWO-SEATER TRACTOR BIPLANES ordered 15.12.15 under Cont No C.P.150907/15 from Sir William Beardmore & Co Ltd, numbered 9201 to 9250 and built Dalmuir. (110-hp Clerget 9Z)**

| | |
|---|---|
| 9201 | Tested 10.5.16 (A Dukinfield Jones); Deld Chingford by lorry 27.5.16; Cranwell 8.8.16; COL 30.4.17 (F/L MA Simpson & FSL HG Tippinge); On nose landing, badly damaged 25.5.17 (F/L MA Simpson & Lt N Lea RNVR); Survey 21.11.17; Deleted 5.12.17 obsolete type |
| 9202 | Converted/built as single-seater; Deld Dover 30.5.16; ADD 18.6.16; Crashed, CW 9.16; Deleted ADD 17.9.16 as spares |
| 9203 | Shipped to Aegean; 2 Wing from 6.16 (7.16?); Shot down by Fokker nr Smyrna 30.3.17 (F/L JE Morgan & S/L A Sandell both killed) |
| 9204 | Deld Dover by rail 8.6.16; ADD 16.6.16; 3 Flt B Sqdn 1 Wing by 18.6.16; ADD by 29.6.16; For survey as spares 14.9.16; Deleted ADD as spares 4.12.16 |

9205 Deld Dover 14.6.16; ADD 17.6.16; 6 Flt A Sqdn 5 Wing 20.10.16; 11 Flt B Sqdn 4 Wing 27.11.16; Became 6 Sqdn 12.16; 10 Sqdn 24.2.17; ADD 4.5.17

9206 Deld Dover 16.6.16; Ready for testing 18.6.16; ADD 22.6.16; 11 Flt B Sqdn 4 Wing 28.11.16; Became 6 Sqdn 12.16; Wrecked 25.2.17; ADD by 1.3.17; Deleted 27.4.17

9207 Deld Dover for erection 18.6.16; ADD 30.6.16; 5 Wing 16.12.16; Dover 20.12.16; Chingford 31.1.17; Cranwell 1.2.17; Surveyed 21.11.17; Deleted 5.12.17 obsolete type

9208 Deld Dover for erection 16.6.16; Accepted 19.6.16; ADD 20.6.16; 10 Flt A Sqdn 4 Wing Dunkerque 20.8.16 - @23.10.16; ADD by 2.11.16; Dover 5.3.17 for erection; Surveyed 16.10.17; Deleted 19.10.17 W&T

9209 Deld Dover for erection 20.6.16; ADD 23.6.16 (repair); 1 Sqdn 5.1.17; ADD 1.2.17; Deleted 27.6.17 general fatigue

9210 Deld Dover 22.7.16; Accepted 9.8.16 (Dukinfield Jones); Deleted 10.3.17

9211 Deld Chingford by lorry 30.6.16; Oakley 29.7.16 (repair longerons); Chingford 18.8.16; Hendon 8.16; Cranwell 31.8.16; Deleted W/E 23.2.18

9212 Deld Dover 26.7.16; Accepted 12.8.16 (Dukinfield Jones); Damaged 23.9.16; Surveyed 16.10.17; Deleted 19.10.17 W&T

9213 Transferred to RFC (Military Wing) 9.16 as A3281 and flown by 46 Sqdn Droglandt

9214 Large fin fitted; Transferred to RFC (Military Wing) 4.9.16 as A3270 and flown by 46 Sqdn Droglandt

9215 Transferred to RFC (Military Wing) 4.9.16 as A3271 and flown by 46 Sqdn Droglandt

9216 Transferred to RFC (Military Wing) 4.9.16 as A3272 and flown by 46 Sqdn Droglandt

9217 Transferred to RFC (Military Wing) 9.16 as A3273 and flown by 46 Sqdn Droglandt

9218 Transferred to RFC (Military Wing) 4.9.16 as A3274 and flown by 46 Sqdn Droglandt

9219 Transferred to RFC (Military Wing) 9.16 as A3275 and flown by 46 Sqdn Droglandt

9220 Transferred to RFC (Military Wing) 9.16 as A3282 and flown by 46 Sqdn Droglandt

9221 Transferred to RFC (Military Wing) 9.16 as A3283 and flown by 46 Sqdn Droglandt

9222 Transferred to RFC (Military Wing) 9.16 as A3284 and flown by 46 Sqdn Droglandt

9223 Transferred to RFC (Military Wing) 9.16 as A3285 and flown by 46 Sqdn Droglandt

9224 Transferred to RFC (Military Wing) 9.16 as A3286 and flown by 46 Sqdn Droglandt

9225 Transferred to RFC (Military Wing) 9.16 as A3287 and flown by 46 Sqdn Droglandt

9226 Transferred to RFC (Military Wing) 9.16 as A3288. Climbing and speed trials at CFS Upavon 3-7.10.16; Flown by 46 Sqdn Droglandt

9227 Transferred to RFC (Military Wing) 9.16 as A3289 and flown by 46 Sqdn Droglandt

9228 Transferred to RFC (Military Wing) 9.16 as A3290 and flown by 46 Sqdn Droglandt

9229 Transferred to RFC (Military Wing) 9.16 as A3291 and flown by 46 Sqdn Droglandt

9230 Transferred to RFC (Military Wing) 9.16 as A3292 and flown by 46 Sqdn Droglandt

9231 Transferred to RFC (Military Wing) 9.16 as A3293 and flown by 46 Sqdn Droglandt

9232 Transferred to RFC (Military Wing) 9.16 as A3294 and flown by 46 Sqdn Droglandt

9233 Deld by rail to Design Flt Eastchurch 18.10.16 (fitted Ranken Dart containers); Accepted 6.11.16 (Dukinfield Jones); Chingford 14.11.16; Incorrectly marked N9233 by 3.17; Deleted W/E 12.2.18

9234 Deld Cranwell for erection 26.10.16; Surveyed 27.11.17; Deleted 6.12.17 wrecked

9235 Deld Cranwell for erection 23.10.16; Tested 2.11.16; Hendon 18.9.17; Cranwell 8.12.17 (now 100-hp Gnome Monosoupape); Surveyed 25.2.18; Deleted 13.3.18 for GI

9236 Deld Cranwell for erection 30.10.16; Surveyed 27.11.17; Deleted 6.12.17 wrecked

9237 Deld Eastchurch Workshops 26.10.16; Awaiting test 1.1.17; Observers School Flt Eastchurch 18.2.17; Eastchurch Workshops 1.4.17 (Fit experimental engine), then retd Observers School Flt; Port wing damaged 6.7.17; Deleted W/E 30.3.18

9238 Deld Eastchurch Workshops 26.10.16; Awaiting test 1.1.17, then to Observers School Flt Eastchurch; Deleted W/E 30.3.18 wrecked

9239 Deld Killingholme store 26.4.17; East Fortune 21.5.17 (arr 22.5.17); Fitted 100-hp Gnome Monosoupape by 10.17; Surveyed 24.12.17; Deleted 3.1.18 as spares

9240 Deld Cranwell store 15.5.17; Surveyed 16.10.17; Deleted 18.10.17 to GI

9241 Built as single-seater; Deld Chingford by rail 18.5.17 - @30.3.18

9242 Deld Dover for erection 23.11.16; Accepted 14.12.16 (Dukinfield Jones); Surveyed 16.10.17; Deleted 19.10.17 W&T

9243 Deld Chingford by lorry 20.12.16; Surveyed 12.3.18; Deleted 16.3.18 DBR

9244 Deld Chingford 23.12.16; Surveyed 12.3.18; Deleted 16.3.18 DBR

9245 Deld Cranwell 30.12.16; Surveyed 21.11.17; Deleted 5.12.17 obsolete type

9246 Deld Cranwell for erection 24.1.17; Accident 9.2.17; Crashed 29.6.17; Surveyed 21.11.17; Deleted 5.12.17 obsolete type

9247 (130-hp Clerget) Deld Cranwell (via Coventry) 30.4.17; Crashed 27.6.17; EAD Grain 18.9.17; Surveyed 25.3.18; Deleted 27.3.18 W&T

9248 (130hp Clerget) Deld Cranwell for erection 12.3.17; Crashed 27.6.17; Became 201/202 TDS Cranwell 1.4.18

9249 Deld Cranwell 8.3.17; Surveyed 3.1.18; Deleted 17.1.18 DBR

9250 Deld Killingholme store 17.4.17; To Killingholme school 3.18 - @5.18; NE Area FIS Redcar 1918
[9239 to 9250 were to have been transferred to RFC (Military Wing) as A5157 to A5168, but not transferred and RFC serials re-issued]

**25 HENRY FARMAN F.27 PUSHER BIPLANES ordered from Brush Electrical Engineering Co Ltd, numbered 9251 to 9275 and built Loughborough. Modified armament ordered 11.16. (Two 150-hp Canton-Unné R.9)**

9251 Deld Cranwell 17.3.17; For deletion by 26.10.17
9252 to 9255 Allocated to Cranwell, cancelled 23.4.17
9256 to 9260 cancelled
9261 to 9275 cancelled by 1.17

**10 AVRO 504E DUAL CONTROL TRACTOR BIPLANES ordered under Cont No C.P.151922/15, numbered 9276 to 9285 and built Manchester. (100-hp Gnome Monosoupape)**

9276 Deld ARD Grain 29.4.16; Tested 29.5.16; Experimental Flt Grain 8.7.16; Avro 28.9.16; Flown Experimental Flt Grain 1.11.16 (Raynham); Renamed Gunnery Experimental Grain 5.12.16; HP Sqdn Manston 12.7.17; Manston FS 14.7.17; COL 31.8.17 (FSL MT McKelvey); War School Manston by 6.10.17; Surveyed 26.10.17; Deleted 29.10.17 W&T

9277 Deld Chingford by lorry 15.5.16; Tested 5.6.16 (Raynham); Avro to redesign plane 21.9.16; Repair by 10.10.16; Avro 25.10.16 (repair); Chingford 10.11.16; Damaged 23.8.17; Deleted W/E 16 23.2.18

9278 Deld Chingford 1.10.16; Avro 3.10.16 (repair); Cranwell on/by 13.2.17; Surveyed 3.1.18; Deleted 17.1.18 W&T

9279 Deld Chingford 1.10.16; Avro 3.10.16 (repair); Hendon 30.4.17; Cranwell 5.5.17; Hendon 6.5.17; ECD Grain 17.6.17; Hendon 26.8.17 (crashed on arrival?); Deleted 14.9.17

9280 Deld Chingford 3.10.16 - @10.17; Possibly the aircraft in which TFSL DR Kerr killed Manston 11.11.17 (or N5313); Surveyed Manston 14.11.17; Deleted 21.11.17 DBR

9281 Deld Yarmouth 30.9.16; Accepted 11.11.16 (Raynham); Freiston 13.5.17; Cranwell by 10.17; Crashed 2.10.17; Freiston by 29.12.17 - @30.3.18

9282 Deld Yarmouth 30.9.16; Accepted 11.11.16 (Raynham); Freiston 16.5.17; Cranwell by 7.17; Eastbourne by rail 27.7.17 (arr 31.7.17); Surveyed 27.11.17; Deleted 5.12.17 W&T

9283     Deld Eastbourne by air 6.10.16; Chingford 16.10.16; Crashed 9.5.17 (PFO DE Penney killed); Deleted 16.5.17

9284     Deld Eastbourne by air 6.10.16; Chingford 16.10.16; Cranwell 8.5.17; Eastbourne by rail 27.7.17 (arr 31.7.17); Surveyed 27.11.17; Deleted 5.12.17 W&T

9285     Deld Chingford by lorry 15.5.16; Cranwell 23.5.17; Freiston 24.5.17; Wrecked Cranwell 26.5.17 (FSL JT Sims killed); Deleted 18.6.17

**20 CAUDRON G.IV TRACTOR BIPLANES ordered from British Caudron (authorised 1.10.15?), numbered 9286 to 9305. (Two 100-hp Anzani)**

9286 to 9305 cancelled 6.16

**50 SHORT BOMBER TRACTOR BIPLANES ordered under Cont No C.P.112793/16, numbered 9306 to 9355 and built Eastchurch. (250-hp Rolls-Royce)** [Gordon Bruce' researches show correct c/n's to be S.249 to S.298]

9306     (RR Mk.II) (short fuselage) Deld Grain 1.4.16 (target for gunnery trials); 12 Flt B Sqdn 4 Wing 3.9.16; Tested, constructional defects reported 20.10.16 (Kemp); ADD 9.11.16 - @14.12.16; B Sqdn 4 Wing by 26.12.16; Became 7 Sqdn 31.12.16; Left for Eastchurch 26.12.16, but returned due to fog; War Flt Eastchurch 23.1.17; Eastchurch Workshops 24.1.17; Deleted 4.5.17

9307     (RR Mk.II) Completed gun trials Grain; Deld and accepted Gunnery School Flts Eastchurch 17.5.16; 3 Wing Manston 23.8.16; ADD 13.9.16; B Sqdn 4 Wing Petite Synthe 16.9.16; Constructional defects reported 31.10.16; ADD 9.11.16; Eastchurch Workshops 26.12.16; Deleted 4.5.17

9308     Accepted Eastchurch 18.7.16; Deld 3 Wing Manston 18.7.16; France 31.7.16; 3 Wing Luxeuil by 25.8.16; Surveyed by HQ Flt Luxeuil 22.1.17

9309     Accepted Eastchurch 18.7.16; Deld 3 Wing Manston 2.8.16; Deleted 16.10.16

9310     Accepted Eastchurch 18.7.16; Deld 3 Wing Manston 20.7.16; COL 2.8.16; Deleted 8.8.16

9311     Accepted Eastchurch 18.7.16; Deld 3 Wing Manston 19.7.16; Transferred to French Govt 31.7.16

9312     Accepted Eastchurch 18.7.16; Deld 3 Wing Manston 15.7.16 (sic); To France but engine seized 3m short of Paris, FL in garden, slightly damage chassis 31.7.16 (FSL CH Butterworth); 3 Wing Luxeuil by 11.8.16; HQ Flt Luxeuil by 1.9.16 (damaged, no engine); Surveyed for deletion 17.11.16

9313     (RR Mk.II) Mkrs Eastchurch by 18.6.16; Tested 29/30.6.16; Deld 3 Wing Manston 22.8.16; 12 Flt B Sqdn 4 Wing 23.8.16; ADD by 14.9.16; 12 Flt B Sqdn 4 Wing Petite Synthe 21.10.16; Constructional defects reported 31.10.16; Became 7 Sqdn Petite Synthe 31.12.16; Eastchurch Workshops 20.12.16; Deleted 4.5.17

9314     (RR Mk.II) Tested Mkrs Eastchurch 29/30.6.16; Accepted Eastchurch 18.7.16; Deld 3 Wing Manston 19.7.16; ADD 13.9.16; 12 Flt B Sqdn 4 Wing 14.9.16; Constructional defects reported 31.10.16; To UK, landed Dunmow 16.12.16; Chingford 18.12.16 (housed); Deleted 25.1.17

9315     Accepted Eastchurch 10.8.16; Deld Eastchurch Workshops 6.9.16; Farnborough 11.10.16 and transferred to RFC (Military Wing) as A5203

9316     Accepted Eastchurch 3.8.16; Deld 3 Wing Manston 8.8.16; Transferred to RFC (Military Wing) 13.11.16 as A5157; Retd Manston by 15.2.17 (no engine); Deleted 28.4.17

9317     Deld PVRS 8.8.16; Design Flt Eastchurch 7.9.16 (bombing trials); Eastchurch Workshops 25.10.16; ADD 15.11.16; 12 Flt B Sqdn 4 Wing 17.11.16; To Eastchurch, but returned due to fog 26.12.16; Eastchurch Workshops 1.1.17; Deleted 4.5.17

9318     (RR Mk.I) Deld 4 Wing (via Dunkerque) 2.9.16; 12 Flt B Sqdn 4 Wing Petite Synthe from/by 6.9.16; Tested 20, 23 & 25.10.16 (centre section cut away to improve tail heaviness); Constructional defects reported 31.10.16; To UK, landed Dunmow 16.12.16

9319     Accepted Eastchurch 10.8.16; Deld Eastchurch Workshops 6.9.16; Allocated Grain for training

17.10.16, but transferred in error to RFC (Military Wing) Farnborough as A5155 19.10.16

9320     Deld Eastchurch Workshops 6.9.16; Farnborough 15.10.16, transferred to RFC (Military Wing) as A5214

9321     (RR Mk.I) Accepted Eastchurch 18.8.16; Deld 3 Wing Manston 20.8.16; ADD 13.9.16; 12 Flt B Sqdn 4 Wing 14.9.16; Constructional defects reported 31.10.16; Hit by flak in raid on Ostende Docks, FL on beach Oost Dunkerque, retd later 15.11.16 (FSL R Darley & AM Kirby); ADD by 23.11.16; Deleted 5.1.17 general fatigue

9322     (RR Mk.III) Accepted Eastchurch 23.8.16; Deld 3 Wing Manston 26.8.16; ADD 13.9.16; 12 Flt B Sqdn 4 Wing 14.9.16; Constructional defects reported 31.10.16; After raid on Ostende Docks, carburettor fire on approach, landed safely 15.11.16 (FSL HG Brackley & LM (G/L) Kent); Repaired on Wing; Became 7 Sqdn 31.12.16; Eastchurch Workshops 24.1.17; Deleted 4.5.17

9323     (RR Mk.III) Accepted Eastchurch 31.8.16; Deld Eastchurch Workshops 7.9.16; Deleted 28.4.17 BUT ADD, allocated Eastchurch storage 23.11.17

9324     (RR Mk.I) Accepted Eastchurch 31.8.16; Deld 3 Wing Manston 2.9.16; ADD 13.9.16; B Sqdn 4 Wing Petite Synthe 14.9.16; Tested 21.10.16 (Kemp); Constructional defects reported 31.10.16; Engine holed by flak in raid on Ostende Docks, FL 50 yds W of Nieuport Pier 17.11.16 (FSL GP Powles & G/L Young); ADD by 28.11.16; Deleted ADD 5.1.17 general fatigue

9325     Deld Eastchurch Workshops 21.9.16; Farnborough 22.9.16; Transferred to RFC (Military Wing) as A4005

9326     (RR Mk.III) Deld Eastchurch Workshops 21.9.16; Accepted 18.10.16 (JL Parker); Design Flt Eastchurch 3.11.16; Eastchurch Workshops 8.12.16; Deleted 4.5.17

9327     (RR Mk.I) Accepted Eastchurch 18.10.16 (JL Parker); Eastchurch Workshops by 2.12.16; Deleted 4.5.17

9328     (RR Mk.I) Accepted Eastchurch 17.10.16 (JL Parker); Eastchurch Workshops to Grain 26.10.16, Engine sent away 23.12.16; LM 28.6.17; Allocated Grain 20.10.17

9329     (RR Mk.I) Accepted 17.10.16 (JL Parker); Eastchurch Workshops by 15.12.16; Deleted 4.5.17 BUT ADD, allocated Eastchurch storage 23.11.17

9330     (RR Mk.I) Accepted 28.10.16 (JL Parker); Design Flt Eastchurch by 15.12.16; Eastchurch Workshops 12.1.17 - @25.2.17 (engine removed); Grain 26.2.17 (ex Allhallows); retd to Design Flt Eastchurch 3.3.17; Eastchurch Workshops 22.3.17 (exptl); Deleted 4.5.17

9331     (RR Mk.I) Accepted 17.10.16 (JL Parker); Eastchurch Workshops by 15.12.16; Deleted 4.5.17

9332     (RR Mk.I) Accepted 28.10.16 (JL Parker); Eastchurch Workshops by 15.12.16; Deleted 4.5.17

9333     (RR Mk.I) Tested, not accepted 18.10.16 (JL Parker); Accepted 2.11.16 (JL Parker); Eastchurch Workshops by 15.12.16; Deleted 4.5.17

9334     (RR Mk.I) Accepted 2.11.16 (JL Parker); Eastchurch Workshops by 15.12.16; Deleted 4.5.17

9335     (RR Mk.IV) Accepted 8.11.16 (JL Parker); Eastchurch to 7 Sqdn 24.12.16 - @16.6.17; Bombed Bruges 3.2.17 (F/L HG Brackley & AM G/L Woolley); Bombed Bruges 5.6.17 (last operational flight); Deleted ADD 27.6.17 general fatigue

9336     (RR Mk.IV) Accepted 8.11.16 (JL Parker); Eastchurch by 12.16; 7 Sqdn 24.12.16; Bombed Ghiselles airfield 16.2.17 (FSL RB Frame - aircraft's last operational flight); Wrecked 15.4.17; Deleted ADD 14.5.17

9337     (RR Mk.IV) Accepted 15.11.16 (JL Parker); Eastchurch by 12.16; 7 Sqdn 24.12.16; Overshot into ditch landing after night raid on Bruges, damaged 3.2.17 (FSL CH Darley & AM G/L Bager); to ADD for survey; Deleted 24.3.17

9338     (RR Mk.IV) Accepted 15.11.16 (JL Parker); Eastchurch Workshops by 1.1.17; Dunkerque 2.1.17; 7 Sqdn 1.17; Landing after night raid on Bruges, hit 9490 4.2.17 (F/L HG Brackley & AM G/L Woolley); Last mention by sqdn 21.6.17; Deleted ADD 27.6.17 general fatigue

9339     (RR Mk.IV) Accepted 13.12.16 (JL Parker); Deld Eastchurch Workshops by 19.12.16; Dunkerque 2.1.17; 7 Sqdn by 2.2.17; FL Le Crotoy after raid on Bruges 3.2.17; retd 11.2.17; Bombed Bruges 5.6.17 (last operational flight); Last mention by sqdn 21.6.17; Deleted ADD 27.6.17 general fatigue

9340     (RR Mk.IV) (Eagle IV) Accepted 20.12.16 (JL Parker);

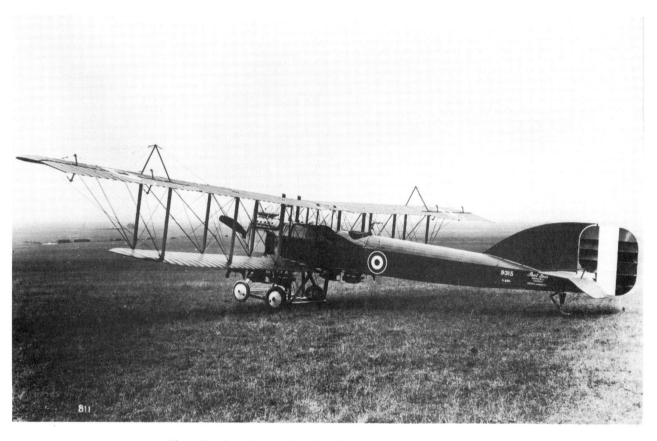

*Short Bomber 9315 at Eastchurch, 1916 (via J.D.Oughton)*

*Nieuport Type 12 9233 with Ranken Dart containers, mispainted as N9233, at Eastchurch 1916. (J.M.Bruce/G.S.Leslie collection)*

*Sopwith 1½ Strutters of 5 Wing, including 9395 'A2' of 5 Sqdn, hangared, probably at Coudekerque. (via Frank Cheesman)*

*Breguet Type V Concours Pusher Biplane 9426, stated to be photographed 9 May 1917. (J.M.Bruce/G.S.Leslie collection)*

*Sage-built Royal Aircraft Factory B.E.2c 9469. (via Philip Jarrett)*

Deld Eastchurch Workshops 19.12.16; Testing Sqdn Martlesham Heath 20.8.17 (dynamometer tests); Grain Armament Dept 9.11.17; Grain Type Test Flt W/E 15.12.17; EAD Grain W/E 16.2.18 - @25.5.18 (Dynamometer tests)

9341 to 9343 cancelled by 1.17
9344 to 9355 cancelled 9.16

## 20 SHORT BOMBER TRACTOR BIPLANES ordered 18.5.16 under Cont Nos C.P.103297/16 & C.P.112535/16 from The Sunbeam Motor Car Co Ltd, numbered 9356 to 9375 and built Wolverhampton. (240-hp Sunbeam)

9356    Deld Chingford by 27.7.16; Tested 31.7.16 (F/L LH Hardstaff); Eastchurch Workshops 23.9.16; Deleted 4.5.17

9357    Deld Chingford by lorry 20.7.16; ADD 16.9.16 - @21.9.16; 12 Flt B Sqdn 4 Wing Petite Synthe by 28.9.16; Eastchurch Workshops 20.12.16; Deleted 4.5.17

9358    Deld Chingford 1.9.16; Eastchurch Workshops 24.9.16; Deleted 4.5.17

9359    Deld Chingford by rail 21.9.16; Gunnery Experimental Grain 5.12.16 (accepted JL Parker); EAD Grain by 10.17; Surveyed 25.3.18 W&T; Deleted 27.3.18

9360    Deld Eastchurch Workshops by lorry 28.9.16; Deleted 4.5.17

9361    Deld Eastchurch Workshops by lorry 2.10.16; Erecting 20.10.16; Accepted 2.11.16; Deleted 4.5.17

9362    Deld Eastchurch Workshops by lorry 7.10.16; Erected 15.10.16; Accepted 11.12.16; Deleted 28.4.17

9363    Deld Eastchurch Workshops for erection 15.10.16; Deleted 4.5.17

9364    Deld Manston 11.11.16; Accepted 17.12.16 (JL Parker); Deleted 28.4.17

9365    Deld Eastchurch Workshops by lorry 10.11.16; Accepted 8.12.16 (JL Parker); Deleted 4.5.17

9366    Deld Manston 11.11.16; Accepted 7.12.16 (JL Parker); Deleted 4.5.17

9367    Deld by lorry to Eastchurch Workshops 22.11.16; Deleted 4.5.17

9368    Deld Manston 19.12.16; Failed test 3.1.17; Retested and accepted 10.1.17 (JL Parker); Deleted 28.4.17

9369    Deld Manston 22.1.17; Deleted 28.4.17

9370    Deld Manston for erection 30.1.17; Deleted 28.4.17

9371 to 9375 cancelled 9.16

## 50 SOPWITH 1½ STRUTTER (ADMIRALTY 9400S TYPE) TRACTOR BIPLANES ordered 23.3.16 under Cont Nos C.P.104237/16 & C.P.106812/16, numbered 9376 to 9425 and built Kingston-on-Thames, delivered from Brooklands. (110 Clerget 9Z).

9376    Brooklands by 2.16; Deld 2.16; Possibly the Sopwith deld Brooklands to 4 Wing 7.2.16, but not listed after 14.2.16; Probably the aircraft which had an accident at Brooklands 10.3.16 (F/L LH Hardstaff); Deld Grain 30.3.16 (F/L LH Hardstaff); 1 Wing by 30.3.16; 5 Flt A Sqdn 5 Wing Coudekerque 11.4.16; ADD W/E 18.5.16; 5 Flt A Sqdn 5 Wing Coudekerque 1.7.16; ADD 9.9.16 (Type 9400S); 8 Flt B Sqdn 5 Wing 29.9.16; Became 5 Sqdn 31.12.16 (Coded 'A5'); EF, FL Oostburg, Zeeland 22.4.17 (FSL DAH Nelles DSC interned); Deleted 11.5.17; Bought for £1,700 23.9.17 and became LA42 of Dutch Air Arm (later S412)

9377    Deld Chingford 18.3.16 (experimental); Tested with Ranken Darts 27.5.16; Design Flt Eastchurch 18.10.16; Hendon 27.11.16; Eastchurch 27.11.16; CFS Upavon 28.11.16; Hendon 30.11.16; Design Flt Eastchurch 4.12.16 (overhaul); To Hendon, but EF, FL Detling 23.1.17; Design Flt Eastchurch 24.1.17; Hendon 9.2.17; Design Flt Eastchurch 15.2.17; ECD Grain 3.3.17; Flown with collapsible floats 2.6.17 (S/Cdr FJ Rutland); Fitted hydrovanes, successfully landed in Sheerness harbour 14.9.17; still ECD Grain 29.9.17

9378    Presentation a/c 'Poverty Bay. New Zealand No.1' 15.12.15. Deld Dover 3.4.16; ADD 6.4.16; 5 Flt A Sqdn 5 Wing Coudekerque by 23.4.16; Wrecked Coudekerque 28.5.16 (FSL GCV Hewson); ADD by 2.6.16 - @27.7.16; 4 Flt B Sqdn 1 Wing Petite Synthe by late 7.16; Camera test 3.8.16; ADD 8.16; C Sqdn 1

Wing 15.8.16; ADD by 14.9.16; C Sqdn 1 Wing 29.9.16; Became 2 Sqdn 12.16; ADD 27.1.17 - @23.2.17; 2 Sqdn by 1.3.17; AP Dover 16.11.17 - @29.12.17; Transport Flt Dover by 3.18 - 7.18 (now 130-hp Clerget); 491 Flt Dover loan 30.7.18; 233 Sqdn Dover; attd 202 Sqdn 5.11.18; 233 Sqdn Dover 19.1.19; SOC 22.2.19

9379    Deld Dover 29.3.16; ADD 6.5.16; 5 Flt A Sqdn 5 Wing Coudekerque by 24.5.16; ADD by 22.6.16; 6 Flt A Sqdn 5 Wing 10.7.16; 5 Flt A Sqdn 5 Wing by 17.8.16; ADD 30.9.16; 5 Wing Coudekerque 17.11.16; Became 5 Sqdn 31.12.16; ADD & deleted 27.4.17, general fatigue

9380    Deld Experimental Flt Grain 27.3.16 (arrived 30.3.16); Visited Kingsnorth 6.4.16 (bombing trials?); HSPP patrol 20.5.16 (F/L P Legh & LM Osbourne); Design Flt Eastchurch 22.6.16; EAD Grain 2.3.17 (engine test); Deleted 23.8.17

9381    Reallocated RFC (Military Wing) W/E 25.3.16; Brooklands by 10.4.16; Transferred to RFC (Military Wing) as 7942 and flown by 70 Sqdn at Fienvillers; Later retd RNAS at Grain, still as 7942

9382    At Brooklands by 10.4.16; Deld Folkestone 20.4.16 (transit); ADD 20.4.16; 5 Wing Coudekerque 2.5.16; 8 Flt B Sqdn 5 Wing Coudekerque by 18.5.16; 5 Flt A Sqdn 5 Wing Coudekerque by 2.6.16; ADD 22.9.16; 8 Flt B Sqdn 5 Wing Coudekerque 17.10.16; Became 5 Sqdn 31.12.16; To ADD & deleted 27.4.17 general fatigue

9383    Presentation a/c 'Britons in Japan No.1' 4.5.16. Brooklands by 10.4.16; Deld Dover 17.4.16; ADD 24.4.16; 8 Flt B Sqdn 5 Wing Coudekerque by 14.5.16 - @17.6.16; ADD by 22.6.16; 8 Flt B Sqdn 5 Wing Coudekerque 14.7.16; Became 5 Sqdn (coded 'A1') 31.12.16; Crashed and DBR Coudekerque 10.2.17 (F/Cdr JCP Wood); For deletion by 15.2.17; Deleted ADD 24.3.17

9384    At Brooklands by 10.4.16; Deld Dover 23.4.16; ADD 27.4.16; 5 Flt A Sqdn 5 Wing Coudekerque by 18.5.16; FTR from raid on Mariakerke aerodrome 21.5.16 (F/L TE Viney DSO killed); For survey by 24.5.16, missing

9385    At Brooklands by 19.4.16; Deld Dover 23.4.16; ADD 24.4.16; 5 Flt A Sqdn 5 Wing Coudekerque 10.5.16; ADD 17.9.16; 5 Flt A Sqdn 5 Wing Coudekerque 29.9.16 - 10.16; 8 Flt B Sqdn 5 Wing Coudekerque by 16.11.16; Became 5 Sqdn 31.12.16; Wrecked 8.2.17; still 5 Sqdn 22.2.17; ADD by 1.3.17; Deleted 27.4.17 general fatigue

9386    Transferred to RFC (Military Wing) as 5719. Farnborough by 20.4.16. Flown by 70 Sqdn at Fienvillers .16

9387    Transferred to RFC (Military Wing) as 5720. At Farnborough 4.16. Flown by 70 Sqdn at Fienvillers .16

9388    Deld 5 Flt A Sqdn 5 Wing Coudekerque on/by 18.5.16; EF, FL, CW 1½m E of Coudekerque 1.8.16 (FSL CD Booker & S/L HJ Roach); For survey by 3.8.16; ADD 17.9.16; Last mention 12.10.16

9389    At Brooklands by 19.4.16; Transferred to RFC (Military Wing) as 5721. To Farnborough 4.16. Flown by 70 Sqdn at Fienvillers .16

9390    At Brooklands by 19.4.16; Deld Chingford 21.4.16; Design Flt Eastchurch 12.10.16; Propeller burst in air, FL, chassis damaged 28.11.16 (F/L LP Openshaw & Lt GH Millar unhurt); ECD Grain 18.3.17; Fitting hook 10.4.17; Fitted hydrovane and flotation gear 8.9.17; Success ditching and flotation tests 9.17; Deleted W/E 8.12.17; Presume rebuilt; Fitted skid undercarriage for arrester gear tests, successfully ditched 22.3.18 & 7.4.18; Fitted arrester gear 9.4.18

9391    At Brooklands by 19.4.16; Transferred to RFC (Military Wing) and flown by 70 Sqdn at Fienvillers .16

9392    At Brooklands by 19.4.16; Transferred to RFC (Military Wing) and flown by 70 Sqdn at Fienvillers .16

9393    At Brooklands by 19.4.16; Transferred to RFC (Military Wing) and flown by 70 Sqdn at Fienvillers .16

9394    At Brooklands by 19.4.16; Deld ADD 30.4.16; 5 Flt A Sqdn 5 Wing Coudekerque 10.5.16; Crashed and DBR Coudekerque 1.7.16 (FSL WE Gardner & G/L F George); ADD 3.7.16 (for survey); 8 Flt B Sqdn 5 Wing Coudekerque 12.9.16; Became 5 Sqdn 31.12.16; ADD 29.4.17; Deleted 27.4.17 (sic) general fatigue

9395 Presentation Aircraft 4.5.16, named 'Tientsin Britons No.1'. Deld Dover (via Tonbridge) 4.5.16; ADD 5.5.16; 8 Flt B Sqdn 5 Wing Coudekerque by 22.6.16; Became 5 Sqdn (coded 'A2') 31.12.16; Sqdn moved to Petite Synthe 1.4.17; Wrecked 21.4.17; ADD by 26.4.17; Deleted 27.4.17 general fatigue

9396 Deld Dover 4.5.16; visited Kingsnorth 11/12.5.16; ADD 23.5.16; 8 Flt B Sqdn 5 Wing Coudekerque (coded 'A4') 14.7.16; Left 05.29; Ran out of fuel during raid on Cognelée Airship Shed, Namur and FL Schoondijke, Zeeland 25.8.16 (FSL CW Jamieson interned); Aircraft interned in Holland; For sale to Netherlands Govt 1.17; Became *LA33* of Dutch Air Arm

9397 Deld ADD 5.16; 5 Flt A Sqdn 5 Wing Coudekerque 10.5.16 - @18.5.16; For survey by 24.5.16; For deletion by 2.6.17, wrecked

9398 Deld Hendon 9.5.16; Cranwell 10.5.16; Propeller and u/c damaged 6.7.17; Surveyed 10.12.17; Deleted 14.12.17 type obsolete

9399 Deld Cranwell 12.5.16; Wrecked by 1.3.17; To Battersea as GI 2.6.17; Surveyed 18.9.17; Deleted 18.10.17

9400 (130-hp Clerget) Accepted Brooklands 5.5.16; Deld Detling 11.5.16; 3 Wing Manston 30.6.16; War Flt Eastchurch 1.7.16; 3 Wing Manston 6.7.16; Tested 21.8.16; AZP, landed Eastchurch 24.8.16 (F/Cdr C Draper & PO Walker); War Flt Eastchurch 5.9.16; 3 Wing Manston 5.9.16; 3 Wing Luxeuil 16.10.16; ADD 1.5.17; Deleted 14.5.17

9401 (130-hp Clerget) Accepted Brooklands 10.5.16; Deld 3 Wing Detling 20.5.16; 3 Wing Manston 8.6.16; Damaged landing 20.6.16 (FSL WJ Sussan); Fairey 13.7.16; Oakley repair 13.7.16; Accepted 3 Wing Manston 30.9.16; 3 Wing Luxeuil 16.10.16; ADD 24.4.17; Dover for survey 24.4.17; Fitted 110-hp Clerget in lieu of 130-hp Clerget; CW 17.6.17; Deleted 30.6.17

9402 Deld Chingford 14.5.16; Villacoublay (via Dunkerque) 5.9.16 (Capt Groves); 5 Wing 24.9.16; Crashed and DBR; ADD 29.9.16; Deleted 5.1.17

9403 Deld Farnborough 14.5.16; Transferred to RFC (Military Wing) and flown by 70 Sqdn at Fienvillers .16

9404 Deld Farnborough 18.5.16; Transferred to RFC (Military Wing) and flown by 70 Sqdn at Fienvillers .16

9405 Presentation a/c 'Alexandria. Britons in Egypt No.1' (4.5.16). Deld Dover (via Eastchurch) 8.6.16; ADD 9.6.16; 5 Flt A Sqdn 5 Wing Coudekerque 9.6.16; Became 4 Sqdn 31.12.16; Fell in sea 4.2.17; For survey 5.2.17; ADD 24.3.17

9406 Transferred to RFC (Military Wing) without engine W/E 3.5.16

9407 (130-hp Clerget) Accepted Brooklands 22.5.16; Deld 3 Wing Detling 25.5.16; 3 Wing Manston 5.16; Damaged Manston 12.6.16; Fairey 13.7.16 (repair); 3 Wing Manston 31.7.16; EF, FL, u/c carried away 11.9.16 (FSL R Collishaw unhurt); Villacoublay 21.9.16; 3 Wing Luxeuil (coded '16') 22.9.16; Claimed Fokker biplane shot down over Rhine during raid on Oberndorf 12.10.16 (FSL R Collishaw); [1 Flt 3 Wing Ochey by 10.11.16; Became A Flt 1 Sqdn 3 Wing 8.12.16]; Fokker D shot down just before reaching target Volklingen & 2-str OOC on homeward journey, retd 12.10 10.11.16 (F/Cdr C Draper & S/L LV Pearkes); still 3 Wing 13.4.17; ADD by 26.4.17; Dover 26.5.17; Cranwell 3.6.17 (arr 4.6.17); Deleted 19.6.17

9408 Accepted Brooklands 24.5.16; Deld Detling 25.5.16; 3 Wing Manston 25.6.16; Badly damaged Manston 5.7.16 (FSL WJ Sussan); Oakley 13.7.16 (repair); Accepted 3 Wing Manston 30.9.16; 3 Wing Luxeuil (coded '20') 16.10.16; ADD 24.4.17; Dover 24.4.17; Fitted 110-hp Clerget in place of 130-hp Clerget 25.4.17; War School Manston 6.10.17; Gunnery School Eastchurch W/E 8.3.18; Leysdown by 4.18; Fleet Observers School Leysdown by 8.18 - 2.19

9409 Transferred to RFC (Military Wing) without engine W/E 13.5.16 and flown by 70 Sqdn at Fienvillers .16

9410 (130-hp Clerget) Accepted Brooklands 24.5.16; Deld 3 Wing Luxeuil (Coded '41') by 11.8.16; Loaned to French for AMF 8.16; B Flt 2 Sqdn 3 Wing Ochey 29.11.16; HA claimed in raid 4.3.17 (FSL CE Pattison & G/L PO HJL Hinkler); to Paris 3.17; 2 Sqdn 1 Wing

17.3.17; ADD 20.4.17; Deleted 27.4.17 general fatigue

9411 Presentation a/c 15.12.15 'Poverty Bay. New Zealand No.2' (15.12.15). Accepted Brooklands 26.5.16; Deld 3 Wing Luxeuil by 10.16; Deleted by 13.11.16 [No trace in 3W Luxeuil reports. Crashed on/before delivery?]

9412 Transferred to RFC (Military Wing) without engine W/E 13.5.16 and flown by 70 Sqdn at Fienvillers .16

9413 Accepted Brooklands 26.5.16; Deld 3 Wing Luxeuil by 11.8.16 - @13.8.16; On loan to French Govt for AMF by 15.9.16 - @24.11.16; Retd 3 Wing for repairs by 1.12.16; Retd French for AMF loan 2.1.17; Transferred to French Govt for AMF 4.17

9414 (130-hp Clerget) Accepted Brooklands 29.5.16; Deld 3 Wing Manston 9.6.16; AZP 3.8.16; AZP, chased *L31* and *L32* 25.8.16 (S/Cdr RLG Marix); 3 Wing Luxeuil 16.10.16 - @2.3.17 (HQ Flt by 10.11.16 - @4.12.16); Dover, restored to commission 9.3.17; ADD by 29.3.17; Dover 26.5.17; Badly damaged 6.8.17; Fitted 110-hp Clerget by 12.17; Visited 17 Sqdn but FL Oxley Wood on return and slightly damaged 16.2.18 (pilot unhurt); Walmer by 3.18; Dover 9.3.18; Fitted 130-hp Clerget by 4.18; Became 491 Flt Dover by 25.5.18; Became 491 Flt/Transport Flt 233 Sqdn Dover 31.8.18; SOC 22.2.19

9415 Transferred to RFC (Military Wing) without engine

9416 Deld Dover 2.6.16; ADD 3.6.16; For survey by 22.6.16; Deleted 7.16 as spares

9417 Deld Dover (via Folkestone) 15.6.16; ADD 16.6.16; 3 Flt B Sqdn 1 Wing St.Pol by 29.6.16 - @8.16; ADD by 14.9.16; C Sqdn 1 Wing St.Pol by 19.9.16 - @9.11.16; 4 Flt B Sqdn 1 Wing St.Pol by 16.11.16; ADD 17.12.16; 2 Sqdn 27.1.17 - @1.3.17; White 2-str biplane sent down smoking nr Wenduyne 1.2.17 (F/L HG Holden & S/L EBC Betts RNVR); ADD by 8.3.17; 2 Sqdn 9.3.17; ADD 5.9.17; Deleted 13.9.17 DBR
ALSO Reported coded 'G' at Houthem, Belgium 1916

9418 Transferred to RFC (Military Wing) without engine

9419 (130-hp Clerget) Deld ADD (via Dover) 3.6.16; 4 Flt B Sqdn 1 Wing St.Pol 23.6.16 - @10.8.16 (camera machine); C Sqdn 1 Wing by 17.8.16; ADD 1.9.16; C Sqdn 1 Wing test 25.9.16; 4 Flt B Sqdn 1 Wing St.Pol W/E 16.11.16; Became 2 Sqdn 12.16 - @26.2.17; ADD by 1.3.17; 2 Sqdn 2.5.17; Crashed Gravelines 13.11.17 (A/F/Cdr J Robinson & OSL WG Anderson); Deleted on squadron 26.11.17

9420 Deld ADD 3.6.16; 8 Flt B Sqdn 5 Wing Coudekerque (coded 'A3') 14.7.16; After raid on St.Denis Westrem aerodrome, hit by ground fire and FL Westkapelle, Zeeland 17.9.16 (FSL DE Harkness DSC wounded and interned); For sale to Dutch Govt 1.17; Became *LA38* of Dutch Air Arm (later *S24* in 1918)

9421 Transferred to RFC (Military Wing) and flown by 70 Sqdn at Fienvillers .16 and shot down by Ltn Wolff nr the Bois Bernard 6.4.17

9422 Deld ADD 9.6.16; 5 Flt A Sqdn 5 Wing Coudekerque 1.7.16 - @8.7.16; ADD by 13.7.16; C Sqdn 1 Wing St.Pol 31.8.16 - @9.11.16; 4 Flt B Sqdn 1 Wing St.Pol by 16.11.16 - @26.12.16; ADD by 28.12.16; 2 Sqdn 7.2.17; Attacked by 5 HA, 1 HA OOC nr Bruges, landed Furnes with battle damage 1.3.17 (F/L ST Edwards wounded, S/L CK Chase DSC unhurt) [but this is not in Edwards' log book!]; To ADD; 2 Sqdn 22.3.17; Dover 9.5.17; War School Manston W/E 3.11.17; Gunnery School Eastchurch/Leysdown W/E 9.3.18 - @30.3.18; East Fortune by 5.18

9423 (later 130-hp Clerget) Presentation a/c 'Peking Britons No.1' (4.5.16). Deld Dover 9.6.16; ADD 16.6.16; 3 Flt B Sqdn 1 Wing St.Pol by 18.6.16; ADD 31.8.16; 8 Flt B Sqdn 5 Wing Coudekerque 11.9.16; FL 16.10.16 (FSL HJT Saint & FSL GMT Rouse); ADD by 19.10.16; 8 Flt B Sqdn 5 Wing Coudekerque 17.11.16; Became 5 Sqdn Coudekerque 31.12.16; ADD by 8.2.17; 5 Sqdn 28.4.17; ADD 11.8.17; Chingford 25.9.17; Cranwell 26.9.17 (now 110-hp Clerget); East Fortune NFS W/E 18.1.18 - @29.8.18; Turnhouse 8.18 - @30.1.19

9424 Transferred to RFC (Military Wing) without engine

9425 Deld Dover 17.6.16; ADD 17.6.16; 3 Flt B Sqdn 1 Wing St.Pol by 25.9.16; C Sqdn 1 Wing 21.10.16 - @9.11.16 ("new photographic Sopwith"); 4 Flt B Sqdn 1 Wing by 16.12.16; Became 2 Sqdn 12.16; ADD 16.4.17; Deleted 27.4.17 general fatigue

**30 BREGUET TYPE V CONCOURS PUSHER BIPLANES ordered under Cont No C.P.107170/16 from Grahame-White Aviation Co Ltd as their Type XIX, numbered 9426 to 9455 and built Hendon for 3 Wing Luxeuil. Stated all still on order 1.17, 13 being packed for 3 Wing. (250-hp Rolls-Royce)**

9426     Due to be ready 27.11.16; Deld Hendon 3.1.17; To CSD by transport 23.3.17, later deleted

9427 to 9435 No evidence of delivery, possibly to store

9436 to 9455 cancelled 11.16

**20 ROYAL AIRCRAFT FACTORY B.E.2c TRACTOR BIPLANES ordered under Cont No C.P.107433/16 from Frederick Sage & Co Ltd, numbered 9456 to 9475 and built Peterborough. W/E 5.11.17 put forward to fit 6 of the 16 [surviving?] B.E.2Cs with 90-hp Curtiss and rest with 150-hp Hispano-Suiza. (All ex RFC without engines, fitted 90-hp Curtiss OX-5 unless stated otherwise)**

9456     Deld CSD White City by 3.16; Chingford 22.3.16; Oakley 3.10.16; Chingford by rail 30.11.16; Beyond repair by 21.8.17; Cranwell without engine W/E 9.11.17 (re-fitted 90hp RAF); Became 201/2 TDS Cranwell 1.4.18

9457     Oakley (repair?) by 1.17 - 3.17. No evidence of delivery. Deleted by 1.17?

9458     (Re-engined 75-hp Hawk) Deld CSD White City by 3.16; Chingford by lorry 22.3.16; Oakley 18.8.16 - @30.12.16; Chingford W/E 13.10.17; Hendon W/E 20.10.17 (repair); Cranwell 22.3.18; Became 201/2 TDS Cranwell 1.4.18

9459     (B.E.2e; 90-hp R.A.F.1a) (Ex RFC A1829) Deld CSD by 30.6.16; Grain 11.9.16; Tested 19.10.16; Yarmouth 24.3.17 (now 75-hp Renault); Burgh Castle 4.5.17; Yarmouth 19.9.17; Surveyed 7.12.17; Deleted 10.12.17

9460     (B.E.2e; 90-hp R.A.F.1a) (Ex RFC A1833) Deld CSD by 30.6.16; To Oakley 10.16 (repair); Hendon W/E 13.10.17 (repair); Cranwell 22.3.18 (now 75- hp RR Mk.I); Became 201/2 TDS Cranwell 1.4.18; Hendon by 25.5.18; 201/2 TDS Cranwell 8.6.18

9461     (B.E.2e; 90-hp R.A.F.1a) (Ex RFC A1835) Deld CSD by 30.6.16; Experimental Flt Grain 1.10.16; Tested after erection 20.11.16; Visited Kingsnorth 30.11.16 (bombing trials?); Renamed Gunnery Experimental Grain 5.12.16; Armament Dept Grain by 29.12.17; Surveyed 25.3.18; Deleted 27.3.18 W&T

9462     (90-hp Curtiss OX-2) Deld CSD by 30.6.16; Cranwell for erection 25.2.17; Wrecked BR 21.7.17; Deleted W/E 5.9.17

9463     (90-hp Curtiss OX-2) Deld CSD by 30.6.16; Eastchurch by rail 6.2.17; G (Exptl) Flt Cranwell 28.3.17 (arr 31.3.17); Became 201/2 TDS Cranwell 1.4.18

9464     (90-hp Curtiss OX-2) Deld CSD by 30.6.16; Cranwell 19.1.17; Deleted 19.5.17

9465     (90-hp Curtiss OX-2) Deld CSD by 30.6.16; Sage by 2.17 (repair?); to Design Flt Eastchurch by road 2.2.17; Observers School Flt Eastchurch by 17.6.17; Possibly the aircraft in which TPFO JP Crawford-Wood & Obs Offr KLC Oxley killed 23.10.17 (or could be N5310); Surveyed 26.10.17; Deleted 29.10.17 wrecked

9466     Deld CSD by 30.6.16; Yarmouth 14.3.17; Surveyed 7.12.17; Deleted 10.12.17

9467     (150-hp Hispano-Suiza) Deld CSD by 30.6.16; Allocated Cranwell 7.9.17; Sage by 29.12.17 (repair); Cranwell W/E 1.2.18; Became 201/2 TDS Cranwell 1.4.18

9468     (150-hp Hispano-Suiza) Deld CSD by 30.6.16; Cranwell W/E 1.2.18; Became 201/2 TDS Cranwell 1.4.18; Became G-EAQR

9469     (90-hp Curtiss OX-2) Deld CSD by 30.6.16; Redcar by rail 25.1.17; Accepted 27.2.17; Deleted 25.6.17

9470     (Re-engined 90-hp R.A.F.1a) Deld CSD by 30.6.16; Experimental Flt Grain 14.11.16; Renamed Gunnery Experimental Grain 5.12.16 (still erecting); Became EAD Grain 9.3.17; Armament Dept Grain from 16.2.18; Hendon 11.6.18; Grain 13.6.18; Dover 18.6.18 (for temp SD); Grain 19.6.18; Romney by 8.18; Eastbourne 9.8.18

9471     (Re-engined 90-hp RAF by 10.17) Deld CSD White City by 30.6.16; East Fortune NFS 9.4.17 (night flying); Crashed on TO, badly damaged 14.12.17 (FSL EW Logsdail); still East Fortune 30.3.18

9472     Deld CSD White City by 30.6.16, unpacked by 4.6.17; Cranwell 21.8.17 (arr 22.8.17) - @30.7.18 (90-hp RAF); Crashed and badly damaged, Bourne, Lincs 28.2.18 (pilot unhurt); Became 201/2 TDS Cranwell 1.4.18; Became 57 TDS Cranwell 17.7.18 - @10.18

9473     Deld CSD White City by 30.6.16, unpacked by 4.6.17; Cranwell 21.8.17 (arr 27.8.17) - 11.17; AGS Freiston by 11.17 - 12.17; Cranwell by 3.18 (now 90-hp RAF); Became 202 TDS Cranwell 1.4.18; Sideslipped on turn, caught fire 2.7.18 (PFO WF Twohey killed)

9474     Deld CSD White City by 30.6.16, unpacked by 4.6.17; Cranwell 21.8.17 (arr 27.8.17) (90-hp RAF); Freiston by 11.17; Cranwell, crashed, CW Potter Hanworth 19.3.18 (pilot unhurt); Deleted W/E 29.3.18

9475     Deld CSD White City by 30.6.16, unpacked by 4.6.17; Cranwell 21.8.17 (arr 27.8.17); Crashed, slightly damaged, Market Deeping 19.12.17 (pilot unhurt); Became 201/2 TDS Cranwell 1.4.18 (90-hp RAF)

**20 SHORT BOMBER TRACTOR BIPLANES ordered 26.6.16 under Cont Nos C.P.104037/16 & C.P.115320/16 from Mann Egerton & Co Ltd as their Type C numbered 9476 and Type CA numbered 9477 to 9495, and built Norwich. 9492 to 9495 cancelled 9.16, but reinstated 11.16. All fitted DC by makers. (250-hp RR Mk.IV)**

9476     (Originally long fuselage version). Accepted Cranwell 17.5.16; Deld 3 Wing Manston 19.7.16; Transferred to RFC (Military Wing) at Farnborough 2.11.16 as A5182

9477     Accepted Eastchurch 25.6.16; Deld 3 Wing Manston 3.7.16; Transferred to RFC (Military Wing) at Farnborough 2.11.16 as A5180

9478     Accepted Eastchurch 18.7.16; Deld 3 Wing Manston 20.7.16; Transferred to RFC (Military Wing) at Farnborough 22.10.16 as A5170

9479     Deld Eastchurch Workshops 6.9.16; Transferred to RFC (Military Wing) at Farnborough 30.9.16 as A5489

9480     Accepted Eastchurch 18.7.16; Deld 3 Wing Manston by 23.7.16; To Dunkerque but retd bad weather 12.9.16; Transferred to RFC (Military Wing) 13.11.16 as A5158; Retd RNAS at Manston, deleted 28.4.17

9481     Accepted Eastchurch 18.7.16; Deld 3 Wing Manston 19.7.16; Transferred to RFC 15.11.16 (Military Wing) as A5159; Retd RNAS at Manston, deleted 28.4.17

9482     Accepted Eastchurch 18.7.16; Deld 3 Wing Manston by 16.7.16 (sic); Tested 5.8.16; Transferred to RFC (Military Wing) at Farnborough 4.11.16 as A5179

9483     Accepted Eastchurch 18.7.16; Deld Eastchurch Workshops 6.9.16; Transferred to RFC (Military Wing) at Farnborough 16.10.16 as A5154

9484     Deld Eastchurch Workshops 6.9.16; Transferred to RFC (Military Wing) at Farnborough 17.11.16; as A5153

9485     Deld and accepted 3 Wing Manston 14.9.16; Transferred to RFC (Military Wing) at Farnborough 23.10.16 as A5173

9486     Deld Eastchurch Workshops (via Hendon) 18.9.16; Deleted 4.5.17; Presume restored to commission; ADD, allocated Eastchurch storage 23.11.17

9487     Deld Eastchurch Workshops 21.9.16; Transferred to RFC (Military Wing) at Farnborough 30.9.16 as A5490

9488     Deld Eastchurch Workshops 27.9.16; Transferred to RFC (Military Wing) at Farnborough 11.10.16 as A5181

9489     Deld Eastchurch Workshops 16.10.16; Grain 2.11.16; Repair 2.17; EAD Grain loan 29.5.17 (overhaul); Hendon 10.8.17 (to remove engine for despatch to CSD); CSD Crystal Palace less engine 13.8.17; Surveyed 30.10.17; Deleted 2.11.17 as GI

9490     Deld Eastchurch Workshops 2.10.16; 7 Sqdn 1.2.17; Crashed into ditch after night raid on Bruges, then hit by 9338 3/4.2.17 (FSL AL Thorne & LM G/L Kent); still 7 Sqdn 22.2.17; ADD by 1.3.17; Deleted 24.3.17

9491     Deld Manston 10.1.17 (Prodger); ADD (ex Hendon, via Dover) 17.3.17; 7 Sqdn 20.4.17; Crashed on roof of 5 Wing CO's office and wrecked 29.4.17 (FSL LA Sands); Deleted ADD 14.5.17

9492     Deld Eastchurch Workshops 7.2.17; 7 Sqdn 26.2.17 - @13.6.17; Deleted ADD 27.6.17 general fatigue

9493     Deld Eastchurch Workshops 9.2.17; 7 Sqdn 1.3.17; Last operational raid to Bruges 5.6.17; Last noted with 7 Sqdn 23.6.17; Deleted ADD 27.6.17 general fatigue

| 9494 | Deld Eastchurch Workshops 13.2.17; Dover 3.17; ADD 17.3.17; 7 Sqdn 9.5.17; Last operational raid to Bruges 5.6.17; ADD 23.6.17; Deleted 27.6.17 general fatigue |
| 9495 | Deld Eastchurch Workshops 20.3.17; Cranwell for instructional purposes 31.5.17; Surveyed 21.11.17; Deleted 5.12.17 DBR; |

**2 SOPWITH PUP TRACTOR BIPLANE PROTOTYPES (became ADMIRALTY 9901 TYPE) ordered under Cont No C.P.109545/16, numbered 9496 and 9497 and built Kingston-on-Thames. (80-hp Clerget)**

| 9496 | Accepted Brooklands 10.7.16; Deld Chingford 9.7.16 (sic); Dover 19.7.16; ADD 20.7.16; C Sqdn 1 Wing 20.7.16; Villacoublay 17.8.16; 3 Wing Luxeuil by 25.8.16; Surveyed 6.4.17 |
| 9497 | FF 5.10.16; Deld Grain 27.10.16; PVRS, tested for Admiralty trials, slightly damaged 31.10.16 (Dukinfield Jones); Put forward 12.16 for modifications by Beardmore; Experimental arrester gear and airscrew guard 22.12.16; Tested after erection 24.12.16 (S/Cdr HM Cave-Brown-Cave); Tested on dummy deck at Grain; Flown off deck 10.1.17 (S/Cdr HM Cave-Brown-Cave); Put forward 1.17 for Sopwith to dismantle and pack for Beardmore; Marked "N9497" at PVRS 2.17; Renamed ECD Grain 26.2.17; 3 deck landings 28.2.17 (F/L CT Freeman); 2 landings on experimental deck 5.3.17 (F/L CT Freeman); 2 deck landings 15.3.17 (S/Cdr HR Busteed then F/L CT Freeman); 2 deck landings 16.3.17 (F/L CT Freeman); 2 deck landings 18.3.17 (F/L EH Dunning then F/L CT Freeman); Deck landings 21.4.17, 1.5.17 & 26.5.17 (all F/L CT Freeman); AGP 13.6.17 (F/L CT Freeman); Steel tipped skids, horns on u/c, tail hook 6.17; Deck landing rail trials 20.7.17; Deck landing trials with skids in toughs 7.9.17; Skid test on deck 6.12.17; EAD Grain by 2.18 (80-hp Le Rhône); Skid test on deck 14.3.18; Stalled on dummy deck 16.3.18; Deck landing skids by 3.18; Still EAD Grain 6.18 |

**2 ROBEY-PETERS Gbs GUN-CARRIER TRACTOR BIPLANES ordered 31.5.16 from Robey & Co Ltd, numbered 9498 and 9499 and built Lincoln (250-hp RR)**

| 9498 | Fitted with Davis gun; Inspected 13.9.16, expected to be ready 20.9.16; Crashed on maiden flight, Bracebridge Heath 5.17 (Capt Hammond); Deleted 23.6.17 |
| 9499 | Not completed |

**1 BRISTOL SCOUT (TYPE D?) TRACTOR BIPLANE numbered 9500 to be built at Filton to replace 1 for Australian Govt (presume 8976)**

| 9500 | Cancelled 7.16 |

**100 CURTISS CANADA MODEL C TRACTOR BIPLANES ordered 5.16 under Cont No C.P.106396/16 from Curtiss, Toronto & numbered 9501 to 9600. (Two 160-hp Curtiss VX)**

9501 to 9600 cancelled

**10 F.B.A. TYPE A PUSHER BIPLANE FLYING BOATS purchase authorised 1.11.16, numbered 9601 to 9610 and built Argenteuil. (100-hp Gnome Monosoupape)**

| 9601 | Deld Dover 19.5.16; Fighting patrol, EF, FL in water 27.5.16 (FSL PS Fisher & AM Norris); HACP 9.7.16 (FSL MR Buckland & LM Robinson); AZP 3.8.16 (F/L GG Hodge & PO Hanna); Deleted 29.10.16 |
| 9602 | Deld Calshot for assembly 9.6.16; Deleted 27.4.17 ["N9602" tested at ADD by 4 Wing pilot 1.8.16 or "9602" on 11.8.16] |
| 9603 | Deld Calshot for assembly 9.6.16; Deleted 9.4.17 |
| 9604 | Deld Windermere for erection 3.7.16; Damaged 19.8.16; Deleted 20.8.16 |
| 9605 | Deld Windermere for erection 3.7.16; COL, CW 29.8.16 (FSL LE Lander injured); Deleted 19.9.16 |
| 9606 | Deld Windermere 29.8.16; Deleted 29.11.16 |
| 9607 | Hull deld Norman Thompson 8.16; Calshot and accepted 15.12.16; Deleted W/E 14.9.17 |
| 9608 | Deld CSD White City 22.5.16; Hull to Norman Thompson 8.16; Rebuild by Norman Thompson 1.17; Possibly the FBA tested by an Admiralty pilot 16.1.17; Deld Calshot 16.3.17; Wings damaged 9.6.17; Deleted W/E 14.9.17 |
| 9609 | Deld CSD White City 6.16; Calshot by lighter 5.9.16; Deleted W/E 14.9.17 |
| 9610 | Deld CSD White City 6.16; Calshot by lighter 5.9.16; Deleted 24.10.16 |

**1 SPAD S.7C.1 TRACTOR BIPLANE SCOUTS built Juvisy and purchased in as pattern aircraft for Mann Egerton production, numbered 9611. (140-hp Hispano)**

| 9611 | Renumbered ex N3399 at ADD 29.11.16; Tested at ADD 6.12.16; Design Flt Eastchurch 24.12.16 (type trials; Tested for 4 Wing by F/L ADW Allen 25.12.16; [Flown direct to Aylsham Road aerodrome]; Mann Egerton Norwich 9.1.17 - 3.17; Transferred to RFC (Military Wing) as B388 |

**24 F.B.A. TYPE B PUSHER BIPLANE FLYING BOATS purchased in France, numbered 9612 to 9635, built Argenteuil & deld from Paris. (100-hp Gnome Monosoupape)**

| 9612 | Deld ex Paris by rail to Killingholme W/E 17.5.17; for deletion by 15.2.18 |
| 9613 | Deld ex Paris by rail to Killingholme W/E 17.5.17; for deletion by 15.2.18 |
| 9614 | Deld ex Paris by rail to Killingholme 17.5.17 (Killingholme Seaplane School by 10.17); 209 TDS Lee-on-Solent W/E 23.6.18; Deleted W/E 25.7.18 |
| 9615 | Deld Killingholme store 10.5.17; Transferred to RFC School Loch Doon by rail 24.7.17, becoming B3984 (survived to 10.18) |
| 9616 | Deld ex Paris by rail to Killingholme store 17.5.17; Hornsea 28.9.17; Killingholme 18.10.17 (base maintenance); Hornsea test 4.12.17; Deleted W/E 20.3.18 |
| 9617 | Deld ex Paris by rail to Killingholme store 17.5.17; at Hornsea by 4.12.17; Killingholme Seaplane School W/E 19.1.18; 209 TDS Lee-on- Solent W/E 13.6.18; Deleted W/E 25.7.18 |
| 9618 | Deld ex Paris by rail to Killingholme store 31.5.17; Left by road for shipment to Malta 17.7.17; Calafrana by 6.10.17; Dismantled for CSD White City by 26.12.17; Retd UK W/E 18.1.18; Killingholme by 30.3.18 - @27.4.18; Killingholme Reserve by 25.5.18; 209 TDS Lee-on-Solent W/E 13.6.18; For deletion by 25.7.18 |
| 9619 | Deld ex Paris by rail to Killingholme store 21.5.17; Left by road for shipment to Malta 17.7.17; Calafrana by 6.10.17; Dismantled for CSD White City by 26.12.17; Retd UK W/E 18.1.18; Killingholme Reserve by 25.5.18; 209 TDS Lee-on-Solent W/E 13.6.18; Deleted W/E 17.10.18 |
| 9620 | Deld ex Paris by rail to Killingholme store 31.5.17; Left by road for shipment to Malta 17.7.17; Calafrana by 6.10.17; Dismantled for CSD White City by 26.12.17; Retd UK W/E 18.1.18; Killingholme Reserve by 25.5.18; 209 TDS Lee-on-Solent W/E 13.6.18; Deleted W/E 25.7.18 |
| 9621 | Deld ex Paris by rail to Killingholme store 30.5.17; To Camper & Nicholson by rail, 11.7.17 (arr 13.9.17); Gosport Aviation Co (for copy); Surveyed 27.3.18; Deleted 27.3.18 W&T |
| 9622 | Deld ex Paris by rail to Killingholme store 30.5.17; Transferred to RFC School Loch Doon by rail 24.7.17 becoming B3985 |
| 9623 | Deld ex Paris to Killingholme store for erection 2.6.17 - LM 25.7.17; Transferred to RFC (Military Wing) as B3986 |
| 9624 | Deld Lee-on-Solent by 11.17; Deleted W/E 21.2.18 |
| 9625 | Deld B Flt Lee-on-Solent for erection by 29.12.17; Became 209 TDS Lee- on-Solent 1.4.18; Deleted W/E 11.7.18 |
| 9626 | Deld Lee-on-Solent by 29.12.17; Killingholme Seaplane School W/E 17.1.18; 209 TDS Lee-on-Solent W/E 13.6.18; Deleted W/E 12.9.18 |
| 9627 | (c/n 827) Deld Killingholme W/E 7.12.17; Lee-on-Solent for erection by 29.12.17; Became 209 TDS 13.6.18; Deleted W/E 12.9.18 |

9628    Deld Le Havre to Calshot for erection W/E 30.11.17; Killingholme Seaplane School 14.12.17; 209 TDS Lee-on-Solent W/E 5.6.18; Deleted W/E 8.8.18

9629    Deld Paris to Calshot W/E 28.12.17 - @27.4.18; 209 TDS Lee-on-Solent by 25.5.18; Calshot School 27.6.18; Deleted W/E 25.7.18

9630    Deld Havre to Calshot for erection W/E 30.11.17; B Flt Lee-on-Solent W/E 8.3.18; Became 209 TDS Lee-on-Solent 1.4.18; Deleted W/E 25.7.18

9631    Deld Lee-on-Solent by 12.17; Killingholme Seaplane School 13.12.17; Deleted W/E 27.6.18

9632    Deld Havre to Calshot for erection W/E 30.11.17; Killingholme Seaplane School by rail W/E 21.12.17; 209 TDS Lee-on-Solent W/E 13.6.18; Deleted W/E 11.7.18

9633    Deld Havre to Calshot for erection W/E 30.11.17; 209 TDS Lee-on-Solent W/E 2.6.18; Deleted W/E 11.7.18

9634    Deld Lee-on-Solent by 12.17; Killingholme W/E 20.12.17; Surveyed 8.4.18; Deleted 15.4.18

9635    Deld Lee-on-Solent W/E 7.12.17; Killingholme W/E 20.12.17; Killingholme Seaplane School by @27.4.18; 209 TDS Lee-on-Solent by W/E 13.6.18; Deleted W/E 12.9.18

**15 serials allocated for purchases in France, but not taken up**

9636 to 9650 not taken up

**100 SOPWITH 1½ STRUTTER TRACTOR BIPLANES (ADMIRALTY 9400S TYPE TWO-SEAT FIGHTERS and 9700 TYPE SINGLE-SEAT BOMBERS) ordered 4.16 under Cont No C.P.104237/16, numbered 9651 to 9750 and built Kingston-on-Thames. Test flown Brooklands by Mkrs, then deld from Brooklands. (110-hp Clerget 9Z standard, but some fitted 130-hp Clerget 9B)**

9651    (Type 9700). Deld Dover 19.6.16; ADD 1.8.16; 8 Flt B Sqdn 5 Wing 6.8.16; 5 Flt A Sqdn 5 Wing by 21.9.16; Paris 22.9.16; 3 Wing Luxeuil (coded '23') [or '33'] by 29.9.16; 3 Flt 3 Wing Ochey by 24.11.16; Transferred to French Govt for AMF 20.4.17

9652    (Type 9700). Accepted Brooklands 21.6.16; Deld 3 Wing Manston 23.6.16; ADD 1.7.16; Loaned AMF 8.16; Retd 3 Wing 10.9.16; HQ Flt 3 Wing 8.12.16; ADD by 26.4.17; Dover 28.5.17; Badly damaged 31.8.17; Manston 20.11.17; Deleted W/E 16.3.18

9653    (Type 9400S). Transferred to RFC less engine; 70 Sqdn Boisdinghem, shot down over Arras 19.7.16 (Lt HR Hele-Shaw & 2/Lt RC Oakes)

9654    (Type 9400L) (130-hp Clerget). Presentation a/c named 'Rio de Janeiro Britons No.1' 4.5.16; Accepted Brooklands 16.6.16; Repaired W/E 30.6.16; Deld Detling 5.7.16 (transit); 3 Wing Manston 6.7.16; To Paris 28.7.16; Put forward W/E 18.8.16 for repair by Sopwith; 3 Wing Luxeuil by 25.8.16; Claimed 2-str biplane OOC Freiburg 15.00-15.30, German observer killed or wounded, then FL St.Argent, 25km S of Luxeuil 12.10.16 (F/Cdr RH Jones & S/L CN Downes awarded Croix de Guerre - but Frankfurter Zeitung claimed there were no German losses); ADD but crashed in transit 7.5.17; Deleted 14.5.17

9655    (Type 9700). Accepted Brooklands 23.6.16; Deld 3 Wing Manston 26.6.16; Le Bourget (via Dunkerque) 1.7.16; 3 Wing Luxeuil (coded '2') 2.8.16; Taxied into tail of F/Cdr RH Jones' a/c and severely damaged its tail 15.9.16 (FSL ST Edwards); 1 Flt 3 Wing Ochey 10.11.16; Became A Flt 1 Sqdn 3 Wing 8.12.16; Transferred to French Govt for AMF 20.4.17

9656    (Type 9400S). Transferred to RFC (Military Wing) less engine

9657    (Type 9700). Accepted Brooklands 26.6.16; Deld 3 Wing Manston 27.6.16; ADD 1.7.16; 3 Wing Luxeuil (coded '3') by 11.8.16; 1 Flt 3 Wing Ochey 10.11.16; Became A Flt 1 Sqdn 3 Wing 8.12.16; Transferred to French Govt for AMF 20.4.17

9658    (Type 9400L). Deld 3 Wing Manston 28.6.16; ADD 29.6.16; C Sqdn 1 Wing St.Pol by 1.7.16; 3 Flt B Sqdn 1 Wing by 13.7.16; ADD by 17.8.16; 8 Flt B Sqdn 5 Wing 11.9.16; Missing from raid on Brussels airship sheds 2.10.16 (FSL AJ Chadwick evaded capture with help of Belgians, retd later to Allied lines); Name 'BUSTER BROWN' below cockpit at one time

9659    (Type 9400S). Transferred to RFC (Military Wing) less engine

9660    (Type 9700). Accepted Brooklands 29.6.16; Deld 3 Wing Manston (coded '1') 6.7.16; ADD 9.7.16; 3 Wing Luxeuil by 21.7.16; Shot down on Oberndorf raid, FL Freiburg aerodrome, by Vzfw Hanstein in Fokker D.II 12.10.16 (FSL CH Butterworth, wounded, PoW)

9661    (Type 9700). Accepted Brooklands 7.16; Deld 3 Wing Manston 7.7.16; ADD 9.7.16; 3 Wing Luxeuil (coded '4') by 11.8.16; Damaged in Oberndorf raid 12.10.16; Luxeuil for repair 17.1.17; 3 Wing Luxeuil (coded '4') .17; Transferred to French Govt for AMF 20.4.17

9662    (Type 9400S). Transferred to RFC (Military Wing) less engine

9663    (Type 9400L). Deld 3 Wing Manston 29.6.16; Dunkerque 29.6.16; 5 Flt A Sqdn 5 Wing by 9.7.16 - @12.11.16; ADD by 16.11.16; AP Dover W/E 13.10.17; Deleted W/E 2.2.18

9664    (Type 9700). Accepted Brooklands 11.7.16; Deld 3 Wing Manston 14.7.16; Paris 28.7.16; 3 Wing Luxeuil (coded '11') by 25.8.16; 2 Flt 3 Wing Ochey 10.11.16; Became B Flt 1 Sqdn 3 Wing 8.12.16; Transferred to French Govt for AMF 20.4.17

9665    (Type 9400S). Transferred to RFC (Military Wing) less engine

9666    (Type 9700). Accepted Brooklands 13.7.16; Deld 3 Wing Manston 15.7.16; ADD 19.7.16; 3 Wing Luxeuil by 11.8.16; 1 Flt 3 Wing Ochey 17.11.16; Became A Flt 1 Sqdn 3 Wing 8.12.16; Transferred to French Govt for AMF 20.4.17

9667    (Type 9400S; 9400L per list). Presentation a/c 'Britons in Tientsin No.2' 4.5.16. Accepted Brooklands 3.7.16; Deld 3 Wing Manston 6.7.16; ADD 9.7.16; 3 Wing Luxeuil (coded '6') by 11.8.16; 3 Flt 3 Wing Ochey 10.11.16; Became A Flt 2 Sqdn 3 Wing 8.12.16; Shot down by AA in reprisal raid on Freiburg 14.4.17 (Lt GRS Fleming PoW, DoW 17.4.17 & AM1 G/L AG Lockyer killed)

9668    (Type 9400S). Transferred to RFC (Military Wing) less engine as A882

9669    (Type 9700). Accepted Brooklands 14.7.16; Deld 3 Wing Manston 18.7.16; ADD 19.7.16; 3 Wing Luxeuil (coded '7') by 30.7.16; 2 Flt 3 Wing Ochey 10.11.16; Became B Flt 1 Sqdn 3 Wing 8.12.16; Transferred to French Govt for AMF 19.4.17

9670    (Type 9700). (130-hp) Accepted Brooklands 15.7.16; Deld 3 Wing Manston but COL 21.7.16; Damaged 26.7.16; Oakley repair 26.7.16; 3 Wing Manston (coded '18') 15.9.16; 3 Wing Luxeuil 21.9.16; 3 Flt 3 Wing Ochey 10.11.16; Became A Flt 2 Sqdn 3 Wing 8.12.16 - LM 13.4.17; Put forward for Westlands to repair engine 1.17; to ADD 4.17; AP Dover by 11.10.17; Manston 29.12.17; Dover 31.12.17 - @23.2.18; Transport Flt Dover by 3.18; Became 491 Flt/Transport Flt Dover by 25.5.18; Became 491 Flt 233 Sqdn 31.8.18; SOC 22.7.19

9671    (Type 9400S). Transferred to RFC (Military Wing) less engine

9672    (Type 9400L). Deld Dover 18.7.16; ADD 20.7.16; A Flt 5 Wing by 7.12.16; 5 Sqdn 31.12.16; ADD 13.8.17; Dover W/E 6.9.17; Hendon by 10.17; Fitted 130-hp Clerget by 29.12.17; SARD Farnborough (via AAP Hendon) W/E 23.2.18; retd AAP Hendon 4.18; No.1 Comm Sqdn Hendon 23.7.18; Grain 10.8.18 (visit) [probably a Hendon runabout]

9673    (Type 9700). Accepted Brooklands 17.7.16; Deld 3 Wing Manston 20.7.16 [Type 9400L]; Grain by 23.7.16 (Anilite bomb dropping trials); 3 Wing Manston 26.9.16; 3 Wing Luxeuil 16.10.16; Loaned French Govt for AMF 7.11.16; Retd 3 Wing Luxeuil 23.1.17; Transferred to French Govt for AMF 20.4.17

9674    (Type 9400S). Transferred to RFC (Military Wing) less engine

9675    (Type 9400S). Transferred to RFC (Military Wing) as A888; To 70 Sqdn

9676    (Type 9400S). Transferred to RFC (Military Wing) as A889; To 70 Sqdn Fienvillers

9677    (Type 9400S). Transferred to RFC (Military Wing) less engine; To 70 Sqdn; Shot down nr Bancourt by Oblt Kimaeir 16.11.16 (Sgt Evans & 2/Lt R Struben)

9678    (Type 9400S). Transferred to RFC (Military Wing) as

**A890**

**9679** (Type 9400S). Transferred to RFC (Military Wing) as A896. To 70 Sqdn

**9680** (Type 9400S). Transferred to RFC (Military Wing) less engine. To 70 Sqdn Fienvillers

**9681** (Type 9400S). Transferred to RFC (Military Wing) as A891. To 70 Sqdn Fienvillers

**9682** (Type 9400S). Transferred to RFC (Military Wing) as A2432

**9683** (Type 9400S). Transferred to RFC (Military Wing) less engine. To 70 Sqdn Fienvillers; Shot down 29.4.17

**9684** (Type 9400S). Transferred to RFC (Military Wing) as A2983; Crashed 12.8.16 (2/Lt Dremon & 2/Lt Preston)

**9685** (Type 9400S). Transferred to RFC (Military Wing) as A897

**9686** (Type 9400S). Transferred to RFC (Military Wing) less engine

**9687** (Type 9400S). Transferred to RFC (Military Wing) as A2988

**9688** (Type 9400S). Transferred to RFC (Military Wing) as A2985

**9689** (Type 9400S). Transferred to RFC (Military Wing) less engine

**9690** (Type 9400S). Transferred to RFC (Military Wing) as A2986

**9691** (Type 9400S). Transferred to RFC (Military Wing) as A2984

**9692** (Type 9400S). Transferred to RFC (Military Wing) as A2989 less engine

**9693** (Type 9400S). Transferred to RFC (Military Wing) as A2987

**9694** (Type 9400S). Transferred to RFC (Military Wing) as A2431; To 43 Sqdn; Shot down (as 9694?) by Ltn Shaefer 4.3.17 (2/Lt P Woods & 2/Lt A Fenton)

**9695** (Type 9400S). Transferred to RFC (Military Wing) less engine as A1903

**9696** (Type 9400S). Transferred to RFC (Military Wing) less engine as A1904

**9697** (Type 9400S). Transferred to RFC (Military Wing) less engine as A1907

**9698** (Type 9400S). Transferred to RFC (Military Wing) less engine

**9699** (Type 9400S). Transferred to RFC (Military Wing) less engine

**9700** (Type 9700). Accepted Brooklands 11.8.16; Deld Design Flt Grain 21.8.16; War Flt Eastchurch 24.8.16; 3 Wing Manston 25.8.16; Design Flt Eastchurch 28.8.16; Westland by rail for examination 20.9.16; 3 Wing Luxeuil (coded '30') by 27.10.16; B Flt 2 Sqdn 3 Wing 15.12.16; Transferred to French Govt for AMF 19.4.17; Deleted 9.11.17

**9701** (Type 9400S). Transferred to RFC (Military Wing) less engine

**9702** (Type 9400S). Transferred to RFC (Military Wing) less engine as A1911

**9703** (Type 9400S). Transferred to RFC (Military Wing) less engine as A1908

**9704** (Type 9400S). Transferred to RFC (Military Wing) less engine

**9705** (Type 9400S). Transferred to RFC (Military Wing) less engine as A1909; To 70 Sqdn; Shot down (as 9705?) 26.9.16 (2/Lt FStJN Echlin killed & AM Grundy)

**9706** (Type 9700) (130-hp Clerget). Accepted Brooklands 30.11.16; Recd 3 Wing Luxeuil (coded '2') 16.12.16; 3 Wing Ochey 24.12.16; Transferred to French Govt 20.4.17 and later captured by Germans

**9707** (Type 9400S). Transferred to RFC (Military Wing) less engine as A1910

**9708** (Type 9400L). Deld Design Flt Eastchurch 23.8.16; 3 Wing Manston 22.9.16; France 24.9.16; 3 Wing Luxeuil (coded '20') by 29.9.16; 3 Flt 3 Wing Ochey 10.11.16; Became A Flt 2 Sqdn 3 Wing 8.12.16; FL advanced aerodrome Malzeville returning from Burbach raid, u/c smashed, engine damaged in combat 22.3.17 (FSL NM MacGregor & AM1 Allen); For ADD 13.4.17; Surveyed 4.17

**9709** (Type 9700). Accepted Brooklands 16.11.16; Deld 3 Wing Luxeuil 27.11.16; CW by 2.3.17; Surveyed 7.3.17

**9710** (Type 9400S). Transferred to RFC (Military Wing) as A1913

**9711** (Type 9700). Accepted Brooklands 16.11.16; Deld 3 Wing Luxeuil (coded '5') 30.11.16; Surveyed 20.3.17; Deleted 4.17

**9712** (Type 9400L). Fitted 140-hp Smith engine

**9713** (Type 9400S). Transferred to RFC (Military Wing) less engine as A1912

**9714** (Type 9700). Accepted Brooklands 20.11.16; Deld 3 Wing Luxeuil 5.12.16; Transferred to French Govt for AMF 20.4.17

**9715** (Type 9700). Deld CSD White City by 30.11.16; Shipped to Aegean; Arr Otranto by 17.2.17

**9716** (Type 9400S). Transferred to RFC (Military Wing) less engine as A1914

**9717** (Type 9400L). Accepted Brooklands 22.8.16; Deld 3 Wing Manston (via Eastbourne) but COL Manston 13.9.16; Retd Sopwith 27.9.16 (replace damaged engine); Oakley repair by 30.11.16; Deleted 10.8.17 (intended for Mudros)

**9718** (Type 9700). CSD White City by 31.12.16; Shipped to 2 Wing Aegean 1.17; Arr Otranto by 17.2.17; Tested Mitylene 26.3.17; Thasos by 1.12.17; Mudros by 1.1.18; Surveyed 19.2.18; Deleted 27.3.18 DBR

**9719** (Type 9400S). Transferred to RFC (Military Wing) as A1915

**9720** (Type 9700). Accepted Brooklands 30.11.16; Deld 3 Wing Luxeuil 15.12.16; Transferred to French Govt for AMF 20.4.17

**9721** (Type 9400S). Allocated CSD 8.6.17 (sic); Transferred to RFC (Military Wing) less engine as A1916

**9722** (Type 9400L). Presentation a/c 'Sao Paulo Britons No.1' 4.5.16; Accepted Brooklands 31.8.16; Deld 3 Wing Manston 14.9.16; 3 Wing Luxeuil (coded '19') 21.9.16; 1 Flt 3 Wing Ochey 10.11.16; HA crashed 14.00-15.15 23.11.16 (F/Cdr C Draper & S/L AT Barker); Became A Flt 1 Sqdn 3 Wing 8.12.16; Dunkerque 9.3.17; Paris 12.3.17 (ex Issy-les-Moulineaux); 2 Sqdn 17.3.17; ADD 7.4.17; Dover 1.5.17; Damaged 7.5.17; Rosyth by rail 18.8.17; HMS *Campania* 11.9.17 - 10.18 (exp purposes); Turnhouse by 11.18; Deleted 18.11.18

**9723** (Type 9700). Accepted Brooklands W/E 7.12.16; Deld 3 Wing Luxeuil by 22.12.16 - @13.4.17; NTO Marseilles by 30.4.17 for 2 Wing Mudros

**9724** (Type 9700). Accepted Brooklands W/E 7.12.16; Deld 3 Wing Luxeuil 26.12.16 - @13.4.17; To ADD by 26.4.17; Dover 28.5.17; Badly damaged 12.8.17; War School Manston W/E 26.10.17; Cranwell 26.3.18; Beverley en route East Fortune 28.3.18

**9725** (Type 9400S). Transferred to RFC (Military Wing) less engine as A1917

**9726** (Type 9400L). Accepted Brooklands 18.8.16; Deld 3 Wing Manston 20.8.16; To France 28.8.16 and to 3 Wing Luxeuil; Flown on Oberndorf Raid 12.10.16 (FSL RF Redpath & AM G/L LA Dell); Deleted 23.10.16 [BUT LM 22.9.16, wrecked]

**9727** (Type 9700). Shipped to Aegean; Arr Otranto by 17.2.17; F Sqdn 2 Wing by 29.4.17 - LM 12.5.17; Deleted 1917

**9728** (Type 9400S). Transferred to RFC (Military Wing) as A1918

**9729** (Type 9700). Deld 3 Wing Manston 28.7.16; Dunkerque 30.7.16; Transferred to French Govt for AMF

**9730** (Type 9400L) (130-hp Clerget). Accepted Brooklands 28.8.16; Deld 3 Wing Manston 31.8.16; 3 Wing Luxeuil (coded '29') 16.10.16; 2 Flt 3 Wing Ochey 10.11.16; Became B Flt 1 Sqdn 3 Wing 8.12.16; ADD 26.4.17; Destroyed by fire on night of 1.10.17; Surveyed 17.10.17; Deleted 23.10.17 burnt

**9731** (Type 9400S). Transferred to RFC (Military Wing) less engine as A1919

**9732** (Type 9700). Accepted Brooklands 24.7.16; Deld 3 Wing Manston 26.7.16; left 22.8.16 [was to go to France 8.16 with 9407]; no further information

**9733** (Type 9700). Deld Chingford for type trials 1.8.16; Retd Brooklands to fit 130-hp Clerget W/E 8.9.16; Dismantled for 3 Wing 15.9.16; 3 Wing Manston by rail 21.9.16; To France 24.9.16 and to 3 Wing Luxeuil (coded '21') by 29.9.16; 3 Flt 3 Wing Ochey 10.11.16; Became A Flt 2 Sqdn 3 Wing 8.12.16; Crashed into N5124 landing from Brebach raid 25.2.17 (FSL H Edwards); LM 16.3.17; Surveyed 20.3.17; Deleted 4.17

*Jenner-Parson standing beside his 3 Wing Sopwith 1½ Strutter 9724. (via Frank Cheesman)*

*Sopwith 1½ Strutter 9742 '10' of 3 Wing, probably McNeil's aircraft, at Ochey early in 1917. (via Frank Cheesman)*

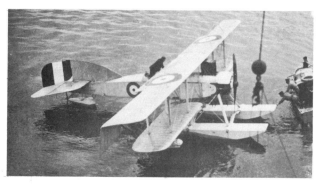

*Short 166 Type 9760, piloted by FSL Fletcher, about to be hoisted aboard HMS Vindex. (IWM Q.73685)*

*Porte F.B.2 Baby Flying Boat 9810. (R.C.Sturtivant collection)*

*Robey-Peters Gun-carrier 9498. (RAE Farnborough)*

| 9734 | (Type 9400S). Transferred to RFC (Military Wing) less engine |
| 9735 | (Type 9400L). Accepted Brooklands 24.7.16; Deld 3 Wing Manston 13.9.16; 3 Wing Luxeuil (coded '28') 21.9.16; 3 Flt 3 Wing Ochey 10.11.16; Became A Flt 2 Sqdn 3 Wing 8.12.16 - @13.4.17; Late starting for Brebach raid, unable to catch patrol, so fighting patrol instead, engaged 4 HA at Chateau Salires, 1 apparently OOC, then damaged in combat, FL Siechamps 25.2.17 (F/L E Potter & AM G/L LA Dell); ADD by 26.4.17; 5 Sqdn by 3.5.17; ADD 25.7.17; Deleted 28.7.17 damage not worth repair |
| 9736 | (Type 9700). Accepted Brooklands 31.7.16; Deld 3 Wing Manston 4.8.16; To France 28.8.16 and to 3 Wing Luxeuil; 2 Flt 3 Wing Ochey 10.11.16 (at local depot); Transferred to French Govt for AMF 20.4.17 |
| 9737 | (Type 9400S). Transferred to RFC (Military Wing) less engine as A1921 |
| 9738 | (Type 9700). Accepted Brooklands 31.7.16; Deld 3 Wing Manston 5.8.16; To France 5.8.16 and to 3 Wing Luxeuil (coded '8'); 1 Flt 3 Wing Ochey 10.11.16; Became 1 Flt A Sqdn 3 Wing 8.12.16; Transferred to French Govt for AMF 19.4.17 |
| 9739 | (Type 9400L). (130-hp Clerget) Presentation Aircraft 4.5.16, named 'Britons in Egypt No.2'; Accepted Brooklands 23.8.16; Deld 3 Wing Manston 28.8.16; Villacoublay 17.9.16; 3 Wing Luxeuil (coded '17') 22.9.16; Participated Dillingen raid, HACP after bombers had retd, HA OOC wings fell off NE of De Lune 24.11.16 (F/L CB Dalison & G/L Fraser); FTR from Brebach raid, shot down Saargemünd by Off St.Vohnacht [Bohlnecht?] of Jasta 24 25.2.17 (FSL LE Smith PoW DoI & G/L AAM1 RS Portsmouth Croix de Guerre killed) [probably the a/c reputed crashed Auesmacher, 17m SSE of Saarbrücken] |
| 9740 | (Type 9400S). Transferred to RFC (Military Wing) less engine as A1922 |
| 9741 | (Type 9700). Accepted Brooklands 1.8.16; Deld France (via 3 Wing Manston) 5.8.16; 3 Wing Luxeuil by 11.8.16 - @13.4.17; After Oberndorf raid, FL in marshy ground, Corbenay, 8km N of Luxeuil 17.40 12.10.16 (FSL GG MacLennan); ADD by 26.4.17; Dover 28.5.17; Cranwell 3.6.17; Became 201/2 TDS Cranwell 1.4.18; Grand Fleet SofAF&G Leuchars by 6.19 |
| 9742 | (Type 9700). Accepted Brooklands 3.8.16; Deld Villacoublay (via 3 Wing Manston) 10.8.16 and to 3 Wing Luxeuil (coded '10'); 3 Flt 3 Wing Ochey 10.11.16; Became A Flt 2 Sqdn 3 Wing 8.12.16 - @4.3.17; Transferred to French Govt for AMF 20.4.17 |
| 9743 | (Type 9400S). Transferred to RFC (Military Wing) less engine as A1923 |
| 9744 | (Type 9400L). (130-hp Clerget) Presentation a/c 4.5.16, named 'Britons in Italy No.1'. Deld 3 Wing Manston 8.9.16 (defective engine); Paris 21.9.16; 3 Wing Luxeuil (coded '12') 22.9.16; 2 Flt 3 Wing Ochey 10.11.16; Became B Flt 1 Sqdn 8.12.16; ADD 9.3.17; Paris to 2 Sqdn 17.3.17; 1 Wing by 22.11.17 - @6.12.17 (depot aircraft); ADD 23.4.17; 2 Sqdn 23.4.17; Seaplane Defence Sqdn St.Pol 29.11.17; Dover 12.12.17 (now 110-hp Clerget); East Fortune by rail 7.1.18 (convtd Ships Strutter); Deleted W/E 15.3.18 |
| 9745 | (Type 9700). Deld Dover 20.8.16; ADD 22.8.16; 8 Flt B Sqdn 5 Wing 11.9.16; 5 Flt A Sqdn 5 Wing by 21.9.16; Paris 22.9.16; 3 Wing Luxeuil by 29.9.16 - @4.17; Transferred to French Govt for AMF 20.4.17 |
| 9746 | (Type 9400S). Transferred to RFC (Military Wing) less engine as A1924 |
| 9747 | (Type 9700). Deld 3 Wing Manston 5.8.16; To France 10.8.16 |
| 9748 | (Type 9400S). Shipped to Aegean; Arr Otranto by 17.2.17; E Flt 2 Wing Hadzi Junas by 4.17; Halberstadt in vertical dive behind enemy lines NW of Lake Doiran 09.05 4.4.17 (TFSL HL Gaskell & 2/Lt J Watt); Shot down by AA, crashed nr Hirsova 2.5.17 (TFSL HL Gaskell & 2/Lt J Watt both killed) |
| 9749 | (Type 9400S). Transferred to RFC (Military Wing) less engine as A1925 |
| 9750 | (Type 9400S). Shipped to Aegean; Arr Otranto by 17.2.17; E Flt 2 Wing Hadzi Junas from 3.4.17 - @22.5.17LM (presume destroyed in explosion) |

**20 SHORT S.90 (ADMIRALTY 166 TYPE) TRACTOR BIPLANE SEAPLANES ordered 28.10.15 under Cont No C.P.105566/16 from Westland Aircraft Works (Petters Ltd), numbered 9751 to 9770, to be built less torpedo gear at Yeovil to A.D. Spec N.2B. (200-hp Salmson/Canton Unné 2.M.7)**

| 9751 | Deld Calshot 10.6.16; Dover 7.7.16; Felixstowe 8.7.16; HMS *Vindex* 10.7.16; Felixstowe 11.8.16; HMS *Vindex* 26.6.17; Felixstowe 1.8.17; Deleted 21.9.17 |
| 9752 | Fitted large radiator 6.16; Calshot to Tilbury for HMS *Ark Royal* 7.16; Shipped to Mudros 2.16; Suda Bay by 1.6.17; Surveyed Mudros 24.9.17; Deleted 16.10.17 DBR |
| 9753 | Deld Calshot and tested 16.6.16; Dover 18.6.16; Felixstowe 19.6.16; HMS *Vindex* 26.6.16; Felixstowe 11.8.16; HMS *Vindex* 21.8.16; Felixstowe 11.12.16; Fouled pier and damaged while being towed by Felixstowe tug 22.12.16 (FSL JA Sadler & PO Jones); Calshot W/E 12.10.17; Killingholme by 29.12.17; Deleted W/E 5.4.18 |
| 9754 | Shipped from Tilbury to Mudros 7.16; HMS *Ark Royal*, tested after erection 3.9.16; Chai Aghirzi 6.9.16; Retd HMS *Ark Royal* in MFA *Princess Ena* 16.9.16; Tested 25.9.16; Aegean by 1.6.17; A Sqdn 2 Wing Thasos by .17; Convtd to landplane at Thasos; Mudros, Surveyed 24.11.17; Deleted 8.12.17 W&T |
| 9755 | Shipped to Mudros; HMS *Ark Royal*, tested after erection 14.9.16; HMS *Empress* 7.10.16; Mudros 23.11.16; HMS *Ark Royal* by 21.2.17; Thasos 19.5.17; Mudros by 1.6.17; Surveyed 24.9.17; Deleted 16.10.17 DBR |
| 9756 | Deld Felixstowe 12.7.16; HMS *Vindex* 19.7.16; Damaged on TO, salved 19.8.16 (F/Cdr HF Towler & PO Fazey rescued); Felixstowe for repair 21.8.16; Westland by road 2.9.16 (repair); Calshot 13.11.16; Surveyed 28.9.17; Deleted 6.10.17 W&T |
| 9757 | Deld Felixstowe 18.7.16; HMS *Vindex* 19.7.16; Drifted and fouled by crane hook 19.7.16 (F/L LP Openshaw); Damaged hoisting in by cruiser HMS *Carysfort* after Operation "R.C.2" (3½ hrs) with 4x16-lb bombs and 1 Lewis gun, 2 magazines, 1 camera 22.10.16 (F/Cdr HF Towler & CPO A Blackwell); HMS *Vindex* 23.10.16; Deleted 3.11.16 |
| 9758 | Shipped to Aegean; Erected HMS *Ark Royal* by 25.10.16; HMS *Empress* 6.11.16; Hit by gunfire on recce nr Karjam 8.1.17 (FSL GS Abbott wounded); Thasos 19.1.17; EF, FL, sank in tow 6.2.17 (crew unhurt) |
| 9759 | Shipped from Calshot (via Plymouth) to Mudros in SS *Egyptian Prince* 9.16; HMS *Ark Royal* by 29.3.17 - @2.4.17; Suda Bay Seaplane Station 2 Wing by 5.17; CW 5.5.17 (pilot slightly injured) |
| 9760 | Deld HMS *Vindex* (via Felixstowe) 11.8.16; Operation "R.C.2", chased by Zeppelin and a Taube, then damaged hoisting in by HMS *Conquest* after operation (3 hrs 40 min) with 4x16-lb bombs, 1 Lewis gun, 2 magazines and 1 camera 22.10.16 (F/L FN Halstead & Lt E Childers); Felixstowe 23.10.16; HMS *Vindex* 14.11.16; Felixstowe 9.5.17; HMS *Vindex* 10.5.17; Killingholme (via Yarmouth) W/E 10.10.17; For deletion by 29.3.18 |
| 9761 | Deld HMS *Vindex* (via Felixstowe) 11.8.16; FL Whitstable 19.10.16 (FSL JA Sadler & Mid FH Isaac); HMS *Vindex* 21.10.16; Felixstowe 9.5.17; HMS *Vindex* 10.5.17; Felixstowe 26.6.17; Calshot 6.10.17; Surveyed 18.12.17; Deleted 28.12.17 DBR |
| 9762 | Shipped to Aegean; HMS *Ark Royal* by 17.2.17; transferred to *Holmesbank* 26.2.17; Suda Bay by 1.6.17 - 5.18; A Sqdn 2 Wing Thasos to 6.18; Disposed by 6.18; Deleted Mudros 9.18 |
| 9763 | Fitted larger radiators 8.16; Shipped from Calshot to Mudros in SS *Kasmir* 10.16; Erected HMS *Ark Royal* and flown 14.11.16; HMS *Empress* 28.12.16; A Sqdn 2 Wing Thasos 19.1.17; Mudros for deletion by 1.19 |
| 9764 | Fitted larger radiators 8.16; Shipped from Calshot to Mudros in SS *Kasmir* 10.16; Tested HMS *Ark Royal* 20.12.16; HMS *Empress* 29.12.16; HMS *Ark Royal* 22.1.17; Transferred to *Holmesbank* 26.2.17; A Sqdn 2 Wing Thasos by .17; Suda Bay by 1.6.17 - @6.18 |
| 9765 | Deld Dover for erection 17.10.16; FL and sank between Folkestone and Deal 18.1.17 (FSL LC Pincott & AM2 Fanshawe); Deleted 6.2.17 |

| | |
|---|---|
| 9766 | Deld Dover 16.10.16; Tested 9.11.16; Calshot 25.5.17; Deleted W/E 14.9.17 |
| 9767 | Deld Felixstowe 25.10.16; Tested 6.2.17; Calshot 9.2.17; Portland 16.3.17; Calshot 10.4.17 (repair); Portland 12.4.17; Calshot 2.5.17; Deleted W/E 14.9.17 |
| 9768 | Deld Felixstowe 26.10.16; Tested 27.11.16; Calshot 9.2.17; Portland 14.2.17; Calshot 5.6.17; Surveyed 28.9.17 W&T |
| 9769 | Deld CSD White City by 31.12.16; Calshot by lighter for erection 7.4.17; Portland 30.4.17; Calshot 9.6.17; Deleted W/E 14.9.17 |
| 9770 | Deld CSD White City by 31.12.16; Calshot 20.4.17; Deleted W/E 14.9.17 |

**10 SHORT BOMBER TRACTOR BIPLANES ordered 31.7.16 under Cont Nos C.P.105536/16 & C.P.120200/16 from George Parnall & Co Ltd (Parnall & Sons), numbered 9771 to 9776 and built Bristol. (250-hp RR)**

| | |
|---|---|
| 9771 | (RR Mk.I) Built as short fuselage version but modified before acceptance. Deld Eastchurch (via Chingford) 7.9.16 (Prodger); Eastchurch Workshops 4.11.16; Deleted 4.5.17 |
| 9772 | (RR Mk.I) Deld 3 Wing Manston 24.9.16; Accepted 26.9.16; Transferred to RFC (Military Wing) at Farnborough 22.10.16 as A5171 |
| 9773 | Deld Manston 13.11.16; Tested 14.11.16 (Prodger); Manston storage 23.11.16; Deleted 19.12.16 |
| 9774 | (RR Mk.I) Deld Eastchurch Workshops by rail 26.11.16; Deleted 4.5.17 |
| 9775 | Deld Manston 6.12.16; Accepted Manston 17.12.16 (JL Parker); Deleted 26.7.17 as spares |
| 9776 | Deld Eastchurch Workshops by rail 14.12.16; Accepted 4.1.17 (JL Parker); 7 Sqdn, tested 1.2.17; Last flown operationally 16.2.17; ADD 20.4.17; Deleted 27.6.17 general fatigue |

9777 to 9780 cancelled 9.16

**10 SHORT ADMIRALTY 830 TYPE TRACTOR SEAPLANES ordered 7.16 under Cont No C.P.118670/16, numbered 9781 to 9790 and built Rochester. (140-hp Canton-Unné) [Not true 830 Types, though officially listed under that designation] [Gordon Bruce's researches show correct c/n's to be S.301 to S.310]**

| | |
|---|---|
| 9781 | Deld Grain 4.11.16; Accepted 15.2.17 (Kemp); Dover 25.5.17 (transit); Calshot school 26.5.17 - @28.9.17; Lee-on-Solent, for deletion by 12.10.17; Surveyed 30.10.17; Deleted 6.11.17 W&T |
| 9782 | Deld Grain 11.11.16; Design Flt Grain 14.1.17; Accepted 14.2.17; still Design Flt Grain 16.3.17; Experimental Design Grain by 24.3.17; Redes Test Depot Grain 30.3.17; Calshot 2.5.17; Grain .17; Calshot 12.6.17; Lee-on-Solent 12.10.17; Surveyed 3.11.17; Deleted 8.11.17 W&T |
| 9783 | Deld Grain 14.11.16 (Kemp); Yarmouth 5.4.17; Killingholme 12.6.17 (transit); South Shields 15.6.17; Calshot FS by rail 3.8.17; Surveyed 3.11.17; Deleted 8.11.17 W&T |
| 9784 | Deld Grain 21.11.16; Tested 22.11.16 (Kemp); Accepted 8.2.17; Felixstowe 5.4.17 (transit); Left for Yarmouth but retd damaged 8.4.17; Yarmouth 13.4.17 (transit); Killingholme 16.4.17; South Shields 20.4.17; HSMPs 1.5.17 (FSL KM Smith x 2, later FSL FH Wallers); by 10.8.17 packed for Calshot (not by 16.8.17); Calshot FS by 26.10.17 (not by 29.9.17); Surveyed 3.11.17; Deleted 8.11.17 W&T |
| 9785 | Deld Grain 14.12.16; Accepted 10.2.17; Calshot by rail 16.4.17; Deleted 5.8.17 |
| 9786 | Deld Grain 19.12.16; Packed 8.4.17; Dundee by rail 12.4.17 (arr 17.4.17); Dismantled for transfer 17.8.17; Calshot FS by rail 19.8.17 (arr 14.9.17); Surveyed 3.11.17; Deleted 8.11.17 W&T |
| 9787 | Deld Grain and accepted 20.12.16 (Kemp); Packed 8.4.17; Dundee by rail 12.4.17 (arr 17.4.17); Calshot FS by rail 18.9.17; Deleted W/E 26.10.17 |
| 9788 | Deld Grain 18.1.17 (Kemp); Packed 8.4.17; Dundee by rail 12.4.17 (arr 17.4.17); Calshot FS by rail 4.9.17; For deletion by 26.10.17 |
| 9789 | Deld Grain 11.1.17 (Kemp); Accepted 13.2.17; Calshot 1.10.17; Lee-on- Solent by 12.10.17; Deleted 6.11.17; Surveyed 30.10.17 wrecked |

| | |
|---|---|
| 9790 | Deld Grain 19.2.17 (Kemp); Dover 1.4.17 (transit); Calshot 4.4.17; Deleted 11.7.17 [C/n's for this batch confirmed by photos] |

**9 SERIAL NUMBERS NOT ALLOTTED**

9791 to 9799 not allotted

**21 PORTE F.B.2 BABY TRACTOR/PUSHER BIPLANE FLYING BOATS ordered 16.2.16 under Cont No C.P.104214/16 from May, Harden & May, numbered 9800 to 9820 and assembled Felixstowe. (Three 250-hp Eagle VIII)**

| | |
|---|---|
| 9800 | Launched Felixstowe but not flown due to trouble with Sunbeam motors; FF 20.11.15 but engines running badly; Slight alterations made; Flown satisfactrily 21.11.15 (F/Cdr JC Porte & F/L RJJ Hope-Vere); Tested Felixstowe 8.1.16; Deld RNAS Felixstowe 1.6.16; Accepted Felixstowe 2.11.16; Tested after reconstructed & fitted 310-hp Sunbeams as left hand tractors & 250-hp Rolls-Royce as left hand pusher 4.11.16 (F/Cdr RJJ Hope-Vere) [turned violently to port, so centre engine changed to right hand pusher]; Launched Bristol Scout D 3028 from top wing; Two 320-hp Sunbeam & one 250-hp RR by 10.17; Felixstowe store by 12.17 (less engines); Deleted W/E 11.7.18 |
| 9801 | (Fitted 260-hp Green as centre engine). Erected Felixstowe by 23.5.16; Grain 25.5.16; Deld Felixstowe for erection 27.7.16; Accepted 27.3.17; Killingholme 12.5.17; Queensferry but stayed South Shields with engine trouble, arr Queensferry 12.7.17; Felixstowe 14.7.17; HMS *Engadine* 18.7.17 (engine repairs); Left 23.7.17; Felixstowe to Queenferry 5.8.17 - @13.10.17; Two 320-hp Sunbeam & one 250-hp RR by 10.17; Fitted Eagle III by 29.12.17; Surveyed Killingholme 9.1.18; Deleted 15.1.18 DBR |
| 9802 | Deld Felixstowe for erection 2.8.16; Queensferry 2.7.17; Felixstowe 6.7.17; Accepted 16.7.17; To Queenferry by 13.10.17; Two 320-hp Sunbeam & one 250-hp RR by 10.17; Felixstowe store by 12.17 (less engines); Deleted W/E 11.7.18 |
| 9803 | Deld Felixstowe for erection 13.10.16; Felixstowe store less engines by 12.17; Deleted W/E 11.7.18 |
| 9804 | Airco by 23.9.16; Deld Felixstowe for erection 11.12.16; Felixstowe store less engines by 12.17; Deleted W/E 11.7.18 |
| 9805 | Airco by 23.9.16; Deld Killingholme for erection 18.12.16; Accepted 3.17; South Shields 17.5.18 (en route Houton Bay); To Dundee by FL, starboard wing and tip float damaged 2m E of Newton Station, towed in to Newton Bewith 25.5.18; Stenness/Houton Bay by 25.5.18 (at Berwick); Deleted W/E 25.7.18 |
| 9806 | Airco by 23.9.16; Deld Killingholme for erection 3.2.17; Accepted 3.17 - 5.18; Killingholme store by 13.6.18; Deleted W/E 19.9.18 |
| 9807 | Airco by 23.9.16; Deld Killingholme for erection 3.2.17; Accepted 3.17; Re-engined 345-hp Rolls-Royce; Dundee 5.18 (transit); Houton Bay 20.5.18 (at Berwick); Catfirth W/E 11.7.18; Deleted W/E 31.12.18 |
| 9808 | Deld Killingholme for erection 24.2.17; Accepted 3.17; Felixstowe store by 4.18; Killingholme store W/E 13.6.18; Deleted W/E 19.9.18 |
| 9809 | Airco by 2.2.17; Deld Killingholme 2.3.17; Felixstowe store by 4.18; Killingholme store W/E 13.6.18; Deleted W/E 19.9.18 |
| 9810 | Airco by 2.2.17; Hull deld Felixstowe 17.4.17; Re-engined three 360-hp Rolls-Royce VIII by 10.17; Attacked by 3 HA nr North Hinder LV, 2 engines disabled, FL on sea, towed Felixstowe by trawler 1.10.17 (W/T operator HM Davies wounded); Tested 9.3.18; Killingholme 17.5.18 (transit); Dundee 18.5.18 (en route Houton Bay); Stenness & Houton Bay by 25.5.18 - @7.18; Houton Bay to Lerwick 10.8.18; Stenness & Houton Bay by 31.10.18; For deletion by 31.12.18 [Reported as Type N.3B at Grain 12.18] |
| 9811 | (Fitted 260-hp Green as centre engine). Airco by 2.2.17; Accepted Killingholme 12.3.17; Hull delivered Felixstowe 28.8.17; Deleted 1.18 |
| 9812 | Airco by 2.2.17; Hull only delivered Killingholme ex Airco 17.8.17; NFT |
| 9813 | Hull only delivered Killingholme ex Airco 17.8.17; NFT |

| | |
|---|---|
| 9814 | Hull only delivered Felixstowe 28.8.17 - @29.9.17 |
| 9815 | Hull only delivered Killingholme ex Airco 17.8.17; NFT |
| 9816 | Hull only delivered Killingholme ex Airco 17.8.17; NFT |
| 9817 | Hull only delivered Killingholme 20.8.17; NFT |
| 9818 | Hull only delivered Killingholme 20.8.17; NFT |
| 9819 | Hull only delivered Felixstowe 26.8.17; NFT |
| 9820 | Hull only delivered Felixstowe 26.8.17; NFT |

**10 AVRO 504B TRACTOR BIPLANES ordered under Cont Nos A.S.19203 & C.P.108003/16 from George Parnall & Co Ltd, numbered 9821 to 9803 and built Bristol. (80-hp Gnome A)**

| | |
|---|---|
| 9821 | Deld Cranwell and tested 26.4.16 (Raynham); Deleted 18.6.17 |
| 9822 | Deld Eastchurch and tested 28.4.16 (Raynham); Eastbourne NFS 10.5.16; Ringmer 14.5.16; Ground collision with Avro 504, wings damaged 19.5.16 (FSL TR Hackman & FSL JA Ramsay); Retd Eastbourne; Chingford 2.3.17; Deleted 22.7.17 |
| 9823 | Deld Eastbourne 12.5.16; Accepted 14.5.16; Ringmer 19.5.16; Eastbourne 20.5.16; Ringmer 22.5.16; Retd Eastbourne; Chingford 2.17; Deleted 22.7.17 |
| 9824 | Deld Eastbourne by rail 9.5.16; Accepted 14.5.16; Deleted 28.9.16 |
| 9825 | Deld Chingford by lorry 15.5.16; Slightly damaged due to bump on field 30.5.16; Deleted 23.8.17 |
| 9826 | Deld Chingford 31.5.16 ; Became 207 TDS Chingford 1.4.18 |
| 9827 | Deld Eastchurch FS 9.6.16; Eastchurch Workshops 10.5.17 - 6.17; Eastchurch FS by 26.6.17; Manston FS 20.8.17; Deleted W/E 22.12.17 |
| 9828 | Deld CSD White City 6.16; Packed for Vendôme by 4.6.17; arr Vendôme ex UK 2.7.17; Became 205 TDS Vendôme 1.4.18 |
| 9829 | Deld CSD White City 6.16; Cranwell 9.6.16; Deleted W/E 18.9.17 |
| 9830 | Deld Cranwell and accepted 11.6.16 (Raynham); Crashed 11.7.17; Deleted W/E 5.9.17 |

**10 SHORT BOMBER TRACTOR BIPLANES (LONG FUSELAGE VERSION) ordered 8.16 under Cont Nos C.P.108243/16 & C.P.117978/16 from The Phoenix Dynamo Manufacturing Co Ltd, numbered 9831 to 9840 and built Bradford. (250-hp RR)**

| | |
|---|---|
| 9831 | (225-hp RR) Crashed on maiden flight; Deld Manston for erection 16.11.16; Accepted 22.12.16 (JL Parker); Deleted 26.7.17 as spares |
| 9832 | Deld 3 Wing Manston 14.9.16; Accepted 18.9.16; Transferred to RFC (Military Wing) at Farnborough 23.10.16 as A6300 [acquired for its RR engine, which was needed for a D.H.4, airframe then burnt] |
| 9833 | Deld Eastchurch Workshops (via Manston) 20.9.16; Transferred to RFC (Military Wing) at Farnborough 22.9.16 as A3932 |
| 9834 | (RR Mk.III) (Serialled N9834 in error). Deld Manston 18.10.16; Failed test with 2-blade propeller 15.12.16 (Prodger) (to retest with 4-bladed propeller); Accepted 15.12.16 (JL Parker) |
| 9835 | (RR Mk.III) Deld 3 Wing Manston 11.11.16; Erecting by Mkrs 13.11.16; Allocated Manston storage 23.11.16 |
| 9836 | (RR Mk.IV) Deld 3 Wing Manston 11.11.16; Erecting by Mkrs 13.11.16; Accepted Manston 14.12.16 (JL Parker); Dover 15.3.17; ADD 17.3.17; 7 Sqdn 30.4.17; ADD 23.6.17; Deleted 27.6.17 general fatigue |
| 9837 to 9840 | cancelled 9.16 |

**20 WIGHT "CONVERTED" TRACTOR BIPLANE SEAPLANES ordered under Cont No C.P.108249/16, numbered 9841 to 9860 and built East Cowes. Wights stated unable to reduce tender 7.16. Work temporarily stopped on batch 12.16, none delivered by then. (250-hp Eagle)**

| | |
|---|---|
| 9841 | (Eagle VII later Eagle VIII) Completed 8.16; Crashed on second flight, Gurnard 7.9.16 (R.Larimer & A.Larimer killed); Rebuilt by Mkrs; Deld Portland W/E 19.10.17; Became 416/7 Flts Portland 25.5.18 (241 Sqdn 20.8.18); Dropped 4 bombs on U-boat 5022N 0157W 25.6.18 (Capt R Jarman & Lt GFF Reid); Deleted W/E 3.10.18 |
| 9842 | (250-hp RR) Completed 3.11.16 as landplane; Deld |

| | |
|---|---|
| | Design Flt Eastchurch 20.12.16; FF 23.12.16; Retd Mkrs 27.5.17 to convert to seaplane under Cont No. A.S.7485/17; NFT |
| 9843 | (250-hp Eagle IC) Deld Observers School Flt Eastchurch 13.4.17 as landplane; Retd Mkrs 15.8.17 to convert to seaplane under Cont No. A.S.7485/17; Redelivered at Mkrs 1.9.17; Portland W/E 14.9.17; Cattewater to Calshot W/E 23.11.17 (now Eagle III); Deleted 8.3.18 |
| 9844 | Deld Eastchurch Workshops 17.3.17 as landplane; Retd Mkrs 26.5.17 to convert to seaplane under Cont No. A.S.7485/17; NFT |
| 9845 | (265-hp Sunbeam Maori). Deld Eastchurch Workshops 24.4.17 as landplane; Retd Mkrs 26.5.17 to convert to seaplane under Cont No. A.S.7485/17; Redeld Calshot 29.7.17; Cherbourg 11.8.17; Fuselage damaged 26.8.17; RR engine by 1.11.17; Refitted Eagle IV by 29.12.17 - 2.18; Eagle VIII by 3.18; Eagle IV by 4.18; Became 414/5 Flts Cherbourg 25.5.18 (in 243 Sqdn Cherbourg from 20.8.18); Deleted W/E 3.10.18 |
| 9846 | FF as seaplane prototype 18.3.17; Accepted Cowes 19.3.17; Deld Calshot 30.3.17; Portland 31.3.17; Calshot 11.7.17; Portland W/E 21.9.17; Fitted modified u/c and enlarged wing tip floats; EF, FL, tried to turn into wind, sideslipped from 200 ft, CW nr Chesil Bank 8.12.17 (FSL JR Ross & Lt FDJ Silwood); Surveyed 11.12.17; Deleted 22.12.17 wrecked |
| 9847 | Trials Calshot 6.17 [no trace in DRs]; Allocated Cattewater 22.3.17 but no evidence of delivery |
| 9848 | Deld Cowes 26.5.17; Calshot 30.5.17; Cattewater 1.6.17; Mkrs by rail 14.7.17; Portland 22.9.17; Dropped 65-lb & 3x100-lb bombs on U-boat 10m W of Portland Bill 23.9.17 (F/Cdr JK Waugh); Dropped 2x100-lb bombs on U-boat 20m SE of Portland Bill 18.10.17 (FSL R Jarman & AM CS Laycock); EF, FL, damaged u/c, sank 26.11.17; Surveyed 6.12.17; Deleted 13.12.17 W&T |
| 9849 | Deld Cowes 2.6.17; Grain Test Dept 12.6.17 (type trials); Damaged 26.6.17; Yarmouth 6.7.17 (transit); South Shields 13.7.17 (transit); Dundee 14.7.17 (transit); Scapa 18.7.17; Crashed 2.2.18; Houton Bay by 3.18, packing for Portsmouth Group; Wings despatched Calshot 8.3.17; Fuselage still Scapa 27.4.18; Patrol Reserve Calshot W/E 1.6.18; ARS Calshot W/E 22.8.18; Deleted W/E 17.10.18 |
| 9850 | (Eagle VII by 29.12.17)(Eagle VIII)(Eagle VI by 8.18) Deld Cowes 9.6.17; Portland 6.7.17; Dropped 4x100-lb bombs on U-boat 4958N 0322 W 11.11.17 (FSL R Jarman awarded DSC & OSL KG Coles); Became 416/7 Flts Portland 25.5.18 (241 Sqdn 20.8.18); Dropped 3x100-lb & 1x65-lb bombs on U-boat, wreckage seen later by trawler 5033N 0155W 26.5.18 (Capt NC Harrison & Cpl Argent); Deleted W/E 26.9.18 |
| 9851 | (Eagle VII to 2.18)(Eagle VI by 4.18 & 8.18) Deld at Cowes 7.17; Portland 12.7.17; Calshot W/E 14.9.17; Cattewater W/E 23.11.17; Portland W/E 24.12.17; Crashed in bad weather outside Portland Harbour 23.1.18 (Lt FDJ Silwood); Became 416/7 Flts Portland 25.5.18 (241 Sqdn 20.8.18) - @30.1.19 |
| 9852 | Deld Calshot 18.7.17; Cherbourg 26.7.17; COL Cherbourg 3.9.17 (FSL CS Mossop); Deleted W/E 14.9.17 |
| 9853 | (265-hp Sunbeam Maori). Deld Grain Type Test Flt 8.9.17 (type trials); Ready for leaving 12.12.17 (to be flown); Grain Acceptance Dept by 29.12.17; Surveyed 27.3.18; Deleted 27.3.18 FW&T |
| 9854 | (Eagle VII) Deld Calshot 16.8.17; Cherbourg 16.8.17 - @23.2.18; Calshot by 8.3.18 (for Cherbourg); Cherbourg W/E 4.5.18; Became 414/5 Flts Cherbourg 25.5.18 (243 Sqdn 20.8.18); Deleted W/E 12.12.18 |
| 9855 | (Eagle VI) Deld Calshot 23.8.17; Portland W/E 7.9.17; Calshot W/E 7.12.17; Portland W/E 15.2.18; Calshot 2.2.18 (u/s) [sic]; Portland W/E 29.3.18; COL 20.4.18; Deleted W/E 25.5.18 |
| 9856 | (Eagle VII to 1.17; Eagle VI by 2.17) Deld at Cowes 25.8.17; Calshot 1.9.17; (Portland) Dropped 3x100-lb bomb on U-boat, all failed to explode 25.3.18 (Ens F Ives USN); Dropped 4x100-lb bombs on U-boat 25.4.18 (Lt FDJ Silwood & Lt EA Sawyer); Became 416/7 Flts Portland 25.5.18; Dropped 4x100-lb bombs on U-boat 24.6.18 (Lt FDJ Silwood & Lt EA Sawyer); Deleted W/E 29.8.18 |

9857 (Eagle VII) Deld Cherbourg W/E 7.9.17; Dropped 3x100-lb bombs on U-boat 20m N of Cape Barfleur 18.3.18 (FSL T Eyre & OSL RE Horton); Dropped bomb on U-boat, failed to explode 26.3.18 (FSL CS Mossop DSC); CW on landing after patrol 26.4.18; Deleted W/E 4.5.18

9858 (Eagle VII) Deld (at Cowes?) 8.9.17; Calshot W/E 21.9.17; Cherbourg W/E 28.9.17 - @19.1.18; Calshot 1.18; to Cherbourg but FL in fog 25m N of Cherbourg, damaged and put on board steamer bound for Cardiff 31.1.18 (FSL CS Mossop and another crew picked up by French destroyer *Admiral Regault de Genouilly* bound for Cardiff); Calshot to Cherbourg W/E 4.5.18; Calshot, On patrol to Cherbourg, badly damaged landing Jersey 29.5.18; Became 414/5 Flts 243 Sqdn Cherbourg 20.8.18; Deleted W/E 12.12.18

9859 (Eagle VII) Deld 10.17; Cherbourg by 12.10.17; Petrol leak, FL in Channel, damaged u/c on TO, landed Bembridge 30.11.17 (FSL CS Mossop); Dropped 100-lb bomb on U-boat 12m N of Cape La Hague 21.12.17 (FSL T Eyre); Dropped 100-lb bomb on white U-boat 5005N 0100W 4.1.18 (FSL WBE Powell); Dropped 65-lb & 2x100-lb bombs on U-boat 5012N 0050W 25.1.18 (F/Cdr CW Scott & AM2 W Ward); Became 414/5 Flts Cherbourg 25.5.18 (in 243 Sqdn from 20.8.18); Tailplane collapsed on TO, crashed Port-en-Bessin 12.8.18 (Lt CS Mossop & Lt RE Horton both killed); Deleetd W/E 29.8.18

9860 Deld Cherbourg (via Calshot) 24.7.17; Dropped 2x100-lb bombs on *UB32*, sunk, 25m NE of Cherbourg 18.8.17 (FSL CS Mossop awarded DSC & AM Ingledew awarded DSM); Dropped 3x100-lb bombs on U-boat 25m NE of Cherbourg 4.9.17 (FSL GS Mossop); Dropped 2 bombs on U-boat 7m S of St.Catherine's, then EF, FL, abandoned, sank 6.12.17 (FSL CS Mossop and another picked up by HMS *P32*); Surveyed 15.12.17; Deleted 28.12.17 TL

**30 AVRO 504B (ADMIRALTY 179 TYPE) TRACTOR BIPLANES ordered 2.6.16 under Cont No A.S.19203 from George Parnall & Co Ltd, numbered 9861 to 9890 and built Bristol. Put forward 8.16 to fit with modified armament for gunnery training. Fitted to carry 4x16-lb bombs for bombing training. (80-hp Gnome A)**

9861 Deld Cranwell 7.11.16; Deleted 2.2.17
9862 FF Filton 11.16; Deld Cranwell for erection 20.11.16; Deleted 16.8.17
9863 Deld Cranwell for erection 20.11.16; Wrecked 31.1.17; FL and wrecked 28.12.17 (sic); Surveyed 21.12.17 wrecked; Deleted 14.1.18
9864 Deld Hendon for erection 23.11.16; Accepted 25.11.16 (Capt Keith Davis); Chingford 9.8.17; Deleted 23.8.17
9865 (DC) Deld Redcar by road 27.11.16; Tested 6.12.16 (Capt Keith Davis); Damaged 6.10.17; Deleted 7.12.17 wrecked
9866 (DC) Deld Redcar by rail 4.12.16; Tested 6.12.16 (Capt Keith Davis); Surveyed 7.12.17 wrecked; Deleted 14.12.17
9867 (DC) Deld Redcar 4.12.16; Tested 6.12.16 (Capt Keith Davis); Run into and damaged by 8949 18.12.16; EF, FL, badly wrecked 16.2.17 (PFO TH Boyd unhurt); Deleted 27.2.17
9868 Deld by road to Eastchurch Workshops 9.12.16; Erected 15.12.16; Eastchurch Gunnery School Flts 7.2.17; Eastchurch FS 7.5.17; Fitted DC 6.7.17; Manston 31.8.17; Hendon to Manston NFS 18.10.17 - @30.3.18
9869 Deld Hendon 9.12.16; Accepted 13.12.16 (Capt Keith Davis); Cranwell 17.3.17; Hendon 18.3.17; Grain ECD 27.4.17; Hendon 9.5.17; Martlesham 27.5.17; Hendon 3.6.17; Grain 16.6.17; Hendon 17.6.17; Manston NFS W/E 27.12.17 - @30.3.18
9870 Deld Cranwell 17.12.16; Wrecked 1.4.17; Deleted 16.8.17
9871 Deld by lorry to Eastchurch Workshops 19.12.16; Awaiting test 1.1.17; Eastchurch FS 4.1.17; Crashed 27.4.17; Surveyed 10.5.17; Deleted 11.5.17
9872 Deld by lorry to Eastchurch Workshops 20.12.16; Awaiting test 1.1.17; Eastchurch FS 4.1.17; Chingford W/E 10.11.17 - @30.3.18
9873 Deld Killingholme 27.12.16 - @10.18; NFT

9874 Deld Killingholme for erection 1.1.17; C Flt Cranwell 9.5.17; Crashed, damaged u/c, propeller etc 7.7.17; Crashed 22.8.17; For despatch by 18.1.18; Redcar School W/E 23.2.18; Crashed, CW 9.3.18 (PFO HJ Clark); Deleted W/E 30.3.18
9875 (DC) Deld Killingholme store 16.1.17; Cranwell 13.4.17; Crashed Cranwell North 6.12.17 (pilot unhurt); Surveyed 10.12.17; Deleted 14.12.17 wrecked
9876 (DC) Deld Killingholme store 16.1.17; Crashed on nose; Deleted 22.8.17
9877 Deld by rail to Chingford 8.1.17; Deleted W/E 6.10.17 BR
9878 Deld by rail to Chingford 8.1.17; Deleted W/E 29.9.17
9879 (DC) Deld Killingholme store 13.1.17; Manston 1.5.17; Chingford 5.5.17 (collected from Bedford); Manston FS (via Eastchurch OFS); FL in field and damaged u/c, nr aerodrome 26.6.17 (PFO AH Lofft); Manston to Manston FS 19.7.17; For deletion by 9.3.18; Deleted W/E 23.3.18
9880 (DC) Deld Killingholme store 1.3.17; War School/Flt Manston 1.5.17 - 3.18; Damaged u/c landing 26.6.17 (FSL Lord Ossulston); FL and damaged 22.9.17
9881 Deld Killingholme store 10.2.17; Cranwell 20.4.17 (arr 21.4.17) - 5.17; at Freiston by 7.17 & 9.17; Cranwell by 8.17; u/c broken 21.8.17; Became 201/2 TDS Cranwell 1.4.18
9882 Deld Killingholme store 10.2.17; C Flt Cranwell 20.4.17; Freiston 23.4.17 - 5.17; Cranwell 7.17; Crashed 22.8.17; Redcar School W/E 19.1.18; Deleted W/E 9.3.18
9883 Deld Killingholme store 10.2.17; Chingford 10.5.17; Badly damaged 25.6.17; Deleted 22.7.17
9884 Deld Killingholme store 24.2.17 - 5.18; Badly damaged 6.7.17;; NFT
9885 Deld Vendôme 14.3.17; BR 1.6.17; Surveyed 12.10.17; Deleted 16.10.17 wrecked
9886 Deld Vendôme 31.3.17; u/c damaged 22.8.17; Surveyed 12.10.17; Deleted 16.10.17 wrecked
9887 Deld Killingholme store 10.2.17; Chingford 9.5.17; EF, FL through hedge, badly damaged 9.6.17 (PFO AM Alexander); Deleted 22.7.17
9888 Deld Chingford by road 7.2.17; Deleted 9.5.17
9889 Deld Cranwell 17.2.17; Deleted 19.5.17
9890 Deld Killingholme store 24.2.17; Chingford 9.5.17 - @23.2.18; B Flt Fairlop by 3.18; Became 207 TDS Chingford/Fairlop 1.4.18

**1 SOPWITH SCHOOL TRACTOR BIPLANE ordered under Cont No C.P.112765/16, numbered 9891 and built Kingston-on-Thames. (80-hp Gnome A)**

9891 Prototype for proposed trainer version of 1½ Strutter; Accepted Brooklands 6.5.16; Deld 3 Wing Detling by 18.5.16; 3 Wing Manston 9.6.16; 3 Wing Detling 11.6.16; 3 Wing Manston 12.6.16; Deleted 25.10.16

**6 SOPWITH 1½ STRUTTER TRACTOR BIPLANES (ADMIRALTY 9400S TYPE TWO-SEAT FIGHTERS) ordered 4.16 under Cont No C.P.113240/16, numbered 9892 to 9897 and built Kingston-on-Thames. Deld from Brooklands. (110-hp Clerget 9Z)**

9892 Transferred to RFC (Military Wing). Used by 70 Sqdn RFC
9893 Deld CSD White City 8.16; Cranwell 25.9.16; Crashed 18.9.17; Surveyed 27.11.17; Deleted 6.12.17 DBR
9894 Deld CSD White City by 12.9.16; Cranwell 23.9.16; Tested 17.11.16; Damaged 5.9.17; Crashed 2.10.17; East Fortune NFS W/E 18.1.18 - @30.3.18; Turnhouse by 29.8.18; Collided with Pup B8012 over Firth of Forth 4.9.18 (2/Lt R Pyne & F/Sgt A Wright both killed) (now 130-hp Clerget)
9895 Deld 3 Wing Manston 12.9.16; Damaged 18.9.16; to 3 Wing Luxeuil but COL Etaples 21.9.16 (FSL GS Harrover); Loaned to French Govt for AMF 7.11.16; Retd 3 Wing Luxeuil 11.2.17; Loaned to French Govt for AMF 23.2.17; Transferred to French Govt for AMF 4.17
9896 Accepted Brooklands 7.9.16; Deld 5 Flt A Sqdn 5 Wing 9.9.16; Detd Sqdn (became B Flt 8 Sqdn) 26.10.16 -

*Wight "Converted" Seaplane 9850, used at Portland. (J.M.Bruce/G.S.Leslie collection)*

*Sopwith Pup 9914 fitted with rocket armament. (RAF Museum P.3197)*

11.16; ADD by 23.11.16; 5 Sqdn 22.12.16; ADD by 11.1.17; 5 Sqdn 26.2.17; Wrecked 29.4.17 (after raid?); ADD by 3.5.17; Deleted 14.5.17

9897   Deld Dover 13.9.16; ADD 16.10.16; C Sqdn 1 Wing 7.11.16; Became 3 Sqdn 12.16 - @26.1.17LM; Held by 9 Sqdn by 1.2.17; Dunkerque by 2.17; 2 Sqdn by 8.2.17; Wrecked 12.5.17; Deleted ADD 14.5.17

**3 SOPWITH PUP (ADMIRALTY 9901 TYPE) TRACTOR BIPLANE PRE-PRODUCTION ordered under Cont No C.P.120390/16, numbered 9898 to 9900 and built Kingston-on-Thames. Deld from Brooklands. Put forward W/E 1.9.16 for French Govt (NTU). (80-hp Clerget)**

9898   Deld Dover 25.11.16; ADD 28.11.16; 3 Sqdn 30.11.16; 8 Sqdn 20.12.16; In action 7.1.17 (FSL AHS Lawson wounded); 3 Sqdn 3.2.17; Roland DD, shared N5188 13.45 16.2.17 (FSL JA Glen); Halberstadt DII OOC nr Menencourt 11.45 4.3.17; 2-str OOC Vaux (confirmed) 10.30 17.3.17; 2-str in flames Ervillers 11.00 17.3.17 (all FSL JJ Malone); ADD W/E 12.4.17; 11 Sqdn 19.5.17; 12 Sqdn 13.6.17; DD on sands by rain, retd aerodrome, COL 14.8.17 (FSL SA Hamilton-Bowyer); Repaired by 21.8.17; AP Dover 23.11.17; Grain ECD 15.12.17; ECD Grain 15.12.17 - @6.18 (expts, fitted 80-hp Le Rhône)

9899   Deld Dover 6.12.16; Dunkerque 11.12.16; 3 Sqdn 11.12.16; ADD by 23.12.16 - @18.1.17; 8 Sqdn by 25.1.17; 3 Sqdn 3.2.17; COL 14.2.17 (FSL JA Glen); ADD by 22.2.17; 4 Sqdn (named "DO-DO") 21.3.17; Scout OOC nr Steenbrugh, S of Bruges 15.30 26.4.17 (FSL AJ Chadwick); Siemens-Schuckert DI crashed in sea 5m E of Zeebrugge 07.20, own a/c shot up 12.5.17 (FSL AJ Enstone); FL on beach 20.5.17 (F/Cdr AM Shook) (flying next day); 2 white 1-strs OOC 5m NE of Dixmude 16.00 6.6.17 (FSL GW Hemming); Marked as 'N9899' 6.17; 11 Sqdn 7.6.17; 4 Sqdn 12.6.17 (temp attd); 11 Sqdn 4.7.17; Albatros, probably 2-str OOC S of Middelkerke 18.45 17.7.17 (FSL HF Airey); Ran into ditch on landing 14.8.17 (FSL HF Airey); still 11 Sqdn by 16.8.17; ADD by 23.8.17 - @27.9.17; Dover by 6.10.17; Surveyed 16.10.17; Deleted 19.10.17 W&T

9900   Deld ADD 12.16; 3 Sqdn 24.12.16 - @15.2.17; Crashed Cormont on aerial gunnery course; ADD by 22.2.17; 9 Sqdn 3.3.17 - @9.3.17; Dover from/by 14.3.17 (repair and overhaul for Dunkerque); Dunkerque 19.4.17; 3 Sqdn Marieux by 4.17; Dover 9.5.17; Walmer 9.5.17; HACP 1.6.17 (FSL WM Lusby); Dover 4.6.17; Wings and propeller damaged 8.6.17; ADD 23.6.17; Seaplane Defence Flt 11.7.17; 12 Sqdn 15.7.17 - @26.8.17; ADD by 30.8.17 - @6.9.17; Dover by 13.9.17; Surveyed 16.10.17; Deleted 19.10.17 W&T; At some time crashed on nose marked 'N9900'

**50 SOPWITH PUP (ADMIRALTY 9901 TYPE) TRACTOR BIPLANES ordered 7.6.16 (updated W/E 3.11.16) under Cont Nos C.P.117318/16 & A.S.11764/17 from Sir William Beardmore & Co Ltd, numbered 9901 to 9950 and built Dalmuir. Fitted with alternative Lewis gun/rocket armament from 9909. 16 a/c fitted with airbags. (9901-9909 & 9911 80-hp Clerget; 9910 & 9912-9959 80-hp Le Rhône)**

9901   (Serial number used as Admiralty Type number for Pup). Deld in crate to Design Flt Eastchurch 1.11.16; Flown 6.11.16 (by Dukinfield Jones, S/Cdr HR Busteed & F/L PA Johnston); Flown 14.11.16 (S/Cdr HR Busteed); ECD Grain 18.3.17; Tested collapsible float 19.4.17 (S/Cdr HR Busteed); Ditching experiments 5.17; Emergency flotation expts 17.6.17; Anchored for 6 hours with airbags for flotation tests 23.6.17; Fitted with detachable u/c; Flown from HMS *Manxman* to HMS *Yarmouth* in Firth of Forth 28.6.17 (S/Cdr FJ Rutland); Detachable chassis repaired after sea landing 12.8.17; With N6440 shot down GoIV No.663, 1 of 10 Gothas, into sea ½m off Margate 22.8.17 (F/Cdr GE Hervey); NFT

9902   FF Grain 23.10.16; Cranwell 30.10.16; Wrecked 24.7.17; Crashed and damaged 6.2.18 (pilot unhurt); Surveyed 25.2.18 wrecked; Deleted 13.3.18

9903   Deld Cranwell 27.11.16; Crashed and badly damaged Cranwell 1.3.18 (pilot unhurt); Became 201/2 TDS

Cranwell 1.4.18

9904   Put forward to fit rocket gear 10.16; Beardmore to fit to fly off deck 11.16 (NTU?); Deld Yarmouth for erection 2.12.16; Accepted 15.12.16 (Dukinfield Jones); HACP 9.3.17 (F/L E Cadbury); AZPs 26.3.17, 24.5.17 & 17.6.17 (all F/L E Cadbury); Became 490 Flt Yarmouth 25.5.18; Burgh Castle by 6.18; HACP, EF, FL Yarmouth 8.6.18; Covehithe by 25.6.18; COL, wrecked 29.6.18 (pilot unhurt)

9905   (80-hp Le Rhône) Put forward to fit rocket gear 10.16; Beardmore to fit to fly off deck 11.16 (NTU?); Deld Yarmouth for erection by 7.12.16; Accepted 15.12.16 (Dukinfield Jones); HACPs 30.3.17 & 4.4.17 (both F/L GWR Fane); Martlesham Heath 8.4.17; Yarmouth 20.4.17; AZP 17.6.17 (F/L GWR Fane); O/t landing 27.6.17 (F/L GWR Fane); HACP 5.9.17 (F/L GWR Fane); Became 490 Flt Yarmouth 25.5.18; Burgh Castle by 5.18?; Covehithe by 25.6.18; EF, FL in sea and sank 5.7.18 (pilot unhurt)

9906   Accepted Dalmuir 7.12.16; Deld Manston 12.12.16; overseas 23.1.17; 3 Wing Luxeuil by 3rd week 2.17; Fighting patrol, celluloid centre section burst in air reducing speed and climb 25.2.17 (F/Cdr C Draper); Surveyed Luxeuil 2.4.17; Deleted 4.17

9907   Deld Manston 7.1.17; Westgate 10.1.17 (repair); Manston 13.2.17; AGPs 25.5.17 (FSL JE Scott), 5.6.17 (FSL JE Scott), 13.6.17 (FSL RH Daly, landed Aldeburgh), 4.7.17, 7.7.17 x 2 & 22.7.17 (FSL CH Fitzherbert); For deletion 2.18; To Greenwich less engine W/E 16.2.18 (presumed for GI use)

9908   Deld Cranwell erection 24.1.17; Lost, FL in field, hit hedge and crashed BR 4.9.17 (FSL SD Culley); Surveyed 22.9.17; Deleted 8.10.17 wrecked

9909   Deld Cranwell 26.1.17; Deleted 28.7.17

9910   (Fitted rocket armament) Accepted 26.12.16; Deld Felixstowe and to Trimley for erection 10.1.17; Flown 13.1.17; Levington NLG 3.2.17; Martlesham 20.2.17; Yarmouth for visit, but EF and stayed 8.4.17; HSPP 16.4.17 (F/L GWR Fane); CSD White City 6.2.18; Surveyed 18.3.18; Deleted 27.3.18 DBR

9911   (80-hp Le Rhône) (Fitted rocket armament) Accepted 26.12.16; Deld Felixstowe and to Trimley for erection 10.1.17; Felixstowe 16.1.17; Trimley 17.1.17; Levington NLG 3.2.17; Martlesham 20.2.17; Yarmouth 26.4.17; Martlesham 28.4.17 (for HMS *Vindex*); Damaged landing 14.6.17 (F/L FN Halstead); [HMS *Vindex*, converted to 80-hp Clerget W/E 2.11.17]; HMS *Vindex* @19.1.18; still at Martlesham 23.2.18; War School Manston by 23.2.18; Deleted W/E 23.3.18

9912   (Fitted rocket armament) Deld PVRS 23.1.17; Renamed ECD Grain 26.2.17; 2 deck landing experiments 4.4.17; War Flt Grain 15.5.17; AGPs 25.5.17, 13.6.17, 7.7.17 x 2 & 12.8.17 (all F/L CT Freeman); Exptl Dept Grain by 29.12.17 (deck landing experiments); Rosyth (via Cranwell & Lincoln) 23.3.18; Grain by 1.4.18; Hendon 10.8.18; Grain 11.8.18

9913   (Fitted rocket armament) Deld East Fortune by rail 26.1.17; Tested by *Manxman* pilot 13.2.17 & 15.2.17; TW in HMS *Manxman* 26.2.17; Deleted 15.3.17

9914   (Fitted rocket armament) Deld East Fortune 28.1.17; Flown 22.2.17; HMS *Manxman* 26.2.17; Damaged by 1.3.17; East Fortune 28.3.17 (u/s); East Fortune 13.5.17; Turnhouse 8.6.17; Crashed on TO 3.7.17; Deleted 7.8.17

9915   Deld Dover 7.2.17; ADD 10.2.17; 9 Sqdn 14.2.17; FL in dense fog, struck hill, lost u/c and propeller nr Suresnil 14.2.17 (FSL CD Crundall); ADD 15.2.17; 11 Sqdn 23.5.17; COL 26.5.17 (FSL TR Swinburne); ADD by 31.5.17; Dover 13.6.17; Walmer 28.9.17; East Fortune NFS W/E 10.11.17; Deleted W/E 6.4.18

9916   (Fitted rocket armament) Deld Dover 7.2.17; ADD 8.2.17; 9 Sqdn 11.2.17; 2-str shot down into sea off Middelkerke shared with N5188 20.30 2.5.17; 2-str OOC Ostende shared with N6188 & N6193 14.15 31.5.17; Crashed Steenwerck 3.6.17 (all FSL HF Stackard); ADD by 7.6.17; Dover 13.6.17; ADD 28.6.17; Seaplane Defence Flt 4.7.17; 12 Sqdn 15.7.17; ADD W/E 30.8.17; Dover W/E 13.9.17; Deleted W/E 1.12.17

9917   Deld East Fortune 10.2.17; HMS *Manxman* 9.3.17; Badly damaged 29.4.17; Turnhouse 29.6.17; Rosyth

7.9.17; Donibristle 15.9.17; Rosyth 16.10.17; Turnhouse W/E 21.3.18; Deleted W/E 11.7.18

9918 (Fitted rocket armament) Deld East Fortune 10.2.17; HMS *Manxman* 28.2.17; Lost at sea 29.4.17 (F/Cdr FJ Rutland - presume later recovered); Deleted 12.5.17

9919 Deld East Fortune 8.2.17; HMS *Manxman* 9.3.17; Badly damaged 29.4.17; Deleted 14.5.17

9920 (Fitted rocket armament); Deld East Fortune 8.2.17; HMS *Manxman* 28.2.17; Lost at sea 29.4.17 (pilot picked by HMS *Patrician*); Deleted 12.5.17

9921 Deld Felixstowe 27.2.17; Martlesham 2.3.17; EF, FL Eye, taken to Pulham Airship Station, then retd Martlesham 11.3.17 (F/L MJG Day); HMS *Vindex* 23.6.17; War School Manston 19.1.18; Exptl Dept Grain, COL Eastbourne, slightly damaged 23.3.18 (pilot unhurt); still at Eastbourne by 6.4.18

9922 (Fitted rocket armament) Deld ECD Grain 5.3.17; Deck landing trials 28.3.17 (F/Cdr LP Openshaw & F/L CT Freeman) & 29.3.17 (F/Cdr LP Openshaw); AGP 25.5.17 (S/Cdr HR Busteed); Fitting deck landing hook and skids by 14.7.17; Tested DL skids 20.7.17 & 23.7.17 x 2 (S/Cdr HR Busteed); Emergency sea landing on skid test flight 30.7.17 (S/Cdr HR Busteed); Rail test 16.8.17; Manston to EC&AD Grain W/E 23.2.18; Launching trials 3.18; Deleted W/E 1.4.18

9923 Deld Cranwell 2.3.17 - 4.17; Freiston by 6.17; Cranwell by 9.17; Crashed, CW Cranwell South 14.1.18 (pilot unhurt); Surveyed 25.2.18; Deleted 13.3.18 W&T

9924 (Fitted rocket armament) Deld Cranwell 2.3.17; Hendon 14.5.17 (repair); HACP, landed Fairlop, then retd Hendon 3.10.17 (F/L MA Simpson); Used by Air Dept officers by 2.18; still at Hendon 4.19 for visits to RAF stations

9925 Deld Cranwell 7.3.17; Wrecked 18.7.17; EF on TO, swerved and blown over 18.10.17 (FSL AC Sharwood); O/t landing, slightly damaged 31.12.17 (pilot unhurt); Crashed, slightly damaged Waddington 16.2.18 (pilot unhurt); Fitted 60-hp Le Rhône by 3.18; Crashed, badly damaged, Cranwell South 14.3.18 (pilot unhurt)

9926 (Fitted rocket armament) Accepted 26.2.17; Deld Felixstowe by rail 17.3.17; HMS *Vindex* 14.4.17; Lost at sea, retd later 28.9.17 (F/L WB Foster); Surveyed 29.9.17; Deleted 8.10.17 TL

9927 Deld Felixstowe by rail 17.3.17; Erected for Martlesham 30.3.17; HMS *Vindex* 4.4.17; Lost at sea 28.9.17 (F/Cdr BD Kilner killed); Surveyed 29.9.17; Deleted 8.10.17 TL

9928 (Fitted rocket armament) Deld Dover 17.3.17 (mispainted as "N9928") ADD 28.3.17; 9 Sqdn 4.4.17 (still as "N9928" initially); COL 22.5.17 (FSL JW Pinder); ADD W/E 14.6.17; Dover 3.7.17; War School Manston for erection 14.10.17; Deleted W/E 2.3.18

9929 Deld Dover 17.3.17; ADD 21.3.17; 4 Sqdn 28.3.17; FL and damaged nr Bergues 23.4.17 (FSL EOA Andrews); ADD by 26.4.17; Dover 2.5.17 (repair, then War Flt); AGPs 5.6.17 & 13.6.17; ADD 23.6.17; Seaplane Defence Flt 3.7.17; ADD 4.8.17 - @23.8.17; 12 Sqdn from/by 25.8.17 - @3.9.17; ADD by 6.9.17; Dover W/E 4.10.17; Surveyed 16.10.17; Deleted 19.10.17 W&T

9930 (Fitted rocket armament) Deld Killingholme for erection 2.3.17; Redcar 25.5.17; Martlesham 12.6.17; HMS *Vindex* 23.6.17; War School Manston by 23.3.18; Deleted 25.3.18

9931 (Convtd to 9901A Ships Pup) Deld Killingholme for erection 2.3.17; Scapa by rail for *Campania* 30.4.17; HMS *Campania* for erection 8.5.17; Scapa/Houton Bay W/E 13.10.17 - @8.12.17; HMS *Campania* by 12.17; HMAS *Sydney* 11.12.17 - @19.1.18; HMS *Dublin* 1.18; Houton Bay for overhaul W/E 2.2.18; Scapa W/E 25.5.18; Smoogroo W/E 18.7.18; Scapa W/E 28.11.18; Smoogroo W/E 12.12.18; Scapa W/E 19.12.18; Smoogroo W/E 31.12.18; Disposed W/E 16.1.19

9932 (Convtd to 9901A Ships Pup) Deld Killingholme for erection 21.3.17; Scapa by rail for *Campania* 30.4.17; HMS *Campania* for erection 8.5.17 - @15.7.17 (LM); [Not Scapa or HMS *Yarmouth* by 29.9.17]; HMS *Yarmouth* to Scapa for overhaul W/E 3.11.17; HMS *Yarmouth* by 23.11.17; Scapa to HMS *Sydney* 7.12.17; HMS *Yarmouth* by 14-21.12.17; Houton Bay Reserve by 29.12.17; Scapa W/E 18.5.18; Smoogroo W/E 11.7.18;

Scapa W/E 12.12.18 - @30.1.19

9933 (Fitted with skid u/c and upward firing Lewis gun) Deld Killingholme for erection 29.3.17; Scapa by rail for erection 30.4.17; HMS *Campania* for erection 8.5.17 - @15.7.17 (LM)

9934 (Fitted rocket armament) Deld Killingholme for erection 29.3.17; HMS *Campania* for erection 8.5.17; Surveyed 20.9.17; Deleted 24.9.17 wrecked

9935 Deld Killingholme for erection 27.3.17; Cranwell 20.4.17 (arr 21.4.17); Wrecked 15.6.17; Still Cranwell 19.10.17; Freiston by 11.17; Cranwell by 1.18 (now 60-hp Le Rhône); Crashed and wrecked Cranwell South 24.1.18 (pilot unhurt); Visited HMS *Eagle* 10.3.18; Freiston 14.3.18; EF, Crashed and badly damaged nr aerodrome 20.3.18 (pilot unhurt); For deletion by 30.3.18

9936 (Fitted rocket armament) Deld Killingholme for erection 4.4.17; B Flt Cranwell 20.4.17 (arr 21.4.17; Wrecked 18.7.17; Crashed Cranwell South 16.2.18 (pilot unhurt); Became 201/2 TDS Cranwell 1.4.18

9937 Deld Killingholme for erection 4.4.17; D Flt Cranwell 24.4.17; Deleted 5.12.17 for GI

9938 (Fitted rocket armament) Deld Killingholme for erection 4.4.17; Cranwell 24.4.17; Parachute dropping 28.10.17; At Freiston 11.17 - 12.17; Deleted W/E 22.2.18

9939 Deld Killingholme for erection 4.4.17; ECD Grain 22.5.17 (engine trials); Repair u/c 23.6.17; Deck landing and arrester gear trials 7.19

9940 (Fitted rocket armament) Deld Killingholme for erection 4.4.17; War Flt Grain 21.5.17 (arr 25.5.17 via Huntingdon & Chingford); AGPs 5.6.17 (F/Cdr RDG Sibley); AGP, attacked Gotha, COL Manston 13.6.17 (F/L FM Fox); Convtd 9901a Ships Pup; East Fortune by rail 14.9.17; Donibristle 22.9.17; HMS *Furious* by lighter 25.9.17; East Fortune 14.11.17; F Sqdn East Fortune by 4.12.17; Donibristle 11.1.18; Turnhouse W/E 21.2.18 (Depot Flt from W/E 22.3.18); HMS *Furious* W/E 20.4.18; Turnhouse W/E 11.7.18; Donibristle W/E 15.8.18; Turnhouse W/E 19.9.18 - @30.1.19

9941 Shipped to Mudros; Stavros by 28-29.10.17; Marsh by 1.2.18; G Sqdn 2 Wing Mudros by 3.18; Became G Sqdn 62 Wing Mudros 1.4.18 - 5.18; Repair Base Mudros by 6.18

9942 (Fitted rocket armament) Shipped to Mudros; Stavros 23.11.17; Imbros (Kephalo) by 1.12.17; Marsh by 1-20.1.18; C Sqdn 2 Wing Mudros; G Sqdn 2 Wing Mudros by 3.18; Became G Sqdn 62 Wing Mudros 1.4.18 - 5.18; F Sqdn 2 Wing Amberkoj by 6.18; Repair Base Mudros by 10.18 - 11.18

9943 Deld East Fortune 13.4.17; HMS *Manxman* 3.5.17; Turnhouse 4.5.17; HMS *Manxman* 29.6.17; u/c, propeller and wings damaged 3.7.17; Turnhouse 3.7.17; HMS *Manxman* 19.7.17; Rosyth 7.9.17; Convtd 9901a Ships Pup; Turnhouse to HMS *Furious* by lighter for erection 12.9.17 East Fortune 14.11.17; Donibristle W/E 11.1.18; Turnhouse W/E 21.2.18; Depot Flt Turnhouse W/E 22.3.18; Turnhouse W/E 30.3.18 - @30.1.19

9944 (Fitted rocket armament) Deld East Fortune 13.4.17; HMS *Manxman* 3.5.17; Turnhouse 7.5.17; HMS *Manxman* 13.5.17 - @15.7.17; HMS *Yarmouth* by 7.17 (for 10 days); HMS *Manxman* 19.7.17 (overhaul); Turnhouse by 7.8.17; HMS *Pegasus* by transport 1.9.17 - @2.9.17; HMS *Manxman* 9.17; HMS *Pegasus* 7.9.17; HMS *Repulse* W/E 14.12.17; Rosyth W/E 20.12.17 - @11.1.18; HMS *Pegasus* by 3-10.1.18; Rosyth to HMS *Pegasus* W/E 10.1.18; HMS *Tiger* W/E 17.1.18; Houton Bay overhaul 2.2.18 (for HMS *Southampton* by 9.3.18); Scapa W/E 18.5.18; Smoogroo W/E 11.7.18; HMS *Vindictive* 26.10.18 - @29.10.18; Smoogroo 10.18; HMS *Vindictive* 1.11.18; Smoogroo 14.11.18; HMS *Vindictive* W/E 21.11.18; Turnhouse 25.11.18; HMS *Vindictive* 11.18 - @30.1.19 (experimental work)

9945 (80-hp Le Rhône) Deld East Fortune 28.4.17; HMS *Manxman* 11.5.17; Rosyth 7.9.17; Donibristle by 5.10.17; HMS *Nairana* by 10.17; Donibristle by 11.17; HMS *Nairana* 8.11.17; HMS *Repulse* W/E 8.11.17; Donibristle W/E 15.11.17; Rosyth W/E 23.11.17; Donibristle to HMS *Nairana* W/E 27.11.17; Rosyth by 29.12.17; to Turnhouse W/E 21.2.18; Deleted W/E 10.10.18

9946    (Fitted rocket armament) Deld Cranwell 5.5.17 (deck practice); Wrecked 27.7.17; Tested 13.8.17; Convtd 9901a Ships Pup; East Fortune NFS by rail for carriers 22.9.17 - @30.3.18; Grand Fleet SoAF&G East Fortune, spun in from 2,000 ft 24.7.18 (2/Lt FA Cash killed)

9947    Deld Dover by rail 4.5.17; Defence Flt Walmer 7.5.17; AGPs 25.5.17 (FSL WH Chisham), also 25.5.17, 5.6.17, 13.6.17 & 7.7.17 (all F/L S Kemball), also 22.7.17 (FSL WM Lusby), also 12.8.17 & 27.8.17 (both F/L RA Little); Attacked Gotha off Holland 12.8.17 (FSL S Kemball); 2 HACPs 3.9.17 (FSL MR Kingsford); HACP 15.9.17 (F/L RA Little); Dover 6.10.17; Donibristle by 5.10.17 (sic); Convtd Type 9901a Ships Pup; Rosyth W/E 13.12.17; HMS *Nairana* W/E 14.12.17; HMS *Renown* W/E 21.12.17; Donibristle W/E 21.12.17; HMS *Nairana* W/E 28.12.17; CW by 11.1.18; Rosyth W/E 18.1.18; To Walmer 7.7.18 - @30.1.19

9948    (Convtd 9901a Ships Pup) (Fitted rocket armament?) Deld Hendon for erection 16.5.17 (launching tests with catapult of Carey design); Removing catapult gear 20.8.17; Badly damaged 1.9.17; East Fortune NFS by rail 1.10.17 - @5.18 (for carriers)

9949    (Convtd 9901a Ships Pup) Fuselage deld Hendon 24.5.17 (catapult launching experiments with 9948); Fuselage to Otis Works 9.6.17; Wings to CSD 13.6.17; Fuselage & wings retd Hendon 14.6.17; Removing catapult gear 13.8.17; East Fortune by rail 1.9.17 (arr 8.9.17); Donibristle 15.9.17; HMS *Nairana* by 29.9.17; HMS *Furious* by 13.10.17 (deck landing experiments with skid u/c); Donibristle by 27.10.17; HMS *Nairana* 8.11.17; HMS *Nairana* to Donibristle W/E 8.11.17; Rosyth W/E 13.12.17; HMS *Nairana* W/E 14.12.17; Rosyth W/E 20.12.17; HMS *Nairana* to HMS *Renown* W/E 20.12.17; HMS *Nairana* to Donibristle W/E 28.12.17; Rosyth W/E 5.1.18; Turnhouse W/E 9.3.18; Rosyth 3.18; Depot Flt Turnhouse W/E 22.3.18; HMS *Furious* by 3.18; Rosyth W/E 28.3.18; Turnhouse W/E 4.4.18; Donibristle W/E 31.10.18; HMS *Argus* W/E 21.11.18; Turnhouse W/E 12.12.18 - @30.1.19; HMS *Argus* by 11.19 (deck landing experiments with skid u/c)

9950    Converted to Beardmore W.B.III (SB3F) prototype. Deld Design Flt Eastchurch by rail for tests 2.2.17; Tested 8.2.17; FL All Hallows, Isle of Grain 10.3.17 (F/L PA Johnston); ECD Grain 12.3.17 (repair); Dismantling 3.5.17; Deleted 19.6.17

**50 ROYAL AIRCRAFT FACTORY B.E.2c TRACTOR BIPLANES ordered 3.11.16 under Cont No C.P.132110/16 from Blackburn Aeroplane & Motor Co Ltd, numbered 9951 to 10000 and built Leeds. Fitted Lewis gun and 4 light or 2 heavy bombs. (90-hp R.A.F.)**

9951    Deld Cranwell 11.5.17; Freiston by 6.17; Yarmouth 28.7.17; Freiston, AZP 19.10.17; Observers School Flt Eastchurch by 3.18; Cranwell by 30.3.18; Lincoln to Cranwell 9.4.18

9952    Wrecked before delivery to Eastchurch; Deleted 21.12.17

9953    Deld Eastchurch Workshops, tested and to Observers School Flt Eastchurch 12.6.17; Deleted from/by 19.8.17

9954    (100-hp R.A.F.) Deld Eastchurch Workshops and to Observers School Flt Eastchurch (coded 'B') 26.6.17; Damaged at Eastbourne 16.7.17, retd 20.7.17; Crashed 29.7.17; Crashed 10.8.17; Gunnery School Eastchurch by 29.12.17; Became 204 TDS Eastchurch 1.4.18 - 6.18; No.1 Observers School Eastchurch by 10.18; Mid-air collision 18.11.18 (Lt CE Wodehouse & 2/Lt RK Little both killed)

9955    Deld Cranwell 25.7.17; Wrecked 23.8.17; FL in pond in middle of aerodrome at 4 AAP Lincoln Racecourse 28.9.17; Crashed 2.10.17; FL and crashed, u/c and propeller damaged Metheringham 19.1.18 (pilot unhurt); Crashed and slightly damaged Scopwick 18.2.18 (pilot unhurt); Became 201/2 TDS Cranwell 1.4.18 - @2.5.18

9956    Deld Cranwell 25.7.17; Crashed, burnt 5.9.17; Surveyed 16.10.17; Deleted 18.10.17 wrecked

9957    Deld Observers School Flt Eastchurch 26.8.17; Became 204 TDS Eastchurch 1.4.18 - @26.5.18; No.1 Observers School Eastchurch by 10.18 - @11.18

9958    Deld Observers School Flt Eastchurch 26.8.17; For deletion by 30.3.18

9959    Deld Observers School Flt Eastchurch 27.9.17; Became 204 TDS Eastchurch 1.4.18; EF on cross-country, FL, crashed Hildeborough 18.5.18 (Lt AM Alexander); No.1 Observers School Eastchurch by 10.18 - @12.18

9960    Deld Observers School Flt Eastchurch 26.8.17; Became 204 TDS Eastchurch 1.4.18 - @7.18

9961    Deld Observers School Flt Eastchurch W/E 13.10.17; Deleted W/E 30.3.18

9962    Deld Observers School Flt Eastchurch (via Chingford) W/E 3.11.17; Became 204 TDS Eastchurch 1.4.18; vensey 1.6.18 (Lt AM Alexander)

9963    Deld Cranwell (coded '1') W/E 19.10.17; Became 57 TDS Cranwell 1.4.18 - 9.18; BUT AAFS Lympne 8.18

9964    Crashed Leeds 26.10.17 (sic), probably on delivery to Cranwell; Surveyed Blackburns 23.10.17; Deleted 14.11.17 wrecked

9965    Deld Cranwell 26.10.17; Lost propeller landing 13.11.17 (FSL LH Pearson); Became 201/2 TDS Cranwell 1.4.18 - @8.5.18

9966    Allocated East Fortune for erection 12.17 - 2.18 (arr by 9.2.18); 4 AAP Lincoln by 30.3.18; Cranwell 13.4.18 (transit); 203 TDS Manston 14.4.18 - @8.18; Wireless School Worthy Down by 9.18

9967    Deld Cranwell W/E 16.11.17 - @30.3.18; Grain by 6.18; Dover 19.6.18 (for temp SD); Grain 20.6.18

9968    Allocated East Fortune for erection 12.17 - 2.18 (arr by 9.2.18); Blackburn by 30.3.18 (allocated War School Manston); 4 AAP Lincoln 4.18; 15 TS Spittlegate 11.5.18

9969    Deld Type Test Flt Grain 17.12.17; Hendon 11.5.18; Martlesham 16.5.18; Hendon 17.5.18; Wyton 18.5.18; Hendon W/E 25.5.18; Grain TD W/E 1.6.18 - @8.18; Detd Dover 19-20.6.18; To French Govt post-war. Preserved Musée de l'Air, Paris (by 1957 to date)

9970    Deld Hendon 13.12.17; Dover 14.12.17; 14 Sqdn 16.12.17; 7 Sqdn by 20.12.17 - @24.1.18; 14 Sqdn by 21.2.18 - @8.3.18; 15 Sqdn by 14.3.18; Became 215 Sqdn 1.4.18; to 214 Sqdn 4.18; Damaged in aerial bombardment 18.6.18

9971    Deld Cranwell 14.12.17 (en route Yarmouth); Yarmouth by 29.12.17 - @30.3.18; Covehithe by 4.18, AZP 12.4.18 (FSL GR Halliday); Burgh Castle by 5.18; Yarmouth by 5.18; Became 490 Flt Yarmouth 25.5.18

9972    Deld RFC Gosport 14.1.18 - @30.3.18 (E & W/T trials)

9973    Deld Yarmouth W/E 2.2.18 - @23.2.18; Bacton by 4.18; AZP 12/13.4.18 (FSL FR Bicknell); Burgh Castle by 5.18; Yarmouth by 5.18; Hendon (ex Aldeburgh) from 25.5.18 - @3.7.18 (compass duties); EF, FL Gosport 3.6.18

9974    Deld Yarmouth W/E 26.1.18; Turnhouse 4.4.18 - @30.1.19; HMS *Furious* by 7.19

9975    Deld Yarmouth W/E 26.1.18; Turnhouse 4.4.18 - @30.1.19 (Observers practice)

9976    Deld Hendon (via Hitchin) 22.1.18 (for Air Dept officers); Orfordness 12.2.18; Chingford 13.2.18 (special service); Mullion, tested 14.3.18; Prawle Point 20.3.18; Padstow by 11.5.18 - @19.11.18

9977    Deld Cranwell W/E 15.2.18; Lost, crashed and badly damaged, Halstead, Essex 23.2.18 (pilot unhurt); Retd 26.2.18; Deleted W/E 22.3.18

9978    Deld Observers School Flt Eastchurch W/E 26.1.18; Became 204 TDS 1.4.18; No 1 Observers School Eastchurch by 12.18; Became 2 MOS 28.12.18

9979    Deld Observers School Flt Eastchurch W/E 26.1.18; Became 204 TDS Eastchurch 1.4.18 - @6.18; No.1 Observers School Eastchurch by 10.18 - @12.18

9980    Deld Yarmouth W/E 2.2.18 (night flying); Turnhouse 4.4.18 (Observers practice); Burgh Castle, AZP, EF, FL 3m E of Beccles 13.4.18 (FSL RC Packe); Deleted W/E 27.4.18

9981    Deld Cranwell (via Hull) 4.2.18 (en route Yarmouth); Yarmouth by 27.2.18 (night flying); Dropped 2x65-lb bombs on U-boat 3m ESE of Lowestoft Harbour 21.3.18 (F/L WL Graham); Burgh Castle, HACP 12.4.18 (F/L CS Iron); Yarmouth by 4.18; Turnhouse W/E 20.4.18 - @30.1.19 (Observers practice)

9982    Deld Yarmouth W/E 2.2.18 (night flying); Turnhouse 4.4.18 (Observers practice); retd Yarmouth 4.18; Burgh Castle, HACP 12.4.18 (F/L CS Iron); Yarmouth, AZP

13.4.18 (F/L CS Iron); Turnhouse W/E 20.4.18; Deleted W/E 12.9.18

9983    Deld Yarmouth W/E 2.2.18 (night flying); Turnhouse 4.4.18 (Observers practice); With HMS *Ouse* sank *UC70* 28.8.18; still Turnhouse 30.1.19

9984    Deld Yarmouth W/e 23.2.18; Turnhouse 4.4.18 (Observers practice); Donibristle W/E 14.11.18 - @30.1.19

9985    Deld Yarmouth W/E 23.2.18; Lost at sea 30.3.18

9986    Deld 1 AAP Coventry by 2.18; D Flt Cranwell W/E 1.3.18; EF, FL Wellingore 5.3.18 (pilot unhurt); Became 201/2 TDS Cranwell 1.4.18; Collided on ground with Pup B6064 and wrecked 3.4.18

9987    Deld 4 AAP Lincoln by 23.2.18; Chingford W/E 8.3.18 (special service); Became 207 TDS Chingford 1.4.18 - @10.5.18

9988    Deld 4 AAP Lincoln 2.18; War School Manston by 30.3.18; 1 TDS Stamford/Wittering by 8.18 - @2.18 (B.E.2d)

9989    Deld 4 AAP Lincoln 2.18; War School Manston by 30.3.18; Became 203 TDS Manston 1.4.18; Stalled on turn, nosedived 2.7.18 (Sgt HR Felton killed)

9990    Deld 4 AAP Lincoln by 30.3.18; Cranwell 31.3.18; Became 202 TDS Cranwell 1.4.18; WO 29.5.18

9991    Deld Grain Type Test Flt 9.11.17 - @25.5.18

9992    Deld Cranwell W/E 2.11.17; Crashed Wildmore, nr New York Village 11.12.17; EF, FL at RFC Boston 24.1.18; Became 201/2 TDS Cranwell 1.4.18

9993    Deld Cranwell (coded 'F') W/E 2.11.17; EF, FL Hanthorpe, Lincs 26.3.18 (retd 27.3.18); Became 201/2 TDS Cranwell 1.4.18 - @6.18

9994    Deld Eastchurch W/E 13.10.17; Hendon 27.4.18; Old Sarum 30.4.18 - @19.5.18; Hendon 20.7.18; No.1 Observers School Eastchurch by 10.18

9995    Deld Brough to Observers School Flt Eastchurch 29.9.17; Became 204 TDS Eastchurch 1.4.18 - 7.18

9996    Deld Brough to Observers School Flt Eastchurch 15.9.17; Became 204 TDS Eastchurch 1.4.18; No.1 Observers School Eastchurch by 10.18; EF, FL 3.10.18 (FSL LH Pearson)

9997    FF 31.8.17; Deld Brough to Observers School Flt Eastchurch 15.9.17 [at Leysdown 10.17]; Became 204 TDS Eastchurch 1.4.18; Starboard wing folded at 500 ft, dived in 31.5.18 (Hon Capt FH McMaster & Lt AF Parker both killed)

9998    Deld Eastchurch Observers School 5.10.17; St.Pol (via Coudekerque and Dover) 23.11.17; Paris Naval Air Station 11.17 (for W/Cdr Spenser DA Grey); For deletion by 29.12.17 - 30.3.18 (wrecked)

9999    (100-hp RAF) Deld Brough to Observers School Flt Eastchurch 25.7.17; Gunnery School Flt by 29.12.17; Became 204 TDS Eastchurch 1.4.18 - @6.18; No.1 Observers School Eastchurch by 10.18

10000    Deld Observers School Flt Eastchurch 19.7.17; Crashed and WO Eastchurch 8.17; Deleted 31.8.17

*Royal Aircraft Factory B.E.2c at Dover with four bombs under the nose. (via Frank Cheesman)*

*Port Victoria P.V.2 N1, at Grain, fitted with Linton Hope floats. (via Philip Jarrett)*

*Port Victoria P.V.4 N8 Pusher Seaplane at Grain 1917. (via J.D.Oughton)*

*Fairey III N9 aboard HMS Slinger for catapult trials, June 1918. (via J.D.Oughton)*

**1 PORT VICTORIA P.V.2 TRACTOR BIPLANE SEAPLANE SCOUT numbered N1 and built at Grain. (100-hp Gnome Monosoupape B-2)**

N1      Completed PVRS Grain 6.16 (pontoon floats) (Linton Hope floats) (fitted movable Davis cannon); Tested 6.6.16; 2 Exptl flights 26.7.16; Under trial 2.8.16; To Maplin Sands 9.8.16 (presume visit for trials); PVRS became ECD Grain 26.2.17 (then being modified to P.V.2 bis); Type Test Dept Grain 21.3.17; ECD Grain for alterations 11.4.17; Retd Type Test Flt Grain 25.4.17; Deleted 27.8.17

**1 MANN EGERTON TYPE F (ADMIRALTY 47 TYPE) TRACTOR BIPLANE to be numbered N2. (130-hp Clerget 9B)**

N2      Cancelled

**SERIAL N3 NOT USED** [possibly N300 used instead]

**2 SOPWITH 1½ STRUTTER TRACTOR BIPLANES, serials N4 and N5 allocated 13.11.16 (130-hp Clerget 9B)**

N4 and N5 cancelled and serials reallocated

**2 SOPWITH FS.1 BABY (IMPROVED) TRACTOR BIPLANE SEAPLANES put forward W/E 1.12.16 and ordered under Cont No A.S.26088 from Sopwith to be numbered N4 and N5 and built at Kingston. (130-hp Clerget 9B)**

N4      Deld Kingston to Type Test Flt Grain 24.3.17 (Hawker); Wrecked on/by 27.3.17; Surveyed 19.11.17 (exptl type unsatisfactory); Deleted 26.11.17

N5      Completed with wheels undercarriage, becoming prototype of 2F.1 Ships Camel; Deld Brooklands to Hendon 3.3.17; Flown 14.3.17; Testing Sqdn Martlesham Heath 15.3.17 (standard Lang propeller); Inverted Lewis gun fitted to centre section; Crashed after TO on second test flight 27.3.17; Rebuilt; ECD Grain 1.4.17 (standard centre-section cut-out, W/T worked from wind-driven generator below port cockpit, 8 Le Prieur rockets on struts 6.17, Admiralty Top Plane mounting for Lewis gun); Visited Eastchurch 4.4.17; W/E 7.4.17 "Arrange split fuselage in N5, originally designed as a seaplane, to convert back to seaplane to allow trials to continue after being interrupted by wrecking of N4; Flown to Brooklands for Sopwith" (sic); Awaiting deck landing hook 19.4.17; Flown 2.6.17; Tested 11.6.17; Under repair 11.8.17; Grain Test Flt W/E 15.12.17; Deleted 13.2.18 (wrecked); Presume rebuilt; Deleted W/E 9.7.18

**N6 AND N7 NOT ALLOTTED**

**1 PORT VICTORIA P.V.4 PUSHER BIPLANE SEAPLANE numbered N8 and built at Grain. (110-hp Clerget 9Z)**

N8      Originally designed for 150-hp Smith static engine, but fitted instead with 110-hp Clerget which proved unsatisfactory. Airframe completed and taken over by Test Dept Grain 9.6.17; Not ready by 28.6.17; Fitted Linton Hope floats. Deleted 27.8.17

**2 FAIREY TYPE III TRACTOR BIPLANE SEAPLANES put forward W/E 1.12.16 to old Admiralty Type 3 Spec, ordered under Cont No A.S.1521 to new A.D. Spec N.2(a), numbered N9 and N10 and built at Hayes. (190-hp Falcon I)**

N9      (C/n F.127). Deld CSD White City to Type Test Dept Grain by road 14.4.17; Damaged float and strut fittings 21.5.17; ECD Grain 10.7.17; Fitting catapult experimental gear from 8.8.17; Grain W/E 24.11.17; Catapult trials HMS *Slinger* 14.5.18 & 13.6.18; Still at Grain 1.19; Bought back by Mkrs; Rebuilt and re-engined 250-hp Maori II, regd K-103 1.5.19; Became G-EAAJ; Sold to Norwegian Navy 5.20; Became N-20 by 1927; Sold to Bjorne Neilson 12.6.28; Scrapped 2.29

N10     (C/n F.128). Fitted 260-hp Maori II. Deld Test Dept Grain by road 31.8.17; FF 14.9.17; Convtd IIIA Landplane to meet Spec N.2(b) under Cont No C.P.136591; Calibration and handling test 2.12.17; Grain Test Dept 5.12.17 - @29.12.17; Reverted seaplane (IIIB wings); Grain 6.2.18 - 11.18 (N.2(a) & N.2(b) type trials); Chassis damaged, towed in to Westgate 31.5.18; Bought back by Mkrs, at Fairey by 31.10.18; Fitted short span single-bay wings and 450-hp Lion; Registered G-EALQ as seaplane 9.19; Participated Schneider Trophy Race at Bournemouth 10.9.19; Mkrs to Grain 14.1.20; Convtd two-bay wings amphibian; Felixstowe 5.9.20; Martlesham Heath 6.9.20; Amphibian Competition 9.20 (various trials: 1,2 or 3 seats; 9 different engines); Croydon 11.10.20; Retd Mkrs; SOC 1922

**N11 TO N13 NOT ALLOTTED** (Blank numbers)

**1 WIGHT TYPE 4 QUADRUPLANE to Admiralty Type 4 Spec, ordered 16.12.16 to Spec N.1 (b), numbered N14 and built at East Cowes. (130-hp Clerget 9B)**

N14     Completed 13.6.17; Flt trials 27.6.17; Hull mods 7.7.17; Deld at Mkrs 16.7.17; Flt trials 18.7.17; Hull mods 9.17; Flt trials 26.9.17; Failed tests, not accepted, still at Wights 12.17 - @23.2.18

     [N14 - triplane substituted for quadruplane W/E 23.2.17] [vice-versa really?]

**1 WIGHT BIPLANE FLYING BOAT, numbered N15 and built at East Cowes. (130-hp Clerget 9B)**

N15     Cancelled, but still on order 1.17. [also reported as Nieuport As14 seaplane]

     [Put forward W/E 1.12.16 for 2 Wight Type 4 to be numbered N14 and N15, and ordered W/E 12.1.17]

**2 WESTLAND TYPE 4 SCOUT SEAPLANE put forward W/E 1.12.16 to Admiralty Type 4 Spec, ordered under Cont Nos C.P.136919/16 & A.S.4684 to A.D. Spec N.1(b), numbered N16 & N17, and built Yeovil. (Ordered with 130-hp Clerget 9B, but delivered with 150-hp B.R.1)**

N16     (C/n W.159?) Variable-camber wing and experimental floats; Deld Test Dept Grain by rail 29.7.17; FF 8.17; Crashed 8.9.17; Deleted W/E 15.9.17

N17     Standard floats; FF 8.17; Later Westland floats; Deld Test Dept Grain 10.17; Westgate W/E 24.11.17; Deleted W/E 6.4.18

**2 NORMAN THOMPSON CRUISER FLYING BOATS ordered 5.1.17 under Cont No A.S.24362 to A.D. Spec N.2(c) and numbered N18 & N19, to be built at Middleton-on-Sea. (Two 320-hp Cossack)**

N18 and N19 Design delayed and finally cancelled

**2 SHORT IMPROVED NAVYPLANE PUSHER BIPLANE PATROL SEAPLANES put forward 2.17, to be numbered N20 & N21. (200-hp Sunbeam)**

N20 and N21 cancelled

**1 PHOENIX P.2 PATROL TRACTOR BIPLANE FLYING BOAT put forward W/E 2.2.17, to be numbered N22. (200-hp Hispano-Suiza 8B)**

N22     Cancelled 1917

**1 PHOENIX PATROL PUSHER BIPLANE SEAPLANE put forward W/E 2.2.17, to be numbered N23.**

N23     Cancelled 1917

*Fairey III N10. (via Philip Jarrett)*

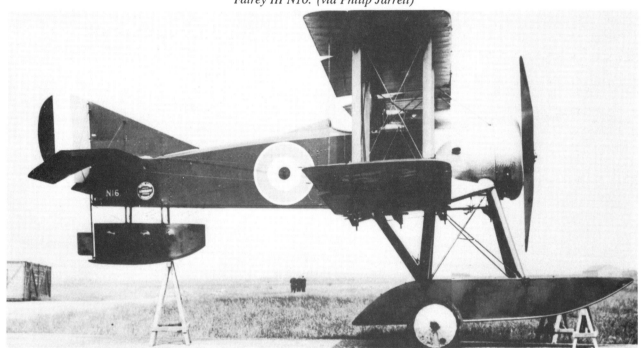

*Westland Seaplane Scout N16. (Westland Aircraft Ltd)*

*Norman Thompson Flying Boat N26 at Grain (via E. Cromie)*

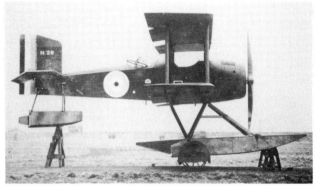

*Handley Page R/200 seaplane N28 at Grain. (via Philip Jarrett)*

*Handley Page R/200 landplane N29 at Grain. (via J.D.Oughton)*

*Short Experimental Scout No.1 Seaplane N36 at Rochester. (J.M.Bruce/G.S.Leslie collection)*

*Norman Thompson N.1B Flying Boat N37. (via Philip Jarrett)*

*Beardmore W.B.IV Fighter N38 at Grain for flotation tests, 27.9.18. (J.M.Bruce/G.S.Leslie collection)*

**2 SUPERMARINE PATROL BIPLANE SEAPLANES put forward 2.17, to be numbered N24 & N25. (200-hp Arab)**

N24 and N25 cancelled

**1 NORMAN THOMPSON TRACTOR BIPLANE FLYING BOAT ordered 6.9.17 (sic) under contract A.S.4682 (BR.255), numbered N26 and built at Middleton-on-Sea. (150-hp Hispano-Suiza)**

N26     Completed 1.17; Deld Calshot 5.4.17, later used for training; 150-hp Hispano-Suiza by 1.18; Deleted 1.3.18 (W&T)

**6 HANDLEY PAGE R/200 RECONNAISSANCE TRACTOR BIPLANE SEAPLANES ordered under Cont A.S.11217 (BR.44) to A.D. Spec N.2(a), numbered N27 to N32 and built at Cricklewood. (200-hp Hispano-Suiza 8B)**

N27     (Completed as seaplane). Allocated Grain 31.5.17 (type trials with 240-hp Hispano-Suiza); Trials on Welsh Harp reservoir, Hendon by 29.12.17 - @27.4.18 BUT Calshot, WO 1.3.18 because of deterioration

N28     (Completed as seaplane). FF 9.17; Deld Cricklewood to ECD Grain W/E 24.11.17; Test Dept Grain 1.12.17; Handling trials 24.12.17; Welsh Harp Hendon 12.17; Grain 12.17, tests delayed by propeller trouble; Deleted W/E 30.3.18

N29     (Completed as landplane). FF 10.17; Issued to Beatty's aerodrome 29.12.17; Type Test Dept Grain 28.1.18; Deleted W/E 30.3.18

N30     (Completed as landplane). Tested Grain 3.18; Cancelled 3.18

N31 and N32. To have been seaplanes. Cancelled 3.18

**3 ROBEY (TRACTOR?) BIPLANE DAVIS & LEWIS GUN-CARRYING SEAPLANES ordered 4.16 [under Cont No C.P.04921/15?] to Spec N.2(a) and numbered N33 to N35, to be built at Lincoln. (200-hp Hispano-Suiza 8B)**

N33     Construction abandoned 7.17
N34 and N35 cancelled 7.17

**1 SHORT EXPERIMENTAL SCOUT NO.1 TRACTOR BIPLANE SEAPLANE ordered under Cont No A.S.9604 to A.D. Spec N.2(a), numbered N36 and built at Rochester. (200-hp Sunbeam Afridi) [Gordon Bruce's researches show correct c/n to be S.313]**

N36     Launched 2.1.17; FF 23.1.17; Deld Test Depot Grain 10.3.17 (type trials); Tested 27.3.17 (JL Parker - described as Short Scout Type 3 - no serial at that stage, c/n only); ECD Grain 27.4.17; Serial number applied 18.5.17; Tested 26.5.17 (F/Cdr MEA Wright); Type Test Dept Grain 1.6.17 - @19.1.18; stated to have been abandoned and mod to Experimental Scout No.2 with 260-hp Maori; Deleted W/E 16.2.18

**1 NORMAN THOMPSON TANDEM-SEATER FIGHTER FLYING BOAT ordered under Cont Nos A.S.10732/17 (BR.64) & A.S.11542 to A.D. Spec N.1(b), numbered N37 and built at Middleton-on-Sea. (150-hp Hispano-Suiza 8Aa)**

N37     Completed W/E 10.12.17; Deld Type Test Dept Grain 20.12.17; Re-fitted 200-hp Hispano-Suiza 8B; Damaged in crash landing 1.18; Deleted W/E 27.6.18

**3 BEARDMORE W.B.IV SINGLE SEAT TRACTOR BIPLANE FIGHTERS ordered under Cont No A.S.11542 (BR.68) to A.D. Spec N.1(a) and numbered N38 to N40, to be built at Dalmuir. (200-hp Hispano-Suiza 8B)**

N38     Completed 11.17; Tested Grain 20.5.18; Martlesham Heath for performance tests 20.5.18 - @13.8.18; Allocated Grain for ditching trials 10.8.18; Flotation tests Grain 27-28.9.18; Tested to destruction, sank under test when flotation chamber stoved in; WO 12.12.18

N39 and N40 not completed

**3 BEARDMORE W.B.V SINGLE SEAT TRACTOR BIPLANE FIGHTERS ordered under Cont No A.S.11542 (BR.68) to A.D. Spec N.1(a) and numbered N41 to N43, to be built at Dalmuir. (200-hp Hispano-Suiza 8B)**

N41     (Fitted 37mm Canon Puteaux quick firing gun; later re-armed with fixed Vickers gun and an upward firing Lewis gun); FF 3.12.17; Ditching tests 17.12.17; Deld Type Test Flt Grain 4.12.17; Crashed and wrecked Kingsferry Bridge 4.1.18 (F/L JW Pinder injured); Surveyed 11.1.18; Deleted 17.1.18 DBR

N42     FF Dalmuir 20.2.18; Project abandoned 4.18

N43     Cancelled (not completed?)

**6 MANN EGERTON TYPE H SHIPBOARD TRACTOR BIPLANE SCOUTS ordered under Cont No A.S.13905/17 (BR.68) to A.D. Spec N.1(a) and numbered N44 to N49, to be built at Norwich. (200-hp Hispano-Suiza 8B)**

N44     Type H1 (fitted buoyancy chambers and jettisonable u/c). Deld Type Test Flt Grain 12.10.17 - @19.1.18

N45     Type H2 (fitted flotation gear). Deld Type Test Flt Grain 19.11.17 - @19.1.18

N46 to N49 not completed

**1 SOPWITH B.1 TRACTOR BIPLANE built at Kingston-on-Thames and numbered N50. Served as prototype for Grain Griffin. (200-hp Hispano-Suiza 8B)**

N50     Tested at Mkrs 23.5.17; Deld ADD by 5.17; 5 Sqdn 16.5.17 - @1.6.17 (went on bombing missions with DH4s - fitted Hispano-Suiza); ADD 6.17; Dover 8.6.17; ECD Grain for type trials W/E 8.12.17; COL 11.12.17 (repaired); 200-hp B.R.1 by 12.17; EC&AD Grain W/E 19.1.18 (for air bag tests); 200-hp Hispano- Suiza 8B by 3.18; Turnhouse W/E 11.7.18 (fitted 200-hp Adder); Grain W/E 3.10.18 - @30.1.19 (fitted hydrovane); Allotted Med Area 31.12.18

**2 KINGSBURY DAVIS-GUN CARRIER TRACTOR TRIPLANES ordered by 4.6.17 under BR.75 to A.D. Spec N.3(a) from Kingsbury Aviation Co and numbered N51 & N52. (275-hp Rolls-Royce)**

N51     Not completed
N52     Cancelled

**2 GRAIN P.V.5 TRACTOR BIPLANE RECONNAISSANCE SEAPLANES built by ECD Grain and numbered N53 & N54. (150/200-hp Hispano-Suiza)**

N53     P.V.5 (150-hp Hispano-Suiza 8A) FF 25.7.17, short preliminary flight, lost float on landing and sank (S/Cdr HR Busteed); Salvaged, FF 29.7.17; Tested 26.8.17 (F/Cdr CT Freeman DSC); Flt tested ECD Grain 6.9.17; Damaged W/E 8.9.17; Deleted W/E 15.9.17

N54     P.V.5A (200-hp Hispano-Suiza 8B) ECD Grain from 12.6.17 (type trials); Test Dept Grain W/E 15.12.17; Repairs after accident 22.12.17; Type Test Dept Grain by 3.18 (150-hp B.R.1); Still Grain 1.19

**1 GRAIN P.V.9 TRACTOR BIPLANE FIGHTER SEAPLANE built by ECD Grain to old Admiralty Type N.1(b) Spec and and numbered N55. (150-hp B.R.1)**

N55     (150-hp B.R.1) Type trials at Grain from 12.6.17; FF 12.17; Felixstowe W/E 3.10.18 - @30.1.19; Felixstowe from 10.19

**3 BLACKBURN SINGLE SEAT BIPLANE PUSHER FLYING BOAT FIGHTERS ordered under Cont No A.S.17278 (BR.105 dated 19.6.17) to A.D. Spec N.1(b) and numbered N56 to N58. (200-hp Hispano-Suiza 8B)**

N56     Hull only built by 11.18; Completed as Pellet with 450-hp Lion. Entered for 1923 Schneider Trophy Race as No.6; Registered G-EBHF 23.7.23; FF 26.9.23; Porpoised and sank in Humber 27.9.23

N57 and N58 cancelled 1917 before completion

*Beardmore W.B.V Fighter N42 at Dalmuir. (via Philip Jarrett)*

*Mann Egerton H.1 N44 shipboard fighter N44. (via J.D.Oughton)*

*Sopwith B.1 N50. (via Philip Jarrett)*

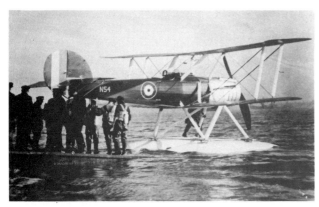

*Grain P.V.5A Reconnaissance Seaplane N54.
(J.M.Bruce/G.S.Leslie collection)*

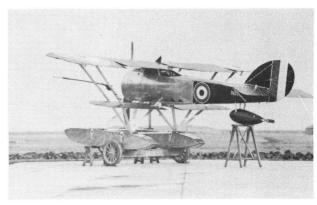

*Grain P.V.9 Fighter Seaplane N55. (via P.H.T.Green)*

*Supermarine Baby Flying Boat Fighter N59. (RAF
Museum P.19388)*

*Felixstowe F.2c Patrol Flying Boat N65 at Felixstowe.
(via E.Cromie)*

*Short N.2B Seaplane N67 with 219 Sqdn at Westgate in 1919. (RAF Museum P.17279)*

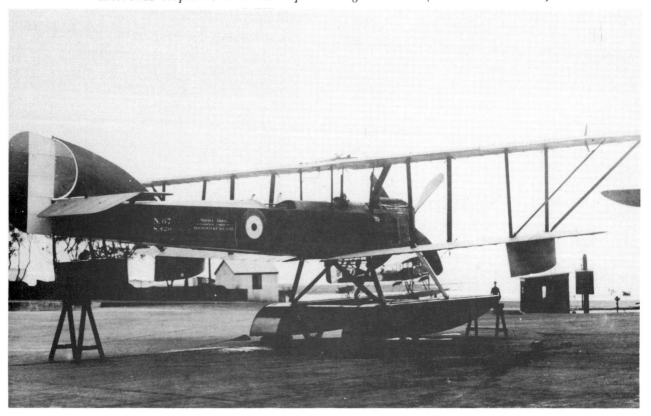

**3 SUPERMARINE BABY PUSHER BIPLANE FLYING BOAT FIGHTERS ordered under Cont Nos A.S.3929 & A.S.22245 (BR.105 dated 19.6.17) to A.D. Spec N.1(b) and numbered N59 to N61, to be built at Woolston. (200-hp Arab)**

N59     FF 2.18; Deld Test Depot Grain 17.4.18 (type & performance trials); To Felixstowe 4.19; (also fitted 200-hp Hispano-Suiza 8B)

N60     To Grain as spares 1918

N61     Cancelled

**2 HANDLEY PAGE TYPE T/400 BIPLANE FLYING BOATS ordered under Cont No A.S.17562 (BR.117 dated 2.7.17) and numbered N62 & N63. (Two 360-hp Eagle VIII)**

N62 and N63. On lines of F3 with experimental folding wings. Cancelled 10.12.17.

**1 FELIXSTOWE F.2c (later F.3) PATROL TRACTOR BIPLANE FLYING BOAT ordered under BR.117 dated 21.6.17, numbered N64 and built at Felixstowe. (Two 360-hp Eagle VIII)**

N64     Completed as F.2c; Wings arrived Felixstowe 8.1.17; Ready at Felixstowe by 3.2.17; FF 10.2.17 (F/Cdr RJJ Hope-Vere); Servo motor tested 15.3.17; Starboard lower plane under repair 14.5.17; Bottom under repair 28.5.17; First patrol as F.2c 9.6.17; Fitting dual control by 6.7.17; War Flt Felixstowe by 7.17; Re-allocated Grain 1.10.17 (presume for conversion to F.3); Retd Felixstowe as F.3, 1st patrol as F.3 31.10.17; Fitted 320-hp Cossack (when?); Hydrophone test 7.1.18; Worn out by 1.4.18; Surveyed 10.5.18; Deleted 15.5.18 FW&T

**1 FELIXSTOWE F.2c PATROL TRACTOR BIPLANE FLYING BOAT ordered under BR.117 dated 21.6.17, numbered N65 and built at Felixstowe. (Two 322-hp Eagle VI)**

N65     Erecting Felixstowe from 19.4.17; Ready 13.5.17; Tested 15.5.17 & 16.5.17; Wings removed, fitting bomb gear 23.5.17; Alterations to rudder controls 3.6.17; Grain 12.6.17; Felixstowe 15.6.17; Grain 23.6.17 (trials); War Flt Felixstowe by 4.7.17; With 8676 & 8689, helped in sinking of *UC1* (dropped 2 bombs) 6m SSW of North Hinder 24.7.17 (W/Cdr JC Porte, F/Cdr AQ Cooper & crew); Fitted 250-hp Sunbeam by 29.12.17; Re-fitted 322-hp Eagle VI; To Grain but retd with engine trouble 18.2.18; Grain 21.2.18; Deleted Grain 18.3.18 DBR

**8 SHORT N.2b TRACTOR BIPLANE SEAPLANES ordered under Cont No No A.S.21847 to A.D. Spec N.2(b) (later RAF Type XXX), numbered N66 to N73 and built at Rochester. (275-hp Maori I) [Originally N66 - N71 to BR.151 and N72 - N73 to BR.221, later all to BR.151] [Gordon Bruce's researches show c/n's to be S.419 to S.426]**

N66     Completed 22.9.17; FF 22.12.17; Deld Type Test Dept Grain W/E 26.1.18; Westgate 20.4.18; Dover 27.4.18 (transit); Calshot TS 4.5.18; Tested 11.5.18; Deleted W/E 13.6.18

N67     Deld Type Test Flt Grain 16.3.18 - @30.3.18 (fitted with 184-type floats); MAD Grain W/E 20.4.18; Felixstowe 9.7.18; Grain 20.7.18; Dover 27.7.18; Le Havre 28.7.18 (retd later); Damaged 17.8.18; New wings and floats fitted 9.18; Felixstowe 31.10.18; FF 2.11.18; To 219 Sqdn Westgate 12.18; Mkrs Rochester 1.3.19; Took Mjr Gen JEB Seely from Rochester to Houses of Parliament, flown through Tower Bridge 9.4.19 (JL Parker); Fitted Eagle VIII; FF 24.5.19 (JL Parker); Grain 27.5.19 (JL Parker); Retd Rochester 28.5.19; Refitted Maori I; Grain 2.1.20

N68 to N73 cancelled, c/n's partially reallotted to N110-N112

**1 SOPWITH T.1 CUCKOO TRACTOR BIPLANE TORPEDO BOMBER ordered under BR.156, numbered N74 and built at Kingston-on-Thames. (200-hp Hispano-Suiza 8B)**

N74     Completed 6.6.17; EAD Grain 7.17; Test flown 2.8.17 prior to air bag test; East Fortune 23.9.17; Donibristle

24.9.17; Rosyth 17.10.17; HMS *Furious* 2.11.17; Rosyth 10.11.17; Test Depot Grain W/E 14.12.17 (fit torpedo gear); Blackburn W/E 2.2.18 (re-engined 200-hp Arab); Cranwell W/E 16.2.18; Type Test Flt Grain for repair 16.3.18 (200hp Arab); East Fortune School W/E 18.7.18; Deleted W/E 29.8.18

**1 KINGSBURY DAVIS-GUN TRACTOR TRIPLANE ordered under BR.75 to A.D. Spec N.3(a), to be numbered N75**

N75     Project cancelled 1.18 due to firm's commitments

**6 FAIREY N.2a TRACTOR BIPLANES ordered under Cont No A.S.30059 (BR.213) to A.D. Spec N.2(a) and numbered N76 to N81. (200-hp Arab)**

N76 to N81 cancelled

**2 NORMAN THOMPSON N.2c TYPE (possibly N.T.4B) PUSHER BIPLANE FLYING BOATS ordered 23.11.17 under Cont No A.S.33477 (BR.237) to A.D. Spec. N.2(c), to be numbered N82 & N83 and built Middleton-on-Sea. Contract closed 8.2.19. (Two 200-hp Arab)**

N82     Initial trials 1.8.18; Tested by Naval Air Section pilot 16.10.18; Allotted Grain 23.10.18; Allotment cancelled W/E 14.11.18; Deleted 31.12.18

N83     Not completed; Deleted 31.12.18

**2 TELLIER FLYING BOATS purchased under BR.233 from France 14.11.17, numbered N84 & N85 and allocated Grain for gun trials. (To have been Lorraine-Dietrich, but deld with 200-hp Hispano-Suiza 8B)**

N84     Deld Grain 6.4.18 - @30.1.19 (gun trials)

N85     Deld Grain 30.4.18- @30.1.19 (gun and camouflage trials)

**2 PHOENIX P.5 CORK TRACTOR BIPLANE FLYING BOATS ordered 28.11.17 under Cont No A.S.37016/17 (BR.256) from The Phoenix Dynamo Mfg Co Ltd to A.D. Spec N.3(b) and numbered N86 & N87. Hulls built by May, Harden & May. (Two 352-hp Eagle VIII)**

N86     Mk.I By road from Hull to Bradford 4.18; Assd Brough; FF 4.8.18, damaged on TO; Deld MAES Grain for type trials 24.8.18; Fitted new wings; FF 17.10.18; Propeller test, wing fabric torn off near blades 22.10.19; Became MAEE Grain 3.20; Overload trials 5.20 - 10.20; still Grain 10.21; Mkrs, Preston by 11.22; Retd MAEE Grain 11.22 (new bottom to hull); MAEE to Felixstowe 17.3.24 (Impact tests 2.4.24 & 4.4.24) (night landing tests); Propeller accident 18.6.24; SOC 11.24

N87     Mk.II By road from Hull to Bradford 5.18; Assd Brough 21.2.19 (P.5A); FF 28.3.19; MAES Grain 27.6.19 performance trials); Hull damaged in water bag trolley tests 29.6.19; Became MAEE Grain 3.20; Re-erected Grain 8.20 after repair by Shorts - @1.21; Preston, re-engined 450-hp Lion IIA as Mk.III; Preliminary flight 31.1.22; Launching and alighting trials 11-12.3.22; FF 2.8.22; Grain to FB Devt Flt 13.7.22; Cruise 4.8.22; Wrecked in gale at Newhaven 18.9.22 (F/L GE Livock); Dismantled 20.9.22; Parts to Grain

**2 FAIREY F.2a PATROL TRACTOR BIPLANE FLYING BOATS ordered under Cont No A.S.37017 (BR.256) to A.D. Spec N.3 and numbered N88 & N89). (2 Sunbeam or Rolls-Royce)**

N88 and N89 (c/n's F.342 and F.343) cancelled

**1 FELIXSTOWE F.5 PATROL TRACTOR BIPLANE FLYING BOAT ordered to Spec N.3, numbered N90 and built at Felixstowe (Two 375-hp Eagle VIII)**

N90     TOC Felixstowe 28.11.17 (type trials); Grain 1.5.18 (hydrophone trials); Felixstowe 20.5.18 (on CTD charge); Visited Copenhagen 19.7.19; Reval 20.7.19; Helsingfors 21.7.19; Retd Grain; Crashed and WO Calshot

*Tellier Flying Boat N85 with C.O.W. gun at Grain. (via Philip Jarrett)*

*Norman Thompson N.T.2c Type Flying Boat N82 at Grain in 1918. (J.M.Bruce/G.S.Leslie collection)*

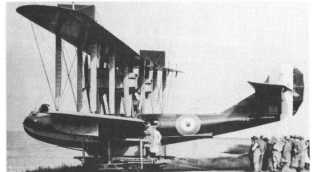

*Phoenix N.86 Cork Mk.I Flying Boat N86. (via Philip Jarrett)*

*Felixstowe F.5 Patrol Flying Boat N90. (via Charles W.Cain)*

*Royal Aircraft Factory C.E.1 Patrol Flying Boat N98. (FAA Museum)*

*Short Shirl N112 fitted with experimental half-ton mail container. (via J.D.Oughton)*

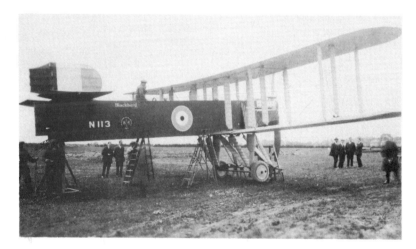

*Blackburn Blackburd Torpedo Bomber N113. (R.C.Sturtivant collection)*

*Sage 4 School Seaplane N117. (R.C.Sturtivant collection)*

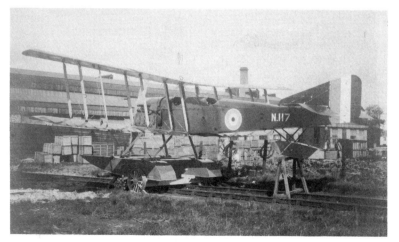

**6 PARNALL PANTHER SHIPBOARD FLEET RECONNAISSANCE TRACTOR BIPLANES ordered 12.17 under Cont No A.S.37023 (BR.267) to A.D. Spec N.2(a), numbered N91 to N96 and built at Yate. (230-hp B.R.2)**

N91 Deld Hendon 20.4.18; AES Martlesham Heath 22.4.18 (performance tests to 24.5.18); Retd Mkrs Filton late 6.18 to fit flotation gear, to at least 1.19

N92 Deld Turnhouse 22.6.18 (fleet trials); To HMS *Campania* in ML *Guide Me* 12.8.18; Scapa 16.8.18; Donibristle 8.18; Turnhouse 10.10.18; Donibristle 11.10.18; HMS *Repulse* 1.11.18 (fleet trials); Rosyth W/E 21.11.18 - @30.1.19

N93 Balanced elevators. Deld MAES Grain 18.9.18 (ditching trials 26.9.18 with flotation gear and jettisonable u/c); Mkrs W/E 24.10.18; Turnhouse W/E 19.12.18 - @30.1.19

N94 Mkrs @25.7.18, prepare for structural tests; Farnborough by 29.8.18 (sand tests, proof loading); left (Mkrs?) W/E 12.12.18; 205 Sqdn HMS *Argus*, crashed in sea 2.11.22

N95 Completed 9.18; Allocated Turnhouse for Fleet trials but not deld by 30.1.19

N96 Fitted Hydrovanes and air bags

**2 SHORT SCHOOL TRACTOR BIPLANE SEAPLANES ordered 1.18 under Cont No A.S.6285 (BR.356) from Fredk Sage & Co Ltd, to be numbered N97 & N98. (200-hp Hispano-Suiza 8B)**

N97 and N98 cancelled and re-allotted

**2 ROYAL AIRCRAFT FACTORY C.E.1 PATROL TRACTOR BIPLANE FLYING BOATS ordered 12.17, numbered N97 & N98 and built at Farnborough**

N97 (230-hp R.A.F.3A) Was to be B9960. FF Hamble 17.1.18; Deld Test Dept Grain 12.3.18 - @30.1.19 (NPL tests)

N98 (260-hp Maori) Was to be B9961. Completed 3.18; Fitted W/T. Deld Test Dept Grain 6.4.18; Westgate 6.1.19; Yarmouth 15.2.19; 219 Sqdn Westgate by 6.19

**N99 - Blank number (more likely a cancelled order?)**

**7 GRAIN GRIFFIN (ADMIRALTY N50 TYPE) TRACTOR BIPLANE ordered 13.3.17, numbered N100 to N106 and built at ECD Grain. (N100-N103 200-hp Arab, later 230-hp B.R.2; N104-N106 230-hp B.R.2 only)**

N100 Recd EC&AD Grain for erection W/E 9.3.18; AES Martlesham Heath 30.3.18 (performance tests); ECD Grain 20.4.18 (modifications); Redcar W/E 26.9.18 (transit); HMS *Vindictive* W/E 3.10.18; Flew off and retd 14.11.18 (to Smoogroo?); Crashed and WO aboard ship; Deleted W/E 12.12.18

N101 Trials 6.18; Tested with skids 31.8.18; Deld Grain 6.9.18; Rosyth W/E 26.10.18; Turnhouse W/E 31.10.18; Donibristle W/E 14.11.18; HMS *Vindictive* W/E 28.11.18; Donibristle W/E 12.12.18; HMS *Vindictive* 19.12.18 - @30.1.19

N102 Deld Test Dept Grain 18.5.18; HMS *Vindictive* Flt, Isle of Grain, swung on downwind TO, hit bank, crashed and destroyed by fire 9.9.18 (Lt AV Lewis killed, 2/Lt GE Durrance injured)

N103 Deld Grain 19.9.18; Turnhouse W/E 17.10.18; Donibristle W/E 12.12.18; HMS *Vindictive* W/E 19.12.18 - @30.1.19

N104 Deld Grain 19.9.18; Rosyth W/E 24.10.18; Turnhouse W/E 31.10.18; Donibristle W/E 21.11.18; HMS *Vindictive* by 11.18- @30.1.19

N105 Deld Grain 19.9.18 - @31.12.18; in transit to Fleet Base W/E 9.1.19 - @W/E 30.1.19; HMS *Vindictive* in Baltic Russia by 30.7.19; FL in sea, salved by tug *St.Ann* from HMS *Larkspur* 13.8.19

N106 Deld Grain W/E 3.10.18; Still completing 4.19; ready for erection 10.19 - 11.19

**3 NORMAN THOMPSON SCHOOL BIPLANE FLYING BOATS ordered 1.18 under Cont Nos A.S.7758 (BR.367) & A.S.35920 and numbered N107 to N109, to be built Middleton-on-Sea. (200-hp Hispano-Suiza 8B or Arab)**

N107 to N109 cancelled

**3 SHORT SHIRL TRACTOR BIPLANE TORPEDO BOMBERS ordered under Cont No A.S.8375 (BR.360) to A.D. Spec N.1(b) (later RAF Type XXII) and numbered N110 to N112. (360-hp Eagle VIII)** [Gordon Bruce's researches show correct c/n's to be S.421 to S.423]

N110 FF Grain 27.5.18 (type trials); V-type u/c; AES Martlesham Heath 3.6.18 (performance tests); Grain 25.6.18; Mkrs 25.6.18 (mods); Tested 1.7.18; Grain 7.18 (ditching trials with flotation gear 7.18); Devonport Docks in transit for Mudros with 186 Sqdn W/E 19.1.19 - @30.1.19 (allocation cancelled)

N111 FF 7.18; Divided u/c; Grain 8.7.18; TAS East Fortune for tests 8.7.18; Became 210 TDS East Fortune 14.8.18; AES Martlesham Heath 24.8.18 (performance); Devt Sqdn Gosport 5.10.18; For Mudros with 186 Sqdn Gosport by 30.1.19, but allocation cancelled

N112 Deld Grain 17.12.18; Devonport Docks in transit for Mudros with 186 Sqdn W/E 19.1.19 - @30.1.19 (allocation cancelled); Gosport by 3.19; Eastchurch 28.3.19; FL, hit stone wall on landing Holyhead, Anglesey while accompanying transatlantic Shirl *Shamrock*, which ditched 18.4.19 (JL Parker); Eastchurch (repair); FF 28.7.19 as 2-str mail carrier fitted with exptl half-ton container under fuselage

**3 BLACKBURN BLACKBURD TRACTOR BIPLANE TORPEDO BOMBERS ordered under Cont No A.S.8376 (BR.370) to A.D. Spec N.1(b) (later RAF Type XXII), numbered N113 to N115. (360-hp Eagle VIII)**

N113 Fitted flotation gear; FF 5.18; AES Martlesham Heath 4.6.18; Crashed Martlesham Heath 2.7.18; To Med 1919

N114 FF 8.18; Deld East Fortune W/E 22.8.18 (torpedo trials); Mkrs Brough; AES Martlesham Heath 16.10.18 (performance, later type trials, intended for 186 Sqdn Mediterranean but allocation cancelled); Gosport 10.12.18 - @30.1.19 (dismantled)

N115 Deld Grain 9.10.18, but retd Mkrs; Devt Sqdn Gosport from 11.18 - @1.19 (NTU?); Devonport Docks for 186 Sqdn W/E 19.1.19 - @30.1.19 (allocation cancelled)

**2 SAGE 4 SCHOOL TRACTOR BIPLANE SEAPLANES ordered under Cont No A.S.6285 (BR.356) to A.D. Spec N.2(a), numbered N116 & N117 and built at Peterborough.**

N116 Sage 4a. Deld Test Dept Grain by rail 30.6.17; FF 3.7.17 with 150-hp Hispano-Suiza; Wrecked 24.7.17; Conv Sage 4b dual control trainer with 200-hp Arab; Deld Grain 13.5.18; FF 17.5.18; Patrol Reserve Calshot W/E 11.7.18; 209 TDS Lee-on-Solent W/E 15.8.18 - @6.19

N117 Sage 4c with 200-hp Hispano-Suiza 8B. Folding wings. Deld Grain 9.10.18 (trials); Westgate 24.1.19 (transit en route 210 TDS Lee-on-Solent); Newhaven 25.1.19; Crashed on flying instruction tests and WO, Newhaven

**1 FAIREY ATALANTA I RECONNAISSANCE TRACTOR BIPLANE FLYING BOAT ordered 5.19 under Cont No 38a/374/C.359 to A.D. Spec N.4 (later RAF Type XXXIII), numbered N118 and built at Gosport. (Four 650-hp Condor IA)**

N118 (C/n F.275) Hull built by Gosport Aviation Co, by road to Bradford for storage 1919; To Grain 2.22 for flotation tests; Assd by Phoenix Dynamo Co; Not flown

**1 FAIREY ATALANTA I RECONNAISSANCE TRACTOR BIPLANE FLYING BOAT ordered 13.5.19 under Cont No 38a/373/C.360 to A.D. Spec N.4 (later RAF Type XXXIII) and numbered N119. Nicholson hull. (Four 650-hp Condor IA )**

Felixstowe Fury Reconnaissance Flying Boat N123 at Grain. (via P.H.T.Green)

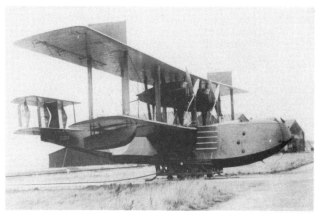

Vickers Valentia Reconnaissance Flying Boat N126. (IWM MH.2925)

Short Cromarty Reconnaissance Flying Boat N120. (via J.D.Oughton)

Fairey N.4 Atalanta I Reconnaissance Flying Boat N119 on Grain slipway, 1923. (via J.D.Oughton)

N119    (C/n F.276) Hull built by May, Harden & May; MAEE Grain by road 1.21 & assd there by Dick Kerr; Taxying trials 22.7.22; Engine runs 27.11.22 & 5.12.22; Preliminary taxying runs 28.5.23; FF 4.7.23; Hull damaged 2.24; MAEE to Felixstowe 3.24; Repaired 3.24; Hull mods 7.24; still Felixstowe 1925

**3   SHORT CROMARTY RECONNAISSANCE TRACTOR BIPLANE FLYING BOATS ordered under Cont No A.S.16772 to A.D. Spec N.3 (later RAF Type XXX), numbered N120 to N122, to be built at Rochester. (Two 650-hp Condor Ia)** [Gordon Bruce's researches show correct c/n's to be S.539, S.544 & S.545 respectively]

N120    Launched 21.3.21; FF 11.4.21 (JL Parker); Deld Grain 13.4.21; Minor mods by Mkrs 11.5.21; Various repairs and mods 8.7.21, completed 19.8.21; Mods to rear cockpit 2.9.21, completed 21.10.21; Type trials at Grain from 21.10.21; Weighed 28.10.21; Repair lower wings 12.12.21; Type trials recommenced 16.1.22; Damaged landing 25.1.22 (F/L ES Goodwin AFC & F/L GE Livock); Repairs to hull completed 9.5.22; Boosted engines installed 17.5.22; Devt Flt Grain 17.7.22; Portland 7.8.22; Cattewater 14.8.22; St.Mary's 21.8.22; Taxied into reef, hull collapsed, beached, St.Mary's, Scilly Is 5.9.22 salved, then BU

N121 and N122 cancelled

**1   FELIXSTOWE FURY RECONNAISSANCE TRACTOR TRIPLANE FLYING BOAT, numbered N123 & built at Felixstowe. (Five 360-hp Eagle VIII).**

N123    Deld Felixstowe 31.10.18; FF 11.11.18; 7-hour flight 24.4.19; 6.19 to be dismantled and shipped to USA to attempt Atlantic Flight (NTU); No.4 Comms Sqdn Felixstowe, crashed on TO for flight to Africa (incorrect landing), Felixstowe 11.8.19 (L/Col PFM Fellowes, Mjr ER Moon, Capt CL Scott, 2/Lt JF Arnold, WO JG

Cockburn & WO HS Locker uninjured; Lt SES McLeod (W/T) drowned)

**3 VICKERS VALENTIA I RECONNAISSANCE FLYING BOATS ordered 5.18 under Cont No A.S.17670 to A.D. Spec N.3 (later RAF Type XXX) and numbered N124 to N126, assembled at Barrow-in-Furness with a Vickers-built superstructure and Saunders hull built at Cowes. Saunders Type No.A.5. (Two Condor IA)**

N124    Launched Cowes 2.3.21; FF 5.3.21; Crashed on flight to Newhaven 3.21; MAEE Grain by 4.21; Prow of hull collapsed on landing 14.6.21; Dismantled Grain 6.21; LM 2.22 (still dismantled)

N125    FL in sea off Bexhill on delivery from Cowes to MAEE 15.3.22 (Vickers test pilot Capt S Cockerell & Capt Brown [probably Arthur Whitten-Brown of transatlantic Vimy fame])

N126    FF 3.23; Deld MAEE Grain 4.23 (type trials); Accepted 12.6.23; Vickers 13.2.24 (repair); (Grain?) COW gun trials 2.24 - 7.24; SOC 11.24

**N127 onwards, post war orders**

**1 SOPWITH BABY TRACTOR BIPLANE SEAPLANE ordered 17.6.16 under Cont Nos C.P.102625, C.P.116706/16 & A.S.10059 from Blackburn Aeroplane & Motor Co Ltd, numbered (out of sequence) as N300 & built at Leeds. (110-hp Clerget 9Z)**

N300    Replacement for 8201 transferred to Japanese Government; HMS *Campania* by 2.17 (from 13.3.17?); ashore for compass adjustment 3.4.17; Tested Scapa 6.4.17; Tested HMS *Campania* 17.4.17; Houton Bay (storage) by 12.17; HMS *Campania* by 29.12.17; Houton Bay (storage) W/E 23.2.18; Surveyed 25.3.18; Deleted 11.5.18 W&T

# EXPERIMENTAL NAVAL MACHINES (N500 onwards)

**1 SOPWITH TRIPLANE SCOUT put forward 9.16 and ordered under Cont No C.P.117520/16, numbered N500 & built at Kingston. (110-hp Clerget 9Z)**

N500    Prototype. Passed by Sopwith's Exptl Dept 28.5.16; FF 30.5.16; Deld Chingford (via Hendon) 16.6.16; Visited Felixstowe 21.6.16 and retd Chingford; A Sqdn 1 Wing RNAS Dunkerque 22.6.16 (service trials); Engaged 2 enemy aircraft 6m N of La Panne recording hits on one 1.7.16 (FSL RS Dallas, who called his a/c 'BROWN BREAD'); 2 Flt A Sqdn 1 Wing Furnes, damaged by flak 28.7.16; Put forward for Sopwith to repair wings W/E 18.8.16; To Sopwith for wing repairs W/E 8.9.16; Presume retd 1 Wing; Shot down small biplane then drove off enemy aircraft attacking a Belgian Maurice Farman 30.9.16 (FSL RS Dallas); HA shot down 21.10.16 (FSL RS Dallas); Became 1 Sqdn RNAS 1.12.16; 8 Sqdn RNAS W/E 15.2.17; Tail fairly high on TO, smashed propeller 16.2.17 (FSL RR Soar); Testing new engine, EF on TO, FL in adjacent field, slightly damaged 26.2.17 (FSL RR Soar unhurt); 10 Sqdn by 26.2.17 - @2.4.17; ADD to 11 Sqdn RNAS but COL 9.6.17; to ADD; 12 Sqdn RNAS 13.6.17; ADD 23.7.17 - @25.10.17; To 12 Sqdn RNAS, burnt 27.10.17; NADD by 1.11.17; Surveyed 17.12.17; Deleted 24.12.17 W&T

**1 WIGHT LANDPLANE TRACTOR BIPLANE ordered 6.16 under Cont No C.P.118196/16, numbered N501 & built at East Cowes. Tender too high 8.16. (225-hp Sunbeam or 225-hp Rolls-Royce)**

N501    Deld Eastbourne 10.7.16; Wrecked 1.9.16 (225-hp RR); Deleted 26.9.16

     [A Wight bomber with 250-hp Rolls-Royce engine cancelled 16.12.16 to release engine to RFC]

**1 BLACKBURN TRIPLANE SINGLE SEAT PUSHER SCOUT ordered 13.8.16 under Cont No C.P.120730/16, numbered N502 & built at Leeds. (110-hp Clerget 9Z)**

N502    Tested Leeds 24.6.16; Ready for further tests 1.8.16; Deld Design Flt Eastchurch for erection 25.9.16 (unnumbered at first); Badly damaged 22.1.17 (S/Cdr HR Busteed); Repaired; Accepted 20.2.17; Re-engined 100-hp Gnome Monosoupape B-2; Deleted 25.2.17

**1 SOPWITH PUP TRACTOR BIPLANE SCOUT numbered N503, to be built at Kingston-upon-Thames. (110-hp Clerget 9Z)** [Put forward W/E 21.7.16 for information of Beardmore]

N503    Not built

**1 SOPWITH TRIPLANE TRACTOR SCOUT ordered 6.16 under Cont No C.P.124352/15, numbered N504 & built at Kingston. (130-hp Clerget 9B)**

N504    Second prototype. Possibly the Triplane flown Brooklands to Chingford and return 2.7.16 (Hawker); Probably the unnumbered Sopwith Triplane fitted 110-hp Clerget 9Z ready for further tests 31.7.16; FF (sic) Brooklands 26.8.16; Hendon 26.8.16; Visited Farnborough 27.8.16 and retd; Under repair 30.8.16; Design Flt Eastchurch 6.9.16 (speed test); Retd Chingford 7.9.16; Brooklands via Hendon for Sopwith to fit 130-hp Clerget 9.9.16 [still unnumbered @21.9.16?]; Chingford 5.10.16; Design Flt Eastchurch 18.10.16 (flown that day by S/Cdr HR Busteed & F/L GH Jackson); Stripped to strengthen tail 25.10.16; Flown 31.10.16 & 3.11.16 (S/Cdr HR Busteed); ADD 15.11.16; 1 Sqdn 23.11.16; ADD .16; 1 Sqdn 15.12.16; ADD 5.2.17; 9 Sqdn by 10.2.17; 8 Sqdn by 2.17; Crashed nr Furnes 26.2.17; Flying again by 28.2.17; Still 8 Sqdn 25.3.17; 10 Sqdn by 30.3.17; ADD 24.4.17; 9 Sqdn 24.4.17; ADD by 6.17; 11 Sqdn

*Wight Trainer N501 at Eastchurch 1916.*
*(J.M.Bruce/G.S.Leslie collection)*

*Blackburn Triplane Scout N502. (via Philip Jarrett)*

*Parnall Zepp-Strafer N505. (via Philip Jarrett)*

*Sopwith Triplane N509, larger machine with 150-hp
engine. (via Philip Jarrett)*

*Phoenix-built Armstrong Whitworth F.K.10 Quadruplane Fighter N511. (R.C.Sturtivant collection)*

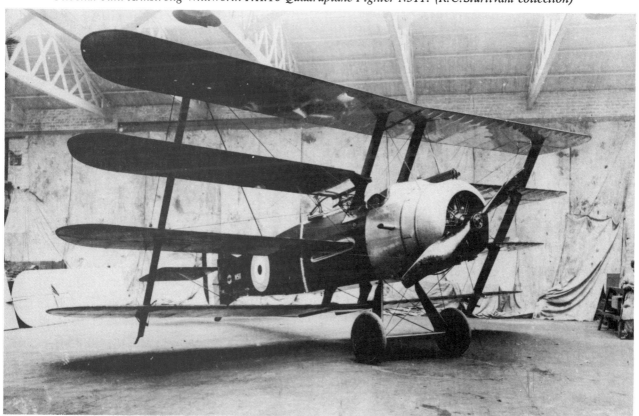

7.6.17; FL 8.6.17 (FSL EC Hillaby); 12 Sqdn 13.6.17 - @19.8.17; ADD, destroyed by fire on night of 1.10.17; Surveyed 17.10.17; Deleted 23.10.17 burnt

**2 PARNALL ZEPP STRAFFER or NIGHT FLYER SCOUT TRACTOR BIPLANES ordered 20.8.16 under Cont Nos C.P.124455/16/24486 & A.S.4683 and numbered N505 and N506, to be built at Bristol. (Originally ordered with 200-hp Afridi)**

N505    (240-hp Maori II) Tested CFS, but did not fly as overweight. Retd Mkrs; Condemned as dangerous

N506    (190-hp Rolls-Royce) Not built

**2 SHORT DAY BOMBER TRACTOR BIPLANES ordered 9.16 and numbered N507 and N508, to be built at Rochester. (Two 200-hp Sunbeam)**

N507 and N508 cancelled 12.16

**2 SOPWITH TRIPLANE SCOUTS ordered under Cont No C.P.133540/16, numbered N509 and N510 and built at Kingston-upon-Thames. (150/200 Hispano-Suiza)**
[New design, not the original triplane]

N509    (150-hp Hispano-Suiza 8Aa) Deld Brooklands to Design Flt Eastchurch 20.10.16; ADD 15.11.16; Design Flt Eastchurch 21.11.16 (S/Cdr HR Busteed); War Flt Manston 13.2.17; Damaged radiator 20.4.17; AGPs 25.5.17 & 13.6.17 (both FSL AC Burt); AGPs 7.7.17 & 22.7.17 (both FSL MA Harker); COL Manston 30.8.17 (F/L AF Brandon); Surveyed 26.10.17; Deleted 29.10.17 W&T

N510    (200-hp Hispano-Suiza 8B) Deld Brooklands to Design Flt Eastchurch 20.10.16 (fitted with modified fuel system); Flown for 10 min that day by F/L PA Johnston, then crashed and CW same day after only 5 minutes flight when tail flutter during speed test caused tail to break away at 100-ft (F/L LH Hardstaff killed)

**2 ARMSTRONG WHITWORTH F.K.10 TRACTOR QUADRUPLANES ordered 29.12.16 under Cont No C.P.135178/16 from The Phoenix Dynamo Manufacturing Co Ltd, numbered N511 and N512 & built at Bradford. (130-hp Clerget 9B)**

N511    Fighter. Deld Bramham Moor to Testing Sqdn Martlesham Heath 3.17 (type trials); Manston 29.3.17; Trials at Boroughbridge 26.4.17; FF Bramham Moor 27.4.17 (same?); Mkrs to Manston for erection 6.5.17; Ready 7.6.17; Deleted Manston 21.8.17

N512    Bomber. Deld Mkrs in/by 11.17; Surveyed at Mkrs 23.11.17 (experimental type, unsatisfactory); Deleted 28.11.17, to Wormwood Scrubbs

**1 ARMSTRONG WHITWORTH FIGHTER RECONNAISSANCE TRACTOR BIPLANE ordered 12.16 under Cont Nos A.S.6285 (BR.241) & AS.27755/1, numbered N513 and built at Gosforth. (200-hp Sunbeam)**

N513    Built but not accepted; Completed 8.3.17; EF, FL nr Beverley en route Martlesham for type trials 7.4.17; Mkrs by 29.12.17 (engine trouble); Scrapped 25.2.18 [Serial H4424 allotted but cancelled]

**1 ARMSTRONG WHITWORTH F.K.10 TRACTOR QUADRUPLANE ordered 1.17 under Cont No C.P.100565/16, numbered N514 & built at Gosforth. (130-hp Clerget 9B)**

N514    Manston on/by 1.4.17; Accepted but unsatisfactory; Engine change 7.6.17; Magneto etc removed 14.8.17; Deleted 25.8.17 unsafe

**2 SUNBEAM BOMBER (ADMIRALTY TYPE 7) (D TYPE) SINGLE-SEATER TRACTOR BIPLANES put forward 1.17 and ordered under Cont No C.P.102580/17, numbered N515 and N516, to be built at Wolverhampton. (200-hp Arab)**

N515    (C/n 171) FF Castle Bromwich 10.17; Deld Testing

Sqdn Martlesham Heath 19.7.18 (performance test); Grain 18.9.18 (comparison trials of mineral and castor oil in engine lubrication)

N516    (C/n 172?) Not completed

**2 SOPWITH F.1 CAMEL TRACTOR BIPLANE SCOUTS numbered N517 and N518 and built at Kingston. (130-hp Clerget 9B) [Put forward W/E 24.2.17, also one for RFC and 1 for French Government]**

N517    Tested Brooklands 26.2.17; ADD 28.2.17 - @29.3.17 (referred to as Camel "F2" in 6 Sqdn daily reports); ADD by 3.5.17; 10 Sqdn by 11-13.5.17; 9 Sqdn from/by 17.5.17; ADD 20.5.17; 11 Sqdn 8.6.17; 12 Sqdn RNAS 13.6.17; Wrecked 29.6.17 (FSL JR Tulley killed); ADD by 5.7.17; Deleted 21.8.17

N518    Tested Brooklands 2.17; Deld Hendon 11.4.17; Testing Sqdn Martlesham 13.4.17 (performance test); Hendon 28.4.17; Tail skid broke 2.5.17; A Flt, Testing Sqdn Martlesham Heath 3.5.17; Rebuilding 7.17; Deld Expeditionary Force W/E 1.9.17 (flown to St.Omer with 150-hp A.R.1 after 17 hrs 20 min flying in England); Retd England by 8.9.17 for engine tests, fitted French Clerget L-S; Type Test Flt Grain by 29.12.17; Fitted 110-hp Le Rhône 9J by 27.4.18; Hendon to AES Martlesham 22.5.18; General work from 10.18; Lost u/c in heavy landing Martlesham 12.18 (Lt Edelston)

**2 HANDLEY PAGE TYPE P/320 RAIDING TRIPLANES ordered 18.7.17 under Cont No A.S.1814, also A.S.7387, to A.D. Spec N.1(a) and numbered N519 to N520, to be built at Cricklewood (320-hp Cossack)**

N519 and N520 cancelled

**2 NIEUPORT TRIPLANE TRACTOR BIPLANE SCOUTS purchased in France and numbered N521 and N522. (130-hp Clerget 9B) [Transferred to RFC per 2.18 official list]**

N521    (c/n N.1946) At ADD by 29.3.17 as "1946"; Serialled N521 at ADD by 5.4.17 - @26.4.17; 11 Sqdn by 3.5.17 - @24.5.17; ADD by 7.6.17; Deleted 27.6.17 (u/s)

N522    Purchase cancelled

**1 AVRO 523 PIKE FIGHTER/BOMBER PUSHER BIPLANE ordered under Cont No A.S.2261, numbered N523, built at Manchester and assembled Hamble. (Two 160-hp Crusader)**

N523    Deld RAE 29.1.16; Was to have been RFC A316, but NTU; Transferred to RNAS; Deld Grain 3 or 4.5.16; Tested 24.5.16 (Raynham); Brooklands 24.5.16 (Raynham); Tested Grain 28.6.16; To Mkrs Manchester 15.7.16 (Raynham & Dobson); Mkrs Hamble, ready by 2.17; Eastchurch Workshops 24.3.17; Surveyed 7.4.17; Deleted 26.4.17

**1 SOPWITH TRIPLANE TRACTOR SCOUT ordered under Cont No A.S.14457, numbered N524 and built Kingston. (130-hp Clerget 9B)**

N524    Loaned French Government; Purchased from France; Allocated Paris-Dunkerque 28.3.17; ADD by 5.4.17; 9 Sqdn 7.5.17; 11 Sqdn 1.6.17; COL 5.6.17 (FSL RG Saunders); ADD by 7.6.17; 12 Sqdn 16.7.17; AP Dover 4.12.17; Surveyed 14.12.17; Deleted 17.12.17 DBR

**1 BEARDMORE W.B.I TRACTOR BIPLANE LONG-RANGE BOMBER ordered under Cont No A.S.7123 and numbered N525, to be built at Dalmuir. (230-hp Adriatic)**

N525    FF 20.9.16; U/c collapsed on landing Inchinnan; Rebuilt; Probably the "RE12" ex Beardmore to Cranwell for erection 16.5.17; Completed 25.5.17; Deld Cranwell for gunnery training 8.6.17 and FF same day but engine unsatisfactory; Re-engined 240-hp Sunbeam; After landing collided with 2 parked B.E.2c's at Cranwell 5.7.17 (W/Cdr REC Peirse); Tested after repair 17.7.17; Crashed BR 18.9.17 (as "RE12"); Surveyed 18.9.17; Deleted 8.10.17 wrecked

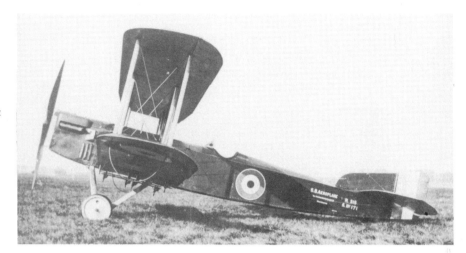

*Sunbeam Bomber N515, (via Philip Jarrett)*

*Nieuport Triplane Scout N521. (J.M.Bruce/G.S.Leslie collection)*

*Avro Pike Fighter/Bomber N523. (via Philip Jarrett)*

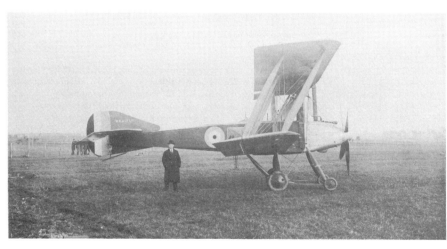

*Beardmore W.B.I Long-Range Bomber N525 at Inchinnan. (via Philip Jarrett)*

**CAPRONI Ca 4 BOMBER TRIPLANES on loan from Italian Government under Cont No A.S.13174 (BR.62), numbered N526 to N531.** This RNAS variant was retrospectively redesignated Ca 52 by the makers around 1930. Urgently required for A/S work in Southern Italy 3.18 (to have been replaced by 6 Caproni biplanes but evidently NTU). (3x400-hp Liberty)

N526    Deld Northern Sqdn 6 Wing Otranto W/E 12.1.18; Retd Italian Govt 30.3.18; 6 Wing at Malpensa by 17.11.18

N527    Deld Northern Sqdn 6 Wing Otranto W/E 12.1.18 (Bulldog insignia with sailor's hat on nose of aircraft); Retd Italian Govt 30.3.18; 6 Wing at Vizzola by 11.11.18

N528    Deld Northern Sqdn 6 Wing Otranto W/E 12.1.18; Retd Italian Govt 30.3.18

N529    Deld Northern Sqdn 6 Wing Otranto W/E 12.1.18; Retd Italian Govt 30.3.18

N530    Deld Northern Sqdn 6 Wing Otranto W/E 26.1.18; Retd Italian Govt 30.3.18

N531    Deld Northern Sqdn 6 Wing Otranto W/E 26.1.18; Retd Italian Govt 30.3.18
[3 more ordered W/E 8.7.18 under BR.610 but cancelled 14.10.18]
[Reported as all attached 227 Sqdn Pizzone, retd 12.18]

**1 NIEUPORT TRACTOR TRIPLANE transferred from RFC (Military Wing) & numberd N532. (110-hp Clerget 9Z)**

N532    [Reported with 11 Sqdn RNAS & 10 Sqdn RNAS but confirmation lacking]; AES Martlesham Heath by 4.17; Allocated Dover for Dunkerque 11.5.17 (NTU?); Deleted by 2.18 [Also reported with Le Rhône] (Ex A6686?)

**6 SOPWITH TRIPLANE SCOUTS ordered 2.9.16 under Cont Nos C.P.125850/16 & A.S.14457 from Clayton & Shuttleworth Ltd, numbered N533 to N538 and built at Lincoln.** Fitted two Vickers guns. (130-hp Clerget 9B)

N533    Deld ADD (via Dover) 12.7.17; 10 Sqdn 21.7.17 (coded 'C', named 'BLACK MARIA', fitted twin Vickers); Albatros DV to pieces in air & another OOC and crashed with pilot shot N of Menin 19.45 27.7.17 (F/L R Collishaw DSC, DSO); ADD 30.8.17 - @6.9.17; 12 Sqdn from/by 10.9.17; AP Dover 4.12.17; Surveyed 14.12.17; Deleted 19.12.17 DBR

N534    Deld ADD (via Eastchurch) 12.7.17; 1 Sqdn 22.7.17; Albatros DV OOC Comines 07.40 10.8.17 (F/L FHM Maynard); Albatros DV crashed Roubaix aerodrome 04.40 16.8.17 (FSL RP Minifie); Scout crashed in hedge Gheluwe 08.45 16.8.17 (S/Cdr RS Dallas); ADD 8.9.17; 12 Sqdn RNAS 3.10.17; AP Dover 4.12.17; Surveyed 14.12.17; Deleted 19.12.17 DBR

N535    Deld War Flt Manston (via Chingford) 25.7.17; Bullet holes in propeller 5.8.17; U/c slightly damaged 8.8.17; AGP 12.8.17 (S/Cdr GL Thomson); Leading edge of top wing damaged bringing out of shed 14.8.17; U/c damaged 20.8.17; Surveyed 26.10.17; Deleted 29.10.17 W&T

N536    Deld ADD by 26.7.17; 10 Sqdn RNAS 28.7.17; Shot down by AA nr Zonnebeke Lake, credited to Ltn Steudel, Jasta 3 at Langemarck 17.00 14.8.17 (FSL SH Lloyd killed); Deleted 1.9.17

N537    Deld Brooklands to ADD (via Dover) 22.8.17 - @6.9.17; 12 Sqdn from/by 10.9.17 - @12.1.18; ADD by 17.1.18 - @24.1.18 for deletion; Not listed at ADD by 31.1.18; [to Dover and deleted with N541?]

N538    Deld London Colney (via Cranwell and Chingford) 17.8.17 (transit); Dover 18.8.17; ADD 19.8.17 - @13.9.17; 12 Sqdn by 15.9.17 - @24.9.17; ADD, for survey by 27.9.17; Destroyed by fire on night of 1.10.17; Surveyed 17.10.17; Deleted 23.10.17 burnt

**1 PORT VICTORIA P.V.7 GRAIN KITTEN TRACTOR BIPLANE ANTI-SUBMARINE SCOUT numbered N539 and built at Grain. (35hp Gnat)**

N539    ECD Grain from 12.6.17; FF 22.6.17; Slightly damaged 5.7.17 (F/Cdr CT Freeman DSC); Awaiting test (after repair?) 26.7.17; EAD Grain by 29.9.17; Grain Test Dept 2.10.17; ECD Grain by 15.12.17; new 30-hp ABC engine tested 21.12.17; Fitting RAF15 wings 22.12.17; still ECD Grain @25.5.18; NFT

**1 PORT VICTORIA P.V.8 EASTCHURCH KITTEN TRACTOR BIPLANE ANTI-SUBMARINE SCOUT numbered N540 and built at Grain. (35-hp Gnat)**

N540    ECD Grain from 12.6.17; FF Grain 7.9.17; Fitted new tailplane; FF at EAD Grain 26.9.17; Under repair 30.9.17; AES Martlesham Heath 19.10.17; Grain ECD 9.11.17 - @15.12.17; EC&AD Grain by 23.2.18; Authorised for transfer to US Government 12.3.18 (Authority No.6048/1918); Packed at Grain; Left for USA W/E 30.3.18

**3 SOPWITH TRIPLANE SCOUTS built for French Government and authorised for transfer to RNAS 2.11.17, re-numbered N541 to N543. (130-hp Clerget 9B)**

N541    Ex French Government as F5; 1 Wing by 8.11.17; Tested Seaplane Defence Squadron St.Pol 19.11.17; 12 Sqdn 6.12.17; Dunkerque 11.1.18; Dover 12.1.18; Surveyed 14.1.18; Deleted 17.1.18 W&T

N542    Ex French Government as F9; 1 Sqdn by 8.11.17; Became N542 16.11.17; 12 Sqdn 4.12.17; To Hendon 19.12.17, but EF, FL Bekesbourne and never reached Hendon (F/Cdr BC Clayton); retd 12 Sqdn (via Dover) 22.12.17; Crashed on aerodrome 30.1.18 (F/Cdr CCR Edwards DSC); Deleted ADD 4.2.18

N543    Ex French Government as F10; 1 Wing by 8.11.17; Tested Seaplane Defence Sqdn St.Pol 28.11.17; AP Dover 4.12.17; Dunkerque; AP Dover 10.12.17; Surveyed 14.12.17; Deleted 19.12.17 DBR

**2 VOISIN "CANON A TITRE DE CESSION" PUSHER BIPLANES loaned by French Government for gun trials at Grain & numberd N544 & N545. (200 Hispano-Suiza).**

N544    (c/n V.1770) Deld EAD Grain 14.11.17 - @3.18; Crashed on nose [date unknown]

N545    (c/n V.1710) Deld ex Paris as V.1710 7.17; London (Hendon?) to EAD Grain as "V.1710" 7.7.17 (Sous Lt Poitou & Mechanic Banzet); Gun trials 16.7.17 (Sous Lt Poitou); Detd Fort George for Anti-submarine trials W/E 29.9.17 - W/E 6.10.17; To St.Pol (named 'DICKY' fitted 37-mm Hotchkiss gun) W/E 10.11.17 (160-hp Peugeot); Retd EAD Grain (via Calais) 30.11.17 (now 220-hp Peugot and serialled N545); For deletion by 15.12.17; No engine by 19.1.18 - @9.3.18

**1 WIGHT QUADRUPLANE FIGHTER ordered under Cont No A.S.35342/17 (BR.255 dated 13.11.17), numbered N546 and built at East Cowes. (110-hp Clerget 9Z)**

    Built as PV (unnumbered). Completed 28.10.16; Testing Sqdn Martlesham Heath by 1.2.17; Dismantled and returned Cowes 8.9.17; Rebuilt and numbered

N546    Brooklands to AES Martlesham Heath; WO Crashed in a cemetery Martlesham Heath 2.2.18; Deleted 2.18

**N547 to N999 never issued**

*Port Victoria P.V.7 Grain Kitten N539. (via M.Davis)*

*Port Victoria P.V.8 Eastchurch Kitten N540
(R.C.Sturtivant collection)*

*Wight Quadruplane Fighter N546. (via M.H.Goodall*

*Caproni Ca 42 Bomber N527. (IWM Q.67620)*

*Voisin 'Canon a Litre de Cession' V1710 (N545), named
'DICKIE' at St.Pol. (J.M.Bruce/G.S.Leslie collection)*

**N1000 to N2999 reserved for Seaplanes, Main Types**

**10 FAIREY CAMPANIA TRACTOR SEAPLANES put forward 12.16, ordered under Cont Nos C.P.115430/16 dated 22.6.16 & C.P.116827 and numbered N1000 to N1009. (Mainly Eagle variants) [C/n's F.16 to F.25]**

N1000     (250-hp Eagle IV) Deld Grain for erection 18.1.17; Exp Design Flt Grain by 29.1.17; Two practice flights 10.2.17; Mkrs 24.2.17 (alterations); NAD Test Flt Grain 27.3.17; Test Depot Grain 1.4.17; Became Type Test Flt Grain by 2.1.18; Rosyth (via East Fortune) W/E 15.2.18; HMS *Pegasus* W/E 21.3.18; Rosyth W/E 4.4.18; Deleted W/E 6.4.18

N1001     (275-hp Eagle V). Revised wing section. Deld Grain 5.5.17; Scapa 7.6.17; Landed South Shields owing to fog 9.6.17 (F/Cdr MEA Wright & CPO Abbott); Scapa 10.6.17 (now 225-hp); HMS *Campania* 17.6.17; Houton Bay on/by 13.10.17.(repair); HMS *Campania* to Scapa for repair W/E 3.11.17 - @30.1.19

N1002     (275-hp Eagle IV, V or VI) Deld Test Depot Grain by road 16.6.17 (type trials); Yarmouth 24.7.17 (transit); South Shields 25.7.17 (transit); Scapa 26.7.17; HMS *Campania* 26.7.17; Crashed, remains salved by HMS *King George V* 11.9.18; Surveyed 18.9.18; Deleted 24.9.18 wrecked

N1003     (275-hp Eagle VI) Deld Grain Test Dept by road 12.7.17; Scapa 30.7.17; Grain to Yarmouth for repair 13.8.17; South Shields 10.9.17 (transit); Yarmouth 11.9.17 (transit); Houton Bay/Scapa W/E 13.10.17 to recover fuselage; HMS *Campania* W/E 21.11.17; Scapa 24.5.18; HMS *Campania* W/E 22.8.18; Deleted W/E 19.9.18

N1004     (275-hp Eagle VI). Deld Grain 14.9.17; Type Test Flt Grain 27.12.17; Surveyed 4.4.18; Deleted 15.4.18 wrecked

N1005     (275-hp Eagle VI) Deld Scapa W/E 20.10.17; HMS *Campania* 26.10.17; Landed and broke strut stranding on North Shore, wreckage salved and retd ship 24.1.18

N1006     (250-hp Maori II) Deld Grain 10.17 (engine trials); To be flown 2.12.17; Dover 8.12.17; Calshot 11.12.17; Portland W/E 21.12.17; Became 416/7 Flts Portland 25.5.18; Deleted W/E 25.7.18

N1007     (345-hp Eagle VII) Deld Scapa for erection W/E 3.11.17; HMS *Campania* 23.12.17; Houton Bay 14.3.18; Scapa W/E 25.5.18; Rosyth WE 31.10.18 - @30.1.19

N1008     (345-hp Eagle VII) Deld Scapa for erection W/E 24.11.17 - @8.12.17; Houton Bay 12.17; HMS *Campania* 29.12.17 (ex Scapa); Scapa 12.1.18; HMS *Campania* 24.1.18; Retd damaged in tow of destroyer *G84* 13.8.18; Deleted W/E 5.9.18

N1009     (345-hp Eagle VII) Deld Scapa for erection 19.11.17; Erecting Houton Bay for 29.12.17; HMS *Campania* 30.1.18; Dropped 2x100-lb bombs on U-boat 10m ahead of ship 10.3.18 (FSL HB Kerruish & WO W Morgan); Crashed on shore, salved 26.6.18; Rosyth W/E 29.8.18 - @30.1.19

**30 SOPWITH BABY TRACTOR BIPLANE SEAPLANES ordered under Cont Nos 115429/16 dated 24.5.16 & C.P.118060/16 from Blackburn Aeroplane & Motor Co Ltd, numbered N1010 to N1039 & built Leeds. Delivered from Brough. (110-hp Clerget 9Z) [W/E 12.1.17 Blackburns completed 25 Babies, including 5 for French Govt]**

N1010     Deld Seaplane Design Flt Grain 5.12.16; Became Experimental Design Grain 2.3.17 (packed for transit); CSD White City by rail 27.3.17; Grain for erection 28.4.17; Erecting Grain for Nore Flt 10.6.17; Felixstowe 11.8.17; Killingholme W/E 29.9.17; Surveyed 6.4.18; Deleted 15.4.18 W&T

N1011     Deld Yarmouth by lorry 29.9.16; Accepted 22.11.16 (Roland Ding); To Dover 30.11.16 but FL en route and towed into harbour; arrived Dover 2.12.16; Tested Dover 6.12.16; Dunkerque 7.1.17; Dover by 8.3.17 (erecting); Dunkerque 24.3.17; Damaged float taxying 28.5.17 (FSL JE Potvin); With 9042 & N1024 attacked U-boat 15m NNE of Nieuport 15.6.17 (FSL JE Potvin);

Dover 15.6.17; AGP 7.7.17 (FSL AC Reid); HMS *Riviera* 14.7.17; Cattewater 10.8.17; Fishguard by road 30.3.18; Yarmouth W/E 13.6.18; Deleted W/E 24.10.18

N1012     Deld Yarmouth by lorry 29.9.16; Accepted 22.11.16 (Ding); LM 25.11.16; en route Port Said 3.17; HMS *Ben-my-Chree*

N1013     Deld HMS *Manxman* for erection 18.1.17; Tested off deck, to HMS *Engadine* and return 24.1.17 (F/Cdr FJ Rutland); still HMS *Manxman* 2.17; Left/deleted by 15.2.17

N1014     Shipped to Mediterranean; Port Said 3.17; HMS *Raven II* 10.3.17 - @11.4.17; HMAS *Brisbane* 4.17; EI&ESS 5.17; HMAS *Brisbane* by 9.5.17; HMS *Raven II* 11.5.17; Port Said 16.5.17; Port Said by 1.12.17

N1015     Deld Dover 30.3.17; Dunkerque 16.6.17; Shot down by enemy seaplane 12m NNE of Nieuport 05.30 19.6.17 (FSL JE Potvin killed); Deleted 4.7.17

N1016     Shipped to Mediterranean; Port Said by 18.3.17; HMS *Anne* 21.3.17; Port Said 23.3.17; 1 Wing Dunkerque by 19.6.17 - @7.17

N1017     Deld Dover and accepted 23.1.17 (Ding); Dunkerque 16.2.17; Dover 21.5.17; Dunkerque 31.5.17; Dover 21.7.17; Calshot FS 14.9.17; For deletion by 26.10.17; Deleted W/E 9.11.17 missing

N1018     Shipped to Aegean; HMS *Ark Royal* to Thasos but EF, FL 30m NW of Cape Murtzephalos (Lemnos), towed to Thasos by patrol boat 4.4.17

N1019     Deld Yarmouth 10.1.17 (transit); Design Flt Grain 13.1.17; Experimental Design Grain by 8.3.17; Dover 28.3.17; Dunkerque 8.4.17; Seaplane DD 10m NE of Nieuport 19.6.17 (F/L R Graham, DSC); Dover 25.6.17 (rebuilt); Dunkerque 22.9.17 [130-hp Clerget by 12.17]; Dover 13.1.18; Westgate 7.2.18; Became 406 Flt Westgate (coded '12') 25.5.18; Became 406 Flt 219 Sqdn 22.7.18 - @11.18

N1020     Deld HMS *Manxman* for erection 1.1.17; Tested off deck but wrecked 24.1.17 (F/L A Gammon); Lost 14.2.17; Deleted 15.2.17

N1021     Deld HMS *Manxman* for erection 18.1.17; Dundee 24.4.17; HMS *Engadine* 1.8.17 (then to Hawkcraig); Rosyth 3.8.17; Surveyed 11.10.17; Deleted 13.10.17 W&T

N1022     Deld HMS *Manxman* for erection 23.1.17; Dundee 31.3.17 (storage); HMS *Engadine* 29.6.17; Rosyth 23.9.17; Dundee 18.10.17; Surveyed 6.1.18; Deleted 15.1.18 DBR

N1023     Deld Newlyn by rail 4.4.17; Erected 5.4.17; Cattewater 30.5.17; Dropped 65-lb bomb on U-boat 10m S of Lands End 16.8.17 (F/L RE Dean); Newlyn W/E 29.12.17; 6 SD Ascot 27.6.18; South Shields 25.7.18 - @30.1.19

N1024     Deld Dover for erection 31.3.17; Dunkerque 15.4.17; Dover 8.6.17; Dunkerque 9.6.17; With 9042 & N1011 attacked U-boat 15m NNE of Nieuport 15.6.17 (S/Cdr HM Cave-Browne-Cave); Dover 24.7.17; Dunkerque 25.7.17; Dover 10.8.17; AGPs 12.8.17 (FSL AC Farquhar) & 22.8.17 (FSL AC Reid); Calshot FS 12.9.17; Surveyed 26.11.17; Deleted 3.12.17 wrecked

N1025     Deld Westgate by rail 24.3.17; AGP, FL in sea, towed to Burnham-on-Crouch 25.5.17 (FSL HC Lemon); Retd Westgate 26.5.17; AGP, damaged by rough sea on TO 5.6.17 (FSL WJ de Salis); AGPs 13.6.17 (FSL LG Maxton later FSL FC Lander); Nore Flt Westgate by 29.12.17; Deleted W/E 20.4.18

N1026     Deld HMS *Campania* 8.3.17; Pierowall 17.6.17; HMS *Campania* 19.6.17; Houton Bay (storage) W/E 30.3.18; Surveyed 25.3.18; Deleted 9.5.18 W&T

N1027     Deld HMS *Campania* 8.3.17; Wrecked by drifter *Volturno* alongside, remains hoisted in 12.3.17; Pierowall 17.6.17; HMS *Campania* 19.6.17; Houton Bay storage by 3.18; Surveyed 25.3.18; Deleted 11.5.18 W&T

N1028     Shipped to Mediterranean; EI&SS Port Said by 9.17; HMS *Empress* by 2.10.17; Port Said 6.11.17; COL Port Said 19.4.18 (FSL CH Biddlecombe); For deletion by 21.4.18

N1029     Shipped to Mudros 4.17; Tested after erection HMS *Ark Royal* 26.6.17; Deleted 1917

N1030    Shipped to Otranto on SS *Arum* for 1 Sqdn (sic) 6 Wing 11.4.17; 6 Wing RNAS Otranto by 28.6.17; Dropped 65-lb bomb on U-boat 20m E of Palascia 12.9.17; Dropped 65-lb bomb on U-boat 25m ENE of Otranto 17.9.17 (both F/Cdr JSF Morrison); Surveyed 31.3.18; Deleted 15.4.18 W&T

N1031    Exp wing modifications; Deld Dover for erection 31.3.17; Dunkerque 15.4.17; Dover 4.6.17; HMS *Riviera* 5.6.17; Dover 8.6.17; Dunkerque 9.6.17; Dover 29.6.17; Seaplane Defence Flt Dunkerque 3.7.17; Dover 10.8.17; Calshot FS 4.9.17; Deleted W/E 8.9.17

N1032    Exp wing modifications; Allocated 6 Wing Otranto 1.5.17; Deleted 1917

N1033    Exp wing modifications. Fishguard on/by 16.4.17 (station's first daily return); Milford Haven 21.4.17; Banked on TO, struck cliff, 2x16-lb bombs exploded, TW 22.4.17 (F/L RE Bush badly burnt); Deleted 24.4.17

N1034    Exp wing modifications. Shipped to Otranto 7.3.17; 6 Wing RNAS Otranto by 14.6.17 - @2.3.18; Deleted by 2.4.18

N1035    Exp wing modifications and synchronised Lewis gun. Shipped to Otranto 8.3.17; 6 Wing RNAS Otranto by 13.6.17 - @12.2.18; Deleted by 8.3.18

N1036    Exp wing modifications; Shipped to Port Said; EI&SS Port Said by 9.17; HMS *Empress* 19.9.17; Port Said 23.9.17; HMS *Empress* 1.11.17; Propeller broke on TO after attempting to rescue crew of N1210, sunk by gunfire from French destroyer *Coutelas* 2.11.17 (F/L TGM Stephens & F/L HdeV Leigh both injured); For deletion by 4.11.17

N1037    Exp wing modifications. Deld Felixstowe for erection 17.4.17; AGP 25.5.17; HACP 13.6.17 (FSL HA Wilson); Killingholme 3.9.17; Hornsea, FL, damaged 2.10.17 (pilot unhurt); Deleted W/E 15.2.18

N1038    Exp wing modifications; Shipped to Port Said; HMS *Empress* 1.11.17; O/t in sea after hoisting out with 2x65-lb bombs aboard, sunk by gunfire from *Empress* 2.11.17 (F/L GD Smith rescued by French destroyer *Coutelas*); For deletion by 4.11.17

N1039    Exp wing modifications. Deld Dundee for erection 20.4.17; CW 30.4.17 (pilot unhurt); Deleted 2.5.17

**20 F.B.A. TYPE B PUSHER BIPLANE FLYING BOAT hulls purchased in Argenteuil, France, numbered N1040 to N1059, and erected and wings fitted by Norman Thompson as their Type N.T.5 under Cont No C.P.120948/16 dated 27.7.16. Deld from Middleton-on-Sea. (Ordered with 100-hp Gnome Monosoupape - but all except three deld with 130-hp Clerget)**

N1040    Modified fuselage; Completed 1.17; Deld Calshot for erection 10.2.17; Deleted W/E 5.10.17

N1041    Completed 3.2.17; Deld Killingholme for erection 27.3.17; Became School m/c; Deleted W/E 5.10.17

N1042    Completed 10.3.17; Deld Killingholme for erection 27.3.17; Became School m/c; Deleted W/E 6.4.18

N1043    Completed 31.3.17; Deld Calshot 4.4.17; Deleted 11.7.17

N1044    Completed 31.3.17; Deld Killingholme for erection 3.4.17; Calshot FS 11.7.17; Crashed 11.10.17 (TFSL BW Whittle killed); Surveyed 8.11.17; Deleted 17.11.17 W&T

N1045    Deld Killingholme for erection 3.4.17; Killingholme School by 23.12.17; 209 TDS Lee-on-Solent W/E 6.6.18; Deleted W/E 25.7.18

N1046    Deld Killingholme for erection 10.4.17; Retd Norman Thompson as seriously damaged by their tester 17.5.17; Calshot TS 26.7.17; Surveyed 28.9.17; Deleted 6.10.17 W&T

N1047    (100-hp Gnome Monosoupape) Completed 21.4.17; Deld Calshot training 8.6.17; Lee-on-Solent W/E 12.10.17; Surveyed 30.10.17; Deleted 6.11.17 W&T

N1048    Completed 4.17; Deld Calshot training 28.6.17; Wrecked 11.9.17; Lee-on-Solent W/E 12.10.17; Surveyed 30.10.17; Deleted 6.11.17 W&T

N1049    Completed 4.17; Deld Calshot training 16.6.17; Wrecked 28.6.17; Surveyed 28.9.17; Deleted 6.10.17 W&T

N1050    Completed 31.3.17; Deld Calshot 4.17; Wrecked landing 12.4.17 (FSL GHT Barnes unhurt); Deleted 25.4.17

N1051    (100-hp Gnome Monosoupape) Completed 31.3.17; Deld Calshot but EF, FL Bembridge 5.4.17; Calshot (coded 'H') 6.4.17 (later Calshot FS); Lee-on-Solent W/E 30.11.17; Deleted W/E 27.3.18

N1052    (c/n 261) [Type C?] Completed 7.4.17; Deld Calshot training 19.4.17; Badly damaged 25.5.17; still Calshot 23.2.18; Lee-on-Solent FS by 3.18; Became 209 TDS Lee-on-Solent 1.4.18; Crash 5.18; Deleted W/E 11.7.18

N1053    Completed 7.4.17; Deld Calshot training 19.4.17; Deleted W/E 1.3.18

N1054    Deld Calshot training 5.4.17; BR by 14.9.17; For deletion by 1.3.18

N1055    Deld Calshot training 8.6.17; BR by 14.9.17; Surveyed 3.11.17; Deleted 8.11.17 W&T

N1056    Completed 28.4.17; Deld Calshot training 12.6.17; Surveyed 28.9.17; Deleted 6.10.17 W&T

N1057    Completed 28.4.17; Deld Calshot training 12.6.17; Crashed BR 11.7.17 (FSL WEN Clark injured); Deleted 15.7.17

N1058    Deld Calshot training 24.5.17; Possibly the a/c in which TFSL JD Grant drowned 3.10.17; Surveyed 7.10.17; Deleted 10.10.17 wrecked

N1059    (100-hp Gnome Monosoupape) Deld Calshot 24.5.17; Damaged wing 6.6.17; Surveyed 3.11.17; Deleted 8.11.17 W&T

**10 SOPWITH BABY TRACTOR BIPLANE SEAPLANES ordered 26.9.16 under Cont Nos C.P.127737 & C.P.133305/16 from Blackburn Aeroplane & Motor Co Ltd, numbered N1060 to N1069 & built Leeds. Deld from Brough. (110-hp Clerget 9Z)**

N1060    Shipped to Mediterranean; Arr EI&SS Port Said for erection by 15.9.17; Still in case 2.2.18; Engine seized 12m N of Port Said, COL in rough sea, sank 3.6.18 (Capt HV Worrall picked up unhurt by sloop)

N1061    Deld Yarmouth 1.5.17; Deleted W/E 5.9.17

N1062    Deld Newlyn by rail 21.4.17; CW on landing 2.6.17 (pilot unhurt); Deleted 14.6.17

N1063    Deld Dundee by rail 28.4.17; Rebuilding from 20.11.17; Became 450 Flt Dundee 5.18; FL on beach & WO 8.18; Deleted W/E 19.9.18

N1064    Deld Yarmouth 23.4.17; Tested 10.5.17; AZP 24.5.17 (FSL GH Bittles); Attacked Zeppelin *L42* 17.6.17 (FSL GH Bittles); Lost at sea 12.17; Surveyed 15.12.17; Deleted 19.12.17 TL

N1065    Deld Westgate 30.4.17; AZP, FL in sea, towed to Grain by *Hopper 15* in damaged condition 24.5.17 (FSL LG Maxton); Dismantled and surveyed at Grain; Deleted 8.6.17

N1066    Deld Yarmouth 1.5.17; HSMP 11.5.17 (F/L CJ Galpin); HMS *Dryad* 11.6.17; Yarmouth 12.6.17; HMS *Dryad* 18.6.17; Yarmouth 19.6.17; HMS *Halcyon* 25.6.17; HACP 27.6.17 (FSL HB Smith); Yarmouth 29.7.17; HMS *Halcyon* 29.7.17; Yarmouth 7.8.17; HMS *Halcyon* 7.8.17; Yarmouth 14.8.17; HMS *Halcyon* 21.8.17; Yarmouth 4.9.17; HMS *Halcyon* 4.9.17; Yarmouth 8.9.17; HMS *Halcyon* 8.9.17; Yarmouth 9.9.17; HMS *Halcyon* 18.9.17; Yarmouth 25.9.17; HMS *Halcyon* 2.10.17; Yarmouth 3.10.17; HMS *Halcyon* 3.10.17; Yarmouth 9.10.17; HMS *Halcyon* 19.10.17; Deleted W/E 23.2.18

N1067    Deld South Shields 14.6.17 (transit); Dundee 16.6.17; Deleted W/E 19.1.18

N1068    Deld Killingholme patrol 1.5.17; AZP 24.5.17; CSD White City, packing for Chilean Govt W/E 24.5.18; Despatched W/E 22.8.18

N1069    Deld Dover for erection 21.4.17; Dunkerque 4.5.17; Dover 3.6.17; Surveyed 5.10.17; Deleted 10.10.17 wrecked; Restored to commission 28.2.18; Became 407 Flt Dover 25.5.18; 6 SD Ascot by 27.6.18; Yarmouth W/E 19.9.18; Deleted W/E 12.12.18

**5 A.D. NAVYPLANE BIPLANE PUSHER SEAPLANES put forward 10.16 and ordered from Supermarine Aviation Works to be numbered N1070 to N1074. (140-hp Smith)**

N1070 to N1074 cancelled

**4 F.B.A. TYPE H PUSHER BIPLANE FLYING BOATS presented to RNAS Otranto by Italian Government, numbered N1075 to N1078. (160-hp Isotta-Fraschini)**

N1075    Recd 6 Wing Otranto 23.6.17 - @8.9.17; Deleted 1917

N1076    Recd 6 Wing Otranto 21.6.17; Became 66/67 Wings 1.4.18 - @21.4.18

N1077    Recd 6 Wing Otranto 23.6.17; Shipped to Malta in SS *Isonzo* 24.6.17; arr Calafrana 27.6.17; Dropped 65-lb bomb on U-boat 30m SE of Malta 20.8.17 (F/L WM Tait & AM Clarke); Repairing by 31.3.18; Deleted 15.5.18 wrecked

N1078    (c/n 283, Italian No 4255). Recd 6 Wing Otranto 23.6.17; Shipped to Malta in SS *Isonzo* 24.6.17; arr Calafrana 27.6.17; FL on A/S patrol, drifted ashore on African coast nr Misurata, Tripoli, destroyed by Italian torpedo boat *Orione* 8.8.17 (F/L WE Robinson & S/L JCA Jenks RNVR both PoWs)

**N1079 SERIAL NUMBER OFFICIALLY NOT ALLOTTED**
- but believed really the projected Short Scout No.3

**20 SHORT ADMIRALTY 184 TYPE TRACTOR BIPLANE SEAPLANES ordered ["prior to Cont A.S.14602/1"], numbered N1080 to N1099 & built Eastchurch. (240-hp Renault-Mercedes)** [Gordon Bruce's researches show correct c/n's to be S.314 to S.333]
[Improved version up to N1089, remainder original version]

N1080    Deld Grain 3.2.17 (with makers); Exptl Design Grain 8.3.17; Became Type Test Depot 31.3.17; Felixstowe 19.6.17 (repair); Test Depot Grain 27.6.17 - @1.8.17; Calshot FS by 10.17; (220-hp Renault by 12.17); For deletion by 1.3.18

N1081    Deld Eastchurch to Grain 12.2.17; Type Test Dept Grain 27.3.17 (fitted Linton-Hope floats and bomb racks); Grain ECD 1.5.17; Grain Test Dept 10.7.17; En route delivery to Calshot, EF, FL Westgate, wrecked by heavy sea 2.9.17 (FSL AR Stack), salvaged; Deleted W/E 8.9.17

N1082    Deld Grain under tow from Queenborough Pier 22.2.17; Accepted 27.2.17 (JL Parker); Type Test Depot Grain 27.3.17; Calshot 28.4.17; Bembridge 29.4.17; Calshot 12.6.17; Deleted W/E 14.9.17

N1083    Deld Grain under tow from Queenborough Pier 3.3.17; Type Test Depot Grain, packed for transit 1.4.17; Calshot 7.5.17; Newhaven 9.5.17; Portland 10.6.17; Calshot 28.7.17 (now 220-hp Renault); Deleted W/E 24.5.18

N1084    Deld Grain under tow from Queenborough Pier 22.3.17; Type Test Depot Grain, packed for transit 1.4.17; Accepted 21.4.17; Dover 28.4.17 (transit); Calshot 1.5.17 (220-hp Renault); Bembridge 3.6.17; Surveyed 28.9.17; Deleted 6.10.17 W&T

N1085    Deld Grain 10.4.17; Accepted 24.4.17 (JL Parker); Calshot 1.5.17; Portland 2.5.17; Calshot, crashed BR 13.7.17

N1086    [240-hp Sunbeam] Deld Grain under tow 5.4.17 (non-standard floats); Fishguard 16.6.17; Westgate to Newhaven 26.7.17 (transit to Fishguard); Calshot to Cattewater 28.7.17 (to Newlyn); Fishguard 31.8.17; Surveyed 20.12.17; Deleted 3.1.18

N1087    Deld Grain 27.4.17; Cattewater 6.6.17; Surveyed 6.10.17; Deleted 13.10.17 W&T

N1088    Deld Grain in tow 14.5.17; Cattewater 27.10.17; Surveyed 5.4.18; Deleted 15.4.18 W&T

N1089    (Fitted with lightened engine bearers) Deld Test Depot Grain 11.5.17 (design trials with Sunbeam engine, light engine bearers and enlarged tail float); Wrecked 17.5.17; Deleted 30.5.17

N1090    Deld Grain in tow 18.5.17; Tested 22.5.17 (JL Parker); Transhipped on lighter waiting for transport 17.6.17; Shipped to Mediterranean; arr El&SS Port Said 9.17; HMS *Empress* 16.9.17; Port Said 24.9.17; HMS *Empress* 25.9.17; Port Said 28.9.17; HMS *City of Oxford* 28.10.17; Port Said 9.11.17; HMS *Empress* 21.1.18; Port Said 18.2.18 - @18.4.18; Alexandria by 22.4.18; Deleted 25.7.18

N1091    Deld Grain 26.5.17; transhipped on lighter waiting for transport 17.6.17; arr El&SS Port Said 9.17; Erecting by 15.9.17; HMS *Empress* 8.10.17; Port Said 13.10.17; HMS *City of Oxford* 3.11.17; Port Said 9.11.17; Alexandria 15.1.18 - @16.4.18; Port Said by 4.18 - @7.18; Alexandria by 8.18; Port Said by 9.18; Became 269 Sqdn Port Said 6.10.18; Obsolete 220-hp Renault

being replaced 12.18; Deleted 1.5.19

N1092    Deld Grain in tow 1.6.17; Yarmouth 4.6.17 (en route Scapa Flow); Dundee (via South Shields) 7.6.17; EF, FL Berwick 8.6.17 (F/Cdr CHC Smith DSC & CPO Forbes); arr Dundee by rail via Berwick coastguards 16.6.17; HMS *Engadine* 1.8.17 - LM30.10.17 (ship at Buncrana 27.9.17 - 18.11.17, retd Liverpool 19.11.17); Packed by 29.12.17; Lee-on-Solent FS W/E 7.2.18; Became 209 TDS Lee-on-Solent 1.4.18; Deleted W/E 11.7.18

N1093    Deld Grain in tow 8.6.17; left 14.6.17; transit 15.6.17; HMS *Manxman* 17.6.17; Surveyed 28.11.17; Deleted 14.12.17 wrecked

N1094    Deld Grain in tow 8.6.17; Packing for Port Said 17.6.17; Left by rail for SS *Hattersee* for Mudros 11.7.17; Tested HMS *Ark Royal* 19.10.17; Talikna 31.10.17; HMS *Ark Royal* 11.17; Collier *John Sanderson* for Suda Bay 13.11.17; Suda Bay by 1.12.17 - @6.18

N1095    Deld Grain in tow 15.6.17; Packing for Port Said 17.6.17; Left by rail for SS *Hattersee* for Mudros 11.7.17; Flown HMS *Ark Royal* 15.10.18 - @18.10.18; Suda Bay by 1.12.17; Deleted 12.17

N1096    (260-hp Maori) Deld Grain in tow from Queenborough Pier 22.6.17; Left by rail to Tilbury for SS *Khiva* to Malta 18.8.17; Calafrana by 10.17; Dropped 65-lb bomb on U-boat 48m SE of Malta 3.1.18; Dropped 2x65-lb bombs on U-boat 18.1.18 (both FSL HL Nunn); Deleted W/E 15.5.18

N1097    (260-hp Maori) Deld Grain 29.6.17; Left by rail to Tilbury for SS *Khiva* to Malta 18.8.17; Calafrana by 10.10.17; Dropped 2x65-lb bombs on U-boat 40m SE of Malta 17.1.18 (FSL DRB Bentley); Dropped 65-lb bomb on U-boat Hurd Bank 10.2.18 (FSL JL Mayer & AM Clarke); For deletion by 5.6.18

N1098    (260-hp Maori) Deld Test Depot Grain in tow 7.7.17 (trials with 260hp Maori; fitted non-droop ailerons, new tail & 4-bladed propeller); Yarmouth 30.9.17; Became 324/6 Flts 25.5.18; Deleted W/E 29.8.18

N1099    Deld Grain in tow 6.7.17; Calshot 16.7.17 (transit); Cattewater 17.7.17; Dropped bomb on U-boat 5m W of Bolt Head, failed to explode 28.7.17 (FSL LGleB Croke & FSL FLB Wood); EF, FL 4m S of Rame Head, towed to Plymouth by *TD105* 7.8.17 (pilot and OSL BE Harrison unhurt); FTR patrol 9.8.17 (FSL BH Bridge & AM2 J Jones both killed); Deleted W/E 10.8.17

**30 SOPWITH BABY TRACTOR BIPLANE SEAPLANES ordered 12.16 under Cont Nos C.P.132111/16 dated 30.10.16 & C.P.133303/16 from Blackburn Aeroplane & Motor Co Ltd, numbered N1100 to N1129 & built Leeds. Delivered from Brough. Built for anti-submarine work. (110-hp Clerget 9Z)**

N1100    Deld HMS *Engadine* 2.5.17; Erected and flown 3.5.17; Rosyth 23.9.17; Dundee W/E 27.10.17; Became 450 Flt Dundee 30.5.18 - @30.1.19

N1101    Deld Killingholme 2.5.17 (engine trouble en route); South Shields 3.5.17; CW on landing 14(10?).5.17 (FSL KM Smith injured); Deleted 9.6.17

N1102    Deld Felixstowe 12.5.17; AGP 25.5.17 & 13.6.17; Still Felixstowe 30.6.17; Hornsea Mere by 7.17; Crashed and sank after mid-air collision with Curtiss H.12 8657 17.7.17 (FSL FM Bryans killed); Deleted 18.7.17

N1103    Deld Felixstowe but FL due to fuel shortage Breydon Water, S of Yarmouth 6.5.17 (F/L W Perham); Felixstowe 7.5.17; Killingholme W/E 16.11.17; Crashed in sea, badly damaged, towed into Grimsby 5.1.18; Deleted 15.1.18 W&T

N1104    Deld South Shields by 1.6.17; CW 10.9.17; Deleted W/E 22.9.17

N1105    Deld Felixstowe 15.5.17; AZP 13.6.17; Hornsea 10.17; South Shields 21.10.17; Wrecked 21.10.17; Surveyed 29.10.17; Deleted 2.11.17 wrecked

N1106    Presented to French Govt (allocated 21.8.17)

N1107    Deld Yarmouth for paddle steamers but FL off Cromer 11.5.17 (FSL HB Brenton); Yarmouth 12.5.17; AZP 4.7.17; Surveyed 2.1.18; Deleted 15.1.18 BR

N1108    Deld Yarmouth for paddle steamers 12.5.17; AZP 17.6.17 (FSL HB Brenton); In HMS *Dryad* 3.7.17 (F/L GH Bittles); HACP 23.7.17 (F/L GWR Fane); Surveyed 10.1.18; Deleted 17.1.18 wrecked

N1109   Deld Yarmouth for paddle steamers 29.5.17; AZPs 4.7.17 & 22.7.17 (F/L LER Murray); FTR from patrol to Cross Sands 27.1.18 (FSL E Morris killed)

N1110   Deld Yarmouth in tow for paddle steamers 27.5.17; AZP 4.7.17; AZP 22.7.17 (FSL FW Dolman); Surveyed 27.12.17; Deleted 27.1.18 DBR

N1111   Deld Killingholme 20.5.17; AZP 24.5.17; HMS *Princess Margaret* 14.8.17; Hornsea to South Shields 22.9.17; Wrecked landing 23.9.17; CW at Seaton Carew 29.9.17; Surveyed 3.10.17; Deleted 18.10.17 wrecked

N1112   Deld Killingholme 8.6.17; U/c damaged landing 25.6.17; HMS *Princess Margaret* 14.8.17; Seaton Carew, damaged in gale 24.10.17; Surveyed 8.12.17; Deleted 22.12.17 DBR

N1113   Deld Killingholme 20.5.17; AZP 24.5.17; Surveyed 20.10.17; Deleted 26.10.17 wrecked

N1114   Deld Killingholme 25.5.17; to Hornsea 11.17; Attempted to return to Killingholme but engine trouble and bad weather 8.12.17, retd later; Deleted W/E 15.2.18

N1115   Shipped to Mudros 1.6.17; HMS *Ark Royal* by 8.17; Thasos 8.8.17 - @23.3.18

N1116   Shipped to Mudros 1.6.17; Flown HMS *Ark Royal* 20.7.17; Thasos 29.7.17; Thasos by 23-26.3.18

N1117   Shipped to Mudros 1.6.17; Flown HMS *Ark Royal* 25.7.17; Z Sqdn 2 Wing Thasos by 8.17; Sideslipped, nosedived, wrecked 11.8.17 (pilot unhurt)

N1118   (Later re-engined 130-hp Clerget) Deld Dover (via Burgh Castle and Yarmouth) 17.6.17 (alterations); Dunkerque 26.6.17; Felixstowe 12.7.17; Dunkerque 13.7.17; Dover 10.8.17; AGP 12.8.17 (FSL AC Reid); Calshot 5.10.17; 6 SD Ascot W/E 25.7.18; South Shields W/E 22.8.18 - @30.1.19

N1119   Deld Yarmouth 2.6.17 ; Felixstowe 7.6.17; Dover 10.6.17; Deleted 4.7.17

N1120   (130-hp Clerget) Deld Dover (via Yarmouth) 9.6.17; Dunkerque 23.6.17; Dover 10.8.17; Calshot 5.10.17; Lee-on-Solent FS W/E 26.1.18; Deleted W/E 3.4.18

N1121   Presented to French Govt (allotted 21.8.17)

N1122   Shipped to Mudros 1.6.17; Flown HMS *Ark Royal* 25.7.17; Thasos 28.8.17; Dropped bomb on U-boat 15m E of Cape Santo 13.1.18 (F/L S Burton); HMS *Ark Royal* 20.1.18; Night bombing raid with N1201 & N1444, FL on landing 22.1.18 (F/L S Burton unhurt); Disposed of by Thasos by 6.18

N1123   (130-hp Clerget) Deld Grain (via Yarmouth) 28.7.17; Dover 31.7.17; Calshot TS 5.8.17; Deleted W/E 8.8.18

N1124   Yarmouth by 6.17; Westgate 26.6.17 (held up by weather); Dover 27.6.17; HMS *Riviera* 14.7.17; Cattewater 10.8.17; HMS *Riviera* (via Portland) W/E 15.11.17; Cattewater 4.1.18; HMS *Riviera* W/E 28.12.'17; Newlyn 27.2.18 (storage); Fishguard by road 30.3.18; Yarmouth W/E 6.6.18; Deleted W/E 12.12.18

N1125   (Later 130-hp Clerget) Deld Yarmouth (via Killingholme) 25.6.17; Dover 26.6.17; Calshot 27.6.17; Deleted W/E 14.9.17

N1126   Shipped to Mediterranean; Arrived EI&ESS Port Said in case by 15.9.17; Port Said by 12.17 (for HMS *City of Oxford* - NTU?); Tested 26.3.18; Alexandria; Ran out of fuel on A/S patrol, FL 4m N of convoy, sank 11.4.18 (FSL CKC Dagg clung to empty petrol tank which he cut adrift, picked up next day by HMS *Rowan*); Deleted 5.18

N1127   (Later re-engined 130-hp Clerget) Deld Fishguard by rail 28.6.17; Bomb frame modified to fit Mk.II 16-lb bomb, tested 19.7.17; With N1683, dropped 65-lb bomb on U-boat 5215N 0445W 22.3.18; Yarmouth W/E 13.6.18; HACP 10.8.18 (2/Lt JC Grant); Wrecked on TO 16.9.18 (pilot unhurt); Deleted W/E 10.10.18

N1128   (Later re-engined 130-hp Clerget) Shipped to Mediterranean; Arrived EI&ESS Port Said for erection by 15.9.17; Erected by 29.12.17; Port Said W/E 3.1.18; Became 269 Sqdn Port Said 6.10.18; EF, FL, towed in by HMS *Heliotrope* then minesweeper HMS *Minerva*, then beached 17.10.18 (Lt GF Hyams); Deleted 1.5.19

N1129   (130-hp Clerget) Shipped to Mediterranean; Arrived EI&ESS Port Said in case by 15.9.17; HMS *Empress* 1.11.17; Port Said 6.11.17; Surveyed 23.11.17; Deleted 21.12.17 wrecked

**10 SHORT ADMIRALTY 184 TYPE (IMPROVED) TRACTOR BIPLANE SEAPLANES ordered 1.17 under Cont Nos C.P.132112/16, A.S.14599/1 & A.S.4247 from Fredk Sage & Co Ltd, numbered N1130 to N1139 & built Peterborough. (240-hp Renault-Mercedes)**
[Improved version up to N1134, remainder original version BUT all Improved per official 1.17 list & AD weekly reports]
[N1130 to N1149 originally to have been all built by Shorts]

N1130   Deld Dover 30.3.17; Deleted 12.7.17

N1131   Deld South Shields for erection 18.4.17; Deleted W/E 23.2.18

N1132   Deld Yarmouth and Accepted 1.5.17 (Desoutter); Felixstowe 29.5.17; Yarmouth 30.5.17; Deleted 7.9.17 for despatch to Farnborough for sand tests, but unsuitable as not standard. BUT Farnborough by 3.18 (strength tests)

N1133   Deld Dundee for erection 4.5.17; Tested 9.5.17 (Desoutter); Dropped 100-lb bomb on U-boat 60m ENE of Bell Rock 13.7.17; EF, FL, crashed in sea, sank on tow 5.1.18 (crew saved); Surveyed 7.1.18; Deleted 19.1.18 TL

N1134   Deld South Shields for erection 9.5.17; Surveyed 11.4.18; Deleted 15.4.18 W&T

N1135   Deld Test Depot Grain by rail 30.5.17; Felixstowe 6.8.17; Yarmouth 7.8.17; South Shields 12.8.17 (transit); Rosyth 13.8.17; Dundee 14.8.17; HMS *Campania* 14.8.17; Dundee 14.8.17; EF, FL 8m SE of May Island 4.10.17 (FSL EOA Andrews & OSL DG McGregor picked up by armed trawler *Strathearn*); Surveyed 4.10.17; Deleted 17.10.17 TL

N1136   Deld Yarmouth 16.6.7; South Shields 20.6.17; HMS *Furious* 2.7.17; Surveyed 24.7.17; Deleted 18.8.17

N1137   Deld South Shields (via Yarmouth) 3.7.17; HMS *Furious* 3.7.17; Rosyth 16.9.17; HMS *Furious* 5.10.17; Rosyth 15.10.17; HMS *Furious* 2.11.17; Wrecked when derrick gear failed while hoisting in 2.11.17; Surveyed 6.11.17; Deleted 15.11.17 wrecked

N1138   (220-hp Renault) Deld HMS *Vindex* (via Yarmouth) 11.7.17; Dundee by 15.10.17; Felixstowe 19.1.18; Grain 28.1.18 (transit); EF, FL Dover 29.1.18; Newhaven 30.1.18 (en route Calshot); Calshot FS W/E 5.2.18; 209 TDS Lee-on-Solent W/E 27.6.18; Deleted 11.18

N1139   Deld Scapa for erection 22.7.17; Surveyed 15.4.18; Deleted 15.4.18 wrecked

**10 SHORT ADMIRALTY 184 TYPE (IMPROVED) TRACTOR SEAPLANES ordered 11.16 under Cont No A.S.10065 from S.E.Saunders Ltd, numbered N1140 to N1149 & built East Cowes. (240-hp Renault-Mercedes)**

N1140   Deld Westgate 13.5.17 (en route Dundee, delayed by weather); Felixstowe 21.5.17; Dundee (via South Shields) 9.6.17; HMS *Manxman* 15.6.17; Dundee by rail 5.7.17; Deleted W/E 12.9.18

N1141   (220-hp Mercedes) Admiralty trials at Cowes 2.5.17; Deld Westgate 23.5.17; Nore Flt Westgate 29.12.17; Deleted W/E 27.4.18

N1142   Deld Cattewater 22.5.17; Damaged, towed in 24.5.17; Calshot FS 24.7.17; Surveyed 18.12.17; Deleted 28.12.17 DBR

N1143   Accepted at Cowes 11.5.17; Deld Cattewater (via Calshot) 4.6.17; Scillies for GI use 20.3.18

N1144   Deld Calshot & accepted 25.5.17; Bembridge 26.5.17; Calshot to Lee-on-Solent W/E 13.12.17; Deleted W/E 11.2.18

N1145   Deld Calshot 2.6.17; Crashed in sea nr Bembridge 4.9.17 (TFSL MS Varden drowned); Deleted W/E 14.9.17

N1146   Deld Newlyn 4.6.17; Calshot (via Cattewater) 29.9.17; Deleted W/E 1.3.18

N1147   Deld Dover 12.6.17; Dunkerque 29.6.17; Dover 13.1.18; Lee-on-Solent TS W/E 8.2.18; Became 209 TDS Lee-on-Solent 1.4.18; Deleted W/E 17.10.18

N1148   Accepted at Cowes 2.6.17; Deld Bembridge 12.6.17; Crashed 14.6.17; Deleted 19.6.17 BR

N1149   (240-hp Sunbeam) Arrived Calshot with engine trouble on delivery to Fishguard 3.7.17; Cattewater 5.7.17; EF, FL 20m S of Start Point, towed to Plymouth by HMS *Porpoise* 10.7.17 (pilot & OSL BE Harrison); Newlyn

14.7.17 (transit); Fishguard 15.7.17; Damaged 25.8.17 (FSL RG Clarke); EF, failed to clear cliff, crashed into Windy Hill, CW, 100-lb bomb failed to explode 28.10.17; Surveyed 29.10.17; Deleted 2.11.17 DBR

## 10 SHORT "320" (ADMIRALTY 310A-4 TYPE) TRACTOR BIPLANE SEAPLANES ordered 11.16 under Cont No A.S.1344, numbered N1150 to N1159 & built Rochester. (320-hp Cossack) [Gordon Bruce's researches show correct c/n's to be S.354 to S.363]

N1150   Deld Type Test Flt Grain 24.3.17 (Parker); Type Test Dept Grain 1.4.17; Shorts Rochester 10.5.17; Test Depot Grain 5.17; Shorts Rochester 26.5.17; Test Depot Grain 27.6.17 (Experimental Aeroplane & Acceptance Dept, packed); Calshot W/E 15.12.17; Shipped to Otranto 2.1.18; Arr 6 Wing RNAS Otranto W/E 18.1.18; Became 66/67 Wings 1.4.18; Surveyed 6.4.18; Deleted 15.4.18 W&T

N1151   Deld Grain and accepted 28.3.17 (Parker); Shipped to Otranto 19.5.17; Recd 6 Wing RNAS Otranto by 28.9.17; Became 66/67 Wings 1.4.18; Deleted 15.4.18 W&T

N1152   Deld Grain and accepted 3.4.17 (Parker); Shipped to Otranto 19.5.17; 6 Wing RNAS Otranto by 21.7.17; Landed at sea, foundered on rocks 17.8.17, BR

N1153   Deld Grain and accepted 3.4.17 (Parker); Accepted 8.4.17 (Parker); Shipped to Otranto 19.5.17; Recd 6 Wing Otranto (coded '3') by 6.7.17; Deleted W/E 7.4.18

N1154   Deld Grain 13.4.17 (Parker); Shipped to Otranto 19.5.17; Recd 6 Wing RNAS Otranto (coded '4') by 18.7.17; Surveyed 7.1.18; Deleted 19.1.18 TL

N1155   Deld Grain 20.4.17; Accepted 24.4.17 (Parker); Shipped to Otranto 19.5.17; Recd 6 Wing RNAS Otranto (coded '5') by 17.8.17; lent HMS *Manxman* 21.1.18; 6 Wing Otranto 5.2.18; Deleted W/E 7.4.18

N1156   Deld Grain 26.4.17; Packing 21.5.17; Transhipped by lighter for 6 Wing RNAS Otranto; Shipped 27.5.17; 6 Wing RNAS Otranto (coded '6') by 2.9.17; CW by 17.8.17

N1157   Deld Grain 1.5.17 (Kemp); Packing 21.5.17; Transhipped by lighter for 6 Wing RNAS Otranto; Shipped 27.5.17; Recd 6 Wing RNAS Otranto (coded '7') by 2.9.17; Lent HMS *Manxman* 21.1.18; 6 Wing RNAS Otranto 15.2.18; Surveyed 31.3.18; Became 66/67 Wings 1.4.18; Deleted 15.4.18 W&T

N1158   Deld Grain 7.5.17 (Kemp); Shorts Rochester 9.5.17 (alterations); Grain 10.5.17; Packing 21.5.17; Transhipped by lighter for 6 Wing RNAS Otranto; Shipped 27.5.17; Recd 6 Wing RNAS Otranto (coded '9') by 2.9.17; Surveyed 19.9.17; Deleted 27.9.17 DBR

N1159   Deld Grain 23.5.17 (Parker); Transhipped by lighter for 6 Wing RNAS Otranto; Shipped 27.5.17; Recd 6 Wing RNAS Otranto by 19.10.17; Surveyed 20.10.17; Deleted 29.10.17 wrecked

## 15 CURTISS H.12 ["IMPROVED H.8"] 'LARGE AMERICA' TRACTOR BIPLANE FLYING BOATS purchased in Canada (tender accepted W/E 9.3.17) & numbered N1160 to N1174. (Two 250-hp RR, later two 250-hp Sunbeam)

N1160 to N1174 not delivered as such

## N1175 to N1179 not allotted

## 10 WHITE & THOMPSON PUSHER BIPLANE FLYING BOATS ordered 11.16 under Cont No A.S.133705/16, numbered N1180 to N1189 & built Middleton-on-Sea. (120-hp Beardmore) [Virtually indistinguishable from N.T.2b's]

N1180   Hull completed 1.17; Deld Calshot FS 8.6.17; Surveyed 18.12.17; Deleted 28.12.17 DBR

N1181   Deld Calshot FS 18.6.17 (no engine by 30.3.18); 209 TDS Lee-on-Solent W/E 27.6.18 (150-hp Hispano-Suiza); Deleted W/E 12.9.18

N1182   Deld Calshot FS 30.6.17; Deleted W/E 1.3.18

N1183   Deld Calshot FS 22.7.17; Cherbourg 24.7.17; CW when hangar destroyed in gale 28.8.17; Deleted W/E 14.9.17 W&T

N1184   Deld Calshot FS 25.7.17; Surveyed 27.10.17; Deleted 29.10.17 wrecked

N1185   (150-hp Hispano-Suiza) Deld Calshot FS 20.7.17; Surveyed 16.11.17; Deleted 21.11.17 wrecked

N1186   (150-hp Hispano-Suiza) Deld Calshot FS W/E 21.9.17; Deleted W/E 30.3.18

N1187   (150-hp Hispano-Suiza) Deld Calshot FS W/E 28.9.17; Deleted W/E 1.3.18

N1188   Deld Calshot FS 8.9.17; Deleted W/E 30.3.18

N1189   (150-hp Hispano-Suiza) Deld Lee-on-Solent TS W/E 12.10.17; Became 209 TDS Lee-on-Solent 1.4.18; Deleted W/E 8.8.18

## 30 FAIREY HAMBLE BABY TRACTOR BIPLANE SEAPLANES put forward 1.17 and ordered under Cont No A.S.7718/17 from George Parnall & Co Ltd, numbered N1190 to N1219 & built Bristol. (130-hp Clerget 9B unless otherwise stated)

N1190   (110-hp Clerget) Deld Test Depot Grain by rail 16.4.17; Felixstowe 3.6.17; Deleted W/E 12.9.18

N1191   Deld Yarmouth (via Calshot) 15.7.17; Newlyn, temp to Scillies 25.7.17; Newlyn 29.7.17; Cattewater 20.12.17; Yarmouth by rail 23.1.18; Killingholme W/E 9.3.18; Deleted W/E 22.3.18

N1192   Deld Calshot FS W/E 9.11.17; Allocated Lee-on-Solent W/E 26.1.18; CSD (packing for Greek Govt) W/E 11.5.18; Despatched W/E 5.9.18; Left England for RHNAS in SS *Piraeus* 27.9.18

N1193   Deld Grain by rail 2.6.17; To Victoria Docks 6.6.17; Shipped to Mudros 12.6.17; Flown HMS *Ark Royal* 5.8.17 - @7.8.17; Mudros by 8.17; Surveyed 18.10.17; Deleted 6.11.17 DBR

N1194   (110-hp Clerget 9Z) Deld Dover (via Calshot) 15.6.17; Dunkerque 28.9.17; Dover 29.9.17; Westgate W/E 16.2.18; Deleted W/E 27.4.18

N1195   (110-hp Clerget 9Z) Mkrs for Mudros by 1.6.17; Shipped to Mudros 10.10.17; HMS *Ark Royal* by 1.12.17; HMS *Peony* by 1.1.18 - @4.3.18

N1196   Shipped to Mudros W/E 10.10.17; Suda Bay 1.12.17 - @21.3.18

N1197   Deld Dundee by road 29.6.17; Deleted W/E 16.3.18

N1198   Deld Bembridge 16.7.17; Wrecked 19.7.17; Deleted

N1199   Still at makers 14.7.17; Assembled Fishguard 6.8.17; Became 426/427 Flts Fishguard 25.5.18 (245 Sqdn 8.18); Dropped 2x65-lb bombs on U-boat 12m NNW of Strumble Head 23.11.17 (FSL HF de la Rue); Deleted W/E 12.12.18

N1200   Calshot by 10.17; BR by 5.10.17

N1201   Shipped to Mudros; Flown HMS *Ark Royal*, then to Imbros, retd later but FL Kharos Bay 24.10.17 (FSL EW Coveney); Salved 25.10.17; HMS *Ark Royal* by 1.12.17; Dropped 2x65-lb bombs on submarine 20m SW of Cape Tigani 20.1.18 (F/L LWE Leage); Talikna 4.3.18 - @9.18; Possibly one of 10 a/c destroyed in enemy air raid on Talikna 24.9.18

N1202   Deld Calshot 23.7.17; Bembridge 24.7.17; Deleted W/E 19.1.18

N1203   Deld Westgate (via Calshot) 13.8.17; Dropped 2x65-lb bombs on U-boat 25-30m NE of North Foreland 23.10.17 (FSL FC Lander); Deleted W/E 27.4.18

N1204   Accepted 26.7.17; Deld Rosyth 10.17; Killingholme store 5.10.17; Hornsea by 2.1.18; Killingholme for erection by 22.2.18; Deleted 20.4.18 DBR

N1205   Still at makers 14.7.17 (for Fishguard); Cattewater to Fishguard (via Newlyn) 13.8.17; Newlyn W/E 10.11.17; Yarmouth by rail 1.2.18 (arr W/E 16.2.18); Became 324/6 Flts Yarmouth 25.5.18; Damaged float on TO 31.5.18; Bombed U-boat 2m NNE Smith's Knoll Pillar Buoy 6.6.18 (Lt AD Pole); Became 324/6 Flts 228 Sqdn Yarmouth 20.8.18; Deleted W/E 12.9.18

N1206   Deld Cattewater (via Portland) 19.8.17; Yarmouth 27.1.18; Deleted W/E 22.3.18

N1207   (110-hp Clerget 9Z) Still at makers 14.7.17 (for Fishguard); Deld Hamble to Calshot (en route Fishguard) 30.8.17; arr Cattewater W/E 15.9.17; Grain by rail 8.2.18; Yarmouth W/E 16.2.18; Killingholme W/E 9.3.18; Deleted 16.3.18 W&T

N1208   Deld Hamble to Calshot 23.8.17 (en route Newlyn); Portland 31.8.17 (en route Plymouth); arr Cattewater W/E 15.9.17; Yarmouth 27.1.18; Killingholme W/E 9.3.18; Deleted W/E 22.3.18

N1209    Shipped to Port Said 7.17; EI&ESS Port Said for erection by 9.17; HMS *Empress* 1.11.17; Port Said 3.11.17 (for HMS *City of Oxford* - NTU?); Surveyed by 29.6.18; Deleted Alexandria 11.18

N1210    Shipped to Port Said 7.17; EI&ESS Port Said for erection by 9.17; HMS *Empress* 1.11.17; EF, FL, attempted to set fire to a/c, rescued by N1036, Haifa Bay 2.11.17 (F/L AE Popham unhurt); For deletion by 4.11.17

N1211    (110-hp Clerget 9Z, re-engined 130-hp Clerget 9B around 2.18) Deld Calshot W/E 9.11.17; Lee-on-Solent TS W/E 26.1.18; CSD (packing for Greek Govt) W/E 11.5.18; Despatched W/E 5.9.18; Left England for RHNAS in SS *Piraeus* 27.9.18

N1212    Deld Westgate (via Calshot) 11.9.17; For deletion by 30.3.18 - @10.18

N1213    Deld Calshot for erection W/E 9.11.17; CSD packing for Greek Govt W/E 6.6.18; Despatched W/E 5.9.18; Left England for RHNAS in SS *Piraeus* 27.9.18

N1214    Mkrs for Mudros by 1.6.17; CSD White City; Shipped to Mudros but sunk in transit; Surveyed 10.11.17; Deleted 15.11.17

N1215    Mkrs for Mudros by 1.6.17; CSD White City; Shipped to Mudros but sunk in transit; Surveyed 10.11.17; Deleted 15.11.17

N1216    Deld Calshot for erection W/E 9.11.17 (to School) CSD packing for Greek Govt W/E 6.6.18; Despatched W/E 5.9.18; Left England for RHNAS in SS *Piraeus* 27.9.18

N1217    In transit to 6 Wing RNAS Otranto by 9.11.17; Sunk in transit, deleted 20.11.17

N1218    In transit to 6 Wing RNAS Otranto by 9.11.17; Sunk in transit, deleted 20.11.17

N1219    Deld by rail to Dundee 21.8.17; Tested 4.9.17; still there @30.1.19

**10 SHORT ADMIRALTY 184 TYPE (IMPROVED?) TRACTOR BIPLANE SEAPLANES put forward 1.17 and ordered under Cont Nos C.P.102693/17 & A.S.3610 from Robey & Co Ltd, numbered N1220 to N1229 & built Lincoln. (240-hp Renault-Mercedes)**

N1220    Deld Rosyth W/E 5.10.17; HMS *Campania* W/E 16.11.17; Scapa for erection on/by 29.12.17 - @9.3.18; Houton Bay for erection 3.18; 430 Flt Houton Bay by 5.18 - @30.1.19

N1221    Deld Scapa for erection W/E 22.9.17; Houton Bay W/E 26.1.18; Propeller accident Houton Bay 23.5.18 (Lt SC Smith injured); 430 Flt Houton Bay 25.5.18 - @30.1.19

N1222    Mkrs by 1.6.17; Shipped to Mudros; HMS *Ark Royal* by 11.17; to collier *John Sanderson* for Suda Bay 13.11.17; Suda Bay by 1.12.17; Surveyed 17.2.18 DBR; Deleted 27.3.18

N1223    Deld HMS *Pegasus* at Rosyth 12.9.17 - @29.9.17; South Shields by 5.1.18; Deleted W/E 3.2.18

N1224    Deld Rosyth W/E 5.10.17; HMS *Furious* 25.10.17; Rosyth 2.11.17; HMS *Pegasus* W/E 3.11.17; HMS *Nairana* W/E 10.11.17; Killingholme W/E 29.12.17; South Shields W/E 29.12.17; Surveyed 11.4.18; Deleted 15.4.18 W&T

N1225    (225-hp Renault) Deld HMS *Nairana* W/E 29.9.17; Killingholme W/E 8.11.17; FL in sea, towed Scarborough; Deleted W/E 20.4.18

N1226    Deld HMS *Pegasus* at Rosyth 28.9.17; Rosyth W/E 11.12.17 - @29.12.17; HMS *Pegasus* by 3.1.18; Killingholme patrol W/E 7.2.18; EF, FL, beached safely off Filey 20.4.18 (pilot unhurt); 405 Flt Hornsea by 13.6.18 (248 Sqdn 20.8.18) - @30.1.19

N1227    Shipped to Mudros 4.10.17; arr Port Said W/E 11.11.17; Re-shipped to Mudros W/E 17.11.17; HMS *Ark Royal* 11.2.18; Talikna 8.3.18; Mudros by 23.3.18; Skyros by 9.18

N1228    Shipped to Mudros .17; Tested HMS *Ark Royal* after erection 30.11.17; Syra in SS *Datchet* 9.12.17 - @23.3.18

N1229    Deld Killingholme W/E 8.9.17; Westgate 27.9.17; Dropped 115-lb on U-boat 4m S of South Falls Head 15.10.17 (FSL AG Hodgson & AM RJ Davis); Dropped 230-lb & 100-lb bomb on *U-48* 2½m NE of Galloper Buoy 23.11.17, U-boat went aground on Goodwin Sands next day as a result of damage (FSL JAE Vowles & AM DA Alderton); Dropped 230-lb & 110-lb bombs on U-

boat, neither exploded, 1m E of Galloper Buoy (5146N 0158W) 5.2.18 (FSL JAE Vowles & AM DA Alderton); EF, towed in by *ML111* 21.3.18 (FSL JAE Vowles & AM DA Alderton); Became 406 Flt Westgate 25.5.18 (219 Sqdn 22.7.18); Tested Foster gun mounting on top plane 30.7.18 (F/L GE Livock); Still Westgate 30.1.19

**10 SHORT ADMIRALTY 184 TYPE (IMPROVED) TRACTOR BIPLANE SEAPLANES put forward 12.16 and ordered 1.17 under Cont Nos C.P.138004/16 & A.S.4247 from Fredk Sage & Co Ltd, numbered N1230 to N1239 & built Peterborough. (240-hp Renault-Mercedes)**

N1230    Deld Scapa for erection 9.8.17; HMS *Campania* W/E 7.2.18; Scapa 8.2.18

N1231    Deld Yarmouth 7.8.17; Killingholme (transit) 7.8.17; South Shields (transit) 9.8.17; Dundee 10.8.17; Deleted W/E 18.5.18

N1232    Deld HMS *Vindex* (via Felixstowe) 7.9.17; FL in Dutch territorial waters 25.9.17, after 6 days brought ashore by Dutch trawler *HD47* to Den Helder, Noord Holland (F/L EG Hopcroft & PO EJ Garner); Aircraft interned in Holland as *K1*; Surveyed 12.12.17; Deleted 15.12.17

N1233    Deld South Shields (via Yarmouth) 5.10.17; Crashed in sea N of Longstone 22.11.17 (TFSL KG MacAloney & AC2 FT Sprules both killed); Surveyed 1.12.17; Deleted 4.12.17 TL

N1234    Mkrs for Mudros by 1.6.17; Shipped to Aegean; Mudros by 10.17; HMS *Ark Royal*, tested after erection 6.11.17; FTR patrol, lost off Cape Murtzephlos, NW of Lemnos 2.12.17 (TFSL LHG Gillespie & TOSL H Odle both drowned); Surveyed 12.12.17; Deleted 19.1.19 TL

N1235    (225-hp Renault) Deld Yarmouth W/E 27.10.17; Killingholme W/E 10.11.17; 405 Flt Hornsea 17.6.18 (248 Sqdn 20.8.18) - @30.1.19

N1236    Mkrs for Mudros by 1.6.17; Shipped W/E 10.10.17; Sunk in transit, deleted 20.11.17

N1237    Deld HMS *Vindex* (via Yarmouth) 31.8.17; Struts gave way owing to sea 28.11.17; Felixstowe by 1.12.17 (u/s); Calshot TS W/E 23.2.18; 209 TDS Lee-on-Solent W/E 20.6.18; Deleted W/E 30.12.18

N1238    Deld HMS *Nairana* W/E 29.9.17; Rosyth 28.10.17; HMS *Nairana* on/by 1.11.17; Deleted W/E 15.11.17

N1239    (225-hp Renault) Deld Rosyth 9.17; HMS *Nairana* 19.9.17 - @29.12.17; Rosyth to South Shields 5.1.18 (transit); Killingholme patrol W/E 25.1.18 (and Hornsea); Deleted W/E 4.7.18

**10 SHORT ADMIRALTY 184 TYPE (IMPROVED) TRACTOR BIPLANE SEAPLANES (Intermediate type) put forward 12.16 and ordered under Cont Nos C.P.138324/16, A.S.1469/1 & A.S.12908/17 from J.Samuel White & Co Ltd, numbered N1240 to N1249 & built East Cowes. (240-hp Sunbeam unless otherwise stated)**
[225-hp Sunbeam per official list 2.18]

N1240    (225-hp Mohawk) Deld Cattewater 30.4.17; Newlyn 27.5.17; Tresco 23.9.17; Newlyn 27.9.17; Cattewater 22.10.17; Calshot 5.11.17; Surveyed 10.3.18 wreck; Deleted 16.3.18

N1241    Shipped to Mudros 3.7.17; arr Mudros W/E 26.9.17; Flown HMS *Ark Royal* 14.9.17; Talikna 31.10.17; HMS *Ark Royal* by 11.11.17 - @26.12.17; Surveyed 8.3.18; Deleted 27.3.18 W&T

N1242    Deld Newlyn 4.6.17 (transit via Cattewater); U/c damaged on TO for Fishguard 5.6.17; Port Mellion, Scillies 12.6.17 (arr 13.6.17) (transit); Fishguard 15.6.17; Deleted W/E 16.2.18

N1243    Deld Westgate 9.6.17; Abandoned, CW 14.6.17; Deleted 15.6.17

N1244    Deld Calshot patrol 19.6.17; Newhaven 20.6.17; Dropped 2x100-lb bombs on U-boat 30m S of Brighton 24.7.17 (FSL AG Bishop); Deleted W/E 1.3.18

N1245    Deld Westgate (via Calshot) 5.7.17; EF, FL in sea and wrecked 22.7.17 (FSL GCB Cotterell & AM Lewis slightly injured); Deleted 31.7.17

N1246    Deld Calshot 5.7.17; Newhaven 7.7.17; Dropped 2x100-lb bombs on U-boat 24m SSE Beachy Head 13.7.17; Surveyed 6.12.17; Deleted 13.12.17 wrecked

N1247    Deld Bembridge 12.7.17; Newhaven 3.8.17; Calshot W/E 7.12.17; Newhaven W/E 14.12.17; Surveyed

N1248    10.1.18; Deleted 15.1.18 W&T

Deld Calshot 26.7.17; Newhaven 13.8.17; U/c carried away, liable to sink, making for Hastings, wreckage brought in by Aux Patrol vessel *Inchgarth* 15.10.17; Surveyed 2.11.17; Deleted 6.11.17 wrecked

N1249    Deld Calshot 16.8.17; Newhaven 21.9.17; COL 5.12.17; Propeller fell off, FL, picked up and retd by transport 7.4.18 (2 crew unhurt); Became 408/9 Flts Newhaven 25.5.18; Deleted W/E 11.7.18

**10 SHORT ADMIRALTY 184 TYPE (IMPROVED) TRACTOR BIPLANE SEAPLANES (Intermediate type) ordered under Cont Nos C.P.138324/16, A.S.12097/1 & A.S.12908/17 from J.Samuel White & Co Ltd, numbered N1250 to N1259 & built East Cowes. (220-hp Renault-Mercedes to N1255, remainder 260-hp Sunbeam Maori]**

N1250    (250-hp Sunbeam) Deld Yarmouth W/E 8.9.17 (sic); FL in English Channel 24.8.17; Dropped 2x100-lb bombs on U-boat 45m E of Yarmouth 21.9.17 (FSL WAN Davern); Became 324/6 Flts Yarmouth 25.5.18; Deleted W/E 1.6.18

N1251    Deld Dundee by rail 29.9.17; Crashed into pier Dundee fish dock, TW 2.18 (S/L JT Cameron slightly injured & AC Peters); Deleted W/E 14.2.18

N1252    Deld Bembridge W/E 1.9.17; Calshot 26.10.17; Surveyed 31.12.17; Deleted 15.1.18 W&T

N1253    Deld Calshot patrol by 26.10.17; Deleted W/E 1.3.18

N1254    Deld Newlyn 9.12.17; Became 424/5 Flts Newlyn 25.5.18; Deleted W/E 8.8.18

N1255    Deld Cattewater (via Portland) 5.11.17; Newlyn W/E 17.11.17; Dropped 100-lb & 65-lb bombs on large U-boat on surface 5032N 0515W 8.5.18 (Ens HT Stanley USN); Became 424/5 Flts Newlyn 25.5.18; Damaged float landing Tresco 26.6.18; Deleted W/E 8.8.18

N1256    Deld Cattewater W/E 16.11.17; Became 347/9 Flts Cattewater 25.5.18; 209 TDS Lee-on-Solent W/E 1.8.18; Deleted W/E 3.10.18 - @30.1.19

N1257    Deld Cattewater W/E 16.11.17; Dropped 2 bombs on U-boat 13m SW of Bolt Head 17.11.17 (F/L JH Woolner & Obs WG Farley); Calshot W/E 8.3.18; Deleted Calshot W/E 29.3.18 wrecked

N1258    Deld Cattewater W/E 16.11.17; Dropped 2x100-lb bombs on U-boat, oil and air seen 4957N 0353W 27.5.18 (2/Lt L Graham & 2/Lt RL Stevenson); Became 347/9 Flts Cattewater 25.5.18; 209 TDS Lee-on-Solent W/E 1.8.18; Deleted W/E 3.10.18

N1259    Deld Portland W/E 19.12.17; Became 416/7 Flts Portland 25.5.18 (241 Sqdn 20.8.18); Bombed U-boat, no results seen 30.9.18 (Lt DR Douglas & Lt EA Sawyer); Still Portland 30.1.19

**15 FELIXSTOWE F.2A TRACTOR BIPLANE FLYING BOATS ordered under Cont No A.S.3610 (BR.17) from Curtiss, Toronto, to be numbered N1260 to N1274. (Eagle VIII)**

N1260 to N1274 presume renumbered N4060 to N4074 and serials reallocated

**12 SHORT ADMIRALTY 184 TYPE (IMPROVED) TRACTOR BIPLANE SEAPLANES ordered under Cont No A.S.14600/1, C.P.138002/16 & C.P.102653 from Robey & Co Ltd, numbered N1260 to N1271 & built Lincoln. (ordered as 225-hp Sunbeam but deld as 240-hp Renault-Mercedes) [23.4.17 to be 225-hp Sunbeam to N1263, remainder 240-hp Renault. Per 2.18 official list all 240-hp]**

N1260    Deld Exptl Design Grain 18.3.17; Erected at Test Depot Grain 31.3.17; ECD Grain 27.4.17; Test Depot Grain 25.6.17; Type Test Flt Grain by 29.12.17; For deletion by 2.2.18
"N1260" FL on beach nr sanatorium N of Zuydcoote 2.10.17; Dunkerque 3.10.17; Dover 10.10.17

N1261    Deld Grain by road 7.4.17; Shipped to Mudros 1.6.17; Flown HMS *Ark Royal* 2.9.17; o/t landing downwind, wrecked 8.10.17 (FSL JA Harman unhurt); Surveyed 10.10.17; Deleted 26.10.17 DBR

N1262    Shipped to Port Said; Erecting EI&ESS Port Said by 15.9.17; HMS *City of Oxford* 28.10.17; HMS *Raglan* 30.10.17; Attacked and badly damaged by Halberstadt 30.10.17 (F/L EJ Burling unhurt & Capt WR Kempson

wounded); Wreckage salved by HMS *Raglan* but subsequently wrecked by blast from her 14" guns; Deleted Port Said 20.12.17 (240-hp Sunbeam)

N1263    (240-hp Sunbeam by 12.17) Shipped to Port Said; EI&ESS Port Said erecting by 9.17; HMS *Raven II* 31.10.17; HMS *Raglan* 2.11.17; HMS *City of Oxford* 4.11.17; U/c smashed in heavy sea on TO, towed back to ship by HM *ML.31* 8.11.17 (F/L GD Smith DSC & 2/Lt LH Pakenham Walsh); Port Said 9.11.17; Surveyed 23.11.17; Deleted 21.12.17 wrecked; Restored to commission; Suez by 2.18; HMS *City of Oxford* 13.2.18; Suez 29.3.18; Port Said by 4.18; HMS *Empress* 8.4.18; Port Said 4.18; Deleted 5.18

N1264    Deld Westgate by road 6.5.17; Nore Flt Westgate by 29.12.17 (240-hp Sunbeam); Became 406 Flt Westgate 25.5.18 (219 Sqdn 22.7.18); COL, on nose, towed to Ramsgate 1.8.18 (2/Lt CP Bristow & AC Sturges unhurt); Lost in mist, crashed 2m out, towed in by motor boat 24.12.18; Deleted W/E 23.1.19

N1265    Deld Bembridge 21.5.17; Calshot patrol 3.6.17; Damaged chassis 1.7.17; Newhaven W/E 1.11.17; Deleted W/E 2.3.18

N1266    Deld Calshot and accepted 25.5.17 (Prodger); Newhaven 28.5.17; Wrecked 16.7.17; Deleted 26.7.17

N1267    Deld Calshot patrol 5.6.17; Bembridge 11.6.17; Calshot patrol 12.7.17 (later training); Deleted W/E 8.3.18

N1268    Deld Killingholme by rail 28.5.17; Whitby 13.6.17 (transit); South Shields 14.6.17; FL 4m E of Seaham and sank 29.12.17 (2 crew taken off by *P52*); Surveyed 3.1.18; Deleted 15.1.18 TL

N1269    Mkrs for Mudros by 1.6.17; Shipped to Mudros; Flown HMS *Ark Royal* 5.10.17; Imbros 24.10.17; HMS *Ark Royal* 5.11.17; Tested 15.12.17 - @22.2.18; Talikna by 3.18; HMS *Ark Royal* 20.3.18; Mudros 4.6.18; Talikna by 6.18; Deleted 1918; Possibly one of 10 Short seaplanes destroyed in enemy air raid on Talikna 24.9.18

N1270    Deld Killingholme by lorry 12.6.17; Dundee 27.6.17 (arr 1.7.17 via South Shields); Deleted W/E 12.9.18

N1271    Deld Killingholme in error by lorry 20.6.17; Ordered to return to Mkrs 21.6.17; Scapa by 22.7.17; to HMS *Campania* but EF, FL off Noss Head 16.8.17; Towed back to Scapa 17.8.17; HMS *Pegasus* 24.8.17; HMS *Campania* 26.8.17; Alighted E of Skerries, lost 16.10.17 (crew saved); Surveyed 18.10.17; Deleted 27.10.17 TL

**8 SHORT ADMIRALTY 184 TYPE (IMPROVED) TRACTOR SEAPLANES ordered under Cont Nos A.S.3610/1 & C.P.138002/16 from Robey & Co Ltd, numbered N1272 to N1279 & built Lincoln. (240-hp Renault-Mercedes)**

N1272    Deld Killingholme by lorry 21.6.17; South Shields 1.7.17; HMS *Furious* 2.7.17; visited Scapa 28.7.17 (survey compass); Scapa 21.8.17 (true up); HMS *Furious* 22.9.17; South Shields 14.11.17; Damaged landing 22.12.17; Deleted W/E 23.2.18

N1273    (220-hp Renault-Mercedes) Deld Killingholme for erection 29.6.17; Yarmouth W/E 29.9.17; Westgate 29.9.17; Damaged at Tongue LV 2.2.18; Became 406 Flt Westgate 25.5.18 (219 Sqdn 22.7.18); Engine caught fire, FL in sea, towed back to Westgate 13.6.18; U/c collapsed on landing, nosed into sea, towed to Ramsgate 1.8.18 (2/Lt CP Bristow); Deleted W/E 12.9.18

N1274    Deld Killingholme for erection 1.7.17; Felixstowe 7.8.17; Dover 11.9.17 (transit); Calshot FS 13.9.17; Surveyed 24.9.17; Deleted 26.9.17 wrecked

N1275    (220-hp Renault-Mercedes) Deld Killingholme for storage 7.7.17; Westgate 7.8.17; EF, FL in sea 29.9.17 (FSL SJ Read); Towed to Newhaven by destroyer 29.9.17 [still there 13.10.17]; Retd Westgate 10.17; Bombed U-boat 11m NE of North Foreland 5.12.17 (F/L AG Hodgson & PO Worthington); EF, FL off Foreness, slightly damaged, towed to Ramsgate 7.1.18; Retd Westgate by road; Hydrophone expts 29-30.1.18; Became 406 Flt Westgate 25.5.18; HSMP, EF, forced to return 4.6.18; Deleted W/E 11.7.18

N1276    Deld Killingholme by lorry 11.7.17; South Shields 21.8.17 (transit); Dundee 30.8.17; Dropped 100-lb bomb on U-boat 14.10.17 (FSL A Holland & OSL L Ritson); Damaged on patrol, dismantled at Berwick on/by 19.10.18; Deleted W/E 21.11.18

N1277    Deld Killingholme by lorry for storage 14.7.17;

Felixstowe (via Yarmouth) W/E 27.10.17; Newhaven W/E 3.11.17; Calshot TS W/E 25.5.18; 209 TDS Lee-on-Solent W/E 6.6.18; Deleted W/E 1.8.18

N1278 Deld Killingholme by lorry for storage 18.7.17; Westgate 20.8.17; Yarmouth 21.8.17 (repair); Westgate 3.9.17; EF, FL in sea 1½m W of South Knock buoy, taken in tow for Sheerness by HMS *Clacton Belle*, but o/t and sank in bad weather, CW of Westgate 6.10.17 (F/L CW Bailey & AM DA Alderton); Surveyed 13.10.17; Deleted 16.10.17 wrecked

N1279 Deld Bembridge 27.8.17; Calshot FS 26.10.17; Lee-on-Solent TS W/E 28.11.17; Became 209 TDS Lee-on-Solent 1.4.18; Deleted W/E 27.6.18

**10 WIGHT CONVERTED TRACTOR BIPLANE SEAPLANES put forward 1.17 and ordered 18.5.17 under Cont No A.S.9336 (BR597), numbered N1280 to N1289 & built East Cowes. (260-hp Maori unless otherwise stated)**

N1280 (250-hp Sunbeam) Accepted at Mkrs 6.10.17; Calshot FS 30.11.17; Experimental fin, offset 9 degrees to port, tested 12.17; Became 210 TDS Calshot 6.18; WO 24.10.18

N1281 (250-hp Sunbeam) Accepted at Mkrs 11.17; Calshot FS 30.11.17; Became 210 TDS Calshot 6.18; ARS Calshot W/E 31.10.18; Deleted W/E 7.11.18

N1282 (250-hp Sunbeam) Accepted at Mkrs 12.17; Calshot FS 7.12.17; Became 210 TDS Calshot 6.18; Deleted W/E 14.11.18

N1283 Accepted at Mkrs 12.12.17; Calshot FS 14.12.17; Became 210 TDS Calshot 6.18; Deleted W/E 14.11.18

N1284 Accepted at Mkrs 19.12.17; Calshot FS 21.12.17; Deleted W/E 13.6.18

N1285 Accepted at Mkrs 12.17; Calshot FS 21.12.17; Deleted W/E 13.6.18

N1286 Accepted at Mkrs 12.17; Calshot FS 6.1.18; Deleted W/E 11.7.18

N1287 Accepted at Mkrs 12.17; Calshot FS 6.1.18; Deleted W/E 13.6.18

N1288 Accepted at Mkrs 12.17; Calshot FS 6.1.18; Became 210 TDS by 6.18; Sideslipped and crashed 10.7.18 (Lt CW Murphy & 2/Lt JA Sutherland both injured); Deleted W/E 25.7.18

N1289 Accepted at Mkrs 1.18; Calshot FS 2.2.18 [11.1.18?]; Deleted W/E 20.6.18

**10 A.D. PUSHER BIPLANE FLYING BOATS ordered under Cont No A.S.14609 (later A.S.1449) from J.Samuel White & Co Ltd (taken over by Pemberton-Billing Ltd), numbered N1290 to N1299 & built Woolston. (Ordered with 190-hp Rolls-Royce but to be deld with 150-hp Hispano-Suiza)**

N1290 No record
N1291 to N1294 cancelled 3.18
N1295 to N1299 delivered as spares

**20 SHORT "320" (ADMIRALTY TYPE SHORT 310-A4) NORTH SEA SCOUT TRACTOR BIPLANE SEAPLANES put forward 2.16 and ordered 12.16 under Cont No A.S.11219, numbered N1300 to N1319 & built Rochester. (310-hp Cossack)**
[Gordon Bruce's researches show correct c/n's S.334 to S.353]

N1300 Allotted CSD to Grain to pack for Otranto 25.9.17; To Otranto W/E 1.12.17; Shipped 12.12.17; Arrived 6 Wing RNAS Otranto W/E 18.1.18; Became 66/67 Wings Otranto 1.4.18; Disposed by 7.18

N1301 Allotted CSD to Grain to pack for Otranto 25.9.17; To Otranto W/E 1.12.17; Shipped 12.12.17; Arrived 6 Wing RNAS Otranto W/E 18.1.18; Dropped 230-lb bomb on U-boat, failed to explode 4015N 1855E 3.6.18; Still 6 Wing Otranto 7.18

N1302 Deld CSD to Grain 27.10.17; Shipped to Malta 20.11.17; Calafrana for erection by 14.2.18; Became 433/4 Flts 268 Sqdn Calafrana (coded 'P') by 8.18 - @12.10.18

N1303 Deld Grain 27.10.17; Yarmouth W/E 10.11.17; Bembridge by 19.1.18; Yarmouth by 23.2.18; Surveyed 8.5.18; Deleted 15.5.18 DBR [a photo shows this clearly painted with c/n S.393, presumably in error]

N1304 Deld Grain W/E 3.11.17; Packed 8.12.17; Despatched W/E 15.12.17; Shipped 31.12.17; To Malta 3.18;

Calafrana for erection by 19.4.18; Became 268 Sqdn Calafrana 27.9.18 - @30.1.19

N1305 Deld Grain W/E 3.11.17; Packed 8.12.17; Despatched W/E 15.12.17; Shipped Otranto 2.1.18; 6 Wing RNAS Otranto by 3.18 - @7.18

N1306 Deld Grain W/E 10.11.17; Packed 14.12.17; Despatched W/E 22.12.17; West India Docks by 15-18.1.18; Shipped Otranto 9.3.18; 6 Wing RNAS Otranto by 3.18; Recd Calafrana W/E 21.4.18 - @9.18; 435/436 Flts 223 Sqdn Otranto by 10.18

N1307 Deld Grain W/E 10.11.17; Packed 14.12.17; Despatched W/E 22.12.17; West India Docks by 15-18.1.18; 6 Wing RNAS Otranto by 3.18; Recd Calafrana W/E 21.4.18; Became 433/4 Flts Calafrana (coded 'A') by 9.18; Bombed U-boat 55m 55° NE of Malta, sighted 12.10, bomb failed to explode 14.11.18 (Lt WR Tapper & 2/Lt WH Hoskin)

N1308 Deld Grain W/E 10.11.17; Despatched W/E 29.12.17; West India Docks by 15-18.1.18; Shipped Otranto 16.3.18; 6 Wing RNAS Otranto by 6.18; Became 435/6 Flts 263 Sqdn Otranto 10.18

N1309 Deld Grain W/E 10.11.17; Shipped 21.3.18; Despatched W/E 29.12.17; West India Docks by 15-18.1.18; To 6 Wing RNAS Otranto 3.18; Calafrana by 6.18 - @9.18; 435/6 Flts 223 Sqdn Otranto by 10.18

N1310 Deld Grain W/E 17.11.17; Despatched CSD W/E 29.12.17; West India Docks by 15-18.1.18; Shipped from Cardiff (sic) to Otranto 29.3.18; Otranto by 6.18; Became 435/6 Flts 263 Sqdn Otranto 10.18

N1311 Deld Grain W/E 24.11.17; Despatched CSD W/E 29.12.17; West India Docks by 15-18.1.18; Shipped to Malta 9.3.18; Calafrana by 5.18 - 9.18; 435/6 Flts Otranto 263 Sqdn by 10.18

N1312 Deld Grain W/E 24.11.17; CSD to Cardiff Docks by 16.1.18; Shipped 28.1.18; To Malta 3.18; Otranto by 5.18; Became 435/6 Flts 263 Sqdn Otranto by 9.18 - @30.1.19

N1313 Deld Grain W/E 24.11.17; CSD to Cardiff Docks by 15.1.18; Shipped 28.1.18; To Otranto 3.18; Calafrana by 5.18; Became 435/6 Flts 263 Sqdn Otranto by 10.18 - @30.1.19

N1314 Deld Grain W/E 1.12.17; CSD to Cardiff Docks by 15.1.18; Shipped 28.1.18; To Otranto 3.18; 66/67 Wing Otranto by 21.4.18 - @7.18

N1315 Deld Grain W/E 8.12.17 - @5.1.18; To CSD; West India Docks by 15-18.1.18; Shipped to Otranto 28.3.18; Otranto by 7.18; Became 435/6 Flts Otranto 263 Sqdn 10.18 - @30.1.19

N1316 Deld Grain 5.12.17; CSD to West India Docks by 16.1.18; Shipped 28.3.18; To Malta 3.18; 435/6 Flts 263 Sqdn Otranto by 10.18 - @30.1.19

N1317 Deld Grain 6.12.17; Trials 28.12.17; To CSD; Left for Malta 2.3.18; Cardiff Docks by 6.3.18; Shipped 29.3.18; Calafrana by 7.18 - @9.18; 435/6 Flts 263 Sqdn Otranto by 10.18 - @30.1.19

N1318 Deld Grain 8.12.17; CSD to West India Docks by 15.1.18 - @6.3.18; Shipped to Otranto 13.4.18; Otranto by 7.18; Became 435/6 Flts 263 Sqdn Otranto 10.18 - @30.1.19

N1319 Deld Grain 11.12.17; To CSD; West India Docks by 1.1.18 - @6.3.18; Shipped to Otranto 10.4.18; Otranto by 8.18; Became 435/6 Flts 263 Sqdn Otranto 10.18 - @30.1.19

**10 FAIREY HAMBLE BABY TRACTOR BIPLANE SEAPLANE put forward 12.16 and ordered 1.17 under Cont No A.S.4765/17, numbered N1320 to N1329 & built Hamble. (110-hp Clerget 9Z) [C/n's F.129 to F.138]**

N1320 Deld Test Depot Grain by road 11.5.17; Flown 2.6.17; Killingholme W/E 29.12.17; Crashed 30.3.18; Deleted 6.4.18

N1321 (Later re-engined 130-hp) Deld Test Depot Grain 17.6.17 (performance trials & propeller trials); ECD Grain 11.8.17; Land chassis fitted from 13.8.17, becoming Hamble Baby Convert (130-hp Clerget); Gunnery School Flts Eastchurch 2.10.17; G Flt Cranwell 4.12.17; Became 201 TDS Cranwell 1.4.18; Became 56 TDS Cranwell 27.7.18; Fuselage to 57 TDS Cranwell for engine instruction 13.8.18; For deletion by 8.1.19

N1322 Probably the Hamble Baby which crashed en route

Hamble to Newlyn 28.7.17; Deld Calshot for erection W/E 7.12.17; Lee-on-Solent W/E 26.1.18; Deleted 1.3.18

N1323    Deld Cattewater (via Portland) 28.10.17; Grain by rail 6.2.18; Yarmouth W/E 16.2.18; Killingholme W/E 9.3.18 (now 130-hp); Yarmouth W/E 16.3.18; Deleted W/E 4.4.18

N1324    Deld Calshot FS 14.9.17; BR by 21.9.17; Deleted W/E 24.10.17

N1325    Deld Houton Bay W/E 10.10.17; Rosyth 15.10.17; Aberdeen for HMS *Campania* 16.10.17; Scapa for erection by 3.11.17; Surveyed Houton Bay 7.12.17; deleted 22.12.17 DBR (crashed)

N1326    (Later re-engined 130-hp) Deld Westgate 6.9.17; Deleted W/E 20.4.18

N1327    Deld Calshot W/E 27.9.17; Westgate 27.9.17; Wrecked 6.11.17 (TFSL GH Herriott killed); Surveyed 17.11.17; Deleted 21.11.17 DBR

N1328    (later re-engined 130-hp Clerget) Deld South Shields 11.8.17; Wrecked 12.8.17; Yarmouth W/E 26.1.18; Deleted W/E 23.2.18 lost at sea

N1329    Deld Calshot TS W/E 29.9.17; COL, wrecked 5.1.18 (FSL TC Gordon slightly injured); Surveyed 6.1.18; Deleted 15.1.18 W&T

**10 FAIREY HAMBLE BABY TRACTOR BIPLANE SEAPLANE put forward 12.16 and ordered 1.17 under Cont No A.S.4765/17, numbered N1330 to N1339 & built Hamble. (130-hp Clerget 9B) [C/n's F.139 to F.148]**

N1330    (110-hp) Still at Makers 14.7.17; Deld Cattewater W/E 27.9.17; Calshot FS 27.9.17; Cattewater W/E 2.11.17 (110-hp); Yarmouth by rail 7.2.18; Deleted W/E 6.4.18

N1331    Deld Lee-on-Solent W/E 1.11.17; Deleted W/E 29.11.17

N1332    Deld Calshot for erection W/E 9.11.17; Lee-on-Solent W/E 26.1.18; Deleted W/E 28.2.18

N1333    Deld Calshot W/E 16.11.17; Bembridge by 19.1.18; Became 412/3 Flts 253 Sqdn Bembridge 25.5.18; Deleted W/E 5.8.18

N1334    Deld Calshot School W/E 16.11.17 - 4.18; CSD White City packing for Greek Govt 25.5.18; Despatched W/E 5.9.18; Left England for RHNAS in SS *Piraeus* 27.9.18

N1335    Deld Calshot School W/E 16.11.17; White City packing for for Greek Govt W/E 11.5.18; Despatched W/E 5.9.18; Left England for RHNAS in SS *Piraeus* 27.9.18

N1336    Shipped to 6 Wing RNAS Otranto 19.1.18; Otranto by 5.18 - @25.8.18; 441 Flt 263 Sqdn St.Maria di Leuca by 8.18 - @12.18; Otranto by 1.19

N1337    Cardiff Docks by 19.1.18; Shipped to Mudros 17.2.18

N1338    Retained by Fairey in Hamble sheds to at least 27.4.18; CSD White City packing for Greek Govt 25.5.18; Despatched W/E 5.9.18; Left England for RHNAS in SS *Piraeus* 27.9.18

N1339    Retained by Fairey in Hamble sheds to at least 27.4.18; CSD White City packing for Greek Govt 25.5.18; Despatched W/E 5.9.18; Left England for RHNAS in SS *Piraeus* 27.9.18

**20 SOPWITH "DAILY MAIL" TWO-SEATER TRACTOR BIPLANE SEAPLANES put forward W/E 22.12.16, to be numbered N1340 to N1359 and built at Kingston-upon-Thames. (100-hp Le Rhône)**

N1340 to N1359 cancelled 1917

**30 SHORT '320' (ADMIRALTY TYPE SHORT 310-A4) TRACTOR BIPLANE SEAPLANES ordered 12.16 under Cont Nos A.S.974 & A.S.3612 from The Sunbeam Motor Co Ltd, numbered N1360 to N1389 & built Wolverhampton. (320-hp Cossack)**

N1360    Deld Yarmouth W/E 29.9.17; FTR patrol 27.10.17 (TFSL PG Shepherd & LM W Fairnie both killed)

N1361    Deld Test Dept Grain by road 1.9.17; Dover 3.10.17 (en route South Shields); Felixstowe 5.10.17; South Shields W/E 10.10.17; Surveyed 15.4.18; Deleted 15.4.18 W&T

N1362    Deld Grain by road 1.9.17; Killingholme (via Felixstowe) 27.10.17; FL, sank nr Flamborough 21.2.18 (pilot and observer rescued by HMS *Ouse*); Deleted W/E 2.3.18

N1363    Deld Grain 25.9.17; Yarmouth W/E 10.11.17; Wrecked 4.11.17; Surveyed 6.11.17; Deleted 14.11.17 wrecked

N1364    Deld Grain 25.9.17; Yarmouth by 10.17; Surveyed 26.11.17; Deleted 3.12.17 wrecked

N1365    Deld Yarmouth W/E 13.10.17; Deleted W/E 23.2.18

N1366    Deld Felixstowe W/E 13.10.17; Calshot (via Newhaven) 31.1.18 (trials); ARS Calshot W/E 29.8.18; Calshot W/E 5.9.18; ARS Calshot W/E 17.10.18; Deleted W/E 7.11.18

N1367    Deld Yarmouth W/E 10.10.17; Surveyed 9.1.18; Deleted 15.1.18 DBR

N1368    Deld Yarmouth W/E 10.10.17; Killingholme W/E 3.11.17; Yarmouth W/E 29.12.17; Killingholme W/E 23.2.18; Felixstowe 28.5.18 (transit); Calshot 29.5.18; Became 210 TDS Calshot 6.18; Deleted W/E 11.7.18

N1369    Deld Grain, tested 11.12.17; Ready to leave 12.12.17; Killingholme W/E 28.12.17; Deleted W/E 6.4.18

N1370    Deld Grain 27.10.17; Yarmouth 15.12.17; Surveyed 30.12.17; Deleted 2.1.18 TL

N1371    Deld Killingholme W/E 2.11.17; EF, FL, TW 24.4.18 (1AM JH Slade passenger injured); Deleted W/E 4.5.18

N1372    Deld Killingholme W/E 2.11.17; Calshot TS (via Lee-on-Solent) 19.5.18; Deleted W/E 11.7.18

N1373    Deld Killingholme for erection W/E 2.11.17 (also used Hornsea); Became USNAS Killingholme 20.7.18 - @30.1.19

N1374    Deld Killingholme for erection W/E 2.11.17 (also used Hornsea); Tees 23.2.18; Killingholme, crashed and salved 27.2.18 (crew unhurt); Surveyed 15.4.18; Deleted 15.4.18 DBR

N1375    Deld Killingholme Patrol for erection W/E 2.11.18; South Shields W/E 27.6.18; USNAS Killingholme W/E 5.9.18 - @30.1.19

N1376    Deld Killingholme Patrol for erection W/E 22.12.17; Deleted W/E 4.7.18

N1377    Deld Killingholme Patrol for erection W/E 9.11.17; Wrecked when fitting broke 4.18; Deleted 15.4.18 DBR

N1378    Deld CSD White City; Shipped to 6 Wing RNAS Otranto 2.1.18; 66/67 Wings Otranto by 21.4.18 - @5.18; NFT

N1379    Deld Grain by 12.17; Tested 14.12.17; Shipped to 6 Wing RNAS Otranto 2.1.18; 6 Wing RNAS Otranto by 24.3.18; Became 66/67 Wings Otranto 1.4.18 - @8.18

N1380    Deld Killingholme for erection W/E 28.12.17 (also used Hornsea); Deleted W/E 27.6.18

N1381    Deld Killingholme for erection W/E 30.11.17; Surveyed 8.4.18; Deleted 15.4.18 DBR

N1382    Deld CSD White City; Cardiff Docks by 15.1.18; Shipped to 6 Wing RNAS Otranto 28.1.18; 66/67 Wings Otranto by 4.18; Lost at sea W/E 21.4.18; Deleted 15.5.18 W&T

N1383    Deld Killingholme patrol W/E 12.12.17; Dropped 2x230-lb bombs on U-boat, 1 failed to explode, 3m E of Flamborough 29.3.18 (FSL AT Maxwell); Deleted W/E 27.6.18

N1384    Deld CSD White City; West India Docks by 15.1.18; Transferred to Cardiff Docks; Shipped to Otranto 2.6.18; 435/436 Flts 263 Sqdn Otranto by 10.18

N1385    Deld CSD White City; West India Docks by 15.1.18; Shipped to Otranto 2.4.18; HMS *Riviera* by 5.18; Sunk by 11.5.18 (6 Gp Taranto); For deletion by 11.5.18; Deleted 10.18

N1386    Deld CSD White City; West India Docks by 15.1.18; Shipped to Otranto 2.4.18; 66/67 Wings Otranto by 7.18 - 8.18; Taranto by 26.9.18; Became 435/6 Flts 263 Sqdn Otranto by 10.18 - @30.1.19

N1387    Deld Killingholme for erection W/E 11.1.18 (also at Hornsea); South Shields 30.6.18; Killingholme W/E 25.7.18; Deleted W/E 26.9.18

N1388    Deld Killingholme for erection W/E 25.1.18; Yarmouth W/E 23.3.18; Deleted 3.18 DBR

N1389    Deld Killingholme for erection W/E 25.1.18; Damaged landing 29.3.18; Deleted W/E 13.4.18

**20 SHORT "320" (ADMIRALTY TYPE SHORT 310-A4) TRACTOR BIPLANE SEAPLANES ordered under Cont No A.S.11219, numbered N1390 to N1409 & built Rochester. (320-hp Cossack) [Gordon Bruce's researches show correct c/n's to be S.399 to S.418]**

N1390    Deld AD Grain W/E 19.12.17; Tested 24.12.17; CSD

White City; Despatched West India Docks for Otranto W/E 26.1.18; Shipped 10.4.18; 435/6 Flts 263 Sqdn Otranto by 10.18 - @30.1.19

N1391 Deld AD Grain 19.12.17; CSD White City; Despatched West India Docks for Otranto W/E 26.1.18; Shipped 10.4.18; 435/6 Flt 263 Sqdn Otranto by 10.18 - @30.1.19

N1392 Deld AD Grain W/E 29.12.17; For Shorts by 19.1.18; Despatched West India Docks (via CSD) for Otranto W/E 26.1.18; Shipped 10.4.18; 435/6 Flts Otranto by 10.18 - @30.1.19

N1393 Deld AD Grain W/E 9.1.18; Dover 24.1.18 (transit); Bembridge 25.1.18; Calshot 27.1.18 - @7.18 (W/T practice for Signals School Portsmouth)

N1394 Deld AD Grain W/E 19.1.18; For Shorts by 19.1.18; Shipped via CSD to Otranto 16.3.18; Otranto by 6.18 - @8.18

N1395 Deld AD Grain W/E 19.1.18; To CSD White City; Shipped to Otranto 16.3.18; Otranto by 6.18; EF, FL in sea, towed Brindisi by destroyer 21.9.18 (2/Lt LA Lewinton & Cpl Murch); Became 435/6 Flts 263 Sqdn Otranto 10.18 - @30.1.19

N1396 Deld AD Grain W/E 19.1.18; To CSD White City; Shipped to Otranto 9.3.18; Otranto by 6.18; Became 435/6 Flts Otranto 10.18 - @30.1.19

N1397 Deld AD Grain W/E 26.1.18; To CSD White City; Cardiff Docks by 15.1.18 (sic); Shipped 9.3.18; Arr Calafrana W/E 21.4.18; Became 268 Sqdn Calafrana 27.9.18 - @10.18

N1398 Deld AD Grain W/E 16.2.18; Westgate 9.7.18 (transit); 210 TDS Calshot 7.18 - @26.9.18; ARS Calshot by 10.18

N1399 Deld AD Grain W/E 2.2.18; To CSD White City; Shipped to Malta 13.3.18; Recd Calafrana by 5.18 - @9.18; 435/6 Flts Otranto by 10.18

N1400 Deld AD Grain W/E 2.2.18; Killingholme patrol W/E 16.2.18 (also at Hornsea); South Shields 26.6.18; USNAS/RAF Killingholme 8.8.18 - @30.1.19

N1401 Deld AD Grain W/E 9.2.18; Killingholme patrol 2.3.18; Deleted W/E 27.8.18

N1402 Deld AD Grain W/E 16.2.18; To 210 TDS Calshot but FL en route off Southsea, drifted into boom defence piles, damaged starboard wingtip towing clear 8.7.18 (2/Lt HG Hitch); ARS Calshot W/E 10.10.18; Deleted W/E 19.12.18

N1403 Deld AD Grain W/E 23.2.18; 210 TDS Calshot 7.7.18; ARS Calshot W/E 12.12.18 - @30.1.19

N1404 Deld AD Grain 20.4.18 (electric starter trials); Felixstowe 21.6.18; Grain 23.6.18 (engine test, later storage); 6 SD Ascot W/E 14.11.18; 3 AAP Norwich W/E 28.11.18 - @30.1.19

N1405 Deld AD Grain W/E 2.3.18; Calshot TS 14.7.18 (From Cherbourg patrol landed Calshot 11.8.18); Grain store W/E 12.9.18; Deleted W/E 7.11.18

N1406 Deld AD Grain W/E 2.2.18; 6 SD Ascot W/E 14.11.18; 3 AAP Norwich W/E 28.11.18 - @30.1.19

N1407 Deld AD Grain W/E 23.3.18; Yarmouth W/E 1.4.18; EF, FL, sank in rough sea off Cross Sands 7.5.18 (2 crew unhurt); Deleted W/E 25.5.18

N1408 Deld AD Grain by 30.3.18; Calshot W/E 11.5.18; Became 410/1 Flts Calshot 25.5.18; Deleted W/E 8.8.18

N1409 Expected for trials 13.4.18; Deld Grain 25.5.18 (exp work); Dover 28.5.18 (transit, bad weather); 410/1 Flt Calshot 29.5.18; Deleted W/E 8.8.18

**40 SOPWITH BABY TRACTOR BIPLANE SEAPLANES put forward 1.17 and ordered under Cont Nos A.S.679, A.S.10059 & C.P.102625 from Blackburn Aeroplane & Motor Co Ltd, numbered N1410 to N1449 & built Leeds. Delivered from Brough. (Fitted Ranken Dart containers for anti-Zeppelin duty). (130-hp Clerget 9B unless otherwise stated)**

N1410 Deld Dover (via Killingholme), COL 6.7.17 (F/L RM Clifford); Deleted 12.7.17

N1411 (110-hp Clerget) Deld Yarmouth (via Killingholme) 28.7.17; Felixstowe 28.7.17; Killingholme 8.9.17; Hornsea 23.9.17; Crashed 29.10.17; Surveyed 8.1.18; Deleted 17.1.18 TL

N1412 (110-hp Clerget) Deld Yarmouth (via Killingholme) 25.7.17; HSMPs 8.12.17 & 21.3.18 (both FSL JC Grant); Became 324/6 Flts Yarmouth 25.5.18; Deleted W/E 15.8.18

N1413 (110-hp Clerget) Deld Killingholme 30.7.17; Hornsea by 10.17 (Teddy bear insignia on fin); Port wing caught by gust on landing, o/t Hornsea 9.10.17 (FSL GF Hyams); Became 453 Flt Hornsea 31.5.18; Became 453 Flt 248 Sqdn Hornsea 8.18; South Shields W/E 23.1.19 - @30.1.19

N1414 (110-hp Clerget) Deld Cattewater by rail 5.7.17; HMS *Riviera* 30.11.17 (temp); Deleted W/E 19.1.18

N1415 (110-hp Clerget) Deld Scapa 27.8.17; To HMS *Pegasus* but fell in sea, CW 30.8.17 (FSL AV Lewis picked up by HMS *Fearless* injured); Deleted

N1416 Deld Scapa for erection 6.8.17; HMS *Pegasus* 24.8.17; HMS *Campania* 27.8.17; Houton Bay 17.3.18; HMS *Campania* 7.5.18; Deleted W/E 11.5.18

N1417 Deld Calshot patrol 9.7.17; Deleted W/E 28.9.17 BR

N1418 Deld Brough Seaplane Depot to Killingholme 28.7.17; Submerged 6.8.17; Hornsea 15.8.17; South Shields, but wrecked nr Whitby, picked up by trawler *Waldorf* 24.10.17 (no sign of pilot); Surveyed 31.10.17; Deleted 6.11.17 wrecked)

N1419 Deld Yarmouth (via Killingholme) 28.7.17; Deleted W/E 23.2.18

N1420 (110-hp Clerget) Deld Newlyn by rail 12.7.17; 6 SD Ascot W/E 20.6.18; South Shields W/E 8.8.18; Deleted W/E 9.1.19

N1421 Deld Brough to South Shields but CW outside harbour, salved 29.7.17 (FSL JHW Clarke unhurt); Remains arr South Shields 4.8.17; Deleted

N1422 Deld Brough to Killingholme 19.8.17; Crashed BR 24.8.17; Deleted W/E 15.9.17

N1423 (110-hp Clerget) Deld Killingholme 21.8.17; Seaton Carew (via South Shields) 15.9.17; Damaged in gale 24.10.17; Re-erecting South Shields 26.1.18; Seaton Carew W/E 6.3.18; South Shields 9.4.18; Became 452 Flt 252 Sqdn South Shields 25.5.18; 451 Flt 252 Sqdn Seaton Carew 7.8.18; Smashed propeller on TO in rough sea 9.9.18; Still 451 Flt 30.1.19

N1424 (110-hp Clerget) Deld Dover (via Yarmouth) 26.6.17; Shipped to Aegean; Tested HMS *Ark Royal* after erection 7.11.17; HMS *Ark Royal* by 1.1.18 - @17.1.18, 2 Wing Imbros; Took part in attack on battlecruiser *Goeben* 20.1.18 (FSL RW Peel); HMS *Ark Royal* by 10.2.18; Talikna by 3.18; HMS *Ark Royal* 24.3.18; Talikna 2.4.18; HMS *Ark Royal* by 19.6.18 (at Mudros); Skyros by 10.18 - @30.1.19; Talikna by 2.11.18

N1425 (110-hp Clerget) Deld Dover (via Yarmouth) 26.6.17; Shipped to Aegean; HMS *Ark Royal* by 11.17; Talikna 5.11.17; To HMS *Ark Royal* 3.18; Disposal by 6.18 (not required); To Greek Navy 6.18 - @30.1.19

N1426 Mkrs for Mudros by 1.6.17; Shipped to Aegean; HMS *Ark Royal* by 11.17; Talikna 5.11.17 - @1.12.17; Syra by 12.18 [or deleted by 1.1.18?]

N1427 Sunk in transit to Port Said, deleted 20.11.17

N1428 Sunk in transit to Port Said, deleted 20.11.17

N1429 Sunk in transit to Port Said, deleted 20.11.17

N1430 To French Govt (allocated 21.8.17)

N1431 To French Govt (allocated 21.8.17)

N1432 (110-hp Clerget) Deld Dundee by rail 3.9.17; Became 450 Flt Dundee 30.5.18 (249 Sqdn 18.8.18) - @30.1.19

N1433 Deld Cattewater W/E 18.9.17; Fishguard by road 30.3.18; Yarmouth W/E 13.6.18; Deleted W/E 12.12.18

N1434 Deld South Shields W/E 10.10.17; Damaged in gale Seaton Carew 24.10.17; War Flt Seaton Carew 8.12.17; Missing on patrol, aircraft found 5451N 0140W and picked up by drifter *No.3153*, taken to Fish Quay, Old Hartlepool, propeller broken, elevators damaged by sea 15.3.18 (FSL CT Greenwood drowned); Deleted W/E 27.3.18

N1435 Deld Seaton Carew W/E 10.10.17; Damaged in gale 24.10.17; Surveyed 8.12.17; Deleted 22.12.17 DBR

N1436 Deld Calshot FS for erection W/E 28.9.17; Caught by gust of wind on TO Sandbanks 7.11.17 (Lt AL Simms unhurt); Surveyed 10.11.17; Deleted 14.11.17 wrecked

N1437 Deld Calshot FS (coded 'C') for erection W/E 28.9.17; South Shields 29.8.18; 451 Flt 246 Sqdn Seaton Carew W/E 14.11.18; South Shields W/E 16.1.19

N1438 Deld Rosyth 21.9.17; Dundee 31.12.17; Became 450 Flt Dundee 30.5.18 (249 Sqdn 18.8.18) - @30.1.19

N1439 Deld Rosyth 21.9.17; HMS *Nairana* 28.9.17; Dundee 21.11.17; Became 450 Flt Dundee 30.5.18 (249 Sqdn

| | |
|---|---|
| | 18.8.18) - @30.1.19 |
| N1440 | Deld Leeds to Rosyth for erection 19.9.17; Dundee by rail 31.12.17; Accepted 17.4.18; Became 450 Flt Dundee 30.5.18; HMS *Nairana* 6.7.18 (to North Russia, arr Kola Inlet 11.7.18) ; Deleted W/E 31.10.18 |
| N1441 | Deld Leeds to Rosyth for erection 19.9.17; Dundee by rail 31.12.17; AD Dundee by 3.18 (for Dundee); Accepted 23.3.18; Became 450 Flt Dundee 30.5.18; Rosyth W/E 4.7.18; HMS *Nairana* 6.7.18 (to North Russia, arr Kola Inlet 11.7.18) ; Deleted W/E 31.10.18 |
| N1442 | Shipped from Mkrs to 6 Wing Otranto W/E 26.9.17; Transit by 9.11.17; 6 Wing RNAS Otranto by 28.12.17; HMS *Ark Royal* by 13.1.18; 6 Wing Otranto, attacked submarine on surface 16m ESE of Palascia 16.1.18 (F/L LG Maxton); Became 66/67 Wings Otranto 1.4.18 - @ 7.18; Otranto, disposed by 10.18 |
| N1443 | Shipped from Mkrs to 6 Wing Otranto W/E 26.9.17; Transit by 9.11.17; 6 Wing RNAS Otranto by 28.12.17; Dropped bomb on U-boat 10m 255° Fana 15.2.18 (FSL G Laws); 66/67 Wings Otranto 1.4.18 - @7.18; Disposed by 10.18 |
| N1444 | Shipped from Mkrs to 6 Wing Otranto W/E 26.9.17; Shipped to Aegean 31.10.17; Tested after erection HMS *Ark Royal* 10.1.18; FTR night bombing raid with N1122 & N1202, EF, FL Lemnos 00.15 22.1.18 (FSL MJB Smith); Found and towed back to harbour mouth by N1668 then to ship by *TB043* 23.1.18; still HMS *Ark Royal* @4.3.18; Talikna to HMS *Peony* 15.6.18; Crashed, TW, salved Port Laki 15.7.18 (pilot rescued unhurt); Talikna 31.7.18 - @30.1.19 |
| N1445 | Shipped from Mkrs to 6 Wing Otranto W/E 26.9.17; Shipped to Aegean 31.10.17; Tested after erection HMS *Ark Royal* 12.1.18; Shot down in flames by Ltn Emil Meinecke while attacking battlecruiser *Goeben* or *Breslau* 20.1.18 (TFSL W Johnston killed) |
| N1446 | Deld South Shields W/E 27.10.17; War Flt Seaton Carew W/E 17.11.17; Dropped 65-lb bomb on U-boat 2m NE of C buoy off Scarborough, then EF, FL, towed in by armed trawler *Minus*, beached South Bay 18.11.17 (FSL EJ Addis); South Shields W/E 23.2.18; Seaton Carew 1.5.18; Landed in fog, collided with buoy, TW 4.5.18 (pilot unhurt); Deleted W/E 25.5.18 |
| N1447 | Deld South Shields W/E 27.10.17; Hornsea (anti U-boat patrols); War Flt Seaton Carew W/E 10.11.17; South Shields W/E 15.12.17; War Flt Seaton Carew 15.1.18; Driven on rocks by high wind ands heavy seas, puncturing float 21.2.18 (pilot unhurt); Still Seaton Carew 30.3.18; 452 Flt 252 Sqdn South Shields 25.5.18; Became 452 Flt 246 Sqdn South Shields 8.18; 252 Sqdn Seaton Carew 28.8.18; South Shields W/E 16.1.19 - @30.1.19 |
| N1448 | Deld Killingholme store from 29.9.17; To Hornsea 4.18; Became 453 Flt Hornsea 25.5.18; Crashed on TO, wrecked 30.6.18 (Ens Burtchart USN injured); Deleted W/E 29.8.18 |
| N1449 | Deld Killingholme store W/E 6.10.17; Hornsea 26.4.18; Became 453 Flt Hornsea 25.5.18 (248 Sqdn 20.8.18); South Shields by W/E 23.1.19 - @30.1.19 |

**30 FAIREY HAMBLE BABY TRACTOR BIPLANE SEAPLANES put forward 1.17 and ordered under Cont No A.S.4765/17, numbered N1450 to N1479 & built Hamble. (130-hp Clerget 9B) [C/n's F.149 to F.178]**

| | |
|---|---|
| N1450 | Deld Westgate by rail 19.9.17; Yarmouth W/E 3.11.17; Deleted W/E 26.1.18 |
| N1451 | Deld Calshot FS W/E 10.10.17; Lee-on-Solent W/E 17.11.17; COL, CW 7.3.18 (FSL FJH Bacon slightly injured); Deleted W/E 3.4.18 |
| N1452 | Deld Calshot FS W/E 10.10.17; Lee-on-Solent W/E 17.11.17; Deleted W/E 3.4.18 |
| N1453 | Deld Calshot W/E 21.9.17; Surveyed 24.9.17; Deleted 26.9.17 wrecked |
| N1454 | Deld Yarmouth W/E 13.10.17; Damaged and capsized landing Southwold, wreckage towed in by trawler 23.1.18 (pilot unhurt); Deleted W/E 23.2.18 |
| N1455 | Deld Calshot patrol W/E 9.11.17; CSD White City packing for Greek Govt W/E 11.5.18; Despatched W/E 5.9.18; Left England for RHNAS in SS *Piraeus* 27.9.18 |
| N1456 | Deld Cattewater (via Portland) 22.9.17; Yarmouth by rail 23.1.18; EF on TO in strong cross-wind, o/t 24.2.18 |

| | |
|---|---|
| | (FSL TC Gordon unhurt); Deleted W/E 2.3.18 |
| N1457 | Deld Fishguard by 24.11.17; Accepted 4.12.17; FL off Cardigan Island, salved by St.Dogmells Lifeboat 21.2.18 (FSL CG Duckworth drowned); Deleted W/E 2.3.18 |
| N1458 | Deld Lee-on-Solent W/E 1.11.17; Surveyed 14.1.18; Deleted 17.1.18 wrecked |
| N1459 | Deld Calshot FS W/E 9.11.17; Surveyed 16.11.17; Deleted 21.11.17 wrecked |
| N1460 | Deld Dundee by rail 6.9.17; Became 450 Flt Dundee 25.5.18 (249 Sqdn 18.8.18) - @30.1.19 |
| N1461 | Deld South Shields W/E 27.10.17; Yarmouth W/E 19.1.18; FTR A/S patrol 20.2.18 (FSL VJ Budd killed); Deleted W/E 23.2.18 |
| N1462 | First aircraft with flaps; Deld Yarmouth W/E 13.10.17; Tested 20.10.17; Deleted 22.12.17 wrecked |
| N1463 | Deld Lee-on-Solent W/E 1.11.17; Deleted W/E 21.2.18 |
| N1464 | In transit to 6 Wing Otranto by 9.11.17; Possibly the a/c which crashed Padua 17.12.17 (F/L J Gorman DoI) - or could be N5229; Surveyed 22.12.17; Deleted 3.1.18 wrecked |
| N1465 | In transit to 6 Wing Otranto by 9.11.17; Arr by 28.12.17; Surveyed 7.1.18; Deleted 19.1.18 TL |
| N1466 | Deld Yarmouth W/E 13.10.17; HACP 14.11.17 (F/L GWR Fane); Deleted 16.3.18 DBR |
| N1467 | Deld Killingholme store 29.9.17; Hornsea 31.10.17; EF, FL 3m NE of Bridlington, towed to Bridlington 1.11.17 (FSL GF Hyams); Killingholme by 27.4.18; Packing at CSD White City for Greek Govt 25.5.18; Despatched W/E 5.9.18; Left England for RHNAS in SS *Piraeus* 27.9.18 |
| N1468 | Deld Killingholme store 29.9.17; Hornsea by 22.11.17; Bombed U-boat Robin Hoods Bay area 26.3.18; Killingholme 26.4.18 (for survey); Packing at CSD White City for Greek Govt 25.5.18; Despatched W/E 5.9.18; Left England for RHNAS in SS *Piraeus* 27.9.18 |
| N1469 | Deld Killingholme store 29.9.17; Hornsea W/E 6.11.17; Dropped 2x65-lb bombs on U-boat 4½m E of Scarborough 8.11.17 (FSL HC Lemon); Tested after fitting 110-hp Clerget 17.12.17; Retested with 130-hp Clerget 29.1.18; Retested with 110-hp Clerget 5.3.18; South Shields, surveyed 11.4.18; Deleted 15.4.18 W&T |
| N1470 | Deld Killingholme store 29.9.17; Killingholme patrol by 3.18; Hornsea 10.5.18; Packing at CSD White City for Greek Govt W/E 6.6.18; Despatched W/E 5.9.18; Left England for RHNAS in SS *Piraeus* 27.9.18 |
| N1471 | Deld Killingholme store 29.12.17 (later patrol); Hornsea 10.5.18; EF on TO, landed heavily on water, float burst and axle bent, beached, Hornsea Mere 16.5.18 (FSL GF Hyams unhurt); Killingholme 27.5.18; Packing at CSD White City for Greek Govt W/E 6.6.18; Despatched W/E 5.9.18 ; Left England for RHNAS in SS *Piraeus* 27.9.18 |
| N1472 | Deld Killingholme store 29.12.17 - @10.5.18; Packing at CSD White City for Greek Govt 25.5.18; Despatched W/E 5.9.18; Left England for RHNAS in SS *Piraeus* 27.9.18 |
| N1473 | Deld Killingholme store 29.9.17; Yarmouth 11.1.18; Deleted W/E 25.5.18 |
| N1474 | Deld Killingholme store 29.9.17; Yarmouth 11.1.18; FL in sea 3m W of Cockle LV, wrecked under tow 26.4.18 (pilot unhurt); Deleted W/E 4.5.18 |
| N1475 | Deld Killingholme store 29.9.17; Yarmouth 11.1.18; Became 324/6 Flts Yarmouth 25.5.18; Deleted W/E 21.11.18 |
| N1476 | Deld Killingholme store by 29.12.17; To CSD White City Left for Mudros 23.1.18; Shipped 2.2.18; HMS *Ark Royal* by 3.18 - @30.1.19 |
| N1477 | Allocated CSD Crystal Palace 27.9.17; Surveyed Crystal Palace 30.10.17; Deleted 2.11.17 as GI |
| N1478 | Allocated RN College Greenwich for GI 26.9.17; Surveyed Crystal Palace 30.10.17; Deleted 2.11.17 as GI |
| N1479 | Allocated RN College Greenwich for GI 26.9.17; Surveyed Crystal Palace 30.10.17; Deleted 2.11.17 as GI |

**25 SHORT "320" (ADMIRALTY TYPE SHORT 310-A4) TRACTOR BIPLANE SEAPLANES put forward 2.17, ordered under Cont No A.S.11219, numbered N1480 to N1504 & built Rochester. (320-hp Cossack)** [Gordon Bruce's researches show correct c/n's to be S.364 to S.388]

*A general view of Taranto/Pizzone around 1916/17. The aircraft coded 'B' is an F.B.A. Type H of the kind used by the RNAS in Malta, the others being Macchi-built Lohners. (Alberto Briganti via Gregory Alegi)*

*Pemberton-Billing A.D. Pusher Flying Boat N1522 at Calshot. (R.C.Sturtivant collection)*

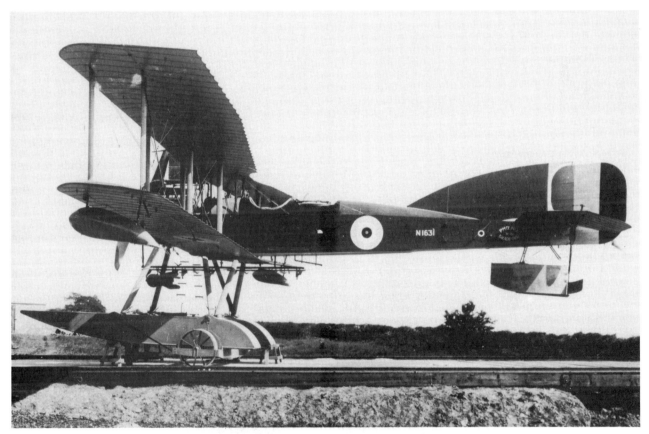

*Phoenix-built Short 184 Type (Improved) Seaplane N1631. (R.C.Sturtivant collection)*

*Maurice Farman Pusher Floatplane N1530. (via J.M.Bruce)*

*Fairey Hamble Baby leaving slipway. (via Philip Jarrett)*

N1480 Prototype; Deld Grain 11.7.17; Retd Shorts 13.7.17 (alterations); Grain 15.7.17 (Kemp); Yarmouth 27.9.17; Deleted W/E 23.2.18

N1481 Deld Grain 19.7.17 (Kemp); Felixstowe 10.9.17; Calshot 12.2.18 (W/T practice for RN Signal School Portsmouth by 5.18); ARS Calshot W/E 5.9.18; Deleted W/E 19.9.18

N1482 Deld Grain 28.7.17; Dundee (via Yarmouth) 20.9.17; RAF/USNAS Killingholme W/E 15.12.17 - @30.1.19

N1483 Deld Grain 15.8.17 (Kemp); Killingholme 20.9.17 (transit); Surveyed 25.9.17; Deleted 8.10.17 wrecked

N1484 Deld Grain 22.8.17; Dundee 1.9.17; Killingholme W/E 2.11.17; Deleted W/E 23.2.18

N1485 Deld Grain 31.8.17; Transferred to Japanese Govt 9.10.17

N1486 Deld Grain 4.9.17; Shipped to 6 Wing Otranto in SS *Perrier* 20.10.17, but ship sunk; Surveyed 29.12.17; Deleted 4.1.18

N1487 Deld Grain 5.9.17; Shipped to 6 Wing Otranto in SS *Perrier* 20.10.17, but ship sunk; Surveyed 29.12.17; Deleted 4.1.18

N1488 Deld Grain 8.9.17; South Shields by 27.10.17; Crashed (collided with N1642?) 28.10.17; Rosyth 28.10.17 (torpedo practice); Surveyed 2.11.17; Deleted 6.11.17 wrecked

N1489 Deld Grain 9.9.17; Rosyth by 3.11.17 (torpedo patrol); Yarmouth W/E 8.2.18; South Shields W/E 16.2.18; Surveyed 11.4.18; Deleted 11.5.18 wrecked; To Agricultural Hall, Islington for preservation by 24.8.18

N1490 Deld Grain 18.9.17 (fit experimental section walnut floats); Yarmouth 27.9.17; Surveyed 9.1.18; Deleted 15.1.18 DBR

N1491 Deld Grain 14.9.17; Left for Malta 27.10.17; Shipped 31.10.17; Arr Calafrana W/E 2.1.18; Dropped 2x230-lb bombs on U-boat attempting to torpedo French battleship 8.2.18 (F/L HL Nunn & AC Hosken); Became 433/4 Flts 268 Sqdn Calafrana (coded 'K') 8.18 - @30.1.19

N1492 Deld Grain 18.9.17; Left for Otranto W/E 27.10.17; Shipped 31.10.17; Wings and u/c lost at sea by 28.12.17 (SS *Perrier*?); For deletion 6 Wing Otranto by 15.1.18, but new wings fitted by 4.18; Became 66/67 Wings Otranto 1.4.18 - 8.18; 435/6 Flts 263 Sqdn Otranto by 10.18 - @30.1.19

N1493 Deld Grain 20.9.17; Left for Malta W/E 27.10.17; Shipped 31.10.17; Arr Calafrana by 26.12.17 - @29.7.18; NFT

N1494 Deld Grain 21.9.17; Shipped 6 Wing RNAS Otranto 3.11.17; (partly?) lost at sea by 28.12.17 (SS *Perrier*?); For deletion by 14.1.18, but rebuilt at 6 Wing Otranto by 25.3.18; Became 66/67 Wings Otranto 1.4.18 - @7.18; NFT

N1495 Deld Grain 21.9.17; Shipped to Malta 19.10.17; Arr Calafrana by 26.12.17; Wrecked 10.1.18

N1496 Deld Grain 22.9.17; Shipped to Otranto 20.10.17; Transit by 28.12.17; 6 Wing Otranto by 20.2.18 - @4.18

N1497 Deld Grain 24.9.17; Shipped to Malta 19.10.17; Arr Calafrana by 26.12.17; Last mention 22.3.18; Deleted by 31.3.18, crashed

N1498 Deld Grain 27.9.17; Felixstowe 1.10.17; Calshot but FL Herne Bay en route, taxied into Westgate 2.2.18; Dover 3.2.18 (transit); Calshot 13.2.18; Deleted W/E 5.4.18

N1499 Deld Grain 28.9.17; Yarmouth 1.10.17; Deleted W/E 23.2.18

N1500 Deld Grain 1.10.17; Left for RNAS Otranto W/E 26.11.17; Shipped Otranto 19.1.18; Arr 6 Wing Otranto by 3.18 - @7.18; 441 Flt 263 Sqdn St.Maria di Leuca by 8.18 - @12.18; 435/6 Flts 263 Sqdn Otranto by @1.19

N1501 Deld Grain 3.10.17; Left for Otranto W/E 24.11.17; Shipped 12.12.17; 6 Wing RNAS Otranto by 24.3.18; Became 66/67 Wings 1.4.18; St. Maria di Leuca by 15.6.18; 435/6 Flts 263 Sqdn Otranto by 10.18 - @30.1.19

N1502 Deld Grain W/E 13.10.17; Shipped to Malta 20.11.17; Arrived Calafrana 12.17? [by 6.2.18]; Dropped 230-lb bomb on U-boat 3602N 0014E 21.4.18 (Capt CR Rischbieth & Pte Clarke); Became 433/4 Flts 268 Sqdn Calafrana (coded 'N') 8.18 - @30.1.19

N1503 Deld Grain W/E 13.10.17; Killingholme W/E 27.10.17; FL Withernsea, slightly damaged 13.12.17; Deleted W/E 23.2.18

N1504 Deld Grain W/E 13.10.17; Shipped to Malta 20.11.17;

arr Calafrana for erection 2.18; Attacked U-boat 28.8.18; Became 433/4 Flts 268 Sqdn Calafrana (coded 'O') 27.9.18; NFT

**15 "LARGE AMERICA" TYPE TRACTOR BIPLANE FLYING BOATS to be ordered from Aircraft Manufacturing Co Ltd & numbered N1505 to N1519. (310/250-hp Rolls-Royce)**

N1505 to N1519 cancelled

**20 "IMPROVED AMERICA" TYPE TRACTOR BIPLANE FLYING BOATS put forward W/E 19.1.17 to be ordered from Aircraft Manufacturing Co Ltd & numbered N1510 to N1529. (310/250-hp Rolls-Royce)**

N1510 to N1519 cancelled 1917
N1520 to N1529 cancelled W/E 2.3.17

**10 A.D. PUSHER BIPLANE FLYING BOATS ordered under Cont No A.S.5388/17 from Pemberton-Billing Ltd, numbered N1520 to N1529 & built Woolston. (200-hp Hispano 8B unless otherwise stated)**

N1520 Deld Grain Test Dept 20.7.17; Tested 5.9.17; Scapa (via Dundee) 15.9.17; Yarmouth to South Shields for Rosyth W/E 27.10.17; Killingholme storage W/E 2.11.17; Deleted W/E 13.6.18

N1521 Deld Calshot School W/E 7.9.17; Deleted W/E 26.1.18

N1522 Deld Calshot School W/E 7.9.17; Deleted W/E 26.1.18

N1523 Mkrs repair by 11.17; To Type Test Flt Grain 15.3.18 (expts); Deleted W/E 5.12.18

N1524 (150-hp Hispano-Suiza) Lost propeller on delivery to Experimental Dept Grain, FL off Margate, towed to Westgate by *MB 1169* 23.5.18 (F/L HL Hitch & AM Bickford); Deleted W/E 30.5.18

N1525 Temp fitted Wolseley Viper; Deld Grain Type Test Flt 2.2.18 (propeller tests); Fitted 200-hp Hispano-Suiza by 3.18; Fitted 210-hp Wolseley Python by 8.18; still Grain @30.1.19

N1526 Deld AD store W/E 30.1.18 - @31.12.18; Became Channel Mk.I G-EAEM with 160-hp Beardmore 6-1B (c/n 969). To Norway as *N-??*

N1527 Allocated Farnborough via CSD for sand tests 4.9.17; Deleted 6.11.17 for Farnborough, sand tested to destruction, no engine

N1528 Deld AD store W/E 19.1.18 - @31.12.18; Became Channel Mk.I G-EAEL with 160-hp Beardmore 6-1B (c/n 970). To Norway as *N-11*

N1529 Allocated for propeller tests at Woolston 17.12.17; Deld AD store by 19.1.18 - @31.12.18; Became Channel Mk.I G-EAED with 160-hp Beardmore 6-1B

**50 MAURICE FARMAN PUSHER BIPLANE FLOATPLANES put forward 1.17 and ordered under BR.71 from The Aircraft Manufacturing Co Ltd & numbered N1530 to N1579, to be built Hendon. (140-hp Hispano-Suiza)**

N1530 Allocated Grain for type trials 28.3.17 (NTU?); Tested Hythe 20-21.5.17 (JL Parker); NFT
N1531 to N1535 cancelled 8.6.17
N1536 to N1569 cancelled .17
N1570 to N1579 cancelled 2.6.17

**10 SHORT ADMIRALTY 184 TYPE TRACTOR BIPLANE SEAPLANES put forward 2.17 and ordered 20.8.17 under Cont No A.S.16063, numbered N1580 to N1589 & built Eastchurch. (240-hp Renault-Mercedes) [Gordon Bruce's researches show correct c/n's to be S.389 to S.398]**

N1580 Launched 16.7.17; Deld Grain 17.7.17; To CSD White City; To Port Said 3.9.17; Arr El&SS Port Said W/E 11.11.17; Reshipped to Malta 19.11.17; Shipped to Otranto 19.11.17; In transit from Port Said to 6 Wing Otranto by 8.2.18 - @22.3.18; stored on HMS *Manxman* by 24.3.18; Calafrana 13.4.18; HMS *Riviera* 16.5.18; Calafrana 19.5.18 - @9.18; HMS *Empress* at Gibraltar .18

N1581 Deld Grain ex Queenborough in tow 19.7.17; To Port Said 3.9.17; Arr El&SS Port Said W/E 7.11.17; HMS *Empress* 3.12.17; Port Said 20.1.18; HMS *Empress*

21.1.18; Port Said 4.2.18; Alexandria 13.3.18; Dropped 2 bombs on U-boat nr outer buoy of North Channel, Alexandria 8.4.18 (Capt EJ Burling & AM H Crisp); Became 270 Sqdn Alexandria 6.10.18; Tested after fitting DC 20.2.19; 268 Sqdn Calafrana 27.8.19

N1582    Deld Grain ex Queenborough in tow 27.7.17; To Port Said 3.9.17; Arr EI&SS Port Said W/E 7.11.17; HMS *City of Oxford* 10.11.17; Port Said 12.11.17; HMS *Empress* 3.12.17; Port Said 20.1.18; HMS *Empress* 21.1.18; During search for battlecruiser *Goeben* shot down by Turkish machine gun fire in Dardanelles 28.1.18 (F/L CG Bronson & O/L LH Pakenham-Walsh Cheshire Regt POW's unhurt)

N1583    Deld Grain ex Queenborough in tow 28.7.17; To Mudros 3.9.17; Arr EI&SS Port Said W/E 11.11.17; Reshipped Mudros W/E 17.11.17; HMS *Ark Royal* by 22-23.2.18

N1584    Deld Grain 10.8.17; Dover 26.9.17; Folkestone in tow of ML 27.9.17 (for Calshot); Dover to Dunkerque 29.9.17; Calshot School W/E 10.10.17; Bembridge W/E 9.1.18; Crashed into wall on mill pond on landing, damaged float and wing 4.5.18 (pilot unhurt); Deleted W/E 11.5.18

N1585    Deld Grain ex Queenborough in tow 17.8.17; Transport to Mudros 15.9.17; Shipped 4.10.17; Arr EI&SS Port Said W/E 11.11.17; Reshipped Mudros 17.11.17; HMS *Ark Royal* by 23.2.18; Damaged, towed to Talikna 26.2.18 (FSL JP Barnes & O/L AO Jones); Still Talikna 6.18; Mudros by 10.18

N1586    (DC) (220-hp Renault) Deld Grain 8.9.17; Westgate 26.9.17 (transit, delayed by weather); Calshot 27.9.17; 209 TDS Lee-on-Solent W/E 6.7.18; Deleted W/E 14.11.18

N1587    (DC) (220-hp Renault) Deld Grain 14.9.17; Dover 3.10.17; Calshot School 5.10.17; 209 TDS Lee-on-Solent W/E 4.7.18; Propeller accident 17.8.18 (F/Cdt WM Jackson injured); Deleted W/E 14.11.18

N1588    Deld Grain ex Queenborough in tow 1.9.17; Cattewater 5.9.17, but arrived Westgate from Ramsgate for repair 6.9.17; Calshot (via Dover) 10.9.17; HMS *Riviera* 12.9.17; Damaged on TO, retd by boat from HMS *Powerful*, wrecked 23.9.17; Cattewater 28.9.17; HMS *Riviera* 30.9.17; Dropped bomb on U-boat 7m E of Start Point 15.10.17 (FSL NI Larter & CPO Mech3 R Nicholson); Cattewater 30.11.17; Surveyed 3.4.18; Deleted 15.4.18 W&T

N1589    Deld Grain 3.9.17; Cattewater 5.9.17; Surveyed 2.12.17; Deleted 5.12.17

**10 SHORT ADMIRALTY 184 TYPE (IMPROVED) TRACTOR BIPLANE SEAPLANES ordered under Cont Nos C.P.105316/17 & A.S.4247/1 dated 3.17 from Fredk Sage & Co Ltd, numbered N1590 to N1599 & built Peterborough. (240-hp Renault to N1592, remainder 260-hp Maori)**

N1590    Shipped to Port Said; Arr EI&SS Port Said 7.11.17; HMS *Empress* 8.11.17; Port Said 27.12.17; HMS *Empress* 21.1.18; Port Said 13.2.18; Wing tip fouled mast of tug, fell in Port Said harbour 28.3.18 (TFSL HE Love DoI & Capt WR Kempson unhurt)

N1591    Shipped to Mudros 4.10.17; Erecting Mudros by 1.1.18; Tested after erection HMS *Ark Royal* 6.1.18; Left 00.20 to bomb battlecruiser *Goeben* but unable to find her, encountered heavy AA and m/g fire so dropped bomb from 1,600ft off Nagara Point 28.1.18 (F/Cdr HGR Malet); Dropped 65-lb & 100-lb bombs on U-boat 3918N 2418E 09.50 GMT 15.2.18 (F/Cdr JBP Ferrand DSO & O/L AE Sole); EF, FL, to Kondia in tow, undamaged 15.2.18 (FSL MJB Smith); Retd ship in tow 22.2.18;

N1592    (240-hp Renault) Deld Scapa for erection W/E 3.11.17; Houton Bay in/by W/E 29.12.17; Dropped 2x100-lb bombs on U-boat 5933N 0159W, then EF, FL Sandoy 17.7.18 (Capt ART Pipon & Lt EJ Garner]; Deleted W/E 21.11.18

N1593    Deld Rosyth by 11.17; HMS *Pegasus* W/E 23.11.17; Dundee 24.2.18 (while ship refitted); Rosyth by 3.18; Dundee 17.3.18 - @30.1.19

N1594    Deld Grain W/E 22.10.17 (W/T tests); Reserve Group Patrol Calshot W/E 24.11.17; Portland W/E 4.5.18; EF on TO, crashed into wreck of coal hulk, wrecked

10.5.18 (Ens R Palmado USN & Cpl Mech CS Laycock both slightly injured); Deleted W/E 25.5.18

N1595    Deld Grain 27.10.17 (W/T tests); To be flown 2.12.17; Calshot 11.12.17; Bembridge W/E 5.4.18; FL, crew taken aboard *P.37*, picking up aircraft on return journey 17.5.18; Became 412/3 Flts 253 Sqdn Bembridge 25.5.18; Deleted W/E 29.8.18

N1596    Deld Yarmouth W/E 20.10.17; Killingholme W/E 20.12.17 (transit); Tees to Rosyth, but damaged float en route at South Shields 23.12.17; HMS *Nairana* W/E 28.12.17; Donibristle W/E 25.1.18; HMS *Nairana* W/E 31.1.18; Dundee 30.3.18 (patrol); Rosyth 4.4.18; HMS *Pegasus* 11.8.18; Deleted

N1597    Shipped to Port Said 3.12.17; Arr EI&SS Port Said for erection W/E 30.12.17; Erected by 12.2.18; O/t landing, sank 25.8.18 (Lt H Wind & AM3 AJ Perry both unhurt), salved; Became 269 Sqdn Port Said 6.10.18; Tested 17.10.18; Sideslipped into water on TO, badly damaged 13.11.18 (2/Lt LF Hill & Chief Mech SC Lay both unhurt); Deleted 23.1.19

N1598    Deld Yarmouth W/E 3.11.17; Felixstowe 11.12.17; HMS *Vindex* W/E 21.12.17; Yarmouth W/E 19.1.18; Landed Margate en route Dover, taxied on to beach, towed into Westgate 19.1.18; Yarmouth 22.1.18; Became 324/6 Flts Yarmouth 25.5.18; HSMP 10.6.18; Deleted W/E 12.9.18

N1599    Deld Felixstowe W/E 15.12.17; Yarmouth 22.1.18 (initially for HMS *Vindex*); Became 324/6 Flts Yarmouth 25.5.18; Dropped 2x100-lb bombs on U-boat, but failed to explode 17.7.18 (Capt JC Grant & Lt E Plowman); still Yarmouth 30.1.19; 219 Sqdn Westgate by 11-12.2.19

**21 SHORT ADMIRALTY 184 TYPE (IMPROVED) TRACTOR BIPLANE SEAPLANES ordered under Cont No A.S.10495/1 dated 3.17 from S.E.Saunders Ltd, numbered N1600 to N1620 & built East Cowes, Isle of Wight. (220-hp Renault unless otherwise stated)**

N1600    Deld Bembridge 20.8.17; Calshot TS W/E 7.12.17; Deleted W/E 1.3.18

N1601    (240-hp Renault) Accepted at Mkrs 7.7.17; Cattewater (via Calshot) 13.7.17; HMS *Riviera* 15.10.17; Cattewater 18.10.17; Newlyn 11.1.18 (to 220-hp Renault 2.18) (at Looe 2.3.18); Became 424/5 Flts Newlyn 25.5.18; Deleted W/E 5.9.18

N1602    Accepted at Mkrs 7.7.17; Cattewater (via Calshot) 16.7.17; EF, FL, broke up, TW, sank 18.8.17 (FSL LGleB Croke & FSL TC Wilkinson brought in by *ML322*); Remains towed in by HM *TB105* 19.8.17

N1603    Deld Cattewater (via Torquay) 3.8.17; In distress, hoisted in to HMS *Riviera*, to Cattewater in launch *No.109* 18.8.17; HMS *Riviera* 8.12.17; Cattewater 10.12.17; Engine caught fire in flight, dived and sideslipped, tail broke off on landing, a/c sank 20.12.17 (pilot and OSL BE Harrison rescued by Greek grain vessel SS *Kanaris* and landed Falmouth); Surveyed 22.12.17; Deleted 29.12.17 TL

N1604    Deld Calshot 27.7.17; Cattewater 28.7.17 (transit); Newlyn (coded '9') 29.7.17; Damaged 15.8.17; Dropped 65-lb & 100-lb bombs on U-boat 16m SE of Wolf Rock 8.9.17 (FSL HJ Horsey); Dropped 100-lb bomb on submarine beneath surface 5012N 0625W 3.12.17 (F/L JW Hobbs & AM RL Hobson); FL, engine trouble, Cattewater 27.3.18; Deleted W/E 18.5.18

N1605    Deld Newlyn (via Calshot & Cattewater 29.7.17); Dropped 100-lb bomb on U-boat 7m E of Wolf Rock 16.8.17 (F/L AT Sketchley & OSL GG Speight); Surveyed 9.10.17; Deleted 10.10.17 wrecked

N1606    Accepted at Mkrs 20.7.17; Newlyn 20.7.17; Calshot 20.8.17 (transit); Newlyn 22.8.17; Bombed and severely damaged U-boat which had missed merchant steamers with torpedo, oil and bubbles seen, 10m SW of The Lizard [4952N 0527W] 19.12.17 (FSL JS Hughes & OSL GG Speight); Dropped 2x100-lb bombs on U-boat, both failed to explode 5013N 0535W 2.1.18 (FSL JS Hughes & OSL KG Styles); FTR from patrol 3.3.18 (Pilot & OSL BG Rowley drowned)

N1607    Deld Newlyn (via Calshot & Cattewater) 12.9.17; Surveyed 30.10.17; Deleted 7.11.17 wrecked

N1608    Deld Yarmouth W/E 13.10.17; Surveyed 26.10.17;

N1609   Deleted 29.10.17 wrecked

N1609   Deld Cattewater W/E 15.9.17; Newlyn W/E 16.11.17; EF, FL 12.4.18; Dropped 2x100-lb bombs on U-boat 29.4.18 (Lt MB Banks & Capt GG Speight); Surveyed 4.5.18; Deleted 11.5.18 wrecked

N1610   (240-hp Renault) Deld Cattewater (via Calshot) 12.9.17; Newlyn 17.9.17 (transit); Fishguard 19.9.17; Became 426/7 Flts Fishguard 25.5.18; Deleted W/E 17.10.18

N1611   Deld Bembridge W/E 14.9.17; Dropped 2x100-lb bombs on U-boat 35m NE of Cape Barfleur, then wrecked and sank 11.11.17 (FSL G Barnes & AM WL Hooper); Presume salved; Calshot TS W/E 22.1.18; 209 TDS Lee-on-Solent W/E 30.5.18; Deleted W/E 12.9.18

N1612   Deld Cattewater W/E 15.9.17; EF, FL, towed by HM TB10 to Dartmouth and hoisted aboard HMS Riviera 20.10.17 (pilot & OSL BE Harrison); Cattewater, EF, FL safely Salcombe 8.11.17 (F/L AT Sketchley & FSL LGleB Croke unhurt); HMS Riviera 15.11.17; Cattewater 26.11.17; HMS Riviera 28.11.17; Cattewater 29.11.17; Newlyn 19.12.17; Towed in and eventually broken up 28.12.17; Surveyed 29.12.17; Deleted 1.1.18 TL

N1613   Deld Bembridge W/E 8.9.17; Dropped 100-lb bomb on U-boat 25m SSE of St.Catherine's 18.10.17 (F/Cdr C McLaurin & AM W/T Dore); EF, FL 2m NE of Selsey Bill, damaged chassis in rough sea, sank in tow 14.12.17 (2 crew unhurt); Deleted 19.12.17 TL

N1614   (240-hp Renault) Deld Cattewater (via Calshot) 27.9.17; Newlyn 5.2.18; EF, FL, nose-dived into sea, towed in, TW 19.3.18 (pilot & F/L BE Harrison rescued by Falmouth trawler Gowan); Deleted W/E 6.4.18

N1615   Deld Bembridge W/E 6.10.17; Surveyed 2.11.17; Deleted 6.11.17 wrecked

N1616   Deld Calshot W/E 20.9.17; Grain 28.9.17 (en route Cattewater); HMS Riviera 6.10.17; Portland 15.10.17 (repair); HMS Riviera 19.10.17; Cattewater 3.11.17; HMS Riviera 8.11.17; Badly strained taxying in heavy sea 27.12.17; Newlyn 17.2.18; Dropped 2x100-lb bombs on U-boat, oil seen 5033N 0520W 16.5.18 (Ens HT Stanley USN & Lt JW Nixon); Became 424/5 Flts Newlyn 25.5.18; Deleted W/E 8.8.18

N1617   Deld Calshot W/E 6.10.17; Bembridge W/E 1.11.17, FL, broke up in tow by patrol boat and sank 25m S of Bembridge 11.12.17 (2 crew saved); Surveyed 13.12.17; Deleted 21.12.17 TL

N1618   Deld Cattewater W/E 19.10.17; Newlyn 20.10.17; Dropped 100-lb & 65-lb bombs on U-boat 24.3.18 (FSL EL MacLeod); Crashed while landing at sea, cartwheeled on to port wing Mounts Bay 28.4.18 (pilot & Capt BE Harrison); Became 424/5 Flts Newlyn 25.5.18; Deleted WE 5.9.18

N1619   Deld Bembridge W/E 26.10.17; Surveyed 12.11.17; Deleted 22.11.17 TL

N1620   Deld Newlyn (via Cattewater) 27.10.17; Deleted W/E 6.4.18

**4 SHORT ADMIRALTY 184 TYPE (IMPROVED) TRACTOR BIPLANE SEAPLANES ordered under Cont No A.S.1247/1 from S.E.Saunders Ltd, numbered N1621 to N1624 & built East Cowes. (220-hp Sunbeam Maori)**

N1621   Deld Calshot W/E 9.11.17 (patrol, later W/T practice for RN Signal School Portsmouth); Became 210 TDS Calshot 6.18 - @30.1.19

N1622   Deld Calshot Cattewater (via Calshot) W/E 23.11.17; HMS Riviera 26.11.17; Cattewater 24.1.18; HMS Riviera 1.2.18; Newlyn 27.2.18; Became 424/5 Flts Newlyn 25.5.18 (235 Sqdn 20.8.18); 418 Flt 239 Sqdn Torquay 9.1.19; Cattewater by 30.1.19

N1623   Deld Calshot W/E 4.12.17 (Patrol reserve, later TS); EF, FL, beached 5m W of Brighton 4.12.17; Became 210 TDS Calshot 6.18; ARS Calshot W/E 8.8.18; 210 TDS Calshot W/E 19.9.18 - @30.1.19

N1624   Deld Cowes to Cattewater (via Calshot) 5.12.17; Dropped 100-lb on U-boat 12m SW of Start Point & another 15m SSW of Start Point in joint attack on U-boat with HMS Oriole 8.12.17 (F/L JH Woolner & PO Connor); 209 TDS Lee-on-Solent 25.6.18 - @30.1.19

**SERIALS N1625 to N1629 NOT ALLOTTED**

**30 SHORT ADMIRALTY 184 TYPE TRACTOR BIPLANE SEAPLANES (IMPROVED VERSION) ordered under Cont No A.S.1247/1 & A.S.10630 from The Phoenix Dynamo Manufacturing Co Ltd, numbered N1630 to N1659 & built Bradford. (Mainly 240-hp Renault-Mercedes to N1652, remainder 260-hp Maori) [C/n's 150 to 179?] [One source says only N1631 and N1653 were Improved version]**

N1630   Deld Killingholme en route Grain, but damaged 9.6.17; Grain for trials (special service) 13.6.17; Test Depot Grain 17.6.17 (type trials); South Shields 21.7.17 (transit); Dundee 23.7.17 (transit); Scapa 26.7.17; HMS Furious 22.8.17; Rosyth 4.10.17; HMS Furious 18.10.17; South Shields 14.11.17; Surveyed 8.12.17; Deleted 22.12.17 DBR

N1631   (C/n 151) Deld Grain for trials 21.6.17; Calshot 13.8.17; Deleted W/E 12.10.17 BR

N1632   Deld Brough to Killingholme by air 11.7.17; Calshot patrol 7.8.17 (arr 9.8.17 via Sheringham); Yarmouth 13.8.17 (repair); Newhaven 26.9.17; C Flt Lee-on-Solent W/E 7.2.18; Became 209 TDS Lee-on-Solent 1.4.18; Lost control in rough air conditions 2.5.18 (2/Lt REW Gwyther seriously injured); Deleted W/E 27.6.18

N1633   Deld Brough to Killingholme by air 15.7.17; Yarmouth 14.8.17; Westgate 16.8.17 (en route Calshot); Newhaven W/E 14.9.17; Calshot patrol W/E 26.10.17; Deleted W/E 2.2.18

N1634   Deld Brough to Killingholme by air 11.7.17; South Shields 21.7.17 (transit); Dundee 22.7.17 (intended for HMS Manxman); HMS Engadine 24.7.17 (ship at Buncrana from 27.9.17); Damaged Trevose Bay, wreckage retd ship by drifter Baden Powell 11.10.17; FL, damaged hoisting up, engine salved 15.10.17; Surveyed 15.10.17; Deleted 19.10.17 DBR

N1635   Deld Cattewater by rail 1.8.17; Newlyn 5.2.18; Became 424/5 Flts Newlyn 25.5.18; Stalled, spun into sea Mounts Bay 29.7.18 (2/Lt TL Harding & 2AM WF Fox both slightly injured); Deleted W/E 12.9.18

N1636   Deld Cattewater by rail 18.7.17; Tested 19.8.17; EF, FL 12m S of Falmouth, towed into Newlyn by ML350 7.9.17 (pilot & OSL BE Harrison); Cattewater 21.9.17; Crashed into US ship landing Whitsand Bay, damaged 30.10.17 (FSL FLB Wood & FSL LGleB Croke unhurt); Sank while being salved by drifter St.Ives Bay 10.12.17 (FSL SG Smith picked up & AM2 FN Scarles missing); Surveyed 22.12.17; Deleted 29.12.17

N1637   Mkrs for Mudros by 1.6.17; Sunk in transit to Mudros, deleted 20.11.17

N1638   Deld Brough to Killingholme by air 23.7.17; Ready 26.7.17; Dundee (via South Shields) 10.8.17; EF, FL, towed by HMS Flying Fish to Aberdeen 31.8.17, dismantled, pieces by rail to Dundee; Re-erecting from 23.10.17; FL in sea 12m SE of Fifeness 24.12.17 (FSL FC Cressman & AM2 GDR Shearer both killed); Deleted 26.12.17 TL

N1639   Shipped to Port Said; arr EI&SS Port Said 7.11.17; HMS Empress 7.11.17; HMS City of Oxford 28.11.17 - @2.12.17; Port Said by 10.1.18 - @27.1.18; Suez by 2.18; HMS City of Oxford 13.2.18; Suez 29.3.18; HMS Empress 29.3.18; Port Said 6.4.18 - @28.4.18; Alexandria by 1.5.18; Dropped 2x65-lb bombs on diving U-boat 8.5.18 (Lt GH Willows & OSL SC Howes); Became 270 Sqdn Alexandria 6.10.18; Deleted 22.3.19

N1640   (220-hp Renault) Deld Bembridge 11.8.17; Calshot FS W/E 16.9.17; Lee-on-Solent TS W/E 26.1.18; Became 209 TDS Lee-on-Solent 1.4.18; Deleted W/E 12.9.18

N1641   (220-hp Renault) Deld HMS Pegasus 31.8.17; Killingholme W/E 23.11.17; Deleted W/E 5.4.18

N1642   Deld Brough to Killingholme by air 21.8.17; South Shields 4.10.17; Crashed [collided N1488?] 28.10.17; Rosyth 28.10.17; East Fortune W/E 9.11.17; Killingholme to HMS Furious W/E 16.11.17; Rosyth by 28.12.17; HMS Pegasus W/E 15.2.18; Rosyth W/E 30.3.18 - @30.1.19

N1643   Deld Grain by rail 21.8.17; HMS Pegasus (via Rosyth) 23.9.17; Rosyth W/E 3.11.17; HMS Pegasus W/E 14.2.18; Dundee 24.2.18 (while ship refitted); Rosyth Depot by 3.18; Dundee 12.3.18 - 10.18

N1644   Deld Rosyth 17.9.17; HMS Furious W/E 9.11.17; South Shields 14.11.17; Deleted W/E 23.2.18

N1645   Deld Scapa W/E 24.11.17; Houton Bay for erection W/E 3.12.17; HMS *Campania* W/E 19.1.18; Houton Bay W/E 20.2.18; Bombed U-boat 5933N 0242W 20.4.18 (Capt ART Pipon & 2/Lt HJ White); Crashed, destroyed W/E 4.5.18

N1646   Deld Westgate (via Killingholme) 6.10.17; Deleted W/E 2.3.18

N1647   Deld Brough to Killingholme by air W/E 13.10.17 (for Hornsea); Crashed on TO for patrol, BO Hornsea 28.2.18 (F/Lt HC Lemon killed & F/Cdr PD Robertson badly injured); Surveyed 6.3.18; Deleted 13.3.18

N1648   Shipped from Mkrs to Mudros W/E 26.9.17; Sunk in CT *Izaston* in transit; Surveyed 28.12.17; Deleted 4.1.18

N1649   Shipped to Port Said; arr EI&SS Port Said W/E 11.11.17; Alexandria 15.1.18 - @10.3.18LM; EF, FL, hoisted in by HMS *Aphis* 9.3.18 (F/Cdr EJ Burling & OSL SC Howes); Port Said by 5.18 - 6.18; Alexandria by 6.18; Deleted 25.7.18

N1650   Deld Rosyth 18.9.17; Hawkcraig W/E 19.1.18; Rosyth W/E 9.5.18 - @30.1.19 (at Hawkcraig by then)

N1651   Shipped to Mudros 15.11.17; Suda Bay by 18.2.18 - 3.18; To Greek Govt deld in Aegean 3.18; 264 Sqdn Suda Bay by 6.18 - @30.1.19

N1652   Shipped to Aegean 31.10.17; HMS *Ark Royal* by 1.1.18 - @9.2.18; Suda Bay by 26.2.18 - @21.3.18; To Greek Govt deld in Aegean 3.18; 264 Sqdn Suda Bay by 6.18 - @30.1.19

N1653   Deld Brough to Killingholme 24.10.17; HMS *Nairana* W/E 23.11.17; HMS *Pegasus* W/E 29.11.17; Rosyth W/E 21.2.18 - @30.1.19

N1654   Shipped to Malta 14.11.17; Arr Calafrana for erection 2.18 - @6.18; To Greek Govt

N1655   Deld Killingholme W/E 23.11.17; Towed into Scarborough, damaged 10.12.17; Crashed in river, CW 13.1.18 (FSL DGB Francis & observer injured) Deleted W/E 26.1.18

N1656   Deld Killingholme 15.12.17 (for Hornsea); South Shields W/E 20.6.18; Deleted W/E 11.7.18

N1657   Deld Killingholme 15.12.17 (for Hornsea); Deleted W/E 22.2.18

N1658   Deld Killingholme W/E 19.12.17; Yarmouth W/E 22.2.18; EF, FL Cromer 17.3.18; Became 324/6 Flts 25.5.18; HSMP 8.6.18; Spun into sea in bad weather after steep turn off Gorleston 9.6.18 (2/Lt CCG Nickels drowned & 2/Lt CJ Lewis slightly injured); Deleted 20.6.18

N1659   Deld AD Killingholme 29.12.17; EF, FL off Flamborough, sank in tow 20.5.18 (crew unhurt); Deleted W/E 27.6.18

**30 SHORT ADMIRALTY 184 TYPE TRACTOR BIPLANE SEAPLANES ordered under Cont No A.S.1249/1 from Brush Electrical Engineering Co Ltd, numbered N1660 to N1689 & built Loughborough. (240-hp Renault-Mercedes to N1671, then 260-hp Maori)**

N1660   Deld Grain by rail 9.7.17; Yarmouth 22.7.17 (184 Dover type); Lost at sea W/E 23.2.18; Deleted W/E 23.2.18

N1661   Deld Dundee for erection 22.7.17; EF, FL off Peterhead 21.8.17; Dropped 100-lb bomb on U-boat nr Bell Rock, then FL, towed to Scapa Flow by HMS *Offa* 14.10.17 (FSL A Holland & OSL L Ritson); Caught fire and crashed in sea in flames 15m NE of St.Abbs Head 8.11.17 (FSL EOA Andrews & AAM1 GW Bickle both killed); Deleted W/E 17.11.17

N1662   Deld Scapa 5.9.17 - @13.10.17; Houton Bay by 12.17; Bombed U-boat 17m SE of Ward Hill 13.3.18 (FSL W Boyd & WO W Dunton); EF, FL 19.3.18; Became 430 Flt Houton Bay 25.5.18; Deleted W/E 21.11.18

N1663   Deld Grain 24.8.17; Yarmouth 9.17 (184 Dover type); detd Westgate W/E 16.1.18; retd Yarmouth W/E 23.3.18; Became 324/6 Flts Yarmouth 25.5.18; Deleted W/E 12.12.18

N1664   Deld Grain by rail 11.8.17; To CSD; Transport for shipment to Malta 13.9.17; Arr EI&SS Port Said 11.11.17; Re-shipped to Malta 19.11.17; HMS *Ark Royal* by 18.1.18; In transit from Port Said to 6 Wing RNAS Otranto by 8.2.18 - @22.3.18; To Calafrana 3.18 - @7.18

N1665   Deld Rosyth 9.17; HMS *Nairana* 13.9.17; Rosyth 7.2.18; to South Shields but elevator damage on slipway in heavy sea 3.3.18 (FSL A Woods); COL, salved 13.3.18 (pilot unhurt); Deleted W/E 13.4.18

N1666   Deld Killingholme W/E 8.9.17; Surveyed 12.10.17; Deleted 16.10.17 wrecked

N1667   Deld Felixstowe by road 4.9.17 (for *Vindex*); Erected 28.9.17; HMS *Vindex* 7.10.17; Felixstowe W/E 23.11.17; HMS *Vindex* W/E 1.12.17; Felixstowe by 22.12.17; Dover 25.1.18 (transit); Newhaven 28.1.18 (transit); Calshot 28.1.18; C Flt Lee-on-Solent W/E 2.2.18; Became 209 TDS Lee-on-Solent 1.4.18; Deleted W/E 8.8.18

N1668   Shipped to Mudros; Tested HMS *Ark Royal* after erection 27.11.17 - @24.1.18; Talikna by 3.18; HMS *Ark Royal* 8.3.18; Talikna 20.3.18; HMS *Ark Royal* 30.3.18; Talikna 3.4.18 - @6.18; HMS *Ark Royal* by 10.18; 266 Sqdn Mudros by 10.18; HMS *Ark Royal* by 31.12.18 - @1.19

N1669   Deld Rosyth 22.9.17; South Shields W/E 9.2.18; Damaged floats on TO 5.4.18 (pilot unhurt); Surveyed 15.4.18; Deleted 15.4.18 wrecked

N1670   Deld Dundee by rail 18.9.17; FL after loss of port aileron control, COL, too dangerous to salvage, sank 20.2.18 (pilot taken aboard destroyer); Deleted W/E 2.3.18

N1671   Deld Dundee by rail 25.9.17; Deleted W/E 21.11.18

N1672   Deld HMS *Vindex* by 10.17; Felixstowe W/E 27.10.17; HMS *Vindex* W/E 19.1.18; Yarmouth 25.1.18; Wrecked 15m ENE of Haisboro LV 27.5.18 (2 crew picked up Lowestoft drifter *Dreadnought*); Deleted W/E 13.6.18

N1673   Shipped to Mudros 16.11.17; Mudros by 30.3.18; Disposed by 6.18 (not reported)

N1674   (250-hp Renault) Deld Bembridge 3.12.17 (transit); Portland 5.12.17 (transit); Cattewater W/E 15.12.17; Deleted W/E 3.5.18

N1675   Deld Yarmouth W/E 3.11.17; Dropped 3 bombs on U-boat 5m NE of Smith's Knoll Pillar Buoy 8.12.17 (F/L BCH Cross); Surveyed 8.5.18; Deleted 15.5.18 wrecked

N1676   Deld Killingholme store by 29.12.17; South Shields 26.6.18 - @30.1.19

N1677   Deld Felixstowe W/E 19.1.18 (for HMS *Vindex*); South Shields W/E 30.1.18; Damaged on slipway owing to heavy swell 28.4.18; 252 Sqdn South Shields 25.5.18 - @30.1.19

N1678   Deld HMS *Riviera* (via Cattewater) 26.11.17; Dropped 2x100-lb bombs on U-boat 3.12.17 (FSL NI Larter & OSL CSA Sivil); FTR A/S patrol 9.12.17 (FSL NI Larter & CPO W/T Op1 Robbins both drowned); Surveyed 14.12.17; Deleted 19.12.17 TL

N1679   Shipped to Port Said 3.12.17; Erected EI&SS Port Said by 26.1.18; EF, FL on A/S patrol 3.2.18; Hit floating object landing, damaged float 29.8.18 (Lt HPD Lane & 2/Lt E Priest both unhurt); Became 269 Sqdn Port Said 6.10.18; Deleted 1.5.19

N1680   Deld Grain Type Test Dept for erection 14.12.17; Dover 24.1.18 (transit); Cattewater (via Calshot) 25.1.18; Deleted W/E 1.3.18

N1681   Deld Grain for erection W/E 24.11.17; Dover 8.12.17; Dunkerque 20.12.17; Dover 12.1.18; Crashed into monitor whilst taxying in harbour, damaged port wing and floats 27.4.18 (FSL LA Westcott); Became 407 Flt Dover 25.5.18; EF, FL 3m NW of Calais, towed into Calais by minesweeper *Lorientais* 31.5.18 (FSL LA Westcott); Became 407 Flt 233 Sqdn Dover 31.8.18; Dunkerque 30.10.18; 407 Flt 233 Sqdn Dover 11.18; Felixstowe 28.3.19

N1682   Deld CSD W/E 19.12.17; Shipped to Aegean 2.1.18; HMS *Ark Royal* by 30.3.18; Talikna 31.3.18; Talikna by 6.18; Possibly one of ten Short seaplanes destroyed in enemy air raid on Talikna 24.9.18

N1683   Deld Fishguard W/E 1.12.17; Accepted 8.12.17; Bombed U-boat 5148N 0541W 8.12.17 (FSL WG Westcott & FSL KF Alford); With N1127, dropped 100-lb bomb on U-boat 5215N 0445W 22.3.18; Became 426/7 Flts Fishguard 25.5.18; Deleted W/E 26.9.18

N1684   Deld Fishguard W/E 8.12.17; HMS *Engadine* 17.1.18; Fishguard 2.18; Cattewater 28.1.18; Lost at sea 8.2.18; Deleted W/E 15.2.18

N1685   Deld Patrol Reserve Calshot for erection W/E 19.12.17; Newhaven 19.1.18; Became 408/9 Flts Newhaven

25.5.18; Crashed into breakwater 21.6.18 (2 crew killed); Deleted W/E 27.6.18

N1686    Deld Patrol Reserve Calshot for erection W/E 12.12.17; Bembridge 19.1.18; Patrol Reserve Calshot W/E 20.3.18; Deleted W/E 1.8.18

N1687    Deld CSD; Shipped to Aegean 28.12.17; Tested HMS *Ark Royal* 2.3.18; Syra 20.3.18; HMS *Ark Royal* 23.4.18; Syra by 6.18; HMS *Ark Royal* by 6.18 - @7.18; Syra by 8.8.18; HMS *Ark Royal* by 12.18 - @30.1.19

N1688    Deld CSD; Cardiff Docks by 19.1.18; Shipped to Aegean 23.1.18; Mudros by 3.18; Suda Bay by 6.18; Talikna by 6.18; HMS *Empress* by 18.11.18 (to Mudros 2.12.18?); Talikna by 30.1.19

N1689    Deld CSD; Cardiff Docks by 19.1.18; Shipped to Mudros 23.1.18; Deleted by 4.3.18

**20 SHORT ADMIRALTY TYPE 310A-4 ("320 TYPE") TRACTOR BIPLANE SEAPLANES ordered under Cont No A.S.3612/1 (BR22) from The Sunbeam Motor Co Ltd, numbered N1690 to N1709 & built Wolverhampton. (320-hp Cossack)**

N1690    Deld MAD Killingholme W/E 1.2.18; Killingholme W/E 10.4.18 (and Hornsea); EF, FL, broke moorings, CW, Staithes 12.5.18; Deleted W/E 27.6.18

N1691    Deld MAD Killingholme W/E 1.2.18; At Mablethorpe 27.4.18; FL, sank, 20m N of Spurn 27.4.18 (pilot unhurt); Deleted Killingholme 18.5.18 TL

N1692    Deld MAD Killingholme W/E 8.2.18; Accepted 1.4.18 (Barrs); Yarmouth W/E 4.4.18; Dropped 230-lb on U-boat 15m SE of Shipwash, believed damaged, landed Felixstowe 15.5.18 (Lt CCG Nickels & Lt ER Munday); Retd Yarmouth 16.5.18; EF, FL, CW 1m E of St.Nicholas LV 23.5.18 (2 crew unhurt); Deleted W/E 13.6.18

N1693    Deld MAD Killingholme W/E 8.2.18; Accepted 1.4.18 (Barrs); Yarmouth W/E 4.4.18; Became 324/6 Flts 25.5.18; With B.E.2c 8417 attacked by 5 Brandenburg seaplanes of 5.C Staffel, shot down and strafed nr Lowestoft, FL on water, sunk by enemy seaplane 7.6.18 (2/Lt RWA Ivermere and AM2 SE Bourne both slightly wounded picked up by motor launches); Deleted W/E 27.6.18

N1694    Deld MAD Killingholme W/E 15.2.18 (for Killingholme); Deleted W/E 27.6.18

N1695    Deld MAD Killingholme W/E 15.2.18 (for RNAS Killingholme) South Shields 27.6.18; Killingholme 8.8.18; EF, FL 6m off Bridlington, sank under tow inside Western boom in River Humber 19.9.18; Deleted 26.9.18

N1696    Deld MAD Killingholme W/E 22.2.18 (for RNAS Killingholme); South Shields 26.6.18; USNAS Killingholme 1.8.18; South Shields W/E 3.10.18; Deleted W/E 14.11.18

N1697    Deld MAD Grain by 30.3.18; 6 SD Ascot W/E 25.7.18; Royal Albert Docks W/E 12.9.18; Shipped to Japanese Navy W/E 3.10.18

N1698    Deld MAD Grain by 30.3.18; 6 SD Ascot W/E 25.7.18; Royal Albert Docks W/E 12.9.18; Shipped to Japanese Navy W/E 3.10.18

N1699    Deld MAD Grain by 30.3.18; Royal Albert Docks W/E 25.7.18; Shipped to Japanese Navy W/E 3.10.18

N1700    Deld MAD Grain by 30.3.18; 6 SD Ascot W/E 25.7.18; Royal Albert Docks W/E 12.9.18; Shipped to Japanese Navy W/E 3.10.18

N1701    Deld MAD Grain 4.18; 6 SD Ascot W/E 25.7.18; Royal Albert Docks W/E 12.9.18; Shipped to Japanese Navy W/E 3.10.18

N1702    Deld MAD Killingholme W/E 27.4.18; Erecting by 31.5.18; USNAS Killingholme 20.7.18 - @30.1.19

N1703    Deld MAD Killingholme 12.3.18 (for RNAS Killingholme); USNAS Killingholme 20.7.18; 402/3 Flts 246 Sqdn Seaton Carew W/E 5.9.18; Deleted W/E 10.10.18

N1704    Deld MAD Killingholme 12.3.18 (for RNAS Killingholme); FL, bad mist and heavy rain, crashed between Spurn and Kilnsea 17.7.18 (2 crew unhurt); USNAS Killingholme 20.7.18; Deleted W/E 10.10.18

N1705    Deld MAD Killingholme W/E 15.5.18; 252 Sqdn South Shields for erection by 25.5.18; USNAS Killingholme

21.8.18; FL of Tyne 6.9.18; Attacked and claimed possibly sank *U156* 25.9.18; Deleted W/E 26.9.18

N1706    Deld MAD Killingholme W/E 15.5.18; 252 Sqdn South Shields, awaiting erection by 25.5.18; USNAS Killingholme 28.8.18; Deleted W/E 26.9.18

N1707    Deld MAD Westgate W/E 18.5.18; Accepted 8.7.18; Patrol Reserve Calshot 13.7.18; 410 Flt 240 Sqdn Calshot by 8.18; ARS Calshot W/E 28.11.18; Deleted W/E 19.12.18

N1708    Deld MAD Westgate W/E 18.5.18; Accepted 8.7.18; ARS Calshot 15.7.18; Calshot (coded 'C' on fin) W/E 12.9.18; Deleted W/E 3.10.18

N1709    Deld MAD Westgate W/E 20.6.18; ARS Calshot 20.7.18; Calshot W/E 17.10.18; ARS Calshot W/E 12.12.18 - @30.1.19

**10 A.D. PUSHER FLYING BOATS ordered under Cont Nos A.S.5388 (provisional) & A.S.20798 from Pemberton-Billing Ltd, numbered N1710 to N1719 & built Woolston. (200-hp Hispano-Suiza 8B)**

N1710    Deld Newport store W/E 19.1.18 - @11.18; Became Channel I G-EAEE

N1711    Deld Newport store W/E 19.1.18 - @11.18; Became Channel I G-EAEK (c/n 971); Later Sheldrake (Channel Type)

N1712    Deld Newport store W/E 16.3.18; Test Depot Grain 19.4.18 - @25.5.18 (propeller test; Odier starter)

N1713    Deld Newport store W/E 12.1.18 - @31.12.18

N1714    Deld Newport store W/E 12.1.18 - @31.12.18; Became Channel I G-EAEJ (c/n 972)

N1715    Deld Newport store W/E 12.1.18 - @31.12.18; Became Channel I G-EAEI (c/n 973); To Norway as *N-10*

N1716    Deld Newport store W/E 12.1.18 - @31.12.18; Became Channel I G-EAEH (c/n 974); To Norway as *N-9*

N1717    Deld Newport store W/E 20.2.18 - @31.12.18

N1718    Deld Newport store W/E 27.2.18 - @11.18

N1719    Deld Type Test Flt Grain 6.4.18 - @3.21 (fitted Wolseley Adder by 12.18) (performance with exptl hydrovanes below hull)

**20 BLACKBURN KANGAROO TWIN-ENGINED TRACTOR BIPLANES ordered under Cont No A.S.7469 from The Blackburn Aeroplane & Motor Co Ltd & numbered N1720 to N1739, to be built Leeds. (250-hp Falcon)**

N1720 to N1739 renumbered B9970 to B9989

**20 SHORT ADMIRALTY 184 TYPE TRACTOR BIPLANE SEAPLANES ordered under Cont No A.S.10630/1 from The Phoenix Dynamo Manufacturing Co Ltd, numbered N1740 to N1759 & built Bradford. (260-hp Maori)**

N1740    Deld Rosyth (via Dundee) W/E 23.11.17; HMS *Nairana* W/E 7.12.17; South Shields 20.2.18; Surveyed 11.4.18; Deleted 15.4.18 W&T

N1741    Deld Rosyth (via Dundee) W/E 23.11.17 - @29.12.17; HMS *Pegasus* by 12.17; Rosyth 11.1.18; HMS *Pegasus* by 19.1.18; Rosyth W/E 14.2.18; Donibristle W/E 16.5.18; Rosyth 5.18; HMS *Pegasus* W/E 23.5.18; Dundee 23.5.18 (storage while ship in dock); Strathbeg 14.9.18; Dundee W/E 26.12.18 - @30.1.19

N1742    Deld Liverpool by 11.17; Steamer to Buncrana by 16.11.17; HMS *Engadine* 31.12.17; Fishguard 12.1.18; Deleted W/E 2.3.18

N1743    Deld Liverpool by 11.17; Steamer to Buncrana by 16.11.17; HMS *Engadine* 29.12.17; Cattewater 28.1.18; Newlyn 9.5.18; Cattewater W/E 11.5.18; 209 TDS Lee-on-Solent W/E 20.6.18; Deleted W/E 14.11.18

N1744    Deld Dundee for erection 30.11.17; HMS *Nairana* W/E 4.1.18 (via Killingholme); Grain W/E 11.1.18; Dundee W/E 25.1.18; HMS *Nairana* W/E 31.1.18; Dundee 23.2.18; HMS *Nairana* 8.3.18; Rosyth 3.18; Dundee 30.3.18; Rosyth 4.4.18; HMS *Nairana* W/E 6.4.18; Rosyth W/E 23.5.18 - @30.1.19

N1745    Deld Dundee for erection 8.12.17; Accepted 11.1.18; HMS *Nairana* 31.1.18; To Rosyth 3.18; Dundee 30.3.18; Rosyth 4.4.18; HMS *Nairana* by 30.4.18; Rosyth W/E 23.5.18; Deleted W/E 19.9.18

N1746    Deld for shipment W/E 19.12.17; Shipped from West India Docks to Mudros 16.3.18; Deld Mudros 6.18;

Talikna by 6.18; Imbros, missing 27/28.8.18 (Mjr JBP Ferrand PoW)

N1747 Deld CSD; Shipped to Aegean 2.1.18; arr Mudros by 3.18; HMS *Ark Royal* by 3.3.18; Talikna 20.3.18; HMS *Ark Royal* 31.3.18; Syra by 6.18; HMS *Ark Royal* by 6.18 - @30.1.19

N1748 Deld CSD; West India Docks by 23.2.18; At Cardiff Docks for Mudros by 27.4.18 - @25.5.18; Shipped 2.6.18; Calafrana by 8.18 - @9.18

N1749 Deld CSD; Shipped to Port Said 26.1.18; Erecting EI&SS Port Said by 16.2.18; HMS *Empress* 19.4.18; Gibraltar 24.5.18; FL in Mediterranean, aircraft destroyed (sic) 24.5.18 (Lt JW Simpson & Lt A Copley interned in Spain unhurt); Presume aircraft returned; HMS *Empress* 17.7.18; HMS *Engadine* 3.8.18?

N1750 Deld CSD; Deld West India Docks by 23.2.18; Shipped to Mudros 23.4.18; HMS *Vindex* by 6.18; To Mudros 6.18; HMS *Ark Royal* by 6.18; HMS *Vindex* by 3.7.18; HMS *Ark Royal* 8.18 - @30.1.19

N1751 Deld CSD; Deld West India Docks by 23.2.18; Shipped to Mudros 4.18; Arr Mudros 6.18; Talikna by 6.18 - @10.18; Possibly one of ten Short seaplanes destroyed in enemy air raid on Talikna 24.9.18

N1752 Deld CSD; West India Docks by 23.2.18; Cardiff Docks for Mudros by 25.5.18; Shipped 2.6.18; Calafrana by 8.18; HMS *Vindex* 16.9.18; Damaged at Mudros 24.9.18

N1753 Deld Cattewater 2.2.18; Tested 4.3.18; 209 TDS Lee-on-Solent W/E 20.6.18 - @30.1.19

N1754 Deld Cattewater 9.2.18; Accepted 6.3.18; Dropped 100-lb bomb on U-boat 5008N 0435W 16.50 11.8.18 (Lt HJ Horsey & AM CH Dixon); Still Cattewater @30.1.19

N1755 Deld Calshot Patrol Reserve 22.2.18; Bembridge W/E 27.4.18; Became 412/3 Flts 253 Sqdn Bembridge 25.5.18; EF, FL in sea and o/t under tow by *TB98* 23.6.18 (Lt L Poulter & AM WT White picked up by *P55*)

N1756 Deld CSD; Cardiff Docks by 23.2.18; Shipped to Port Said 8.3.18; Alexandria by 11.6.18; EF, FL on road nr Balloon Base, CW 23.7.18 (Lt RA Fearnley & 3AM T Sanders both injured); Deleted 5.8.18

N1757 Deld CSD; Cardiff Docks; Shipped to Port Said 23.3.18; Port Said by 5.18; Alexandria by 23.5.18; EF, FL in Gulf of Kenais, beached 31.7.18; Became 270 Sqdn Alexandra 6.10.18; Landed, TO again but floats carried away, sank 1.8.19 (2/Lt CM Galletly & 2/Lt EV Parrish swam ashore, severe exposure); Deleted 4.8.19

N1758 Deld Calshot Patrol Reserve W/E 30.3.18; Portland by 4.18; Became 416/7 Flts Portland 25.5.18 (241 Sqdn 20.8.18) - @30.1.19

N1759 Deld CSD; Shipped to Mudros 29.3.18; HMS *Ark Royal* by 5.18; Talikna by 6.18; Possibly one of ten Short seaplanes destroyed in enemy air raid on Talikna 24.9.18

**20 SHORT ADMIRALTY 184 TYPE TRACTOR BIPLANE SEAPLANES ordered under Cont No A.S.10495/1 from S.E.Saunders, numbered N1760 to N1774 & built East Cowes. (260-hp Maori)**

N1760 Deld Bembridge W/E 19.12.17; Landing chassis and floats damaged landing 30.1.18; Deleted W/E 6.4.18

N1761 (250-hp) Deld Portland (via Calshot) 14.12.17; Cattewater 15.12.17; 209 TDS Lee-on-Solent W/E 15.8.18 - @30.1.19

N1762 Retained Mkrs; Deld Cattewater (via Portland) 23.6.18; Deleted W/E 2.9.18

N1763 Deld Bembridge W/E 29.12.17; Landed in fog, collided with buoy, caught fire 4.5.18 (pilot unhurt); Deleted W/E 25.5.18

N1764 Deld Bembridge W/E 19.1.18; Became 412/3 Flts 253 Sqdn Bembridge 25.5.18; Deleted W/E 8.8.18

N1765 Deld Portland W/E 19.1.18; Surveyed 20.3.18; Deleted 27.3.18 wrecked

N1766 Deld Newhaven 2.2.18; Became 408/9 Flts Newhaven 25.5.18; Deleted W/E 25.7.18

N1767 Deld Cattewater W/E 20.4.18; Newlyn 4.5.18; Dropped 2x100-lb bombs on U-boat, 1 failed to explode 5037N 4058W 6.5.18 (Lt AB Blanksby & 2/Lt R Nicholson); Became 424/5 Flts Newlyn 25.5.18 (235 Sqdn 20.8.18); 418 Flt 239 Sqdn Torquay 9.1.19; Cattewater W/E 16.1.19 - @30.1.19

N1768 Deld Calshot W/E 25.1.18; HMS *Riviera* (via Cattewater) 28.1.18; Cattewater 29.1.18; 209 TDS Lee-on-Solent W/E 18.8.18 - @30.1.19

N1769 Deld Portland (via Calshot) 5.1.18; Cattewater (coded 'A') 7.1.18; Deleted W/E 25.7.18

N1770 Deld Portland 12.2.18; Cattewater 14.2.18; EF, FL Newlyn 23.3.18; Newlyn 30.4.18; Became 424/5 Flts Newlyn 25.5.18 (235 Sqdn 20.8.18); 418 Flt 239 Sqdn Torquay 9.1.19; Cattewater W/E 16.1.19 - @30.1.19

N1771 Deld Portland W/E 23.2.18 (no engine); Became 416/7 Flts Portland (coded 'P No.3' on fin) 25.5.18; Struck tree, FL in field 1m inland from Budleigh Salterton 31.5.18 (Lt HG Burrell & Ens EA Wenz USN both injured); Deleted W/E 27.6.18

N1772 Deld Bembridge W/E 23.2.18 (no engine); Surveyed 8.3.18; Deleted 13.3.18 DBR

N1773 Deld Newhaven W/E 8.3.18; Bembridge W/E 15.3.18; EF, FL 5023N 0100W, lost 16.3.18 (Ens EA Stone USN & OSL EJT Moore both injured); Deleted W/E 30.3.18

N1774 Deld Calshot W/E 23.2.18; Cattewater 1.3.18; HMS *Orotava* (named 'AVATORO') W/E 6.3.18 (to Dakar); Cattewater 23.7.18; HMS *Orotava* 8.8.18; Damaged hoisting aboard 8.8.18 (replaced by N1790); Hit air pocket on TO, CW, wreckage hoisted aboard ship 20.8.18 (Lt VW Lamb unhurt & OSL LG Catherall slightly injured); Deleted W/E 26.9.18

**SERIALS N1775 to N1779 NOT ALLOTTED**

**20 SHORT ADMIRALTY 184 TYPE TRACTOR BIPLANE SEAPLANES ordered under Cont No A.S.4247/1 from Fredk Sage & Co Ltd, numbered N1780 to N1799 & built Peterborough. (260-hp Maori)**

N1780 Shipped to Mudros 19.12.17; HMS *Ark Royal* by 30.3.18; Talikna 9.4.18 - @8.18; Possibly one of ten Short seaplanes destroyed in enemy air raid on Talikna 24.9.18

N1781 Shipped to Mudros 19.12.17; HMS *Ark Royal* by 30.3.18; Talikna 17.4.18 - @30.4.18; Mudros by 10.18; Possibly one of ten Short seaplanes destroyed in enemy air raid on Talikna 24.9.18

N1782 (250-hp Sunbeam) Deld Yarmouth W/E 1.12.17; Damaged by gunfire at Shoeburyness while en route from Yarmouth to Westgate W/E 15.12.17; Dismantled and to Westgate by rail for repair W/E 20.12.17; EF, FL nr South Knock Buoy, towed back by torpedo boat 21.3.18; Became 406 Flt Westgate (coded '5') 25.5.18 (219 Sqdn 22.7.18); HACP 5.11.18; Still 406 Flt @30.1.19

N1783 Deld CSD W/E 12.12.17; West India Docks by 19.1.18; Shipped to Mudros 12.2.18; Otranto by 5.18 - 8.18; 435 or 436 Flt 263 Sqdn Otranto by 10.18; 437 Flt 266 Sqdn Talikna by 2.19

N1784 Deld CSD; Shipped to Port Said 1.1.18; Erecting Port Said by 16.2.18; HMS *Empress* 8.4.18; Port Said 21.4.18; HMS *Empress* 24.4.18; Gibraltar 3.8.18; HMS *Engadine* 11.8.18; To "Payloss" (sic) and retd 12.8.18

N1785 (250-hp Sunbeam) Deld Cattewater W/E 14.12.17; HMS *Riviera* 14.2.18; Newlyn 27.2.18 (stored initially during ship refit); Became 424/5 Flts Newlyn 25.5.18 (235 Sqdn 20.8.18); Cattewater 30.12.18 - @30.1.19

N1786 Deld CSD; Cardiff Docks by 19.1.18; Shipped to Mudros 9.2.18; HMS *Ark Royal* by 3.18; HMS *Ark Royal* by 6.18; Talikna by 6.18 - @2.11.18; HMS *Manxman* @13.11.18; To HMS *Manxman* again at Ismid 14.11.18; HMS *Empress* 16.11.18; Mudros 2.12.18

N1787 Deld CSD; West India Docks by 23.2.18; Shipped to Mudros 3.18; BUT Shipped 6.5.18; Skyros by 6.18; Possibly one of ten Short seaplanes destroyed in enemy air raid on Talikna 24.9.18

N1788 Deld CSD; West India Docks by 23.2.18; Shipped to Mudros 10.4.18; Calafrana by 6.18; HMS *Manxman* 22.8.18 - @9.18; Detd Sqdn Thasos by 28.10.18; Mudros by 1.19

N1789 Deld Cattewater W/E 12.1.18 - @30.1.19

N1790 Deld CSD; Cattewater W/E 19.1.18; Dropped 230-lb bomb on U-boat 5013N 0320W, failed to explode 30.5.18 AH (Lt AH Partner & 2/Lt RL Stevenson); HMS *Orotava* 8.8.18 (replaced N1774); Cattewater 25.11.18 - @30.1.19

N1791  Deld CSD; Cardiff Docks by 23.2.18; Shipped to Mudros 9.3.18; Otranto by 6.18 - @7.18; 441 Flt St.Maria di Leuca by 8.18 - @10.18

N1792  Deld Calshot W/E 23.1.18; Bembridge W/E 24.4.18; Became 412/3 Flts 25.5.18; Deleted W/E 11.7.18

N1793  (250-hp Sunbeam) Deld Calshot W/E 23.1.18; Cherbourg W/E 1.3.18; Became 414/5 Flts Cherbourg 25.5.18 (243 Sqdn 20.8.18); 242 Sqdn Newhaven W/E 28.11.18 - @30.1.19

N1794  Deld Calshot W/E 2.2.18; Portland W/E 22.3.18; Dropped 100-lb & 230-lb bombs on U-boat 5028N 0155W, oil and bubbles seen 25.3.18 (Ens McNamara USN & OSL EA Sawyer); Deleted W/E 4.5.18

N1795  Deld Calshot W/E 15.2.18; Cherbourg W/E 9.3.18; Became 414/5 Flts Cherbourg 25.5.18 (243 Sqdn 20.8.18) - @30.1.19

N1796  Deld Cattewater W/E 23.2.18; Dropped 2x100-lb bombs on U-boat 5000N 0004W, red substance on water 10.4.18 (Lt JL Stocks & Lt ER Owen); still Cattewater @30.1.19

N1797  Deld Fishguard by rail W/E 23.2.18; Became 426/7 Flts Fishguard 25.5.18; EF, FL in crosswind and crashed, TW, salved 11.6.18 (pilot and observer unhurt); Deleted W/E 27.6.18

N1798  Deld Reserve Group Patrol Calshot W/E 15.3.18; Bembridge W/E 25.5.18; Became 412/3 Flts Bembridge 25.5.18 (253 Sqdn 7.6.18); ARS Calshot W/E 18.7.18; Bembridge W/E 19.9.18 - @30.1.19

N1799  Deld Reserve Group Patrol Calshot W/E 15.3.18; Newhaven W/E 25.5.18; Became 408/9 Flts Newhaven 25.5.18; Deleted W/E 27.6.18

**20 Unidentified aircraft cancelled**

N1800 to N1819 cancelled

**20 SHORT ADMIRALTY 184 TYPE TRACTOR BIPLANE SEAPLANES ordered under Cont Nos A.S.3610/1 & A.S.14600 from Robey & Co Ltd, numbered N1820 to N1839 & built Lincoln. (240-hp Renault-Mercedes to N1826, then 260-hp Maori)**

N1820  Deld Killingholme store 22.9.17; Westgate 8.12.17; EF, FL nr the South Falls, collapsed under tow, sank 10.5.18; Deleted W/E 25.5.18

N1821  Shipped to Malta; Arr Calafrana for erection, ready 9.11.17; Dropped 2x65-lb bombs on U-boat 3550N 1522E, N1493 & N1504 also investigated 4.4.18 (FSL DRB Bentley & LAC Chapman); HMS Riviera 11.5.18; Calafrana 19.5.18; Deleted 1918

N1822  Shipped from Mkrs to Malta W/E 26.9.17; Arr Calafrana for erection, ready 9.11.17 - @3.18; Syra by 2-26.3.18; Respray at Calafrana by 31.3.18; 433/4 Flts 268 Sqdn Calafrana 27.9.18; NFT

N1823  Shipped to Malta; Arr Calafrana for erection, ready 9.11.17 - @6.18; 266 Sqdn Mudros by 10.18; NFT

N1824  Deld Cattewater 20.8.17 (transit); Newlyn 21.8.17; Shipped to Mudros 4.10.17; Tested after erection HMS Ark Royal 9.12.17; Syra to SS Datchet 9.12.17; Syra by 31.12.17; HMS Ark Royal by 1.2.18; Suda Bay by 2.3.18; Syra by 3.18; HMS Ark Royal (at Syra), damaged, brought in by trawler 4.6.18; Syra by 10.18 - @30.1.19; To Greek Govt

N1825  Shipped to Mudros 5.10.17; Tested after erection HMS Ark Royal 19.1.18; Talikna 30.1.18; Thasos by 3.18

N1826  Shipped to Mudros 20.11.17; Tested after erection HMS Ark Royal 13.1.18; A Sqdn 6 Wing Thasos 17.1.18; HMS Ark Royal 20.1.18; A Sqdn 6 Wing Thasos by 28.2.18 & 3-25.3.18; Talikna by 6.18

N1827  Shipped to Port Said 12.17; EI&SS Port Said by 8.12.17; EF, beached Basata 9.1.18 (F/L GD Smith & LM Phillips); In storage for engine overhaul 1.18 - 12.18; 268 Sqdn Calafrana 27.8.19

N1828  Shipped to Malta; Calafrana for erection by 12.12.17 - 6.18; HMS Manxman by 25.7.18; 433/4 Flts 268 Sqdn Calafrana 10.11.18 - @16.4.19; HMS Ark Royal by 11.19; Calafrana 10.11.19

N1829  Deld Killingholme, tested 31.10.17 (and flown Hornsea); South Shields W/E 1.6.18; 402/3 Flts 246 Sqdn Seaton Carew 24.8.18; South Shields W/E 26.9.18; Deleted W/E 12.12.18

N1830  Deld Killingholme, tested 3.11.17 (and flown Hornsea); South Shields 31.5.18; Killingholme W/E 5.12.18 - @30.1.19

N1831  Deld Rosyth W/E 9.11.17; HMS Pegasus W/E 10.11.17; Rosyth W/E 11.1.18; HMS Pegasus W/E 7.2.18; Dundee 24.2.18; Rosyth W/E 9.3.18; Dundee 14.3.18; Dropped 2x100-lb bombs on U-boat 5616.30N 0217W 26.7.18 (Capt WR Kenny & Capt DG McGregor); still Dundee @30.1.19

N1832  Deld Rosyth W/E 9.11.17; HMS Pegasus W/E 16.11.17; Dundee 21.11.17; HMS Pegasus 10.12.17; Rosyth W/E 10.1.18; Cattewater W/E 25.2.18 (transit); South Shields 25.2.18; Surveyed 11.4.18; Deleted 15.4.18 W&T

N1833  Shipped to Aegean 14.11.17; HMS Manxman from 1.18 - @13.3.18; To Otranto 3.18; HMS Manxman by 2.4.18 - @7.5.18; Otranto by 5.18 - 7.18; Dropped 230-lb bomb on U-boat, direct hit, off Durazzo 23.5.18 (Lt JHW Clarke & AM Bramham); Deleted 1918

N1834  Shipped to Aegean 14.11.17; HMS Manxman by 12.17; To Otranto 20.2.18; 66/67 Wings Otranto by 21.4.18 - @6.18

N1835  Deld to Dundee W/E 24.11.17; Strathbeg 11.10.18; Dundee W/E 30.12.18 - @30.1.19

N1836  By rail to Liverpool 19.11.17; HMS Engadine 27.12.17; Cattewater 28.1.18; Dropped 230-lb & 100-lb bombs on U-boat, oil seen 4957N 0457W 7.6.18 (Lt AH Partner & Obs W/T CH Nixon); 209 TDS Lee-on-Solent W/E 26.9.18 - @30.1.19

N1837  Deld CSD by 11.17; By rail to Liverpool 19.11.17; HMS Engadine 27.12.17; Wrecked on breakwater 10.1.18; Surveyed 10.1.18; Deleted 15.1.18 DBR

N1838  Deld CSD by 11.17; Shipped to Port Said 3.12.17; Tested after erection Port Said 18.1.18; Controls became unmanageable, FL, o/t, CW, sank in tow 6.5.18 (Lt GW Morey & Lt RStH Clarke rescued by drifter; Deleted 12.5.18

N1839  Deld for shipment W/E 19.11.17; Shipped to Port Said 10.1.18; Recd EI&SS Port Said for erection W/E 9.2.18; EF, FL Lake Menzala, E of Port Said 1.4.18 (Lt GD Smith & Lt AD Ferguson); Landed nr trawler, port float smashed on TO in rough sea, o/t, sank in tow, CW 30.7.18 (Lt RStH Clarke & 3AM H Crisp unhurt); Deleted 1.8.18

**50 FAIREY CAMPANIA TRACTOR BIPLANE SEAPLANES ordered under Cont No A.S.3591 from Barclay, Curle & Co Ltd to be numbered N1840 to N1889 & built Glasgow. (345-hp Eagle VIII)**

N1840  Deld MAD Dundee W/E 30.3.18; Accepted 3.4.18; HMS Nairana W/E 20.4.18; Sideslipped and crashed on TO Turnhouse 12.6.18

N1841  Deld MAD Dundee W/E 27.4.18; Accepted 3.5.18; Rosyth W/E 6.6.18; HMS Pegasus 11.7.18; Rosyth 22.8.18 - @30.1.19

N1842  Deld Dundee W/E 4.5.18; HMS Nairana W/E 23.5.18; Rosyth by 13.6.18; HMS Campania W/E 17.10.18; Rosyth W/E 30.11.18 - @31.12.18

N1843  Deld Rosyth W/E 4.5.18; Accepted Dundee 12.5.18; Rosyth to HMS Pegasus W/E 12.5.18; Dundee 23.5.18 (storage while ship in dock); Rosyth W/E 4.7.18; HMS Campania 18.7.18; Deleted W/E 3.10.18

N1844  Deld MAD Dundee W/E 4.5.18; HMS Nairana W/E 18.5.18 (to North Russia 6.7.18); Dundee W/E 12.12.18; HMS Nairana W/E 9.1.19 - @30.1.19

N1845  Deld MAD Dundee W/E 18.5.18 - Accepted 22.5.18; HMS Nairana W/E 1.6.18 (to North Russia 6.7.18); Rosyth W/E 15.8.18; HMS Campania W/E 30.10.18; Rosyth W/E 28.11.18; Deleted W/E 19.12.18

N1846  Deld MAD Dundee W/E 18.5.18; Accepted 30.5.18; Rosyth W/E 20.6.18; Turnhouse Depot by 7.18; HMS Renown by 7.18; HMS Pegasus 11.7.18 (hoisted in 7.8.18); Rosyth by 29.8.18; Turnhouse Depot W/E 19.9.18; Rosyth W/E 17.10.18 - @30.1.19

N1847  Deld MAD Dundee W/E 25.5.18; Accepted 3.6.18; Rosyth W/E 20.6.18; HMS Nairana 6.7.18 (to North Russia, arr Kola Inlet 11.7.18); Brought down, landed in river Wolympi 17.8.18 (Lt Thompson & Lt WJ Umpleby); Deleted W/E 31.10.18

N1848  Deld MAD Dundee by 7.6.18; Accepted 10.6.18;

Rosyth W/E 4.7.18; HMS *Nairana* W/E 11.7.18; Rosyth W/E 25.7.18; HMS *Nairana* W/E 17.10.18; Dundee W/E 7.11.18; Deleted W/E 14.11.18

N1849 Deld MAD Dundee and accepted 17.6.18; Rosyth W/E 11.7.18; HMS *Nairana* W/E 11.7.18 (to North Russia); Dundee W/E 12.12.18; HMS *Nairana* (North Russia) W/E 9.1.19 - @30.1.19

N1850 Deld MAD Dundee W/E 27.6.18; HMS *Campania* 29.8.18; Crashed 14.10.18 (Lt FG Aplin & Lt CS Collingwood retd in SS *Rowena*); Deleted W/E 21.11.18

N1851 Deld MAD Dundee and accepted 11.7.18; HMS *Pegasus* W/E 25.7.18; HMS *Campania* 26.10.18; HMS *Pegasus* 29.10.18; Dundee W/E 19.12.18 - @19.3.19

N1852 to N1889 cancelled

**60 CURTISS H.16 PATROL TRACTOR BIPLANE FLYING BOATS ordered from Curtiss under BR.50. Serials N1890 to N1949 allotted by 4.6.17, but renumbered N4890 to N4949 and serials reallocated**

N1890 to N1949 cancelled

**10 FELIXSTOWE F.3 TRACTOR BIPLANE FLYING BOATS ordered, to be serialled N1950 to N1959. Serials "hung up" by 16.7.17**

N1950 to N1959 cancelled

**70 FAIREY CAMPANIA TRACTOR BIPLANE SEAPLANES ordered from The Sunbeam Motor Car Co Ltd and Fredk Sage & Co Ltd to be numbered N1890 to N1959 & built Wolverhampton and Peterborough. (345-hp Rolls-Royce?)**
[Not known how many from each company]

N1890 to N1959 cancelled

**26 FAIREY HAMBLE BABY TRACTOR BIPLANE FLOATPLANES ordered under Cont Nos A.S.10058 & A.S.37123 from George Parnall & Co Ltd, numbered N1960 to N1985 & built Bristol. (130 Clerget 9B unless stated otherwise)**

N1960 Allocated 17.12.17 HMS *Beryl* to Calshot school via Queenstown; Deld Calshot W/E 19.1.18; Lee-on-Solent W/E 26.1.18; CSD White City packing for Greek Govt W/E 11.5.18; Despatched W/E 5.9.18; Left England in SS *Piraeus* for RHNAS 27.9.18

N1961 Allocated 17.12.17 HMS *Beryl* to Calshot school via Queenstown; Deld Calshot W/E 19.1.18; Lee-on-Solent W/E 26.1.18; CSD White City packing for Greek Govt W/E 11.5.18; Despatched W/E 5.9.18; Left England in SS *Piraeus* for RHNAS 27.9.18

N1962 Deld Westgate W/E 20.12.17; Became 406 Flt Westgate 27.5.18 (219 Sqdn 22.7.18); Deleted W/E 19.12.18

N1963 Deld Calshot W/E 9.11.17; Cattewater W/E 16.11.17; Surveyed 12.12.17; Deleted 17.12.17 wrecked

N1964 (110-hp Clerget) Deld Scapa for erection 3.11.17; Calshot 10.12.17; Scapa W/E 19.1.18; Lee-on-Solent W/E 31.1.18; CSD White City packing for Greek Govt W/E 11.5.18; Despatched W/E 5.9.18; Left England in SS *Piraeus* for RHNAS 27.9.18

N1965 (110-hp Clerget) Deld Scapa for erection 3.11.17; Calshot 10.12.17; Scapa W/E 19.1.18; Lee-on-Solent W/E 31.1.18; CSD White City packing for Greek Govt W/E 11.5.18; Despatched W/E 5.9.18; Left England in SS *Piraeus* for RHNAS 27.9.18

N1966 Shipped to Aegean; HMS *Ark Royal* by 1.18 - @3.18

N1967 Shipped to Malta W/E 26.9.17; Calafrana for erection by 7.11.17 - @26.12.17; Packing for HMS *Manxman* by 23-30.1.18; HMS *Manxman* by @5.3.18 - @19.3.18; For deletion by 27.4.18

N1968 Shipped to Malta W/E 26.9.17; Calafrana for erection by 26.12.17; Packing for HMS *Manxman* by 23-30.1.18; HMS *Manxman* by @5.3.18 - @19.3.18; Calafrana by 1.5.18; Deleted W/E 8.5.18

N1969 Deld Calshot 26.10.17; Lee-on-Solent W/E 26.1.18; For deletion by 21.2.18 [Possibly the aircraft whose wing broke away, fell 5,000ft, Hamble 18.2.18 (PFO AE Gullett killed) - or N1971]; Deleted W/E 2.3.18

N1970 (110-hp Clerget) Deld Calshot W/E 9.11.17; Became 410/1 Flts Calshot 25.5.18; Deleted W/E 29.8.18

N1971 Deld Calshot FS W/E 9.10.17; Lee-on-Solent W/E 26.1.18; For deletion by 21.2.18 [see N1969]; Deleted W/E 2.3.18

N1972 Deld Calshot 26.10.17; Surveyed Lee-on-Solent 18.12.17; Deleted 28.12.17 DBR

N1973 Deld Calshot 11.17; Sideslipped, crashed and wrecked 19.1.18 (pilot uninjured); Deleted W/E 23.1.18

N1974 Deld Calshot 2.11.17; Surveyed 6.12.17; Deleted 8.12.17 wrecked

N1975 Deld Calshot 11.17; Surveyed 10.11.17; Deleted 14.11.17 wrecked

N1976 Shipped to 6 Wing RNAS Otranto 31.10.17; Lost in SS *Perrier* sunk en route Otranto; Surveyed 29.12.17; Deleted 4.1.18

N1977 Deld Killingholme store W/E 7.12.17; Yarmouth W/E 16.2.18; Deleted W/E 23.2.18

N1978 Deld Scapa for erection 3.11.17 (Houton Bay by 12.17); Lee-on-Solent School for erection W/E 8.2.18; CSD White City packing for Greek Govt W/E 11.5.18; Despatched W/E 5.9.18; Left England in SS *Piraeus* for RHNAS 27.9.18

N1979 Deld Killingholme store 29.9.17; Hornsea 10.11.17; Killingholme patrol W/E 29.12.17; Hornsea 10.5.18; CSD White City packing for Greek Govt by 25.5.18; Despatched W/E 5.9.18; Left England in SS *Piraeus* for RHNAS 27.9.18

N1980 Shipped to 6 Wing RNAS Otranto 31.10.17; Lost in SS *Perrier* sunk en route Otranto; Surveyed 29.12.17; Deleted 4.1.18

N1981 Shipped to 6 Wing RNAS Otranto 27.10.17; arr 6 Wing RNAS Otranto by 15.1.18; 359 Flt 271 Sqdn Otranto by 10.18 - @30.1.19

N1982 Shipped to 6 Wing RNAS Otranto 10.11.17; 6 Wing RNAS Otranto by 20.2.18; HMS *Riviera*; 441 Flight St.Maria di Leuca by 10.18; Deleted 10.18

N1983 Shipped to 6 Wing RNAS Otranto 10.11.17; 6/66 Wing RNAS Otranto by 20.2.18 - @7.18; HMS *Riviera*; 441 Flight St.Maria di Leuca by 10.18; Deleted 10.18

N1984 Deld Killingholme store W/E 13.10.17; Left for Mudros (via CSD) 23.1.18; Shipped 2.2.18; HMS *Ark Royal* by 3.18; HMS *Ark Royal* by 6.18; HMS *Peony* 25.7.18; Talikna 12.8.18; HMS *Peony* 17.8.18; Talikna 26.9.18 - @30.1.19

N1985 Deld Killingholme store W/E 13.10.17; Left for Mudros (via CSD) 23.1.18; Shipped 2.2.18; HMS *Ark Royal* by 3.18; HMS *Ark Royal* by 6.18; HMS *Peony* 25.7.18; Talikna 12.8.18; HMS *Ark Royal* 8.18 - @30.1.19

**74 FAIREY HAMBLE BABY CONVERT TRACTOR BIPLANE LANDPLANES ordered under Cont Nos. A.S.10058 & A.S.37123 from George Parnall & Co Ltd, numbered N1986 to N2059 & built Bristol. (130 Clerget 9B)**
[C/n's P.1/1 to P/1/74? N2002 was P.1/17]

N1986 Deld CSD; Shipped to 6 Wing RNAS Otranto 10.12.17; Sunk in transit, Surveyed 15.1.18; Deleted 19.1.18

N1987 Deld CSD; Shipped to 6 Wing RNAS Otranto 10.12.17; Sunk in transit, Surveyed 15.1.18; Deleted 19.1.18

N1988 Deld CSD; Shipped to 6 Wing RNAS Otranto 10.12.17; Sunk in transit, Surveyed 15.1.18; Deleted 19.1.18

N1989 Deld CSD; Shipped Otranto 14.12.17; 6 Wing RNAS Otranto by 3.18; Became 66/67 Wings Otranto 1.4.18; 225 Sqdn Andrano by 23.4.18 - @11.5.18; 6 Group Taranto by 10.18

N1990 Deld CSD; Shipped to Otranto 11.12.17; 6 Wing RNAS Otranto by 24.3.18; Became 66/67 Wings Otranto 1.4.18; 225 Sqdn Andrano by 23.4.18 - @11.5.18; 6 Group Taranto by 10.18

N1991 Deld CSD; Shipped Otranto 11.12.17; 6 Wing RNAS Otranto by 24.3.18; Became 66/67 Wings Otranto 1.4.18; 225 Sqdn Andrano by 23.4.18 - @11.5.18; 6 Group Taranto by 10.18

N1992 Deld Killingholme store W/E 3.11.17; Yarmouth W/E 8.3.18 (at Burgh Castle by 12.5.18); Became 490 Flt Yarmouth 25.5.18 (still Burgh Castle @27.6.18)

N1993 Deld Killingholme store W/E 3.11.17; Yarmouth W/E 16.3.18 (to Burgh Castle 3.5.18); Became 490 Flt Yarmouth 25.5.18; Burgh Castle by 11.6.18 - @13.6.18

N1994 Deld Killingholme store W/E 3.11.17; Yarmouth 12.3.18; Became 490 Flt Yarmouth 25.5.18; Deleted

N1995    W/E 13.6.18
Deld Killingholme store W/E 3.11.17; Yarmouth 12.3.18; Became 490 Flt Yarmouth 25.5.18; Deleted W/E 13.6.18

N1996    Deld Cranwell for School 30.11.17; To E Flt 201 TDS Cranwell 1.4.18; Became 57 TDS Cranwell 27.7.18

N1997    Deld Cranwell W/E 30.11.17; Became 201/2 TDS Cranwell 1.4.18

N1998    Deld Cranwell for erection W/E 30.11.17; Became 201/2 TDS Cranwell 1.4.18

N1999    Deld Cranwell for erection W/E 30.11.17; Became 201/2 TDS Cranwell 1.4.18

N2000    Deld Cranwell for erection W/E 30.11.17; Became 201/2 TDS Cranwell 1.4.18

N2001    Deld Cranwell for erection W/E 7.12.17; Became 201/2 TDS Cranwell 1.4.18

N2002    Deld Cranwell 27.11.17; Became 201/2 TDS Cranwell 1.4.18

N2003    Deld Cranwell W/E 7.12.17; Surveyed 25.2.18; Deleted 13.3.18 for GI

N2004    Deld Killingholme store W/E 8.12.17 - @30.3.18
N2005    Deld Killingholme store W/E 8.12.17 - @30.3.18
N2006    Deld Killingholme store W/E 8.12.17 - @30.3.18
N2007    Deld Killingholme store W/E 23.2.18; Yarmouth 12.3.18; Became 490 Flt Yarmouth 25.5.18; Deleted W/E 1.6.18

N2008    Deld Killingholme store W/E 15.12.17; Yarmouth 12.3.18; To TO on to Camel and Bristol F.2b outside hangar 5.18; Deleted W/E 25.5.18

N2009    Deld Killingholme store W/E 15.12.17; Yarmouth W/E 22.3.18; Deleted W/E 6.6.18

N2010    Deld Killingholme store W/E 12.12.17 - @30.3.18
N2011    Deld Killingholme store W/E 12.12.17 - @30.3.18
N2012    Deld Killingholme store W/E 12.12.17 - @30.3.18
N2013    Deld Killingholme store W/E 12.12.17 - @30.3.18
N2014    Deld Killingholme store W/E 12.12.17 - @30.3.18
N2015    Deld Killingholme store W/E 12.12.17 - @30.3.18
N2016    Deld Killingholme store W/E 19.12.17 - @30.3.18
N2017    Deld Killingholme store W/E 19.12.17 - @30.3.18
N2018    Deld Killingholme store W/E 5.1.18 - @30.3.18
N2019    Deld Killingholme store W/E 5.1.18 - @30.3.18
N2020    Deld Killingholme store W/E 5.1.18 - @30.3.18
N2021    Deld Killingholme store W/E 5.1.18 - @30.3.18
N2022    Deld Killingholme store W/E 5.1.18 - @30.3.18
N2023    Deld Killingholme store W/E 5.1.18 - @30.3.18
N2024    Deld Killingholme store W/E 12.1.18 - @30.3.18
N2025    Deld Killingholme store W/E 12.1.18 - @30.3.18
N2026    Deld Killingholme store W/E 12.1.18 - @30.3.18
N2027    Deld Killingholme store W/E 19.1.18 - @30.3.18
N2028    Deld Killingholme store W/E 8.2.18 - @30.3.18
N2029    Deld Killingholme store W/E 8.2.18 - @30.3.18
N2030    Deld Killingholme store W/E 8.2.18 - @30.3.18
N2031    Deld Killingholme store W/E 19.1.18 - @30.3.18
N2032    Deld Killingholme store W/E 26.1.18 - @30.3.18
N2033    Deld Killingholme store W/E 1.2.18 - @30.3.18
N2034    Deld Killingholme store W/E 26.1.18 - @30.3.18
N2035    Deld Killingholme store W/E 26.1.18 - @30.3.18
N2036    Deld Killingholme store W/E 26.1.18 - @30.3.18
N2037    Deld Killingholme store W/E 1.2.18 - @30.3.18
N2038    Deld Killingholme store W/E 1.2.18 - @30.3.18
N2039    Deld Killingholme store W/E 8.2.18 - @30.3.18
N2040    Deld Killingholme store W/E 8.2.18 - @30.3.18
N2041    Deld Killingholme store W/E 8.2.18 - @30.3.18
N2042    Deld Killingholme store W/E 8.2.18 - @30.3.18
N2043    Deld Killingholme store W/E 22.2.18 - @30.3.18
N2044    Deld Killingholme store W/E 22.2.18 - @30.3.18
N2045    Deld Killingholme store W/E 22.2.18 - @30.3.18
N2046    Deld Killingholme store W/E 22.2.18 - @30.3.18
N2047    Deld Killingholme store W/E 22.2.18 - @30.3.18
N2048    Deld Killingholme store W/E 22.2.18 - @30.3.18
N2049    Deld Killingholme store W/E 1.3.18 - @30.3.18
N2050    Deld Killingholme store W/E 1.3.18 - @30.3.18
N2051    Deld Killingholme store W/E 8.3.18 - @30.3.18
N2052    Deld Killingholme store W/E 8.3.18 - @30.3.18
N2053    Deld Killingholme store W/E 8.3.18 - @30.3.18
N2054    Deld Killingholme store W/E 8.3.18 - @30.3.18
N2055    Deld Killingholme store W/E 8.3.18 - @8.3.18
N2056    Deld Killingholme store W/E 8.3.18 - @29.3.18
N2057    Deld Killingholme store W/E 8.3.18 - @29.3.18
N2058    Deld Killingholme store W/E 22.3.18 - @29.3.18
N2059    Deld Killingholme store W/E 22.3.18 - @29.3.18

**75 SOPWITH BABY TRACTOR BIPLANE SEAPLANES ordered under Cont Nos A.S.10059 (BR.59) & C.P.102625 from The Blackburn Aeroplane & Motor Co Ltd, numbered N2060 to N2134 & built Leeds. (130-hp Clerget 9B)**

N2060    Deld Killingholme store W/E 13.10.17; Deleted 21.12.17 as spares

N2061    Deld Killingholme store W/E 13.10.17; Deleted 21.12.17 as spares

N2062    Deld Killingholme store W/E 13.10.17; Deleted 21.12.17 as spares

N2063    Deld Killingholme store W/E 2.11.17; South Shields for erection 19.3.18; Seaton Carew W/E 27.3.18; South Shields W/E 24.4.18; 451/2 Flts 252 Sqdn Seaton Carew 24.5.18 (246 Sqdn 15.8.18); EF, FL, dismantling 29.8.18; South Shields W/E 5.9.18 - @30.1.19

N2064    Deld Killingholme store W/E 13.10.17; South Shields for erection 19.3.18; Seaton Carew W/E 27.3.18; South Shields W/E 27.4.18; Seaton Carew 8.5.18; Became 452 Flt 252 Sqdn Seaton Carew 25.5.18; EF, FL Sunderland, dismantled and returned 28.5.18; FL Whitby owing to part of u/c breaking 10.6.18; South Shields by 13.6.18; 451 Flt 246 Sqdn Seaton Carew 29.9.18; South Shields W/E 9.1.19 - @30.1.19

N2065    Deld Killingholme store W/E 20.10.17; Deleted 21.12.17 as spares

N2066    Deld Killingholme store W/E 20.10.17; Deleted 21.12.17 as spares

N2067    Deld Killingholme store W/E 2.11.17; South Shields for erection 19.3.18; Seaton Carew by 30.3.18; South Shields by 27.4.18; 252 Sqdn South Shields 25.5.18; Seaton Carew, but EF, FL off Seaham, towed into Tees by armed trawler 7.6.18; 452 Flt 252 Sqdn Seaton Carew W/E 20.6.18; Dropped 65-lb bomb on U-boat 6/8m ENE of Scarborough 30.6.18 (Lt EJ Addis); Dropped bomb 10 yds ahead of conning tower of *U77* 14/16m E of Skinningrove 26.7.18 (Lt EJ Addis); EF, FL in sea and damaged 2.9.18 (pilot unhurt); Deleted W/E 24.9.18

N2068    Deld Killingholme store W/E 2.11.17; Yarmouth patrol W/E 16.3.18; Became 324/6 Flts Yarmouth 25.5.18 (228 Sqdn 20.8.18); HSMP 9.6.18 & 10.6.18; Deleted W/E 14.11.18

N2069    Deld Killingholme store W/E 2.11.17; Yarmouth patrol W/E 16.3.18; Became 324/6 Flts 25.5.18; HSMP 9.6.18; Crashed on TO, wrecked, sank 16.8.18 (crew unhurt); Deleted W/E 29.8.18

N2070    Deld Killingholme store W/E 20.10.17; Deleted 21.12.17 as spares

N2071    Deld Killingholme store W/E 2.11.17; Yarmouth (coded 'K') W/E 16.3.18; Towed into Felixstowe 9.5.18; Retd Yarmouth 12.5.18; Became 324/6 Flts Yarmouth 25.5.18 (228 Sqdn 20.8.18); Tested with Hamble floats 26.5.18; Felixstowe 3.7.18 (fitted 2 Lewis guns); Yarmouth W/E 8.8.18; Deleted W/E 12.12.18

N2072    Deld CSD 11.17; Recd EI&SS Port Said in packing case by 22.12.17; Controls failed, hit Arab landing, CW 20.5.18 (Lt CH Biddlecombe slightly injured); Deleted 27.5.18

N2073    Deld CSD 11.17; Recd EI&SS Port Said in packing case by 22.12.17; Became 431/2 Flts 269 Sqdn Port Said 6.10.18; Deleted 27.1.19

N2074    Deld CSD 11.17; Shipped to Mudros 20.11.17; HMS *Ark Royal* for erection by 6.12.17; Suda Bay by 6.18; HMS *Ark Royal* by 6.18; Talikna by 27.10.18

N2075    Deld CSD 11.17; Shipped to Mudros 20.11.17; HMS *Ark Royal* for erection by 6.12.17 - @6.18

N2076    Deld CSD 11.17; Shipped to Mudros 1.12.17; HMS *Ark Royal* for erection by 6.12.17; Syra by 6.18; HMS *Ark Royal* 3.10.18; Syra 4.10.18; Talikna by 31.10.18 - @4.11.18; Syra by 12.18 - @30.1.19

N2077    Deld CSD 11.17; Shipped to Mudros 6.12.17; HMS *Ark Royal* for erection by 6.12.17; Tested 19.2.17 - @25.3.18; Surveyed 63 Wing 17.4.18; Deleted 15.5.18 DBR

N2078    Deld Hornsea (named 'THE JABBERWOCK') 25.1.18; Bombed U-boat 10m NE of Scarborough 26.3.18 (FSL GF Hyams); FL in fog and damaged 1m NW of Air Station 23.4.18 (Lt DCS Bland slightly injured), retd 24.4.18; Became 453 Flt Hornsea 25.5.18; Deleted W/E 25.7.18 [Replica now in FAA Museum]

*Sopwith Baby N2071 'K' at Yarmouth, 1918.*
*(J.M.Bruce/G.S.Leslie collection)*

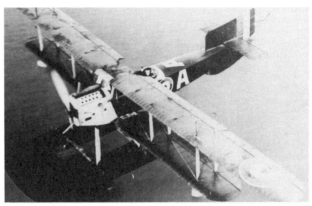

*Fairey IIIB (possibly N2243) coded 'A' of 219 Sqdn,*
*1919 (RAF Museum P.17273)*

*Wight 'Converted' Seaplane N2183 at Cowes.*
*(M.H.Goodall)*

*Fairey IIIA N2850, the first production machine of the*
*many Fairey III variants. (R.C.Sturtivant collection)*

*Norman Thompson N.T.2B Flying Boat Trainer N256x. (via Philip Jarrett)*

*Gosport Aviation-built F.B.A. Type B Flying Boat Trainer N2682. (via J.D.Oughton)*

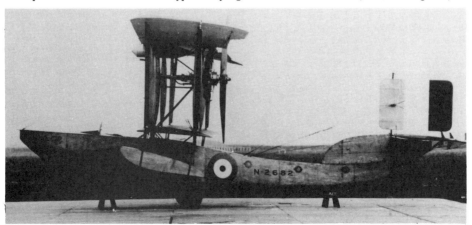

N2079   Due Killingholme W/E 19.1.18; Hornsea by 16.3.18; EF, FL, o/t 1m E of Hornsea, salved 26.3.18 (pilot unhurt)

N2080   Deld CSD 11.17; Shipped to Otranto 1.12.17; In transit by 21.12.17; Arrived 6 Wing RNAS Otranto by 24.3.18

N2081   Deld CSD 11.17; Shipped to Otranto 6.12.17; In transit by 28.12.17; Arrived 6 Wing RNAS Otranto by 24.3.18; 441 Flt 263 Sqdn St.Maria di Leuca by 8.18 - @9.18; 435/6 Flts 263 Sqdn Otranto by 1.19

N2082   Deld CSD 11.17; Shipped to Aegean 1.12.17; Recd HMS *Ark Royal* for erection 3.18; HMS *Peony* by 6.18

N2083   Deld CSD 11.17; Shipped to Aegean 1.12.17; Tested HMS *Ark Royal* after erection then to Talikna 28.2.18; Talikna by 6.18

N2084   Deld CSD 11.17; Shipped 10.12.17; Sunk in transit to Mudros; Surveyed 15.1.18; Deleted 19.1.18

N2085   Deld CSD 11.17; Shipped 10.12.17; Sunk in transit to Mudros; Surveyed 15.1.18; Deleted 19.1.18

N2086   Deld CSD 11.17; Shipped to Aegean 14.12.17; Recd HMS *Ark Royal* for erection by 13.3.18

N2087   Deld Hornsea W/E 16.2.18; Dropped 65-lb bomb on U-boat 10m ESE of Scarborough 26.3.18 (FSL GF Hyams); Bridlington by 4.18; Hornsea 12.4.18 (overhaul); Became 453 Flt Hornsea 25.5.18; Became 453 Flt 248 Sqdn Hornsea 20.8.18; South Shields W/E 17.10.18 - @30.1.19

N2088   Deld Hornsea W/E 25.1.18; Tested 17.3.18; EF, FL in sea, picked up 5m E of Hornsea by steamer *Hans Just (C.T.9)* 20.3.18; Became 453 Flt Hornsea 25.5.18 (248 Sqdn 20.8.18); South Shields W/E 12.12.18 - @30.1.19

N2089   Deld Hornsea W/E 23.2.18; Became 453 Flt Hornsea 25.5.18 (248 Sqdn 20.8.18); South Shields W/E 9.1.19 - @30.1.19

N2090   Deld CSD 11.17; Shipped to Otranto 14.12.17; arr 6 Wing RNAS Otranto 3.18 - @25.9.18; 435/6 Flts 263 Sqdn Otranto by 10.18; 441 Flt 263 Sqdn St.Maria di Leuca

N2091   Deld CSD 11.17; Shipped to Otranto 19.12.17; In transit by 18.1.18; arr 6 Wing RNAS Otranto by 24.3.18 - @7.18; 441 Flt St.Maria di Leuca by 8.18; 435/6 Flts 263 Sqdn Otranto by 1.19

N2092   Deld CSD 11.17; Shipped to Otranto 19.12.17; In transit by 18.1.18; arr 6 Wing RNAS Otranto by 24.3.18 - @7.18; 441 Flt St.Maria di Leuca by 8.18

N2093   Deld CSD 11.17; Shipped to Otranto 19.12.17; In transit by 18.1.18; arr 6 Wing RNAS Otranto by 24.3.18; 441 Flight St.Maria di Leuca by 15.6.18 - @8.18

N2094   Deld AD Killingholme for erection W/E 12.12.17; Hornsea 25.4.18; Became 453 Flt Hornsea 25.5.18; Retd from Bridlington with damaged wing 29.5.18; EF on TO, FL from 50 ft, port float and fuselage bent 5.6.18 (pilot unhurt); Deleted W/E 22.8.18

N2095   Deld AD Killingholme for erection W/E 19.2.18; Hornsea 13.4.18; Became 453 Flt Hornsea 25.5.18 (248 Sqdn 20.8.18); Bombed U-boat 5m E of Scarborough, slight wreckage seen 9.8.18 (Lt FC Sherwood); Deleted W/E 24.10.18

N2096   Deld AD Killingholme for erection W/E 19.12.17; Hornsea by 14.3.18; EF, FL, crashed in rough sea and wrecked, Bridlington, trawler unable to salve 14.4.18 (Ens Gastin USN slightly injured); Deleted W/E 24.10.18

N2097   Deld AD Killingholme for erection W/E 19.12.17; Hornsea by 3.18; Tested 1.4.18; EF after TO, struck fence on waters edge and crashed, wrecked 8.5.18 (pilot unhurt); Became 453 Flt Hornsea 25.5.18; Deleted W/E 25.7.18

N2098   Deld AD Killingholme for erection W/E 19.12.17; War Flt Seaton Carew W/E 8.2.18; South Shields W/E 6.3.18; Seaton Carew 3.4.18; 252 Sqdn South Shields 25.5.18; 452 Flt Seaton Carew 8.6.18 (246 Sqdn 15.8.18) - @30.1.19

N2099   Deld AD Killingholme for erection W/E 28.12.17; War Flt Seaton Carew W/E 9.2.18; South Shields W/E 10.4.18; COL after patrol 26.4.18 (pilot unhurt); Became 252 Sqdn South Shields 25.5.18 - @10.10.18; 453 Flt 248 Sqdn Hornsea by 15.10.18 - @30.1.19

N2100   Deld AD Killingholme for erection W/E 28.12.17; War Flt Seaton Carew 19.3.18; Became 252 Sqdn South Shields 25.5.18 - @30.1.19

N2101   Deld AD Killingholme for erection W/E 28.12.17; Seaton Carew 19.3.18; Dropped 65-lb bomb on U-boat 15m S of Hartlepool 25.3.18 (FSL EF Waring); South Shields 26.3.18; War Flt Seaton Carew 25.4.18; Dropped 65-lb bomb on U-boat SE of Sunderland 5455N 0114W 1.5.18 (Lt RR Richardson); Became 452 Flt Seaton Carew 25.5.18; Caught fire taxying, fuselage badly damaged 11.6.18 (Lt LCF Clutterbuck unhurt); South Shields W/E 20.6.18 - @30.1.19

N2102   Deld AD Killingholme for erection for Killingholme School W/E 19.1.18; Deleted W/E 27.4.18

N2103   Deld AD Killingholme for erection for Killingholme School W/E 28.12.17; CSD White City packing for Chilean Government W/E 24.5.18; Shipped to Chile W/E 22.7.18; Talcahuano 3.7.19 - .21

N2104   Due 29.11.17; Deld AD Killingholme for erection for Killingholme School W/E 28.12.17; CSD White City packing for Chilean Government W/E 24.5.18; Shipped to Chile W/E 22.7.18; Crashed into cruiser *O'Higgins* while taking off, Mejillones harbour, 8.20

N2105   Deld AD Killingholme for erection for Killingholme School W/E 19.1.18; Crashed in water 3.18 (PFSL GE Tugwell); Deleted W/E 5.4.18

N2106   Deld AD Killingholme for erection W/E 11.1.18; War Flt Seaton Carew W/E 22.3.18; South Shields 21.3.18; Seaton Carew W/E 27.3.18; Driven on to sandbank by strong wind while taxying, capsized on TO and sank Tees Fairway 27.4.18 (pilot unhurt); Deleted W/E 29.5.18

N2107   Deld AD Killingholme for erection W/E 11.1.18; War Flt Seaton Carew W/E 22.3.18; South Shields 20.3.18; Seaton Carew W/E 27.3.18; South Shields W/E 27.4.18; Seaton Carew 3.5.18; Became 452 Flt 252 Sqdn Seaton Carew 25.5.18; EF, FL Whitby, repaired 13.6.18; Bombed U-boat 2m SE of Whitby, then EF, collided with support of seaplane hangar, CW 27.7.18 (Lt LCF Clutterbuck shaken); South Shields W/E 8.8.18; 451/2 Flts 252 Sqdn Seaton Carew W/E 3.9.18; Deleted W/E 12.9.18

N2108   Deld AD Killingholme for erection W/E 19.1.18; War Flt Seaton Carew W/E 22.3.18; South Shields 20.3.18; Seaton Carew W/E 27.3.18; South Shields W/E 14.4.18; Seaton Carew 21.4.18; EF, FL Seahaven 13.5.18, dismantled to return; 252 Sqdn South Shields 25.5.18; Seaton Carew 24.9.18; EF, FL in sea 5m NE of Whitby, capsized by strong and gusty wind, damaged and salved 25.9.18 (pilot unhurt); South Shields W/E 7.11.18 - @30.1.19

N2109   Deld Killingholme for erection W/E 19.1.18; South Shields 22.3.18; War Flt Seaton Carew W/E 27.3.18; South Shields W/E 27.4.18; Seaton Carew 3.5.18; Dropped 65-lb bomb on U-boat 4m SE of Skinningrove 10.5.18 (F/L RR Richardson); Became 451/2 Flts Seaton Carew 25.5.18; South Shields 7.6.18; 451 Flt Seaton Carew 1.7.18 (246 Sqdn 15.8.18); Dropped 65-lb bomb on U-boat 5m SE of South Cheek, Robin Hood Bay 12.8.18 (Lt GE Taylor); Dropped 65-lb bomb on U-boat 5426N 0020W 27.8.18 (Lt LCF Clutterbuck); Collided with wreckage and damaged tail float 8.9.18; still 451 Flt 30.1.19

N2110   Deld AD Killingholme for erection 19.1.18; War Flt Seaton Carew 26.3.18; Dropped 65-lb bomb on U-boat 5m E of Sunderland, oil seen 6.4.18 (2/Lt EJ Addis); South Shields 21.4.18 (overhaul); Seaton Carew 1.5.18; EF, FL 12m E of Redcar, o/t and sank 1.5.18 (pilot picked up by *TB.741*); Deleted W/E 11.5.18

N2111   Deld AD Killingholme for erection W/E 19.1.18 (due 11.1.18); South Shields 24.3.18; War Flt Seaton Carew 22.4.18; Became 452 Flt 252 Sqdn Seaton Carew 25.5.18; EF, FL 4½m ESE of Tyne 27.5.18; Dropped 65-lb bomb on U-boat 10m SE of Sunderland, slight oil patch 30.5.18 (Lt EJ Addis); Dropped 65-lb bomb on U-boat 7m NNE of Whitby, oil seen 31.5.18 (Lt LCF Clutterbuck); Fog, EF, FL, collided with buoy on TO, badly wrecked off Tees, salved 20.6.18 (pilot slightly injured); Deleted W/E 27.6.18

N2112   Deld AD Killingholme for erection W/E 26.1.18; Hornsea 11.5.18; Became 453 Flt Hornsea 25.5.18 (248 Sqdn 20.8.18); EF, FL, badly damaged, picked up by trawler and taken South Shields 18.9.18; Still at South Shields 30.1.19

N2113   Deld AD Killingholme for erection W/E 25.1.18; to

Hornsea 4.18; Killingholme by 3.5.18; 453 Flt Hornsea 31.5.18 (248 Sqdn 20.8.18); South Shields W/E 23.1.19 - @30.1.19

N2114    Deld AD Killingholme for erection W/E 25.1.18; Yarmouth patrol (coded 'A') W/E 8.3.18; Became 454/5 Flts Yarmouth 25.5.18; HSMP 10.6.18; Deleted W/E 25.7.18

N2115    Deld AD Killingholme for erection W/E 25.1.18; Yarmouth patrol W/E 8.3.18; Tested 20.3.18; HSMPs 2.4.18 & 15.5.18 (Lt JC Grant); Became 454/5 Flts Yarmouth 25.5.18; Felixstowe 3.7.18; HSMP and HACP 12.8.18 (Lt JC Grant); 454/5 Flts Yarmouth 12.8.18 (229 Sqdn 20.8.18); Deleted W/E 10.10.18

N2116    Deld AD Killingholme for erection W/E 25.1.18; Yarmouth patrol W/E 8.3.18; Became 454/5 Flts Yarmouth 25.5.18; HSMP 10.6.18; EF, FL in sea, CW, returned by trawler *Isernia* 17.6.18 (pilot unhurt); Deleted W/E 27.6.18

N2117    Deld AD Killingholme for erection W/E 23.2.18; Yarmouth patrol W/E 8.3.18; Became 454/5 Flts 25.5.18 (229 Sqdn 20.8.18); Deleted W/E 12.12.18

N2118    Due 2.2.18; Deld CSD; Shipped to Malta 8.2.18; arr Calafrana for erection 3.18 - @8.18

N2119    Due 2.2.18; Deld CSD; Shipped to Malta 8.2.18; arr Calafrana for erection 3.18 - 4.18; HMS *Manxman* by 7.5.18 - @8.18; not listed by 9.18

N2120    Due 2.2.18; Deld CSD; Shipped to Malta 8.2.18; arr Calafrana for erection 3.18 - 4.18; HMS *Manxman* by 5.18 - @7.18; Calafrana by 8.18 - @10.18

N2121    Allocated Mkrs to Albert Dock for New York Exhibition 2.2.18; To USA 2.18

N2122    Due 9.2.18; Deld CSD; Shipped to Malta 12.2.18; Calafrana for erection by 24.4.18; HMS *Manxman* for deletion by 7.5.18

N2123    Due 9.2.18; Deld CSD; Shipped to Malta 17.2.18; Calafrana for erection by 24.4.18 - @10.18

N2124    Due 9.2.18; Deld CSD; Shipped to Malta 17.2.18; Calafrana for erection by 24.4.18; HMS *Riviera* 17.5.18; Calafrana 19.5.18 - @10.18

N2125    Allocated Brough store in case 9.2.18; Transferred to foreign government by 30.3.18

N2126    Allocated Brough store in case 9.2.18; Transferred to foreign government by 30.3.18

N2127    Allocated Brough store in case 9.2.18; Transferred to foreign government by 30.3.18

N2128    Allocated Brough store in case 9.2.18; Transferred to foreign government by 30.3.18

N2129    Allocated Brough store in case 9.2.18; Transferred to foreign government by 30.3.18

N2130    Allocated Brough store in case 9.2.18; Transferred to foreign government by 30.3.18
     [N2125 to N2130 possibly part of 20 Babies to Japan in 1918, or of 10 to Norway]

N2131    Deld CSD; Cardiff Docks by 6.1.18; Shipped to Port Said 13.3.18; Alexandria from/by 17.5.18; Became 270 Sqdn Alexandria 6.10.18; Deleted 30.4.19

N2132    Deld CSD; Cardiff Docks by 6.1.18; Shipped to Port Said 13.3.18; Alexandria by 5.18; Tested 12.5.18; To 269 Sqdn Port Said 12.18; 268 Sqdn Calafrana 27.8.19

N2133    Deld CSD 2.18; Shipped to Malta 13.3.18; arr Calafrana for erection 3.18 and retained to at least 10.18; 269 Sqdn Port Said by 8.19; 268 Sqdn Calafrana 27.8.19

N2134    Deld CSD 2.18; Shipped to Malta 13.3.18; arr Calafrana for erection 3.18; still there 10.18

**20 NORMAN THOMPSON N.T.4A "SMALL AMERICA" ANTI-SUBMARINE RECONNAISSANCE FLYING BOATS ordered under Cont Nos A.S.12528 (BR.63) & A.S.32477 from Norman Thompson Flight Co Ltd, numbered N2140 to N2159 & built Middleton-on-Sea. (Two 200-hp Hispano-Suiza)**

N2140    Deld Calshot W/E 7.12.17; Cattewater W/E 28.12.17; Deleted W/E 27.6.18

N2141    Deld Calshot W/E 23.11.17; EF, FL St.Catherines Point, towed to Calshot 26.11.17; EF, FL, towed Poole, lower starboard plane washed away by heavy seas 14.12.17 (Lt MO Fairhurst unhurt); Portland 2.1.18; Cattewater 7.1.18; Deleted W/E 27.6.18

N2142    Deld Calshot TS W/E 9.11.17; Deleted 2.3.18

N2143    Deld Calshot TS W/E 16.11.17; Deleted 2.3.18

N2144    Deld Calshot TS W/E 19.10.17; Deleted 2.3.18

N2145    Deld at Mkrs 15.12.17 for Cattewater (NTU); Deleted at Mkrs W/E 9.5.18

N2146    Deld at Mkrs 1.1.18; Cowes 13.3.18; Leaking radiator, FL Brixham 18.3.18; Torquay to Cattewater 20.3.18; Deleted W/E 27.6.18

N2147    Deld at Mkrs 19.1.18; Cattewater (via Portland) 5.4.18; Deleted W/E 27.6.18

N2148    Deld at Mkrs 2.2.18; Calshot by 30.3.18 for Cattewater (NTU); Deleted W/E 24.4.18

N2149    Deld at Mkrs 9.3.18; Newhaven by 30.3.18; Dover 7.4.18 (transit); MAD Grain 12.4.18; Deleted W/E 26.9.18

N2150    Deld at Mkrs 30.3.18; Killingholme Seaplane School W/E 20.4.18; Felixstowe Seaplane School 9.5.18; Deleted W/E 29.8.18

N2151    Deld at Mkrs 20.4.18; Westgate, towed from Ramsgate Harbour (transit) 4.5.18; Felixstowe Seaplane School W/E 25.5.18; Deleted W/E 29.8.18

N2152    Deld at Mkrs 4.5.18; Allocated Killingholme (NTU?)

N2153    Deld at Mkrs 11.5.18; Probably never reached RAF

N2154    Deld at Mkrs 18.5.18; Probably never reached RAF

N2155    Deld at Mkrs 25.5.18; Became G-EAOY

N2156    Probably not completed

N2157    Probably not completed

N2158    Probably not completed

N2159    Probably not completed

**20 FELIXSTOWE F.3 PATROL TRACTOR BIPLANE FLYING BOATS ordered under Cont No A.S.11426 (BR.22) from Handley Page Ltd, to be numbered N2160 to N2179. Renumbered N4160 to N4179**

N2160 to N2179 renumbered

**50 WIGHT CONVERTED RECONNAISSANCE TRACTOR BIPLANE SEAPLANES ordered under Cont No A.S.9336/17, numbered N2180 to N2229 & built East Cowes. (260-hp Maori)**

N2180    Deld Calshot TS 25.1.18; Became 210 TDS Calshot 6.18; Deleted W/E 11.7.18

N2181    Deld Calshot TS 26.1.18; Became 210 TDS Calshot 6.18; Deleted W/E 13.6.18

N2182    Deld Calshot TS W/E 2.2.18; Became 210 TDS Calshot 6.18; Deleted W/E 8.8.18

N2183    Deld Calshot TS W/E 8.2.18; Deleted W/E 13.6.18

N2184    Deld Calshot TS W/E 8.2.18; Became 210 TDS Calshot 6.18; Deleted W/E 11.7.18

N2185    Deld Calshot TS W/E 22.2.18; Became 210 TDS Calshot 6.18; ARS Calshot W/E 8.8.18; Deleted W/E 7.11.18

N2186    Deld Calshot TS W/E 22.2.18; Became 210 TDS Calshot 6.18; Deleted W/E 11.7.18

N2187    Deld Calshot TS 27.2.18; Became 210 TDS Calshot 6.18; Deleted W/E 8.8.18

N2188    Deld Calshot TS 27.2.18; Became 210 TDS Calshot 6.18; Deleted W/E 11.7.18

N2189    Deld Calshot TS 8.3.18; Became 210 TDS Calshot 6.18; Deleted W/E 11.7.18

N2190    Deld Calshot TS 14.3.18; Deleted W/E 13.6.18

N2191    Deld Calshot TS W/E 22.3.18; Deleted W/E 13.6.18

N2192    Deld 'C' Flt Calshot TS W/E 22.3.18; to 'B 'Flt 209 TDS Lee-on-Solent 4.18; Deleted W/E 11.7.18

N2193    Deld Calshot TS 22.3.18; EF, FL Lee-on-Solent 19.5.18 (FSL L Poulter); Became 210 TDS Calshot 6.18; Deleted W/E 11.7.18

N2194    Deld Calshot TS W/E 30.3.18; Deleted W/E 27.4.18

N2195    to N2199 delivered as spares

N2200    to N2229 cancelled

**30 FAIREY IIIB SHIPBOARD BOMBER TRACTOR BIPLANE SEAPLANES under Cont Nos 38a/392/C374 & A.S.16660 (BR.475) & numbered N2230 to N2259. (260-hp Maori II) [C/n's F.277 to F.306]**

N2230    Deld Grain 16.8.18 (type trials); 442 Flt 219 Sqdn Westgate, tested 9.11.18; Tested 26.11.18 (Mjr GE Livock); still Westgate 30.1.19

N2231    Deld 1(S)MAD Hamble W/E 17.10.18 - @30.1.19; HMS *Pegasus* (South Russia) by 11.20; shore base 2.11.20; HMS *Pegasus* 11.20 (to Malta 15.11.20, arr 18.11.20); HMS *Pegasus* 24.1.21; Calafrana 28.8.21

N2232    Deld 1(S)MAD Hamble W/E 10.10.18; Westgate W/E 17.10.18 - 6.19 (based Hastings from W/E 7.11.18; to Newhaven W/E 28.11.19 - @30.1.19); HMS *Pegasus* (South Russia) by 10.20; Shore base 10.20; HMS *Pegasus* 16.10.20; Shore base 2.11.20; HMS *Pegasus* 11.20 (to Malta 15.11.20, arr 18.11.20); HMS *Pegasus* 24.1.21; Calafrana 28.8.21

N2233    (IIIC) Deld 1(S)MAD Hamble W/E 19.9.18; Portsmouth W/E 17.10.18 (for Yarmouth - NTU?); 1(S)MAD Hamble W/E 24.10.18 - @30.1.19; Archangel by .19; Captured and used by Bolsheviks

N2234    Deld 1(S)MAD Hamble W/E 19.9.18; 408/9 Flts 242 Sqdn Newhaven W/E 17.10.18; Deleted W/E 28.11.18

N2235    Deld 1(S)MAD Hamble W/E 26.9.18; Newhaven W/E 17.10.18; ARS Westgate W/E 24.10.18; 408/9 Flts 242 Sqdn Newhaven W/E 31.10.18; Deleted W/E 21.11.18

N2236    Deld 1(S)MAD Hamble by 26.9.18; Mkrs W/E 17.10.18; 1(S)MAD Hamble W/E 14.11.18 - @30.1.19; Convtd IIIC; HMS *Ark Royal* (South Russia) by 26.9.21 - @2.3.22

N2237    Deld 1(S)MAD Hamble W/E 10.10.18; Mkrs W/E 17.10.18; 1(S)MAD Hamble W/E 24.10.18; 408/9 Flts 242 Sqdn Newhaven W/E 7.11.18; Deleted W/E 28.11.18

N2238    Deld 1(S)MAD Hamble W/E 3.10.18; Mkrs W/E 17.10.18; 1(S)MAD Hamble W/E 21.11.18 - @30.1.19; Convtd IIIC; Feneraki, Constantinople by 7.21 - @9.21

N2239    Deld 1(S)MAD Hamble W/E 10.10.18; Mkrs W/E 17.10.18; 1(S)MAD Hamble W/E 7.11.18 - @30.1.19; HMS *Pegasus* (South Russia) by 10.20; shore base 10.20; HMS *Pegasus* 16.10.20 (to Malta 15.11.20, arr 18.11.20); HMS *Pegasus* (coded 'Z') 24.1.21; Calafrana 28.8.21

N2240    Deld 1(S)MAD Hamble W/E 10.10.18; Mkrs W/E 24.10.18 - @30.1.19; Calafrana to HMS *Pegasus* 1.2.22

N2241    Deld 1(S)MAD Hamble W/E 10.10.18; Mkrs W/E 24.10.18; 1(S)MAD Hamble W/E 31.10.18 - @30.1.19; Convtd IIIC; HMS *Ark Royal* (South Russia) by 21.7.21; Feneraki, Constantinople by 7.21 - @9.21

N2242    Deld 1(S)MAD Hamble W/E 24.10.18 - @30.1.19

N2243    Deld 1(S)MAD Hamble W/E 17.10.18; Westgate 22.10.18 (transit); Felixstowe W/E 24.10.18; 442 Flt 219 Sqdn Westgate W/E 14.11.18 - @5.19; Convtd IIIC; HMS *Ark Royal* (South Russia) by 14.2.22 - @8.3.22

N2244    Deld 1(S)MAD Hamble W/E 17.10.18; Lee-on-Solent W/E 24.10.18 (for Yarmouth, but NTU); Deleted W/E 21.11.18

N2245    Deld 1(S)MAD Hamble W/E 17.10.18; Westgate 24.10.18; Yarmouth (via Felixstowe) 26.10.18-@30.1.19

N2246    Laid down as IIIB; Built as IIIC with 375-hp Eagle VIII (first conversion to this standard); Completed 9.18; Deld Grain 18.10.18 (type tests & balanced ailerons; performance with 4-bladed propeller 3.19 - 4.19); Allocated Cape-Cairo Flight (NTU?); Convtd landplane 6.20; AEE W/E 10.7.20 (performance and calibration); Gosport 15.7.20 (deck landing trials on HMS Eagle)

N2247    Deld 1(S)MAD Hamble W/E 17.10.18 - @30.1.19

N2248    Deld 1(S)MAD Hamble W/E 17.10.18 - @30.1.19

N2249    Deld 1(S)MAD Hamble W/E 17.10.18 - @30.1.19; Convtd IIIC; Feneraki, Constantinople by 7.21 - 9.21; HMS *Ark Royal* (South Russia) by 4.11.21

N2250    Deld 1(S)MAD Hamble W/E 24.10.18 - @30.1.19; Convtd IIIC; HMS *Ark Royal* (South Russia) by 29.6.21

N2251    Deld 1(S)MAD Hamble W/E 31.10.18; Newhaven 21.11.18 - @30.1.19 (for Yarmouth)

N2252    Deld 1(S)MAD Hamble W/E 31.10.18 - @30.1.19

N2253    Deld 1(S)MAD Hamble W/E 31.10.18 - @30.1.19; Convtd IIIC; HMS *Ark Royal* (South Russia) by 9.6.21 - @1.7.21

N2254    Deld 1(S)MAD Hamble W/E 7.11.18 - @30.1.19

N2255    Built as IIIB (375-hp Eagle VIII); Fairey Hayes 2.11.18 - @30.1.19 for trials; Became G-EAPV; To Sweden

N2256    Built as IIIB (375-hp Eagle VIII); Fairey Hayes 2.11.18 - @30.1.19 for trials as school machine

N2257    Built as IIIB (375-hp Eagle VIII); Fairey Hayes 9.11.18 - @30.1.19 for trials; Lee-on-Solent to HMS *Argus* 20.2.21; Lee-on-Solent 29.5.22

N2258    Built as IIIB (375-hp Eagle VIII); Fairey Hayes 9.11.18 - @30.1.19 for trials; Lee-on-Solent to HMS *Argus* 20.2.21; Lee-on-Solent 29.5.22

N2259    Built as IIIB (375-hp Eagle VIII); Fairey Hayes 11.18 - @30.1.19 for trials; Lee-on-Solent to HMS *Argus* 20.2.21; Lee-on-Solent 29.5.22

**100 NORMAN THOMPSON N.T.2B PUSHER BIPLANE FLYING BOAT TRAINERS ordered under Cont Nos 38a/554/C567 & A.S.24906/18 (BR.535), numbered N2260 to N2359 & built Middleton-on-Sea. (212-hp Arab)**

N2260    Deld 209 TDS Lee-on-Solent 2.11.18 - @30.1.19

N2261    Deld 209 TDS Lee-on-Solent 2.11.18 - @30.1.19

N2262    Deld 209 TDS Lee-on-Solent 9.11.18 - @30.1.19

N2263    Deld 209 TDS Lee-on-Solent 9.11.18 - @30.1.19

N2264    Deld 209 TDS Lee-on-Solent 16.11.18 - @30.1.19

N2265    Deld 209 TDS Lee-on-Solent 16.11.18 - @30.1.19

N2266    Deld AAP South Shotwick for store 23.11.18 - @30.1.19; Exported to Norway

N2267    Deld 209 TDS Lee-on-Solent 23.11.18 - @30.1.19

N2268    Deld 209 TDS Lee-on-Solent 23.11.18 - 10.19

N2269    Deld 209 TDS Lee-on-Solent 23.11.18 - @30.1.19

N2270    Deld 209 TDS Lee-on-Solent 3.12.18 - @30.1.19

N2271    Deld 209 TDS Lee-on-Solent 3.12.18 - @30.1.19

N2272    Deld 209 TDS Lee-on-Solent 3.12.18 - @30.1.19

N2273    Deld 209 TDS Lee-on-Solent 3.12.18 - @30.1.19

N2274    Mkrs 14.12.18 - @30.1.19 for SW Area

N2275    Still at Mkrs 30.1.19 for SW Area; To Norwegian Air Force as *N-12*, later *N-27*

N2276    Deld 209 TDS Lee-on-Solent W/E 9.1.19 - @30.1.19

N2277    Deld 209 TDS Lee-on-Solent W/E 9.1.19 - @30.1.19

N2278    Deld 209 TDS Lee-on-Solent 17.1.19 (JL Parker) - @30.1.19

N2279    Still at Mkrs 30.1.19 for SW Area

N2280    Still at Mkrs 30.1.19 for SW Area

N2281    Deld AAP South Shotwick 1.19; Possibly exported

N2282    Deld AAP South Shotwick 1.19; Exported

N2283    Still at Mkrs 30.1.19; To Japanese Government

N2284    Still at Mkrs 30.1.19; To Peruvian Air Force .19; Exhibited at Atlantic City Exposition 1919

N2285    Still at Mkrs 30.1.19; Exported

N2286    Still at Mkrs 30.1.19; To Esthonian Air Force 5.19

N2287    Still at Mkrs 30.1.19; To Esthonian Air Force 5.19

N2288    Still at Mkrs 30.1.19; To Norwegian Air Force as *N-13*

N2289    No information

N2290    Became G-EAQO; To Canada as G-CACG

N2291    Probably exported

N2292    Exported

N2293    To Peruvian Air Force .19

N2294    (Beardmore, later 200-hp Arab). Exhibited Harrods 1919

N2295    to N2359 cancelled 1.19

**30 FELIXSTOWE F.2A PATROL TRACTOR BIPLANE FLYING BOATS ordered under Cont No A.S.14154 (BR.80) from S.E.Saunders Ltd & numbered N2280 to N2304. Renumbered N4280 to N4309**

N2280 to N2304 renumbered N4280 to N4309

**3 FELIXSTOWE F.3 PATROL TRACTOR BIPLANE FLYING BOATS ordered under BR.80 from May, Harden & May & numbered N2305 to N2307. (230-hp Rolls-Royce)**

N2305 to N2307 In abeyance 16.7.17 (later cancelled)

**12 FELIXSTOWE F.3 PATROL TRACTOR BIPLANE FLYING BOATS ordered under BR.86 to be built by Malta Dockyard & numbered N2310 to N2321. Renumbered N4310 to N4321**

N2310 to N2321 renumbered N4310 to N4321

**24 CURTISS H.12 PATROL TRACTOR BIPLANE FLYING BOATS ordered under BR.106 from Curtiss & numbered N2330 to N2353. Renumbered N4330 to N4353**

N2330 to N2353 renumbered N4330 to N4353

**40 FAIREY CAMPANIA RECONNAISSANCE TRACTOR BIPLANE SEAPLANES ordered under Cont No A.S.18939 (BR.131), numbered N2360 to N2399 & built Hayes, erected & tested Hamble. (Eagle to N2374, remainder 260-hp Maori II) [C/n's F.180 to F.219]**

N2360 (Eagle IV) Deld Houton Bay for erection W/E 22.12.17; HMS *Campania* 30.1.18; lent Scapa 14.2.18; HMS *Campania* 19.2.18 - @23.6.18; Scapa by 27.6.18 - @30.1.19

N2361 (Eagle VI, VII or VIII) Deld Houton Bay for erection W/E 22.12.17; Scapa 21.2.18; Erecting HMS *Campania* 10.3.18; Scapa 11.3.18; HMS *Campania* 14.3.18; Houton Bay 14.5.18; HMS *Campania* 31.5.18; Retd in tow of drifter *N389* 26.8.18; Rosyth W/E 26.9.18 - @30.1.19

N2362 (Eagle VII) Deld Houton Bay for erection W/E 26.1.18; Scapa W/E 4.5.18; HMS *Campania* (coded 'PC4') 7.5.18; Wrecked, salved 23.9.18 (ship to Scapa); Deleted

N2363 (Eagle VIII) Deld Grain Type Test Flt 10.12.17 (handling and calibration); Tested 17.12.17; Calshot (via Westgate) 6.1.18; Portland 17.1.18; Dropped 2x230-lb bombs on suspected U-boat 5000N 0253W, oil seen 16.5.18 (Lt FDJ Silwood & Lt EA Sawyer); Became 416/7 Flts Portland 25.5.18 (241 Sqdn 20.8.18) - @30.1.19

N2364 (Eagle IV) Deld AD Dundee for erection 4.12.17; Fairey Hayes W/E 23.3.18 (repair); MAD Dundee W/E 29.8.18; HMS *Pegasus* 11.10.18; HMS *Campania* 29.10.18; HMS *Pegasus* 29.10.18; Dundee 8.12.18 - @30.1.19; To Russia with North Russian Expeditionary Force [ship?]

N2365 (Eagle VIII) Deld Grain Type Test Flt 12.12.17; Dover 12.2.18 (en route Newhaven); Calshot to Cherbourg W/E 22.2.18; Picked up French seaplane *CH2* which had been adrift all night 7.3.18 (FSL CS Mossop DSC); EF, FL, towed into Port en Bessin 11.3.18; Became 414/5 Flts Cherbourg 25.5.18; Became 414/5 Flt 243 Sqdn Cherbourg 20.8.18 - @30.1.19

N2366 (Eagle IV) Deld Dundee for erection 13.12.17; HMS *Pegasus* 8.3.18; Rosyth W/E 21.3.18; HMS *Campania* 17.7.18; Retd in tow of HMS *Violent* 5.9.18; Dundee 9.18; HMS *Campania* 15.10.18; Deleted W/E 28.11.18

N2367 (Eagle VIII) Deld Dundee for erection 18.12.17; HMS *Pegasus* 6.3.18; Rosyth 25.5.18; Turnhouse W/E 3.10.18; Rosyth W/E 21.11.18 - @30.1.19

N2368 (Eagle VIII) Deld Dundee for erection 20.12.17; HMS *Pegasus* (coded 'LB9') 6.3.18; Rosyth W/E 23.5.18; Deleted W/E 20.6.18

N2369 (Eagle VIII) Deld Dundee for erection 23.12.17; HMS *Pegasus* 6.3.18; Dundee (via Rosyth) 23.5.18 (stowed while ship in dock); HMS *Pegasus* 8.7.18; HMS *Campania* 26.10.18; HMS *Pegasus* 29.10.18; Dundee 8.12.18 - @30.1.19; 266 Sqdn Russia

N2370 (Eagle VIII) Deld Dundee by rail 1.1.18; Accepted 4.2.18; Rosyth 16.2.18; HMS *Nairana* 23.2.18; To Dundee 3.18; HMS *Nairana* to Rosyth W/E 4.4.18; HMS *Nairana* W/E 2.5.18; Rosyth by 27.6.18; HMS *Nairana* 6.7.18 (to North Russia) - @30.1.19

N2371 (Eagle VIII) Deld Dundee for erection 7.1.18; HMS *Pegasus* 20.2.18; Dundee 24.2.18 (stored during refit); HMS *Nairana* 3.4.18; Rosyth W/E 2.5.18; HMS *Nairana* 2.5.18; Rosyth by 23.5.18; Dundee by 13.6.18; HMS *Nairana* W/E 11.6.18 (sic); Rosyth W/E 11.7.18 - @30.1.19

N2372 (Eagle VI) Deld Houton Bay for erection 1.18 (still awaited 19.1.18); Scapa to HMS *Campania* 7.5.18; Scapa 10.5.18; HMS *Campania* 24.5.18; Deleted 11.18 (now Eagle VIII)

N2373 (Eagle VIII) Deld Houton Bay for erection 1.18 (still awaited 19.1.18); Scapa 4.5.18; HMS *Campania* 7.5.18; Wrecked 30.5.18, remains retd in SS *Snipe*; Rosyth W/E 29.8.18; HMS *Campania* W/E 19.9.18 - @31.10.18; Deleted 11.18

N2374 (Eagle VIII) Deld Brush 6.3.18 for erection and trials; Dundee W/E 28.3.18; HMS *Pegasus* W/E 4.4.18; Dundee 23.5.18 (storage, ship in dock); HMS *Pegasus* 8.7.18; Rosyth W/E 17.10.18 - @30.1.19

N2375 Deld Newhaven W/E 23.3.18 - 4.18; 416/7 Flts Portland 25.5.18 (241 Sqdn 20.8.18) - @30.1.19

N2376 Deld Calshot W/E 30.3.18; Became 410 Flt Calshot 25.5.18; ARS Calshot W/E 29.8.18; 410 Flt 240 Sqdn Calshot W/E 12.9.18 - @30.1.19

N2377 Deld Calshot W/E 30.3.18; Became 410 Flt Calshot 25.5.18 (240 Sqdn 20.8.18); Bembridge W/E 5.9.18; Deleted W/E 3.10.18

N2378 Deld Patrol Reserve Calshot W/E 30.3.18; 412 Flt Bembridge xx.5.18 (253 Sqdn 7.6.18); ARS Calshot W/E 31.10.18 - @30.1.19

N2379 Deld Patrol Reserve Calshot W/E 30.3.18 (later TS); Became 210 TDS Calshot 6.18 - @30.1.19

N2380 Deld Patrol Reserve Calshot W/E 30.3.18; 408/9 Flts Newhaven W/E 18.7.18 (242 Sqdn 20.8.18); Deleted W/E 3.10.18

N2381 Deld Patrol Reserve Calshot W/E 30.3.18; Hamble Sheds by 27.4.18; 210 TDS Calshot W/E 20.6.18; Patrol Reserve Calshot W/E 8.8.18 - @30.1.19

N2382 Deld Patrol Reserve Calshot W/E 11.5.18; Portland W/E 23.5.18; Became 416/7 Flt Portland 25.5.18 (241 Sqdn 20.8.18); Deleted W/E 12.9.18

N2383 Deld Patrol Reserve Calshot W/E 18.5.18; 412 Flt 253 Sqdn Bembridge 25.5.18; Deleted W/E 8.8.18

N2384 Deld Patrol Reserve Calshot W/E 11.5.18; Portland W/E 18.5.18; Became 416/7 Flts Portland 25.5.18 (241 Sqdn 20.8.18); 209 TDS Lee-on-Solent W/E 12.9.18; Deleted W/E 10.10.18

N2385 Hamble Sheds by 27.4.18 - @25.5.18; Deld Patrol Reserve Calshot by 13.6.18; 412 Flt Bembridge W/E 18.7.18; ARS Calshot W/E 31.10.18; 412 Flt 253 Sqdn Bembridge W/E 28.11.18 - @30.1.19

N2386 Deld Patrol Reserve Calshot 12.3.18; 416/7 Flts Sqdn Portland W/E 1.8.18 (241 Sqdn 20.8.18); ARS Calshot W/E 12.9.18; 210 TDS Calshot W/E 24.10.18 - @30.1.19

N2387 Deld Patrol Reserve Calshot 12.3.18; ARS Calshot W/E 29.8.18; 210 TDS Calshot W/E 17.10.18 - @30.1.19

N2388 Deld Patrol Reserve Calshot W/E 22.3.18; 412 Flt Bembridge W/E 6.6.18; Deleted W/E 25.7.18

N2389 Deld Hamble Sheds W/E 27.4.18; 210 TDS Calshot W/E 20.6.18; ARS Calshot W/E 7.11.18; Deleted W/E 12.12.18

N2390 Deld 410/1 Flts Calshot W/E 27.4.18; Deleted W/E 13.6.18

N2391 Deld Hamble Sheds W/E 27.4.18; Deleted W/E 29.8.18

N2392 Deld Hamble Sheds W/E 27.4.18; 408/9 Flts Newhaven W/E 27.6.18 (242 Sqdn 15.8.18); ARS Calshot W/E 14.11.18; Deleted W/E 5.12.18

N2393 Deld 1(S)MAD Hamble W/E 6.6.18; 210 TDS Calshot W/E 8.8.18 - @30.1.19

N2394 Deld Patrol Reserve Calshot 18.3.18; 414/5 Flts Cherbourg 25.5.18; 408/9 Flts Newhaven W/E 25.7.18 (242 Sqdn 15.8.18); COL 26.10.18; Deleted W/E 14.11.18

N2395 Deld Patrol Reserve Calshot 18.3.18; 410/1 Flts Calshot W/E 11.7.18; 210 TDS Calshot W/E 15.8.18; ARS Calshot W/E 12.9.18; 410/1 Flts 240 Sqdn Calshot W/E 10.10.18; ARS Calshot W/E 16.1.19 - @30.1.19

N2396 Deld 1(S) MAD Hamble W/E 13.6.18; 210 TDS Calshot W/E 18.7.18; ARS Calshot W/E 3.10.18; 210 TDS Calshot W/E 10.10.18; Deleted W/E 17.10.18

N2397 Deld 1(S)MAD Hamble W/E 20.6.18; 210 TDS Calshot W/E 1.8.18; Deleted W/E 29.8.18

N2398 Deld MAD Westgate 25.5.18; Bembridge (via Calshot) 7.6.18; 408/4 Flts Newhaven W/E 13.6.18 (242 Sqdn 15.8.18); Deleted W/E 19.12.18

N2399 Deld MAD Westgate and accepted 16.6.18; Calshot 17.6.18; 408/9 Flts Newhaven W/E 20.6.18; 210 TDS Calshot W/E 1.8.18; ARS Calshot W/E 12.9.18; 210 TDS Calshot W/E 28.by 11.18 - @30.1.19
[One unidentified a/c was coded 'X.L.8' in HMS *Pegasus*]

**50 FELIXSTOWE F.3 PATROL BIPLANE FLYING BOATS ordered 7.17 from The British & Colonial Aeroplane Co Ltd, to be numbered N2400 to N2449 & built Filton**

N2400 to N2429 cancelled and serials reallotted

**30 NORMAN THOMPSON N.T.2B PUSHER FLYING BOAT TRAINERS ordered from Norman Thompson under Cont Nos 38a/400/C396, A.S.14449 & A.S.17694/18 (BR.447), numbered N2400 to N2429 & built Middleton-on-Sea. (212-hp Arab)**

N2400 Deld at Mkrs 7.18; Grain 4.8.18 (Type & propeller tests); To be disposed of 8.20

N2401 Deld 1(S)MAD Hamble W/E 22.8.18; 209 TDS Lee-on-Solent W/E 29.8.18 - @30.1.19

N2402    Deld 209 TDS Lee-on-Solent 24.8.18 - @30.1.19

N2403    Deld at Mkrs 24.8.18; MAD Sherburn-in-Elmet 17.10.18 - @30.1.19

N2404    Deld at Mkrs 31.8.18; AAP Brockworth W/E 5.9.18 - @30.1.19 [still in transit 31.12.18]

N2405    Deld at Mkrs 31.8.18; AAP South Shotwick W/E 5.9.18 - @30.1.19

N2406    Deld at Mkrs 31.8.18; AAP South Shotwick W/E 5.9.18 - @30.1.19

N2407    Deld at Mkrs 31.8.18; AAP South Shotwick W/E 12.9.18 - @30.1.19

N2408    Deld at Mkrs 14.9.18; AAP South Shotwick W/E 19.9.18 - @30.1.19

N2409    Deld at Mkrs 14.9.18; AAP South Shotwick W/E 19.9.18 - @30.1.19

N2410    Deld at Mkrs 14.9.18; AAP South Shotwick W/E 19.9.18 - @30.1.19

N2411    Deld at Mkrs 21.9.18; AAP South Shotwick W/E 26.9.18 - @30.1.19

N2412    Deld at Mkrs 21.9.18; MAD Sherburn-in-Elmet W/E 3.10.18 - @30.1.19

N2413    Deld at Mkrs 21.9.18; MAD Sherburn-in-Elmet W/E 3.10.18 - @30.1.19

N2414    Deld at Mkrs 28.9.18; 3 AAP Norwich W/E 3.10.18 - @30.1.19

N2415    Deld at Mkrs 28.9.18; 3 AAP Norwich W/E 10.10.18 - @30.1.19

N2416    Deld at Mkrs 28.9.18; 3 AAP Norwich W/E 10.10.18 - @30.1.19

N2417    Deld MAD Sherburn-in-Elmet W/E 17.10.18 - @30.1.19

N2418    Deld MAD Sherburn-in-Elmet W/E 17.10.18 - @30.1.19

N2419    Deld MAD Sherburn-in-Elmet W/E 17.10.18 - @30.1.19

N2420    Deld MAD Sherburn-in-Elmet W/E 17.10.18 - @30.1.19

N2421    Deld 209 TDS Lee-on-Solent 5.10.18 - @30.1.19

N2422    Deld 209 TDS Lee-on-Solent 5.10.18 - @30.1.19

N2423    Deld MAD Sherburn-in-Elmet 5.10.18 - @30.1.19

N2424    Deld MAD Sherburn-in-Elmet W/E 17.10.18 - @30.1.19

N2425    Deld 209 TDS Lee-on-Solent W/E 7.11.18 - @30.1.19

N2426    Deld 209 TDS Lee-on-Solent W/E 24.10.18 - @30.1.19

N2427    Deld 209 TDS Lee-on-Solent W/E 7.11.18 - @30.1.19

N2428    Deld 209 TDS Lee-on-Solent 2.11.18 - @30.1.19

N2429    Deld 209 TDS Lee-on-Solent W/E 7.11.18 - @30.1.19

**30 TYPE? ordered under Cont No A.S.18936, numbered N2430 to N2459**

N2430 to N2459 cancelled and partially reissued

**50 A.D. PATROL PUSHER BIPLANE FLYING BOATS ordered from Pemberton-Billing Ltd under Cont No AS.18936 (BR.133), numbered N2450 to N2499 & built Woolston. (150/200-hp Hispano-Suiza, but stored without engines)**

N2450    Deld Newport store W/E 27.4.18 - @11.18

N2451    Deld Newport store W/E 27.4.18 - @31.12.18; Convtd to Supermarine Channel I as G-EAEG (c/n 975)

N2452    Deld Newport store W/E 27.4.18 - @31.12.18; Convtd to Supermarine Channel I as G-EAEF

N2453    Deld Newport store W/E 27.4.18 - @11.18

N2454    Deld Newport store W/E 27.4.18 - @11.18

N2455    No evidence of delivery

N2456    to N2461 cancelled 12.17

N2462    to N2499 cancelled [N2462 onwards may have been a separate contract]

**24 NORMAN THOMPSON N.T.2B PUSHER FLYING BOAT TRAINERS ordered 16.11.17 from S.E.Saunders Ltd under Cont No AS.22028/1/17 (BR.154), numbered N2500 to N2523 & built East Cowes. (212-hp Arab)**

N2500    Deld 209 TDS Lee-on-Solent W/E 21.11.18 - @30.1.19

N2501    (200-hp Hispano-Suiza) Deld Calshot TS 18.5.18; Calshot store W/E 18.7.18 - @30.1.19

N2502    Still at Mkrs 30.1.19

N2503    Mkrs for disposal by 31.12.18

N2504    Deld 209 TDS Lee-on-Solent W/E 12.11.18 - @30.1.19

N2505    Deld 1(S)MAD Hamble W/E 10.10.18; 209 TDS Lee-on-Solent 29.10.18 - @30.1.19

N2506    Deld 209 TDS Lee-on-Solent 5.10.18 - @30.1.19

N2507    Deld 1(S)MAD Hamble W/E 12.10.18 - @30.1.19

N2508    Deld 209 TDS Lee-on-Solent 19.10.18 - @30.1.19

N2509    Deld 1(S)MAD Hamble 26.10.18; 209 TDS Lee-on-Solent W/E 14.11.18 - @30.1.19

N2510    to N2514 deld by 1.1.19 but probably retained at Mkrs

N2515    to N2523 cancelled 6.19

**N2524 to N2529 not allotted**

**25 FELIXSTOWE F.2A PATROL TRACTOR BIPLANE FLYING BOATS ordered under BR.74 & BR.90 from The Aircraft Manufacturing Co Ltd & numbered N2530 to N2554. Renumbered N4530 to N4554 (Eagle VIII)**

N2530 to N2554 renumbered N4530 to N4554

**24 NORMAN THOMPSON N.T.2B PUSHER FLYING BOAT TRAINERS ordered under Cont No AS.25834/18 (BR.177), numbered N2555 to N2579 & built Middleton-on-Sea. (200-hp Hispano-Suiza unless otherwise stated)**

N2555    Deld Calshot TS 19.12.17; Deleted W/E 5.4.18

N2556    Deld Calshot TS 29.12.17; Calshot store W/E 4.7.18 - @30.1.19

N2557    Deld Calshot TS 15.1.18; Calshot store W/E 4.7.18; AAP Eastleigh W/E 25.7.18; AAP South Shotwick W/E 19.9.18 - @30.1.19

N2558    Deld Calshot 19.1.18; Calshot store W/E 4.7.18; AAP Eastleigh W/E 18.7.18; 209 TDS Lee-on-Solent W/E 25.7.18 - @30.1.19

N2559    Deld Dover (via Folkestone) 27.1.18; Tested then to Type Test Flt Grain 28.1.18 (type tests, propeller tests and fabric evaluation tests); Deleted W/E 12.12.19

N2560    Deld at Mkrs 2.2.18; Type Test Flt Grain 5.2.18 (type tests); For disposal 8.20

N2561    Deld at Mkrs 9.2.18; Calshot School W/E 8.3.18; Calshot store W/E 4.7.18; AAP Eastleigh W/E 18.7.18; AAP South Shotwick W/E 19.9.18 - @30.1.19

N2562    Deld at Mkrs 23.2.18; Grain 24.2.18; Calshot TS 24.2.18; Became 210 TDS Calshot 1.4.18; Calshot store W/E 4.7.18; AAP Eastleigh W/E 18.7.18; 209 TDS Lee-on-Solent W/E 25.7.18; Deleted W/E 7.11.18

N2563    Deld at Mkrs 23.2.18; Calshot TS W/E 8.3.18; Became 210 TDS Calshot 1.4.18; Calshot store W/E 4.7.18; AAP Eastleigh W/E 11.7.18; AAP South Shotwick W/E 19.9.18 - @30.1.19

N2564    Deld Calshot TS 2.3.18; Became 210 TDS Calshot 1.4.18; Calshot store W/E 4.7.18; AAP Eastleigh W/E 11.7.18; AAP South Shotwick W/E 19.9.18 - @30.1.19

N2565    Deld Calshot TS 9.3.18; Became 210 TDS Calshot 1.4.18; Calshot store W/E 4.7.18; AAP Eastleigh W/E 11.7.18; AAP South Shotwick W/E 19.9.18 - @30.1.19

N2566    Deld Calshot TS 16.3.18; Became 210 TDS Calshot 1.4.18; Calshot store W/E 4.7.18; AAP Eastleigh W/E 11.7.18; AAP South Shotwick W/E 19.9.18 - @30.1.19

N2567    Deld Calshot TS 23.3.18; Became 210 TDS Calshot 1.4.18; Calshot store W/E 4.7.18; AAP Eastleigh W/E 11.7.18; AAP South Shotwick W/E 19.9.18 - @30.1.19

N2568    Deld Calshot TS 23.3.18; Became 210 TDS Calshot 1.4.18; Calshot store W/E 4.7.18 - @30.1.19

N2569    First machine to have slewed engine installation; Deld Calshot TS 30.3.18; Became 210 TDS Calshot 1.4.18; Calshot store W/E 4.7.18 - @30.1.19

N2570    Deld Portsmouth 12.3.18; 210 TDS Calshot 6.4.18; Calshot store W/E 4.7.18; AAP Eastleigh W/E 11.7.18; AAP South Shotwick W/E 12.9.18 - @30.1.19

N2571    Deld Portsmouth 12.3.18; 210 TDS Calshot 13.4.18; Calshot store W/E 4.7.18; AAP Eastleigh W/E 11.7.18; AAP South Shotwick W/E 12.9.18 - @30.1.19

N2572    Deld 210 TDS Calshot 20.4.18; Calshot store W/E 4.7.18; AAP Eastleigh W/E 11.7.18; AAP South Shotwick W/E 12.9.18 - @30.1.19

N2573    Deld 210 TDS Calshot 27.4.18; Calshot store W/E 4.7.18; AAP Eastleigh W/E 11.7.18; AAP South Shotwick W/E 4.9.18 - @30.1.19

N2574    Deld 210 TDS Calshot 27.4.18 - @25.5.18; 209 TDS Lee-on-Solent by 13.6.18 - @30.1.19

N2575    Deld 210 TDS Calshot 4.5.18 - @25.5.18; 209 TDS

N2576    Lee-on-Solent by 13.6.18 - @30.1.19
Deld 210 TDS Calshot 4.5.18; Calshot store W/E 4.7.18 - @30.1.19

N2577    Deld 210 TDS Calshot 11.5.18; Calshot store W/E 4.7.18 - @30.1.19

N2578    (Arab) Deld 210 TDS Calshot 18.5.18; AAP South Shotwick W/E 26.9.18 - @30.1.19

N2579    (Arab) Deld 210 TDS Calshot 18.5.18; AAP South Shotwick W/E 19.9.18 - @30.1.19

**50 FAIREY CAMPANIA RECONNAISSANCE TRACTOR BIPLANE SEAPLANES ordered under BR.177 to be built by Robey & Co Ltd, Lincoln & numbered N2580 to N2629**

N2580 to N2629 cancelled

**30 SHORT ADMIRALTY 184 TYPE RECONNAISSANCE TRACTOR BIPLANE SEAPLANES ordered 12.17 under Cont No A.S.42581 (BR.318) from Brush Electrical Engineering Co Ltd, numbered N2600 to N2629 & to be built Loughborough. (260-hp Maori)**

N2600 to N2629 cancelled

**30 SHORT ADMIRALTY 184 TYPE RECONNAISSANCE TRACTOR BIPLANE SEAPLANES ordered 12.17 under Cont No A.S.42581 (BR.177 & BR.310) from Brush Electrical Engineering Co Ltd, numbered N2630 to N2659 & built Loughborough. (260-hp Maori)**

N2630    Deld Cattewater for erection 26.4.18; Tested 4.5.18; 418 Flt Torquay 27.7.18 (239 Sqdn 20.8.18) - @30.1.19

N2631    Deld Cattewater for erection 1.5.18; Accepted 4.5.18; Newlyn 10.5.18; Became 424/5 Flts Newlyn 25.5.18 (235 Sqdn 20.8.18); Dropped 2 bombs on U-boat 30.6.18; 418 Flt 239 Sqdn Torquay 6.1.19

N2632    Deld Cattewater 5.5.18 - @30.1.19

N2633    Left West India Docks in HMS *Vindex*; Ship arr Malta 4.6.18, arr Mudros 13.6.18; still HMS *Vindex* 5.7.18

N2634    Left West India Docks in HMS *Vindex*; Ship arr Malta 4.6.18, arr Mudros 13.6.18; still HMS *Vindex* 5.7.18; Talikna by 8.18; Probably one of ten Short seaplanes destroyed in enemy raid on Talikna 24.9.18

N2635    Accepted at Mkrs 15.5.18; Deld 406 Flt Westgate (via Yarmouth) 16.5.18 (219 Sqdn 22.7.18); Stalled from 150ft, wrecked 26.10.18 (2/Lt OMD Rochs & Sgt Gregory unhurt); Deleted W/E 14.11.18

N2636    Deld MAD Dundee W/E 15.5.18; Strathbeg 11.10.18 - @30.1.19

N2637    Deld MAD Dundee W/E 18.5.18; Strathbeg 14.9.18; Dundee 27.9.18; Crashed on TO 11.10.18 (Lt Clarke & O/L PA Sainsbury); Deleted W/E 17.10.18

N2638    Deld MAD Westgate W/E 21.5.18; Accepted 21.5.18; Killingholme W/E 24.5.18; South Shields W/E 31.5.18; 403 Flt Seaton Carew W/E 26.9.18; Killingholme W/E 12.12.18 - @30.1.19

N2639    Deld MAD Westgate 23.5.18; Accepted 23.5.18; South Shields (via Yarmouth & Killingholme) 25.5.18 (arr 26.5.18); 402/3 Flts 246 Sqdn Seaton Carew 28.8.18; Killingholme W/E 5.12.18 - @30.1.19

N2640    Deld MAD Westgate W/E 25.5.18; Accepted 30.5.18; Killingholme en route, caught fire after landing, slightly damaged 31.5.18 (Lt AH Pearce & AM Knight unhurt); South Shields 4.6.18; 402 Flt 246 Sqdn Seaton Carew 30.7.18; EF, FL 20m SE of Whitby, towed to Whitby 26.9.18 (repaired and retd 2.10.18); still Seaton Carew 30.1.19

N2641    Deld 400/1 Flts Dundee W/E 6.6.18; 400 Flt Strathbeg 14.9.18; 400/1 Flts Dundee 26.9.18 - @30.1.19

N2642    Deld MAD Westgate, accepted and to 406 Flt 219 Sqdn Westgate (coded '13') 6.6.18; Deleted 4.4.19

N2643    Deld MAD Westgate & accepted 9.6.18; Killingholme 11.6.18; South Shields 13.6.18; To Berwick but EF, FL off Newbiggin, towed back to base by motor boat 20.6.18; 402/3 Flts 246 Sqdn Seaton Carew 30.7.18 (246 Sqdn 15.8.18) - @30.1.19

N2644    Deld Dundee & accepted 15.6.18; 400 Flt Strathbeg 11.10.18; Dundee W/E 31.12.18 - @30.1.19

N2645    Deld MAD Westgate & accepted 16.6.18; Killingholme 20.6.18 (retd due to fog); Killingholme 25.6.18; South Shields 26.6.18; 402 Flt 246 Sqdn Seaton Carew 21.8.18

N2646    - @30.1.19
Deld MAD Westgate & accepted 19.6.18; Patrol Reserve Calshot 20.6.18; 412 Flt 253 Sqdn Bembridge W/E 27.6.18; Deleted W/E 12.12.18

N2647    Deld 6 SD Ascot W/E 27.6.18; Shipped from Newport Docks 23.7.18; arr Alexandria 12.8.18; Became 270 Sqdn Alexandria 6.10.18; 268 Sqdn Calafrana 27.8.19

N2648    Deld 6 SD Ascot W/E 27.6.18; Docks W/E 29.8.18; Shipped 19.9.18; arr 'X' AD Abu Qir 16.10.18; 431 Flt 269 Sqdn Port Said 21.10.18; 268 Sqdn Calafrana 27.8.19

N2649    Deld 6 SD Ascot W/E 27.6.18 for Gibraltar; Milwall Docks W/E 25.7.18; Shipped 8.18; Gibraltar by 9.18; HMS *Engadine* 1.10.18; Gibraltar 3.12.18; Recd 'X' AD Abu Qir 27.1.19; 269 Sqdn Port Said 4.2.19; 268 Sqdn Calafrana 27.8.19

N2650    Deld Patrol Reserve Calshot W/E 4.7.18; 253 Sqdn Bembridge W/E 18.7.18; Crashed on TO Bembridge 18.7.18 (FSL L Poulter & AM White); Deleted W/E 1.8.18

N2651    Deld MAD Dundee W/E 4.7.18; 430 Flt Houton Bay W/E 1.8.18 - @30.1.19 (detd Kirkwall 8.18)

N2652    Deld MAD Dundee W/E 11.7.18; 430 Flt Houton Bay W/E 8.8.18 (detd Kirkwall 8.18); Dropped 100-lb and 230-lb bombs on U-boat 31.8.18 (Capt HL Macro & Lt W Sanderson); still Houton Bay @30.1.19

N2653    Deld 6 SD Ascot W/E 11.7.18; Docks W/E 29.8.18; Shipped to Port Said 19.9.18; Recd 'X' AD Abu Qir 16.10.18; 431 Flt 269 Sqdn Port Said 29.10.18; 268 Sqdn Calafrana 27.8.19

N2654    Deld 6 SD Ascot W/E 11.7.18; Docks W/E 29.8.18; Shipped to Port Said 14.10.18; Recd 'X' Abu Qir 4.11.18; 270 Sqdn Alexandria 8.11.18; 268 Sqdn Calafrana 27.8.19;

N2655    Deld MAD Westgate & accepted 19.7.18; Patrol Reserve Calshot 20.7.18; 418 Flt 239 Sqdn Torquay by 29.8.18 - @26.1.19

N2656    Deld MAD Westgate & accepted 23.7.18; Calshot 30.7.18; 418 Flt 239 Sqdn Torquay 31.8.18; Bombed U-boat 29.8.18 (sic); still Torquay @30.1.19

N2657    Deld 426/7 Flts Fishguard W/E 18.7.18 - @30.1.19 (245 Sqdn 20.8.18)

N2658    Deld 426/7 Flts Fishguard W/E 18.7.18 - @30.1.19 (245 Sqdn 20.8.18)

N2659    Deld 426/7 Flts Fishguard W/E 18.7.18 - @30.1.19 (245 Sqdn 20.8.18)

**20 UNIDENTIFIED cancelled aircraft**

N2660 to N2679 cancelled

**30 F.B.A. TYPE B PUSHER BIPLANE FLYING BOAT TRAINERS ordered under Cont No A.S.16491 from Gosport Aviation Co Ltd, numbered N2680 to N2709 & built Gosport. (100-hp Gnome Monosoupape)**

N2680    Deld Woolston to Calshot W/E 23.11.17; Climbed too steeply, nosedived into water 12.12.17 (FSL JL Moran killed); Surveyed 13.12.17; Deleted 17.12.17 wrecked

N2681    Deld Woolston to Calshot W/E 16.11.17; Lee-on-Solent School W/E 23.11.17; COL, CW 22.12.17 (TFSL VH Littleboy killed); Surveyed 14.1.18; Deleted 17.1.18

N2682    Deld Woolston to Calshot W/E 30.11.17; Westgate 8.12.17 (transit); Type Test Flt Grain 14.12.17 (Handling and calibration); Killingholme School W/E 26.1.18; Deleted W/E 25.4.18

N2683    Deld Woolston to Calshot School 14.12.17; Lee-on-Solent W/E 17.1.18; Crashed in field Lee-on-Solent 30.1.18 (PFO E Bradley injured); Deleted W/E 21.2.18

N2684    Deld Calshot W/E 19.1.18; Lee-on-Solent School W/E 31.1.18; Became 209 TDS Lee-on-Solent 1.4.18; Deleted W/E 25.7.18

N2685    (Fitted DC) Deld Grain 14.12.17 (exptl); Calshot W/E 30.5.18; Westgate by 9.6.18; 209 TDS Lee-on-Solent W/E 13.6.18; Deleted W/E 8.8.18

N2686    Deld Calshot W/E 2.2.18; B Flt Lee-on-Solent W/E 21.2.18; Became 209 TDS Lee-on-Solent 1.4.18; Struck water landing, bounced, nosedived 30.5.18 (PFO GB Summers slightly injured); Deleted W/E 11.7.18

N2687    Deld Calshot W/E 8.2.18; B Flt Lee-on-Solent W/E

21.2.18; Became 209 TDS Lee-on-Solent 1.4.18; Deleted W/E 25.7.18

N2688    Deld Calshot W/E 8.2.18; B Flt Lee-on-Solent W/E 28.2.18; Became 209 TDS Lee-on-Solent 1.4.18; Deleted W/E 4.5.18

N2689    Deld Lee-on-Solent School W/E 27.3.18; Became 209 TDS Lee-on-Solent 1.4.18; Deleted W/E 25.7.18

N2690    Deld Calshot W/E 15.2.18; Lee-on-Solent School 10.3.18; Became 209 TDS Lee-on-Solent 1.4.18; Nosedived, wrecked 5.4.18, salved (PFO HC Lake killed); Deleted W/E 4.5.18

N2691    Deld Calshot TS W/E 27.4.18; 209 TDS Lee-on-Solent W/E 13.6.18; Deleted W/E 25.7.18

N2692    Deld Killingholme Reserve W/E 27.4.18; 209 TDS Lee-on-Solent W/E 13.6.18; Deleted W/E 26.9.18

N2693    Deld Killingholme Reserve W/E 27.4.18; 209 TDS Lee-on-Solent W/E 13.6.18; Deleted W/E 3.10.18

N2694    Deld 209 TDS Lee-on-Solent W/E 13.4.18; Deleted W/E 27.6.18

N2695    Deld Calshot TS W/E 4.5.18; 209 TDS Lee-on-Solent W/E 5.6.18; Stalled, nosedived, crashed on open ground, CW 5.6.18; Deleted W/E 25.7.18

N2696    Deld Calshot TS W/E 4.5.18; 209 TDS Lee-on-Solent W/E 13.6.18; Deleted W/E 25.7.18

N2697    Deld Calshot TS W/E 4.5.18; 209 TDS Lee-on-Solent W/E 13.6.18 - @30.1.19

N2698    For Brazilian Government by 30.3.18; Expected for trials 4.5.18

N2699    For Brazilian Government by 30.3.18; Expected for trials 4.5.18

N2700    Deld Calshot TS W/E 18.5.18; 209 TDS Lee-on-Solent W/E 13.6.18; Deleted W/E 8.8.18

N2701    Deld Calshot TS WE 25.5.18; 209 TDS Lee-on-Solent W/E 13.6.18; Deleted W/E 8.8.18

N2702    Deld Calshot TS W/E 18.5.18; 209 TDS Lee-on-Solent W/E 13.6.18; Deleted W/E 8.8.18

N2703    Deld Calshot TS W/E 18.5.18; 209 TDS Lee-on-Solent W/E 13.6.18; Deleted W/E 9.1.19

N2704    Deld Calshot TS W/E 18.5.18; 209 TDS Lee-on-Solent W/E 13.6.18 - @30.1.19

N2705    Deld Calshot TS W/E 18.5.18; 209 TDS Lee-on-Solent W/E 13.6.18; Deleted W/E 25.7.18

N2706    Deld 209 TDS Lee-on-Solent W/E 20.6.18; Drifted overland and sideslipped into ground 4.9.18 (PFO TJ Gardiner injured); Deleted W/E 3.10.18

N2707    Deld 209 TDS Lee-on-Solent W/E 20.6.18; Deleted W/.E 19.8.18

N2708    Deld 210 TDS Calshot TS W/E 27.6.18; 209 TDS Lee-on-Solent W/E 11.7.18; Sideslipped into water after TO 16.8.18 (F/Cdt WC Gaskin); Deleted W/E 19.9.18

N2709    Deld 210 TDS Calshot W/E 27.6.18; 209 TDS Lee-on-Solent W/E 11.7.18; Deleted W/E 8.8.18

**30 F.B.A. TYPE B PUSHER BIPLANE FLYING BOAT TRAINERS ordered under Cont No A.S.30729 (BR.226) from Gosport Aviation Co Ltd, numbered N2710 to N2739 & built Gosport. (100-hp Gnome Monosoupape)**

N2710    Deld 210 TDS Calshot W/E 27.6.18; 209 TDS Lee-on-Solent W/E 11.7.18 - @30.1.19

N2711    Deld 210 TDS Calshot W/E 27.6.18; 209 TDS Lee-on-Solent W/E 11.7.18 - @30.1.19

N2712    Deld 209 TDS Lee-on-Solent W/E 11.7.18 - @30.1.19

N2713    Deld 209 TDS Lee-on-Solent W/E 11.7.18; Deleted W/E 26.9.18

N2714    Deld 209 TDS Lee-on-Solent W/E 11.7.18; Hull collapsed after bounced on TO 6.7.18 (F/Cdt A Waller injured); Deleted W/E 8.8.18

N2715    Deld 209 TDS Lee-on-Solent W/E 11.7.18; Deleted W/E 14.11.18

N2716    Deld 209 TDS Lee-on-Solent W/E 11.7.18; Deleted W/E 29.8.18

N2717    Deld 1(S) MAD Hamble W/E 1.8.18; 209 TDS Lee-on-Solent 8.18; Sideslipped on turn, hit beach, nosed over 22.8.18 (PFO RO Cutler injured); Deleted W/E 12.9.18

N2718    Deld 1(S) MAD Hamble W/E 1.8.18; 209 TDS Lee-on-Solent W/E 15.8.18; Deleted W/E 31.12.18

N2719    Deld 1(S) MAD Hamble W/E 1.8.18; 209 TDS Lee-on-Solent W/E 15.8.18 - @30.1.19

N2720    Deld 1(S) MAD Hamble W/E 1.8.18; 209 TDS Lee-on-Solent W/E 22.8.18 - @30.1.19

N2721    Deld 1(S) MAD Hamble W/E 1.8.18; 209 TDS Lee-on-Solent W/E 22.8.18; Deleted W/E 5.12.18

N2722    Deld 1(S) MAD Hamble W/E 1.8.18; 209 TDS Lee-on-Solent W/E 22.8.18 - @30.1.19

N2723    Deld 209 TDS Lee-on-Solent W/E 22.8.18 - @30.1.19

N2724    Deld 209 TDS Lee-on-Solent W/E 22.8.18 - @30.1.19

N2725    Deld 209 TDS Lee-on-Solent W/E 22.8.18 - @30.1.19

N2726    Deld 209 TDS Lee-on-Solent W/E 22.8.18; Deleted W/E 3.10.18

N2727    Deld 1(S) MAD Hamble W/E 22.8.18; 209 TDS Lee-on-Solent W/E 29.8.18; Deleted W/E 7.11.18

N2728    Deld 1(S) MAD Hamble W/E 1.8.18; 209 TDS Lee-on-Solent W/E 29.8.18 - @30.1.19

N2729    Deld 209 TDS Lee-on-Solent W/E 29.8.18; Deleted W/E 14.11.18

N2730    Deld 209 TDS Lee-on-Solent W/E 29.8.18; Steep glide with engine full on, nosedived in 29.10.18 (1 killed); still on strength 30.1.19

N2731    Deld 209 TDS Lee-on-Solent W/E 5.9.18; Nosedived into sea 29.10.18 (F/Cdt WL James killed); Deleted W/E 14.11.18

N2732    Deld 209 TDS Lee-on-Solent W/E 5.9.18 - @30.1.19

N2733    Deld 209 TDS Lee-on-Solent W/E 12.9.18 - @30.1.19

N2734    Deld 209 TDS Lee-on-Solent W/E 12.9.18 - @30.1.19

N2735    Deld 209 TDS Lee-on-Solent W/E 12.9.18 - @30.1.19

N2736    Deld 209 TDS Lee-on-Solent W/E 26.9.18; Deleted W/E 7.11.18

N2737    Deld 209 TDS Lee-on-Solent W/E 26.9.18; Sideslipped and nosedived to ground 19.10.18 (F/Cdt JW Wood killed); Deleted W/E 31.10.18

N2738    Deld 209 TDS Lee-on-Solent 24.9.18 - @30.1.19

N2739    Deld 209 TDS Lee-on-Solent W/E 26.9.18 - @30.1.19

**20 NORMAN THOMPSON N.T.4A ANTI-SUBMARINE RECONNAISSANCE TRACTOR BIPLANE FLYING BOATS ordered under Cont Nos A.S.30729 & A.S.32477 (BR.225), to be numbered N2740 to N2759 & built Middleton-on-Sea. (Two 200-hp Hispano-Suiza)**

N2740 to N2746 cancelled 1.6.18
N2747 to N2759 cancelled 1.18

**25 NORMAN THOMPSON N.T.2B PUSHER BIPLANE FLYING BOATS ordered under Cont Nos A.S.34279/18 (BR.248) & A.S.10732 from Pemberton Billing Ltd, numbered N2760 to N2784 & built Woolston. (150 or 200-hp Hispano-Suiza)**

N2760    (200-hp) Deld at Mkrs Woolston 4.4.18; Calshot TS W/E 25.5.18; Calshot store W/E 4.7.18 - @30.1.19

N2761    to N2778 Deld Newport Store 5.8.18 - @30.1.19

N2779    to N2784 Deld to store (with Mkrs?) 5.8.18

N2785 to N2789 not allotted

**30 SHORT ADMIRALTY 184 TYPE TRACTOR SEAPLANES ordered under Cont No A.S.31674 from Brush Electrical Engineering Co Ltd, numbered N2790 to N2819 & built Loughborough. (260-hp Maori)**

N2790    Deld Fishguard 19.1.18; Became 426 Flt Fishguard 25.5.18 (245 Sqdn 20.8.18); Deleted W/E 12.9.18

N2791    Deld West India Docks by 29.12.17 - @19.1.18; Shipped to Mediterranean; En route Port Said 26.1.18; Erecting Port Said by 16.2.18; Became 431 Flt 269 Sqdn Port Said 6.10.18; Failed to climb on TO, stalled, floats struck stone breakwater, crashed in sea, sank in tow, Port Said 13.10.18 (FSL GF Hyams & Capt HW Eades unhurt); Deleted 15.10.18

N2792    Shipped to Mediterranean; En route Port Said 26.1.18; Erecting Port Said by 16.2.18; Became 431 Flt 269 Sqdn Port Said 6.10.18; 268 Sqdn Calafrana 27.8.19

N2793    Deld Dundee W/E 2.2.18; To Montrose, then sank 1.4.18; Deleted W/E 13.4.18

N2794    Deld Dundee by rail 28.1.18; Accepted 11.2.18; Became 400/1 Flts Dundee 25.5.18; Strathbeg 11.10.18; Crashed on TO 15.10.18 (2/Lt JE West & 2/Lt WG Leathwood both injured); Deleted W/E 7.11.18

N2795    Deld Dundee by rail 24.1.18; Fishguard for erection 2.2.18; Dropped 100-lb which failed to explode, and 1 100-lb bomb which exploded, on U-boat 5153N 0535W

29.4.18 (Lt ES Smith & 2AM FG Hayward); FL in fog, smashed tail float 10.5.18; Became 426 Flt Fishguard 25.5.18; Deleted W/E 29.8.18

N2796 Deld Fishguard W/E 1.2.18; CW landing in strong wind 13.5.18 (2 crew unhurt); Deleted W/E 25.5.18

N2797 Deld Cattewater 9.2.18; Newlyn 21.3.18 (transit); Tresco 23.3.18; Returning from patrol, fire caused by broken petrol pipe 10.5.18 (Capt CR Morrish DSC & Lt JL Feather both slightly burnt); Deleted W/E 22.5.18

N2798 Deld Cattewater 9.2.18; Newlyn 25.4.18; Became 424/5 Flts Newlyn 25.5.18 (235 Sqdn 20.8.18); 418 Flt 239 Sqdn Torquay W/E 16.1.19 - @30.1.19

N2799 Deld Cattewater 15.2.18; Became 420/1 Flts Cattewater 30.5.18 (237 Sqdn 20.8.28); 424/4 Flts 235 Sqdn Newlyn 2.9.18; 418 Flt 239 Sqdn Torquay W/E 16.1.19 - @30.1.19

N2800 Deld Dundee 15.2.18; Became 400/1 Flts Dundee 25.5.18; Dropped 2x230-lb bombs on U-boat 3.6.18 (FSL ECB Wright & OSL RB Hunter); 400 Flt Strathbeg 6.11.18; Dundee W/E 31.12.18 - @9.1.19

N2801 Deld Calshot patrol W/E 1.3.18; Bembridge W/E 16.3.18; Became 412 Flt Bembridge 25.5.18 (253 Sqdn 7.6.18); Deleted W/E 12.9.18

N2802 Deld Cattewater patrol 28.2.18; Became 420/1 Flts Cattewater 30.5.18; Deleted W/E 4.7.18

N2803 Deld CSD 2.18; Shipped HMS *Manxman* 9.3.18; Calafrana by 6.18; HMS *Manxman* by 7.18 - @9.18; 15 Group Mudros by 10.18 - @30.1.19; HMS *Manxman* by 13.11.18; (266 Sqdn?) Talikna by 1.19

N2804 Deld Calshot patrol 8.3.18; Newhaven W/E 13.4.18; Dropped 230-lb & 100-lb bombs on suspected U-boat 5043N 0020W 16.5.18 (Lt JFR Kitchen); Became 408 Flt Newhaven 25.5.18; Collided with house on seashore 16.7.18 (Lt JE Greenwell killed); Deleted W/E 8.8.18

N2805 Deld Calshot patrol 8.3.18; Cherbourg W/E 20.4.18; Became 414/5 Flts Cherbourg 25.5.18 (243 Sqdn 20.8.18) - @30.1.19

N2806 Deld Dover for erection 9.3.18; Flown 20.3.18; Became 407 Flt Dover 25.5.18 (233 Sqdn 31.8.18); Caught fire on TO returning from Calais 14.11.18 (Lt ID Richardson & Sgt Mech HAM Ball); still Dover 30.1.19; MAES Grain by 3.19; EF, FL off Edinburgh LV, taken in tow by HMS *Nizam* but CW 31.3.19 (Lt PR Crowe); SOC 7.4.19

N2807 Deld Westgate by rail W/E 9.3.18; Became 406 Flt Westgate 25.5.18 (219 Sqdn 26.7.18); Felixstowe 23.11.18; Westgate 8.12.18 - @24.12.18; HMS *Pegasus* 12.18 (briefly); 406 Flt 219 Sqdn Westgate by 3.1.19 - 25.1.19LM

N2808 Deld Dundee 16.3.18; Accepted 28.3.18; Deleted W/e 4.5.18

N2809 Deld Cardiff Docks by 4.18; Shipped HMS *Manxman* 13.4.18; Calafrana by 6.18; HMS *Manxman* 22.8.18 - @9.18; 15 Group Mudros by 10.18 - @30.1.19; HMS *Manxman* by 12-13.11.18

N2810 Shipped Cardiff Docks to Port Said 30.3.18; Port Said by 5.18; Alexandria by 12.5.18; Became 270 Sqdn Alexandria 6.10.18; 268 Sqdn Calafrana 27.8.19

N2811 Shipped Newport Docks 29.3.18; Arr Port Said by 16.5.18FM; EF at 100-150 ft, FL downwind in harbour, COL, u/c carried away, wreckage towed in by *ML240* 2.6.18 (Capt EM King & Lt AD Ferguson unhurt); Fuselage only in storage; Became 269 Sqdn Port Said 6.10.18; Deleted 1.5.19

N2812 Shipped Newport Docks 29.3.18; Arr Port Said by 5.18; Became 431 Flt 269 Sqdn Port Said 6.10.18; 268 Sqdn Calafrana 27.8.19

N2813 Shipped from Cardiff Docks for Mudros 10.4.18; Mudros by 6.18; HMS *Ark Royal* by 6.18 - 10.18; Mudros 10.18; HMS *Empress* 11.10.18; Mudros 30.11.18 - 12.18; Talikna by 2.1.19

N2814 Allocated Mudros 3.18; HMS *Vindex* at West India Docks 18.5.18 (arr Mudros 13.6.18); HMS *Ark Royal* by 8.18; HMS *Vindex* 17.8.18

N2815 Deld 4.4.18 for Taranto; Shipped 20.4.18; Talikna by 6.18; Tested HMS *Ark Royal* 21.7.18; Talikna 19.8.18 - @26.10.18; Possibly one of ten Short seaplanes destroyed in enemy raid on Talikna 26.9.18

N2816 Deld Cattewater 4.4.18; Tested after erection 25.4.18; HMS *Mantua* 28.4.18; Cattewater 18.7.18; HMS *Mantua* 1.8.18; Cattewater 10.9.18; HMS *Orotava*

29.9.18; French seaplane base Dakar 11.11.18; HMS *Orotava* 13.11.18; Calshot W/E 25.11.18; ARS Calshot W/E 12.12.18 - @30.1.19

N2817 Deld Cattewater 4.4.18; HMS *Mantua* 28.4.18; Cattewater 18.7.18; HMS *Mantua* 1.8.18; Cattewater 10.9.18; HMS *Mantua* 29.9.18; Cattewater 1.11.18; HMS *Mantua* 9.11.18; Cattewater 20.11.18 - @30.1.19

N2818 Deld Cattewater 4.4.18; 418 Flt 239 Sqdn Torquay W/E 15.8.18 - @30.1.19

N2819 Deld Yarmouth 12.3.18; MAD Westgate for erection 27.4.18; Accepted 2.5.18; Yarmouth 4.5.18; Became 324/6 Flts Yarmouth 25.5.18; Bombed U-boat but failed to explode 8.6.18 (Lt JG Simpson); HSMP 10.6.18; Deleted 29.8.18

## 30 SHORT ADMIRALTY 184 TYPE TRACTOR SEAPLANES ordered under Cont No A.S.31667/17 from Robey & Co Ltd, numbered N2820 to N2849 & built Lincoln. (260-hp Maori)

N2820 Deld Calshot for erection W/E 19.12.17; Newhaven W/E 22.2.18; Became 408 Flt Newhaven 25.5.18; Deleted W/E 11.7.18

N2821 Deld Calshot for erection W/E 19.12.17; Newhaven W/E 30.3.18; Became 408 Flt Newhaven 25.5.18 (242 Sqdn 15.8.18); ARS Calshot W/E 7.11.18 - @30.1.19

N2822 Deld CSD 11.17; Shipped to Port Said W/E 19.12.17; Erecting Port Said by 16.2.18; HMS *Empress* 9.4.18; Gibraltar 11.6.18; HMS *Engadine* 7.8.18; Gibraltar 29.11.18 - @12.18

N2823 In transit to Port Said 1.1.18; Erecting Port Said by 16.2.18; Tested after erection 30.3.18; Lost returning from convoy, fuel shortage, FL El Arish, u/c badly damaged in rough sea 23.8.18 (Lt GW Morey & 2/Lt LT Harris unhurt); Dismantled, retd Port Said by rail 27.8.18; EF, FL in sea, taxied then o/t and sank, TW 31.10.18 (FSL GF Hyams & 2/Lt CF Standish rescued by destroyer HMAS *Swan* and conveyed to Salonika); Deleted 4.11.18

N2824 Deld CSD 11.17; Shipped to Port Said 26.1.18; Port Said by 4.18; HMS *Empress* 14.4.18; EF, FL, towed to Port Said by HMT *Eroican* 19.4.18 (Lt GAA Pennington & Lt RC Kennedy both unhurt); Gibraltar 3.6.18; HMS *Engadine* 4.8.18; Gibraltar 24.9.18; HMS *Engadine* 10.12.18; Cattewater 20.12.18 - @30.1.19

N2825 Deld CSD 11.17; Cardiff Docks by 19.1.18; Shipped to Mudros 28.1.18; Suda Bay by 6.18 - @10.18; Mudros by 11.18 - @30.1.19

N2826 Deld Calshot for erection 19.1.18; Cherbourg W/E 15.2.18; Surveyed Calshot 6.3.18; Deleted 13.3.18 DBR

N2827 Deld Calshot 19.1.18 (W/T training for RN Signal School Portsmouth); Operating from, Newhaven, dropped 230-lb bomb on U-boat, oil seen 7.7.18 (Lt JB Ackroyd & Lt B Dangerfield MC); Deleted W/E 15.8.18

N2828 Deld Calshot for erection W/E 25.1.18; Tresco (via Milford Haven and Newlyn) 24.2.18; FL off Cornish coast, picked up 7.3.18 (2 crew unhurt); Fishguard by 3.18; Newlyn 17.3.18 (en route Tresco); Tresco by 20.3.18; Became 350/3 Flts Tresco 25.5.18; 424/5 Flts Newlyn 3.8.18 (235 Sqdn 20.8.18); Floats damaged TO in swell 11.8.18; 418 Flt 239 Sqdn Torquay W/E 9.1.19 - @30.1.19

N2829 Deld CSD 12.17; West India Docks 19.1.18; Shipped from Cardiff Docks to Mudros 2.6.18; HMS *Engadine* (based Malta) .18; Calafrana by 8.18 - @9.18; Talikna by 6.18 - @30.1.19; Syra 9.18

N2830 Deld Fishguard W/E 26.1.18; Became 426 Flt Fishguard 25.5.18; Dropped 230-lb bomb on U-boat 5208N 0552W (nr The Smalls), oil and bubbles seen 6.7.18 (Lt EA Eames & 2AM FG Hayward); Deleted W/E 29.8.18

N2831 Deld CSD 1.18; West India Docks by 23.2.18; Shipped to Mudros 10.4.18; Calafrana by 6.18; HMS *Engadine* 28.7.18; Gibraltar 4.8.18; Mudros by 10.18

N2832 Deld Cattewater 5.2.18; Dropped 230-lb & 100-lb bombs on U-boat 5003N 0315W 22.4.18 (Lt S Graham & Lt FR Allen); Became 420/1 Flts Cattewater 25.5.18 (237 Sqdn 20.8.18) - @30.1.19

N2833 Deld Patrol Reserve Calshot W/E 22.2.18; Cherbourg W/E 11.5.18; Became 414/5 Flts Cherbourg 25.5.18 (243 Sqdn 20.8.18); 241 Sqdn Portland W/E 5.12.18 - @30.1.19

N2834 Deld Calshot W/E 22.3.18; Cherbourg W/E 18.5.18;

N2835 | Deld Cardiff Docks 9.2.18; Shipped to Mudros 9.3.18; Otranto by 5.18 - @8.18; 435/6 Flts 263 Sqdn Otranto by 10.18; HMS *Vindex* by 1.19; Sebastapol by 4.19

Became 414/5 Flts Cherbourg 25.5.18 (243 Sqdn 20.8.18); Deleted W/E 12.9.18

N2836 | Deld Cattewater 9.2.18; Dropped 230-lb bomb which failed to exploded, and 100-lb exploded, on U-boat 5018N 0322W 9.5.18 (Ens Macauley USN & 3AM W/T Hibberth); Became 420/1 Flts Cattewater 25.5.18 (237 Sqdn 20.8.18) - 30.1.19

N2837 | Deld CSD 1.18; Cardiff Docks 16.2.18; Shipped to Mudros 16.3.18; Syra by 6.18 - @30.1.19

N2838 | Deld CSD 1.18; Cardiff Docks 23.2.18; Shipped to Port Said 8.3.18; Port Said by 5.18; Alexandria by 11.6.18 - 10.18; 431 Flt 269 Sqdn Port Said by 2.11.18; 270 Sqdn Alexandria by 25.11.18 (test); 431 Flt 269 Sqdn Port Said 10.2.19; 270 Sqdn Alexandria 13.2.19; 431 Flt 269 Sqdn Port Said 2.19; 268 Sqdn Calafrana 27.8.19; HMS *Ark Royal* 2.3.20; Calafrana 5.3.20

N2839 | Deld Killingholme patrol W/E 4.3.18 (and Hornsea); Deleted W/E 27.6.18

N2840 | Deld CSD 2.18; Shipped to Mudros 9.3.18; Otranto by 6.18; Became 435/6 Flts 263 Sqdn Otranto 27.9.18 - @10.18; HMS *Vindex* by 1.19

N2841 | Deld CSD 2.18; Cardiff Docks by 23.2.18; Shipped to Mudros 9.3.18; Otranto by 6.18; Became 435/6 Flts 263 Sqdn Otranto 27.9.18 - @10.18; Mudros by 1.19

N2842 | Deld Fishguard for erection W/E 9.3.18; Became 426 Flt Fishguard 25.5.18 (245 Sqdn 20.8.18); Deleted W/E 10.10.18

N2843 | Deld Fishguard for erection 9.3.18; HSMP, fired on by U-boat 6.3.18 (pilot & AM2 FG Hayward); Became 426 Flt Fishguard 25.5.18; Visited Wexford 28.7.18; Became 426 Flt 245 Sqdn Fishguard 20.8.18 - @30.1.19

N2844 | Deld AD Killingholme 12.3.18; Killingholme Training Division 4.4.18; FL off Whitby and damaged 14.5.18 (Ens Phelan Allen USN); Reached South Shields 19.5.18; Killingholme 5.18; 252 Sqdn South Shields, picked up at sea and towed in by trawler 25.5.18; Deleted W/E 13.6.18

N2845 | Deld Cattewater without engine 21.3.18; Became 420/1 Flts Cattewater 25.5.18 (237 Sqdn 20.8.18) - @30.1.19

N2846 | Deld AD Killingholme W/E 22.3.18; Westgate (via Yarmouth) 7.4.18; Cattewater 12.4.18; Became 420/1 Flts Cattewater 25.5.18; 418 Flt 239 Sqdn Torquay W/E 1.8.18 - @30.1.19

N2847 | Deld AD Grain 23.3.18; Left Grain for Alexandria 4.4.18; Shipped from Royal Albert Docks 7.5.18; Arr Port Said 25.6.18; Smashed float on landing 31.8.18 (Lt G Waugh & 2/Lt WT Ward); Became 431 Flt 269 Sqdn Port Said 6.10.18; 268 Sqdn Calafrana 27.8.19

N2848 | Deld AD Grain 23.3.18; Left Grain for Alexandria 4.4.18; Shipped from Royal Albert Docks 7.5.18; Alexandria, EF, FL in sea, CW 14.7.18 (Lt GAF Hudson & observer injured); Deleted 64 Wing 1.8.18

N2849 | Deld AD Grain 23.3.18; Left Grain for Alexandria 4.4.18; Shipped from Royal Albert Docks 7.5.18; Erecting Port Said by 29.6.18; Became 431 Flt 269 Sqdn Port Said 6.10.18; 268 Sqdn Calafrana 27.8.19

**50 FAIREY IIIA SHIPBORNE RECONNAISSANCE TRACTOR BIPLANES ordered under Cont No A.S.35160 (BR.257), numbered N2850 to N2899 & built Hayes. N2853 to N2862 fitted skid u/c. N2864 to N2874, and possibly N2875 to N2888, fitted skid u/c and air bags. N2889 to N2899 fitted wheel undercarriage. (260-hp Maori II)**
C/n's F.220 to F.269]
[Some to Luce Bay in 10.18] [N2853 - N2877, N2882 intended for Turnhouse, but probably never reached there]

N2850 | Deld AES Martlesham Heath 30.4.18 (performance); U/c and wings changed W/E 27.7.18; Grain 18.9.18 (type trials); 523 Flt 258 Sqdn Luce Bay W/E 21.11.18; Deleted W/E 19.12.18

N2851 | Deld MAD Grain W/E 18.5.18 (conversion); Crashed on nose 17.5.18 (repaired); On delivery, overshot on attempting to gain height, crashed, WO Hylton 14.7.18 (Capt AL Simms DoI)

N2852 | Deld Grain 18.5.18 (conversion) (type test, also castor and mineral oil tests) to at least 1.19

N2853 | Deld 6 AAP Renfrew W/E 25.5.18 - @31.12.18

N2854 | Deld 6 AAP Renfrew W/E 25.5.18 - @31.12.18
N2855 | Deld 6 AAP Renfrew W/E 25.5.18 - @31.12.18
N2856 | Deld 6 AAP Renfrew W/E 25.5.18 - @31.12.18
N2857 | Deld 6 AAP Renfrew W/E 25.5.18 - @31.12.18
N2858 | Deld 6 AAP Renfrew W/E 25.5.18 - @31.12.18
N2859 | Deld 6 AAP Renfrew W/E 25.5.18 - @31.12.18
N2860 | Deld 6 AAP Renfrew W/E 25.5.18 - @31.12.18
N2861 | Deld 6 AAP Renfrew W/E 6.6.18 - @31.12.18
N2862 | Deld 6 AAP Renfrew W/E 6.6.18 - @31.12.18
N2863 | (Skid u/c, 6 air bags and a hydrovane) Deld 6 AAP Renfrew by 13.6.18 - @31.12.18
N2864 | Deld 6 AAP Renfrew W/E 13.6.18 - @31.12.18
N2865 | Deld 6 AAP Renfrew W/E 13.6.18 - @31.12.18
N2866 | Deld 6 AAP Renfrew W/E 13.6.18 - @31.12.18
N2867 | Deld 6 AAP Renfrew W/E 20.6.18 - @31.12.18
N2868 | Deld 6 AAP Renfrew W/E 13.6.18 - @31.12.18
N2869 | Deld 6 AAP Renfrew W/E 20.6.18 - @31.12.18
N2870 | Deld 6 AAP Renfrew W/E 27.6.18 - @31.12.18
N2871 | Deld 6 AAP Renfrew W/E 27.6.18 - @31.12.18
N2872 | Deld 6 AAP Renfrew W/E 27.6.18 - @31.12.18
N2873 | Deld 6 AAP Renfrew W/E 27.6.18 - @31.12.18
N2874 | Deld 6 AAP Renfrew W/E 27.6.18 - @31.12.18
N2875 | Deld 6 AAP Renfrew W/E 27.6.18 - @31.12.18
N2876 | Allotted RAE 9.9.18 (for engine tests, but not arrived by 30.1.19); Became three-seater G-EADZ; Convtd to IIIC and re-regd G-EAMY; To Sweden
N2877 | Deld 6 AAP Renfrew by 10.18 - @21.11.18
N2878 | Deld 6 AAP Renfrew by 10.18 - @31.12.18
N2879 | Deld 6 AAP Renfrew by 10.18 - @31.12.18
N2880 | Deld 6 AAP Renfrew by 10.18 - @31.12.18
N2881 | Deld 6 AAP Renfrew by 26.9.18 - @19.12.18
N2882 | Deld 6 AAP Renfrew by 26.9.18 - @19.12.18
N2883 | Deld 6 AAP Renfrew W/E 25.7.18 - @31.12.18
N2884 | Deld 6 AAP Renfrew W/E 25.7.18 - @31.12.18
N2885 | Deld 6 AAP Renfrew W/E 25.7.18 - 11.18
N2886 | Deld 6 AAP Renfrew W/E 25.7.18 - @31.12.18
N2887 | Deld 6 AAP Renfrew W/E 25.7.18 - @31.12.18
N2888 | Deld 6 AAP Renfrew W/E 25.7.18 - @31.12.18
N2889 | Deld 6 AAP Renfrew W/E 25.7.18; Turnhouse W/E 15.8.18 - @30.1.19
N2890 | Deld 6 AAP Renfrew W/E 1.8.18 - @31.12.18
N2891 | Deld 6 AAP Renfrew W/E 1.8.18; Turnhouse W/E 26.9.18; Deleted W/E 19.12.18
N2892 | Deld 6 AAP Renfrew W/E 1.8.18 - @31.12.18
N2893 | Deld 6 AAP Renfrew W/E 8.8.18 - @31.12.18
N2894 | Deld 6 AAP Renfrew W/E 8.8.18 - @31.12.18
N2895 | Deld 6 AAP Renfrew W/E 15.8.18 - @31.12.18
N2896 | Deld 6 AAP Renfrew W/E 15.8.18 - @31.12.18
N2897 | Deld 6 AAP Renfrew W/E 15.8.18 - @31.12.18
N2898 | Deld 6 AAP Renfrew W/E 15.8.18 - @31.12.18
N2899 | Deld 6 AAP Renfrew W/E 22.8.18 - @31.12.18

**50 SHORT ADMIRALTY 184 TYPE RECONNAISSANCE TRACTOR BIPLANE SEAPLANES ordered under Cont Nos A.S.37022/17 & A.S.9791/18 (BR.266) from Robey & Co Ltd, numbered N2900 to N2949 & built Lincoln. (260-hp Maori)**

N2900 | Deld Calshot W/E 5.4.18; Cherbourg W/E 30.4.18; Became 414/5 Flts Cherbourg 25.5.18 (243 Sqdn 20.8.18) - @30.1.19

N2901 | Deld AD Killingholme 12.3.18; Yarmouth W/E 4.4.18; Became 428/9 Flts Yarmouth 25.5.18; Felixstowe W/E 15.8.18; 428/9 Flts 229 Sqdn Yarmouth W/E 12.9.18 - @30.1.19

N2902 | Deld AD Killingholme W/E 8.3.18; Yarmouth 12.3.18; Fuel shortage, FL on sea, taken in tow minesweeper but sunk in rough sea off Winterton 3.5.18; Deleted W/E 11.5.18

N2903 | Deld Calshot 12.3.18; Shipped to Alexandria 24.4.18; Alexandria by 5.18; Port Said 5.6.18; Spun in from 200 ft nr 8-mile buoy Port Said 16.6.18 (Lt GW Murray & Lt FA Gill picked up by *ML242*, both injured); Deleted 25.6.18

N2904 | Deld Calshot 12.3.18; Shipped from Avonmouth 1.5.18; Alexandria by 11.6.18; Became 270 Sqdn Alexandria 6.10.18; 431 Flt 269 Sqdn Port Said 24.11.18; 270 Sqdn Alexandria 27.11.18; Searching for missing N1757, EF, FL in heavy sea, wrecked, Marsa Kheneine 1.8.19 (Lt EE Smith & 2/Lt RAG Beschen-Kawsky); Deleted 4.8.19

N2905 | Deld Calshot 12.3.18; Shipped from Avonmouth 1.5.18;

Alexandria by 9.6.18; FL in sea El Amariah, 40m W of Alexandria 30.7.18 (2/Lt LF Hill); SOC 1.8.18

N2906   Deld Calshot 12.3.18; Barry Docks by 27.4.18; Shipped from Cardiff 25.5.18; Otranto by 6.18; Became 435/6 Flts 263 Sqdn Otranto 27.9.18; HMS *Riviera* 12.11.18; Mudros 30.11.18 - @30.1.19

N2907   Deld Fishguard W/E 20.4.18; Became 426 Flt Fishguard 25.5.18 (245 Sqdn 20.8.18); Deleted W/E 7.11.18

N2908   Deld Fishguard W/E 20.4.18; Became 426 Flt Fishguard 25.5.18 (245 Sqdn 20.8.18); Bombed suspected U-boat 3.9.18 (pilot & AM2 FG Hayward); Deleted W/E 17.10.18

N2909   Deld Calshot TS W/E 27.4.18; Became 210 TDS Calshot 6.18; Deleted W/E 29.8.18

N2910   At Devonport by 25.5.18; Shipped to Malta 29.6.18; NFT

N2911   At Devonport by 25.5.18; Shipped to Malta 29.6.18; Syra by 6.18; HMS *Ark Royal* by 8.18; Syra 7.8.18; HMS *Vindex* 21.11.18; Talikna 12.12.18; Syra by 30.1.19

N2912   Allotted Malta 4.18; At Devonport 25.5.18; Shipped to Malta 29.6.18; Talikna by 10.18; Detd Sqdn Thasos by 28.10.18; HMS *Empress* to 13.11.18 (at San Stephano); Tested Mudros 30.11.18 for HMS *Campania*

N2913   Deld Cattewater 3.5.18; Became 421 Flt Cattewater 25.5.18 (237 Sqdn 20.8.18); Dropped 230-lb bomb on U-boat 4933N 0440W 0915 8.8.18 (Lt SG Robinson & Lt J Whitehead); still Cattewater 30.1.19

N2914   At Devonport by 25.5.18; Shipped to Malta 29.6.18; HMS *Campania*; HMS *Ark Royal* by 6.18; HMS *Engadine* at Gibraltar 24.9.18 (N2944 intended?)

N2915   Shipped from West India Docks to Gibraltar in HMS *Vindex* 18.5.18; HMS *Empress* 31.5.18; Gibraltar 13.7.18; HMS *Empress* 18.7.18; Gibraltar 3.8.18; HMS *Engadine* by 19.8.18; Gibraltar by 6.9.18; HMS *Engadine* by 10.18; Gibraltar to 431 Flt 269 Sqdn Port Said 4.2.19; Calafrana to 269 Sqdn Port Said 12.8.19; Deleted 12.8.19

N2916   Deld Barry Docks by 25.5.18; Shipped 14.6.18; Calafrana by 7.18; HMS *Engadine* 28.7.18; Gibraltar 12.8.18; HMS *Engadine* 19.8.18 - @9.1.19LM; Cattewater by 30.1.19

N2917   Deld Newport Docks W/E 11.5.18; Shipped to Port Said 29.5.18; Alexandria by 30.6.18; Became 270 Sqdn Alexandria 6.10.18; Deleted 13.6.19 ('Dover' Type)

N2918   Deld Cattewater W/E 18.5.18; Became 421 Flt Cattewater 25.5.18 (237 Sqdn 20.8.18); 418 Flt 239 Sqdn Torquay 29.8.18; Deleted W/E 30.1.19

N2919   Deld Cattewater 23.5.18; 424/5 Flts Newlyn (via Falmouth) 29.5.18 (235 Sqdn 20.8.18); 418 Flt 239 Sqdn Torquay 6.1.19 - @30.1.19

N2920   Deld Cattewater W/E 18.5.18; Dropped 230-lb & 100-lb bombs on U-boat 5008N 0350W 0650 12.8.18 (2/Lt AH Partner & 3AM LW Barber); Deleted W/E 29.8.18

N2921   Deld MAD Westgate W/E 25.5.18; Accepted 30.5.18; 406 Flt Westgate 6.18; EF, FL 4m NE of Tongue LV, towed to Westgate 17.6.18; EF, FL 3½m ENE of North Foreland, sank, salved by trawler *TB.90* 2.8.18 (Lt J Prescott & Sgt Pitt rescued by trawler *Aries II*) ; Deleted W/E 12.9.18

N2922   Deld MAD Westgate W/E 25.5.18; Accepted 10.6.18; Killingholme 10.6.18 (transit); South Shields 11.6.18; 404/5 Flts 248 Sqdn Hornsea 11.8.18 - @30.1.19

N2923   Deld 421 Flt Cattewater W/E 6.6.18 (237 Sqdn 20.8.18) - @30.1.19

N2924   Deld 421 Flt Cattewater W/E 6.6.18; 424/5 Flts 235 Sqdn Newlyn 19.7.18; 418 Flt 239 Sqdn Torquay 30.12.18 - @30.1.19

N2925   Deld 421 Flt Cattewater W/E 13.6.18 (235 Sqdn 20.8.18); EF on TO, FL crosswind, crashed 3.10.18 (2 crew unhurt); Deleted W/E 24.10.18

N2926   Deld Cattewater W/E 13.6.18; 424/5 Flts 235 Sqdn Newlyn 17.6.18; 418 Flt 239 Sqdn Torquay 30.12.18 - @30.1.19

N2927   Deld MAD Westgate W/E 13.6.18; Accepted 16.6.18; 406 Flt Westgate 6.18; With N2937 and 2 Camels attacked by 7 German seaplanes, shot down in sea 4m SE of Kentish Knock by Brandenburg seaplane, BO 18.7.18 (Lt JAH Pegram & 2/Lt LA Thrower both killed); Deleted W/E 25.7.18

N2928   Deld MAD Westgate W/E 13.6.18; Accepted 16.6.18;

Dover 19.6.18 (en route Calshot); 408/9 Flts Newhaven 20.6.18; Calshot, crashed in sea 4.7.18; 412 Flt 253 Sqdn Bembridge W/E 11.7.18; Landed Cherbourg 25.7.18, retd; Stalled and crashed on turning to land 27.10.18 (2/Lt JHC Wake seriously injured & Sgt AA Smith slightly injured); Deleted W/E 21.11.18

N2929   Deld 6 SD Ascot W/E 13.6.18; Shipped 14.7.18; Calafrana by 8.18; HMS *Riviera* 19.9.18; Taranto 5.10.18; 435/6 Flts 263 Sqdn Otranto by 11.18; HMS *Riviera* 12.11.18; Mudros 30.11.18 - @30.1.19

N2930   Deld 6 SD Ascot W/E 13.6.18; Shipped 14.7.18; Calafrana 8.18; HMS *Riviera* 19.9.18; 435/6 Flts 263 Sqdn Otranto 5.10.18; HMS *Riviera* 12.11.18; Mudros 30.11.18 - @30.1.19

N2931   Deld 6 SD Ascot for Malta W/E 20.6.18; Shipped 14.7.18; HMS *Ark Royal* by 7.18; Mudros 10.18; HMS *Riviera* 12.10.18; Mudros 14.10.18; Talikna by 13-14.11.18

N2932   Deld 6 SD Ascot for Malta W/E 20.6.18; Salford Docks for Malta by 25.7.18; Shipped 1.8.18; Calafrana by 9.18

N2933   Deld 6 SD Ascot for Malta W/E 20.6.18; Shipped 14.7.18; HMS *Ark Royal* by 7.18; Mudros 10.18; HMS *Riviera* 12.10.18; Mudros 14.10.18; Talikna by 27.10.18 - @15.11.18; Mudros by 11.18; HMS *Ark Royal* by 1.19

N2934   Deld 6 SD Ascot for Malta W/E 27.6.18; Shipped 14.7.18; HMS *Ark Royal* by 7.18; Mudros 10.18; HMS *Riviera* 3.10.18; Mudros 14.10.18; Talikna by 28.10.18 - @15.11.18; HMS *Ark Royal* by 1.19

N2935   Deld 6 SD Ascot for Malta W/E 27.6.18; Salford Docks for Malta by 25.7.18; Shipped 1.8.18; Calafrana by 9.18

N2936   Deld MAD Westgate W/E 27.6.18; Accepted 30.6.18; Yarmouth 2.7.18; EF, FL, sank in tow of HMS *Cricket* 21.8.18 (2 crew retd in trawler); Deleted W/E 29.8.18;

N2937   Deld MAD Westgate W/E 27.6.18; Accepted 4.7.18; 406 Flt Westgate 4.7.18; With N2927 and 2 Camels attacked by 7 German seaplanes, shot down in sea 4m SE of Kentish Knock by Brandenburg seaplane, BO 18.7.18 (Lt JAE Vowles & 2/Lt JGM Farrall); Deleetd W/E 1.8.18

N2938   Deld 406 Flt Westgate and accepted (coded '14') 4.7.18; Became 406 Flt 219 Sqdn Westgate 22.7.18 - @7.19 (mine spotting patrols in North Sea 7.19)

N2939   Deld MAD Westgate W/E 4.7.18; Accepted 8.7.18; 407 Flt Dover 9.7.18 (233 Sqdn 31.8.18); detd Dunkerque 23.10.18; 407 Flt 233 Sqdn Dover 29.10.18 - @30.1.19; Westgate by 4.19 - @7.19 (mine spotting patrols in North Sea 6.19)

N2940   Deld 426/7 Flts Fishguard W/E 18.7.18 (245 Sqdn 20.8.18) - @30.1.19

N2941   Deld 426/7 Flts Fishguard W/E 18.7.18 (245 Sqdn 20.8.18) - @30.1.19

N2942   Deld 426/7 Flts Fishguard W/E 18.7.18 (245 Sqdn 20.8.18) - @30.1.19

N2943   Deld 6 SD Ascot W/E 25.7.18; Shipped 18.8.18; Calafrana by 9.18; HMS *Riviera* 19.9.18; Taranto 5.10.18

N2944   Deld 6 SD Ascot W/E 25.7.18; Shipped 18.8.18; Gibraltar by 9.18; HMS *Engadine* 25.9.18 - 9.11.18LM; HMS *Riviera* .18 (based Malta)

N2945   Deld 6 SD Ascot W/E 25.7.18; Shipped 18.8.18; Gibraltar by 9.18; HMS *Engadine* 25.9.18; Damaged 9.10.18; Gibraltar 10.10.18; HMS *Engadine* 10.12.18; Cattewater 20.12.18 - @30.1.19

N2946   Deld MAD Dundee W/E 27.6.18; 400/1 Flts 249 Sqdn Dundee W/E 8.8.18; FL, badly damaged in North Sea, salved 11.9.18 (2/Lt FWC Body & O/L PA Sainsbury picked up unhurt by N1276)

N2947   Deld MAD Dundee W/E 27.6.18; 400/1 Flts 249 Sqdn Dundee W/E 8.8.18; 400 Flt Strathbeg W/E 14.11.18; 400/1 Flts 249 Sqdn Dundee W/E 31.12.18 - @30.1.19

N2948   Deld 6 SD Ascot W/E 25.7.18; Calafrana by 9.18; HMS *Riviera* 19.9.18; Taranto 5.10.18; 435/6 Sqdn 263 Sqdn Otranto by 10.18 - @30.1.19

N2949   Deld 6 SD Ascot W/E 25.7.18; Docks by 26.9.18; Shipped to Malta 11.10.18, damaged on *Hazlemere*

**50 SHORT ADMIRALTY 184 TYPE RECONNAISSANCE TRACTOR BIPLANE SEAPLANES ordered 30.11.17 under Cont No A.S.36727 (BR.263) from J.Samuel White & Co Ltd, numbered N2950 to N2999 & built East Cowes. (260-hp Maori)**

N2950 Deld Calshot TS 4.4.18; Became 210 TDS Calshot 6.18; Deleted W/E 8.8.18

N2951 Deld Calshot TS W/E 27.4.18; Became 210 TDS Calshot 6.18; ARS Calshot W/E 15.8.18; 210 TDS Calshot W/E 3.10.18; ARS Calshot W/E 9.1.19 - @30.1.19

N2952 Deld Calshot TS W/E 27.4.18; Became 210 TDS Calshot 6.18; ARS Calshot W/E 3.10.18 - @30.1.19

N2953 Deld Cattewater 22.5.18 but EF, FL en route at Portland; arr 420/3 Flts Cattewater 26.5.18 (237 Sqdn 20.8.18) - @30.1.19

N2954 Deld Cattewater W/E 10.5.18; Tresco (via Newlyn) 18.5.18; Became 350/1 Flts Tresco 25.5.18; 420/3 Flts Cattewater 12.8.18 (237 Sqdn 20.8.18); 350/1 Flts 234 Sqdn Tresco W/E 22.8.18; 420/3 Flts 237 Sqdn Cattewater (via Newlyn) 25.9.18; 350/1 Flts 234 Sqdn Tresco 28.10.18 - @30.1.19
BUT seaworthiness tests at Grain by W/E 25.5.18 - @W/E 15.6.18

N2955 Deld Cowes 18.5.18; Cattewater 19.5.18; 350/1 Flts Tresco 25.5.18 (234 Sqdn 20.8.18) - @30.1.19 (numerous visits to Newlyn)

N2956 Deld 420/3 Flts Cattewater (via Calshot) W/E 6.6.18 (237 Sqdn 20.8.18) - @30.1.19

N2957 Deld Cattewater 10.5.18; HMS *Engadine* 10.5.18; Devonport 25.5.18 for Malta; Shipped 20.6.18; Talikna by 6.18; Syra by 8.18; HMS *Ark Royal* 8.18; Phoenika 26.8.18; HMS *Vindex* 29.9.18; Talikna 30.9.18 - @13.11.18; Mudros by 11.18 - @12.18

N2958 Deld Cattewater 21.5.18; 424/5 Flts Newlyn 25.5.18; Dropped 230-lb & 100-lb bombs on U-boat 4927N 0623W 30.6.18 (Capt WB Callaway & 2/Lt JW Nixon); FL, compass failure and darkness, drifted 3 days, CW 2.7.18 (2/Lt RA Jacquot & 2/Lt JW Nixon rescued by HMS *Active* 5.7.18); Deleted W/E 29.8.18

N2959 Deld Newlyn W/E 18.5.18; Became 424/5 Flts Newlyn 25.5.18; 420/3 Flts Cattewater (coded 'B1') 29.5.18; Dropped 100-lb & 230-lb bombs on U-boat 5010N 0310W 11.6.18 (2/Lt RL Pallett & Lt AG Bishop); Became 420/3 Flts 237 Sqdn Cattewater 20.8.18 - @30.1.19

N2960 Deld 420/3 Flts Cattewater W/E 18.5.18 (237 Sqdn 20.8.18); 424/5 Flts 235 Sqdn Newlyn 2.9.18; 418 Flt 239 Sqdn Torquay 2.1.19 - @30.1.19

N2961 Deld 420/3 Flts 237 Sqdn Cattewater 31.5.18; To 424/5 Flts 235 Sqdn Newlyn but FL in heavy sea 1.9.18 (Lt FF Smith & Lt J Whitehead both drowned); Deleted W/E 19.9.18

N2962 Deld Cattewater 5.6.18; 350/1 Flts Tresco W/E 20.6.18; 418 Flt 239 Sqdn Torquay 19.8.18; Dropped 2x100-lb bombs on U-boat, oil and bubbles seen 0523N 0242W 24.8.18 (Lt WEN Growden & Lt AG Bishop); Missing from patrol, error of judgment 3.9.18 (Lt AG Bishop & 2/Lt FA Huycke both killed); Deleted W/E 3.10.18

N2963 Deld Calshot W/E 13.6.18; 350/1 Flts Tresco W/E 20.6.18; FL in sea after lost and ran out of petrol 6.7.18; Washed up Audienne, Brittany, taken to Pont l'Abbé 21.7.18 (Lt JCS Hendry & Lt CW Capes buried Guilvines, nr Quimper); Deleted W/E 25.7.18

N2964 Deld 414/5 Flts Cherbourg 25.5.18 (243 Sqdn 20.8.18); 408/9 Flts 242 Sqdn Newhaven W/E 5.12.18 - @30.1.19

N2965 Deld Cattewater 15.6.18; Patrol Reserve Calshot W/E 20.6.18; 416/7 Flts Portland W/E 11.7.18; Deleted W/E 1.8.18

N2966 Deld 407 Flt Dover 25.6.18 (233 Sqdn 31.8.18); Collided with minelayer *P.48 Biarritz* and damaged starboard wing 3.7.18 (Lt LA Westcott); detd Dunkerque 27.10.18; 407 Flt 233 Sqdn Dover 1.11.18 - @30.1.19; Tested Westgate 8.4.19; Tested after overhaul 20.8.19

N2967 Deld Newhaven 22.6.18 (transit); 407 Flt Dover 24.6.18; EF on TO, sideslipped and crashed avoiding ships and pier Dover Harbour 2.7.18 (Lt GA Wright & Pte Tilby unhurt); Deleted W/E 25.7.18

N2968 Deld 407 Flt Dover 26.6.18; EF on TO, sideslipped and crashed 1½m SW of Dover Harbour, o/t and sank under tow 29.7.18 (Lt LA Westcott & 3AM HAM Ball rescued unhurt); Deleted W/E 8.8.18

N2969 Deld 407 Flt Dover 27.6.18 (233 Sqdn 31.8.18) - @2.19

N2970 Deld Patrol Reserve Calshot W/E 11.7.18; 408/9 Flts 242 Sqdn Newhaven W/E 15.8.18 - @30.1.19; HMS *Nairana* (Syren Force, North Russia) by 15.9.19

N2971 Deld 412/3 Flts Bembridge W/E 11.7.18; Landed too fast, went on to beach, tipped on nose, Bembridge inner harbour 27.7.18 (FSL L Poulter); Deleted W/E 29.8.18

N2972 Deld 407 Flt Dover (via Calshot) 16.7.18 (233 Sqdn 31.8.18); detd Dunkerque 23.10.18; 407 Flt 233 Sqdn Dover 29.10.18 - @30.1.19

N2973 Deld Patrol Reserve Calshot W/E 25.7.18; 416/7 Flts Portland W/E 1.8.18 (241 Sqdn 20.8.18) - @30.1.19

N2974 Deld 1(S)MAD Hamble W/E 25.7.18; 408/9 Flts 242 Sqdn Newhaven W/E 1.8.18; Deleted W/E 7.11.18

N2975 Deld 1(S)MAD Hamble W/E 25.7.18; 412/3 Flts 253 Sqdn Bembridge W/E 1.8.18 - @30.1.19

N2976 Deld 1(S)MAD Hamble W/E 15.8.18; 209 TDS Lee-on-Solent W/E 29.8.18; Became RAF & Naval Cooperation School Lee-on-Solent 16.6.19; Became RAF Seaplane Establishment Lee-on-Solent 14.7.19 - @10.19

N2977 Deld 407 Flt Sqdn Dover W/E 25.7.18 (233 Sqdn 31.8.18) - @31.12.18; 219 Sqdn Westgate by 5.19 - @7.19 (mine spotting patrols in North)

N2978 Deld 1(S)MAD Hamble W/E 29.8.18; Portland 6.9.18 (transit); 418 Flt 239 Sqdn Torquay 15.9.18; Spun in sea, sank 2m E of Torquay Signal Station 24.9.18 (2 crew slightly injured); Deleted W/E 5.10.18

N2979 Deld 424/5 Flts 235 Sqdn Newlyn (via Cattewater) 16.10.18; EF, FL in sea, sank in tow to Newlyn 17.12.18 (presume salved); 418 Flt 239 Sqdn Torquay 2.1.19 - @30.1.19

N2980 Deld 412/3 Flts 253 Sqdn Bembridge W/E 15.8.18; 408/9 Flts 242 Sqdn Newhaven W/E 7.11.18 - @30.1.19

N2981 Deld Calshot W/E 15.8.18; 414/5 Flts 243 Sqdn Cherbourg W/E 29.8.18; Deleted W/E 16.1.19

N2982 Deld 209 TDS Lee-on-Solent W/E 5.9.18 - @30.1.19

N2983 Deld 1(S)MAD Hamble W/E 12.9.18; 209 TDS Lee-on-Solent 28.9.18 - @30.1.19

N2984 Deld 209 TDS Lee-on-Solent W/E 29.8.18; Became RAF & Naval Cooperation School Lee-on-Solent 16.6.19; Became RAF Seaplane Establishment Lee-on-Solent 14.7.19 - @10.19

N2985 Deld 1(S)MAD Hamble W/E 26.9.18; Calshot W/E 3.10.18; 408/9 Flts 242 Sqdn Newhaven W/E 10.10.18 - @30.1.19

N2986 Deld 1(S)MAD Hamble W/E 26.9.18; 412/413 Flights 253 Sqdn Bembridge W/E 3.10.18 - @30.1.19; Became G-EAJT

N2987 Deld 1(S)MAD Hamble W/E 26.9.18; 209 TDS Lee-on-Solent W/E 3.10.18; Became RAF & Naval Co-operation School Lee-on-Solent 16.6.19; Became RAF Seaplane Establishment 14.7.19 - @9.19

N2988 Deld 424/5 Flts 235 Sqdn Newlyn (via Cattewater) 11.10.18; Deleted W/E 9.1.19

N2989 Deld 1(S)MAD Hamble W/E 3.10.18; Torquay 4.10.18 (transit); Cattewater 8.10.18 (transit); 424/5 Flts 235 Sqdn Newlyn W/E 17.10.18; 418 Flt 239 Sqdn Torquay 2.1.19 - @30.1.19

N2990 Deld 1(S)MAD Hamble W/E 10.10.18; 210 TDS Calshot W/E 30.1.19

N2991 Deld Portland W/E 10.10.18; Cattewater W/E 17.10.18; HMS *Mantua* W/E 21.11.18; Cattewater W/E 28.11.18 - @30.1.19

N2992 Deld MAD Hamble W/E 10.10.18; Cattewater W/E 24.10.18 - @30.1.19

N2993 Deld 1(S)MAD Hamble by 10.18; Cattewater W/E 17.10.18 - @30.1.19

N2994 Deld 1(S)MAD Hamble W/E 17.10.18; Cattewater W/E 24.10.18 - @30.1.19

N2995 Deld Westgate 24.10.18; Tested 27.10.18; 406 Flt 219 Sqdn Westgate 10.18 - @7.19

N2996 Deld 1(S)MAD Hamble Yarmouth 28.10.18 (via Westgate); 403 Flt 246 Sqdn Seaton Carew W/E 6.11.18 - @30.1.19; Became G-EBGP

N2997 Deld 1(S)MAD Hamble W/E 24.10.18; Westgate 28.10.18 (transit); 404/5 Flts 248 Sqdn Hornsea 29.10.18 - @30.1.19; RAF(R) HMS *Pegasus* (Dvina River) from 22.9.19; ship arrived Dundee 3.10.19

N2998 Deld 1(S)MAD MAD Hamble W/E 24.10.18; Calshot W/E 31.10.18; 408/9 Flts 242 Sqdn Newhaven (coded 'N' on fin) 6.11.18; Patrol, landed Fécamp 9.11.18; Still Newhaven 30.1.19; Became G-EALC

N2999 Deld 1(S)MAD Hamble W/E 24.10.18; 210 TDS Calshot W/E 31.10.18 - @30.1.19; still Calshot 2.20 - @3.20

*Henry Farman F.27, probably N3017, with 2 Wing at Imbros 1917. (J.M.Bruce/G.S.Leslie collection)*

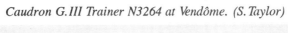

*Caudron G.III Trainer N3264 at Vendôme. (S.Taylor)*

**50 HENRY FARMAN F.27 (TROPICAL TYPE) PUSHER BIPLANES** authorised 1.4.16 for purchase from Aéroplanes Henry et Maurice Farman, Billancourt (Seine) and numbered N3000 to N3049. (150-hp Canton Unné R.9). Initially earmarked for Russia, but shipped to Aegean instead. By 1.17, delivered to N3022, N3023 - N3048 being packed and retained in Paris.

N3000  Deld 2 Wing Mudros; Deleted by 1.17
N3001  Deld 2 Wing Mudros; C Flt 2 Wing Imbros by 13.12.16 - @10.1.17
N3002  Deld 2 Wing Mudros; C Flt A Sqdn 2 Wing Imbros by 13.12.16 - @4.1.17
N3003  Deld 2 Wing Mudros; C Flt 2 Wing Imbros by 13.12.16 - @4.1.17; Mitylene by 23.4.17
N3004  Deld 2 Wing Mudros; 2 Wing Mudros; To Roumanian Government, Bucharest 21.11.16
N3005  Deld 2 Wing Mudros; Deleted by 1.17
N3006  Deld 2 Wing Mudros; Deleted by 1.17
N3007  Deld 2 Wing Mudros; 2 Wing Thasos from 13.10.16; Imbros by 25.10.16; To Roumanian Government, Bucharest 21.11.16
N3008  Deld 2 Wing Mudros; Imbros by 10.16; To Roumanian Government, Bucharest 25.10.16
N3009  Deld 2 Wing Mudros; G Flt 2 Wing Marsh (Mudros) by 1.12.17 - @21.1.18; Became G Flt 62 Wing Marsh (Mudros) 1.4.18
N3010  Deld 2 Wing Mudros; A Sqdn 2 Wing Thasos by @10.2.17 - @1.5.17
N3011  Deld 2 Wing Mudros; G Flt 2 Wing Marsh (Mudros) by 1.12.17 - @21.1.18; Became G Flt 62 Wing Marsh (Mudros) 1.4.18 - @5.18; To Greek AF for training by 6.18 - @1.19
N3012  Deld 2 Wing Mudros; Surveyed 13.12.17; Deleted 27.12.17 DBR
N3013  Deld 2 Wing Mudros; Mudros Base by 1.12.17 (not listed by 1.1.18); To Greek Government
N3014  Deld 2 Wing Mudros
N3015  Deld 2 Wing Mudros; G Flt 2 Wing Marsh (Mudros) by 1.12.17; Surveyed 8.3.18 DBR; Deleted 27.3.18
N3016  Deld 2 Wing Mudros
N3017  Deld 2 Wing Mudros; A Sqdn 2 Wing Thasos by 5.2.17 - @1.5.17
N3018  Deld 2 Wing Mudros; Convtd seaplane; HMS *Ark Royal* by 21.12.17 - @3.18; Greek AF by 6.18 - @1.19
N3019  Deld 2 Wing Mudros; G Flt 2 Wing Marsh (Mudros) by 1.12.17 - @21.1.18
N3020  Deld 2 Wing Mudros; D Sqdn 2 Wing Stavros, tested 24.10.17; Flown to at least @14.1.18
N3021  Deld 2 Wing Mudros and tested on erection 15.1.17; C Sqdn 2 Wing Imbros 11.2.17; Shot down nr Chanak by Fokker flown by Ltn Meinecke 12.2.17 (F/L CA Maitland-Heriot & O/L WC Jameson both PoWs unhurt, but Jameson killed as PoW 15.9.18)
N3022  Deld 2 Wing Mudros; B Sqdn 2 Wing Thermi by 4.6.17 - @16.6.17; G Sqdn 2 Wing Marsh, collided with Camel B3722, CW 19.10.17 (FSL JH Wild)
N3023  Deld 2 Wing Mudros; A Sqdn 2 Wing Thasos by 1.12.17 - @1.1.18; D Sqdn 2 Wing Stavros by 17.1.18; G Flt 2 Wing Marsh (Mudros); Became G Flt 62 Wing Marsh (Mudros) 1.4.18 - @5.18; To Greek AF for training by 6.18 - 1.19
N3024  Deld 2 Wing Mudros; Shot down nr Smyrna by Fokker 30.3.17 (FSL BA Trechmann & LM WA Jones RFC both PoWs)
N3025  to N3028 transferred to RFC (Military Wing) as A8976 to A8979
N3029  transferred to RFC (Military Wing) as A8969 (and B3969 NTU)
N3030  to N3034 transferred to RFC (Military Wing) as A8980 to A8984
N3035  transferred to RFC (Military Wing) as A8968 (and B3970 NTU)
N3036  to N3049 transferred to RFC (Military Wing) as A8985 to A8998
       [N3025 to N3049 also allotted B3959 to B3983, but NTU]

**50 CAUDRON G.III TRACTOR BIPLANE TRAINERS** purchased from Aéroplanes Caudron and numbered N3050 to N3099 for use at Vendôme. Delivered from Villacoublay. (100-hp Anzani) [C/n's consecutively 2004 to 2013, 2021 to 2050 & 2081 to 2090]

N3050  Deld RNASTE Vendôme by air 9.11.16; Became 205 TDS Vendôme 1.4.18; To 212 TDS Vendôme 5.18; Struck ridge landing, o/t, slightly damaged 19.5.18 (F/Cdt D Welsh & Capt HJ Lloyd); Bounced, stalled and sideslipped on TO after heavy landing, wrecked 10.8.18 (F/Cdt JD Fleming slightly injured & Lt HE Forrow)
N3051  Deld RNASTE Vendôme by air 16.11.16; Dismantled 4.6.17; Became 205 TDS Vendôme 1.4.18; To 212 TDS Vendôme 5.18; Badly damaged 7.6.18 (F/Cdt HJ Turner & Capt HJ Lloyd)
N3052  Deld RNASTE Vendôme by air 9.11.16; Became 205 TDS Vendôme 1.4.18; To 212 TDS Vendôme 5.18; Ran into N3264, wrecked 14.5.18 (PFO RO Cutler & Lt R Furnes); Badly damaged landing 12.6.18 (F/Cdt WM Jackson & Lt MA Sams)
N3053  Deld RNASTE Vendôme by air 10.11.16; FL in wheatfield, o/t, dismantled 4.6.17 (Lt AJ Furlow slightly injured); Became 212 TDS Vendôme 1.4.18; Lost, FL, bad bump 30ft from ground, crashed, nr Blains 7.4.18 (PFO AG MacDonald injured); EF, FL, wheatfield, o/t, slightly damaged 28.6.18 (Lt AJ Furlow injured & Lt R Turner); O/t landing, badly damaged 16.8.18 (PFO CB Lymington & Lt NP Playford)
N3054  Deld RNASTE Vendôme by air 19.11.16; Heavy landing 23.5.17; Became 205 TDS Vendôme 1.4.18; Taxied into by N3240 12.4.18; Bounced landing, badly damaged 21.5.18 (F/Cdt WLD Curette & Capt HJ Lloyd); Crashed and wrecked La Bruère 29.6.18 (F/Cdt WJ Wedlake injured & 2/Lt CV Lacey)
N3055  Deld RNASTE Vendôme by air 9.11.16; Hit tree landing and wrecked 29.11.16 (Capt Steele & 2/Lt Collins); Flew into ground 28.1.18 (PFO JA McFadden); Badly smashed landing in heavy wind and rain 25.2.18 (PFO RH Andrews); Became 205 TDS Vendôme 1.4.18; To 212 TDS Vendôme 5.18; Stalled landing, crashed and wrecked 27.7.18 (PFO G Cowell)
N3056  Deld RNASTE Vendôme by air 15.11.16; Repairing by 25.4.17; U/c wrecked and rudder damaged 9.6.17; Surveyed 31.10.17; Deleted 17.11.17 DBR
N3057  Deld RNASTE Vendôme by air 17.11.16; EF, Crashed 6.6.17 (PFO WB Woodland); Crashed and wrecked 13.7.17 (FSL AC Getley); Became 205 TDS Vendôme 1.4.18; Pancaked landing, damaged 12.4.18 (F/L EM Morgan); Pancaked landing, badly damaged 27.6.18 (F/Cdt FHR Trevor & Capt HJ Lloyd); Landed on Avro 8659, wrecked 12.8.18 (F/Cdt RER Wynn & Lt NP Playford)
N3058  Deld RNASTE Vendôme by air 23.11.16; Became 205 TDS Vendôme 1.4.18; To 212 TDS Vendôme 5.18; EF, FL, o/t on Vendôme-Blois road 21.5.18 (PFO I Rubovinid seriously injured and Lt R Turner unhurt); Slightly damaged landing 29.6.18 (PFO LJ Evans & Lt R Turner)
N3059  Deld RNASTE Vendôme by air 23.11.16; Became 205 TDS Vendôme 1.4.18; To 212 TDS Vendôme 5.18; Hit ridge landing, o/t, slightly damaged 2.6.18 (PFO WFVOJ Fitzgerald injured & 2/Lt CV Lacey); Damaged landing in bad weather 17.6.18 (PFO CF Phillips & Lt R Turner); Badly damaged Montoire 13.7.18 (F/Cdt CH Burgess & Lt R Turner); Pancaked landing 17.10.18 (F/Cdt A Colin & Capt AE Best both unhurt)
N3060  Deld RNASTE Vendôme by air 17.11.16; Crashed, CW nr Chateau Renault 4.12.16 (FSL WD Jackson unhurt); Repaired by 25.4.17; Became 205 TDS Vendôme 1.4.18; Failed to flatten out Vendôme, CW 10.4.18 (PFO WJ Costello injured)
N3061  Deld RNASTE Vendôme by air 11.11.16; CW 21.11.16; Deleted 18.1.17
N3062  Deld RNASTE Vendôme by air 15.11.16; Wrecked 23.2.17; Dismantled 5.10.17; Stalled and dived on TO, CW 18.2.18 (2/Lt WE Hall injured); Surveyed 7.3.18

wreck; Deleted 13.3.18

N3063   Deld RNASTE Vendôme by air 15.11.16; FL after EF 15.11.16 (2/Lt AS Bourinot); CW 1.12.16; Deleted 27.3.17

N3064   Deld RNASTE Vendôme by air 16.11.16; COL, CW 11.1.17 (PFO L Mackay); Deleted W/E 3.2.17

N3065   Deld RNASTE Vendôme by air 16.11.16; FL and damaged 17.3.17; Struck wire fence landing, o/t 5.1.18 (PFO ACG Anderson); Heavy landing 22.1.18 (PFO HH Coulson); Bounced and pancaked landing, CW 27.1.18 (PFO WG Illingworth); Deleted W/E 15.2.18

N3066   Deld RNASTE Vendôme by air 15.11.16 (marked as "3066"); Dismantled 5.10.17; Became 205 TDS Vendôme 1.4.18; Damaged landing in rainstorm 27.4.18 (PFO S Dixon); Bounced and stalled landing 9.5.18 (F/Cdt AE Cuthbert); To 212 TDS Vendôme; Heavy landing, wrecked 8.6.18 (PFO ND Hume & Lt HD Reid); Heavy landing, slightly damaged 26.9.18 (F/Cdt H Small & 2/Lt CV Lacey both unhurt); Badly damaged landing 28.10.18 (F/Cdt PA Morton & Lt CV Lacey both slightly injured)

N3067   Deld RNASTE Vendôme by air 16.11.16; Wrecked by 14.5.17; FL and dismantled 9.7.17; Wrecked 20.8.17; Stalled landing 9.1.18 (PFO CB Hatton); O/t on rough ground 24.2.18 (PFO CG Scampton); Nosedived from 250 ft into field nr aerodrome, CW 16.3.18 (PFO WJ Allen); For deletion by 30.3.18

N3068   Deld RNASTE Vendôme by air 23.11.16; Awaiting survey 27.11.16; Re-erecting 28.11.16; Collided with another a/c taxying Chateaudun 12.3.17 (PFO RL Kent); Became 205 TDS Vendôme 1.4.18

N3069   Deld RNASTE Vendôme by air 23.11.16; damaged landing 2.3.17; Wrecked BR 25.5.17; Deleted 14.6.17; Rebuilt and restored to commission 9.17; Became 205 TDS Vendôme 1.4.18; Damaged chassis, boom, propeller landing 2.4.18 (PFO SW Stewart); Flew into ground 4.5.18 (PFO HF Turner stunned)

N3070   Deld RNASTE Vendôme by air 23.11.16; CW 2.12.16; Deleted 18.1.17

N3071   Deld RNASTE Vendôme by air 23.11.16; CW 24.11.16; Deleted 18.1.17

N3072   Deld RNASTE Vendôme by air 4.12.16; Wrecked 21.7.17; Stalled and o/t landing 14.1.18 (PFO LC Townsend); Pancaked landing 27.1.18 (PFO AWG Crosby); O/t landing 10.3.18 (PFO HE Richardson); Became 212 TDS Vendôme 1.4.18; Stalled on TO, badly damaged, Pezow 23.5.18 (PFO K Stuart-Smith & Capt HJ Lloyd)

N3073   Deld RNASTE Vendôme by road 20.12.16; Damaged on cross-country 1.5.17; FL and damaged 1.6.17; Surveyed 24.10.17; Deleted 29.10.17 DBR

N3074   Deld RNASTE Vendôme by road 4.12.16; Deleted 18.3.17

N3075   Deld RNASTE Vendôme by air 4.12.16; Wrecked by 26.2.17; Deleted 28.2.17

N3076   Deld RNASTE Vendôme by road 10.12.16; Deleted 18.3.17

N3077   Deld RNASTE Vendôme by road 18.12.16; CW 27.6.17; Dismantled 5.10.17; Surveyed 12.10.17; Deleted 16.10.17 wrecked

N3078   Deld RNASTE Vendôme by road 18.12.16; FL, o/t on aerodrome 14.6.17 (Lt JH Colbert); Dismantled 28.9.17; Became 205 TDS Vendôme 1.4.18; To 212 TDS Vendôme 5.18; Failed to flatten out landing, damaged 6.9.18 (2/Lt E Williams seriously injured & Lt HE Forrow slightly injured)

N3079   Deld RNASTE Vendôme by road 10.12.16; Wrecked 18.1.17; Deleted 26.2.17

N3080   Deld RNASTE Vendôme by road 4.12.16; Crashed, CW on landing 22.1.17 (2/Lt McKenzie); Deleted W/E 3.2.17

N3081   Deld RNASTE Vendôme by road 8.1.17; COL, wrecked 21.4.17 (2/Lt FW Byrne injured); O/t landing, wrecked 2.2.18 (2/Lt Drobashian injured); EF, FL, ran into fence Ruille-sur-le-Loire 18.3.18 (PFO RM Morris slightly injured); Became 205 TDS Vendôme 1.4.18; Undershot landing, damaged 11.4.18 (PFO C Bottomley); Bounced and stalled landing, badly damaged 17.5.18 (F/Cdt TV Callard & Capt EE Maitland-Heriot); To 212 TDS Vendôme 5.18; Heavy landing, slightly damaged 7.6.18 (F/Cdt JR Price & Capt HJ Lloyd); EF, FL in wheat

field, o/t, slightly damaged, Pouline 25.6.18 (PFO L Walters slightly injured & Capt HJ Lloyd); Pancaked landing, slightly damaged 19.7.18 (F/Cdt DA Boulton injured & Capt HJ Lloyd unhurt); O/t landing, badly damaged 15.9.18 (2/Lt CF Weedon & Capt NP Playford unhurt)

N3082   Deld RNASTE Vendôme by road 29.12.16; Wrecked by 14.5.17; TW landing in poor light 23.3.18 (PFO HRF Richardson); Became 205 TDS Vendôme 1.4.18; Flew into ground, damaged 7.4.18 (PFO A Holden); Landed in hayfield, o/t, slightly damaged, Ponce 29.6.18 (F/Cdt LW Kersley & Capt HJ Lloyd); Later 212 TDS Vendôme; Stalled from 20 ft landing, o/t, wrecked 22.10.18 (F/Cdt A Colin injured & 2/Lt CV Lacey unhurt)

N3083   Deld RNASTE Vendôme by air 24.12.16; FL, crashed 3.2.17; Stalled avoiding two other aircraft on TO, crashed, BO 4.5.17 (2/Lt GL Newman injured); Deleted 14.6.17

N3084   Deld RNASTE Vendôme by road 24.12.16; Deleted 15.2.17

N3085   Deld RNASTE Vendôme by road 22.12.16; Became 205 TDS Vendôme 1.4.18; FL in wheat field, o/t, CW 29.6.18 (2/Lt E Rostedt injured)

N3086   Deld RNASTE Vendôme by road 12.1.17; Wrecked 23.5.17; Ran into crashed machine while taxying 23.7.17; Surveyed 22.9.17; Deleted 26.9.17 wrecked

N3087   Deld RNASTE Vendôme by road 24.12.16; CW 9.6.17; Became 205 TDS Vendôme 1.4.18; To 212 TDS Vendôme 5.18; Hit ridge and o/t landing, badly damaged 22.5.18 (F/Cdt AG Thackeray injured & 2/Lt CV Lacey)

N3088   Deld RNASTE Vendôme by road 22.12.16; Flew into ground, CW landing Vendôme 24.2.17 (2/Lt EV Bayley killed); Deleted 6.3.17

N3089   Deld RNASTE Vendôme by road 24.12.16; Crashed and damaged 11.7.17; EF, propeller smashed 24.2.18 (PFO RAH Hamilton); Became 205 TDS Vendôme 1.4.18; Hit building on aerodrome while landing in ground mist 10.4.18 (PFO SH Thornton injured), for deletion

N3090   Deld RNASTE Vendôme by air 24.12.16; Spun on turn after TO, dived in from 150 ft, CW 22.1.18 (F/Cdt C Murray killed & PFO EC Chesterton injured); Deleted W/E 8.2.18

N3091   Deld RNASTE Vendôme by road 29.12.16; Wrecked 21.7.17; Became 205 TDS Vendôme 1.4.18 - @5.4.18

N3092   Deld RNASTE Vendôme by air 24.1.17 after FL en route from Paris; Became 205 TDS Vendôme 1.4.18; To 212 TDS Vendôme 5.18; Heavy landing, badly damaged 7.6.18 (PFO GRC Soutar & Lt HD Reid); Taxied into ditch landing, slightly damaged 15.8.18 (F/Cdt CA Doney & 2/Lt CV Lacey); EF, FL, o/t, slightly damaged 1.9.18 (F/Cdt A Hore & Lt HE Forrow)

N3093   Deld RNASTE Vendôme by air 11.1.17; Became 205 TDS Vendôme 1.4.18

N3094   Deld RNASTE Vendôme by road 11.1.17; Struts and u/c damaged 30.7.17; Pancaked from 6 ft landing 14.1.18 (PFO JA McFadden); Became 205 TDS Vendôme 1.4.18; To 212 TDS Vendôme 5.18; Slightly damaged landing 28.9.18 (Lt RC Hill & Capt EM Morgan unhurt)

N3095   Deld RNASTE Vendôme by road 24.1.17; Damaged tailplane and engine 4.6.17; Dismantled 5.11.17; Became 205 TDS Vendôme 1.4.18; To 212 TDS Vendôme 5.18; FL nr aerodrome, u/c caught in wheat, o/t 8.6.18 (Capt D Wemyss Gorman died of injuries 9.7.18 & Lt PG Stokes-Rees seriously injured)

N3096   Deld RNASTE Vendôme by road 19.1.17; Became 205 TDS Vendôme 1.4.18; To 212 TDS Vendôme 5.18; O/t landing, wrecked 6.7.18 (F/Cdt DA Boulton & Capt HJ Lloyd)

N3097   Deld RNASTE Vendôme by road 12.1.17; Became 205 TDS Vendôme 1.4.18; To 212 TDS Vendôme 5.18; Failed to flatten out, went into ground, badly damaged 24.5.18 (F/Cdt JW Brown & Capt HJ Lloyd); EF, FL, o/t, slightly damaged, nr Montoire Lavasin 8.8.18 (F/Cdt RP Llewellyn & Lt HE Forrow); EF, landed in wood, badly damaged Monnaie 21.11.18 (F/Cdt H Findlay-Ferguson unhurt)

N3098   Deld RNASTE Vendôme by road 14.1.17; FL in ploughed field nr Montoire 15.3.18 (PFO FW Dodman); Became 205 TDS Vendôme 1.4.18; To 212 TDS Vendôme 5.18; Landed in ploughed field under water, o/t, St.Jean Froidmentel 17.5.18 (Lt HD Reid & Lt R Turner); still 212 TDS Vendôme @11.18

N3099    Deld RNASTE Vendôme by road 10.1.17; Became 205 TDS Vendôme 1.4.18; To 212 TDS Vendôme 5.18; Propeller shaft broken in mid-air, pancaked in ploughed field, o/t, wrecked, St.Nicholas des Motels 7.6.18 (PFO RG Spencer & Lt HD Reid)

**Unidentified order for 70 aircraft to be serialled N3100 to N3169. Cancelled but partially reallocated**

**5 NIEUPORT TYPE 17bis TRACTOR BIPLANE SCOUTS purchased from Établissements Nieuport and delivered 4.17 from Issy-les-Moulineaux, Paris (130-hp Le Rhône) [all except N3100 fitted with overwing Lewis gun and Vickers gun]**

N3100    Deld ADD by 4.17; 11 Sqdn 19.4.17 (only mention by sqdn); 6 Sqdn by 26.4.17 - @7.6.17; ADD by 14.6.17 - @9.8.17; For survey at CSD with view to despatch abroad 28.7.17 (NTU?)

N3101    Deld ADD by 19.4.17; 11 Sqdn 20.4.17 [only mention]; 6 Sqdn by 26.4.17; Albatros DV OOC & another shot down crashed NW of Cambrai 6.6.17 (S/Cdr C Draper); Crashed and wrecked nr aerodrome 14.6.17 (F/L GA Gooderham); ADD for survey 15.6.17; Deleted 27.6.17

N3102    Deld ADD by 19.4.17; 2 AD 4.17; 6 Sqdn 23.4.17; ADD 13.6.17 - @9.8.17; Deleted 1917

N3103    ADD by 7.6.17 - @9.8.17; For survey at CSD with view to despatch abroad 28.7.17 (NTU?)

N3104    ADD by 7.6.17 - @9.8.17; For survey at CSD with view to despatch abroad 28.7.17 (NTU?)

**4 NIEUPORT TYPE 12 TWO-SEATER TRACTOR BIPLANES purchased from Établissements Nieuport and built at Issy-les-Moulineaux, numbered N3170 to N3173. (110-hp Clerget 9Z)**

N3170    Deld Paris to 1 Wing St.Pol 8.9.16; Eastchurch 9.9.16; Cranwell 12.9.16; Deleted 11.3.17

N3171    Deld Chingford 27.9.16 (transit); Cranwell 28.9.16; Surveyed 21.11.17; Deleted 5.12.17 obsolete type

N3172    Shipped to Aegean?

N3173    Shipped to Aegean; B Sqdn 2 Wing Thermi by 13.2.17; Burst petrol tank, landed in water nr aerodrome on return 13.2.17 (F/L HE Morgan & S/L AEH Roberts), presume salved; Mitylene by 10.4.17; Surveyed 21.9.17; Deleted 6.10.17 W&T

**10 NIEUPORT TYPE 12 TWO-SEATER TRACTOR BIPLANES purchased from Établissements Nieuport and built at Issy-les-Moulineaux, numbered N3174 to N3183. (130-hp Clerget 9B)**

N3174    Shipped to Aegean?

N3175    Shipped to Aegean; D Sqdn 2 Wing Stavros by 2.17; 1 Albatros shot down smoking nr Angista 11.2.17 (F/L CE Wood & 2/Lt EP Hyde RFC); 2 Wing Mudros, for deletion by 1.12.17

N3176    Shipped to Aegean; B Sqdn 2 Wing Thermi by 13.2.17; 11 Sqdn by 4.17; Surveyed 21.9.17; Deleted 6.10.17 wrecked

N3177    Shipped to Aegean?

N3178    Shipped to Aegean?

N3179    Shipped to Aegean?

N3180    Shipped to Aegean; Surveyed Mudros 21.9.17; Deleted 6.10.17 DBR

N3181    Shipped to Aegean?

N3182    Shipped to Aegean; A Sqdn 2 Wing Thasos, shot down by Halberstadt Scout over Drama-Mavala road, credited von Eschwege 22.3.17 (F/L SG Beare and Lt EP Hyde RFC both PoWs)

N3183    Shipped to Aegean; Mudros by 4.17; Crashed and wrecked Mudros 26.4.17; B Sqdn 2 Wing Thermi by 6.17; Surveyed Mudros 6.11.17; Deleted 26.11.17 DBR

**4 NIEUPORT TYPE 17bis SINGLE-SEATER SCOUT TRACTOR BIPLANES purchased from Établissements Nieuport and built at Issy-les-Moulineaux, numbered N3184 to N3187. (130-hp Clerget 9B)**

N3184    Deld ADD by 25.1.17; 6 Sqdn by 1.2.17 - @16.3.17; Aviatik C OOC smoking Houthulst Forest 8.2.17 (F/L EW Norton DSC); Large 2-str last seen in vertical dive Ghistelles 1.3.17 (Lt JdeC Paynter); Tested against Sopwith Triplane 3.3.17; 11 Sqdn by 27.3.17; Wrecked 4.5.17; ADD 4.5.17; 11 Sqdn W/E 14.6.17; Surveyed 27.6.17

N3185    England by 25.2.17; Allocated Nieuport England for trials 31.3.17 - @23.2.18

N3186    Deld Paris to ADD 15.2.17 - @1.3.17; 6 Sqdn by 4.3.17; 1 AD St.Omer 6.3.17; 6 Sqdn 9.3.17; Crashed on TO 11.3.17 (FSL CL Bailey); ADD by 15.3.17; 11 Sqdn 1.4.17 - @20.4.17; 6 Sqdn by 26.4.17; Crashed & DBR Guizancourt 1.6.17 (FSL VC Holyman); ADD 2.6.17; Deleted 27.6.17

N3187    Deld Paris to ADD 15.2.17 - @22.2.17; 6 Sqdn by 24.3.17; Albatros DII shot down & another OOC W of Douai 17.00 5.4.17; Albatros DII in flames and another OOC W of Douai 17.00, then FL Bouquemaison 5.4.17 (retd 7.4.17); Albatros DIII OOC 11.45 and another OOC 12.00, both Cambrai 9.4.17 (all F/Cdr EW Norton); Crashed and burnt Maricourt 9.4.17 (F/Cdr EW Norton injured); Deleted ADD 27.4.17

**1 NIEUPORT TYPE 12 TWO-SEATER TRACTOR BIPLANE SCOUTS purchased from Établissements Nieuport and built at Issy-les-Moulineaux, numbered N3188. (130-hp Clerget 9B)**

N3188    Deld from Versailles by rail to ADD 22.2.17

**9 NIEUPORT TYPE 17bis SINGLE-SEATER TRACTOR BIPLANE SCOUTS purchased from Établissements Nieuport and built at Issy-les-Moulineaux, numbered N3189 to N3197. (130-hp Clerget 9B)**

N3189    Ready at makers 25.2.17; Deld ADD by 1.3.17 - @8.3.17; 6 Sqdn by 11.3.17; Albatros DIII dived and crashed NW of Fresnoy-le-Grand 15.15 10.5.17 (FSL OJ Gagnier); Shot down by 4 HA and o/t in No Mans Land at Villers Outreaux 19.30 11.5.17 (FSL OJ Gagnier seriously wounded, hid in shell hole); Deleted ADD 14.5.17

N3190    At Villacoublay 27.2.17; Deld ADD by 8.3.17; 6 Sqdn 9.3.17; Crashed Hinges 9.4.17 (FSL JdeC Paynter injured); ADD by 12.4.17; Deleted 25.4.17; Presumed restored to commission; ADD by 28.6.17 - @9.8.17 (LM); For survey at CSD with view to despatch abroad 28.7.17 (NTU?)

N3191    At Villacoublay 27.2.17; Deld ADD W/E 8.3.17; 6 Sqdn 11.3.17; EF, crashed from 200ft after combat 5.4.17 (FSL MR Kingsford injured in action); ADD W/E 12.4.17; 11 Sqdn W/E 3.5.17; Wrecked 10.6.17; ADD by 14.6.17; Deleted 27.6.17

N3192    At Villacoublay 27.2.17; Deld ADD W/E 8.3.17; 6 Sqdn (coded '15') by 24.3.17; Albatros D.III OOC 7m E of Honnecourt 13.15, shared N3208 then own m/c shot down E of Harcourt 29.4.17 (FSL AHV Fletcher PoW wounded); Deleted 11.5.17

N3193    At Villacoublay 27.2.17; Deld ADD 4.3.17; 6 Sqdn 12.3.17; Crashed, CW Guizancourt 24.5.17 (FSL P Wood); ADD by 31.5.17 for survey; Deleted ADD 27.6.17

N3194    At Villacoublay 27.2.17; Deld Paris to ADD 4.3.17; 6 Sqdn 10.3.17; Crashed and damaged Guizancourt 28.4.17 (FSL H Lawson); ADD by 3.5.17 - @9.8.17 (LM); For survey at CSD with view to despatch abroad 28.7.17 (NTU?)

N3195    At Villacoublay 27.2.17; Deld ADD W/E 8.3.17; 6 Sqdn (coded '1') 9.3.17; Crashed, CW 52 Sqdn RFC aerodrome Citadel, SE of Albert 3.5.17 (FSL RW Berridge DoI); ADD 5.17; Deleted 27.6.17

N3196    At Villacoublay 27.2.17; Deld ADD W/E 8.3.17; 6 Sqdn 10.3.17 - @31.5.17; AD by 7.6.17 - @28.6.17; For survey at CSD with view to despatch abroad 28.7.17 (NTU?)

N3197    At Villacoublay 27.2.17; Deld ADD W/E 8.3.17; 6 Sqdn 11.3.17 - @7.6.17; FL, slightly damaged, Sus St.Leger 28.3.17; ADD by 14.6.17; For survey at CSD with view to despatch abroad 28.7.17 (NTU?)

**1 NIEUPORT TYPE 17bis SINGLE-SEATER TRACTOR BIPLANE SCOUTS purchased from Établissements Nieuport, built Issy-les-Moulineaux & numbered N3198. (130-hp Clerget 9B)**

N3198    Nieuport Works Issy by 25.2.17 ready for Villacoublay; Deld ADD W/E 8.3.17; 6 Sqdn 9.3.17; Crashed 18.3.17 (FSL RK Slater); ADD by 22.3.17; Deleted 24.3.17

**11 NIEUPORT TYPE 17bis SINGLE-SEATER TRACTOR BIPLANE SCOUTS purchased Établissements from Nieuport, built Issy-les-Moulineaux & numbered N3199 to N3209. (130-hp Clerget 9B)**

N3199    Ready 27.2.17; Deld ADD W/E 8.3.17; 6 Sqdn (coded '8') by 15.3.17; Albatros DIII OOC Guise 18.50, own m/c shot up 29.4.17 (FSL RR Winter); Albatros OOC NE of St.Quentin 11.50-12.00 19.5.17 (FSL CL Bailey); HA OOC 1.6.17 (FSL AMcB Walton); ADD W/E 14.6.17 - @9.8.17; For survey at CSD with view to despatch abroad 28.7.17 (NTU?)

N3200    Ready 27.2.17; Deld ADD W/E 8.3.17; 6 Sqdn (coded '9') 11.3.17; COL Chipilly 23.4.17 (FSL ST Edwards); ADD by 26.4.17; Deleted 15.5.17; Presumed restored to commission; ADD by 28.6.17 - @9.8.17; For survey at CSD with view to despatch abroad 28.7.17 (NTU?)

N3201    Ready 27.2.17; Deld ADD W/E 8.3.17; 6 Sqdn 10.3.17; Stalled at 400 ft, Savy 17.3.17 (FSL FC Walker killed); ADD 22.3.17; Deleted 24.3.17

N3202    Ready 1.3.17; Deld ADD W/E 8.3.17; 6 Sqdn 11.3.17; COL 13.3.17 (FSL AHV Fletcher); ADD by 15.3.17; 6 Sqdn W/E 29.3.17; Shot down nr Arras 18.45 5.4.17 (FSL RK Slater POW); Deleted 11.5.17

N3203    Ready 1.3.17; Deld ADD W/E 8.3.17; 6 Sqdn 22.3.17; Crashed and wrecked Guizancourt aerodrome 20.5.17 (FSL AMcB Walton); ADD by 24.5.17; Deleted 27.6.17

N3204    Ready 2.3.17; Deld ADD W/E 8.3.17; 6 Sqdn 14.3.17 (large band behind cockpit, possibly red); Shot down, lost wings nr Moevres by Vzfw Reisinger, Jasta 12 c.12.00-12.15 6.6.17 (F/L FP Reeves killed); ADD 7.6.17 (for survey); Deleted 25.6.17

N3205    Ready 2.3.17; ADD after 8.3.17; 6 Sqdn 15.3.17; HA OOC 5.4.17; HA OOC 9.4.17 (both FSL AL Thorne); "FSL AL Thorne killed by storm" 9.4.17; Crashed 25.4.17; ADD by 26.4.17; 11 Sqdn ; COL 11.5.17 (FSL VC Holyman); Deleted 14.5.17

N3206    Deld ADD W/E 14.3.17; 6 Sqdn by 24.3.17; Crashed 13.4.17 (S/Cdr JJ Petre DSC killed); ADD by 19.4.17 (for survey); Deleted 27.4.17

N3207    ADD by 22.3.17; 6 Sqdn 27.3.17 - @31.5.17; ADD by 14.6.17 (u/s); Deleted 27.6.17

N3208    6 Sqdn by 5.4.17; Albatros D.III OOC 7m E of Honnecourt shared with N3192 13.15 29.4.17; Albatros D.III shot down in flames and another OOC Guise 18.55 29.4.17 (all F/Cdr EW Norton); ADD W/E 14.6.17 - @28.6.17; For survey at CSD with view to despatch abroad 28.7.17 (NTU?)

N3209    2 AD by 19.4.17 - @26.4.17; 6 Sqdn by 3.5.17; Albatros C OOC smoking Elincourt, NW of Bohain 11.40 20.5.17 (F/L BPH de Roeper wounded); Badly shot up in combat 1.6.17 (S/Cdr CD Breese slightly wounded); ADD by 5.6.17 - @9.8.17; Deleted 27.6.17 (sic)

**30 HENRY FARMAN F.40 PUSHER BIPLANES purchased from Henry & Maurice Farman, built Paris & numbered N3210 to N3239. (160-hp Renault)**

N3210    Deld Eastchurch Workshops for erection by rail ex France 20.1.17 - @31.1.17; Bomb Flt Eastchurch by 18.2.17; Observers School Flt Eastchurch 15.3.17; Surveyed 8.11.17; Deleted 17.11.17 DBR

N3211    Deld Eastchurch 5.7.17; Deleted 31.8.17

N3212    Deld by road from Nine Elms to Eastchurch Workshops for erection 1.5.17; Deleted W/E 8.9.17

N3213    Deld by rail from Paris to Eastchurch Workshops for erection 24.3.17; Deleted 31.8.17

N3214    (c/n 4004) Deld by rail to Eastchurch Workshops for erection 17.1.17; Bomb Flt Eastchurch 3.3.17; Observer School Flt 14.3.17; Deleted 31.8.17

N3215    Deld Chingford by rail for erection 1.5.17; Deleted 31.8.17

N3216    Deld Chingford for erection 23.3.17; Observers School Flt Eastchurch 25.5.17; AGP 5.6.17 (F/L EM Pizey & F/L AHS Lawson); For repair 28.6.17; Deleted 21.8.17

N3217    Deld Chingford for erection 23.3.17; Observers School Flt Eastchurch 25.5.17; Surveyed 8.11.17; Deleted 17.11.17 W&T

N3218    Deld CSD White City 1.17; Chingford by rail for erection 13.3.17; Hendon 31.5.17; Dunkerque 2.6.17; Hendon (via Grain) 11.7.17; Gunnery School Eastchurch 15.8.17; Deleted 31.8.17

N3219    Deld Chingford by road 8.3.17; Eastchurch 25.5.17; Deleted 31.8.17

N3220    Deld Cranwell 10.3.17; Chingford for erection 23.3.17; Kingsnorth 21.4.17 (exptl); Gunnery School Flts Eastchurch W/E 2.3.18

N3221    Deld from Paris to Cranwell for erection 18.4.17; Eastchurch Workshops by rail for Gunnery School Eastchurch 12.5.17 (arr 1.6.17); Deleted 31.8.17

N3222    Deld from Paris to Cranwell for erection 18.4.17; Observers School Flt Eastchurch 15.5.17; Deleted 18.9.17 BR

N3223    (c/n 4052) Deld Cranwell 10.3.17; Eastchurch Workshops by rail, arr 1.6.17; Cranwell 11.7.17; Gunnery School Eastchurch 28.8.17 (arr 30.8.17); Surveyed 8.11.17; Deleted 17.11.17 W&T

N3224    Deld from Paris to Cranwell for erection 18.4.17; Eastchurch Workshops by rail for Gunnery School Eastchurch, arr 1.6.17; Deleted 31.8.17

N3225    Deld Manston (via Dover) for erection 12.5.17; Eastchurch (via Eastchurch) 16.8.17; Deleted W/E 22.9.17 BR

N3226    Deld Manston (via Dover) by rail for erection 5.5.17; Observers School Flt Eastchurch W/E 8.9.17; Damaged W/E 15.9.17; Surveyed 8.11.17; Deleted 17.11.17 W&T

N3227    Deld Redcar 1.6.17; Eastchurch Workshops by rail for Gunnery School Eastchurch 4.6.17 (arr 9.6.17); Deleted 31.8.17

N3228    Deld Paris to Eastchurch W/E 3.11.17; Surveyed 8.11.17; Deleted 17.11.17 W&T

N3229    (c/n 4066) Deld Hendon 3.5.17; Observers School Flt Eastchurch 16.8.17; Surveyed 8.11.17; Deleted 17.11.17 W&T

N3230    Deld Paris to Cranwell for erection 18.4.17; Eastchurch Workshops for Gunnery School Eastchurch 16.8.17 (arr 1.6.17); Deleted 31.8.17

N3231    Deld Paris to Cranwell for erection 27.4.17; Eastchurch Workshops by rail for Gunnery School Eastchurch , arr 1.6.17, but to Observers School Flt Eastchurch; Surveyed 8.11.17; Deleted 17.11.17 W&T

N3232    Deld Paris to Cranwell for erection 30.4.17; Desp Eastchurch Workshops 19.5.17, then to Observers School Flt Eastchurch; Surveyed 8.11.17; Deleted 17.11.17 W&T

N3233    Deld Paris to Cranwell for erection 27.4.17; Desp Eastchurch Workshops 22.5.17, then Observers School Flt Eastchurch; Surveyed 8.11.17; Deleted 17.11.17 W&T

N3234    (150-hp Renault) (c/n 3426?) Deld Paris to Grain EAD 4.7.17; Surveyed 25.3.18; Deleted 27.3.18 W&T

N3235    Allocated Paris to EAD Grain 7.4.17; Allocated Chingford to Gunnery School Eastchurch 7.8.17; Deld Observers School Flt Eastchurch W/E 13.10.17; Surveyed 8.11.17; Deleted 17.11.17 W&T

N3236    Allocated Paris to Manston 7.4.17; re-allocated Chingford 8.6.17; re-allocated Hounslow for Cdr Perron, French Liaison Officer 5.10.17 (arr by 29.12.17) - @30.3.18

N3237    Deld Manston for erection 7.6.17; Observers School Flt Eastchurch W/E 8.9.17; Surveyed 8.11.17; Deleted 17.11.17 W&T

N3238    Deld Paris to Cranwell for erection 1.5.17; To Eastchurch Workshops 22.5.17 (not arrived until 7.7.17); Observers School Flt Eastchurch by 22.9.17; Surveyed 8.11.17; Deleted 17.11.17 W&T

N3239    Deld Eastchurch for Observers School Flt 5.7.17; Surveyed 8.11.17; Deleted 17.11.17 W&T

**30 CAUDRON G.III TRACTOR BIPLANES purchased by Aéroplanes Caudron and built Rue, numbered N3240 to N3269 & deld from Villacoublay. (100-hp Anzani)**

N3240    (c/n 2075/4024) Deld RNASTE Vendôme by road 31.12.16; repair by 25.4.17; FL and dismantled 27.5.17; Became 205 TDS Vendôme 1.4.18; Taxied into N3054 landing, damaged 12.4.18 (PFO JLF Creighton); Bounced and stalled landing, TW 17.4.18 (PFO JLF Creighton)

N3241    (c/n 3249/4000) Deld RNASTE Vendôme by air 7.1.17; Wrecked landing 24.3.17; Dismantled 25.3.17; CW 11.6.17; Crashed landing in poor light 23.3.18 (PFO CC Crossley); Became 205 TDS Vendôme 1.4.18; O/t landing, damaged 22.4.18 (PFO WA Crick); U/c collapsed landing 6.5.18 (PFO FL Southgate); O/t on TO 10.5.18 (F/Cdt FR Eveleigh); To 212 TDS Vendôme 5.18; O/t landing, badly damaged 21.5.18 (F/Cdt R Bower & Capt EE Maitland-Heriot)

N3242    (c/n 2073/4022) Deld RNASTE Vendôme by air 7.1.17; Dismantled, awaiting survey 4.3.17; Deletion recommended 6.3.17; Evidently rebuilt; Became 205 TDS Vendôme 1.4.18; Taxied into 5296 damaging tail boom 10.5.18 (PFO RH Barker)

N3243    (c/n 2836/4025) Deld RNASTE Vendôme by road 8.1.17; Wings and u/c damaged 6.7.17; Became 205 TDS Vendôme 1.4.18; To 212 TDS Vendôme 5.18; O/t landing, badly damaged 23.5.18 (F/Cdt A Waller & 2/Lt CV Lacey)

N3244    (c/n 2115/4049) Deld RNASTE Vendôme by road 8.1.17; Wrecked by 30.4.17

N3245    (c/n 2059/4008) Deld RNASTE Vendôme by air 11.1.17; Deleted 28.2.17

N3246    (c/n 4013) Deld RNASTE Vendôme by road 19.1.17; Wrecked 2.6.17; Wrecked 26.7.17; Wrecked 28.9.17; Failed to flatten out 12.1.18 (PFO JJ Sullivan); FL nr St.Amand-de-Vendôme 14.2.18 (PFO CE Sherlock); Became 205 TDS Vendôme 1.4.18; To 212 TDS Vendôme 5.18; Stalled and sideslipped in, o/t, wrecked 14.5.18 (F/Cdt RD Bird injured & Capt HJ Lloyd)

N3247    (c/n 4026) Deld RNASTE Vendôme by road 19.1.17; Wrecked at Tours 16.7.17

N3248    (c/n 4009) Deld RNASTE Vendôme by road 24.1.17; Crashed on TO 12.7.17 (PFO FW Barton); Bad landing 24.2.18 (PFO L Joslin); Stalled on TO, Chateaudun 19.3.18 (PFO FW Mills); Became 205 TDS Vendôme 1.4.18; To 212 TDS Vendôme 5.18; Overshot into fence, damaged, Pont-du-Gennes 16.5.18 (PFO AE Hounsom); O/t landing, slightly damaged 9.10.18 (Lt RC Hill unhurt)

N3249    (c/n 4023) Deld RNASTE Vendôme by road 24.1.17; CW 31.5.17; Deletion recommended by 22.6.17; Evidently rebuilt; Stalled landing 30.1.18 (PFO SA Kemp); Crashed on TO 12.2.18 (PFO HG Thompson); Bad landing 23.2.18 (PFO J Prescott); Became 205 TDS Vendôme 1.4.18; To 212 TDS Vendôme 5.18; O/t landing 28.4.18 (PFO AV Davis); Flew into ground 16.6.18 (2/Lt WH Saunders injured)

N3250    (c/n 4028) Deld RNASTE Vendôme by road 31.1.17; Dismantled 4.6.17; Bad landing, CW 14.1.18 (PFO FS Russell); Pilot fainted in air, CW 9.2.18 (PFO AH Fitton slightly injured); Became 205 TDS Vendôme 1.4.18

N3251    Deld RNASTE Vendôme by road 24.2.17; Dismantled 25.8.17; O/t landing in bad weather 9.1.18 (2/Lt Kent); Bad landing 12.2.18 (PFO MS Smith); FL, wing hit tree, CW, between Trôo and Montoire 25.3.18 (PFO HJ Greenland); For deletion by 30.3.18

N3252    Deld RNASTE Vendôme by road 19.2.17; FL nr aerodrome and hit trees 2.10.17 (2/Lt GF Baker injured); Surveyed 7.10.17; Deleted 13.10.17 wrecked

N3253    (c/n 4029) Deld RNASTE Vendôme by road 31.1.17; Damaged landing 1.5.17; To dismantle 7.6.17; Rebuilding 13.7.17; Broke tail and u/c landing 14.1.18 (PFO FC Sanderson); FL in plough on aerodrome 31.1.18 (PFO HC Price); Damaged landing Pouline 19.2.18 (PFO AA Caney); Stalled on TO, CW 16.3.18 (PFO CB Smith); For deletion by 30.3.18

N3254    Deld RNASTE Vendôme 10.2.17; Wrecked 22.8.17 (TPFO WF Ferrier DoI 26.8.17)

N3255    Deld RNASTE Vendôme by road 3.3.17; Deleted 19.12.17 wreck

N3256    Deld RNASTE Vendôme 10.2.17; O/t landing 22.8.17; but still at Vendôme 30.3.18

N3257    (c/n 4041) Deld RNASTE Vendôme 8.2.17; Wrecked BR 25.4.17; Deletion recommended 22.6.17

N3258    Deld RNASTE Vendôme by road 19.2.17; Damaged 7.9.17; Became 212 TDS Vendôme 1.4.18; COL 3.6.18 (F/Cdt TH Houghton, slightly injured)

N3259    Deld RNASTE Vendôme by road 13.2.17; Wrecked 29.5.17; Surveyed 11.11.17; Deleted 21.11.17 wrecked

N3260    Deld RNASTE Vendôme by road 13.2.17; BR by 25.4.17; Deleted 28.6.17

N3261    Deld RNASTE Vendôme by road 13.2.17; Deletion recommended 7.4.17

N3262    Deld RNASTE Vendôme by road 13.2.17; CW 23.3.17; Deletion recommended 29.3.17

N3263    Deld RNASTE Vendôme by road 24.2.17; O/t landing 5.8.17 (PFO CW Emmett & 2/Lt GFE Harrison both injured); Surveyed 19.12.17; Deleted 31.12.17 wrecked

N3264    Deld RNASTE Vendôme by road 24.2.17; Became 205 TDS Vendôme 1.4.18; EF, undershot, struck u/c on ground, wrecked 3.4.18 (PFO SH Thornton); Ran into N3052 on landing 14.5.18 (PFO RO Cutler); To 212 TDS; Badly damaged landing 7.6.18 (PFO TH Hall & Lt R Turner); Bounced landing 15.9.18 (F/Cdt A Hore & Lt HE Forrow unhurt)

N3265    Deld RNASTE Vendôme 28.1.17; Crashed Vendôme 25.7.17 (T/S/L FW Barton); CW 2m W of St.Amand-du-Vendôme 10.1.18 (F/L PH Martin & mechanic); Hit ridge landing 18.1.18 (2/Lt CH Wilson); FL in ploughed field Lance 24.2.18; Became 205 TDS Vendôme 1.4.18; Hit soft ground, o/t 9.4.18 (PFO WF Twohey); Retd Mkrs?; Paris to Vendôme by air 23.6.18 - @10.18

N3266    Deld RNASTE Vendôme 28.1.17; Retd Mkrs?; Paris to Vendôme 11.7.17; Wrecked 16.7.17; To dismantle 25.8.17; Flew into telegraph wires, CW, Orleans 12.1.18 (PFO JH Green); Became 205 TDS Vendôme 1.4.18; To 212 TDS Vendôme 5.18; Pancaked landing, wrecked 17.6.18 (F/Cdt RD Bird & Capt HJ Lloyd); For deletion by 12.18

N3267    Deld RNASTE Vendôme 23.3.17; Retd Mkrs 8.5.17; Paris to Vendôme by air 23.6.17; Wrecked 26.7.17; Dismantled 5.10.17; O/t landing 5.2.18 (PFO VJ O'Neil); TW 9.2.18 (WO CV Lacey & PFO MH Tench);

N3268    Deld RNASTE Vendôme 23.3.17; Retd Mkrs 8.5.17; Paris to Vendôme by air 26.6.17; Damaged 7.9.17; Dismantled 5.10.17; Deleted W/E 23.11.17

N3269    Deld RNASTE Vendôme 23.3.17; Wrecked 7.9.17; Failed to flatten out landing, flew into ground, football ground 18.1.18 (2/Lt HA Robinson killed); Deleted W/E 1.3.18

**N3270 to N3279 numbers not used**

**20 CAUDRON G.III TRACTOR BIPLANES purchased by Aéroplanes Caudron and built Rue, numbered N3280 to N3299 & deld by road from Paris. (100-hp Anzani)**

N3280    (c/n 4528) Deld RNASTE Vendôme for erection 15.5.17; Wrecked when struck tree avoiding another aircraft 21.7.17 (2/Lt GFE Harrison injured); Caught slipstream of another aircraft and flew into ground 24.3.18 (PFO WE Willday slightly injured); Became 205 TDS Vendôme 1.4.18; To 212 TDS Vendôme 5.18; O/t landing, wrecked 2.7.18 (F/Cdt WF Howard & 2/Lt CV Lacey); Slightly damaged landing 16.9.18 (F/Cdt WR Godard unhurt)

N3281    (c/n 4529) Deld RNASTE Vendôme for erection 15.5.17; Damaged 16.8.17; Damaged 7.9.17; Surveyed 31.10.17; Deleted 17.11.17 DBR

N3282    (c/n 4530) Deld RNASTE Vendôme for erection 15.5.17; Tail and rudder wrecked 16.6.17; O/t landing, propeller smashed 10.9.17 (PFO KHG Tilley unhurt); Wrecked 21.9.17; Surveyed 4.1.18; Deleted 17.1.18 wrecked

N3283    (c/n 4531) Deld RNASTE Vendôme for erection 23.5.17; Wrecked 20.8.17; O/t landing 14.1.18 (PFO SJ Saunders); O/t landing 30.1.18 (PFO HF Mulhall); Bumped, stalled, sideslipped, wrecked 3.2.18 (PFO HF

Mulhall); Deleted W/E 2.3.18

N3284  (c/n 4532) Deld RNASTE Vendôme for erection 23.5.17; Ready 31.5.17; Crashed and damaged 11.7.17; Dismantled 5.10.17; Re-erected; O/t landing 21.3.18 (PFO JW Pears); Landed on ridge, CW 27.3.18 (PFO HN Farncomb); Became 205 TDS Vendôme 1.4.18; CW landing 2.5.18 (PFO CW Taylor); To 212 TDS; O/t landing, slightly damaged 27.8.18 (F/Cdt F Eppinger & Capt NP Playford); EF, stalled on gliding turn, dived in, wrecked, farm nr aerodrome, Pauline 10.10.18 (F/Cdt AL Brice injured & Capt RD Best unhurt)

N3285  (c/n 4535) Deld RNASTE Vendôme for erection 24.5.17; Wrecked on cross-country Chateaudun 13.6.17; Became 205 TDS Vendôme 1.4.18; O/t landing, damaged 12.4.18 (PFO HPN Gubbins); Struck ridge landing, o/t 5.5.18 (PFO DP Brennan); To 212 TDS Vendôme 5.18; Hit ridge, o/t, wrecked 24.5.18 (F/Cdt WM Jackson & Capt EE Maitland-Heriot)

N3286  Deld RNASTE Vendôme by road 21.5.17; Wrecked BR 16.8.17; Surveyed 22.9.17; Deleted 26.9.17; Caudron repair; Presume restored to commission; Vendôme W/E 14.12.17; Deleted W/E 29.12.17

N3287  Deld RNASTE Vendôme by road 21.5.17; To rebuild 14.6.17; Wrecked 28.9.17; Became 212 TDS 1.4.18; Crashed on TO, badly damaged, Villerable 22.5.18 (F/Cdt FC Ferrier & 2/Lt CV Lacey); Stalled on TO, wrecked 6.7.18 (PFO LHK Ingham & Capt HJ Lloyd)

N3288  Deld RNASTE Vendôme by road 21.5.17; O/t St.Amand 4.7.17; Wrecked BR 22.8.17

N3289  Deld RNASTE Vendôme 28.1.17; Wrecked 21.7.17; Bad landing 10.1.18 (PFO CG Prior); O/t landing 16.3.18 (PFO AM Stevens); FL in ploughed field, o/t NW of aerodrome 27.3.18 (PFO SW Stewart); Became 205 TDS Vendôme 1.4.18; To 212 TDS 5.18; Hit tree landing, TW 10.4.18 (PFO MD Macpherson); Hit ridge landing, badly damaged 16.8.18 (PFO R StJ Sheppard & 2/Lt CV Lacey both slightly injured)

N3290  Deld RNASTE Vendôme by road 21.6.17; Surveyed 11.12.17; Deleted 21.12.17 wrecked

N3291  Deld RNASTE Vendôme by road 21.6.17; Dismantled 5.10.17; Became 205 TDS Vendôme 1.4.18; Flew into ground landing, TW 17.4.18 (PFO WF Twohey); Heavy landing, wrecked 3.6.18 (F/Cdt RD Bird & Capt HJ Lloyd)

N3292  Deld RNASTE Vendôme by road 21.6.17; To repair 21.8.17; Deleted W/E 7.9.17 BR

N3293  Deld RNASTE Vendôme by road 24.6.17; Wrecked 13.7.17; Lost propeller landing, landed on main road to Vendôme, CW 2.2.18 (PFO GW Wilson); still at Vendôme 30.3.18

N3294  Deld RNASTE Vendôme by road 24.6.17; U/c damaged 22.8.17; Dismantled 5.10.17; Surveyed 30.11.17 wrecked; Deleted 13.12.17

N3295  Deld RNASTE Vendôme by road 24.6.17; Wrecked 28.9.17; Became 205 TDS Vendôme 1.4.18; O/t landing, damaged 24.4.18 (PFO CEJ Jones); To 212 TDS Vendôme 5.18; Struck ridge landing, slightly damaged 19.7.18 (Lt AE Kennedy & Capt HJ Lloyd)

N3296  Deld RNASTE Vendôme 25.6.17; Damaged 7.9.17; FL on aerodrome 12.1.18 (2/Lt MA Toomey); Stalled from 5 ft 28.1.18 (PFO WE Lewis); FL, Les Roches, nr Montaire 9.2.18 (PFO AE Lloyd); Wing tip struck while landing 24.2.18 (PFO RE Keys); O/t landing 9.3.18 (PFO L Poulter); Hit mound landing, badly damaged 28.3.18 (PFO GK Lucas); Became 205 TDS Vendôme 1.4.18; FL in corn, o/t, slightly damaged, Coulommiers, nr Vendôme 28.5.18 (F/Cdt FA Taylor & Lt R Turner); Tested 8.6.18

N3297  Deld RNASTE Vendôme 6.7.17; Surveyed 11.11.17; Deleted 21.11.17 wrecked

N3298  Deld RNASTE Vendôme 6.7.17; Bad landing 9.3.18 (PFO CN Shaw); Became 205 TDS Vendôme 1.4.18; Landed steeply, CW 3.4.18 (PFO AJ Parker); To 212 TDS Vendôme 5.18; O/t landing in bad weather, badly damaged 12.6.18 (F/Cdt OS Holmes & Lt R Turner); Stalled and nose dived into hangar on TO, Vendôme 19.11.18 (F/Cdt SF Bladwell killed)

N3299  Deld RNASTE Vendôme by road 12.7.17; Bounced and went on nose 27.1.18 (PFO HJ Bradley injured); For deletion by 8.2.18

**75 NORMAN THOMPSON N.T.2B PUSHER BIPLANE FLYING BOATS ordered from Supermarines under Cont Nos 38a/612/C641 & A.S.26371/18 (BR.627) and numbered N3300 to N3374, to be built at Woolston. (Engine?)**

N3300  to N3314 built in 1919? (none delivered to 2.12.18 and no evidence of delivery in 1919)

N3315  to N3374 cancelled 12.18

**Reservation for 24 unidentified aircraft to be serialled N3375 to N3398 not taken up**

**1 SPAD S.7C.1 purchased from France and numbered N3399. (140-hp Hispano-Suiza)**

N3399  (C/n S.211) For Admiralty evaluation; Montreuil to St.Pol 23.11.16 (transit); ADD 23.11.16; Renumbered 9611 29.11.16

**N4000 to N4999 reserved for large flying boats**

**38 FELIXSTOWE F.3 PATROL TRACTOR BIPLANE FLYING BOATS ordered on Cont No AS.32421 from Short Bros Ltd, numbered N4000 to N4037 & built Rochester. (350-hp Eagle VIII) [Gordon Bruce's researches show correct c/n's to be S.588 to S.625. Originally to have been S.528 to S.565]**

N4000  Deld 350/1 Flts Tresco (via Cattewater) 29.7.18 (234 Sqdn 20.8.18); Bounced on TO, port side of hull gave way, beached on Samson Is 7.8.18 (Lt WL Anderson); still Tresco @30.1.19

N4001  Deld 350/1 Flts 234 Sqdn Tresco (via Cattewater) 3.8.18; Engine trouble, FL and crashed outside Tresco Harbour, sank in tow, 22.8.18 (crew saved); Deleted W/E 29.8.18

N4002  Deld 350/1 Flts 234 Sqdn Tresco (via Cattewater) 26.8.18 - @30.1.19

N4003  Deld Cattewater W/E 26.9.18 - @30.1.19

N4004  Deld Cattewater 23.8.18 - @30.1.19

N4005  Deld Cattewater W/E 26.9.18 - @30.1.19

N4006  Deld Cattewater W/E 26.9.18 - @30.1.19

N4007  Deld Feltham store W/E 26.9.18 - @30.1.19

N4008  Deld Feltham Store W/E 26.9.18 - @30.1.19

N4009  Deld 3 AAP Norwich W/E 30.10.18 - @30.1.19; [To G-CYDH?]

N4010  Deld 3 AAP Norwich W/E 7.11.18 - @30.1.19; Imperial Gift to Canada; Became G-CYDI; TOC 13.4.21; SOC 12.9.23

N4011  Deld 3 AAP Norwich W/E 21.11.18 - @30.1.19; Imperial Gift to Canada; Became G-CYDJ; TOC 13.4.21; SOC 12.9.23

N4012  Allocated 3 AAP Norwich but not arr by 30.1.19; Imperial Gift to Canada; Not registered; TOC 8.7.21; Held spare at Halifax, NS, SOC 4.1.23

N4013  Deld 3 AAP Norwich W/E 28.11.18 - @30.1.19; Imperial Gift to Canada; Not registered; TOC 8.7.21; Held spare at Vickers (Canada); SOC 3.1.23

N4014  Deld 3 AAP Norwich W/E 28.11.18 - @30.1.19; Imperial Gift to Canada; Became G-CYDQ; TOC 13.4.21; SOC 12.9.23

N4015  Deld 3 AAP Norwich W/E 5.12.18 - @30.1.19; Imperial Gift to Canada; Became G-CYEN; TOC 13.4.21; SOC 12.9.23

N4016  Deld 3 AAP Norwich W/E 23.11.19 - @30.1.19; Imperial Gift to Canada; Became G-CYBT; TOC 13.4.21; SOC 12.9.23

N4017  Deld 3 AAP Norwich W/E 19.12.18 - @30.1.19

N4018  Deld 3 AAP Norwich W/E 9.1.19 - @30.1.19

N4019  Deld 3 AAP Norwich W/E 31.12.18 - @30.1.19; Became G-EAQT

N4020  Deld 1(S) MAD Hamble W/E 19.12.18 - @30.1.19

N4021  Deld 1(S) MAD Hamble W/E 19.12.18 - @30.1.19

N4022  Deld 1(S) MAD Hamble W/E 19.12.18 - @30.1.19

N4023  Deld 1(S) MAD Hamble W/E 19.12.18 - @30.1.19

N4024  Deld AAP Sherburn W/E 23.1.19 - @30.1.19

*A Curtiss H.12 at anchor. (via Philip Jarrett)*

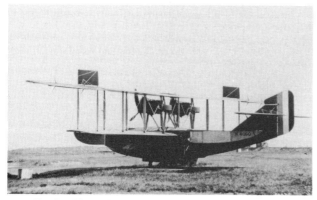

*Curtiss H.16 "Large America" Patrol Flying Boat
N4060. (J.M.Bruce/G.S.Leslie collection)*

*Felixstowe F.2A Patrol Flying Boat N4287 at
Killingholme. (J.M.Bruce/G.S.Leslie collection)*

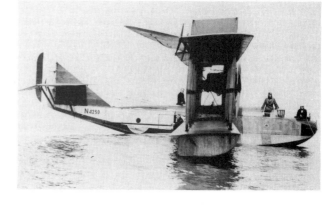

*Felixstowe F.3 Patrol Flying Boat N4230.
(J.M.Bruce/G.S.Leslie collection)*

*Curtiss H.12B "Large America" Patrol Flying Boat
N4332. (J.M.Bruce/G.S.Leslie collection)*

| | |
|---|---|
| N4025 | Allocated storage but not arr by 30.1.19 |
| N4026 | Allocated storage but not arr by 30.1.19 |
| N4027 | Allocated storage but not arr by 30.1.19 |
| N4028 | Allocated storage but not arr by 30.1.19 |
| N4029 | Allocated storage but not arr by 30.1.19 |
| N4030 | FF Rochester 3.2.19 (JL Parker); For storage |
| N4031 | FF Rochester 17.2.19 (JL Parker); For storage |
| N4032 | FF Rochester 21.2.19 (JL Parker); For storage |
| N4033 | FF Rochester, not accepted 25.2.19 (EAG Robinson); Tested Rochester 26.2.19 (JL Parker); Accepted 4.4.19 (EAG Robinson); For storage |
| N4034 | FF Rochester 25.2.19 (JL Parker); For storage |
| N4035 | FF Rochester 28.2.19 (JL Parker); For storage |
| N4036 | For storage |
| N4037 | For storage |

**12 FELIXSTOWE F.5 PATROL TRACTOR BIPLANE FLYING BOATS ordered on Cont No AS.32421 from Short Bros Ltd, numbered N4038 to N4049 & built Rochester. (375-hp Eagle VIII)** [Gordon Bruce's researches show correct c/n's to be S.626 to S.637. Originally to have been S.566 to S.577]

| | |
|---|---|
| N4038 | FF Rochester 10.7.19 (JL Parker); FB Devt Flt (coded 'E') 12.21 - 9.22; MAEE Grain by 1.23 - @6.23 |
| N4039 | Flown Rochester 1.9.19 (JL Parker); Deld MAES Grain 9.9.19 - @11.19 (performance trials and comparison with N4040); 480 Flt; Crashed at night and caught fire on impact, Calshot, 16.8.25 BO (1 killed) |
| N4040 | Flown Rochester 3.1.19 & 4.1.19 (JL Parker); Deld Grain 8.1.19 (type test); MAEE Grain (store) 22.5.19; MAEE Grain (flying) 29.3.20; Tested with modified rudder against N4038 with normal rudder 21.2.21 |
| N4041 | Tested Rochester 11.1.19 & 18.1.19 (JL Parker); Deld CTD Felixstowe by EAG Robinson 29.1.19 (tests for Grain); 232 Sqdn Felixstowe; No.4 Comm Sqdn Felixstowe - was to tour Scandinavia with N4044, FL in thick fog Orford Bay, Suffolk 11.7.19; Dundee 12.7.19 (arr 13.7.19); Left for Christiansund, but retd bad weather 20.7.19; Retd Felixstowe 25.7.19; Calshot 7.24; Withdrawn 10.7.24; AP Flt Calshot 5.25 |
| N4042 | FF Rochester 23.1.19 (JL Parker); Deld CTD Felixstowe by EAG Robinson 25.1.19 (tests for Grain); No.4 Comms Sqdn by 7.19 - @8.19; Grain by 4.22 - @5.22; Calshot by 5.22; FB Devt Flt Grain from 4.23; EF, FL off Mouse LV, sank under tow, 27.7.23, wreck salved 28.7.23; Visit to Sweden via Felixstowe and Calshot 30.7.23 - 25.8.23 (still FB Devt Flt) |
| N4043 | FF Rochester 3.2.19 (JL Parker); Tested 7.2.19 (EAG Robinson); 230 Sqdn Calshot .22 - .23; Calshot 11.2.24 |
| N4044 | FF Rochester 3.3.19 (JL Parker); 232 Sqdn Felixstowe; No.4 Comm Sqdn Felixstowe; Dundee 11.7.19; Christiansund 21.7.19; Copenhagen 28.7.19; Stockholm 5.8.19; Retd Felixstowe 6.8.19 (Scandinavian tour, flew 2,450 miles in 27 days, piloted by Mjr CJ Galpin); 230 Sqdn, spun in from 1,800ft ¼m from shore, Felixstowe, 29.4.20 (S/Ldr ER Moon) |
| N4045 | FB Devt Flt Grain by 5.22; Docked on RAF floating dock under own power 11.5.22; Felixstowe 29.7.23 for Swedish cruise; Visit to Sweden via Felixstowe and Calshot 30.7.23 - 25.8.23; still FB Devt Flt Grain 11.23 |
| N4046 | Saunders (Rebuilt); AP Flt Calshot 4.2.24; Saunders .24; AP Flt; 1.5.24; Stalled on turn nr water and landed heavily, nr Calshot, 19.5.24 |
| N4047 | Trial flight Rochester 26.3.19 (JL Parker); AP Flt Calshot 16.4.24 - @7.25 |
| N4048 | FF Rochester 17.6.19 (JL Parker); AP Flt Calshot 3.3.24 - @10.26 |
| N4049 | FF Rochester 27.6.19 (JL Parker); RAF Base Calshot 6.24; Propeller accident, 21.7.24; EF, FL in English Channel, 4.11.24 WOC |

**10 serials not allotted**

N4050 to N4059 not allotted

**15 CURTISS H.16 "LARGE AMERICA" PATROL TRACTOR BIPLANE FLYING BOATS ordered to N.3B Type Specification under Cont Nos B.1387/1137 & A.S.6731, numbered N4060 to N4074 (probably to have been N1160 to N1174) & built Hammondsport. (All deld without engines for erection, fitted 375-hp Eagle VIII)**

| | |
|---|---|
| N4060 | Deld AD Felixstowe W/E 9.3.18; Test Dept Grain 4.5.18; Tested @31.5.18 (hydrophone tests); Became MAES Grain 6.18 - @9.18 (fitted Cooper night landing stick equipt); 230 Sqdn Felixstowe (c/s AX21) W/E 26.9.18 - @30.1.19 |
| N4061 | Deld AD Felixstowe W/E 23.3.18; Killingholme, but fog, FL Mablethorpe 24.4.18; 318/9 Flts Dundee 27.4.18 (arr 1.5.18) (249 Sqdn 18.8.18) - @30.1.19 |
| N4062 | Deld AD Felixstowe W/E 30.3.18; US Navy dett Killingholme 26.7.18; Bombed U-boat 5m NE of Flamborough, then landed South Shields 30.7.18 (Lt Lynch); 318/9 Flts Dundee 15.8.18 (249 Sqdn 18.8.18); Deleted W/E 17.10.18 |
| N4063 | Deld AD Felixstowe W/E 30.3.18; 324/6 Flts Yarmouth 1.6.18 (228 Sqdn 20.8.18); Crashed on TO 29.7.18 (crew unhurt); still Yarmouth 30.1.19 |
| N4064 | Deld AD Felixstowe W/E 30.3.18; Seaplane School Felixstowe W/E 13.6.18 - @30.1.19 (Painted N1164 on delivery, but repainted N4064) |
| N4065 | Deld AD Felixstowe W/E 30.3.18; Dundee 30.7.18 (transit); 306 Flt Houton Bay 1 8.18 - @30.1.19 |
| N4066 | Deld AD Felixstowe W/E 30.3.18; South Shields 28.5.18 (transit); 318/9 Flts Dundee 29.5.18 (249 Sqdn 20.8.18); Dropped 2x230-lb bombs on U- boat 25m E of Montrose 20.45 3.6.18 (Capt WR Kenny, Capt NH Woodhead, AM1 CG Allred & AAM1E CP Denton); still Dundee 30.1.19 |
| N4067 | Deld MAD Felixstowe 4.4.18; Killingholme 5.6.18; US Navy dett Killingholme 20.7.18; Crashed en route Dundee 28.10.18 (1st pilot and engineer missing, 2nd pilot seriously injured, W/T operator unhurt); Deleted W/E 31.10.18 |
| N4068 | Deld MAD Felixstowe W/E 30.3.18; Killingholme W/E 17.5.18; US Navy dett Killingholme 20.7.18; Deleted W/E 5.9.18 |
| N4069 | For MAD Felixstowe W/E 27.4.18; To Dundee but engine trouble, FL Yarmouth 25.6.18; 318/9 Flts Dundee 28.6.18 (249 Sqdn 20.8.18) - @30.1.19; Sank River Tay [date unknown] |
| N4070 | Deld MAD Felixstowe W/E 25.7.18; Houton Bay (via Scarborough) 6.8.18; 318/9 Flts Dundee W/E 8.8.18 (249 Sqdn 20.8.18); Hit ship's mast on River Tay, crashed and burst into flames 21.9.18 (Capt A Holland, 2AM FE Wilson & 2AM E Marriott all killed; 2/Lt FI Atkins injured) |
| N4071 | Deld MAD Felixstowe W/E 29.8.18; ARS Calshot W/E 28.11.18 - @30.1.19 |
| N4072 | Deld MAD Felixstowe W/E 19.6.18; South Shields 25.6.18 (transit); 318/9 Flts Dundee 26.6.18 (249 Sqdn 20.8.18) - @30.1.19 |
| N4073 | Deld Liverpool (Docks?) W/E 5.12.18 - @30.1.19 |
| N4074 | Deld MAD Felixstowe W/E 29.8.18; Seaplane School Felixstowe W/E 19.9.18 - @31.1.19 |

**5 serials not allotted (or cancelled order?)**

N4075 to N4079 not allotted

**20 FELIXSTOWE F.2A PATROL TRACTOR BIPLANE FLYING BOATS ordered from S.E.Saunders Ltd under Contract No A.S.14154, numbered N4080 to N4099 & built East Cowes. (375-hp Eagle VIII)**

| | |
|---|---|
| N4080 | Deld Yarmouth (via Westgate) 15.8.18; Struck wreckage on TO, damaged hull, reached shore in sinking condition 18.9.18; still Yarmouth 30.1.19 |
| N4081 | Deld 345/6 Flts 240 Sqdn Calshot W/E 29.8.18; Dundee W/E 28.11.18; 345/6 Flts 240 Sqdn Calshot W/E 9.1.19 - @30.1.19 |
| N4082 | Deld US Navy dett Killingholme - @30.1.19 |
| N4083 | Deld Felixstowe 22.8.18 - @25.2.19 |
| N4084 | Deld 318/9 Flts 257 Sqdn Dundee W/E 29.8.18 - @30.1.19 |
| N4085 | Deld 3 AAP Norwich W/E 19.12.18 - @30.1.19; 267 Sqdn Calafrana (named *Neptune*), trip with *Sirius* to Gibraltar, during return flight, crashed on TO and disintegrated, Bizerta, North Africa, 22.6.23; Remains retd Malta by destroyer HMS *Tuscan* 27.6.23 |
| N4086 | Deld 3 AAP Norwich W/E 19.12.18 - @30.1.19; 267 Sqdn Calafrana (Named *Sirius*, c/s 4AK) by 1.21 - @7.22 |

N4087    Deld 3 AAP Norwich W/E 19.12.18 - @30.1.19

N4088    Deld 3 AAP Norwich W/E 19.12.18 - @30.1.19; 267 Sqdn Calafrana by 1.21; Crashed, 4.22

N4089    Deld 3 AAP Norwich W/E 19.12.18 - @30.1.19; 267 Sqdn Calafrana (Named *Neptune*) by 11.21; Lost at sea, 26.5.22 (replaced by an F.5)

N4090    Deld 3 AAP Norwich W/E 19.12.18 - @30.1.19; Calshot by 4.24

N4091    Deld 3 AAP Norwich W/E 19.12.18 - @30.1.19; 480 Flt Calshot by 1.24; Saunders 4.2.24; Modified to F.5; AP Flt Calshot by 3.24

N4092    Mkrs 14.9.18 - @11.18; 3 AAP Norwich store by 31.12.18 - @1.19; 1 SD storage; 267 Sqdn Calafrana by 2.22 (Named *Venus*, c/s 4AF); FL in Mediterranean, 19.2.23

N4093    Still at Mkrs 30.1.19 for SE Area

N4094    Still at Mkrs 30.1.19 for SE Area

N4095    Deld Felixstowe W/E 15.11.18 - @30.1.19

N4096    Deld Felixstowe W/E 15.11.18 - @30.1.19

N4097    Deld Felixstowe W/E 15.11.18 - @30.1.19

N4098    Deld Felixstowe W/E 15.11.18 - @30.1.19

N4099    Deld Felixstowe W/E 17.10.18; Propeller accident 10.11.18 (Sgt Shales injured); still Felixstowe 30.1.19; Calshot, Crashed and CW in Solent 1924 (WOPs body found inside after salvaged)

**50 FELIXSTOWE F.3 (11) and F.5 (39) PATROL TRACTOR BIPLANE FLYING BOATS ordered on Cont Nos 38a/1090/C & A.S.4499/18 (BR.347) from Dick, Kerr & Co, & numbered N4100 to N4149, to be & built Preston. (375-hp Eagle VIII)**

N4100    No information

N4101    to N4111 Deld at Mkrs by 11.12.18 (presumed all to store)

**Built as F.5 from here** (2 aircraft and 10 superstructures delivered by 11.12.18)

N4112    Deld at Mkrs by 11.12.18 (presumed to store)

N4113    Deld at Mkrs by 11.12.18 (presumed to store)

N4114    to N4119 no information

N4120    AP Flt Calshot by 2.24; FL Cowes, IoW 14.7.24; Reconditioned by Shorts (c/n S.639)

N4121    Calshot; FB Devt Flt Felixstowe 21.6.24 - @8.24; MAEE 10.26 (towed EEC Kingston N9712)

N4122    No information

N4123    No information

N4124    to N4149 cancelled 12.18

      [N4113 to N4149 (37 a/c) officially recorded as cancelled 12.18, but at least two of the 10 additional superstructures were completed and saw service]

      [Supposedly only N4100-4110 and N4120, N4121 completed]

      [Cont A.S.4499 was 18 F.3 up to N4117, then 32 F.5 N4118 onwards]

**10 serials not allotted (or cancelled order?)**

N4150 to N4159 not allotted

**20 FELIXSTOWE F.3 PATROL TRACTOR BIPLANE FLYING BOATS ordered on Cont Nos A.S.11426, A.S.30303 & A.S.30620 (BR.22) from The Phoenix Dynamo Manufacturing Co Ltd, numbered N4160 to N4179 (were to be N2160 to N2179) & built Bradford. (375-hp Eagle VIII)**

N4160    Allocated Grain for type trials 3.12.17 (NTU); Deld AAP Sherburn W/E 10.10.18 - @30.1.19

N4161    Deld AAP Sherburn W/E 10.10.18 - @30.1.19

N4162    Deld AAP Sherburn W/E 17.10.18 - @30.1.19

N4163    Deld AAP Sherburn W/E 17.10.18 - @30.1.19

N4164    Deld AAP Sherburn W/E 7.11.18 - @30.1.10

N4165    Deld AAP Sherburn W/E 7.11.18 - @30.1.19

N4166    Deld AAP Sherburn W/E 7.11.18 - @30.1.19

N4167    Deld AAP Sherburn W/E 14.11.18 - @30.1.19

N4168    Deld AAP Sherburn W/E 7.11.18 - @30.1.19

N4169    Deld AAP Sherburn W/E 7.11.18 - @30.1.19

N4170    Deld AAP Sherburn W/E 14.11.18 - @30.1.19

N4171    Deld AAP Sherburn W/E 12.12.18 - @30.1.19

N4172    Deld AAP Sherburn W/E 12.12.18 - @30.1.19

N4173    Allocated AAP Sherburn by 30.1.19

N4174    Allocated AAP Sherburn by 30.1.19

N4175    Deld AAP Sherburn W/E 5.12.18 - @30.1.19

N4176    Deld 3 AAP Norwich W/E 23.1.19 - @30.1.19

N4177    Deld AAP Sherburn W/E 31.12.18 - @30.1.19; Became G-EBDQ

N4178    Mkrs for storage by 30.1.19; To Canada (Imperial Gift); TOC CAF 8.7.21; Held spare; SOC 4.1.23

N4179    Mkrs for storage by 30.1.19; To Canada (Imperial Gift); TOC CAF 8.7.21; Held spare; SOC 4.1.23

**50 FELIXSTOWE F.3 (11) & F.5 (39) PATROL TRACTOR BIPLANE FLYING BOATS ordered on Cont No AS.4496/18 (BR.348) from The Phoenix Dynamo Manufacturing Co Ltd, numbered N4180 to N4229 & built at Bradford. (375-hp Eagle VIII)**

N4180    Deld at Mkrs by 11.12.18; Storage at Mkrs by 30.1.19

N4181    Deld at Mkrs by 11.12.18; Storage at Mkrs by 30.1.19; To Canada; Became G-CYEO; TOC 13.4.21; SOC 12.9.23

N4182    to N4188 no information

N4189    Conv F.5?; FB Devt Flt by 7.24 - @8.24

N4190    No information

N4191    (c/n 261?) Conv F.5?; Calshot by 2.24 - @3.25

**Built as F.5 from here** (9 aircraft and 10 superstructures deld by 11.12.18)

N4192    Calshot by 6.24 - @5.25

N4193    230 Sqdn Calshot 1922/3; Calshot 14.11.23 - @2.24; Shorts, Rochester; AP Flt Calshot 5.10.24 - @7.25; Reconditioned by Shorts (c/n S.643)

N4194    Calshot by 4.24 - @5.24

N4195    Calshot by 3.24 - @6.26; Reconditioned by Shorts (c/n S.640)

N4197    FB Devt Flt by 7.24 - @8.24

N4198    Grain by 26.9.18; RAF Base Calshot by 9.24; Hit mast of light on TO and crashed, Portland Harbour, 8.11.24

N4199    480 Flt by 1.25 - @6.25

N4200    480 Flt by 9.23; Hit dolphin on TO, Calshot, 15.1.24; Wreck salved

N4201    to N4229 cancelled 12.18, but 10 superstructures completed and delivered (presumed N4201 - N4210)

**50 FELIXSTOWE F.3 PATROL TRACTOR BIPLANE FLYING BOATS ordered 22.5.17 to N.3B Type Specification under Cont No AS.13823 (BR.72) from Dick, Kerr & Co Ltd, numbered N4230 to N4279 & built Preston. (375-hp Eagle VIII)**

N4230    Deld MAD South Shields 2.3.18; Killingholme 14.3.18; Type Test Flt Grain 16.3.18; Hydrophone trials at Shoeburyness 7.5.18 & 15.5.18, completed 25.5.18; Houton Bay W/E 20.6.18; Dropped 2x230-lb bombs on U-boat 7.7.18 (Capt HW Kendall & Lt WBE Powell); Attacked U-boat 20.7.18; Still Houton Bay 30.1.19

N4231    Deld MAD South Shields, tested 20.2.18; Came adrift from moorings, o/t and sank in harbour, wreck brought ashore 28.2.18 (crew unhurt); Deleted W/E 2.3.18

N4232    Deld MAD South Shields W/E 11.5.18; Dundee 10.6.18; Houton Bay W/E 20.6.18; 301 Flt Catfirth W/E 1.8.18; Stenness/Houton Bay W/E 24.10.18; 301 Flt Catfirth W/E 21.11.18; Deleted W/E 19.12.18

N4233    Deld MAD South Shields 8.4.18 for Houton Bay; Scapa (via Dundee) 28.6.18; Stenness/Houton Bay W/E 4.7.18 - @30.1.19

N4234    Deld MAD South Shields for erection W/E 15.5.18; Cattewater 1.7.18 (transit); 350/3 Flts Tresco 4.7.18 (painted in turquoise and white dazzle); Cattewater 5.7.18; Tresco 7.18; Petrol leak, FL, sank in swell under tow 8.7.18 (Capt CRH Stewart, Lt FH Prime and crew saved unhurt by hospital ship *Braemar Castle*)

N4235    Deld MAD South Shields 4.4.18; Tested 25.4.18; Dundee 3.5.18 (delayed by weather in transit); Houton Bay W/E 11.5.18; Became 306 Flt Houton Bay 31.7.18; 318/9 Flts 257 Sqdn Dundee W/E 14.11.18 - @30.1.19

N4236    Deld MAD South Shields for erection W/E 15.5.18; MAES Grain by rail 7.8.18 (arr 8.8.18) (navigation trials); Hull damaged 8.19; For disposal 8.20

N4237    Deld MAD South Shields W/E 18.5.18; Dundee 25.7.18 (transit); 306 Flt Houton Bay by 28.7.18 - @30.1.19

N4238    Deld MAD South Shields W/E 4.5.18; Tested 8.5.18; Killingholme 15.5.18 (transit); Cattewater 17.5.18 (transit); 350/3 Flts Tresco W/E 6.6.18 (234 Sqdn 20.8.18); Seriously damaged landing on water 14.6.18; Dropped 2x230-lb bombs on submarine 5103N 0550W

09.10 30.8.18 (Lt MO Fairhurst, Capt CRH Stewart, Cpl Mech P Durrant & Cpl Mech D Mackenzie); Ran out of fuel, FL, damaged 23.10.18; Retd in tow *ML319* 24.10.18; Still Tresco 30.1.19

N4239    Deld MAD South Shields W/E 25.5.18; Felixstowe 9.7.18 (transit); Patrol Reserve Calshot 13.7.18; 347/9 Flts 238 Sqdn Cattewater W/E 15.8.18 - @30.1.19

N4240    Deld MAD South Shields W/E 25.5.18; Felixstowe en route Cattewater but retd engine trouble 30.7.18; Cattewater 8.8.18; 350/3 Flts Tresco 13.8.18 (234 Sqdn 20.8.18) - @30.1.19

N4241    Deld MAD South Shields W/E 27.6.18; Patrol Reserve Calshot by 25.7.18; 350/3 Flts Tresco (via Newlyn) 28.7.18; Cattewater (via Newlyn) 21.8.18; 350/3 Flts 234 Sqdn Tresco 4.9.18 - @30.1.19

N4242    Deld MAD South Shields but crashed and sank taxying outside harbour 6.4.18; Salved, beached and stored in shed by 7.4.18

N4243    Felixstowe W/E 25.5.18; Cattewater 26.5.18; Newlyn 27.5.18 (en route Tresco); 350/3 Flts Tresco W/E 6.6.18 (234 Sqdn 8.18) - @30.1.19

N4244    MAD South Shields W/E 27.6.18; Dundee 1.8.18; Kirkwall by 8.18; 306 Flt Houton Bay by 6.8.18 - @30.1.19

N4245    Deld MAD South Shields 8.4.18 for re-allotment; Dundee 3.5.18 (delayed weather in transit); Houton Bay W/E 11.5.18; 309/310 Flts Stenness by 25.5.18 - @29.8.18); Kirkwall by 9.18; Advanced Base Pierowall to Houton Bay 12.10.18 - @30.1.19

N4246    Deld Stenness/Houton Bay W/E 18.5.18; MAD South Shields W/E 13.6.18 - @30.1.19

N4247    Deld MAD South Shields 8.4.18; Dundee 12.5.18 (transit); Attacked U-boat 20.5.18; Houton Bay W/E 20.5.18; Dropped 2x230-lb bombs on U-boat 12m E of Dennis Head 3.6.18 (Capt HA Wilson); Became 306 Flt Houton Bay 31.7.18 - @30.1.19

N4248    Deld MAD South Shields W/E 25.7.18; Killingholme 10.8.18 (transit); 347/9 Flts Cattewater 12.8.18 (238 Sqdn 20.8.18) - @30.1.19

N4249    Deld MAD South Shields W/E 4.5.18; Scapa (via Dundee) 28.6.18; Stenness/Houton Bay W/E 4.7.18 (detd Pierowall 28.8.18 - @31.8.18); Deleted W/E 14.11.18

N4250    Deld MAD South Shields W/E 27.6.18; Tested 2.8.18; Killingholme 10.8.18 (transit); 347/9 Flts Cattewater W/E 15.8.18 (238 Sqdn 20.8.18); Killingholme W/E 14.11.18; Felixstowe W/E 31.12.18 - @30.1.19

N4251    Deld MAD South Shields W/E 27.6.18; Tested 2.8.18; Killingholme 2.9.18; Felixstowe W/E 26.9.18 - @30.1.19

N4252    Deld MAD South Shields W/E 27.6.18; Dundee 13.8.18; 306 Flt Houton Bay by 19.8.18; Orkneys, lost at sea 4m NE of Fair Island 16.9.18 (Lt WM Shoesmith, Lt AJ Reith and crew rescued); Deleted W/E 14.11.18

N4253    Deld MAD South Shields W/E 18.5.18; Left for Stenness but crashed in harbour, salvaging 3.6.18 (Lt FI Jacks and crew saved)

N4254    Deld MAD South Shields W/E 27.6.18; Tested 27.8.18; Killingholme 3.9.18 (transit); Cattewater W/E 17.10.18 - @30.1.19

N4255    Deld MAD South Shields W/E 25.7.18; Cattewater W/E 29.8.18 - @30.1.19

N4256    Deld MAD South Shields W/E 25.7.18; Tested 4.9.18; Killingholme 18.9.18 (transit); 347 Flt 238 Sqdn Cattewater W/E 26.9.18; Calshot 6.11.18; Cattewater W/E 14.11.18 - @30.1.19

N4257    Deld MAD South Shields W/E 25.7.18; Tested 27.9.18 & 1.10.18; still MAD South Shields 30.1.19

N4258    Deld MAD South Shields W/E 25.7.18; Tested 18.9.18; Felixstowe 27.9.18 - @30.1.19

N4259    Deld MAD South Shields W/E 29.8.18; Tested 4.10.18; still MAD South Shields 30.1.19

N4260    Deld MAD South Shields W/E 1.8.18; Tested 8.9.18; Killingholme 18.9.18 (en route Cattewater); Newhaven by 26.9.18; Wrecked in transit, deleted W/E 31.10.18

N4261    Deld MAD South Shields W/E 8.8.18; Tested 22.10.18; still MAD South Shields 30.1.19

N4262    Deld MAD South Shields W/E 15.8.18 - @30.1.19

N4263    Deld MAD South Shields W/E 29.8.18; Tested 23.10.18; still MAD South Shields 30.1.19

N4264    Deld MAD South Shields W/E 5.9.18 - @30.1.19

N4265    Deld MAD South Shields W/E 5.9.18 - @30.1.19

N4266    Deld MAD South Shields W/E 12.9.18 - @30.1.19

N4267    Deld MAD South Shields W/E 12.9.18 - @30.1.19

N4268    to N4273 no delivery record

N4274    Deld MAD South Shields W/E 19.9.18 - @30.1.19

N4275    Deld MAD South Shields W/E 19.9.18 - @30.1.19

N4276    No delivery record

N4277    No delivery record

N4278    Deld MAD South Shields W/E 26.9.18 - @30.1.19

N4279    Deld MAD South Shields W/E 19.9.18 - @30.1.19

**30 FELIXSTOWE F.2A PATROL TRACTOR BIPLANE FLYING BOATS ordered under Cont Nos A.S.14154 (BR.80) & A.S.34426 from S.E.Saunders Ltd, numbered N4280 to N4309 & built East Cowes. (375-hp Eagle VIII unless otherwise stated)**

N4280    (Eagle VII) Deld Seaplane School Felixstowe (via Calshot) W/E 17.11.17; Deleted W/E 20.6.18

N4281    Deld Seaplane School Felixstowe 6.1.18; Crashed on TO for patrol to Terschelling 6.4.18; Repaired; Still Felixstowe 30.1.19

N4282    Deld Calshot School 28.1.18; Felixstowe patrol 3.2.18; Shot 2-str which crashed 12.3.18; With 8661 met 5 enemy seaplanes on water 7m E of old position of North Hinder LV 14.00 12.3.18; With N4513 & 8677 sighted 2 German seaplanes at 08.31, 1 biplane shot down in flames by Ens Stephen Potter USN, whose pilot was Capt NA Magor 19.3.18 [During WW.2, the US Navy Fletcher-class destroyer DD-538 was named *Stephen Potter* after him]; Yarmouth 26.3.18; 324/6 Flts Yarmouth 25.5.18; Deleted W/E 25.7.18

N4283    Deld Type Test Flt Grain 21.2.18; Yarmouth patrol 19.3.18; Dazzle-painted black and white 3.18; AZP 13.4.18 (Capt GE Livock & Capt R Leckie DSC); Became 324/6 Flts Yarmouth 25.5.18 (228 Sqdn 20.8.18); Hull holed landing 26.4.18 (Capt GE Livock); still Yarmouth 30.1.19; MAES Grain .19; Felixstowe .19

N4284    Deld Seaplane School Felixstowe (via Calshot) 8.3.18; HACP 10.6.18; Burned in shed, faulty wandering lead 6.8.18; Deleted W/E 29.8.18

N4285    Deld Calshot patrol W/E 1.3.18; Became 345/6 Flts Calshot 25.5.18; ARS Calshot W/E 29.8.18; 345/6 Flts 240 Sqdn Calshot 26.9.18; 318/9 Flts 257 Sqdn Dundee W/E 7.11.18; Calshot W/E 12.12.18 - @1.19

N4286    Deld Calshot patrol 26.3.18; Became 345/6 Flts Calshot 25.5.18 (240 Sqdn 20.8.18); Dropped 230-lb bomb on U-boat which was under attack by *SSZ.28* 8.7.18 (Capt HA Mumford, Lt CA Stephenson, Ens JJ Schieffelin USN & Ens Staub USN); ARS Calshot 21.11.18; Deleted W/E 19.12.18

N4287    Deld Killingholme patrol (via Felixstowe) 20.3.18; Dropped bombs on U-boat 5338N 0059E 26.6.18 (Ens JJ Schieffelin USN); Dropped 2x230-lb bombs on U-boat 33m E of Whitby 28.6.18 (Lt FRV Lynch, Ens Grosvenor USN, Ens JJ Schieffelin USN, Ens Staub USN & Engineer LMM Bernstein); Dropped 2 bombs on U-boat 13.7.18 (Lt Lawrence & Ens GS Hodges USN); USNAS dett Killingholme 20.7.18; Deleted W/E 5.9.18

N4288    Deld Felixstowe patrol 26.3.18; Crashed in harbour during night flying 26.4.18 (crew saved); Surveyed 10.5.18; Deleted 15.5.18 wrecked

N4289    Deld Yarmouth (via Felixstowe) W/E 6.4.18 (Dazzle painted red and yellow); Westgate 12.5.18; Yarmouth 20.5.18; Became 324/6 Flts Yarmouth 25.5.18 (228 Sqdn 20.8.18); HACP, FL off Dutch coast 4.6.18; Deleted W/E 7.11.18

N4290    Deld Killingholme patrol W/E 20.4.18; Struck wreckage on TO 8.6.18; USNAS dett Killingholme 20.7.18; Dundee 29.10.18

N4291    Deld Killingholme 20.4.18 (named "OLD BLACKEYE"); Shot down Zeppelin *L62* over Heligoland, nr Borkum Deep 10.5.18 (Capt TC Pattinson & Capt AH Munday); USNAS dett Killingholme 20.7.18; To Dundee but leaking radiator, FL South Shields 29.10.18; Deleted W/E 7.1.19

N4292    Deld Calshot TS 4.4.18; Became 210 TDS Calshot 6.18; ARS Calshot W/E 22.8.18; Deleted W/E 19.12.18

N4293    Deld Felixstowe 4.5.18; HACP 10.6.18; EF, FL, COL from special operation, complete loss 30.6.18; Deleted

N4294  W/E 11.7.18
Deld Felixstowe (via Calshot) 12.5.18; Crashed on TO, complete loss 30.6.18; Deleted W/E 11.7.18

N4295  Deld Dover 9.5.18 (transit); Retd Dover, engine trouble 10.5.18; Yarmouth 11.5.18; Fired at U-boat 5435N 0430W 17.5.18 (Capt BCH Cross & Lt LC Beaver); Became 324/6 Flts (228 Sqdn 20.8.18) Yarmouth 25.5.18; Deleted W/E 24.10.18

N4296  Deld Felixstowe 11.5.18; On lighter after crash; Deleted W/E 12.12.18

N4297  Deld Felixstowe 18.5.18; With N4513 and N4540 attacked approx 20m SE of North Hinder LV by 4 Brandenburg W.29 seaplanes of 1.C Staffel and forced down Aldeburgh 4.7.18; Repaired; Still Felixstowe 30.1.19

N4298  Deld Felixstowe and tested 18.5.18; Became 327/8 Flts Felixstowe 30.5.18 (230 Sqdn 20.8.18) (coded 'AM') to at least 30.1.19

N4299  Deld Felixstowe 27.5.18; FL nr Terschelling LV while chasing Zeppelin with 5 other aircraft, picked up by Dutch fishing smack, interned in Holland 2.8.18 (Capt LW Wilson, 3AM RA Wootton, 3AM HB May & Lt LC Bower); Deleted W/E 8.8.18 [BUT also reported as crashed on TO, locked ailerons 2.8.18]

N4300  Deld Felixstowe 16.6.18; Became 230 Sqdn Felixstowe 8.18 - @30.1.19

N4301  Deld Felixstowe 8.6.18; @12.2.19

N4302  Deld Felixstowe 4.6.18; Yarmouth 12.6.18; HACP, forced down off Vlieland 2.10.18 (Capt AT Barker, Lt VFA Galvayne killed, Pte Hopkins); Deleted W/E 24.10.18
BUT Wrecked on TO, beached 24.10.18 (crew unhurt)

N4303  Deld Felixstowe 11.6.18; 324/6 Flts Yarmouth (named 'THE SUICIDE CLUB') W/E 11.7.18 (228 Sqdn 20.8.18); AZP 5.8.18 (Capt SJ Fetherston & Capt EA Mossop); HACP 24.9.18 (Capt JC Grant); still Yarmouth 30.1.19

N4304  Deld 19.6.18 but FL Eastbourne with engine trouble; Dover 23.6.18 (transit); Felixstowe 25.6.18; still Felixstowe 30.1.19

N4305  Deld Felixstowe 17.6.18; Yarmouth 22.7.18; HACP 29.7.18 (Lt JC Grant); Attacked by 5 Brandenburg W29 seaplanes of 1.C Staffel and shot down off Lowestoft, burned on water, sank 31.7.18 (Capt EA Mossop, Lt G Hodson & Pte G/L Greenwood rescued by HMS *Halcyon*; Pte RRN Cooper & Pte WHD Dingley drowned); Deleted W/E 8.8.18

N4306  Deld Dover 28.6.18 (transit); Felixstowe Seaplane School 29.6.18 - @30.1.19

N4307  Deld Felixstowe Seaplane School 16.7.18 - @30.1.19

N4308  Deld Felixstowe 6.7.18 - @30.1.19

N4309  Deld Patrol Reserve Calshot W/E 10.7.18; 210 TDS Calshot W/E 8.8.18; ARS Calshot W/E 5.9.18; 210 TDS Calshot W/E 31.10.18 - @30.1.19

**12 FELIXSTOWE F.3 PATROL TRACTOR BIPLANE FLYING BOATS ordered under Cont No A.S.14835 (BR.86) from Malta Dockyard, numbered N4310 to N4321. (375-hp Eagle VIII)**

N4310  Tested 22.3.18; Under repair by 31.3.18; Deld Calafrana by 24.4.18; NFT from 25.5.18

N4311  Deld Calafrana by 24.4.18; Became 360/3 Flts 267 Sqdn Calafrana 27.9.18 - @11.18; Mkrs for Calafrana 1.19; 267 Sqdn Calafrana by 6.20 - @6.21

N4312  Deld Calafrana by 1.5.18; Became 360/3 Flts 267 Sqdn Calafrana 27.9.18 - @30.1.19

N4313  Deld Calafrana W/E 16.5.18; Became 360/3 Flts 267 Sqdn Calafrana 27.9.18 - @30.1.19

N4314  Mkrs 5.18; Calafrana by 27.6.18; Became 360/3 Flts 267 Sqdn Calafrana 27.9.18 - @30.1.19

N4315  Otranto by 7.18 - 8.18

N4316  Allocated Otranto, later Calafrana, but wrecked by 8.18; Rebuilding to at least 30.1.19

N4317  Deld Otranto by 7.18; Became 359 Flt 271 Sqdn Otranto 27.9.18; 268 Sqdn Calafrana to 270 Sqdn Alexandria 7.3.19; Deleted 7.7.19

N4318  Mkrs by 6.18; Deld Calafrana by 7.18 - @8.18; Otranto by 8.18 (359 Flt 271 Sqdn 27.9.18) - @11.18; 268 Sqdn Calafrana to 270 Sqdn Alexandria 7.3.19; Deleted 27.4.19

N4319  Mkrs by 6.18; Deld Calafrana 360/3 Flts 267 Sqdn by 9.18 - @30.1.19

N4320  Mkrs by 6.18; Deld Calafrana by 6.18; Otranto by 8.18; 359 Flt 271 Sqdn Otranto by 9.18 - @30.1.19

N4321  Deld Calafrana by 6.18; Became 360/3 Flts 267 Sqdn Calafrana 27.9.18 - @16.1.19

**8 serials not allotted**

N4322 to N4329 not allotted

**24 CURTISS H.12B "LARGE AMERICA" PATROL TRACTOR BIPLANE FLYING BOATS (Type N.3B) ordered 21.6.17 under Cont No A.S.6734 (BR.106) from Curtiss, numbered N4330 to N4353 and built at Hammondsport. Originally to have been serialled N2330 to N2353 but serials ordered to be changed on arrival. N2330 to N2350 delivered as such to Felixstowe for erection. (Two 375-hp Eagle VIII)**
[Some converted to F.2A standard after arrival]

N4330  Shipped to UK 22.11.17; Arr MAD Felixstowe for erection W/E 29.12.17; To Mediterranean W/E 19.1.18; 263 Sqdn Port Said

N4331  Shipped to UK 5.12.17; Arr MAD Felixstowe for erection W/E 5.1.18; To Mediterranean W/E 19.1.18

N4332  Shipped to UK W/E 5.12.17; Arr MAD Felixstowe for erection W/E 29.12.17; Tested 21.1.18; Type Test Flt Grain 28.1.18; Yarmouth patrol 17.3.18; Deleted W/E 25.5.18

N4333  Shipped to UK 17.12.17 and erected MAD Felixstowe; Deld Felixstowe for erection 18.1.18 - @30.1.19 (Reallocated for W/T tests 3.6.18)

N4334  Shipped to UK 9.1.18; MAD Felixstowe by 23.2.18; Calshot 26.3.18; Became 345/6 Flts Calshot 25.5.18 (240 Sqdn 20.8.18); ARS Calshot W/E 14.11.18; Crashed Calshot 12.12.18; Deleted W/E 19.12.18

N4335  Shipped to UK 19.12.17; Arr MAD Felixstowe W/E 19.12.17; To Mediterranean W/E 19.1.18; NFT

N4336  Shipped to UK 17.12.17; Arr MAD Felixstowe W/E 19.12.17; Killingholme 3.2.18; FL 5m N of Hornsea, beached, damaged wing tip and float 2.5.18; Bombed U-boat, and destroyers dropped DCs, oil and large air bubbles seen, considered successful 9.7.18; EF, FL 12.7.18; Petrol failure, FL in sea, wrecked, 12m E of Hornsea 19.7.18 (4 men clung to wreckage, including Ens AW Hawkins USNRF), wreckage taken in by 2 trawlers; USNAS dett Killingholme 20.7.18; Deleted W/E 5.9.18

N4337  Shipped to UK 8.12.17; Recd MAD Felixstowe W/E 19.12.17; Calshot (coded 'C') 3.2.18; Became 345/6 Flts Calshot 25.5.18 (240 Sqdn 20.8.18); ARS Calshot W/E 16.1.19 - @30.1.19

N4338  Shipped to UK 11.12.17; Arr MAD Felixstowe W/E 19.12.17 (convtd F.2A); While escorting convoy with N4339 nr North Hinder LV, attacked by 3 Zeebrugge-based fighters (probably Brandenburg W12s or W29s), shot down by aircraft crewed by Flugobermaat Urban and Lt d R Ehrhard of 1.C Staffel of Seeflugstation Flanders 1, Zeebrugge 15.2.18 (T/F/L CC Purdy, Ens AD Sturtevant USNR, Boy Mech AH Stephenson & AAM1 SJ Hollidge all killed) [Sturtevant, the co-pilot, was the first US Navy aircrew to be killed in WW1; he was awarded posthumous Navy Cross, and two successive American destroyers were named USS *Sturtevant* after him]

N4339  Shipped to UK 11.12.17; Recd MAD Felixstowe W/E 19.12.17 (convtd F.2A); Attacked by 10 seaplanes 20m SE of North Hinder, but fled 15.2.18 (crew unhurt); Worn out, hull strained by 1.7.18; still Felixstowe 30.1.19

N4340  Shipped to UK 21.12.17; Recd MAD Felixstowe W/E 19.1.18; Calshot patrol W/E 22.2.18; Dropped 2x230-lb bombs on U-boat 5013N 0027W 6.3.18 (F/L GMF O'Brien & OSL AJ Price); EF, FL, adrift in Channel 14.5.18 (crew picked up by another aircraft and taken to Cherbourg); Aircraft salved?; Became 345/6 Flts Calshot 25.5.18; Deleted W/E 29.8.18

N4341  Shipped to UK 21.12.17; Recd MAD Felixstowe W/E 19.1.18; Tresco (via Calshot) 8.3.18; Arr Cattewater 9.3.18; Scilly, dropped 2x230-lb bombs on *U-103* (which was later sunk) 4947N 0625W 10.5.18 (Lt MO

Fairhurst); Became 350/3 Flts Tresco 25.5.18; Cattewater 16.7.18; 350/3 Flts Tresco 21.7.18 (234 Sqdn 20.8.18); Dropped 2x230-lb bombs on U-boat, oil seen 11.10.18; Still Tresco 30.1.19

**N4342** Shipped to UK 21.12.17; Recd MAD Felixstowe W/E 19.1.18; To Calshot by FL, towed into Littlehampton 27.2.18; Cattewater 28.2.18; Felixstowe by 3.18; Surveyed 21.3.18; Deleted 27.3.18 (lost)

**N4343** Shipped to UK 21.12.17; Recd MAD Felixstowe W/E 19.1.18; Killingholme patrol 28.2.18; Dropped 2x230-lb bombs on U-boat which was then sunk by destroyers off Spurn Head 13.6.18 (Lt WF Cleeve & Ens Plehan Allen USN); Bombed U-boat 25m NE of Whitby 19.7.18; USNAS dett Killingholme 20.7.18; Attacked U-boat 9.9.18; still Killingholme 30.1.19

**N4344** Shipped to UK 9.1.18; Recd MAD Felixstowe W/E 2.2.18; Felixstowe Seaplane School W/E 13.3.18; Deleted W/E 31.12.18

**N4345** Shipped to UK 9.1.18; Recd MAD Felixstowe W/E 2.2.18; Felixstowe School W/E 6.3.18; Attacked by 4 Brandenburg seaplanes of 3.C Staffel and shot down by Obermaatrose Metzing and Flugmaat Walker, FL, o/t, CW, nr the Inner Gabbard 6.6.18 (L/Col EDM Robertson [Station CO] & Mjr CJ Galpin rescued next day by flying boats from Felixstowe); Deleted W/E 13.6.18

**N4346** Shipped to UK 9.1.18; Recd MAD Felixstowe W/E 9.2.18; Calshot 22.4.18; Became 345/6 Flts Calshot 25.5.18 (240 Sqdn 20.8.18); Deleted W/E 12.9.18

**N4347** Shipped to UK 9.1.18; Recd MAD Felixstowe W/E 9.2.18; Calshot patrol 9.3.18; Became 345/6 Flts Calshot 25.5.18; Deleted W/E 1.8.18

**N4348** Shipped to UK 9.1.18; Recd MAD Felixstowe W/E 9.2.18; Killingholme patrol 16.3.18; COL, salving 29.7.18 (crew unhurt); Converted to H.12 during repair; USNAS Killingholme 20.7.18; Deleted W/E 12.9.18

**N4349** Shipped to UK 12.1.18; Recd MAD Felixstowe W/E 9.2.18 (convtd F.2A); Calshot TS 24.4.18; 345/6 Flts Calshot W/E 18.7.18 (240 Sqdn 20.8.18); ARS Calshot W/E 21.11.18; Deleted W/E 31.12.18

**N4350** Shipped to UK 12.1.18; Recd MAD Felixstowe W/E 9.2.18; To Killingholme patrol but EF, FL Yarmouth 22.4.18 (to Killingholme later); FL in rough weather, undamaged 4.6.18; Bombed U-boat 15m E of Spurn Head 8.6.18 (Capt AH Munday & Ens RU Mill USN); Crashed, bounced, broke back, sank in tow 10.6.18 (Lt HL Madge, Ens W Jackson USNRF & 2AM PN Payne all slightly injured; 2AM G Pelling unhurt); Deleted W/E 27.6.18

**N4351** to N4353 cancelled

**6 serials not allotted (or cancelled order?)**

N4354 to N4359 not allotted

**38 FELIXSTOWE F.3 TRACTOR PATROL BIPLANE FLYING BOATS ordered under Cont No A.S.14835 (BR.Adm.1269) from Malta Dockyard, numbered N4360 to N4397. (375hp Eagle VIII)**

**N4360** Deld 9.18; 266 Sqdn Mudros; 270 Sqdn Alexandria from 6.10.18; 431 Flt 269 Sqdn Port Said 13.1.19; 270 Sqdn Alexandria 15.1.19; 268 Sqdn Calafrana 27.8.19

**N4361** Deld Calafrana by 9.18; 15 Group in transit 11.18 - @30.1.19

**N4362** Deld Calafrana by 9.18; 15 Group in transit 11.18; Calafrana by 1.19

**N4363** Deld Calafrana by 9.18; 15 Group in transit 11.18; Calafrana by 1.19

**N4364** Deld Calafrana 11.18 - @30.1.19

**N4365** Deld Calafrana 11.18 - @30.1.19

**N4366** Deld Calafrana by 1.19; 270 Sqdn Alexandria 6.8.19

**N4367** Malta Dockyard 10.18 - 11.18; in transit to 270 Sqdn Alexandria by 21.12.18; Engines etc salved 30.1.19; "Certificate of transfer 22.2.19"

**N4368** Malta Dockyard 10.18 - @30.1.19; "Certificate of transfer 4.4.19"

**N4369** Malta Dockyard 10.18 - @30.1.19

**N4370** "Certificate of transfer 14.5.19"; 267 Sqdn 3.21 - @4.21

**N4371** "Certificate of transfer 28.5.19"

**N4372** Calafrana to 270 Sqdn Alexandria 3.7.19; 268 Sqdn Calafrana 27.8.19

**N4373** to N4377 no information

**N4378** (DC) 267 Sqdn by 6.20 - @6.21

**N4379** to N4385 no information

**N4386** Calafrana to Alexandria 6.8.19

**N4387** no information

**N4388** to N4397 cancelled 1.19

**2 serials not allotted (or cancelled order?)**

N4398 to N4399 not allotted

**30 FELIXSTOWE F.3 PATROL TRACTOR BIPLANE FLYING BOATS ordered on Cont No. A.S.30620 (BR.199) & A.S.4496/18 from The Phoenix Dynamo Manufacturing Co Ltd, numbered N4400 to N4429 & built Bradford. (375-hp Eagle VIII)**

**N4400** Deld AD Killingholme to Type Test Flt Grain 11.3.18; Cooper servo motor fitted to ailerons 7.18; Cooper "autoflare" landing stick device tested W/E 17.8.18; Aveline starter tests W/E 5.10.18; Tested stabilizer 9.11.18; For hull pressure trials with Coates impact measuring device 3.4.19; Shorts for reconditioning 12.2.20; Sold to the Portuguese Govt 23.4.20; Became C-PAON

**N4401** Deld AD Killingholme W/E 11.4.18; Dundee 13.4.18 (transit); Houton Bay 14.4.18; Deleted W/E 27.6.18 wrecked

**N4402** Deld MAD Brough 8.4.18; AD Killingholme W/E 24.4.18; South Shields 26.4.18 (en route Dundee); Left for Dundee but capsized in heavy swell and sank, 27.4.18; salved, retd MAD South Shields for reconstruction; Dick, Kerr W/E 28.11.18 - @30.1.19

**N4403** Deld MAD Brough 8.4.18; Houton Bay W/E 25.5.18 (306 Flt 31.7.18) - @30.1.19

**N4404** (C/n 201?). Deld MAD Brough 8.4.18; Houton Bay (via Dundee) 19.5.18; Wrecked when hull struck unseen object on TO 23.5.18; Deleted W/E 27.6.18

**N4405** Deld 2(N) MAD Brough W/E 27.6.18; Houton Bay W/E 18.7.18 (306 Flt 31.7.18); FL E of Auskerry 28.6.18 (sic); Catfirth W/E 8.8.18; Deleted W/E 12.12.18

**N4406** Deld Houton Bay W/E 13.6.18 (306 Flt 31.7.18) - @31.10.18

**N4407** Deld 2(N) MAD Brough 8.4.18; Houton Bay W/E 4.7.18; At Kirkwall when dropped 2 bombs on U-boat 5927N 0219W 13.7.18 (Capt W Man & Lt WM Shoosmith); 300 Flt Catfirth W/E 1.8.18; 306 Flt Houton Bay W/E 12.9.18; Deleted W/E 12.12.18

**N4408** Deld Dundee W/E 20.6.18; Houton Bay W/E 17.7.18 (306 Flt 31.7.18) - @30.1.19

**N4409** Deld 2(N) MAD Brough W/E 27.6.18; MAES Grain 2.7.18 - @30.1.19 (expts)

**N4410** Deld 2(N) MAD Brough W/E 27.6.18; Houton Bay W/E 18.7.18 (306 Flt 31.7.18); Dundee W/E 14.11.18 - @30.1.19

**N4411** Deld 2(N) MAD Brough W/E 27.6.18; 306 Flt Houton Bay W/E 1.8.18 (at Adv Base Pierowall 10.8.18 - @31.8.18); Dropped bomb on U-boat 29.8.18 (Capt P Brend & Lt AJ Reith); Deleted W/E 21.11.18

**N4412** Deld 2(N) MAD Brough by 27.6.18; 'F' Training Flt Houton Bay W/E 29.8.18 (at Kirkwall 9.18); Crashed, wrecked 30.9.18 (pilot and observer slightly injured); Deleted W/E 14.11.18

**N4413** Deld 2(N) MAD Brough W/E 27.6.18; 347/8 Flts 238 Sqdn Cattewater W/E 22.8.18; 234 Sqdn 350/3 Flts Tresco 26.9.18; 347/9 Flts 238 Sqdn Cattewater 6.11.18 - @30.1.19

**N4414** Deld 2(N) MAD Brough W/E 11.7.18; For Cattewater, but spun in landing Calshot 2.9.18 (Capt T O'Connor killed; Lt BB Ball, Lt FW Fox & Sgt W Robinson all injured); Deleted W/E 12.9.18

**N4415** Deld 2(N) MAD Brough W/E 11.7.18; 347/8 Flts 238 Sqdn Cattewater W/E 22.8.18; 350/3 Flts 234 Sqdn Tresco 11.10.18 - @30.1.19

**N4416** Deld 2(N) MAD Brough W/E 11.7.18; 347/9 Flts 238 Sqdn Cattewater W/E 15.8.18 - @30.1.19

**N4417** Deld 2(N) MAD Brough W/E 4.7.18; 318/9 Flts 257 Sqdn Dundee W/E 5.9.18 - 11.18

**N4418** Deld 2(N) MAD Brough W/E 25.7.18; 318/9 Flts 257 Sqdn Dundee W/E 5.9.18 - @30.1.19

N4419    Deld 2(N) MAD Brough W/E 25.7.18; Grain W/E 12.9.18 (transit); 347/8 Flts 238 Sqdn Cattewater W/E 19.9.18 - @30.1.19

N4420    Deld 2(N) MAD Brough W/E 25.7.18; 347/9 Flts 238 Sqdn Cattewater W/E 26.9.18 - @30.1.19

N4421    Deld 2(N) MAD Brough W/E 25.7.18; 347/9 Flts 238 Sqdn Cattewater W/E 10.10.18 - @30.1.19

N4422    Deld 2(N) MAD Brough W/E 1.8.18; Deleted W/E 17.10.18

N4423    Deld 2(N) MAD Brough W/E 29.8.18 - @30.1.19

N4424    Deld 2(N) MAD Brough W/E 29.8.18 - @30.1.19

N4425    Deld 2(N) MAD Brough W/E 5.9.18 - @30.1.19

N4426    Deld 2(N) MAD Brough W/E 22.8.18 - @30.1.19

N4427    Deld 2(N) MAD Brough W/E 12.9.18 - @30.1.19

N4428    Deld 2(N) MAD Brough W/E 26.9.18 - @30.1.19

N4429    Deld MAD Sherburn W/E 31.10.18 - @30.1.19

**50 FELIXSTOWE F.2A PATROL TRACTOR BIPLANE FLYING BOATS ordered on Cont No AS.4498/18 (BR.349) from S.E.Saunders, numbered N4430 to N4479 & built East Cowes. (375-hp Eagle VIII)**

N4430    Deld 230 Sqdn Felixstowe W/E 24.10.18 - @28.1.19

N4431    Deld 318/9 Flts 257 Sqdn Dundee (via Felixstowe) W/E 31.10.18; Escorting convoy *H264*, landed in position 26UUQ, sank 6.11.18 (crew saved by trawler); Deleted W/E 14.11.18

N4432    Deld South Shields 24.10.18 (transit via Killingholme); 318/9 Flts 257 Sqdn Dundee 25.10.18 - @30.1.19

N4433    Deld 318/9 Flts 257 Sqdn Dundee (via Killingholme) 29.10.18; Killingholme 4.3.19

N4434    Deld Calshot W/E 21.11.18; Newhaven W/E 12.12.18; Felixstowe W/E 9.1.19 - @30.1.19

N4435    Deld Calshot W/E 21.11.18; Newhaven W/E 12.12.18; ARS Calshot W/E 31.12.18; Calshot by 7.23 - @10.23

N4436    Still at Mkrs 30.1.19; 267 Sqdn Calafrana

N4437    Still at Mkrs 30.1.19; Calshot by 5.22 (Named *Cuttle*); Became Air Pilotage Flt 5.2.23; EF, FL 2m SE of Portland Bill 16.10.23

N4438    Deld Felixstowe W/E 28.11.18 - @30.1.19; 267 Sqdn Calafrana (named *Saturn*, c/s 4AR) by 9.20 - 9.22

N4439    Deld Felixstowe W/E 21.11.18 - @23.2.19; Felixstowe by 10.21

N4440    Deld Felixstowe W/E 28.11.18 (transit); 318/9 Flts 257 Sqdn Dundee W/E 5.12.18 - @30.1.19

N4441    Deld Felixstowe W/E 28.11.18 - @30.1.19

N4442    Deld Calshot 11.18; Retd Mkrs 16.11.18; Felixstowe W/E 31.12.18 - @30.1.19

N4443    Deld Felixstowe W/E 19.12.18 - @30.1.19

N4444    Deld Yarmouth W/E 9.1.19 - @30.1.19

N4445    Deld Felixstowe W/E 23.1.19 - @30.1.19

N4446    Still at Mkrs 30.1.19

N4447    Still at Mkrs 30.1.19

N4448    Still at Mkrs 30.1.19

N4449    Deld 347/9 Flts 238 Sqdn Cattewater W/E 23.1.19 - @30.1.19

N4450    Still at Mkrs 30.1.19

N4451    Still at Mkrs 30.1.19

N4452    to N4459 no delivery record

N4460    238 Sqdn Cattewater by 9.20; EF, FL in sea 15m from starting point, hull badly damaged 17.1.21 (F/L GE Livock picked up by trawler *Verity*)

N4461    No delivery record

N4462    Convtd F.5

N4463    No delivery record

N4464    No delivery record

N4465    Killingholme .18 (balanced ailerons, but no cabin)

N4466    No delivery record

N4467    Convtd F.5

N4468    to N4474 No delivery record

N4475    Calshot by 5.21 - 10.21; Felixstowe by 10.21

N4476    230 Sqdn Felixstowe by 12.20

N4477    No delivery record

N4478    230 Sqdn Calshot by .22

N4479    No delivery record

**25 FELIXSTOWE F.2A PATROL TRACTOR BIPLANE FLYING BOATS ordered on Cont No AS.4502/18 (BR.350) from May, Harden & May to be numbered N4480 to N4504 and built at Hythe. (375-hp Eagle VIII)**

N4480    Tested Hythe 13.10.18; Deld Felixstowe W/E 7.11.18 - 2.19

N4481    Deld Felixstowe W/E 8.10.18 - @30.1.19

N4482    Deld 230 Sqdn Felixstowe W/E 7.11.18 - @30.1.19

N4483    Retd Mkrs for tests 23.11.18; Deld Felixstowe W/E 12.12.18 - @30.1.19

N4484    Deld South Shields (via Killingholme) 11.11.18 (transit); 318/9 Flts 257 Sqdn Dundee W/E 28.11.18 - @30.1.19

N4485    Deld Calshot W/E 21.11.18 (transit); Felixstowe W/E 28.11.18 - @30.1.19

N4486    Deld Felixstowe W/E 21.11.18 - @30.1.19

N4487    Still at Mkrs 30.1.19

N4488    Still at Mkrs 30.1.19; 267 Sqdn Calafrana by 5.21 (Named *Mercury*, c/s 4AM) - @8.22

N4489    Deld Calshot W/E 9.1.19 - @30.1.19

N4490    Deld Felixstowe 22.1.19; 267 Sqdn Calafrana by 11.21 (Named *Aquila*, c/s 4AP) - @9.22

N4491    to N4493 No delivery record

N4494    238 Sqdn Cattewater by 9.20 - @5.21

N4495    No delivery record

N4496    No delivery record

N4497    Flown (238 Sqdn?) Cattewater 26.8.20 (first flight for a year)

N4498    267 Sqdn Calafrana by 10.21

N4499    Cattewater .19; (238 Sqdn?) Cattewater, tested 14.2.21 (first flight for a year) - @4.21; Seaplane Training Sqdn by 1.23; FL, tail heavy, Solent, 15.5.24 WOC

N4500    238 Sqdn Cattewater

N4501    to N4504 no evidence of delivery

**5 serials not allotted (or cancelled order?)**

N4505 to N4509 not allotted

**10 FELIXSTOWE F.2A PATROL TRACTOR BIPLANE FLYING BOATS ordered under Cont No A.S.2697 to Spec N.3B from May, Harden & May, numbered N4510 to N4519 & built Hythe. (375-hp Eagle VIII)**

N4510    Deld Type Test Flt Grain (via Calshot) 25.1.18 (type trials); Felixstowe patrol 20.3.18; EF, FL, sank in tow in heavy seas 8.4.18; Deleted W/E 20.8.18

N4511    Deld Yarmouth patrol W/E 2.2.18; EF, FL 50m E of Yarmouth, broke adrift & sank in tow of HMS *Glowworm* 15.2.18 (F/Cdr FW Walker DSC & F/L EA Bolton saved); Deleted W/E 23.2.18

N4512    Deld Calshot W/E 15.2.18; Yarmouth patrol W/E 22.2.18 (324/6 Flts 25.5.18); Dropped 2 bombs on U-boat 8.6.18 (Capt EA Bolton & Ens Teulon USN); Crashed in sea, sank, attempting to rescue Camel N6608 21.6.18 (crew safe); Deleted W/E 27.6.18

N4513    Deld Calshot 15.2.18; Felixstowe patrol 18.2.18; With N4282 & 8677 (q.v.) sighted 2 seaplanes at 08.31, 1 shot down in flames 19.3.18; With N4297 and N4540 attacked by 4 Brandenburg W.29 seaplanes of 1.C Staffel, claimed 1 shot down, then forced down, sank under tow approx 20m SE of North Hinder LV 4.7.18 (Lt S Anderson, Lt KL Williams & Boy Mech AEV Hilton all wounded; 2AM AC Cokeley killed); Deleted W/E 18.7.18

N4514    Deld Calshot W/E 22.2.18; Felixstowe School 8.3.18; Crashed 25.10.18 (Lt J Hunt & 3AM FC Kale slightly injured; 2/Lt HJW Locke, 2/Lt M Gardiner & F/Cdt WR Godard unhurt); Deleted W/E 21.11.18

N4515    Deld Calshot W/E 30.3.18; To Felixstowe Patrol but FL off Dungeness, taken to Dover by trawler 11.3.18; Towed to Felixstowe from Ramsgate 17.3.18; Propeller accident 14.6.18 (2AM Lealand killed); Stalled on landing and wrecked 3.8.18 (2/Lt JSA Forest, Lt AH Lye and Lt LG Frust all injured) ; Deleted W/E 29.8.18

N4516    Deld Killingholme patrol W/E 15.2.18; Broke tail on leaving slipway 3.6.18; Elevator shot away 19.7.18; USNAS dett Killingholme 20.7.18; Dropped 2 bombs on U-boat off Scarborough 5416N 0002W 23.7.18 (Ens B Lee); Crashed off Immingham 14.8.18 (crew unhurt); Deleted W/E 5.9.18

N4517    Deld Dover (via Calshot) Dover 19.3.18 (transit, towed into harbour after EF); Yarmouth 20.3.18; Surveyed 8.5.18; Deleted 15.5.18 wreckage

N4518    Deld Felixstowe (via Calshot) but EF, FL Dover 26.3.18; Felixstowe 27.3.18; Yarmouth 1.6.18;

Westgate 2.6.18; HACP 8.6.18; Felixstowe 20.6.18; 324/6 Flts 228 Sqdn Yarmouth W/E 27.6.18 - @30.1.19

N4519    Deld Felixstowe (via Calshot) 2.4.18; Seaplane School Felixstowe 1.7.18; Deleted W/E 7.11.18

**10 FELIXSTOWE F.2A PATROL TRACTOR BIPLANE FLYING BOATS ordered from May, Harden & May under Cont No A.S.24912 (BR.74 & BR.90) & numbered N4520 to N4529, to be built Hythe. (375-hp Eagle VIII)**

N4520 to N4529 cancelled

**25 FELIXSTOWE F.2A PATROL TRACTOR BIPLANE FLYING BOATS ordered from Aircraft Manufacturing Co Ltd under Cont No A.S.21558, numbered N4530 to N4554 (to have been N2530 to N2554), to be built by May, Harden & May at Hythe. (375-hp Eagle VIII)**

N4530    Deld Felixstowe 14.5.18; Killingholme 3.6.18; Bombed U-boat 15m E of Spurn, oil and bubbles seen 8.6.18 (Capt AH Munday); Felixstowe, HACP 19.7.18 (Lt JC Grant); Seaplane School Felixstowe W/E 12.12.18 - @30.1.19

N4531    Deld Felixstowe 18.5.18; Deleted W/E 16.1.19

N4532    Deld Dundee W/E 1.6.18 - @30.1.19

N4533    Deld Felixstowe 15.6.18; EF, FL 10m from Terschelling, Frisian Islands, taxied to Terschelling but when 200 yards off shore attacked and set on fire by Ltn Christiansen in Brandenburg W19 No.2239, 4.6.18 (Capt RFL Dickey DSO, Capt RJ Paul, Lt AG Hodgson, 2AM EPC Burton & F/W(?) ACH Russell all interned); Deleted W/E 20.6.18

N4534    Deld Calshot TS W/E 18.5.18; Became 210 TDS Calshot (coded 'G') 6.18; Patrol Reserve Calshot W/E 1.8.18; ARS Calshot W/E 29.8.18; 210 TDS Calshot W/E 12.9.18; ARS Calshot W/E 9.1.19 - @30.1.19

N4535    Deld 345/6 Flts Calshot W/E 18.5.18; Newhaven W/E 6.6.18; 345/6 Flts 240 Sqdn Calshot W/E 29.8.18; ARS Calshot W/E 12.9.18; 345/6 Flts 240 Sqdn Calshot W/E 24.10.18; Dundee W/E 7.11.18; Calshot W/E 12.12.18; ARS Calshot W/E 10.1.19; RAF Base Calshot by 11.23

N4536    Deld Calshot TS (via Felixstowe) 22.4.18; Became 210 TDS Calshot 6.18; ARS Calshot W/E 5.9.18; 210 TDS Calshot W/E 31.10.18; ARS Calshot W/E 31.12.18 - @30.1.19; RAF Base Calshot by 11.22 (as F.5?)

N4537    Deld Felixstowe 30.5.18; Damaged in battle 4.10.18 (Capt TWS Harris killed; Cpl MB Blackadder injured; 2/Lt LW Morwick, 2/Lt W Galloway & 1AM AW Goodey uninjured) [or crashed in harbour after TO]; Deleted W/E 17.10.18

N4538    Deld Felixstowe (via Calshot) 5.6.18; HSMP 7.7.18 (Lt JC Grant); Heavy landing in harbour during night flying 16.7.18 (W/O 3AM TA Snell & 3AM C Methem both killed); Deleted W/E 25.7.18

N4539    Deld Felixstowe 6.6.18; HACP 9.7.18 (Lt JC Grant); still Felixstowe 30.1.19

N4540    Deld Felixstowe 12.6.18; With N4297 and N4513 attacked approx 20m SE of North Hinder LV by 4 Brandenburg W29 seaplanes of 1.C Staffel, but N4540 escaped and landed Yarmouth for repair 4.7.18 (2AM W Blacklock, the engineer, climbed out on wing in flight and stopped oil leak in starboard engine); EF, FL, destroyed by crew 1.10.18; Deleted W/E 10.10.18

N4541    Deld 333/5 Flts Felixstowe (via Calshot) 27.6.18; Became 333/5 Flts 232 Sqdn Felixstowe 20.8.18; Crashed 30.10.18 (Lt JS Hughes slightly injured; 4 crew unhurt); Deleted W/E 28.11.18

N4542    Deld Yarmouth (via Felixstowe) 7.8.18 - @30.1.19

N4543    Deld Newhaven via Calshot 5.7.18 (transit); 230 Sqdn Felixstowe 6.7.18; Dropped bomb on U-boat 25m 30° Whitby 19.7.18 (Ens JJ Schieffelin USN & Lt RO Cutler) [stated to be from Killingholme !]; Fuel shortage, FL in sea, sank SE of Smith's Knoll 9.11.18 (2/Lt OE Coleman, 2/Lt FB Candy, 2/Lt J Freeman, Sgt RH Thomas & 2AM LA Christmas picked up by Dutch trawlers *Corrie & Zeepard*); Deleted W/E 28.11.18

N4544    Deld 210 TDS Calshot W/E 8.8.18; ARS Calshot W/E 24.10.18 - @30.1.19; Calshot Group Workshop & Repair Depot .20

N4545    Deld 327/8 Flts Felixstowe 8.7.18 (230 Sqdn 20.8.18) (coded 'AM', open cockpit, dazzle painted) - @30.1.19;

Modified as F.2B

N4546    Deld Felixstowe 28.7.18; EF during bank, crashed in sea 21.8.18 (2/Lt RH Bullock killed; 2/Lt W Pendleton injured; Lt A Woods, 2/Lt DM Crater & 2AM RJ Kinshaw all uninjured); Deleted W/E 12.9.18

N4547    Deld 210 TDS Calshot W/E 1.8.18; ARS Calshot W/E 9.1.19 - @30.1.19; 230 Sqdn Felixstowe by 2.22; Hull struck submerged object, towed back to air station, 14.2.22

N4548    Deld Seaplane School Felixstowe W/E 15.8.18; Fishguard (transit via Cattewater and Newlyn) 4.10.18; Lytham 11.10.18 - @30.1.19 repair for Seaplane School Felixstowe

N4549    Deld Yarmouth 16.8.18; With N4550, D.H.9 D5709 and D.H.4 N6395 fought the station's last engagement with 5 Brandenburg seaplanes of 1.C Staffel, badly damaged, 16.9.18 (Lt VS Green); still Yarmouth 30.1.19

N4550    Deld Yarmouth W/E 15.8.18; With N4549, DH9 D5709 and DH4 N6395 fought the station's last engagement with 5 Brandenburg seaplanes of 1.C Staffel 16.9.18 (Capt J Hodson); Deleted W/E 31.10.18

N4551    Deld 232 Sqdn Felixstowe W/E 29.8.18; EF, FL 10m NNW of Nordwijk, drifted ashore, salved by Dutch, interned 2.10.18 (2/Lt TN Enright, 2/Lt W Pendleton, 1AM HL Curtis & 3AM WA Mitchell unhurt; Lt JC Stockman injured, all interned); Deleted W/E 10.10.18; Retained and re-serialled *L.2* by Dutch

N4552    Deld Felixstowe 3.9.18 - @1.2.19

N4553    Deld 228 Sqdn Yarmouth W/E 19.9.18 - @30.1.19

N4554    In transit to Dundee W/E 26.9.18; No evidence of arrival, presume crashed on delivery

**5 FELIXSTOWE F.2A PATROL TRACTOR BIPLANE FLYING BOATS ordered under Cont No A.S.24912 & numbered N4555 to N4559. (375-hp Eagle VIII)**

N4555 to N4559 cancelled

**20 FELIXSTOWE F.2A PATROL TRACTOR BIPLANE FLYING BOATS ordered from May, Harden & May under Cont Nos 38a/551/C564 & A.S.24912/18 (BR.589), numbered N4560 to N4579 & built Hythe. (375-hp Eagle VIII)**

N4560    to N4563 No information

N4564    Calshot by 3.20 - @11.20; Seaplane Training Sqdn Calshot by 11.22 - @2.23

N4565    No information

N4566    Calshot 1919; Calshot c.1924 (Convtd F.5?)

N4567    To Chile as *Guardamarine Zamartu*

N4568    Deld Calshot 12.19

N4569    Deld Calshot 9.12.19 - @2.20; Seaplane Training Sqdn Calshot by 3.23 - @11.23

N4570    Deld Calshot 12.12.19; Cattewater by 10.20 - @1.21; Seaplane Training Sqdn Calshot by 3.23 - @11.23; 480 Flt 11.23; Crashed on TO from glassy water, port wing tip damaged off Cowes, IoW, 12.12.23

N4571    Deld Calshot 12.19; Grain, tow line broke after landing, drifted on to beach 30.2.22 (F/L GE Livock)

N4572    Completed by 4.20; Calshot by 5.21 - 10.21

N4573    to N4579 cancelled 12.19

**50 FELIXSTOWE F.5 PATROL TRACTOR BIPLANE FLYING BOATS ordered from S.E.Saunders Ltd under Cont Nos 38a/550/C563 & A.S.24911/18 (BR.590), to be numbered N4580 to N4629 & built East Cowes. (375-hp Eagle VIII)**

N4580 to N4589 no evidence of delivery
N4590 to N4629 cancelled 1.19

**50 FELIXSTOWE F.5 TRACTOR BIPLANE FLYING BOATS ordered from Gosport Aviation Co Ltd under Cont Nos 38a/552/C565 & A.S.24910/18 (BR.591), numbered N4630 to N4679 & built Gosport. (375-hp Eagle VIII)**

N4630    Recond Shorts, Rochester (c/n S.641); Calshot 2.6.24; APF Calshot by 3.25

N4631    No information

N4632    Recond; Calshot 10.11.21; FB Devt Flt Grain by 6.22; MAEE Grain from 4.23 - @6.23 (recond); Visit to Sweden via Felixstowe and Calshot 30.7.23 - 25.8.23; Calshot by 5.25

N4633    No information

N4634    Calshot by 7.23; Recond Shorts, Rochester (c/n S.642) 7.2.24; ARS Calshot 5.24; RAF Base Calshot by 7.24 - @2.25; Saunders; Calshot 6.3.25 - @7.25; SoNC Lee-on-Solent 7.25; Became G-EAIK "Gosport Flying Boat" (c/n G.6/100)

N4635    Calshot by 12.20 - @2.21; AP Flt Calshot by 3.25

N4636    AP Flt Calshot by 11.22; 480 Flt 1.4.23 - @6.25; SoNC Lee-on-Solent 7.25 - @8.25

N4637    Seaplane Training Sqdn; Starboard propeller came adrift over English Channel, FL in sea, 14m off Alderney, 6.10.21; 480 Flt; Rudder bar carried away in air, made heavy landing and hull collapsed, Calshot, 25.4.23

N4638    No information

N4639    Seaplane Training Sqdn, EF on TO, FL downwind, o/t and sank, off Swanage, Dorset, 12.9.22 WOC

N4640    to N4679 cancelled 1.19

**50 FELIXSTOWE F.5 PATROL TRACTOR BIPLANE FLYING BOATS ordered from May, Harden & May under Cont Nos 38a/599/C627 & A.S.26345/18 (BR.620), to be numbered N4680 to N4729 & built Hythe. (375-hp Eagle VIII)**

N4680 to N4729 cancelled 12.18

**50 FELIXSTOWE F.5 PATROL TRACTOR BIPLANE FLYING BOATS ordered from Dick, Kerr & Co under Cont Nos 38a/604/C633 & A.S.26344/18 (BR.621), to be numbered N4730 to N4779 & built Preston. (375-hp Eagle VIII)**

N4730 to N4779 cancelled 12.18

**50 FELIXSTOWE F.5 PATROL TRACTOR BIPLANE FLYING BOATS ordered from Phoenix Dynamo Co under Cont Nos 38a/598/C628 & A.S.26343/18 (BR.622), numbered N4780 to N4829 & built Bradford. (375-hp Eagle VIII)**

N4780 to N4829 cancelled 12.18

**50 FELIXSTOWE F.5 PATROL TRACTOR BIPLANE FLYING BOATS ordered from Short Bros Ltd under Cont Nos 38a/600/C629 & A.S.26368/18 (BR.623), to be numbered N4830 to N4879 & built Rochester. (375-hp Eagle VIII)** [Gordon Bruce's researches show correct c/n's to be S.528 to S.537]

N4830    FF Rochester 24.9.19

N4831    FF Rochester 30.10.19; Collided with ferry boat, Felixstowe Harbour, Suffolk, 29.6.21

N4832    FF Rochester 12.9.19; Deld Training School Calshot 9.19

N4833    FF Rochester 6.11.19; Calshot by 10.20; AP Flt Calshot 2.23; FL, Cherbourg, 5.3.23; Repaired; AP Flt 3.23 - @10.23

N4834    FF Rochester 9.1.20; Calshot by 9.20 - @2.21; AP Flt Calshot 7.23 - @9.23

N4835    FF Rochester 20.1.20; Calshot by 7.20; AP Flt Calshot 12.22 - @10.23

N4836    FF Rochester 29.1.20; AP Flt Calshot 12.22 - @10.23

N4837    Flown Rochester 6.2.20; AP Flt Calshot 12.22

N4838    (Eagle VIIIs) FF Rochester 26.2.20; MAEE Grain from 12.20 - @3.22 (stability tests); Tested with Avro aileron balance 12.20; Tested with standard rudder against N4040 with modified rudders 21.2.21; 230 Sqdn Calshot; Caught fire in H Shed, partially burnt Calshot 1924; Saunders; Cowes by 3.25; AP Flt Calshot 6.3.25 - @7.25

N4839    (Lions) FF Rochester 23.3.20; MAEE Grain (Exp ailerons); Shorts 10.21 (fit Lions); MAEE Grain FF 5.22; Trials with 4-bladed propellers 6.22; FB Devt Flt Grain 13.7.22 (before trials complete); Tested 16.8.22; still MAEE Grain 6.23

N4840    to N4879 cancelled 1.19

**10 serials not allotted (or cancelled order?)**

N4880 to N4889 not allotted

**110 CURTISS H.16 "LARGE AMERICA" TRACTOR BIPLANE FLYING BOATS ordered under Cont No A.S.6731 (BR.50), numbered N4890 to N4999 (to have been N1890 to N1949) & built Hammondsport. (Two 375-hp Eagle VIII)**

N4890    Deld AAP Brockworth 26.9.18 - @30.1.19

N4891    Deld MAD Felixstowe W/E 25.5.18; South Shields 6.7.18 (transit); Strathbeg 7.18 (transit); Dundee 13.7.18; COL, CW at dusk on River Tay 27.8.18 (F/L NH Woodhead)

N4892    Deld MAD Felixstowe W/E 25.5.18; MAES Grain 27.7.18 (type trials); Flown with Wright stabilizers 21.11.18 - 2.12.18 but unsatisfactory; Rubber paint tests; Tested with Aveline stabiliser 3.19 - 4.19; Hull repaired 6.19; Redes MAEE Grain 3.20; Flown until 10.20 then disposed of

N4893    Deld MAD Felixstowe W/E 8.8.18; Seaplane School Felixstowe 26.9.18 - @30.1.19

N4894    Deld MAD Felixstowe W/E 8.8.18 - @31.10.18; ARS Calshot W/E 28.11.18 - @30.1.19

N4895    Deld MAD Felixstowe W/E 13.6.18; South Shields (delayed by fog in transit); 306 Flt Houton Bay 25.7.18; Bombed U-boat 1.8.18 (Capt P Brend & Lt HL Macro); Dropped 2x230-lb bombs on U-boat 5835N 0107W 12.8.18 (Capt EPM Davis & Lt W Sanderson); still Houton Bay (Group?) by 29.8.18 - @30.1.19

N4896    Deld MAD Felixstowe W/E 6.6.18; Dundee 17.7.18 (transit); 306 Flt Houton Bay W/E 25.7.18 - @30.1.19

N4897    Deld MAD Felixstowe W/E 4.7.18; 'F' Training Flt Houton Bay W/E 29.8.18; Dropped 2 bombs on U-boat but 1 failed to explode 29.8.18 (Capt HW Kendall & 2/Lt JR Cox); Deleted W/E 12.12.18

N4898    Deld MAD Felixstowe W/E 4.7.18; Cattewater (via Calshot) 6.8.18 - @30.1.19

N4899    Deld MAD Felixstowe W/E 25.7.18; Cattewater W.E 29.8.18 (detd Brest W/E 19.9.18 - @26.9.18); South Shields late 10.18 (transit via Calshot); Orkney by 1.11.18; Calshot W/E 7.11.18 (transit); Killingholme W/E 14.11.18; South Shields W/E 21.11.18; Killingholme W/E 31.12.18; Deleted W/E 9.1.19

N4900    Deld MAD Felixstowe W/E 22.8.18; AAP Sherburn W/E 5.12.18 - @30.1.19; Scrapped

N4901    Deld MAD Felixstowe W/E 22.8.18; AAP Sherburn W/E 31.12.18 - 30.1.19; Scrapped

N4902    Arr Southampton Docks W/E 22.8.18; AAP Brockworth W/E 19.9.18 - @30.1.19; Imperial Gift to Canada; Not registered; TOC 20.4.21; Used as spares for G-CYEP; SOC 7.11.24

N4903    Arr Avonmouth Docks W/E 22.8.18; AAP Brockworth W/E 26.9.18 - @30.1.19; Scrapped

N4904    Arr Portsmouth Docks W/E 5.9.18; AAP Brockworth W/E 19.9.18 - @30.1.19; Scrapped

N4905    Deld AAP Brockworth 19.9.18 - @30.1.19; Imperial Gift to Canada; Became G-CYEP; TOC 22.2.22; SOC 21.1.24

N4906    Arr Southampton Docks W/E 22.8.18; AAP Brockworth W/E 19.9.18 - @30.1.19; Scrapped

N4907    Arr Southampton Docks W/E 22.8.18; AAP Brockworth W/E 26.9.18 - @30.1.19; Scrapped

N4908    Arr Portsmouth Docks W/E 5.9.18; AAP Brockworth W/E 26.9.18 - @30.1.19; Scrapped

N4909    Deld AAP Sherburn W/E 7.11.18 - @30.1.19; Scrapped

N4910    Deld AAP Sherburn W/E 12.12.18 - 30.1.19; Scrapped

N4911    Arr Avonmouth Docks W/E 22.8.18; AAP Brockworth W/E 29.8.18 - @30.1.19; Scrapped

N4912    Arr Avonmouth Docks W/E 22.8.18; AAP Brockworth W/E 29.8.18 - @30.1.19; Scrapped

N4913    Arr Southampton Docks W/E 29.8.18; AAP Brockworth W/E 12.9.18 - @30.1.19; Scrapped

N4914    Deld AAP Sherburn W/E 28.11.18 - @30.1.19; Scrapped

N4915    Deld AAP Sherburn W/E 7.11.18 - @30.1.19; Scrapped

N4916    Deld AAP Sherburn W/E 5.12.18 - @30.1.19; Scrapped

N4917    Deld AAP Brockworth W/E 29.8.18 - @30.1.19; Scrapped

N4918    Deld AAP Brockworth W/E 22.8.18 - @30.1.19; Scrapped

N4919    Arr Portsmouth Docks W/E 5.9.18; AAP Brockworth W/E 12.9.18 - @30.1.19; Scrapped

N4920    Deld AAP Brockworth W/E 5.9.18 - @30.1.19; Scrapped

N4921    Deld AAP Sherburn W/E 31.10.18 - @30.1.19; Scrapped

N4922    Arr Portsmouth Docks W/E 5.9.18; AAP Brockworth W/E 26.9.18 - @30.1.19; Scrapped

N4923    Deld AAP Sherburn W/E 16.12.18 - @30.1.19;

N4924    Deld MAD Felixstowe W/E 29.8.18; AAP Sherburn W/E 16.1.19 - @30.1.19; Scrapped

N4925    Deld MAD Felixstowe W/E 29.8.18; AAP Sherburn W/E 19.12.18 - @30.1.19; Scrapped

N4926    Deld MAD Felixstowe W/E 29.8.18; AAP Sherburn W/E 19.12.18 - @30.1.19; Scrapped

N4927    Arr Avonmouth Docks W/E 22.8.18; AAP Brockworth W/E 5.9.18 - @30.1.19; Scrapped

N4928    Deld MAD Felixstowe W/E 29.8.18; AAP Sherburn W/E 5.12.18 - @30.1.19; Scrapped

N4929    Arr Glasgow Docks W/E 22.8.18; AAP Sherburn W/E 31.10.18 - @30.1.19; Scrapped

N4930    Deld AAP Brockworth W/E 5.9.18 - @30.1.19; Scrapped

N4931    Deld AAP Brockworth W/E 19.9.18 - @30.1.19; Scrapped

N4932    Deld AAP Brockworth W/E 26.9.18 - @30.1.19; Scrapped

N4933    Deld AAP Brockworth W/E 3.10.18 - @30.1.19; Scrapped

N4934    Deld 3 AAP Norwich W/E 3.10.18 - @30.1.19; Scrapped

N4935    Deld 3 AAP Norwich W/E 3.10.18 - @30.1.19; Scrapped

N4936    Deld 3 AAP Norwich W/E 3.10.18 - @30.1.19; Scrapped

N4937    Deld 3 AAP Norwich W/E 3.10.18 - @30.1.19; Scrapped

N4938    Deld AAP Sherburn W/E 10.10.18 - @30.1.19; Scrapped

N4939    Deld 3 AAP Norwich W/E 3.10.18 - @30.1.19; Scrapped

N4940    Deld AAP Sherburn W/E 3.10.18 - @30.1.19; Scrapped

N4941    Deld AAP Sherburn W/E 3.10.18 - @30.1.19; Scrapped

N4942    Deld AAP Sherburn W/E 3.10.18 - @30.1.19 - damaged; Scrapped

N4943    Deld AAP Sherburn W/E 31.10.18 - @30.1.19 - damaged; Scrapped

N4944    Deld AAP Sherburn W/E 31.10.18 - @30.1.19; Scrapped

N4945    Arr damaged at Manchester W/E 7.11.18 - @30.1.19 (still damaged)

N4946    Deld AAP Sherburn W/E 21.11.18 - @31.12.18; Scrapped

N4947    Arr damaged at Glasgow Docks W/E 7.11.18; AAP Sherburn W/E 12.12.18 - @30.1.19 (wrecked); Scrapped

N4948    Arr damaged at Glasgow Docks W/E 7.11.18; AAP Sherburn W/E 12.12.18 - @30.1.19 (wrecked); Scrapped

N4949    Deld AAP Sherburn W/E 7.11.18 - @30.1.19; Scrapped

N4950    to N4999 cancelled

---

**N5000 to N8999 reserved for Aeroplanes, Main Types**

---

**30 MAURICE FARMAN S.7 LONGHORN PUSHER BIPLANES ordered 19.5.16 under Cont No CP.114825/16 from Robey & Co Ltd, numbered N5000 to N5029 & built Lincoln. (75-hp Hawk)**

N5000    Deld Killingholme for erection 1.17; Cranwell by 21.1.17; Eastbourne 14.5.17 (now 90-hp Curtiss OX-2); Deleted W/E 2.3.18 (now 80-hp Renault)

N5001    Deld Chingford 3.2.17; Accepted 9.2.17 (JL Parker); Surveyed 26.11.17; Deleted 5.12.17 as spares

N5002    Deld Killingholme store 30.1.17; Deleted 12.11.17 as spares

N5003    Deld Killingholme store 10.2.17; Redcar 22.4.17 (for erection by makers); Surveyed 7.12.17; Deleted 14.12.17 as spares

N5004    Deld Killingholme store for erection 30.1.17; Killingholme service 2.18; Deleted 2.18

N5005    Deld Killingholme store 10.2.17; Deleted 12.11.17 as spares

N5006    Deld Killingholme store 24.2.17; Eastbourne (via Hendon) 31.7.17; Surveyed 27.11.17; Deleted 5.12.17 wrecked

N5007    Deld Killingholme store 24.2.17; Accepted 8.3.17 (JL Parker); Deleted 12.11.17 for spares

N5008    Deld Killingholme store and accepted 9.3.17 (JL Parker); Crashed Killingholme [No date]; Eastchurch to fit Curtiss 18.6.17 (arr 25.6.17 via Huntingdon, damaged); Eastbourne, Crashed & WO 2.18

N5009    Deld Killingholme store and accepted 8.3.17 (JL Parker); Killingholme service 2.18; Scrapped due to deterioration 21.4.18 (now 90-hp Curtiss)

N5010    Transferred RFC (Military Wing) as A9978

N5011    Transferred RFC (Military Wing) as A9979

N5012    Transferred RFC (Military Wing) 4.17 as B393

N5013    Transferred RFC (Military Wing) 4.17 as B399

N5014    Transferred RFC (Military Wing) 4.17 as B398

N5015    Transferred RFC (Military Wing) 4.17 as B400

N5016    Transferred RFC (Military Wing) 4.17 as B397

N5017 to N5029 in abeyance 10.4.17, later cancelled

**30 MAURICE FARMAN S.7 LONGHORN PUSHER BIPLANES ordered 22.8.16 under Cont No CP.114826/16 from Brush Electrical Engineering Co Ltd, numbered N5030 to N5059 & built Loughborough. Delivered initially to CSD White City. (80-hp Renault)**

N5030    Deld Eastchurch Workshops 16.10.16; Eastchurch FS 19.10.16; Eastchurch Workshops for repair 8.1.17; Eastchurch FS 11.1.17; Crashed 26.2.17; Eastchurch Workshops 27.2.17; Deleted 3.4.17

N5031    Deld Eastchurch Workshops 19.10.16; Eastchurch FS 21.10.16; Eastchurch Workshops for repair 8.1.17; Eastchurch FS 18.2.17; Eastchurch Workshops 26.5.17, then retd Eastchurch FS; Crashed 24.7.17; Surveyed 26.11.17; Deleted 5.12.17 as spares

N5032    Deld Cranwell 2.11.16; Eastbourne 4.4.17; Surveyed 21.12.17 DBR; Deleted 15.1.18

N5033    Deld Cranwell 25.12.16; Eastbourne 5.4.17; CW 25.5.17 (pilot unhurt); Deleted 2.6.17

N5034    Deld Chingford 30.12.16; Explosion at 5/6,000ft, dived into Edmonton sewage farm 11.5.17 (F/L L Morgan & TPFO RH Seed both killed); Surveyed 12.5.17; Deleted 19.5.17

N5035    (DC) Deld Redcar by transport 15.11.16; Tested 11.1.17; Wrecked landing 6.7.17; Deleted 9.9.17 BR

N5036    (DC) Deld Redcar by road 27.11.16; Tested 11.1.17; COL 27.2.17 (PFO FA Frost); Severely damaged 6.7.17; Deleted 8.9.17 BR

N5037    (DC) Deld Redcar 4.11.16; Tested 10.11.16; Propeller and top plane damaged taxying 21.11.16 (F/L LMB Weil & FSL HLE Tyndale-Biscoe); Ran into 3304 and 3440 taxying, all damaged 21.12.16 (PFO CR Derington-Turner unhurt); U/c damaged landing 6.1.17 (PFO WJ Coast unhurt); Badly damaged 22.8.17; Surveyed 7.12.17; Deleted 14.12.17 as spares

N5038    Deld Cranwell 9.11.16; Deleted 25.2.17

N5039    Deld Chingford by road 1.12.16; Deleted 31.7.17

N5040    Deld Chingford for erection 1.1.17; visited Cranwell (via Hendon) 19.8.17; Redcar 20.8.17; retd Chingford but crashed Selby en route 23.8.17; Deleted 24.8.17

N5041    Deld Eastchurch Workshops by road 5.12.16 (erecting by makers by 1.1.17); Eastchurch FS 12.1.17; U/c and wing damaged 26.6.17; U/c broken 15.8.17; Eastbourne W/E 3.11.17; Retd Eastchurch?; Crashed nr Mayfield 19.12.17 (PFO GW Cooper slightly hurt); Deleted W/E 26.1.18

N5042    Deld Cranwell 23.11.16; Eastbourne 15.4.17; Deleted 18.6.17

N5043    Deld Cranwell 1.1.17; Eastbourne 15.4.17; Surveyed 27.11.17; Deleted 5.12.17 wrecked

N5044    Deld Eastchurch FS 3.1.17; Manston FS W/E 5.9.17; Surveyed 14.12.17; Deleted 19.12.17 wrecked

N5045    Deld Eastchurch Workshops by road 2.1.17; Eastchurch FS 31.1.17; Manston 7.8.17; For deletion by 30.3.18

N5046    Deld Cranwell 2.1.17: Eastbourne 4.4.17; Mkrs Loughborough 30.5.17 (repair); Eastbourne 10.6.17; Surveyed 27.11.17; Deleted 5.12.17 wrecked

N5047    Deld UK to RNASTE Vendôme 16.2.17; Surveyed 12.10.17; Deleted 16.10.17 DBR

N5048    Deld UK to RNASTE Vendôme 1.5.17; Surveyed 7.3.18;

Deleted 13.3.18 DBR

N5049  Deld UK to RNASTE Vendôme 16.2.17; COL 30.4.17; Surveyed 7.3.18; Deleted 13.3.18 DBR

N5050  Deld Chingford by rail for erection 16.1.17; Crashed and damaged 20.7.17; to Redcar but crashed at St.Albans en route 15.8.17; Surveyed 27.10.17; Deleted 2.11.17 wrecked

N5051  Deld Killingholme 13.1.17; Redcar 14.3.17; COL 1.4.17; Surveyed 7.12.17; Deleted 14.12.17 as spares

N5052  Deld UK to RNASTE Vendôme 16.2.17; Manston FS for erection W/E 8.12.17; Deleted 26.1.18

N5053  Deld Eastchurch Workshops by rail 26.1.17 (fitted DC); Eastchurch FS by 2.2.17; Eastchurch Workshops 3.2.17; Chingford 25.5.17; Eastchurch FS 26.5.17; U/c damaged 7.7.17; Eastbourne W/E 27.10.17; Surveyed 15.11.17; Deleted 21.11.17 wrecked

N5054  Deld Killingholme 10.2.17; Redcar 14.3.17; Surveyed 7.12.17; Deleted 14.12.17 as spares

N5055  Deld Killingholme 17.2.17; Redcar 14.3.17; Crashed on cross-country flight 15.4.17 (PFO FHY Titcomb killed); COL 18.7.17; Deleted 8.9.17 BR

N5056  (DC) Deld Killingholme 1.3.17; Redcar 14.3.17; COL by 17.4.17; Surveyed 20.4.17; Deleted 4.5.17

N5057  Deld Killingholme 17.2.17; Redcar 14.3.17; Crashed [NO DATE] (PFO R Sykes); Deleted 8.9.17

N5058  Deld Killingholme 24.2.17; Redcar 22.4.17; Crashed 4.7.17; Surveyed 7.12.17; Deleted 14.12.17 as spares

N5059  Deld Killingholme 24.2.17; Redcar 22.4.17; COL, CW 9.5.17 (PFO LL Stanyon); Deleted 16.5.17

**20 MAURICE FARMAN S.11 SHORTHORN PUSHER (EASTCHURCH TYPE) BIPLANES ordered 20.5.16 under 1.17 Cont No C.P.114966/16 from Eastbourne Aviation Co Ltd, numbered N5060 to N5079 & built Eastbourne. (160-hp Renault unless otherwise stated)**

N5060  (C/n 124) Deld Chingford 20.12.16; Eastchurch 24.8.17 (for conversion); Gunnery School Flt Eastchurch W/E 1.10.17 (75-hp Renault); Became 204 TDS Eastchurch 1.4.18 - @8.18

N5061  (C/n 125) Deld PVRS for alterations 1.1.17; Became ECD Grain 26.2.17; Eastchurch Workshops 7.7.17, for Gunnery School (125-hp Anzani); Observers School Flt Eastchurch by 10.17; Gunnery School Flt Eastchurch by 29.12.17; Became 204 TDS Eastchurch 1.4.18

N5062  (C/n 126) Deld Gun Flt Eastchurch 13.2.17; Eastchurch Workshops 14.2.17; Gunnery School Flt Eastchurch 8.3.17; Leysdown 25.4.17 - @1.6.17; Gun Flt Eastchurch, port wing damaged 23.6.17; Crashed 25.7.17; Deleted 4.8.17

N5063  (C/n 127) (70-hp Renault) Accepted Eastbourne but flight cut short due to snowstorm 13.1.17 (JL Parker); Deld Eastchurch Workshops (via Eastbourne) 29.1.17; Eastchurch Gun Flt 30.1.17; Damaged 5.4.17; to Eastchurch Workshops; Eastchurch Gun Flt 22.6.17; To convert 6.10.17; Gunnery School Flt Eastchurch by 29.12.17; Observers School Flt Eastchurch by 3.18; Became 204 TDS Eastchurch 1.4.18; Gunnery School Eastchurch, collided with Avro while ascending 19.7.18 (2/Lt JF Grady & Boy Mech LH Sampson both killed) (170-hp Renault)

N5064  (C/n 128) (160-hp Renault) Deld Eastchurch Workshops 29.1.17; Gun Flt Eastchurch 30.1.17; Gun Flt at Leysdown 25.4.17 - @1.6.17; Gunnery School Flt Eastchurch by 29.12.17; Became 204 TDS Eastchurch 1.4.18 (now 150-hp Renault)

N5065  (C/n 129) Deld Gun Flt Eastchurch 8.3.17; Eastchurch Workshops 5.4.17; Gun Flt at Leysdown 25.4.17 - @22.6.17; Eastchurch by 10.17; Gunnery School Flt Eastchurch by 29.12.17; Became 204 TDS Eastchurch 1.4.18

N5066  (C/n 130) (70-hp Renault) Accepted Eastbourne 8.2.17 (JL Parker); Deld Gun Flt Eastchurch 28.2.17; Gun Flt at Leysdown 25.4.17; Eastchurch Workshops 22.6.17; Observers School Flt Eastchurch by 12.17; Gunnery School Flt Eastchurch by 29.12.17; Deleted W/E 2.3.18

N5067  (C/n 131) (70-hp Renault) Accepted Eastbourne 21.2.17 (JL Parker); Deld Eastchurch Workshops by air 13.3.17; Crashed 19.3.17; Gun Flt Eastchurch by 8.4.17; Gun Flt Leysdown by 25.4.17 - @2.6.17; Eastchurch for conversion by 29.9.17; Gunnery School Flt Eastchurch

N5068  by 29.12.17; Became 204 TDS Eastchurch 1.4.18 - 8.18 (C/n 132) Accepted Eastbourne 21.2.17 (JL Parker); Deld Eastchurch Workshops 5.4.17; Eastchurch 11.5.17; Converting by 25.7.17; Gunnery School Flt Eastchurch by 29.12.17; Became 204 TDS Eastchurch 1.4.18

N5069  (C/n 133) Deld Eastchurch Workshops 7.4.17; Gun Flt Leysdown 25.4.17; Caught fire in air, BO 2.5.17 (two crew unhurt); Deleted Eastchurch Workshops 10.5.17

N5070  (C/n 134) Accepted Eastbourne 17.3.17 (JL Parker); Deld Eastchurch Workshops by air for Gunnery School Flt 21.4.17 - @30.6.17; Observers School Flt Eastchurch by 10.17; Became 204 TDS Eastchurch 1.4.18

N5071  (C/n 135) Accepted Eastbourne 22.4.17 (JL Parker); Deld Eastchurch Workshops for Gunnery School Flt 27.4.17 - @30.6.17; Observers School Flt Eastchurch by 10.17; Gunnery School Flt Eastchurch by 29.12.17; Became 204 TDS Eastchurch 1.4.18

N5072  (C/n 136) (75-hp Renault) Deld Eastbourne 30.4.17; Accepted 1.5.17 (JL Parker); Deld EAC to Eastchurch Workshops 1.6.17 (arr 2.6.17) - @30.6.17; Observers School Flt by 10.17 - 12.17; Gunnery School Flt Eastchurch by 29.12.17; Became 204 TDS Eastchurch 1.4.18

N5073  (C/n 137) (70-hp Renault) Deld Eastchurch Workshops by air for Gunnery School Flt 21.4.17; Accepted 24.4.17; Observers School Flt Eastchurch 4.17; Fitting experimental nacelle designed by F/Cdr IGV Fowler & F/L EM Pizey 5.6.17 (marked 'Fowzey 1'); Surveyed 12.12.17; Deleted 19.12.17 DBR

N5074  (C/n 138) (70-hp Renault) Accepted Eastbourne 22.4.17 (JL Parker); Deld Eastchurch Workshops 24.4.17; Eastchurch FS 27.4.17; Crashed 8.6.17; Eastchurch Workshops 12.6.17; Deleted 17.12.17

N5075  (C/n 139) (80-hp Renault) Deld Eastchurch Workshops 18.5.17 (JL Parker); Gunnery School Flt Eastchurch by 29.12.17; Became 204 TDS Eastchurch 1.4.18 - @8.18

N5076  (C/n 140) (80-hp Renault) Accepted and deld Eastbourne 7.5.17 (JL Parker); Eastchurch Workshops for Gunnery School Flt 24.5.17 (JL Parker); Converting by 29.9.17; Gunnery School Flt Eastchurch by 29.12.17; Became 204 TDS Eastchurch 1.4.18

N5077  (C/n 141) (160-hp Renault) Deld Eastchurch Workshops 8.6.17, then to Gun Flt; Eastchurch Workshops 26.6.17; Dunkerque 7.7.17; Dover 8.7.17; Eastchurch 9.7.17; Damaged by water 10.7.17; Observers School Flt Eastchurch by 10.17; Gunnery School Flt Eastchurch by 29.12.17; 150-hp Renault by 1.18; Became 204 TDS Eastchurch 1.4.18

N5078  (C/n 142) Deld Eastchurch Workshops 14.6.17 - @26.8.17; Observers School Flt Eastchurch by 8.17; Gunnery School Flt Eastchurch by 29.12.17; Became 204 TDS Eastchurch 1.4.18

N5079  (C/n 143) Deld Eastchurch Workshops by air for Gunnery School Flt 23.6.17 - @26.6.17; Observers School Flt Eastchurch by 10.17; Gunnery School Flt Eastchurch by 29.12.17; Deleted W/E 30.3.18

**40 SOPWITH 1½ STRUTTER 9400S and 9700 TYPES TRACTOR BIPLANES put forward 10.16 and ordered under Cont No C.P.115639/16, numbered N5080 to N5119 & built Kingston-upon-Thames. Deld from Brooklands. (110-hp Clerget 9Z unless otherwise stated)**

N5080  (Type 9400S) Deld Dover 13.9.16; ADD 15.9.16; 5 Flt A Sqdn 5 Wing 17.9.16; Detd Sqdn 22 Wing 26.10.16, becoming B Flt 8 Sqdn; 3 Sqdn 17.11.16; [9 Sqdn by 1.2.17 ?]; 2 Sqdn by 3.2.17; Dover 29.4.17; Chassis wrecked and wings damaged 13.5.17; still Dover 29.9.17; War School Manston W/E 20.10.17; Gunnery School Flt Eastchurch 2.3.18; Became 204 TDS Eastchurch 1.4.18 - @7.18

N5081  (Type 9400S) Deld ADD (via Dover) 17.9.16; 8 Flt B Sqdn 5 Wing 1.11.16; 7 Flt B Sqdn 5 Wing by 16.11.16; Became 5 Sqdn 31.12.16; ADD 13.2.17; 5 Sqdn 7.5.17; ADD 13.8.17; 2 Sqdn 5.10.17; Shot down by AA over enemy line Lombartzyde by Flakbattery 514 6.11.17 (FSL HP Salter & OSL HW White both PoWs); Surveyed 13.11.17; Deleted 16.11.17 TL

N5082  (Type 9400S) (130-hp Clerget) Brooklands 10.10.16;

Deld Chingford 14.10.16; Brooklands 16.10.16; ADD by 2.11.16; 5 Flt A Sqdn 5 Wing by 6.11.16; Became 4 Sqdn 31.12.16 - @11.3.17; 2 Sqdn by 13.3.17; Dover 29.4.17; Slightly damaged 21.5.17; AP Dover by 8.12.17; 491 Flt/Transport Flt Dover by 25.5.18 (233 Sqdn 31.8.18); EF on TO, FL Duke of York's Military School and crashed, badly damaged 17.10.18 (Lt AW Goodale & 2/Lt Miller unhurt); WOC 24.10.18

**N5083** (Type 9400S) (130-hp Clerget) CSD White City by 30.8.16 (not by 31.10.16); Shipped to Aegean; Mitylene by 12.3.17 - @11.4.17; Imbros (Kephalos) by 1.12.17; Mudros by 1.1.18; Marsh by 17.1.18; Greek training by 3.18 - 4.18; Imbros by 4.18 - 10.18; Transferred Greek Govt (2-str) 10.18 - 1.19

**N5084** (Type 9400S) Presentation a/c named 'Sao Paulo Britons No.2' (presented 4.5.16). Deld Dover 18.9.16; ADD 21.9.16; 5 Flt A Sqdn 5 Wing 22.9.16; B Flt 8 Sqdn 26.10.16; Hit plough, Vert Galand 11.16; Deleted by RFC by 23.11.16

**N5085** (Type 9400S) Deld CSD White City for packing 10.16; Shipped to Aegean

**N5086** (Type 9400S) (130-hp Clerget) Deld CSD White City for packing 10.16; Shipped to Aegean; A Flt 2 Wing Thasos by 9.1.17 - @24.1.17; E Flt 2 Wing Hadzi Junas by 28.3.17 - @30.4.17 (LM); Engaged HA but badly shot up 28.3.17 (FSL EP Hicks & AM1 AE King); Stavros by 1.12.17 - @1.1.18; 2 Wing Mudros by 3.18; Became 62 Wing Mudros 1.4.18

**N5087** (Type 9400) Deld CSD White City for packing 10.16; Shipped to Aegean; E Flt 2 Wing Hadzi Junas from 11.4.17; Engaged HA 22.4.17 (FSL WV Simonds unhurt & AM1 A Carder seriously wounded); LM 22.5.17; Surveyed Mudros 10.10.17; Deleted 26.10.17 W&T

**N5088** (Type 9700) Deld CSD White City for packing by 30.9.16; 3 Wing Luxeuil (coded '1') by 13.10.16; Dropped bombs, then Fokker EI OOC Brebach, became lost, FL, damaged, Fontenoy 25.2.17 (FSL JE Sharman slightly injured); Transferred French Govt for AMF 19.4.17

**N5089** (Type 9700) Arr 3 Wing Luxeuil (coded '25') by 13.10.16 [1 or 2 Sqdn 3 Wing by 4.3.17]; To ADD by 26.4.17; To UK 13.9.17; War School Manston by 6.10.17; Cranwell 26.3.18 (transit); Beverley en route Redcar 28.3.18; East Fortune W/E 30.3.18; Freiston

**N5090** (Type 9400S) (130-hp Clerget) Deld ADD 1.10.16; 5 Flt A Sqdn 5 Wing 23.10.16; B Flt 8 Sqdn 26.10.16; ADD 17.11.16; Cowl came off in air, FL in ploughed field W of Depot 11.2.17 (FSL GMT Rouse - a/c coded 'P'); 2 Sqdn 4.3.17; AP Dover 16.11.17 - @24.2.18; 8 Sqdn by 8.3.18; Dover 16.3.18; Became 491 Flt Dover by 25.5.18/Transport Flt Dover by 5.18 to 8.18; EF, FL in sea and sank 5m SE of Dungeness 13.7.18 (Capt E Anthony & 2/Lt LA Churchill picked up by trawler); WOC 17.7.18

**N5091** (Type 9700) Deld CSD White City by 30.9.16; Arr 3 Wing Luxeuil (coded '24') by 13.10.16; 1 Flt Ochey 10.11.16; Became A Flt 1 Sqdn 8.12.16; Transferred French Govt for AMF 19.4.17

**N5092** (Type 9700) Arr 3 Wing Luxeuil 13.10.16; 2 Flt Ochey 10.11.16; Became B Flt 1 Sqdn 8.12.16; Transferred French Govt for AMF 20.4.17 (less engine)

**N5093** (Type 9400S) Deld ADD 10.16; 5 Flt A Sqdn 5 Wing 1.11.16; Became 4 Sqdn 31.12.16; ADD 28.3.17; Crashed Dunkerque 23.8.17 (FSL GMT Rouse of 4 Sqdn); To ADD; For survey 27.9.17; Destroyed by fire on night of 1.10.17; Surveyed 17.10.17; Deleted 23.10.17 TL

**N5094** (Type 9700) Arr 3 Wing Luxeuil (coded '32') 3.11.16; 2 Flt Ochey 10.11.16; Transferred French for AMF 20.4.17

**N5095** (Type 9700) Arr 3 Wing Luxeuil by 10.11.16; to 4 Flt 3 Wing Luxeuil until 13.4.17 (LM); Transferred French Govt for AMF 19.4.17

**N5096** (Type 9400S) Deld ADD by 19.10.16; 5 Flt A Sqdn 5 Wing 23.10.16; B Flt 8 Sqdn 28.10.16; C Flt 1 Sqdn 17.11.16; ADD 30.11.16; 4 Sqdn by 1.2.17 - @9.3.17; 2 Sqdn by 13.3.17; Dover 23.5.17

**N5097** (Type 9700) Arr 3 Wing Luxeuil by 3.11.16; loaned French Govt for AMF (no engine) 7.11.16 - @13.4.17; Transferred French Govt 4.17

**N5098** (Type 9700) Deld 4 Flt 3 Wing Luxeuil (coded '32') by 10.11.16; 5 Flt 3 Wing by 1.12.16; Reserve Flt 3 Wing Luxeuil by 8.12.16; B Flt 1 Sqdn 3 Wing Ochey by 15.12.16; Transferred French Govt for AMF 20.4.17

**N5099** (Type 9400S) Deld CSD White City by 31.10.16; Shipped to Aegean; Stavros to E Flt Sqdn 2 Wing Hadzi Junas 23.4.17 - @22.5.17 (LM); F Sqdn 2 Wing Marian by 25.5.17

**N5100** (Type 9700) Deld 5 Flt 3 Wing Luxeuil by 10.11.16; Transferred French Govt for AMF 20.4.17

**N5101** (Type 9700) Arr 3 Wing Luxeuil by 3.11.16; Loaned French Govt for AMF (no engine) by 10.11.16 - @13.4.17; Transferred French Govt 4.17

**N5102** (Type 9400S) Deld ADD (via Dover) 16.10.16; 5 Flt A Sqdn 5 Wing 23.10.16; B Flt 8 Sqdn 26.10.16; B or C Sqdn 17.11.16; ADD 30.11.16; 4 Sqdn (coded '1') 22.12.16; Shot down by Vizeflugmeister Wirtz at Roxem 7.2.17 (F/L CR Blagrove & AM2 G/L J Milne both killed); Deleted 24.3.17

**N5103** (Type 9700) Arr 3 Wing Luxeuil by 3.11.16; loaned French Govt for AMF (no engine) by 10.11.16; Transferred French Govt 4.17

**N5104** (Type 9700) Arr 3 Wing Luxeuil (coded '34') by 3.11.16; 4 Flt 3 Wing Luxeuil by 10.11.16; 5 Flt 3 Wing Luxeuil by 1.12.16; Reserve Flt 3 Wing Luxeuil by 8.12.16 - @13.4.17; Transferred French Govt for AMF (no engine) 20.4.17

**N5105** (Type 9400S) FL Eastbourne on delivery 25.10.16; ADD 26.10.16 - @2.11.16; 3 Sqdn by 16.11.16; ADD 30.12.16; 3 Sqdn by 4.1.17; 9 Sqdn 1.2.17; 2 Sqdn by 7.2.17 - @27.2.17; Crashed and burnt BR at French aerodrome 1.3.17; ADD by 8.3.17; Deleted 24.3.17

**N5106** (Type 9700) Deld 5 Flt 3 Wing Luxeuil (coded '35') by 10.11.16; Reserve Flt 3 Wing by 8.12.16; B Flt 1 Sqdn 3 Wing Ochey by 15.12.17 - @13.4.17; Surveyed 4.17

**N5107** (Type 9700) Arr 3 Wing Luxeuil 13.10.16; 5 Flt 3 Wing Luxeuil (coded '36') by 10.11.16; 6 Flt 3 Wing Luxeuil by 1.12.16; Reserve Flt 3 Wing Luxeuil by 8.12.16; B Flt 1 Sqdn 3 Wing Ochey by 15.12.16 - @13.4.17; Damaged 1.17; [Flown Luxeuil to Vendôme 23.4 17, then to Paris 25.4.17]; ADD 16.5.17 (u/s); Deleted 20.8.17

**N5108** (Type 9400S) Shipped to Aegean; Mitylene by 15.3.17 - @22.4.17; Reported as Von Eschwege's 4th victory

**N5109** (Type 9700) Deld 5 Flt 3 Wing Luxeuil (coded '37') by 10.11.16; 6 Flt 3 Wing Luxeuil by 1.12.16; Reserve Flt 3 Wing Luxeuil by 8.12.16 - @13.4.17; COL 1.17; ADD by 26.4.17; Dover W/E 6.9.17; War School Manston 11.9.17; Surveyed 28.11.17; Deleted 3.12.17 wrecked

**N5110** (Type 9700) Shipped to Aegean; A Flt 2 Wing Thasos by 9.1.17; Convtd 1-str bomber at Thasos; Stavros (coded 'F') by 4.17

**N5111** (Type 9400S) Deld CSD White City by 31.10.16; Shipped to Aegean; E Flt (later E Sqdn) 2 Wing Hadzi Junas by 28.3.17 - @22.5.17; Engaged HA but damaged and put out of action 5.4.17 (F/L CE Wood & Capt Hicks RFC); Presumed destroyed in accidental explosion when flight wiped out 27.5.17; Deleted Mudros 1.12.17

**N5112** (Type 9700) (130-hp Clerget) Deld Design Flt Eastchurch 10.11.16; By rail to Southampton for 3 Wing Luxeuil 18.1.17 (arr by 2.2.17); Surveyed 12.4.17

**N5113** (Type 9700) Arr 3 Wing Luxeuil by 17.11.16; Transferred French Govt for AMF 20.4.17

**N5114** (Type 9400S) (130-hp Clerget) Deld Design Flt Eastchurch 15.11.16; 1 Wing 28.11.16; ADD 30.11.16; 5 Flt A Sqdn 5 Wing 11.12.16; Became 5 Sqdn (coded 'B3') 31.12.16; Crashed, o/t 27.2.17; ADD 2.17; For survey 8.3.17; Deleted 24.3.17

**N5115** (Type 9700) Arr 3 Wing Luxeuil (coded '44') 15.11.16; 4 Flt 3 Wing Luxeuil by 1.12.16; A Flt 2 Sqdn 3 Wing 8.12.16; Transferred French Govt for AMF 20.4.17

**N5116** (Type 9700) Arr 3 Wing Luxeuil (coded '43') 15.11.16; 4 Flt 3 Wing Luxeuil by 1.12.16; A Flt 2 Sqdn 3 Wing 8.12.16; Transferred French Govt for AMF 19.4.17

**N5117** (Type 9400S) Arr 3 Wing Luxeuil 15.11.16; 3 Flt 3 Wing Luxeuil by 24.11.16; B Flt 2 Sqdn 3 Wing Ochey by 8.12.16; Shot down on Freiburg reprisal raid by Vzfw Rudolf Rath, Jasta 35 nr Schlettstadt, 13m NE of Colmar 14.4.17 (FSL H Edwards PoW & G/L AAM1 JL Coghlan killed)

N5118   (Type 9700) (130-hp Clerget) Deld CSD White City by 31.10.16; arr 3 Wing 21.11.16; loaned French Govt for AMF (no engine) by 1.12.16; Transferred French Govt 4.17 (less engine)

N5119   (Type 9700 convtd to Type 9400) (130-hp Clerget) Shipped to Aegean; F Sqdn 2 Wing Amberkoj/Marian by 29.4.17 - @26.5.17 (With composite RFC/RNAS unit); Reconstructed; to 2 Wing Marsh 28.10.17 - @1.1.18; G Sqdn 2 Wing Mudros by 3.18; Became G Sqdn 62 Wing Mudros 1.4.18; Disposed by 6.18 (details not reported)

**50 SOPWITH 1½ STRUTTER 9700 TYPE TRACTOR BIPLANE BOMBERS ordered 13.7.16 under Cont No C.P.119334/16 from Westland Aviation Works, numbered N5120 to N5169 & built Yeovil. (110-hp Clerget 9Z)**

N5120   Performance trials at Mkrs, then modifications; Deld Design Flt Eastchurch by lorry 3.10.16; Accepted 6.10.16 (Hawker); Packing for transport 2.12.16; By rail to Southampton for shipment to 3 Wing 6.12.16; arr 3 Wing Luxeuil 23.12.16 - @13.4.17 (LM); For shipment to Mediterranean 4.17; Allocated from 3 Wing to Mudros 11.6.17

N5121   Deld Hendon for erection 4.10.16; Accepted 10.10.16; to 3 Wing Luxeuil (coded '38') 19.10.16; 5 Flt 3 Wing Luxeuil by 10.11.16; 6 Flt 3 Wing Luxeuil by 1.12.16; Reserve Flt 3 Wing Luxeuil by 8.12.16; A Flt 1 Sqdn 3 Wing Ochey by 15.12.16; Wrecked by 26.1.17; Retd from raid on Burbach with a bomb which exploded killing 2 mechanics and injuring 3 more 27.1.17 (FSL MH Stephens severely injured & FSL TR Shearer injured) [23.1.17 per Edwards log]; Surveyed 23.2.17

N5122   Deld Hendon 11.10.16; Accepted 13.10.16; to 3 Wing Luxeuil by rail (coded '39') 26.10.16; Transferred French Govt for AMF 19.4.17

N5123   Deld Hendon 14.10.16; Accepted 18.10.16 (Prodger); Dismantled, to 3 Wing 7.11.16; arr 3 Wing Luxeuil (coded '48') 21.11.16; Transferred French Govt for AMF 20.4.17

N5124   Deld Hendon for erection 19.10.16; Accepted 24.10.16 (Hawker); to 3 Wing Luxeuil (coded '54') 14.11.16 (arr 29.11.16); On landing from raid on Brebach, crashed into by 9733 25.2.17 (FSL HDM Wallace); Deleted 4.17

N5125   Accepted at Mkrs 1.11.16; Arr 3 Wing Luxeuil 11.16; Loaned French Govt for AMF (no engine) by 10.11.16; Retd 3 Wing 2.2.17; Re-loaned French Govt 2.3.17; Transferred French Govt 4.17 (less engine)

N5126   Accepted at Mkrs 1.11.17; Arr 3 Wing Luxeuil (coded '50') 19.10.16 (arr 15.11.16); Transferred French Govt for AMF 20.4.17 (less engine)

N5127   Accepted at Mkrs 1.11.16; Arr 3 Wing Luxeuil 16.11.16; Reserve Flt 3 Wing Luxeuil by 15.12.16; Loaned French Govt for AMF 29.11.16; Transferred French Govt 4.17 (less engine)

N5128   Accepted at Mkrs W/E 11.11.16; Arr 3 Wing Luxeuil (coded '49') 16.11.16; 6 Flt 3 Wing Luxeuil by 1.12.16; Reserve Flt 3 Wing Luxeuil by 8.12.16; Transferred French for AMF 19.4.17

N5129   Accepted at Mkrs W/E 11.11.16; Arr 3 Wing Luxeuil 11.16; Loaned French Govt for AMF (no engine) 16.12.16 - @13.4.17; Transferred French Govt for AMF 4.17

N5130   Accepted at Mkrs W/E 11.11.16; Arr 3 Wing Luxeuil 27.11.16; Loaned French Govt for AMF (no engine) by 27.12.16; Transferred French 4.17

N5131   Accepted at Mkrs W/E 11.11.16; Arr 3 Wing Luxeuil 21.11.16; Loaned French Govt for AMF (no engine) by 29.11.16; Destroyed by fire 15.1.17; Surveyed 7.3.17

N5132   Accepted at Mkrs W/E 11.11.16; Arr 3 Wing Luxeuil 27.11.16; Loaned French Govt for AMF (no engine) 5.1.17; Transferred French 4.17 (less engine)

N5133   Accepted at Mkrs W/E 2.12.16; Arr 3 Wing Luxeuil 29.11.16; Loaned French Govt for AMF (no engine) 11.12.16; Surveyed 23.2.17

N5134   Accepted at Mkrs W/E 2.12.16; Arr 3 Wing Luxeuil 12.16; Loaned French Govt for AMF (no engine) by 14.12.16; Shot down by Ltn Kaemmel, Jasta 23 16.3.17 (Serg Louis Pivette)

N5135   Accepted at Mkrs W/E 2.12.16; Arr 3 Wing Luxeuil 28.11.16; Loaned French Govt for AMF (no engine) by 5.1.17; Retd 3 Wing Luxeuil 9.3.17; Transferred French 20.4.17 (less engine)

N5136   Accepted at Mkrs W/E 2.12.16; Arr 3 Wing Luxeuil 12.16; Loaned French Govt (no engine) 9.1.17; Transferred French for AMF 4.17 (less engine)

N5137   Accepted at Mkrs 21.12.16; Arr 3 Wing Luxeuil 23.12.16; Loaned French Govt for AMF (no engine) 9.1.17 - @13.4.17; Transferred French for AMF 4.17 (less engine)

N5138   Deld Hendon and accepted 4.12.16; To dismantle for despatch 6.12.16; Desp 3 Wing Luxeuil 3.1.17; Loaned French Govt for AMF (no engine) 19.3.17 - @13.4.17; Transferred French 4.17 (less engine)

N5139   Accepted at Mkrs 21.12.16; Arr 3 Wing Luxeuil 22.12.16; Loaned French Govt for AMF (no engine) 9.1.17 - @13.4.17; Transferred French 4.17 (less engine)

N5140   Accepted at Mkrs 21.12.16; Arr 3 Wing Luxeuil 12.16; Loaned French Govt for AMF (no engine) 16.1.17 - @13.4.17; Transferred French 4.17 (less engine)

N5141   Accepted at Mkrs 21.12.16; Arr 3 Wing Luxeuil 12.16; Loaned French Govt (no engine) 27.1.17 - @13.4.17; Transferred French 4.17 (less engine)

N5142   Accepted at Mkrs 21.12.16; Arr 3 Wing Luxeuil 22.12.16; Loaned French Govt for AMF (no engine) by 11.1.17 - @13.4.17; Transferred French 4.17 (less engine)

N5143   Accepted at Mkrs 21.12.16; Arr 3 Wing Luxeuil 26.12.16; Loaned French Govt for AMF (no engine) by 9.2.17 - @13.4.17; Transferred French 4.17 (less engine)

N5144   Accepted at Mkrs 21.12.16; Deld 3 Wing Luxeuil 12.16; Transferred French Govt for AMF 20.4.17 (less engine); also coded (B)

N5145   Accepted at Mkrs 21.12.16; Deld 3 Wing Luxeuil 12.16; Transferred French Govt for AMF 20.4.17 (less engine)

N5146   Accepted at Mkrs 29.12.16; Deld 3 Wing Luxeuil 12.16; Loaned French Govt (no engine) 3.3.17 - @13.4.17; Transferred French Govt for AMF 4.17 (less engine)

N5147   Accepted at Mkrs 29.12.16; Deld 3 Wing Luxeuil 12.16 (less engine); Loaned French Govt (no engine) 19.3.17 - @13.4.17; Transferred French Govt for AMF 4.17

N5148   Accepted at Mkrs 29.12.16; Deld 3 Wing Luxeuil 12.16; Loaned French Govt (no engine) 19.3.17 - @13.4.17; Transferred French Govt for AMF 4.17

N5149   Accepted at Mkrs W/E 13.1.17; Deld 3 Wing Luxeuil 1.17; Loaned French Govt (no engine) 2.3.17 - @13.4.17; Transferred French Govt for AMF 4.17

N5150   (130-hp Clerget) Deld Dover for erection 15.1.17; ADD 26.2.17; 5 Sqdn 3.3.17; ADD 11.8.17; Dover 20.8.17; Brooklands 21.8.17; Manston 21.8.17; Dover 22.8.17; 2 Sqdn 3.9.17; Crashed on TO 4.9.17 (F/Cdr LM Jordan); ADD by 6.9.17; 2 Sqdn 5.10.17 (Depot a/c with 1 Wing by 28.10.17); AD Dover 13.11.17; 2 Sqdn 15.11.17; Seaplane Defence Sqdn 20.11.17; ADD by 22.11.17; Seaplane Defence Sqdn by 23.11.17; AP Dover 29.11.17; Manston 2.12.17; Dover 12.17; Seaplane Defence Sqdn W/E 6.12.17; Dover 19.12.17 - @29.12.17; East Fortune NFS by 1.1.18 - @30.3.18 (convtd Ships Strutter with 110-hp Clerget); Fleet Practice Sqdn Turnhouse by 11.5.18 - @25.11.18

N5151   Deld Dover for erection 15.1.17; FL after pilots flying boots caught petrol lever and closed it 26.1.17; Deleted 12.3.17

N5152   Deld Dover for erection 15.1.17; ADD 14.2.17; 5 Sqdn 30.3.17; Wrecked 13.7.17 (FSL NS Wright); Deleted ADD 16.7.17

N5153   Deld Dover for erection by 20.1.17; ADD by 1.2.17; 7 Sqdn 14.2.17 - @9.3.17; 5 Sqdn by 5.4.17 - @10.5.17; ADD by 21.6.17; Dover 27.6.17; Badly damaged 29.7.17; War School Manston 24.11.17 - @3.18; Marine Observers School Leysdown by 8.18 - @2.19

N5154   (110-hp Clerget 9Z) Deld Dover for erection 15.1.17; Awaiting test 3.2.17; ADD 6.2.17; 2 Sqdn (named 'FIREFLY') 24.2.17; EF, FL Cadzand 12.5.17 (FSL N Von L Tapscott & O/L GA Richardson both interned); Deleted 21.5.17; Aircraft taken over by Dutch as *LA34* (2C) (later *S-413*)

N5155   Deld Dover for erection 15.1.17; ADD 26.2.17; Badly

damaged 20.7.17

N5156   Deld Dover for erection 15.1.17; ADD 14.2.17; 5 Sqdn 3.3.17 - @26.4.17

N5157   Accepted at Mkrs 13.1.17; Arr 3 Wing Luxeuil 1.17; Loaned French Govt 7.4.17; Transferred French Govt for AMF 20.4.17 (less engine)

N5158   Accepted at Mkrs 13.1.17; Arr 3 Wing Luxeuil 1.17; Loaned French Govt 7.4.17; Transferred French Govt for AMF 20.4.17 (less engine)

N5159   Accepted at Mkrs 17.1.17; Arr 3 Wing Luxeuil 1.17 - @13.4.17; Shipped to Aegean; Arr Mudros 30.6.17 - @1.12.17; Greek Unit Marsh by 1.1.18; Greek training by 3.18

N5160   Accepted at Mkrs 17.1.17; Arr 3 Wing Luxeuil 1.17; Transferred French Govt for AMF 20.4.17 (less engine)

N5161   Accepted at Mkrs 1.2.17; Deld 3 Wing Luxeuil 1.17 - @13.4.17 (no engine); Shipped to Aegean; Arr Mudros 30.6.17 - @1.12.17; Marsh by 1.1.18 - @14.2.18; Mudros 14.2.18; G Flt 2 Wing Mudros 25.3.18; Became G Flt 62 Wing Mudros 1.4.18 (Convtd to Type 9400)

N5162   Accepted at Mkrs 1.2.17; Desp 3 Wing Luxeuil 29.1.17 (sic); ADD by 26.4.17; Dover 11.8.17; War School Manston W/E 27.10.17; Cranwell 26.3.18; Beverley en route East Fortune (via Redcar) 28.3.18

N5163   Accepted at Mkrs 1.2.17; 3 Wing Luxeuil 15.3.17 - @13.4.17; Shipped to Aegean; Marsh by 7.7.17; Smyrna by 1.8.17 - @29.8.17; Mudros by 1.12.17 - @1.1.18

N5164   Deld Dover for erection 8.2.17; Cranwell for erection 5.9.17; Convtd to Ships Strutter (when/where?); ECD Grain 19.1.18; Turnhouse W/E 11.5.18; HMS *Furious* W/E 31.5.18 - @27.6.18; Turnhouse by 7.18 - @11.18

N5165   Deld Dover for erection 14.2.17; Cranwell W/E 2.11.17; Surveyed 21.12.17; Deleted 14.1.18 DBR

N5166   Wrecked on delivery to Cranwell 15.2.17; repaired; Deleted 19.6.17

N5167   Deld Dover for erection 20.2.17; Cranwell 11.9.17; COL Cranwell South 11.12.17 (pilot unhurt); Surveyed 21.12.17; Deleted 14.1.18

N5168   Accepted at Mkrs 15.2.17; 3 Wing Luxeuil 2.4.17; For shipment to Aegean 4.17; Arr Mudros 30.6.17 (conv Type 9400); Imbros by 1.12.17; Surveyed 19.2.18; Deleted 13.3.18 wrecked

N5169   Accepted at Mkrs 16.2.17; Desp 3 Wing Luxeuil 17.2.17; Dunkerque to Dover 11.8.17; War School Manston 27.10.17; East Fortune NFS (via Redcar) 26.3.18 - @6.18

**10 SOPWITH 1½ STRUTTER 9400S TYPE TRACTOR BIPLANE FIGHTERS ordered 6.16 under Cont No C.P.118231/16 with money donated by Patriotic League, numbered N5170 to N5179 & built Kingston-upon-Thames. (110-hp Clerget 9Z or 130-hp Clerget 9B)**

N5170   (130-hp) Presentation a/c (probably 'Tientsin Britons No.1', replacing 9395). Allocated Mkrs to 3 Wing Luxeuil 25.10.16; CSD White City by 31.10.16; 3 Wing Luxeuil by 16.11.16; 3 Wing Ochey by 15.12.16; (fitted 110-hp Clerget in lieu of 130-hp Clerget 25[?].4.17); ADD 24.4.17; Dover 4.17; Badly damaged 22.8.17; War Flt Manston 6.10.17; Hendon W/E 27.10.17 (for use of Air Dept officers, fitted with 130-hp Clerget); Left for Turnhouse 4.4.18; Crashed and WO at Stevenage, Herts en route Turnhouse 6.4.18 (pilot unhurt) [SARD 4.18, allotted Rosyth]

N5171   (130-hp) Presentation a/c (probably 'Tientsin Britons No.2', replacing 9667). 3 Wing Luxeuil (coded '46'), arr 15.11.16; 3 Wing Ochey by 15.12.16 [1 or 2 Sqdn 3 Wing by 3.17]; Shot down nr Markirch, 14½m NW of Colmar by Albatros Vzfw Gustav Schindler, Jasta 35 14.4.17 (W/Cdr CEH Rathborne PoW later escaped & AM1 G/L V Turner killed)

N5172   (110-hp by 12.17 - 1.18) Presentation a/c (probably 'Sao Paolo No.1', replacing 9722). Deld Brooklands to Eastchurch Design Flt 9.11.16; ADD ('camera machine') 10.11.16; 2 or 3 Sqdn 17.12.16; 2 Sqdn by 1.2.17 - @18(?).3.17; ADD by 15.3.17; 2 Sqdn 20.4.17; Dunkerque to Dover and return 2 Sqdn 7.7.17; Dover 2.9.17; Chingford 4.9.17 (photo training duties); Became 207 TDS Chingford 1.4.18

N5173   (130-hp) Presentation a/c (probably 'Sao Paolo No.2',

replacing N5084). Accepted Brooklands 6.11.16; Arr 3 Wing Luxeuil (coded '51') by 1.12.16; B Flt 1 Sqdn 3 Wing Ochey by 15.12.16 - @9.3.17; HA claimed on Brebach raid 4.3.17 (FSL H Edwards & G/L PO Walker); Paris to 2 Sqdn 17.3.17; Wrecked 20.6.17; ADD 21.6.17; Deleted 27.6.17

N5174   (130-hp) Presentation a/c 'Rio de Janeiro Britons No.1', replaced 9654. Accepted Brooklands 8.11.16; Arr 3 Wing Luxeuil (coded '53'), 29.11.16; 3 Wing Ochey by 15.12.16; Villacoublay 10.3.17; 2 Sqdn 17.3.17; ADD 7.4.17; Dover 9.6.17; St Pol and back 12.7.17 ("ex Hendon"); COL Dover 22.7.17; War School Manston (named 'WILL O' THE WISP') 6.10.17; AGP 31.10.17/1.11.17; Gunnery School Flt Eastchurch W/E 2.3.18; Surveyed 18.3.18; Deleted 22.3.18 DBR

N5175   (130-hp) Presentation a/c (probably 'Peking Britons No.1', replacing 9423). Deld ADD (via Shoreham) 28.11.16; Crashed by 14.12.16; Deleted 5.1.17 DBR

N5176   (110-hp) Presentation a/c (probably 'Britons in Egypt No.1', replacing 9405). Shipped to Aegean; Arr Otranto by 17.2.17; F Sqdn 2 Wing by 29.4.17 - @26.5.17; Mudros by 1.12.17; Marsh by 1.1.18; A Sqdn 2 Wing Thasos; To Greek Govt for training (2 str) by 10.18 - 1.19

N5177   (130-hp) Presentation a/c (probably 'Britons in Egypt No.2', replacing 9739). Shipped to Aegean; Arr Otranto by 17.2.17; F Sqdn 2 Wing by 29.4.17 - @15.5.17LM

N5178   (130-hp) Presentation a/c (probably 'Britons in Italy No.1', replacing 9744). Shipped to Aegean?

N5179   (???-hp) Presentation a/c (probably 'Britons in Japan No.1', replacing 9383). Deld CSD White City by 30.11.16; Shipped to Aegean; Arr Otranto by 17.2.17; F Sqdn 2 Wing by 29.4.17 - @26.5.17;

**20 SOPWITH PUP (ADMIRALTY 9901 TYPE) TRACTOR BIPLANE SCOUTS put forward 7.16 and ordered under Cont No C.P.119901/16, numbered N5180 to N5199 & built Kingston-upon-Thames. Delivered from Brooklands. (Ordered with 80-hp Le Rhône but some fitted 80-hp Gnôme)**

N5180   (80-hp Le Rhône) Deld Chingford 31.8.16 (transit); ADD (via Dover) 6.9.16; C Sqdn 1 Wing 7(11?).9.16; Crashed, CW 9.16 (last mention 16.9.16); ADD by 21.9.16 (repair) Deleted W/E 19.10.16.
[The spurious serial number 'N5180' was later carried by converted Sopwith Dove G-EBKY, which was not this aircraft]

N5181   (80-hp Gnôme) Deld Chingford 31.8.16; Dover 7.9.16; ADD 11.9.16; 4 Flt B Sqdn 1 Wing 11.9.16; 8 Sqdn (coded 'T') 10.11.16; Halberstadt shot down nr Remy 10.50 and 2-str nr Fontaine 11.30 20.12.16 (FSL RR Soar); FL after combat, wrecked Picquigny, NW of Amiens 26.1.17 (F/L RR Soar); 3 Sqdn 3.2.17; Dover 28.3.17 (overhaul); War School Manston 6.10.17 - 3.18; Freiston

N5182   Deld Chingford 5.9.16; ADD (via Dover) 6.9.16; Allocated to RFC (Military Wing) as A8736 at Dunkerque but not taken up; C Sqdn 1 Wing 7.9.16; Seaplane BU & into sea 6m off Ostende c.12.00 25.9.16 (FSL ER Grange) [Sablatnig SF2 Nr609, Seeflug 1 (Lt ZS Soltenborn & Lt ZS Rothig killed]; C Flt 8 Sqdn 26.10.16 (detd flt initially); Allotted FSL RA Little 14.11.16 and named 'LADY MAUD'; Roland or LVG 2-str shot down in flames, crashed nr wood N of Courcelette 09.50 23.11.16; Halberstadt D shot down SE of Bapaume 11.30 4.12.16; Albatros DII OOC Fontaine 11.15 20.12.16 (all FSL RA Little); 3 Sqdn 3.2.17; ADD 10.2.17; 9 Sqdn 27.2.17 - @16.3.17; ADD by 22.3.17 (repair); Dover 28.3.17 - @30.4.17; Walmer Defence Flt by 5.17; 2 AZPs 23.5.17; AGP 25.5.17 (all FSL WH Chisam); Dover Defence Flt 5.6.17 - 9.17; AGP 5.6.17; Wings, propeller and u/c damaged 6.7.17; Walmer, badly damaged 11.8.17; War Flt/School Manston W/E 20.10.17; Deleted W/E 23.2.18

N5183   Deld Dover (via Chingford) 13.9.16; ADD 15.9.16; Allocated to RFC (Military Wing) as A8735 at Dunkerque but not taken up; C Sqdn 1 Wing by 17.9.16; Attacked by HA and damaged by AA, EF, FL Malo 25.9.16 (F/L SV Trapp), flying again 26.9.16; Brown seaplane into sea 10m off Ostende 16.00 23.10.16 (F/L N Keeble); 8 Sqdn 26.10.16 (detd flt initially);

Damaged Fienvillers 28.10.16 (F/L SJ Goble); For ADD repair (NTU?); 3 Sqdn 3.2.17; COL Rue, N of mouth of Somme 14.2.17 (FSL AT Whealy, retd 15.2.17; ADD 2.17; Dover 23.2.17 (repair and overhaul); ADD 17.3.17; 4 Sqdn 21.3.17; COL 26.4.17; ADD by 28.4.17; AP Dover 2.5.17 (repair); ADD 31.5.17; 9 Sqdn 19.6.17; 2 AD by 28.6.17 - @5.7.17; ADD (ex 3 Sqdn) 12.7.17; Deleted 16.7.17 Not worth repair

N5184    Deld Chingford (via Hendon) 9.9.16; Dover 13.9.16; ADD 15.9.16; C Sqdn 1 Wing by 17.9.16; Deld Vert Galant 23.10.16; ADD by 9.11.16; C Sqdn 1 Wing 11.11.16; 8 Sqdn 16.11.16; White biplane dived smoking NE of Bapaume 20.12.16 (F/L GE Hervey); 3 Sqdn 3.2.17; ADD 10.2.17; 4 Sqdn by 1.3.17; Wrecked on ground 10.4.17; For survey by 12.4.17; Deleted ADD 27.4.17

N5185    Deld ADD (via Manston) 15.9.16 - @21.9.16; C Sqdn 1 Wing by 23.9.16; Hit flare lorry landing in strong wind 3.11.16; ADD (defects reported 26.10.16); ADD by 9.11.16 - @9.11.16; 3 Sqdn (named 'BINKY II') 30.11.16; 8 Sqdn 20.12.16; 3 Sqdn 3.2.17; FL Filescamp Farm 25.2.17 (FSL LH Rochford); Crashed and o/t in soft ground 4.3.17 (FSL E Pierce); Still 3 Sqdn 8.3.17; 2 AD by 29.3.17 (overhaul); 3 Sqdn by 5.4.17; Wrecked 11.4.17; ADD by 12.4.17; Deleted 27.4.17

N5186    (80-hp Le Rhône) Deld Chingford 16.9.16; Design Flt Eastchurch 12.10.16; Fitted with Le Prieur rocket and mg armament and wide centre section cut-out at Eastchurch; Flown 17.10.16; ADD 23.10.16; 4 Flt B Sqdn 1 Wing 4.11.16; Became 2 Sqdn 5.11.16; 8 Sqdn (coded '4') 16.11.16 (faulty assembly workmanship reported 4.11.16 & 7.1.17); "Type K (Albatros?)" shot down Ypres 26.12.16 (F/Cdr BL Huskisson); 2-str shot down Arras 23.1.17 (F/Cdr BL Huskisson injured); 3 Sqdn 3.2.17, COL nr Talmus, S of Vert Galant 14.2.17 (FSL R Collishaw unhurt); still 3 Sqdn 22.2.17; ADD 1.3.17; 4 Sqdn 21.3.17; Wrecked 10.4.17; ADD by 12.4.17; Deleted 27.4.17

N5187    Deld Dover 22.9.16; ADD 23.9.16; 4 Flt B Sqdn 1 Wing 24.9.16 - @9.11.16; EF, FL on beach La Panne 24.9.16 (FSL HR Wambolt); ADD (defects reported 26.10.16); C Sqdn 1 Wing by 16.11.16; 8 Sqdn (named 'TICKIE' or 'VICKIE', believed with 8 Sqdn) 20.12.16; 3 Sqdn 3.2.17 - @13.2.17; ADD by 15.2.17; 4 Sqdn 16.3.17; Wrecked 10.4.17; For survey by 12.4.17; Deleted ADD 27.4.17

N5188    (80-hp Gnôme); Deld Chingford (via Northolt and Hendon) 24.9.16; Hendon to Dover for Dunkerque 14.10.16 but damaged Harty Ferry (Isle of Sheppey); Tested Hendon 20.10.16; ADD (via Eastchurch and Dover) 2.11.16; C Sqdn 1 Wing 4.11.16; Became 3 Sqdn 5.11.16; 8 Sqdn 20.12.16; 3 Sqdn 3.2.17; Roland DD Bapaume, shared 9898 13.45 16.2.17 (FSL HF Beamish); COL 4.3.17 (FSL HF Beamish unhurt); Dover 16.3.17 (repair and overhaul); ADD 7.4.17; 9 Sqdn 16.4.17; HA shot down off Middelkerke, shared 9916 20.30 2.5.17 (FSL HE Mott); FL on beach E of Calais 2.5.17; retd 3.5.17; 11 Sqdn 3.6.17; 12 Sqdn 13.6.17 - @28.6.17; ADD by 7.17; Dover 4.7.17; War School Manston 23.9.17 - @30.3.18; EF, FL on beach 4.12.17 (repaired)

N5189    (80-hp Le Rhône) Deld ADD (via Dover) 9.11.16; 3 Sqdn 10.11.16; Chased enemy seaplane from Ghistelles, then EF, FL in sea, picked up by French patrol boat *Capricorn* and towed into Calais 12.11.16 (FSL N Keeble); ADD by 16.11.16; 3 Sqdn 5.1.17; 8 Sqdn, crashed 5m from Vert Galant on delivery 7.1.17 (FSL HG Travers); 3 Sqdn 3.2.17; Crashed 15.2.17; For survey by 22.2.17; Deleted ADD 24.3.17 DBR

N5190    (80-hp Le Rhône) Deld Dover 16.10.16; ADD 17.10.16; Allocated to RFC (Military Wing) as A8734 at Dunkerque but not taken up; C Sqdn 1 Wing (coded '2') 23.10.16; Defects reported 26.10.16; 8 Sqdn 26.10.16; Shot down nr Moeuvres by Ltn Mohr, Jasta 3 23.11.16 (F/L W Lush-Hope PoW, DoW 24.11.16)

N5191    Deld Dover 16.11.16; ADD 21.11.16; 3 Sqdn 28.11.16; 8 Sqdn 20.12.16; Shot down nr Hennies by Offrstlvtr Kosmahl & Ltn d R Schultz, Fl.A(A).261 2.2.17 (FSL WE Traynor killed - he was 3 Sqdn, attd 8 Sqdn); For survey by 8.2.17; Deleted 11.5.17 BUT

Surveyed 17.10.17; Deleted 23.10.17 TL

N5192    (80-hp Le Rhône) Deld ADD (via Dover) 20.10.16; Allocated to RFC (Military Wing) as A8737 at Dunkerque but not taken up; C Sqdn 1 Wing 23.10.16; C Flt 8 Sqdn 26.10.16 (detd flt initially); 2-str in flames 1m NE of La Bassée 09.50 23.11.16 (FSL RA Little); Wings collapsed over aerodrome pulling out of dive in test flight Vert Galant 10.12.16 (FSL SV Trapp killed); Deleted 5.1.17

N5193    (80-hp Le Rhône) Deld Dover 21.10.16; ADD 22.10.16; Allocated to RFC (Military Wing) as A8732 at Dunkerque but not taken up (defects reported 26.10.16); C Sqdn 1 Wing 23.10.16; C Flt 8 Sqdn 26.10.16 (detd flt initially); Roland D OOC nr Bapaume 14.50 10.11.16; LVG C OOC Pys-Miraumont 15.30 16.11.16 (both FSL DMB Galbraith); "Type K" (Albatros?) shot down OOC in spinning nose dive 20.12.16 (FSL AS Todd); Shot down nr Bapaume by Ltn M von Richtofen, Jasta Boelcke 4.1.17 (F/L AS Todd killed); For survey 11.1.17; Deleted 24.3.17

N5194    Deld Dover 19.10.16; ADD 20.10.16; Allocated to RFC (Military Wing) as A8733 at Dunkerque but not taken up (defects reported 26.10.16); C Sqdn 1 Wing 23.10.16; C Flt 8 Sqdn 26.10.16 (detd flt initially); LVG 2-str OOC Gommecourt 10.55 16.11.16; 2-str dest Bapaume 15.35 17.11.16; 2-str down on fire SE of Bapaume 09.50 27.11.16; Halberstadt DII shot down SE of Bapaume 11.00 4.12.16 (all F/L SJ Goble); Albatros DII OOC S of Bapaume 15.00 4.1.17 (FSL ER Grange DSC); Albatros DII OOC Grévillers 11.00 7.1.17 (FSL RA Little DSC); 3 Sqdn 3.2.17; FL Cramont 26.2.17 (FSL ST Hosken); HA down smoking behind Bapaume on 12.30 - 13.45 patrol, then lost, ran out of fuel, FL, crashed Le Crotoy 4.3.17 (FSL HEP Wigglesworth unhurt); 2 AD by 15.3.17 - @29.3.17 (rebuilt); 3 Sqdn by 5.4.17; Albatros DIII OOC Croiselles 06.30 23.4.17 (FSL GB Anderson); 2 AD by 26.4.17; 3 Sqdn to ADD 28.4.17; Dover 12.5.17; AGP 25.5.17; Wings and u/c slightly damaged 15.6.17; CW 20.8.17 (TFSL CB Cook); Deleted in field 20.8.17

N5195    (80-hp Gnôme) Deld ADD by 11.16 (not by 2.11.16); 3 Sqdn 5.11.16; FL Oost Dunkerque 7.1.17; retd sqdn on/by 18.1.17; 8 Sqdn 25.1.17; 3 Sqdn 3.2.17; ADD by 15.3.17; Dover 16.3.17 (repair and overhaul); U/c damaged 25.4.17; Wrecked 24.5.17; Damaged 24.7.17; War School Manston 29.9.17 - @30.3.18

N5196    Deld ADD by 9.11.16; 3 Sqdn 10.11.16; 8 Sqdn (coded 'T') 16.11.16; LVG C crashed E of Cambrai 14.40 23.11.16 (FSL DMB Galbraith); 2-str OOC E of Bucquoy 10.10 11.12.16 (F/L SJ Goble); 3 Sqdn 3.2.17; Attacked by 3 Halberstadts 4.3.17 (FSL E Percy); 2 AD 21.3.17 - @29.3.17; ADD by 5.4.17; 4 Sqdn 24.4.17; Orange 2-str (Aviatik?) with green and brown wings & 260-hp Maybach engine BU at 9,000ft Rosendael, shared N6462 12.20 2.5.17 (FSL FV Hall); Seaplane OOC Blankenberghe 07.45 12.5.17; Gotha crashed in sea 15m N of Westende, shared N6168, N6176 & N6198 18.30 25.5.17; 2-str OOC Ostende, shared N6462 17.35 28.5.17 (all FSL EW Busby); 11 Sqdn 7.6.17; 12 Sqdn 13.6.17; Wrecked 7.7.17; ADD by 12.7.17; Deleted 16.7.17

N5197    (80-hp Gnôme) Deld Brooklands direct to 3 Sqdn 10.11.16; 8 Sqdn 16.11.16; Halberstadt shot down N of Bapaume, shared 3691 26.12.16 (F/L GE Hervey); Albatros C OOC smoking NE of Bapaume 11.35 23.1.17 (F/L CD Booker); 3 Sqdn 3.2.17; COL Campigneulles, SW of Montreuil 14.2.17 (FSL LH Rochford unhurt); ADD 15.2.17; Dover 23.2.17 (repair and overhaul); ADD 11.3.17 (damaged in transit); Dover 28.3.17; AGP 25.5.17; Crashed and damaged 25.7.17; War Flt Manston 23.9.17 - 3.18; Freiston

N5198    (80-hp Le Rhône) Deld ADD (via Dover) 22.11.16; 3 Sqdn 30.11.16; 8 Sqdn 20.11.16 (sic); "Type L" shot down Achiet le Petit 27.12.16 (F/L CR Mackenzie); In combat 7.1.17 (FSL AHS Lawson wounded); Shot down nr Favreuil by Ltn H von Keudall, Jasta 1 24.1.17 (F/Cdr CR Mackenzie DSO killed); Deleted ADD 24.3.17

N5199    Deld Dover 26.11.16; ADD 28.11.16; 3 Sqdn 30.11.16; 8 Sqdn 5.1.17; In combat 7.1.17 (FSL ER Grange wounded); 3 Sqdn 3.2.17; Albatros DI spun

OOC and crashed nr Manoncourt 11.15 4.3.17 (FSL LH Rochford); Halberstadt DII crashed nr Bourlon Wood 10.20 6.4.17 (F/Cdr LS Breadner); Shot up 11.4.17 (FSL S Bennett); ADD 12.4.17; Deleted 27.4.17

**20 SOPWITH 1½ STRUTTER TYPE 9700 TRACTOR BIPLANES ordered 25.6.16 under Cont Nos C.P.119038/16 & A.S.14814 from Mann, Egerton & Co Ltd, Norwich and numbered N5200 to N5219. (110-hp Clerget 9Z unless stated otherwise)**

N5200    Shipped to Aegean; 2 Wing Thasos by 1.12.17; Surveyed 19.2.18; Deleted 13.3.18 wreck

N5201    Shipped to Aegean; F Sqdn 2 Wing by 29.4.17 - @26.5.17

N5202    Shipped to Aegean?

N5203    Accepted at Mkrs 10.1.17; Arrived 3 Wing Luxeuil 1.17; Allocated 2 Wing Mudros 23.3.17; Thasos by 6.17; Marsh by 12.7.17 - @21.7.17

N5204    Accepted at Mkrs 4.1.17; Arrived 3 Wing Luxeuil 1.17; Convtd to Type 9400; Shipped to Aegean; Stavros by 16.10.17 - @1.12.17; Mudros by 1.1.18 - @4.18

N5205    Accepted at Mkrs 15.1.17; Arrived 3 Wing Luxeuil 1.17; Shipped to Aegean; Marsh by 1.12.17 - @1.1.18; Mudros by 3.18; Marsh by 20.3.18; Thasos by 6.18 - @10.18; To Greek Govt

N5206    Accepted at Mkrs 15.1.17; Arrived 3 Wing Luxeuil 1.17; Shipped to Aegean; Arr Otranto by 17.2.17; Thasos by 28.10.17 - @1.12.17; Mudros by 1.1.18

N5207    Deld ADD by 8.3.17; to UK 13.9.17; War Flt Manston W/E 15.9.17; East Fortune NFS (via Redcar) 26.3.18

N5208    Deld ADD by 8.3.17; Dover 6.7.17; Wings and u/c damaged 21.7.17; War School Manston W/E 26.10.17; Cranwell 26.3.18 (transit); Redcar (via Beverley) 28.3.18 (transit); East Fortune NFS W/E 30.3.18

N5209    Accepted at Mkrs 15.2.17; To 5 Wing Coudekerque 2.17; Presumed shipped to Aegean; Surveyed Mudros 23.9.17; Deleted 6.10.17 wrecked

N5210    Accepted at Mkrs 15.2.17; To 5 Wing Coudekerque from 2.17; Shipped to Aegean; Mudros by 1.12.17 (repair); Lemnos, surveyed 5.12.17 wrecked; Deleted 15.1.18

N5211    Allocated Mkrs to 3 Wing Luxeuil 11.1.17 (NTU?); Shipped to Aegean; Mudros by 7.17

N5212    Allocated 3 Wing 11.1.17 (NTU); Shipped to Aegean; Mudros by 1.12.17 - @1.1.18; 6 Wing Otranto by 10.2.18; Greek training by 3.18; Repair Base by 6.18

N5213    Allocated 3 Wing 18.1.17 (NTU); Convtd to Type 9400; Assembling Pembroke 4.5.17; Shipped to Aegean; C Flt 2 Wing Imbros by 11.17 - @1.1.18 (130-hp Clerget); A Sqdn 2 Wing Thasos; Mudros by 3.18 - 4.18; Greek training by 6.18 - 10.18; To Greek Govt

N5214    Deld Pembroke and flown 4.5.17; Presumed lost on sea patrol 31.7.17 (FSL W Allaway killed) BUT Pembroke, packed for transit by 6.12.17; SW Group, for deletion by 29.12.17; Mullion by 1.18 (?)

N5215    Deld Pembroke for erection 4.5.17; East Fortune NFS 1.1.18 (Mod to Ships Strutter); Stalled from 25ft on landing 23.5.18 (Lt GW Stallard)

N5216    Allocated Mkrs to 3 Wing Luxeuil 25.1.17 (cancelled?); Shipped to Aegean; Tested Mudros 24.6.17; Thasos by 1.12.17; Deleted 1.18

N5217    Allocated Mkrs to 3 Wing Luxeuil 25.1.17 (cancelled?)

N5218    Allocated Mkrs to 3 Wing Luxeuil 25.1.17 (cancelled 20.2.17); Sunk in transit to Mudros 6.17

N5219    Allocated Mkrs to 3 Wing Luxeuil 1.2.17 (cancelled 20.2.17); Presented to Russia 1917

**30 SOPWITH 1½ STRUTTER TYPE 9400S TRACTOR BIPLANES ordered 25.6.16 under Cont No C.P.119038/16 from Mann Egerton & Co Ltd as their Type D, numbered N5220 to N5249 & built Norwich. (110-hp Clerget 9Z or 130-hp Clerget 9B)**

N5220    Deld Design Flt Eastchurch by rail 7.12.16; ADD 8.2.17; 5 Sqdn 1.3.17; ADD 11.8.17; for UK by 27.9.17; Dover by 29.9.17; Hendon 6.10.17 (for Cdr CR Samson); War School Manston W/E 27.10.17 - @3.18; 204 TDS Eastchurch by 8.18; Marine Observers School Eastchurch by 8.18 - 2.19

N5221    Deld Dover for erection 8.12.16; ADD 24.12.16; 5

Sqdn 11.2.17 - @2.7.17; AD by 5.7.17; Wrecked 3.8.17; Deleted ADD 20.8.17

N5222    Deld Dover for erection 8.12.16; ADD 20.12.16; 4 Sqdn by 4.1.17; ADD 28.3.17; Dover 23.5.17; CW 5.6.17; Deleted 6.6.17

N5223    Shipped to Aegean; Arr Otranto by 17.2.17; A Sqdn 2 Wing Thasos by 3.17; Shot down Xanthi-Phillippopolis road during reconnaissance of Philloppolis area, by Ltn von Eschwege, Borido, FA 30 30.3.17 (FSL JM Ingham & S/L JE Maxwell both killed)

N5224    Shipped to Aegean; E Flt 2 Wing Hadzi Junas 28.3.17 - @22.5.17; Twin-engined HA crashed nr Pataros 07.00 8.4.17 (F/L ET Bradley & 2/Lt CT Repton RFC); F Sqdn 2 Wing by 25.5.17; Transferred Russian Govt

N5225    Shipped to Aegean?

N5226    Shipped to Aegean?

N5227    Deld Killingholme by 2.17; Transit to Mudros 20.2.17

N5228    Shipped to Aegean?

N5229    (110-hp) Shipped to Aegean 5.4.17; 6 Wing Otranto by 13.6.17; Smyrna by 8.8.17 - @15.8.17; Possibly the a/c crashed Padua 17.21.17 (F/L J Gorman DoI) - or could be N1464; Surveyed 21.12.17 (now 130-hp); Deleted 3.1.18 wrecked

N5230    (130-hp) Deld Cranwell 23.4.17; East Fortune 25.5.18

N5231    (110-hp) Allocated Mkrs to 3 Wing Luxeuil 4.1.17 (NTU); Special Duty Flt 55 Wing RFC from 1.17; Shipped to Aegean 5.4.17; 6 Wing Otranto by 17.8.17; Surveyed 5.12.17; Deleted 13.12.17 DBR

N5232    (110-hp) Allocated Mkrs to 3 Wing Luxeuil 4.1.17 (NTU); Special Duty Flt 55 Wing RFC from 1.17; Shipped to Aegean 5.4.17; 6 Wing Otranto by 7.7.17; Dropped 2x65-lb bombs on U-boat 20m NE of Otranto 7.11.17; Surveyed 5.12.17 DBR (now 130-hp); Deleted 13.12.17; Restored to commission by 13.1.18; Became 66/67 Wing Otranto 1.4.18 - @21.4.18; 225 Sqdn Italy by 28.4.18 - @18.7.18; Taranto by 10.18 - @30.1.19

N5233    (110-hp) Allocated Mkrs to 3 Wing Luxeuil 4.1.17 (NTU); Shipped to Aegean 5.4.17; 6 Wing Otranto by 18.7.17 (now 130-hp); Dropped 2x65-lb bombs on U-boat 25m NE of Otranto 19.11.17; Surveyed 11.12.17; Deleted 3.1.18 DBR

N5234    (110-hp) Deld Pembroke by 5.17; Assembling 4.5.17; Eastchurch by rail 5.10.17 for Gunnery School Flt; Fitted 100-hp Monosoupape 2.18; Became 204 TDS Eastchurch 1.4.18

N5235    Transferred Belgian Aviation Militaire less engine as *S1*

N5236    Transferred Belgian Aviation Militaire less engine as *S2*

N5237    Transferred Belgian Aviation Militaire less engine as *S3*

N5238    Transferred Belgian Aviation Militaire less engine as *S4*

N5239    Transferred Belgian Aviation Militaire less engine as *S5*

N5240    Transferred Belgian Aviation Militaire less engine as *S6*; Flown for a time by Belgian 'ace' Sergeant Willy Coppens of 4me Escadrille

N5241    Allocated Felixstowe store 22.3.17; Transferred Belgian Aviation Militaire less engine as *S7*

N5242    Transferred Belgian Aviation Militaire less engine as *S8*

N5243    Allocated Mkrs to 3 Wing Luxeuil 25.1.17 (NTU); Shipped to Aegean in SS *Arum* for Aeroplane Flt 6 Wing 24.3.17; 6 Wing Otranto by 14.6.17 - @23.8.17

N5244    Presented to Imperial Russian Air Force 1917

N5245    (110-hp) Deld Felixstowe 15.4.17; Grain TD for erection 21.6.17, then to ECD Grain (air bag trials); Hendon (via Chingford) 21.7.17; Grain 29.7.17; Chingford 31.7.17; Hendon 7.8.17; (HD duties for Derby 10.17); Grain 10.2.18 (arr 11.2.18); Convtd Ships Strutter and fitted W/T; Hendon (via Dover & Martlesham Heath) 23.2.18 (for use of Air Dept Officers); Rosyth 6.4.18 (arr 7.4.18, transit); Turnhouse W/E 27.4.18 - @30.1.19

N5246    (130-hp) Deld Felixstowe store 2.5.17; Grain TD for erection 19.6.17 (fitted air bags), then to ECD to at least 20.6.18

N5247    (110-hp) Deld Felixstowe store 15.4.17; Grain EAD by 26.7.17 (gun trials); Calais 26.8.17; Le Tréport to Grain 27.8.17; St.Pol 24.9.17; still in France 29.9.17; Paris to St.Pol 11.10.17; Grain EAD 12.10.17; Chingford 28.12.17; Grain 29.12.17; Grain EAD from 20.3.18; Hendon 16.5.18; Grain 17.5.18; Hendon 19.5.18; Grain .18; Hendon 29.6.18; Grain 30.6.18; Hendon 2.7.18; Orfordness 3.7.18; Hendon 4.7.18; Grain 5.7.18; Hendon by 1.8.18; Grain 2.8.18; Hendon 6.8.18

N5248 (130-hp) Deld Felixstowe store 15.4.17; Desp by rail for Mudros 16.8.17; F Sqdn Erecting Mudros by 1.12.17 - @1.1.18; 2 Wing Hadzi Junas; Stavros by 3.18 - @4.18; F Sqdn 62 Wing Mudros by 6.18 - @1.19

N5249 (110-hp) Deld Felixstowe store 15.4.17; Desp by rail for Mudros 16.8.17; Erecting Mudros by 1.12.17; Mitylene by 1.3.18 - 4.18; Thasos by 6.18 - 1.19

**30 AVRO 504B (ADMIRALTY 179 TYPE DUAL) TRACTOR BIPLANES ordered 22.7.16 under Cont Nos C.P.120735/16 and C.P.121726 from The Sunbeam Motor Car Co Ltd, numbered 5250 to 5279 & built Wolverhampton. Fitted for 4 x 16-lb bombs. (80-hp Gnôme)**

N5250 Deld Cranwell 23.11.16; Wrecked 5.12.16; Deleted 30.12.16

N5251 (DC) Deld Eastchurch Workshops by rail 23.11.16; Eastchurch FS 12.4.17; Manston 20.8.17; Deleted 19.9.17

N5252 Deld Cranwell 30.11.16; Redcar School W/E 19.1.18 (504C); For deletion by 23.3.18

N5253 Deld Cranwell 30.11.16; Freiston by 7.17; Deleted W/E 18.9.17

N5254 Deld Cranwell 5.12.16; Crashed, CW 8.8.17; Deleted W/E 18.9.17

N5255 Deld Cranwell 14.2.17; Freiston by 3.17; Crashed and wrecked by 16.4.17; Deleted 19.5.17

N5256 (DC) (Convtd 504H) Deld Redcar by rail 4.12.16; Scarborough 29.1.17; Redcar 30.1.17; Wrecked landing 3.2.17; repaired; Crashed, CW nr Potts 13.12.17 (PFO S Castle-Smith unhurt); For deletion by 15.12.17

N5257 Deld Eastchurch Workshops by road for erection 11.12.16; Gun Flt Eastchurch 3.1.17; Eastchurch Workshops 7.2.17; Gun Flt Eastchurch 19.2.17 - @8.3.17 (u/s); Bomb Flt Eastchurch by 24.3.17; Gun Flt Leysdown 25.4.17; EAD Grain by rail 21.7.17; Eastchurch to Manston FS 21.8.17; Convtd 504H by 12.17; Surveyed 6.4.18; Deleted 15.4.18 DBR

N5258 (Convtd 504H by 12.17) Deld Eastchurch Workshops by road for erection 11.12.16; Manston FS 22.8.17; Deleted W/E 2.2.18

N5259 Deld ex Avro to Eastchurch Workshops 14.12.16; Chingford 7.5.17; Surveyed 2.9.17; Deleted 2.11.17 wrecked

N5260 Deld ex Avro to Eastchurch Workshops 14.12.16; Eastchurch FS 1.5.17; Chingford 7.5.17; U/c smashed 5.7.17; BR by 21.8.17

N5261 (Convtd 504H) Deld CSD White City 2.17; Fitted with interrupter gear; Twin floats (?); Hendon 22.5.17 - @25.5.18 (catapult expts)

N5262 (DC) (Convtd 504H) Deld Killingholme for erection 27.12.16; Chingford 25.5.17 (arr 26.5.17) - 3.18

N5263 (DC) Deld Killingholme for erection 27.12.16; Eastchurch Workshops 22.6.17 (arr 23.6.17); Manston 20.8.17; Surveyed 5.10.17; Deleted 6.10.17 wrecked

N5264 (DC) (Convtd 504H) Deld Killingholme for erection 27.12.16; Redcar 9.5.17; Damaged 21.7.17; Damaged 22.9.17; Deleted W/E 5.1.18

N5265 (DC) Deld Killingholme for erection 27.12.16; Redcar 9.5.17; DBR 23.7.17; Deleted 8.9.17

N5266 (DC) Deld Killingholme for erection 27.12.16; Redcar 16.6.17; BR by 21.8.17; Deleted 8.9.17

N5267 (DC) (Convtd 504H) Deld CSD White City 2.17; Fitted with interrupter gear; Killingholme for erection 9.3.17; Redcar 18.6.17; Damaged 6.10.17; Deleted W/E 26.1.18

N5268 (DC) (Convtd 504H) Deld Killingholme for erection 26.1.17; Redcar 23.6.17 (arr 24.6.17); Damaged 8.9.17; Deleted W/E 26.1.18

N5269 Deld CSD White City 2.17 (Convtd 504H); Hendon for erection 31.5.17 (catapult expts); Brough 1.6.18; Hendon 3.6.18

N5270 (Convtd 504H) Tested Hendon 23.4.17; Elswick works 26.4.17; Hendon for erection 23.6.17 - @25.5.18 (catapult expts)

N5271 (Convtd 504H by 29.12.17) Deld C Flt Cranwell 10.1.17; Crashed, damaged u/c, wings and propeller 14.8.17; Crashed and badly damaged Cranwell North 21.1.18 (pilot unhurt); FL in mist, wheel damaged, Beckering 20.3.18 (pilot unhurt); A Flt Cranwell by 4.18; Freiston by 10.18

N5272 (DC) Deld Killingholme for erection 24.1.17; Eastbourne 25.4.17; Broke u/c 2.5.17; CW 11.9.17; Surveyed 26.9.17; Deleted 26.9.17 DBR

N5273 (Convtd 504H) Deld Eastchurch Workshops for erection 20.3.17; Chingford 7.5.17; Surveyed 15.1.18 DBR; Deleted 19.1.18

N5274 (DC) Deld Killingholme for erection 16.1.17; Cranwell 24.4.17; Crashed 5.7.17; Crashed 22.8.17; Deleted W/E 18.9.17

N5275 Deld UK to Vendôme for erection 10.3.17; Wrecked BR 21.5.17; Surveyed 12.10.17; Deleted 16.10.17 wrecked

N5276 Deld UK to Vendôme for erection 10.3.17; Surveyed 12.10.17; Deleted 16.10.17 DBR

N5277 Deld Killingholme 26.2.17; Cranwell 24.4.17; Deleted W/E 26.10.17

N5278 Deld Killingholme for erection 27.3.17; Cranwell 24.4.17; Crashed, CW 13.7.17; Wrecked BR 15.8.17; For deletion by 2.11.17

N5279 Deld Killingholme store 17.4.17; Eastbourne 7.5.17; CW 9.5.17; Deleted 17.5.17

**30 SAGE N.3 SCHOOL TRACTOR BIPLANE DUAL CONTROL TRAINERS ordered 16.7.16 under Cont No C.P.120734/16 (to Specification N.3?), numbered N5280 to N5309, to be built Peterborough. (75-hp Hawk)**

N5280 Deld Cranwell 27.12.16; Retd Makers 15.1.17 - @26.8.17; Allocated Cranwell 20.10.17; Condemned by F/L RR Soar; (Ground?) instructional by 10.17; Surveyed 3.1.18; Deleted 17.1.18; Crashed and rebuilt 23.5.18 (sic)

N5281 Mkrs by 29.12.17; For Cranwell by 19.1.18 but contract cancelled 25.2.18

N5282 to N5309 cancelled 25.2.18

**20 AVRO 504G (ADMIRALTY 179 DUAL TYPE) TRACTOR BIPLANES ordered 16.7.16 under Cont No A.S.120731 from The Regent Carriage Co Ltd [and British Caudron Co per 1.17 official list], numbered N5310 to N5329 & built Fulham. Fitted to carry 4x16-lb bombs. Delivered from Hendon? (80-hp Gnôme unless otherwise stated)**

**504G from here**

N5310 (DC) Deld Hendon to Eastbourne 25.8.17; Possibly the m/c which crashed 23.10.17 (TPFO JP Crawford-Wood & Obs Off KLC Oxhey both killed) [or 9465]; Surveyed 26.10.17; deleted 29.10.17 DBR

N5311 (DC) Deld Hendon to Eastbourne 25.8.17; Became 206 TDS Eastbourne 1.4.18

N5312 (75-hp Renault) Deld Hendon for erection 26.8.17; Manston FS 15.9.17 - @3.18 (refitted 80-hp Gnôme by 12.17)

N5313 Deld Hendon for erection 28.8.17; Manston FS 15.9.17; Possibly the m/c in which TFSL DR Kerr killed 11.11.17 [or 9780]; Surveyed 15.11.17; Deleted 21.11.17 wrecked

N5314 Deld Hendon for erection 15.9.17; Cranwell by 11.17; Became 201/2 TDS Cranwell 1.4.18

N5315 Deld Hendon for erection 24.9.17; Huntingdon 3.10.17 (transit); Cranwell 5.10.17 (FL Market Deeping en route); Crashed, u/c and propeller damaged, Brauncewell 14.1.18; Crashed and badly damaged, Cranwell North 11.3.18 (pilot unhurt); Became 201/2 TDS Cranwell 1.4.18

N5316 Deld Hendon for erection 29.9.17; Chingford by 29.12.17; Became 207 TDS Chingford 1.4.18

N5317 Deld Chingford by 9.17 (not by 29.9.17); EF, FL ploughed field 29.11.17 (PFO LF Pendred); Became 207 TDS Chingford/Fairlop 1.4.18

N5318 Convtd fighter with Vickers & Lewis guns (when/where?); Deld Hendon W/E 27.10.17; Chingford W/E 9.11.17; Surveyed 17.1.18; Deleted 19.1.18 wrecked

N5319 Deld Hendon W/E 27.10.17; Chingford W/E 9.11.17; B Flt Fairlop by 3.18; Became 207 TDS Chingford/Fairlop 1.4.18

N5320 Deld Hendon W/E 27.10.17; Chingford W/E 3.11.17 - @29.12.17; B Flt Fairlop by 3.18; Became 207 TDS Chingford/Fairlop 1.4.18

N5321 Deld Hendon W/E 3.11.17; Chingford W/E 24.11.17; For deletion by 30.3.18

*Sage 3 Dual Control Trainer N5280. (via J.D.Oughton)*

*Sopwith Triplane N5431 of 2 Wing flown at Mudros by Flt Lt J.W. Alcock, later Sir John Alcock of Transatlantic Vimy fame. (via Frank Cheesman)*

*C.D.Booker's Sopwith Triplane N5482 'MAUD' with 8 Sqdn around April-May 1917. (via Frank Cheesman)*

*Sopwith Triplane N5468 'ANGEL' and others of 'C' Flight No.8 Squadron at Mont St.Eloi. (RAF Museum P.18144)*

*Avro 504G Trainer N5810 'A' at Cranwell. (A.Hogarth Savage via Peter Green)*

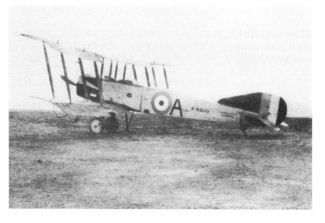

N5322    Deld Hendon W/E 24.11.17; Chingford 8.12.17; Fairlop by 2.18; Chingford/Fairlop by 3.18; Became 207 TDS Chingford/Fairlop 1.4.18

N5323    Deld Hendon W/E 24.11.17; Chingford 8.12.17 - 3.18

N5324    Convtd fighter with Vickers & Lewis guns (when/where?); Deld Hendon W/E 1.12.17; Chingford 8.12.17; Surveyed 21.2.18; Deleted 27.3.18

N5325    Deld Hendon W/E 8.12.17; Chingford 15.12.17; For deletion by 2.2.18

N5326    Deld Hendon for erection W/E 29.12.17; Manston FS 12.1.18 - @30.3.18

N5327    Deld Hendon for erection W/E 29.12.17; Eastbourne 10.1.18; became 206 TDS Eastbourne 1.4.18

N5328    Deld Hendon for erection W/E 29.12.17; Eastbourne 7.1.18; became 206 TDS Eastbourne 1.4.18

N5329    Deld Hendon by 1.18 (not by 29.12.17); Chingford 10.1.18; Became 207 TDS Chingford/Fairlop 1.4.18

## 20 MAURICE FARMAN S.7 LONGHORN PUSHER BIPLANES ordered 27.8.16 under Cont No C.P.120727/16 from Phoenix Dynamo Co Ltd, numbered N5330 to N5349 & built Bradford. (75-hp Hawk unless otherwise stated)

N5330    Deld Eastchurch Workshops 28.12.16; Accepted 4.3.17 (JL Parker); Manston FS 7.8.17; Deleted W/E 23.3.18

N5331    Deld Chingford by rail 4.1.17; Awaiting test 23.1.17; Accepted 27.2.17 (JL Parker); Surveyed 26.11.17; Deleted 5.12.17 as spares

N5332    Deld Eastchurch Workshops by rail 8.1.17; Accepted 4.3.17 (JL Parker), then to Eastchurch FS; Eastchurch Workshops 22.5.17; Retd Eastchurch FS; U/c damaged 7.7.17; Eastbourne W/E 10.11.17; Surveyed 8.2.18; Deleted 17.1.18

N5333    Deld Eastchurch Workshops by rail 10.1.17; Accepted 4.3.17 (JL Parker) then to Eastchurch FS; Eastbourne W/E 10.11.17; For deletion by 19.1.18

N5334    Deld Killingholme store 5.2.17 (JL Parker); Redcar 22.4.17; Crashed, wings and u/c smashed 26.7.17; Surveyed 7.12.17; Deleted as spares 14.12.17

N5335    Left Bradford 27.1.17-28.1.17, then to Killingholme store 6.2.17 (JL Parker), failed test; Failed acceptance test 13.3.17 (JL Parker); Accepted 15.3.17 (JL Parker); To service at Killingholme 2.18; For deletion by 30.3.18 (now 90-hp Curtiss)

N5336    (Convtd) Tested on delivery to Killingholme store but not accepted 31.1.17 (JL Parker); Accepted 14.3.17 (JL Parker); Deleted W/E 22.2.18

N5337    (Convtd) Tested on delivery to Killingholme store 3.2.17 (JL Parker); Deleted W/E 22.2.18

N5338    (Convtd) Deld Killingholme store 24.2.17; Deleted W/E 22.2.18

N5339    Deld Killingholme store 24.2.17; Eastchurch FS 18.6.17 (arr 20.6.17 via Huntingdon & Chingford) (to fit Curtiss); Manston FS 26.7.17; Surveyed 6.12.17 wrecked; Deleted 10.12.17

N5340    Deld Killingholme store 14.2.17 (JL Parker); To service at Killingholme 2.18; For deletion by 30.3.18 (90-hp Curtiss)

N5341    Deld Killingholme store 4.3.17; Deleted 12.11.17 for spares

N5342    Deld Killingholme store 16.1.17 (JL Parker); Redcar 27.10.17; Surveyed 7.12.17; Deleted 14.12.17 as spares

N5343    Accepted en route to Killingholme store 18.2.17 (JL Parker); Eastchurch 18.6.17 (arr 21.6.17); Fitting 90-hp Curtiss 29.9.17; Manston FS W/E 10.11.17; Deleted W/E 23.3.18

N5344    Deld Killingholme store 9.3.17; Redcar W/E 27.10.17; Surveyed 7.12.17; Deleted as spares 14.12.17

N5345    Deld Killingholme store 8.3.17; Eastchurch FS 14.6.17 (arr 15.6.17); Eastchurch Workshops 19.6.17; U/c broke 15.8.17; Fitted 90-hp Curtiss 29.9.17; Manston FS W/E 10.11.17; Deleted W/E 23.3.18

N5346    Deld Killingholme store 8.3.17; Accepted 9.3.17 (JL Parker); Eastchurch FS 14.6.17 (arr 15.6.17); Eastchurch Workshops 19.6.17; Fitted 90hp Curtiss 29.9.17; Manston FS W/E 10.11.17; Deleted W/E 23.3.18

N5347    (Convtd) Acceptance test en route Killingholme store 8.3.17 (JL Parker); Further acceptance test 15.3.17 (JL Parker); Deleted W/E 23.2.18

N5348    Deld Killingholme store and then accepted 11.3.17 (JL Parker); Deleted for spares 12.11.17

N5349    Deld Killingholme store and accepted 13.3.17 (JL Parker); Eastchurch 14.6.17; Fitting 90-hp Curtiss 29.9.17; Manston FS W/E 10.11.17 - 12.18 (Fitted 80-hp Renault by 3.18)

## 40 SOPWITH TRIPLANE SCOUTS ordered 23.7.16 under Cont Nos C.P.120945/16 & 87/A/1086 from Clayton & Shuttleworth Ltd, numbered N5350 to N5389 & built Lincoln. (130-hp Clerget 9B)

N5350    Deld 4 AAP Lincoln 2.12.16 for testing; Chingford, under repair 7.12.16; Design Flt Eastchurch 11.12.16; Dover 1.3.17 (engine trouble en route to Dunkerque); ADD 4.3.17; 10 Sqdn 16.3.17; EF, ditched nr Boulogne 23.4.17 (FSL RF Collins); Pilot and a/c rescued by French patrol boat *Joyeuse* and taken to DNT Office building Dunkerque; Furnes by 25.4.17 (for deletion); Deleted 13.10.17

N5351    Deld ADD (via Dover) 13.2.17; 8 Sqdn by 16.2.17; Crashed in field on TO 11.3.17 (FSL JAMcD Allan); ADD by 15.3.17; 10 Sqdn 13.4.17 - @7.5.17; ADD by 10.5.17; 11 Sqdn by 5.6.17; Crashed 8.6.17 (FSL ECR Stoneman); ADD by 14.6.17; 12 Sqdn 12.7.17 - @14.8.17; ADD by 16.8.17; Dover by 13.10.17; Chingford 7.1.18; Possibly the a/c in which F/L LEB Wimbush crashed 27.3.18 (DoI 28.3.18) - or could be N6151; Surveyed 30.3.18; Deleted 15.4.18 wrecked

N5352    Deld ADD by 2.17; 1 Sqdn 7.2.17 - @8.2.17; ADD by 15.2.17 (repair); 10 Sqdn by 28.2.17; Crashed on TO 9.5.17 (FSL LG Steel); Deleted ADD 14.5.17

N5353    Wrecked on delivery to Cranwell 5.3.17; Dover for repair by 25.3.17; Deleted 1.4.17

N5354    Deld ADD by 22.3.17; 10 Sqdn by 28.3.17; ADD 9.5.17; 9 Sqdn 9.5.7; ADD 29.5.17; 10 Sqdn 5.7.17; Albatros DIII OOC Roulers 07.45 12.8.17; Albatros DIII Ledeghem 08.30 17.8.17 (both FSL GL Trapp); FL, crashed and damaged E of Elverdinghe 19.8.17 (FSL GL Trapp unhurt); ADD 19.8.17; 1 Sqdn 1.10.17; Sideslipped on TO in gusty wind 13.10.17 (FSL AJ Binks injured, DoI 9.2.18), to ADD; Surveyed 22.11.17; Deleted 28.11.17 DBR

N5355    Left for ADD by EF, FL, burst tyre nr Spalding 11.3.17 (FSL RA Little); Felixstowe 12.3.17; Dover 14.3.17; ADD 17.3.17; 10 Sqdn by 28.3.17 - @4.4.17; ADD by 5.4.17; 11 Sqdn by 23.5.17; COL 29.5.17 (FSL JN McAllister); ADD by 31.5.17; 10 Sqdn 10.8.17; Attacked by 5 Albatros nr Langemarck and shot down by Ltn Jacobs, Jasta 7, 20.8.17 (FSL CH Weir PoW, DoI 21.8.17) [nr Ramscapelle per Germans - too far away!]; Deleted 1.9.17

N5356    Deld Hendon 17.3.17; ADD 18.3.17 - @22.3.17; 10 Sqdn by 28.3.17; ADD, hit tree, left for repair 23.4.17 - @26.4.17; Flying again with 10 Sqdn by 30.4.17; ADD by 3.5.17; 10 Sqdn 5.5.17; ADD 30.5.17; 9 Sqdn 11.7.17; ADD 4.8.17; 10 Sqdn 22.8.17; ADD 27.8.17 - @30.8.17; 12 Sqdn from/by 4.9.17; ADD 16.9.17, deleted 17.9.17 damaged BR

N5357    Deld ADD by 29.3.17; 10 Sqdn 5.4.17; Damaged landing 21.4.17 (FSL E Dickson); Repaired locally by 26.4.17; still 10 Sqdn by 13.5.17; ADD by 17.5.17; 10 Sqdn (coded 'K') 17.6.17; Shot down Wervicq-Comines by Ltn W Blume, Jasta 26, 21.00 11.7.17 (FSL RL Kent POW unhurt); Deleted 8.8.17

N5358    Deld Dover 23.3.17; ADD 25.3.17; 10 Sqdn 24.4.17; ADD 10.5.17; 9 Sqdn 11.5.17; ADD 3.6.17; 10 Sqdn (coded 'Q') 11.6.17; Damaged landing Oost Capelle 14.6.17 (FSL CRM Prewett); Shot down Zonnebeke-Moorslede by Ltn Allmenröder, Jasta 11, 08.05 24.6.17 (FSL RG Saunders killed); Deleted 2.7.17

N5359    Deld Dover 4.4.17; ADD 5.4.17; 10 Sqdn by 12.4.17; Aviatik C OOC 3m SE of Ypres, shared N6294 07.15 1.6.17; Albatros DIII crashed W of Polygon Wood c.11.00 6.6.17; Albatros DIII OOC Zonnebeke 19.20 14.6.17; 2-str OOC Houthem 09.40 15.6.17; 2-str OOC Houthem 09.40 18.6.17; (all FSL JA Page); EF, FL and wrecked Chateau Lovie 25.6.17 (FSL CR Pegler); ADD 26.6.17; Deleted in field 27.6.17

N5360    Deld Hendon 11.4.17; Dover 12.4.17; ADD by 19.4.17; 10 Sqdn 26.4.17; ADD 10.5.17; 9 Sqdn 11.5.17; ADD by 17.5.17; 9 Sqdn 26.5.17; COL 11.6.17 (FSL AF

MacDonald); ADD by 14.6.17; 12 Sqdn from/by 16.7.17; Crashed 3.9.17; ADD 5.9.17; Surveyed 17.10.17; Deleted 23.10.17 wrecked

**N5361** Deld ADD by 26.4.17; 10 Sqdn 9.5.17; Albatros DIII OOC W of Polygon Wood c.11.10 6.6.17 (FSL JH Keens); Damaged, landed Chateau Lovie 7.6.17 (FSL JH Keens wounded), retd sqdn 8.6.17; Crashed and damaged Droglandt 22.7.17 (FSL AMO McLachlen); ADD 23.7.17 - @30.8.17; 12 Sqdn from/by 2.9.17; AP Dover 4.12.17; CSD White City W/E 15.12.17: Deleted 17.12.17 for War Museum Exhibition at Royal Academy

**N5362** Deld Chingford for erection 17.4.17; Wrecked 19.4.17; Surveyed 2.5.17; Deleted 9.5.17

**N5363** Deld ADD by 3.5.17; 10 Sqdn 5.5.17; ADD 14.5.17; ADD; 9 Sqdn 1.6.17 - @5.7.17; ADD by 12.7.17; Deleted 16.7.17

**N5364** Flt tested Farnborough 15.5.17; Deld ADD by 6.17; 10 Sqdn 16.6.17; FL at 306 Siege Battery after pilot shot in leg 12.7.17 (FSL JAMcD Allan injured); Wings folded in dive when shot down by Ltn H Dilthey, Jasta 27, S of Passchendaele 24.7.17 (FSL TC May killed); Deleted 8.8.17

**N5365** Deld Dover (via Cranwell and Hendon) 25.4.17; ADD 29.4.17; 10 Sqdn 13.5.17; Crashed Clairmarais 20.5.17; ADD 22.5.17 - @21.6.17; 9 Sqdn by 27.6.17; FL 27.6.17 (FSL KG Macdonald); Retd 28.6.17; Engine cut on TO, FL in cornfield, damaged 7.7.17 (FSL AF MacDonald unhurt); ADD by 12.7.17; Deleted 24.7.17

**N5366** Deld Dover 29.4.17; ADD 2.5.17; 10 Sqdn 13.5.17; Albatros Scout OOC am, FL, slightly damaged La Lovie 20.5.17 (FSL CE Pattison wounded); ADD 29.5.17; 10 Sqdn, tested 7.6.17; Albatros DV BU Zonnebeke 08.10 24.6.17 (F/L JE Sharman DSC); 2-str OOC nr Wervicq 19.45 26.6.17 (FSL HW Taylor); COL Droglandt 20.7.17 (FSL AMO McLachlen); ADD 21.7.17; 10 Sqdn 19.8.17; Albatros DIII OOC E of Menin 18.35 21.8.17 (FSL GL Trapp); 8 Sqdn 30.8.17; COL in thick mist Mont St.Eloi 5.9.17 (FSL SH McCrudden severely injured); ADD 6.9.17; AP Dover 25.1.18; Gunnery School Flts Eastchurch 1.2.18; Became 204 TDS Eastchurch 1.4.18 - @6.18

**N5367** Deld Dover (via Lincoln and North Weald) 30.5.17; ADD 31.5.17; 10 Sqdn 6.6.17; Landed too fast on uneven ground, o/t, wrecked Droglandt 15.6.17 (FSL CR Pegler); ADD 17.6.17; 10 Sqdn 19.7.17; FL in water Ghyvelde 9.8.17; Retd sqdn 10.8.17; Shot down nr Roulers by Ltn Georg von der Osten, Jasta 11 on 25.8.17 (FSL ADM Lewis PoW) [Langemarck per Germans]; Deleted 7.9.17

**N5368** Deld Chingford 3.5.17; Dover 5.5.17; ADD 23.5.17; 10 Sqdn 7.6.17; FL 12.6.17 (FSL QS Shirriff); Flying again 15.6.17; Shot down Zillebeke by Ltn Güttler, Jasta 24, 08.50 12.7.17 (FSL CR Pegler killed) Deleted 8.8.17

**N5369** Deld Chingford (via Bourne & Cranwell) 5.6.17; ADD 5.6.17 - @21.6.17; 12 Sqdn by 25.6.17; Crashed 12.7.17 (FSL DH Daly minor injuries); Deleted ADD 16.7.17

**N5370** Deld Dover (via Lincoln) 2.5.17; ADD 21.7.17; 10 Sqdn 10.8.17; EF, FL, wrecked between Oostvleteren and Westvleteren, N of Poperinghe 15.8.17 (FSL JG Manuel); ADD 16.8.17; Deleted ADD 20.8.17

**N5371** Deld Dover (via Bekesbourne) 7.6.17; ADD 7.6.17; 9 Sqdn 13.6.17; EF after 5 minutes of practice flight, crashed 16.6.17 (FSL HE Mott unhurt); still 9 Sqdn 5.7.17; Deleted ADD 16.7.17

**N5372** Deld Dover 23.5.17; ADD 23.5.17; 10 Sqdn 30.5.17; FL, damaged nr aerodrome 8.6.17 (FSL CRM Prewett); Crashed and damaged Droglandt 14.6.17 (FSL CR Pegler); ADD 15.6.17 - @19.7.17; 1 Sqdn by 23.7.17; COL downwind 10.8.17 (FSL SS Flook); ADD 10.8.17; 8 Sqdn 6.9.17; ADD 10.9.17 - @8.10.17; 1 Sqdn by 11.10.17; FL Luneville 14.10.17; AP Dover 23.11.17; Surveyed 14.12.17; Deleted 19.12.17 W&T

**N5373** Deld ADD (via Eastchurch and Dover) 25.5.17; 1 Sqdn 8.6.17; Albatros Scout OOC Gheluvelt - Ten-Brielen 18.35 3.7.17; Albatros DV OOC 4m E of Messines, shared N5455, N5479, N5485, N6296, N6300, N6304 & N6308 20.05 17.7.17; Albatros DV OOC Houthulst Forest 16.00 8.8.17; Albatros DV OOC nr Moorslede 07.40 9.8.17 (all FSL CG Brock); EF, FL, wrecked nr

Dranoutre 13.8.17 (FSL CG Brock slightly injured); ADD 13.8.17; Deleted 20.8.17

**N5374** Deld ADD (via Huntingdon and Dover) 25.5.17; 9 Sqdn 9.6.17; Spun into ground 3m from aerodrome 13.6.17 (FSL TR Shearer killed); Deleted ADD 27.6.17

**N5375** Deld ADD by 14.6.17; 10 Sqdn 15.6.17; FL and wrecked nr Droglandt 6.7.17 (FSL JAMcD Allan unhurt); ADD 7.7.17; 10 Sqdn 5.8.17; ADD 27.8.17; 12 Sqdn from/by 2.9.17 - @17.9.17 [LM]; ADD 9.17; Destroyed by enemy bombs 1.10.17; Surveyed 17.10.17; Deleted 23.10.17 wrecked

**N5376** Deld Hendon (via Cranwell) 30.5.17; Dover 4.6.17; ADD 5.6.17; 10 Sqdn 17.6.17 (named 'BLACK SHEEP'); FL due to flak 21.6.17 (FSL HW Taylor); Local repair, flying again 24.6.17; Shot down E of Messines by Ltn C Allmenrder, Jasta 11 on 25.6.17 (FSL GE Nash, wounded, PoW) [N of Quesnoy per Germans]; Deleted 9.7.17

**N5377** Deld Chingford (via Cranwell) 30.5.17 (transit); ADD (via Dover) 31.5.17; 9 Sqdn 9.6.17; 1-str OOC Oost Dunkerque, shared N5378, N5459, N5475 & N5489 05.10 17.7.17 (FSL EK Pierce); Aviatik C OOC Middelkerke, shared N5462 17.35 28.7.17 (FSL FJW Mellersh); ADD 29.7.17; 1 Sqdn (coded '4') 27.9.17; Shot down Dadizeele by Ltn Wilde, Jasta 4, 06.50 patrol on 5.10.17 (FSL MJ Watson PoW); Surveyed 17.10.17; Deleted 23.10.17 TL

**N5378** Deld Hendon 8.6.17 (transit); ADD (via Dover) 9.6.17; 9 Sqdn 13.6.17; COL 16.6.17 (F/Cdr GE Hervey); 1-str OOC Oost Dunkerque, shared N5377, N5459, N5475 & N5489 05.10 17.7.17 (FSL AF MacDonald); ADD 4.8.17; 1 Sqdn 27.9.17; 12 Sqdn 30.11.17; COL 8.12.17 (FSL HStJE Youens); Flying again 10.12.17; Deletion requested 4.1.18, but still 12 Sqdn 10.1.18; ADD 1.18; Dover 13.1.18; Chingford 28.1.18; Became 207 TDS Chingford 1.4.18

**N5379** Deld ADD (via Dover) 12.6.17; 10 Sqdn 25.6.17; Albatros Scout OOC nr Lille 09.40 7.7.17 (FSL JA Page); Engine trouble, FL les Moëres 15.7.17 (F/Cdr R Collishaw); COL Clairmarais North 21.8.17; ADD 27.8.17; Damaged by fire on night of 1.10.17; Salved; 12 Sqdn 25.10.17 (for storage initially, but sqdn a/c by 29.11.17); Crashed 8.12.17; Deleted 31.12.17 BUT still 12 Sqdn to 10.1.18, for deletion by 17.1.18

**N5380** Deld ADD (via Dover) 12.6.17; 10 Sqdn 25.6.17; EF, FL in field, struck ridge, o/t, wrecked 3.7.17 (F/L JA Page unhurt); ADD 4.7.17; 10 Sqdn 23.7.17; Albatros DIII OOC Polygon Wood 12.10 9.8.17; Red Albatros DIII crashed in flames Houthulst Forest 16.15 14.8.17 (both FSL HJT Saint); Albatros DV OOC 18.30 & another 18.35 Menin (FSL JG Manuel); ADD 27.8.17; 12 Sqdn W/E 2.9.17; To AP Dover but crashed 4.12.17

**N5381** Deld ADD (via Dover) 16.6.17; 10 Sqdn 26.6.17; Albatros DV OOC then FL and wrecked SE of Polygon Wood 06.45 17.7.17 (FSL C Lowther); ADD 18.7.17; 10 Sqdn 15.8.17; Damaged landing 15.8.17; Albatros DV OOC & another crashed E of Menin 18.30-18.35 21.8.17 (FSL JG Manuel); 1 Sqdn 27.8.17; Attacked by formation of Albatros Scouts, shot down Wytschaete by Ltn Stapenhorst, Jasta 11 3.9.17 (FSL GBG Scott killed); Deleted ADD 3.9.17

**N5382** Deld War Flt Manston (via Eastchurch( (named 'OOSLUMBIRD') 13.6.17; FL nr Minster 14.6.17 (FSL JE Scott); AGPs 4.7.17 & 7.7.17 x 2 (FSL RH Daly); One of two Gotha GIII shot down in flames 15m off Ostende 11.30 7.7.17 (FSL RH Daly awarded DSC); O/t landing, damaged 11.7.17 (FSL HC Lemon unhurt); AGPs 22.7.17, 12.8.17 (FSL HC Lemon); Possibly the aircraft which collided with N6466 26.10.17 (F/L AF Brandon DSC killed); Surveyed 7.11.17; Deleted 14.11.17 DBR

**N5383** Deld War Flt Manston 18.6.17; AGP 4.7.17; AGP, COL, damaged tail and wings 7.7.17 (FSL AC Burt); Cranwell W/E 1.3.18; Became 201/2 TDS Cranwell 1.4.18

**N5384** Deld Dover 20.6.17; Transferred French Govt as F11 23.6.17; Retd ADD W/E 11.10.17; 1 Sqdn 16.10.17; EF, FL on beach, sank in soft sand Coxyde Bains 6.11.17 (FSL JO Simpson); NADD W/E 8.11.17; Dover 28.1.18; Gunnery School Flts Eastchurch 29.1.18; Became 204 TDS Eastchurch 1.4.18 - @7.18

N5385     Deld Dover 20.6.17; Transferred French Govt as *F12* 23.6.17; Naval Escadrille de Chasse, Dunkerque, crashed 13.7.17

N5386     Deld Dover 20.6.17 (via Lincoln); Transferred French Govt as *F13* 21.6.17; Retd at ADD W/E 11.10.17; 1 Wing HQ St.Pol W/E 25.10.17 (Depot storage); Seaplane Defence Sqdn W/E 29.11.17; 12 Sqdn 10.12.17; Seaplane Defence Sqdn 12.1.18; Dover 13.1.18; Chingford by 17.1.18 (Fairlop LG by 19.1.18); Chingford by 23.3.18; Became 207 TDS Chingford/Fairlop 1.4.18 - @5.18; Selected for Museum (NTU?)

N5387     Deld Dover 14.7.17; Transferred French Govt as *F14* 24.6.17 [sic] (Lt Nungesser); Flown Dover to Dunkerque 15.7.17 & 21.7.17 (French pilot); Retd ADD; Damaged by fire on night of 1.10.17; 1 Sqdn (coded '15', named 'PEGGY') 15.10.17; 2-str OOC S of Comines 11.00 21.10.17 (FSL HleR Wallace); 12 Sqdn 6.12.17; Dover 13.1.18 but retd Walmer with engine trouble; Dover 14.1.18; Deleted W/E 23.2.18

N5388     Deld Dover (via Huntingdon) 16.7.17; Dunkerque 21.7.17 (French pilot); Transferred French Govt (as *F15*?) (fitted 110-hp Clerget). Claimed destroyed with pilot, per Flugsport 9.17, presumably the a/c shot down by Ltn Altemeier, Jasta 24 on 26.9.17

N5389     Earmarked for French Govt, but with N5932-N5934 replaced by N5384-N5387; Deld ADD (via Dover) 12.7.17; 10 Sqdn 23.7.17; Albatros Scout OOC N of Polygon Wood 19.30 25.8.17 (FSL DF FitzGibbon); ADD 27.8.17 - @13.9.17; 12 Sqdn by 15.9.17 - @27.9.17LM; To ADD; Burnt in fire on night of 1.10.17; Surveyed 17.10.17; Deleted 23.10.17 burnt

**30 BRISTOL SCOUT D TRACTOR BIPLANES ordered under Cont Nos C.P.127042/16 & C.P.130592/16/X, numbered N5390 to N5419 & built Filton. N5400 to N5419 cancelled 10.16, presume later reinstated. (100hp Gnôme Monosoupape to N5399; N5400 80-hp Le Rhône [80-hp Gnôme per 1.17 official list], N5401 onwards 80-hp Gnôme)**

N5390     (C/n 1837) Deld Eastchurch Workshops by road 2.11.16 (arrived 11.11.16); War Flt Eastchurch 27.11.16; Grain by 2.17; War Flt Manston 18.3.17; AGPs 25.5.17 (FSL RH Daly), 5.6.17 (FSL AC Burt), 13.6.17 (FSL AC Burt) & 12.8.17 (FSL HJ Nelson); War School Manston W/E 6.10.17; Surveyed 26.10.17; Deleted 29.10.17 W&T

N5391     (C/n 1838) Deld Eastchurch Workshops by road 10.11.16; War Flt Eastchurch to Grain 21.11.16; HSPP 1.3.17 (FSL GMF O'Brien); War Flt/School Manston 21.3.17; AGP 13.6.17 (FSL AC Burt later F/Cdr GL Thomson); AGP, engine tail and wings damaged landing 7.7.17 (FSL Lord Ossulston unhurt); AGP 12.8.17 (FSL S Quayle); For deletion by 30.3.18

N5392     (C/n 1839) Deld Eastchurch Workshops by rail 13.11.16; Spotting Flt Eastchurch 22.11.16; Detling 15.2.17; War Flt Manston 1.4.17; AGP 5.6.17 (FSL HR de Wilde); AGP 7.7.17 (FSL S Quayle); Run into by Avro 504 (RFC) B966 20.7.17; Dawn patrol, FL, ran into dyke, o/t and damaged, Sandwich 23.9.17 (FSL WF Crundall unhurt); For deletion by 30.3.18

N5393     (C/n 1840) Awaiting engine at Mkrs by 10.11.16; Shipped to Aegean; 2 Wing Mudros; B Sqdn 2 Wing Thermi by 4.6.17; Marsh by 5.10.17 - @6.10.17; 2 Wing Imbros

N5394     (C/n 1841) (100-hp Gnôme Mono) Deld East Fortune NFS by rail 27.11.16; To British & Colonial W/E 7.1.17 (repair); East Fortune for erection by 1.4.17 - @30.3.18

N5395     (C/n 1842) Deld Eastchurch Workshops by rail 10.12.16; Detling 15.2.17; Manston 28.3.17; O/t landing 5.5.17 (F/L EP Hardman unhurt); Grain 14.6.17 for special duties; Manston 10.8.17; Cylinder head flew off 6.9.17; Deleted W/E 8.9.17

N5396     (C/n 1843) Awaiting engine at Mkrs by 10.11.16; Shipped to Aegean; 2 Wing Mudros & Imbros

N5397     (C/n 1844) (60-hp Le Rhône) Deld Chingford by lorry 14.12.16; Awaiting test 1.4.17; Rudder damaged 10.7.17; 100-hp Gnôme Mono by 10.7.17; 60-hp Le Rhône by 12.17; Became 207 TDS Chingford 1.4.18

N5398     (C/n 1845) Deld Chingford by lorry 14.12.16; War Flt Manston 23.1.17; Hit by Avro 1484 taxying, wings

damaged 16.3.17; AGPs 25.5.17 (FSL AC Burt), 7.7.17 (FSL HC Lemon) & 12.8.17 (FSL CFD Ash); Badly damaged on TO 16.8.17 (FSL JA Piquet unhurt); Surveyed 21.12.17 (now War School); Deleted 28.12.17 DBR

N5399     (C/n 1846) Fitted with overwing Lewis gun; Awaiting engine at Mkrs by 10.11.16; Deld Cranwell by 2.17 (not by 31.12.16); Redcar War Flt 16.3.17; U/c damaged landing 12.6.17 (F/L NWG Blackburn); Surveyed 7.12.17 wrecked; Deleted 14.12.17

N5400     (C/n 1847) (80-hp Le Rhône) Deld East Fortune by rail 13.11.16 - @30.3.18; U/c damaged landing 29.6.17; COL, u/c and propeller wrecked 12.12.17 (FSL PK Glazebrook); Grand Fleet AG&FS East Fortune [formed 19.7.18], WO 20.8.18

N5401     (C/n 1848) Deld East Fortune NFS by rail 13.11.16 - @30.3.18

N5402     (C/n 1849) Deld Eastchurch Workshops by rail 14.11.16; Chingford 9.2.17; Cranwell by lorry 9.5.17 (arrived 15.5.17); Crashed and damaged 18.7.17; Crashed 2.10.17; Crashed nr east gate, badly damaged 2.12.17 (pilot unhurt); Became 201/2 TDS Cranwell 1.4.18

N5403     (C/n 1850) Deld Redcar by rail 14.11.16; B Flt Cranwell by transport 22.4.17 (arrived 26.4.17); CW 17.7.17; Crashed, u/c and propeller damaged 4.12.17 (pilot unhurt); Crashed, slightly damaged Cranwell South 21.2.18 (pilot unhurt); Became 201/2 TDS Cranwell 1.4.18

N5404     (C/n 1851) Deld Redcar by rail 14.11.16; Cranwell by transport 3.6.17 (arrived 7.6.17); U/c smashed 25.6.17; Wrecked 22.7.17; U/c broken 11.8.17; Crashed 2.10.17; Became 201/2 TDS Cranwell 1.4.18

N5405     (C/n 1852) Deld Redcar by rail 16.11.16; U/c wrecked landing 26.12.16 (PFO HF Stackard); Cranwell by transport 3.6.17 (arr 7.6.17); Crashed 21.8.17; Crashed and badly damaged, Cranwell South 19.12.17 (pilot unhurt); Became 201/2 TDS Cranwell 1.4.18; Crashed and damaged 4.4.18 (pilot unhurt)

N5406     (C/n 1853) Deld Redcar by rail 16.11.16; Cranwell by transport 10.5.17 (arrived 15.5.17); Damaged 5.9.17; Became 201/2 TDS Cranwell 1.4.18

N5407     (C/n 1854) Deld by rail to Eastchurch Workshops 23.11.16; Chingford 8.2.17; Cranwell by lorry 10.5.17 (arrived 12.5.17); Crashed 13.7.17; COL Cranwell South 29.1.18 (pilot unhurt); Became 201/2 TDS Cranwell 1.4.18

N5408     (C/n 1855) Deld by rail to Eastchurch Workshops 22.11.16; Chingford 9.2.17; Cranwell by lorry 31.3.17 (arrived 3.4.17); Became 201/2 TDS Cranwell 1.4.18

N5409     (C/n 1856) Deld by rail to Eastchurch Workshops 24.11.16; Eastchurch FS 14.12.16; For deletion by 30.3.18

N5410     (C/n 1857) Deld Cranwell 30.11.16; Crashed 1.3.17; Deleted 12.3.17

N5411     (C/n 1858) Deld Filton to RNASTE Vendôme for erection 8.1.17; Became 205 TDS Vendôme 1.4.18; 212 TDS by 5.18; COL, damaged 20.5.18 (PFO WA Souter & Capt RH Martin)

N5412     (C/n 1859) (100-hp Gnôme Monosoupape) Deld Filton to RNASTE Vendôme for erection 3.1.17; Awaiting test 8.1.17; Wing and u/c damaged 28.9.17; Crashed Vendôme 25.1.18; EF, swung into ground, badly damaged 25.6.18 (F/Cdt CA Matthews slightly injured)

N5413     (C/n 1860) Deld RNASTE Vendôme by road 14.1.17; Landed in semi-darkness, CW 13.2.18 (F/L EE Maitland-Heriot injured); For deletion by 22.2.18

N5414     (C/n 1861) Deld Redcar by rail 4.12.16; Tested 1.3.17; B Flt Cranwell by transport 22.4.17 (arrived 26.4.17); CW 12.7.17; Became 201/2 TDS Cranwell 1.4.18

N5415     (C/n 1862) Deld Redcar by rail 4.12.16; Tested 1.3.17; B Flt Cranwell by transport 10.5.17 (arrived 15.5.17); Crashed and wrecked, Cranwell North 12.1.18 (pilot unhurt); Crashed and slightly damaged 22.3.18 (pilot unhurt); Became 201/2 TDS Cranwell 1.4.18

N5416     (C/n 1863) Deld Hendon for erection 15.12.16; Tested 19.12.16; Accepted 24.12.16; Damaged by 7.2.17; EF, FL Northolt 28.5.17 (FSL EB Freeland); Retd Hendon 30.5.17; Deleted 15.6.17

N5417     (C/n 1864) Deld by rail to Eastchurch Workshops 18.12.16; Chingford 9.2.17; Cranwell by lorry 31.3.17

N5418 (arrived 3.4.17); COL 16.6.17; Crashed and slightly damaged Ermine Street 14.3.18 (pilot unhurt); Became 201/2 TDS Cranwell 1.4.18

N5418 (C/n 1865) Fitted with overwing Lewis gun; Deld Chingford by lorry 19.12.16; Cranwell 11.4.17; Wrecked 1.5.17 (pilot unhurt); Became 201/2 TDS Cranwell 1.4.18

N5419 (C/n 1866) Deld Chingford by lorry 16.12.16 (arrived 19.12.16); Cranwell 11.4.17; Wrecked 1.5.17 (TPFO HE Grundy DoI); Rebuilt; Crashed nr RFC Waddington 10.12.17 (pilot unhurt); Crashed, Cranwell South 20.3.18 (pilot unhurt); Became 201/2 TDS Cranwell 1.4.18

**75 SOPWITH TRIPLANE SCOUTS ordered 1.9.16 under Cont No C.P.125849/16, numbered N5420 to N5494 & built Kingston-upon-Thames. Delivered from Brooklands (130-hp Clerget 9B)**
[Per 1.17 official list N5420/3, 5425/37, 5339 - 130-hp Clerget, presume rest 110-hp]

N5420 Deld Brooklands to ADD (via Dover) 8.11.16; A Sqdn 1 Wing Furnes 9.11.16; Became 1 Sqdn 1.12.16 - @14.12.16; Crashed and DBR St.Omer; To ADD; For survey 28.12.16; Deleted by ADD 5.1.17
[Supposedly to Clayton & Shuttleworth as pattern a/c, but this must have been N5421]

N5421 Deld Lincoln to Hendon 7.2.17; Grain 8.2.17 (transit); ADD (via Dover) 14.2.17; 8 Sqdn (named 'HIGH JINKS') 15.2.17; In action 23.5.17 (FSL HV Hall wounded); Ran into wires, crashed and damaged in dusk landing 5.6.17 (FSL WL Jordan); ADD 6.6.17; 8 Sqdn (still named 'HIGH JINKS') 5.8.17; Albatros DV OOC Hénin-Lietard shared N5460 & N5465 18.30 19.8.17 (F/Cdr RB Munday); Still 8 Sqdn 20.9.17; 1 Sqdn by 9.17; Shot down Houthulst Wood by Ltn Bongartz, Jasta 36, 26.9.17 (FSL JC Akester PoW wounded); Surveyed 3.10.17; Deleted 8.10.17 TL

N5422 Deld ADD by 11.16; A Sqdn 1 Wing 17.11.16; Became 1 Sqdn 1.12.16; HA OOC 4m NE of St.Quentin 11.45 6.4.17 (F/Cdr BC Clayton) [but shown as indecisive in his log book]; ADD rebuild and overhaul 9.5.17; 1 Sqdn 13.6.17; COL 11.7.17 (FSL RP Minifie); Deleted ADD 16.7.17 general fatigue

N5423 Deld Design Flt Eastchurch and tested 28.11.16; Tested with larger chord wings (area 257 sq ft) 11.12.16; FTR from altitude test, lost in sea off Dieppe 3.1.17 (F/L PA Johnston picked by French trawler)

N5424 Deld Manston but FL en route in fog Brede, Sussex 4.12.16; Manston War Flt 5.12.16; Anti Gotha patrols 16.2.17, 25.5.17, 5.6.17 & 13.6.17 (all S/Cdr CH Butler DSC); AGP 4.7.17; AGP, engaged 2 HA, one fell in sea and sank 20m W of Ostende 7.7.17 (S/Cdr CH Butler DSC awarded DSO); AGP, bullets hit propeller at 18,000ft FL Fort Darland, Chatham 22.7.17 (FSL GK Cooper); still Manston War Flt @29.9.17; War School Manston by 10.17 (used for HD duties); Cranwell W/E 2.3.18

N5425 Deld Dover 22.12.16; ADD 24.12.16 (4 Wg pilot); 1 Sqdn (coded '16') 23.1.17; HA OOC Villers-lès-Cagnicourt shared N5437 11.50, then EF, FL, o/t in soft ground nr Béthune 29.4.17 (FSL HV Rowley); ADD by 3.5.17; 9 Sqdn 1.6.17; EF, crashed 11.6.17 (FSL AF MacDonald); ADD 14.6.17; 1 Sqdn 10.7.17; Fought enemy scouts, FL and damaged nr Messines 21.7.17 (FSL SW Rosevear); ADD 21.7.17; 10 Sqdn 16.8.17; Shot down OOC Ypres-Frezenberg by Ltn Hess, Jasta 28, 18.40 21.8.17 (FSL C Lowther killed); Deleted 7.9.17

N5426 Deld ADD (via Dover) 28.11.16; 1 Sqdn 15.12.16; Comparison test with Nieuport 3184 of 6 Sqdn 7.2.17; Albatros C OOC W of Douai 08.00 23.4.17 (F/L TG Culling DSC); 2-str shot down SW of Douai 11.30 7.5.17; Albatros D OOC nr Douai 10.25 19.5.17 (both FSL HK Millward); In combat against Offstlvtr M Müller, Jasta 28 (FSL HK Millward wounded); ADD 11.7.17; Deleted 20.8.17 general fatigue

N5427 Presentation a/c named 'Philippine Island Britons No.1' 20.10.16; Deld ADD; 1 Sqdn (coded '13') 24.12.16; 1-str OOC Fresnoy 19.00 29.4.17 (F/L FHM Maynard); ADD 30.5.17; temp 1 Sqdn 3-4.6.17; ADD; 8 Sqdn

1.7.17; ADD 6.7.17; 9 Sqdn 11.7.17; ADD 29.7.17; Deleted 20.8.17 general fatigue

N5428 1 Wing RNAS, en route ADD, engine choked after TO, CW 24.12.16; Deleted ADD 5.1.17

N5429 Deld ADD 12.16; 1 Sqdn 24.12.16; ADD by 11.1.17; 1 Sqdn 23.1.17 - @8.2.17; 8 Sqdn by 15.2.17 - @22.3.17; 10 Sqdn by 29.3.17; ADD 24.5.17; 10 Sqdn 27.6.17; 2-str OOC nr Moorslede 7.7.17 (FSL CR Pegler); Albatros scout BU Polygon Wood 18.00 16.7.17 (FSL HW Taylor); Became detached from flight, sent [down?] a scout which collided with another, not credited 20.7.17 (FSL HW Taylor); ADD 5.8.17; 1 Sqdn (coded '2') 20.8.17; Shot down Wervicq by Ltn Wüsthoff, Jasta 4, 07.45 13.9.17 (FSL JR Wilford, PoW wounded); Deleted ADD 17.9.17

N5430 Evaluated by RFC (Military Wing); Deld Testing Sqdn Martlesham Heath by 11.16 (Trial Report No.25); CFS Upavon by 1.17; Hendon 15.1.17; Martlesham Heath 17.1.17; AES Orfordness by 6.17 (fitted armament and Aldis sight, also G expts); AGP 13.6.17 (Lt AL Howarth); AGP 7.7.17, 12.8.17 & 22.8.17 (all Capt Vernon Brown); visited RAE 1.10.18 [Only Triplane to serve with the RFC]

N5431 Deld CSD White City by 31.12.16; Shipped to Aegean 1.17; 2 Wing Mudros (coded 'L'); E Flt 2 Wing Hadzi Junas by 3.17; Crashed, o/t, badly damaged Salonika 26.3.17 (F/L JW Alcock); B Sqdn 2 Wing Thermi 18.6.17 - @8.17; Halberstadt DD N of Illkeli-Pergama road 20.6.17; C Sqdn 2 Wing Mudros, shot down an Albatros W4 into sea nr Lemnos c.08.00 30.9.17 [also reported as 2 Rumpler seaplanes]; Albatros DIII dived in from 12,000 ft, crashed on nose in marsh nr Zanoscw 19.11.17; Rumpler C in flames dived in Drama 25.11.17; Albatros DIII crashed 29.11.17 (all FSL HT Mellings); Thasos (repair) @1.12.17 - @3.18; Hit wall landing, o/t [Date unknown] (Nightingale?); Repair Base by 6.18; Bits used to construct Alcock A.1

N5432 Deld ADD by 28.12.16; 1 Sqdn 5.1.17 (tested Pott's Carburettor 16.1.17); EF, FL and crashed nr aerodrome 23.3.17 (F/L CA Eyre); ADD by road 24.3.17 - @29.3.17 (repair); 2 AD by 19.4.17; 1 Sqdn 20.4.17; Crashed at Croisy 23.4.17; ADD 23.5.17; 1 Sqdn 11.6.17; FL with parts of machine shot through nr Wagnonlieu 16.6.17 (FSL EC Hillaby); ADD 4.8.17; 1 Sqdn 20.9.17; AP Dover 23.11.17; Surveyed 14.12.17; Deleted 19.12.17 W&T

N5433 Deld ADD 12.16; 1 Sqdn on/by 27.12.16; Crashed in ploughed field next to Furnes aerodrome 27.12.16 (FSL TG Culling); For survey 28.12.16 DBR; Deleted ADD 5.1.17

N5434 Deld ADD by 28.12.16; 1 Sqdn 23.1.17; O/t landing 27.2.17; ADD by 8.3.17; 8 Sqdn 7.4.17; 08.40 patrol, Albatros shot down and crashed on enemy side of lines Vimy, then attacked by 7 Albatros single-seaters and spun down OOC into No Mans Land, Rouvroy, nr Vimy Ridge, credited to Ltn Von Doering, Jasta 11 4.5.17 (FSL DM Shields wounded, hid in shell hole 10.00 - 16.00); Deleted 11.5.17

N5435 Deld Dover 22.12.16; ADD 24.12.16; 1 Sqdn 27.12.16; Albatros DIII OOC E of Wancourt 08.30 4.5.17; Albatros DIII OOC Hénin-Lietard 19.45 19.5.17 (both F/L CA Eyre); ADD 23.5.17; 1 Sqdn 25.6.17; Shot down Reckem by Flm Heinrich, Marine Jasta 1, 16.50 6.7.17 (FSL EC Hillaby killed); Deleted 8.8.17

N5436 Deld Dover 22.12.16; ADD 24.12.16; 1 Sqdn 27.12.16; Shot down HA 27.1.17; Aviatik C destroyed ½m N of Dixmude 1.2.17; Attacked 2-str then shot down Albatros DIII 2m ESE of St.Quentin 12.00 5.4.17; 2-str OOC in vertical dive 2m E of Cambrai 14.45 8.4.17; Albatros shot down 17.22 & another on fire Arleux 17.25 22.4.17; Albatros C OOC W of Douai 08.00 23.4.17; Albatros DIII OOC SE of Lens 08.15 24.4.17; Rumpler crashed Haynecourt 08.30-08.50 & Albatros DIII OOC Haynecourt 09.25 30.4.17 Albatros DIII OOC 3m E of Lens 19.00-19.30 5.5.17; (all F/Cdr RS Dallas DSC); COL Bailleul 3.6.17 (FSL JF Nalder); ADD 3.6.17; 1 Sqdn 4.8.17; Albatros DV OOC NE of Ypres 08.40 14.8.17 (F/L CB Ridley); DFW C OOC nr Zillebeke 17.05 10.9.17 (FSL CB Ridley); AP Dover 8.11.17; Deleted 26.11.17

N5437 Deld ADD by 28.12.16 BUT Deld ADD (via Dover)

2.1.17; 1 Sqdn 5.1.17; HA OOC Villers-lès-Cagnicourt shared N5426 11.50 29.4.17 (FSL CB Ridley); FL Dainville 1.5.17 (F/Cdr RS Dallas); ADD 3.6.17; 10 Sqdn 20.7.17; Albatros Scout crashed Wervicq 11.30 12.8.17 (FSL H Day); Albatros DV NE of Zonnebeke OOC 08.00 16.8.17 (FSL JA Cole); ADD 27.8.17; Deleted 3.9.17 general fatigue

N5438    Damaged at Brooklands before delivery, repaired by Mkrs; Deld Dover 16.3.17; ADD 17.3.17; 10 Sqdn on/by 19.3.17; Bumped landing from OP, TO again but stalled, sideslipped in from 50ft, wrecked 28.4.17 (FSL RF Collins DoI); Wreckage to ADD; Deleted 14.5.17

N5439    Deld ADD by 16.1.17; 1 Sqdn 28.1.17 - @9.2.17; ADD by 15.2.17; 8 Sqdn (named 'WHITFIELD') 11.3.17; O/t on landing 4.4.17 (FSL DM Shields unhurt); ADD 5.4.17; Deleted 14.5.17

N5440    Presentation a/c 'Britons in Siam No.1' 20.10.16. Deld Design Flt Eastchurch 23.1.17 (first to be fitted with smaller tailplane and elevators); ADD 2.2.17; 1 Sqdn 6.2.17; HA OOC Epinoy 08.20 14.4.17; Albatros DIII crashed in houses nr Noyelles 11.00 and another DD S of Wancourt 11.20 24.4.17; Albatros DIII DD Epinoy aerodrome 11.10 29.4.17; Albatros DIII OOC Hénin-Lietard 19.45 19.5.17 (all F/Cdr TFN Gerrard); Damaged in combat 26.5.17; General engagement with 15/20 HA, Albatros DIII crashed nr Moorslede and another OOC shared a Nieuport at Moorslede 07.45, then FL Moorslede after badly shot up 4.6.17 (F/Cdr TFN Gerrard); ADD by 7.6.17; 1 Sqdn 10.8.17; Shot down over lines by Ltn Quant, Jasta 36 26.9.17 (FSL WJ Burnett killed); Surveyed 3.10.17; Deleted 8.10.17 TL

N5441    Deld Dover 25.1.17; Dunkerque 26.1.17; 1 Sqdn 28.1.17; Wheels sank into soft ground, o/t, landing after test flight 27.2.17 (FSL NDM Hewitt unhurt); ADD by 1.3.17; 2 AD 3.17; 1 Sqdn 25.3.17; EF, FL S of Béthune, set fire to a/c as believed in enemy territory 29.4.17 (FSL HDM Wallace); Deleted 14.5.17

N5442    Deld ADD 23.1.17; 1 Sqdn 1.2.17; 8 Sqdn (named 'PIP') by 15.2.17; Albatros C OOC E of Douai 07.30 10.5.17; Aviatik C on fire E of Lens, shared N5465 & N5471 09.45 4.6.17 (both FSL EA Bennetts); Wing collapsed in spin, crashed and wrecked Neuville St.Vaast 23.6.17 (FSL JN MacAllister killed); Deleted ADD 27.6.17

N5443    Deld Dover 26.1.17; ADD 29.1.17; 1 Sqdn 1.2.17; FL Calais 9.2.17 (retd 10.2.17); ADD 18.5.17 (repair and overhaul); 9 Sqdn 3.6.17; COL 7.6.17 (FSL AF MacDonald); ADD 8.6.17; Deleted 27.6.17

N5444    Presentation a/c 'Canary Island Britons No.1' 20.10.16. ADD by 2.17; 1 Sqdn 5.2.17; Albatros C OOC 4m NE of St.Quentin 11.50 6.4.17; Albatros DIII OOC Arleux 17.20 22.4.17; Albatros DIII OOC 3-4m E of Lens 19.00-19.30 5.5.17; Albatros DIII OOC Estrées, S of Douai 10.30 19.5.17; Albatros C crashed E of Hénin-Lietard 09.30 20.5.17 (all F/L TG Culling DSC); Albatros C crashed St.Jean, NE of Ypres 12.00 15.6.17 [Ltn d R Friedrich Reichstein & Lt Johann Raddatz of FA7, both killed]; Black/white Albatros DV shot down nr St.Julien 17.45 20.6.17 (both F/Cdr CA Eyre); ADD 24.6.17; Deleted 27.6.17 general fatigue

N5445    Deld Brooklands to EAD Grain 14.8.17 (allocated 15.12.16); Fitted twin Vickers gun and non-standard rudder; Part of engine broke away 17.4.18 (Capt LAT Pritchard slightly injured)

N5446    Presentation a/c 'Manaos Britons No.1' 20.10.16. Due ADD by 27.1.17, arr by 8.2.17; 1 Sqdn 9.2.17; COL Bethencourt 5.4.17 (retd 6.4.17); Albatros DIII crashed Ercourt-Epinoy 11.10 29.4.17; Red Albatros DV crashed on Douai aerodrome, shared N5493 19.15 patrol 29.4.17; Albatros DII OOC nr Vitry-en-Artois, shared N5488 19.40 11.5.17; Albatros DIII OOC Hénin-Lietard 19.45 19.5.17; Albatros DV apparently OOC Warneton-Deulemont 06.15 12.6.17 (all FSL RP Minifie); ADD 3.7.17; 10 Sqdn 5.8.17; COL 9.8.17 (FSL H Day); ADD 9.8.17; 8 Sqdn 2.9.17; ADD 7.9.17; 1 Sqdn 12.9.17; In combat nr Westroosebeke 18.00 19.9.17 (FSL CFD Ash wounded); Crashed on TO 25.9.17 (FSL JC Akester); ADD by 27.9.17; Surveyed 3.10.17; Deleted 8.10.17 W&T

N5447    Presentation a/c 'Presented by the Government of the

Dominican Republic' 27.2.17. Deld Hendon 8.2.17; ADD via Dover 9.2.17; 8 Sqdn 10.2.17, last mention 24.3.17; Stood on nose landing 27.3.17 (F/L RJO Compston); ADD by 29.3.17; 2 AD Candas 6.4.17; 1 Sqdn 13.4.17; Engine damaged in combat, FL Boiry-St.Martin 19.5.17 (FSL HDM Wallace); Damaged on landing Steenwerck 3.6.17 (FSL JF Nalder); ADD by 7.6.17; 10 Sqdn 11.8.17; 1 Sqdn 27.8.17; Landed too fast, hit N6295 5.9.17 (FSL H Winn); ADD by 6.9.17; For survey 27.9.17; Destroyed by fire on night of 1.10.17; Surveyed 17.10.17; Deleted 23.10.17

N5448    Due ADD by 27.1.17; 1 Sqdn 9.2.17; Attacked 2 Halberstadts, rescued by N5444, then last seen climbing over enemy lines at 7,000 ft, shot down nr Malalow (Malahow?) Stn by Hptm Paul von Osterroht, Jasta 12 6.4.17 (F/L LMB Weil killed); Deleted 11.5.17

N5449    Deld Dover 15.2.17; ADD 26.2.17; 8 Sqdn Auchel (named 'JOAN') 28.2.17; COL 15.3.17 (FSL JAM Allen), to ADD; 8 Sqdn (named 'BINKY') 16.4.17; Albatros with red fuselage and red and green wings OOC smoking Douai 18.10 3.5.17 (F/Cdr PA Johnston); ADD 6.7.17; 8 Sqdn 5.8.17 (still named 'BINKY'); FL after hit by ground m/g fire, m/c shelled for 8hrs by enemy nr Bailleul 10.8.17 (FSL ED Crundall); ADD 10.8.17; 1 Sqdn (coded '13') 8.9.17; 2-str OOC S of Comines 11.00 21.10.17; 2-str OOC Passchendaele-Moorslede 10.10 26.10.17 (both FSL AGA Spence); AP Dover 23.11.17; Surveyed 18.12.17; Deleted 22.12.17 W&T

N5450    Deld Brooklands to ADD 14.2.17; 1 Sqdn 26.2.17; O/t landing, extensively damaged 5.4.17 (FSL AW Kay unhurt); ADD by road 9.4.17; 8 Sqdn (named 'TIKI') 2.5.17; Shot down Flers, N of Douai by Ltn Maashoff, Jasta 11 24.5.17 (FSL HL Smith killed); Deleted 29.5.17

N5451    Deld from Brooklands to ADD 11.2.17; 1 Sqdn 26.2.17; ADD 9.5.17 (repair and overhaul); 9 Sqdn 3.6.17; Albatros DIII OOC Dixmude 11.45 but starboard rudder controls shot away, FL, crashed nr Furnes-Coxyde road 8.6.17 (FSL HF Stackard wounded); ADD by 14.6.17; Deleted 27.6.17

N5452    Deld ADD (via Dover) 26.2.17; 8 Sqdn 11.3.17, last mention 25.3.17; 10 Sqdn by 29.3.17; ADD 3.6.17 - @5.7.17; 1 Sqdn by 11.7.17; Shot down nr Pérenchies by Flakzug 43 29.7.17 (FSL VG Austen POW, wounded); Deleted 15.8.17

N5453    Deld Dover 16.3.17; Damaged 17.3.17; ADD 18.6.17; 1 Sqdn 3.7.17; ADD 12.9.17; C Flt 12 Sqdn 25.10.17 (held for Depot at first, then training with C Flt by 8.11.17); AP Dover 21.2.18; Wormwood Scrubbs without engine W/E 2.3.18

N5454    Deld Dover 15.2.17; ADD 16.2.17; 8 Sqdn (named 'HILDA' by F/L RR Soar) 26.2.17; FL Sachin 8.4.17; ADD by 12.4.17; 9 Sqdn 4.5.17; COL 23.5.17 (FSL AT Whealy); ADD by 24.5.17; 1 Sqdn (coded '6') by 12.7.17; Crashed 16.7.17 (FSL LA Philip injured); To ADD; 1 Sqdn (coded '1') 14.8.17; Albatros Scout OOC E of Ypres 08.15 15.8.17; Albatros DV BU NE of Messines 18.25 16.9.17; Albatros DV shot down nr Westroosebeke 18.00 19.9.17; 2-str crashed S of St.Julien 12.25 26.9.17; Aviatik C crashed intact S of Polygon Wood 10.55 17.10.17 [possibly numbered G82 - or G83]; Gotha OOC in vertical dive N of Passchendaele 14.30 18.10.17; Albatros DV OOC S of Comines 11.00 20.10.17; Fokker DV OOC Westroosebeke 08.45 27.10.17; 2-str shot down E of Gheluvelt 18.55 31.10.17 (all F/L RP Minifie); AP Dover 8.11.17; Deleted 26.11.17

N5455    Due ADD by 10.2.17, arr by 23.2.17; 8 Sqdn (named 'WILLA') 26.2.17; Albatros DII OOC Lens 17.45-19.30 patrol 7.4.17 (F/Cdr CD Booker); Aviatik intact 06.50-08.45 patrol 24.4.17 (F/L RA Little) [presume numbered G25]; Albatros DIII OOC nr Vitry 12.5.17 (F/Cdr CD Booker) ADD 24.5.17; 1 Sqdn 10.7.17; Albatros DV OOC 4m E of Messines shared N5373, N5479, N5485, N6296, N6300, N6304 & N6308 20.05 17.7.17 (F/L HL Everitt); Hit by 10 Sqdn a/c whilst stationery after landing in mist Chocques 20.8.17 (F/L HL Everitt); ADD 20.8.17; 1 Sqdn 21.9.17; COL 14.10.17 (FSL MA Harker); Shot up by Ltn Kurt Wüsthoff, Jasta 4 27.10.17 (FSL W Clapperton wounded); AP Dover 8.11.17; Deleted 26.11.17

N5456    Deld Dover 16.3.17; ADD 17.3.17; 10 Sqdn on/by

19.3.17; Halberstadt down in flames Zarren 6.5.17 (FSL MWW Eppstein); Shot down by AA fire over Zeebrugge and crashed in sea nr Blankenberghe 12.5.17 (FSL MWW Eppstein killed) [believed Flakzug 72 nr Laventie]; Deleted 2.6.17

N5457 Deld Dover 26.2.17; ADD 27.2.17; 1 Sqdn 4.3.17; FL nr Mons after combat at 12,000ft over Doignies at 08.00 with Ltn K Schäfer, Jasta 11 on 6.4.17 (FSL NDM Hewitt PoW); Deleted 11.5.17

N5458 Deld Dover 28.2.17; ADD 1.3.17; 8 Sqdn 6.3.17; Albatros DIII OOC Beaumont 15.30 8.4.17; Green/red Albatros DIII shot down, wings folded and broke off nr Thelus, N of Arras 17.40-19.25 patrol 21.4.17 (both F/Cdr AR Arnold); Shot up by Vzfw K Menckhoff, Jasta 3, crashed Nouex-les-Mines 9.5.17 (FSL LEB Wimbush wounded); ADD by 10.5.17; 10 Sqdn (coded 'Q') 9.6.17; Halberstadt DII OOC N of St.Julien c.10.55 15.6.17; Albatros DV OOC Moorslede 17.40 15.6.17; Halberstadt OOC nr St.Julien 10.50 18.6.17; Crashed nr aerodrome 23.7.17 (all FSL DF FitzGibbon); ADD 24.7.17; 12 Sqdn from/by 13.8.17; AP Dover 4.12.17; CSD White City W/E 8.12.17; Deleted 21.12.17 and sent to USA for Lady Drogheda's exhibition

N5459 Deld Dover 1.3.17; ADD 4.3.17 - @22.3.17; 2 AD Candas on/by 24.3.17; 1 Sqdn 6.4.17; Wrecked in collision with 59 Sqdn R.E.8 taking off Bellevue 20.4.17 (FSL WH Chisam); ADD by 26.4.17; 9 Sqdn 23.5.17; LVG C OOC 5m off Ostende 16.30 26.5.17; Albatros DIII OOC 3m off Ostende 19.00-9.30 5.6.17;(all FSL OC Le Boutillier); Propeller smashed landing on rough ground 19.6.17 (FSL OC Le Boutillier); 2-str NW of Nieuport 19.30 16.7.17; 1-str OOC Oost Dunkerque, shared N5377, N5378, N5475 & N5489 05.10 17.7.17 (both FSL OC Le Boutillier); ADD 23.7.17; 1 Sqdn 14.8.17; Albatros DV OOC Becelaere shared N6292 10.10 19.9.17 (FSL EW Desbarats); Shot down nr Passchendaele by Vzfw Kosmahl, Jasta 26, 09.30 patrol 20.9.17 (FSL EW Desbarats, PoW unhurt); Surveyed 22.9.17; Deleted 27.9.17 TL

N5460 Deld Dover 16.3.17; ADD 17.3.17; 8 Sqdn 17.3.17; Albatros DIII OOC Sailly 08.40 24.4.17; Aviatik C OOC in vertical dive nr Douai 09.45 2.5.17; Red Albatros DIII OOC & another in flames E of Douai 19.50 11.5.17; Albatros DIII OOC Douai 18.00 23.5.17 (all FSL GG Simpson); 2-str captured E of Izel, shared N6292 17.30-18.10 patrol 11.7.17 (FSL JH Thompson); Albatros DV OOC Hénin-Lietard, shared N5421 & N5465 18.30 19.8.17 (F/Cdr CD Booker); ADD 7.9.17; 12 Sqdn 25.10.17; ADD 8.11.17; AP Dover 25.1.18; Chingford 29.1.18; Gunnery School Flts Eastchurch by 2.2.18; Became 204 TDS Eastchurch 1.4.18

N5461 Deld Dover 26.2.17; ADD 27.2.17; 1 Sqdn 4.3.17; Attacked by 3 HA and shot down in flames Eterpigny-Dury by Oblt Ritter Adolf von Tutschek, Jasta 12 08.00 19.5.17 (FSL GG Bowman killed); Deleted 2.6.17

N5462 Deld Dover for erection 9.3.17; ADD 15.3.17; 8 Sqdn 16.3.17; FL 7.4.17; ADD by 12.4.17; 9 Sqdn 19.5.17; Albatros Scout OOC 3m off Ostende 19.00-19.30 5.6.17 (FSL JW Pinder); 2-str OOC Leffinghe 06.35 24.7.17; Aviatik C OOC Middelkerke shared N5377 17.35 28.7.17 (both F/Cdr GG Simpson); ADD 4.8.17; 10 Sqdn 21.8.17; ADD 27.8.17; 12 Sqdn 24.10.17; AP Dover 19.2.18; Wormwood Scrubs without engine W/E 2.3.18

N5463 Deld Dover for erection 7.3.17; ADD 11.3.17; 8 Sqdn 17.3.17; Shot down nr Courrières 29.4.17 (FSL AE Cuzner killed) [believed nr Billy-Montigny by Rittm Frhr von Richthofen, Jasta 11]; Deleted 11.5.17

N5464 Deld Dover 16.3.17; ADD 17.3.17; 8 Sqdn (named 'DORIS' by F/L ED Crundall) by 4.17; Albatros C OOC nr Hénin-Lietard & another OOC 4m E of Douai 09.05 14.4.17 (F/L ED Crundall); Brought down in lines by flak, FL nr Béthune 10.5.17 (F/L ED Crundall wounded); ADD 10.7.17; 2 AD by 12.7.17; 10 Sqdn 23.7.17; OOC, FL, CW 19.8.17 NE of Proven (FSL TL Glasgow killed); wreckage ADD 19.8.17; Surveyed 17.10.17; Deleted 23.10.17 wrecked

N5465 Deld Dover 16.3.17; ADD 17.3.17; 8 Sqdn 23.3.17; Albatros Scout shot down NE of Arras 18.00 - 19.35 26.4.17; Aviatik C on fire E of Lens shared N5471 &

N5442 09.45 4.6.17; Albatros DV OOC Hénin-Lietard 10.15 7.6.17; 2-str probably destroyed Hénin-Lietard 12.6.17; DFW CV brought down intact NE of Ypres shared N6299 (q.v.) 08.30 16.6.17 (all FSL RR Thornely); ADD 2.7.17; 8 Sqdn 12.8.17; Albatros DV OOC Hénin-Lietard, shared N5421 & N5460 18.30 19.8.17; O/t landing 19.8.17 (both FSL ED Crundall), repaired; ADD 7.9.17; 1 Sqdn 20.9.17; DFW CV OOC Comines 11.45 17.10.17; DFW C OOC E of Poelcappelle, shared N5479 10.30 18.10.17; 2-str crashed Comines-Wervicq 13.30 24.10.17; Albatros DIII OOC Gheluvelt 17.15 29.10.17; Pfalz DIII down in flames nr Dixmude shared Camel B5651 15.45 12.11.17 (all F/L SM Kinkead); AP Dover 23.11.17; Surveyed 14.12.17; Deleted 19.12.17 W&T

N5466 Deld Dover 16.3.17; ADD 17.3.17; 8 Sqdn 23.3.17 - @30.3.17; ADD by 5.4.17; 10 Sqdn 23.5.17; Albatros C in flames Wervicq-Poelcapelle shared N5478, N5490 & N6302 08.50 & Albatros DIII OOC NW of Poelcapelle shared N5490 09.40 5.6.17 (FSL DF FitzGibbon); Crashed and damaged Droglandt 8.6.17 (FSL DF FitzGibbon); ADD 9.6.17; 1 Sqdn 17.7.17; Aviatik C OOC E of Lille 09.30 22.7.17 (S/Cdr RS Dallas DSC & Bar); O/t landing in long grass at edge of aerodrome 27.7.17 (FSL SS Flook); to ADD; 1 Sqdn 8.9.17; Wing came off during practice flight and crashed 1m SW of Bailleul 30.9.17 (FSL WJ Beattie killed); Surveyed 17.10.17; Deleted 23.10.17

N5467 Deld Dover for erection 16.3.17; ADD 21.3.17; 8 Sqdn (named 'MINCOL') 23.3.17; COL 3.4.17; In combat with 3 Albatros Scouts, shot down Bailleul by Ltn d R Heinrich Gontermann, Jasta 5 08.05 24.4.17 (FSL EBJ Walter killed); Deleted ADD 27.4.17

N5468 Deld Dover for erection 7.3.17; ADD 11.3.17; 8 Sqdn (named 'ANGEL' by Jenner-Parson) 16.3.17; Albatros Scout OOC Douai 20.00-21.00 28.5.17; Aviatik crashed nr Arras shared N5482 & N6292 (q.v.) 08.55 12.6.17 (all F/Cdr CHB Jenner-Parson); ADD 2.9.17; C Flt 12 Sqdn 25.10.17 for storage, used for training by 29.10.17; AP Dover 21.2.18; For survey 28.2.18; Wormwood Scrubs without engine W/E 2.3.18

N5469 Deld Dover for erection 18.3.17; ADD 25.3.17; 8 Sqdn 28.3.17; Halberstadt D OOC E of Arras 19.30 7.4.17 Halberstadt DII OOC Noyelles-Lens 12.00 9.4.17; Halberstadt D OOC south of Lens 18.55, then FL Bouvignises 21.4.17; Retd 22.4.17; Aviatik C photographing Auchel aerodrome brought down intact inside British lines nr Béthune 12.30 24.4.17 (numbered G25) (all F/L RA Little); ADD by 26.4.17; 9 Sqdn 3.6.17; Albatros Scout OOC off Ostende 19.00-19.30 5.6.17 (FSL JC Tanner); EF in mid-Channel, landed Dominion Camp 13.6.17; ADD 14.6.17; 1 Sqdn 4.8.17; Crashed on TO 20.8.17 (FSL JH Winn); ADD 20.8.17; 1 Sqdn 27.9.17; AP Dover 8.11.17; Deleted 26.11.17

N5470 Presentation a/c 'Government of Dominica' 27.2.17. Deld Dover 18.3.17; ADD 4.4.17; 8 Sqdn 4.4.17; COL 14.4.17; ADD 14.4.17; 10 Sqdn 23.5.17; Albatros DIII OOC Menin-St.Julien 08.45 7.6.17 (FSL R Collishaw); Shot down Zonnebeke-Moorslede by Vzfw F Krebs, Jasta 6 c.19.20 14.6.17 (FSL LH Parker killed); Deleted by 21.6.17

N5471 Deld Dover for erection 20.3.17; ADD 28.3.17; 8 Sqdn 30.3.17; Aviatik C OOC E of Douai 06.45 & Aviatik C OOC 1m W of Douai 07.00 30.4.17; Aviatik C OOC OOC NE od Douai 07.00 30.4.17; Albatros C OOC E of Douai shared N5442 07.30 10.5.17; Aviatik C on fire E of Lens, shared N5442 & N5465 09.45 4.6.17 (all F/L RJO Compston - F/Cdr from 12.5.17); Shot down by m/g fire E of Vermelles, FL in front line trenches 28.6.17 (FSL WL Jordan unhurt); For survey 5.7.17; ADD 9.7.17; Deleted 19.7.17

N5472 Deld Dover for erection 20.3.17; ADD 13.4.17; 8 Sqdn (named 'PEGGY' - but some doubts, see N5387) 26.4.17; Damaged in combat 3.5.17; Damaged in combat, COL 27.5.17; Albatros DIII OOC W of Douai 20.30 28.5.17 (all FSL R McDonald); ADD; 8 Sqdn 25.6.17; ADD 6.7.17; 9 Sqdn 11.7.17; Scout OOC Leke 05.30 29.7.17 (FSL EB Freeland); Damaged 29.7.17 (FSL EB Freeland unhurt); ADD by 2.8.17; 1 Sqdn (coded '17') by 25.8.17; Aviatik C OOC SE of Nieuport

12.10 13.11.17 (F/Cdr HV Rowley); AP Dover 23.11.17; Surveyed 14.12.17; Deleted 19.12.17 W&T

N5473 Deld Dover for erection 20.3.17; Wing broke off in dive from 2,500 ft, BO 24.3.17 (FSL W Oliver killed)

N5474 Deld Dover 21.3.17; ADD 25.3.17; 8 Sqdn (named 'GWEN') 3.4.17; Shot down S of Seclin by Ltn Kurt Wolff, Jasta 11 1.5.17 (FSL ED Roach killed); Deleted 11.5.17

N5475 Deld Dover 18.3.17; Tested 21.3.17; ADD 23.3.17; 8 Sqdn 25.3.17; FL, o/t in muddy field nr Aix 28.3.17 (FSL D Hammond); ADD 30.3.17; 9 Sqdn 24.4.17; EF, FL les Möeres 30.4.17 (retd sqdn 1.5.17); Manston but engine trouble, FL 13.5.17 (FSL HF Stackard); retd 9 Sqdn 20.5.17; 1 Sqdn by 6.17; 9 Sqdn 8.6.17; 1-str OOC Oost Dunkerque, shared N5377, N5378, N5459 & N5489 05.10 17.7.17; EF after flak burst nr propeller, FL on beach, o/t in soft sand N of Nieuport 20.7.17 (FSL AF MacDonald unhurt); ADD by 26.7.17; 1 Sqdn (coded '18') 20.8.17; 12 Sqdn 30.11.17; Deleted 11.1.18

N5476 Deld Dover 23.3.17; ADD 22.4.17 - @26.4.17; 1 Sqdn by 5.17; 2-str crashed SW of Douai 11.30 7.5.17 (FSL HK Millward); 2 AD Candas by 10.5.17; 1 Sqdn 18.5.17; While avoiding Nieuport Scout landing cross-wind nose dived into aerodrome 16.7.17 (FSL LA Philip injured); ADD 16.7.17; 1 Sqdn 20.8.17; FTR 11.15 patrol Houthulst Forest, shot down Ten-Brielen by Ltn Blume, Jasta 26, 24.10.17 (FSL JEC Hough killed); Surveyed 31.10.17; Deleted 2.11.17 TL

N5477 Deld Dover for erection 22.3.17; ADD 24.3.17; 8 Sqdn 28.3.17; Albatros Scout OOC E of Oppy 07.30 22.4.17; Albatros Scout OOC Douai 20.00-20.50 28.5.17; Albatros Scout OOC Douai aerodrome 13.6.17; COL 5.7.17 (all FSL AR Knight); ADD by 12.7.17; 10 Sqdn 29.7.17; COL Houthem 10.8.17 (FSL CH Weir); ADD 11.8.17; 1 Sqdn 4.9.17; Shot down Langemarck-Poelcapelle by Oblt Oskar Freiherr von Bönigk, Jasta 4 on 9.9.17 (FSL LE Adlam killed); Deleted ADD 17.9.17

N5478 Deld Dover 23.3.17; ADD 4.4.17; via 2 AD Candas to 1 Sqdn Chipilly 8.4.17; COL Dancourt 9.4.17; ADD by 12.4.17; 10 Sqdn 23.5.17; Albatros C in flames Wervicq-Poelcapelle shared N5466, N5490 & N6302 08.50 5.6.17 FSL KG Boyd); 2-str in flames Nieuport-Dixmude 14.10 5.6.17 (FSL HW Taylor); FL and damaged nr Bailleul 13.6.17 (FSL CR Pegler); AD 14.6.17; 10 Sqdn 13.7.17; 2 Albatros DV destroyed, then shot down Becelaere by Ltn Otto Brauneck, Jasta 11 11.00 22.7.17 (F/L JA Page killed); Deleted 8.8.17

N5479 Presentation a/c 'Britons in Spain No.1' 20.10.16. Deld Dover by 4.3.17; ADD 5.4.17; 1 Sqdn (coded '8') 8.4.17; Albatros Scout OOC Epinoy aerodrome 17.30 6.5.17 (FSL LH Cockey); Albatros DIII down on fire NE of Ypres 20.56 14.6.17; 2-str OOC E of Warneton shared N6300 & N6308 10.25 13.7.17; Albatros DV OOC 4m E of Messines shared N5373, N5455, N5485, N6296, N6300, N6304 & N6308 20.05 17.7.17 (all F/Cdr FHM Maynard); ADD 22.7.17; 1 Sqdn (coded '18') by 15.8.17; DFW C OOC E of Poelcappelle shared N5465 10.30 18.10.17 (FSL JH Forman); AP Dover 8.11.17; Deleted 26.11.17

N5480 Deld Dover for erection 29.3.17; ADD 7.4.17 - @12.4.17; 2 AD Candas by 19.4.17; 1 Sqdn 30.4.17; With AA shot down HA on British side of lines Arras-Bapaume 11.05 27.5.17 (FSL DW Ramsay); Shot down over Dadizeele by Vzfw F Altemeier, Jasta 24 7.7.17 (FSL DW Ramsay killed) [S of Bousbecque per Germans); Deleted 8.8.17

N5481 Deld Dover for erection 29.3.17; ADD 5.4.17; 8 Sqdn 10.4.17; LVG spun in nr Gavrelle 7.5.17 (F/L HA Pailthorpe); Shot down nr Faschoda by Ltn d R Hans Hinsch, Jasta 11 23.5.17 (F/L HA Pailthorpe killed); Deleted 22.6.17

N5482 Deld Dover for erection 29.3.17; 10 Sqdn 5.4.17; ADD 4.17; 8 Sqdn (named 'MAUD' by F/Cdr CD Booker), zig-zag stripe aft of roundel) 10.4.17; Brown and green LVG (red crosses on white square) OOC Courrières - Hénin-Lietard 08.00-10.00 patrol 14.4.17; Albatros DIII OOC Drocourt 17.20 26.4.17; Albatros DIII shot down Douai 18.25-20.05 patrol 30.4.17; Large 2-str OOC Hénin-Lietard 13.35 4.5.17; 2-str OOC E of Douai 07.30 10.5.7; Albatros DIII OOC 1m W of Douai,

shared N5493 15.45 23.5.17; Albatros DIII crashed nr Douai 07.15 & another on fire E of Willerval 08.35 24.5.17; Albatros DIII W of Douai 20.20 28.5.17 (all F/Cdr CD Booker DSC); DFW CV C9045/16 (numbered G44) crashed nr Arras shared N5468 & N6292 (q.v.) 12.6.17 (F/Cdr CHB Jenner-Parson); Albatros DV OOC Arras-Cambrai 20.15 14.6.17; Albatros DV OOC Quiéry la Motte shared N6292 19.55-21.15 patrol, o/t landing 17.7.17; Rumpler C OOC Thelus 08.30 20.7.17 (all F/Cdr CD Booker DSC); Albatros DV OOC Fresnoy 19.30, then FL, crashed Farbus Wood, destroyed by artillery, credited Ltn Schöbinger, Jasta 12 11.8.17 (F/Cdr CD Booker DSC unhurt)

N5483 Deld Dover for erection 30.3.17; ADD 7.4.17; 10 Sqdn (named 'BLACK ROGER') 24.4.17; Albatros C shot down in flames SW of Wervicq 09.15 1.6.17; 2-str OOC St.Julien shared N5490, N5487 & N5492 09.00 2.6.17; Albatros DIII crashed nr Roubaix 20.25 3.6.17; Halberstadt DII crashed N of Polygon Wood 11.00 6.6.17; Albatros C shot down, pilot killed, seen to crash Clercken 09.15 7.6.17; Albatros DIII OOC & Halberstadt OOC Moorslede 17.45 15.6.17; HA probably Halberstadt OOC nr Roulers 19.10 17.6.17 (all FSL EV Reid); FL and damaged 24.6.17 (F/L JE Sharman DSC); Albatros DVII OOC Deulemont 11.00 6.7.17; Albatros DIII BU in air, crashed Polygon Wood and Albatros DIII shot down, pilot shot, seen to crash Veldhoek 07.45 12.7.17; Albatros DV OOC Menin-Messines 08.05 20.7.17; Fokker DV seen to crash edge of wood N of Becelaere 20.30 21.7.17; Albatros DV OOC Polygon Wood 20.25 23.7.17; Albatros DIII shot down Menin 19.50 & Albatros DV OOC with pilot shot Courtrai-Menin 20.00 & another BU in air Menin 20.05 27.7.17; Albatros DV shot down Becelaere 20.00 28.7.17 (all FSL EV Reid DSC); Albatros DV destroyed Dadizeele-Becelaere 20.00, then last seen 20.40 shot down by K FLAK No.21 down nr Armentiéres [nr Moorslede] 28.7.17 (FSL EV Reid DSC killed) [or Moorslede area by Lt Frhr von Boenigk, Jasta 4]; Deleted 15.8.17

N5484 Deld ADD .17; 1 Sqdn by 11.3.17 per Clayton log [by 15.2.17 per ADR, but seems too early]; HA OOC E of Lens 18.00, then EF, FL S of Béthune 29.4.17 (FSL AP Heywood wounded); retd 30.4.17; Engine trouble, FL Boiry St.Martin 11.5.17, retd sqdn 12.5.17; Fight with 2 HA, 1 shot down E of Ypres 06.15, then FL and damaged nr Ten-Brielen 7.6.17 (FSL JF Nalder wounded); ADD by 14.6.17; 9 Sqdn 23.7.17; Albatros DIII crashed Leke 05.30 29.7.17 (FSL OC Le Boutillier); ADD 4.8.17; 10 Sqdn 20.8.17; ADD 27.8.17; 12 Sqdn 9.7.17; Crashed, CW on aerodrome 15.11.17 (FSL HW McCumming); Deleted 26.11.17

N5485 Deld Dover 1.4.17; ADD 5.4.17; 10 Sqdn 24.4.17; Crashed Clairmarais 20.5.17; AD by 25.5.17; 1 Sqdn 10.7.17; Albatros DV OOC 4m E of Messines shared N5373, N5455, N5479, N6296, N6300, N6304 & N6308 18.05 17.7.17; Scout OOC probable N of Menin 14.8.17 (both FSL GBG Scott); EF, FL and damaged on aerodrome 15.8.17 (FSL GBG Scott); ADD 15.8.17; 1 Sqdn 21.9.17; EF on TO 15.10 17 (FSL MA Harker); ADD 16.10.17 (overhaul); AP Dover 25.1.18; Chingford 29.1.18; Gunnery School Flts Eastchurch by 23.2.18; Became 204 TDS Eastchurch 1.4.18 - @6.18

N5486 Deld CSD White City 4.17; Desp Russian Govt 5.17; Survives in Russia

N5487 Deld Dover 3.4.17; ADD 8.4.17; 10 Sqdn (named 'BLACK PRINCE') 24.4.17; 2-str OOC St.Julien shared N5490, N5492 & N5493 09.00 2.6.17; Albatros DIII crashed NE of Ypres salient 08.45 11.00 4.6.17; Albatros DIII OOC Polygon Wood area 11.50 6.6.17; Albatros DIII crashed Deulemont 11.00 6.7.17; Albatros DV OOC Polygon Wood 20.45 11.7.17; Albatros DV in flames Menin-Messines 08.05 20.7.17; Albatros DV OOC Dadizeele 19.50 28.7.17 (all FSL WM Alexander); ADD 5.8.17; 1 Sqdn 27.8.17; Hit ridge and o/t on aerodrome 11.9.17 (FSL CFD Ash); ADD by 13.9.17; Destroyed by fire on night of 1.10.17; Surveyed 17.10.17; Deleted 23.10.17 burnt

N5488 Deld Dover 28.2.17; ADD 7.4.17; 2 AD Candas by 26.4.17; 1 Sqdn 30.4.17; Albatros DII OOC nr Vitry-en-

Artois shared N5446 19.40 11.5.17 (FSL OB Ellis); Albatros Scout BU in air Hénin-Lietard c.19.45, then shot down in flames from 12,000 ft E of Arleux by Ltn GW Groos, Jasta 4 19.5.17 (FSL OB Ellis killed); Surveyed 11.12.17; Deleted 14.12.17 TL

N5489   Deld Dover 4.4.17; ADD 6.4.17; 10 Sqdn by 10.4.17 - @12.5.17; ADD by 17.5.17; 9 Sqdn 3.6.17; O/t landing bad ground 17.6.17 (FSL KG Macdonald); Albatros DIII OOC Nieuport shared N5377, N5378, N5459 & N5475 05.10 17.7.17 (FSL EB Freeland); 12 Sqdn 17.7.17 - @16.8.17; ADD by 30.8.17; 1 Sqdn 20.9.17; DFW Aviatik 2-str shot down intact (possibly numbered G82 - or G83) S of Polygon Wood 10.45 17.10.17; Albatros DV OOC SE of Wervicq 09.40 21.10.17; Albatros C crashed on fire Comines 12.00 24.10.17 (all FSL SW Rosevear); AP Dover 8.11.17; Deleted 26.11.17

N5490   Deld Dover 4.4.17; ADD 20.4.17; 10 Sqdn (named 'BLACK MARIA') 26.4.17; Albatros DII crashed nr railway junction E of Courtemarcke 17.30 30.4.17; Halberstadt OOC E of Dixmude 19.30 9.5.17; Seaplane crashed into water Ostende 07.45 11.5.17; Albatros DIII in flames S of Wervicq 09.20 1.6.17; 2-str OOC St.Julien shared N5483, N5487 & N5492 09.00 2.6.17; Albatros DIII in flames nr Roubaix 20.15 3.6.17; Albatros C in flames Wervicq-Poelcapelle shared N5466, N5478 & N6302 08.50 & Albatros DIII OOC NW of Poelcapelle shared N5466 09.40 5.6.17; Albatros DIII in flames 10.50, another in flames 11.05 & another OOC 11.10, all Polygon Wood area 6.6.17; Albatros DIII OOC Menin-St.Julien 08.45 7.6.17; Crashed and damaged Droglandt 8.6.17 (all FSL R Collishaw); ADD 9.6.17; 9 Sqdn 20.7.17; Albatros DV OOC Leke 05.20 29.7.17; Albatros DV on fire Lombartzyde 18.10 29.7.17 (both F/L AT Whealy); ADD 4.8.17; 1 Sqdn 17.8.17; Albatros OOC SW of Douai 18.00, then FL in enemy territory NE of St.Julien 19.9.17 (FSL RE MacMillan, PoW unhurt) [claimed Passchendaele by Vzfw Kosmahl, Jasta 26]; Surveyed 22.9.17; Deleted 27.9.17 TL

N5491   Deld Dover 4.4.17; ADD 23.4.17 - @26.4.17; 2 AD Candas by 10.5.17; 1 Sqdn 19.5.17; Took off for special mission 09.40, shot down Moorslede by Ltn Mettlich, Jasta 8 8.6.17 (F/L TG Culling DSC killed) [also suggested nr Warneton by Flugmeister Bossler, Marinefeldjasta 1]; Deleted 25.6.17

N5492   Deld Dover 6.4.17; ADD 23.4.17; 10 Sqdn (named 'BLACK MARIA') 9.5.17; Albatros DIII dest Ypres-Staden 10.30 21.5.17; 2-str OOC St.Julien shared N5483, N5487 & N5490 09.00 2.6.17; Badly shot about 4.6.17; Halberstadt crashed on fire 11.00 & Albatros DIII OOC 11.15, both Polygon Wood area 6.6.17; Albatros DIII OOC St.Julien 09.00 7.6.17 (all FSL GE Nash); Halberstadt [or Aviatik] C OOC Menin 17.15, Albatros DIII OOC & Albatros DV crashed 17.40 N of Moorslede 15.6.17; HA probably Halberstadt OOC Roulers 19.10 17.6.17; Albatros DV crashed Moorslede 08.10 24.6.17; Aviatik C crashed nr Poelcapelle Stn 11.10, m/c damaged by gunfire 2.7.17; 2 Albatros Scout OOC Deulemont 09.40-11.30 6.7.17; Albatros DV OOC Moorslede 20.40 11.7.17; Albatros DV OOC S of Polygon Wood 07.45 12.7.17; Damaged by flak, FL La Lovie 14.7.17 (unhurt); Albatros DV OOC Menin-Messines 08.00 20.7.17; 2 Albatros DV OOC Passchendaele 08.00-08.40 21.7.17 (all F/L R Collishaw DSC, DSO); Shot down S of Moorslede 19.45 27.7.17 (FSL G Roach killed) [claimed Benthem 20.40 by Lt K.von Schönebeck, Jasta 11]; Deleted 8.8.17 [Collishaw only 1 21.7.17? - none in his log book!]

N5493   Deld Dover 6.4.17; ADD 20.4.17; 8 Sqdn (named 'BLYMP' - nickname of RA Little's son) 26.4.17; Aviatik C crashed Oppy 12.25 28.4.17; Albatros DIII crashed Douai aerodrome, shared N5446 of 1 Sqdn 19.15 29.4.17; 2 Albatros DIII OOC E of Arras 07.10 & 07.25 30.4.17; Albatros DIII OOC Vitry 19.30 2.5.17; LVG C OOC SE of Lens 10.10 9.5.17; DFW Aviatik C OOC Douvrin 11.00 18.5.17; Albatros DIII OOC 1m W of Douai, shared N5482 15.45 23.5.17; Albatros DIII OOC Quierry-la-Motte 08.10 25.5.17 Aviatik crashed Vendin-le-Vieil, shared N6295 09.35 16.6.17; Albatros DV crashed 1m E of Hénin-Lietard 10.25 21.6.17; DFW

Aviatik C crashed on fire 1m E of Acheville 17.40-8.25 patrol 26.6.17 [possibly Gefr E Bittorf & Ltn P Schweizer]; Albatros DV OOC E of Lens, shared N6292 06.55 29.6.17; Albatros DV OOC Lens 11.00 3.7.17; DFW C crashed N of Izel 11.15 6.7.17 (all FSL RA Little, later A/F/Cdr DSO DSC); Badly shot about in general engagement 28.7.17 (FSL ED Crundall unhurt); ADD 5.8.17; 1 Sqdn W/E 6.9.17; Collided with SPAD VII B3503 of 19 Sqdn RFC [Capt J Manley killed] on British side of lines nr Neuve Eglise 18.9.17 (FSL NS Wright killed); Surveyed 17.10.17; Deleted 23.10.17 wrecked

N5494   Presentation a/c 'Peking Britons No.2' 20.10.16. Deld Dover 14.4.17; ADD 29.4.17; 1 Sqdn 9.5.17; Choked engine and COL on aerodrome 11.7.17 (FSL E Nicholls); ADD by 12.7.17; 8 Sqdn 12.8.17; ADD 7.9.17; 1 Sqdn 14.9.17; AP Dover 8.11.17; War School Manston W/E 30.11.17; Surveyed 19.12.17; Deleted 28.12.17 W&T

**N5495 to N5499 blank numbers**

**50 SOPWITH 1½ STRUTTER 9700 TYPE TRACTOR BIPLANE BOMBERS ordered 11.16 under Cont No C.P.127493/16, numbered N5500 to N5549 and built Kingston-upon-Thames. Deld from Brooklands. (110-hp Clerget 9Z or 130-hp Clerget 9B)**

N5500   Deld CSD White City by 31.12.16; Shipped to Aegean; F Sqdn 2 Wing by 29.4.17 - @24.5.17; Amberkoj to Stavros 11.5.18; Marian 12.5.18 - @27.5.18

N5501   (130-hp) Accepted at Mkrs W/E 7.12.16; Arr 3 Wing Luxeuil 26.12.16; Hit by flak in Freiburg reprisal raid, dead engine, FL just behind French lines, shelled 14.4.17 (FSL AC Dissette); Deleted

N5502   (110-hp) Accepted at Mkrs W/E 7.12.16; Arr 3 Wing Luxeuil 26.12.16; Transferred to French Govt less engine for AMF 20.4.17

N5503   (110-hp) Accepted at Mkrs W/E 7.12.16; Arr 3 Wing Luxeuil 26.12.16 - LM 13.4.17; To ADD 4.17; 2 Sqdn 12.7.17; ADD 17.7.17; Dover on/by 9.8.17; Badly damaged 13.8.17; War School Manston W/E 24.11.17 - @30.3.18

N5504   (110-hp) Deld Dover 26.1.17; ADD 27.1.17; 7 Sqdn 3.2.17; 5 Sqdn 1.4.17; ADD 2.6.17; Eastbourne 5.6.17; Brooklands 6.6.17; Allocated Eastbourne 8.6.17; Eastbourne by 10.17 [quoted as "L.C.T.L."]; Chingford 8.1.18; Detling 24.1.18; Chingford by 23.2.18 - @3.18 (special service); Became G-EAVB (c/n 5341) [Reported as transferred by 7.6.17 to French Govt as Type 1B.2, but does not appear to fit]

N5505   (110-hp) Deld ADD by 1.1.17; 7 Sqdn by 18.1.17; Crashed and DBR 4.2.17; ADD by 1.2.17 (sic); For deletion 15.2.17; Deleted 24.3.17

N5506   (130-hp) Shipped to Aegean; Convtd to Type 9400; Stavros by 1.12.17 - @1.1.18; Repair Base Mudros by 3.18 - 6.18 & 10.18; Transferred to Greek Govt

N5507   (110-hp) Arr 3 Wing Luxeuil by 5.1.17; Transferred to French Govt less engine for AMF 20.4.17 (retained serial)

N5508   Deld Dover 29.1.17; ADD 1.2.17; Dover 9.6.17; Badly damaged 8.17; Dived in from great height and crashed on rocks on coast 14.9.17 (FSL AA Bishop killed)

N5509   Deld ADD by 2.17 (not by 25.1.17); 7 Sqdn 1.2.17; 5 Sqdn 1.4.17; Wrecked 7.5.17; ADD by 17.5.17; Deleted 27.6.17

N5510   (110-hp) Accepted at Mkrs 21.12.16; Allocated 3 Wing Luxeuil 9.12.16 (arr 12.16) - @13.4.17(LM); For shipment to Eastern Mediterranean 4.17; Arr Mudros 30.6.17

N5511   (110-hp) Accepted at Mkrs 21.12.16; Allocated 3 Wing Luxeuil 19.12.16 (arr 12.16); Transferred to French Govt less engine for AMF 20.4.17

N5512   (110-hp) Accepted at Mkrs 30.12.16; Arr 3 Wing by 19.1.17 [1 or 2 Sqdn 3 Wing by 3.17]; ADD, COL 16.5.17; Deleted 27.6.17

N5513   (130-hp) Accepted at Mkrs 30.12.16; Arr 3 Wing Luxeuil 1.17 - LM 13.4.17; Surveyed 12.4.17

N5514   (110-hp) Deld CSD White City by 31.12.16 - @31.1.17; Arr 3 Wing Luxeuil by 22.2.17; Transferred to French Govt for AMF 19.4.17

N5515 (110-hp) Accepted at Mkrs 4.1.17; Deld CSD White City 1.17; 3 Wing Luxeuil by 2.2.17 - LM13.4.17; For shipment to Eastern Mediterranean 4.17; Convtd to Type 9400; Mudros by 1.12.17 - @1.1.18 (now 130-hp); A Sqdn 2 Wing Thasos; Marsh by 26.2.18 & @19.3.18; Mudros by 3.18; Transferred to Greek Govt for training by 6.18 - 1.19

N5516 (110-hp) Accepted at Mkrs 4.1.17; Arr 3 Wing Luxeuil by 9.3.17 - @13.4.17; For shipment to Eastern Mediterranean 4.17; Arr Mudros 30.6.17; Transferred to Greek Govt; Total loss in transit to Mudros; Deleted 28.11.17

N5517 (110-hp) Accepted at Mkrs 4.1.17; Arr 3 Wing Luxeuil by 9.3.17 - @13.4.17; For shipment to Eastern Mediterranean 4.17; Smyrna by 12-13.9.17; Marsh by 1.12.17 - @1.1.18; G Flt 2 Wing Mudros by 3.18; Became G Flt 62 Wing Mudros 1.4.18; Repair Base Mudros by 6.18

N5518 (110-hp) Accepted at Mkrs 4.1.17; Arr 3 Wing Luxeuil by 9.2.17 - @13.4.17; ADD by 26.4.17; 2 Sqdn 9.7.17; ADD 17.7.17; Dover 9.8.17; Badly damaged 1.9.17; Manston W/E 10.11.17; Cranwell 26.3.18 (transit); East Fortune (via Beverley) 28.3.18

N5519 (110-hp) Deld ADD (not by 25.1.17); 7 Sqdn on/by 1.2.17; 5 Sqdn 1.4.17; Crashed and wrecked 1.5.17 (FSL OR Griffin); Deleted ADD 14.5.17

N5520 (110-hp) Deld Dover 6.1.17; ADD 27.1.17; 7 Sqdn by 1.2.17; 5 Sqdn 1.4.17 - @21.6.17; Dunkerque to Brooklands (via Eastchurch) 25.6.17; Prawle Point but damaged wing landing 27.6.17; Cranwell 26.10.17; Surveyed 10.12.17 type obsolete; Deleted 14.12.17

N5521 (130-hp) Crashed and DBR on landing new from England, ADD 13.2.17; Deleted 24.3.17

N5522 (110-hp) Accepted at Mkrs 11.1.17; Arr 3 Wing Luxeuil by 9.2.17; Transferred to French Govt less engine for AMF 20.4.17

N5523 (110-hp) Accepted at Mkrs 11.1.17; Arr 3 Wing Luxeuil by 23.3.17; Transferred to French Govt less engine for AMF 20.4.17

N5524 (130-hp) Accepted at Mkrs 15.1.17; arr 3 Wing Luxeuil 17.2.17 - LM14.4.17; ADD by 26.4.17; 2 Sqdn 11.7.17; AP Dover 23.11.17; War School Manston 10.12.17 (now 110-hp); Deleted W/E 23.2.18

N5525 (110-hp) Deld Design Flt Eastchurch 14.2.17; Dunkerque 1.3.17; Dover 15.6.17; Badly damaged 21.8.17; War School Manston W/E 17.11.17; For deletion by 16.2.18

N5526 (130-hp) Accepted at Mkrs 15.1.17; arr 3 Wing Luxeuil by 9.2.17 - LM14.4.17; For shipment to Eastern Mediterranean 4.17; Arr Mudros 30.6.17

N5527 (110-hp) Shipped to Aegean; Convtd to Type 9400; 2 Wing Mudros; Mitylene by 1.12.17 - @3.18; Transferred to Greek Govt; Repair Base Mudros by 6.18 & 10.18 - 1.19

N5528 (130-hp) Deld ADD by 25.1.17; 7 Sqdn by 1.2.17; 5 Sqdn 1.4.17; ADD 2.6.17; Dover 7.6.17; U/c and wings damaged 21.7.17; Manston W/E 20.10.17; AGPs 31.10.17 & 11.11.17; Surveyed 18.12.17; Deleted 24.12.17 wreck

N5529 (110-hp) Arr 3 Wing Luxeuil 12.3.17 - LM13.4.17; For shipment to Eastern Mediterranean 4.17; Arr Mudros 30.6.17; Marsh by 1.12.17; A Sqdn 2 Wing Thasos; Mudros by 3.18; Transferred to Greek Govt for training by 10.18 - @1.19

N5530 (130-hp) Accepted at Mkrs 19.1.17; arr 3 Wing Luxeuil 30.3.17; Vendôme 22.4.17 (transit); Paris 23.4.17; ADD by 26.4.17; Hendon 3.9.17; War Flt Manston 10.9.17 - @3.3.18 (now 110-hp); Marine Observers School Leysdown by 8.18 - @2.19

N5531 Accepted at Mkrs 31.1.17; Arr 3 Wing Luxeuil 15.3.17 - LM14.4.17; ADD by 26.4.17; 5 Sqdn by 29.4.17; Wrecked 14.6.17; ADD 14.6.17; Deleted 27.6.17

N5532 Allocated Mkrs to 3 Wing Luxeuil 18.1.17 (cancelled); Shipped to Aegean; Stavros to Adv Base Amberkoj 9.5.17; F Sqdn 2 Wing, during raid on Drama air station, pilot hit in head by AA fire over Angista, knocked out but recovered control and landed safely 18.5.17 (FSL GA Magor wounded)

N5533 (110-hp) Allocated to 3 Wing Luxeuil 18.1.17 (cancelled 22.2.17); Deld CSD White City 4.4.17

N5534 (110-hp) Allocated to 3 Wing Luxeuil 8.2.17 (cancelled 22.2.17); Shipped to Aegean; Mitylene by 1.12.17; Surveyed 8.3.18 wrecked; Deleted 27.3.18

N5535 Allocated to 3 Wing Luxeuil 8.2.17 (cancelled 22.2.17); War School Manston (unconfirmed)

N5536 (110-hp) Shipped to Aegean; Thasos by 1.12.17 - @1.1.18; Marsh by 26.1.18 (with Greeks); Thasos by 3.18; Disposed by 6.18 (fate not reported)

N5537 (110-hp) Shipped to Aegean; Mitylene to Mudros 17.9.17; Mudros by 1.12.17; Marsh by 1.1.18; Surveyed 19.2.18; Deleted 13.3.18 wrecked

N5538 to N5549 cancelled

**10 SOPWITH 1½ STRUTTER 9700 TYPE TRACTOR BIPLANE BOMBERS to be numbered N5550 to N5559 and built Kingston-upon-Thames.**

N5550 to N5559 cancelled 12.16 (8 aircraft for Belgium also cancelled at same time). Serials re-allocated

**10 SOPWITH TRIPLANE FIGHTERS to be numbered N5550 to N5559 and built Kingston-upon-Thames.**

N5550 to N5559 cancelled

**40 NIEUPORT XV BOMBARDMENT TRACTOR BIPLANE put forward 9.16, to be N5560 to N5599. (230-hp Renault)**

N5560 to N5599 cancelled 2.17 and serials partially re-allocated

**25 ROYAL AIRCRAFT FACTORY B.E.2C TRACTOR BIPLANES ordered 11.16 from Oakley & Co, to be numbered N5570 to N5594. (150-hp Hispano-Suiza)**

N5570 to N5594 cancelled 11.16

**25 SOPWITH 1½ STRUTTER LONG RANGE DAY BOMBER TRACTOR BIPLANES ordered 25.9.16 under Cont Nos C.P.119334/16, C.P.128263/16, C.P.129281/16 & C.P.135963/16 from Westland Aircraft Works, numbered N5600 to N5624 and built Yeovil. Order changed 12.16, last 20 now to be fighter variant instead of bombers. Built as 9700 Type single seat bomber to N5604, remainder 9400S Type two seat fighter. (110-hp Clerget 9Z)**

**9700 Type**
N5600 Accepted at Mkrs 21.2.17; Deld 3 Wing Luxeuil 21.2.17; ADD by 12.4.17; Dover 9.8.17 - 9.17; CW 18.8.17; LM 22.8.17

N5601 Deld Felixstowe store for erection 29.3.17; Mullion 16.4.17; Grain EC&AD 9.2.18 (for flotation expts); Grain ECD by 1.4.18 - @27.6.18 (now Ship Strutter); Flown off deck of HMS *Vindex* 3.4.18; Naval Flt Manston by 6.18 - 7.18; HMS *Vindex* (launched from railed deck on skids)

N5602 Deld Felixstowe store for erection 29.3.17; Mullion 16.4.17; TW 2.5.17 (FSL AF Buck seriously injured); Deleted 2.5.17

N5603 Deld Felixstowe store for erection 29.3.17; Mullion for unpacking 16.4.17; Prawle Point 23.4.17; fitted flotation bags 24.4.17; CW 26.4.17 (FSL CR Lupton injured); Deleted 7.5.17

N5604 Deld Felixstowe store for erection 29.3.17; Mullion for unpacking 16.4.17; Prawle Point 23.4.17; fitted flotation bags 25.4.17; Ready 4.5.17; HSMP 10.6.17; Retd from patrol, nosedived into sea from 1,500ft and sank 22.6.17 (FSL HL Crowe drowned); Wreckage salved by trawler *Lois* and taken to Plymouth 23.6.17; Deleted 25.6.17

**9400S Type from here**
N5605 Deld B Flt Cranwell for erection 5.3.17; Collided with N5636 and damaged 22.8.17; East Fortune W/E 18.1.18 - @30.3.18 (convtd Ships Strutter)

N5606 Deld B Flt Cranwell for erection 7.3.17; Crashed and damaged 17.7.17; Convtd Ships Strutter; East Fortune W/E 18.1.18; Donibristle W/E 15.2.18; Rosyth W/E 15.2.18; HMS *Repulse* 13.2.18; Rosyth 13.2.18; HMAS *Australia* W/E 15.2.18; Rosyth W/E 21.2.18; Donibristle by 23.2.18; Rosyth W/E 9.3.18; Fleet AD Turnhouse W/E 6.4.18 - @30.1.19

N5607 (Type 9700) (100-hp Monosoupape) Deld Felixstowe store 29.3.17; Mullion 16.4.17; Ready 30.4.17; Gunnery School Flt Eastchurch W/E 13.10.17; Became

N5608 — 204 TDS Eastchurch 1.4.18
(Type 9700) (110-hp Clerget) Deld Felixstowe store 29.3.17; Mullion for unpacking 21.4.17; Gunnery School Flt Eastchurch W/E 13.10.17; Eastchurch NFS by 3.18 - @29.8.18; To Fleet AD Turnhouse by 8.18 - @30.1.19

N5609 — Deld Felixstowe store 29.3.17; To Messrs Mathwin, Cardiff for shipment 29.3.17; Shipped to Aegean in SS *Arum* for Aeroplane Flt 6 Wing 5.4.17; 6 Wing Otranto by 20.6.17 [LM]

N5610 — Deld Felixstowe store 29.3.17 (for Cattewater but NTU); Left by rail for Mudros 13.8.17; Lost in transit by 15.11.17

N5611 — (130-hp) Deld Felixstowe store 29.3.17; Left by rail for shipment 13.8.17; Shipped to 8.17 or 9.17; Mudros by 1.12.17; Imbros by 1.18; Stavros by 3.18 - 6.18; Imbros by 6.18; Stavros by 10.18 - 1.19

N5612 — (100-hp Monosoupape) Deld Felixstowe store 29.3.17; Pembroke for unpacking 22.4.17; Tested 29.5.17; U/c and propeller damaged landing 4.6.17 (FSL W Allaway & FSL CF Brewerton); still Felixstowe @10.17; Gunnery School Flts Eastchurch by 29.12.17 (from 10.17?) - @23.2.18; East Fortune NFS W/E 16.3.18 (now 100-hp Gnôme Monosoupape); Became 208 TDS East Fortune 6.18; Collided with stationery aircraft on ground 17.6.18 (Lt J McFadden & Lt FI Bradley both injured)

N5613 — Deld Felixstowe store 29.3.17; Pembroke for unpacking 22.4.17; Gunnery School Flt Eastchurch 6.10.17; AGP 31.10.17/1.11.17, landed Dunkerque then retd Eastchurch; 100-hp Monosoupape by 12.17 - 1.18; 110-hp Clerget by 2.18; East Fortune NFS W/E 16.3.18 - @30.3.18

N5614 — Deld Felixstowe store 29.3.17; Desp Mudros 8.4.17; Convtd to Type 9700; Tested Mudros 6.7.17; Surveyed 19.9.17; Deleted 2.10.17 wrecked

N5615 — Deld Felixstowe store 29.3.17; Desp Mudros 8.4.17

N5616 — Deld Felixstowe store 29.3.17; Desp Mudros 8.4.17; C Sqdn 2 Wing Imbros by 8.17 - @8.9.17; EF, FL Salt Lake sand, went on nose and damaged 30.8.17 (FSL AB Hill)

N5617 — (110-hp Clerget) Deld Felixstowe store 29.3.17; Desp 8.4.17; Mullion for unpacking 30.4.17 - @9.17; Gunnery School Flts Eastchurch by 10.17; AGP 31.10.17/1.11.17; East Fortune NFS by 3.18 - @29.8.18; To Fleet AD Turnhouse 9.18 - @11.18; Donibristle by 31.12.18 - @30.1.19

N5618 — Deld Felixstowe store 4.4.17; Desp Mudros 8.4.17; D Sqdn 2 Wing Stavros by 8.10.17; COL after combat 10.12.17 (F/Cdr PC Douglass DoI & OSL W Hinsley injured); Deleted 24.12.17; Deleted 15.1.18 wrecked

N5619 — Deld Felixstowe store 4.4.17; Mullion for unpacking 30.4.17; Prawle Point but FL Thurlestone 11.7.17; FL and damaged nr Salcombe 12.7.17 (FSL FH McMaster); Prawle Point 12.7.17; Mullion W/E 7.11.17; Padstow 21.4.18; Mullion 1.5.18; Padstow 2.5.18; Became 493 Flt 254 Sqdn Padstow by 25.5.18

N5620 — Deld Felixstowe store 4.4.17; left by rail for Mudros 13.8.17; Lost in transit by 15.11.17

N5621 — Deld Felixstowe store 4.4.17; left by rail for Mudros 13.8.17; Lost in transit by 15.11.17

N5622 — Deld Felixstowe store 4.4.17; Yarmouth by 31.7.17; Surveyed 9.1.18 DBR; Deleted 15.1.18

N5623 — Convtd to Type 9700; Deld Mullion for erection 21.4.17; Prawle Point 24.4.17; Ready 4.5.17 (Type 9400S); Badly damaged 9.5.17; Deleted 5.6.17

N5624 — Convtd to Type 9700; Deld Mullion for erection 21.4.17; Ready 10.5.17; Prawle Point 11.5.17; CW 27.5.17 (deletion recommended but evidently rebuilt); Mullion W/E 7.11.17 (tested 3.12.17); Surveyed 26.3.18; Deleted 15.4.18

**NOT ALLOTTED N5625 to N5629**

**25 SOPWITH 1½ STRUTTER LONG RANGE DAY BOMBER TRACTOR BIPLANES** ordered 25.9.16 under Cont Nos C.P.128262/16 & C.P.129602/18 from Mann, Egerton & Co Ltd as their Type D, numbered N5630 to N5654 and built Norwich. Order placed 11.16 to convert from bomber to fighter. Built as 9700 Type to N5634, remainder 9400S Type. (130-hp Clerget 9B)

N5630 — Deld Felixstowe store 31.3.17; To Cranwell (via Norwich) 19.4.17 (arr 23.4.17); Surveyed 10.12.17 (now 110-hp Clerget); Deleted 14.12.17 type obsolete

N5631 — Deld Felixstowe store 31.3.17; To Cranwell (via Norwich) 19.4.17 (arr 25.4.17); Deleted 16.8.17

N5632 — Deld Felixstowe store 31.3.17; Cranwell (via Norwich) 28.4.17; Crashed and damaged 17.7.17; Crashed and damaged u/c and wing 4.12.17 (pilot unhurt); 110-hp Clerget by 12.17 - 1.18; fitted 130-hp Clerget by 2.18; FL, u/c broken Gosberton 20.3.18 (pilot unhurt); Became 201/2 TDS Cranwell 1.4.18; Redcar 11.5.18; Cranwell 5.18; Freiston 17.5.18; Cranwell by 6.18; Became 56/57 TDS Cranwell 27.7.18; East Fortune W/E 8.8.18; Convtd Ship Strutter; AFG Turnhouse, EF, FL hit tree 10.8.18 (Lt DB Adamson & Capt CN Downes both injured); Deleted W/E 10.10.18

N5633 — Deld Felixstowe store 31.3.17; Left 19.4.17; [Convtd Ships Strutter (when?)]; Yarmouth trg 2.8.17; to NSO Liverpool W/E 6.4.18; Houton Bay Reserve W/E 13.4.18; Scapa W/E 18.5.18; HMS *Campania* W/E 13.6.18; For deletion W/E 28.11.18

N5634 — Deld Felixstowe store 31.3.17; Yarmouth trg 2.8.17; [Convtd to Ships Strutter (when?)]; Felixstowe store W/E 30.3.18; to NSO Liverpool W/E 6.4.18; Houton Bay W/E 13.4.18; Scapa W/E 18.5.18; Smoogroo W/E 1.6.18; HMS *Campania* W/E 11.7.18; Smoogroo W/E 17.8.18; Scapa W/E 28.11.18 - @30.1.19

N5635 — Deld Felixstowe store 31.3.17 for Mudros (NTU); Not listed from 19.4.17; Yarmouth from 3.8.17; HACP 23.12.17; still Yarmouth @29.1.18; Convtd Ships Strutter; Yarmouth 6.2.18; Felixstowe store for Liverpool W/E 30.3.18; to Liverpool W/E 6.4.18; To Houton Bay 4.18; Scapa by 5.18; Smoogroo by 1.6.18; HMS *Campania* by 6.18; Deleted 11.18

N5636 — Deld B Flt Cranwell 9.5.17; Collided with N5605 and damaged 22.8.17; Wrecked 18.9.17; Convtd to Ships Strutter; East Fortune NFS W/E 18.1.18 - @3.18; To Houton Bay Reserve 3.18 - @4.18; Turnhouse by 11.5.18 - @6.18; Turnhouse W/E 17.10.18; Donibristle W/E 21.11.18; Turnhouse W/E 12.12.18 - @30.1.19 ALSO HMS *Indomitable*

N5637 — Deld B Flt Cranwell 7.5.17; U/c and propeller broken 13.8.17; Deleted W/E 15.25.9.17 BR

N5638 — Deld Felixstowe store 14.5.17; Convtd to Ships Strutter (when?); Yarmouth trg 2.8.17; Felixstowe store W/E 30.3.18; NSO Liverpool W/E 6.4.18; Houton Bay Reserve W/E 13.4.18; Scapa W/E 18.5.18; HMS *Campania* W/E 13.6.18; For deletion W/E 28.11.18

N5639 — (110-hp) Deld Felixstowe store 14.5.17; Left by rail for Otranto 11.8.17; Shipped to Aegean; 6 Wing Otranto by 9.11.17; EF, FL in sea nr minelayer, machine lost 7.1.18 (FSL AC Gatley); Surveyed 10.1.18; Deleted 19.1.18 TL

N5640 — (110-hp) Deld Felixstowe store 18.5.17; Left by rail for Otranto 11.8.17; 6 Wing Otranto by 9.11.17; Became 66 Wing Otranto 1.4.18; Surveyed 1.4.18; Deleted 15.5.18 wrecked

N5641 — (110-hp) Deld Felixstowe store 18.5.17; Left by rail for Otranto 11.8.17; 6 Wing Otranto by 9.11.17; Surveyed 5.12.17 wrecked; Deleted 13.12.17

N5642 — (110-hp) Deld Felixstowe store 21.5.17; Left by rail for Otranto 11.8.17; 6 Wing Otranto by 9.11.17; Surveyed 10.1.18; Deleted 19.1.18 TL

N5643 — Deld Felixstowe store 21.5.17; Mann Egerton 18.7.17; Cranwell for erection 20.7.17; Badly damaged 6.8.17; Convtd to Ships Strutter; East Fortune 5.1.18 - @3.18 & 6.18; Donibristle by 6.18 - @8.18; East Fortune by 8.8.18; Turnhouse W/E 19.8.18 - @30.1.19

N5644 — Deld Felixstowe store 21.5.17; Mann Egerton 18.7.17; Cranwell for erection 21.7.17; Wrecked 15.8.17; Convtd to Ships Strutter; East Fortune 5.1.18 - @3.18; Donibristle by 1.3.18; HMAS *Australia* W/E 16.3.18; Rosyth 3.18; HMS *Repulse* 14.3.18; Rosyth 24.3.18; Turnhouse W/E 4.4.18; HMS *Repulse* 8.4.18; ashore 19.4.18; HMS *Repulse* 19.4.18; HMS *Furious* W/E 27.4.18; Turnhouse W/E 10.5.18; Donibristle W/E 23.5.18; Turnhouse W/E 19.9.18; Donibristle W/E 17.10.18; HMS *Glorious* 26.10.18; Donibristle 15.12.18 - @30.1.19 ALSO HMS *New Zealand*

N5645 — (Type 9700) Deld Felixstowe store 4.5.17; Mann Egerton 18.7.17; Cranwell for erection 22.7.17; To

HMS *Eagle* but crashed 10.3.18 (Capt RF Redpath); Surveyed 12.3.18; Deleted 16.3.18 wrecked

N5646 Deld Felixstowe store 4.5.17; Mann Egerton 18.7.17; Chingford for erection 23.7.17; Cranwell by 9.17; Convtd Ships Strutter at Cranwell; 110-hp Clerget by 12.17; East Fortune NFS W/E 18.1.18 - @3.18; Turnhouse by 7.18 - @30.1.19

N5647 Deld Felixstowe store 4.5.17; Mann Egerton 18.7.17; Cranwell for erection 21.7.17; Damaged 5.9.17; East Fortune W/E 25.1.18 - @5.18; Turnhouse by 11.11.18

N5648 Allocated Mudros 29.5.17; Shipped to Aegean; Thasos by 1.12.18 (110-hp Clerget)

N5649 Deld Felixstowe store 25.5.17; Mann Egerton 18.7.17; Chingford for erection 20.7.17; Crashed 5.9.17; Cranwell W/E 12.10.17 (now 110-hp Clerget); East Fortune W/E 18.1.18 - @5.18; Turnhouse by 7.18 - @1.19

N5650 Allocated Mudros 29.5.17; Shipped to Aegean; Thasos by 1.12.17 (now 110-hp Clerget); Stavros by 3.18 & 6.18 & 10.18 - @1.19; Transferred to Greek Govt

N5651 Allocated Mudros 29.5.17; Shipped to Aegean; Mitylene by 1.12.17 - 3.18

N5652 Allocated Mudros 29.5.17; Shipped to Aegean; Mudros by 1.12.17 - @1.1.18; Mitylene by 20.1.18; Imbros by 10.2.18; C Sqdn 62 Wing Mudros by 4.18

N5653 Allocated Mudros 29.5.17; Shipped to Aegean; Mudros by 1.12.17 - @1.1.18; Stavros by 3.18; Repair Base by 6.18

N5654 (110-hp Clerget) Allocated Mudros 29.5.17; Shipped to Aegean; Mudros by 1.12.17; C Sqdn 2 Wing Imbros by 12.1.18 - @6.18

**N5655 TO N5659 NOT ALLOTTED (BLANK NUMBERS)**

**CURTISS J.N.4 (IMPROVED) ordered from Canada 11.16, to be numbered N5660 to N5709. (90-hp Curtiss OX-5)**

N5660 to N5709 not delivered

**N5710 to N5719 NOT ALLOTTED (BLANK NUMBERS)**

**30 MAURICE FARMAN S.7 LONGHORN PUSHER BIPLANES ordered 11.16 (tender accepted 1.17) under Cont No C.P.132301/16 from Brush Electrical Engineering Co Ltd, numbered N5720 to N5749 and built Loughborough. (80-hp Renault unless otherwise stated)**

N5720 Deld Killingholme store for erection 21.3.17; Erected by 21.3.17; Manston FS (via Chingford) 3.5.17; Deleted 26.1.18

N5721 Deld Killingholme store for erection 21.3.17; Erected by 21.3.17; Manston FS (via Chingford) 3.5.17; BR 21.6.17

N5722 Deld Killingholme store for erection 15.3.17; Manston FS (via Chingford) 3.5.17; Surveyed 15.10.17; Deleted 18.10.17 wrecked

N5723 (75-hp Renault) Deld Killingholme store for erection 15.3.17; Erected by 21.3.17; Manston FS (via Chingford) 3.5.17; For deletion by 23.2.18

N5724 (75-hp Renault) Deld Killingholme store for erection 23.3.17; Chingford 4.6.17 (transit); Manston FS 5.6.17; Surveyed 16.1.18; Deleted 19.1.18 wrecked

N5725 (75-hp Renault) Deld Killingholme store for erection 9.4.17; Manston FS 4.6.17 then to Chelmsford for repair; Chingford 2.7.17; Surveyed 14.11.17; Deleted 21.11.17 DBR

N5726 (75-hp Renault) Deld Killingholme store for erection 29.3.17; Manston FS 9.7.17 (arr via Huntingdon 12.7.17); Surveyed 1.1.18; Deleted 15.1.18 exposure

N5727 (75-hp Renault) Deld Killingholme store for erection 29.3.17; Manston FS 4.6.17; Dived in from 1,000ft, CW, BR 5.7.17 (PFO HJ Flynn killed); Deleted 15.7.17

N5728 (75-hp Renault) Deld Killingholme store for erection 31.3.17; Manston FS 4.6.17 - @30.3.18

N5729 (75-hp Renault) Deld Eastchurch Workshops by road 31.3.17; Eastchurch FS 29.5.17; Crashed 8.8.17; Surveyed 26.11.17; Deleted 5.12.17

N5730 Deld Eastchurch Workshops by road 31.3.17; Eastchurch FS 31.5.17; Surveyed 26.11.17; Deleted 5.12.17 for spares

N5731 Deld Eastchurch Workshops by road 4.4.17; Surveyed 26.11.17; Deleted 5.12.17 for spares

N5732 Deld Eastchurch Workshops for erection 6.4.17; Chingford by road 15.4.17; Eastbourne 27.10.17; Deleted W/E 8.12.17

N5733 Deld Chingford by road 18.4.17; Wing collapsed in mid-air 28.7.17 (TPFO RM Denholm killed); Deleted 8.8.17

N5734 Deld Chingford 25.5.17; Crashed and damaged 20.7.17; Surveyed 26.11.17; Deleted 5.12.17 for spares

N5735 Deld Eastbourne for erection 30.4.17; Surveyed 6.12.17; Deleted 19.12.17

N5736 Deld Eastbourne by erection 1.5.17; Deleted W/E 2.3.18

N5737 Deld Eastbourne for erection 5.5.17; Burst tyre landing, afterwards destroyed 11.1.18 (pilot unhurt); Deleted W/E 26.1.18

N5738 Deld Killingholme store 28.4.17; Surveyed 9.9.17; Deleted 12.9.17 for spares

N5739 Deld Killingholme store 30.4.17; Surveyed 12.11.17; Deleted 19.11.17 for spares

N5740 Deld Cranwell store 7.5.17; Manston FS (via Grain and Huntingdon) 8.6.17; CW 13.7.17 (PFCdt DO Mulholland seriously injured)

N5741 Deld Cranwell store 7.5.17; Manston FS 3.7.17 (arr 6.7.17 via Huntingdon); Deleted W/E 23.2.18

N5742 Deld Cranwell store 7.5.17; Ready 12.6.17; Manston FS 3.7.17; Deleted W/E 23.2.18

N5743 Deld Cranwell store 7.5.17 (later Cranwell School); Surveyed 27.11.17; Deleted 6.12.17 W&T

N5744 Deld Killingholme store by road 11.5.17; Cranwell 23.6.17; Manston FS (via Chingford) 26.6.17; U/c damaged 11.7.17; Surveyed 28.11.17; Deleted 5.12.17 W&T

N5745 Deld Eastbourne 30.5.17; Deleted W/E 26.1.18

N5746 Deld Eastbourne 11.7.17; Deleted W/E 2.2.18

N5747 Deld Eastbourne and fitting DC 14.6.17; Surveyed 18.12.17 wrecked; Deleted 28.12.17

N5748 Deld Eastbourne 2.6.17; For deletion by 30.3.18

N5749 Deld Hendon 23.6.17; Manston FS (via Killingholme and Chingford 26.6.17); Wrecked 14.7.17, deletion recommended

**10 MAURICE FARMAN S.7 LONGHORN PUSHER BIPLANES ordered 19.7.16 under Cont No C.P.132300/16 from Phoenix Dynamo Co Ltd, numbered N5750 to N5759 & built Bradford. (75-hp Hawk)**

N5750 (Convtd) Deld Killingholme store (landed Bellasize en route) and accepted 19.3.17 (JL Parker); Deleted W/E 23.2.18

N5751 (Convtd) Accepted en route Killingholme store 19.3.17 (JL Parker); Deleted 14.12.17 for spares

N5752 Deld and erected Killingholme 31.3.17; Redcar W/E 27.10.17; Surveyed 7.12.17; Deleted 14.12.17 as spares

N5753 (90-hp Curtiss) Deld Killingholme store 27.3.17; For deletion by 30.3.18

N5754 (90-hp Curtiss); Deld Killingholme store 27.4.17; for deletion by 30.3.18

N5755 (Convtd) Deld Killingholme store 28.4.17; Deleted W/E 23.2.18

N5756 Deld Eastchurch Workshops 30.3.17; Eastchurch FS 17.4.17; Crashed 25.4.17; Eastchurch Workshops 26.4.17 (repair); Manston FS 26.7.17; Damaged 15.9.17; Surveyed 19.9.17; Deleted 24.9.17 wrecked

N5757 Deld Eastchurch Workshops by rail 5.4.17; Eastchurch FS 4.17; Crashed 21.8.17; Eastbourne W/E 10.11.17; Surveyed 20.11.17 (now 80-hp Renault); Deleted 26.11.17 wrecked

N5758 Deld Killingholme store via Brough, EF, FL en route, then contd to Killingholme and accepted 26.4.17 (JL Parker); Eastbourne 23.6.17 (arr 26.7.17 after FL nr Sleaford en route 25.7.17); EF, FL Dicker 8.12.17; Deleted W/E 15.12.17

N5759 (Curtiss OX-2) Deld Killingholme store after FL en route nr Barton Airship Sheds 27.4.17 (JL Parker); Redcar 20.12.17; Surveyed 22.12.17; Deleted W/E 26.1.18

**N5760 to N5769 NOT ALLOTTED (BUT N5760 - N5799 OFFICIALLY BLANK NUMBERS)**

**25 ROYAL AIRCRAFT FACTORY B.E.2c ordered 11.16 from Robey & Co Ltd, numbered N5770 to N5794 and to be built Lincoln. (150-hp Hispano)**

N5770 to N5794 cancelled 11.16

**N5795 to N5799 NOT ALLOTTED**

**30 AVRO 504G (ADMIRALTY 179 TYPE DUAL) TRACTOR BIPLANE TRAINERS ordered 11.16 (amended 29.7.17) under Cont Nos C.P.121501, C.P.133706/16 & A.S.19207 from A.V.Roe & Co Ltd, numbered N5800 to N5829 and built Hamble & Manchester. Fitted to carry 4x16-lb bombs (80-hp Gnôme)**

N5800  (fitted gun) Deld C Flt Cranwell 12.6.17; EF,FL Leadenham, undamaged, retd, 23.2.18; Became 201/2 TDS Cranwell 1.4.18

N5801  (fitted gun) Deld C Flt Cranwell for erection 13.6.17; Collided with R.E.7 2260, both damaged 18.12.17 (pilot injured); Crashed, slightly damaged, Byard's Leap 13.3.18 (pilot unhurt); Became 201/2 TDS Cranwell 1.4.18

N5802  (fitted gun) Deld Cranwell 19.6.17; Became 201/2 TDS Cranwell 1.4.18

N5803  (fitted gun) Deld Cranwell for erection 13.6.17; Became 201/2 TDS Cranwell 1.4.18; Stalled, spun in wrecked 18.5.18 (2/Lt JM Johnston killed)

N5804  (fitted gun) Deld Cranwell for erection 26.6.17; Freiston 7.17; Cranwell by 10.17; Became 201/2 TDS Cranwell 1.4.18

N5805  Deld Cranwell for erection 26.6.17; Crashed 5.7.17; Surveyed 16.10.17; Deleted 18.10.17 wrecked

N5806  Deld C Flt Cranwell 2.7.17; Crashed nr east gate, slightly damaged 6.12.17 (pilot unhurt); Became 201/2 TDS Cranwell 1.4.18

N5807  Deld Cranwell for erection 7.7.17; Chingford 20.7.17 (transit); Damaged 22.7.17; Manston FS 26.7.17; Became 203 TDS Manston 1.4.18; EF, FL, stalled on turn 25.4.18 (2/Lt LF Joyne slightly injured)

N5808  (Fitted gun) Deld Cranwell for erection 10.7.17; Manston FS (via Chingford) 20.7.17; Surveyed 31.3.18; Deleted 15.4.18 DBR

N5809  (Fitted gun) Deld Cranwell for erection 14.7.17; Redcar School 22.7.17 - @3.18

N5810  Deld Cranwell (coded 'A') for erection 28.7.17; Lost, FL, slightly damaged 10.3.18 (PFO HH Martin unhurt); Became 201/2 TDS Cranwell 1.4.18

N5811  Deld Cranwell 1.8.17; Slightly damaged 5.9.17; For deletion by 9.11.17

N5812  Deld Cranwell for erection 2.8.17; Became 201/2 TDS Cranwell 1.4.18

N5813  (fitted gun) Deld C Flt Cranwell for erection 10.8.17; Became 201/2 TDS Cranwell 1.4.18

N5814  (fitted gun) Deld C Flt Cranwell for erection 10.8.17; Crashed and damaged Ancaster 20.3.18 (pilot unhurt); Became 201/2 TDS Cranwell 1.4.18

N5815  (fitted gun) Deld A Flt Cranwell 22.8.17; Freiston by 9.17; Cranwell 31.10.17; COL, slightly damaged 8.12.17; Became 201/2 TDS Cranwell 1.4.18

N5816  Deld C Flt Cranwell for erection 25.8.17; Crashed, propeller and u/c smashed, Plungar 4.1.18; Became 201/2 TDS Cranwell 1.4.18

N5817  Deld C Flt Cranwell for erection 29.8.17; Spun in 16.5.18 (PFO HP Smith seriously injured); Became 201/2 TDS Cranwell 1.4.18

N5818  Deld Manston FS (coded '7') W/E 8.9.17 - @30.3.18

N5819  Deld Manston FS W/E 8.9.17 - @30.3.18

N5820  Deld Hamble to Chingford 13.10.17; B Flt Fairlop by 2.18 - @30.3.18

N5821  Deld Hamble to Chingford 13.10.17; B Flt Fairlop by @30.3.18

N5822  Deld Hamble to Chingford 13.10.17; B Flt Fairlop by 2.18 - @30.3.18

N5823  Deld Hamble to Chingford 13.10.17; Broke port wheel landing 16.11.17 (PFO LF Pendred); O/t landing downwind 2.18 (Lt CL Bailey); B Flt Fairlop by @30.3.18

N5824  Deld Hamble to Chingford 13.10.17; B Flt Fairlop by 2.18; Became 207 TDS Chingford/Fairlop 1.4.18

N5825  Deld Manchester to Redcar School by rail 1.10.17 - @30.3.18

N5826  Deld Manchester to Redcar School by rail 1.10.17 - @30.3.18

N5827  Deld Manchester to Manston FS by rail 4.10.17;

Surveyed 22.10.17; Deleted 26.10.17 wrecked

N5828  Deld Manchester to Manston FS by rail 4.10.17 - 3.18

N5829  (DC) Deld Manchester to Eastbourne by rail 3.10.17; Became 206 TDS Eastbourne 1.4.17

**N5830 to N5859 NOT ALLOTTED (BLANK NUMBERS)**

**50 NIEUPORT TYPE 17bis TRACTOR BIPLANE SCOUTS put forward 12.16, ordered 1.17 under Cont Nos C.P.10093/16 & C.P.100633/16 from Nieuport & General Aircraft Co Ltd, numbered N5860 to N5909 and built Cricklewood. (Ordered with 130-hp Clerget 9B, some delivered with 110 Clerget 9Z)**

N5860  (130-hp) Deld Hendon for erection 24.3.17; Tested 26.3.17; ADD 29.3.17 - @5.4.17; 11 Sqdn by 8.4.17 - @21.4.17; 6 Sqdn by 26.4.17; Wrecked 21.6.17; ADD 21.6.17; Deleted 27.6.17

N5861  (130-hp) Deld Hendon 1.4.17; Tested 7.4.17; ADD 8.4.17; 11 Sqdn 20.4.17; 6 Sqdn 22.4.17; Albatros DV OOC NW of Cambrai 12.00-12.15 6.6.17 (FSL RF Redpath) [but not in his log book!]; still 6 Sqdn 14.6.17; ADD by 21.6.17; Deleted 30.6.17

N5862  (130-hp) Deld Hendon 10.4.17; Accepted 13.4.17; ADD 16.4.17 - @26.4.17; 6 Sqdn by 3.5.17; ADD 5.6.17 (u/s); Allocated CSD survey with view to despatch abroad 28.7.17; still ADD 9.8.17

N5863  (130-hp) Deld Hendon 14.4.17; Tested 26.4.17; Accepted 30.4.17; New centre section fitted on site by Nieuport 17.6.17; Chingford 3.7.17 (transit); Gunnery School Flt Eastchurch 4.7.17; For deletion by 9.2.18

N5864  (130-hp) Deld Hendon for erection 2.5.17; New centre section fitted on site by Nieuport 17.6.17; Gunnery School Flts Eastchurch 23.7.17; Deleted W/E 9.2.18

N5865  Deld Hendon for erection 21.4.17; Accepted, then to ADD 26.4.17; 6 Sqdn W/E 10.5.17; Albatros DV OOC NW of Cambrai 12.15 6.6.17 (F/L GLE Stevens); ADD by 21.6.17; Allocated CSD survey with view to despatch abroad 28.7.17; still ADD 9.8.17

N5866  (130-hp) Deld Hendon for erection 31.5.17; New centre section fitted on site by Nieuport 17.6.17; Cranwell 22.6.17 (arr 23.6.17); Surveyed 16.10.17; Deleted 18.10.17 as GI

N5867  (130-hp) Deld Hendon for erection 14.6.17; New centre section fitted on site by Nieuport 17.6.17; Cranwell 14.7.17 (arr 18.7.17); Surveyed 21.11.17; Deleted 5.12.17 obsolete type

N5868  (130-hp) Deld Hendon for erection 12.6.17; New centre section fitted on site by Nieuport 17.6.17; Gunnery School Flts Eastchurch W/E 24.11.17; For deletion by 9.2.18

N5869  Deld Hendon for erection 20.7.17; Observers School Flt Eastchurch 20.7.17; Destroyed by fire 30.8.17

N5870  (110-hp) Deld Hendon for erection 14.7.17; Gunnery School Flts Eastchurch 20.7.17; Deleted W/E 9.2.18

N5871  (110-hp) Deld Hendon for erection 2.7.17; Observers School Flt Eastchurch 21.7.17 (for defence); Deleted W/E 9.2.18

N5872  (110-hp) Deld Hendon for erection 11.7.17; Observers School Flt Eastchurch 20.7.17 (for defence); Deleted W/E 9.2.18

N5873  (130-hp) (Nieuport 'Baby') Deld Hendon for erection 28.7.17; Dismantling for transport 10.8.17; East Fortune by rail 15.8.17 (arr 17.8.17) (for defence); Surveyed 24.12.17; Deleted 3.1.18 as spares

N5874  (130-hp) Deld Hendon 9.8.17; East Fortune W/E 22.9.17 (for defence); Deleted 3.1.18 as spares; Selected for Museum preservation 4.18, to Agricultural Hall, Isington by 24.8.18, but destroyed post-war

N5875  (110-hp) Deld Hendon for erection 18.8.17; Chingford 27.8.17 (for defence); Became 207 TDS Chingford 1.4.18

N5876  (110-hp) Deld Hendon for erection 26.8.17; Chingford 10.9.17 (for defence); Became 207 TDS Chingford 1.4.18; Old Sarum

N5877  (110-hp) Deld Hendon for erection 1.9.17; Beyond repair by 29.9.17; Surveyed 27.12.17 DBR; Deleted 15.1.18

N5878  (110-hp) (17B) Deld Hendon W/E 8.9.17; Eastbourne 17.9.17; CFS Upavon 19.5.18

N5879  (110-hp) Deld Hendon store 8.9.17; Surveyed 27.12.17 DBR; Deleted 15.1.18

*Nieuport 17bis, possibly N5878, at Yatesbury. (RAF Museum P.8607)*

*Mann, Egerton-built Spad S.VII N6210, probably at Martlesham Heath. (RAF Museum P.4832)*

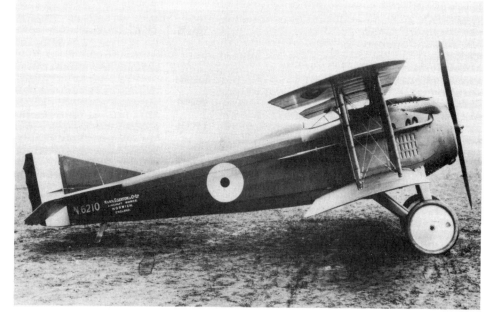

*Maurice Farman Shorthorn N6310, probably at Eastchurch (RAF Museum P.3438)*

N5880 Deld Hendon for erection 14.9.17; Cranwell 29.9.17 (arr 2.10.17); Surveyed 21.11.17; Deleted 5.12.17 obsolete type

N5881 Deld Hendon for erection 14.9.17; Cranwell 29.9.17 (arr 2.10.17); Surveyed 21.11.17; Deleted 5.12.17 obsolete type

N5882 Deld Hendon for erection W/E 22.9.17; Cranwell 30.9.17; Surveyed 21.11.17; Deleted 5.12.17 obsolete type

N5883 Deld Hendon for erection W/E 22.9.17; Cranwell 2.10.17; Surveyed 21.11.17; Deleted 5.12.17 obsolete type

N5884 (130-hp) Deld Hendon store 23.9.17; Surveyed 27.12.17; Deleted 15.1.18 DBR

N5885 (110-hp) Deld Hendon store 27.9.17; Surveyed 27.12.17; Deleted 15.1.18 DBR

N5886 (110-hp) Deld Hendon store 28.9.17; Surveyed 27.12.17; Deleted 15.1.18 DBR

N5887 (110-hp) Deld Hendon store W/E 5.10.17; Surveyed 27.12.17; Deleted 15.1.18 DBR

N5888 (110-hp) Deld Hendon store W/E 5.10.17; Surveyed 27.12.17; Deleted 15.1.18 DBR

N5889 (110-hp) Deld Hendon store W/E 12.10.17; Surveyed 27.12.17; Deleted 15.1.18 DBR

N5890 (110-hp) Deld Hendon store W/E 12.10.17; Surveyed 27.12.17; Deleted 15.1.18 DBR

N5891 Deld Hendon store W/E 12.10.17; Surveyed 27.12.17; Deleted 15.1.18 DBR

N5892 Deld Hendon store W/E 12.10.17; Surveyed 27.12.17; Deleted 15.1.18 DBR

N5893 Deld Hendon store W/E 12.10.17; Surveyed 27.12.17; Deleted 15.1.18 DBR

N5894 Deld Hendon store W/E 12.10.17; Surveyed 27.12.17; Deleted 15.1.18 DBR

N5895 Deld Hendon store W/E 12.10.17; Surveyed 27.12.17; Deleted 15.1.18 DBR

N5896 Deld Hendon store W/E 12.10.17; Surveyed 27.12.17; Deleted 15.1.18 DBR

N5897 Deld Hendon store W/E 12.10.17; Deleted 22.12.17 and to CSD Crystal Palace without engine as GI for carpenters classes

N5898 Deld Hendon store W/E 12.10.17; Surveyed 27.12.17 DBR; Deleted 15.1.18

N5899 Deld Hendon store ex Gosport Works W/E 26.10.17; Surveyed 27.12.17; Deleted 15.1.18 DBR

N5900 Deld Hendon store ex Gosport Works W/E 26.10.17; Surveyed 27.12.17; Deleted 15.1.18 DBR

N5901 Deld Hendon store ex Gosport Works W/E 26.10.17; Surveyed 27.12.17; Deleted 15.1.18 DBR

N5902 Deld Hendon store ex Gosport Works W/E 26.10.17; Surveyed 27.12.17; Deleted 15.1.18 DBR

N5903 Deld Hendon store ex Gosport Works W/E 26.10.17; Surveyed 27.12.17 DBR; Deleted 15.1.18

N5904 Allocated Hendon store 15.10.17; Allocated cancelled 31.10.17

N5905 Allocated Hendon store 15.10.17; Allocated cancelled 31.10.17

N5906 Deld Hendon store W/E 8.12.17; CSD White City 15.12.17; Deleted 21.12.17 and to USA for Lady Drogheda's Exhibition

N5907 Deld Hendon store W/E 8.12.17; Surveyed 27.12.17; Deleted 15.1.18 DBR

N5908 Deld Hendon store W/E 8.12.17; Surveyed 27.12.17; Deleted 15.1.18 DBR

N5909 Deld Hendon store W/E 8.12.17; Surveyed 27.12.17; Deleted 15.1.18 DBR

**25 SOPWITH 1½ STRUTTER TRACTOR BIPLANES to be numbered N5910 to N5934.**

N5910 to N5934 cancelled and 25 Sopwith Triplanes ordered in lieu with same numbers

**25 SOPWITH TRIPLANE SCOUTS ordered 22.12.16 under Cont Nos C.P.138322/16, C.P.21645/17, A.S.1397/17 & A.S.2571/17 from Oakley & Co, numbered N5910 to N5934 & built Ilford. (130-hp Clerget 9B)**

N5910 (Fitted twin Vickers guns) Allocated Dunkerque 12.7.17 (NTU); Deld Hendon W/E 13.10.17; War School Manston W/E 27.10.17 - @6.18 (War Flt)

N5911 (Fitted twin Vickers guns) Deld Hendon W/E 27.10.17;

War School Manston W/E 3.11.17 - @6.4.18; SE Area FIS Shoreham by mid-1918

N5912 Deld Hendon 19.10.17; War School Manston 21.2.18 - 3.18; No.2 Fighting School Marske (coded '94') to at least 12.18; Redcar .19; Preserved post-war; Remains discovered on dump at 2 ASU Cardington 1936; Restored for 1936 Hendon Pageant by F/L Buckle & F/Sgt Scott, also 1937; In store at 5 MU Kemble by 1945; To 39 MU Colerne for refurbishing 1950; SBAC Show Farnborough 9.50; Displayed at Hendon 1951; To Historic Aircraft Store Fulbeck; Renovated by Hawker Siddeley at Dunsfold 1961; Air Historical Branch by 1961; Participated Royal Tournament at Earls Court 1962; To Biggin Hill for storage; FAA Museum Yeovilton by 1964; Refurbished and to RAF Museum Hendon 1972 to date

N5913 to N5929 cancelled 1.11.17 on A.S.28219/17

N5930 to N5931 cancelled by 11.17

N5932 to N5934 for French Govt. N5932 - N5934 (also N5389) cancelled 30.5.17 and replaced by N5384 - N5386 (also N5387)

**N5935 to N5939 NOT ALLOTTED (BLANK NUMBERS)**

**15 SOPWITH 1½ STRUTTER (ADMIRALTY 9700 TYPE) TRACTOR BIPLANES ordered from Sopwith, numbered N5940 to N5954**

N5940 to N5954 cancelled 11.16 (yet tender received W/E 5.1.17)

**N5955 to N5959 NOT ALLOTTED (BLANK NUMBERS)**

**50 AIRCO D.H.4 TRACTOR BIPLANE BOMBERS put forward 1.17 and ordered under Cont No C.P.101977/17 from Westland Aircraft Works, numbered N5960 to N6009 & built Yeovil. (275-hp Eagle) [N5995 onwards had higher u/c]**

N5960 (Twin Vickers guns) Deld Hendon 20.3.17; Martlesham Heath 30.3.17; ADD by 26.4.17; 2 Sqdn 2.5.17; Crashed and wrecked 19.5.17 (FSL JF Chisholm & S/L CS Fox injured); ADD by 24.5.17; Deleted 27.6.17

N5961 (Eagle V) Deld Dover 7.4.17; ADD 7.4.17; 2 Sqdn 16.4.17 - @21.10.17; ADD by 24.10.17 - @24.1.18; 12 Sqdn by 29.1.18 - @23.2.18; ADD by 28.2.18; 5 Sqdn 28.2.18; Albatros OOC in raid on Busigny aerodrome 11.02 18.3.18 (F/Cdr CPO Bartlett & G/L W Naylor); Became 205 Sqdn 1.4.18; Ran into hole on aerodrome landing, wrecked 7.4.18 (Lt L Jolly injured & G/L L James unhurt); Rep Pk 2 ASD 8.4.18; SOC 26.4.18

N5962 (275-hp Eagle VII/V/VII) Deld ADD 4.17; 5 Sqdn 14.5.17 - @15.6.17; ADD by 21.6.17; 5 Sqdn 11.8.17 (Eagle V by 12.17]; Albatros D.V OOC Aertrycke aerodrome 11.40 8.12.17 (FSL E Dickson & AC1 AGL R Shaw); ADD 12.1.18; 2 Sqdn 12.3.18; Became 202 Sqdn 1.4.18; Missing, last seen nr Engel Dump 28.9.18 (Lt R Ringrose & 2/Lt H Hollings both killed); Deleted 15.10.18

N5963 Deld Dover 16.4.17; ADD 20.4.17; 2 Sqdn 29.4.17; Spotting for warship shoot on Zeebrugge, attacked by yellow biplane with dark green crosses, which was shot down into sea 12.5.17 (FSL LN Glaisby & OSL V Greenwood); Escort to 3696 on recce to Ostende, last seen over Oost Dunkerque Bains 1m astern heading for shore 26.5.17 (FSL W Houston-Stewart & OSL CL Haines both killed)

N5964 (Eagle V) Deld ADD 4.17; 2 Sqdn 26.4.17; ADD by 24.5.17; 2 Sqdn 26.6.17; ADD by 9.9.17; 2 Sqdn 23.9.17; ADD by road 7.12.17; 12 Sqdn W/E 7.2.18; 2 Sqdn 8.3.18; COL 12.3.18 (FSL AG Storey); Wrecked, 18.3.18; Still 2 Sqdn 21.3.18; ADD 25.3.18; 4 ASD Guines 28.3.18; Deleted 8.4.18

N5965 (Eagle V) Deld ADD by 3.5.17; 2 Sqdn 10.5.17; COL 22.8.17 (FSL ECR Stoneman); ADD by 23.8.17; 2 Sqdn 8.9.17; Fuel tank holed by flak, FL on beach, nosed up La Panne 24.1.18 (FSL FS Russell & Observer unhurt); Flying escort to N5997 contact lost at 16.45 and went in sea off La Panne 11.3.18 (FSL CG Macdonald & G/L AAM1 PJ Capp both drowned); Wreckage picked up 16.3.18; Deleted 18.3.18

N5966 (Eagle V) Deld ADD (via Bournemouth and Dover) 29.4.17; 2 Sqdn 19.5.17 - @2.6.17; ADD by 7.6.17; 2

N5967 Sqdn 24.7.17 - @3.9.17; ADD by 6.9.17; 2 Sqdn (coded 'E') by 4.10.17; Became 202 Sqdn 1.4.18; LM 6.4.18; NFT

N5967 (Eagle VI) Deld ADD (via Dover) 29.4.17; 5 Sqdn 30.4.17; COL 9.9.17 (FSL CH Pownall & AC2 CS Osborn); ADD by 13.9.17; 5 Sqdn (coded 'A1') 23.9.17; Eagle V by 12.17; Swung on TO, hit bomb dump, wrecked 10.3.18 (FSL NA Taylerson & AGL GE Daffey unhurt); still 5 Sqdn 21.3.18; 4 ASD Guines by 30.3.18; 2 ASD 4.18; Rep Pk 1 ASD 4.18; SOC 8.4.18

N5968 (Eagle VII) Deld ADD 5.8.17; 5 Sqdn 9.8.17; Crashed and destroyed by fire nr Houthulst Forest 13.1.18 (FSL H Willis DoI & AGL AM2 A Foster injured); Deleted 21.1.18

N5969 (Eagle V later VI) Deld ADD by 10.5.17; 2 Sqdn (coded 'K') by 12.5.17; HA OOC 8.8.17 (F/L FE Sandford & F/L OGL Pickup); Became 202 Sqdn 1.4.18; HA OOC 2.5.18 (FSL LF Pendred & Lt NH Jenkins); Albatros DV in flames 17.45 9.5.18 (Lt RHV Fowler & Lt IH McClure) [but this aircraft also claimed by C66 of 213 Sqdn]; Ferried to 98 Demobilisation Sqdn but EF at 1,000 ft en route, FL Setques Pool Pilots' Range, u/c sank in hole 15.3.19 (2/Lt PR Spivey); Retd 1 AD salvage 17.3.19

N5970 Transferred to RFC (Military Wing) as B3955

N5971 (Eagle VI) Deld ADD by 5.17; 5 Sqdn 10.5.17; Attacked by HA during raid on Aertrycke aerodrome 20.7.17 (FSL LN Glaisby & AM2 LV Saw both wounded); ADD by 26.7.17; 5 Sqdn (coded 'G') by 2.8.17; ADD W/E 30.8.17; 5 Sqdn by 4.10.17; Damaged in collision with Capt Bailey 12.3.18; ADD by 14.3.18; 4 ASD Guines 28.3.18; Deleted 8.4.18

N5972 (Fitted twin Vickers and Lewis gun) (Eagle VI) Deld ADD by 5.17; 2 Sqdn (coded 'J') 23.5.17 - @27.5.17; ADD by 31.5.17; 2 Sqdn 5.7.17; Crashed on ridge landing Bergues 6.3.18 (FSL LH Pearson); Smashed in collision 21.3.18; ADD 23.3.18; 4 ASD Guines 28.3.18; Deleted 8.4.18

N5973 Deld Eastbourne 16.5.17 (transit); Dover 17.5.17; ADD 19.5.17; 2 Sqdn 9.6.17; COL 27.6.17 (FSL AC Jones killed & OSL CB Orfeur DoI 1.7.17); Deleted ADD 20.8.17

N5974 (Eagle VI to 12.17; To Eagle V 1.18) Deld ADD by 5.17; 5 Sqdn 23.5.17; Attacked by Albatros returning from raid on Ghistelles aerodrome 7.7.17 (Pilot unhurt & LM WJ Edwards wounded); Attacked by HA returning from raid on Aertrycke aerodrome 20.7.17 (FSL WF Cleghorn unhurt & AM1 G/L WR Burdett wounded); ADD by 26.7.17; 5 Sqdn 30.7.17; Crashed 27.1.18; ADD by 31.1.18; Deleted 18.2.18 wrecked

N5975 Shipped to Aegean; 2 Wing Imbros by 1.12.17 - @1.1.18; Marsh by 13.3.18; Imbros by 24.3.18; Mudros by 3.18 - 4.18; C Sqdn 2 Wing Imbros; Repair Base Mudros by 6.18; F Sqdn 62 Wing, tested 22.7.18; Mudros 24.7.18; Mudros by 7.18 - @30.1.19

N5976 Shipped to Aegean; Imbros by 1.12.17; Marsh by 1.1.18 - @2.3.18 (250-hp Eagle); Imbros by 24.3.18 - 4.18; Repair Base by 6.18; C Sqdn 2 Wing Imbros; F Sqdn 62 Wing Mudros by 8.18; 62 Wing Marsh by 10.18; Repair Base Mudros by 10.18; 222 Sqdn Mudros/San Stefano by 14.11.18

N5977 (Twin Vickers guns) (Eagle VIII later V) Deld Dover 25.5.17; ADD 26.5.17; 5 Sqdn 28.5.17 - @6.7.17; ADD by 12.7.17; 5 Sqdn 30.7.17 - @11.8.17; ADD by 16.8.17; 5 Sqdn 11.9.17 - @4.12.17; Damaged and forced down at Frontier airfield 21.9.17 (FSL NP Playford slightly wounded); NADD by 13.12.17 - @31.12.17; 12 Sqdn by 7.2.18; 17 Sqdn 8.3.18; Became 217 Sqdn 1.4.18; Crashed 4.5.18; 4 ASD Guines 5.5.18; 11 AP to 202 Sqdn 15.3.19 (transit); 98 Sqdn 16.3.19; 1 ASD 18.3.19; To England 18.3.19

N5978 (Twin Vickers guns) Deld ADD (via Dover) 26.5.17; 5 Sqdn (coded 'B3') 28.5.17; Yellow Albatros shot down after bombing Aertrycke aerodrome 20.7.17 (F/Cdr INC Clarke DSC & O/L RS St.John); ADD by 26.7.17 - @23.8.17; 5 Sqdn by 30.8.17; Crashed 19.11.17; ADD 20.11.17 - @22.11.17; Deleted 29.11.17

N5979 Deld ADD by 31.5.17; 2 Sqdn 2.6.17; Crashed and wrecked on TO 8.6.17 (F/L GE Harvey & AAM1 G/L W Bowman); ADD by 14.6.17; Deleted 27.6.17

N5980 Transferred to RFC (Military Wing) as B3956

N5981 Deld ADD by 31.5.17; 2 Sqdn 5.6.17; Crashed on TO, landed on French Sopwith Triplane F17, both wrecked 27.6.17 (FSL LN Glaisby & OSL V Greenwood); ADD 28.6.17; Deleted 20.8.17

N5982 (Eagle VI) Deld ADD by 14.6.17; 5 Sqdn 18.6.17; Shot away 2 propeller blades testing gun after raid on Sparappelhoek aerodrome 23.7.17 (F/Cdr RJ Slade and observer killed); Shot down during raid on Oostcamp 30.1.18 (FSL FTP Williams & AC1 G/L CA Leitch both killed); Deleted 4.2.18

N5983 Deld ADD by 7.6.17; 2 Sqdn 13.6.17; COL and wrecked 21.8.17 (F/L CJ Wyatt & OSL AI Hutt both killed); Deleted ADD 3.9.17

N5984 Allocated Mudros 1.5.17; Shipped to Aegean; D Sqdn 2 Wing Stavros by 29.11.17 - @1.1.18; Marsh by 13.3.18; Imbros by 20.3.18; G Sqdn by 3.18 - 5.18; F Sqdn by 6.18

N5985 (Eagle VI) Deld Hendon (via Eastbourne) 15.6.17; ADD 17.6.17; 2 Sqdn 20.6.17; ADD 6.17; 2 Sqdn 25.6.17; Fuel tank hit by shrapnel, FL La Panne 24.1.18 (retd 25.1.18); Became 202 Sqdn 1.4.18; Attacked by 2 Albatros, FL Bray Dunes, o/t in water, badly damaged 18.20 4.5.18 (Lt JP Everitt seriously wounded & Lt WR Stennett killed); Salved, to 4 ASD, still there 31.5.18; Taken in hand at 4 ASD 15.10.18; Awaiting reconstruction 26.10.18; NFT

N5986 Transferred to RFC (Military Wing) as B3957
N5987 Transferred to RFC (Military Wing) as B3958
N5988 (Eagle VI later VIII) Deld ADD by 7.17; 5 Sqdn 2.7.17 - @28.2.18; ADD by 3.18; 2 Sqdn (coded 'K') 12.3.18; FL on beach W of Nieuport 24.3.18; Became 202 Sqdn (coded 'K') 1.4.18; To 233 Sqdn Dover but arrived in dark, FL, damaged Westcliffe Golf Links, St.Margarets Bay 6.3.19 (2/Lt E Tompkins unhurt); WOC 19.3.19

N5989 (Eagle VII) Deld Hendon 21.6.17; Dover 23.6.17; ADD 24.6.17; 2 Sqdn (coded 'L') by 28.6.17; Became 202 Sqdn (coded 'L') 1.4.18; In action with EA nr Zeebrugge, petrol tank hit, badly damaged 4.5.18 (Capt GW Biles uninjured, Lt EE Gowing seriously wounded); For repair; Retd 202 Sqdn, COL 18.7.18 (2/Lt AC Reeman unhurt); 4 ASD 20.7.18

N5990 Transferred to RFC (Military Wing) as B3959
N5991 Transferred to RFC (Military Wing) as B3960
N5992 (Eagle VI) Deld Dover 1.7.17; ADD 2.7.17; 5 Sqdn 14.7.17; ADD by 26.7.17; 5 Sqdn (coded 'B5') 20.8.17; Crashed W/E 15.11.17; EF en route bombing raid on Aertrycke aerodrome, FL on beach, crashed 1,000 yds W of Nieuport 27.1.18 (FSL FTP Williams); Crashed in action 30.3.18 (FSL CJ Heywood uninjured, AGL TW Jones wounded); SOC Repair Pk 2 ASD 4.4.18

N5993 (Eagle V) Deld Dover 1.7.17; ADD 2.7.17; 5 Sqdn 20.7.17; Eagle VI by 12.17; ADD 27.2.18; 2 Sqdn 13.3.18; Became 202 Sqdn 1.4.18; Scout OOC smoking 19.15 4.6.18 (Lt HS Round & Pte1 AE Humphrey); Dived into sea 2km E of Loon Plage, nr Calais road 10.8.18 (2/Lt AC Reeman & Pte1 WG Shepherd both killed); Wreckage to 4 ASD 11.8.18; Deleted 15.8.18

N5994 Transferred to RFC (Military Wing) as B3961
N5995 Transferred to RFC (Military Wing) as B3962
N5996 (Eagle V) Deld ADD by 12.7.17; 5 Sqdn 13.7.17; Crashed W/E 5.11.17; Crashed W/E 15.11.17; NADD W/E 6.12.17; 5 Sqdn 22.2.18; ADD W/E 7.3.18; 4 ASD Guines 28.3.18; 202 Sqdn (coded 'E') 18.5.18; 1 black scout shot down into sea 1m off Zeebrugge Mole 19.15 4.6.18 (Lt AL Godfrey & 2/Lt E Darby DSM); Combat with 5 Pfalz at Middelkerke 27.6.18 (Lt JF Moffett USNR unhurt & Lt WD Jeans wounded); FL beach 500 yds E of Zuydcoote Semaphore 28.6.18; Retd 4 ASD 28.6.18 (now Eagle VII)

N5997 (Eagle VI) Deld ADD 7.17; 2 Sqdn (coded 'M', with zig-zag on fuselage and nose-thumbing devil on fin) 12.7.17; Became 202 Sqdn (coded 'M') 1.4.18; Albatros D.V OOC 6m WNW of Ostende 06.55 2.4.18 (Capt CR Vaughan & Lt IH McClure); Seaplane in sea 10m off Ostende 10.10 3.6.18 (Lt AL Godfrey & 2/Lt C Taylor); In combat off Zeebrugge 4.6.18 (Lt JP Everitt unhurt & Lt IH McClure seriously wounded); Repaired on sqdn; 1-str into sea off Ostende, then EF, FL ½m E of La Panne 17.6.18 (Lt HS Round & 2/Lt W Taylor); Shot down into sea by m/g fire over Zeebrugge Mole during bombing raid on Zeebrugge 18.10.18 (F/L R Coulthard

& 2/Lt L Timmins); Deleted 31.10.18

N5998    Transferred to RFC (Military Wing) as B3963

N5999    Transferred to RFC (Military Wing) as B3964

N6000    (Eagle VI) Deld ADD (via Dover) 10.7.17; 5 Sqdn (coded 'B1') 13.7.17; Albatros DV OOC Ostende-Blankenberghe 12.10 17.2.18; Albatros DV OOC St.Pierre Capelle c.13.00 18.2.18 (both F/L E Dickson & AGL W Naylor); Tested after crash 9.3.18; HA OOC Honnecourt 21.3.18; Albatros DV crashed 10.45 27.3.18 (both F/Cdr CPO Bartlett DSC & AGL W Naylor); Became 205 Sqdn 1.4.18; Pfalz OOC 10.15 1.4.18 (Capt CPO Bartlett DSC & AGL W Naylor); Attacked by 2 scouts, 1 red/black/white Pfalz with stripes over wings sent down in steep dive smoking 13.50 7.4.18 (Capt CR Lupton DFC & AGL 1AM AG Wood); Crashed 12.4.18 (Capt CPO Bartlett & G/L Jackson); Rudder controls shot away, FL, hit telegraph wires nr Corbie 17.4.18 (Capt CR Lupton DFC & AGL AG Wood both unhurt); For 2 ASD

N6001    (Eagle VI) Deld ADD 23.7.17; 5 Sqdn 24.7.17; Albatros DV crashed & another OOC Busigny aerodrome and dump c.11.00 16.3.18 (F/L SR Watkins & S/Cdr SJ Goble DSO, DSC); Attacked by 5 Pfalz, 1 shot down by rear gun, then 2 Fokker DrIs manoeuvring on to its tail collided and fell locked together, catching fire on crashing Rannecourt 10.00 28.3.18 (F/Cdr CPO Bartlett & AGL W Naylor); Became 205 Sqdn 1.4.18; Retd early with engine trouble, COL 16.15 12.4.18 (Lt R Chalmers & Lt JEH Chadwick unhurt); To 2 Salvage Dump 15.4.18; SOC Rep Pk 2 ASD 26.4.18

N6002    Transferred to RFC (Military Wing) as B3965

N6003    Transferred to RFC (Military Wing) as B3966

N6004    (Twin Vickers guns) (Eagle VI) Deld ADD (via Dover) 24.7.17; 5 Sqdn (coded 'B35') 24.7.17; Fokker DrI destroyed 09.12 30.3.18 (F/Lt J Gamon & OSL FH Stringer); Became 205 Sqdn 1.4.18; Fokker Dr.I in flames, then Pfalz OOC Chaulnes Rly Stn 19.50 23.4.18 (Capt J Gamon & Lt R Scott); Pfalz DIII crashed nr Mericourt, brought down by concerted fire from rear gunners of 8 machines in tight formation 08.30 20.5.18 (Capt J Gamon & Sgt J Jones); Crashed into by D9620 on aerodrome 11.6.18 (Capt J Gamon & Sgt PL Richards unhurt); 2 ASD 12.6.18; SOC 26.6.18 NWR

N6005    (Eagle VI) Deld ADD (via Eastchurch & Dover) 29.7.17; 5 Sqdn 30.7.17 - @4.12.17; NADD by 6.12.17; 5 Sqdn 17.2.18; 1 NAP Dunkerque 21.2.18; 5 Sqdn, 27.2.18; Albatros DV OOC Mont D'Origny aerodrome 10.30-10.45 9.3.18 (FSL GE Siedle & Sgt AGL WJH Middleton); Combat damage, FL nr Doullens after raid on Busigny Dump 16.3.18 (FSL GM Cartmel & AGL AM1 RB Wilcox both injured); For survey by 21.3.18; SOC 8.4.18 NWR

N6006    Transferred to RFC (Military Wing) as B3967

N6007    Transferred to RFC (Military Wing) as B3968 (NTU); Deld ADD by 8.17; 5 Sqdn 9.8.17; Crashed 16.8.17 (FSL AH Garland & G/L EG Symonds injured); ADD by 23.8.17; Destroyed by fire on night of 1.10.17; Surveyed 17.10.17; Deleted 23.10.17 burnt

N6008    Deld ADD (via Dover) 9.8.17; 5 Sqdn 9.8.17; Crashed in sea on bombing raid 19.12.17 (FSL SS Richardson & AC1 G/L RA Furby both killed); Surveyed 24.12.17; Deleted 28.12.17 lost

N6009    (Eagle VII by 12.17 - 2.18, later Eagle VIII) Deld ADD by 2.8.17; 5 Sqdn by 13.8.17; Crashed by 10.1.18; 2 HA shot down in raid on Busigny aerodrome & dump, shared A7644 09.44-11.48 16.3.18 (F/Cdr CR Lupton DSC & AGL Smith); HA claimed shot down (endorsed indecisive) 18.3.18 (FSL GE Siedle & Sgt AGL WJH Middleton); Albatros DV OOC SW of Vendhuile 15.20 22.3.18 (F/Cdr CR Lupton DSC & 1AM AGL AG Wood); Became 205 Sqdn 1.4.18; BU over Amiens returning from raid on Chaulnes Rly Stn 9.5.18 (Capt CR Lupton DSC & G/L 1AM AG Wood both killed)

**20 AVRO 504B (ADMIRALTY 179 DUAL TYPE) TRACTOR BIPLANES** ordered 1.17 (later 29.7.17) under Cont Nos A.S.19202 & C.P.139233/16 from George Parnall & Co Ltd, numbered N6010 to N6029 & built Bristol. Fitted to carry 4x16-lb bombs. (80-hp Gnome)

N6010    (fitted gun) Deld Killingholme 24.2.17; Cranwell 24.4.17; Crashed 17.8.17; U/c damaged 2.10.17; Deleted W/E 2.11.17

N6011    Deld Killingholme 26.2.17; Cranwell 10.7.17 (transit); Chingford 11.7.17; Crashed 21.7.17; Deleted 23.7.17

N6012    Deld Killingholme 9.3.17; Chingford 8.5.17; Deleted W/E 26.1.18

N6013    Deld Killingholme by 4.17; Chingford 9.5.17; Deleted 22.7.17

N6014    Deld Killingholme for erection 31.3.17; Chingford 29.4.17 (transit); Manston 30.4.17; Deleted 29.9.17

N6015    Transferred to RFC (Military Wing) as A9975

N6016    Transferred to RFC (Military Wing) as A9976

N6017    Transferred to RFC (Military Wing) as A9977

N6018    Transferred to RFC (Military Wing) as B382

N6019    Transferred to RFC (Military Wing) as B383

N6020    Transferred to RFC (Military Wing) as B384

N6021    Transferred to RFC (Military Wing) as B385

N6022    Transferred to RFC (Military Wing) as B389

N6023    Transferred to RFC (Military Wing) as B390

N6024    Transferred to RFC (Military Wing) as B391

N6025    Transferred to RFC (Military Wing) as B392

N6026    Transferred to RFC (Military Wing) as B395

N6027    (C/n P.79?) Transferred to RFC (Military Wing) as B396

N6028    Transferred to RFC (Military Wing) 4.17 as B1390

N6029    Transferred to RFC (Military Wing) 4.17 as B1391

**50 SPAD S.7C.1 TRACTOR BIPLANE SCOUTS** ordered 12.16 from Nieuport & General Aircraft Co Ltd, to be numbered N6030 to N6079 & built Cricklewood. (150-hp Hispano-Suiza 8A)

N6030 to N6079 cancelled and serials reallotted

**50 ROYAL AIRCRAFT FACTORY S.E.5a TRACTOR BIPLANE FIGHTERS** ordered 2.17 from The British Caudron Co Ltd, to be numbered N6030.

N6030 to N6079 cancelled and serials reallotted

**50 NIEUPORT TYPE 17bis TRACTOR BIPLANE SCOUTS** ordered 3.17 from Nieuport & General Aircraft Co Ltd, to be numbered N6030 to N6079 & built Cricklewood (130-hp Clerget)

N6030 to N6079 cancelled

**50 SPAD S.7C.1** ordered mid 12.16 from Man, Egerton & Co Ltd, to be numbered N6080 to N6129 and built Norwich. (150-hp Hispano-Suiza)

N6080 to N6129 cancelled and apparently superseded by N6210 to N6284

**30 SOPWITH PUP TRACTOR BIPLANE SCOUTS** ordered 7.6.16 under Cont No C.P.128681 from Sir William Beardmore & Co Ltd, to be numbered N6100 to N6129 & built Dalmuir

N6100 to N6129 cancelled and order changed to W.B.III

**30 BEARDMORE W.B.III TRACTOR BIPLANE SHIP-PLANES** ordered 12.2.17 under Cont Nos A.S.775/17 & A.S.14757 from Sir William Beardmore & Co Ltd, numbered N6100 to N6129 & built Dalmuir. (80-hp Le Rhône 9c unless otherwise stated) [N6101 and N6102 S.B.IIIF with folding u/c, remainder S.B.IIID with dropping u/c. These designations promulgated in AWO 2499/17 dated 6.7.17] [N6100 to N6112 believed originally to have been S.B.IIIF with folding wings]

N6100    Allocated Vickers 5.6.17; Deld Rosyth W/E 3.11.17; Donibristle W/E 9.11.17; HMS *Cassandra* 3.12.17; Donibristle 21.3.18; HMS *Nairana* W/E 27.4.18; Rosyth W/E 2.5.18; HMS *Nairana* W/E 2.5.18; Donibristle to HMS *Nairana* W/E 2.5.18; To Turnhouse 5.18; Rosyth to HMS *Nairana* W/E 9.5.18; Donibristle W/E 9.5.18; For deletion by 15.8.18

N6101    Deld East Fortune 15.7.17; HMS *Manxman* 24.7.17; East Fortune 27.7.17; U/c broken on landing 10.10.17 (F/Cdr JCP Wood); Deleted W/E 9.3.18

N6102    Deld ECD Grain for erection 24.7.17; Type test 6.8.17 (S/Cdr HR Busteed); Tested with jettisonable u/c; Acceptance Dept Grain W/E 1.12.17; Rosyth by rail 12.12.17; Donibristle W/E 28.12.17; Turnhouse W/E 21.2.18 - @30.1.19

N6103    Accepted at Mkrs 10.7.17 (Dukinfield Jones); Erecting Grain from/by 26.7.17; Tested 28.7.17; Fitting 100hp Gnome Monosoupape 27.8.17; Acceptance Dept Grain W/E 1.12.17; Rosyth by 18.1.18 (ex Port Victoria); East Fortune W/E 31.1.18 (training); Deleted W/E 27.6.18

N6104    Allocated HMS *Cassandra* 21.6.17 (NTU?); Deld HMS *Pegasus* W/E 27.8.17; Transport to Turnhouse 1.9.17; Donibristle by 5.10.17; Rosyth W/E 8.11.17

N6105    Deld HMS *Pegasus* W/E 27.8.17; Transport to Turnhouse 1.9.17; Donibristle by 5.10.17; Rosyth W/E 8.11.17; Surveyed 2.11.17; Deleted 6.11.17 for spares

N6106    Deld HMS *Pegasus* W/E 27.8.17; Transport to Turnhouse 1.9.17; Donibristle by 25.10.17; Rosyth W/E 8.11.17; Surveyed 2.11.17; Deleted 6.11.17 for spares

N6107    Deld HMS *Pegasus* W/E 27.8.17; Transport to Turnhouse 1.9.17; Donibristle by 5.10.17; Rosyth W/E 27.10.17; Surveyed 2.11.17; Deleted 6.11.17 for spares

N6108    Deld Donibristle W/E 5.10.17; Beardmore 18.10.17 (ex??); Rosyth by 2.11.17; Surveyed 2.11.17; Deleted 6.11.17 for spares

N6109    Deld by rail to East Fortune 10.10.17; Donibristle W/E 3.11.17; HMS *Pegasus* (via Rosyth) W/E 10.11.17; Rosyth W/E 16.11.17; Donibristle to HMS *Nairana* 7.12.17; Rosyth to HMS *Nairana* W/E 7.11.17; HMS *Renown* W/E 14.12.17; Unsuccessful attempt to fly from ships forecastle 12.17; Rosyth W/E 21.12.17; Surveyed 16.12.17; Deleted 22.12.17 wrecked

N6110    Deld Donibristle W/E 5.10.17; Rosyth W/E 27.10.17; Surveyed 2.11.17; Deleted 6.11.17 for spares

N6111    Deld Donibristle W/E 27.10.17; Rosyth W/E 13.12.17; Surveyed 12.12.17; Deleted 19.12.17 wrecked

N6112    Deld Donibristle W/E 27.10.17; Turnhouse W/E 9.3.18; HMS *Nairana* W/E 20.4.18; Donibristle W/E 2.5.18; Turnhouse W/E 2.5.18; Donibristle W/E 23.5.18; For deletion by 29.8.18

N6113    Donibristle by 27.10.17; HMS *Nairana* W/E 25.1.18; Donibristle W/E 7.2.18; Rosyth W/E 16.2.18; HMS *Nairana* W/E 28.2.18; Donibristle W/E 16.3.18; Rosyth W/E 16.5.18; HMS *Pegasus* W/E 23.5.18; Donibristle W/E 23.5.18; For deletion W/E 15.9.18

N6114    Deld Rosyth W/E 10.10.17; Donibristle W/E 15.11.17; Rosyth W/E 23.11.17; Donibristle W/E 28.12.17; HMS *Pegasus* 15.3.18; Rosyth 18.3.18 Donibristle W/E 21.3.18; Rosyth 3.18; Donibristle W/E 4.4.18; Rosyth W/E 20.4.18; HMS *Nairana* W/E 2.5.18; Rosyth W/E 2.5.18; HMS *Nairana* W/E 9.5.18; Rosyth W/E 9.5.18; HMS *Nairana* to Donibristle W/E 9.5.18; HMS *Nairana* W/E 16.5.18; Rosyth W/E 16.5.18; HMS *Nairana* W/E 16.5.18; HMS *Pegasus* W/E 16.5.18; Rosyth W/E 16.5.18; Donibristle to Rosyth W/E 16.5.18 (twice); Rosyth to Donibristle W/E 23.5.18; Deleted W/E 1.8.18

N6115    Deld Donibristle W/E 10.10.17; HMS *Nairana* W/E 30.11.17; HMS *Renown* 11.17; Rosyth W/E 7.12.17; HMS *Nairana* 20.12.17; HMS *Princess Royal* by 1.18; HMS *Pegasus* 1.18; Donibristle W/E 4.1.18; Rosyth W/E 18.1.18; Donibristle to Rosyth again W/E 18.1.18; HMS *Nairana* W/E 17.1.18; Donibristle W/E 31.1.18; For deletion W/E 15.8.18

N6116    Donibristle by 27.10.17; HMS *Nairana* W/E 30.11.17; ALSO Rosyth to HMS *Nairana* W/E 30.11.17; HMS *Renown* 14.12.17; Rosyth W/E 21.12.17; HMS *Nairana* to Rosyth W/E 20.12.17; Donibristle W/E 11.1.18 - @23.2.18; HMS *Nairana* 2.18; Rosyth W/E 28.2.18; Turnhouse by 30.3.18; Deleted 1.8.18; To Agricultural Hall, Islington by 24.8.18

N6117    Deld Grain Test Depot 17.10.17; Deleted 3.1.18 wrecked

N6118    Deld Rosyth W/E 27.10.17; Turnhouse W/E 21.3.18; Deleted W/E 11.7.18

N6119    Deld Donibristle W/E 27.10.17; Rosyth W/E 23.11.17; HMS *Pegasus* 12.17; Rosyth W/E 20.12.17; Surveyed 22.12.17; Deleted 31.12.17 wrecked

N6120    Deld Rosyth W/E 27.10.17; Donibristle W/E 22.11.17; Rosyth W/E 28.3.18; HMS *Nairana* W/E 28.3.18; Rosyth to HMS *Pegasus* W/E 28.3.18; Donibristle 4.4.18; Turnhouse by 4.18; HMS *Nairana* by 4.18;

Donibristle W/E 4.4.18; HMS *Nairana* by 5.4.18; Rosyth 5.18; Turnhouse W/E 9.5.18; Deleted W/E 4.7.18

N6121    Deld Donibristle W/E 27.10.17; HMS *Pegasus* W/E 13.12.17; Rosyth to HMS *Pegasus* W/E 14.12.17 - @17.12.17; Rosyth W/E 20.12.17; HMS *Nairana* W/E 21.12.17; Donibristle W/E 28.12.17; HMS *Pegasus* to Donibristle W/E 28.12.17; Rosyth W/E 4.4.18; Donibristle W/E 2.5.18; For deletion W/E 15.8.18

N6122    Deld Rosyth W/E 27.10.17; Donibristle W/E 15.11.17; HMS *Nairana* W/E 30.11.17; Rosyth W/E 7.12.17; Donibristle 11.1.18; East Fortune NFS W/E 31.1.18 (training); For deletion W/E 27.6.18

N6123    Deld Rosyth for erection W/E 27.10.17; Donibristle W/E 25.1.18; HMS *Pegasus* W/E 15.2.18 [@15.2.18]; Rosyth W/E 15.2.18; HMS *Dublin* to Rosyth W/E 15.2.18; HMS *Pegasus* W/E 15.2.18; Donibristle W/E 21.2.18; HMS *Pegasus* by 15.3.18; Donibristle 18.3.18; HMS *Nairana* W/E 28.3.18; Donibristle W/E 4.4.18; Rosyth W/E 4.4.18; HMS *Pegasus* W/E 4.4.18; W/E 4.4.18 = Donibristle ex *Nairana*, *Nairana*, *Pegasus*, *Nairana*, *Pegasus* ALSO Donibristle to Rosyth, *Nairana*, *Pegasus*, *Nairana* [i.e a series of movements to and from Donibristle, exact details not clear in records]; Rosyth to HMS *Nairana* W/E 2.5.18; Rosyth W/E 2.5.18; HMS *Nairana* W/E 9.5.18; Donibristle W/E 9.5.18; HMS *Nairana* W/E 9.5.18; Donibristle to Rosyth W/E 16.5.18 (twice); to HMS *Nairana* W/E 16.5.18; Donibristle W/E 16.5.18; Rosyth to HMS *Pegasus* W/E 16.5.18; Rosyth W/E 16.5.18; HMS *Nairana* to Donibristle W/E 23.5.18; HMS *Pegasus* W/E 23.5.18; HMS *Pegasus* to Donibristle W/E 23.5.18 (twice); Donibristle to Rosyth W/E 23.5.18 (twice); Rosyth to HMS *Pegasus* W/E 23.5.18; Rosyth by 6.18; Donibristle 8.18 W/E 15.8.18; Deleted W/E 12.9.18

N6124    Deld Rosyth W/E 3.11.17; Donibristle W/E 25.1.18; ALSO Rosyth to HMS *Nairana* W/E 25.1.18; Donibristle W/E 26.1.18; HMS *Nairana* W/E 31.1.18; Donibristle W/E 21.2.18 - @23.2.18; HMS *Nairana* to Donibristle W/E 28.2.18; For deletion W/E 15.8.18

N6125    (80-hp Clerget) Deld Rosyth W/E 3.11.17; Donibristle W/E 15.11.17; HMS *Pegasus* W/E 13.12.17 - @17.12.17; Rosyth W/E 20.12.17; Donibristle W/E 28.12.17; HMS *Nairana* W/E 8.2.18; Turnhouse W/E 9.3.18 (for HMS *Nairana*); HMS *Nairana* from 3.18; Turnhouse by 30.3.18; Donibristle W/E 4.4.18; Rosyth W/E 20.4.18; Turnhouse W/E 9.5.18; Deleted W/E 27.6.18

N6126    Deld Rosyth W/E 3.11.17; Donibristle W/E 15.11.17; HMS *Pegasus* W/E 28.12.17; Donibristle to Rosyth W/E 28.12.17; Donibristle @29.12.17; HMS *Pegasus* by 31.12.17 - @7.1.18; Rosyth by @11.1.18 - @18.1.18; For deletion W/E 19.1.18

N6127    Deld Rosyth W/E 3.11.17; Donibristle W/E 15.11.17; HMS *Pegasus* W/E 13.12.17; HMS *Phaeton* 11.12.17; Rosyth W/E 20.12.17; Donibristle W/E 31.1.18; East Fortune W/E 16.2.18 (training); Deleted W/E 2.3.18

N6128    Deld Rosyth W/E 3.11.17; Rosyth by 28.12.17 - @19.1.18; Donibristle by 8.2.18; HMS *Pegasus* W/E 15.2.18 - @16.3.18; Donibristle @23.2.18; HMS *Pegasus* by 3.18; Donibristle 18.3.18; HMS *Cassandra* 21.3.18; HMS *Cassandra* 29.3.18; Donibristle W/E 9.5.18; HMS *Cassandra* W/E 9.5.18; Rosyth to HMS *Cassandra* W/E 9.5.18; Donibristle by 25.5.18; HMS *Cassandra* W/E 13.6.18; Turnhouse W/E 11.7.18; Deleted W/E 25.7.18

N6129    Deld Rosyth W/E 9.11.17; Donibristle W/E 28.12.17; HMS *Nairana* W/E 4.1.18; HMS *Pegasus* to Donibristle W/E 3.1.18; HMS *Pegasus* 3.1.18; HMS *Yarmouth* W/E 31.1.18; HMS *Nairana* W/E 7.2.18; Scapa W/E 7.2.18; Houton Bay W/E 16.2.18 (overhaul) Scapa W/E 18.5.18; Smoogroo W/E 12.9.18; Scapa W/E 21.11.18 - @30.1.19

**30 AVRO 504B (ADMIRALTY 179 DUAL TYPE) DUAL CONTROL TRACTOR BIPLANES** ordered 22.7.16 as armament trainers from The Sunbeam Motor Co Ltd under Cont No C.P.139209/16 dated 30.12.16, numbered N6130 to N6159 & built Wolverhampton. Fitted to carry 4x16-lb bombs. Interrupter gear. (80-hp Gnome)

N6130    Deld Killingholme store for erection 10.2.17; Chingford 30.4.17 (transit); Manston FS 1.5.17; Deleted 31.7.17 (ex overhaul)

N6131    Deld Killingholme store for erection 10.2.17; Chingford 30.4.17 (transit); Manston FS 1.5.17; Wrecked 21.8.17; Deleted 1.9.17

N6132    Deld Killingholme store for erection 10.2.17; Manston FS (via Chingford) 3.5.17; Damaged 22.8.17; Surveyed 27.9.17; Deleted 1.10.17 wrecked

N6133    Deld Chingford by rail 31.1.17; Surveyed 24.3.17; Deleted 1.4.17

N6134    Deld Chingford 31.1.17; EF, FL in field nr reservoir, EF and crashed on TO from field over hedge and railway lines 1.3.17 (FSL EW Keesey); Deleted 23.7.17

N6135    Deld Chingford 3.2.17; EF, FL in field nr lower reservoir 27.2.17 (FSL EW Keesey); Badly damaged 25.6.17; W/E 29.9.17

N6136    Deld Chingford 3.2.17; Deleted 22.7.17

N6137    Deld Chingford 5.2.17; Deleted 9.5.17

N6138    Deld Killingholme store for erection 24.2.17; Manston FS 30.4.17; Wrecked 7.8.17; Deleted 18.8.17

N6139    Deld Killingholme store for erection 24.2.17; Chingford 30.4.17 (transit); Manston FS 1.5.17 - @30.3.18

N6140    Deld Killingholme store for erection 24.2.17; Manston (via Chingford) 3.5.17; Surveyed 22.10.17; Deleted 26.10.17 wrecked

N6141    Deld Killingholme store for erection 18.2.17; Manston FS 30.4.17; Wrecked 7.8.17; Deleted 18.8.17

N6142    Deld Killingholme store for erection 18.2.17; Manston FS 30.4.17 (via Chingford); Deleted W/E 23.3.18

N6143    Deld Killingholme store for erection 18.2.17; Manston FS 30.4.17; Wrecked 26.7.17; Deleted 3.8.17

N6144    Deld Killingholme store for erection 24.2.17; Chingford 9.5.17 - @30.3.18; Fuselage and wings damaged 15.7.17

N6145    Deld Killingholme store for erection 24.2.17; Chingford 25.5.17; Deleted 22.7.17

N6146    Deld Killingholme store for erection by 26.2.17; Chingford 25.5.17 (arr 26.5.17); Deleted 22.7.17

N6147    Deld Eastchurch Workshops by road 27.2.17; Eastchurch FS 12.4.17; Manston FS 31.8.17 - @30.3.18

N6148    (DC) Deld Redcar by road 8.3.17; Tested 28.3.17 (Barrs); FL, u/c wrecked and propeller broken 21.5.17 (PFO EHS Low unhurt); Fuselage and wings damaged 5.7.17; Damaged 8.9.17; Surveyed 7.12.17; Deleted 14.12.17 wrecked

N6149    (DC) Deld Redcar 10.3.17; Tested 28.3.17 (Barrs); FL and wrecked 7m NW of Bishop Auckland 26.5.17 (PFO H Day unhurt); Deleted 25.6.17

N6150    (DC) Deld Killingholme store for erection 21.3.17; Eastbourne 2.5.17 (arr 4.5.17); CW 12.9.17 (S/Cdr AF Bettington killed); Surveyed 20.9.17; Deleted 26.9.17 DBR

N6151    (DC) Deld Killingholme store for erection 1.5.17; Chingford (via Huntingdon) 9.5.17; Badly damaged 31.7.17; Possibly the a/c in which F/L LER Wimbush killed 27.3.18 - or N5351; Surveyed 30.3.18; Became 207 TDS Chingford 1.4.18; Deleted 15.4.18 wrecked

N6152    Deld Killingholme store for erection 4.4.17; Chingford (via Huntingdon) 9.5.17; Became 207 TDS Chingford 1.4.18

N6153    Deld Killingholme store for erection 27.3.17; Chingford 10.5.17; Surveyed 28.12.17; Deleted 15.1.18 wrecked

N6154    Deld Killingholme store for erection 4.4.17; Cranwell 26.5.17; Surveyed 10.12.17; Deleted 14.12.17 wrecked

N6155    Deld Killingholme store for erection 4.4.17; Cranwell 26.5.17; Crashed, u/c damaged, Brauncewell 22.1.18 (pilot unhurt); CW 25.1.18 (PFO O Drew injured); Deleted W/E 23.2.18

N6156    Deld Killingholme store for erection 4.4.17; Cranwell 4.6.17; Freiston 6.6.17; C Flt Cranwell by 9.17; Damaged 5.9.17; Damaged by fire 2.10.17; Redcar School W/E 19.1.18; For deletion by 5.4.18

N6157    Deld Cranwell 3.5.17; U/c broken 11.8.17; Redcar School W/E 19.1.18 - @30.3.18

N6158    Deld Parnall to Cranwell 23.5.17 - @27.6.17; Freiston by 6.17 - 8.17; Cranwell, u/c broken 11.8.17; Freiston @6.9.17; For deletion by 26.10.17

N6159    Deld Cranwell 3.5.17; CW 21.7.17; Deleted W/E 11.9.17

**50 SOPWITH PUP (ADMIRALTY 9901 TYPE) TRACTOR BIPLANE SCOUTS put forward 1.17, ordered under Cont No C.P.100785/16, numbered N6160 to N6209 & built Kingston-upon-Thames. (80-hp Le Rhône)**

N6160    Deld Dover for erection 22.1.17; ADD 29.1.17; 3 Sqdn 1.2.17; Halberstadt DII down in spin Bapaume, then EF, FL 12.10 15.2.17; FL at RFC aerodrome 25.2.17; Halberstadt DII OOC in spin nr Hermies 11.05 4.3.17 (all FSL R Collishaw); Albatros C OOC Cambrai 19.00 22.4.17; 2 Halberstadt collided taking evasive action Le Pave 17.30 23.4.17 (all FSL HS Kerby); ADD 18.5.17; AP Dover 21.8.17 (overhaul); Cranwell 27.10.17; Became 201/2 TDS Cranwell 1.4.18; Freiston 24.4.18 (now 80-hp Gnome); Became 4 SoAF&G Freiston 6.5.18; Mid-air collision 18.5.18 (Capt JC Tanner killed)

N6161    Deld Dover 22.1.17; ADD 25.1.17; 3 Sqdn 25.1.17; Shot down nr Blankenberghe 1.2.17 (FSL GL Elliott PoW); Aircraft captured and given German markings

N6162    Deld Dover for erection 4.4.17; ADD 8.4.17; 3 Sqdn by 26.4.17; Damaged by explosive bullet 29.4.17 (FSL ET Hayne); In action 11.5.17 (FSL HS Broad); Large 2-str seaplane in sea smoking 6-12m N of Ostende, shared N6183, N6465, N6477 & N6479 c.11.10 7.7.17 (F/L LH Rochford); FL on delivery to 11 Sqdn 24.7.17 (FSL WH Chisam); 11 Sqdn by 26.7.17; ADD by 2.8.17 - @27.9.17; Dover by 4.10.17; Surveyed 16.10.17; Deleted 19.10.17 W&T

N6163    Deld Dover for erection 24.1.17; ADD 29.1.17; 9 Sqdn 1.2.17; Wrecked Malo 13.2.17 (FSL S Bennett); ADD by 15.2.17; 3 Sqdn by 15.3.17; Halberstadt DII OOC N of Bapaume 10.40, then FL nr Contalmaison Chateau 17.3.17 (FSL FD Casey unhurt); Deleted 20.3.17

N6164    Deld Dover for erection 24.1.17; ADD 29.1.17; 9 Sqdn 6.2.17; Dunkerque; Damaged by shell splinters after fight with 2 HA, 1 of which he shot down, then FL in sea, o/t, nr Cadzand, Zeeland 1.3.17 (FSL FV Branford interned); Deleted 11.5.17; Interned by Dutch as *LA41* (later *S212*)

N6165    Deld Hendon for erection 26.1.17; Accepted 6.2.17; Dover en route ADD 8.2.17 - @15.2.17; Slightly damaged at RFC aerodrome, Dover 9.2.17; 3 Sqdn by 22.2.17; Shot down by Oblt Hans Kummetz, Jasta 1 nr Vis-en-Artois 4.3.17 (FSL JP White killed); Deleted 11.5.17

N6166    Deld Hendon for erection 26.1.17; Dover en route ADD 6.2.17; ADD (via Dover) 6.2.17; 3 Sqdn W/E 15.2.17; In action, landed Bertangles 4.3.17 (FSL LA Powell DoW 7.3.17); Albatros D OOC Cambrai 09.00 11.4.17 (FSL PG McNeil); FL Allonville 11.5.17 (FSL OC Le Boutillier); ADD 22.5.17; 9 Sqdn 19.6.17; 11 Sqdn 13.7.17 - @25.8.17; ADD by 30.8.17 - @4.10.17; AP Dover by 13.10.17; Surveyed 16.10.17; Deleted 26.10.17 W&T

N6167    Deld Hendon for erection 26.1.17; Accepted 6.2.17; ADD 9.2.17; 9 Sqdn 14.2.17; FL 15.2.17 (FSL JC Tanner); ADD by 22.2.17; 9 Sqdn 26.2.17; Halberstadt DII OOC 12.30 (FSL AT Whealy); 11 Sqdn 19.5.17; 4 Sqdn 6.6.17 (tempy); 11 Sqdn 8.6.17 - @10.6.17; 12 Sqdn by 21.6.17; AP Dover 4.12.17; Grain ECD 15.12.17 - 6.18

N6168    Deld Hendon for erection 26.1.17; Accepted 6.2.17; Dover (transit) 8.2.17; ADD 9.2.17; 9 Sqdn 10.2.17; 4 Sqdn 22.4.17; Orange Albatros DIII OOC E of Nieuport 12.45 30.4.17; KB DD Ghistelles 08.00 9.5.17; Aviatik C crashed ½m SE of Ghistelles aerodrome shared N6200 17.15 9.5.17; Albatros DIII dest off Zeebrugge 07.30 12.5.17; Gotha BU & spun into sea 15m N of Westende shared N5196, N6176 & N6198 18.30 25.5.17; KB fell to ground Ostende 04.40 5.6.17; Albatros DV crashed and another OOC N of Handzaeme 15.20 6.6.17 (all FSL LFW Smith); ADD 24.6.17 - @7.7.17; 11 Sqdn by 11.7.17 - @26.7.17; FL, damaged 23.7.17 (FSL EGA Eyre); ADD by 2.8.17; AP Dover W/E 27.9.17; Cranwell 27.10.17 (later 80-hp Gnome); Became 201/2 TDS Cranwell 1.4.18

N6169    (80-hp Gnome) Deld Hendon for erection 26.1.17; Accepted 3.2.17; ADD (via Dover) 6.2.17; 3 Sqdn 10.2.17; HA OOC Vaux 11.30 11.3.17; Albatros in flames NE of Bapaume 10.35 & Halberstadt OOC Ecoust-St.Mein 10.50 17.3.17; Blue Halberstadt OOC E of Arras 11.30 24.3.17 (all F/Cdr BC Bell); Albatros DIII OOC NE of Pronville 15.10 8.4.17; DFW CV forced down Morchies-Louverval 16.50 21.4.17 (numbered G22, Uffz M Haase & Lt R Kelm of FA26); Albatros DIII OOC Cagnicourt 17.30 21.4.17; Albatros OOC Cagnicourt to S of Havrincourt Wood, shared N6182 & N6208 (q.v.) 06.30 23.4.17; DFW CV forced to land, captured Morchies-Louveral 16.50 24.4.17 (all F/L HG Travers); Albatros Scout OOC map ref 11.30-11.45 13.5.17 (FSL LS Breadner); Crashed 20.6.17 (FSL MG Woodhouse); ADD by 21.6.17; Dover 4.7.17; Damaged 31.8.17; War School Manston W/E 20.10.17 - @30.3.18; 204 TDS Eastchurch by 9.18; Stalled in on turn after TO 18.9.18 (F/Cdt MH Bottomley slightly injured)

N6170 Deld Hendon for erection 26.1.17; Accepted 6.2.17; ADD (via Dover) 10.2.17 - @22.2.17; 3 Sqdn by 27.2.17; Shot down by Ltn Schröder, Jasta 1 Inchy - Sains-lés-Marquion 4.3.17 (F/L HR Wambolt killed); [For survey, missing" 8.3.17]; M/c recovered by Germans (sic); BUT 2 AD RFC by 22.3.17; 3 Sqdn 19.3.17; N6170 tested 22.3.17 (Rochford); Crashed and wrecked Hesdigncul 30.4.17 (FSL J Bampfylde-Daniell); ADD 1.5.17; Deleted 14.5.17 [Either the m/c was recovered by British or it was a mispainted m/c. It was unlikely to have been A6170, however, as 2/Lt A Robertson of 66 Sqdn RFC was injured in a crash in this 18.4.17]

N6171 Deld ADD by @6.2.17 - @8.2.17; 3 Sqdn Marieux by 1.3.17 (coded 'P', named 'BLACK ARROW'); Damaged in storm; Albatros DII OOC Pronville, shared N6178 10.30 12.4.17; Albatros DIII OOC nr Cambrai 19.15 22.4.17; Albatros DIII OOC Croiselles 06.30 23.4.17; Albatros in flames Bourlon Wood, shared N6178 & N6194 07.00 2.5.17 (All FSL E Pierce); COL Ficheaux 6.5.17 (FSL OC Le Boutillier); ADD by 10.5.17; Dover W/E 31.5.17; ADD 27.6.17; Seaplane Defence Flt St.Pol 3.7.17; ADD 17.8.17; Dover W/E 6.9.17; Cranwell 27.10.17 (later 80-hp Gnome); Became 201/2 TDS Cranwell 1.4.18

N6172 Deld ADD 1.17; 3 Sqdn 10.2.17 (coded 'M') (named 'BLACK TULIP'); 2-str DD in dive nr Warlencourt 13.35 14.2.17 (F/L RG Mack); HA shot down then himself shot down Quéant-Pronville by Hptm Paul von Osterroht, Jasta 12 [Marquion-Bourlon per Germans] 12.4.17 (A/F/Cdr RG Mack, PoW wounded); Deleted 11.5.17

N6173 Deld Hendon for erection 31.1.17; FL on aerodrome on acceptance test 7.2.17 (F/Cdr TD Hallam DSC); To repair 24.3.17; Surveyed, deletion recommended 20.4.17; Instead restored & fitted 100-hp Monosoupape early 1918; Hendon by 25.1.18 [ex works?] (for use by Air Dept officers who made visits to stations in UK and GHQ France) to at least 4.7.18; Expeditionary Force to Lympne 31.7.18; Retd Marquise but COL 1.8.18; To 1 ASD; SOC 11.8.18 NWR

N6174 Deld ADD 2.17; 3 Sqdn Marieux by 15.2.17; 2-str OOC E of Arras (probably indecisive) 11.30 24.3.17 (FSL FD Casey); COL 2.4.17 (FSL FD Casey); Albatros DIII crashed Pronville 15.00 8.4.17 (FSL FD Casey); ADD 22.5.17; 9 Sqdn 19.6.17; Albatros DV OOC SW of Haynecourt 16.00-18.37 patrol 7.7.17 (FSL JW Pinder); 11 Sqdn 13.7.17; Albatros OOC S of Nieuport 18.45 17.7.17 (FSL AR Brown); Engine cut out while diving on HA at 7,000ft, FL in sea 17m N of Ostende 27.7.17 (FSL EJK Buckley; aircraft and pilot salved and to Dunkerque on board TBD *Francis Garnier*); Dover by 13.10.17; Surveyed 16.10.17; Deleted 19.10.17 W&T

N6175 Deld Dover (via Hastings) 7.2.17; ADD 8.2.17; 3 Sqdn 11.2.17; Albatros C OOC Vaux 11.50 11.3.17; Albatros DIII OOC nr Pronville 10.50 17.3.17 (both F/L HG Travers); COL 2.4.17 (FSL G Anderson); To AD for repair; 3 Sqdn 26.4.17; Shot down Roumaucourt, W of Cambrai by Ltn Paul Billik, Jasta 12 19.15 30.4.17 (FSL JJ Malone DSO killed); Deleted 2.6.17

N6176 Deld ADD 2.17; 3 Sqdn; ADD by 5.17; 4 Sqdn 12.5.17; Albatros C BU, in sea 10m N of Bray Dunes 05.35 25.5.17; Gotha in sea 15m N of Westende, shared

N5196, N6168, & N6198 18.30 25.5.17; 2-str crashed SW of Furnes, shared N6187 08.45 26.5.17; White Albatros DV crashed nr Courtemarck 16.40 3.6.17 (all FSL AJ Chadwick); FL in mist nr Calais, dismantled and retd by road 29.6.17; ADD 26.8.17; 12 Sqdn 25.9.17; Dover 23.11.17; ECD Grain 10.12.17 - @6.18

N6177 Deld ADD (via Dover) 26.2.17; 9 Sqdn tested 28.2.17; Seaplane dest Wenduyne 24.3.17 (FSL HS Kerby); 4 Sqdn 22.4.17; White 1-str (Siemens-Schuckert DI?) into sea 5m E of Zeebrugge 07.20 12.5.17 (FSL GW Hemming); LM with sqdn 26.5.17; ADD 5.17; Dover 13.6.17; AGP 7.7.17; Crashed 11.7.17; War School Manston W/E 20.10.17; Deleted W/E 2.3.18

N6178 Deld ADD 2.17; 3 Sqdn 15.2.17; COL 4.3.17 (FSL FC Armstrong); Halberstadt DII OOC (possibly indecisive) Bourlon Wood 10.20 6.4.17; HA OOC, then Albatros DII OOC Pronville, shared N6171 10.30 12.4.17; Albatros C in flames Bourlon Wood, shared N6171 & N6194 07.00 2.5.17; Albatros DIII OOC Bourlon Wood, shared N6465 19.05 6.5.17 (all FSL FC Armstrong); ADD 22.5.17; 9 Sqdn 9.7.17; 11 Sqdn 13.7.17; COL 16.7.17 (FSL LA Sands); Crashed on TO 10.8.17 (FSL LA Sands); Dover W/E 13.10.17; Surveyed 16.10.17; Deleted 19.10.17 W&T

N6179 (80-hp Gnome) Deld ADD 2.17; 3 Sqdn 15.2.17 (named 'BABY MINE'); "Type K" fell vertically Achiet-le-Grand 4.3.17 (F/Cdr TC Vernon); Albatros DIII OOC Epinoy 17.30 & another OOC Epinoy 18.00 23.4.17; Albatros DIII down smoking S of Cambrai 10.30 29.4.17 (all FSL AW Carter); ADD by 5.17; Dover 9.5.17 (repair); ADD 24.6.17; Seaplane Defence Flt St.Pol 3.7.17; ADD 4.8.17; Dover 21.8.17; Seaplane Defence Flt 31.8.17; ADD 1.9.17; Seaplane Defence Flt 4.9.17; Gotha damaged and forced to land 29.9.17 (FSL LH Slatter); Dover 12.10.17; War School Manston W/E 27.10.17 - @30.3.18 (for another station by 3.18)

N6180 Deld ADD (via Dover) 2.6.17; 11 Sqdn 20.7.17; COL 25.7.17 (FSL WC Wilson injured); LM on sqdn 22.8.17, but sqdn disbanded 27.8.17 - still 11 Sqdn in ADR 6.9.17 !; ADD by 13.9.17; 12 Sqdn 2.10.17; AP Dover, but on arrival crashed in cemetery W of Dover, CW 4.12.17 (FSL OP Adam injured); Deleted W/E 15.12.17

N6181 Deld ADD (via Dover) 9.3.17; 3 Sqdn by 15.3.17 (named 'HAPPY'); Albatros DIII BU & Albatros C in flames Cambrai 09.00 11.4.17; Gotha G.IV Nr G610/16 landed intact SE of Vron 10.30 23.4.17 (numbered G23, Lt K Schweren, Lt O Wirsch & Offstlvtr A Hecher of KG III/15 PoWs); Albatros DIII down smoking Bourlon Wood 17.30 23.4.17; Albatros DIII OOC Bois du Gaard, SE of Cambrai 11.15 29.4.17 (all F/L LS Breadner); LM 2.5.17; ADD 5.17; Dover 8.5.17 (repair); ADD 31.5.17; 3 Sqdn 4.6.17; Dived in from 1000ft into wheat field nr Furnes, between Oost Dunkerque and Coxyde 6.7.17 (FSL H Allan killed); ADD 10.7.17; For survey 12.7.17; Deleted 3.9.17

N6182 Deld Dover 24.3.17; ADD 25.3.17; 3 Sqdn by 29.3.17; Albatros DIII OOC NE of Pronville 15.00; Albatros DIII OOC Villers-lez-Cagnicourt 18.40 21.4.17; Albatros DIII OOC Saudemont 17.15-18.30 & Albatros C OOC Pronville 18.40 23.4.17; Forced DFW CV to land Morchies-Louverval, shared N6169 & N6208 (q.v) 16.50 24.4.17; Albatros DIII OOC N of Cambrai 19.15 26.4.17; Albatros DIII in flames Bantouzell-Cambrai 11.00 29.4.17; Albatros DIII OOC Moeuvres 11.10 2.5.17 (all FSL FD Casey); ADD 12.5.17; 12 Sqdn from/by 11.7.17; To Dover but shot down in sea nr Kentish Knock LV 4.12.17 (FSL JA Morell rescued by MTB); Deleted 14.12.17 TL

N6183 Deld Dover 24.3.17; ADD 16.4.17; 3 Sqdn (via Candas) (named 'MILDRED H') 30.4.17; Albatros DIII OOC, pilot believed shot Bourlon-Fontaine-Notre-Dame 13.40 23.5.17; Albatros DIII crashed & burnt Ecourt-St.Quentin 07.30 27.5.17; 2 seaplanes in sea 6-12m off Ostende, 1 shared N6162, N6465, N6477 & N6479 c.11.10 7.7.17 (all FSL JA Glen); ADD 16.7.17; 11 Sqdn by 30.7.17; FL in water 14.8.17 (FSL FR Johnson rescued); ADD by 16.8.17; Deleted 20.8.17

N6184 Deld Dover 24.3.17; ADD 4.4.17; 9 Sqdn 5.4.17; 11 Sqdn 19.5.17; 4 Sqdn 6.6.17 - @21.6.17 (temp attd); 11 Sqdn by 28.6.17; FL, damaged 17.7.17 (FSL ECR

Stoneman); Dover by 26.7.17; Surveyed 13.10.17; Deleted 18.10.17 wrecked

N6185 Tested Brooklands 2.3.17; Deld Dover 16.3.17; ADD 17.3.17; 4 Sqdn 22.3.17 (coded 'A', named 'ANZAC'); HA dest SE of Dixmude 19.15 26.4.17; HA OOC over floods S of Nieuport 19.00 30.4.17 (both FSL CJ Moir); Shot down nr Zeebrugge 10.5.17 (T/F/L CJ Moir killed); Deleted 21.5.17

N6186 Deld Dover for erection 7.3.17; ADD 17.3.17; 3 Sqdn from/by 21.3.17 (test of new machine); COL Marieux 28.3.17 (FSL S Bennett); 2 AD, RFC by 5.4.17; 3 Sqdn RFC by 26.4.17; Shot down nr Ecourt-St.Quentin [nr Cantaing per Germans] by Obltn Ritter von Tutschek, Jasta 12 1.5.17 (FSL AS Mather PoW); Deleted 11.5.17

N6187 Deld Dover for erection 7.3.17; ADD 23.3.17; 4 Sqdn 28.3.17; Aviatik C OOC Westende 07.30 9.5.17; 2-str crashed Furnes, shared N6176 08.45 26.5.17; 1-str BU off Ostende, crashed 2m NE of Nieuport 19.15 5.6.17 (all FSL AJ Enstone); ADD 17.6.17 - @7.7.17; 11 Sqdn by 11.7.17; HA down in spin 18.7.17 (FSL ND Hall); Last mention with sqdn 30.8.17; 12 Sqdn, wrecked; Retd ADD 12.9.17; Deleted 17.9.17

N6188 (80-hp Gnome) Deld Dover for erection 7.3.17; ADD 23.3.17; 9 Sqdn 25.3.17; 2-str OOC Furnes-Nieuport, shared 9916 & N6193 09.15 31.5.17; LVG OOC Westende-Ghistelles 09.15 1.6.17 (both FSL FE Banbury); 11 Sqdn 11.6.17; 4 Sqdn 13.6.17 (temp attd); 11 Sqdn 4.7.17; ADD 24.7.17; Dover 26.8.17 (overhaul); War School Manston W/E 20.10.17 - @30.3.18

N6189 Deld Dover for erection 10.3.17; ADD 15.3.17; 9 Sqdn 18.3.17 - @1.4.17; ADD by 5.4.17; Dover 10.5.17 (repair); ADD by 31.5.17; Dover War Flt 25.6.17 - @13.10.17; AGPs 13.6.17 & 22.8.17; War School Manston by 20.10.17, for deletion by 30.3.18

N6190 Deld Dover for erection 9.3.17; ADD 17.3.17; 4 Sqdn 24.4.17; ADD 24.6.17 - @5.7.17; 11 Sqdn by 11.7.17 - @30.8.17; Damaged 12.7.17; COL 17.8.17 (FSL LA Sands); Dover by 6.9.17; War School Manston W/E 20.10.17; EC&AD Grain W/E 2.3.18 (deck arrester gear experiments); DL expts with skids & wheel u/c; DL expts with staggered 15-in wing struts 16.3.18; DL expts with skids 13.9.18

N6191 Deld Dover for erection 10.3.17; ADD 15.3.17; 9 Sqdn 18.3.17; Unsuccessfully attacked U-boat 15m off Ostende 7.5.17 (F/Cdr GE Hervey); COL 9.6.17 (FSL FJW Mellersh); ADD by 14.6.17; Dover War Flt W/E 5.7.17; AGPs 22.7.17, 12.8.17 & 22.8.17 (all F/Cdr GE Hervey); War School Manston 27.10.17; Deleted W/E 23.3.18

N6192 Deld Dover for erection 10.3.17; ADD 15.3.17; 9 Sqdn 25.3.17; 11 Sqdn 3.6.17; 4 Sqdn 6.6.17 (temp attd); 2-str OOC 4m NE of Dixmude shared N6476 16.00 6.6.17 (FSL EJK Buckley); 11 Sqdn (coded 'A-C') 4.7.17; O/t on sands St.Pol 15.8.17; ADD 16.8.17; Dover by 6.9.17; Cranwell 27.10.17 (later 80-hp Gnome); Became 201/2 TDS Cranwell 1.4.18

N6193 Deld Dover for erection 14.3.17; ADD 15.3.17; 9 Sqdn 16.3.17; Halberstadt OOC Zeebrugge 07.15 12.5.17; 2-str down in near vertical dive 5m off Nieuport 09.20 28.5.17; 2-str OOC Furnes-Nieuport, shared 9916 & N6188 16.15 31.5.17 (both FSL TR Shearer); 2-str on fire off Ostende 17.00 5.6.17 (both FSL HE Mott); Badly shot up 6.6.17 (FSL HF Stackard); ADD 7.6.17; Dover 4.7.17; Badly damaged 22.8.17; War Flt Manston 29.9.17; Surveyed 3.1.18; Deleted 15.1.18 W&T

N6194 Deld Dover for erection 14.3.17; ADD 15.3.17; 3 Sqdn by 18.3.17; Halberstadt OOC Queant-Bourlon 10.30 12.4.17; Albatros DIII OOC N of Cambrai-Arras road 18.00 23.4.17; Albatros C in flames Bourlon Wood, shared N6178 & N6171 07.00 2.5.17 (all FSL AT Whealy); In action, lost control landing, crashed Frémicourt ALG, believed credited Fl-Maat Künstler, Marine Jasta 1 12.6.17 (FSL WE Orchard PoW DoW); Crashed 3 or 5.7.17; Surveyed 17.10.17; Deleted 23.10.17 wrecked

N6195 Deld Dover for erection 15.3.17; ADD 17.3.17; 9 Sqdn by 17.3.17; Blown over on landing 23.3.17 (FSL J Bampfylde-Daniell unhurt); ADD by 29.3.17; 3 Sqdn Marieux (coded 'G', named GAB...' [not clear in photo]) 12.5.17 - @7.7.17; Crashed on nose St.Pol

5.17; ADD by 12.7.17; Dover W/E 26.7.17; War School Manston 23.9.17; Deleted W/E 23.3.18

N6196 Deld Dover for erection 16.3.17; ADD 18.3.17; 9 Sqdn 21.3.17; 4 Sqdn 22.4.17; 11 Sqdn 7.6.17; 12 Sqdn 15.6.17 - @14.7.17; ADD by 19.7.17; Dover W/E 27.9.17; Cranwell 27.10.17 (fitted 80-hp Gnome); Became 201/2 TDS Cranwell 1.4.18

N6197 (80-hp Gnome) Deld Dover for erection 13.4.17; ADD 20.4.17; 3 Sqdn 1.5.17; FL nr Doullens 11.5.17; Albatros DII OOC Awoingt-Bourlon 13.30-14.00 23.5.17; COL 2.6.17 (all FSL LS Breadner) [flown again 4.6.17]; ADD by 18.6.17; Dover W/E 26.7.17; War School Manston 6.10.17 - @30.3.18

N6198 (80-hp Gnome) Deld Dover for test 21.3.17; ADD 30.3.17; 4 Sqdn from 9.4.17; Gotha spun into sea 15m N of Westende, shared N5196, N6168, N6176 & N6198 18.30 25.5.17; Caught by wind after landing, o/t 3.6.17 (both FSL GMT Rouse); ADD by 7.6.17; Dover 4.7.17; Dover by 10.17; War School Manston 13.10.17 - 3.18

N6199 (80-hp Gnome) Deld Dover for erection 20.3.17; ADD 23.3.17; 9 Sqdn 25.3.17; 11 Sqdn 25.5.17; Siemens-Schuckert DI dest & another OOC NE of Dixmude 16.00 6.6.17 by FSL GW Hemming of 4 Sqdn (sic); 4 Sqdn 15.6.17 (temp attd); 11 Sqdn 4.7.17; Dover 9.8.17; War School Manston 13.10.17; Eastbourne 8.5.18 - @29.5.18; SE Area FIS Shoreham .18

N6200 (80-hp Gnome) Deld Dover for erection 21.3.17; ADD 30.3.17; 4 Sqdn Bray Dunes (name 'BOBS') 8.4.17; Fokker DII OOC Ghistelles 10.10 24.4.17; Aviatik C crashed ½m SE of Ghistelles, shared N6168, and 1-str OOC down in spin Westende 17.15 9.5.17 (all F/L later A/F/Cdr AM Shook); EF, FL in sea 4m N of Bray Dunes 08.40, picked up by French destroyer Oriflamme and towed into Dunkerque, brought ashore 19.5.17 (A/F/Cdr AM Shook unhurt); ADD 19.5.17; Dover 4.6.17; Crashed 11.7.17; AGP 22.7.17; Spun twice, COL 12.8.17 (FSL AM Alexander); War Flt Manston 29.9.17; For deletion by 30.3.18

N6201 (80-hp Gnome) Deld Dover for erection 23.3.17; ADD 30.3.17; 9 Sqdn 5.4.17 - @8.4.17; Believed the a/c which crashed on TO 9.4.17; ADD by 12.4.17; Dover 2.5.17 (repair); ADD 31.5.17; 12 Sqdn 18.6.17; ADD by 21.6.17; Dover 4.7.17; Badly damaged 7.8.17; War School Manston 6.10.17; For deletion by 30.3.18

N6202 (80-hp Gnome) Deld Dover for erection 25.3.17; ADD Dunkerque by 5.4.17; 3 Sqdn W/E 12.4.17; Albatros DIII OOC Croiselles 06.30 23.4.17 (FSL HF Beamish); Albatros DIII crashed N of Cambrai (probably Vzfw Emil Eisenhuth, Jasta 3, killed) 19.15 26.4.17 (FSL JJ Malone DSO); ADD by 3.5.17; Dover 8.5.17 (repair); AGP 13.6.17; Badly damaged 19.6.17; 12 Sqdn by 25.8.17; Dover by 9.17; War School Manston W/E 20.10.17 - @30.3.18 [with Testing Sqdn Martlesham Heath 29.12.17]; Freiston

N6203 Deld Dover for erection 24.3.17; ADD 4.4.17; 3 Sqdn 13.4.17; Albatros OOC Hendicourt 17.50 21.4.17; Albatros down smoking S of Cambrai 10.30 29.4.17 (both FSL HS Broad); LM with sqdn 5.5.17; ADD by 10.5.17; Dover by 31.5.17; ADD 25.6.17; Seaplane Defence Flt St.Pol (coded 'S', named 'MINA') 3.7.17; ADD 4.8.17; 12 Sqdn by 25.8.17; AP Dover 23.11.17; ECD Grain 10.12.17 - 6.18; [Deck landing set fitted to first of new batch of Pups 15.12.17]; Crashed on nose at one time

N6204 Transferred to Russian Government (allocated 21.3.17) BUT allocated to store 3.12.17

N6205 Deld Dover for erection 31.3.17; ADD 13.4.17; 3 Sqdn (named 'BETTY') by 19.4.17; Albatros DIII OOC Bourlon Wood, SE of Cambrai 17.30 23.4.17; Albatros DIII crashed Bois du Gaard 11.00 29.4.17; Albatros DIII OOC NE of Cambrai 10.45 1.5.17; Damaged Marieux 11.5.17 (all FSL JST Fall); ADD 12.5.17 - @24.5.17; Dover by 11.5.17 (sic); Badly damaged 6.8.17; Walmer 6.10.17; Eastbourne (via Dover) W/E 9.11.17; Grain, fitting deck landing gear from 22.12.17 [therefore became Ships Pup]; BUT East Fortune NFS from/by 24.11.17 - @3.18 (training)

N6206 Deld Dover for erection 31.3.17; ADD 4.6.17; Seaplane Defence Flt 21.7.17; COL 8.8.17 (F/L GW Price); ADD 17.8.17; Dover W/E 13.10.17; Surveyed

16.10.17; Deleted 19.10.17 W&T

N6207 Deld Dover for erection 31.3.17; ADD 7.4.17; 3 Sqdn 13.4.17 (named 'BLACK BESS'); Shot down Fresnes-Vitry by Oblt Ritter von Tutschek, Jasta 12 4.5.17 (FSL HS Murton PoW); Deleted 21.5.17

N6208 Deld Dover for erection 31.3.17; ADD 8.4.17; 3 Sqdn 13.4.17; 2-str OOC 5m N of Quéant 17.40 21.4.17; 3 Albatros DIII, 1 dest Croisilles 06.30, 1 OOC Croisilles 07.15 & 1 OOC Croisilles-Havrincourt 07.45 23.4.17; With N6169 & N6182 forced DFW C5297/16 of FA26 to land Morchies-Louverval 16.50, then EF, landed alongside HA then both destroyed by German shell fire 24.4.17 (all FSL JJ Malone DSO) [numbered G25, Uffz Max Haase slightly wounded, observer Ltn Karl Keim died after 10 min]; Deleted ADD 26.4.17

N6209 Deld Oxted to Hendon for erection 10.2.17; Ready 19.2.17; Dover 26.2.17; ADD 27.2.17; 3 Sqdn 13.3.17; EF, FL Beauvais 5.4.17 (FSL HF Beamish unhurt); to 2 AD; 3 Sqdn 9.5.17; 11 Sqdn 11.7.17; ADD 20.7.17; Dover 26.8.17; Cranwell 27.10.17 (fitted 80-hp Gnome); Became 201/2 TDS Cranwell 1.4.18

**75 SPAD S.7C.1 ordered 1.17 under Cont No A.S.30438 from Mann, Egerton & Co Ltd, numbered N6210 to N6284 & built Norwich (150-hp Hispano-Suiza)**

N6210 Sample aircraft recd and being stripped down W/E 19.1.17; Testing Sqdn Martlesham Heath, tested 4.17 - 5.17; Transferred to RFC (Military Wing) as A9100

N6211 to N6271 transferred to RFC as A9101 to A9161

N6272 to N6284 transferred to RFC as B1351 to B1363

**N6285 TO N6289 NOT ALLOTTED (blank numbers)**

**20 SOPWITH TRIPLANE SCOUTS ordered 1.17 under Cont No C.P.138323/16, numbered N6290 to N6309 & built Kingston-on-Thames. (130-hp Clerget 9B)**

N6290 Deld Dover 14.4.17; ADD 24.4.17; To 8 Sqdn (named 'DIXIE') 1.5.17; Albatros DIII with red fuselage and green wings OOC Hénin-Lietard 18.10 3.5.17 (F/Cdr AR Arnold); Albatros DIII shot down Neuvireuil 20.55 28.5.17 (F/L PA Johnston); temp 1 Sqdn by 8.6.17; 8 Sqdn 12.6.17; Albatros DV Douai OOC 20.00 13.6.17 (F/Cdr AR Arnold); ADD 10.7.17; 10 Sqdn 24.7.17; FL and damaged NW of Proven 4.8.17 (FSL KR Munro uninjured); Shot down over Polygon Wood by Ltn Güttler, Jasta 24 12.10 9.8.17 (FSL KR Munro killed) [nr Eessen per Germans]; Deleted 1.9.17 [Replica completed 1990, named 'DIXIE II', regd G-BOCK]

N6291 Deld Dover 15.4.17; Badly damaged 29.4.17; ADD 28.5.17; 1 Sqdn 4.6.17; Albatros DIII OOC E of Ypres 06.15 7.6.17 (F/Cdr TFN Gerrard); Albatros Scout OOC smoking NE of Ypres 20.30 14.6.17 (F/L FHM Maynard); DFW C OOC Ten-Brielen, SE of Ypres 09.45 3.7.17; Albatros DIII OOC E of Gheluvelt 18.35 3.7.17 (both F/Cdr CA Eyre); Shot down by Ltn de R Richard Krüger, Jasta 4 over Dadizeele 7.7.17 (F/Cdr CA Eyre killed) [W of Wervicq per Germans]; Deleted 8.8.17

N6292 Deld Dover 15.4.17; ADD 1.5.17; 8 Sqdn 3.5.17 (named 'LILY' by F/L RR Soar "because it was hard to get into" (sic)); LVG C OOC La Bassée 10.00 23.5.17; Aviatik C OOC Arras 08.35, then DFW CV C9045/16 of FAA288 OOC N of Arras, shared N5468 & N5482 08.55 OOC 12.6.17 (numbered G44, Ltn von Pieveling & Ltn Nieberie); Aviatik OOC Esquerchin 09.10-10.30 patrol 27.6.17; Albatros DIII OOC E of Lens, shared N5493 06.55 29.6.17; Albatros OOC Pont-à-Vendin 08.00-09.10 patrol 3.7.17; Aviatik C OOC Pont-à-Vendin 18.30 6.7.17; 2-str captured E of Izel, shared N5460 17.30-18.10 patrol 11.7.17; Albatros DIII OOC Quiéry la Motte, shared N5482 19.55-21.15 patrol 17.7.17 (all F/L RR Soar DSC); ADD 5.8.17 - @30.8.17; 1 Sqdn by 6.9.17; Albatros DV OOC Becelaere, shared N5459 10.10 19.9.17 (FSL JH Winn); In action with 2 HA, shot down 09.00-10.00 by Ltn Wendelmuth, Jasta 8 20.9.17 (FSL JH Winn killed); Surveyed 22.9.17; Deleted 27.9.17 TL

N6293 Deld Dover for erection 17.4.17; ADD 30.4.17; 10 Sqdn 9.5.17 - @10.5.17; ADD by 17.5.17; 11 Sqdn by

23.5.17; Crashed into ditch on landing 28.5.17 (FSL EJK Buckley); ADD by 31.5.17; 1 Sqdn 7.6.17; Shot down nr Quesnoy by Offz St Max Müller, Jasta 28 8.6.17 (FSL TR Swinburne killed); Deleted 25.6.17

N6294 Deld Dover for erection 18.4.17; ADD 1.5.17; 10 Sqdn (coded 'B') 9.5.17; Aviatik C OOC 3m SE of Ypres, shared N5359 07.15 1.6.17 (FSL AC Dissette); Left 11.17 on PR escort, shot down over Coxyde by Ltn Gustav Nolte, Jasta 18, BU, crashed in wood, BO, nr Proven 2.6.17 (FSL AC Dissette killed); ADD 2.6.17; Deleted 3.9.17

N6295 Deld Dover for erection 19.4.17; ADD 2.5.17; 8 Sqdn (coded 'B') 10.5.17; Loaned 1 Sqdn 12.6.17; 8 Sqdn 16.6.17; Aviatik C crashed Vendin-le-Vieil, shared N5493 09.35 16.6.17 (F/L PA Johnston); ADD 10.7.17; 10 Sqdn 25.7.17; Albatros C OOC 1m S of Roulers 07.40 21.8.17; Albatros DV OOC S of Roulers 07.00 25.8.17 (both F/L HJT Saint); 1 Sqdn 27.8.17; Collided into by N5447 landing 5.9.17; ADD 6.9.17; 12 Sqdn 31.12.17; For survey by 17.1.18; Deleted by ADD 21.1.18

N6296 Presentation a/c 'Britons in France No.1' 20.10.16. Deld Dover for erection 23.4.17; ADD 5.5.17; 1 Sqdn 10.5.17; Albatros DIII OOC S of Hénin-Lietard 19.45 19.5.17 (F/Cdr RS Dallas); Rumpler scout OOC nr Ghistelles 7.7.17; Albatros DV OOC 4m E of Messines, shared N5373, N5455, N5479, N5485, N6300, N6304 & N6308 20.05 17.7.17 (both FSL E Anthony); ADD 28.8.17; Dest by fire on night of 1.10.17; Surveyed 17.10.17; Deleted 23.10.17 burnt

N6297 Deld Dover for erection 23.4.17; ADD 2.5.17; 10 Sqdn 14.5.17; Halberstadt D OOC E of Armentières 09.50 20.5.17 (FSL PG McNeil); Flown to Cassel 21.5.17 by FSL Reid for comparative tests with Albatros Scout, Baby Nieuport and Pup: Triplane proved superior both in speed and climbing power and seemed to handle equally quickly with any other; Halberstadt D OOC 15m of Ostende 19.45 25.5.17 (FSL PG McNeil); Shot down by Offstvtr St Klein, Jasta 27 nr Moorslede 3.6.17 (FSL PG McNeil killed) [Sopwith 1-str nr Wervicq per Germans]; Deleted 25.6.17

N6298 Deld Dover for erection 7.5.17; ADD 20 or 21.5.17; 2 AD by 31.5.17; 1 Sqdn 4.6.17; Engine choked on TO, sideslipped, nosedived, Bailleul 7.6.17 (FSL HDM Wallace killed); ADD by 14.6.17; For survey by 28.6.17

N6299 Deld Dover for erection 25.4.17; ADD 25.5.17; 8 Sqdn 7.6.17; Albatros DIII crashed nr Lens 09.50 12.6.17; DFW C.V C5046/16 of FAA211 brought down intact nr Loos, shared N5465 08.30 16.6.17 (numbered G47, Vzfw Helmuth Tosch killed & Ltn K Riegel PoW); 2 Aviatiks forced to land 3.7.17 (all F/Cdr RJO Compston); ADD 10.7.17; 1 Sqdn 28.7.17; Albatros DV OOC NE of Ypres 08.40 14.8.17; Albatros DV crashed Menin 07.00 16.8.17; DFW C OOC W of Deûlémont, shared N6301 07.50 26.8.17; Albatros DV crashed Zandvoorde-Becelaere 10.10 19.9.17 (all FSL SW Rosevear); EF, FL nr La Sythe 27.10.17; ADD by 29.10.17; Surveyed 31.10.17; Deleted 2.11.17 DBR

N6300 Deld Dover for erection 27.4.17; ADD 27.5.17; 1 Sqdn 30.5.17; Albatros DV OOC NE of Gheluvelt 10.00 7.7.17; 2-str OOC E of Warneton, shared N5479 & N6308 10.25 13.7.17; Albatros DV OOC 4m E of Messines, shared N5373, N5455, N5479, N5485, N6296, N6304 & N6308 20.05 17.7.17; Albatros DV OOC Moorslede 07.40 9.8.17 (all FSL AGA Spence); ADD 20.8.17; 1 Sqdn 10.9.17; Attacked troops nr Zandvoorde 20.9.17 (FSL E Anthony); EF, FL, crashed N of Kemmel 31.10.17 (F/L WS MacGrath); ADD 1.11.17; Deleted 5.11.17 DBR

N6301 Deld Dover for erection 27.4.17; ADD 24.5.17; 8 Sqdn 28.5.17 (named 'DUSTY II'); 10 Sqdn 7.6.17; 8 Sqdn 12.6.17; ADD 7.7.17; 1 AD 7.17; 1 Sqdn 13.7.17; Albatros DV OOC nr Moorslede 07.40 9.8.17 (F/L FHM Maynard); DFW C OOC W of Deûlémont, shared N6299 07.50 26.8.17 (FSL HV Rowley); ADD 8.9.17; Dest by fire on night of 1.10.17; Surveyed 17.10.17; Deleted 23.10.17 burnt

N6302 Deld Dover for erection 29.4.17; ADD 21.5.17; 10 Sqdn 4.6.17; Albatros C in flames Wervicq-Poelcapelle, shared N5466, N5478 & N5490 08.50 5.6.17 (FSL FVL

*Maurice Farman Shorthorn ("Fowzey Type") N6314 with balanced rudder at Eastchurch. (J.M.Bruce/G.S.Leslie collection)*

*Westland-built Airco D.H.4 N6416 'MOORQ', probably Sorley's aircraft, with 2 Wing at Imbros, 1917 (via Tim Mason)*

*Sopwith Ships Pup N6452 being brought back to HMS Furious on a lighter. This machine made the world's first deck landing on 2 August 1917, piloted by Sqdn Cdr E.H.Dunning DSC, who was drowned in this machine a few days later. (IWM Q.96516)*

*Beardmore S.B.IIID shipboard aircraft N6708 with jettisonable undercarriage. (via J.D.Oughton)*

Boyd); Crashed and damaged Droglandt 7.6.17 (FSL R Collishaw); ADD 7.6.17; 10 Sqdn 7.7.17; Albatros DV OOC Roulers 20.00 17.7.17; Albatros D.V Houthulst Forest 20.25 23.7.17; Albatros DV OOC Langemarck 12.40 24.7.17; General engagement, Albatros DV OOC W of Tourcoing 19.30 27.7.17 (all FSL AW Carter); Albatros Scout OOC Wervicq 08.00 16.8.17; Albatros DV OOC Roubaix 15.30 20.8.17; Albatros DV OOC E of Menin 18.30 21.8.17 (all FSL WM Alexander); ADD 27.8.17; Destroyed by fire on night of 1.10.17; Surveyed 17.10.17; Deleted 23.10.17 burnt

N6303    Deld Dover for erection 29.4.17; ADD 23.5.17; 10 Sqdn by 3.6.17; EF, FL and damaged landing Poperinghe 5.6.17 (FSL QS Shirriff); ADD 5.6.17; 1 Sqdn 11.7.17; Albatros DV OOC Quesnoy 09.10 12.7.17; Albatros DV down in flames S of Houthulst Forest 16.00 8.8.17 (all/both F/L RP Minifie); EF, FL and crashed S of Crucifix Hill 13.8.17 (F/L RP Minifie); ADD 13.8.17; 1 Sqdn 12.9.17; EF, FL, damaged nr Locre 20.9.17 (FSL AJ Binks); ADD W/E 27.9.17; AP Dover W/E 13.10.17; To Chingford but EF, FL en route at Eastchurch 13.1.18; Became 207 TDS Chingford 1.4.18

N6304    Deld Dover 2.5.17; ADD 24.5.17; 9 Sqdn 28.5.17; COL Furnes 2.6.17 (A/F/Cdr GG Simpson); ADD by 7.6.17; 1 Sqdn (coded 'K') 10.7.17; Albatros DV OOC 4m E of Messines, shared N5373, N5455, N5479, N5485, N6296, N6300 & N6308 20.05 17.7.17 (FSL CB Ridley); EF, FL Neuve-Eglise 7.8.17 (retd same day); Shot down Zillebeke Lake, nr Hollebeke by Ltn Groos, Jasta 11 11.00 16.8.17 (FSL AT Gray killed) Deleted 1.9.17

N6305    Deld Dover for erection 7.5.17; ADD 23.5.17; 9 Sqdn 27.5.17; EF on TO, stalled on turning back, dived in 13.7.17 (F/Cdr KG Macdonald injured); Deleted ADD 16.7.17

N6306    Deld Dover for erection 7.5.17; ADD 21.5.17; 10 Sqdn 24.5.17; "Halberstadt-type" 1-str scout OOC 15m off Ostende 19.45 25.5.17 (FSL LH Parker); Visited 20 Sqdn RFC Ste Marie Cappel 29.5.17 for comparative tests with FE and Nieuports; Albatros Scout OOC Ypres-Courtrai 18.00 3.6.17 (FSL LH Parker); Shot down nr Zonnebeke by Ltn Gross, Jasta 11 08.05 24.6.17 (FSL AB Holcroft, PoW wounded); Deleted 2.7.17

N6307    Deld Dover for erection 7.5.17; ADD 31.5.17; 10 Sqdn (named 'BLACK DEATH') 3.6.17; Albatros DIII shot down OOC Polygon Wood area 11.10 6.6.17; Albatros DIII shot down nr Roulers, then Albatros DIII OOC, crashed nr Moorslede 09.00 7.6.17; Albatros DIII OOC nr Zonnebeke 19.15 14.6.17; 2-str OOC St.Julien-Houthem 09.40 15.6.17; Albatros D.V dest Zonnebeke 08.10 24.6.17; Albatros DIII BU Polygon Wood 12.25 12.7.17 (all FSL, later F/Cdr JE Sharman DSC); Hit by AA while in combat, BU, crashed W of Comines 22.7.17 (F/Cdr JE Sharman DSC killed) [Credited by Germans to Oblt Reinhardt, Jasta 11, but another source says Flakbatterie 503]; Deleted 8.8.17

N6308    Deld Dover for erection 5.5.17; ADD 23.5.17; 1 Sqdn 4.6.17; 2-str OOC E of Warneton, shared N5479 & N6300 10.25 13.7.17; Albatros DV OOC 4m E of Messines, shared N5373, N5455, N5479, N5485, N6296, N6300 & N6304 20.05 17.7.17 (both FSL HV Rowley); Albatros DV shot down E of Wervicq 08.00 12.8.17 (F/Cdr RS Dallas); Shot down E of Ploegsteert Wood by Oblt Hartmann, Jasta 28, 21.8.17 (FSL FC Lewis killed) [at Terhand per Germans]; Deleted 7.9.17

N6309    Deld Dover for erection 5.5.17; ADD 24.5.17; 1 Sqdn 3.6.17; Shot down over Dadizeele, believed down at Comines by Ltn Kurt Wolff, Jasta 11 7.7.17 (FSL HK Millward killed); Deleted 8.8.17

**20 MAURICE FARMAN S.11 SHORTHORN ordered 1.17 under Cont Nos C.P.103698/17 & A.S.18919 from Eastbourne Aviation Co Ltd & numbered N6310 to N6329. (80/170-hp Renault)**

N6310    (C/n 144) (160-hp later 150-hp) Deld Eastbourne 12.7.17; Observers School Flt Eastchurch 13.7.17; "Eastchurch" type by 29.12.17; Became 204 TDS Eastchurch 1.4.18

N6311    (C/n 145) (160-hp later 170-hp) Deld Eastbourne

12.7.17; Observers School Flt Eastchurch 13.7.17; Converting to "Eastchurch" type 25.7.17; Became 204 TDS Eastchurch 1.4.18

N6312    (C/n 146) (160-hp later 170-hp) Deld Eastbourne 12.7.17; Observers School Flt Eastchurch 6.8.17; Conv to "Eastchurch" 14.8.17; Bullets hit propeller, m/c caught fire, crashed 20.3.18 (F/L HJ Arnold DSO & A/B GHG Walker both killed); For deletion by 30.3.18

N6313    (C/n 147) (150-hp Renault-Mercedes) Deld Eastbourne 5.9.17; For deletion by 30.3.18

N6314    (C/n 148) (160-hp) Deld Eastbourne 1.8.17; Observers School Flt Eastchurch 16.8.17; For conv to "Eastchurch" type 24.8.17 [Fowzey type]; Became 204 TDS Eastchurch 1.4.18

N6315    (C/n 149) Deld Eastbourne 15.8.17; Manston War Flt 20.8.17; Manston FS 2.10.17; Surveyed 11.10.17; Deleted 16.10.17 wrecked

N6316    (C/n 150) (80-hp) Deld Eastbourne 15.8.17; Manston 22.8.17; Surveyed 9.1.18; Deleted 15.1.18 BR

N6317    (C/n 151) (80-hp, to 170-hp "Eastchurch type 2.18) Deld Eastbourne 23.8.17; Gunnery School Flt Eastchurch 27.10.17; Became 204 TDS Eastchurch 1.4.18 - @7.18

N6318    (C/n 152) (80-hp, to 170-hp "Eastchurch type 2.18) Deld Eastbourne 23.8.17; Gunnery School Flt Eastchurch W/E 10.11.17; Became 204 TDS Eastchurch 1.4.18 - @6.18

N6319    (C/n 153) (80-hp, to 150-hp "Eastchurch type 1.18) Deld Eastbourne 5.9.17; Gunnery School Flt Eastchurch W/E 3.11.17; Became 204 TDS Eastchurch 1.4.18 - @6.18

N6320    (C/n 154) (80-hp Renault) Deld Eastbourne 13.8.17; Surveyed 27.11.17; Deleted 5.12.17 DBR

N6321    (C/n 155) (160-hp, to 170-hp "Eastchurch type 1.18) Deld Eastbourne 7.9.17; Observers School Flt Eastchurch 21.9.17; Became 204 TDS 1.4.18

N6322    (C/n 156) (160-hp, to 170-hp "Eastchurch type 1.18) Deld Eastbourne 28.9.17; Observers School Flt Eastchurch 28.9.17; Became 204 TDS Eastchurch 1.4.18

N6323    (C/n 157) (160-hp, to 170-hp "Eastchurch type 1.18) Deld Eastbourne 28.9.17; Observers School Flt Eastchurch 28.9.17; Became 204 TDS Eastchurch 1.4.18

N6324    (C/n 158) (to 170-hp "Eastchurch type 1.18) Deld Eastbourne 3.10.17; Gunnery School Flt Eastchurch 10.17; Became 204 TDS Eastchurch 1.4.18 - @6.18

N6325    (C/n 159) (to 170-hp "Eastchurch type 2.18) Deld Eastbourne W/E 9.10.17; Gunnery School Flt Eastchurch W/E 13.10.17; Became 204 TDS Eastchurch 1.4.18 - @6.18

N6326    (C/n 160) (to 170-hp "Eastchurch type 2.18) Deld Gunnery School Flt Eastchurch W/E 20.10.17; Deleted W/E 8.3.18

N6327    (C/n 161) (to 170-hp "Eastchurch type 2.18) Deld Gunnery School Flt Eastchurch 27.10.17; Became 204 TDS Eastchurch 1.4.18

N6328    (C/n 162) (80-hp Renault) Deld Eastbourne W/E 27.10.17; Surveyed 18.12.17 DBR; Deleted 18.12.17 DBR

N6329    (C/n 163) (80-hp Renault) Deld Eastbourne W/E 3.11.17; Surveyed 18.12.17 DBR; Deleted 18.12.17 DBR

**50 SOPWITH F.1 CAMEL TRACTOR BIPLANE SCOUTS put forward 1.17 & ordered under Cont No C.P.102581/17, numbered N6330 to N6379 & built Kingston-upon-Thames. Delivered from Brooklands. (Mostly 130-hp Clerget 9B but 11 with 150-hp BR.1)**

[Engines not identified for N6333, 38, 40, 44, 54, 66]
[W/E 2.2.17 put forward for Sopwith to prepare presentation plates "Presented by Colony of Mauritius" - NTU?]

N6330    (130-hp Clerget) Deld 7.5.17; ADD by 17.5.17; 6 Sqdn 22.8.17; 10 Sqdn 30.8.17; Albatros DV OOC NE of Westroosebeke 16.10 27.9.17 (FSL SA Bowyer); After combat with Albatros scouts shot down OOC 8m E of Dixmude by Ltn P Billik, Jasta 7, 12.12.17 (FSL JG Clark, PoW) [at Kenem per Germans]; Surveyed 17.12.17; Deleted 22.12.17 TL

N6331    (130-hp Clerget) Deld Dover 14.5.17; ADD 15.5.17; 6 Sqdn 19.6.17; O/t landing, wrecked 11.7.17 (FSL EH Kendall); Deleted ADD 16.7.17

N6332    (130-hp Clerget) Deld ADD by 24.5.17; Transferred to RFC (Military Wing) St.Omer 25.5.17; 2 AD Candas

26.5.17; Tested with Sopwith/Kauper Mk.III interrupter gear 26.6.17; 70 Sqdn 28.6.17; Shot down nr Waterdamhoek by Vzfw Franke, Jasta 8 17.7.17 (Lt WE Grossett PoW)

N6333 Deld Eastchurch 28.6.17; AGP 22.7.17; Engaged Gotha off SE coast but guns jammed and own engine hit 12.8.17 (F/L AA Wallis); AZP 22.8.17 (F/L AA Wallis); Deleted W/E 22.9.17

N6334 (130-hp Clerget) Deld ADD by 24.5.17; 6 Sqdn 16.6.17; Albatros DV dest E of Dixmude 20.30 23.7.17 (F/L P Wood); Shot down nr Zevecote 17.8.17 (FSL FS Strathy killed); Deleted 1.9.17

N6335 (BR.1) Deld Dover 30.5.17; ADD 31.5.17; 4 Sqdn 4.6.17; Crashed on TO 11.7.17 (FSL RAG Hill); ADD by 12.7.17; Seaplane Defence Flt 11.9.17; Became Seaplane Defence Sqdn 23.9.17; Aviatik C OOC shared B6357 15.35 4.12.17; Albatros C in sea 4m NW of Wenduyne, shared B6357, B6391 & B6407 15.05 5.12.17 (both FSL GC Mackay); Became 13 Sqdn 13.1.18; Crashed, wrecked 18.1.18; 1 NAP Dunkerque 18.1.18; Surveyed 4.3.18; Deleted 13.3.18

N6336 (B.R.1) Deld A Flt AES Martlesham Heath for engine tests 30.5.17 (tested away from Martlesham Heath at various places); Hendon 6.17; Martlesham Heath 9.6.17; Hendon 12.6.17; Dunkerque 12.6.17; Grain ECD 15.6.17; Biggin Hill 16.6.17; Eastbourne 25.6.17; Biggin Hill 26.6.17; Hendon 3.7.17 (Capt HBR Rowell RFC); Brooklands 10.7.17; Hendon but damaged top wings and engine bearers 16.7.17 (Capt HBR Rowell RFC); Cranwell by rail 20.7.17; Surveyed 18.9.17; Deleted 8.10.17 to GI

N6337 (BR.1) Deld ADD by 7.6.17; 4 Sqdn 9.6.17; Gotha 3-str OOC 30m NW of Ostende 08.30 4.7.17; Albatros C BU SW of Ghistelles, shared N6370 14.40 6.7.17; 2-str seaplane OOC off Ostende 11.10-11.15 7.7.17 (all FSL SE Ellis); Spun into ground after TO 12.7.17 (FSL SE Ellis killed); Deleted ADD 16.7.17

N6338 To RFC (Military Wing) as B3977; 65 Sqdn by 3.7.17; Allocated Martlesham Heath trials 7.5.18 (NTU?)

N6339 (130-hp Clerget) Deld Dover for storage 16.5.17; Damaged on lorry during delivery to Dunkerque (per letter dated 29.5.17); ADD 12.6.17; 6 Sqdn 26.6.17; Albatros DV OOC W of Steene 17.50 22.7.17; Albatros DV OOC Middelkerke 07.20 20.8.17 (Both FSL MH Findlay); 10 Sqdn 30.8.17; ADD 29.9.17; Dover by 12.10.17; War School Manston 15.2.18; Became Pool of Pilots Manston 1.4.18; ALSO Cranwell by 16.5.18 (prefix?)

N6340 Deld RAF Farnborough 12.5.17 for sandbag tests, tested to destruction BUT Deld Farnborough from T.1 for sand test 6.11.17

N6341 (130-hp Clerget) Deld Dover for storage 18.5.17; ADD 29.6.17; 6 Sqdn 12.7.17; DFW C OOC in spin 3m NE of Dixmude 20.40 22.7.17 (F/L BPH de Roeper); FL in field, o/t, damaged 25.7.17 (F/L BPH de Roeper); ADD 26.7.17; 10 Sqdn 30.8.17; Albatros DV OOC Westroosebeke 11.30 23.9.17; Albatros DV nr Praet Bosch Wood, NE of Dixmude 13.40 20.10.17 (both F/Cdr HJT Saint); Albatros Scout OOC NW of Dixmude 13.15, m/c damaged, landed Droglandt 5.11.17 (FSL AA Cameron); 2-str OOC W of Dixmude, shared N6351 13.00 15.11.17 (FSL WM Alexander); Dover 4.1.18; EC&AD Grain 23.2.18 (ditching experiments with hydrovane); Ditching tests without air bags or hydrovanes 25.7.18

N6342 (130-hp Clerget refitted BR.1) Deld Dover for storage 18.5.17; ADD 8.6.17; 6 Sqdn 17.6.17; 10 Sqdn 30.8.17; Albatros DV OOC SE of Dixmude 08.00 6.9.17 (FSL WA Curtis); Crashed and damaged nr aerodrome 10.9.17 (FSL P Wood); ADD 11.9.17; 4 Sqdn 2.10.17 (storage for AD?); 9 Sqdn 19.10.17; Albatros Dr OOC S of Dixmude, shared B6230 12.20 23.11.17 (FSL JP Hales); 1 NAP Dunkerque 13.1.18 (refitted BR.1); Frontier 8.3.18; AD St.Pol 23.3.18; 4 ASD Guines 29.3.18; 8 Sqdn 31.3.18; Became 208 Sqdn 1.4.18; Burnt to prevent capture, La Gorgue 9.4.18

N6343 (130-hp Clerget) Deld Dover for storage 18.5.17; ADD 23.6.17; 8 Sqdn 6.7.17; Albatros DII in flames Lens-Noyelles 20.15-21.45 15.7.17 (FSL EA Bennetts); In action 24.9.17 (FSL WL Jordan wounded): 1 NAP Dunkerque 29.11.17; AP Dover 4.12.17 (for repair,

completed W/E 12.1.18, retd Dover Repair Shop, completed W/E 2.2.18); War School Manston W/E 9.2.18; Deleted W/E 23.3.18

N6344 Allocated Boulton & Paul as pattern aircraft for RFC production 1.8.17 - @23.2.18; To RFC School of Instruction, Henley 2.18 as B9990

N6345 (B.R.1) Deld Dover for storage 18.5.17; ADD 28.5.17; 4 Sqdn 5.6.17 (named 'CHU CHIN CHOW'); Albatros C in flames Roulers 10.30 25.6.17 (FSL AJ Chadwick); Seaplane Defence Sqdn 17.10.17 (still named 'CHU CHIN CHOW'); Became 13 Sqdn 13.1.18; 2-str seaplane in sea in flames 1m E of Ostende shared B3773, B3782, N6345 & N6349 13.55 19.2.18 (FSL GD Smith); With B3782, N6349 & N6363 attacked U-boat, forced it to submerge ½m E of North Middelkerke Buoy 06.40-08.25 patrol 23.2.18 (FSL GD Smith); Dover 5.3.18; 13 Sqdn 8.3.18; 1 NAP Dunkerque 9.3.18; 4 ASD Guines 28.3.18; Deleted 8.4.18 general fatigue

N6346 (BR.1) Deld Dover for storage 18.5.17; ADD 27.5.17; 4 Sqdn 4.6.17; Engine trouble, COL, wrecked 11.7.17 (A/F/Cdr GMT Rouse injured); Deleted ADD 16.7.17

N6347 (BR.1) Deld Dover for storage 18.5.17; ADD 25.5.17; 4 Sqdn 26.5.17; 1-str OOC 15m off Nieuport 15.00 4.6.17 (A/F/Cdr AM Shook); Albatros DIII crashed on beach & 2-str OOC Ostende 19.00-19.30 5.6.17 (A/F/Cdr AM Shook); 2-str OOC Nieuport 07.15 27.6.17; Attacked Gotha last seen low over Holland 08.30 4.7.17; 2-str seaplane into sea 19m off Ostende 11.15 7.7.17 (all FSL AJ Enstone); Albatros DV OOC SE of Ostende 09.45 22.8.17 (FSL CRR Hickey); 9 Sqdn 31.12.17; 10 Sqdn 4.2.18; Crashed British side of lines, CW 18.2.18 (FSL RE Burr DoW 20.2.18) [credited Obltn B Lörzer, Jasta 26]; ADD W/E 25.2.18; Surveyed 25.2.18; Deleted 13.3.18

N6348 (BR.1) Deld Dover for storage 21.5.17; AZP 25.5.17; ADD by 31.5.17; 4 Sqdn 5.6.17; FL Oost Dunkerque 3.9.17 (FSL GEC Howard wounded by shrapnel); ADD 9.17; Seaplane Defence Flt 21.9.17; Became Seaplane Defence Sqdn 23.9.17; Seaplane BU, into sea nr Ostende 17.00 25.9.17 (FSL LH Slatter) [Vzflgm Plattenburg, Seeflug 1 wounded]; Wrecked by enemy bombing 20.10.17; ADD by 25.10.17; Surveyed 31.10.17; Deleted 2.11.17

N6349 (BR.1) Deld Dover for storage 21.5.17; ADD 8.6.17; 4 Sqdn 11.6.17 - @11.8.17; ADD by 30.8.17; Seaplane Defence Flt 11.9.17; Became Seaplane Defence Sqdn 23.9.17; 2-str seaplane into sea off Zeebrugge, shared B6239 07.30 17.10.17 (FSL JW Pinder); White Albatros C OOC nr Bruges 13.30 3.1.18 (F/L MJG Day); Became 13 Sqdn 13.1.18; 2-str seaplane into sea in flames 1m E of Ostende shared B3773, B3782, N6345 & N6363 13.55 19.2.18 (FSL FC Stovin); Attacked U-boat, which was forced to submerge ½m E of North Middelkerke Buoy, with B3782, N6345 & N6363 06.40-08.25 patrol 23.2.18; Rumpler 2-str crashed Dixmude-Cockelaere, shared B3782 & B3935 15.00 8.3.18 (both FSL EV Bell); Became 213 Sqdn 1.4.18; Seaplane shot down Zeebrugge c.14.30 1.4.18 (Lt GC Mackay); Last seen when left formation at 15,000 ft 10m NW of Zeebrugge 10.50 7.4.18 (Lt KR Cole, PoW); Deleted 8.5.18

N6350 (130-hp Clerget) Deld Dover for storage 21.5.17; ADD 9.6.17; 6 Sqdn 16.6.17; Shot down in flames from 13,000ft by Albatros nr Slype 10.50 12.7.17 (FSL EH Kendall killed) [has been suggested as 11th victory of Lt. Osterkamp of Marine Jasta 1 at Zandvoorde at 21.05, but the time does not fit; more likely Lt Gotte, Jasta 20 nr Slype or Oblt Dostler, Jasta 6 who had 2 victories that day, one Houthem-Hollebeke & one Zillebeke]; Deleted 8.8.17

N6351 (130-hp Clerget) Deld Dover for storage 21.5.17; ADD 12.6.17; 6 Sqdn 16.6.17; Aviatik crashed 1m E of Westende, shared B3833 & B3882 18.15 17.8.17 (FSL ED Carroll); COL after wheel came off 19.8.17 (FSL EA Abbott); Sqdn disbanded 27.8.17; 10 Sqdn 30.8.17; Crashed & damaged nr aerodrome 9.9.17 (FSL RE Carroll); ADD 10.9.17; 10 Sqdn 27.10.17; 2-str OOC W of Dixmude, shared N6341 13.00 15.11.17 (FSL HB Maund); Tested 22.12.17; Shot down in general engagement with Albatros scouts W of Lille 3.1.18 (FSL AG Beattie PoW) [credited Vzfw Oberlander, Jasta 30 at

Provin); Deleted 7.1.18

**N6352** (130-hp Clerget) Allocated Imbros 21.5.17; Shipped to Aegean; 2 Wing by 8.17; Repair Base Mudros by 1.12.17 - @8.18; D Sqdn Stavros by 10.18; 220 Sqdn Imbros by 22.10.18 - @1.11.18; Stavros @1.19; RAF South Russia to Russian Air Corps 8.19

**N6353** (130-hp Clerget) Shipped to Aegean; Stavros by 1.12.17 - @1.1.18; Repair Base Mudros by 3.18 - @5.18; F Sqdn 62 Wing Mudros by 6.18 - @30.1.19

**N6354** Allocated Mudros 21.5.18; No evidence of delivery

**N6355** (130-hp Clerget) Deld Dover for storage 23.5.17; ADD 16.6.17; 6 Sqdn 26.6.17; Albatros DV OOC in flames E of Nieuport 20.05 21.7.17 (FSL RE Carroll); 10 Sqdn 30.8.17; Shot down, last seen SE of Houthulst Forest 15.10 27.9.17 (FSL JS de Wilde killed) [suggested by Ltn Dannhuber, Jasta 26]; Surveyed 3.10.17; Deleted 8.10.17 TL

**N6356** (130-hp Clerget) Deld Dover for storage 24.5.17; ADD 27.5.17; 6 Sqdn 8.6.17; In action 26.7.17 (FSL AC Campbell-Orde wounded); FL in field, o/t and damaged 13.8.17 (FSL ED Abbott); ADD 15.8.17; 9 Sqdn 10.9.17; 2-str OOC Leffringhe-Snaeskerke 13.00 15.9.17 (FSL EM Knott); NAP Dunkerque 19.10.17; 8 Sqdn 28.11.17; 2 Albatros OOC N of Scarpe, nr Vitry 11.30 28.12.17 (FSL WF Crundall); Albatros DV OOC Neuvireuil, shared B6319, B6369 & B6377 11.30 24.1.18 (FSL RL Johns); Albatros DV OOC S of Hénin-Lietard c.15.30 29.1.18 (FSL PM Dennett); Albatros DV OOC Carvin, shared B6328, B6371 & B6340 12.15 2.2.18 (FSL WF Crundall); Albatros DV OOC S of Pont-à-Vendin, shared N6379, B6387 & B3832 12.45 5.2.18 (FSL WH Sneath); Albatros DV crashed in flames nr Thonville, shared B6379 & B3832 11.15 16.2.18 (FSL WH Sneath); NAP Dunkerque 17.2.18; AP Dover 18.2.18 - @23.2.18; East Fortune NFS by 2.3.18 - 31.3.18 (transit); At one time coded 'W' with white circle aft of roundel

**N6357** (130-hp Clerget) Deld Dover for storage 24.5.17; Erected 31.5.17; ADD 2.6.17; 6 Sqdn W/E 14.6.17; Crashed in field 18.8.17 (F/L GD Kirkpatrick); ADD 20.8.17; 10 Sqdn 11.9.17; Scout OOC Ten-Brielen 16.30 14.9.17; Albatros Scout OOC E of Hooge 10.00 19.9.17 (both FSL RE Carroll); AP Dover 23.11.17; 12 Sqdn 28.11.17; Crashed & wrecked 24.3.18; 4 ASD Guines 28.3.18; Deleted W/E 22.4.18

**N6358** (130-hp Clerget) Deld Dover for storage 24.5.17; ADD 2.6.17; 6 Sqdn W/E 14.6.17; Albatros OOC St.George 17.50 26.7.17; Albatros DV in flames into sea NE of Nieuport 17.10 27.7.17 (both FSL JH Forman); Albatros OOC, then FL in field, o/t, CW S of Wilskerke 16.15 28.7.17 (FSL JH Forman wounded); ADD by 30.7.17; 9 Sqdn 21.9.17; Left with flight 14.00 but lost formation, believed shot down by 3 HA nr Zarren 11.10.17 (FSL N Black DoW 12.10.17); Surveyed 25.10.17; Deleted 29.10.17 TL

**N6359** (130-hp Clerget) Deld Dover for storage 25.5.17; ADD 1.6.17; 6 Sqdn W/E 14.6.17; HA BU over Nieuport 16.45-18.35 patrol 15.8.17 (FSL FS Strathy); Crashed in field, CW 19.8.17 (FSL GE Siedle); ADD 21.8.17; 10 Sqdn 22.9.17; Albatros C OOC NE of Houthulst Forest 16.10 24.9.17 (FSL RH Daly); Albatros DIII OOC crashed NE of Houthulst 16.10, then hit by AA, FL Bray Dunes, damaged 26.9.17 (FSL RH Daly wounded); ADD 27.9.17; Destroyed by fire on night of 1.10.17; Surveyed 17.10.17; Deleted 23.10.17 burnt

**N6360** (130-hp Clerget) Deld Dover for storage 25.5.17; ADD 1.6.17; 6 Sqdn W/E 14.6.17; Aviatik C sent down spinning NW of Wilskerke c.14.30, then shot down by Ltn d R Hugo Jöns, Jasta 20 20.7.17, BO (A/F/Cdr GG MacLennan killed); Deleted 8.8.17

**N6361** (BR.1) Deld Dover for storage 25.5.17; ADD 4.6.17; 4 Sqdn 9.6.17; Shot down by 4 HA nr Ramscapelle, probably c.19.50 10.7.17 (FSL EW Busby killed) [probably the Sopwith claimed by Germans Coxyde-Furnes]; Deleted ADD 16.7.17

**N6362** (BR.1) Deld Dover for storage 26.5.17; ADD 4.6.17; 4 Sqdn 12.6.17; BU after intercepting Gothas, crashed Neumunster, 5m NW of Bruges 12.00 13.6.17 (FSL LFW Smith DSC killed); For survey 14.6.17; Deleted 26.7.17

**N6363** (BR.1) Deld Dover for storage 26.5.17; ADD 7.6.17; 4

Sqdn 9.6.17; 3-str Gotha smoking 30m NW of Ostende 08.30 4.7.17; Albatros DV BU Ghistelles 09.10 18.8.17; Albatros DIII OOC S of Ghistelles 10.25, but wounded 21.10.17 (all F/Cdr AM Shook); AP Dover 23.11.17; SD Sqdn 13.1.18; Became 13 Sqdn 15.1.18; Fokker DrI OOC Staden 15.25 25.1.18; All-black 2-str exploded in air 2m N of Ostende, shared B3782 14.20 30.1.18; Rumpler C BU, fell Oostkerke 12.45 2.2.18; 2-str seaplane into sea on fire 1m E of Ostende shared B3773, B3782, N6345 and N6349 13.55 19.2.18; With B3782, N6345 & N6349 attacked U-boat, forcing it to submerge ½m E of North Middelkerke Buoy 06.40-08.25 patrol 23.2.18 (all F/Cdr MJG Day); Led attack on 6 seaplanes but forced down in sea in flames 25m N of Dunkerque 13.00 27.2.18 (F/Cdr MJG Day, DSC clung to wreckage but drowned); Surveyed 4.3.18; Deleted 13.3.18

**N6364** (BR.1) Deld Dover for storage 26.5.17; ADD 9.6.17; 3 Sqdn 28.6.17; Seaplane crashed in sea 3m N of Ostende, shared B3781, B3782, B3805 & N6377 14.15 27.7.17; Albatros DV OOC S of Ostende 18.20 17.8.17 (both F/L JST Fall); Albatros DV OOC nr Thourout 11.00 11.9.17 (FSL WH Chisam); 4 Sqdn 2.11.17; Became 204 Sqdn 1.4.18; 4 ASD Guines 8.5.18; Deleted 8.5.18 general fatigue

**N6365** (130-hp Clerget) Allocated Mudros 21.5.17; Shipped to Aegean; G Sqdn 2 Wing Mudros from 30.10.17; C Sqdn 2 Wing Imbros 15.11.17 - @2.18; HA probable 2.12.17 (Lt G Donald); FF seaplane dest 5m S V Smola C.D.1 (sic) 17.1.18 (both Lt G Donald); G Sqdn 2/62 Wing Mudros by 3.18

**N6366** (130-hp Clerget?) Allocated Mudros 21.5.17; CSD White City (packed) by 4.6.17; Shipped to Aegean 6.6.17; Claimed by Germans on "Russian" front 9.17; Surveyed Mudros 21.9.17; Deleted 4.10.17 TL

**N6367** (130-hp Clerget) Allocated Mudros 21.5.17; CSD White City (packed) by 4.6.17; Shipped to Aegean 6.6.17; F Sqdn 2 Wing Mitylene by 9.17; D Sqdn 2 Wing Stavros by 25.11.17 - @1.1.18; Mudros by 3.18; F Sqdn 62 Wing Mudros by 5.18; To RHNAS for training by 10.18 - @11.18

**N6368** (BR.1) Deld Dover for storage 28.5.17; ADD 7.6.17; 4 Sqdn 23.6.17; Albatros DV OOC Ghistelles, shared N6369 19.50 10.7.17 (FSL RM Keirstead); Lost in mist, FL in sea nr Calais 24.7.17 (FSL J Gamon uninjured), salved and to ADD; Seaplane Defence Flt 6.9.17; Became Seaplane Defence Sqdn 23.9.17; Wrecked by enemy bombing 20.10.17; ADD by 25.10.17; Surveyed 31.10.17; Deleted 2.11.17

**N6369** (BR.1) Deld Dover for storage 30.5.17; ADD 2.6.17; 4 Sqdn 27.6.17; 2 Albatros DVs OOC Ghistelles, shared N6362 19.50 10.7.17; Seaplane crashed 20m N of Middelkerke, shared B3841 & N6370 19.30 25.7.17 (all A/F/Cdr AJ Chadwick DSC); Wrecked off La Panne 28.7.17 (A/F/Cdr AJ Chadwick DSC killed, last seen swimming towards wreckage); Deleted 15.8.17

**N6370** (BR.1) Deld Dover for storage 30.5.17; ADD 5.6.17; 4 Sqdn 23.6.17; 2-str OOC Ghistelles 18.00 3.7.17; 2-str BU SW of Ghistelles, shared N6337 14.40 6.7.17 (both F/L AJ Chadwick); 2-str BU 1m SE of Ghistelles 04.20 14.7.17 (FSL AJ Enstone); Seaplane crashed 20m N of Middelkerke, shared N6369 & B3841 19.30 25.7.17; Albatros DV OOC E of Dixmude 09.10 18.8.17; Albatros DV OOC and another shot down in flames St.Pierre Capelle 18.10 24.9.17 [2nd possibly Oblt John, Jasta 28]; Albatros OOC BU S of Ghistelles 10.25 and another OOC S of Ghistelles 10.30 21.10.17 (all FSL RM Keirstead); 9 Sqdn 31.12.17; Crashed nr Houthulst Forest probably hit by AA 22.1.18 (FSL JE Beveridge wounded); Deleted ADD 28.1.18

**N6371** (130-hp Clerget, later BR.1) Deld Dover for storage 30.5.17; ADD 16.6.17; 6 Sqdn 26.6.17; Albatros DV shot down nr Dixmude 17.45 (F/Cdr HD McLaren); 10 Sqdn 30.8.17; FL, Crashed and damaged nr aerodrome 3.9.17 (FSL HJ Emery); ADD 4.9.17; 10 Sqdn 1.10.17; Shot down in flames by Albatros NE of Dixmude 13.20 27.10.17 (FSL GH Morang killed); Surveyed 31.10.17; Deleted 2.11.17 TL

**N6372** (130-hp Clerget later BR.1) Deld Dover for storage 30.5.17; ADD 20.6.17; 8 Sqdn 6.7.17; Rumpler C fell on house, Montigny shared B3757 10.40 13.7.17; Albatros DV OOC Lens-La Bassée 09.15 28.7.17; 2-str forced to land nr Le Ban, 09.00-09.25 patrol 27.10.17; FL Léalvillers 21.11.17 (all FSL WL Jordan); AP Dover 23.11.17 - @24.1.18; 12 Sqdn by 30.1.18; Sqdn disbanded 1.4.18; 491 Flt Dover by 25.5.18 (EF duties); 4 ASD W/E 1.6.18; 4 ASD Audembert to 213 Sqdn 27.8.18; 212 Sqdn Yarmouth, airship experiments at Pulham; 4 ASD Pilots Pool by 4.10.18; WOC 31.10.18 general fatigue

N6373 (130-hp Clerget) Deld Dover for storage 31.5.17; ADD 17.6.17; 6 Sqdn 26.6.17; Albatros DV OOC nr Moere 20.15, but own m/c badly shot up 23.7.17 (F/L GA Gooderham); 10 Sqdn 30.8.17; FL, damaged (map ref given) 3.9.17 (FSL HS Broughall MC); ADD 4.9.17; RNAS Dover W/E 1.11.17; AP Dover W/E 23.11.17; RNAS Dover W/E 9.2.18; War School Manston W/E 16.2.18; For deletion by 2.3.18

N6374 (130-hp Clerget) Deld Dover for storage 31.5.17; ADD 20.6.17; 8 Sqdn 4.7.17; O/t landing 15.7.17; ADD by 19.7.17; 10 Sqdn 11.9.17; Shot down in flames SE of Houthulst Wood, believed by Ltn Adam, Jasta 6 soon after 10.00 19.9.17 (FSL EVJ Grace missing); Surveyed 22.9.17; Deleted 27.9.17 TL

N6375 (130-hp Clerget) Deld Dover for storage 31.5.17; ADD 23.6.17; 8 Sqdn 10.7.17; DFW C dest Lens, shared B3760, N6376 & N6378 18.40 20.7.17; Aviatik C crashed E of Loos, shared B3877 16.00 27.7.17; DFW C OOC E of Lens, shared B3845 & B3921 08.50 19.8.17 (all FSL R McDonald); 2-str OOC Hénin-Lietard, shared B6318, B6340 & N6376 09.00 6.12.17 (FSL PM Dennett); ADD 28.12.17; AP Dover 29.12.17; EC&AD Grain (unarmed) 26.2.18; Crashed, o/t Grain 8.3.18; still EC&AD Grain 25.5.18

N6376 (130-hp Clerget later BR.1) Deld CSD for storage by 5.17; Dover for storage 1.6.17; ADD 20.6.17; 8 Sqdn 7.7.17 (nicknamed 'NAP'); DFW C dest Pelves, shared N6378 10.15 13.7.17 (FSL RR Soar); DFW CV dest Lens, shared B3760, N6375 & N6378 18.40 20.7.17 (FSL WM Davidson); Crashed on TO, damaged 22.7.17 (FSL WM Davidson); ADD by 26.7.17; 10 Sqdn 30.8.17; EF on TO, FL in field nr aerodrome, badly damaged 6.9.17 (FSL EVJ Grace); ADD 6.9.17; 8 Sqdn 9.10.17; COL 18.10.17 (F/Cdr CD Booker); Flying again 24.10.17; FL Bailleul 20.11.17 (FSL EG Johnstone); Flying again 26.11.17; DFW C Hénin-Lietard, shared B6318, B6340 & N6375 09.00 6.12.17; Albatros DV OOC Bailleul, shared B6447 & N6448 15.00 1.1.18; DFW C crashed Gavrelle, shared B6278, B6319 & B6447 11.30 4.1.18 (all FSL EG Johnstone); ADD 8.1.18 - @10.1.18; 1 NAP by 17.1.18 (re-engined BR.1 W/E 28.2.18); 10 Sqdn 13.3.18; Pfalz DIII OOC Roulers 09.30 16.3.18; Pfalz DIII in flames BU & another OOC Menin-Roulers 09.20 24.3.18 (both F/L HT Mellings DSC); Became 210 Sqdn 1.4.18; Albatros C crashed La Bassée 17.15 9.4.18 (F/L HT Mellings); In action 15.4.18 (F/L HT Mellings wounded); COL in high wind, badly damaged 19.4.18 (FSL CW Payton unhurt); 4 ASD Dunkerque 19.4.18; 213 Sqdn 30.6.18; LVG C crashed on fire S of Zevecote, shared D3341 & D9649 16.50 21.8.18 (Lt DS Ingalls USNR); Detd from formation, attacked by 8 DVII biplanes, spun down to 80-ft, stalled, then shot down one NW of Roulers, then attacked by another which overshot and dived into ground Lampernisse 4.10.18 (2/Lt EB Holden); 2-str on fire nr Zevecote shared D3341 & D9649, but damaged in combat 0930, FL Lampernisse 4.10.18 (Lt DS Ingalls USNR); Retd by lorry 8.10.18; To 4 ASD; Deleted 15.10.18 general fatigue

N6377 (BR.1) Deld CSD for storage by 5.17; Dover for storage 1.6.17; ADD 7.6.17; 3 Sqdn (named 'TIKI') 16.6.17; Seaplane crashed in sea 3m N of Ostende, shared B3781, B3782, B3805 & N6364 14.15 27.7.17; Albatros DV OOC SE of Middelkerke 18.40 5.9.17; DFW forced to land Furnes-Adinkerke, shared B3785, B3858, B3866 & B3895 18.00 10.9.17; Albatros DV probably OOC Middelkerke 11.00 23.9.17 (all FSL later F/L HF Beamish); Repair Shop Dover W/E 22.12.17; AP Dover W/E 26.1.18; 1 Sqdn W/E 9.2.18; COL, damaged RFC Dover/Swingate Down 6.3.18 (S/Cdr RS Dallas DSC unhurt); Became 201 Sqdn 1.4.18; Left 10.20, last seen nr Hangard 22.4.18 (2/Lt WH Easty killed); Deleted 23.4.18

N6378 (130-hp Clerget) Deld CSD for storage by 5.17; Dover for storage 1.6.17; ADD 26.6.17; 8 Sqdn 10.7.17; Albatros DV OOC E of Oppy 13.00 12.7.17; DFW C dest Pelves 10.15, shared N6376 & Albatros DV crashed nr Croiselles 11.30 13.7.17; Albatros DIII OOC S of Lens 20.45 15.7.17; DFW Aviatik OOC Izel-Gavrelle 08.20 16.7.17; DFW CV shot down Lens, shared B3760, N6375 & N6376 18.40 20.7.17; Albatros DV OOC E of Oppy 19.30 21.7.17; DFW Aviatik OOC Rouvroy 06.20 19.45 22.7.17 (all F/Cdr RA Little DSO DSC); COL, wrecked Petit Sains 27.10.17 (FSL WM Davidson injured); ADD by 1.11.17; Deleted 3.12.17

N6379 (130-hp Clerget) Deld CSD for storage by 5.17; Dover for storage 1.6.17; ADD 18.6.17; 6 Sqdn 26.6.17; Crashed and damaged on aerodrome 14.7.17 (FSL WH Wilmot); Albatros DV BU Westende 20.05 21.7.17 (FSL RR Winter); 10 Sqdn 30.8.17; ADD 6.9.17; 10 Sqdn 7.10.17; O/t landing, wrecked 14.10.17; ADD 19.10.17; 8 Sqdn 28.1.18; Albatros DV OOC S of Pont-à-Vendin, shared B3832, B6387 & N6356, then m/c BU while diving on HA at excessive speed 12.45 5.2.18 (FSL H Day DSC killed); Deleted 11.2.18

**50 AIRCO D.H.4 TRACTOR BIPLANE BOMBERS put forward 1.17 and ordered under Cont Nos C.P.102623 & C.P.103711/17 from Westland Aircraft Works, numbered N6380 to N6429 & built Yeovil (200-hp Siddeley-Deasy)**

N6380 Transferred to RFC (Military Wing) as B3987 (RAF3A)

N6381 Deld Eastbourne 19.8.17 (transit); 2 Sqdn 20.8.17 (via Dover); ADD 23.8.17; 2 Sqdn by 25.8.17; ADD by 30.8.17; 2 Sqdn by 3.9.17; ADD 9.9.17; 2 Sqdn 23.9.17; 12 Sqdn 12.1.18 - @2.2.18; NADD by 7.2.18; 12 Sqdn W/E 14.3.18; Crashed, wrecked 28.3.18; 4 ASD Guines 28.3.18; Deleted 8.4.18

N6382 Transferred to RFC (Military Wing) as B9434 (RAF3A)

N6383 Transferred to RFC (Military Wing) as B9435 (RAF3A)

N6384 Transferred to RFC (Military Wing) as B9436 (RAF3A)

N6385 Transferred to RFC (Military Wing) as B9437 (RAF3A)

N6386 Transferred to RFC (Military Wing) as B9438 (RAF3A)

N6387 Transferred to RFC (Military Wing) as B9439

N6388 Deld ADD (via Dover) 26.8.17 - @6.9.17; 2 Sqdn by 9.9.17 - @14.9.17; ADD by 20.9.17; Dest by fire on night of 1.10.17; Surveyed 17.10.17; Deleted 22.10.17 burnt

N6389 Deld Dunkerque (via Eastbourne) 3.9.17 - @6.9.17; 2 Sqdn by 11.9.17; In action 21.10.17 (S/Cdr PFM Fellowes & FSL WR Stennett wounded); Crashed into searchlight in mist on landing and badly damaged St.Pol 27.1.18 (FSL LH Pearson); ADD 21.2.18; Dover W/E 28.3.18; Became 491 Flt Dover by 25.5.18 - @31.5.18; 4 ASD by 6.18; 5 Group (Dunkerque?); 2 SS Richborough 9.18

N6390 Deld ADD by 6.9.17; 2 Sqdn 15.9.17; FL Clacton after special operation 5.12.17; Hendon 6.12.17; AAP Dover 11.3.18 (repair); 6 Sqdn 20.3.18; Became 206 Sqdn 1.4.18 [left by 6.4.18]; 218 Sqdn by 3.5.18; Dover W/E 24.5.18; 4 ASD by 6.18; Pilots Pool; 4 ASD; WOC 30.9.18 general fatigue

N6391 Deld Hendon 12.9.17; ADD 13.9.17; 2 Sqdn 19.9.17 - @30.9.17; ADD by 4.10.17 - @23.2.18; 12 Sqdn by 28.2.18; Crashed in field nr aerodrome, BO 15.3.18 (FSL CW Emmett killed); Remains ADD 18.3.18; 4 ASD Guines 28.3.18; For deletion by 31.3.18

N6392 Deld Hendon 12.9.17; ADD 13.9.17; 2 Sqdn 2.10.17; EF, FL Yarmouth after special operation 5.12.17; Dover 6.12.17; Dunkerque 8.12.17; 2 Sqdn by 29.12.17; 12 Sqdn 6.3.18; Became 212 Sqdn 1.4.18; 218 Sqdn by 3.5.18; Slightly damaged landing Dover 20.5.18 (Lt JB Palmer & Sgt G/L G Barlow unhurt); AAP Dover W/E 24.5.18; 4 ASD Audembert 17.6.18; 4 ASD Pilots Pool by 28.9.18; 2 SS Richborough 9.18

N6393 Transferred to RFC (Military Wing) as B9456

N6394 Deld ADD by 27.9.17; 2 Sqdn 2.10.17; ADD by 11.17; 2 Sqdn 21.11.17 (comparison of 2 and 4 blade propellers); Dover 11.12.17 (overhaul); to 12 Sqdn but thick weather, sideslipped to ground trying to ascertain whereabouts, badly damaged nr Hardingham (nr Cape Gris Nez) 28.2.18 (FSL J Hardman slightly injured); 12 Sqdn W/E 7.3.18 - @28.3.18; 4 ASD Guines by 30.3.18; Deleted 8.4.18

N6395   Deld Hendon W/E 21.9.17; Burgh Castle 19.9.17; Yarmouth 23.9.17; HACP 12.12.17 (F/L GWR Fane DSC); Became 490 Flt Yarmouth 25.5.18; Covehithe by 6.18; With F.2As N4549 & N4550 & D.H.9 D5209 engaged 5 HA 12m E of Shipwash LV 16.9.18

N6396   Deld Hendon 21.9.17; Yarmouth 24.9.17; Became 490 Flt Yarmouth by 25.5.18 - @6.18; Burgh Castle by 12.6.18

N6397   Transferred to RFC (Military Wing) as B9458

N6398   Deld CSD White City 19.9.17; To 2 Wing Otranto (less engine) 24.9.17; Shipped 4.10.17; Mudros Repair Base without engine by 1.12.17 - @1.1.18; Mudros by 3.18; Possibly the Mudros machine on reconnaissance which EF, FL, sideslipped to ground, burnt out ½m from aerodrome 26.2.18 (T/F/L J Moore & Lt CE Palmer both killed)

N6399   Deld CSD White City for 2 Wing 3.10.17; Shipped to Aegean 31.10.17; arr Mudros by 1.12.17 - @1.1.18; 2 Wing by 3.18; Became 62 Wing 1.4.18 - @6.18; 62 Wing Stavros by 10.18 - @30.1.19; Transferred to Greek Government

N6400   Deld CSD White City for 2 Wing 3.10.17; Shipped to Aegean 31.10.17; arr Mudros by 1.12.17 - @1.1.18; 2 Wing Stavros by 3.18; Became 62 Wing Stavros 1.4.18 - 6.18; Repair Base Mudros by 5.18; F Sqdn 62 Wing Mudros by 7.18; Repair Base Mudros by 10.18; 220 Sqdn Imbros by 28.10.18; F Sqdn 62 Wing Mudros by 11.18 - @30.1.19

N6401   Transferred to RFC (Military Wing) as B9460

N6402   Deld ADD by 27.9.17; 2 Sqdn 2.10.17; Crashed nr Fort Mardyck, BO 7.1.18 (FSL CR Barber & S/L HR Easby killed); Deleted 4 ASD 21.1.18

N6403   Deld Dover W/E 6.10.17; 2 Sqdn 26.11.17; Landed Little Bentley after special operation 5.12.17; Hendon by 6.12.17; Dover W/E 9.2.18; 17 Sqdn 16.2.18; Crashed, wrecked 27.2.18; NADD 27.2.18; 4 ASD Guines 28.3.18; Deleted 8.4.18

N6404   Deld Hendon W/E 27.10.17 (ex Gosport Works); Grain W/E 3.11.17; Dover 10.12.17; 2 Sqdn 12.12.17; Hendon (via Dover) 3.1.18; 6 Sqdn Dover by 17.1.18; 11 Sqdn 7.3.18; 12 Sqdn W/E 14.3.18 - @30.3.18; Petite Synthe to 218 Sqdn 21.4.18; Overshot, went round again hit flagstaff, CW Guston Road 1.5.18 (Lt EA Lawson injured & Lt LH Herridge); Deletion recommended 3.5.18

N6405   Felixstowe to Hendon W/E 15.12.17; Transferred to RFC (Military Wing) as B9461

N6406   Shipped to Aegean 27.10.17; arr Mudros for erection by 1.12.17 - @1.1.18; Marsh by 18.1.18; Imbros by 3.18 - @5.18

N6407   Deld Hendon W/E 13.10.17; Cranwell W/E 9.11.17; Freiston by 11.17; Cranwell by 1.18; Crashed, badly damaged Spittlegate 4.3.18 (pilot unhurt); Became 201/2 TDS Cranwell 1.4.18 - @5.18

N6408   Deld Dover W/E 13.10.17; 2 Sqdn 23.11.17; Became 202 Sqdn 1.4.18; 218 Sqdn 3.5.18; Dover W/E 24.5.18; 491 Flt Dover by 25.5.18 - @31.5.18; 4 ASD by 25.10.18 for Pool; 217 Sqdn by 3.19; HQ RAF with 11 AP 20.3.19

N6409   Transferred to RFC (Military Wing) as B9470

N6410   Shipped to Aegean 27.10.17; arr 2 Wing Mudros for erection by 1.12.17 - @1.1.18; Marsh by 18.1.18; Mudros, shot down on reconnaissance of battlecruiser *Goeben* 22.3.18 (F/Cdr TR Hackman & O/L TH Piper PoWs)

N6411   Shipped to Aegean 10.11.17; C Sqdn 2 Wing Mudros by 3.18; Marsh by 13.3.18; Mudros by 3.18; Became 62 Wing Mudros 1.4.18 - @5.18; Repair Base Mudros by 6.18; 226 Sqdn Pizzone; Transferred to Greek Government by 10.18 - @11.18

N6412   Deld W/E Hendon 3.11.17; Observers School Flt Eastchurch W/E 10.11.17; HP Sqdn Manston 28.11.17; DH4 School Manston (coded '1') 19.1.18; Became 203 TDS Manston 1.4.18; Became 55 TDS Manston 14.7.18 - @11.18

N6413   Deld Hendon W/E 10.10.17; Observers School Eastchurch W/E 10.11.17; HP Sqdn Manston 28.11.17; DH4 School Manston 19.1.18; Collided with Pup landing Manston 5.1.18 (FSL LH Pearson)

N6414   Deld War School Manston W/E 20.10.17; HP Sqdn Manston 2.1.18; DH4 School Manston 19.1.18; Became

N6415   203 TDS Manston 1.4.18 - @7.18
Deld War Flt Manston W/E 27.10.17; HP Sqdn Manston 28.10.17; DH4 School Manston 19.1.18 - @30.3.18; DH4 Sqdn Manston by 5.4.18; Controls failed, dived in 16.6.18 (F/Cdt PK Mason injured)

N6416   Deld War School Manston W/E 27.10.17; HP Sqdn Manston on/by 27.10.17; AGP 31.10.17/1.11.17; Shipped to Aegean 10.11.17; arr 2 Wing Mudros for erection by 1.1.18; Marsh by 3.3.18; Mudros by 3.18; Became 62 Wing Mudros 1.4.18 - @5.18; F Sqdn 62 Wing Imbros by 6.18 - @7.18 (large sunburst on fuselage with 'SULTAN SELIM II' written on sun; also with 'MOORQ' written on sun)

N6417   Deld CSD White City 29.10.17; Shipped to Aegean 14.11.17; in transit to 6 Wing by 28.12.17; 6 Wing Otranto by 1.2.18; 224 Sqdn (named 'BOUNCING BERTIE') 1.4.18 - @16.12.18; AD Taranto by 6.19; 'X' AD Abu Qir 28.6.19; WOC 25.8.19

N6418   Deld CSD White City 10.17; Shipped to Aegean 14.11.17; In transit to 6 Wing by 28.12.17; 6 Wing Otranto by 1.2.18; 224 Sqdn (coded '8') 1.4.18; Shot down in flames returning from bombing attack in Gulf of Cattaro 6.9.18 (Lt RB Picken & Lt AF Hodgskin both killed)

N6419   Deld CSD White City 10.17; Shipped to Aegean 20.11.17; In transit to 6 Wing Otranto by 28.12.17; Marsh by 19.3.18; Imbros by 3.18 - @6.18; C Sqdn 62 Wing Imbros by 5.18 - @28.6.18; Taranto by 1.19

N6420   Deld CSD White City 10.17; Shipped to Aegean 14.11.17; In transit to 6 Wing by 28.12.17; 2 Wing Mudros by 29.1.18 - @29.1.18 (F/Cdr LA Hervey & S/L S Chryssids); G Sqdn 2 Wing Mudros by 3.18; Became G Sqdn 62 Wing Mudros 1.4.18 - @5.18; Repair Base Mudros by 6.18; 226 Sqdn Pizzone; Repair Base Mudros by 10.18 - @30.1.19

N6421   Deld CSD White City 10.17; Shipped to Otranto 12.12.17 - @18.1.18; 224 Sqdn (coded '1') by 21.4.18 - @7.18; 496/8 Flts 224 Sqdn Andrano by 2.10.18 - @11.10.18; Taranto by 1.19; AD Taranto by 6.19; 'X' AD Abu Qir 28.6.19; WOC 25.8.19

N6422   Deld CSD White City 10.17; Shipped to Aegean 12.12.17; In transit to Taranto by 18.1.18; 6 Wing Otranto by 24.3.18; Became 66/67 Wing Otranto 1.4.18 - @21.4.18; 224 Sqdn by 28.4.18 - @13.6.18; AD Taranto by 8.18; 496/8 Flts 224 Sqdn 23.10.18 - @23.12.18; Taranto by 1.19; AD Taranto by 6.19; 'X' AD Abu Qir 28.6.19; WOC 25.8.19

N6423   Deld CSD White City 10.17; Shipped to Aegean 12.12.17; arr Mudros for erection by 1.1.18; G Sqdn 2 Wing Mudros by 24.3.18; Became G Sqdn 62 Wing Mudros 1.4.18; Mudros Base by 4.18 - @5.18; Stavros by 6.18; Repair Base Mudros by 10.18 - @30.1.19

N6424   Deld CSD White City 10.17; Shipped to Aegean 12.12.17; arr Mudros for erection by 1.1.18; 2 Wing Mudros by 2.18; Became 62 Wing Mudros 1.4.18 - 5.18; Imbros by 6.18

N6425   Deld AAP Brooklands to Eastchurch 10.11.17; HP Sqdn Manston 28.11.17; DH4 School Manston (coded '4') 17.1.18; Became 203 TDS Manston 1.4.18

N6426   Deld Observers School Flt Eastchurch W/E 10.11.17; Manston W/E 1.12.17; Gunnery School Flt Eastchurch by 29.12.17; Became 204 TDS Eastchurch 1.4.18 - @28.7.18

N6427   Deld Cranwell W/E 23.11.17; Freiston by 11.17; Cranwell by 1.12.17 (training); Crashed, propeller and u/c damaged Cranwell North 16.1.18 (pilot unhurt); Became 201/2 TDS Cranwell 1.4.18 - @5.18

N6428   Deld Cranwell 19.11.17 (W/T trials); Detd Wireless Experimental Establishment Biggin Hill 6.3.18; Retd Cranwell; Became 201/2 TDS Cranwell 1.4.18; WT Establishment Biggin Hill 29.5.18

N6429   Deld Cranwell W/E 7.12.17 (training) [Oxford to Cranwell 28.1.18]; Became 201/2 TDS Cranwell 1.4.18

**30 SOPWITH SHIPS PUP (ADMIRALTY 9901a TYPE) TRACTOR BIPLANE SCOUTS ordered 16.2.17 (later 14.3.17) under Cont Nos A.S.19598/17 & A.S.775 from Sir William Beardmore & Co Ltd, numbered N6430 to N6459 & built Dalmuir. Fitted airbags and alternative Lewis gun and rocket armament. (80-hp Le Rhône) [wheel u/c, but some later converted to skid u/c]**

N6430    Deld East Fortune 4.5.17; HMS *Manxman* 11.5.17 but damaged in transit and retd East Fortune (Turnhouse?); HMS *Manxman* 8.6.17 [Turnhouse @8-9.6.17]; HMS *Yarmouth* 23.7.17?; Shot down *L23* in sea in flames off Lodbjerg, Denmark 21.8.17 (FSL BA Smart picked up by TBD *Prince*, retd next day); Rosyth 7.9.17; NFT

N6431    Deld East Fortune 4.5.17; HMS *Manxman* 11.5.17; HMS *Yarmouth* 23.8.17; Rosyth 7.9.17; Scapa 29.9.17 for recovery and trueing up for HMS *Yarmouth*; HMS *Yarmouth* 29.9.17; Scapa 29.10.17; HMS *Dublin* 10.12.17; Houton Bay on/by 13.12.17; Fairey to Rosyth W/E 15.12.17; HMS *Sydney* by 12.17; HMS *Campania* W/E 22.12.17; Houton Bay W/E 29.12.17; HMS *Dublin* 26.1.18; Rosyth 4.2.18; FP Sqdn Turnhouse W/E 16.3.18; Deleted W/E 19.12.18

N6432    Allocated Aegean 12.4.17; Shipped to Aegean; Tested Stavros 9.10.17; Marsh 26.11.17 - @9.12.17; Mudros Base by 1.1.18; G Sqdn 2 Wing Mudros by 3.18; Became G Sqdn 62 Wing Mudros 1.4.18; F Sqdn Hadzi Junas; Marsh by 10.18; Transferred RHNAS for training by 1.19

N6433    Allocated Aegean 12.4.17; Shipped to Aegean; Stavros by 1.12.17; Mudros Base by 1.1.18; C Sqdn 2 Wing Mudros; Transferred to RHNAS for training by 10.18 - @30.1.19

N6434    Deld Killingholme store 22.5.17; East Fortune by rail 15.9.17 (for carriers); Deleted W/E 30.3.18; ALSO HMS *Renown* (unconfirmed)

N6435    Deld Killingholme store 22.5.17; ADD (via Eastchurch) 17.7.17; Seaplane Defence Flt St.Pol 31.7.17 - @2.9.17; ADD by 6.9.17; Dover by 13.9.17; Cranwell W/E 1.11.17; Crashed, badly damaged, Cranwell South 11.3.18 (pilot unhurt)

N6436    Deld Killingholme store 27.5.17; ADD 3.7.17 - @19.7.17; Seaplane Defence Flt by 24.7.17; ADD 17.8.17 - @30.8.17; Dover by 6.9.17; Cranwell W/E 1.11.17

N6437    Deld Killingholme store 27.5.17; Wyton 16.7.17 (transit); ADD (via Chingford) 18.7.17; Seaplane Defence Flt 31.7.17; Seaplane dest off Ostende, shared N6459 & N6478 17.45 12.8.17 (F/L PS Fisher) [FF33L No.1246 (Flgm Walter Paatz & Vzfw Putz, Seeflug 1 both killed)]; Badly damaged landing 5.9.17 (FSL FG Horstmann); ADD 5.9.17; Deleted 13.9.17 DBR

N6438    Deld Dover 1.6.17; Walmer Defence Flt 5.6.17; HACP 8.6.17 & 16.6.17x2 (all FSL WH Chisam); Badly damaged landing Dover 11.8.17 (F/L RA Little); remained Dover for repair; HACP from Dover, landed Walmer 21.8.17 (F/Cdr CT MacLaren); HACP at Walmer 8.9.17 (F/L RA Little); Dover 29.9.17; Donibristle by 5.10.17; Rosyth W/E 13.12.17; HMS *Pegasus* W/E 20.12.17 (by 17.12.17); HMS *Repulse* W/E 20.12.17; HMS *Pegasus* to HMS *Tiger* 27.12.17; HMS *Pegasus* 6.1.18; Donibristle by 1.18 (for HMS *Tiger*); Rosyth W/E 18.1.18; HMS *Nairana* W/E 8.2.18; [also Donibristle to HMS *Nairana* W/E 7.2.18]; Turnhouse W/E 9.3.18 (for HMS *Nairana*) (with Depot Flt to W/E 30.3.18); Surveyed 3.5.18; Deleted 15.5.18 wrecked
ALSO HMS *Furious* (marked 'EXCUSE ME') for DL experiments with skid u/c ALSO Grain 1918 (arrester gear experiments)

N6439    Deld Dover 1.6.17; Walmer Defence Flt 4.6.17; 2 HACPs 7.6.17 (FSL WM Lusby); HACP 14.6.17 (FSL JA Shaw); AGP 7.7.17; AGP 22.7.17 (F/L S Kemball); HACPs 12.8.17, 21.8.17, 22.8.17 & 9.9.17 (all FSL MR Kingsford); Dover 29.9.17; Donibristle by 5.10.17; Dover by 23.10.17; Donibristle by 27.10.17 - @3.11.17; Rosyth to HMS *Pegasus* W/E 10.11.17; Donibristle to HMS *Pegasus* W/E 15.11.17; Rosyth W/E 27.12.17; Turnhouse W/E 21.3.18 - @30.1.19

N6440    Deld Dover 1.6.17; Walmer Defence Flt 27.7.17; AGP 12.8.17 (F/L HS Kerby); Gotha GIV 656/16 dest off Southend c.20.00 12.8.17 (F/L HS Kerby) (Lt Kurl Rolin, Uffz Rudi Stolle & Uffz Otto Rosinsky, 16 Staffel, Kampfgeschwader all killed); HACP, with 9901 shot down Gotha GIV 663/16 of KG3 off Margate c.10.45 22.8.17 [Ltn d R Werner Joschkowitz & Lt Walter Latowsky killed; Uffz Bruno Schneider PoW]; HACPs 3.9.17x2, 5.9.17 & 9.9.17 (all F/L HS Kerby); Dover 30.9.17; Rosyth by 22.10.17 - @3.11.17;

Donibristle W/E 9.11.17; HMS *Nairana* W/E 7.12.17; HMS *Princess Royal* by 12.17; Rosyth W/E 14.12.17; HMS *Pegasus* 13.1.18; Rosyth W/E 8.2.18; FP Sqdn Turnhouse @16.4.18; Deleted W/E 12.9.18 ALSO HMS *New Zealand*

N6441    Deld Dover 1.6.17; Walmer Defence Flt 6.6.17; AGP 7.7.17; AGP 22.7.17 (F/Cdr TC Vernon); 2 AGPs (F/Cdr TC Vernon then FSL S Kemball); HACPs 3.9.17x2 & 9.9.17 (F/Cdr CT MacLaren); Dover 6.10.17; Donibristle by 27.10.17 (@5.10.17?); Turnhouse W/E 21.2.18 (to Depot Flt W/E 22.3.18); HMS *Furious* to Rosyth to W/E 28.3.18; Turnhouse W/E 4.4.18 - @3.5.18; Deleted W/E 27.4.18

N6442    Deld Dover 1.6.17; Walmer Defence Flt 3.6.17; HACP 16.6.17 (FSL JA Shaw); AGP 7.7.17; AGP 22.7.17 (FSL JA Shaw); Taxied into by RFC B.E.2 (2/Lt Rice) and badly damaged 26.7.17; Dover 28.7.17 (repair); [Walmer Defence Flt by 3.11.17?]; East Fortune by 29.12.17 - 2.18 (training)

N6443    Acceptance test 30.5.17; Deld Turnhouse 9.7.17 (for HMS *Manxman*); transported to HMS *Pegasus* 1.9.17; HMS *Repulse* 7.11.17; Flew off turret at anchor 14.11.17; HMS *Pegasus* 14.11.17; Donibristle 14.11.17; *Pegasus* W/E 22.11.17; HMS *Tiger* .17; HMS *Renown*, ditched after TO from forecastle ramp 1.12.17; Flew off HMS *Repulse* turret at anchor 8.12.17; HMS *Pegasus* by 8.12.17; HMS *Yarmouth* 11.12.17; Rosyth to HMS *Yarmouth* 15.12.17; Rosyth by 28.12.17 - @29.12.17; *Pegasus* 1.18; Rosyth W/E 11.1.18; Donibristle 1.18; Rosyth W/E 17.1.18; HMS *Nairana* by 17.1.18; Donibristle 22.1.18; HMS *Nairana* by 2.18; HMS *Princess Royal* W/E 7.2.18; HMS *Nairana* 2.18; Rosyth W/E 8.2.18; Turnhouse W/E 28.2.18; Donibristle W/E 20.4.18; Rosyth W/E 20.6.18; Turnhouse W/E 11.7.18; Deleted W/E 15.8.18

N6444    Deld Turnhouse 9.7.17 (for HMS *Manxman*); Rosyth 7.9.17; Donibristle by 5.10.17; HMS *Renown* by 11.17; Rosyth W/E 9.11.17; Donibristle W/E 7.12.17; HMS *Pegasus* W/E 13.1.18; Engine trouble, retd aerodrome 31.1.18; HMS *Pegasus* to HMS *Campania* W/E 7.2.18; Houton Bay (overhaul ex HMS *Pegasus*) W/E 16.2.18; DBR when Bessonneau tent blew down in gale 2.3.18; Deleted W/E 9.3.18

N6445    Deld Grain 14.6.17 (deck landing trials); U/c collapsed 24.6.17; Packed for East Fortune 8.9.17; arr East Fortune 14.9.17 (not listed 22.9.or 29.9) Donibristle by 5.10.17 - @3.11.17; HMS *Manxman*; Rosyth to HMS *Nairana* W/E 30.11.17; HMS *Princess Royal* 11.12.17; Lost overboard in heavy squall 15.12.17; Surveyed 19.12.17; Deleted 28.12.17 TL

N6446    Deld Grain W/E 1.7.17 (deck landing trials); Hendon 20.8.17; Grain 22.8.17; East Fortune by rail 1.9.17 (arr 8.9.17); Donibristle 15.9.17; Rosyth 16.9.17; Donibristle W/E 15.11.17; Rosyth W/E 13.12.17; HMS *Pegasus* W/E 14.12.17; Rosyth to Donibristle W/E 14.12.17; HMAS *Australia* W/E 20.12.17; HMS *Pegasus* 1.18; HMS *Repulse* W/E 3.1.18; Donibristle W/E 18.1.18; Rosyth W/E 18.1.18; HMS *Pegasus* 13.2.18; Donibristle by 2.18; Turnhouse W/E 21.2.18 - @1.3.18; Rosyth to HMS *Furious* W/E 4.4.18; Rosyth W/E 2.5.18; HMS *Furious* W/E 11.5.18; Rosyth W/E 18.5.18; Deleted W/E 20.6.18 ALSO HMAS *Sydney*

N6447    Deld War Flt Grain 14.6.17 (Fleet use); Deleted W/E 25.5.18

N6448    Deld East Fortune 27.6.17; Donibristle 25.9.17; HMS *Nairana* by 29.9.17; HMS *Renown* W/E 30.11.17; FL in sea on TO, capsized, sank 1.12.17 (F/Cdr RE Penny); Surveyed 4.12.17; Deleted 8.12.17 wrecked

N6449    Deld East Fortune 27.6.17; Donibristle 24.9.17; HMS *Dublin* 7.11.17; Houton Bay W/E 14.12.17 (overhaul); HMS *Campania* W/E 22.12.17; HMS *Dublin* 1.18; *Campania* W/E 19.1.18; Houton Bay @2.2.18; HMS *Chatham* to Scapa W/E 23.2.18; For deletion by 9.3.18 ALSO HMAS *Sydney*

N6450    Deld HMS *Furious* 9.7.17; HZP, ditched on return 11.9.17 (S/Cdr WG Moore rescued by *Mystic*); Deleted W/E 22.9.17

N6451    Deld HMS *Furious* 9.7.17; East Fortune 10.11.17 (for carriers); Rosyth W/E 18.1.18; Turnhouse W/E 9.3.18; Deleted W/E 11.7.18 ALSO HMS *Furious*

N6452    Deld HMS *Furious* 11.7.17 (deck landing experiments);

World's first deck landing on carrier under way 2.8.17 (S/Cdr EH Dunning DSC); Stalled on overshoot and crashed in sea 7.8.17 (S/Cdr EH Dunning DSC drowned); Deleted 20.8.17

N6453   Deld HMS *Furious* 11.7.17; Tail damaged 7.8.17 (S/Cdr EH Dunning DSC); Deck landing expts 27.8.17 (F/Cdr HR Busteed); 'F' Sqdn East Fortune 10.11.17; Donibristle W/E 12.1.18; Rosyth W/E 16.2.18; Turnhouse W/E 16.3.18; HMS *Furious* to Rosyth W/E 21.3.18; Turnhouse W/E 4.4.18; Deleted W/E 11.7.18 ALSO HMS *Repulse* 2.18

N6454   Deld HMS *Furious* 11.7.17; Surveyed 14.11.17; Deleted 21.11.17 wrecked

N6455   Deld Turnhouse 9.7.17; HMS *Pegasus* 1.9.17; HMS *Lion* 8.11.17 - @26.11.17; HMS *Pegasus* 16.11.17 - @26.11.17 (at Rosyth for erection by 29.11.17); Donibristle to HMS *Nairana* W/E 30.11.17; HMS *Pegasus* to HMS *Tiger* 10.12.17; HMS *Pegasus* 17.12.17; Rosyth 19.12.17; HMS *Tiger* to Rosyth W/E 21.12.17; HMS *Pegasus* 13.1.18 [@19.1.18]; HMS *Repulse* to Donibristle W/E 18.1.18; HMS *Pegasus* W/E 8.2.18; Donibristle 24.2.18 (storage during ship's refit); HMS *Pegasus* 13.3.18; Donibristle W/E 21.3.18; Turnhouse by 6.4.18 - @10.5.18; HMS *Furious* W/E 15.8.18; Turnhouse W/E 17.10.18 - @30.1.19

N6456   Deld Turnhouse 9.7.17; HMS *Pegasus* 1.9.17; Donibristle W/E 30.11.17; HMS *Pegasus* W/E 7.12.17; HMS *Repulse* 11.12.17; Rosyth W/E 20.12.17; HMS *Pegasus* 22.12.17 - @3.1.18; Flew off HMS *Tiger* at anchor 3.1.18; HMS *Tiger* to HMS *Pegasus* W/E 17.1.18 - @24.1.18; Rosyth by 2.18; HMS *Pegasus* W/E 2.2.18; Turnhouse 24.2.18 (storage during ship's refit); HMS *Pegasus* 15.3.18; Turnhouse 8.4.18; Donibristle W/E 9.5.18; HMS *Pegasus* W/E 9.5.18; Donibristle W/E 16.5.18; HMS *Pegasus* 16.5.18; Donibristle W/E 16.5.18; HMS *Pegasus* 16.5.18; Donibristle W/E 16.5.18; Rosyth W/E 16.5.18; Donibristle 5.18; HMS *Pegasus* W/E 23.5.18 Rosyth W/E 23.5.18; HMS *Pegasus* 8.7.18; Rosyth W/E 22.9.18; Donibristle W/E 17.10.18; Turnhouse W/E 30.1.19; HMS *Furious* by 7.19

N6457   Deld Felixstowe by rail 5.7.17 (to erect for Martlesham for HMS *Vindex*); Yarmouth 20.7.17; HMS *Vindex* 21.7.17 - @9.9.17; Martlesham Heath by 22.9.17 (for HMS *Vindex*); HMS *Vindex* by 28.9.17; Cranwell by 31.10.17 - @1.11.17; Martlesham Heath by 3.11.17 - @23.2.18 (for HMS *Vindex*); BUT Cranwell by 29.12.17 & @19.1.18 & @23.2.18; Crashed and wrecked 25.2.18 (pilot unhurt); Cranwell from 4.18

N6458   Deld Felixstowe by rail for erection 5.7.17; Martlesham Heath 25.8.17 - @23.2.18 (for HMS *Vindex*); Allocated Manston; 204 TDS Eastchurch by 7.18; Propeller accident 20.7.18 (2/Lt WP Wemple seriously injured)

N6459   Deld Dover 11.7.17; ADD 15.7.17; Seaplane Defence Flt 31.7.17; FF33L No.1246 dest off Ostende, shared N6437 (q.v.) & N6478 17.45 12.8.17 (FSL LH Slatter); COL 8.9.17; ADD 20.9.17 - @4.10.17; Dover 10.17; Surveyed 16.10.17; Deleted 19.10.17 W&T

## 70 SOPWITH PUP (ADMIRALTY 9901 TYPE) TRACTOR BIPLANE SCOUTS ordered 27.7.17 under Cont No C.P.102622, numbered N6460 to N6529 & built Kingston-upon-Thames. Delivered from Brooklands. (80-hp Le Rhône)

N6460   Deld Dover 15.4.17; ADD 29.4.17; 3 Sqdn 5.5.17; (To Manston overnight 4.7.17; Walmer 6.7.17 then returned Furnes); Went up to intercept returning aircraft from raid on London by 22 Gothas, EF, FL in sea and sank 1m SW of Nieuport 7.7.17 (FSL LL Lindsay rescued by French TBD) [believed by Ltn G Sachsenberg, Marinejasta 1]; Deleted 8.8.17

N6461   Deld Dover for erection 17.4.17; ADD 11.5.17; 3 Sqdn 19.5.17; Albatros DIII OOC NE of Bullecourt 09.30 20.5.17 (FSL LH Rochford); Hit another aircraft on TO, crashed in ditch 3.7.17; To ADD; Surveyed 17.10.17; Deleted 23.10.17 wrecked

N6462   Deld Dover 18.4.17; ADD 22.4.17; 4 Sqdn 30.4.17; HA BU Rosendale, shared N5196 (q.v) 12.20 2.5.17; 2-str OOC Ostende, shared N5196 17.35 28.5.17 (both F/Cdr JD Newberry); ADD 18.6.17; 9 Sqdn 19.6.17; Albatros DV OOC SW of Haynecourt, shared N6469 &

N6475 c.17.30 7.7.17 (F/Cdr GE Hervey); 2-str crashed Bullecourt 16.00-18.00 patrol, then spun in from 1,500/2,000ft landing 7.7.17 (FSL JC Tanner DoI) [believed by Obltn K von Döring, Jasta 4]; Deleted ADD 16.7.17

N6463   Shipped to Aegean; Deld Mudros 30.6.17

N6464   Deld Dover 24.4.17; ADD 25.4.17; 3 Sqdn (coded 'D') 3.5.17; Shot down by Vzfw Reissinger, Jasta 12, last seen nr Bourlon 11.5.17 (FSL J Bampfylde-Daniell, POW wounded) [nr Haynecourt per Germans]; Deleted 21.5.17

N6465   Deld Dover 29.4.17; ADD 1.5.17; 3 Sqdn 5.5.17; Albatros DIII OOC Bourlon Wood shared N6178 & Albatros DIII OOC Lagnicourt 19.05 6.5.17; Albatros DIII crashed and burnt Villers 07.50 27.5.17 (all FSL HS Kerby); Large 2-str seaplane in sea 6-12m off Ostende, shared N6162, N6183, N6477 & N6479 c.11.10 7.7.17 (F/L FC Armstrong); ADD 16.7.17; 12 Sqdn by 19.7.17; ADD 23.8.17; Dover by 13.9.17; Cranwell 27.10.17 (fitted 80-hp Gnome); Became 201/2 TDS Cranwell 1.4.18

N6466   Deld Dover for erection 29.4.17; ADD 2.5.17; 3 Sqdn 12.5.17; COL Dunkerque Bains 19.6.17 (F/L FC Armstrong); still at ADD 21.6.17; Dover 4.7.17; Walmer, badly damaged 11.8.17; War School Manston 6.10.17; Possibly collided N5382 26.10.17 (F/L AF Brandon DSC killed); Surveyed 10.11.17; Deleted 14.11.17 wrecked

N6467   Deld Dover 30.4.17; ADD 10.5.17; 3 Sqdn 19.5.17; ADD 16.7.17; 12 Sqdn by 19.7.17; Dover W/E 13.9.17; Cranwell 27.10.17 (fitted 80-hp Gnome); Became 201/2 TDS Cranwell 1.4.18

N6468   Deld Dover 2.5.17; ADD 29.6.17 - @12.7.17; 11 Sqdn by 17.7.17; ADD W/E 6.9.17; 12 Sqdn 25.9.17; AP Dover 23.11.17; ECD Grain 10.12.17 (conversion to Ships Pup); Skid chassis completed 19.12.17; Deck landing gear fitted 21.12.17; Deleted 13.3.18 DBR, but still on charge 6.18

N6469   Deld Dover for erection 30.4.17; ADD 2.6.17; 9 Sqdn 19.6.17; Albatros DV OOC SW of Haynecourt, shared N6462 & N6475 c.17.30 7.7.17 (FSL HE Mott); 11 Sqdn 13.7.17; AD Dover W/E 6.9.17; War School Manston W/E 3.11.17; Surveyed Manston 4.1.18; Deleted 15.1.18 W&T

N6470   Allocated Mudros 23.4.17; Shipped to Aegean; Mudros by 9.17; Marsh 29.9.17; On nose landing 4.10.17 (F/L JLA Sinclair); C Sqdn 2 Wing Mudros by 1.12.17 - @1.1.18; Transferred to Greek Government for training by 3.18 - @30.1.19

N6471   Allocated Mudros 23.4.17; Shipped to Aegean; Mudros by 7.17; C Sqdn 2 Wing Imbros 13.7.17; Tipped on nose by ratings at Tenedos 4.8.17; Retd Imbros 13.8.17 (repair); Tested after re-erection 10.9.17; Transferred to Greek Government for training 3.18 - @30.1.19

N6472   Deld Cranwell 12.5.17; Redcar 6.7.17; Cranwell 8.7.17; Caught by gust, u/c collapsed 22.10.17 (A/F/L WW Wakefield); Parachute dropping 12.12.17; Crashed and badly damaged Waddington 9.3.18 (pilot unhurt); Became 201/2 TDS Cranwell 1.4.18; Freiston 20.4.18

N6473   Deld Cranwell 12.5.17; Deleted W/E 23.11.17

N6474   Deld Dover for erection 18.4.17; ADD 23.4.17; 3 Sqdn (named 'EXCUSE ME' by FSL AW Carter) 3.5.17; Albatros DIII OOC E of Bullecourt 07.40 27.5.17 (FSL AW Carter); Fouled kite balloon rope at 300ft on TO, crashed on back 4.6.17 (FSL AW Carter unhurt); ADD by 7.6.17; Dover 4.7.17; War School Manston 6.10.17; Deleted W/E 2.3.18

N6475   Deld Dover for erection 18.4.17; ADD 25.4.17; 4 Sqdn 29.4.17; Albatros DIII crashed in field 2m SE of Ghistelles 16.00 25.5.17 (FSL SE Ellis); 2-str [or Albatros DIII?] dest 3-4m E of Dixmude 08.30 4.6.17 (FSL SE Ellis); 9 Sqdn 18/19.6.17; Albatros DIII OOC SW of Haynecourt 17.30 7.7.17 (FSL JW Pinder); To 11 Sqdn (coded '9') but nosed up on landing Hondschoote 13.7.17 (FSL ECR Stoneman); last mention on sqdn 16.7.17; Dover by 26.7.17; War School Manston 6.10.17; For deletion by 30.3.18 (now fitted 80-hp Gnome)

N6476   Deld Dover 30.4.17; ADD 2.5.17; 4 Sqdn 20.5.17; 2-str OOC 4m NE of Dixmude shared N6192 16.00 6.6.17 (F/L GMT Rouse); ADD 3.9.17; 12 Sqdn 3.10.17; AP

Dover 4.12.17; Eastbourne W/E 15.12.17; Dover but COL 3.2.18 (pilot unhurt); Deleted 9.2.18

N6477   Deld Dover for erection 19.4.17; ADD 25.4.17; 3 Sqdn 1.5.17; Large 2-str seaplane in sea 6-12m N of Ostende, shared N6162, N6183, N6465 & N6479 c.11.10 7.7.17 (FSL RFP Abbott); 11 Sqdn 11.7.17; LM by sqdn 24.7.17; Dunkerque to Dover 26.7.17; Cranwell 27.10.17 (fitted 80-hp Gnome); Became 201/2 TDS Cranwell 1.4.18

N6478   Deld Dover for erection 19.4.17; ADD 22.4.17; 4 Sqdn 29.4.17 - @10.5.17; Dover by 31.5.17; ADD 20.6.17; Seaplane Defence Flt 4.7.17; FF33L No.1246 dest off Ostende, shared N6437 (q.v.) & N6459 17.45 12.8.17 (FSL R Graham); Became Seaplane Defence Sqdn 23.9.17; Dover 15.10.17; East Fortune 17.11.17 (practice); Ran into post turning, badly damaged 1.3.17 (FSL DH Lees); Surveyed 23.3.18; Deleted 27.3.18 wreck

N6479   Deld Dover for erection 19.4.17; ADD 20.4.17; 3 Sqdn 13.5.17; Albatros DIII OOC W of Bourlon 13.45 23.5.17 (FSL JST Fall); DFW C OOC NE of Ypres, landed 06.30 17.6.17 (FSL JA Glen); Large 2-str seaplane in sea 6-12m N of Ostende, shared N6162, N6183, N6465 & N6477 c.11.10 7.7.17; Landed from previous patrol, TO again, Albatros DV in sea smoking 1m NW of Ostende Piers 12.20 7.7.17 (both FSL JST Fall); ADD 30.7.17; Dover W/E 20.9.17; Cranwell 27.10.17; RN College Greenwich 15.12.18 without engine as GI

N6480 to N6529 cancelled

## 50 NIEUPORT TYPE 17bis TRACTOR BIPLANE SCOUTS ordered 2.17 from Nieuport & General Aircraft Co Ltd & numbered N6530 to N6579, to be built at Cricklewood

N6530 to N6579 cancelled and replaced by SOPWITH CAMEL order

## 50 SOPWITH F.1 CAMEL TRACTOR BIPLANE SCOUTS ordered under Cont No C.P.102627/17 & numbered N6530 to N6579, to be built at Kingston

N6530 to N6579 cancelled

## 25 SPAD S.7C.1 TRACTOR BIPLANE SCOUTS put forward W/E 19.1.17, ordered under Cont No A.S.30438 from Mann, Egerton & Co Ltd as their Type G & numbered N6580 to N6604. (150-hp Hispano-Suiza)

N6580 to N6604 transferred to RFC (Military Wing) and renumbered B1364 to B1388

## 40 BRISTOL TRACTOR BIPLANE SCOUTS put forward 1.17, to be numbered N6610 to N6649

N6610 to N6649 cancelled 3.17

## 50 SOPWITH 2F.1 SHIP'S CAMEL TRACTOR BIPLANES ordered under Cont Nos A.S.7862 & C.P.103733/17, numbered N6600 to N6649 & built Kingston. Originally to have been B6151 to B6200 for RFC (Military Wing). Accepted 10 AAP Brooklands (150-hp B.R.1 unless otherwise stated)

N6600   Deld Yarmouth W/E 13.10.17; Donibristle W/E 18.1.18; Rosyth to HMS *Yarmouth* W/E 19.1.18; Donibristle by 8.2.18 - @23.2.18; Turnhouse by 3.18; HMS *Lion* 16.3.18; Crashed 21.3.18; Rosyth W/E 28.3.18; Turnhouse W/E 28.3.18; Rosyth by 30.3.18; Donibristle to Turnhouse W/E 5.4.18; Rosyth, wrecked 27.4.18; Turnhouse by 3.5.18 (deletion recommended)

N6601   Deld 10 AAP Brooklands to Rosyth W/E 16.11.17; Donibristle W/E 30.11.17; Rosyth W/E 13.12.17; HMS *Pegasus* 15.12.17; Donibristle W/E 3.1.18; HMS *Pegasus* 3.1.18; HMS *Tiger* W/E 7.2.18; Donibristle W/E 28.2.18; HMS *Tiger* W/E 28.2.18; Crashed in sea, salved by HMS *Pegasus*, salved 21.3.18; Rosyth W/E 28.3.18; Turnhouse W/E 28.3.18 - 4.18; Rosyth to HMS *Furious* W/E 4.4.18; Turnhouse by 3.5.18, deletion recommended ALSO HMS *Campania* by 1.3.18

N6602   Deld 10 AAP Brooklands to Donibristle 22.11.17; Rosyth to HMS *Nairana* W/E 21.12.17; HMS *Lion* W/E

11.1.18; Rosyth W/E 19.1.18; HMS *Furious* W/E 6.4.18; HMS *Glorious* W/E 20.4.18; Turnhouse by 4.18; Rosyth W/E 9.5.18 [by 2.5.18]; Turnhouse W/E 18.5.18; Donibristle W/E 29.8.18; HMS *Caroline* 19.9.18; Donibristle 12.10.18; Rosyth 11.18; HMS *Caledon* 11.18; ashore 2.12.18; HMS *Caledon* 12.18 - @30.1.19; HMS *Nairana* by 1.19

N6603   (130-hp Clerget) Deld Grain Test Depot W/E 15.12.17; Rosyth for erection W/E 18.1.18; Rosyth by 23.2.18; Donibristle W/E 15.8.18; HMS *Undaunted* W/E 19.9.18; HMS *Tiger* W/E 3.10.18; HMAS *Melbourne* W/E 21.11.18; HMS *Tiger* by 12.18; ashore 9.1.19; HMS *Dublin* 9.1.19; HMAS *Melbourne* W/E 23.1.19 - @30.1.19 ALSO HMS *Pegasus* 1918

N6604   (130-hp Clerget) Deld Donibristle W/E 3.11.17; HMS *Nairana* W/E 8.11.17; Rosyth W/E 23.11.17; Donibristle W/E 7.12.17; Rosyth W/E 13.12.17; HMS *Nairana* W/E 14.12.17; HMS *Lion* 19.12.17; Rosyth W/E 20.12.17; Donibristle W/E 28.12.17; Rosyth by 11.1.18; HMS *Pegasus* 11.1.18; Donibristle to Rosyth 8.2.18; Donibristle W/E 16.3.18; Rosyth W/E 21.3.18; HMS *Princess Royal* by 25.4.18; HMS *Nairana* to Rosyth W/E 9.5.18; Yarmouth by 5.18; HMS *Glorious* by 5.18; For deletion at Rosyth by 16.5.18; Crashed HMS *Nairana*, engine to Donibristle by 23.5.18; Deleted W/E 4.7.18

N6605   (130-hp Clerget) Deld Cranwell W/E 16.11.17; Rosyth by 28.12.17 - @18.1.18; HMS *Pegasus* to HMS *Repulse* 7.2.18; Rosyth by 23.2.18; HMS *Nairana* W/E 28.3.18; HMS *Glorious* W/E 2.5.18; HMS *Nairana* W/E 11.5.18; HMS *Glorious* W/E 18.5.18; Rosyth W/E 13.6.18; HMS *Furious* 8.7.18; Flown in raid on Tondern airship base, FL Scallinger, Nr Esbjerg, Denmark, m/c interned 19.7.18 (Lt NE Williams interned)

N6606   Farnborough to Killingholme (via Hendon) W/E 6.11.17; Hendon to Donibristle W/E 6.11.17; HMS *Nairana* W/E 15.11.17; Rosyth W/E 23.11.17; Donibristle W/E 7.12.17; Rosyth W/E 20.12.17; HMS *Pegasus* W/E 20.12.17; Donibristle W/E 3.1.18; HMS *Pegasus* 3.1.18; Donibristle 2.18; Rosyth W/E 8.2.18; HMS *Repulse* 6.2.18; Donibristle 13.2.18; Rosyth W/E 15.2.18; HMS *Renown* W/E 21.2.18 (named 'SHALL US'); Rosyth @23.2.18; HMS *Pegasus* by 3.18; HMS *Tiger* 25.3.18; Donibristle W/E 4.4.18; Rosyth W/E 4.4.18; HMS *Tiger* W/E 4.4.18; Donibristle to HMS *Tiger* W/E 4.4.18; HMS *Tiger* by 25.4.18 - @9.5.18; HMS *Tiger* to Rosyth W/E 9.5.18; HMS *Tiger* W/E 9.5.18; HMS *Tiger* to Donibristle W/E 9.5.18; Rosyth W/E 9.5.18; Donibristle W/E 18.5.18; Rosyth W/E 13.6.18; Possibly the m/c which fell in sea on TO from HMS *Tiger* 29.5.18 (pilot & engine rescued by destroyer); Deleted W/E 20.6.18

N6607   (130-hp Clerget) Deld Cranwell W/E 16.11.17; Donibristle W/E 23.11.17; Rosyth by 28.12.17; Donibristle W/E 15.2.18; Rosyth by 15.2.18; Donibristle W/E 15.2.18; Rosyth @23.2.18; HMS *Southampton* to Houton W/E 30.3.18; Rosyth 8.4.18; Donibristle W/E 20.4.18; HMS *Southampton* to Donibristle 8.5.18; East Fortune W/E 9.5.18; Turnhouse from W/E 24.5.18; Donibristle W/E 17.10.18; HMS *Lion* W/E 21.11.18; Donibristle W/E 31.12.18 - @30.1.19

N6608   Deld 10 AAP Brooklands to HMS *Vindex* W/E 2.11.17; Yarmouth 19.1.18; HACP, EF, FL Aldeburgh 2.6.18; HACPs 9.6.18 & 10.6.18; On patrol, EF, FL nr lightship on water and sank 21.6.18 (Lt RC Packe drowned); For deletion by 27.6.18

N6609   Deld 10 AAP Brooklands to HMS *Vindex* W/E 2.11.17; Yarmouth W/E 26.1.18; Wrecked 23.3.18; For deletion by 23.3.18

N6610   (130-hp Clerget) Deld War School Manston W/E 3.11.17 - 5.18; 205 TDS Vendôme by 6.18 - @30.1.19

N6611   Deld 10 AAP Brooklands to Rosyth W/E 30.11.17; Donibristle W/E 7.12.17; HMS *Pegasus* 3.1.18; Rosyth W/E 18.1.18 (and ex Donibristle); Donibristle W/E 28.2.18; Rosyth W/E 16.3.18; HMS *Royalist* W/E 21.3.18; ashore 29.3.18; HMS *Campania* by 1.4.18; HMS *Royalist* to Rosyth W/E 4.4.18; Turnhouse W/E 20.4.18; HMS *Renown* by 25.4.18; Donibristle W/E 11.7.18; Rosyth W/E 15.8.18; Donibristle W/E 29.8.18;

HMS *Royalist* 20.9.18; Rosyth 20.9.18; HMS *Royalist* 21.9.18; Rosyth 12.10.18; HMS *Royalist* 12.10.18; Rosyth 17.10.18; Deleted W/E 31.10.18

**N6612** Deld 10 AAP Brooklands to Rosyth W/E 30.11.17; Donibristle W/E 7.12.17; Rosyth W/E 13.12.17; HMS *Pegasus* W/E 20.12.17; Turnhouse 24.2.18 (stowed during ships refit); HMS *Pegasus* by 16.3.18; Turnhouse W/E 13.4.18; HMS *Pegasus* W/E 20.4.18; Rosyth W/E 19.9.18; Turnhouse W/E 3.10.18 - @30.1.19; Rosyth to HMS *Phaeton* 12.9.19; Ashore while ship in Biörkö Sound [Latvia?] 29.9.19; HMS *Vindictive*, Baltic Russia (Koivisto); Dropped 2 bombs on railway station nr Petrograd 6.10.19 (F/L SD Culley)

**N6613** (130-hp Clerget) Deld War School Manston W/E 10.11.17 - @5.18, photographed standing on nose; HACP 28.1.18 (FSL SA Hamilton-Bowyer); 205 TDS Vendôme by 6.18 - @30.1.19

**N6614** Deld Rosyth W/E 30.11.17; HMS *Nairana* W/E 20.12.17; Turnhouse W/E 9.3.18; Rosyth W/E 20.4.18; HMS *Nairana* W/E 27.4.18; Rosyth by 9.5.18; HMS *Glorious* to Rosyth W/E 16.5.18; Donibristle to Rosyth W/E 23.5.18; Donibristle W/E 23.5.18; Rosyth W/E 23.5.18; Donibristle W/E 23.5.18; HMS *Comus* 23.5.18; Scapa by 27.6.18; Smoogroo W/E 12.9.18; Scapa W/E 12.9.18; HMS *Indomitable* 9.9.18; ashore 19.9.18; HMS *Indomitable* 19.9.18; ashore 28.9.18; HMS *Indomitable* 28.9.18; Smoogroo W/E 4.11.18; Scapa W/E 28.11.18; HMS *Indomitable* W/E 23.1.19 - @30.1.19

**N6615** (130-hp Clerget) Deld Cranwell W/E 16.11.17; Inverkeithing by rail W/E 23.11.17 (to Rosyth); Rosyth for erection by 28.12.17; Donibristle 18.1.18; Rosyth W/E 31.1.18; HMS *Pegasus* W/E 8.2.18 - @24.2.18; Turnhouse W/E 28.2.18 - @9.3.18 (stowed during ships refit); HMS *Pegasus* W/E 16.3.18 - @21.3.18; HMS *Campania* by 1.4.18; on a ship by 5.4.18 - @8.4.18; Donibristle 13.4.18; Turnhouse by 27.4.18 (while HMS *Pegasus* out of action); HMS *Pegasus* W/E 2.5.18; Turnhouse to Donibristle W/E 9.5.18; HMS *Pegasus* W/E 9.5.18; Turnhouse to HMS *Pegasus* W/E 9.5.18; Turnhouse W/E 16.5.18; HMS *Pegasus* W/E 1.7.18; Turnhouse repair W/E 15.8.18; For 2(N) ARD W/E 3.10.18

**N6616** En route Brooklands to East Fortune, EF, FL Ancaster 6.12.17 (undamaged); Cranwell W/E 14.12.17 (for Rosyth); East Fortune W/E 5.1.18; Donibristle by 11.1.18; Cranwell by 18.1.18 (temp); Donibristle to Rosyth W/E 18.1.18 [- @19.1.18]; HMS *Pegasus* W/E 18.1.18; Donibristle to Rosyth W/E 8.2.18 - @3.18; Donibristle to Turnhouse W/E 28.3.18; Rosyth to HMS *Galatea* 1.4.18; Donibristle 3.4.18; Rosyth W/E 4.4.18; HMS *Chatham* 14.4.18; Donibristle 8.5.18; HMS *Chatham* 8.5.18; Donibristle 9.5.18; Turnhouse by 5.18; HMS *Chatham* by 16.5.18; ashore 16.5.18; HMS *Chatham* 18.5.18; Turnhouse 3.7.18; Donibristle W/E 14.11.18 - @30.1.19; To Estonian AF 1919, stationed Koivisto with Estonian markings over standard scheme

**N6617** Landed Redcar en route to East Fortune 11.12.17; Houton Bay by 12.17; Rosyth to HMS *Nairana* 21.12.17; HMS *Renown* W/E 4.1.18; Houton Bay W/E 16.2.18 (overhaul); Rosyth 2.18; Houton Bay W/E 2.3.18 (overhaul); Scapa W/E 18.5.18; HMS *Caroline* W/E 6.7.18; HMS *New Zealand* 10.8.18; Smashed on Q-turret by heavy sea 23.8.18; Deleted W/E 12.9.18

**N6618** Beardmore factory 4.2.18; deld Rosyth store 2.18; Donibristle W/E 8.2.18; Rosyth by 16.3.18; Turnhouse W/E 6.4.18; Donibristle W/E 21.11.18 - @30.1.19

**N6619** Deld W/E 19.12.17; Howden, left for East Fortune, landed Shipton, broke propeller 20.12.17; HMS *Pegasus* by 29.12.17; Brooklands to Rosyth by 11.1.18 - @18.1.18; Donibristle by 8.2.18; HMS *Renown* by 8.2.18; Rosyth W/E 21.2.18; Turnhouse W/E 6.4.18; HMS *Inflexible* 25.7.18; Donibristle 2.8.18; HMS *Courageous* 27.8.18; Rosyth 30.8.18; HMS *Campania* to HMS *Pegasus* 26.10.18; Rosyth by 31.10.18; Scapa W/E 14.11.18 - @30.1.19

**N6620** Deld Yarmouth W/E 3.11.17 - @17.6.18; HACP 10.6.18; 273 Sqdn Burgh Castle by 6.18; AZP, missing in action 5.8.18 (Lt G F Hodgson killed)

**N6621** Deld Yarmouth W/E 3.11.17; HACP 9.6.18; 273 Sqdn Burgh Castle by 25.6.18; Became 486 Flt 273 Sqdn Burgh Castle on/by 26.9.18 - @28.10.18; 212 Sqdn Yarmouth by 10.18 - @30.1.19

**N6622** Deld Yarmouth W/E 3.11.17; Used for air launching experiments with HMA *R.23* at Pulham 6.18 (successfully dropped in flight, Lt RE Keys DFC); AZP 5.8.18 (Capt GD Kirkpatrick); Became 212 Sqdn Yarmouth 20.8.18

**N6623** Deld Yarmouth W/E 3.11.17 - 5.18; Felixstowe by 5.18; Fitted skid u/c, lost at sea in unsuccessful attempt by Cdr CR Samson to TO from lighter *H3* towed by destroyer HMS *Truculent* off Orfordness 30.5.18; For deletion by 27.6.18

**N6624** Deld War School Manston W/E 3.11.17; Covehithe by 10.6.18 - @1.7.18; HACP 10.6.18; 486 Flt Sqdn Burgh Castle by 7.7.18 (273 Sqdn 20.8.18) - @9.10.18; AZP 5.8.18 (Lt J Tomkins); Yarmouth by 31.12.18

**N6625** Deld War School Manston for erection W/E 3.11.17 - @25.5.18; Yarmouth by 16.6.18; Became 212 Sqdn Yarmouth 26.6.18 - @29.8.18; AZP, landed Bacton 5.8.18 (Lt GW Stafford); Felixstowe by 26.9.18; Martlesham Heath 3.3.19 - @7.4.19; Cranwell @30.7.19 (unarmed) ALSO HMS *Galatea* by 5.18 (doubtful?)

**N6626** Deld War School Manston W/E 3.11.17; Became Scout School Manston 5.18; Pool of Pilots Joyce Green 5.10.18; Crashed with stalling engine on climbing turn nr ground 21.10.18 (Lt R Welsh injured)

**N6627** Deld War School Manston W/E 3.11.17; Deleted W/E 23.3.18

**N6628** Deld War School Manston W/E 3.11.17; Depot (CSD White City?) to War School Manston 3.18 - @5.18; 205 TDS Vendôme (130-hp Clerget) by 6.18; Stalled on turn and spun in 25.6.18 (F/Cdt JES Denham)

**N6629** Deld CSD White City by 29.12.17; Rosyth W/E 11.1.18; Donibristle W/E 18.1.18; HMS *Nairana* W/E 8.2.18; Rosyth W/E 15.2.18; HMAS *Sydney* W/E 15.2.18; Rosyth by 23.2.18; HMS *Lion* by 28.2.18; Houton Bay W/E 30.3.18; (overhaul); HMS *Comus* 17.6.18; ashore 20.6.18; HMS *Comus* 20.6.18; ashore 27.6.18; HMS *Comus* 27.6.18; ashore 4.7.18; HMS *Comus* 4.7.18; Smoogroo 9.7.18; Scapa W/E 25.7.18; Smoogroo W/E 1.8.18; Scapa W/E 15.8.18; Smoogroo W/E 12.9.18 - @30.1.19

**N6630** Deld CSD White City by 29.12.17; Rosyth W/E 11.1.18; Donibristle W/E 18.1.18; HMS *Pegasus* W/E 8.2.18 (and ex Rosyth W/E 8.2.18) [by 5.2.18 - @24.2.18]; Turnhouse W/E 28.2.18 (stowed during ships refit); HMS *Pegasus* W/E 16.3.18; Turnhouse W/E 13.4.18 (while ship out of action); HMS *Pegasus* W/E 9.5.18; Turnhouse to Donibristle W/E 9.5.18; HMS *Pegasus* W/E 9.5.18; Turnhouse W/E 16.5.18; Cranwell W/E 25.5.18; Redcar 3.6.18; HMS *Furious* 8.7.18; HMS *Renown* W/E 15.8.18; Rosyth W/E 19.9.18; For deletion W/E 17.10.18

**N6631** Deld CSD White City W/E 5.1.18; Rosyth W/E 18.1.18; Donibristle W/E 31.1.18; Rosyth W/E 8.2.18; HMS *Lion* 13.2.18; Rosyth 13.2.18; HMAS *Sydney* W/E 15.2.18; Rosyth W/E 15.2.18; Donibristle W/E 16.3.18; Rosyth W/E 21.3.18; HMS *Royalist* 29.3.18; Rosyth 16.4.18; Turnhouse W/E 27.4.18; HMS *Phaeton* 6.9.18; Rosyth 17.9.18; Donibristle W/E 24.11.18; HMS *Inconstant* W/E 23.1.19 - @30.1.19

**N6632** Deld CSD White City W/E 19.1.18; Rosyth W/E 25.1.18; Donibristle W/E 8.2.18; Rosyth W/E 15.2.18 - @9.3.18; HMS *Comus* to Houton Bay W/E 30.3.18 (overhaul); Scapa W/E 18.5.18; Smoogroo W/E 1.6.18; Deleted W/E 20.6.18

**N6633** Deld CSD White City 1.18; Rosyth W/E 18.1.18; Donibristle W/E 8.2.18; Rosyth W/E 8.2.18; HMS *Princess Royal* 7.2.18; Donibristle 25.2.18; HMS *Princess Royal* 27.2.18; Donibristle 24.3.18; Rosyth W/E 4.4.18; Donibristle 4.18; HMS *Renown* 24.4.18; Donibristle 3.5.18; For deletion W/E 15.8.18

**N6634** Deld Yarmouth 16.1.18 @3.- 5.18; Tongue Patrol Flt Manston by 25.5.18 - @27.6.18; Attacked U-boat 31.5.18; Manston (470 Flt?) by 27.6.18 [Naval Flt 219 Sqdn?]; Throwley 27.10.18; Felixstowe by 11.18 - @30.1.19

**N6635** Deld CSD White City W/E 19.1.18; Rosyth W/E 25.1.18; Donibristle W/E 15.2.18; Rosyth W/E 15.2.18;

Donibristle by 23.2.18; HMAS *Sydney* by 27.2.18; Donibristle 27.2.18; HMAS *Sydney* to Donibristle W/E 21.3.18; Turnhouse to Donibristle W/E 28.3.18; HMAS *Sydney* W/E 28.3.18; Turnhouse from W/E 23.5.18; HMS *Phaeton* 8.6.18; ashore 13.6.18; Rosyth by 25.7.18 (repair); 2(N) ARD W/E 3.10.18 - @17.10.18

N6636    Deld CSD White City W/E 19.1.18; Rosyth W/E 31.1.18 - @23.2.18; Donibristle W/E 28.2.18; HMS *Calliope* 4.3.18; Houton Bay 11.3.18 (overhaul); Smoogroo 25.5.18; Scapa by 13.6.18; Hit air pocket while turning at low altitude, dived in Kirkwall 3.8.18 (Lt JP Walker killed); For deletion by 29.8.18

N6637    Deld CSD White City W/E 19.1.18; Rosyth W/E 31.1.18; Donibristle W/E 15.2.18 - @23.2.18; Rosyth W/E 28.2.18; Donibristle W/E 28.3.18; HMS *Caroline* to Houton Bay W/E 30.3.18 (overhaul); HMS *Repulse* 10.7.18; Rosyth 31.7.18; HMS *Repulse* 22.8.18; Donibristle (fitted W/T) 25.9.18 - @30.1.19

N6638    Mkrs @19.1.18; Deld CSD White City 1.18; Rosyth W/E 31.1.18; Donibristle W/E 15.2.18; Rosyth W/E 15.2.18; HMS *Repulse* 13.2.18; Donibristle 17.2.18; Rosyth W/E 21.2.18; HMS *Repulse* 18.2.18; Rosyth by 23.2.18; HMS *Repulse* 23.3.18; HMS *Pegasus* 24.3.18; Donibristle W/E 28.3.18 - @1.4.18; BUT HMS *Campania* by 1.4.18 - @8.4.18; Turnhouse by 4.18; Donibristle to Rosyth W/E 4.4.18; Turnhouse by 13.4.18 (while HMS *Pegasus* out of action); HMS *Pegasus* by 5.18; Donibristle W/E 9.5.18; Turnhouse to Donibristle W/E 9.5.18; Rosyth W/E 13.6.18; Turnhouse W/E 11.7.18; HMAS *Sydney* W/E 21.11.18; HMAS *Melbourne* W/E 16.1.19; HMAS *Sydney* W/E 23.1.19 - @30.1.19

N6639    Deld CSD White City W/E 19.1.18; Rosyth 1.18; Crashed on TO in snow from Rosyth football ground 20.1.18 (FSL AC Sharwood); Donibristle W/E 15.2.18; HMS *Phaeton* W/E 16.3.18; Rosyth 14.3.18; HMS *Royalist* to Donibristle 15.3.18; Rosyth to HMS *Royalist* W/E 4.4.18; Rosyth to HMS *Furious* W/E 4.4.18; Deleted W/E 15.8.18

N6640    Deld CSD White City W/E 26.1.18; Rosyth W/E 15.2.18; Turnhouse W/E 6.4.18; Donibristle W/E 15.8.18; HMS *Inconstant* 19.8.18; Rosyth 24.8.18; Deleted W/E 5.9.18

N6641    Deld CSD White City W/E 19.1.18; Rosyth W/E 15.2.18; HMS *Renown* W/E 16.3.18; HMS *Furious* by 5.18; HMS *Renown* 29.5.18; Donibristle W/E 13.6.18; HMS *Royalist* 13.6.18; Donibristle 20.6.18; HMS *Furious* 8.7.18; Donibristle W/E 22.8.18; Turnhouse W/E 12.9.18; Donibristle W/E 17.10.18; Turnhouse W/E 22.11.18; Deleted W/E 5.12.18

N6642    Deld CSD White City W/E 26.1.18; Rosyth W/E 15.2.18; Turnhouse W/E 6.4.18; Rosyth W/E 2.5.18; Turnhouse W/E 2.5.18; Donibristle W/E 2.5.18; Rosyth W/E 2.5.18; HMS *Princess Royal* 4.5.18; Rosyth 10.7.18; HMS *Inconstant* 10.7.18; Rosyth 31.7.18; *Comus* 24.8.18; Deleted W/E 5.9.18

N6643    Deld CSD White City W/E 26.1.18; Rosyth W/E 15.2.18; HMS *Pegasus* W/E 21.3.18; HMS *Campania* by 1.4.18 - @8.4.18; Turnhouse W/E 13.4.18; HMS *Pegasus* W/E 20.4.18; Turnhouse by 2.5.18 (while HMS *Pegasus* out of action); HMS *Pegasus* W/E 9.5.18; Turnhouse to Donibristle W/E 9.5.18; HMS *Pegasus* W/E 9.5.18; Turnhouse W/E 16.5.18; HMS *Pegasus* W/E 11.7.18; Turnhouse 19.9.18 - @30.1.19

N6644    Deld CSD White City W/E 26.1.18; Rosyth W/E 15.2.18; Donibristle W/E 28.2.18; Rosyth W/E 16.3.18; HMS *Phaeton* 14.3.18; Donibristle 23.3.18; Rosyth W/E 28.3.18; HMS *Phaeton* 2.4.18; Rosyth 16.4.18; Turnhouse W/E 27.4.18; Deleted W/E 27.5.18

N6645    Deld CSD White City W/E 26.1.18; Rosyth W/E 23.2.18; Turnhouse W/E 6.4.18; Rosyth W/E 20.4.18; HMS *Courageous* 26.4.18; Turnhouse 18.5.18; Donibristle W/E 31.10.18 - @30.1.19

N6646    Deld CSD White City W/E 26.1.18; Rosyth W/E 15.2.18; HMS *Pegasus* to Rosyth W/E 15.2.18 - @30.3.18; Turnhouse to Donibristle W/E 4.4.18; Rosyth W/E 4.4.18; HMS *Nairana* W/E 13.4.18; Rosyth W/E 11.7.18; Donibristle W/E 22.8.18; HMS *Penelope* W/E 17.10.18; HMS *Nairana* W/E 16.1.19

N6647    Deld CSD White City W/E 26.1.18; Rosyth W/E 15.2.18 - @9.3.18; Donibristle to Rosyth W/E 21.3.18;

Turnhouse to Donibristle W/E 4.4.18; HMS *Lion* W/E 13.4.18; Turnhouse from W/E 10.5.18; HMS *Lion* 17.7.18; Turnhouse 5.9.18; Donibristle W/E 14.11.18; HMS *Indomitable* W/E 12.12.18 - @30.1.19; ashore at Rosyth; HMS *Inconstant* 7.2.19; ashore at Rosyth 2.4.19

N6648    Deld CSD White City W/E 26.1.18; Rosyth W/E 15.2.18 - @23.2.18; Donibristle to Rosyth W/E 21.3.18; HMS *Nairana* W/E 4.4.18; HMS *Tiger* W/E 11.7.18; Turnhouse W/E 19.9.18 - @30.1.19

N6649    Mkrs @19.1.18; Deld CSD White City by 2.18; Rosyth W/E 15.2.18; Turnhouse W/E 6.4.18; HMS *Phaeton* 24.7.18; Turnhouse 27.7.18; HMS *Phaeton* 28.7.18; Turnhouse 11.8.18; HMS *Phaeton* 11.8.18; Turnhouse 17.8.18; HMS *Phaeton* 18.8.18; Turnhouse 24.8.18; HMS *Phaeton* 25.8.18; Turnhouse 2.9.18; HMS *Phaeton* 2.9.18; Turnhouse 6.9.18; Donibristle W/E 2.11.18; HMS *Phaeton* 23.12.18; ashore 15.1.19 - @30.1.19

**30 AVRO 504B TRACTOR BIPLANES put forward 1.17 & ordered under Cont No C.P.103733/17 from George Parnall & Co Ltd, numbered N6650 to N6679 & built Bristol. Fitted to carry 4x16-lb bombs. Interrupter gear. (80-hp Gnome) [all DC?]**

N6650    Transferred to RFC (Military Wing) 4.17 as B1392
N6651    Transferred to RFC (Military Wing) 4.17 as B1393
N6652    Transferred to RFC (Military Wing) 4.17 as B1394
N6653    Transferred to RFC (Military Wing) 4.17 as B1397
N6654    Transferred to RFC (Military Wing) 4.17 as B1398
N6655    Transferred to RFC (Military Wing) 4.17 as B1399
N6656    Transferred to RFC (Military Wing) 4.17 as B1400
N6657    Deld C Flt Cranwell 18.5.17; U/c smashed 25.6.17; U/c smashed 11.8.17; Crashed, CW Cranwell South 14.3.18 (pilot unhurt); For deletion by 30.3.18
N6658    Deld Cranwell 11.5.17; Deleted 27.7.17
N6659    (DC) Deld Eastbourne by rail 12.5.17; Crashed, damaged 2.1.18 (pilot unhurt); Became 206 TDS Eastbourne 1.4.18
N6660    (DC) Deld Eastbourne by rail 12.5.17; For deletion by 19.1.18
N6661    (DC) Deld Eastbourne by rail 12.5.17; Crashed and wrecked 12.12.17 (pilot unhurt); For deletion by 15.12.17
N6662    (DC) Deld Eastbourne by rail for erection 25.5.17; For deletion by 19.1.18
N6663    (DC) Deld Eastbourne by rail for erection 26.5.17; Became 206 TDS Eastbourne 1.4.18
N6664    (DC) Deld Eastbourne by rail for erection 28.5.17; Deleted 25.8.17
N6665    (DC) Deld Eastbourne by rail 5.6.17; Deleted 25.7.17
N6666    Deld C Flt Cranwell 9.6.17; Crashed 21.8.17; Redcar for evaluation W/E 19.1.18; For deletion by 30.3.18
N6667    Deld Cranwell for erection 13.6.17; Crashed and damaged 14.7.17; Crashed and CW Rauceby gun station 29.1.18 (TPFO NC Collett killed); For deletion by 1.2.18
N6668    Deld Chingford for erection 14.6.17; Fell in reservoir, CW 4.9.17 (TPFO AS Coombe killed & PFO C Saunders serisously injured)
N6669    Deld Chingford for erection 19.6.17 - @2.18; Fairlop by 30.3.18; Became 207 TDS Chingford/Fairlop 1.4.18
N6670    (DC) Deld Eastbourne 31.5.17; Crashed and damaged, Cooden Golf Links 13.1.18 (pilot unhurt); For deletion by 30.3.18
N6671    Deld Eastbourne for erection 8.6.17; Deleted 25.7.17
N6672    (DC) Deld Eastbourne by rail for erection 2.7.17; Crashed and damaged on TO 31.1.18 (pilot unhurt); Became 206 TDS Eastbourne 1.4.18
N6673    (DC) Deld Eastbourne by rail for erection 2.7.17; Became 206 TDS Eastbourne 1.4.18
N6674    (DC) Deld Eastbourne by rail for erection 10.7.17; EF in sideslip, crashed 5.1.18 (pilot unhurt); Surveyed 8.1.18 DBR; Deleted 17.1.18
N6675    Deld Eastbourne by rail for erection 14.7.17; Deleted 21.8.17
N6676    (DC) Deld Eastbourne by rail for erection 16.7.17; Surveyed 6.12.17; Deleted 19.12.17 wrecked
N6677    (DC) Deld Eastbourne by rail for erection 20.7.17; Crashed and wrecked 16.3.18 (pilot unhurt); Deleted W/E 30.3.18

N6678    Deld Manston FS by road 25.7.17; Became Pilots Pool Manston 1.4.18

N6679    Deld Manston FS by rail 28.7.17 (coded '2'); Became Pilots Pool Manston 1.4.18

**70 BEARDMORE W.B.III (SBIIID with jettisonable u/c) TRACTOR BIPLANE SHIPBOARD AIRCRAFT ordered under Cont Nos A.S.775 & A.S.12856, numbered N6680 to N6749 & built Dalmuir. 42 cancelled 5.2.18, presume reinstated but mostly to storage. (80-hp Le Rhône)**

N6680    Deld Donibristle W/E 9.11.17; Rosyth W/E 16.11.17; Donibristle W/E 22.11.17; Rosyth W/E 21.3.18; Donibristle 3.18; HMS *Pegasus* W/E 21.3.18; Donibristle W/E 21.3.18; Rosyth W/E 28.3.18; HMS *Pegasus* W/E 28.3.18; Donibristle W/E 28.3.18; HMS *Pegasus* W/E 28.3.18 [@26-28.3.18]; Donibristle W/E 28.3.18; Rosyth W/E 13.6.18; Donibristle W/E 11.7.18; Deleted W/E 12.9.18

N6681    Deld Donibristle W/E 9.11.17; Rosyth W/E 16.11.17 - @28.12.17; HMS *Pegasus* 1.18; Donibristle W/E 11.1.18; HMS *Pegasus* W/E 21.3.18 [@18.3.18]; Donibristle W/E 21.3.18; Rosyth W/E 28.3.18; HMS *Pegasus* W/E 28.3.18; Donibristle W/E 28.3.18; For deletion by 15.8.18

N6682    Deld Donibristle W/E 9.11.17; Rosyth W/E 16.11.17; Donibristle W/E 8.2.18; Rosyth W/E 21.3.18; HMS *Nairana* W/E 28.3.18; Donibristle 30.3.18; HMS *Nairana* 30.3.18; Donibristle 4.4.18; Rosyth W/E 4.4.18; Donibristle to HMS *Nairana* W/E 4.4.18 (three times); Donibristle to HMS *Pegasus* W/E 4.4.18; a ship (*Pegasus*?) by 5.4.18; Rosyth by 2.5.18; Donibristle W/E 9.5.18; Rosyth W/E 16.5.18; HMS *Pegasus* to Donibristle W/E 23.5.18 (twice); Rosyth W/E 23.5.18 (twice); HMS *Pegasus* to Rosyth W/E 23.5.18; Donibristle by 6.18; Rosyth W/E 11.7.18; Donibristle W/E 15.8.18; Rosyth W/E 24.10.18; Donibristle W/E 31.10.18 - @30.1.19

N6683    Deld HMS *Campania* for erection 22.12.17; Houton Bay (erection) W/E 29.12.17; Damaged when Bessonneau tent blown down in gale 27.2.18; Surveyed 2.3.18 (repairable); Deleted W/E 27.4.18

N6684    Deld HMS *Campania* for erection 22.12.17; Houton Bay (erection) W/E 29.12.17; Deleted W/E 27.4.18

N6685    Deld Houton Bay W/E 29.12.17; Scapa W/E 18.5.18; Smoogroo W/E 18.8.18; Scapa W/E 28.11.18 - @30.1.19

N6686    Deld Houton Bay W/E 29.12.17 (repair wing by 23.2.18) (ex HMS *Royalist* by 9.3.18); Scapa W/E 18.5.18; Smoogroo W/E 1.8.18; Scapa W/E 19.12.18 - @30.1.19

N6687    Deld Rosyth for erection W/E 16.11.17; Donibristle W/E 5.1.18; HMS *Nairana* W/E 11.1.18; Donibristle but smashed u/c landing on snow 15.1.18; Rosyth W/E 18.1.18 (ex HMS *Pegasus*); Turnhouse W/E 21.3.18; Deleted W/E 11.7.18

N6688    Deld Rosyth for erection W/E 16.11.17; East Fortune W/E 16.2.18 (for carriers); Became 208 TDS East Fortune 6.18; Deleted W/E 11.7.18

N6689    Deld Houton Bay for erection W/E 2.2.18; Damaged when Bessonneau tent blown down in gale 27.2.18; Surveyed 2.3.18 (repairable); Deleted W/E 27.4.18

N6690    Deld Rosyth for erection W/E 23.11.17; Donibristle 11.1.18; HMS *Pegasus* 13.2.18; Rosyth 15.2.18; For deletion by 21.2.18

N6691    Deld Rosyth W/E 23.11.17; Donibristle W/E 28.12.17; HMS *Pegasus* W/E 18.1.18; HMS *Nairana* W/E 17.1.18; Donibristle W/E 25.1.18; Rosyth W/E 25.1.18; Turnhouse W/E 21.3.18; Deleted W/E 11.7.18

N6692    Deld Rosyth W/E 23.11.17 - @29.12.17; HMS *Pegasus* W/E 3.1.18 - @10.1.18; Donibristle to HMS *Pegasus* W/E 11.1.18 [HMS *Pegasus* @7-11.1.18]; Donibristle W/E 17.1.18 - @19.1.18; HMS *Nairana* to Rosyth W/E 28.1.18; Donibristle to HMS *Pegasus* W/E 8.2.18 [by 8.2.18 at anchor]; Rosyth W/E 15.2.18; HMS *Pegasus* 13.2.18; Donibristle 15.2.18; HMS *Nairana* by 23.2.18; Donibristle W/E 28.2.18; HMS *Nairana* from 3.18; Donibristle by 30.3.18; HMS *Pegasus* to Donibristle W/E 4.4.18; HMS *Nairana* to Donibristle W/E 4.4.18 - @30.1.19

N6693    Deld Houton Bay for erection W/E 23.2.18; Scapa for erection W/E 4.5.18; Smoogroo W/E 8.8.18; HMS *Vindictive* 29.10.18; Scapa W/E 28.11.18; Smoogroo W/E 12.12.18; Scapa W/E 23.1.19 - @30.1.19

N6694    Deld Houton Bay for erection W/E 29.12.17; Escaped damage when Bessonneau tent blown down in gale 27.2.18; Deleted W/E 27.4.18

N6695    Deld Houton Bay (via Aberdeen) for erection W/E 12.12.17; Damaged when Bessoneau tent blown down in gale 27.2.18; Surveyed 2.3.18 (repairable); Deleted W/E 27.4.18

N6696    Deld Rosyth for erection W/E 30.11.17; Donibristle W/E 16.2.18; Rosyth W/E 21.3.18; Donibristle 3.18; HMS *Pegasus* W/E 28.3.18 [by 26.3.18]; Donibristle W/E 4.4.18; Rosyth W/E 4.4.18; HMS *Nairana* W/E 4.4.18; Donibristle W/E 4.4.18; HMS *Pegasus* by 3-5.4.18; Donibristle by 2.5.18; HMS *Cassandra* 29.7.18; Donibristle 9.8.18; Deleted W/E 21.11.18

N6697    Deld Rosyth for erection W/E 30.11.17; Donibristle W/E 8.2.18 - @16.5.18; Rosyth 5.18; *Pegasus* W/E 23.5.18; Donibristle W/E 23.5.18; Rosyth W/E 23.5.18; Donibristle W/E 23.5.18; Rosyth W/E 23.5.18; Turnhouse W/E 11.7.18; Deleted W/E 15.8.18

N6698    Deld Houton Bay for erection W/E 29.12.17; Scapa from W/E 4.5.18; Smoogroo W/E 8.8.18; Scapa W/E 28.11.18 - @30.1.19

N6699    Deld Rosyth for erection W/E 30.11.17; East Fortune NFS W/E 8.2.18 (for carriers); Deleted W/E 27.6.18

N6700    Deld Rosyth for erection W/E 30.11.17; Donibristle by 3.1.18; Rosyth by 18.1.18; Donibristle W/E 8.2.18; Turnhouse W/E 20.4.18; Donibristle W/E 23.5.18; HMS *Pegasus* W/E 1.8.18; Rosyth W/E 15.8.18; Donibristle W/E 21.11.18 - @30.1.19

N6701    Tested Dalmuir 10.12.17; Deld Houton Bay for erection W/E 29.12.17; Scapa for erection from W/E 4.5.18; Smoogroo W/E 15.8.18; Scapa W/E 28.11.18; Smoogroo W/E 12.12.18; Scapa W/E 23.1.19 - @30.1.19

N6702    Deld Killingholme Reserve W/E 14.12.17; 6 AAP Renfrew W/E 27.4.18; Turnhouse W/E 13.6.18; Donibristle W/E 11.7.18; Rosyth W/E 29.8.18; Donibristle W/E 29.8.18 - @30.1.19

N6703    Deld Killingholme Reserve W/E 14.12.17; 6 AAP Renfrew W/E 27.4.18; Turnhouse W/E 13.6.18; HMS *Pegasus* W/E 1.8.18; Donibristle W/E 15.8.18; Rosyth W/E 22.8.18; Donibristle W/E 2.9.18; Rosyth W/E 24.10.18 - @30.1.19

N6704    Deld Killingholme Reserve W/E 14.12.17; 6 AAP Renfrew W/E 27.4.18; Turnhouse W/E 13.6.18; HMS *Pegasus* W/E 1.8.18; Rosyth W/E 15.8.18; Donibristle W/E 29.8.18; Rosyth W/E 26.9.18; Donibristle W/E 3.10.18; Rosyth W/E 17.10.18; Deleted W/E 31.10.18

N6705    Deld Killingholme Reserve W/E 14.12.17; 6 AAP Renfrew W/E 27.4.18; Turnhouse W/E 13.6.18; Donibristle W/E 11.7.18; Rosyth W/E 24.10.18; Donibristle W/E 31.10.18 - @30.1.19

N6706    Deld Killingholme Reserve W/E 12.12.17; 6 AAP Renfrew W/E 27.4.18; Turnhouse W/E 13.6.18; Donibristle W/E 15.8.18 - @30.1.19

N6707    Deld Killingholme Reserve W/E 12.12.17; 6 AAP Renfrew W/E 27.4.18; Turnhouse W/E 13.6.18; Donibristle W/E 17.10.18 - @30.1.19

N6708    Deld Grain Type Test Flt without engine 13.12.17; Weighed 20.12.17; Rosyth W/E 15.2.18; Donibristle W/E 28.3.18; HMS *Nairana* W/E 13.4.18; Rosyth W/E 20.4.18; HMS *Nairana* W/E 22.4.18; Rosyth W/E 2.5.18; HMS *Nairana* W/E 11.5.18; Donibristle W/E 16.5.18; Rosyth W/E 23.5.18; For deletion W/E 15.8.18

N6709    Deld Killingholme Reserve W/E 12.12.17; 6 AAP Renfrew W/E 27.4.18; transit W/E 13.6.18; Turnhouse W/E 11.7.18; Donibristle W/E 22.8.18; Rosyth W/E 3.10.18; Donibristle W/E 17.10.18; Rosyth W/E 24.10.18; Donibristle W/E 14.11.18 - @30.1.19

N6710    Deld Killingholme Reserve W/E 12.12.17; 6 AAP Renfrew WE 27.4.18; transit W/E 13.6.18; Turnhouse W/E 11.7.18 (for HMS *Pegasus*); Donibristle W/E 15.8.18; Rosyth W/E 26.9.18; Donibristle W/E 3.10.18; Rosyth W/E 17.10.18; Donibristle W/E 31.10.18 - @30.1.19

N6711    Deld Killingholme Reserve W/E 12.12.17; 6 AAP Renfrew W/E 27.4.18; transit W/E 13.6.18; Turnhouse W/E 11.7.18; Donibristle W/E 15.8.18; Rosyth W/E

3.10.18; Donibristle W/E 17.10.18; Rosyth W/E 24.10.18; Donibristle W/E 14.11.18 - @30.1.19

N6712 Deld Killingholme Reserve W/E 12.12.17; 6 AAP Renfrew W/E 27.4.18; transit W/E 13.6.18; Turnhouse W/E 11.7.18; Donibristle W/E 15.8.18; Rosyth W/E 26.9.18; Donibristle W/E 3.10.18; Rosyth W/E 17.10.18; Deleted W/E 21.11.18

N6713 Deld Killingholme Reserve W/E 12.12.17; 6 AAP Renfrew W/E 27.4.18; transit W/E 13.6.18; Donibristle W/E 11.7.18; Rosyth W/E 22.8.18; Donibristle W/E 29.8.18; Flew under Forth Bridge 28.8.18 (Capt WW Wakefield); Rosyth W/E 26.9.18; Donibristle W/E 3.10.18; Rosyth W/E 17.10.18; Donibristle W/E 31.10.18 - @30.1.19

N6714 Deld Killingholme Reserve W/E 19.12.17; 6 AAP Renfrew W/E 27.4.18; transit W/E 13.6.18; Turnhouse W/E 11.7.18 (for HMS *Pegasus*); Donibristle W/E 15.8.18; Rosyth W/E 22.8.18; Donibristle W/E 29.8.18; Deleted W/E 21.11.18

N6715 Deld Killingholme Reserve W/E 12.12.17; 6 AAP Renfrew W/E 27.4.18; transit W/E 11.7.18; Donibristle W/E 15.8.18 - @30.1.19

N6716 Deld Killingholme Reserve W/E 19.12.17; 6 AAP Renfrew W/E 27.4.18; transit W/E 11.7.18; Donibristle W/E 15.8.18 - @30.1.19

N6717 Deld Killingholme Reserve W/E 19.12.17; 6 AAP Renfrew W/E 27.4.18; transit W/E 11.7.18; Donibristle W/E 15.8.18 - @30.1.19

N6718 Deld Killingholme Reserve W/E 19.12.17; 6 AAP Renfrew W/E 27.4.18; transit W/E 11.7.18; Donibristle W/E 15.8.18 - @30.1.19

N6719 Deld Killingholme Reserve W/E 19.12.17; 6 AAP Renfrew W/E 27.4.18; transit W/E 11.7.18; Donibristle W/E 15.8.18 - @30.1.19

N6720 Deld Killingholme Reserve W/E 19.12.17; 6 AAP Renfrew W/E 27.4.18; transit W/E 11.7.18; Donibristle W/E 15.8.18 - @30.1.19

N6721 Deld Killingholme Reserve W/E 5.1.18; 6 AAP Renfrew W/E 27.4.18; transit W/E 11.7.18; Donibristle W/E 15.8.18 - @30.1.19

N6722 Deld Killingholme Reserve W/E 5.1.18; 6 AAP Renfrew W/E 27.4.18; transit W/E 11.7.18; Donibristle W/E 15.8.18 - @30.1.19

N6723 Deld Killingholme Reserve W/E 5.1.18; 6 AAP Renfrew W/E 27.4.18; transit W/E 11.7.18; Donibristle W/E 15.8.18 - @30.1.19

N6724 Deld Killingholme Reserve W/E 5.1.18; 6 AAP Renfrew W/E 27.4.18; transit W/E 11.7.18; Donibristle W/E 15.8.18 - @30.1.19 BUT 6 AAP Renfrew by 31.12.18

N6725 Deld Killingholme Reserve W/E 5.1.18; 6 AAP Renfrew W/E 27.4.18; transit W/E 11.7.18; Donibristle W/E 15.8.18; Turnhouse W/E 19.9.18 - @30.1.19

N6726 Deld Killingholme Reserve W/E 5.1.18; 6 AAP Renfrew W/E 27.4.18; transit W/E 11.7.18; Turnhouse W/E 15.8.18 - @30.1.19

N6727 Deld Killingholme Reserve W/E 5.1.18; 6 AAP Renfrew W/E 27.4.18; transit W/E 11.7.18; Turnhouse W/E 15.8.18 - @30.1.19

N6728 Deld Killingholme Reserve W/E 5.1.18; 6 AAP Renfrew W/E 27.4.18; transit W/E 11.7.18; Turnhouse W/E 15.8.18 - @30.1.19

N6729 Deld Killingholme Reserve W/E 5.1.18; 6 AAP Renfrew W/E 27.4.18; transit W/E 11.7.18; Turnhouse W/E 15.8.18 - @30.1.19

N6730 Deld Killingholme Reserve W/E 5.1.18; 6 AAP Renfrew W/E 27.4.18; transit W/E 11.7.18; Turnhouse W/E 15.8.18 - @30.1.19

N6731 Deld Killingholme Reserve W/E 26.1.18; 6 AAP Renfrew W/E 27.4.18 - @30.1.19 [HMS *Inconstant* 17.1.19 - 23.1.19? - listed as aeroplane 6371]

N6732 Deld Killingholme Reserve W/E 26.1.18; 6 AAP Renfrew W/E 27.4.18 - @30.1.19

N6733 Deld Killingholme Reserve W/E 26.1.18; 6 AAP Renfrew W/E 27.4.18 - @30.1.19

N6734 Deld Killingholme Reserve W/E 26.1.18; 6 AAP Renfrew W/E 27.4.18 - @30.1.19

N6735 (110-hp Le Rhône) Deld Killingholme Reserve W/E 26.1.18; 6 AAP Renfrew W/E 27.4.18; 6 SD Ascot 25.7.18; Transferred to Japanese Govt W/E 29.8.18

N6736 Deld Killingholme Reserve 26.1.18; 6 AAP Renfrew W/E 27.4.18; 6 SD Ascot W/E 18.7.18; Transferred to Japanese Govt W/E 29.8.18

N6737 Deld Killingholme Reserve W/E 26.1.18; 6 AAP Renfrew W/E 27.4.18 - @30.1.19

N6738 Deld Killingholme Reserve W/E 26.1.18; 6 AAP Renfrew W/E 27.4.18 - @30.1.19

N6739 Deld Killingholme Reserve W/E 26.1.18; 6 AAP Renfrew W/E 27.4.18 - @30.1.19

N6740 Deld Killingholme Reserve W/E 26.1.18; 6 AAP Renfrew W/E 27.4.18 - @30.1.19

N6741 Deld Killingholme Reserve W/E 26.1.18; 6 AAP Renfrew W/E 27.4.18 - @30.1.19

N6742 Deld Killingholme Reserve W/E 26.1.18; 6 AAP Renfrew W/E 27.4.18 - @30.1.19

N6743 Deld Killingholme Reserve W/E 23.2.18; 6 AAP Renfrew W/E 27.4.18 - @30.1.19

N6744 Deld Killingholme Reserve W/E 23.2.18; 6 AAP Renfrew W/E 27.4.18 - @30.1.19

N6745 Deld Killingholme Reserve W/E 23.2.18; 6 AAP Renfrew W/E 27.4.18 - @30.1.19

N6746 Deld Killingholme Reserve W/E 23.2.18; 6 AAP Renfrew W/E 27.4.18 - @30.1.19

N6747 Deld Killingholme Reserve W/E 23.2.18; 6 AAP Renfrew W/E 27.4.18 - @30.1.19

N6748 Deld Killingholme Reserve W/E 23.2.18; 6 AAP Renfrew W/E 27.4.18 - @30.1.19

N6749 Deld Grain Type Test Flt W/E 23.2.18 (engine test); 6 AAP Renfrew W/E 8.8.18 - @30.1.19

**50 SOPWITH 2F.1 SHIP'S CAMEL TRACTOR BIPLANE SCOUTS ordered under Cont No A.S.35920 from Sir William Beardmore & Co Ltd, numbered N6750 to N6799 & built Dalmuir. (150-hp B.R.1)**

N6750 FF 20.2.18. Deld Rosyth store W/E 16.3.18; Donibristle to Rosyth W/E 21.3.18; HMS *Galatea* 8.4.18; Rosyth 18.4.18; Turnhouse W/E 27.4.18; Scapa W/E 31.10.18 - @7.11.18; Donibristle by 21.11.18; HMS *Tiger* W/E 16.1.19 - @30.1.19; Transferred to Lettish Govt

N6751 Deld Rosyth W/E 16.3.18; Turnhouse W/E 16.4.18; Donibristle W/E 2.5.18; Rosyth W/E 2.5.18; HMS *Renown* 4.5.18; Rosyth W/E 16.5.18; HMS *Royalist* 13.5.18; Donibristle 18.5.18; HMS *Renown* 25.7.18; Donibristle 13.8.18; Rosyth W/E 22.8.18; HMS *Courageous* 15.9.18; Donibristle 15.10.18 - @30.1.19 ALSO HMS *Iron Duke*

N6752 Deld Rosyth W/E 16.3.18; Turnhouse W/E 6.4.18; Donibristle W/E 13.4.18; HMS *Courageous* 21.4.18; Rosyth 26.4.18; HMS *Courageous* 5.18; ashore 5.18; HMS *Southampton* W/E 9.5.18; Rosyth 19.5.18; Turnhouse 3.7.18; Donibristle 1.10.18; Rosyth W/E 24.10.18; Donibristle W/E 14.11.18; HMS *Princess Royal* 8.1.19; Not listed by W/E 23.1.19 ALSO HMS *Royal Sovereign*

N6753 Deld Rosyth by rail W/E 21.3.18; Turnhouse W/E 21.3.18; Donibristle W/E 16.5.18; Rosyth W/E 16.5.18; HMS *Birkenhead* 18.5.18; HMS *Furious* by W/E 11.7.18; Deleted W/E 15.8.18

N6754 Deld Rosyth by rail W/E 21.3.18; Turnhouse W/E 21.3.18; Donibristle W/E 16.5.18; Rosyth W/E 16.5.18; HMS *Royalist* 16.5.18; FL in sea, attended by HMS *Vega* 20.5.18; Rosyth, For deletion by 27.6.18

N6755 Deld Rosyth by rail W/E 30.3.18; Turnhouse W/E 6.4.18; HMS *Galatea* 18.4.18; Rosyth 9.5.18; HMS *Southampton* 19.5.18; Turnhouse W/E 13.6.18; HMS *Furious* W/E 11.7.18; Turnhouse W/E 15.8.18 (repair); 2(N) ARD W/E 3.10.18 - @17.10.18

N6756 Deld Rosyth by rail W/E 30.3.18; Turnhouse to Donibristle W/E 4.4.18; HMAS *Melbourne* 16.4.18; Turnhouse W/E 24.5.18; Rosyth by 25.5.18; HMS *Galatea* by 6.18; Turnhouse by 27.6.18; HMS *Aurora* 3.7.18; CW by force of weather in North Sea 23.8.18; Remains put ashore at Rosyth 24.8.18

N6757 FF 20.3.18; Deld Rosyth by rail W/E 30.3.18; Turnhouse W/E 6.4.18 - @25.5.18; HMS *Cordelia* by 6.18; Donibristle W/E 17.10.18; HMS *Iron Duke* W/E 24.10.18; Rosyth W/E 31.10.18; Donibristle W/E 31.12.18 - @30.1.19; HMS *Eagle* Flt RAF Base Gosport, EF on TO while testing Fort Grange 26.3.20 (F/O WF Dickson injured) (only flown 6 hrs)

N6758 Deld Rosyth by rail W/E 30.3.18; Turnhouse W/E 6.4.18; HMS *Phaeton* W/E 20.4.18; Turnhouse W/E

18.5.18; Donibristle W/E 15.8.18; Rosyth W/E 29.8.18; HMS *Princess Royal* W/E 19.9.18; Rosyth 15.10.18; Donibristle W/E 14.11.18 - @30.1.19

N6759 Deld Rosyth store by rail W/E 30.3.18; Turnhouse to Donibristle W/E 4.4.18; Rosyth W/E 13.4.18; Donibristle W/E 16.4.18; HMS *Birkenhead* 22.4.18; Donibristle 8.5.18; HMS *Birkenhead* 9.5.18; Donibristle 18.5.18; HMS *Birkenhead* 18.5.18; Donibristle 24.5.18; Rosyth 24.5.18; HMS *Birkenhead* 5.18; Rosyth 31.5.18; HMS *Indomitable* 26.8.18; Scapa 9.9.18; HMS *Inflexible* 3.11.18; Disposed W/E 23.1.19

N6760 Deld Turnhouse W/E 23.3.18; Rosyth W/E 30.3.18; Turnhouse 4.18; Donibristle W/E 4.4.18; HMS *Comus* 16.4.18; Rosyth 29.4.18; HMS *Comus* W/E 11.5.18; Rosyth 18.5.18; Donibristle W/E 23.5.18; Rosyth W/E 11.7.18; HMS *Lion* W/E 15.8.18; Rosyth W/E 29.8.18; Deleted W/E 5.9.18

N6761 Deld Turnhouse 3.18; Rosyth W/E 30.3.18; Turnhouse to Donibristle W/E 4.4.18; HMS *Furious* 9.4.18; Deleted W/E 5.9.18

N6762 Deld Turnhouse 3.18; Rosyth W/E 30.3.18; Donibristle W/E 4.4.18; HMS *Royalist* 16.4.18; Turnhouse 16.5.18; Rosyth W/E 15.8.18; Turnhouse W/E 19.9.18; Rosyth W/E 31.10.18; Deleted W/E 5.12.18 ALSO HMS *Barham*

N6763 Deld Turnhouse 3.18; Rosyth W/E 30.3.18; Turnhouse W/E 6.4.18; Donibristle W/E 20.4.18; Rosyth W/E 27.4.18; HMS *Courageous* 2.5.18; Rosyth 9.5.18; HMS *Courageous* 18.5.18; Turnhouse 13.7.18; Deleted W/E 18.7.18

N6764 Deld Turnhouse 3.18; Rosyth W/E 30.3.18; Turnhouse W/E 6.4.18; Donibristle W/E 20.4.18; Rosyth W/E 20.4.18; HMS *Lion* by 25.4.18; Rosyth by 4.18; HMS *Lion* 4.5.18; Rosyth by 9.5.18; Donibristle to HMS *Lion* W/E 9.5.18; Donibristle W/E 9.5.18; HMS *Lion* 7.6.18; Turnhouse 11.7.18; Donibristle W/E 21.11.18 - @30.1.19

N6765 Deld Turnhouse 3.18; Rosyth W/E 30.3.18; Turnhouse W/E 6.4.18; Rosyth W/E 27.4.18; Turnhouse by 3.5.18; For deletion W/E 13.6.18

N6766 Deld Turnhouse 3.18; Rosyth W/E 30.3.18; Turnhouse W/E 6.4.18; Rosyth W/E 20.4.18; HMS *Caroline* 21.4.18; Rosyth 1.5.18; HMS *Galatea* 9.5.18; Turnhouse to Donibristle W/E 16.5.18; HMS *Galatea* 16.5.18; to Donibristle but struck treetop landing and spun in 18.5.18 (FSL MHW Trendall DoI 19.5.18)

N6767 Deld Rosyth W/E 30.3.18; Turnhouse W/E 13.4.18; Rosyth W/E 20.4.18; HMS *Cordelia* 29.4.18; ashore 28.5.18; HMS *Furious* 8.7.18; Donibristle 12.12.18; HMS *Furious* W/E 16.1.19; ashore 3.2.19; HMS *Vindictive*, Korvisto, South Russia; Attacked Kite Balloon 25.10.19 (F/L SD Culley)

N6768 Deld Turnhouse W/E 6.4.18; Rosyth W/E 20.4.18; Donibristle 4.18; HMS *Calliope* 23.4.18; Rosyth 26.4.18; Donibristle W/E 11.5.18; HMS *Calliope* W/E 11.5.18; ashore 5.18; HMS *Comus* 5.18; Rosyth W/E 23.5.18; Donibristle W/E 23.5.18; Rosyth W/E 23.5.18; HMS *Caroline* 25.6.18; Scapa 4.7.18; Smoogroo 3.10.18; HMS *Penelope* W/E 10.10.18; Donibristle 12.10.18; HMS *Princess Royal* 15.10.18; Scapa W/E 31.12.18; HMS *Princess Royal* W/E 23.1.19 - @30.1.19

N6769 Deld Turnhouse 3.18; Rosyth W/E 30.3.18; Turnhouse W/E 6.4.18; Donibristle W/E 9.5.18; HMS *Lion* 4.5.18; Rosyth W/E 18.5.18; Scapa by 23.5.18; HMS *Lion* 7.6.18; Flown off, landed nr HMS *Verulam*, seriously damaged, salved by HMS *Campania*, retd base 13.6.18 (Mjr RDG Sibley); Scapa W/E 27.6.18; ashore; HMS *Valiant* 20.12.18; ashore; HMS *Valiant* 16.1.19, lost speed, sideslipped in 29.1.19 (Lt W Smith drowned)

N6770 Deld Turnhouse Rosyth W/E 6.4.18; Turnhouse W/E 13.4.18; Donibristle W/E 27.4.18; Rosyth W/E 2.5.18; HMS *Nairana* W/E 2.5.18; Donibristle W/E 11.5.18; HMS *Nairana* W/E 18.5.18; HMS *Princess Royal* 14.7.18; Donibristle 24.8.18; Rosyth W/E 29.8.18; HMS *Galatea* 10.9.18; Rosyth W/E 27.10.18; HMS *Campania* to HMS *Pegasus* 26.10.18; Rosyth 27.10.18; Scapa W/E 14.11.18; HMS *Aurora* 30.12.18; Disposed W/E 30.1.19

N6771 Deld Turnhouse W/E 13.4.18; Donibristle W/E 16.5.18; HMS *Furious* 24.5.18; Flown in raid on Tondern airship base, FL Bramminge, Denmark, pilot burned aircraft

19.7.18 (Capt WD Jackson interned)

N6772 Deld Turnhouse W/E 13.4.18 - @13.5.18; HMS *Pegasus* 5.18; Turnhouse to Donibristle W/E 9.5.18; Rosyth W/E 16.5.18; HMS *Pegasus* 15.5.18; Donibristle W/E 16.5.18; Rosyth W/E 23.5.18; HMS *Galatea* W/E 23.5.18; ashore 10.7.18; HMS *Furious* 12.7.18; Turnhouse W/E 15.8.18; 2(N) ARD W/E 3.10.18 (repair)

N6773 Deld Turnhouse W/E 13.4.18; Donibristle W/E 16.5.18; Rosyth W/E 16.5.18; Turnhouse 5.18; HMS *Courageous* 23.5.18; Rosyth W/E 18.7.18; HMS *Chatham* W/E 25.7.18; ashore 17.8.18; HMS *Chatham* 17.8.18; HMS *Pegasus* W/E 26.9.18; Donibristle W/E 3.10.18; Rosyth W/E 17.10.18; HMS *Undaunted* 21.10.18; Rosyth W/E 24.10.18; Donibristle W/E 31.12.18; HMS *Lion* W/E 23.1.19 - @30.1.19

N6774 Deld Turnhouse W/E 13.4.18; Donibristle W/E 2.5.18; Turnhouse W/E 9.5.18; Rosyth W/E 9.5.18; HMS *Phaeton* 12.5.18; Rosyth 22.5.18; HMS *Phaeton* 22.5.18; Donibristle W/E 23.5.18; HMS *Phaeton* 6.18; For deletion by 13.6.18

N6775 Deld Turnhouse W/E 13.4.18; HMS *Comus* 4.18; Donibristle W/E 27.4.18; Rosyth W/E 2.5.18; HMS *Comus* W/E 2.5.18; Donibristle W/E 11.5.18; HMS *Comus* W/E 25.5.18; Rosyth W/E 13.6.18; Turnhouse W/E 1.8.18; 2(N) ARD W/E 3.10.18 (repair) ALSO HMS *Courageous* 5.18; HMS *Calliope*

N6776 Deld Turnhouse W/E 6.4.18; Donibristle W/E 16.5.18; Rosyth W/E 23.6.18; HMS *Glorious* by 7.18; Turnhouse W/E 11.7.18; Donibristle W/E 21.11.18; HMS *Lion* 16.12.18 - @30.1.19; HMS *Argus*?; Crashed and salved 2.7.19

N6777 Deld Turnhouse W/E 13.4.18; Donibristle W/E 16.5.18; Rosyth W/E 23.5.18; HMS *Royalist* 4.6.18; Rosyth 5.6.18; HMS *Royalist* 5.6.18; Rosyth 17.6.18; HMS *Furious* W/E 15.8.18; Donibristle W/E 22.8.18; HMS *Furious* 29.9.18; Donibristle W/E 11.12.18; HMS *Furious* W/E 23.1.19 - @30.1.19; Grand Fleet SoAF&G Leuchars by 7.19

N6778 Deld Turnhouse W/E 20.4.18; Donibristle W/E 2.5.18; Rosyth W/E 9.5.18; HMS *Glorious* W/E 16.5.18; Rosyth W/E 20.6.18; Scapa W/E 18.7.18; HMS *Penelope* by 1.10.18; Scapa W/E 10.10.18 for deletion

N6779 Deld Turnhouse 4.18; Donibristle 4.18; HMS *Calliope* 4.18 - 5.18; Turnhouse to 5.18; Donibristle W/E 2.5.18; Rosyth W/E 2.5.18; HMS *Calliope* W/E 2.5.18; Donibristle W/E 11.5.18; HMS *Calliope* W/E 18.5.18; Rosyth W/E 13.6.18; HMS *Furious* 8.7.18; Donibristle W/E 22.8.18; Deleted W/E 12.9.18

N6780 Deld Turnhouse 3.4.18; Donibristle W/E 27.4.18; Rosyth W/E 2.5.18; HMS *Comus* W/E 2.5.18; Donibristle by 16.5.18; HMS *Comus* to Rosyth W/E 23.5.18; Turnhouse W/E 1.8.18; 2(N) ARD W/E 3.10.18 (repair)

N6781 Deld Turnhouse W/E 20.4.18; Lost control stunting, went into spinning nose dive 17.4.18 (Lt BB Palmer); Deleted W/E 3.5.18

N6782 Deld Turnhouse W/E 20.4.18; Donibristle W/E 9.5.18; Rosyth 23.5.18; HMS *Royalist* 4.6.18; Rosyth 5.6.18; HMS *Galatea*, flown off after 2-str seaplane, attacked it unsuccessfully, FL Denmark 19.6.18 (Capt GG Simpson DSC); Deleted W/E 18.7.18 [Aircraft was to have been retd after war, but NFT]

N6783 Deld Turnhouse by 4.18; Donibristle W/E 16.5.18; HMS *Sydney* W/E 16.5.18; Donibristle 18.5.18; HMS *Sydney* W/E 23.5.18; Chased 2 2-strs & a 1-str, latter believed to have been brought down, then landed by Harwich Force, picked up the Sharps (sic) 1.6.18 (2/Lt AC Sharwood); Donibristle by 27.6.18; For deletion W/E 18.7.18

N6784 Deld Turnhouse W/E 20.4.18; Donibristle W/E 16.5.18; Rosyth W/E 23.5.18; HMS *Southampton* W/E 23.5.18; Rosyth W/E 13.6.18; HMS *Southampton* W/E 18.7.18; For deletion W/E 15.8.18; Turnhouse by 29.8.18; 2(N) ARD W/E 3.10.18 (repair)

N6785 Deld Turnhouse W/E 27.4.18; Donibristle W/E 16.5.18; Rosyth W/E 16.5.18; HMS *Pegasus* 18.5.18; Donibristle 23.5.18; Rosyth W/E 23.5.18; Rosyth to HMS *Melbourne* W/E 23.5.18; Deleted W/E 20.6.18

N6786 Deld Donibristle 15.5.18; Turnhouse to Donibristle W/E 23.5.18; Rosyth W/E 23.5.18; HMS *Inflexible* 21.5.18;

Rosyth W/E 13.6.18; Scapa W/E 11.7.18; HMAS *Australia* W/E 31.10.18; Rosyth W/E 21.11.18; Donibristle W/E 19.12.18 - @30.1.19 ALSO briefly HMS *Inflexible* from 23.10.18? [listed as N6286]

N6787 Deld Turnhouse W/E 27.4.18; HMS *Phaeton* 13.6.18; Turnhouse 17.6.18; HMS *Phaeton* 17.6.18; HMS *Phaeton* 20.6.18; Turnhouse 26.6.18; HMS *Phaeton* 26.6.18; ashore 5.7.18; HMS *Phaeton* 5.7.18; ashore 10.7.18; HMS *Phaeton* 16.7.18; ashore 24.7.18; Rosyth W/E 15.8.18; Turnhouse W/E 14.9.18; HMS *Southampton* W/E 21.11.18; ashore 28.11.18; HMS *Inflexible* 5.12.18; ashore 24.1.19 - @30.1.19

N6788 Deld Turnhouse W/E 27.4.18; Donibristle W/E 16.5.18; HMS *Glorious* W/E 18.5.18; Turnhouse 5.18; Rosyth W/E 23.5.18; HMS *Furious* W/E 23.5.18; Turnhouse 31.5.18; Donibristle W/E 22.8.18; HMS *Pegasus* W/E 29.8.18; Deleted W/E 28.11.18

N6789 Deld Turnhouse by 4.18; Donibristle W/E 18.5.18; Rosyth W/E 23.5.18; HMS *Furious* W/E 23.5.18; HMAS *Sydney* by 5.18; HMS *Furious* by 6.18; Turnhouse W/E 21.9.18; HMS *Phaeton* 30.9.18; Turnhouse 10.18; HMS *Phaeton* 17.11.18; Donibristle 2.12.18; HMS *Malaya* W/E 16.1.19; Donibristle W/E 23.1.19 - @30.1.19

N6790 Deld 6 AAP Renfrew W/E 20.5.18; Turnhouse W/E 1.6.18; Smoogroo W/E 27.6.18; HMS *Comus* W/E 18.7.18; HMAS *Australia* W/E 15.8.18; Smoogroo W/E 31.10.18; HMS *Indomitable* 4.11.18; Smoogroo W/E 28.11.18; HMS *Indomitable* W/E 5.12.18; Donibristle W/E 12.12.18 - @30.1.19 ALSO HMS *Barham*

N6791 Deld Turnhouse W/E 27.4.18; Donibristle W/E 16.5.18; HMS *Indomitable* 14.5.18; Rosyth 16.5.18; HMS *Indomitable* 16.5.18; Rosyth 5.18; HMS *Indomitable* W/E 23.5.18; Rosyth W/E 13.6.18; Donibristle W/E 15.8.18; Rosyth W/E 2.9.18; HMS *Iron Duke* 11.10.18; Donibristle 21.10.18; HMS *Iron Duke* 22.10.18; Donibristle 14.11.18 - @30.1.19

N6792 Deld Turnhouse W/E 15.5.18; Donibristle W/E 23.5.18; Rosyth W/E 23.5.18; HMS *Indomitable* 11.6.18; Smoogroo W/E 18.7.18; Scapa W/E 25.7.18; HMS *Inflexible* 28.9.18; ashore 16.10.18; HMS *Inflexible* 16.10.18; Smoogroo 22.10.18; Scapa W/E 28.11.18; HMS *Royal Sovereign* 17.12.18; Scapa 13.1.19; HMS *Inflexible* W/E 23.1.19 - @30.1.19

N6793 Deld Turnhouse W/E 18.5.18; Rosyth W/E 13.6.18; Donibristle W/E 15.8.18; HMS *Pegasus* 20.8.18; Donibristle 28.8.18; Rosyth W/E 19.9.18; HMS *Courageous* W/E 17.10.18; Donibristle 30.10.18; Rosyth W/E 21.11.18; HMS *Comus* 23.12.18 - @30.1.19

N6794 Deld Turnhouse W/E 18.5.18; HMAS *Melbourne* W/E 17.10.18; Rosyth W/E 24.10.18; Donibristle W/E 19.11.18; HMS *Cassandra* W/E 5.12.18; Disposed W/E 23.1.19

N6795 Deld Turnhouse W/E 15.5.18; Rosyth W/E 13.6.18; Turnhouse W/E 1.8.18; Donibristle W/E 15.8.18; Turnhouse W/E 17.10.18; HMS *Royalist* W/E 24.10.18; Rosyth W/E 31.10.18; Donibristle W/E 14.11.18; HMS *Valiant* 30.1.19

N6796 Deld Turnhouse W/E 18.5.18; HMS *Courageous* W/E 1.8.18; Turnhouse W/E 15.8.18; 2(N) ARD W/E 3.10.18 (repair)

N6797 Deld Donibristle W/E 15.5.18; HMS *Sydney* 19.5.18; Turnhouse to Donibristle W/E 23.5.18; HMS *Tiger* W/E 13.6.18; Turnhouse W/E 1.8.18; 2(N) ARD 3.10.18 (repair)

N6798 Deld Turnhouse W/E 15.5.18; HMS *Sydney* 19.5.18; Turnhouse to Donibristle W/E 23.5.18; Rosyth W/E 13.6.18; HMS *Furious* 8.7.18; Surveyed W/E 15..8.18; Deleted W/E 5.9.18

N6799 Deld Turnhouse W/E 15.5.18; Donibristle W/E 19.9.18; Rosyth W/E 17.10.18; HMS *Penelope* 27.10.18; HMS *Iron Duke* 14.11.18 - @30.1.19

**50 SOPWITH 2F.1 SHIP'S CAMEL TRACTOR BIPLANE SCOUTS ordered 1.17 under Cont No A.S.2301/18 (BR.319) from Sir William Beardmore & Co Ltd, numbered N6800 to N6849 & built Dalmuir. (150-hp B.R.1)**

N6800 Deld Turnhouse W/E 18.5.18; Donibristle W/E 23.5.18; Rosyth W/E 23.5.18; HMS *Phaeton* 23.5.18; Rosyth

5.6.18; ashore 8.7.18; HMS *Furious* 8.7.18; Deleted W/E 18.7.18

N6801 Deld Turnhouse W/E 18.5.18; Deleted W/E 11.7.18

N6802 Deld Renfrew W/E 18.5.18; Turnhouse W/E 25.5.18; HMS *Phaeton* 2.6.18; Turnhouse 6.18; HMS *Inflexible* 19.6.18; Turnhouse 24.6.18; Deleted W/E 11.7.18

N6803 Shipped Malta 30.5.18; Aegean Group by 8.18 - 9.18; 220 Sqdn Imbros by 28.10.18; Mudros Repair Base by 10.18 - @30.1.19; 222 Sqdn Mudros by 1.11.18; RAF South Russia to Russian Air Corps 8.19

N6804 Shipped Malta 30.5.18; Aegean Group by 8.18 - 9.18; 220 Sqdn Imbros by 10.18 - @30.1.19; To White Russian Forces .19

N6805 Shipped Malta 30.5.18; Aegean Group by 8.18 - 9.18; 220 Sqdn Imbros by 27.10.18 - @1.11.18; Mudros by 10.18 - @30.1.19

N6806 Shipped Malta 12.6.18; HMS *Manxman* at Malta @30.6.18 - @31.12.18

N6807 Shipped Malta 12.6.18; HMS *Manxman* at Malta from 7.18 - @31.12.18

N6808 Shipped Malta 12.6.18; HMS *Manxman* at Malta @30.6.18 - @31.12.18

N6809 Deld 6 AAP Renfrew W/E 25.5.18; Turnhouse W/E 1.6.18; HMS *Birkenhead* W/E 1.8.18; Rosyth W/E 15.8.18; 2(N) ARD W/E 3.10.18 (repair)

N6810 Deld 6 AAP Renfrew W/E 25.5.18; Turnhouse W/E 1.6.18; HMS *Furious* 6.18; With another a/c, went up after 2 seaplanes bombing a ship, attacked 2-str unsuccessfuly, then FL in sea, salved by destroyer HMS *Wolfhound* 19.6.18 (Lt MW Basedon); Deleted W/E 18.7.18

N6811 Deld 6 AAP Renfrew W/E 25.5.18; Turnhouse W/E 1.6.18; HMS *Lion* W/E 1.8.18; Donibristle W/E 18.8.18; Rosyth W/E 19.9.18; HMS *Comus* 1.10.18; Donibristle W/E 12.12.18 - @30.1.19; HMS *Argus* 1919 (deck trials)

N6812 Deld Yarmouth by 27.6.18; Felixstowe by 25.7.18; Successful launch from lighter towed by TBD HMS *Truculent*, landed Martlesham Heath 31.7.18 (Lt SD Culley); Flown off lighter *H3*, unsuccessfully chased Zeppelin 5.8.18 (Lt SD Culley); AES Martlesham 8.18; Fitted non-standard fixed twin Lewis guns, towed on lighter behind HM TBD *Redoubt*, flown off by Lt SD Culley who attacked and shot Zeppelin *L53* down in flames off Heligoland Bight (5340N 0546E), both Culley and N6812 being picked up by HMS *Redoubt's* lighter after ditching 11.8.18; Felixstowe by 29.8.18; 212 Sqdn Great Yarmouth by 10.18 - @30.1.19; Preserved Imperial War Museum, marked "F3043" in 1960; To FAA Museum 1974; Later retd IWM & repainted N6812; extant

N6813 Deld Turnhouse W/E 20.6.18; Rosyth W/E 11.7.18; HMS *Indomitable* W/E 9.7.18; Rosyth 2.8.18; Donibristle W/E 15.8.18; HMS *Indomitable* 16.8.18; ashore 26.8.18; Deleted W/E 5.9.18

N6814 Deld Yarmouth by 27.6.18; 212 Sqdn Great Yarmouth 10.18; Airworthiness trials under HMA *R.23* 3.10.18; Successful launch from HMA *R.23* 6.11.18 at Pulham (Lt R E Keys); still Yarmouth @30.1.19

N6815 Deld 6 AAP Renfrew W/E 1.6.18; shore base 7.18; HMS *Furious* 11.8.18; Donibristle 11.12.18; HMS *Furious* W/E 23.1.19 - @30.1.19

N6816 Deld 6 AAP Renfrew W/E 1.6.18; Rosyth W/E 15.8.18; HMS *Inconstant* 17.8.18; Rosyth 19.8.18; HMS *Aurora* 24.8.18; Damaged by force of weather, to Rosyth 8.11.18; Donibristle W/E 14.11.18; HMS *Aurora* W/E 21.11.18; Smoogroo W/E 9.1.19; HMS *Aurora* W/E 23.1.19 - @30.1.19

N6817 Deld 6 AAP Renfrew W/E 1.6.18; shore base 7.18; HMS *Inconstant* 6.7.18; ashore 8.7.18; HMS *Inconstant* 10.7.18; ashore 20.7.18; HMS *Inflexible* 3.8.18; ashore 10.8.18; HMS *Inflexible* 12.8.18; ashore 14.8.18; HMS *Inflexible* 16.8.18; ashore 19.9.18; HMS *Inflexible* 19.9.18; Scapa 29.9.18; HMS *Inflexible* 17.10.18; Scapa W/E 31.10.18; Smoogroo W/E 21.11.18; Scapa W/E 28.11.18; Disposed W/E 23.1.19

N6818 Deld 6 AAP Renfrew W/E 1.6.18; Turnhouse W/E 20.6.18; HMS *Royalist* 20.6.18; Turnhouse 26.6.18; HMS *Royalist* 26.6.18; Turnhouse 6.7.18; HMS *Royalist* 6.7.18; Turnhouse 8.7.18; HMS *Royalist* 8.7.18; Turnhouse 10.7.18; HMS *Royalist* 10.7.18; Turnhouse

27.7.18; HMS *Indomitable* 3.8.18; Rosyth 10.8.18; Donibristle W/E 22.8.18; Turnhouse W/E 19.9.18; Deleted W/E 3.10.18

**N6819** Deld 6 AAP Renfrew W/E 1.6.18; Rosyth W/E 11.7.18; Donibristle W/E 19.9.18; HMS *Lion* W/E 24.10.18; Donibristle W/E 31.10.18; HMS *Orion* 21.11.18; Donibristle W/E 19.12.18 - @30.1.19 ALSO HMS *Royal Oak* 1919

**N6820** Deld 6 AAP Renfrew W/E 13.6.18; HMS *Pegasus* W/E 15.8.18; Scapa W/E 14.11.18; Disposed W/E 23.1.19 ALSO HMAS *Sydney* 1918; HMAS *Melbourne* 1918

**N6821** Deld 6 AAP Renfrew W/E 20.6.18; Smoogroo 8.18; HMAS *Melbourne* W/E 15.8.18; Smoogroo W/E 29.8.18; HMAS *Melbourne* W/E 19.9.18; Rosyth W/E 17.10.18; Turnhouse W/E 12.12.18 - @30.1.19

**N6822** Deld 6 AAP Renfrew W/E 20.6.18; HMAS *Sydney* 7.18; Smoogroo 31.7.18; HMAS *Sydney* 8.18; Smoogroo 13.8.18; Turnhouse 9.18; Donibristle W/E 26.9.18; HMAS *Sydney* W/E 17.10.18; Donibristle W/E 21.11.18 - @30.1.19
ALSO HMAS *Australia* 1918; HMAS *Melbourne* 1918

**N6823** Deld 6 AAP Renfrew W/E 27.6.18 (for Turnhouse); HMS *Furious* by 7.18; Flown in raid on Tondern airship base, FL Holmslands Klit, Denmark, interned 19.7.18 (Lt S Dawson interned)

**N6824** Deld 6 AAP Renfrew W/E 20.6.18; Scapa 18.7.18; HMS *Dublin* W/E 12.9.18; Scapa W/E 19.9.18 ; HMS *Undaunted* W/E 10.10.18; HMS *Penelope* W/E 24.10.18; Turnhouse for tests W/E 31.10.18 - @30.1.19; Grand Fleet SoAG&F Leuchars by 1.19; Stalled and crashed after flat turn 4.2.19 (2/Lt RWS Winter killed)

**N6825** Deld 6 AAP Renfrew W/E 20.6.18; Rosyth 6.18; HMS *Inflexible* 25.6.18; Rosyth 2.7.18 - @26.9.18; HMS *Furious* 9.18; Donibristle W/E 12.12.18; HMS *Furious* W/E 23.1.19 - @30.1.19; Grand Fleet SoAF&G Leuchars by 6.19; HMS *Vindictive*, crashed 13.8.19 (Lt WS Taylor killed)

**N6826** Deld 6 AAP Renfrew W/E 20.6.18; Rosyth W/E 11.7.18; HMS *Royalist* 11.8.18; Rosyth 15.8.18; HMS *Pegasus* W/E 29.8.18; Donibristle W/E 19.12.18; HMS *Furious* W/E 16.1.19; HMS *Pegasus* W/E 23.1.19 - @30.1.19 ALSO HMAS *Australia*

**N6827** Deld 6 AAP Renfrew W/E 20.6.18; Rosyth W/E 11.7.18; Turnhouse W/E 22.8.18; 2(N) ARD for repair W/E 3.10.18 - @17.10.18

**N6828** Transit W/E 27.6.18; Deld Turnhouse W/E 11.7.18; HMS *Dublin* W/E 22.8.18; Smoogroo W/E 29.8.18; Scapa W/E 12.9.18; HMS *Dublin* W/E 19.9.18; Donibristle W/E 14.11.18; HMAS *Australia* W/E 28.11.18 - @30.1.19 (Capt Fox)

**N6829** Deld 6 AAP Renfrew W/E 27.6.18; Turnhouse W/E 11.7.18; HMS *Galatea* W/E 15.8.18; Crashed 20yds ahead of ship on TO 6.9.18 (2/Lt FC Hamilton injured, rescued by HMS *Inconstant*'s whaler)

**N6830** Deld 6 AAP Renfrew W/E 27.6.18; Turnhouse 7.18; HMS *Phaeton* 10.7.18; Turnhouse 16.7.18; Rosyth 15.8.18; *Princess Royal* W/E 22.8.18; Deleted W/E 5.9.18

**N6831** Transit by 27.6.18; Deld Turnhouse W/E 11.7.18; Donibristle W/E 22.8.18; HMS *Caroline* W/E 29.8.18; HMS *Royalist* W/E 27.10.18; Donibristle W/E 21.11.18 - @30.1.19

**N6832** Deld 6 AAP Renfrew W/E 27.6.18; Turnhouse 7.18; HMS *Furious* 7.18; Turnhouse W/E 21.11.18; Donibristle W/E 21.11.18; Turnhouse W/E 5.12.18; Donibristle W/E 12.12.18; HMS *Furious* W/E 16.1.19 - @30.1.19; Grand Fleet SoAF&G Leuchars 6.19 ALSO HMS *New Zealand* 1918

**N6833** Deld 6 AAP Renfrew W/E 27.6.18; Turnhouse W/E 11.7.18; HMS *Birkenhead* W/E 15.8.18; Rosyth W/E 29.8.18; HMS *Birkenhead* W/E 29.8.18; HMS *New Zealand* W/E 19.9.18; Donibristle W/E 19.12.18 - @30.1.19

**N6834** Deld 6 AAP Renfrew W/E 27.6.18 (for Turnhouse); Rosyth by 8.18; HMS *Inconstant* 4.8.18; FL in sea, recovered by HMS *Viscount* 10.8.18; HMS *Lion* W/E 22.8.18; Turnhouse W/E 16.9.18; HMS *Undaunted* 2.10.18; Turnhouse 12.10.18; Donibristle W/E 14.11.18; HMS *Ajax* 4.12.18; Donibristle W/E 16.1.19 - @30.1.19

**N6835** Transit W/E 4.7.18; Deld Donibristle by 8.18; HMS *Glorious* W/E 15.8.18; Donibristle W/E 3.10.18; Rosyth W/E 17.10.18; Turnhouse W/E 13.12.18; HMS *Tiger* W/E 23.1.19 - @30.1.19

**N6836** Deld 6 AAP Renfrew W/E 4.7.18; Rosyth W/E 15.8.18; HMS *Pegasus* W/E 12.9.18; Donibristle W/E 19.12.18; HMS *Pegasus* W/E 23.1.19 - @30.1.19

**N6837** Deld Turnhouse W/E 11.7.18; Deleted W/E 1.8.18

**N6838** Deld 6 AAP Renfrew W/E 4.7.18; Transit W/E 11.7.18; Donibristle W/E 15.8.18; HMS *Renown* 12.9.18; Donibristle 31.10.18; HMS *Valiant* W/E 31.12.18 - @30.1.19; ashore 5.19; HMS *Phaeton* 20.5.19; ashore 28.5.19; HMS *Phaeton* 31.5.19 ALSO HMAS *Sydney* 1918

**N6839** Deld 6 AAP Renfrew W/E 4.7.18; shore base 7.18; HMS *Inconstant* 31.7.18; Rosyth 4.8.18; HMS *Princess Royal* W/E 22.8.18; ashore 11.9.18; Deleted W/E 5.9.18 (sic)

**N6840** Deld 6 AAP Renfrew W/E 4.7.18; Transit W/E 18.7.18; Rosyth W/E 15.8.18; Turnhouse W/E 19.9.18; HMS *Furious* W/E 17.10.18; Donibristle W/E 12.12.18; HMS *Furious* W/E 16.1.19 - @30.1.19

**N6841** Deld 6 AAP Renfrew W/E 4.7.18; Transit W/E 18.7.18; Rosyth W/E 15.8.18; HMS *Inconstant* W/E 22.8.18; Donibristle W/E 29.8.18; Rosyth W/E 19.9.18; Donibristle W/E 26.9.18; Rosyth W/E 24.10.18; Turnhouse W/E 12.12.18 - @30.1.19

**N6842** Deld 6 AAP Renfrew W/E 4.7.18; Transit W/E 18.7.18; HMS *Southampton* W/E 15.8.18; HMS *Courageous* W/E 26.9.18; Donibristle W/E 17.10.18; Rosyth W/E 21.11.18; Turnhouse W/E 12.12.18 - @30.1.19

**N6843** Deld 6 AAP Renfrew W/E 11.7.18; HMS *Inconstant* W/E 15.8.18; Rosyth W/E 29.8.18; Turnhouse W/E 19.9.18; Deleted W/E 3.10.18

**N6844** Transit W/E 1.8.18; Donibristle W/E 15.8.18; Rosyth W/E 22.8.18; HMS *Birkenhead* W/E 29.8.18; Rosyth W/E 26.9.18; Turnhouse W/E 12.12.18 - @30.1.19

**N6845** Transit W/E 1.8.18; Turnhouse W/E 15.8.18; Rosyth W/E 22.8.18; HMS *Penelope* W/E 29.8.18; Deleted W/E 12.9.18

**N6846** Deld 6 AAP Renfrew W/E 1.8.18; Transit W/E 8.8.18; Donibristle W/E 22.8.18; Rosyth W/E 29.8.18; HMS *Comus* W/E 19.9.18; Rosyth W/E 3.10.18; HMS *Campania* to Scapa 26.10.18; Rosyth by 31.10.18; Scapa W/E 14.11.18 - @30.1.19

**N6847** Transit W/E 8.8.18; Rosyth W/E 22.8.18; HMS *Undaunted* W/E 29.8.18; HMS Rosyth W/E 19.9.18; *Birkenhead* 23.9.18; Rosyth W/E 17.10.18; Donibristle W/E 14.11.18; HMS *Renown* 7.1.19; Donibristle W/E 23.1.19 - @30.1.19

**N6848** Deld 6 AAP Renfrew W/E 8.8.18; Donibristle W/E 29.8.18; HMS *Chatham* W/E 19.9.18; HMAS *Sydney* W/E 16.1.19; HMS *Chatham* W/E 23.1.19 - @30.1.19

**N6849** Deld 6 AAP Renfrew by 6.8.18; Transit W/E 15.8.18; Donibristle W/E 29.8.18; HMS *Princess Royal* W/E 19.9.18 - @14.11.18; Rosyth 11.18; Donibristle W/E 21.11.18 - @30.1.19

**N6850 TO N6899 NOT ALLOTTED** [or cancelled?]

**30 SOPWITH T.1 CUCKOO TRACTOR BIPLANE TORPEDO BOMBERS ordered from Blackburn under Cont Nos 38a/245/C240, A.S.6799 (BR.275) & A.S.10375/18, numbered N6900 to N6929 (were to be D3276 to D3325) & built Leeds. (225-hp Arab)** [N6900 to N6949 originally to have been D3276 to D3325 from Pegler under Cont No A.S.35976. As the firm could not deliver until 1919, N6900 to N6929 was built by Blackburns, who delivered them after N6930 to N6949]

**N6900** Deld 9 AAP Newcastle W/E 10.10.18; East Fortune W/E 31.10.18 (for carriers); Donibristle W/E 21.11.18 - @30.1.19

**N6901** Deld 9 AAP Newcastle W/E 10.10.18; East Fortune W/E 24.10.18 (for carriers); Donibristle W/E 14.11.18 - @30.1.19

**N6902** Deld 9 AAP Newcastle W/E 17.10.18; East Fortune W/E 31.10.18 (for carriers); Turnhouse W/E 21.11.18 - @30.1.19

**N6903** Deld 9 AAP Newcastle W/E 17.10.18; East Fortune W/E 31.10.18 (for carriers) - @30.1.19

**N6904** Deld 9 AAP Newcastle W/E 24.10.18; East Fortune

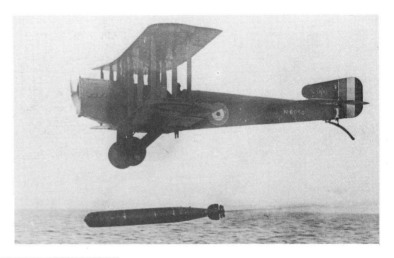

*Sopwith Cuckoo Torpedo Bomber N6950 dropping a torpedo. (via J.D.Oughton)*

*Bristol-built Parnall Panther N7426 landing on HMS Eagle, June 1920. (J.M.Bruce/G.S.Leslie collection)*

*Sopwith 2F.1 Camels N7149 'SWILLINGTON' and N7146 at Turnhouse, 1919. (RAF Museum P.245)*

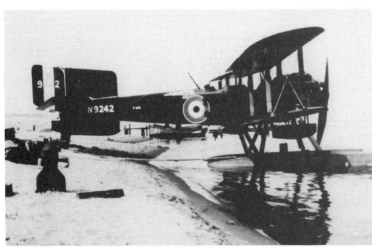

*Fairey IIIC N9242 from HMS Pegasus moored on the banks of the Dvina River in 1919 (RAF Museum P.22182)*

W/E 31.10.18 (for carriers) - @30.1.19

N6905 Deld 9 AAP Newcastle W/E 31.10.18; East Fortune W/E 7.11.18 (for carriers); Donibristle W/E 14.11.18; 185 Sqdn HMS *Argus* W/E 28.11.18; Gosport W/E 24.12.18 - 30.1.19

N6906 Deld 9 AAP Newcastle by 7.12.18 (for manoeuvrability tests Martlesham Heath - NTU)

N6907 Deld 9 AAP Newcastle W/E 31.10.18; SD Flt Gosport W/E 14.11.18 - @30.1.19

N6908 Deld 9 AAP Newcatsle W/E 7.11.18; transit to Donibristle W/E 21.11.18 (not arrived by 30.1.19)

N6909 Deld East Fortune W/E 31.10.18 (for carriers) - @30.1.19

N6910 Deld 9 AAP Newcastle W/E 31.10.18; in transit W/E 7.11.18 - @31.12.18; 1(S) ARD Farnborough by 1.19 - @30.1.19; to Gosport, convtd Mk.II (200-hp Viper)

N6911 Deld 9 AAP Newcastle W/E 31.10.18; SD Flt Gosport 6.11.18 (arr 17.11.18 via York, Retford & Shoreham) - @30.1.19

N6912 Deld 9 AAP Newcastle by W/E 31.10.18; SD Flt Gosport W/E 12.12.18 - @30.1.19

N6913 Deld 9 AAP Newcastle W/E 7.11.18 - @30.1.19

N6914 Deld 9 AAP Newcastle W/E 7.11.18; East Fortune W/E 14.11.18 (for carriers) - @30.1.19

N6915 Deld 9 AAP Newcastle W/E 7.11.18; Donibristle W/E 12.12.18 - @30.1.19

N6916 Deld 9 AAP Newcastle W/E 7.11.18; transit to Donibristle/Turnhouse W/E 28.11.18 (not arrived by 30.1.19_

N6917 Deld 9 AAP Newcastle W/E 7.11.18; in transit W/E 12.12.18; Turnhouse W/E 16.1.19 - @30.1.19

N6918 Deld 9 AAP Newcastle W/E 7.11.18; in transit W/E 21.11.18; Turnhouse W/E 5.12.18 - @30.1.19

N6919 Deld 9 AAP Newcastle W/E 14.11.18; Donibristle W/E 12.12.18 - @30.1.19

N6920 Deld 9 AAP Newcastle W/E 14.11.18 - @30.1.19; RAE Farnborough from 3.10.19 (rudder tests); Martlesham Heath 21.6.21

N6921 Deld 9 AAP Newcastle W/E 14.11.18 - @30.1.19

N6922 Deld 9 AAP Newcastle W/E 14.11.18; Turnhouse W/E 31.12.18 - @30.1.19

N6923 Deld 9 AAP Newcastle W/E 14.11.18; Donibristle W/E 19.12.18 - @30.1.19; No.1 Trg Flt Gosport by 11.21; 210 Sqdn Gosport by 3.22

N6924 Deld 9 AAP Newcastle W/E 21.11.18; in transit W/E 19.12.18; Turnhouse W/E 16.1.19 - @30.1.19

N6925 Deld 9 AAP Newcastle W/E 21.11.18; Turnhouse W/E 16.1.19 - @30.1.19

N6926 Deld 9 AAP Newcastle W/E 28.11.18; 185 Sqdn W/E 9.1.19; 1(S)ARD Farnborough W/E 23.1.19 - @30.1.19; Convtd Mk.II (200-hp Viper); D Flt Development Sqdn/186 Sqdn Gosport by 6.19

N6927 Deld 9 AAP Newcastle W/E 28.11.18; 185 W/E 31.12.18 - @30.1.19; 186 Sqdn, stalled and spun on slow turn Gosport 3.5.19 (2/Lt C Harrison)

N6928 Deld 9 AAP Newcastle W/E 5.12.18; 201 TDS East Fortune W/E 13.1.19 - @30.1.19

N6929 Deld 9 AAP Newcastle W/E 5.12.18; 185 Sqdn W/E 23.1.19 - @30.1.19; Convtd Mk.II (200-hp Viper); Deld 2.19

**20 SOPWITH T.1 CUCKOO TRACTOR BIPLANE TORPEDO BOMBERS ordered from Pegler under Cont Nos A.S.35976/17 (BR.275) & A.S.10375/18, numbered N6930 to N6949 and built Doncaster. (225-hp Arab) [N6938 to N6949 cancelled 1.19 - but presumably after they had mostly been built?]**

N6930 Deld 9 AAP Newcastle W/E 24.10.18; 201 TDS East Fortune W/E 7.11.18 - @30.1.19

N6931 On delivery to 9 AAP Newcastle, crashed at Ossett, Yorks 19.11.18

N6932 Crashed on delivery to 9 AAP Newcastle 12.18

N6933 to N6940 For storage but still at Mkrs 30.1.19

N6940 to N6947 due for delivery to 9 AAP Newcastle 12.18 (NTU?)

N6948 probably not completed

N6949 probably not completed

**50 SOPWITH T.1 CUCKOO TRACTOR BIPLANE TORPEDO BOMBERS ordered 1.18 from Blackburn Aeroplane & Motor Co Ltd under Cont No A.S.3298/18/13 (BR.327), numbered N6950 to N6999 (were to be F8231 to F8280), and built at Leeds. (225-hp Arab)**

N6950 Deld Grain Test Depot 22.5.18 (via Yarmouth 25.5.18, arr W/E 1.6.18); 201 TDS East Fortune W/E 1.8.18; Deleted W/E 26.9.18

N6951 Deld 4 AAP Lincoln W/E 25.5.18; 201 TDS East Fortune W/E 18.7.18; Deleted W/E 21.11.18

N6952 Deld 4 AAP Lincoln for East Fortune W/E 20.6.18; Marske W/E 22.8.18 (for East Fortune) [crashed en route?]; Deleted W/E 9.1.19

N6953 Deld 4 AAP Lincoln W/E 20.6.18; Cramlington W/E 22.8.18 (transit); 201 TDS East Fortune W/E 12.9.18 - @30.1.19; HMS *Furious*

N6954 Deld 4 AAP Lincoln W/E 27.6.18; 201 TDS East Fortune W/E 18.7.18; Deleted W/E 17.10.18

N6955 Deld 4 AAP Lincoln W/E 11.7.18; NARD for repair W/E 29.8.18; Deleted W/E 24.10.18

N6956 Deld 4 AAP Lincoln W/E 18.7.18; Marske W/E 22.8.18 (transit); 201 TDS East Fortune W/E 29.8.18 - @30.1.19

N6957 Deld 4 AAP Lincoln for East Fortune W/E 27.6.18; 9 AAP Newcastle W/E 11.8.18; 201 TDS East Fortune W/E 19.9.18 - @30.1.19

N6958 Deld 4 AAP Lincoln W/E 11.7.18; in transit W/E 22.8.18; 201 TDS East Fortune W/E 26.9.18 - @30.1.19

N6959 Deld 4 AAP Lincoln W/E 18.7.18; 201 TDS East Fortune 14.8.18 - @30.1.19

N6960 Deld 9 AAP Newcastle W/E 25.7.18; 201 TDS East Fortune W/E 1.8.18 - @30.1.19

N6961 Deld 9 AAP Newcastle W/E 25.7.18; 201 TDS East Fortune W/E 1.8.18; Deleted W/E 26.9.18

N6962 Deld 9 AAP Newcastle W/E 25.7.18; 201 TDS East Fortune W/E 22.8.18; Deleted W/E 7.11.18

N6963 Deld 9 AAP Newcastle W/E 1.8.18; 201 TDS East Fortune W/E 7.11.18 - @30.1.19

N6964 Deld 9 AAP Newcastle W/E 8.8.18; East Fortune W/E 15.8.18; Deleted W/E 22.8.18

N6965 Deld 201 TDS East Fortune W/E 22.8.18 - @30.1.19

N6966 Deld 9 AAP Newcastle W/E 15.8.18; 201 TDS East Fortune W/E 22.8.18 - @10.18

N6967 Deld 9 AAP Newcastle W/E 8.8.18; 201 TDS East Fortune W/E 22.8.18 - @30.1.19

N6968 Deld 9 AAP Newcastle W/E 15.8.18; 201 TDS East Fortune W/E 12.9.18; Deleted W/E 21.11.18

N6969 Deld 9 AAP Newcastle W/E 15.8.18; 201 TDS East Fortune W/E 5.9.18; Deleted W/E 7.11.18

N6970 Deld 9 AAP Newcastle W/E 1.8.18; 201 TDS East Fortune W./E 12.9.18; Hit water during torpedo drop 24.10.18 (2/Lt PW Lynch Blosse injured); Deleted W/E 7.11.18

N6971 Deld 9 AAP Newcastle W/E 22.8.18; 201 TDS East Fortune W/E 12.9.18 - @30.1.19; Convtd Mk.II (200-hp Viper)

N6972 Deld 9 AAP Newcastle W/E 22.8.18; FL Doncaster en route Gosport W/E 12.9.18; Gosport (SD Flt?) W/E 26.9.18 - @31.12.18; 1(S)ARD Farnborough by 1.19 [convtd Mk.II (200-hp Viper) ]

N6973 Deld 9 AAP Newcastle W/E 29.8.18; On delivery to Gosport, caught fire in air, FL, sideslipped, hit trees Selby 31.8.18 (Lt GR Whitaker unhurt); Deleted W/E 12.9.18

N6974 Deld 9 AAP Newcastle W/E 29.8.18; FL Retford en route Gosport W/E 12.9.18; SD Flt Gosport by 26.9.18 - @30.1.19

N6975 Deld 9 AAP Newcastle W/E 5.9.18; East Fortune W/E 12.9.18; Donibristle W/E 24.10.18; 185 Sqdn HMS *Argus* W/E 14.11.18; left W/E 23.1.19; CAAD test 14.10.21; 210 Sqdn by 5.22; No.1 Torpedo Bomber Flt Gosport by 6.22

N6976 Mkrs by 31.8.18; Deleted at Mkrs W/E 28.11.18

N6977 Deld East Fortune W/E 5.9.18; Donibristle W/E 24.10.18; 185 Sqdn HMS *Argus* W/E 14.11.18, damaged; Deleted W/E 31.12.18

N6978 Deld 9 AAP Newcastle W/E 5.9.18; East Fortune W/E 19.9.18; FL Penston 3.10.18; Donibristle W/E 24.10.18; 185 Sqdn HMS *Argus* W/E 14.11.18 - @12.18; 1(S)ARD Farnborough 1.19

N6979 Deld 9 AAP Newcastle W/E 19.9.18; East Fortune W/E 3.10.18; Donibristle W/E 24.10.18; 185 Sqdn HMS *Argus* W/E 14.11.18, damaged; 1(S) ARD Farnborough 1.19

N6980 Deld 9 AAP Newcastle W/E 5.9.18; East Fortune W/E 12.9.18; Donibristle W/E 24.10.18; HMS *Furious* W/E 14.11.18 - @31.12.18 (trials); Gosport for carriers by 19.1.19 - @30.1.19

N6981 Deld 9 AAP Newcastle W/E 19.9.18; East Fortune W/E 3.10.18; Donibristle W/E 24.10.18; Gosport for carriers W/E 9.1.19 - @30.1.19

N6982 Deld 9 AAP Newcastle by W/E 26.9.18; East Fortune W/E 3.10.18; Donibristle W/E 24.10.18; 185 Sqdn HMS *Argus* W/E 21.11.18, damaged; Deleted W/E 31.12.18

N6983 Deld 9 AAP Newcastle W/E 26.9.18; East Fortune W/E 3.10.18; Donibristle W/E 24.10.18; 185 Sqdn HMS *Argus* W/E 21.11.18; Gosport for carriers W/E 24.12.18 - 30.1.19

N6984 Deld 9 AAP Newcastle W/E 26.9.18; East Fortune W/E 3.10.18; Donibristle W/E 24.10.18; 185 Sqdn HMS *Argus* W/E 14.11.18 - @31.12.18; 1(S)ARD Farnborough 1.19

N6985 Deld 9 AAP Newcastle W/E 10.10.18; East Fortune W/E 17.10.18; Donibristle W/E 24.10.18; HMS *Furious* W/E 14.11.18; Gosport for carriers W/E 24.12.18 - 30.1.19

N6986 Deld 9 AAP Newcastle W/E 26.9.18; East Fortune W/E 17.10.18; Donibristle W/E 24.10.18; 185 Sqdn HMS *Argus* W/E 14.11.18; ashore W/E 23.1.19

N6987 Deld 9 AAP Newcastle W/E 26.9.18; East Fortune W/E 3.10.18; Donibristle W/E 24.10.18; 185 Sqdn HMS *Argus* W/E 14.11.18 - @31.12.18; 1(S)ARD Farnborough 1.19

N6988 Deld 9 AAP Newcastle W/E 31.10.18; 201 TDS East Fortune W/E 14.11.18; Turnhouse W/E 12.12.18; 201 TDS East Fortune W/E 9.1.19; Donibristle W/E 16.1.19 - @30.1.19

N6989 Deld 9 AAP Newcastle by 31.12.18; 185 Sqdn W/E 9.1.19; 1(S)ARD Farnborough W/E 23.1.19 - @30.1.19 for conv Mk.II (200-hp Viper); CAAD test 13.9.21

N6990 Deld 9 AAP Newcastle W/E 19.9.18; East Fortune W/E 3.10.18; Donibristle W/E 24.10.18; 185 Sqdn HMS *Argus* W/E 14.11.18 - @31.12.18; Donibristle by 30.1.19; 1(S)ARD Farnborough, for conv Mk.II (200-hp Viper)

N6991 Deld 9 AAP Newcastle W/E 26.9.18; East Fortune W/E 3.10.18; Donibristle W/E 24.10.18; 185 Sqdn HMS *Argus* W/E 14.11.18; ashore W/E 23.1.19

N6992 Deld Donibristle W/E 24.10.18; 185 Sqdn HMS *Argus* W/E 14.11.18 - @31.12.18; 1(S)ARD Farnborough 1.19, for conv Mk.II (200-hp Viper)

N6993 Deld Donibristle W/E 24.10.18; HMS *Furious* W/E 14.11.18; Gosport for carriers 24.12.18 - @ 30.1.19

N6994 Deld 9 AAP Newcastle W/E 31.10.18; East Fortune for carriers W/E 31.10.18 - @30.1.19

N6995 Deld East Fortune for carriers W/E 19.9.18; Donibristle W/E 24.10.18; 185 Sqdn HMS *Argus* from 11.18 - @31.12.18; 1(S)ARD Farnborough 1.19 (?)

N6996 Deld 9 AAP Newcastle W/E 17.10.18; Donibristle W/E 31.10.18; East Fortune for carriers W/E 7.11.18 - @30.1.19

N6997 Convtd Mk.II at 1(S)ARD Farnborough (200-hp Viper). Deld 6 AAP Newcastle W/E 28.11.18; 185 Sqdn W/E 16.1.19 - @30.1.19

N6998 Deld 9 AAP Newcastle W/E 14.11.18 - @30.1.19

N6999 Deld 9 AAP Newcastle W/E 19.9.18; East Fortune for carriers W/E by 26.9.18; Donibristle W/E 24.10.18; left W/E 14.11.18; Convtd Mk.II (200-hp Viper)

**100 SOPWITH T.1 CUCKOO TRACTOR BIPLANE TORPEDO BOMBERS** ordered 16.10.17 from **Fairfield Engineering** under Cont No AS.27863/17 (BR.187), numbered **N7000 to N7099 & built Glasgow. (225-hp Arab)** [originally to have been C7901 to C8000]

N7000 Deld 6 AAP Renfrew W/E 8.8.18; 201 TDS East Fortune W/E 12.9.18 - @31.12.18; 1(S)ARD Farnborough by 12.18; 201 TDS East Fortune by 30.1.19; A Flt Development Sqdn Gosport by 6.19

N7001 Deld 6 AAP Renfrew W/E 18.7.18; 201 TDS East Fortune W/E 12.10.18 - @30.1.19

N7002 Deld 6 AAP Renfrew W/E 15.8.18; 201 TDS East Fortune W/E 12.10.18 - @30.1.19

N7003 Deld 6 AAP Renfrew W/E 22.8.18; 201 TDS East Fortune W/E 12.10.18 - @30.1.19

N7004 Deld 201 TDS East Fortune W/E 12.9.18 - @30.1.19

N7005 Deld 6 AAP Renfrew W/E 5.9.18; 201 TDS East Fortune W/E 26.9.18 - @30.1.19

N7006 Deld 6 AAP Renfrew W/E 5.9.18; 201 TDS East Fortune W/E 12.9.18 - @30.1.19

N7007 Deld 6 AAP Renfrew W/E 26.9.18; Deleted W/E 17.10.18

N7008 Deld 6 AAP Renfrew W/E 19.9.18; 201 TDS East Fortune W/E 3.10.18 - @30.1.19

N7009 Deld 6 AAP Renfrew W/E 26.9.18; Deleted W/E 17.10.18

N7010 Deld 6 AAP Renfrew W/E 4.10.18; East Fortune W/E 24.10.18; Donibristle W/E 14.11.18 - @30.1.19

N7011 Deld 6 AAP Renfrew W/E 26.9.18; East Fortune W/E 31.10.18; Donibristle W/E 21.11.18; 185 Sqdn HMS *Argus* W/E 12.12.18; 1(S) ARD Farnborough W/E @30.1.19

N7012 Deld 6 AAP Renfrew W/E 4.10.18; East Fortune W/E 31.10.18; Donibristle W/E 21.11.18; East Fortune for carriers by @30.1.19

N7013 Deld 6 AAP Renfrew W/E 4.10.18; East Fortune for carriers W/E 31.10.18; Donibristle W/E 14.11.18; Turnhouse W/E 21.11.18 - @30.1.19

N7014 Deld 6 AAP Renfrew W/E 31.10.18; East Fortune W/E 7.11.18 - @30.1.19

N7015 Deld 6 AAP Renfrew W/E 31.10.18; East Fortune W/E 7.11.18 - @30.1.19

N7016 Deld 6 AAP Renfrew W/E 7.11.18 (for Martlesham Heath); 9 AAP Newcastle W/E 5.12.18 - @30.1.19; For East Fortune 2.19

N7017 Deld 6 AAP Renfrew W/E 14.11.18; 201 TDS East Fortune W/E 12.12.18 - @30.1.19

N7018 Deld 6 AAP Renfrew W/E 7.11.18; Donibristle W/E 14.11.18 - @30.1.19

N7019 Deld 6 AAP Renfrew W/E 7.11.18; East Fortune for carriers W/E 14.11.18 - @30.1.19

N7020 Deld 6 AAP Renfrew W/E 14.11.18; in transit 12.12.18 (for Turnhouse/Donibristle - NTU?)

N7021 Deld 6 AAP Renfrew W/E 21.11.18; 201 TDS East Fortune W/E 12.12.18 - @30.1.19

N7022 Deld 6 AAP Renfrew W/E 5.12.18; 185 Sqdn W/E 31.12.18 - @30.1.19

N7023 Deld 6 AAP Renfrew W/E 28.11.18; 185 Sqdn W/E 19.12.18 - @30.1.19

N7024 Deld 6 AAP Renfrew W/E 28.11.18; 185 Sqdn W/E 19.12.18 - @30.1.19

N7025 Deld 6 AAP Renfrew W/E 5.12.18; 185 Sqdn W/E 19.12.18 - @30.1.19

N7026 Deld 6 AAP Renfrew W/E 16.1.19
N7027 Deld 6 AAP Renfrew W/E 16.1.19
N7028 Deld 6 AAP Renfrew W/E 16.1.19
N7029 Deld 6 AAP Renfrew W/E 16.1.19
N7030 Deld 6 AAP Renfrew W/E 16.1.19
N7031 Deld 6 AAP Renfrew W/E 16.1.19
N7032 Deld 6 AAP Renfrew W/E 16.1.19
N7033 Deld 6 AAP Renfrew W/E 16.1.19
N7034 Deld 6 AAP Renfrew W/E 16.1.19
N7035 Deld 6 AAP Renfrew W/E 16.1.19
N7036 Deld 6 AAP Renfrew W/E 30.1.19
N7037 Deld 6 AAP Renfrew W/E 30.1.19
N7038 Deld 6 AAP Renfrew W/E 30.1.19
N7039 to N7049 Still at Mkrs @30.1.19
N7050 to N7099 cancelled 1.19

**40 SOPWITH 2F.1 SHIP'S CAMEL TRACTOR BIPLANE SCOUTS** ordered 2.2.18 (later 27.6.18) from **Sir William Beardmore & Co Ltd** [and **Arrol-Johnston Ltd, Dumfries**] under Cont Nos 38a/383/C273 & A.S.3458/18 (BR.329 later BR.520), numbered **N7100 - N7139 & built Dalmuir** [and **Dumfries?**]. Accepted 6 AAP Renfrew. (150-hp Bentley B.R.1)

N7100    Deld Rosyth W/E 29.8.18; HMS *Inconstant* 24.8.18; Donibristle 2.9.18; HMS *Inconstant* 2.9.18; Donibristle 20.9.18; HMS *Inconstant* 17.11.18; Donibristle 2.12.18; HMS *Inconstant* 1.19; Donibristle 15.1.19 - @30.1.19

N7101    Deld 6 AAP Renfrew W/E 15.8.18; transit W/E 22.8.18; Turnhouse W/E 29.8.18; Donibristle W/E 19.9.18; HMAS *Sydney* W/E 3.10.18; Rosyth W/E 17.10.18; HMS *Renown* 24.10.18; Turnhouse 9.12.18; HMS *Renown* 7.1.19 - @30.1.19

N7102    Deld 6 AAP Renfrew W/E 15.8.18; transit W/E 22.8.18; Turnhouse W/E 29.8.18; Donibristle W/E 19.9.18; Rosyth W/E 24.10.18; HMS *Nairana* W/E 31.10.18; Rosyth W/E 21.11.18; Donibristle W/E 12.12.18; Deleted W/E 19.12.18

N7103    Deld Turnhouse W/E 29.8.18; Donibristle W/E 19.9.18; HMS *Tiger* W/E 26.9.18; Rosyth W/E 3.10.18; HMS *Campania* 10.18; HMS *Pegasus* 26.10.18; Rosyth 27.10.18; Scapa W/E 14.11.18 - @30.1.19 ALSO HMS *Barham*; HMS *Royal Sovereign* (damaged by vibration from 15-inch guns)

N7104    Deld 6 AAP Renfrew W/E 15.8.18; transit W/E 22.8.18; Turnhouse W/E 29.8.18; Donibristle W/E 19.9.18; HMAS *Melbourne* W/E 24.10.18; Rosyth W/E 14.11.18; Donibristle W/E 21.11.18; Turnhouse W/E 12.12.19 - @30.1.19; joined HMS *Royal Sovereign* at Scapa 11.6.19

N7105    Deld 6 AAP Renfrew W/E 22.8.18; Turnhouse W/E 29.8.18; Donibristle W/E 26.9.18; HMS *Repulse* 19.10.18; Donibristle @25.11.18 - @30.1.19

N7106    Deld 6 AAP Renfrew W/E 22.8.18; Turnhouse W/E 29.8.18; Donibristle W/E 26.9.18; HMS *Repulse* 30.9.18; Rosyth 23.10.18; HMS *Campania* 10.18; HMS *Pegasus* 26.10.18; Rosyth 27.10.18; Scapa W/E 14.11.18 - @30.1.19; HMS *Vindictive*, Koivisto, Baltic Russia by 10.19; Bombed Bolshevik destroyer off Krasnaya Gorka 16.10.19 (F/L SD Culley)

N7107    Deld 6 AAP Renfrew W/E 22.8.18; Turnhouse W/E 29.8.18; HMS *Undaunted* by 27.9.18; Scapa 1.10.18; HMS *Southampton* 23.10.18; Scapa 1.11.18; Disposed W/E 23.1.19

N7108    Deld 6 AAP Renfrew W/E 22.8.18; Turnhouse W/E 29.8.18; Donibristle W/E 26.9.18; Rosyth 13.10.18; HMS *Caroline* 13.10.18; Scapa 18.10.18; Donibristle W/E 31.10.18; Scapa W/E 31.12.18; HMS *Royal Sovereign* 13.1.19 - @30.1.19

N7109    Transit W/E 29.8.18; Deld Donibristle W/E 12.9.18; Rosyth W/E 26.9.18; HMS *Penelope* 28.9.18; Scapa 1.10.18; HMS *New Zealand* 22.10.18; Donibristle 9.12.18 - @30.1.19

N7110    Deld 6 AAP Renfrew W/E 29.8.18; Turnhouse 29.8.18; HMS *Penelope* 2.10.18; Rosyth 12.10.18; HMS *Penelope* 19.10.18; Rosyth 26.10.18; HMS *Birkenhead* 6.11.18; HMS *Chatham* W/E 16.1.19; HMS *Birkenhead* W/E 23.1.19 - @30.1.19

N7111    Transit W/E 29.8.18; Donibristle W/E 26.9.18; HMS *Birkenhead* 2.10.18; Rosyth 10.10.18; Deleted W/E 31.10.18

N7112    Transit W/E 29.8.18; HMS *Southampton* 8.9.18; Smoogroo W/E 21.11.18; Scapa W/E 19.12.18; HMS *Southampton* W/E 23.1.19 - @30.1.19

N7113    Deld 6 AAP Renfrew W/E 29.8.18; transit W/E 5.9.18; Turnhouse W/E 26.9.18; HMS *Royalist* 17.10.18; ashore 14.11.18; HMS *Royalist* 14.11.18; ashore 2.12.18; HMS *Royalist* 28.12.18 - @30.1.19

N7114    Transit W/E 5.9.18; Donibristle W/E 26.9.18; Rosyth W/E 17.10.18; HMS *Princess Royal* 13.10.18; Scapa 7.12.18; HMS *Princess Royal* 8.1.19 - @30.1.19

N7115    Deld 6 AAP Renfrew W/E 5.9.18; For deletion by W/E 26.9.18; Deleted W/E 10.10.18

N7116    Deld 6 AAP Renfrew W/E 5.9.18; Turnhouse W/E 12.9.18; HMS *Inconstant* W/E 3.10.18; ashore 8.10.18; HMS *Galatea* 13.10.18; Donibristle 23.10.18; HMS *Canada* W/E 5.12.18 [possibly the aircraft which crashed in sea on TO from *Canada*'s X-turret 5.12.18]; Scapa W/E 19.12.18; HMS *Canada* 29.12.18; Scapa 9.1.19; HMS *Canada* W/E 23.1.19 - @30.1.19

N7117    Deld 6 AAP W/E 5.9.18; Turnhouse W/E 12.9.18; HMS *Glorious* 29.9.18; Donibristle W/E 31.10.18; HMS *Penelope* W/E 21.11.18; Scapa 23.11.18; HMS *Penelope* 25.11.18; Scapa 16.12.18; HMS *Penelope*

19.12.18; Donibristle 30.12.18 - @30.1.19

N7118    Deld 6 AAP Renfrew W/E 12.9.18; Turnhouse W/E 26.9.18; Donibristle W/E 17.10.18; Rosyth W/E 24.10.18; HMS *Nairana* W/E 31.10.18; HMS *Argus* W/E 14.11.18; Turnhouse W/E 12.12.18 - @30.1.19

N7119    Deld Turnhouse W/E 12.9.18; HMS *Undaunted* 27.9.18; ashore 9.10.18; HMS *Inconstant* 10.18; Donibristle 12.10.18; HMS *Comus* W/E 12.12.18; HMS *Orion* W/E 31.12.18; Donibristle W/E 16.1.19 - @30.1.19; HMS *Vindictive*, South Russia by 10.19; Bombed *Andrei Pervosvanny* in dry dock at Kronstadt 2.10.19 (F/L SD Culley)

N7120    Transit W/E 12.9.18; Turnhouse W/E 19.9.18; Donibristle W/E 17.10.18; HMS *Lion* 21.10.18; Donibristle 28.10.18; Rosyth W/E 21.11.18; Donibristle W/E 28.11.18; HMS *Warspite* 1.12.18; ashore 28.1.19 ALSO HMS *Queen Elizabeth*

N7121    Transit W/E 12.9.18; Turnhouse W/E 19.9.18; Donibristle W/E 7.10.18; HMS *Caroline* 13.10.18; ashore 19.10.18; HMS *Glorious* 26.10.18; Donibristle 15.12.18 - @30.1.19

N7122    Deld 6 AAP Renfrew W/E 12.9.18; Turnhouse W/E 19.9.18; HMS *Cassandra* 11.10.18; Donibristle W/E 12.12.18 - @30.1.19

N7123    Deld 6 AAP Renfrew W/E 12.9.18; Turnhouse W/E 19.9.18; HMS *Inconstant* 13.9.18; Donibristle 23.9.18; HMS *Inconstant* 25.10.18; Donibristle W/E 31.10.18; HMS *Inconstant* W/E 14.11.18; Donibristle 17.11.18 - @30.1.19

N7124    Deld Turnhouse W/E 19.9.18; Donibristle W/E 21.11.18 - @30.1.19

N7125    Deld Turnhouse W/E 19.9.18; Donibristle W/E 17.10.18; HMS *Iron Duke* 11.10.18; Donibristle 21.10.18; HMS *Iron Duke* 22.10.18 - @30.1.19

N7126    Transit W/E 19.9.18; Turnhouse W/E 26.9.18; Rosyth W/E 17.10.18; HMS *Galatea* 24.10.18; Donibristle 25.10.18; HMS *Lion* 9.11.18; Scapa 29.11.18; HMS *Lion* 4.12.18 - @30.1.19

N7127    Deld Turnhouse W/E 26.9.18; HMS *Phaeton* 20.9.18; Turnhouse 23.9.18; Rosyth W/E 24.10.18; HMS *Pegasus* 11.11.18; Donibristle 8.12.18; HMS *Pegasus* W/E 31.12.18; Donibristle 2.1.19; HMS *Pegasus* W/E 23.1.19 - @30.1.19

N7128    Deld Turnhouse W/E 26.9.18; Donibristle W/E 17.10.18; HMS *Courageous* 19.10.18; Donibristle 13.12.18; HMS *Courageous* 15.12.18; Donibristle W/E 16.1.19 - @30.1.19

N7129    Deld Turnhouse W/E 26.9.18; Donibristle W/E 14.11.18; HMS *Empress of India* 21.11.18; Smoogroo 1.1.19; Donibristle W/E 23.1.19 - @30.1.19

N7130    Deld 6 AAP Rosyth W/E 26.9.18; Transit W/E 3.10.18; Turnhouse W/E 17.10.18; Rosyth W/E 31.10.18; Donibristle W/E 31.12.18 - @30.1.19; HMS *Vindictive*, Koivisto, Baltic Russia by 10.19; Tested 29.10.19

N7131    Transit W/E 3.10.18; Turnhouse W/E 17.10.18; Donibristle W/E 31.10.18; Turnhouse W/E 19.12.18 - @30.1.19

N7132    Beardmore 21.9.18 (Constantinesco-gear tests from 17.10.18); Sherburn-in-Elmet (in transit) 23.1.19

N7133    Transit W/E 3.10.18; Deld Turnhouse W/E 10.10.18; HMS *Undaunted* 24.10.18; Donibristle 26.10.18; Rosyth 23.11.18; Turnhouse W/E 12.12.18 - @30.1.19

N7134    Deld 6 AAP W/E 6.10.18; Turnhouse W/E 10.10.18; Rosyth W/E 24.10.18; HMS *Nairana* 10.18; HMS *Argus* W/E 14.11.18; Turnhouse W/E 12.12.18; HMS *New Zealand* 19.12.18; Donibristle 27.12.18 - @30.1.19

N7135    Deld Turnhouse W/E 14.10.18; Donibristle W/E 31.10.18 - @30.1.19

N7136    Test flown 4.10.18 at Dalmuir; Deld 6 AAP Renfrew 4.10.18; Transit W/E 17.10.18; Turnhouse W/E 24.10.18; Donibristle W/E 14.11.18; HMS *Galatea* W/E 21.11.18; Donibristle 8.12.18; HMS *Barham* W/E 16.1.19; Donibristle W/E 23.1.19 - @30.1.19

N7137    Deld Turnhouse W/E 24.10.18 - @30.1.19

N7138    Deld Turnhouse W/E 24.10.18; Donibristle W/E 31.10.18; HMS *Dublin* W/E 21.11.18; HMS *Galatea* W/E 16.1.19; HMS *Dublin* W/E 23.1.19 - @30.1.19

N7139    Deld 6 AAP Renfrew 11.10.18; Turnhouse W/E 24.10.18; HMS *Penelope* 27.10.18; ashore 1.11.18; HMS *Undaunted* 1.12.18; Scapa 16.12.18; HMS *Undaunted* 17.12.18; ashore 27.1.19 - @30.1.19

**10 SOPWITH 2F.1 SHIP'S CAMEL TRACTOR BIPLANE SCOUTS** ordered 2.2.18 (amended 27.6.18) and built by Arrol Johnson (sub-let from Beardmore) under Cont A.S.3458/18 (BR.329 later BR.520), numbered N7140 to N7149 & built Dumfries. (150-hp Bentley B.R.1)

N7140   Deld 6 AAP Renfrew by 31.10.18; Donibristle 11.18; HMS *New Zealand* W/E 31.12.18; HMS *Princess Royal* W/E 16.1.18; Donibristle W/E 23.1.19 - @30.1.19; HMS *Vindictive*, Koivisto, Baltic Russia by 10.19; Bombed Krasnaya Gorka 14.10.19; Bombed Krasnaya Gorka and gunned fort 15.10.19; Bombed No.5 Fort at Kronstadt 18.10.19; Bombed Krasnaya Gorka then attacked kit balloon 19.10 19; Bombed Krasnaya Gorka 20.10.19 (all F/L SD Culley)

N7141   Deld 6 AAP Renfrew 2.11.18; Turnhouse W/E 5.12.18 - @30.1.19

N7142   Deld 6 AAP Renfrew 2.11.18; Turnhouse W/E 12.12.18 - @30.1.19

N7143   Deld 6 AAP Renfrew W/E 28.11.18; Turnhouse W/E 12.12.18 - @30.1.19; HMS *Vindictive*, Baltic Russia by 10.19; Tested 10.11.19; To Lettish Government

N7144   Deld 6 AAP Renfrew W/E 5.12.18; Turnhouse W/E 12.12.18 - @30.1.19

N7145   Deld 6 AAP Renfrew W/E 5.12.18 - @30.1.19

N7146   Deld 6 AAP Renfrew W/E 19.12.18; Turnhouse @30.1.19 (in transit); HMS *Malaya*

N7147   Deld 6 AAP Renfrew W/E 19.12.18 - @23.1.19; HMS *Furious*; Spun into Firth of Forth from 200ft, E of Forth Bridge 2.7.19 (2/Lt FN Underwood drowned)

N7148   Deld 6 AAP Renfrew W/E 31.12.18 - @23.1.19; HMS *Malaya*

N7149   Presentation a/c "Swillington". Mkrs by 30.1.19; Deld 6 AAP Renfrew .19; Turnhouse .19

**50 SOPWITH T.1 CUCKOO TRACTOR BIPLANE TORPEDO BOMBERS** ordered under Cont Nos 38a/527/C550 & A.S.23688/18 (BR.560) from Blackburn Aeroplane & Motor Co Ltd, numbered N7150 to N7199 & built Leeds. (Mk.I with Arab & Mk.II with 200-hp Viper) (all deld by mid 1919)

N7150   Deld 9 AAP Newcastle W/E 12.12.18; 185 Sqdn W/E 9.1.19 - @30.1.19

N7151   Deld 9 AAP Newcastle W/E 12.12.18; 185 Sqdn W/E 31.12.18 - @30.1.19; Convtd to Mk.II

N7152   Deld 9 AAP Newcastle W/E 12.12.18; 185 Sqdn W/E 31.12.18 - @30.1.19; C Flt Devt Sqdn Gosport by 6.19; 210 Sqdn by 7.20; EF, crashed in Solent 27.7.20

N7153   Deld 9 AAP W/E 19.12.18; 185 Sqdn W/E 23.1.19

N7154   Deld 9 AAP Newcastle W/E 19.12.18; 185 Sqdn East Fortune W/E 16.1.19 - @30.1.19; A Flt Development Sqdn 6.19; CAAD Turnhouse test 10.10.21

N7155   Deld 9 AAP Newcastle W/E 19.12.18; Convtd Mk.II; 1(S) ARD Farnborough by 12.18 - @30.1.19; No.1 Training Flt Gosport by 8.22 - @11.22; 210 Sqdn by 11.22

N7156   Deld 9 AAP Newcastle W/E 31.12.18 - @30.1.19; For East Fortune 2.19

N7157   Deld 9 AAP Newcastle W/E 31.12.18 - @30.1.19; For East Fortune 2.19

N7158   Deld 9 AAP Newcastle W/E 16.1.19 - @30.1.19; For East Fortune 2.19

N7159   Mkrs 12.18, convtd Mk.II; Grain from 13.1.19 - @30.1.19

N7160   Deld 6 AAP Renfrew W/E 16.1.19 - @30.1.19

N7161   Deld 6 AAP Renfrew 2.19; 210 Sqdn by 2.21; No.1 Training Flt Gosport by 8.21 - @11.21

N7162   Deld 4 AAP Lincoln by 30.1.19

N7163   Deld AES Martlesham Heath 31.3.19 (manoeuvrability tests over camera obscura); Not listed from 23.6.19

N7164   Deld 3 AAP Norwich W/E 30.1.19

N7165   On delivery to AAP Sherburn-in-Elmet by 30.1.19

N7166 to N7171 Still at Mkrs, allotted for storage 30.1.19

N7172   No evidence of delivery

N7173   No.1 Training Flt Gosport by 9.21 - @10.21; 210 Sqdn by 2.22

N7174 to N7186 No evidence of delivery

N7187   CAAD Turnhouse test 13.9.21; No.1 Training Flt Gosport by 11.21

N7188   B Flt Development Beardmore Sqdn Gosport 6.19

N7189 to N7191 No evidence of delivery

N7192   Convtd Mk.II (to Type XXII Spec); Grain by 7.19; U/c collapsed landing with torpedo; Damaged radiator 10.19; Fitted modified tail attachment 2.20; still Grain 6.20

N7193   Mk.II, deld Grain 6.5.19; For repair by 17.5.19; Radiator trouble 18.10.19 (sic); B Flt Development Sqdn Gosport 6.19; Grain to 7.19, u/c damaged 6.19; 186 Sqdn Gosport, spun in from 2000ft 1.8.19 (Lt AH Paull seriously injured)

N7194   No.1 Training Flt Gosport by 10.22

N7195   210 Sqdn by 4.22 - 9.22/No.1 Training Flt Gosport by 5.22 - @9.22

N7196   No evidence of delivery

N7197   210 Sqdn by 3.22

N7198   B Flt Development Sqdn Gosport 6.19

N7199   No evidence of delivery

**100 SOPWITH 2F.1 SHIP'S CAMEL TRACTOR BIPLANE SCOUTS** ordered from Fairey Aviation Co Ltd, numbered N7200 to N7299 to be built at Hayes.

N7200 to N7299 cancelled

**50 SOPWITH 2F.1 SHIP'S CAMEL TRACTOR BIPLANE SCOUTS** ordered from Pegler under Cont Nos 38a/553/C566 & A.S.24904/18 (BR.593), numbered N7300 to N7349. (150-hp Bentley B.R.1)

N7300 to N7349 cancelled 11.18

**50 SOPWITH 2F.1 SHIP'S CAMEL TRACTOR BIPLANE SCOUTS** ordered from Sir William Beardmore & Co Ltd and sub-let to Arrol Johnston Ltd under Cont Nos 38a/663/C695 & A.S.24907/18 (BR.594), numbered N7350 to N7399 & built Dumfries. Accepted 6 AAP Renfrew. (150-hp Bentley B.R.1)

N7350   No evidence of delivery

N7351   No evidence of delivery

N7352   MAEE Grain by 2.21 (fitted with airship and overhead wire landing gear for small craft)

N7353   No evidence of delivery

N7354   No evidence of delivery

N7355   203 Sqdn by 11.21; Struck concrete post on TO, Leuchars 16.11.21 (F/O T Brewin)

N7356   Experimental, 3-position ignition switch; To Canada; TOC 12.8.25; Held spare; SOC 18.11.28

N7357   RAF Base Leuchars by 6.21

N7358   To Canada; TOC 12.8.25; Held spare; SOC 18.10.28

N7359   203 Sqdn by 6.22

N7360   203 Sqdn by 6.22 - @9.22

N7361   No evidence of delivery

N7362   Painted all-white

N7363   To Canada; TOC 12.8.25; Held spare; SOC 7.6.27

N7264   No evidence of delivery

N7365   203 Sqdn by 5.22 - 10.22

N7366   To Canada; TOC 12.8.25; Held spare; SOC Camp Borden 18.11.28

N7367   203 Sqdn Leuchars by 4.22; EF while diving under Forth Bridge during gun trials against HMS *Agamemnon*, crashed in sea, wrecked 29.5.22

N7369 to N7373 No evidence of delivery

N7374   203 Sqdn by 5.22

N7375 to N7399 cancelled 12.18

**150 PARNALL PANTHER FLEET RECONNAISSANCE TRACTOR BIPLANES** ordered from Geo Parnall and Co Ltd under Cont Nos 38a/601/C630 & AS.26370 (BR.627), numbered N7400 to N7549 & built Bristol. (230-hp Bentley B.R.2) [Work ceased at Parnall 15.2.19 and transferred to Bristol under Cont No 38a/388/C1035 with c/n's 5715 to 5864] [50 cancelled 1.19 - presume reinstated]

N7400   Deld Grain on/by 8.19; Possibly the a/c used for trials with Edwards hook 18.12.19; Flotation gear ditching trials, completed W/E 26.6.20

N7401 to N7405 No evidence of delivery

N7406   (C/n P.877). 205 Sqdn HMS *Argus* by 5.22 - 8.22

N7407   No evidence of delivery

N7408   205 Sqdn by 11.21; EF, ditched in Moray Firth flying from HMS *Argus* 3.11.21 TL (salved?)

N7409   205 Sqdn - crashed on deck of HMS *Argus* (date?); 205

Sqdn *Argus* by 2.21, disembarked 13.11.21; 205 Sqdn HMS *Argus* by 5.22; 441 Flt, EF failed on TO, FL, o/t Leuchars 26.5.24

N7410 to N7416 No evidence of delivery

N7417 Gosport by 3.20 - @11.20

N7418 & N7419 No evidence of delivery

N7420 Mobile Flight Delney by 6.20

N7421 to N7425 No evidence of delivery

N7426 (C/n P.897?) *Eagle* Flight Gosport by 4.20; Flown by 203 Sqdn from Henlow via Farnborough to Gosport 23.6.20

N7427 No evidence of delivery

N7428 1 FTS Leuchars by 12.21

N7429 Gosport (coded 'P1') 1919 (deck trials in HMS *Argus* 1920); AEE Martlesham Heath 13.5.20

N7430 205 Sqdn HMS *Argus* from 15.1.22, FL in sea 24.3.22

N7431 205 Sqdn HMS *Argus* from 20.1.21 - @3.21

N7432 205 Sqdn HMS *Argus* by 3.21

N7433 *Argus* Flight (205 Sqdn?), stalled on TO, wrecked Fort Rowner, Gosport 20.5.21

N7434 to N7448 No evidence of delivery

N7449 205 Sqdn HMS *Argus* by 6.21; Crashed on deck 15.6.21

N7450 205 Sqdn HMS *Argus* - crashed on nose on deck (date?)

N7451 205 Sqdn HMS *Argus* from 20.1.21, disembarked 13.11.21; 205 Sqdn HMS *Argus* from Gosport 21.3.23 - @6.23

N7452 205 Sqdn HMS *Argus* from 20.1.21; Crashed on port side 29.6.21; disembarked 13.11.21

N7453 205 Sqdn HMS *Argus* (coded 'B') from 20.1.21, disembarked 13.11.21. (Crashed on deck 1921). HMS *Argus* at Malta (code 'B' in black on white fin) 1924

N7454 CAAD Turnhouse, tested 8.9.21

N7455 No evidence of delivery

N7456 205 Sqdn HMS *Argus* from 20.1.21; COL 25.2.21; disembarked 13.11.21

N7457 205 Sqdn HMS *Argus* by 2.21, disembarked 13.11.21

N7458 205 Sqdn HMS *Argus* from 20.1.21, disembarked 13.11.21

N7459 205 Sqdn HMS *Argus* by 2.21, disembarked 13.11.21; RAF Base Leuchars on 20.6.24 when FL near Gosport and badly damaged

N7460 442 Flt Leuchars when propeller accident 20.9.23; 442 Flt by 2.24; Crashed on deck of HMS *Argus* 27.5.24

N7461 442 Flt by 2.24; Slewed over side of HMS *Argus* on TO near Balearic Islands 11.3.24

N7462 441 Flt by 5.24 - @6.24; Propeller accident 28.5.24

N7463 No evidence of delivery

N7464 442 Flt Leuchars by 11.23; 441 Flt (?) Leuchars by 11.23; Propeller accident Leuchars 3.1.24; RAF Base Leuchars on 29.5.24 when lost speed and crashed in sea after dummy landing alongside HMS *Argus*

N7465 CAAD Turnhouse by 5.21 - @6.21; 442 Flt by 2.24

N7466 442 Flt by 1.24; Crashed on deck of HMS *Argus* 27.4.24

N7467 MAEE Grain from 2.20 - @4.20 (u/c hook trials)

N7468 HMS *Argus*, toppled off turret platform when about to launch from HMS *Repulse*, wrecked 9.11.21

N7469 CAAD Turnhouse by 5.21; 205 Sqdn HMS *Argus* from 15.1.22, Became 441 Flt 1.4.23; EF on TO, wrecked Leuchars 24.5.23

N7470 CAAD Turnhouse until 5.4.21 when EF, FL, o/t in ploughed field

N7471 205 Sqdn by 12.20 ('B' on fin) until crashed on deck (F/O EC Usher No.3 - date unknown)

N7472 No evidence of delivery

N7473 DLT in HMS *Argus* 31.8.21 (oleo u/c and large rudder); 205 Sqdn HMS *Argus* from 15.1.22; Ditched 1.6.22

N7474 205 Sqdn HMS *Argus* by 3.22

N7475 205 Sqdn HMS *Argus* by 3.22; 205 Sqdn HMS *Argus* from Gosport 21.3.23; Became 441 Flt 1.4.23; Disembarked Gosport 26.7.23; 442 Flt by 6.24 - @9.24

N7476 Grain for disposal by 8.20; 205 Sqdn by 12.22; 442 Flt by 9.24

N7477 205 Sqdn by 3.22 - @5.22; 405 Flt pilot 24.6.24 when crashed on TO Leuchars after EF and wrecked

N7478 205 Sqdn until 27.3.22 when EF, FL, wrecked Leuchars

N7479 442 Flt by 12.23; FL, badly damaged Kilmany, Fife 31.10.24

N7480 CAAD Turnhouse test 16.9.21; 205 Sqdn HMS *Argus* from 15.1.22 - @2.22

N7481 CAAD Turnhouse test 13.9.21; 205 Sqdn HMS *Argus* from 15.1.22, disembarked to Gosport 15.5.22

N7482 CAAD Turnhouse test 15.9.21; 205 Sqdn HMS *Argus* from 15.1.22; Crashed on TO at Newcastle, BO 15.10.22

N7483 RAF Base Leuchars by 11.21, also 22.5.23 when propeller accident; 441 Flight, o/t landing in bad weather Leuchars 17.7.23

N7484 205 Sqdn HMS *Argus* from 15.1.22

N7485 442 Flt HMS *Argus* by 11.23; HMS *Hermes* (441 Flt?) by 3.24; RAF Base Leuchars, FL, wrecked Alnwick 14.8.24

N7486 442 Flt HMS *Argus* by 12.23; Crashed on deck 27.5.24; Hit funnel casing landing, crashed over side, sank 19.6.24

N7487 441 Flt by 2.24?; 442 Flt by 2.24 - @5.24

N7488 No evidence of delivery

N7489 442 Flt by 12.23

N7490 205 Sqdn Leuchars until 9.3.23 when FL near Leuchars and wrecked (but see also N7494); 442 Flt by 12.23; HMS *Hermes* (441 Flt?) by 1.24 - @3.24

N7491 No evidence of delivery

N7492 No evidence of delivery

N7493 205 Sqdn Leuchars by 1.22; Swung on TO, hit building, wrecked 6.2.22

N7494 205 Sqdn Leuchars by 1.22; 205 Sqdn when EF, FL nr Leuchars 9.3.23

N7495 205 Sqdn HMS *Argus* from Gosport 21.3.23; Became 442 Flt 1.4.23; Disembarked to Gosport 26.7.23;

N7496 205 Sqdn by 3.22 - @4.22; Damaged when FL on beach at Leuchars 20.3.22

N7497 RAF Base Leuchars 12.21; 441 Flt 26.7.23 when crashed over side of HMS *Argus* on TO for Gosport in gusty weather, salved; 441 Flt by 5.24 (?). 442 Flt by 9.24

N7498 205 Sqdn HMS *Argus* from Gosport 21.3.23; Became 442 Flt 1.4.23; Disembarked to Gosport 26.7.23

N7499 205 Sqdn HMS *Argus* from Gosport 21.3.23; Became 442 Flt 1.4.23; Disembarked to Gosport 26.7.23; 442 Flt from 12.6.24

N7500 to N7502 No evidence of delivery

N7503 Gosport by 6.20 - @10.20; 205 Sqdn, crashed on HMS *Argus* 25.2.21 as "No.3". Disembarked at Rosyth 13.11.21; HMS *Argus* at Malta 1924 (date seems unlikely - *Argus* not at Malta 1924?)

N7504 & N7505 No evidence of delivery

N7506 205 Sqdn HMS *Argus* by 5.22; EF on TO, FL in field, Park Farm, wrecked, Guardbridge, Fife, 9.11.22

N7507 No evidence of delivery

N7508 205 Sqdn by 5.22 - crashed on deck of HMS *Argus* (date?)

N7509 205 Sqdn when EF shortly after TO, sideslipped and went in from 60ft, wrecked Donibristle 17.7.22

N7510 406 Flt pilot - EF, FL and wrecked Leuchars 12.8.24

N7511 205 Sqdn by 5.22; 205 Sqdn HMS *Argus* from Gosport 21.3.23; Became 441 Flt 1.4.23; Disembarked to Gosport 26.7.23; 441 Flight, heavy landing, wrecked, Leuchars 27.8.23

N7512 205 Sqdn by 5.22; 205 Sqdn HMS *Argus* from Gosport 21.3.23; Became 441 Flt 1.4.23; Disembarked to Gosport 26.7.23; Overshot arresting gear landing, slewed to port, went over side, salved 8.5.23

N7513 Leuchars (442 Flt?) by 7.24 - @11.24

N7514 No evidence of delivery

N7515 442 Flt by 9.24 - @10.24

N7516 AEE Martlesham from 5.20 (calibration); Gosport 11.7.20 for DL trials in HMS *Eagle*; Gosport by 2.21

N7517 To GI at Halton workshops by 1921/22

N7518 No evidence of delivery

N7519 Gosport by 5.22

N7520 441 Flt by 8.24; EF, FL, o/t, Broomhill, Northumb 4.8.24; EF, crashed Alnwick, Northumberland 14.8.24

N7521 Leuchars by 9.22; 205 Sqdn HMS *Argus* from Gosport 21.3.23; Became 441 Flt 1.4.23; Disembarked to Gosport 26.7.23

N7522 Gosport by 5.22

N7523 to N7526 No evidence of delivery

N7527 442 Flt by 6.24 - @10.24

N7528 CAAD Turnhouse test 9.9.21; RAF Base Leuchars by 12.21; 205 Sqdn by 3.22 - @11.22

N7529 CAAD Turnhouse test 16.9.21; 205 Sqdn HMS *Argus* from 15.1.22 - @3.22

N7530 Completed Filton 23.6.20; 205 Sqdn HMS *Argus* from

15.1.22 - @3.22; Became G-EBCM and first flown Croydon as such 13.4.22

N7531    205 Sqdn HMS *Argus* from 15.1.22 - @3.22

N7532 to N7534 No evidence of delivery

N7535    442 Flt, EF on TO, wrecked, Leuchars 15.6.23; 442 Flt by 6.24 - @9.24

N7536    No evidence of delivery

N7537    205 Sqdn by 10.22; Propeller accident Leuchars 4.1.23; 205 Sqdn HMS *Argus* from Gosport 21.3.23; Became 442 Flt 1.4.23; Disembarked to Gosport 26.7.23; 442 Flt @9.24

N7538 to N7540 No evidence of delivery

N7541    205 Sqdn by 10.22 and 7.23

N7542    No evidence of delivery

N7543    442 Flt by 7.24

N7544 to N7548 No evidence of delivery

N7549    CAAD Turnhouse test 13.9.21; 205 Sqdn by 2.22; Tipped on nose landing 8.6.22, also accident 9.6.22

**100 SHORT SHIRL TRACTOR BIPLANE TORPEDO BOMBERS ordered under Cont No A.S.26372 to Specification XXX (Type 3), numbered N7550 to N7649, to be built at Rochester. (360-hp Eagle VIII)**

N7550 to N7649 cancelled

**30 SOPWITH 2F.1 SHIP'S CAMEL TRACTOR BIPLANE SHIPBOARD SCOUTS ordered under Cont No 38a/662/C694 from Sir William Beardmore & Co Ltd, numbered N7650 - N7679, to be built at Dalmuir. (150-hp Bentley B.R.1)**

N7650 to N7679 cancelled 11.18

**162 PARNALL PANTHER FLEET RECONNAISSANCE TRACTOR BIPLANES ordered under Cont Nos 38a/719/C747 & A.S.30982/18 (BR.658) from Geo Parnall and Co Ltd, numbered N7680 to N7841, to be built at Bristol. (230-hp Bentley B.R.2)**

N7680 to N7841 cancelled 2.19

**N7842 TO N7849 NOT ALLOTTED (or cancelled order?)**

**130 SOPWITH 2F.1 SHIP'S CAMEL TRACTOR BIPLANES ordered under Cont No 38a/720/C748 & A.S.30981 (BR.657) from Fredk Sage & Co Ltd, numbered N7850 to N7979, to be built at Peterborough. (150-hp Bentley B.R.1)**

N7850 to N7979 cancelled 12.18

**100 SOPWITH T.1 CUCKOO TORPEDO BOMBER TRACTOR BIPLANES ordered from Blackburn Aeroplane & Motor Co Ltd under Cont Nos 38a/769/C793 & A.S.32641/18 (BR.677), numbered N7980 to N8079 & built Leeds. (Ordered with 200-hp Arab but deld with 200-hp Viper)** [AIR.1/35/15/1/217 refers to 14 Cuckoos at RAE, fitting Viper for Gosport/*Argus*]

N7980    No evidence of delivery

N7981    No evidence of delivery

N7982    B Flt Development Sqdn Gosport by 6.19

N7983    No evidence of delivery

N7984    No.1 Training Flt Gosport by 9.21 - @5.22

N7985    No evidence of delivery

N7986    A Flt Development Sqdn Gosport by 6.19

N7987    No evidence of delivery

N7988    Forced landed (no details)

N7989    No evidence of delivery

N7990    Convtd by Mkrs to Mk.III (Falcon III); Deld MAES Grain 11.9.19 (type and performance trials); Allocated Gosport 6.12.19; For deletion by 13.2.20

N7991    No evidence of delivery

N7992    C Flt Development Sqdn Gosport by 6.19; No.1 Training Flt Gosport by 9.21 - @10.21

N7993    B Flt Development Sqdn Gosport by 6.19; No.1 Training Flt Gosport by 8.22 - @11.22

N7994    210 Sqdn by 7.22; No.1 Training Flt Gosport by 10.22

N7995    210 Sqdn by 6.22 - @8.22; No.1 Training Flt Gosport by 8.22

N7996    210 Sqdn by 6.22; No.1 Training Flt Gosport by 8.22

N7997    210 Sqdn by 7.9.20; Crashed during formation torpedo attack on HMS *Queen Elizabeth*, 4m E of Sandown Bay 7.9.20

N7998    No evidence of delivery

N7999    Mk.II (Viper)

N8000    No.1 Training Flt Gosport by 10.22 - @11.22

N8001    No.1 Training Flt Gosport by 10.21; HMS *Argus* by 6.22; Went on nose on deck of *Argus* 10.6.22

N8002    No evidence of delivery

N8003    No.1 Training Flt Gosport by 10.21 - @11.21; 210 Sqdn by 11.21 - 6.22; EF on TO Gosport 7.6.22

N8004    No evidence of delivery

N8005    Mk.II. Deld Martlesham Heath 23.6.20 (parachute tests); To MAEE Grain W/E 24.7.20 (tests with new type rudder); Met flts 9.20; Tested adjustable rudder crank W/E 17.11.20; MAEE from 4.23 - 6.23 (recondition and mods for met observations)

N8006    No.1 Training Flt Gosport by 8.22 - @11.22

N8007 to N8010 No evidence of delivery

N8011    Deld 1919; 210 Sqdn by .20

N8012 to N8079 cancelled 1.19

**N8080 TO N8129 cancelled (or not allocated)**

**50 SOPWITH 2F.1 SHIP'S CAMEL TRACTOR BIPLANES ordered from Hooper & Co Ltd under Cont Nos 38a/906/C947 & A.S.37354/18 (BR.729), numbered N8130 to N8179 & built London. (130-hp Clerget)**

N8130    Presentation a/c 'Tamworth'. Mkrs 11.18 - @30.1.19; HMS *Vindictive* (Koivisto, Baltic Russia) .19; 203 Sqdn by 5.22; HMS *Argus*

N8131    Mkrs by 28.11.18 - @30.1.19

N8132    Mkrs by 28.11.18 - @30.1.19

N8133    Mkrs by 28.11.18 - @30.1.19

N8134    Mkrs by 28.11.18 - @30.1.19; *Eagle* Flt by 5.20 - 10.20 (shore base Gosport)

N8135    Mkrs by 28.11.18 - @30.1.19

N8136    Mkrs by 28.11.18 - @30.1.19; To Latvia with B.R.1

N8137    Mkrs by 28.11.18 - @30.1.19; To Latvia with B.R.1

N8138    No evidence of delivery

N8139    No evidence of delivery

N8140    Grand Fleet S of AF&G Leuchars by 7.19 - @8.19

N8141    Grand Fleet S of AF&G Leuchars by 7.19 - @8.19

N8142    Grand Fleet S of AF&G Leuchars by 8.19

N8143    Grand Fleet S of AF&G Leuchars, tested 14.8.19

N8144 & N8145 No evidence of delivery

N8146    203 Sqdn by 5.22

N8147 & N8148 No evidence of delivery

N8149    203 Sqdn by 5.22 - @6.22

N8150    203 Sqdn by 5.22 - @6.22

N8151    To Canada; TOC 12.8.25; Held spare; SOC 22.7.29

N8154    No evidence of delivery

N8153    To Canada; TOC 12.8.25; Held spare; SOC 22.7.29

N8154 & N8155 No evidence of delivery

N8156    To Canada; TOC 12.8.25; Held spare; To Museum, preserved in 45 Sqdn markings; Displayed Trenton 1959; Restored to flying condition and flown by W/Cdr Paul Hartman in 1967 Centennial Year, then retd to Canadian War Museum

N8157 to N8164 no evidence of delivery

N8165 to N8179 cancelled 1.19

**50 SOPWITH 2F.1 SHIP'S CAMEL TRACTOR BIPLANES ordered 17.5.18 from Clayton & Shuttleworth Ltd under Cont Nos 38a/911/C952, 38a/1153/C1109 & A.S.37750/18 (BR.738), numbered N8180 to N8229 & built Lincoln. Accepted 4 AAP Lincoln. (150-hp Bentley B.R.1)**

N8180 to N8183 no evidence of delivery

N8184    HMS *Vindictive*, Baltic Russia by 10.19; Dropped 4 bombs on Bolshevik destroyer, then EF, FL on beach at Fort xxxxx 4.10.19 (F/L SD Culley); Dropped 4 bombs on Bolshevik destroyer off Greyhound Battery and machine gunned it 29.10.19 (F/L SD Culley)

N8185    No evidence of delivery

N8186    No evidence of delivery

N8187    HMS *Vindictive*, Baltic Russia, left at Libau 11.19, then sent to Riga for Latvian use; To Latvian Air Force as 9 to at least 7.20

N8188 to N8190 no evidence of delivery

N8191    CARD Leuchars by 5.21 - 6.21; 205 Sqdn by 4.22; EF

on TO, stalled on to roof of house nr Leuchars 3.4.22

N8192 to N8201 no evidence of delivery

N8202    CARD Leuchars; Tested 4.6.21 prior to despatch

N8203    No evidence of delivery

N8204    To Canada; TOC 12.8.25; Held spare; SOC 18.11.28

N8205 to N8229 cancelled 1.19

## N8230 TO N8999 NOT ALLOTTED

## N9000 to N9999 reserved for Seaplanes, Main Types
(contd from N2999)

**60 SHORT ADMIRALTY 184 TYPE TRACTOR BIPLANE SEAPLANES ordered from Robey & Co Ltd under Cont Nos 38a/183/C178 & A.S.9791/18 (BR.440), numbered N9000 to N9059 & built Lincoln. (260-hp Sunbeam Maori)**

N9000    Deld 6 SD Ascot W/E 1.8.18; Shipped 27.8.18; Docks by 29.8.18 for Gibraltar; Gibraltar by 10.18; HMS *Engadine* 10.10.18 - @5.12.18LM; Arr 'X' AD Abu Qir 29.1.19; 270 Sqdn Alexandria 3.2.19; 268 Sqdn Calafrana 27.8.19

N9001    Deld 1(S)MAD Hamble W/E 1.8.18; 407 Flt 233 Sqdn Dover 3.8.18 (detd Dunkerque 23.10.18 - 29.10.18) - @30.1.19; 406 Flt 219 Sqdn Westgate by 1.19 - @7.19 (mine spotting patrols in North Sea 5.19)

N9002    Deld 1(S)MAD Hamble W/E 1.8.18; 407 Flt 233 Sqdn Dover 9.8.18; Hit harbour wall and sideslipped in on TO, o/t in water in harbour, CW, towed in 25.9.18 (2/Lt I Winskill and another unhurt); Deleted 3.10.18

N9003    Deld 1(S)MAD Hamble W/E 1.8.18; Calshot W/E 8.8.18; ARS Calshot W/E 15.8.18; 412/3 Flts 253 Sqdn Bembridge W/E 19.9.18; EF, FL in sea 11.11.18 (2/Lt L Poulter & Lt Shaw) (towed back); still Bembridge 30.1.19

N9004    Deld 1(S)MAD Hamble W/E 8.8.18; 209 TDS Lee-on-Solent W/E 10.10.18 - @30.1.19

N9005    Deld 1(S)MAD Hamble W/E 8.8.18; 209 TDS Lee-on-Solent by 26.9.18 - @30.1.19

N9006    Deld 1(S)MAD Hamble W/E 22.8.18; Calshot 26.9.18; 412/3 Flts 253 Sqdn Bembridge W/E 3.10.18 - @30.1.19

N9007    Deld 1(S)MAD Hamble W/E 22.8.18; 416/7 Flt 241 Sqdn Portland W/E 3.10.18 - @30.1.19; 406 Flt 219 Sqdn Westgate by 5.19 - @7.19 (mine spotting patrols in North Sea 6.19); Killingholme by 7.19; HMS *Argus* 24.7.19 (to Archangel)

N9008    Deld 1(S)MAD Hamble W/E 22.8.18; Calshot 6.9.18; 416/7 Flt 241 Sqdn Portland W/E 10.9.18 - @30.1.19

N9009    Deld 6 SD Ascot W/E 29.8.18; To docks W/E 31.10.18; Shipped to Gibraltar 12.11.18; 269 Sqdn Port Said 4.2.19; 268 Sqdn Calafrana 27.8.19; HMS *Engadine*

N9010    Deld 6 SD Ascot W/E 29.8.18; Shipped to Malta 19.10.18; HMS *Ark Royal* by 11.18; Calafrana 10.11.19

N9011    Deld 6 SD Ascot W/E 29.8.18; Docks W/E 1.9.18; Shipped to Malta 11.10.18 (Damaged on SS *Hazlemere*)

N9012    Deld 6 SD Ascot W/E 29.8.18; Docks W/E 1.9.18; Shipped to Malta 11.10.18; Recd RAF South Russia Instructional Mission 3.11.19; To Russian Aviation Corps 10.11.19

N9013    Deld 6 SD Ascot W/E 29.8.18; Shipped to Malta 11.10.18; Recd RAF South Russia Instructional Mission 3.11.19; To Russian Aviation Corps 10.11.19

N9014    Deld 6 SD Ascot W/E 5.9.18; Docks W/E 1.9.18; Mudros by 6.18 - @11.18; Talikna by 2.11.18 - @10.1.19 (266 Sqdn?)

N9015    Deld 426/7 Flts 235 Sqdn Fishguard W/E 12.9.18 - @30.1.19; Calshot by 2.20

N9016    Deld 1(S)MAD Hamble W/E 12.9.18; 416/7 Flst 241 Sqdn Portland W/E 20.9.18; Overshot landing at dusk, crashed into breakwater 28.10.18 (Lt FSS Wates slightly injured); Deleted W/E 14.11.18

N9017    Deld 1(S)MAD Hamble W/E 19.9.18; Calshot 26.9.18; 414/5 Flt 243 Sqdn Cherbourg W/E 17.10.18 - @30.1.19 (detd Fécamp by 1.11.18 - @8.11.18)

N9018    Deld 1(S)MAD Hamble W/E 19.8.18; Calshot 24.9.18 - @30.1.19; Calshot, tested with DC 27.2.20 - @6.20

N9019    Deld 2(N)MAD Brough W/E 26.9.18; 403 Flt 246 Sqdn Seaton Carew 15.10.18 - @30.1.19

N9020    Deld 2(N)MAD Brough W/E 26.9.18; 403 Flt 246 Sqdn Seaton Carew 13.10.18 - @30.1.19

N9021    Deld 1(S)MAD Hamble W/E 26.9.18; Calshot W/E 3.10.17; 414/5 Flts 243 Sqdn Cherbourg W/E 24.10.18 - @30.1.19

N9022    Deld 1(S)MAD Hamble W/E 26.9.18; 209 TDS Lee-on-Solent 28.9.18 - @30.1.19

N9023    Deld 1(S)MAD Hamble W/E 3.10.18; Cattewater W/E 24.10.18 - @30.1.19

N9024    Deld 2(N)MAD Brough W/E 3.10.18; 402 Flt 246 Sqdn Seaton Carew W/E 31.10.18 - @30.1.19; Syren Force, HMS *Nairana* (North Russia) by 1.9.19 - @24.9.19

N9025    Deld 2(N)MAD Brough W/E 3.10.18; 402 Flt 246 Sqdn Seaton Carew W/E 24.10.18 - @30.1.19

N9026    Deld 2(N)MAD Brough W/E 10.10.18; 402 Flt 246 Sqdn Seaton Carew by 17.10.18; Killingholme W/E 5.12.18 - @30.1.19

N9027    Deld 2(N)MAD Brough W/E 10.10.18; South Shields 19.10.18 (transit, weather); 400/1 Flts 249 Sqdn Dundee 21.10.18; Rosyth 14.6.19 (for HMS *Vindictive*)

N9028    Deld 2(N)MAD Brough W/E 3.10.18; 1(S)MAD Hamble W/E 10.10.18; 418/9 Flts 239 Sqdn Torquay W/E 17.10.18 - @30.1.19

N9029    Deld 2(N)MAD Brough W/E 3.10.18; 1(S)MAD Hamble W/E 10.10.18; 418/9 Flts 239 Sqdn Torquay W/E 17.10.18 - @30.1.19; 2(N)MAD Brough by 2.19; Yarmouth 12.2.19; Killingholme by 7.19; HMS *Argus* 23.7.19; RAF(R) HMS *Pegasus* 31.7.19 (at Archangel); ashore 9.19; HMS *Pegasus* 4.9.19; ashore 9.19; HMS *Pegasus* 11.9.19

N9030    Deld MAD Dundee W/E 10.10.18; 400/1 Flts 249 Sqdn Dundee W/E 21.11.18 - @30.1.19

N9031    Deld MAD Dundee W/E 10.10.18; Accepted 19.10.18; 400/1 Flts 249 Sqdn Dundee W/E 24.10.18 - @30.1.19

N9032    Deld 426/7 Flts 245 Sqdn Fishguard W/E 17.10.18 - @30.1.19;

N9033    Deld 426/7 Flts 245 Sqdn Fishguard 16.10.18 - @30.1.19

N9034    Deld 6 SD Ascot W/E 17.10.18; 1(S)MAD Hamble W/E 31.12.18 - @30.1.19; Syren Force, HMS *Nairana* (North Russia) by 17.9.19

N9035    Deld 6 SD Ascot W/E 17.10.18; 2(N)MAD Brough W/E 12.12.18; Felixstowe 24.2.19

N9036    Deld 6 SD Ascot W/E 24.10.18; 2(N)MAD Brough W/E 5.12.18 - @30.1.19; Allotted Dundee by 30.1.19; RAF(R) HMS *Pegasus* Dvina River by 8.19 - 9.19

N9037    Deld 6 SD Ascot W/E 24.10.18; 2(N)MAD Brough W/E 12.12.18 - @30.1.19

N9038    Deld 6 SD Ascot W/E 24.10.18; 2(N)MAD Brough W/E 5.12.18 - @30.1.19

N9039    Deld 6 SD Ascot W/E 31.10.18; 1(S)MAD Hamble W/E 28.11.18; 210 TDS Calshot W/E 31.12.18 - @30.1.19; RAF(R) HMS *Pegasus* Dvina River by 9.19

N9040    Deld 6 SD Ascot W/E 31.10.18; 2(N)MAD Brough W/E 21.11.18; Killingholme W/E 12.12.18 - @30.1.19

N9041    Deld 6 SD Ascot W/E 24.10.18; 2(N)MAD Brough W/E 12.12.18 - @30.1.19

N9042    Allocated 6 SD Ascot W/E 31.10.18; 1(S)MAD Hamble W/E 21.11.18; 210 TDS Calshot W/E 28.11.18 - @7.19; SoNC Lee-on-Solent by 8.21

N9043    Deld 6 SD Ascot W/E 31.10.18; 2(N)MAD Brough W/E 21.11.18; Killingholme W/E 12.12.18; Yarmouth W/E 16.1.19 - @30.1.19; Westgate by 3.5.19 - @10.6.19

N9044    Deld 6 SD Ascot W/E 31.10.18; 2(N)MAD Brough W/E 14.11.18; South Shields 1.12.18 (transit); 400/1 Flts 249 Sqdn Dundee 5.12.18 - @30.1.19

N9045    Deld 2(N)MAD Brough W/E 31.10.18; Killingholme W/E 14.11.18 - @30.1.19; Syren Force, HMS *Nairana* (North Russia) by 5.9.19 - @21.9.19

N9046    Deld 2(N)MAD Brough W/E 14.11.18; 400/1 Flts 249 Sqdn Dundee W/E 28.11.18 - @30.1.19; HMS *Vindictive*, Baltic Russia by 23.11.19

N9047    Deld 2(N)MAD Brough W/E 7.11.18; Killingholme W/E 14.11.18 - @30.1.19; HMS *Pegasus* Dvina River by 9.19; HMS *Ark Royal* by 7.20; HMS *Pegasus* 28.7.20

N9048    Deld 2(N)MAD Brough 2.11.18; Killingholme W/E 14.11.18 - @30.1.19; RAF(R) HMS *Pegasus* Dvina River by 9.19; ashore 9.19; HMS *Pegasus* 19.9.19

N9049    Deld 2(N)MAD Brough 2.11.18; 401/1 Flts 249 Sqdn Dundee W/E 21.11.18 - @30.1.19

N9050    Deld 1(S)MAD Hamble W/E 14.11.18; 210 TDS Calshot W/E 28.11.18 - @30.1.19

N9051  Deld 1(S)MAD Hamble W/E 14.11.18; 209 TDS Lee-on-Solent W/E 28.11.18 - @30.1.19

N9052  Deld 1(S)MAD Hamble W/E 14.11.18 - @30.1.19; SoNC Lee-on-Solent by 10.21

N9053  Deld 2(N)MAD Brough W/E 21.11.18; 400/1 Flts 249 Sqdn Dundee W/E 19.12.18 - @30.1.19

N9054  Deld 2(N)MAD Brough W/E 21.11.18; South Shields 14.12.18 (transit); Rosyth 16.12.18 - @30.1.19

N9055  Deld 2(N)MAD Brough W/E 28.11.18; South Shields (via Hornsea) 25.1.19 (transit); Dundee 1.2.19; HMS *Vindictive* at Rosyth 30.6.19 - @24.7.19 (Baltic Russia)

N9056  Deld 2(N)MAD Brough W/E 21.11.18; 400/1 Flts 249 Sqdn Dundee W/E 19.12.18 - @30.1.19; HMS *Vindictive* by 27.6.19

N9057  Deld 2(N)MAD Brough W/E 28.11.18; Seaton Carew W/E 19.12.18 (transit); 400/1 Flts 249 Sqdn Dundee W/E 31.12.18 - @30.1.19; HMS *Vindictive* (Baltic Russia) by 23.11.19

N9058  Deld 2(N)MAD Brough W/E 28.11.18; 406 Flt 219 Sqdn Westgate (coded '7' on fin) W/E 19.12.18; To South Shields via Killingholme, but landed Warkworth owing to fog, FL, dismantled 11.19 (T/Capt AH Pearce)

N9059  Deld 2(N)MAD Brough W/E 28.11.18 - @30.1.19

**40 SHORT ADMIRALTY 184 TYPE TRACTOR BIPLANE SEAPLANES ordered under Cont Nos 38a/182/C177 & A.S.9790/18 (BR.318 & BR.417) from The Brush Electrical Engineering Co Ltd, numbered N9060 to N9099 & built Loughborough. (260-hp Sunbeam Maori)**

N9060  Deld 1(S)MAD Hamble W/E 1.8.18; 412/3 Flts 253 Sqdn Bembridge W/E 5.9.18 - @30.1.19

N9061  Deld 1(S)MAD Hamble W/E 1.8.18; Calshot W/E 8.8.18; 408/9 Flts 242 Sqdn Newhaven W/E 15.8.18 - @11.18

N9062  Deld 1(S)MAD Hamble W/E 8.8.18; Calshot W/E 15.8.18; 416/7 Flts 241 Sqdn Portland W/E 22.8.18; ARS Calshot W/E 14.11.18 - @30.1.19

N9063  Deld Houton Bay W/E 12.9.18 - @30.1.19

N9064  Deld 1(S)MAD Hamble W/E 15.8.18; 209 TDS Lee-on-Solent W/E 22.8.18 - @31.10.18

N9065  Deld 1(S)MAD Hamble W/E 29.8.18; 209 TDS Lee-on-Solent W/E 5.9.18 - @30.1.19; Syren Force, HMS *Nairana* (North Russia) by 20.9.19

N9066  Deld 6 SD Ascot W/E 22.8.18; Docks W/E 26.9.18; Shipped 26.9.18; Arrived 'X' AD Abu Qir 19.10.18; 269 Sqdn Port Said 27.10.18; 270 Sqdn Alexandria by 21.12.18; 269 Sqdn Port Said 27.1.19; 270 Sqdn Alexandria 30.1.19; 268 Sqdn Calafrana 27.8.19

N9067  Deld 6 SD Ascot W/E 22.8.18; Docks W/E 26.9.18; Shipped to Alexandria 26.9.18

N9068  Deld 6 SD Ascot W/E 22.8.18; Docks W/E 12.9.18; Shipped to Malta 11.10.18; Calafrana by 3.20; HMS *Ark Royal* 6.3.20; Damaged hoisting out 16.3.20

N9069  Deld MAD Dundee W/E 29.8.18 for Stenness/Houton Bay (NTU?); Not listed from W/E 5.9.18; HMS *Pegasus* by 26.9.18; HMS *Campania* 26.10.18; HMS *Pegasus* by 12.18; Dundee by 31.12.18; HMS *Pegasus* W/E 23.1.19 - @30.1.19

N9070  Deld 1(S)MAD Hamble W/E 19.9.18; Calshot 18.9.18; 209 TDS Lee-on-Solent W/E 26.9.18 - @30.1.19; Syren Force, HMS *Nairana* (North Russia) by 14.9.19

N9071  Deld 1(S)MAD Hamble W/E 5.9.18; 209 TDS Lee-on-Solent W/E 19.9.18 - @30.1.19

N9072  Deld 1(S)MAD Hamble W/E 5.9.18; 209 TDS Lee-on-Solent W/E 19.9.18 - @30.1.19

N9073  Deld MAD Dundee, accepted 18.9.18; 400/1 Flts 249 Sqdn Dundee W/E 26.9.18; EF, FL, sank 15m E of Montrose 14.10.18 (Lt Trynde & observer picked up by destroyer HMS Lydiard)

N9074  Deld 1(S)MAD Hamble W/E 26.9.18; 418/9 Flts 239 Sqdn Torquay 28.9.18 - @30.1.19

N9075  Deld 2(N)MAD Brough W/E 26.9.18; 402 Flt 246 Sqdn Seaton Carew (via Scarborough) 17.10.18 - @30.1.19

N9076  Deld 6 SD Ascot W/E 3.10.18; To docks W/E 31.10.18; Shipped to Gibraltar 12.11.18; arr 'X' AD Abu Qir 27.1.19; 270 Sqdn Alexandria 21.2.19; 268 Sqdn HMS Calafrana 27.8.19; HMS *Engadine*; To HMS *Ark Royal* at Constantinople 15.3.20 (to South Russia); HMS *Pegasus* 26.6.20; HMS *Ark Royal* 28.7.20; Left ship at Haida Pasha 31.8.20

N9077  Deld 6 SD Ascot W/E 3.10.18; To docks W/E 31.10.18; Shipped to Malta 14.11.18; HMS *Ark Royal* at Constantinople 10.9.19; Calafrana by 3.20; HMS *Ark Royal* (South Russia) 5.3.20; HMS *Pegasus* 26.6.20; HMS *Ark Royal* 28.7.20; Left ship at Haida Pasha 31.8.20

N9078  Deld 6 SD Ascot W/E 10.10.18; Devonport W/E 9.1.19; left W/E 23.1.19; HMS *Engadine* W/E 31.1.19; 266 Sqdn Petrovsk by 28.5.19; HMS *Orlionoch* 17.7.19; Petrovsk 25.7.19

N9079  Deld 6 SD Ascot W/E 31.10.18; Devonport W/E 9.1.19; Left W/E 23.1.19; HMS *Engadine* W/E 31.1.19; 266 Sqdn Petrovsk/HMS *Engadine* by 4.19; Petrovsk by 5.19; HMS *Alader Yousanoff* 19.5.19; Crashed on turn during bombing raid to Alexandrovsk, FL in sea, sank (bombs did not explode) 20.5.19 (2/Lt RGK Morrison & Lt HG Pratt rescued);

N9080  Deld 6 SD Ascot W/E 31.10.18; Devonport W/E 9.1.19; left W/E 23.1.19; HMS *Engadine* by 31.1.19; 266 Sqdn Petrovsk/HMS *Engadine* by 4.19; Embarked HMS *Alader Yousanoff* 12.5.19; FL in fog outside Fort Alexandrovsk, sank while taxying, CW 23.5.19 (Capt JA Sadler & Lt F Kingham picked up 32 hrs later by HMS *Asian*)

N9081  Deld 6 SD Ascot W/E 31.10.18; Devonport W/E 9.1.19; left W/E 23.1.19; HMS *Engadine* by 31.1.19; 266 Sqdn Petrovsk/HMS *Engadine* by 4.19; Crashed on TO 25.4.19; Repaired; Petrovsk by 7.19; HMS *Orlionoch* 17.7.19; Petrovsk 25.7.19

N9082  Deld 6 SD Ascot W/E 10.10.18; Devonport W/E 9.1.19; left W/E 23.1.19; HMS *Engadine* by 28-31.1.19; Dropped 112-lb bomb to lighten a/c as unable to TO, bomb exploded, a/c wrecked 28.1.19 (2 slightly injured); 266 Sqdn Petrovsk/HMS *Engadine* by 4.19 - @12.6.19; Embarked HMS *Alader Yousanoff* 12.5.19; Badly damaged landing 17.5.19 (2/Lt RGK Morrison & Lt HG Pratt); Petrovsk 19.5.19; *Alader Yousanoff* 6.19

N9083  Deld 6 SD Ascot W/E 17.10.18 (packed by 9.1.19) - @30.1.19

N9084  Deld 6 SD Ascot W/E 17.10.18; 2(N)MAD Brough W/E 5.12.18 - @30.1.19

N9085  Deld 6 SD Ascot W/E 24.10.18; Devonport W/E 9.1.19; left W/E 23.1.19; HMS *Engadine* W/E @30.1.19; 266 Sqdn Petrovsk by 4.19; HMS *Orlionoch* 21.7.19

N9086  Presentation a/c 'Saltcoats Drakemyre'. Deld 6 SD Ascot W/E 24.10.18; 2(N)MAD Brough W/E 4.12.18 - @30.1.19

N9087  Deld 6 SD Ascot W/E 24.10.18; 2(N)MAD Brough W/E 12.12.18 - @30.1.19; Killingholme to Brough 27.2.19; To Felixstowe but landed crosswind and sank, Felixstowe Harbour 1.3.19 (2/Lt L Poulter)

N9088  Deld 1(S)MAD Hamble W/E 24.10.18; 405 Flt 248 Sqdn Hornsea W/E 14.11.18 - @30.1.19

N9089  Deld MAD Dundee W/E 31.10.18; Accepted 9.11.18; 400/1 Flts 249 Sqdn Dundee W/E 21.11.18 - @30.1.19

N9090  Deld MAD Dundee, accepted 21.11.18; HMS *Pegasus* W/E 23.1.19 (later to Dvina River); Spun in on test flight 20.8.19 (2/Lt CM LeMoine killed & F/Sgt HW Quantrell severely shaken)

N9091  Deld 6 SD Ascot W/E 31.10.18; 1(S)MAD Hamble W/E 14.11.18; 210 TDS Calshot W/E 21.11.18 - @30.1.19; 'CT' on fin at Lee-on-Solent 1920

N9092  Deld 6 SD Ascot W/E 31.10.18; 2(N)MAD Brough W/E 14.11.18; left W/E 5.12.18 (at Bridlington); Killingholme W/E 12.12.18; 400/1 Flts 249 Sqdn Dundee W/E 31.12.18 - 30.1.19; HMS *Argus*

N9093  Deld MAD Dundee W/E 14.11.18; Accepted 28.11.18; HMS *Pegasus* W/E 9.1.19 - @30.1.19

N9094  Deld MAD Dundee W/E 21.11.18; Accepted 5.12.18; HMS *Pegasus* W/E 23.1.19 - @30.1.19

N9095  Deld 2(N)MAD Brough W/E 21.11.18; Wrecked in transit to 6 SD Ascot W/E 19.12.18

N9096  Deld 2(N)MAD Brough W/E 28.11.18; Yarmouth W/E 31.12.18 - @30.1.19; Became G-EBBM

N9097  Deld 2(N)MAD Brough W/E 5.12.18; 400/1 Flts 249 Sqdn Dundee W/E 31.12.18

N9098  Deld 2(N)MAD Brough W/E 5.12.18 - @30.1.19

N9099  Deld 2(N)MAD Brough W/E 5.12.18 - @30.1.19

**40 SHORT ADMIRALTY 184 TYPE TRACTOR BIPLANE SEAPLANES** ordered under Cont No 38a/184/C179 & A.S.9792 (BR.423 & BR.441) from J.S.White & Co Ltd, numbered N9100 to N9139 & built East Cowes. (260-hp Sunbeam Maori)

N9100    Deld 1(S)MAD Hamble W/E 7.11.18; Cattewater W/E 14.11.18 - @30.1.19

N9101    Deld 1(S)MAD Hamble W/E 21.11.18; Cattewater W/E 12.12.18 - 30.1.19

N9102    Deld 1(S)MAD Hamble W/E 21.11.18; 418/9 Flts 239 Sqdn Torquay W/E 21.11.18 - @30.1.19

N9103    Deld 209 TDS Lee-on-Solent W/E 28.11.18 - @30.1.19

N9104    Deld 1(S)MAD Hamble W/E 14.11.18; 209 TDS Lee-on-Solent W/E 28.11.18 - @30.1.19

N9105    Deld Calshot W/E 14.11.18 - @30.1.19

N9106    Deld 1(S)MAD Hamble W/E 5.12.18; 209 TDS Lee-on-Solent W/E 12.12.18 - @30.1.19

N9107    Deld 1(S)MAD Hamble W/E 5.12.18; 209 TDS Lee-on-Solent W/E 19.12.18 - @30.1.19; Grain, to be disposed by 8.20

N9108    Deld 1(S)MAD Hamble W/E 12.12.18; 209 TDS Lee-on-Solent W/E 31.12.18 - @30.1.19

N9109    Deld 1(S)MAD Hamble W/E 19.12.18 - @30.1.19

N9110    Deld 1(S)MAD Hamble W/E 19.12.18; 210 TDS Calshot W/E 9.1.19 - @30.1.19; Westgate by 10.7.19

N9111    Deld 1(S)MAD Hamble W/E 9.1.19; 210 TDS Calshot W/E 16.1.19 - @30.1.19; Tested Westgate 10.7.19

N9112 to N9115 Mkrs by 30.1.19 for storage

N9116 & N9117 No evidence of delivery

N9118    Grain (coded 'G' on fin); Became G-EBBN

N9119    Syren Force, HMS *Nairana* (North Russia) by 29.8.19 - @21.9.19

N9120 to N9124 No evidence of delivery

N9125    HMS *Ark Royal* (South Russia) by 26.3.20; HMS *Pegasus* 26.6.20; HMS *Ark Royal* 28.6.20; HMS *Pegasus* 28.7.20 - @2.9.20

N9126    No evidence of delivery

N9127    To Estonian Government

N9128    Free issue to Chile

N9129    To Estonian Government

N9130    To Estonian Government as *No.39*

N9131 to N9135 cancelled 1.19 but evidently reinstated

N9131    HMS *Ark Royal* (South Russia) by 7.7.20; HMS *Pegasus* 28.7.20; ashore 16.10.20

N9132    To Estonian Government; Became *No.40*

N9133    Killingholme by 7.19; HMS *Argus* 24.7.19

N9134    To Estonian Government; Became *No.41*

N9135    Deld Grain 3.19 (type trials with 300-hp Sunbeam Manitou; first aircraft to be fitted with this engine)

N9136 to N9139 cancelled 1.19

**30 SHORT ADMIRALTY 184 TYPE TRACTOR BIPLANE SEAPLANES** ordered under Cont Nos 38a/295/C285 & A.S.11688/18 (BR.422) from Robey & Co Ltd, numbered N9140 to N9169 & built Lincoln. (260-hp Sunbeam Maori)

N9140    Deld 2(N)MAD Brough W/E 28.11.18 - @30.1.19; 4 Comms Sqdn Felixstowe by 5.19; EF, FL on a pier, crashed 23.5.19 (Capt HL Nunn & Lt CJT Boys both injured)

N9141    Deld 1(S)MAD Hamble W/E 12.12.18 - @30.1.19

N9142    Deld 1(S)MAD Hamble W/E 12.12.18 - 30.1.19; SoNC Lee-on-Solent .19

N9143    Deld 1(S)MAD Hamble W/E 12.12.18 - @30.1.19; SoNC Lee-on-Solent 7.21 - @11.21

N9144    Deld 1(S)MAD Hamble W/E 19.12.18 - @30.1.19; SoNC Lee-on-Solent 8.21 - @11.21

N9145    Deld 1(S)MAD Hamble W/E 19.12.18 - @30.1.19; SoNC Lee-on-Solent 9.21

N9146    Deld 1(S)MAD Hamble W/E 19.12.18 - @30.1.19

N9147    Deld 1(S)MAD Hamble W/E 31.12.18 - @30.1.19

N9148    Deld 1(S)MAD Hamble W/E 31.12.18 - @30.1.19

N9149    Allocated AAP Sherburn-in-Elmet by 30.1.19

N9150    Deld 3 AAP Norwich W/E 30.1.19; SoNC Lee-on-Solent by 11.21

N9151    Allocated AAP Sherburn-in-Elmet by 30.1.19

N9152    (275-hp Sunbeam) Allocated AAP Sherburn-in-Elmet by @30.1.19

N9153    Allocated AAP Sherburn-in-Elmet by 30.1.19

N9154    Allocated AAP Sherburn-in-Elmet by 30.1.19

N9155    Allocated AAP Sherburn-in-Elmet by 30.1.19

N9156    Mkrs by 30.1.19 for storage; HMS *Ark Royal* by 8.20; Left ship in tow at Haida Pasha 31.8.20; HMS *Pegasus* by 23.9.20; Calafrana 8.11.20

N9157    No evidence of delivery

N9158    Mkrs by 30.1.19 for storage

N9159    Mkrs by 30.1.19 for storage

N9160    Mkrs by 30.1.19 for storage; HMS *Ark Royal* by 26.8.20; Left ship at Haida Pasha 31.8.20; HMS *Pegasus* by 25.9.20; Calafrana 8.11.20

N9161    Mkrs @30.1.19 for 1 SD store

N9162 & N9163 No evidence of delivery

N9164    Calafrana by 3.20; HMS *Ark Royal* 5.3.20; HMS *Pegasus* 26.6.20; HMS *Ark Royal* (South Russia) 28.7.20 - @31.8.20

N9165 to N9169 No evidence of delivery, but contract reported to have been completed

**30 SHORT ADMIRALTY 184 TYPE TRACTOR BIPLANE SEAPLANES** ordered under Cont Nos 38a/296/C286 & A.S.11686/18 (BR.424) from Supermarine Aviation Works, numbered N9170 to N9199 & built Woolston. (260-hp Sunbeam Maori III)

N9170    Deld 1(S)MAD Hamble W/E 12.9.18; 414/5 Flts 243 Sqdn Cherbourg W/E 3.10.18 - @30.1.19

N9171    Deld 1(S)MAD Hamble W/E 3.10.18; Cattewater 8.10.18 - @30.1.19

N9172    Deld 1(S)MAD Hamble W/E 17.10.18; Westgate 29.10.18 (transit); Hornsea 30.10.18 (transit); 402/3 Flts 246 Sqdn Seaton Carew by 31.10.18 - @30.1.19

N9173    Deld 1(S)MAD Hamble W/E 24.10.18; Westgate 29.10.18 (transit); Hornsea 30.10.18 (transit); 402/3 Flts 246 Sqdn Seaton Carew by 31.10.18 - @30.1.19

N9174    Deld 1(S)MAD Hamble W/E 31.10.18; 210 TDS Calshot 9.11.18 - @30.1.19

N9175    Deld 1(S)MAD Hamble W/E 7.11.18; 210 TDS Calshot W/E 12.12.18 - @30.1.19

N9176    Deld 1(S)MAD Hamble W/E 14.11.18; 210 TDS Calshot W/E 5.12.18 - @30.1.19; HMS *Pegasus* (Archangel) by 5.9.19; Trotsky 6.9.19; HMS *Pegasus* 8.9.19

N9177    Deld 1(S)MAD Hamble W/E 28.11.18; 209 TDS Lee-on-Solent W/E 12.12.18 - @30.1.19

N9178    Deld 1(S)MAD Hamble W/E 5.12.18; Lee-on-Solent W/E 23.1.19 - @30.1.19

N9179    Deld 1(S)MAD Hamble W/E 12.12.18 - 30.1.19

N9180    Deld 1(S)MAD Hamble W/E 19.12.18; 210 TDS Calshot W/E 9.1.19; Killingholme by 7.19; HMS *Argus* 23.7.19; HMS *Pegasus* (Archangel) by 6.9.19

N9181    Deld 1(S)MAD Hamble W/E 31.12.18 - @30.1.19; Lee-on-Solent .19

N9182    Deld AAP Sherburn-in-Elmet W/E 30.1.19; Killingholme to Seaton Carew 4.9.19 (weather); Dundee 5.9.19

N9183    Deld 3 AAP Norwich W/E 30.1.19

N9184    Allocated AAP Sherburn-in-Elmet by 30.1.19

N9185    Mkrs by 30.1.19 for storage; HMS *Vindictive* 30.6.19 (to Baltic Russia); HMS *Argus* 14.11.19

N9186 to N9189 Mkrs by 30.1.19 for storage

N9190    To Estonian Government; Became *No.24*

N9191 & N9192 To Estonian Government

N9193    HMS *Ark Royal* 8.19; Syren Force, HMS *Nairana* (North Russia) by 27.8.19 - @23.9.19

N9194 & N9195 No evidence of delivery

N9196    Killingholme by 9.19; Seaton Carew 4.9.19 (weather); Dundee 5.9.19

N9197 & N9198 No evidence of delivery

N9199    HMS *Pegasus* by 25.3.20; HMS *Ark Royal* 26.6.20; HMS *Pegasus* 28.6.20; HMS *Ark Royal* 28.7.20

**30 SHORT ADMIRALTY 184 TYPE TRACTOR BIPLANE SEAPLANES** ordered under Cont No A.S.30729 (BR.484) to be numbered N9200 to N9229. Cancelled 6.18

N9200 to N9229 cancelled 6.18

**30 FAIREY IIIB TRACTOR BIPLANE SEAPLANES** ordered under Cont Nos 38a/513/C522 & A.S.22394/18 (BR.522), numbered N9230 to N9259 & built Hayes. Deld as IIIC. (260-hp Sunbeam Maori II or III) [C/n's F.307 to F.336]

**NB** (1) *Nairana* aircraft left Murmansk 2.6.19; arr Medveji-Goru 6.6.19. (2) 2 a/c crashed by 1.7.19. 1 was N9235 on 30.6.19 (q.v.); the other (N9236?) FL in water (crew unhurt) (3) 6 a/c required 2.19 for London-Cape Flight (NTU?) - one was N2246

N9230    Deld 1(S)MAD Hamble W/E 28.11.18 - @31.1.19; Syren Force, HMS *Nairana* (to North Russia) 18.5.19 - @16.9.19; Captured and used by Bolsheviks

N9231    Deld 1(S)MAD Hamble W/E 12.12.18 - @30.1.19; Syren Force, HMS *Nairana* (North Russia) by 28.8.19 - @23.9.19

N9232    Deld 1(S)MAD Hamble W/E 19.12.18 - @30.1.19; Syren Force, HMS *Nairana* (North Russia), FL off Shunga 21.6.19 (Lt Haines & Lt Thursfield); HMS *Pegasus* by 31.8.21; Calafrana 28.9.21

N9233    Deld 1(S)MAD Hamble W/E 19.12.18 - @30.1.19; Syren Force, HMS *Nairana* (North Russia) by 8.6.19 - @31.8.19

N9234    Deld 1(S)MAD Hamble W/E 19.12.18 - @30.1.19; Syren Force, HMS *Nairana* (North Russia) by 11.8.19 - @22.9.19

N9235    Deld 1(S)MAD Hamble W/E 31.12.18 - @30.1.19; Syren Force, HMS *Nairana* (to North Russia) by 18.5.19; Hit by AA & MG fire at 2000ft, FL in trees in forest 2m SSE of Uniza Bridge 30.6.19 (2/Lt BG Blampied & Lt Harvey unhurt); Still flying 9.7.19

N9236    Deld 1(S)MAD Hamble W/E 31.12.18 - @30.1.19; Syren Force, HMS *Nairana* (North Russia) by 18.5.19 - @5.9.19; EF, FL while bombing Petrozavodsk 5.8.19 (Lt Hooton & 2/Lt Pell)

N9237    Deld 1(S)MAD Hamble W/E 16.1.19 - @30.1.19; Syren Force, HMS *Nairana* (North Russia) by 18.5.19 - @18.8.19

N9238    Deld 1(S)MAD Hamble W/E 9.1.19 - @30.1.19; Syren Force, HMS *Nairana* (North Russia) by 18.5.19 - @2.10.19; FL, towed by N9236 21.6.19

N9239    Deld 1(S)MAD Hamble W/E 9.1.19 - @30.1.19; Syren Force, HMS *Nairana* (North Russia) by 18.5.19; Flown 11.6.19 only

N9240    Mkrs @30.1.19; Syren Force, HMS *Nairana* (North Russia) 18.5.19 - @9.19; EF, towed back by *Beresnik* to Khorobritsoe 16.9.19

N9241    Deld 1(S)MAD Hamble W/E 30.1.19; Syren Force, HMS *Nairana* (North Russia) 18.5.19 - @17.9.19

N9242    Deld 1(S)MAD Hamble W/E 30.1.19; RAF(R) HMS *Pegasus* (Dvina River) by 27.4.19 - 9.19

N9243    Mkrs @30.1.19; RAF(R) HMS *Pegasus* (Dvina River) 27.4.19 - @8.19; Syren Force, HMS *Nairana* (North Russia) by 14.9.19

N9244    Mkrs @30.1.19; RAF(R) HMS *Pegasus* (Dvina River) 27.4.19 - @8.19

N9245    Mkrs @30.1.19

N9246    Mkrs @30.1.19; Base (Constantinople) by 10.20; HMS *Pegasus* 15.10.20; Calafrana 15.11.20; HMS *Pegasus* (South Russia) by 24.1.21; Calafrana 28.8.21

N9247    Mkrs @30.1.19; RAF(R) HMS *Pegasus* (Dvina River) 27.4.19 - @6.19; Crashed, towed in

N9248    Mkrs @30.1.19; RAF(R) HMS *Pegasus* (Dvina River) 27.4.19 - @8.19

N9249    Mkrs @30.1.19; RAF(R) HMS *Pegasus* (Dvina River) 27.4.19; Attack on Bolsheviks, petrol tank hit by bullet but retd safely 8.7.19 (Lt LM Hilton & Lt GJ Reid unhurt); Shot down near Advanced Bolshevik Gunboats, crashed in enemy lines 14.7.19 (2/Lt HL Marshall & Lt G Lansdowne both PoW)

N9250    RAF(R) HMS *Pegasus* (Dvina River) 27.4.19 - @6.19; HMS *Ark Royal* by 17.6.21

N9251    RAF(R) HMS *Pegasus* (Dvina River) 27.4.19; Crashed into ammunition lighter on TO, WO 20.7.19 (2/Lt AJ Rankin unhurt, 2/Lt J Gondré drowned)

N9252    RAF(R) HMS *Pegasus* (Dvina River) 27.4.19 - @6.19

N9253    RAF(R) HMS *Pegasus* (Dvina River) 27.4.19; Ashore 14.9.19

N9254    RAF(R) HMS *Pegasus* (Dvina River) 27.4.19 - @6.19

N9255    Grain from 21.3.19 (type trials); RAF(R) HMS *Pegasus* (Dvina River) 27.4.19 - @9.19

N9256    Imp Gift to Canada; Became G-CYCF; TOC 4.10.20; SOC 7.10.20 (Mod as Transatlantic contender)

N9257    HMS *Pegasus* by 10.20; Spun into sea after TO, wreckage salved, Fenerakis(?), Constantinople 18.10.20

(F/O FH Isaac injured & Obs Officer EJ Garner AFC killed)

N9258    Deld by 30.6.19; HMS *Ark Royal* (South Russia) by 19.5.21; HMS *Pegasus* (coded 'Z') by 14.7.21; Calafrana 28.9.21; HMS *Pegasus* 30.1.22; Damaged, retd Calafrana 1.2.22

N9259    HMS *Pegasus* by 2.22; Became G-EBDI

**30 SHORT ADMIRALTY 184 TYPE TRACTOR BIPLANE SEAPLANES ordered under Cont No 38a/528/C588 & A.S.23694 (BR.559) from Brush Electrical Engineering Co Ltd, numbered N9260 to N9289 & built Loughborough. (275hp Maori III)**

N9260    Deld AAP Sherburn-in-Elmet W/E 30.1.19; HMS *Pegasus* (South Russia) by 5.20; Ashore 25.5.20; HMS *Ark Royal* (South Russia) by 25.7.20; HMS *Pegasus* 29.7.20 - @23.9.20

N9261    Deld 1(S)MAD Hamble W/E 9.1.19 - @30.1.19; SoNC Lee-on-Solent by 9.21 - @11.21

N9262    Deld AAP Sherburn-in-Elmet W/E 30.1.19

N9263    Deld AAP Sherburn-in-Elmet W/E 30.1.19

N9264    Allocated AAP Sherburn-in-Elmet W/E 30.1.19; Free issue to Chile

N9265    Allocated AAP Sherburn-in-Elmet W/E 30.1.19; Free issue to Chile

N9266    Mkrs by 30.1.19 for storage; Free issue to Chile

N9267    Mkrs by 30.1.19 for storage

N9268    Mkrs by 30.1.19 for storage; Free issue to Chile

N9269    HMS *Nairana* by 5.19; HMS *Vindictive* (Baltic Russia) by 23.11.19

N9270    Dundee by 1.20

N9271    Grain, to be disposed of 8.20

N9272 to N9275 No evidence of delivery

N9276    HMS *Pegasus* (South Russia) by 27.3.20 - @18.4.20

N9277    HMS *Pegasus* (South Russia) by 26.3.20; HMS *Ark Royal* 26.8.20

N9278 and N9279 No evidence of delivery

N9280 to N9289 cancelled 12.18

**60 SHORT ADMIRALTY 184 TYPE TRACTOR BIPLANE SEAPLANES ordered under Cont Nos 38a/603/C632 & A.S.26369/18 (BR.624) from Robey & Co Ltd, numbered N9290 to N9349 & built Lincoln. (260-hp Sunbeam)**

N9290    RAF(R) HMS *Pegasus* (Dvina River) 27.4.19

N9291    RAF(R) HMS *Pegasus* (Dvina River) 27.4.19

N9292    RAF(R) HMS *Pegasus* (Dvina River) 27.4.19

N9293    RAF(R) HMS *Pegasus* (Dvina River) 27.4.19 - @7.19

N9294    RAF(R) HMS *Pegasus* (Dvina River) 27.4.19 - @8.19

N9295    RAF(R) HMS *Pegasus* (Dvina River) 27.4.19 - @9.19; Dvina River 9.19; HMS *Pegasus* 11.9.19; Dvina River 14.9.19

N9296    Ashore (South Russia) by 5.20; HMS *Pegasus* 25.5.20

N9297 to N9301 No evidence of delivery

N9302    HMS *Pegasus* by 25.3.20; HMS *Ark Royal* 28.6.20; HMS *Pegasus* 28.7.20 - @5.10.20; Dvina River 10.20; HMS *Pegasus* 2.11.20; Calafrana 18.11.20; HMS *Ark Royal* by 6.1.21

N9303    HMS *Vindictive* (Baltic Russia) by 23.11.19

N9304    No evidence of delivery

N9305 to N9349 cancelled 12.18

**50 SHORT ADMIRALTY 184 TYPE SEAPLANES ordered under Cont Nos 38a/831/C857 & A.S.34425 (BR.696) from Brush Electrical Engineering Co Ltd, numbered N9350 to N9399, to be built Loughborough. (Engine?)**

N9350 to N9399 cancelled 12.18

**50 SHORT ADMIRALTY 184 TYPE TRACTOR BIPLANE SEAPLANES ordered under Cont Nos 38a/830/C856 & A.S.34421/18 (BR.997) from J.S.White & Co Ltd, numbered N9400 to N9449, to be built East Cowes. (260hp Maori)**

N9400 to N9449 cancelled 1.19

**N9450 onwards, post-war contracts**

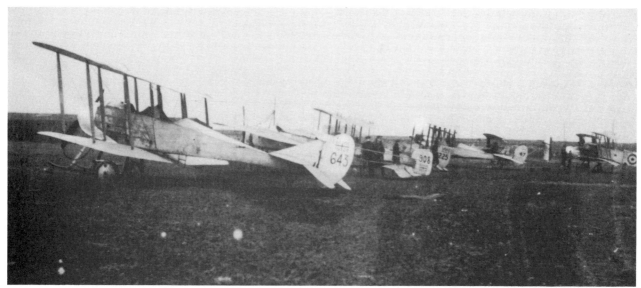

*Royal Aircraft Factory B.E.8 643 and other RNAS aircraft including Bleriot XI 908, Bristol T.B.8 and B.E.2A 47. These 2 Sqdn machines were all detached to Dover for a mass raid on Zeebrugge and Ostende on 10 February 1915. (FAA Museum)*

*Royal Aircraft Factory R.E.7 2260 served at Cranwell after transfer from the RFC. (J.M.Bruce/G.S.Leslie collection)*

*Avro 504A 2930, seen here, probably after it crashed on landing at Redcar on 21 November 1916, is fitted with vertical tail surfaces taken from 504C 3307, which had been deleted four months earlier (via Peter Green)*

# AIRCRAFT TRANSFERRED FROM RFC (MILITARY WING) OR ISSUED TO RNAS FROM RFC PRODUCTION BUT NOT RENUMBERED

**1 ROYAL AIRCRAFT FACTORY B.E.8 TRACTOR BIPLANE built at Farnborough under Cont No C.P.59384/14. (80-hp Gnome)**

643    Ex RFC (Military Wing). Arrived Eastchurch 23.9.14; Partially wrecked on TO 26.9.14 (F/L REC Peirse); 3 Sqdn Morbecque 30.9.14; Shipped to Sheerness in SS *Princess* 2.11.14; Handley Page repair; to 2 Sqdn Eastchurch 2.15; Detd Dover for raids on Zeebrugge and Ostende 10.2.15; 2 Sqdn Dover dett at Westgate 10.2.15; Became 2 Wing Dover dett 13.7.15; 4 Wing 4.8.15; 4 Wing dett Westgate 7.9.15; Westgate 10.15 - 4.16; Wheel came off in air 19.11.15 (FSL JA Carr); Deleted 24.5.16

**2 ROYAL AIRCRAFT FACTORY B.E.2c TRACTOR BIPLANES from batches 1652-1697 and 1698-1747, built by The British & Colonial Aeroplane Co Ltd, transferred from RFC less engine**

1688    (c/n 384) Farnborough to Hendon 19.4.18 - @11.8.18 (for use of Air Ministry officers)

1738    (c/n 440) 28 Sqdn RFC by 11.15; CFS Upavon 1916; to Cranwell 8.4.16 (less engine); Fitted 90-hp Curtiss OX-2; EF, FL among cattle, Kirkby-la-Thorpe 10.7.16 (PFSL RG Gardner); Crashed and damaged 14.7.17; Wrecked 9.10.17; Surveyed 15.10.17; Deleted 26.10.17 wrecked

**7 ROYAL AIRCRAFT FACTORY R.E.7 TRACTOR BIPLANES from various batches transferred from RFC**

2191    (120-hp Austro-Daimler) Ex RFC Netheravon to Cranwell 16.4.16; Overturned [no date]; Deleted 24.8.16

2201    (120-hp Austro-Daimler) Ex RFC Ascot to Cranwell 13.5.16; Surveyed 3.1.18; Deleted for spares 17.1.18

2241    (120-hp Austro-Daimler) Ex RFC to Cranwell 3.4.16; Crashed on TO, killed 2 sheep, wrecked 23.6.16; Deleted 5.7.16

2242    (120-hp Austro-Daimler) Ex RFC to Cranwell 3.4.16; Deleted 10.1.17

2260    (200-hp Sunbeam) Deld ex RFC to Cranwell for erection 15.8.16; To Sunbeam, Wolverhampton 25.11.16 - @16.3.17; Coventry to ECD Grain 15.6.17; Deld Hendon to Cranwell 6.7.17; Hit by Avro 504 N5801 taxying and damaged 18.12.17 (pilot injured); Became 201/2 TDS Cranwell 1.4.18 - @5.18

2324    For transfer from RFC by 1.17 but never delivered

2362    (200-hp Sunbeam) Presentation a/c 'Dominica'. Deld Cranwell 1.12.16; Wrecked 7.8.17; Deleted W/E 5.9.17

**6 ROYAL AIRCRAFT FACTORY B.E.2c TRACTOR BIPLANES earmarked for transfer from RFC as "A2564" to "A2569". Wolseley-built under Cont No A.3062. 2564 to 2566 reported as B.E.2f at Cranwell, but only 2564 confirmed as being there. (90-hp RAF.1a)**

2564    (transferred less engine) (Fitted 150-hp Hispano-Suiza) Presentation a/c 'Tai-Yan Bank, Hong Kong'. Allocated Sage 20.12.16, arrived 1.17 (by 31.1.17) - @28.2.17; Sage repair by 29.12.17; Cranwell W/E 1.2.18; Became 201/2 TDS Cranwell 1.4.18

2565    (transferred less engine) Ex presentation a/c 'Punjab No.38. Amritsar', but this removed on reallocation. Not delivered by 1.17 and later cancelled

2566    South Shields by 2.18; Hendon W/E 1.3.18; Test Dept Grain 17.3.18 (listed as "A2566")

2567    Not transferred

2568    Not transferred

2569    Not transferred

**2 ROYAL AIRCRAFT FACTORY B.E.2c TRACTOR BIPLANES from batch 2670 to 2769 built by Ruston, Proctor & Co Ltd. (90-hp RAF.1a)**

2735    Ex RFC to D Flt Cranwell 22.3.16; AZP 28.11.16 (S/Cdr REC Peirse); Wrecked 1.3.17; Deleted 15.3.17

2737    Ex RFC to D Flt Cranwell 22.3.16; AZP 25/26.9.16; AZP 28.11.16 (F/Cdr FHM Maynard); At Freiston 5.17; Became 201/2 TDS Cranwell 1.4.18; WO 29.5.18

**4 AVRO 504A (ADMIRALTY 179 TYPE) TRACTOR BIPLANES from batch 2890-2939 built by S.E.Saunders Ltd, transferred from RFC. (80-hp Gnome)**

2929    (DC) Deld Redcar 11.5.16; FL nr Darlington, damaged 14.5.17 (PFO CT Greenwood unhurt); Surveyed 7.12.17 wrecked; Deleted 14.12.17

2930    (DC) Deld Redcar 11.5.16; Fitted with fin of 3307; COL, damaged 21.11.16 (FSL N Black); Deleted 29.1.17

2933    (DC) Deld Redcar 21.5.16; Damaged 7.1.17; Fuselage and u/c damaged 21.7.17; Wings and chassis damaged 6.10.17; For deletion by 26.1.18

2934    (DC) Deld Redcar 21.5.16; Fuselage and u/c damaged 4.7.17; Fuselage damaged 1.9.17; Surveyed 7.12.17; Deleted 14.12.17 wrecked

**3 MAURICE FARMAN S.7 LONGHORN TRACTOR BPLANE TRAINERS from batch 2960-3000 built by The Aircraft Manufacturing Co Ltd at Hendon. (70-hp Renault)**

2973    Deld Hendon to Chingford 15.7.15; DC removed 5/6.4.16; Deleted 22.4.16

2983    Deld Hendon to Chingford by lorry 20.8.15; Crashed into 983 and damaged 3.6.16 (PFSL RJES Dawson slightly injured); Deleted 11.11.16

2984    Deld CSD White City to Eastbourne 27.8.15; FL and broke chassis 9.10.15 (Mr Fraser & Mr German); Wrecked 25.11.15 (FSL L Edwards); Deleted 13.3.16

**1 ROYAL AIRCRAFT FACTORY B.E.2c TRACTOR BIPLANE from batch 4070-4219 built by The British & Colonial Aeroplane Co Ltd, transferred from Farnborough**

4122    (c/n 673) RAE Farnborough (trials with RAF variable pitch airscrew); Hendon 20.4.18; 1 Comms Sqdn Hendon 23.7.18 - @10.8.18

**9 ROYAL AIRCRAFT FACTORY B.E.2c TRACTOR BIPLANES from batch 4300-4599 built by Weir Group, transferred from RFC and re-engined**

4336    (G.& J.Weir build) (90-hp Curtiss OX-5). Deld ex Zoo Buildings Glasgow to Cranwell 1.4.16; Awaiting erection by 23.5.16; Ruston Proctor to fit engine 26.5.16; Cranwell 17.7.16; Lost in mist, EF, FL in field, ran into thick hedge, wrecked 4.2.17 (PFO FTP Williams); Deleted 12.2.17

4337    (G.& J.Weir build) (90-hp Curtiss OX-5, later 100-hp RAF). Deld ex Zoo Buildings Glasgow to Cranwell 1.4.16; Awaiting erection by 23.5.16; Ruston Proctor to fit engine 26.5.16; Retd Cranwell 29.8.16; At Freiston 3.17; Wrecked by 16.4.17; Freiston by 4.5.17; Surveyed 12.9.17; Deleted 8.10.17 wrecked

4426    (Denny build) (90-hp Curtiss OX-5). (DC). Deld ex Zoo Buildings Glasgow to Cranwell 1.4.16; Awaiting erection 23.5.16; D Flt Cranwell by 8.16 (a/w erection); Fitted 90-hp RAF.1a by 29.12.17; FL, damaged u/c, Retford 20.1.18 (pilot unhurt); Crashed, slightly damaged, Scopwick 18.2.18 (pilot unhurt); Became 201/2 TDS Cranwell 1.4.18; Became 56/57 TDS Cranwell 27.7.18 - @25.9.18

4524    [A.Stephens build] (90-hp Curtiss OX-5). Deld ex Zoo Buildings Glasgow to Cranwell 1.4.16; Ruston Proctor to fit engine 23.5.16; Cranwell 5.8.16 (Freiston @ 2.3.17); Deleted W/E 5.9.17

4525    [A.Stephens build] (75-hp Renault). Deld ex Zoo Buildings Glasgow to Cranwell 1.4.16; Fitting DC 23.5.16; Fitted 90-hp RAF.1a by 29.12.17; Became 202/1 TDS Cranwell 1.4.18

4526    [A.Stephens build] (75-hp Renault). Deld ex Zoo Buildings Glasgow to Cranwell 1.4.16; Fitting DC 23.5.16; Manston NFS 23.3.18 (became 203 TDS?)

4570    [North British Loco build] (90-hp Curtiss OX-2). Deld

|      | |
|------|-|
|      | ex Zoo Buildings Glasgow to Cranwell 1.4.16; Ruston Proctor to fit engine 23.5.16; Cranwell .16; Retd safely ex Leadenham (FL?) 4.12.17; Became 201/2 TDS Cranwell 1.4.18 |
| 4571 | [North British Loco build] (75-hp Renault). Deld ex Zoo Buildings Glasgow to Cranwell 1.4.16; Fitting DC 18.4.16; Manston NFS 23.3.18 (became 203 TDS?) |
| 4572 | [North British Loco build] (90-hp Curtiss OX-5). Deld Cranwell 4.16; Awaiting erection 23.5.16; Ruston Proctor to fit engine 26.5.16; Cranwell 27.7.16; [flown Farnborough to Hendon 12.5.17]; Damaged on TO 26.7.17; Deleted W/E 5.9.17 |

**2 BRISTOL SCOUT TYPE D TRACTOR BIPLANES from batch 5554-5603 built by The British & Colonial Aeroplane Co Ltd, transferred from RFC. (80-hp Gnome)**

| 5564 | (c/n 1054) Deld Cranwell 5.4.16; Crashed 8.9.16 [presume collision with 8975 in which S/Cdr I-HWS Dalrymple-Clark killed]; Deleted 3.10.16 |
|------|-|
| 5565 | (c/n 1055) Deld E Flt Cranwell 5.4.16; Wrecked 1.4.17; Crashed 6.7.17; Became 201/2 TDS Cranwell 1.4.18 |

**6 ROYAL AIRCRAFT FACTORY B.E.2e TRACTOR BIPLANES from batch 6228-6327 built by Ruston, Proctor & Co Ltd, transferred from RFC less engines**

| 6233 | (B.E.2c) Hendon by 23.2.18 (station communications aircraft, made numerous visits to other stations); 1 Comms Sqdn Hendon 23.7.18 |
|------|-|
| 6259 | Deld Cranwell 21.8.16 (fitted "Experimental Engine No.1 75-hp Rolls- Royce"); Damaged Claypole 24.1.17; Became 202 TDS Cranwell 1.4.18 (now 150-hp Hispano-Suiza); Chingford to Cranwell 8.5.18; Stalled and dived in 19.6.18 (PFO J Erskine) |
| 6324 | (Fitted 75-hp RR Hawk) Deld Cranwell 8.1.17; Wyton 1.4.18 (transit); Manston (via Chingford) 2.4.18 (still 75-hp RR Hawk) |
| 6325 | (Fitted 75-hp RR Hawk) Deld D Flt Cranwell 15.3.17; Crashed landing 22.8.17; Became 201/2 TDS Cranwell 1.4.18 |
| 6326 | (Fitted 75-hp RR Hawk) Deld D Flt Cranwell 15.3.17; Crashed landing 22.8.17; Manston NFS 23.3.18 (became 203 TDS?) |
| 6327 | (Fitted 75-hp RR Hawk) Deld Lincoln to Cranwell 21.4.17; Crashed, wrecked Ingleby, Lincs 28.2.18 (pilot unhurt); Became 201/2 TDS Cranwell 1.4.18 |

**1 ROYAL AIRCRAFT FACTORY B.E.2e TRACTOR BIPLANE from batch 6728-6827 built by Vulcan Motor & Engineering Co (1906) Ltd**

| 6802 | Presentation a/c "Presented by the Associated Commercial Travellers Association of Australia". 20 Trg Wing 2.9.18; 269 Sqdn (Submarine Flt) Port Said by 1.11.18; To 'X' AD Aboukir 10.3.19; 5 FS 14.3.19; WO 1.4.19 |
|------|-|

**1 BRISTOL SCOUT TYPE D TRACTOR BIPLANE from batch 7028-7057 built by The British & Colonial Aeroplane Co Ltd**

| 7053 | (c/n 1119) AES Orfordness (fitted synchronised Vickers gun); Hendon by 25.5.18 (station comms aircraft); 1 Comm Sqdn Hendon 23.7.18 - @18.8.18 |
|------|-|

**1 MAURICE FARMAN S.11 SHORTHORN PUSHER BIPLANE from batch 7346-7395 built by The Aircraft Manufacturing Co Ltd under Cont No 878/A/109, transferred from RFC. (80-hp Renault)**

| 7385 | Deld Cranwell 23.5.16; Surveyed 15.10.17; Deleted 26.10.17 DBR |
|------|-|

**1 SOPWITH 1½ STRUTTER 9400 TYPE TRACTOR BIPLANE from batch 7762-7811 built by Ruston, Proctor & Co Ltd. (110-hp Clerget)**

| 7811 | CFS by 4.16 - 4.17; NARD from W/E 15.8.18; Turnhouse W/E 5.9.18 - @30.1.19 |
|------|-|

**1 SOPWITH 1½ STRUTTER 9400 TYPE TRACTOR BIPLANE transferred from RNAS (ex 9381) and numbered 7942, later returned to RNAS but not renumbered again. (110-hp Clerget)**

| 7942 | (ex 9381) 34 RS Tern Hill by 17.7.17; 52 Sqdn; 70 Sqdn; Orfordness by 3.18; EAD Grain 2.3.18 - @9.3.18 |
|------|-|

**3 MAURICE FARMAN S.11 SHORTHORN PUSHER BIPLANES from batch A324-A373 built by The Aircraft Manufacturing Co Ltd, transferred from RFC without engines. (Later fitted 80-hp Renault)**

| A324 | Deld ex RFC to Cranwell 5.6.16; Wrecked 4.10.16; Deleted 25.10.16 |
|------|-|
| A334 | Deld Ex RFC to Cranwell 9.6.16; Flown 9.6.16; Freiston 6.16; Cranwell 28.6.16; Surveyed 12.9.17; Deleted 8.10.17 W&T |
| A354 | Deld Cranwell 26.6.16; Surveyed 12.9.17; Deleted 8.10.17 W&T |

**1 SOPWITH PUP TRACTOR BIPLANE from batch A626-A675 built by Standard Motor Co Ltd, transferred from RFC in France**

| A626 | CFS Test Sqdn by 10.16; To France 4.11.16; 2 AD to 70 Sqdn RFC; To 8 Sqdn RNAS late 12.16; 2-str shot down S of Bapaume 26.12.16 (F/L JC Croft); Shot down nr Bapaume, believed by Ltn Mallinckrodt, Jasta 10 4.1.17 (F/L JC Croft PoW); Aircraft captured by Germans; For deletion by 11.1.17 TL |
|------|-|

**2 ROYAL AIRCRAFT FACTORY F.E.2b PUSHER BIPLANES from batch A778-A877 built by G & J Weir**

| A793 | From 100 Sqdn RFC to A Sqdn RNAS 16.11.17; Became 16 Sqdn RNAS 8.1.18; Wrecked by HA 21.1.18 |
|------|-|
| A826 | Ex RFC by rail to EAD Grain for erection 29.3.17; Spiral nose dive, CW 13.7.17 (TFSL RB Morrison DoI); Deleted 29.8.17 |

**1 SOPWITH 1½ STRUTTER TRACTOR BIPLANE from batch A954-A1053 built by The Fairey Aviation Co Ltd**

| A1053 | (c/n F.126) 45 Sqdn by 8.17; South Shotwick from W/E 12.9.18; CTD Grain from 21.9.18 - 1.19 (mods) |
|------|-|

**3 SOPWITH 1½ STRUTTER TRACTOR BIPLANES from batch A1054-A1153 built by Vickers Ltd at Crayford**

| A1067 | Orfordness by 3.18; Experimental Dept Grain W/E 2.3.18; Deleted end 5.18 |
|------|-|
| A1114 | (130-hp Clerget) 30 TS from 4.11.17; CFS; NARD from W/E 25.7.18; To Turnhouse W/E 1.8.18 - @30.1.19 |
| A1148 | (Type 9400) (100-hp Gnome Monosoupape, later 130-hp Clerget) Deld ex RFC Islington to Gunnery School Flt Eastchurch for erection 24.10.17 - @30.3.18 |

**13 ROYAL AIRCRAFT FACTORY B.E.2e TRACTOR BIPLANES from batches A1261-A1310 (Barclay, Curle & Co), A1311-A1360 (Napier & Miller) & A1361-A1410 (Denny). (90-hp RAF1A)**

| A1284 | Shipped to Mudros 5.17; Imbros 1917; Marsh by 1.12.17 - @1.1.18; Surveyed 18.2.18; Deleted 13.3.18 wrecked |
|------|-|
| A1285 | Shipped to Mudros 5.17; Marsh by 1.12.17 - @1.1.18; Surveyed 13.2.18; Deleted 13.3.18 wrecked |
| A1286 | Deld ex G & J Weir to Cranwell for erection 23.5.17; Fitting for night duty by 9.6.17; AZP 25.9.17; Freiston 14.12.17; Cranwell by 1.18; Crashed and slightly damaged Cranwell South 2.3.18 (pilot unhurt); Crashed and wrecked, Mattersey, nr Retford, Notts 9.3.18 (pilot unhurt); Surveyed 13.3.18; Deleted 15.4.18 |
| A1287 | Deld ex G & J Weir to Cranwell for erection 25.5.17; FL in mist, propeller damaged, Spilsby, Lincs 23.1.18; Crashed and damaged 28.1.18 (pilot unhurt); Collided with A1328 landing and badly damaged, Cranwell, 15.3.18 (pilot unhurt); 211 TDS Portholme Meadow by |

*Royal Aircraft Factory B.E.2e A1285 of 2 Wing after overturning at Marsh aerodrome early in 1918. (W.J.Evans)*

*Royal Aircraft Factory R.E.9 A3910 was flown at Grain for a time in 1918. (W.J.Evans)*

*Martinsyde F.1 prototype A3933 was briefly at Hendon in the summer of 1918. (J.M.Bruce/G.S.Leslie collection)*

*Vickers F.B.11 A4814, which joined the Eastchurch Design Flight on 16 November 1916 is pictured here the next day. (J.M.Bruce/G.S.Leslie collection)*

A1306    8.5.18 - @8.18
East Africa to 'X' AD 3.6.18; 20 Trg Wing 8.7.18; 269 Sqdn (Submarine Flt) Port Said 28.10.18; 18 TDS 21.2.19; WO 1.3.19

A1326    Shipped to Mudros 5.17; Surveyed Mudros 18.10.17; Deleted 21.11.17 TL

A1327    Shipped to Mudros 5.17; Marsh by 1.12.17 - @1.1.18; Mudros for Greek training by 3.18 - 11.18

A1328    Deld ex G & J Weir to Cranwell for erection 26.5.17 - @16.11.17; Freiston by 12.17; Cranwell by 1.18; Collided with A1287 on landing and badly damaged, Cranwell, 15.3.18 (pilot unhurt); Became 201/2 TDS Cranwell 1.4.18; 58 TDS Cranwell, went in on turn after TO 19.9.18 (Lt HE Barry injured)

A1329    Deld ex G & J Weir to Cranwell for erection 26.5.17; COL 22.8.17; Crashed 5.9.17; Crashed 2.10.17; Lost, FL, broke u/c and left wing running into ditch and hedge 16.10.17 (PFSL GA Pitt)

A1382    Deld Redcar School without engine by transport for erection 15.5.17 (for night flying); Fitted 90-hp RAF; still Redcar 6.4.18

A1383    Deld Redcar School without engine for erection 25.5.17 (for night flying); U/c wrecked and propeller broken; Fitted 100-hp RAF; Deleted W/E 6.4.18

A1384    Deld without engine; Shipped to Aegean; Fitted 100-hp RAF; G Flt 2 Wing Marsh by 1.12.17 - @3.18; Mudros, deleted by 6.18

A1385    Deld without engine; Shipped to Aegean; Fitted 100-hp RAF; Imbros by 1.12.17 - @1.1.18; Marsh for Greek training by 19.1.18 - @11.18

**6 BRISTOL SCOUT D TRACTOR BIPLANES from batch A1742-A1791 built by The British & Colonial Aeroplane Co Ltd. (80-hp Gnome)**

A1769    Deld Cranwell 5.12.16; Wrecked 24.4.17; Deleted 19.5.17

A1770    Deld Cranwell 8.12.16; Wrecked 31.1.17; Deleted 15.2.17

A1771    Deld Cranwell 8.12.16; CW 21.8.17 (TPFO HS Holroyd killed); Deleted W/E 5.9.17

A1772    Deld Cranwell 8.12.16; Deleted W/E 15.2.18

A1790    Deld Cranwell 5.12.16; Crashed in field W of aerodrome, TW 7.6.17 (TPFO WW Pitt killed); Deleted 18.6.17

A1791    Deld Cranwell 5.12.16; Burst tyre landing, o/t 12.1.17 (FSL EJK Buckley injured); Wrecked 4.4.17; Wrecked 8.8.17; O/t, badly damaged, Cranwell South 23.1.18 (pilot unhurt); Crashed, propeller and wing damaged 21.3.18 (pilot unhurt); Became 201/2 TDS Cranwell 1.4.18

**6 ROYAL AIRCRAFT FACTORY B.E.2e TRACTOR BIPLANES from batch A1792-A1891 built by Vulcan Motor & Engineering Co (1906) Ltd, transferred from RFC for night flying (Fitted 90-hp RAF1A)**

A1829    Transferred less engine; Deld Cranwell for erection 31.3.17 - 5.17; Freiston by 7.17 - 8.17; Cranwell, crashed 6.8.17; Freiston by 10.17 - 11.17; Deleted W/E 16.11.17
Supposedly to RNAS less engine as 9459 (seems unlikely)

A1830    Deld Cranwell 31.3.17; to Freiston 7.17; Surveyed 18.9.17; Deleted 8.10.17 wrecked

A1831    Deld Yarmouth 26.4.17; to Freiston, but landed California, nr Ormesby due to mist 15.5.17 (F/Cdr V Nicholl & F/Cdt JI Harrison); arr Freiston 16.5.17; retd Yarmouth 17.5.17 - @10.17; Burgh Castle by 29.12.17; Deleted W/E 2.2.18

A1832    Deld Yarmouth 21.5.17; Burgh Castle W/E 8.9.17; Yarmouth W/E 15.9.17; Burgh Castle 29.9.17; Hendon to Yarmouth 8.12.17; HACPs 23.12.17, 27.12.17 & 28.12.17; Surveyed 2.1.18; Deleted 15.1.18 BR

A1833    Transferred less engine; Deld Redcar 31.3.17; O/t and damaged by heavy gust of wind 21.5.17 (F/L AM Blake unhurt); Cranwell 14.7.17 (arr 15.7.17); Crashed 17.7.17; Surveyed 3.1.18; Deleted 17.1.18 wrecked
Supposedly to RNAS less engine as 9460 (seems unlikely)

A1835    Transferred less engine; Deld Redcar for erection 11.4.17; Cranwell 14.7.17 (arr 15.7.17); Crashed and damaged 18.7.17; still Cranwell 11.11.17; to Freiston 11.17; D Flt Cranwell by 12.17; Became 201/2 TDS Cranwell 1.4.18 - @5.18
Supposedly to RNAS less engine as 9461 (seems unlikely)

**1 AIRCO D.H.4 TRACTOR BIPLANE BOMBER from batch A2125-A2174 built by The Aircraft Manufacturing Co Ltd, for trials.**

A2168    Tested CFS Upavon 10.4.17; Orfordness @12.8.17; EAD Grain by 25.5.18 [not by 9.3.18] (fitted 1½-pdr COW gun firing upwards through centre section); Tested with 200-hp RAF 3A with modified exhaust; Later to USA

**1 ROYAL AIRCRAFT FACTORY B.E.2e TRACTOR BIPLANE from batch A2733-A2982 built by The British & Colonial Aeroplane Co Ltd. (90-hp RAF1A)**

A2982    (c/n 1736) Hendon to Martlesham 23.2.18; Hendon 12.4.18; Eastbourne 4.5.18; Hendon 18.5.18 (station aircraft); to Brooklands but landed Eton 8.6.18

**1 ROYAL AIRCRAFT FACTORY R.E.9 TRACTOR BIPLANE conversion from R.E.8 batch A3832-A3931 built by D.Napier & Son, for trials. (140-hp RAF 4A)**

A3910    EAD Grain by 25.5.18 [not by 9.3.18]

**1 MARTINSYDE F.1 TRACTOR BIPLANE PROTOTYPE, for trials. (250-hp Rolls-Royce Mk.III)**

A3933    Tested at CFS Upavon 11.6.17 - 22.7.17; Orfordness, HD duty 22.8.17; AP Hendon by 4.18; Hendon 9.4.18; Orfordness 12.4.18; Hendon .18; Farnborough 21.6.18 - .19

**3 MAURICE FARMAN S.7 LONGHORN PUSHER BIPLANES from batch A4061 to A4160 built by The Aircraft Manufacturing Co Ltd, transferred from RFC less engines. (Fitted 75-hp Renault)**

A4144    Deld RNASTE Vendôme 28.2.17; Manston FS for erection W/E 8.12.17; Deleted W/E 2.3.18

A4145    Deld RNASTE Vendôme by road 16.1.17; Erected 18.1.17; Deleted 7.18; To American Air School Tours 7.18, but unsafe, used for GI only

A4146    Deld RNASTE Vendôme by road 16.1.17; Erected 18.1.17; Deleted 7.18

**1 ROYAL AIRCRAFT FACTORY R.E.8 TRACTOR BIPLANE from batch A4664-A4763 built by The Coventry Ordnance Works Ltd. (150-hp RAF 4A)**

A4714    Deld from Coventry to Cranwell 6.6.18

**1 VICKERS F.B.11 TRACTOR BIPLANE FIGHTER ["VICKERS COMPETITION"] for trials (250-hp Eagle III)**

A4814    FF 6.16; Joyce Green to Eastchurch Design Flt 16.11.16; Left/deleted 17.3.17

**7 SOPWITH SHIP STRUTTER conversions from 1½ Strutter batch A5238-A5337 built by Wells Aviation Co Ltd which was partially cancelled. (various engines)**

A5238    78 Sqdn Suttons Farm by 11.17; Turnhouse W/E 20.4.18; Deleted W/E 3.10.18

A5253    (Type 9400) (100-hp Gnome Monosoupape) Ex RFC Islington to Gunnery School Flt Eastchurch 24.10.17; East Fortune NFS W/E 11.3.18

A5254    (130-hp Clerget) Kenley 1918; ECD Grain by 25.5.18; Donibristle W/E 15.8.18; HMS *Furious* W/E 14.11.18 - @30.1.19

A5257    (130-hp Clerget) NARD from W/E 25.5.18; Group Headquarters Turnhouse W/E 4.7.18; Stalled on flat spin turning down wind 6.7.18 (Lt DJJ de Villiers & CPO WM Garner killed)

A5260    (Type 9400) (100-hp Gnome Monosoupape) Ex RFC Islington to Gunnery School Flt Eastchurch 24.10.17; East Fortune NFS W/E 26.3.18

A5261    (Type 9400) (100-hp Gnome Monosoupape) Ex RFC Islington to Gunnery School Flt Eastchurch 24.10.17; Became 204 TDS Eastchurch 1.4.18 - @5.18

A5262    (Type 9400) (130-hp Clerget) Ex RFC Islington to Gunnery School Flt Eastchurch 24.10.17; Pilots & Observers AG&AFS Leysdown by 4.18

## 1 ROYAL AIRCRAFT FACTORY F.E.2b PUSHER BIPLANE from batch A5500-A5649 built by G & J Weir Ltd. (120-hp Beardmore)

A5546    SARD by 20.10.17 for EF; 2 AD Candas by 11.17; A Sqdn 19.11.17 - @4.1.18; 16 Sqdn by 1.3.18; 100 Sqdn RFC 5.3.18; SOC 3 AD 9.18

## 2 ROYAL AIRCRAFT FACTORY F.E.2b PUSHER BIPLANES from batch A5650-A5799 built by Weir Group. (120-hp Beardmore)

A5664    100 Sqdn RFC by 3.18; 16 Sqdn 5.3.18; Became 216 Sqdn 1.4.18; 100 Sqdn 10.5.18

A5671    100 Sqdn RFC by 3.18; 16 Sqdn 5.3.18; Became 216 Sqdn 1.4.18; 100 Sqdn 10.5.18; AAF Orly from 9.18

## 26 SOPWITH SHIP STRUTTER (9700 TYPE) TRACTOR BIPLANE conversions from batch A5950-A6149 built by Morgan & Co. (130-hp Clerget 9B unless otherwise stated)

A5951    Deld Mullion for erection 30.6.17; Exptl Dept Grain 9.2.18; Turnhouse W/E 11.7.18; HMS *Furious* 11.8.18; HMS *Argus* 12.12.18; Donibristle W/E 31.12.18 - @30.1.19

A5952    Deld Mullion for erection 30.6.17; Exptl Dept Grain 9.2.18 (expts with additional struts and bracing); Turnhouse W/E 25.5.18; HMS *Furious* W/E 1.6.18; Turnhouse W/E 29.8.18; Donibristle W/E 12.9.18; Turnhouse W/E 19.9.18 - @30.1.19

A5982    Deld ex RFC Islington to F Sqdn East Fortune by rail 21.12.17; Donibristle W/E 21.3.18; HMS *Furious* W/E 23.3.18 (by 22.3.18); Turnhouse 25.3.18; HMS *Furious* .18; Rosyth W/E 28.3.18; Turnhouse 4.18; Donibristle 3.4.18; Rosyth 4.4.18; HMS *Furious* by 27.4.18; HMS *Repulse* W/E 10.5.18; Deleted W/E 15.8.18 [probably the aircraft which fell in sea on TO 25.7.18]

A5983    Deld ex RFC Islington to F Sqdn East Fortune by rail 21.12.17 - 2.18; Donibristle by 3.18; HMS *Furious* W/E 21.3.18; Donibristle W/E 9.5.18; Rosyth W/E 16.5.18; HMS *Furious* W/E 16.5.18; Turnhouse 3.7.18 - @30.1.19

A5984    Deld ex RFC Islington to F Sqdn East Fortune by rail 28.12.17; Donibristle W/E 21.3.18; HMS *Furious* W/E 21.3.18; Turnhouse W/E 19.9.18 - @30.1.19; HMS *Bellerophon* (1.19?)

A5985    Deld ex RFC Islington to F Sqdn East Fortune by rail 28.12.17; Donibristle 16.3.18; HMS *Furious* by 22.3.18; Turnhouse to Donibristle W/E 21.3.18; HMAS *Australia* W/E 28.3.18; HMS *Furious* by 6.4.18; HMAS *Australia* by 27.4.18; Rosyth W/E 9.5.18; Donibristle W/E 9.5.18; Rosyth W/E 9.5.18; HMAS *Australia* W/E 9.5.18; Turnhouse W/E 11.7.18; HMS *Bellerophon* W/E 21.11.18; Rosyth W/E 5.12.18; Turnhouse W/E 12.12.18; HMS *Bellerophon* W/E 23.1.19 - @30.1.19

A5986    Deld ex RFC Islington to F Sqdn East Fortune by rail 28.12.17 - @3.18; Donibristle by 3.18; Rosyth W/E 21.3.18; HMS *Furious* W/E 21.3.18 (by 22.3.18); Lost speed turning sharply in gusty wind and crashed 29.4.18 (Lt HF Mears & Capt GH Miller both killed); wreckage to Donibristle; Deleted W/E 15.8.18

A5987    Deld ex RFC Islington to F Sqdn East Fortune by rail 28.12.17 - @3.18; HMS *Furious* by 22.3.18; Turnhouse W/E 20.4.18; Donibristle W/E 9.5.18; Rosyth W/E 9.5.18; HMS *Renown* W/E 16.5.18; Turnhouse 29.5.18; Donibristle 29.5.18; Turnhouse 6.18; Scapa by 22.6.18 (landed Smoogroo); HMS *Renown* by 7.18; Turnhouse 10.7.18; Donibristle 10.7.18; HMS *Renown* 7.18; ashore 17.7.18; HMS *Renown* 7.18; Turnhouse 25.7.18; Donibristle 25.7.18; HMS *Renown* by 29.8.18; Turnhouse W/E 19.9.18; Donibristle W/E 26.9.18; Turnhouse W/E 21.11.18; Donibristle W/E 28.1.18; Turnhouse W/E 31.12.18; HMS *Warspite* 17.1.19; ashore 28.1.19

A5988    Deld ex RFC Islington to F Sqdn East Fortune by 19.1.18 - @3.18; HMS *Furious* by 22.3.18; Turnhouse W/E 13.4.18; Donibristle W/E 9.5.18; Rosyth W/E 9.5.18; *Repulse* W/E 9.5.18; Rosyth 5.18; HMS *Indomitable* 14.5.18; Turnhouse W/E 13.6.18; Donibristle 9.18; HMS *Barham* 6.9.18; Rosyth 1.10.18; Donibristle W/E 21.11.18 - @30.1.19

A5989    Deld ex RFC Islington to F Sqdn East Fortune by 19.1.18; Rosyth W/E 21.3.18; HMS *Furious* W/E 21.3.18 (by 22.3.18) - @4.18; Donibristle by 5.18; Rosyth W/E 2.5.18; To HMS *Furious* W/E 2.5.18; Donibristle W/E 2.5.18; HMS *Furious* W/E 11.5.18; Turnhouse W/E 11.7.18; Deleted W/E 31.10.18

A5990    Deld ex RFC Islington to F Sqdn East Fortune by 19.1.18; HMS *Furious* W/E 21.3.18 (by 22.3.18); Donibristle W/E 23.5.18; HMS *Furious* by 6.18; Donibristle by 27.6.18; HMS *Glorious*, flying from port turret, capsized hitting deck and fell into sea 5.7.18 (Lt HW Adam killed); Salved, to Scapa 5.7.18; Deleted W/E 31.10.18

A5991    Deld ex RFC Islington to F Sqdn East Fortune by 19.1.18; Donibristle W/E 21.3.18; HMS *Furious* W/E 21.3.18 (by 22.3.18); Turnhouse W/E 25.7.18 - @30.1.19

A5992    Deld ex RFC Islington to F Sqdn East Fortune by 1.18; Rosyth W/E 21.3.18; HMS *Furious* W/E 23.3.18 (coded 'J.D.8') (by 22.3.18); HMS *New Zealand* W/E 1.8.18; Donibristle W/E 15.8.18; Turnhouse W/E 29.8.18; Donibristle W/E 28.11.18; HMS *Argus* W/E 12.12.18; Donibristle W/E 31.12.18; HMS *Furious* 16.1.19 - @30.1.19

A5993    Deld ex RFC Islington to F Sqdn East Fortune by 19.1.18; Donibristle W/E 21.3.18; HMS *Furious* W/E 21.3.18 (by 22.3.18) - @5.18; ashore by 24.5.18; Turnhouse 5.18; Donibristle W/E 23.5.18; Turnhouse W/E 6.6.18; HMS *Renown* W/E 11.7.18; Turnhouse W/E 18.7.18; Deleted W/E 22.8.18

A5994    Deld ex RFC Islington to F Sqdn East Fortune by 19.1.18; Donibristle W/E 21.3.18; HMS *Furious* W/E 21.3.18 (by 22.3.18); Donibristle W/E 23.5.18; HMS *Courageous* W/E 1.8.18; Turnhouse W/E 15.8.18; Donibristle W/E 22.8.18; HMS *Courageous* W/E 29.8.18; Turnhouse W/E 19.9.18; Deleted W/E 24.10.18

A5995    Deld ex RFC Islington to F Sqdn East Fortune 1.18; Exptl Dept Grain (without engine) 2.2.18 (for mods); Turnhouse W/E 2.5.18; Donibristle W/E 2.5.18; Rosyth W/E 9.5.18; HMAS *Australia* W/E 9.5.18; Turnhouse 5.18; HMS *Furious* W/E 10.5.18; Turnhouse W/E 11.7.18; Donibristle W/E 26.9.18; HMS *Campania* W/E 31.10.18; For deletion by 28.11.18; ALSO HMS *Renown*?

A5996    Deld ex RFC Islington to F Sqdn East Fortune 1.18; Exptl Dept Grain (without engine) 2.2.18 (mods); Turnhouse W/E 2.5.18; Donibristle W/E 2.5.18; Rosyth W/E 2.5.18; Turnhouse 5.18; HMS *Furious* W/E 10.5.18 (by 9.5.18); Donibristle W/E 23.5.18; HMS *Furious* W/E 23.5.18; Turnhouse W/E 19.9.18; Donibristle W/E 28.11.18; Turnhouse W/E 12.12.18 - @30.1.19

A5997    Deld ex RFC Islington to F Sqdn East Fortune 1.18; Exptl Dept Grain (without engine) 2.2.18 (mods); Turnhouse W/E 20.4.18; HMS *Furious* W/E 27.4.18; Turnhouse by 4.18; Donibristle W/E 2.5.18; Turnhouse to HMS *Furious* W/E 3.5.18; Donibristle W/E 2.5.18; Donibristle W/E 2.5.18; HMS *Furious* 5.18; Turnhouse 14.5.18; HMS *Furious* by 25.5.18; Turnhouse W/E 31.5.18; Rosyth by 27.6.18; HMS *Furious* 11.7.18; Turnhouse 13.9.18; HMS *Furious* 17.10.18 - @30.1.19; Turnhouse by 3.19

A5998    Deld ex RFC Islington to to F Sqdn East Fortune by 19.1.18; Rosyth W/E 21.3.18; HMS *Furious* W/E 21.3.18 (by 22.3.18); Turnhouse by 4.18; HMS *Furious* W/E 3.5.18; Donibristle W/E 2.5.18; Turnhouse to HMS *Furious* W/E 31.5.18; Donibristle W/E 15.8.18; Turnhouse W/E 19.9.18; Donibristle W/E 3.10.18; HMS *Courageous* W/E 17.10.18; Donibristle W/E

*Martinsyde G.102 Elephant A6286 (Presentation aircraft 'Rhodesia III') was flown as a station aircraft at Hendon in the Spring of 1918. (RAF Museum)*

*Royal Aircraft Factory F.E.2b A6536 during flotation gear trials at Grain 30 May 1918. (J.M.Bruce/G.S.Leslie)*

*Airco D.H.4 A7864 was tested at Felixstowe with RAF.3a and RAF.4d engines in 1918. (via Frank Cheesman)*

21.11.18 - @30.1.19

A5999    Deld ex RFC Islington to to F Sqdn East Fortune 1.18; Exptl Dept Grain (without engine) 2.2.18 (mods); Turnhouse W/E 27.4.18; Rosyth W/E 18.5.18 (by 16.5.18); Donibristle W/E 23.5.18; HMS *Furious* W/E 23.5.18; Donibristle W/E 31.10.18; HMS *Furious* W/E 14.11.18 - @30.1.19; Turnhouse by 3.19

A6000    (160-hp Clerget) Deld ex RFC Islington to to EC&AD Grain 26.1.18 (mods); Turnhouse W/E 20.4.18; HMS *Furious* W/E 27.4.18; Turnhouse W/E 25.7.18; HMS *Furious* W/E 29.8.18; Deleted W/E 14.11.18

A6006    Ex RFC Brook Green by road to Turnhouse for conv Ship Strutter 18.3.18; Donibristle W/E 15.8.18; HMS *Barham* 12.8.18; Turnhouse 29.8.18 - @30.11.19; Also HMS *Queen Elizabeth*

A6010    Ex RFC Brooks Green by road to Turnhouse for conv to Ship Strutter 18.3.18; HMS *Inflexible* 3.8.18; ashore 10.8.18; for deletion W/E 12.9.18

A6014    Ex RFC Ascot 3.18; Houton Bay via NSO Aberdeen for HMS *Campania* 3.18; HMS *Campania* by 30.3.18; Houton Bay W/E 13.4.18; HMS *Campania* W/E 27.4.18; Houton Bay W/E 4.5.18; HMS *Campania* W/E 25.5.18; Scapa W/E 1.6.18 - @30.1.19

A6015    Ex RFC Ascot 3.18; Houton Bay via NSO for HMS *Campania* 3.18; HMS *Campania* by 30.3.18; Houton Bay W/E 13.4.18; HMS *Campania* W/E 27.4.18; Houton Bay W/E 4.5.18; HMS *Campania* W/E 25.5.18; Scapa W/E 1.6.18 - @30.1.19; Reported supplied to White Russians 1919

A6019    Ex RFC Ascot by road to EC&AD Grain (without engine) 26.1.18 for conv Ship Strutter 21.3.18; Turnhouse W/E 25.5.18; Donibristle W/E 11.7.18; HMS *Furious* W/E 15.8.18; Donibristle W/E 31.10.18; HMS *Furious* W/E 14.11.18 - @30.1.19; Turnhouse by 3.19; Donibristle 11.3.19

## 2 SOPWITH PUP TRACTOR BIPLANES from batch A6150 to A6249 built by Whitehead, Richmond

A6158    RAE Farnborough on/by 17.2.17; ADD by 15.3.17; 3 Sqdn by 16.3.17 - @14.4.17 (but gap); Halberstadt DII OOC Bourlon Wood 10.20 6.4.17 (FSL JST Fall); Albatros OOC, Albatros DII crashed & Halberstadt crashed Cambrai 08.45, then badly shot up, FL Savy 11.4.17 (FSL JST Fall); 2 AD Candas by 19.4.17; 3 Sqdn (coded 'WB') 3.5.17; Last seen Ecourt St.Quentin, shot down by Obltn H Lorenz, Jasta 33 14.5.17 (FSL WR Walker PoW) [S of Estrées per Germans]

A6160    66 Sqdn RFC from 24.2.17; ADD .17; 3 Sqdn by 15.3.17; Halberstadt DIII OOC Bourlon Wood 10.20 6.4.17 (FSL AW Carter); Shot down by Ltn Schneider, Jasta 5 29.4.17 (TFSL SL Bennett killed)

## 2 MARTINSYDE G.102 ELEPHANT TRACTOR BIPLANES from batch A6250-A6299 built by Martin and Handasyde

A6257    Ex RFC Hounslow to Hendon 7.4.18 - @11.8.18 (station aircraft)

A6286    (160-hp Beardmore) Presentation a/c 'Rhodesia III'. Tested Martlesham 7.17 - 12.8.17; Hendon (station aircraft) by 14.3.18; AES Orfordness W/E 11.5.18; Farnborough by 2.7.18 - @1.19 [but still Orfordness 13.9.18]

## 2 ROYAL AIRCRAFT FACTORY F.E.2b PUSHER BIPLANES from batch A6351-A6600 assembled by Boulton & Paul Ltd

A6536    EC&AD Grain by 25.5.18; Tested with flotation gear 30.5.18; Successfully ditched for 2nd time, revised skid chassis with wooden hydrovane, undamaged 29.6.18

A6573    AAP Lympne by 29.1.18; 2 AD Candas by 2.18; 16 Sqdn 26.2.18; 100 Sqdn RFC 5.3.18; 2 ASD Fienvillers 10.3.18

## 27 SOPWITH SHIP STRUTTER (9700 TYPE) TRACTOR BIPLANE conversions from batch A6901-A7000 built by Hooper & Co Ltd. (110-hp Clerget 9Z unless otherwise stated)

A6905    Ex RFC Brook Green to Turnhouse for Ship Strutter conversion 18.3.18; HMS *Glorious* W/E 15.8.18;

Donibristle W/E 21.11.18 - @30.1.19

A6910    (130-hp Clerget by 12.17) Deld by rail for erection to Prawle Point 2.7.17; Cranwell 2.10.17; Hendon 12.1.18 (en route EC&AD Grain but NTU); While on ground hit by DH6 B2738, badly damaged 21.1.18 (pilot unhurt); For deletion by 9.2.18

A6911    (130-hp Clerget, later 110-hp Clerget) Deld by rail for erection to Prawle Point 2.7.17; Cranwell 2.10.17; EC&AD Grain for modifications 13.1.18 (engine trouble, FL RFC Stamford en route); DL trials with unsprung skids 28.2.18 - 4.6.18; HMS *Vindex* 19.3.18; Grain 20.3.18; Turnhouse by 27.4.18; Grain by 5.18; Turnhouse W/E 18.5.18; Donibristle W/E 11.7.18; HMS *Furious* W/E 15.8.18 - @30.1.19

A6912    Deld by rail for erection to Prawle Point 2.7.17; Hendon (via New Malden) W/E 26.10.17; Surveyed 25.10.17; Deleted 29.10.17 DBR

A6913    (130-hp Clerget 9.17, 110-hp Clerget by 12.17) Deld by rail for erection to Prawle Point 2.7.17; Badly damaged 14.8.17; Cranwell 2.10.17; Hendon 12.1.18; EC&AD Grain 26.1.18 (expts); Turnhouse W/E 18.5.18; HMS *Furious* W/E 15.8.18; HMS *Argus* W/E 19.12.18; Donibristle W/E 31.12.18 - @30.1.19

A6917    Deld Mullion for erection 30.6.17; EC&AD Grain 16.2.18 (expts); Turnhouse W/E 19.9.18 - @30.1.19

A6918    (110-hp Clerget) Deld Mullion for erection 30.6.17; EC&AD Grain 16.2.18 (expts); Left W/E 4.7.18; Grain, tested with DL gear with hydrovane, then to Fleet 4.19

A6919    Deld Farnborough to Pembroke 30.6.17; Packed for transit by 8.11.17; Houton Bay by 29.12.17; HMS *Campania* W/E 30.3.18; Donibristle W/E 31.10.18; Scapa W/E 14.11.18; Disposed W/E 23.1.19

A6920    Deld Farnborough to Pembroke 30.6.17; Packed for transit by 8.11.17; Houton Bay for HMS *Campania* 29.12.17; HMS *Campania* W/E 30.3.18; Scapa W/E 21.11.18; Houton Bay, propeller accident 5.3.19

A6921    Deld Farnborough to Pembroke 30.6.17; Packed for transit by 8.11.17; Houton Bay for HMS *Campania* by 29.12.17; HMS *Campania* W/E 30.3.18; Scapa W/E 14.11.18 - @30.1.19; Delney by 10.19

A6922    (130-hp Clerget) Deld Farnborough to Pembroke 30.6.17; Packed for transit by 8.11.17; Houton Bay for HMS *Campania* by 29.12.17; HMS *Campania* W/E 30.3.18; EF, crashed, wreckage hoisted aboard 14.5.18; Rosyth W/E 14.11.18; HMS *Campania* W/E 21.11.18; For deletion W/E 28.11.18; BUT Donibristle W/E 12.12.18 - @30.1.19

A6952    Ex RFC Islington by road to Turnhouse for Ship Strutter conversion and fit 130-hp Clerget 18.3.18; HMS *Indomitable* W/E 1.8.18; Turnhouse W/E 19.9.18; HMS *Valiant* 20.12.18; ashore 10.1.19; HMS *Valiant* 16.1.19; ashore 29.1.19

A6966    (130-hp Clerget) Deld ex RFC Islington to EC&AD Grain for conv Ship Strutter 26.1.18; Turnhouse W/E 18.5.18 - @25.7.18; Rosyth by 29.8.18; HMS *Indomitable* 16.9.18; ashore 19.9.18; HMS *Indomitable* 19.9.18; ashore 9.10.18; HMS *Indomitable* 10.10.18; ashore 16.10.18; HMS *Indomitable* 16.10.18; ashore 31.10.18; HMS *Indomitable* 3.11.18; Donibristle W/E 19.12.18 - 30.1.19

A6967    Ex RFC Islington by road to Turnhouse for Ship Strutter conversion and fit 130-hp Clerget 18.3.18; HMS *Repulse* W/E 26.9.18; Rosyth W/E 3.10.18; HMS *Repulse* W/E 21.11.18; HMS *Malaya* W/E 5.12.18; Donibristle W/E 31.12.18 - @30.1.19

A6968    Ex RFC Islington by road to Turnhouse for Ship Strutter conversion and fit 130-hp Clerget 18.3.18; HMAS *Australia* W/E 1.8.18; 10.18; Scapa W/E 31.10.18; Deleted W/E 1.11.18

A6969    Ex RFC Islington by road to Turnhouse for Ship Strutter conversion and fit 130-hp Clerget 18.3.18; East Fortune W/E 11.5.18; Deleted W/E 29.8.18

A6970    Ex RFC Islington by road to Turnhouse for Ship Strutter conversion and fit 130-hp Clerget 18.3.18; to HMS *Indomitable* 6.18; FL in sea 3.6.18

A6971    (130-hp Clerget) Ex RFC Islington by road to EC&AD Grain for Ship Strutter conversion 21.3.18; Turnhouse W/E 25.5.18; HMS *Furious* W/E 11.7.18; Donibristle W/E 22.8.18; HMS *Furious* W/E 3.10.18; Turnhouse W/E 5.12.18; HMS *Furious* W/E 12.12.18 - @30.1.19

A6972    Ex RFC Islington by road to EC&AD Grain for Ship

Strutter conversion 16.2.18; Turnhouse W/E 25.5.18; HMS *Furious* W/E 11.7.18 - @30.1.19

A6980 Ex RFC Brooks Green by road to Turnhouse for Ship Strutter conversion 3.18; HMS *Inflexible* 25.6.18; Turnhouse 7.18; HMS *Inflexible* 5.7.18; Donibristle 2.8.18; Turnhouse W/E 29.8.18; HMS *Inflexible* 16.9.18; ashore 10.18; HMS *Inflexible* 10.10.18; ashore 16.10.18; HMS *Inflexible* 16.10.18; ashore 26.10.18; ashore W/E 21.11.18; Smoogroo W/E 12.12.18; HMS *Inflexible* W/E 23.1.19 - @30.1.19

A6981 Ex RFC Brooks Green by road to Turnhouse for Ship Strutter conversion 3.18; HMS *New Zealand* W/E 15.8.18; Turnhouse W/E 19.9.18; HMS *Barham* W/E 16.1.19; Donibristle W/E 23.1.19 - @30.1.19

A6985 Ex RFC Ascot to EC&AD Grain by road for Ship Strutter conversion 23.3.18; Turnhouse W/E 1.6.18; HMS *Furious* W/E 15.8.18 - @30.1.19

A6986 Ex RFC Ascot to EC&AD Grain by road for Ship Strutter conversion 23.3.18; Turnhouse W/E 1.6.18; Donibristle W/E 11.7.18; HMS *Furious* W/E 15.8.18; Rosyth W/E 29.8.18; HMS *Furious* W/E 3.10.18; Turnhouse W/E 17.10.18; Deleted W/E 31.10.18

A6987 Ex RFC Ascot to EC&AD Grain by road for Ship Strutter conversion 23.3.18 (skid u/c, mod wing bracing, X-type struts and Grain flotation gear); Turnhouse W/E 13.6.18; Donibristle W/E 11.7.18; HMS *Furious* W/E 15.8.18 - @30.1.19

A6988 Ex RFC Ascot to EC&AD Grain by road for Ship Strutter conversion 23.3.18; Turnhouse W/E 18.5.18; Rosyth W/E 13.6.18; Turnhouse W/E 11.7.18; HMS *Furious* W/E 15.8.18; Deleted W/E 14.11.18

A6989 Ex RFC Ascot to EC&AD Grain by road for Ship Strutter conversion 23.3.18; Turnhouse W/E 18.5.18; HMS *Furious* W/E 11.7.18 - @30.1.19

A6990 Ex RFC Ascot to EC&AD Grain by road for Ship Strutter conversion 23.3.18; Turnhouse W/E 11.7.18; Donibristle W/E 19.9.18; HMS *Furious* W/E 17.10.18; Donibristle W/E 12.12.18; HMS *Furious* W/E 23.1.19 - @30.1.19

## 8 MAURICE FARMAN S.11 SHORTHORN PUSHER BIPLANES from batch A7001-A7100 built by The Aircraft Manufacturing Co Ltd, diverted from RFC order. Originally to be A7041 to A7048, but A7043 to A7050 sent instead. (75-hp Renault)

A7043 Deld RNASTE Vendôme 9.2.17; Deleted 7.18
A7044 Deld RNASTE Vendôme by road 21.1.17; Deleted 7.18
A7045 Deld RNASTE Vendôme by road 21.1.17; Deleted 7.18
A7046 Deld RNASTE Vendôme 3.2.17 - @22.2.18; Deleted 2.18
A7047 Deld RNASTE Vendôme ex UK 2.3.17; Deleted 7.18
A7048 Deld RNASTE Vendôme ex RFC Ascot 27.1.17; Deleted 7.18
A7049 Deld RNASTE Vendôme ex UK 2.3.17; Deleted 7.18
A7050 Deld RNASTE Vendôme ex UK 2.3.17; Deleted 7.18

## 117 AIRCO D.H.4 TRACTOR BIPLANE BOMBERS from batch A7401-A8090 built The Aircraft Manufacturing Co Ltd. Many delivered direct to RNAS. (mainly 200-hp B.H.P. or 375-hp Eagle VIII)

A7446 (Eagle VIII) Testing Sqdn Martlesham Heath 9.8.17; Mkrs 17.9.17; 5 Sqdn 24.10.17; 2 Sqdn 24.10.17; Officially allocated 14.3.18; Became 202 Sqdn 1.4.18; Pfalz DIII, wing came off, crashed N of Eessen 12.00 5.6.18; Fokker DVII OOC over Bruges 14.25 10.8.18; Fokker DVII in flames Dudzeele & Pfalz crashed Beukemaere Farm, Lisseweghe 11.05-11.25 16.9.18 (all Capt N Keeble DFC DSC & Capt EBC Betts DFC); COL Ghistelles 17.10.18 (Lt LF Pendred & Lt NH Jenkins both killed); Salved; 4 ASD 22.10.18 - @25.10.18

A7457 (200-hp RAF.3a) Deld Hendon for Special Service 12.6.17; Eastchurch 16.6.17; Flown Hendon 25.6.17; Bacton 9.8.17, AZP (named 'NON STARTER'); AZP, landed Bacton 22.8.17 (F/L GWR Fane); retd Yarmouth 26.8.17; Experimental Constructive Dept Grain 30.9.17 (air bag trials); later EC&AD; Test Dept Grain W/E 26.1.18 (flotation tests 28.1.18); EC&AD Grain by W/E 9.2.18; Test Dept Grain 3.18; EC&AD Grain W/E

9.3.18 - @25.5.18 (hydrovane and flotation gear experiments)

A7459 (200-hp RAF.3a) Deld Hendon for Special Service 12.6.17; Bacton 9.8.17; crashed in North Sea, BR 5.9.17; Surveyed 12.9.17; Deleted 24.9.17 TL

A7464 (Eagle V) Presentation a/c 'Mauritius No.1'. 57 Sqdn RFC, COL 24.6.17; 25 Sqdn, FL Clairmarais 28.11.17 (crew unhurt); to 1 ASD; 2 AI to 205 Sqdn 3.6.18; COL 5.6.18 (Lt JG Kerr & 2/Lt HW Hopton); 2 ASD 7.6.18; Rebuilt as F6119 3.7.18

A7486 (Eagle V) 2 AAP Hendon by 6.17; 25 Sqdn RFC, crashed on TO 8.7.17; to 2 AD; 57 Sqdn RFC, COL 8.11.17; 1 AD 10.11.17; 2 ASD by 3.18; 205 Sqdn 31.3.18; Crashed returning from bombing raid, Dampiere 12.4.18 (Lt RC Day & 2/Lt McKay); 2 ASD 13.4.18; SOC Rep Pk 1 ASD 19.4.18

A7487 (Eagle VIII) Presentation a/c 'Gold Coast No.2'. 57 Sqdn RFC by 7.17; 25 Sqdn RFC, 1 victory 27.10.17 (Lt JA McCudden & AM J Harris); 55 Sqdn RFC; 25 Sqdn RFC, engine cut on TO, crashed 3.1.18 (crew unhurt); to Rep Pk 1 ASD; 2 ASD 2.4.18; 2 AI by 6.18; to 205 Sqdn but FL en route at Sains-les-Pernes 3.6.18; arr 205 Sqdn 4.6.18; COL 4.7.18 (Lt GC Matthews & Sgt L Murphy unhurt); 2 ASD Rep Pk 7.7.18; SOC 2 ASD 31.7.18 NWR

A7518 (Eagle VI) 57 Sqdn RFC, FL, damaged 9.9.17; to 1 AD; 55 Sqdn RFC, collided with tender on landing 24.12.17 (crew unhurt); to 2 AD; 2 AI by 6.18; 205 Sqdn 3.6.18; Direct hit by flak in raid on Barleux, FL, COL nr Villers-Bretonneux 23.8.18 (Lt EO Danger & 2/Lt AD Hollingsworth unhurt)

A7561 57 Sqdn RFC by 8.17; Albatros shot down 18.8.17 (2/Lt AB Cook & 2/Lt RN Bullock); COL 21.10.17; 1 AD 22.10.17; 25 Sqdn RFC, FL, wrecked 5.2.18; to Rep Pk 1 ASD; 205 Sqdn by 17.4.18 (FM); HA OOC 23.4.18 (Lt W Elliott & AGL AM G Smith); Pfalz DIII OOC Chaulnes 10.30 15.5.18 (Lt W Elliott unhurt & 2/Lt HP Bennett wounded); 2 ASD 14.8.18 (time expired); Rebuilt as F6512 in error 28.8.18, later changed to H7119

A7573 (Eagle VI) 18 Sqdn RFC, COL 15.10.17 (2/Lt D Richardson & 2/Lt F Folliott); to 2 AD; 25 Sqdn RFC, stalled on landing 11.3.18; to 1 AD; Rep Pk 1 ASD to 2 AI 4.6.18; 205 Sqdn 9.6.18; Fokker DVII OOC Chaulnes-Brie Bridge 15.40 10.8.18 (Lt WE Clarke & 2/Lt CN Witham); Missing in action 13.8.18 (Lt T Fattorini & 2/Lt SJ Parkes both killed); SOC in field 14.8.18

A7587 (250-hp RR) Presentation a/c 'Gold Coast No.2'. 2 AD to 5 Sqdn 10.3.18; EF, FL 16.3.18 (FSL GE Siedle & Sgt AGL WJH Middleton); Damaged when attacked by 3 triplanes, claimed HA shot down, then FL Estrees 18.3.18 (FSL CE Wodehouse wounded & AGL L James unhurt); Rep Pk 1 ASD by 1.4.18; 2 AI 27.5.18; 205 Sqdn 3.6.18; Pfalz DIII on tail of D8412 sent down OOC nr Chaulnes 15.50 10.8.18; Pfalz DIII last seen in vertical dive c.08.00 11.8.18 (both Lt R Chalmers & 2/Lt SH Hamblin); Left 08.30, FTR 7.9.18 (Lt DJT Mellor killed & 2/Lt JC Walker PoW); SOC in field 7.9.18

A7619 (Eagle VI) 57 Sqdn RFC, FL, wrecked 1.1.18; to Rep Pk 2 ASD by 4.18; 205 Sqdn 5.4.18; 2 ASD 3.6.18 (cracked longeron); Rebuilt as F6077 3.7.18

A7620 (Eagle VI) Ex RFC Ascot via CSD White City to Dover 25.9.17; Arrived and left Dover on/by 13.10.17; ADD from W/E 7.12.17; 5 Sqdn 11.1.18; Red Albatros DV with plain black crosses OOC Busigny aerodrome 10.45 18.3.18 (F/L E Dickson DSO wounded & OSL WH Scott); Pfalz DIII left wing folded, crashed Rainecourt 15.30 27.3.18; Pfalz DIII OOC Proyart-Foucaucourt 09.50 28.3.18 (both F/L E Dickson DSC & OSL W Stewart); EF, FL Bertangles 30.3.18; Became 205 Sqdn 1.4.18; Left 15.14, FTR raid on La Motte aerodrome 6.4.18 (Lt GM Cartmel & AM1 G/L A Lane both killed); SOC in field 7.4.18

A7629 Deld AAP Hendon for erection 28.8.17; For RNAS Dunkerque, but to RFC instead as fitted with Galloway BHP; 2 TDS Lake Down 9.9.17

A7632 (Eagle VIII) Deld RFC Ascot via CSD White City to Dover 25.9.17; Hendon W/E 13.10.17; AP Dover W/E 1.12.17; 2 Sqdn (via ADD) 16.2.18; Became 202 Sqdn

1.4.18; Hit by AA over Ostende 12.6.18 (Capt CF Brewerton unhurt & Lt MG English slightly wounded); Pfalz DIII OOC inland of Ostende 17.00 16.7.18 (Capt AV Bowater & 2/Lt E Darby DSM); Monoplane OOC over Nieuport 11.35 14.8.18 (Lt LH Pearson & 2/Lt E Darby); Pfalz DIII OOC 16.9.18 (Lt LH Pearson & 2/Lt E Darby DSM); Missing last seen at 16,500 ft over Ostende pursued by 5 HA 11.00 26.9.18 (Lt FAB Gasson & 2/Lt S King both killed); Deleted 15.10.18

A7644   (Eagle VII) Hendon by 9.17; ADD 27.9.17; 5 Sqdn 3.10.17; After raid on Guise dump landed Villers-Bretonneux 8.3.18 (FSL BR Carter wounded & AGL HF Watson unhurt); 2 HA shot down in raid on Busigny aerodrome & dump, shared N6009 09.44-11.48 16.3.18 (F/Cdr CPO Bartlett & AGL W Naylor); COL 18.3.18 (F/L E Dickson DSC & OSL WH Scott both unhurt); to 2 ASD; 4 ASD by 30.3.18 - @27.4.18; For deletion by 25.5.18

A7647   (Eagle VI by 12.17, Eagle VII by 1.18) Deld Dover (via Hendon) W/E 13.10.17; 5 Sqdn 23.11.17; Crashed, CW Petite Synthe 11?.3.18; Deleted in squadron 18.3.18

A7652   RNAS to RFC Hendon by 27.10.17; Rep Pk 1 ASD to 2 AI; 12.8.18; 205 Sqdn 14.8.18; 2 ASD 26.9.18

A7653   Allocated RNAS to RFC Hendon 22.10.17 as spares or to fit engine

A7657   RNAS to RFC Hendon by 27.10.17 (allocated 22.10.17 as spares or to fit engine)

A7663   (Eagle VII) Deld Hendon for erection 26.9.17; AP Dover 3.10.17; 5 Sqdn 4.12.17; FTR raid on Busigny aerodrome, last seen diving nr Premont 18.3.18 (FSL RB Ransford & AM1 G/L G Smith DSM both killed); for deletion by 30.3.18

A7665   (Eagle VII) Deld Hendon W/E 6.10.17; AES Martlesham Heath 25.10.17 (tested with exptl u/c & larger propeller); Dunkerque 18.11.17; Hendon to Dover 23.11.17; 2 Sqdn 4.12.18; Hit searchlight on landing 4.1.18 (FSL FS Russell & observer unhurt); ADD 5.1.18; 2 Sqdn 18.3.18; Shot down by AA fire nr Sassenbrug [?] 22.3.18 (FSL FEA Bembridge seriously injured, AM1 G/L HG Lovelock DSM killed); Recovered badly damaged; Deleted 17.4.18

A7670   Allocated Dunkerque 10.9.17 (NTU)

A7671   (200-hp B.H.P) Tested Martlesham Heath 3.10.17 - 28.12.17; RFC Hendon by 3.18; Hendon 8.3.18; Yeovil 23.3.18; Farnborough by 5.18; Crashed Trimley 8.5.18

A7680   (Eagle V) NADD; (ex?) Dover by transport W/E 3.1.18; 25 Sqdn shot down 5.2.18

A7688   (200-hp RAF 3a) 49 Sqdn RFC by 2.18; 5 Sqdn RNAS from 6.3.18; 1 ASD SOC 8.4.18 NWR

A7701   (200-hp RAF 3a) Tested CFS Upavon 10.11.17; EC&AD Grain W/E 26.1.18; ECD Grain by 25.5.18 (for deletion by 23.3.18)

A7726   (190-hp Renault) Deld RFC Ascot to Hendon W/E 3.11.17; Cranwell by rail W/E 10.11.17; Became 201/2 TDS Cranwell 1.4.18

A7737   (Eagle VII) Deld Hendon ex Gosport Works W/E 27.10.17; AP Dover W/E 24.11.17; 202 Sqdn 8.4.18; 4 ASD 6.11.18

A7739   (Eagle VII later VI) Deld Hendon ex Gosport Works W/E 27.10.17; AP Dover W/E 24.11.17; NADD 18.2.18; 5 Sqdn W/E 7.3.18; Albatros DV crashed Busigny aerodrome 1100 16.3.18 (F/L E Dickson DSC & OSL WH Scott); Became 205 Sqdn 1.4.18; Attacked by 6 HA over Peronne, green & yellow Pfalz DIII OOC nr Villers-Bretonneux 2.4.18 (Capt E Dickson DSC & 2/Lt WH Scott); Attacked nr Abancourt by 3 triplanes and black Pfalz with crosses on white background, sent down the Pfalz DIII OOC 15.50 6.4.18 (Capt E Dickson DSC & 2/Lt WH Scott); Fokker DrI OOC Chaulnes 16.15 22.4.18 (Capt E Dickson DSC & AGL CV Robinson DSM); Fokker DrI OOC Chaulnes Rly Stn 1930-1940 23.4.18 (Capt E Dickson DSC & Sgt AGL CV Middleton); COL 8.6.18 (Lt JC Wilson & Sgt SM MacKay both unhurt); Rep Pk 2 ASD 11.6.18; SOC 21.6.18 NWR

A7742   (Eagle VII) Deld Hendon by 2.12.17; AP Dover 8.12.17; 5 Sqdn 15.12.17; Albatros DV, tailplane broke off nr Promour 10.55 18.3.18 (FSL GBS McBain & AM1 AGL W Jones); In combat, lost wing on landing and crashed 27.3.18 (FSL GBS McBain & AM1 AGL W Jones both injured); 2 ASD by 1.4.18; 57 Sqdn, shot

down 23.6.18 (Lt CW Peckham & 2/Lt AJ Cobbin missing); SOC 23.6.18

A7744   (Eagle VII) Deld Hendon W/E 3.11.17; AP Dover W/E 1.12.17; Grain 12.17; AP Dover 13.12.17; 5 Sqdn 19.12.17; HA OOC 30.1.18 (FSL JM Mason & AGL CV Robinson DSM); Became 205 Sqdn 1.4.18; 2 ASD 4.6.18 (cracked longeron); Rebuilt as F6099 3.7.18

A7751   (190-hp Renault) Deld RFC Ascot to Hendon W/E 3.11.17; Cranwell by rail W/E 10.11.17 - @30.3.18

A7757   Grain (ditching and hydrovane trials); WO at 31 Wing AP 10.6.19

A7760   (Eagle VIII) Ex RFC Lilbourne to Hendon, then Brooklands W/E 17.11.17; 1(S)ARD Farnborough to EC&AD Grain W/E 2.3.18 (fit flotation gear); 217 Sqdn 11.6.18; En route raid on Zeebrugge, EF, FL beach, Mardyck 29.7.18 (Lt GC Matthews & Sgt E Farley); Collided with A7772 on landing, badly damaged, Crochte 16.8.18 (1/Lt AL Grimme USA slightly injured & 2/Lt F Sutherland unhurt); to 4 ASD; 2 SS Richborough 15.9.18

A7761   Ex RFC to Tregantle & Withnoe by 30.3.18

A7762   (Eagle VIII) 1(S)ARD Farnborough by 27.4.18 allocated Dunkerque; 491 Flt Dover by 25.5.18; 217 Sqdn by 31.5.18; COL 7.6.18 (Lt JH Hardman & Sgt Mech G/L FW Shufflebottom); 4 ASD repair 8.6.18 - @27.10.18

A7764   (Eagle VIII) 1(S)ARD Farnborough to East Fortune for erection W/E 9.3.18; Dunkerque 28.3.18; Turnhouse by 31.3.18; Deleted W/E 4.7.18

A7768   (Eagle VII later VI) Deld Hendon W/E 3.11.17; AP Dover W/E 24.11.17 - @4.18; To 202 Sqdn by 27.4.18; Last seen between Ostende & Zeebrugge 14.5.18 (Lt F Titchener & Pte 1 G/L JG Waller)

A7772   (Eagle VIII) 1(S)ARD Farnborough to AAP Dover W/E 9.3.18 (erected in Repair Shops 13.3.18); NADD 21.3.18; Became 4 ASD Guines by 28.3.18; 217 Sqdn 1.4.18; With A7935 dropped 2x230-lb bombs each on U-boat 25m NNE of Dunkerque 30.5.18; With A7846 dropped 2x230-lb bombs each on U-boat 3m N of Ostende 1.6.18; Taxied into bomb hole 7.6.18 (Lt H Rudd & AM HA Child unhurt); Repaired on sqdn; With A8050 dropped 4 bombs each on U-boat NNE of Middelkerke 12.8.18; Collided A7760 on landing, badly damaged, Crochte 16.8.18 (Lt HS Stidston injured & Pte1 G/L MC Day unhurt); To 4 ASD Guines; Deleted 31.8.18 general fatigue

A7773   (Eagle VIII) 1(S)ARD Farnborough to AAP Dover 15.2.18; 17 Sqdn 27.2.18; Became 217 Sqdn 1.4.18; Damaged in enemy air raid 5/6.6.18; With A8059 attacked U-boat with 2x250-lb bombs each 12m N of Zeebrugge 23.4.18; With A8013 dropped 2x230-lb bombs on U-boat nr CI Buoy, East Dyke 29.6.18 (Lt GR Judge); Run into by A8067, Crochte 30.7.18; 4 ASD 30.7.18 - @25.10.18

A7790   (Eagle IV) 2 AI by 5.18; 205 Sqdn 19.5.18; COL 31.5.18 (Lt BW Fletcher & Sgt FL Roberts both unhurt); for 2 ASD; SOC 2 Salvage Dept 4.6.18

A7811   (Eagle VI) 2 AI by 4.18; 205 Sqdn 21.4.18; Pfalz DIII OOC Chaulnes 1030 15.5.18 (Lt W Grossart & Sgt PL Richards); Damaged by flak then attacked by 2 Fokker DrI and a Fokker DVII, observer shot down the biplane, but rudder controls shot away, spun in from 200/300 ft on approach, TW 09.15 19.7.18 (Lt JC Wilson severely wounded & 2/Lt JB Leach unhurt); Remains to 2 ASD 20.7.18; SOC in field

A7817   (RAF) RFC Islington to Eastchurch NAS by road W/E 8.3.18; Became 204 TDS Eastchurch 1.4.18 - @27.6.18

A7829   (Eagle VIII) Deld Hendon W/E 1.12.17; AAP Dover 15.12.17; 17 Sqdn 17.2.18 [deld Bergues ex Calais 21.2.18]; Became 217 Sqdn 1.4.18; Badly shot up 27.4.18; 4 ASD Guines 30.4.18 - @25.10.18

A7830   (Eagle VIII) Deld Hendon W/E 1.12.17; Yarmouth 8.12.17 (special service); Dropped 2x65-lb bombs on U-boat 6½m ESE of Lowestoft 21.3.18 (W/Cdr CR Samson DSO & AM Radcliffe); Became 490 Flt Yarmouth by 25.5.18; Martlesham Heath 16.7.18; 25 Sqdn by 10.18; Crashed 7.10.18 (2/Lt F Sneed & 2/Lt M Shires both injured)

A7831   (RAF) RFC Islington to Eastchurch NAS by road W/E 8.3.18; Became 204 TDS Eastchurch 1.4.18; Manston W/E 27.6.18 - @8.18

A7832   (RAF) RFC Islington to Eastchurch NAS by road W/E

8.3.18; Became 204 TDS Eastchurch 1.4.18; Cranwell 29.5.18

A7841 (RAF) RFC Islington to Eastchurch NAS by road W/E 8.3.18; Became 204 TDS Eastchurch 1.4.18

A7843 (190-hp Renault) RFC Islington to Eastchurch NAS by road W/E 8.3.18; Became 204 TDS Eastchurch 1.4.18 - @22.5.18

A7844 (RAF) RFC Islington to Eastchurch NAS by road W/E 8.3.18; Became 204 TDS Eastchurch 1.4.18

A7845 (Eagle VIII) Deld Hendon for erection W/E 1.12.17; AAP Dover 15.12.17; NADD 29.12.17; 2 Sqdn by 2.1.18; Became 202 Sqdn (coded 'R') 1.4.18; Lost u/c landing 25.5.18 (Capt CF Brewerton & Lt MG English both unhurt); to 4 ASD Guines; 202 Sqdn 28.6.18; 98 Sqdn 16.3.19; 1 ASD 18.3.19

A7846 (Eagle VIII) Deld Hendon for erection W/E 1.12.17; To AAP Dover but FL Twickenham, damaged, retd Hendon by road 29.12.17 (pilot unhurt); AAP Dover 16.2.18; 17 Sqdn RFC 28.2.18; Became 217 Sqdn 1.4.18; With A7867 attacked U-boat, each dropped 2x230-lb bombs 8 miles NE of Dunkerque 3.4.18 (Lt G Dymore-Brown & AC G/L Harper); With A8065 dropped 2x230-lb bombs each on 4 destroyers 15m NNW Ostende 19.40 19.5.18; With A7772 dropped 2x230-lb bombs each on U-boat 3m N of Ostende 1.6.18; Damaged in enemy air raid 5/6.6.18; Albatros driven down OOC into sea 19.35 28.6.18 (Lt CW Bragg & 1/Pte G/L EE Hunnisett); Seaplane on water attacked last seen smoking 28.6.18 [possibly the same victory]; Claimed direct hit on trawler 24.7.18 (Lt AM Phillips & Lt NS Dougall); Hit by A7863 when standing on aerodrome, BO 22.8.18; Deleted 31.8.18

A7848 (Eagle VIII) Deld Hendon W/E 1.12.17; To Yarmouth but landed Northolt 28.12.17; retd Hendon 31.12.17; arr Yarmouth (special service); AZP 13.4.18 (Mjr V Nicholl DSC & 2/Lt HG Owen); Became 490 Flt Yarmouth (coded '11') by 25.5.18 - @25.9.18

A7849 (Eagle VIII, later VI) Deld Hendon W/E 1.12.17; AAP Dover 15.12.17; 2 Sqdn 2.1.18; Became 202 Sqdn 1.4.18 - @25.4.18 (LM); 4 ASD Dunkerque by 25.5.18 - @31.5.18; 4 ASD Wissant to 202 Sqdn 17.9.18; Shot down by 5 HA, crashed Engel Dump 28.9.18 (Lt AM Stevens & 2/Lt WHL Halford both killed); Deleted 15.10.18

A7863 (Eagle VIII) Deld Hendon for erection W/E 1.12.17; AP Dover 13.1.18; ADD 16.2.18; 12 Sqdn 2.18; 17 Sqdn 17.2.18; Dropped 230-lb bomb on U-boat NE of Dunkerque 13.3.18 (FSL JN Rutter & LAC G/L AW Vidler); Crashed and damaged nr Bergues aerodrome 19.3.18 (FSL GD Brown, AC1 GL HG Groves); 4 ASD Guines 23.3.18; 217 Sqdn 26.5.18; Damaged in enemy air raid 5/6.6.18; 2-str monoplane seaplane crashed in sea 29.7.18 (Lt AM Phillips & Lt NS Dougall); Crashed on TO, BO 22.8.18 (Ens E Schoonmaker USNRF & Q/M2 GE Sprague USNRF both unhurt)

A7864 (200-hp RAF.4d) Deld AAP Dover W/E 22.12.17; Felixstowe (inscribed 'FELIXSTOWE' on nose) (exptl engine fitting RAF 3a and RAF 4d); Rebuilt as F5836 7.8.18

A7867 (Eagle VIII) Deld Hendon W/E 7.12.17; AAP Dover W/E 7.1.18; 17 Sqdn 3.2.18; ADD 2.18; 17 Sqdn 16.2.18; ADD 2.18; 17 Sqdn 28.2.18; Became 217 Sqdn 1.4.18; With A7846 attacked U-boat, each dropped 2x230-lb bombs 8m NE of Dunkerque 3.4.18 (Capt HH Gonyou & Lt JF Reid); With A8022 dropped 2x230-lb bombs on U-boat 2m off Ostende Piers 27.6.18; Spun into sea 3m NE of Dunkerque 06.45 20.8.18 (Yeoman 1st Class ME O'Gorman USNRF & Ens TN McKinnon USNRF both drowned); Deleted 31.8.18

A7868 (Eagle VIII) Deld Hendon W/E 1.12.17; AAP Dover 18.12.17; 2 Sqdn after FL Calais 4.1.18; Became 202 Sqdn 1.4.18 (segmented circle marking on fin); Halberstadt 1-str OOC over Meetkerke aerodrome 11.10 18.5.18; Attacked 5 Albatros off Ostende, 1 shot down in flames and 1 OOC in sea 3m off Ostende 19.20 21.5.18 (all Lt LA Ashfield & G/L Cpl LA Allen); Attacked by 5 HA nr Middelkerke, landed safely 27.6.18 (Lt LA Ashfield unhurt & Lt NH Jenkins DSM seriously wounded); FTR photo recce 16.7.18 (Lt LA Ashfield, DFC & Lt MG English both killed) [credited Flgm Goerth, Marine Jasta 3 at Zevecote 18.10]; Deleted

31.8.18

A7870 (Eagle VIII) Deld Hendon W/E 22.12.17; Airco W/E 16.2.18 (expts); Hendon 2.18; AAP Dover 21.2.18; 17 Sqdn (via ADD) 5.3.18; Became 217 Sqdn 1.4.18; FL on beach at Mardyck 22.4.18; Badly damaged after bombing raid 19.5.18 (Lt JH Hardman & A/G H Tallboys unhurt); 4 ASD 19.5.18; 217 Sqdn 24.9.18; Crashed 23.10.18; 4 ASD 25.10.18; Deleted 31.10.18

A7875 1(S)ARD Farnborough to 4 ASD 25.10.18; 217 Sqdn by 2.11.18 (FM); COL 20.11.18 (2/Lt SJ Saunders & 2/Lt TC Tyers both unhurt); 11 AP 28.11.18; To be WOC 4.1.19

A7878 (Eagle VIII) Deld Hendon W/E 7.12.17; AAP Dover 10.1.18; ADD 16.2.18; 17 Sqdn 18.2.18; Dover 8.3.18 (visit?); 17 Sqdn 9.3.18; Became 217 Sqdn 1.4.18; Ran into lorry on landing, badly damaged 12.6.18 (Lt HS Matthews & 1/Pte G/L E Farley both injured); 4 ASD 13.6.18; 2 SS Richborough 15.9.18

A7893 (Eagle VIII) To 1(S)ARD Farnborough (for HMS *Argus*) W/E 16.1.19 - @30.1.19; TO NZPAF Sockburn by 1921

A7908 (250-hp RR) 2 AD RFC Candas by 3.18; 5 Sqdn 12.3.18; Missing nr St.B(?)enin 16.3.18 (F/Cdr LW Ormerod, DSC & FSL WLH Pattison, DSC both killed, buried Le Cateau)

A7915 (Eagle V) 1(S)ARD Farnborough by 2.5.18; Rec Pk 5.18; 2 AI 27.5.18; 205 Sqdn 31.5.18; Bumped on landing, wings damaged 16.6.18 (Lt HG Kirkland & 2/Lt JC Walker both unhurt); 2 ASD 18.6.18; SOC 22.6.18 NWR

A7917 217 Sqdn by 20.9.18 (FM); FL Maxenzeal, nr Alost 17.12.18 (2/Lt RW Woodhead & 2/Lt GC Paish); Retd sqdn 19.12.18; 233 Sqdn Dover 27.2.19

A7920 France to Lympne (via Dover) 13.9.18; 4 ASD Wissant to 217 Sqdn 24.9.18; Tail skid post bent on TO, ran into ditch 27.9.18 (Lt TW Whittaker & Sgt E Farley); 233 Sqdn Dover 27.2.19; 2 Comms Sqdn Kenley by 4.19 (special duty with King of the Belgians); FL successfully Evère 22.4.19

A7924 (Eagle VIII) 4 ASD Wissant to 217 Sqdn 24.9.18; Attacked by 16 HA, shot down in flames 28.9.18 (1/Lt JE Gregory USAS & 2/Lt E Martin-Bell both killed)

A7925 4 ASD Wissant to 217 Sqdn 4.11.18; 233 Sqdn Dover 1.3.19

A7926 1(S)ARD Farnborough to 4 ASD 25.10.18

A7929 4 ASD by 11.18; 202 Sqdn 4.11.18; SAD Farnborough for HMS *Argus* 6.1.19; 6 SD Ascot (for HMS *Argus*) W/E 16.1.19 - @30.1.19; NZPAF Sockburn (coded 'J') by 1921

A7930 (Eagle VIII) 1(S)ARD Farnborough by 4.18; Dover 4.4.18; 202 Sqdn 8.5.18; 2 D-types OOC, rudder shot away in combat, crash landed on beach, wings and u/c damaged, nr Fort Mardyck 4.6.18 (FSL LH Pearson & G/L SE Allatson); to 4 ASD; 2 SS Richborough 15.9.18

A7933 (Eagle V) 2 AI to 5 Sqdn 24.3.18; Became 205 Sqdn 1.4.18; Badly shot up while bombing Chaulnes Rly Stn, FL Bellevue 23.4.18 (Lt LF Cocks wounded & Lt HF Taylor unhurt); 2 ASD 27.4.18; Rebuilt as F6059 2.7.18

A7934 (Eagle VIII) 1(S)ARD Farnborough by 4.18; Dover by 27.4.18; 217 Sqdn 9.5.18; With A8067 dropped 2x230-lb bombs each on U-boat escorted by 4 destroyers 15m NNW Ostende 1910 19.5.18; 2-str biplane seaplane shot down in steep dive 08.30 1.6.18 (Lt AE Bingham & G/L H Tallboys); Damaged in hangar by A8082 taking off, Crochte 18.7.18; 4 ASD 19.7.18 - @25.10.18

A7935 (Eagle VIII) 1(S)ARD Dunkerque by 4.18; Dover 4.18; 217 Sqdn (coded 'E') by 27.4.18; With A7772 dropped 2x230-lb bombs each on U-boat 25m NNE of Dunkerque 30.5.18; Attacked by 4 Pfalz DIII over Zeebrugge, shot down 1 in flames 31.5.18 (2/Lt GB Coward & AAM1 1/Pte G/L GF Briggs observer unhurt); Damaged in enemy air raid 5/6.6.18; After raid on Zeebrugge, patrol chased by 4 Pfalz, aircraft then shot down by Dutch troops, o/t on landing Souburg airfield, Vlissingen, Zeeland 17.6.18 (2/Lt GB Coward & Lt JF Reid interned); Retained by Dutch as *deH432*

A7941 (Eagle VIII) 1(S)ARD Farnborough by 4.18; 217 Sqdn W/E 27.4.18; Damaged in enemy air raid 5/6.6.18; Combat with 8 enemy seaplanes nr Zeebrugge, shot down 2-str monoplane seaplane into sea 19.40 29.7.18 (Lt RG Shaw & Lt UGA Tonge); still 217 Sqdn 31.7.18;

4 ASD by 9.18; 2 SS Richborough 15.9.18; 217 Sqdn by 28.9.18

**A7942** (Eagle VIII) 1(S)ARD Farnborough to Dunkerque Naval Wing 4.4.18; 2 AI by 5.18; 55 Sqdn 17.5.18; 491 Flt Dover by 25.5.18; 3 ASD 7.9.18

**A7945** (Eagle VIII) 1(S)ARD Farnborough by 4.18; Dunkerque Naval Wing 4.4.18; Dover by 27.4.18; 217 Sqdn by 15.5.18; With A7996 dropped 2x230-lb bombs each on U-boat escorted by 4 destroyers 15m NNW of Ostende 19.05 19.5.18; Monoplane seaplane apparently OOC 08.30 1.6.18 (Lt FE Bridges & G/L HG Groves); Bounced landing after raid, u/c collapsed, went on nose 23.6.18 (Lt AM Phillips & AM2 G/L H Tourlamain); 4 ASD 25.6.18 - @25.10.18

**A7964** (Eagle VI) 1(S)ASD Farnborough by 2.5.18; 2 AI to 205 Sqdn 12.6.18; Hit on ground by D9234 landing 11.8.18; Fokker DVII OOC W of St.Quentin 18.40 7.9.18 (2/Lt HF Taylor & 2/Lt J Golding); Fokker DVII OOC St.Quentin 17.50 15.9.18 (2/Lt HF Taylor & 2/Lt HS Mullen); 2 ASD 23.9.18; Rebuilt as H6858 3.10.18

**A7969**(Eagle VIII) 1(S)ARD Farnborough by 25.5.18 for Dunkerque; Dover W/E 1.6.18; 4 ASD by 6.18; 217 Sqdn 18.6.18; Badly shot about 22.7.18 (Capt DW Davies & Sgt GI White); Crashed on TO, badly damaged 22.8.18 (2/Lt LH Nesbitt & 2/Lt W Spranklin both unhurt); 4 ASD 23.8.18; 2 SS Richborough 15.9.18

**A7976** 2 AI to 5 Sqdn 24.3.18; Left 09.35, FTR 28.3.18 (FSL JG Carroll killed & AGL GE Daffey MPK)

**A7985** (Eagle VII) 1(S)ARD Farnborough by 1.5.18; 2 AI by 6.18; 205 Sqdn 6.6.18; EF, FL nr aerodrome 4.7.18 (Lt RLMcK Barbour & 2/Lt JH Preston); Pfalz DIII in flames between Marcelcave and the lines 20.00 31.7.18 (Lt RLM Barbour & 2/Lt JH Preston); COL, u/c collapsed 29.8.18 (2/Lt FF Anslow & AM Cleverley); COL 17.9.18 (2/Lt AN Hyde & 2/Lt WW Harrison unhurt); to 2 ASD; SOC 20.9.18

**A7992** Dover by 10.18; Pool of Pilots 5.10.18

**A7993** (325-hp RR) HAAP by 4.18; Medical Flt Hendon 2.4.18; AES Martlesham Heath 24.4.18 - @20.5.18; Convtd to D.H.4A (RR ungeared); AEE Martlesham Heath by 6.19 (performance and climb)

**A7996** (Eagle VIII) 1(S)ARD Farnborough by 23.2.18; AAP Dover W/E 9.3.18 (erected in Repair Shop 13.3.18); 17 Sqdn 20.3.18; Became 217 Sqdn 1.4.18; With A7945 dropped 4x230-lb bombs on U-boat escorted by 4 destroyers 15m NNW of Ostende 19.05 19.5.18; 1 Pfalz sent down vertically OOC smoking between Zeebrugge & Ostende 20.15 17.6.18 (Lt AM Phillips & Sgt GI White); EF on TO, damaged 30.7.18 (2/Lt HA Pank & 2/Lt EM Ball both unhurt); to 4 ASD, to at least 25.10.18

**A8006** (Eagle VIII) 1(S)ARD Farnborough by 23.2.18; AAP Dover W/E 9.3.18 (erected in Repair Shop); 217 Sqdn 25.4.18; Damaged in enemy air raid 5/6.6.18; Crashed on TO, badly damaged 15.7.18 (Lt SJ Saunders & 2/Lt WA Spranklin both slightly injured); 4 ASD 16.7.18; 217 Sqdn by 9.18; Crashed 9.18; 4 ASD 14.9.18 - @25.10.18

**A8012** (Eagle VIII) 1(S)ARD Farnborough by 5.18; 491 Flt Dover by 25.5.18 (W/E 1.6.18); 217 Sqdn 1.6.18; Participated in raid on Zeebrugge, retd safely 5.6.18; Damaged in enemy air raid 5/6.6.18; 4 ASD by 9.6.18; 202 Sqdn by 3.10.18; Pilot's gun muzzle attachment hit propeller, FL beach La Panne 5.10.18 (Lt NH Witter & 2/Lt AEE Lee); 4 ASD 5.10.18 - @25.10.18

**A8013** (Eagle VIII) 1(S)ARD Farnborough by 5.18; 491 Flt Dover by 25.5.18 (W/E 1.6.18); 217 Sqdn 7.6.18; With A7773 dropped 2x230-lb bombs on U-boat nr CI Buoy, East Dyke 29.6.18 (Lt RM Berthe); While raiding Zeebrugge, shot down OOC by HA, BU in air 5m N of Ostende 19.45 30.6.18 (Lt CJ Moir & 1/Pte G/L EE Hunnisett killed) [credited Flgm Goerth, Marine Jasta 3]

**A8022** (Eagle VIII) 1(S)ARD Farnborough by 5.18; 491 Flt Dover by 25.5.18 (W/E 1.6.18); 4 ASD Audembert 7.6.18; 217 Sqdn 8.6.18; Broke wing landing 15.6.18 (Capt DW Davies & Sgt GJ Wilson); Pfalz DIII shot down OOC 17.6.18 (Capt DW Davies & Sgt G/L GI White); With A7867 dropped 2x230-lb bombs on U-boat 2m off Ostende Piers 27.6.18; Crashed, to 4 ASD 29.6.18; retd 217 Sqdn; COL after A/S patrol, wings and u/c damaged 9.18 (Lt SW Whittaker & Sgt G/L GI

White unhurt); 4 ASD 16.9.18 - @25.10.18

**A8023** (Eagle VIII) 1(S)ARD Farnborough by 5.18; 491 Flt Dover by 25.5.18 (W/E 1.6.18); 4 ASD Audembert to 217 Sqdn 13.6.18; Shot down by HA, last seen in water 5m off Ostende 06.00 28.6.18 (Lt AE Bingham & Lt LJ Smith PoWs) [credited Ltn Puss of Seefrontstaffel]

**A8025** (Eagle VIII) 1(S)ARD Farnborough by 5.18; 491 Flt Dover by 25.5.18 (W/E 1.6.18); 4 ASD 6.18; 202 Sqdn (coded 'Z') 6.6.18; Attacked by 5 HA off Middelkerke, damaged, landed safely 27.6.18 (Lt LH Pearson & 2/Lt E Darby DSM unhurt); Repaired on sqdn; Lost over enemy lines, last seen nr Engel Dump 06.35 28.9.18 (Capt AV Bowater & Lt DL Melvin both PoW); Deleted 15.10.18

**A8029** (Eagle VI) Deld 2 AAP Hendon by 9.5.18; 2 AI by 6.18; 205 Sqdn 18.6.18; Pfalz DIII shot down Bray 19.57 5.7.18; Pfalz DIII OOC La Flaguye 10.15 30.7.18 (both Lt EH Johnson & 2/Lt AR Crosthwaite); Pfalz DIII OOC Peronne, also attacked by D8387 c.08.00 11.8.18 (Lt EH Johnson & Lt HF Taylor); 2 ASD 21.8.18 (longerons strained); Rebuilt as H7125 17.9.18

**A8030** (Eagle V) Deld 2 AAP Hendon by 9.5.18; 2 AI 22.5.18; 205 Sqdn 28.5.18; 2 ASD 30.6.18 (poor performance); Rebuilt as F6187 12.7.18

**A8032** (Eagle VIII, later 200-hp RAF 3a) 1(S)ARD Farnborough by 25.5.18 for Dunkerque; Yarmouth by 29.6.18 - @10.8.18; AZP, shot down L70 nr the Blakeney Overfalls buoy and damaged L65, landed Sedgeford 5.8.18 (Mjr E Cadbury & Capt R Leckie); 534 Flt 273 Sqdn Covehithe by 8.18 - @5.11.18

**A8033** (Eagle VIII) 1(S)ARD Farnborough by 25.5.18 - @31.5.18 for Dunkerque (NTU?); Covehithe by 1.7.18 - @18.8.18; Became 534 Flt 273 Sqdn Covehithe by 8.18 - 10.18; 534 Flt 273 Sqdn Burgh Castle, 2 HACPs 9.11.18; 534 Flt 273 Sqdn Covehithe, HACP 10.11.18; still Covehithe 27.11.18

**A8039** (Eagle VIII) 1(S)ARD Farnborough by 25.5.18 - @31.5.18 for Dunkerque (NTU?); Yarmouth by 29.6.18; AZP 5.8.18 (Lt RE Keys & AM AT Harman); AZP from Burgh Castle, FL nr Louth 6.8.18 (2 crew unhurt)

**A8040** (Eagle VIII) 1(S)ARD Farnborough by 25.5.18 - @31.5.18 for Dunkerque (NTU?); Yarmouth by 25.6.18 - @17.9.18

**A8044** (Eagle VIII) 1(S)ARD Farnborough by 25.5.18 - @31.5.18 for Dunkerque (NTU?); Covehithe by 9.7.18; AZP 5.8.18 (Lt WR Plaskitt & Sgt Keeling); Became 534 Flt 273 Sqdn Covehithe 8.18 - 10.18

**A8046** (Eagle VIII) 1(S)ARD Farnborough by 25.5.18; AAP Dover 14.6.18; 4 ASD by 7.18; 217 Sqdn 2.7.18; Crashed on TO 8.8.18 (Lt SW Whittaker & 2/Lt PJ Holmes); Crashed on TO, badly damaged 9.10.18 (Lt SW Whittaker & 2/Lt PJ Holmes both unhurt); 4 ASD by 25.10.18; Deleted 31.10.18 DBR

**A8050** (Eagle VIII) 4 ASD by 7.18; 217 Sqdn 30.7.18; With A7772 dropped 4 bombs each on U-boat 150° off Middelkerke 12.8.18; COL, badly damaged 16.8.18 (2/Lt GC Paish unhurt); to 4 ASD; 2 SS Richborough 15.9.18

**A8056** (Eagle VIII) 217 Sqdn by 9.8.18; Landed in cornfield nr aerodrome and smashed 16.8.18 (Capt DW Davies & Sgt GJ Wilson); Badly shot about in raid on Thourout, FL Morshoek, nr Abincourt 28.9.18 (Capt DW Davies & Sgt GJ Wilson); Flying again 4.10.18; Hit by ground fire 7.10.18 (Pilot unhurt & Sgt G/L GI White wounded); 98 Sqdn 15.3.19 (arr 17.3.19); 1 ASD 25.3.19

**A8059** (Eagle VIII) Deld 2 AAP Hendon 2.18; AAP Dover 23.2.18; 17 Sqdn 5.3.18; Became 217 Sqdn 1.4.18; With A7773 dropped 2x230-lb bombs each on U-boat 12m N of Zeebrugge 23.4.18; COL 5.5.18 (Lt JN Rutter & G/L HG Groves both unhurt); 4 ASD Guines 5.5.18 - @31.5.18; 4 ASD Audembert to 202 Sqdn 17.7.18; Attacked by 5 HA, 1 sent down OOC Lisseweghe 17.05 16.9.18 (Lt NH Witter & 2/Lt AEE Lee); 2-str (probably Rumpler) Zele-Termonde 13.05 30.10.18 (Lt NH Witter & 2/Lt AEE Lee); Crashed Zerkegen 10.12.18 (repaired locally); 98 Sqdn 16.3.19; 1 ASD 18.3.19 (for 11 AP)

**A8061** (Eagle VIII) 4 ASD by 8.18; 217 Sqdn 25.8.18; FL in water just off beach nr La Panne 16.9.18 (2/Lt SJ

Saunders & 2/Obs AM Turnbull USA both unhurt); 4 ASD 18.9.18 - @25.10.18

A8063 (Eagle VIII) Deld 2 AAP Hendon by 2.18; AAP Dover 24.2.18; 17 Sqdn 13.3.18; Became 217 Sqdn 1.4.18; While attempting to bomb enemy trawler spun in sea and wrecked 2½m N of Zeebrugge Mole 22.4.18 (Lt CF Parsons & AC1 G/L GS Gladwin captured by enemy trawler, PoW); Deleted 13.5.18

A8065 (Eagle VIII) Deld 2 AAP Hendon by 2.18; AAP Dover 26.2.18; 17 Sqdn 8.3.18; Became 217 Sqdn 1.4.18; With A7846 dropped 2x230-lb bombs each on 4 destroyers 15m NNW Ostende 19.40 19.5.18; Attacked destroyer 21.5.18 (Lt GB Coward & Ptel A/G SF Briggs); FTR from raid on Zeebrugge lock gates 28.5.18 (L/Col PFM Fellowes PoW wounded & Sgt FH Pritchard PoW) [credited Flgm Bieber of Seefrontstaffel]

A8066 (Eagle VIII) Deld 2 AAP Hendon by 2.18; AAP Dover 11.3.18; 17 Sqdn 16.3.18; Became 217 Sqdn 1.4.18; COL 22.4.18 (LM); 4 ASD Dunkerque by 25.5.18 - @31.5.18; Rep Pk 1 ASD by 8.18; 2 ASD 23.8.18; 4 ASD by 9.18; 202 Sqdn 15.9.18; Missing, last seen over Nieuport 06.25 28.9.18 (Lt CR Moore & 2/Lt E Darby both PoW); Deleted 15.10.18
BUT 534 Flt 273 Sqdn Covehithe by 9.18

A8067 (Eagle VIII) Deld 2 AAP Hendon 2.18; AAP Dover 23.2.18; 17 Sqdn 8.3.18; Became 217 Sqdn 1.4.18; With A7934 dropped 2x230-lb bombs each on U-boat escorted by 4 destroyers 15m NNW Ostende 1910 19.5.18; EF on TO, crashed into 2 aircraft 29.7.18 (Lt HS Matthews & Sgt E Farley); Repaired on sqdn; 98 Sqdn 16.3.19; 1 ASD 18.3.19

A8071 (Eagle VII) 5 Sqdn by 25.3.18; Became 205 Sqdn 1.4.18; Triplane OOC Chaulnes Rly Stn 19.30 23.4.18 (Lt GE Siedle & Sgt CV Middleton); Shot about by AA, landed Bertangles 31.5.18 (Lt GE Siedle & Sgt CV Middleton unhurt); 2 ASD 1.6.18; Rebuilt as F6114 3.7.18

A8072 (Eagle VIII) 4 ASD by 8.18; 217 Sqdn 19.8.18; 98 Sqdn 6.3.19; 1 ASD 19.3.19

A8074 (Eagle VIII) Flown Lympne to 4 ASD Audembert 4.8.18; 217 Sqdn by 14.8.18; TW by explosion while stationary on aerodrome 22.8.18; Wreckage to 4 ASD 23.8.18; 2 SS Richborough 15.9.18

A8079 (Eagle VIII) Deld 2 AAP Hendon by 3.18; AAP Dover 9.3.18; NADD 20.3.18; 4 ASD Guines 28.3.18; 202 Sqdn by 7.4.18; Attacked by 5 Pfalz DIII over Donkerklok Battery, slightly damaged 27.6.18 (Capt J Robinson DFC uninjured & Lt FS Russell, DSC slightly wounded); to 4 ASD; 202 Sqdn 28.9.18; FL in mist on beach at low tide, crashed, DBR, salvaging 27.1.19 (2/Lt GC Cole & 2/Lt GP Muffey); WOC 6.2.19

A8080 (Eagle VII) Rec Pk by 4.18; 205 Sqdn 10.4.18; Crashed into D8405 on TO, CW 18.4.18 (Lt WE MacPherson unhurt); 2 ASD 18.4.18; SOC Adv Salvage Dump 19.4.18

A8081 (Eagle VIII) 4 ASD by 8.18; 217 Sqdn 19.8.18; Hit ridge landing after A/S patrol and broke off u/c 5.9.18 (Capt DW Davies & Sgt GJ Wilson both unhurt); 4 ASD 9.9.18 - @25.10.18

A8082 (Eagle VIII) 1(S)ARD Farnborough by 25.5.18; AAP Dover by 12.6.18; 4 ASD Audembert 13.6.18; 217 Sqdn 2.7.18; Crashed into hangar on TO, wrecking A7934 & D8353, badly damaged 18.7.18 (Lt RM Berthe & Lt AC Lester unhurt); to 4 ASD, to at least 25.10.18

A8083 Exp - fitted 400-hp Sunbeam Matabele; Allocated from RFC 16.2.18 for experiments; Deld 14 AAP Castle Bromwich to Hendon 5.5.18; Farnborough 27.6.18; Tested CFS 16.12.18 - 31.12.18

A8084 (Eagle V) 2 AI to 5 Sqdn 24.3.18; Became 205 Sqdn 1.4.18; EF on TO, badly damaged 9.4.18 (Lt HD Evans & Sgt PL Richards unhurt); 2 ASD 11.4.18 (repair)

A8089 (Eagle VI) 2 AI by 9.18; 205 Sqdn 18.9.18; Left 17.35 to bomb Villers Outréaux, dived steeply with 2 Fokker DVIIs HA on tail, BU over Le Catelat 18.45 21.9.18 (2/Lt AN Hyde & 2/Lt WW Harrison both killed)

A8090 Rep Pk 1 ASD to 2 AI 13.9.18; 205 Sqdn 18.9.18; 4 ASD 24.9.18; 2 ASD to 57 Sqdn 26.9.18; Shot down in flames 2.10.18 (Lt F Neale & 2/Lt E Preece both killed)

**9 SOPWITH 1½ STRUTTER TRACTOR BIPLANES from batch A8141-A8340 built by Ruston, Proctor & Co Ltd. (various engines)**

A8204 (Type 9400) (100-hp Gnome Monosoupape) Ex RFC Islington to Gunnery School Flights Eastchurch for erection 24.10.17 - @30.3.18

A8224 (Clerget) Ex RFC (Convtd Ship Strutter) Turnhouse W/E 27.4.18; HMS *Inflexible* 12.8.18; Turnhouse 14.8.18; HMS *Inflexible* 16.8.18; ashore 13.9.18; Deleted W/E 12.9.18 (sic)

A8233 (Clerget) Ex RFC (Convtd Ship Strutter); Turnhouse W/E 20.4.18; Deleted W/E 3.10.18

A8255 (130-hp Clerget) Orfordness by 7.17; Allocated Rosyth 4.4.18 (Convtd Ship Strutter); ECD Grain by 27.4.18 - @13.6.18, allocated Rosyth (DL tests with skids; hydrovane ditching trials); transit by 20-27.6.18; Turnhouse by 25.7.18; Donibristle W/E 3.10.18; Rosyth W/E 13.10.18; Turnhouse W/E 12.12.18 - @30.1.19

A8275 (Clerget) Ex RFC (Convtd Ship Strutter) Turnhouse W/E 20.4.18; Deleted W/E 3.10.18

A8277 (130-hp Clerget) Ex RFC (Convtd Ship Strutter) Turnhouse W/E 20.4.18; Donibristle W/E 15.8.18 - @30.1.19; ALSO HMS *Malaya*; HMS *Indomitable* 8.18

A8288 (Type 9400)(110-hp Clerget) Ex RFC Islington to Gunnery School Flights Eastchurch for erection 24.10.17; Became 204 TDS Eastchurch 1.4.18 - @7.18

A8300 (Clerget) Ex RFC (Convtd Ship Strutter) Turnhouse W/E 20.4.18; HMS *Repulse* W/E 22.8.18; Rosyth 19.9.18; Donibristle W/E 7.11.18; Deleted W/E 28.11.18

A8317 (130-hp Clerget) (Convtd Ship Strutter) Brook Green by 2.18; EC&AD Grain W/E 23.2.18; ECD Grain by 1.4.18; Turnhouse from W/E 10.5.18; Donibristle W/E 16.5.18; Rosyth W/E 16.5.18; HMS *Furious* W/E 16.5.18; Donibristle W/E 23.5.18; HMS *Furious* W/E 23.5.18; Turnhouse W/E 11.7.18; Donibristle W/E 15.8.18; HMS *Furious* W/E 3.10.18; Rosyth W/E 17.10.18; Deleted W/E 31.10.18

**9 ROYAL AIRCRAFT FACTORY B.E.2E TRACTOR BIPLANES from batch A8626-A8725 built by The British & Colonial Aeroplane Co Ltd. (90hp RAF 1a)**

A8692 Allocated for transfer from RFC to Cranwell 1.6.17 (NTU); To 47 Sqdn Salonika instead

A8693 Allocated for transfer from RFC to Cranwell 1.6.17 (NTU); To 47 Sqdn Salonika instead

A8694 Ex RFC to D Flt Cranwell for erection 12.6.17; Freiston by 7.8.17 - @10.17; Cranwell by 10.17; AGS Freiston by 11.17 - @12.17; Cranwell, crashed and slightly damaged 18.12.17 (pilot unhurt); Cranwell to Freiston 15.2.18; Capsized taxying 23.2.18 (2 crew unhurt); Cranwell by 3.18; Became 201/2 TDS Cranwell 1.4.18; 211 TDS Portholme Meadow 1.5.18; FL en route Scopwick at Baston, dismantled 13.10.18 (F/Cdr CHB Jenner-Parson)

A8695 Ex RFC, Milton to D Flt Cranwell for erection 8.6.17 - 10.17; Freiston by 12.17; D Flt Cranwell by 2.18; Became 201/2 TDS Cranwell 1.4.18; 211 TDS Scopwick by 10.18 - @12.18

A8696 Ex RFC, Milton to D Flt Cranwell for erection 9.6.17; Crashed 2.10.17; Crashed, propeller and tail damaged, Cranwell South 20.12.17 (PFO Fearn slightly injured); Surveyed 3.1.18 wrecked; Deleted 17.1.18

A8697 Ex RFC, Milton to D Flt Cranwell for erection 9.6.17; AZP, landed RFC Waddington 19.10.17 (F/Cdr MA Simpson); Became 201/2 TDS Cranwell 1.4.18; Became 56/57 TDS Cranwell 27.7.18 - @13.9.18

A8698 Ex RFC, Milton to D Flt Cranwell for erection 8.6.17; Freiston by 7.17 - @10.17; D Flt Cranwell by 10.17; Surveyed 21.11.17; Deleted 5.12.17 wrecked

A8699 Ex RFC, Milton to D Flt Cranwell for erection 8.6.17; Broke u/c 14.8.17; Smashed up on ground in dense fog 30.1.18 (PFO FP Pemble) [or may have been B3710]; For deletion by 1.2.18

A8713 Ex RFC; Cranwell by 11.7.18 - @23.7.18 (prefix?)

**3 SOPWITH 1½ STRUTTER TRACTOR BIPLANES from batch A8744-A8793 built by Vickers Ltd.**

A8760 EAD Grain by 25.5.18
A8779 (140-hp Clerget) (Convtd Ship Strutter) At Chester W/E 5.9.18; Turnhouse W/E 19.9.18 - @30.1.19
A8781 (Clerget) Ex RFC (Convtd Ship Strutter) to Turnhouse W/E 20.4.18 - 26.9.18

**SPAD S.7C.1 TRACTOR BIPLANE SCOUTS from batch A8794-A8893 built by The Air Navigation Co Ltd. (180-hp Hispano)**

A8834 Ascot by 28.8.17 for EF; 1 AD by 19.10.17; 19 Sqdn RFC 25.10.17; 1 ASD to England 15.2.18; RFC Lympne to War School Manston 3.18; Became Scout School, Pool of Pilots Manston 1.4.18; Stalled and nose-dived 2.7.18 (Lt EPJ Hull killed)

**7 SPAD S.7C.1 TRACTOR BIPLANE SCOUTS from batch A9100-A9161 built by Mann, Egerton & Co Ltd. (Allocated from RFC less engines 13.3.18. Fitted 180-hp Hispano)**

A9114 Ex RFC 3.18; Tregantle & Withnoe store by 30.3.18
A9115 Ex RFC 3.18; Tregantle & Withnoe store by 30.3.18
A9116 Ex RFC 3.18; Tregantle & Withnoe store by 30.3.18
A9145 Ex RFC 3.18; Tregantle & Withnoe store by 30.3.18
A9146 Ex RFC 3.18; Tregantle & Withnoe store by 30.3.18
A9149 Ex RFC 3.18; Tregantle & Withnoe store by 30.3.18
A9153 Ex RFC 3.18; Tregantle & Withnoe store by 30.3.18

**AIRCO D.H.6 TRACTOR BIPLANES in batch A9563-A9762 built by The Grahame-White Aviation Co Ltd. (Deld without engines. Fitted 90-hp RAF unless otherwise stated)**

A9565 68 TDS Tadcaster by 1.18 - 3.18; Cullercoates by 7.18; D Flt Tees 1.8.18/509 Flt 252 Sqdn Seaton Carew by 8.18
A9569 (Curtis OX-5) 502/3 Flts 260 Sqdn Westward Ho! from 5.9.18
A9570 Cramlington by 16.4.18 (only mention)
A9571 76 Sqdn Copmanthorpe; 68 TS Tadcaster/Bramham by 1.18 - 3.18; Cramlington by 4.18; EF, FL off 'C' Buoy 7.4.18 (LM); 507 Flt Cramlington by 5.18
A9573 68 TS Bramham; 252 Sqdn Cramlington by 14.4.18 - @24.5.18; 252 Sqdn Redcar by 25.5.18; Towed into Redcar 17.6.18 (pilot believed safe)
A9575 Cramlington by 30.5.18
A9593 252 Sqdn Cramlington by 27.5.18
A9598 Deld Chingford for erection 3.7.17; Erected by 20.7.17; Damaged 9.8.17; Became 207 TDS Chingford 1.4.18; EF, stalled in, caught fire Chingford 19.5.18 (2/Lt WR Burdett killed)
A9599 Deld Chingford for erection 9.7.17; Erected by 20.7.17; Became 207 TDS Chingford 1.4.18; Hendon 24.7.18; Hounslow 25.7.18
A9600 Deld Eastchurch Observer School by rail 5.7.17; Hendon 20.7.17; Eastchurch OS 8.8.17; Chingford 9.8.17; For deletion by 6.4.18
A9601 Deld Eastchurch Observer School by rail 5.7.17 (no engine); Hendon 24.7.17; Eastchurch 8.8.17; Chingford 9.8.17; Surveyed 20.12.17 wreck; Deleted 28.12.17
A9602 Deld Cranwell 7.7.17; Chingford 29.7.17; Deleted W/E 26.1.18
A9603 Deld Cranwell 12.7.17; Chingford 7.8.17; Fairlop by 8.17 - 9.17; Chingford by 10.17; Became 207 TDS Chingford 1.4.18
A9612 Deld Chingford by lorry without engine for erection 12.7.17; Erected 20.7.17; Became 207 TDS Chingford 1.4.18; Eastbourne .18; 207 TDS Chingford 19.5.18; 98 Sqdn Old Sarum by .18
A9613 Deld Chingford by lorry without engine for erection 13.7.17; Erected 20.7.17; Became 207 TDS Chingford 1.4.18; Became G-EAMT
A9622 Deld Manston FS by road 20.7.17; Surveyed 28.11.17; Deleted 5.12.17 DBR
A9628 203 TDS Manston by 7.18
A9629 Deld Chingford 27.7.17; Surveyed 16.9.17; Deleted 21.9.17 DBR
A9633 SMOP Dover by 11.18
A9634 (90-hp RAF.1a to 2.18, then 100-hp RAF) Deld Chingford 30.7.17; Became 207 TDS Chingford 1.4.18
A9640 Deld Chingford 10.8.17; Awaiting erection by 16.8.17; Became 207 TDS 1.4.18

A9641 Deld Hendon for test 9.8.17; Chingford 11.8.17; Became 207 TDS Chingford 1.4.18
A9649 Deld Hendon for test 14.8.17; Chingford 15.8.17; For deletion by 23.2.18
A9650 Deld Chingford 15.8.17; Awaiting test by 16.8.17; Became 207 TDS Chingford 1.4.18
A9659 502/3 Flts 260 Sqdn Westward Ho! by 21.8.18 - @28.11.18
A9672 Deld 1 TDS Stamford 28.9.17; Hastings to Eastbourne 14.7.18
A9694 252 Sqdn Cramlington by 28.4.18; 252 Sqdn Redcar 30.5.18; EF, FL in sea, towed to beach 3m N of Whitby, salving 7.6.18 (pilot unhurt); Flown 17-22.7.18
A9696 252 Sqdn Cramlington by 1.5.18
A9697 252 Sqdn Redcar/West Ayton by 18.7.18 - @27.7.18

**4 REBUILDS from batch B701 to B900 by 1(S)ARD Farnborough**

B744 (Ship Strutter) (Clerget) Deld AES Martlesham Heath by 1.18; ECD Grain W/E 18.5.18; Donibristle W/E 12.8.18; Turnhouse W/E 19.9.18; Donibristle W/E 26.9.18; HMS *Furious* W/E 17.10.18; HMS *Glorious* W/E 3.12.18; Donibristle W/E 16.1.19 - @30.1.19
B812 (1½ Strutter) 78 Sqdn Sutton's Farm by 12.17; Turnhouse from W/E 20.4.18; Deleted W/E 3.10.18
B862 (1½ Strutter) 78 Sqdn Sutton's Farm by 11.17; Turnhouse from W/E 20.4.18; Deleted W/E 3.10.18
B895 (Camel) Rep Pk 1 ASD to 1 AI 29.7.18; 208 Sqdn 1.8.18; Wrecked, to 1 ASD 15.9.18; Rebuilt as H7236 5.11.18

**2 BRISTOL F.2B FIGHTER RECONNAISSANCE TRACTOR BIPLANES from batch B1101 to B1350 built by The British & Colonial Aeroplane Co Ltd**

B1206 (c/n 2374) Deld AES Martlesham Heath 27.1.18 (tested with 230-hp Siddeley Puma 2.18); left 3.4.18; Chingford to Hendon 12.4.18 - @9.6.18 (station aircraft)
B1290 (c/n 2458) (Falcon) Erecting EAD Grain by 25.5.18; Dover 18.6.18 (temp for Special Duty); Grain 20.6.18; Hendon 6.7.18; Grain 8.7.18; Hendon 10.7.18; Grain 12.7.18

**1 SPAD S.7C.1 TRACTOR BIPLANE SCOUT purchased by GHQ, BEF. (150-hp Hispano)**

B1622 Ex RFC Lympne 3.18; War School Manston W/E 9.3.18; Became Pool of Pilots (Scouts School) Manston 1.4.18

**10 SOPWITH PUP TRACTOR BIPLANE SCOUTS from batch B1701 to B1850 built by Standard Motor Co Ltd**

B1816 Deld Dover without engine 20.7.17; ADD 11.8.17; 11 Sqdn by 14.8.17; ADD 31.8.17; 12 Sqdn from/by 4.9.17, wrecked; ADD 19.9.17; Surveyed 22.9.17; Deleted 27.9.17 DBR
B1817 Deld Dover without engine 20.7.17; ADD 9.8.17; 11 Sqdn by 14.8.17; ADD 31.8.17; 12 Sqdn from/by 4.9.17 - @22.11.17; RNASTE Vendôme (by rail via Abbeville) W/E 29.11.17 - @30.3.18
B1818 Deld Dover without engine 20.7.17; ADD 11.8.17; 11 Sqdn by 16.8.17; ADD 31.8.17; 12 Sqdn from/by 4.9.17 - @22.11.17; RNASTE Vendôme (by rail via Abbeville) W/E 29.11.17 - @31.3.18
B1819 Deld Dover without engine 22.7.17; ADD 11.8.17; Seaplane Defence Sqdn 5.9.17; Dover 22.10.17; Hendon W/E 3.11.17; Cranwell W/E 10.11.17; Surveyed 21.11.17; Deleted 5.12.17 DBR
B1820 Deld Dover without engine 22.7.17; ADD 11.8.17; Seaplane Defence Sqdn 15.8.17; 12 Sqdn 16.11.17; RNASTE Vendôme W/E 6.12.17; Became 205 TDS Vendôme 1.4.18; Went on nose landing, slightly damaged 23.6.18 (F/Cdt RB Mumford unhurt); EF on TO, swerved, hit 8635 outside Bessonneau hangar, wrecked 29.7.18 (2/Lt JAVM Robert unhurt); still 205 TDS 11.18
B1821 Deld Dover without engine 22.7.17; ADD 16.8.17; Seaplane Defence Sqdn 5.9.17; Dover 27.10.17; Eastchurch W/E 10.1.18; Eastbourne NFS W/E 19.1.18;

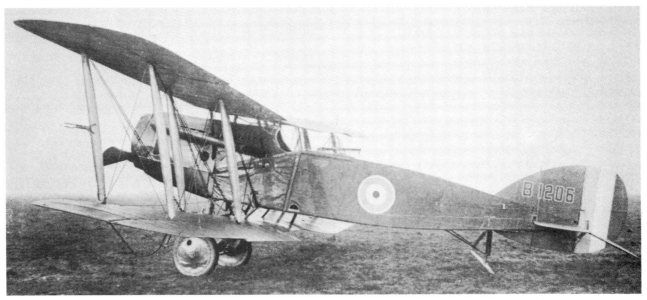

*Bristol Fighter F.2b B1206 was used as a station aircraft at Hendon in 1918. (via B.Robertson)*

*Spad S.7 B1622 was flown at Manston in the Spring of 1918. (via M Burrow)*

*Sopwith Pup B2218, which was flown late in 1918 by 506 (D.H.6) Flight at Owthorne, here carries a spitting cat representation on a white fin. (RAF Museum)*

B1822 Deld Dover without engine 25.7.17; Walmer Defence Flt 30.9.17; Dover 5.11.17; East Fortune NFS by 24.11.17 - @30.3.18; COL 9.12.17 (FSL AC Sharwood)

B1823 Deld Dover without engine 25.7.17; ADD 16.8.17; Walmer Defence Flt 29.9.17; East Fortune by 24.12.17; Deleted W/E 9.2.18

B1824 (80-hp Le Rhône) Deld Cranwell store 24.7.17; Surveyed 14.9.17; Deleted 8.10.17 wrecked

B1825 (80-hp Gnome) Deld Cranwell store 25.7.17; Became 201/2 TDS Cranwell 1.4.18; East Fortune W/E 6.4.18

**13 AIRCO D.H.4 TRACTOR BIPLANE BOMBERS from batch B2051 to B2150 built by F.W.Berwick & Co Ltd. (200-hp B.H.P)**

B2115 Lympne by 6.18; Eastbourne W/E 25.6.18

B2122 Deld CSD White City by 1.2.18; Shipped to Otranto 28.2.18; 224 Sqdn Otranto by 11.5.18; Swung landing after raid on Cattaro seaplane base, hit hangar, damaged 2/Lt RB Picken's machine 23.8.18 (2/Lt SJ Chamberlain & Lt J Ellingham unhurt)

B2125 Deld CSD White City by 1.2.18; Cardiff Docks by 23.2.18; Shipped to 6 Wing Otranto 1.3.18; 224 Sqdn Otranto by 28.4.18 - @1.5.18

B2128 Deld CSD White City by 1.2.18; Cardiff Docks by 23.2.18; Shipped to 6 Wing Otranto 1.3.18; 224 Sqdn Otranto by 7.4.18 - @1.5.18

B2131 Deld CSD White City by 23.2.18; Shipped to 6 Wing Otranto 28.3.18; 224 Sqdn Otranto by 11.5.18 - @6.18; 226 Sqdn by 15.6.18; 224 Sqdn by 1.7.18 - @17.8.18; AD Taranto by 6.19; 'X' AD 28.6.19; WOC at ASD 25.8.19

B2134 Deld CSD White City by 1.2.18; Shipped to 6 Wing Otranto 9.3.18; 224 Sqdn Otranto by 7.4.18 - @1.5.18

B2137 Deld CSD White City 2.18; Shipped to Otranto 28.3.18; 224 Sqdn Otranto by 11.5.18 - @17.8.18

B2142 Deld CSD White City 3.18; Shipped to Otranto 28.3.18; 224 Sqdn Otranto by 11.5.18 - @15.6.18; Deleted by 13.7.18

B2143 Deld CSD White City by 30.3.18; Shipped to Otranto 10.4.18; AR&ED Pizzone .18; AD Adriatic Group by 8.18; 224 Sqdn Taranto by 27.9.18 - @31.1.19

B2146 Deld CSD White City by 7.3.18; Shipped to Otranto 25.3.18; AD Adriatic Group by 8.18; 224 Sqdn Taranto by 25.9.18 - @4.10.18; Mudros by 12.18

B2147 Deld CSD White City by 7.3.18; Shipped to Otranto 25.3.18; AR&ED Pizzone .18; AD Taranto by 13.6.18; Deld Valona 5.9.18; 224 Sqdn 5.9.18 - @31.1.19; AD Taranto by 6.19; 'X' AD 28.6.19; WOC at ASD 25.8.19

B2148 Deld CSD White City by 7.3.18; Shipped to Otranto 21.4.18; AR&ED Pizzone .18; AD Adriatic Group by 8.18; 226 Sqdn by 2.10.18; Mudros by 10.18 - @1.19

B2149 Deld CSD White City by 7.3.18; Shipped to Otranto 9.4.18; 224 Sqdn Otranto by 11.5.18 - @15.6.18

**14 SOPWITH PUP TRACTOR BIPLANE SCOUTS from batch B2151 to B2250 built by Whitehead Aircraft Ltd**

B2173 (80-hp Le Rhône) Deld Cranwell for erection 10.9.17; Crashed and badly damaged Cranwell South 10.3.18 (pilot unhurt); Became 201/2 TDS Cranwell 1.4.18

B2181 (80-hp Le Rhône) Deld Cranwell 18.9.17; Collided with B2208 and slightly damaged 16.2.18 (pilot unhurt); Became 201/2 TDS Cranwell 1.4.18

B2183 (80-hp Le Rhône) Deld Cranwell 18.9.17; Became 201/2 TDS Cranwell 1.4.18 - @5.18

B2202 (80-hp Gnome) Deld Cranwell without engine W/E 5.9.17; Became 201/2 TDS Cranwell 1.4.18; 211 TDS Portholme Meadow by 6.18

B2203 (80-hp Gnome) Deld Cranwell without engine W/E 5.9.17; Crashed and damaged propeller and u/c 11.1.18 (pilot unhurt); Crashed and damaged axle, Cranwell South 26.3.18 (pilot unhurt); Became 201/2 TDS Cranwell 1.4.18; Crashed and damaged 4.4.18 (pilot unhurt); Castle Bromwich 2.6.18

B2204 (80-hp Gnome) Deld Cranwell without engine 11.9.17; EF, FL, undamaged, Ballisford 13.3.18 (pilot unhurt); Became 201/2 TDS Cranwell 1.4.18

B2205 Deld Cranwell without engine W/E 5.9.17; Surveyed

B2208 (80-hp Gnome) Deld G (Exptl) Flt Cranwell by road W/E 5.9.17; Collided with B2181 and CW 16.2.18 (pilot unhurt); Surveyed 25.2.18; Deleted 13.3.18

B2211 (80-hp Gnome) Deld Cranwell for erection 11.9.17; Crashed on aerodrome and badly damaged 1.3.18 (pilot unhurt); Became 201/2 TDS Cranwell 1.4.18; East Fortune W/E 6.4.18; Grand Fleet SoAF&G Leuchars by 7.19 - @8.19

B2212 (80-hp Le Rhône) Deld Manston War Flt W/E 15.9.17; EC&AD Grain W/E 23.2.18 (expts); Eastbourne 23.3.18 (remained, engine trouble); EC&AD Grain 25.3.18 - @7.9.18 (expts)

B2213 (80-hp Le Rhône) Manston War Flt W/E 15.9.17; Eastbourne 25.4.18; Upper Heyford 1.8.18

B2217 (80-hp Le Rhône) Deld Killingholme store 15.9.17; ECD Grain 16.12.17 (Expts); Rosyth 23.3.18 (via Cranwell and Lincoln); retd ECD Grain (via Cranwell) 3.4.18; Northolt by 5.18; Hendon 14.5.18; Salisbury 18.5.18; Stonehenge to Grain (via Hendon) 19.5.18; Hendon 4.6.18; Grain 5.6.18; Hendon by 4.7.18; Grain by/to 2.20 (W/Cdr HR Busteed's aircraft)

B2218 506 Flt 251 Sqdn Owthorne by 10.18 - @6.11.18 (white fin with spitting cat)

B2226 (80-hp Le Rhône) Deld Cranwell for erection 11.9.17; Became 201/2 TDS Cranwell 1.4.18

**11 SOPWITH CAMELS from batch B2301-B2550 built by Ruston Proctor & Co Ltd. (130-hp Clerget 9B unless otherwise stated)**

B2488 4 Sqdn AFC to 2 AI; 205 TDS Vendôme 30.6.18; Caught by gust, badly damaged 19.7.18 (Lt JF Meek unhurt); 84 ARS 11.18

B2537 Deld NAP Lincoln 11.17; Cranwell W/E 30.11.17; EF, crashed and slightly damaged Guyhirne 14.3.18 (pilot unhurt); Became 201 TDS Cranwell 1.4.18; Became 56 TDS Cranwell 27.7.18 - @12.18

B2538 Deld NAP Lincoln 11.17; AES Orfordness 28.11.17 - @30.3.18 (gun sight tests)

B2539 Deld NAP Lincoln by 12.17; G Flt Cranwell W/E 14.12.17; Crashed and slightly damaged on aerodrome 27.2.18 (pilot unhurt); Became 201/2 TDS Cranwell 1.4.18

B2540 Deld NAP Lincoln by 12.17; G Flt Cranwell W/E 14.12.17; O/t and slightly damaged, Cranwell South [date?] (pilot unhurt); Became 201/2 TDS Cranwell 1.4.18; Became 56 TDS Cranwell 27.7.18 - @11.18

B2541 Deld NAP Lincoln 11.17; Cranwell W/E 7.2.18; To workshops 7.2.18 to fit 150-hp Gnome Monosoupape; Hendon 10.3.18 (flown by W/Cdr the Master of Sempill); Hendon to Yeovil 23.3.18 (but returned Hendon; AAP Hendon by 30.3.18 (allocated Cranwell); AES Martlesham Heath 12.4.18 (Engine expts); Orfordness 26.4.18

B2542 Deld NAP Lincoln 11.17; Cranwell W/E 7.12.17; Fitted 150-hp Gnome Monosoupape; Became 201/2 TDS Cranwell 1.4.18; Became 56/57 TDS Cranwell 27.7.18 - @24.3.19

B2543 Shipped to 2 Wing Mudros 4.1.18; Erecting Mudros by 3.18 - @4.18; Marsh by 20.3.18; Imbros by 6.18; D Sqdn Stavros; Marsh by 10.18; To Greek Government; Greek Air Force by 1.19

B2544 Shipped to 2 Wing Mudros 4.1.18; Erecting Mudros by 3.18; Marsh by 13.3.18; Surveyed 14.3.18; Deleted 15.4.18 wrecked

B2545 Cardiff Docks by 1.1.18; Shipped to 2 Wing Mudros 12.1.18; Erecting Mudros by 3.18 - @4.18; Imbros by 6.18; Repair Base Mudros by 10.18 - @1.19

B2546 Cardiff Docks by 1.1.18; Shipped to 2 Wing Mudros 28.1.18; Erecting Mudros by 3.18 - @4.18; Stavros by 6.18

**11 SOPWITH 1½ STRUTTER (9400 TYPE) TRACTOR BIPLANES from batch B2551 to built by Ruston Proctor & Co Ltd**

B2551 Ex RFC Islington less engine to Gunnery School Flts Eastchurch 24.10.17 (100-hp Gnome Monosoupape); Fleet Observers School Leysdown by 8.18 - @2.19

B2552 Turnhouse W/E 20.4.18; Deleted W/E 3.10.18

B2562    Deld South Shotwick W/E 12.9.18; Grain W/E 21.9.18 - @30.1.19 (mods)

B2566    (Convtd Ship Strutter) Hendon by 3.18; Grain 17.3.18; Turnhouse W/E 15.8.18; Donibristle W/E 17.10.18; Rosyth W/E 24.10.18; HMS *Campania* W/E 31.10.18; Deleted W/E 25.11.18

B2578    2(N)ARD Coal Aston from W/E 18.7.18; Turnhouse W/E 1.8.18; Deleted W/E 24.10.18

B2582    222 Sqdn Mudros by 2.11.18

B2583    45 Sqdn by 6.17 - @7.17; Turnhouse from W/E 20.4.18; Deleted W/E 3.10.18

B2591    Maidstone to Eastbourne 10.8.18

B2593    78 Sqdn by 9.17; Eastbourne

B2597    Deld South Shotwick W/E 12.9.18; Grain 21.9.18 - @1.19 (mods); Grand Fleet SoAF&G Leuchars by 6.19

B2600    Deld South Shotwick W/E 12.9.18; Grain 27.9.18 - @1.19 (mods)

**225 AIRCO D.H.6 TRACTOR BIPLANES from batch B2601-B3100 built by Airco. (90-hp RAF 1A unless otherwise stated)**

B2612    (100-hp RAF) Deld Hendon for erection 15.9.17; Chingford 19.9.17; Became 207 TDS Chingford 1.4.18; Hendon 24.7.18; Hounslow 25.7.18

B2613    (100-hp RAF) Deld Hendon to Chingford 23.9.17; Became 207 TDS Chingford 1.4.18

B2614    Deld Chingford 21.9.17; Became 207 TDS Chingford 1.4.18

B2615    Deld Hendon to Chingford 22.9.17 (at Fairlop 3.18); Became 207 TDS Chingford/Fairlop 1.4.18

B2616    Deld Hendon to Chingford 23.9.17; Became 207 TDS Chingford 1.4.18

B2622    Deld Redcar School by rail 3.10.17; School closed 1.4.18

B2623    (80-hp Renault) Deld Hendon W/E 29.9.17; Eastbourne NFS W/E 13.10.17; Became 206 TDS Eastbourne 1.4.18; Manston 2.5.18

B2624    (80-hp Renault) Deld Eastbourne NFS W/E 13.10.17 - @30.3.18

B2625    Deld Hendon to Chingford W/E 13.10.17; Became 207 TDS Chingford 1.4.18

B2626    Deld CSD White City by 10.17; Hendon W/E 13.10.17; Chingford 13.10.17; Became 207 TDS Chingford 1.4.18; Hendon 17.7.18

B2637    Deld Chingford W/E 13.10.17; Became 207 TDS Chingford 1.4.18; SMOP Dover by 2.19

B2638    Deld Chingford W/E 13.10.17; Became 207 TDS Chingford 1.4.18

B2639    (80-hp Renault to 12.17; 90-hp RAF from 2.18) Deld Chingford W/E 13.10.17; Became 207 TDS Chingford 1.4.18

B2640    Deld Chingford W/E 13.10.17; Became 207 TDS Chingford 1.4.18

B2641    Deld Chingford W/E 13.10.17; Became 207 TDS Chingford 1.4.18

B2645    26 TS Narborough by 3.18; SMOP Dover by 12.18 - @2.19

B2647    Deld Chingford W/E 25.10.17; Became 207 TDS Chingford 1.4.18

B2648    Deld Chingford W/E 25.10.17; Became 207 TDS Chingford 1.4.18; Hendon 17.7.18

B2649    Deld Chingford W/E 25.10.17; Deleted W/E 1.2.18

B2650    Deld Chingford 25.10.17; Became 207 TDS Chingford 1.4.18

B2651    Deld Chingford W/E 25.10.17; Became 207 TDS Chingford 1.4.18

B2657    Deld Chingford W/E 27.10.17; Became 207 TDS Chingford 1.4.18; Deleted W/E 6.4.18

B2658    Shipped to 2 Wing Mudros without engine 14.11.17; Mudros Base without engine by 1.1.18; Erecting Mudros for Greek training by 3.18; Mudros Repair Base by 6.18 - @1.19

B2659    Shipped to 2 Wing Mudros without engine 22.11.17; Mudros Base without engine by 1.1.18; Erecting Mudros by 3.18; F Sqdn by 6.18; Stavros by 17.8.18; Marsh by 10.18 - @1.19

B2660    Shipped to 2 Wing Mudros without engine 14.11.17; Mudros Base without engine by 1.1.18; Erecting Mudros by 3.18 - @4.18; Mudros Repair Base by 6.18 - @1.19

B2661    Deld CSD White City 11.17; Shipped to 2 Wing Mudros without engine 14.11.17; Mudros Base without engine

by 1.1.18; Erecting Mudros by 3.18 - @4.18; F Sqdn Mudros by 6.18 - @1.19; To Greek Government

B2678    Deld Hendon W/E 10.11.17; Cranwell W/E 16.11.17; Became 201/2 TDS Cranwell 1.4.18 - @19.7.18; Chingford, Crashed & WO 1918

B2679    Deld Hendon W/E 10.11.17; Cranwell W/E 23.11.17; Became 201/2 TDS Cranwell 1.4.18

B2680    Deld Hendon W/E 10.11.17; Chingford W/E 17.11.17; Became 207 TDS 1.4.18

B2681    Deld Hendon W/E 10.11.17; Chingford W/E 24.11.17; Became 207 TDS Chingford 1.4.18

B2682    Deld Hendon W/E 10.11.17; Chingford W/E 24.11.17; Became 207 TDS Chingford 1.4.18

B2683    52 TS Cramlington by 3.18; SD Flt 252 Sqdn Cramlington by 24.5.18; FL 29.6.18; SD Flt 252 Sqdn Redcar by 2.7.18; EF, FL in sea 2.7.18

B2686    Chingford by 1.18; Cramlington by 16.4.18; FL Harley Barracks 26.4.18; Became 252 Sqdn Cramlington by 24.5.18; 252 Sqdn Redcar 30.5.18

B2687    Deld Hendon W/E 10.11.17; Chingford 5.12.17; Became 207 TDS Chingford 1.4.18

B2688    Deld Hendon W/E 10.11.17; Chingford W/E 24.11.17; Surveyed 15.1.18; Deleted 19.1.18 wreck

B2689    Deld Hendon W/E 10.11.17; Chingford W/E 24.11.17; Became 207 TDS Chingford 1.4.18; Became G-EAMS

B2690    Deld Hendon W/E 10.11.17; Chingford W/E 24.11.17; Became 207 TDS Chingford 1.4.18

B2691    Deld Hendon W/E 17.11.17; Chingford W/E 24.11.17; Deleted W/E 16.2.18

B2697    Deld Hendon W/E 17.11.17; Chingford W/E 1.12.17; Became 207 TDS Chingford 1.4.18

B2698    Deld Redcar School by road W/E 17.11.17; Deleted W/E 16.2.18

B2699    Deld Redcar School by road W/E 22.11.17; Crashed, CW 9.12.17 (F/L HLE Tyndale-Biscoe injured); Deleted W/E 22.12.17

B2700    Deld Redcar School by road W/E 24.11.17; 52 TS Catterick 25.4.18 - @6.18

B2701    (100-hp RAF) Deld Redcar School by road W/E 24.11.17; 52 TS Catterick 25.4.18; 49 TDS Catterick 15.7.18 - @9.18

B2708    Deld Redcar School by road W/E 24.11.17; Closed 1.4.18

B2709    Deld Redcar School by road W/E 1.12.17; For deletion by 16.2.18 - @23.3.18; Closed 1.4.18; Presumably rebuilt; 252 Sqdn Redcar by 7.18 - @8.18; 507/8 Flts 252 Sqdn Tynemouth by 1.8.18

B2710    Deld Redcar School by road W/E 1.12.17; Closed 1.4.18; SD Flt 252 Sqdn Cramlington by 6.6.18

B2711    Deld Redcar School by road W/E 24.11.17; Closed 1.4.18; SD Flt 252 Sqdn Cramlington 27.4.18; 507/8 Flt Tynemouth .18 (unit move?)

B2717    Deld Redcar School by road W/E 1.12.17; Closed 1.4.18; SD Flt 252 Sqdn Cramlington 27.4.18

B2718    Deld Redcar School by road W/E 1.12.17; Closed 1.4.18

B2719    Deld Redcar School by road W/E 17.12.17; Closed 1.4.18; SD Flt 252 Sqdn Cramlington 27.4.18; MAD South Shields by 5.18; 507/8 Flts 252 Sqdn Cramlington 31.5.18; 507/8 Flts 252 Sqdn Tynemouth 8.6.18; MAD South Shields 18.9.18

B2720    Deld Redcar School by road W/E 17.12.17; Closed 1.4.18; SD Flt 252 Sqdn Cramlington 27.4.18; 507 Flt 252 Sqdn Tynemouth 8.6.18; EF, FL in sea off Coquet 24.8.18 (pilot saved by trawler)

B2721    Deld Redcar School by road W/E 17.12.17; Closed 1.4.18

B2725    Deld Redcar School by road W/E 17.12.17; Closed 1.4.18; SD Flt Cramlington 27.4.18

B2726    Deld Redcar School W/E 17.12.17; Closed 1.4.18

B2727    Deld Redcar School by 29.12.17; Crashed 31.12.17 (PFO FM Anderson killed); Deleted W/E 16.1.18

B2728    Deld Redcar School W/E 17.12.17; Closed 1.4.18; to Catterick but engine trouble, FL Thornaby 25.4.18

B2729    Deld Redcar School W/E 17.12.17; Closed 1.4.18; Cramlington 27.4.18

B2735    (100-hp Renault) Deld Redcar School for erection W/E 24.12.17; Closed 1.4.18

B2736    (re-engined 80-hp Renault) Deld Hendon for erection W/E 1.12.17; Eastbourne NFS 25.1.18; Became 206 TDS Eastbourne 1.4.18

B2737    (80-hp Renault) Deld Hendon for erection W/E 1.12.17; Eastbourne NFS 1.12.17; Became 206 TDS Eastbourne 1.4.18; Chingford 17.5.18

B2738    Deld Hendon W/E 1.12.17; In air, collided with 1½ Strutter A6910 on ground, badly damaged 21.1.18 (pilot unhurt); Eastbourne NFS 8.3.18; Landed on 504A D1604, slightly damaged 21.3.18 (pilot unhurt); Became 206 TDS Eastbourne 1.4.18

B2739    (80-hp Renault) Deld Hendon W/E 1.12.17; Eastbourne NFS 8.1.18; Became 206 TDS Eastbourne 1.4.18

B2740    Deld Hendon W/E 1.12.17; Chingford 19.12.17; Became 207 TDS Chingford 1.4.18; Hendon 24.7.18; Hounslow 25.7.18

B2741    (Re-engined 80-hp Renault) Deld Hendon W/E 8.12.17; Eastbourne NFS 17.12.17; Became 206 TDS Eastbourne 1.4.18

B2745    (Re-engined 80-hp Renault) Deld Hendon W/E 8.12.17; Eastbourne NFS 28.1.18; Became 206 TDS Eastbourne 1.4.18; 6 TDS Boscombe Down

B2746    (Re-engined 80-hp Renault) Deld Hendon W/E 8.12.17; Eastbourne NFS 3.1.18; Became 206 TDS Eastbourne 1.4.18; to Lympne but FL and crashed 8.6.18 (pilot unhurt); 6 TDS Boscombe Down

B2750    Deld Hendon W/E 12.12.17; Eastbourne NFS 21.1.18; Crashed & CW 11.3.18 (pilot unhurt); Surveyed 13.3.18; Deleted 16.3.18

B2751    Deld Hendon W/E 12.12.17; Eastbourne NFS 27.12.17; Became 206 TDS Eastbourne 1.4.18; Manston 25.4.18

B2755    Deld Hendon W/E 15.12.17; Eastbourne 23.12.17; Deleted W/E 23.3.18

B2756    (Re-engined 80-hp Renault) Deld Hendon W/E 15.12.17; Eastbourne NFS 22.12.17; Became 206 TDS Eastbourne 1.4.18

B2760    (Re-engined 80-hp Renault) Deld Hendon W/E 15.12.17; Eastbourne NFS 24.1.18; Became 206 TDS Eastbourne 1.4.18; 50 TDS Eastbourne 15.7.18; WO 23.7.18

B2761    Deld Hendon W/E 22.12.17; Eastbourne NFS W/E 23.3.18; Became 206 TDS Eastbourne 1.4.18; Chingford 17.5.18

B2767    (Re-engined 80-hp Renault) Deld Hendon W/E 22.12.17; Eastbourne NFS 4.1.18; Crashed East Grinstead 21.2.18 (pilot unhurt); Became 206 TDS Eastbourne 1.4.18

B2768    Deld Hendon W/E 22.12.17; Eastbourne NFS 31.12.17; EF, FL Pevensey 21.1.18; 203 TDS Manston 2.5.18 - @7.18

B2771    519/520 Flts 255 Sqdn Pembroke by 21.10.18

B2772    (Re-engined 80-hp Renault) Deld Hendon W/E 22.12.17; Eastbourne NFS (via Bexhill) 24.1.18; Became 206 TDS Eastbourne 1.4.18; 207 TDS Chingford 17.5.18

B2773    Deld Hendon W/E 22.12.17; Eastbourne NFS 3.1.18; Crashed into Avro B3268 and slightly damaged 4.1.18; Became 206 TDS Eastbourne 1.4.18; 203 TDS Manston 2.5.18 - @6.18

B2777    Deld Hendon W/E 29.12.17; Eastbourne NFS 21.1.18; Became 206 TDS Eastbourne 1.4.18

B2778    Deld Cranwell by road by 19.1.18 (at Freiston 15.2.18 - @30.3.18); 201/2 TDS Cranwell by 5.18 - @7.18

B2781    519/520 Flts 255 Sqdn Pembroke by 9.18

B2782    Deld Cranwell by road by 19.1.18; Became 202 TDS Cranwell 1.4.18; Stalled, nosedived, BO 10.7.18 (F/Cdt HA Nord killed)

B2783    Deld Cranwell by road by 19.1.18; Became 202 TDS Cranwell 1.4.18; Became 57 TDS Cranwell 27.7.18; Collided with E2929 19.8.18

B2784    MAD South Shields by 9.18; 505 Flt 251 Sqdn West Ayton 5.9.18; Crashed nr Ravenscar Station 11.9.18

B2786    519/520 Flts 255 Sqdn Pembroke by 9.18

B2787    Deld Cranwell by road W/E 18.1.18; Became 201/2 TDS Cranwell 1.4.18; 58 TDS Cranwell 7.18; Collided with 504 2929 19.8.18 (Lt NCS Campbell & F/Cdt CE Wiltshire both killed)

B2788    Deld Redcar School by road 30.3.18; School closed 1.4.18

B2789    519/520 Flts 255 Sqdn Pembroke by 24.8.18; With F3351, dropped 1 bomb on U-boat, failed to explode 12.30 24.8.18 (Lt R Nicholson); still Pembroke 20.10.18

B2791    521/2 Flts 244 Sqdn Bangor by 15.8.18 - 9.18

B2792    Deld Hendon W/E 12.1.18; Chingford 26.1.18; Became 207 TDS Chingford 1.4.18; 211 TDS Portholme Meadow by 6.18 - @10.18

B2793    Deld Hendon W/E 19.1.18; Chingford 26.1.18; Became 207 TDS Chingford 1.4.18; 211 TDS Portholme Meadow by 5.18 - @9.18; Crashed and damaged propeller, u/c and 2 mainplanes 12.6.18 (F/Cdr CHB Jenner Parson)

B2800    Deld 2 AAP Hendon by 27.4.18 (for A/S work); 251 Sqdn Atwick W/E 25.5.18 - @8.18

B2805    272 Sqdn Luce Bay by 10.18

B2808    SD Flt 252 Sqdn Cramlington by 2.4.18; FL in Sunderland Harbour 3.4.18; Disposed of by RNAS Cramlington W/E 25.5.18; 52 TS Cramlington by 8.18

B2809    SD Flt 252 Sqdn Cramlington by 3.4.18 - @4.6.18; 507/8 Flts Tynemouth by 5.18; EF, FL Blyth 10.6.18

B2818    SD Flt 250 Sqdn Padstow by 9.8.18

B2819    528 Flt 256 Sqdn Sea Houses by 10.18

B2840    Hendon by 15.5.18 (visited RAE); RAE Farnborough 29.8.18 (test modified wings)

B2842    Seaton Carew by 7.18; MAD South Shields by 8.18; A Flt/527 Flt 256 Sqdn Sea Houses 8.8.18 - @9.8.18

B2843    MAD South Shields to 507 Flt 252 Sqdn Tynemouth 1.8.18 - @21.8.18; 508 Flt Tynemouth, EF, FL in sea off Sunderland 24.8.18

B2844    MAD South Shields to A Flt 256 Sqdn Sea Houses 9.8.18; New Haggerston 9.8.18

B2845    MAD South Shields to A Flt/527 Flt 256 Sqdn Sea Houses by 7.18; New Haggerston 9.8.18; 527 Flt Sea Houses by 24.8.18

B2846    MAD South Shields to C Flt Sea Houses 8.8.18; New Haggerston 9.8.18; Sea Houses, Crashed, CW by strong gale on turn 14.8.18 (pilot unhurt)

B2847    500/1 Flts 250 Sqdn Padstow by 8.18 - @13.11.18

B2848    500/1 Flts 250 Sqdn Padstow by 24.9.18 - @1.11.18

B2851    500/1 Flts 250 Sqdn Padstow by 8.18 - @9.18

B2852    500/1 Flts 250 Sqdn Padstow by 13.11.18

B2853    MAD South Shields to 527 Flt 256 Sqdn Sea Houses 29.8.18 - @18.11.18; COL 26.9.18 (pilot unhurt)

B2856    MAD South Shields to Tyne 3.9.18; 510 Flt Redcar, FL, u/c & bottom wing damaged Whitby 10.9.18 (pilot unhurt); 517 Flt Sea Houses by 12.9.18

B2857    500/1 Flts Sqdn Padstow by 5.18 - @18.10.18

B2861    Dundee; Became G-EANJ

B2862    Dundee

B2871    SD Flt Cramlington by 4.18; FL in sea 3.4.18

B2883    MAD South Shields to 527 Flt 256 Sqdn Sea Houses 7.9.18 - @12.11.18

B2889    500/1 Flts 250 Sqdn Padstow by 27.10.18

B2891    MAD South Shields to 528 Flt 256 Sqdn Sea Houses 7.9.18 - @18.11.18

B2894    MAD South Shields to 527/8 Flts 256 Sqdn Sea Houses 13.9.18

B2895    MAD South Shields to 527 Flt 256 Sqdn Sea Houses 7.9.18 - @13.11.10

B2896    500/1 Flts 250 Sqdn Padstow by 7.18 - @7.11.18

B2897    500/1 Flts 250 Sqdn Padstow by 29.9.18 - @13.11.18

B2903    Redcar to MAD South Shields 20.9.18; Grain (flotation gear expts); 519/520 Flts 255 Sqdn Pembroke; 517/8 Flts 254 Sqdn Prawle Point by 24.10.18

B2905    517/8 Flts 254 Sqdn Prawle Point by 4.10.18 - @27.10.18

B2909    507/8 Flts 252 Sqdn Tynemouth .18

B2912    South Shields by 9.18; 528 Flt 256 Sqdn Sea Houses 4.9.18 - @14.11.18

B2913    South Shields by 9.18; 528 Flt 256 Sqdn Sea Houses 4.9.18 - @3.11.18

B2916    MAD South Shields by 9.18; 528 Flt 256 Sqdn Sea Houses 13.9.18; FL and wrecked nr New Haggerston aerodrome 1.10.18 (crew unhurt)

B2919    528 Flt 256 Sqdn Sea Houses by .18

B2929    Grain (flotation gear expts)

B2933    MAD South Shields by 9.18; 510 Flt 252 Sqdn Redcar 16.9.18 - @5.10.18; 510 Flt 252 Sqdn West Ayton by 11.10.18; EF, FL off Whitby, salved 13.10.18; still on strength 12.11.18

B2937    521/2 Flt 244 Sqdn Bangor by 14.11.18

B2944    Ex RFC to Tregantle & Withnoe store W/E 30.3.18

B2945    Ex RFC to Tregantle & Withnoe store W/E 30.3.18

B2946    Ex RFC to Tregantle & Withnoe store W/E 30.3.18

B2947    Ex RFC to Tregantle & Withnoe store W/E 30.3.18

B2948    Ex RFC to Tregantle & Withnoe store W/E 30.3.18

B2949    Ex RFC to Tregantle & Withnoe store W/E 30.3.18

B2960    531/3 Flts 272 Sqdn Machrihanish by 19.10.18; FL in

B2961 field 22.10.18; 523/4 Flts 258 Sqdn Luce Bay by 10.18
531/3 Flts 272 Sqdn Machrihanish by 17.10.18 - @6.11.18

B2962 531/3 Flts 272 Sqdn Machrihanish by 10.18 - @11.11.18

B2963 RAE Farnborough by 17.6.18 (modified wings); Hendon 3.7.18; RAE Farnborough 29.8.18

B2964 500/1 Flts 250 Sqdn Padstow by 4.10.18; 531/3 Flts 272 Sqdn Machrihanish by 23.10.18; EF, FL in sea 27.10.18 (pilot rescued by drifter)

B2965 500/1 Flts 250 Sqdn Padstow, collided with B7611 on landing and slightly damaged 18.9.18 (pilot unhurt); 524/529 Flts 258 Sqdn Luce Bay by 21.10.18 - @23.10.18

B2966 500/1 Flts 250 Sqdn Padstow, COL 16.7.18; 524/529 Flts 258 Sqdn Luce Bay by 4.10.18 - @28.10.18

B2967 524/529 Flts 258 Sqdn Luce Bay by 17.10.18 - @6.11.18

B2968 517/8 Flts 254 Sqdn Prawle Point by 14.8.18; FL Portleworth 29.10.18

B2969 517/8 Flts 254 Sqdn Prawle Point by 26.8.18 - @29.10.18

B2970 21 TDS Driffield by 6.18; 524/529 Flt 258 Sqdn Luce Bay by 16.10.18 - @6.11.18

B2971 521/2 Flts 244 Sqdn Bangor, EF, FL and crashed, towed to base 7.9.18 (pilot unhurt)

B2972 524/529 Flts 258 Sqdn Luce Bay by 3.11.18 - @6.11.18

B2973 521/2 Flts 244 Sqdn Bangor by 10.18 - @12.18

B2976 521/2 Flts 244 Sqdn Bangor by 9.18 - @4.10.18

B2977 521/2 Flts 244 Sqdn Bangor by 31.8.18 - @14.11.18

B2978 521/2 Flts 244 Sqdn Bangor by 29.10.18 - @1.11.18

B2979 521/2 Flts 244 Sqdn Bangor by 1.11.18 - @18.12.18

B2982 521/2 Flts 244 Sqdn Bangor by 6.11.18 - @18.11.18

B2983 528 Flt 256 Sqdn Sea Houses by .18; 521/2 Flts 244 Sqdn Bangor by 23.11.18 - @8.12.18

B2995 528 Flt 256 Sqdn Sea Houses by .18

B3003 MAD South Shields to Redcar 26.9.18; 510 Flt 252 Sqdn West Ayton by 13.10.18 - @13.11.18; Became G-EARL

B3005 510 Flt 252 Sqdn West Ayton by 6.11.18 - @7.11.18

B3010 2 WS Penshurst by 5.18; 521/2 Flt 244 Sqdn Bangor by .18

B3011 507 (?) Flt Yarmouth by .18

B3018 76 Sqdn Catterick by 7.18; D Flt/509 Flt 252 Sqdn Seaton Carew 1.8.18 - 11.18; Crashed and damaged on TO 17.8.18 (pilot unhurt)

B3019 509 Flt 252 Sqdn Seaton Carew by 11.9.18 - @11.11.18

B3020 521/2 Flts 244 Sqdn Bangor by 14.8.18 - @8.12.18

B3021 B Flt 244 Sqdn Bangor by 8.8.18; EF, crashed on patrol 14.8.18 (Lt JR Johnstone killed)

B3023 B Flt 244 Sqdn Bangor by 9.8.18; Became 522 Flt 244 Sqdn Bangor 15.8.18; Crashed on rigging test 26.8.18 (Lt AC Bencher & AM Nicholls); Stalled on turn, spun in 18.9.18 (Capt DA Tuck slightly injured & 3AM EW Shaw killed)

B3025 521/2 Flts 244 Sqdn Bangor by 29.10.18 - @8.12.18

B3026 MAD South Shields by 10.18; 507/8 Flt 252 Sqdn Tynemouth 21.10.18; FL off Blythe and sank 4.11.18

B3028 MAD South Shields to 507/8 Flts 252 Sqdn Tynemouth 29.9.18

B3029 MAD South Shields to 507/8 Flts 252 Sqdn Tynemouth 18.9.18; EF, FL in sea, salved 29.9.18 (pilot safe)

B3030 MAD South Shields to 507/8 Flts 252 Sqdn Tynemouth 18.9.18 - @11.18

B3031 MAD South Shields to 507/8 Flts 252 Sqdn Tynemouth 23.9.18 - @11.18

B3032 Tynemouth by 10.8.18 (third digit of serial uncertain); MAD South Shields to Sea Houses 2.10.18; 504 Flt 251 Sqdn Atwick by 10.18

B3033 MAD South Shields to Sea Houses 2.10.18 - @11.10.18; 526 Flt 256 Sqdn New Haggerston by 31.10.18 - @14.11.18

B3034 528 Flt 256 Sqdn Sea Houses by 13.10.18 - @18.11.18

B3035 526 Flt 256 Sqdn New Haggerston by 13.10.18 - @12.11.18

B3036 509 Flt 252 Sqdn Seaton Carew by 10.18

B3037 MAD South Shields to 509 Flt 252 Sqdn Seaton Carew 21.9.18 - @11.11.18

B3038 519/520 Flts 255 Sqdn Pembroke by 28.9.18 - @5.11.18

B3039 519/520 Flts 255 Sqdn Pembroke by 30.9.18 - @5.11.18

B3040 MAD South Shields to C Flt (528 Flt) Sea Houses 4.8.18

B3051 46 TS Catterick; 504 Flt 251 Sqdn Atwick by 11.18

B3054 46 TS Catterick by 29.5.18; 507/8 Flts 252 Sqdn Tynemouth by 7.18 - @30.8.18

B3056 SMOP Dover by 10.18 - @2.19

B3061 504 Flt 251 Sqdn Atwick by 30.7.18 - @6.11.18; Became G-EARJ

B3062 D Flt/509 Flt 252 Sqdn Seaton Carew by 1.8.18; FL in sea and badly damaged 9m NE of H Buoy, Hartlepool 18.9.18 (pilot unhurt)

B3063 MAD Killingholme by 8.18; C Flt/510 Flt 252 Sqdn Redcar (via Stallingborough) 8.8.18; FL in sea and wrecked 2m S of Saltburn 14.8.18

B3064 505 Flt 251 Sqdn West Ayton by 29.9.18 - @6.11.18

B3065 505 Flt 251 Sqdn West Ayton by 28.9.18 - @12.11.18; Became G-EARK

B3066 D Flt/509 Flt 252 Sqdn Seaton Carew by 1.8.18; EF, FL in sea and sank 8m ESE of Tyne 7.8.18 (crew rescued)

B3067 505 Flt 251 Sqdn West Ayton by 8.18 - @11.18; Became G-EARR

B3068 505 Flt 251 Sqdn West Ayton by 8.18; 506 Flt 251 Sqdn Owthorne by 10.18; Became G-EARM

B3069 D Flt/509 Flt 252 Sqdn Seaton Carew by 8.18 - @9.11.18; 246 Sqdn Seaton Carew by 1.19; EF, FL in sea 11.1.19

B3071 MAD South Shields by 7.18; C Flt 256 Sqdn Sea Houses 11.7.18; Fell in sea 5545N 0146W 25.7.18

B3072 MAD South Shields by 7.18; 507/8 Flts 252 Sqdn Tynemouth 17.7.18; EF, FL in sea and sank off St.Mary's Island 6.9.18 (pilot saved)

B3073 MAD South Shields to C Flt/528 Flt 256 Sqdn Sea Houses 11.7.18 - @12.8.18

B3074 MAD South Shields to A Flt/527 Flt 256 Sqdn Sea Houses 26.7.18; 526 Flt 252 Sqdn New Haggerston 2.8.18; 527 Flt 256 Sqdn Sea Houses, Fell in sea 5m E of "64EFK" 24.8.18 (pilot saved by destroyer)

B3075 MAD South Shields to C Flt 252 Sqdn Redcar 14.7.18; Became 510 Flt 252 Sqdn 15.8.18; FL in sea SE of Runswick Bay, towed into Whitby 21.8.18 (pilot saved)

B3076 MAD South Shields by 7.18; SD Flt 252 Sqdn Tynemouth 16.7.18; D Flt Flt 252 Sqdn Tees & Seaton Carew by 18.7.18; EF, FL Dalton Percy 12.8.18

B3077 MAD South Shields by 7.18; SD Flt 252 Sqdn Tynemouth 12.7.18; FL 20m E of Tyne, salved by destroyer 12.7.18 (crew saved)

B3078 MAD South Shields by 7.18; SD Flt 252 Sqdn Tynemouth 13.7.18; MAD South Shields by 9.18; 507/8 Flts 252 Sqdn Tynemouth 2.9.18 - @6.11.18; FL 1m NW of aerodrome 5.10.18 (aircraft and pilot safe)

B3079 C Flt 252 Sqdn Redcar by 18.7.18; Became 510 Flt 252 Sqdn Redcar 15.8.18 - @5.10.18; 505/510 Flts 252 Sqdn West Ayton by 11.10.18; MAD South Shields 6.11.18

B3080 MAD South Shields by 7.18; SD Flt Sea Houses 27.7.18

B3081 MAD South Shields by 25.5.18; 508 Flt 252 Sqdn Tynemouth 17.6.18 - @11.11.18; EF, FL and beached between Blyth and Newbiggin 6.7.18, retd 7.7.18

B3082 Allocated MAD South Shields for 256 Sqdn by 25.5.18; 507/8 Flts 252 Sqdn Tynemouth by 13.7.18 - @17.8.18; Dropped 100-lb bomb on U-boat 5517N 0122W 17.8.18 (Lt Whitmore); 504 Flt 251 Sqdn Atwick by 17.10.18 - @11.11.18; Became G-EAQY

B3083 Allocated MAD South Shields for 256 Sqdn by 25.5.18; SD Flt 252 Sqdn Seaton Carew 21.6.18; EF, FL in sea 29.6.18

B3084 Allocated MAD South Shields for 256 Sqdn by 25.5.18; SD Flt Tynemouth 11.6.18; Crashed on aerodrome, CW 20.6.18 (2 crew safe)

B3085 Allocated MAD South Shields for 256 Sqdn by 25.5.18; 508 Flt 252 Sqdn Tynemouth by 6.7.18; FL 16.7.18

B3086 Allocated MAD South Shields for 256 Sqdn by 25.5.18; 510 Flt 252 Sqdn Redcar 7.6.18 - @17.6.18; D Flt/509 Flt 252 Sqdn Seaton Carew by 8.18; FL Easington 11.10.18

B3087 Allocated MAD South Shields for 256 Sqdn by 25.5.18; 509 Flt 252 Sqdn Seaton Carew 11.6.18; Spun in and caught fire 18.7.18 (Capt CD Danby & 2AM EA Bannister killed)

B3088 Allocated MAD South Shields for 256 Sqdn by 25.5.18; SD Flt 252 Sqdn Seaton Carew 21.6.18; EF, FL in sea of Easington 30.6.18

B3089 Allocated MAD South Shields for 256 Sqdn by 25.5.18; D Flt 252 Sqdn Seaton Carew 21.6.18; Became 509 Flt 252 Sqdn 15.8.18 - @9.11.18

B3090    Allocated MAD South Shields for 256 Sqdn by 25.5.18; 509 Flt 252 Sqdn Seaton Carew 11.6.18; 508 Flt 252 Sqdn Tynemouth by 17.6.18 - @24.8.18

B3091    Allocated MAD Killingholme for 256 Sqdn by 25.5.18; SD Flt 251 Sqdn Atwick by 30.6.18; EF, FL 3½m SW of Robin Hoods Bay, undamaged 8.7.18 (pilot unhurt)

B3092    Allocated MAD Killingholme for 256 Sqdn by 25.5.18; SD Flt 251 Sqdn Atwick by 30.6.18; FL and crashed 3½N of Bridlington 23.7.18 (pilot unhurt)

B3093    Allocated MAD Killingholme for 256 Sqdn by 25.5.18; 256 Sqdn by 7.18; EF, FL and CW on TO, Ellington Colliery nr Ashington 5.7.18 (Lt JO McLellan DoI & 2AM H Suttle killed)

B3094    Allocated MAD Killingholme for 256 Sqdn by 25.5.18; Became G-EALT

B3095    Allocated MAD Killingholme for 256 Sqdn by 25.5.18; A Flt Sea Houses by 2.8.18; Fell in sea, in tow by trawler, E of Emmanuel Head 2.8.18 (2 crew rescued by convoy)

B3096    Allocated MAD Killingholme for 256 Sqdn by 25.5.18; 506 Flt 251 Sqdn Owthorne by 19.7.18 - @7.11.18

B3097    Allocated MAD Killingholme for 256 Sqdn by 25.5.18; 527 Flt 256 Sqdn Sea Houses by 6.8.18 - @13.10.18

B3098    Allocated MAD Killingholme for 256 Sqdn by 25.5.18; MAD South Shields by 7.18; SD Flt Tynemouth 10.7.18; 527/8 Flts 256 Sqdn Sea Houses by 7.18

B3099    Allocated MAD Killingholme for 256 Sqdn by 25.5.18

B3100    Allocated MAD Killingholme for 256 Sqdn by 25.5.18; 505/510 Flts 251 Sqdn West Ayton by 28.9.18 - @18.10.18; 504 Flt 251 Sqdn Atwick by 11.18; 505/510 Flts 251 Sqdn West Ayton 18.11.18; Became G-EAPG

## 41 AVRO 504A TRACTOR BIPLANE TRAINERS from batch B3251-B3300 built by Humber Ltd. (80-hp Gnome)

B3251    Deld Chingford W/E 13.10.17; Became 207 TDS Chingford 1.4.18

B3252    Deld Chingford W/E 13.10.17; Became 207 TDS Chingford 1.4.18

B3253    Deld by road to Manston NFS 15.10.17; Became 203 TDS Manston 1.4.18

B3254    Deld by road to Manston NFS 18.10.17; Became 203 TDS Manston 1.4.18

B3255    (DC) Deld Eastbourne 27.10.17; Surveyed 27.11.17; Deleted 5.12.17 DBR

B3256    (DC) Deld Eastbourne 27.10.17; EF, FL and wrecked 29.1.18 (PFO FCD Bridle slightly injured)

B3257    Deld Redcar School W/E 3.11.17 - @30.3.18; School closed 1.4.18; Became 2 SoSF 5.18; Became NE Area FIS Redcar 1.7.18 - @8.18

B3258    Deld Redcar School W/E 3.11.17 - @30.3.18; School closed 1.4.18

B3259    Deld Chingford 3.11.17; Became 207 TDS Chingford 1.4.18

B3260    Deld Chingford 3.11.17; Became 207 TDS Chingford 1.4.18

B3261    Deld Redcar School by road W/E 10.11.17; For deletion W/E 22.12.17

B3262    Deld Redcar School by road W/E 29.12.17; Closed 1.4.18

B3263    Deld Manston NFS by road W/E 29.12.17 - @30.3.18

B3264    (Balanced rudder) Deld Manston NFS by road W/E 17.11.17; Became 203 TDS Manston 1.4.18; 50 TDS by Eastbourne 10.18 (prefix?)

B3265    Deld Manston NFS by road WE 17.11.17; Became 203 TDS Manston 1.4.18; 53 TDS Dover by 8.18, EF while flying low, turned into wind, crashed 20.8.18 (F/Cdt WE Smith seriously injured)

B3266    Deld Manston NFS W/E 29.12.17; Deleted W/E 23.2.18

B3267    Deld Eastbourne NFS for erection W/E 24.11.17; Crashed & WO 23.4.18

B3268    Deld Eastbourne W/E 24.11.17; Deleted W/E 12.1.18

B3269    Deld Chingford for erection W/E 24.11.17 (with B Flt Fairlop 3.18); Became 207 TDS Chingford/Fairlop 1.4.18; Half ARS Shotwick by 6.18; 98 Sqdn 19.6.18

B3270    Deld Chingford for erection W/E 24.11.17; Became 207 TDS Chingford 1.4.18

B3271    Deld Chingford for erection W/E 29.12.17; Became 207 TDS Chingford 1.4.18

B3272    Deld Chingford for erection W/E 29.12.17; Became 207 TDS Chingford 1.4.18

B3273    Deld Chingford for erection W/E 29.12.17; Became 207 TDS Chingford 1.4.18

B3274    Deld Chingford for erection W/E 29.12.17 (with B Flt Fairlop 3.18); Became 207 TDS Chingford/Fairlop 1.4.18

B3275    Deld Redcar School W/E 12.12.17; For deletion by 30.3.18

B3278    4 TDS Hooton Park from 30.11.17; Chingford for erection W/E 29.12.17; Became 207 TDS Chingford 1.4.18

B3279    4 TDS Hooton Park from 30.11.17; B Flt Fairlop W/E 29.12.17; Became 207 TDS Chingford/Fairlop 1.4.18

B3280    4 TDS Hooton Park from 30.11.17; Manston NFS for erection W/E 19.12.17; Became 203 TDS Manston 1.4.18

B3281    Deld Manston NFS for erection W/E 19.12.17; Became 203 TDS Manston 1.4.18

B3282    Deld Manston NFS for erection W/E 19.12.17; Became 203 TDS Manston 1.4.18

B3283    Deld Manston NFS for erection W/E 19.12.17; Surveyed 31.3.18; Deleted 15.4.18 DBR

B3284    Deld Redcar School for erection W/E 19.12.17; For deletion by 30.3.18

B3285    Deld Redcar School for erection W/E 29.12.17; Crashed 27.2.18 (PFO EP McIndoe killed); For deletion by 30.3.18

B3286    Deld Redcar School by road W/E 29.12.17; Became SoSF Redcar 1.4.18; Became 2 SS Redcar 5.18 - @7.18

B3287    Deld Redcar School by road W/E 29.12.17; Became SoSF Redcar 1.4.18; Became 2 SoSF 5.18 - @6.18

B3288    Deld Redcar School by road W/E 29.12.17; Deleted W/E 30.3.18

B3289    Deld Chingford by road W/E 29.12.17; Became 207 TDS Chingford 1.4.18

B3290    Deld Chingford by road W/E 29.12.17; Became 207 TDS Chingford 1.4.18

B3291    Deld Eastbourne NFS by road W/E 29.12.17; Became 206 TDS Eastbourne 1.4.18 - @6.18

B3292    Deld Manston NFS by road W/E 29.12.17; Became 203 TDS Manston 1.4.18; Northolt by 11.19; RAE Farnborough 20.11.19; RAF Display Hendon 1920

B3293    Deld Redcar School W/E 12.1.18; Deleted W/E 16.2.18

## 1 SPAD S.7C.1 TRACTOR BIPLANE SCOUT. GHQ BEF purchase in France. (150-hp Hispano-Suiza)

B3563    1 AD to 19 Sqdn RFC 26.2.17; Mid-air collision with B1593 8.17; 1 AD repair 12.8.17; 19 Sqdn RFC 3.12.17; Marquise 28.12.17; England 15.2.18; War School Manston by 3.18; Became Pool of Pilots Manston 1.4.18

## 51 ROYAL AIRCRAFT FACTORY B.E.2E TRACTOR BIPLANES from batch B3651 to B3750 built by Vulcan Motor & Engineering Co (1906) Ltd at Southport to Cont No 87A/1871. B3701 onwards all to RNAS (90hp R.A.F.1A)

B3657    269 Sqdn (Submarine Flt) Port Said by 1.11.18; 'X' AD 9.3.19

B3701    Deld Cranwell 24.8.17 - 10.17 (W/T expts); (at Freiston 12.17); (at Howden 3.18); Became 201/2 TDS Cranwell 1.4.18 - @6.18

B3702    Deld Cranwell 21.8.17; Crashed and burnt Cranwell South 3.12.17 (PFO EH Dyson killed); Deleted 10.12.17

B3703    Deld Cranwell 21.8.17 (at Freiston 11.17 - 2.18); D Flt Cranwell by 3.18; Manston NFS 24.3.18; Became 203 TDS Manston 1.4.18 - @7.18

B3704    Deld Cranwell 21.8.17; FL due to darkness on cross-country and badly damaged 21.9.17; Surveyed 16.10.17; Deleted 18.10.17

B3705    (BE.2c) Deld Chingford 20.8.17; Cranwell 29.12.17; Freiston by 3.18; Cranwell 8.3.18; Became 201/2 TDS Cranwell 1.4.18 - @8.10.18

B3706    (BE.2c) Deld Chingford 20.8.17; Cranwell 29.12.17; Became 201/2 TDS Cranwell 1.4.18

B3707    Deld Cranwell 21.8.17 (at Freiston by 2.18); Deleted 12.3.18 wreck; Presume rebuilt; Freiston by 21-22.3.18; Became 201/2 TDS Cranwell 1.4.18; Cranwell by 5.18 - @5.7.18

B3708    (OX-2, later 90-hp RAF.1a by 3.18) Deld Cranwell 21.8.17 (at Freiston 3.18); Became 201/2 TDS Cranwell

B3709 Deld Cranwell 21.8.17; Surveyed 12.3.18; Deleted 16.3.18 wrecked

B3710 Deld Cranwell 21.8.17 (at Freiston by 5.9.17 - @26.1.18) Deleted W/E 16.2.18 [Possibly the m/c smashed up on ground in dense fog 30.1.18 (PFO FP Pemble) - or could be A8699]

B3711 Shipped to Mudros in CT *Izaston* 23.9.17; sunk in transit; Surveyed 28.12.17; Deleted 4.1.18

B3712 Shipped to Mudros in CT *Izaston* 23.9.17; sunk in transit; Surveyed 23.9.17; Deleted 4.1.18

B3713 Deld Cranwell 21.8.17; Became 201/2 TDS Cranwell 1.4.18 - @20.7.18

B3714 Deld Cranwell 21.8.17; Became 201/2 TDS Cranwell 1.4.18

B3715 Deld Cranwell 23.8.17; Surveyed 14.9.17; Deleted 8.10.17

B3716 Deld Cranwell 27.8.17 (at Freiston 10.17); Became 201/2 TDS Cranwell 1.4.18

B3717 Deld Cranwell 26.8.17 (at Freiston 11.17 - @8.12.17); Surveyed 25.2.18; Deleted 13.3.18 DBR

B3718 Deld Cranwell 26.8.17 (at Freiston 11.17 - 12.17); Crashed and slightly damaged Rawston 11.1.18 (PFO Turton slightly injured); Deleted W/E 15.2.18

B3719 Deld Cranwell for erection 28.8.17 (at Freiston from 14.12.17 & from 7.2.18); Became 201/2 TDS Cranwell 1.4.18 - @8.4.18

B3720 Deld Cranwell for erection 28.8.17; Crashed & CW Cranwell South 13.3.18 (PFO FR Carlin slightly injured); Deleted W/E 23.3.18

B3721 Deld Cranwell for erection 28.8.17; Deleted W/E 26.10.17

B3722 Deld Cranwell 5.9.17 (at Freiston 12.17); Crashed, slightly damaged South Collingham, nr Newark 14.3.18 (pilot unhurt); retd 15.3.18; Chingford 27.3.18; Became 207 TDS Chingford 1.4.18 - @1.6.18; 55 TDS Manston by 7.18

B3723 Deld Cranwell for erection 28.8.17; Became 201/2 TDS Cranwell 1.4.18

B3724 (90-hp Curtiss OX-2, later 90-hp R.A.F.) Deld Cranwell for erection 29.8.17; Used by G (Exptl) Flt; FL 27.3.18 (pilot unhurt); Became 201/2 TDS Cranwell 1.4.18

B3725 Shipped to Mudros in CT *Izaston* 23.9.17; Sunk in transit; Surveyed 28.12.17; Deleted 4.1.18

B3726 Deld Eastchurch Observers School by rail 4.9.17; Manston NFS W/E 30.3.18; Became 203 TDS Manston 1.4.18 - 6.18

B3727 Deld Eastchurch Observers School by rail 4.9.17; Became 204 TDS Eastchurch 1.4.18; 55 TDS Manston 14.7.18

B3728 Deld Eastchurch Observers School by rail 4.9.17; Became 204 TDS Eastchurch 1.4.18; 203 TDS Manston by 5.18

B3729 Deld Eastchurch Observers School by rail 4.9.17; Became 204 TDS Eastchurch 1.4.18; 203 TDS Manston W/E 6.4.18 - @6.18

B3730 Deld Eastchurch Observers School W/E 15.9.17; Became 204 TDS Eastchurch 1.4.18; 203 TDS Manston by 6.18; Became 55 TDS Manston 15.7.18

B3731 Deld Redcar by rail 8.9.17; F Sqdn East Fortune W/E 1.12.17 - @30.3.18

B3732 Deld Redcar by rail 8.9.17; F Sqdn East Fortune by rail, arr 29.11.17; Deleted 15.4.18 DBR

B3733 Deld Redcar by rail 8.9.17; F Sqdn East Fortune W/E 1.12.17 - @30.3.18

B3734 Deld Redcar by rail 8.9.17; F Sqdn East Fortune W/E 1.12.17 - @30.3.18

B3735 Deld Redcar by rail 9.9.17; F Sqdn East Fortune W/E 1.12.17 - @30.3.18

B3736 Deld Cranwell 2.10.17 (at Freiston 12.17); Crashed, CW Cranwell South 18.2.18 (pilot unhurt); Became 201/2 TDS Cranwell 1.4.18

B3737 Deld Cranwell 2.10.17 (at Freiston 10.17 - 2.18); Became 201/2 TDS Cranwell 1.4.18 - @18.9.18

B3738 Deld Cranwell without engine 18.9.17 (at Freiston 12.17); Crashed, badly damaged Wilford 18.2.18 (pilot unhurt); Became 201/2 TDS Cranwell 1.4.18 - @11.8.18

B3739 Deld Cranwell without engine 18.9.17 (at Freiston 11.17); Became 201/2 TDS Cranwell 1.4.18 - @10.5.18

B3740 Deld Cranwell without engine 18.9.17 (at Freiston 12.17); Crashed, badly damaged Bloxholm 27.12.17 (pilot unhurt); FL North Hykeham 14.3.18 (pilot unhurt); retd 15.3.18; Manston 29.3.18; Became 203 TDS Manston 1.4.18

B3741 Deld Cranwell without engine 25.9.17; Crashed, badly wrecked 6.2.18 (pilot unhurt); Became 201/2 TDS Cranwell 1.4.18

B3742 Deld Cranwell without engine 25.9.17; Became 201/2 TDS Cranwell 1.4.18; Crashed, wings and propeller damaged, Cranwell South 1.4.18 (pilot unhurt)

B3743 Deld Cranwell without engine 25.9.17; Crashed, TW Cranwell North 21.2.18 (pilot unhurt); Surveyed 25.2.18; Deleted 13.3.18 DBR

B3744 Deld Cranwell without engine 25.9.17 (at Freiston 2.18); Became 201/2 TDS Cranwell 1.4.18

B3745 Deld Cranwell without engine 25.9.17; Became 201/2 TDS Cranwell 1.4.18

B3746 Deld Eastchurch Observers School by rail 3.10.17; Manston FS W/E 30.3.18; Became 203 TDS Manston 1.4.18 - @6.18

B3747 Deld Eastchurch Observers School by rail 3.10.17; Manston FS W/E 30.3.18; Became 203 TDS Manston 1.4.18 - @6.18

B3748 Deld Eastchurch Observers School by rail 4.10.17; Manston FS W/E 6.4.18; Eastbourne 30.5.18; 203 TDS Manston by 6.18

B3749 Deld Eastchurch Observers School by rail W/E 1.12.17; Manston FS W/E 30.3.18; Became 203 TDS Manston 1.4.18; Became 55 TDS Manston 14.7.18

B3750 Deld Donibristle W/E 27.10.17; East Fortune W/E 11.1.18; Donibristle W/E 18.1.18; Turnhouse W/E 21.2.18; Donibristle W/E 2.3.18; Turnhouse W/E 6.4.18; Deleted W/E 4.7.18

**200 SOPWITH F.1 CAMEL TRACTOR BIPLANE SCOUTS numbered B3751 to B3950 built at Kingston-upon-Thames to Cont A.S.6175 and accepted at Brooklands. 104 to RNAS. (130-hp Clerget 9B or 150-hp BR.1)**

B3751 Deld Brooklands to Hendon 13.6.18; Brooklands by 16.6.18; London Colney 18.6.18; Hendon 19.6.18; Westlands Yeovil 8.7.18; Hendon by 31.7.18 ('hack' ?)

B3757 (130-hp Clerget) Deld CSD White City by 4.6.17; Dover 5.6.17; ADD 25.6.17; 8 Sqdn 7.7.17; Aviatik C OOC Cuincy 09.40 13.7.17; Rumpler C fell on house Montigny, shared N6372 10.40 13.7.17; Albatros DIII dest Gavrelle-Hamblain 08.30 22.7.17; (both F/Cdr PA Johnston); Collided mid-air with B3877 during combat over Lens 17.8.17 (F/Cdr PA Johnston killed); Deleted 7.9.17

B3758 (130-hp Clerget) Deld Dover 5.6.17; ADD 28.6.17; 8 Sqdn 6.7.17; 19.00 patrol, shot down in flames Loison-Harnes by Obltn Bethge, Jasta 30 15.7.17 (FSL F Bray killed); Deleted 8.8.17

B3759 (130-hp Clerget later BR.1) Deld CSD White City by 4.6.17; Dover 5.6.17; ADD 27.6.17; 8 Sqdn 10.7.17; 1 NAP Dunkerque 15.12.17; 12 Sqdn 18.12.17; COL 8.3.18 (FSL WH Easty); Deleted in Sqdn 11.3.18

B3760 (130-hp Clerget) Deld CSD White City by 4.6.17; Dover 5.6.17; ADD 26.6.17; 8 Sqdn 10.7.17; DFW C dest Lens, shared N6375, N6376 & N6378 18.40 20.7.17 (FSL JH Thompson); FL 22.11.17 (FSL WF Crundall); retd 23.11.17; 1 NAP Dunkerque 26.11.17 (overhaul); 10 Sqdn 19.1.18; Crashed and badly damaged Argues 3.2.18 (FSL AL Jones); 1 NAP Dunkerque 4.2.18 (overhaul); 12 Sqdn 26.3.18; Became 212 Sqdn 1.4.18; Crashed, wrecked 5.4.18; Surveyed 4 ASD 28.4.18; Deleted 15.5.18

B3761 (BR.1 later 130-hp Clerget) Deld Dover 5.6.17; Manston War Flt by 19.6.17; AGP, retd engine trouble made bad landing 7.7.17 (FSL AH Lofft); Attacked Gotha 20m off North Foreland, fired 420 rounds no result 12.8.17 (S/Cdr CH Butler); AGP, enemy bullet in crankcase, FL nr Manston 22.8.17 (S/Cdr CH Butler); O/t landing 29.11.17 (FSL GS Smith); Became Pool of Pilots Manston 1.4.18; Freiston 3.5.18; Manston by 1.19

B3762 (110-hp Clerget) Deld CSD White City 6.6.17; Packed for Mudros 15.6.17; Shipped to 2 Wing Mudros 6.17; Marsh by 6.10.17; Mudros 13.11.17 - @9.12.17; Marsh by 1.1.18; Surveyed 12.2.18; Deleted 13.3.18 wrecked

B3769 (BR.1) Deld CSD White City by 5.6.17; Shipped to 2

Wing Mudros 6.17; F Sqdn 2 Wing Mitylene by 9.17; G Sqdn 2 Wing Marsh by 10.17; D Sqdn 2 Wing Stavros by 1.12.17 - @1.1.18; Repair Base Mudros by 3.18 - @11.18; 222 Sqdn Mudros by 2.11.18; To Greek Air Force by 10.18 - 11.18

B3770  Deld CSD White City by 5.6.17; Shipped to Mudros 6.17; G Flt 2 Wing Mudros by 8.17; F Flt 2 Wing Mitylene 10.9.17; Collided with Henry Farman 3022, CW 19.10.17 (F/Cdr G Donald)

B3771  Deld CSD White City by 5.6.17; Shipped to Mudros 6.17; Marsh by 12.17 - @1.1.18

B3772  (130-hp Clerget) Deld CSD White City by 5.6.17 for RNAS but transferred RFC for US Government (authorised 19.6.17); To Canadian Air Force Beamsville 2.10.18; CAF Camp Borden 1918

B3773  (130-hp Clerget, later BR.1) Deld Manston War Flt 16.6.17; AGP, FL, crashed nr Manningtree 7.7.17 (FSL AH Lofft unhurt); ADD 20.8.17; Seaplane Defence Flt 11.9.17; Became Seaplane Defence Sqdn 23.9.17; Became 13 Sqdn 15.1.18; 2-str seaplane into sea in flames 1m E of Ostende, shared B3782, N6345, N6349 & N6363 13.55 19.2.18 (FSL E Bell); Crashed and damaged 19.2.18 (FSL E Bell); 1 NAP Dunkerque 21.2.18; 4 ASD Guines 28.3.18; 8 Sqdn 31.3.18; Became 208 Sqdn 1.4.18; Burnt to prevent capture, La Gorgue 9.4.18

B3774  (BR.1) Deld Manston War Flt 20.6.17; Shot Gotha into sea in spinning nosedive 35m off Kent coast 7.7.17 (FSL JE Scott DSC); AGP 12.8.17 (FSL CH FitzHerbert); Dover 18.8.17; ADD 19.8.17; 4 Sqdn 26.8.17; ADD 8.9.17; 1 NAP Dunkerque (overhaul) W/E 29.11.17; 13 Sqdn W/E 24.1.18; EF, landed 1 NAP 18.2.18; Retd 13 Sqdn 21.2.18; Shot down in sea OOC by Pfalz DIII, sank West Deep, nr Nieuport 11.00 24.3.18 (FSL LC Messiter rescued by French TB318); Deleted 8.4.18

B3781  (BR.1) Deld Dover for storage 13.6.17; ADD 2.7.17; 3 Sqdn 10.7.17; Seaplane into sea 3m N of Ostende, shared N6364, N6377, B3782, B3805 14.15 27.7.17 (FSL AB Ellwood); Crashed nr St.Pol 27.8.17 (FSL JWP Amos); ADD by 30.8.17; 1 NAP by 25.10.17; 9 Sqdn 22.12.17; Fokker DrI dest SW of Roulers, shared B6430 14.00 3.2.18 (FSL MA Harker); 10 Sqdn 4.2.18; Wheel in ditch taxying after landing, on nose, damaged 8.3.18 (FSL SC Joseph); Lost E of Roulers, believed over Houthulst Forest 18.3.18 (FSL GT Steeves PoW); Deleted 18.3.18

B3782  (BR.1 later 170-hp CR.1) Deld Dover for storage 13.6.17; ADD 2.7.17; 3 Sqdn 13.7.17; Seaplane into sea 3m N of Ostende, shared N6364, N6377, B3781 & B3805 14.15 27.7.17 (FSL JA Glen); FL nr Coxyde 18.8.17, Albatros DV OOC Stalhille 07.15 & another BU, wings off Belhutte 07.25 3.9.17; Albatros DV OOC Thourout 11.50 11.9.17 (all F/Cdr LS Breadner); AP Dover 20.11.17; Seaplane Defence Sqdn 12.1.18; Became 13 Sqdn 15.1.18; Seaplane in flames 100yds off Blankenberghe Piers, shared B3909, B6407, B6410 & B7186 14.00 29.1.18; 2-str exploded in air 2m N of Ostende, shared N6363 14.20 30.1.18 (both FSL JdeC Paynter); 2-str seaplane into sea in flames 1m E of Ostende, shared B3773, N6345, N6349 and N6363 13.55 19.2.18; With N6345, N6349 & N6363 attacked U-boat which was forced to submerge ½m E of North Middelkerke Buoy 06.40-08.25 patrol 23.2.18; Rumpler C crashed Dixmude-Cockelaere, shared B3935 & N6349 15.00 8.3.18 (all F/L JdeC Paynter); Fitted 170-hp CR.1 by 28.3.18; Became 213 Sqdn 1.4.18; Hit ridge landing and wrecked Bergues 20.4.18 (Lt FL Cattle injured); To 4 ASD; Surveyed 28.4.18; Deleted 15.5.18

B3783  (130-hp Clerget) (BR.1 per ADR) Deld Dover for storage 14.6.17; ADD 29.6.17; 3 Sqdn 10.7.17 - @9.9.17; In combat over Nieuport Piers 17.8.17 (FSL RFP Abbott wounded); ADD by 13.9.17; dest by enemy bombs 1.10.17; Surveyed 17.10.17; Deleted 23.10.17 wrecked

B3784  (130-hp Clerget) (BR.1 per ADR) Deld Dover for storage 14.6.17; ADD 2.7.17; 4 Sqdn 14.7.17; FL on beach Bray Dunes 22.7.17; ADD by 26.7.17; 4 Sqdn 8.8.17; Seaplane Defence Sqdn 16.10.17; Wrecked by enemy bombs 20.10.17; ADD by 24.10.17; Surveyed 31.10.17; Deleted 21.11.17

B3785  (BR.1) Deld Dover for storage 14.6.17; ADD 5.7.17; 11

Sqdn 22.7.17; 3 Sqdn 4.9.17; DFW C forced down intact Furnes-Adinkerke, shared N6377, B3858, B3866 & B3895 18.00 10.9.17 (F/Cdr RF Redpath); DFW C OOC Houthulst Forest, shared B6401 & B6408 11.05 28.1.18 (FSL CS Devereaux); 1 NAP Dunkerque 27.2.18; 4 ASD Guines 28.3.18; 8 Sqdn 30.3.18; Became 208 Sqdn 1.4.18; Burnt to prevent capture La Gorgue 9.4.18

B3786  (BR.1) Deld Dover for storage 15.6.17; ADD 5.7.17; 3 Sqdn 26.7.17; COL 3.9.17 (FSL HR de Wilde); 1 NAP Dunkerque 23.2.18; 4 ASD Guines 28.3.18; 1 ASD Rely to 203 Sqdn (named 'ALINE') 10.4.18; 2 Fokker DrI OOC Armentières-Neuve Eglise 11.40 3.5.18 (F/L ET Hayne); LVG C crashed nr Salomé, E of La Bassée, shared B3855, B7198,, B7231, D3376 & D3384 11.45, then COL 15.5.18 (FSL AN Webster); Rep Pk 1 ASD 18.5.18; Rec Pk 1 ASD 26.6.18; 2 ASD 24.7.18; 5 AI 7.18; 2 AI 28.7.18; 73 Sqdn 31.7.18; Crashed, to 1 ASD 13.9.18; Rebuilt as H7234 5.11.18

B3793  (BR.1) Deld Dover for storage without engine 16.6.17; ADD 5.7.17; 3 Sqdn 17.7.17; FL Coxyde Bains 28.7.17; Albatros apparently OOC N of Nieuport 18.30, then shot up, FL damaged Coxyde Bains 28.7.17 (FSL RFP Abbott unhurt); ADD by 2.8.17; Seaplane Defence Flt St.Pol 6.9.17; Seaplane on fire 12m NE of Nieuport, shared B3794 19.10 15.9.17 (FSL LH Slatter); Became Seaplane Defence Sqdn 23.9.17; Wrecked by enemy bombs 20.10.17; ADD by 24.10.17; Surveyed 31.10.17; Deleted 2.11.17

B3794  (BR.1) Deld Dover for storage without engine 16.6.17; ADD 6.7.17; 3 Sqdn 15.7.17 - @26.7.17; ADD by 2.8.17; Seaplane Defence Flt St.Pol 6.9.17; Seaplane on fire 12m NE of Nieuport, shared B3793 19.10 15.9.17 (F/Cdr R Graham); Became Seaplane Defence Sqdn 23.9.17; FL in Dunkerque harbour, salved 31.10.17 (FSL GP Brown and machine picked up by monitor HMS Prince Eugene); ADD by 8.11.17; 1 NAP 18.2.18; 8 Sqdn 21.2.18; 3 Sqdn 3.3.18; COL Mont St.Eloi 7.3.18 (FSL SE Wise); 1 NAP 9.3.18; 4 ASD Guines 28.3.18; 208 Sqdn 5.4.18; Burnt to prevent capture La Gorgue 9.4.18

B3795  (BR.1) Deld Observers School Flts Eastchurch by air 21.6.17; AGP 7.7.17 (F/Cdr C Draper); AGPs 22.7.17 & 22.8.17 (F/L EM Pizey); HAP 14.8.17 (F/L GA Cox); ADD (via Dover) 26.8.17; 4 Sqdn 5.9.17; Albatros C crashed in sea 2m NE of Ostende 13.45 1.10.17 (FSL RAG Hill); EF, FL on beach Coxyde 11.3.18; 4 ASD Guines 28.3.18; 3 Sqdn 31.3.18; Became 203 Sqdn 1.4.18; Sideslipped and spun in while formating, CW 21.4.18 (Lt LD Bawlf DoI); To 4 ASD 22.4.18; Surveyed 28.4.18; Deleted 11.5.18

B3796  (BR.1) Completed W/E 17.6.17; Deld ADD by 28.6.17; 3 Sqdn 2.7.17; FTR 05.45 patrol 3.9.17 (FSL ND Hall PoW); Deleted 3.9.17

B3797  (BR.1) Completed W/E 17.6.17; Deld ADD by 21.6.17; 3 Sqdn 5.7.17; COL, wrecked 13.7.17 (F/L JST Fall); Deleted ADD 16.7.17

B3798  (BR.1) Deld Observers School Flts Eastchurch by air 21.6.17; AGP 7.7.17 (F/L SR Watkins); Attacked Gotha off Kent coast wounding a gunner, but broke off action when own engine hit 12.8.17; AGP 22.8.17 (both F/Cdr AF Bettington); ADD 22.8.17; 3 Sqdn 5.9.17; Albatros DV OOC nr Thourout 11.10 11.9.17 (F/L LH Rochford); 1 NAP Dunkerque 12.1.18 - @14.2.18 (overhaul); 8 Sqdn by 19.2.18; 3 Sqdn 3.3.18; DFW Aviatik in flames Hénin-Lietard, shared B7185 11.20 9.3.18 (FSL WH Chisam); Albatros C crashed in flames 4m E of Bapaume, shared B7203 & flight 16.45 21.3.18 (FSL OP Adam); Became 203 Sqdn 1.4.18; Crashed then shelled N of Loos 1.4.18 (2/Lt OP Adam killed); SOC in field 1.4.18

B3805  (Clerget, later BR.1) Deld Dover 26.6.17; ADD 26.6.17; 3 Sqdn 2.7.17; Attacked by HA, engine shot away, FL beach E of Coxyde Bains 26.7.17 (FSL WH Chisam); Seaplane in sea 3m N of Ostende 14.15, shared B3781, B3782, N6364 & N6377 27.7.17 (FSL LD Bawlf); COL 28.7.17 (FSL DL Bawlf); Crashed nr aerodrome on test flight, wrecked 10.8.17 (F/Cdr FD Casey DSC DoI); Deleted ADD 20.8.17

B3806  (BR.1) Completed W/E 24.6.17; Deld ADD by 28.6.17; 4 Sqdn 14.7.17; Shot down by 2 HA nr Ostende

20.7.17 (FSL FW Akers killed) [credited Ltn Joens, Jasta 20]; Deleted 8.8.17

B3807 (BR.1) Completed W/E 24.6.17; Deld ADD by 28.6.17; 3 Sqdn 2.7.17; EF, FL on beach Zuydcoote 10.8.17; Albatros DIII OOC smoking nr Leke 18.20 5.9.17; COL 6.9.17 (al F/L LH Rochford); Seaplane Defence Sqdn 16.10.17; Wrecked by enemy bombs 20.10.17; ADD by 24.10.17; Surveyed 31.10.17; Deleted 2.11.17

B3808 (BR.1) Completed W/E 24.6.17; Deld ADD by 28.6.17; 3 Sqdn 5.7.17; EF, FL on beach 9.8.17; Albatros DV dest and another OOC probable nr Thourout 11.40 16.9.17 (all F/Cdr FC Armstrong); COL 24.10.17 (F/L LH Rochford); 1 NAP 25.10.17; 9 Sqdn 22.12.17; FL in fog nr Mardyke 28.1.18 (FSL AP Squire); 10 Sqdn 4.2.18; Became 210 Sqdn 1.4.18; COL from patrol 2.4.18 (FSL AL Jones unhurt); 4 ASD 3.4.18; SOC in field 8.4.18

B3809 (BR.1) Completed W/E 24.6.17; Deld ADD by 5.7.17; 3 Sqdn 9.7.17; FL, crashed on beach Coxyde Bains 24.7.17 (FSL HM Ireland); ADD by 26.7.17; 11 Sqdn 18.8.17; ADD 3.9.17 - @18.10.17; AP Dover by 1.11.17; 3 Sqdn 15.12.17 (coded 'II', named 'NIBS'); U/c damaged on landing 6.1.18; Flying again 13.1.18; DFW C OOC SE of Dixmude, 1m behind lines 11.15 28.1.18 (FSL KD Macleod); Crashed nr Ouderdom, SE of Poperinghe 21.2.18 (FSL KD Macleod); 1 NAP Dunkerque 22.2.18; 13 Sqdn 23.3.18; 10 Sqdn 28.3.18; Became 210 Sqdn 1.4.18; 2-str OOC Merville 12.30 22.4.18 (FSL HL Nelson); Shot down by flak 14.15 29.4.18 (Lt HL Nelson killed); SOC in field 29.4.18

B3810 (130-hp Clerget) Completed W/E 24.6.17; Deld ADD by 5.7.17; 9 Sqdn 13.7.17; Albatros C OOC Middelkerke-Nieuport, shared B3818, B3829, B3832 & B3897 08.00 5.9.17 (FSL OW Redgate); COL 12.9.17 (FSL W Ingleson unhurt); ADD 20.9.17; Dover by 13.10.17; 1 NAP W/E 25.10.17; 9 Sqdn 1.11.17; 1 NAP by 8.11.17; 1 Sqdn 9.11.17; EF on edge of aerodrome, crashed and damaged 5.12.17 (FSL AR McAfee); 1 NAP Dunkerque (overhaul) 6.12.17; Propeller accident 18.3.18 (PO RC Morris injured); 12 Sqdn 23.3.18; Became 212 Sqdn 1.4.18; 4 ASD Guines 18.4.18 (used by Pilots Pool); WOC 31.7.18

B3817 (BR.1) CSD White City without engine by 15.6.17; Deld Brooklands to ADD (via Dover) 6.7.17; 4 Sqdn 17.7.17; EF, FL, crashed attempting to return to aerodrome 19.8.17 (FSL RM Keirstead); ADD by 30.8.17; Seaplane Defence Flt 21.9.17; Became Seaplane Defence Sqdn 23.9.17 - @20.10.17; ADD by 24.10.17; 9 Sqdn 30.1.18; 10 Sqdn (coded 'A') 4.2.18; Became 210 Sqdn (coded 'A') 1.4.18; Lost, FL in field nr Hazebrouck, CW 11.4.18 (FSL E Swale unhurt); 4 ASD 12.4.18; Deleted in field 22.4.18

B3818 (130-hp Clerget later BR.1) Deld CSD White City by 15.6.17; Dover without engine 24.6.17; ADD 3.7.17; 9 Sqdn 13.7.17; Albatros C OOC off Westende, shared B3820 05.30 25.7.17 (FSL OW Redgate); ADD by 2.8.17; 9 Sqdn 26.8.17; Albatros C OOC Middelkerke-Nieuport, shared B3810, B3829, B3832 & B3897 08.00 5.9.17 (FSL AR Brown); DFW C OOC nr Zarren, shared B6217 17.00 21.9.17; Albatros DIII dest N of Dixmude, shared B3832, B5652, B6217 & B6230 16.10 28.9.17; 2-str OOC over Slype, shared B6230 14.50 2.10.17; Albatros DIII crashed S of Ostende, shared B3830 12.30 15.10.17; Albatros DV spinning down OOC S of Middelkerke 11.00 17.10.17; Albatros DV shot down S of Pervyse, crashed 3m behind enemy lines 15.00 20.11.17; DFW C on fire 4m E of Pervyse, shared B3844 & B6288 15.15 10.12.17 (all FSL OW Redgate); 1 NAP 13.1.18; 4 Sqdn 15.3.18; 1 NAP Dunkerque 19.3.18; 4 Sqdn 24.3.18; 4 ASD Guines 28.3.18; 210 Sqdn 19.4.18; Albatros C crashed in field N of La Bassée 14.20 20.4.18 (Capt ES Arnold); EF, FL, badly damaged Bavinchove, nr Cassel 6.5.18 (Capt ES Arnold unhurt); 4 ASD 8.5.18; Deleted 13.5.18 general fatigue

B3819 (BR.1) Deld CSD White City by 15.6.17; Dover without engine 24.6.17; ADD 3.7.17; 9 Sqdn 15.7.17; COL 15.7.17; Damaged 29.7.17 (FSL WEB Oakley unhurt); ADD 21.9.17; AP Dover, crashed and damaged RFC Dover 4.12.17 (FSL KG Boyd); Deleted 15.12.17; Presume rebuilt & restored; War School Manston

29.12.17; Tyre burst landing, on nose 5.2.18 (PFO SC Joseph); Became Pool of Pilots Manston 1.4.18 (130-hp Clerget); Eastbourne 27.5.18; COL, badly damaged 12.8.18 (pilot unhurt); 4 SoAF&G Freiston; 50 TDS Eastbourne .18

B3820 (130-hp Clerget) Deld CSD White City by 15.6.17; Dover without engine 24.6.17; ADD 3.7.17; 9 Sqdn 13.7.17; Albatros C OOC over sea off Westende, shared B3818 05.30 25.7.17 (FSL JW Pinder); Shot down in spin by Albatros D nr Nieuport pm 14.8.17 (FSL MN Baron killed); Deleted 1.9.17

B3821 (130-hp Clerget) Deld CSD White City by 15.6.17; Dover without engine 24.6.17; ADD 11.7.17; 6 Sqdn 21.7.17; DFW C crashed nr Nieuport, shared B3833 16.00 28.7.17 (FSL RR Winter); COL 23.8.17; ADD 27.8.17; 8 Sqdn 28.9.17; Hit by AA 2.10.17 (FSL JH Thompson); Flying again 16.10.17; DFW C shot down Sallaumines, shared 2 others [not confirmed] 27.10.17 (F/Cdr CD Booker); COL 17.11.17 (FSL WH Sneath); Flying again 26.11.17; Albatros C in flames Wingles 13.55 5.12.17 (both FSL WH Sneath); 1 "new-type, twin tail" OOC 5m N of Bourlon Wood 11.15-11.20 4.1.18 (FSL H Day); Albatros DV crashed E of Lens 15.00 24.1.18 (FSL WH Sneath); 10 Sqdn 4.2.18 (temp custody); 1 Sqdn 15.2.18 (temp); War School Manston (via Dover) 20.2.18; Deleted W/E 9.3.18

B3822 (130-hp Clerget) Deld CSD White City by 15.6.17; Dover without engine 26.6.17; ADD 11.7.17; 12 Sqdn from/by 16.7.17; Possibly wrecked 17.7.17 (maybe the a/c in which FSL DH Daly killed 17.7.17); For survey 19.7.17; Surveyed ADD 17.10.17; Deleted 23.10.17 wrecked

B3829 (130-hp Clerget later 110-hp Le Rhône) Allocated Martlesham for gun trials 25.6.17; Martlesham Heath to Eastchurch 7.8.17; Dover 8.8.17; Calais 8.8.17 (weather); ADD 9.8.17; 9 Sqdn 15.8.17; Albatros C OOC Middelkerke-Nieuport, shared B3810, B3818, B3832 & B3897 08.00 5.9.17 (F/Cdr ST Edwards); Albatros DV crashed 1m NW of Leke, shared B3898 & B3905 17.15 14.9.17 (FSL AC Campbell-Orde); FL, crashed and CW in flooded area of No Mans Land nr Pervyse, abandoned 14.9.17 (FSL AC Campbell-Orde saved); Surveyed 22.9.17; Deleted 27.9.17

B3830 (130-hp Clerget) Deld ADD by 5.7.17; 9 Sqdn 16.7.17; COL 2.9.17 (FSL EB Freeland), repaired; Albatros DIII crashed S of Ostende, shared B3818 12.30 15.10.17 (FSL FJW Mellersh); AP Dover for repair 23.11.17; War School Manston W/E 7.2.18; Became Pool of Pilots Manston 1.4.18

B3831 (130-hp Clerget) Deld ADD (via Dover) 5.7.17; 9 Sqdn 13.7.17; COL 17.7.17 (FSL FE Banbury); Test after repair 24.7.17; EF, FL Furnes 26.7.17; EF, FL, crashed 3m after TO 4.8.17 (FSL EH Snell bruised); ADD 4.8.17; Deleted 20.8.17

B3832 (130-hp Clerget) Deld ADD 6.7.17; 9 Sqdn 13.7.17; Albatros C OOC Middelkerke-Nieuport, shared B3810, B3818, B3829 & B3897 08.00 5.9.17 (F/L FE Banbury); Albatros DIII dest N of Dixmude, shared B3818, B5652, B6217 & B6230 16.10 28.9.17 (FSL JP Hales); 1 NAP Dunkerque 1.11.17; 8 Sqdn 19.1.18; Albatros DV shot down S of Pont-à-Vendin, shared N6356, N6379 & B6387 12.45 5.2.18; Albatros DV crashed in flames Thonville, shared B6379 & N6356 11.15 16.2.18 (FSL HHS Fowler); 1 NAP Dunkerque 17.2.18; War School Manston (via Dover) 19.2.18; Spun into sea nr Westgate 30.3.18 (TFSL N Mallard killed); Deleted W/E 6.4.18

B3833 (130-hp Clerget later BR.1) Deld Dover 7.7.17; ADD 8.7.17; 6 Sqdn 12.7.17; Aviatik C crashed 1m E of Westende, shared N6351 & B3882 18.15 17.8.17; Albatros DV OOC Moere, shared B3882 10.50 20.8.17; Albatros DIII dest N of St.Pierre Capelle 09.45 22.8.17; DFW C crashed Nieuport, shared B3821 16.00 28.7.17; 10 Sqdn 30.8.17; Fokker DrI shot down in flames over Wervicq 16.50 15.9.17 [Oblt Kurt Wolff, Jasta 11]; Albatros DIII down smoking, probably decisive E of Hooge 10.00-10.15 19.9.17; Damaged by gunfire, crashed nr Ypres 21.9.17 (all FSL NM MacGregor); ADD for survey 22.9.17; Dest by fire on night of 1.10.17; Surveyed 17.10.17; Deleted 23.10.17

B3834 (130-hp Clerget) Deld Manston War Flt 10.7.17; AGP

*Sopwith Camel B3843 of Manston War Flight attacked a Gotha over Ramsgate on 22 August 1917 when being flown by FSL CH FitzHerbert. (via Frank Cheesman)*

*Sopwith Camels of 'A' and 'B' Flights of 8 Sqdn around the time of re-equipment from Triplanes at Mont St.Eloi in July-August 1917. B3757, the nearest machine, was lost in a mid-air collision during combat on 17 August 1917, Flight Commander PA Johnston being killed. (via Frank Cheesman)*

*Sopwith Camels of 'A' Flight 8 Sqdn in the snow at Mont St.Eloi early in the winter of 1917/18. B3921 'A' was flown by Flight Commander R.B.Munday. (via Frank Cheesman)*

22.7.17; AGP 12.8.17 (FSL RH Daly); Helped shoot down Gotha G.IV/663/16 in flames off Margate, landed damaged, bullet in No.6 cylinder 22.8.17 (F/L AF Brandon); Deleted W/E 9.2.18

B3835  (130-hp Clerget later BR.1) Deld A Flt AES Martlesham Heath (tests with 130-hp Clerget, later BR.1); Crashed Martlesham

B3841  (BR.1) Deld ADD (via Dover) 7.7.17; 4 Sqdn 16.7.17; Seaplane crashed 20m N of Middelkerke, shared N6369 & N6370 19.30 25.7.17 (A/F/Cdr AJ Enstone); 3 Albatros DV OOC SE of Ostende 09.45-09.50 22.8.17 (FSL GW Hemming); 2-str in sea Westende 16.25 10.9.17 (A/F/L AJ Enstone); Yellow-fuselage Albatros DV OOC Ratteville 12.00 30.9.17; DFW C OOC S of Pervyse 14.35 9.11.17; Albatros DV all-black fuselage, camouflaged wings in flames S of Thourout 11.40 24.3.18 (all A/F/Cdr AJ Enstone); Became 204 Sqdn 1.4.18; 4 ASD Guines 16.5.18 - @25.5.18

B3842  (BR.1) Deld War School Manston 10.7.17; AGP 22.7.17; EF, FL and wrecked nr aerodrome 13.8.17 (FSL CH FitzHerbert); Dover 18.8.17; ADD by 23.8.17; 3 Sqdn 5.9.17; COL, DBR Hawkeshill, Walmer 12.12.17 (FSL KD MacLeod unhurt); Surveyed 17.12.17 DBR; Deleted 24.12.17 DBR

B3843  (130-hp Clerget later BR.1 by 10.17) Deld War School Manston 11.7.17 (named 'WONGO BONGO'); AGP 12.8.17 (FSL MA Harker); Attacked Gotha over Ramsgate 22.8.17 (FSL CH FitzHerbert); Bullet in propeller 25.9.17; O/t Manston 28.9.17 (FSL FV Hall); Became Pool of Pilots Manston 1.4.18 - @1.19; HAPs 31.5.18 & 1.6.18 (both FSL SA Hamilton-Bowyer)

B3844  (130-hp Clerget later BR.1) Deld War School Manston 12.7.17; AGPs 22.7.17; Attacked Gotha off North Foreland but guns jammed, and on return FL 1m from Manston 12.8.17 (FSL AC Burt); Attacked Gotha at 15,000 ft over Herne, Deal and Dover and shot it down nr Dover 11.20 22.8.17 (FSL EB Drake) [probably the m/c from which Unteroff Bruno Schneider, Kampfgeschweder 3, Staffel 15 taken PoW); Deleted W/E 24.11.17

B3845  (130-hp Clerget) Deld ADD 11.7.17; 8 Sqdn 16.7.17; Albatros DIII OOC SE of Gavrelle 08.30 22.7.17; Albatros DIII OOC Lens-La Bassée 09.15 28.7.17; Albatros DIII OOC Lens 20.15 15.8.17; DFW OOC E of Lens, shared N6375 & B3921 08.50 19.8.17; Aviatik C OOC probably on fire Pont-à-Vendin - Courrières 11.49 11.9.17 (all FSL RR Thornely); FL, crashed, damaged Olhain 27.10.17 (F/L MR Kingsford); ADD by 1.11.17; 12 Sqdn 19.2.18; EF, dived vertically, CW Loon Plage 12.3.18 (FSL GJW Goodwin killed); Deleted ADD 18.3.18

B3846  (130-hp Clerget) Deld ADD by 12.7.17; 8 Sqdn 16.7.17; AP Dover for repair 26.11.17; War School Manston W/E 7.2.18; Became Pool of Pilots Manston 1.4.18 - @5.18

B3851  (130-hp Clerget) Presentation a/c named 'Majara' (Ex RFC aircraft); Tested Martlesham Heath 23.8.17; Hendon 8.9.17; Brooklands 15.9.17; Medical Flt Hendon 24.4.18 - @31.5.18; 4 ASD WOC 31.8.18 general fatigue BUT to Medical Flt Hendon with 29 TS 1.1.19

B3853  (BR.1) Deld ADD by 12.7.17; 4 Sqdn 16.7.17; Rumpler fighter seaplane crashed in sea, BU 12m N of Wenduyne 18.00 10.9.17 (A/F/Cdr PS Fisher); In action 24.9.17 (A/F/Cdr PS Fisher seriously wounded); AZP from Walmer 29.1.18 (S/Cdr BL Huskisson); EF following combat with V-strutters, FL Bulscamp 11.3.18 (F/L GW Hemming); 4 ASD Guines 28.3.18; 1 AI to 208 Sqdn 7.4.18; Burnt La Gorgue to prevent capture 9.4.18

B3854  (BR.1) Deld ADD by 7.17; 4 Sqdn 17.7.17; Crashed, wrecked Bray Dunes 9.8.17 (FSL GHB Smyth injured); ADD by 16.8.17; Deleted 3.9.17

B3855  (BR.1) Deld ADD (via Dover) by 13.7.17; 4 Sqdn 21.7.17; FL Frontier 13.3.18; 1 NAP Dunkerque by 21.3.18; 4 ASD Guines 28.3.18; 203 Sqdn 22.4.18; Fokker DrI OOC Armentières-Neuve Eglise 11.35 3.5.18; Fokker DrI 1m E of Herlies 11.40 9.5.18; LVG C crashed into hedge nr Salomé, E of La Bassée, shared B3786, B7198, B7231, D3376 & D3374 11.45 15.5.18; Pfalz DIII crashed N of La Bassée 11.20 16.5.18; Attacked Pfalz DIII which was diving on rear of flight, it

crashed into house S of Merville (flight comprised B6212, B6378, B7231 & D3384) 11.20 17.5.18; Rumpler C in flames Merville, shared D3384 11.20 18.5.18 (all Capt HF Beamish); RP 1 ASD 13.7.18 (unfit for further service); Rebuilt as F5992 (completed 29.7.18 and SOC as B3855)

B3856  (BR.1) Deld ADD (via Dover) 14.7.17; 4 Sqdn 24.7.17; Albatros DV OOC SE of Ostende 09.45 22.8.17 (FSL AJB Tonks); Albatros DV OOC Zeebrugge 13.45 1.10.17; Albatros C dest 20m NE of Zeebrugge 14.45 4.11.17; Albatros C OOC SE of Dixmude 11.30 13.11.17 (all FSL GHD Gossip); Became 204 Sqdn 1.4.18; Crashed, badly damaged 21.4.18; To 4 ASD; Surveyed 6.5.18; Deleted 18.5.18 wrecked

B3857  (BR.1) Deld ADD by 19.7.17; 3 Sqdn 24.7.17; 4 Sqdn 2.11.17; 9 Sqdn 31.12.17; Joined 3 Sqdn formation by mistake, EF, FL in sea, CW nr No.3 Buoy 30.1.18 (FSL AR McAfee); Deleted 4.2.18

B3858  (BR.1) Deld ADD by 19.7.17; 3 Sqdn 27.7.17; Albatros DIII OOC St.Pierre Capelle 15.50 22.8.17; COL nr DFW C forced down intact, shared B3785, B3866, B3895 & N6377 Furnes-Adinkerke 18.00 10.9.17 (both FSL GB Anderson); ADD by 13.9.17 - @25.10.17; 1 NAP by 25.10.17; 3 Sqdn 26.10.17; EF, FL and crashed nr Woeston 5.2.18 (FSL E Pierce); 1 NAP (overhaul) 7.2.18 (flying again 9.2.18); 9 Sqdn 24.3.18; Became 209 Sqdn 1.4.18 (had green/mauve striped fuselage); Albatros believed crashed, shared B6311, B7200 & D3328 12.4.18 (pilots not listed); Albatros C in flames Beaucourt-Ignaucourt, shared B7200 & D3338 (q.v.) 10.25 21.4.18; Albatros DV crashed E of Villers-Bretonneux, shared B7270 14.45 27.4.18; Pfalz DIII OOC 1m S of Hamel 15.55 4.5.18; LVG C down smoking nr Bayonvillers, shared D3338 09.40 16.5.18; Albatros DV OOC NW of Meulte 11.30 30.5.18; Rumpler C claimed forced down, shared B6398 08.30 6.6.18, not credited; LVG CV shot down N of Ailly-sur-Noye, shared D3328 08.30 17.6.18 (numbered G/5Bde/18); White-finned Fokker DVII BU N of Harbonnières 20.10 29.6.18 (all Lt later Capt RM Foster); Shot down from 1,000 ft by Fokker DVIIs S of Mourcourt 13.15 4.7.18 (2/Lt HR Frank unhurt)

B3865  (BR.1) Presentation a/c 'Basutoland No.1, Peete' 4.17. Deld Dover store 23.7.17; ADD 24.7.17; 4 Sqdn 5.8.17; FL, o/t landing on beach nr Calais 5.9.17 (FSL RAG Hill); ADD by 13.9.17; AP Dover by 13.10.17; 3 Sqdn 21.12.17; 4 Sqdn 6.3.18; Became 204 Sqdn 1.4.18; COL, CW 19.7.18 (Lt WA Pomeroy); 4 ASD WOC 31.7.18

B3866  (BR.1) Presentation a/c 'Basutoland No.2, Mokhachane' 4.17; Deld ADD by 26.7.17; 3 Sqdn (named 'SYBIL') 30.7.17; EF, FL nr Pervyse 4.9.17; DFW C forced down intact, shared B3785, B3858, B3895 & N6377 Furnes-Adinkerke 18.00 10.9.17 (both FSL GS Harrover); Lost port wheel on TO, COL 27.10.17 (F/L GB Anderson); 1 NAP Dunkerque W/E 1.11.17; 9 Sqdn 22.12.17; 1-str OOC probably nr Staden 3.2.18 (F/Cdr OW Redgate); 10 Sqdn 4.2.18; Crashed, wrecked St.Sixte, N of Poperinghe 16.2.18 (FSL GO Smith); 1 NAP Dunkerque W/E 21.2.18; Surveyed 4.3.18; Deleted 13.3.18 wrecked

B3867  (BR.1) Presentation a/c 'Basutoland No.3, Moshoeshoe' 4.17; Deld ADD by 26.7.17; 4 Sqdn 29.7.17; Albatros C OOC 1m W of Ghiselles 16.50 3.9.17; 2-str seaplane in sea 22m NE of Ostende, shared B3879 & B6213 08.15 22.9.17 (all FSL KV Turney); Collided B3934 at 15,000 ft and fell locked together into sea 6m N of Nieuport 17.15 27.9.17 (FSL KV Turney killed); Surveyed 17.10.17; Deleted 23.10.17 TL

B3868  (130-hp Clerget) Presentation a/c 'Basutoland No.4, Letsie I' 4.17; Deld Dover 31.8.17 - @1.9.17; 1 NAP Dunkerque by 6.9.17; 8 Sqdn 9.9.17; 10 Sqdn 4.2.18 (temp custody); 1 Sqdn 15.2.18 (temp); War School Manston (via Dover) 19.2.18; Crashed inverted 23.2.18; Deleted W/E 30.3.18

B3869  (130hp Clerget later BR.1) Presentation a/c 'Basutoland No.5, Lerotholi' 4.17; Deld Dover store 23.7.17; ADD 25.7.17; 6 Sqdn 30.7.17; ADD 27.8.17; 10 Sqdn 17.10.17; Albatros DV crashed nr Keyem 12.45 15.11.17 (FSL JG Manuel); 1 NAP (overhaul) 24.1.18; 9 Sqdn 24.3.18; 4 ASD Guines 28.3.18; 204 Sqdn

11.4.18; FL 15.6.18 (Lt SCJ Askin unhurt); 4 ASD 17.6.18; Deleted

**B3870** (130-hp Clerget) Presentation a/c 'Basutoland No.6, Letsie II' 4.17; Deld Dover 20.7.17; ADD 22.7.17; 9 Sqdn 4.8.17; Shot down in flames SE of Nieuport by Vzfw Buckler, Jasta 17 06.45 9.8.17 (FSL MG Woodhouse killed); Deleted 1.9.17

**B3877** (130-hp Clerget) Presentation a/c 'Basutoland No.7, Griffith' 4.17; Deld ADD 20.7.17; 8 Sqdn 24.7.17; Aviatik C crashed E of Lens, shared N6375 16.00 27.7.17 (F/Cdr RA Little), shelled by British guns, crew killed; Mid-air collision B3757 during combat over Lens 17.8.17 (FSL EA Bennetts killed); Deleted 7.9.17

**B3878** (130-hp Clerget) Presentation a/c 'Basutoland No.8, Makhaola' 4.17; Deld Dover 31.8.17 - @1.9.17; ADD by 6.9.17; 8 Sqdn (coded 'Z') by 9.9.17; 1 NAP Dunkerque 25.1.18; Dover 28.1.18; EC&AD Grain 23.2.18 - @8.2.18 (still coded 'Z') (ditching trials with hydrovane & tail vane 9.8.18)

**B3879** (BR.1) Presentation a/c 'Basutoland No.9, Bereng' 4.17; Deld ADD by 26.7.17; 4 Sqdn 5.8.17; Albatros C OOC 1m SW of Ghistelles 16.50 3.9.17; 2-str in sea 22m NE of Ostende, shared B3867 & B6213 08.15, then seaplane in sea 25m NE of Zeebrugge 08.35 22.9.17; V-strutter OOC Coxyde-Keyem 16.30-16.40 11.3.18; Pfalz DIII probably crashed 5m off Middelkerke 08.25 21.3.18; Pfalz DIII crashed 1½m NE of from Dixmude 17.00 26.3.18 (all F/L JEL Hunter); Became 204 Sqdn 1.4.18; Rumpler C OOC S of Dixmude 13.15 2.5.18; Rumpler C last seen going down on back at 10,000ft S of Dixmude 8.5.18 (both Capt JEL Hunter); 4 ASD Guines 21.5.18 - @25.5.18; Deleted?

**B3880** (130-hp Clerget) Presentation a/c 'Basutoland No.10, Maama' 4.17; Deld Dover store 23.7.17; ADD 25.7.17; 9 Sqdn 29.7.17; Aviatik OOC Westende 13.00 15.9.17 (FSL WEB Oakley); Shot down by 2 HA S of Ostende c12.30 15.10.17 (FSL WEB Oakley PoW); Surveyed 25.10.17; Deleted 29.10.17 TL

**B3881** (130-hp Clerget) Deld ADD (via Dover) 21.7.17; 9 Sqdn 29.7.17 (cut-out head of comedian George Robey on fin); COL 29.7.17; EF, COL 9.9.17 (FSL EM Knott); to ADD; Seaplane Defence Sqdn by 24.10.17; ADD W/E 8.11.17; 4 ASD 3.4.18 - @23.4.18; 4 ASD Pilots Pool Guines by 25.5.18 - 21.11.18LM

**B3882** (130-hp Clerget) Deld ADD (via Dover) 21.7.17; 6 Sqdn 26.7.17; Albatros DIII OOC Ghistelles 17.40 15.8.17; Aviatik C crashed 1m E of Westende, shared B3833 & N6351 18.15 17.8.17; Albatros C OOC Moere, shared B3833 10.50 20.8.17 (all F/Cdr BPH de Roeper); 10 Sqdn 30.8.17; Albatros DV OOC E of Zonnebeke 16.30 9.9.17, Albatros DV crashed N of Moorslede 10.45 28.9.17 (both FSL GL Trapp); Damaged by gunfire, petrol tank hit 18.10.17 (FSL HWM Cumming); Damaged by storm 20.10.17; 1 NAP Dunkerque 3.11.17; 12 Sqdn 19.12.17; Sqdn disbanded 1.4.18; Dover, engine choked on TO, crashed avoiding shed, badly damaged 14.5.18 (Lt FP Pemble unhurt); Dover store by 25.5.18; 4 ASD Pilots Pool Audembert 17.6.18; Spun in after flat turn while landing, crashed Le Crotoy 18.6.18 (Lt J Douglas killed)

**B3883** (130-hp Clerget) Deld Dover store 23.7.17; ADD 26.7.17; 9 Sqdn 29.7.17; Crashed, damaged 14.8.17 (FSL OC Le Boutillier); ADD 14.8.17; 9 Sqdn 10.9.17; Albatros DV crashed just W of Leke, shared B3884, B3898 & B3905 17.30 11.9.17 [probably Lt ZS Gotz, MFJ1]; Aviatik C crashed on fire NE of Nieuport, shared B3892 & B3905 16.45 16.9.17; Albatros DV Nieuport-Westende 16.25 21.9.17; Albatros DIII OOC Leke, shared B3892 & B3898 15.45 24.9.17; Albatros C dest Middelkerke, shared B3884, B3892, B3898 & B5652 10.55 30.9.17; Albatros C dest Middelkerke 11.55 10.9.17 (all FSL HF Stackard); Albatros C OOC Slype 13.45 & another dest Pervyse, shared B3884 14.35 13.11.17 (F/Cdr JST Fall); AP Dover 23.11.17; War School Manston 31.12.17; Became Pool of Pilots Manston 1.4.18 (130-hp Clerget); Crashed 27.4.18

**B3884** (130-hp Clerget later BR.1) Deld ADD by 26.7.17; 9 Sqdn 4.8.17; Albatros DV crashed 1m behind trenches SE of Pervyse, shared B3898, B3907 & B6204 c19.35 3.9.17; Aviatik C OOC W of Middelkerke 09.40 4.9.17; Albatros C OOC Middelkerke, shared B3892, B3898,

B3907 & B6204 13.35 6.9.17; Albatros DV crashed just W of Leke, shared B3883, B3898 & B3905 17.30 11.9.17 [probably Lt ZS Gotz, MFJ1]; Albatros C dest Middelkerke, shared B3883, B3892, B3898 & B5652 10.55 30.9.17; 2-str in flames E of Slype, shared B3898 13.00 21.10.17; Albatros C dest Pervyse, shared B3883 14.35 13.11.17; DFW C on fire 4m E of Pervyse, shared B3818 & B6288 15.15 10.12.17 (all FSL AW Wood); 1 NAP Dunkerque 13.1.18; 3 Sqdn 27.2.18; 8 Sqdn 1.3.18 - @21.3.18; Walmer to AAP Dover 2.4.18; 4 ASD Guines 4.18; 201 Sqdn 23.4.18; Albatros DV shot down Bapaume-Mory, shared D1852 & flight 06.45 16.5.18; Albatros DV BU Haucourt, 6m SE of Arras 19.00 17.5.18 (all Lt MH Findlay); General engagement S of Armentières, petrol tank holed, FL nr Boeschepe c.08.30 1.8.18 (2/Lt BL McCarthy wounded); Rep Pk 1 ASD 2.8.18; Deleted 8.9.18

**B3888** Ex Kingston Works to Hendon for erection 19.7.17; Martlesham 13.8.17

**B3892** (130-hp Clerget) Deld ADD by 26.7.17; 9 Sqdn 4.8.17; EF, COL 5.8.17 (FSL HleR Wallace); Tested after repair 7.8.17; Albatros C OOC Middelkerke, shared B3884, B3898, B3907 & B6204 13.35 6.9.17; Aviatik crashed on fire nr Nieuport, shared B3883 & B3905 16.45 16.9.17 [serial uncertain] (both FSL HLeR Wallace); Albatros DIII OOC Leke, shared B3883 & B3898 15.45 24.9.17 (FSL AW Wood); Albatros C dest Middelkerke, shared B3883, B3884, B3898 & B5652 10.55 30.9.17 (FSL CA Narbeth); COL 7.11.17 (FSL MS Taylor); 1 NAP Dunkerque (overhaul) 9.11.17; 8 Sqdn 19.1.18; 1 NAP Dunkerque (overhaul) 2.2.18 (refitted BR.1 c.28.2.18-1.3.18); 4 Sqdn 17.3.18; Pfalz DIII crashed in floods 2m NE of Dixmude & another (all-white) OOC NE of Dixmude 17.00 26.3.18 (FSL CRR Hickey); Became 204 Sqdn 1.4.18; Crashed and badly damaged 6.5.18; 4 ASD Guines 8.5.18; Deleted 13.5.18 general fatigue

**B3893** (130-hp Clerget) Deld ADD by 26.7.17; 9 Sqdn 29.7.17; Albatros DV OOC Westende 13.05 15.9.17; Albatros DV OOC Leke 15.10 20.9.17; DFW C OOC on fire Ostende 09.00 13.10.17 (all F/L AR Brown); 1 NAP Dunkerque 1.11.17 (overhaul); 8 Sqdn 19.1.18; 10 Sqdn 4.2.18 (temp custody); 1 Sqdn 15.2.18; War School Manston (via Dover) 19.2.18; Deleted 30.3.18

**B3894** (BR.1) Deld Dover 23.7.17; ADD 24.7.17; 3 Sqdn 5.8.17; Albatros DV OOC Middelkerke 11.00 23.9.17 (FSL GS Harrover wounded); ADD 10.10.17; Seaplane Defence Squadron 16.10.17; Became 13 Sqdn 15.1.18; 1 NAP Dunkerque (overhaul) 31.1.18; 4 Sqdn 9.3.18; Crashed 11.3.18 (FSL GEC Howard); 1 NAP Dunkerque by 14.3.18; 4 ASD Guines 28.3.18; 204 Sqdn 25.4.18; Albatros DIII DD 3m off Ostende 27.5.18; Fokker DVII OOC Blankenberghe 14.45 30.6.18; Fokker DVII OOC pilot fell out & another BU over Roulers down in sea [Lombartzyde-Roulers] 19.00-19.30, then FL Coxyde 31.7.18 (all Capt JEL Hunter DSC); 2 Fokker DVII in flames & another OOC Blankenberghe 10.55 12.8.18 (Capt JEL Hunter DSC wounded); Fokker DVII OOC SE of Ypres 19.00 15.8.18 (Lt BE Barnum); COL 30.8.18 (2/Lt JR Chisman); 4 ASD Guines 31.8.18; WOC 12.9.18 general fatigue

**B3895** (BR.1) Deld ADD (via Dover) 27.7.17; 3 Sqdn 5.8.17; Albatros DV OOC S of Middelkerke 15.50 22.8.17; DFW C forced down intact, shared B3785, B3858, B3866 & N6377 Furnes-Adinkerke 18.00 10.9.17; Albatros Scout dest Couckelaere 10.45 11.9.17; FL nr Oost Dunkerque 23.9.17 (all FSL ET Hayne), flying again by 27.9.17; 4 Sqdn 3.11.17; Became 204 Sqdn 1.4.18; 4 ASD Guines 20.5.18 - @25.5.18

**B3896** (130-hp Clerget) Deld ADD 25.7.17; 9 Sqdn 4.8.17; Hit hangar and aircraft on landing 11.9.17 (FSL W Ingleson unhurt); to 1 NAP Dunkerque; 9 Sqdn 1.11.17; ADD 19.11.17 - @29.12.17; 1 NAP Dunkerque (overhaul) by 3.1.18 (refitted BR.1 c.14-21.2.18); 8 Sqdn 21.2.18; 3 Sqdn 3.3.18 - @10.3.18; 1 NAP Dunkerque by 14.3.18; 4 ASD Guines 28.3.18; 213 Sqdn 13.4.18; In action 9.5.18 (Lt RT Whiteley wounded); To 4 ASD; Deleted 13.5.18 general fatigue

**B3897** (130-hp Clerget later BR.1) Deld ADD (via Dover) 25.7.17; 9 Sqdn 30.7.17; Shot down and FL 1½m W of

*Brightly painted Sopwith Camel B3926 of Manston War Flight. On the starboard side it had the inscription 'HAPPY HAWKINS' the full depth of the fuselage. (via Frank Cheesman)*

*Sopwith Camels B5655 and B6308 of 2 Wing in the Aegean. (via Frank Cheesman)*

*Sopwith Camel B3782 of 213 Sqdn was flown by Flight Lieutenant J.de C. Paynter early in 1918. (F.L.Cattle via Frank Cheesman)*

*Striped Sopwith Camel B3858 of 3 Sqdn was flown at Walmer by FSL E Pierce in November-December 1917 while the squadron was resting. (via Frank Cheesman)*

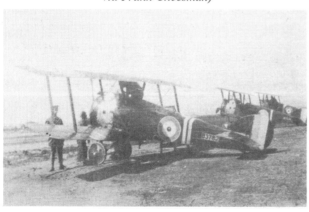 

Nieuport 8.8.17; Albatros C OOC Middelkerke-Nieuport, shared B3810, B3818, B3829 & B3832 08.00 5.9.17 (FSL AW Wood); Flying again 10.9.17; COL 12.9.17 (FSL W Ingleson); HA in steep dive probably dest 11.00 17.10.17 (F/Cdr JST Fall); LM28.12.17; 1 NAP Dunkerque (overhaul) by 3.1.18 - @9.3.18; 12 Sqdn by 11.3.18; Sqdn disbanded 1.4.18; 4 ASD to 2 AI 17.5.18; Rep Pk 2 ASD 17.5.18; 2 AI 18.5.18; 209 Sqdn 25.5.18; Hit French wagon on approach, CW 27.5.18 (Capt CN Jones unhurt); 2 ASD by 31.5.18 ; SOC 11.6.18 NWR

**B3898** (130-hp Clerget) Deld ADD (via Dover) 26.7.17; 9 Sqdn 4.8.17; Albatros DV crashed 1m behind trenches SE of Pervyse, shared B3884, B3907 & B6204 c19.35 3.9.17; DFW C OOC nr Middelkerke, shared B3905 & B6204 09.40 4.9.17; Albatros C OOC Middelkerke, shared B3884, B3892, B3907 & B6204 13.35 6.9.17; Albatros DV OOC Middelkerke, shared B6204 19.05 9.9.17; Albatros DV crashed just W of Leke, shared B3883, B3884 & B3905 17.30 11.9.17 [probably Lt ZS Gotz, MFJ1]; Albatros DV crashed 1m NW of Leke, shared B3829 & B3905 17.15 14.9.17; Albatros DIII OOC Leke, shared B3883 & B3892 15.45 24.9.17; Albatros DV OOC Middelkerke 16.25 24.9.17; Albatros C dest Middelkerke, shared B3883, B3884, B3892 & B5652 10.55 30.9.17; Albatros C OOC E of Slype, shared B6217 14.50 2.10.17; 2-str in flames E of Slype, shared B3884 13.00 21.10.17 (all F/Cdr JST Fall); 1 NAP Dunkerque 3.11.17; 10 Sqdn 18.1.18; 9 Sqdn 4.2.18; Dover 17.2.18; War School Manston 19.2.18; Became Pool of Pilots Manston 1.4.18; ARS Vendôme by 11.18

**B3905** (130-hp Clerget) Deld ADD 27.7.17; 9 Sqdn 4.8.17 (named 'MURYEL'); DFW C OOC nr Middelkerke, shared B3898 & B6204 09.40 4.9.17 (FSL JE Scott); Albatros DV crashed just W of Leke, shared B3883, B3884 & B3898 17.30 11.9.17 [probably Lt ZS Gotz, MFJ1]; Albatros DV crashed 1m NW of Leke, shared B3829 & B3898 17.15 14.9.17 (both FSL CA Narbeth); Aviatik C crashed on fire NE of Nieuport, shared B3883 & B3892 16.45 16.9.17 (FSL AW Wood); 12 Sqdn 22.12.17; Shot down nr Menin Sleyhage by Ltn von Haebler, Jasta 36 8.3.18 (FSL HR Casgrain PoW); Deleted 11.3.18

**B3906** (130-hp Clerget) Deld Dover 7.8.17; ADD 9.8.17; 9 Sqdn 15.8.17; Patrol 17.25-18.55, chased by 4 Albatros DV, 1 OOC St.Pierre Capelle, then own m/c shot down and FL in No Mans Land, St.Pierre Capelle 20.9.17 (FSL R Sykes wounded); Surveyed 22.9.17; Deleted 27.9.17

**B3907** (130-hp Clerget) Deld ADD by 2.8.17; 9 Sqdn 9.8.17; Albatros DV crashed 1m behind trenches SE of Pervyse, shared B3884, B3898 & B6204 c19.35 3.9.17; Albatros C OOC Middelkerke, shared B3892, B3898, B3907 & B6204 13.35 6.9.17 (both FSL JE Scott); COL 24.9.17 (FSL MS Taylor unhurt); ADD 24.9.17; Dest by fire night of 1.10.17; Surveyed 17.10.17; Deleted 23.10.17 burnt

**B3908** (BR.1) Deld ADD by 2.8.17 - @9.8.17; 11 Sqdn by 18.8.17 - @30.8.17; 3 Sqdn by 4.9.17; COL 26.9.17 (S/Cdr RH Mulock); Dest by fire night of 1.10.17; Surveyed 27.9.17; Deleted 23.10.17 burnt

**B3909** (BR.1) Deld ADD (via Dover) 28.7.17; 3 Sqdn 11.8.17; Albatros DV OOC nr Stalhille 07.30 3.9.17; ADD by 6.9.17; 4 Sqdn 30.9.17; Seaplane Defence Squadron St.Pol 17.10.17; EF, FL on beach, damaged one wing Malo les Bains 10.10.17 (A/F/Cdr CJ Price); Became 13 Sqdn 15.1.18; 2-str seaplane in flames 100yds off Blankenberghe Pier, shared B3782, B6407, B6410 & B7186 14.00 29.1.18; Pfalz DIII OOC Ostende 10.30 24.3.18 (both FSL JE Greene); 4 ASD Guines 28.3.18; 13 Sqdn 30.3.18; Became 213 Sqdn 1.4.18; Seaplane dest Zeebrugge c14.30 1.4.18 (2/Lt JE Greene); 4 ASD Guines 20.5.18 - @25.5.18; Deleted?

**B3910** (130-hp Clerget) Deld ADD 16.8.17; 10 Sqdn 30.8.17; Albatros DV OOC NE of Houthulst Forest 11.25 23.9.17 (A/F/Cdr WM Alexander); Albatros DV apparently OOC 2m W of Lille 22.12.17 (FSL WH Wilmot); 9 Sqdn 4.2.18; Dover 16.2.18; War School Manston 19.2.18; Became Pool of Pilots Manston 1.4.18; Freiston 3.5.18; Became 4 SoAF&G Freiston 6.5.18; Starboard wing folded up pulling out after firing

at ground target 14.5.18 (2/Lt CF Mossman killed)

**B3912** (130-hp Clerget) Deld ADD (via Dover) 7.8.17; 6 Sqdn 17.8.17; 10 Sqdn 30.8.17; 1-str OOC Ten-Brielen 16.30 14.9.17; Crashed, damaged Vlamertinghe 23.9.17 (both FSL WC Johnston); ADD for survey 24.9.17; dest by fire night of 1.10.17; Surveyed 17.10.17; Deleted 23.10.17 burnt

**B3919** (130-hp Clerget) Deld Dover 7.8.17; ADD 9.8.17; 6 Sqdn, RNAS 14.8.17; Fokker DVII OOC 06.10-08.10 patrol 17.8.17; Crashed and damaged in field 22.8.17 (both FSL ED Abbott); ADD 23.8.17; 10 Sqdn 27.9.17; In combat 21.10.17 (FSL WN Fox wounded); Collided B5666 on aerodrome, damaged 5.11.17 (FSL JG Clark); NADD 6.11.17; 10 Sqdn 2.2.18 (storage for AD); 9 Sqdn 4.2.18; Dover 12.3.18; Chingford 13.3.18; Became 207 TDS Chingford 1.4.18; Turnhouse by 12.18 [Once coded '10']

**B3920** (130-hp Clerget) Deld Dover 23.8.17; ADD 26.8.17; 10 Sqdn 6.9.17; FL, crashed E of Ypres, CW 25.9.17 (FSL AF MacDonald injured); ADD 26.9.17; Surveyed 3.10.17; Deleted 8.10.17 DBR

**B3921** (130-hp Clerget) Deld ADD (via Dover) 9.8.17; 8 Sqdn 18.8.17; DFW OOC E of Lens, shared N6375 & B3845 08.50 19.8.17 (FSL WL Jordan); KB dest 22.8.17; In moonlight, set alight a shed containing a KB Quiéry-la-Motte - Brebières 20.45 29.9.17; 2-str OOC 27.10.17; Grounded KB destroyed N of Meurchin 06.10 7.11.17 (all F/Cdr RB Munday); 1 NAP Dunkerque W/E 10.1.18 (fitted BR.1 W/E 21.2.18); 13 Sqdn 21.2.18; 10 Sqdn 28.3.18; Became 210 Sqdn 1.4.18; Time expired, to Rec Pk 4 ASD 4.6.18 unfit for further service in field; Flown to England 11.6.18

**B3922** (BR.1) Deld ADD (via Walmer) 9.8.17; 8 Sqdn (coded 'D') 19.8.17; Ran into bank landing, slightly damaged 29.9.17 (F/Cdr C Draper); ADD 1.10.17 - @4.10.17; Dover by 13.10.17; War School Manston (coded 'D') 31.12.17; Became Pool of Pilots Manston 1.4.18 - @5.18; Crashed 17.4.18; 470 Flt/Tongue Defence Flt Manston from 10.6.18; Burgh Castle 15.11.18

**B3923** (130-hp Clerget) Presentation a/c 'The Springbok'; Deld War Flt Manston 10.8.17; AGPs 12.8.17 (FSL EB Drake); AGP, bullet through propeller 22.8.17 (F/L AF Brandon); Surveyed 28.10.17; Deleted 29.10.17

**B3924** (130-hp Clerget) Deld War Flt Manston 10.8.17; AGP 12.8.17 (FSL AH Lofft); Exptl airscoops fitted 7.9.17; Greenwich Naval College W/E 16.2.18 for GI purposes

**B3925** (130-hp Clerget) Deld War Flt Manston 11.8.17; Attacked Gotha off North Foreland without result 12.8.17 (FSL HR de Wilde); Repairing bullet through propeller 15.8.17; Surveyed 24.12.17; Deleted 3.1.18

**B3926** (130-hp Clerget) Deld War Flt Manston 13.8.17; AGP 22.8.17 (FSL MA Harker); Crashed 27.9.17 (FSL FV Hall); Became Pool of Pilots Manston (named 'HAPPY HAWKINS') 1.4.18 (BR.1); Yarmouth by 12.6.18 - @9.18 (Burgh Castle)

**B3933** (BR.1 later 130-hp Clerget) Deld ADD (via Dover) 9.8.17; 6 Sqdn 18.8.17; 10 Sqdn 30.8.17; During engagement W of Roulers 07.10, shot down Terhand-Becelaere by Ltn W von Bülow, Jasta 36 13.9.17 (FSL ED Abbott PoW); Possibly the a/c being salved by S/Cdr TC Vernon of 9 Sqdn when he crashed 14.9.17 (DoI 15.9.17); Deleted 17.9.17

**B3934** (BR.1) Deld ADD (via Walmer) 9.8.17; 11 Sqdn 15.8.17; 4 Sqdn 2.9.17; Collided B3867 at 15,000 ft and fell locked together into sea 6m N of Nieuport 17.15 27.9.17 (FSL EJK Buckley killed); Surveyed 17.10.18; Deleted 23.10.17 TL

**B3935** (BR.1) Deld ADD 8.17; 11 Sqdn by 16.8.17; 3 Sqdn 3.9.17; 1-str OOC nr Thourout 11.10 11.9.17 (FSL LA Sands); O/t landing, damaged Walmer 24.12.17 (FSL WH Chisam unhurt); AP Dover 28.12.17 (repair); NADD W/E 7.2.18 - @23.2.18; 13 Sqdn by 28.2.18; Rumpler C crashed Dixmude-Cockelaere, shared B3782 & N6349 15.00 8.3.18 (FSL FC Stovin); Became 213 Sqdn 1.4.18; 4 ASD Guines 20.5.18 - @25.5.18

**B3936** (BR.1) Deld Dover 9.8.17; ADD 10.8.17; 4 Sqdn 19.8.17 - @4.9.17; ADD by 13.9.17; Seaplane Defence Squadron 19.10.17; Albatros DIII crashed in sea NW of Ostende c15.15 27.10.17 (FSL LH Slatter); Crashed while taxying 4.11.17; ADD 4.11.17; 1 NAP (overhaul) 29.12.17; 3 Sqdn 23.1.18; Fokker DrI OOC SE of

Dixmude 12.00, but own m/c badly shot up 5.2.18 (FSL RC Berlyn); 8 Sqdn 1.3.18; Became 208 Sqdn 1.4.18; Burnt to prevent capture La Gorgue 9.4.18

**B3937** (BR.1) Deld AAP Hendon 8.17; ADD (via Dover) 10.8.17; 11 Sqdn 15.8.17; 4 Sqdn 2.9.17; Albatros Scout in flames S of Ghistelles c10.25, then shot down nr Ichteghem 21.10.17 (FSL EGA Eyre killed); Surveyed 31.10.17; deleted 2.11.17 TL

**B3938** (130-hp Clerget) Deld AAP Hendon 8.17; ADD (via Dover) 10.8.17; 4 Sqdn by 18.8.17; Shot down OOC smoking E of Dixmude 09.10 18.8.17 (FSL CRW Hodges killed) [believed by Ltn P Billik]

**B3939** (BR.1) Deld AAP Hendon 8.17; ADD (via Dover) 14.8.17; 4 Sqdn 26.8.17; Crashed and awaiting survey by 7.3.18; 1 NAP W/E 14.3.18; 4 ASD Guines 28.3.18; 204 Sqdn 10.4.18; Crashed on TO, TW 20.6.18 (Lt GEC Howard unhurt); 4 ASD 20.6.18; WOC 30.6.18 general fatigue

**B3940** (BR.1) Deld AAP Hendon 8.17; ADD (via Dover) 10.8.17; 3 Sqdn 18.8.17; COL 6.9.17 (FSL ET Hayne); Flying again by 9.9.17; Albatros DV OOC, possibly indecisive Thourout 11.100 11.9.17 (FSL GB Anderson); AP Dover 29.12.17; ADD 21.2.18; 10 Sqdn 23.2.18; Became 210 Sqdn 1.4.18; Port wheel came on TO, o/t landing, practice flight 28.5.18 (Lt DM McGregor unhurt); Rep Pk 1 ASD 28.5.18; Deleted 8.6.18 NWR

**B3947** (130-hp Clerget) Deld Brooklands to CSD White City 21.8.17; Despatched 2 Wing Mudros 27.8.17; Sunk in transit, deleted 28.11.17

**B3948** (130-hp Clerget) Deld Brooklands to CSD White City 21.8.17; Despatched 2 Wing Mudros 27.8.17; Sunk in transit, deleted 28.11.17

**B3949** (130-hp Clerget) Deld Brooklands to CSD White City 11.9.17 for 2 Wing RNAS; Marsh by 30.11.17; C Flt 2 Wing Imbros by 12-19.1.18; Stavros by 3.18 - @4.18 (repair); Repair Base Mudros by 6.18

**B3950** (130-hp Clerget later BR.1) Deld AAP Hendon; ADD (via Dover) 11.8.17; 6 Sqdn 23.8.17; 10 Sqdn 30.8.17; 2-str forced down Houthulst Forest & strafed on ground, neither pilot nor observer came out 11.15 20.9.17; FL, damaged Middle aerodrome 4.11.17 (both FSL JG Manuel); Flying again 8.11.17; Albatros DV OOC Staden 14.50 23.1.18 (F/Cdr WM Alexander); 1 NAP Dunkerque (overhaul) 24.1.18; 12 Sqdn 25.3.18; Became 212 Sqdn 1.4.18; 4 ASD 4.18; 201 Sqdn 27.4.18; OP, EF, FL, crashed nr Remaisnil 14.50 25.5.18 (Lt BL McCarthy unhurt); 2 ASD 27.5.18; Rebuilt as F6063 2.7.18

## 1 ROYAL AIRCRAFT FACTORY N.E.1 PUSHER BIPLANE NIGHT FIGHTER. (200-hp Hispano-Suiza)

**B3975** Fifth a/c, sent for final inspection 21.12.17; Deld EAD Grain W/E 23.2.18

## 3 F.B.A. PUSHER BIPLANE FLYING BOATS. (150-hp Gnome Monosoupape)

**B3984** Ex 9615; In store Bogton for RNAS by 26.9.18 - 11.18; AAP Renfrew by 1.19

**B3985** Ex 9622; In store Bogton for RNAS by 26.9.18 - 11.18; AAP Renfrew by 1.19

**B3986** Ex 9623; In store Bogton for RNAS by 26.9.18 - 11.18; AAP Renfrew by 1.19

## 3 SOPWITH SHIP STRUTTER TRACTOR BIPLANES rebuilt at 2(N)ARD Coal Aston

**B4012** Turnhouse by 3.5.18 (prefix assumed)

**B4016** 78 Sqdn by 12.17; Convtd Ship Strutter; Turnhouse W/E 26.4.18; Deleted W/E 3.10.18

**B4044** (130-hp Clerget) Grain ECD by 25.5.18; Convtd Ship Strutter; Turnhouse W/E 11.7.18 - @23.1.19

## 11 AVRO 504A TRACTOR BIPLANE TRAINERS from batch B4301 to B4400 built by Avro. (B4309/10, B4338/9 transferred without engines, others with 80-hp Gnome)

**B4309** (80-hp Gnome, later 100-hp Gnome Monosoupape) Deld Cranwell 2.10.17; Redcar 14.3.18; Deleted W/E 30.3.18

**B4310** (80-hp Gnome, later 80-hp Le Rhône). Deld Cranwell 9.10.17; Became 201/2 TDS Cranwell 1.4.18 - @14.5.18

**B4311** Deld Cranwell 9.10.17; Crashed nr aerodrome, u/c smashed 23.1.18 (pilot unhurt); Crashed, CW Rauceby 22.3.18 (PFO AL Stephens shock); Pool of Pilots Joyce Green by 4.19 - @6.19 (prefix?)

**B4312** Deld Cranwell 9.10.17, allocated Redcar by 30.3.18

**B4313** Deld Cranwell 9.10.17; Crashed and badly damaged 1m E of Rauceby Gun Station 19.12.17 (pilot unhurt); Redcar 14.3.18 (now 100-hp Gnome Monosoupape); Became 2 SSF 5.18; Spun in 3.5.18 (Lt EG Rice & Lt LR Thacker both killed)

**B4314** Deld Redcar School by rail 3.10.17; For deletion by 9.3.18 (NTU?); NE Area FIS Redcar by 8.18; Crashed [NO DATE] (PFO Foote)

**B4315** Deld Redcar School 10.10.17 - @30.3.18

**B4316** (DC) Deld Eastbourne NFS by rail 7.10.17; Became 206 TDS Eastbourne 1.4.18; Crashed into B6100 9.5.18 (pilot unhurt)

**B4317** (504J)(100-hp Gnome Monosoupape) (DC) Deld Eastbourne NFS (80-hp Gnome) by rail 7.10.17; Became 206 TDS Eastbourne 1.4.18 - @23.5.18

**B4338** Deld Bristol to Manston FS for erection W/E 8.12.17; Became 203 TDS Manston 1.4.18

**B4339** (80-hp Gnome) Deld Bristol to Manston FS for erection W/E 8.12.17; Became 203 TDS Manston 1.4.18

**B4361** Chingford/Fairlop

**B4362** Chingford/Fairlop

**B4363** Chingford/Fairlop

**B4373** Chingford/Fairlop

## 20 ROYAL AIRCRAFT FACTORY B.E.2E TRACTOR BIPLANES from batch B4401 to B4600 built by The British & Colonial Aeroplane Co Ltd (c/n 2519-2718). (90hp R.A.F.)

**B4529** 55 TDS Manston by 8.18

**B4535** Exp Flt Gosport by 5.18 - 1.19 (for RN Signal School Portsmouth)

**B4537** Exp Flt Gosport by 5.18 - 10.18 (for RN Signal School Portsmouth)

**B4549** Deld Observers School Eastchurch W/E 27.10.17; Manston FS W/E 30.3.18; Became 203 TDS Manston 1.4.18; Became 55 TDS Manston 14.7.18 - @8.18

**B4550** 110 Sqdn Sedgford; 203 TDS Manston by 6.18

**B4555** Deld Donibristle W/E 3.11.17; Turnhouse W/E 21.2.18; Donibristle W/E 2.3.18; Turnhouse W/E 6.4.18; Donibristle W/E 23.5.18; Turnhouse W/E 13.6.18; Donibristle W/E 11.7.18 - @30.1.19

**B4556** Deld to Rosyth 18.10.17; Donibristle W/E 9.11.17; Turnhouse W/E 30.3.18; Crashed 25.4.18 (Lt NP Davies killed & Lt GA Bird injured); Deleted W/E 3.5.18

**B4558** Deld Observers School Eastchurch for erection by 29.12.17 - @30.3.18; 203 TDS Manston by 7.6.18 - @7.18

**B4560** Deld to Rosyth W/E 3.11.17; East Fortune NFS for erection W/E 9.2.18 - @30.3.18

**B4563** Deld to Rosyth W/E 3.11.17; East Fortune NFS for erection W/E 9.2.18 - @30.3.18

**B4565** Deld Observers School Flt Eastchurch W/E 3.11.17 - @30.3.18; 203 TDS Manston by 10.6.18

**B4572** Deld Mkrs by road to RFC Gosport 13.12.17 - @5.18 (W/T trials with RN Signal School Portsmouth)

**B4573** Deld Observers School Flts Eastchurch for erection W/E 10.11.17; Manston NFS W/E 30.3.18; Became 203 TDS Manston 1.4.18 - @8.4.18

**B4574** Deld Observers School Flts Eastchurch W/E 10.11.17; Paris NAS W/E 22.12.17 - @30.3.18 (special service with W/Cdr Spenser DA Gray)

**B4575** Deld Observers School Flts Eastchurch W/E 10.11.17; Manston NFS by 30.3.18; Became 203 TDS Manston 1.4.18 - @5.18

**B4578** Deld Observers School Flts Eastchurch for erection W/E 10.11.17; to Manston NFS W/E 30.3.18; Became 203 TDS Manston 1.4.18

**B4579** Deld Gunnery School Eastchurch for erection W/E 10.11.17; Manston NFS W/E 30.3.18; Became 203 TDS Manston 1.4.18; Became 55 TDS Manston 14.7.18 - @8.18

**B4580** Deld Gunnery School Eastchurch W/E 1.12.17; Manston

NFS W/E 30.3.18; Became 203 TDS Manston 1.4.18;
Became 55 TDS Manston 14.7.18 - @8.18

B4586   Deld D Flt Cranwell W/E 23.11.17; 203 TDS Manston
FS W/E 6.4.18 - @6.18

B4596   269 Sqdn (Submarine Flt) Port Said by 9.11.18; X' AD
28.2.19

## 27 MAURICE FARMAN S.11 SHORTHORN PUSHER BIPLANE TRAINERS from batch B4651 to B4580 built by The Aircraft Manufacturing Co Ltd. (mainly 80-hp Gnome)

B4655   Eastchurch by 3.18; Cranwell 11.3.18 (prefix?)

B4674   (80-hp Renault later 75-hp RR) Deld Eastbourne by rail
/21.7.17; Gunnery School Flts Eastchurch W/E 10.11.17
- @30.3.18; Became G-EAAZ

B4675   (80-hp Renault later 75-hp RR) Deld Eastbourne by road
23.7.17; Gunnery School Flts Eastchurch W/E 10.11.17
- @30.3.18

B4676   Deld Redcar School for erection 24.7.17; Surveyed
7.12.17; Deleted 14.12.17 as spares

B4677   Deld Redcar School for erection 24.7.17; Surveyed
7.12.17; Deleted 14.12.17 as spares

B4678   Deld Redcar School for erection 24.7.17; Surveyed
7.12.17; Deleted 14.12.17 as spares

B4687   (80-hp Renault) Deld Chingford for erection 3.8.17;
Gunnery School Flts Eastchurch W/E 13.10.17 -
@30.3.18

B4690   (75-hp Renault) Deld Eastbourne NFS by rail 30.7.17;
Gunnery School Flts Eastchurch W/E 3.11.17 -
@30.3.18

B4695   (75-hp Renault) Deld Eastbourne NFS by rail 1.8.17;
Gunnery School Flts Eastchurch W/E 3.11.17 -
@30.3.18; 204 TDS Eastchurch by 8.18

B4700   (75-hp Renault) Deld Eastbourne NFS by rail 13.10.17;
Gunnery School Flts Eastchurch W/E 17.11.17 - @3.18;
8 TDS Netheravon, WO 18.5.18

B4705   Deld Manston FS by road 9.8.17; Surveyed 9.1.18;
Deleted 15.1.18 BR

B4710   Deld Manston FS by road 15.8.17; Surveyed 9.1.18;
Deleted 15.1.18 BR

B4713   Deld Redcar School by rail 14.8.17; Damaged 21.9.17;
Surveyed 7.12.17; Deleted 14.12.17 as spares

B4714   Deld Redcar School by rail 14.8.17; Surveyed 7.12.17;
Deleted 14.12.17 as spares

B4728   Deld Redcar School 30.8.17; Surveyed 7.12.17; Deleted
14.12.17 as spares

B4729   Deld Redcar School by rail 30.8.17; Surveyed 7.12.17;
Deleted 14.12.17 as spares

B4730   Deld Redcar School by rail 30.8.17; Surveyed 7.12.17;
Deleted 14.12.17 as spares

B4745   Deld Redcar School W/E 8.9.17; Surveyed 7.12.17;
Deleted 14.12.17 as spares

B4746   Deld Redcar School W/E 8.9.17; Surveyed 7.12.17;
Deleted 14.12.17 as spares

B4747   (80-hp Renault) Deld Gunnery School Flts Eastchurch by
rail 8.9.17; Surveyed 12.3.18; Deleted 16.3.18 wrecked

B4748   (80-hp Renault) Deld Gunnery School Flts Eastchurch by
rail 8.9.17 - @30.3.18

B4755   Deld Redcar School by rail 26.9.17; Surveyed 7.12.17;
Deleted 14.12.17 as spares

B4756   Deld Redcar School by rail 26.9.17; Surveyed 7.12.17;
Deleted 14.12.17 as spares

B4763   (80-hp Renault) Deld Manston by road 3.10.17;
Surveyed 9.1.18; Deleted 15.1.18 BR

B4764   (80-hp Renault) Deld Manston by road 3.10.17;
Surveyed 9.1.18; Deleted 15.1.18 BR

B4771   Deld Redcar School by 13.10.17; Surveyed 7.12.17;
Deleted 14.12.17 as spares

B4772   Deld Redcar School by 13.10.17; Surveyed 7.12.17;
Deleted 14.12.17 as spares

## 19 SOPWITH F.1 CAMEL TRACTOR BIPLANE SCOUTS from batch B5551 - B5650 built by Ruston Proctor & Co Ltd. (130-hp Clerget 9B unless otherwise stated) [Appears to be every fifth aircraft initially to up to B5616]

B5551   Deld 4 AAP Lincoln by 8.11.17; Hendon W/E 1.12.17;
War School Manston W/E 1.12.17; Deleted W/E 9.3.18

B5556   Deld 4 AAP Lincoln by 8.11.17; Chingford W/E
29.12.17; Rebuilt and reserialled F9548 allocated
5.8.18, but cancelled and reverted to B5556

B5560   204 TDS Eastchurch, spun in OOC 21.5.18 (2/Lt LE
Pocock seriously injured)

B5561   Deld 4 AAP Lincoln by 8.11.17; Chingford W/E
29.12.17; Allocated War School Manston by 30.3.18

B5565   Cranwell, wrecked 18.9.18

B5566   Deld 10 AAP Brooklands by 19.1.18; Gunnery School
Flts Eastchurch 23.2.18 - @3.18; Wrecked .18

B5571   Naval aircraft at Clayton & Shuttleworth, Deleted
13.12.17 wreck

B5576   Deld AAP Lincoln by 12.17; Gunnery School Flts
Eastchurch W/E 8.12.17; Became 204 TDS Eastchurch
1.4.18; Engine trouble on TO, stalled in on turn
23.11.18 (2/Lt HV Perrin seriously injured)

B5581   Deld Rosyth W/E 7.12.17; Donibristle W/E 28.12.17;
Turnhouse W/E 21.2.18 - @30.1.19 (W/T expts)

B5586   Deld Rosyth W/E 7.12.17; Donibristle W/E 28.12.17;
Turnhouse W/E 28.2.18 - @1.19

B5591   Deld Rosyth W/E 7.12.17; Donibristle W/E 20.12.17;
Rosyth W/E 25.1.18; Turnhouse W/E 21.3.18; Stalled at
200ft, spun in 18.7.17 (Lt WD Baird slightly injured)

B5596   Deld 4 AAP Lincoln to Yarmouth W/E 20.12.17;
Became 490 Flt Yarmouth 25.5.18; 28 TDS Weston-on-
the-Green by 8.18

B5600   Rep Pk 1 ASD to England W/E 12.4.18; Yarmouth by
8.18; 470 Flt 273 Sqdn Burgh Castle .18

B5601   (150-hp B.R.1) Deld AAP Lincoln to Yarmouth W/E
29.12.17 - @5.18; 470 Flt (Tongue Defence Flt)
Manston by 25.5.18 (detd from Yarmouth); With B7269
and seaplanes N2927 & N2937 engaged by 7 enemy
seaplanes, 1 seen to crash vertically in sea off Kentish
Knock 18.7.18 (Lt FC Vincent); Naval Flt 219 Sqdn
Manston by 10.8.18; Throwley 26.10.18

B5606   Deld 4 AAP Lincoln to Yarmouth W/E 29.12.17;
Became 490 Flt Yarmouth 25.5.18 [at Burgh Castle];
Naval Flt 219 Sqdn Manston 1.10.18

B5611   Deld 4 AAP Lincoln to Cranwell 22.12.17; Became
201/2 TDS Cranwell 1.4.18 - @11.18

B5616   Deld Cranwell W/E 29.12.17; Crashed nr W/T station
and wrecked 20.2.18 (PFO RH Adcock injured);
Surveyed 25.2.18; Deleted 13.3.18 DBR

B5621   1 AI by 5.18; 208 Sqdn 16.5.18; Lost, FL, o/t, CW
28.5.18 (Lt WE Holland unhurt); Rep Pk 1 ASD
29.5.18; SOC in field 31.5.18

B5642   2 AI to 10.18; 5 AI 8.10.18; 1 ASD to 204 Sqdn
30.10.18; Damaged on landing 22.11.18; 1 ASD
14.1.19

## 100 SOPWITH F.1 CAMEL TRACTOR BIPLANE SCOUTS ordered 4.8.17 under Cont No A.S.7861 from Clayton & Shuttleworth Ltd, numbered B5651 to B5750 & built Lincoln. All deld to RNAS (Ordered with BR.1 but all except two delivered with 130-hp Clerget 9B)

B5651   Deld Dover W/E 8.9.17; ADD 15.9.17; 9 Sqdn
27.9.17; 1 NAP Dunkerque 21.10.17; 1 Sqdn 6.11.17;
Pfalz DIII in flames nr Dixmude, shared N5465 15.45
12.11.17 (FSL JH Forman); 12 Sqdn 6.12.17 -
@23.12.17; ADD by 27.12.17; 1 NAP Dunkerque by
3.1.18 - @7.3.18; 12 Sqdn by 11.3.18; Became 212
Sqdn 1.4.18; 4 ASD 3.4.18; 210 Sqdn 28.4.18; Stalled
landing & spun in from 50ft, CW 4.5.18 (Lt WL
Davidson USAS injured); 4 ASD 6.5.18; Surveyed
6.5.18; Deleted 18.5.18

B5652   Deld ADD by 13.9.17; 9 Sqdn 25.9.17; Albatros DIII
destroyed N of Dixmude, shared B3818, B3832, B6217
& B6230 16.10 28.9.17; Albatros C shot down
Middelkerke, shared B3883, B3884, B3892 & B3904
10.55 30.9.17 (both FSL MS Taylor); 1 NAP
Dunkerque 21.10.17; 12 Sqdn 10.12.17; Crashed,
wrecked Petite Synthe 18.12.17 (FSL JA Morell);
Surveyed 24.12.17; Deleted 3.1.18

B5653   Deld Dover W/E 8.9.17; ADD 15.9.17; 9 Sqdn
21.9.17; 1 NAP Dunkerque 21.10.17; 12 Sqdn
10.12.17; Crashed, wrecked 700yds N of Petite Synthe
23.12.17 (FSL TM Greeves); Surveyed 24.12.17;
Deleted 3.1.18

B5654   Deld AP Dover (via Cranwell) 20.9.17; War School
Manston 31.12.17 (Scouts Pool); Spun into ground from
1,500 ft 12.2.18 (2/Lt DR Glen killed); For deletion by
16.2.18

B5655   Shipped to Mudros 6.12.17; G Sqdn 2 Wing by 3.18;

Marsh by 13.3.18

**B5656** Shipped to Mudros by 1.1.18; B Sqdn 2 Wing Imbros by 3.18; 15 Gp Repair Base Mudros by 6.18 - 11.18

**B5657** Shipped to Mudros 6.12.17; 2 Wing Mudros for erection by 30.3.18; 15 Gp Repair Base Mudros by 6.18 - 1.19; To Greek Air Force

**B5658** Deld Dover 15.9.17; 1 NAP Dunkerque by 27.9.17; 10 Sqdn 19.11.17; Missing after engagement with Albatros Scouts W of Lille 13.45 3.1.18 (FSL F Booth killed) [believed shot down Meurchin by Uffz Liebert, Jasta 30]; Deleted 7.1.18

**B5659** Deld ADD by 4.10.17; 1 NAP Dunkerque by 25.10.17; 10 Sqdn 3.11.17; 2-str crashed Cockelaere, shared B6341 08.00 12.11.17 (FSL AG Beattie); 9 Sqdn 4.2.18; Chingford (via Dover) 14.3.18; Became 207 TDS Chingford 1.4.18; Became 54 TDS Chingford 20.7.18; Diving on target wheels hit water, o/t, sank Chingford reservoir 30.7.18 (2/Lt HC Curtiss injured)

**B5660** Deld ADD by 27.9.17; 1 NAP Dunkerque by 25.10.17; 1 Sqdn 6.11.17; Crashed, wrecked Middle aerodrome 8.11.17 (FSL AGA Spence); 1 NAP Dunkerque 8.11.17; Surveyed 13.11.17; Deleted 19.11.17 CW

**B5661** Deld ADD by 27.9.17; AP Dover by 29.9.17; War School Manston 15.2.18; Deleted 23.3.18

**B5662** Deld Cranwell W/E 19.10.17; Crashed Cranwell South 26.3.18 (pilot unhurt); Became 201/2 TDS Cranwell 1.4.18; Freiston 22.5.18; Cranwell by 6.18; 4 FS Freiston, lost speed on turn nr ground 17.12.18 (2/Lt WF Howett killed)

**B5663** Deld AP Dover W/E 13.10.17; To 10 Sqdn, COL 23.11.17 (FSL FV Hall); Red Albatros DV smoking crashed Keyem-Leke, shared B6320 15.35 5.12.17 (F/L WA Curtis); Gen engagement 9 HA, collided Albatros Scout, crashed OOC locked together nr Staden, claimed by Ltn Wandelt, Jasta 36 14.50 23.1.18 (FSL RA Blyth killed); Deleted 28.1.18

**B5664** Deld AP Dover (via Cranwell) 30.9.17; Walmer by 12.10.17; Dover by 27.10.17; 10 Sqdn 26.11.17; 9 Sqdn 4.2.18; Chingford (via Dover) 13.3.18; Became 207 TDS Chingford 1.4.18

**B5665** Deld AP Dover W/E 20.10.17; To ADD but EF, FL in English Channel nr Dieppe 2.1.18 (F/Cdr CD Booker); Deleted 14.1.18

**B5666** Deld Hendon (via Cranwell) 3.10.17; ADD 5.10.17; 10 Sqdn 20.10.17; Collided B3919 on aerodrome 5.11.17; Crashed, damaged 18.12.17 (FSL AA Cameron); ADD 19.12.17; 1 NAP Dunkerque by 29.12.17; 12 Sqdn 3.3.18; Became 212 Sqdn 1.4.18 - @2.4.18; 4 ASD to 2 AI 7.5.18; 209 Sqdn 10.5.18; Shot down, probably in combat with Albatros nr Beaufort 11.15 15.5.18 (2/Lt OG Brittorous killed)

**B5667** Deld AP Dover W/E 13.10.17; ADD by 29.12.17; 10 Sqdn 3.1.18; 9 Sqdn 4.2.18; Chingford (via Dover) 13.3.18; Became 207 TDS Chingford 1.4.18

**B5668** Shipped to Mudros 10.11.17; C Sqdn 2/62 Wing Imbros by 1.18; F Sqdn 62 Wing Mudros 15.4.18 - @6.18

**B5669** Shipped to Mudros 10.11.17

**B5670** Shipped to Mudros 26.11.17; Mudros for erection by 30.3.18; Imbros by 6.18

**B5671** Deld Cranwell 9.10.17; COL, damaged 23.2.18 (pilot unhurt); Became 201/2 TDS Cranwell 1.4.18

**B5672** Deld Cranwell 9.10.17; Spun in, CW Cranwell South 22.1.18 (PFO LG Huddlestone killed)

**B5673** Deld 4 AAP Lincoln to G (Exp) Flt Cranwell 6.10.17 Became 201/2 TDS Cranwell 1.4.18; Freiston 10.5.18; Cranwell by 6.18

**B5674** Deld 4 AAP Lincoln to G (Exp) Flt Cranwell 5.10.17; Collided with Pup C262 and badly damaged, Cranwell South 28.2.18 (pilot unhurt) Became 201/2 TDS Cranwell 1.4.18 - @6.18

**B5675** Deld 4 AAP Lincoln to Cranwell 9.10.17; Crashed and slightly damaged Cranwell South 28.2.18 (pilot unhurt); Became 202 TDS Cranwell 1.4.18; Crashed and damaged 4.4.18 (pilot unhurt); Became 57 TDS Cranwell 27.7.18 - @11.18

**B5676** Deld 4 AAP Lincoln to Cranwell 26.10.17; O/t landing 23.2.18 (pilot unhurt); Crashed, wrecked Cranwell South 9.3.18; Became 201/2 TDS Cranwell 1.4.18 Became 56/57 TDS Cranwell 27.7.18 - @11.18

**B5677** Deld 4 AAP Lincoln to Cranwell 19.10.17; Crashed &badly damaged 25.2.18 (pilot unhurt) Became 201/2

TDS Cranwell 1.4.18; Freiston 22.4.18; Cranwell by 11.18

**B5678** Deld 4 AAP Lincoln to Cranwell 26.10.17; Crashed Freiston 13.12.17; Cranwell by 12.17; Crashed S of Rauceby Gun Position 13.12.17 (F/L EE Blake killed); Surveyed 21.12.17; Deleted 15.1.18 wrecked

**B5679** Shipped to 2 Wing Mudros 19.12.17; Marsh by 26.2.18; Imbros by 24.3.18; 15 Group Repair Base Mudros by 6.18; 220 Sqdn Imbros by 27.10.18 - @1.19; RAF South Russia to 'A' dett RAF Instructional Mission South Russia 8.19; To White Russian Forces 1919

**B5680** Shipped to 2 Wing Mudros 14.12.17; Mudros for erection by 3.18; Stavros by 6.18 & 10.18 - @1.19; RAF South Russia to 'A' dett RAF Instructional Mission South Russia 8.19; To White Russian Forces 1919

**B5681** Shipped to 2 Wing Mudros 14.12.17; G Sqdn 2/62 Wing by 3.18; Mudros Repair Base by 6.18

**B5682** Shipped to 2 Wing Mudros 9.1.18; Mudros for erection by 30.3.18; Imbros by 6.18; Repair Base Mudros by 10.18 - @11.18; 220 Sqdn Imbros by 7.11.18; To RHNAS by 10.18 - 1.19

**B5683** Shipped to Aegean 4.1.18; arr 6 Wing Otranto by 3.18; Became 66/67 Wing 1.4.18; 225 Sqdn by 28.4.18 - @7.18; AD Taranto by 8.18; 481/3 Flts 225 Sqdn Andrano by 9.18; AD Taranto by 10.18

**B5684** Deld Cranwell W/E 16.11.17; Wrecked on/by 21.11.17; Surveyed 27.11.17; Deleted 6.12.17

**B5685** Wrecked at Mkrs by 29.12.17; Deld 4 AAP Lincoln by 2.18; Cranwell W/E 23.2.18 [ALSO RFC a/c ex Mansfield 23.3.18 !]

**B5686** Wrecked at Mkrs by 29.12.17; Allocated for delivery to Cranwell by 23.2.18 - @30.3.18; Deld Cranwell 4.18

**B5687** (130-hp Clerget later B.R.1) Deld AP Dover W/E 10.11.17; 10 Sqdn 29.12.17; O/t landing and damaged 30.1.18 (FSL HA Patey); 1 NAP Dunkerque (overhaul) 1.2.18 (re-fitted B.R.1 c.14-21.3.18); 3 Sqdn 23.3.18; Crashed Mont St.Eloi 31.3.18 (F/Cdr RA Little); Became 203 Sqdn 1.4.18; Petrol tank and engine shot through in combat 7.4.18 (FSL RC Berlyn slightly wounded); 4 ASD 9.4.18; 213 Sqdn 3.5.18; Albatros DV OOC 3m N of Middelkerke 19.55 15.5.18; Pfalz DIII OOC Moorslede, shared C65 & D3409 19.35 2.6.18 (both Lt JAC Tayler); Into ditch landing 28.7.18 (Lt AF Chick unhurt); To 4 ASD; WOC 15.8.18 general fatigue

**B5688** Deld Hendon (via Cranwell) W/E 17.11.17; War School Manston (coded 'F') W/E 24.11.17; Crashed 6.3.18 (FSL HR Gillett killed)

**B5689** Deld War School Manston W/E 22.12.17; Became Pilots Pool Manston 1.4.18 - @7.5.18

**B5690** Deld War School Manston W/E 22.12.17; Tested 14.1.18; Deleted 16.2.18

**B5691** Shipped to 2 Wing Mudros 9.1.18; Mudros for erection by 30.3.18; Repair Base Mudros 4.18; Imbros by 6.18

**B5692** Presentation a/c 'Punjab No.1, Bahawalpur'; Shipped to 2 Wing Mudros 19.12.17; Mudros by 3.18; Repair Base Mudros by 6.18; 220 Sqdn Imbros by 28.10.18 - @1.19

**B5693** Deld CSD White City 12.17; Hendon repair 12.17; East Fortune NFS for erection W/E 1.1.18; Redcar 22.3.18; 2 SSF Redcar, spun in 20.5.18 (Capt JAMcD Allan killed)

**B5694** Deld CSD White City 12.17; Hendon W/E 22.12.17; East Fortune NFS for erection W/E 1.1.18; Turnhouse W/E 9.3.18; East Fortune W/E 5.4.18

**B5695** Deld CSD White City 11.17; Cardiff Docks by 1.1.18; Shipped to 2 Wing Mudros 17.2.18; Repair Base Mudros by 6.18 & 10.18 - @11.18

**B5696** Deld CSD White City 11.17; Hendon W/E 29.12.17 (repair); East Fortune W/E 1.1.18 - @2.18

**B5697** Deld CSD White City 11.17; Cardiff Docks by 1.1.18; Shipped to 2 Wing Mudros 17.2.18; Repair Base Mudros by 6.18; Mudros for deletion 10.18

**B5698** Deld CSD White City 11.17; Hendon W/E 29.12.17 (repair); East Fortune NFS W/E 1.1.18; Turnhouse @1-3.3.18; Ground collision with another Camel, East Fortune 4.3.18; Grand Fleet SoAF&G East Fortune by 9.18 - @8.19

**B5699** Deld 4 AAP Lincoln to Cranwell W/E 23.11.17; Became 201/2 TDS Cranwell 1.4.18; Crashed, wings damaged 4.4.18 (pilot unhurt)

**B5700** Deld 4 AAP Lincoln to G (Experimental) Flt Cranwell

W/E 30.11.17 - @3.18; Crashed 5m NE of Doncaster 19.2.18 (pilot unhurt)

**B5701** Deld 4 AAP Lincoln to Cranwell W/E 16.11.17; Crashed, wings and u/c damaged, Ewerby 20.3.18 (pilot unhurt); Became 201 TDS Cranwell 1.4.18; Spun in from 300 ft 24.6.18 (PFO EA Appleby killed)

**B5702** Deld 4 AAP Lincoln to Cranwell W/E 23.11.17; Freiston @12.17; F Flt Cranwell 5.1.18; Crashed, wings and u/c damaged, Cranwell South 22.1.18 (pilot unhurt); Crashed and badly damaged, Cranwell South 21.2.18 (pilot unhurt); Became 201/2 TDS Cranwell 1.4.18

**B5703** Deld 4 AAP Lincoln to Cranwell W/E 23.11.17; Became 201/2 TDS Cranwell 1.4.18 - @6.18

**B5704** Deld 4 AAP Lincoln to Cranwell W/E 23.11.17; Crashed, propeller and wing damaged 23.1.18 (pilot unhurt); COL 1.3.18 (pilot unhurt); Became 201 TDS Cranwell 1.4.18; WO 3.7.18

**B5705** Deld Yarmouth W/E 17.11.17; Deleted W/E 30.3.18

**B5706** Deld Yarmouth W/E 17.11.17; Burgh Castle 23.11.17; Yarmouth 12.17 - @4.18; 470 Flt Manston by 25.5.18 (detd from Yarmouth); EF, FL off Lowestoft 1.6.18 (pilot picked up by minesweeper); presume salved; HAP 4.6.18; still Yarmouth 16.6.18; Covehithe by 18.6.18 - @21.6.18; 273 Sqdn Burgh Castle by 8.18; AZP 5.8.18 (Capt GWR Fane)

**B5707** Deld Yarmouth 20.11.17; Became 490 Flt Yarmouth 25.5.18; Lost at sea, for deletion by 1.6.18

**B5708** Deld 4 AAP Lincoln to Cranwell W/E 23.11.17; Crashed Rowston, nr Digby 6.1.18 (pilot unhurt); Surveyed 8.1.18; Deleted 17.1.18

**B5709** Deld 4 AAP Lincoln to Cranwell W/E 23.11.17; Crashed & CW Willoughby 21.3.18 (pilot unhurt)

**B5710** Deld 4 AAP Lincoln 11.17; Transferred to Belgian Govt 11.17

**B5711** Deld 4 AAP Lincoln 11.17; Transferred to Belgian Govt 11.17

**B5712** Deld Cranwell W/E 23.11.17; Wrecked on/by 21.11.17; Surveyed 27.11.17; Deleted 6.12.17

**B5713** (Convtd 2-str) Deld Observers School Flt Eastchurch by 29.12.17; Became 204 TDS Eastchurch (coded '13') 1.4.18 - @19.12.18

**B5714** Deld Hendon to Observers School Flt Eastchurch 24.11.17; AZP 28.1.18; still Eastchurch by 1.8.18

**B5715** Deld CSD White City 11.17; Shipped to 6 Wing Otranto 19.12.17; 6 Wing Otranto by 3.18; Became 66/67 Wing Otranto 1.4.18 - @21.4.18; 225 Sqdn by 28.4.18 - @8.18; 481/3 Flts 225 Sqdn Andrano 8.18; (225 Sqdn?) Taranto by 10.18 - @1.19

**B5716** Deld CSD White City 11.17; Shipped to 6 Wing Otranto 8.1.18; in transit by 18.1.18; 66/67 Wing Otranto by 21.4.18; 225 Sqdn by 28.4.18 - 6.18

**B5717** Deld 4 AAP Lincoln to Gunnery School Flts Eastchurch W/E 8.12.17; Eastbourne 27.2.18; Became 206 TDS Eastbourne 1.4.18; Eastchurch 20.5.18; 60 TDS Eastbourne by 7.18 - @11.18

**B5718** Deld 4 AAP Lincoln to Cranwell 5.12.17; Crashed and o/t, CW 23.2.18 (PFO JW McVean seriously injured); Surveyed 28.2.18; Deleted 13.3.18 DBR

**B5719** Deld 4 AAP Lincoln to Gunnery School Flts Eastchurch W/E 7.12.17; Became 204 TDS Eastchurch 1.4.18; Eastbourne 15.5.18

**B5720** Deld East Fortune by road 12.11.17; Redcar 22.3.18; Hit telegraph wires on racecourse, crashed, BO 3.4.18 (F/Lt CE Pattison DoI); Deleted W/E 13.4.18

**B5721** Deld East Fortune by road 12.11.17; Redcar 29.3.18 - @4.18

**B5722** Deld East Fortune NFS by road 15.11.17; detd Turnhouse W/E 1.3.18; East Fortune W/E 5.4.18; Grand Fleet SoAF&G East Fortune by 8.18

**B5723** Deld East Fortune NFS by road 15.11.17; Turnhouse W/E 9.3.18; 208 TDS East Fortune, slewed on TO, TW 17.6.18 (2/Lt D Reekie slightly injured)

**B5724** Deld East Fortune by rail 18.11.17; Deleted (or left) W/E 2.2.18

**B5725** Deld East Fortune by rail 18.11.17; Left W/E 16.2.18; 6 Wing Otranto by 24.3.18

**B5726** Deld CSD White City 11.17; Shipped to Aegean 4.1.18; Mudros for erection by 30.3.18; Repair Base Mudros 6.18 & 10.18 - @1.19; To Greek Government

**B5727** Deld CSD White City 11.17; Shipped to Aegean 4.1.18; Mudros for erection by 30.3.18; Stavros by 6.18; 220 Sqdn by 28.10.18 - @2.11.18; Repair Base Mudros 10.18 - @1.19; RAF Instructional Mission South Russia by 11.19; To White Russian Forces 1919

**B5728** Deld CSD White City 11.17; Cardiff Docks by 1.1.18; Shipped to Mudros 28.1.18; Mudros by 3.18; Repair Base Mudros by 6.18; Stavros by 10.18; Repair Base Mudros by 10.18 - @11.18

**B5729** Deld CSD White City 11.17; Shipped to 6 Wing 4.1.18; 66/67 Wing Otranto by 21.4.18; 225 Sqdn by 28.4.18 - @8.18; 481/3 Flts 225 Sqdn Andrano 8.18; 225 Sqdn Taranto by 10.18 - @11.18

**B5730** Deld CSD White City 11.17; Cardiff Docks by 15.1.18; Shipped to 6 Wing 28.1.18; 226 Sqdn by 28.4.18 - @6.18; AD Taranto by 7.18 - @8.18, 10.18 - @11.18

**B5731** Deld 4 AAP Lincoln; Tested 3.12.17; Cranwell W/E 14.12.17; O/t landing, slightly damaged 24.2.18 (Lt AR Talbot unhurt); Became 201 TDS Cranwell 1.4.18; Became 56 TDS Cranwell 15.7.18; Crashed when wings collapsed in dive from 2,800 to 2,000 ft 17.7.18 (F/Cdt AWW Goodwin killed)

**B5732** Deld CSD White City 11.17; Cranwell W/E 14.12.17; Became 201/2 TDS Cranwell W/E 1.4.18 - @6.18

**B5733** Deld CSD White City 11.17; Cranwell 5.12.17; Crashed, slightly damaged, Rauceby 19.2.18 (pilot unhurt); Pool of Pilots Manston 4.4.18 - @7.18

**B5734** Deld War School Manston (via Chingford) 22.12.17; EF after TO, FL in ploughed field, o/t 19.2.18 (FSL GW Stallard unhurt); Crashed, CW 6.3.18 (FSL WN Cross killed); Deleted W/E 15.3.18

**B5735** Deld Lincoln to Chingford 31.12.17; Became 207 TDS Chingford 1.4.18; Became 54 TDS Chingford/Fairlop 20.7.18; Spun in Fairlop 25.11.18

**B5736** Deld Lincoln to Cranwell 18.12.17; Chingford W/E 29.12.17; Became 207 TDS Chingford 1.4.18

**B5737** Deld Rosyth W/E 7.12.17; Donibristle W/E 13.12.17; Turnhouse W/E 21.2.18 - @30.1.19

**B5738** Deld Rosyth W/E 7.12.17; Turnhouse W/E 28.2.18 - @30.1.19

**B5739** Deld Rosyth W/E 7.12.17; Turnhouse W/E 21.2.18 - @30.1.19 (W/T expts); CSSP(sic) Crail, stalled, crashed into building, BO nr Crail 4.5.19

**B5740** Deld Yarmouth W/E 29.12.17; Became 490 Flt Yarmouth 25.5.18 - @17.6.18; 273 Sqdn Burgh Castle by 6.18 - @9.18

**B5741** Deld Yarmouth W/E 15.12.17; Became 490 Flt Yarmouth 25.5.18; Covehithe, HAP, then EF, FL Orfordness 8.6.18

**B5742** Deld 4 AAP Lincoln to Yarmouth W/E 29.12.17; Surveyed 19.12.17; Deleted 3.1.18 DBR [crashed on delivery?]

**B5743** Deld Chingford to EAD Grain 29.12.17 - @25.5.18

**B5744** Deld 4 AAP Lincoln to Gunnery School Flts Eastchurch W/E 22.12.17; Became 204 TDS Eastchurch 1.4.18; Stall turn nr ground, spun in from 20ft 2.6.18 (2/Lt H Norman killed)

**B5745** Deld 4 AAP Lincoln to Cranwell 18.12.17; Grain AD W/E 29.12.17 for Belgian Government; To Belgian Military Air Arm; To Belgian War Museum

**B5746** Deld 4 AAP Lincoln to HMS *Vindex* (via Martlesham Heath) W/E 21.12.17; Yarmouth W/E 26.1.18; Became 490 Flt Yarmouth by 25.5.18; 273 Sqdn Burgh Castle by 5.18 - @25.6.18; Yarmouth @17.6.18 BUT Oakley Park to Manston (via Hendon) 22.12.17

**B5747** Deld Cranwell W/E 21.12.17; Chingford W/E 29.12.17; With B5748 to Manston but landed 1½m south of Cliffe Fort 31.12.17; Eastchurch to Dover 3.1.18; Calais but landed Beau Marais 4.1.18; Transferred to Belgian Govt

**B5748** Deld Chingford W/E 29.12.17; to Manston 31.12.17 but landed 1½m south of Cliff Fort; Grain to Dover 3.1.18; Calais 4.1.18; Transferred to Belgian Govt

**B5749** (B.R.1) Deld 4 AAP Lincoln to .17; Hendon 18.12.17; AAP Dover 23.12.17; 9 Sqdn 14.1.18; 10 Sqdn 4.2.18; COL 11.3.18 (FSL HA Patey); 1 NAP Dunkerque 12.3.18; 4 ASD Guines 28.3.18; 2 AI 7.5.18; 201 Sqdn 9.5.18; Albatros DV OOC E of Albert 17.45 15.5.18; Albatros DV shot down Bapaume-Mory, shared D1862 & flight 06.45 16.5.18 (both Lt HLeR Wallace); Pancaked landing, broke axle, wheel and propeller 27.5.18; KB in flames Achiet Le Grand, shared D3419 17.35, engine hit by m/g fire, FL, crashed Sus St.Leger 16.7.18 (both 2/Lt RSS Orr); Fokker DVII OOC

332

Bailleul-Armentières 11.20 29.7.18 (Capt SM Kinkead DSC DFC); Fokker DVII shot down in flat spin apparently OOC SW of Armentières 08.30 1.8.18 (2/Lt RS Orr); 2 Fokker DVII OOC St.Christ, shared C143 & C196 11.00 12.8.18 (Lt R Sykes); EF, FL nr Bayonvillers 13.8.18 (Lt R Sykes unhurt); Rep Pk 2 ASD 17.8.18; Rebuilt as F6263 22.8.18

**B5750** (B.R.1) Deld 4 AAP Lincoln to Chingford (via Cranwell) 21.12.17; AAP Dover 23.12.17; 3 Sqdn 6.1.18; COL 22.1.18 (FSL CS Devereaux); 1 NAP Dunkerque (overhaul) 23.1.18; 10 Sqdn 12.3.18; Became 210 Sqdn 1.4.18; Shot down, last seen E of Armentières 14.30 11.4.18 (2/Lt MT McKelvey PoW wounded)

## 65 SOPWITH PUP (ADMIRALTY 9901 TYPE) BIPLANE TRACTOR SCOUTS from batch B5901 to B6150 built by Standard Motor Co Ltd. (80-hp Gnome unless otherwise stated)

**B5928** Deld Cranwell 11.9.17; Became 201/2 TDS Cranwell 1.4.18

**B5929** (80-hp Gnome, later 60-hp Le Rhône) Deld Cranwell 11.9.17; Crashed & badly damaged Cranwell South 19.3.18 (pilot unhurt); Became 201/2 TDS Cranwell 1.4.18; 'G' (Experimental) Flt Cranwell, propeller accident 3.6.18 (3AM LF Baker killed)

**B5930** (80-hp Le Rhône) Deld Dover W/E 29.9.17; War School Manston W/E 3.11.17; To Eastbourne but COL 17.6.18 (pilot unhurt)

**B5938** (80-hp Le Rhône) Deld Dover W/E 29.9.17; War School Manston W/E 3.11.17; Became Pool of Pilots Manston 1.4.18; Eastbourne to Manston 22.5.18

**B5939** (80-hp Le Rhône) Deld Killingholme store for erection 15.9.17; ECD Grain 15.12.17; TD Grain to Grain W/E 1.6.18; Grain from 7.19 (deck landing and arrester gear)

**B5940** (80-hp Le Rhône) Deld Killingholme store for erection 15.9.17; ECD Grain 22.12.17 - @11.19 (fitted attachments to centre section for overhead landing wires 19.4.19)

**B5948** Deld Cranwell for erection 25.9.17; Became 201/2 TDS Cranwell 1.4.18

**B5949** Deld Cranwell for erection 18.9.17; Became 201/2 TDS Cranwell 1.4.18

**B5950** Deld Cranwell for erection 25.9.17; Became 201/2 TDS Cranwell 1.4.18

**B5958** (80-hp Le Rhône) Deld Dover W/E 29.9.17; War School Manston W/E 3.11.17; Became Pool of Pilots Manston 1.4.18 - @12.5.18

**B5959** Deld Dover W/E 29.9.17; War School Manston W/E 3.11.17; Deleted W/E 30.3.18

**B5960** (80-hp Le Rhône) Deld Dover W/E 29.9.17; War School Manston W/E 3.11.17; Became Pool of Pilots Manston 1.4.18

**B5968** (80-hp Le Rhône) Deld Killingholme store for erection by 10.17 [not by 29.9.17]; Grain ECD 13.12.17; Repairing 4.18

**B5969** (80-hp Le Rhône) Deld Killingholme store for erection W/E 6.10.17; Grain ECD 13.12.17 - @1.4.18

**B5970** (80-hp Le Rhône) Deld Killingholme store for erection W/E 6.10.17; ECD Grain 13.12.17; Hendon 17.5.18; Grain 18.5.18; Hendon 6.6.18; Yarmouth 4.7.18; Hendon .18; Norwich 1.8.18; Hendon 8.18 - @8.8.18

**B5978** (60-hp Le Rhône) Deld Cranwell 9.10.17; Crashed and u/c smashed, Cranwell South 14.1.18 (pilot unhurt); O/t landing, slightly damaged 27.2.18 (pilot unhurt); Became 201/2 TDS Cranwell 1.4.18

**B5979** (60-hp Le Rhône) Deld Cranwell 9.10.17; Crashed and wrecked, Cranwell South 6.1.18 (pilot unhurt); Became 201/2 TDS Cranwell 1.4.18

**B5980** Deld Cranwell 10.17; Tyre burst landing in snowstorm 26.11.17 (FSL LH Pearson); Completely dest by engine fire 11.3.18; Surveyed 12.3.18; Deleted 16.3.18

**B5988** (80-hp Gnome later 60-hp Le Rhône) Deld Cranwell (coded '1') W/E 12.10.17; To Freiston by 3.18; FL in marshes, propeller and u/c damaged 1.4.18 (pilot unhurt); still Freiston 11.5.18

**B5989** Deld Cranwell for erection W/E 20.10.17; Became 201/2 TDS Cranwell 1.4.18

**B5990** (80-hp Clerget) Deld Cranwell W/E 12.10.17; Became 201/2 TDS Cranwell 1.4.18

**B5991** (80-hp Le Rhône) Deld War School Manston W/E 6.10.17; Became Pool of Pilots Manston 1.4.18; Eastbourne by 21.6.18

**B5992** (80-hp Le Rhône) Deld War School Manston W/E 6.10.17; Became Pool of Pilots Manston 1.4.18; Mid-air collision with "5455" 17.7.18 (Sgt EH Sayers killed; Sgt JD Bishop killed in other a/c)

**B5993** (80-hp Le Rhône) Deld War School Manston W/E 6.10.17; Deleted W/E 30.3.18

**B5994** (80-hp Le Rhône) Deld War School Manston W/E 6.10.17; Became Pool of Pilots Manston 1.4.18; Eastbourne 16.5.18; EF, crashed Groombridge, nr Tunbridge Wells 17.5.18 (pilot unhurt)

**B6001** (80-hp Le Rhône) Deld War School Manston by road 19.10.17; (ground?) looped, o/t 4.12.17 (FSL GD Smith); Became Pool of Pilots Manston 1.4.18; 206 TDS Eastbourne 8.5.18 - @7.18

**B6002** (80-hp Le Rhône) Deld Killingholme store by road W/E 2.11.17; ECD Grain 15.12.17 - @25.5.18

**B6003** (80-hp Le Rhône) Deld Killingholme store by road W/E 2.11.17; ECD Grain 16.12.17; Hendon 12.6.18; Grain 24.7.18 (expts & DL trials); Centre section reported loose 8.11.20 (flown 57½ hours)

**B6004** (80-hp Le Rhône) Deld Killingholme store by road W/E 2.11.17; ECD Grain 17.12.17 - @25.5.18

**B6011** (Convtd Ships Pup) Deld Rosyth W/E 9.11.17; Donibristle W/E 30.11.17; Rosyth W/E 5.1.18; Donibristle 1.2.18; Turnhouse W/E 21.2.18; Deleted W/E 25.5.18

**B6012** (Convtd Ships Pup) Deld Rosyth by road W/E 9.11.17; Donibristle W/E 22.11.17; Rosyth W/E 5.1.18; Donibristle W/E 8.2.18; Rosyth W/E 16.3.18; Turnhouse W/E 21.3.18; Deleted W/E 19.9.18

**B6013** (60-hp Le Rhône) Deld Cranwell W/E 1.11.17; Became 201/2 TDS Cranwell 1.4.18

**B6014** Deld Cranwell W/E 1.11.17; Crashed, damaged 25.2.18 (pilot unhurt); FL, o/t 2m from aerodrome 25.3.18 (pilot unhurt); Became 201/2 TDS Cranwell 1.4.18

**B6021** Deld Cranwell for erection W/E 1.11.17; Crashed and slightly damaged 5.3.18 (pilot unhurt); Crashed, slightly damaged, Cranwell South 9.3.18 (pilot unhurt); Became 201/2 TDS Cranwell 1.4.18; Collided with B.E.2c 3716 26.4.18 (2/Lt NV Grimsditch slightly injured)

**B6022** Deld Cranwell W/E 1.11.17; Crashed, badly damaged 22.3.18 (pilot unhurt)

**B6023** (to 60-hp Le Rhône 2.18) Deld Cranwell for erection W/E 1.11.17 - @30.3.18

**B6024** Deld Cranwell for erection 1.11.17 - @30.3.18

**B6031** Deld Cranwell W/E 3.11.17; Crashed, wrecked Cranwell South 3.1.18 (pilot unhurt); Surveyed 3.1.18; Deleted 17.1.18

**B6032** Deld Cranwell W/E 1.11.17; Crashed, slightly damaged, Cranwell South 28.2.18 (pilot unhurt); Became 201/2 TDS Cranwell 1.4.18

**B6033** Deld Cranwell W/E 1.11.17; Became 201/2 TDS Cranwell 1.4.18

**B6034** Deld Cranwell W/E 1.11.17; Crashed, u/c damaged, Cranwell South 22.1.18 (pilot unhurt); Became 201/2 TDS Cranwell 1.4.18

**B6049** Deld Redcar School for erection W/E 17.11.17; 201/2 TDS Cranwell 26.4.18; NE Area FIS Redcar by 8.18

**B6050** Deld Redcar School for erection W/E 17.11.17; Deleted W/E 19.1.18

**B6051** Deld Redcar School for erection W/E 17.11.17; 201/2 TDS Cranwell 8.5.18

**B6052** Deld Redcar School for erection W/E 17.11.17; Deleted W/E 6.4.18

**B6061** (to 60-hp Le Rhône 1.18) Deld Cranwell for erection W/E 23.11.17; Became 201/2 TDS Cranwell 1.4.18; Became 56 TDS Cranwell 15.7.18 - @9.1.19

**B6062** (80-hp Le Rhône) Deld Cranwell for erection W/E 23.11.17; Became 201/2 TDS Cranwell 1.4.18; Became 56 TDS Cranwell 15.7.18 - @9.18

**B6063** (to 80-hp Le Rhône) Deld Cranwell for erection W/E 23.11.17; Crashed, slightly damaged 1½m N of Heckington 2.4.18 (pilot unhurt); Became 201/2 TDS Cranwell 1.4.18; Crashed, Cranwell South 3.4.18 (pilot unhurt); Became 56 TDS Cranwell 15.7.18 - @9.18

**B6064** (to 60-hp Le Rhône) Deld Cranwell for erection W/E 23.11.17; Became 201/2 TDS Cranwell 1.4.18; Hit on ground by B.E.2c 9966, CW 3.4.18 (pilot unhurt)

**B6073** (100-hp Gnome Monosoupape) Deld AAP Hendon for

erection W/E 1.11.17, and used by Air Dept officers to at least 25.5.18

B6074 (100-hp Gnome Monosoupape) Deld AAP Hendon for erection W/E 1.11.17, and used by Air Dept officers - @23.2.18; Medical Flt Hendon by 5.18; 70 TS Beaulieu

B6075 (to 80-hp Le Rhône) Deld Cranwell W/E 30.11.17; Became 201/2 TDS Cranwell 1.4.18

B6076 (to 60 HP Le Rhône 2.18) Deld Cranwell W/E 12.12.17; Became 201/2 TDS Cranwell 1.4.18

B6085 Deld Chingford W/E 8.12.17; Became 207 TDS Chingford 1.4.18

B6086 Deld Chingford for erection W/E 8.12.17; Became 207 TDS Chingford 1.4.18

B6087 Deld Chingford for erection W/E 8.12.17; Became 207 TDS Chingford 1.4.18

B6088 (80-hp Le Rhône) Deld Chingford for erection W/E 12.12.17; Became 207 TDS Chingford 1.4.18

B6097 Deld Chingford for erection W/E 12.12.17; Became 207 TDS Chingford 1.4.18

B6098 Deld Chingford for erection W/E 15.12.17; Became 207 TDS Chingford 1.4.18

B6099 Deld Eastbourne NFS W/E 15.12.17; Became 206 TDS Eastbourne 1.4.18

B6100 Deld Eastbourne NFS W/E 12.12.17; Became 206 TDS Eastbourne 1.4.18; COL, then crashed into by 504A B4316 9.5.18 (pilot unhurt)

B6143 (80-hp Le Rhône) Deld Cranwell for erection W/E 11.1.18; Became 201/2 TDS Cranwell 1.4.18

B6146 (80-hp Le Rhône) Deld Coventry W/E 11.1.18; ARS to 4 TDS Hooton Park 26.1.18 BUT Cranwell W/E 12.1.18; Became 201/2 TDS Cranwell 1.4.18

B6149 Deld Cranwell for erection W/E 11.1.18; Became 201/2 TDS Cranwell 1.4.18

## 131 SOPWITH F.1 CAMEL TRACTOR BIPLANE SCOUTS from batch B6201 to B6450 built at Kingston-upon-Thames. (130-hp Clerget 9B or 150-hp B.R.1)

B6201 (130-hp Clerget) Deld ADD (via Dover) 13.8.17; 10 Sqdn 26.8.17; Scout OOC Wervicq 11.10 21.9.17 (FSL HJT Saint); Returning in mist and low cloud, lost control, spun out of clouds and CW on aerodrome, BO 23.12.17 (FSL DRC Wright killed); Deleted 31.12.17

B6202 (130-hp Clerget) Deld ADD by 16.8.17; 10 Sqdn 30.8.17; Albatros DV OOC Ten-Brielen 16.30 14.9.17; Albatros DV OOC Westroosebeke-Passchendaele 11.10 26.9.17; Albatros DV OOC smoking NE of Westroosebeke 16.10 27.9.17 (all FSL DF FitzGibbon); 2-str OOC SE of Zarren 13.45 15.10.17; 2-str in flames NE of Dixmude 13.30 & Albatros DV crashed NE of Dixmude 13.50, both shared D6203 & D6289 21.10.17; Albatros DV NE of Dixmude, shared B6225 13.20 27.10.17; Albatros DV OOC & another crashed NW of Dixmude 15.00-15.05 4.11.17; Albatros DV OOC nr Keyem 12.45 15.11.17 (all FSL WA Curtis); 1 NAP Dunkerque (overhaul) 26.11.17; 10 Sqdn 24.1.18; 9 Sqdn 4.2.18; AAP Dover 19.3.18; 213 Sqdn 7.4.18; 4 ASD 16.4.18 - @27.4.18; 4 ASD Pilots Pool; 4 ASD Wissant by 1.8.18; WOC 31.8.18 general fatigue

B6203 (130-hp Clerget) Deld ADD (via Dover) 21.8.17; 10 Sqdn 4.9.17; 2-str in flames NE of Dixmude 13.30 & Albatros DV crashed NE of Dixmude 13.50, both shared B6202 & B6289 21.10.17 (FSL HJ Emery); AP Dover 23.11.17; War School Manston 31.12.17; Deleted W/E 30.3.18

B6204 (130-hp Clerget) Deld ADD (via Dover) 19.8.17; 9 Sqdn 26.8.17; Albatros DIII crashed 1m behind trenches SE of Pervyse, shared B3884, B3898 & B3907 c19.35 3.9.17; DFW C OOC nr Middelkerke, shared B3898 & B3905 09.40 4.9.17; Albatros C OOC Middelkerke, shared B3884, B3892, B3898 & B3907 13.35 6.9.17; Albatros DV OOC E of Middelkerke, shared B3898 19.05, COL, unhurt 9.9.17 (all FSL HF Stackard); 4 Sqdn 2.10.17 (presume for storage); 9 Sqdn 19.10.17; 1 NAP Dunkerque (overhaul) 20.12.17; 10 Sqdn (named 'ALLO! LIL BIRD') 24.1.18; After raid on Rumbeke aerodrome red-nosed Albatros C seen to crash into tree SW of aerodrome 15.15 3.2.18 (F/L WGR Hinchliffe); 9 Sqdn 4.2.18; Manston (via Dover) 26.2.18; Dover 27.2.18; Chingford 15.3.18; Became 207 TDS Chingford 1.4.18; Dived in from 2,000ft 30.4.18 (2/Lt

CFS Jackson killed)

B6211 (130-hp Clerget, later B.R.1) Deld Brooklands to ADD (via Dover) 26.8.17; 10 Sqdn 7.9.17; Albatros DV OOC E of Hooge 10.00 19.9.17; EF, FL N of Ypres 13.1.18 (both FSL HB Maund); 1 NAP Dunkerque (overhaul) 19.1.18 (fitted B.R.1 c.28.2.18-7.3.18); 1 Sqdn 12.3.18; Albatros DV OOC Roulers 1625 16.3.18; Albatros DV OOC Slype 14.10 22.3.18; (both F/Lt SM Kinkead); Became 201 Sqdn 1.4.18; Wheel came off on TO, went on nose landing 23.4.18 (FSL CB Ridley); Albatros DV shot down Bapaume-Mory, shared D1862 and flight 06.45 16.5.18 (Lt RH Hemmens); Landed fast in cornfield nr aerodrome, overshot, crashed 16.5.18 (Lt RH Hemmens unhurt); 4 ASD Guines 17.5.18 - @25.5.18

B6212 (B.R.1) Deld Brooklands to ADD (via Dover) 22.8.17; 11 Sqdn to ADD 2.9.17 [per Redpath log]; 1 NAP Dunkerque to Seaplane Defence Squadron 22.10.17; Became 13 Sqdn (coded 'M', named 'BLACK PRINCE') 15.1.18; Crashed and damaged Bergues 19.2.18 (FSL WJ Mackenzie); 1 NAP Dunkerque 21.2.18; 4 ASD Guines by 28.3.18; 1 AI to 203 Sqdn 10.4.18; See B3855 17.5.18 (1/Lt WW Goodnow USAS); 1 ASD 25.6.18 (time expired); 8 AAP Lympne 27.6.18; Farnborough 30.6.18

B6213 (B.R.1) Deld ADD by 23.8.17; 4 Sqdn 4.9.17; 2-str seaplane in sea 22m NE of Ostende, shared B3867 & B3879 08.15, then FL in sea off Zeebrugge 22.9.17 (FSL AC Burt picked up by British destroyer); Surveyed 3.10.17; Deleted 8.10.17 TL

B6214 (130-hp Clerget) Deld CSD White City 1.9.17; Left for 6 Wing 6.9.17; Shipped to Aegean; 6 Wing Otranto by 9.11.17; transferred on loan to RFC 7th Brigade by 28.12.17 - @ 8.3.18; 224 Sqdn by 28.4.18

B6215 (130-hp Clerget) Deld CSD White City 1.9.17; Left for 6 Wing 6.9.17; Shipped to Aegean; 6 Wing Otranto by 9.11.17; transferred on loan to RFC 7th Brigade by 28.12.17; Surveyed 6 Wing 29.12.17; Deleted 19.1.18 wrecked

B6216 (130-hp Clerget) Deld Grain to ADD 2.9.17; 10 Sqdn 20.9.17; Albatros DIII OOC Westroosebeke 11.30, own machine shot up, crashed Westroosebeke 23.9.17 (FSL EJ Bussell); ADD 24.9.17; Destroyed by fire on night of 1.10.17; Surveyed 17.10.17; Deleted 23.10.17 burnt

B6217 (130-hp Clerget) Deld ADD by 6.9.17; 9 Sqdn 11.9.17; DFW C OOC nr Zarren, shared B3818 17.00 21.9.17; Albatros DV into sea off Ostende 07.50 & another crashed ½m N of Dixmude 08.20 23.9.17; Albatros DV dest N of Dixmude, shared B3818, B3832, B5652 & B6230 16.10 28.9.17; Albatros C OOC E of Slype, shared B3898 11.50 2.10.17 (all F/Cdr ST Edwards); HA probably dest nr Pervyse 12.20 28.10.17 (F/Cdr AR Brown); War School Manston (via AP Dover) 22.1.18; Became Pool of Pilots Manston 1.4.18; Freiston 3.5.18

B6218 (130-hp Clerget) Deld Brooklands to Hendon 11.9.17; AES Martlesham 14.9.17 - 3.18 (tested Gwynne-built Clerget engine); Brooklands as Experimental Trench Fighter with Lewis guns firing downwards aimed by mirror sight; To France 7.3.18; 3 Sqdn RFC Warloy at first; Rep Pk 1 ASD by 4.18; England 11.4.18; Orfordness 26.4.18, ready for SOC; Convtd 2-str instead

B6225 (130-hp Clerget) Deld Dover W/E 8.9.17; ADD by 13.9.17; 10 Sqdn 14.9.17; FL Elverdinghe road 24.9.17; Damaged by gunfire 25.9.17; Albatros DV crashed NE of Dixmude, shared B6202 13.20 27.10.17 (FSL KV Stratton); Dover 4.1.18; War School Manston 19.2.18; Eastbourne 16.5.18

B6226 (130-hp Clerget) Deld ADD by 30.8.17; 10 Sqdn 4.9.17; Albatros DV OOC SE of Dixmude 08.00 6.9.17 (FSL HS Broughall); Shot down NE of Ypres, last seen 11.35 20.9.17 (FSL HS Broughall PoW); Surveyed 22.9.17; Deleted 27.9.17

B6227 (130-hp Clerget) Deld Brooklands to ADD (via Dover) 1.9.17; 8 Sqdn by 9.9.17; Albatros DV D2284/17 [became G45] forced down intact Souchez, shared Lt JH Tudhope in Nieuport B3617 of 40 Sqdn RFC & FSL JH Thompson (serial?) of 8N Sqdn, 18.55 (Oblt Hans Waldhausen, Jasta 37, PoW), then hit by AA fire, FL in shell hole, o/t, lost u/c Souchez 27.9.17 (F/Cdr CD Booker); ADD 29.9.17; Destroyed by fire 1.10.17; Deleted 5.11.17

B6228 (130-hp Clerget, later B.R.1) Deld Brooklands to ADD (via Dover) 1.9.17; 8 Sqdn 9.9.17 (arrived 11.9.17 after two forced landings); EF, FL Neuville St.Vaast 23.11.17 (FSL BW Broatch), retd by 26.11.17; DFW OOC Loison, E of Lens, shared B6311 10.45 6.12.17; DFW C OOC Hénin-Lietard, shared B6379 14.35 27.12.17; Black and white Albatros DV crashed in flames and exploded on hitting ground Cité St.Auguste, shared B6311 (q.v.) 11.15 2.1.18 (all FSL H Day); 1 NAP Dunkerque (overhaul) 25.1.18 (re-fitted B.R.1 by 3.18); 10 Sqdn 20.3.18; Became 210 Sqdn 1.4.18; LVG C crashed and burnt Neuf-Berquin, crew PoW 12.45 10.4.18 (F/Cdr AW Carter) [Presume numbered in G161-G164 range, for which details are sparse]; Albatros DV OOC Armentières 10.50 8.5.18; Rumpler C OOC on back Bailleul (pilot killed, observer wounded), shared B7227 & D3364 11.45 9.5.18; (both Lt SC Joseph); FL in mist 1km E of Esquelbecq, CW avoiding tree 11.5.18 (Lt SC Joseph unhurt); Rep Pk 4 ASD 12.5.18; Deleted 20.5.18 general fatigue

B6229 (130-hp Clerget) Deld AP Dover 31.8.17; ADD 1.9.17; 8 Sqdn 11.9.17; Damaged by flak 23.11.17, flying again by 29.11.17; Albatros OOC 5.12.17 (both FSL JH Thompson); DFW OOC Vitry, shared B6379 11.00 28.12.17 (F/Cdr GW Price); NAP Dover 3.1.18; EC&AD Grain 23.2.18 - @6.18 (fitted hydrovane and flotation gear for ditching experiments)

B6230 (130-hp Clerget) (B.R.1) Deld ADD by 9.17; 9 Sqdn 13.9.17 (named 'RETA IV'); Albatros DV dest N of Dixmude, shared B3818, B3832, B5652 & B6217 16.10 28.9.17; 2-str OOC Ostende-Slype, shared B3818 14.50 2.10.17; Albatros DV OOC Slype shared 10.40 27.10.17; Albatros DV shot down and crashed Schoore 12.20 28.10.17; Albatros DV OOC S of Dixmude, shared N6342 12.20 23.11.17 (all F/Cdr FE Banbury); War School Manston (via AP Dover) 22.1.18; Became Pool of Pilots Manston 1.4.18; Eastbourne 8.5.18

B6231 (130-hp Clerget) Deld Battersea Exptl Works (fitted Constantinescu gun gear) by 9.17; Hendon 27.9.17; AP Dover W/E 13.10.17 (for CC gun gear trials with 9, 10 & 3 sqdns); 9 Sqdn by 29.10.17; Albatros C seen to crash SE of Quesnoy 15.30 22.12.17 (F/Cdr JST Fall); 10 Sqdn 21.1.18; 3 Sqdn 4.2.18; NAP Dunkerque 7.3.18; 4 ASD Guines 28.3.18; 201 Sqdn 23.4.18; Failed to pull out of dive on practice target and CW nr Nouex-les-Auxi 10.30 25.4.18 (Capt SW Rosevear DSC DoI); 4 ASD Guines 25.4.18; Surveyed 28.4.18; Deleted 15.5.18 wrecked

B6232 (B.R.1) Deld Brooklands to AP Dover 26.8.17; ADD 27.8.17; 4 Sqdn 8.9.17; Badly damaged in combat 8.9.17; Badly damaged in combat 24.9.17 to ADD; Dest by fire night of 1.10.17; Surveyed 17.10.17; Deleted 23.10.17 burnt

B6239 (B.R.1) Deld ADD by 6.9.17; Seaplane Defence Flt 21.9.17; Shared with N6349 one of two seaplanes shot down into sea, sank 17.10.17 (F/Cdr CJ Price); Became 13 Sqdn 15.1.18; Became 213 Sqdn 1.4.18; Albatros DV in flames (Vzfw Triebswetter, Jasta 16 killed after he had shot down a KB), shared C65 1m S of Woumen 17.35 19.5.18 (Lt WE Gray); 4 ASD 27.5.18

B6240 (B.R.1) Deld ADD by 6.9.17; Seaplane Defence Flt 21.9.17; Patrol 16.53-18.22, FF33L No.1582, Seeflud I (Vzflgm Plattenburg WIA & Lt Brettman) shot down in sea, then EF, FL in sea 10m N of Malo-les-Bains, salved by destroyer and brought into Dunkerque 25.9.17 (F/Cdr R Graham rescued); ADD 25.9.17 (for survey); Dest by fire night of 1.10.17; Surveyed 17.10.17; Deleted 23.10.17 burnt

B6241 (B.R.1) Deld Brooklands to AP Dover 31.8.17; ADD 1.9.17; 3 Sqdn 11.9.17 (named 'KLON'); DFW OOC SE of Houthulst Forest 15.00 23.1.18 (F/L GB Anderson); 8 Sqdn 1.3.18; Walmer 28.3.18; AAP Dover by 4.18 - @5.18 (no engine); 4 ASD by 31.5.18; 4 ASD Pilots Pool by 9.18 (no engine)

B6242 (B.R.1) Deld Brooklands to AP Dover 31.8.17; ADD 1.9.17; 3 Sqdn 11.9.17 (named 'FIDGETY PHIL' at Walmer 11.17-12.17); 2 Albatros DV OOC, shared B6401 and B6408 Gheluvelt 10.45 30.1.18 (F/L AB Ellwood); 8 Sqdn 1.3.18; Walmer Defence Flt W/E 30.3.18; Dover by road 2.4.18; 4 ASD Guines 4.18; 210 Sqdn 25.4.18; Albatros C crashed 1m N of Aubers,

shared C62 & D3364 16.15 9.5.18 (Capt ES Arnold); FL Belle Houllefort 11.5.18; KB in flames Armentières 08.35 9.6.18 (both Lt CJ Shackell); COL 23.6.18 (Lt HR Hughes unhurt); 1 ASD 25.6.18; Rebuilt as F6027 19.7.18

B6243 (B.R.1) Deld ADD by 6.9.17; 4 Sqdn 12.9.17; Albatros DV OOC E of Kayem 14.00 23.11.17 (FSL AJB Tonks); Became 204 Sqdn (named 'TSING TAU') 1.4.18 - @6.4.18; 4 ASD Guines by 20.5.18 - @25.5.18;

B6244 (130-hp Clerget) Deld ADD by 13.9.17; 10 Sqdn 26.9.17; Albatros DV OOC NE of Westroosebeke 16.05 27.9.17; Albatros DV OOC NE of Passchendaele 14.15 1.10.17 (both FSL WA Curtis); AP Dover 4.1.18; EC&AD Grain 24.2.18 - @6.18 (ditching trials with hydrovane?)

B6245 (130-hp Clerget) Deld Brooklands to CSD White City 8.9.17; Packed 24.9.17; Shipped to Otranto 9.10.17; arr 6 Wing Otranto W/E 18.1.18 (by 15.1.18); Became 66/67 Wings Otranto 1.4.18; 225 Sqdn by 28.4.18 - 8.18; 481/3 Flts 225 Sqdn Andrano .18; 225 Sqdn Taranto by 10.18 - @1.19

B6246 (130-hp Clerget) Deld Brooklands to CSD White City 8.9.17; Packed 24.9.17; Shipped to Otranto 9.10.17; arr 6 Wing Otranto W/E 28.12.17; Became 66/67 Wings 1.4.18; Surveyed 27.3.18; Deleted 15.4.18 damaged beyond repair

B6253 (130-hp Clerget) Deld CSD White City 12.9.17; Shipped to 2 Wing Mudros 21.9.17; Imbros by 1.12.17 - @1.1.18; Repair Base Mudros by 3.18

B6254 (130-hp Clerget) Deld CSD White City 12.9.17; Shipped to 2 Wing Mudros 21.9.17; C Sqdn Gliki by 12.17; Imbros by 1.12.17 - @12.1.18; Marsh by 17-19.1.18 & @26.2.18; Imbros by 3.18; F Sqdn Mudros by 6.18; Repair Base Mudros by 10.18 - @1.19

B6255 (130-hp Clerget) Deld CSD White City 12.9.17; Shipped to 2 Wing Mudros 21.9.17 - @1.12.17; Stavros by 1.1.18 - @3.18; F Sqdn Mudros by 6.18 & 10.18; To Greece

B6256 (B.R.1) Deld ADD W/E 13.9.17; 4 Sqdn 25.9.17 - @10.12.17; DFW C OOC N of Pervyse 13.30 9.11.17 (FSL AJB Tonks); Crashed 11.12.17; 1 NAP Dunkerque (overhaul) 11.12.17; 10 Sqdn 18.2.18; Became 210 Sqdn 1.4.18; FL in mist, wrecked 2km from Wormhout 11.5.18 (Lt MF Sutton unhurt); 4 ASD 12.5.18; Deleted 20.5.18 general fatigue

B6257 (B.R.1) Deld ADD W/E 20.9.17; 3 Sqdn 26.9.17; 4 Sqdn 6.3.18; FL Soex 13.3.18; 4 ASD Guines 28.3.18 - @31.3.18; 1 AI to 209 Sqdn by 3.4.18; Albatros DV smoking E of Villers-Bretonneux 14.45 27.4.18 (Lt MS Taylor); 1 AI to 209 Sqdn 10.5.18; Last seen engaging enemy triplane 15.5.18 (Lt G Wilson killed); Deleted 15.5.18

B6258 (130-hp Clerget) Deld AP Dover W/E 8.9.17; ADD by 13.9.17; 9 Sqdn 15.9.17; COL 20.9.17 (FSL EM Knott); TO on special mission 05.53, shot down 26.9.17 (FSL W Ingleson PoW); Surveyed 3.10.17; Deleted 8.10.17 TL

B6259 (130-hp Clerget) Deld ADD W/E 13.9.17; 10 Sqdn 24.9.17; Crashed and damaged Nieuport-Dixmude line OP 15.11.17 (FSL RE Carroll); 1 NAP 16.11.17; 12 Sqdn 29.12.17; Became 212 Sqdn 1.4.18; Transit to 4 ASD, FL in mist Gravelines 17.4.18; Téteghem 18.4.18; arr 4 ASD 20.4.18; 213 Sqdn 5.6.18 (only mention), probably one of two aircraft badly damaged in enemy raid on aerodrome that day; TOC 4 ASD but deleted 15.6.18 TW

B6260 (130-hp Clerget, later B.R.1) ADD by 20.9.17; 10 Sqdn 24.9.17; Crashed on TO 26.10.17 (FSL GH Morang unhurt); AD (later NAP) Dunkerque 28.10.17; 8 Sqdn 28.1.18; EF, FL in shell hole S of aerodrome 3.2.18 (FSL CRC Walworth); 1 NAP Dunkerque (overhaul) by 7.2.18; 4 ASD Guines by 28.3.18; 208 Sqdn (coded 'A') 7.4.18; Burnt to prevent capture La Gorgue 9.4.18

B6269 Martlesham Heath by 28.3.18

B6272 Walmer Defence Flight (named 'ABE')

B6276 (B.R.1) Deld ADD by 13.9.17; 4 Sqdn 23.9.17; Albatros C apparently OOC 20m NE of Zeebrugge 14.45 4.11.17 (FSL AC Burt); 9 Sqdn 31.12.17; 10 Sqdn 4.2.18; Became 210 Sqdn 1.4.18; Badly shot about by EA in gen engagement nr Armentières 8.5.18 (Capt

*Sopwith Camel B6230 of 9 Sqdn was flown in late 1917 by Flight Commander FE Banbury with the name 'RETA IV'.
(A.W.Woods via Frank Cheesman)*

*Sopwith Camel B6242, named 'FIDGETY PHIL', with 3 Sqdn at Walmer late in 1917. (via Frank Cheesman)*

*Sopwith Camel B6243, named 'TSING TAU', was flown by FSL AJB Tonks of 4 Sqdn. (A.N.Ferry via Frank
Cheesman)*

ES Arnold unhurt?); 4 ASD 9.5.18; Deleted 20.5.18 NWR (general fatigue)

**B6277** (B.R.1) Probably Bxx77 collected by 8 Sqdn pilot from Brooklands but which crashed Mardyck 10.9.17 (FSL WL Jordan); ADD by 13.9.17; For survey by 27.9.17; Dest by fire night of 1.10.17; Surveyed 17.10.17; Deleted 23.10.17 burnt

**B6278** (130-hp Clerget) Deld ADD by 27.9.17; 8 Sqdn 8.11.17; Rumpler C OOC towards Cambrai, shared B6340 5.12.17 (FSL AJ Dixon); DFW C crashed Gavrelle, shared N6376, B6319 & B6447 11.30, then shot down Neuvireuil-Oppy 4.1.18 (FSL AJ Dixon killed); Deleted 14.1.18

**B6279** (130-hp Clerget) Deld ADD by 20.9.17; 10 Sqdn 22.9.17; Shot down, last seen N of Houthulst Forest 24.9.17 (Lt B Foster PoW) [believed by Ltn K Wüsthoff, Jasta 4]; Surveyed 3.10.17; Deleted 8.10.17 TL

**B6280** (130-hp Clerget) Deld Brooklands to Observers School Flt Eastchurch for defence 7.9.17; Became 204 TDS Eastchurch 1.4.18 - @9.18

**B6281** (130-hp Clerget) Deld Brooklands to Observers School Flt Eastchurch W/E 3.11.17 (for defence); Became 204 TDS Eastchurch 1.4.18 - @10.18

**B6288** (130-hp Clerget) Deld AP Dover by 25.9.17; ADD by 27.9.17; 9 Sqdn 14.10.17; Albatros C smoking/dest Zarren 09.50 16.10.17 (F/Cdr JST Fall); Albatros C OOC 4m W of Courtrai, shared B6317 (which got the credit) 13.45 6.12.17; Albatros C OOC probably dest W of Courtrai 8.12.17; DFW C on fire 4m E of Pervyse, shared B3818 & B3884 15.15 10.12.17 (all FSL EM Knott); LM 22.12.17; 12 Sqdn by 24.12.17; Crashed and CW 16.2.18 (FSL JL Allison); ADD 2.18; Deleted 18.2.18

**B6289** (130-hp Clerget) Deld ADD by 20.9.17; 10 Sqdn (flight letter 'A' on fuselage) 26.9.17; 2-str in flames NE of Dixmude 13.30 & Albatros DV crashed NE of Dixmude 13.50, both shared B6202 & B6203 21.10.17 (FSL HL Nelson); 9 Sqdn 4.2.18; With 9 Sqdn at Dover, to Martlesham but o/t landing and badly damaged 26.2.18 (pilot unhurt); still Testing Flt Martlesham Heath 9.3.18; AAP Dover 19.3.18; Eastchurch W/E 30.3.18; Lost control, crashed 24.6.18 (2/Lt RG Haye DoI)

**B6290** (130-hp Clerget) Deld ADD by 27.9.17; 8 Sqdn 9.10.17; Attacked Moncheux aerodrome 17.55, on return unable to find own aerodrome at dusk, FL in field, o/t, Corbie, 18km E of Amiens 23.10.17 (F/Cdr RB Munday); Flying again 5.11.17; Lost on OP nr Lens 10.15 9.11.17 (F/Lt HS Magrath PoW) [believed by Ltn H Brzenk]; Captured intact and used by Germans for technical evaluation, fitted with bomb racks; Surveyed 13.11.17; Deleted 16.11.17 TL

**B6291** (130-hp Clerget) Deld ADD (via Dover) 21.9.17; 10 Sqdn 28.9.17; FL, wrecked Droglandt 30.9.17 (FSL CE Bramhall injured); ADD 1.10.17; AP Dover by 12.10.17; War School Manston 31.12.17; Became Pool of Pilots Manston 1.4.18; 206 TDS Eastbourne 5.6.18; Stalled on TO, crashed, o/t, wrecked 7.6.18 (2/Lt JB Risk slightly injured); Became 50 TDS 15.7.18 - @1.11.18

**B6297** (130-hp Clerget) Deld ADD 9.17; 10 Sqdn 29.9.17; Damaged by m/g fire 13.45 15.10.17 (FSL IP Sutherland); COL 20.10.17 (FSL HWM Cumming injured); ADD 21.10.17; NAP Dunkerque W/E 8.11.17; 12 Sqdn W/E 13.12.17; Sqdn disbanded 1.4.18; 4 ASD to 2 AI 7.5.18; 201 Sqdn 9.5.18; Albatros DV crashed NE of Villers-Bretonneux 19.50 10.5.18; Albatros DV crashed OOC NE of Villers-Bretonneux 17.45, then engaged by Fokker DrI, ran out of fuel, FL, damaged Freschevillers, unhurt 15.5.18; Albatros DV shot down Bapaume-Mory, shared D1862 & flight 06.45 16.5.18 (all Capt SM Kinkead DSC); 2 ASD 19.5.18; Rebuilt as F6153 3.7.18

**B6298** (130-hp Clerget) Deld AP Dover W/E 15.9.17; 1 NAP Dunkerque by 27.9.17; 8 Sqdn 13.11.17; Crashed on test flight, wrecked La Bellevue 23.11.17 (FSL GS Smith killed); Deleted ADD 3.12.17

**B6299** (130-hp Clerget) Deld AP Dover W/E 15.9.17; 1 NAP Dunkerque by 27.9.17; 10 Sqdn (coded 'B') 16.11.17; Albatros DV in flames W of Roulers 11.20, previously shot at by B5268 10.12.17; Albatros DV OOC E of Dixmude 14.40 12.12.17; 2 Albatros DV engaged, 1 DD in vertical dive, other in gentle glide seen to within 1,000ft of ground 2m W of Lille 10.50 22.12.17 (all F/Cdr NM MacGregor); 9 Sqdn 4.2.18; Chingford (via Dover) 13.3.18; Became 207 TDS Chingford 1.4.18

**B6300** (130-hp Clerget later B.R.1) Deld ADD by 9.17; 4 Sqdn 30.9.17; Albatros DV OOC E of Dixmude 14.00 23.11.17 (FSL CRR Hickey); Albatros DV OOC Coxyde-Keyem 16.30-16.40 11.3.18 (F/Cdr AM Shook); Albatros DV OOC nr St.Pierre Capelle 17.00 16.3.18 (S/Cdr BL Huskisson); 2 Albatros DV on fire 12.10 22.3.18 [First of these believed Ltn Bertram Heinrich, MJF1]; Albatros DV OOC Slype 14.30 22.3.18 (all F/Cdr AM Shook); Became 204 Sqdn 1.4.18; COL Téteghem 15.5.18 (Capt AC Burt unhurt); To 4 ASD; Deleted 20.5.18 TW

**B6301** (130-hp Clerget); Deld ADD (via Dover) 21.9.17; For survey by 27.9.17; Dest by fire night of 1.10.17; Surveyed 17.10.17; Deleted 23.10.17 burnt

**B6307** (130-hp Clerget) Deld CSD White City 8.9.17; Packed 24.9.17; Shipped to Mudros 27.9.17; 2 Wing Mudros by 1.12.17; Marsh by 1.1.18; Thasos by 13-14.1.18; Marsh by 10.2.18; Mitylene by 3.18; F Sqdn 2 Wing Mudros 4.18; Repair Base Mudros by 6.18

**B6308** (130-hp Clerget) Deld CSD White City 27.9.17; Shipped to Mudros 5.10.17; 2 Wing Mudros by 1.12.17; Marsh by 1.1.18; Thasos by 14.1.18; Stavros by 30.3.18; Repair Base Mudros by 6.18 & 10.18 - @11.18

**B6309** (130-hp Clerget) Deld CSD White City 27.9.17; Shipped to Mudros 27.9.17; 2 Wing Mudros by 1.12.17; Marsh by 1.1.18 (repair); G Sqdn 2 Wing by 30.3.18

**B6310** (130-hp Clerget) Deld CSD White City 24.9.17; Shipped to Otranto 9.10.17; arr 6 Wing Otranto W/E 28.12.17; Became 66/67 Wing 1.4.18; 225 Sqdn Andrano by 28.4.18; Left 07.15, HA shot down Tirana aerodrome 28.8.18 (Lt JG Nash); Became 481/3 Flts 225 Sqdn Andrano/Taranto by 10.18 - @1.19

**B6311** (130-hp Clerget, later B.R.1) Deld AD/1 NAP Dunkerque by 27.9.17; 8 Sqdn 8.11.17; DFW OOC Loison, SE of Lens, shared B6228 10.45 6.12.17; Black and white Albatros DV crashed in flames, exploded on hitting ground nr Cité St.Auguste, shared B6228 11.15 2.1.18 [Ltn Gunther Auffahrt, Jasta 29 killed - possibly G122]; "New-type" 2-str crashed Fresnes les Montauban 12.50 6.1.18 (all F/Cdr GW Price); 1 NAP Dunkerque (overhaul) W/E 31.1.18 (re-engined B.R.1 c.7-14.3.18); 9 Sqdn 23.3.18; Became 209 Sqdn 1.4.18; Albatros DV believed crashed, shared B3858, B7200 & D3328 12.4.18 (pilot?); FL 21.4.18 (Lt AW Aird); Left 16.45 on special mission, shot down 24.4.18 (Lt FC Stovin killed)

**B6317** (130-hp Clerget) Deld AP Dover W/E 15.9.17; ADD by 27.9.17; 3 Sqdn 2.10.17; 9 Sqdn 19.10.17; Albatros C dest 4m W of Courtrai, shared B6288 13.45 6.12.17 (F/Lt RR Winter); 12 Sqdn 22.12.17; Sqdn disbanded 1.4.18; 491 Flt Dover, damaged 25.5.18 (Lt Darlington); still 491 Flt @31.5.18; Pilots Pool; 4 ASD WOC 30.6.18 general fatigue

**B6318** (130-hp Clerget) Deld AP Dover W/E 15.9.17; Walmer by 29.9.17; Dover 27.10.17; ADD to 8 Sqdn (via Chocques) 31.10.17; DFW C OOC Hénin-Lietard, shared N6375, N6376 & B6340 09.00 6.12.17; Dropped 2x20-lb bombs on Metallurgique Works at Pont-à-Vendin 2.1.18; Albatros DV OOC Epinoy Wood, shared B6321, B6340 & B6371 4.1.18 (all F/Cdr RB Munday); 1 NAP 17.2.18; AP Dover 2.18; War School Manston 21.2.18; Became Pool of Pilots Manston 1.4.18; Eastbourne 9.5.18 - 8.18 [Convtd to 2-seater by then]

**B6319** (130-hp Clerget, later B.R.1) Deld ADD by 9.17 (not by 29.9.17); 8 Sqdn 1.10.17; DFW C on fire Harnes - Pont-à-Vendin 12.40 28.12.17; Albatros DV OOC Neuvireuil, shared B6340 15.30 1.1.18 (both FSL RJO Compston); Hannover C crashed W of Arras, shared B6340 (q.v.) & B6447 10.05 3.1.18 (FSL WL Jordan); DFW C crashed Gavrelle, shared N6376, B6278 & B6447 11.30 4.1.18 (Lt PM Dennett); Crashed 19.1.18; Albatros DV OOC Neuvireuil, shared N6356, B6369 & B6377 11.30 24.1.18 (both FSL CRC Walworth); LM 29.1.18; 1 NAP Dunkerque (overhaul) by 31.1.18; 4 ASD Guines 28.3.18; 1 AI 12.4.18; 203 Sqdn 13.4.18; Pfalz DIII OOC Vieux Berquin 15.00, controls shot

*Sopwith Camel B6289 'A' Flight, 10 Sqdn carries its flight letter on the fuselage. (via Frank Cheesman)*

*Sopwith Camel B6340 'P' of 8 Sqdn has the white wheel discs of 'A' Flight. This machine gained many victories when flown by Flight Commander RJO Compston. (via Frank Cheesman)*

*Sopwith Camel B6401 of 3 Sqdn was flown by Flight Commander LH Rochford. (via Frank Cheesman)*

away, FL, N of Lillers, CW 21.4.18 (F/Cdr RA Little unhurt); 4 ASD Guines 22.4.18 (still 130-hp Clerget 27.4.18, re-fitted B.R.1 by 25.5.18); 204 Sqdn 16.8.18; HA dest 5m NE of Dixmude c10.20, m/c shot up, FL British side of lines, CW 20.9.18 (2/Lt DF Tysoe slightly wounded); 4 ASD 21.9.18; WOC 30.9.18 general fatigue

B6320 (130-hp Clerget) Deld ADD by 27.9.17; 10 Sqdn 28.10.17; Albatros DV OOC NNE of Dixmude 13.00 15.11.17; Red Albatros DV OOC crashed smoking, shared B5663 15.35 5.12.17; Wheels and axles shot off while strafing trenches nr Mariakerke 11.12.17 (all FSL FV Hall); 9 Sqdn 4.2.18; AAP Dover 19.3.18; 491 Flt Dover 25.5.18 - @6.18

B6321 (130-hp Clerget) Deld Brooklands to AP Dover W/E 10.11.17; ADD 19.12.17; 8 Sqdn 22.12.17; Hannover C BU Fampoux (numbered G121), shared B6340 & SE5A B665/Capt EC Mannock of 40 Sqdn RFC 11.38 1.1.18 [Vzfw Fritz Korbacher & Ltn d R Wilhelm Klein, FAA288 both killed] ; Albatros DV OOC Epinoy Wood, shared B6318, B6340 & B6371 4.1.18 (both FSL GK Cooper); Albatros DV crashed Vitry-en-Artois - Fresnes 11.30 24.1.18; Albatros DV OOC Fresnes 12.30 3.2.18 (both FSL JB White); 1 NAP Dunkerque 17.2.18; 12 Sqdn 20.2.18; Sqdn disbanded 1.4.18; Dover, EF, FL rough ground, o/t and wrecked 25.5.18 (Lt RMcI Gordon); Deletion recommended 27.5.18; To ARS Guston Road, Dover instead; WOC 7.9.18

B6327 (130-hp Clerget) Deld ADD by 29.7.17; 3 Sqdn 2.10.17; 9 Sqdn 19.10.17; War School Manston (via AP Dover) 22.1.18; Became Pool of Pilots Manston 1.4.18; Freiston 3.5.18

B6328 (130-hp Clerget) Deld 1 NAP Dunkerque by 25.10.17; 8 Sqdn 28.11.17; Albatros DV OOC Carvin 12.15, shared B6340 & B6371 2.2.18 (FSL RL Johns); 1 NAP Dunkerque 16.2.18; AP Dover 17.2.18; War School Manston 19.2.18; Deleted W/E 23.3.18

B6329 (150-hp Gnome Monosoupape) Deld Hendon 10.17 (engine trials); Testing Sqdn Martlesham Heath 16.11.17 - @3.18 (Exp engine fitting)

B6330 (130-hp Clerget, later B.R.1 by 6.18) Deld ADD by 27.9.17; 1 NAP Dunkerque by 25.10.17; 9 Sqdn 1.11.17; 10 Sqdn 24.1.18; 9 Sqdn 4.2.18; AAP Dover 19.3.18; 213 Sqdn 3.4.18; Survey Flt 4 ASD 12.4.18; 213 Sqdn 4.6.18; EF, FL in beach 2m S of Bray Dunes, o/t, badly damaged 7.6.18 (Lt JE Greene unhurt); to 4 ASD

B6331 (130-hp Clerget) Deld CSD White City 1.10.17; Shipped to Mudros 5.10.17; 2 Wing Mudros by 1.12.17 - @1.1.18; Marsh by 13.3.18; Thasos 14.3.18; Repair Base Mudros by 30.3.18

B6337 (130-hp Clerget) Deld CSD White City 27.9.17; Shipped to 2 Wing Mudros 5.10.17; C Sqdn 2 Wing Imbros by 1.1.18 - @14.1.18; G Sqdn Mudros by 3.18; 2 Wing Mudros, nose dived into sea during low stunting 16.5.18 (Lt PA Enright injured)

B6338 (130-hp Clerget) Deld CSD White City 27.9.17; Shipped to 2 Wing Mudros 9.10.17; Mudros by 1.12.17; Imbros by 3.18; Repair Base Mudros by 6.18; RHNAS from/by 1.10.18 - @1.19

B6339 (130hp Clerget) Deld CSD White City 27.9.17; Shipped to Otranto 9.10.17; arr 6 Wing Otranto W/E 28.12.17; Became 66/67 Wings 1.4.18 - @21.4.18; 225 Sqdn by 28.4.18 - @10.8.18; Top plane torn off when D.H.4 "9437" landed on top of it [No date]

B6340 (130-hp Clerget) Deld ADD by 27.9.17; 8 Sqdn (coded 'P') 28.10.17; Albatros DIII crashed on fire just over lines nr Oppy 08.20 8.11.17; LVG Aviatik OOC Vitry-en-Artois 10.55 22.11.17; Rumpler C towards Cambrai, shared B6278 5.12.17; DFW C OOC Hénin-Lietard, shared N6375, N6376 & B6318 09.00 6.12.17; DFW C OOC Drocourt-Douai, shared B6379 & FSL HM Reid 11.25 6.12.17; Hannover C BU Fampoux, shared B6340 (q.v.) & SE5A B665 of 40 Sqdn RFC 11.38 1.1.18; Albatros DV OOC Neuvireuil, shared B6340 15.30 1.1.18; DFW C crashed W of Arras, shared B6319 & B6447 10.05 3.1.18 (probably Ltn J.Lampart & Ltn A.Zipper, Fl.Abt 46 both killed); DFW C OOC smoking Epinoy Wood 11.20 3.1.18; Albatros DV OOC Epinoy Wood, shared B6318, B6321 & B6371 4.1.18; Albatros DV OOC S of La Bassée, shared B6447 11.50 6.1.18; 2-

tailed 2-str OOC Douai-Ostricourt 11.30 & Albatros DV OOC Carvin 12.15, the 2nd shared N6356, B6328 & B6371 2.2.18; DFW C OOC SE of Douai 11.25 3.2.18; DFW C shot down Sallaumines 12.25 3.2.18 (all F/Cdr RJO Compston); 10 Sqdn 4.2.18 (temp custody); 1 Sqdn 15.2.18; AP Dover 16.2.18; War School Manston 21.2.18; Became Pool of Pilots Manston 1.4.18; 50 TDS Eastbourne 27.5.18; Spun in 4.8.18 (2/Lt LL de Jaen injured)

B6341 (130-hp Clerget) Deld ADD by 10.17; 10 Sqdn 7.10.17; 2-str crashed Couckelaere, shared B5659 08.00 12.11.17 (A/F/L GL Trapp); Patrol left 15.10, BU in air diving to attack 2-str 12.11.17 (A/F/L GL Trapp killed); Deleted 27.11.17

B6342 ASD to 8 Sqdn 31.3.18; Became 208 Sqdn 1.4.18; Burnt to prevent capture 9.4.18

B6345 (B.R.1) 213 Sqdn by 7.18 - returned for overhaul

B6346 Shipped to Aegean; arr 6 Wing Otranto W/E 28.12.17 BUT 28 Sqdn, stalled, crashed 21.10.17 (Lt D Skelton killed)

B6347 (130hp Clerget) Deld AP Dover W/E 3.11.17; COL, CW 23.11.17 (TFSL HF Airey killed); Surveyed 5.12.17; Deleted ADD 28.11.17

B6348 (130-hp Clerget) Deld ADD by 20.9.17; 1 NAP Dunkerque by 25.10.17; 12 Sqdn 10.12.17; Shot down over lines in flames 25.1.18 (FSL JHT Carr PoW); Deleted 4.2.18

B6349 (130-hp Clerget) Deld AP Dover W/E 3.11.17; 8 Sqdn 6.1.18; Albatros DV OOC in steep dive Fresnes-Vitry 11.40 24.1.18 (F/L GK Cooper); 1 NAP 17.2.18; Dover 17.2.18; East Fortune 23.2.18 - @30.3.18

B6350 (130-hp Clerget) Deld Dover W/E 6.10.17; Walmer by 12.10.17; Dover by 27.10.17; 8 Sqdn (coded 'E') 28.11.17; O/t on TO strong wind 6.12.17; O/t by strong gust while taxying 28.12.17 (both FSL GK Cooper); 1 NAP 3.1.18 (overhaul); 3 Sqdn 28.2.18; 4 Sqdn 6.3.18; EF, FL on beach Bray Dunes 11.3.18; FL Moere 13.3.18; Became 204 Sqdn 1.4.18; Drove down Rumpler C previously attacked by B6389, forced it to land nr Wulpen 12.00, British pilot then landed alongside but Rumpler exploded killing several Belgians, German crew taken PoW 21.4.18 (Lt CRR Hickey superficial burns); Crashed on TO, CW 22.4.18 (2/Lt GW Graham injured); To 4 ASD; Surveyed 6.5.18; Deleted 18.5.18

B6351 (B.R.1) Deld AP Dover W/E 6.10.17; 1 Sqdn 23.11.17; 9 Sqdn 10.12.17; Albatros DV sent spinning down but lost in mist 15.05 19.12.17; Shot up KB forcing observer to bale out 22.12.17 (both FSL FJW Mellersh); Albatros C OOC Staden 08.40 3.2.18 (F/Cdr ST Edwards); 10 Sqdn 4.2.18; Albatros DV crashed S of Menin 09.50 18.2.18; Became 210 Sqdn 1.4.18; Pfalz DIII crashed Bac St.Maur 10.55 8.5.18 (all Lt FV Hall); Hit sandbags attempting to TO sidewind, damaged 22.5.18 (Lt GA Learn unhurt); Rep Pk 1 ASD 23.5.18; Rebuilt as F5933 25.6.18, later rebuilt as H7108 14.9.18

B6357 (B.R.1) Deld AP Dover W/E 6.10.17; Seaplane Defence Sqdn 21.10.17; Aviatik C OOC Houthulst Forest, shared N6335 15.35 4.12.17 (FSL JW Pinder); Albatros C shot down into sea 15.05 4m NW of Wendyne after it had previously been attacked by B6391, B6407 & N6335 5.12.17 (FSL JW Pinder); Albatros DV DD in nose dive, possibly in flames but could have been reflection of sun, not seen to crash 10.12.17 (FSL JW Pinder); LM 31.12.17; ADD to 1 NAP Dunkerque W/E 3.1.18; 10 Sqdn 4.2.18; Albatros DV OOC N of Ypres 16.45 28.2.18; Albatros DV crashed SE of Dixmude 16.00 10.3.18 (both FSL HT Mellings); Crashed on TO and CW nr aerodrome 12.3.18 (FSL HT Mellings bruised); 1 NAP Dunkerque 13.3.18; Deleted 18.3.18

B6358 (B.R.1) Deld AP Dover W/E 6.10.17; Seaplane Defence Sqdn 21.10.17; Shot down KB then lost in fog, ran out of fuel, FL in marsh and crashed Pitgam, 4.12.17 (FSL JE Greene); ADD by 6.12.17; 1 NAP Dunkerque by 13.12.17 (overhaul); 9 Sqdn 23.1.18; DFW DD Pervyse 28.1.18 (FSL MS Taylor); 10 Sqdn 4.2.18; Pfalz DIII OOC smoking Menin-Roulers 09.20 24.3.18 (FSL LP Coombes); Became 210 Sqdn 1.4.18; Albatros DV in flames N of La Bassée 15.45 9.4.18 (FSL LP Coombes); EF, FL in ploughed field nr aerodrome, damaged 21.4.18 (2/Lt CJ Shackell unhurt); 4 ASD 21.4.18; 213 Sqdn 30.6.18; HA OOC off Wenduyne,

shared B6448, B7270, D3326, D9627 & D9647 11.40
7.7.18 (Lt GD Smith); Last seen 10m S of Ostende
25.8.18 (Lt EC Toy); Deleted 15.9.18

**B6359** (B.R.1) Deld AP Dover W/E 6.10.17; 1 Sqdn 26.11.17;
AZP from Dover 28/29.1.18; Albatros DV OOC E of
Armentières 10.05-12.10 patrol 11.3.18; Albatros DV
OOC in dive NE of Roulers, shared B6419 16.35
16.3.18 (both FSL HleR Wallace); Became 201 Sqdn
1.4.18; Albatros C OOC SE of Albert, shared B6421,
B6429, B7225, B7267 & B7278 shot down 10.10 2.5.18
(Lt HdeR Wallace); 4 ASD Guines 9.5.18 (overhaul,
later Pilots Pool); WOC 31.10.18 general fatigue

**B6360** (130-hp Clerget) Deld CSD White City 13.10.17;
Shipped to Mudros 31.10.17; 2 Wing Mudros by
1.12.17 - @1.1.18; C Sqdn 2 Wing Imbros Stavros by
3.18; Repair Base Mudros by 6.18 & 10.18 - @1.19; To
Greece Air Force

**B6361** (130-hp Clerget) Deld CSD White City 13.10.17;
Shipped to Mudros 31.10.17; 2 Wing Mudros by
1.12.17 - @1.1.18; Marsh by 10.2.18; Mitylene by
3.18; F Sqdn 2 Wing Mudros 4.18; Imbros by 6.18

**B6367** (130-hp Clerget) Shipped to Mudros 26.11.17; 2 Wing
Mudros for erection by 1.1.18 - @3.18; Imbros by 6.18;
F Sqdn Mudros; To RHNAS

**B6368** (130-hp Clerget) Allotted CSD White City for 6 Wing
Otranto by 9.11.17; Shipped to Aegean 20.11.17; arr 6
Wing Otranto by 28.12.17; Became 66/67 Wings 1.4.18
- @21.4.18; 225 Sqdn by 28.4.18 - 6.18

**B6369** (130-hp Clerget) Deld AP Dover W/E 13.10.17; ADD
2.1.18; 8 Sqdn 3.1.18; Albatros DV OOC Wingles,
shared B6377 & B6447 11.25 19.1.18; 2 Albatros DV
OOC Neuvireuil, the 1st shared B6369 & the 2nd shared
N6356, B6319 & B6377 11.30 24.1.18; Albatros DV
crashed nr Beaumont, shared B6377 13.15 25.1.18;
Albatros DV OOC Beaumont-Drocourt 11.35 28.1.18
(all F/L WL Jordan); 1 NAP Dunkerque 17.2.18; 12
Sqdn 23.2.18 - @21.3.18; 4 ASD Guines 28.3.18; 209
Sqdn 27.4.18; Pfalz DIII shot down S of wood nr
Fignières 08.00 3.6.18; LVG C OOC Cappy 08.30
6.6.18; LVG C OOC Proyart 11.30 & another crashed
in flames S of Morcourt 11.35 9.6.18 (all Lt JH Siddall);
Left 18.05 with 3 others, attacked by 3 HA, last seen
going down in flames S of Albert 1.7.18 (Lt LC Story
killed)

**B6370** (130-hp Clerget) Deld AP Dover W/E 3.11.17; 9 Sqdn
23.11.17; DFW C mottled yellow & brown crashed
Moorslede, 4/5m W of Courtrai 10.30 6.12.17; Albatros
DV OOC 2m W of Staden 11.45 6.12.17; Albatros DV
with blue and white fuselage and broad white wing tips
broke up in air NE of Houthulst Forest 14.45 8.12.17
(all F/Cdr JST Fall); 10 Sqdn 25.1.18; Shot down by
Vzfw Fruhner of Jasta 26, SW of Rumbeke, probably
c15.15 3.2.18 (FSL WH Wilmot killed); Deleted 4.2.18

**B6371** (130-hp Clerget) AP Dover W/E 13.10.17; 8 Sqdn
4.1.18; Albatros DV OOC Epinoy Wood, shared B6318,
B6321 & B6340 4.1.18 (FSL HHS Fowler); Twin-tailed
2-str with pink squares on top plane crashed Fresnoy
13.00 6.1.18 (FSL H Day); Albatros DV OOC Sailly, S
of Vitry 12.10-12.15 19.1.18 (FSL GW Price); Albatros
DV OOC Vitry 11.20 22.1.18; Albatros DV OOC S of
Scarpe River 11.40 29.1.18; Albatros DV OOC Carvin
12.15, shared N6356, B6328 & B6340 2.2.18 (all FSL
H Day); 1 NAP Dunkerque 17.2.18; 12 Sqdn by
20.2.18; Became 212 Sqdn 1.4.18; 4 ASD Guines
8.4.18; 209 Sqdn 27.4.18; Blue LVG C in flames
crashed in river S of Méricourt sur Somme 08.30 9.6.18;
Damaged landing 2.7.18; Fokker DVII crashed
Assévillers 08.40 11.8.18; (all Lt CG Edwards DFC);
Direct hit by shell at 200 ft, BU in air SE of Jig-Saw
Wood 12.15 27.8.18 (Lt CG Edwards DFC killed); SOC
in field 27.8.18

**B6377** (130-hp Clerget) Deld AP Dover W/E 6.10.17; Walmer
by 12.10.17; AP Dover by 27.10.17; Walmer by 11.17;
NAP Dover by 17.12.17; Manston 9.1.18; 8 Sqdn (via
AP Dover) 12.1.18; Albatros DV OOC Wingles, shared
B6369 & B6447 11.25 19.1.18; Albatros DV OOC
Hénin-Lietard 15.00 19.1.18; 2 Albatros DV OOC
Neuvireuil, 1st shared B6369, 2nd shared N6356, B6319
& B6369 11.30 24.1.18; Albatros DV crashed nr
Beaumont, shared B6369 13.15 25.1.18 (all FSL EG
Johnstone); 1 NAP Dunkerque 17.2.18; Dover 17.2.18;

East Fortune 23.2.18 - @30.3.18

**B6378** (130-hp Clerget, later B.R.1) Deld Walmer by 10.17;
AP Dover 27.10.17; ADD 12.1.18; 8 Sqdn 13.1.18;
KB attacked on ground after dark, in flames Godault
Farm, Beaumont - Hénin-Lietard 18.00 21.1.18;
Albatros DV OOC vertically Fresnes-Vitry, 11.40
24.1.18; Albatros Scout OOC Beaumont-Auby 12.30
29.1.18; Albatros DV OOC Fresnes 12.20 3.2.18 (all
F/Cdr RB Munday); 3 Sqdn 18.2.18; 1 Sqdn by
21.2.18; 1 NAP Dunkerque 20.3.18; 213 Sqdn 1.4.18; 4
ASD 11.4.18; 203 Sqdn 16.5.18; see B3855 17.5.18;
Fokker DVII DrI Fournes-en-Weppes 30.5.18 (both Capt
R Sykes); 2 ASD unfit for further service in field
16.8.18; Rep Pk 1 ASD 17.8.18; to England 18.8.18

**B6379** (130-hp Clerget) Deld AP Dover W/E 5.10.17; 8 Sqdn
5.12.17; DFW OOC Drocourt-Douai, shared B6340 &
FSL HM Reid 6.12.17 (FSL WL Jordan); DFW C OOC
Hénin-Lietard, shared B6228 14.35 27.12.17 (both FSL
H Day DSC); DFW C OOC Vitry, shared B6229 1.00
28.12.17; Albatros DV OOC Vitry 11.20 22.1.18;
Roland crashed La Bassée 24.1.18; Small new type 2-str
in flames La Bassée 11.05 28.1.18; Albatros DV crashed
in flames nr Thonville, shared B3832 & N6356 11.15
16.2.18 (all F/Cdr GW Price); 3 Sqdn 18.2.18; 1 Sqdn
by 21.2.18; ADD 5.3.18 - @28.3.18; 213 Sqdn
@1.4.18; 4 ASD Guines by 12.4.18 - @27.4.18; 2 ASD
by 5.18; 209 Sqdn 20.5.18; LVG CV No.3871 shot
down in flames in British lines S of Albert, crew killed
12.00 27.5.18 [numbered G/5Bde/11]; Fokker DrI OOC
E of Albert 20.20 20.7.18 (both Lt WR May); EF, FL,
crashed 4.7.18 (Lt DY Hunter); EF at 50 ft on TO,
stalled, spun in, CW 25.7.18 (Lt JP Naish killed); 1
ASD 25.7.18; SOC in field 28.7.18

**B6380** (130-hp Clerget) Deld AP Dover W/E 13.10.17; 10
Sqdn 12.1.18; EF, FL, slightly damaged La Lovie
15.1.18 (FSL AA Cameron unhurt), retd 16.1.18;
Turned with insufficient speed and spun in from 200 ft
immediately after TO, CW 18.1.18 (FSL AA Cameron
seriously injured); ADD 18.1.18; Deleted 21.1.18

**B6381** (130-hp Clerget) Deld AP Dover W/E 3.11.17; 9 Sqdn
(named 'DAPHNE') 23.11.17; War School Manston (via
AP Dover) 22.1.18; Deleted W/E 16.2.18

**B6387** (130-hp Clerget) Deld Brooklands to AP Dover W/E
10.11.17; 8 Sqdn 25.1.18; Albatros DV shot down S of
Pont-à-Vendin, shared B3832, N6356 & N6379 12.45
5.2.18; Albatros OOC 15.2.18 (both F/Cdr R
McDonald); 3 Sqdn 18.2.18; ADD by 21.2.18; 4 ASD
Guines 28.3.18; 213 Sqdn 1.4.18; 4 ASD Guines (later 4
ASD Wissant); 213 Sqdn 17.10.18; EF, FL, hit E4406,
badly damaged 17.10.18 (2/Lt WG Fleming injured); 4
ASD 23.10.18

**B6388** (130-hp Clerget) Deld AP Dover W/E 20.10.17; COL,
CW 23.11.17 (FSL RE Carroll); Deleted 28.1.18

**B6389** (B.R.1) Deld Dover by 12.10.17; 4 Sqdn 23.11.17;
DFW C crashed N of Nieuport Piers 13.30 6.12.17;
Pfalz DIII crashed W of Dixmude, another OOC
Pervyse-Dixmude & another OOC shared with Belgian
Spad 17.00 26.3.18; Became 204 Sqdn 1.4.18; Rumpler
C DD to 8/9,000ft nr Bergues, then engine misfiring,
HA then forced down by B6350 21.4.18; Pfalz DIII in
sea Middelkerke-Coxyde area 15.30 12.6.18 (all A/F/L
later A/F/Cdr later Capt RM Keirstead); Collided with
D3386 over Zeebrugge, fell in sea in flames 16.40
13.7.18 (Lt GW Graham killed); WOC 31.7.18

**B6390** (B.R.1) Deld AP Dover W/E 13.10.17; Seaplane
Defence Flt 21.10.17; Albatros DV OOC Ostende,
13.30-15.00 patrol 19.12.17 (F/Cdr R Collishaw);
Became 13 Sqdn 15.1.18; FL in sea, sank 10m N of
Nieuport 28.3.18 14.00 (FSL EG Wilkinson picked up
destroyer HMS *Myngs*); Deleted 8.4.18

**B6391** (B.R.1) Deld AP Dover W/E 13.10.17; Seaplane
Defence Sqdn 29.11.17; Albatros C in sea 4m NW of
Wenduyne, shared N6335, B6357 & B6407 15.05
5.12.17 (FSL JdeC Paynter); ADD W/E 27.12.17; 1
NAP Dunkerque W/E 3.1.18; 10 Sqdn 4.2.18; Night
bombed Abeele aerodrome with 4x16-lb bombs 27.2.18
(FSL MT McKelvey); Crashed and CW on bomber
escort to Bruges 23.3.18 (FSL HA Patey); 4 ASD
25.3.18; 204 Sqdn 20.4.18; COL 21.5.18 (Lt WJP
Jenner unhurt); 4 ASD 21.5.18; WOC 30.6.18 general
fatigue

*Sopwith Camels B6410 and B6397 of the Seaplane Defence Squadron at St.Pol in December 1917. (via Frank Cheesman)*

*Sopwith Camel B7230 'T' of 3 Sqdn after being forced to land behind German lines on 10 March 1918, FSL KD Campbell being taken prisoner. (via Frank Cheesman)*

*Sopwith Camel B7234 of 204 Sqdn, named 'LAURA', was shot down on 31 July 1918. (via Frank Cheesman)*

*A patrol of Sopwith Camels of 3 Sqdn about to leave Mont St.Eloi. 'Kiwi' Beamish is running up B7275 'P'. (via Frank Cheesman)*

B6397   (B.R.1?) Deld AP Dover W/E 20.10.17; Seaplane Defence Sqdn 12.12.17; Crashed, CW 12.17 (S/Cdr R Graham DSC); Deleted ADD 31.12.17

B6398   (B.R.1) Deld AP Dover W/E 20.10.17; 1 Sqdn 9.11.17; Albatros DV crashed Beerst 13.00 & another OOC N of Dixmude 13.15 15.11.17; DFW C OOC SE of Dixmude 16.00 4.12.17; Albatros DV OOC Houthulst Forest 06.45 6.12.17; Albatros DV OOC probably dest N of Passchendaele 11.00 6.12.17; 2-str Scout OOC 2m NW Menin 15.30 10.3.18; Collided with 10 Sqdn aircraft (B5749) on aerodrome 11.3.18 (all FSL SM Kinkead, DSC); Became 201 Sqdn 1.4.18; Practice flight, collided with cow and killed Frenchman on edge of aerodrome, badly damaged 7.4.18 (2/Lt DJ Hartle injured); 4 ASD 7.4.18; 1 AI by 5.18; 209 Sqdn 5.5.18; Albatros DV OOC Belloy-Pozières 10.15 15.5.18 (Lt WR May); Fokker DrI (Ltn Hübner, Jasta 4, PoW) shot down W of Corbie, shared B7199 & D3329 16.15 16.5.18 (Lt WR May) [numbered G/5Bde/8]; Rumpler C claimed forced down, shared B3858, not credited 08.30 6.6.18 (Lt LJ Descon); EF, FL, drifted, crashed Ailly-sur-Somme 24.6.18 (2/Lt RN Wellington unhurt); 2 ASD 25.6.18; 2 AI by 8.18; 201 Sqdn 9.8.18; Fokker DVII OOC smoking Heudicourt 06.30 and another crashed Lagnicourt 07.15 2.9.18; Fokker DVII OOC Cambrai 18.45 6.9.18; Pfalz DIII Scout crashed in flames Fontaine-Notre-Dame, W of Cambrai 08.45 15.9.18 (all Capt RCB Brading DFC); TO crosswind, crashed 14.12.18 (2/Lt VSG Hawkins unhurt); to 2 ASD; ALSO 1 FS Turnberry (named 'SYLVESTA')

B6399   (B.R.1) Presentation a/c 'Punjab No.43. Jhang-Gujaret-Si'. Deld AP Dover W/E 20.10.17; Seaplane Defence Sqdn 4.1.18; Became 13 Sqdn 15.1.18; Became 213 Sqdn 1.4.18; 4 ASD Pilots Pool Guines 8.5.18; WOC 31.7.18

B6400   (B.R.1, later 170-hp CR.1 by 23.3.18) Presentation a/c 'Hong Kong, Lady Ho Tung'. Deld AP Dover W/E 20.10.17; Seaplane Defence Flt 21.10.17; Became 13 Sqdn 15.1.18; Albatros CII DD in vertical dive damaged Ramscapelle 12.25 16.2.18; Rumpler C in flames 1m to sea Ostende-Wenduyne, shared B6407, B6410 & B7276 09.05 12.3.18; Rumpler C damaged 16.3.18 (all F/Cdr LH Slatter); Became 213 Sqdn 1.4.18; Albatros DV crashed in sea & another OOC in sea 5m W of Westende 14.45 11.5.18 (Capt LH Slatter); 4 ASD 2.6.18; WOC 15.6.18

B6401   (B.R.1) Deld AP Dover W/E 20.10.17; 3 Sqdn 20.11.17 (rising sun painted on fin); DFW C OOC Houthulst Forest, shared B3785 & B6408 11.05 28.1.18; 2 Albatros DV OOC nr Gheluvelt, shared B6242 & B6408 10.45 30.1.18 (all F/L later F/Cdr LH Rochford); 8 Sqdn 1.3.18; Walmer 28.3.18; AAP Dover by road 2.4.18 - 5.18; 4 ASD Guines by 25.5.18; 213 Sqdn 30.6.18; Fokker DVII OOC 4m SE of Ypres 12.15 12.8.18 (Lt GC Mackay); 4 ASD 16.9.18; WOC 30.9.18 general fatigue

B6407   (B.R.1) Deld AP Dover W/E 20.10.17; Seaplane Defence Flt 21.10.17; Albatros C crashed in sea 4m NE of Wenduyne, shared B6357, B6391 & N6335 15.05 5.12.17 (FSL ML Cooper); Albatros C observer fell out, then OOC Ostende-Zeebrugge 14.45 19.12.17 (FSL GC Mackay); Became 13 Sqdn 15.1.18; 2-str seaplane in flames 100yds from Blankenberghe Piers, shared B3782, B3909, B6410 & B7186 14.00 29.1.18 (FSL GC Mackay); Rumpler C in flames 1m to sea Ostende-Wenduyne, shared B6400, B6410 & B7226 09.05 12.3.18 (FSL JE Greene); Became 213 Sqdn 1.4.18; 4 ASD 22.5.18 - @25.5.18

B6408   (B.R.1) Deld AP Dover W/E 20.10.17; 3 Sqdn 29.12.17; DFW OOC Houthulst, shared B3785 & B6401 11.05 28.1.18; 2 Albatros DV OOC nr Gheluvelt, shared B6242 & B6401 10.45 30.1.18 (all F/L JA Glen); 1 NAP Dunkerque 27.2.18; 4 ASD Guines 28.3.18; 203 Sqdn 12.4.18; Left 10.30, FTR, flight attacked by 15 triplanes and Pfalz, flight shot down Pfalz DIII in flames shared B7197, C61 & D3362 11.15, soon afterwards a Camel seen OOC nr Merville 17.5.18 (2/Lt ER Prideaux killed)

B6409   (B.R.1) Deld AP Dover W/E 20.10.17; 1 Sqdn 23.11.17; Albatros DV OOC nr Middelkerke 11.15 29.11.17 (FSL JH Forman); AZP from Dover 28/29.1.18; Albatros DV OOC Nieuport 15.50 21.3.18 (F/Lt SM Kinkead, DSC); Dropped 2x16-lb bombs on Uytkerke aerodrome 21.3.18 (FSL JH Forman); COL Fienvillers 28.3.18 (FSL JH Forman); Became 201 Sqdn 1.4.18; Damaged by flak, FL, COL Ste.Marie Capelle 11.4.18 (2/Lt F Newton); 4 ASD 11.4.18; 201 Sqdn 17.4.18; 2 AI 9.6.18; Rec Pk 10.6.18; Flown to England 13.6.18

B6410   (B.R.1) Deld AP Dover W/E 20.10.17; Seaplane Defence Sqdn 21.10.17; Became 13 Sqdn 15.1.18; 2-str seaplane in flames 100yds off Blankenberghe Piers, shared B3782, B3909, B6407 & B7186 14.00 29.1.18 (FSL ML Cooper); Rumpler C in flames 1m to sea Ostende-Wenduyne, shared B6400, B6407 & B7226 09.05 12.3.18 (FSL GC Mackay); Became 213 Sqdn 1.4.18; 2-str seaplane on fire Zeebrugge c.14.30 1.4.18 (Lt ML Cooper) [Flobmt M Behrendt & Ltn DR Hauptugel, Seeflug 1 both killed]; 4 ASD 26.5.18

B6411   (B.R.1) Deld Dover W/E 27.10.17; 1 Sqdn 23.11.17; AZP from Dover 28/29.1.18; AZP from Dover 29.1.18 (F/Cdr RP Minifie); Became 201 Sqdn 1.4.18; Albatros DV OOC SE of Albert 10.30 2.5.18; Fokker DrI OOC S of Albert 19.20 16.5.18 (both Lt HP Guard); Rep Pk 1 ASD 22.5.18; 2 ASD 22.5.18; Flown Marquise to Farnborough 27-28.5.18

B6417   (B.R.1) Deld AP Dover W/E 27.10.17; 3 Sqdn 29.12.17; Albatros DV OOC Thourout-Dixmude 11.40 18.2.18 (F/L DA Bawlf); 8 Sqdn 1.3.18; Became 208 Sqdn 1.4.18; General engagement, shot down, FL NE of Loos 12.10 7.4.18 (2/Lt DC Hopewell PoW) [believed by Ltn P.Billik, Jasta 52]

B6418   (B.R.1) Deld AP Dover W/E 27.10.17; 1 Sqdn 9.11.17; Albatros DV OOC probably dest N of Passchendaele 11.00 6.12.17 (F/Cdr CB Ridley); Dover with sqdn 10.12.17; Brooklands 12.12.17; Dover 13.12.17; Retd France with sqdn 16.12.17; 2-str in flames Dixmude-Nieuport, then shot down decoy KB nr Kemmel, shared B6429 15.15, then EF, FL and CW 12.3.18 (F/Cdr CB Ridley); 1 NAP Dunkerque by 14.3.18; Deleted W/E 21.3.18

B6419   (B.R.1) Deld AP Dover W/E 27.10.17; 1 Sqdn 9.11.17; Albatros DV OOC NE of Dixmude 13.55 15.11.17; Albatros DV OOC probably dest Houthulst Forest 11.15 4.12.17; Albatros DV OOC Roulers 15.00 8.3.18; Albatros DV crashed 2m NW of Menin 15.30 10.3.18; Albatros DV red/yellow tail crashed E of Roulers 11.55 16.3.18; Albatros DV OOC in dive NE of Roulers, shared B6359 16.35 16.3.18 (all FSL MH Findlay); Pfalz DIII in flames 3m SE of Nieuport 07.15 21.3.18; Became 201 Sqdn 1.4.18; Controls shot away in strenuous fight against 8 Fokker DrI, FL, crashed nr Mericourt 18.05 6.4.18 (2/Lt MH Findlay DSC unhurt); SOC in field 7.4.18 dest

B6420   (B.R.1) Deld AP Dover W/E 27.10.17; 1 Sqdn 9.11.17; Albatros DV OOC nr Middelkerke 14.15 29.11.17; DFW CV shot down E of Dixmude 11.15 8.12.17 (both F/Cdr RP Minifie); AZP from Dover 29.1.18 (F/Lt CB Ridley); Albatros DV OOC then another but crashed in floods SE of Dixmude 07.25 13.3.18 (all F/Cdr RP Minifie); Shot down in combat with Pfalz scouts nr Houthulst Forest 17.3.18 (A/F/Cdr RP Minifie, DSC PoW); Deleted 18.3.18

B6421   (B.R.1) Deld AP Dover W/E 27.10.17; 1 Sqdn 23.11.17; With sqdn to Dover 10.12.17?; Retd France with sqdn 16.2.18; COL Fienvillers 28.3.18 (FSL RE Bright); Became 201 Sqdn 1.4.18; Albatros C OOC N of Albert, shared B6359, B6429, B7225, B7267 & B7278 10.10 2.5.18; Scout OOC E of Albert 17.45 15.5.18; Albatros DV dest Bapaume-Mory, shared D1862 & flight 06.45 16.5.18; Overshot landing, caught bump, o/t, unhurt 22.5.18 (all Lt RCB Brading); 2 ASD 23.5.18; 2 ASD by 15.8.18; 54 Sqdn by 8.18; FTR 27.9.18 (Lt P McCaig killed)

B6427   (B.R.1) Deld AP Dover W/E 27.10.17; 1 Sqdn 9.11.17; DFW C crashed Roggevelde 09.15 15.11.17 (S/Cdr RS Dallas DSC); Albatros DV OOC NE of Dixmude 13.55 15.11.17 (FSL HR de Wilde); Rumpler C in flames Dixmude 11.15 12.3.18 (S/Cdr RS Dallas DSC); Became 201 Sqdn 1.4.18; Caught wind on TO for practice flight, swung round, tipped on nose 8.5.18 (Lt BL McCarthy); 4 ASD 9.5.18; WOC 31.10.18 general fatigue

**B6428** (B.R.1) Deld AP Dover W/E 27.10.17; 1 Sqdn 9.11.17; Albatros DV OOC Vladsloo, E of Dixmude 14.10 5.12.17; 2-str OOC Ostende 06.25 6.12.17; Albatros DV crashed on fire S of Zillebeke Lake, shared B7202 11.45 19.2.18; 1-str OOC Menin 15.30 10.3.18; 2-str OOC Comines-Warneton 12.00 11.3.18; Albatros DV crashed in floods SE of Dixmude 07.25 13.3.18; With B7233 attacked 8 Pfalz DIII, shot down 1 which crashed in floods & another in flames Dixmude 11.45 15.3.18; Albatros DV crashed E of Roulers 11.55 16.3.18; Albatros DV OOC NE of Roulers 16.25 16.3.18; Albatros DV in sea in flames SE of Nieuport, Pfalz DIII crashed in flames 4m S of Nieuport & HA (Albatros DV?) OOC nr Nieuport 07.15 21.3.18; Became 201 Sqdn 1.4.18; Fokker DrI OOC Bouchoir 13.15 6.4.18 (all FSL:F/Lt:Capt SW Rosevear, DSC); Left 10.20, last seen nr Hangard 22.4.18 (Capt GA Magor killed); SOC in field 23.4.18

**B6429** (B.R.1) Deld AP Dover (via) Eastchurch W/E 27.10.17; 1 Sqdn 23.11.17; AZP from Dover 29/30.1.18; Decoy KB shot down nr Kemmel, shared B6418 15.15 12.3.18; DFW C OOC Dixmude 11.45 16.3.18; Albatros DV crashed on beach 6m NE of Nieuport 15.50 21.3.18; Became 201 Sqdn 1.4.18; Albatros DV OOC Arras-Albert 13.00 1.4.18 (all F/L:F/Cdr:Capt HV Rowley); Fokker DrI OOC Bouchoir 13.15 6.4.18; Albatros C OOC N of Albert, shared B6359, B6421, B7225, B7267 & B7278 10.10 2.5.18 (both Capt SM Kinkead); 4 ASD Guines 9.5.18 (overhaul, later Pilots Pool); SOC 31.7.18

**B6430** (B.R.1) Deld AP Dover W/E 3.11.17; 1 Sqdn 9.11.17; Badly shot up 15.11.17; 9 Sqdn 10.12.17; Fokker DrI dest 2m SW of Roulers, shared B3781 14.00, then shot down nr Roulers, believed folded up 3.2.18 (A/F/Cdr RR Winter killed); Deleted 4.2.18

**B6431** (B.R.1) Deld AP Dover W/E 27.10.17; 1 Sqdn 23.11.17; DFW C OOC Ostende 07.30 6.12.17; AZP from Dover 29/30.1.18 (both S/Cdr RS Dallas); Became 201 Sqdn 1.4.18; Pfalz DIII E of Villers-Bretonneux 12.50 2.5.18 (Capt CB Ridley); Pfalz DIII OOC Bapaume 13.15 9.5.18 (Lt R McLaughlin); 2 AI 31.5.18; Rec Pk 1 ASD and flown to England 1.6.18 (for overhaul)

**B6437** (130-hp Clerget) Deld CSD White City by 29.10.17; Shipped to 2 Wing Mudros 10.11.17; Mudros by 1.12.17 - @1.1.18; Marsh by 26.2.18; G Sqdn 2 Wing by 3.18; Mobile Sqdn Mudros, lost control, spinning nose dive Mudros harbour 3.6.18 (Lt AJ Nightingale killed) (now 110-hp Clerget)

**B6438** (130-hp Clerget) Deld CSD White City 10.17; Shipped to Mudros 20.11.17; 2 Wing Mudros for erection by 1.1.18 - @3.18; Repair Base Mudros by 5.18; 221 Sqdn Stavros by 6.18 & 8.18; Repair Base Mudros by 10.18; Stavros by 10.18 - @11.18

**B6439** (130-hp Clerget) Deld CSD White City by 29.10.17; Shipped to 2 Wing Mudros 10.11.17

**B6440** (130-hp Clerget) Deld CSD White City by 29.10.17; Shipped to 2 Wing Mudros 10.11.17; Mudros by 1.12.17 - @1.1.18; Imbros by 3.18; Repair Base Mudros by 6.18

**B6441** (130-hp Clerget, later 110-hp Clerget) Deld CSD White City by 29.10.17; Shipped to 6 Wing Otranto 20.11.17; arr 6 Wing Otranto by 28.12.17; Became 66/6 Wing Otranto 1.4.18 - @21.4.18; 225 Sqdn by 28.4.18; Became 481/3 Flts 225 Sqdn Andrano/Taranto by 10.18 - @11.18

**B6446** 50 TDS Eastbourne by 6.18 (red overall); Crashed 21.8.18 (2/Lt CA Manzetti killed)

**B6447** (130-hp Clerget, later B.R.1) Deld AP Dover W/E 3.11.17; 8 Sqdn 23.11.17; Grey-green Albatros DV OOC Mericourt 11.25 28.12.17; Albatros DV possibly OOC Bailleul, shared N6376 & B6448 15.00 1.1.18 (both FSL WL Jordan); Hannover C crashed W of Arras, shared B6319 & B6340 10.05 3.1.18 (Lt PM Dennett); DFW C crashed Gavrelle, shared N6376, B6278 & B6319 11.30 4.1.18; Albatros DV OOC S of La Bassée, shared B6340 (q.v.) 11.50 6.1.18 (all FSL WL Jordan); Albatros DV OOC Wingles, shared B6369 & B6377 11.25 19.1.18; Albatros DV OOC Hénin-Liétard 15.15 19.1.18 (both Lt PM Dennett); FL and crashed Bergues, unhurt 25.1.18 (F/L WL Jordan); 1

NAP Dunkerque 27.1.18 (overhaul; re-engined B.R.1 by 7.3.18); 4 Sqdn 12.3.18; Became 204 Sqdn 1.4.18; 4 ASD Guines 17.6.18 (later Audembert, used by Pilots Pool) - @9.18

**B6448** (130-hp Clerget) Deld AP Dover W/E 17.11.17; 8 Sqdn 4.12.17; Albatros DV possibly OOC Bailleul, shared N6376 & B6447 15.00 1.1.18 (FSL HM Reid); 10 Sqdn 4.2.18 (temp custody); 1 Sqdn 15.2.18; COL 15.2.18 (FSL RE Bright); to 1 NAP; Hendon 26.3.18; 4 ASD Guines 29.3.18 (arr 30.3.18); 213 Sqdn 30.6.18; EA OOC off Wenduyne, shared B6358, B7270, D3326, D9627 & D9647 11.40 7.7.18; COL, unhurt 10.7.18 (both Lt PC Jenner); to 4 ASD

**B6449** (130-hp Clerget) Deld AP Dover W/E 3.11.17; 10 Sqdn 12.11.18; 9 Sqdn 4.2.18; Crashed, CW Great Mongehem 10.3.18 (FSL JSJ Craigen); AAP Dover 15.3.18; Deleted ADD 18.3.18

**B6450** (130-hp Clerget) Deld Brooklands to Dover W/E 1.12.17; 10 Sqdn 4.1.18; Albatros DV OOC E of Houthulst Forest 11.35 14.1.18; 2-str BU Staden 14.50 23.1.18 (both F/Cdr WA Curtis); 9 Sqdn 4.2.18; AAP Dover 19.3.18 - @28.3.18; Dover by 4.18 - 5.18 (at Manston by 27.4.18); Practice flight, stalled on climbing turn, nosedived, CW Dover 17.5.18 (Lt WB Hughes killed); Surveyed 22.5.18; Deleted 24.5.18

## 21 SOPWITH F.1 CAMEL TRACTOR BIPLANE SCOUTS from batch B7131 by B7180 built by Portholme Aerodrome Ltd. (150-hp B.R.1 or 130-hp Clerget 9B)

**B7148** 1 AI to 210 Sqdn 25.5.18; 2-str crashed E of Bailleul, shared B7153 17.45 1.6.18; Albatros DV OOC SE of Kemmel 18.30 15.6.18 (both Lt CW Payton); Spun in OOC on practice flight, believed fainted nr St.Sylvestre-Cappel 18.6.18 (Lt CJ Shackell killed); to 1 ASD; SOC 21.6.18 NWR

**B7150** (B.R.1) Deld 3(W)ARD Yate by 11.4.18; 206 TDS Eastbourne by 5.18; COL Stonecross 9.5.18 (pilot unhurt); To USA

**B7152** (B.R.1) Deld 3(W)ARD Yate by 11.4.18; 201 Sqdn to 2 ASD 13.5.18; 4 ASD 25.5.18; 2 AI to 201 Sqdn (coded 'X') 30.5.18; 2 ASD 13.8.18; Rep Pk 1 ASD 14.8.18; To England for overhaul 14.8.18

**B7153** Rec Pk to 1 AI 16.5.18; 210 Sqdn (coded 'X' and 'V') 22.5.18; Pfalz DIII OOC Bailleul, shared C672 08.10 27.5.18; 2-str crashed S of Bailleul, shared B7148 17.45 1.6.18 (both Lt LP Coombes); Pfalz DIII OOC Ploegsteert Wood 08.30 9.6.18 (Lt SC Joseph); Pfalz DIII OOC SE of Ypres 20.15 23.6.18; Fokker DVII crashed, another OOC then 2 Pfalz DIII OOC 1m W of Armentières, all shared D3387 & D9608 (q.v.) 19.20 26.6.18 (Lt IC Sanderson); 4 ASD for survey 3.8.18; 210 Sqdn 8.9.18; Caught by wind landing, o/t, badly damaged 11.9.18 (Lt HH Whitlock unhurt); to 4 ASD; WOC 30.9.18 general fatigue

**B7154** (B.R.1) Deld 3(W)ARD Yate by 11.4.18; 4 ASD Guines by 4.18; 213 Sqdn 16.5.18; Hannover C OOC Poperinghe, shared B7229 & C65 17.45 15.6.18 (Lt AR Talbot); 4 ASD 7.8.18; WOC 31.10.18 general fatigue

**B7155** (B.R.1) Deld 3(W)ARD Yate by 11.4.18; 1 AI to 210 Sqdn 20.5.18; Wings folded back when pulled up sharply from vertical dive in practice flight 11.6.18 (2/Lt N Mason killed); to Rep Pk 1 ASD; SOC in field 13.6.18

**B7157** Rec Pk to 2 ASD 19.5.18; 201 Sqdn 22.5.18; Left 11.20 low flying patrol, FTR 8.8.18 (2/Lt W Cox PoW); SOC in field 8.8.18

**B7159** Rec Pk to 2 AI 11.5.18; 201 Sqdn 16.5.18; Lost direction, FL, o/t, wrecked nr Doullens 10.6.18 (Lt J Paton unhurt); Rebuilt as F6246 15.8.18

**B7160** Rec Pk to 1 AI 8.5.18; 210 Sqdn 14.5.18; HOP, collided D3385, wings came off, crashed British side of lines 15.5.18 (Lt MS Kelly killed); Not salved; SOC in field 20.5.18

**B7162** (B.R.1) Deld 3(W)ARD Yate by 26.4.18; Rec Pk to 1 AI 22.5.18; 203 Sqdn by 31.5.18; Crashed on TO from uneven LG 1.9.18 (2/Lt T Nolan injured); 2 ASD 3.9.18; SOC in field 9.9.18 NWR

**B7163** (B.R.1) Deld 3(W)ARD Yate by 26.4.18; 1 AI to 210 Sqdn 20.5.18; Last seen OOC S of Estaires after general engagement over Ploegsteert Wood 08.30 9.6.18 (2/Lt C

Marden PoW); SOC in field 9.6.18

B7165 Ex RFC to RNAS Tregantle & Withnoe store by 30.3.18; 80 Sqdn

B7166 Ex RFC to RNAS Tregantle & Withnoe store by 30.3.18

B7167 Ex RFC to RNAS Tregantle & Withnoe store by 30.3.18; 45 Sqdn; 80 Sqdn; 66 Sqdn (coded 'S'), lost on action 22.10.18 (2/Lt JM Kelly, PoW)

B7168 Ex RFC to RNAS Tregantle & Withnoe store by 30.3.18

B7169 Ex RFC to RNAS Tregantle & Withnoe store by 30.3.18

B7170 Ex RFC to RNAS Tregantle & Withnoe store by 30.3.18

B7175 Deld 3(W)ARD Yate by 27.4.18; 4 ASD by 25.5.18; 213 Sqdn 3.6.18; Dest by fire in enemy bombing raid 29.6.18; WOC 31.7.18

B7176 (130-hp Clerget) AAP Dover to 1 NAD 23.3.18; 3(W)ARD Yate by 27.4.18; 4 ASD Guines by 25.5.18; 204 Sqdn 8.6.18; Rumpler C crashed into shell hole 5m S of Ypres 15.30 22.7.18; Sea green Pfalz DIII crashed nr Roulers 11.30 31.7.18 (both Lt TW Nash); Fokker DVII OOC 6m E of Ypres 08.25 15.8.18 (Lt JR Robinson wounded); Crashed on TO 21.8.18 (Lt CL Kelly unhurt); 4 ASD 22.8.18 - @25.10.18

B7177 208 TDS East Fortune by 6.18; AAP Whitley Abbey to 32 TDS 25.7.18

B7180 (130-hp Clerget) Norwich to Yarmouth 26.4.18; Norwich 27.4.18; Rec Pk to 1 AI but retd bad weather 14.5.18; flown France to England 29.7.18

**100 SOPWITH F.1 CAMEL TRACTOR BIPLANE SCOUTS ordered under Cont No A.S.7861 from Clayton & Shuttleworth Ltd and numbered B7181 to B7280, to be built at Lincoln. All delivered to RNAS (except B7235-B7237 to Belgium). (150-hp B.R.1 or 130-hp Clerget 9B)**

B7181 (130-hp Clerget) Deld CSD White City 12.17; Cardiff Docks by 1.1.18; Shipped to 2 Wing Mudros 25.1.18; Repair Base Mudros by 3.18; Repair Base Mudros 6.18; 220 Sqdn by 10.18; Repair Base Mudros by 10.18 - 1.19; RAF South Russia to Russian Air Corps 8.19

B7182 (130-hp Clerget) Deld CSD White City 12.17; Cardiff Docks by 1.1.18; Shipped to 2 Wing Mudros 25.1.18; Repair by 3.18; F Sqdn 62 Wing Mudros by 4.18; Imbros by 6.18; Marsh by 10.18; Mudros, with RHNAS by 10.18 - @1.19

B7183 (130-hp Clerget) Deld CSD White City 12.17; Shipped to 2 Wing Mudros 30.1.18; Mudros for erection by 3.18

B7184 (B.R.1) Deld 4 AAP Lincoln W/E 12.12.17; AP Dover 27.12.17; Loon Plage, Calais 13.1.18; 3 Sqdn by road 14.1.18; 14.00 patrol, shot down W of Zarren by Ltn C.Degelow, Jasta 7 23.1.18 (FSL HStJE Youens PoW); Deleted 28.1.18

B7185 (B.R.1) Deld 4 AAP Lincoln W/E 19.12.17; Hendon 5.1.18 (transit); Dover 10.1.18; 10 Sqdn 2.2.18 (temp custody); 8 Sqdn 4.2.18; 3 Sqdn 3.3.18; DFW Aviatik in flames Hénin-Lietard, shared B3798 11.20 9.3.18; Hannover C on fire Gavrelle-Fresnes, shared B7203 & B7220 11.20 16.3.18; Albatros DV OOC nr Douai, shared B7222 11.15 21.3.18 (all FSL JA Glen); Albatros C crashed 4m E of Bapaume, shared B7203 & flight 21.3.18 (FSL JA Glen wounded); Pfalz DIII crashed Vaulx-Beugnâtre 17.00 23.3.18 (F/Cdr FC Armstrong); Became 203 Sqdn 1.4.18; Albatros C crashed nr Givenchy, shared B7229 & B7231 16.10 9.4.18; Albatros C crashed in flames nr Lavantie, shared Camel with green wing tips & elevators from another sqdn 18.30 11.4.18 (both Capt JA Glen); COL due to high wind, damaged 15.45 18.4.18 (Capt AB Ellwood unhurt); 4 ASD 19.4.18; 1 AI by 5.18; 203 Sqdn 22.5.18; DFW C dest Estaires, shared D3371, D3414, D3417 & D9585 06.10 16.6.18 (pilot?); 1 AI 6.7.18 (time expired); 1 RP 1 ASD 7.7.18; Rebuilt as F5966 9.7.18

B7186 (B.R.1) Deld 4 AAP Lincoln W/E 12.12.17; Chingford (via Cranwell) 21.12.17 (transit); AP Dover 23.12.17; 13 Sqdn 21.1.18; 2-str seaplane in flames 100 yards off Blankenberghe Piers, shared B3782, B3909, B6407 & B6410 14.00 29.1.18 (F/Cdr LH Slatter); Pfalz DIII OOC in sea 2m N of Ostende 10.30 24.3.18 (FSL GC MacKay); 4 ASD Guines 28.3.18; 213 Sqdn 9.6.18; Last seen in spin after attacked by HA 4m N of Blankenberghe 27.6.18 (Lt WG Evans killed) [credited Flgm Zenses, Marine Jasta 2]; WOC 31.7.18

B7187 (B.R.1) Deld 4 AAP Lincoln W/E 19.12.17; AP Dover 29.12.17; 3 Sqdn 6.1.18; 8 Sqdn 3.3.18; Became 208 Sqdn 1.4.18; Fokker DrI OOC in general engagement nr Lens, shared B7189 & B7196 11.15, then shot down in flames by Ltn Hertz, Jasta 59 11.30 6.4.18 (FSL WH Sneath killed)

B7188 (B.R.1) Deld 4 AAP Lincoln W/E 19.12.17; Cranwell 12.17 (crashed in transit); AP Dover 13.1.18; 10 Sqdn 2.2.18 (temp custody); 8 Sqdn 4.2.18; Shot down by HA nr Arleux 18.2.18 (FSL CRC Walworth killed); Deleted 11.3.18

B7189 (B.R.1) Deld 4 AAP Lincoln W/E 19.12.17; AP Dover 28.12.17; 3 Sqdn 27.1.18; 8 Sqdn 1.3.18; Became 208 Sqdn 1.4.18; Fokker DrI OOC Lens, shared B7187 & B7196 11.15 6.4.18 (Lt GK Cooper); Burnt to prevent capture La Gorgue 9.4.18

B7190 (B.R.1) Deld 4 AAP Lincoln to Chingford 22.12.17 (transit); AP Dover 12.17; 9 Sqdn 12.1.18; 10 Sqdn 4.2.18; Dropped 4x16-lb bombs in night attack on Abeele aerodrome 26/27.2.18 ; Dropped 4x16-lb bombs on Zeebrugge 7.3.18; 2-str OOC nr Roulers 15.45 10.3.18 (all F/L WGR Hinchliffe); Became 210 Sqdn 1.4.18; 2-str crashed in flames nr Roulers 11.30 3.4.18 (Capt WGR Hinchliffe); FL, COL nr Cassel 11.4.18 (2/Lt CW Payton unhurt); 4 ASD Guines 12.4.18; 2 AI 17.5.18; 201 Sqdn 18.5.18; Albatros DV OOC nr Aubigny, shared D1862 08.45 23.5.18; Pfalz DIII OOC SE of Albert 10.55 30.5.18; Albatros DV OOC Achiet-le-Grand 19.55 30.5.18; Hit by D6520 on landing 15.7.18; Flying again 17.7.18; KB nr Bray, SE of Albert, shared D9586 12.20 19.7.18; Fokker DVII OOC S of Armentières 10.20 30.7.18; Damaged by flak 1.8.18; Fokker DVII OOC SE of Dickebusch Lake 20.30 1.8.18; After bombing ammunition trains engaged 2-str which glided to ground 8.8.18; Fokker DVII OOC Foucaucourt 09.00 10.8.18; Fokker DVII crashed Rosières, nr Fouquescourt 16.15 11.8.18; Fokker DVII forced to land nr Bayonvillers c.17.10 12.8.18 (numbered G/5Bde/20 and sent to UK, Ofstvtr Blumenthal, Jasta 23 PoW); 60 Fokker DVII encountered of which 20 were attacking DH4s returning from raid on Peronne, one OOC nr Lihons and another crashed Rosières 11.10 13.8.18 (all Capt SM Kinkead DSC DFC); EF, FL, o/t by storm after landing 7.9.18 (Capt R McLaughlin DFC unhurt); 2 ASD 11.9.18; SOC 2 Salvage Dump 24.9.18

B7191 (B.R.1) Deld 4 AAP Lincoln W/E 19.12.17; Chingford 27.12.17 (transit); 1 Sqdn Dover 29.12.17; 9 Sqdn 23.1.18; 10 Sqdn 4.2.18; Became 210 Sqdn 1.4.18; Lost, FL soft ground, badly damaged Houdain 10.4.18 (2/Lt HB Maund); 4 ASD Guines 11.4.18, 2 AI 7.5.18; 201 Sqdn 10.5.18; Albatros DV shot down Bapaume-Mory, shared D1862 & flight 06.45 16.5.18; Badly shot about 16.5.18 (both Lt R McLaughlin); Albatros DV D OOC nr Albert 19.30 17.5.18 (Lt HleR Wallace); Albatros DV OOC Achiet le Grand 19.15 30.5.18 (Lt R McLaughlin); Ran out of fuel, crashed, wrecked nr Nouex 3.6.18 (Lt JA Parkinson injured); 2 ASD 3.6.18; Rebuilt as F6111 3.7.18

B7192 (B.R.1) Deld 4 AAP Lincoln W/E 12.12.17; Chingford 12.17 (transit); 1 Sqdn 29.12.17; 10 Sqdn 10.1.18; AZP from Dover 28.1.18 (S/Cdr RS Dallas); 8 Sqdn 4.2.18; 3 Sqdn 3.3.18; Albatros DV OOC Marquion 12.30 22.3.18; Albatros OOC Vaulx, shared B7218 and flight 15.30 24.3.18 (both F/L LD Bawlf); 4 ASD Guines to 213 Sqdn 25.4.18; Shot down by HA, last seen 4m N of Middelkerke 11.5.18 (2/Lt JA Reid killed); Deleted 20.5.18

B7193 (B.R.1) Deld 4 AAP Lincoln W/E 12.12.17; AP Dover 19.12.17; 3 Sqdn 6.1.18; Albatros DV OOC Roulers 13.15 29.1.18 (F/Cdr FC Armstrong); 8 Sqdn 1.3.18; Became 208 Sqdn 1.4.18; Burnt to prevent capture La Gorgue 9.4.18

B7194 (B.R.1) Deld 4 AAP Lincoln W/E 12.12.17; Hendon (via Godmanchester) W/E 19.1.18; Deleted 11.1.18 [crashed on delivery?]

B7195 (B.R.1) Deld 4 AAP Lincoln W/E 12.12.17; Stonehenge to Hendon 3.1.18; AP Dover 7.1.18; 9 Sqdn 23.1.18; 10 Sqdn 4.2.18; Albatros DV shot down S of Menin 09.50 18.2.18 (FSL FV Hall); Albatros DV OOC 10m NE of Roulers 15.00 19.2.18; Albatros DV crashed SE of Dixmude 16.00 10.3.18; Became 210 Sqdn 1.4.18; 2-str and Albatros DV crashed Fleurbaix 14.30-14.35 12.4.18 (all F/L JG Manuel); Damaged by AA fire 29.4.18 (T/Lt HA Patey unhurt); 4 ASD Dunkerque 30.4.18; WOC 30.6.18 general fatigue

B7196 (B.R.1) Deld 4 AAP Lincoln W/E 19.12.17; AP Dover 31.12.17; 3 Sqdn 27.1.18; Albatros DV OOC Quesnoy 10.55 17.2.18 (F/L AT Whealy); 8 Sqdn Walmer 1.3.18; Became 208 Sqdn 1.4.18; Fokker DrI OOC Lens, shared B7187 & B7189 11.15 6.4.18 (Lt TFN Gerrard); Burnt to prevent capture La Gorgue 9.4.18

B7197 (BR.1) Deld 4 AAP Lincoln W/E 19.12.17; Dover W/E 26.1.18; 1 NAP 16.2.18; 8 Sqdn 17.2.18; 2-str OOC nr Drocourt 11.30 21.2.18 (F/Cdr RB Munday); 3 Sqdn 3.3.18; DFW C crashed into houses 1m E of Hénin-Lietard, shared B7224 12.40 18.3.18 (F/L ET Hayne); COL in gale 28.3.18 (F/Cdr HF Beamish DFC); 4 ASD Guines 31.3.18; 203 Sqdn 19.4.18; EF after fight with Albatros Scouts after bombing Merville, crashed La Belle Hôtesse 2.5.18 (F/Cdr LH Rochford); Pfalz DIII crashed in flames Estaires-Merville, shared B6408, C61 & D3362 11.15 17.5.18 (both F/Cdr LH Rochford); EF, FL La Belle Hôtesse, wrecked 20.5.18 (2/Lt YES Kirkpatrick unhurt); 1 ASD 22.5.18; Rebuilt as F5915 25.6.18

B7198 (BR.1) Deld 4 AAP Lincoln W/E 19.12.17; AP Dover (via Cranwell) 12.1.18; 10 Sqdn 30.1.18 (temp custody); 8 Sqdn 4.2.18; Albatros DV OOC 2m NE of Vitry 11.15 18.2.18 (FSL WL Jordan); 3 Sqdn 2/3.3.18; Albatros DV crashed Haubourdin c.11.00 18.3.18 (FSL S Smith); Became 203 Sqdn 1.4.18; Fokker DrI BU & crashed 3m E of Oppy 14.00 1.4.18 (F/Cdr RA Little); LVG C crashed nr Salomé, N of La Bassée, shared B3786, B3855, B7231, D3376 & D3384 11.45 15.5.18 (1/Lt W Goodnow USAS); Burst tyre after landing Acq 16.5.18 (F/Cdr RA Little); 4 ASD Guines (overhaul) 17.5.18 after landing in fog en route at Boisdinghem; still 4 ASD 25.5.18

B7199 (BR.1) Deld 4 AAP Lincoln W/E 19.12.17; AP Dover 23.2.18 (sic); 9 Sqdn Dover 17.2.18; To France 20.3.18; Became 209 Sqdn 1.4.18; Albatros DIII shot down S of Halluin 11.15 (Uffz Wenn, Jasta 57 killed) & another OOC S of Halluin 11.15, the 2nd shared Lt JH Siddall (who usually flew B3327) 2.4.18; Rumpler C shot down W of Amiens 12.4.18 [numbered G/5Bde/1]; Albatros DV OOC Brie 18.15 & another crashed Cayeux 18.45 2.5.18; Pfalz DIII OOC E of Rosières 10.45 15.5.18; Fokker DrI shot down & captured W of Corbie [numbered G/5Bde/8, Ltn Hübner, Jasta 4 PoW], shared B6398 & D3329 16.15, then lost, landed nr Corbie 16.5.18 (all Capt ST Edwards DSC); While stationary, hit by D3402 taxying out 19.5.18; 2 ASD 20.5.18; 80 Sqdn, crashed 13.8.18 (Lt AW Chadwick); to ASD; Rebuilt as F6261 22.8.18

B7200 (BR.1) Deld 4 AAP Lincoln W/E 19.12.17; Hendon (via London Colney) 29.1.18; 9 Sqdn Dover from 17.2.18; Hendon 23.2.18 (visit?); 9 Sqdn Dover W/E 2.3.18; To France 20.3.18; Aviatik C OOC 1m S of Becelaere, shared B7247, B7250 & D3328 07.25 26.3.18 (FSL MS Taylor); Became 209 Sqdn 1.4.18; Albatros DV believed crashed, shared B3858, B6311 & D3328 12.4.18 (pilot?); See D3328 21.4.18 (Lt MS Taylor); Crashed in field on TO 6.5.18 (Lt R Crabtree injured); 4 ASD 6.5.18; 213 Sqdn 26.6.18; Dest by fire in enemy bombing raid 29.6.18; WOC 31.7.18

B7201 (B.R.1) Deld 4 AAP Lincoln W/E 19.12.17; Hendon (via London Colney) 29.1.18; AP Dover W/E 9.2.18; NADD 21.2.18; 3 Sqdn 23.2.18; 8 Sqdn 1.3.18; Became 208 Sqdn 1.4.18; Albatros DV shot down 6.4.18 (2/Lt RL Johns); Burnt to prevent capture La Gorgue 9.4.18

B7202 (BR.1) Deld 4 AAP Lincoln W/E 19.12.17; Hendon 9.1.18 (transit); AP Dover 10.1.18; 9 Sqdn 23.1.18; 10 Sqdn 4.2.18; Albatros C crashed and burnt S of Zillebeke Lake, shared B6428 11.45 19.2.18 (F/L AW Carter) (Baron von Putkamer wounded); Became 210 Sqdn 1.4.18; 2 KB shot down, own m/c damaged 12.4.18 (Capt AW Carter DSC); Hit rut landing, lost wheel, nosed up 25.4.18 (Lt WL Davidson unhurt); 4 ASD Guines 26.4.18; 213 Sqdn 12.6.18; Stalled on TO, spun in from 200ft, TW 7.8.18 (Lt JAC Tayler killed);

B7203 To 4 ASD; WOC 15.9.18

(BR.1) Deld 4 AAP Lincoln W/E 19.12.17; Cranwell (transit) 16.1.18; AP Dover 18.1.18; 10 Sqdn 2.2.18 (temp custody); 8 Sqdn 4.2.18; Albatros DV OOC Douai 11.15 18.2.18 (F/Cdr RJO Compston); 3 Sqdn 3.3.18; DFW C Hénin-Lietard (possibly indecisive), shared B7185 11.20 9.3.18 (F/L WH Chisam); Albatros C OOC nr Brebières 11.00 12.3.18; Hannover C in flames Gavrelle-Fresnes, shared B7185 and B7229 11.20 16.3.18; Albatros DV in flames crashed 4m E of Bapaume, nr Vaulx, shared B3798, B7185, B7216, B7222, B7223, B7224, B7228, B7229 & B7231 16.45 21.3.18; Albatros DV crashed nr Boursies 12.30 22.3.18; Albatros DV OOC nr Beaumetz, shared flight 17.15 24.3.18 (all A/F/Cdr LH Rochford); Became 203 Sqdn 1.4.18; Albatros C crashed, with B & A Flts nr Vaulx 1.4.18; Albatros DV crashed nr Boursies 2.4.18; Albatros DV OOC nr Beau 4.4.18; Hit through petrol tank and main spar by m/g fire while shooting up trenches around Bapaume 5.4.18; Caught in ground mist, FL in ploughed field 13.4.18 (all Lt LH Rochford); COL 2.5.18 (2/Lt FG Gibbons); 4 ASD Guines 4.5.18; 213 Sqdn 28.6.18; Destroyed by fire in enemy bombing raid 29.6.18; WOC 31.7.18

B7204 (BR.1) Deld 4 AAP Lincoln to Cranwell 20.1.18; Hendon 22.1.18; AP Dover 24.1.18; 1 NAP 16.2.18; 8 Sqdn 17.2.18; Shot down 18.2.18 (F/Cdr GW Price DSC & Bar killed); Deleted 11.3.18

B7205 (130-hp Clerget) Deld CSD 12.17; Cardiff Docks by 15.1.18; Shipped to 6 Wing 17.2.18; 66/67 Wings Otranto by 21.4.18; 226 Sqdn by 28.4.18 - @6.18; AD Taranto by 7.18 - @10.18

B7206 (130-hp Clerget) Deld CSD 12.17; Cardiff Docks by 15.1.18; Shipped to Mudros 30.1.18; Mudros for erection by 3.18; Repair Base Mudros by 6.18 & 10.18 - @11.18

B7207 (130-hp Clerget) Deld CSD 12.17; Cardiff Docks by 15.1.18; Shipped to Mudros 30.1.18; Mudros for erection by 3.18; Repair Base Mudros by 6.18; F Sqdn Mudros; D Sqdn Stavros; 222 Sqdn Stavros by 10.18; To RHNAS by 10.18 - @1.19

B7208 (130-hp Clerget) Deld CSD 12.17; Cardiff Docks by 15.1.18; Shipped to 2 Wing Mudros 30.1.18; 66/67 Wings Otranto by 21.4.18; 226 Sqdn by 28.4.18 - @6.18; AD Taranto by 7.18 - @8.18; 28 Sqdn Italy

B7209 (130-hp Clerget) Deld CSD 12.17; Cardiff Docks by 1.1.18; Shipped to 6 Wing Otranto in SS Hesleyside 25.1.18; Repair Base Mudros by 6.18 F Sqdn Mudros; H.2 Flt, RHNAS Stavros by 10.18; Repair Base Mudros 10.10.18 - @1.19

B7210 (130-hp Clerget) Deld CSD 12.17; Cardiff Docks by 1.1.18; Shipped to 6 Wing Otranto in SS Hesleyside 25.1.18; Repair Base Mudros by 6.18; Imbros by 9.18 - 10.18; 220 Sqdn

B7211 (130-hp Clerget) Deld Cardiff Docks by 1.1.18; Shipped to 2 Wing Mudros 28.1.18; In transit from Mudros to 66/67 Wings by 21.4.18; 222 Sqdn; Thasos by 6.18 & 10.18 - 1.19; To Greek Air Force

B7212 (130-hp Clerget) Deld CSD 12.17; Cardiff Docks by 1.1.18; Shipped to 6 Wing Otranto in SS Hesleyside 25.1.18; Repair Base Mudros by 6.18; D Sqdn Stavros by 6.18 & 10.18 - 1.19

B7213 (130-hp Clerget) Deld Cardiff Docks by 1.1.18; Shipped to 2 Wing Mudros 30.1.18; Mudros for erection by 3.18; Marsh by 20.3.18

B7214 (130-hp Clerget) Deld Cardiff Docks by 1.1.18; Shipped to 2 Wing Mudros 28.1.18; In transit from Mudros to 66/67 Wings by 21.4.18; Repair Base Mudros by 6.18

B7215 (BR.1) Deld AP Dover W/E 12.1.18; 9 Sqdn 23.1.18; 10 Sqdn 4.2.18; Albatros DV OOC SE of Dixmude 08.30 16.3.18; 2-str OOC Roulers 15.45 10.3.18; Pfalz DIII OOC Menin-Roulers 09.20 24.3.18 (F/Cdr WM Alexander); Became 210 Sqdn 1.4.18; 2-str dest Roulers 11.30 3.4.18; Albatros C OOC E of Estaires 17.15 11.4.18 (both Capt WM Alexander); O/t landing after OP, badly damaged 8.5.18 (Lt A Baird unhurt); 4 ASD 9.5.18; 213 Sqdn 25.6.18; Dest by fire in enemy bombing raid 29.6.18; WOC 31.7.18

B7216 (BR.1) Deld AP Dover W/E 12.1.18; 1 NAP 16.2.18; 8 Sqdn 17.2.18; 3 Sqdn 3.3.18; See B7203 21.3.18 (F/L LA Sands); Collided B7219 in combat, crashed nr

St.Quentin, 13.00 patrol 22.3.18 (F/L LA Sands killed);
For deletion by 30.3.18

B7217 (BR.1) Deld AP Dover W/E 12.1.18; to 10 Sqdn for temp custody but overshot and o/t landing on arrival 30.1.18 (FSL E Burton unhurt); 1 NAP 1.2.18 (overhaul); 3 Sqdn 15.3.18; Lost nr Haubourdin last seen in nose dive with HA on tail 18.3.18 (FSL JL Allison killed); Deleted 8.4.18

B7218 (BR.1) Deld AP Dover W/E 26.1.18; 10 Sqdn 2.2.18 (temp custody); 8 Sqdn 4.2.18; Albatros DV OOC 2m NE of Vitry 11.15 18.2.18 (FSL EG Johnstone); 3 Sqdn 3.3.18; Albatros DV BU nr Drocourt 11.20 11.3.18; Albatros DV crashed nr Marquion 12.30 22.3.18; Albatros DV OOC Vaulx, shared B7192, B7220, B7224, B7227, B7228, B7231 & B7274 15.30 24.3.18 (all F/Cdr FC Armstrong); Fell in flames after trench strafe S of Ervillers 25.3.18 (F/Cdr FC Armstrong DSC killed); Deleted 8.4.18

B7219 (BR.1) Deld 4 AAP Lincoln 1.18; AP Dover W/E 26.1.18; 1 NAP 16.2.18; 8 Sqdn 17.2.18; 3 Sqdn 3.3.18; Collided B7216 in combat, crashed S of St.Quentin, 13.00 patrol 22.3.18 (FSL WA Moyle killed); For deletion by 30.3.18 [Temp convtd to 2-str at one time]

B7220 (BR.1) Deld 4 AAP Lincoln to AP Dover 19.1.18; 10 Sqdn 2.2.18 (temp custody); 8 Sqdn 4.2.18; 3 Sqdn 3.3.18; Albatros DV OOC 2m E of Lens 13.15 10.3.18; Aviatik C OOC 2m W of Haubourdin 10.50 17.3.18 (both F/L AT Whealy); Pfalz DIII OOC nr Esquerchin 11.50 21.3.18 (F/Cdr FC Armstrong); Albatros DV crashed Marquion 12.30 22.3.18; Pfalz DIII OOC Vaulx 16.55 23.3.18; Albatros OOC Vaulx, shared B7218 and flight 15.30 24.3.18; Became 203 Sqdn 1.4.18; LVG C crashed into canal S of Sailly-sur-la-Lys, 1m E of Estaires 14.20 11.4.18; Albatros DV crashed nr Merville & Pfalz DIII crashed into building nr Merville-Estaires road 09.30 22.4.18; DFW C crashed into house 1m NE of Lens 11.10 3.5.18; Pfalz DIII crashed 1m E of Herlies; 11.30 9.5.18; LVG C crashed E of Richebourg, N of La Bassée 19.50 14.5.18; DFW C crashed 1m E of Pont du Hem, shared B7251 10.50 15.5.18; Pfalz DIII OOC ½m N of La Bassée 11.20 & LVG C OOC Bucoy 11.35 16.5.18 (all F/L:A/F/Cdr:Capt AT Whealy); Pfalz DIII OOC N of Neuf Berquin, shared D3376 19.50 18.5.18 (Capt RA Little); Shot down spinning OOC nr Richebourg St.Vaast, NW of La Bassée 11.10 5.6.18 (2/Lt AN Webster killed) [by Fl.Maat Zenses of Marine Jasta 2 at Pervyse-Avelkappelle]; SOC in field 5.6.18

B7221 (BR.1) Deld 4 AAP Lincoln to AP Dover 19.1.18; 1 NAP 17.2.18 (overhaul); 10 Sqdn 24.3.18; Became 210 Sqdn 1.4.18; Hit rut landing, o/t, badly damaged 23.4.18 (2/Lt A Baird unhurt); 4 ASD 24.4.18; Tested 26.5.18; 4 ASD Pilots Pool 22.6.18; Failed to pull out of dive 9.8.18 (Lt TRA May killed); WOC 15.8.18 BR

B7222 (BR.1) Deld 4 AAP Lincoln to AP Dover W/E 2.2.18; ADD to 8 Sqdn 18.2.18; 3 Sqdn 3.3.18; Albatros C in flames nr Tortequesne, shared B7229 & B7230 12.00 8.3.18 (FSL KD Macleod); Albatros C crashed Hermies 10.35 16.3.18 (F/L WH Chisam); Albatros DV OOC nr Douai, shared B7185 11.15 21.3.18 (F/Cdr LH Rochford); See B7203 16.45 21.3.18; Pfalz DIII crashed Noreuil, shared B7229 17.25 23.3.18; Shot down RE8 with British markings seen firing on British troops 27.3.18 (all FSL KD Macleod); Became 203 Sqdn 1.4.18; COL rough ground 21.4.18 (2/Lt ER Prideaux unhurt); 4 ASD 22.4.18; 204 Sqdn 17.6.18; FL in floods, CW 2.7.18 (Lt HWM Cumming; to 4 ASD; 210 Sqdn 14.8.18; Fokker DVII OOC over Zeebrugge 19.15 15.8.18; Fokker DVII crashed nr Roulers, shared D3357, D3379, D9655 & E1405 18.30 3.9.18 (both Lt HR Hughes); 1 AD 16.1.19 surplus

B7223 (BR.1) Deld 4 AAP Lincoln to AP Dover W/E 12.1.18; 1 NAP 16.2.18; 8 Sqdn 17.2.18; 3 Sqdn 2/3.3.18; Albatros DV OOC E of Lens 13.15 10.3.18; See B7203 21.3.18; Albatros DV OOC nr Beaumetz 17.15 24.3.18 (both F/L WH Chisam); In action 26.3.18 (F/L WH Chisam wounded); COL in gale 28.3.18 (FSL R Sykes); 4 ASD Guines 31.3.18; 209 Sqdn 1.5.18. Left 18.25, hit by AA, wings broke off, spun in from 8,000ft W of Méaulte 14.5.18 (Lt EV Bell killed)

B7224 (BR.1) Deld 4 AAP Lincoln to AP Dover W/E 26.1.18 -
@16.2.18; 3 Sqdn 2.18 (transit); 8 Sqdn 18.2.18; 3 Sqdn 3.3.18; DFW C OOC Bellecourt-Nauroy, shared B7197, B7216 & B7231 11.3.18; DFW C crashed in houses 1m E of Hénin-Lietard, shared B7197 12.40 18.3.18; See B7203 21.3.18; Albatros DV OOC Vaulx, shared B7218 and flight 15.30 24.3.18; Crashed at 1 AD St.Omer 31.3.18 (all FSL RC Berlyn); Became 203 Sqdn 1.4.18; Flying again by 6.4.18; O/t on TO 12.4.18 (2/Lt HW Skinner); 4 ASD 14.4.18; 2 ASD by 5.18; 209 Sqdn 20.5.18; EF, FL, o/t in long grass, damaged, nr Mericourt 10.6.18 (Lt LC Story unhurt); 2 ASD 11.6.18; Rebuilt as F6135 3.7.18

B7225 (BR.1) Deld 4 AAP Lincoln by 19.1.18; Hendon 29.1.18 (transit); AP Dover 15.2.18; 1 NAP 21.2.18; 1 Sqdn 28.2.18; Albatros DV OOC 16.3.18 (FSL MT Spence); FL Haute Visée aerodrome 30.3.18; Became 201 Sqdn 1.4.18; Albatros C OOC N of Albert, shared B6359, B6421, B6429, B7267 & B7278 10.10 2.5.18 (Lt H Riddell); Albatros DV crashed Bapaume-Mory, shared D1862 & flight 06.45 16.5.18 (Lt RSS Orr); Albatros DV OOC SE of Albert 10.55 30.5.18 (Lt RE Bright); 2 AI 30.5.18; Rep Pk 1 ASD 31.5.18 (overhaul); Flown to UK 5.6.18

B7226 (BR.1) Deld 4 AAP Lincoln by 19.1.18; Cranwell 25.1.18 (transit); Hendon after EF, FL Huntingdon 10.2.18 (transit); AP Dover 15.2.18 (repair); NADD 27.2.18; 13 Sqdn 28.2.18; Rumpler C in flames 1m to sea Ostende-Wenduyne, shared B6400, B6407 & B6410 09.05 12.3.18 (FSL EV Bell); Became 213 Sqdn 1.4.18; Albatros DIII OOC Wenduyne 19.50 8.5.18 (Lt CP Brown); COL bad weather 26.5.18 (Lt HER Nelson unhurt); EF, FL 1m from Bergues, CW 4.6.18 (Lt FP Pemble unhurt); to 4 ASD; 204 Sqdn 9.8.18 - LM15.8.18; To 4 ASD; Deleted 31.8.18 general fatigue

B7227 (BR.1) Deld 4 AAP Lincoln by 19.1.18; Hendon 27.1.18 (transit); AP Dover 28.1.18; 1 NAP 16.2.18; 8 Sqdn 17.2.18; 3 Sqdn 2/3.3.18; Albatros DV crashed nr Boursies 13.00 22.3.18; Albatros DV OOC Vaulx, shared B7218 and flight 15.30 24.3.18 (both F/L E Pierce); 4 ASD Guines 31.3.18; 210 Sqdn (coded 'C') 30.4.18; Rumpler C OOC on back, pilot killed, observer wounded, Bailleul, shared B6228 & D3364 11.45 9.5.18 (Capt ES Arnold); Halberstadt C OOC Ypres 19.45 & another OOC 2m E of Ypres 20.15 14.5.18 (Lt AL Jones); KB in flames and 2 others DD Ploegsteert, shared B7249 & D3410 11.20 21.5.18 (Lt GB Wootten); KB dest E of Pont Riqueul, E of Lestrem shared C62 & D3401 17.10 21.5.18 (Lt AL Jones); Left 12.40, attacked by 4 Fokker DVII Bousbecque, shot down by Josef Jacobs 21.6.18 (2/Lt RG Carr PoW, escaped 1.7.18); SOC in field 22.6.18

B7228 (BR.1) Deld 4 AAP Lincoln by 19.1.18; Cranwell to Brooklands 11.2.18; AAP Dover 19.2.18; ADD 12.3.18; 3 Sqdn 17.3.18; Albatros DV in flames 4m E of Bapaume 16.45 21.3.18 (FSL CS Devereaux); Albatros OOC Vaulx, shared B7218 and flight 15.30 24.3.18 (FSL FJS Britnell); Became 203 Sqdn 1.4.18; Badly shot about by enemy m/g fire over Merville, FL Floringhem 09.30 22.4.18 (2/Lt NC Dixie slightly wounded); 4 ASD Guines 23.4.18 - @31.5.18; 204 Sqdn by 2.6.18; Fokker DVII OOC over Ostende 14.45 30.6.18 (Lt WA Pomeroy); COL, CW 28.7.18 (Lt BE Barnum unhurt); 4 ASD 28.7.18; 213 Sqdn 3.9.18; Fokker DVII shot down and crashed 1m SE of Beveren Rly Stn 09.30 4.10.18 (Lt AF Chick); EF, COL 14.10.18 (Lt AF Chick unhurt); 4 ASD 24.10.18

B7229 (BR.1) Deld 4 AAP Lincoln by 19.1.18; Spittlegate (via Cranwell) 6.2.18; Hendon 7.2.18; AP Dover 2.18; 1 NAP 17.2.18; 8 Sqdn 18.2.18; 3 Sqdn 3.3.18; Albatros C in flames nr Tortequesne, shared B7222 & B7230 12.00 8.3.18; Albatros DV OOC Lens 13.15 10.3.18; Hannover C on fire Gavrelle-Fresnes, shared B7185 & B7203 11.20 16.3.18; Albatros DV OOC Marquion 12.30 22.3.18; Pfalz DIII crashed nr Noreuil, shared B7222 17.25 23.3.18; Became 203 Sqdn 1.4.18; Albatros C crashed nr Giverchy, shared B7185 & B7231 16.10 9.4.18; Bad weather, FL, crashed Nédonchele 13.4.18 (all F/L:Capt AB Ellwood); 4 ASD 16.4.18; 213 Sqdn 22.5.18; Hannover C OOC Poperinghe, shared B7154 & C65 17.45 15.6.18 (Lt CP Sparkes); EF, FL in sea 7m off Nieuport 16.7.18 (Lt BA Hewett picked up unhurt); Deleted 15.9.18

**B7230** (BR.1) Deld 4 AAP Lincoln by 19.1.18; Cranwell 26.1.18 (transit); AP Dover 6.2.18; ADD 17.2.18; 8 Sqdn 18.2.18; 3 Sqdn (coded 'T') 3.3.18; Albatros C in flames nr Tortequesne, shared B7222 & B7229 12.00 8.3.18 (FSL CS Devereaux); 09.30 patrol, shot down by Vzfw Edgar Scholz, Jasta 11, spun down from 14,000ft nr Lens, but landed safely behind enemy lines 10.3.18 (FSL KD Campbell PoW); Deleted 11.3.18

**B7231** (BR.1) Deld 4 AAP Lincoln by 19.1.18; Cranwell 4.2.18 (for Dover); Lympne to Dover 12.2.18; 1 NAP 17.2.18; 8 Sqdn 18.2.18; 3 Sqdn 3.3.18; Albatros DV OOC Haubourdin-Seclin 11.05 18.3.18; See B7203 21.3.18; Albatros OOC Vaulx, shared B7218 and flight 15.30 24.3.18; COL in gale, unhurt 28.3.18 (all F/L ET Hayne); Became 203 Sqdn 1.4.18; DFW C in flames 3m NE of Lens 12.30 6.4.18; Fokker DrI crashed 1m SE of Violaines 13.00 7.4.18; Albatros C crashed nr Givenchy, shared B7185 & B7229 16.10 9.4.18; Albatros DV in flames Neuve Eglise 14.30 11.4.18 (all F/Cdr RA Little); LVG C crashed nr Salomé, N of La Bassée, shared B3786, B3855, B7231, D3376 & D3384 11.45 15.5.18; See B3855 17.5.18 (both 2/Lt HW Skinner); COL from OP, wheel came off 25.5.18 (2/Lt HW Skinner unhurt); 4 ASD 26.5.18; Rebuilt as F5939 25.6.18

**B7232** (BR.1) Deld 4 AAP Lincoln by 19.1.18; AP Dover (via Hendon) 16.2.18; NADD 26.2.18; 3 Sqdn 27.2.18; 8 Sqdn 5.3.18; Became 208 Sqdn 1.4.18; Albatros DV shot down 6.4.18; EF on TO 7.4.18 (both 2/Lt EG Johnstone DSC); 4 ASD 7.4.18; 213 Sqdn by 6.18; Hit by D3378 while stationery, badly damaged 3.6.18; To 4 ASD; 204 Sqdn 25.7.18; Fokker DVII OOC Ostende-Zeebrugge 10.55 12.8.18 (Lt WJP Jenner); Fokker DVII OOC Roulers 17.55 14.8.18; Pale green Fokker DVII yellow stripes OOC Menin 19.05 15.8.18; Hit by AA, FL, sideslipped into ground, CW Lampernisse 24.9.18 (all Lt OJ Orr); 4 ASD 25.9.18; Deleted 30.9.18 DBR

**B7233** (BR.1) Deld 4 AAP Lincoln to Cranwell 4.2.18; AP Dover 6.2.18; ADD 28.2.18; 1 Sqdn 5.3.18; With B6428 attacked 8 Pfalz DIII, he claimed 1 OOC Dixmude 11.45 15.3.18 (FSL GB Gates); Became 201 Sqdn 1.4.18; Crashed on TO 17.4.18 (2/Lt WH Easty unhurt); 4 ASD 18.4.18; 213 Sqdn 5.6.18; Lost propeller at 2,500ft, crashed E of Bergues 21.6.18 (Capt JW Pinder); 4 ASD 21.6.18; 213 Sqdn 18.8.18; EF on TO, FL, hit telephone wire, o/t, badly damaged 23.8.18 (Lt GC Mackay unhurt); To 4 ASD; 213 Sqdn 16.10.18; Crashed on practice flight Audembert 11.1.19 (Lt WS McLean injured); 1 ASD 11.1.19

**B7234** (BR.1, later 170-hp CR.1 by 28.3.18, later BR.1 by 31.7.18) Deld 4 AAP Lincoln by 19.1.18; AP Dover (via North Weald) 15.2.18; ADD 27.2.18; 13 Sqdn but COL 5.3.18; Flying by 16.3.18; Became 213 Sqdn 1.4.18; COL 11.4.18 (FSL RT Whiteley); To 4 ASD; 204 Sqdn 22.5.18 (named 'LAURA'); Missing, hit by ground m/g fire after combat with 10 Fokkers over Roulers 31.7.18 (Lt RL Hollingsworth PoW)

**B7235** (130-hp Clerget) Deld AP Dover W/E 23.2.18 for Belgian Government; To Belgian aerodrome Calais 24.2.18

**B7236** (130-hp Clerget) (130-hp Clerget) Deld 4 AAP Lincoln 1.18; AP Dover W/E 9.2.18 for Belgian Government; To Belgian aerodrome Calais 24.2.18

**B7237** (130-hp Clerget) Deld 4 AAP Lincoln by 19.1.18; Hendon (via Grantham) 7.2.18; AP Dover 23.2.18 for Belgian Government; To Belgian aerodrome, Calais 18.2.18

**B7238** (130-hp Clerget) Deld 4 AAP Lincoln 1.18; Cranwell W/E 15.2.18; Became 201 TDS 1.4.18; Spinning nose dive 28.6.18 (2/Lt AC Davis killed)

**B7239** (Convtd 2-str) (130-hp Clerget) Deld 4 AAP Lincoln 1.18; Cranwell W/E 15.2.18; Crashed west gate of aerodrome, TW 28.2.18 (PFO GC Crowley injured); repaired; Became 201 TDS Cranwell 1.4.18; Became 56 TDS 27.7.18 - @24.3.19

**B7240** (130-hp Clerget) Deld 4 AAP Lincoln 1.18; Cranwell 7.2.18; Crashed and slightly damaged, Wyberton, nr Freiston 8.3.18 (pilot unhurt); Became 201 TDS Cranwell 1.4.18; Freiston by 5.18; Became 4 FS Freiston 7.18; Crashed 16.8.18

**B7241** (130-hp Clerget) Deld 4 AAP Lincoln by 23.2.18 - @3.18; Cranwell by 21.3.18; Became 201 TDS Cranwell 1.4.18; Became 56 TDS Cranwell 27.7.18; Spun in diving on ground target 16.10.18 (Lt B Morgan killed)

**B7242** (130-hp Clerget) Deld Cranwell W/E 1.3.18; Crashed 4m NW of aerodrome, CW 23.3.18 (PFO AV Jones killed); repaired; Became 201 TDS 1.4.18 - @8.6.18

**B7243** (130-hp Clerget) Deld 4 AAP Lincoln to Cranwell W/E 15.2.18; Crashed on aerodrome, slightly damaged 20.2.18 (pilot unhurt); Became 201 TDS 1.4.18; Cranwell Workshops 3.5.18; NE Area FIS Redcar 8.5.18 - @15.10.18

**B7244** (Convtd 2-str) (130-hp Clerget) Deld Cranwell W/E 1.3.18; Crashed and wrecked on aerodrome 27.2.18 (PFO HJ Dyer injured); Became 201 TDS 1.4.18; Became 56 TDS Cranwell 27.7.18; Freiston 5.3.19 - @24.3.19

**B7245** (BR.1) Deld 4 AAP Lincoln to AP Dover (via Fairlop) 28.2.18; 9 Sqdn Dover by 17.3.18; Became 209 Sqdn 1.4.18; Badly damaged in Richtofen combat 21.4.18 (Lt WJ Mackenzie wounded, probably by Vzfw Edgar Scholz); 4 ASD 21.4.18; 213 Sqdn 4.6.18; Last seen 7m NE of Nieuport at 19,000ft 14.45 21.6.18 (Lt KWJ Hall PoW); Deleted 30.6.18

**B7246** (BR.1) Deld 4 AAP Lincoln to 2 AAP Hendon by 23.2.18; Wrecked on/by 7.3.18; Deleted 13.3.18

**B7247** (BR.1) Deld 4 AAP Lincoln 2.18; FL Fairlop en route Dover 23.2.18; AP Dover 24.2.18; 9 Sqdn Dover 27.2.18; Aviatik OOC 1m S of Becelaere, shared B7200, B7250 & D3328 07.25 26.3.18 (F/Cdr FE Banbury); Became 209 Sqdn 1.4.18; Pilot fainted, believed suffered heart attack in flight on TO, stalled and spun in 2.4.18 (Capt FE Banbury DSC killed); Wreckage 4 ASD 4.4.18; Deleted 8.4.18

**B7248** (BR.1) Deld 4 AAP Lincoln to Cranwell by 23.2.18 (transit); AAP Dover (via Huntingdon) 29.2.18; NADD 12.3.18; 1 Sqdn 15.3.18; Became 201 Sqdn 1.4.18; KB shot down in flames E of Boyelles, shared C6730/Capt DJ Bell of 3 Sqdn 06.45 8.4.18; Fokker DrI BU S of Albert 19.20 16.5.18 (both F/Cdr CB Ridley); Albatros DV OOC Achiet-le-Grand 30.5.18 (Lt HP Guard); Fokker DrI over Pozières 08.15 30.6.18; Blue Fokker DVII white tail OOC nr Foucaucourt 19.15 4.7.18 (both Capt CB Ridley DSC); Fokker DVII OOC Bailleul-Armentières 11.20 29.7.18 (Lt CL Wood); Rep Pk 1 ASD 30.7.18 unfit for further flying; Rebuilt as F6330 in error 12.8.18, later changed to H7000

**B7249** (BR.1) Deld 4 AAP Lincoln 2.18; to Cranwell then EF, FL Stamford 16.2.18; Left 16.2.18 for Dover; arr AAP Hendon 28.2.18; Dover 6.3.18; 9 Sqdn by 15.3.18; Became 209 Sqdn 1.4.18; EF, FL, crashed nr Locre 2.4.18 (Lt AP Squire injured); 2 ASD 3.4.18; 210 Sqdn 30.4.18; FL Lederzele 14.5.18 (Lt HA Patey unhurt); KB in flames & 2 DD Ploegsteert, shared B7227 & D3410 11.20 21.5.18 (Lt HA Patey); Collided with D9590 when both dived to attack HA over Neuve Chapelle, last seen in pieces between Neuve Chapelle and Laventie 18.15 10.6.18 (Capt JG Manuel DSC killed); SOC in field 11.6.18

**B7250** (BR.1) Deld 4 AAP Lincoln 2.18; FL Fairlop en route Dover 23.2.18; AP Dover 24.2.18; 9 Sqdn by 17.3.18; Became 209 Sqdn 1.4.18; Albatros DIII OOC S of Halluin 11.15 2.4.18; Albatros DIII OOC Albert, shared D3327 17.05 11.4.18; Pfalz DIII shot down SE of Hangard 19.20 23.4.18; Aviatik C OOC 1m S of Becelaere, shared B7200, B7247 & D3328 07.25 26.3.18 (all Capt OW Redgate); Dived on 2-str, unable to regain control, crashed in flames N of Lamotte-Warfusée, 500m S of le Hamel 09.00 23.5.18 (2/Lt AW Aird killed); SOC in field 24.5.18

**B7251** (BR.1) Deld 4 AAP Lincoln to AP Dover 16.2.18; NADD 28.2.18; 3 Sqdn 8.3.18; Albatros DV OOC 2m SE of Lens 13.15 10.3.18; COL in gale 28.3.18; Became 203 Sqdn 1.4.18; DFW CV crashed 1m E of Pont du Hem, shared B7220 10.50 15.5.18; Pfalz DIII OOC N of La Bassée 11.20 16.5.18 (all FSL:Lt FJS Britnell); 4 ASD 12.6.18; Rebuilt as F5936 25.6.18, later again rebuilt as H7220 5.11.18

**B7252** (BR.1) Deld 4 AAP Lincoln to AP Dover 16.2.18; ADD 27.2.18; 3 Sqdn 11.3.18; FTR from patrol (later retd)

11.3.18 (FSL BE Wise); 1 NAP by 14.3.18; 4 ASD Guines 28.3.18; 210 Sqdn 22.4.18; Albatros DV OOC Armentières 10.55 8.5.18; Albatros DV OOC Armentières 19.25, then FL in mist, wrecked, unhurt 11.5.18 (both Lt LP Coombes); Rep Pk 4 ASD 12.5.18; 213 Sqdn 3.7.18; Albatros C OOC 3m ESE of Dixmude, shared D3409, D8189 & D9664 19.40 11.8.18; Fokker DVII OOC 6 m E of Dixmude, shared D8189, D8217 & D9678 14.25 23.9.18 (both Lt CP Sparkes); Last seen when patrol attacked by 7 Fokker DVII 3m W of Thourout 17.45 25.9.18 (Lt CP Sparkes PoW) [credited Flgm Zenses, Marine Jasta 2 at Wijnendaele 14.45 (sic)]; Deleted 30.9.18

B7253 (B.R.1) Deld 4 AAP Lincoln to AP Dover 23.2.18; 9 Sqdn by 15.3.18; collided and damaged Dover 20.3.18 (F/L EB Drake); AP Dover by 28.3.18; 4 ASD Guines 31.3.18; 8 Sqdn 31.3.18; Became 208 Sqdn 1.4.18; Burnt to prevent capture La Gorgue 9.4.18

B7254 (BR.1) Deld 4 AAP Lincoln 2.18; Hendon 19.2.18 (transit); AP Dover 21.2.18; NADD 27.2.18 - @7.3.18; 1 NAP by 14.3.18; 4 ASD Guines 28.3.18; 213 Sqdn 11.4.18; Albatros DV shot down Wenduyne 19.50 6.5.18; 3 Albatros DIII shot down, one of them in flames, in sea nr Wenduyne 19.50 8.5.18; 2 Pfalz DIII OOC 14.20, shared C66, C73, D1866 & D3333 14.20 1.6.18 (all Capt JdeC Paynter); Probably one of two aircraft badly damaged in German raid on aerodrome 5.6.18[LM]; To 4 ASD; 204 Sqdn 16.8.18; 2-str into sea Blankenberghe-Zeebrugge 19.00 16.9.18; COL 18.9.18 (both Lt PF Cormack); To 4 ASD; 4 ASD WOC 30.9.18 general fatigue

B7255 (130-hp Clerget) Shipped to 6 Wing 17.2.18; 66/67 Wings Otranto by 21.4.18; 226 Sqdn by 28.4.18 - @6.18; AD Taranto by 7.18 - @11.18

B7256 (130-hp Clerget) Shipped to 6 Wing 17.2.18; 66/67 Wings Otranto by 21.4.18; 226 Sqdn by 28.4.18 - @6.18; AD Taranto by 7.18 - @1.19

B7257 (130-hp Clerget) Shipped to 6 Wing 23.2.18; Stavros by 6.18

B7258 (130-hp Clerget) Shipped to 6 Wing 23.2.18; Repair Base Mudros by 6.18 & 10.18 - @1.19

B7259 (130-hp Clerget) Deld 4 AAP Lincoln to Cranwell by 23.2.18; Crashed, slightly damaged, Cranwell South 7.3.18 (pilot unhurt); Became 201 TDS Cranwell 1.4.18 - @5.18

B7260 (130-hp Clerget) Deld 4 AAP Lincoln 2.18; Cranwell by 23.2.18; For deletion by 30.3.18; BUT NE Area FIS Redcar by 30.8.18

B7261 (130-hp Clerget) Deld 4 AAP Lincoln 2.18; Cranwell W/E 1.2.18; Became 201/2 TDS Cranwell 1.4.18; Freiston 17.4.18; 201 TDS Cranwell by 8.6.18

B7262 (130-hp Clerget) Deld 4 AAP Lincoln 2.18; Cranwell by 23.2.18; Crashed and slightly damaged, Cranwell South 14.3.18 (pilot unhurt); Became 201 TDS Cranwell 1.4.18; Became 56 TDS Cranwell 27.7.18; Spun in 4.12.18

B7263 (130-hp Clerget) Deld 4 AAP Lincoln 2.18; Cranwell by 23.2.18; FL and badly damaged Alnwick 23.2.18 (pilot unhurt); Became 201 TDS Cranwell 1.4.18; 4 SoAF&G Freiston 1.6.18; Became 4 FS Freiston 7.18; Spun in diving on ground target 14.8.18 (Lt JF Meek)

B7264 (130-hp Clerget) Deld 4 AAP Lincoln 2.18; Cranwell by 23.2.18; Crashed, CW, Cranwell South 11.3.18 (PFO WJ Stevens killed); Deleted W/E 22.3.18

B7265 (130-hp Clerget) Deld East Fortune NFS by 23.2.18; Redcar 26.4.18; NE Area FIS Redcar by 21.8.18 - @9.18

B7266 (130-hp Clerget) Deld East Fortune 19.1.18 - @23.2.18; Redcar School 29.3.18 - @4.18; NE Area FIS Redcar by 12.8.18 - @27.11.18

B7267 (BR.1) Deld 4 AAP Lincoln by 23.2.18; AAP Dover 12.3.18; NADD 17.3.18; 1 Sqdn 18.3.18; COL Fienvillers 28.3.18 (FSL RSS Orr); Became 201 Sqdn 1.4.18; Fokker DrI shot down Mericourt 13.15 6.4.18 (Lt AGA Spence); Albatros C OOC N of Albert, shared B6359, B6421, B6429, B7225 & B7278 10.10 2.5.18 (Lt RE Bright); Albatros DV D OOC Achiet-le-Grand 19.55 30.5.18 (Lt LH Riddell); EF, FL downwind in cornfield, o/t, wrecked Beauvoir 25.6.18 (Lt LH Riddell unhurt); to 2 ASD; Rebuilt as F6058 2.7.18

B7268 (130-hp Clerget) Deld 4 AAP Lincoln by 23.2.18; War

School Manston 3.18; Tested 11.3.18; Tongue Defence/Patrol Flt Manston from 10.6.18 - 8.18; 470 Flt 219 Sqdn Manston by 3.8.18; Martlesham Heath 13.8.18; Also unarmed training aircraft, red/white quartered disc wheels

B7269 (130-hp Clerget) Deld 4 AAP Lincoln by 23.2.18; War School Manston 3.18; Became Pool of Pilots Manston 1.4.18; 470 Flt/Tongue Defence Flt Manston 10.6.18; 491 Flt Dover, with B5601 and seaplanes N2927 & N2937 engaged 6 enemy seaplanes off Kentish Knock 18.7.18 (Lt CFA Wagstaff)

B7270 (BR.1) Deld 4 AAP Lincoln 2.18; AAP Dover (via Fairlop) 28.2.18 [but by 23.2.18!]; 9 Sqdn Dover 13.3.18; 2-str sent down NE of Houthulst Forest 15.30 22.3.18 (F/Cdr AR Brown); Became 209 Sqdn 1.4.18; Petrol tank shot through, FL Bois l'Abbé 10.4.18, retd 11.4.18; Fokker DrI OOC c.17.00 Albert 11.4.18; Fokker DrI on fire Warfusée-Abancourt, shared D3326 08.30 12.4.18; Dived on red Fokker DrI attacking Lt WR May, DrI (No.425/17) dived down vertically and crashed Vaux-sur-Somme 10.45, wreckage shelled for some hours, given number G/5Bde/2, pilot Rittm M Baron von Richtofen, Cdr Jasta 1 killed 21.4.18 (all Capt AR Brown DSC) [Richtofen killed by single bullet. Victory also claimed by Australian ground machine gunners]; Albatross DV crashed E of Villers-Bretonneux, shared B3858 14.45 27.4.18; Fokker DrI OOC 1m S of Cerisy 12.15 2.5.18 (all Capt OW Redgate); Fuel shortage, COL, unhurt 3.5.18 (all Capt OW Redgate); 4 ASD Guines 4.5.18; 213 Sqdn 30.6.18; HA OOC off Wenduyne, shared B6358, B6448, B7270, D3326 & D9647 11.40 7.7.18; Tyre came off landing, unhurt 29.7.18 (both Lt WA Rankin); 4 ASD 29.7.18; 213 Sqdn 17.9.18; Fokker DVII crashed 2m E of Roulers 09.30 4.10.18; Fokker DVII crashed & another burst into flames Roulers-Iseghem 15.55 4.10.18; Fokker DVII crashed into houses Thourout, shared D3409 10.15 14.10.18 (all Capt JE Greene); 4 ASD 5.11.18

B7271 (BR.1, later 170-hp CR.1 by 28.3.18) Deld 4 AAP Lincoln to AAP Dover 11.3.18; NADD 17.3.18; 13 Sqdn 18.3.18; Became 213 Sqdn 1.4.18; Crashed 21.4.18 (Lt J Reid); Engine trouble, damaged landing 21.5.18 (Lt WG Evans unhurt); 4 ASD Guines 21.5.18; 210 Sqdn 7.8.18; Fokker DVII crashed W of Roulers 09.30 11.8.18 (Lt GA Welsh); Last seen at 14,000ft over Bruges 09.25 16.9.18 (2/Lt EB Markquick killed) [credited Flgm Goerth, Marine Jasta 3 at Zorkeghem]; Deleted 15.10.18

B7272 (BR.1) Deld 4 AAP Lincoln by 27.2.18; Cranwell 6.3.18; AAP Dover (via Cranwell) 8.3.18; 9 Sqdn Dover by 15.3.18; flown to France 20.3.18; Became 209 Sqdn 1.4.18; Lost, FL, lost u/c, damaged, French aerodrome Montigny 24.4.18 (Lt EV Bell unhurt); 4 ASD 24.4.18; 213 Sqdn 4.6.18; Albatros DV OOC 4m S of Dixmude, shared C65, D3397, D3409 & D3411 (but probably only C65) 18.00 7.6.18 (Lt CP Sparkes); Shot down, crashed, badly damaged nr Pervyse 12.6.18 (Lt JN Nelson DoW 14.6.18); to 4 ASD; 213 Sqdn 31.8.18; Fokker DVII OOC N of Ostende 18.10 6.9.18 (Lt PC Jenner); With D3331 attacked Fokker DVII which collided with another Fokker DVII 5m SW of Ostende 18.35 25.9.18; 2 Fokker DVII and another OOC crashed Leke 14.30 14.10.18; KB shot down 5m NNE of Ghent 10.25 9.11.18 (all Lt CJ Sims); 11 AP 24.2.19; ECD Grain from 7.19 (deck landing expts)

B7273 (BR.1) Deld 4 AAP Lincoln by 27.2.18; AAP Dover 15.3.18; 9 Sqdn 16.3.18; Became 209 Sqdn 1.4.18; DFW C crashed British side of lines Armentières-Poperinghe 12.00 1.4.18; Lost wheel on TO, COL 14.5.18 (both Lt MA Harker); 4 ASD 14.5.18; 4 ASD Pilots Pool Guines by 8.18; WOC 4 ASD 30.9.18 general fatigue

B7274 (BR.1) Deld 4 AAP Lincoln by 27.2.18; AAP Dover W/E 9.3.18; 3 Sqdn 21.3.18; Albatros OOC Vaulx, shared B7218 and flight 15.30 24.3.18 (F/L S Smith); COL in gale 28.3.18; 4 ASD Guines 31.3.18; 213 Sqdn 21.4.18; Albatros DV OOC Uytkerke 15.15 27.4.18 (Lt CP Brown); LM27.5.18; 4 ASD by 31.5.18; 213 Sqdn 7.6.18; Destroyed by fire in enemy bombing raid 29.6.18; WOC 31.7.18

**B7275** (BR.1) Deld 4 AAP Lincoln by 27.2.18; AAP Dover 12.3.18; NADD 17.3.18; 3 Sqdn (coded 'P') 23.3.18; Became 203 Sqdn 1.4.18; COL uneven ground, o/t 7.6.18 (2/Lt WAW Carter unhurt); to 1 ASD; Rebuilt as F5948 25.6.18; Again rebuilt as F6476 31.8.18

**B7276** (BR.1) Deld 4 AAP Lincoln 2.18; AAP Dover 17.3.18; ADD 23.3.18; 3 Sqdn 26.3.18; COL in gale 28.3.18; 4 ASD 31.3.18; 213 25.4.18; Last seen over Zeebrugge Mole during raid 2.5.18 (Lt EF Bensly PoW); Surveyed 6.5.18; Deleted 18.5.18

**B7277** (BR.1) Deld 4 AAP Lincoln by 27.2.18; AAP Dover 20.3.18; 4 ASD Guines 24.3.18; 3 Sqdn 31.3.18; Became 203 Sqdn 1.4.18; Flight attacked by 6 Albatros DV over Neuve Eglise, shot down in flames 11.4.18 (2/Lt S Smith killed); SOC in field 11.4.18

**B7278** (BR.1) Deld 4 AAP Lincoln by 27.2.18; AAP Dover 18.3.18; 4 ASD Guines 24.3.18; 1 Sqdn 30.3.18; Became 201 Sqdn 1.4.18; Fokker DrI dest Bouchoir 13.15 6.4.18; Albatros C OOC N of Albert, shared B6359, B6421, B6429, B7225 & B7267 10.10 2.5.18 (both Lt AGA Spence); Shot down in flames during fight with 7 HA E of Villers-Bretonneux 19.00 25.6.18 (Lt E Nightingale killed); SOC 25.6.18

**B7279** (BR.1) Deld 4 AAP Lincoln by 30.3.18 for Dover-Dunkerque Command

**B7280** (BR.1) Deld 4 AAP Lincoln to AAP Dover 15.3.18; 4 ASD Guines 24.3.18; 1 Sqdn 30.3.18; Became 201 Sqdn 1.4.18; Fokker DrI completely OOC SE of Albert 15.00, then COL Le Crotoy 12.4.18; Flying again 20.4.18; Pfalz DIII OOC over Bapaume 13.15, but own m/c badly shot up by AA fire, FL Bertrancourt aerodrome 9.5.18 (all Lt JH Forman); 4 ASD Guines 11.5.18; 210 Sqdn 11.7.18; Fokker DVII OOC over Zeebrugge 11.55 16.7.18; Pfalz DIII OOC SE of Ostende 09.45 20.7.18; 2-str crashed into hedge S of Ostende, shared F5914 08.30 22.7.18; 2-str crashed into floods N of Dixmude 11.15 31.7.18; Fokker DVII in flames NE of Lille 19.25 1.8.18; Fokker DVII crashed SW of Ghistelles 19.15 6.8.18; Fokker DVII crashed in flames NE of Roulers 18.30 3.9.18 (all T/Capt HA Patey DSC); Last seen nr Abeele aerodrome at 2,000ft, shot down by Ltn Beckmann, Jasta 56 17.30 5.9.18 (T/Capt HA Patey DSC PoW); Deleted 15.9.18; Captured by Germans and fitted with wicker seat; Exhibited in Berlin, but removed during WW2 to avoid damage by Allied bombing (fuselage only?); To Polish National Aircraft Museum, Krakow after WW2 & extant

## 6 SOPWITH F.1 CAMEL TRACTOR BIPLANE SCOUTS from batch B7281 to B7480 built by Ruston, Proctor & Co Ltd. (130-hp Clerget 9B)

**B7295** 201 TDS Cranwell, caught hedge stunting nr ground, Ancaster 8.7.18 (2/Lt WW Meddings killed)

**B7296** (Clerget L-S) Deld 4 AAP Lincoln to Dover 23.3.18; Rec Pk to 1 AI 8.4.18; 208 Sqdn 10.4.18; Crashed on TO, CW Serny 16.4.18 (2/Lt H Goodwin injured); 1 ASD 17.4.18

**B7300** 204 TDS Eastchurch by 8.18; Spun in 6.8.18 (2/Lt TF Kesterton killed)

**B7390** France to England 21.4.18; 206 TDS Eastbourne by 7.18; Stalled at 50ft, crashed 2.7.18 (2/Lt AK Smithells)

**B7470** War School Manston by 4.18; 1 School of Aerial Fighting Ayr by 4.18

**B7471** 70 Sqdn, Albatros DV shot down 12.3.18; 2 2-str dest 23.3.18 (all 2/Lt J Aldred); Crashed 17.5.18; 2 ASD 18.5.18; 2 AI to 209 Sqdn 5.7.18; Lost, o/t damaged Soncamp aerodrome 19.7.18 (Lt AGS Blake unhurt); Fokker DVII OOC Comines, shared C198 & D6495 07.20 26.7.18 (Lt KM Walker); HA crashed Caix, shared C1672 19.15 8.8.18; Fokker DVII crashed NW of Rosières 19.15 9.8.18 (both Capt JK Summers MC); Last seen in combat Fokker biplanes E of Peronne 08.30 12.8.18 (2/Lt DK Leed killed); SOC in field 12.8.18

## 83 AIRCO D.H.9 TRACTOR BIPLANE BOMBERS from batch of 100 ordered under Cont Nos A.S.17570 & A.S.22860 from Westland Aircraft Works and numbered B7581 to B7680, to be built at Yeovil. All originally intended for use by naval units. (B7581 to B7590 250-hp F.I.A.T., but refitted 200-hp B.H.P. for overseas, remainder 200-hp B.H.P)

**B7581** Deld 10 AAP Brooklands 1.18 (refitted B.H.P.); AP Dover 24.1.18; 4 ASD Guines 1.4.18; 211 Sqdn 12.4.18; Shot up 7.7.18 (2/Lt NG Breeze wounded); HA OOC in flames 11.00 1.11.18 (Lt JF Drake & 2/Lt GJ Moore); 2 ASD 2.2.19 (unfit to fly Channel)

**B7582** Deld 10 AAP Brooklands by 13.1.18 (refitted B.H.P.); Cranwell to AAP Hendon 28.1.18 (comms work); B.H.P. by 2.18; 1 Comm Sqdn Hendon 23.7.18; Martlesham 10.8.18

**B7583** Deld AP Dover 21.1.18; 6 Sqdn 16.2.18; Became 206 Sqdn 1.4.18; Went on nose landing 21.4.18 (Lt LN Warren & Pte1 JT O'Brien unhurt); to 1 ASD; 206 Sqdn 27.4.18; Rep Pk 1 ASD 29.5.18 (overhaul); 2 ASD 25.6.18; SOC 1 ASD 13.8.18 NWR

**B7584** Deld 10 AAP Brooklands 2.18 (refitted B.H.P.); AP Dover W/E 9.2.18; 202 Sqdn 4.5.18; 4 ASD 24.7.18

**B7585** Deld 10 AAP Brooklands 2.18 (refitted B.H.P.); AP Dover 19.2.18; 217 Sqdn 16.5.18; Damaged in enemy air raid 5/6.6.18; 4 ASD Guines 27.7.18 - @3.10.18

**B7586** Deld 10 AAP Brooklands 2.18 (refitted B.H.P.); AP Dover W/E 9.2.18; 6 Sqdn 23.2.18; Became 206 Sqdn 1.4.18; FL nr Busnes after bombing raid, BO 23.4.18 (2/Lt LM Whittington injured & A/G Pte1 S Jones wounded); SOC in field 27.4.18

**B7587** Deld 10 AAP Brooklands (refitted B.H.P.); AP Dover W/E 9.2.18; 6 Sqdn 19.2.18; Became 206 Sqdn 1.4.18; Bombing raid to Armentières railway station, attacked by 2 Fokker DrI, EF, FL Winnezeele 18.15 11.5.18 (Lt GA Pitt unhurt & 2/Lt CE Anketell MM killed); Rep Pk 1 ASD 14.5.18; SOC in field 15.5.18

**B7588** Deld 10 AAP Brooklands 2.18 (refitted B.H.P.); AP Dover 2.18; 6 Sqdn 21.2.18 - @28.3.18; 211 Sqdn by 6.4.18; Hit rut landing, nose up 25.4.18 (2/Lt ETM Routledge & 2/Lt IAB McTavish); Rep Pk 1 ASD 25.4.18; Rebuilt; 2 ASD 26.6.18; 104 Sqdn .18

**B7589** Deld 10 AAP Brooklands 2.18 (refitted B.H.P.); AP Dover W/E 9.2.18; 6 Sqdn 18.2.18; EF, FL Bray Dunes 10.3.18; Became 206 Sqdn 1.4.18; COL from raid 20.4.18 (Lt EJ Stedman & A/G CG Smith); Rep Pk 1 ASD 20.4.18; SOC 5.5.18

**B7590** Deld 10 AAP Brooklands 2.18 (refitted B.H.P.); AP Dover 28.2.18; 11 Sqdn 16.3.18; 6 Sqdn 29.3.18; Crashed 1.4.18; Deleted ADD 3.4.18

**B7591** Deld 10 AAP Brooklands to AP Dover 15.2.18; 6 Sqdn 27.2.18; Shot down 1 of 6 Albatros DV, spiral nosedive, crashed & burnt in floods between St.Pierre Capelle & the lines 14.40 9.3.18 (F/Cdr TF Le Mesurier DSC & PO AGL JJ Ryan); Became 206 Sqdn 1.4.18; FL Sally, then Bruigny 25.4.18; EF, FL in ploughed field, o/t Beutin, nr Etaples 29.4.18 (Lt JV Turner & 2/Lt EW Tatnall); 1 ASD 2.5.18; SOC 4.5.18

**B7592** Deld 10 AAP Brooklands to AP Dover 15.2.18; ADD by 23.2.18; 6 Sqdn 26.2.18; FL on beach Oost Dunkerque-Coxyde 9.3.18 (FSL AM Bannatyne & AC1 AGL RA Hollingsbee both wounded); Became 206 Sqdn 1.4.18 4 ASD Dunkerque by 6.4.18 (Pilots Pool by 18.6.18); 2 SS Richborough 2.10.18

**B7593** Deld 10 AAP Brooklands to AP Dover 21.2.18; Damaged 17.3.18; 202 Sqdn 4.5.18; Bounced on ridge on TO, on nose 14.9.18 (Lt LF Pendred & 2/Lt HS Saunder unhurt); 4 ASD 15.9.18 - @25.10.18

**B7594** Deld 10 AAP Brooklands to AP Dover 26.2.18; 11 Sqdn 20.3.18; 6 Sqdn 29.3.18; Became 206 Sqdn 1.4.18; Last seen over Menin 08.15 19.5.18 (2/Lt FG Reddie & 2/Lt AC Howell-Jones both killed); SOC in field 20.5.18

**B7595** Deld 10 AAP Brooklands to AP Dover 16.2.18; 6 Sqdn 26.2.18; 6 Sqdn by 18.3.18; 11 Sqdn 20.3.18; 6 Sqdn 29.3.18; Became 206 Sqdn 1.4.18; Badly damaged by flak nr Merville 9.5.18 (Lt EA Burn & 2/Lt AH Mitchener both unhurt); Rep Pk 1 ASD 11.5.18; SOC in field 14.5.18

**B7596** Deld 10 AAP Brooklands to AP Dover W/E 23.2.18; ADD to 6 Sqdn 23.2.18 (but retd bad weather, arr 26.2.18); Became 206 Sqdn 1.4.18; HA in flames 3.5.18 (Lt LN Warren & Pte1 JT O'Brien); HA OOC thick smoke Halvin 1.7.18; HA OOC & HA DD Roulers 29.7.18; Pfalz DIII Scout crashed 2m N of Menin & Pfalz DIII in flames 19.20-19.35 29.7.18; Pfalz DIII OOC & Pfalz DIII BU in air Menin-Wervicq 08.30 1.8.18 (all Lt LN Warren & Lt LA Christian); Wrecked by 30.9.18, to be retd; 206 Sqdn by 12.18; EF, FL

Lissendorf on ferry flight 19.12.18 (2/Lt NE Latham & Cpl Lloyd both unhurt); 8 SS repair

**B7597** Deld 10 AAP Brooklands to AP Dover W/E 23.2.18; 6 Sqdn 28.2.18; Became 206 Sqdn 1.4.18; EF on TO, FL 4.7.18 (2/Lt RH Stainbank & 2/Lt CO Shelswell both unhurt); 1 ASD 7.7.18

**B7598** Deld 10 AAP Brooklands to AP Dover 19.2.18; Left Dover for 6 Sqdn but landed Manston, then returned to Dover but COL 27.2.18(FSL VCM Tiarks); 4 ASD 5.4.18; 211 Sqdn 15.4.18; Damaged by AA fire Bruges-Ostende 9.7.18 (Lt H Axford & Cpl F Wilkinson both unhurt); 1 ASD 10.7.18

**B7599** Deld 10 AAP Brooklands to AP Dover W/E 23.2.18; 6 Sqdn by 21.2.18; Became 206 Sqdn 1.4.18; Ferried Boisdinghem-Alquines but COL 17.4.18 (Lt VCM Tiarks & AGL Pte1 HW Williams both unhurt); 1 ASD 17.4.18

**B7600** Deld 10 AAP Brooklands to AP Dover 21.2.18; 6 Sqdn 27.2.18; Crashed 18.3.18 (FSL LE Oakeshott & AGL Dray); Flying by 22.3.18; Became 206 Sqdn 1.4.18; 211 Sqdn 6.4.18; EF nr aerodrome, tried to turn, spun in, BO 15.5.18 (2/Lt CK Flower & 2/Lt IAB McTavish both killed); Salvage to 1 ASD 16.5.18; SOC 18.5.18 NWR

**B7601** Deld 10 AAP Brooklands to AP Dover 26.2.18; 218 Sqdn Dover 24.4.18; EF, damaged 30.5.18 (Lt BH Stata); 4 ASD 31.5.18 (Pilots Pool by 1.7.18)

**B7602** Deld 10 AAP Brooklands to AP Dover 23.2.18; 6 Sqdn 8.3.18; Became 206 Sqdn 1.4.18; Crashed nr Wylder due to mist 11.5.18 (Lt CM Hyslop & 2/Lt FS Ganter both unhurt); Rep Pk 1 ASD 14.5.18; SOC 17.5.18

**B7603** Deld 10 AAP Brooklands to AP Dover 21.2.18; 6 Sqdn 6.3.18; Became 206 Sqdn 1.4.18; 211 Sqdn 6.4.18; In combat, FL Zuydcoote 16.9.18 (Obs 2/Lt HM Moodie DoW); HA OOC 11.00 4.11.18 (Capt WD Gairdner & Lt BJ Paget); 98 Sqdn 26.2.19

**B7604** Deld 10 AAP Brooklands to AP Dover 23.2.18; 6 Sqdn 8.3.18; ADD 12.3.18 (engine test); 6 Sqdn by 14.3.18 - @21.3.18; ADD by 26.3.18; 4 ASD Guines 1.4.18; 211 Sqdn 6.4.18; Left 10.20 for bombing raid on Varssenaere aerodrome, in combat with 5 HA then caught by heavy AA, crashed 21.5.18 (Lt RFC Metcalfe & 2/Lt DR Bradley unhurt); Rep Pk 1 ASD 23.5.18; Rebuilt as F5847 25.6.18

**B7605** Deld 10 AAP Brooklands to AP Dover 23.2.18; 6 Sqdn 8.3.18; Became 206 Sqdn 1.4.18; COL after bombing raid 25.4.18 (Lt WL Coleridge & 2/Lt RW Brigstock both unhurt); Rep Pk 1 ASD 27.4.18; SOC in field 28.4.18

**B7606** Deld 10 AAP Brooklands to DH4 School Manston 23.2.18; Became 203 TDS Manston 1.4.18; Crashed 12.4.18 (2/Lt JH Evierson & 2/Lt JH Holland both injured)

**B7607** Deld 10 AAP Brooklands to DH4 School Manston 23.2.18; Became 203 TDS Manston 1.4.18

**B7608** Deld 10 AAP Brooklands to DH4 School Manston 23.2.18; Became 203 TDS Manston (coded '3A') 1.4.18; Became 55 TDS Manston 14.7.18: Wings collapsed, dived into sea 24.7.18 (F/Cdt TT Whitley & 1AM A Capes both killed)

**B7609** Deld 10 AAP Brooklands by 23.2.18; DH4 Sqdn Manston W/E 8.3.18; Became 203 TDS Manston (coded '4A') 1.4.18; Became 55 TDS 14.7.18; Crashed 20.11.18

**B7610** Deld 10 AAP Brooklands to DH4 Sqdn Manston W/E 8.3.18; Pancaked landing 11.3.18 (FSL KHG Tilley & FSL EE Ward unhurt); Became 203 TDS Manston 1.4.18; EF at 150 ft on TO, turned back, sideslipped, crashed, BO 2.5.18 (2/Lt SP Inman injured)

**B7611** Deld Mullion (via Prawle Point) 23.3.18; Padstow by 12.4.18; Mullion, tested 17.4.18; Padstow 19.5.18; Became 494 Flt 250 Sqdn Padstow 30.5.18; Hit by DH.6 B2965 landing 18.9.18 (2 crew unhurt)

**B7612** Deld 10 AAP Brooklands to Mullion by rail 26.3.18; Prawle Point 27.4.18; COL 26.5.18; Became 492 Flt Prawle Point 30.5.18; 236 Sqdn Mullion by 8.18

**B7613** Deld 10 AAP Brooklands to Mullion 18.3.18; Prawle Point W/E 2.5.18; 493 Flt Mullion 5.18; Padstow 17.5.18; Dropped 100-lb bomb on U-boat, but no results seen 5036N 0511W 17.20 18.9.18 (Lt HW Whale & Lt T Terrell); Became 494 Flt 250 Sqdn Padstow 30.5.18 -

**B7614** @11.10.18
Deld 10 AAP Brooklands to AP Dover 6.3.18; Calais 16.3.18; 11 Sqdn 17.3.18; Became 211 Sqdn 1.4.18; Left 14.35, attacked by 6 HA on PR mission, badly shot up, FL and crashed, CW nr Oudecappelle 13.8.18 (Lt CH Miller wounded & Cpl SJ Bence killed); 1 ASD 14.8.18; SOC 17.8.18 NWR

**B7615** Deld 10 AAP Brooklands to AP Dover 8.3.18; 11 Sqdn 20.3.18; 6 Sqdn 31.3.18; Became 206 Sqdn 1.4.18; Bombing raid, FL, o/t 1m SE of aerodrome 12.4.18 (Lt H Mitchell & AM CF Costen unhurt); Rep Pk 1 ASD 12.4.18; SOC 19.4.18

**B7616** Deld 10 AAP Brooklands to AP Dover 11.3.18; 11 Sqdn 20.3.18; 4 ASD Guines (crashed) 28.3.18 - @25.10.18

**B7617** Deld 10 AAP Brooklands to AP Dover 8.3.18; 11 Sqdn 20.3.18; 6 Sqdn 29.3.18; Became 206 Sqdn 1.4.18; Crashed nr aerodrome on landing, caught fire, bombs exploded 12.4.18 (Lt R Robinson killed & A/G G Woodgate unhurt); Wreckage to Rep Pk 1 ASD; SOC 19.4.18

**B7618** Deld 10 AAP Brooklands to AP Dover 15.3.18; 11 Sqdn 24.3.18; 6 Sqdn 29.3.18; Became 206 Sqdn 1.4.18; COL from bombing raid 17.4.18 (Lt LM Whittington & Pte1 S Jones both unhurt); Adv Salvage to Rep Pk 1 ASD 17.4.18; SOC 25.4.18

**B7619** Deld 10 AAP Brooklands to AP Dover 15.3.18; 11 Sqdn 23.3.18; 6 Sqdn 29.3.18; Became 206 Sqdn 1.4.18; COL 12.4.18 (Lt EHP Bailey & 2/Lt CE Anketell both unhurt); Rep Pk 1 ASD 12.4.18; SOC 19.4.18

**B7620** Deld 10 AAP Brooklands to AP Dover 15.3.18; Crashed and damaged RFC Dover 26.3.18; 4 ASD 30.3.18; 211 Sqdn (coded 'A') by 6.4.18; Left 14.00, hit by AA fire after bombing Bruges, FL Nummer Een, nr Breskens, Zeeland 27.6.18 (Capt JA Gray & 2/Lt JJ Comerford both interned); Aircraft later taken over by Dutch as *deH433* and stationed Soesterberg for training KNIL pilots (Dutch East Indies Army)

**B7621** Deld 10 AAP Brooklands to AP Dover 16.3.18; 4 ASD Guines 3.4.18; 211 Sqdn 12.4.18, crashed 29.4.18 (Lt JF Drake & 2/Lt NG Breeze); COL 13.6.18 (Lt JF Drake & 2/Lt NG Breeze both unhurt); 1 ASD 13.6.18; SOC 5.7.18 NWR

**B7622** Deld 10 AAP Brooklands to AP Dover 15.3.18; 11 Sqdn 23.3.18; 6 Sqdn 29.3.18; Flat turn into wind, crashed, CW 31.3.18 (FSL LE Oakeshott & FSL HW Day both DoI); 4 ASD 2.4.18; Deleted 8.4.18

**B7623** Deld 10 AAP Brooklands to AP Dover 16.3.18; 4 ASD Guines to 211 Sqdn (coded 'L', later 'B' by 8.18) 7.4.18; COL 10.7.18 (1/Lt DR Harris USAS & 2/Lt WL Bing); Badly hit by AA fire NE of Bruges, FL Zoudekerque, Zeeland 16.8.18 (1/Lt DR Harris USAS & 2/Lt J Munro both interned); SOC in field 16.8.18; Became Dutch *deH438*

**B7624** Deld 10 AAP Brooklands to AP Dover 16.3.18; 4 ASD Guines 1.4.18; 211 Sqdn 7.4.18; Engine damaged in combat, FL on beach La Panne 20.7.18 (Capt HM Freland unhurt & Mjr R Loraine wounded); Raid on Bruges Docks, fired on by German and Dutch coastal guards, engine hit, FL and burnt by crew, Sas van Gent (Hoofdplaat), Zeeland 8.8.18 (2/Lt LK Davidson & 2/Lt WL Bing both interned); SOC in field 8.8.18

**B7625** Deld 10 AAP Brooklands to AP Dover 15.3.18; 211 Sqdn 20.4.18; Struck bump landing, wiped off u/c 6.5.18 (Lt GH Baker & 2/Lt TB Dodwell both unhurt); Rep Pk 1 ASD 7.5.18; SOC 11.5.18

**B7626** Deld 10 AAP Brooklands to AP Dover 16.3.18; 4 ASD Guines 3.4.18; 211 Sqdn 12.4.18; In action 3.10.18 (2/Lt DJ Avery); HA BU in air, shared D551 & E8962 11.00 4.11.18 (2/Lt CH Dickins & 2/Lt AM Adams); 2 ASD 22.2.19 unfit for further service in field

**B7627** Deld 5 AAP Filton by 30.3.18; AP Dover by 3.4.18; 202 Sqdn 4.5.18; 4 ASD Pilots Pool 24.7.18; EF, FL, stalled, wrecked 21.10.18 (Lt RC Treen slightly injured); 4 ASD by 25.10.18; Deleted 31.10.18 DBR

**B7628** Deld 5 AAP Filton to AP Dover but landed RFC Dover and crashed 26.3.18 (Lt Game, RFC), then to Dover; 491 Flt Dover 25.5.18; 4 ASD Audembert 7.6.18; 218 Sqdn by 1.8.18; Pfalz DIII OOC 07.55 13.8.18 (Lt AWE Reeves & 2/Lt GM Worthington); Fokker DVII OOC Stalhille aerodrome 09.43 20.9.18 (Lt AM Anderson & Sgt J Harris); 4 ASD by air 11.10.18 (time

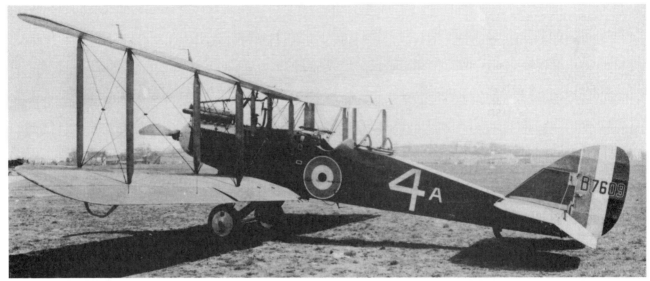

*Airco D.H.9 B7609 '4A' of 203 TDS at Manston in 1918. (RAF Museum P.16195)*

*Airco D.H.9 B7620 '9' with Dutch serial number de H.433 after being interned following its forced landing in Holland after being hit by flak on 27 June 1918. (via Frank Cheesman)*

*Royal Aircraft Factory A.E.3 Ram II B8783, which was fitted with armour, was tested by 201 Sqdn in July 1918. (R.A.Lynes)*

B7629    expired)
Deld 5 AAP Filton to AP Dover 29.3.18; 4 ASD Guines 1.4.18; 211 Sqdn 7.4.18; Hit railway signal post on TO 2.6.18 (Lt GT Scott & 2/Lt PR Thornton both unhurt); 1 ASD 3.6.18; SOC 6.6.18 NWR

B7630    Deld 5 AAP Filton by 30.3.18; AAP Dover 2.4.18; 202 Sqdn 4.5.18; 4 ASD 25.6.18 (later Pilots Pool); EF, FL, starboard wing hit tree, nosed in 3.10.18 (Sgt J Stewart slightly injured); 4 ASD by 25.10.18

B7632    Deld 5 AAP Filton by 30.3.18; AAP Dover 2.4.18; 211 Sqdn 7.4.18; COL 12.4.18 (Lt NA Taylersen & A/G LC Norman); 4 ASD Guines 13.4.18 - @27.4.18; Rep Pk 1 ASD by 5.18; 1 AI 7.5.18; 4 ASD by 25.5.18 - @31.5.18; 211 Sqdn by 9.18, crashed; 4 ASD 29.9.18; To England 2.4.19 [BUT not mentioned in sqdn record, and 211 did not send its aircraft to 4 ASD]

B7635    Deld 5 AAP Filton by 30.3.18; AAP Dover 2.4.18 - 5.18; 217 Sqdn by 16.5.18; 218 Sqdn 24.9.18; FL on sqdn transfer to Vert Galant 16.11.18 (Lt JA Eyres & AM Dawson); Marquise 30.12.18; SOC 1 ASD 21.1.19

B7636    Mkrs by 30.3.18 for Dunkerque; RP 1 ASD 4.18; 49 Sqdn 30.4.18; 2 ASD 23.5.18; Rebuilt as F6171 3.7.18

B7637    Deld 5 AAP Filton by 30.3.18; AAP Dover 2.4.18; 4 ASD Guines 7.4.18; 211 Sqdn 7.4.18; Badly shot up in bombing raid between Ostende & Nieuport 9.5.18 (Lt FJ Islip unhurt & 2/Lt E Cooke wounded); Rep Pk 1 ASD 11.5.18; SOC in field 14.5.18

B7638    Deld 5 AAP Filton by 30.3.18; Dover to Lympne W/E 4.5.18; 1 AI 5.18; 211 Sqdn 11.5.18; FL in field 12.6.18 (Lt JF Drake & 2/Lt NG Breeze both unhurt); Rep Pk 1 ASD 13.6.18; SOC 5.7.18 MWR

B7639    Deld Mullion (via Helston) 4.18; Tested 23.4.18; Prawle Point 28.4.18; Became 492 Flt 254 Sqdn Prawle Point by 25.5.18; COL 26.5.18

B7640    Deld Mullion (via Helston) W/E 27.3.18; Prawle Point 28.4.18; Surveyed 10.5.18 wrecked; Deleted 18.5.18

B7642    Deld 5 AAP Filton W/E 27.3.18; 10 AAP Brooklands by 4.18; Yarmouth 6.4.18 (anti-sub); Dropped 2x100-lb bombs on U-boat 8m NE of Shipwash LV 9.5.18; 490 Flt Yarmouth by 25.5.18 - @18.6.18; HACP 10.6.18; Covehithe by 6.18

B7643    Deld 5 AAP Filton W/E 27.3.18; AAP Dover 2.4.18; 211 Sqdn 7.4.18; COL 13.4.18 (2/Lt GH Baker & Pte2 HW Newsham) both unhurt; 4 ASD Guines 14.4.18; 2 SS Richborough 15.9.18

B7647    Deld 10 AAP Brooklands 28.3.18; Yarmouth 6.4.18 (anti-sub); 490 Flt Yarmouth 25.5.18 - @6.7.18

B7654    Deld 10 AAP Brooklands by 15.4.18; RP 1 ASD by 5.18; 1 AI 4.5.18; 206 Sqdn 4.5.18; COL 19.5.18 (Lt S Gillott & 2/Lt FS Ganter both unhurt); To Rep Pk 1 ASD; SOC 21.5.18 NWR

B7655    Deld 10 AAP Brooklands by 22.4.18; Mullion by 5.18; Padstow 24.5.18; Rec Pk by 7.18; 2 AI 2.7.18; 3 ASD 4.7.18

B7656    Deld 5 AAP Filton by 25.4.18; 218 Sqdn by 29.5.18; Damaged landing 29.5.18 (Lt WF Purvis unhurt), repaired on sqdn; Overshot landing, damaged u/c and wings 8.6.18 (Capt MG Baskerville & Chief Mech SH Newton), repaired on sqdn; Crashed, CW on local flight Capelle 24.6.18 (Lt HVM Hoskins seriously injured); to 4 ASD

B7658    Deld 10 AAP Brooklands by 22.4.18; Rec Pk to 1 AI 7.5.18; 206 Sqdn 14.5.18; Sqdn move, EF, COL Alquines 5.6.18 (Lt CM Hyslop & AG JW Pacey unhurt); Rep Pk 1 ASD 8.6.18; SOC 11.6.18 NWR

B7659    Deld 10 AAP Brooklands by 25.4.18; AAP Dover W/E 15.5.18; Shipped to Italy?; 226 Sqdn Pizzone by 28.5.18; Became 472/4 Flts 226 Sqdn Pizzone 9.18

B7660    Deld AAP Dover W/E 15.5.18; 218 Sqdn W/E 24.5.18 - @31.5.18; Damaged by AA fire Ostende 12.6.18 (Capt JF Chisholm & G/L LH Lecke unhurt); to 4 ASD; 218 Sqdn 27.9.18; Fokker DrI OOC Thourout 09.35-09.40 29.9.18 (Capt CS Iron & 2/Lt C Ford); 98 Sqdn 21.1.19; to England 15.2.19

B7661    Deld 10 AAP Brooklands by 22.4.18; Rec Pk to 1 AI 4.5.18; 211 Sqdn 8.5.18; Left 10.15, last seen behind formation over target Varssanaere aerodrome 21.5.18 (2/Lt HE Tansley & 2/Lt NB Harris PoWs); SOC in field 21.5.18

B7662    Deld Mullion W/E 11.5.18; 493 Flt 236 Sqdn Mullion by 25.5.18; Prawle Point 12.6.18; On return from patrol

crashed Gaspell, BO 19.6.18 (Lt FStP Harran DoI & A/C F Fairbrother killed)

B7663    Deld Mullion W/E 11.5.18; 493 Flt 236 Sqdn Mullion by 25.5.18 - @3.6.18; Padstow by 17.7.18

B7665    Deld Mullion W/E 11.5.18; 494 Flt 250 Sqdn Padstow 24.5.18, FL in sea, towed in by trawler 14.6.18 (crew saved)

B7666    Deld Mullion W/E 11.5.18; 493 Flt 236 Sqdn Mullion by 25.5.18; 492 Flt Prawle Point 254 Sqdn 12.6.18 - @23.10.18; 493 Flt 236 Sqdn Mullion by 29.10.18 - @30.10.18

B7667    Deld 5 AAP Filton by 27.4.18; 218 Sqdn by 31.5.18; Crashed in sea, last seen above clouds at 12/14,000ft off Nieuport 10.6.18 (Lt RW Robinson & G/L 1/Pte HA Claydon both drowned); WOC 30.6.18

B7668    Deld 5 AAP Filton by 26.4.18; Rec Pk by 23.5.18; 206 Sqdn 25.5.18; Left 17.35, seen over Courtrai 29.7.18 (Lt G Cheston USAS killed & Cpl JW Pacey wounded?); SOC in field 31.7.18

B7669    Deld 5 AAP Filton by 27.4.18; AAP Dover by 5.18; 217 Sqdn 18.5.18; Damaged in enemy air raid 5/6.6.18; 4 ASD Pilots Pool 13.6.18; 2 SS Richborough 15.9.18

B7670    Deld 5 AAP Filton by 26.4.18; Shipped to Italy; 226 Sqdn Pizzone by 28.4.18; Became 472/4 Flts 226 Sqdn Pizzone 9.18 - @1.19; Taranto to 'X' AD 28.6.19; 55 Sqdn by 7.20 - @25.9.20

B7671    Deld 5 AAP Filton by 5.18; 491 Flt Dover W/E 24.5.18; Despatched 2.6.18; 218 Sqdn by 1.8.18; Hit by AA Bruges Docks 15.9.18 (Lt HD McLaren & Sgt G Barlow); 4 ASD 16.9.18 - @25.10.18

B7672    'Presented by Patrick Burns Esq of Calgary, Alberta'. AAP Dover W/E 15.5.18; 218 Sqdn W/E 24.5.18; Fokker DVII crashed in sea 07.30 14.7.18; Pfalz DIII OOC S of Ostende 07.55 13.8.18 (Lt AC Lloyd & Sgt J Harris); Pfalz DIII in flames Ghistelles aerodrome 13.25 15.8.18 (both Lt AWE Reeves & 2/Lt GM Worthington); Lympne 14.1.19

B7673    Deld 5 AAP Filton by 27.4.18; AAP Dover to 218 Sqdn W/E 24.5.18; Hit by flak Zeebrugge 07.30 14.7.18 (Lt AM Anderson unhurt & 2/Lt CJ Swatridge slightly wounded); Raid on Zeebrugge, lost Blankenberghe-Zeebrugge 16.7.18 (Lt JA Pugh & 2/Lt J Ankers both PoW) [credited Ltn Poss of Seefrontstaffel]; Deleted 31.7.18

B7676    Deld AAP Dover W/E 15.5.18; 218 Sqdn W/E 24.5.18; Overshot landing from raid, hit lorry 23.6.18 (Lt H Fawdry & 2/Lt JS Cryan); To 4 ASD; 2 SS Richborough 2.10.18

B7677    Deld AAP Dover W/E 15.5.18; 218 Sqdn W/E 1.6.18; Badly damaged in raid on Ostende 5,7.18 (Lt BH Stata & 2/Lt CVR Browne); 4 ASD Guines 8.7.18; 4 ASD Audembert by 9.18; 218 Sqdn 29.9.18; Fokker DVII OOC Cortemarcke 09.40 29.9.18 (Lt FP Mulcahy USMC & Cpl TL McCullough); 98 Sqdn 21.1.19; to England W/E 15.2.19

B7678    Deld 5 AAP Filton by 6.5.18; Rec Pk to 1 AI 22.5.18; 206 Sqdn 27.5.18; Pfalz DIII crashed nr Ledeghem 19.40 29.7.18 (Lt Schlotzhauer USAS & Cpl HW Williams); Left 07.40, FTR 5.10.18 (2/Lt C Hancock & 2/Lt LH Prime both PoW)

B7679    Deld 5 AAP Filton by 20.5.18; Rec Pk to 1 AI 11.6.18; 211 Sqdn 14.6.18; In action 16.8.18 (Lt GH Baker wounded); 2 ASD 22.2.19 (unfit to fly Channel)

B7680    Deld 5 AAP Filton by 20.5.18; Rec Pk to 1 AI 12.6.18; 206 Sqdn 13.6.18; Burst radiator, FL, crashed Elseghem 22.11.18 (Lt GA Pitt & Lt HOFB Blew both unhurt); 8 SS for repair

## Various rebuilds by 1(S)ARD Farnborough

B7764    (D.H.4) (F.I.A.T.) 1(S)ARD by 11.4.18 for A/S for Cdr HA Williamson; 2 AI by 8.18; 205 Sqdn 14.8.18; Shot about by HA in raid on Busigny, FL nr Germaine 16.9.18 (Lt GC Matthews & Lt AG Robertson killed); 2 ASD 20.9.18; SOC 2 Salvage Dump 2 ASD W/E 24.9.18

B7769    (Camel) (140-hp Clerget) 1(S)ARD Farnborough by 25.5.18; Rec Pk to 2 AI 2.7.18; 208 Sqdn 19.7.18; DFW C OOC E of Oppy, shared D1923, D8168 & F5933 06.00 14.8.18; 2-str OOC Pont-à-Vendin, shared "D8115"/Lt WV Skall 19.00 25.9.18 (both Lt RCD'A

Gifford); EF, FL, crashed 1.9.18 (2/Lt TH Pyke unhurt); Rep Pk 1 ASD 3.9.18; Rebuilt as H7112 17.9.18

B7859 (Camel) 2 AI to 208 Sqdn 14.11.18; 2 ASD 22.11.18

B7860 (Camel) (130-hp Clerget) 1(S)ARD Farnborough by 25.5.18; Dover 11.6.18; 4 ASD Guines 21.6.18; 210 Sqdn 24.7.18; Pfalz DIII OOC E of Dixmude 10.00 30.7.18; Fokker DVII OOC N of Lille 19.25 1.8.18; Fokker DVII crashed nr Zonnebeke 07.25 & another spun and crashed 2m SE of Staden 07.30, then EF, FL successfully Hospital Farm 9.8.18 (all Capt ED Crundall); Struck beach in darkness trying to land St.Pol, badly damaged Mardyck 00.35 15.8.18 (Capt ED Crundall injured); To 4 ASD Audembert (fitted BR.1); 204 Sqdn 1.10.18; Fokker DVII crashed outskirts of Ghent 09.10 27.10.18 (Lt HG Clappison); Fokker DVII on fire Nazareth 13.15 30.10.18 (Capt ED Crundall); EF, left formation, FL, hit tree, spun in Rousbrugge 1.11.18 (2/Lt HA Argles injured); Wreckage 8 SS, SOC in field

B7862 (Camel) (Clerget L-S) 1 ASD to 208 Sqdn 8.7.18; FL, hit trees, unhurt 17.7.18 (Lt RCD'A Gifford); to Rep Pk 1 ASD; SOC 21.7.18 NWR

B7889 (Camel) 50 TDS Eastbourne by 7.6.18 - @1.11.18

B7903 (1½ Strutter) Deld AAP Brockworth W/E 5.9.18; Turnhouse W/E 26.9.18 - @30.1.19

B7914 (Ship Strutter) Deld AAP Brockworth W/E 12.9.18; Grain 27.9.18 - @30.1.19 (for Turnhouse by 11.18 but still Grain 1.19)

B7915 (1½ Strutter) Deld AAP Brockworth W/E 5.9.18; Turnhouse W/E 26.9.18 - @30.1.19

B7916 (1½ Strutter) Deld AAP Brockworth W/E 5.9.18; Turnhouse W/E 26.9.18 - @30.1.19

B7937 (D.H.4) 4 ASD Wissant to 202 Sqdn 14.11.18; 1(S)ARD Farnborough for HMS *Argus* 6.1.19; 6 SD Ascot (for HMS *Argus*) W/E 16.1.19 - @30.1.19

B7941 (D.H.4) (Eagle VIII) 4 ASD Wissant to 217 Sqdn 16.10.18; 98 Sqdn 6.3.19; 1 ASD 19.3.19

B7964 (D.H.4) (Eagle VIII) 4 ASD Wissant to 217 Sqdn 22.10.18; 98 Sqdn 6.3.19; 1 ASD 19.3.19

B7985 (D.H.4) 495 Flt 246 Sqdn Seaton Carew by 6.11.18

B7986 (D.H.4) 4 ASD to 202 Sqdn 4.11.18; 233 Sqdn Dover 6.3.19; 2 Comms Sqdn Buc from 26.4.19 (special duty with HM King of the Belgians)

B8012 (Pup) FPS Turnhouse, collided with 1½ Strutter 9894 over Firth of Forth 4.9.18 (2/Lt HA Sutherland killed)

B8179 (Camel) 471 Flt 233 Sqdn Walmer by 10.8.18

**62 AVRO 504J TRACTOR BIPLANE TRAINERS from batch B8581 to B8780 built by Parnall & Sons Ltd. Many delivered to RNAS. (100-hp Gnome Monosoupape)**

B8581 Deld Manston NFS W/E 17.11.17; Redes 203 TDS Manston 1.4.18

B8582 Deld Manston NFS W/E 17.11.17; Deleted W/E 30.3.18

B8583 Deld Manston NFS for erection W/E 17.11.17; Eastchurch W/E 30.3.18

B8584 Deld Manston NFS W/E 10.11.17; Eastchurch W/E 30.3.18

B8585 Deld Manston NFS for erection W/E 10.11.17; Eastchurch W/E 30.3.18; Became 204 TDS Eastchurch 1.4.18; Collided with Farman when gliding down to land 19.7.18 (Lt RM Collingwood killed)

B8586 Deld Manston NFS W/E 17.11.17; Eastchurch W/E 30.3.18; Became 204 TDS Eastchurch 1.4.18 - @6.18

B8587 Deld Manston NFS W/E 17.11.17; Eastchurch W/E 30.3.18

B8588 Deld Manston NFS for erection W/E 17.11.17; Eastchurch W/E 30.3.18

B8589 Deld Manston NFS for erection W/E 17.11.17; Eastchurch W/E 30.3.18; Became 204 TDS Eastchurch 1.4.18

B8590 Deld Manston NFS for erection W/E 1.12.17; Eastchurch W/E 30.3.18; Became 204 TDS Eastchurch 1.4.18 - @6.18

B8596 Deld Chingford for erection W/E 1.12.17; Became 207 TDS Chingford 1.4.18

B8597 Deld Redcar School by road W/E 1.12.17; Became SSF Redcar 1.4.18

B8598 Deld Redcar School by road W/E 1.12.17 - @30.3.18; Became SSF Redcar 1.4.18; Became 2 SSF Redcar 5.18;

B8599 Became NE Area FIS Redcar 1.7.18 - @19.12.18
Deld Redcar School by road W/E 1.12.17; Tested 25.1.18; Became SSF Redcar 1.4.18; Became 2 SSF Redcar 5.18; Became NE Area FIS Redcar 1.7.18 - @8.18; Crashed [NO DATE] (Reynolds)

B8600 Deld Redcar School by road W/E 15.12.17; Deleted W/E 30.3.18

B8601 Deld Chingford for erection W/E 12.12.17; Became 207 TDS Chingford 1.4.18

B8602 Deld Chingford for erection W/E 15.12.17; Burst into flames on landing Fairlop 21.1.18 (PFO WE Floyd killed)

B8603 Deld Chingford for erection W/E 12.12.17; Became 207 TDS Chingford 1.4.18; 5 Group Dover (RR) by 5.18; Crashed 21.5.18 (Lt/Col DH Hyde-Thomson killed)

B8616 Deld Redcar School for erection W/E 12.1.18; Deleted W/E 30.3.18

B8617 Deld Redcar School for erection W/E 12.1.18; Became SSF Redcar 1.4.18; Became 2 SSF Redcar 5.18; Became NE Area FIS Redcar 1.7.18 - @14.12.18

B8618 Deld Redcar School for erection W/E 12.1.18; Became SSF Redcar 1.4.18; EF on climbing turn nr ground, turned back, sideslipped, spun in 22.4.18 (Pte WAC Easter killed & Lt CR Moore injured); Presume rebuilt; Became 2 SSF Redcar 5.18; Became NE Area FIS Redcar 1.7.18 - @28.11.18

B8619 Deld Redcar School for erection W/E 12.1.18; Became SSF Redcar 1.4.18; Became 2 SSF Redcar 5.18

B8620 Deld Redcar School for erection W/E 19.1.18; Tested 16.2.18; Became SSF Redcar 1.4.18; Became 2 SSF Redcar 5.18; Became NE Area FIS Redcar 1.7.18 - @3.12.18

B8621 Deld Redcar School for erection W/E 19.1.18 - @30.3.18; Became SSF Redcar 1.4.18; Became 2 SSF Redcar 5.18; Became NE Area FIS Redcar 1.7.18 - @7.9.18

B8622 Deld RNASTE Vendôme W/E 1.2.18; Became 205 TDS Vendôme 1.4.18; FL, stalled and spun, wrecked 27.6.18 (PFO RH Boyden)

B8623 Deld RNASTE Vendôme W/E 1.2.18; Became 205 TDS Vendôme 1.4.18; Slightly damaged landing 3.5.18 (PFO KP Kirkwood); Accident 15.5.18 (F/Cdt RB Mumford); EF, landed in wheat field, nosed up, slightly damaged 5.7.18 (PFO AJ O'Neil); To 212 TDS Vendôme 7.18; Hit ridge landing, slightly damaged 15.9.18 (2/Lt C Hooper & Lt AD Reid unhurt)

B8624 Deld RNASTE Vendôme W/E 8.2.18; EF, FL 21.3.18 (PFO HJ McLeod); Damaged landing 13.3.18 (FSL WR Reid); Became 205 TDS Vendôme 1.4.18; Bounced landing, slightly damaged 12.6.18 (PFO EBF Auld); EF, stalled on turn, spun in 9.9.18 (Lt LV Evans seriously injured & F/Cdt EW Hutchinson injured)

B8625 Deld RNASTE Vendôme W/E 22.2.18; Became 205 TDS Vendôme 1.4.18; Badly damaged landing 3.5.18 (PFO HA Sutherland); Crashed 19.8.18 (Lt C Keith-Johnstone unhurt); FL 3km SE of Montoire 25.8.18 (F/Cdt RE Lindsay unhurt); EF, FL 28.10.18 (Lt R MacLean unhurt)

B8626 Deld RNASTE Vendôme W/E 8.2.18; Became 205 TDS Vendôme 1.4.18; 212 TDS by 8.18; Pancaked landing, slightly damaged 27.8.18 (F/Cdt FC Maugham & Lt FW Wright); ARS 84 Wing Vendôme by 11.18

B8627 Deld RNASTE Vendôme W/E 22.2.18; Damaged landing 12.3.18 (PFO HJ McLeod); Became 205 TDS Vendôme 1.4.18; 212 TDS Vendôme by 6.18; Slightly damaged landing 3.6.18 (PFO SR Pragnall & Capt PH Martin); Crashed Chemille 4.7.18 (F/Cdt EJ Weaver)

B8628 Deld RNASTE Vendôme W/E 8.2.18; U/c, propeller and wings broken on TO 18.3.18 (PFO JG Davidson); Became 205 TDS Vendôme 1.4.18; Crashed 25.8.18 (F/Cdt CE Eastgate unhurt); Crashed 19.9.18 (F/Cdt CE Eastgate unhurt); ARS 84 Wing Vendôme by 11.18

B8629 Deld RNASTE Vendôme W/E 15.2.18; Became 205 TDS Vendôme 1.4.18; 212 TDS Vendôme on/by 20.5.18; Stalled and crashed, slightly damaged 26.5.18 (F/Cdt NH Wallace & Capt PH Martin); 205 TDS Vendôme by 7.18; Pancaked landing, slightly damaged 2.7.18 (Capt JH Green); 212 TDS Vendôme by 9.18; Lost control, badly damaged 14.9.18 (F/Cdt BS Pearce & Lt AD Reid both unhurt); Crashed on TO, slightly damaged 23.11.18 (F/Cdt TEJ Pearl unhurt)

B8630 Deld RNASTE Vendôme W/E 8.2.18; Became 205 TDS Vendôme 1.4.18; Badly damaged landing 27.6.18 (PFO FC Hamilton); 212 TDS Vendôme by 7.18; Stalled landing, u/c and leading edge damaged 17.8.18 (Lt WR Bell & Lt FW Wright); ARS 84 Wing Vendôme, tested 16.10.18 - @11.18

B8631 Deld RNASTE Vendôme W/E 15.2.18; Became 205 TDS vendome 1.4.18; Hit tree in ditch while landing, badly damaged 18.6.18 (PFO EA Gaunt); FL on unsuitable ground Monnaie (?) 30m from aerodrome 12.8.18 (2/Lt WS Pennington slightly injured); ARS 84 Wing Vendôme by 11.18

B8632 Deld RNASTE Vendôme W/E 22.2.18; Became 205 TDS Vendôme 1.4.18; Fuel shortage, FL, overshot into hedge, badly damaged 7.6.18 (F/Cdt JES Dunham); EF, FL, dived in, wrecked nr Chateau Renault 26.7.18 (F/Cdt WG Coulthard)

B8633 Deld RNASTE Vendôme W/E 22.2.18; Became 205 TDS Vendôme 1.4.18; Pancaked landing 12.8.18 (Lt AF MacDonald & pupil unhurt); EF, FL St.Anne Crucheray road, just outside aerodrome 1.10.18 (F/Cdt S Thornley slightly injured & 2/Lt AE Betts unhurt)

B8634 Deld RNASTE Vendôme W/E 25.1.18; Became 205 TDS Vendôme 1.4.18; Badly damaged on landing 12.6.18 (PFO J Wood); To 212 TDS Vendôme; Went into depression taxying, badly damaged 9.7.18 (Lt LN Nash & Lt AD Reid); To 205 TDS Vendôme; EF, FL on unsuitable ground nr St.Amand 15.8.18 (F/Cdt AEJ Camfield injured); ARS 84 Wing Vendôme by 11.18

B8635 Deld RNASTE Vendôme W/E 25.1.18; Became 205 TDS Vendôme 1.4.18 - @9.18; ARS 84 Wing Vendôme by 11.18

B8636 Deld RNASTE Vendôme W/E 25.1.18; U/c and wings damaged landing 27.3.18 (PFO WR Reid); Became 205 TDS Vendôme 1.4.18; FL 1km NW of Blois 10.8.18 (Lt LV Evans unhurt)

B8637 Deld Chingford/Fairlop W/E 1.2.18; Became 207 TDS Chingford 1.4.18

B8638 Deld Chingford W/E 9.2.18; Deleted W/E 2.3.18

B8639 Deld Chingford/Fairlop W/E 8.2.18; Became 207 TDS Chingford 1.4.18

B8640 Deld Chingford W/E 25.1.18; Became 207 TDS Chingford 1.4.18

B8641 Deld Eastbourne NFS W/E 26.1.18; Became 206 TDS Eastbourne 1.4.18; Crashed & wrecked 17.4.18 (2 crew unhurt)

B8642 Deld Eastbourne NFS W/E 2.2.18; Became 206 TDS Eastbourne 1.4.18; COL 30.7.18 (2/Lt JG Stitt slightly injured)

B8643 Deld Eastbourne NFS W/E 2.2.18; Became 206 TDS Eastbourne 1.4.18; Ran into hollow on TO, u/c wrecked 4.7.18; Became 54 TDS Eastbourne 15.7.18 - @23.8.18

B8644 Deld Eastbourne NFS W/E 9.2.18; Became 206 TDS Eastbourne 1.4.18; Became 54 TDS Eastbourne 15.7.18

B8645 Deld Eastbourne NFS 9.2.18; Became 206 TDS Eastbourne 1.4.18 - @29.5.18; SE Area FIS Shoreham .18; 45 TDS Rendcombe by 8.18

B8646 Deld RNASTE Vendôme W/E 29.2.18; Became 205 TDS Vendôme 1.4.18; To 212 TDS Vendôme; Ran into another aircraft, damaged wing 6.7.18 (Lt AD Reid); Flew into ground, badly damaged 1.8.18 (2/Lt FE Capon); ARS 84 Wing Vendôme by 11.18

B8647 Deld RNASTE Vendôme W/E 22.2.18; Became 205 TDS Vendôme 1.4.18; To 212 TDS Vendôme; FL in field, badly damaged la Chapelle Vendômoise 29.6.18 (2/Lt PT Hopkins & Lt GR Hake); Propeller stopped while spinning, sideslipped into ground, badly damaged Chateau-Renault 27.8.18 (PFO J Masterton unhurt); still 212 TDS Vendôme 10.18; ARS 84 Wing Vendôme by 11.18

B8648 Deld RNASTE Vendôme W/E 29.2.18; Became 205 TDS Vendôme 1.4.18; Landed on slope in rough ground, slightly damaged 8.7.18 (F/Cdt AEJ Camfield); ARS 84 Wing Vendôme by 11.18

B8649 Deld RNASTE Vendôme W/E 22.2.18; Became 205 TDS Vendôme 1.4.18; EF, FL, CW Blois road 18.6.18 (F/Cdt GR Sachey)

B8650 Deld RNASTE Vendôme W/E 29.2.18; Became 205 TDS Vendôme 1.4.18; FL St.Amand 16.9.18 (F/Cdt JA Fraser unhurt); Crashed on TO 17.10.18 (F/Cdt PG Lee injured)

B8651 Deld RNASTE Vendôme W/E 29.2.18; Became 205 TDS Vendôme 1.4.18; Slightly damaged landing after looping Tours 29.6.18 (Lt SE Brewster); To 212 TDS Vendôme; Crashed 22.8.18 (2/Lt HF Fleming unhurt); 205 TDS by 10.18; Crashed 17.10.18 (F/Cdt PG Lee unhurt)

B8652 Deld RNASTE Vendôme W/E 29.2.18; Became 205 TDS Vendôme 1.4.18; 212 TDS on/by 20.5.18; EF on TO, slightly damaged 26.5.18 (F/Cdt WF McCann & Capt PH Martin); Caught slipstream of another a/c while landing, badly damaged 2.7.18 (F/Cdt AA Garlick); ARS 84 Wing Vendôme by 11.18

B8653 Deld RNASTE Vendôme W/E 22.2.18; Became 205 TDS Vendôme 1.4.18; Slightly damaged landing 24.6.18 (PFO C Shaw); Spun in on football ground, wrecked 26.7.18 (F/Cdt JH Coulthurst unhurt)

B8654 Deld RNASTE Vendôme W/E 8.3.18; Became 205 TDS Vendôme 1.4.18; To 212 TDS Vendôme; FL, overshot into wheat field, slightly damaged 19.7.18 (F/Cdt R Pearce slightly injured); Landed bad ground, badly damaged 27.8.18 (F/Cdt J Smith & Lt C Ouseley-Smith); still 212 TDS 10.18; ARS 84 Wing Vendôme by 11.18

B8655 Deld RNASTE Vendôme W/E 1.3.18; Became 205 TDS Vendôme 1.4.18; Hit a Curtiss while landing 18.6.18 (F/Cdt HC Hammond slightly injured); To 212 TDS Vendôme; Stalled attempting to clear hedge, badly damaged Courdemanche 8.8.18 (PFO FB Candy & Capt PH Martin); Bounced landing, badly damaged 10.11.18 (F/Cdt FT Allaway & Lt C Ouseley-Smith unhurt); ARS 84 Wing Vendôme by 11.18

B8656 Deld RNASTE Vendôme W/E 1.3.18; Became 205 TDS Vendôme 1.4.18; Crashed 10.8.18 (F/Cdt GE Black unhurt); Crashed 25.8.18 (Lt SJ Fisher unhurt)

B8657 Deld RNASTE Vendôme W/E 8.3.18; Became 205 TDS Vendôme 1.4.18; 212 TDS Vendôme by 7.18; ARS 84 Wing Vendôme by 11.18

B8658 Deld RNASTE Vendôme W/E 1.3.18; Became 205 TDS Vendôme 1.4.18; Badly damaged landing 31.5.18 (PFO RG Stephens); ARS 84 Wing Vendôme by 11.18

B8659 Deld RNASTE Vendôme W/E 1.3.18; Became 205 TDS Vendôme 1.4.18; To 212 TDS Vendôme; Landed on by Caudron N3057 12.8.18 (F/Cdt A Huxley slightly injured & Lt AD Reid unhurt)

B8660 Deld RNASTE Vendôme W/E 1.3.18; Became 205 TDS Vendôme 1.4.18; U/c and propeller broken landing 6.6.18 (PFO SR Pragnall); Crashed 1.11.18 (F/Cdt C Forrest unhurt); To ARS 84 Wing Vendôme 11.18

## 1 ROYAL AIRCRAFT FACTORY A.E.3 RAM II ARMOURED PUSHER BIPLANE. (230-hp Bentley BR.1)

B8783 To France 30.6.18; St.Andre to 201 Sqdn 1.7.18 (not on strength); to 209 Sqdn 13.7.18

## 1 AIRCO D.H.6 TRACTOR BIPLANE rebuilt by 27 Wing

B8790 Cramlington/North Shields by 4.18; FL in sea 2m SE of Sunderland Pier 28.4.18 (Lt Turner & Sig Checksfield)

## 7 HANDLEY PAGE O/400 TRACTOR BIPLANE HEAVY BOMBERS from batch B8802 to B8813 built by the Royal Aircraft Factory at Farnborough. (Two 320-hp Sunbeam Cossack unless otherwise stated)

B8804 Lympne by 8.18; Rec Pk 10.8.18; 207 Sqdn 12.8.18; Crashed, o/t, on return from night raid, 19.9.18 (2/Lt LR Blacking, Lt RJ Mesney & Sgt JS Taylor unhurt); to 2 ASD

B8806 Lympne to Rec Pk 24.9.18; 3 AD 25.9.18; 216 Sqdn 27.9.18; Fitted for mail carrying by 1.19; FL in fog, crashed at Düren en route Marquise to Cologne 20.1.19 (Lt GW Moore & Lt FD Taylor unhurt); SOS 21.1.19; Collected by 10 SS

B8807 (Eagle VIII) England to Rec Pk 20.9.18; 3 AD 20.9.18 (arr 21.9.18); 216 Sqdn (coded 'Y') 20.9.18; Flown Hucqueliers to Guines 12.12.18; 4 ASD 20.12.18 (fit out as mail carrier); 216 Sqdn 1.10; To carry mail to Valenciennes, but crashed into trees on TO, Forques, nr Marquise, TW 29.3.19 (2/Lt FH Sullivan killed, 2/Lt A

*Birds-eye view of Handley Page O/400 B8811 'A2' of 207 Sqdn around October 1918*

*Blackburn Kangaroo B9970, used for trials at Martlesham Heath, later joined the British civil register as G-EAOW.*

*Airco D.H.9 C1385 'A' of No.2 Marine Observers School, Eastchurch in 1919 (RAF Museum P.15587)*

Westall DoI & AC1 GW Tucknott injured); 1 ASD 31.3.19

B8810 England to 4 ASD by 25.10.18; 207 Sqdn (coded 'H' later 'A') 10.18; Permission given to SOS 15.1.19; to be salved by convenient Salvage Section

B8811 England to 4 ASD by 25.10.18; 207 Sqdn (coded 'A-2' in 10.18, 'G' in 11.18) by 10.18 - @10.11.18; 58 Sqdn (coded 'A-2') by 5.19; To ME with 216 Sqdn; Buc by 25.8.19; Pisa by 26.9.19; WO at St.Raphael en route

B8812 England to Rec Pk 8.10.18; 3 AD 9.10.18; 100 Sqdn 9.10.18 - @1.19; 216 Sqdn by 3.19

B8813 3 AD by 10.18; 100 Sqdn 27.10.18; 216 Sqdn 28.1.19; 207 Sqdn to Buc 31.7.19 allocated Egypt, but RTP 25.8.19

## 1 SOPWITH 1½ STRUTTER TRACTOR BIPLANE rebuilt by 3(W)ARD Yate

B8911 Deld 2(N)ARD Coal Aston W/E 18.7.18; Turnhouse W/E 8.8.18 - @30.1.19

## 1 BRISTOL F.2b TRACTOR BIPLANE rebuilds by 3(W)ARD Yate

B8937 (250-hp RR) No.1 Torpedo Sqdn East Fortune, spun in on TO 13.7.18 (Lt EF Kerruish killed)

B8942 201 TDS East Fortune, stalled in climbing turn, sideslipped to ground, smoke bombs exploded 31.10.18 (Lt JN Bissell & Lt EW Bragg killed)

B8943 Grand Fleet SoAF&G by 9.19 - @10.19

## 1 AIRCO D.H.9 TRACTOR BIPLANE BOMBERS from batch B9331 to B9430 built by Vulcan Motor & Engineering Co (1906) Ltd.

B9346 1 AI to 211 Sqdn but COL 26.6.18 (Lt CM Ducking); Flying again 28.6.18; Hit by AA nr Zeebrugge, FL in sea 4m N of Nieuport 17.35 13.7.18 (2/Lt W Gilman & Pte1 WJ Atkinson both drowned) [BUT credited Flgm Blaass, Marine Jasta 3]; SOC in field 13.7.18

B9348 1 AI to 211 Sqdn 24.6.18; 2 ASD 22.2.19

B9369 (230-hp Puma) Deld 1 AAP Coventry 7.18; 491 Flt 233 Sqdn Dover 9.7.18; EF, FL in sea and sank, attempted salve Dover Harbour 8.8.18 (Lt HG Sullivan & 2/Lt CD Churchill unhurt); WOC 1.9.18

B9370 Deld 1 AAP Coventry 7.18; 491 Flt Dover 26.7.18; Stalled landing, port wing hit ground, u/c collapsed, badly damaged 29.8.18 (Lt DL Melvin); ARS Dover by 30.8.18; Retd 491 Flt 233 Sqdn Dover by 12.18

B9371 Deld 1 AAP Coventry by 7.18; 491 Flt 233 Sqdn Dover 20.7.18

B9386 Deld 6 SD Ascot W/E 18.7.18; Shipped to Adriatic Group 10.8.18; Mudros by 10.18 - @1.19; 226 Sqdn Otranto

B9387 Deld 6 SD Ascot W/E 18.7.18; Shipped to Adriatic Group 10.8.18; 226 Sqdn Otranto; Taranto by 10.18 - @1.19

B9388 Deld 6 SD Ascot W/E 18.7.18; Shipped to Adriatic Group 15.8.18; AD Taranto by 17.8.18; 226 Sqdn Otranto; Mudros by 10.18 - @1.19. To White Russian Forces

B9389 Deld 6 SD Ascot W/E 25.7.18; Shipped to Adriatic Group 15.8.18; 226 Sqdn Otranto; Mudros by 10.18 - @1.19

B9390 Deld 6 SD Ascot W/E 25.7.18; Shipped to Adriatic Group 15.8.18; 226 Sqdn by 2.10.18; Mudros by 10.18 - @1.19

B9391 Deld 6 SD Ascot W/E 25.7.18; Shipped to Adriatic Group 15.8.18; AD Taranto by 17.8.18; 226 Sqdn by 2.10.18; Taranto by 10.18; Mudros by 10.18 - @1.19

B9392 Deld 6 SD Ascot W/E 1.8.18; Shipped to Aegean Group 15.8.18; 226 Sqdn Pizzone; Taranto by 10.18; AD Taranto to 'X' AD 28.6.19

B9393 Deld 6 SD Ascot W/E 1.8.18; To Docks W/E 12.9.18; Shipped to Mudros 13.9.18; Mudros by 10.18 - @1.19; To White Russian Forces

B9418 1 Observers School Eastchurch by 10.18; Became 2 MOS Eastchurch 28.12.18 - @1.19

B9419 2 MOS Eastchurch by 3.19 - @7.19

## 6 HANDLEY PAGE O/400 TRACTOR BIPLANE HEAVY BOMBERS from batch B9446 to B9451 built at Cricklewood. (Two 320-hp Sunbeam Cossack)

B9446 Deld Kingsbury Works to Hendon 7.1.18; Cranwell 8.1.18 (D/F wireless devt trials); Hendon 16.2.18; Cranwell 21.2.18 (continuing trials); Stonehenge 23.3.18 (transit); Biggin Hill 24.3.18; Hendon 2.4.18; Netheravon 24.4.18; 97 Sqdn; 115 Sqdn from 12.7.18; 1 SoN&BD Stonehenge

B9447 Deld Kingsbury Works to Hendon 12.1.18; On nose taxying, slightly damaged 21.1.18 (Gordon Bell unhurt); HP Works, Cricklewood 4.3.18; For delivery by 30.3.18, allocated HP Sqdn Stonehenge

B9448 Deld HP Sqdn Stonehenge 16.2.18 - @1.3.18; 1 SoN&BD Stonehenge by 7.6.18 - @16.6.18

B9449 HP for schools by 23.2.18; Deld 2 AAP Hendon 3.18; Cranwell by 22.3.18; Became 201/2 TDS Cranwell 1.4.18; 213 TDS Cranwell 17.6.18; Became 58 TDS Cranwell 27.7.18 - @31.7.18

B9450 HP for schools by 23.2.18; Deld 2 AAP Hendon 3.18; Cranwell by 3.18; Became 201/2 TDS Cranwell 1.4.18 - @13.5.18

B9451 HP for schools by 23.2.18; Deld Hendon to Cranwell W/E 8.3.18; Became 201/2 TDS Cranwell 1.4.18; COL 21.5.18 (PFO HC Price & F/L JLA Sinclair)

## 25 AIRCO D.H.4 TRACTOR BIPLANE BOMBERS ordered under Cont No A.S.29679 from Westland Aircraft Works and numbered B9476 to 9500, to be built at Yeovil. All to RNAS. (200-hp B.H.P unless otherwise stated)

B9476 Deld CSD White City 11.17; Shipped to 2 Wing Mudros 19.12.17 (no engine); Mudros by 3.18; Surveyed 2.3.18 (wrecked and burnt); Deleted 15.4.18

B9477 Deld CSD White City 11.17; Shipped to 2 Wing Mudros 2.1.18 (no engine); Mudros for erection by 4.3.18 - @24.3.18; Stavros by 6.18 & @4.8.18; Stavros by 10.18; Andrano by 10.18; Mudros by 10.18 (with Greeks); 220 Sqdn Imbros by 20.10.18 - @2.11.18

B9478 Deld Hendon W/E 17.11.17; Cranwell W/E 1.12.17; Became 201/2 TDS Cranwell 1.4.18; To Redcar but FL nr Redcar 5.5.18

B9479 Deld Cranwell W/E 7.12.17 - @30.3.18; Crashed 28.1.18 (pilot unhurt); Became 201/2 TDS Cranwell 1.4.18; 202 TDS 17.6.18 Cranwell; Became 57 TDS Cranwell 27.7.18 - @11.18

B9480 Deld Observers School Flt Eastchurch W/E 24.11.17; HP Sqdn Manston 28.11.17; DH4 School Manston 19.1.18; Became 203 TDS Manston 1.4.18; Became 55 TDS Manston (coded '6') 14.7.18; 55 TDS Narborough 9.18 - @10.18

B9481 Deld HP Sqdn Manston by 21.12.17; DH4 School Manston 19.1.18; Deleted W/E 26.1.18

B9482 Deld HP Sqdn Manston 28.11.17; DH4 School Manston 19.1.18; Became 203 TDS Manston 1.4.18 - @7.18

B9483 Deld CSD White City 12.17; Hendon W/E 8.12.17; Collided with searchlight, badly damaged 11.12.17 (W/Cdr AM Longmore & PO Lee both injured); Surveyed 14.12.17; Deleted 19.12.18 DBR

B9484 Deld CSD White City 12.17; Hendon W/E 8.12.17; Dover 22.12.17; Paris 23.12.17; In transit by air to Otranto by 18.1.18; DH Flt 6 Wing Otranto by 21.3.18; Became 224 Sqdn Otranto 1.4.18; Became 496/8 Flts 224 Sqdn Otranto 9.18 - @10.18; Taranto by 10.18 - @1.19

B9485 Deld CSD White City 11.17; Shipped to 2 Wing Mudros 2.1.18; recd Mudros for erection by 24.3.18; 63 Wing 1.4.18; Nosedived after TO, BO 17.4.18 (2/Lt JH Taylor & 2/Lt CC Betts both killed); Surveyed 20.4.18 wrecked; Deleted 11.5.18 wrecked

B9486 Deld HP Sqdn Manston by road/rail W/E 26.11.17; DH4 School Manston (coded '8') 19.1.18; Became 203 TDS Manston 1.4.18 - @7.18

B9487 Deld HP Sqdn Manston by road/rail by 26.11.17; DH4 School Manston (coded '9') 19.1.18; Became 203 TDS Manston 1.4.18; Became 55 TDS Manston (coded '9') 14.7.18; 55 TDS Narborough 9.18 - @11.18

B9488 (190-hp Renault) Deld Cranwell for erection W/E 30.11.17; Became 201/2 TDS Cranwell 1.4.18 - @6.18

B9489 Deld Cranwell for erection W/E 30.11.17 - @23.2.18;

|  | Became 202 TDS Cranwell 1.4.18; Became 57 TDS Cranwell 27.7.18 - @10.18 |
| --- | --- |
| B9490 | Deld HP Sqdn Manston by road/rail W/E 27.11.17; DH4 School Manston (coded '10') 19.1.18; Became 203 TDS Manston 1.4.18 - @5.18; 4 ASD by 25.10.18 |
| B9491 | Deld HP Sqdn Manston by road/rail W/E 30.11.17; DH4 School Manston (coded '9') 19.1.18; Became 203 TDS Manston 1.4.18; Landed on port wing and crashed 12.6.18 |
| B9492 | Deld CSD by 1.12.17; Shipped to 2 Wing Mudros 19.1.18 (no engine); arr Mudros by 3.18; 220 Sqdn Imbros by 19.6.18 - @25.6.18; Mudros Repair Base by 10.18 |
| B9493 | Deld CSD White City 11.17; Shipped to 2 Wing Mudros 2.1.18 (no engine); Mudros (coded 'Z') by 3.18 |
| B9494 | (190-hp Renault) Deld Cranwell for erection W/E 22.12.17; Became 201/2 TDS Cranwell 1.4.18 |
| B9495 | (190-hp Renault) Deld Cranwell for erection W/E 7.12.17; Crashed, u/c damaged Cranwell North 5.4.18 (pilot unhurt); Flat spin, then spinning nose dive into ground 9.5.18 (PFO RJW Taylor killed) |
| B9496 | Deld Cranwell W/E 7.12.17; Crashed landing, slightly damaged 28.3.18 (pilot unhurt); Became 202 TDS 1.4.18; Crashed nr Avro 13.6.18 (PFO HE Foster slightly injured) |
| B9497 | Deld EAD Grain W/E 7.12.17 (fit Stokes gun); AP Dover 22.2.18; 11 Sqdn 8.3.18; 12 Sqdn 19.3.18; Crashed 30.3.18; To ADD; Deleted 8.4.18 |
| B9498 | Deld EAD Grain W/E 15.12.17 (fit Stokes gun); AP Dover 27.2.18; 11 Sqdn 20.3.18; Became 211 Sqdn 1.4.18; Overshot landing 8.4.18 (Lt N Haigh & Lt CL Bray both unhurt); 4 ASD Guines 8.4.18; Deleted 8.4.18 |
| B9499 | Deld AP Dover (via Chingford) 11.12.17; 6 Sqdn 19.1.18; 11 Sqdn 11.3.18; Became 211 Sqdn 1.4.18; 4 ASD Guines 9.4.18; 218 Sqdn by 3.5.18; Dover W/E 24.5.18; 4 ASD Pilots Pool 26.6.18 - @9.7.18 |
| B9500 | Deld Hendon (via Brooklands) 14.12.17; Dover 22.12.17; Paris 23.12.17; Transit by air to 6 Wing by 18.1.18; DH4 Flt 6 Wing Otranto by 3.18; Became 224 Sqdn 1.4.18 - @8.18; Damaged by seaplanes 13.6.18 (Lt EL Bragg & Lt PE Linder unhurt) |

**1 SOPWITH 7F.1 SNIPE TRACTOR BIPLANE FIGHTER PROTOTYPE. (230-hp BR.2)**

| B9963 | RAE from 23.11.17; Brooklands by 3.18; Hendon 20.3.18 (for use of Air Department officers); 1 (Comms) Sqdn Hendon 23.7.18 - @12.18 |
| --- | --- |

**20 BLACKBURN R.T.1 KANGAROO TRACTOR BIPLANE TORPEDO PATROL BOMBERS ordered under Cont No A.S.7469 (BR.33) and numbered B9970 to B9989, to be built at Leeds. Originally to have been N1720 to N1739. (Two 250-hp Falcon II)**

| B9970 | Deld AES Martlesham Heath 3.1.18 (performance tests); FF 3.1.18; u/c collapsed 19.1.18; Dismantled and packed from 9.3.18; retd Mkrs by rail 27.4.18; 4 AAP Lincoln by 9.5.18 for Seaton Carew (NTU?); Became G-EAOW |
| --- | --- |
| B9971 | Deld 4 AAP Lincoln by 27.4.18 for No.18 Group; Tadcaster 2.5.18 (transit); 252 Sqdn Seaton Carew by 9.5.18 (495 Flt from 30.5.18); Dropped 2 bombs on U-boat submarine 1½m ENE of H Buoy, Robin Hood's Bay, oil and bubbles seen 10.5.18 (Lt EF Waring & Lt AP Knightbridge); Fuel failure, FL on sea 1½m NE of North Cheek, Robin Hood's Bay, towed to Robin Hood's Bay 31.5.18 (Lt ES Dean unhurt & Sig WC Hazelwood slightly injured) |
| B9972 | Deld 4 AAP Lincoln by 5.18; 252 Sqdn Seaton Carew 10.5.18 (495 Flt from 30.5.18); Visit to Killingholme 4.6.18 but landed Stallingborough; Dropped 2x230-lb bombs on U-boat 18m SE of South Hartlepool 8.6.18 (Lt RR Richardson & 2/Lt J Hirst); Bombed U-boat 5445N 0042W, oil and bubbles seen 9.6.18 (Lt RR Richardson); Dropped 2x230-lb bombs on U-boat 5m SE of North Buoy 5448N 0110W 13.6.18 (Lt RR Richardson); Dropped 2 bombs on U-boat 5439N 0055W 28.7.18 (Lt ES Dean & Lt AP Knightbridge); Became 495 Flt 246 Sqdn 8.18 - @17.10.18; Became G-EAKQ |
| B9973 | Deld 4 AAP Lincoln 8.5.18; 252 Sqdn Seaton Carew |

|  | 10.5.18 (495 Flt from 30.5.18); Dropped 2x230-lb bombs on U-boat 5425N 0025W 30.5.18 (Lt ES Dean & Lt AP Knightbridge); Became 495 Flt 246 Sqdn Seaton Carew 8.18 - @16.10.18; Became G-EAIU; Scrapped 1930 |
| --- | --- |
| B9974 | Deld 4 AAP Lincoln 5.18; 252 Sqdn Seaton Carew 17.5.18 (495 Flt from 30.5.18); Damaged landing 25.5.18 (2 crew unhurt); Anti-Submarine Inshore Patrol Observers School Aldeburgh |
| B9975 | Deld 4 AAP Lincoln .18; 495 Flt 252 Sqdn Seaton Carew by 6.18; Dropped 2 bombs on U-boat 5425N 020W, failed to explode, HMS *Kempenfelt* to position 28.7.18 (Lt RR Richardson & 2/Lt J Hirst); Became 495 Flt 246 Sqdn Seaton Carew 8.18; Dropped 2x230-lb bombs on U-boat 5438N 0052W, bubbles seen 3.9.18 (Lt RR Richardson & AM Taplin) |
| B9976 | Deld 4 AAP Lincoln 6.6.18; 495 Flt 252 Sqdn Seaton Carew 6.6.18; Dropped 2x230-lb bombs on U-boat 12m SE of Seaham 28.7.18 (Lt EF Waring & Lt DL Brocklesby); Became 495 Flt 246 Sqdn Seaton Carew 8.18; Crashed landing in bad visibility, TW 26.8.18 (2 crew unhurt) |
| B9977 | Deld 4 AAP Lincoln 18.6.18; 495 Flt 252 Sqdn Seaton Carew 23.6.18; Became 495 Flt 246 Sqdn Seaton Carew 8.18 - @19.10.18; Became G-EAMJ |
| B9978 | Deld 4 AAP Lincoln 6.18; 495 Flt 252 Sqdn Seaton Carew 29.6.18; Became 495 Flt 246 Sqdn Seaton Carew by 16.8.18 - @30.10.18; Bombed U-boat 5423N 022W oil and bubbles seen, and another 5420N 022W oil and bubbles seen 27.8.18 (Lt CH Cooper & AM Twigg); Became G-EAIT; Crashed & WO Brough 25.5.25 |
| B9979 | Deld 4 AAP Lincoln 7.18; 495 Flt 252 Sqdn Seaton Carew 13.7.18; Tested 14.7.18; Became 495 Flt 246 Sqdn Seaton Carew by 16.8.18 - @16.10.18 |
| B9980 | Deld 4 AAP Lincoln 7.18; 495 Flt 252 Sqdn Seaton Carew 25.7.18; Became 495 Flt 246 Sqdn Seaton Carew by 16.8.18 - @10.18 |
| B9981 | Deld 4 AAP Lincoln 7.18; 495 Flt 252 Sqdn Seaton Carew 7.18; Tested 1.8.18; Became 495 Flt 246 Sqdn Seaton Carew by 16.8.18 - @30.10.18; Sold to Grahame-White Aviation Co Ltd, to Hendon 11.5.19; Became G-EADE; Crashed & WO 7.19 |
| B9982 | Deld 4 AAP Lincoln 8.18; 495 Flt 246 Sqdn Seaton Carew by 28.8.18 - @10.18; Sold to Grahame-White Aviation Co Ltd, to Hendon 11.5.19; Became G-EADF; Crashed on TO, wrecked Hendon 31.5.19 |
| B9983 | Deld 4 AAP Lincoln 8.18; 495 Flt 246 Sqdn Seaton Carew 8.18 - @18.10.18; Dropped 520-lb bomb on *UC70* in Runswick Bay (5431N 0040W), oil and bubbles seen, later sunk by DCs dropped by destroyer HMS *Ouse* 28.8.18 (Lt EF Waring recommended DFC, 2/Lt HJ Smith & Sig Reed); Crashed at Seaton Carew, WO |
| B9984 | MOS Aldeburgh by 9.18; Became Anti-Submarine Inshore Patrol Observers School Aldeburgh 28.12.18; Became 1 MOS Aldeburgh 1.1.19 - @2.19 |
| B9985 | Sold to Grahame-White Aviation Co Ltd, to Hendon 11.5.19; Became G-EADG |
| B9986 | MOS Aldeburgh by 11.18; Became Anti-Submarine Inshore Patrol Observers School Aldeburgh 28.12.18; Became 1 MOS Aldeburgh 1.1.19 |
| B9987 | 1 MOS Aldeburgh from 1.19 - 2.19 |
| B9988 | Not deld by 11.18. In service 1.19 |
| B9989 | Not deld by 11.18. No details of service |

NB. 495 Flt transferred to 256 Sqdn at Sea Houses by 1.3.19, but no serials have come to light for this period

**81 SOPWITH F.1 CAMEL TRACTOR BIPLANE SCOUTS from batch C1 to C200 built by Nieuport & General Aircraft Co Ltd at Cricklewood. (130-hp Clerget LS, some re-engined)**

| C1 | 42 TS Wye by 2.18; Shipped to Aegean; 220 Sqdn Imbros by 1.11.18 |
| --- | --- |
| C17 | Deld 2 AAP Hendon for erection W/E 16.2.18; War School Manston W/E 23.3.18; Became Pool of Pilots Manston 1.4.18; FL Sandwich, Kent 10.5.18 (FSL SA Hamilton-Bowyer); 205 TDS Vendôme by 6.18; Port wheel came off taxying, went on nose, damaged 29.6.18 (Mjr BPH de Roeper); Stalled at 400ft on gliding turn, spun in 1.11.18 (F/Cdt GH Reeks seriously injured) |

C18 Deld 2 AAP Hendon for erection W/E 16.3.18; To Pool of Pilots Manston 4.18; Freiston 3.5.18

C19 (Convtd 2-seater) Deld 2 AAP Hendon for erection W/E 16.3.18; Pool of Pilots Manston 6.4.18; Eastbourne 3.6.18; U/c smashed 4.6.18 (2/Lt LB Irish unhurt); 50 TDS Eastbourne by @1.11.18

C20 Deld 2 AAP Hendon for erection W/E 16.2.18; Cranwell 20.3.18; To USA

C21 Deld 2 AAP Hendon for erection W/E 16.2.18; Cranwell W/E 23.3.18; 4 FS Freiston by 10.18

C22 Deld 2 AAP Hendon W/E 16.2.18; Cranwell 4.5.18

C23 Deld 2 AAP Hendon for erection W/E 16.2.18; Cranwell W/E 23.3.18; Became 201/2 TDS Cranwell 1.4.18; Became 56/57 TDS Cranwell 27.7.18 - @11.18

C24 Deld 2 AAP Hendon for erection W/E 16.2.18; Cranwell 21.3.18; Became 201/2 TDS Cranwell 1.4.18; Freiston (coded 'C') 4.5.18; Overturned; 56/57 TDS Cranwell by 7.18

C25 Deld 2 AAP Hendon for erection W/E 16.2.18; Cranwell 21.3.18; Became 201/2 TDS Cranwell 1.4.18; Crashed, wings damaged 4.4.18 (pilot unhurt); 4 SoAF&G Freiston 20.5.18; Spun in while turning nr ground 26.6.18 (2/Lt JW Dowling killed)

C26 Deld 2 AAP Hendon for erection W/E 16.2.18; War School Manston W/E 23.3.18; Became Pool of Pilots Manston 1.4.18 - @9.18

C27 Deld 2 AAP Hendon for erection W/E 16.2.18; War School Manston W/E 9.3.18; 4 SoAF&G Freiston 3.5.18; Became 4 FS Freiston 7.18; Lost speed turning nr ground, crashed 10.8.18 (2/Lt SR Pragnall)

C28 Deld 2 AAP Hendon for erection W/E 23.2.18; War School Manston; W/E 9.3.18; For deletion by 30.3.18; Presume rebuilt; 485/6 Flts 273 Sqdn Burgh Castle; HMS *Argus* by 6.20; Delny 4.6.20; HMS *Argus* 25.6.20 - @8.20; Bought for American Expeditionary Force; To USA and became civil NC3938

C29 Deld 2 AAP Hendon for erection W/E 23.2.18; War School Manston 10.3.18; Went into ground during low stunting 26.3.18 (2/Lt JE Pullen killed); Deleted W/E 30.3.18

C30 Deld 2 AAP Hendon for erection W/E 23.2.18; Cranwell 14.3.18; CFS Upavon by 15.5.18; Cranwell 201/2 TDS by 8.6.18

C31 (80-hp Le Rhône) Deld 2 AAP Hendon for erection W/E 23.2.18; Cranwell 22.3.18; FL, u/c damaged, Metheringham, Lincs 27.3.18 (pilot unhurt); Became 201/2 TDS Cranwell 1.4.18

C32 Deld 2 AAP Hendon for erection W/E 23.2.18, for Cranwell

C33 Deld 2 AAP Hendon for erection W/E 23.2.18; Cranwell 15.3.18; Crashed, propeller and wings damaged, Cranwell South 23.3.18 (pilot unhurt); Became 201/2 TDS Cranwell 1.4.18; E Flt Freiston

C34 Deld 2 AAP Hendon for erection W/E 23.2.18; Cranwell 20.3.18; Became 201/2 TDS Cranwell 1.4.18; 4 FS Freiston (coded 'E'), crashed

C35 Deld 2 AAP Hendon for erection W/E 23.2.18; Cranwell 14.3.18; Became 201/2 TDS Cranwell 1.4.18

C36 Deld 2 AAP Hendon for erection W/E 23.2.18; Cranwell 14.3.18; Became 201/2 TDS Cranwell 1.4.18

C37 Deld CSD 3.18; Shipped to Mudros 13.3.18; Repair Base Mudros by 25.7.18

C38 Deld CSD 3.18; Shipped to Mudros 13.3.18; Repair Base Mudros by 25.7.18

C39 Deld CSD 3.18; Shipped to Mudros 13.3.18; F Sqdn 2 Wing Mudros by 5.18; Repair Base Mudros by 25.7.18

C40 Deld CSD 3.18; Shipped to Mudros 13.3.18; Repair Base Mudros by 5.18; Repair Base Mudros by 25.8.18 - @1.19; 222 Sqdn Mudros by 28.10.18

C41 Deld CSD 3.18; Shipped to Mudros 13.3.18; D Sqdn Stavros .18; Repair Base Mudros by 25.7.18 - @10.18; Stavros @25.9.18 - @1.19; RAF South Russia to HQ Russian Aviation Corps 8.19

C42 Deld CSD 3.18; Shipped to 6 Wing 18.3.18; 226 Sqdn by 28.4.18; Became 472/4 Flts 226 Sqdn Pizzone 9.18 - @1.19; BUT Convtd 2-seater CFS Upavon .18 (painted all white and named 'WHITE FEATHER'); Grand Fleet SoAF&G Leuchars by 7.19

C43 Deld CSD 3.18; Shipped to 6 Wing 13.3.18; 226 Sqdn by 28.4.18; Became 472/4 Flt 226 Sqdn Pizzone 9.18 - @1.19; COL Durazzo 22.10.18 (FSL AC Getley)

C44 Deld CSD 3.18; Shipped to 6 Wing 18.3.18; 66 Wing by 7.4.18; 226 Sqdn by 28.4.18; Became 472/4 Flts 226 Sqdn Pizzone 9.18 - @1.19

C45 Deld CSD 3.18; Shipped to 6 Wing 18.3.18; 66 Wing by 7.4.18; 226 Sqdn by 28.4.18; Became 472/4 Flts 226 Sqdn Pizzone 9.18 - @10.18

C46 Deld CSD 3.18; At docks by 30.3.18 for shipment to Otranto; Shipped to 66 Wing 21.4.18 (diverted?); 14 Wing Taranto by 8.18; 66 Sqdn by 1.8.18 - @27.10.18; 2 HA shot down 1.8.18 (Lt TH Timmis); 2-str shot down 5.8.18 (Capt CE Maude)

C47 Deld CSD 3.18; At docks by 30.3.18 for shipment to Mudros; Shipped to Mudros 21.4.18

C48 Deld CSD 3.18; At docks by 30.3.18 for shipment to Mudros; Shipped to Mudros 21.4.18

C49 Deld CSD 3.18; At docks by 30.3.18 for shipment to Mudros; Shipped to Mudros 21.4.18; Mudros by 7.18 - @1.19; D Sqdn Stavros by 25.9.18; H.2 Flt RHNAS Stavros by 10.18

C50 Deld CSD 3.18; At docks by 30.3.18 for shipment to Mudros; Shipped to Mudros 21.4.18

C51 Deld CSD 3.18; Shipped to Mudros 25.3.18; Mudros by 7.18; Stavros by 8.18 - @9.18; 220 Sqdn Imbros by 28.10.18 - @2.11.18; Mudros by 10.18 - @1.19; RAF South Russia to HQ Russian Aviation Corps 8.19

C52 Deld CSD 3.18; Shipped to 6 Wing Otranto 25.3.18 (diverted?); Taranto by 5.18 - @8.18

C53 Deld CSD 3.18; At docks by 30.3.18 for shipment to Otranto; Shipped to 66 Wing 9.4.18; 226 Sqdn by 25.5.18; Became 472/4 Flt 226 Sqdn Pizzone 9.18 - @11.18

C54 Deld CSD 3.18; At docks by 30.3.18 for shipment to Otranto; Shipped to 66 Wing 9.4.18; 226 Sqdn by 25.5.18 - @6.18; Disposed of by 25.7.18; 45 Sqdn Italy by 8.18; 2-str shot down Fodalti 10.8.18; 2-str shot down 20.8.18 (both Lt EH Masters); 45 Sqdn France by 11.18

C55 Deld CSD 3.18; At docks by 30.3.18 for shipment to Otranto; Shipped to 66 Wing 9.4.18; 226 Sqdn by 25.5.18 - @6.18; Disposed of by 25.7.18; 14 Wing Taranto by 8.18

C56 Deld CSD 3.18; At docks by 30.3.18 for shipment to Otranto; Shipped to 66 Wing 9.4.18; 226 Sqdn by 25.5.18 - @6.18; AD Taranto by 7.18; 481/3 Flts 225 Sqdn Andrano by 8.18 (and 10.18 - @11.18?); Taranto by 11.18

C57 (DC) Deld 7 AAP Kenley by 30.3.18 for Eastbourne NFS; Convtd 2-str; 206 TDS Eastbourne 2.5.18; Became 50 TDS Eastbourne 15.7.18 - @1.11.18

C58 Deld 1 SD 3.18; Rec Pk to 209 Sqdn 7.5.18; Returning from visit to French aerodrome at Vignacourt, sideslipped on TO, nosedived, CW 22.5.18 (Lt CT Evans USAS injured); 2 ASD 24.5.18; SOC 24.5.18 Not worth repair

C59 (BR.1) Deld 1 SD 3.18; Rec Pk to 2 AI 18.5.18; 209 Sqdn 25.5.18; Turned to starboard on TO, o/t 1.6.18 (Lt RW Snoke USAS unhurt); to 2 ASD; 2 AI to 209 Sqdn 12.8.18; Overshot, crashed into hangars Bertangles 21.8.18 (Lt L Belloc unhurt); 1 ASD 23.8.18; Rebuilt as H7093 6.9.18

C60 Deld 1 SD 3.18; 6 SD Ascot W/E 15.8.18; Shipped to Mudros 6.9.18; Mudros by 10.18 - @11.18

C61 (refitted BR.1) Deld Dover W/E 30.3.18; 1 AI to 203 Sqdn 22.4.18; DFW CV OOC N of Estaires, shared D3353 11.40 15.5.18; Pfalz DIII in flames Estaires-Merville, shared B6408, B7197 & D3362, 11.15 badly shot about 17.5.18 (both 2/Lt CF Brown); Rep Pk 1 ASD 23.6.18; Rec Pk 1 AD 24.6.18; 2 AI by 7.18; 209 Sqdn 5.7.18; Fokker DVII crashed Bailleul, shared F5925 09.45 1.8.18; Halberstadt C in flames Harbonnières, shared C142, C199, D9588 & D9625 19.05 8.8.18; Fokker DVII down SW of Froyart 09.05, pilot surrendered to British infantry 12.8.18 [numberd G/5Bde/20] (all Capt RM Foster DFC); Collided with Lt JE Gibbons and buckled centre section 23.8.18 (Capt RM Foster DFC uninjured); Fokker DVII OOC smoking Récourt-Dury 10.40 30.8.18; Fokker DVII crashed just N of Rumilly 17.00 & Fokker DVII crashed nr Saudemont, pilot wounded 17.15 15.9.18; Pfalz DXII OOC Athies 07.30 4.11.18 (all Capt RM Foster DFC); 1 ASD 14.1.19

358

*Lt R Stone and Capt LH Rochford standing in front of Sopwith Camel C61 of 203 Sqdn. (via Frank Cheesman)*

*Airco D.H.6 C5194 of 250 Sqdn Padstow, seen at Newlyn after being salved by a collier following a ditching in the sea on 4 July 1918. (via Frank Cheesman)*

*Boulton & Paul P.3 Bobolink C8655, an unsuccessful shipboard fighter flown at Hendon and Martlesham Heath.*

C62 (refitted BR.1) Deld Dover W/E 30.3.18; 4 ASD Guines to 210 Sqdn 20.4.18; Albatros C crashed 1m N of Aubers, shared B6242 & D3364 16.15 9.5.18 (Lt FV Hall); Albatros DV OOC Menin-Courtrai 07.10 20.5.18; KB dest Pont Riqueuel, E of Lestrem, shared B7227 & D3401 17.10 21.5.18; Albatros DV crashed E of Bailleul 17.00 26.5.18; Pfalz DIII OOC Bailleul, shared B7153 08.10 27.5.18 (all Lt CW Payton); FL nr 32 KBS 3.6.18 (Lt A Baird); Night patrol, attempt to TO from FL, but port tyre came off, swerved and o/t, badly damaged nr 32 KBS 3.6.18 (Capt WGR Hinchliffe injured); 1 ASD 3.6.18; Rebuilt as F5945 25.6.18

C63 (refitted BR.1) Deld Dover W/E 30.3.18; 1 AI by 4.18; EF on TO, ran into side of hangar, badly damaged 21.4.18 (2/Lt CBH Lefroy unhurt); 4 ASD Guines by 27.4.18 - @31.5.18; Rec Pk 1 ASD to 2 ASD 11.6.18; 201 Sqdn 26.6.18; COL, hit trees 8.8.18 (Lt CE Hill injured); 2 ASD 10.8.18

C64 (refitted BR.1) Dover W/E 30.3.18; 4 ASD Guines to 201 Sqdn 20.4.18; LVG C crashed nr Tilloy, SE of Arras 08.15 13.6.18 (Capt HR de Wilde); Fokker DVII OOC Bray, believed crashed in River Somme 15.20 8.8.18 (Lt RCB Brading); 2 ASD 8.10.18 (fabric soggy etc)

C65 (refitted BR.1) Deld Dover W/E 30.3.18; 4 ASD Guines to 213 Sqdn 22.4.18; Albatros DV in flames after it had shot down a Belgian KB, 1m S of Woumen, shared B6239 17.35 19.5.18 (Vzfw Triebswetter, Jasta 16 killed); Pfalz DIII OOC Moorslede, shared B5687 & D3409 19.35 2.6.18; Albatros OOC in spin smoking 4m S of Dixmude, officially shared B7272, D3397, D3409 & D3411 (but probably only C65 in reality) 18.00 7.6.18; Hannover C, violet wings, white markings on tail OOC over Dickebusch Lake, S of Poperinghe, shared B7154 & B7229 17.45 15.6.18; Fokker DVII spun into sea after shooting down D.H.9 D5687 of 218 Sqdn Blankenberghe-Ostende 10.20 27.6.18 (all Capt JW Pinder); Spun on landing, CW 29.7.18 (2/Lt EC Toy unhurt); to 4 ASD; 4 ASD, test 6.9.18 - @11.18

C66 (Refitted BR.1) Mkrs by 30.3.18 for Dunkerque; 4 ASD to 213 Sqdn 22.4.18; Albatros DV in flames 15m N of Ostende 17.55 9.5.18 [BUT probably same a/c as claimed by N5969/McClure]; 2 Pfalz OOC, shared B7254, C73, D1866 & D3333 14.20 1.6.18 (all Lt GD Smith); Crashed on TO 25.6.18 (Lt WG Upton); 4 ASD 25.6.18; 204 Sqdn 4.8.18; Fokker DVII OOC at 11,000ft over Ghistelles 18.45 10.8.18; Fokker DVII OOC SE of Bailleul, shared D9628 19.15 13.8.18; Pfalz DIII crashed 5m E of Ypres & 2 HA (Fokker DVIIs?) OOC 3m E of Ypres 08.30 15.8.18 (all Capt AJB Tonks); Fokker DVII crashed 5m NE of Dixmude 10.25 20.9.18 (2/Lt FR Brown); Last seen 4/5m SE of Dixmude 18.50 25.9.18 (2/Lt T Warburton PoW); Deleted 30.9.18

C67 Deld 2 AAP Hendon W/E 3.3.18; Yarmouth W/E 4.4.18 - @5.18; 470 Flt Manston by 25.5.18 (detd from Yarmouth); Tongue Defence Flt by 6.18; Yarmouth 10.6.18; 80 Sqdn (coded 'R'), shot down in German lines by Jasta 11 pilot

C68 Deld 2 AAP Hendon W/E 3.3.18; Yarmouth W/E 4.4.18; Became 490 Flt Yarmouth by 25.5.18; HACP 10.6.18; Covehithe by 12.6.18 - @1.7.18; 273 Sqdn Burgh Castle by 30.7.18 - 16.8.18; 28 TDS Weston-on-the-Green by 12.18 (dual control)

C69 Deld 2 AAP Hendon by 3.3.18; Yarmouth W/E 4.4.18 - @5.18; detd 470 Flt Manston/Tongue Defence Flt by 25.5.18; Yarmouth 10.6.18 - @11.8.18; 28 TDS Weston-on-the-Green by 8.10.18 - @28.10.18 (tested)

C70 Deld 2 AAP Hendon W/E 3.3.18; Yarmouth W/E 4.4.18; Burgh Castle to Yarmouth 3.5.18; EF, FL, slightly damaged Westleton, nr Saxmundham 9.5.18; FL, Therberton Hall, 1m from Leiston 16.5.18; Became 490 Flt Yarmouth by 25.5.18 - @1.7.18; HACP 10.6.18

C71 Deld 2 AAP Hendon W/E 27.3.18; Dover by 27.4.18; 4 ASD Guines (fit BR.1) W/E 4.5.18; 213 Sqdn 2.6.18; 4 ASD 3.6.18; 4 ASD to 204 Sqdn 20.9.18; Fokker DVII in vertical dive believed hit, Melle 08.45 4.11.18 (2/Lt WE Baxter); 203 Sqdn 25.1.19; RTP W/E 23.2.19

C72 Deld 2 AAP Hendon W/E 27.3.18 - @27.4.18; 4 ASD Guines (fit BR.1) by 25.5.18; 204 Sqdn 17.6.18; 2 Fokker DVIIs Menin 19.05 15.8.18; Crashed on TO,

CW 22.8.18 (both Lt TW Nash); 4 ASD 22.8.18 - @25.10.18; Air Council Inspection Sqdn Croydon by 8.19 (L/Col ER Ludlow-Hewitt CMG, DSO, MC)

C73 Deld 2 AAP Hendon W/E 27.3.18; Dover by 27.4.18; 4 ASD Guines 3.5.18 (fit BR.1); 213 Sqdn 25.5.18; 2 Pfalz DIII OOC Bruge, shared B7254, C66, D1866 & D3333 14.20 1.6.18 (Lt FL Cattle); Albatros C OOC 7m NE of Dixmude, shared with D9649 09.55 11.8.18 (2/Lt DS Ingalls USNR) [but 5 Group reports 2 shared]; LM 15.8.18; 204 Sqdn from 4.10.18; Crashed on TO, o/t 26.10.18 (2/Lt EH Coote unhurt); 1 ASD 28.10.18

C74 Deld 2 AAP Hendon W/E 27.3.18; Dover by 27.4.18; 4 ASD Guines (fit BR.1) W/E 4.5.18; 204 Sqdn 21.5.18; Albatros DIII OOC Ostende 19.20 27.5.18; Pfalz DIII shot down into sea when attacking a D.H.4 200-300yds N of Nieuport Piers 15.30 12.6.18; Fokker DVII OOC 10m NE of Ypres 19.00 & Fokker DVII crashed 5m NE of Thourout 19.30 31.7.18; Fokker DVII OOC 5m E of Dixmude, shared D8187 11.00 14.8.18; Fokker DVII DD Varsennaere-Dixmude 08.30 15.8.18; Fokker DVII crashed, another OOC & a third in flames SE of Ypres, shared D8146 19.00 15.8.18; Fokker DVII OOC Blankenberghe-Zeebrugge 14.00, then severely damaged by flak 15.9.18 (all Capt CRR Hickey DFC); 4 ASD 15.9.18; Deleted 30.9.18 general fatigue

C75 Deld 2 AAP Hendon W/E 27.3.18; 4 ASD Guines (fitted BR.1) by 27.4.18; 204 Sqdn 5.5.18; Fokker DVII OOC Blankenburghe 14.45 30.6.18 (Capt AC Burt); Fokker DVII DD N of Roulers 11.15 31.7.18 (Capt AC Burt); LVG C, grey and black striped fuselage into sea Middelkerke 19.10 16.9.18; Light grey and yellow Fokker DVII OOC 5m NE of Dixmude 10.25 20.9.18 (both Lt GEC Howard); Missing 26.9.18 (Lt GEC Howard killed) [credited Flgm Engelfried, Marine Jasta 5 at Wenduyne]

C76 Deld 2 AAP Hendon W/E 27.3.18 - @27.4.18; 4 ASD Guines (fitted BR.1) by 25.5.18; 213 Sqdn 28.6.18; 4 ASD 12.8.18; 213 Sqdn 26.9.18; EF, FL rough ground N of Bergues 29.9.18 (2/Lt KG Ibison); 4 ASD 11.10.18 - @25.10.18; 11 AP by 1.19; 213 Sqdn 31.1.19; 11 AP 23.2.19; WOC 23.2.19

C93 Deld 2 AAP Hendon 4.18; 201/2 TDS Cranwell 25.4.18 - @6.18

C94 201/2 TDS Cranwell by 5.18

C124 (BR.1 later Clerget) Deld 2 AAP Hendon by 11.5.18; Rec Pk to 2 ASD 20.6.18; 209 Sqdn 7.7.18; O/t landing 12.7.18 (Lt DB Griffith); 2 ASD 19.7.18; 5 AI 3.10.18; 208 Sqdn 9.10.18; Landed cross-wind, turned on nose 1.11.18 (2/Lt TF McGuire); 7 SS 2.11.18 for 2 ASD

C125 Deld 2 AAP Hendon by 9.5.18; Rec Pk to 2 ASD 10.7.18; 201 Sqdn (coded 'H') 8.8.18; Last seen in combat with Fokker DVII S of Bourlon Wood, crashed nr Seronvillers 07.30 20.9.18 (2/Lt J Mill killed)

C138 Deld 6 SD Ascot by 25.5.18; Shipped from Liverpool to Mudros 26.6.18; 15 Group by 6.18; 221 Sqdn (D Sqdn) Stavros by 25.9.18 - @1.19

C139 (BR.1) Deld 2 AAP Hendon by 25.5.18 - @31.5.18; Rec Pk to 2 ASD 27.6.18; 201 Sqdn 2.7.18; Sideslipped landing in field, crashed 29.7.18 (2/Lt AC Forrest killed); SS 1 ASD 1.8.18 & deleted

C140 Deld 15.5.18; 6 SD Ascot by 25.5.18; Shipped from Liverpool to Mudros 26.6.18; 15 Group by 6.18; 221 Sqdn/D Sqdn Stavros by 8.18 - @1.19; 12 Sqdn Germany by 4.19 - @3.20

C141 (BR.1) Deld 2 AAP Hendon by 17.5.18; Rec Pk to 2 ASD 3.6.18; 2 AI by 6.18; 201 Sqdn 9.6.18; COL in corn, o/t 1.7.18 (Lt JA Parkinson unhurt); 2 ASD 2.7.18; 17th Aero Sqdn USAS by 8.18; Lost in action 24.8.18 (Lt HB Frost PoW); SOC 26.8.18

C142 (BR.1) Deld 2 AAP Hendon by 18.5.18; 2 AI to 209 Sqdn 10.7.18; Halberstadt C crashed in flames Harbonnières, shared C61, C199, D9588 & D9625 19.05 8.8.18 (Lt JE Gibbons); COL, o/t 10.8.18 (Lt JE Gibbons unhurt); 2 ASD 11.8.18; Rebuilt as F6250 17.8.18

C143 (BR.1) Deld 2 AAP Hendon by 20.5.18; Rec Pk to 2 ASD 4.6.18; 2 AI by 6.18; 201 Sqdn 11.6.18; 2 Fokker DVII OOC St.Christ, shared B5749 & C196 11.00 12.8.18 (Capt HR de Wilde); Badly shot up by Fokkers 13.8.18 (2/Lt GH Fowles); Hit rut landing 3.10.18 (2/Lt J Paton unhurt); to 2 ASD

C144 (BR.1) Deld 2 AAP Hendon by 18.5.18; Rec Pk to 1 AI 8.6.18; 210 Sqdn 10.6.18; 2-str seaplane crashed in sea 3m N of Ostende 19.00-19.10 7.8.18 (Lt AS Highstone); Crashed on TO avoiding telegraph wires after engine choked 13.8.18 (Lt AS Highstone); 4 ASD Audembert to 204 Sqdn 9.10.18; Last seen in dogfight with 30/40 Fokker DVII over St.Denis Westrem 09.10 27.10.18 (2/Lt N Smith PoW)

C191 Rec Pk to 2 AI 13.8.18; 2 AI to 201 Sqdn 2.9.18; Fokker DVII crashed in flames Bois de Pincemaille 14.50 9.11.18 (2/Lt MI Ashley); To 203 Sqdn Boisdinghem but FL St.Quentin en route 23.1.19; Boisdinghem 27.1.19 for breaking up

C192 Rec Pk to 2 AI 16.8.18; To 203 Sqdn but engine trouble landing on arrival, hit weather vane 16.8.18 (Lt CA Bouchier unhurt); to RP 1 ASD (salvage) 26.8.18; Rebuilt as F6468 26.8.18

C193 201 Sqdn by 2.7.18; Rep Pk 1 ASD to 2 AI 7.7.18; 209 Sqdn 13.7.18; Left 04.15, shot down nr Cappy aerodrome by Flakbatterie 82, 19.7.18 (Lt DB Griffith killed); SOC 19.7.18

C194 2 AI to 209 Sqdn 5.7.18; Hit by ground m/g fire, FL No Mans Land nr Beaucourt, CW 8.8.18 (Lt WA Rollason unhurt); Collected by 22 Wing SS 8.8.18; Salved by No.6 SS, 5 Brigade 8.18

C195 Rec Pk to 2 ASD 9.8.18; 201 Sqdn 12.8.18; O/t on landing, badly damaged 2.1.19 (2/Lt VSG Hawkins unhurt)

C196 (BR.1) Deld 2 AAP Hendon by 13.6.18; Rec Pk 1 to 2 ASD 9.7.18; 201 Sqdn 8.8.18; Fokker DVII OOC St.Christ, shared B5749 & C143 11.00 12.8.18 (Lt R McLaughlin); Fokker DVII OOC Cambrai 18.45 6.9.18 (2/Lt HJ Ewan); Fokker DVII BU SE of Cambrai 17.35 16.9.18 (Capt RCB Brading DFC); Hannover C, orange fuselage & white tail crashed E of Bavai 16.10 4.11.18; Fokker DVII crashed Bois de Clermont 11.40 10.11.18 (both Lt JA Parkinson); 203 Sqdn Boisdinghem 23.1.19; RTP W/E 9.2.19

C197 (BR.1) Deld 2 AAP Hendon by 13.6.18; Rec Pk to 2 ASD 10.8.18; 203 Sqdn 16.8.18; Hannover C spun OOC from 7,000ft Bois Bernard, crashed SE of Lens, shared D9597 09.00 24.9.18; Fokker DVII OOC almost certainly crashed Hem-Lenglet 08.30 28.9.18; Fokker DVII crashed nr Naves 13.30 1.10.18; Rumpler C in flames nr St.Aubert 16.30 9.10.18; Fokker DVII OOC, & another OOC shared D9597, both nr Vertain 16.35 23.10.18; Fokker DVII OOC Cauroir 08.45 2.10.18 (all Lt W Sidebottom); RTP W/E 9.2.19

C198 (BR.1) Deld 2 AAP Hendon by 13.6.18; Rec Pk to 2 AI 30.6.18; 209 Sqdn 7.7.18; Albatros C OOC crashed Grivesnes-le Plessier, shared D1891 11.00 18.7.18; Fokker DVII OOC N of Comines, shared B7471 & D6495 07.20 26.7.18 (both Capt JK Summers MC); Hit by ground m/g fire, returned damaged 8.8.18 (Capt JK Summers MC unhurt); 2 ASD 9.8.18; Rebuilt as F6240 14.8.18

C199 (BR.1) Deld 2 AAP Hendon by 13.6.18; Rec Pk to 2 AI 30.6.18; 209 Sqdn 6.7.18; Halberstadt C in flames N of Harbonnières, shared C61, C142, D9588 & D9625 19.05 8.8.18 (Lt MA Toomey); Longeron shot through S of Somme 10.8.18 (Lt MA Toomey unhurt); 2 ASD 11.8.18; Rebuilt as F6258 17.8.18

C200 (BR.1) Deld 2 AAP Hendon by 13.6.18; Rec Pk to 1 AI 6.7.18; 210 Sqdn 18.7.18; Halberstadt DD, observer shot NE of Dixmude 10.40 1.8.18; Fokker DVII OOC SE of Ostende 16.40 1.8.18 (both Lt AL Jones); Fokker DVII crashed nr Zonnebeke 07.25 9.8.18 (Lt WW Gyles); 4 ASD for survey 18.9.18; AP 4 ASD by 10.18, crashed; 4 ASD 18.10.18; 213 Sqdn 14.11.18; 11 AP 24.2:19; WOC 24.2.19

## 77 SOPWITH PUP TRACTOR BIPLANE SCOUTS from batch C201 to C550 built by the Standard Motor Co Ltd at Coventry. (90-hp Le Rhône unless otherwise stated)

C201 Deld Cranwell W/E 20.3.18; FL, u/c damaged nr Ancaster 20.3.18 (pilot unhurt); Became 201/2 TDS 1.4.18

C202 (80-hp Gnome) Deld Cranwell for erection W/E 19.1.18; Became 201/2 TDS 1.4.18; 95 Sqdn by 17.4.18

C205 (60-hp Le Rhône) Deld Cranwell for erection W/E 19.1.18; Became 201/2 TDS 1.4.18

C208 (80-hp Gnome) Deld Cranwell for erection W/E 18.1.18; Became 201/2 TDS 1.4.18

C211 Deld F Flt East Fortune NFS 11.1.18 - @30.3.18

C214 Deld F Flt East Fortune NFS 11.1.18; Donibristle W/E 21.3.18; HMS Furious W/E 21.3.18 (skid u/c tests with 9949; flown by W/Cdr HR Busteed); Rosyth W/E 20.3.18; Surveyed 18.3.18 (wrecked); Deleted 27.3.18 BUT to Turnhouse W/E 4.4.18; Deleted W/E 17.5.18

C217 Deld F Flt East Fortune W/E 19.1.18; Rosyth W/E 21.3.18; Turnhouse W/E 4.4.18 - @30.1.19

C220 Deld F Flt East Fortune NFS W/E 19.1.18 - @3.18

C223 Deld F Flt East Fortune NFS W/E 19.1.18 - @3.18; Manston by 4.18; Eastbourne 25.4.18; Grand Fleet SoAF&G Leuchars by 6.19

C226 Deld F Flt East Fortune NFS W/E 19.1.18; COL 15.4.18 (Lt SJN Haigh seriously injured)

C229 Deld War School Manston W/E 25.1.18; Became Pool of Pilots Manston 1.4.18; Eastbourne 25.4.18; COL 7.8.18 (pilot unhurt)

C232 Deld Cranwell W/E 9.2.18; Freiston, crashed and badly damaged 22.3.18 (pilot unhurt)

C235 (80hp Le Rhône) Deld Cranwell W/E 2.2.18 - @20.3.18; 32 TDS by 7.18; 36 Sqdn 6.7.18

C238 (60-hp Le Rhône later 80-hp Gnome) Deld Cranwell W/E 25.1.18; Became 201/2 TDS 1.4.18; Grand Fleet SoAF&G Leuchars by 3.19

C240 Pool of Pilots Manston by 6.18

C241 (80-hp Gnome) Deld Cranwell W/E 25.1.18; Became 201/2 TDS Cranwell 1.4.18

C244 Deld War School Manston W/E 25.1.18; Became Pool of Pilots Manston 1.4.18

C247 Deld War School Manston W/E 23.2.18; Became Pool of Pilots Manston 1.4.18 - @6.18; Shipped to Egypt?; 19 TDS El Rimal

C250 Deld War School Manston W/E 16.2.18; Became Pool of Pilots Manston 1.4.18 - @6.18; Shipped to Egypt; 'X' AD by 8.18; 19 TDS 5.8.18

C253 Deld War School Manston W/E 16.2.18; Became Pool of Pilots Manston 1.4.18; Eastbourne 3.5.18

C256 Deld War School Manston W/E 16.2.18; Became Pool of Pilots Manston 1.4.18

C257 Eastbourne, crashed and wrecked 29.6.18

C259 (60-hp Le Rhône) Deld Cranwell W/E 22.2.18

C262 (80-hp Le Rhône) Deld Cranwell W/E 15.2.18; Collided with B5674, crashed, badly damaged Cranwell South 28.2.18 (pilot uninjured); Became 201/2 TDS Cranwell 1.4.18

C265 (80-hp Le Rhône) Deld Cranwell W/E 22.2.18; Lost, landed, damaged propeller Hubberts' Bridge 20.3.18 (pilot unhurt); Became 201/2 TDS 1.4.18 - @6.18

C268 (80-hp Le Rhône) Deld Cranwell W/E 8.3.18; Freiston 1.4.18

C269 MOS Leysdown by 8.18 - @2.19

C271 Deld War School Manston W/E 2.3.18; Became Pool of Pilots Manston 1.4.18

C274 Deld War School Manston W/E 23.2.18; Became Pool of Pilots Manston 1.4.18 - @6.18

C277 Deld War School Manston W/E 23.2.18; Became Pool of Pilots Manston 1.4.18; Stalled at 50ft and nosedived in 5.7.18 (Lt W Towen seriously injured)

C280 Deld War School Manston W/E 2.3.18; Became Pool of Pilots Manston (coded '18') 1.4.18; Eastbourne 17.6.18

C283 Deld East Fortune NFS W/E 23.2.18 - @30.3.18 (practice landings); Grand Fleet SoAF&G Leuchars by 5.19

C286 Deld East Fortune NFS W/E 23.2.18 - @30.3.18 (practice landings)

C289 Deld East Fortune NFS W/E 2.3.18 - @30.3.18 (practice landings)

C292 Deld East Fortune NFS W/E 23.2.18 - @30.3.18

C295 (80-hp Le Rhône) Deld Cranwell W/E 8.3.18; Crashed, slightly damaged, Cranwell South 21.3.18 (pilot unhurt); Became 201/2 TDS Cranwell 1.4.18

C298 Deld Cranwell W/E 8.3.18; EF, FL, axle damaged, nr Grantham 20.3.18 (pilot unhurt); Became 201/2 TDS Cranwell 1.4.18

C301 Deld Cranwell Workshops 3.18; Cranwell School 14.3.18; Crashed and damaged 26.3.18 (pilot unhurt); Became 201/2 TDS 1.4.18 - @14.5.18

C304 Deld Chingford W/E 11.3.18; Became 207 TDS

Chingford 1.4.18

| | |
|---|---|
| C307 | Deld Vendôme W/E 30.3.18; Became 205 TDS Vendôme 1.4.18; EF, FL, slightly damaged on aerodrome 1.7.18 (PFO SR Pragnell); Crashed 16.9.18 (Lt SJ Fisher unhurt) |
| C310 | Deld Vendôme W/E 30.3.18; Became 205 TDS Vendôme 1.4.18; Badly damaged avoiding another aircraft 8.6.18 (PFO FW Wright unhurt); Machine collapsed after nose put down for loop 30.9.18 (Lt SJ Fisher killed) |
| C313 | Deld Vendôme W/E 30.3.18; Became 205 TDS Vendôme 1.4.18; Swung landing, badly damaged 24.6.18 (PFO AE Betts unhurt); Crashed 13.8.18 (2/Lt AH Williams); Crashed landing downwind 5.9.18 (F/Cdt R Coombes-White unhurt) |
| C314 | Deld 3 AAP Norwich W/E 27.3.18; 206 TDS Eastbourne 4.18; EF diving on target, crashed, damaged 3.7.18 (2/Lt AE Wilson injured) |
| C316 | Deld Vendôme W/E 30.3.18; Became 205 TDS Vendôme 1.4.18; Crashed on Wing football ground 17.10.18 (Capt SB Joyce slightly injured) |
| C317 | Deld 1 SD 3.18 for naval use |
| C319 | Deld Vendôme W/E 30.3.18; Became 205 TDS Vendôme 1.4.18; Crashed on TO, badly damaged 29.6.18 (PFO AE Betts unhurt); Crashed 13.8.18 (F/Cdt CSG Davies unhurt) |
| C320 | Deld 1 SD 3.18; 206 TDS Eastbourne by 8.6.18 |
| C322 | Deld Vendôme W/E 30.3.18; Became 205 TDS Vendôme 1.4.18; Went on nose landing, badly damaged 17.6.18 (PFO CM Pinkerton); Hit top wing of Avro on TO, damaged propeller, o/t landing, badly damaged 18.7.18 (PFO RM Barron slightly injured) |
| C325 | Deld Vendôme late 3.18; Became 205 TDS Vendôme 1.4.18; Drifted landing due to gust of wind, badly damaged 18.5.18 (PFO JJ McLeod & Capt PH Martin unhurt); Caught fire at 300 ft, pilot thrown out at 150 ft nr Crucheray, BO 21.6.18 (PFO WSG Barker killed) BUT 84 Wing Vendôme by 8.8.18; ALSO 56 TDS Cranwell by 5.8.18 - @13.9.18 |
| C326 | 56 TDS Cranwell by 7.9.18 - @11.18 |
| C331 | Deld Rosyth by rail W/E 30.3.18; Turnhouse W/E 11.4.18 - @4.5.18; ½ARS Shotwick to 96 Sqdn 19.5.18 |
| C332 | Deld Rosyth by rail W/E 30.3.18; Turnhouse W/E 11.4.18 - @5.18 |
| C333 | Deld Rosyth by rail W/E 30.3.18; Turnhouse W/E 6.4.18; Yate W/E 24.5.18 (no engine) |
| C334 | Deld Rosyth by rail W/E 30.3.18; Turnhouse W/E 6.4.18 - @4.5.18 |
| C336 | Deld Rosyth by rail W/E 30.3.18; Turnhouse W/E 6.4.18; Yate W/E 24.5.18 (no engine) |
| C338 | Deld Rosyth by rail W/E 30.3.18; Turnhouse W/E 6.4.18; Yate W/E 24.5.18 (no engine) |
| C340 | Allocated Eastchurch by 30.3.18 |
| C342 | Allocated Eastchurch by 30.3.18 |
| C343 | Allocated Eastchurch by 30.3.18 |
| C344 | Allocated Eastchurch by 30.3.18 |
| C345 | Allocated Eastchurch by 30.3.18 |
| C350 | Deld Chingford W/E 6.4.18 |
| C351 | Deld Turnhouse by rail W/E 11.4.18 - @4.5.18 |
| C352 | Deld Turnhouse by rail W/E 11.4.18; Yate 24.5.18 (no engine) |
| C353 | Deld Turnhouse by rail W/E 11.4.18 - @4.5.18 |
| C357 | Deld Turnhouse by rail W/E 11.4.18 - @4.5.18 |
| C359 | Deld Turnhouse by rail W/E 11.4.18 - @4.5.18 |
| C361 | Deld Turnhouse by rail W/E 11.4.18 - @4.7.18 |
| C363 | Allocated 207 TDS Chingford by 1.4.18 |
| C365 | Allocated 207 TDS Chingford by 1.4.18 |
| C367 | Allocated 207 TDS Chingford by 1.4.18 |
| C368 | Allocated 207 TDS Chingford by 1.4.18 |
| C369 | Allocated 207 TDS Chingford by 1.4.18 |
| C370 | Allocated 207 TDS Chingford by 1.4.18 |
| C406 | 56 TDS Cranwell by 9.18 |
| C423 | 56 TDS Cranwell by 9.18 |
| C424 | 56 TDS Cranwell by 9.18 |

## 3 AVRO 504A TRACTOR BIPLANE TRAINERS from batch C551 - C750 built by Humber Ltd

| | |
|---|---|
| C721 | 56 TDS Cranwell by 11.18 |
| C722 | 201/2 TDS Cranwell by 6.18 |
| C725 | 201/2 TDS Cranwell by 6.18 |

## 6 BRISTOL FIGHTER F.2b TRACTOR BIPLANES from batch C751 - C1050 built by parent company

| | |
|---|---|
| C770 | (c/n 3170) Hendon by 21.6.18 - @8.7.18 |
| C902 | (c/n 3302) 21 TDS Driffield to Pool of Pilots Manston 28.6.18 |
| C903 | (c/n 3303) 59 TS Rendcombe by 3.18 - @5.5.18; 50 TDS Catterick by 8.18; 45 TDS Rendcombe by 11.18 - @12.18; 2 MOS Eastchurch by 3.19 - @7.19; Served post-war |
| C905 | (c/n 3305) Pool of Pilots Manston by 6.18 - @27.7.18 |
| C907 | (c/n 3307) Pool of Pilots Manston by 6.18 - @27.7.18 |
| C910 | (c/n 3310) Pool of Pilots Manston by 5.18 - @6.18 |

## 41 AIRCO D.H.9 TRACTOR BIPLANE BOMBERS from batch C1151 to C1450 built by G & J Weir Ltd at Glasgow. (200-hp B.H.P.)

| | |
|---|---|
| C1168 | Rec Pk to 1 AI 12.6.18; 211 Sqdn 14.6.18; In action 17.6.18 (2/Lt J Steel Muir wounded); Lost way, landed Yarmouth, then landed Manston due to storm 7.9.18; Retd sqdn 9.9.18; Damaged by flak, FL Möeres 7.10.18 (Lt JL McAdam & Sgt Mech H Lindsay both wounded); 2 ASD 22.2.19 (unfit to fly Channel) |
| C1175 | Rec Pk to 206 Sqdn 1.5.18; Crashed into telephone wires Boisdinghem 15.5.18 (Lt EA Burn & 2/Lt AH Mitchener unhurt) [credited Obltn Kahler of Seefrontstaffel]; 1 ASD 19.5.18; SOC wrecked |
| C1177 | 98 Sqdn, crashed 2.3.18 (Capt Bell & Lt Malcolm); Rep Pk 1 ASD to 98 Sqdn 30.4.18; Rec Pk 1 ASD 6.5.18 wrecked; 1 AI 24.6.18; 206 Sqdn 28.6.18; Left 14.15 on long reconnaissance, FTR 29.6.18 (Lt C Eaton & 2/Lt EW Tatnall both PoW); SOC in field 1.7.18 |
| C1181 | Rec Pk to 1 AI 19.5.18; 206 Sqdn 21.5.18; Fokker DrI crashed and burnt Bac St.Maur, shared C6240 12.00 7.6.18 (Lt LA Christian & 2/Lt EW Tatnall); Collided "B7413" on TO, CW 17.6.18 (Lt FA Brock & Cpl LH Hartford USAS); 1 ASD 19.6.18; SOC 22.6.18 NWR |
| C1206 | Deld 4 AAP Lincoln by 5.18; 491 Flt Dover 15.5.18 - @14.6.18; Despatched 2.6.18 (sic); 218 Sqdn by 6.18; Damaged 18.6.18 (Lt BH Stata & 2/Lt CVR Browne); Yellow 2-str in flames shared by formation Ostende 18.25 5.7.18 (Capt WF Cleghorn & 2/Lt GJL Potts); Damaged in combat 28.9.18 (2/Lt F Nelms USMCR wounded & 2/Lt CC Barr DoW 6.10.18); 4 ASD 6.10.18 repair; Deleted 15.10.18 general fatigue |
| C1207 | Deld Dover by 15.5.18; 218 Sqdn W/E 1.6.18; Hit by flak, down in flames off Zeebrugge 11.8.18 (Lt H Fawdry & 2/Lt JS Cryan both killed); Deleted 31.8.18 |
| C1208 | Deld 491 Flt Dover by 5.18; Despatched 2.6.18; 98 Sqdn by 12.6.18; SOC missing 12.6.18? |
| C1210 | Deld 491 Flt Dover W/E 24.5.18; AAP Dover to 218 Sqdn 7.6.18; COL 15.6.18 (Lt CF Smith & Sgt G/L RS Joysey); To 4 ASD; 2 SS Richborough 2.10.18 |
| C1211 | Deld 491 Flt Dover W/E 24.5.18; 218 Sqdn (Code 'V1') by 6.18; During raid on Zeebrugge Mole, hit by AA over Belgian coast, FL and damaged u/c and lower wing Breskens, Zeeland 29.6.18 (Lt WF Purvis & 2AM LH Locke both interned) [credited Flgm Zenses, Marine Jasta 2] ; Deleted 31.7.18; Became Dutch *deH434*; Retd RAF 20.3.20 |
| C1244 | 57 TDS Cranwell, propeller accident 6.8.18 (Cpl Mech Davis injured) |
| C1250 | Deld ECD Grain by 1.4.18 - @25.5.18; Cranwell, nosed up in rough ground 9.18 |
| C1261 | Deld Turnhouse W/E 13.6.18; Crashed 19.9.18 (Lt JC Ambler injured & 2/Lt W Smith slightly injured); Deleted W/E 10.10.18 |
| C1264 | Deld Turnhouse W/E 13.6.18 - @30.1.19 |
| C1286 | Deld Dover 5.18; 219 Sqdn W/E 1.6.18 |
| C1294 | Renfrew to AAP Dover 26.6.18; 4 ASD Audembert 28.6.18; 218 Sqdn 29.6.18; Fokker DrI OOC off Zeebrugge 07.20 14.7.18 (Lt CLW Brading & G/L Sgt F Smith); Heavily damaged in attack by HA on Belgian coast, FL Vrouwenpolder, Zeeland 5.9.18 (Lt JG Munro & 2/Lt TW Brodie both interned unhurt); Deleted 15.9.18; Became Dutch *deH441* |
| C1295 | 218 Sqdn to 4 ASD 25.7.18; 4 ASD Pilots Pool, crashed; 4 ASD by 25.10.18 |
| C1296 | 1 AI to Alquines 18.6.18 (by Rec Pk 1 ASD); 492 Flt 254 Sqdn Prawle Point by 18.8.18 - @27.10.18; To |

Australian Government

| | |
|---|---|
| C1297 | Deld 492 Flt 254 Sqdn Prawle Point by 6.10.18 - @19.10.18; COL 8.10.18 (2/Lt RJ Thompson seriously injured & 3AM AHW Busby injured) |
| C1298 | Deld 492 Flt 254 Sqdn Prawle Point by 8.18 - @7.11.18 |
| C1299 | Deld 492 Flt 254 Sqdn Prawle Point by 8.18 - @31.10.18 |
| C1300 | Padstow by 4.10.18; EF, FL, damaged Harlyn Bay 21.10.18 (pilot unhurt) |
| C1301 | Deld Padstow by 12.4.18; Became 494 Flt 250 Sqdn Padstow by 25.5.18; COL 17.9.18 (2 crew unhurt) |
| C1302 | Deld 493 Flt 236 Sqdn Mullion by 11.18; East Fortune by 20.11.18 |
| C1303 | 494 Flt 250 Sqdn Padstow by 28.10.18 - @31.10.18 |
| C1304 | 494 Flt 236 Sqdn Mullion, EF, stalled and spun in on TO 18.1.18 (2/Lt RJ Cotterell killed) |
| C1305 | Mullion by 11.18; To Prawle Point but missing en route 7.11.18 (Lt Lamb & AM Lownes) |
| C1306 | 493 Flt 236 Sqdn Mullion by 25.9.18 - @28.10.18 |
| C1307 | East Fortune by 12.18; Lake Down 15.12.18 (arr 18.12.18) |
| C1326 | Deld Yarmouth by 1.8.18; 555/6 Flts 219 Sqdn Manston 13.8.18; Crashed 23.9.18 (Lt SW Orr & 2/Lt JW Davies); 218 Sqdn (via Dover) 29.9.18; Returning from raid on Melle Siding, FL, crashed Wulveringhem 14.10.18 (Lt SW Orr slightly injured & 2/Lt JW Davies seriously injured); 4 ASD 17.10.18; Deleted 31.10.18 DBR |
| C1327 | Deld Yarmouth by 8.18; 555/6 Flts 219 Sqdn Manston 10.8.18; 218 Sqdn (via Dover) 29.9.18; Returning from bombing raid, FL on beach and crashed nr Dunkerque 18.10.18 (2/Lt J Jackson & Sgt J Mathers); 4 ASD 19.10.18 - @25.10.18 |
| C1328 | Deld Yarmouth by 8.18; 555/6 Flts 219 Sqdn Manston 12.8.18; 218 Sqdn (via Dover) 29.9.18; Engine burnt out over Bruges during raid, FL 200 yds inside British lines, crashed, shelled 18.10.18 (2/Lt CM Arias unhurt & 2/Lt MJ Clark injured); Deleted 31.10.18 |
| C1329 | Deld Yarmouth by 11.8.18; 555/6 Flts 219 Sqdn Manston 13.8.18 - @9.18 |
| C1330 | Deld 555/6 Flts 219 Sqdn Manston by 10.8.18 - @9.18 |
| C1331 | Deld 219 Sqdn Westgate/Manston by 12.4.18; 555/6 Flts 219 Sqdn Manston 26.6.18 - @9.18 |
| C1332 | Deld 219 Sqdn Westgate/Manston by 12.4.18; 555/6 Flts 219 Sqdn Manston 26.6.18; 218 Sqdn (via Dover) 29.9.18; Returning from raid, COL St.Pol 16.10.18 (2/Lt J Jackson & Sgt R Mathers); 4 ASD 16.10.18 - @25.10.18 |
| C1341 | Rec Pk 1 ASD by 8.18; 1 AI 22.8.18; 206 Sqdn 24.8.18; COL from bombing raid in high wind and heavy rain 29.9.18 (Lt H McLean & 2/Lt HP Hobbs unhurt?); to Rep Pk 1 ASD 30.9.18 |
| C1380 | MOS Aldeburgh by 11.18 (prefix?) |
| C1381 | MOS Aldeburgh by 9.18 - @10.18 (prefix?) |
| C1385 | 2 MOS Eastchurch (coded 'A') by 3.19 - @7.19 |
| C1387 | Deld 493 Flt Mullion by 6.18; Damaged in storm 8.6.18; 493 Flt 236 Sqdn Mullion 20.8.18; COL, slightly damaged 1.9.18 (pilot unhurt) |

**13 SOPWITH PUP TRACTOR BIPLANE SCOUTS from batch C1451 to C1550 built by Whitehead Aircraft Ltd at Richmond, Surrey. (80-hp Le Rhône)**

| | |
|---|---|
| C1502 | Deld Turnhouse W/E 11.5.18 - @30.1.19 |
| C1503 | Deld Turnhouse W/E 11.5.18 - @30.1.19 |
| C1508 | Deld Turnhouse W/E 11.5.18 - @30.1.19 |
| C1515 | 54 TDS Fairlop, spun into ground 16.10.18 (2/Lt FW Halliwell severely injured |
| C1516 | Deld Turnhouse W/E 11.5.18 - @30.1.19 |
| C1517 | Deld Turnhouse W/E 11.5.18: Deleted W/E 19.12.18 |
| C1518 | Deld Turnhouse W/E 11.5.18: Deleted W/E 19.12.18 |
| C1519 | Deld 207 TDS Chingford 31.5.18 - @10.18 |
| C1523 | Deld Turnhouse W/E 11.5.18 - @30.1.19 |
| C1532 | Deld Turnhouse W/E 11.5.18 - @30.1.19 |
| C1533 | Deld Turnhouse W/E 11.5.18 - @30.1.19 |
| C1535 | Deld Turnhouse W/E 11.5.18: Deleted W/E 19.12.18 |
| C1537 | Deld Turnhouse W/E 11.5.18 - @30.1.19 |
| C1541 | Deld Turnhouse W/E 11.5.18 - @30.1.19 |

**2 SOPWITH F.1 CAMEL TRACTOR BIPLANE SCOUTS from batch C1601 - C1700 built by Boulton & Paul at Norwich**

| | |
|---|---|
| C1614 | W/T School Biggin Hill (R/T tests 22.3.18 as receiving aircraft for B6303); 204 TDS Eastchurch from 18.1.19 |
| C1672 | 70 Sqdn, crashed 9.5.18; 2 ASD 10.5.18; 2 AI to 209 Sqdn 4.7.18; Fokker DVII crashed Caix, shared B7471 19.15 8.8.18 (Capt EB Drake); EF, FL 2000 yds N of Le Quesnel 10.8.18 (Capt EB Drake unhurt); Collected by 22 Wing SS 10.8.18; salved by No.6 SS, 5 Bde 8.18 |

**43 AIRCO D.H.6 TRACTOR BIPLANES built by The Grahame-White Aviation Co Ltd at Hendon. (90-hp R.A.F.1A)**

| | |
|---|---|
| C2016 | SD Flt 252 Sqdn Cramlington by 28.4.18 - @1.6.18; 507/8 Flts 252 Sqdn Tynemouth by 6.18; FL off St.Mary's Island, sank attempting tow into harbour in heavy sea 2.7.18 (2 crew saved) |
| C2021 | 521/2 Flts 255 Sqdn Anglesey, FTR from patrol 14.8.18 |
| C2027 | 507/8 Flts 252 Sqdn Tynemouth by 4.8.18 |
| C2035 | 510 Flt 251 Sqdn Ayton by 1.11.18 |
| C2067 | A or B Flt, later 519/520 Flts 255 Sqdn Pembroke by 11.8.18 - @29.9.18 |
| C2074 | 521/2 Flts 244 Sqdn Bangor by 12.9.18; Crashed Carnarvon Bay 11.10.18 (Lt DJ Wilks) |
| C2076 | 519/520 Flts 255 Sqdn Pembroke by 9.18 |
| C2078 | 507/8 Flts 252 Sqdn Tynemouth by 10.18 |
| C2079 | 507 Flt 252 Sqdn Tynemouth (coded 'II') by 6.8.18; Dropped bomb on U-Boat 3m SE of Sunderland, oil seen 1950 21.8.18 (Lt CB Gibson); EF, FL off Souter Point, towed Milldam jetty by Island Prince (T.R.62) 3.9.18 (pilot unhurt) |
| C2080 | C Flt/528 Flt 256 Sqdn Sea Houses by 7.18; 526 Flt 256 Sqdn New Haggerston 6.8.18; 272 Sqdn Campbeltown by 12.18; Propeller accident 5.12.18 (2AM JJ O'Donnell slightly injured) |
| C2081 | Deld South Shields by 7.18; 507 Flt 252 Sqdn Tynemouth 26.7.18 - @4.9.18 |
| C2082 | Deld South Shields by 7.18; 507 Flt 252 Sqdn Tynemouth 9.7.18; South Shields 7.18; 507 Flt 252 Sqdn Tynemouth 29.7.18; EF, FL in sea ENE of Souter Point, towed into Tyne 4.8.18 (pilot unhurt); repaired; 531/3 Flts 272 Sqdn Machrihanish by 23.10.18 |
| C2083 | Deld South Shields by 7.18; 508 Flt 252 Sqdn Tynemouth 11.8.18; South Shields 21.10.18 |
| C2084 | Deld South Shields by 7.18; 528 Flt 256 Sqdn Sea Houses 27.7.18; 526 Flt 256 Sqdn New Haggerston 9.8.18 - @16.11.18 |
| C2085 | 531/3 Flts 272 Sqdn Machrihanish by 16.10.18 - @19.10.18 |
| C2087 | 502/3 Flts 260 Sqdn Westward Ho! by 8.18; FL in sea, sank 3.9.18 (pilot unhurt); Salved; EF, FL Lundy Island 19.9.18 |
| C2088 | 502/3 Flts 260 Sqdn Westward Ho! by 9.18; FL in sea 3.9.18 |
| C2098 | Deld Hendon to ECD Grain 24.1.18 (gun expts); Surveyed 25.3.18; Deletion authorised 27.3.18 but still in use for ditching trials 6.18; Ditched without hydrovane, undamaged 14.6.18 |
| C2101 | Deld Hendon W/E 19.1.18; EF, FL Stanford-le-Hope en route Grain 24.1.18; arr EAD Grain 25.1.18 - @25.5.18 (gun expts); Became G-EAGG (Airco 7.19) |
| C2104 | Deld Hendon W/E 19.1.18; Manston FS 16.2.18; Became 203 TDS Manston 1.4.18 - @8.18 |
| C2107 | Deld Hendon 19.1.18; Manston FS 28.1.18; Became 203 TDS Manston 1.4.18 |
| C2110 | Deld Hendon 19.1.18; Manston FS 24.2.18; Deleted W/E 23.3.18 |
| C2111 | 531/3 Flts 272 Sqdn Machrihanish by 15.10.18; EF, FL in sea 26.10.18 (pilot and aircraft rescued by SS Agate) |
| C2112 | 502/3 Flts 260 Sqdn Westward Ho! by 21.8.18 - @25.10.18 |
| C2113 | Deld Hendon W/E 19.1.18; Manston FS 12.2.18; For deletion by 23.3.18 |
| C2114 | 500/1 Flts 250 Sqdn Padstow by 19.9.18 - @13.10.18 |
| C2115 | 531/3 Flts 272 Sqdn Machrihanish by 17.10.18 - @6.11.18 |
| C2116 | Deld Hendon W/E 19.1.18; Manston FS 18.2.18; Cranwell W/E 30.3.18; Became 201/2 TDS Cranwell 1.4.18 - @7.18 |
| C2119 | Deld Hendon W/E 19.1.18; Manston FS 6.2.18; Became 203 TDS Manston 1.4.18 - @5.18; 507/8 Flts 252 Sqdn Tynemouth by 6.11.18 |

| | |
|---|---|
| C2120 | 531/3 Flts 272 Sqdn Machrihanish, EF, FL Rathlin Island 27.10.18 |
| C2121 | 531/3 Flts 272 Sqdn Machrihanish, FL in sea 17.10.18 |
| C2122 | Deld Hendon W/E 19.1.18, retd ex Barnet 28.1.18; Manston FS W/E 9.2.18; For deletion by 23.3.18 |
| C2123 | 531/3 Flts 272 Sqdn Machrihanish by 26.10.18; FL in sea and sank 5521N 0620W 5.11.18 (Lt Knight rescued by drifter) |
| C2125 | Deld Hendon W/E 19.1.18; Manston FS W/E 9.2.18; Became 203 TDS Manston 1.4.18 - @6.18 |
| C2128 | Deld Hendon W/E 19.1.18; Manston FS 12.2.18; Cranwell (via Chingford) 26.3.18; Became 202 TDS Cranwell 1.4.18; Became 57 TDS Cranwell 27.7.18 - @10.18 |
| C2131 | Deld Hendon W/E 19.1.18; Manston FS W/E 9.2.18; 201/2 TDS Cranwell (via Chingford and Huntingdon) 3.4.18 |
| C2134 | Deld Hendon 19.1.18; Manston FS 18.2.18; 201/2 TDS Cranwell (via Chingford and Huntingdon) 2.4.18 |
| C2137 | Deld Hendon 19.1.18; Manston FS 12.2.18; Cranwell W/E 23.3.18; Became 201/2 TDS Cranwell 1.4.18 |
| C2140 | Deld Manston NFS for erection W/E 26.1.18; Became 203 TDS Manston 1.4.18 - @6.18 |
| C2143 | Deld Manston NFS for erection W/E 26.1.18; Became 203 TDS Manston 1.4.18 |
| C2146 | Deld Manston NFS for erection 23.2.18; Became 203 TDS Manston 1.4.18 - @8.18 |
| C2147 | SMOP Dover from 10.18 - @11.18 |
| C2149 | Deld Manston NFS for erection W/E 9.2.18; Became 203 TDS Manston 1.4.18 - @8.18 |

**17 D.H.9 TRACTOR BIPLANE BOMBERS from batch C2151 to C2230 built by F.W.Berwick & Co Ltd. (200-hp B.H.P)**

| | |
|---|---|
| C2153 | Martlesham to Hendon 1.8.18 - @10.8.18 |
| C2154 | Rec Pk to 1 AI 3.5.18; 206 Sqdn 8.5.18; EF on TO, FL nr aerodrome, wrecked 10.5.18 (Lt L Childs slightly injured & 2/Lt FW Chester unhurt); Rep Pk 1 ASD 14.5.18; SOC in field 17.5.18 |
| C2156 | Rec Pk to 206 Sqdn 25.4.18; COL after raid 14.5.18 (Lt EA Burn & AG Blyth both unhurt); 1 ASD 17.5.18; 206 Sqdn by 9.6.18 |
| C2157 | Rec Pk to 206 Sqdn 21.4.18; Missing believed shot down in flames between Bailleul and Kemmel between 18.00 & 19.00 3.5.18 (Lt AE Steele & 2/Lt AE Slinger both killed); SOC in field 3.5.18 |
| C2158 | Rec Pk to 1 AI 17.5.18; 97 Sqdn; 98 Sqdn; 4 ASD to 218 Sqdn 6.9.18; Attacked by 2 HA Zeebrugge-Ostende, FL Deutsche Bank Channel, mouth of River Schelde 15.9.18 (Lt WS Mars & 2/Lt HE Power both interned both slightly injured); Deleted 31.10.18 |
| C2160 | Shipped to Otranto 20.4.18; 226 Sqdn by 25.5.18 |
| C2161 | Shipped to Otranto 20.4.18; 224 Sqdn by 9.6.18; Missing en route Taranto 20.10.18 (2/Lt JTR Proffitt killed) |
| C2162 | Shipped to Otranto 20.4.18; 226 Sqdn by 25.5.18 - @6.18; Disposed of by 25.7.18 |
| C2174 | Deld 2 AAP Hendon by 29.4.18; Rec Pk to 1 AI 21.5.18; 98 Sqdn by 5.18; HA shot down 29.5.18 (Lt AM Phillips & Lt NC MacDonald); 4 ASD to 491 Flt 233 Sqdn Dover 25.10.18 - @12.18 |
| C2175 | Deld 2 AAP Hendon by 1.5.18; Rec Pk to 206 Sqdn 25.5.18; Defective 11.6.18, for Rep Pk 1 ASD; Recommended to be retd, not suitable 21.6.18; to 1 ASD, flown to England 26.6.18 |
| C2176 | Deld 2 AAP Hendon by 1.5.18; Rec Pk 5.18; 1 AI to 206 Sqdn 19.5.18; EF [on TO?], FL, CW 6.6.18 (Lt F Daltrey slightly injured & 2/Lt MG Penny unhurt); Missing last seen at 5,000ft in heavy AA 2m E of Ostende 25.6.18 (2/Lt F Daltrey PoW & 1/Pte R Sheppard killed); SOC in field 25.6.18 |
| C2180 | Rec Pk to 1 AI 20.5.18; 211 Sqdn 22.5.18; Pancaked landing, crashed 1.6.18 (2/Lt HH Palmer & 2/Lt JS Muir); 1 ASD 2.6.18 |
| C2186 | Deld Hendon to Dover W/E 24.5.18; 218 Sqdn by 20.5.18; COL 12.6.18 (Lt JRA Barnes & G/L Sgt RJ Williams unhurt); COL after raid on Bruges 9.7.18 (Capt EF Chamberlain USMC & 2/Lt FH Bugge); to 4 ASD; 2 SS Richborough 15.9.18 |
| C2187 | Rec Pk to 1 AI 27.5.18; 206 Sqdn 30.5.18; CW, SOC in field 8.6.18 |

| | |
|---|---|
| C2193 | 1 ASD by 6.18; 206 Sqdn 1.8.18; Fokker DVII in flames, crashed E of Messines 18.50 13.8.18 (Lt D Stainbank & 2/Lt EW Richardson); Hit by AA, crashed 0935 5.10.18 (Sgt Mech G Packman slightly injured & 2/Lt JW Kennedy unhurt); to Rep Park 1 ASD |
| C2199 | Rec Pk to 1 AI 4.8.18; 206 Sqdn 9.8.18; Left 05.05, FTR 11.8.18 (Lt EHP Bailey & 2/Lt R Milne both killed); SOC in field 11.8.18 |
| C2210 | Mkrs, packed for EF 29.5.18; 1 ASD to 211 Sqdn 28.6.18; Travelling flight, hit ridge landing, u/c collapsed 6.12.18 (2/Lt HC Thomas & 3AM EW Morgan both unhurt); No.7 SS 7.12.18 |

**1 ROYAL AIRCRAFT FACTORY B.E.12 TRACTOR BIPLANE from batch C3081 to C3280 built by The Daimler Co Ltd**

| | |
|---|---|
| C3180 | 1 ASD to 207 Sqdn 6.9.18; En route Liegescourt to Estrées-en-Chaussée, EF, FL, crashed, TW nr Abbeville 29.9.18 (2/Lt WFA Snell unhurt & Sgt Mech JA Forsythe injured); SOC in field |

**15 SOPWITH F.1 CAMEL TRACTOR BIPLANE SCOUTS from batch C3281 to C3380 built by Boulton & Paul Ltd at Norwich. (130-hp Clerget 9B unless stated otherwise)**

| | |
|---|---|
| C3294 | 50 TDS Eastbourne, collided in formation 5.9.18 (Lt ES Possolo killed) |
| C3296 | 206 TDS Eastbourne by 6.18; Became 50 TDS Eastbourne 15.7.18; Crashed and badly damaged 13.8.18 (pilot unhurt); Left 1.11.18 |
| C3316 | Rec Pk to 1 AI 23.8.18; 208 Sqdn 3.9.18; 2 AI 22.11.18 |
| C3320 | Rec Pk to 2 ASD 10.8.18; 43 Sqdn 24.8.18; 2 AI 30.8.18; 205 TDS Vendôme FS 4.9.18; Crashed 9.10.18 (F/Cdt SW Geagan unhurt) |
| C3326 | Deld 6 SD Ascot W/E 5.9.18; To docks W/E 19.9.18; Shipped to Mudros 11.10.18; Repair Base Mudros by 1.19; To White Russian Forces 1919 |
| C3328 | Deld 6 SD Ascot W/E 5.9.18; To docks W/E 19.9.18; Shipped to Mudros 11.10.18; To White Russian Forces 1919 |
| C3330 | Deld 6 SD Ascot W/E 5.9.18; To docks W/E 19.9.18; Shipped to Mudros 11.10.18; Mudros by 1.19; To White Russian Forces 1919 |
| C3332 | Deld 6 SD Ascot by 29.8.18; Shipped to Mudros 11.10.18; Mudros by 1.19; To White Russian Forces 1919 |
| C3334 | Deld 6 SD Ascot W/E 5.9.18; To docks W/E 19.9.18; Shipped to Mudros 11.10.18; Mudros by 1.19; To White Russian Forces 1919 |
| C3336 | Shipped 4.9.18; Taranto by 11.18; 'X' AD 11.4.19; WOC 21.5.19 |
| C3338 | Deld 6 SD Ascot W/E 5.9.18; Shipped 12.9.18; Taranto by 10.18; 'X' AD 11.4.19; WOC 21.5.19 |
| C3340 | Deld 6 SD Ascot W/E 5.9.18; Shipped 12.9.18; Taranto by 10.18; 'X' AD 11.4.19; WOC 21.5.19 |
| C3342 | Shipped 4.9.18; Taranto by 11.18; 'X' AD 11.4.19; WOC 21.5.19 |
| C3344 | Shipped 4.9.18; Taranto by 11.18; 'X' AD 11.4.19; WOC 21.5.19 |

**6 HANDLEY PAGE O/400 TRACTOR BIPLANE HEAVY BOMBERS from batch C3487 to C3498 built by the Royal Aircraft Factory at Farnborough. (Eagle)**

| | |
|---|---|
| C3487 | Completed 3.18; Farnborough by 10.4.18; 214 Sqdn 20.4.18; Shot down bombing Solwey Works, Zeebrugge and captured 18/19.5.18 (Capt VE Sieveking killed, Lt HA Havilland-Roe killed & A/G F Spencer PoW wounded); SOC 19.5.18 |
| C3488 | Deld RAE Farnborough for acceptance 20.4.18; Rec Pk to 214 Sqdn 4.5.18 - @1.6.18; Probably the a/c wrecked in enemy air raid 9.6.18 |
| C3489 | Deld RAE Farnborough for acceptance 27.4.18; Rec Pk to 214 Sqdn 6.5.18; Participated bombing raid 13/14.6.18 (Cpl WH Neve seriously wounded); Port engine caught fire returning from raid on Thourout, FL outside aerodrome 8/9.10.18 (Lt [PAF?] Belton); To Buc for Egypt but crashed en route in bad visibility nr Pontoise 6.7.19 |
| C3490 | 215 Sqdn by 11.6.18 - @24.6.18; 207 Sqdn by 6.18; |

C3492    Tested 8 AAP Lympne 31.7.18; Dest by HA at Rep Pk 1 ASD 23.9.18

C3492    (Eagle VIII) Deld 8 AAP Lympne 5.18; 214 Sqdn 2.5.18; Attacked Solwey Works Zeebrugge, hit by AA, lost fuel, FL in sea 4m S of Nieuport, stayed afloat 9 hrs 22.8.18 (2/Lt J Hetherington unhurt, 2/Lt EC Fletcher drowned & Elec3 CW Kennedy USN unhurt - 2 picked up next day by US seaplane after 9hrs in sea); WOC 31.8.18

C3493    215 Sqdn by 6.6.18 - @8.18

## 2 SOPWITH 5F.1 DOLPHIN TRACTOR BIPLANES from batch C3777 to C4276 built at Kingston-on-Thames. (200-hp Hispano-Suiza)

C3785    Deld Brooklands by 29.12.17; Dover 6.1.18; Became 491 Flt Dover by 25.5.18 - @1.6.18; Shark teeth markings at one time, with a training unit

C3786    Deld Brooklands to AP Dover 6.12.17; 1 Sqdn RNAS Dover W/E 15.12.17; RNAS Dover 9.2.18; 4 Sqdn 23.3.18; Became 204 Sqdn 1.4.18; Wrecked 7.4.18; 1 AI 7.4.18; 2 ASD by 6.18; 23 Sqdn 9.6.18; 1 HA shared nr Hangard 29.6.18; 1 Albatros OOC 1.7.18 (Lt A Pearson)

## 1 MAURICE FARMAN S.7 LONGHORN PUSHER BIPLANE TRAINER built under Cont No A.S.24483 by The Brush Electrical Engineering Co Ltd at Loughborough from spares made by Robey and Phoenix Dynamo. (90-hp Curtiss)

C4279    Deld Killingholme W/E 25.1.18; Deleted W/E 16.2.18

## 9 AVRO 504J TRACTOR BIPLANE TRAINERS from batch C4301 to C4500 built by parent firm at Hamble. (100-hp Gnome Monosoupape)

C4322    (504K) Donibristle by 6.19

C4361    Deld Cranwell to Chingford for erection W/E 17.11.17; Became 207 TDS Chingford 1.4.18 - @2.6.18

C4362    Deld Cranwell to Chingford for erection W/E 24.11.17; Became 207 TDS Chingford 1.4.18

C4363    Deld Cranwell to Chingford for erection W/E 12.11.17; Became 207 TDS Chingford 1.4.18

C4373    Deld Chingford W/E 1.12.17; Became 207 TDS Chingford by 1.4.18

C4383    Deld Cranwell W/E 7.12.17; Crashed and badly damaged Potter Hanworth 8.3.18 (pilot unhurt); Crashed and damaged Cranwell South 26.3.18 (pilot unhurt); 2 SSF Redcar, struck airman while landing 29.6.18 (2AM HJ Wright killed); still 2 SSF Redcar 7.18

C4393    Deld Cranwell W/E 7.12.17; Crashed, u/c and propeller damaged 25.1.18 (pilot uninjured); Redcar School 14.3.18; Deleted W/E 23.3.18

C4403    Deld Chingford for erection W/E 1.12.17; Became 207 TDS Chingford by 1.4.18

C4413    Deld Chingford for erection W/E 8.12.17; Became 207 TDS Chingford by 1.4.18

## 1 AIRCO D.H.4 TRACTOR BIPLANE from batch C4501 to C4540 built by parent company

C4523    1(S)ARD Farnborough by 27.4.18 - @27.5.18 for Killingholme anti-submarine (use of W/Cdr HA Williamson); UK to Rec Pk 14.10.18; 3 AD 17.10.18 - @18.10.18

## 7 BRISTOL F.2b FIGHTER TRACTOR BIPLANES from batch C4601 to C4900 built by parent company

C4700    Hounslow to Hendon 21.6.18 - @17.8.18; Hangelar by 8.19; 48 Sqdn

C4721    Eastbourne by 5.18; Grain 27.5.18; Hendon 30.5.18

C4733    Ex RFC without engine to Tregantle & Withnoe store W/E 30.3.18

C4769    201/2 TDS Cranwell from 5.18 (first F.2b on station)

C4800    Hounslow to Hendon 21.6.18 - @24.7.18; Hounslow by 8.19

C4885    Hendon by 5.18; 1 Comms Sqdn Hendon 23.7.18

C4889    Deld HAAP to Hendon Medical Flt 4.4.18 - @9.6.18

## 44 AIRCO D.H.6 TRACTOR BIPLANES from batch C5126 to C5275 built by The Kingsbury Aviation Co Ltd at Kingsbury. (various engines)

C5130    (90-hp RAF) Cramlington by 3.18; FL in sea 4m off Blyth 5.4.18; Salved; C Flt 252 Sqdn Redcar 30.5.18 - @13.7.18

C5150    (80-hp Renault) Ex RFC to 2 AAP Hendon for erection by 23.2.18; Eastbourne 28.2.18

C5151    (80-hp Renault) Ex RFC to 2 AAP Hendon for erection by 23.2.18; Eastbourne NFS 8.3.18; Deleted W/E 30.3.18

C5159    504 Flt 251 Sqdn Atwick by 23.7.18

C5166    250 Sqdn Padstow .18

C5170    504 Flt 251 Sqdn Atwick by 31.7.18 - @11.11.18

C5171    SD Flt 251 Sqdn Stallingborough by 7.18; D Flt/509 Flt 252 Sqdn Seaton Carew 28.7.18; FL in sea Blackhills, towed to Tyne 20.9.18

C5172    Deld South Shields by 7.18; A Flt/527 Flt 256 Sqdn Sea Houses 28.7.18; Dropped bomb on U-boat 5535N 0130W, nothing seen 24.8.18 (F/Sgt Douglas); FL in sea and sank off Coquet Island 6.9.18 (2/Lt MR Shier killed)

C5173    Deld South Shields by 7.18; C Flt/528 Flt 256 Sqdn Sea Houses 28.7.18 - @12.8.18; 526 Flt 256 Sqdn New Haggerston by 26.8.18 - @12.11.18

C5174    Deld South Shields by 7.18; A Flt/527 Flt 256 Sqdn Sea Houses 30.7.18; 526 Flt 256 Sqdn Sqdn New Haggerston 6.8.18; Crashed on TO 19.9.18 (2/Lt CW Kerr injured & 3AM T Mackenzie killed)

C5178    Deld 2 AAP Hendon by 5.18; Hendon Medical Flt 24.5.18

C5183    (90-hp Curtiss) Deld 2 AAP Hendon by 18-25.5.18 for 18 Group; 504 Flt 251 Sqdn Atwick by 13.7.18

C5184    (90-hp Curtiss) Deld 2 AAP Hendon by 18-25.5.18 for 18 Group; 504 Flt 251 Sqdn Atwick by 6.18 - @11.18

C5185    (90-hp Curtiss) Deld 2 AAP Hendon by 18-25.5.18 for 18 Group; 504 Flt 251 Sqdn Atwick by 15.6.18 - @31.8.18

C5186    (90-hp Curtiss) Deld 2 AAP Hendon by 18-25.5.18 for 18 Group; 504 Flt 251 Sqdn Atwick by 30.6.18 - @11.11.18; FL in wheat field 1½m NW of Hunmanby 10.7.18 (pilot unhurt)

C5187    (90-hp Curtiss) Deld 2 AAP Hendon by 18-25.5.18 for 18 Group; 504 Flt 251 Sqdn Atwick by 9.18

C5188    (90-hp Curtiss) Deld 2 AAP Hendon by 18.5.18; Killingholme W/E 25.5.18; 504 Flt 251 Sqdn Atwick by 3.9.18

C5189    (90-hp Curtiss) Deld 2 AAP Hendon by 25.5.18 for 18 Group; 504 Flt 251 Sqdn Atwick by 15.6.18 - @6.11.18; Bombed U-boat 26.7.18 (Lt S Markussen)

C5190    (90-hp Curtiss OX-5) Allocated 250 Sqdn HQ Padstow by 25.5.18

C5191    (90-hp Curtiss OX-5) Allocated 250 Sqdn HQ Padstow by 25.5.18; 500/1 Flts 250 Sqdn Padstow by 16.6.18; FL and crashed 30.6.18; Still Padstow 4.7.18

C5192    (90-hp Curtiss OX-5) Deld 250 Sqdn Padstow by 25.5.18 - @7.7.18

C5193    (90-hp Curtiss OX-5) Allocated 250 Sqdn HQ Padstow by 25.5.18; 500/1 Flts 250 Sqdn Padstow by 12.6.18; FL, crashed 24.7.18; 528 Flt 256 Sqdn Sea Houses by 17.11.18

C5194    (90-hp Curtiss OX-5) Allocated 250 Sqdn HQ Padstow by 25.5.18; 500/501 Flts 250 Sqdn Padstow by 11.6.18; FL in sea, badly damaged, salved by collier Brook and taken to Newlyn 4.7.18 (pilot unhurt)

C5195    (90-hp Curtiss OX-5) Allocated South Shields by 25.5.18; Seaton Carew 29.6.18; Crashed on TO in strong wind, struck telegraph wires, lower wings and u/c broke away 21.7.18 (pilot unhurt); 528 Flt 256 Sqdn Sea Houses by 11.18

C5196    (90-hp Curtiss OX-5) Allocated South Shields by 25.5.18; Elford 17.6.18; 'C' Flt/528 Flt 256 Sqdn Sea Houses by 31.7.18 - @18.11.18

C5197    (90-hp Curtiss OX-5) Allocated South Shields by 25.5.18; Redcar 9.7.18

C5198    (90-hp Curtiss OX-5) Allocated South Shields by 25.5.18; 507/8 Flts 252 Sqdn Tynemouth 19.6.18; FL 16.7.18

C5199    517/8 Flts 254 Sqdn Prawle Point by 7.18; FL in sea, sank 1.8.18 (pilot rescued by drifter)

C5200   517/8 Flts 254 Sqdn Prawle Point by 4.7.18; Crashed Gara Rock 6.7.18

C5201   517/8 Flts 254 Sqdn Prawle Point by 2.7.18 - @3.8.18

C5202   517/8 Flts 254 Sqdn Prawle Point by 8.7.18; Boscombe Down 18.12.18

C5203   517/8 Flts 254 Sqdn Prawle Point by 3.7.18; Boscombe Down 18.12.18

C5204   517/8 Flts 254 Sqdn Prawle Point by 3.7.18; EF, FL in sea 13.11.18 (2 crew rescued by steamer); Boscombe Down 18.12.18

C5205   500/1 Flts 250 Sqdn Padstow by 7.18; Collided with C7858 and went in sea, TW 23.7.18 (2 crew unhurt)

C5206   500/1 Flts 250 Sqdn Padstow by 1.7.18 - @10.11.18; Dropped 85-lb bomb on U-boat 3m W of Trevose Head 23.7.18 (Capt H Goodfellow)

C5207   500/1 Flts 250 Sqdn Padstow by 23.7.18; Dropped 60-lb bomb on U-boat 2m off Newquay 13.8.18 (Lt HH Shorter); FL in sea 23.8.18

C5208   517/8 Flts 254 Sqdn Prawle Point by 8.18; FL in sea, broke up 14.11.18 (2 crew unhurt)

C5209   517/8 Flts 254 Sqdn Prawle Point by 19.9.18; EF, FL in sea, sank 14.11.18 (2 crew saved by steamer)

C5210   517/8 Flts 254 Sqdn Prawle Point by 28.7.18 - @25.10.18

C5211   504 Flt 251 Sqdn Atwick by 4.7.18; EF, FL in sea 1m E of Atwick, towed to Bridlington 12.9.18 (crew unhurt)

C5212   506 Flt 251 Sqdn Owthorne by 31.8.18 - @9.18

C5213   506 Flt 251 Sqdn Owthorne by 28.7.18 - @17.11.18

C5214   506 Flt 251 Sqdn Owthorne by 18.7.18 - @9.18

C5215   506 Flt 251 Sqdn Owthorne by 18.7.18 - @1.8.18

## 25 CAUDRON G.III PUSHER BIPLANE TRAINERS purchased from Caudron Works under BR.167 dated 24.9.17 and numbered C5276 to C5300. All delivered from Paris to RNAS for use at Vendôme. (100-hp Anzani)

C5276   Deld RNASTE Vendôme 16.11.17; Tested 19.11.17; Surveyed 11.12.17; Deleted 21.12.17 wrecked

C5277   Deld RNASTE Vendôme 16.11.17; Failed to flatten out on landing 22.1.18 (PFO JD McLaren); Deleted W/E 8.2.18

C5278   Deld RNASTE Vendôme 16.11.17; Heavy landing, o/t, badly damaged 29.1.18 (PFO DR McLachrie unhurt); CW landing 18.3.18 (PFO JW Peers); Became 205 TDS Vendôme 1.4.18; To 212 TDS Vendôme FL in wheat field, o/t, badly damaged nr Blois 22.7.18 (PFO LHK Ingham injured)

C5279   Deld RNASTE Vendôme for erection W/E 23.11.17; Starting accident, o/t 27.1.18 (PFO CJ Sims); Failed to flatten out, wrecked 3.2.18 (PFO TW Whittaker unhurt); Became 205 TDS Vendôme 1.4.18; To 212 TDS Vendôme; O/t landing, nacelle and rudder damaged 21.5.18 (F/Cdt BT Humphreys & Lt R Turner); Slightly damaged landing 7.7.18 (F/Cdt DA Boulton & Capt HJ Lloyd); Stalled on steep turn nr ground 22.8.18 (F/Cdt JF Harrison slightly injured)

C5280   Deld RNASTE Vendôme for erection W/E 30.11.17; Lost on cross-country, FL, went into trees, TW Marray 13.3.18; (PFO REW Gwyther unhurt); For deletion by 30.3.18

C5281   Deld RNASTE Vendôme W/E 23.11.17; O/t landing 18.3.18 (PFO CT Lewinton); Became 205 TDS Vendôme 1.4.18; To 212 TDS Vendôme; O/t landing, slightly damaged 12.6.18 (F/Cdt SE Wood & Lt R Turner); O/t landing, badly damaged 6.9.18 (Lt TC Knowles & Capt NP Playford unhurt); Ran into wheelbarrow after landing, o/t, badly damaged 12.10.18 (F/Cdt AT Smooker & 2/Lt CV Lacey unhurt)

C5282   Deld RNASTE Vendôme W/E 30.11.17; Heavy landing 6.2.18 (2/Lt Littlewood); FL, TW St.Laurent 19.4.18 (PFO WJ Lowndes unhurt); Became 205 TDS Vendôme 1.4.18; To 212 TDS Vendôme; O/t landing, slightly damaged 16.5.18 (PFO PLJ Lewin & Capt HJ Lloyd); O/t landing 13.6.18 (F/Cdt CM Hallett); Bounced landing, slightly damaged 24.7.18 (F/Cdt NJ Harley & Capt HJ Lloyd); Hit ridge, o/t, badly damaged 16.9.18 (F/Cdt RHJ Affleck & Capt NP Playford unhurt)

C5283   Deld RNASTE Vendôme 23.11.17; Heavy landing in dark 6.1.18 (PFO PWF Mills unhurt); Stalled, CW 30.1.18 (PFO KN Knapp); Deleted W/E 22.3.18

C5284   Deld RNASTE Vendôme W/E 6.12.17; Mid air collision with C5290, CW 22.1.18 (PFO HC Langstone killed); Deleted W/E 8.2.18

C5285   Deld RNASTE Vendôme W/E 30.11.17; Became 205 TDS Vendôme 1.4.18; Hit ridge landing, o/t 18.4.18 (PFO WJ Lowndes unhurt); To 212 TDS Vendôme; Caught in slipstream of another aircraft on TO, wrecked 12.6.18 (PFO GRC Soutar slightly injured & Lt MA Sams unhurt)

C5286   Deld RNASTE Vendôme W/E 22.12.17; Stalled on TO 18.2.18 (PFO GV Key injured); Deleted W/E 8.3.18

C5287   Deld RNASTE Vendôme for erection W/E 6.12.17; Became 205 TDS Vendôme 1.4.18; To 212 TDS; Pancaked, wrecked 27.6.18 (Lt JM Davies & Capt HJ Lloyd); Pancaked landing, wrecked 22.10.18 (F/Cdt WH Gill & 2/Lt CV Lacey unhurt)

C5288   Deld RNASTE Vendôme W/E 30.11.17; Struck wire fence landing, o/t 5.1.18 (PFO ACG Anderson unhurt); Became 205 TDS 1.4.18; Stalled over trees, wrecked 10.5.18 (PFO FVF Bennett)

C5289   Deld RNASTE Vendôme W/E 6.12.17; FL on aerodrome, hit tree, CW 27.1.18 (PFO AH Fitton unhurt); Deleted W/E 8.3.18

C5290   Deld RNASTE Vendôme W/E 6.12.17; Mid air collision with C5284, CW 22.1.18 (PFO HT Coo killed); Deleted W/E 8.2.18

C5291   Deld RNASTE Vendôme W/E 6.12.17; Collided with plough while landing Blois 7.1.18 (PFO EW Harland unhurt); FL into ditch landing on aerodrome 18.2.18 (2/Lt EEA Mills); O/t landing 24.2.18 (PFO GM Hughes unhurt); O/t landing Crucheray 9.3.18 (PFO N Thomas); Bounced landing, CW 27.3.18 (PFO EG Crier injured)

C5292   Deld RNASTE Vendôme W/E 19.1.18; Became 205 TDS 1.4.18; Bounced and stalled landing 25.5.18 (F/Cdt DV Tandy seriously injured)

C5293   Deld RNASTE Vendôme W/E 4.1.18; Lost, FL, damaged Ruille-sur-Loir, nr Montoire 19.2.18 (2/Lt AF Millar unhurt); Flew into trees on Vendôme road, CW 9.3.18 (PFO BH Whiting killed); Deleted W/E 22.3.18

C5294   Deld RNASTE Vendôme W/E 4.1.18; Choked, stalled and nosedived, CW 9.1.18 (PFO WJ Irwin unhurt); Deleted W/E 8.2.18

C5295   Deld RNASTE Vendôme W/E 19.1.18; Tested 19.1.18; Bumpy landing, o/t 30.1.18 (PFO F Kirk); Bad landing, CW 9.3.18 (PFO CH Porter); Hit ridge landing and o/t 27.3.18 (WO2 FC Layton unhurt); Became 205 TDS Vendôme 1.4.18; O/t landing, wrecked 8.8.18 (F/Cdt W Holtham & Lt HE Forrow)

C5296   Deld RNASTE Vendôme W/E 19.1.18; Tested 5.2.18; Stalled landing, CW 18.2.18 (PFO HF Mulholland); Became 205 TDS 1.4.18; Hit ridge landing, damaged 2.4.18 (PFO JM Johnston unhurt); Taxied into by N3243, wing and tail boom damaged 10.5.18; To 212 TDS Vendôme; Stalled attempting to clear trees, badly damaged Seillac, nr Blois 22.5.18 (F/Cdt BT Humphreys & Lt R Turner)

C5297   Deld RNASTE Vendôme W/E 12.1.18; Tested 12.1.18; Stalled landing, CW 10.2.18 (PFO WB Craig); Became 205 TDS Vendôme 1.4.18; Lost control landing, nosedived into ground 11.4.18 (PFO FB Hyndman slightly injured); To 212 TDS Vendôme; Stalled landing, wrecked 17.8.18 (F/Cdt JF Harrison slightly injured)

C5298   Deld RNASTE Vendôme W/E 18.1.18; Sideslipped and fell to ground in park at rear of church in Vendôme, wrecked 29.1.18 (PFO C Mortimer injured); Deleted W/E 22.3.18

C5299   Deld RNASTE Vendôme W/E 1.2.18; Bad landing 11.3.18 (PFO MS Smith); Became 205 TDS 1.4.18; CW landing 27.4.18 (PFO FL Salmon unhurt)

C5300   Deld RNASTE Vendôme W/E 25.1.18; Stalled on TO, CW 31.1.18 (PFO CB Crowther); Deleted W/E 1.3.18

## 15 AIRCO D.H.6 TRACTOR BIPLANES from batch C5451 to C5750 built by Harland & Wolff Ltd at Belfast.

C5460   (90-hp R.A.F.) SD Flts 252 Sqdn Cramlington by 15.4.18; Became 507/8 Flts 252 Sqdn Cramlington 25.5.18; 507/8 Flts 252 Sqdn Tynemouth 3.6.18 - @30.6.18

C5461   507/8 Flts 252 Sqdn Cramlington by 2.6.18

| | |
|---|---|
| C5463 | 530 Flt 244 Sqdn Tallaght by 8.18 |
| C5477 | SD Flt Cramlington by 28.4.18 |
| C5478 | 507/8 Flts 252 Sqdn Cramlington by 2.6.18 |
| C5497 | 494 Flt 250 Sqdn Prawle Point by 8.10.18; Crashed landing in thick mist Bee Sands, Torcross 29.10.18 (pilot unhurt) |
| C5499 | 531/3 Flts 272 Sqdn Machrihanish by 19.10.18 - @11.11.18 |
| C5520 | 524/559 Flts 258 Sqdn Luce Bay by 23.8.18 - @3.11.18 |
| C5521 | A & B Flts 255 Sqdn Pembroke by 7.7.18 |
| C5542 | 524/559 Flts 258 Sqdn Luce Bay by 21.10.18 |
| C5694 | SD Flt Cramlington by 3.18 |
| C5700 | C Flt 244 Sqdn Tallaght by 12.18 |
| C5706 | 500/1 Flts 250 Sqdn Padstow by 7.18 |
| C5730 | C Flt/510 Flt 252 Sqdn Redcar by 6.18 |
| C5740 | 515/6 Flts 236 Sqdn Mullaghmore by 5.11.18 |

**7 AVRO 504J TRACTOR BIPLANE TRAINERS from batch C5751 to C6050 built by Harland & Wolff Ltd at Belfast. (100-hp Gnome Monosoupape)**

| | |
|---|---|
| C5801 | Shoreham 1918; 204 TDS Eastchurch, mid air collision 15.9.18 (Lt LA Philip killed & F/Cdt WF Ashfield injured) |
| C5803 | 204 TDS Eastchurch by 6.18 |
| C5807 | 204 TDS Eastchurch; EF, FL, crashed, u/c damaged 17.6.18 |
| C5809 | 204 TDS Eastchurch by 6.18 |
| C5813 | 206 TDS Eastbourne by 19.6.18; 54 TDS Fairlop by 9.18 |
| C5843 | 207 TDS Chingford, spun in from 300 ft 8.7.18 (2/Lt C Homewood) |
| C5844 | 207 TDS Chingford; FL on golf links, hit horse on TO, o/t and caught fire 4.7.18 (Lt GR Ashton & F/Cdt J Pedley both injured) |

**47 AIRCO D.H.9 TRACTOR BIPLANE BOMBERS from batch C6051 to C6350 built by parent company at Hendon. (200-hp B.H.P.)**

| | |
|---|---|
| C6060 | Deld Martlesham 31.1.18; Hendon 23.2.18; Farnborough 2.3.18; 98 Sqdn |
| C6121 | 1 AI to 206 Sqdn 20.6.18; Left 18.29, last seen 2m N of Gheluve 25.7.18 (Lt FT Heron & 2/Lt CJ Byrne both killed); SOC in field 26.7.18 |
| C6122 | Fairlop to Hendon 12.5.18; Martlesham Heath 15.5.18 |
| C6136 | Rec Pk to 206 Sqdn 26.4.18; Left 18.15, badly shot about by HA, FL Téteghem 20.5.18 (Lt PW Birkbeck uninjured & 2/Lt W Susman wounded); 2 ASD 22.5.18; Rebuilt as F5850 25.6.18 |
| C6138 | 4 ASD Dunkerque by 25.5.18 - @31.5.18 |
| C6152 | Rec Pk to 1 AI 1.4.18; 206 Sqdn 1.4.18; COL 21.5.18 (Lt RH Stainbank & 2/Lt FC Taylor); SOC 24.5.18 NWR |
| C6158 | 1 AI to 206 Sqdn 18.4.18; Overshot landing, crashed into trailer 12.6.18 (Sgt R Jackson & Pte1 WS Blyth); 1 Rep Pk 1 ASD 14.6.18; 4 ASD 17.6.18; SOC 1 ASD 5.7.18 NWR |
| C6159 | Rec Pk to 206 Sqdn 16.5.18; FTR bombing raid, last seen W of Roulers 07.10 19.5.18 (2/Lt BF Dunford & 2/Lt FF Collins); SOC 20.5.18 |
| C6161 | Rec Pk to 1 AI 15.5.18; 206 Sqdn 17.5.18; Left 08.15, last seen nr Menin 19.5.18 (2/Lt H Mitchell & AM CF Costen both PoW); SOC 20.5.18 |
| C6163 | 206 Sqdn from 21.5.18; Damaged by shrapnel in bombing raid, FL Acquin 23.5.18 (Capt GLE Stevens & Lt LA Christian unhurt); Rep Pk 1 ASD 23.5.18; SOC 27.5.18 |
| C6167 | Rec Pk to 1 AI 27.5.18; 211 Sqdn 30.5.18; Hit by AA, EF on bombing raid, FL beach 3.6.18 (Lt GH Baker & 2/Lt TB Dodwell); COL 16.6.18 (2/Lt ETM Routledge & 2/Lt JFJ Peters unhurt); Rep Pk 1 ASD 16.6.18; SOC 20.6.18 NWR |
| C6180 | Rec Pk to 1 AI 23.4.18; 206 Sqdn 25.4.18; EF, FL Clairmarais 6.6.18 (Capt JW Mathews & Lt C Knight unhurt); Rep Pk 1 ASD 10.6.18; SOC 1 ASD 5.7.18 NWR |
| C6196 | AI to 218 Sqdn 2.11.18 - @2.1.19 |
| C6201 | Shipped to Mudros 20.4.18 |
| C6205 | Shipped to Mudros 20.4.18; Imbros by 25.5.18; 220 Sqdn by 10.18; 222 Sqdn Imbros by 14-16.11.18; Repair Base Mudros by 10.18 - @1.19 |
| C6208 | Shipped to Mudros 20.4.18; 226 Sqdn by 25.5.18 - @7.18; AD Taranto by 29.8.18 |
| C6212 | Rec Pk to 1 AI 14.5.18; 98 Sqdn by 6.18; HA scout OOC 1.6.18 (Capt FA Laughlin & Lt H Tasker); 4 ASD by 8.18; 218 Sqdn 9.8.18; In combat 11.8.18 (Lt KR Campbell unhurt & Sgt AE Powell slightly wounded); COL, damaged 29.8.18 (Lt GF Smith & 2/Lt B Archer); 4 ASD 1.9.18; 2 SS Richborough 2.10.18 |
| C6213 | Shipped to Mudros 20.4.18 |
| C6220 | Deld 2 AAP Hendon by 8.5.18; Rec Pk to 1 AI 1.7.18; 206 Sqdn 2.7.18; Pfalz DIII down smoking, crashed Neuve Eglise 07.25 7.8.18 (Lt H Stier USAS & Sgt J Chapman DSM); EF, COL 23.8.18 (Lt JD Russell & 2/Lt B Knee unhurt); 1 ASD 24.8.18; SOC 12.9.18 NWR |
| C6221 | Shipped to Mudros 20.4.18; 226 Sqdn by 25.5.18 - @8.18 |
| C6222 | Shipped to Mudros 20.4.18; Repair Base Mudros by 25.5.18; 220 Sqdn by 3-4.7.18; Stavros by 10.18 - @1.19 |
| C6224 | Shipped to Mudros 20.4.18; 226 Sqdn by 25.5.18 - @2.10.18; Taranto by 10.18 - @1.19 |
| C6240 | Deld 2 AAP Hendon by 30.4.18; 1 AI to 206 Sqdn 14.5.18; Fokker DrI crashed and burnt, shared C118 Bac St.Maur 12.00 7.6.18 (Capt GLE Stevens & Lt C Eaton); Pfalz DIII crashed Zonnebeke 12.32 12.6.18 (Capt GLE Stevens & Lt LA Christian); Hit in radiator by AA approaching target, unable to keep up with formation on return flight, running fight (15.25-15.40) Nazareth, nr Ghent with 3 Fokker biplanes, one of which BU in air, then crashed Aeltre-Pucques 30.10.18 (Sgt Mech G Packman & 2/Lt JW Kennedy unhurt); to Rep Pk 1 ASD |
| C6245 | 6 Wing Otranto by 18.3.18 (or C6255?) |
| C6248 | Deld 2 AAP Hendon by 30.4.18; 4 ASD; 2 SS Richborough 2.10.18 |
| C6250 | Deld Hendon to Dover W/E 24.5.18; 218 Sqdn by 20.5.18; Slightly damaged after raid 12.6.18 (Lt JW Kennedy & G/L Pte1 EWS Curtis unhurt); COL 18.6.18 (Lt JW Kennedy & Pte1 EWS G/L Curtis unhurt); Yellow Pfalz DIII DD 18.15 5.7.18; Albatros DV down in sea shared by formation Zeebrugge 07.10 14.7.18 (both Capt JF Chisholm & G/L Sgt RJ Williams); Engine cut, landed crosswind, badly damaged 18.8.18 (Bos CJ O'Connor USN & QM C Van Galder unhurt); 4 ASD 20.8.18; 2 SS Richborough 15.9.18 |
| C6265 | Deld 2 AAP Hendon by 26.4.18; Rec Pk to 206 Sqdn 4.5.18; COL, CW 19.6.18 (Lt FT Heron & 2/Lt CO Shelswell unhurt); 1 ASD 21.6.18; SOC 23.6.18 NWR |
| C6270 | Rec Pk to 1 AI 13.7.18; 211 Sqdn 15.7.18; Stalled landing from bombing raid, CW 17.10.18 (2/Lt J Hart and 2/Lt TE Drake both slightly injured); Remains to Rep Pk 1 ASD 17.10.18 |
| C6273 | Rec Pk to 1 AI 27.5.18; 4 ASD by 9.18; 2 SS Richborough 15.9.18 |
| C6275 | Rec Pk to 206 Sqdn 25.5.18; COL 16.6.18 (Lt AJ Garside & 2/Lt MG Perry unhurt); 1 ASD 18.6.18; SOC 25.6.18 NWR |
| C6280 | 204 TDS Eastchurch by 13.7.18 - @11.18; 2 MOS Eastchurch by 2.19 |
| C6281 | 'X' AP Qantara by 9.18; 144 Sqdn 6.9.18; Mudros by 10.18 - @11.18 |
| C6282 | Deld 2 AAP Hendon by 8.5.18; 1 AI to 211 Sqdn 27.5.18; Sideslipped on landing 29.6.18 (2/Lt CO Carson & Cpl H Lindsay unhurt); 1 ASD 30.6.18; SOC 3.7.18 NWR |
| C6283 | Deld 6 SD Ascot W/E 15.8.18; At docks W/E 19.9.18; Shipped to Mudros in SS *Hazlemere* W/E 17.10.18, but damaged en route |
| C6286 | 2 MOS Eastchurch by 3.19 - @7.19 |
| C6287 | Rec Pk to 211 Sqdn 1.6.18; EF, FL on beach Gravelines 24.6.18 (2/Lt ETM Routledge & 2/Lt JFJ Peters unhurt); 1 ASD 24.6.18 |
| C6289 | Rec Pk by 6.18; 1 AI 1.7.18; 206 Sqdn 8.7.18; Pfalz DIII OOC 20.00-20.15 25.7.18 (2/Lt FA Brock & Sgt Mech LH Rowe); Left on bombing raid 05.30, last seen Neuve Eglise 7.8.18 (2/Lt FA Brock & Pte CH Cullimore both killed); SOC in field 8.8.18 |
| C6292 | 1 Observers School Eastchurch by 10.18 - @11.18 |
| C6310 | 6 Wing Otranto by 18.3.18 |

| | |
|---|---|
| C6321 | 218 Sqdn by 20.5.18; Damaged in combat nr Ostende 12.6.18 (Lt CLW Brading & G/L Sgt RS Joysey); EF on overshoot, CW 7.7.18 (Lt CLW Brading & G/L Sgt F Smith unhurt); to 4 ASD for repair; 2 SS Richborough 15.9.18 |
| C6322 | 218 Sqdn by 20.5.18; 4 ASD Pilot Pool by 25.6.18; Crashed; WOC 30.9.18 DBR |
| C6326 | 4 ASD to 491 Flt 233 Sqdn Dover 23.10.18 - @16.12.18 |
| C6327 | Deld 6 SD Ascot W/E 15.8.18; At docks W/E 19.9.18; Shipped to Mudros in SS *Hazlemere* W/E 17.10.18, but damaged en route |
| C6328 | Deld 6 SD Ascot W/E 15.8.18; At docks W/E 19.9.18; Shipped to Mudros in SS *Hazlemere* W/E 17.10.18, but damaged en route |
| C6329 | Deld 6 SD Ascot W/E 15.8.18; At docks W/E 19.9.18; Shipped to Mudros in SS *Hazlemere* W/E 17.10.18, but damaged en route |
| C6348 | Rec Pk to 1 AI 24.6.18; 211 Sqdn (coded 'C') 26.6.18; EF on TO, FL, crashed in corn, o/t 7.8.18 (Capt RM Wynne-Eyton & 2/Lt TB Dodwell unhurt); Badly damaged by flak over Bruges, FL in the Wielingen, 2m from coast, sank 16.8.18 (Capt RM Wynne-Eyton unhurt & 2/Lt TB Dodwell both badly wounded, both rescued by Dutch guard boat, interned); SOC 16.8.18 |

**75 AIRCO D.H.6 TRACTOR BIPLANES from batch C6501 to C6700 built by Morgan & Co & built Leighton Buzzard. (80-hp Renault up to at least C6636, 90-hp Curtiss OX-5 by at least C6660)**

| | |
|---|---|
| C6508 | Cramlington by 4.18; FL in sea off Sunderland 3.4.18; FL in sea Cullercoats 6.4.18 |
| C6513 | 513 Flt 241 Sqdn Chickerell by 8.18 - @11.18 |
| C6514 | 517/8 Flts 254 Sqdn Prawle Point by 8.18; EF, FL in sea, towed Dartmouth by drifter 23.8.18 (pilot unhurt) |
| C6515 | 517/8 Flts 254 Sqdn Prawle Point by 6.18; Crashed on TO after landing Stoke Church 24.6.18 (pilot unhurt) |
| C6516 | 17 TS Yatesbury by 6.18; 515/6 Flts 236 Sqdn Mullion by 30.8.18; 517/8 Flts Prawle Point 28.11.18 |
| C6519 | 515/6 Flts Mullion by 31.7.18; Became 515/6 Flts 236 Sqdn Mullion by 8.18 - @25.11.18 |
| C6521 | 517/8 Flts 254 Sqdn Prawle Point by 20.8.18 - @10.11.18 |
| C6522 | HAAP to Medical Flt Hendon W/E 6.4.18 - @25.5.18 |
| C6553 | 507/8 Flts 252 Sqdn Cramlington by 10.6.18 |
| C6557 | Deld 2 AAP Hendon for erection by 23.2.18; Eastbourne NFS 28.2.18; Left station 22.7.18 |
| C6559 | Deld 2 AAP Hendon for erection by 23.2.18; Eastbourne NFS 26.3.18; 11 TDS Old Sarum by 7.18 |
| C6560 | 521/2 Flts 244 Sqdn Bangor by 2.9.18; 530 Flt 244 Sqdn Tallaght 23.10.18; 521/2 Flts 244 Sqdn Bangor 10.12.18 |
| C6561 | 515/6 Flts 236 Sqdn Mullion by 9.9.18 - @17.11.18 |
| C6562 | 517/8 Flts 254 Sqdn Prawle Point by 28.7.18 - @1.10.18 |
| C6563 | 517/8 Flts 254 Sqdn Prawle Point by 7.18; 515/6 Flts 236 Sqdn Mullion 19.7.18 - @27.11.18 |
| C6564 | 517/8 Flts 254 Sqdn Prawle Point by 23.7.18; Boscombe Down 18.12.18 |
| C6565 | 511/2 Flts 253 Sqdn Bembridge by 7.18 |
| C6566 | 511/2 Flts 253 Sqdn Bembridge by 7.18 - @9.18 |
| C6567 | Unit?, Stalled and spun in on climb, Duxford 28.7.18 (F/O RK Hardy, RN) |
| C6568 | Deld 2 AAP Hendon for erection by 23.2.18; Eastbourne NFS 27.3.18 |
| C6570 | Deld 2 AAP Hendon for erection by 23.2.18; Eastbourne NFS 1.4.18; Chingford 7.5.18 |
| C6571 | 211 TDS Portholme by 10.18 |
| C6577 | SMOP Dover by 11.18 - @12.18 |
| C6578 | 511/2 Flts 253 Sqdn New Bembridge by 8.18; SMOP Dover by 11.18 |
| C6581 | 211 TDS Portholme Meadow by 7.8.18 |
| C6582 | 511/2 Flts 253 Sqdn New Bembridge by 8.18 |
| C6587 | 511/2 Flts 253 Sqdn New Bembridge by 7.18 - @8.18 |
| C6588 | 17 TS Yatesbury by 6.18; SD Flt 254 Sqdn Mullion by 21.8.18 (sic); Became 515/6 Flts 236 Sqdn Mullion 15.8.18; EF, FL in sea, damaged, towed harbour 2.9.18 (pilot unhurt) |
| C6590 | 511/2 Flts 253 Sqdn New Bembridge by 7.18 |
| C6591 | 511/2 Flts 253 Sqdn New Bembridge by 7.18 - @11.18 |
| C6592 | 511/2 Flts 253 Sqdn New Bembridge by 9.18 |
| C6593 | 511/2 Flts 253 Sqdn New Bembridge by 9.18 |
| C6617 | 513 Flt 241 Sqdn Chickerell by 12.6.18 - @13.6.18 |
| C6618 | 513 Flt 241 Sqdn Chickerell by 13.6.18 - @5.7.18 |
| C6631 | Allocated 1 SD for RNAS use 21.3.18 |
| C6632 | Allocated 1 SD for RNAS use 21.3.18 |
| C6633 | Allocated 1 SD for RNAS use 21.3.18; 10 TDS Harling Road by 6.18 |
| C6634 | Allocated 1 SD for RNAS use 21.3.18 |
| C6635 | Allocated 1 SD for RNAS use 21.3.18; 10 TDS Harling Road by 6.18 |
| C6636 | Allocated 1 SD for RNAS use 21.3.18; 10 TDS Harling Road by 6.18 |

**(90-hp Curtiss OX-5 from about here)**

| | |
|---|---|
| C6640 | (engine?) 211 TDS Portholme Meadow by 29.7.18 |
| C6653 | South Shields by 8.18; 507/8 Flts 252 Sqdn Tynemouth 28.8.18 |
| C6655 | (engine?) 521/2 Flts 244 Sqdn Bangor by 29.8.18; EF, FL in sea, sank under tow 8m NW of Holyhead 18.9.18 (pilot unhurt) |
| C6656 | (engine?) 521/2 Flts 244 Sqdn Bangor by 15.8.18 - @15.11.18 |
| C6657 | 517/8 Flts 254 Sqdn Prawle Point by 1.10.18 |
| C6660 | 2 AAP Hendon by 27.4.18 for 18 Group anti-submarine - @18.5.18 |
| C6661 | 515/6 Flts 236 Sqdn Mullion by 9.18; EF, FL in sea, towed in by tug 19.9.18 (pilot unhurt) |
| C6664 | 515/6 Flts 236 Sqdn Mullion by 1.10.18 - @3.12.18 |
| C6666 | 517/8 Flts 254 Sqdn Prawle Point by 28.9.18 - @14.11.18; 515/6 Flts 236 Sqdn Mullion by 11.18 |
| C6667 | 517/8 Flts 254 Sqdn Prawle Point by 28.9.18 - @8.10.18; Dropped 65-lb bomb on U-boat 5015N 0334W 23.9.18 (Lt R Wimpenny); 515/6 Flts 236 Sqdn Mullion by 10.18 |
| C6671 | 502/3 Flts 250 Sqdn Westward Ho! by 11.10.18 - @14.11.18 |
| C6672 | 502/3 Flts 250 Sqdn Westward Ho! by 13.10.18 - @14.11.18 |
| C6677 | 511/2 Flts 253 Sqdn Bembridge by 11.18 |
| C6678 | Deld W/E 15.5.18; 254 Sqdn Mullion by 18-25.5.18; 500/1 Flts 250 Sqdn Padstow by 5.18; Ran out of petrol, FL in sea, towed in undamaged 20.5.18 (pilot unhurt); Missing 29.5.18 |
| C6679 | Deld W/E 15.5.18; 254 Sqdn Mullion by 18-25.5.18; 500/1 Flts 250 Sqdn Padstow .18 |
| C6680 | Deld W/E 15.5.18; 254 Sqdn Mullion by 18-25.5.18; 500/1 Flts 250 Sqdn Padstow by 29.5.18 - @6.7.18; 502/3 Flts Westward Ho! by 23.7.18 - @8.18; 526 Flt 256 Sqdn New Haggerston by 10.18 |
| C6681 | 254 Sqdn Mullion by 18-25.5.18; 500/1 Flts 250 Sqdn Padstow by 29.5.18; Crashed 26.6.18; C Flt Redcar by 7.7.18 |
| C6682 | 254 Sqdn Mullion by 18-25.5.18; 500/1 Flts 250 Sqdn Padstow by 15.6.18 - @8.18; FL, crashed, wrecked 3m S of Bude 6.7.18 (pilot unhurt) |
| C6683 | 254 Sqdn Mullion by 18-25.5.18; 500/1 Flts 250 Sqdn Padstow by 27.5.18; FL in sea 28.5.18 |
| C6685 | C Flt/510 Flt 252 Sqdn Redcar by 28-29.6.18 |
| C6686 | South Shields by 9.18; 527 Flt 256 Sqdn Sea Houses 23.9.18 - @6.11.18; 509 Flt 252 Sqdn Seaton Carew by 11.11.18; 527 Flt 256 Sqdn Sea Houses by 14.11.18; Crashed, WO Cullercoats 30.11.18 (both crew unhurt) |
| C6687 | 527 Flt 256 Sqdn Sea Houses by 12.11.18 |
| C6688 | South Shields by 9.18; 509 Flt 252 Sqdn Seaton Carew 20.9.18 - @11.11.18 |
| C6689 | C Flt/510 Flt 252 Sqdn Redcar by 29.6.18 |
| C6690 | Deld MAD South Shields W/E 25.5.18; 252 Sqdn Seaton Carew 29.6.18 - @4.7.18 |
| C6691 | Deld MAD South Shields W/E 25.5.18; To 507/8 Flts 252 Sqdn Tynemouth but crashed in harbour on arrival, salved 9.7.18 (pilot unhurt); Still Tynemouth 11.11.18 |
| C6692 | Deld MAD South Shields W/E 25.5.18; C Flt/510 Flt 252 Sqdn Redcar 6.7.18 - @16.7.18 |
| C6693 | Deld MAD South Shields for erection 23.5.18; Seaton Carew 23.5.18; 507/8 Flts 252 Sqdn Tynemouth by 8.6.18; MAD South Shields 11.8.18; 507/8 Flts 252 Sqdn Tynemouth by 9.18; EF, FL on beach Whitburn 8.9.18 (pilot safe); South Shields 18.9.18; 507/8 Flts 252 Sqdn Tynemouth 29.9.18 - @19.10.18 |
| C6694 | Deld MAD South Shields for erection 23.5.18; C Flt/510 Flt 252 Sqdn Redcar 11.7.18; FL in sea 24.7.18 (two crew picked up by motor launch) |

C6695    Deld MAD South Shields W/E 25.5.18; C Flt/510 Flt 252 Sqdn Redcar 7.6.18; EF, FL in sea off Whitby, CW in tow 8.7.18 (pilot unhurt)

C6696    Deld MAD South Shields W/E 25.5.18; C Flt/510 Flt 252 Sqdn Redcar 18.6.18 - @7.18; FL in sea off Redcar, salving by steamer 30.6.18

C6697    Deld MAD South Shields W/E 25.5.18; C Flt/510 Flt 252 Sqdn Redcar 18.6.18; MAD South Shields 16.9.18; 507/08 Flts 252 Sqdn Tynemouth 29.9.18 - @11.11.18

C6698    Deld MAD South Shields W/e 25.5.18; 507/8 Flts 252 Sqdn Tynemouth by 7.18; MAD South Shields 9.7.18; 507/8 Flts 252 Sqdn Tynemouth by 17.7.18; MAD South Shields 18.9.18; Seaton Carew

C6699    Deld MAD South Shields W/E 25.5.18; 507/8 Flts 252 Sqdn Tynemouth 12.6.18 - @19.6.18; MAD South Shields by 7.18; 510 Flt 252 Sqdn Redcar 14.7.18 - @16.8.18; 509 Flt 252 Sqdn Seaton Carew by 30.8.18; MAD South Shields 20.9.18; 510 Flt 252 Sqdn Redcar 29.10.18

C6700    Deld MAD South Shields W/E 25.5.18; SD Flt 252 Sqdn Cramlington 31.5.18; 507/8 Flts 252 Sqdn Tynemouth 8.6.18; FL Friars Mead Farm 20.6.18; C Flt/510 Flt 252 Sqdn Redcar by 8.18; 509 Flt 252 Sqdn Seaton Carew by 8.18 - @9.18

**5 SOPWITH F.1 CAMEL TRACTOR BIPLANE SCOUTS from batch C6701 to C6800 built by The British Caudron Co Ltd at Alloa. (100-hp Le Rhône)**

C6718    78 Sqdn by 17.2.18; 2 ASD to 65 Sqdn 18.5.18; 2 ASD 23.5.18; Rec Pk 2 ASD by 7.18; 2 AI 22.7.18; 201 Sqdn 9.8.18; Fokker DVII OOC Lihons 19.45 11.8.18 (Lt FTS Sehl); Taxying after return from low flying practice, ran into D9653 8.10.18 (Lt FTS Sehl); to 2 ASD

C6727    Grand Fleet S of AF&G Leuchars by 7.19

C6735    (110-hp Le Rhône) Turnhouse by 5.18; EF, spun in 24.7.18 (Lt JIA Rossington-Barnett killed)

C6736    (110-hp Le Rhône) Deld 6 AAP Renfrew W/E 25.5.18; Turnhouse W/E 13.6.18 - @30.1.19

C6737    (110-hp Le Rhône) Deld 6 AAP Renfrew W/E 25.5.18; Turnhouse W/E 13.6.18 - @30.1.19

**34 AIRCO D.H.6 TRACTOR BIPLANES from batch C6801 to C6900 built by Savages Ltd.**

C6804    SD Flt Cramlington by 8.4.18 - @18.4.18LM

C6815    A Flt/527 Flt 256 Sqdn Seahouses by 8.18; 526 Flt 256 Sqdn New Haggerston 9.8.18

C6832    (90-hp R.A.F.) SD Flt Cramlington by 1.4.18; FL Belsay 2.4.18; FL at Blyth & South Shields 6.4.18; MAD South Shields W/E 25.5.18 & disposed of

C6838    Harling Road (10 TDS?) to 211 TDS Portholme Meadow 8.7.18 - @10.18

C6860    526 Flt 256 Sqdn Sea Houses by 12.11.18

C6861    (engine?) 211 TDS Portholme Meadow by 7.18; 1 MOS Aldeburgh, collided at 300 ft with C7829 24.5.19 (2/Lt W Wyatt DoI 26.5.19 and Sgt LD Adcock injured)

C6862    'C' Flt/510 Flt 252 Sqdn Redcar by 7.18

C6871    252 Sqdn by 7.18 - @8.18; 510 Flt 252 Sqdn Redcar by 29.8.18; FL in high wind, u/c smashed Whitby 11.9.18 (pilot unhurt)

C6872    252 Sqdn by 7.18 - @8.18; 502/3 Flts Westward Ho! .18; MAD South Shields to 507/8 Flts 252 Sqdn Tynemouth 26.8.18 - @12.10.18

C6873    252 Sqdn by 7.18 - @8.18; MAD South Shields to 510 Flt 252 Sqdn Redcar 23.8.18 - @29.9.18; 251 Sqdn West Ayton by 16.10.18 - @12.11.18; BUT 501 Flt 250 Sqdn Padstow by 7.11.18

C6874    MAD South Shields to 528 Flt 256 Sqdn Sea Houses 4.9.18

C6875    MAD South Shields to B Flt 256 Sqdn Sea Houses 8.8.18; D Flt/509 Flt 252 Sqdn Seaton Carew by 12.8.18; 526 Flt 256 Sqdn New Haggerston by 9.18; Crashed in sea, salved 9.9.18 (crew unhurt)

C6876    256 Sqdn by 7.18 - @8.18; MAD South Shields by 8.18; B Flt 256 Sqdn Sea Houses 6.8.18; 526 Flt 256 Sqdn New Haggerston 6.8.18; D Flt/509 Flt 252 Sqdn Seaton Carew, FL in bad position ½m S of Blackhalls Coastguard Station 21.8.18 (pilot unhurt); 528 Flt 256 Sqdn Sea Houses by 26.8.18 - @5.9.18

C6877    MAD South Shields to 527/8 Flts 256 Sqdn Sea Houses 9.8.18 - @26.8.18; 511/2 Flts Bembridge .18

C6878    MAD South Shields (via Cullercoats) to 'D' Flt/509 Flt Seaton Carew 1.8.18

C6879    C Flt/528 Flt 256 Sqdn Sea Houses by 3.8.18; A Flt/527 Flt 256 Sqdn Sea Houses, wrecked on TO 16.8.18 (pilot unhurt)

C6880    MAD South Shields by 8.18; 'A' Flt/527 Flt 256 Sqdn Sea Houses 6.8.18; To 526 Flt 256 Sqdn New Haggerston but smashed u/c landing 6.9.18 (pilot unhurt); still New Haggerston @16.11.18

C6881    (Curtiss OX-5) Deld MAD South Shields W/E 25.5.18; 'C' Flt/510 Flt 252 Sqdn Redcar 7.6.18; Dropped 100-lb bomb on U-boat 1m E of P Buoy, Runswick Bay, the U-boat being also attacked by HMS Calvier (ML401) 14.7.18 (Lt FR Giradot); MAD South Shields 18.9.18; 528 Flt 256 Sqdn Sea Houses 2.10.18 - @18.11.18

C6882    (Curtiss OX-5) Deld MAD South Shields W/E 25.5.18; 'C' Flt/510 Flt 252 Sqdn Redcar by 5.6.18; Dropped bomb on U-boat off H Buoy, Tees 24.6.18 (Lt LM Burton); EF, FL, crashed 25.6.18 (pilot unhurt); Bombed U-boat 15.7.18; 513 Flt 241 Sqdn Chickerell by 8.18 (??)

C6883    (Curtiss OX-5) Deld MAD South Shields W/E 25.5.18; SD Flt Seaton Carew 30.5.18; SD Flt Cramlington, dropped bomb on U-boat 7m SE of Cresswell 3.6.18 (Capt FW Walker DSC); 507/8 Flts 252 Sqdn Tynemouth 8.6.18; FL in sea 6m E of Sunderland, towed into Tyne 28.6.18

C6884    (Curtiss OX-5) Deld MAD South Shields W/E 25.5.18; 507/8 Flts 252 Sqdn Tynemouth 11.6.18; FL 16.7.18

C6885    (Curtiss OX-5) Deld MAD South Shields W/E 25.5.18; 'C' Flt/510 Flt 252 Sqdn Redcar by 6.18 - @27.6.18

C6886    (Curtiss OX-5) For delivery to 253 Sqdn by 25.5.18; 514 Flt Telscombe by 7.18 - @8.18

C6887    (90-hp R.A.F.) Allocated Killingholme by 25.5.18; 504 Flt 251 Sqdn Atwick by 18.6.18 - @25.6.18

C6888    (90-hp R.A.F.) Allocated Killingholme by 25.5.18; 504 Flt 251 Sqdn Atwick by 15.6.18; EF, FL, propeller and starboard wing damaged, 2m S of Withernsea, rtd by lorry 24.6.18 (pilot unhurt); still Atwick @29.9.18 - @1.10.18

C6889    (90-hp R.A.F.) Allocated Killingholme by 25.5.18; 512/513 Flts 253 Sqdn Bembridge by 5.11.18; Became G-EAHI

C6890    (90-hp R.A.F.) Allocated Killingholme by 25.5.18; 504 Flt 251 Sqdn Atwick by 6.18; EF, FL in sea 7m NE of Scarborough, sank in tow 17.6.18 (pilot to Scarborough in drifter Venus)

C6891    514 Flt Telscombe by 6.18; Became 514 Flt 242 Sqdn Telscombe 15.8.18 - @1.11.18; 511/2 Flts 253 Sqdn New Bembridge by 10.11.18

C6892    513 Flt 241 Sqdn Chickerell by 8.18 - @11.18

C6893    514 Flt Telscombe by 6.18; Became 514 Flt 242 Sqdn Telscombe 15.8.18 - @11.18

C6895    514 Flt Telscombe by 7.18

C6897    Bembridge by 7.18; Became 511/2 Flts 253 Sqdn New Bembridge 8.18 - @9.18

C6899    513 Flt 241 Sqdn Chickerell by 8.18 - @11.18

C6900    513 Flt 241 Sqdn Chickerell by 9.18

**3 ROYAL AIRCRAFT FACTORY B.E.2e TRACTOR BIPLANES from batch C7001 to C7100 built by Barclay, Curle & Co Ltd**

C7081    55 TDS Manston by 7.18 - @8.18

C7082    ARS to 55 TDS Manston 21.8.18

C7083    55 TDS Manston from 8.18

**37 AIRCO D.H.6 TRACTOR BIPLANES from batch C7201 to C7600 built by Ransomes, Sims & Jeffries at Ipswich. (90-hp R.A.F.)**

C7203    SD Flt Cramlington, FL in sea off Tynemouth 2.4.18

C7205    AP Hendon to Hendon by road 17.4.18; Yate W/E 4.5.18

C7217    Shawbury to 521/2 Flts 244 Sqdn Bangor 18.8.18

C7284    211 TDS Portholme Meadow by 7.18 - @8.18

C7311    Ex RFC to 1 SD allocated by 30.3.18

C7312    Ex RFC to 1 SD allocated by 30.3.18

C7313    Ex RFC to 1 SD allocated by 30.3.18

C7314  Ex RFC to 1 SD by 30.3.18

C7315  Ex RFC to 1 SD by 30.3.18

C7316  Ex RFC to 1 SD by 30.3.18

C7331  Ex RFC to 1 SD allocated by 30.3.18

C7332  Ex RFC to 1 SD allocated by 30.3.18

C7333  Ex RFC to 1 SD allocated by 30.3.18

C7334  Ex RFC to 1 SD allocated by 30.3.18; MAD South Shields by 9.18; 527 Flt 256 Sqdn Sea Houses 13.9.18 - @11.18; 526 Flt 256 Sqdn New Haggerston by 14.11.18

C7335  Ex RFC to 1 SD allocated by 30.3.18; MAD South Shields by 9.18; Seaton Carew 1.9.18; 505 Flt 251 Sqdn West Ayton by 11.9.18 - @13.11.18

C7336  Ex RFC to 1 SD allocated by 30.3.18; MAD South Shields by 9.18; 526 Flt 256 Sqdn New Haggerston 2.9.18 - @12.18; Dropped bomb on U-boat, results unobserved 11.9.18 (2/Lt WU Kennedy)

C7337  Ex RFC to 1 SD allocated by 30.3.18; 506 Flt 251 Sqdn Owthorne by 10.18 - @13.11.18

C7338  Ex RFC to 1 SD allocated by 30.3.18; MAD South Shields by 9.18; 527 Flt 256 Sqdn Sea Houses 4.9.18 - @17.11.18

C7339  Ex RFC to 1 SD allocated by 30.3.18; MAD South Shields by 9.18; 505 Flt 251 Sqdn West Ayton 5.9.18; FL in sea at Petard, towed to Tyne 16.9.18

C7340  Ex RFC 1 SD Depot allocated by 30.3.18; 505 Flt 251 Sqdn West Ayton by 11.9.18 - @16.9.18

C7346  519/520 Flts 255 Sqdn Pembroke by 24.10.18 - @7.11.18

C7348  South Shields store by 9.18; 505 Flt 251 Sqdn West Ayton 5.9.18

C7350  519/520 Flts 255 Sqdn Pembroke .18

C7378  SMOP Dover by 11.18 - @1.19

C7401  (80-hp Renault) Deld Turnhouse 24.5.18

C7402  (80-hp Renault) Deld Turnhouse 24.5.18- @10.18

C7403  Deld Turnhouse 24.5.18

C7413  500/1 Flts 250 Sqdn Padstow by 28.9.18

C7417  502/3 Flts 250 Sqdn Westward Ho! by 28.9.18; Crashed on beach S of Hartland Quay 21.10.18

C7418  502/3 Flts 250 Sqdn Westward Ho! by 28.9.18; FL and crashed 21.10.18; EF, FL in sea, aircraft and pilot picked up in convoy 23.10.18 (pilot unhurt)

C7419  502/3 Flts 250 Sqdn Westward Ho! by 27.9.18; FL Abbotshaw, aircraft and pilot picked up 14.11.18

C7422  502/3 Flts 250 Sqdn Westward Ho! by 27.10.18 - @13.11.18

C7423  502/3 Flts 250 Sqdn Westward Ho! by 28.9.18 - @14.11.18

C7431  502/3 Flts 250 Sqdn Westward Ho! by 28.9.18 - @1.10.18

C7432  502/3 Flts 250 Sqdn Westward Ho! by 13.11.18

C7547  236 Sqdn Mullion

C7554  502/3 Flts 250 Sqdn Westward Ho! by 6.18; 506 Flt 251 Sqdn Owthorne by 19.11.18

**151 AIRCO D.H.6 TRACTOR BIPLANES from batch C7601 to C7900 built by The Grahame-White Aviation Co Ltd & built Hendon. (90-hp RAF.1A from C7601)**

C7602  Deld Hendon W/E 26.1.18; Manston NFS 15.2.18; Cranwell W/E 29.3.18; Became 202 TDS Cranwell 1.4.18; Became 57 TDS Cranwell 27.7.18; MAD South Shields 11.18; 252 Sqdn West Ayton 6.11.18

C7605  Deld Hendon W/E 26.1.18; Manston NFS 18.2.18; Cranwell (via Stamford) 23.3.18

C7608  Deld Hendon W/E 26.1.18; Manston NFS 15.2.18; Cranwell W/E 23.3.18

C7611  Deld Hendon W/E 26.1.18; Manston NFS 21.2.18; Cranwell W/E 23.3.18

C7613  500/1 Flts 250 Sqdn Padstow by 4.10.18

C7614  Deld Hendon W/E 26.1.18; Manston NFS 18.2.18; Cranwell (via Chingford and Huntingdon) 2.4.18

C7617  Deld Hendon W/E 26.1.18; Manston NFS 21.2.18; Became 203 TDS Manston 1.4.18

C7620  Deld Hendon W/E 9.2.18; Manston NFS for erection W/E 16.2.18; Became 203 TDS Manston 1.4.18 - @7.18; Became G-EALS

C7623  Deld Hendon W/E 9.2.18; Manston NFS for erection W/E 16.2.18; Became 203 TDS Manston 1.4.18 - @7.18

C7626  Deld Hendon W/E 9.2.18; Manston NFS for erection W/E 16.2.18; Became 203 TDS Manston 1.4.18

**80-hp Renault from here unless otherwise stated**

C7628  203 TDS Manston by 7.18

C7629  Deld Manston NFS 3.18; Became 203 TDS Manston 1.4.18

C7632  Deld Manston NFS W/E 30.3.18; Became 203 TDS Manston 1.4.18 - @5.18

C7635  Deld Manston NFS W/E 16.3.18; Became 203 TDS Manston 1.4.18

C7638  (90-hp R.A.F.) Deld 2 AAP Hendon W/E 2.2.18; Manston NFS 16.2.18; Became 203 TDS Manston 1.4.18

C7641  (90-hp R.A.F.) Deld 2 AAP Hendon W/E 16.2.18; Manston NFS W/E 2.3.18; Cranwell (via Chingford and Huntingdon) 2.4.18

C7644  Deld Manston NFS W/E 16.3.18; Became 203 TDS Manston 1.4.18 - @5.18; 256 Sqdn by 11.18?

C7645  515/6 Flts 236 Sqdn Mullion by 9.18; EF, FL, crashed, slightly damaged 11.11.18 (pilot unhurt)

C7647  Deld 2 AAP Hendon for erection W/E 23.2.18; Manston NFS W/E 16.3.18; Became 203 TDS Manston 1.4.18; Surveyed 5.4.18 (wrecked); Deleted 15.4.18; Presume rebuilt; 515/6 Flts 236 Sqdn Mullion by 6.11.18 - @2.12.18

C7649  515/6 Flts 236 Sqdn Mullion by 29.10.18 - @2.12.18

C7650  Deld 2 AAP Hendon by 30.3.18; to 203 TDS Manston 4.18 - @7.18

C7652  MAD South Shields by 8.18; 528 Flt 256 Sqdn Sea Houses 29.8.18; Crashed and wrecked on TO Sea Houses 4.9.18 (pilot unhurt)

C7653  Deld 2 AAP Hendon for erection W/E 23.2.18; Manston NFS W/E 2.3.18; Became 203 TDS Manston 1.4.18; 205 TDS Vendôme by 5.18

C7654  MAD South Shields by 8.18; 528 Flt 256 Sqdn Sea Houses 1.9.18 - @15.11.18

C7655  MAD South Shields by 9.18; 510 Flt 251 Sqdn West Ayton 5.9.18; still West Ayton @29.9.18; 505 Flt 251 Sqdn West Ayton by 8.11.18; 251 Flt 506 Sqdn Owthorne 1.1.19

C7656  Deld 2 AAP Hendon for erection W/E 23.2.18; Manston NFS W/E 9.3.18; Became 203 TDS Manston 1.4.18

C7657  MAD South Shields by 9.18; 510 Flt 252 Sqdn Redcar 17.9.18; Dropped 100-lb bomb on U-boat 5428N 0030W c14.55 29.9.18 (2/Lt HC Cook); West Ayton by 11.10.18 - @4.11.18

C7659  Deld 2 AAP Hendon for erection W/E 23.2.18; Manston NFS W/E 9.3.18; Deleted W/E 30.3.18

C7662  Deld 2 AAP Hendon for erection W/E 23.2.18; Manston NFS W/E 9.3.18; Cranwell W/E 30.3.18 - @6.18

C7663  SD Flt Mullion by 5.18

C7665  Deld 2 AAP Hendon for erection by 23.2.18; Manston NFS W/E 9.3.18; Cranwell W/E 30.3.18; Became 201/2 TDS Cranwell 1.4.18 - @5.18; 58 TDS Cranwell, crashed 9.8.18 (PFO CCF Walker slightly injured)

C7666  515/6 Flts 254 Sqdn (later 236 Sqdn) Mullion by 5.18 - @23.10.18 BUT 7 TDS Feltwell by 7.18; 37 TDS Yatesbury 15.7.18 - @8.18

C7668  Deld 2 AAP Hendon for erection W/E 23.2.18; Manston NFS W/E 9.3.18; Cranwell 2.4.18; 203 TDS Manston tested 29.5.18 - @8.18

C7671  Deld 2 AAP Hendon to Manston NFS W/E 23.2.18; Became 203 TDS Manston 1.4.18

C7674  Deld 2 AAP Hendon for erection W/E 23.2.18; Chingford W/E 16.3.18; Became 207 TDS Chingford 1.4.18; 211 TDS Portholme Meadow by 5.18 - @6.18

C7677  Deld 2 AAP Hendon for erection W/E 23.2.18; Chingford W/E 9.3.18; Became 207 TDS Chingford 1.4.18; 211 TDS Portholme Meadow by 5.18; Norwich 27.5.18; 126 Sqdn Fowlmere by 7.18; 5 TDS Stamford .18

C7679  517/8 Flts 254 Sqdn Prawle Point by 21.11.18

C7680  Deld 2 AAP Hendon for erection W/E 23.2.18; 207 TDS Chingford 4.18

C7681  500/1 Flts 250 Sqdn Padstow by 28.9.18 - @18.11.18

C7683  Deld 2 AAP Hendon for erection W/E 23.2.18; Chingford W/E 8.3.18; Became 207 TDS Chingford 1.4.18; 211 TDS Portholme Meadow by 6.18; Spun in on turn nr aerodrome 1.7.18 (Lt JH Caudell killed)

C7686  Deld 2 AAP Hendon W/E 9.3.18; Eastbourne NFS 24.3.18; Became 206 TDS Eastbourne 1.4.18

C7689  Deld 2 AAP Hendon for erection W/E 23.2.18;

Eastbourne NFS W/E 14.3.18; Surveyed 12.3.18 (wrecked); Deleted 13.3.18

C7692 Deld 2 AAP Hendon W/E 9.3.18; Eastbourne NFS 25.3.18; Became 206 TDS Eastbourne 1.4.18

C7695 Deld 2 AAP Hendon for erection W/E 23.2.18; Eastbourne NFS 6.3.18

C7698 Deld 2 AAP Hendon W/E 9.3.18; Eastbourne NFS W/E 30.3.18; Became 206 TDS Eastbourne 1.4.18

C7701 Deld 2 AAP Hendon W/E 9.3.18; Eastbourne NFS 22.3.18; Became 206 TDS Eastbourne 1.4.18

C7704 Deld 2 AAP Hendon W/E 16.3.18; Eastbourne NFS 22.3.18; Became 206 TDS Eastbourne 1.4.18; Left station 22.7.18

C7707 Deld 4 AAP Lincoln W/E 16.3.18; Eastbourne NFS 24.3.18; Became 206 TDS Eastbourne 1.4.18

C7710 Deld 4 AAP Lincoln W/E 16.3.18; Eastbourne NFS 21.3.18; Became 206 TDS Eastbourne 1.4.18

C7713 Deld 4 AAP Lincoln W/E 16.3.18; Eastbourne NFS 20.3.18; Became 206 TDS Eastbourne 1.4.18

C7716 Deld 2 AAP Hendon W/E 16.3.18; Cranwell W/E 30.3.18; Became 201/2 TDS Cranwell 1.4.18 - @5.18

C7719 Deld 2 AAP Hendon W/E 16.3.18; Cranwell 23.3.18; Became 201/2 TDS Cranwell 1.4.18 - @20.7.18

C7722 Deld 2 AAP Hendon W/E 16.3.18; Cranwell W/E 30.3.18; Became 201/2 TDS Cranwell 1.4.18 - @5.18

C7725 Deld 3 AAP Norwich W/E 16.3.18; Cranwell W/E 30.3.18; Became 201/2 TDS Cranwell 1.4.18

C7726 Deld 201/2 TDS Cranwell 4.18 - @6.18

C7728 Deld 3 AAP Norwich W/E 16.3.18; Cranwell 3.18; Became 201/2 TDS Cranwell 1.4.18 - @7.18

C7731 Deld Eastchurch W/E 30.3.18; Became 204 TDS Eastchurch 1.4.18

C7732 Deld 204 TDS Eastchurch by 5.18

C7734 Deld Eastchurch W/E 30.3.18; Became 204 TDS Eastchurch 1.4.18; 1 TDS Stamford by 9.18

C7737 Deld Eastchurch W/E 30.3.18; Became 204 TDS Eastchurch 1.4.18

C7740 Deld Eastchurch W/E 30.3.18; Became 204 TDS Eastchurch 1.4.18

C7743 Deld Eastchurch W/E 30.3.18; Became 204 TDS Eastchurch 1.4.18

C7746 Deld Eastchurch W/E 30.3.18; Became 204 TDS Eastchurch 1.4.18

C7749 Allocated for delivery to Eastchurch by 30.3.18

C7752 Deld Eastchurch W/E 30.3.18; Became 204 TDS Eastchurch 1.4.18 - @5.18

C7754 Deld 204 TDS Eastchurch by 5.18; To US Navy

C7755 Deld 204 TDS Eastchurch 4.18

C7758 Deld 204 TDS Eastchurch 4.18

C7761 Deld Eastchurch W/E 30.3.18; Became 204 TDS Eastchurch 1.4.18 - @5.18

C7764 Deld Eastchurch W/E 30.3.18; Became 204 TDS Eastchurch 1.4.18

C7767 Deld Eastchurch W/E 30.3.18; Became 204 TDS Eastchurch 1.4.18; Eastchurch by 11.18; 2 MOS (233 Sqdn?) Eastchurch by 1.19

C7770 Deld Eastchurch W/E 30.3.18; Became 204 TDS Eastchurch 1.4.18

C7773 Deld Eastchurch W/E 30.3.18; Became 204 TDS Eastchurch 1.4.18

C7774 507 Flt 252 Sqdn Tynemouth by 21.8.18; MAD South Shields 23.9.18

C7775 Deld 3 AAP Norwich W/E 27.3.18, allocated Eastbourne NFS

C7777 Deld 206 TDS Eastbourne 4.18

C7778 507/8 Flts 252 Sqdn Tynemouth by 3.9.18

C7779 Deld 206 TDS Eastbourne 4.18

C7780 531/3 Flts 272 Sqdn Machrihanish by 16.10.18 - @23.10.18

C7782 531/3 Flts 272 Sqdn Machrihanish by 16.10.18; EF, FL 23.10.18

C7786 530 Flt 244 Sqdn Tallaght .18

C7794 Visited Ayr 11.18, anti-sub patrol (from Luce Bay?)

C7796 530 Flt 244 Sqdn Bangor by 10.18; C Flt/530 Flt 244 Sqdn Tallaght 18.10.18; 530 Flt 244 Sqdn Bangor 8.12.18

C7799 (90-hp Curtiss OX-2) SD Flt 254 Sqdn Mullion W/E 25.5.18; FL, crashed on cliffs Lizard Point 8.7.18 (Lt Ticein missing)

C7800 530 Flt 244 Sqdn Bangor .18; C Flt/530 Flt 244 Sqdn Tallaght by 23.10.18; 530 Flt 244 Sqdn Bangor 8.12.18

C7811 Allocated Cranwell by 30.3.18

C7815 Allocated Cranwell by 30.3.18; Became G-EAQB

C7817 Allocated Cranwell by 30.3.18

C7819 Allocated Cranwell by 30.3.18

C7821 Allocated Cranwell by 30.3.18

C7823 Deld 3 AAP Norwich W/E 30.3.18 for Cranwell; Became G-EBPN

C7825 Allocated Cranwell by 30.3.18

C7827 Deld 3 SD for RNAS 21.3.18

C7829 (90-hp RAF) Deld 1 SD 21.3.18; 1 MOS Aldeburgh, mid-air collision with C6861 24.5.19 (Lt CVC Wright DoI & Lt EWS Jacobi killed)

C7831 Deld 1 SD for RNAS 21.3.18

C7832 (90-hp Curtiss OX-2) Deld 493 Flt 254 Sqdn Mullion W/E 25.5.18 - @21.8.18; 515/6 Flts 236 Sqdn Mullion by 8.18 - @9.18

C7833 Deld 1 SD for RNAS 21.3.18; 10 TDS Harling Road by 6.18

C7834 (90-hp Curtiss OX-2) Deld 493 Flt 254 Sqdn Mullion W/E 25.5.18 - @21.8.18; 236 Sqdn Mullion by 11.10.18 - @2.12.18

C7835 Deld 1 SD for RNAS 21.3.18; 500/1 Flts 250 Sqdn Padstow by 10.10.18 - @16.10.18

C7836 (90-hp Curtiss OX-2) Allocated 254 Sqdn Mullion W/E 25.5.18; 493 Flt 254 Sqdn Mullion by 6.18 - @19.10.18

C7837 Deld 1 SD for RNAS 21.3.18

C7838 (90-hp Curtiss OX-2) Allocated 254 Sqdn Mullion W/E 25.5.18; 493 Flt 254 Sqdn Mullion by 6.18 - @7.18; 254 Sqdn Mullion by 21.8.18; 515/516 Flts 236 Sqdn Mullion by 9.18 - @27.11.18

C7839 Deld 1 SD for RNAS 21.3.18

C7840 (90-hp Curtiss OX-2) Allocated 254 Sqdn Mullion W/E 25.5.18; 493 Flt 254 Sqdn Mullion by 23.6.18 - @8.18; 236 Sqdn Mullion by 1.10.18 - @27.11.18

C7841 Deld 1 SD for RNAS 21.3.18

C7842 (90-hp Curtiss OX-2) Allocated 254 Sqdn Mullion W/E 25.5.18; 493 Flt 254 Sqdn Mullion by 6.18; EF, FL, towed in by French trawler 14.8.18

C7843 Deld 1 SD for RNAS 21.3.18; Mullion by 31.7.18

C7844 (90-hp Curtiss OX-2) Allocated 254 Sqdn Mullion W/E 25.5.18; 493 Flt 254 Sqdn Mullion by 6.18; EF, FL, sank 30.6.18 (crew rescued)

C7845 Ex RFC to 1 SD 21.3.18

C7846 (90-hp Curtiss OX-2) Allocated 254 Sqdn Mullion W/E 25.5.18; 493 Flt 254 Sqdn Mullion by 6.18; Tested 13.7.18 - @28.10.18

C7847 (90-hp Curtiss OX-2) Allocated 254 Sqdn Mullion W/E 25.5.18; 493 Flt 254 Sqdn Mullion by 30.6.18 - @9.18; 515/516 Flts 236 Sqdn Mullion by 29.10.18 - @3.12.18

**90-hp Curtiss OX-5 from here**

C7848 (90-hp Curtiss OX-5) Allocated 250 Sqdn HQ Padstow by 25.5.18; 500/1 Flts Padstow by 6.18 - @9.8.18; 502/3 Flts 260 Sqdn Westward Ho! by 13.8.18; EF, FL in sea 15.8.18

C7849 (90-hp Curtiss OX-5) Allocated 250 Sqdn HQ Padstow by 25.5.18; 500/1 Flts Padstow by 16.6.18; Dropped 65-lb bomb on U-boat 5055N 0450W 27.7.18 (Lt AC Tremellen); 502/3 Flts 260 Sqdn Westward Ho! by 15.8.18; Stalled on turn, spun Westward Ho! 4.9.18 (2/Lt HC Kibby DoI)

C7850 (90-hp Curtiss OX-5) Allocated 250 Sqdn HQ Padstow by 25.5.18; 500/1 Flts 250 Sqdn Padstow by 17.6.18 - @14.7.18; 502/3 Flts 250 Sqdn Westward Ho! by 23.7.18; Stalled on gliding turn & spun in landing at dusk from A/S patrol 13.8.18 (2/Lt C Waine injured); 500/1 Flts 250 Sqdn Padstow by 8.18

C7851 (90-hp Curtiss OX-5) Allocated 250 Sqdn HQ Padstow by 25.5.18; 500/1 Flt 250 Sqdn Padstow by 7.18

C7852 (90-hp Curtiss OX-5) Allocated 250 Sqdn HQ Padstow by 25.5.18; 502/3 Flt 260 Sqdn Westward Ho! by 23.7.18 - @31.7.18

C7853 (90-hp Curtiss OX-5) Allocated 250 Sqdn HQ Padstow by 25.5.18; 500/1 Flts 250 Sqdn Padstow by 9.8.18 - @14.8.18

C7854 (90-hp Curtiss OX-5) Allocated 250 Sqdn HQ Padstow by 25.5.18; 500/501 Flts 250 Sqdn Padstow by 4.7.18 - @17.7.18; 502/503 Flts 260 Sqdn Westward Ho! by 18.8.18 - @11.18

C7855 (90-hp Curtiss OX-5) Allocated 250 Sqdn HQ Padstow by 25.5.18; 500/1 Flts 250 Sqdn Padstow by 30.6.18 -

@15.7.18; 260 Sqdn Westward Ho! by 3.8.18 - @1.11.18; FL 9.8.18

C7856 (90-hp Curtiss OX-5) Allocated 250 Sqdn HQ Padstow by 25.5.18; 500/1 Flts 250 Sqdn Padstow by 30.6.18 - @18.11.18; Propeller accident 21.9.18 (Sgt H Newton killed)

C7857 (90-hp Curtiss OX-5) Allocated 250 Sqdn HQ Padstow by 25.5.18; 500/1 Flts 250 Sqdn Padstow by 19.8.18 - @28.9.18

C7858 (90-hp Curtiss OX-5) Allocated 250 Sqdn HQ Padstow by 25.5.18; 500/1 Flts 250 Sqdn Padstow by 7.18 - @1.11.18; Collided with C5205 on landing, lower wing broken 23.7.18 (2 crew unhurt)

C7859 (90-hp Curtiss OX-5) Allocated 250 Sqdn HQ Padstow by 25.5.18; 500/1 Flts 250 Sqdn Padstow by 7.18 - @13.11.18

C7861 B Flt/530 Flt 244 Sqdn Bangor by 7.8.18; 'C' Flt/530 Flt 244 Sqdn Tallaght 18.10.18; 530 Flt 244 Sqdn Bangor 10.12.18

C7862 521/522 Flt 244 Sqdn Bangor by 19.8.18 - @11.18

C7863 530 Flt 244 Sqdn Bangor by 9.6.18; 'C' Flt/530 Flt 244 Sqdn Tallaght 18.10.18; 530 Flt 244 Sqdn Bangor 10.12.18

C7864 131 Sqdn Shawbury by 5.18; B Flt later 521/2 Flts 244 Sqdn Bangor by 9.8.18 - @11.18; 51 TS Waddington by 12.18

C7871 252 Sqdn Tynemouth by 7.18; MAD South Shields 26.8.18; 527/8 Flts 256 Sqdn Sea Houses by 11.10.18

C7875 Allocated by 25.5.18 for delivery to 253 Sqdn; 511/2 Flts 253 Sqdn Bembridge by 6.18 - @8.18

C7876 Allocated by 25.5.18 for delivery to 253 Sqdn

C7877 Allocated by 25.5.18 for delivery to 253 Sqdn; 511/2 Flts 253 Sqdn Bembridge by 8.18 - @9.18

C7878 Allocated by 25.5.18 for delivery to 253 Sqdn; 511/2 Flts 253 Sqdn Bembridge by 11.18

C7879 Allocated by 25.5.18 for delivery to 253 Sqdn

C7880 Allocated by 25.5.18 for delivery to 253 Sqdn

C7881 Allocated by 25.5.18 for delivery to 253 Sqdn

C7882 Allocated by 25.5.18 for delivery to 253 Sqdn

C7883 Allocated by 25.5.18 for delivery to 253 Sqdn; 511/2 Flts 253 Sqdn New Bembridge by 11.18

C7884 Allocated by 25.5.18 for delivery to 253 Sqdn

C7885 Allocated by 25.5.18 for delivery to 253 Sqdn; 511/2 Flts 253 Sqdn New Bembridge by 10.11.18

C7886 Allocated by 25.5.18 for delivery to 253 Sqdn

C7887 Allocated by 25.5.18 for delivery to 253 Sqdn

C7888 Allocated by 25.5.18 for delivery to 253 Sqdn

C7889 Allocated by 25.5.18 for delivery to 253 Sqdn; 511/2 Flts New Bembridge by 10.11.18

C7890 242 Sqdn Newhaven by 9.18; Sideslipped, caught fire 13.9.18 (2/Lt RT Stewart killed)

C7891 511/2 Flts 253 Sqdn New Bembridge by 8.18 - @9.18

C7892 511/2 Flts 253 Sqdn New Bembridge by 8.18 - @9.18

C7893 511/2 Flts 253 Sqdn New Bembridge by 8.18

C7896 511/2 Flts 253 Sqdn New Bembridge by 8.18; Crashed, TW 23.10.18 (pilot unhurt)

C7897 511/2 Flts 253 Sqdn New Bembridge by 9.18 - @11.18

C7899 517/8 Flts 254 Sqdn Prawle Point by 28.9.18 - @13.11.18

C7900 507/8 Flts 252 Sqdn Tynemouth by 3.9.18 - @6.11.18

## 7 SOPWITH F.1 CAMEL TRACTOR BIPLANE SCOUTS from batch C8201 to C8300 built by Ruston, Proctor & Co Ltd at Lincoln. (130-hp Clerget 9B)

C8266 (140-hp Clerget) Rec Pk to 208 Sqdn 11.4.18; Albatros DV OOC Provin 11.15 8.5.18; Red Albatros DV OOC Phalempin 13.45 9.5.18; Silver Pfalz DIII OOC S of Merville 11.50 18.5.18; 2-str OOC NE of Lens, shared D1813, D1853, D1873, D1879, D1889 & D6544 08.00 22.5.18; (all Lt HHS Fowler); EF on TO 16.6.18 (Lt G Swannell unhurt); To 1 ASD; Rebuilt as F5957 27.6.18

C8267 Deld Lincoln to Cranwell 14.3.18 (transit); Hendon 15.3.18; To RFC instead; 43 Sqdn, shot down by Ltn P Billick, Jasta 52, 28.3.18 (2/Lt H Adams)

C8276 43 Sqdn by 3.8.18 - @12.8.18; 2 ASD by 9.18; 205 TDS Vendôme 4.9.18 - @11.18; Crashed 12.10.18 (F/Cdt SWG Eagan unhurt)

C8279 70 Sqdn, crashed 20.4.18 (2/Lt J Gower); 2 AI to 209 Sqdn 28.6.18; Left 10.00, last seen in combat with enemy scout, driven down NE of Warfusée 7.7.18 (Lt

DY Hunter killed); SOC 7.7.18

C8285 1 AI to 208 Sqdn 7.7.18; In combat (no details), with D6638 08.35-10.10 patrol 29.7.18 (Lt JW Marshall); O/t landing 4.8.18 (Lt CH Living); 1 ASD 5.8.18; SOC 7.8.18

C8287 (B.R.1) 4 ASD Dunkerque by 25.5.18 - @31.5.18; 205 TDS Vendôme, wings folded in dive 12.7.18 (F/Cdt SP Thompson killed)

C8291 FF 23.3.18; 43 Sqdn Avesnes-le-Comte; Clairmarais to 65 Sqdn 27.3.18 (Lt EG Brookes 4 victories); Flown from France to England 25.7.18; 50 TDS Eastbourne (130-hp Clerget), wrecked when fabric stripped in roll 29.8.18

## 1 ARMSTRONG WHITWORTH F.K.8 TRACTOR BIPLANE from batch C8401 to C8651 built by parent company

C8464 9 AAP Gosforth to Cranwell 20.3.18

## 3 BOULTON & PAUL P.3 BOBOLINK TRACTOR BIPLANE SHIPBOARD FIGHTERS numbered C8655 to C8657. (230-hp Bentley B.R.2)

C8655 Deld Hendon 18.6.18; Norwich 19.6.18; Hendon 21.6.18; Martlesham Heath 3.7.18; Norwich by 22.7.18 [This machine was referred to as the Hawk, although that should correctly have referred to the unbuilt Type P.5, serials C8652 to C8654]

C8656 and C8657 cancelled

## 25 MAURICE FARMAN S.7 LONGHORN PUSHER BIPLANE TRAINERS ordered under Cont No A.S.24483 from The Brush Electrical Engineering Co Ltd and numbered C9311 to C9335, to be built at Loughborough. All to RNAS. (Various engines)

C9311 (90-hp Curtiss OX-2) Deld Manston FS by road W/E 17.11.17; Deleted W/E 23.3.18

C9312 (90-hp Curtiss OX-2) Deld Manston FS by road W/E 17.11.17; Deleted W/E 23.3.18

C9313 (90-hp Curtiss OX-2) Deld Manston FS by road W/E 17.11.17; Deleted W/E 23.3.18

C9314 (90 Curtiss OX-2) Deld Eastbourne NFS by road W/E 24.11.17; Deleted W/E 9.2.18

C9315 (90-hp Curtiss OX-2) Deld Eastbourne NFS by road W/E 24.11.17; Taxied into ditch 11.1.18 (Pilot uninjured); Deleted W/E 9.2.18

C9316 (90-hp Curtiss OX-2 later 80-hp Renault) Deld Eastbourne NFS by road W/E 24.11.17 - @3.18

C9317 Deld Manston FS by road W/E 24.11.17; Deleted W/E 23.3.18

C9318 Deld Manston FS by road W/E 8.12.17; Deleted W/E 23.3.18

C9319 Deld Manston FS by road W/E 1.12.17; Deleted W/E 23.3.18

C9320 (Curtiss OX-2) Deld Eastbourne NFS by road W/E 1.12.17; Deleted W/E 9.2.18

C9321 (80-hp Renault) Deld Eastbourne NFS by road W/E 8.12.17 - @30.3.18

C9322 Deld Eastbourne NFS by road W/E 8.12.17; Deleted W/E 23.3.18

C9323 Deld Manston FS by road W/E 8.12.17; Deleted W/E 23.3.18

C9324 Deld Manston FS by road W/E 12.12.17; Deleted W/E 23.3.18

C9325 Deld Manston FS by road W/E 12.12.17; Deleted W/E 23.3.18

C9326 Deld Eastbourne NFS by road W/E 12.12.17; Deleted W/E 23.3.18

C9327 (80-hp Renault) Deld Eastbourne NFS by road W/E 12.12.17 - @30.3.18

C9328 (80-hp Renault) Deld Eastbourne NFS by road W/E 19.12.17 - @30.3.18

C9329 (80-hp Renault) Deld Eastbourne NFS by road W/E 19.12.17 - @30.3.18

C9330 Deld Eastbourne NFS by road W/E 19.12.17; Deleted W/E 23.3.18

C9331 Deld Eastbourne NFS by road 29.12.17; Deleted W/E 23.3.18

C9332 (80-hp Renault) Deld Eastbourne NFS W/E 29.12.17; Deleted W/E 23.3.18

C9333     Deld Manston FS for erection W/E 29.12.17; Deleted W/E 23.3.18

C9334     Deld Manston FS for erection W/E 29.12.17; Deleted W/E 23.3.18

C9335     (90-hp Curtiss OX-2) Deld Manston FS for erection W/E 19.1.18; Deleted W/E 23.3.18

**36 AIRCO D.H.6 TRACTOR BIPLANES from batch C9336 to C9485 built by The Gloucestershire Aircraft Co Ltd & built Cheltenham.**

C9336     (RAF.1A) 68 TS Bramham by 12.17; SD Flt Cramlington, FL at Sunderland 6.4.18; Became 507 Flt 252 Sqdn Cramlington 25.5.18

C9380     SD Flt 252 Sqdn Redcar by 2.6.18

C9383     (RAF.1A) RFC, FL Harlaxton 23.3.18; C Flt 252 Sqdn Cramlington by 20.4.18; SD Flt 252 Sqdn Redcar 30.5.18 - @5.7.18

C9402     524/529 Flts 258 Sqdn Luce Bay by 24.10.18

C9403     (RAF.1A) SD Flt Cramlington by 3.18; Became SD Flt 252 Sqdn Cramlington by 28.4.18; SD Flt 252 Sqdn Redcar 30.4.18 - @14.6.18

C9404     SD Flt Cramlington by 2.4.18; FL in Sunderland Harbour 3.4.18; 509 Flt 252 Sqdn Seaton Carew by 3.9.18; FL in sea, towed to harbour 22.9.18 (pilot rescued by *Coble*)

C9407     524/529 Flts 258 Sqdn Luce Bay by 29.8.18 - @24.10.18

C9408     524/529 Flts 258 Sqdn Luce Bay by 1.10.18 - @28.10.18

C9409     524/529 Flts 258 Sqdn Luce Bay by 24.8.18 - @6.11.18

C9410     524/529 Flts 258 Sqdn Luce Bay by 16.8.18 - @11.10.18

C9411     524/529 Flts 258 Sqdn Luce Bay by 16.8.18 - @6.11.18

C9412     A/B Flts later 519/520 Flts 255 Sqdn Pembroke by 20.7.18 - @5.11.18

C9413     524/529 Flts 258 Sqdn Luce Bay by 24.8.18 - @3.11.18

C9414     524/529 Flts 258 Sqdn Luce Bay by 23.8.18 - @3.11.18

C9415     A/B Flts later 519/520 Flts 255 Sqdn Pembroke by 14.7.18 - @27.9.18

C9416     524/529 Flts 258 Sqdn Luce Bay by 16.8.18 - @6.11.18

C9418     A/B Flts 255 Sqdn Pembroke by 4.7.18 - @13.7.18

C9420     524/529 Flts 258 Sqdn Luce Bay by 8.18 - @21.10.18

C9423     A/B Flts later 519/520 Flts 255 Sqdn Pembroke by 7.7.18 - @28.9.18

C9436     524/529 Flts 258 Sqdn Luce Bay by 26.10.18

C9438     524/529 Flts 258 Sqdn Luce Bay by 23.8.18

C9439     A/B Flts later 519/520 Flts 255 Sqdn Pembroke by 29.7.18 - @5.11.18; Bombed U-boat, bubbles seen 0935 14.8.18 (Lt AJD Peebles)

C9440     A/B Flts later 519/520 Flts 255 Sqdn Pembroke by 4.7.18 - @12.18

C9442     524/529 Flts 258 Sqdn Luce Bay by 24.8.18 - @11.18

C9443     519/520 Flts 255 Sqdn Pembroke by 12.18

C9444     C Flt 244 Sqdn Tallaght from 24.10.18; Crashed Dalkui 6.11.18 (Lt HF Monypeny)

C9447     521/2 Flts 244 Sqdn Bangor by 11.18; C Flt/530 Flt 244 Sqdn Tallaght by 23.11.18; 521/2 Flts 244 Sqdn Bangor 8.12.18

C9452     524/529 Flts 258 Sqdn Luce Bay by 24.8.18 - @12.9.18

C9460     SD Flt 252 Sqdn Cramlington by 20.6.18

C9473     SD Flt Cramlington by 30.4.18 - @3.5.18

C9477     (RAF.1A) SD Flt Cramlington by 3.18; FL in sea, picked up by armed trawler 10.5.18

C9478     (RAF.1A) SD Flt 252 Sqdn Cramlington by 3.4.18; 507/8 Flts 252 Sqdn Tynemouth 14.6.18; MAD South Shields 30.7.18; 507/8 Flts 252 Sqdn Tynemouth 28.8.18 - @5.9.18; MAD South Shields 9.18; 507/8 Flts 252 Sqdn Tynemouth 18.9.18 - @16.10.18

C9479     (RAF.1A) SD Flt 252 Sqdn Cramlington by 28.4.18; FL in sea 10.5.18 (pilot saved by trawler)

C9480     (RAF.1A) SD Flt 252 Sqdn Cramlington by 1.5.18; 507/8 Flts 252 Sqdn Tynemouth 2.6.18 - @12.6.18

C9481     (RAF.1A) 252 Sqdn Cramlington by 24.5.18; 507/8 Flts 252 Sqdn Tynemouth 10.6.18 - @10.18; EF, FL in sea 4.7.18

C9482     507/8 Flts 252 Sqdn Tynemouth by 9.18; MAD South Shields 18.9.18; 255 Sqdn by 12.18; Became G-EAMK

**50 HANDLEY PAGE O/400 TRACTOR BIPLANE HEAVY BOMBERS from batch C9636 to C9785 built at Cricklewood.**

**(Eagle, Maori or Liberty)**

C9643     Deld 2 AAP Hendon 25.4.18; Lympne 1.5.18; AP Marquise 5.18; 214 Sqdn 8.5.18; Dropped first 1650-lb SN bomb, on Middelkerke 24/25.7.18; Tail damaged in mid-air collision 1.10.18 (Lt HRW Ellison); To Middle East with sqdn, to Buc 6.7.19; arr Cairo 31.7.19; 216 Sqdn (coded 'P') 1.2.20; Withdrawn 10.21

C9644     (Eagle VIII) Deld 2 AAP Hendon by 5.18; Lympne 2.5.18; AP Marquise 5.18; 214 Sqdn 16.5.18; Tested 30.5.18; Returning from raid on Melle railway sidings, stbd engine caught fire at 3,000 ft, FL safely on beach Wenduyne, but only engines salved 13/14.10.18 (Lt GS Lewtas, Lt FC Sumner & Sgt Mech G Conley)

C9646     Deld 2 AAP Hendon 4.18; To Lympne but FL Ragfield Farm, nr Sittingbourne, Kent 1.5.18; AP Marquise 15.5.18; 214 Sqdn 15.5.18; TO uphill, wheels caught wheat crop, o/t St.Inglevert 17.7.18 (Lt DR Tullis, Lt R Binckes DoI 21.7.18 & Ens RM Stocker USNRF all injured); 4 ASD 17.7.18; 214 Sqdn 9.10.18; To Middle East with sqdn, to Buc 4.7.19; Arr Cairo 31.7.19 - @7.12.19

C9648     (Eagle VIII) Deld 2 AAP Hendon 1.5.18; AP Marquise 5.18; 214 Sqdn 8.5.18; After raid on Mariakerke aerodrome, FL on beach between Valkenisse and Koudkerke, Zeeland 30.6.18 (Lt JD Vance, 2/Lt SB Potter & Sgt Plt RG Kimberley interned); SOC in field 1.7.18; Became Dutch *HP703*; Retd RAF 20.3.20

C9649     Deld 2 AAP Hendon 5.18; To Netheravon but EF, FL Boscombe Down 12.5.18; Andover 13.5.18 [207 Sqdn]; 215 Sqdn Andover by 18.6.18 - @24.6.18; 2 SoN&BD Andover 3.8.18 - @15.8.18

C9657     Deld 2 AAP Hendon 17.5.18; 207 Sqdn (coded 'W' 8.18, then 'A' by 9.18) by 8.18; EF on way to raid St.Quentin, FL, CW Famechon 6/7.9.18 (Lt LG Semple shaken, 2/Lt GNG Hamilton injured & Pte HH Phillips shaken); 2 ASD 8.9.18; SOC 2.10.18

C9658     Deld 2 AAP Hendon 5.18; 215 Sqdn by 13.6.18; Shot down in raid on Frescaty 16/17.9.18 (Lt HR Dodd killed, Lt EC Jeffkins PoW & 2/Lt A Fairhurst PoW)

C9659     Deld 2 AAP Hendon 5.6.18; 215 Sqdn by 4.7.18; FTR raid on Folpesweiler aerodrome 22/23.8.18 (2/Lt FE Rees killed, 2/Lt J Stott killed & G/L Sgt GW Hare PoW); SOC 17.9.18 missing

C9660     215 Sqdn by 6.18; To 207 Sqdn (coded 'D' 8.18, then 'N' 9.18) 6.18; EF, FL, engine cut at 100 ft, crashed with bombs into haystack 29.9.18 (Capt WA Scott, Lt TG Fawcett & G/L AH Vickers all unhurt); Awaiting write-off by 30.9.18

C9661     (Eagle VIII) FF 27.5.18; Deld 2 AAP Hendon 6.18; 1 SoN&BD Stonehenge by 5.7.18 - @6.7.18; 216 Sqdn from 26.7.18, left behind when sqdn went to France; 1 SoN&BD Stonehenge by 8.18; COL fast at night on bumpy ground 2.9.18 (Mjr JH Tyssen and Capt NL Garston uninjured)

C9662     (Eagle VIII) Mkrs by 10.6.18; Rec Pk by 7.18; 3 ASD 17.7.18; 216 Sqdn 20.7.18; FTR from bombing raid on Metz-Sablon railway junction 16/17.9.18 (Lt B Norcross killed, 2/Lt RH Cole PoW, DoW 30.9.18 & Sgt Mech G Hall PoW); SOC in field 17.9.18

C9664     Deld 2 AAP Hendon 31.5.18; 207 Sqdn by 6.18; 215 Sqdn by 9.6.18; Tanks damaged during raid on Boulay aerodrome, COL, TW 31.8.18 (Pilot 2/Lt GW Wilson slightly injured); SOC 31.8.18 in field

C9665     (Eagle VIII) Deld 2 AAP Hendon 5.18; Andover 25.5.18; 207 Sqdn by 6.18; Missing from night raid, left 22.51 18/19.7.18 (Lt F Kemp, Lt WMF Bayless & Lt G Rose all PoW); SOC 19.7.18

C9666     (Eagle VIII) Mkrs allocated SW Area for 207 Sqdn, changed to 216 Sqdn 10.6.18; 4 ASD by 7.18; 214 Sqdn 28.7.18; Returning from bombing raid, FL soft sand, o/t Zuydcoote Bains 14.8.18 (2/Lt JMcK Young slightly injured, Capt GH Russell unhurt & 2/Lt AW Steward unhurt); Rep Pk 4 ASD 14.8.18; 214 Sqdn 29.10.18; To Middle East with sqdn, to Buc 1.7.19; Arr Cairo 27.7.19; 216 Sqdn (coded 'Z') 1.2.20; Crashed on nose .21; Withdrawn 10.21

ALSO 214 Sqdn, participated night raid on Zeebrugge locks 28.5.18 (Capt CH Darley) [aircraft given and retained name 'Zeebrugge' as a consequence]. This does not fit - wrong date?

*Handley Page O/400 C9643 'P' of 216 Sqdn is seen here with wings folded after arrival in the Middle East. (via Frank Cheesman)*

*This Sopwith Camel was unofficially converted by 208 Sqdn at Serny in June 1918 to a two-seater, but only survived in this form for a few days before higher authority ordered that it be reverted to standard. It is thought to have been Draper's original aircraft, D1928. (via Frank Cheesman)*

*Airco D.H.9 D3007 '11' of 203 Sqdn at Mudros in late 1918. (via A.S. Thomas/Frank Cheesman)*

C9668    215 Sqdn by 8.6.18; Returning from raid on Cambrai, shot down 2-str OOC 3m S of Marquion 01.00 17.8.18 (Lt MC Purvis, Lt WE Crombie MC & Sgt Mech PJ Sprange); After raid on Boulay aerodrome, EF, FL nr Rambervillers, CW 31.8.18 (Lt MC Purvis seriously injured, Lt WE Crombie MC killed, 2/Lt F Caton DoW, Sgt G/L EB Wade wounded, 2/Lt CN Yelverton slightly injured); SOC in field 31.8.18

C9669    (Eagle VIII) Mkrs, allocated SW Area for 215 Sqdn Netheravon 10.6.18 (NTU, changed to 216 Sqdn); 58 TDS Cranwell by 1.10.18 - @8.10.18

C9672    215 Sqdn by 17.6.18 - @18.6.18

C9673    (Eagle VIII) Mkrs Cricklewood for 2 AAP Hendon for EF by 22.5.18; UK to Rec Pk 10.8.18; 3 ASD 15.8.18; 215 Sqdn 1.9.18; FTR bombing raid on Kaiserslautern Rly Junction 14/15.9.18 (2/Lts AG Harrison, HD Davies, C Guild all PoW); SOC in field 15.9.18

C9674    (Eagle VIII) Mkrs Cricklewood for 2 AAP Hendon for EF by 22.5.18; 2 AAP Hendon by 1.6.18 - @11.6.18; 207 Sqdn by 6.18; 214 Sqdn (coded 'C') by 7.18; For Rep Pk 27.2.19 (unfit for further service); to Carvin 3.4.19

C9675    (Eagle VIII) 8 AAP Lympne to Rec Pk 13.6.18; Paris 7.7.18; 3 ASD 8.7.18; 216 Sqdn (coded 'N') 31.7.18; 4 ASD 16.1.19 (fit out as mail carrier); 216 Sqdn 25.1.19; Left in open for several weeks, declared unfit 10.4.19, for 1 ASD

C9676    (Eagle VIII) HP by 4.6.18 for 2 AAP Hendon for EF; 2 ASD by 7.18; 207 Sqdn (coded 'P' 9.18, then 'J' by 11.18) 19.7.18; Hit goal post on TO Guines 5.4.19 (Lt R Pughe & 2/Lt S Pike), for 1 ASD

C9680    (Eagle VIII) Mkrs Cricklewood by 1.6.18 - @18.6.18 for 2 AAP Hendon; Rec Pk by 7.18; 3 ASD 17.7.18; 216 Sqdn (coded 'Z') by 25.7.18; 4 ASD 21.12.18 (fit out as mail carrier); 216 Sqdn 4.1.19; FL in field Romsee 30.4.19 (Lt FB Shaw & Sgt EE Scott both unhurt), dismantled by 2 ELG
Rebuilt as F6285 8.9.18 ???

C9682    (Eagle VIII) Mkrs Cricklewood by 5.6.18 for 2 AAP Hendon; Rec Pk to 214 Sqdn 30.6.18; TO downwind for raid, o/t in crops, caught fire, bombs exploded, TW 24.7.18 (Lt HA McCormick, Cpl EA Barber & Lt JC Foster USNRF all injured); Deleted 15.8.18

C9683    Mkrs Cricklewood for 2 AAP Hendon by 5.6.18; 8 AAP Lympne to Rec Pk 6.7.18; 215 Sqdn 15.7.18; FTR from raid on Courcelles 14/15.9.18 (2/Lt A Tapping, 2/Lt JB Richardson & Lt WJN Chalklin all PoW); SOC in field 15.9.18

C9684    207 Sqdn Andover by 6.18; 215 Sqdn Andover by 8.6.18 - @11.6.18; 2 SoN&BD Andover by 20.8.18

C9685    215 Sqdn by; 3 ASD 24.8.18 (fitted mail dropping apparatus); 216 Sqdn 14.11.18; 4 ASD 4.12.18 (fit as mail carrier); Retd 216 Sqdn 12.18; While carrying mail, wrecked Geyen 12.2.19 (Lt ET Primrose unhurt, Lt CJ Clarke injured, Gen Hogg injured, Lt Weston unhurt, 1 airman unhurt, 1 batman unhurt)

C9690    7 AAP Kenley by 9.18; Rec Pk 13.9.18; 3 AD 15.9.18; 215 Sqdn 15.9.18; COL 00.50 1.10.18 (Lt LR McKenna, 2/Lt WH Seeburgher & Lt W Hutchings) BUT 116 Sqdn by 6.18 - @7.18

C9699    Uk to Rec Pk 23.9.18; 3 ASD 24.9.18; 215 Sqdn 25.9.18; 97 Sqdn 17.1.19; Became G-EASL

C9708    UK to Rec Pk 4.8.18; 3 ASD (via Paris & Courban) 14-16.8.18; 216 Sqdn 20.8.18; COL from raid 17.9.18 (2/Lt BC Cotter injured); 3 ASD 17.9.18

C9709    UK to Rec Pk 29.7.18; 3 ASD (via Paris) 1.8.18; 216 Sqdn 13.8.18; Returning from raid on Morhange aerodrome, FL, damaged, Lunéville 5/6.11.18 (Lt LR Fox DFC, 2/Lt FR Gibson & Lt LR McKenna); 3 AD 6.11.18

C9714    UK to Rec Pk 9.8.18; 3 AD 11.8.18; 215 Sqdn 26.8.18; 97 Sqdn 18.1.19; With 214 Sqdn to Egypt, to Buc 10.7.19; En route, crashed on TO in soft ground nr Albenga 27.7.19

C9715    Hendon by 8.18 (demonstration for Canadian journalists); 58 TDS Cranwell by 5.9.18 - @26.10.18 (prefix?)

C9718    58 TDS Cranwell by 27.10.18

C9720    U/s, replaced by C9673 15.8.18; UK to Rec Pk 13.9.18; 3 ASD (via Paris) 24.9.18; 215 Sqdn 25.9.18; Missing nr Thionville Rly Junction on bombing raid 29/30.10.18

(2/Lt JB Vickers PoW, 2/Lt SJ Goodfellow PoW & Sgt RE Culshaw all PoWs); SOC in field 30.10.18

C9721    1 ASD by 9.18; 207 Sqdn (coded 'L') 7.9.18 - @30.9.18

C9722    58 TDS Cranwell by 2.10.18 - @8.10.18

C9723    8 AAP Lympne by 9.18; Rec Pk 13.9.18; 3 ASD 15.9.18 (arr 16.9.18); 215 Sqdn 17.9.18; FTR raid on Frescaty aerodrome, shot down in flames nr Metz 20.9.18 (2/Lt ACG Fowler, 2/Lt JS Ferguson & 2/Lt CC Eaves all killed); SOC in field 21.9.18

C9724    UK to Rec Pk 15.9.18; 3 ASD 16.9.18; 215 Sqdn 18.9.18; FL on aerodrome returning from night raid, wrecked 6.10.18 (2/Lt FA Rowe unhurt, 2/Lt WJ Boon wounded & 2/Lt JJ Snow unhurt); 3 ASD 6.10.18

C9727    Deld 2 AAP Hendon 8.18; Left Hendon 31.8.18; UK to Rec Pk 1.9.18; 3 ASD 4.9.18 (arr 5.9.18); 215 Sqdn 15.9.18; En route Cologne, port engine believed hit by AA nr Bonn, FL Oosterhout, nr Breda, m/c fired 16/17.9.18 (2/Lt CC Fisher, 2/Lt RS Oakley & 2/Lt CJ Locke interned by Dutch); SOC in field 17.9.18

C9733    58 TDS Cranwell by 19.8.18 - @19.10.18

C9734    UK to Rec Pk 29.8.18; 2 ASD 3.9.18; 3 ASD 4.9.18 (arr 7.9.18); 215 Sqdn 7.9.18; FTR raid on Kaiserslautern railway junction 23.10.18 (Lt E Lorimer, 2/Lt RH Bruce & Lt CE Thompson)

C9743    Deld 2 AAP Hendon 24.4.18; Rec Pk 13.9.18 (arr 16.9.18); 3 ASD 17.9.18 (arr 18.9.18); 215 Sqdn 20.9.18; 97 Sqdn 19.1.19; 214 Sqdn, to Buc for Egypt 31.7.19; Fréjus St.Raphael 1.8.19 (new engine needed); Destroyed there in gale 13.8.19

C9744    3 AD by 11.18; 115 Sqdn 9.11.18 - @1.19; FL St.Valéry-en-Caux 21.11.18; With 216 Sqdn France to Egypt - arr Buc 17.7.19; Vienne 13.8.19; Suda Bay 24.9.19; Egypt 11.10.19; Crashed & WO 26.3.20

C9746    UK to Rec Pk 24.10.18; Paris 30.10.18; 3 ASD 1.11.18; 216 Sqdn 6.11.18 - @20.1.19; 214 Sqdn by 3.19; With 216 Sqdn France to Egypt - arr Buc 17.7.19; Taranto by 13.8.19; Cairo 15.9.19

C9750    58 TDS Cranwell by 27.10.18; 58 Sqdn by 10.18 (confusion with 58 TDS?); Taranto by .19 (coded 'C')

C9753    UK to Rec Pk 13.10.18; 3 AD 17.10.18 (arr 18.10.18); 215 Sqdn 21.10.18; 207 Sqdn 18.1.19

C9755    'H' Flt 1 SoN&BD Stonehenge .18; 215 Sqdn by 11.18

C9758    UK to Rec Pk 15.10.18; 3 AD 17.10.18; 115 Sqdn 27.10.18 - @end 1.19; 207 Sqdn to Buc 31.7.19, allocated for Egypt & 216 Sqdn; Lyons 4.8.19; Rome 10.8.19; Athens 13.8.19; Suda Bay 26.8.19; arr Cairo 15.9.19

C9771    (Eagle VIII) Deld 2 AAP Hendon for EF by 6.12.18; 1 ASD to 215 Sqdn 3.1.19; 97 Sqdn 17.1.19

C9780    216 Sqdn by 25.3.19 (mail run to Valenciennes)

**4 AVRO 504J & 504K TRACTOR BIPLANE TRAINERS from batch D1 to D200 built by parent company at Hamble**

D30    (504J) Eastchurch by 10.18

D162    54 TDS Fairlop, stalled on turn, spun in 16.6.18 (2/Lt J Herries)

D163    208 TDS Leuchars by 7.18

D186    (100-hp Gnôme Monosoupape) 254 Sqdn "Queensferry", hit hedge pulling out of spin 11.5.18 (Lt A Crozier & C/Sgt AF Lew USAS both injured)

**30 AIRCO D.H.9 TRACTOR BIPLANE DAY BOMBERS from batch D451 to D950 built by Cubitt Ltd/NAF No.2 at Croydon. (200-hp B.H.P.)**

D459    Deld 4 AAP Hendon by 8.5.18; Rec Pk to 1 AI 20.5.18; 206 Sqdn 21.5.18; COL 10.6.18 (Lt EHP Bailey & 2/Lt WD McKinnon unhurt); Wrecked, to Rep Pk 1 ASD 11.6.18

D472    203 TDS Manston by 6.18; Became 55 TDS Manston 14.7.18; 55 TDS Narborough 12.9.18 - @11.18

D473    55 TDS Manston by 9.18; 1 Observers School by 10.18 - @11.18

D474    108 Sqdn by 6.18 - @12.18; Pool of Pilots Manston/Joyce Green by 3.19 - 8.19

D476    Pool of Pilots Manston; Observers School .18

D479    Pool of Pilots Manston by 7.18; EF, FL and crashed Sandwich, Kent 3.9.18 (Capt SA Hamilton-Bowyer); Air Observers School .18

D482    1 AI to 211 Sqdn 30.6.18; Direct hit by AA between

Ypres & Roulers, FL, crashed, TW 29.9.18 (2/Lt JL McAdam unhurt & 2/Lt TW Kelly killed); Salvage to 1 ASD 1.10.18

| | |
|---|---|
| D495 | 203 TDS Manston by 7.18; Became 55 TDS 14.7.18 - @11.18 |
| D517 | Deld 7 AAP Kenley by 9.18; 1 AI to 211 Sqdn 30.9.18; Left 11.00, attacked by 4 HA at 14,000 ft over Maubeuge 1.11.18 (2/Lt PM Keary unhurt & 2/Lt A Robinson slightly wounded); 7 SS 2.11.18 for 2 ASD |
| D547 | 6 AI to 211 Sqdn 1.12.18; 98 Sqdn 24.2.19 |
| D551 | Rep Pk to 1 AI 7.9.18; 211 Sqdn (coded 'X') 30.9.18; HA BU in air, shared B7626 & E8962 11.00 4.11.18 (2/Lt WG Watson & Sgt Obs C Lamont); 98 Sqdn 25.2.19; 1 ASD 3.3.19 |
| D555 | Deld 7 AAP Kenley by 10.18; 4 ASD to 218 Sqdn 16.10.18; 98 Sqdn 21.1.19; Retd UK 15.2.19 |
| D559 | Rec Pk to 1 AI 4.10.18; 206 Sqdn by 11.18 |
| D560 | Deld 7 AAP Kenley by 9.18; Rec Pk to 1 AI 1.10.18; 206 Sqdn by 10.18; Left 07.45, shot down nr Aelbecke by Oblt H Auffahrt (his 23rd) 5.10.18 (Lt CT Knight USAS & 2/Lt JH Perring both PoW) |
| D562 | Arr 'X' AD ex UK 18.11.18; 269 Sqdn Port Said 23.11.18; 142 Sqdn 18.3.19; ASD 12.8.19 |
| D565 | 1 AI to 211 Sqdn 26.9.18; Shot down in flames in running fight Cambrai - Ypres 11.30 29.9.18 (1/Lt WH Mooney USAS, PoW wounded & 2/Lt VA Fair MC killed) |
| D568 | Rec Pk to 1 AI 26.9.18; 211 Sqdn 30.9.18; Hit by AA over Menin, badly damaged, COL 2.10.18 (2/Lt PM Keary & 2/Lt RM Alston unhurt); to Rep Pk 1 ASD |
| D569 | Rec Pk to 1 AI 2.10.18; 206 Sqdn (coded 'A') 10.18; Fokker DVII in flames nr Lendelede, shared D5782 14.40 14.10.18 (Capt RNG Atkinson MC & 2/Lt JS Blanford); Badly smashed Jahlay-Saart 19.4.19; to 1 ASD |
| D573 | 1 Observers School Eastchurch by 10.18 - @12.18 BUT Arr 'X' AD ex UK 18.11.18; 269 Sqdn Port Said 23.11.18; 142 Sqdn 18.3.19 |
| D576 | Deld 7 AAP Kenley by 10.18; SMOP Dover by 11.18 |
| D580 | Deld 7 AAP Kenley by 10.18; Naval Flt 219 Sqdn Manston 30.10.18 - @16.12.18 |
| D587 | 491 Flt 233 Sqdn Dover |
| D590 | 2 ASD to 218 Sqdn 14.12.18; 98 Sqdn 21.1.19; Retd UK 15.2.19 |
| D592 | 491 Flt 233 Sqdn Dover, FL in bad weather, slightly damaged Dungeness 20.12.18 (both crew uninjured) |
| D597 | At Burton-on-Trent W/E 10.10.18; 6 SD Ascot W/E 31.10.18 for Mudros; Shipped W/E 21.11.18; Presumably not shipped; 491 Flt 233 Sqdn Dover by 16.12.18; Bad weather, FL Dungeness, damaged 20.12.18 (2/Lt HH Lewis & 2/Lt RA Darby); 212 Sqdn by 2.19 |
| D598 | Deld 7 AAP Kenley .18; 73 Wing Yarmouth, stalled and crashed 5.12.18 (2/Lt L Leeming DoI & 2/Lt ED Warren killed) |
| D605 | 4 ASD by 10.18; 218 Sqdn 16.10.18; Left at Fréthun 27.10.18 |
| D606 | From France to 206 Sqdn Egypt 10.8.19 |
| D612 | 534 Flt 273 Sqdn Covehithe by 5.11.18 - @22.11.18; HACPs 5.11.18 & 7.11.18 |
| D636 | 226 Sqdn Pizzone by 10.18 BUT 103 Sqdn by 3.19; 1 ASD 17.3.19; From France to 206 Sqdn Egypt 29.7.19; WO at ASD 13.11.19 |

**41 AIRCO D.H.9 TRACTOR BIPLANE DAY BOMBERS** from batch D1001 to D1500 built by National Aircraft Factory No.2 [Crossley] at Heaton Chapel. (200-hp B.H.P.)

| | |
|---|---|
| D1006 | Deld 491 Flt Dover W/E 24.5.18; Bercq 7.6.18; 218 Sqdn, COL from raid 21.6.18 (Lt W Bentley & 2/Lt AJ Cunningham both unhurt); To 4 ASD; 2 SS Richborough 2.10.18 |
| D1010 | Deld 4 AAP Lincoln 5.18; 491 Flt Dover by 25.5.18 (W/E 1.6.18); 98 Sqdn, crashed 16.6.18 (Lt W Strugnell & Sgt C Lomax both killed) |
| D1012 | Deld 4 AAP Lincoln by 27.5.18; Rec Pk to 1 AI 1.6.18; 206 Sqdn 7.6.18; Left 03.30 on long reconnaissance, FTR 24.6.18 (Lt WC Cutmore & 2/Lt WG Duncan both killed); SOC in field 25.6.18 |
| D1015 | 1 ASD to 206 Sqdn 25.6.18; Pfalz DIII shot down 1½m E of Ypres 19.20-19.35 29.7.18; Pfalz crashed 2m SW |

of Menin 08.30 1.8.18 (both 2/Lt JFS Percival & 2/Lt FJ Paget); COL 9.8.18 (Lt AJ Garside & 2/Lt C Hancock unhurt); Rep Pk 1 ASD 10.8.18; SOC 13.8.18 NWR; Rebuilt as F6453 23.8.18

| | |
|---|---|
| D1017 | 218 Sqdn, COL after raid on Ostende 5.7.18 (Lt W Bentley & 2/Lt AJ Cunningham); 4 ASD 5.7.18; 2 SS Richborough 15.9.18 |
| D1021 | Deld 4 AAP Lincoln by 30.5.18; 1 AI by 31.5.18; 211 Sqdn (coded 'K') 2.6.18; Sideslipped, COL 25.6.18 (2/Lt HH Palmer & Pte1 WJ Atkinson); Rep Pk 1 ASD 26.6.18; SOC 29.6.18 NWR |
| D1024 | 1 AI to 206 Sqdn 18.6.18; Fokker DVII in flames W of Sotteghem 15.25-15.40 30.10.18 (Lt AJ Garside & Sgt J Chapman DFM); Left in open when sqdn arrived Nivelles, wings and fuselage became warped, for 8 SS overhaul 14.4.19 |
| D1028 | 4 ASD to 218 Sqdn 31.7.18; Hit by AA, FL on beach 2m E of Zeebrugge, wrecked, submerged by tide 11.8.18 (Lt WS Mars & 2/Lt HE Power both unhurt); 4 ASD 12.8.18; 2 SS Richborough 15.9.18 |
| D1047 | 109 Sqdn Stonehenge by 7.18; 491 Flt 233 Sqdn Dover 31.7.18 - @12.18 |
| D1049 | Lympne to Rec Pk 6.7.18; 1 AI 7.7.18; 491 Flt 233 Sqdn Dover by 5.9.18 |
| D1051 | Presentation a/c 'Zanzibar 12'; 1 ASD by 7.18; 206 Sqdn 28.7.18; Pfalz DIII BU in air Neuve-Eglise 07.25 7.8.18 (Lt EA Burn & Capt WA Carrothers); Throttle came off in air, FL nr aerodrome 1.10.18 (Lt HW Campbell & 2/Lt CO Thompson) |
| D1052 | 491 Flt 233 Sqdn Dover by 15.8.18; 218 Sqdn 29.9.18; Returning from raid on railway junction nr Bruges, EF, FL on beach, crashed, badly damaged, W of Mardyck 17.10.18 (Sgt GM Rowley & Sgt IIG Pearce both unhurt); 4 ASD 19.10.18 - @25.10.18 |
| D1053 | 534 Flt 273 Sqdn Covehithe by 30.8.18 - @28.10.18; Imperial Gift to India 8.20 |
| D1058 | 203 TDS Manston by 7.18 |
| D1078 | 557/8 Flts 212 Sqdn Yarmouth by 21.8.18 - @10.18 |
| D1079 | 534 Flt 273 Sqdn Covehithe by 5.8.18 - @12.18; AZP 5.8.18 (Lt FR Bicknell, Sgt Bull) |
| D1081 | 557/8 Flts 212 Sqdn Yarmouth by 14.8.18 - @10.18 |
| D1082 | 4 ASD to 218 Sqdn 31.8.18; COL from raid, CW 7.9.18 (Lt HP Brumell & Sgt RS Joysey both unhurt); 4 ASD 8.9.18; 2 SS Richborough 15.9.18 |
| D1083 | 4 ASD to 218 Sqdn 16.8.18; COL from raid 31.8.18 (Lt WS Mars & 2/Lt HE Power both unhurt); 4 ASD 1.9.18; 2 SS Richborough 2.10.18 |
| D1085 | 4 ASD to 218 Sqdn 27.8.18; Fokker DVII OOC NW of Bruges 16.35 15.9.18 (Lt BH Stata & 2/Lt CVR Brown); Met storm returning from raid, BU, spun in, CW, Wulveringhem 28.9.18 (Lt BH Stata & 2/Lt CVR Brown both killed) |
| D1086 | 109 Sqdn by 6.18; 211 Sqdn by 1.11.18; 6 AI by 2.19; 211 Sqdn 12.2.19; 98 Sqdn 23.2.19; 1 ASD 5.3.19; To England 6.3.19; from France to 206 Sqdn Egypt 10.8.19 |
| D1088 | 218 Sqdn by 29.9.18; FL 1.10.18 (Lt KR Campbell & 2/Lt LA Churchill), retd later; Left at Frethun when sqdn moved 23.10.18, still there 31.10.18 |
| D1089 | 4 ASD to 218 Sqdn 16.8.18; COL from raid on Bruges, badly damaged 22.8.18 (Lt FJ Burslem & 2/Lt B Hutchinson); 4 ASD 23.8.18; 218 Sqdn 9.10.18; 98 Sqdn 21.1.19; Retd UK 15.2.19 |
| D1096 | MOS Aldeburgh by 10.18; Became 1 ASIPOS Aldeburgh 29.12.18; Became 1 MOS Aldeburgh 1.1.19 - @3.19 |
| D1098 | MOS Aldeburgh by 10.18; Became 1 ASIPOS Aldeburgh 29.12.18; Became 1 MOS Aldeburgh 1.1.19 |
| D1121 | AAP Coventry to Dover 23.9.18 |
| D1122 | 491 Flt 233 Sqdn Dover to 4 ASD Audembert 26.9.18; 218 Sqdn 29.9.18; Fokker DVII OOC Lichtervelde 0935 29.9.18 (Lt JH Sprott & 2/Lt SJ Lewin); 98 Sqdn 21.1.19; Retd UK 15.2.19 |
| D1123 | 202 Sqdn for evaluation by 10.18, crashed; AP 4 ASD 24.10.18 (then taken in hand 4 ASD) |
| D1137 | 4 ASD Audembert to 218 Sqdn 29.9.18 - @LM 18.10.18 |
| D1149 | Arr 'X' AD ex UK 24.11.18; 206 Sqdn 16.7.19; WO 22.11.19 |
| D1165 | 2 ASD to 218 Sqdn 2.11.18; Pfalz DIII in flames NW of Hautmont 11.35 4.11.18 (Lt JRA Barnes & Sgt F Smith); 8 AAP Lympne 14.1.19; SOC |

| D1167 | 206 Sqdn, ferry flight, crashed Sitault 1.12.18 (Sgt Mech JW Duffield Harding & Sgt G Woodgate both injured [killed?]) |
|---|---|
| D1171 | 119 Sqdn by 22.10.18; 25 TS Thetford by 12.18; 6 AI by 1.19; 211 Sqdn 2.1.19; 98 Sqdn 23.2.19; to 1 ASD 8.3.19 |
| D1218 | 54 TDS Fairlop by 11.18; Crashed in fog Catterick 24.11.18 |
| D1224 | 52 TDS Cramlington, spun in on gliding turn 30.7.18 (2/Lt FA Bird & F/Sgt WG Daiber injured). [prefix not given. C1224 or F1224 possible] |
| D1243 | 491 Flt 233 Sqdn Dover |
| D1330 | 219 Sqdn Naval Flt Manston by 8.18 |
| D1331 | 219 Sqdn Naval Flt Manston by 8.18 |
| D1332 | 219 Sqdn Naval Flt Manston by 8.18 |
| D1354 | Covehithe; 47 Sqdn by 9.19 - @10.19 |
| D1355 | Covehithe |

### 33 AVRO 504A TRACTOR BIPLANE TRAINERS from batch D1601 to D1650 built by The Eastbourne Aviation Co Ltd and built Eastbourne. (Mainly 80-hp Gnôme)

| D1601 | Deld Eastbourne NFS for erection W/E 26.1.18; FL and damaged nr Hampden Park 31.1.18 (pilot uninjured); Became 206 TDS Eastbourne 1.4.18; EF on TO, crashed and damaged 11.5.18 (pilot unhurt) |
|---|---|
| D1602 | Deld Eastbourne NFS W/E 23.2.18; Became 206 TDS Eastbourne 1.4.18; Became 50 TDS 15.7.18 - @1.8.18 |
| D1603 | (Gnôme) Deld Eastbourne NFS W/E 2.2.18; Became 206 TDS Eastbourne 1.4.18; EF, nosedived 8.4.18 (2/Lt MD Moore seriously injured) |
| D1604 | Deld Eastbourne NFS W/E 9.2.18; Landed on by D.H.6 B2738 and CW 21.3.18 (PFO L Brown killed); Surveyed 21.3.18; Deleted 26.3.18 |
| D1605 | Deld Eastbourne NFS W/E 9.2.18; COL and wrecked 13.2.18 (pilot uninjured); Deleted W/E 9.3.18 |
| D1606 | Deld Eastbourne NFS W/E 9.2.18; Became 206 TDS Eastbourne 1.4.18; Lost speed on turn nr ground, spinning nose dive, wrecked 12.6.18 (2/Lt WS Pullen killed) |
| D1607 | Deld Eastbourne NFS W/E 9.2.18; Became 206 TDS Eastbourne 1.4.18; Disb into 50 TDS Eastbourne 15.7.18 - @14.9.18 |
| D1608 | (DC) Deld Eastbourne NFS W/E 16.2.18; Became 206 TDS Eastbourne 1.4.18 - @6.6.18 |
| D1609 | Deld Chingford W/E 16.2.18; Became 207 TDS Chingford 1.4.18 |
| D1610 | Deld Chingford 23.2.18; Became 207 TDS Chingford 1.4.18 |
| D1611 | Deld Chingford for erection 23.2.18; Became 207 TDS Chingford 1.4.18 |
| D1612 | Deld Chingford for erection 23.2.18; Became 207 TDS Chingford 1.4.18 |
| D1613 | Deld Chingford 23.2.18; Became 207 TDS Chingford 1.4.18 |
| D1614 | (504B)(DC) Deld Eastbourne NFS for erection W/E 2.3.18; Became 206 TDS Eastbourne 1.4.18; Disb into 50 TDS Eastbourne 15.7.18 - @14.8.18 |
| D1615 | (504B)(DC) Deld Eastbourne NFS W/E 2.3.18; Became 206 TDS Eastbourne 1.4.18; Disb into 50 TDS Eastbourne 15.7.18; HMS *Argus*, EF on TO, crashed in sea 16.4.19 (Capt SE Ritchie killed) (now 110-hp Le Rhône) |
| D1616 | Deld Eastbourne NFS W/E 9.3.18; SoAF&G Leuchars by 5.19 |
| D1617 | Deld Eastbourne NFS W/E 9.3.18; Became 206 TDS Eastbourne 1.4.18; Disb into 50 TDS Eastbourne 15.7.18; Crashed 10.8.18 (2/Lt G Dutton slightly injured) |
| D1618 | Deld Eastbourne NFS W/E 9.3.18; Became 206 TDS Eastbourne 1.4.18; Disb into 50 TDS Eastbourne 15.7.18 - @24.9.18; SE Area FIS Shoreham .18 |
| D1619 | Deld Eastbourne NFS W/E 9.3.18; Became 206 TDS Eastbourne 1.4.18; Disb into 50 TDS Eastbourne 15.7.18 |
| D1620 | Deld Eastbourne NFS W/E 9.3.18; Became 206 TDS Eastbourne 1.4.18; Disb into 50 TDS Eastbourne 15.7.18 - @3.8.18 |
| D1621 | (Monosoupape) Deld Eastbourne NFS W/E 16.3.18; Became 206 TDS Eastbourne 1.4.18 - @21.6.18; SE Area FIS Shoreham .18 |

| D1622 | Deld Eastbourne NFS W/E 16.3.18; Became 206 TDS Eastbourne 1.4.18 |
|---|---|
| D1623 | (Monosoupape) Deld Eastbourne NFS W/E 30.3.18; Became 206 TDS Eastbourne 1.4.18 - @4.6.18 |
| D1624 | Deld 206 TDS Eastbourne by 5.18; Disb into 50 TDS Eastbourne 15.7.18 |
| D1625 | Deld 206 TDS Eastbourne by 29.5.18; 212 TDS Vendôme by 8.18 - @9.18 |
| D1626 | (504K)(110-hp Le Rhône) Deld 201/2 TDS Cranwell 4.18; Freiston by 5.18 |
| D1627 | (504K)(110-hp Le Rhône) Allocated Cranwell by 30.3.18; 212 TDS Vendôme by 8.18; Hit ridge, broke u/c 3.9.18 (F/Cdt C Harrington & Lt O Smith) |
| D1629 | 212 TDS Vendôme by 9.18 |
| D1631 | (504K) Deld 2 AAP Hendon by 5.18; Medical Flt Hendon 11.5.18; 471 Flt 233 Sqdn Dover 19.9.18; Manston 20.9.18; AES Martlesham Heath by 11.18 |
| D1641 | (Le Rhône) Cricklewood to Hendon Air Station 25.6.18; 1 Comm Sqdn Hendon 23.7.18 - @28.7.18 |
| D1646 | Pool of Pilots Manston by 6.18 - @7.18 |
| D1647 | (Le Rhône) Deld 206 TDS Eastbourne by 12.6.18 |
| D1648 | (Le Rhône) Deld 206 TDS Eastbourne by road 31.5.18 - @7.18 |

### 38 AIRCO D.H.9 TRACTOR BIPLANE DAY BOMBERS from batch D1651 to D1750 built by Mann, Egerton & Co Ltd and built Norwich. (200-hp B.H.P. unless otherwise stated)

| D1653 | Deld AAP Norwich 3.18; Yarmouth W/E 23.3.18; Became 490 Flt Yarmouth by 25.5.18; EF, FL in sea, sank 14.8.18 (crew rescued by F.2A N4542) |
|---|---|
| D1654 | Deld AAP Norwich 3.18; Yarmouth W/E 23.3.18; Became 490 Flt Yarmouth by 25.5.18; 534 Flt 273 Sqdn Covehithe by 25.6.18 - @9.18 |
| D1655 | Deld AAP Norwich 3.18; Yarmouth W/E 30.3.18; AZP 13.4.18 (F/Cdr E Cadbury & OSL FL Wills); Became 490 Flt Yarmouth by 25.5.18 - @15.6.18; HSMP 10.6.18; Covehithe by 6.18; Manston Naval Flt by 7.18; 534 Flt 273 Sqdn Covehithe by 1.8.18 - @15.11.18; 2x100-lb bombs dropped on British submarine *C.25*, missed 8.8.18; 534 Flt 273 Sqdn Burgh Castle, HACP 9.11.18 |
| D1656 | Deld AAP Norwich 3.18; Yarmouth W/E 30.3.18; AZP 13.4.18 (Capt GWR Fane & OSL S Plowman); Became 490 Flt Yarmouth 25.5.18 (212 Sqdn 20.8.18) - @15.10.18 |
| D1657 | Shipped from West India Docks to Otranto 27.4.18; AD Taranto by 7.18; 472/4 Flts 226 Sqdn Pizzone by 8.18 |
| D1658 | Shipped from West India Docks to Otranto 27.4.18; AD Taranto by 7.18; 472/4 Flts 226 Sqdn Pizzone by 8.18 |
| D1659 | Shipped from West India Docks to Otranto 27.4.18; AD Taranto by 7.18; 472/4 Flts 226 Sqdn Pizzone by 8.18; In sea 30m NE of Brindisi during raid on Durazzo 08.05 26.8.18 (Lt IF George & Pte1 W Copley) |
| D1660 | Shipped from West India Docks to Otranto 27.4.18; AD Taranto by 7.18; 224 Sqdn by 8.18; 66/67 Wing, EF, FL in sea after raid on Durazzo, sank 17.9.18 (2 crew picked up unhurt by Italian destroyer) |
| D1661 | Shipped from West India Docks to Otranto 27.4.18; AD Taranto by 7.18 - @8.18; 224 Sqdn by 2.10.18 - @23.10.18; Pizzone by 10.18; 472/4 Flts 226 Sqdn Pizzone |
| D1662 | Shipped from West India Docks to Otranto 27.4.18; 226 Sqdn Pizzone by 7.18; Became 472/4 Flts 226 Sqdn Pizzone 9.18 - @2.10.18; Mudros by 10.18 - @1.19 |
| D1663 | 1 AI to 206 Sqdn 19.4.18; Badly damaged by AA 3.5.18 (Lt T Roberts & Sgt J Chapman DFM unhurt); Rep Pk 1 ASD 6.5.18; Rebuilt as F5843 25.6.18 |
| D1681 | Deld 492 Flt 254 Sqdn Prawle Point 24.5.18; Landed and CW Paignton, Devon 9.6.18 |
| D1682 | Deld 492 Flt 254 Sqdn Prawle Point 22.5.18 - @27.10.18; Longside by 15.11.18 |
| D1683 | Deld 492 Flt 254 Sqdn Prawle Point by 25.5.18; 494 Flt 250 Sqdn Padstow W/E 30.5.18 |
| D1684 | Deld 492 Flt 254 Sqdn Prawle Point 24.5.18 - @6.18; Tested 27.5.18 |
| D1685 | Deld 492 Flt 254 Sqdn Prawle Point 24.5.18; Tested 27.5.18; Dropped 2x230-lb bombs on U-boat 5017N 0305W 9.6.18 (Capt RR Thornely DSC & AM Ford) |
| D1686 | Deld 492 Flt 254 Sqdn Prawle Point 24.5.18; Tested 27.5.18; FL, slightly damaged Hallsands 6.6.18; still |

there 25.6.18

D1687   Deld 3 AAP Norwich by 30.4.18; Rec Pk to 1 AI 10.5.18; SOC 1 ASD 5.7.18 NWR

D1688   Deld 3 AAP Norwich 27.4.18 - @31.5.18 for Dunkerque; Rec Pk to 1 AI 6.18; 206 Sqdn 13.6.18; Hit rut landing 23.11.18 (Lt GW Welch & 2/Lt TH Lowe unhurt); retd 8 SS for repair

D1689   Deld 3 AAP Norwich by 3.5.18; Rec Pk by 5.18; 1 AI 9.5.18; 206 Sqdn 12.5.18; HA shot down OOC when squadron attacked by 8 Pfalz DIII E of Ypres 28.7.18 (Lt GA Pitt & G/L Sgt G Betteridge); Returning from bombing Courtrai Rly Stn, attacked by 20 Pfalz DIII, 1 in flames crashed W of Courtrai & 1 in spin 19.20-19.35, then thick fog nr aerodrome, EF, FL in wood, lost wings in treetops, W of Quercamp 28.7.18 (Lt GA Pitt & G/L Sgt G Betteridge unhurt); 1 ASD 15.8.18; SOC 19.8.18

D1690   491 Flt Dover by 5.18 (transit?); En route 3 AAP Norwich to 103 Sqdn Salisbury, FL in mist and low cloud, spun in on landing, CW, Guston Road 6.5.18 (Lt GF Townsend); Surveyed 7.5.18; For deletion by 24.5.18; WOC Dover 21.7.18

D1691   Deld Dover W/E 15.5.18; 218 Sqdn by 20.5.18; After raid on Ostende, EF, FL on sands on French/Belgian border 25.6.18 (Lt EH Dixon & 2/Lt PK Wilson unhurt); repaired on sqdn; Overshot, hit D7241 1.8.18; Badly shot up by HA 12.8.18; 4 ASD 12.8.18; 233 Sqdn Dover by 16.10.18; France 18.10.18; 4 ASD 10.18; 218 Sqdn 24.10.18; 98 Sqdn 21.1.19; Retd UK 15.2.19

D1693   Deld 3 AAP Norwich by 8.5.18; Rec Pk to 1 AI 14.5.18; 211 Sqdn 16.5.18; Port wing folded up crossing over trenches at 20 ft Pervyse, CW 26.5.18 (Capt TF Le Mesurier DoW & 2/Lt R Lardner killed); Salvaged to 8 AP 27.5.18; SOC in field

D1694   Deld 491 Flt Dover W/E 24.5.18; Bergue 7.6.18; 98 Sqdn by 6.18; Missing 16.6.18 (Lt D McCartney & Lt J Jackman both killed); SOC 17.6.18

D1695   Deld 3 AAP Norwich by 9.5.18; Rec Pk to 206 Sqdn 21.5.18; Stalled on turn after TO and spun in, BO 22.5.18 (2/Lt EP Morgan DoI & 2/Lt F Taylor killed); Rep Pk 1 ASD 23.5.18; SOC 27.5.18

D1699   Deld 3 AAP Norwich by 13.5.18; Rec Pk to 1 AI 18.5.18; 206 Sqdn 21.5.18; EF, FL Droglandt 23.6.18 (Lt T Roberts & 2/Lt RW Brigstock unhurt); Rep Pk 1 ASD 25.6.18; SOC 27.6.18 NWR

D1701   Deld 3 AAP Norwich by 13.5.18; Rec Pk to 1 AI 5.18; 211 Sqdn (coded 'V') 25.5.18; Attacked by 6 Fokker biplanes on PR mission, FL and crashed between Forthem & Loo, SE of Furnes 13.8.18 (1/Lt AF Bonnalie USAS & 2/Lt TB Dodwell both unhurt); Rec Pk 1 ASD 14.8.18; SOC 27.8.18 NWR

D1708   Deld 3 AAP Norwich by 25.5.18; Dover (via Eastbourne) 29.6.18; 4 ASD Audembert 30.6.18; 218 Sqdn 2.7.18; Yellow Albatros in flames Ostende, shared formation 18.25 5.7.18 (Capt MG Baskerville & Sgt J Harris); EF, FL and wrecked, Groede, Zeeland 16.8.18 (Lt AC Lloyd & 2/Lt MG Wilson both interned) [credited Ltn Osterkap, Marine Jasta 1]; Aircraft interned

D1711   Allocated 250 Sqdn HQ Padstow by 25.5.18; 492 Flt 254 Sqdn Prawle Point by 23.7.18; 493 Flt 236 Sqdn Mullion 15.8.18 - @18.10.18

D1712   Allocated 250 Sqdn HQ Padstow by 25.5.18; 492 Flt 254 Sqdn Prawle Point by 23.7.18; 493 Flt 236 Sqdn Mullion by 8.18; Crashed owing to broken drift wire Poldhu Creek 15.10.18 (pilot unhurt)

D1713   494 Flt 250 Sqdn Padstow by 25.5.18; Retd with engine trouble, COL 18.10.18

D1714   494 Flt 250 Sqdn Padstow by 25.5.18; COL 16.6.18 (2/Lt AEN Ashford & 2/Lt JD Davidson both injured)

D1718   1 ASD to 206 Sqdn 6.6.18; Fokker DVII crashed NW of Nieppe 11.15 30.8.18; KB shot down Frelinghem-Deulemont 4.9.18 (both Capt RNG Atkinson MC & 2/Lt FS Ganter); Hit by AA, all controls shot away, crashed in shell holes nr Ypres 5.10.18 (Capt RNG Atkinson MC & 2/Lt JS Blanford); to Rep Pk 1 ASD

D1728   1 AI by 6.18; 206 Sqdn 20.6.18; COL 16.8.18 (Lt TC Story unhurt); Rep Pk 1 ASD 17.8.18

D1730   1 AI by 6.18; 206 Sqdn 25.6.18; Left 0440 on long recce, FTR 7.7.18 (Lt JR Harington & 2/Lt CL Bray both killed) [credited Flgm Goerth, Marine Jasta 3, in

D1747   sea]; SOC in field 8.7.18

D1747   MOS Aldeburgh by 8.18; Became ASIPOP Aldeburgh 28.12.18; Became 1 MOS Aldeburgh 1.1.19 - 2.19

D1749   MOS Aldeburgh by 8.18 - @12.18

D1750   4 ASD to 218 Sqdn 3.8.18; Fokker DVII OOC Cortemarcke, shared U.S. D.H.4 A3205 (Lt R Talbot USMC & Cpl RG Robinson USMC) 08.15 8.10.18 (Lt HW Matthews & 2/Lt HW Murray); 98 Sqdn 21.1.19; To UK 15.2.19

**25 AIRCO D.H.4 TRACTOR BIPLANE DAY BOMBERS ordered 12.10.17 under Cont No A.S.29679 from Westland Aircraft Works, numbered D1751 to D1775 & built Yeovil. Many delivered initially to AAP Brooklands. All to naval units. (200-hp B.H.P. unless otherwise stated)**

D1751   Deld Dover 2.1.18; 6 Sqdn 13.1.18; 11 Sqdn 11.3.18; Hendon (via Dover) 15.3.18; Dunkerque 16.3.18; EF, FL ADD 17.3.18; 11 Sqdn 18.3.18; Became 211 Sqdn 1.4.18; 4 ASD 8.4.18?; 218 Sqdn 24.4.18; Crashed, damaged 8.5.18 (Lt BH Stata & Capt FET Hewlett); AP Dover repair 10.5.18; 491 Flt Dover by 25.5.18; 4 ASD 25.6.18; 2 SS Richborough 2.10.18

D1752   Deld Dover 22.12.17 - @12.1.18; ADD by 17.1.18; 6 Sqdn 19.1.18; 11 Sqdn 11.3.18; Became 211 Sqdn 1.4.18; 4 ASD 8.4.18; 218 Sqdn 25.4.18; Dover W/E 24.5.18; Rec Pk 1 ASD by 7.18; 5 AI 19.7.18; 49 Sqdn 20.7.18; Pilots Pool, crashed, to 4 ASD 25.10.18

D1753   Deld NAP Brooklands W/E 29.12.17; Dover 4.1.18; 6 Sqdn 3.1.18; 11 Sqdn 11.3.18; EF, FL, crashed 23.3.18 (FSL AG Storey & AGL HW Newsham); 4 ASD Guines 24.3.18; Deleted 8.4.18

D1754   Deld NAP Brooklands 1.18; Dover 13.1.18; 6 Sqdn 27.1.18; 11 Sqdn 11.3.18; Became 211 Sqdn 1.4.18; 202 Sqdn 16.4.18; Crashed on TO, BO 21.4.18 (Lt GH Whitmill killed); Surveyed 28.4.18; Deleted 15.5.18

D1755   Deld W/E 12.12.17 to Sunbeams Moorfield Works, Wolverhampton for expts

D1756   Deld NAP Brooklands W/E 19.12.17; Dover 16.2.18; Deleted 15.5.18 DBR; Restored to commission; 491 Flt Dover by 25.5.18; 4 ASD by 13.10.18

D1757   Deld NAP Brooklands W/E 19.12.17; AAP Dover 18.2.18; 11 Sqdn 6.3.18; Became 211 Sqdn 1.4.18; 202 Sqdn 16.4.18; 218 Sqdn 25.4.18 - @27.4.18; 202 Sqdn (retd?) to Dover 28.4.18; COL Guston Rd, Dover 1.5.18 (Lt JH Eyres & 1AM RH Peters uninjured); Broke propeller and crashed over edge of aerodrome Dover 9.5.18 (Lt JH Eyres injured); AP Dover repair 10.5.18; Surveyed 15.5.18; Deletion recommended 17.5.18; 491 Flt Dover by 24.5.18 (for deletion); 4 ASD 25.6.18; Deleted 5.7.18

D1758   Deld NAP Brooklands W/E 19.12.17; AAP Dover 21.2.18; 11 Sqdn 12.3.18; 12 Sqdn 16.3.18 - @30.3.18; Surveyed Dover 10.5.18; Deleted 15.5.18 DBR; Restored to commission; 491 Flt Dover by 25.5.18; Rec Pk 1 ASD 6.18; 2 ASD 18.6.18; 4 ASD Audembert 21.6.18; 4 ASD Pilots Pool by 3.7.18 - @13.7.18; 491 Flt Dover by 15.8.18; Pilots Pool to 4 ASD by road by 25.10.18

D1759   Deld CSD White City by 1.12.17; Shipped to 2 Wing Mudros 19.1.18; Mudros by 4.18; Repair Base Mudros by 25.7.18; F Sqdn 62 Wing Mudros by 8.18 - @11.18; 220 Sqdn Imbros by 28.10.18 - @1.19

D1760   Deld CSD White City by 1.12.17; Shipped to 2 Wing Mudros 19.1.18; 220 Sqdn Imbros 7.6.18 - @1.19

D1761   Deld CSD White City by 15.1.18; Shipped to Mudros 30.1.18; 224 Sqdn by 21.4.18 - @8.18

D1762   Deld CSD White City by 1.12.17; Shipped to 2 Wing Mudros 19.1.18; Stavros by 6.18 - @1.19

D1763   Deld CSD White City by 1.12.17; Shipped to 2 Wing Mudros 30.1.18; Mudros by 3.18 - @4.18; Stavros by 6.18 - @2.8.18; Mudros Repair Base by 10.18 - @1.19

D1764   Deld Exptl Flt Gosport 11.1.18 - @10.18 (E/WT expts with RN Signal School, Portsmouth)

D1765   Deld CSD White City by 1.1.18; Shipped to Mudros 30.1.18; 224 Sqdn by 7.4.18 - @11.5.18

D1766   Deld CSD White City by 1.1.18; Shipped to Mudros 30.1.18; Mudros by 3.18 - @4.18; Stavros by 6.18 & @10.9.18 - @1.19; 220 Sqdn Imbros by 20.10.18

D1767   Deld AAP Hendon 1.18; Cranwell 8.1.18 - @3.18; Crashed on nose Cranwell North 17.1.18

D1768    Deld AAP Hendon 1.18; Cranwell W/E 18.1.18 - @4.18; O/t in wind and slightly damaged 26.2.18 (F/Cdr NR Cook DSC & PFO GC Bladon uninjured)

D1769    (re-engined Puma) Deld NAP Brooklands by 19.1.18; ECD Grain 25.1.18 - @1.4.18 (hydrovane and fittings for flotation gear experiments); Grain Test Dept by 25.5.18; Tested with flotation gear 20.7.18; Ditching trials with double hydrovane 16.8.18; Ditching trials with wooden hydrovane 21.8.18; Martlesham Heath by 10.18; Grain by 11.18 (continue flotation trials)

D1770    Deld CSD White City by 15.1.18; Shipped to Mudros 30.1.18; G Sqdn 2 Wing Mudros by 3.18; 66/67 Wings by 21.4.18; 226 Sqdn by 25.5.18; F Sqdn Mudros by 10.18

D1771    Deld CSD White City by 15.1.18; Shipped to Mudros 30.1.18; Mudros by 24.3.18 - @3.6.18; F Sqdn Mudros by 6.18 - @1.19; H.2 Flt RHNAS Stavros by 2.11.18

D1772    Deld CSD White City by 15.1.18; Shipped to Mudros 30.1.18; 224 Sqdn by 7.4.18 - @13.6.18; AD Taranto by 7.18; 496/8 Flts 224 Sqdn 2.9.18; FL 3,000yds inside enemy lines NW of Fieri 21.9.18 (2/Lt Mawer & 2/Lt GE Hughes PoWs)

D1773    Deld CSD White City by 15.1.18; Shipped to Mudros 30.1.18; 224 Sqdn by 7.4.18; Crashed on TO for raid 9.6.18 (Lt WF Salter killed & 2AM SW James injured); Deleted 27.6.18

D1774    Deld CSD White City by 15.1.18; Shipped to Mudros 30.1.18; Mudros by 24.3.18 - @4.18; Mobile Sqdn Mudros, wingtip hit flagstaff landing and caught fire 10.6.18 (Lt GM Scott & Boy W/T H Boyles both killed)

D1775    Deld CSD White City by 15.1.18; Shipped to Mudros 30.1.18; 224 Sqdn Otranto by 7.4.18 - @30.4.18; Disposed of by 25.5.18 (not reported)

## 51 SOPWITH F.1 CAMEL TRACTOR BIPLANE SCOUTS from batch D1776 to D1975 built by Ruston, Proctor & Co Ltd at Lincoln. (150-hp B.R.1 or 130-hp Clerget 9B)

D1779    4 ASD Guines by 31.5.18; Rec Pk to 2 ASD 13.6.18

D1781    2 AI to 208 Sqdn 10.4.18; Pfalz DIII with brown fuselage and yellow tail shot down Merville 12.00 18.5.18 (Capt HGW Debenham); Lost in mist, FL nr Engine Repair Section, Vernon, crashed on TO 30.6.18 (Lt J Mollison unhurt); SOC 2 ASD 30.6.18

D1804    Rec Pk to 2 ASD 7.4.18; 70 Sqdn, crashed 11.6.18 (2/Lt OA Heron injured); 2 AI 6.18; 201 Sqdn 20.6.18; Bombed railway sidings E of Merincourt, presumed aircraft spun into ground E of Proyart 11.05 8.8.18 (2/Lt NOM Foggo PoW); Rebuilt as F6089 3.7.18 (sic)

D1812    (130-hp Clerget) Presentation a/c 'Shanghai Race Club No.4'; 73 Sqdn RFC by 4.18; Fokker DrI OOC 7.4.18; HA destroyed 12.4.18 (both Capt GAH Pidcock); Marquise by 7.18; Lympne 15.7.18; Farnborough 24.7.18; 204 TDS Eastchurch by 24.9.18; Flew into hill in fog 28.10.18 (Lt JA Smee killed)

D1813    (130-hp Clerget) Deld Hendon W/E 30.3.18; 9 AAP Lympne 31.3.18; Rec Pk to 208 Sqdn 11.4.18; Albatros DV OOC crashed nr Meurchin 11.15 8.5.18; 2-str OOC 2m E of Lens, shared C8266, D1853, D1873, D1879, D1889 & D6544 08.00 22.5.18 (both Lt EG Johnstone); Shot up in combat 8.7.18 (Lt WA Crundall unhurt); 1 AD 8.7.18; Rebuilt as F6022 25.7.18

D1824    (BR.1) Deld AAP Dover W/E 4.5.18; 4 ASD Guines W/E 4.5.18; 204 Sqdn 19.5.18 - @25.5.18; 4 ASD Guines by 31.5.18; 204 Sqdn by 6.18; Fokker DVII OOC over Blankenberghe 14.45 30.6.18 (Capt AJB Tonks); EF, FL on aerodrome, CW 24.7.18 (Capt AJB Tonks unhurt); 4 ASD 25.7.18; 213 Sqdn 29.8.18; Left formation at 14,500ft, shot down by 2 HA 10m SE of Ostende 5.9.18 (2/Lt CE Francis PoW) [credited Flgm Mayer, Marine Jasta 3 at Stalhille]; Deleted 15.9.18

D1834    (140-hp Clerget) 1 AI to 208 Sqdn 20.5.18; Rumpler C dest 1m SW of Estaires, shared D1928 08.10 8.7.18; Albatros DV dest SW of Douai, shared D6490 20.20 31.7.18; Fokker DVII OOC Nesle 11.25 9.8.18 (all Lt WEG Mann); Badly shot up by EA and ground m/g fire 12.00 9.8.18 (Lt WEG Mann unhurt); 2 ASD 12.8.18; Rebuilt as F6264 22.8.18

D1836    (130-hp Clerget) 73 Sqdn, Albatros OOC 7.4.18 (2/Lt JH Drewry); Rec Pk by 4.18; 208 Sqdn 11.4.18; Petrol tank shot through, FL, caught by high wind on TO, o/t

D1840    14.4.18 (2/Lt EG Johnstone unhurt); 1 AD repair 15.4.18; Rec Pk 1 ASD to 2 ASD 25.6.18; 65 Sqdn, crashed 8.7.18 (2/Lt W Standring)

D1840    (130-hp Clerget) Rec Pk to 208 Sqdn 11.4.18; Bullet through tank while firing on enemy transport, FL, o/t E of St.Venant 13.4.18 (2/Lt WEG Mann unhurt); Depot 13.4.18; Rebuilt as F5919 25.6.18

D1845    (130-hp Clerget) Rec Pk to 208 Sqdn (coded 'C') 11.4.18; In action 15.4.18 (2/Lt JG Glazier wounded by bullet); Albatros DV OOC Provin 11.15 8.5.18; Albatros DV OOC Phalempin 13.45 9.5.18 (both Lt WEG Mann); FL, o/t Acq 18.5.18 (Lt JH Smith unhurt); Rebuilt and retd 208 Sqdn strength; 2-str OOC NE of La Bassée, shared D8144 & D8149 07.30 20.7.18 (Lt RCD'A Gifford); 2 Pfalz DIII OOC Estaires 09.30 31.7.18; Fokker DrI OOC Meurchin 11.50 7.8.18 (both Capt WL Jordan DSC DFC); Lost wheel on TO, o/t on landing 15.8.18 (Capt WL Jordan DSC DFC unhurt); 1 ASD 16.8.18; Rebuilt as F6347 in error 23.8.17, changed to H7016

D1852    (130-hp Clerget) Rec Pk to 208 Sqdn 11.4.18; 2-str shot down SW of Hénin-Lietard 09.35 21.4.18 (Capt R McDonald) (Ltn Heinrich Grabhorn & Ltn Otto Baltzer, FAA 268 both killed); Shot down by Vzfw Julius Trortsky, Jasta 43 nr Provin, last seen 11.15 8.5.18 (Capt R McDonald killed); SOC in field 8.5.18

D1853    (130-hp Clerget) Rec Pk to 208 Sqdn 11.4.18; Albatros DV crashed 1m S of Merville 07.15 17.4.18; 2-str OOC 2m E of Lens, shared C8266, D1813, D1873, D1879, D1889 & D6544 08.00 22.5.18; Albatros DV shot down N of Lestrem, shared D1879, D1889 & D6698 12.15 2.6.18 (all 2/Lt PM Dennett); EF, FL, damaged 7.7.18 (Lt HK Scrivener unhurt); 1 ASD 7.7.18; Rebuilt as F6036 24.7.18

D1854    (130-hp Clerget) Rec Pk to 208 Sqdn 11.4.18; Albatros shot down 21.4.18; Fokker DrI OOC Merville, shared D1889, D1923 & D6698 11.10 31.5.18 (both Lt PM Dennett); Shot down Merville-Estaires 12.15 2.6.18 (Lt PM Dennett killed)

D1856    (130-hp Clerget) Rec Pk to 208 Sqdn 11.4.18; Lost, FL in field Colembert 29.4.18 (Lt GA Wightman); 1 ASD repair 1.5.18; 148th US Aero Sqdn by 6.7.18; 1 ASD 9.7.18; 148th US Aero Sqdn 4.8.18, but u/s; 1 AI 8.18; 2 AI 2 ASD 22.8.18; 148th US Aero Sqdn 25.8.18; 2 ASD 28.8.18 (defective rigging); 73 Sqdn by 10.18; Shot down by Ltn K Plauth, Jasta 51 8.10.18 (Lt GDL Snyman missing)

D1860    (130-hp Clerget) Deld 4 AAP Lincoln by 5.4.18; Hendon 5.4.18; Lympne 7.4.18; Rep Pk to 208 Sqdn 11.4.18; Albatros DV crashed nr Provin 11.15 8.5.18 (Lt GA Cox); Reported defective 8.6.18 (Lt GA Cox); AI 1 ASD 9.6.18; Rec Pk 12.6.18; 2 ASD 26.6.18; 205 TDS Vendôme 30.6.18; O/t by gust of wind when landing, badly damaged 17.7.18 (F/Cdt RB Mumford); 84 Wing ARS Vendôme by 11.18

D1862    (Clerget L-S later BR.1) Deld 4 AAP Lincoln 3.18; 4 ASD Guines 30.3.18; 201 Sqdn 17.4.18; Albatros DV shot down Bapaume-Mory, shared B3884, B5749, B6211, B6297, B6421, B7191, B7225 & D3393 06.45 16.5.18; Albatros DV OOC nr Aubigny, shared B7190 08.45 23.5.18 (both Mjr CD Booker DSC); 2 ASD 13.7.18 (unfit for further flying); RP 1 ASD 7.8.18; To England 8.8.18 ALSO "D1862" 208 Sqdn, Pfalz DIII shot down 1m S of Estaires 09.30 31.7.18 (Lt RCD'A Gifford) [Neither this, nor B7862 which he usually flew, fit at that date]

D1865    (130-hp Clerget) Deld 4 AAP Lincoln by 30.3.18; 4 ASD Guines 30.3.18; Rec Pk to 208 Sqdn 11.4.18; Struck shed landing 19.4.18 (2/Lt JS McDonald); Rep Pk 1 ASD 20.4.18; 2 ASD 13.6.18; 70 Sqdn by 5.7.18; Wrecked 9.7.18; Rep Pk 1 ASD 11.7.18; SOC 14.7.18

D1866    (130-hp Clerget) Deld 4 AAP Lincoln 3.18; 4 ASD Guines 30.3.18; 213 Sqdn 1.6.18; 2 Pfalz OOC Bruge, shared B7254, C66, C73 & D3333 14.20 1.6.18 (Lt PC Jenner); Destroyed by fire in enemy bombing raid 29.6.18; WOC 31.6.18

D1867    (130-hp Clerget) Rec Pk by 4.18; 208 Sqdn 11.4.18; Albatros DV OOC Provin 11.15 8.5.18 (2/Lt JB White); 1 AI 14.7.18 (unfit for further service); Rec Pk 1 ASD by 8.18; Lympne 9.8.18

D1868    (130-hp Clerget) Deld 4 AAP Lincoln by 30.3.18; 4

ASD Guines 30.3.18; Dover by 27.4.18 - @5.18; 204 Sqdn by 1.6.18; 2-str OOC 14.30 & Fokker DVII OOC 14.40 Zeebrugge-Blankenberghe 30.6.18 (Lt RMcI Gordon); 4 ASD Guines to 4 ASD Audembert 14.8.18; to 210 Sqdn 3.10.18; Fokker DVII crashed 4m NE of Roulers 09.23, then shot down by a Fokker DrI 09.25 8.10.18 (Lt CF Pineau PoW); Deleted 31.10.18

D1869    (130-hp Clerget) Deld 4 AAP Lincoln 3.18; 4 ASD Guines 3.18; Rec Pk by 4.18; 208 Sqdn 11.4.18; 2-str dest 1m NW of La Bassée 17.40 12.4.18; Pfalz DIII OOC 1m SE of La Bassée 4.5.18 (both Capt WL Jordan); Collided with stationery D.H.9 while landing 16.5.18 (Lt LC Gilmour unhurt); 1 ASD 16.5.18; Rebuilt as F5925 25.6.18; SOC 1 ASD 30.8.18

D1870    Deld 4 AAP Lincoln 3.18 - @11.5.18; Rec Pk to 2 ASD 27.5.18; 43 Sqdn, shot down by Ltn C Bolle, Jasta B 25.7.18 (Lt RE Meredith killed)

D1871    (130-hp Clerget L-S) Deld 4 AAP Lincoln by 30.3.18; 4 ASD Guines 30.3.18; 4 AAP Lincoln by 27.4.18; 4 ASD Guines by 25.5.18; 213 Sqdn 25.6.18; Attacked by 15 HA and shot down over lines Dixmude-Ypres 15.8.18 (Lt CH Denny killed); Deleted 15.9.18

D1872    (130-hp Clerget) Rec Pk to 208 Sqdn 11.4.18; EF, FL, crashed 23.4.18 (2/Lt H Bayly); Rep Pk 1 ASD 26.4.18; 1 AI 9.6.18; 210 Sqdn 11.6.18; Fokker DVII blue fuselage and red tail OOC E of Dixmude 20.30 24.7.18; Halberstadt C BU in air SE of Kemmel Hill 12.40 31.7.18; Fokker DVII yellow fuselage, white tail, red nose OOC N of Lille 19.25 1.8.18 (all Lt L Yerex); 4 ASD 13.8.18; WOC 15.9.18 general fatigue

D1873    (130-hp Clerget) Rec Pk to 1 AI 12.4.18; 208 Sqdn 13.4.18; Albatros DV OOC Provin - Pont-à-Vendin 11.15 8.5.18; Albatros C OOC 2m NE of Lens, shared C8266, D1813, D1853, D1879, D1889 & D6544 08.00 22.5.18 (both Capt GK Cooper); Left 09.30, patrol heavily attacked by HA, FTR 2.9.18 (2/Lt JW Marshall wounded); SOC 2.9.18

D1877    (130-hp Clerget L-S) Deld 4 AAP Lincoln by 30.3.18; Rec Pk to 208 Sqdn 11.4.18; 1 AI 22.7.18 (unfit for further service); Flown to England 24.7.18; Stored Agricultural Hall, Islington 1918 for permanent preservation; Presume later scrapped

D1879    Rec Pk by 4.18; 208 Sqdn 20.4.18; 1 DFW OOC 11.5.18 (Lt JS McDonald); C-type OOC 2m NE of Lens 08.00, shared C8266, D1813, D1853, D1873, D1889 & D6544 08.00 22.5.18 (Lt JS McDonald); Propeller broke on operational patrol, FL Tonnay 22.5.18 (Lt JS McDonald unhurt) [presumably same patrol]; Albatros DV N of Lestrem, shared D1853, D1889, D6698 12.15 2.6.18 (Lt JS McDonald); Rebuilt as F5916 25.6.18 ALSO Rebuilt as F6243 23.8.18

D1883    Tested Rec Pk 16.6.18; 1 AI 18.6.18; to 210 Sqdn 24.6.18; Hit standing corn on edge of aerodrome while landing, o/t 7.8.18 (Lt W Stephenson); 4 ASD 7.8.18; 210 Sqdn 28.9.18; Last seen engaged by 12-15 EA over Houthulst Forest, believed crashed in forest 09.50 1.10.18 (Mjr RDG Sibley killed); Deleted 15.10.18

D1889    (140-hp Clerget) Deld 4 AAP Lincoln 4.18; Northolt 24.4.18; Rec Pk 25.4.18 (via Lympne); 1 AI 2.5.18; 208 Sqdn 16.5.18; C-type OOC 2m NE of Lens, shared C8266, D1813, D1853, D1873, D1879 & D6544 08.00 22.5.18; Fokker DrI OOC E of Lens 06.45 23.5.18; Fokker DrI OOC Merville, shared D1854, D1923 & D6698 11.10 31.5.18; Albatros DV dest N of Lestrem, shared D1853, D1879, & D6698 12.15 2.6.18; Albatros DV OOC 2m E of Merville, shared D1955 18.35 4.6.18 (all Capt WL Jordan DSC); Shot down over Wytschaete by Ltn C Degelow, Jasta 29 25.7.18 (2/Lt WA Carveth, PoW); SOC 25.7.18

D1891    8 AAP Lympne by 5.18; Rec Pk 1.5.18; 2 AI 3.5.18; 43 Sqdn 10.5.18; 2 AI to 209 Sqdn 29.6.18 [6.7.18?]; Albatros 2-str OOC, crashed Grivesnes-le-Plessier, shared C198 11.00 18.7.18 (Lt KM Walker); Shot down N of Comines by Uffz Körner & Ltn Schultz, Fl-Abt A258 0720-0740 26.7.18 (2/Lt G Travers PoW); SOC 27.7.18

D1906    Deld 4 AAP Lincoln by 15.4.18; Rec Pk to 1 AI 2.5.18; 208 Sqdn 3.5.18; Aviatik C dest 1½m ESE of Calonne 20.00 12.5.18 (Capt WL Jordan DSC); Crashed on TO, o/t 16.5.18 (Capt WL Jordan DSC unhurt); SOC in field 16.5.18

D1914    (130-hp Clerget) Shipped to Otranto 22.4.18; 226 Sqdn by 25.5.18 - @6.18; AD Taranto by 7.18; 481/3 Flts 225 Sqdn Andrano by 8.18 - @9.18; Taranto by 10.18 - @11.18 (225 Sqdn?)

D1915    (130-hp Clerget) Shipped to Otranto 22.4.18; 226 Sqdn by 25.5.18 - @6.18; AD Taranto by 7.18; Acceptance test 30.7.18; 481/3 Flts 225 Sqdn Andrano 30.7.18 - @10.18; Taranto by 10.18 - @1.19 (225 Sqdn?)

D1916    (130-hp Clerget) Shipped to Otranto 20.4.18; 226 Sqdn by 25.5.18 - @6.18; AD Taranto by 7.18; 481/3 Flts 225 Sqdn Andrano by 8.18 - @9.18; Taranto by 10.18 - @1.19 (225 Sqdn?)

D1919    (Clerget L-S) Deld 4 AAP Lincoln by 18.4.18; 1 AI to 208 Sqdn 17.5.18; Pfalz DIII OOC S of Merville 11.50 18.5.18 (Capt GK Cooper); EF, FL, crashed nr Lillers 9.7.18 (Lt MC Howell unhurt?); 1 ASD 10.7.18; SOC 17.7.18 NWR

D1923    (Clerget) Rec Pk by 5.18; 1 AI 14.5.18; 208 Sqdn 24.5.18; Fokker DrI OOC Merville, shared D1854, D1889 & D6698 11.10 31.5.18; Albatros DV shot down N of Lestrem 12.15 2.6.18; Fokker DrI OOC Meurchin-Epinoy 07.50 8.7.18; Albatros DV OOC Neuve Chapelle 11.25 16.7.18 (all 2/Lt JS McDonald); HA OOC Merville 0730-08.30 patrol 28.7.18; DFW C OOC E of Oppy, shared B7769, D8168 & F5933 06.00 14.8.18 (both Lt WR Allison); 1 ASD 24.8.18 (unfit for further service); Flown to England 5.9.18 (overhaul)

D1928    (Clerget L-S) Deld 4 AAP Lincoln by 20.4.18; Rec Pk to 1 AI 2.5.18; 208 Sqdn 4.5.18; DFW C OOC River Scarpe 19.45 8.5.18 (Mjr C Draper DSC); Rumpler C dest 1m SW of Estaires, shared D1834 08.10 8.7.18 (Lt J Mollison); FL Candas 19.8.18 (Lt J Mollison); Patrol attacked by Fokker DVIIs 07.50, shot down OOC, went down on back from 4,000 ft followed by 4 HA Arras-Cambrai road, E of Vis-en-Artois 27.8.18 (Lt J Mollison killed)

D1949    (130-hp Clerget) Deld 6 SD Ascot W/E 11.7.18; Shipped to Mudros 17.7.18; Calafrana by 9.18 - @1.19

D1950    (130-hp Clerget) Deld 6 SD Ascot W/E 11.7.18; Shipped to Mudros 17.7.18; Calafrana by 9.18 - @1.19

D1951    Deld 6 SD Ascot W/E 25.7.18; To docks W/E 1.8.18; Shipped 17.8.18; 222 Sqdn Mudros by 28.10.18; Mudros by 10.18 - @1.19

D1952    Shipped to Mudros 17.7.18; Mudros by 10.18 - @1.19

D1955    (140-hp Clerget) Shipping via Southampton to 1 ASD by 26.4.18; Rec Pk to 1 AI 14.5.18; 208 Sqdn 24.5.18; Albatros DV OOC 2m E of Merville, shared D1889 18.35 4.6.18 (Lt EG Johnstone); Missing after engagement at 07.50 but improbable brought down by HA as all below; more likely EF, FL 8.7.18 (Lt HK Scrivener PoW); SOC 8.7.18

D1956    (Clerget) 43 Sqdn France to UK 8.10.18; 222 Sqdn Mudros by 2.11.18

D1966    (130-hp Clerget) Deld Islington by 13.6.18; 6 SD Ascot W/E 20.6.18; Shipped from West India Docks 18.7.18; Mudros by 9.18; D Sqdn Stavros; Stavros by 10.18 - @1.19; RAF South Russia to 'A' Dett RAF Instructional Mission South Russia 8.19

D1967    (130-hp Clerget) Deld Islington by 13.6.18; 6 SD Ascot W/E 20.6.18; Shipped from West India Docks 18.7.18; Mudros by 9.18; H.2 Flt RHNAS Thasos/Stavros by 10.10.18; Repair Base Mudros by 10.18 - @1.19

D1968    (130-hp Clerget) Deld Islington by 13.6.18; 6 SD Ascot W/E 20.6.18; Shipped from West India Docks 18.7.18; Mudros by 9.18; H.2 Flt RHNAS Thasos/Stavros by 10.10.18; Repair Base Mudros by 10.18 - @1.19

D1969    (130-hp Clerget) Deld Islington by 13.6.18; 6 SD Ascot W/E 20.6.18; Shipped from West India Docks 18.7.18; Mudros by 9.18; D Sqdn Stavros; Stavros by 10.18

D1970    (130-hp Clerget) Deld Islington by 13.6.18; 6 SD Ascot W/E 20.6.18; Shipped from West India Docks 18.7.18; Mudros by 9.18; 220 Sqdn Imbros by 10.18 - @1.19

D1971    (130-hp Clerget) Deld Islington by 13.6.18; 6 SD Ascot W/E 20.6.18; Shipped from West India Docks 18.7.18; Mudros by 9.18; 220 Sqdn Imbros by 10.18 - @1.19; RAF South Russia to 'A' Dett RAF Instructional Mission South Russia 8.19

D1972    (130-hp Clerget) Deld Islington by 13.6.18; 6 SD Ascot W/E 20.6.18; Shipped from West India Docks 17.7.18; AD Taranto by 8.18; Taranto by 11.18 - @1.19 (ARD?); AP Taranto by 4.19; 'X' AD 11.4.19; WO

D1973 (130-hp Clerget) Deld Islington by 13.6.18; 6 SD Ascot W/E 20.6.18; Shipped from West India Docks 17.7.18; AD Taranto by 8.18; Taranto by 11.18 - @1.19 (ARD?); AP Taranto by 4.19; 'X' AD 11.4.19; WO 21.5.19; ASD Egypt by 4.11.19

**11 AVRO 504K TRACTOR BIPLANE TRAINERS from batch D1976 to D2125 built by Frederick Sage & Co Ltd at Peterborough (130-hp Clerget 9B)**

D1998 56 TDS Cranwell, spun in after flat turn 3.9.18 (F/Cdt FE Wallis seriously injured)
D2000 Deld 4 AAP Lincoln 8.8.18; 57 TDS Cranwell 9.8.18 - @12.18; Propeller accident 16.10.18 (2AM WE Lowe slightly injured)
D2001 56 TDS Cranwell by 7.18 - @8.18
D2002 56 TDS Cranwell, stalled on turn with failing engine 1.8.18 (Capt JC Tanner killed & Lt EG Amatt injured)
D2009 57 TDS Cranwell by 10.18 - @12.18
D2021 204 TDS Eastchurch .18
D2026 204 TDS Eastchurch .18
D2027 57 TDS Cranwell by 10.18
D2031 56 TDS Cranwell by 11.18 - @1.19 (prefix?)
D2069 (504K) 50 TDS Eastbourne; 204 TDS Eastchurch .18; 2 MOS Eastchurch by 3.19; 143 Sqdn 16.7.19
D2110 54 TDS Chingford/Fairlop, crashed while stunting 2.9.18 (Capt IG Davies killed)

**2 BRISTOL F.2B TRACTOR BIPLANES from batch D2126 to D2625 built by National Aircraft Factory at Aintree**

D2208 Cranwell, o/t late 1918 or early 1919
D2607 Exptl Flt Gosport by 3.19 - 4.19 (for RN Signal School, Portsmouth)

**46 AIRCO D.H.9 TRACTOR BIPLANE DAY BOMBERS from batch D2776 to D2875 built by Short Bros and built Rochester. (200-hp B.H.P.)**

D2781 Deld 2 AAP Hendon 3.18; AAP Dover 18.3.18; 11 Sqdn 23.3.18; Became 211 Sqdn (coded 'M') 1.4.18; HA claimed OOC 13.7.18 (Lt ES Morgan & 2/Lt R Simpson); Left 11.35, hit over Zeebrugge, FL Groede, Zeeland 25.7.18 (Sgt RS Gude interned & Sgt HM Partridge DoW); SOC 25.7.18
D2782 Deld 2 AAP Hendon 3.18; Chingford 18.3.18 (transit); AAP Dover 20.3.18; 11 Sqdn 23.3.18; Became 211 Sqdn 1.4.18; Flak damage 14.7.18 (2/Lt HH Palmer wounded & 2/Lt WC Snowden unhurt); 2 ASD 22.2.19 (unfit to fly Channel)
D2783 Deld 2 AAP Hendon 3.18; AAP Dover 21.3.18; 6 Sqdn 24.3.18; Became 206 Sqdn 1.4.18; Rep Pk 1 ASD 30.5.18 (overhaul); 1 AI by 6.18; 206 Sqdn 16.6.18; Hit by EA fire, FL Estrée Blanche 26.6.18 (Lt C Eaton & Lt EW Tatnall unhurt); Rep Pk 1 ASD 26.6.18; SOC 2.7.18 NWR
D2784 Deld 2 AAP Hendon 3.18; AAP Dover 23.3.18; 4 ASD Guines 1.4.18; 211 Sqdn 7.4.18; Last seen Ostende-Nieuport in formation believed crashed nr Uytkerke 12.00 19.5.18 (Lt NA Taylerson & 2/Lt CL Bray both killed) [credited Flgm Engelfried of Seefrontstaffel]
D2785 Deld 2 AAP Hendon 3.18; Cranwell 24.3.18 - @4.18
D2786 (Puma) Deld EAD Grain 12.3.18; ECD Grain by 1.4.18 - @23.6.18 (flotation gear expts); 2 ASD, SOC 24.8.18 NWR
D2787 Deld 2 AAP Hendon 3.18; Cranwell (coded '111') 24.3.18; Became 202 TDS Cranwell 1.4.18; Spun in from 500 ft 12.7.18 (2/Lt WL Lanigan killed)
D2788 Deld 2 AAP Hendon 3.18; Cranwell 24.3.18; Became 201/2 TDS Cranwell 1.4.18
D2789 Deld 7 AAP Kenley 12.3.18 (for D of T); Cranwell (via Lympne) 31.3.18
D2790 Deld 7 AAP Kenley 12.3.18 (for D of T); Cranwell (via Lewes) 29.3.18 - @5.18
D2791 Deld 7 AAP Kenley 12.3.18 (for D of T); Cranwell (via Lewes) 29.3.18; Chingford 14.4.18; Cranwell 24.4.18
D2792 Deld 7 AAP Kenley 12.3.18 (for D of T); Cranwell (via Lewes) 29.3.18; Stalled in 24.4.18 (PFO CM Bates)
D2793 Shipped to Otranto 10.4.18; AD Taranto by 7.18; 226 Sqdn by 8.18; FTR raid on Cattaro 30.8.18 (2/Lt JE

Watkins & Gnr WA Easiman both killed)
D2794 Shipped to Otranto 10.4.18; AD Taranto by 7.18; 224 Sqdn by 29.7.18; Stalled and o/t on landing Valona 29.8.18 (FSL SJ Chamberlain & Lt MI Brockbank both unhurt)
D2795 Deld 12.3.18; Shipped to Otranto 10.4.18; 224 Sqdn by 7.18; Raid on Cattaro 6.9.18 (2/Lt RT Gray, observer, wounded); Taranto by 10.18 - @1.19; AP Taranto by 6.19; 'X' AD 28.6.19
D2796 Deld 12.3.18; Shipped to Otranto 10.4.18; AD Taranto by 7.18; 224 Sqdn by 7.18 - @20.10.18
D2797 Deld 12.3.18; Shipped to Mudros 22.4.18; 220 Sqdn Imbros by 30.6.18 - @4.11.18; Stavros by 11.18 - @1.19
D2798 Deld 12.3.18; Shipped to Otranto 10.4.18; AD Taranto by 7.18; 226 Sqdn by 8.18; Taranto by 1.19; AP Taranto by 6.19; 'X' AD 28.6.19; 'Z' Unit British Somaliland by 1.20 - 5.4.20
D2799 8 AAP Lympne by 30.3.18; Cranwell 6.4.18; En route 12 TS Thetford crashed Sproughton, Suffolk 20.4.18; Cranwell by 1.19
D2800 Shipped from West India Docks to Otranto 27.4.18; 268 Sqdn Calafrana by 6.18 - @1.19
D2801 Shipped from West India Docks to Otranto 27.4.18; 268 Sqdn Calafrana by 6.18 - @1.19
D2802 Shipped from West India Docks to Otranto 27.4.18; 226 Sqdn by 7.18; FTR raid on Cattaro 30.8.18 (Lt J McDonald DFC, PoW & Pte GLE Sutcliffe killed)
D2803 Shipped from Cardiff to Mudros 7.5.18; Shipped to Mudros 18.7.18; Stavros by 10.18 - @1.19; 553 Flt 221 Sqdn (coded '1') by 2.19; Crashed 3.2.19 (Capt JWP Grigson)
D2804 Shipped from Cardiff to Mudros 7.5.18; Shipped to Mudros 18.7.18; Stavros by 7.8.18 - @15.5.18; 2xx Sqdn, lost 5.9.18 (Lt HT Williams)
D2805 Pilots Pool, crashed, to 4 ASD by road by 25.10.18
D2821 221 Sqdn Petrovsk .18; Became G-EALJ
D2825 (F.I.A.T.) RAE by 1.20 (short wave radio coils); HMS Eagle 1920/1 (deck landing trials); Last flown RAE 7.11.27
D2830 203 TDS Manston by 6.18; Became 55 TDS Manston 14.7.18; Spun in from 500 ft 22.8.18 (F/Cdt H Marshall injured)
D2831 201/2 TDS Cranwell by 5.18
D2835 Deld 6 SD Ascot W/E 1.7.18; Shipped 25.8.18; Mudros by 10.18 - @1.19
D2836 Deld 6 SD Ascot W/E 1.7.18; Shipped 25.8.18; Mudros by 10.18 - @1.19
D2838 Deld 6 SD Ascot W/E 1.7.18; Shipped 25.8.18; Mudros by 10.18 - @1.19
D2841 Shipped to Mudros 18.5.18; Repair Base Mudros by 6.18; G Sqdn 2 Wing Mudros by 6.18; F Sqdn 62 Wing Mudros by 11.18; Imbros by 10.18 - @1.19; 16 Wing AP by 4.19; 47 Sqdn 21.4.19; To White Russian Forces 1919;
D2842 Shipped to Mudros 18.5.18; Repair Base Mudros by 6.18; F Sqdn 62 Wing Mudros by 7.18; 220 Sqdn Imbros by 27.10.18; 221 Sqdn Imbros 23.12.18 - @1.19; 16 Wing AP by 4.19; 47 Sqdn 21.4.19; RAF South Russia to Russian Air Corps 8.19
D2843 Shipped to Mudros 18.5.18; Repair Base Mudros by 6.18; F Sqdn 62 Wing Mudros by 9.18 - @11.18; Taranto by 10.18; 220 Sqdn Imbros by 27.10.18 - @16.11.18; 16 Wing AP by 4.19; 47 Sqdn 21.4.19; RAF South Russia to Russian Air Corps 8.19
D2844 Shipped to Mudros 18.5.18; Repair Base Mudros by 6.18; Stavros by 29.8.18; Imbros 14.10.18; 222 Sqdn Mudros by 1.11.18; 222 Sqdn San Stephano 14.11.18 - @1.19; 16 Wing AP by 4.19; 47 Sqdn 21.4.19; To White Russian Forces 1919
D2847 Deld 6 SD Ascot W/E 13.6.18; Salford Docks W/E 25.7.18; Shipped to Mudros 1.8.18; Repair Base Mudros by 10.18 - @1.19; To White Russian Forces 1919; 47 Sqdn by 3.20
D2848 Deld 6 SD Ascot W/E 13.6.18; To West India Docks W/E 11.7.18; Shipped to Mudros 18.7.18; Mudros by 9.18; Repair Base Mudros by 10.18 - @1.19; 222 Sqdn Mudros by 2.11.18; 222 Sqdn San Stephano 14.11.18
D2849 Deld 6 SD Ascot W/E 13.6.18; Salford Docks W/E 25.7.18; Shipped to Mudros 1.8.18; Deleted Mudros 10.18

D2850    Deld 6 SD Ascot W/E 13.6.18; Salford Docks W/E 25.7.18; Shipped to Mudros 1.8.18; Deleted Mudros 10.18

D2851    Deld 6 SD Ascot W/E 13.6.18; Salford Docks W/E 25.7.18; Shipped to Mudros 1.8.18; 222 Sqdn Mudros by 28.10.18; Repair Base Mudros by 10.18 - @1.19

D2852    Deld 6 SD Ascot W/E 13.6.18; Salford Docks W/e 25.7.18; Shipped to Mudros 1.8.18; Repair Base Mudros by 10.18

D2853    Deld 6 SD Ascot W/E 13.6.18; Shipped West India Docks to Mudros 18.7.18; Mudros by 9.18; 478/480 Flts 222 Sqdn Mudros by 28.10.18; Repair Base Mudros by 10.18 - @1.19; 16 Wing AP by 4.19; 47 Sqdn 21.4.19

D2854    Deld 6 SD Ascot W/E 13.6.18; Shipped West India Docks to Mudros 18.7.18; Mudros by 9.18; Repair Base Mudros by 10.18 - @1.19; 478/480 Flts 222 Sqdn Mudros by 28.10.18; 222 Sqdn San Stephano 14.11.18; 221 Sqdn by .19

D2855    Rec Pk to 1 AI 1.6.18; 206 Sqdn 11.6.18; Last seen over Menin 08.40 1.8.18 (Capt JW Mathews & 2/Lt WA John both killed); SOC 1.8.18

D2875    Shorts Rochester by 20.6.18 for conversion for ships aeroplane

## 90 AIRCO D.H.9 TRACTOR BIPLANE DAY BOMBERS from batch D2876 to D3275 built by parent company at Hendon

D2877    Deld 2 AAP Hendon for EF by 25.5.18; 222 Sqdn Mudros by 1.11.18

D2883    Deld 6 SD Ascot W/E 13.6.18; Salford Docks W/E 25.7.18; Shipped to Mudros 1.8.18; Repair Base Mudros by 10.18 - @1.19; To White Russians 1919

D2884    Deld 6 SD Ascot W/E 13.6.18; Salford Docks W/E 25.7.18; Shipped to Mudros 1.8.18; Repair Base Mudros by 10.18; With Greeks by 1.19; Became G-EALJ

D2885    Deld 6 SD Ascot W/E 13.6.18; Salford Docks W/E 25.7.18; Shipped to Mudros 1.8.18; 222 Sqdn Mudros by 29.10.18; Repair Base Mudros by 10.18 - @1.19

D2886    Deld 6 SD Ascot W/E 13.6.18; Salford Docks W/E 25.7.18; Shipped to Mudros 1.8.18; Mudros by 10.18 - @1.19; To White Russians 1919

D2887    Deld 6 SD Ascot W/E 27.6.18; Salford Docks W/E 25.7.18; Shipped to Mudros 1.8.18; Mudros by 10.18 - @1.19; 222 Sqdn Mudros by 11.18; 222 Sqdn San Stephano 14.11.18

D2888    Deld 6 SD Ascot W/E 13.6.18; Salford Docks W/E 25.7.18; Shipped to Mudros 1.8.18; Repair Base Mudros by 10.18 - @1.19; To White Russians 1919

D2889    Islington by 13.6.18; 6 SD Ascot W/E 20.6.18; West India Docks 11.7.18; Shipped to Mudros 18.7.18; Mudros by 9.18

D2890    Islington by 13.6.18; 6 SD Ascot W/E 20.6.18; West India Docks 11.7.18; Shipped to Mudros 18.7.18; Mudros by 9.18; Mudros, deleted 10.18

D2891    Deld 6 SD Ascot W/E 15.8.18; Shipped 21.9.18; Taranto by 11.18 - @1.19; AP Taranto by 6.19; 'X' AD 28.6.19; ASD by 10.19; 142 Sqdn 7.10.19; 5 Sqdn by 8.20

D2892    Deld 6 SD Ascot W/E 15.8.18; Shipped 21.9.18; Taranto by 1.19; 'X' AD 1.4.19; RAF South Russia to Russian Air Corps 24.11.19

D2893    Deld 6 SD Ascot W/E 15.8.18; Shipped 21.9.18; Taranto by 11.18; 'X' AD 1.4.19; RAF South Russia to Russian Air Corps 8.19

D2894    Deld 6 SD Ascot W/E 15.8.18; Shipped 21.9.18; Taranto by 11.18; 'X' AD 1.4.19; RAF South Russia to Russian Air Corps 8.19

D2895    Deld 6 SD Ascot W/E 15.8.18; Shipped to Taranto 21.9.18; 'X' AD 1.4.19; To White Russians 1919

D2896    Deld 6 SD Ascot W/E 15.8.18; Shipped to Taranto 21.9.18; Taranto by 11.18; 'X' AD 1.4.19; RAF South Russia to Russian Air Corps 8.19

D2906    Shipped to Aegean; 226 Sqdn by 2.10.18

D2907    Shipped to Aegean; 226 Sqdn .18

D2910    Shipped to Otranto 24.5.18; AR&ED Pizzone .18; AD Taranto by 7.18; 224 Sqdn Andrano 17.8.18 - @2.10.18; Taranto by 11.18 - @1.19; AP Taranto by 7.19; 'X' AD 1.7.19

D2911    Shipped to Otranto 24.5.18; AR&ED Pizzone .18; AD Taranto by 7.18 - @8.18; 226 Sqdn by 2.10.18; Mudros

D2912    by 10.18 - @1.19
Shipped to Otranto 24.5.18; AR&ED Pizzone .18; AD Taranto by 8.18; 224 Sqdn by 2.10.18; Mudros by 10.18 - @1.19; 47 Sqdn by 11.18; To White Russians 1919

D2913    Shipped to Otranto 24.5.18; AR&ED Pizzone .18; AD Taranto by 7.18 - @8.18; Mudros by 10.18 - @1.19

D2914    Deld Barry Docks 24.5.18; Shipped to Otranto 14.6.18; Repair Base Mudros by 10.18

D2915    Deld Barry Docks 24.5.18; Shipped to Mudros 14.6.18; Mudros by 9.18

D2918    Rec Pk to 211 Sqdn (coded 'D') 28.7.18; Shot down on bombing raid, wreckage in sea 7/9m N of Gravelines 7.9.18 (Lt ES Morgan DFC & 2/Lt R Simpson both killed, picked up by French in sea); SOC in field 7.9.18

D2919    Hendon, crashed 8.8.18 (Lt CR Perring DoI); 211 Sqdn by 9.18

D2921    Deld Yarmouth by 7.18; 555/6 Flts 219 Sqdn Manston 28.7.18; EF, FL, starboard wing & u/c smashed 15.8.18 (Lt EWT Fussell & Sgt Mech DA Alderton); 218 Sqdn (via Dover) 29.9.18; Landed St.Pol after hit by AA fire in raid on Melle 13/14.10.18 (Lt W Bentley pilot wounded); Spun after TO, CW 20.10.18 (Lt CS Oegger & Sgt Paschal USA both unhurt); 4 ASD 21.10.18 - @25.10.18

D2922    Deld Yarmouth by 7.18; 555/6 Flts 219 Sqdn Manston 30.7.18; FL nr Minster 10.8.18; 218 Sqdn (via Dover) 29.9.18; In action 2.10.18 (Lt FG Burden wounded); U/s, burnt on squadron, SOC 22.1.19

D2923    555/6 Flts 219 Sqdn Manston by 3.8.18 - @9.18

D2924    Deld Yarmouth by 7.18; 555/6 Flts 219 Sqdn Manston 30.7.18; Overshot, side slipped into field and caught fire 12.8.18 (Lt JW Ratcliffe & Sgt Mech DA Alderton both injured)

D2925    Deld Yarmouth by 7.18; 555/6 Flts Manston 30.7.18 - @9.8.18

D2927    Recd 'X' AD ex UK 19.10.18; left; 'X' AD 1.1.19; 5 FS Egypt .19; 'X' AP 4.6.19; 206 Sqdn 9.8.19

D2940    Deld 6 SD Ascot W/E 15.8.18; Shipped to Mudros 11.10.18; To White Russians 1919

D2941    Deld 6 SD Ascot W/E 15.8.18; Shipped 27.9.18; Taranto by 11.18 - @1.19; AP Taranto by 3.19; 'X' AD 1.4.19

D2948    Deld 6 SD Ascot W/E 15.8.18; To docks W/E 19.9.18; Shipped to Mudros 11.10.18; Repair Base Mudros by 1.19; To White Russians 1919

D2951    Recd 'X' AD ex UK 24.11.18; Mudros, crashed 19.12.18 (Lt BH Church seriously injured & Lt RB Poole killed); 'X' AD by 7.19; 206 Sqdn 16.7.19

D2954    Recd 'X' AD ex UK 24.11.18; 206 Sqdn 16.7.19; WO 11.12.19

D2958    Deld 6 SD Ascot W/E 15.8.18; To docks W/E 19.9.18; Shipped to Mudros 11.10.18; Repair Base Mudros by 1.19; To White Russians 1919

D2962    Deld 6 SD Ascot W/E 15.8.18; To docks W/E 19.9.18; Shipped on SS *Hazlemere* W/E 17.10.18 but damaged en route Mudros

D2963    Deld 494 Flt 250 Sqdn Padstow by 29.6.18; EF, FL in sea, 1 bomb exploded on hitting water 24.7.18 (Capt N Wadham & 2/Lt AGV Reeves both slightly injured)

D2964    Deld 494 Flt 250 Sqdn Padstow 6.18; Landed with broken wing 13.7.18; Bombed U-boat 5028N 0515W 28.7.18; still Padstow 23.10.18

D2965    Deld 494 Flt 250 Sqdn Padstow by 25.5.18 - @31.9.18

D2966    Deld 494 Flt 250 Sqdn Padstow 6.18 - @8.7.18

D2967    Deld 6 SD Ascot W/E 15.8.18; To docks W/E 19.9.18; Shipped on SS *Hazlemere* W/E 17.10.18 but damaged en route Mudros

D2968    Deld 494 Flt 250 Sqdn Padstow by 25.5.18; 492 Flt Prawle Point by 8.18; Dropped 230-lb bomb on U-boat 5011N 0343W 20.35 10.8.18 (2/Lt RJ Thompson & 3AM AHW Busby); COL Gara Rock owing to thick mist 29.10.18 (2 crew unhurt)

D2969    Allocated 250 Sqdn HQ Padstow by 25.5.18; 492 Flt 254 Sqdn Prawle Point by 9.18

D3002    Deld 6 SD Ascot W/E 20.6.18; Shipped to Taranto 4.7.18; AD Taranto by 8.18; AR&ED Pizzone by .18; 224 Sqdn Taranto by 11.18 - @1.19; AP Taranto by 6.19; 'X' AD 28.6.19; 'Z' Unit British Somaliland by 1.20 - @4.20 (used as spares)

D3003    Deld 6 SD Ascot W/E 20.6.18; West India Docks W/E 11.7.18; Shipped to Mudros 18.7.18; Mudros by 9.18;

Stavros, tested 11.10.18; 222 Sqdn Mudros by 31.10.18; Repair Base Mudros by 10.18 - @1.19

**D3004** Deld 6 SD Ascot W/E 20.6.18; West India Docks W/E 11.7.18; Shipped to Mudros 18.7.18; Mudros by 9.18; Repair Base Mudros by 10.18 - @1.19

**D3005** Deld 6 SD Ascot W/E 20.6.18; Shipped to Taranto 4.7.18; AD Taranto by 8.18; 226 Sqdn by 2.10.18; Taranto by 10.18; 224 Sqdn by 4.12.18; Taranto to 'X' AD 28.6.19 - .20 (then at Ismailia)

**D3006** Deld 6 SD Ascot W/E 20.6.18; Shipped to Taranto 4.7.18; AD Taranto by 8.18; AR&ED Pizzone by .18; Taranto by 10.18; Mudros by 10.18 - @1.19

**D3007** Deld 6 SD Ascot W/E 20.6.18; Shipped to Taranto 4.7.18; AD Taranto by 8.18; AR&ED Pizzone by .18; 226 Sqdn by 2.10.18; 223 Sqdn Mudros (coded '11') by 10.18 - @1.19

**D3008** Deld 6 SD Ascot W/E 20.6.18; Shipped to Taranto 4.7.18; AD Taranto by 8.18; 224 Sqdn by 2.10.18; Mudros by 10.18 - @1.19

**D3009** Deld 6 SD Ascot W/E 20.6.18; Shipped to Taranto 4.7.18; AD Taranto by 8.18

**D3010** Deld 6 SD Ascot W/E 20.6.18; Shipped to Taranto 17.7.18; AD Taranto by 8.18; 226 Sqdn by 2.10.18; Mudros by 10.18 - @1.19

**D3011** Deld 6 SD Ascot W/E 20.6.18; Shipped to Taranto 17.7.18; Mudros by 10.18 - @1.19

**D3012** Deld 6 SD Ascot W/E 20.6.18; Shipped to Taranto 4.7.18; AD Taranto by 8.18; AR&ED Pizzone by .18

**D3028** Pool of Pilots Manston/Joyce Green by 8.18 - @10.18

**D3061** Deld 6 SD Ascot W/E 20.6.18; Shipped to Taranto 17.7.18; AD Taranto by 8.18

**D3062** Deld 6 SD Ascot W/E 20.6.18; Shipped to Taranto 17.7.18; AD Taranto by 8.18; Repair Base Mudros by 10.18; 224 Sqdn 17.10.18 - @1.19

**D3063** Deld 6 SD Ascot W/E 20.6.18; Shipped to Taranto 17.7.18; AD Taranto by 8.18

**D3093** Rec Pk to 1 AI 7.7.18; 211 Sqdn 10.7.18; Bombing raid, shot down smoking OOC at 11.30 in running fight when formation attacked by 40/50 HA Ypres-Cambrai 29.9.18 (2/Lt AG White & 2/Lt JB Blundell both killed)

**D3094** 4 ASD to 218 Sqdn 13.7.18; EF, FL on beach Hooglade 6.10.18 (Lt HW Matthews & 2/Lt B Archer); 4 ASD 6.10.18 (repair)

**D3095** 218 Sqdn by 28.7.18; After raid on Ostende harbour crashed nr Beaumaris 4.8.18 (2/Lt EH Attwood & 2/Lt FK Wilson both injured); 4 ASD 4.8.18; 2 SS Richborough 2.10.18

**D3099** 218 Sqdn by 1.8.18; U/c collapsed landing, badly damaged 11.8.18 (Lt HW Matthews & 2/Lt B Archer both unhurt); 4 ASD 12.8.18; 2 SS Richborough 15.9.18

**D3117** 110 Sqdn by 6.18 - @8.18; Pilots and Observers AF & AGS Leysdown by 8.18 - @2.19; Propeller accident 26.11.18 (1AM FW Parsons injured); 'Z' Unit British Somaliland (coded '6') by 12.19 - @5.4.20 (Used as ambulance)

**D3118** 55 TDS Manston by 7.18; Stalled on turn, spun in from 500 ft 30.7.18 (F/Cdt RT Wickham seriously injured & 1AM GD Frost killed)

**D3119** 203 TDS Manston by 7.18

**D3152** Deld 6 SD Ascot W/E 25.7.18; To docks W/E 29.8.18; Shipped to Mudros 6.9.18 - @10.18; Repair Base Mudros by 1.19; To White Russians 1919

**D3153** Deld 6 SD Ascot W/E 25.7.18; To docks W/E 29.8.18; Shipped to Mudros 6.9.18 - @10.18; Repair Base Mudros by 1.19; To White Russians 1919

**D3154** Deld 6 SD Ascot W/E 25.7.18; To docks W/E 29.8.18; Shipped to Mudros 6.9.18 - @10.18; Repair Base Mudros by 1.19; To White Russians 1919

**D3155** Deld 6 SD Ascot W/E 25.7.18; To docks W/E 29.8.18; Shipped to Mudros 6.9.18 - @10.18; Repair Base Mudros by 1.19

**D3210** Rec Pk to 1 AI 31.8.18; 211 Sqdn 12.9.18; Hit by AA returning from raid on Bruges, EF, FL by railway N of aerodrome, crashed into hedge 15.9.18 (2/Lt JM Payne unhurt & Lt CT Linford slightly wounded); 1 ASD 17.9.18; SOC 20.9.18

**D3221** 203 TDS Manston by 7.18

**D3224** Rec Pk to 1 AI 13.8.18; 206 Sqdn 14.8.18 - @30.9.18

**D3226** Rec Pk to 1 AI 12.8.18; 206 Sqdn 13.8.18; Left 07.20, last seen nr Dunkerque 2.9.18 (2/Lt HA Scrivener PoW wounded & Sgt CH Davidson PoW DoW same day);

SOC in field 3.9.18

**D3232** 73 Wing Yarmouth by 11.8.18; Swung, stalled and crashed on TO, CW 21.8.18 (Lt JW Ritch & Lt TFP Llewellyn both injured)

**D3233** Rec Pk to 1 AI 8.18; 211 Sqdn 12.8.18; While stationery, hit by 20 Sqdn Bristol Fighter (E2603?) 23.11.18; 2 ASD 24.11.18

**D3234** 4 ASD by 8.18; 218 Sqdn 18.8.18; Pfalz DIII OOC Blankenberghe 16.20 24.8.18 (Lt W Bentley & 2/Lt AJ Cunningham); FL 21.12.18 (local repair); 98 Sqdn 21.1.19

**D3240** 219 Sqdn Manston by 9.8.18

**D3241** Rec Pk to 1 AI 15.8.18; 211 Sqdn 17.8.18; Left 1100 last seen going down S of Maubeuge with 10 HA attacking 1.11.18 (2/Lt JM Payne & 2/Lt WG Gadd both PoW)

**D3242** Naval Flt 219 Sqdn Manston by 3.8.18 - @21.11.18

**D3249** Rec Pk to 1 AI 8.18; 206 Sqdn 10.8.18; Thick ground mist, crashed, CW 6.9.18 (2/Lt SM Desmond & 3AM A Helliwell both DoI); SOC in field 8.9.18 wrecked

**D3251** 1 AI to 211 Sqdn 17.8.18; Left 13.30, bombed Bruges docks, engine hit by AA, FL Breskens, Zeeland 24.9.18 (2/Lt J Olorenshaw & 2/Lt RL Kingham both interned unhurt); Became Dutch *deH444*

**D3252** RP 1 ASD to 1 AI 14.8.18; 211 Sqdn 14.8.18; Landed fast, overshot, o/t 26.9.18 (2/Lt GC Hope & 2/Lt AB Bedford unhurt); Rep Pk 1 ASD 26.9.18

**D3253** 4 ASD to 218 Sqdn 18.8.18; 98 Sqdn 21.1.19; Retd UK 15.2.19

**D3256** Rec Pk to 1 AI 15.8.18; 206 Sqdn 17.8.18; COL from bombing raid, into tree in thick mist 29.9.18 (Lt AL Seddon & 1/Pte AF Bailey unhurt), to be retd

**D3257** Rec Pk to 1 AI 14.8.18; 206 Sqdn 15.8.18; EF, FL 11.10.18 (Lt CH Denny & Pte1 S Jones unhurt); to Rep Pk 1 ASD

**D3259** Rec Pk to 1 AI 23.8.18; 211 Sqdn 25.8.18; Returning ferry pilot to Marquise, FL Teteghem aerodrome in strong wind, hit bump, o/t 7.10.18 (2/Lt EJ Stevenson & Lt Wetham both unhurt), for Rep Pk 1 ASD; 8 AP 8.10.18; 1 ASD 8.10.18

**D3271** 4 ASD to 218 Sqdn 21.8.18; Fokker DVII OOC Bruges 09.20 20.9.18 (Capt JF Chisholm DSC DFC & Sgt RJ Williams); Engine hit by AA after bombing Bruges Docks, EF, broke propeller landing Vlissingen, Zeeland 26.9.18 (Capt JF Chisholm DSC DFC & Sgt RJ Williams interned); Deleted 15.10.18; Repaired and became Dutch *deH446*

**D3272** 4 ASD to 218 Sqdn 21.8.18; Raid on Bruges, attacked by 4 Fokker DVII and a 2-str, 1 Fokker DVII OOC smoking W of Bruges 09.30 20.9.18 (Lt EH Attwood & 2/Lt AE Smith); Last seen in steep dive with 5 HA on tail, Lichtervelde 09.45 29.9.18 (2/Lt JL Pritchard & 2/Lt AE Smith both killed); Deleted 15.10.18

**100 SOPWITH F.1 CAMEL TRACTOR BIPLANE SCOUTS ordered under Cont No A.S.7861 from Clayton & Shuttleworth Ltd and numbered D3326 to D3425, to be built at Lincoln. All to naval units. (150-hp B.R.1 unless otherwise stated)**

**D3326** Deld 4 AAP Lincoln 3.18; AAP Dover 12.3.18; 9 Sqdn 15.3.18; Became 209 Sqdn 1.4.18; Fokker DrI on fire Warfusée-Abancourt, shared B7270 08.30 12.4.18 (Lt FJW Mellersh); O/t landing 9.5.18 (2/Lt DY Hunter); 4 ASD Guines 10.5.18; 213 Sqdn 30.6.18; HA OOC off Wenduyne, shared B6358, B6448, B7270, D9627 & D9647 11.40 7.7.18; Albatros DV OOC over Bruges, shared D9490 11.50 30.7.18 (both Lt ML Cooper); In action 31.7.18 (Lt ML Cooper wounded); Lost over enemy lines 28.9.18 (2/Lt A Fletcher PoW); Deleted 15.10.18

**D3327** Deld 4 AAP Lincoln 3.18; AAP Dover 18.3.18; 4 ASD Guines 24.3.18; 9 Sqdn 30.3.18; Became 209 Sqdn 1.4.18; See B7199 2.4.18; Albatros DV OOC Albert 17.05 11.4.18; Albatros DV OOC Cayeux 18.30 2.5.18; Albatros DV OOC smoking over Marcelcave (possibly indecisive) 20.35 19.5.18 (all Lt JH Siddall); Shot up in combat with HA 28.6.18 (Lt LC Story unhurt); 2 ASD 29.6.18; Rebuilt as F6177 7.7.18

**D3328** Deld 4 AAP Lincoln 3.18; AAP Dover 12.3.18; 9 Sqdn 15.3.18 (to France 20.3.18); Aviatik OOC 18m S of Becelaere, shared B7200, B7247 & B7250 07.25 26.3.18

(FSL AP Squire); Became 209 Sqdn 1.4.18; Albatros believed crashed, shared B3858, B6311 & B7200 12.4.18 (pilot unknown); Flown in von Richthofen combat 21.4.18 (2/Lt WR May); LVG C crashed N of Ailly-sur-Noye, shared B3858 08.30 17.6.18 (Lt RD Gracie USAS) [numbered G/5Bde/18]; EF, FL nr aerodrome 3.7.18 (Lt E Scadding); FL Pont Noyelles, dismantled as ground unsuitable for TO 6.7.18 (Lt DB Griffith); 2 ASD 8.7.18 (war worn); 17th US Aero Sqdn by 8.10.18; Missing 14.10.18 (2/Lt HC Knotts killed)

D3329 Deld 4 AAP Lincoln 3.18; AAP Dover 15.3.18; 4 ASD Guines 24.3.18; 9 Sqdn by 28.3.18; Became 209 Sqdn 1.4.18; Forced to return from patrol with engine trouble 21.4.18; DFW C dest SW of Cerisy 13.55 23.4.18 (both Lt FJW Mellersh); White Fokker DrI crashed 1m S of Cerisy 12.00 2.5.18 [Ltn Hans Weiss, Jasta 11 killed]; Hit by AA 13.5.18; Fokker DrI captured W of Corbie, shared B6398 & B7199 16.15 16.5.18 [numbered G/5Bde/8; Lt Hübner, Jasta 4 PoW]; EF, FL, retd by road 22.5.18 (all Lt MS Taylor); Shot down by HA from 1,500 ft, down in spiral, crashed nr Hamel 11.15 7.7.18 (Lt MS Taylor killed), unsalveable, heavily shelled; SOC 7.7.18

D3330 Deld 4 AAP Lincoln 3.18; AAP Dover 17.3.18; 4 ASD Guines 24.3.18; 8 Sqdn 29.3.18; Became 208 Sqdn 1.4.18; Burned to prevent capture Le Gorgue 9.4.18

D3331 Deld 4 AAP Lincoln 3.18; AAP Dover 18.3.18; 4 ASD Guines 24.3.18; 9 Sqdn 30.3.18; Became 209 Sqdn 1.4.18; Albatros DIII OOC Albert, shared B7250 17.05 11.4.18; Fokker DrI OOC Cléry 11.00 20.4.18; Pfalz DIII crashed Warfusée-Abancourt 18.50 but own a/c badly shot about, retd, crashed 19.15 24.4.18 (all Lt CG Edwards); 4 ASD Guines 24.4.18; 213 Sqdn 13.7.18; With B7272 attacked a Fokker DVII which collided with another Fokker biplane 5m SW of Ostende 18.35 25.9.18 (2/Lt RA Pearce); Badly shot up 1.10.18 (2/Lt RA Pearce); 4 ASD 14.10.18; 11 AP by 12.18; 213 Sqdn 17.12.18; EF on TO, caught telegraph pole 14.1.19 (Lt CJ Sims DFC unhurt); 11 AP 17.1.19; WOC 31.1.19

D3332 Deld 4 AAP Lincoln 3.18; AAP Dover 12.3.18; 9 Sqdn 15.3.18 (to France 20.3.18); Crashed Bulscamp 24.3.18 (A/F/Cdr OC Le Boutillier); 4 ASD Guines by 31.3.18; 204 Sqdn by 20.5.18; Albatros Scout OOC at 17,000ft nr Ghistelles 18.45 20.5.18 (Capt GHD Gossip); Fokker DVII OOC S of Ghistelles 14.45 29.6.18 (Lt CP Allen); Fokker DVII OOC SE of Ostende 10.55 31.7.18 (Lt HH Blanchard); Crashed 1.8.18 (Lt RC Hirst unhurt); 4 ASD 2.8.18; 210 Sqdn 20.9.18; Fokker DVII crashed S of St.Pierre Capelle 14.40 24.9.18; Fokker DVII crashed SE of Roulers & another OOC Roulers 17.15 1.10.18; White tailed Fokker DVII crashed in flames 4m NE of Roulers 09.20 8.10.18 (all Capt E Swale); 203 Sqdn 24.1.19; RTP W/E 23.2.19

D3333 (130-hp Clerget) Deld 4 AAP Lincoln 3.18; AAP Dover 18.3.18; 4 ASD Guines 24.3.18; 3 Sqdn 30.3.18; Became 203 Sqdn 1.4.18; COL uneven ground, o/t, damaged Lièttres 10.4.18 (2/Lt NC Dixie unhurt); 4 ASD 12.4.18; 213 Sqdn 14.5.18; 2 Pfalz DIII OOC Bruge, shared B7254, C66, C73 & D1866 14.20 1.6.18 (Lt CH Denny); Collided with D3383 and crashed nr les Möeres 29.6.18 (Lt FP Pemble DoI); 4 ASD Guines 29.6.18

D3334 Deld 4 AAP Lincoln 3.18; AAP Dover 15.3.18; NADD 23.3.18; 3 Sqdn 26.3.18; COL, CW Izel-le-Hameau 26.3.18 (FSL W Archer); To 4 ASD Guines; Deleted 8.4.18

D3335 Deld 4 AAP Lincoln 3.18; AAP Dover 21.3.18; 8 Sqdn Walmer 27.3.18 (to France 30.3.18); Became 208 Sqdn 1.4.18; Albatros DV shot down 1m E of Oppy 11.10 6.4.18 (Capt WL Jordan, DSC & Bar); Burned to prevent capture La Gorgue 9.4.18

D3336 Deld 4 AAP Lincoln 3.18; AAP Dover 20.3.18; 4 ASD Guines 26.3.18 - @31.3.18; 1 AD Rely to 203 Sqdn 2.4.18; Shot up, FL Beauvais aerodrome 7.4.18 (FSL AN Webster unhurt); 4 ASD Guines 9.4.18; 204 Sqdn 16.5.18; Fokker DVII OOC Zeebrugge 14.30 30.6.18 (Lt JG Lumley); Crashed on TO, TW 8.8.18 (Lt RC Hirst injured); 4 ASD 8.8.18; 210 Sqdn 28.9.18; Fokker DVII OOC 4m NE of Dixmude 14.45 28.9.18; Fokker DVII OOC NE of Dixmude 17.50 29.9.18 (both Lt KR

Unger); Fokker DVII crashed Rombies-Estreux 11.15 30.10.18 (Capt SC Joseph); 203 Sqdn 24.1.19; RTP W/E 2.2.19

D3337 Deld 4 AAP Lincoln by 30.3.18 for Dunkerque

D3338 Deld 4 AAP Lincoln 3.18; AAP Dover 16.3.18; NADD 23.3.18; Became 4 ASD Guines 24.3.18; 9 Sqdn (named 'JEAN') 25.3.18; COL 31.3.18 (F/Cdr AR Brown DSC); Became 209 Sqdn 1.4.18; Participated von Richtofen combat; Albatros C in flames Beaucourt-Ignaucourt, shared B3858 & B7200 [Ltn d R Kurt Fischer & Ltn d R Rudolph Rolinius, FAA 203], 10.25 21.4.18; Albatros C captured Albert, shared Taylor/Harker/Brock/Foster 06.10 22.4.18 [possibly numbered G/5Bde/3]; Pfalz DIII OOC 4-5m E of Villers-Bretonneux 15.55 4.5.18; Fokker DrI crashed S of Bray 11.45 9.5.18 [Ltn Johann Janzen unhurt]; LVG C down smoking nr Bayonvillers, shared B3858 09.40 16.5.18; Albatros DV OOC Vauvillers 19.20 31.5.18 (all Capt OC Le Boutillier); LVG C OOC Martinpuich-Delville Wood, shared D3396 07.10 23.6.18 (Capt JK Summers); Stalled on approach, dived in, o/t 30.6.18 (Lt KM Walker unhurt); 2 ASD 1.7.18; Rebuilt as F6180 7.7.18

D3339 Deld 4 AAP Lincoln 3.18; AAP Dover 23.3.18; 8 Sqdn Walmer 29.3.18 (to France 30.3.18); Became 208 Sqdn 1.4.18; Burned to prevent capture La Gorgue 9.4.18

D3340 Deld 4 AAP Lincoln 3.18; AAP Dover 17.3.18; NADD 23.3.18; 4 ASD Guines 24.3.18; 209 Sqdn 2.4.18; Opened up to go round again, EF, stalled and nosedived in clearing trees 1.7.18 (Lt AL Porter unhurt); 2 ASD 2.7.18; SOC 8.7.18 NWR

D3341 Deld 4 AAP Lincoln 3.18; AAP Dover 15.3.18; 9 Sqdn Dover 16.3.18; Collided and damaged Dover 20.3.18 (F/L FE Banbury); AAP Dover @28.3.18; 4 ASD Guines to 204 Sqdn 25.4.18; Badly shot up in combat 15.5.18 (Lt WF Robinson unhurt); 4 ASD 17.5.18; 213 Sqdn 30.6.18; Rumpler C crashed in sea 8m NNE of Nieuport 10.40 31.7.18 (Lt CP Brown) (German crew rescued by RN destroyer); LVG C crashed on fire S of Zevecote, shared N6376 & D9649 16.50 21.8.18; KB in flames, which set fire to 3 hangars nr La Barrière, shared D3378 & D9649 10.50 18.9.18 (both Lt HC Smith); Fokker DVII OOC & another turned on back and crashed on road 1m W of Mitswe [Mitswaere?] 14.45 24.9.18; Rumpler C in flames over St.Pierre Capelle, shared D9649 17.30 24.9.18 (all Lt GS Hodson); Last seen in flames after attacked by 20 HA NW of Roulers 4.10.18 (2/Lt WG Upton killed)

D3342 Deld 4 AAP Lincoln 3.18; to Cranwell but wings damaged on landing 31.3.18 (pilot unhurt); Dover 29.4.18; 4 ASD Guines W/E 4.5.18; 213 Sqdn 8.5.18; Both ailerons shot away by 2 HA, crashed into hangar on landing 15.5.18 (Lt AR Talbot unhurt); To 4 ASD; 204 Sqdn by 7.18; Fokker DVII OOC S of Ostende 10.55 30.7.18 (Capt GHD Gossip); To 4 ASD; 213 Sqdn 22.8.18; Crashed nr aerodrome after TO 14.10.18 (Lt FCA Thorpe seriously injured); To 4 ASD 10.18 - @25.10.18

D3343 Deld 4 AAP Lincoln 3.18; AAP Dover 17.3.18; 4 ASD Guines 24.3.18; 3 Sqdn 30.3.18; Became 203 Sqdn 1.4.18; Damaged in combat Auchy, nr La Bassée 0740 1.7.18 (2/Lt NC Dixie); 1 ASD 1.7.18; Rebuilt as F5965 2.7.18

D3344 Deld 4 AAP Lincoln by 30.3.18 for Dunkerque; Rec Pk to 1 AI 21.4.18; 203 Sqdn 22.4.18; Propeller hit mound on TO, crashed in ploughed field 29.5.18 (2/Lt CF Brown injured); 4 ASD 30.5.18; Rebuilt as F5941 25.6.18

D3345 Deld 4 AAP Lincoln 3.18; AAP Dover 20.3.18; 4 ASD Guines 26.3.18; 9 Sqdn 27.3.18; Became 209 Sqdn 1.4.18; Participated von Richtofen combat 21.4.18; Albatros DV OOC Cayeux 18.30 2.5.18; Fokker DrI OOC 3m NW of Montdidier 20.00 3.6.18; Pfalz DIII in flames nr Warfusée, Ltn Steinbrecher, Jasta 46 made world's first operational parachute escape 20.05 27.6.18 (all Capt EB Drake); Badly damaged by ground m/g fire, FL bad ground, o/t Oresmaux 4.7.18 (Lt JE Fenton unhurt); 2 ASD 5.7.18

D3346 Deld 4 AAP Lincoln by 30.3.18 - @6.4.18; 4 ASD Guines 4.18; Landed on a hill at St.Englebert 17.4.18 (pilot unhurt) - probably on abortive delivery to 204

Sqdn; 204 Sqdn 20.4.18; Crashed on TO 19.5.18 (Lt BE Barnum unhurt); 4 ASD 20.5.18; Halberstadt C crashed S of Stalhille, on N bank of Bruges-Ostende canal 14.40 30.8.18 (Capt LH Slatter DSC of 4 ASD Pilots Pool); 4 ASD Pilots Pool 14.10.18 - @25.10.18; Crashed; To 471 Flt 233 Sqdn Walmer; 11 AP 22.2.19; WOC 22.2.19

**D3347** Deld AAP Dover 23.3.18; 4 ASD Guines 26.3.18 - @31.3.18; 1 ASD Rely to 203 Sqdn 2.4.18; COL, TW, burnt on site 13.4.18 (2/Lt J Denison DoI); SOC

**D3348** Deld 4 AAP Lincoln by 30.3.18 - @6.4.18; 4 ASD 4.18; 210 Sqdn 17.4.18; Albatros DV in flames Armentières 19.25 11.5.18; Pfalz DIII crashed nr Bac St.Maur 20.05 18.5.18; Pfalz DIII OOC Bailleul 08.20 27.5.18 (all Capt WM Alexander); Last seen S of Estaires after general engagement over Ploegsteert Wood 08.30 9.6.18 (2/Lt W Breckenridge PoW) [credited Ltn Katzenstein, Jasta 30]; SOC 9.6.18

**D3349** Deld 4 AAP Lincoln 3.18; Cranwell 31.3.18 (transit); AAP Dover (via Hendon) 1.4.18; 4 ASD Guines 2.4.18; 210 Sqdn 3.4.18; EF, FL, badly damaged Hesdigneul 18.4.18 (FSL ES Arnold unhurt); 4 ASD Guines 19.4.18; 204 Sqdn 25.5.18; Fokker DVII OOC off Blankenberghe 14.30 30.6.18 (Lt CRR Hickey); Crashed Möeres 1.7.18 (Lt RL Hollingsworth); 4 ASD Guines 1.7.18; 4 ASD Audembert 14.8.18; 213 Sqdn 18.8.18; Fokker DVII OOC 10m S of Ostende 07.30 25.8.18; Rumpler C crashed 1m N of Zevecote, shared F5913 15.00 6.9.18 (both Lt AH Turner); After landing, taxied into small ditch 26.9.18 (2/Lt GC Garner); 4 ASD 28.9.18; Deleted 30.9.18 general fatigue

**D3350** Deld 4 AAP Lincoln by 30.3.18; AAP Dover 2.4.18; 4 ASD Guines 3.4.18; 1 AI by 8.4.18; 201 Sqdn 11.4.18; Fokker DrI OOC S of Albert 19.20 16.5.18 (Lt GB Gates); Sideslipped in on landing, wrecked 30.5.18 (Lt GB Gates unhurt); 2 ASD 31.5.18; Rebuilt as F6122 3.7.18

**D3351** Deld 4 AAP Lincoln by 30.3.18 - @6.4.18; 4 ASD 4.18; 213 Sqdn 20.4.18; Albatros DV into sea 5m N of Westende, shared D3357 14.45 11.5.18 (Lt GC Mackay); 4 ASD 20.6.18; 210 Sqdn 8.8.18; Overshot, swung, hit hedge, badly damaged 16.8.18 (Lt W Stephenson); To 4 ASD

**D3352** Deld 4 AAP Lincoln by 30.3.18; AAP Dover 2.4.18; 4 ASD Guines 3.4.18; 208 Sqdn 5.4.18; Burnt to prevent capture La Gorgue 9.4.18 (only 1 hours flying time)

**D3353** Deld 4 AAP Lincoln by 30.3.18; AAP Dover 12.4.18 (via Hendon); Rec Pk to 1 AI 22.4.18; 203 Sqdn 23.4.18; DFW CV OOC N of Estaires, shared C61 11.40 15.5.18 (Capt LH Rochford); Last seen when flight attacked by 6 Pfalz DIII N of La Bassée 16.5.18 (Capt PR White PoW)

**D3354** Deld 4 AAP Lincoln by 30.3.18; AAP Dover 2.4.18; 4 ASD Guines 3.4.18; 1 AI by 8.4.18; 210 Sqdn 11.4.18; 2-str OOC Bethune 14.05-16.05 patrol 11.5.18 (Lt HB Maund) (unconfirmed); Hannover C OOC smoking Armentières 19.25 11.5.18 (Lt HB Maund); FL in mist, wrecked 11.5.18 (Lt HB Maund unhurt); 4 ASD 12.5.18; 204 Sqdn 2.7.18; Fokker DVII crashed in flames Roulers 19.30 31.7.18 (Lt RM Bennett wounded by ground fire); Fokker DVII into sea Blankenberghe & another OOC crashed in sea Zeebrugge - Ostende 10.55 12.8.18 (Lt OJ Orr); Fokker DVII [or Pfalz DIII], starboard wing gave way Menin 19.00 & Fokker DVII black and white tail OOC SE of Ypres 19.05 15.8.18 (Lt RM Bennett); FL Calais 15.8.18; 4 ASD 16.8.18; 213 Sqdn 16.10.18; Hit by wheels of another aircraft when in flight, crashed on coast 4m W of Ostende 15.00 27.10.18 (2/Lt C Shaw unhurt); To 4 ASD

**D3355** Deld 4 AAP Lincoln by 30.3.18; AAP Dover 2.4.18; 4 ASD Guines 3.4.18; 204 Sqdn 10.4.18; Fokker DVII OOC over Zeebrugge 14.40 30.6.18 (Capt GHD Gossip); Last seen in combat 12.8.18 (Lt SCJ Askin PoW); Deleted 15.9.18

**D3356** Deld 4 AAP Lincoln by 30.3.18 - @6.4.18; 4 ASD to 213 Sqdn 20.4.18; Destroyed by fire in enemy bombing raid 29.6.18; WOC 30.6.18

**D3357** Deld 4 AAP Lincoln by 30.3.18 - @6.4.18; 4 ASD to 213 Sqdn 11.4.18; Albatros DV into sea 5m N of Westende, shared D3351 [maybe another probable, not credited by Combat Reports to any particular pilot] 14.45 11.5.18 (Lt JE Greene); O/t landing in strong wind 4.6.18 (Lt RWI Hall unhurt); to 4 ASD; 210 Sqdn 15.8.18; Fokker DVIII crashed nr Roulers, shared B7222, D3379, D9655 & E1405 18.30 3.9.18 (2/Lt JA Lewis); Last seen in combat with 15 HA at 18,000ft over Zeebrugge 11.05 16.9.18 (2/Lt JA Lewis killed) [credited Ltn Wilhelm, Marine Jasta 4, at sea]

**D3358** Deld 4 AAP Lincoln by 30.3.18; AAP Lympne by 6.4.18; 4 ASD to 213 Sqdn 11.4.18; Crashed on TO 21.4.18 (Capt FG Horstmann DSC) LM; 4 ASD Audembert to 213 Sqdn 15.6.18; Damaged in enemy bombing raid 29.6.18; 4 ASD 4.7.18 (repair); 204 Sqdn from 27.9.18; Hit by AA fire while raiding Lichtervelde 4.10.18 (Lt HJ Gemmel unhurt); 4 ASD 11.10.18 - @25.10.18; 11 AP by 2.19; WOC 22.2.19

**D3359** Deld 4 AAP Lincoln by 30.3.18; AAP Dover (via Cranwell) 5.4.18; 4 ASD to 204 Sqdn 10.4.18; Collided with HA in general dogfight between Zeebrugge and Blankenberghe, 14.40 onwards 30.6.18 (Lt JM Wilson missing)

**D3360** Deld 4 AAP Lincoln by 30.3.18; AAP Hendon 5.4.18; AAP Dover 7.4.18; 4 ASD to 203 Sqdn 17.4.18; Bullet in tank during combat with Fokker DrI, FL, hit ditch, nr Armentières 11.55 3.5.18 (Lt JD Breakey); 4 ASD Guines 4.5.18; 213 Sqdn 30.6.18; Seaplane DD on to water 17.30 31.7.18 (Lt PC Jenner); Shot up in combat, FL on beach Malo 21.8.18 (Lt LC Scroggie); Last seen 5m SE of Ostende attacking HA at 10,000ft 18.35 25.9.18 (2/Lt JC Sorley) [credited LtzS Achilles, Marine Jasta 5, NW of Roulers]; Deleted 15.10.18

**D3361** Deld 4 AAP Lincoln by 30.3.18; AAP Dover 3.4.18; 4 ASD Guines 4.18; To 204 Sqdn, COL, retd 4 ASD 10.4.18; 204 Sqdn 20.4.18; 4 ASD Guines 5.18; 204 Sqdn 23.5.18; Last seen spinning and diving in combat in Nieuport/Ypres sector 29.6.18 (Lt S Harston killed)

**D3362** Deld 4 AAP Lincoln by 30.3.18; 4 ASD to 203 Sqdn 17.4.18; Pfalz DIII in flames Estaires-Merville, shared B6408, B7197 & C61 11.15, damaged in combat, FL St.Venant 17.5.18 (Lt R Stone unhurt); 4 ASD 18.5.18; 2 AI by 7.18; 5 AI 14.7.18; SOC 1 ASD 14.8.18 NWR [14.9.18?]

**D3363** Deld 4 AAP Lincoln by 30.3.18; AAP Dover 2.4.18; 4 ASD Guines 3.4.18; 1 AI 7.4.18; 201 Sqdn 11.4.18; Pfalz DIII crashed Hangard 11.10 22.4.18 (Capt SW Rosevear DSC); 1 Rep Pk 1 ASD 3.8.18 unfit time expired

**D3364** Deld 4 AAP Lincoln by 30.3.18 - @4.4.18; 1 ASD to 210 Sqdn 12.4.18; General engagement, Albatros DV OOC Armentières 10.55 8.5.18; Rumpler C OOC on back Bailleul (pilot killed, observer wounded), shared B6228 & B7227 11.45 9.5.18; Albatros C at 17,000ft, crashed 1m N of Aubers, shared B6242 & C62 16.15 9.5.18 (all Capt AW Carter); Very pistol exploded blowing out left side of cockpit 9.5.18 (Capt JG Manuel DSC injured); FL in fog, sideslipped, crashed avoiding house Ledringhem 11.5.18 (Capt AW Carter slightly injured); 4 ASD 12.5.18; 213 Sqdn 26.6.18; Destroyed by fire in enemy bombing raid 29.6.18; WOC 31.6.18

**D3365** Mkrs by 30.3.18 - @6.4.18; Rec Pk to 1 AI 6.5.18; 210 Sqdn 14.5.18; Rumpler C crashed NE of Bailleul, shared D3391 11.05 17.5.18 (Lt AL Jones); Engine choked, FL nr aerodrome, damaged 22.5.18 (Lt AS Highstone unhurt); Rep Pk 1 ASD 23.5.18; SOC 25.5.18 NWR

**D3366** Deld 4 AAP Lincoln by 30.3.18 - @4.4.18; 1 ASD to 210 Sqdn 12.4.18; Albatros DV crashed NE of Hollebeke 14.45 29.4.18 (Capt JG Manuel); Pfalz DIII OOC E of Estaires 12.10 20.5.18 (Lt GB Wootten); On TO ran into D.H.9 standing between two hangars, damaged 20.5.18 (T/Lt C Marsden shaken); Rep Pk 1 ASD 21.5.18; SOC 23.5.18 NWR

**D3367** Deld 4 AAP Lincoln by 30.3.18 for Dunkerque; Rec Pk to 1 AI 1.6.18; 210 Sqdn 9.6.18; Left 09.00, wings folded up and crashed NE of Zillebeke Lake after combat with 3 HA 24.6.18 (Lt GA Learn killed); SOC in field 24.6.18

**D3368** Deld 4 AAP Lincoln by 30.3.18 - @6.4.18; Rec Pk to 1 AI 21.4.18; 209 Sqdn 22.4.18; Scout OOC Bray 19.40 1.7.18 (Lt WA Stead); Collided stationery D9606 on TO, CW 4.7.18 (Lt WA Stead injured); 2 ASD 5.7.18; SOC No.2 Salvage Dump 6.7.18

**D3369** Mkrs by 30.3.18; Deld 4 AAP Lincoln by 27.4.18 for

Dunkerque; AAP Dover to 4 ASD Guines W/E 4.5.18; 213 Sqdn 14.5.18; Destroyed by fire in enemy bombing raid 29.6.18; WO 30.6.18

**D3370** Deld 4 AAP Lincoln 4.18; 4 ASD to 203 Sqdn 17.4.18; Shot down 2m E of Ypres 08.55 4.7.18 (Lt AJ Fricker PoW); SOC 4.7.18

**D3371** Deld 4 AAP Lincoln 4.18; Rec Pk by 5.18; 1 AI 1.5.18; 203 Sqdn 2.5.18; DFW CV crashed E of Nieppe Forest 10.15 19.5.18 (Capt LH Rochford); DFW C dest Estaires, shared B7185, D3414, D3417 & D9585 06.10 16.6.18 (Lt R Stone); Wheel came off on landing 2.7.18 (Capt LH Rochford unhurt); Rep Pk 1 ASD 3.7.18; Rebuilt as F6035 24.7.18

**D3372** Deld 4 AAP Lincoln 4.18; AAP Dover by 27.4.18; 4 ASD Guines W/E 4.5.18; 204 Sqdn 8.5.18 - @6.6.18 (then to Depot?); 204 Sqdn from 29.7.18; COL, CW 21.8.18 (Lt N Smith unhurt); 4 ASD 21.8.18; 213 Sqdn 26.9.18; Shot down by Ltn M Lampel 28.9.18 (Lt PC Jenner)

**D3373** Deld 4 AAP Lincoln 4.18; Rec Pk to 1 AI 23.4.18; 209 Sqdn 29.4.18; Albatros DV crashed nr Flaucourt 10.15 15.5.18 (Capt OW Redgate wounded); Damaged in combat, retd 07.00 4.7.18 (Capt JK Summers); 2 ASD 7.7.18; SOC 17.7.18; Rebuilt as F6192

**D3374** Deld WARD by 12.4.18; Rec Pk to 1 AI 2.5.18; 210 Sqdn 6.5.18; Controls shot away by flak, FL, wrecked nr Zuyhuis 6.5.18 (Lt J Hollick unhurt); 4 ASD Guines 7.5.18; 204 Sqdn 25.6.18; COL after patrol, badly damaged 3.8.18 (Lt GEC Howard unhurt); 4 ASD 4.8.18; To 204 Sqdn 9.18; Fokker DVII lost lower port wing and 2 more OOC Ostende-Blankenberghe 19.00-19.10 16.9.18; 2 Fokker DVII OOC 5m E of Dixmude 10.25 20.9.18; Fokker DrI in flames NE of Dixmude 18.45 24.9.18 (all Lt WB Craig); Shot down over Blankeberghe 26.9.18 (Lt WB Craig killed) [credited Flgm Engelfried, Marine Jasta 5]; Deleted 15.10.18

**D3375** (170-hp BR.1) Deld WARD by 12.4.18; Rec Pk to 1 AI 2.5.18; 201 Sqdn 4.5.18; Left 10.30, last seen in combat with 8 Pfalz DIII over Bapaume 9.5.18 (2/Lt F Newton killed)

**D3376** Deld WARD by 12.4.18; Rec Pk to AI 3.5.18; 203 Sqdn 4.5.18; LVG C dest nr Salomé, E of La Bassée, shared B3786, B3855, B7198, B7231 & D3384 11.45 15.5.18; DFW C crashed nr Steenkerke 11.50 17.5.18; Pfalz DIII in flames Merville-Estaires 10.40 18.5.18; Pfalz DIII OOC N of Neuf Berquin, shared B7220 19.50 18.5.18; Pfalz DIII crashed E of Merville 10.35 19.5.18; Albatros DV white fuselage & tailplane, grey upper wing OOC Fournes-en-Weppes 18.10 30.5.18 (all Lt ET Hayne); 2 ASD 16.8.18 (unfit for further service); 1 ASD to England 17.8.18

**D3377** (BR.1) Deld 4 AAP Lincoln by 15.4.18; Rec Pk by 5.18; 1 AI 2.5.18; 210 Sqdn 7.5.18; FL in mist, TW nr Rubrouck 11.5.18 (Lt BAPL d'Etchegoyen DoI 13.5.18); Rep Pk 4 ASD 12.5.18; Surveyed 13.5.18; Deleted 20.5.18

**D3378** (130-hp Clerget) Deld 4 AAP Lincoln by 27.4.18 for Dunkerque; 4 ASD to 213 Sqdn 22.5.18; O/t landing 27.5.18 (Lt CH Denny); Hit another aircraft on TO, badly damaged 3.6.18 (Lt PC Jenner unhurt); To 4 ASD; 213 Sqdn 22.8.18; Rumpler C in flames E of Ostende Piers, shared D9649 14.00 15.9.18; KB in flames which fell on hangar setting that on fire and spreading to two other hangars La Barrière, shared D3341 & D9649 10.50 18.9.18 (both Lt HC Smith); Last seen being attacked by 17 HA nr La Barrière 10.15 14.10.18 (Lt WT Owen killed)

**D3379** Deld 4 AAP Lincoln by 16.4.18; Rec Pk to 1 AI 3.5.18; 210 Sqdn 14.5.18; Broke tail skid taxying for TO, swung round, on nose, damaged 15.5.18 (Lt MF Sutton unhurt); 4 ASD 16.5.18; 210 Sqdn 13.8.18; Fokker DVII crashed SE of Bruges 16.20 15.8.18 (Lt SC Joseph); Leading C Flt, Fokker DVII crashed nr Roulers, shared B7222, D3357, D9455 & E1405 18.30, but aileron shot away and strut shot through 3.9.18 (Capt SC Joseph unhurt); 4 ASD 6.9.18; 213 Sqdn 2.10.18; 11 AP 24.2.19; WOC 24.2.19

**D3380** Deld 4 AAP Lincoln by 16.4.18; Rec Pk to 1 AI 6.5.18; 210 Sqdn 9.5.18; FL in mist, crashed Bolleszeele 11.5.18 (Capt ES Arnold injured); Rep Pk 4 ASD 12.5.18; 213 Sqdn 30.6.18; Last seen in combat with 11

HA along coast 21.8.18 (Lt J Wooding PoW)

**D3381** Deld 4 AAP Lincoln by 16.4.18; Rec Pk to 1 AI 14.5.18; 210 Sqdn 16.5.18; KB in flames & 2 DD nr Estaires 10.00 5.6.18 (Lt AL Jones); 2-str W/T m/c crashed nr Vieux-Berquin, shared D3401 08.25 6.6.18 (2/Lt KT Campbell); Shot down British side of lines, CW 17.6.18 (2/Lt KT Campbell killed) [An Albatros DV BU Zillebeke Lake 08.00 this day, but uncertain whether by D3381/Campbell or D3424/Strickland]; SOC in field 17.6.18

**D3382** Deld 4 AAP Lincoln by 16.4.18; Rec Pk to 1 AI 1.5.18; 210 Sqdn 2.5.18; FL in fog, crashed 1 km E of Esquelbecq 11.5.18 (Lt HB Frost badly shaken); 4 ASD 12.5.18; 210 Sqdn 25.8.18; Missing 8.10.18 (2/Lt RW Hopper); Deleted 31.10.18

**D3383** Presentation aircraft 'City of Hull, Australia' [but see B3383]. Deld AAP Dover W/E 23.3.18; 4 ASD 4.18; 213 Sqdn 1.5.18; Collided D3333, crashed nr les Möeres 14.45 29.6.18 (Lt FL Cattle DoI) [credited Vzfw Wadowski, Jasta 52?]; 4 ASD 29.6.18; 210 Sqdn 25.8.18

**D3384** Deld AAP Dover W/E 23.3.18; 4 AAP Lincoln by 20.4.18; Rec Pk to 1 AI 3.5.18; 203 Sqdn 4.5.18; LVG C dest Salomé, E of La Bassée, shared B3786, B3855, B7198, B7231 & D3376 11.45 15.5.18; Pfalz DIII OOC N of La Bassée 11.20 16.5.18; See B3855 17.5.18; Rumpler C in flames Merville, shared B3855 11.20 18.5.18 (all FSL JD Breakey); DFW crashed E of Lens 18.15 13.7.18 (Lt FTS Sehl); 2 ASD 16.8.18 (unfit for further service); RP 1 ASD to 2 ASD 17.8.18; To England 21.8.18

**D3385** Deld AAP Dover W/E 23.3.18; 4 AAP Lincoln by 20.4.18; Rec Pk to 1 AI 6.5.18; 210 Sqdn 9.5.18; Pfalz DIII OOC 2m E of Ypres 20.15 14.5.18 (Lt FV Hall); On HOP, collided B7160 which had been hit by AA fire, tail came off, crashed British side of lines 15.5.18 (Lt FV Hall killed); 4 ASD 15.5.18; SOC 20.5.18

**D3386** (130-hp Clerget) Presentation a/c 'Punjab 19. Hissar'. Deld 4 AAP Lincoln by 27.4.18; 4 ASD to 204 Sqdn 16.5.18; Albatros DV OOC nr Ghistelles 18.45 20.5.18 (Lt S Harston); Collided B6389 over Zeebrugge, BU, dived steeply towards Holland 16.40 13.7.18 (2/Lt JH Mesham killed); SOC 31?.7.18

**D3387** Deld AAP Dover W/E 23.3.18; 4 AAP Lincoln by 20.4.18; Rec Pk to 1 AI 8.5.18; 210 Sqdn 14.5.18; Albatros C crashed and burst into flames nr Bailleul 11.45 16.5.18; Albatros DV OOC Neuve-Eglise area 10.45 18.5.18; 2-str spun & crashed NE of Armentières 10.45 19.5.18 (all Capt WGR Hinchliffe); Fokker DVII OOC SE of Kemmel 08.15 10.6.18; Fokker DVII crashed 3m SW of Armentières 20.00 23.6.18; Fokker DVII crashed, Fokker DVII OOC, 2 Pfalz DIII OOC 1m W of Armentieres, shared B7153 & D9608 (q.v.) 19.20 26.6.18; Pfalz DIII in flames Lestrem 11.15 6.7.18 (all Capt LP Coombes); 4 ASD for survey 28.7.18; 204 Sqdn 25.8.18; Last seen with flight in combat 5m NE of Dixmude 20.9.18 (2/Lt EG Rolph PoW); Deleted 30.9.18

**D3388** Presentation aircraft 'City of Hull, Australia'. Deld AAP Dover W/E 23.3.18; Rec Pk to 1 AI 1.6.18; 210 Sqdn 5.6.18; Flying low in misty conditions hit sea 5m off Nieuport/Ostende 29.7.18 (2/Lt WS Jenkins shock); SOC 29.7.18

**D3389** (130-hp Clerget) Deld 4 AAP Lincoln by 27.4.18; 4 ASD to 204 Sqdn 16.5.18; Albatros Scout OOC Ghistelle 18.45 20.5.18 (Lt RAG Hill); 4 ASD 13.8.18; WOC 15.9.18 general fatigue

**D3390** Deld 4 AAP Lincoln by 23.4.18; Rec Pk to 1 AI 8.5.18; 210 Sqdn 14.5.18; Left 09.30, FTR 18.5.18 (Lt J Hollick killed) [credited Uffz Pech, Jasta 29]; SOC 19.5.18

**D3391** Deld 4 AAP Lincoln by 22.4.18; Rec Pk by 5.18; 1 AI 14.5.18; 210 Sqdn 16.5.18; Rumpler C crashed NE of Bailleul, shared D3365 11.05 17.5.18 (Lt HA Patey); Left 0930, FTR 18.5.18 (Lt MF Sutton PoW wounded) [credited Uffz Pech, Jasta 29]; SOC 19.5.18

**D3392** Deld 4 AAP Lincoln by 22.4.18; Rec Pk to 1 AI 3.5.18; 210 Sqdn 8.5.18; FL in fog 11.5.18; Pfalz DIII crashed Ypres-Merville 11.30 30.5.18; KB in flames nr Estaires 10.00 5.6.18 (both Lt E Swale); Starboard wheel came off landing, o/t badly damaged

28.6.18 (Lt HR Hughes unhurt); Rep Pk 1 ASD 29.6.18; SOC 17.7.18; Rebuilt as F6028 26.7.18

**D3393** Deld 4 AAP Lincoln by 22.4.18; Rec Pk to 2 ASD 7.5.18; 201 Sqdn 10.5.18; Albatros DrI crashed Bapaume-Mory, shared D1862 & flight 06.45 16.5.18; Fokker DrI OOC Smoking S of Albert 19.20 16.5.18 (both Lt JH Forman); Fokker DVII BU SE of Bailleul 11.20 29.7.18 (Capt RCB Brading); Rep Pk 2 ASD 18.8.18; Rep Pk 1 ASD 18.8.18; flown to England for overhaul 19.8.18

**D3394** (130-hp Clerget) Presentation a/c 'St.Catherine's, Ontario'; Deld 4 AAP Lincoln by 27.4.18; 4 ASD to 204 Sqdn 21.5.18; Fokker DVII OOC into sea Zeebrugge-Blankenberghe 14.30 30.6.18 (Lt JH Mesham); Shot down by m/g fire after combat with 10 Fokker DVII over Roulers 31.7.18 (Lt JE Gow unhurt)

**D3395** Presentation a/c 'Mayurbhanj'. Deld 4 AAP Lincoln by 30.4.18; Rec Pk to 1 AI 18.5.18; 210 Sqdn 25.5.18; Overshot landing, crashed into hedge avoiding 2 stationery aircraft, damaged 4.7.18 (Lt GA Welsh unhurt); Rep Pk 1 ASD 5.7.18; Rebuilt as F6318 in error 9.8.18, changed to H7284

**D3396** Presentation a/c 'Gold Coast Aborigines No.1'. Deld 4 AAP Lincoln by 29.4.18; Rec Pk to 2 ASD 8.5.18; 209 Sqdn 15.5.18; LVG C OOC Martinpuich-Delville Wood 07.10 23.6.18 (Lt WJ Armstrong USAS); Main spar buckled, FL nr Allonville 28.6.18 (2/Lt WJ MacKenzie); 2 ASD 29.6.18; 17th US Aero Sqdn 23.9.18 - @14.10.18

**D3397** (130-hp Clerget) Deld W/E 15.5.18; 4 ASD Guines to 213 Sqdn 25.5.18; Albatros OOC smoking 4m S of Dixmude, officially shared B7272, C65, D3409 & D3411 (but probably only C65 in reality) 18.00 7.6.18 (Lt WE Gray); EF, FL, badly damaged les Möeres aerodrome 9.6.18 (Lt JN Nelson unhurt); to 4 ASD; 210 Sqdn 13.8.18; Fokker DVII OOC over Roulers 17.10 1.10.18; Fokker DVII crashed 4m NE of Roulers 09.20 8.10.18 (both Lt WW Gyles); Rep Pk 1 ASD Marquise 16.1.19 surplus

**D3398** (130-hp Clerget) Presentation a/c 'Residents (British) Netherlands East Indies No.2'. Deld 4 AAP Lincoln by 27.4.18; 4 ASD Guines by 25.5.18; 213 Sqdn 7.6.18; Destroyed by fire in enemy bombing raid 29.6.18; WOC 30.6.18

**D3399** (BR.1 later 130-hp Clerget) Presentation a/c 'Imperial Order of Daughters of the British Empire (USA)'. Deld 4 AAP Lincoln by 29.4.18; Rec Pk to 1 AI 14.5.18; 210 Sqdn 14.5.18; Fokker DrI (gen V Rautter Viktor von Pressentin, JG1) crashed 2m S of Estaires 11.30 31.5.18; Fokker DrI crashed S of Bailleul 10.10 5.6.18 (all Capt AW Carter); Pfalz DIII OOC Estaires, 16.40 patrol 28.6.18 (Lt AL Jones); 4 ASD Guines for survey 24.7.18; 213 Sqdn 22.9.18; COL in gusty wind, badly damaged 2.9.18 (Lt JC Sorley unhurt); To 4 ASD; WOC 15.9.18 general fatigue

**D3400** Presentation a/c 'Baroda No.4'. Deld 4 AAP Lincoln by 27.4.18; 4 ASD to 213 Sqdn 20.5.18; Attacked 4 HA nr Ostende, blue Rumpler C crashed nr Steene 14.15 1.6.18 (Lt GC Mackay); O/t landing trying to avoid another aircraft, wings and engine damaged 3.6.18 (Lt GC Mackay); 4 ASD 3.6.18; 204 Sqdn 13.8.18; Fokker DVII OOC Menin 19.05 15.8.18 (Lt HH Blanchard); COL, damaged 25.8.18 (Lt RC Pattulo); 4 ASD 26.8.18; 213 Sqdn 2.10.18; LVG C crashed E of Gits 06.30 14.10.18 (Lt HC Smith wounded); Fokker DVII wing came off, crashed Beerst 14.30 14.10.18 (Lt GS Hodson); Fokker DVII destroyed 10m NE of Ghent 10.30 9.11.18 (Lt HC Smith); 11 AP 25.2.19; WOC 25.2.19

**D3401** Deld 4 AAP Lincoln by 25.4.18; Rec Pk to 1 AI 14.5.18; 210 Sqdn 16.5.18; KB dest Pont Riqueul, E of Lestrem, shared B7227 & C62 17.10 21.5.18; 2-str, probably Rumpler, OOC Neuf Berquin 07.50 6.6.18; 2-str W/T m/c crashed nr Vieux-Berquin, shared D3381 08.25 6.6.18 (all Lt SC Joseph); EF, FL, wrecked nr Wirquin 23.6.18 (2/Lt GC Sutcliffe unhurt); 1 ASD 24.6.18; Rebuilt as F5987 14.7.18

**D3402** Deld 4 AAP Lincoln by 29.4.18; Rec Pk to 2 ASD 11.5.18; 209 Sqdn 15.5.18; Lost control, swung taxying out, crashed into stationery B7199 19.5.18 (Lt CT Evans USAS unhurt); 2 ASD 20.5.18; Rebuilt as F6150 3.7.18

**D3403** Rec Pk to 1 AI 16.5.18; 203 Sqdn 18.5.18; DFW C E of Vieux-Berquin, shared D3413 05.30 21.5.18 (2/Lt RC Berlyn); Landed on rough ground, o/t 6.6.18 (Lt CF Brown); 1 ASD 7.6.18

**D3404** Deld 4 AAP Lincoln by 29.4.18; Rec Pk to 1 AI 16.5.18; 210 Sqdn 21.5.18; Albatros DV crashed into shellhole E of Ypres 19.20 27.5.18 (Lt WS Jenkins); EF, FL, o/t, badly damaged Abeele 3.6.18 (Lt CJ Shackell unhurt); Rep Pk 1 ASD 5.6.18; Rebuilt as F5946 25.6.18 (again rebuilt, as H6874 17.10.18)

**D3405** Deld 4 AAP Lincoln by 28.4.18; Rec Pk to 2 AI 11.5.18; 209 Sqdn 16.5.18; Left 17.25 for HOP Proyart, FTR 20.6.18 (2/Lt H Mason PoW); SOC 20.6.18

**D3406** Deld 4 AAP Lincoln by 29.4.18; Rec Pk by 9.5.18; 1 AI to 210 Sqdn 14.5.18; Albatros DV OOC 2m E of Ypres, then landed with tail shot away by 5 HA 20.15 14.5.18 (Lt SC Joseph); FL Arques 21.5.18 (Lt HB Frost unhurt); 1 ASD 22.5.18; 70 Sqdn (coded 'C') by 9.18; Lost in action 4.9.18 (2/Lt WM Herriott DoW)

**D3407** (130-hp Clerget) Deld 4 AAP Lincoln by 27.4.18; 4 ASD to 213 Sqdn 25.5.18; Destroyed by fire in enemy bombing raid 29.6.18; WOC 30.6.18

**D3408** Rec Pk to 2 AI 11.5.18; 209 Sqdn 16.5.18; Crashed on TO, CW (Lt DY Hunter); 2 ASD 5.7.18; SOC 10.7.18 NWR

**D3409** (130-hp Clerget) Deld W/E 15.5.18; 4 ASD by 25.5.18; 213 Sqdn 26.5.18; Pfalz DIII OOC Moorslede, shared B5687 & C65 19.35 2.6.18; Albatros DV OOC smoking 4m S of Dixmude, officially shared B7272, C65, D3397 & D3411 (but probably only really C65) 18.00 7.6.18 (both Lt WE Gray); Albatros C OOC 3m ESE of Dixmude, shared B7252, D8189, & D9664 19.40 11.8.18 (2/Lt EC Toy); 4 ASD Guines 13.9.18; 4 ASD Audembert 4.10.18; 213 Sqdn 5.10.18; Red-tailed Fokker DVII dest E of Aertrycke 12.05 8.10.18 (Capt JE Greene DFC); HA crashed into houses Thourout, shared B7270 10.15 14.10.18 (Lt K McLeish USNRF); Last seen attacked by 17 Fokker DVII Pervyse, possibly shot down in flames 14.30 14.10.18 (Capt JE Greene DFC killed)

**D3410** Rec Pk to 1 AI 8.5.18; 210 Sqdn 14.5.18; Pfalz DIII OOC 3m E of Ypres 19.45 16.5.18; Pfalz DIII crashed nr Bac St.Maur 20.05 18.5.18; Pfalz DIII OOC E of Estaires 12.10 20.5.18; KB in flames & 2 DD Ploegsteert, shared B7227 & B7249 11.20 21.5.18; Pfalz DIII OOC Bailleul 08.10 27.5.18 (all Capt HB Maund); In action 28.5.18 (Capt HB Maund wounded?); 2-str crashed le Doulieu, shared D9590 08.25 6.6.18; Pfalz DIII OOC & another crashed NE of Ploegsteert Wood 08.35 9.6.18 (both Capt JG Manuel); Fokker DVII shot down SE of Zillebeke Lake 15.00 17.6.18 (Capt HA Patey); Shot up by AA fire 21.6.18 (Capt HA Patey unhurt); Rep Pk 1 ASD 22.6.18; Rebuilt as F6315 in error 9.8.18, changed to H6993

**D3411** (130-hp Clerget) 4 ASD to 213 Sqdn 20.5.18; Pfalz DIII OOC E of Estaires 12.10 20.5.18; Shot up in combat, FL nr Berques 26.6.18 (both Lt BA Hewett); 4 ASD by 9.18; 213 Sqdn 29.9.18; EF, FL, o/t 1m SW of Lichtervelde 1.11.18 (Lt RA Pearce unhurt); Tested 2.11.18 (LM)

**D3412** (130-hp Clerget) 4 ASD by 25.5.18; 213 Sqdn 26.5.18; Destroyed by fire in enemy bombing raid 29.6.18; WOC 30.6.18

**D3413** Deld 4 AAP Lincoln by 7.5.18; Rec Pk to 1 AI 14.5.18; 203 Sqdn 17.5.18; DFW CV crashed E of Vieux-Berquin, shared D3403 05.30 21.5.18 (Capt LH Rochford); EF, FL and crashed nr Acq 29.5.18 (Capt LH Rochford unhurt); 4 ASD 30.5.18; 213 Sqdn by 6.18; Attacked by 4 Fokkers, FL, slight wing damage nr Wormhout 27.6.18 (Lt BA Hewett unhurt); 4 ASD 27.6.18; Rebuilt and renumberd F5942 25.6.18 (sic)

**D3414** Deld 4 AAP Lincoln by 14.5.18; Rec Pk to 1 AI 17.5.18; 203 Sqdn 17.5.18; Killed observer in LVG, 2 indecisive combats S of Arras 19.30 patrol 10.6.18; Pfalz DIII crashed E of Outtersteene and another OOC W of Armentières 18.35 11.6.18; Escorting RE8, Fokker DVII dest nr Ervillers 20.40 and another indecisive Bailleul (all Mjr R Collishaw); DFW C dest Estaires, shared B7185, D3371, D3417 & D9585 06.10 16.6.18 (Lt YES Kirkpatrick); Engine failed to restart after cut on landing, landed in cornfield 19.6.18 (Lt FG

*Sopwith Camel D3417 of 203 Sqdn nearest the camera had numerous victories while being flown by Major R.Collishaw, and was inherited by his successor, Major TF Hazell. In the background is B3809 'NIBS'. (via Frank Cheesman)*

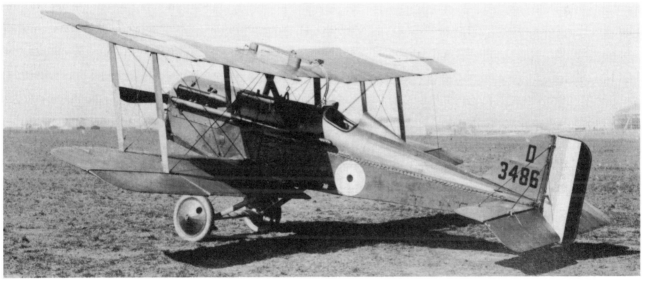

*Royal Aircraft Factory S.E.5a D3486 was one of three of its type flown by the War School at Manston. (J.M.Bruce/G.S.Leslie collection)*

*Sopwith Camels of 226 Sqdn at Pizzone (Taranto), including D6610, D6614 and C45. (via Frank Cheesman)*

Black); 1 ASD 20.6.18; SOC 5.7.18 NWR

**D3415** Deld 3 AAP Norwich by 10.5.18; Rec Pk to 1 AI 16.5.18; 203 Sqdn 17.5.18; Fokker DVII OOC 2m S of Ypres 20.55 4.7.18 (Lt IW Hunter); DFW C crashed Bauvin 06.45 22.7.18 (Capt LD Bawlf); COL uneven ground 20.8.18 (2/Lt MG Cruise); 2 ASD 17.8.18 (sic); Rebuilt as H6853 3.10.18

**D3416** Deld 4 AAP Lincoln by 7.5.18; Rec Pk to 1 AI 14.5.18; 203 Sqdn 17.5.18; DFW C crashed nr Morchies, then Albatros C crashed railway cutting nr St.Léger 11.40 22.5.18 (Capt RA Little DSO & Bar, C de G & Palm); Left 22.30 27.5.18, shot down Noeex-les-Auxi, found 05.00 28.5.18 (Capt RA Little DSO & Bar, C de G & Palm killed); remains to Rep Pk 1 ASD; SOC in field 31.5.18

**D3417** Deld 4 AAP Lincoln by 17.5.18; Rec Pk to 1 AI 27.5.18; 203 Sqdn 29.5.18; LVG C OOC La Bassée 5.6.18; Fokker Dr.1 OOC nr Neuve Eglise 12.00 7.6.18 (both Capt LH Rochford); Pfalz DIII BU & another OOC shared 2 others Outtersteene 18.35 11.6.18; Fokker DVII crashed nr Ervillers, E of Arras-Bapaume railway line, possibly shared R.E.8 20.40 15.6.18 (both Mjr R Colishaw); DFW C dest Estaires, shared B7185, D3371, D3414 & D9585 06.10 16.6.18 (Capt ET Hayne); Fokker DVII shot down Dixmude-Nieuport 18.00 patrol 25.6.18; Fokker DVII crashed Bussy, N of Noyon 20.00 26.6.18; Pfalz DIII OOC Houthulst Wood after it had been attacked by 4 other a/c of the patrol 19.05 30.6.18; Fokker DVII crashed into house nr Hollebeke 20.55 4.7.18; 2 DFC C collided when attacked, fell locked together NE of Dixmude 21.30 4.7.18; DFW crashed into canal SE of Merville 11.00 & another OOC over Miraumont 11.40 20.7.18; Dropped from 150ft on Dorignies aerodrome in dawn raid with F/Cdr Rochford, dropped bombs and fired 1,400 rounds m/g, hangar set on fire, 2-str recce a/c shot down in flames while landing 03.55 22.7.18; Retd for recce of damaged hangars, Albatros DV crashed nr Scarpe River 05.35 22.7.18; Dark brown DFW C crashed 2,000yds NE of Locon 15.20 9.8.18; Fokker DVII crashed S of River Somme & another OOC W of Bray 19.25, then FL with damaged engine at Bertangles 10.8.18; Fokker DVII crashed 1m S of Damery 20.00 15.8.18; FL nr Bray 05.00 patrol 26.8.18; FL nr Albert 28.8.18; okker DVII shot down Bapaume 19.00 29.8.18; Fokker DVII OOC Epinoy 07.05 24.9.18; Fokker DVII crashed, BO, dest Lieu-St.Amand aerodrome 13.05 & another crashed 2m W of Lieu-St.Amand aerodrome 13.38 26.9.18; (all Mjr R Collishaw); still 203 Sqdn 1.19 (COs machine)

**D3418** Deld 4 AAP Lincoln by 17.5.18; Crashed and damaged at Sandwich while en route Lympne 23.5.18 (Lt RD Williams USAS); Guston Rd, Dover 24.5.18 (repair); 7 AAP Lympne 6.18; Rec Pk 6.6.18; 1 AI 7.6.18; 210 Sqdn 19.6.18; O/t landing after patrol 29.7.18 (Lt HH Whitlock); to 1 ASD; Rebuilt as F6323 in error 9.8.18, changed to H7286

**D3419** Deld 4 AAP Lincoln by 17.5.18; Rec Pk to 1 AI 27.5.18; 201 Sqdn (via 2 ASD) 31.5.18; Rumpler C BU, in flames, SE of Villers-Bretonneux, own m/c badly damaged 19.45 16.6.18; KB in flames E of Achiet-le-Grand, shared B5749 17.35 16.7.18; KB in flames Fricourt, E of Albert 12.20 19.7.18 (all Lt GB Gates); Missing, last seen nr Harbonnières 10.30 8.8.18 (Lt RH Hemmens PoW); Salved by 6 SS 5 Brigade 8.18; SOC 8.8.18

**D3420** Deld 4 AAP Lincoln by 23.5.18; 2 ASD to 209 Sqdn 9.6.18; Shot up in engagement with 2-strs Lamotte 28.6.18 (Lt JP Naish); 2 ASD 28.6.18; Rebuilt as F6197 17.7.18

**D3421** Rec Pk by 5.18; 2 ASD 4.6.18; 209 Sqdn 11.6.18; Damaged by ground m/g fire 8.8.18 (Lt WM Wormald wounded); 2 ASD 9.8.18; Rebuilt as F6247 15.8.18

**D3422** 4 ASD by 7.18; 210 Sqdn 31.7.18; Pfalz DIII OOC 2m S of Westende 10.50 11.8.18; Engine hit by m/g fire, FL, damaged nr Woesten 24.8.18; Flying again 5.9.18; Fokker DVII crashed in sea 6m N of Zeebrugge 11.15 16.9.18; General engagement with 15 Fokker DVII nr Staden, 1 crashed W of Wijnendaele Wood 07.55 & 1 OOC Wijnendaele Wood 08.05 29.9.18 (all Lt A Buchanan); 4 ASD for survey 11.10.18 - @25.10.18;

471 Flt 233 Sqdn Walmer by 2.19; 11 AP by road 21.2.19; WOC 21.2.19

**D3423** Presentation a/c 'Tirisdeach', presented by people of Island of Tiree. Rec Pk to 1 AI 8.8.18; 209 Sqdn 9.8.18; Crashed in lines after engagement with 5 HA, FO Peronne (Bayonvillers) 11.8.18 (2/Lt JA Watt slightly wounded); brought in by 22 Wing SS 11.8.18; 6 SS 5 Brigade 8.18; SOC

**D3424** Deld 4 AAP Lincoln by 16.5.18; Rec Pk to 1 AI 10.6.18; 210 Sqdn 11.6.18; FL after combat c.08.00 17.6.18 (Lt CH Strickland wounded) [An Albatros DV BU Zillebeke Lake 08.00 this day, but uncertain whether by D3381/Campbell or D3424/Strickland]; Rep Pk 1 ASD 18.6.18; SOC 21.6.18 NWR

**D3425** Rec Pk to 1 AI 30.7.18; 201 Sqdn 3.8.18; Attacked by 4 Fokker DVII, FL on fire 300yds behind lines Harbonnières 8.8.18 (Lt JM Mackay PoW); SOC 8.8.18

**3 ROYAL AIRCRAFT FACTORY S.E.5A TRACTOR BIPLANE SCOUTS from batch D3426 to D3575 built by Vickers at Weybridge. (200-hp Hispano-Suiza)**

**D3485** Ex RFC to War School Manston W/E 16.3.18; Deleted W/E 30.3.18

**D3486** 10 AAP Brooklands to War School Manston W/E 9.3.18; Became Pool of Pilots (Scout School) Manston 1.4.18

**D3487** 10 AAP Brooklands allocated War School Manston by 30.3.18; SMOP Dover by 12.18

**5 SOPWITH PUP TRACTOR BIPLANES from batch D4011 to D4210 built by Whitehead Aircraft Ltd at Richmond.**

| | |
|---|---|
| **D4016** | Eastbourne (painted white) |
| **D4018** | Cranwell |
| **D4027** | East Fortune by 6.4.18 |
| **D4028** | 208 TDS Leuchars by 7.18 |
| **D4034** | 208 TDS Leuchars by 25.7.18 |

**24 AVRO 504J & 504K TRACTOR BIPLANE TRAINERS from batch D4361 to D4560 built by The Sunbeam Motor Car Co Ltd at Wolverhampton. (110-hp Gnôme Monosoupape or 130-hp Clerget 9B)**

**D4361** (Mono) 55 TS Lilbourne, Crashed 19.6.18; 55 TS Shotwick by 9.8.18 BUT Eastbourne to 93 Sqdn 1.8.18

**D4367** (Mono) Eastbourne by 8.18; 93 Sqdn 1.8.18; 55 TS Shotwick by 26.8.18

**D4393** Pool of Pilots Manston by 3.19 - @4.19

**D4414** Pool of Pilots Manston by 6.18 - @10.8.18

**D4415** 203 TDS Manston by 6.18; Became 55 TDS Manston 14.7.18; 55 TDS Narborough 11.9.18 - @11.18

**D4416** 55 TDS Manston by 8.18

**D4417** 55 TDS Manston by 7.18

**D4445** (130-hp Clerget) 56 TDS Cranwell by 9.18; Spun in 3.10.18 (F/Cdt AS Rogers seriously injured)

**D4446** 56 TDS Cranwell by 9.18 - @10.18

**D4447** 56 TDS Cranwell by 11.18

**D4450** 56 TDS Cranwell by 8.18 - @1.19

**D4454** (130-hp Clerget) 2 Observers School Manston, turned close to ground while landing, wing hit ground 19.10.18 (F/Cdt RH Read slightly hurt & 2/Lt HA Young injured)

**D4490** 55 TDS Manston test 24.10.18

**D4493** ARS to 55 TDS Manston 3.8.18

**D4494** 55 TDS Manston by 8.18; 55 TDS Narborough 11.9.18 - @1.19

**D4496** 55 TDS Manston from 8.18

**D4497** 55 TDS Manston by 9.18

**D4498** ARS to 55 TDS Manston 3.8.18 - @2.19

**D4499** ARS to 55 TDS Manston 4.8.18; 55 TDS Narborough 11.9.18 - @11.18

**D4500** 55 TDS Manston by 9.18

**D4501** 55 TDS Manston by 9.18; 55 TDS Narborough 11.9.18 - @2.19

**D4503** 55 TDS Narborough by 9.18 - @11.18

**D4504** ARS to 55 TDS Manston 8.18; 55 TDS Narborough 11.9.18 - @10.18

**D4505** 55 TDS Manston by 9.18 - @10.18

**20 HANDLEY PAGE O/400 TRACTOR BIPLANE HEAVY BOMBERS from batch D4561 to D4660 built by The Metropolitan Carriage, Wagon & Finance Co at Birmingham. (Eagle or Liberty)**

D4563  1 S of N&BD Stonehenge by 6.18 - @5.7.18; 207 Sqdn (coded 'B1') by 8.18

D4564  207 Sqdn (coded 'N') by 15.6.18; EF, FL, wing struck tree taking off again, into ditch, CW 27.10.18 (2/Lt PC Crovat & 2/Lt A Wichelow both injured)

D4565  (Eagle VIII) 207 Sqdn (coded 'F' 8.18 - @9.18, then 'B' 11.18, then 'M' 11.18) by 15.6.18; Rebuilt on sqdn 10.18; Reported totally unfit due to exposure to weather, Carvin 30.12.18 (Capt FCB Savile)

D4566  215 Sqdn by 8.6.18; Shot down in raid on Cologne 16/17.9.18 (Lt HB Monaghan, Lt HE Hyde & Lt GW Mitchell all PoWs); SOC in field 17.9.18

D4567  215 Sqdn by 12.6.18; Missing, left 23.50 to bomb Fives Railway Sidings 3/4.8.18 (Lt HL Hammond, 2/Lt WH Brinkworth, G/L Sgt HT Pheby all killed)

D4568  (Eagle VIII) 14 AAP Castle Bromwich by 12.6.18; Rec Pk to 215 Sqdn 7.8.18; Raid, starboard propeller shaft shot off, engine on fire, FL crashed nr Baccarat 27.9.18 (2/Lt SG Jary slight shock, 2/Lt E Anderson contusions & 2/Lt J Durien injured); 3 ASD 27.9.18

D4569  (Eagle VIII) Mkrs by 5.6.18 to accept at works; 8 AAP Lympne by 6.18; Rec Pk 11.6.18; Verton 11.6.18; 2 AI 6.18; 207 Sqdn (coded 'R') 17.6.18; EF on TO, into trenches, on nose, badly damaged 29.10.18 (Lt AJ Court unhurt)

D4570  (Eagle VIII) Mkrs by 5.6.18 - @1.6.18 to accept at works; 8 AAP Lympne to 214 Sqdn (via Marquise) (coded 'C') 2.7.18; With 214 to ME, to Buc 1.7.19; Arr Cairo 22.7.19 - @2.8.19

D4578  (Eagle VIII) 8 AAP Lympne by 7.18; 4 ASD 15.7.18; 214 Sqdn 1.8.18 ('terrier' insignia on nose); With 214 Sqdn to ME 30.7.19; At Cairo by 2.8.19

D4579  (Eagle VIII) 8 AAP Lympne by 7.18; 215 Sqdn 1.8.18; 4 ASD 3.8.18; 214 Sqdn 15.8.18; EF after leaving for raid on Zeebrugge, FL, went on nose in ploughed field 24.9.18 (Capt GH Russell, 2/Lt JMcK Young both unhurt & Lt HA McCormick USNRF walked into propeller, DoI); Rep Pk 4 ASD 29.9.18; Rebuilt as J4592 3.1.19

D4580  (Eagle VIII) 8 AAP Lympne by 10.18; Tested 4.10.18; Rec Pk 17.10.18; 3 ASD 18.10.18; 215 Sqdn 28.10.18; Overbanked on coming in to land, hit ground in vertical nose dive, CW 24.12.18 (2/Lt JH O'Grady & 2/Lt WR Dallas both killed, 3AM W Morton seriously injured); to 4 ASD for disposal 26.12.18

D4581  (Eagle VIII) 4 ASD to 214 Sqdn 9.8.18; With 214 Sqdn to ME, to Buc 6.7.19; Arr Cairo 28.7.19 - @2.8.19

D4582  58 TDS Cranwell by 16.7.18 - @19.8.18

D4585  115 Sqdn from 1.9.18; Crashed 14.9.18 (2/Lt RJ Whitaker & 2/Lt TE Greer both injured); 3 ASD 15.9.18; 207 Sqdn by .19

D4591  (Eagle VIII) 4 ASD to 214 Sqdn 25.9.18; With 214 to ME, to Buc 1.7.19; EF, FL, crashed in mountains Trets, nr Draguignan, between Toulon & Marseilles, BO 08.00 9.7.19 (Lt FC Sumner, Lt C Hall, Cpl JH Jaffe & Cpl EH Flintoff all killed)

D4596  England to Rec Pk 2.10.18; 207 Sqdn (coded 'D') 3.10.18; For 216 Sqdn Egypt; Arr Fréjus 14.8.19; Arr Taranto 17.9.19; Damaged in gale Valona 25.9.19

D4597  England to 3 ASD (via Paris) 17.10.18; 216 Sqdn 19.10.18; With 216 Sqdn to ME, to Buc 21.7.19

D4598  England to 3 ASD (via Paris) 14.10.18; 216 Sqdn 21.10.18; Returning from raid on Saarbrucken, sideslipped from 500 ft, Roville 29/30.10.18 (Capt AG Cable USAS, 2/Lt W Hutchings & Lt JE Kemshall all injured); 3 AD 30.10.18

D4621  (Eagle VIII) 216 Sqdn, crashed Roubruck 11.4.19 (2/Lt P McNaughton, 2/Lt DE Haighton and 1 airman all unhurt); SOC

D4626  (Eagle VIII) Deld 14 AAP Castle Bromwich by 11.1.19; 216 Sqdn by 23.1.19; With 216 Sqdn to ME, to Buc 21.7.19; En route, broke tail skid & lower elevators, Pisa 26.7.19; left 6.8.19; At Taranto by 13.8.19; Arr Cairo 27.8.19

**3 ROYAL AIRCRAFT FACTORY R.E.8 TRACTOR BIPLANES from batch D4661 to D4810.**

D4713  Deld 201/2 TDS Cranwell 7.6.18
D4715  Deld 201/2 TDS Cranwell 11.6.18
D4720  Deld 201/2 TDS Cranwell 11.6.18

**3 ARMSTRONG WHITWORTH F.K.8 RECONNAISSANCE TRACTOR BIPLANES from batch D5001 to D5200 built by Sir W.G.Armstrong Whitworth & Co Ltd at Gosforth, Newcastle-on-Tyne.**

D5082  7 AAP Kenley by 25.5.18 for 253 Sqdn (NTU); Exptl Flt Gosport by 5.18 - @4.19 (for RN Signal School, Portsmouth); To Agricultural Hall, Islington for preservation in error for B9599 23.8.18, presume retd

D5090  7 AAP Kenley by 25.5.18 for 253 Sqdn (NTU); Exptl Flt Gosport by 10.18 - 12.18 (for RN Signal School, Portsmouth); D Flt Devt Sqdn Gosport by 6.19

D5117  7 AAP Kenley by 25.5.18 for 253 Sqdn (NTU); Exptl Flt, Gosport Calshot by 28.5.18 - @9.18 (for RN Signal School, Portsmouth)

**24 HANDLEY PAGE O/400 TRACTOR BIPLANE HEAVY BOMBERS from batch D5401 to D5450 built by The Birmingham Carriage Co at Birmingham. (Two 375-hp Eagle VIII)**

D5401  Mkrs by 12.4.18; Accepted Smethwick 14.4.18; Petrol trouble, FL in field on delivery to Upper Heyford 19.4.18 (Lt H Shaw); Petrol trouble, FL Port Meadow 22.4.18; Farnborough 24.4.18; Lympne (via Penshurst) 27.4.18; Rec Pk 4.5.18; 214 Sqdn 4.5.18; Badly damaged by AA during raid on Bruges Docks, FL on beach Oostdunkerque Bains, destroyed by enemy shipping, set on fire 16.6.18 (Lt WSB Freer, Cpl Wardrop & Lt R Binckes); WOC 30.6.18

D5402  Mkrs for acceptance by 20.4.18; Rec Pk to 214 Sqdn 10.5.18; CW landing after raid on Ostende 17.6.18 (Lt AMG Cosgrave, Lt AR Clark & AG H Williamson unhurt); Deleted

D5404  207 Sqdn by 15.6.18; After night raid, EF, FL Domart, TW 10.8.18 (Lt G Roberts injured, Lt RJ Mesney injured & Lt LG Semple); Rep Pk 2 ASD 13.8.18; SOC 27.8.18

D5405  215 Sqdn by 22.5.18 - @30.5.18; 207 Sqdn by 15.6.18; Shot up in night raid on Peronne, EF, FL in field, o/t, CW 7.8.18 (Mjr TA Batchelor seriously injured; Lt AW Robinson & Capt C Gilmour both slightly injured); Rep Pk 2 ASD 9.8.18; SOC 20.8.18

D5406  215 Sqdn by 27.5.18 - @30.5.18; 207 Sqdn by 15.6.18; 58 Sqdn 30.8.18, used as training machine as unable to climb with loads, until earmarked for ASD for training in England 10.12.18

D5407  215 Sqdn by 11.6.18; Lost, landed Reclinghem, asked way but landed Matringhem in error, taxying out to TO again, struck bank, lost u/c, CW 18.7.18 (Lt J Lorimer & 2/Lt JP Armitage unhurt); SOC 19.7.18 wrecked

D5408  207 Sqdn by 15.6.18; Wrecked 20.6.18; SOC Rep Pk 2 ASD 20.8.18

D5409  207 Sqdn (coded 'X' 8.18 - 9.18, then 'C' 11.18) by 15.6.18 - @10.11.18

D5410  Deld 14 AAP Castle Bromwich by 12.6.18; Lympne 6.18; Coudekerque (via Audembert) 16.6.18; 214 Sqdn by 9.18; Rep Pk 4 ASD 3.9.18 (rebuild, out of true); Fitted out for mail carrying; 216 Sqdn 15.12.18; While carrying mail, CW Cognelée, 7m NNW of Namur 9.1.19 (2/Lt R Logan & 2/Lt E Conning both slightly injured); 4 ASD 13.1.19

D5411  Deld 14 AAP Castle Bromwich by 12.6.18; 214 Sqdn by 1.7.18; Reported out of true and badly damaged by AA fire 28.10.18; to 2 ASD

D5415  97 Sqdn by 6.18; Crashed on practice flight 14.8.18 (Lt RG Hornby, Lt LC Baker, Lt JA Porter, Lt JS Andrews, AG Fleming & AG Aldridge); 3 ASD 14.8.18; 100 Sqdn 31.10.18 - end 1.19; With 216 Sqdn to ME, to Buc 17.7.19, left 28.7.19; Left Rome 2.8.19; Mersa Matruh by 13.8.19; Arr Cairo 27.8.19; still 216 Sqdn @1.20

D5416  58 TDS Cranwell by 1.7.18 - @27.11.18

D5418  97 Sqdn by 6.18; Crashed 18.8.18 (Lt GA Box, Lt

Grundy), Lt Kilby, Cpl Skipper & AM Walpole); 3 ASD 19.8.18; 100 Sqdn 1.11.18; FL in bad weather, unable to TO again owing to condition of ground Charleroi 9.1.19 (Lt EC Middleton, 2/Lt HG Shaw, 2/Lt CHBPrice & AC2 PF Hobbs); Retd 14.1.19 - @end 1.19; to dismantle for 4 ASD; With 216 Sqdn to ME, to Buc 10.7.19; Istres 12.7.19; Blown from moorings in gale, CW, Istres 17.7.19

| | |
|---|---|
| D5419 | 58 TDS Cranwell by 20.7.18 - @7.8.18 |
| D5420 | 58 TDS Cranwell by 15.7.18 - @26.10.18 |
| D5421 | 58 TDS Cranwell by 19.7.18 - @20.11.18 |
| D5422 | Rec Pk to 207 Sqdn (coded 'A' 8.18, then 'S' 9.18) 10.8.18; Lost after night raid on Namur, COL French aerodrome 1.11.18 (Capt JS Harvey, 2/Lt GNG Hamilton & Sgt LCS Boshier unhurt) |
| D5429 | Lympne by 9.18; Rec Pk 13.9.18; 3 AD 14.9.18 (arr 24.9.18); 207 Sqdn (coded 'Z' 9.18, then 'L' by 11.18) 18.9.18; To Egypt, arr Fréjus 14.8.19; arr Lyons 13.9.19; Wrecked in gale en route 23.11.19 |
| D5431 | UK to Rec Pk 23.8.18; 3 ASD 25.8.18; 215 Sqdn 27.8.18; COL after raid on Ehrang Rly Junction 2.9.18 (Capt GS Buck MC DFC killed, 2/Lt CC Fisher shaken & 2/Lt AK Barter DFC severely injured); SOC in field 3.9.18 |
| D5433 | Rec Pk to 207 Sqdn (coded 'D') 1.9.18; Left for night raid on Grimcourt, stbd propeller came off, FL, badly damaged Famechon aerodrome 29.9.18 (Lt Dd'H Humphreys, 2/Lt SA Garratt & Pte1 JA Dornan all unhurt); Awaiting write-off by 30.9.18 |
| D5440 | Rec Pk by 10.18; 207 Sqdn 4.10.18; COL from night raid, went into bomb store, CW 23.10.18 (Lt FB Champress, 2/Lt AP Roberts & NCO HJ Taylor all unhurt); SOC in field |
| D5441 | 3 ASD by 10.18; 216 Sqdn 3.10.18; FL Bayon 10/11.10.18 (Lt L Tilden-Smith, Lt JE Kemshall & Lt GJ Holdcroft); 3 ASD 10.10.18 |
| D5444 | UK to Rec Pk 23.10.18; To 3 AD but bad weather, FL Boran 23.10.18; 2 AD 31.10.18; 216 Sqdn 1.11.18 (coded 'Q'); 97 Sqdn 1.1.19 - end 1.19; With 216 Sqdn to Buc 21.7.19; Left Rome 2.8.19; Mersa Matruh by 13.8.19; Arr Cairo 23.8.19; Still 216 Sqdn 6.3.20; Became G-EASO |
| D5446 | 214 Sqdn by 6.18; To IAF 9.11.18; Paris to Marquise but FL N of Beauvais 14.12.18 |

**39 AIRCO D.H.9 TRACTOR BIPLANE DAY BOMBERS from batch D5551 to D5850 built by Waring & Gillow Ltd (some under sub-contract by Wells Aviation Co, Chelsea). (200-hp B.H.P.)**

| | |
|---|---|
| D5582 | Rec Pk to 1 AI 12.4.18; to 206 Sqdn but crashed on arrival, bad ground Drionville 15.4.18 (Lt AE Steele & 1Pte A/G FC Bevis both injured); 1 ASD 15.4.18; to Adv Salvage, then SOC Rep Pk 1 ASD 25.4.18 |
| D5590 | Deld 2 AAP Hendon by 15.4.18; Rec Pk to 1 AI 10.5.18; 206 Sqdn 15.5.18; Pfalz DIII OOC 1½m E of Ypres 19.20-19.35 29.7.18 (Lt EA Burn & Capt WA Carrothers); Pfalz DIII OOC Menin-Wervicq 08.30 1.8.18 (Lt CS Johnston & 2/Lt AB Sangster); Missing 13.8.18 (Lt CS Johnson & 2/Lt AB Sangster both killed); SOC in field 14.8.18 |
| D5606 | Rec Pk to 1 AI 12.4.18; 206 Sqdn 18.4.18; Wrecked, to Rep Pk 1 ASD 28.5.18 |
| D5609 | Deld 2 AAP Hendon by 17.4.18; Rec Pk to 206 Sqdn 4.5.18; Left 14.14, engagement with HA, FL in shell hole No Mans Land, unable to salve 30.6.18 (Lt EA Burn injured & 2/Lt CO Shelswell unhurt); SOC in field |
| D5624 | Rec Pk by 4.18; 211 Sqdn 1.5.18; Forced to land crosswind as 2 other aircraft in way on ground, starboard wing hit ground, on nose 29.5.18 (Lt ETM Routledge & Cpl H Lindsay unhurt); 1 ASD 30.5.18 |
| D5625 | Martlesham Heath to Hendon 5.6.18; Villacoublay 6.6.18; Hendon 7.6.18 |
| D5638 | MOS Leysdown by 8.18 - @2.19 |
| D5646 | 233 Sqdn; 1 Observers School Eastchurch by 10.18; Became 2 MOS Eastchurch 28.12.18 - @7.19 |
| D5654 | Deld 2 AAP Hendon by 21.4.18; Rec Pk to 1 AI 29.5.18; 4 ASD by 9.18; 218 Sqdn 13.9.18; FTR from raid on Thourout 28.9.18 (2/Lt TM Steele missing & 2/Lt G Gedge PoW); Deleted 15.10.18 |
| D5661 | Deld 2 AAP Hendon 5.18; AAP Dover W/E 24.5.18; |

218 Sqdn by 31.5.18; Ran into ditch landing after raid 15.6.18 (Lt WF Purvis & 2AM G/L TR Barber unhurt); To 4 ASD; 218 Sqdn 19.10.18; FL Oye 22.10.18 (Lt JRA Barnes & 2/Lt FE Green unhurt)

| | |
|---|---|
| D5667 | AAP Dover by 3.18; Chingford 13.3.18; 4 ASD to 218 Sqdn 1.8.18; Returning from raid, spun in from 800ft on aerodrome, BO 19.8.18 (Lt JE Wase & 2/Lt JC Cavanagh both killed); WOC 31.8.18 |
| D5672 | Pool of Pilots Manston/Joyce Green 8.18 - @10.18; Became G-EAMX |
| D5683 | Deld 2 AAP Hendon 5.18; AAP Dover W/E 24.5.18; 218 Sqdn W/E 1.6.18; Pfalz DIII OOC Bruges-Ostende 16.50-17.20 5.9.18; Fokker DVII BU Bruges 16.30 15.9.18 (both Lt GH Howarth & 2/Lt FJ Gallant); u/s, burnt on site, SOC 22.1.19 |
| D5686 | 110 Sqdn by 6.18; MOS Leysdown by 8.18 - @2.19; Imperial Gift to India 8.20, became G-IAAS later VT-AAS |
| D5687 | Deld 2 AAP Hendon 5.18; AAP Dover W/E 24.5.18; 218 Sqdn by 20.5.18; COL 10.6.18 (Lt EH Dixon & G/L Sgt RJ Williams unhurt); Repaired on sqdn; Dived in combat with Fokker, BU in air over Blankenberghe, Fokker then shot down by C65 27.6.18 (Lt C Briggs & 2/Lt WH Warner both killed) [credited Flgm Kutschke, Seefrontstaffel] |
| D5689 | 110 Sqdn by 6.18; MOS Leysdown by 8.18 - @2.19 |
| D5696 | Deld 2 AAP Hendon by 23.5.18; 1 ASD to 206 Sqdn 7.6.18; EF, FL, crashed on sunken road running through aerodrome 12.6.18 (Lt H Stier USAS & 2/Lt WG Duncan); Rep Pk 1 ASD 15.6.18; SOC 5.7.18 NWR |
| D5709 | 557 Flt 212 Sqdn Yarmouth by 1.8.18 - @27.9.18; AZP 5.8.18 (Lt WK Prendergast & 2/Lt E Gray); With F.2A N4549, N4550 & D.H.4 N6395 engaged 5 HA 12m off Shipwash LV 16.9.18; Imperial Gift to India 8.20 |
| D5712 | 4 ASD to 218 Sqdn 9.8.18; Fokker OOC Cortemarck 17.50, but badly shot up 28.9.18 (Lt ER Brewer USMC & Sgt ER Wershiner USMC both wounded); 4 ASD 6.10.18 - @25.10.18 |
| D5713 | 1 Observers School Eastchurch by 12.18; Became 2 MOS Eastchurch 28.12.18 - @2.19 |
| D5714 | Rec Pk to 1 AI 14.8.18; 211 Sqdn 16.8.18; Damaged by flak returning from bombing raid, FL, COL Ypres-Courtrai 29.9.18 (2/Lt VGH Phillips & 2/Lt AF Taylor both unhurt); Rep Pk 1 ASD 30.9.18 |
| D5717 | 218 Sqdn, engine hit by AA fire during raid on Zeebrugge Mole, EF, FL Biggekerke, Zeeland 31.7.18 (Lt LWC Pearce & 2/Lt FH Bugge unhurt); Deleted 15.8.18 |
| D5721 | Pool of Pilots Manston/Joyce Green by 7.18 - @8.18 |
| D5727 | 204 TDS Eastchurch by 6.18 |
| D5728 | 1 Observers School Eastchurch by 10.18; Became 2 Marine Observers School Eastchurch 28.12.18 - @7.19 |
| D5731 | 1 Observers School Eastchurch by 11.18 - @12.18 |
| D5742 | Erected by Wells Aviation Co; 491 Flt 233 Sqdn Dover by 20.7.18 - @15.8.18; Eastbourne repair 8.18; 491 Flt 233 Sqdn Dover 13.9.18; 218 Sqdn 24.9.18; FTR from raid 26.9.18 (2/Lt JT Aitken & 2/Lt OR Hibbert PoWs) |
| D5750 | Rec Pk to 1 AI 31.8.18; 206 Sqdn 3.9.18; Took off crosswind, stalled, crashed 20.9.18 (2/Lt C Knight USAS & 2/Lt JH Perring both unhurt); Rep Pk 1 ASD 21.9.18; SOC 23.9.18 |
| D5753 | Rec Pk to 1 AI 31.8.18; 206 Sqdn 7.9.18 - @30.9.18 |
| D5754 | 493 Flt 236 Sqdn Mullion by 9.18; Tested 28.9.18; East Fortune 5.11.18 (arr 11.11.18) |
| D5756 | MOS Leysdown by 8.18 - @2.19; Imperial Gift to India |
| D5782 | Rec Pk to 1 AI 7.8.18; 206 Sqdn 9.8.18; Fokker DVII OOC E of Messines 18.50 13.8.18 (Capt T Roberts & 2/Lt CO Shelswell); Fokker DVII in flames crashed nr Lendelede, shared D569 14.40 14.10.18 (Lt H McLean & 2/Lt HP Hobbs); Collided with taxying Snipe while landing 9.2.19 (Capt T Roberts & Sgt Pugh unhurt); to 9 SS for repair |
| D5793 | 109 Sqdn by 6.18; 557/8 Flts 212 Sqdn Yarmouth by 19.8.18 - @7.9.18; AZP, attacked *L70* which was later brought down by A8032, COL Sedgeford 5.8.18 (Capt CS Iron, Lt HG Owen unhurt); Imperial Gift to India 8.20 |
| D5802 | 109 Sqdn by 6.18; Yarmouth, AZP, FTR 5.8.18 (Capt DGB Jardine & Lt ER Munday both killed; Jardine's body washed up Verduse, W coast of Jutland 26.9.18) |
| D5807 | 557/8 Flts 212 Sqdn Yarmouth by 19.9.18 - @15.10.18 |

D5809    109 Sqdn by 6.18; Yarmouth, AZP 5.8.18 (Capt CB Sproatt & Capt J Hodson); COL, wrecked 10.8.18 (2 crew unhurt)

D5816    Presentation a/c 'Faridkot No.3', fitted modified engine cowling. Rec Pk to 1 AI 1.8.18; 206 Sqdn 4.8.18; Left 05.30, crashed through enemy action nr Grasse-Payelle, CW 7.8.18 (Lt JFS Percival & 2/Lt J Lowthian both injured); Rep Pk 1 ASD 9.8.18; SOC 11.8.18

D5838    Rec Pk to 1 AI 4.10.18; 206 Sqdn 6.10.18; Hit rut landing 12.11.18 (Lt AL Seddon & 2/Lt EW Richardson both unhurt)

D5849    Deld 6 SD Ascot for Mudros W/E 17.10.18

## 3 AVRO 504A/J/K TRACTOR BIPLANE TRAINERS from batch D6201 to D6250 built by Humber Ltd at Coventry.

D6210    Redcar, o/t, wrecked 1918

D6216    56/57 TDS Cranwell by 8.18 - @18.9.18

D6235    (Monosoupape) Shoreham to Telscombe but engine caught fire on landing, TL 20.7.18 (pilot unhurt)

## 13 AVRO 504A/J/K TRACTOR BIPLANE TRAINERS from batch D6251 to D6400 built by Brush at Loughborough. (100-hp Gnôme Monosoupape)

D6251    (DC) Deld Eastbourne NFS W/E 2.3.18; Became 207 TDS Eastbourne 1.4.18; FL and wrecked 13.6.18 (2/Lt JTJ McA'nulty unhurt); Became 50 TDS Eastbourne 15.7.18 - @8.18

D6252    (DC) Deld Eastbourne NFS W/E 2.3.18; Became 207 TDS Eastbourne 1.4.18 - @8.18

D6253    (DC) Deld Eastbourne NFS W/E 2.3.18; ; Became 207 TDS Eastbourne 1.4.18; Became 50 TDS Eastbourne 15.7.18; Crashed & WO 26.7.18

D6254    (DC) Deld Eastbourne NFS W/E 2.3.18; ; Became 207 TDS Eastbourne 1.4.18; Became 50 TDS Eastbourne 15.7.18 - @9.18

D6255    (DC) Deld Eastbourne NFS W/E 2.3.18; ; Became 207 TDS Eastbourne 1.4.18; Became 50 TDS Eastbourne 15.7.18 - @9.18

D6256    Deld Chingford W/E 8.3.18; Became 207 TDS Chingford by 1.4.18

D6257    Deld Chingford W/E 8.3.18; Became 207 TDS Chingford by 1.4.18

D6258    Deld Chingford W/E 8.3.18; Became 207 TDS Chingford by 1.4.18

D6259    Deld Chingford W/E 8.3.18; Became 207 TDS Chingford by 1.4.18

D6260    Deld Chingford W/E 8.3.18; Became 207 TDS Chingford by 1.4.18

D6270    Gosport by 6.18; Hendon 25.6.18

D6334    (504K) 55 TDS Manston 25.8.18; Eastchurch

D6352    (504K) 55 TDS Manston from 8.18 - @9.18

## 27 SOPWITH F.1 CAMEL TRACTOR BIPLANE SCOUTS from batch D6401 to D6700 built by Boulton & Paul Ltd at Norwich. (130-hp Clerget 9B or 110-hp Le Rhône)

D6434    (140hp Clerget) 1 AI to 208 Sqdn 25.4.18; Lost, FL, went into ditch, wrecked at 2 ASD Verton 3.5.18 (Lt LC Gilmour unhurt); 2 ASD 3.5.18 for rebuild; 2 AI by 8.18; 201 Sqdn (coded 'D') 9.8.18; In action 6.9.18 (Lt LG Tearle wounded); 203 Sqdn 23.1.19

D6446    1 AI to 208 Sqdn 17.6.18; Albatros DV shot down SW of Douai, shared D1834 20.20 31.7.18 (Lt LFA Green); COL, wrecked 14.9.18 (2/Lt GV Snell); 1 ASD 15.9.18; Rebuilt as H7239 5.11.18

D6490    (Clerget) Rec Pk to 1 AI 12.4.18; 208 Sqdn 17.4.18; Albatros dest SW of Douai, shared D1834 20.20 31.7.18 (Lt LFA Green); Rep Pk 1 ASD 16.8.18 (unfit for further service); Rebuilt as H7239 5.11.18

D6494    (Clerget) Rec Pk to 1 AI 12.4.18; 208 Sqdn 15.4.18; Rep Pk 1 ASD 30.4.18 (wrecked); Rec Pk to AI 26.6.18; 54 Sqdn by 4.7.18; Down in spin after combat 4.7.18 (2/Lt CH Atkinson killed)

D6495    Rec Pk to 2 AI 6.4.18; 2 ASD by 7.18; 209 Sqdn 1.7.18; Fokker DVII OOC N of Comines, shared B7471 & C198 07.20 26.7.18 (Lt AL Porter wounded); Pancaked landing, tyre burst, tilted on to wing, up on nose 29.7.18 (2/Lt EG Gaff unhurt); 1 ASD 30.7.18; Rebuilt as F6327 in error 10.8.18, later changed to

H6998

D6516    1 AI to 208 Sqdn 9.5.18; On TO, hit D.H.9 taxiing in 15.5.18 (Lt MC Howell slightly injured); 1 ASD 16.5.18, SOC in field

D6520    4 Sqdn AFC by 5.18; Wrecked, to 1 ASD 15.5.18; 2 ASD by 7.18; 201 Sqdn 5.7.18; Collided with B7190 15.7.18 (2/Lt WA Hall); Flying again 19.7.18; O/t landing in strong wind 24.7.18 (2/Lt NOM Foggo unhurt); Flying again 28.7.18; Left 14.45, attacking troops in wood just N of Rosières, sent into spin by Fokker DVIIs, crashed on road, BO 9.8.18 (Lt R Stone killed); SOC 9.8.18

D6534    1 AI to 208 Sqdn 24.5.18; Rumpler C shot down S of Estaires 09.50 28.7.18 (Lt MC Howell); Stalled and crashed on TO 31.8.18 (2/Lt E Munro unhurt); 1 ASD 31.8.18; SOC 3.9.18

D6544    (Clerget) Rec Pk to 1 AI 11.4.18; 208 Sqdn 16.4.18;2-str OOC 2m E of Lens, shared D1813, D1853, D1873, D1879, D1889 08.00 22.5.18 (Lt EG Johnstone); Crashed 9.7.18 (Lt WR Allison); 1 ASD 10.7.18, wrecked; SOC 1.8.18 Rebuilt with new serial (unidentified)

D6555    6 SD Ascot by 23.8.18; 212 TDS Vendôme by 9.18; COL 16.9.18 (2/Lt JGT Jenkins)

D6556    (Clerget) 1 RP Marquise by 4.18; 208 Sqdn 11.4.18 - @13.4.18; 4 ASD by 25.5.18 - @31.5.18; 2 ASD by 7.18; 70 Sqdn 4.7.18 - @26.7.18

D6590    1 AI to 208 Sqdn 30.4.18; Red Albatros DV OOC Phalempin, shared C8266, then FL Isberques 13.45 9.5.18 (Lt GA Wightman); 4 ASD 18.5.18; Rebuilt as F5917 25.6.18

D6596    1 AI to 208 Sqdn 24.5.18; COL, wrecked Serny 6.9.18 (Lt E Munro); 1 ASD 7.9.18; Rebuilt as H7214 14.10.18

D6606    1 AI to 208 Sqdn 17.5.18; Wrecked 29.8.18; 1 ASD 29.8.18; SOC 10.9.18

D6610    (130-hp Clerget) Deld 6.4.18; Shipped to Otranto 22.4.18; 226 Sqdn by 25.5.18 - @8.18; 472/4 Flts 226 Sqdn by 8.18 - @1.19

D6612    (130-hp Clerget) Deld 6.4.18; Shipped to Mudros 20.4.18; Repair Base Mudros by 6.18; 220 Sqdn Imbros by 10.18

D6614    (130-hp Clerget) Deld 6.4.18; Shipped to Otranto 22.4.18; 226 Sqdn by 25.5.18 - @10.18; Taranto by 10.18 - @1.19 (226 Sqdn?)

D6616    (130-hp Clerget) Deld 6.4.18; Shipped to Otranto 22.4.18; 226 Sqdn by 25.5.18 - @8.18; Taranto by 10.18 - @1.19

D6618    (130-hp Clerget) Deld 6.4.18; To docks 8.4.18; Shipped to Otranto 22.4.18; 226 Sqdn by 25.5.18 - 7.18; AD Taranto by 7.18 - @8.18

D6620    (130-hp Clerget) Deld 6.4.18; To docks 8.4.18; Shipped to Mudros 20.4.18; Stavros by 6.18

D6622    (130-hp Clerget) Deld 6.4.18; To docks 8.4.18; Shipped to Mudros 20.4.18; Imbros by 6.18

D6624    Dover by 27.4.18 - 5.18; 4 ASD by 25.5.18; 204 Sqdn 27.5.18; Fokker DVII in flames 5m N of Blankenberghe, another spun & collided with a 204 Sqdn m/c (probably D6359) & both fell together S of Blankenberghe 14.45 30.6.18 (Capt AJ Enstone); Attacked 3 seaplanes off Middelkeke, Brandenburg W12 crashed in sea 10m N of Blankenberghe 11.20 1.7.18 (Capt AJ Enstone); Shot down in sea 12.8.18 (Lt RAG Hill wounded); Deleted 15.9.18

D6626    (BR.1) Deld 4 AAP Lincoln by 27.4.18; AAP Dover W/E 4.5.18; 4 ASD by 25.5.18; 204 Sqdn 27.5.18; Fokker DVII crashed in flames Roulers 11.15 31.7.18 (Lt SA Robinson); COL 31.7.18 (Lt SA Robinson unhurt); To 4 ASD; 204 Sqdn 15.9.18; Fokker DVII down smoking Blankenberghe & another DD 10.50 26.9.18; Fokker DVII crashed NW of Wercken 12.25 28.9.18; Rumpler C white fin and rudder crashed E of Lichtervelde 16.30 1.10.18 (all Capt CRR Hickey DFC); Collided with D8188 at 12,000ft over Nieuport after diving through cloud and both fell SW of Ramscapelle 3.10.18 (Capt CRR Hickey killed); Remains to 4 ASD 4.10.18; Deleted 15.10.18 DBR

D6628    Rec Pk to 1 AI 20.5.18; 208 Sqdn 24.5.18; Engine trouble, COL 6.7.18 (Lt LC Gilmour); 1 AD 10.7.18; Rebuilt as F6304 26.7.18

D6634    (Clerget) 1 AI to 208 Sqdn 24.5.18; Hannover C dest

Oppy 09.05 16.8.18 (Lt WEG Mann); 1 ASD 25.8.18 (unfit for further service); Flown to England 1.9.18

D6638    Presentation a/c 'British Residents in Siam'. Deld 3 AAP Norwich 19.4.18; 70 Sqdn; 1 AI to 208 Sqdn 29.5.18; In combat (no details), with C8285, 08.35-10.10 patrol 29.7.18 (Lt GA Wightman); Crashed 15.9.18 (2/Lt EMunro); Wrecked, to 1 ASD 17.9.18; Rebuilt as H7237 5.11.18

D6698    1 AI to 208 Sqdn 24.5.18; Fokker DrI OOC Merville, shared D1854, D1889 & D1923 11.10 31.5.18; Albatros shot down N of Lestrem, shared D1853, D1879 & D1889 12.15 & another OOC Merville-Estaires 12.20 2.6.18 (Lt RL Johns); COL 11.6.18 (Lt RL Johns killed); SOC 11.6.18

**13 AVRO 504K TRACTOR BIPLANE TRAINERS from bnatch D7051 to D7200 built by Hewlett & Blondeau Ltd at Leagrave. (130-hp Clerget 9B)**

D7073    204 TDS Eastchurch by 6.18
D7086    Grand Fleet SoAF&G Leuchars by 7.19
D7089    201 TDS East Fortune, propeller accident 27.11.18 (3AM W Highet injured)
D7091    56 TDS Cranwell by 8.18
D7092    56 TDS Cranwell by 8.18
D7093    56 TDS Cranwell by 8.18
D7096    55 TDS Manston by 8.18 - @9.18
D7097    Eastchurch to 55 TDS Manston 9.8.18
D7098    55 TDS Manston by 8.18; 55 TDS Narborough 11.9.18 - @2.19
D7099    55 TDS Manston by 9.18; 55 TDS Narborough 11.9.18
D7189    MAES Grain by 8.20 - @9.20
D7197    Pool of Pilots by 10.18 - @3.19
D7199    Pool of Pilots by 10.18 - @3.19; Dover by 18.6.19

**14 AIRCO D.H.9 TRACTOR BIPLANE BOMBERS from batch D7201 to D7300 built at Westland Aircraft Works, Yeovil. (230-hp B.H.P.)**

D7204    Deld 5 AAP Filton by 17.5.18; Rec Pk to 1 AI 12.6.18; 211 Sqdn (coded 'J') 16.6.18; Badly shot up 26.6.18 (Lt HN Lett & Pte2 HW Newsham); Hit by AA over Bruges Docks, FL Zuidzande, Zeeland 24.8.18 (Lt JA Dear & 2/Lt JFJ Peters both interned); SOC 24.8.18

D7211    Shipped to Mudros 18.5.18; Repair Base Mudros by 6.18 & 10.18 - @1.19; H.2 Flt RHNAS Thasos/Stavros by 10.10.18 - @2.11.18

D7212    Shipped to Mudros 18.5.18; Repair Base Mudros by 6.18

D7213    Deld 6 SD Ascot W/E 25.5.18; Shipped to Mudros 15.6.18; Aegean Group, FL and captured 17.10.18 (Lt W Bamber & Lt KG Withers both PoWs)

D7214    Deld 6 SD Ascot W/E 25.5.18; Shipped to Mudros 15.6.18; Stavros by 19.8.18 - @1.19; Crashed 5.11.18 (2/Lt RC Morrison & 2/Lt JR Barrett)

D7239    Bristol to AAP Dover 7.6.18; 4 ASD Audembert 7.6.18; 218 Sqdn 6.18; COL from raid 26.6.18 (Lt JA Pugh & 2/Lt MG Wilson unhurt); 4 ASD by 10.18; 2 SS Richborough 2.10.18

D7240    Bristol to AAP Dover 7.6.18; 218 Sqdn by 30.6.18; Returning from raid, crashed nr Calais, engines damaged 19.7.18 (Lt HP Brumell & Sgt RS Joysey); Crashed on beach nr Calais after raid, badly damaged 29.8.18 (Lt HP Brumell & 2/Lt G Gedge); To 4 ASD; 2 SS Richborough 2.10.18

D7241    Bristol to AAP Dover 7.6.18; 218 Sqdn by 5.7.18; HA in flames, shared formation 18.25 5.7.18 (Lt GWE Hanmer & Sgt AE Powell); Hit by D1691 overshooting, badly damaged 1.8.18; 4 ASD 3.8.18; 491 Flt 233 Sqdn Dover by 8.10.18; 4 ASD 13.10.18; 218 Sqdn 21.10.18; Returning from bombing raid, FL, crashed Bisseghem 9.11.18 (2/Lt CM Arias & Sgt RG Pearce unhurt); to 2 ASD

D7242    Bristol to AAP Dover 12.6.18; 4 ASD Audembert 13.6.18; 218 Sqdn by 2.7.18; Probably accounted for the Pfalz DIII OOC 2.7.18 (Lt H Fawdry & 2/Lt JS Cryan); Albatros crashed 2/3m N of Nieuport 18.35 5.7.18 (Lt H Fawdry & 2/Lt JS Cryan); Pfalz DIII OOC Ghistelles aerodrome 13.25 15.8.18 (Lt HP Brumell & Sgt RS Joysey); 4 ASD 20.10.18 - @25.10.18 (overhaul, time expired)

D7243    Bristol to AAP Dover 12.6.18; 491 Flt Dover 16.6.18; EF, FL Maidstone 31.7.18; Became 491 Flt 233 Sqdn Dover 31.8.18 - @16.12.18

D7245    Bristol to AAP Dover 13.6.18; 491 Flt Dover 16.6.18; Landed on rough ground at edge of aerodrome, u/c wrecked, wings damaged 18.8.18 (Lt LG Sullivan unhurt); To ARS Guston Road; 491 Flt 233 Sqdn Dover by 9.18; 218 Sqdn loan 24.9.18; Tested 491 Flt 26.9.18; Retd 218 Sqdn by 1.19; 98 Sqdn 21.1.19; Retd UK 15.2.19

D7246    Bristol to AAP Dover 13.6.18; 491 Flt Dover 16.6.18; En route to Lee-on-Solent, EF, FL in sea 3m SE of Folkestone, badly damaged by fire 9.8.18 (Lt DL Melvin & Lt GL Comba both rescued) AND/OR EF, FL in sea and sank 8m SW of Beachy Head 25.8.18 (Lt DL Melvin & Lt GL Comba picked up unhurt by HMS *Orion*); WOC 5.9.18

D7248    Bristol to AAP Dover 13.6.18; 491 Flt Dover 16.6.18 (233 Sqdn 31.8.18); 218 Sqdn 29.9.18; Returning from raid, EF, FL in sea off Ostende, sank 18.10.18 (2/Lt MJ Carroll & Sgt AJ Oliver both unhurt); Deleted 31.10.18

D7250    Deld 3 AAP Norwich 6.18; Lympne (via AAP Dover) 18.6.18; SOC 1 ASD 6.7.18 NWR

**11 AIRCO D.H.9 TRACTOR BIPLANE BOMBERS from batch D7301 to D7400 built by F.W.Berwick & Co Ltd, London. (240-hp B.H.P.)**

D7308    Prawle Point by 30.11.18; 14 TDS Lake Down 18.12.18
D7315    Rec Pk to 1 AI 28.7.18; 206 Sqdn 30.7.18; Left 08.55, FTR 12.8.18 (Lt JC Ivens & 2/Lt CA Atkins PoWs); SOC in field 14.8.18; Salvaged in No Mans Land by 103 Sqdn 7.9.18; SOC 7.9.18
D7322    Rec Pk to 1 AI 11.8.18; 206 Sqdn 11.8.18; Badly shot up by AA fire Armentières 29.8.18 (Lt CL Cumming unhurt & 2/Lt B Knee slightly wounded); 1 ASD 31.8.18; SOC 2.9.18
D7338    1 AI to 211 Sqdn 16.9.18; Left aileron shot away by HA, FL outside aerodrome, hit bump, o/t 29.9.18 (2/Lt JM Payne & Lt WG Gadd); 1 ASD 29.9.18
D7358    6 AI to 211 Sqdn 9.12.18; to 98 Sqdn 26.2.19; 1 ASD 5.3.19
D7362    Rec Pk to 1 AI 29.9.18; 211 Sqdn 30.9.18; Left 09.45, hit by AA, seen to land in enemy territory SW of Charleroi 10.11.18 (2/Lt HC Thomas & 2/Lt JHR Smith both killed)
D7368    557/8 Flts 212 Sqdn Yarmouth by 15.10.18 - @31.10.18
D7369    Rec Pk to 1 AI by 10.18; 211 Sqdn (coded 'V') 7.10.18 but FL Petite Synthe en route; Thick mist, landed Boussières, crashed 30.11.18 (Lt DF Taber & 2/Lt JM McLellan both unhurt) (for 1 ASD); 7 SS Behain 1.12.18
D7372    3 FS Sedgeford by 3.19; 206 Sqdn by 5.19
D7373    2 ASD to 218 Sqdn 14.11.18; Stalled on landing 9.12.18 (2/Lt MJ Carroll & 2/Lt James both unhurt); to 2 ASD; SOC 16.12.18
D7380    206 Sqdn, flying accident 14.5.19 (2/Lt SH Gibbs DoI & Sgt A Page killed)

**57 AVRO 504J (100-hp Gnôme Monosoupape) & 504K (110-hp Le Rhône) TRACTOR BIPLANE TRAINERS from batch D7501 to D7800 built by parent company at Manchester**

D7392    208 TDS Eastchurch, WO 25.7.18
D7511    (504J) Deld Cranwell by road for expts W/E 8.3.18; 2 AAP Hendon (via Chingford) 20.3.18 - @25.5.18 (for use of Air Dept officers)
D7512    (504J) Deld RNASTE Vendôme W/E 30.3.18; Became 205 TDS Vendôme 1.4.18; ARS 84 Wing Vendôme by 30.11.18
D7513    (504J) Deld RNASTE Vendôme W/E 30.3.18; Became 205 TDS Vendôme 1.4.18; 212 TDS Vendôme 5.18 - @10.18; COL 13.8.18 (PFO FB Candy & Capt PH Martin); ARS 84 Wing Vendôme by 30.11.18
D7514    (504J) Deld RNASTE Vendôme W/E 303.18; Became 205 TDS Vendôme 1.4.18; 212 TDS Vendôme 5.18 - @10.18; Hit ridge landing, badly damaged 4.9.18 (F/Cdt AH Murphy & Lt GR Hake unhurt)
D7515    (504J) Deld RNASTE Vendôme W/E 30.3.18; Became 205 TDS Vendôme 1.4.18; ARS 84 Wing Vendôme by 11.18

D7516 (504J) Deld 205 TDS Vendôme W/E 30.3.18; ARS 84 Wing Vendôme by 11.18

D7527 (504J) Deld 205 TDS Vendôme W/E 30.3.18; 212 TDS Vendôme, mid-air collision with Caudron "6265", badly damaged 30.7.18 (Lt TC Beeken & Lt FW Wright); ARS 84 Wing Vendôme by 11.18

D7528 (504J) Deld RNASTE Vendôme W/E 30.3.18; Became 205 TDS Vendôme 1.4.18; 212 TDS Vendôme, badly damaged 5.7.18 (Lt AD Reid); contd post-war

D7529 (504J) Deld RNASTE Vendôme W/E 30.3.18; Became 205 TDS Vendôme 1.4.18; Crashed 16.10.18 (F/Cdt WH Palmer unhurt); ARS 84 Wing Vendôme by 11.18

D7530 (504J) Deld RNASTE Vendôme W/E 30.3.18; Became 205 TDS Vendôme 1.4.18; 212 TDS Vendôme by 6.18 - @10.18; Landed in pit, damaged u/c, St.Amand 28.6.18 (Lt GR Hake); ARS 84 Wing Vendôme by 11.18

D7533 (504J) Deld Redcar School W/E 30.3.18; Became SoSF Redcar 1.4.18; Became 2 SoSF Redcar 5.18; Became NE Area FIS Redcar 1.7.18 - @24.3.19; contd post-war

D7536 (504J) Deld Redcar School W/E 30.3.18; Became SoSF Redcar 1.4.18; Became 2 SoSF Redcar 5.18; Became NE Area FIS Redcar 1.7.18 - @2.19; contd post-war

D7539 (504J) Deld Redcar School W/E 30.3.18; Became SoSF Redcar 1.4.18; Became 2 SoSF Redcar 5.18; Became NE Area FIS Redcar 1.7.18 - @5.3.19

D7541 (504J) Deld 205 TDS Vendôme W/E 30.3.18; Crashed 25.8.18 (2/Lt HF Fleming); Crashed 27.10.18 (F/Cdt F Fraser unhurt); ARS 84 Wing Vendôme by 11.18

D7542 (504J) Deld 205 TDS Vendôme W/E 30.3.18; ARS 84 Wing Vendôme by 11.18; contd post-war

D7543 (504J) Deld Redcar School W/E 23.3.18; Became SoSF Redcar 1.4.18; Became 2 SoSF Redcar 5.18 - @6.18; contd post-war

D7544 (504J) Deld Redcar School W/E 30.3.18; Became SoSF Redcar 1.4.18; Became 2 SoSF Redcar 5.18; Became NE Area FIS Redcar 1.7.18 - @19.9.18

D7545 (504J) Deld Eastbourne NFS W/E 30.3.18; Became 206 TDS Eastbourne 1.4.18; Became 50 TDS Eastbourne 15.7.18; COL, wrecked 13.8.18 (pilot unhurt)

D7546 (504J) Deld Eastbourne NFS W/E 30.3.18; Became 206 TDS Eastbourne 1.4.18 - @17.5.18

D7547 (504J) Deld Eastbourne NFS W/E 30.3.18; Became 206 TDS Eastbourne 1.4.18; Stalled and spun in from 150ft 13.5.18 (2/Lt AM Broad injured)

D7548 (504J) Deld Eastbourne NFS W/E 30.3.18; Became 206 TDS Eastbourne 1.4.18 - @7.18

D7549 (504J) Deld Eastbourne NFS W/E 30.3.18; Became 206 TDS Eastbourne 1.4.18; Crashed & WO 22.4.18

D7550 (504J) Deld Eastbourne NFS W/E 30.3.18; Became 206 TDS Eastbourne 1.4.18; Crashed and wrecked 27.7.18 (pilot unhurt)

D7574 (504K) (110-hp Le Rhône) Deld 201/2 TDS Cranwell by road 4.18 - @5.18

D7575 (504K) (110-hp Le Rhône) Deld 201/2 TDS Cranwell by road 4.18

D7581 (504J) (110-hp Le Rhône) Deld 201/2 TDS Cranwell 4.18 - @5.7.18

D7582 (504J) (110-hp Le Rhône) Deld ex Brooklands to Hendon 26.1.18; Deld Avro to Cranwell 28.3.18; 24 Sqdn to Croydon for DofR 1.7.19; Air Council Inspection Sqdn 22.8.19

D7588 (504J) (110-hp Le Rhône) Deld Cranwell 28.3.18; Became 201 TDS Cranwell 1.4.18; Became 56 TDS Cranwell 27.7.18 - @9.18; To G-EADQ; Became Irish Air Corps VI

D7589 (504J) (110-hp Le Rhône) Deld Cranwell 28.3.18; Became 201 TDS Cranwell 1.4.18; Became 56 TDS Cranwell 27.7.18 - @11.18

D7595 (504J) (110-hp Le Rhône) Deld Cranwell 28.3.18

D7596 (504J) (110-hp Le Rhône) Deld Cranwell 28.3.18; Became 201 TDS Cranwell 1.4.18; Became 56 TDS Cranwell 27.7.18 - @8.18; NE Area FIS Redcar 8.18

D7617 (504K) Eastchurch

D7636 207 TDS Chingford by 2.6.18

D7643 2 SoSF Redcar by 5.18

D7651 RNAS Hendon by 3.18; Medical Flt Hendon 1.4.18 - @25.5.18

D7656 (504K) Deld Chingford W/E 23.3.18; Became 207 TDS Chingford 1.4.18

D7657 (504K) Deld Chingford W/E 23.3.18; Became 207 TDS Chingford 1.4.18; 207 TDS Fairlop, propeller accident 28.5.18 (Lt FBG Smith, MC DoI & 2/Lt C Homewood unhurt)

D7658 (504K) Deld Chingford W/E 23.3.18; Became 207 TDS Chingford 1.4.18 - @2.6.18

D7659 (504K) Deld Chingford W/E 23.3.18; Became 207 TDS Chingford 1.4.18

D7660 (504K) Deld Chingford W/E 23.3.18; Became 207 TDS Chingford 1.4.18 - @2.6.18; 54 TDS Fairlop, mid-air collision with Camel F2104 30.7.18 (2/Lt HB Hatcher & Sgt AB Bean both killed)

D7664 London Colney to Hendon 3.5.18; London Colney to Hendon W/E 1.6.18

D7676 (504J) Deld Redcar School W/E 23.3.18; NE Area FIS Redcar by 8.18 - @21.9.18

D7677 (504J) Deld Redcar School W/E 23.3.18; NE Area FIS Redcar by 8.18 - @13.12.18

D7678 (504J) Deld Redcar School W/E 23.3.18; NE Area FIS Redcar by 8.18 - @2.11.18

D7679 (504J) Deld Redcar School W/E 23.3.18; Became SoSF Redcar 1.4.18; Became 2 SoSF Redcar 5.18

D7680 (504J) Deld Redcar School W/E 23.3.18; Became SoSF Redcar 1.4.18; Became 2 SoSF Redcar 5.18; Became NE Area FIS Redcar 1.7.18 - @24.9.18

D7707 (504J) (100-hp Monosoupape) Deld Eastchurch by road W/E 30.3.18; Became 204 TDS Eastchurch 1.4.18; Stalled at 25ft and dived to earth 31.5.18 (2/Lt WM Sinclair slightly injured)

D7708 (504J) (100-hp Monosoupape) Deld Eastchurch by road W/E 30.3.18; Became 204 TDS 1.4.18

D7709 (504J) (100-hp Monosoupape) Deld Eastchurch by road W/E 30.3.18; Became 204 TDS 1.4.18 - @6.18

D7710 (504J) (100-hp Monosoupape) Deld Eastchurch by road W/E 30.3.18; Became 204 TDS 1.4.18 - @7.18

D7726 (504J) (100-hp Monosoupape) Deld Cranwell by road W/E 30.3.18; Became 201 TDS Cranwell 1.4.18; Became 56 TDS Cranwell 27.7.18 - @2.19

D7727 (504J) (100-hp Monosoupape) Deld Cranwell by road W/E 30.3.18; Became 201 TDS Cranwell 1.4.18 - @5.18

D7728 (504J) (100-hp Monosoupape) Deld Cranwell by road W/E 30.3.18; Became 201 TDS Cranwell 1.4.18; Became 56 TDS Cranwell 27.7.18 - @11.18

D7729 (504J) (100-hp Monosoupape) Deld Cranwell by road W/E 30.3.18; Became 201 TDS Cranwell 1.4.18 - @5.18

D7730 (504J) (100-hp Monosoupape) Deld Cranwell by road W/E 30.3.18; Became 201 TDS Cranwell 1.4.18; Became 56 TDS Cranwell 27.7.18

D7756 (504J) 50 TDS Eastbourne by 7.18; 93 Sqdn 1.8.18

**2 BRISTOL FIGHTER F.2b TRACTOR BIPLANES from batch D7801 to D8100 built by parent company**

D7859 Test Dept Grain from 9.19 (meteorological tests)

D7910 Grain by 9.18 (flotation gear & hydrovane); Floated off slipway 18.9.18, to be tested again off HMS *Slinger*

**48 SOPWITH F.1 CAMEL TRACTOR BIPLANE SCOUTS from batch D8101 to D8150 built by Ruston, Proctor & Co Ltd at Lincoln. (130-hp Clerget LS)**

D8115 1 AI to 208 Sqdn 7.7.18; DFW C OOC Merville 7.30-08.30 patrol 28.7.18; Pfalz DIII OOC Estaires 09.30 31.7.18 (both Lt EG Johnstone DSC); Lost wheel on TO, on nose landing 31.7.18 (Lt EG Johnstone DSC unhurt); 1 ASD 1.8.18; Rebuilt as F6332 16.8.18, later changed to H7001

D8130 51 TDS Shotwick by 8.18; Propeller accident 4.2.19 (Capt JH Tudhope slightly injured)

D8133 Tested Tadcaster 24.6.18, then to 4 AAP Lincoln; Dover, despatched 2.6.18 (sic)

D8137 Deld Devonport W/E 25.5.18; Shipped to Mudros 29.6.18; Mudros by 8.18 - @1.19 with RHNAS

D8138 Deld Devonport W/E 25.5.18; Shipped to Mudros 29.6.18; Imbros by 10.18

D8139 Deld Devonport W/E 25.5.18; Shipped to Mudros 29.6.18; 222 Sqdn Mudros by 27.10.18 - @31.10.18; Marsh by 10.18 - @1.19; RAF South Russia to 'A' Dett RAF Instructional Mission South Russia 8.19 - 12.19

D8140 Deld Devonport W/E 25.5.18; Shipped to Mudros

29.6.18; 222 Sqdn Mudros by 2.11.18; 220 Sqdn Imbros by 10.18 - @1.19; RAF South Russia to HQ Russian Aviation Corps 8.19

**D8141** Deld Devonport W/E 25.5.18; Shipped to Mudros 29.6.18; Repair Base Mudros by 10.18; 220 Sqdn Imbros by 27.10.18 - @2.11.18

**D8142** Deld Devonport W/E 25.5.18; Shipped to Mudros 29.6.18; 220 Sqdn Imbros by 27.10.18 - @1.19

**D8143** Deld 4 AAP Lincoln by 9.5.18; Rec Pk to 1 AI 1.6.18; 208 Sqdn 9.6.18; Undershot, crashed into hangars 18.7.18 (Lt AB Ollerenshaw unhurt); 1 AD 22.7.18; Rebuilt as F6320 in error 9.8.18, later changed to H6994

**D8144** Deld 4 AAP Lincoln by 10.5.18; 1 AI to 208 Sqdn 3.6.18; Fokker DrI OOC 2m E of La Bassée 19.40 7.7.18; Fokker DrI OOC Meurchin-Epinoy 07.50, then Pfalz DIII OOC Metalurgique Works 08.00 8.7.18; DFW C shot down Richebourg St.Vaast 11.50, then crashed 9.7.18; LVG C shot down Merville, shared D8149 & Lt WE Carveth c.11.45 16.7.18; 2-str OOC NE of La Bassée, shared D1845 & D8149 07.30 20.7.18; Axle broke on landing, o/t 2.8.18 (all Capt WL Jordan DSC DFC); SS 1 AD 3.8.18; Rebuilt as F6331 in error 16.8.18, later changed to H7288

**D8146** (140-hp Clerget) Deld 4 AAP Lincoln 5.18; Walmer store 5.18; 491 Flt Dover on/by 25.5.18; Walmer storage to 4 ASD (via AAP Dover) 16.6.18; 204 Sqdn 4.7.18; Fokker DVII bright red fuselage OOC NE of Ypres 19.00-19.30 31.7.18; 2 Fokker DVII in flames Hénin, 1 shared C74 19.05 15.8.18; White tailed Fokker DVII OOC Gheluvelt 11.50 3.9.18 (all Lt RMcI Gordon); Salmon Fokker DVII in sea off Zeebrugge Mole, shared F3922 14.00 15.9.18; Salmon Fokker DVII in flames Blankenberghe-Zeebrugge, shared D8183, D8187, D8188 & F3922 18.55-19.00 16.9.18 (both Lt FG Bayley); Spun in on TO, u/c collapsed, CW 3.10.18 (Lt HW Connop unhurt); 4 ASD 4.10.18; Deleted 15.10.18 general fatigue

**D8147** (140-hp Clerget) Deld 4 AAP Lincoln 5.18; Walmer store 5.18; 491 Flt Dover on/by 25.5.18; Walmer storage to AAP Dover 12.6.18; 4 ASD 6.18; 213 Sqdn 30.6.18; Propeller accident 18.7.18 (1AM HR Foden DoI 19.7.18); Swung and crashed starting for patrol 30.7.18 (Lt CP Sparkes unhurt); to 4 ASD; 210 Sqdn 7.9.18; Shot up, FL 24.9.18 (T/Capt SC Joseph DSC wounded) [credited Ltn Wilhelm, Marine Jasta 4]; M/c flying again 27.9.18; Fokker DVII crashed 1m W of Lichtervelde 07.55 29.9.18; Fokker DVII OOC Roulers 17.10 1.10.18 (all Lt WS Jenkins); Landed in main square of Ostende, first "Englishman" into town after Germans left 11.45 17.10.18 (Lt A Buchanan); 1 AD 16.1.19 (surplus)

**D8149** (Clerget LS) Deld 4 AAP Lincoln by 14.5.18; 1 AI by 6.18; 208 Sqdn 12.6.18; LVG C shot down Merville, shared D8144 & Lt WE Carveth c.11.45 16.7.18; 2-str OOC NE of La Bassée, shared D1845 & D8144 07.30 20.7.18 (both Lt PC Richards); Fokker DVII OOC 3.10.18 (2/Lt HJ Philp); 2 AI 9.10.18 (rebuild, fit to cross Channel); Rep Pk 2 ASD 26.10.18

**D8154** Deld 6 SD Ascot by 25.5.18; Shipped to Mudros 12.6.18; Imbros by 10.18 - @1.19 (220 Sqdn?); To White Russians 1919

**D8155** Deld 6 SD Ascot by 25.5.18; Shipped to Mudros 12.6.18; Repair Base Imbros by 8.18; 220 Sqdn Imbros by 10.18?; Mudros by 10.18 - @1.19, with Greeks

**D8156** Deld 6 SD Ascot by 25.5.18; Shipped to Mudros 12.6.18; Repair Base Mudros by 10.18 - @11.18

**D8157** Deld 6 SD Ascot by 25.5.18; Shipped to Mudros 12.6.18

**D8162** (Clerget LS) Deld 4 AAP Lincoln by 15.5.18; Rec Pk to 1 AI 29.7.18; 208 Sqdn 3.8.18; LVG C OOC 1½m NE of Pacaut Wood 12.20 12.8.18 (Capt WL Jordan DSC DFC); HA shot down 6.9.18 (2/Lt RE Goodfellow); COL 7.9.18 (2/Lt E Jackson unhurt); 1 ASD 7.9.18; Rebuilt as H7215 14.10.18

**D8166** (Clerget LS) Deld 4 AAP Lincoln by 17.5.18; Rec Pk to 1 AI 4.8.18; 148th Aero Sqdn; Rep Pk 1 ASD by 10.18; 2 AI by 29.10.18; 201 Sqdn 17.12.18; 203 Sqdn 23.1.19

**D8168** (Clerget LS) Deld 4 AAP Lincoln by 18.5.18; 1 AI by 8.18; 208 Sqdn 1.8.18; DFW C OOC E of Oppy, shared B7769, D1923 & F5933 06.00 14.8.18; Fokker DVII on fire Arras-Cambrai road 18.30 6.9.18 (both Capt JB

White); Left 14.00, engaged by HA, FL Villechottes, wrecked 26.9.18 (Hon Capt A Storey wounded); 2 ASD 29.9.18, 208 Sqdn by 3.10.18 - @4.11.18

**D8177** (140-hp Clerget LS) Deld 4 AAP Lincoln 5.18; Walmer 5.18; 491 Flt Dover on/by 25.5.18; Walmer storage to AAP Dover 12.6.18; 4 ASD Guines 16.6.18; 213 Sqdn 30.6.18; Fokker DVII in flames, crashed Ostende, shared D9649, but probably only D8177 09.25 14.7.18 (Lt CP Brown); Fokker DVII smoking nr Varssenaere 10.45 20.9.18 (Lt DS Ingalls USNRF); Fokker DVII wings folded up, crashed & another dived and crashed into trees 1m SW of Thourout 14.45 24.9.18; Fokker DVII spinning OOC E of Roulers 12.00 29.9.18; Fokker DVII in flames and 2 more crashed nr Rumbeke 09.30 4.10.18 (all Capt CP Brown); Last seen under attack by 17 Fokker DVII Pervyse 14.30 14.10.18 (2/Lt FRL Allen killed)(now BR.1)

**D8179** (Clerget L-S) Deld 4 AAP Lincoln 5.18; 491 Flt Dover 25.5.18; AAP Dover to 471 Flt Walmer 16.6.18 (233 Sqdn 31.8.18); 11 AP 23.2.19; WOC 23.2.19

**D8180** Deld 4 AAP Lincoln 5.18; 471 Flt 233 Sqdn Dover by 31.7.18; Dunkerque by 31.8.18; 148th Aero Sqdn (coded 'S'), crashed 16.9.18 (Lt Moore)

**D8181** Deld 4 AAP Lincoln 5.18; Walmer store 27.5.18; 471 Flt Walmer 16.6.18; EF, FL 1m W of Deal 29.7.18 (Capt RM Keirstead); Became 471 Flt 233 Sqdn Walmer 31.8.18 - @13.10.18

**D8182** (140-hp Clerget) Deld 4 AAP Lincoln 5.18; 491 Flt Dover 25.5.18; Walmer storage to AAP Dover 12.6.18; 4 ASD Guines 16.6.18; 204 Sqdn 4.7.18; Shot down by ground m/g fire after combat with 10 Fokker DVII over Roulers 31.7.18 (Lt J Farquhar DoW 1.8.18)

**D8183** (BR.1) Deld 4 AAP Lincoln 5.18; 471 Flt Walmer 25.5.18; Depot to 204 Sqdn 31.8.18; See D8187 16.9.18 (2/Lt JR Chisman); Spun in from 150 ft on TO 24.10.18 (2/Lt JWG Price injured); Wreckage to 1 ASD, SOC in field

**D8185** Deld 4 AAP Lincoln 5.18; Walmer storage by on/25.5.18; 471 Flt Walmer 16.6.18; O/t by wind taxying after landing 24.7.18 (Lt JW Mackenzie); Guston Rd repair 24.7.18; 471 Flt Walmer 19.8.18; Became 471 Flt 233 Sqdn Walmer 31.8.18 - @13.10.18; Dover 10.18; 471 Flt 233 Sqdn Walmer 30.10.18; 11 AP 21.2.19 by road

**D8186** Deld 4 AAP Lincoln 5.18; 471 Flt Walmer on/by 25.5.18; Walmer storage by 6.18; AAP Dover 12.6.18; 4 ASD Audembert 21.6.18; Tested 24.9.18; 204 Sqdn, In action 28.9.18 (Lt RMcI Gordon wounded)

**D8187** Deld 4 AAP Lincoln 5.18; 471 Flt Walmer on/by 25.5.18; Dover, despatched 2.6.18; 4 ASD to 204 Sqdn 1.8.18; Fokker DVII OOC 5m E of Dixmude, shared C74 11.00 14.8.18; (Lt HH Blanchard); 2 Fokker DVII in sea Blankenberghe-Zeebrugge, 1st one shared D8146, D8183, D8188 & F3942 18.55-19.00 16.9.18 (Lt RM Bennett); Crashed after TO 17.9.18 (Lt RM Bennett); Last seen behind formation returning in heavy rain nr Ypres 29.9.18 (Lt RM Bennett killed) [credited Flgm Pfeiffer, Marine Jasta 3 at Woumen 18.15]

**D8188** Deld 4 AAP Lincoln 5.18; 491 Flt Dover on/by 25.5.18; Walmer storage to AAP Dover 12.6.18; 4 ASD Audembert 21.6.18; 204 Sqdn 16.8.18; Fokker DVII OOC Blankenberghe-Zeebrugge, shared D8146, D8183, D8187 & F3942 18.55-19.00 16.9.18 (2/Lt N Smith); Fokker DVII OOC Blankenberghe 10.50 26.9.18 (both 2/Lt SE Matthey); Collided with D6626 at 12,000ft over Nieuport, both fell SW of Ramscapelle 3.10.18 (2/Lt SE Matthey killed); Remains to 4 ASD 4.10.18; Deleted 15.10.18 DBR

**D8189** Deld 4 AAP Lincoln 5.18; 471 Flt Walmer on/by 25.5.18; Rec Pk to 1 AI 8.6.18; ?? Sqdn, crashed into wood in Belgium 7.18; 4 ASD by 8.18; 213 Sqdn 9.8.18; Albatros C OOC 3m ESE of Dixmude, shared B7252, D3409 & D9664 19.40 11.8.18; Fokker DVII into sea 2m NW of Zeebrugge, pilot baled out but parachute failed to open 19.15 21.8.18; Fokker DVII OOC 6m ENE of Dixmude, shared B7252, D8217 & D9678 14.25 23.9.18; Fokker DVII OOC 4m W of Thourout 17.45 25.9.18; Fokker DVII OOC, FL in Houthulst Forest 1.10.18 (all Lt WE Gray); Then crashed Houthulst Forest, unable to salve 1.10.18 (Lt WE Gray unhurt); Deleted 15.10.18

| | |
|---|---|
| D8190 | Deld 4 AAP Lincoln 5.18; 491 Flt Dover on/by 25.5.18; Walmer store to 471 Flt 233 Sqdn Walmer 16.6.18 - @30.10.18; 11 AP by 1.19; SOC 23.1.19 |
| D8191 | Deld 4 AAP Lincoln 5.18; 471 Flt Walmer on/by 25.5.18; 4 ASD by 25.10.18 |
| D8192 | Rec Pk to 2 ASD 6.6.18; 43 Sqdn by 8.18; 2 ASD 30.8.18; Rec Pk 4.9.18; 1 AI 7.9.18; 208 Sqdn 12.9.18 [& @29.9.18]; 4 ASD by 9.18; 208 Sqdn?, HA shot down 25.10.18 (2/Lt PFT Luckham); 2 AI 3.11.18 |
| D8205 | 4 ASD to 204 Sqdn 16.8.18; Fokker DVII OOC Blankenberghe-Zeebrugge 19.00 16.9.18 (2/Lt CL Kelly); Last seen in flight combat 5m NE of Dixmude 20.9.18 (2/Lt CL Kelly killed) [credited Ltn Osterkamp, Marine Jasta 2]; Deleted 30.9.18 |
| D8216 | 4 ASD to 213 Sqdn 17.7.18; Albatros DV OOC 3m SW of Ostende 12.05 30.7.18 (Capt JW Pinder); Pfalz DIII OOC Dixmude 10.50 13.8.18 (Lt GC Mackay); Last seen when patrol attacked by 7 Fokker DVII 3m W of Thourout 25.9.18 (Lt LC Scroggie killed) [credited LtzS Achilles, Marine Jasta 5 at Hooglede 17.50]; Deleted 15.10.18 |
| D8217 | (BR.1) 4 ASD by 7.18; 213 Sqdn 29.7.18; Fokker DVII OOC 6m ENE of Dixmude, shared B7252, D8189 & D9678 14.25 23.9.18 (Lt MN Hancocks); Damaged by enemy fire, FL les Möeres 28.9.18 (Lt MN Hancocks); Rep Pk 4 ASD by 10.18; 69 AP 26.10.18; 471 Flt Walmer to 11 AP 22.2.19; WOC 22.2.19 |
| D8218 | (BR.1) Lympne to 4 ASD Audembert 11.8.18; 204 Sqdn 25.9.18; Crashed escorting bombing scouts, FL, CW Wolsten 28.9.18 (2/Lt FR Brown severely injured); 4 ASD by 25.10.18; 213 Sqdn 30.10.18; LVG C crashed 7m SE of Ghent, shared D9648, D9675 & F8505 10.40 10.11.18 (Lt AB Rosevear); 11 AP 23.2.19; WOC 23.2.19 |
| D8219 | (BR.1) 4 ASD by 22.7.18; 204 Sqdn 24.7.18; Crashed on TO 8.8.18 (Lt WB Craig unhurt); 4 ASD 8.8.18; 213 Sqdn 28.9.18; Badly shot up 1.10.18 (Capt JR Swanston); 4 ASD 3.10.18; 210 Sqdn by 23.10.18; DFW C crashed Merbes le Chateau 08.40 10.11.18; Fokker DVII crashed E of Binche 13.15 10.11.18 (both Lt WS Jenkins); 2 ASD 19.1.19 (surplus) |
| D8220 | (BR.1) 4 ASD to 213 Sqdn 31.7.18; Fokker DVII ailerons shot away 2m N of Wenduyne 15.50 11.8.18; Fokker DVII crashed & burnt Ouckene 18.45 5.9.18; Caught by gust after landing, o/t 28.9.18 (all Capt JR Swanston); To 4 ASD; 213 Sqdn 25.10.18; 11 AP 24.2.19; WOC 24.2.19 |
| D8221 | 4 ASD to 204 Sqdn 13.8.18; Shot down by ground m/g fire Nieuport-Dixmude, crashed, CW nr Nieuport 15.9.18 (Lt RE Hodgson killed); Wreckage to 4 ASD 15.9.18; 210 Sqdn 14.10.18; Damaged 14.1.19; Started rebuilding but RTP by 24.1.19; Produce to 2 AD 30.1.19 |
| D8222 | 4 ASD to 204 Sqdn 3.8.18; Fokker DVII OOC Menin 19.05 15.8.18; Fokker DVII white fin and wheels OOC Pervyse 18.50 24.9.18 (Lt CP Allen); COL, wrecked 17.10.18 (2/Lt S Barker unhurt); 4 ASD 19.10.18 - @25.10.18 |
| D8223 | 4 ASD to 204 Sqdn 1.8.18; Fokker DVII OOC Menin 19.05 15.8.18 (Lt WJP Jenner); In action 3.10.18 (Lt WJP Jenner wounded); Missing after sqdn attacked by 12 HA nr Termande 23.10.18 (Sgt CMA Mahon killed) |
| D8224 | 4 ASD to 213 Sqdn 31.7.18; Lost wheel on TO, COL, badly damaged 21.8.18 (Lt WG Upton unhurt); To 4 ASD to at least 25.10.18 |
| D8231 | 4 Sqdn AFC; Grand Fleet SoAF&G Leuchars by 8.18 - @1.19 |
| D8234 | Grand Fleet SoAF&G Leuchars by 10.18; Stalled and spun in 18.1.19 (2/Lt CT Dempsey injured) |
| D8247 | 1 AI to 208 Sqdn 1.7.18 - @31.10.18 |

## 2 AVRO 504K TRACTOR BIPLANE TRAINERS from batch D8251 to D8300 built by parent company at Manchester.

| | |
|---|---|
| D8253 | (504K) 2 MOS Eastchurch by 3.19 - @7.19 |
| D8285 | Deld Eastbourne 14.7.18 |

## 9 HANDLEY PAGE O/400 TRACTOR BIPLANE HEAVY BOMBERS from batch D8302 to D8350 built by parent company at Cricklewood. (Eagle VIII)

| | |
|---|---|
| D8305 | UK to Rec Pk 20.9.18; 3 ASD 24.9.18 (arr 25.9.18); 215 Sqdn 26.9.18; En route Xaffévillers to Alquines, EF, FL in thick mist, collided with farm buildings nr St.Pol 30.11.18 (Lt JA Philips unhurt, Lt AVW Church DoI 1.12.18, Cpl RJ Forward unhurt & 3AM W Wellard unhurt); 2 ASD 1.12.18 |
| D8307 | UK to Rec Pk 28.8.18; 3 ASD 29.8.18; 215 Sqdn 4.9.18; Wrecked landing after raid on Morhange aerodrome 6.11.18 (Lt JB Baldie killed; 2/Lt RO Hughes & 2/Lt H Ricketts shaken); 3 AD 6.11.18 |
| D8309 | Hendon to Rec Pk 13.9.18; 3 ASD 18.9.18 (arr 19.9.18); 216 Sqdn 21.9.18 - @2.19; Dropped 1,650-lb SN bomb on Metz 23.10.18 |
| D8311 | UK to Rec Pk 27.9.18; 3 ASD 27.9.18 (arr 29.9.18); 215 Sqdn 1.10.18; 97 Sqdn 17.1.19 - @31.1.19 |
| D8315 | UK to Rec Pk 13.10.18; 3 AD 17.10.18 (slightly damaged landing); 97 Sqdn 2.11.18; 216 Sqdn 17.12.18; 4 ASD to fit as mail carrier, retd 216 Sqdn 14.1.19; While carrying mail, crashed in snowstorm at La Lacque, S of St.Omer 5.2.19 (Lt JHV Wood & Lt IB Boyce both unhurt); SOC 5.2.19 |
| D8317 | 207 Sqdn by 9.11.18 - @11.11.18; Istres by 13.8.19; At St.Raphael 13.9.19 (214 Sqdn); En route to 216 Sqdn Egypt crashed Valona 27.11.19 |
| D8319 | UK to Rec Pk 23.10.18; St.Inglevert for store 27.10.18; 3 ASD 30.10.18; 100 Sqdn 13.11.18; 216 Sqdn 28.1.19; Crashed into hedge while landing Ans aerodrome 9.4.19 (Lt SH Griffiths & Lt AC Taylor unhurt); to 2 ELG Ans for ASD |
| D8321 | UK to Rec Pk 29.10.18; 3 AD 30.10.18; 215 Sqdn 6.11.18; EF, FL, Wrecked Attainville, nr Paris 29.11.18 (Lt SH Griffiths unhurt, 2/Lt DF Harrison, Cpl Smith, AM Hinder & AM Smith all unhurt); SOC 29.11.18; Collected by Le Bourget 30.11.18; SOC in field |
| D8323 | UK to Rec Pk 9.11.18; 207 Sqdn 13.11.18; Permission to be SOS 15.1.19, to be salved by a convenient SS, but rebuilt; With 214 Sqdn (Named 'IVY' on nose after Dell's wife, with ivy leaf insignia) to Buc 6.7.19 for Egypt; Tyre burst landing in heat at Marseilles 10.7.19; Pisa 13.7.19; Rome 14.7.19; Taranto 18.7.19; To Crete but FL on beach nr Armyro 22.7.19; Suda Bay 24.7.19; Mersa Matruh 26.7.19; Heliopolis 28.7.19; Abu Sueir 29.7.19; Still 214 Sqdn 31.12.19 |

## 40 AIRCO D.H.4 TRACTOR BIPLANE DAY BOMBERS from batch D8351 to D8430 built by parent company at Hendon. (230-hp B.H.P.)

| | |
|---|---|
| D8351 | Deld 2 AAP Hendon .18; Hendon 30.7.18; Cranwell 10.8.18; Orfordness 8.18; Hendon 11.8.18 |
| D8352 | Deld 2 AAP Hendon .18; Hendon 30.7.18; UK to Paris 13.10.18 |
| D8353 | 4 ASD to 217 Sqdn 17.7.18; Damaged in hangar by A8082 taking off Crochte 18.7.18; 4 ASD 22.7.18; 4 ASD Wissant to 217 Sqdn 1.10.18; Dropped 2x230-lb bombs, 1 failed to explode on U-boat 5129N 0237W 5.10.18; 233 Sqdn Dover 1.3.19 |
| D8354 | (Eagle IV) Deld 2 AAP Hendon W/E 11.7.18; Turnhouse W/E 15.8.18 - @1.19 |
| D8355 | Deld 2 AAP Hendon .18; Hendon 30.7.18 |
| D8358 | (Eagle IV) Deld 2 AAP Hendon W/E 11.7.18; Turnhouse W/E 15.8.18 - @1.19 |
| D8359 | Deld 2 AAP Hendon .18; Hendon 30.7.18; RAF GHQ 10.8.18 |
| D8360 | (Eagle IV) Deld Islington W/E 15.8.18; Turnhouse by 8.18 - @1.19 |
| D8361 | (Eagle IV) Deld Islington W/E 15.8.18; Turnhouse by 8.18 - @1.19 |
| D8363 | (Eagle VIII) 4 ASD to 217 Sqdn 22.7.18; Burnt out when hit by A7863 while standing on aerodrome 22.8.18 |
| D8366 | 4 ASD to 217 Sqdn but wings damaged and u/c wrecked on arrival 30.7.18 (Lt RF Johnson USN unhurt); retd 4 ASD; 4 ASD Wissant to 217 Sqdn 16.10.18; 233 Sqdn Dover 1.3.19 |
| D8370 | (Eagle VIII) Allocated for transfer from RFC Hendon to Dover-Dunkerque Command by 30.3.18; 4 ASD Wissant to 217 Sqdn 22.7.18; Seaplane shot down 17.9.18 (Lt AM Phillips & Lt NS Dougall); To Mjr Boid 1.3.19 |
| D8371 | (Eagle VIII) Allocated for transfer from RFC Hendon to Dover-Dunkerque Command by 30.3.18; Yarmouth by |

25.6.18 - @28.9.18 (at Covhithe 6.18)

**D8374** (Eagle VIII) Allocated for transfer from RFC Hendon to Dover-Dunkerque Command by 30.3.18; 217 Sqdn for erection by 10.9.18; Crashed, caught fire, nr Crochte aerodrome, BO 28.9.18 (2/Lt AF Tong killed & Sgt Mech G/L M Connolly injured)

**D8376** (Eagle VIII) Allocated for transfer from RFC Hendon to Dover-Dunkerque Command by 30.3.18; 4 ASD to 217 Sqdn 17.7.18; COL, badly damaged 19.8.18 (Lt H Rudd and 2/Lt F Elliott both unhurt); 4 ASD by 9.18; 2 SS Richborough 15.9.18

**D8379** 5 Sqdn RNAS by 25.3.17; Left on bombing raid 15.29, FTR 27.3.18 (FSL EC Stocker & AAM1 CM Rendle both killed)

**D8381** (Eagle VIII) Allocated for transfer from RFC Hendon to Dover-Dunkerque Command by 30.3.18

**D8384** (Eagle VI later VIII) Allocated for transfer from RFC Hendon to Dover-Dunkerque Command by 30.3.18; 8 AAP Lympne by 31.5.18; 2 AI to 3 ASD 1.7.18; 55 Sqdn 8.7.18; 3 ASD 7.8.18; 55 Sqdn 14.9.18; Shot down 6.11.18

**D8387** (Eagle VI) 8 AAP Lympne by 31.5.18; 2 ASD by 6.18; 205 Sqdn 30.6.18; Damaged by flak 25.7.18 (observer 2/Lt PS Hartley wounded); flying again by 2.8.18; Engaged Pfalz DIII 08.00, afterwards OOC 11.8.18 (Lt WH Clarke & Lt CN Witham); FL after engaged by heavy AA 21.8.18 (Lt AN Hyde & 2/Lt WW Harrison unhurt); Retd 22.8.18; 2 AI 1.9.18

**D8390** (Eagle VIII) Dunkerque by 9.18; 4 ASD by rail 3.9.18; 202 Sqdn 3.11.18; 98 Sqdn 15.3.19; Crashed & WO Bruges 19.3.19; 1 ASD 19.3.19 WOC

**D8391** (Eagle VIII) 4 ASD to 202 Sqdn 13.10.18; 98 Sqdn 16.3.19; 1 ASD 19.3.19

**D8393** (Eagle VIII) 217 Sqdn by 18.10.18; 98 Sqdn 17.3.19; 1 ASD 19.3.19; to England 23.3.19

**D8394** 217 Sqdn by 22.8.18; FL due to failing light Bergues 7.9.18; Crashed 23.10.18; 4 ASD 25.10.18; Deleted 31.10.18 DBR

**D8399** Deld 1(S)ARD Farnborough by 27.4.18 for Dunkerque; AAP Dover to 217 Sqdn 18.5.18; EF, FL Nieuport Bains, abandoned, destroyed by enemy shellfire 30.5.18 (Capt HH Gonyou injured & Lt JF Reid unhurt); Deleted 15.6.18

**D8400** (Eagle VII later VIII) Deld 1(S)ARD Farnborough by 27.4.18; Dover W/E 4.5.18; 491 Flt Dover by 25.5.18; 4 ASD Audembert 17.6.18; 217 Sqdn by 29.6.18; COL Crochte 13.7.18 (Lt DW Davies & A/G H Tallboys unhurt); 4 ASD 18.7.18; 202 Sqdn by 1.10.18; Flown from Varsennaere to 233 Sqdn Dover, but crashed on FL in dark Wanston Court Farm, nr Swingate Downs aerodrome, damaged 6.3.19 (2/Lt LS Clarke); WOC 19.3.19 (for RTP)

**D8401** (Eagle V) 2 AI to 205 Sqdn 21.4.18; Left 09.55, FTR raid on Chaulnes Rly Stn, NW of Quesnel 18.5.18 (2/Lt HCR Conron & 2/Lt J Finnigan); SOC 19.5.18

**D8402** Deld 1(S)ARD Farnborough by 27.4.18; Dover to 4 ASD Guines W/E 24.5.18; 202 Sqdn 26.5.18; Damaged in action 4.6.18 (Lt TA Warne-Browne unhurt & G/L Cpl Mech W Bowman slightly wounded); repaired on sqdn; U/c smashed on landing 22.7.18 (Lt FS Russell + another unhurt); While escorting A7632, both attacked by 7 HA, shot up, but observer 2 HA OOC firing spare gun from shoulder, FL Rousbrugge railhead 29.7.18 (1/Lt W Chalaire USNR & AGL Pte1 AE Humphreys both badly wounded); 4 ASD repair 31.7.18; Dismantling from 24.10.18

**D8403** (Eagle VIII) Deld 1(S)ARD Farnborough by 27.4.18; Hendon to Dover 22.5.18; 4 ASD Guines W/E 24.5.18; 217 Sqdn 25.6.18; 2-str OOC 30.6.18 (Lt AM Phillips & G/L Toulamaine); Wrecked landing nr Crochte 6.7.18 (Lt AM Phillips & Sgt Mech FW Shufflebottom unhurt); Repaired on sqdn; Damaged German destroyer 10.8.18; COL, badly damaged 16.8.18 (Lt SJ Saunders & 2/Lt C Fenteman-Coates both unhurt); to 4 ASD, still there 25.10.18

**D8404** Deld 1(S)ARD Farnborough by 27.4.18 - @31.5.18 for Dunkerque

**D8405** 2 ASD to 205 Sqdn 31.3.18; Hit by A8080 on TO 18.4.18; 2 ASD 19.4.18 & SOS

**D8407** (Eagle VIII) Deld 1(S)ARD Farnborough 6.4.18 - @27.4.18; 491 Flt Dover by 25.5.18; 4 ASD Wissant by 8.18; 202 Sqdn (coded 'S') 16.8.18; 98 Sqdn 6.3.19; 1 ASD 18.3.19

**D8409** (Eagle VIII) Deld 1(S)ARD Farnborough 6.4.18 - @27.4.18; Dover by 31.5.18; 4 ASD Audembert by 6.18; 202 Sqdn 23.6.18; FL Leffrinckhouke 16.11.18 (Lt WAE Pepler & 2/Lt JC Castle); FL Leffrinckhouke 24.12.18, flying again 30.12.18; SAD Farnborough for HMS *Argus* 6.1.19

**D8412** (Eagle VI) Rec Pk to 2 ASD 8.4.18; 205 Sqdn 12.4.18; Pfalz DIII OOC Warfusée-Abancourt 11.15-11.30 7.7.18 (Lt RLMcK Barbour & 2/Lt JH Preston); Shot up Pfalz DIII on its tail Chaulnes - Pont-les-Brie 15.40, which was later down OOC by A7597 10.8.18 (Lt JG Kerr unhurt; 2/Lt HW Hopton DoW 12.8.18); Rebuilt as F6511 in error 28.8.18, changed later to H7118

**D8417** (Eagle VIII) Deld 1(S)ARD Farnborough 6.4.18 - @27.4.18; 491 Flt Dover by 25.5.18 - @31.5.18; 4 ASD Wissant by 25.10.18; 217 Sqdn 4.11.18; 233 Sqdn Dover 27.2.19

**D8418** (Eagle VIII later VII) Deld 1(S)ARD Farnborough 6.4.18 - @27.4.18; 4 ASD Guines by 25.5.18; Dover by 31.5.18; 4 ASD to 202 Sqdn 28.6.18; 6 Sqdn 15.3.19; 1 ASD Marquise 18.3.19

**D8420** (Eagle VIII) Deld 1(S)ARD Farnborough 6.4.18 - @27.4.18; 491 Flt Dover by 25.5.18 - @31.5.18; 4 ASD Wissant to 202 Sqdn (coded 'F') 31.7.18; Attacked and badly shot up by Fokker DVII Blankenberghe-Zeebrugge 13.10 21.8.18 (Lt GR Hurst unhurt & Sgt LA Allen seriously wounded) [credited Ltn Osterkamp, Marine Jasta 2]; squadron repair; Hit by m/g fire 22.10.18; flying again by 28.10.18; SAD Farnborough for HMS *Argus* 6.1.19; 6 SD Ascot by 1.19 for HMS *Argus*

**D8421** (Eagle VI) Rec Pk to 2 AI 16.7.18; 205 Sqdn 19.7.18; During raid on Peronne station, one of its 112-lb bombs knocked off the port wing of a Pfalz which was climbing 200 ft directly underneath it but did not explode 11.8.18 (Lt W Grossart & 2/Lt JB Leach); Badly shot about by HA in bombing raid on Busigny, then damaged by storm after landing 17.9.18 (Lt HF Taylor unhurt & 2/Lt HS Millen wounded); 2 ASD 20.9.18

**D8422** (Eagle VIII) Deld 1(S)ARD Farnborough 6.4.18 - @27.4.18; Dover by 31.5.18; 4 ASD Wissant to 202 Sqdn 13.8.18; COL 6.9.18 (1/Lt JF Moffett USNR & Cpl RK Hooper both unhurt); 4 ASD by lorry 7.9.18; 202 Sqdn, crashed, to 4 ASD 7.10.18 - @25.10.18

**D8423** (Eagle VIII) 4 ASD to 202 Sqdn 1.9.18; 98 Sqdn 6.3.19; 1 ASD 19.3.19

**D8429** (Eagle VI) Rec Pk to 2 ASD 31.7.18; 205 Sqdn 7.8.18; Pfalz DIII crashed W of Peronne during raid on Peronne station 07.58 11.8.18 (Lt GC Matthews & Sgt L Murphy); Damaged in combat with Fokker DVIIs during raid on Peronne station 11.00 13.8.18 (Lt FO McDonald seriously wounded & Sgt FG Manning killed); General engagement, Fokker DVII leader (red nose, black fuselage with white diagonal stripe) crashed NW of Peronne 10.05 23.8.18 (2/Lt FO McDonald & Sgt L Murphy); Shot about by HA in raid on Busigny 16.9.18 (Lt EO Danger wounded & Lt AD Hollingsworth unhurt); 2 ASD 20.9.18

**26 AVRO 504K TRACTOR BIPLANE TRAINERS from batch D8781 to D9080 built by The Grahame-White Aviation Co Ltd & built Hendon. [c/n's G.W.3051 to G.W.3350?]**

**D8797** (130-hp Clerget) 204 TDS Eastchurch by 12.18; Flat turn at 200ft, stalled and spun in 7.12.18 (Sgt A Radnor killed)

**D8840** 204 TDS Eastchurch 1918

**D8844** (130-hp Clerget) 204 TDS Eastchurch by 10.18; Flat turn at 150ft, nosedived in 16.10.18 (F/Cdt EB Rayner DoI)

**D8851** 55 TDS Manston by 7.18 - @8.18

**D8861** 54 TDS Fairlop, stalled on turn with engine off at 500ft 8.10.18 (F/Cdt FS Everett)

**D8901** 56 TDS Cranwell by 8.18

**D8908** 56 TDS Cranwell by 8.18 - @9.18

**D8909** 56 TDS Cranwell by 8.18

**D8910** 10 TDS Harling Road by 6.18; 57 TDS Cranwell by 9.18 - @12.18

**D8911** 56 TDS Cranwell by 8.18 - @9.18

| | |
|---|---|
| D8912 | 56 TDS Cranwell by 9.18 |
| D8913 | 56 TDS Cranwell by 9.18 |
| D8914 | (130-hp Clerget) 56 TDS Cranwell by 18.9.18; Propeller accident 23.9.18 (F/Cdt JBP Scott slightly injured) |
| D8915 | 56 TDS Cranwell by 9.18 |
| D8916 | 56 TDS Cranwell by 8.18; Mid-air collision with B.E.2c 8409 4.11.18 (Lt HM De-Bathe killed) |
| D8917 | 56 TDS Cranwell by 9.18 |
| D8918 | 57 TDS Cranwell by 10.18 |
| D8919 | 56 TDS Cranwell by 9.18 |
| D8920 | (130-hp Clerget) 56 TDS Cranwell by 9.18; 57 TDS Cranwell by 10.18; Crashed 18.11.18 (F/Cdt W Newton seriously injured & F/Cdt C Chapman killed) |
| D8921 | 56 TDS Cranwell by 9.18 |
| D8923 | 204 TDS Eastchurch, EF, crashed 15m from aerodrome practising aerial fighting 14.11.18 (2/Lt AE Rayner slightly injured & F/Cdt Hoskins) |
| D8937 | FF 19.9.18; 204 TDS Eastchurch; Engine fell out on TO before leaving ground 20.12.18 (Capt L Cunningham & Sgt Sharman unhurt) |
| D8944 | (130-hp Clerget) 54 TDS Fairlop by 1.19; EF, sideslipped in 8.1.19 (Capt NB Starbuck slightly injured & Sgt RJ Courd killed) [? - listed as D9844] |
| D8980 | 57 TDS Cranwell by 9.18 - @2.19 |
| D8981 | 56 TDS Cranwell by 9.18 |
| D8982 | 57 TDS Cranwell by 9.18 |

## 1 ROYAL AIRCRAFT FACTORY F.E.2b TRACTOR BIPLANES from batch D9081 to D9230 built by Alex Stephen & Sons

| | |
|---|---|
| D9152 | (160hp Beardmore) 58 TDS Cranwell, stalled and spun in 28.10.18 (PFO MF Thwaite killed) |

## 13 AIRCO D.H.4 TRACTOR BIPLANE DAY BOMBERS from batch D9231 to D9280 built by parent company at Hendon.

| | |
|---|---|
| D9232 | (Eagle VII) Deld 2 AAP Hendon by 22.4.18; Rec Pk to 205 Sqdn 25.4.18; Pfalz DIII OOC in vertical dive Chaulnes-Rosières 17.42 3.5.18 (Capt E Dickson & AGL CV Robinson); COL, pilot fainted 15.5.18 (2/Lt WE MacPherson injured & 2/Lt JA Whalley unhurt); 2 ASD 17.5.18; Rebuilt as F6103 3.7.18 |
| D9234 | (Eagle V) Deld 2 AAP Hendon by 10.5.18; 2 AI to 205 Sqdn 6.6.18; Crashed into D.H.4 A7964 landing 11.8.18 (2/Lt FO MacDonald & 2/Lt JC Walker both unhurt); SOC in field 14.8.18 |
| D9238 | (Eagle) Rec Pk to 2 AI 12.4.18; 205 Sqdn (coded 'P') 15.4.18; Albatros DV in flames 4-6m W of Chaulnes during raid on Chaulnes Rly Stn 11.25-11.30 18.5.18 (Capt E Dickson & AGL CV Robinson); Pfalz DIII in flames S of Bray 19.58 5.7.18 (Lt CJ Heywood unhurt & 2/Lt EA Dew wounded); Fokker DVII crashed E of Chaulnes 11.00-11.10 13.8.18 (Lt CJ Heywood & Sgt SF Langstone); 2 AI 1.9.18; Rec Pk 2.9.18; Lympne 4.9.18 |
| D9241 | Rec Pk to 2 AI Sqdn 10.4.18; 205 Sqdn but crashed on arrival, new u/c fitted 11.4.18; Crashed 16.6.18 (Lt JC Wilson & Sgt SM MacKay); Crashed 30.6.18 (Lt JC Wilson & Sgt SF Langstone); 2 ASD 26.9.18 |
| D9243 | (Eagle VI) 2 AI to 205 Sqdn 13.4.18; Left 16.10, down in flat spin over Chaulnes Rly Stn 3.5.18 (Lt R Scott & 2/Lt TA Humphreys both killed); SOC in field 4.5.18 |
| D9250 | (Eagle VII later VI) Deld 2 AAP Hendon by 26.4.18; Rec Pk to 2 AI 3.5.18; 205 Sqdn 14.5.18; Left 07.30, FTR raid on Busigny 16.9.18 (2/Lt FF Anslow PoW & Sgt L Murphy killed) |
| D9253 | (Eagle VI) Deld 2 AAP Hendon by 24.4.18; Rec Pk to 2 AI 1.5.18; 205 Sqdn 2.5.18; EF, FL, crashed nr Bellancourt 9.5.18 (Lt HCR Conron unhurt & 2/Lt Deacon slightly injured); 2 ASD 10.5.18; Rebuilt as F6167 3.7.18 |
| D9255 | (Eagle VI) Deld 2 AAP Hendon by 29.4.18; Rec Pk to 2 ASD 1.5.18; 205 Sqdn 4.5.18; Yellow and green Fokker DrI in flames W of Chaulnes 16.05 17.5.18; COL 15.7.18 (both Lt R Chalmers & 2/Lt SH Hamblin); Pfalz DIII in flames crashed Chaulnes 15.50 10.8.18 (Capt JM Mason & Sgt WJH Middleton); Fokker DVII OOC NW of Busigny 09.30 16.9.18 (2/Lt KG Nairn & 2/Lt KR McKinley); RD 27.9.18; 2 ASD by 10.18; RP 1 ASD |

| | |
|---|---|
| | 19.10.18; Lympne 22.10.18 |
| D9256 | (Eagle VII) Deld 2 AAP Hendon by 30.4.18; Rec Pk to 2 ASD 5.5.18; 205 Sqdn 11.5.18; Shot about by triplane, landed Cagny 11.05 5.6.18 (Lt WV Theron & Sgt HF Monday both unhurt); 2 ASD 7.6.18; Shot about SS 7.6.18; Rebuilt as F6139 3.7.18 |
| D9260 | Deld 2 AAP Hendon by 30.4.18; 2 AI to 205 Sqdn 16.5.18; Pfalz DIII OOC by observer Rosières 08.25 20.5.18 (Lt R Chalmers & 2/Lt SH Hamblin); COL on or W/E 24.5.18 (repaired); Crashed into N6064 on aerodrome 11.6.18 (Lt WE Macpherson & Lt CF Ambler unhurt); 2 ASD 12.6.18; SOC 26.6.18 NWR |
| D9264 | 205 Sqdn, Fokker DVII dest NE of Peronne 23.8.18 (2/Lt FO MacDonald & Sgt SM MacKay) [serial suspect] |
| D9269 | Rec Pk to 2 AI 5.6.18; 205 Sqdn 16.6.18; Pfalz DIII OOC 11.00-11.10 13.8.18 Peronne (Lt WH Clarke & 2/Lt CN Witham); Fokker DVII OOC 4.9.18 (Lt DJT Mellor & Sgt WJH Middleton); 2 ASD 26.9.18 |
| D9277 | Deld 3 AAP Norwich by 10.5.18; 2 AI to 205 Sqdn 12.6.18; Hit by flak 17.6.18 (Capt J Gamon wounded); Red Fokker DVII, spun in, crashed into trees 1m NE of Bethencourt 15.05 21.8.18 (Lt WH Clarke & 2/Lt CN Witham); Light green, white tailed Fokker DVII OOC & another DD St.Quentin-Brie 09.00-09.15 6.9.18 (Lt EH Johnson & 2/Lt AR Crosthwaite); Damaged by storm 17.9.18; 2 ASD 17.9.18 |

## 17 SOPWITH F.1 CAMEL TRACTOR BIPLANE SCOUTS from batch D9381 to D9530 built by Boulton & Paul Ltd at Norwich. (130-hp Clerget 9B or 110-hp Le Rhône)

| | |
|---|---|
| D9402 | Deld 3 AAP Norwich by 8.5.18; Rec Pk to 1 AI 17.5.18; 208 Sqdn 19.5.18; Pfalz DIII shot down Hénin-Lietard 11.45 31.7.18 (Lt MC Howell); O/t landing 6.9.18 (2/Lt G Lovett injured); 1 ASD 7.9.18; Rebuilt as H7235 5.11.18 |
| D9424 | Deld 3 AAP Norwich by 10.5.18; Rec Pk to 1 AI 16.7.18; 208 Sqdn 22.7.18; Fell OOC from 1,000 ft, crashed Ambricourt 17.9.18 (2/Lt S Clark killed); To 1 ASD; SOC 20.9.18 |
| D9430 | Deld 3 AAP Norwich by 10.5.18; Rec Pk to 1 AI 25.5.18; Rec Pk to 1 AI 14.6.18; Walmer by 8.18; Dover 19.8.18; Rep Pk 2 ASD by 10.18; 2 AI 16.10.18 |
| D9434 | Deld 491 Flt Dover on/by 25.5.18; Walmer store to 471 Flt 233 Sqdn Walmer 16.6.18; EF on FL, crashed nr Morely Farm, Dargate 15.8.18 (Capt GW Hemming unhurt); ARS Guston Road by 24.8.18; WOC 5.9.18 |
| D9436 | (140-hp Clerget) Deld 491 Flt Dover on/by 25.5.18; Walmer store to 471 Flt 233 Sqdn Walmer 16.6.18; Wheel collapsed landing, badly damaged 15.8.18 (Lt AL Jones); to ARD Guston Rd for repair; 233 Sqdn Dover by 10.18; 471 Flt 233 Sqdn Walmer 30.10.18; Crashed on TO, badly damaged Varssenaere 30.11.18 (2/Lt AC Davern); 11 AP repair by 20.12.18 |
| D9484 | Rec Pk to 1 AI 25.5.18; Rec Pk to 1 AI 23.8.18; 208 Sqdn 28.8.18; Left 17.00, patrol attacked by large number of Fokker biplanes 6.9.18 (2/Lt AH Hiscox killed); Presume a/c recovered; Halberstadt shot down Gouy 17.50 25.9.18; Fokker DVII OOC SE of St.Quentin 18.40 26.9.18 (both Capt WEG Mann); 2 AI 31.10.18 |
| D9488 | Deld 491 Flt Dover on/by 25.5.18; Walmer store to 4 ASD Audembert 21.6.18; 204 Sqdn 1.8.18; EF landing, crashed on aerodrome, badly damaged 22.8.18 (Lt HG Clappison unhurt); 4 ASD 23.8.18; 80 Sqdn by 9.18 |
| D9490 | (150-hp Clerget) Deld 491 Flt Dover on/by 25.5.18; Walmer store to 4 ASD Audembert 21.6.18; 213 Sqdn 13.7.18; Albatros OOC over Bruges, shared D3326 11.50 30.7.18; Seaplane crashed in sea 15m NW of Ostende 19.35 31.7.18; Fokker DVII shot down 5m SE of Ostende 15.50 11.8.18 (all Lt CJ Sims); 4 ASD 31.8.18 |
| D9496 | (150-hp Clerget) Deld 3 AAP Norwich 5.18; Acc 25.5.18; Deld 471 Flt Walmer on/by 25.5.18; Rec Pk to 2 ASD 10.6.18; Walmer store 6.18; 4 ASD Audembert 21.6.18; 204 Sqdn 1.8.18; Fokker DVII crashed in sea Blankenberghe 10.55 12.8.18 (Lt RMcI Gordon); Hit by AA fire Nieuport-Dixmude, FL, crashed Ramscappelle, severely damaged 15.9.18 (2/Lt LP Worthington slightly injured); To 4 ASD; 210 Sqdn (named 'DOT') 14.10.18; |

Fokker DVII crashed Binche 13.15 10.11.18 (2/Lt JE Berry); 203 Sqdn 24.1.19; RTP by 16.2.19

D9506    Deld 3 AAP Norwich by 27.5.18; Rec Pk to 2 ASD 24.7.18; 43 Sqdn .18; 2 AI 30.8.18; 205 TDS Vendôme 4.9.18; Crashed on landing in gale 5.9.18 (F/Cdt PH Jenner unhurt)

D9517    (110-hp Le Rhône) Deld Turnhouse W/E 13.6.18 - @1.19

D9519    (110-hp Le Rhône) Deld Turnhouse W/E 13.6.18 - @1.19

D9521    (110-hp Le Rhône) Deld Turnhouse W/E 13.6.18 - @1.19

D9523    (110-hp Le Rhône) Deld Turnhouse W/E 13.6.18; to HMS *Tiger* 10.18; Collapsed in air on flattening out suddenly 16.10.18 (2/Lt PR Hale)

D9525    (110-hp Le Rhône) Lincoln to Marske 2.6.18 (on delivery?); Deld Turnhouse 6.18; Nosedived and spun in 1.10.18 (2/Lt HIM Monk killed)

D9527    (110-hp Le Rhône) Deld Turnhouse W/E 13.6.18 - @1.19

D9529    (110-hp Le Rhône) Deld Turnhouse W/E 13.6.18 - @1.19

## 15 SOPWITH F.1 CAMEL TRACTOR BIPLANE SCOUTS
from batch D9531 to D9580 built by Portholme Aerodrome Ltd & built Huntingdon. (130-hp Clerget LS unless otherwise stated)

D9533    Shipped to Aegean; 222 Sqdn Mudros by 27.10.18

D9540    Rec Pk to 1 AI 23.4.18; 208 Sqdn 30.4.18; Left 06.30, last seen at 500 ft N of La Bassée apparently under control with 2 HA on tail 16.5.18 (Lt WE Cowan PoW) [credited Ltn von Marwitz, Jasta 30]; SOC in field 16.5.18

D9542    (140-hp Clerget) 255 Sqdn Tenby by 29.10.18 (flown by Lt RR Soar)

D9546    56 TDS Cranwell by 8.9.18

D9552    Deld 6 SD Ascot W/E 11.7.18; Shipped to Mudros 17.8.18; 222 Sqdn Mudros by 28.10.18; Repair Base Mudros by 10.18 - @1.19; To White Russian Forces 1919

D9553    Deld 6 SD Ascot W/E 11.7.18; Shipped to Mudros 17.7.18; Mudros by 10.18 - @1.19; To White Russians 1919

D9554    Deld 6 SD Ascot W/E 11.7.18; Shipped to Taranto 17.7.18; AD Taranto by 8.18; (AD?) Taranto by 10.18 - @1.19

D9557    Deld 6 SD Ascot W/E 15.8.18; To docks W/E 19.9.18; Shipped to Mudros 11.10.18; Mudros by 1.19; To White Russian Forces 1919

D9558    Deld 6 SD Ascot W/E 11.7.18; Shipped to Taranto 17.7.18; AD Taranto by 8.18; (AD?) Taranto by 10.18 - @1.19

D9559    Deld 6 SD Ascot W/E 25.7.18; Shipped 8.8.18; (AD?) Taranto by 10.18 - @1.19

D9560    Deld Southport by 13.6.18; 6 SD Ascot W/E 20.6.18; Shipped to Taranto 17.7.18; AD Taranto by 8.18; (AD?) Taranto by 10.18 - @1.19

D9561    Deld Southport by 13.6.18; 6 SD Ascot W/E 20.6.18; Shipped to Taranto 17.7.18; AD Taranto by 8.18; (AD?) Taranto by 10.18 - @1.19

D9562    Deld Southport by 13.6.18; 6 SD Ascot W/E 20.6.18; Shipped to Taranto 17.7.18; AD Taranto by 8.18; (AD?) Taranto by 10.18 - @1.19

D9563    Deld Southport by 13.6.18; 6 SD Ascot W/E 20.6.18; Shipped to Taranto 17.7.18; AD Taranto by 8.18; (AD?) Taranto by 10.18 - @1.19

D9579    Deld 3 AP Norwich for EF by 23.5.18; 204 TDS Eastchurch by 16.10.18 (may have been F9579 but unlikely)

## 100 SOPWITH F.1 CAMEL TRACTOR BIPLANE SCOUTS
ordered under Cont No 87/A/1836 & A.S.17929 from Clayton & Shuttleworth Ltd and numbered D9581 to D9680, to be built at Lincoln. Accepted 4 AAP Lincoln. All except D9602 to D9605 Mostly to naval units. (130-hp Clerget LS unless otherwise stated)

D9581    (BR.1) Deld 4 AAP Lincoln by 16.5.18; 1 ASD to 203 Sqdn 6.6.18; Pfalz DIII crashed Auchy, nr La Bassée 07.25 1.7.18 (Lt WAW Carter); Hit by AA 09.00 nr Monchy, FL in shellhole and trenches Fosse Farm 9.10.18 (2/Lt P Calder unhurt); to 1 ASD

D9582    (BR.1) Deld 4 AAP Lincoln by 23.5.18; Rec Pk to 2 AI 2.6.18; 201 Sqdn 3.6.18; Engine seized up, crashed and wrecked nr Rougefay 5.7.18 (Lt L Mortimore injured); SOC No.2 Salvage Dump 6.7.18

D9583    1 ASD to 203 Sqdn 9.6.18; DFW C crashed SE of Lestrem, shared D9618 06.00 20.7.18; Fokker DVII crashed nr Carvin 10.35 22.7.18; Fokker DVII probably crashed 3m SE of La Bassée 07.45 25.7.18 (all Lt W Sidebottom); COL uneven ground 16.8.18 (Lt W Sidebottom unhurt); 2 ASD 17.8.18; Rebuilt as F6478 in error 31.8.18, changed to H7089

D9584    1 AI to 210 Sqdn 29.5.18; Port wheel came off on landing, u/c broke away, badly damaged 27.6.18 (Lt CF Pineau unhurt); Rep Pk 1 ASD 28.6.18; Rebuilt as F6030 21.7.18

D9585    (BR.1) Deld 4 AAP Lincoln by 17.5.18; 1 ASD to 203 Sqdn 6.6.18; DFW C Estaires, shared B7185, D3371, D3414 & D3417 06.10 16.6.18 (Lt CF Brown); Fokker DVII OOC and another crashed nr Carvin 10.35 22.7.18 (Capt LH Rochford); Shot down Goudecourt Military Cemetery, nr La Bassée 25.7.18 (Lt CF Brown DoW 26.8.18) [credited Ltn P Billik, Jasta 52]

D9586    (BR.1) Deld 4 AAP Lincoln by 15.5.18; Rec Pk 5.18; 2 AI to 201 Sqdn 22.5.18; DFW C OOC SE of Arras 12.00 9.6.18; Albatros CV OOC Bois de Tailles, shared Dolphin with white circle behind fuselage roundel, 09.45 28.6.18 (both Lt RCB Brading); KB down in flames nr Bray-sur-Somme, SE of Albert, shared B7190 12.20, then petrol tank hit by flak, FL nr Aveluy Wood 19.7.18 (Lt RSS Orr unhurt); Rep Pk 1 ASD 22.7.18

D9587    (BR.1) Deld 4 AAP Lincoln by 21.5.18; Rec Pk to 2 AI 27.5.18; 201 Sqdn 31.5.18; EF after hit by flak in raid on Bancourt aerodrome, FL and wrecked Acheux 19.6.18 (Lt R McLaughlin unhurt); 2 ASD 21.6.18; Rebuilt as F6056 27.6.18

D9588    (BR.1) Deld 4 AAP Lincoln by 18.5.18; 2 AI to 209 Sqdn (coded 'K') 28.5.18; Halberstadt C crashed in flames Harbonnières, shared C61, C142, C199 & D9625 19.05 8.8.18 (Lt CG Edwards); EF, FL nr Mercatel 3.9.18 (2/Lt EH Stubbs unhurt); 1 ASD 5.9.18; Rebuilt as H7115 17.9.18

D9589    Rec Pk to 201 Sqdn 26.5.18; Albatros C OOC NE of Albert 10.15 30.5.18; Albatros CV OOC Achiet-Le Grand 19.45 30.5.18; (both Capt MH Findlay); Badly damaged by ground fire 8.8.18; Left 17.00, last seen in combat with Fokker DVIIs E of Foucaucourt 9.8.18 (Lt MS Misener killed); SOC 9.8.18

D9590    Deld 4 AAP Lincoln by 21.5.18; 1 AI to 210 Sqdn 4.6.18; 2-str crashed le Doulieu, shared D3410 08.25 6.6.18 (Lt WS Jenkins); Collided with B7249 while both diving to attack HA 10.6.18 (2/Lt FC Dodd killed); SOC in field 11.6.18

D9591    (BR.1) Deld 4 AAP Lincoln by 22.5.18; 1 AI to 210 Sqdn 4.6.18; Ran into trench landing, o/t, badly damaged 18.6.18 (Lt WJ Saunders injured); Rep Pk 1 ASD 19.6.18; SOC 21.6.18 NWR

D9592    Rec Pk to 1 AI 14.6.18; 203 Sqdn 6.18; Fokker DVII spun in Morenchies 08.50 2.10.18 (Capt JD Breakey); 1 ASD for overhaul 24.11.18 (fit to fly Channel)

D9593    Deld 4 AAP Lincoln by 27.5.18; Rec Pk to 2 ASD 10.5.18 (sic); 209 Sqdn 2.6.18; Lost, landed French aerodrome Beauvais, TO again, stalled, o/t 7.6.18 (Lt JP Nash unhurt); 2 ASD 9.6.18

D9594    (BR.1) Deld 4 AAP Lincoln by 23.5.18; Rec Pk to 1 AI 29.5.18; 203 Sqdn (coded 'H') 30.5.18; Fokker DrI OOC 1m SE of Lestrem 11.45 7.6.18 (Capt AT Whealy); On TO, hit and killed a man on outfield in game of cricket, TW 31.7.18 (Lt CW Sutcliffe injured); To 1 ASD; SOC 6.8.18

D9595    (BR.1) Deld 4 AAP Lincoln by 27.5.18; Lympne to Rec Pk 27.5.18; 1 AI 29.5.18; 203 Sqdn 30.5.18; LVG C crashed into canal nr Merville 06.20 20.7.18 (Lt AE Rudge); Fokker DVII OOC nr Carvin 10.35 22.7.18 (Lt R Stone); Fokker DVII OOC E of Bray 19.30 11.8.18 (Lt W Sidebottom); After encountering several HA new type monoplanes, seen going down apparently under control nr Peronne 11.35 16.8.18 (Sgt PM Fletcher, PoW) ALSO 203 Sqdn, DFW C dest S of Mericourt, shared D9641 22.8.18 (Lt W Sidebottom) - serial not possible at that date

D9596 1 ASD to 204 Sqdn 30.10.18; Fokker DVII with black stripes on wings and white tail sent down in uncontrollable spin over Soffeghem 13.50 1.11.18 (2/Lt HG Clappison); 203 Sqdn 25.1.19; RTP by 16.2.19

D9597 Rec Pk to 2 ASD 11.8.18; 203 Sqdn by 24.8.18; Hannover C spun OOC from 7,000ft Bois Bernard, crashed SE of Lens, shared C197 09.00 24.9.18 (2/Lt WH Coghill); Fokker DVII OOC Escaudoevres 13.30 1.10.18; Fokker DVII OOC Vertain, shared C197 16.35 23.10.18 (both Lt DB Barbour); COL Tournai 1.1.19 (Lt DB Barbour injured)

D9598 (BR.1) Rec Pk to 2 AI 27.5.18; 209 Sqdn 28.5.18; Rec Pk to 2 ASD 9.8.18; 203 Sqdn 16.8.18; O/t landing 17.9.18 (Sgt AG Taylor unhurt); To 1 ASD; Rebuilt as H7206 5.11.18

D9599 (BR.1) Rec Pk to 2 AI 9.8.18; 209 Sqdn 11.8.18; Fokker DVII dest Buissy 14.30 25.8.18; Halberstadt C crashed Monchy 13.05, then Hannover C BU & crashed in woods E of Remy, CW 13.10 27.8.18; Fokker DVII E of Epinoy 17.15 15.9.18; Fokker DVII OOC Sauchy Lestrée, shared F3233 16.40 20.9.18 (all Lt later Capt WR May); Fokker DVII Ecourt St.Quentin 18.35, badly shot about in combat S of River Scarpe 21.9.18 (Capt WR May unhurt); 1 ASD 27.9.18; Rebuilt as H7210 5.11.18

D9600 4 ASD to 210 Sqdn 3.8.18; Fokker DVII destroyed Dixmude 11.8.18 (Lt CW Payton); Engine trouble, FL on aerodrome, hit haystack, o/t 14.8.18 (Lt KR Unger); To 4 ASD; 204 Sqdn 27.9.18; Fokker DVII destroyed & another OOC Wercken 12.30 28.9.18 (Capt AJB Tonks DFC); Fokker DVII port wing folded up & another OOC S of Ghent 09.10 27.10.18 Fokker DVII in flames Nazareth 13.15 30.10.18 (Capt CP Allen); Fokker DVII down in spin Melle 08.45 4.11.18 (Capt CP Allen); RTP 23.2.19

D9601 4 ASD by 8.18; 204 Sqdn 9.8.18; Fokker DVII in flames & another seen to crash E of Ypres 08.25 15.8.18 (Lt WB Craig); COL from patrol, CW 1.9.18 (Lt FR Brown unhurt); To 4 ASD; 213 Sqdn 1.10.18; Last seen Roulers 16.00 4.10.18 (2/Lt KG Ibison killed)

D9606 Deld 4 AAP Lincoln by 31.5.18; Lympne 3.6.18; Marquise 4.6.18; 2 AI to 209 Sqdn 25.6.18; Hit on ground by D3368, wrecked 4.7.18; 2 ASD 5.7.18; SOC 5.7.18

D9607 Deld 4 AAP Lincoln by 31.5.18; 2 AI to 209 Sqdn 23.6.18; Albatros DV OOC Bray 19.40 1.7.18 (Capt JK Summers MC); Engine badly damaged by m/g fire, FL Corbie 8.7.18 (Capt JK Summers MC wounded); Rep Pk 2 ASD 9.7.18; 5 AI 1.10.18

D9608 1 AI to 210 Sqdn 19.6.18; Fokker DVII crashed, another OOC, then 2 Pfalz DIII OOC 1m W of Armentières, shared B7153 & D3387 19.20 26.6.18 [Crashed Fokker believed Obflgm Kurt Schoenfelder, Jasta]; General engagement, Fokker DVII OOC SE of Ostende 09.45 20.7.18; Fokker DVII OOC Nieuport-Dixmude 11.15 31.7.18; Fokker DVII DD Wervicq 18.30 31.7.18 (all Lt KR Unger); Damaged by flak 12.8.18 (2/Lt HR Hughes slightly wounded); To 4 ASD; 204 Sqdn 24.9.18; Fokker DVII crashed in flames Lichtervelde 11.05 & another DD forced to land nr Roulers 9.10.18 (Capt TW Nash DFC); FTR after sqdn attacked by 12 HA nr Termonde 23.10.18 (Capt TW Nash DFC killed)

D9609 Rec Pk to 2 AI 14.6.18; 210 Sqdn 24.6.18; KB in flames N of Estaires 11.10 30.6.18; Fokker DVII OOC pilot killed SE of Ostende, shared F5914 09.45 20.7.18; Fokker DVII crashed NW of Wervicq 18.25 31.7.18 (both Lt A Buchanan); 4 ASD 31.8.18 for survey; 4 ASD Pilots Pool, crashed in sea off Wimereux, wrecked 30.10.18 (2/Lt JB Fast slightly injured)

D9610 Rec Pk to 1 AI 8.6.18; 210 Sqdn 27.6.18; Stalled and spun after TO, badly damaged 20.8.18 (2/Lt JG Hojel killed)

D9611 Rec Pk to 1 AI 10.6.18; 203 Sqdn 11.6.18; DFW CV crashed S of Combles, shared D9641 12.10 27.8.18; Fokker DVII in flames nr Haynecourt c.18.40 16.9.18; Fokker DVII OOC Haynecourt 15.30 20.9.18; Fokker DVII in flames at 3,000ft in general engagement E of Cambrai 13.18, then FL Mory aerodrome 26.9.18; Engine seized up after attacked Lieu St.Amand aerodrome, FL in trenches N of Bapaume-Cambrai road,

machine under enemy observation 26.9.18 (all Lt FJS Britnell); SOC in field

D9612 Rec Pk to 2 ASD 11.6.18; To 201 Sqdn but engine trouble, overshot on landing, crashed in cornfield and wrecked 25.6.18 (2/Lt T Burns unhurt); Rec Pk 1 ASD 2.8.18; SOC 5.8.18

D9613 (BR.1) Flown Doncaster-Lincoln-Hounslow 6.6.18; Rec Pk (via Lympne) 7.6.18; 2 AI 8.6.18; 210 Sqdn 12.6.18; Albatros DV crashed SE of Zillebeke Lake 08.00 17.6.18; General engagement, 2 Fokker DVII OOC, 1 smoking, SE of Ostende 09.45 20.7.18; Fokker DVII OOC SE of Ostende 17.55 22.7.18 (all Lt E Swale); 2 Fokker DVII OOC, 1 smoking, SE of Ostende 19.45-20.00 1.8.18; While taxying, hit by D9622 landing into sun 6.8.18 (all 2/Lt HH Whitlock); To 4 ASD; 210 Sqdn 25.9.18; 2-str OOC Westende-Nieuport 13.15 14.10.18 (Lt OJ Orr); Shot down nr Termonde after sqdn attacked by 12 HA 23.10.18 (Lt OJ Orr killed)

D9614 Rec Pk to 1 AI 8.6.18; 210 Sqdn 18.6.18; Shot down nr Armentières 26.6.18 (2/Lt CD Boothman killed); SOC in field 28.6.18

D9615 (BR.1) Mkrs for 4 AAP Lincoln by 4.6.18; Rec Pk to 2 AI 18.6.18; 210 Sqdn 24.6.18; LVG C in flames 2m N of Armentières 19.25 26.6.18; Pfalz DIII crashed nr Armentières 19.35 29.6.18; Fokker DVII crashed 1-2m W of Ostende 19.20 6.8.18 (all Lt SC Joseph); Fokker DVII OOC Zonnebeke 09.35 11.8.18; Fokker DVII in flames Vladsloo-Eessen 18.35 11.8.18; Caught rut on TO, swung into haystack 13.8.18 (all 2/Lt P Boulton); To 4 ASD; Deleted 30.9.18 general fatigue

D9616 (BR.1) Rec Pk to 1 AI 15.6.18; 210 Sqdn 18.6.18; Albatros DV in flames Armentières, shared D9622 19.30 29.6.18 (Lt WW Gyles); Overshot into sandbags while landing, badly damaged 16.7.18 (Lt WW Gyles unhurt); To 4 ASD; Rebuilt as F6301 26.7.18

D9617 1 AI to 210 Sqdn 25.6.18; COL cross-wind, on nose 6.7.18 (Lt GC Sutcliffe unhurt); Rep Pk 1 ASD 6.7.18; Rebuilt as F6023 25.7.18

D9618 (BR.1) Mkrs for 4 AAP Lincoln by 4.6.18; Rec Pk to 1 AI 18.6.18; 203 Sqdn 21.6.18 (red cowling and wheel discs in 6.18; Named 'WAACAL' and aluminium cowl and white wheel discs by 8.8.18); DFW C crashed SE of Lestrem, shared D9583 06.00 20.7.18; Pre-dawn raid on Dorignies aerodrome with Mjr Collishaw 22.7.18; Fokker dest E of La Bassée 07.40 25.7.18; Fokker DVII OOC E of Bray 19.30 11.8.18; EF, FL, crashed nr Chuynolles 2.9.18; EF, FL, wrecked in trenches nr Peronne 5.9.18 (all Capt LH Rochford DSC, DFC unhurt); SOC 5.9.18

D9619 (BR.1) Mkrs for 4 AAP Lincoln by 4.6.18; Rec Pk to 1 AI 21.6.18; 209 Sqdn 29.6.18; Left 09.30, last seen N of railway Warfusée-Marcelcave 8.8.18 (2/Lt L Thompson killed); SOC 8.8.18

D9620 (BR.1) Mkrs for 2 AAP Lincoln by 4.6.18; Rec Pk to 1 AI 25.6.18; 210 Sqdn 27.6.18; EF, FL, damaged 1m from aerodrome 6.7.18 (Lt HH Whitlock unhurt); 1 ASD 7.7.18; SOC 10.7.18 NWR

D9621 (BR.1) Mkrs for 4 AAP Lincoln by 4.6.18; Rec Pk to 2 ASD 20.5.18; Rec Pk to 2 ASD 21.6.18; 4 Sqdn 6.18; 1 ASD 29.6.18; 209 Sqdn 29.6.18; Shot down W of Houthem, last seen 08.40 25.7.18 (2/Lt AGS Blake PoW) [credited Ltn Beckmann, Jasta 56]; SOC in field 27.7.18

D9622 (BR.1) Mkrs for 2 AAP Lincoln by 4.6.18; Rec Pk to 1 AI 19.6.18; 210 Sqdn 22.6.18; Halberstadt C in flames 3m SW of Armentières 19.20 26.6.18; Fokker DVII in flames Armentières, shared D9616 19.30 29.6.18 (both Capt HA Patey); Collided D9613 landing into sun 6.8.18 (Lt GA Welsh); 4 ASD to 204 Sqdn 15.9.18; Fokker DVII in flames Melle 08.45 4.11.18 (2/Lt PAH King); Fog, FL in field, fuselage broke in two and fell back, Menin-Wervicq road 1.12.18 (Lt WOG Fenton shaken); 11 SS 9.12.18 wreck

D9623 (BR.1) Mkrs for 4 AAP Lincoln by 4.6.18; Norwich by 6.18; Cranwell 19.6.18 (transit); Lympne 20.6.18; Rec Pk 21.6.18; 2 AI 25.6.18; 210 Sqdn 6.7.18; Guns jammed in combat at about 10,000ft, dived, pilot fell out of seat but clung to centre section struts as aircraft fell OOC, got back in cockpit and regained control at 2,000ft 20.7.18 (Lt W Stephenson unhurt); Tyre burst landing after patrol, went on nose 29.7.18 (Lt GC Sutcliffe

*Sopwith Camel D9638 'III' of 203 Sqdn crashed on its nose at Morenchies after Lt HW Skinner was severely wounded in combat on 2 October 1918. (via Frank Cheesman)*

*Sopwith Snipe E8102 of 201 Sqdn exhibits the damage it suffered during Major Barker's epic single-handed combat against a horde of enemy aircraft on 27 October 1918, a feat for which he was later awarded a well-merited Victoria Cross. (via Frank Cheesman)*

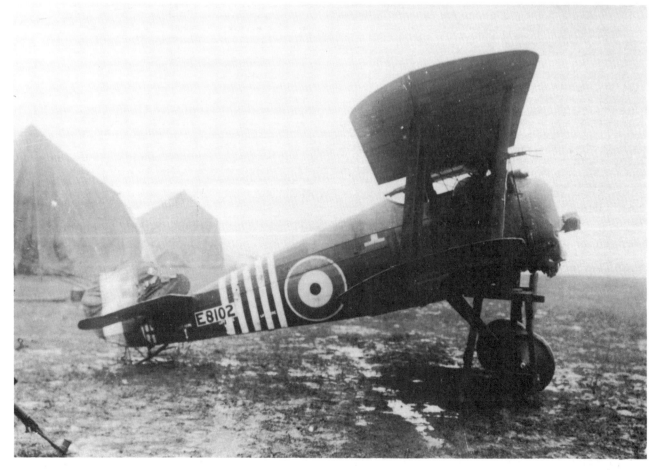

unhurt); Retd 1 ASD; Rebuilt as F6324 in error 9.8.18, later changed to H7287

**D9624** (BR.1) Mkrs for 2 AAP Lincoln by 4.6.18; Rec Pk to 1 AI 25.6.18; 203 Sqdn 6.7.18; Fokker DVII in flames Carvin 10.35, then FTR, last seen in combat with Fokker DVIIs over Carvin 22.7.18 (Lt AE Rudge killed); SOC 22.7.18

**D9625** (BR.1) Mkrs for 4 AAP Lincoln by 4.6.18; Rec Pk to 2 ASD 27.6.18; 209 Sqdn 1.7.18; Halberstadt C crashed in flames N of Harbonnières, shared C61, C142, C199 & D9588 19.05 8.8.18 (2/Lt MA Harker); FL Peronne 11.8.18 (2/Lt MA Harker); 22 Wg SS 11.8.18; Salved by No.6 SS, 5th Bde 21.8.18; To 2 ASD; Rebuilt as F6479 in error 31.8.18, later changed to H7090

**D9626** (BR.1) Mkrs for 4 AAP Lincoln by 4.6.18; Rec Pk to 1 AI 1.7.18; 210 Sqdn 5.7.18; Shot down, last seen fighting 2 HA at 7,000 ft nr Roulers 16.15 22.7.18 (2/Lt EH Bullen, USAS killed)

**D9627** 4 ASD by 30.6.18; 213 Sqdn 30.6.18; HA OOC off Wendyne, shared B6358, B6448, B7270, D3326 & D9647 11.40 7.7.18 (Lt CJ Sims); Crashed in sea 7m N of Nieuport 18.40 15.7.18 (Lt W Dawson DoI); Deleted 15.7.18

**D9628** 204 Sqdn by 8.18; Fokker DVII OOC SE of Bailleul, shared C66 19.15 13.8.18; HA crashed E of Ypres 08.25 15.8.18; Badly shot up in combat Nieuport-Ypres 15.8.18 (all Lt HWM Cummings unhurt); 4 ASD 15.8.18; 204 Sqdn 22.9.18; Fokker DVII OOC Blankenberghe 10.45 26.9.18 (2/Lt FR Brown); COL, badly damaged 29.9.18 (Lt AH Williams unhurt); 4 ASD 29.9.18; 213 Sqdn 18.10.18; EF over Ostende, retd aerodrome but COL 24.10.18 (Lt AH Pownall unhurt); to 4 ASD

**D9629** Rec Pk to 2 AI 4.7.18; 209 Sqdn (coded 'F') 4.7.18; Left 04.15, shot down nr Cappy aerodrome 19.7.18 (2/Lt E Scadding PoW) [credited Flakbatterie 764]; SOC 19.7.18

**D9630** 4 ASD by 7.18; 204 Sqdn 7.7.18; Shot down E of Ypres 15.8.18 (Lt CD Darlington killed)

**D9631** Rec Pk to 1 AI 25.6.18; 210 Sqdn 29.6.18; Last seen diving steeply with HA on tail in general engagement with 5 Pfalz scouts nr Lestrem 11.55 6.7.18 (2/Lt WJ Saunders PoW wounded); SOC in field 6.7.18

**D9632** Rec Pk to 1 AI 29.6.18; 203 Sqdn 1.7.18; Fokker DVII OOC 2m S of Ypres 08.55 4.7.18 (2/Lt NC Dixie); Probably hit by AA attacking Lieu St.Amand aerodrome, EF on return, FL trenches 26.9.18 (2/Lt NC Dixie unhurt); SOC 26.9.18

**D9633** Rec Pk to 1 AI 27.6.18; 203 Sqdn 3.7.18; COL, caught by wind, slewed round, on nose 10.7.18 (Lt YES Kirkpatrick unhurt); To 1 ASD; Rebuilt as F6039 25.7.18

**D9634** Rec Pk to 1 AI 28.7.18; 209 Sqdn 27.8.18; Engine shot through, FL, crashed nr Arras 16.9.18 (Lt G Knight unhurt); 1 ASD 17.9.18; Rebuilt as H7224 5.11.18

**D9635** 1 AI to 209 Sqdn 27.7.18; Lost, FL long grass Rumberes 7.8.18 (Lt HV Peeling unhurt); 2 ASD 9.8.18; 80 Sqdn, missing 4.11.18 (2/Lt HC Grant)

**D9636** 2 AI to 209 Sqdn 2.7.18; Last seen in combat SW of Houthem 08.40 25.7.18 (Lt JH Siddall killed) [credited Ltn D Collins, Jasta 56]; in field SOC 27.7.18

**D9637** Rec Pk to 2 AI 9.7.18; 209 Sqdn 8.8.18; Fokker DVII crashed E of Bouchier, shared D9657 11.55 10.8.18 [probably Ltn Muhs(?), Jasta 12]; Fokker DVII OOC Peronne 07.55 11.8.18 (both Capt JK Summers MC); Fokker DVII crashed nr Buissy 14.30 25.8.18 (Capt TC Luke MC); Low flying patrol, badly damaged by ground fire, crashed in shell hole, caught fire NW of Monchy 26.8.18 (Capt TC Luke MC slightly injured); Unsalvageable, SOC in field

**D9638** Rec Pk to 2 ASD 9.8.18; 203 Sqdn (coded 'III') 16.8.18; Fokker DVII crashed nr Haynecourt 15.30 20.9.18 (Lt HW Skinner); General engagement 08.50, shot down Fokker DVII at Noyelles-sur-Escaut then crashed on nose Morenchies 2.10.18 (Lt HW Skinner wounded); Crashed and WO Noyelles 8.10.18

**D9639** 5 AI to 201 Sqdn 9.10.18 - @1.12.18

**D9640** (BR.1) Mkrs by 17.6.18 for 4 AAP Lincoln; Rec Pk to 1 AI 7.7.18; 203 Sqdn 26.7.18; Fokker DVII, wings folded up W of Haynecourt 15.30 20.9.18 (2/Lt WH Coghill); Attacked Lieu St.Amand, Fokker DVII in

flames at 2,500ft E of Cambrai 13.15, then shot down in flames by Fokker DVII NE of Cambrai 26.9.18 (2/Lt WH Coghill PoW)

**D9641** (BR.1) Mkrs by 17.6.18 for 4 AAP Lincoln; Rec Pk to 2 AI 6.7.18; 203 Sqdn 6.7.18; DFW C dest S of Mericourt, shared "D9595" 06.30 22.8.18; DFW C crashed S of Combles, shared D9611 12.10 27.8.18; Fokker DVII crashed Trescault, just E of Havrincourt Wood 16.15 4.9.18 (all Capt AT Whealy); COL 9.11.18 (Sgt Lindsay); RTP by 9.2.19

**D9642** (BR.1) Mkrs by 17.6.18 for 4 AAP Lincoln; Rec Pk to 2 AI 7.7.18; 201 Sqdn 11.7.18; Fokker DVII BU SW of Armentières 20.45 31.7.18 (Mjr CD Booker DSC); Crashed in lines after combat with large number of Fokker DVIIs W of Rosières 11.00 13.8.18 (Mjr CD Booker DSC DoI) [credited Ltn Ulrich Neckel, Jasta 11] [Booker claimed to have shot down 3 Fokker DVII before being shot down himself]; SOC 13.8.18; Salved by No.6 SS, 5th Bde 21.8.18

**D9643** (BR.1) Mkrs by 17.6.18 for 4 AAP Lincoln; Rec Pk to 2 ASD 15.8.18; 201 Sqdn, into hole landing, o/t 4.11.18 (2/Lt CMK Morrison unhurt); for 2 ASD

**D9644** (BR.1) Mkrs by 17.6.18 for 4 AAP Lincoln; Rec Pk to 1 AI 1.7.18; 209 Sqdn 29.7.18; Left 09.55, last seen at 200ft over Guillaucourt 8.8.18 (2/Lt WL Brookes killed); SOC 8.8.18; Salved by No.6 SS, 5th Bde 21.8.18

**D9645** (BR.1) Mkrs by 17.6.18 for 4 AAP Lincoln; Rec Pk to 1 AI 6.7.18; 201 Sqdn 22.7.18; Fokker DVII probably OOC over Bailleul 29.7.18 (Lt RSS Orr); Fokker DVII OOC Armentières 20.45 31.7.18 (Lt RSS Orr); Left 06.00, down in flames E of Villers-Brettonneux 8.8.18 (Lt RSS Orr killed)

**D9646** (BR.1) Mkrs by 17.6.18 for 4 AAP Lincoln; Rec Pk to 1 AI 7.7.18; 209 Sqdn 20.7.18; Stalled landing, badly damaged 29.7.18 (Lt WA Rollason); 1 ASD 30.7.18; Rebuilt as F6329 in error 10.8.18, later changed to H6999

**D9647** 4 ASD to 213 Sqdn 4.7.18; Albatros DV OOC off Wendyne, shared B6358, B6448, B7270, D3326 & D9627 11.40 7.7.18 (Lt EN Allott); COL 13.7.18 (Lt RA Pearce); to 4 ASD; Rec Pk by 10.18; Pool 8.10.18

**D9648** (BR.1) 4 ASD to 204 Sqdn 15.7.18; 2 Fokker DVII OOC Blankenberghe 10.55, but aircraft severely shot up in combat, FL on beach Mardyke 12.8.18 (Lt WA Pomeroy); 4 ASD 12.8.18; 204 Sqdn 6.9.18; Fokker DVII DD Pervyse 18.50 24.9.18 (Lt SA Robinson); Hit by m/g fire raiding Lichtervelde 4.10.18 (Lt JR Robinson unhurt); Rep Pk 4 ASD by 25.10.18; 69 Aerodrome 26.10.18; to 213 Sqdn [to La Baraque 31.10.18; Bergues 1.11.18]; Fokker DVII OOC 10m SE of Ghent 15.15 9.11.18; LVG crashed 7m SE of Ghent, shared D8218, D9675 & F8505 10.40 10.11.18 (both Capt GC Mackay); 11 AP 23.2.19; WOC 23.2.19

**D9649** 4 ASD to 213 Sqdn 6.7.18; Fokker DVII in flames crashed Ostende, with D8177, probably by D8177 only 09.25 14.7.18 (Lt GFC Hopewell); Albatros C OOC 7m NE of Dixmude, shared C73 09.55 11.8.18 [5 Group record says 2 shared]; LVG C crashed on fire S of Zevecote, shared D3341 & N6376 16.50 21.8.18 (all Capt CP Brown); Rumpler C in flames E of Ostende Piers, shared D3378 14.00 15.9.18; KB in flames, fell on hangar setting it alight, then fire spread to 2 other hangars nr La Barrière, shared D3341 & D3378 10.50 18.9.18; Rumpler C in flames over St.Pierre Capelle, shared D3341 17.30 24.9.18; HA OOC in flames over Nieuport, own m/c badly damaged 25.9.18 (all Lt DS Ingalls USNRF); To 4 ASD; 210 Sqdn 17.10.18; FL S of Bruges 19.10.18 (Lt WA Pomeroy) [LM]

**D9650** (BR.1) Mkrs by 17.6.18 for 4 AAP Lincoln; Rec Pk to 1 AI 20.7.18; 209 Sqdn 20.7.18; Landed cross-wind Izel-le-Hameau, ran down bank on to sunken road, o/t 24.10.18 (2/Lt WP James unhurt); to 1 ASD

**D9651** (BR.1) Mkrs by 17.6.18 for 4 AAP Lincoln; 1 ASD to 203 Sqdn 13.7.18; DFW C shot down N of Hem 13.00 25.8.18; Left 19.30, DFW C crashed Hem 28.8.18; Fokker DVII OOC Haynecourt 15.30 20.9.18; Fokker DVII took off and crashed in field SW of Lieu St.Amand aerodrome 13.00 26.9.18; LVG C crashed nr Sensée Canal, nr Hem-Lenglet 07.30 29.9.18; Left 12.00, Fokker DVII dest Morenchies 2.10.18 (all Capt JD

Breakey); COL 9.11.18 (2/Lt Willy); 1 ASD 4.12.18

**D9652** (BR.1) Rec Pk to 2 AI 9.7.18; 2 AI 10.7.18; 201 Sqdn 2.8.18; Low flying patrol, shot down by ground fire E of Bayonvillers 09.05 8.8.18 (Lt LH Riddell PoW); SOC 8.8.18

**D9653** Rec Pk to 2 ASD 10.7.18; 201 Sqdn 10.8.18; Fokker DVII crashed N of Ligny 11.00 3.10.18 (2/Lt GK Green); After low flying patrol, collided with C6718 on landing in semi-darkness, both aircraft seriously damaged 8.10.18 (2/Lt GK Green); To 2 ASD; Rebuilt as H6890 [H6892?] 1.11.18

**D9654** Rec Pk to 1 AI 8.7.18; 203 Sqdn 13.7.18; Possibly the aircraft in which Lt FG Black wounded 3.9.18; COL on road nr edge of aerodrome 21.9.18 (Lt FG Black injured); 1 ASD 22.9.18; SOC 25.9.18

**D9655** 4 ASD to 210 Sqdn 24.7.18; Fokker DVII crashed S of Slype 18.45 11.8.18; Fokker DVII crashed nr Roulers, shared B7222, D3357, D3379 & E1405 18.30 3.9.18; Fokker DVII crashed E of Roulers 17.10 1.10.18 (all Lt CW Payton); EF, FL, badly damaged N of Herzeele 3.10.18 (2/Lt WS Jenkins minor injuries); 4 ASD 4.10.18 - @25.10.18

**D9656** Rec Pk to 1 AI 28.7.18; 201 Sqdn 29.7.18; Left 11.20 on low flying patrol, shot down in flames in front of advancing troops, destroyed by fire Harbonnières 8.8.18 (Lt R McLaughlin unhurt); SOC 8.8.18; Salved by No.6 SS, 5th Bde 21.8.18

**D9657** Rec Pk to 1 AI 14.7.18; 209 Sqdn 25.7.18; Fokker DVII crashed E of Bouchoir, shared D9637 11.55 10.8.18 [probably Ltn Muhs(?), Jasta 12]; Fokker DVII in flames Peronne 08.10 11.8.18 [probably Ltn Festler, Jasta 11] (both Lt KM Walker); Last seen in combat with 4 Fokker DVII E of Peronne 08.30 12.8.18 (Lt KM Walker killed); SOC 12.8.18

**D9658** 4 ASD to 204 Sqdn 15.7.18; COL, badly damaged 29.8.18 (Lt FG Bayley unhurt); To 4 ASD; 210 Sqdn 1.10.18; After attacking and silencing AA position, shot down in flames by ground m/g fire Courtrai 10.00 2.10.18 (Lt CW Payton killed)

**D9659** (BR.1) 4 ASD to 213 Sqdn 17.7.18; Fokker DVII OOC 4m SE of Ypres 12.15 12.8.18; Pfalz DIII OOC 3m W of Ostende 10.40 13.8.18 (both Lt JE Greene); Attacked by 11 HA, shot up, FL, crashed nr aerodrome 21.8.18 (Lt WA Rankin unhurt); To 4 ASD, still there 25.10.18

**D9660** (BR.1) Deld 2 AAP Hendon W/E 29.8.18; Turnhouse W/E 12.9.18; Donibristle W/E 31.10.18; Turnhouse W/E 21.11.18 - @30.1.19

**D9661** (BR.1) Deld 2 AAP Hendon W/E 29.8.18; Turnhouse W/E 12.9.18; Donibristle W/E 31.10.18; Turnhouse W/E 21.11.18 - @30.1.19

**D9662** (BR.1) Deld 2 AAP Hendon W/E 29.8.18; Turnhouse W/E 12.9.18 - @30.1.19

**D9663** (BR.1) Deld 2 AAP Hendon W/E 29.8.18; Turnhouse W/E 12.9.18 - @30.1.19

**D9664** 4 ASD to 213 Sqdn 7.8.18; Albatros OOC 3m ESE of Dixmude, shared B7252, D3409 & D8189 19.40 11.8.18 (Lt AH Turner); 4 ASD 16.8.18; 210 Sqdn 12.9.18; Last seen diving on HA in general engagement with 15 HA Zarren-Wijnendaele Wood 08.00 29.9.18 (2/Lt JF Stafford killed); Deleted 15.10.18

**D9665** (BR.1) Deld 2 AAP Hendon W/E 29.8.18; Turnhouse W/E 20.9.18 - @30.1.19

**D9666** (BR.1) Lympne to 4 ASD Guines 13.7.18; 2 AAP Hendon W/E 29.8.18; Turnhouse W/E 20.9.18 - @30.1.19

**D9667** 5 AI to 201 Sqdn (coded 'B', named 'ROSSLYN CASTLE') 4.10.18 (presentation a/c?); 203 Sqdn 23.1.19; RTP W/E 9.2.19

**D9668** 1 ASD to 209 Sqdn 8.8.18; Last seen in combat with Fokker DVIIs E of Peronne 12.8.18 (Capt JK Summers MC PoW) [credited Ltn Lothar von Richtofen, Jasta 11]; SOC 12.8.18

**D9669** Rec Pk to 2 ASD 15.8.18; 201 Sqdn (coded 'B') 11.8.18; Fokker DVII crashed Lagnicourt 07.15 2.9.18 (Capt R Sykes); Low flying patrol, crashed in shell hole at ALG, o/t, wrecked 9.10.18 (Lt RD Hambrook unhurt); To 2 ASD; Rebuilt as H6898 25.11.18

**D9670** (BR.1) Rec Pk to 1 AI 22.7.18; 209 Sqdn 25.7.18; Left 14.00, hit by ground m/g fire, FL French area nr Conty 8.8.18 (Lt MA Toomey); Brought in by 22 Wg SS for 2 ASD 8.8.18; SOC 8.8.18

**D9671** (BR.1) Rec Pk to 1 AI 22.7.18; 203 Sqdn 24.7.18; Fokker DVII OOC E of Bray 19.30 11.8.18 (Capt JP Hales); Left 12.10, hit by AA fire, spun in N of Bray 23.8.18 (Capt JP Hales killed)

**D9672** Rec Pk to 2 AI 10.7.18; 201 Sqdn 8.8.18; LVG C crashed in flames 2m SE of Haynecourt, 2 crew baled out successfully. shared F5941 09.05 16.9.18; Fokker DVII crashed in flames 9.10.18; Albatros C OOC Forêt de Mormal 12.30 29.10.18; Fokker DVII in flames SE of Montifiure 14.50 9.11.18 (all Lt JM Mackay); still 201 Sqdn 23.11.18

**D9673** (BR.1) 4 ASD to 210 Sqdn 24.7.18; Fokker DVII OOC Nieuport-Dixmude, shared E1405 11.15 31.7.18; Fokker DVII OOC Wervicq, shared E1405 18.25 31.7.18 (both Capt LP Coombes); Tail skid broke landing, swung, hit tree 13.8.18 (Lt SC Joseph); to 4 ASD; 201 Sqdn 26.9.18; Shot down in flames, last seen 14.30 in single combat with 7 Fokker DVIIs after patrol attacked by 14 HA 2m N of Dixmude 14.10.18 (Lt K McLeish USNRF killed, body found nr Ghistelles)

**D9674** 1 ASD to 210 Sqdn 30.7.18; Propeller shot through by AA, FL, badly damaged nr Poperinghe 23.8.18 (Lt L Yerex unhurt); to 4 ASD; Tested 25.9.18 - @4.10.18

**D9675** (BR.1) 1 ASD to 210 Sqdn 30.7.18; Fokker DVII OOC N of Lille 19.25 1.8.18; Fokker DVII crashed W of Roulers 11.8.18; Fokker DVII crashed SE of Bruges 16.20 15.8.18 (all Lt E Swale); Overshot landing, crashed just off aerodrome 7.9.18 (2/Lt JE Harrison unhurt); to 4 ASD; 213 Sqdn 6.11.18; LVG C crashed 7m SE of Ghent, shared D8218, D9648 & F8505 10.40 10.11.18 (Lt AF Chick); 11 AP 23.2.19; WOC 23.2.19

**D9676** Rec Pk to 2 AI 8.8.18; 209 Sqdn 9.8.18; Low flying patrol, BU in air, crashed nr Monchy unsalveable 26.8.18 (2/Lt RW Whalley wounded); SOC in field 27.8.18

**D9677** (BR.1) 4 ASD to 213 Sqdn 29.7.18; Badly shot up in low level bombing raid 14.10.18 (Mjr R Graham unhurt); 4 ASD 14.10.18; 213 Sqdn 12.11.18; 11 AP 25.2.19; WOC 25.2.19

**D9678** 4 ASD to 213 Sqdn 31.7.18; Fokker DVII OOC 6m ENE of Dixmude, shared B7252, D8189 & D8217 14.25 23.9.18 (Lt AR Talbot); EF, FL in sea and ran into side of monitor *General Craufurd*, sank 2.10.18 (2/Lt WH Herd rescued unhurt); deleted 15.10.18

**D9679** Rec Pk to 1 AI 5.9.18; 203 Sqdn 28.9.18; RTP W/E 16.2.19

**D9680** Rec Pk to 2 ASD 9.8.18; 201 Sqdn 13.8.18; O/t landing cross-wind through corn, wrecked Noeux 14.8.18 (2/Lt HJ Ewan unhurt); For 2 ASD; 204 Sqdn, ex Bisseghem 28.10.18 (visit?)

**13 HANDLEY PAGE O/400 TRACTOR BIPLANE HEAVY BOMBERS from batch D9681 to D9730 built by Clayton & Shuttleworth Ltd at Lincoln. (Eagle VIII)**

**D9681** England to 216 Sqdn (via Paris) 10.5.18; 3 ASD 16.9.18 (wrecked)

**D9682** 215 Sqdn

**D9683** 215 Sqdn by 12.6.18; 207 Sqdn 18.1.19; Exposed to weather, declared unfit 19.4.19; for overhaul by 8 SS

**D9684** Mkrs 16.4.18 for EF; 215 Sqdn from/by 19.8.18; Missing on bombing raid on Mannheim 16/17.9.18 (2/Lt JB Lacy, 2/Lt CN Yelverton & 2/Lt RT Down all PoW); SOC in field 17.9.18

**D9691** 58 TDS Cranwell by 4.7.18 - @22.7.18

**D9694** (Eagle VIII) Lympne to 4 ASD 11.8.18; 214 Sqdn 3.9.18; EF returning from raid, crashed into wood, caught fire, BO, St.Inglevert 4.10.18 (Lt C Burgener, Sgt AA Parker & Elec Magee USA all unhurt); SOC in field 5.10.18; WOC 30.11.18

**D9696** 214 Sqdn by 24.10.18 [COs machine at St.Inglevert]; With 214 Sqdn to ME, to Buc 6.7.19; Arr 31.7.19 - @2.8.19

**D9700** UK to Rec Pk 11.8.18; 3 AD 12.8.18; 216 Sqdn 22.8.18; 97 Sqdn 26.8.18; Rec Pk to 3 AD 15.9.18; 97 Sqdn by 11.18; EF, FL Breteuil 30.11.18 (Lt Gunther, Lt Neil, AM Horridge & AM Wishart all unhurt?); To have been repaired 2 AI, but SOC in field 23.12.18

**D9701** (Eagle VIII) Lympne to Rec Pk 13.9.18; 3 AD 15.9.18 (arr 16.9.18); 216 Sqdn 17.9.18; Turned at low altitude, sideslipped in, wrecked in field adjoining aerodrome,

Quilen 9.12.18 (Lt CE Mott & Lt IB Boyce unhurt); 2 ASD 9.12.18

D9714    UK to Rec Pk 18.10.18; 3 AD 23.10.18; 215 Sqdn 1.11.18; 207 Sqdn 18.1.19

D9718    58 TDS Cranwell by @27.10.18 - @22.11.18

D9719    58 TDS Cranwell by 2.11.18

D9720    UK to Rec Pk 30.10.18; Paris 4.11.18 (weather); contd to 3 AD 11.18; 216 Sqdn by 4.19; Crashed Aachen 30.4.19 (Lt LG Semple and observer unhurt)

## 1 ROYAL AIRCRAFT FACTORY R.E.8 TRACTOR BIPLANES from batch E1 to E300 built by The Siddeley-Deasy Motor Car Co Ltd at Coventry

E32    207 TDS Chingford, propeller accident 2.4.18 (Pte Corti injured); 10 TDS Harling Road by 10.18

## 12 AIRCO D.H.9 TRACTOR BIPLANE DAY BOMBERS from batch E601 to E700 built by Whitehead Aircraft Co Ltd at Richmond. (230-hp Puma)

E601    Acceptance tests Brooklands 27/28.6.18; Yarmouth by 8.7.18; Covehithe 29.7.18; Became 534 Flt 273 Sqdn Covehithe by 1.9.18 - @31.10.18

E603    Manston to 557/8 Flts 212 Sqdn Yarmouth 22.7.18 - @31.10.18

E604    Manston to Yarmouth 13.8.18; FL Walberswick, nr Southwold, wrecked 19.8.18 (2 crew unhurt)

E606    Eastchurch to Manston 6.7.18 - @8.18

E612    Covehithe by 11.18

E635    Rec Pk to 2 ASD 6.8.18; 49 Sqdn 9.8.18; 2 AI by 1.19; 211 Sqdn 13.2.19; 98 Sqdn 23.2.19; 1 AD 5.3.19; To England 6.3.19

E686    Deld 6 SD Ascot for Mudros W/E 17.10.18; Shipped/left W/E 7.11.18; Base Depot RAF Novorossisk to Russian Air Corps 14.2.20

E687    Deld 6 SD Ascot for Mudros W/E 17.10.18; Shipped/left W/E 7.11.18; Base Depot RAF Novorossisk to Russian Air Corps 14.2.20

E688    Deld 6 SD Ascot for Mudros W/E 17.10.18; Shipped/left W/E 7.11.18; TOC Base Depot RAF Novorossisk 14.2.20; SOC 5.3.20

E689    Deld 6 SD Ascot for Mudros W/E 31.10.18; Shipped/left W/E 7.11.18; TOC Base Depot RAF Novorossisk 14.2.20; SOC 5.3.20

E690    Deld 6 SD Ascot for Mudros W/E 17.10.18; Shipped/left W/E 21.11.18; TOC Base Depot RAF Novorossisk 14.2.20; SOC 5.3.20

E691    Rec Pk to 1 AI 16.10.18; 211 Sqdn 18.10.18; Hit on ground by another m/c 27.10.18; to 7 SS 28.10.18; SOC in field

## 2 AIRCO D.H.9A TRACTOR BIPLANE DAY BOMBERS from batch E701 to E1100 built by Whitehead Aircraft Co Ltd at Richmond.

E764    221 Sqdn .19; To Anti-Bolsheviks

E766    221 Sqdn by 7.19; To Anti-Bolsheviks

## 43 SOPWITH F.1 CAMEL TRACTOR BIPLANE FIGHTERS from batch E1401 to E1600 built by Ruston, Proctor & Co Ltd at Lincoln. (130-hp Clerget LS)

E1404    1 AI to 208 Sqdn 10.7.18; Hit by AA, fell OOC behind lines 06.30 18.7.18 (Lt WSK Scudamore killed); SOC in field 18.7.18

E1405    4 ASD to 210 Sqdn 28.7.18; Fokker DIII OOC 5m E of Dixmude 09.55 30.7.18 (Lt SC Joseph); Fokker DVII OOC Nieuport-Dixmude 11.15 & another OOC Wervicq, both shared D9673 18.25 31.7.18; Fokker DVII crashed SE of Dixmude 18.35 11.8.18; Fokker DVII OOC Nieuport-Westende 09.05 12.8.18; Fokker DVII crashed nr Roulers, shared B7222, D3357, D3379 & D9655 18.30 3.9.18; Fokker DVII crashed SE of Roulers 17.30 5.9.18 (all Lt IC Sanderson); In action 17.9.18 (Lt IC Sanderson wounded); 4 ASD 5.10.18; Deleted 15.10.18 general fatigue

E1406    4 ASD to 213 Sqdn 16.8.18; Fokker DVII lost starboard wing 10m S of Ostende 07.30 25.8.18; Fokker DVII crashed in wood 2½m S of Varssenaere 14.40 5.9.18 (both Lt JE Greene); 4 ASD 17.9.18; 210 Sqdn

E1408    12.10.18; 4 ASD 13.10.18; 204 Sqdn 7.11.18; 203 Sqdn 25.1.19; RTP W/E 23.2.19

E1408    Hendon to Lympne 27.6.18; 1 AI to 208 Sqdn 18.7.18; Left 08.00, last seen over Lillers on outward journey 28.7.18 (Sgt D Tottman PoW); SOC 28.7.18

E1417    Lympne to Rec Pk 6.7.18; 1 AI 9.7.18; 208 Sqdn 20.7.18; 2-str OOC S of Estaires 20.40 29.7.18; Pfalz DIII shot down S of Pont-à-Vendin 11.40 31.7.18 (both Lt JB White); DFW C OOC 13.9.18 (2/Lt EA Kenny); Crashed 8.10.18 (2/Lt PFT Luckham); 2 AI 3.11.18

E1419    54 TDS Fairlop, crashed on approach 4.8.18 (2/Lt SA Grimmride)

E1420    (140-hp RAF) 54 TDS Fairlop, turned slowly into wind and spun in from 500 ft 25.7.18 (2/Lt W Meff killed)

E1433    Deld AAP Whitley Abbey/Coventry W/E 11.7.18; 6 SD Ascot by 13.7.18; Shipped to Taranto 30.7.18; AD Taranto by 9.18 - @30.1.19

E1436    4 FS Freiston, spar broke while diving on target, landed safely 29.7.18 (2/Lt EA Kenny unhurt) [only 1 hrs flying from new]

E1438    4 FS Freiston .18

E1440    Deld 4 AAP Lincoln by 7.18; 208 TDS Leuchars 25.7.18

E1447    2 SoSF Redcar, petrol shortage, FL, o/t 19.6.18 (Capt GleB Diamond injured)

E1465    Deld 6 SD Ascot W/E 29.8.18; Shipped 6.9.18; Mudros by 10.18 - @11.18

E1466    Deld 6 SD Ascot W/E 29.8.18; To Docks W/E 19.9.18; Shipped 11.10.18; Mudros by 1.19; To White Russian Forces

E1468    Rec Pk to 1 AI 8.7.18; 208 Sqdn 8.7.18; Left 19.00, badly shot about by ground m/g fire bombing Jigsaw Wood, nr St.Léger, FL nr lines 20.15 26.8.18 (Lt JW Marshall); 1 ASD 29.8.18; SOC in field

E1489    66 Sqdn by 10.18; ARS 84 Wing Vendôme by 11.18

E1490    205 TDS Vendôme, crashed 13.9.18 (2/Lt JB Fast); ARS 84 Wing Vendôme by 11.18

E1491    205 TDS Vendôme, crashed 16.9.18 (2/Lt AH Williams unhurt)

E1492    205 TDS Vendôme, engine choked at 6 ft after TO, slightly damaged 17.8.18 (F/Cdt CSP Davis unhurt)

E1493    205 TDS Vendôme, spun in on back Nourray 21.11.18 (PFO AM McElhinney killed)

E1504    205 TDS Vendôme, swung on TO and badly damaged 27.8.18 (2/Lt JAV McRobert unhurt)

E1510    205 TDS Vendôme, crashed 16.8.18 (F/Cdt GR Gaches unhurt); Crashed St.Ouen 4.10.18 (F/Cdt JA Fraser unhurt)

E1511    To EF 8.18 for Vendôme, but burnt at Depot and SOC

E1512    ARS 84 Wing Vendôme by 11.18

E1513    205 TDS Vendôme, crashed 16.8.18 (PFO WA Hammerton unhurt); ARS 84 Wing Vendôme by 11.18

E1514    205 TDS Vendôme, engine choked on TO, struck road, stalled and o/t, badly damaged 25.7.18 (F/Cdt HW Clark); ARS 84 Wing Vendôme by 11.18

E1515    205 TDS Vendôme, u/c collapsed when swung on TO, badly damaged 30.7.18 (PFO C Shaw); Crashed 14.10.18 (F/Cdt AW Gilbert unhurt); ARS 84 Wing Vendôme by 11.18

E1516    Naval Flt 219 Sqdn Manston by 21.11.18

E1518    Naval Flt 219 Sqdn Manston by 3.8.18; 28 Sqdn

E1520    204 TDS Eastchurch by 29.9.18

E1523    32 TDS Montrose to 204 TDS Eastchurch 29.7.18 - @12.10.18

E1524    204 TDS Eastchurch by 3.9.18

E1526    210 Sqdn by 10.18

E1529    Deld Eastbourne 19.7.18

E1536    (BR.1) 43 Sqdn to 2 ASD 30.8.18; 209 Sqdn, COL in strong gusty wind, o/t 7.1.19 (2/Lt LH Parson unhurt); to 1 ASD

E1538    Lympne to Rec Pk 30.7.18; 1 AI 24.8.18; 208 Sqdn 28.8.18; Fokker DVII OOC Marquin-Ecourt St.Quentin 17.50 1.9.18; Fokker DVII OOC N of St.Quentin 26.9.18 (both Capt GK Cooper); 2 ASD 22.11.18

E1545    (140-hp Clerget) Rec Pk to 1 AI 4.8.18; 208 Sqdn 5.8.18; Left 09.00, FTR after patrol attacked heavily by HA 2.9.18 (2/Lt CH Living PoW); SOC 2.9.18

E1546    Rec Pk to 1 AI 4.8.18; 208 Sqdn 5.8.18; 2 ASD 30.10.18

E1556    485/6 Flts 273 Sqdn Burgh Castle by 1.8.18 - @17.9.18

E1558    486 Flt 273 Sqdn Burgh Castle by 8.18 - @4.11.18

E1559    Yarmouth by 7.18; 470 Flt 219 Sqdn Manston 1.10.18; 148th US Aero Sqdn

E1588    Hendon to Martlesham 28.6.18; Rec Pk by 8.18; 1 AI 13.8.18; 208 Sqdn 16.8.18; Fokker DVII in flames S of River Scarpe 07.50 27.8.18; DFW C OOC N of Gloster Wood 10.00 1.9.18; Fokker DVII OOC Marquin 14.25 3.9.18; Fokker DVII in flames & another OOC Canal du Nord 18.30 6.9.18 (all Capt WEG Mann); 2 ASD 30.10.18

E1589    Rec Pk to 2 ASD 9.8.18; 201 Sqdn 14.8.18; 148th US Aero Sqdn

**24 AVRO 504J & 504K TRACTOR BIPLANE TRAINERS from batch E1601 to E1900 built by parent firm at Hamble**

E1611    Grand Fleet SoAF&G East Fortune/Leuchars by 10.18 - @3.19. Became G-EAHU

E1612    Grand Fleet SoAF&G East Fortune/Leuchars by 9.18 - @5.19

E1613    Grand Fleet SoAF&G East Fortune/Leuchars by 9.18 - @8.19

E1614    Grand Fleet SoAF&G East Fortune/Leuchars by 7.19

E1615    Grand Fleet SoAF&G Leuchars by 3.19

E1616    Grand Fleet SoAF&G Leuchars by 1.19 - @5.19

E1620    212 TDS Vendôme, fuel shortage, FL in dark, badly damaged Lisle 5.10.18 (Lt AD Reid unhurt)

E1624    (504K) (Monosoupape) 212 TDS Vendôme, landing wire broke and engine trouble, landed on top of wood, badly damaged Chateau-Renault 10.11.18 (F/Cdt W Henry & Lt AD Reid unhurt); ARS 84 Wing Vendôme 11.18

E1625    (504K) ARS 84 Wing Vendôme by 11.18; 205 TDS Vendôme by 30.11.18

E1627    (504K) ARS 84 Wing Vendôme by 11.18; 212 TDS Vendôme

E1628    (504K) (Le Rhône) 205 TDS Vendôme, accidentally opened throttle 12.10.18 (F/Cdt RE Lindsay slightly injured); ARS 84 Wing Vendôme by 11.18

E1672    Grand Fleet SoAF&G Leuchars by 8.19

E1675    Grand Fleet SoAF&G Leuchars by 4.19 - @5.19; Became G-EAIG

E1678    Grand Fleet SoAF&G East Fortune/Leuchars by 5.19

E1698    56 TDS Cranwell by 9.18; 57 TDS Cranwell by 12.18

E1699    55 TDS Manston by 10.18

E1700    56 TDS Cranwell by 10.18; Midland Area FIS Lilbourne 4.10.18

E1712    East Fortune by 9.18

E1795    55 TDS Manston by 10.18

E1798    56 TDS Cranwell by 8.18 - @12.18

E1799    56 TDS Cranwell by 8.18

E1800    57 TDS Cranwell by 18.9.18 - @3.19

E1806    (504K) (110-hp Le Rhône) 1(S)MAD Hamble, EF after TO, turned back, crashed 5.7.18 (Capt EL Pralle & Lt WF Cleeve both slightly injured)

E1860    205/212 TDS Vendôme by 12.18

**3 BRISTOL F.2B TRACTOR BIPLANES from batch E1901 to E2150 built by Sir W.G.Armstrong Whitworth & Co Ltd at Gosforth. (215-hp Arab)**

E1902    Grand Fleet SoAF&G Leuchars, crashed 10.7.19 (Lt EJ Campbell Kirby & 2/Lt KC McKenzie injured)

E1969    On delivery Cranwell to Liverpool, crashed on TO, BO 31.7.19 (Lt WA Roberts & Lt E Ireland both killed)

E1971    Cranwell by 6.19

**15 AVRO 504K TRACTOR BIPLANE TRAINERS from batch E2901 to E3050 built by Morgan & Co at Leighton Buzzard**

E2910    Special Station Fairlop by 10.18

E2924    57 TDS Cranwell by 11.18

E2927    57 TDS Cranwell by 9.18 - @11.18

E2928    56 TDS Cranwell by 8.18

E2929    (130-hp Clerget) 58 TDS Cranwell, collided with D.H.6 B2787 19.8.18 (F/Cdt SA Scott & 2/Lt CE Shirlwell both killed)

E2969    57 TDS Cranwell by 11.18

E3001    Grand Fleet SoAF&G Leuchars by 5.19 - @6.19

E3005    Grand Fleet SoAF&G Leuchars by 5.19 - @6.19

E3006    Grand Fleet SoAF&G Leuchars by 5.19 - @6.19

E3007    Grand Fleet SoAF&G Leuchars by 5.19 - @6.19

E3010    Grand Fleet SoAF&G Leuchars by 5.19 - @6.19

E3027    57 TDS Cranwell by 9.18

E3037    201 TDS East Fortune, EF, FL, crashed 13.1.19 (2/Lt JL Rolston slightly injured & 2/Lt GG Daddell unhurt)

E3038    57 TDS Cranwell by 11.18

E3041    (80-hp Le Rhône) 57 TDS Cranwell by 11.18; Became RAF (Cadet) College Cranwell 5.2.20 - 4.20

**13 AVRO 504K TRACTOR BIPLANE TRAINERS from batch E3051 to E3150 built by Savages Ltd at Kings Lynn**

E3057    (130-hp Clerget) 56 TDS Cranwell, spun in 17.8.18 (F/Cdt WC Spriggs seriously injured)

E3058    56 TDS Cranwell by 8.18

E3059    56 TDS Cranwell by 8.18 - @9.18; 57 TDS Cranwell by 10.18 - @11.18

E3060    56 TDS Cranwell by 8.18

E3062    55 TDS Manston by 8.18 - @9.18

E3063    55 TDS Manston by 8.18; 55 TDS Narborough 11.9.18

E3070    55 TDS Manston by 10.18

E3104    55 TDS Narborough by 10.18 - @1.19

E3109    55 TDS Narborough by 11.18 - @2.19

E3123    Grand Fleet SoAF&G Leuchars by 6.19

E3126    Grand Fleet SoAF&G Leuchars by 9.19

E3135    55 TDS Narborough by 2.19

E3140    Pool of Pilots Joyce Green, tested new 11.2.19 - @3.19

**1 ROYAL AIRCRAFT FACTORY F.E.2H TRACTOR BIPLANES from trial batch E3151 to E3153**

E3151    EAD Grain by 25.5.18 (awaiting wings and tail)

**8 AVRO 504K TRACTOR BIPLANE TRAINERS from batch E3254 to E3403 built by Parnall & Sons Ltd at Bristol**

E3390    Deld Turnhouse W/E 12.12.18 - @30.1.19

E3391    Deld Turnhouse W/E 12.12.18 - @30.1.19

E3392    Deld Turnhouse W/E 12.12.18 - @30.1.19; Grand Fleet SoAF&G Leuchars by 5.19 - @11.19; CAAD Leuchars by 2.21 - @5.21

E3393    Deld Turnhouse W/E 12.12.18 - @30.1.19

E3394    Deld Turnhouse W/E 12.12.18 - @30.1.19; Leuchars by .19 - .20

E3395    Deld Turnhouse W/E 12.12.18 - @10.19; BUT Gullane @6.19

E3396    Deld Turnhouse W/E 12.12.18 - @8.19; BUT Gullane @6.19

E3397    Deld Turnhouse W/E 12.12.18; Stalled 50ft from ground 4.3.19 (2/Lt JE Badgeley unhurt & 2/Lt AW Green seriously injured)

**25 AVRO 504K TRACTOR BIPLANE TRAINERSS from batch E3404 to E3903 built by parent company at Hamble**

E3404    205 TDS Vendôme by 11.18; ARS 84 Wing Vendôme by 11.18

E3405    205 TDS Vendôme by 9.18; ARS 84 Wing Vendôme by 11.18; 205 TDS Vendôme by 30.11.18

E3406    (Monosoupape) 212 TDS Vendôme, FL, badly damaged Hourray 23.9.18 (2/Lt W Pye & Lt ED Reid unhurt); ARS 84 Wing Vendôme by 11.18; 205 TDS Vendôme by 11.18; CFS Upavon by 12.23

E3407    (Monosoupape) 212 TDS Vendôme, EF, FL, ran into vine wires, o/t nr aerodrome, slightly damaged 1.9.18 (Lt CS Kent unhurt); Pancaked from 40ft, badly damaged 1.10.18 (2/Lt W Pye & Lt ED Reid unhurt); ARS 84 Wing Vendôme by 11.18; 205 TDS by 11.18

E3408    (Monosoupape) 205 TDS, FL Nazelles 25.9.18 (F/Cdt F Lythgoe unhurt); To ARS 84 Wing Vendôme 11.18; Became G-EADY

E3409    205 TDS by 11.18; ARS 84 Wing Vendôme by 11.18

E3521    55 TDS Manston test 24.10.18

E3531    55 TDS Narborough by 1.19 - @2.19

E3548    EAF Contingent Bereznik 8.19

E3582    EAF Contingent Bereznik 8.19

E3583    Syren Force, North Russia by 15.9.19 - @29.9.19

E3620    ARS 84 Wing Vendôme by 11.18

E3621    ARS 84 Wing Vendôme by 11.18

E3622    ARS 84 Wing Vendôme by 11.18

E3623    205 TDS Vendôme by 11.18; ARS 84 Wing Vendôme by 11.18

E3624    ARS 84 Wing Vendôme by 11.18

E3626   ARS 84 Wing Vendôme by 11.18
E3627   ARS 84 Wing Vendôme by 11.18
E3628   ARS 84 Wing Vendôme by 11.18
E3629   ARS 84 Wing Vendôme by 11.18
E3630   205 TDS Vendôme by 11.18
E3632   205 TDS Vendôme by 11.18
E3797   (Monosoupape) MAES Grain by 23.6.20 [504L at one time]
E3800   Development Sqdn Gosport 1919
E3808   (Monosoupape) FF 18.3.19; Devt Flt Gosport, spun into sea while spotting for torpedo drop by Sopwith Cuckoo 23.3.20 (F/O GH Boyce)

## 10 AVRO 504K TRACTOR BIPLANE TRAINERS   from batch E4104 to E4303 built by Humber Ltd at Coventry

E4144   (Monosoupape) 55 TDS Manston by 4.8.18
E4232   56 TDS Cranwell by 11.18
E4285   57 TDS Cranwell by 4.19
E4286   57 TDS Cranwell by 1.19 - @3.19
E4287   57 TDS Cranwell by 5.19
E4292   56 TDS Cranwell by 1.19
E4293   56/57 TDS Cranwell by 1.19 - @4.19
E4296   57 TDS Cranwell by 1.19
E4297   57 TDS Cranwell by 4.19 - @5.19
E4298   57 TDS Cranwell by 4.19 - @5.19

## 1 AVRO 504J TRACTOR BIPLANE TRAINER  from batch E4324 to E4373 built by Eastbourne Aviation Co

E4332   (Le Rhône) (c/n 332) 206 TDS Eastbourne by 13.7.18

## 50 SOPWITH F.1 CAMEL TRACTOR BIPLANE SCOUTS ordered under Cont No A.S.7861 from Clayton & Shuttleworth Ltd, Lincoln and numbered E4374 to E4423. Accepted 4 AAP Lincoln. All to naval units. (150-hp B.R.1 unless otherwise stated)

E4374   Deld 3.6.18; Rec Pk to 1 AI 30.7.18; 203 Sqdn 1.8.18; Struck by ground fire over Peronne, crashed in front line, under shell fire, TW 31.8.18 (2/Lt DH Woodhouse slightly injured); SOC in field 31.8.18

E4375   2 AI to 201 Sqdn 9.8.18; Fokker DVII OOC Assévillers 18.45 10.8.18 (Lt WAW Carter); Fokker DVII OOC E of Cambrai 18.45 6.9.18 (2/Lt GH Fowles); Low flying patrol, fuel tank hit by m/g fire, crashed, o/t nr British tanks in midst of the barrage, unsalveable 27.9.18 (Lt WAW Carter escaped through lines unhurt)

E4376   Rec Pk to 1 AI 28.7.18; 209 Sqdn 27.8.18; Low flying patrol, last seen over Cambrai 13.15 29.9.18 (Capt EB Drake killed)

E4377   Rec Pk to 2 ASD 9.8.18; 203 Sqdn 16.8.18; Patrol attacked by Fokker DVIIs, last seen in combat over Haynecourt 15.30 20.9.18 (2/Lt CG Milne PoW)

E4378   Rec Pk to 2 ASD 9.8.18; 209 Sqdn 12.8.18; Last seen diving W over Abancourt with Fokker DVII on tail 8.10.18 (2/Lt F Cornwell PoW)

E4379   Rec Pk to 2 ASD 9.8.18; 201 Sqdn 10.8.18; Fokker DVII OOC over Lihons 19.45, then tyre burst landing, o/t 11.8.18 (Lt JA Parkinson unhurt); 2 ASD 12.8.18; Rebuilt as F6281 4.9.18

E4380   Rec Pk to 1 AI 3.8.18; 209 Sqdn 27.8.18; Fokker DVII down in flames Thun-l'Evêque 13.40 8.10.18 (Lt FA Giles); Practising rolls and spins, spun in on aerodrome from 500ft 11.10.18 (2/Lt M Heard killed); to 1 ASD, SOC in field

E4381   Lympne to Rec Pk 26.7.18; 1 AI 30.7.18; 209 Sqdn 27.8.18; Last seen 07.30 Ecourt St.Quentin, probably one of two aircraft seen down in flames [the other probably F5970] 2.9.18 (2/Lt WM Wormald killed)

E4382   Rec Pk to 1 AI 7.8.18; 209 Sqdn 27.8.18; Last seen over Emerchourt 06.30 17.9.18 (2/Lt JE Walker killed)

E4383   4 ASD to 210 Sqdn 13.8.18; Fokker DVII crashed S of Pierre Capelle 14.40 24.9.18; Fokker DVII crashed E of Staden 17.25 28.9.18; Fokker DVII OOC Wijnendaele Wood 08.00 29.9.18; Fokker DVII attacking British KBs shot down Ardoye, NE of Roulers 14.15 14.10.18 (all Lt P Boulton); Overshot on landing, o/t down bank, badly damaged 28.10.18 (T/2/Lt KW Akers unhurt); 2 ASD 29.10.18

E4384   Depot to 204 Sqdn 30.10.18; Patrol attacked 08.45 by 24

Fokker DVIIs with red noses and white tails, shot about then hit by AA, FL then shelled Moulin de Voorde 4.11.18 (Lt JR Chisman unhurt); Salved by 8 SS 5.11.18; Depot 6.11.18, deletion recommended

E4385   4 ASD to 213 Sqdn 10.8.18; Last seen 17.45 when patrol attacked by 7 Fokker DVIIs 3m W of Thourout 25.9.18 (2/Lt G Iliff killed)

E4386   8 AAP Lympne by 8.18; Rec Pk to 1 AI 1.9.18; 203 Sqdn 15.9.18; Rumpler C dest nr St.Aubert, shared C187 16.30 9.10.18; Green/white Fokker DVII OOC E of Bray 15.15 29.10.18 (both Capt LH Rochford); still 203 Sqdn @12.18

E4387   Presentation a/c 'Leatherhead'. 204 Sqdn by 16.8.18; COL, badly damaged 21.8.18 (Lt DF Tysoe unhurt); 4 ASD 21.8.18; 204 Sqdn 28.9.18; Last seen 09.10 in dog fight over St.Denis Westrem with 30/40 Fokker DVIIs 27.10.18 (2/Lt PF Cormack presumed killed)

E4388   Rec Pk to 2 AI 9.8.18; 209 Sqdn 11.8.18; Left 15.00, last seen under control at 10,000 ft nr Hamblin 1.9.18 (2/Lt HV Peeling PoW); SOC 5.9.18

E4389   Rec Pk to 2 AI 8.8.18; 209 Sqdn 9.8.18; Left 14.15, hit by heavy ground m/g fire, fuel tank shot through, FL and stood on nose Villers-lès-Roye, nr Bouchoir 10.8.18 (Lt JW Sole); 22 Wing SS 10.8.18; SOC 10.8.18

E4390   4 ASD to 210 Sqdn 7.8.18; Fokker OOC NE of Roulers 17.20, then last seen diving from 2,000ft nr Abeele aerodrome, probably shot down in engagement SE of Roulers 17.30  5.9.18 (Lt L Yerex PoW); Deleted 15.9.18

E4391   Rec Pk to 2 ASD 9.8.18; 201 Sqdn 14.8.18; Apparently hit by flak, FL, o/t Flesquières 11.55 14.9.18 (2/Lt WA Johnston PoW); SOC 1 ASD 14.9.18

E4392   Rec Pk to 1 AI 7.8.18; 209 Sqdn 22.8.18; Low flying patrol, left 19.10, retd with bottom right hand longeron shot through 20.00 26.8.18 (Lt RL Scharff unhurt); 1 ASD 27.8.18; Rebuilt as H7107 14.9.18

E4393   Rec Pk to 1 AI 7.8.18; 209 Sqdn 26.8.18; Left 15.00, last seen diving on 7 Fokker DVIIs over Boiry-Notre Dame 1.9.18 (2/Lt RL Scharff PoW) [credited Ltn Quandt, Jasta 36]; SOC in field 1.9.18

E4394   Rec Pk to 209 Sqdn 27.9.18 (ferrying work); O/t on landing after wheel came away 18.1.19 (2/Lt EL Edwards unhurt); 203 Sqdn 24.1.19; RTP W/E 23.2.19

E4395   1 AD to 204 Sqdn 2.11.18; 203 Sqdn 25.1.19; RTP W/E 23.2.19

E4396   Rec Pk to 2 AI, collided on arrival, badly damaged 6.8.18 (Lt HH Whitlock unhurt); Crashed & WO on ferry flight 6.8.18

E4397   4 ASD to 213 Sqdn 12.8.18; COL on turn 28.9.18 (Lt GS Sutcliffe); 4 ASD 28.9.18 - @25.10.18; 1 AI to 209 Sqdn 4.11.18; to 203 Sqdn, RTP W/E 23.2.19

E4398   Rec Pk to 2 ASD 13.8.18; 203 Sqdn 30.8.18; Overshot landing from operational patrol 11.10.18 (Sgt AC Fidgen unhurt); to 1 ASD

E4399   Rec Pk to 2 ASD 10.8.18; 201 Sqdn 14.8.18; Last seen nr ground going E over Bouries 2.9.18 (2/Lt WA Hall PoW); SOC 2.9.18

E4400   Rec Pk to 2 ASD 10.8.18; 203 Sqdn 17.8.18; COL in dark 28.8.18 (2/Lt CRR Horton injured); 2 ASD 30.8.18; Rebuilt as H6864 13.10.18

E4401   4 ASD to 210 Sqdn 20.9.18; Fokker DVII crashed 4m NE of Roulers 09.23 8.10.18 (2/Lt JE Berry); 203 Sqdn 24.1.19; RTP 9.2.19

E4402   Rec Pk to 2 ASD 11.8.18; 201 Sqdn 18.8.18; 203 Sqdn 23.1.19; RTP W/E 2.2.19

E4403   Rec Pk to 2 ASD 15.8.18; 201 Sqdn 21.9.18; Fuel tank pierced, FL in shell hole 3.10.18 (2/Lt AH Griffiths wounded); To 2 ASD; Rebuilt as H6884 25.10.18

E4404   Deld 4 AAP Lincoln by 8.18; Rec Pk 11.8.18; 2 ASD to 203 Sqdn 3.9.18; Attacked by 4 Fokker DVII while attacking balloons over Cambrai, down in flames NE of Bourlon Wood 15.9.18 (Sgt RR Lightbody killed); SOC in field 15.9.18

E4405   4 ASD to 204 Sqdn 13.8.18; Shot down E of Ypres 15.8.18 (2/Lt DE Culver missing); Deleted 31.8.18

E4406   4 ASD, tested 16.8.18; 210 Sqdn 18.8.18; Fokker DVII OOC E of Ypres 18.30 1.9.18; Fokker DVII crashed Courtrai 18.30 3.9.18; Fokker DVII crashed W of Ostende 18.35 6.9.18; Badly damaged by AA fire, landed Teteghem 18.35 17.9.18 (all Capt E Swale); 4 ASD 17.9.18; 213 Sqdn 16.10.18; Flown into by B6387

E4407     on aerodrome, badly damaged 17.10.18 (2/Lt EJ
Whitmell slightly injured); 4 ASD 23.10.18 - @25.10.18

E4407     4 ASD to 210 Sqdn 13.8.18; KB deflated (not destroyed)
NE of Zarren 12.20 14.8.18; Albatros DV shot down
and crashed W of Warneton 12.20 21.8.18; Fokker DVII
OOC Wijnendaele Wood, SE of Dixmude 16.25
31.8.18; Fokker DVII OOC over Lille 18.10 3.9.18;
Fokker DVII crashed in flames and another crashed nr
canal bank S of Ostende 18.30 17.9.18; Fokker DVII in
general engagement E of canal Schoore-Keyem 14.40
24.9.18 (all Lt WS Jenkins); Hit by AA fire, spun in 1m
S of Wulpen, wrecked 27.9.18 (2/Lt HE Light injured);
To 4 ASD; Deleted 31.10.18 general fatigue

E4408     Deld 4 AAP Lincoln W/E 8.8.18; Turnhouse W/E
29.8.18 - @30.1.19

E4409     Rec Pk to 2 ASD 13.8.18; 203 Sqdn 21.8.18; Patrol
attacked formation, last seen over Haynecourt 15.30
20.9.18 (2/Lt MG Cruise killed)

E4410     Rec Pk to 2 ASD 13.8.18; 203 Sqdn 2.9.18; Landed at
dusk, o/t 1.10.18 (2/Lt DH Woodhouse unhurt); for 1
ASD

E4411     Deld 8 AAP Lympne by 8.18; Rec Pk 9.8.18; 201 Sqdn
by 21.8.18; 2 AI by 9.18; 201 Sqdn 3.9.18; FL and
wrecked in field inundated with shell holes nr Bapaume
26.9.18 (2/Lt GH Fowles slightly injured); 2 ASD
29.9.18; 201 Sqdn by 1.19

E4412     Deld 4 AAP Lincoln W/E 8.8.18; Turnhouse W/E
29.8.18 - @30.1.19

E4413     Deld 4 AAP Lincoln W/E 8.8.18; Turnhouse W/E
19.9.18 - @30.1.19; Grand Fleet SoAF&G Leuchars by
9.19

E4414     Deld 4 AAP Lincoln W/E 8.8.18; Turnhouse W/E
29.8.18; EF, FL, crashed nr aerodrome 20.8.18 (Lt G
Heath killed)

E4415     Deld 4 AAP Lincoln W/E 8.8.18; Turnhouse W/E
29.8.18 - @30.1.19; Grand Fleet SoAF&G Leuchars by
2.19

E4416     Deld 4 AAP Lincoln W/E 8.8.18; Turnhouse W/E
12.9.18 - @30.1.19

E4417     Deld 4 AAP Lincoln W/E 8.8.18; Turnhouse W/E
29.8.18 - @30.1.19

E4418     4 ASD to 204 Sqdn 29.8.18; Fokker DVII OOC
Dixmude-Ypres 11.50 3.9.18 (2/Lt RC Pattulo); Shot
down in sea in flames nr Blankenberghe 15.9.18 (2/Lt
RC Pattulo killed); Deleted 30.9.18

E4419     (BR.1) 4 ASD to 210 Sqdn 18.8.18; EF, FL on beach,
damaged La Panne 19.10.18 (2/Lt LS Gillett unhurt); 4
ASD 24.10.18 - @25.10.18; 11 AP by 1.19; 213 Sqdn
16.1.19; 11 AP 24.2.19; WOC 24.2.19

E4420     69 Aerodrome 4 ASD to 204 Sqdn 31.8.18; Fokker
DVII OOC Courtrai 11.20 9.10.18 (Lt FG Bayley);
Missing after sqdn attacked by 12 HA nr Termoule
23.10.18 (Lt FG Bayley killed)

E4421     4 ASD to 210 Sqdn 17.9.18; Fokker DVII crashed
Wijnendaele Forest, nr Staden 08.00 29.9.18; Fokker
DVII crashed Houthulst Forest 09.55 1.10.18 (both Lt
CW Payton); 4 ASD 1.10.18 for survey; 213 Sqdn
21.10.18; Lost, landed Bray Dunes, EF on TO, FL
outside aerodrome 28.10.18 (Lt FJT Fenn); 4 ASD by
31.10.18

E4422     (BR.1) Rec Pk to 1 ASD 16.10.18; 203 Sqdn 18.10.18;
Spun in Aubry-du-Hainaut, nr Valenciennes 12.11.18
(Sgt Mech JA Nicholls DoI)

E4423     Deld 30.7.18; Rec Pk to 1 AI 23.9.18; 209 Sqdn by
10.18; Collided with H7278 W of Bourlon 15.00 8.10.18
(Capt DGA Allen killed);

**1 AIRCO D.H.4 TRACTOR BIPLANE DAY BOMBER from
batch E4624 to E4628 built by parent company**

E4624     2 ASD to 5 Sqdn 31.3.18; Became 205 Sqdn 1.4.18;
COL from raid aborted by bad visibility, caught fire,
bomb exploded 24.4.18 (Lt RC Day injured & Sgt SM
MacKay unhurt); to Rep Pk 1 ASD; SOC Adv Salvage
Dump 2 ASD 26.4.18

**6 SOPWITH 7F.1 SNIPE TRACTOR BIPLANE FIGHTERS
from batch E6137 to E6536 built by Boulton & Paul Ltd at
Norwich**

E6173     1 ASD to Stree, retd weather 29.4.19; 208 Sqdn by
9.5.19 - @21.8.19

E6175     1 ASD to 208 Sqdn Stree (coded 'S') 18.3.19 -
@21.8.19

E6350     RAF Contingent Bereznik 1919 (Mjr Kazakov killed)

E6351     RAF Contingent Bereznik 1919

E6360     RAF Contingent Bereznik 1919

E6375     RAF Contingent Bereznik 1919

**5 SOPWITH 7F.1 SNIPE TRACTOR BIPLANE FIGHTERS
from batch E6787 to E6936 built by D.Napier & Son**

E6864     Grand Fleet SoAF&G Leuchars by 6.19 - @8.19

E6865     Grand Fleet SoAF&G Leuchars by 6.19 - @8.19

E6866     Grand Fleet SoAF&G Leuchars by 7.19 - @8.19

E6884     RAF Contingent Bereznik 1919

E6896     Grand Fleet SoAF&G Leuchars by 5.19 - @11.19

**SOPWITH F.1 CAMEL TRACTOR BIPLANE FIGHTERS
from batch E7137 to E7336 built by Ruston, Proctor & Co Ltd
at Lincoln. (130-hp Clerget 9B unless otherwise stated)**

E7142     (130-hp Clerget LS) Deld 6 SD Ascot W/E 15.8.18;
Shipped 6.9.18; Mudros by 10.18 - @30.1.19

E7144     Grand Fleet SoAF&G Leuchars, tested 21.6.19

E7164     Rec Pk to 1 AI 23.8.18; 208 Sqdn 25.8.18; 2 AI
31.10.18

E7165     Deld 4 AAP Lincoln by 8.18; Lympne 11.8.18 (transit);
Rec Pk Marquise 12.8.18; 1 AI 23.8.18; 208 Sqdn
28.8.18; Pfalz DXII shot down Gouy 12.20 26.9.18;
Fokker DVII shot down N of Lesdains 12.30 29.9.18;
Fokker DVII dest Brancourt 18.10 & another in flames
Premont 18.15 OOC 3.10.18 (all Capt JB White); 2
ASD 19.11.18

E7166     (BR.1) Rec Pk to 1 AI 14.8.18; 208 Sqdn 16.8.18;
Fokker DVII OOC NE of Fresnoy 11.45 2.10.18 (Capt
JS McDonald); COL, on nose 26.10.18 (2/Lt CE
Metcalfe unhurt); 7 SS 30.10.18

E7172     Rec Pk to 1 AI 1.9.18; 208 Sqdn 3.9.18; DFW C OOC
probably crashed S of Hénin-Lietard 07.50 13.9.18;
Fokker DVII OOC Croix-Fonsommes 12.50 5.10.18 (Lt
MC Howell); 2 ASD 3.11.18

E7175     Rec Pk to 1 AI 5.9.18; 208 Sqdn 7.9.18; 2 ASD
31.10.18

E7177     Rec Pk to 1 AI 1.9.18; 208 Sqdn 3.9.18; Fokker DVII
OOC Lesdain 12.30 29.9.18; Fokker DVII shot down
2m NE of Brancourt 18.30 3.10.18 (both Lt RCD'A
Gifford); 2 AI 19.11.18; to England 20.12.18

E7179     Rec Pk to 1 AI 31.8.18; 208 Sqdn 31.8.18; COL
1.10.18 (Lt WV Skall); 2 AI 3.11.18

E7181     (140-hp Clerget) 1 AI to 208 Sqdn 4.9.18; COL 7.9.18
(2/Lt G Lovett injured); To 1 ASD; SOC 12.9.18

E7194     (140-hp Clerget) Rec Pk to 1 AI 6.9.18; 208 Sqdn
8.9.18; EF, FL nr lines 11.10.18 (2/Lt CE Metcalfe
unhurt); to 2 ASD

E7195     Rec Pk to 1 AI 5.9.18; 208 Sqdn 8.9.18; 2 AI 3.11.18

E7206     Rec Pk to 2 ASD 22.9.18; 208 Sqdn 1.10.18; 2 ASD
22.11.18

E7207     Rec Pk to 1 AI 6.9.18; 208 Sqdn 8.9.18; Landed in
dark, o/t 9.10.18 (Lt GA Wightman unhurt); SOC in
field

E7220     Rec Pk to 1 AI 5.9.18; 208 Sqdn 7.9.18; Crashed Mont
St.Eloi 19.9.18 (Lt HJ Botterell); 2 ASD 22.11.18

E7232     4 FS Freiston .18 (named 'DIMPS III' and painted red
and white with sunbursts on upper wing and tailplane)

E7252     Deld 4 AAP Lincoln by 9.18; 56/57 TDS Cranwell
11.9.18 - @17.9.18

E7255     Grand Fleet SoAF&G Leuchars by 9.18 - @11.18

E7258     Grand Fleet SoAF&G Leuchars by 9.18 - @10.18
BUT Rec Pk to 1 ASD 29.9.18

E7263     Rec Pk to 1 AI 26.9.18; 5 AI 1.10.18; 208 Sqdn
14.10.18; COL 21.10.18 (Mjr C Draper); 2 ASD
22.11.18

E7264     56/57 TDS Cranwell by 10.18

E7274     MAES Grain by 14.4.21 (modifications)

E7297     51 TDS Shotwick, spun in on landing 2.10.18 (2/Lt AL
Fachnie slightly injured)

E7311     Rec Pk to 2 AI 26.9.18; 208 Sqdn 1.10.18; Starboard
axle broke landing, on nose 14.11.18 (2/Lt CR Curry
unhurt); to 2 ASD

## 6 SOPWITH 7F.1 SNIPE TRACTOR BIPLANE FIGHTERS from batch E7337 to E7836 built by Ruston Proctor & Co Ltd at Lincoln

E7343 2 ASD to 208 Sqdn 19.11.18; COL 20.1.19 (2/Lt EA Kenny); Flying again 6.2.19; LM 20.6.19
E7356 208 Sqdn by 24.1.19 (FM); EF, FL in ploughed field, o/t nr Donstiennes 24.4.19 (Lt JS Clarke); to 1 SS
E7361 208 Sqdn by 17.3.19FM - LM20.6.19
E7363 208 Sqdn by 16.5.19FM - LM14.8.19
E7364 208 Sqdn by 27.6.19FM - LM14.8.19
E7416 56/57 TDS Cranwell by 8.3.19

## 38 SOPWITH 7F.1 SNIPE TRACTOR BIPLANE FIGHTERS from batch E7987 to E8286 built by parent company at Kingston. (200-hp B.R.2)

E7988 208 Sqdn by 30.7.19FM - LM7.8.19
E7996 1 ASD to 43 Sqdn 12.8.18; 208 Sqdn by 19.4.19 FM - LM22.8.19
E8042 Rec Pk to 2 ASD 14.9.18; 5 AI 4.10.18; 2 AI 10.18; 208 Sqdn 30.10.18; COL 17.1.19 (2/Lt GV Snell); Wreckage to 7 SS 17.1.19 & WOC
E8048 Rec Pk to 2 ASD 16.9.18; 2 AI 14.10.18; 208 Sqdn 30.10.18
E8051 Rec Pk to 2 ASD 16.9.18; 5 AI 4.10.18; 2 AI to 208 Sqdn 30.10.18; Crashed on TO, CW 22.1.19 (Lt WV Skall unhurt); Wreckage to 7 SS 24.1.19 & WOC
E8054 Rec Pk to 2 ASD 17.9.18; 2 AI 14.10.18; 208 Sqdn 30.10.18; Crashed 17.6.19 (Lt HJ Walden) LM
E8066 Rec Pk to 2 ASD 16.9.18; 2 AI to 208 Sqdn 30.10.18; Fast landing, hit stationery E8162 20.1.19 (Capt WEG Mann unhurt); to 7 SS 25.1.19
E8068 Grain, hydrovane & wheel jettison ditching tests 19.10.18; Martlesham Heath 21.12.18; Retd Grain; Flotation gear removed 3.19; Fitted hydrovane gear 4.19
E8085 4 Sqdn AFC; Grain from 7.19 (tests with slinging gear & flotation gear)
E8102 St.Omer to 201 Sqdn 17.10.18; Shot down 3 Fokker DVIIs and 1 2-str: 1 a/c BU up in air NE of Forêt de Mormal, Snipe went into spin, came out amid 15 Fokkers, 2 of which were sent spinning down, then another shot down in flames, the Snipe was then smoking but shot down another Fokker in flames, before crashing on British side of lines 08.25-08.30 27.10.18 (Mjr WG Barker wounded, awarded VC for this); Request recd 26.11.18 from Canadian Govt to secure aircraft, without repair; Desp 6 SS to SS Fienvillers 21.11.18 (still in transit 29.11.18); Fuselage preserved and shipped to Leaside Aerodrome, Toronto 6.19; Displayed Canadian National Exhibition 8.19, then to Camp Borden; Officially TOC CAF 2.6.21; Cat B Camp Borden 2.6.21; SOC 24.6.21; Stored/displayed by National Research Council 1930s onwards to at least 1956. Displayed Canadian War Museum by 1959 to date
E8108 2 AI to 208 Sqdn 31.10.18; COL 11.2.19 (Lt E Jackson unhurt); to 2 ASD
E8110 Deld Brooklands to 8 AAP Lympne 26.10.18
E8111 Deld Turnhouse W/E 17.10.18 - @30.1.19
E8112 Deld Turnhouse W/E 17.10.18 - @30.1.19
E8129 2 AI to 208 Sqdn 3.11.18; O/t landing 8.4.19 (2/Lt EK Dashwood unhurt); 1 SS repair
E8132 2 AI to 208 Sqdn (coded 'D') 3.11.18; Crashed Donstiennes 24.4.19 (Lt CR Davidson MC injured); SOC in field
E8134 2 AI to 208 Sqdn 3.11.18; Landed slowly, crashed 10.3.19 (Lt RS Carey); SOC in field
E8135 2 AI to 208 Sqdn 3.11.18; Caught hole landing 23.11.18 (2/Lt RA Gibbs); 7 SS 27.11.18
E8140 2 AI to 208 Sqdn 19.11.18; EF, FL Stree 12.2.19 (Lt G Swannell unhurt); to 2 ASD
E8143 6 AI to 208 Sqdn 25.1.19; Mist, heavy rain, hit trees 14.4.19 (Lt E Jackson injured); SOC
E8151 208 Sqdn by 12.8.19FM - @13.8.19LM
E8154 208 Sqdn by 7.4.19FM; Crashed on TO 25.7.19 (Lt E Jackson); Flying again 7.8.19; Still 208 Sqdn 20.8.19
E8162 2 ASD to 208 Sqdn 27.11.18; Hit by E8066 while stationery 20.1.19 (Mjr HG Smart unhurt); 7 SS 27.1.19
E8167 4 Sqdn AFC (coded '1-0'); 2 ASD to 208 Sqdn 19.11.18; Sqdn move, overshot landing new aerodrome, stalled avoiding telephone wires, CW nr camp

Donstiennes 15.3.19 (Lt G Smith unhurt)
E8171 204 TDS Eastchurch by 18.11.18
E8176 Acc 10 AAP Brooklands 9.10.18; 6 AI to 208 Sqdn 21.1.19 - @14.8.19
E8177 2 ASD to 208 Sqdn 19.11.18; Wheels collapsed landing 6.2.19 (Capt DM Faure unhurt); to 2 ASD
E8178 6 AI to 208 Sqdn 25.1.19 - @14.8.19
E8180 208 Sqdn by 2.8.19FM - @18.8.19
E8181 2 AI to 208 Sqdn (coded 'M') 31.10.18 - @18.8.19
E8183 2 ASD to 208 Sqdn 16.11.18; O/t landing 24.11.18 (2/Lt GL Smith unhurt); 7 SS 27.11.18
E8184 6 AI to 208 Sqdn 4.1.19; EF, FL Strée 25.1.19 (Lt LFA Green unhurt); to 2 ASD
E8185 2 AI to 208 Sqdn 3.11.18 - @11.8.19
E8188 6 AI to 208 Sqdn 25.1.19 - @13.8.19
E8200 208 Sqdn by 4.7.19FM - @21.8.19
E8201 2 ASD to 208 Sqdn 17.11.18 - @4.7.19LM
E8269 2 ASD to 208 Sqdn 22.11.18; Spun in on practice flight Thuilles, BO 21.12.18 (2/Lt TF McGuire killed); WOC 21.12.19 burnt
E8270 208 Sqdn (coded 'V') by 5.4.19FM - @21.8.19

## 1 SOPWITH 7F.1 SNIPE TRACTOR BIPLANE FIGHTER from batch E8307 to E8406 built by Portholme Aerodrome Ltd at Huntingdon. (200-hp B.R.2)

E8313 2 ASD to 208 Sqdn 27.11.18; Landed slowly, wheels stuck in mud, o/t 1.3.19 (Lt FK Hope unhurt); SOC in field

## 23 AIRCO D.H.9A TRACTOR BIPLANE DAY BOMBERS from batch E8407 to E8806 built by parent company at Hendon. (400-hp Liberty)

E8411 2 AI to 205 Sqdn 27.9.18; EF after raid on Wassigny, FL, crashed Bois de Buire 9.10.18 (2/Lt HF Taylor & 2/Lt MLV Hill unhurt); to 2 ASD
E8413 205 Sqdn from 9.10.18; COL from raid on Charleroi 4.11.18 (Lt RJV Pulvertoft & 2/Lt WM Newton unhurt); U/c crashed on landing new aerodrome Mauberge 27.11.18 (2/Lt PJ Baker unhurt); to 2 ASD
E8418 Rec Pk to 205 Sqdn 18.9.18; COL after raid on Wassigny 8.10.18 (2/Lt RJV Pulvertoft unhurt & 2/Lt W Haviland injured); to 2 ASD
E8419 Rec Pk to 205 Sqdn 23.9.18; Recce 29.9.18 (Lt HG Kirkland wounded & 2/Lt CO'N Daunt killed); Flying again 8.10.18; COL from bombing raid on Wassigny 9.10.18 (Lt AL Monger & 2/Lt WM Newton unhurt); to 2 ASD
E8437 2 AI to 205 Sqdn 25.9.18; EF, COL on aerodrome 7.1.19 (Lt Gould unhurt); to 2 ASD
E8438 1 AP to 5 AI 5.10.18; 205 Sqdn 13.10.18; EF, FL nr Tournai 5.2.19 (2/Lt SJ Furze); Salved by 10th Bde for 2 ASD
E8444 MAEE Grain, flotation tests off Nore LV from HMS *Slinger*, CW, beached 27.11.20
E8457 ECD Grain, fitted detachable wings, flotation gear & detachable wheels, air tested, then to Fleet 4.19
E8458 Twickenham from W/E 12.9.18; Turnhouse W/E 24.10.18; Disposed 1.19
E8459 Twickenham from W/E 12.9.18; Turnhouse W/E 24.10.18; Disposed 1.19
E8489 Deld Turnhouse W/E 24.10.18; Disposed 1.19
E8490 Deld Turnhouse W/E 24.10.18; Disposed 1.19
E8491 Deld Turnhouse W/E 24.10.18; Disposed 1.19; Grand Fleet SoAF&G by 9.19; 39 Sqdn (coded '1' & '11') by 6.23 - @7.23; CFS by 2.31
E8492 Deld Turnhouse W/E 24.10.18 - @30.1.19
E8508 205 Sqdn by 27.11.18 - @3.1.19
E8510 Deld Turnhouse W/E 24.10.18 - @30.1.19; 24 Sqdn, stalled on turn on TO and crashed Kenley 4.1.23
E8512 Deld Turnhouse W/E 24.10.18 - @30.1.19; served post-war
E8513 Deld Turnhouse W/E 24.10.18 - @30.1.19; served post-war
E8514 Deld Turnhouse W/E 24.10.18 - @30.1.19; served post-war
E8515 Deld Turnhouse W/E 24.10.18 - @12.18; Disposed 1.19
E8516 Turnhouse from 10.18 - @12.18; Disposed by 1.19
E8537 205 Sqdn to Sart 26.2.19
E8653 205 Sqdn to Hesdin (via Valenciennes) 21.2.19

*Sopwith Snipe E8132 'D' of 208 Sqdn at Maretz in November 1918. (via Frank Cheesman)*

*Sopwith Snipe E8176 of 208 Sqdn early in 1919. (via Frank Cheesman)*

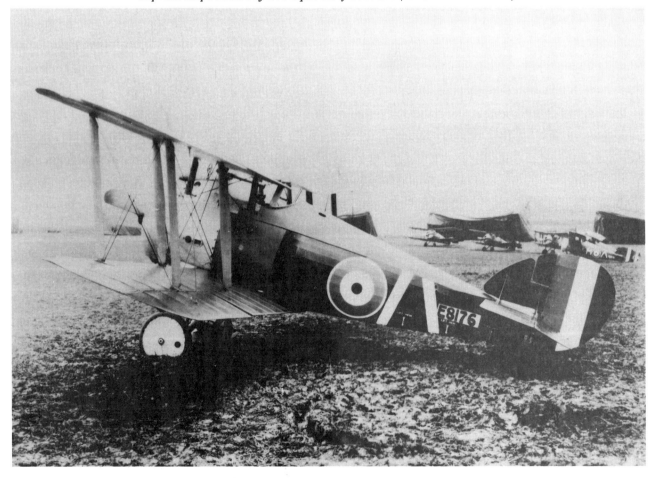

**66 AIRCO D.H.9 TRACTOR BIPLANE DAY BOMBERS from batch E8857 to E9056 built by parent company at Hendon. (230-hp Puma)**

| | |
|---|---|
| E8872 | 1 AI to 211 Sqdn 29.9.18; Hit by HA on return from target, FL W of Roulers 5.10.18 (2/Lt VGH Phillips & 2/Lt AF Taylor both wounded); Remains to 1 ASD, only engine and gun salved; 8 AP 8.10.18 & WOC |
| E8873 | Rec Pk to 206 Sqdn 13.10.18 - @30.1.19 |
| E8874 | 206 Sqdn by 18.10.18; Fokker DVII in flames Sotteghem Ghent 10.00-10.15 4.11.18 (2/Lt H McLean & 2/Lt HP Hobbs) |
| E8877 | Rec Pk to 1 AI 23.8.18; 206 Sqdn 30.8.18; Caught fire in air Buschbell 31.1.19 (Lt CL Cumming & 2/Lt AJ Waters both killed); SOC in field |
| E8878 | Rec Pk 23.8.18; 206 Sqdn 21.9.18 - @19.10.18 |
| E8880 | Rec Pk to 2 ASD 27.9.18; 211 Sqdn 30.9.18; Fokker DVII destroyed S of Charleroi 15.15 9.11.18 (Lt WF Blanchfield & 2/Lt TR Lole); 98 Sqdn 23.2.19; 1 ASD 8.3.19 |
| E8881 | 4 ASD to 218 Sqdn 25.9.18; Attacked 7 HA over Cortemarck, Fokker DrI in flames & another OOC 17.50, m/c badly shot up 28.9.18 (Lt HD McLaren DFC unhurt & Sgt G Barlow wounded); 4 ASD 4.10.18 |
| E8883 | Rec Pk by 13.9.18; 4 ASD Audembert 18.9.18; 218 Sqdn 25.9.18; Lost over enemy lines 12.00 28.9.18 (Lt HP Brumell & Sgt RS Joysey both PoW); Deleted 15.10.18 |
| E8888 | 'F' Flt 186 Development Sqdn Gosport 1919 |
| E8896 | Deld Brockworth W/E 10.10.18 for Taranto; Left/shipped W/E 14.11.18 |
| E8897 | Deld Brockworth W/E 10.10.18 for Taranto; Left/shipped W/E 14.11.18 |
| E8898 | Deld Brockworth W/E 10.10.18 for Taranto; Left/shipped W/E 14.11.18 |
| E8899 | Deld Brockworth W/E 10.10.18 for Taranto; Left/shipped W/E 14.11.18 |
| E8900 | Deld Brockworth W/E 10.10.18 for Taranto; Left/shipped W/E 14.11.18 |
| E8901 | Deld Brockworth W/E 10.10.18 for Taranto; Left/shipped W/E 14.11.18 |
| E8902 | Deld Brockworth W/E 10.10.18 for Taranto; Left/shipped W/E 14.11.18 |
| E8913 | Deld Brockworth W/E 10.10.18 for Taranto; Left/shipped W/E 14.11.18 BUT Rec Pk to 5 AI 4.10.18 |
| E8914 | Deld Brockworth W/E 17.10.18; 6 SD Ascot W/E 24.10.18 for Mudros; Left/shipped W/E 21.11.18 |
| E8915 | Deld Brockworth W/E 17.10.18; 6 SD Ascot W/E 24.10.18 for Mudros; Left/shipped W/E 28.11.18 |
| E8916 | Deld Brockworth W/E 17.10.18; 6 SD Ascot W/E 24.10.18 for Mudros; Left/shipped W/E 28.11.18 |
| E8917 | Deld Brockworth W/E 17.10.18; 6 SD Ascot W/E 24.10.18 for Mudros; Left/shipped W/E 28.11.18 |
| E8924 | Deld 6 SD Ascot W/E 12.9.18; Shipped to Taranto 14.11.18; 'A' dett RAF South Russia Instructional Mission to storage 3.11.19 |
| E8925 | Deld 6 SD Ascot W/E 12.9.18; Shipped to Taranto 14.11.18; RAF South Russia to Russian Air Corps 8.19 |
| E8926 | Deld 6 SD Ascot W/E 12.9.18; Shipped to Taranto 14.11.18; To Anti-Bolsheviks |
| E8927 | Deld 6 SD Ascot W/E 12.9.18; Shipped to Taranto 14.11.18; To Anti-Bolsheviks |
| E8928 | Deld 6 SD Ascot W/E 12.9.18; Shipped to Taranto 14.11.18; To Anti-Bolsheviks |
| E8929 | Deld 6 SD Ascot W/E 12.9.18 for Taranto; Left/shipped W/E 21.11.18 |
| E8936 | 1 AI to 211 Sqdn 25.9.18; Left 11.30 to bomb Staden, not seen after raid 28.9.18 (2/Lt WJ Johnson killed & Sgt Mech WE Jones MM PoW) |
| E8937 | 2 AI by 11.18; 211 Sqdn 4.11.18; 98 Sqdn 26.2.19; 8 AAP Lympne 13.3.19 |
| E8940 | Deld 6 SD Ascot W/E 12.9.18; Shipped to Taranto W/E 21.11.18 |
| E8942 | Deld 6 SD Ascot W/E 15.10.18; To Docks W/E 31.10.18; Shipped to Taranto 14.11.18; RAF South Russian Instructional Mission to Russian Aviation Corps 24.11.19 |
| E8944 | Deld 6 SD Ascot W/E 17.10.18; Shipped to Taranto 14.11.18; To Anti-Bolsheviks |
| E8945 | Deld 6 SD Ascot W/E 12.9.18; Left Shipped to Mudros |
| E8946 | Deld 6 SD Ascot W/E 17.10.18; To docks W/E 31.10.18; Shipped to Taranto 14.11.18 |
| E8947 | Deld 6 SD Ascot W/E 12.9.18; To docks W/E 31.10.18; Shipped to Taranto 14.11.18; RAF South Russia to Russian Air Corps 8.19 |
| E8948 | Deld 6 SD Ascot W/E 12.9.18; To docks W/E 31.10.18; Shipped to Mudros 14.11.18; To Anti-Bolsheviks |
| E8949 | Deld 6 SD Ascot W/E 12.9.18; To docks W/E 31.10.18; Shipped to Mudros 14.11.18; RAF South Russia to Russian Air Corps 8.19 |
| E8950 | Deld 6 SD Ascot W/E 12.9.18; To docks W/E 31.10.18; Shipped to Mudros 14.11.18; RAF South Russian Instructional Mission to Russian Aviation Corps 24.11.19 |
| E8951 | Deld 6 SD Ascot W/E 12.9.18; To docks W/E 31.10.18; Shipped to Mudros 14.11.18; RAF South Russian Instructional Mission to Russian Aviation Corps 24.11.19 |
| E8952 | Deld 6 SD Ascot W/E 12.9.18; To docks W/E 31.10.18; Shipped to Mudros 14.11.18; RAF South Russian Instructional Mission to Russian Aviation Corps 24.11.19 |
| E8953 | Deld 6 SD Ascot W/E 12.9.18; At docks 10.18; Shipped to Mudros 14.11.18; 47 Sqdn by 2.20; Crashed landing on bad ground at height 12.3.20 |
| E8954 | Rec Pk to 1 AI 1.10.18; 211 Sqdn 3.10.18; HA OOC 1.11.18 (2/Lt CC Brouncker & Sgt Mech PC Siverton); Overshot landing, failed to clear sunken road, crashed 14.12.18 (Lt MF Mousley & 2/Lt W Norrie unhurt); 7 SS Bohain 16.12.18 |
| E8957 | 4 ASD by 10.18; 218 Sqdn 19.10.18; COL 14.1.19 (Lt Whitehead & AM Barnes unhurt); to 2 ASD |
| E8958 | 4 ASD Audembert to 218 Sqdn 29.9.18; Lost over enemy lines when dropping rations at Stadenburg 2.10.18 (Capt WF Cleghorn DFC killed & 2/Lt FH Stringer DSC, PoW); Deleted 15.10.18 |
| E8960 | 4 ASD to 218 Sqdn 9.10.18; COL after bombing raid, badly damaged 18.10.18 (Lt JRA Barnes & 2/Lt FE Green both unhurt); 4 ASD 20.10.18 - @25.10.18 |
| E8962 | Rec Pk to 1 AI 5.10.18; 211 Sqdn 8.10.18; HA BU in air, shared B7626 & E8962 11.00 4.11.18 (both Lt EG Gaff & 2/Lt WJ Large); EF on TO, swung avoiding rut 30.11.18 (2/Lt EJ Stevenson & Sgt J Smith unhurt); 7 SS Bohain 1.12.18; for 2 ASD |
| E8986 | Deld docks W/E 19.9.18; Shipped to Mudros W/E 3.10.18 - @30.1.19; To Anti-Bolsheviks |
| E8987 | Deld 6 SD Ascot W/E 12.9.18; To docks W/E 31.10.18; Shipped to Mudros 14.11.18; To Anti-Bolsheviks |
| E8988 | Deld docks W/E 19.9.18; Shipped to Mudros W/E 3.10.18 - @30.1.19; To Anti-Bolsheviks |
| E8990 | To docks W/E 19.9.18; Shipped to Mudros W/E 3.10.18 - @30.1.19; 222 Sqdn Mudros/San Stefano by 14.11.18; To Anti-Bolsheviks |
| E8991 | Deld docks W/E 19.9.18; Shipped to Mudros W/E 3.10.18 - @30.1.19; To Anti-Bolsheviks |
| E8992 | Deld docks W/E 19.9.18; Shipped to Mudros W/E 3.10.18 - @30.1.19; To Anti-Bolsheviks |
| E8996 | 269 Sqdn Port Said to 'X' AP Kantara 14.3.19 |
| E8997 | 269 Sqdn Port Said to 'X' AP Kantara 14.3.19 |
| E8998 | 269 Sqdn Port Said to 142 Sqdn 14.3.19 |
| E8999 | 269 Sqdn Port Said to 142 Sqdn 14.3.19 |
| E9001 | 206 Sqdn, lost in fog, FL in Holland 3.3.19 (Lt C Workman & AM E Rogan both injured) |
| E9021 | SMOP Dover by 10.18 - @11.18; 212 Sqdn by 2.19 - @3.19 (A/S training) |
| E9022 | Deld 555/6 Flts 219 Sqdn Manston 13.10.18; HACP 5.11.18 |
| E9025 | Deld 555/6 Flts 219 Sqdn Manston 8.10.18 - @11.18 |
| E9029 | Rec Pk to 1 AI 5.10.18; 206 Sqdn (coded 'J') 6.10.18-@4.19 |
| E9031 | Deld 555/6 Flts 219 Sqdn Manston 8.10.18; HACP 4.11.18 |
| E9032 | Deld 557/8 Flts 212 Sqdn Yarmouth by 15.10.18 - @28.10.18 |
| E9036 | SMOP Dover by 10.18; Landed in dark, ran into bank, damaged propeller, tailskid and lower wings, Lympne 13.11.18 (Lt GW Stallard) |
| E9037 | SMOP Dover by 10.18 - @11.18; 212 Sqdn by 3.19 (A/S training) |

The column heading W/E 21.11.18; TOC Base Depot RAF Novorossisk 14.2.20; To Anti-Bolsheviks appears at the top of the second column under E8945.

E9049    4 ASD by 10.18; 218 Sqdn 23.10.18; FL on delivery at French aerodrome Calais 24.10.18 (Lt KR Campbell & Lt LA Churchill both unhurt); to 4 ASD 24.10.18

## 11 AVRO 504K TRACTOR BIPLANE TRAINERS from batch E9207 to E9506 built by The Graham-White Aviation Co Ltd at Hendon

E9254    (80-hp Le Rhône) 58 TDS Cranwell by 11.18
E9255    (80-hp Le Rhône) 58 TDS Cranwell by 11.18
E9256    56 TDS Cranwell by 12.18
E9257    (80-hp Le Rhône) Cranwell by 7.19
E9288    56 TDS Cranwell by 11.18 - @1.19
E9293    56 TDS Cranwell, crashed and wrecked late 1918 (2/Lt PG Deedes)
E9295    56 TDS Cranwell by 12.18
E9317    55 TDS Narborough by 1.19
E9323    55 TDS Narborough by 1.19
E9326    55 TDS Narborough by 1.19
E9334    55 TDS Narborough by 1.19

## 11 AIRCO D.H.9A TRACTOR BIPLANE DAY BOMBERS from batch E9657 to E9756 built by Mann, Egerton & Co Ltd at Norwich

E9657    Grain by 2.19 - @8.19 (fit flotation gear)
E9662    Rec Pk to 205 Sqdn 12.8.18; COL 1.10.18 (2/Lt G Bannerman unhurt); to 2 ASD
E9673    212 Sqdn Yarmouth, swung on TO and crashed into fence 28.8.18 (Lt GW Stallard); 2 MOS Eastchurch by 3.19 - @7.19; PD Ascot; AD Hinaidi 3.24
E9689    Fitted exp flotation gear by JS White at Cowes; Grain 26.3.20; Repairs 19.4.20; Ready for trials 3.5.20; Declared surplus 3.8.20
E9697    Grain, fitting Gratze hydrovane wing floats & air bags 3.19 - @8.19
E9707    5 ASD to 205 Sqdn 29.10.18; COL new aerodrome Maubeuge 27.11.18 (Lt WH Clarke & 2/Lt CN Witham); flying again 8.12.18; Still 205 Sqdn 2.19
E9713    Rec Pk to 5 AI 5.10.18; 205 Sqdn 14.10.18 - @3.1.19
E9716    Rec Pk to 5 AI 5.10.18; 205 Sqdn 14.10.18 - @3.1.19
E9721    Rec Pk to Paris for IAF 17.10.18; 205 Sqdn from 8.12.18; COL 7.2.19 (Capt PJ Barnett unhurt); to 2 ASD
E9731    2 AI to 205 Sqdn, COL with D.H.9 F6074 of 107 Sqdn, WO 10.11.18 (2/Lt SJ Furze); SOC in field
E9756    Grain by 7.19

## 4 SOPWITH F.1 CAMEL TRACTOR BIPLANE SCOUTS from rebuilds by 3 ARD Yate to cover the losses of the German Offensive of 3.18 and numbered E9964 to E9983.

E9978    50 TDS Eastbourne (coded 'F') by 7.6.18 - @1.11.18
E9979    50 TDS Eastbourne (coded 'F') by 7.6.18 - @1.11.18
E9980    Deld Bristol to Dover (via Eastbourne) 1.7.18
E9981    Wye to 50 TDS Eastbourne 1.7.18

## 4 HANDLEY PAGE O/400 TRACTOR BIPLANE HEAVY BOMBERS from batch F301 to F320 built by The Birmingham Carriage Co at Birmingham. (Eagle)

F302    With 216 Sqdn to ME, arr Buc 17.7.19; Left 20.7.19; Left Rome, FL Mulaos, Greece 2.8.19; Still there 13.8.19; Crashed Abu Hamed, Egypt 12.4.20 BO
F304    14 AAP to 115 Sqdn 18.1.19; With 216 Sqdn to ME, to Buc 10.7.19; Left 12.7.19; Crashed in sea off Monterosso, nr Spezia, CW 28.7.19 (L/Col Dins killed; Lt Adams, AM Balfour & Sgt Ashley all injured)
F305    14 AAP to 115 Sqdn 18.1.19; With 216 Sqdn to Egypt, to Buc 10.7.19; Left 12.7.19; Damaged by gales Istres 15.7.19; San Remo 23.8.19; Crashed & wrecked when elevator controls jammed at 400ft, Pisa 3.9.19 (crew unhurt); 214 Sqdn 1920
F316    With 214 Sqdn to Egypt, arr Taranto 13.9.19; Probably destroyed in gale 26.9.19

## 26 AIRCO D.H.9A TRACTOR BIPLANE DAY BOMBERS from batch F951 to F1100 built by Westland Aircraft Works at Yeovil

F955    557/8 Flts Yarmouth by 7.18
F956    555/6 Flts Manston to 557/8 Flts 212 Sqdn Yarmouth 22.7.18; Attacked U-boat which rose to surface and attacked aircraft W of Smith's Knoll Pillar Buoy, engine disabled, FL in sea, taken in tow 12.8.18 (2 crew rescued)
F958    555/6 Flts 219 Sqdn Manston 1918
F959    557/8 Flts 212 Sqdn Yarmouth by 21.8.18
F990    Rec Pk to 205 Sqdn 1.9.18; Fokker DVII OOC Busigny 15.20 15.9.18 (Lt CJ Heywood & Sgt SF Langstone); EF, FL struck fence Dinant 20.1.19 (Lt RE Morton unhurt); to 2 ASD
F996    2 AI to 205 Sqdn 8.12.18; COL 19.1.19 (Lt RLMcK Barbour unhurt); to 2 ASD; To England 11.3.19
F1007    Rec Pk to 2 ASD 3.9.18; 205 Sqdn 7.9.18; Photo recce, red-nosed Fokker DVII in flames Le Cateau 15.30 9.10.18 (Lt JG Kerr & 2/Lt G Gardner); COL from raid, u/c collapsed 4.11.18 (Capt W Grossart & 2/Lt CN Witham both unhurt); COL Halluin West 24.11.18 (Lt RK Rose unhurt); to 2 ASD
F1008    Rec Pk to 205 Sqdn (coded 'G') 1.9.18; 2 ASD 1.2.19 (poor condition)
F1009    Rec Pk to 205 Sqdn 1.9.18; 2-str in flames W of Roisel 17.00 15.9.18 (2/Lt FO McDonald & 2/Lt JB Leach); Damaged by storm 17.9.18; 2 ASD 26.9.18
F1013    Rec Pk to 2 AI 16.9.18; 205 Sqdn 18.9.18; COL 23.10.18 (2/Lt FO McDonald & 2/Lt RM Allen); Crashed in fog Bertangles 7.12.18 (2/Lt FO McDonald & Capt W Grossart unhurt)
F1014    Rec Pk to 205 Sqdn 10.9.18; White-tailed Fokker DVII crashed nr Neuvillette-Mont d'Origny 16.40 3.10.18 (Lt RLMcK Barbour & Capt MEM Wright); COL 10.10.18 (2/Lt WB Esplin & 2/Lt W Wilson unhurt); flying again by 23.10.18; Fokker DVII OOC nr Charleroi 10.35 9.11.18 (2/Lt WB Esplin & 2/Lt CHL Needham); still 205 Sqdn 2.1.19; Travelling flight to Louveterie, COL Ans 7.1.19 (2/Lt WB Esplin & 2/Lt CHL Needham unhurt); To England 11.3.19
F1015    Rec Pk to 2 AI 16.9.18; 205 Sqdn 17.9.18; Crashed on TO 27.10.18 (2/Lt AM Duggan & 2/Lt LA Drain unhurt); NFT
F1016    Rec Pk to 205 Sqdn 1.9.18; Hannover C in flames 2m N of St.Quentin, then Fokker DVII BU in air S of St.Quentin c.08.45 16.9.18 (Lt WE MacPherson & 2/Lt CF Ambler); Damaged by storm 19.9.18; 2 ASD 24.9.18
F1017    Rec Pk to 205 Sqdn 1.9.18; EF, crashed nr aerodrome, TW 6.9.18 (Lt WE MacPherson unhurt & 2/Lt CF Ambler cut); SOS 6.9.18
F1019    Rec Pk to 2 AI 18.9.18; 205 Sqdn 21.9.18; Silver grey Fokker DVII crashed into small wood Vaux-le-Prêtre, N of Brancourt-le-Grand 13.40 29.9.18 (Lt RLMcK Barbour & Capt MEM Wright); COL Valenciennes 18.1.19 (Lt HF Taylor unhurt); to 2 ASD
F1022    Rec Pk to 2 AI 9.18; 205 Sqdn 23.9.18; Left 08.35, last seen going E nr Florennes 9.11.18 (Lt EH Johnson & Sgt Mech GE Grundy both killed); SOC in field 9.11.18
F1024    Rec Pk to 2 AI 23.9.18; 205 Sqdn 23.9.18; In action 3.10.18 (observer Sgt Mech WJH Middleton DoW 4.10.18); 1 ASD 10.18; 205 Sqdn 13.10.18; White-tailed green fuselage Fokker DVII in flames N of Namur 10.11 9.11.18 (2/Lt FO McDonald & Sgt AP Pearce); 1 ASD by 11.18; 205 Sqdn 12.11.18; LM 2.1.19
F1025    205 Sqdn by 3.10.18; Fokker DVII OOC Maubeuge 15.35 4.11.18 (Mjr EG Joy & 2/Lt LA Drain); COL Germund 7.1.19 (Lt WH Clarke & Lt WR McKinlay unhurt); SOC
F1040    UK to Rec Pk 25.9.18; 2 AI 25.9.18; 205 Sqdn 27.9.18; COL 1.10.18 (2/Lt RE Morton & 2/Lt LA Drain)
F1043    UK to Rec Pk 25.9.18; 2 AI 25.9.18; 205 Sqdn 27.9.18; Green Fokker DVII in flames Grougis 16.08 11.10.18 (Capt AR McAfee & Sgt W Jones); LM 27.11.18
F1044    UK to Rec Pk 25.9.18; 2 AI 26.9.18; 205 Sqdn 27.9.18; Crashed into F.2B E2255 of 20 Sqdn 13.10.18 (Lt KG Nairn & 2/Lt G Bannerman unhurt); to 2 ASD
F1048    UK to Rec Pk 25.9.18; 2 AI 25.9.18; 205 Sqdn (coded 'T') 27.9.18; Crashed u/c landing new aerodrome Maubeuge 27.11.18 (2/Lt EB Fielden & Sgt Pawley); To England 23.2.19
F1049    Rec Pk to 2 AI 27.9.18; 205 Sqdn 1.10.18; Fokker DVII OOC Charleroi 9.11.18 (Lt RJV Pulvertoft & 2/Lt WM

Newton) [presumed F1049, but last digit of serial indistinct]; U/c crashed new aerodrome Maubeuge 27.11.18 (2/Lt G Gardner & Lt PN Melitus); Engine cut, crashed on aerodrome 17.1.19 (Lt WE Dipple); to 2 ASD To England 11.3.19

F1074 205 Sqdn, FL nr Spa 7.2.19 (Capt AR McAfee unhurt); to 2 ASD
F1094 552 Flt 221 Sqdn (coded 'G') .19; To Anti-Bolsheviks
F1095 552 Flt 221 Sqdn .19

## 24 AIRCO D.H.9 TRACTOR BIPLANE DAY BOMBERS from batch F1101 to F1300 built by Waring & Gillow Ltd. (230-hp Puma)

F1106 557/8 Flts 212 Sqdn Yarmouth by 17.10.18
F1109 557/8 Flts 212 Sqdn Yarmouth by 10.18
F1111 Deld 6 SD Ascot W/E 24.10.18; Shipped to Mudros W/E 21.11.18; TOC Base Depot RAF Novorossisk 14.2.20; To White Russian Forces
F1115 Deld 6 SD Ascot W/E 24.10.18; Shipped to Mudros W/E 21.11.18
F1117 Manston, HACP 4.11.18; still Manston 3.19
F1126 RAF North Russia by 8.19
F1127 6 AI to 211 Sqdn 8.12.18; 98 Sqdn 23.2.19; 1 ASD 5.3.19
F1133 Deld 6 SD Ascot W/E 24.10.18; Shipped to Mudros W/E 21.11.18; RAF North Russia by 8.19
F1142 Deld 6 SD Ascot W/E 24.10.18; Shipped to Mudros W/E 21.11.18; RAF North Russia by 13.8.19 - @23.8.19
F1143 Deld 6 SD Ascot W/E 24.10.18; Shipped to Mudros W/E 21.11.18; RAF North Russia by 8.19
F1149 2 AI to 211 Sqdn 10.11.18; 98 Sqdn 23.2.19; 1 ASD 5.3.19; to England 6.3.19
F1157 2 AI to 211 Sqdn 29.10.18; Left 11.30, FTR 4.11.18 (2/Lt CC Brouncker & 2/Lt CD Macdonald both killed); SOC in field
F1159 Rec Pk to 206 Sqdn 1.10.18; Last seen British side of lines nr Deulemont 3.10.18 (Sgt Mech R Walker wounded PoW & Pte1 AF Bailey missing)
F1168 RAF North Russia by 8.19
F1174 Deld Hendon to Manston Naval Flt 3.10.18
F1191 Manston, HACP 10.11.18 (prefix?)
F1206 Deld Hendon to Manston Naval Flight 26.11.18 - @1.19
F1210 RAF North Russia .19
F1232 Deld 6 SD Ascot W/E 24.10.18; Shipped to Mudros W/E 21.11.18; TOC Base Depot RAF Novorossisk 14.2.20; To White Russian Forces
F1233 Deld 6 SD Ascot W/E 24.10.18; Shipped to Mudros W/E 21.11.18
F1247 Deld 6 SD Ascot W/E 24.10.18; Shipped to Mudros W/E 21.11.18
F1248 Deld 6 SD Ascot W/E 24.10.18; Shipped to Mudros W/E 21.11.18
F1250 Deld 6 SD Ascot W/E 24.10.18; Shipped to Mudros W/E 21.11.18
F1279 6 AI by 2.19; 211 Sqdn 11.2.19; 98 Sqdn 23.2.19; 1 ASD 5.3.19; to England 6.3.19

## 23 SOPWITH F.1 CAMEL TRACTOR BIPLANE FIGHTERS from batch F1301 to F1550 built by Boulton & Paul Ltd. (130-hp Clerget 9B or 110-hp Le Rhône)

F1301 (110-hp Le Rhône) Deld Turnhouse by 27.6.18. Left W/E 25.7.18; To USAS as training aircraft (IWM photo Q66688)
F1303 (110-hp Le Rhône) Deld Turnhouse by 27.6.18 - @30.1.19; Grand Fleet SoAF&G Leuchars by 3.19
F1305 (110-hp Le Rhône) Deld Turnhouse by 27.6.18 - @30.1.19
F1312 148th US Aero Sqdn to 1 AI 4.8.18; 208 Sqdn 28.8.18; COL 14.9.18 (2/Lt E Jackson); 1 ASD 16.9.18; Rebuilt as H7207 5.11.18
F1314 1 AI to 208 Sqdn 13.7.18; Left 10.45, last seen spinning down after combat nr La Bassée 31.7.18 (Lt LC Gilmour PoW); SOC in field 31.7.18
F1398 Rec Pk to 1 AI 18.8.18; 208 Sqdn 24.8.18; Hit mound on TO 1.10.18 (2/Lt E Jackson unhurt); 7 Adv SS 3.10.18
F1399 (140-hp Clerget) Rec Pk to 1 AI 15.7.18; 208 Sqdn 12.8.18; Left 14.50 on wireless patrol nr Lens, FTR

10.9.18 (Lt JP Lloyde PoW)

F1405 Grand Fleet SoAF&G by 8.18 - @9.18
F1406 Grand Fleet SoAF&G by 8.18 - @2.19
F1411 (140-hp Clerget) Deld Eastbourne 26.6.18; Spun in 17.7.18 (Lt EM Parson killed)
F1412 50 TDS Eastbourne by 16.7.18
F1417 (130-hp Clerget) 54 TDS Fairlop, stalled, cartwheeled, sideslipped into ground 18.10.18 (Capt FB Sedgewick killed) (prefix?)
F1518 470 Flt 219 Sqdn Manston by 10.8.18; EF, FL in sea, lost 15.8.18 (pilot picked up by Short N2635 from Westgate)
F1520 470 Flt 219 Sqdn Manston (coded 'C') by 2.9.18 (broad white fuselage band, stripped cowling, white outlined field disc); Burgh Castle 15.11.18
F1522 470 Flt 219 Sqdn Manston (coded 'W') by 2.9.18; Burgh Castle 15.11.18
F1524 Acc test 3 AAP 28.7.18; 470 Flt 219 Sqdn Manston by 10.8.18 - @2.9.18
F1526 (Clerget) Deld 3 AAP Norwich 7.18; 471 Flt 233 Sqdn Walmer 28.7.18; 11 AP 23.2.19; WOC 23.2.19
F1528 Presentation a/c "A Siege Battery, 2nd Siege Artillery Reserve Brigade". Deld 3 AAP Norwich 7.18; Acceptance test 28.7.18; 471 Flt 233 Sqdn Walmer 28.7.18; 471 Flt Eringhem 25.10.18; Badly strained 1.11.18 (Lt AC Davern); 4 ASD 2.11.18 (overhaul)
F1530 (Clerget) Deld 3 AAP Norwich 7.18; 471 Flt 233 Sqdn Walmer 28.7.18 - @30.10.18; Tested Ghistelles 7.12.18 (4 ASD?); 11 AP from 13.12.18; WOC 14.1.19
F1534 (Clerget) Deld 3 AAP Norwich 7.18; 471 Flt 233 Sqdn Walmer 31.7.18; To 11 AP 11.18; WOC 23.1.19
F1536 (130-hp Clerget) Deld 3 AAP Norwich 7.18; 471 Flt 233 Sqdn Walmer 28.7.18 - @29.10.18; Tested Ghistelles 10.12.18 (4 ASD?); 11 AP, stalled and spun in on turn from 500ft while circling after TO, TW Ghistelles 14.12.18 (2/Lt JB Fast killed); WO 15.12.18 (authorised 21.12.18)
F1537 Deld 3 AAP Norwich 7.18; 471 Flt 233 Sqdn Walmer by 8.18
F1550 Presentation a/c 'Ontario'. Rec Pk to 2 AI 27.9.18; 5 AI 2.10.18; 208 Sqdn 2.10.18; 2 AI 16.11.18; 209 Sqdn 19.11.18; 2 AI 19.11.18

## 2 AIRCO D.H.9A TRACTOR BIPLANE BOMBERS from batch F1603 to F1652 built by Westland Aircraft Works

F1618 6 AI to 205 Sqdn, COL 13.2.19 (Lt Sox); to 2 ASD
F1626 552 Flt 227 Sqdn Petrovsk by .19

## 1 AIRCO D.H.4 TRACTOR BIPLANE BOMBERS from btach of tow built by Aircraft Manufacturing Co Ltd to replace D8408 and D9231, numbered F1551 and F1552

F1551 (Eagle V) (Replaced D8408) Rec Pk to 2 AI 30.5.18; 205 Sqdn 3.6.18; COL from bombing raid on Chaulnes Rly Stn 19.6.18 (Lt EO Danger & 2/Lt AD Hollingsworth unhurt); 2 ASD 19.6.18

## 13 SOPWITH F.1 CAMEL TRACTOR BIPLANE SCOUTS from batch F1883 to F1957 built by Boulton & Paul Ltd. (130-hp Clerget)

F1920 Rec Pk to 1 AI 7.9.18; 208 Sqdn 16.9.18; 2 AI 30.10.18
F1931 Rec Pk to 1 AI 13.9.18; 208 Sqdn 16.9.18; O/t landing 13.11.18 (2/Lt CR Curry unhurt); to 2 ASD
F1937 Rec Pk to 1 AI 13.9.18; 208 Sqdn 15.9.18; Crashed avoiding workman on TO 29.9.18 (2/Lt A Haybittle unhurt); 2 ASD 30.9.18; SOC in field
F1943 Grand Fleet SoAF&G East Fortune/Leuchars by 10.18 - @4.19 (prefix?)
F1949 Deld 6 SD Ascot W/E 12.9.18; Shipped to Taranto without engine 19.9.18; Taranto by 11.18 - @30.1.19 (Fitted 130-hp Le Rhône)
F1950 Deld 6 SD Ascot W/E 12.9.18; To docks W/E 26.9.18; Shipped to Mudros 11.10.18; Mudros by 1.19; To White Russian Forces 1919
F1951 Deld 6 SD Ascot W/E 12.9.18; To docks W/E 26.9.18; Shipped to Mudros W/E 3.10.18 Mudros by 10.18 - @30.1.19; To White Russian Forces 1919
F1952 Deld 6 SD Ascot W/E 12.9.18; To docks W/E 26.9.18; Shipped to Mudros W/E 3.10.18; Mudros by 10.18 -

F1953 @30.1.19 (with Greeks by 1.19)
Deld 6 SD Ascot W/E 12.9.18; To docks W/E 26.9.18; Shipped to Mudros W/E 3.10.18; Mudros by 10.18 - @30.1.19 (with Greeks); RAF South Russia Instructional Mission by 11.19

F1954 Deld 6 SD Ascot W/E 12.9.18; To docks W/E 26.9.18; Shipped to Mudros 11.10.18; Mudros by 11.18 - @30.1.19; To White Russian Forces 1919

F1955 Deld 6 SD Ascot W/E 12.9.18; To docks W/E 26.9.18; Shipped to Mudros W/E 3.10.18; Mudros by 10.18 - @30.1.19; RAF South Russia, to 'A' dett South Russia Instructional Mission 8.19; To White Russian Forces 1919

F1956 Deld 6 SD Ascot W/E 12.9.18; To docks W/E 26.9.18; Shipped to Mudros W/E 3.10.18; Mudros by 10.18 - @30.1.19; 222 Sqdn Mudros/San Stefano by 14.11.18; To White Russian Forces 1919

F1957 Deld 6 SD Ascot W/E 12.9.18; To docks W/E 26.9.18; Shipped to Mudros W/E 3.10.18. Mudros by 11.18 - @30.1.19; RAF South Russia, to 'A' dett South Russia Instructional Mission 8.19; To White Russian Forces 1919

## 15 SOPWITH F.1 CAMEL TRACTOR BIPLANE FIGHTERS from batch F2008 to F2082 built by Ruston, Proctor & Co Ltd at Lincoln. (130-hp Clerget)

F2027 FF 22.10.18; 50 TDS Eastbourne by 10.18; Wings collapsed when pulled out too suddenly diving on ground target 9.11.18 (F/Cdt HE Crook killed)
F2028 50 TDS Eastbourne, pilot hit rudder bar, crashed (date?)
F2071 Deld 6 SD Ascot W/E 10.10.18; Shipped Mudros W/E 7.11.18
F2072 Deld 6 SD Ascot W/E 10.10.18; Shipped Mudros W/E 7.11.18
F2073 Deld 6 SD Ascot W/E 17.10.18; Shipped Mudros W/E 7.11.18
F2074 Deld 6 SD Ascot W/E 17.10.18; Shipped Mudros W/E 7.11.18
F2075 Deld 6 SD Ascot W/E 24.10.18; Shipped Mudros W/E 7.11.18
F2076 Deld 6 SD Ascot W/E 17.10.18; Shipped Mudros W/E 7.11.18
F2077 Deld 6 SD Ascot W/E 17.10.18; Shipped Mudros W/E 7.11.18
F2078 Deld 6 SD Ascot W/E 17.10.18; Shipped Mudros W/E 7.11.18
F2079 Deld 6 SD Ascot W/E 17.10.18; Shipped Taranto W/E 7.11.18
F2080 Deld 6 SD Ascot W/E 17.10.18; Shipped Taranto W/E 7.11.18
F2081 Deld 6 SD Ascot W/E 17.10.18; Shipped Taranto W/E 7.11.18
F2082 Deld 6 SD Ascot W/E 17.10.18; Shipped Taranto W/E 7.11.18
F2084 (110-hp Le Rhône) Deld 7 AAP Kenley by 23.5.18; 1 AI by 6.18; attd 208 Sqdn 29.6.18 - @14.9.18 (Wing Commander's aircraft); 40 Sqdn to 203 Sqdn, RTP W/E 23.2.19

## 2 SOPWITH F.1 CAMEL TRACTOR BIPLANE SCOUTS from batch F2083 to F2182 built by Hooper & Co Ltd, London. (110-hp Le Rhône)

F2101 FF 25.6.18; Acc Brooklands 28.6.18; 50 TDS Eastbourne by 7.18 - @11.18
F2104 54 TDS Fairlop, mid-air collision with 504K D9660 29.7.18 (2/Lt L Bell killed)

## 20 SOPWITH SHIP STRUTTER TRACTOR BIPLANES ex French-built 1½ Strutters "à titre de cession" from French Government for Strutter conversion. 4 deld W/E 4.5.18 & 16 W/E 11.5.18. (130-hp Clerget)

F2210 (Ex S7034) Deld Turnhouse W/E 25.5.18; HMS *Courageous* W/E 31.10.18; Donibristle W/E 12.12.18 - @30.1.19
F2211 (Ex S7083) Deld Turnhouse W/E 25.5.18; Fitted 9 hook-on clips and tested HMS *Argus* by L/Col R Bell-Davies, VC, DSO 1.10.18; HMS *Argus* 1.10.18; Deleted W/E 12.12.18

F2212 (Ex S7084) Deld Turnhouse W/E 25.5.18 - @30.1.19
F2213 (Ex S7096) Deld Turnhouse W/E 25.5.18 - @30.1.19
F2214 (Ex S7100) Deld Turnhouse W/E 25.5.18; Donibristle W/E 17.10.18; Rosyth W/E 31.10.18 - @30.1.19
F2215 (Ex S7107) Deld Turnhouse W/E 25.5.18; Donibristle W/E 16.9.18; HMS *Renown* W/E 17.10.18; Donibristle 12.10.18; HMS *Renown* to Donibristle 23.10.18 - @26.10.18; HMS *Renown* to Donibristle 30.10.18; Smoogroo by 3-4.12.18; HMS *Renown* to Donibristle W/E 19.12.18 - @30.1.19
F2216 (Ex S7108) Deld Turnhouse W/E 25.5.18; HMS *Furious* W/E 14.11.18; HMS *Indomitable* W/E 12.12.18 - @30.1.19; ashore; HMS *Royal Sovereign* 12.3.19; ashore 24.3.19
F2217 (Ex S7109) Deld Turnhouse W/E 25.5.18 - @30.1.19
F2218 (Ex S7110) Deld Turnhouse W/E 25.5.18 - @30.1.19
F2219 (Ex S7111) Deld Turnhouse W/E 25.5.18 - @30.1.19
F2220 (Ex S7112) Deld Turnhouse W/E 25.5.18; Donibristle W/E 29.8.18; HMS *New Zealand* W/E 19.9.18; HMS *Argus* W/E 14.11.18; Donibristle W/E 12.12.18 - @30.1.19
F2221 (Ex S7119) Deld Turnhouse W/E 25.5.18; Donibristle W/E 3.12.18; HMS *Malaya* W/E 16.1.19 - @30.1.19
F2222 (Ex S7120) Deld Turnhouse W/E 25.5.18; HMS *Courageous* W/E 26.9.18; Rosyth W/E 17.10.18; HMS *Courageous* W/E 24.10.18; Rosyth W/E 31.10.18; Turnhouse W/E 28.11.18; Rosyth W/E 5.12.18 - @30.1.19; HMS *Argus* by 25.11.19 - 7.20; U/c collapsed landing 12.3.20 (F/O EC Usher)
F2223 (Ex S7121) Deld Turnhouse W/E 25.5.18; NARD W/E 14.11.18 - @30.1.19
F2224 (Ex S7124) Deld Turnhouse W/E 25.5.18; Donibristle W/E 5.9.18; HMS *Repulse* W/E 19.9.18; Donibristle W/E 26.9.18; Turnhouse W/E 10.10.18; HMS *Repulse* W/E 17.10.18; Rosyth W/E 24.10.18; Deleted W/E 31.10.18
F2225 (Ex S7116) Deld Turnhouse W/E 25.5.18; Donibristle W/E 5.9.18; HMS *Renown* to Donibristle 30.9.18; Turnhouse W/E 16.10.18; Deleted W/E 14.11.18
F2226 (Ex S7098) Deld Turnhouse W/E 25.5.18 - @30.1.19; HMS *Argus* 1919
F2227 (Ex S7099) Deld Turnhouse W/E 25.5.18; Donibristle W/E 28.11.18; HMS *Courageous* W/E 3.12.18; Donibristle W/E 16.1.19 - @30.1.19
F2228 (Ex S7103) Deld Turnhouse W/E 25.5.18; HMS *Repulse* W/E 3.10.18; HMS *Barham* 12.10.18; Donibristle 27.10.18; To HMS *Renown* 1.19; ashore 9.1.19; Disposed by 23.1.19
F2229 (Ex S7104) Deld Turnhouse W/E 25.5.18; HMS *Renown* 12.9.18; Donibristle 21.9.18; HMS *Renown* 21.9.18; Donibristle 27.9.18; HMS *Renown* 9.10.18; Donibristle W/E 17.10.18; Disposed W/E 23.1.19 ALSO HMS *Malaya*

## 9 AVRO 504K TRACTOR BIPLANE TRAINERS from batch F2233 to F2332 built by The Brush Electrical Engineering Co Ltd at Loughborough.
### (100-hp Gnome Monosoupape)

F2234 54 TDS Fairlop, hit by bullet from another aircraft 13.10.18 (2/Lt EA Freitag uninjured; F/Cdt GSC Barron injured); contd post-war
F2241 50 TDS Eastbourne by 9.18 - @10.18
F2242 50 TDS Eastbourne by 9.18 - @10.18
F2270 (80-hp Le Rhône) 52 TDS Cramlington, stalled nr ground and dived in 14.1.19 (2/Lt HH Smith & F/Cdt RB Earley both injured) (or H2270?)
F2309 Deld Turnhouse W/E 12.12.18 - @30.1.19; RAF Base Leuchars by 1.20; EF, stalled on turn 23.1.20
F2310 Deld Turnhouse W/E 12.12.18 - @30.1.19
F2311 56 TDS Cranwell by 18.11.18 - @30.1.19
F2312 57 TDS Cranwell by 19.11.18
F2314 56 TDS Cranwell by 11.18 - @12.18

## 5 SOPWITH 7F.1 SNIPE TRACTOR BIPLANE FIGHTERS from batch F2333 to F2532 built by the parent company at Kingston-on-Thames.

F2336 208 Sqdn by 7.8.19FM - @21.8.19
F2343 208 Sqdn by 17.3.19FM; COL 31.7.19 (Lt BH Matthews) LM

| | |
|---|---|
| F2344 | 208 Sqdn by 18.3.19FM; FL, blown over in storm, Aachen 31.3.19 (Lt CR Davidson unhurt); to 2 ASD |
| F2378 | 208 Sqdn by 3.5.19FM; Crashed 28.5.19 (Lt AE Woodbridge) LM |
| F2404 | 208 Sqdn by 17.3.19FM - @20.8.19 |

## 5 AIRCO D.H.4 TRACTOR BIPLANE DAY BOMBERS from batch F2633 to F2732 built by The Glendower Aircraft Co Ltd, London

| | |
|---|---|
| F2633 | Rec Pk to 2 AI 15.9.18; 205 Sqdn 18.9.18; Fokker DVII dest 21.9.18 (Lt EH Johnson & Sgt Mech WJH Middleton); 2 ASD 25.9.18; 57 Sqdn 27.9.18 |
| F2640 | (Eagle VIII) Rec Pk to 217 Sqdn (via 202 Sqdn) 25.10.18; 98 Sqdn 16.3.19; 1 ASD 17.3.19; to England 18.3.19 |
| F2643 | (Eagle VIII) 202 Sqdn to 217 Sqdn 25.10.18; 202 Sqdn to 98 Sqdn 16.3.19; 1 ASD 18.3.19 (to OC 91 Wing) |
| F2650 | 205 Sqdn by 3.19 |
| F2657 | Rec Pk to 2 ASD 22.10.18; 1 ASD by 1.19; 216 Sqdn 3.1.19 |

## 36 SOPWITH F.1 CAMEL TRACTOR BIPLANE SCOUTS from batch ordered under Cont No A.S.7861 from Clayton & Shuttleworth Ltd, Lincoln and numbered F3096 to F3145. (150-hp B.R.1)

| | |
|---|---|
| F3097 | Deld 4 AAP Lincoln W/E 29.8.18; Turnhouse (coded '1') W/E 12.9.18 - @30.1.19 |
| F3098 | Rec Pk to 1 AI 16.9.18; 203 Sqdn by 10.18; Fokker DVII OOC smoking Bruay 15.15 29.10.18 (Sgt WG Jones); Crashed Rue de Marais, Raismes 9.11.18 (Sgt WG Jones); Crashed on practice flight, nr Auby 9.12.18 (2/Lt RH Thompson killed); SOC in field |
| F3099 | Deld 2 AAP Hendon by 10.18; 4 ASD 25.10.18; 213 Sqdn 7.11.18; 11 AP 25.2.19; WOC 25.2.19 burnt Ghistelles |
| F3100 | 1 ASD to 204 Sqdn 30.10.18; Fokker DVII OOC Melle 08.40 4.11.18 (2/Lt T Whittaker); EF landing, overshot 17.1.19 (Lt T Whittaker unhurt?); RTP |
| F3101 | 4 ASD Audembert to 204 Sqdn 21.9.18; Attacked by 12 HA after dropping bombs, probably one of two RAF a/c seen to collide nr Termonde 23.10.18 (2/Lt G Sutcliffe killed) |
| F3102 | 4 ASD to 204 Sqdn (named 'FUMS UP I') 15.9.18; Fokker DVII into sea NE of Ostende 10.45 26.9.18 (Lt N Smith); Engine choked, FL, o/t marshes nr Téteghem 24.10.18 (Lt JR Chisman unhurt); 1 ASD 27.10.18 |
| F3103 | 4 ASD Audembert to 204 Sqdn 21.9.18; 2 Fokker DVII OOC NE of Dixmude 18.50 24.9.18 (Lt PF Cormack); HA OOC Melle, shared F3928 08.30-11.00 patrol 23.10.18; Fokker DVII OOC Ghent 09.10 27.10.18 (both 2/Lt AH Williams); Overshot landing after raid, opened up to go round again, hit top of chimney stack, spun in 31.10.18 (2/Lt AH Williams killed); to 1 ASD |
| F3104 | Deld 4 AAP Lincoln W/E 29.8.18; Turnhouse W/E 19.9.18; Tested 1.5.19 |
| F3105 | Rec Pk to Rep Pk 2 ASD 26.9.18; 5 AI 8.10.18; 204 Sqdn to 1 ASD 1.11.18; 2 AI to 204 Sqdn, COL 7.11.18 (Lt C Byron); 203 Sqdn 25.1.19; RTP W/E 16.2.19 |
| F3106 | 4 ASD to 210 Sqdn (coded 'N') 6.9.18; Fokker DVII OOC nr St.Pierre Capelle/5m SE of Nieuport 14.40 24.9.18; Black & yellow Fokker DVII crashed and another OOC 7m SE of Nieuport 17.45 28.9.18; Fokker DVII crashed W of Wijnendaele Forest, pilot fell out 07.50-08.00 29.9.18 (all Lt GA Welsh); Fokker DVII crashed E of Binche 13.15 10.11.18 (Lt RG Burns); Overshot landing, hit sunken road, damaged 19.11.18 (Lt RG Burns injured); Rebuilt by sqdn, flying again by 7.12.18; 203 Sqdn 24.1.19; RTP W/E 23.2.19 |
| F3107 | 4 ASD to 210 Sqdn 18.9.18; Ran into hedge landing to report position of enemy troops to 59 Bde RFA at Aulnois 9.11.18 (T/Capt FC Gorringe MC unhurt); 2 ASD 11.11.18 |
| F3108 | 4 ASD to 204 Sqdn 4.10.18; In combat 17.10.18 (2/Lt AE Robertson wounded); EF, FL, o/t Furnes 23.10.18 (Lt JWG Price); 1 ASD 25.10.18; Rebuilt as H7241 5.11.18 |
| F3109 | 204 Sqdn by 27.9.18 (FM); Fokker DVII with red tail OOC Courtrai 11.20 9.10.18; 2 Fokker DVII shot down Thermonde 10.05 23.10.18; Fokker DVII OOC S of |

| | |
|---|---|
| | Ghent 09.10 27.10.18; Fokker DVII OOC Nazareth 13.15 30.10.18 (all 2/Lt JD Lightbody); 1 ASD 14.1.19 |
| F3110 | 4 ASD to 213 Sqdn 29.9.18; Badly shot up, landed Petite Synthe (2/Lt WH Herd); 4 ASD 2.10.18; 213 Sqdn 30.10.18; 11 AP 24.2.19; WOC 24.2.19 |
| F3111 | Rec Pk to St.Omer 24.9.18; Rec Pk by 10.18; 1 AI 2.10.18; 209 Sqdn 9.10.18; Crashed on TO, damaged wings, propeller & u/c Berck-sur-Mer 20.1.19 (2/Lt R Snaith unhurt); 203 Sqdn, RTP W/E 23.2.19 |
| F3112 | Rec Pk to 1 AI 1.10.18; 204 Sqdn 26.10.18; Last seen in dog fight with 30/40 Fokker DVII over St.Denis Westrem 09.10 27.10.18 (2/Lt AJH Ross killed); SOC in field |
| F3113 | Deld 4 AAP Lincoln by 29.8.18; Turnhouse W/E 12.9.18 - @30.1.19 |
| F3114 | UK to 4 ASD 25.10.18; 213 Sqdn 7.11.18; Overshot landing, hit fence 9.11.18 (2/Lt FW Radford unhurt); 4 ASD 14.11.18 |
| F3116 | 4 ASD by 9.18; 210 Sqdn 28.9.18; Fokker DVII crashed nr Courtemarcke 08.00 29.9.18 (Capt E Swale DFC); Last seen 07.30 over Pitthem low bombing and shooting up 14.10.18 (2/Lt CC Fountain killed) |
| F3117 | 4 ASD to 210 Sqdn 4.10.18; Last seen 07.30 over Pitthem low bombing and shooting up 14.10.18 (2/Lt HH Whitlock PoW) |
| F3118 | 4 ASD to 213 Sqdn 28.9.18; Crash landed after going over lines 29.9.18 (2/Lt JD Redmond); 4 ASD 10.18; 213 Sqdn 21.10.18; 11 AP 25.2.19; WOC 25.2.19 |
| F3120 | 4 ASD to 213 Sqdn 3.10.18; COL 3.10.18 (2/Lt FW Radford); flying again 7.10.18; Last seen when patrol attacked by 17 HA Pervyse-Thourout 14.10.18 (Lt JCJ McDonald killed) |
| F3121 | 4 ASD to 213 Sqdn 29.9.18; Badly shot up 2.10.18 (Capt ML Cooper); 4 ASD 2.10.18; 213 Sqdn 25.10.18; 11 AP 25.2.19; WOC 25.2.19 burnt |
| F3122 | 4 ASD to 213 Sqdn 2.10.18; Fokker DVII OOC over Eessen 14.30 14.10.18; EF, FL, crashed, CW Ruysselede, unable to salve 24.10.18 (both 2/Lt FW Radford); Deleted 31.10.18 |
| F3123 | 8 AAP Lympne by 9.18; 4 ASD Audembert 1.10.18 |
| F3124 | 4 ASD to 210 Sqdn 10.10.18; 2 ASD as surplus but FL en route 17.1.19; retd 210 Sqdn 20.1.19 (D8219 sent in lieu); 203 Sqdn, RTP W/E 16.2.19 |
| F3126 | Presentation a/c 'Punjab No.19. Hissar' 3.10.18. 4 ASD to 213 Sqdn 13.10.18; EF circling to land, FL in field, crashed 1m W of Bergues aerodrome 30.10.18 (2/Lt JC Stone slightly injured); to 4 ASD |
| F3127 | 4 ASD to 210 Sqdn 10.10.18; 203 Sqdn 24.1.19; RTP W/E 16.2.19 |
| F3128 | 487 Flt 230 Sqdn Felixstowe (steel u/c, 1 Vickers, mounts for 2 Lewis); 486 Flt 273 Sqdn Burgh Castle by 22.10.18 [jettisonable u/c] |
| F3129 | Deld Lincoln to Manston by 8.10.18; Burgh Castle 15.11.18 |
| F3130 | 4 ASD to 213 Sqdn 8.10.18; 11 AP 25.2.19; WOC 25.2.19 |
| F3132 | 4 ASD to 210 Sqdn 22.10.18; Fokker DVII crashed S of Onnezies 11.20 30.10.18; Fokker DVII destroyed over Marcke 15.15 30.10.18 (both Capt VF Symondson); While on practice flight nr aerodrome attempted turn at low speed, spun in 13.11.18 (Capt VF Symondson killed); Wreckage to 2 ASD 14.11.18; SOC in field |
| F3133 | 486 Flt 273 Sqdn Burgh Castle 22.10.18 - @9.11.18 |
| F3134 | 485/6 Flts 273 Sqdn Burgh Castle by 9.11.18 |
| F3136 | 213 Sqdn by 2.19; To 11 AP 2.19 |
| F3138 | 213 Sqdn by 2.19; To 11 AP 2.19 |

## 36 SOPWITH F.1 CAMEL TRACTOR BIPLANE SCOUTS from batch ordered under Cont Nos A.S.14412 & A.S.17565 from The Nieuport & General Aircraft Co, Cricklewood and numbered F3196 to F3245. (130-hp Clerget 9B unless otherwise stated)

| | |
|---|---|
| F3196 | Mkrs by 17.6.18 for 2 AAP Hendon; 486 Flt 273 Sqdn Burgh Castle by 10.9.18 |
| F3197 | Mkrs by 17.6.18 for 2 AAP Hendon; 557/8 Flts 212 Sqdn Yarmouth by 21.8.18 |
| F3198 | 557/8 Flts 212 Sqdn Yarmouth by 8.18; 470 Flt/Manston Naval Flt 219 Sqdn (coded 'C') 1.10.18 |
| F3199 | 50 TDS Eastbourne by 1.11.18 |
| F3207 | 50 TDS Eastbourne by 1.11.18 |

F3209    50 TDS Eastbourne by 1.11.18

F3213    (B.R.1) Deld 2 AAP Hendon W/E 29.8.18; Turnhouse W/E 19.9.18 - @30.1.19

F3214    (B.R.1) Deld 2 AAP Hendon W/E 29.8.18; Turnhouse W/E 19.9.18 - @30.1.19

F3215    (B.R.1) Deld 2 AAP Hendon W/E 29.8.18; Turnhouse W/E 19.9.18 - @30.1.19

F3216    (B.R.1) Deld 2 AAP Hendon W/E 29.8.18; Turnhouse W/E 19.9.18 - @30.1.19

F3217    (B.R.1) Deld 2 AAP Hendon W/E 29.8.18; Turnhouse W/E 19.9.18 - @30.1.19

F3218    (B.R.1) Deld 2 AAP Hendon W/E 29.8.18; Turnhouse W/E 19.9.18 - @30.1.19

F3219    (B.R.1) Rec Pk to 1 AI 2.9.18; 209 Sqdn 3.9.18; Went into hole on landing 26.10.18 (2/Lt GT Porter slightly injured); to 1 ASD

F3220    Rec Pk to 1 AI 1.9.18; 203 Sqdn 25.9.18; Last seen in general engagement with 16 Fokker DVII over Hem Langlet 08.30 28.9.18 (Sgt Mech WN Mayger MM killed?)

F3221    Rec Pk to 1 AI 18.9.18 - @30.9.18; 203 Sqdn by 10.18; Caught by gust landing, crashed 9.10.18 (Lt E Stanton unhurt); to 1 ASD

F3222    Rec Pk to 1 AI 16.9.18; 204 Sqdn 30.10.18; Crashed 4.11.18 (Lt Hobson); 1 ASD 14.1.19

F3223    Rec Pk to 1 AI 19.9.18; 209 Sqdn 29.9.18; Collided with balloon cable 9.10.18 (2/Lt JE Gibbons killed)

F3224    (BR.1) Rec Pk to 2 ASD 15.8.18; 4 Sqdn AFC 23.8.18; Rep Pk 1 ASD by 10.18; 2 AI to 5 AI 4.10.18; 210 Sqdn 1.11.18; Fokker DVII OOC Binche 13.15 10.11.18 (Lt HR Hughes); 203 Sqdn 24.1.19; RTP W/E 2.2.19

F3225    1 AI to 209 Sqdn 30.8.18; Sideslipped low flying, crashed on aerodrome 26.9.18 (2/Lt J Shaw unhurt); 1 ASD 27.9.18

F3226    Rec Pk to 1 AI 3.9.18; 209 Sqdn 5.9.18; Fokker DVII crashed S of Marcoing 16.15 8.10.18; After landing, oil obscured view, taxied into F5923 1.11.18 (both 2/Lt CL Hurst unhurt); to 1 ASD   BUT Rec Pk to St.Omer 24.9.18

F3227    Rec Pk to 2 ASD 15.10.18; 201 Sqdn (coded 'F') 29.9.18; 203 Sqdn, RTP W/E 9.2.19

F3228    209 Sqdn by 10.18; Fokker DVII crashed SE of Marcoing 14.15 8.10.18 (2/Lt CL Hurst); 1 AI to 203 Sqdn 23.11.18; RTP W/E 9.2.19

F3230    Rec Pk to 1 AI 23.9.18; 203 Sqdn by 27.10.18 - @22.12.18

F3231    1 AI to 209 Sqdn 3.9.18; Crashed 9.11.18 (Lt ET Wales); 2 AI 18.11.18 (unfit for war flying but fit to fly Channel)

F3232    Rec Pk to 1 AI 27.8.18; 209 Sqdn 31.8.18; Collided tree tops landing, spun in, CW 11.10.18 (2/Lt BM Carter injured); to 1 ASD and SOC

F3233    Rec Pk to 1 AI 1.9.18; 209 Sqdn 17.9.18; Fokker DVII OOC Sauchy-Lestrée, shared D9599 16.40 20.9.18; Attacked by 7 Fokker DVII, 1 Fokker DVII crashed in flames between Ecourt St.Quentin & canal 18.35 21.9.18 (both Lt G Knight); 203 Sqdn 21.1.19; RTP W/E 9.2.19

F3235    4 ASD to 210 Sqdn 31.8.18; Fokker DVII crashed N of Wijnendaele Wood, BO 08.00 29.9.18 (Lt GW Hopkins); Missing after general engagement with 11 HA over Roulers 17.10 1.10.18 (2/Lt RW Johnson killed) [18.10 per sqdn. 1 Camel seen 2,000ft E of Roulers]; Deleted 15.10.18

F3236    (BR.1) Rec Pk to 2 ASD 2.8.18; 2 AI by 10.18; 4 ASD Audembert 2.10.18; 213 Sqdn 3.10.18; 11 AP 24.2.19; WOC 24.2.19

F3238    (BR.1) 4 ASD to 210 Sqdn 22.8.18; Fokker DVII OOC nr Ostende 18.35 6.9.18; Fokker DVII in sea 3m NW of Zeebrugge 11.10 16.9.18; Fokker DVII crashed N of St.Pierre Capelle 14.40 & another OOC 3m SE of Nieuport 14.45 24.9.18; Fokker DVII in flames E of Roulers 17.10 1.10.18 (all Lt CF Pineau); EF, FL on Belgian aerodrome Hondschoote 14.10.18 (Sgt AT Shepherd); 4 ASD 16.10.18; 213 Sqdn 14.11.18; 11 AP 23.2.19; WOC 23.2.19

F3239    (BR.1) 4 ASD to 213 Sqdn 10.18; Fokker DVII crashed S of Roulers 15.55 4.10.18 (Lt GS Hodson); Caught by wind landing, o/t 7.10.18 (Lt WT Owen); Rep Pk 4 ASD by 25.10.18; 4 ASD Audembert 26.10.18; 213 Sqdn by 11.18; Pilot apparently fainted while landing,

dived in, badly damaged nr Varssenaere 4.11.18 (Lt ER Huston injured); to 4 ASD

F3240    4 ASD to 204 Sqdn 22.8.18; KB in flames 5m SE of Ostende 11.35 16.9.18; Fokker DVII crashed & another OOC Pervyse 18.50 24.9.18 (all Capt TW Nash DFC ); 4 ASD by 10.18; 213 Sqdn 16.10.18; Landed in thick mist, went on nose 29.10.18 (Lt AH Turner); to 4 ASD

F3241    486 Flt 273 Sqdn Burgh Castle by 8.18 - @9.11.18

F3242    4 ASD to 204 Sqdn 22.8.18; Spun in formating after TO, CW 3.9.18 (Lt HWM Cumming DoI 5.9.18); 4 ASD 5.9.18; 210 Sqdn, FL en route at Hoog Huis 13.10.18; arr 14.10.18; Last seen 11.15, missing after 7 Fokker DVII engaged E of Valenciennes 30.10.18 (Lt A Buchanan DFC PoW)

F3243    4 ASD to 204 Sqdn 22.8.18; Yellow-tailed Fokker DVII in flames 5m NE of Dixmude 10.25 20.9.18; Fokker DVII OOC Blankenberghe 10.45 26.9.18; Fokker DVII OOC Termonde 10.05 23.10.18 (all Lt HG Clappison); Ran into brick building on landing 29.10.18 (Lt HG Clappison unhurt); for 1 ASD

F3244    (B.R.1) Deld 2 AAP Hendon W/E 15.8.18; To Turnhouse W/E 29.8.18; Not arrived by 30.1.19 (crashed on delivery?)

F3245    (B.R.1) 4 ASD to 1 AI 7.9.18; 203 Sqdn 25.9.18; Caught by gust landing, o/t 5.10.18 (Sgt AC Fidgen unhurt); to 1 ASD

**65 AIRCO D.H.6 TRACTOR BIPLANES from batch ordered under Cont Nos 87/A/1844 & A.S.17567, numbered F3346 to F3445 & built at Hendon. (90-hp RAF 1A or 90-hp Curtiss OX-5)**

F3346    Deld MAD South Shields by 7.18; B/C Flts 256 Sqdn Sea Houses 9.7.18; Fell in sea off Berwick 22.7.18 (Lt Roberts)

F3347    C Flt/528 Flt Sea Houses by 14.7.18; FL, crashed Holy Island 25.7.18

F3348    Deld MAD South Shields by 7.18; B/C Flts 256 Sqdn Sea Houses 9.7.18; FL on Holy Island, bottom wing and u/c destroyed 25.7.18 (pilot unhurt); still 256 Sqdn Sea Houses 2.8.18

F3349    A/B Flts 255 Sqdn Pembroke (named 'KITTY') by 3.8.18; Propeller accident 23.8.18 (3AM Gosling injured); Became 519/520 Flts 255 Sqdn Pembroke Dock on/by 24.8.18 - @3.11.18

F3350    255 Sqdn Pembroke by 20.7.18 - @9.8.18; B Flt 244 Sqdn Bangor, fell in sea 23.8.18 (Lt CWS Hall picked up by destroyer)

F3351    A/B Flts 255 Sqdn Pembroke by 4.7.18; Became 519/520 Flts 255 Sqdn Pembroke by 4.7.18 - @13.10.18; With B2789, dropped bomb on U-boat 14.45 24.8.18 (Lt AJD Peebles)

F3352    A/B Flts 255 Sqdn Pembroke Dock by 7.18

F3353    D Flt/509 Flt Tees & Seaton Carew by 6.18; A/B Flts 255 Sqdn Pembroke by 4.7.18 - @28.9.18; 519/520 Flts Pembroke by 9.18 - 11.18

F3354    A/B Flts 255 Sqdn Pembroke by 4.7.18 - @24.7.18

F3355    527/8 Flts 256 Sqdn Sea Houses by 9.18

F3357    519/520 Flts 255 Sqdn Pembroke by 9.18

F3366    SD Flt 251 Sqdn Atwick by 13.7.18; Became 504 Flt 251 Sqdn 15.8.18 - @15.10.18

F3367    SD Flt 251 Sqdn Atwick, FL in sea, picked by armed trawler 14.7.18

F3368    506 Flt 251 Sqdn Owthorne by 29.9.18 - @13.11.18; Became O-BAQQ

F3369    506 Flt 251 Sqdn Owthorne by 4.9.18; Fell in sea 1.10.18 (pilot picked up by destroyer)

F3370    Deld MAD South Shields by 7.18; B/C Flt Sea Houses 3.7.18; Fell in sea 24.7.18 (Lt GCW Petersen unhurt)

F3371    Deld MAD South Shields by 7.18; B/C Flt Sea Houses 3.7.18; Fell in sea 24.7.18

F3372    Deld MAD South Shields by 7.18; B Flt/528 Flt 256 Sqdn Sea Houses 5.7.18 - 8.18

F3373    Deld MAD South Shields by 7.18; D Flt/509 Flt 252 Sqdn Seaton Carew 22.7.18 - @11.11.18; FL Blackhall Rocks 23.8.18 (pilot and machine safe)

F3376    Seaton Carew by 31.7.18

F3380    272 Sqdn Machrihanish by 17.10.18 - @11.18

F3384    272 Sqdn Machrihanish by 11.18

F3386    Deld Hendon to RAE 24.7.18 - @29.8.18 (Exp - modified wings with 10 degrees back stagger)

F3389 MOS Aldeburgh by 10.18; Became ASIPOS Aldeburgh 28.12.18; Became 1 MOS Aldeburgh 1.1.19

F3390 Seaton Carew by 13.7.18; 272 Sqdn Luce Bay 10.18; MOS Aldeburgh by 10.18

F3391 MOS Aldeburgh, dived into ground off sideslip 17.10.18 (F/Cdt S Gosney slightly injured & Sgt H Woods unhurt)

F3392 506 Flt 251 Sqdn Owthorne by 27.7.18 - @13.11.18

F3393 Atwick by 23.7.18 - @31.7.18; 506 Flt 251 Sqdn Owthorne by 7.18 - @11.18; 504 Flt 251 Sqdn Atwick by 3.9.18; EF, FL crashed u/c Flamborough 20.9.18

F3394 506 Flt 251 Sqdn Owthorne by 31.7.18 - @11.18

F3395 Deld MAD South Shields by 8.18; 526 Flt 256 Sqdn New Haggerston 6.8.18

F3396 Deld MAD South Shields by 8.18; 507 Flt 252 Sqdn Tynemouth 2.8.18 - @6.11.18

F3397 Deld MAD South Shields by 8.18; 507/8 Flts 252 Sqdn Tynemouth 4.8.18 - @11.18

F3398 Deld MAD South Shields by 8.18; 507 Flt 252 Sqdn Tynemouth 30.7.18 - @11.11.18

F3399 Deld MAD South Shields by 8.18; 526/7 Flts 256 Sqdn Sea Houses 6.8.18

F3400 (90-hp Curtiss) Deld MAD South Shields by 8.18; 507/8 Flts 252 Sqdn Tynemouth 2.8.18; Port mainplanes folded up out of short dive, spun in Cullercoats 23.8.18 (Lt AG Blundell killed)

F3401 B Flt 256 Sqdn Sea Houses by 7.18; C Flt/528 Flt Sea Houses by 12.8.18; COL 20.8.18 (pilot unhurt)

F3402 Deld MAD South Shields by 7.18; A Flt/527 Flt 256 Sqdn 30.7.18 - @8.18; B Flt Sea Houses by 8.18

F3403 Deld MAD South Shields by 8.18; To Sea Houses but crashed on TO, slightly damaged 4.8.18 (pilot unhurt); 505 Flt 251 Sqdn West Ayton 5.9.18 - @11.11.18

F3404 Deld MAD South Shields by 8.18; C Flt/528 Flt 256 Sqdn Sea Houses by 12.8.18; 507/8 Flt 252 Sqdn Tynemouth by 11.10.18 - @11.18

F3405 Deld MAD South Shields by 8.18; 256 Sqdn Sea Houses 6.8.18

F3406 D Flt/509 Flt 252 Sqdn Seaton Carew by 8.18; FL 9m NE H Buoy, Hartlepool, badly damaged 18.9.18 (pilot unhurt)

F3407 Deld MAD South Shields by 9.18; Scarborough 1.9.18; 505 Flt 251 Sqdn West Ayton by 11.9.18 - @13.11.18

F3408 D Flt/509 Flt 252 Sqdn Seaton Carew by 8.18 - @11.11.18

F3409 506 Flt 251 Sqdn Owthorne by 29.9.18

F3410 Deld MAD South Shields by 8.18; 507/8 Flts 252 Sqdn Tynemouth 3.9.18

F3411 MAD South Shields by 9.18; 527 Flt 256 Sqdn Sea Houses 4.9.18 - @18.11.18

F3412 Deld MAD South Shields by 8.18; 507/8 Flts 252 Sqdn Tynemouth by 4.9.18 - @12.11.18

F3413 511/2 Flts 252 Sqdn Bembridge by 11.18

F3414 513 Flt 241 Sqdn Chickerell by 9.18; 507/8 Flts 252 Sqdn Tynemouth by 10.18; 513 Flt 241 Sqdn Chickerell by 11.18

F3415 513 Flt 241 Sqdn Chickerell by 9.11.18

F3417 511/2 Flts 252 Sqdn Bembridge by 11.18

F3420 514 Flt 242 Sqdn Telscombe by 11.18

F3421 513 Flt 241 Sqdn Chickerell by 11.18; 514 Flt 242 Sqdn Telscombe 1918

F3422 Bembridge by 9.18; FL, towed Bembridge 15.9.18

F3424 511/2 Flts 252 Sqdn Bembridge by 11.18

F3425 514 Flt 242 Sqdn Telscombe by 11.18

F3426 514 Flt 242 Sqdn Telscombe by 11.18

F3428 Deld MAD South Shields by 9.18; 509 Flt 252 Sqdn Seaton Carew 26.9.18; Crashed, wing, propeller and u/c smashed 25.10.18 (pilot unhurt)

F3429 509 Flt 252 Sqdn Seaton Carew by 6.11.18 - @18.11.18

F3430 Deld MAD South Shields by 9.18; 510 Flt 252 Sqdn Redcar 20.9.18; 510 Flt 252 Sqdn West Ayton 8.10.18; Killingholme 30.12.18

F3431 Deld MAD South Shields by 9.18; 256 Sqdn Sea Houses 23.9.18; 526 Flt 256 Sqdn New Haggerston by 4.10.18 - @3.11.18

F3432 507/8 Flt 252 Sqdn Tynemouth by 11.18

F3433 Deld MAD South Shields by 9.18; 510 Flt 252 Sqdn Redcar 17.9.18; 510 Flt 252 Sqdn West Ayton 11.10.18 - @16.10.18

F3435 Deld MAD South Shields by 9.18; 510 Flt 252 Sqdn Redcar 26.9.18 - @2.10.18; 510 Flt 252 Sqdn West Ayton by 12.10.18 - @2.12.18; Became G- EAHH

F3440 B Flt 255 Sqdn Pembroke by 4.7.18

**41 SOPWITH F.1 CAMEL TRACTOR BIPLANE SCOUTS ordered under Cont Nos A.S.14412 & A.S.17565 from The Nieuport & General Aircraft Co, Cricklewood and numbered F3918 to F3967. (130-hp Clerget 9B unless otherwise stated)**

F3918 Yarmouth by 21.8.18; 470 Flt/Manston Naval Flight 219 Sqdn (coded 'D') 1.10.18; Yarmouth by 1.19

F3919 (150-hp B.R.1) Deld 2 AAP Hendon W/E 15.8.18; Turnhouse W/E 19.9.18 - @30.1.19

F3920 Rec Pk to 1 AI 4.9.18; 203 Sqdn 16.9.18; RTP W/E 9.2.19

F3921 Rec Pk to 2 AI 18.9.18; 201 Sqdn (coded 'C') 8.10.18; 203 Sqdn 23.1.19; RTP W/E 9.2.19

F3922 4 ASD to 204 Sqdn 26.8.18; Fokker DVII grey green with white elevators and tail OOC Gheluvelt 11.50 3.9.18; 2-str DD E of Ypres 13.30 5.9.18; Salmon Fokker DVII into sea just off Zeebrugge Mole, shared D8146 14.00 15.9.18 (all Lt BE Barnum); Salmon Fokker DVII in flames Blankenberghe-Zeebrugge, shared D8146, D8183, D8187 & D8188, also Fokker DVII in flames & another OOC (neither shared) 18.55-19.00 16.9.18 (Capt CRR Hickey DFC); Fokker DVII OOC Blankenberghe 10.50 26.9.18 (Lt BE Barnum); 1 ASD 14.1.19

F3923 (B.R.1) Deld 2 AAP Hendon W/E 22.8.18; Turnhouse W/E 12.9.18 - @30.1.19

F3924 (B.R.1) Deld 2 AAP Hendon W/E 22.8.18; Turnhouse W/E 5.9.18 - @30.1.19

F3925 (B.R.1) Deld 2 AAP Hendon W/E 22.8.18; Turnhouse W/E 19.9.18; Deleted W/E 14.11.18

F3926 Yarmouth by 9.18; Manston Naval Flight 219 Sqdn 1.10.18; Yarmouth by 1.19 BUT Rec Pk to 1 AI 2.10.18; 203 Sqdn 18.10.18; RTP W/E 2.2.19

F3927 Rec Pk to 2 ASD 18.9.18; 2 AI to 5 AI 8.10.18; 1 AI by 11.18; 204 Sqdn 2.11.18; 1 ASD 14.1.19

F3928 Rec Pk to 4 ASD Audembert 10.18; 204 Sqdn 4.10.18; HA OOC Melle, shared F3103, then last seen going down, FL 3m E of Deynze, believed engine hit by ground m/g fire 08.30-11.00 patrol 23.10.18 (2/Lt HJ Gemmel PoW)

F3929 4 ASD to 204 Sqdn (named 'FUMS UP III') 28.9.18; Fokker DVII shot down in flames over St.Denis Westrem 09.10 27.10.18 (Lt RMcI Gordon wounded); KB destroyed Huysee 07.25 31.10.18; Fokker DVII OOC flapping leaf 08.45 Melle 4.11.18 (both Capt CL Morley DFC); 1 ASD 14.1.19

F3930 4 ASD to 210 Sqdn 17.9.18; Fokker DVII OOC nr St.Pierre Capelle 14.40 24.9.18; Halberstadt C spun in E of floods SE of Nieuport 17.45 27.9.18; Separated from patrol, joined fight between 8 Spad/6 Hanriot and about 15 HA, Fokker DVII in flames 8m NE of Ypres 09.45 1.10.18 ("believed new type Fokker"); All black Fokker DrI OOC 2m S of Lichtervelde 10.40 14.10.18; Fokker DVII crashed 2m W of Locquignol 10.30 27.10.18; Fokker DVII crashed 200yds E of Rombies 11.15 30.10.18; KB in flames Estreux 12.10 1.11.18; Damaged by AA 8.11.18 (all T/Lt KR Unger)

F3931 4 ASD to 210 Sqdn 6.9.18; Last seen in combat with 2 HA over Ghistelles 18.30 17.9.18 (2/Lt JE Harrison) [credited Flgm Hubrick, Marine Jasta 4]

F3932 Rec Pk to 2 AI 18.9.18; 5 AI 2.10.18; 201 Sqdn 4.10.18; 203 Sqdn 23.1.19; RTP W/E 9.2.19

F3933 (B.R.1) 1 ASD to 203 Sqdn 26.9.18; Wheels into trench landing 30.10.18 (Capt HA MacKay unhurt); to 1 ASD

F3934 Rec Pk to 1 AI 23.9.18; 209 Sqdn 29.9.18; 1 ASD 14.1.19

F3935 Rec Pk to 1 AI 7.9.18; 209 Sqdn 26.9.18; Hit overhead wires landing, wrecked 19.12.18 (2/Lt J Bradbury injured); to 1 ASD

F3936 Rec Pk to 1 AI 9.10.18; 209 Sqdn by 14.11.18

F3939 Rec Pk to 1 AI 17.10.18; 209 Sqdn 27.10.18; FL, hit overhead wires St.Waast-Wargnies 10.11.18 (2/Lt AP Murray unhurt); 1 ASD 16.11.18

F3940 Rec Pk to 1 AI 1.10.18; 204 Sqdn 26.10.18; Last seen 09.10 in dog fight with 30/40 Fokker DVII over St.Denis Westrem 27.10.18 (2/Lt HG Murray killed)

F3941 Rec Pk to 2 AI 18.9.18; 5 AI 8.10.18; 210 Sqdn 30.10.18; FL 1.1.19 (2/Lt ES McNames); Retd by 6.1.19; 203 Sqdn 24.1.19; RTP W/E 23.2.19

F3942    (B.R.1) Rec Pk to 1 AI 23.9.18; 209 Sqdn 9.10.18; EF, FL strong cross-wind, o/t nr aerodrome 2.1.19 (2/Lt GT Parker unhurt); to 1 ASD

F3943    Rec Pk to 1 AI 23.9.18; 148th US Aero Sqdn; 203 Sqdn by 22.10.18; RTP W/E 9.2.19

F3944    (B.R.1) 4 ASD to 213 Sqdn (coded '6', also black 'A' on white fin) 6.9.18; Fokker DVII in flames E of Roulers & Rumpler C DD and landed badly 2m E of Thourout 09.30 4.10.18 (Lt AH Turner); Fokker DVII OOC 7m S of Ghent 14.15, then shared Albatros C crashed S of Ghent with F3966 & F5913 14.30 1.11.18 (Lt GC Mackay); Wheels stuck in mud after landing, went on nose 20.1.19 (Mjr AG Taylor AFC unhurt); 11 AP 29.1.19 (for repair); WOC 2.2.19

F3945    4 ASD to 213 Sqdn 13.9.18; 4 ASD 13.10.18 - @25.10.18; 11 AP by 1.19; 213 Sqdn 16.1.19; 11 AP 24.2.19; WOC 24.2.19

F3946    (B.R.1) Rec Pk to 1 AI 9.10.18; 209 Sqdn 11.10.18; Pfalz DXII OOC Athies, shared C61 & H6998 07.30 4.11.18 (Lt EW Mills); Into shell hole on TO, o/t 9.12.18 (2/Lt CR Campbell unhurt); to 1 ASD; 209 Sqdn by 24.1.19

F3947    Rec Pk to 1 AI 23.9.18; 209 Sqdn 9.10.18; Delivery La Paye to Bruille after FL La Paye, lost, crashed between Tergnier & Laon 10.11.18 (Lt ET Walls injured); SOC in field 10.11.18

F3948    4 ASD by 9.18; 213 Sqdn 13.9.18; Shot down 28.9.18 (Lt WA Rankin PoW); Deleted 15.10.18

F3949    Rec Pk to 1 AI 1.10.18; 203 Sqdn, propeller caught mound of earth on TO, then hit telegraph wires, CW 28.10.18 (2/Lt LM Pickwick unhurt)

F3950    4 ASD to 213 Sqdn 27.9.18; Lost, FL Bray Dunes, went on nose on TO 28.9.18 (Lt JC Stone); to 4 ASD; 204 Sqdn 18.10.18; Fokker DVII black stripes on wing and white tail OOC Sotteghem 13.50 1.11.18 (2/Lt S Barker); 204 Sqdn by 1.19; 203 Sqdn 25.1.19; RTP W/E 9.2.19

F3951    4 ASD to 213 Sqdn 26.9.18; Spun in from 200ft on train being bombed 1m NE of Gitsberg, CW 2.10.18 (Capt ML Cooper DFC killed)

F3956    471 Flt 233 Sqdn Walmer by 2.19; To 11 AP 2.19

F3959    1 AI to 203 Sqdn 16.11.18; RTP W/E 9.2.19

F3960    Rec Pk to 1 AI 13.10.18; 204 Sqdn from 19.10.18; Fog, FL in field, hit telegraph post, o/t on Menin-Wervicq road, Varssenaere 1.12.18 (Lt CA Morris unhurt); 11 SS 9.12.18 (wreck)

F3961    1 AI to 203 Sqdn 23.11.18 - @16.1.19

F3963    204 Sqdn by 3.10.18 (FM); 1 ASD 14.1.19

F3964    (B.R.1) 4 ASD to 213 Sqdn 5.10.18; Swung on TO 24.10.18 (2/Lt RN Webster unhurt); to 4 ASD; 204 Sqdn Heule

F3965    (B.R.1) 4 ASD to 213 Sqdn 29.9.18; Fokker DVII DD Isseghem-Roulers 15.55, then hit by AA fire 4.10.18 (Lt AF Chick); to 4 ASD; 471 Flt by 2.19; 11 AP 21.2.19; WOC 21.2.19

F3966    (B.R.1) 4 ASD to 213 Sqdn 29.9.18; Fokker DVII crashed nr Beveren Rly Stn 09.30 4.10.18; Albatros C crashed 7m S of Ghent 14.15 14.30, shared F3944 & F5913 1.11.18 (Lt MN Hancocks); 11 AP 23.2.19; WOC 23.2.19

F3967    (B.R.1) Rec Pk to 4 ASD Audembert 10.18; 213 Sqdn 14.10.18; O/t landing in mist and darkness in ploughed field Uxem 25.11.18 (2/Lt JPS Burton unhurt); 11 AP repair 27.11.18; WOC 22.2.19

**3 SOPWITH F.1 CAMEL TRACTOR BIPLANE SCOUTS from batch F3968 to F4067 built by Ruston, Proctor & Co Ltd at Lincoln**

F4017    204 TDS Eastchurch 1918 (dazzle scheme)

F4018    204 TDS Eastchurch 1918

F4019    204 TDS Eastchurch 1918 (2-str conversion)

**11 SOPWITH F.1 CAMEL TRACTOR BIPLANE SCOUTS from mixed batch F4170 to F4220 rebuilds by 3(W)ARD Yate**

F4189    53 TDS Dover, floated to ground after got on back in half roll 13.9.18 (F/Cdt EH Evans killed)

F4193    (130-hp Clerget) 204 TDS Eastchurch by 25.9.18; Crashed 30.11.18 (2/Lt C Morris killed)

F4199    204 TDS Eastchurch by 24.9.18 (chequered turtle deck)

F4200    204 TDS Eastchurch by 10.10.18

F4201    204 TDS Eastchurch by 25.9.18

F4204    56 TDS Cranwell by 9.18

F4210    Grand Fleet SoAF&G Leuchars by 2.19

F4211    Grand Fleet SoAF&G East Fortune/Leuchars by 10.18 - @30.1.19

F4212    57 TDS Cranwell by 8.18 - @12.18

F4213    56 TDS Cranwell by 15.10.18 - @14.11.18

F4214    56/57 TDS Cranwell by 9.18 - @11.18 (possibly 2-str conversion)

**1 AVRO 504 TRACTOR BIPLANE TRAINER from batch F4170 to F4220 of rebuilds by 3(W)ARD Yate**

F4217    207 TDS Chingford/Fairlop 1918

**4 BRISTOL F.2B TRACTOR BIPLANES from batch F4271 to F4970 built by parent firm**

F4322    Deld 5 AAP Filton W/E 21.11.18; Turnhouse W/E 12.12.18 - @30.1.19; Grand Fleet SoAF&G Leuchars by 6.19

F4410    208 Sqdn by 8.8.19 - @20.8.19

F4446    208 Sqdn by 23.5.19 - @7.8.19 (presume replaced by F4410)

F4656    Deld 5 AAP Filton W/E 21.11.18; Turnhouse W/E 12.12.18 - @30.1.19

**19 SOPWITH F.1 CAMEL TRACTOR BIPLANE SCOUTS from batch F4974 to F5073 built by Clayton & Shuttleworth at Lincoln**

F4983    Deld War School Manston (coded 'V') 13.10.18 (broad white fuselage band); Burgh Castle 15.11.18

F4985    Rec Pk to 204 Sqdn 30.12.18; Crashed on TO 14.1.19 (Lt AB Ollerenshaw); 203 Sqdn 25.1.19; RTP W/E 16.2.19

F4986    Rec Pk to 204 Sqdn 14.12.18; 203 Sqdn 25.1.19; RTP W/E 16.2.19

F4987    (B.R.1) Deld 4 AAP Lincoln W/E 21.11.18; Turnhouse W/E 12.12.18 - @30.1.19; Grand Fleet SoAF&G Leuchars by 1.19; Hit ground during contour chasing 6.2.19 (Lt RL Bateman injured)

F4988    Rec Pk by 11.18; 2 AI to 204 Sqdn 7.11.18; 203 Sqdn 25.1.19; RTP W/E 16.2.19

F4990    Rec Pk to 204 Sqdn 15.12.18; COL, overshot 21.1.19 (Lt WR Stewart unhurt); SOC in field & burnt on station 23.1.19

F4991    (B.R.1) Deld 4 AAP Lincoln W/E 21.11.18; Turnhouse W/E 12.12.18 - @30.1.19

F4992    (B.R.1) Deld 8 AAP Lympne W/E 21.11.18; Turnhouse W/E 16.1.19 - @30.1.19

F5014    (B.R.1) Deld 4 AAP Lincoln W/E 21.11.18; Donibristle by W/E 16.1.19 - @30.1.19; Grand Fleet SoAF&G Leuchars by 7.19; Stalled, spun in from 1,500ft 1.8.19 (Lt PH Smith killed)

F5015    (B.R.1) Deld 4 AAP Lincoln W/E 21.11.18; Donibristle W/E 12.12.18 - @30.1.19

F5016    (B.R.1) Deld 4 AAP Lincoln W/E 28.11.18; Donibristle W/E 12.12.18 - @30.1.19

F5017    (B.R.1) Deld 4 AAP Lincoln W/E 21.11.18; Donibristle W/E 16.1.19 - @30.1.19; Grand Fleet SoAF&G Leuchars by 6.19 - @8.19

F5018    (B.R.1) Deld 4 AAP Lincoln W/E 21.11.18; Turnhouse W/E 12.12.18 - @30.1.19

F5019    (B.R.1) Deld 4 AAP Lincoln W/E 21.11.18; Donibristle W/E 12.12.18 - @30.1.19; Grand Fleet SoAF&G Leuchars 5.19 - @7.19

F5020    (B.R.1) Deld 4 AAP Lincoln W/E 21.11.18; Donibristle W/E 12.12.18 - @30.1.19

F5021    (B.R.1) Deld 4 AAP Lincoln W/E 21.11.18; Turnhouse W/E 12.12.18 - @30.1.19

F5022    (B.R.1) Deld 4 AAP Lincoln W/E 21.11.18; Donibristle W/E 16.1.19 - @30.1.19; Grand Fleet SoAF&G Leuchars by 5.19

F5024    (B.R.1) Deld 4 AAP Lincoln W/E 21.11.18; Donibristle W/E 16.1.19 - @30.1.19

F5025    (B.R.1) Deld 4 AAP Lincoln W/E 21.11.18; Donibristle W/E 16.1.19 - @30.1.19; Grand Fleet SoAF&G Leuchars by 8.19

## 7 AIRCO D.H.4 TRACTOR BIPLANE BOMBERS from batch F5699 to F5798 built by Palladium Autocars Ltd, London

F5704 (Eagle VIII) 217 Sqdn by 19.9.18; Returning from bombing raid on Ostende, crashed, TW, W of Furnes 28.9.18 (2/Lt AR Padmore & Sgt Mech G/L FW Shufflebottom both killed); remains to 4 ASD; Deleted 31.10.18 DBR

F5706 (Eagle VIII) 202 Sqdn (coded 'T') by 30.9.18; 98 Sqdn 6.3.19; 1 ASD 17.3.19

F5707 4 ASD to 202 Sqdn 9.10.18; 233 Sqdn Dover 6.3.19

F5708 217 Sqdn by 20.9.18 (FM); Engine trouble, FL Wusburgh 28.9.18 (Lt HS Stidston & Sgt Mech MC Day); COL 20.11.18 (2/Lt RW Woodhead & Pte1 PG Bradley); 233 Sqdn Dover 1.3.19

F5715 (Eagle VIII) 4 ASD Wissant to 217 Sqdn 29.9.18; Sank into rut taxying for TO, damaged 29.9.18 (Lt LH Nesbitt & Sgt E Farley); flying again next day; 98 Sqdn 16.3.19; 1 ASD 19.3.19

F5721 202 Sqdn (transit ex 4 ASD?) to 217 Sqdn 25.10.18; Propeller accident 9.11.18 (AM1 H Joseph slightly injured); 233 Sqdn Dover 1.3.19

F5796 (Eagle VIII) 202 Sqdn by 3.19; 98 Sqdn 15.3.19

**Various rebuilds in France numbered between F5801 and F6300 (in practice batch overlapped in error to F6308)**

## 2 AIRCO D.H.9 TRACTOR BIPLANE DAY BOMBER rebuilds

F5841 (ex A8019, TOC 25.6.18) 1 AI to 206 Sqdn 30.6.18; SOC 2.9.18 BUT Collided with telegraph wires ferrying to Linselles 24.10.18 (Lt RH Stainbank & 2/Lt EW Richardson unhurt); to Rep Pk 1 ASD

F5848 (ex C6186, TOC 25.6.18) 1 AI to 206 Sqdn 6.7.18; Left 17.35, crashed due to enemy activity in vicinity of Rousbrugge-Haringhe 29.7.18 (Lt RH Stainbank & 2/Lt EW Richardson unhurt); 1 ASD 3.8.18; SOC 7.8.18 NWR

## 56 SOPWITH F.1 CAMEL TRACTOR BIPLANE FIGHTER rebuilds

F5913 (ex B2432, TOC 25.6.18) (BR.1) Rep Pk 1 ASD to 1 AI 1.7.18; 210 Sqdn 7.7.18; FL, damaged 10.7.18 (2/Lt HH Whitlock unhurt); To 4 ASD; 213 Sqdn 24.8.18; Fokker DVII pilot killed S of Ostende 07.30 25.8.18 (Lt GC Mackay); Fokker DVII down spinning on back 8-10m from Ostende 18.40 25.8.18 (Capt CP Brown); Fokker DVII 4m S of Varssenaere aerodrome 14.40 5.9.18; Rumpler C crashed 1m N of Zevecote, shared D3349 15.00 6.9.18 (both Lt GC Mackay); Albatros C crashed 2m S of Ghent, shared F3944 & F3966 14.30 1.11.18 (Lt AH Turner); EF, FL, battle damage, NE of Courtrai 9.11.18 (2/Lt GC Garner unhurt); 4 ASD 14.11.18

F5914 (ex B5229, TOC 25.6.18) (BR.1) Rep Pk 1 ASD to 1 AI 2.7.18; 210 Sqdn (coded 'S') 7.7.18; General engagement over Ostende, Fokker shot down in sea pilot killed, shared D9609 & HA OOC SE of Ostende 09.45 20.7.18 (all Capt HT Mellings); 2-str crashed into hedge S of Ostende, shared B7280 08.30, then at 08.45 separated from flight, attacked by 4 Fokker DVIIs, one of which crashed 1m E of Ypres, then aircraft went missing, last seen fighting about 12 HA at 200ft 5m S of Ostende 18.20 22.7.18 (Capt HT Mellings DSC killed); Deleted 31.7.18

F5915 (ex B7197, TOC 25.6.18) (BR.1) Rep Pk 1 ASD to 2 ASD 9.7.18; 2 AI by 8.18; 201 Sqdn 8.8.18; Swung and hit trees on TO and wrecked 9.8.18 (Lt RD Hambrook unhurt); 2 ASD 10.8.18; SOC 20.8.18 NWR

F5918 (ex B2527, TOC 25.6.18) (130-hp Clerget) Rep Pk 1 ASD to 1 AI 2.7.18; 208 Sqdn 22.7.18; O/t on rough ground landing 4.8.18 (Lt AH Hiscox); 1 ASD 5.8.18; Rebuilt as F6335 in error 16.8.18, changed to H7003

F5923 (ex C1581, TOC 25.6.18) 2 AI by 8.18; 209 Sqdn 10.8.18; FL S of Franvillers 6.9.18 (2/Lt JW Sole); O/t landing 24.9.18 (Lt Beebe); While taxying, crashed into by F3226 1.11.18 (2/Lt JW Sole); to 1 ASD

F5925 (ex D1869, TOC 25.6.18) Rep Pk 1 ASD to 1 AI 28.7.18; 209 Sqdn 30.7.18; Fokker DVII crashed

Bailleul, shared C61 09.45 1.8.18 (Capt WR May); Petrol tank shot through, FL, crashed nr Agny 26.8.18 (Lt JE Walker unhurt); Rep Pk 1 ASD 27.8.18; SOC 30.8.18 NWR

F5928 (ex B2529, TOC 25.6.18) 43 Sqdn to 2 AI 30.8.18; 205 TDS Vendôme 4.9.18; FL nr Amand 29.10.18 (2/Lt AE Betts unhurt)

F5933 (ex B6351, TOC 25.6.18) Rep Pk 1 ASD to 1 AI 29.7.18; 208 Sqdn 29.7.18; Pfalz DIII OOC Meurchin, 11.50 7.8.18; DFW C OOC E of Oppy, shared B7769, D1923 & D8168 06.00 14.8.18 (both Lt EG Johnstone); COL, axle broke 27.8.18 (Lt TH Pyke); Rep Pk 1 ASD 29.8.18; Rebuilt as H7108 14.9.18

F5934 (ex B7406, TOC 25.6.18) Rep Pk 1 ASD to 1 AI 28.7.18; 201 Sqdn 29.7.18; Last seen over Assévillers during combat with 10 HA 10.8.18 (Lt CL Wood killed); SOC 20.8.18

F5936 (ex B7251, TOC 25.6.18) Rep Pk 1 ASD to 1 AI 7.8.18; 2 ASD 8.8.18; 209 Sqdn 9.8.18; Lost wheel on TO, COL 29.8.18 (Lt JE Gibbons unhurt); 1 ASD 31.8.18; Rebuilt as H7220 5.11.18

F5937 (ex B5213, TOC 25.6.18) Rep Pk 1 ASD to 2 AI 9.8.18; 209 Sqdn 12.8.18; Low flying patrol, last seen 07.45 after dropping bombs S of River Scarpe 28.9.18 (Lt JE Fenton killed)

F5939 (ex B7231, TOC 25.6.18) Rep Pk 1 ASD to 2 ASD 9.8.18; 201 Sqdn 10.8.18; 203 Sqdn 23.1.19; RTP by 9.2.19

F5941 (ex D3344, TOC 25.6.18) Rep Pk 1 ASD to 1 AI 30.7.18; 201 Sqdn (coded 'E') 3.8.18; 2 Halberstadt C down in flames SE of Rosières 16.15 & 16.20 10.8.18; Hannover C in flames dived in Moeuvres-Bourlon Wood 13.10 3.9.18; Albatros C crashed in flames E of Metz en Couture 19.25 3.9.18; Hannover C BU and dived in Noyelles-Herlincourt 10.20 7.9.18; Albatros C in flames BU nr Cantaing 06.50 8.9.18; LVG C in flames, crashed E of Villers-Plouich 13.25 14.9.18; LVG C crew baled out successfully crashed in flames 2m SE of Haynecourt, shared D9672 09.05 16.9.18; Rumpler or LVG C crashed OOC N of Bourlon Wood 17.25 23.9.18 (all Capt GB Gates DFC); KB in flames SE of Canderon(?) [map ref] 11.30 27.9.18 (Capt GB Gates DFC wounded); Fokker OOC nr Bois de Pincemaille 14.45 9.11.18 (Capt GB Sykes DFC); 203 Sqdn 23.1.19; RTP W/E 9.2.19

F5944 (ex D6659, TOC 25.6.18) (BR.1) Rep Pk 1 ASD to 1 AI 24.7.18; 209 Sqdn 26.7.18; Fokker DVII OOC W of Proyart 09.00 12.8.18 (Capt WR May); O/t landing 14.9.18 (Lt EW Mills); O/t landing new aerodrome Bruille 24.10.18 (2/Lt EL Edwards unhurt); to 1 ASD

F5953 (ex D6687, TOC 26.6.18) Rep Pk 1 ASD to 2 ASD 9.8.18; 209 Sqdn 10.8.18; 203 Sqdn 21.1.19; RTP W/E 2.2.19

F5957 (ex C8266, TOC 27.6.18) Rep Pk 1 ASD to 2 ASD 10.8.18; 1 AI to 208 Sqdn 18.9.18; 2 AI 30.10.18

F5965 (ex D3343, TOC 2.7.18) Rep Pk 1 ASD to 2 AI 8.8.18; 209 Sqdn 9.8.18; Hit by AA, crashed N of Feuchy Chapél 29.8.18 (Lt MA Toomey wounded); 1 ASD 31.8.18; SOC 4.9.18 NWR

F5970 (ex D1828, TOC 9.7.18) (BR.1) Rep Pk 1 ASD to 2 AI 9.8.18; 209 Sqdn 11.8.18; Last seen 07.30 St.Quentin - 2 a/c seen down in flames probably F5970 and E4381 2.9.18 (Capt RC Grant); SOC in field 2.9.18

F5982 (ex C6727, TOC 12.7.18) 203 Sqdn, RTP W/E 9.2.19

F5983 (ex C8262, TOC 12.7.18) Rep Pk 1 ASD to 2 ASD 17.8.18; 201 Sqdn 29.9.18; Caught by gust landing, o/t 24.10.18 (2/Lt JFG Gaffrey unhurt); to 2 ASD

F5986 (ex D1839, TOC 14.7.18) 1 AI to 209 Sqdn 18.9.18; Last seen in combat with Fokker DVIIs over Ecourt St.Quentin 16.45 20.9.18 (Lt DC Ware killed)

F5987 (ex D3401, TOC 14.7.18) Rep Pk 1 ASD to 2 ASD 22.8.17; 4 ASD by 10.17; 213 Sqdn 3.10.18; Last seen when patrol attacked by 17 HA Pervyse-Thourout 14.10.18 (2/Lt LB McMurty killed)

F5990 (Ex F1316, TOC 14.7.18) 2 AI to 209 Sqdn (coded 'B') 18.11.18; 203 Sqdn 21.1.19; RTP W/E 9.2.19

F5991 (ex F1310, TOC 14.7.18) (BR.1) Rep Pk 1 ASD to 2 AI 8.8.18; 201 Sqdn 9.8.18; Fuel shortage, FL Wavrans 2.9.18 (Lt J Mill unhurt); 2 ASD 4.9.18; SOC 7.9.18 NWR

F5994 (ex D9422, TOC 17.7.18) Rep Pk 1 ASD to 2 AI

*Airco D.H.9A F1048 'T' during the winter of 1918/19. (J.M.Bruce/G.S.Leslie collection)*

*Sopwith Camel rebuild F5914 'S' of 210 Sqdn in which Captain H.T.Mellings was killed on 22 July 1918 (via Frank Cheesman)*

*Sopwith Camel rebuild F5953 (minus the prefix letter) with 209 Sqdn in late 1918. (via Frank Cheesman)*

*Sopwith Camel 'X' of 201 Sqdn, probably F6240, has extra cooling slots in its engine cowling, a local modification introduced for low level ground strafing work. (via Frank Cheesman)*

14.8.18; 201 Sqdn 9.9.18; Fokker DVII OOC SE of Cambrai 17.35 16.9.18 (Capt R McLaughlin DFC); 2 ASD 9.11.18 (overhaul)

**F6022** (ex D1813, TOC 25.7.18) Rep Pk 1 ASD to 2 ASD 22.8.18; 201 Sqdn (coded 'S') 4.10.18 (black/white chequered tailplane, white fin and wheels discs); 203 Sqdn 23.1.19

**F6025** (ex D9464, TOC 25.7.18) Rep Pk 1 ASD to 2 ASD 31.7.18; 203 Sqdn by 22.12.18; RTP W/E 9.2.19

**F6027** (ex B6242, TOC 18.7.18) 1 ASD to 203 Sqdn 27.9.18 - @16.1.19

**F6028** (ex D3392, TOC 21.7.18) Rep Pk 1 ASD to 1 AI 11.8.18; 209 Sqdn 23.8.18; Crashed into trees nr Remy 07.30 26.8.18 (Lt L Belloc killed); SOC in field 26.8.18

**F6030** (ex D9584, TOC 21.7.18) 1 AI to 209 Sqdn (coded 'G') 4.9.18; 203 Sqdn 21.1.19; RTP W/E 9.2.19

**F6033** (ex various, TOC 24.7.18) Rep Pk 1 ASD to 1 AI 29.8.18; to 203 Sqdn but crashed on delivery 22.9.18 (Sgt JD Parkinson slightly injured); 1 ASD 22.9.18

**F6036** (Ex D1853, TOC 24.7.18) (BR.1) 1 ASD to 204 Sqdn 30.10.18; EF, FL into tree nr Desselghem on Courtrai-Ghent road 21.12.18 (Lt AB Ollerenshaw injured); To 1 ASD; SOC in field 23.12.18

**F6037** (Ex D1929, TOC 24.7.18) Rep Pk to St.Omer 24.9.18; Rep Pk 1 ASD to 1 AI 2.10.18; 204 Sqdn 26.10.18 (coded '16', named 'FUMS UP IV' by Chisman); Fokker DVII crashed Wondelgem, NW of Ghent 09.10 27.10.18 (2/Lt PAH King); Fokker DVII dest Melle 08.40 4.11.18 (2/Lt S Green); Destroyed in fire 26.1.19 (203 Sqdn)

**F6039** (ex D9633, TOC 25.7.18) Rep Pk 1 ASD to 1 AI 29.8.18; To 203 Sqdn, COL 22.9.18 (Sgt W Nader unhurt); retd 1 ASD

**F6098** 209 Sqdn; RTP 203 Sqdn W/E 2.2.19 [BUT this serial was D.H.9 ex D5701]

**F6100** (ex D9440, TOC 12.7.18) 2 AI to 209 Sqdn 10.8.18; Engine choked on TO, o/t 22.8.18 (2/Lt AV Redwood unhurt); 1 ASD 23.8.18; Rebuilt as H7094 6.9.18

**F6126** (ex B2389, TOC 3.7.18) 4 ASD to 213 Sqdn 3.10.18; FL in sea, pilot seen hanging on to tail off Zeebrugge 19.10.18 (Lt AR Talbot swam ashore, believed PoW); Deleted 31.10.18

**F6155** (ex D1825, TOC 3.7.18) 2 AI to 5 AI 18.7.18; ARS 84 Wing Vendôme by 11.18; RTP 11.18

**F6159** 2 ASD to 205/212 TDS Vendôme 4.9.18 [BUT this was F.K.8 serial]

**F6193** (Ex D1782 17.7.18) Rep Pk 2 ASD by 9.18; 5 AI 8.10.18; 2 AI by 11.18; 210 Sqdn 8.11.18; Fokker DVII DD 1400 10.11.18 (Lt KR Unger); 203 Sqdn 24.1.19; RTP by 9.2.19

**F6223** (ex B9175, TOC 2.8.18) 2 ASD to 201 Sqdn (coded 'Y') 11.9.18; Rep Pk 2 ASD to 5 AI 3.10.18; 201 Sqdn (coded 'Y') by 11.18; Fokker DVII smoking E of Bavai 16.00 4.11.18 (2/Lt EP Nicholson); Black Fokker DVII OOC NE of Maubeuge 14.45 9.11.18; Fokker OOC Bois de Pincemaille 9.11.18 (both Lt RD Hambrook); 203 Sqdn 23.1.19

**F6228** (ex B3345, TOC 2.8.18) 2 ASD to 5 AI 10.10.18; 208 Sqdn 13.10.18; Crashed on TO 17.11.18 (2/Lt CR Curry); 7 SS 19.11.18

**F6238** (ex D6484, TOC 10.8.18) 209 Sqdn 14.11.18; To 203 Sqdn 1.19; RTP W/E 9.2.19

**F6240** (ex C198, TOC 14.8.18) 2 ASD to 201 Sqdn (coded 'X') 9.11.18; 203 Sqdn 23.1.19

**F6243** (ex F5916, TOC 23.8.18) 2 AI to 210 Sqdn 12.11.18; 203 Sqdn 24.1.19; RTP W/E 23.2.19

**F6244** (ex D1875, TOC 15.8.18) Crashed in 80 Sqdn 9.10.18?; 201 Sqdn by 1.19; 203 Sqdn 23.1.19 for disposal (F6264 intended?)

**F6246** (ex B7159, TOC 15.8.18) Rep Pk 2 ASD to 2 AI 13.10.18; 210 Sqdn 15.11.18; Crashed Bavai, badly damaged 3.1.19 (Lt EJ Dearlove, slightly injured); To have been rebuilt on sqdn, but RTP 24.1.19; Produce to 2 AD 30.1.19

**F6250** (ex C142, TOC 17.8.18) Rep Pk 2 ASD to 5 AI 3.10.18; 201 Sqdn 9.10.18; KB DD damaged Bois d'Amfroipret 13.50 4.11.18 (Lt FTS Sehl); 203 Sqdn 23.1.19; RTP by 9.2.19

**F6256** (ex B2448, TOC 18.8.18) Rep Pk 2 ASD to 5 AI 13.10.18; Rep Pk 2 ASD to 2 AI 24.10.18; 201 Sqdn 15.12.18; 203 Sqdn 23.1.19; RTP W/E 9.2.19

**F6257** (ex D8204, TOC 17.8.18) (BR.1) Rep Pk 2 AD to 5 AI 8.10.18; 1 AI to 204 Sqdn 31.10.18; Formation attacked 08.45 at 12,000 ft by 24 Fokker DVIIs with red noses and white tails, last seen over Melle 4.11.18 (2/Lt JD Lightbody killed)

**F6258** (ex C199, TOC 17.8.18) Rep Pk 2 ASD to 5 AI 8.10.18; 2 ASD to 201 Sqdn 9.11.18; 203 Sqdn 23.1.19

**F6259** (ex D8107, TOC 19.8.18) Rep Pk 2 ASD to 2 AI 14.10.18; 210 Sqdn 12.11.18; 203 Sqdn 24.1.19; RTP W/E 16.2.19

**F6263** (ex B5749, TOC 22.8.18) Rep Pk 2 ASD to 203 Sqdn 5.10.18 - @18.1.19

**F6264** (ex D1834, TOC 22.8.18) Rep Pk 2 ASD to 5 AI 4.10.18; 2 ASD to 201 Sqdn 26.10.18 - @7.1.19; [to 203 Sqdn 23.1.19 ?]

**F6265** (ex B7875, TOC 22.8.18) Rep Pk 2 ASD to 5 AI 19.10.18; 1 ASD to 204 Sqdn 30.10.18; EF, FL Bisseghem 1.11.18 (Lt WOG Fenton); Gunnery practice, EF, stalled, nosedived Berck-sur-Mer 14.12.18 (2/Lt CA Morris injured); 1 ASD 15.12.18; SOC in field 6.1.19

**F6311** (ex D6544, TOC 1.8.18) Rep Pk 1 ASD to 1 AI 1.9.18; 209 Sqdn 3.9.18; Serial issued in error, renumbered H7278 retrospectively

## 6 AIRCO D.H.4 TRACTOR BIPLANE DAY BOMBER rebuilds

**F6070** (ex B884, TOC 2.7.18) (Eagle VIII) 2 AI to 205 Sqdn 5.7.18; Pfalz DIII crashed and burnt Rosières-Chaulnes 19.15 8.8.18 (Lt AR McAfee & Sgt L Murphy); Photo recce, COL 25.8.18 (Lt W Grossart & 2/Lt JT Rowe unhurt) 25.8.18; SOS 26.8.18

**F6077** (ex A7619?, TOC 3.7.18) 2 AI to 205 Sqdn 18.9.18; 2 AI 24.9.18

**F6104** (ex D9247, TOC 3.7.18) 2 AI to 205 Sqdn 14.8.18; Fokker DVII OOC in raid on Rochy 19.05 30.8.18 (Lt GC Matthews & 2/Lt JB Leach); 2 AI 1.9.18; 57 Sqdn 2.9.18

**F6119** (ex A7464, TOC 3.7.18) (Eagle V) 2 AI to 205 Sqdn 18.9.18; COL when u/c struck top of RE hangar after returning from raid on Villers Outréaux with engine trouble, bomb exploded 20.9.18 (Lt WV Theron DoI & 2/Lt JT Rowe injured); SOC 2 Salvage Dump, 2 ASD 23.9.18

**F6136** (ex D9242, TOC 3.7.18) (Eagle V) 2 AI to 205 Sqdn 7.8.18; COL from bombing raid on Doingt station 25.8.18; 1 ASD 25.8.18; Rebuilt as H7122 6.9.18

**F6169** (ex A2144, TOC 3.7.18) (Eagle VI) Rec Pk 2 ASD to 2 AI 22.7.18; 205 Sqdn 12.8.18; O/t landing from bombing raid, stalled, nosedived into ground, TW 1820 22.8.18 (Lt JB Cunningham killed & Sgt EB England injured); SOC 22.8.18

## 2 AIRCO D.H.9 TRACTOR BIPLANE DAY BOMBER rebuilds

**F6095** (ex C6175, TOC 3.7.18) 2 AI to 211 Sqdn 4.11.18; 98 Sqdn 24.2.19

**F6196** (Ex C6133 17.7.18) 2 ASD to 218 Sqdn 2.11.18; 98 Sqdn 21.1.19; Retd UK 15.2.19

## 5 SOPWITH F.1 CAMEL TRACTOR BIPLANE SCOUTS from batch F6301 to F6500 built by Boulton & Paul Ltd at Norwich

**F6301** Deld 6 SD Ascot W/E 12.9.18; Shipped to Taranto without engine 26.9.18; Fitted 130-hp Clerget; Taranto by 11.18 - @30.1.19

**F6302** Deld 6 SD Ascot W/E 12.9.18; Shipped to Taranto without engine 26.9.18; Fitted 130-hp Clerget; 226 Sqdn Taranto by 11.18 - @30.1.19; AP Taranto to 'X' AD 11.4.19; WOC 21.5.19; Presume rebuilt; 4 FTS; Became G-EBER regd F/O WJ McDonagh 9.8.22 (regn not carried); Crashed 4.11.22 (W Burns-Thompson)

**F6303** Deld 6 SD Ascot W/E 12.9.18; Shipped to Taranto without engine 26.9.18; Taranto by 11.18 - @30.1.19; 3 Sqdn?

**F6304** Deld 6 SD Ascot W/E 12.9.18; Shipped to Taranto W/E 7.11.18

**F6356** Grand Fleet SoAF&G Leuchars by 4.19 - @5.19

**50 SOPWITH SHIP STRUTTER TRACTOR BIPLANE FIGHTERS ex French Government 1½ Strutter fuselages for conversion for shipboard use, to be numbered F7547 to F7596. (130-hp Clerget 9B)**

F7547   Deld 6 AAP Renfrew W/E 12.9.18; Grain for conversion 27.9.18; Turnhouse W/E 5.12.18 - @30.1.19

F7548   Deld 6 AAP Renfrew W/E 12.9.18; Grain for conversion 27.9.18; Turnhouse W/E 5.12.18 - @30.1.19

F7549   Deld 6 AAP Renfrew W/E 12.9.18; Grain for conversion 27.9.18; Turnhouse W/E 12.12.18 - @30.1.19

F7550   Deld 6 AAP Renfrew W/E 12.9.18; Grain for conversion 27.9.18; Turnhouse W/E 5.12.18 - @30.1.19

F7551   Deld 6 AAP Renfrew W/E 22.8.18; Turnhouse W/E 19.9.18 - @30.1.19

F7552   Deld 6 AAP Renfrew W/E 5.9.18 - @30.1.19 (for Turnhouse)

F7553   Deld 6 AAP Renfrew W/E 12.9.18; Grain for conversion 27.9.18; Turnhouse W/E 28.11.18 - @30.1.19

F7554   Deld 6 AAP Renfrew W/E 22.8.18; Turnhouse W/E 19.9.18 - @30.1.19

F7555   Deld 6 AAP Renfrew W/E 5.9.18 - @30.1.19 (for Turnhouse)

F7556   Deld 6 AAP Renfrew W/E 5.9.18 - @30.1.19 (for Turnhouse)

F7557   Deld 6 AAP Renfrew W/E 22.8.18; Turnhouse W/E 19.9.18 - @30.1.19

F7558   Deld 6 AAP Renfrew W/E 5.9.18 - @30.1.19 (for Turnhouse)

F7559   Deld 6 AAP Renfrew W/E 5.9.18 - @30.1.19 (for Turnhouse)

F7560   Deld 6 AAP Renfrew W/E 12.9.18; Grain for conversion 27.9.18; Turnhouse W/E 5.12.18 - @30.1.19

F7561   Deld 6 AAP Renfrew W/E 22.8.18; Turnhouse W/E 19.9.18; HMS *Emperor of India* W/E 21.11.18; Scapa W/E 19.12.18; HMS *Emperor of India* W/E 23.1.19; ashore 26.1.19 - @30.1.19

F7562   Deld 6 AAP Renfrew W/E 22.8.18; Turnhouse W/E 19.9.18; HMAS *Australia* W/E 28.11.18; HMS *Furious* W/E 16.1.19; HMAS *Australia* W/E 23.1.19 - @30.1.19

F7563   Deld 6 AAP Renfrew W/E 12.9.18; Grain for conversion 27.9.18 - @30.1.19

F7564   Deld 6 AAP Renfrew W/E 12.9.18; Grain for conversion 27.9.18 - @30.1.19

F7565   Deld 6 AAP Renfrew W/E 12.9.18; Grain for conversion 27.9.18 - @30.1.19

F7566   Deld 6 AAP Renfrew W/E 5.9.18 - @30.1.19 (for Turnhouse)

F7567   Deld 6 AAP Renfrew W/E 12.9.18; Grain for conversion 1.10.18 - @30.1.19

F7568   Deld 6 AAP Renfrew W/E 5.9.18 - @30.1.19 (for Turnhouse)

F7569   Deld 6 AAP Renfrew W/E 5.9.18 - @30.1.19 (for Turnhouse)

F7570   Deld 6 AAP Renfrew W/E 5.9.18; Turnhouse W/E 21.11.18 - @30.1.19

F7571   Deld 6 AAP Renfrew W/E 5.9.18 - @30.1.19 (for Turnhouse)

F7572   Deld 6 AAP Renfrew W/E 12.9.18; Grain for conversion 28.9.18 - @30.1.19

F7573   Deld 6 AAP Renfrew W/E 5.9.18 - @30.1.19 (for Turnhouse)

F7574   Deld 6 AAP Renfrew W/E 5.9.18 - @30.1.19 (for Turnhouse)

F7575   Deld 6 AAP Renfrew W/E 12.9.18; Grain for conversion 28.9.18 - @30.1.19

F7576   Deld 6 AAP Renfrew W/E 22.8.18; Turnhouse W/E 19.9.18 - @30.1.19

F7577   Deld 6 AAP Renfrew W/E 5.9.18 - @30.1.19 (for Turnhouse)

F7578   Deld 6 AAP Renfrew W/E 12.9.18; Grain for conversion 28.9.18 - @30.1.19

F7579   Deld 6 AAP Renfrew W/E 12.9.18; Grain for conversion 1.10.18 - @30.1.19

F7580   Deld 6 AAP Renfrew W/E 5.9.18; Turnhouse W/E 12.12.18 - @30.1.19

F7581   Deld 6 AAP Renfrew W/E 5.9.18; Turnhouse W/E 12.12.18 - @30.1.19

F7582   Deld 6 AAP Renfrew W/E 5.9.18; Turnhouse W/E 12.12.18 - @30.1.19

F7583   No information

F7584   Deld 6 AAP Renfrew W/E 12.9.18; Grain for conversion 3.10.18 - @30.1.19

F7585   No information

F7586   No information

F7587   2(N)ARD Coal Aston by 7.19; Leuchars 10.7.19; Donibristle 15.7.19

F7588   No information

F7589   No information

F7590   2(N)ARD Greenhill by 11.18; To Japanese Government (or Latvia?)

F7591   to F7596 No information

**24 SOPWITH F.1 CAMEL TRACTOR BIPLANE SCOUTS from batch F8496 to F8595 built by The Nieuport & General Aircraft Co Ltd at Cricklewood**

F8496   (BR.1) Deld 2 AAP Hendon W/E 21.11.18; Donibristle W/E 16.1.19 - @30.1.19

F8497   (BR.1) Deld 2 AAP Hendon W/E 21.11.18; Donibristle W/E 19.12.18 - @30.1.19; Grand Fleet SoAF&G Leuchars by 5.19; Attempted slow roll too nr ground 9.5.19 (Lt DG Cooper killed)

F8501   (BR.1) 1 ASD to 204 Sqdn 26.10.18; Fokker DVII down in spin Melle 08.40 4.11.18 (Lt E Stanton); Hit small bank landing Heule 6.1.19 (Lt RE Baty MC unhurt); 1 ASD by rail 13.1.19

F8502   (BR.1) 4 ASD to 213 Sqdn 5.10.18; Last seen nr Zeebrugge 11.45 19.10.18 (Lt AH Pownall); he was flying again by 23.10.18

F8503   (BR.1) 4 ASD to 213 Sqdn 3.10.18; Fokker DVII DD smoking 3m E of Thielt 11.15 14.10.18 (Lt GW Hopkins); 203 Sqdn 24.1.19; RTP W/E 9.2.19

F8504   (BR.1) 4 ASD to 213 Sqdn 14.10.18; LVG C down in flames Somergem 15.20 19.10.18 (Mjr R Graham DSO DFC); 11 AP 24.2.19; WOC 24.2.19 burned

F8505   (BR.1) 4 ASD to 213 Sqdn (coded 'A') 17.10.18; LVG C crashed 7m SE of Ghent, shared D8218, D9648 & D9675 10.40 10.11.18 (Lt HH Gilbert); 11 AP 23.2.19; WOC 23.2.19

F8508   (BR.1) 4 ASD to 213 Sqdn 8.10.18; Fokker DVII tail broke off over Zevecote 14.30 14.10.18 (Lt WJ Mackenzie); Fokker DVII OOC 10m E of Ghent 10.30 9.11.18 (Capt WJ Mackenzie); 11 AP 25.2.19; WOC 25.2.19

F8509   (BR.1) 8 AAP Lympne to Rec Pk 4.10.18; 4 ASD 6.10.18; 210 Sqdn 9.10.18; Last seen flying SE at 2,000 ft nr Bois de Wauhu over Mons 09.10 10.11.18 (2/Lt JE Pugh killed)

F8510   (BR.1) UK to 4 ASD 25.10.18; 471 Flt 233 Sqdn Walmer by 2.19; 11 AP 21.2.19; WOC 21.2.19

F8511   (BR.1) 4 ASD to 213 Sqdn (coded 'G') 17.10.18; 11 AP 25.2.19; WOC 25.2.19

F8512   (BR.1) UK to 4 ASD 25.10.18; 213 Sqdn 7.11.18; 11 AP 23.2.19

F8524   (BR.1) 1 AI to 203 Sqdn, COL uneven ground 14.11.18 (2/Lt DH Woodhouse unhurt); for 1 ASD

F8525   1 AI to 203 Sqdn 1.11.18; RTP W/E 23.2.19

F8527   486 Flt 273 Sqdn Burgh Castle by 31.10.18 - @6.11.18

F8528   (BR.1) Deld 2 AAP Hendon W/E 21.11.18; Donibristle W/E 19.12.18 - @30.1.19

F8529   (BR.1) Deld 2 AAP Hendon W/E 21.11.18; Donibristle W/E 16.1.19 - @30.1.19; Grand Fleet SoAF&G Leuchars by 3.19 - @7.19

F8541   (B.R.1) Deld 2 AAP Hendon W/E 21.11.18; Donibristle W/E 16.1.19 - @30.1.19; Grand Fleet S of AF & G Leuchars by 6.19

F8542   Yarmouth by 1.19; Grand Fleet SoAF&G Leuchars by 7.19

F8544   (B.R.1) Deld 2 AAP Hendon W/E 21.11.18; Donibristle W/E 16.1.19 - @30.1.19

F8545   (BR.1) Deld 2 AAP Hendon W/E 31.12.18; In transit for carriers by 31.1.19; Grand Fleet SoAF&G Leuchars by 6.19 - @9.19; BUT Gullane @8.19

F8546   (B.R.1) Deld 2 AAP Hendon 11.18; Donibristle W/E 19.11.18 - @31.1.19; Grand Fleet SoAF&G Leuchars by 2.19 - 7.19

F8547   Deld 2 AAP Hendon W/E 19.12.18; Donibristle W/E 19.12.18 - @30.1.19; Grand Fleet SoAF&G Leuchars by 5.19 - @6.19

F8548      Grand Fleet SoAF&G Leuchars by 9.19

**5 SOPWITH F.1 CAMEL TRACTOR BIPLANE SCOUTS from batch F8646 to F8695 built by Portholme Aerodrome Ltd at Huntingdon.**

F8646      (BR.1) 4 ASD to 204 Sqdn 29.9.18; EF on TO, attempted to make aerodrome, CW 10.1.19 (Lt E Stanton unhurt); 1 ASD by rail 15.1.19; Grand Fleet SoAF&G Leuchars by 4.19

F8647      4 ASD to 213 Sqdn 18.10.18; Hit by AA, tail broke off, spun in, CW nr Belgian coast 23.10.18 (Lt FJT Fenn unhurt); Deleted 4 ASD 30.11.18

F8671      (BR.1) Deld 3 AAP Norwich W/E 21.11.18; Donibristle W/E 19.1.19 - @30.1.19

F8672      (BR.1) Deld 3 AAP Norwich W/E 21.11.18; Donibristle W/E 19.12.18 - @30.1.19; Grand Fleet SoAF&G Leuchars by 4.19 - @5.19

F8673      (BR.1) Deld 3 AAP Norwich W/E 21.11.18; Donibristle W/E 19.12.18 - @30.1.19; Grand Fleet SoAF&G Leuchars by 5.19

**4 AVRO 504K TRACTOR BIPLANE TRAINERS from batch F8696 to F8845 built by Parnall & Sons Ltd at Bristol**

F8754      56 TDS Cranwell by 8.18; Became RAF (Cadet) College 5.2.20 - @1.22

F8758      56 TDS Cranwell by 8.18; contd post-war

F8759      56 TDS Cranwell by 6.18; Became RAF (Cadet) College (coded 'B7') 5.2.20; contd post-war

F8760      56 TDS Cranwell by 6.18 - @7.18; contd post-war

**1 AVRO 504K TRACTOR BIPLANE TRAINER from batch F8846 to F8945 built by Frederick Sage & Co Ltd at Peterborough**

F8881      (80-hp Le Rhône) 56 TDS Cranwell, propeller accident (Pte2 15.1.19 HE Smith seriously injured)

**1 SOPWITH F.1 CAMEL TRACTOR BIPLANE FIGHTER from assorted rebuilds F9496 to F9545 by 5(E)ARD Henlow**

F9548      (Ex B5556 5.8.18) 207 TDS Chingford; Fatal crash 19.12.18

**5 CAUDRON G.III PUSHER BIPLANE TRAINER rebuilds from spares in France in batch F9551 to F9565.**

F9556      212 TDS Vendôme, ran into airman after landing 16.9.18 (Lt RD Best & F/Cdt Dunlop unhurt & 1AM Sinclair injured); Bounced landing, skid broke, badly damaged 25.9.18 (Lt RD Best & F/Cdt C Boliver unhurt)

F9558      212 TDS Vendôme, contaminated fuel, slightly damaged 23.11.18 (F/Cdt AL Auerhaan & Cpl Vincent unhurt)

F9560      212 TDS Vendôme, stalled on turn nr ground, wrecked Pouline 29.8.18 (Capt NP Playford & PFO RE Sutton)

F9562      (Ex French 6375) (100-hp Anzani). 212 TDS Vendôme, failed to flatten out 24.6.18 (F/Cdt RHJ Affleck injured)

F9565      (Ex French 6378) 212 TDS Vendôme by 8.18 - @11.18; Bad landing, slightly damaged 17.8.18 (PFO LC Lertts & Capt NP Playford)

**1 SOPWITH F.1 CAMEL TRACTOR BIPLANE FIGHTER from rebuilds F9573 to F9622 by 3(W)ARD Yate**

F9579      204 TDS Eastchurch by 16.10.18

**1 AVRO 504K TRACTOR BIPLANE TRAINER from batch F9746 to F9845 built by Hewlett & Blondeau Ltd**

F9782      213 Sqdn Scopwick by 7.4.19 - @10.4.19

**2 AVRO 504K TRACTOR BIPLANE TRAINERS from batch H201 to H350 built by Scottish Aviation**

H226      Turnhouse by 5.19; BUT Gullane @5.19

H246      Turnhouse by 5.19; BUT Gullane @5.19

**4 AVRO 504K TRACTOR BIPLANE TRAINERS from batch H1896 to H2145 built by The Sunbeam Motor Car Co Ltd at Wolverhampton**

H1917    2 Observers School Manston by 2.12.18

H1918    2 Observers School Manston by 3.1.19

H1922    2 Observers School Manston by 24.12.18

H1932    (130-hp Clerget) 204 TDS Eastchurch by 2.19; Dived into ground on steep turn 10.2.19 (2/Lt GE McLeod DoI & Capt FG Garrett slightly hurt)

**16 AVRO 504K TRACTOR BIPLANE TRAINERS from batch H2146 to H2645 built by parent company**

H2160      Deld Turnhouse W/E 7.11.18 - @30.1.19

H2161      Deld Turnhouse W/E 7.11.18 - @30.1.19

H2165      57 TDS Cranwell by 12.18 (propeller tests)

H2167      56 TDS Cranwell by 11.18 - @2.19

H2168      56 TDS Cranwell by 11.18

H2169      56 TDS Cranwell by 11.18

H2235      to H2244 Allotted Turnhouse W/E 31.10.18, but not listed W/E 7.11.18 (NTU?)

H2296      Grand Fleet SoAF&G Leuchars by 1.19 - @8.19

H2297      Tested 8.7.19; Grand Fleet SoAF&G Leuchars by 7.19; Became G-EAHV

H2298      Grand Fleet SoAF&G Leuchars by 2.19

H2299      Grand Fleet SoAF&G Leuchars by 2.19

H2300      Grand Fleet SoAF&G Leuchars, propeller accident 25.3.19 (2/AM CE Tatam seriously injured)

H2311      56 TDS Cranwell by 11.18

H2314      56 TDS Cranwell by 11.18

H2391      3 Sqdn by 2.22; 203 Sqdn by 7.22 - @4.23

H2537      204 TDS Eastchurch, controls broke on firing practice 18.1.19 (Lt WH Hughes slightly hurt)

**2 SOPWITH F.1 CAMEL TRACTOR BIPLANE SCOUTS from batch H2646 to H2745 built by Boulton & Paul Ltd at Norwich**

H2705      RAF North Russia

H2740      Cranwell by 9.18

**10 AVRO 504K TRACTOR BIPLANE TRAINERS from batch H2946 to H3195 built by The Brush Electrical Engineering Co Ltd at Loughborough. (100-hp Gnome Monosoupape)**

H3001      Grand Fleet SoAF&G Leuchars by 5.19 - @6.19

H3002      Grand Fleet SoAF&G Leuchars by 5.19 - @6.19

H3003      Grand Fleet SoAF&G Leuchars by 6.19

H3005      Grand Fleet SoAF&G Leuchars by 7.19; Became RAF Base Leuchars 18.3.20 - @6.22

H3006      Grand Fleet SoAF&G Leuchars by 6.19 (at Gullane 10.19); Became RAF Base Leuchars 18.3.20 - @9.22; Sank in sand and badly damaged 14.6.22 (F/O F Kirk of 205 Sqdn & F/O EC Usher)

H3007      Grand Fleet SoAF&G Leuchars by 6.19; Became RAF Base Leuchars 18.3.20; EF on landing, collided with railway signal and crashed Guardbridge, Fife 23.8.21

H3008      Grand Fleet SoAF&G Leuchars by 6.19; Crashed 17.6.19 (2/Lt J Golman slightly injured); 24 Sqdn by 9.23; EF, stalled and crashed in meadow, Wickham Rd, Shirley, Surrey 7.9.23

H3009      Grand Fleet SoAF&G Leuchars by 6.19

H3010      Grand Fleet SoAF&G Leuchars by 6.19

H3123      Grand Fleet SoAF&G Leuchars by 7.19

**7 AIRCO D.H.9A TRACTOR BIPLANE BOMBERS from batch H3396 to H3545 built by Westland Aviation Works at Yeovil**

H3414      MOS Leysdown by 8.18 - 2.19

H3488      Cranwell by 9.19

H3510      Grand Fleet SoAF&G Leuchars by 10.19 (at Delnu 10.19); Became RAF Base Leuchars 3.20 - 5.20; Cont post-war

H3514      Grand Fleet SoAF&G Leuchars by 9.19

H3516      Delney by 10.19

H3518      (Convtd 3-str) Grand Fleet SoAF&G Leuchars by 12.19; Became RAF Base Leuchars 3.20 - 5.20; 205 Sqdn, FL in sea en route Durness-Invergordon 6.10.20

H3541      (Built for ship use) Grand Fleet SoAF&G Leuchars by

10.19; Rebuilt c/n.144; Contd post-war

## 1 AIRCO D.H.9A TRACTOR BIPLANE BOMBER from batch H3546 to H3795 built by Vulcan Motor & Engineering Co (1906) Ltd at Southport

H3596    Delney by 10.19 (3-seat conversion; 3 Sqdn?)

## 18 AIRCO D.H.9 TRACTOR BIPLANE BOMBERS from batch H4216 to H4315 built by parent company

H4218    6 AI to 211 Sqdn 9.12.18; 98 Sqdn 24.2.19; 8 AAP Lympne 12.3.19
H4223    555/6 Flts 219 Sqdn Manston, HACP 10.11.18
H4229    Eastbourne
H4231    59 TDS Cranwell, nosed in landing 5.18; Propeller accident 22.1.19 (3AM D Edwards injured)
H4245    2 ASD to 211 Sqdn 15.11.18; 98 Sqdn 23.2.19; 1 ASD 5.3.19; to England 6.3.19
H4249    206 Sqdn by 12.18; EF, FL Andrimont, E of Verviers 1.1.19 (Lt CL Cumming & 2/Lt Brown unhurt); for 8 SS repair
H4256    206 Sqdn by 12.18; Hangar collapsed on it during night, Nivelle 20-21.12.18; to 7 SS repair
H4259    Deld Naval Flt 219 Sqdn Manston 26.10.18 - @2.12.18; HACPs 5.11.18 & 10.11.18; To Poland 19.3.20
H4262    Deld Naval Flt 219 Sqdn Manston 31.10.18 - @11.18
H4264    Deld Naval Flt 219 Sqdn Manston by 21.11.18
H4267    Deld Naval Flt 219 Sqdn Manston 31.10.18 - @7.12.18
H4268    Deld 534 Flt 273 Sqdn Covehithe by 4.11.18 @2.12.18; HACP 4.11.18
H4272    Deld 534 Flt 273 Sqdn Covehithe, HACP 10.11.18
H4279    Deld 534 Flt 273 Sqdn Covehithe by 9.11.18 - @22.11.18; HACPs 9.11.18 & 10.11.18; To Poland 19.3.20
H4282    206 Sqdn by 4.19
H4284    Deld Mullion by 12.18; Padstow by 12.18
H4287    Deld Padstow by 11.18 - @12.18
H4291    206 Sqdn by 12.18 - @30.1.19

## 2 AIRCO D.H.9 TRACTOR BIPLANE BOMBERS from batch H5541 to H5890 built by The Alliance Aeroplane Co Ltd, London.

H5556    St.Omer to Tourignies 17.1.19; 6 AI to 211 Sqdn 7.2.19; 98 Sqdn 23.2.19
H5559    Cranwell by 4.19

## 4 AVRO 504K TRACTOR BIPLANE TRAINERS from batch H6543 to H6842 built by Humber Ltd at Coventry.

H6543    56/57 TDS Cranwell by 1.19 - @13.5.19; Became G-EAFX later G-EASG
H6545    56/57 TDS Cranwell by 2.19 - @5.19
H6550    56/57 TDS Cranwell by 1.19
H6586    Cranwell by 4.20

**H6843 to H7342 were allocated for the renumbering of aircraft rebuilt in France, a few of which went to naval units. Many such numbers were given to rebuilds which had originally been incorrectly reserialled in the range F6320 onwards**

## 14 SOPWITH F.1 CAMEL TRACTOR BIPLANE FIGHTERS

H6997    (Ex F6320, ex D8143, TOC 9.8.18) 6 AI to 209 Sqdn 23.11.18 (named 'DIMPS', personal m/c of Col S. "Crasher" Smith); 203 Sqdn, RTP by 9.2.19
H6998    (Ex F6327, ex D6495, TOC 10.8.18) 1 AI to 209 Sqdn 13.10.18; Pfalz DXII OOC Athies, shared C61 & F3946 07.30 4.11.18 (Lt EK Langton); 203 Sqdn 21.1.19; RTP by 9.2.19
H7000    (Ex F6330, ex B7248, TOC 12.8.18) Rep Pk 1 ASD to 1 AI 16.10.18; Rep Pk 1 ASD 22.10.18; 1 AI to 209 Sqdn (coded '3') 1.11.18; To 203 Sqdn 1.19; RTP by 9.2.19
H7004    (Ex F6336, ex E1473, TOC 16.8.18) Rep Pk 1 ASD to 1

AI 16.10.18; RTP 203 Sqdn W/E 9.2.19
H7008    (Ex F6341, ex B5630, TOC 20.8.18) Rep Pk 1 ASD to 2 ASD 3.10.18; 2 AI 13.10.18; 208 Sqdn 14.11.18; 2 AI 19.11.18
H7009    (Ex F6342, ex B8206, TOC 20.8.18) 1 AI to 209 Sqdn (coded '4') 14.11.18; 203 Sqdn 21.1.19
H7082    (ex F6471, ex B1469, TOC 26.8.18) Rep Pk 1 ASD to 1 AI 16.10.18; 204 Sqdn 26.10.18; Chased by 3 Fokker DVIIs at 20-100ft, Fokker DVII hit tree and wrecked, own m/c completely shot up 27.10.18 (2/Lt HA Argles unhurt); 1 ASD 28.10.18
H7084    (ex F6473, ex C3298, TOC 31.8.18) 6 AI to 209 Sqdn 24.12.18; RTP 203 Sqdn W/E 9.2.19
H7104    (ex D9504, TOC 10.9.18) 2 AI to 204 Sqdn 4.11.18; 203 Sqdn 25.1.19; RTP W/E 23.2.19
H7105    (ex D6648, TOC 11.9.18) 1 AI to 203 Sqdn 14.12.18; RTP W/E 23.2.19
H7278    (ex F6311, ex D6544, TOC 1.8.18) 1 AI to 209 Sqdn 3.9.18; Mid-air collision with E4423 W of Bourlon 1500 8.10.18 (2/Lt RGA Bingham killed)
H7280    (ex F6313, ex B5599, TOC 9.8.18) Rep Pk 1 ASD to 5 AI 17.10.18; 204 Sqdn by 1.19; 203 Sqdn 25.1.19; RTP by 9.2.19
H7284    (ex F6318, ex D3395, TOC 9.8.18) 1 AI to 209 Sqdn 13.10.18; 203 Sqdn 21.1.19; RTP by 9.2.19
H7286    (ex F6323, ex D3419 TOC 9.8.18) (BR.1) 2xx Sqdn, probably hit by AA, FL in shell holes Wancourt 14.10.18 (2/Lt RB Wiggins injured); SOC in field [NOT NAVAL?]

## 24 CAUDRON G.III PUSHER BIPLANE TRAINERS purchased in France for naval training use and numbered H8265 to H8288. Probably all to Vendôme. (100-hp Anzani)

H8265    (ex French 6553) No information
H8266    (ex French 6554) No information
H8267    (ex French 6555) 212 TDS Vendôme, bounced landing, o/t, badly damaged 16.9.18 (2/Lt JG Jenkins & Lt HE Forrow unhurt)
H8268    (ex French 6556) No information
H8269    (ex French 6557) 212 TDS Vendôme, FL, overshot, ran into ditch, slightly damaged Sarigny-sur-Braye 4.10.18 (F/Cdt WL Barber & Lt HE Forrow unhurt)
H8270    (ex French 6558) 212 TDS Vendôme by 10.18 - @11.18
H8271    (ex French 6559) No information
H8272    (ex French 6560) 212 TDS Vendôme by 10.18; Stalled landing, wrecked 4.10.18 (F/Cdt WW Inskip slightly injured & Lt GRB Smyth unhurt))
H8273    (ex French 6561) 212 TDS Vendôme, fast landing, badly damaged Tours 19.11.18 (F/Cdt WH Gell & 2/Lt CV Lacey unhurt)
H8274    (ex French 6562) No information
H8275    (ex French 6563) 212 TDS Vendôme by 10.18 - @11.18
H8276    (ex French 6564) 212 TDS Vendôme, slightly damaged landing 29.10.18 (F/Cdt HS White & Capt FJ Vincent unhurt)
H8277    (ex French 6565) 212 TDS Vendôme by 8.18; Struck ridge landing, slightly damaged 28.10.18 (F/Cdt HF Ferguson unhurt)
H8278    (ex French 6566) 212 TDS Vendôme by 8.18 - @11.18
H8279    (ex French 6573) No information
H8280    (ex French 6574) No information
H8281    (ex French 6575) No information
H8282    (ex French 6576) No information
H8283    (ex French 6577) 212 TDS Vendôme by 8.18
H8284    (ex French 6578) No information
H8285    (ex French 6568) 212 TDS Vendôme, o/t landing, slightly damaged 25.9.18 (F/Cdt GF Elliott & Lt HE Forrow)
H8286    (ex French 6569) 212 TDS Vendôme, badly damaged landing 27.10.18 (F/Cdt PA Martin & 2/Lt CV Lacey unhurt)
H8287    (ex French 6672) 212 TDS Vendôme by 8.18
H8288    (ex French 6680) No information

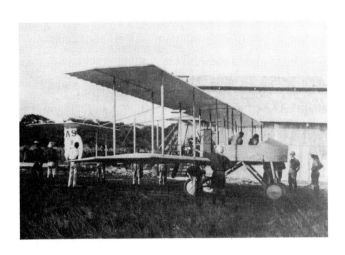

Henry Farman F.27 (all steel) "AS/8/HF" flown in East Africa during the Königsberg campaign. (J.M.Bruce/G.S.Leslie collection)

This Henry Farman F.27 (all-steel) was one of the aircraft used by Gordon and FSL HJ Arnold to range the guns of the monitors 'Mersey' and 'Severn' on the German battlecruiser Königsberg in the Rufiji river delta. (via Frank Cheesman)

Curtiss Model F flying boat at Simon's Bay, November 1914. This aircraft was later hired by the Admiralty for use during the Königsberg campaign. (Green Collection, South African State Archives G.313)

# MISCELLANEOUS AIRCRAFT

## AIRCO D.H.4 (American built; 400-hp Liberty)

A3269    US Northern Bombing Group; attd 491 Flt Dover 9.10.18; Retd US Northern Bombing Group 13.10.18

A3295    US Northern Bombing Group; Attd 218 Sqdn 29.9.18; Fokker DVII OOC Cortemarke 08.15 8.10.18 (Lt R.Talbot USMC & Cpl R.G.Robinson USMC); Retd US Northern Bombing Group 11.10.18

## 1 ALBATROS DIII acquired 4.6.17 and later brought to England where fitted with engine from G39

G42    (Ex D2015/16) Forced down by 29 Sqdn RFC. St.Omer by 6.17; Ste.Marie Capell 19.6.17 (1 Sqdn pilot, F/Cdr TFN Gerrard); ADD by 8.17; Dover 11.8.17 (F/Cdr RFS Leslie); Manston 20.8.17; St.Albans 21.8.17 (en route Cranwell); Chingford 23.8.17; to Cranwell 26.8.17 but crashed in aerodrome (S/L TPM Alexander); Dover to Cranwell for erection 25.9.17 - @23.2.18

## CAUDRON G.III TRACTOR BIPLANE TRAINERS

2941    212 TDS Vendôme, slightly damaged 27.9.18 (Capt AT Smooker unhurt)

6259    212 TDS Vendôme by 8.18; Bounced landing, badly damaged 14.8.18 (F/Cdt JF Harrison & Lt NP Playford)

6261    212 TDS Vendôme by 8.18; Bad landing, wrecked 13.8.18 (F/Cdt CA Doney DoI 13.8.18 & 2/Lt CV Lacey injured)

6262    212 TDS Vendôme by 8.18; Wheel off on TO, badly damaged 13.8.18 (Lt FW Letzig & 2/Lt CV Lacey)

6263    212 TDS Vendôme by 5.18; Skid broke landing, badly damaged 19.5.18 (Capt E Maitland-Heriot & F/Cdt FC Andrews both unhurt); FL in wheat field 2.7.19 (2/Lt KC Brown injured)

6265    205 TDS Vendôme by 7.18; Collided with Avro D7527 and wrecked 30.7.18 (F/Cdt PM Barr killed (injured?)? & Capt R Turner killed)

6267    205 TDS Vendôme by 6.18; COL, wrecked, BO 18.6.18 (Lt PG Stokes-Rees killed & PFO HC Densham badly burnt)

6680    212 TDS, crashed on TO, badly damaged 9.10.18 (F/Cdt JM Steele & Capt RD Best unhurt); Propeller smashed on TO 11.10.18 (F/Cdt JM Steele unhurt); Stalled on TO, crashed on stbd wing 31.10.18 (Capt AL Bree & Capt RD Best unhurt)

## CURTISS MODEL F FLYING BOAT

-    (90-hp) Hired from Mr Gerard Hudson at Durban for Kônigsberg operations; Left Simonstown in SS *Kinfauns Castle* 6.11.15; Mafia Island 15.11.15; EF, FL in mouth of Kikunja River 10.12.15 (FSL HD Cutler PoW); Aircraft retrieved and retd SS *Kinfauns Castle*, but badly damaged so retd South Africa

## HENRI FARMAN PUSHER BIPLANES

4003    (140 hp Canton Unné) 2 Sqdn 2 Wing St.Pol by 8.8.15

AS/8/HF    Mafia Island 6.15; Crashed on test flight, WO 6.15 (F/L JT Cull) [SAAC serial?]

SA/9/HF    Mafia Island 6.15; Shot down Rufiji Delta 11.7.15 (F/L JT Cull & FSL HJ Arnold both rescued unhurt) [SAAC serial?]

## MAURICE FARMAN PUSHER BIPLANE

1347    1 Sqdn, St.Pol, AZP 17.5.15 (W/Cdr AM Longmore)

## FOKKER D.VII

4453/18    1 ASD to 204 Sqdn 10.1.19; WO 23.1.19 burnt

D7/6539    (Engine No.32897) War booty flown by 208 Sqdn; Caught telegraph wires, stalled, COL Donstiennes 30.4.19 (Mjr CE Bryant DSO unhurt?); SOC in field

## FRIEDRICHSHAFEN FF33F SEAPLANE

536    HMS *Ark Royal* at Mudros by 11.5.17

## NIEUPORTS

c/n 104    1 Sqdn St.Pol by 3.5.15 - @14.5.15

c/n 110    2 Wing Imbros - COL 29.9.15 (FSL MA Simpson)

c/n 114    1 Sqdn St.Pol by 16.5.15

c/n 120    1 Sqdn St.Pol by 15.5.15 - @20.5.15 (became 3168?)

c/n 140    2 Wing Imbros by 4.11.15(FM) - @8.11.15

c/n 141    2 Wing Imbros by 5.11.15(FM)

c/n 339    Northern Aircraft FS Windermere for erection by 1.5.16

## At least 17 SOPWITH TRIPLANES to France. First 10 authorised 11.8.16, at rate of 1 per week from production line. Next 4 allocated 31.5.17 ex N5384 - N5387 (were to have been N5392 - N5394 & N5389). N5388 apparently also allocated.

F1    Deld Brooklands to Dover 28.11.16; ADD 11.12.16 (French pilot)

F2    Deld Brooklands to Dover 4.12.16; ADD 11.12.16 (French pilot)

F3    Deld Brooklands to Dover 20.12.16; ADD 30.12.16

F4    Deld Brooklands to Dover 6.12.16; ADD 11.12.16 (French pilot)

F5    Deld Brooklands to Dover 24.12.16; ADD 15.1.17 (French pilot); French Aviation to ADD W/E 11.10.17 - @18.10.17; 1 Wing by 25.10.17 - @1.11.17; Became N541 on repurchase W/E 8.11.17

F6    Deld Dover for erection 27.1.17; Awaiting test by 3.2.17; ADD 14.2.17

F7    Deld Dover 25.1.17; ADD 29.1.17

F8    Deld Dover 26.1.17; ADD 1.3.17 (French pilot)

F9    Deld Dover 29.1.17; ADD 1.17; To French; Retd ADD W/E 11.10.17; 1 Sqdn 11.10.17; Became N542 on repurchase 16.11.17

F10    Deld Dover 26.2.17; ADD 1.3.17 (French pilot); French Aviation to ADD W/E 11.10.17; 1 Wing W/E 25.10.17; Became N543 on repurchase W/E 8.11.17

F11    (ex N5384) To French 23.6.17; Retd ADD as N5384 W/E 11.10.17

F12    (ex N5385) To French 23.6.17

F13    (ex N5386) To French 21.6.17; Retd ADD as N5386 W/E 11.10.17

F14    (ex N5387) To French 24.6.17; Retd ADD by 10.17; 1 Sqdn 16.10.17; Last mention 20.10.17 (then reverted to N5387)

F15    (ex N5388) To French 21.7.17

F16    No information

F17    Landed on by D.H.4 N5981 of 2 Sqdn, wrecked, St.Pol 27.6.17

## VOISINS

V551    1 Sqdn St.Pol by 6.5.15 (only entry)

V552    1 Sqdn St.Pol by 9.5.15; detd 4 Sqdn Dover 24.5.15 (spotting work)

V555    1 Sqdn St.Pol by 1.5.15; 1 Wing by 22.6.15; HZP from Furnes 17.5.15 (FSL BL Huskisson); 4 Sqdn Dover 24.5.15

V556    1 Sqdn St.Pol by 10.5.15 - @14.6.15

V558    1 Sqdn St.Pol by 15.5.15 - @28.5.15

[These six were 3821 - 3826, all 1 Sqdn by 30.4.15]

V929    Dunkerque to Grain 11.5.16; Retd France 26.6.16 (French crew)

V1540    Arr Basrah for RFC Force D Mesopotamia 8.2.16; Food drops siege of Kut; Wrecked 10.4.16; Flying again 16.4.16 (F/L WH Dunn); Deleted 23.1.17

V1541    Arr Basrah 8.2.16; Fell in Turkish lines, shot down by m/g fire 5.3.16 (2/Lt RH Peck & Capt WG Palmer both killed)

V1602    Paris to Grain 9.6.16 (became 9154)

V1721    (220 hp Peugeot) BAC Paris to EAD Grain W/E 23.2.18 - @25.5.18

V1887    EAD Grain by 25.5.18

V2010    (140 hp Peugeot) ECD Grain by 7.17; Fitting air bags 26.7.17; Lost float 12.8.17; to France W/E 10.11.17

*Fokker DVII D7/6539 after being surrendered to 208 Sqdn at Cologne. Left to right, 'Poppy' Pope, Reg Smart and mechanic. (via Frank Cheesman)*

*Fokker DVII D7/6539 with 208 Sqdn after being painted in British colours. It was written off at Donstiennes on 30 April 1919 after catching telegraph wires while being flown by Major CE Bryant DSO. (via Frank Cheesman)*

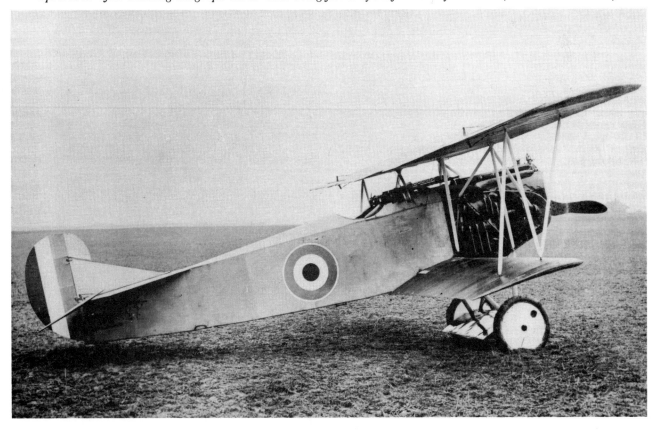

*Captured Albatros DIII at the RNAS Aircraft Depot, Dunkerque (St.Pol) had been flown by Ltn Simon of Jasta 11, and was probably the machine numbered G42, flown to Dover by Flight Commander RFS Leslie on 11 August 1917. (via Frank Cheesman)*

*Friedrichshafen FF.33F 536, captured intact at Gallipoli, was flown for a time from the seaplane carrier HMS Ark Royal. (via Frank Cheesman)*

*French Sopwith Triplane 'F3'. (J.M.Bruce/G.S.Leslie collection)*

*French Sopwith Triplane 'F17' after being landed on by D.H.4 N5981 of 2 Sqdn at St.Pol 27.6.17. (via Frank Cheesman)*

# UNIDENTIFIED INCIDENTS

20.2.14 Short, Eastchurch, engine trouble, FL, stalled, sideslipped. o/t St.Margaret's Hill, Dover 20.2.14 (L/Seaman Andrews unhurt).

19.3.14 Bombs exploded, aircraft fell in sea (Lt CF Lan Davis unhurt; PO Tel JC Hendry thrown out, rescued).

23.6.15 3 Wing, German a/c brought down, probably wrekced by British aeroplane, nr Gaba Tepe.

29.7.15 Avro FTR from coastal reconnaissance to Zeebrugge (S/L Dalzell & S/L CH Dolling-Smith).

10.12.15 2 Wing a/c crashed nr aerodrome in gusty weather, CW (pilot seriously injured, observer killed).

14.6.16 2 Wing, radiator punctured by bullets, FL in sea off Long Island (F/L LA Hervey & Sassoon).

30.9.16 Bristol Scout, 2 Wing, LVG C OOC Chakli, nr Smyrna (FSL HT Mellings).

12.11.16 Bristol Scout, 2 Wing, LVG or Aviatik 2-str crashed nr Chikli (FSL HT Mellings).

16.11.16 Henry Farman, 2 Wing, attacked by Fokker monoplane, EF, FL in sea close to HM ships (F/L IHW Barnato & S/L AEH Roberts rescued unhurt).

13.12.16 Bristol Scout, C Flt 2 Wing Imbros, EF, FL in slat lake, wrecked, Kephalo (pilot unhurt).

19.3.17 2 Wing, Albatros 2-str, observer killed (FSL HT Mellings).

20.5.17 2 Wing, Halberstadt 2-str, observer killed (FSL HT Mellings).

1.6.17 Henry Farman, A Flt 2 Wing, shot down into sea 3m N of Kojen Nakla while escorting Schneider which had landed nearby but overturned (FSL AF Brandon shaken in Schneider; S/L D Argyropous drownd & S/L Psychas unhurt in Farman).

9.6.17 Nieuport fighter, 2 Wing Stavros, on photo reconnaissance and spotting, spun near ground (FSL JW Chuter & S/L AW Henton both killed).

12.6.17 F Sqdn 2 Wing Thasos, 4 Sopwith 1½ fighters on photo reconnaissance, 1 shot down by Halberstadt nr Bulgarian coast (F/L EP Hicks picked up by French MB & AAM1 AE King drowned swimming ashore).

18.6.17 Henry Farman, 2 Wing Marsh, overbanked on TO, sideslipped, nosedived from 600ft, BO (Greek trainee pilot killed).

27.7.17 Newly erected Camel, 2 Wing, encountered large seaplane and 2 small SS scouts at 7,000ft, shot down 1 scout in nose dive into water off Seddul Bahr (F/L JW Alcock).

28.6.17 Sopwith, 2 Wing Stavros, reconnaissance, attacked by HA, both fell OOC (FSL BJ Braby & O/L L Marsh both killed).

5.7.17 Nieuport, 2 Wing Imbros, EF, FL in sea while spotting, sank (pilot and observer picked up).

8.7.17 Henry Farman, 2 Wing Imbros, FTR raid on Nagara (S.H.Chalblias & O Lazaris missing).

1.8.17 F Sqdn 2 Wing Thermi, a fighter FTR from raid on lorry workshops at Halka Bounan, 2m E of Smyrna. Descended from 7,000 ft and crashed on rocks behind Mount Pagus (F/L WH Richardson and Mid JR Barry RNR both killed).

2.8.17 Pup, Z Sqdn 2 Wing Thasos, L/Cdr Moraitinis attacked by 1 of 3 enemy aircraft (a seaplane) attacking Thasos and drove it down into water nr Kavalla.

6.8.17 Bristol Scout, F Sqdn 2 Wing Thermi, damaged by shelling in hangar at Chios.

11.8.17 Schneider, A & Z Sqdns 2 Wing Thasos, During raids on Drama and Gereviz, (raiding Geraviz?), pilot attempted to clear jamb, sideslipped, nosedived and wrecked aircraft (pilot unhurt).

16.8.17 Henry Farman, G Flt 2 Wing, EF, FL while attacking submarine 3m S of Capre Tigani, crashed (F/L C Gilmour & OSL TH Piper unhurt).

17.8.17 Sopwith 2-str, A & Z Sqdns 2 Wing Thasos, seriously damaged landing after photo recce.

20.8.17 Z Sqdn 2 Wing Thasos, a/c shot about in fight with HA attacking Thasos (S/L Meletopoulos wounded).

28.8.17 A Pup flown from Mudros to join A Sqdn 2 Wing Thasos, having been erected in *Ark Royal*.

2-3.9.17 B & F Sqdns Thermi, An H.Farman from Mudros force landed Karu Burnu (FSL WE Foster & S/L H Burns both PoW).

2.9.17 Henry Farman, 2 Wing Mudros, returning from reprisal raid on 3 ships in Sarisgalar Bay, FL, hit submerged wall, CW nr Avlonari (FSL H Wild & OSL TH Piper both unhurt?).

10.9.17 3 Camels from Mudros to Thermi to reinforce B and F Sqdns 2 Wing.

12.9.17 Camel, D Sqdn 2 Wing Stavros, shot down by a scout piloted by Ltn Eschwege nr Tasli (F/Cdr CE Wood killed).

18.9.17 Sopwith fighter, B & F Sqdns Thermi, on recce, EF, FL in sea, 2 crew rescued.

19.9.17 Henry Farman, 2 Wing Mudros, dropped 2x100-lb bombs on submarine 23m W of Dardanelles (FSL GW Parker & OSL RW Greenwood).

30.9.17 2 Wing Mudros, Sopwith Triplane N5431 (F/Lt HT Mellings DSC) shot down 1 of 3 "Blue Bird" seaplanes into sea nr Lemnos. Also involved were Mudros Camel (F/Lt JW Alcock) and Tenedos Pup (FSL PK Fowler). Alcock shot down another "Blue Bird". Fowler attacked an HA and probably hit observer. Not very clear report, but Mellings saw an HA on water, pilot picked up wounded by destroyer HMS *Acheron* (joint Camel/Pup victory?).

18.10.17 H.Farman, A & Z Sqdns 2 Wing Thasos, on Chanak raid, FL in sea, parts salved (2 crew rescued).

12.11.17 Sopwith 2-str, D Sqdn 2 Wing Stavros, shot down Albatros DIII in flames Serres, nr Drama. (F/Lt HT Mellings).

25.11.17 Camel, 2 Wing Stavros, shot down Rummpler C NE of Stavros, landed Drama.

11.17 2 Wing Mudros, 1 seaplane lost in month, occupants picked up by Greek fishing boat.

7.1.18 2 Wing, a/c wrecked on TO for reconnaissance, (pilot saved by HMS *Peony*).

17.1.18 C Sqdn 2 Wing, shot down Friedrichshafen FF33 into water from 1,000ft nr Suda, both occupants killed, wreck salved by a monitor (F/Cdr G Donald).

23.1.18 1½ Strutter shot down in flames in harbour off Chanak-Kale by Ltn Emil Meinecke (FSL Spyros Hambas, a Greek, killed).

21.7.18 DH4, 224 Sqdn, shot down by chaser into sea nr Platamona Point, S of Cattaro (Lt EC Bragg & Lt PE Lindner).

2.8.18 DH, 67 Wing, in raid on Cattaro, damaged by gunfire, FL on shore SE side of Malaluka Bay, 20m SE of Cattaro (Capt EP Hardman & Gnr Hartney PoWs).

26.8.18 D.H.4, 67 Wing, FL in sea 30m NE of Brindisi during raid on Tirana aerodrome (not found).

30.8.18 DH, 67 Wing, COL after raid on Cattaro (Lt Kendall & Pte Wynn both killed).

30.8.18 DH9 "2793", 67 Wing, left Pizzone 05.30, FTR raid on Cattaro (2/Lt GW Cooper, Lt HB Hubbard & Pte WCL Easman all killed).

W/E 2.9.18 DH, 67 Wing, seen to spiral down to water apparently under control off Trieste Bay (2/Lt Corkery & Lt EC Bragg).

5.9.18 DH9, FTR patrol Aegean (Lt NT Williams missing & Lt EC Finzi drowned).

24.10.18 "N4302", Yarmouth, wrecked on TO, beached, crew unhurt.

c.26.1.19 Short, Dvina River, crashed in No Man's Land, CW (Lt WV Lamb & Lt AJ Redman unhurt).

16.6.19 DH9a, 221 Sqdn, FTR raid on Astrakhan, EF, FL Ouvaree (2/Lt AJ Mantle & 2/Lt H Ingram PoWs unhurt).

7.19 or 8.19 Seaplane lost, Dvina River (Lt JS Prouse wounded).

# UNIDENTIFIED RNAS CASUALTIES

## OFFICERS

| | |
|---|---|
| 21.4.13 | Berne, Payr R. Eastchurch. Aircraft suddenly started forward on ground, DoI. (pilot Lt G.V.Wildman-Lushington, RMA unhurt) |
| 10.3.15 | Shepherd, PFSL AG. Eastbourne, fell in sea en route seaplane sheds to aerodrome |
| 3.8.15 | Watson, F/L KF. Med, missing from patrol, drowned |
| 10.8.15 | Johnston, F/L DK. C Flt 2 Sqdn/Shot down off Ostende |
| 14.10.15 | Davis, F/L CF Lan. HMS Ark Royal, between Kephalo and Malta |
| 26.11.15 | Rose, FSL JH. Imbros, at Kephalo Advanced Base |
| 1.12.15 | Hughes, TFSL BFM. North Front, drowned in seaplane accident off Gibraltar |
| 6.1.16 | Busk, F/Cdr HA. Dardanelles |
| 8.1.16 | Black, TFSL SA. Imbros |
| 11.1.16 | Bolas, TFSL JS. Farman. Imbros - shot down Sedd-el-Bahr, off Hellespont, Turkey by a/c of FFA6 |
| 11.1.16 | Brinsmead, TFSL CH. Imbros - as above |
| 10.6.16 | Williams, TFSL GK. Luxeuil |
| 20.9.16 | Scott, TFSL JD. 3 Wing Luxeuil |
| 20.10.16 | Greenwell, TPFSL AR. Cranwell, dived in from 200ft |
| 29.11.16 | Mann, TFSL ATO. 3 Wing Luxeuil |
| 13.1.17 | Vallings, TFSL RKJ. Mudros/ FTR photo recce over Orfano Valley, fell from 1000ft [also 2/Lt AC Panting killed] |
| 12.3.17 | Knight, TFSL RV. Cranwell (Instructor) |
| 30.3.17 | Conby, TLt HB, DSC.Shot down on bombing expedition, died 3.6.17 as PoW Constantinople |
| 20.5.17 | Haig, TFSL JD. Shot down in sea nr Thasos by Lt Eschwege while spotting for HMS Raglan |
| 20.5.17 | Keightley, TSL G - as above |
| 9.6.17 | Chuter, TFSL JW. Nieuport (130-hp). D Sqdn 2 Wing Stavros - PR and spotting, spun near ground |
| 9.6.17 | Henton, T/S/L AW (RNVR) - as above |
| 28.6.17 | Brady, FSL BJ. 1½ Strutter. Stavros/Shot down OOC by HA which also crashed |
| 28.6.17 | Marsh, O/L L - as above |
| 17.7.17 | Begg, TFSL RG. Adriatic (buried Otranto) |
| 17.7.17 | Planterose, TOSL EA - as above |
| 22.7.17 | Brett, TFSL LH. Mudros, flying accident |
| 1.8.17 | Barry, Ty Midmn JR (RNR). 1½ Strutter. F Sqdn 2 Wing, FTR raid on Halka Dounan Rly Workshops, crashed on Mount Pagus from 7,000ft |
| 1.8.17 | Richardson, T/F/L WH - as above, both buried Smyrna |
| 3.9.17 | Thomas, TFSL JE, ferry pilot of RNAS Air Dept N.I.Section. Dived in from 300-400ft nr Yeovil. (Mr Robert Norton seriously inj) |
| 24.9.17 | Lockie, TPFO K. Vendome |
| 26.11.17 | Blake, TPFO IH (DoI). Vendome |
| 7.1.18 | Jones, TFObs WBL. 6 Wing Taranto, drowned after came down in sea in heavy weather [N1154 or N1465] |
| 7.1.18 | Phillips, TFSL GH as above |
| 7.1.18 | Fox, TFSL CE - as above |
| 7.1.18 | Gordon, TOSL A - as above |
| 22.1.18 | Burden, T/F/L CE. Manston, EF, FL, crashed Thanet |
| 30.1.18 | Brearley, TFSL HB. East Fortune |
| 8.2.18 | Jewell, TFSL C. Crashed Basingstoke |
| 23.2.18 | Chapman, T/F/L CHM. Eastchurch (also AC1 Brady), collided TFSL Reid |
| 23.2.18 | Reid, TFSL HM. Eastchurch (also AM RG Arrowsmith), collided T/F/L Chapman |
| 13.3.18 | Anderson, FSL WS. D Sqdn 2 Wing Stavros, COL on delivery from Mudros |
| 18.3.18 | Harland, TPFO EW. Cranwell, EF, stalled, dived in |
| 31.3.18 | Connop, TFSL HA. Dunkerque |

## RATINGS

| | |
|---|---|
| 21.8.14 | Statham, AM1 CE. Ostende |
| 31.10.14 | Ferguson, AM1 A. HMS Hermes |
| 8.10.15 | Wright, PO Mech PR. Dunkerque |
| 26.11.15 | Bostowe. Imbros (with FSL Rose) |
| 2.12.15 | Brandon, AM1 WCNB. Buried Hendon Park Cemetary |
| 17.1.16 | Beard, AM2 CE. |
| 5.2.16 | Wynter, AM1 EC. Eastchurch |
| 13.2.16 | Haynes, AM2 FG. Buried Gosport |
| 24.2.16 | Careless, AM1 F. HMS Espiègle - Mesopotomia |
| 17.3.16 | Ball, LM F. East Fortune |
| 30.3.16 | Biddlecombe, AAM1 F. Buried Veille Chapelle |
| 28.5.16 | Leggett, AM1 SL. |
| 28.8.16 | Hornby, AM1 S. |
| 15.9.16 | Langford, AC2 OB. |
| 20.9.16 | Taylor, AM2 FWG, 3 Wing Luxeuil (with TFSL JD Scott) |
| 21.11.16 | Thompson, AM1 LCdE. |
| 5.1.17 | Hollidge, LM WT. Mudros |
| 29.1.17 | Dawes, AM1 WDS. Buried Deal |
| 31.1.17 | Hart, AM1 WH. Mullion |
| 5.2.17 | Helps, AM1 HT. Cranwell |
| 14.2.17 | Depper, CPO Mech3 G. AD Dunkerque |
| 14.2.17 | Gill, AM2 VJA. AD Dunkerque |
| 3.3.17 | Boyland, AM1 CD (USA). Killingholme |
| 3.4.17 | Carney, AM1 RH. Dunkerque |
| 27.5.17 | Leslie, AC1 O. Mudros |
| 28.4.17 | Dear, AM1 P. Buried Cambridge |
| 8.5.17 | Beckett, AC2 F |
| 27.5.17 | Woolhead, CPO Mech2 WH. Mudros |
| 27.5.17 | Gibson, AC2 HNJ. Mudros |
| 31.5.17 | Ellingworth, AM2 C. Tresco |
| 1.6.17 | Shephard, AC2 AL. Thasos |
| 2.6.17 | Wiseman, AM1 GI. Dunkerque |
| 6.6.17 | Creasy, AM2 W. Tresco |
| 4.7.17 | Austins, AM1 A. Felixstowe |
| 22.7.17 | Allen, AAM1 W. Felixstowe |
| 25.7.17 | Carter, AM2 DW. RNAS Peterborough |
| 10.8.17 | Currington, AM1 S. DoW. Dunkerque, Aeroplane fight 5.8.17 |
| 14.8.17 | Egleshaw, AC2 JG. Calshot |
| 9.10.17 | Leyland, AM2 WE. Cranwell |
| 19.10.17 | Evans, LM HJ. Mudros |
| 19.10.17 | Housden, LM AA. Dunkerque |
| 20.10.17 | Day, AAM1 VE. Dunkerque |
| 15.11.17 | Dolley, AM2 BF. A Sqdn Autreville |
| 26.11.17 | Allen, AAM1 E |
| 28.11.17 | Wainwright, AAM1 F. Westgate |
| 10.12.17 | Wood, AM2 RW. Killingholme |
| 14.12.17 | Campbell, AM2 JA. AD Dunkerque |
| 13.1.18 | Jeffries, AAM1 AL (DoI). 5 Sqdn - bombing raid |
| 13.1.18 | Mason, LM HW. 5 Sqdn - bombing raid |
| 23.2.18 | Brady, AC1 WCE. Eastchurch (with T/F/L/ Chapman) |
| 23.2.18 | Arrowsmith AM RG. Eastchurch (with TFSL Reid) |
| 12.3.18 | Cole, AC2 AS. Killingholme |
| 13.3.18 | Anderson, FSL WS. 2 Wing |
| 21.3.18 | Jones, AM1 FR. (D1604?) |
| 22.3.18 | Johnson, AC1 EW. Manston |

*Short 184 and Fairey Campania seaplanes at Portland in July 1918. Fin markings were carried on all local machines by that time, the nearest machine being N2965 with marking 'P No.9'. (IWM Q.84284)*

The local Portland fin marking 'P No.3' is clearly seen on Short 184 N1771, which had struck a tree during a forced landing near Budleigh Salterton on 31 May 1918, injuring both crew members. (via Frank Cheesman)

*Fairey Campania N2368 with HMS Pegasus marking 'L.B.9' The significance of this type of marking, used by several seaplane carriers in 1918, is unclear. (via FAA Museum)*

*Short 184 with Newhaven local marking 'N-A3'. (RAF Museum P.21707)*

# MISCELLANY

## No.3 Wing, Tenedos (No.3 Sqdn until 21.6.15)
(aircraft disembarked ex France 26-27.3.15)

Fin codes:

| | |
|---|---|
| 1 | (1369) (100 hp Renault) M Farman tested 31.3.15 |
| 2 | (1241) (100 hp Renault) H Farman tested 7.4.15 |
| 3 | H Farman tested 7.4.15; later B.E.2c by 1.5.15 |
| 4 | B.E.2c, to Imbros 3.8.15 |
| 5 | B.E.2c tested 16.5.15 |
| 6 | Voisin by 27.5.15 |
| 7 | Voison (130 hp Canton-Unné) tested 26.5.15 |
| 8 | Voison tested 27.5.15; EF, flight abandoned 22.6.15 (F/L GL Thomson) [LM] |
| 9 | [could this be Sopwith 1205?] |
| 10 | Voisin by 18.6.15; later Nieuport tested 29.8.15 |
| 11 | H Farman by 2.5.15 |
| 12 | H Farman by 5.5.15 |
| 13 | number not used? |
| 14 | H Farman by 2.5.15 |
| 15 | H Farman by 29.5.15 |
| 16 | H Farman by 2.6.15 |
| 17 | H Farman by 8.6.15 |
| 18 | no information |
| 19 | Voisin by 28.6.15 |
| 20 | H Farman by 19.7.15 |
| 21 | no information |
| 22 | H Farman by 5.7.15 |
| 23 | H Farman tested 4.8.15 (became H7) |
| 24 | H Farman (130 hp Canton-Unné) at Imbros by 7.8.15; to Tenedos 11.8.15; Came down Suvla 19.8.15 (Cdr CR Samson) |
| 25 | M Farman by 7.8.15 |
| 26 | Nieuport tested Tenedos 3.9.15, then to Imbros (became N1?) |
| 27 | Nieuport (90 hp Le Rhône) tested Imbros 29.8.15; to Tenedos 3.9.15 (became N2?) |
| 28 | Nieuport tested 3.9.15 (became N3?) |
| 1205 | Tabloid by 9.5.15 - @4.6.15 |
| 1206 | Tabloid by 28.6.15 |

### Revised system of local numbers from 10.15

| | |
|---|---|
| BE2 | BE2c (1111) by 5.10.15 |
| H3 | (Originally HF.3) H Farman Ex 2 Wing 15.10.15 - @19.11.15 |
| H4 | (Originally HF.4) H Farman Ex 2 Wing 18.10.15 |
| H5 | (Originally HF.5) H Farman Ex 2 Wing 21.10.15 |
| H4 | H Farman by 25.10.15 - @31.12.15 |
| H5 | H Farman by 9.11.15; Shot down in bombing attack on Ferejik Rly Stn, FL in marshes nr Maritza River, pilot set fire to a/c 19.11.15 (FSL GF Smylie rescued by Bell-Davies who was awarded VC) |
| H6 | (Originally HF.6) H Farman (130 hp) Ex 2 Wing 30.10.15 - @5.11.15 |
| H7 | H Farman (ex 23) by 4.9.15 - @31.12.15 |
| H8 | H Farman tested 17.12.15 - @30.12.15 |
| M1 | M Farman by 25.10.15 - @30.10.15 |
| M2 | (Originally MF.2) by 25.10.15 - @29.12.15 |
| M3 | (Originally MF.3) M Farman (110 hp) by 25.10.15 - @25.12.15 |
| M4 | M Farman. No information |
| M5 | M Farman by 27.12.15 |
| M6 | M Farman by 1.12.15; EF, FL in sea, picked up by trawler, towed Kephalo 20.12.15 (F/L PEH Wakeley & Mid EK St.Aubyn) |
| N1 | Nieuport (3172 q.v) (ex 26?) by 1.11.15 |
| N2 | Nieuport (ex 27?) by 9.10.15 (Cdr Samson's machine) - @14.12.15 |
| N3 | Nieuport (ex 28?) by 16.12.15 - @29.12.15 |
| N4 | Nieuport tested new 18.12.15 - @25.12.15 |

An unidentified Sopwith Triplane on the Western Front was coded '7' and named 'KANOPIT'.

## Captured German airmen (AIR.1/544/16/5/6) - possible RNAS victories

| | |
|---|---|
| 1.5.17 | Flugmaat Karl Berghoff and Leutnant Richard Freude of Seeflugstation Flandern I. North Sea. |
| 11.6.17 | Flugmeister Alfred Burgstaller of Seeflieger Abt.II, Nr 355. Channel. |
| 11.6.17 | Flieger Leutnant Paul Strang of Seeflieger Abt.II. Dover. |
| 9.7.17 | Leutnant Hermann Becker of Seeflugstation Flandern I. At sea |
| 9.7.17 | Leutnant Wilhelm Heinrich Ludwig Löwe of Seeflugstation Zeebrügge 13. At sea. |
| 9.7.17 | Leutnant Joseph Mallman & Leutnant z.See (Joachim) Thousen of Seeflugstation Zeebrügge 532. At sea. |
| 4.9.17 | Hauptmann Claus August Hempel & Oblt Herbert Knigge of Kampfgeschwader 4. Dunkirk. |
| 10.9.17 | Vizefeldwebel (Flugzeugführer) Friedrich Eckardt-Bay of Flieger - Abt.293. Dunkirk. |

## RNAS SEAPLANE REQUIREMENTS as laid down 11.16

| | |
|---|---|
| Type 1 | Torpedo-carrying 2-str seaplane fitted 1 x 450-hp Sunbeam or 2 x 310-hp Sunbeam. |
| Type 2 | North Sea scouting 2-str seaplane fitted 310-hp Sunbeam. |
| Type 3 | Carrier type scouting 2-str seaplane fitted 200-hp Sunbeam or 190-hp Rolls-Royce. |
| Type 4 | Seaplane for attacking Zeppelins fitted 130-hp Clerget or 140-hp Smith. |
| Type 5 | Fleet reconnaissance and spotting 2-str seaplane fitted 150-hp pusher Smith. |

## SEAPLANE STATION CODES PAINTED ON AIRCRAFT

| | |
|---|---|
| B | Bembridge |
| C | Calshot |
| CH | Cherbourg |
| G | Grain |
| K | Killingholme (see below) |
| N | Newhaven |
| P | Portland (P No.1, P No.2, P No.3 etc) |
| TN | Tynemouth/South Shields (e.g.Short 184 'TNZ') |
| Y? | Yarmouth |
| - | Westgate (large fin number surrounded by circle |
| - | Cattewater (fin letter/number codes, e.g. A7, B5, L2) [Could LB = Lee-on-Solent, or PC = Portland? See ships codes below] |

Killingholme - markings carried by US Navy aircraft:

| | |
|---|---|
| F.2A | K32, K33, K41, K42, K45 |
| H.16 | K2, K4-K7, K10-K13, K16, K21, K25, K26, K28-K30, K33, K37-K40, K42, K43 |

H.16 K10 - Bombed oil patch near Scarborough, EF, FL inside Spurn 8.9.18

H.16 K21 - Bombed U-boat 20m off Flamborough, FL, towed Scarborough 14.10.18

H.16 K28 - EF, FL off Flamborough Head 14.9.18

H.16 K38 - Crashed nr Immingham 1.10.18 (2nd pilot, engineer and W/T operator all killed)

H.16 K42 - FL 6m NE of Scarborough 6.9.18

H.16 A1062 - Bombed U-boat 21.8.18

H.16 ??? - Crashed, glassy water, crew saved 6.11.18

## SEAPLANE CARRIER CODES

| | |
|---|---|
| HMS *Campania* | Schneider/Baby e.g. C, C.4 etc? Campania e.g. P.C.4 (N2362), B.X.3 |
| HMS *Furious* | 1½ Strutter e.g. J.D.8 (A5992) |
| HMS *Pegasus* | Campania e.g. O.H.8, K.G.8, L.B.9 (N2368), X.L.8 |
| HMS *Vindictive* | Fairey III e.g. E.D.9 (or F.D.9 or T.D.9) and K.T.T. (or X.T.T. - in sea) |
| Unknown | Short 184 e.g. L.M.6 |
| Unknown | Short 184 e.g. N-A3 (could this signify 3rd a/c of 'A' Flt at Newhaven?) |

# NAVAL AIRCRAFT UNITS 1911 - 1919

The correct titles and movements of RNAS units is not always clear in surviving records, but the following list is believed to be essentially accurate. Parent formations and additional information are given in round brackets. Where appropriate, anomolies have been noted as such, generally in square brackets. Commanding officers are listed where known.

## HQ RNAS (with BEF)
At Dunkerque (?) by 1.9.14; Morbecque 17.9.14; Then to go to Douai (NTU?); Whole force to go to Thourout 12.10.14; [Regrouped as Naval Wing 15.10.14?].
ALSO HQ RNAS Dunkerque to Spycker 9.2.18

## NAVAL SQUADRONS
NOTE - Parent Wings are given in most instances. Up to 31.3.18 these could be RNAS Wings (Nos.1 to 6) or RFC Wings. In the case of RFC Wings the controlling Brigade is also given. From 1.4.18 all Wings were RAF, the former RNAS Wings having 60 added to their numbers. Home-based Wings were now usually controlled by Groups.

### Eastchurch (Mobile) Squadron

BASES
Formed Eastchurch 8.8.14 [initial aircraft = 33 (Bell-Davies), 43 (Dalrymple-Clark), 46 (Briggs), 49 (Sippe), 50 (Samson), 66 (Beevor)]; Immingham 9.8.14; Skegness 11.8.14; Eastchurch 24.8.14; Ostende Racecourse 27.8.14; Became No.3 Sqdn 1.9.14.

COMMANDING OFFICERS
S/Cdr R Bell-Davies 8.14 (did not take up post?); W/Cdr CR Samson by 27.8.14 - 1.9.14.

AIRCRAFT -
Short S.38, BE2a, T.B.8, Sopwith Tractor, DFW

### No.185 Squadron

BASES
Formed East Fortune 21.10.18 (as Torpedo Bomber Unit for service in HMS Argus); To cadre 9.4.19; Disbanded 14.4.19.

AIRCRAFT - Cuckoo

### No.186 Squadron

BASES
Formed HMS Argus 31.12.18 (for intended anti-shipping operations in Caspian, based at Baku, but NTU); Gosport 17.2.19 (became Torpedo Devt Unit); Became 210 Sqdn 1.2.20.

AIRCRAFT - Cuckoo.

### No.1/201 Squadron

BASES
Formed as 1 Sqdn at Antwerp 1.9.14; Ostend 3.9.14; Dunkerque 14.9.14; Antwerp 16.9.14; Ostende 9.10.14; Disb in retreat 14.10.14.

Refd as 1 Sqdn at Gosport (Grange Field) 15.10.14 (Naval Wing, RFC); A Flt detd Dover 29.12.14 (Relieved A Flt 1 Sqdn); B Flt to Dover 2.1.15 (Relieved Defence Flt 2 Sqdn); Dover 28.1.15; A Flt (2x504B) detd Westgate 2-5.2.15; Dett Westgate by 8.2.15 gone by 15.2.15 (F/Cdr JT Babington); St.Pol 22.2.15 "[relieved 3 Sqdn, completed move 1.3.15]"; Became No.1 Wing 21.6.15.
Detts: C Flt (4 T.B.8) to Farnborough 18.11.14; Gosforth 19.11.14; Whitley Bay 18.12.14 (2 a/c were left at Newcastle to form C Flt. They were detached from 1 Sqdn 2.2.15 to become an independent unit).
[One source says: "1 Sqdn refd as Wing 8.15 and transferred to Dover preparatory to transferring to Dardanelles"]
[A disposition list has: "Dardanelles week 22-28.9.15 = 1 Sqdn of 1 Wing (Morane/Le Rhone)"].

Refd ex A Sqdn as 1 Sqdn at Furnes 1.12.16 (1 Wing) [appears to have been effective 6.12.16] [201 Sqdn history notes in Castle Cornet, Guernsey state A Sqdn 1 Wing became Detd Sqdn 3.7.16, then 1 Sqdn 6.12.16]; Chipilly 15.2.17 (14 Wing 4 Bde) [here became known as No.1 (Naval) Squadron to avoid confusion with No.1 Squadron, RFC]; La Bellevue 11.4.17 (13 Wing 3 Bde); Bailleul 1.6.17 (11 Wing 2 Bde); Bray Dunes (Middle Aerodrome)

2.11.17 (4 Wing); Dover (refit) 10.12.17 (4 Wing); Teteghem 16.2.18 (1 Wing); Ste.Marie Cappel 27.3.18 (11 Wing 2 Bde); Fienvillers 28.3.18 (13 Wing 3 Bde); Became 201 Sqdn 1.4.18; Noeux lès Auxi 12.4.18 (13 Wing 3 Bde); Ste.Marie Cappel 20.7.18 (11 Wing 2 Bde); Poulainville 6.8.18 (22 Wing 5 Bde); Noeux lès Auxi 14.8.18 (13 Wing 3 Bde); Baizieux 19.9.18 (13 Wing 3 Bde); Beugnatre 14.10.18 (13 Wing 3 Bde); La Targette 27.10.18 (13 Wing 3 Bde); Bethencourt 22.11.18 (13 Wing 3 Bde); To cadre 23.1.19 (a/c to 203 Sqdn); Lake Down 15.2.19 (33 Wing 2 Group); Eastleigh 2.9.19 7 Group); Disbanded 31.12.19.

COMMANDING OFFICERS
S/Cdr EL Gerrard 1.9.14; Disbanded 13.10.14.

S/Cdr AM Longmore 15.10.14 (W/Cdr by 1.15); Became 1 Wing 21.6.15.

S/Cdr FK Haskins DSC 6.12.16; S/Cdr RS Dallas DSO DFC 14.6.17; S/Cdr CD Booker DFC 18.3.18 (became Mjr wef 1.4.18); Mjr CM Leman MC DFC 18.8.18; - ? - 15.2.19; Disbanded 31.12.19.

AIRCRAFT - Henry Farman, B.E.2a, T.B.8, Sopwith 3-Seater.

Sopwith Sociable, Sopwith Gordon Bennett, BE2a, BE8, Tabloid, T.B.8, Avro 504B, Morane Parasol, Bleriot Parasol, Vickers F.B.5, Curtiss N (Mod), Bristol Scout C, Voisin Biplane, Shorthorn, Nieuport 10, Nieuport 11, White & Thompson Flying Boat,

Sopwith Triplane, F.1 Camel.

### No.2/202 Squadron

BASES
Formed as 2 Sqdn at Eastchurch 10.9.14; Dunkerque 16.9.14; Antwerp 17.9.14; Ostende 10.10.14; England & disb 10.10.14.

Refd as 2 Sqdn at Eastchurch 17.10.14 (training duties); Became 2 Wg 21.6.15
Detts:
Defence Flight (TB.8's 1223 & 1224): Dover 24.12.14 to 2.1.15 (relieved by B Flt 1 Sqdn)
Dett: Dover 10.2.15 (or 26.3.15) to 6.15 (4 Bleriot Parasol) [not part of 2 Sqdn?]
Defence Flight: Westgate (fd) 3.15 to .15
A Flt: Westgate end 4.15 [@18.6.15 = F/Cdr A B Gaskell]
B Flt: Eastchurch by W/E 10.5.15
C Flt: Eastchurch by W/E 10.5.15

Refd ex B Sqdn 1 Wing as 2 Sqdn at St.Pol 5.11.16 (1 Wg RNAS) [effective 12.16] [also reported as fd ex 1 Wing 1.2.17]; Bergues 26.1.18; Became 202 Sqdn 1.4.18 (61 Wing 5 Group); Varssenaere 20.11.18 (61 Wing 5 Group) (reported detached from Group early 12.18 to work with Grand Fleet); Castle Bromwich late 1.19 (was to move to Leuchars when room); Dover (cadre) 24.3.19 (but still at Dunkerque to 1.3.19 !); Driffield 26.3.19 8 Wing 16 Trg Group); Spittlegate 10.19; Disbanded 22.1.20.

COMMANDING OFFICERS
S/Cdr SDA Grey 1.9.14; Disbanded 13.10.14.

S/Cdr EL Gerrard 17.10.14 (became W/Cdr 1.15) to 21.6.15.

F/Cdr DCS Evill 5.11.16; S/Cdr DCS Evill 31.12.16; S/Cdr PFM Fellowes 1.4.17; S/Cdr FE Sandford 1.11.17; F/Cdr BS Wemp W/E 8.2.18 (became Mjr wef 1.4.18); Mjr RW Gow DSO DFC 7.4.18; Capt J Robinson 1.1.19; Capt RM Bayley 23.3.19; Disbanded 22.1.20.

AIRCRAFT - Tabloid, Sopwith 3-seater, Sopwith Pusher Seaplane, B.E.2a.

Bleriot XI, Morane Monoplane, Morane BB, Curtiss N (Mod), Bristol T.B.8, Avro 501, Avro 504B, BE8, Bleriot Parasol, Bristol

Scout C, Short Long Range Pusher, Henry Farman F.40, BE2c.

1½ Strutter, D.H.4.

## No.3/203 Squadron

BASES

Formed ex Eastchurch (Mobile) Sqdn as 3 Sqdn at St.Pol 1.9.14; Morbecque 19.9.14; Adv party Lille 29.9.14; Lille on/by 1.10.14; Dunkerque 3.10.14; Antwerp 5.10.14; Ostend 7.10.14; Roulers 12.10.14; St.Omer 14.10.14 (absorbed remains of 1 & 2 Sqdns?); Poperinghe 18.10.14; St.Pol (by?) 7.11.14; Dover 26.2.15; sailed to Dardanelles 11.3.15; arr Marseilles 16.3.15; embarked SS *Abda* 17.3.15; Tenedos 24.3.15 (ALG at Cape Hellas 5.15 - 29.6.15); Became 3 Wing 21.6.15.

Refd ex C Sqdn 1 Wing as 3 Sqdn at St.Pol 5.11.16 (1 Wing); Vert Galant 3.2.17 (22 Wing 5 Bde) (B Flt detd Cormont for weeks Aerial Musketry Range course, retd 18.2.17); Bertangles 28.2.17 (22 Wing 5 Bde); Marieux (22 Wing 5 Bde, later 13 Wing 3 Bde); Furnes 15.6.17 (4 Wing); St.Pol 26.8.17 (4 Wing); Furnes 27.8.17 (4 Wing); Bray Dunes 6.9.17 (4 Wing); Walmer 1.11.17 [some from 27.10.17] (rest period); Bray Dunes (Middle Aerodrome) 3.1.18 (retd 4 Wing) [B Flt (3 a/c) at Berck-sur-Mer 8.2.18 - 15.2.18 for course on RFC Aerial Gunnery Range]; Mont St.Eloi 1.3.18 (10 Wing 1 Bde); Treizennes (Aire) 28.3.18 (10 Wing 1 Bde); Became 203 Sqdn 1.4.18 (10 Wing 1 Bde); Estree Blanche (Liettres) 10.4.18 (10 Wing 1 Bde); Izel-le-Hameau (Filescamp Farm) 16.5.18 (10 Wing 1 Bde); Allonville 14.8.18 (22 Wing 5 Bde); Izel-le-Hameau 6.9.18 (10 Wing 1 Bde); Bruille 24.10.18 (10 Wing 1 Bde); Auberchicourt 24.11.18 (10 Wing 1 Bde); Orcq 22.12.18 (10 Wing 1 Bde) [or Tournai 21.12.18 - @1.19 per 10 Wing records]; Boisdinghem 18.1.19 (91 Wing 1 Bde); Waddington as cadre 27.3.19 (3 Group by 11.19); Scopwick (Digby) 12.19; Disbanded 21.1.20.

COMMANDING OFFICERS

S/Cdr R Bell-Davies 1.9.14 - 22.1.15 (wounded); S/Cdr AM Longmore by 2.10.14 [until temp replaced Samson 8.10.14]; W/Cdr CR Samson DSO 10.14 or 11.14; Became 3 Wing 21.6.15

F/Cdr RH Mulock DSO 5.11.16 (became S/Cdr 21.5.17); S/Cdr LS Breadner 10.17; S/Cdr R Collishaw DSO DSC DFC 23.1.18; (became Mjr wef 1.4.18); Mjr TF Hazell, DSO, MC, DFC 21.10.18; - ? - 24.3.19; Disbanded 21.1.20.

AIRCRAFT - Henry Farman, Short Tractor Seaplane, T.B.8, BE2a, BE2c, BE8, Bleriot Parasol, Bleriot XI, Sopwith Pusher Seaplane, RE5, Sopwith 3-str, Short Triple Twin, Breguet de Chasse, Maurice Farman, Morane BB, Nieuport 10, Nieuport 11, Nieuport 17bis, Nieuport 21, Henry Farman F.20, Bristol Scout, Morane Parasol.

1½ Strutter, Pup, F.1 Camel.

## No.4/204 Squadron

BASES

Formed as 4 Sqdn at Dover 25.3.15 (ex Defence Flt Dover, which had formed earlier that month) [this is confirmed, yet a Defence Flt Dover still existed alongside 4 Sqdn 31.3.15] [BUT another source says 4 Sqdn formed ex 4 Wing at Dover 29.7.15]; Eastchurch 3.8.15; Became 4 Wg W/E 11.10.15 [BUT another source says attd Eastchurch FS from fortnight ending 25.10.15 (S/Cdr A Ogilvie) - @27.12.15].

Refd as 4 Sqdn at Coudekerque 31.12.16 (4 Wing) [as A Sqdn !]; Bray Dunes (Frontier) 1.4.17; Walmer 2.1.18 (rest/refit); Bray Dunes 1.3.18 retd (4 Wing); Became 204 Sqdn 1.4.18 (64 Wing 7 Bde); Teteham 13.4.18 (61 Wing 5 Group); Cappelle 30.4.18; Teteghem 9.5.18 (now 64 Wing 7 Bde, later (61 Wing 5 Group); Heule 24.10.18 (65 Wing 2 Bde to 17.11.18, then 65 Wing 10 Bde); Waddington (cadre) 6.2.19 (27 Wing, later 3 Group); Disbanded 31.12.19.

COMMANDING OFFICERS

S/Cdr CL Courtney 25.3.15; S/Cdr CE Risk W/E 9.8.15 (to 5 Sqdn W/E 6.9.15); Disbanded 11.10.15.

F/Cdr JCP Wood (temp) 31.12.16; S/Cdr JWK Allsop 15.2.17; S/Cdr BL Huskisson DSC 13.3.17 (became Mjr wef 1.4.18); Mjr

EW Norton DSC 27.7.18; Mjr LS Breadner 18.11.18; Mjr EW Norton DSC 21.11.18; Mjr P Huskinson MC 10.12.18; Mjr RS Lucy 10.1.19; Capt HB Maund 23.1.19; Disbanded 31.12.19.

AIRCRAFT - F.B.5, Avro 504B, BE2c, BE8, Henry Farman F.27, Bleriot Parasol, Nieuport 10.

1½ Strutter, Pup, F.1 Camel.

## No.5/205 Squadron

BASES

Formed 2.8.15 as 5 Sqdn from a nucleus of 4 Sqdn left at Dover; Disb into RNAS Dover between 11.10.15 & 25.10.15 (soon became 5 Wing?).

Refd from B Sqdn 5 Wing at Coudekerque 31.12.16 (5 Wing); Flez by 2.17 (22 Wing 5 Bde) (retreated, various moves, details unknown); Petite Synthe 1.4.17 (ex Coudekerque?) (4 Wing; 5 Wing by 25.4.17) (took over half flt of 7 Sqdn 2.4.17); Villers-Bretonneux 6.3.18 (22 Wing 5 Bde); Mons-en-Chaussee 11.3.18 (shelled out); Champien 21.3.18; Bertangles 23.3.18; Conteville (Bois de Roche) 28.3.18; Became 205 Sqdn 1.4.18; Bovelles 25.8.18; Proyart East 16.9.18; Moislains 7.10.18 (still 22 Wing); 25.10.18 (51 Wing 9 Bde); Maubeuge 27.11.18 (9 Wing 5 Bde); La Louveterie 12.1.19 15 Wing 5 Bde) [Another source says 1 Flt moved there 2-3.1.19, other 2 Flts 4-5.1.19]; Sart 11.2.19; Hucknall (cadre) 18.3.19 (3 Group by 11.19); Scopwick 12.19; Disbanded 22.1.20.

COMMANDING OFFICERS

S/Cdr CE Risk 2.8.15; W/Cdr CL Lambe W/E 6.9.15; Disbanded.

S/Cdr ET Newton-Clare 31.12.16; S/Cdr SJ Goble DSO DSC 15.7.17 (became Mjr wef 1.4.18); Mjr JF Gordon DFC 28.8.18; Mjr JB Elliott 2.11.18; Disbanded 22.1.20.

AIRCRAFT - 504B, Sopwith Spinning Jenny.

1½ Strutter, D.H.4, D.H.9A.

## No.6/206 Squadron

BASES

6 Sqdn nucleus assembled at Dover 1.11.16; Petite Synthe 12.12.16 (sqdn officially formed here 31.12.16 from A Sqdn 4 Wing; La Bellevue 11.3.17 (13 Wing 3 Bde); Chipilly 11.4.17 (14 Wing 4 Bde); Flez (Guizencourt) 26.4.17 (14 Wing 4 Bde); Bray Dunes (Frontier aerodrome) 18-19.6.17 (3 Wing 4 Bde to 29.6.17, then 14 Wing 4 Bde); Dunkerque 26-27.8.17 & disbanded (aircraft & crews to 9 & 10 Sqdns).

Refd as 6 Sqdn at Dover 1.1.18 (from personnel of Defence Flight Walmer & 11 Sqdn RNAS); Petite Synthe 14.1.18 (5 Wing); Ste.Marie Cappel 30.3.18 (11 Wing 2 Bde); Became 206 Sqdn 1.4.18 (11 Wing 2 Bde); Boisdinghem 11.4.18 (11 Wing 2 Bde); Alquines 15.4.18 (11 Wing 2 Bde); Boisdinghem 29.5.18 (11 Wing 2 Bde); Alquines 5.6.18; Ste Marie Cappel 5.10.18 (65 Wing 5 Bde); Linselles East 24.10.18 (11 Wing 2 Bde); Nivelles East 26.11.18 (11 Wing 2 Bde) [moved 9.12.18 per Pitt log book]; Bickendorf 18-21.12.18 (11 Wing 2 Bde); Mauberge 27.5.19 (11 Wing 2 Bde?); in transit 7.6.19 via Marseilles; Alexandria 19.6.19; Heliopolis 24.6.19; Helwan 27.6.19 (Training Bde, Middle East); Became 47 Sqdn 1.2.20.

COMMANDING OFFICERS

S/Cdr JJ Petre DSC 31.12.16; S/Cdr CD Breese 14.4.17; Disbanded 27.8.17.

S/Cdr CT MacLaren 1.1.18 (became Mjr wef 1.4.18); Mjr GRM Reid DSO MC 23.5.19; Disbanded 1.2.20.

AIRCRAFT - Nieuport 10, Nieuport 11, Nieuport 12, Nieuport 12, Nieuport 17bis, F.1 Camel.

D.H.4, D.H.9.

## "RNAS Squadron" (same as 7 Sqdn?)

To Mbyuni 28.1.16; to go to Maktak 2.16.
(per S/Cdr ET Cull's report 26.3.16 - 1.6.16)

434

## No.7/207 Squadron

### BASES
Formed as 7 Sqdn in UK and shipped out; Kondoa Irangi 4.16 (German East Africa); Arr M'buyuni 5.5.16? (2 a/c); Lolkissale 30.5.16 (2 a/c in transit); Masaie Steppe (30m ESE of Ufiome) 30.5.16 (FL, petrol, undamaged); Salim (12m N of Kondoa Irangi) 12.6.16 (3rd a/c soon joined them here); Aheti 23.7.16; Mpapua 15.8.16; Kilossa 22.8.16 [Adv Base Manamanga 14.11.16 to 23.12.16] [Adv Base Alt Iringa 30.11.16 to 7.12.16]; Alt Iringa 7.12.16 [1 a/c detd Dar-es-Salaam from/by 20.12.16]; [1 a/c detd Ubena (Njombe) 20.12.16]; Officially disbanded 12.1.17 [personnel to return UK, to be replaced by RFC 28.1.17].

Refd from B Sqdn 4 Wing as 7 Sqdn at Petite Synthe wef 31.12.16; Coudekerque 3.4.17 (5 Wing) [A 1½ Strutter flt then handed to 5 Sqdn to complete it; took over half flight of HPs then assembling at Coudekerque under S/Cdr Allsop, who then took over 7 Sqdn which now comprised 5 HP and 7 Short Bomber] [Flight of 4 a/c ex HP Sqdn Manston under F/Cdr Buss] [Reduced to 10 a/c 28.7.17; the other 8 a/c became 7A Sqdn] [Dett 4 a/c (3123/3126/3127/3136) to UK 3.9.17 (BUT this was flt of 7A Sqdn per 207 Sqdn history); Redcar 5.9.17; Manston 2.10.17 (5.10.17?); Became A Sqdn 5.10.17]; Sqdn became 207 Sqdn 1.4.18 (65 Wing 7 Bde, later 64 Wing 7 Bde); Netheravon 22.4.18 (5 Group) (refit O/400); Andover 13.5.18; Ligescourt 6-7.6.18 (54 Wing 9 Bde) (with O/100 & O/400); Estrees-en-Chaussee 26.10.18 (54 Wing 9 Bde); Carvin 1.12.18; Merheim 29.12.18 (11 Wing 2 Bde); Hangelar 10.5.19 (9 Wing 9 Bde until 21.7.19, then 2 Wing); All a/c to 100 Sqdn St.Inglevert for duty in Middle East 22.8.19; Tangmere (cadre) 23.8.19; Croydon 8.10.19; Kenley 10.1.20; Uxbridge 16.1.20; Disbanded 20.1.20.

### COMMANDING OFFICERS
S/Cdr ERC Nanson 4.16; Disbanded 12.1.17.

S/Cdr CL Courtney 12.16; S/Cdr JWK Allsop 5.4.17; S/Cdr JT Babington DSO 27.6.17; S/Cdr HA Buss 1.1.18; S/Cdr H Stanley-Adams 20.2.18 (became Mjr wef 1.4.18); Mjr GL Thomson DSC 24.5.18; Mjr TA Batchelor DSC 26.7.18; Mjr GR Elliot 7.8.18; Mjr MHB Nethersole 5.6.19; Disbanded 20.1.20.

### AIRCRAFT - Voisin Biplane, BE2c, Henry Farman F.27, Short 827.

Caudron G.IV, 1½ Strutter, Short Bomber, O/100, O/400.

## No.7A Squadron

### BASES
Formed as 7A Sqdn at Coudekerque 28.7.17 (5 Wing) (formed out of 7 Sqdn when decided HP squadrons should have only 10 a/c); Became 14 Sqdn RNAS 9.12.17.

### AIRCRAFT - O/100.

## No.8/208 Squadron

### BASES
Formed as 8 Sqdn in UK (Grain?) 3.1.16? [first 4 a/c left Grain 18.1.16 for F/Cdr Nansen's Sqdn - but this was 7 Sqdn!]; In transit in SS *Laconia* .16; arr Chukwani Bay (Zanzibar) 3.16 [referred to as Cape Sqdn by 7.16; East Africa Force by 7.17]; Disbanded wef 12.17.
Detts: Kilwa; HMS *Himalaya* @1.11.16; HMS *Manica* @9.2.17; HMS *Princess* 1.3.17; Lindi 12.3.17; HMS *Manica* 28.3.17; Lindi @7.7.17; Mtua @17.11.17 (Voisins); a dett embarked; HMFA *Trent* 27.5.17; arr Lindi 1.6.17.
(The last batch of personnel and material left Zanzibar on or about 17.4.18)

(A detached sqdn with no number was attached 22 Wing 5 Bde by 11.10.16, and formed the nucleus of another 8 Sqdn, operating at the same time as the 8 Sqdn in East Africa, as follows)

Reformed from flights of 1, 4 and 5 Wings as 8 Sqdn at St.Pol 25.10.16 [comprised A Flt ex 4 Wing with 6 Nieuport "17B" (80-hp Le Rhone), B Flt ex 1 Wing with 6 Pup (80-hp Le Rhone) & C Flt ex 5 Wing with 6 Strutter (110-hp Clerget)]; Vert Galant 26.10.16 (22 Wing 5 Bde); St.Pol 3.2.17 (Dunkerque Command & Dover Patrol) (for a rest and re-equipment. A/c split into 8 & 9

Sqdns. Relieved by 3 Sqdn); Furnes 14.2.17 (22 Wing 5 Bde); Lozinghem (Auchel) 27.3.17 (10 Wing 1 Bde); Mont St.Eloi 16.5.17 (10 Wing 1 Bde) (attd 22 Wg 10.17?); Bray Dunes (Middle aerodrome) 1.3.18 (Dunkerque Command & Dover Patrol); Walmer 3.3.18 (Dunkerque Command & Dover Patrol) (for a rest and reformed); Bray Dunes (Middle aerodrome) 28.3.18 (4 Wing); Teteghem 30.3.18 (4 Wing); Became 208 Sqdn 1.4.18 (64 Wing 7 Bde); La Gorgue 2.4.18 (10 Wing 1 Bde); Serny 9.4.18 (10 Wing 1 Bde); Tramecourt 30.7.18 (10 Wing 1 Bde); Foucacourt 23.9.18 (10 Wing 1 Bde, to 22 Wing 5 Bde 29.9.18); Estreés-en-Chaussée 9.10.18 (22 Wing 5 Bde); Maretz 26.10.18 (22 Wing 5 Bde); Stree 3.12.18 (22 Wing 5 Bde); Donstiennes by 25.12.18 (22 Wing 5 Bde); Heumer 19.5.19 (22 Wing 5 Bde, to 11 Wing 2 Bde 20.5.19); Eil 7.8.19; Netheravon 29.8.19 (absorbed into Flying School Netheravon 5.9.19); Disbanded 7.11.19.

### COMMANDING OFFICERS
S/Cdr FW Bowhill by 31.5.16 (later W/Cdr); Disbanded in East Africa 12.17.

F/Cdr GR Bromet DSO 25.10.16 (became S/Cdr 31.12.16); S/Cdr C Draper 28.10.17 (became Mjr wef 1.4.18); Mjr HG Smart 14.1.19; - ? - 27.8.19; Disbanded 7.11.19

### AIRCRAFT - Voisin Biplane, Short 827.
Nieuport 11, Nieuport 17bis, Nieuport 21, 1½ Strutter, Pup, Sopwith Triplane, F.1 Camel, Snipe.

## No.9/209 Squadron

### BASES
Formed as 9 Sqdn from a nucleus of 8 Sqdn at St.Pol 1.2.17 (1 Wing); Furnes 2.4.17 (4 Wing); Flez 15.6.17 (14 Wing 4 Bde); Guizancourt 16.6.17 (14 Wing to 1.7.17, then 13 Wing 3 Bde); Izel-le Hameau 5.7.17 (13 Wing 3 Bde); Bray Dunes (Frontier aerodrome) 10.7.17 (14 Wing 4 Bde); Leffrinckhoucke 25.7.17 (14 Wing 4 Bde); Bray Dunes (Frontier aerodrome) 28.9.17 (4 Wing); Bray Dunes (Middle aerodrome) 10.10.17 (4 Wing); Dover (for a rest) 8.2.18; Bray Dunes (Middle aerodrome) 19-21.3.18 (4 Wing); Cappelle 23.3.18 (4 Wing); Bailleul (Asylum aerodrome) 27.3.18 (11 Wing 2 Bde); Clairmarais North 29.3.18 (11 Wing 2 Bde); Became 209 Sqdn 1.4.18; Bertangles 7.4.18 (22 Wing 5 Bde); Quelmes 20.7.18 (11 Wing 2 Bde); Bertangles 6.8.18 (22 Wing 5 Bde); Izel-le-Hameau 14.8.18 (10 Wing 1 Bde); Bruille 24.10.18 (10 Wing 1 Bde to 1.11.18 then 91 Wing 1 Bde); Saultain 22.11.18 (91 Wing 1 Bde); Froidmont (cadre) 11.12.18 (91 Wing 1 Bde to 17.1.19, then 11 Wing 2 Bde); Scopwick (cadre) 13.2.19 (59 Wing); Disbanded 24.6.19.

### COMMANDING OFFICERS
S/Cdr H Fawcett 1.2.17; S/Cdr TC Vernon 23.8.17; S/Cdr EW Norton 15.9.18; S/Cdr CH Butler 31.1.18 (became Mjr wef 1.4.18); Mjr JO Andrews DSO MC 6.5.18; Mjr TFN Gerrard DSC 12.9.18; Mjr RF Redpath 18.11.18.

### AIRCRAFT - Nieuport 10, Nieuport 11, Nieuport 12, Nieuport 17bis, Nieuport 21, 1½ Strutter, Pup, Sopwith Triplane, F.1 Camel.

## No.10/210 Squadron

### BASES
Formed as 10 Sqdn at St.Pol 12.2.17 (4 Wing); Furnes 28.3.17; Droglandt 15.5.17 (11 Wing 2 Bde, to 22 Wing 5 Bde 13.6.17); Leffrinckhoucke 5.10.17 (14 Wing 5 Bde); Téteghem 20.11.17 (4 Wing) [dett 3 a/c Berck-sur-Mer 28.2.17 to 4.1.18]; Eringhem 30.3.18 (1 Wing); Treizennes 31.3.18 (10 Wing 1 Bde); Became 210 Sqdn 1.4.18; Liettres 9.4.18 (10 Wing 1 Bde); St.Omer 27.4.18 (11 Wing 2 Bde); Ste Marie Capelle 30.5.18 (11 Wing 2 Bde, to 22 Wing 5 Bde 13.6.18); Téteghem 8.7.18 (61 Wing 5 Gp); Eringhem 22.7.18 (61 Wing 5 Gp); Boussieres 23.10.18 (13 Wing 3 Bde); Scopwick (Digby) 17.2.19; Disbanded 24.6.19.

### COMMANDING OFFICERS
S/Cdr CD Breese 12.2.17; 21.4.17; S/Cdr BC Bell DSO DSC 21.4.17; A/S/Cdr RF Redpath 28.9.17; S/Cdr BC Bell DSO DSC 1.10.17 (became Mjr wef 1.4.18); Capt FC Gorringe 8.1.19; Capt AW Carter DSC 2.19; Disbanded 24.6.19.

### AIRCRAFT - Nieuport 12, Sopwith Triplane, F.1 Camel.

## No.11/211 Squadron

BASES
As 11 Sqdn at Maktau (German East Africa) 1.9.15(?) to at least 4.16. [this designation appears to have been briefly used for Cull's party]

Refd as 11 Sqdn at Petite Synthe 8.3.17 (4 Wing); Hondschoote 20.4.17 (4 Wing); Bray Dunes (Frontier aerodrome) 6.7.17 (4 Wing); Disbanded 27.8.17 (owing to shortage of pilots)

Refd as 11 Sqdn at Petite Synthe 11.3.18 (5 Wing); Became 211 Sqdn 1.4.18 (65 Wing 7 Bde; Wing to 5 Bde 5.18; under SHQ by 8.6.18; to 10 Bde 18.6.18); Clary (Iris Farm) 24.10.18 (22 Wing 5 Bde); Thuillies 3.12.18 (22 Wing 5 Bde); Wyton 15.3.19; Thetford 4.19; Disbanded 24.6.19.

COMMANDING OFFICERS
S/Cdr JT Cull by 12.15 - @4.16.

F/Cdr HG Travers 8.3.17; S/Cdr H Stanley-Adams 6.17; Disbanded 27.8.17.
S/Cdr HG Travers DSC 1.10.17 (became Mjr wef 1.4.18); Mjr R Loraine DSO MC 26.5.18; Mjr GRM Reid DSO MC 25.7.18; Capt HN Lett 10.3.19; Disbanded 24.6.19.

AIRCRAFT - Caudron G.III.

Nieuport 10, Nieuport 11, Nieuport 17bis, Nieuport 21, Sopwith Triplane, Pup, F.1 Camel.

D.H.4, D.H.9, D.H.9A

## No.12/212 Squadron

BASES
Formed as 12 Sqdn at Hondschoote 8.6.17 (5 Wing) [formed from No.1 Wing as a training squadron]; Petite Synthe 1.7.17 (5 Wing); Disbanded 1.4.18.
Refd as 212 Sqdn at Yarmouth 20.8.18; Disbanded 9.2.20

COMMANDING OFFICERS
S/Cdr EW Norton 1.7.17; S/Cdr AR Arnold 15.9.17 - @3.1.18; Disbanded 1.4.18
Mjr E Cadbury DSC DFC 20.8.18 - @1.19; Disbanded 9.2.20.

AIRCRAFT - Pup, Sopwith Triplane, F.1 Camel.

D.H.4, D.H.9A.

## No.13/213 Squadron

BASES
Formed as 13 Sqdn from Seaplane Defence Squadron at St.Pol 15.1.18 (1 Wing); Bergues 23.1.18 (1 Wing); Varssenaere 28.10.18 (1 Wing); Became 213 Sqdn 1.4.18 (61 Wing 5 Group); Eringhem 11.18 (5 Group); Stalhille 27.11.18 (5 Group); Sherburn-in-Elmet (cadre) 1.19 (16 Group); Scopwick 19.3.19 (3 Group); Disbanded 31.12.19.

COMMANDING OFFICERS
S/Cdr R Collishaw DSO DSC 15.1.18; Mjr R Graham DSO DFC 5.18; Disbanded 31.12.19.

AIRCRAFT - F.1 Camel.

## No.14/214 Squadron

BASES
Formed ex 7A Sqdn as 14 Sqdn at Coudekerque 9.12.17 (5 Wing); Alquines 10.3.18 (5 Wing) (became training squadron); Coudekerque 26.3.18 (5 Wing); Became 214 Sqdn 1.4.18 (65 Wing 7 Bde, to 82 Wing 5 Group 4.6.18); St.Inglevert 29.6.18 (82 Wing 5 Group); Quilen 24.10.18 (82 Wing 9 Bde); Chemy 30.10.18 (82 Wing 9 Bde to 22.10.18, then 54 Wing 9 Bde to 28.4.19, then 9 Wing 9 Bde); Posted to Egypt [aircraft left Paris/Buc from 6.7.19; arrived from 29.7.19 via Marseilles, Pisa, Rome, Taranto, Suda Bay, Mersa Matruh]; Heliopolis 29.7.19 (Palestine Brigade); Abu Sueir by 4.9.19 (Palestine Brigade); Disbanded 1.2.20 (absorbed into 216 Sqdn).

COMMANDING OFFICERS
S/Cdr HG Brackley DSO DSC 9.12.17 (became Mjr wef 1.4.18); Mjr WL Welsh DSC 26.3.19 - 8.19; Mjr Brown @ 7.19?

AIRCRAFT - O/100, O/400.

## No.15/215 Squadron

BASES
Formed as 15 Sqdn from personnel of 7 & 14 Sqdn at Coudekerque 10.3.18 (5 Wing); Became 215 Sqdn 1.4.18 (65 Wing 7 Bde); Netheravon 23.4.18 (4 Wing); Andover 13.5.18 (33 Wing); Alquines 4.7.18 (54 Wing 9 Bde); Xaffévillers 19.8.18 (83 Wing 8 Bde); Alquines 17.11.18 (83 Wing 8 Bde); Ford Junction 2.2.19 (21 Wing); Disbanded 18.10.19.

COMMANDING OFFICERS
F/Cdr JF Jones DSC 10.3.18 (became Mjr wef 1.4.18); Mjr GL Thomson DSC DFC 27.7.18.

AIRCRAFT - O/100, O/400.

## No.16/216 Squadron

BASES
Formed ex A Sqdn RNAS as 16 Sqdn at Ochey 8.1.18 (41 Wing GHQ Brigade - Wing to 8 Bde 1.2.18); Ochey Woods 15.3.18; Villeneuve 30.3.18 (41 Wing 8 Bde); Became 216 Sqdn 1.4.18 (dett Cramaille 20.4.18 - 13.5.18); Ochey 9.5.18 (41 Wing 8 Bde, to 83 Wing 8 Bde 2.7.18); Autreville 12.8.18 (83 Wing 8 Bde); Roville-aux-Chenes 28.9.18 (83 Wing 8 Bde); Quilen 17.11.18 (83 Wing 8 Bde); Marquise 14.12.18 (83 Wing 8 Bde, to 89 Wing HQ Wing by 2.19); In transit to Egypt 5.19; Kantara 8.7.19 (Palestine Brigade) [Continued as Transport squadron until 1975].

COMMANDING OFFICERS
S/Cdr KS Savory DSO 8.1.18; S/Cdr HA Buss DSC 19.1.18 (became Mjr wef 1.4.18); Mjr WR Read MC DFC AFC 1.9.18; Mjr HA Buss DSC 5.3.19; S/Ldr CH Nicholas AFC by 12.19 - 12.20.

AIRCRAFT - FE2b, O/100, O/400.

## No.17/217 Squadron

BASES
Formed as 17 Sqdn to replace RNAS Seaplane Base Dunquerke at Dunkerque 14.1.18 (1 Wing); Bergues 1.2.18 (1 Wing); Became 217 Sqdn 1.4.18 (61 Wing 5 Group); Crochte 5.7.18 (61 Wing 5 Group); Varssenaere 23.10.18 (1 Wing? 5 Group); Dover 20.2.19 (5 Group); Dunkerque by 3.19 (5 Group); in transit 25-26.3.19; Dover (Guston Road) 27.3.19 (5 Group); Disbanded 19.10.19; Driffield (cadre) 28.3.19; Disbanded 19.10.19.

COMMANDING OFFICER
S/Cdr WL Welsh DSC 14.1.18 - @4.19 (became Mjr wef 1.4.18) .

AIRCRAFT - D.H.4, D.H.9.

## No.218 Squadron

BASES
Formed at Dover (Guston Road) 24.4.18 (7 Bde); Petite Synthe 23.5.18 (61 Wing 5 Group); Fréthun 7.7.18 (82 Wing 5 Group); Reumont 23.10.18 8 (9 Wing 5 Bde); Vert Galant 16.11.18 (90 Wing 3 Bde); Hucknall (cadre) 7.2.19 (27 Wing); Disbanded 24.6.19.

COMMANDING OFFICERS
Mjr BS Wemp DFC 24.4.18; Mjr CH Hayward 28.12.18 - @1.19.

AIRCRAFT
D.H.4, D.H.9

## No.219 Squadron
Formed at Westgate 22.7.18 (included 406, 442, 470, 555 & 556 Flts); Disbanded 7.2.20.

COMMANDING OFFICER
Mjr GE Livock 22.7.18 to 7.19.

AIRCRAFT - Baby, Hamble Baby, H.12, Short 184, IIIB, D.H.9, B.E.2c, 504, Camel, CE1, N.2B, H.16.

## No.220 Squadron

BASES
Formed ex C Sqdn 2 Wing at Imbros wef 1.4.18 (62 Wing) [ex Recce Sqdn Aegean]; mobile 9.18 (62 Wing 15 Group) (included 475, 476 & 477 Flts) (dett San Stephano); Did not actively adopt 220 Sqdn numberplate until 9.18; Pizzone 11.18 (62 Wing); Mudros 12.18 (62 Wing); Imbros 12.18 (by 14.11.18); Mudros 2.19 (as cadre); Disbanded 21.5.19.

COMMANDING OFFICERS
Mjr FJE Feeney @ 7.18 - @18.9.18; Mjr JO Andrews 10.18.

AIRCRAFT - F.1 Camel, D.H.4, D.H.9.

## No.221 Squadron

BASES
Formed ex D Sqdn 2 Wing at Stavros wef 1.4.18 (62 Wing; to 15 Group 9.18) [ex Anti-submarine Sqdn (Aegean)] (included 552, 553 & 554 Flts from 9.18); Did not actively adopt 221 Sqdn numberplate until 9.18; Absorbed into 222 Sqdn Mudros 15.10.18.

Reformed as mobile sqdn at Lemnos 20.12.18 - @23.12.18; Mudros 12.18; HMS *Riviera* 29.12.18 (first flight embarked for service in South Russia remainder of sqdn mobilising; also embarked HMS *Empress*); Batum 5.1.19; Baku 9.1.19 (flt arrived); Petrovsk Kaskar 12.1.19 (D.H.9 flt arrived 14.1.19) (detts Chechen & Lagan) (joined up with "Norperforce" from Persia 3.19); Began evacuating 18.8.19; Disbanded 1.9.19.

COMMANDING OFFICERS
- ? - 1.4.18; Mjr AFF Jacob 8.18; Disbanded 10.18

Mjr JO Andrews 20.12.18; Mjr Baron de Ville 4.19; Disbanded 1.9.19.

AIRCRAFT - D.H.4, D.H.6, D.H.9, F.1 Camel.

D.H.4, D.H.9A.

## No.222 Squadron

BASES
Formed ex A & Z Sqdns 2 Wing at Thasos wef 1.4.18 (63 Wing; 62 Wing 15 Group by 22.9.18) [ex No.1 Fighter Sqdn (Aegean)] (dett Stavros by 1.5.18); Marian 13.5.18; Mudros 22.5.18; Imbros 6.7.18; Mudros 7.7.18; Did not actively adopt 222 Sqdn numberplate until 9.18 (included 478, 479 & 480 Flts from 9.18); Mudros by 27.10.18 (Adv Base Dedea Gatch by 27-28.10.18); San Stephano 14.11.18; Mudros 23.11.18; Disbanded 27.2.19.

COMMANDING OFFICER
W/Cdr REC Peirse DSO 1.4.18.

AIRCRAFT - F.1 Camel, 1½ Strutter, D.H.4, D.H.6, D.H.9.

## No.223 Squadron

BASES [very complex, but appears to be as follows]
Formed ex B Sqdn 2 Wing at Mitylene wef 1.4.18 (62/63 Wing) [ex No.2 Fighter Sqdn (Aegean)]; Stavros 21.4.18; Mitylene by 1.5.18; Disbanded .18 (Did not actively adopt 223 Sqdn numberplate)

Refd at Stavros .18 (62/63 Wing); Disbanded 7.18.

Refd from Seaplane Unit Otranto at Otranto 7.18 (66 Wing); Redes 263 Sqdn 27.9.18.

Refd as mobile bombing sqdn 9.18 (62 Wing 15 Group); to Lemnos Is (Mudros) 11.18 (62 Wing 15 Group) (included 559, 560 & 561 Flts from 9.18); Disbanded 16.5.19.

COMMANDING OFFICERS
Mjr AB Gaskell DSC @18.9.18; Mjr HF de la Rue DFC @ 10.18.

AIRCRAFT - F.1 Camel, D.H.4, D.H.9, D.H.9A, Short 184.

## No.224 Squadron

BASES
Formed from the D.H.4 bombing flights of 6 Wing at Alimini (Otranto) wef 1.4.18 - @20.6.18 (67 Wing) [ex Anti-submarine sqdn, Otranto]; Andrano 14.6.18 (included 496, 497 & 498 Flts from 9.18); Pizzone 9.12.18; Disbanded 15.4.19.

COMMANDING OFFICER
Mjr JSF Morrison 1.4.18 - @10.18.

AIRCRAFT - 1½ Strutter, D.H.4, D.H.9, F.1 Camel.

## No.225 Squadron

BASES
Formed from part of 6 Wing at Alimini (Otranto) wef 1.4.18 (67 Wing Adriatic Group) [ex Fighter sqdn, Otranto]; Andrano 14.6.18 (included 481, 482 & 483 Flts from 9.18); Pizzone 9.11.18; Disbanded 19.12.18.

COMMANDING OFFICER
Mjr T Hinshelwood 1.4.18; Disbanded 19.12.18.

AIRCRAFT - 1½ Strutter, F.1 Camel, Hamble Baby Convert.

## No.226 Squadron

BASES
Formed from the D.H.4 bombing unit [or Bombing Sqdn] at Pizzone wef 1.4.18 (67 Wing); to Otranto 5.18 (67 Wing); to Pizzone 19?.6.18 (67 Wing) (included 472, 473 & 474 Flts from 9.18); Andrano 1.10.18 (detd for ops); Pizzone 3.10.18; Andrano 9.10.18; Marsh (Lemnos) by 14.10.18 [now 62 Wing]; Albania 13.10.18 (en route for Macedonian front); Mudros 10.18; Pizzone 11.11.18 (63 Wing 15 Group); Disbanded 18.12.18.

COMMANDING OFFICERS
Mjr MS Marsden 1.4.18; Mjr RFS Leslie DSC DFC AFC 19.4.18; Disbanded 18.12.18.

AIRCRAFT - 1½ Strutter, D.H.4, D.H.9, D.H.9A.

## No.227 Squadron

BASES
Formed from comms sqdn 6 Wing at Pizzone wef 1.4.18 66 Wing (later 67 Wing Adriatic Group) [OR ex Caproni sqdn, Taranto] (included 499, 550 & 551 Flts from 9.18); Disbanded 9.12.18. [Squadron never fully established. Various conflicting reports. One dated 8.9.18 said sqdn not yet formed, to be twin-engined Caproni biplane, but under consideration to be D.H.9 unit. Another says formed 1.7.18 but never operational. Yet another says not formed by 1.11.18]

AIRCRAFT - Caproni Ca.4, 1½ Strutter, D.H.4, D.H.9.

## No.228 Squadron

BASES
Formed from Boat Flight at Yarmouth 20.8.18 (73 Wing 4 Group) - @1.3.19 (included 324, 325 & 326 Flts); to Killingholme .19; Disbanded 30.6.19.

COMMANDING OFFICERS
Mjr R Leckie DSO DSC DFC 20.8.18; Mjr SJ Fetherston 1.19; Disbanded 30.6.19.

AIRCRAFT - H.16, F.2A.

## No.229 Squadron

BASES
Formed from Short & Schneider Flights at Yarmouth 20.8.18 (73 Wing 4 Group) (inc 428, 429, 454 & 455 Flts); Disb 31.12.19.

COMMANDING OFFICERS
Capt BCH Cross (temp) 20.8.18; Mjr AB Gaskell DSO 21.9.18; Mjr H Stewart by 10.18; Mjr AB Gaskell DSO by 1.19.

AIRCRAFT - Short 184, Schneider, Baby, Fairey IIIC.

## No.230 Squadron

BASES
Formed out of the Anti Submarine Patrol Unit at Felixstowe
20.8.18 (70 Wing 4 Group) (included 327, 328 & 487 Flts);
Calshot 7.5.22; Became 480 Flt 1.4.23.

COMMANDING OFFICERS
Capt CJ Clayton 20.8.18; W/Cdr CE Risk OBE 9.10.19; S/L FGD
Hards DSC DFC 21.5.20; W/Cdr IT Courtney 12.20; Disbanded
1.4.23.

AIRCRAFT - H.12, H.16, F.2A, F.3, F.5, Short 184, F.1 Camel.

## No.231 Squadron

BASES
Formed out of the Anti Submarine Patrol Unit Felixstowe 20.8.18
70 Wing 4 Group) (included 329, 330 & 487 Flts); Disbanded
7.7.19.

COMMANDING OFFICER
Mjr JO Galpin 20.8.18; Disbanded 7.7.19.

AIRCRAFT - F.2A

## No.232 Squadron

BASES
Formed at Felixstowe 20.8.18 (76 Wing 4 Group, to 70 Wing 4
Group 11.18) (included 333, 334 & 335 Flts); Redes 4 Comms
Sqdn 5.1.19.

COMMANDING OFFICER
Mjr J Gordon DFC 20.8.18; Disbanded 5.1.19.

AIRCRAFT - F.2A.

## No.233 Squadron

BASES
Formed at Dover 31.8.18 (5 Group) (included 407, 471 & 491
Flts); Disbanded 15.5.19.

COMMANDING OFFICERS
Capt HV German (temp) 31.8.18 - @27.10.18; Capt AC Reid by
10.11.18; Mjr R Graham DSO DSC DFC 21.11.18; Disbanded
15.5.19.

AIRCRAFT - F.2A, Wight SP, Short 184, F.1 Camel, D.H.4,
D.H.9.

## No.234 Squadron

BASES
Formed ex RAF Seaplane Base Scillies at Tresco 20.8.18 (71
Wing 9 Group) (included 350, 351, 352 & 353 Flts); Disbanded
15.5.19.

COMMANDING OFFICERS
Mjr RB Maycock 20.8.18; Mjr GH Cox 1.19; Disbanded 15.5.19.

AIRCRAFT - F.3, Short 184, H.12B.

## No.235 Squadron

BASES
Formed at Newlyn 20.8.18 (71 Wing 9 Group) (included 424 &
425 Flts); Disbanded 22.2.19.

COMMANDING OFFICER
Mjr AK Robertson 20.8.18; Disbanded 15.5.19.

AIRCRAFT - Short 184.

## No.236 Squadron

BASES
Formed at Mullion 20.8.18 (71 Wing 9 Group) (included 493,
515 & 516 Flts); Disbanded 15.5.19.

COMMANDING OFFICERS
Mjr RBB Colmore 20.8.18; Disbanded 15.5.19

AIRCRAFT - 1½ Strutter, D.H.6, D.H.9.

## No.237 Squadron

BASES
Formed at Cattewater 20.8.18 (72 Wing 9 Group) (included 421,
422 & 423 Flts); Disbanded 15.5.19.

AIRCRAFT - Short 184.

## No.238 Squadron

BASES
Formed at Cattewater 20.8.18 (74 Wing 9 Group) (included 347,
348 & 349 Flts); Disbanded 15.5.19.

COMMANDING OFFICER
Mjr RH Kershaw 20.8.18; Disbanded 15.5.19.

AIRCRAFT - H.16, F.3, F.5.

## No.239 Squadron

BASES
Formed at Torquay 20.8.18 (72 Wing 9 Group) (included 418
Flt); Disbanded 15.5.19.

COMMANDING OFFICER
Capt NG Stewart Dawson DSC 20.8.18; Disbanded 15.5.19.

AIRCRAFT - Short 184.

## No.240 Squadron

BASES
Formed at Calshot 20.8.18 (74 Wing 10 Group) (included 345,
346 & 410 Flts); Disbanded 15.5.19.

COMMANDING OFFICER
Mjr CW Scott 20.8.18; Disbanded 15.5.19.

AIRCRAFT - Short 320, Short 184, Campania, H.12, F.2A.

## No.241 Squadron

BASES
Formed at Portland 20.8.18 (75 Wing 10 Group) (included 416,
417 & 513 Flts); Disbanded 18.6.19.

COMMANDING OFFICER
Mjr JK Waugh DSC 20.8.18; Disbanded 18.6.19.

AIRCRAFT - Wight SP, Short 184, Campania, D.H.6, F.2A.

## No.242 Squadron

BASES
Formed at Newhaven 15.8.18 (75 Wing 10 Group) (included 408,
409 & 514 Flts); Disbanded 15.5.19.

COMMANDING OFFICER
Mjr TW Elsdon 20.8.18; Disbanded 15.5.19.

AIRCRAFT - Short 184, Campania, D.H.6.

## No.243 Squadron

BASES
Formed at Cherbourg 20.8.18 (75 Wing 10 Group) (included 414
& 415 Flts); Disbanded 15.3.19.

COMMANDING OFFICERS
Mjr CW Scott 20.8.18; Disbanded 15.3.19.

AIRCRAFT - Wight SP, Short 184.

## No.244 Squadron

BASES
Formed at Bangor 15.8.18 (77 Wing 14 Group) (included 521, 522 & 530 Flts); Disbanded 22.1.19.

COMMANDING OFFICERS
Mjr H Probyn 15.8.18; Disbanded 22.1.19.

AIRCRAFT - D.H.6.

## No.245 Squadron

BASES
Formed at Fishguard 20.8.18 (77 Wing 14 Group) (included 426 & 427 Flts); Disbanded 19.5.19.

COMMANDING OFFICERS
Mjr FD Till 20.8.18; Mjr LF Forbes MC 4.19; Disbanded 19.5.19.

AIRCRAFT - Hamble Baby, Short 184.

## No.246 Squadron

BASES
Formed at Seaton Carew 15.8.18 (68 Wing 18 Group) (included 402, 403, 451, 452 & 495 Flts); Disbanded 31.5.19.

COMMANDING OFFICERS
Capt GC Deans 15.8.18; Mjr MA Simpson 18.12.18; Disbanded 31.5.19.

AIRCRAFT - D.H.6, Baby, Short 184, Kangaroo.

## No.247 Squadron

BASES
Formed at Felixstowe 20.8.18 (76 Wing later 40 Wing 4 Group) (included 336, 337 & 338 Flts); Disbanded 22.1.19.

COMMANDING OFFICER
Capt AT Barker 20.8.18; Disbanded 22.1.19.

AIRCRAFT - F.2A.

## No.248 Squadron

BASES
Formed at Hornsea 20.8.18 (79 Wing 18 Group) (included 404, 405 & 453 Flts); Disbanded 6.3.19.

COMMANDING OFFICER
Capt HC Mallet 20.8.18; Disbanded 6.3.19.

AIRCRAFT - Baby, Schneider, Short 184.

## No.249 Squadron

BASES
Formed at Dundee 18.8.18 (78 Wing 18 Group) (included 400, 401 & 450 Flts); Disbanded 8.10.19.

COMMANDING OFFICERS
Mjr (later L/Col) EVS Wilberforce 18.8.18; Mjr JEB MacLean 8.19; Disbanded 8.10.19.

AIRCRAFT - Short 184, Baby.

## No.250 Squadron

BASES
Formed at Padstow 1.5.18 (71 Wing 9 Group) (included 494, 500 & 501 Flts); Disbanded 15.5.19.

COMMANDING OFFICERS
Mjr RE Orton 31.5.18 - @22.6.18; Mjr FW Merriam AFC @ 11.18; Disbanded 15.5.19.

AIRCRAFT - D.H.6, D.H.9.

## No.251 Squadron

BASES
Formed at Hornsea 1.5.18 (79 Wing 18 Group) (included 504, 505, 506 & 510 Flts); Disbanded 30.6.19.

COMMANDING OFFICER
Mjr JD Maude 1.5.18 - @8.18; Disbanded 30.6.19.

AIRCRAFT - D.H.6.

## No.252 Squadron

BASES
Formed at Tynemouth 1.5.18 (68 Wing 18 Group) (included 451, 452, 495, 507, 508, 509 & 510 Flts); Killingholme (cadre) 31.1.19; Disbanded 30.6.19.

COMMANDING OFFICER
Mjr RM Everett 7.5.18; Disbanded 8.10.19.

AIRCRAFT - D.H.6, Baby, Kangaroo.

## No.253 Squadron

BASES
Formed at Bembridge 7.6.18 (75 Wing 18 Group) (included 412, 413, 511, 512 & 513 Flts); Disbanded 5.5.19.

COMMANDING OFFICER
Mjr A Durston 7.6.18; Disbanded 5.5.19.

AIRCRAFT - D.H.6, Short 184.

## No.254 Squadron

BASES
Formed at Prawle Point 31.5.18 (72 Wing 9 Group) (included 492, 515, 516, 517 & 518 Flts); Disbanded 22.2.19.

COMMANDING OFFICER
Mjr FG Andreae 31.5.18; Disbanded 22.2.19.

AIRCRAFT - D.H.6, D.H.9.

## No.255 Squadron

BASES
Formed at Pembroke by 25.5.18 (77 Wing 14 Group) (included 519, 520, 521, 522, 523 & 524 Flts); Disbanded 14.1.19.

COMMANDING OFFICERS
Capt RR Soar 11.6.18; Mjr RG Gould by 7.9.18 - @3.11.18; Disbanded 8.10.19.

AIRCRAFT - D.H.6.

## No.256 Squadron

BASES
Formed at Sea Houses 6.18 (68 Wing 18 Group) (included 495, 525, 526, 527 & 528 Flts); Disbanded 30.6.19.

COMMANDING OFFICERS
- ? - 7.18; Mjr JCP Wood by 18.12.18; Disbanded 8.10.19.

AIRCRAFT - D.H.6, Kangaroo.

## No.257 Squadron

BASES
Formed at Dundee 7.18 (78 Wing 22 Group); (included 318 & 319 Flts); Disbanded 30.6.19.

COMMANDING OFFICERS
- ? - 7.18; Mjr HdeV Leigh by 12.18; Disbanded 30.6.19.

AIRCRAFT - H.16, F.2A.

## No.258 Squadron

BASES
Formed at Luce Bay  15.8.18 (18 Group)  (included 523, 524 & 529 Flts); Sqdn demobilized 9.12.18; Disbanded 5.3.19.

COMMANDING OFFICERS
Mjr EE Clarke 15.8.18; Disbanded 5.3.19.

AIRCRAFT - D.H.6.

## No.259 Squadron

BASES
Formed at Sea Houses  7.18 (76 Wing 4 Group, later 70 Wing 4 Group)  (included 342, 343 & 344 Flts); Disbanded 13.8.19.
[though probably only ever existed on paper]

COMMANDING OFFICERS
- ? - 7.18; Capt EJ Webster by 1.19; Disbanded 13.8.19.

AIRCRAFT - F.2A.

## No.260 Squadron

BASES
Formed at Westward Ho!  15.8.18 (71 Wing 9 Group)  (included 502 & 503 Flts); Disbanded 22.2.19.

AIRCRAFT- D.H.6.

## No.261 Squadron

BASES
Formed at Felixstowe  20.8.18 (76 Wing 4 Group later 70 Wing 4 Group)  (included 339, 340 & 341 Flts); Disbanded 13.9.19.
[though probably only ever existed on paper]

COMMANDING OFFICERS
Capt CL Scott 20.8.18; Disbanded 13.9.19.

AIRCRAFT - F.2A.

## No.263 Squadron

BASES
Formed at Otranto  27.9.18 (66 Wing 6 Group)  (included 359, 435, 436 & 441 Flts); to Taranto 11.18; Disbanded 16.5.19.

AIRCRAFT - Short 320, Short 184, Baby, F.3.

## No.264 Squadron

BASES
Formed at Suda Bay  27.9.18 (63 Wing 15 Group)  (included 439 & 440 Flts); Disbanded 1.3.19.

COMMANDING OFFICER
Mjr RM Field 27.9.18; Disbanded 1.3.19.

AIRCRAFT - Short 184.

## No.265 Squadron

BASES
To form at Gibraltar  .18 (HQ RAF Mediterranean)  (was to include 364, 365 & 366 Flts); Sqdn never actually came into existence.

AIRCRAFT - F.3 intended.

## No.266 Squadron

BASES
Formed at Mudros  27.9.18 (66 Wing 6 Group)  (included 437 & 438 Flts); to South Russia; Talikna by 24.1.19; HMS *Engadine* 18.2.19; Petrovsk 12.3.19  (2nd flt disembarked 20.3.19; HMS *Alader Youssanoff* 18.5.19; Petrovsk 11.7.19; HMS *Orlionoch* 27.7.19; transit 27.8.19; Novorossisk 29.8.19; HMS *Grafton* 30.8.19; Disbanded 1.9.19; Ship arr home 17.10.19

COMMANDING OFFICER
Capt JA Sadler 1.2.19; Disbanded 1.9.19.

AIRCRAFT - Short 320, Short 184.

## No.267 Squadron

BASES
Formed at Calafrana  27.9.18 (17 Wing)  (included 360, 361, 362 & 363 Flts); Redes 481 Flt 1.8.23.

COMMANDING OFFICERS
Mjr AE Pettingell 27.9.18; - ? - 3.19; S/L E Osmond CBE by 6.20; S/L AJ Miley OBE 6.2.23; Disbanded 1.8.23.

AIRCRAFT - Short 184, F.2A, F.3, IIID.

## No.268 Squadron

BASES
Formed at Calafrana  27.9.18 (17 Wing)  (included 433 & 434 Flts); Disbanded 11.10.19.

COMMANDING OFFICERS
Mjr AM Cave 27.9.18; Disbanded 11.10.19.

AIRCRAFT - Short 184, Short 320.

## No.269 Squadron

BASES
Formed at Port Said  6.10.18 (64 Wing)  (included 431 & 432 Flts); Alexandria 15.9.19 (64 Wing); Redes 481 Flt 15.11.19.

COMMANDING OFFICERS
Mjr PL Holmes DSC 6.10.18; F/L H Stewart by 9.19; S/Ldr KC Buss 10.19; Disbanded 15.11.19.

AIRCRAFT - Short 184, BE2e, D.H.9.

## No.270 Squadron

BASES
Formed at Alexandria  6.10.18 (64 Wing)  (included 360, 361, 362 & 363 Flts); Disbanded 15.9.19 (merged into 269 Sqdn).

COMMANDING OFFICER
Mjr EJ Hodsoll 6.10.18; Disbanded 15.9.19.

AIRCRAFT - Short 184, F.3, D.H.9.

## No.271 Squadron

BASES
Formed at Taranto  27.9.18 (66 Wing Adriatic Group)  (included 357, 358 & 367 Flts); (dett Otranto); Disbanded 9.12.18.

AIRCRAFT - Short 184, F.3.

## No.272 Squadron

BASES
Formed at Machrihanish  15.8.18 (25 Group)  (included 531, 532 & 533 Flts); Disbanded 5.3.19.

COMMANDING OFFICERS
Mjr TV Lister 15.8.18; Disbanded 5.3.19.

AIRCRAFT - D.H.6.

## No.273 Squadron

BASES
Formed at Yarmouth  20.8.18 (HQ 4 Wing)  (included 470, 485, 486 & 534 Flts); To cadre 14.3.19; Disbanded 5.7.19.

COMMANDING OFFICERS
Mjr AS Maskell 8.18 - @1.19; Disbanded 5.7.19.

AIRCRAFT - D.H.4, D.H.9, D.H.9A, F.1 Camel, B.E.2c.

## No.274 Squadron

To have formed 11.18 for anti-submarine work with Vimies at Seaton Carew (68 Wing 18 Group). Formed instead as bomber sqdn at Bircham Newton 15.6.19 with V/1500s and a few O/400s.

## A Squadron

BASES
Formed at Manston 5.10.17 (with 10 HPs = 4 from Redcar, 4 from Hendon, 2 from 7 Sqdn Coudekerque); Autreville 11.10.17 (41 Wing GHQ Bde); Ochey 20.11.17; Redes 16 Sqdn 8.1.18.

COMMANDING OFFICER
S/Cdr KS Savory DSO 5.10.17; Redes 16 Sqdn 8.1.18.

AIRCRAFT - O/100, O/400, F.E.2b.

## Seaplane Defence Flight/Squadron

BASES
Formed as Seaplane Defence Flight at St.Pol 30.6.17; Became Seaplane Defence Squadron 23.9.17; Redes 13 Sqdn 15.1.18.

COMMANDING OFFICERS
S/Cdr R Graham 30.6.17; S/Cdr R Collishaw DSO DSC 29.12.17; Redes 13 Sqdn 15.1.18.

AIRCRAFT - Baby, Sopwith Triplane, Pup, F.1 Camel.

## Handley Page Squadron

BASES
Formed at Manston 1.7.16; Luxeuil 21.12.16; Disbanded?
Refd at Manston late .17; Stonehenge 1.2.18 (attached 2 TDS); Disbanded 4.18 into 1 SoAN&BD.

COMMANDING OFFICER
S/Cdr GL Thomson DSC @1.2.18.

AIRCRAFT - O/100, O/400.

## NUMBERED NAVAL FLIGHTS

On or about 25 May 1918, coastal based flights of the Royal Air Force were grouped into small flights, most of which either formed part of squadrons or were later absorbed into newly formed squadrons. This system gradually fell into disuse during 1919, though the 400-series was later resurrected for use by small Fleet Air Arm units when these began to form in April 1923. Numbers were allocated in blocks, as follows

```
300 - 358  Large flying boats [333-344 for Special Service]
400 - 442  Float seaplanes
450 - 455  Sopwith Baby seaplanes
470 - 487  Land fighters
           (against attack of hostile torpedo seaplanes)
490 - 499  Light bombers (anti-submarine patrol)
500 - 533  Special duties (D.H.6 anti-submarine patrols)
           [15 of these planned to be replaced by D.H.9 flights from
           10.18, but NTU]
534        as 490 - 499
550 - 561  as 490 - 499
562        Malta Anti-submarine
```

## 300 (FB) Flight
Formed 15.6.18 at Catfirth (in 28 Group) to at least 3.19, with F.3. Never attached to a squadron.

## 301 to 305 (FB) Flights
Were to have joined 300 Flt at Catfirth, also with F.3, but never formed.

## 306 (FB) Flight
Formed 31.7.18 at Houton Bay (in 28 Group) to at least 3.19, with H.16, F.3 and Short 184. A detachment based at Pierowall for a time from 10.8.18, and another at Dundee from 13.11.18. Never attached to a squadron.

## 307 & 308 (FB) Flights
Due to form at Houton Bay 15.8.18 and 31.8.18 respectively, but NTU.

## 309 to 311 (FB) Flights
Formed at Stenness in 28 Group) 5.18, 31.5.18 and 15.7.18 respectively, with F.3. Never attached to a squadron.

## 312 to 317 (FB) Flights
Were to have formed at Strathbeg (in 22 Group) between 15.7.18 and 15.10.18, but NTU.

## 318 & 319 (FB) Flights
Both formed 30.5.18 at Dundee with F.2A. Joined 257 Sqdn when it formed 7.18. COs were respectively Captains JG Ireland and NH Woodhead in 1918. Both disbanded 30.6.19.

## 320 to 323 (FB) Flights
320 to 322 Flts formed 5.18 at East Halton, Killingholme in 18 Group) with F.2A, H.12, H.12A and H.16, and 323 Flt was to have formed by 31.10.18, but all ceased to exist when the station and aircraft were handed over the US Navy 20.7.18.

## 324 to 326 (FB) Flights
324 and 325 Flts formed 5.18 at Yarmouth, followed by 326 Flt on 15.7.18, all with F.2A. Joined 228 Sqdn when it formed 20.8.18, and all disbanded 30.6.19. COs in 1.19 were respectively Captains J Hodson, AM FitzRandolph and EA Bolton.

## 327 & 328 (FB) Flights
Both formed around 25-30.5.18 at Felixstowe, each with 3+1 F.2A. Joined 230 Sqdn when it formed 20.8.18. Existed to at least 2.19, the CO of 327 Flt in 1.19 being Capt H Rampling.

## 329 & 330 (FB) Flights
Both formed 30.5.18 at Felixstowe, each with 3+1 F.2A. Joined 231 Sqdn when it formed 20.8.18. Both disbanded 7.7.19, the CO of 330 Flt in 1.19 being Capt CW Bailey.

## 331 & 332 (FB) Flights
Were to have formed at Felixstowe 30.9.18 and 15.10.18 (later 15.11.18) respectively, but NTU.

## 333 to 335 (FB) Flights
Formed at Felixstowe 31.5.18, 31.5.18 and 15.6.18 respectively, each with 3+1 F.2A. Joined 232 Sqdn when it formed 20.8.18, this unit becoming No.4 Communications Sqdn 5.1.19. 335 Flt disbanded on that date, but 333 and 334 Flts continued to at least 3.19, the respective COs in 1.19 being Capt JP Barnes and Lt JS Hughes.

## 336 to 338 (FB) Flights
336 Flt formed at Felixstowe 31.7.18, followed by 337 Flight 15.9.18, each with 3+1 F.2A, but 338 Flt never formed (was to have formed 15.9.18). Joined 247 Sqdn when it formed 20.8.18 and both disbanded 22.1.19. Respective COs in 1.19 were Captains LG Maxton and LV Kahn.

## 339 to 341 (FB) Flights
To have formed in 261 Sqdn at Felixstowe on 30.9.18, 15.10.18 and 15.10.18 respectively, each with 3+1 F.2A, but only 339 and 341 Flts existed by 1.19, the former being commanded by Capt HA Wilson. No details of disbandment.

## 342 to 344 (FB) Flights
To have formed in 259 Sqdn at Felixstowe on 31.10.18, 31.10.18 and 15.11.18 respectively, each with 3+1 F.2A, but only a nucleus of 341 Sqdn existed by 1.19. No details of disbandment.

## 345 & 346 (FB) Flights
Formed 5.18 at Calshot, with H.12B and F.2A. Joined 240 Sqdn when it formed 20.8.18, and probably ceased to exist when that unit disbanded 15.5.19.

## 347 to 349 (FB) Flights
Formed at Cattewater on 15.6.18, 15.7.18 and later 15.10.18 respectively, with H.16 and F.3, joining 238 Sqdn when it formed 20.8.18. 347 Flt was to detached to Holy Island mid 11.18, and was at Killingholme 12.18, moving to Calshot 11.12.18, later returning to Cattewater. All existed to at least 3.19, and probably until squadron disbanded 15.5.19,

## 350 to 353 (FB) Flights
Formed at Tresco, Scillies on 31.5.18, 30.6.18, 15.9.18 and 30.9.18 respectively, with F.3, Short 184 and a few H.12, H.12A and FBA. Joined 234 Sqdn when it formed 20.8.18, and all existed to at least 3.19, and 352 and 353 Flts are known to have ceased to exist when squadron disbanded 15.5.19.

## 354 to 356 (FB) Flights
Were to have been part of 270 Sqdn when it formed 6.10.18 at Alexandria with F.3, but no evidence that they ever existed in practice.

## 357 & 358 (FB) Flights
At Taranto in 271 Sqdn when it formed 27.9.18, with F.3. Ceased to exist when squadron disbanded 9.12.18.

## 359 (FB) Flight
Was to have been in 271 Sqdn, but instead joined 263 Sqdn when it formed at Otranto 27.9.18. Moved to January by 1.1.19, probably ceasing to exist when that unit disbanded 16.5.19.

## 360 to 363 (FB) Flights
In 267 Sqdn when it formed at Calafrana 27.9.18, with F.3. All existed to at least 3.19, being subsequently absorbed into the squadron and ceasing to exist.

## 364 to 366 (FB) Flights
To have formed in 265 Sqdn at Gibraltar, but flights and squadron never actually existed.

## 367 (FB) Flight
At Taranto in 271 Sqdn when it formed 27.9.18, with F.3. Ceased to exist when squadron disbanded 9.12.18.

## 400 & 401 (Seaplane) Flights
Formed 30.5.18 at Dundee, with Short 184, joining 248 Sqdn it formed 18.8.18. 401 Flt left 248 Sqdn on moving to Strathbeg 8.18, but rejoined it on returning to Dundee, probably soon after the Armistice; to Killingholme as cadre 3.19, and disbanded there. 401 Flt still at Dundee 3.19, its CO in 1918 being Capt OR Griffin.

## 402 (Seaplane) Flight
Formed 30.6.18 at Seaton Carew, joining 246 Sqdn when it formed 15.8.18, with Short 184. Disbanded 24.3.19.

## 403 (Seaplane) Flight
Formed 5.18 at East Halton, Killingholme with Short 184, Short 320 and Hamble Baby. To Seaton Carew 15.8.18 and joined 246 Sqdn, probably ceasing to exist when that unit disbanded 31.5.19.

## 404 (Seaplane) Flights
Formed 5.18 at East Halton, Killingholme with Short 184. To Hornsea Mere 15.8.18 and joined 248 Sqdn, then to North Coates Fitties 26.9.18, ceasing to exist when the sqdn disbanded 6.3.19.

## 405 (Seaplane) Flight
Formed 15.6.18 at Hornsea Mere with Short 184. Joined 248 Sqdn when it formed 20.8.18, and ceased to exist when the sqdn disbanded 6.3.19.

## 406 (Seaplane) Flight
Formed 25.5.18 at Westgate with Short 184, Baby and Hamble Baby. Became part of 219 Sqdn when it formed 22.7.18. Was to have been re-equipped with Fairey IIIB 30.9.18, but NTU. Commanded by Capt AH Pearce 1.19, and existed to at least 7.19, and possibly until sqdn disbanded 7.2.20.

## 407 (Seaplane) Flight
Formed 20.5.18 at Dover with Short 184 and Baby. Joined 233 Sqdn when it formed 31.8.18, commanded by Capt HV German. Disbanded 31.3.19.

## 408 (Seaplane) Flight
Formed 5.18 at Newhaven with Short 184 and Campania. Joined 242 Sqdn when it formed 15.8.18, still at Newhaven 3.19 and possibly until sqdn disbanded 15.5.19.

## 409 (Seaplane) Flight
Formed 15.8.18 at Newhaven in 242 Sqdn with Short 184. Appears to have disbanded 11.18. To reform 30.11.18 but NTU.

## 410 (Seaplane) Flight
Formed 31.5.18 at Calshot with Short 184, Short 320 and Campania. Joined 240 Sqdn when it formed 20.8.18 and existed to at least 3.19 and possibly ceasing until sqdn disbanded 15.5.19.

## 411 (Seaplane) Flight
To form at Calshot on/by 31.8.18 with Short 184 in 240 Sqdn, but postponed to 9.18, then 15.12.18 and finally cancelled.

## 412 (Seaplane) Flight
Formed 20.5.18 at Bembridge with Short 184 and Campania. Joined 253 Sqdn when it formed 7.6.18 and existed to at least 3.19 and possibly until sqdn disbanded 5.5.19.

## 413 (Seaplane) Flight
Formed 15.9.18 at Bembridge in 253 Sqdn with Short 184, disb around 11.18. To reform 21.12.18 with Short 184 but NTU.

## 414 & 415 (Seaplane) Flights
Formed 5.18 at Cherbourg with Short 184 and Wight seaplanes, becoming part of 243 Sqdn when it formed 20.8.18. Ceased to exist when sqdn disbanded 15.3.19.

## 416 & 417 (Seaplane) Flights
Formed 5.18 and 31.5.18 respectively at Portland with Short 184, Campania and Wight seaplanes, becoming part of 241 Sqdn when it formed 20.8.18. Existed to at least 3.19 and possibly until sqdn disbanded 18.6.19.

## 418 (Seaplane) Flight
Formed 15.6.18 at Torquay with Short 184, becoming part of 239 Sqdn when it formed 20.8.18. Existed to at least 3.19 and possibly until sqdn disbanded 15.5.19.

## 419 (Seaplane) Flight
Was to form at Torquay 31.7.18 but postponed to 8.18 then cancelled. Eventually formed 15.11.18 at Torquay in 239 Sqdn, moving almost immediately to Strathbeg, but instead to Dundee in 249 Sqdn and existed to at least 3.19.

## 420 to 423 (Seaplane ) Flights
All due to form 5.18 at Cattewater with Short 184, but in the event only 420 and 421 Flights actually formed. Became part of 237 Sqdn when it formed 20.8.18, and existed to at least 3.19 and possibly until sqdn disbanded 15.5.19.

## 424 & 425 (Seaplane) Flights
Formed 20.5.18 at Newlyn with Short 184, becoming part of 235 Sqdn when it formed 20.8.18. Ceased to exist when sqdn disbanded 22.2.19.

## 426 & 427 (Seaplane) Flights
Formed 20.5.18 at Fishguard with Short 184, becoming part of 235 Sqdn when it formed 20.8.18. Both existed 11.18 but disbanded soon afterwards.

## 428 & 429 (Seaplane) Flights
Formed 5.18 at Yarmouth each with 6+2 Short 184 and 320, becoming part of 229 Sqdn when it formed 20.8.18. To have received Fairey IIIB 10.18, but never arrived. Existed to at least 1.19.

## 430 (Seaplane) Flight
Formed 5.18 at Houton Bay with Short 184 (in 28 Group), but not attached to a sqdn. Authorised to disband 19.9.18 though still shown on official list dated 1.3.19.

## 431 & 432 (Seaplane) Flights
Authority dated 6.6.18 for both to form at Port Said, and 431 Flt formed there 22.7.18 with Short 184. Doubts as to whether 432 Flt actually formed (or it may have been at Alexandria). Became part of 269 Sqdn when it formed 6.10.18 and existed to at least 3.19.

## 433 & 434 (Seaplane) Flights
Formed around 10.18 at Calafrana, Malta, probably with Short 184, as part of 268 Sqdn. Existed to at least 3.19.

## 435 & 436 (Seaplane) Flights
Formed around 10.18 at Otranto as part of 263 Sqdn, with Short 184 and 320, and Baby. With sqdn to Taranto 11.18, until sqdn disbanded 16.5.19.

**437 (Seaplane) Flight**
Formed around 10.18 at Mudros as part of 266 Sqdn, with Short 184. Also operated from Talikna. Commanded by Capt JA Sadler when absorbed into 266 Sqdn on going to South Russia 1.2.19

**438 (Seaplane) Flight**
Formed around 10.18 at Skyros as part of 266 Sqdn, with Short 184. Ceased to exist 2.19.

**439 (Seaplane) Flight**
Formed around 10.18 at Suda Bay as part of 264 Sqdn, with Short 184. Ceased to exist when sqdn disbanded 1.3.19.

**440 (Seaplane) Flight**
Formed around 10.18 at Syra as part of 264 Sqdn, with Short 184. Ceased to exist when sqdn disbanded 1.3.19.

**441 (Seaplane) Flight**
Formed around 1.10.18 at St.Maria di Leuca as part of 263 Sqdn, with Short 184 and 320, Baby and Hamble Baby. With sqdn to Taranto 11.18, until sqdn disbanded 16.5.19.

**442 (Seaplane) Flight**
Formed 15.10.18 at Felixstowe as part of 219 Sqdn with Fairey IIIB. To Westgate 11.18 and commanded by F/Cdr GH Bittles 1.19. Ceased to exist when sqdn disbanded 7.2.20.

**450 (Baby Seaplane) Flight**
Formed 30.5.18 at Dundee with Baby and Hamble Baby. Joined 249 Sqdn when it formed 18.8.18, and commanded by Lt GAA Pennington. Disbanded 30.9.18.

**451 & 452 (Baby Seaplane) Flights**
Formed 25.5.18 at Seaton Carew as part of 252 Sqdn with Baby. Transferred to 246 Sqdn when it formed 15.8.18, then disbanded 10.10.18 and 31.10.18 respectively.

**453 (Baby Seaplane) Flight**
Formed 30.5.18 at Hornsea Mere with Baby and became part of 248 Sqdn when it formed 20.8.18. Disbanded 30.11.18.

**454 and 455 (Baby Seaplane) Flights**
Formed 25.5.18 and 15.6.18 respectively at Yarmouth with Baby. Became part of 229 Sqdn when it formed and disbanded 30.9.18 and 31.10.18 respectively.

**470 (Fighter) Flight**
Formed 27.5.18 at Manston with 6+2 Camel, also referred to as Tongue Defence Flight or Manston Naval Flight. Became part of 219 Sqdn when it formed 22.7.18, transferring to 273 Sqdn 13.11.18; 3 aircraft detached Bacton 11.11.18 and 3 aircraft detached Burgh Castle 12.11.18. Existed to at least 1.19 when commanded by Capt FC Vincent.

**471 (Fighter) Flight**
Formed 14.6.18 under Capt W.M.Alexander at Walmer with Camel, and joined 233 Sqdn when it formed 31.8.18. Detached to Stalhille (Belgium) 25.10.18, returning to Walmer around 21.1.19. Disbanded 17.3.19, personnel being absorbed into 233 Sqdn Dover.

**472 to 474 (Fighter) Flights**
Formed 9.18 at Pizzone within 226 Sqdn with Camel, D.H.9 and later D.H.9A. Ceased to exist when sqdn disbanded 18.12.18.

**475 to 477 (Fighter) Flights**
Formed 9.18 at Mudros within 220 (Mobile) Sqdn with Camel. Still listed 3.19 but probably ceased to exist when sqdn disbanded 1.19.

**478 to 480 (Fighter) Flights**
Formed 9.18 at Mudros within 222 Sqdn with Camel. Ceased to exist when sqdn disbanded 27.2.19.

**481 to 483 (Fighter) Flights**
Formed 9.18 at Andrano within 225 Sqdn with Camel, 1½ Strutter and Hamble Baby Convert. Ceased to exist when sqdn disbanded 19.12.18.

**485 & 486 (Fighter) Flights**
Formed 7.8.18, originally known as Temporary 'A' & 'C' Flts respectively, at Burgh Castle each with 6+2 Camel. Within 273 Sqdn from it formation 20.8.18, but detached to 212 Sqdn. Commanded 1.19 by Captains GD Kirkpatrick and GWR Fane respectively, and both existed to at least 3.19.

**487 (Fighter) Flight**
Formed 1.9.18 at Butley as Supernumary Camel Flight, becoming 487 Flt 3.9.18 as part of 230 Sqdn. Disbanded 1.19.

**490 (Light Bomber) Flight**
Formed 25.5.18 at Yarmouth with 6+2 D.H.4 and D.H.9A, joining 212 Sqdn when it formed 20.8.18. Commanded 1.19 by Capt CB Sproatt. To Dover 3.19 and ceased to exist when sqdn disbanded 9.2.20.

**491 (Light Bomber) Flight**
Formed 25.5.18 at Guston Road, Dover with D.H.9, being commanded by Capt CF Brewerton DSC from 16.6.18. Joined 233 Sqdn when it formed 31.8.18. Disbanded 1.3.19, it personnel being absorbed into 233 Sqdn.

**492 (Light Bomber) Flight**
Formed 30.5.18 at Prawle Point with D.H.9, within 254 Sqdn from 15.8.18. Ceased to exist when sqdn disbanded 22.2.19.

**493 (Light Bomber) Flight**
Formed 30.5.18 at Mullion with D.H.9, joining 236 Sqdn when it formed 20.8.18. Existed until 3.19, and possibly until sqdn disbanded 15.5.19.

**494 (Light Bomber) Flight**
Formed 2.5.18 at Padstow as D.H.9 Flight within 250 Sqdn, becoming 494 Flt 30.5.18. Existed until 3.19, and possibly until sqdn disbanded 15.5.19.

**495 (Light Bomber) Flight**
Formed 30.5.18 at Seaton Carew with Kangaroo within 252 Sqdn. Transferred to 246 Sqdn when it formed 15.8.18. Authrised 10.18 to be divided between Sea Houses & West Ayton, to make way for intended F.I.A.T.-engined Vimy squadron. At Sea Houses by 1.3.19. Possibly existed until sqdn disbanded 30.6.19.

**496 to 498 (Light Bomber) Flights**
Formed 9.18 at Otranto with D.H.4 within 224 Sqdn. Later at Taranto, probably moving there with sqdn from 9.12.18. Still listed 3.19 but probably ceased to exist when sqdn disbanded 3.1.19.

**499 (Light Bomber) Flight**
Formed 9.18 on paper at Pizzone with Caproni bombers within 227 Sqdn, but had not appeared by 11.18. Squadron disbanded 9.12.18.

**500 & 501 (Special Duty) Flights**
Formed 31.5.18 at Padstow with D.H.6 within 250 Sqdn. Existed to at least 3.19, and possibly until sqdn disbanded 15.5.19.

**502 & 503 (Special Duty) Flights**
Formed 6.6.18 at Westward Ho! with D.H.6 within 260 Sqdn, to 250 Sqdn 15.8.18. Existed to at least 3.19, and possibly until sqdn disbanded 15.5.19.

**504 (Special Duty) Flight**
Formed 31.5.18 at Atwick with D.H.6 within 251 Sqdn. Existed to at least 3.19, and possibly until sqdn disbanded 30.6.19.

**505 (Special Duty) Flight**
Formed 31.5.18 at Greenland Top with D.H.6 within 251 Sqdn. To West Ayton 11.18, then to Killingholme as cadre 3.19, possibly until sqdn disbanded 30.6.19.

**506 (Special Duty) Flight**
Formed 7.6.18 at Owthorne with D.H.6 within 251 Sqdn. To Killingholme as cadre 3.19. Possibly existed until sqdn disbanded 30.6.19.

**507 & 508 (Special Duty) Flights**
Formed 24.5.18 at Cramlington with D.H.6 within 252 Sqdn. Moved to Tynemouth 8.6.18, then to Killingholme as cadre 3.19, possibly until sqdn disbanded 30.6.19.

**509 (Special Duty) Flight**
Formed 7.6.18 at Cramlington under Capt HA Furniss with D.H.6 within 252 Sqdn, being also known as 'D' Flt. Ceased to exist by 1.3.19, possibly disbanding soon after the Armistice.

**510 (Special Duty) Flight**
Formed 7.6.18 at Redcar with D.H.6 within 252 Sqdn, being also known as 'C' Flt. Moved to West Ayton and joined 251 Sqdn by 11.18, then to Killingholme as cadre 3.19, possibly until sqdn disbanded 30.6.19.

**511 & 512 (Special Duty) Flights**
Formed 7.6.18 at Brading with D.H.6 within 253 Sqdn. Moved to New Bembridge 8.8.18, then disbanded 21.1.19.

**513 (Special Duty) Flight**
Formed 7.6.18 at Chickerall with D.H.6 within 253 Sqdn, being also known as 'D' Flt initially. Transferred to 241 Sqdn when it formed 20.8.18, then disbanded 23.1.19.

**514 (Special Duty) Flight**
Formed 7.6.18 at Telscombe Cliffs with D.H.6 within 253 Sqdn, being also known as 'A' Flt. Transferred to 242 Sqdn when it formed 15.8.18, then disbanded 20.1.19.

**515 & 516 (Special Duty) Flights**
SD Flt formed 16.5.18 at Mullion with D.H.6. Further flight formed 6.6.18 and became 515 & 516 Flts within 254 Sqdn, to 236 Sqdn 20.8.18. Ceased to exist when sqdn disbanded 15.5.19.

**517 & 518 (Special Duty) Flights**
Formed 6.6.18 at Prawle Point with D.H.6 within 254 Sqdn. Ceased to exist when sqdn disbanded 22.2.19.

**519 & 520 (Special Duty) Flights**
Formed 6.6.18 under Capt RR Soar at Pembroke with D.H.6 within 255 Sqdn, being also known as 'A' and 'B' Flts. Ceased to exist when sqdn disbanded 14.1.19.

**521 & 522 (Special Duty) Flights**
Formed 6.6.18 at Anglesey with D.H.6 within 255 Sqdn. Moved to Bangor 15.8.18 and joined 244 Sqdn, being also known as 'A' and 'B' Flts. Ceased to exist when sqdn disbanded 22.1.19.

**523 & 524 (Special Duty) Flights**
Formed 6.6.18 at Luce Bay with D.H.6 within 255 Sqdn, being also known as 'A' and 'B' Flts. Transferred to 258 Sqdn when it formed 15.8.18. 523 Flt was to have received Fairey IIIA 10.18. Ceased to exist when sqdn disbanded 5.3.19.

**525 (Special Duty) Flight**
Formed 6.6.18 at Prawle Point with D.H.6 within 254 Sqdn. Moved to Ashinton 28.6.18. Still existed 3.19

**526 (Special Duty) Flight**
Formed 30.5.18 at New Haggerston with D.H.6 within 256 Sqdn, being possibly also known as 'B' Flt. Also reported at Seahouses 10.18 - 12.18. Still existed 3.19.

**527 & 528 (Special Duty) Flights**
Formed 6.6.18 at Seahouses with D.H.6 within 256 Sqdn, being also known as 'A' and 'C' Flts. To Killingholme as cadre 3.19.

**529 (Special Duty) Flight**
Formed 15.8.18 at Luce Bay with D.H.6 within to 258 Sqdn. Ceased to exist when sqdn disbanded 5.3.19.

**530 (Special Duty) Flight**
Formed 15.8.18 at Bangor with D.H.6 within 244 Sqdn, being also known as 'C' Flight. Moved to Tallaght 18.10.18, returning to Bangor 11.11.18; Ceased to exist when sqdn disbanded 22.1.19.

**531 to 533 (Special Duty) Flights**
Formed 15.8.18 at Machrihanish with D.H.6 within 272 Sqdn. 531 and 532 Flts were to have received Fairey IIIA 10.18. Ceased to exist when sqdn disbanded 5.3.19.

**534 (Light Bomber) Flight**
Formed 8.18 ex Temporary D Flt at Covehithe with D.H.4 and D.H.9 in 273 Sqdn. Part or all of flt at Burgh Castle by 11.19, but based Covehithe by 3.19. Commanded by Capt A Scarrisbrick.

**550 & 551 (Light Bomber) Flights**
Formed 9.18 at Pizzone on paper with Caproni bombers in 227 Sqdn, but had not appeared by 11.18. Disbanded 9.12.18.

**552 to 554 (Light Bomber) Flights**
Formed 9.18 at Mudros in 221 Sqdn, with D.H.9 (552 & 554 Flts) and D.H.9A (553 Flt). 552 and 553 Flts with sqdn to Petrovsk Zaskar 1.19 to at least 2.19.

**555 & 556 (Light Bomber) Flights**
Formed 26.6.18 at Manston each with 6+2 D.H.9 or D.H.9A, receiving aircraft which had had been intended for 146 Sqdn when it was to have formed in Egypt. Joined 219 Sqdn when it formed 22.7.18, 555 Flt being commanded by Lt W.Windrum 1.19. Both disbanded 17.6.19.

**557 & 558 (Light Bomber) Flights**
Formed 26.6.18 at Yarmouth each with 6+2 D.H.9/D.H.9A, joining 212 Sqdn when it formed 20.8.18. 558 operated briefly from Holt 8.18. Both to Dover 3.19, probably until sqdn disbanded 9.2.20.

**559 to 561 (Light Bomber) Flights**
Formed 9.18 at Mudros in 223 (Mobile) Sqdn with D.H.9. to at least 3.19 and possibly until sqdn disbanded 16.5.19.

**562 (Malta Anti-Submarine) Flight**
Formed 8.18 at Marsa Racecourse, Malta under 17 (Malta) Wing with D.H.9, disbanding 1.1.19.

## NAVAL WINGS

**RFC (Naval Wing)**
Renamed RNAS 1.7.14.

**No.1/61 Wing**
Formed by renaming 1 Wing Sqdn as 1 Wing RNAS at St.Pol 21.6.15 (comprised A, B, C & D Sqdns) [but another source says 1 Wing left for St Pol 26.2.15 - @30.6.15]; (Rearranged 3.7.15: A, B & C Sqdns to work together under S/Cdr Spenser Grey DSO & D, E & F Sqdns to work together under S/Cdr Bigsworth. Sqdn equipment: A-Henry Farman; B-B.E.2c; C-Nieuport & Morane; D-Henry Farman & Voisin; E-Avro & Nieuport; F-Seaplanes); Eastchurch 1.8.15 (B Sqdn temp at Furnes @20.6.15) [OR Dover 2.8.15 [1-4.8.15] - intended for Dardanelles but cancelled]; St.Pol 12-14.8.15; Divided 1.3.16 into A and B Squadrons [also C Sqdn per 201 Sqdn history, Castle Cornet, Guernsey]; Renamed Dunkerque Headquarters 1.3.16 (comprising 3, 4 & 5 Sqdns); Reverted to 1 Wing W/E 7.4.16 (with 1 & 2 Sqdns); Became 61 Wing RAF 1.4.18 (5 Group) 1.4.18; Disbanded 13.11.18
(As 61 Wing controlled 202, 204, 210, 213, 217, 218 Squadrons)

COMMANDING OFFICERS
- ? - .15; W/Cdr AM Longmore W/E 11.10.15; W/Cdr RM Groves 19.1.16; S/Cdr FK Haskins DSC 23.4.16; Cdr EC Chambers 26.5.16; W/Cdr RH Clark-Hall 15.2.17 - @9.17; W/Cdr PFM Fellowes by 2.1.18 (became L/Col 1.4.18); Mjr BL Huskisson, DSC (temp) 28.5.18; L/Col E Osmond 4.6.18; Wing disbanded 13.11.18.

AIRCRAFT - Morane Parasol, FBA Flying Boat, Avro 504B, Sopwith Gordon Bennett, Caudron G.IV, Morane BB, Nieuport 10, Nieuport 11, Nieuport 12, Nieuport 21, Henry Farman F.27, Henry Farman F.40, BE2c, REP Parasol, Bristol Scout C, Voisin Biplane, Breguet de Chasse, Bleriot XI, Sopwith Triplane, 1½ Strutter, Pup.

Sub-units included the following:

**A Flight 1 Wing [A Group)?]**
Formed at Dover 11.15; St.Pol 29.11.15; Became A Sqdn 1.3.16.

**HQ Sqdn 1 Wing**
Formed at St.Pol by 7.10.15.

**Eastchurch Group 1 Wing**
Formed at St.Pol by 6.10.15 - @30.12.15 (CO F/Cdr RJ Bone).

**A Group 1 Wing**
Formed St.Pol by 6.10.15 - @31.12.15 (CO F/Cdr FK McLean)

## B Group 1 Wing
Formed at St.Pol by 22.11.15 - @31.12.15 (CO F/Cdr JJ Petre by 30.12.15 ?). AIRCRAFT - Nieuport Scout, Nieuport 12.

## A Sqdn 1 Wing
Formed ex A Flight at St.Pol 1.3.16 (Comprised No.1 Flt, 2-str Nieuport (recce); No.2 Flt, 1-str Nieuport (fighting & anti-Zeppelin); Bombing Flt (temp attd), Caudron (sub patrol & bomb dropping)); Furnes 10.6.16 (16.6.16?); Became known as Detached Sqdn 3.7.16, then 1 Sqdn 6.12.16.

COs - S/Cdr IT Courtney by 20.3.15; F/Cdr FK Haskins DSC 1.3.16; S/Cdr FK Haskins DSC 10.6.16; Became 1 Sqdn 6.12.16.

AIRCRAFT - 504, M Farman, Henry Farman, Nieuport, Nieuport Scout (1 & 2 Flts), Nieuport 12 (2 Flt), Triplane N500 (2 Flight)

## B Sqdn 1 Wing
Formed at St.Pol 1.3.16 (Comprised No.3 Flt, 2-str Nieuport (W/T spotting) & No.4 Flt, B.E.2c (night spotting)); Became 2 Sqdn 5.11.16. (CO F/Cdr DCS Evill 1.3.16 - 5.11.16).

AIRCRAFT - B.E.2c (4 Flt, later 3 Flt for night spotting), Nieuport Scout (3 Flt later 4 Flt), Nieuport 12 (3 & 4 Flts), 1½ Strutter (4 Flt), Farman F.40 (3 Flt), Pup (4 Flt)

## C Sqdn 1 Wing
Refd ex 14 Flt at St.Pol 6.16 (with fighting element & recce/camera element); Became 3 Sqdn 5.11.16.

AIRCRAFT - Nieuport Scout, Nieuport 12, 1½ Strutter, Pup.

## 3 Sqdn 1 Wing
Formed St.Pol by 24.5.16 (ex Experimental Flight AD ?) (included No.14 Flight); Became C Sqdn 6.16 (W/E 17.7.16). (CO S/Cdr RH Mulock DSO by 3.7.16)

## No.2/62 Wing
Formed ex 2 Sqdn as 2 Wing RNAS at Eastchurch 21.6.15 (dett at Westgate, to 4 Wing 4.8.15); St.Pol 1-4.8.15 (intended to relieve 1 Wing, but 1 Wing remained Dunkerque) (dett remained Eastchurch to at least 10.8.15); Dover 12-14.8.15; Embarked for Dardanelles 15.8.15; Imbros (Kephalo Point) 31.8.15 (Tenedos?); Evacuated 18.1.16? (absorbed 3 Wing that date).
(Reformed?) at Mudros by 5.16; Disbanded 1.4.18 (expanded to form 62 and 63 Wings).
62 Wing formed at Mudros 1.4.18 (Aegean Group (later 15 (Aegean) Group); Petrovsk by 8.19; Disbanded .19.
(Controlled 220, 221, 222, 223, 226 Squadrons)

COMMANDING OFFICERS
It is not always clear from surviving records who was in overall command, but the following has been gleaned mainly from disposition lists:
W/Cdr EL Gerrard 21.6.15 - @5.8.15; Appears to have been under CE Risk (5 Sqdn CO) at Dover); W/Cdr EL Gerrard @22.9.15 (he arrived Imbros in command on/by 22.9.15 with 16 officers and 196 ratings); Wg Capt FR Scarlett W/E 3.3.16 - @9.17 (i/c RNAS ships and units in E.Med); BUT W/Cdr FH Sykes @31.8.15 - @30.11.15 (also in command 3 Wing); S/Cdr JRW Smyth-Pigott DSO @ 5.16 (listed from W/E 16.6.16 - @22.9.16); S/Cdr PA Shepherd 3.6.16 - @14.8.16 [ALSO S/Cdr CF Kilner DSO 26.6.16 - @14.8.16]; S/Cdr RJ Bone 10.10.16; W/Cdr JW Seddon detailed for 2Wg 23.9.17 (to be in command?) Col R Gordon DSO (OC 62/63 Wings) @9.18; L/Col FET Hewlett OBE (OC 62/63 Wings) @12.18; L/Col FW Bowhill @1.19 - @8.19.

AIRCRAFT - Tabloid, Morane Parasol, Caudron G.IV, Bristol Scout C, Curtiss N (Mod), Avro 504B, BE2c, Sopwith Seaplane, Short Type C Seaplane, Shorthorn, Nieuport 10, Nieuport 12, Nieuport 17bis, 1½ Strutter, Sopwith Triplane, O/100, Henry Farman F.27, Henry Farman F.40, F.1 Camel, Short 166, BE2e, Baby, Bristol Scout D.

Sub-units included the following:

## A Flight/Squadron 2 Wing
Formed as A Flight at Imbros 5.16? [by 3.16?]; Thasos 29.5.16; Became A Sqdn 1.1.17 (1 British and 1 Greek flight); Combined with Z Sqdn to form 222 Sqdn RAF 1.4.18 (CO S/Cdr PA Shepherd by 2.17; None? 5.17 - @9.17). AIRCRAFT - Nieuport 12, Scout C, Henry Farman, 1½ Strutter, Short 166, Pup.

## B Flight/Squadron 2 Wing
Formed as B Flight at Imbros 5.16(??); Mitylene 3.16 (Advanced dett of 2 a/c at Long Island; moved to Thermi 16.5.16) (Second advanced base opened Khios 6.16); Became B Sqdn 1.1.17 [or 2.17?]; Kalloni (Mitylene) 9.10.17; Became 223 Sqdn RAF 1.4.18. (S/Cdr RJ Bone DSO 10.10.16 - @24.9.17). AIRCRAFT - Henry Farman, 1½ Strutter, D.H.4, Nieuport 12, Scout D, F.1 Camel.

## C Flight/Squadron
Formed as C Flight at Mudros 5.16?; Imbros by 6.10.16; Became C Sqdn 1.1.17; Kephalo (Imbros Island) 1.2.17 [Thasos @2.7.17 - @24.9.17]; Gliki (Imbros Island) 9.10.17; Became 220 Sqdn RAF wef 1.4.18. (COs F/Cdr RH Kershaw @12.2.17; S/Cdr AC Barnby 17.3.17 - @24.9.17). AIRCRAFT - Henry Farman, Nieuport Scout, Scout C, Caudron G.IV, BE.2c, 504B, Scout D, 1½ Strutter, D.H.4, Nieuport 12, BE2e, F.1 Camel, D.H.9.

## D Flight/Squadron 2 Wing
Formed as D Flight at Imbros by 12.15; Mudros (Marsh aerodrome) 2.6.16; Stavros 8.16; Thasos @27.9.16?; Stavros @6-13.10.16?; Became D Sqdn .17 (still D Flight 24.9.17); Became 221 Sqdn RAF 1.4.18. (COs S/Cdr, later W/Cdr JRW Smyth-Pigott DSO @2.4.17 - @24.9.17; F/Cdr PC Douglass until killed 10.12.17). AIRCRAFT - 1½ Strutter, D.H.4, Nieuport 12, F.1 Camel, Henry Farman.

## E Flight 2 Wing
Formed as E Flight at Mudros 3.17 (Mobile fighting squadron); Hadzi Junas 28.3.17 (Attd 17 Sqdn RFC); Destroyed in accidental explosion at Hadzi Junas just before due to move to Thasos; Remnants to Marian, then refd at Hadzi Junas. (COs FSL HL Gaskell 28.3.17; F/L ET Bradley 2.5.17). AIRCRAFT - 1½ Strutter (4 a/c), Triplane (N5431 only).

## F Squadron 2 Wing
Formed out of B Flt at Stavros 4.17 (Mobile squadron, 1-str bomber); Amberkoj 29.4.17; Stavros 11.5.17; Marian 12.5.17; Destroyed in accidental explosion 12.5.17.
Refd at Mudros from remnants of E & F Sqdns with new aircraft 6.17; Thasos 3.6.17; Mudros 18.6.17; Thermi 30.7.17 (Bomber a/c retd to Mudros 17.9.17); Mitylene 10.9.17; Mudros 17.9.17; Stavros (when?); Mudros @ 7.18 - 11.18. [Not given RAF squadron number?]. (COs F/L ET Bradley 3.6.17; later Lt JRW Smyth-Pigott, DSO). AIRCRAFT - 1½ Strutter, F.1 Camel, Pup, D.H.4, D.H.9.

## G Squadron 2 Wing
At Imbros @4.17 - @6.17; Mudros (Marsh aerodrome) by 19.7.17 until 1.4.18.

AIRCRAFT - Henry Farman F.27 (4 a/c), D.H.4, D.H.9.

## Z (Greek) Squadron 2 Wing
Formed at Mudros 1.7.17; Thasos 18.7.17; Combined with A Sqdn to form 222 Sqdn RAF 1.4.18.

## Roumanian Flight 2 Wing
Left Mudros for Bucharest 21.11.16. AIRCRAFT - Henry Farman (4 night a/c).

## No.3/63 Wing
Formed ex 3 Sqdn as 3 Wing RNAS at Tenedos 21.6.15; Imbros (Kephalo Point) 4.8.15; Disb into 2 Wing 18.1.16 (COs W/Cdr CR Samson by 20.6.15; W/Cdr FH Sykes by 31.8.15; Disbanded 18.1.16).
AIRCRAFT - Tabloid, FB.5, Breguet Biplane, Shorthorn, BE2c, Henry Farman, Voisin Biplane, Maurice Farman, Tabloid.

Strategic Bombing Wing formed at Detling 2.16; Became 3 Wing RNAS W/E 28.4.16; Manston 29.5.16 (remnants still Manston 6.11.16?); Luxeuil-les-Bains (nr Nancy) 16.10.16 (detts from 7.16; constructional party left England 16.6.16) (Adv Base Ochey); Disbanded 30.6.17. (CO W/Cdr WL Elder 14.6.16 - 30.6.17).
AIRCRAFT - Short Bomber, Curtiss R.2, BE2c, Sopwith School, Henry Farman F.27, Breguet Concours, 1½ Strutter, Pup, J.N.3, J.N.4, Morane Parasol, Bristol Scout C, Voisin Biplane, Shorthorn, Nieuport 10, Breguet de Chasse, Avro 504B, O/100.

63 Wing RAF formed at Mudros 1.4.18 (Aegean Grp, later 15 (Aegean) Grp); Disbanded .19 (still existed 1.3.19).
(Controlled 144, 222, 226, 264, 266 Squadrons)

### No.4/64 Wing

Formed ex 4 Sqdn as 4 Wing RNAS at Dover 29.7.15 (dett ex 2 Wing at Westgate 4.8.15) (dett Dunkerque @23.9.15 - @31.10.15) (dett 4 Nieuports attd RFC Abeele 29.3.16 for 18 days, then to Dunkerque); Petite Synthe 11.4.16 (adv pty arrived) (last Eastchurch entry 14.4.16; aircraft remaining behind became War Flt Eastchurch by 16.4.16); From W/E 23.6.16 comprised 1 Sqdn F/L RGA Baudry with 9, 10 & 11 Flts (only 9 & 10 Flts by W/E 30.6.16) & 2 Sqdn F/L FT Digby with 11 & 12 Flts; From W/E 14.7.16 became A Sqdn F/L RGA Baudry with 9 & 10 Flts (F/L ADW Allen from W/E 14.8.16) & B Sqdn F/L FT Digby with 11 & 12 Flts (F/Cdr DG Young from 9.16); Dett sent to co-operate with RFC on Somme 8.16 (became 8 Sqdn); Coudekerque by 12.16; A & B Sqdns became 6 & 7 Sqdns 31.12.16 (aircraft now on squadron strength); La Panne from/by 4.17 (replaced by 5 Wing?) [23.3.18 HQ to be temp at Frontier]; Became 64 Wing 1.4.18 (7 Bde); Maidstone/Netheravon 22.4.18 (5 Group) (to UK with 207 & 215 Sqdns) and disbanded.
(COs S/Cdr CL Courtney W/E 1.10.15 - @9.17 [to 1918?]; W/Cdr E Osmond @ 2.1.18; L/Col E Osmond 1.4.18 - 22.4.18).

AIRCRAFT - 504B, RE5, Voisin Biplane, REP Parasol, Tabloid, Scout C, Nieuport 21, Caudron G.IV, JN.3, BE2c, Henry Farman F.40, Bleriot Parasol, Morane Parasol, Burgess, 1½ Strutter, Shorthorn, Avro 504C, Nieuport 10, Nieuport 11, Nieuport 12.
(As 64 Wing controlled 29, 74, 204, 208 Squadrons)
Reformed 6.6.18 as 64 (Egypt) Wing from Port Said & Alexandria seaplane stations with HQ at Alexandria; Disbanded 15.9.19. (CO L/Col CE Risk 6.18)

### No.5/65 Wing

Formed (initially as 5 Sqdn until 1.16?) at Dover 31.7.15 (Took over Westgate Defence Flight) [30.12.15 to be transferred to Coudekerque by flights as required, leaving Defence Flights at Dover with 6 pilots]; Coudekerque 3.3.16; Disbanded 31.12.16 Became 4 & 5 Sqdns. (COs S/Cdr CE Risk @ 10.15; S/Cdr SDA Grey DSO 1.3.16; S/Cdr GR Bromet (temp) 26.6.16; S/Cdr SDA Grey DSO 15.8.16 - 31.12.16)

AIRCRAFT - Dyott Monoplane, BE2c, Scout C, 504B, Morane Parasol, J.N.3, Tabloid, F.B.5, Morane-Saulnier BB, Nieuport 10, Nieuport 12, Caudron G.IV, Pup.

Reformed from nucleus of 4 Sqdn at Dover 31.12.16 (took over Petite Synthe 1.4.17); Coudekerque end 3.17 (replaced 4 Wing there); Rosendael by 16.9.17 to at least 17.1.18; Malo-les-Bains by 11.2.18; Became 65 Wing 1.4.18 (7 Brigade); Petite Synthe by 5.18 (7 Brigade until 18.6.18, then 10 Brigade); Malo-les-Bains 10.18 (10 Brigade); Heule @11.11.18 (2 Brigade); To cadre 6.2.19. (As 65 Wing controlled 204, 206, 211, 214, 215 Sqdns and numerous other RAF and US squadrons]

COMMANDING OFFICERS: S/Cdr SDA Grey DSO 31.12.16; W/Cdr JT Cull DSO (temp) 1.9.17; L/Col JA Cunningham DSO DFC 1.4.18; L/Col TAE Cairnes DSO 24.10.18; Mjr EW Norton MC by 12.18; Mjr HV Champion de Crespigny MC DFC 3.12.18; Mjr KL Caldwell MC DFC 7.12.18; Mjr GC Bowman DSO MC 13.12.18; Mjr HV Champion de Crespigny MC DFC 18.12.18; L/Col JA Cunningham DSO DFC 28.12.18; L/Col AABT Lowison MC 17.1.19; Mjr HV Champion de Crespigny MC DFC 31.1.19 Wing to cadre 6.2.19.

AIRCRAFT - Henry Farman F.40, Breguet de Chasse, Breguet Concours, Breguet de Bombe, 1½ Strutter.

[Per Weekly Lists, 5 Wing refd W/E 7.4.16 under S/Cdr SDA Grey DSO comprising
1 Sqdn = 5 Flt, also 6 Flt from W/E 12.5.16 (F/Cdr SV Sippe DSO; F/Cdr GR Bromet from 26.6.16)
2 Sqdn F/Cdr ET Newton-Clare = 7 & 8 Flts (later F/L TE Viney)
W/E 14.7.16 became (to @30.9.16) A Sqdn F/Cdr AG Andreae & B Sqdn F/Cdr ET Newton-Clare].

### No.6/66 Wing

6 Wing RNAS formed ex RNAS Otranto with 1 & 2 Sqdns, HQ at Otranto 13.3.17; Expanded to form 66 and 67 Wings 1.4.18.
(CO S/Cdr (later) W/Cdr CHK Edmonds, DSO 13.3.17 (RNAS Otranto) - 1.4.18) (comprised 224 to 227 Sqdns).
[Unconfirmed report that the following units formed at Otranto 2.16, later joining 6 Wing: 1 Squadron (6 Sopwith Baby), 2 Squadron (6 Short 184, 6 Short 320) & Aeroplane Flight (6 1½ Strutter)]

66 Wing RAF formed at Otranto 1.4.18 - @10.18 (Adriatic Group, becoming No.6 (Adriatic) Group by 27.9.18); to Taranto late 18 (still Taranto 1.3.19); Disbanded 19. (CO L/Col DA Oliver, DSO, OBE 1.4.18 - @11.18).
[66 Wing controlled 223, 224, 225, 263 Squadrons]

AIRCRAFT - FBA Flying Boat, 1½ Strutter, Short 320, F.1 Camel, Hamble Baby Convert, Caproni Ca.4, Baby, Short 184, D.H.4 , D.H.9, F.1 Camel.

### No.67 Wing

Formed out of 6 Wing RNAS at Taranto 1.4.18 (Adriatic Group, became No.6 (Adriatic) Group by 27.9.18); Disb into 66 Wing 6.12.18. (CO L/Col RP Ross DSO 1.4.18) (controlled 226, 227, 271 Squadrons)

### No.68 (Operations) Wing

BASES
Formed with HQ at The Gables, Seaton Carew 11.7.18 (18 Group); Disbanded .19 (still existed 6.19). (CO L/Col CEH Rathborne by 18.12.18). (Controlled 246, 252, 256, 274 Squadrons and stations at Ashington, New Haggerston, Redcar, Sea Houses, Seaton Carew, Tynemouth).

### No.70 (Operations) Wing

Formed at Felixstowe 20.8.18 (4 Group); Disbanded .19 (still existed .6.19). (CO L/Col EDM Robertson from 20.8.18). (Controlled 230, 231, 232, 247, 259, 261 Squadrons at Felixstowe and School for Anti-Submarine Patrol Observers at Aldeburgh).

### No.71 (Operations) Wing

Formed at Penzance 8.8.18? (9 Group); Disbanded .19 (still existed 6.19). (Controlled 234, 235, 236, 250, 260 Squadrons and stations at Mullion, Newlyn, Padstow, Tresco, Westward Ho!)

### No.72 (Operations) Wing

Formed at Cattewater 8.8.18? (9 Group); Disbanded .19 (still existed 3.19). (Controlled 237, 238, 239, 254 Squadrons and stations at Cattewater, Prawle Point, Torquay).

### No.73 (Operations) Wing

Formed at Great Yarmouth 20.8.18 (4 Group); Disbanded .19 (still existed 6.19). (COs L/Col V Nicholl DSO DFC 20.8.18; L/Col ETR Chambers by 1.19). (Controlled 212, 228, 229 Squadrons and station at Yarmouth).

### No.74 (Operations) Wing

Formed at Calshot 8.8.18? (10 Group); Disbanded .19 (still existed 6.19). (Controlled 240 Squadron and station at Calshot).

### No.75 (Operations) Wing

Formed at Warsash 8.8.18? (10 Group); Disbanded .19 (still existed 3.19); (Controlled 241, 242, 243, 253 Squadrons and stations at Bembridge, Cherbourg, Newhaven, Portland).

### No.76 (Operations) Wing

Formed at Felixstowe 20.8.18 (4 Group); Disbanded into 70 Wing 1.12.18. (Controlled 232, 247, 259, 261 Squadrons at Felixstowe).

### No.77 (Operations) Wing

Formed at Milford Haven 8.8.18? (14 Group); Disbanded by 1.11.18. (Controlled 244, 245, 255 Squadrons and stations at Bangor, Fishguard, Pembroke).

### No.78 (Operations) Wing

Formed at Dundee 8.8.18? (22 Group); Disbanded .19. (Controlled 249, 257 Squadrons, 1 Torpedo Training Squadron and Grand Fleet School of Aerial Fighting and Gunnery and stations at Dundee, East Fortune and Leuchars)

## No.79 (Operations) Wing
Formed at Hornsea 26.8.18 (18 Group); Disbanded .19 (still existed 6.19). (CO L/Col FK McClean from 26.8.18). (Controlled 248, 251 Squadrons and station at Hornsea).

## COASTAL GROUPS
After the formation/Remarks of the Royal Air Force, coastal work came mainly under Operations Groups, as follows:

### No.4 (Operations) Group)
Formed 1.4.18 at Great Yarmouth, moving by 6.18 to Cliff House, Felixstowe, where it disbanded in 1919. (Controlled 70, 73 & 76 Wings, and stations at Aldeburgh, Burgh Castle, Covehithe, Felixstowe, Hickling Broad, Lowestoft (Kite Balloon Section), Manston, Pulham (Airship Station), Shotley, Westgate, Yarmouth.

### No.5 (Operations) Group)
Formed 1.4.18 at 18 Marine Parade, Dover where it disbanded in 1919. It had an advanced headquarters at Spycker Camp, Dunkerque until this closed down 14.4.19. Controlled 61, 65 & 82 Wings, and stations at Capel le Ferne/Folkestone (Airship Station), Dover (Guston Rd), Dover (Swingate Down), Dunkerque, Godmersham Park (Airship Station), Hythe, Walmer.

### No.9 (Operations) Group)
Formed 1.4.18 at Mount Wise, Devonport, where it disbanded in mid-1919. Controlled 71 & 72 Wings, stations at Bath, Blandford, Bridport (Airship Station), Bude (Airship Staton), Cattewater, Laira (Airship Station), Merifield, Mullion (Aeroplanes), Mullion (Airship Station), Newlyn, Padstow, Prawle Point, Torquay, Tresco (Scilly), Westward Ho! and the aircraft carriers HMS *Mantua* & HMS *Oratava*.

### No.10 (Operations) Group)
Formed 1.4.18 at Calshot, moving c.6.18 to Warsash (Southampton), and 12.7.20 to Lee-on-Solent, where it remained until being disbanded into Coastal Area 18.1.32. Controlled 74 & 75 Wings, and stations at Bembridge, Calshot, Cherbourg, Chickerall, Lee-on-Solent, Fecamp (France), Moreton/ Dorchester (Airship Station), New Bembridge, Newhaven, Polegate (Airship Station), Portland, Sandbanks, Shindon (Airship Station), Telscombe Cliffs, Tipnor (Balloon Base), Upton (Airship Station).

### No.14 (Operations) Group)
Formed 1.4.18 at St.Mary's Street, Haverfordwest, where it disbanded around 3.19. Controlled 77 Wing, also stations at Anglesey (Airship Station), Bangor, Dublin, Fishguard, Malahide, Milford Haven, Pembroke (Airship Station), Pembroke Dock, Wexford.

### No.18 (Operations) Group)
Formed 1.4.18 at Immingham, moving in 5.18 to Habrough where it disbanded 18.10.19. (NB Habrough originally known as Killingholme, but renamed to avoid confusion with the RAF station there). Controlled 68 & 79 Wings, and stations at Atwick, Ashington, Cramlington (Aeroplanes), Cramlington (Airship Station), Flamborough, Greenland Top, Hornsea, Howden (Airship Station), Immingham, Killingholme, Kirkleatham, Lowthorpe, New Hagerston, North Coates Fitties, Owthorne, Redcar, Sea Houses, Seaton Carew, South Shields, Tees & Tynemouth, West Ayton.

### No.22 (Operations) Group)
Formed 1.7.18 at East Fortune, moving by 7.18 to Station Hotel, Stirling, where it disbanded 5.19. Controlled 78 Wing, and stations at Auldbar, Chathill (Airship Station), Dundee, East Fortune, Kirkwall/Orkney, Longside (Airship Station), Luce Bay, Machrihanish, Peterhead, Strathbeg.

### No.25 (Operations) Group)
Formed 12.8.18 out of No.22 Group at Luce Bay, where it disbanded in 1919. No Wings. Controlled stations at Ayr, Ballycastle, Ballywalter, Inchinnan, Luce Bay (Aeroplanes), Luce Bay (Airship Station), Machrihanish, Renfrew, Turnberry.

### No.28 (Orkney & Shetland Islands) Group)
Formed 1918 at Stenness, Orkney, where it disbanded in 1919. No Wings. Ccontrolled stations at Caldale (Balloon Base), Catfirth, Houton (Seaplanes), Houton (Balloon Base), Lerwick (Balloon Base), Scapa, Smoogroo, Stenness.

### No.29 (Fleet) Group)
Formed 27.11.18 at North Queensferry, where it disbanded into Coastal Area 31.3.22. No Wings. Controlled stations at Donibristle, Dundee, Leuchars, Turnhouse (and postwar Dundee, Felixstowe, Houton Bay, Smoogroo).

## ROYAL HELLENIC NAVAL AIR SERVICE (attached RNAS)

**H.1 Flight.** At Thasos by 2.11.18 - @16.11.18

**H.2 Flight.** Formed at Thasos by 10.18; Stavros 10.10.18; Mudros by 2.11.18; Ramanos by 16.11.18.

*Cattewater Short 184 N2959 'B1', which attacked a U-boat on 11 June 1918. (via Bruce Robertson)*

# MISCELLANEOUS RELEVANT RNAS/RFC/RAF UNITS

**ARMY AIRCRAFT PARKS** (one attached to each Army)
1st AAP - formed 15.12.15. Based Aire by 7.16. Lillers by 17.2.17 - @1.6.17. Houdain by 19.6.17; Became 1 AP 1.1.18.
2nd AAP - formed 15.12.15. Based Hazebrouck by 7.16 until became 2 AP 1.1.18 (at Droglandt).
3rd AAP - formed 15.12.15 at Beauval. At Frevent by 17.2.17 until split 6.17.
3rd (Northern) AAP - formed 6.17. At Puchevillers by 19.6.17 until rejoined 11.17.
3rd (Southern) AAP - formed 6.17. At Eterpigny by 19.6.17 until rejoined 11.17.
3rd AAP - reformed 11.17 at Puchevillers. Became 2 AP 1.1.18
4th AAP - at Beauval by 7.16. Daours by 17.2.17 - @31.3.17. Harbonnières by 22.4.17. Eterpigny by 15.5.17 - @19.6.17; Coudekerque by 11.7.17. Guillacourt 21.12.17. Became 4 AP 1.1.18.
5th AAP - Puchevillers by 17.2.17 - @1.6.17. Herzeele by 7.17 - 11.17. Disbanded around 12.18?
6th AAP - formed 11.17 at Vézelise - @1.12.17. Disbanded c.12.18?? (was this ex 3rd (Southern) AAP?).

## AIRCRAFT PARKS

[AP with Expeditionary Force]. At St.Omer. Became 1 AP 17.3.15
[AP in England] Became 2 AP 17.3.15.

1 AP. Formed 17.3.15 ex AP St.Omer. Became 1 AD 13.12.15.
2 AP. Formed 17.3.15 ex AP in England.
3 AP. Formed 7.15 at Candas. Became 3 AD 13.12.15.
[should this be 2 AD?]
4 AP. Formed in Mesopotamia.

1 AP. Reformed 1.1.18 in 1 Brigade ex 1 AAP Houdain - @11.4.18. Ouve-Wirquin by 8.6.18. Liettres to Lugy 16.6.18- @8.18. Somain by 11.18.
2 AP. Reformed 1.1.18 in 2 Brigade ex 2 AP Droglandt. Eecke by 7.3.18 - @11.4.18. Houlle by 8.6.18; To Bavichove 16.9.18. Bisseghem by 11.18.
3 AP. Reformed 1.1.18 in 3 Brigade ex 3 AAP Puchevillers. To Candas 30.3.18 - @22.7.18. Bihucourt by 11.18.
4 AP. Reformed 1.1.18 in 5 Brigade ex 4 AAP Guillacourt. Villers Carbonnel by 7.3.18. To Vron 29.3.18. St.Riquier by 11.4.18 - 8.18. Cagny to Villers Carbonnel 29.9.18. Premont by 11.18.
5 AP. Formed .18 in 2 Brigade. At Herzeele by 7.3.18 - @11.4.18. Arneke by 8.6.18 - @22.7.18. Wevelghem by 11.18.
6 AP. Formed .18 in 8 Brigade. At Vézelise by 11.4.18 - @22.7.18.
8 AP. Formed in 7 Brigade at Armbouts-Cappel (nr Dunkerque) by 10.3.18 - @22.7.18.
9 AP. Formed .18 in 9 Brigade at . Ouve-Wirquin by 11.4.18. To Beauvais area 3.6.18. Left 21.6.18. Fontenay (5m WNW of Rozoy) by 22.7.18. At Vacquerie-le-Boucq by 8.18. Noyelles-sur-Escaut by 11.18.
10 AP. Formed .18 in ? Brigade (not formed by 8.6.18). At Ouve-Wirquin by 22.7.18 - @8.18. Faubourg-des-Poste by 11.18.
11 AP. Formed 7.5.18 at Coudekerque as (61 Wing AP in 5 Group), becoming 11 AP 30.5.18, to at least 8.18. At Rambervillers by 11.18. At Ghistelles from/by 24.3.19.

## AIRCRAFT DEPOTS

1 AD. Formed 13.12.15 ex 1 AP at St.Omer to at least 7.16. Lillers by 4.17. St.Omer by 6.17, until to Guines (near Calais) 18.5.18. To Docks de Petite Synthe 31.10.18.
2 AD. At Candas by 7.16. To Rang-du-Fliers 25-30.3.18. Groffliers by 8.6.18; Vron by 11.18.
3 AD. Formed at Courban (nr Chattilon-sur-Seine) 3.18 - @11.18.
4 AD. Formed 21.8.18 at Balinghem (in 5 Group), vacated by 28.12.18.

## SALVAGE SECTIONS

No.2. Richborough.
No.7. Behain by 12.18.

## AEROPLANE SUPPLY DEPOTS

1 ASD. At St.Omer by 11.17. To Marquise 22.4.18 - @3.19 (Pilots Pool at Setques).
2 ASD. At Fienvillers by 11.17; Hesdin by 31.5.18 - @25.8.18; Berck-sur-Mer by 8.6.18 (by 4.18?) - @11.18 (On 25.3.18, Issue Section to St.Andre-aux-Bois, and Repair Section to Verton) (Pilots Pool at Berck-sur-Mer by 8.6.18 - @22.7.18; to Wissant by 6.18 - @7.18).
3 ASD. Formed at Courban 3.18 - 11.18 (for HP aircraft).
4 ASD. Left Dover 19.3.18 for Dunkerque in PMS *Plumpton*, and main party followed 20.3.18 in HMS *General Craufurd*. Set up at Guines by 24.3.18 (Issue and Reception Section based 69 Aerodrome, Audembert from 8.5.18 (officially opened 26.5.18), later to Wissant). Vacated Guines by 28.12.18 (5 Group), aircraft then went to 11 AP instead.

## AIR ISSUES SECTIONS
(Referred to as Air Issues or Issues Sections)
No.1. Rely by 4.18 - 11.18 (in 1 ASD).
No.2. St.André-aux-Bois by 4.18 - @9.18; Fienvillers by 11.18 (in 2 ASD).
No.5. Le Bourget by 22.7.18.
No.6. Bickendorff @7.19 - @9.19 (in 1 ASD).

## AIRCRAFT REPAIR PARKS
No.1. Marquise by 6.18 - @11.18.
No.2. Bahot by 4.18 - @11.18.

## AIRCRAFT SUPPLY PARKS
No.1. St.Omer by 4.18; Closed by 23.6.18.

## RECEPTION PARK
Unnumbered. At Marquise by 4.18 - @11.18 (attd 1 ASD).
(Received aircraft ex UK)

## NAVAL SUPPORT UNITS
Aircraft Depot formed St.Pol by 26.9.16 (eventually becoming Naval Aircraft Depot?). Absorbed into 4 ASD on formation.
Subsidiary Depot forming at Hippodrome Wellington, Ostende 12.10.14.
No.1 Naval Aircraft Park. First mentioned 22.10.17. Merged into 4 ASD on formation.
Naval Aircraft Supply Depot - 20.4.18 "Will cease to exist".

## VARIOUS U.K. ODDMENTS

Central Store Depot, Wormwood Scrubbs existed by 19.4.15.

RNAS Central Depot at White City by 25.10.15 - @27.12.15. (replaced Wormwood Scrubbs?)

Grain Island Repair Depot by 24.10.14 - @27.12.15.

Manston - HP Sqdn became D.H.4 School 19.1.18.

Dover Defence Flight existed by 24.7.16 (F/L TC Vernon). Became 15 Flight, Dover Defence Sqdn by 7.8.16 - still under Vernon, but he had left by 21.8.16.

Seaplane Base Dunkerque formed 2.15. Became 217 Sqdn 1.4.18.

Fleet Aeroplane Repair Dept at Donibristle (otherwise Naval Aeroplane Repair Depot).

(Southern) Aeroplane Repair Depot at Farnborough.

## VARIOUS OVERSEAS ODDMENTS

RNAS Durban by 31.3.16 - @30.4.16 [see 11 Sqdn]. Became East Africa Field Force by 31.5.16 - @31.8.16. (CO S/Cdr JT Cull to 9.15, then S/Cdr FW Bowhill by 10.15)

RNAS Mombasa by 31.3.16 - @30.4.16. Became Cape Station by 31.5.16 - @31.8.16 (S/Cdr ERC Nansen)

RFC Force D, Mesopotamia (naval element). (CO W/Cdr R Gordon DSO by 3.7.16. No CO by 24.7.16).

# UNITED KINGDOM NAVAL AIR STATIONS 1911 TO 1919

The following are the main airfields and landing grounds used for naval purpose in the United Kingdom between 1911 and 1919. More detailed information on the units concerned will be found elsewhere. Airship stations, being outside the scope of this book, are only listed where also used at some stage by aeroplanes.

**ALDEBURGH**, Suffolk - NLG sub-station for Yarmouth from 8.15. No.1 Anti-Submarine Inshore Patrol Observers School formed 1918, became Marine Observers School, then No.1 Marine Observers School 1.1.19, disbanded 1919.

**ANGLESEY/LLANGEFNI**, Anglesey - Airship station. Also 521 & 522 Flts (otherwise A & C Flts) formed in 255 Sqdn 6.6.18, to 244 Sqdn Bangor 15.8.18.

**ASHINGTON**, Northumberland - RFC station. Also 525 Flt 256 Sqdn from 28.6.18, still existed 3.19.

**ATWICK/HORNSEA**, Yorks - RFC station, naval units attached. RNAS HD flight from 8.15 for a time. 504 Flt formed in 251 Sqdn 31.5.18, sqdn disbanded 30.6.19.

**BACTON**, Norfolk - NLG sub-station for Yarmouth from 8.15. 557 & 558 Flts formed in 212 Sqdn 20.8.18. 3 a/c of 470 Flt 273 Sqdn from 11.11.18.

**BANGOR**, Caernarvonshire - SD station opened 7.18. 521, 522 & 530 Flts (otherwise A, B & C Flts) formed in 244 Sqdn 7.8.18. 530 Flight left 18.10.18, but returned 11.11.18. Sqdn disbanded 22.1.19

**BARROW IN FURNESS/WALNEY ISLAND**, Lancashire - Airship station. Aeroplane dett attached 1.16 - 4.16.

**BARRY/CARNOUSTIE**, Forfarshire. Temp LG for RNAS Dundee 5.15.

**BEMBRIDGE HARBOUR**, Isle of Wight - Seaplane sub-station for Calshot from 1915. 412 Flt from 30.5.18, in 253 Sqdn from 7.6.18, joined by 413 Flt from 15.9.18 until 11.18, disbanded 5.5.19.

**BEMBRIDGE/FORELAND/NEW BEMBRIDGE**, Isle of Wight - SD airfield opened 8.18. 511 & 512 Flts (otherwise A & B Flts) arrived in 253 Sqdn 8.8.18, disbanded 21.1.19.

**BOWNESS ON WINDERMERE**, Westmorland - private marine base. Northern Aircraft Co trained RNAS seaplane pilot 1.15, becoming RNAS Windermere before closing 8.16.

**BRADING**, Isle of Wight - RFC DLG from 12.17. 511 & 512 Flts (otherwise A & B Flts) formed in 253 Sqdn 7.6.18, left 8.8.18.

**BURGH CASTLE**, Suffolk - NLG sub-station for Yarmouth from 11.15. 485 & 486 Flts (otherwise A & C Flts) formed 7.8.18, in 273 Sqdn from 7.8.18, also 534 Flt from 10.18, plus 3 a/c of 470 Flt from 12.11.18. Also part/all of 534 Flt in 11.18. Sqdn disbanded 5.7.19.

**BUTLEY**, Suffolk - Experimental station. Supernumary Camel Flight from 1.9.18, became 487 Flt 230 Sqdn 3.9.18, disbanded 1.19.

**CAIRNCROSS**, Berwickshire - RFC NLG. SD Flt 256 Sqdn formed 6.6.18, to Seahouses as 528 Flt 15.8.18.

**CALSHOT**, Hampshire - Seaplane station opened 22.3.13. 345, 346 & 410 Flts formed 30.5.18, became part of 240 Sqdn 20.8.18. 411 Flt planned but not formed. Sqdn disbanded 15.5.19. 210 TDS formed 6.18, disbanded into RAF & Naval Co-operation School, became School of Naval Co-operation 23.12.19.

**CATFIRTH**, Shetland Isles - Flying boat base opened 11.17. 300 Flt formed 15.6.18, disbanded 1919.

**CATTEWATER**, Devon - Marine base opened 3.17. 420 & 421 Flts formed 30.5.18, absorbed into 237 Sqdn 20.8.18. 422 & 423 Flts planned but not formed. 347, 348 & 349 Flts formed 15.6.18 onwards, becoming part of 238 Sqdn 20.8.18. All disbanded 15.5.19.

**CHICKERELL**, Dorset - SD station from 6.18. 513 Flt (otherwise D Flt) formed in 253 Sqdn 7.6.18, to 241 Sqdn 20.8.18, disbanded 23.1.19.

**CHINGFORD**, Essex - RNAS school opened 4.15. 207 TDS formed 1.4.18, became 54 TDS 20.7.18, disbanded 7.2.19.

**CLACTON**, Essex - Seaplane station, advanced base for Westgate 8.14.

**COVEHITHE**, Suffolk - Night sub-station for Yarmouth from 3.15. Temp D Flt from 30.5.18, became 534 Flt in 273 Sqdn 20.8.18, disbanded 1919.

**CRAMLINGTON (EAST)**, Northumberland - SD station from 5.18. 507 & 508 Flts formed 23.5.18 in 252 Sqdn. Joined by 509 Flt (otherwise D Flt) 2.6.18. Disbanded after Armistice.

**CRANWELL (NORTH)/HMS DAEDALUS**, Lincolnshire - Training station opened 1.4.16. 213 TDS formed for Handley Page training 7.6.18, became 58 TDS 27.7.18, disbanded 1919.

**CRANWELL (SOUTH)/HMS DAEDALUS**, Lincolnshire - RNAS Training Establishment opened 1916. 201 & 202 TDS formed 1.4.18, became 56 & 57 TDS 27.7.18, both disbanded 13.3.19.

**CROMARTY**, Ross & Cromarty - Seaplane station 1913 to 1915.

**DETLING**, Kent - NLG for Eatchurch War Flight from 5.15. Strategic Bombing Wing formed 2.16, became 3 Wing 4.16, to Manston 29.5.16. RNAS NLG from 7.8.16. To RFC 3.4.17

**DONIBRISTLE**, Fife - Ships aeroplane base 1918/19.

**DOVER HARBOUR**, Kent - Marine base from 11.14. 407 Flt from 30.5.18, absorbed into 233 Sqdn 31.8.18, disbanded 3.19.

**DOVER/GUSTON ROAD**, Kent - Landplane base from 8.14. Various sqdns 1914-1918. 491 Flt from 25.5.18, absorbed into 233 Sqdn 31.8.18 to 3.19. 490, 557 & 558 Flts 212 Sqdn 3.19 to 2.20.

**DUNDEE/STANNERGATE**, Forfar - Opened 3.14 as seaplane & flying base on transfer from Port Laing. 400, 401 & 450 Flts formed 30.5.18, in 249 Sqdn from 18.8.18. 400 Flt left 8.18 & others 3.19. 318 & 319 Flts formed 30.5.18, in 257 Sqdn from 7.18, disbanded 30.6.19. 'G' BST Flt formed 15.8.18, disb 1919.

**EASTBOURNE**, Sussex - Fowler Flying School taken over 8.14 as Naval Flying School. Temporarily closed 9.11.16 on transfer of school to Vendôme. Re-opened by 1.5.17. Became 206 TDS 1.4.18, then 50 TDS 15.7.18, left 1919.

**EASTCHURCH**, Isle of Sheppey, Kent - Opened 11.11 (3.11?) as first RN Air Station, later becoming a Naval Flying School. Also used for test flying by Shorts. Used by various RNAS squadrons and wings 1914/16. Other units included Gunnery Schools Flight from 1.5.16 (comprising, Bomb, Gun & Miscellaneous Flights), Observers School Flight from 25.12.16, Design Flight from 14.8.16. Gun Flight to Leysdown 25.4.17. Design Flight to Grain 17.3.17. Miscellaneous Flight became Spotting Flight 15.9.16. Station became 204 TDS 1.4.18, disbanded 1919.

**EAST FORTUNE**, East Lothian - opened 8.16 as airship station, also used by home defence detachments. 'F' Sqdn for aircraft ashore from HMS Furious by 1.17. 208 TDS from 6.18, to Leuchars 7.18. Torpedo Aeroplane School formed 3.7.18, became 201 TDS 14.8.18, became Torpedo Training Sqdn 30.4.19, disbanded 1920. Grand Fleet School of Aerial Fighting & Gunnery formed out of 208 TDS 19.7.18, to Leuchars 10.11.18. 185 Sqdn formed 21.10.18, disbanded 14.4.19.

**FAIRLOP**, Essex - sub-station for Chingford from 1916, became part of 207 TDS 1.4.18, renumbered as 54 TDS 20.7.18, disbanded 7.2.19.

**FELIXSTOWE**, Suffolk - Opened as seaplane & flying boat station 15.4.13. Nore Defence Flight 1917. 327 to 344 Flts formed or planned from 30.5.18, becoming part of 230, 231, 232, 247, 259 & 261 Sqdns 20.8.18. 442 Flt formed 15.10.18 in 219 Sqdn, leaving 11.18. All disbanded by 9.19, except 333 & 334 Flts which became No.4 Comms Sqdn 5.1.19, disbanding 1919. C, D & E BST Flts also existed 1918.

**FISHGUARD**, Pembrokeshire - Seaplane station opened 11.4.17. 426 & 427 Flts formed 30.5.18, in 245 Sqdn from 20.8.18, disbanding 19.5.19.

**FORT GEORGE/ARDERSIER**, Inverness-shire - opened as seaplane temp sub-station 1913. Moved to Dundee 7.14.

**FREISTON**, Lincolnshire - opened mid 1916 as sub-station to Cranwell for and bomb dropping gunnery training. School of Aerial Fighting & Gunnery formed 6.5.18, became No.4 Fighting School, disbanded 3.20.

**GOSFORTH**, Northumberland - Armstrong Whitworth aerodrome used by RNAS elements 11.14 - 3.15.

**GOSPORT**, Hants - used by RNAS from 17.10.14 until 1.15. Development Sqdn formed 17.8.18, became 186 (Development) Sqdn 1.1.19 for torpedo training, became 210 Sqdn 1.2.20.

**GRAIN & PORT VICTORIA**, Kent - experimental station opened 3.12.12. Nore War Flt formed 24.4.16. Experimental Flt formed 4.16, became Gunnery Experimental 5.1.16. Seaplane Design Flt formed 5.12.16. Design Flt ex Eastchurch 16.3.17, also Experimental Design Flt, became Test Depot 30.3.17, became Marine Aircraft Experimental Station 5.18, later Marine Aircraft Experimental Establishment. Type Test Dept ex Southampton 4.4.17, became Type Test Flt. Port Victoria Aeroplane Repair Station, became Experimental Constructive Dept 1.2.17. Experimental Armament Dept by 1.2.17. Nore Patrol Flt 1918.

**GREENLAND TOP/STALLINGBOROUGH**, Lincs - RFC/RAF NLG used from SD from 5.18. 505 Flt formed in 251 Sqdn 31.5.18, to West Ayton 11.18.

**HAWKCRAIG POINT**, Fife - experimental station 1917/18.

**HENDON**, Middx - Pre-war civil aerodrome used by RNAS from 8.14. Flying school and later aeroplane park.

**HOLT**, Norfolk - NLG sub-station for Yarmouth. Used by 558 Flt 212 Sqdn 8.18 - 3.19.

**HORNSEA MERE**, Yorks - opened 7.15 as seaplane sub-station of Killingholme. 453 Flt formed 30.5.18 & 405 Flt 15.6.18, joined by 404 Flt 15.8.18, all in 248 Sqdn from 20.8.18, disbanding by 6.3.19. Also HQ 251 Sqdn.

**HOUTON BAY**, Orkney - opened 7.17 as seaplane & flying boat station. 430 Flt formed 3.5.18, also 306 Flt 31.7.18 & F BST Flt 15.8.18. 307 & 308 Flts planned but not formed. Closed 1919.

**IMMINGHAM**, Lincs - used briefly by Eastchurch (Mobile) Sqdn and other aircraft until 1.15. Later kite balloon base.

**KILLINGHOLME**, Lincs - opened 7.14, some landplane use, but mainly seaplane & flying boat base, later including Acceptance Park. 403, 404, 320, 321 & 322 Flts formed from 30.5.18, leaving or disbanding by 20.7.18 on arrival of US Navy flying boat squadron. 323 Flt planned but not formed. Various SD Flt cadres from 3.19 prior to disbandment.

**LEE-ON-SOLENT**, Hants - opened 7.17 as seaplane training station, initially to relieve pressure at Calshot. Became 209 TDS 1.4.18, then RAF & Naval Co-operation School 16.6.19, and RAF Seaplane Establishment 14.7.19, to Calshot 12.19.

**LEUCHARS**, Fife - opened 7.18 as 208 (Temporary) TDS, became No.1 Torpedo Training Sqdn 19.7.18, left 8.18. Grand Fleet School of Aerial Fighting & Gunnery formed 10.11.18, disbanded 1920.

**LEVINGTON**, Suffolk - storage sub-station for Felixstowe.

**LEYSDOWN**, Isle of Sheppey, Kent - LG for RNAS Eastchurch from 1911. Gun Flight detached from Eastchurch 25.4.17, became Marine Observers School 1.4.18

**LUCE BAY**, Wigtown - opened 15.7.15 as airship station, used for SD from 6.18. 523 & 524 Flts (otherwise A & B Flts) formed in 255 Sqdn 6.18, to 258 Sqdn & joined by 529 Flt 15.8.18, disbanded 5.3.19.

**MACHRIHANISH**, Argyll - opened 8.18 as airship and SD station. 531-533 Flts formed 15.8.18 in 272 Sqdn, sqdn disbanded 5.3.19.

**MANSTON**, Kent (initially known as MANSTONE) - opened Spring 1916 as a sub-station for Westgate. Nucleus of 3 Wing from 29.5.16 until 14.10.16. Other units included Handley Page Training Flight (formed 4.1.16, to Stonehenge 19.1.18), Handley Page Sqdn (formed 1.7.16, to Luxeuil 21.12.16), RNAS War School (formed 11.9.17, became Pilots Pool 1.4.18), D.H.4 School (formed 19.1.18), A Sqdn (formed 5.10.17 from a flight of 7 Sqdn, to France 11.10.17), 203 TDS (formed 1.4.18, became 55 TDS 15.7.18, to Sedgeford 1.9.18). 470 Flt (otherwise Tongue Defence Flt) formed 27.5.18, and 555 & 556 Flts formed 26.6.18, all in 219 Sqdn from 22.7.18, all being disbanded by 7.2.20, except 470 Flt to 273 Sqdn 13.11.18. No.2 Observers School formed 14.9.18, became No.1 (Observers) School of Aerial Gunnery.

**MARTLESHAM HEATH**, Suffolk - RFC NLG, also used as DLG for RNAS Felixstowe (ex Trimley) from 23.2.17.

**MULLION**, Cornwall - opened as airship station. 515 & 516 Flts formed 16.5.18 & 6.6.18, also 493 Flt 30.5.18, all in 254 Sqdn, until to 236 Sqdn 20.8.18. All disbanded by 15.5.19.

**NEW HAGGERSTON**, Northumberland - former RFC NLG. 526 Flt of 256 Sqdn from 30.5.18, to at least 3.19.

**NEWHAVEN**, Sussex - opened 9.5.17 as seaplane sub-station to Calshot. 408 Flt formed 30.5.18, also 409 Flt when joined 242 Sqdn 15.8.18, sqdn disbanded 15.5.19.

**NEWLYN**, Cornwall - opened 1.17 as seaplane station, with 424 & 425 Flts from 30.5.18, becoming part of 235 Sqdn 20.8.18, disbanded 22.2.19.

**NORTH COATES FITTIES**, Lincs - opened 4.16 as RFC NLG, used by 404 SD Flt from 26.9.18, disbanded 6.3.19.

**OWTHORNE**, E.Yorks - opened 12.16 as RFC NLG. 506 Flt formed in 251 Sqdn 7.6.18, left 3.19.

**PADSTOW**, Cornwall - opened 2.18 for marine operations. DH9 Flt formed 2.5.18, became 494 Flt in 250 Sqdn 30.5.18. 500 & 501 Flts formed 30.5.18 in 250 Sqdn. Sqdn disbanded 15.5.19.

**PEMBROKE**, Pembs - airship station opened 1.16. 519 & 520 Flts (or 'A' & 'B' Flts) formed 6.6.18 in 255 Sqdn, dis 14.1.19.

**PIEROWALL/WESTRAY**, Orkney - Flying boat moorings, advanced base for Houton Bay from 10.8.18. Closed 9.12.18.

**PORTHOLME MEADOW**, Hunts - Portholme Aerodrome Ltd testing station. 211 TDS formed 1.4.18, became 59 TDS 7.18, left 15.10.18.

**PORTLAND HARBOUR**, Dorset - opened 9.16 as a seaplane sub-station to Calshot. 416 & 417 Flts formed by 31.5.18, in 241 Sqdn from 20.8.18, disbanded 18.6.19.

**PRAWLE POINT**, Devon - opened 4.17 for marine operations. DH9 Flight formed 18.4.18, became 492 Flt 30.5.18, in 254 Sqdn from 15.8.18. 517 & 518 Flts formed in 254 Sqdn 6.6.18, squadron disbanded 22.2.19.

**REDCAR**, N Yorks - opened 4.7.15 as RNAS HD station and flying school. Flt of 7 Sqdn 5.9.17 - 2.10.17 for A/S duties. 510 Flt (otherwise 'C' Flight) formed in 252 Sqdn 7.6.18, left 11.18. School of Special Flying formed 4.18, becoming 2 SoSF 5.18, then NE Area Flying Instructors School 1.7.18, disbanded 1919.

**RENNINGTON**, Northumberland - opened 3.17 as RFC NLG. 525 Flt Formed in 256 Sqdn 6.6.18, left 28.6.18.

**RINGMER**, Sussex - opened 4.16 as NLG for RNAS Eastbourne. Used by occasional detachments for Army co-operation.

**ROCHFORD**, Essex - RNAS for home defence 5.15 , to 4.16.

**ROSYTH**, Fife - opened 1917 as kite balloon station and storage depot. Used by disembarked ships aircraft.

**SCAPA**, Orkney - Opened 11.8.14 as seaplane station, later Fleet Aircraft Repair Base & Storage Depot.

**SCARBOROUGH**, N Yorks - opened 8.15 for RNAS home defence. Closed 8.2.17 and all aircraft to Redcar.

**SEAHOUSES**, Northumberland - opened 2.17 as RFC NLG. Renamed ELSWICK 7.10.18. 527 & 528 Flts formed 6.6.18 in 256 Sqdn, also 495 Flt 14.11.18. Sqdn disbanded 30.6.19

**SEATON CAREW/WEST HARTLEPOOL**, Durham - opened 5.16 as RFC home defence station. Kangaroo Flt formed 9.5.18, became 495 Flt in 252 Sqdn 30.5.18, to 246 Sqdn 15.8.18. 509 Flt formed in 252 Sqdn 7.6.18, left 3.19.

**SEATON CAREW/TEES**, Durham - opened 12.17 as seaplane station. 402, 451 & 452 Flts formed in 252 Sqdn 25.5.18, and 403 Flt arrived 15.8.18, then flts to 246 Sqdn, disbanded by 5.19.

**SKEGNESS**, Lincs - used by Eastchurch Sqdn 8.14.

**SMOOGROO**, Orkney - opened 6.18 as Fleet Practice Station.

**SOUTH SHIELDS**, Durham - seaplane station/ depot from 7.16.

**STENNESS LOCH**, Orkney - opened 5.18 as flying boat station, with 309, 310 and later 311 Flts. Closed 1919.

**STONEHENGE**, Wilts - opened 11.17 as RFC TDS. RNAS Handley Page Squadron ex Manston 19.1.18, soon disbanding into No.1 School of Navigation & Bomb Dropping.

**STRATHBEG LOCH**, Aberdeenshire - opened 12.17 as seaplane sub-station of RN Peterhead. 400 Flt formed 30.5.18, in 249 Sqdn from 18.8.18, left 3.19. 312 to 317 Flts planned but never formed.

**TALLAGHT**, Co.Dublin - opened 8.18 as RAF TDS. 530 Flt (otherwise C Flt) in 244 Sqdn arrived 18.10.18, left 11.11.18.

**TELSCOMBE CLIFFS**, Sussex - opened 4.16 as RFC NLG. 514 Flt (otherwise A Flt) formed in 253 Sqdn 7.6.18, to 242 Sqdn 15.8.18, disbanded 20.1.19.

**TORQUAY HARBOUR**, Devon - opened 1918 as seaplane & kite balloon station. 418 Flt formed 30.5.18, in 239 Sqdn from 20.8.18, disbanded 15.5.19. 419 Flt formed 15.11.18, but soon left.

**TREGANTLE**, Cornwall - opened 1918, storage of naval aircraft.

**TRESCO**, Scillies - opened 2.17 as seaplane & flying boat station. 350 to 353 Flts formed from 30.5.18, in 234 Sqdn from 20.8.18, disbanded 15.5.19.

**TRIMLEY**, Suffolk - opened 1916 as DLG for Felixstowe. Facility transferred to Martlesham Heath 23.2.17.

**TURNHOUSE**, West Lothian - opened 1.5.16 as RFC home defence. Fleet Aeroplane Depot from 1918, becoming Coastal Area Aircraft Depot 1920.

**TYNEMOUTH**, Northumberland - opened 12.16 as RFC NLG. 507 & 508 Flts formed in 252 Sqdn 8.6.18, left 3.19.

**WALMER**, Kent - opened 5.17, used by resting RNAS Western Front squadrons. 471 Flt formed 14.6.18, in 233 Sqdn from 31.8.18, plus 491 Flt 21.1.19. Sqdn disbanded 15.5.19.

**WESTGATE/MUTRIX FARM**, Kent - opened 4.15 as landplane base, closed 27.6.16 and replaced by Manston.

**WESTGATE/St.MILDRED'S BAY**, Kent - opened 6.14 as seaplane station. 406 Flt formed 25.5.18, in 219 Sqdn from 22.7.18. Also 442 Flt from 11.18. Both disbanded 7.2.20.

**WESTWARD HO!**, Devon - opened 6.6.18 when 502 & 503 Flts formed in 260 Sqdn, they transferred to 250 Sqdn 15.8.18, disbanded 2.2.19

**WHITLEY BAY**, Northumberland - coastal defence station from 2.15 until 1916.

**WITHNOE**, Cornwall - opened 1918 for storage of naval aircraft.

**YARMOUTH (GREAT)**, Norfolk - opened 15.4.13 for seaplane & landplane operations. Various flights formed from 25.5.18: 324-326, 428, 429, 454, 455, 485, 486, 490, 534, 557, 558 being grouped as 212, 228, 229 & 273 Sqdns from 20.8.18. Closed 1.20.

# INDEX OF BRITISH AND AMERICAN AIRMEN IN SERIAL & UNIT LISTS

# A RECONCILIATION OF SHORTS' CONSTRUCTOR'S NUMBERS WITH ACTUAL AND REPORTED NAVAL SERIALS

This Appendix has been contributed by Gordon Bruce and summarises his researches over many years into Shorts archives, the Public Record Office and other sources. Linkage of c/n's to Naval serials and Type descriptions are taken from direct references in Shorts Order Book (which was lost for many years) and from contemporary Shorts written records unless shown otherwise by the use of brackets. In most of the bracketed cases, however, linkage can be made by the use of other sources. The reference to H M Lists are to the PRO Lists of H M Naval Aircraft Built, Building and under Repair (noting that the historical parts of the March 1918 List are not entirely reliable).

## SAMSON'S SERIALS
### 2 April - August 1911

In March 1911 Lieuts C.R.Samson, R.Gregory and A.M. Longmore RN and Lieut E.L.Garrard RMLI reported to Short Brothers' aircraft works at Eastchurch, Isle of Sheppey for a course of flying instruction and aeronautical engineering under the aegis of the Royal Aero Club. A patriot, Frank McClean, provided two of his own aircraft - Shorts S.26 and S.28 - free of charge for the Officers' instruction save that the Admiralty was to foot any bill for repairs. Each aircraft was then secondhand:

    S.26 - originally G.Colmore's Short-Sommer.
    S.28 - originally J.T.C.Moore-Brabazon's Short-Sommer
Additionally McClean gave instructions to Shorts for a third aircraft [S.34] to be built and allotted to the Naval task.

When flying training started on 16 March 1911 Samson's log and reports to the Admiralty referred to S.26 and S.28 as the older" and "newer" aircraft respectively. On 2 April, after S.34 became available [completed 8 March and allotted to the Naval task on 31 March] Samson evolved his private numbering system for his log and reports to the Admiralty:

    Naval Biplane No.1 was the oldest machine.
    Naval Biplane No.2 was a machine under repair after a crash by Cockburn (the Club's instructor) and Longmore on 31 March when they failed to clear a dyke.
    Naval Biplane No.3 was the newest machine.
Cross-references to Short' archives show conclusively that these were respectively S.26, S.28 and S.34.

S.26 [sometimes called "The Dud" or "The Owd Bitch" suffered frequent damage and Samson reported that he "paid off" this aircraft at the end of April. S.28 [dubbed "The Dyke machine"] after the Longmore crash on 31 March] also suffered badly and was assessed as beyond economical repair following a crash on 1 May. The Admiralty then authorised use of an imprest fund provided by McClean for a total rebuild of S.28; Shorts allotted a new c/n [S.38] to the rebuild, but Samson continued to use the style "Naval Biplane No.2" because the engine and parts of S.28 had been used in the rebuild. Shorts Order Book records delivery of S.38 to the Naval task at 10.45 on 23 May 1911 in complete condition and ready for engine test".

Samson's private series continued until at least August 1911:

    Naval Biplane No.1: S.26 ["The Dud", "The Owd Bitch"], McClean, ex Colmore; withdrawn April 1911.
    Naval Biplane No.2: S.28 ["The Dyke machine"] McClean, ex Moore-Brabazon; rebuilt as S.38 May 1911. On 19 August 1911 Samson flew S.38 for 4hrs 58 mins 30 seconds, setting a British Duration Record.
    Naval Biplane No.3: S.34; McClean, completed 8 March 1911. Samson's log 24 April 1911: gained certificate on No.3 machine".

Although styled "Naval Biplane" all these aircraft remained the property of Frank McClean.

## ADMIRALTY SERIALS: FIRST NUMBERING SYSTEM
### November 1911 - 22 February 1912

This series was establised by the Admiralty in the Autumn of 1911 to identify the aircraft it was then buying. The first two aircraft bought were S.34 and S.38, purchased from McClean for £550 and £600 respectively. Samson's log for 29 November 1911 identifies S.38 as "No.2 Biplane" so that S.34 was clearly "No.1 Biplane" - i.e.the Admiralty established a sensible progression of c/n and Service serial which reversed the seniority of Samson's private list.

    No.1 Biplane: S.34; ex Naval Biplane No.3; ex McClean No.2 Biplane: S.38; ex Naval Biplane No.2; ex McClean. On 1 December 1911, Longmore "splashed-down" into the Medway with S.38 to lay the foundations of Shorts long association with marine aircraft; 10 January 1912 Samson flew S.38 from HMS *Africa* at anchor off Grain Island.

No.3 Biplane: S.39 Triple Twin; first flown by Samson on 22 November 1911.
No.4 Biplane: S.27 Tandem Twin; Cecil Grace's single-engined S.27 Short-Sommer converted for McClean to two Gnomes [same c/n retained]. First flown by Samson 2 December 1911 and wrecked by him 11 March 1912.

## ADMIRALTY SERIALS: FIRST ALPHA/NUMERICAL SYSTEM 23 February - 18 April 1912

In February 1912 the Admiralty introduced a more flexible system to identify biplanes (B), monoplanes (M) and hydro-aeroplanes (H) [the handier term "seaplanes" was invented later by Winston Churchill, then First Lord of the Admiralty].

In mid April 1912 the 'B' designation for biplanes was changed to 'T'; no reason has been traced but it may be surmised that the change was to avoid confusion with the Royal Engineers' Air Battalion's designation of tractor aircraft from B1 onwards.

For clarity, the 'B' designations are listed below [all 'H' designations and probably all 'M' designations had been issued before the change from 'B' to 'T'].

    B1: S.34, ex No.1 Biplane. Samson's log 24 February 1912: flew "B1 (34)". 12 April 1912 Samson dropped 98-lb bomb from B1.
    B2: S.38, ex No.2 Biplane.
    B3: S.39 Triple Twin.
    B4?: It is possible that S.27 Tandem Twin may have held this designation briefly before Samson wrecked this aircraft on 11 March 1912.

## ADMIRALTY SERIALS: SECOND ALPHA/NUMERICAL SYSTEM 19 April 1912 - September 1912

Following creation of the 'T' designation for biplanes the Admiralty's system survived the formation of the Royal Flying Corps on 13 May 1912 and remained in use by the Naval Wing until September 1912 when a simple numerical system, not classified by aircraft layout or function, was introduced. Ray Sturtivant's theory that the new 'T' designation for biplanes indicated "Twin-planes" can not be faulted.

    T1: S.34 [ex B1]. Later 1
    T2: S.38 [ex B2]. Later 2. Samson's log 28 April 1912: "T2 (38)". On 2 May 1912 Samson flew T2 [70-hp Gnome] from HMS *Hibernia* under weigh at 10½ knots in Weymouth Bay, landing at Lodmoor. During the Naval Review of May 1912 Gregory dropped a dummy bomb of 300-lb from S.38 at an altitude of 500ft, striking his target. Later the same day Gregory demonstrated that a pilot could detect a submerged submarine. S.38 was also flown in the Royal Navy's bombing trials.
    T3: S.39 [ex B3]. Later 3.
    T4: S.47 Triple Tractor, delivered 24 July 1912.Later 4.
    T5: S.45 70-hp Gnome tractor seaplane; delivered and first flown (by Samson) 23 May 1912. Later 5.
    T6: Breguet. Later 6.

## NAVAL WING R.F.C. NUMERICAL SERIES
### From September 1912

This series recognised the formation of the Royal Flying Corps on 13 May 1912 Nos.1 to 200 were allotted to the Naval Wing and Nos.201 to 800 to the Military Wing, Central Flying School etc.

Samson's log book shows that the new system, which survived the formation of the Royal Naval Air Service on 1 July 1914, was in use by 3 September 1912.

This series ran up to 10000 in 1916, when a new alpha/numerical series, commencing N1, was introduced.

| Navy | C/n | Type | Notes |
|------|-----|------|-------|
| [1] | S.34 | Short-Sommer (50-hp Gnome) | Bought second-hand from Frank McClean; there is therefore no direct Order Book linkage of Naval serial to c/n. Deld 8.3.11. Was T1. |
| 1 | S.86 | S.38 nacelle type (50-hp Gnome) | Delivered 8.12.13. |

[It used to be thought that S.34 "soldiered on" until the early part of WW1. The Order Book, however, shows S.34 was replaced by S.86 which was delivered on 8.12.13 as a "50-hp School biplane to replace Naval No.1". Obviously, under the accounting convention of the time, the Naval Serial No.1 was retained for S.86 thus giving rise to the belief that S.34 "soldiered on" after an imputed reconstruction]

| 2 | S.38 | Short-Sommer (50-hp Gnome) | Was T2. Delivered 23.5.11. |

[Flown by Samson from HMS *Africa* at anchor 10.1.12 and under weigh 2.5.12. Reconstructed by Naval Wing 4.13. On 29.11.13 WS Churchill, then First Lord of the Admiralty, flew as a passenger. The pilot, Lt GV Wildman-Lushington, RMA, allowed Churchill to take the controls and thus became the first Cabinet Minister anywhere in the World to control his own aircraft. In later months Churchill took flying lessons from Lieutenant DA Spenser Grey RN and Lieutenant JW Seddon RN]

| 3 | S.39 | Triple Twin | Was T3. Deld 18.9.11. |

[15.2.13 order to be rebuilt identical to Naval aeroplane No.28, to incorporate as much as possible of Triple Twin. (Two 50-hp Gnome)]

| 3 | S.78 | S.38 nacelle type | Rebuild of S.39. Deld by 4.6.13. |
| 4 | S.47 | Triple Tractor | Was T4. Deld 24.7.12. |
| 5 | S.45 | Tractor seaplane | Was T5. Deld 23.5.12 |
| 8 | S.42 | Monoplane (50-hp Gnome) | Was M2. Deld by 24.2.12. |

['8' sometimes wrongly reported as an S.38 but is specifically given by e.g. HM List June 1914 as a 50-hp Short monoplane]

| 10 | S.41 | 100-hp seaplane, "HMS Amphibian" | Was H1 . Deld by 27.3.12. |

[Samson: No.10 "never broke a strut or a float which was a rare testimony of its strength and reliability"]

| 12 | S.46 | Tandem seaplane (70-hp Gnome) | Was H2. Deld by 23.9.12. Flown by Samson late 1912/early 1913. |
| [14] | S.52 | Hydromonoplane,2x140-hp Gnome | Cancelled. |

[Not, as sometimes reported, the Short monoplane. HM List for June 1914 shows the 50-hp Short monoplane as Navy aircraft No.8 as do other sources. Although the Order Book does not describe as No.14 the link is inescapable]

| [19] | S.54 | 140/160-hp Gnome seaplane | S.54 ordered 2.8.12 as 140-hp seaplane. |

[No.19 listed in HM Lists and Air Department correspondence as 160-hp seaplane. S.54 is the only aircraft in the Order Book which fits Navy 19. No.19 deleted 12.15, sometimes wrongly reported as an S.38]

| 20 | S.56 | 100-hp Gnome seaplane | 20 & 21 Improved S.41s. Initially H8 and H9, deld respectively 21.4.13 and 17.10.12 [sic]. |
| 21 | S.57 | 100-hp seaplane | Despite the Order Book there is photographic proof that 20 was S.57. |
| [28] | S.55 | S.38 nacelle type | Deld 2.11.12. Linkage of Naval serial to c/n deduced. |
| 34 | S.61 | S.38 nacelle type | Deld 14.4.13 |
| 42 | S.61 | Olympia PV 80-hp seaplane | Purchased by the Admiralty after the Show. |
| 62 | S.66 | S.38 nacelle type (80-hp Gnome) | |
| 63 | S.67 | S.38 nacelle type (80-hp Gnome) | |
| 64 | S.76 | S.38 nacelle type (80-hp Gnome) | |
| 65 | S.75 | S.38 nacelle type (80-hp Gnome) | |
| 66 | S.77 | S.38 nacelle type (80-hp Gnome) | Maxim gun aircraft |
| 74 - 77 | S.69 to S.72 | Type 74 seaplane (100-hp Gnome) | |
| 78 & 79 | S.73 & S.74 | 160-hp seaplanes | Order Book and HM Lists specific. Attributions as 100-hp wrong. |
| 80 | S.79 | Two-seat pusher biplane (100-hp Gnome) | |
| 81 & 82 | S.64 & S.65 | 160-hp Gnome seaplanes | The first Folders |
| 89 & 90 | - | - | Often referred to as 160-hp Short seaplanes. |

[No Shorts built with these serials: may have been allotments not taken up, or may have been two Borel seaplanes, for "Flight" magazine reported in July 1913 that eight Borels had been ordered but the immediately preceding six Borels 83 to 88 are the only known run]

| 119 - 122 | S.82 to S.85 | 160-hp Gnome seaplane | 121 first to launch torpedo, Calshot 28.7.14. 119 & 120 in Cuxhaven raid 25.12.14, 120 came down. |
| 126 | S.81 | 160-hp Gnome pusher seaplane | Gun carrier |
| 135 | S.88 | 135-hp Canton-Unné seaplane | Lost in Cuxhaven raid 25.12.14 |

| 136 | S.87 | 200-hp Canton-Unné seaplane | In Cuxhaven raid 25.12.14. |

[The Order Book is specific as to the horsepowers and reversal of serial and constructor's numbers of 135 and 136]

| [140] | - | - | Sometimes referred to as a Short. HM Lists are specific that this was a Henry Farman. |

| 145 | ? | ? |

[HM Lists in late 1914 give as a 65-hp Austro-Daimler single-seater without specifying manufacturer. If this aircraft was a Short, as sometimes said, there is no Order Book evidence for a direct sale by Short to the Admiralty. If, however, it was Short acquired second-hand by the Naval Wing a suitable candidate is S.63, a nacelle-type S.38 ordered by the War Office at the same time as S.62, both aircraft being noted in the Order Book as delivered on 21st April 1913. Delivery is confirmed by a Director Military Aeronautics letter dated 8th September 1913 which records a C.F.S. establishment of four Short "propellers" (i.e. pushers), three on strength and one under reconstruction. Three of the four are clearly S.38s 401, 402 and 446 and the fourth must have been the previously unpublished 443 which a Sefton Brancker letter of 19th September 1913 records as a Short propeller "under orders for reconstruction at makers" (cf 8th September letter), but that it was not "intended to purchase more 50-hp Gnome Short Propellers". Following the crash of 446 that aircraft was struck off and it is therefore possible that the newly identified 443 was transferred to the Naval Wing as surplus to requirements and reconstructed as a single seat test-bed for the recently announced 65-hp Austro-Daimler. The serial 145 would have come up for allotment shortly after February 1914]

| 152 | S.89 | S.38 nacelle type | 80-hp Gnome |

| 161 - 166 | S.90 to S.95 | Type 166 seaplanes | 200-hp Canton-Unné |

| [178] | None allotted | [Proposed 200-hp Canton-Unné tractor seaplane B Type] - Not built; not listed in Order Book. |

[Naval number deduced. HM Lists are consistent in describing as an aeroplane (i.e. landplane) with Canton-Unné. See Navy 190 to 198]

| [180] | None allotted | [100-hp Gnome tractor aeroplane] | Does not appear in Order Book. Although HM Lists in 1914 show as "an order" and "proposed" there is no evidence of construction. |

| [181] | None allotted | [50-hp Gnome pusher biplane] | No aircraft in the Order Book was built as 181 although HM Lists in 1914 show as a proposed 50-hp Gnome pusher biplane. |

| [182] | None allotted | [100-hp Gnome Type 74 seaplane, dual control - A major problem!] |

[Not listed in the Order Book yet HM Lists show as an order (June 1914) and delivered as at September 1914. Possibly the serial was allotted and an aircraft built up from spares by the RNAS. Alternatively the aircraft might have been Frank McClean's Green-engined 1913 competition seaplane re-engined with a Gnome and impressed against this previously allotted serial as a Type 74 analogue. Support for this theory id that an April 1914 impressment survey records McClean's seaplane as "about to be fitted with a different engine" and an impressment file talks of the price for F/Lt McClean's seaplanes (NB plural: 905 and another) ]

| 183 | S.128 | Type 74 seaplane | 100-hp Gnome |

| 184 & 185 | S.106 & S.107 | Prototypes of the Type 184 "225" torpedo carrier. |

| [186] | - | | (a) Wight Seaplane 200-hp Canton-Unné in HM Lists June & July 1914 (see 187) |
| | None allotted | No record in Order Book | (b) Proposed Short 200-hp Canton-Unné seaplane in August-December 1914 and September 1915 Lists with same characteristics as 184 and 185 - a third prototype 184? Twin 200-hp Canton-Unné Short tractor seaplane in March 1916 List. See 187, also 1448-1449. |

| [187] | None allotted | No record in Order Book | (a) HM Lists June and July 1914: proposed as 200-hp Canton-Unné Short torpedo seaplane (see 186). (b) August 1914 and thereafter: identity switched to Wight seaplane (see 186). |

| [190 - 198] | None allotted | [Two-seater landplanes] | HM Lists June-December 1914: proposed as 200-hp Canton-Unné - production models of 178. Abandoned in 1915. Serials 191-198 sometimes wrongly reported as "not allotted". No record in Order Book. |

| 811 - 818 | S.108 to S.115 | Type 74 (100-hp Gnome) | 811, 814 & 815 in Cuxhaven raid 25.12.14. 814 & 815 lost. |

| 819 - 821 | S.119 to S.121 | Type 830 seaplane | 135-hp Canton-Unné |

| 822 - 827 | S.122 to S.127 | Type 827 seaplane | 150-hp Sunbeam |

| 828 - 830 | S.116 to S.118 | Type 830 seaplane | 135-hp Canton-Unné |

| 841 - 850 | S.129 to S.138 | Type 184 (225-hp Sunbeam) | HM Lists show first ordered with 200-hp Canton-Unné. |

| 904 | S.58 | S.38 nacelle type (70-hp Gnome) | 904 & 905 acquired from McClean on outbreak of War. Order Book was annotated to show the new identities. |

| 905 | S.80 | 160-hp Gnome seaplane | McClean's "Nile". |

| 1268 - 1279 | S.139 to S.150 | | [Described in HM Lists as "Tractor 126 Type gun armed". - Proposed".] - [Proposed in HM List December 1914. Order Book: "tractor, gun carrying, not built". 1268 and 1279 sometimes reported as S.45: no authority traced for this] |

| 1335 - 1346 | S.151 to S.162 | Type 830 seaplane | 135-hp Canton-Unné |

| | | | |
|---|---|---|---|
| **[1373]** | None allotted | [Wright "Sqdn Cdr Ogilvie"] | Description in HM Lists varies but Ogilvie's Short-Wright No.6 is the best fit. A secondary candidate is the Wright Model F or H imported in 1915 with which Ogilvie's name is associated. |
| **[1448 - 1449]** | None allotted | [Short 186 Type, 2x200 C-Unné] | Proposed in September 1915 List; "postponed" in March 1916 List. Not built. Serials sometimes wrongly reported as "not allotted". |
| **3063 - 3072** | S.163 to S.172 | Short 827 seaplane | 150-hp Sunbeam |
| **[3093 - 3112]** | - | [Short 827 seaplane | 150-hp Sunbeam. Sometimes wrongly reported as Short-built. |

[HM Lists are specific that these were Sunbeam-built, while the Order Book does not list them]

| | | | |
|---|---|---|---|
| **3706** | S.248 | Short bomber prototype | 225-hp Sunbeam/250-hp Rolls-Royce. |
| **8031 - 8105** | S.173 to S.247 | Type 184 seaplane | 225-hp Sunbeam |
| **8317 & 8318** | S.299 & S.300 | 310-hp Type 'A' tractor aeroplane | HM List September 1915 - these serials were originally allotted to 2 x Hewlett & Blondeau with 2 x 100-hp Clerget. |
| **8319 & 8320** | S.311 & S.312 | 310-hp Type B tractor seaplane | As 8317 & 8318 |
| **9306 - 9355** | S.249 to S.298 | Short bomber | 250-hp Rolls-Royce. |
| **9781 - 9790** | S.301 to S.310 | Tractor seaplane | 140-hp Canton-Unné |
| **[N20 & N21]** | None allotted | [Short pusher anti-submarine a/c] | Reported by historians as ordered and cancelled. No Order Book evidence or c/n. |
| **[N36]** | S.313 | [200-hp two-seat exptl seaplane] | Order Book does not confirm that S.313 was N36, the linkage is, however, inescapable as Scout No.1. |
| **N66 - N73** | S.419 to S.426 | Short N.2b (275-hp Sunbeam) | Eight serials and eight c/n's were allotted in the Order Book. |

[N66 and N67 built. When the last six were cancelled, c/n's S.421 to S.423 were reallotted to Shirls N110 to N112. C/n's S.424 to S.426 were not reallotted]

| | | | |
|---|---|---|---|
| **[N97 & N98]** | None allotted | [Short School seaplane] | Reported by historians. No Order Book evidence or c/n's. The project became Short Shrimp sporting seaplane c/n's S.540-S.542. |
| **N110 - N112** | S.421 to S.423 | Short Shirl (375-hp Rolls-Royce) | C/n's originally allotted to N.2b's (see N66 to N73). Short's first order for Air Board. |
| **N120 - N122** | S.539, S.544 & S.545 | | Short Cromarty - Only N120 built. |
| **[N507 & N508]** | None allotted | [Short Day Bomber (22 x 200-hp Sunbeam)] - Listed in AIR.1/152/15/119 October 1916 to January 1917 but no entry in Order Book. | |

**[N1079]**    S.364a    200-hp two-seat tractor
[Short Scout No.3 was photographed with the c/n S.364 but no Service serial visible. The Order Book shows specifically that c/n S.364 was duplicated - S.364a to the Scout and S.364 to a Short 310 which was the lead machine of batch N1480 to N1504. Histories do not record an allotment for N1079: perhaps this was intended for Scout S.364a noting that this appeared in March 1917 and N1080 (next in line to the suggested allocation) was an Eastchurch-built Short 184 which appeared late January/early February 1917. S.364a also Eastchurch-built.

| | | | |
|---|---|---|---|
| **N1080 - N1097** | S.314 to S.331 | Type 184 seaplane | 240-hp Renault-Mercedes |
| **N1098** | S.332 | Type 184 seaplane | 260-hp Sunbeam |
| **N1099** | S.333 | Type 184 seaplane | 240-hp Renault-Mercedes |
| **N1150 - N1159** | S.354 to S.363 | 310-hp Sunbeam torpedo carrier | |
| **N1300 - N1319** | S.334 to S.353 | 310-hp Sunbeam torpedo carrier | C/n's originally allotted to 20 Short 184s N1130 to N1149 which were actually built by Sage and by Saunders - presumably transferred to allow Shorts to concentrate on the later type |
| **N1390 - N1409** | S.399 to S.418 | Short 310 seaplane | |
| **N1480 - N1504** | S.364 to S.388 | Short 310 seaplane | |
| **N1580 - N1589** | S.389 to S.398 | Type 184 seaplane | 240-hp Renault-Mercedes |
| **N4000 - N4037** | S.588 to S.625 | Felixstowe F.3 | Built at Rochester for Air Board. Originally allotted c/n's S.528 to S.565. |
| **N4038 - N4049** | S.626 to S.638 | Felixstowe F.5 | Built at Rochester for Air Board. Originally allotted c/n's S.566 to S.577. |
| **N4830 - N4839** | S.528 to S.537 | Felixstowe F.5 | Built at Rochester for Air Board. |
| **[N4840 - N4879]** | - | Felixstowe F.5 | |

[Historians report that the serials for the preceding batch ran to N4879. No Order Book evidence or c/n's' for reported N4840 to N4879]

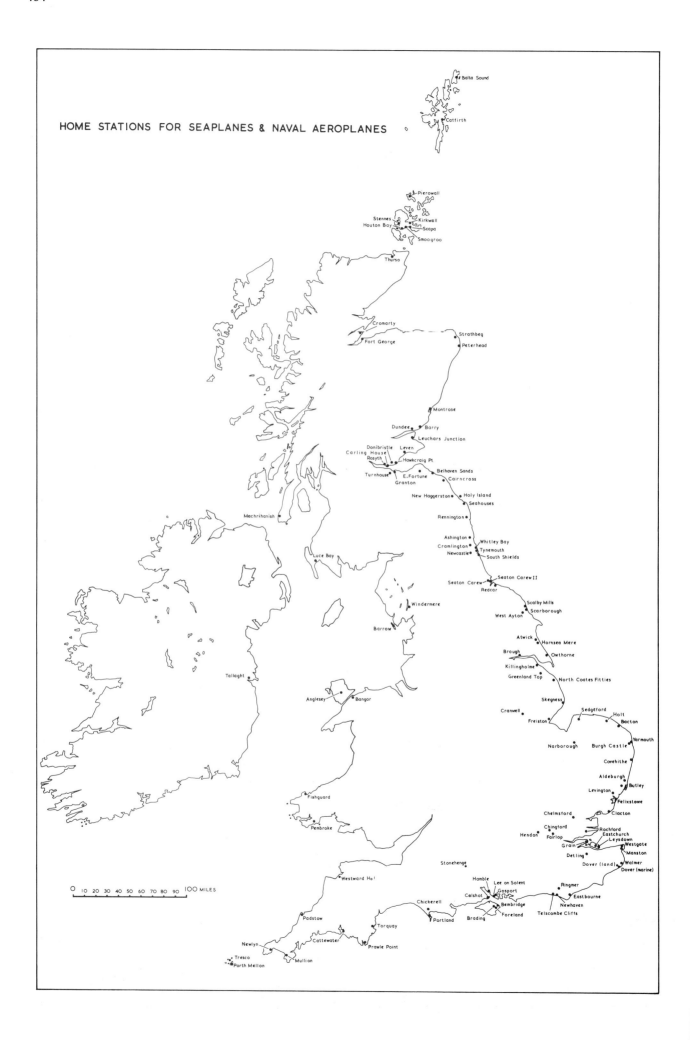

HOME STATIONS FOR SEAPLANES & NAVAL AEROPLANES

## MAPS OF HOME STATIONS FOR SEAPLANES AND NAVAL AEROPLANES

These World War I maps have been drawn by Mick Davis to various scales,
and are based on documents in the AIR.1 series at the Public Record Office.

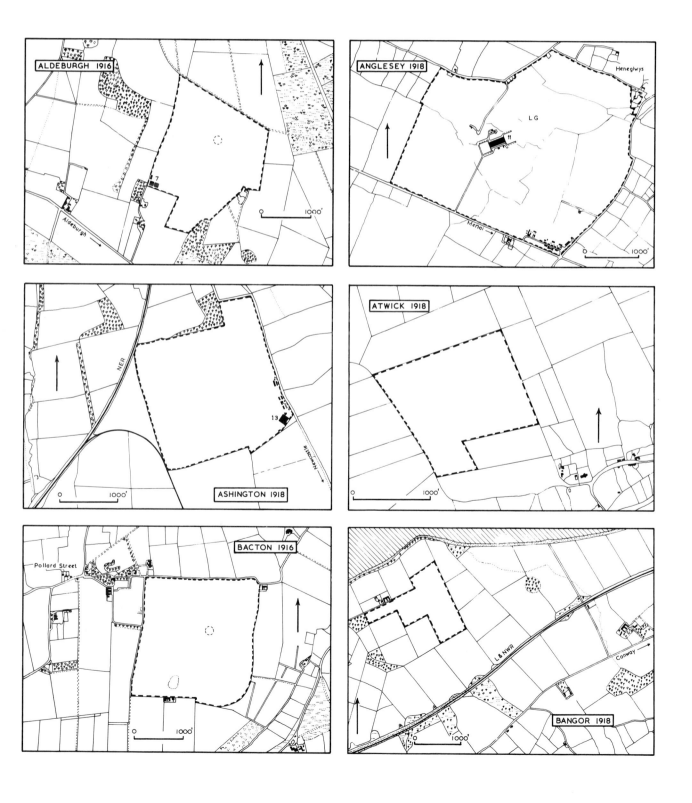

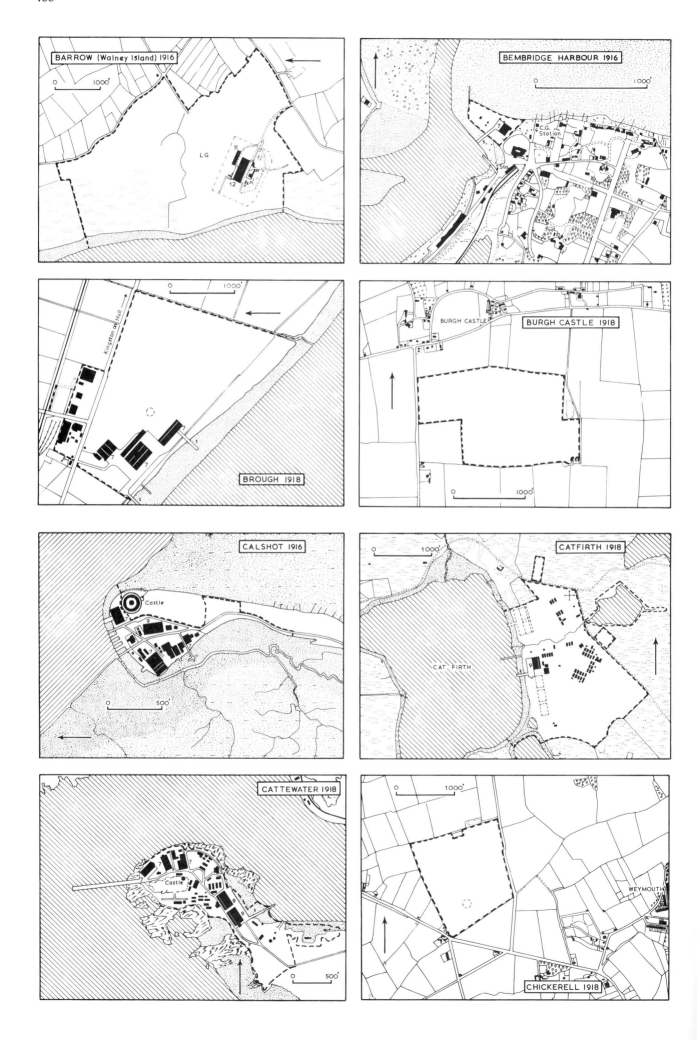

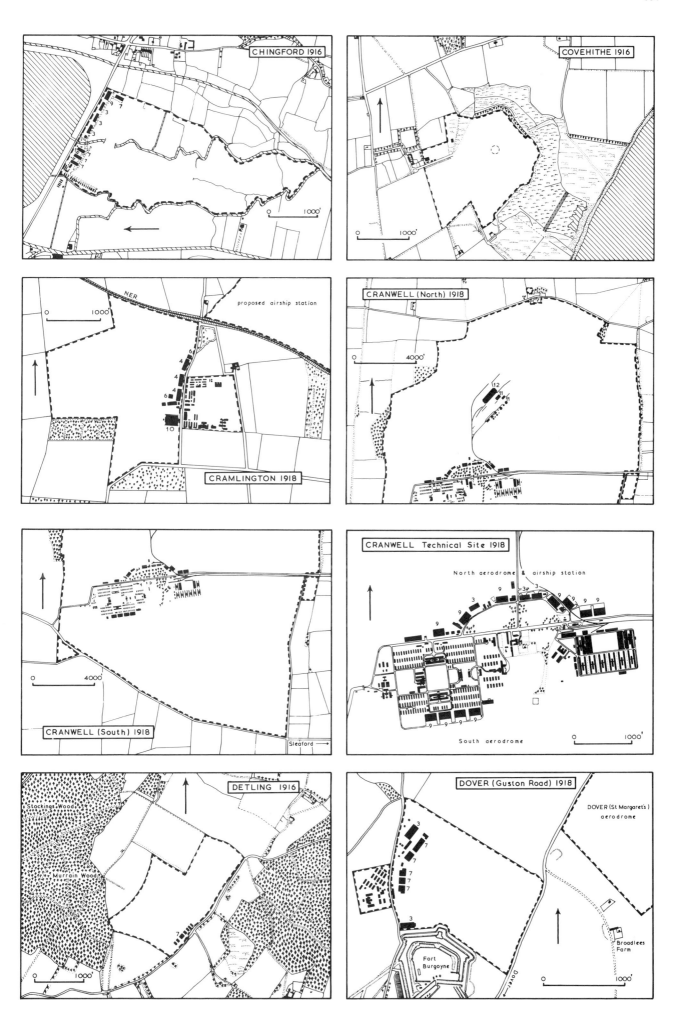

CHINGFORD 1916

COVEHITHE 1916

CRAMLINGTON 1918

proposed airship station

NER

1000'

CRANWELL (North) 1918

4000'

CRANWELL (South) 1918

Sleaford →

CRANWELL Technical Site 1918

North aerodrome & airship station

South aerodrome

1000'

DETLING 1916

Stockings Wood

Murrain Wood

1000'

DOVER (Guston Road) 1918

DOVER (St Margaret's) aerodrome

Broadlees Farm

Fort Burgoyne

Dover

1000'

468

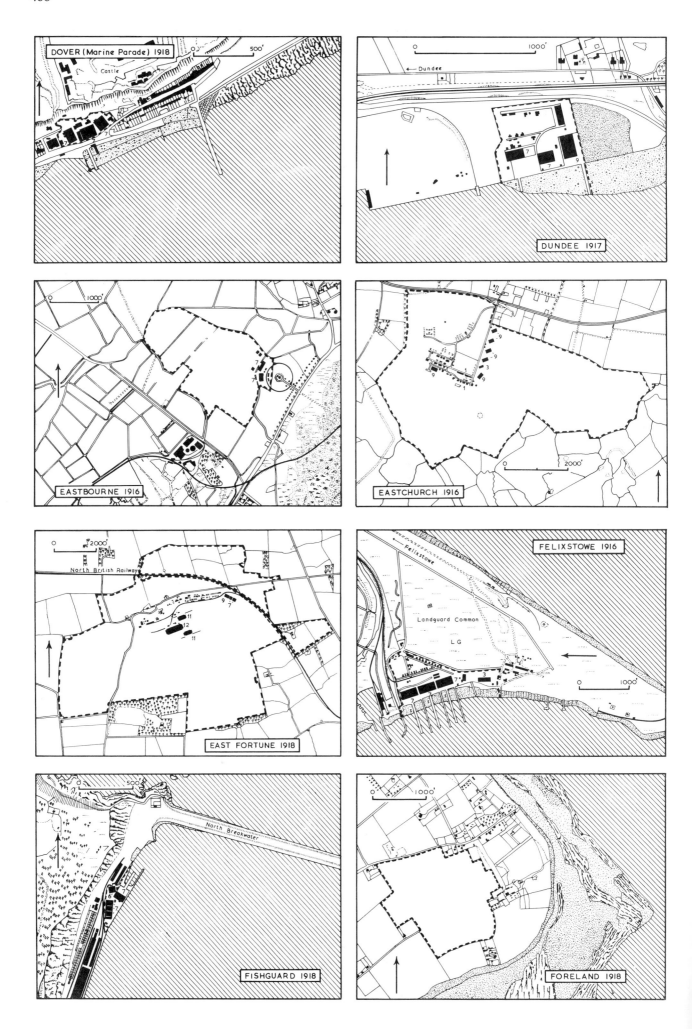

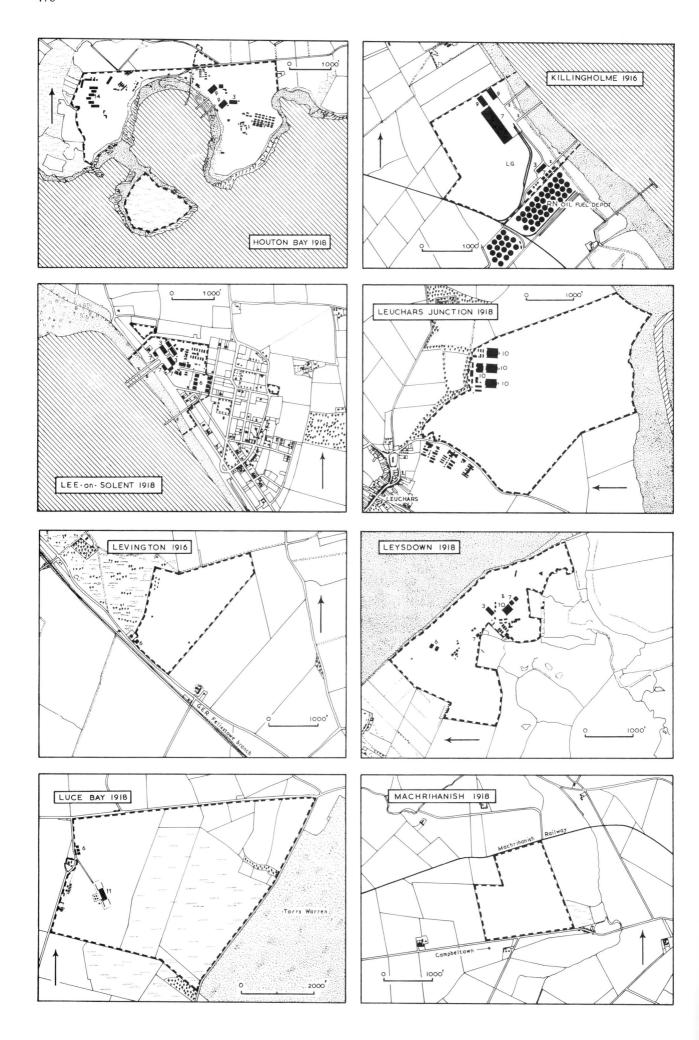

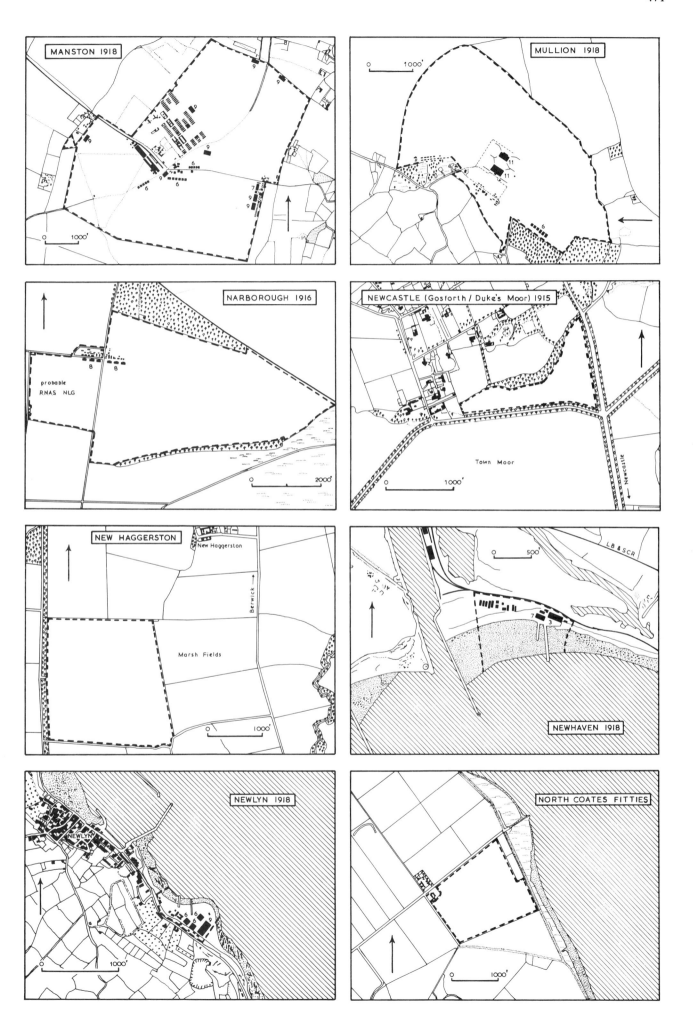

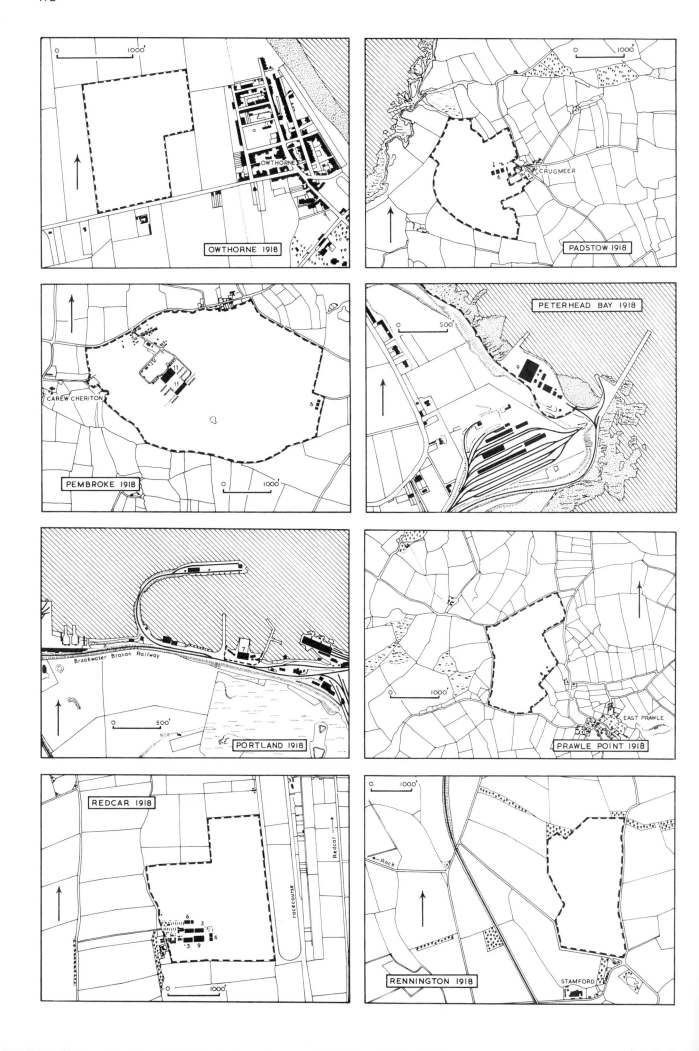

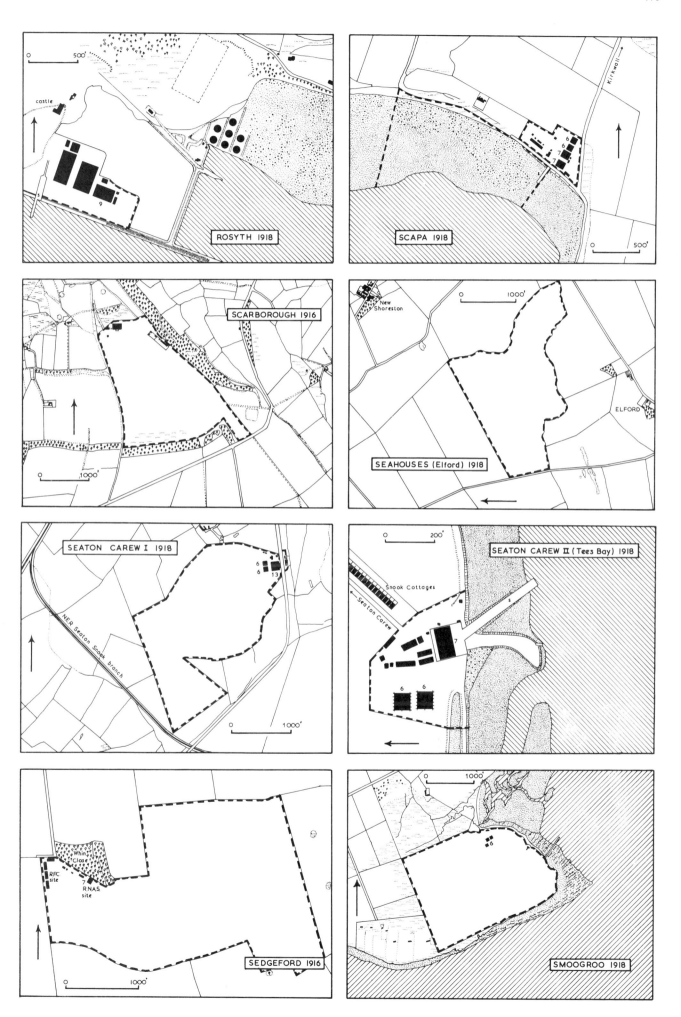

ROSYTH 1918

SCAPA 1918

SCARBOROUGH 1916

SEAHOUSES (Elford) 1918

SEATON CAREW I 1918

SEATON CAREW II (Tees Bay) 1918

SEDGEFORD 1916

SMOOGROO 1918

474

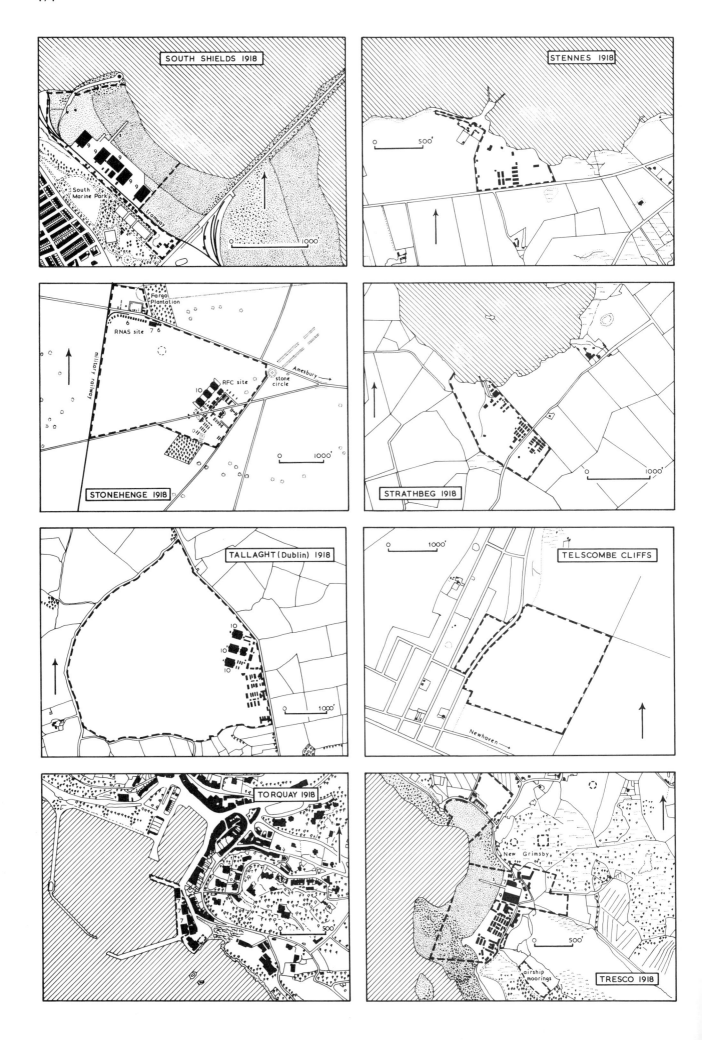

475

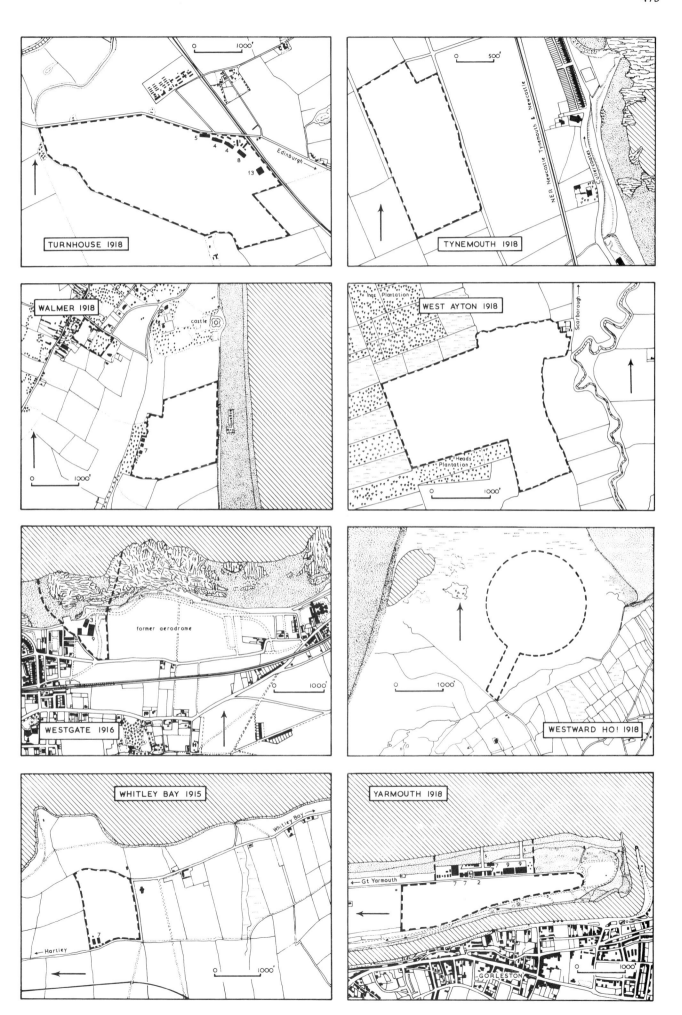

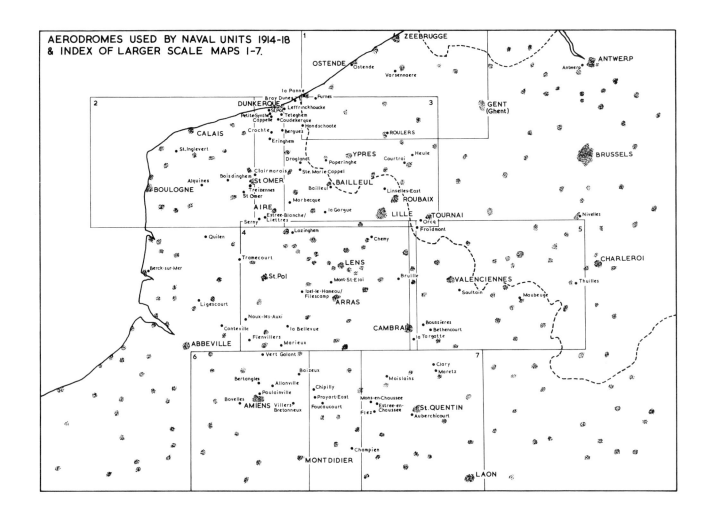

AERODROMES USED BY NAVAL UNITS 1914-18
& INDEX OF LARGER SCALE MAPS 1-7.

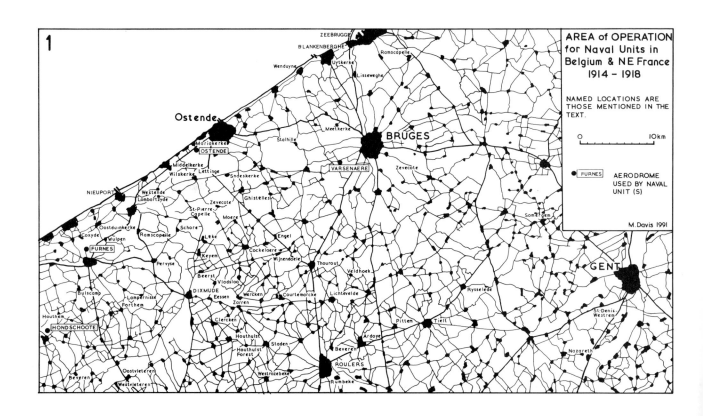

1

AREA of OPERATION
for Naval Units in
Belgium & NE France
1914 - 1918

NAMED LOCATIONS ARE
THOSE MENTIONED IN THE
TEXT.

0                    10km

●  FURNES    AERODROME
            USED BY NAVAL
            UNIT (S)

M. Davis 1991

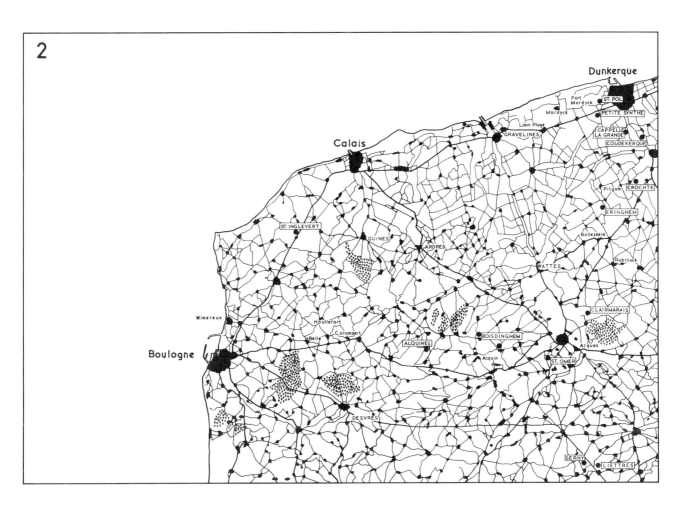

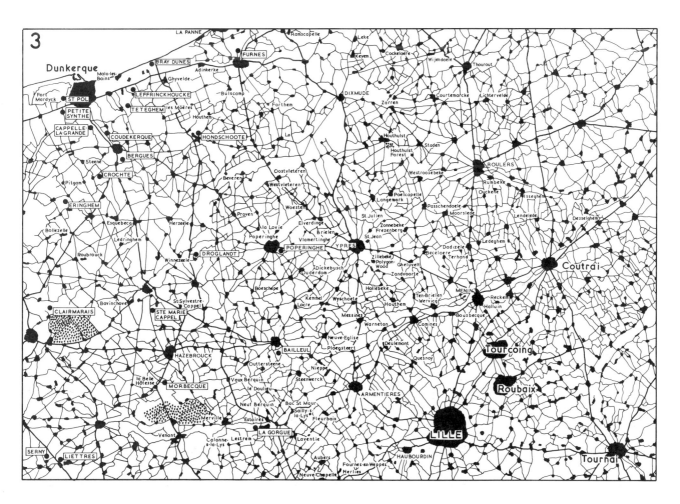

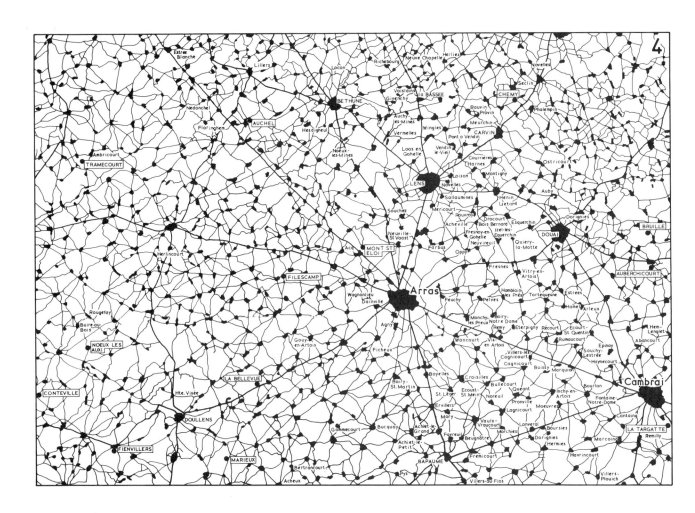

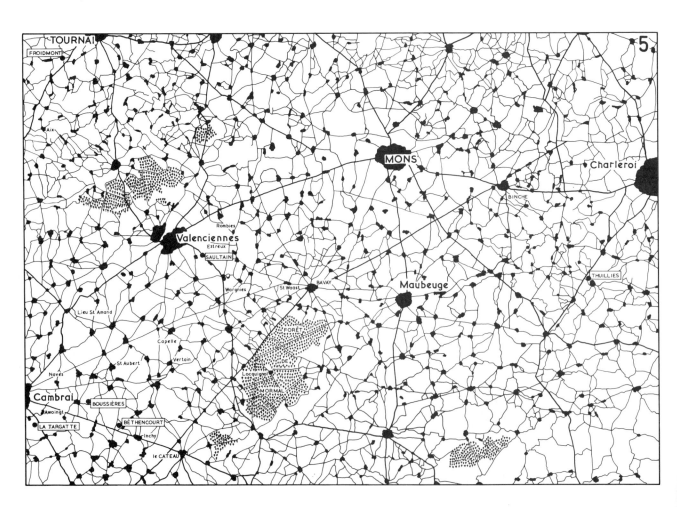

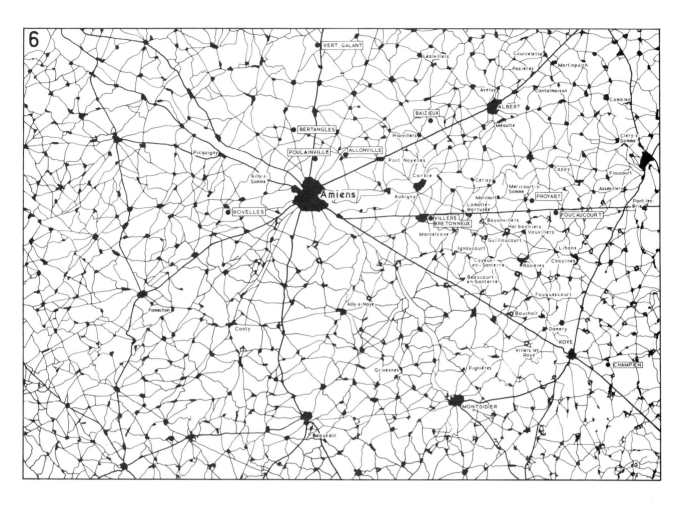

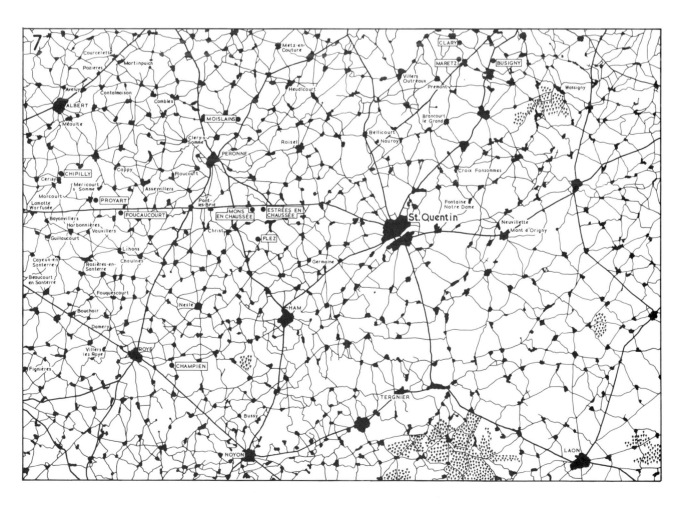